Hymns and Tunes
— an Index

by

Katharine Smith Diehl

The Scarecrow Press, Inc.
New York and London   1966

To

William and Annetta Kraushaar

HYMNALS ANALYZED

ARRANGED ACCORDING TO SYMBOLIC CITATION CODE

CODE

A   The Hymnal 1940 (Episcopal)

B   The Hymnal 1916 (Episcopal)

C   The Hymnal 1916, with variant tunes, c1936 (Episcopal)

D   The Church hymnal 1892 (Episcopal)

E   The English hymnal (Anglican)

F   Hymns ancient and modern (Anglican)

G   The Methodist hymnal 1935

H   The Methodist Protestant hymnal 1921

I   The Methodist hymnal 1925, c1905

J   Service book and Hymnal of the Lutheran Church in America

K   Common service book (Lutheran)

L   Book of worship (Evangelical Lutheran)

M   American Lutheran hymnal

N   The Hymnal and Order of service (Augustana Lutheran)

O   The Lutheran hymnary (Evangelical Lutheran)

P   The Concordia hymnal (Lutheran)

Q   The Lutheran hymnal (Missouri Synod)

R   The Hymnbook 1955 (Presbyterian)

S   The Hymnal 1933 (Presbyterian U.S.A.)

T   The Psalter hymnal 1927 (United Presbyterian)

U   The Presbyterian hymnal 1927 (Presbyterian U.S.)

V   The New Psalms and hymns 1901 (Presbyterian U.S.)

W   The Church hymnary (Church of Scotland)

X   Songs of praise (Anglican)

Y   The American student hymnal (unaffiliated)

Z   Christian worship (Baptists and Disciples)

AA   Evangelical Lutheran hymnbook (Missouri Synod)

AB   The Student hymnary (unaffiliated)

AC   The New Hymnal for American youth (unaffiliated)

AD   The New Church hymnal (unaffiliated)

AE   The Hymnal (Evangelical United Brethren)

AF   Pilgrim hymnal (Congregational)

AG   Hymnal for Christian worship (Presbyterian U.S.)

AH   The Hymnal, Army and Navy

AI   The New Christian hymnal ("orthodox, evangelical faith")

AJ   The Psalter (Reformed)

AK   The Hymnal (Evangelical Reformed)

AL   The Hymnary (United Church of Canada)

AM   Trinity hymnal (Orthodox Presbyterian)

AN   Hymns of the Spirit (Universalist Unitarian)

AO   The Book of worship (Re-

v

	formed)	BH	Union hymnal (Jewish)
AP	The Book of praise (Presbyterian Church of Canada)	BI	Liturgy and hymnal (Swedenborgian: General Church)
AQ	Hymns for the celebration of life (Universalist Unitarian)	BJ	Hymns: The Yattendon hymnal (Anglican)
AR	The Brethren hymnal (Church of the Brethren)	BK	A Hymnal for Friends (Quaker)
AS	Hymnal 1925 (Church of the Brethren)	BL	Hymnal of Christian unity (Catholic-Protestant)
AT	Baptist hymnal 1956 (Southern Baptist)	BM	Our parish prays and sings (Catholic, especially schools)
AU	The Broadman hymnal (Baptist)	BN	The New Saint Basil hymnal
AV	New Baptist hymnal c1926, 1958 printing (American Baptist)	BO	St. Basil's hymnal 1935 (Catholic)
AW	The Mennonite hymnary (Mennonite General Conference)	BP	The Monastery hymnal (Catholic)
AX	Christian hymnal (Mennonite General Conference)	BQ	The St. Gregory hymnal (Catholic)
AY	Church and Sunday School hymnal (Eastern Mennonite)	BR	The Magnificat (New-Church)
AZ	The Liturgy and Offices of worship (Moravian)	BS	Twenty four Psalms (Catholic)
BA	Hymnal and Liturgies (Moravian)	BT	The Handbook to the Lutheran Hymnal (Missouri Synod)
BB	The Church hymnal (Seventy-Day Advent)	BU	Ausbund (Amish Mennonite, full German text)
BC	Hymns (Mormon)	BV	Anglican hymn book
BD	The Beacon hymnal (Universalist Unitarian)	BW	Handbook to the Mennonite hymnary (Mennonite General Conference)
BE	Christian Science hymnal	BX	The New hymn and tune book 1914 Unitarian
BF	Christian worship (Reformed Church in America)	BY	The Baptist hymn book 1962 (British Baptist)
BG	Oxford book of carols (Anglican)	BZ	Final report, Methodist hymnal 1966

The hymnals, arranged by date and with fuller citation, will be found in Appendix I.

Indexes I and II

The first and second indexes are concerned with the hymns, the refrains, the variant first lines of both hymns and refrains; the authors; and the hymnals within which these hymns by these authors may be found quickly.

Here are four related quotations from Index I: First lines and variants, with citations:

> O Christian, haste, thy mission high fulfilling (Thomson)
>   AB367 X O Sion, haste   106630
>
> O Sion, haste, thy mission high fulfilling (Thomson)
>   A261; B474; D249; G475; [etc]; AB367   107557
>
> O Zion, haste, thy mission (Thomson) G475 X O Sion,
>   haste, thy mission   107887
>
> Publish glad tidings (Thomson) R O Sion, haste, thy mission high fulfilling   108398

And here is the relevant quotation from Index II: Authors and first first lines:

> Thomson, Mary Ann, 1834-1923 O Sion, haste, thy mission;
>   X106630 O Christian, haste; X107887 O Zion, haste;
>   R108398 Publish glad tidings

- - - - - - - -

Question: Where can I find the hymn beginning "O Zion, haste"?

Answer: Find the words alphabetically in Index I. The hymn is reported to be in Book G, as #475; the author is Thomson. Because G is the only book named, this is the first time the phrase (as you quote it) is found. You are told that other hymnals quote it differently. G475 is also mentioned at the standard entry which follows the X. (Refer to serial number for the information). Notice that all except one of the serial numbers are repeated in each index.

Question: Who wrote the hymn "O Sion, haste", and does it

begin that way?

Answer: Find the phrase alphabetically, as above. The auth-
or is Thomson. Scan the Thomsons in Index II until you
find that one credited with the first line fragment. The
information you wish follows the author's name and dates.

Question: Mary Ann Thomson wrote something that has "Sion"
in the first line. Can you find the poem for me?

Answer: Scan the entry "Thomson, Mary Ann", at Index II.
If the word appears, refer to one of the hymnals noticed.
If the word had not appeared, reference to either
Julian or to the Judson Concordance may be helpful.
Concordances to secular poetry are useful in identifying
poetry by well-known writers who usually have some
religious writings to their credit.

Indexes III, IV, and V

The third, fourth, and fifth indexes are concerned with the melodies,
the refrains, their variant opening melodies and refrains; the names
of those melodies (these names are here called tune names); the
composers; and the hymnals within which these tunes by these composers may be found quickly.

Here are six related quotations from Index III: Tune names
and variants, with citations:

Carol melody, 14th c (Hohenfurth ms. 1410) X Quem
pastores   1546

Dearmer (Hohenfurth ms.) X Quem pastores   2427

Quem pastores (Hohenfurth ms.) [DMSMFSLSR, MFSFM]
A35; B506; C506; E543; F456; N195; O500; Q90; W349;
[etc]   8754

-----. V [DMSMFSLSR, MSFMR] Q90   8754a

Quem pastores laudavere (Hohenfurth ms. 1410)
X Quem pastores   8755

Shepherds left their flocks astraying (Hohenfurth ms. 1410)
X Quem pastores   9966

And this is the relevant quotation from Index IV: Composers and
tune names:

<u>Hohenfurth ms.</u> 1410 Quem pastores; X1546 Carol melody,
14c; X2427 Dearmer; X8755 Quem pastores laudavere;
X9966 Shepherds left their flocks astraying

Finally this, from <u>Index V: Melodies,</u> a systematic index:

        DMSMFSLSR,MFSFM   8754
        DMSMFSLSR,MSFMR   8754a

- - - - - -

Question: In what hymnal is the melody, "Quem pastores",
printed?

Answer: Find the tune name, "Quem pastores", in Index
III. The information identifies seventeen hymnals, with
the number of the melody in each; as, A35 means
Book A, #35.

Question: "Quem pastores" is sometimes called "Quem pastores
laudavere". Are there other names?

Answer: From Index III, the source of the melody is <u>Hohen-
furth ms.</u>, 1410. Look alphabetically in Index IV for
this source name, and then again alphabetically for
"Quem pastores". The several names are given, but not
the books making use of these names.

Question: Does "Quem pastores" have a refrain?

Answer: Refer to the answer just above. There are several
X serial numbers; but no R serial number. This indicates
that no refrain is associated.

Question: Does "Quem pastores" always have the same notation?

Answer: The information in Index III includes one ditto
entry, and the symbol V followed by a melody. Examine
the melody at #8754 and at #8754a. There is a slight
difference. This variant reading may be examined in
Q90.

Question: How do I use Index V?

Answer: A long answer is required for this.

<u>Index V: Melodies,</u> a systematic index is arranged alphabetically by
a special symbolic alphabet, that of the syllables of the diatonic
scale which reads: Do, Re, Mi, Fa, Sol, La, Ti, Do, Re, etc.
In this book the syllables are recorded as D R M F S L T D R,

etc. No adjustment is made for low and high positions.

This diatonic scale has seven primary syllabic names and tones, but it has additional intermediate values which are produced by lowering or raising the basic tones by a musical half step. Lowering is indicated by use of the symbol ♭ (flat), and raising is indicated by use of the symbol # (sharp). Both lowered and raised notational values occur in hymn tunes. However <u>Hymns</u> and <u>tunes:</u> <u>an index</u> NEVER USES FLATS. Instead, a conversion table has been followed in translating the printed notes to the related raised, or sharped, rendering. It reads:

♭ D	becomes	T	♭ S	becomes	F#	
♭ R	"	D#	♭ L	"	S#	
♭ M	"	R#	♭ T	"	L#	
♭ F	"	M	♭ D	"	T	etc

When using Index V, the tonal value of D is low; and that of T is high. Low values precede high values; and a low tone repeated precedes any mention of the next higher tone. All tones with sharps (#) follow the simple tone, and precede any mention of the tone next above. Within Index V the readings range from DDDDDDD DDDTRD, LLL to TTTDTLTDR, DRMLTDR. If this were converted to numerals (values One to Seven) it would be the range from 1,111, 111,111, 721,666 to 7,771,767,121,236,712. No attempt or intention is made to perform the conversions. For non-musicians the example is more clear than the unfamiliar symbolic language of DoReMi.

> Question: What melody is this: MFSMRDLS, DRMD, FSL
> when written in syllables?

> Answer: Index V begins with the D entries; continues with R; then to the MD sections. Move ahead to MR ... to MM ... on to MF ... to MFM ... to MFS. Repeat this procedure until you find the proper sequence. It will be serially numbered 12058.

> Refer to Index III; serial number 12058 should be identified by the tune name "Westridge" by Shaw; and the identical syllabic reading should be repeated as from the question above and from Index V. Four books contain this tune. Further information may be secured by reference to "Shaw" in Index IV.

The question just above may require more complicated identification
if neither the inquirer nor the respondent can translate the musical
sounds into syllables of the diatonic scale. The simplest recourse
is to go to a piano with an illustration such as the one in Appendix
E. Pick out the tune by using (if possible) no black keys whatsoever.
If you know the names of the piano keys, there will be little trouble
reporting the melody in names of the keys struck. The schedule
for conversion of notes on the piano to the symbolic musical language will help you create the tune in the form reported by Index
V. After the conversion, proceed as indicated just above. Trace the
serial number in Index III; find a hymnal in which it is contained;
have someone play it for you. Good luck!

Back to the "Quem pastores" illustration, for more ques-
tions:

Question: A melody is going around in my head. In syllables
it is Do Mi Sol Mi Fa Sol La Sol Re, Mi Fa Sol Fa
Mi. Can I find it in print through these indexes?

Answer: Proceed by first changing the full syllable names
to initials. Continue by tracing from DDD ... to DRD
... to DMD ... Thence to DMSM ... Serial number
8754 should be indicated.
Return to Index III, to #8754. You are back at "Quem
pastores". But this time the search began with melody
only, and led to the discovery of books in which the
melody was printed, to the source of the tune, to its
tune names as here standardized, and to the cluster of
variants associated with it.

Question: In this new hymnal, tune names are not used.
Help me find information. The tune is in the key with
neither sharps nor flats.

Answer: Refer to the illustration in Appendix D for basic tone
names in all keys. Record the melody by using the syllable names reduced to the single initial letter. (That
is, Do becomes D, Re becomes R, etc.)
Assume the record reads: DMSSSLSFMRDD,DMS;
and the supposed source is "1st publ. Paris Proces-
cessional, 1697".
The first approach will be to verify existence of this
source in Index IV. There is no mention, so another
method must be used.

Use Index V, and identify the tune through tracing the recorded syllables. You should reach #166. Turn, at Index III, to #166: "Adoro te devota", a Benedictine plainsong, Mode 5. Specific hymnals containing it are mentioned; and entries #167-168 give further information.

Question: Sometimes melodies are written in Key of F (one flat), and sometimes in Key of G (one sharp).. Does this make any difference in the syllables?

Answer: None. "Leoni", a Jewish traditional melody is found in many hymnals (as at AD70) written in Key of A Flat (four flats); but in others (as at AL25) written in Key of A (three sharps). This is a difference of a half tone throughout. Melodically there is no difference in the sequences. The tune is the same tune -- only the physical measurements of tonality vary. And singability! Church musicians are accepting the fact that congregations expect low-pitched songs in their church books.

In summary:

1. Citation symbols in Indexes I and III refer by letters to the hymnals, and by numbers to the specific items within these specific hymnals, to the place at which the words (or the melody, respectively) by any form of its words (or its melody, and under any tune name) are printed.

2a. Reference symbols include X, which in Index I refers from a non-standard first line and its single first identified citation to the standard form, and in Index III from a non-standard tune name without citation to the standard tune name;

2b. Reference symbols include R, which in Indexes I and III present the standard reading of the refrain of the hymn or of the melody without citations. These are the same as the citations to the standard first lines and melodies, and need not be repeated. Also;

2c. Reference symbols include V which, in Index III only, identifies a variant melody or a variant melodic refrain and cites its first appearance only. Reference to the standard readings is unnecessary because the tune name remains constant, and the variants file immediately below the standard forms.

3. Though but the first appearance of any hymn or melody in a hymnal is recorded, others within the book may be identified

by use of the hymnal's own indexes (in all but a very few instances. Cf. the Chart in Appendix G).

4. Indexes II and IV serve to gather all the primary sources (here defined as the author or composer originally responsible for the words or the music, respectively); and those intermediate sources responsible for renderings which vary considerably from the standard form and which frequently (but not always) appear under words, melody, or tune name differing from the standard form.

5. The symbols of reference -- R, V, and X -- are used correlatively within Indexes I-II and Indexes III-V. They cannot be used between these two sets of indexes.

6. Indexes I-IV are alphabeted by the roman alphabet, using all letters, in simple word-by-word order.

7. Indexes I and III use initial articles in all languages and observe these articles in alphabeting (contrary to usual library practice).

8. Indexes II and IV may use the initial articles, but they are totally disregarded (following the usual library practice).

9. Citations in Indexes I and III are to the "Hymnals analyzed".

10. References by R, V, and X in Indexes II and IV are to the relative serial numbers in Indexes I and III.

11a. Indexes I and II provide virtually identical information, but by inverted approaches. The serial numeration of Index I is used for reference purposes in Index II. Citations within specific hymnals are recorded only in Index I;

11b. Accompanying Index V (arranged by the symbolic alphabet of the syllables of the diatonic musical scale) are both Indexes III and IV, referring respectively to the tune names and to the composers. The melody is repeated in Indexes III and V. The source (composer) is repeated in Indexes III and IV, The citations are indicated but once, in Index III. The serial numbers are repeated in Indexes III and V; and are used for reference purposes only in Index IV.

12. In other words, everything within the entire sequence of five indexes can be approached in two ways except the item numbers within the individual hymnals. To have repeated these would have caused undue and unnecessary increase in the bulk of the book.

TABLE OF CONTENTS

I
HYMNS AND TUNES

Hymns and tunes: an index is a catalog to congregational song found
in seventy-eight hymnals officially adopted for use at public worship
during some part of this 20th century, chiefly in the English language, chiefly containing both words and music, and always repre-
senting United Kingdom and North American Jewish-Christian institutions.

Specifically it is an attempt to (1) identify hymns (the poems)
published in these seventy-eight hymnals analyzed, to (2) associate
each with its author (source), and with the variant readings or segments of the hymn, to (3) locate the printed texts within these books
which were used during this 20th century through December 31, 1965.
It further attempts to (4) identify melodies (the sung tune) used as
hymn tunes published in these same seventy-eight hymnals analyzed
(always exclusive of books symbolized by letters BT, BU, and BW
which contain no music), to (5) associate each tune with its composer
(source), and with the variant readings or segments of the tune, to
(6) identify the names associated with these tunes, no matter the
variety and number of such names, and to (7) locate the scores of
these melodies within these books which were used during the 20th
century through December 31, 1965.

Indirectly this catalog forms a literary first-line and author index
to the poetry of these hymnals -- a segment of poetry whose analysis is incidental to secular first-line and author indexes; and a corresponding tune name, melodic, and composer index to the scores
within the hymnals -- a segment of musicology whose published
analysis is almost non-existent.

Further and indirectly, each of these five indexes may be helpful
for identification of materials in books not here analyzed; it may
clarify texts and tunes not yet properly associated; and provide a
basis for further clarification of the sources here stated as standard

but about which there remains irresolution.

There is no place within this introduction, and no place within the indexes, to pass judgment. Occasional comments are made after extremely close reading of these hymnals by a librarian who, for almost thirty years, has been closely associated with college and university students and who, for a bit more than one-third of that time, was organist in small parishes.

As a guide to bio-bibliography, by the simple inclusion of full personal names and dates of birth and death, dates of individual hymns and tunes (especially when source dates are not available), publication dates of anthologies from which hymns have been borrowed, this index provides a greater cumulation than any individual hymnal indexes can offer. It brings to the present time many facts cited in Julian's Dictionary of hymnology; and it blends the information presented by Baker's Biographical dictionary with that within the hymnals.

Confusion is recognized in some of the early books cited as sources. To untangle the gesang-buchs, the geistliche gesang-buchs, harps, and companions -- and then to do likewise with the publications issued by see and diocese, sometimes cited by diocesan name and other times by given form name as breviary, ritual, and sometimes by the compiler -- would have been an impossible task. The same may be said for traditional materials. Where does German traditional cease and Swiss tune begin; when does an English tune become a Devon melody; and when did a White spiritual cease being an English traditional and become an American folk hymn? It has seemed more important to do the preliminary sorting ên masse than to make tiny delineation for a tiny number of these items.

Information is more readily accessible on the literary portion of any hymnal than on its musical portion. Though they have not limited their functions to the hymns, apparently both the Hymn Society of America and the British Hymn Society are more involved in the literary studies, the hymnody, than in the music as they proceed in their Dictionary of American hymnology (under preparation) and revision of Julian's Dictionary of hymnology (under preparation).

Hopefully the search in each aspect of congregational song is now a little less tedious. It is certainly not ended.

Hymns and tunes: an index could be compiled and completed only because the hymnals analyzed were immediately in hand; and a few very hard-fact additional references close by.

All books indexed were secured rather easily except those cited as C, BI, and BJ. Book C was at the organ bench in little Saints Andrew and Stephen Mission Church (Episcopal), Douglas, Georgia, where the project was begun. On the day this editing was completed it was received as part of the collection! Book BI was on long loan from Perkins School of Theology Library, Southern Methodist University. Book BJ was also on long loan -- from the Chicago Theological Seminary Library, University of Chicago. Strangely, copies are in everybody's hands while the books are in official institutional adoption; and as suddenly they disappear from the face of the local earth. To "missions", summer camps, local less wealthy sister congregations, etc.   -- but not to the book market, not to the specialized dealers, and rarely are they retained within the family more than a single generation!

Although this working collection is not available for public use, copies may be consulted in music libraries at colleges and universities which emphasize choral work, and at some of the larger theological seminaries where church music is a major study. Princeton Seminary's Benson Collection has many of these books; Yale, Chicago, Union (in New York), Catholic University of America, Washington Cathedral, and the Library of Congress may be mentioned. Smaller seminary libraries will offer some books, especially those related to the immediate denomination and its close associates. One library, Andover-Harvard, had received sometime in 1964 fifty boxes of hymnals from another of the Harvard libraries which (according to a letter under their date June 22, 1965) they doubt they can "get around to processing ... anytime soon. "

Few public libraries will provide these books. Hymnals are considered -- at least by librarians -- to be too closely associated with religion to be included in the humane materials of society in community. Church and parish and temple libraries will have some books. Church organists, choir directors, ministers of music will have personal collections or will know of choir-owned copies in the neighborhood. Music librarians will be collectors, especially of the more highly liturgical and poetically sophisticated books. Denominational archives will have sample copies, occasional second and third copies for consultation, but few copies for home use.

Here, then, is a large body of literature one time plentiful as were the carrier pigeons, as quickly gone: part of the heritage of man in society -- man, perhaps at his humblest and his greatest moments, worshiping and praising his Maker.

A glance at the Symbolic Citation List of books indexed disposes one to believe they have been chosen at great random: It is hoped that this is not fact. They have come to the compiler's attention at various times, have been analyzed in denominational blôc when possible; but it was far more important to do the indexing than to be dilatory because one of the members of the Presbyterian (or other) family of churches had not yet made the book. Such delay would postpone any compilation.

Included are the full music editions of hymnals (i.e., books of congregational song) officially published by religious bodies in the Judaeo-Christian tradition, and approved for use at the chief services of worship by these bodies since 1900 and through December 31, 1965;

Also companions, or handbooks, to two of the hymnals: selected because of the wealth of additional poetry included in its original language;

Also three student hymnals, representative of the worship of the younger generation at university and college;

Also the tri-liturgical Army and Navy hymnal;

Also the Oxford Book of carols and the Yattendon hymnal, both representative of books used within the Anglican Communion and of the new materials (or old materials discovered anew) which are being incorporated into more and more general hymnals within and without the Anglican Communion;

Also one book without musical notation, Ausbund: notation does not exist. This is said to be the "oldest hymn book officially in use by any church in America," dating from 1570 and little changed, according to The handbook to the Mennonite hymnary (p. xxx). It is commonly said in the Lancaster County (Pennsylvania) musical circles that the Amish plainchant continues the 16th century singing tradition more truly than does institutional singing that is far more sophisticated.

Usually several distinctly different hymnals have been chosen for a single denominational family. Range in date of publication has been a selection factor.

These hymnals bear Canadian, United States, and United Kingdom imprints; they are principally in the English language. Ausbund was originally prepared for the South German and Swiss Mennonites, and is today somewhat removed from the idiom commonly called "Pennsylvania Dutch." Several Catholic hymnals contain the Latin text to hymns used at the Mass in addition to many simpler hymns for lesser services and meetings.

The oldest of the truly 20th century books is the Moravian Offices of worship and Hymns (3d ed., rev. and enl.) from 1891.

The newest published hymnal is Anglican hymn book, released 30 June, 1965.

And finally, there are included the contents of an unpublished hymnal. Editor Carlton R. Young provided the Report of the Hymnal Committee of the Commission on Worship to the 1964 General Conference of the Methodist Church. By closely comparing the 1935 edition (The Methodist hymnal) with the indexes and contents of this Report, a record of the whole new book has been made. In this instance only, a book symbol (BZ) is used without hymn number. Sorry, but we could do no other.

Hopefully, and despite an apparently complicated set of indexing determinants, you can find the poem or its author, the song or its composer, the name of the tune and the very book in which it has been printed. If this be true the book will have served its purpose. Many references are given; many citations are recorded: all of them within these books which represent a generous cross section of western man's religious institutions at worship sometime during the first two-thirds of the Twentieth Century. If your question refers to the hymn or the tune used by a congregation at high worship (where books in official adoption are invariably used) it is probable you will find its answer. The denominations or faiths included are:

Amish (BU)
Anglican Communion (U.S.A., Canada, U.K., Commonwealth countries) (A, B, C, D, E, F, X, BG, BJ, BV)
Army and Navy (U.S.A.) (AH)
Baptists (U.S.A., U.K.) (Z, AT, AU, AV, BY)
Carolers (BG)
Catholic (Bl, BM, BN, BO, BP, BQ, BS)
Christian Church (Z)
Christian Reformed (AI, AJ)
Christian Science (BE)
Church of the Brethren (AR, AS)
Congregationalists (AF)
Disciples (Z)
Evangelical-United Brethren (AE)
General Church of the New Jerusalem (BI)
Jewish (Central Conference) (BH)
Lutherans (U.S.A. only) J, K, L, M, N, O, P, Q, AA, BT)
Mennonites (AW, AX, AY, BW, also BU)
Methodists (U.S.A. only) (G, H, I, BZ)
Moravians (AZ, BA)
Mormons (BC)
New Church (BR)
Presbyterians (U.S.A., Canada, U.K., Commonwealth countries) (R, S, T, U, V, W, AG, AM, AP)
Protestant Episcopal (A, B, C, D)
Quakers (BK)
Reformed (AK, AO, BF)
Seventh Day Adventists (BB)
Students (University groups) (Y, AB, AC)
Unitarian-Universalist (AN, AQ, BD, BX)
Unaffiliated (AD)
United Church of Canada (AL)

II

THE HYMNAL: SEVERAL OF ITS CHARACTERISTICS

Though it would be difficult to secure statistics, I would believe that the telephone directory is the most frequently used reference book in the western world, and the church hymnal is the second most used reference book. Falling into the natural "directory" category, the telephone book serves countless uses beyond that of indicating telephone number. Falling into the natural "anthology" category, the hymnal has uses far beyond that of presenting hymns used at worship services.

The hymnal I knew as a child, Book of worship (L), contains the liturgy and prayer book materials for public and private worship, the Augsburg Confession, and the Formula for the Government and Discipline of the Evangelical Lutheran Church, as revised in 1888. The hymnal portion in this full music edition begins on p. 267 and closes on p. 781. Its pp. 745-81 contain: Index of subjects, Index of first lines of hymns, Index of first lines of all stanzas [including the first], Alphabetical index of tunes, and Metrical index of tunes. The authors and composers were neglected.

This pattern of prayer book and hymnal bound together (either with or without distributive subtitle pages) has been fairly common in certain traditions. The Liturgy and the Offices of worship and Hymns (AZ) contains 119 pages of liturgies, thirty-two of Offices, and 479 pages of hymns on which are printed 1523 numbered hymns and additional chants.

Liturgy and hymnal for the use of the General Church of the New Jerusalem (BI) is far more complete. Its 420 pages of liturgy, 150 pages of hymns, and its twenty-seven anthems (13 in English, 11 in Hebrew with text and tune reading properly from right to left, and 2 in Greek) indicates the broadest language range of any book analyzed.

Hymns for the celebration of life (AQ) is arranged in three distinct sections, using a major title page and two subtitle pages -- each featuring a tree-of-life design. The first section has 327 hymns with tunes; the second numbered 328-558 is called "Celebrations and praise", being readings; then follow sixty pages of "Notes on hymns, tunes, and readings," and a final thirty-nine pages of various indexes.

Anglican hymn book (BV) has no liturgic material, and only eleven Amens. However, as the Hymnal for the celebration of life (AQ) is exquisite in its entire form and text, so is this in its sharp black print on bright white light-weight opaque paper, its modern layout at the "Acknowledgments" and its wealth of information displayed for easy access at the indexes. In the style long familiar to instrumental music, the metrical index gives the opening score for women's voices.

Trinity hymnal (AM) is dignified, simple, academically correct, It pursues the uses of the Orthodox Presbyterians in terminology, Biblical quotation at the head of each hymn, inclusion of a great many Psalms in meter and a large number of gospel songs. Always, however, in clear and unadorned typography, abounding in quarter notes. Guide lines are centered at the foot of the facing pages.

One pair of books (AZ and BA), both Moravian, shows a continuity of musical thinking which began in mid-18th century with the Grimm and Gregor patterns of numbering all tunes of a single meter by a single identification number, and the various tunes designated by an accompanying letter. In this index there are citations to "Gregor's 217th Metre-B" and to "Grimm's 253d Metre-A". Hymnals preceding these two had used the system, the choirs and musicians and people were accustomed to it. When Book BA was being edited, the numeration was continued, as secondary; a tabular schedule was included to show related tunes; but -- and in the fashion of the 1920s -- the tune name took precedence over the metre number.

A similar intercoding is indicated in English hymnal (E), p. xxxxi, with its parent volume which has not been indexed. However, no recent U.S. publications illustrate this kind of continuity. Rather there has seemed to be deliberate change for the sake of change. Whether the 1935 and the 1966 Methodist books (G and BZ) will be intercoded cannot be stated. The Report (BZ) which is representative of the 1966 volume does contain much related matter, but for purposes of compilation and not for purposes of exposition to the congregations. Certainly in this pair the intention to return Wesley's hymns to the literature of congregational song is illustrated.

An interesting comparison is the study of books prepared by large committees or commissions, and others prepared by a very small number of editors under guidance of their chief. The Rev. Canon Percy Dearmer edited and had published numerous hymnals. When his Songs of praise (X) came in hand the acknowledgements had a peculiar ring: hymns cited as written by persons known by initial only, and the initials sounded like the letters symbolizing names of books! A letter to Oxford University Press confirmed suspicions: Most of the initials referred to hymns by the Canon himself. There had come to be so many over the years that he hesitated to publish the fact. Now, as this Songs of praise (X) is being reprinted the Press is publishing the author's name.

The music editors of Songs of praise (X) were Ralph Vaughan and Martin Shaw. They used a joint pseudonym, also an initialism: S.M.W.V.R.

Small committees and lone editors show yet another kind of modesty: hesitation to indicate their own or their immediate superior's birth dates. This may be fine for the moment, but it creates a genuine nuisance after a quarter century or more has passed. People wonder who these folks were, when they lived, and at what point in time and place to set them.

The institutional church is somewhat in agreement that a hymnal will be viable for approximately twenty-five years. Another point of general agreement is its size: approximately 600 hymns, with sufficient tunes to serve the usual needs of the congregations. Some books are lavishly supplied with tunes; some are meager; some use a few melodies over and over again; others rarely repeat a tune. The Psalter (AJ), for example, repeated few melodies.

Influence of one book on another can be seen in several pairs of books: Yattendon hymnal (BJ) strongly influenced the American Student hymnal (Y); Oxford Book of carols (BG) seemed reflected in it. I was a student of the editor of American Student hymnal and of some of his co-editors at the time this book was being compiled and published, and the excitement about the Oxford University Press's hymnology contributions was generally known. Book BG had had more evident influence on The Hymnal 1940 (A), Service book and Hymnal (J), Book of praise (X), and Anglican hymn book (BV). Passage of an additional ten or twelve years' time caused the greater use of carols.

Among the older books, those which were prepared by and for institutional churches having headquarters in the same city were uncommonly similar. The Book of worship (L) and Book of worship (AO) were used by two major bodies whose congregations regularly used the same places of worship on alternate Sundays: the Lutheran and the Reformed congregations of Bucks, Berks, Lebanon and adjacent counties of Pennsylvania. Headquarters for both were in Philadelphia, local congregational communities were almost identical -- certainly the Sunday Schools were attended by the same people -- and historically both had similar German antecedents. The liturgies in these hymnals vary, the confessions vary, but the hymns are from one tradition and not from two. Hymnal and Liturgies (BA), also from the region but specifically from the city of Bethlehem, Pennsylvania, likewise bears almost as strong resemblance to these Lutheran and Reformed hymnals as it does to its own predecessor (AZ) -- simply because of the cross-fertilization of locale.

Contrast the texts of the Baptist hymn book (BY) and any of the Anglican books. Now contrast it with any of the Baptist books from an American press. The relationship between the British volumes will be close, though doctrinal differences be great; the relationship between the Baptist books on both sides of the Atlantic will be slight, though the doctrinal views be similar.

Another comparison may be made among all books coming from the continental reformation institutional churches (i.e., excluding the Anglican tradition). Continental tradition weighted the hymnals with stately music, with German or Scandinavian hymns -- whose translations show variously effective style; and they use little 20th century material. Until, of course, you come to Service book and hymnal (J) which profited greatly from the editorial searches made by the people who did The Hymnal 1940 (A), Hugo E. Gibson (deceased) told me one day that the "Lutherans would like to have been the creators of The Hymnal 1940", a statement he had received from one of the Evangelical Lutheran leaders (also deceased). They made of their own hymnal (J)a fine book. Its solidity and scholarship is in sharp contrast to books symbolized as K, L, M, N, O, and P. The Lutheran hymnal (Q) is from the Missouri Synod tradition, and is parallel rather than in contrast to J.

Issue of Hymnal of Christian unity (BL) in 1964 shows yet another coming together. It carries the nihil obstat of Rt. Rev. Ignatius T. Kelly, censor deputatus, and imprimatur of the Bishop of Toledo, George J. Rehring, S.T.D., dated April 24, 1964. On the list of individuals whose assistance was gratefully acknowledged are Rev. Leonard W. Ellenwood, who was chiefly responsible for the Hymnal 1940, Companion (not indexed), Rabbi Elliot D. Rosenstock, and the research staff of the British Museum! Most certainly the usual Roman Catholic congregation would, at first, be at rather a complete loss when many of the hymns were sung; and just as certainly congregations from the liturgical Protestant traditions would be quite at home.

One meets all sorts of folks in a bibliography: personal friends, teachers, community acquaintances. Within Hymns and tunes: an index there are musical giants: Wagner, Beethoven, Brahms, the folk tunes of England and Germany, Negro spirituals, and at least 131 of the melodies which Bach used in his chorales. Probably all of the melodies in the first Protestant hymnal, published in Wittenberg, 1524, are included.

Poetically there are the Brownings, Edmund Spenser, Lord Tennyson, Christina Rossetti, Jan Struther, Robert Bridges, Goethe, and Robert Frost. Translations by John Mason Neale from the classical Greek and Latin, and by Catherine Winkworth from the German are legion. Unfortunately, because the intermediate author is not recognized in the indexes, these latter are apparently neglected.

The most unexpected event occurred on the evening of 23 April 1964. It was the 400th anniversary of Shakespeare's birth, and one of his sonnets was found: "Poor soul, the centre of my sinful earth." It is the only truly Shakespearean poem discovered, though a year later the song he quotes in Act 2 of As you like it was found: "Blow, blow, thou winter wind."

It might be true that the song of the congregation at worship will be the place where true brotherhood will begin. Jew, Catholic, Protestant can sing together all of "The God of Abraham praise," except the doxology which tends to be trinitarian rather than unitarian; all can sing together, "O God, our help in ages past." Catholic and Protestant have, in the Hymnal of Christian unity, one hundred hymns mutually useful. The overtones found in Walter Chalmers Smith's "Immortal, invisible, God only wise," one of these hundred, are Vedantic. Inter-relations far beyond these suggested are frequent, and the books resulting from this hard musical and poetical thinking indicate that hymnologists and musicians pursue what is vital to their institutions' good.

In the manner of librarians critically examining books of reference, the hymnals were studied. (See Appendix G for details). Some important points may be considered in the light of these explanatory notes.

Title page, with authority symbol

"Authority" here means "auspices", either institutional or personal. Several books were sent to press without such identification, or with it stated vaguely. Most institutional approval is clearly indicated.

Table of contents

Usually complete. In several instances there was simply an outline of the hymns and no indication of preface, indexes, etc. Here and there a book showed weak editorial and press supervision through the evidence of the table of contents being printed on the verso (i. e. the left page) rather than recto page.

Sources fully acknowledged within the preface, or within its formal
  counterpart

Indicates a differentiation between those books which do, and do
not, give specific acknowledgement for use of all new and copyright
material somewhere within the formal preface or index section of
the hymnal. Generally speaking, those books which contain full acknowledgements were bibliographically more regular throughout. They
showed evidence of careful scholarship, and of steady editorial
supervision; citations were exact, names regularly spelled, and the
text of both hymn and tune had little alteration.

Birth and death dates of author and composer

Essential to either literary or musical studies are dates when the
texts were created. Humanly speaking, people like to know when
other folks lived. Tracing the elements of plainsong to its modern
adaptations, or of folksong to its modern form, is a bit easier if
dates are given to the intermediate renderings. Inclusion of this
element was seen to be one of the evidences of careful editing.

Hymns (Poetry): First line index

Few poems used as hymns have names. The substitute is the
opening phrase, or first line. Several of the early books contain indexes to first lines of all stanzas: a boon, but not fashionable at
mid-century.

Author index

That any book of poetry should be published without a list of the
men and women who wrote the poems is hard to understand! But
twenty of these hymnals (exclusive of Ausbund, some of whose authors are named within the hymn, and others not yet identified) lack
an author index.

Hymns of the historical faith

Intended as indication of the choice of strong theological and
doctrinal orientation in the hymnal; a trait more characteristic of
the 19th century books than of most of these indexed. Perhaps the
best illustration of change is the Hymnal of Christian unity (BL)
which bears the proper Catholic signatures and which is almost

totally like the hymnals coming from the highly liturgical non-Roman Catholic institutions.

Psalter in meter

Most books contain some Psalms in meter. "The Lord is my Shepherd", "All people that on earth do dwell", and others are so well-known that their Psalter origin is forgotten. This category implies a full or certainly moderate use of the Psalms from the Scottish Psalter, 1650, etc.

19th - 20th century hymns

In most books these dominate. The 19th century was the period when the English hymn waxed important over its European counterpart and predecessor. It was the century of great evangelistic crusades; of fine translators; and of the proletarian awakening. It was the century of missionary expansion around the world.

The corresponding social awakening of religious organizations in the 20th century is evident, especially, in hymnals representative of strong liturgical traditions.

Children's hymns named

That church musicians find words and tunes for use by children at worship, fitting properly into the scheme of the church hymnal, indicates the historic thesis that the literature for life's use must be learned early, repeated often. The profound need not be esoteric. It may be as simple as Hey's "Can you count the stars?"

Tunes (Music): Tune name index, alphabetical

This is the counterpart to a first line index. At the extremes of the Roman Catholic and the very evangelistic-fundamental sects using gospel songs, this information and this index have not been traditional. A tendency towards more general use is evident in such books as The Hymnal (AE) and Hymnal of Christian unity. (BL).

Tune name index, metrical

Probably the least used index of any contained in any hymnal is this one! Congregations are musically handicapped, they are outspoken with their desire to sing the familiar words to the familiar tunes. Few in any congregation realize that the metrical index is prepared to discourage singing the familiar combinations. Fewer people realize that this index is indeed a classification of the poetry (hymn) by the number of feet in its line, and number of lines in its stanza. Still fewer do anything about it. Book AZ, the earlier Moravian hymnal index, uses the poetical/musical meter as its guide to general arrangement. The economy thus achieved permitted publication of a great anthology of hymns: there was absolutely no place for reprinting even one tune. Grimm and Gregor, mid-18th century, introduced this practice.

Anglican hymn book (BV) is the most helpful of any book musically. The metrical index (1) names and describes each meter, (2) records the tune name, (3) records the item numbers of hymns set to this tune, (4) indicates presence of a descant, faux bourdon, or special setting, (5) quotes several measures of the opening score for soprano and also voices, and (6) names item numbers where the tune is used in a different key. This innovation may encourage congregational participation, and use of variant melodies to the hymn. Surely it is far easier to sing a sample tune, than to sing a list of words called "tune names".

Composer index

Why should not mention of the musical source be just as technically and ethically essential as mention of literary source? Comparison of the record shows close association of these indexes in the books examined.

Plainsongs included

Tally is as accurate as modern settings and notation allow it to be. Many of the tunes which Luther and Walther used in their first books, issued in Wittenberg in 1524, were derived from plainsongs. Little trace remains of them in the congregational hymn, though a great deal is evident in liturgical portions of hymnals. English chant dominates the service music "at the back of the book." When Hymnal 1940 (A) introduced four settings for the Holy Communion (one of which was Gregorian from the 9th-12th centuries) tradition was broken. And when the trail-blazing Hymnal of Christian unity (BL) included Isaac Watts', "O God, our help in ages past" reverse tradition was broken. "Of the Father's love begotten" has been part of Protestant Christmas song so long that people do not associate it with plainsong!

Some of these crooked places are being made straight. Melodies from early temple and church are finding their ways back to the books.

Reformation tunes

Men active at this period in the Church's history were steeped in traditional learning and wanted the best retained. From Luther's small 1524 hymnal containing eight hymns (four by Luther, three by Paul Speratus, and one probably by Justus Jonas) and the Walther Geistliche Gesangkbuchleyn with five-part music, through the years of Bourgeois' Psalter music to about 1650 is the era implied here.

Hymnals of this 20th century with heavy liturgical and reformation heritage are the books which contain Reformation tunes in great abundance: Lutheran, Anglican, Calvinist. The Yattendon hymnal (BJ) and The Lutheran hymnal (Q) have influenced other volumes.

Folk tunes, all cultures

Folk music is quite old, somewhat weather-beaten and healed of its weaknesses; it has no known composer; and it is of the people as an act of celebration.

"Innsbruck" was a folk tune, arranged by numerous musicians -- including Bach. We are far removed from the words originally associated with it. Closer is "Harlech" and some congregations may find it difficult to use this latter melody as praise to God in song.

The prison songs, work songs, soldiers' marching songs, boating songs, and hymns of troubled people everywhere carry their own weight as part of the song of temple and church. So with the songs of the land, of the nursery, of the natural events of living: childhood, courtship, love and marriage, babies, the infant and puberty rites, old age, death. Oxford book of carols (BG) is to the fore in this literature, and the American student hymnal (Y) includes much of the same spirit.

From the U.S.A., folk contributions have come through the Appalachian mountain musicians (mostly probably almost directly from the English immigrants of many years ago), from the Southwest (none of which is apparently herein), and from the American Negro. This latter music is rushing into books headlong.

Gospel songs

Folk song and gospel song are closely associated. The primary differences are (1) age, or date of composition and (2) intention, or use of the text and tune.

The gospel song is an evangelistic teaching device, easily learned, with emotional and sometimes fearful overtones, and with very close association of words and tune; it is of recent known authorship (though frequently the writing has been done by some of the little people whose poems or tunes are purchased and published by evangelistic agents -- either anonymously or under the names of the editor); and it is intended to encourage man to praise God through his offering of honor and worship.

The intention of the folk song is celebration. This opens its way for use in the liturgical tradition. Several journalists exercised displeasure at exclusion of "Nearer my God to Thee" from Anglican Hymn book (BV). Inclusion of "The holly and the ivy" was not heralded! The latter is pure folk song, celebration of birth, one of the wonders of life; the former can boast no such wonderment.

Again, this index is passing no judgment; the examples mentioned are given as examples only.

Editorial policies, etc.: Prefatory statement on congregational song

Except as the institutional church's stated attitude towards participation by the congregation in its song, it is anomalous to find a course of lessons in "how to sing" within a hymnal. Liturgy and hymnal (BI) devotes pages 629-32 to this purpose.

Other books include general musical directions; liturgical directions for best use of the hymns presented; and several hymnals make historical statements about hymnody within the immediate denomination. This may be presented in an enlarged preface, or separately. Any of these items indicate jurisdictional interest in congregational participation.

Specialties of the book

Certain committees, while cumulating the materials for the hymnals, have studiedly or inadvertantly accumulated materials of interest to themselves. The notes, Nos. 1-30, accompanying the chart indicate some of these special features which are published and which are among the peculiarly useful specialties librarians frequently require.

Liturgical section

Institutional worship, as with all institutional activity, includes some formally organized services. The Mass is the largest and the most complex. Stage follows stage in regularly ordered steps. Variations are permitted occasionally. Some of the hymnals examined contain these elements of public worship which are regularly the responsibility of the congregation. A portion of this material is sung, a portion is spoken; some of it may be either sung or spoken.

The liturgical materials are: responsive readings (biblical and other), canticles, portions or the whole of the Mass (by any name: Holy Communion, Lord's Supper, Eucharist, Mass); responses to prayers or lessons; certain ritual acts. However, if the whole book of worship is included (and only this whole book, with its separate title page, etc.) in this category it is considered a "bound-with" book and is not tallied. An example would be the one-book edition of the Book of Common prayer and The Hymnal 1940. Only The Hymnal 1940 is considered herein.

Prayer book section (or substitute)

Reread the paragraph just above.

If, within the regulation hymnal, there are full services of worship (no matter how brief they be) this is implied within the category. The Brethren hymnal (AR) includes several brief litanies. A litany is a complete, though short, service; it is not part of traditional Church of the Brethren worship. It belongs to be counted here.

In contrast, most of the books coming from the old German or Scandinavian tradition do contain almost complete prayer books, and certain of the rituals too. Those descending from Swedenborgian origins (BI and BR), from Unitarian and Universalist origins (AN,

AQ, BD, and BX) contain the prayer books. So does Our parish prays and sings (BM) which is in the vanguard of the people's books for use in Catholic worship.

The Anglican Communion, world-wide in its use of an almost-uniform liturgy, directs -- rather than dominates -- congregational song. It will be interesting to follow the Roman Catholic hymnals during the latter third of this century. Will they be in the Lutheran pattern (as Our parish prays and sings) or the Anglican (as Hymnal of Christian unity)?

Documents of the historical faith

Surveying Notes Nos. 31-41, the range of true document relating to the faith in its early years will be noticed. The Confessions are secular documents, and are thus part of the political history of Europe in the 16th-17th centuries. The Catechisms are educational documents, essential to the initiatory lessons for the children of the church. Both sorts are binding today.

THE INDEXES

Several definitions, quite descriptive, must accompany these indexes. They are:

> The Hymn (poem)
> The Authors/Composers
> The Tune name
> The Melody

Following the four definitive statements are formal descriptions of each index. They are:

> Index I: First lines and variants, with citations
> Index II: Authors and first lines
> Index III: Tune names, and variants, with citations
> Index IV: Composers and tune names
> Index V: Melodies, a systematic index

THE HYMN (POEM)

Hymn: a song of praise to God; specifically a metrical composition adapted to be sung in a religious service, sometimes distinct from psalm or anthem, as not being part of the text of the Bible. (O.U.D.)

Within certain limits this definition has been followed. Psalms and anthems which are printed apart from the hymns have been excluded from the Index. However a metrical version of a psalm or anthem is usually within the physical portion of the book which is called "hymnal", and is therefore indexed. The objective being identification (cataloging) of the contents of these hymnals, everything reasonably located within the section of congregational song has been included. Judgment as to whether or not they are songs of praise to God has not been passed.

Many changes are made to poems before they pass the editorial and theological scrutiny. Such simple variations as spelling cause confusion: Saviour, Savior; Sion, Zion; Alleluia, Hallelujah, Alleluja; and O, Oh. These can be arbitrarily controlled in an index (and they have been) by predetermining the spelling form.

It is impossible to control the entire text of a poem as the X references show. Which form of the first line (and only the first line as printed is here studied) was the original cannot be determined from this Index. Many variations are not here evident, because they come at second or later line.

Likewise no attempt can be made to certify that the lines are in proper order. As example, Edna St. Vincent Millay's poem, "Renascence" was used in the predecessor to AC, and began: "O God, thou canst not hide from me." In AC and in Y it was quoted; "O God, I cried, no dark disguise." And about thirty-five years later in AQ it is quoted as: "The world stands out on either side." The AQ first line stood at opening of third stanza in Y, and opening of second stanza in AC, as it had in the predecessor edition (to AC). These books were edited less than two city blocks apart -- but separated by thirty-five years in time. No wonder the careful editors to Hymns for the celebration of life remarked in a letter (dated January 11, 1965), "We wanted [the book] to be perfect. Ah, me."

A change made by John Wesley many years ago to Watts' metrical version of Psalm 90 cannot be discovered except by knowing the text. Watts wrote, "Our God, our help." Wesley changed it to read, "O God, our help." Julian says, ". . . of Watts's original it would be difficult to write too highly. It is undoubtedly one of his finest compositions, and his best paraphrase."

Refrains are frequently better known than the stanzas they accompany, perhaps because the refrain is repetitive. Sometimes it seems that the hymn is attached to the refrain, rather than the reverse. These irregularities are noticed. The regular first line is recorded with citations; but regular first line of the refrain is recorded without citations, but with a reference R to the parent text.

It is a pity that so many poems and melodies have been edited, garbles, altered, parodied, and emasculated -- and then inserted into the books used at public worship. This happens in all quarters, and without question. The originals are legally in the public domain, and theological prerogative is commonly accepted! Poet and organist did something to correct this in Yattendon hymnal (BJ), as later poet and musicians did in the Oxford Book of carols (BG). Fine scholarship has come into general acceptance, and hymnals have coincidentally become books to which both theologians and scholars can look with pride.

THE AUTHORS AND COMPOSERS

The author/composer is here defined as that person, institution, publisher, or tradition who wrote, approved, published, or transmitted to others the earliest verified text of the hymn or tune;

Editors, arrangers -- all intermediate people -- are rarely credited;

Translators are not considered, unless the work is by itself a peculiar contribution to the literature of hymnody in which event the translator is author of the version;

Compilers and hymnals are frequently cited as agents responsible for publication of the hymn or tune in some language or in some musical key;

Classical and anonymous sources (as Bible, Breviary, etc.) are accepted; the Anonymous category precedes both Index I and III normal alphabeting;

Traditional hymns and tunes are sorted by region or country of origin. "The holly and the ivy" is English traditional; whereas "Innsbruck" is associated with Heinrich Isaak's name, though he used a popular German melody as its foundation. Actually in this matter of tradition, had the decision been to become a purist there would have been added more confusion than aid. The course laid by the best hymnologists, editors, and musicians has been followed, and several fine scholars are represented by this collection of books. The part reserved for our share was that of the well-read librarian who catalogs specialist materials for the library patrons.

When the text was not a close variant -- as when the metrical rendering, the translation, or the editing caused a difference in more than a few words (but not necessarily in the quotation of the same stanzas) -- an entirely new entry was established under this second reading. Variants which became attached to this second reading were cited here only, and not with the version established as the first standard first line.

Non-English text of a hymn quoted is indexed within its alphabetic position as an independent standard first line. References follow the usual order.

No references are made from one standard reading to another standard reading, except through Index II; "Authors and first lines." Here it is hoped that these variations and versions may be collected practically -- and, hopefully, properly! Authorship and renderings of the early hymns has been especially difficult to establish consistently and accurately.

Serial numbers have little value within Index I alone. They are the means of cumulating the materials through Index II.

Reference from variants to accepted standard form of first line is given in Index I. Its converse, reference from accepted form of first line to the variants, is indicated in Index II. Similar reference pattern is established in the musical sections of this work.

In summary: First lines are always recorded, cited at first appearance within each hymnal; first line variants are always recorded, cited the first time they appear, reference (X) is made to the standard first line, citation is made at standard first line; refrains are never cited, but are always recorded and reference (R) to standard first line is made; refrain variants are cited at the time of first appearance, reference (X) is made to the standard refrain; occasionally an asterisk (*) after citation number indicates use of a variant refrain. All alphabeting is word-by-word.

THE TUNE NAME

As secular musical compositions have distinctive names, so does
the music to which congregations sing their hymns. The words used
to name the tune come from various sources, and are normally
quite overlooked by the singer.

Placed above the score (centered, to the left, or to the right
margin) will be such words as Wetterling, Deliverance, Lura, Message, Aethelwold, Second Parish, Old Hundred, St Petersburg,
Olivet, Down Ampney, Pange Lingua. They form a vocabulary that
is unexplored, and they offer hints of biographical worth: the bio-
graphy of the melody, or of the hymn and tune together, or of the
author and his assignment at the time of composition, or a friend
to whom it is dedicated, or an unused middle name (as "Othello",
by E.O. Excell); or pseudonymous name (as "El Nathan"). Perhaps
the greatest single source of tune names has been the first lines
of the hymns associated with the tunes as used at the several offices, or services, in the early and middle years of church history.
Another source has been the names of saints associated with the
composition of the melody, or with the hymn which it was to accompany. In Catholic circles the word Saint (usually reduced to St.)
is used with tune names; in communities where the word Saint is
looked on with less favor it may be omitted. This produces a variant for the indexer!

Mention has been made of the use of the first phrases of the
Latin office hymns as tune names. These are the old literature. A
still older musical literature is included within these indexes: that
which has come from Jewish tradition. Though only one Jewish
hymnal was included, Union hymnal (BH), plus a portion of another
Army and Navy Hymnal (AH), thirty-three distinct Jewish traditional
melodies are given. Many of these have long been associated with
Jewish feasts and fasts and holy days.

Another similar literature is that which has come from the
years known as the Reformation Period. A great number of these

xl

tunes are known by the first phrase of the usual hymn it accompanied, almost invariably in the German language. J.S. Bach used many of these tunes as the basis for chorales which he inserted into his many oratorios: again, the citation is normally to the first line- though much tampering has occurred to these tune names.

Traditional folk song, or other secular names are usual tune names for melodies which have long been known by "everybody", without identified composer, and usually associated with political or geographical regions or folk enclaves. "Londonderry Air" is an illustration. There are many others.

Gospel songs are known variously: by the first line, the repeti- tive phrase in the refrain, by the closing lines of either the first stanza or the refrain. They have, however far more frequently than have the more staid hymns, a close association of words and music. Whereas the formal hymnody is likely to interchange text and tune from service to service, and certainly from denomination to denomination, the gospel song is usually a consistent union of words and music. Consequently words from the text are logical tune name.

As these books indexed increased in number, it became more and more frequently necessary to use first lines for tune identifica- tion. Several hymnals from the less liturgic of the institutional churches had many unnamed melodies. The people using these hymnals call the tunes by the first lines of the hymn: our decision was theirs. Reference to other names was always made when neces- sary, but citations are given only to the standard tune name.

THE MELODY

Melody: A series of single notes arranged in musically expressive
         succession.

Tune: A musical setting of a hymn or psalm, usually in four-part
         harmony, intended for use in public worship. (O.U.D.)

The musical portion of these indexes is concerned with the melody, its source and its identification as a unique composition. The materials which were studied to secure the melodies were the tunes, the arrangements or settings of hymns for use in public worship. The names applied to these melodies are therefore called tune names, but the final index in the series is called "Melodies, a systematic index."

Music, in all its pleasing variations, is produced by many instruments animate and inanimate. The worth or meaning of music is symbolic of every intensity of every human emotion. This symbolic meaning is not considersd in Hymns and tunes. Rather, the sequence of the physical phenomena of tones within the musical octave (eight-tone scale) are the important element.

Musical traditions have developed several tonal patterns. One is prominent in the usual congregational song of the western world. The tonal scale, be it the major or its relative minor, is the combination of whole and half step intervals. The tones of the major scale have accepted syllable names: Do, Re, Mi, Fa, Sol, La, Ti and Do (which closes one sequence and opens the next).

These symbols -- Do, Re, Mi, Fa, Sol, La, Ti -- are the musical syllables used in the solmization of any diatonic scale.

These symbols -- Do, Re, Mi, Fa, Sol, La, Ti -- are not identical with the notes on a clef or the position at which a musical instrument is played. A diatonic scale has relative values only, relative to the initial tone which is to form the base of the eight-tone octave. The opening tone is always Do, according to the major scale; and La, according to the minor scale. The key in which the tune is written affects the printed notation, but does not affect the solmization.

For these reasons it is possible to write the symbols: Do Do Re Ti Do Re/Mi Mi Fa Mi Re Do/Re Do Ti Do and, however high or low it be sung, it will always sound like "My country 'tis of thee."

The stability of the tonic values of syllables make it possible to display the opening phrases of the musical literature of congregational song. The display is symbolic. There is, in fact, a chain effect of musical symbolism which begins with the five-line staff and its intervening spaces. Each line, each space has its particular and permanent name.

The diatonic scale can begin anywhere on this staff, it will close

xlii

an octave higher or lower. Its initial and terminal points are determined by the key signature of the score: the number of sharps or the number of flats to be regularly observed. These sharps and flats regulate the intervals; they regulate the position for recording the melody on the five-line staff; they regulate the key tone (Do); they do not regulate the solmization of the melody.

Conversion of the notational record to sol-fa notation (Solmization) is the next symbolic act, symbolic because no music need be sounded to perform the act.

Symbolism is carried to yet another degree by reducing the syllable names of the tones from Do Re Mi Fa Sol La Ti to D R M F S L T -- possible only because there is no repetition.

A musical score may contain tones which are modified by raising or lowering them one-half step. Indication is marked by the use of sharps (#) or flats (♭). This index does not change the syllable name of the tone, but uses the sharp (#) as indicative of change. It must be carefully noticed that, in the interests of practicality, all tones affected by either flats or sharps have been written with the relative syllable followed by its sharp. This means that a flatted note is called by the syllable name next lower in the scale with a sharp. The conversion scale reads:

♭ D	becomes	T	♭ S	becomes	F#
♭ R	"	D#	♭ L	"	S#
♭ M	"	R#	♭ T	"	L#
♭ F	"	M	♭ D	"	T	etc.

The musical notation is affected by the flat/sharp conversion. Melodic reproductions on instruments with determined intervals (as the piano) will not be affected. However melodic reproduction on a stringed instrument (as the violin) or a wind instrument (as a slide trombone) will be affected. Melodic reproduction by the human voice will be affected. The true tonic intervals differ slightly in color when a note is flatted or its companion is raised the half-step interval.

Because our subject is congregational song -- that is, community singing -- these niceties of tonal values do not obtain. The music is usually sung by folks whose voices are untrained; the range of tone is about one and one-third octaves. Many, many of the tunes cluster about a four or five tone range. This has not always been true. Plainsongs permitted and utilized more melodic range. The dramatic (pseudo-operatic) melodies of the 19th century have passed. The twentieth century tunes are simple, though they vary from the blithe to the solemn.

In recording melodies it was quickly apparent that a brief quotation was all that was essential for raw identification -- except in a few instances where the sounds used for singing the first line of the hymn were repeated by several composers. The record of the second line of the setting was sufficient to enforce a decision to quote sixteen successive musical syllables (terms used to name the relative tones in the diatonic scale). A very few times it has been necessary to record more than sixteen syllables; and in a mere handful of instances has it been essential to indicate the length of the poem being set to music. In this latter situation it was always the late portion of the music which varied. "Old hundred twenty fourth", by Louis Bourgeois (1551) was reduced by one ten-syllable phrase to form "Toulon". A note is given with each to indicate the metrical length: 10.10.10.10.10 for the original, and 10.10.10. 10 for the reduction.

The fact that melodic quotation exceeds actual needs for identification does assist in finding the variants printed in several books. Occasionally a single hymnal will quote the melody in two different ways without indication of editor. The Bach arrangements are usually properly cited, but most variations and harmonizations are anonymous (that is, the fact of the change is neither indicated nor credited). Taking place now, however, is a real improvement in this respect. The fine companions prepared by several of the musical editorial committees have led to far greater exactitude in quoting sources (authors, composers, etc.) and in indication of editorial changes within the texts of both tunes and hymns. Greater care concerning biographical detail is being exercised.

Within this Index, the melody is quoted twice, just as are the tune names and the first lines. It was possible in cataloging the poems attributed to an author to shorten the first line, because

words are a very familiar means of communication. Melodies of
the tunes attributed to a composer have not been shortened beyond
the length given in Index V. They are quoted in an unfamiliar language, in the musical syllables beginning with Do (written D); and
they are subject to great variation from book to book. The same
is true of tune names, they have been quoted in full in Indexes III
and IV. Tune names are words, but unfamiliar words and coined
words.

Just as concert music has several themes within a single composition, so with hymns. A hymn tune is short, offers little opportunity for variety, but distinctive airs are present. Koschat's melody
known as "Poland" has a dual melody throughout. It is difficult to
decide which is primary and which secondary. Normally the soprano
line would be treated as primary, and the alto line as secondary;
that decision is followed here.

Other melodies have preliminary phrases which are distinctive,
but which may not always be quoted. Palestrina's "Victory" is illustrative. Beginning with a triple Alleluia, the body of the hymn is a
sequence of five or more four-line stanzas. The tune, because it
may or may not utilize the preliminary phrase, must have quotation
from both vantage points.

Still another congregational song is that which uses the antiphonal
statement of stanza, followed by refrain which is repetitive. Gospel
songs are nearly always written in this way; so are many out-going
and bright hymns as well as a large number of processional and
recessional compositions.

In each of these instances involving a second theme, the record
of that theme has been made just as accurately and at as great
length (sixteen tones) as was the primary theme. The difference lies
alone in the citations recorded. Because the name of the refrain or
of the secondary melody will be that of its parent standard melody,
there is no alphabetical gap between them in the index. The filing
order has usually been: standard primary tune (with melodic quotation, source, and citations), followed by secondary entry bearing
quotation of refrain (without citations), and this followed by variants
to either standard or refrain melodies. Citations are always made

xlv

to the first appearance of a variant as well as to its relative standard entry.

INDEX DESCRIPTIONS

INDEX I: First lines and variants, with citations

This is a list in simple word-by-word alphabetic order of the first lines of every first stanza, of the first lines of every refrain (chorus), and of every variation of these first lines and refrains found in all the books analyzed.

The first line is followed, in parentheses, by its source (author). Citations to the item numbers (hymn numbers) within the hymnals where it is quoted are then given, as AZ290 means Book AZ, Hymn 290. The final information is serial numeration, beginning with 100001: this being the simplest way to completely differentiate the hymn numeration from the melodic numeration which begins with One (1).

Citations are not given for refrain first lines, rather a reference (R) is made to the related standard first line.

Citations are given to the first appearance of a variant reading of the first line, or a variant reading of the refrain first line, and reference (X) is made to the related standard first line or related standard refrain first line. This citation is also recorded within the standard first line entry.

The literary problems involved in the first line identification were many. Julian's Dictionary of hymnology helped considerably. Personal knowledge helped. Many hundreds of times, however, reference to previously cited renderings of the hymn was necessary to confirm identity; other times reference to the author file was helpful.

When the text was a close variant, it was handled as above. This might be described as reference to the standard first line, for purposes of this Index.

INDEX II: Authors and first lines

This is a list in simple word-by-word alphabetic order of the accepted personal, institutional, anthology, and traditional sources of the standard first lines found within these books analyzed.

The author's name, with dates when available, is followed by a brief quotation of the first line of the first stanza of the hymn and occasionally by date associated with the text when that date is useful for identification purposes. Then follows an item number preceded by letter R or V (being refrains and variant readings) and a brief redaction of each such refrain or variant.

This index II does not identify the accepted form of the first line by serial number. That may be readily found alphabetically in Index I. Variants, refrains, etc. are numerically coded, however, to make reference both more rapid and more accurate.

The literary problems in Index II were many. Again, <u>Julian's Dictionary</u> and the indexes within each hymnal aided identification of dates, full personal or compilation (anthology) names, etc. The everlasting objective has been the original source: who wrote this poem (hymn) in its original form and language? Hymnal editors have frequently given the credit to the intermediate arranger, or translator. A "traditional" source has had to be used when no individual agent could be found. A kind of "Potter's Field" -- a place for the strangers: first lines of unknown origin -- was established: "Anonymous". This has been fitted into the index at the very beginning of the file (before A).

Authors of religious poetry are legion and from time immemorial. If the hymn be of biblical origin, in traditional antiphonal psalm form and text, the biblical source is used. But if the psalm be re - written to conform to western poetical practice, then either the book in which the metrical psalm was published or the human agent (author) is credited. Notice the large number of hymns with the general source, Scottish Psalters.

There is no established relation between Indexes I-II and Indexes III-IV. An accidental relation is occasionally made because a hymn tune is not given a tune name. The first line of the first stanza is substituted.

INDEX III: <u>Tune names and variants, with citations</u>
This is a list in simple word-by-word alphabetic order of all the

tune names, or of first lines substituted for tune names not
given, and of all variants of either the tune names or the first
line substitutes which are associated with the particular melodies
found in all the books examined.

The tune name is followed, in parentheses, by its source (composer). Then follows the quotation in syllables of the diatonic scale,
approximately sixteen tones of the beginning melody. This is within brackets. Citations refer to the item numbers within each hymnal
where the melody is repeated -- its first quotation only within each
book. BC13 means Book BC, Hymn Tune at Hymn 13. Final information is the serial numeration, beginning with One (1): this being
a separate and distinct series from that found in Index I where the
numeration begins differently.

Notice carefully that a hymn tune is identified but once within
a hymnal, except where variants occur. This variant would be
treated either with the variant tune names, or as a absolute variant
with its own associated citations. Simple repetition which occurs frequently can be discovered by reference to the Tune Name Index
within the individual hymnal.

The musicological problems in Index III compilation have been
legion.

This section has been two-pronged. It has involved the verbal
form of the name of the melody (tune name), and it has involved
the musical form that melody takes when sung (by the diatonic scale).
Then there have been the many and quite variant sources which apparently belong to the song as we know it.

The tune name accepted here as standard is that name first
found to be associated with the given melody, in the chronological
cataloging of the hymnals. The melody is actually the pivotal item,
but a systematic way of identifying it has been through its peculiar
tune name.

The source accepted here as standard is the earliest cited person,
institution, publication, or culture associated with the particular
melody.

The melody here accepted as standard is the form in which it first appeared in the actual examination of the hymnals.

Notice carefully that no attempt is made to identify the reasons or the sources for the creation of the tune names. It is the melody which is being traced.

When tune name variants were found, references to the accepted (standard) name were prepared using X. No citations to variant names have been included. This would have added confusion to confusion, and anyone wishing to sort it out may do so from the citations which are recorded at the standard tune name entry.

When melodic variants have been close, a reference (V) with standard tune name, variant melodic reading, and single citation was prepared. Because melodic variants and refrains carry the standard tune name identification tag, it has been unnecessary to make actual references to the information anywhere. R, in this Index III, indicates refrain melody.

There is no reference from accepted tune name to the alternate tune name in Index III. Such information may be readily found through Index IV, "Composers and tune names." Virtually the only references herein are those inter-relating the unused to the used tune names. Infrequently one of the old tunes has been edited, the source is quite distinct and so is the tune name. A clear reference from each to other is made.

Serial numeration in Indexes III and V is interdependent. Index III is true sequence, from Number One. Index V is true melodic sequence, with the serial number indicating the numbered item in Index III. Thus the sung tune points to the tune name, to its composer, to verification of the melody, to citations within printed books, and to variant renderings.

Within Index III, serial numbers serve simply to display items. Through Index IV, serial numbers collect variant tune names and refrain tune names in the same way that variants and refrains are collected in Index II to the words of the hymns quoted as Index I. It is hoped that the patterns of Indexes I-II and III-IV are parallel.

In summary: Tune names are always recorded; cited at their first appearance within a hymnal; related melodies are always recorded with the standard tune names; variant tune names are always re-

corded but location of that variant is never cited, however a reference (X) is made to the established or standard tune name; refrains
are recorded melodically, are never cited, but a reference (R) to
the established standard tune name (actually, the standard melody)
is made; variants to the melody are cited one time only, parallel
citation at the established tune name is made, and reference V to
that established tune name is prepared. The established source is
quoted within the actual working file and implied within the published
file at each time a tune name or its related melody is named. Variant and intermediate sources are ignored for the purposes of this
Index. All alphabeting within Index III is word-by-word according
to the standard tune name or its variants.

INDEX IV: Composers and tune names

This is a list in simple alphabetic word-by-word order of the accepted (established) personal, institutional, anthology, and traditional
sources of the accepted (standard) melodies and associated tune
names as found in the books examined.

The name of the composer of the melody, with dates when available, is followed by the tune name and associated dates when appli-
cable, and finally by whatever variant tune names are associated
with it. These variant tune names are preceded by X and the serial
numbers from Index III.

Index IV does not cite serial numbers of standard tune names,
nor does it repeat melodic symbolism. Both these are available
alphabetically in Index III.

The literary and musicological problems of Index IV are those already named for its parallel Index III. Related to this Fourth was
the very close reading of the melodic solmization each time it appeared under its (possible) seventy-five variants: Seventy-five books
examined were full melody hymnals -- all except BT, BU, and BW.
More complicated, and far more elusive, were melodies which bore
nothing relevant to materials already indexed: tune name, source,
related words, etc. A great many of these awaited the garner and
sorting which came when Index V was created.

Church musicians and composers of music that has become classical are as legion as their brother hymnists (poets). Melodies from the early centuries of the Christian Era were usually handed down as plain song. So they are here, except where a more personal or exact name is associated with the melody. Some are traditional to a culture, as are many of the Jewish melodies. A few are from manuscript sources, as from the Herrnhut ms -- obviously Unitas Fratrum and here called Bohemian Brethren.

In passing: So much of practical dependence has been placed on the manuscript scores by the Moravians in our own U.S.A. that only within the recent four or five years have the choristers and trombone choir at the Lititz (Pennsylvania) Moravian Church retired their manuscripts to the vault and taken to the use of photoduplicates for the festal services of Christmas and Easter according to information from one of the Brethren (officers).

Revision of plainsong to modern setting has nearly always permitted indication of a human agent as proper source. In many instances it is a hymnal published by a diocese, a city, or an individual. A great number of the chorales which Bach arranged came from plain songs -- yet within this Index they are cited otherwise. The modern rendering is quite different enough to cite the original source with the Mode number when the plain chant is meant, and to cite the mediary when the modern rendering is indicated. With reference to Bach as composer, he is less responsible for hymn tune creation than for hymn tune arrangement. For that reason some of his better known arrangements are identified in a secondary manner only; but his own musical creations are listed under his own name at Index IV. Many of the chorales for which he did either the figured bass or the full arrangement are included in the index, and may be completely identified by comparison with the 371 chorales, named in the accompanying bibliography.

The tune name, the source, and the melody accepted as standard within Index III are the same within Index IV.

INDEX V: Melodies, a systematic index
This is a simple reproduction according to the increasing values of the syllables of the diatonic scale of every distinctive melody and

each of its variants, of every distinctive refrain and each of its
variants, with the proper and corresponding item number attached
to its standard tune name in Index III.

For a description of the diatonic scale, see p. 1158.

The portion of melody recorded is the syllables necessary to
sing approximately, and nearly always, the first sixteen vocal
sounds according to the words at the beginning of hymns; the corresponding syllables to the words of the refrains; and musical in-
vocations (which are refrains in reverse: as at Palestrina's "Victory"). Natural phrasing, that is the line endings, is indicated
by commas. A very few quite brief melodies close before the end
of sixteen syllables. These are punctuated by a full stop (period).

Melody which seems to be in the form of English chant is usually set to the number of syllables necessary to sing stanza one.
But note well, the melodies of Father Joseph Gelineau, S.J. (found
in Twenty four Psalms, book BS) are quoted as printed because the
poetry retains its original antiphonal form. Only because Twenty-
four Psalms is a true hymnal, and not intended as liturgy, is it
included. Similar materials in many hymnals have been excluded
because they are not intended for use except within the stated or
liturgical portion of congregational worship.

Many uses will be found for this fifth index, but it has served
the purposes of the entire Hymns and tunes; an index as definitive
medium for identifying tunes which bore no relation to each other
through diatonic or label similarities. It was thus that the fourteen
tune names to the melody here called "Cana" by Vulpius were
gathered. It was here that many tunes, usually cited as German,
or English traditional, or Anonymous were identified and found to
be duplicates. One tune attributed to J.S.B. Monsell (a poet, not a
musician) was identified as of Slovak origin.

IV

ACKNOWLEDGMENTS

From 10 April 1957, over the signature of Richard L. Evans with indication that a copy of Hymns, the official hymnal of the Church of Jesus Christ of Latter-Day Saints, was being presented for the Index, until almost the day when these final pages of manuscript were being taken to the Scarecrow Press Editorial Office at New Brunswick, New Jersey, people and institutions have helped make this book possible. These mentioned below have been known through correspondence, personal friendship, library affiliation, the library school classrooms at both the University of Tennessee and Rutgers - The State University of New Jersey, and other sections of Rutgers jurisdiction.

It has been necessary to have the entire library of books analyzed constantly at hand. These publishers have provided gift copies of their publications: Augsburg Publishing House, Augustana Book Concern, Broadman Press, The Christian Science Board of Directors, Church of God in Christ - Mennonite, The Church of Jesus Christ of Latter-Day Saints, Concordia Publishing House, The Otterbein Press, The Presbyterian Church - U.S. through its General Assembly's Training School, The United Lutheran Publication House, and The Westminster Press.

The friends include three clergymen: Norman B. Bucher, Jr., Irving Decker, and Howard A. Merkey. Lay friends to name are: Abram Beck, Alois Braun (deceased), Rose Burges Breustedt, Georgia Moe Gibson, Luella Gish, George L. Heiges, David W. Landis, Ena B. Minchew, Bernice Schneider, and Jane Smith.

Three students in my Rutgers Library School course, "Advanced reference sources," added useful books: Sister Mary Raymund, O. S.B., Joseph H. DaRold, and Joseph N. Swab. Several others were extremely interested, and offered books which were quite outside the defined limits of the work.

Libraries and librarians (glad that someone was -- for yet another time in her life "the fool in the forest" and having a marvelous time!) were willing to assist: Mennonite Library and Archives, of Lancaster (Pennsylvania) provided Amish Ausbund sources and information, Salem College, of Salem (North Carolina) quickly sent a copy of the earlier Moravian hymnal which Lititz (Pennsylvania) friends could not provide because of legal restrictions. Elizabeth Hughey (Methodist Publishing House), Jean W. Steele (Westminster Press), and Emily M. Chandler (Wesleyan Theological Seminary, Westminster, Md) each provided necessary historical information. Theodosia Hotch (one of the Regional Librarians, Georgia) and Barbara LaMont (Douglass College Librarian) discovered books and places to secure others.

Member libraries in the American Theological Library Association quickly offered books on long loan: Bridwell Library (Perkins Theological Seminary of Southern Methodist University) and Hammond Library (Chicago Theological Seminary of the University of Chicago) could send books which were very hard to find. Andover-Harvard Theological Library and New Church Theological School (through its president, Dr. Edwin G. Capon) offered and sent hymnals which could be retained.

Credit for assistance far beyond rule by law must be fully expressed to three men: F.P. Gough, Secretary, Anglican Hymn Book Committee, for prepublication air shipment of a copy of this book which is not for sale within the U.S.A.; the Rev. R.W. Thomson, Baptist Union of Great Britain and Ireland, for air shipment of a copy of the Baptist Hymn Book just before my closing deadline for indexing; and Dr. Carlton R. Young, editor of the hymnal being published by the Methodist Church in 1966, for a copy of the Final Report of his committee. This latter gift made it possible to include the text and melodies of a not-yet-published book authorized by a major denomination in our country. To have been forced to omit this would have been unfortunate indeed.

The Knox County (Tennessee) librarians, through their chief librarian, Emma Suddath, made Julian's Dictionary of Hymnology a gift. Isabel Stouffer (Cataloger, Speer Library at Princeton Theological Seminary), Lorena Garloch and Marylouise Meder (fellow faculty at Rutgers, Graduate School of Library Service), Grace Mostue (Douglass College Reference Librarian, Rutgers), and Mary M. Andrews (briefly at Rutgers, now at the Graduate School of Library Studies, University of Hawaii) -- to each of you six librarians I am grateful for technical suggestions.

Through the offices of my dean, Neal Harlow (Graduate School of Library Service, Rutgers - The State University) a small grant from the Rutgers Research Council was secured. This made possible the assistance which Virginia High has given. If the Melodic Index (Section V) be in proper order, it is to her credit. If there be error, it is my fault. Let it never be said there is no joy in preparing exact results. The Computer will say neither "Excelsior" when the task is to be done, nor "Eureka" when it is successfully completed. The human mind and heart are still essential.

My commercial artist niece, Anne Diehl, prepared the illustrations. And Ralph Shaw gave further of his encouragement. Bless them both!

KATHARINE S. DIEHL

New Brunswick, N. J.

PART ONE: THE HYMNS

First Lines and Variants, With Citations

A

A babe is born all of a May (English carol, 15th c) BG 116 100001

A babe is born in Bethlehem (German carol, 14th c) M612; O194; 100002

A babe is born of high nature (English trad carol, 15th c) BG40 100003

A babe lies in the cradle (Geistliche nachtigal, 1649 German carol) A 39 100004

A boy was born in Bethlehem (German trad carol) BG85 100005

A brighter dawn is breaking (Dearmer) E126; X435 100006

A broken heart, my God, my King (Watts) I266; M75; V289 100007

A charge to keep I have (Wesley,) C D501; F328; G287; H312; I388; L527; N501; R301; U289; V472; W518; Y379; Z373; AE274; AG161; AH419; AL362; AO485; AP 593; AR312; AS328; AT358; AU157; AV203; AW214; AX 163; AY38; AZ1340; BA449; BR378; BV602; BY461; BZ 100008

A child is born in Bethlehem (Latin carol, 14th c) BG73; BL6; BM82 100009

A child this day is born (English trad carol) BG2; BR554; BV102 100010

A city awaits us we soon shall behold (Newell) AY403 100011

A debtor to mercy alone (Toplady) W703; AM99 100012

A few more years shall roll

(Bonar) B443; D203; E361; H524; I578; K480; L195; M365; N592; O352; V631; AI 332; AM609; AP610; AS475; AX576; AY252; AZ1490; BA 739; BB372 100013

A fierce unrest seethes at the core (Marquis) AQ53 100014

A full surrender I have made (Oatman) AX399; AY109 100015

A gentle hand unseen by us (Warner) AX626 100016

A gladsome hymn of praise we sing (Blatchford) W28; AL593; AP715; AW403 100017

A glorious day is dawning (---) BE2 100018

A glory gilds the sacred page (Cowper) G388; H94; I198; K 170; L310; R260; U135; V75; W197; AB102; AI157; AL184; AM258; AP290; AR238; AS 176; AT186; AV74; BE334; BR235; BV310; BY252 100019

A glory in the word we find (Campbell Hymnbook.) BB656 100020

A gospel others daily see (Naylor) R The world of sinners ibid 100021

A grateful heart a garden is (Dennis) BE3 100022

A great and mighty wonder (St Germanus) A18; B82; E19; F 68; J18; K17; M363; N30; O 182; P128; Q76; X70; AW526; BB672; BV90; BY87 100023

A great and mighty wonder, Our Christmas Festal brings (St Anatolius) AA149 100024

A haze on the far horizon (Car-

ruth) Y9;   AB300;   AC533
                            100025
A herald voice the lonely desert
   cheers (Pope) BR129   100026
A holy air is breathing round
   (Livermore) Z467; AN445; AR
   501; BE4; BX480   100027
A holy stillness breathing calm
   (---) S38app   100028
A hymn of glory let us sing
   (St Bede) J110; K122; M453;
   Q212; AA235; AM212; AS153
                            100029
A King might miss the guiding
   Star (Benson) Y329; AC453
                            100030
A Lamb goes forth our griefs to
   share (Gerhardt) M396; O165
                            100031
A Lamb goes uncomplaining forth
   (Gerhardt) O301; AA191
                            100032
A late lark twitters from the
   quiet skies (Henley) AC537
                            100033
A little child, a Joy of Heart
   (Bates) AC458   100034
A little child on the earth has
   been born (Flemish trad car-
   ol) X352; BG74   100035
A little child the Saviour came
   (Robertson) B341; W305; AK
   332; AL217; AM352; AP348;
   AW300; AZ290; BA284
                            100036
A little child there is y-born
   (German trad carol, 15th c)
   BG118;   100037
A little kingdom I possess (Al-
   cott) BH251   100038
A little seed lay fast asleep
   (Writer) AL610; AW406
                            100039
A little that the righteous hold
   (U. P. Psalter, 1912) T63; AJ
   97   100040
A message came to a maiden
   young (Dutch trad & Dearmer)
   A317; X226; BG100   100041
A message from the Sacred
   Heart (Russell) BQ68 100042
A message sweet the breezes
   bring (Switton) BH133 100043

A messenger of peace (Zinzen-
   dorf N. L.)   AZ1193   100044
A messenger within the grave
   (Latin, 4th-5th c) X148 100045
A mighty fortress is our God
   (Luther) A551; B213; G67; H
   405; I101; J150; K195; L343;
   M486-7; N266; O270; P239; Q
   262; R91; S266; U308; V530;
   Y351; Z155; AA273; AB243;
   AC210; AD289; AE59; AF363;
   AG41; AH378; AI309; AK281;
   AM81; AN304; AO606; AQ16;
   AR75; AS258; AT40; AU38;
   AV37; AW549; BB261; BC3;
   BD78; BE10*; BF396; BI9;
   BK75; BR365; BX314; BZ
   *deliberate variant   100046
A mighty fortress is our Lord
   (Luther) M487 X A mighty
   fortress is our God
                           100047
A mighty stronghold is our God
   (Luther) L343 X A mighty
   fortress is our God
                           100048
A new shrine stands in beauty
   reared (Marshall) BH213
                           100049
A noble life, a simple faith
   (Isaacs) Z512; AN296; AQ106;
   BD104; BH225   100050
A parting hymn we sing (Wolfe)
   R443; S362; Z469; AD408; AE
   335; AK343; AM363; AO445;
   AS468; AT397; AU292; AV
   256; AZ1305; BF605 100051
A pilgrim and a stranger, I jour-
   ney here below (Gerhardt) K
   517; M319; O504; Q586
                           100052
A poor wayfaring Man of grief
   (Montgomery) BC153   100053
A priestly Heart the Sacred Heart
   Latin BQ337   100054
A ransom for all my Saviour
   once came (Helphingstone) AX
   319   100055
A rest remaineth for the weary
   (Kunth) Q615   100056
A ruler once came to Jesus by
   night (Sleeper) AT215; AU68;
   AW461; AX326; AY509 100057

A safe stronghold our God is
still (Luther) E362; F183;
W526; X 436; AL397; AP542;
AZ1028; BA679; BV402; BY
562   100058

A servant of God, the Apostle
of old (Hostetter) AY299
                             100059

A shepherd band their flocks are
keeping (---) BR546   100060

A shining city, one happy in
snow and sun (Drinkwater)
Y65   100061

A sinful man am I (Bonar) AZ
1312   100062

A slumber I know in Jesus' name
(Landstad) AA565   100063

A solis ortus cardine (Sedulius)
BT104   100064

A song of spring once more we
sing (Groser) Z591   100065

A sovereign Protector I have
(Toplady) W560 X Inspirer and
Hearer of prayer   100066

A Star is moving through the sky
(Jonae??) K542; M376 100067

A stranger and a pilgrim, I
(Hammond) AZ574   100068

A stranger once did bless the
earth (Clare) BY633   100069

A temple of the Lord I saw
(Tarrant) X I saw the city of
the Lord, Pt. II   100070

A thing of beauty is a joy forever
(Keats) AC491   100071

A thousand oracles divine (Wesley, C) I75   100072

A thousand years have come and
gone (Lynch) S128   100073

A time to watch, a time to pray
(Neale) BV171; BY136 100074

A tower of strength, our God
doth stand (Luther) D416
                             100075

A virgin most pure as the prophets
did tell (English trad carol)
BQ12 X A virgin most pure
as the prophets do tell
                             100076

A virgin most pure, as the
prophets do tell (English trad
carol) BG4; BP14; BQ12
                             100077

A voice, a heavenly voice I hear
(Wallin) J270; N238 100078

A voice by Jordan's shore
(Longfellow) AN210; BX219
                             100079

A voice from heaven we have
heard (Tomlinson) BE5
                             100080

A voice hath spoken from the
dust (Jensen) BC291   100081

A voice upon the midnight air
(Martineau) X124; AN184
                             100082

A way to Calvary leadeth (Liander) P176   100083

A week within the sukko green
(Hess) BH189   100084

A wonderful Saviour is Jesus my
Lord (Crosby) AE283; AI270;
AM675; AS289; AT272; AX
510; BB651   100085

A work hath Christ for thee to
do (Sedding) F430; BV35
                             100086

A year again is now descending
(Rambach) P141   100087

A year of precious blessings
(Crosby) BB480   100088

Abide among us, we implore
thee (Grundtvig) O142; P95
                             100089

Abide among us with thy grace
(Stegmann) AO140   100090

Abide in grace, Lord Jesus
(Stegmann) O57; P57; AZ25;
BA590   100091

Abide in me, O Lord, and I in
thee (Stowe) AO703; BX283;
BY775   100092

Abide in me, o'ershadow by thy
love (Stowe) BX283 X Abide
in me, O Lord . . . 100093

Abide in me, the true and living
vine (Fillmore) AY87 100094

Abide not in the realm of dreams
(Burleigh) AN297; AQ222; BE
6; BX346   100096

Abide, O dearest Jesus (Stegmann) Q53; AA9   100096

Abide with me, fast breaks the
morning light (Woods) BE7 X
Abide with me, fast falls the
eventide (Lyte)   100097

Abide with me, fast falls the eventide (Lyte) A467; B18; D12; E363; F27; G520; H34; I50; J576; K476; L16; M289; N550; O552; P340; Q552; R64; S33; T306; U470; V42; W286; X437; Y368; Z138; AA40; AB31; AC 20; AD61; AE42; AF209; AG 23; AH169; AI49; AK51; AL 550; AM335; AN127; AO25; AP663; AQ79; AR417; AS35; AT295; AU179; AV296; AW40; AX356; AY293; AZ457; BA516; BB50; BC51; BE7,8*; BF193; BI62; BJ20; BK72; BR326; BV500; BX163; BY686; BZ
*var. by Woods   100098

Abide with me, I need thee every day (Dietrick) AX368; AY70   100099

Abide with me, my Saviour blest (Timm) M286   100100

Abide with me; 'tis eventide (Hofford) BC2   100101

Abide with us, Lord Jesus! Thy grace sustain (Stegmann) M13 X Abide with us, our Saviour, nor let . . .   100102

Abide with us, O Saviour dear (Selnecker) N268   100103

Abide with us, our Saviour, Nor let thy mercy cease (Stegmann) J192; K433; L60; N358; AK34; AW559   100104

Abide with us, the day is waning (Boye) O333; Q194   100105

Abode of peace, my Father's home forever (Rosenius) N624   100106

About the field they piped full right (English trad carol, ca 1450) BG169   100107

Above the clear blue sky (Chandler) B353; D570; W37; AP714; AZ 1191; BA811; BD195   100108

Above the heavens, eternal God! (Watts) BI68   100109

Above the hills of time the cross is gleaming (Tiplady) G145 Z236   100110

Above the trembling elements (Price) AY49   100111

Abundant fields of grain shall wave (U.P. Psalter, 1912)

AJ195 X Blest be the Lord our Father's God   100112

Accept from human hands anointed (Brucker) BL48   100113

Accept, kind Father, bread and wine (Mary Francis, Sr.) BN206   100114

Accept this host, O God of Love (Brucker) BL47   100115

According to thy gracious word (Montgomery) B320; D233; E300; G410; H443; I234; J266; K191; L324; M49; N239; O151; P102; R444; S358; T363; U380; V557; W313; X259; Z456; AE 337; AF284; AG242; AI164; AK338; AL227; AM360; AO 438; AP360; AR510; AS466; AW305; AX176; AZ172; BV 367; BY306; BZ   100116

Ach bleib bei uns, Herr Jesu Christ (Selnecker) AY22d; BT292; BW557   100117

Ach bleib mit deiner Gnade (Stegmann) BT53; BW559   100118

Ach frölich will ich singen (Ausbund) BU25   100119

Ach Gott, ein manches herzeleid (Zions harfe) 1803 AY9d   100120

Ach Gott und Herr, Wie gross und schwer (Rutilius) BT317   100121

Ach Gott Vater im Höchsten Thron (H. Loch & L. Meister) BU40   100122

Ach Gott, verlass mich nicht (Franck) BT402   100123

Ach Gott! verleih mir dein Genad (Rogel) BU53   100124

Ach Gott vom Himmel, sieh darein (Luther) BT260   100125

Ach Gott vom Himmelreich (Ausbund) BU27   100126

Ach, wie gross ist deine Gnade (Olearius) BT384   100127

Across the sky the shades of night (Hamilton) D202; O206; Q110; AA164; BX181; BY710   100128

Ad Coenam Agni providi (Latin)
BJ30b   100129
Ad regias Agni dapes (Latin, 4th
c) BO288   100130
Ad te Rex summe (Latin) X
Attende, Domine, et miserere
          100131
Adam lay abounden Bounden in a
bond (English trad carol, 15th
c) BG180   100132
Adeste, fideles (Latin text) (Latin
18th c) Y298; AD120; AF133;
AH123; AK112b; AN156; BM
64; BN10; BO150; BP12; BQ
158; BT102; BW80   100133
Adeste fideles (English text)
(Latin, 18th c) X Come hither,
ye faithful X O come, all ye
faithful X Ye faithful, with
gladness   100134
Adon olom a'sher molach (Jewish
trad) AH154; BH276   100135
A'do-noy, A'do-noy, Ayl ra-
chum (Jewish traditional) BH
313   100136
A-do-noy, mo o-dom va-tay-do-
hu (Jewish traditional) BH334
          100137
A'do-noy yim-loch l'o-lom vo-ed
(Jewish traditional) BH294
          100138
Adoramus te Christe, et Benedici-
mus tibi (Breviary) BQ190
          100139
Adoramus te, panem coelitum
(Latin) BQ232   100140
Adoro te devote (St Thomas
Aquinas) BM30; BN88; BO32;
BP48; BQ227   100141
Advent tells us Christ is near
(Hankey) A235; B348; E586
          100142
Afar on the mountain the Shep-
herd (Pratt) AX253   100143
Afar upon a foreign shore
A martyr's crown (---) BQ107
          100144
After thy loving kindness, Lord
(Scottish Psalter, 1650) AL652;
AP45; AW589   100145
Again as daylight fades and night
draws near (Burgess) BD7
          100146

Again, as evening's shadow falls
(Longfellow) G42; I48; R62;
W275; Z139; AB27; AF46;
AL209; AN119; AO34; AP332;
AQ271; AW280; AZ369; BA
777; BB56; BF199; BH11;
BR126; BX138   100147
Again is come the new church-
year (Olearius) AA140
          100148
Again, O Lord and Saviour
(Neumann) AK140   100149
Again, our dear redeeming Lord
(Curtis) BC251   100150
Again our earthly cares we
leave (Newton) BB25 X Great
Shepherd of thy people, hear
          100151
Again returns the day of holy
rest (Mason) AO11; AW286;
BB466; BR98   100152
Again the day returns of holy
rest (Mason) BB466 X Again
returns the day of holy rest
          100153
Again the Lord's own day is
here (St Thomas à Kempis??)
F40; BV67   100154
Again the morn of gladness
(Ellerton) B352; U440; V746;
W237; AH163; AL193; AP802
          100155
Again the slowly circling year
(St Hilary) BN54; BO188
          100156
Again thy glorious sun doth rise
(Wallin) M561; N545   100157
Again we meet around the board
(Snow) BC242   100158
"Against my second coming"
(Wattles) Y266   100159
Ah, dearest Jesus, holy Child,
make thee a bed (Luther) R173;
S118; AD123; AF75; BV98
          100160
Ah, dearest Jesus, holy Child
(Luther) X From heaven high
X Give heed, my heart
          100161
Ah, dearest Jesus, how hast
thou offended (Heermann) M413
X Ah holy Jesus...   100162

Ah, holy Jesus, how hast thou
offended (Heermann) A71; B
155; E70; J85; K100; M413;
N115; O300; P192; R191;
S158; X99; AD147; AF163;
AK147; AM179; AP201; AW
534; BJ42; BV151; BY137;
BZ   100163
Ah, how shall fallen man (Watts)
AZ1295   100164
Ah! Lord our God, let them not
be confounded (Heermann) AA
280   100165
Ah! think not, the Lord delayeth
(Dearmer) X59; AF112 100166
Ah, this heart is void and chill
(Spitta) AZ861   100167
Ah, well it is that God should
read (Aguilar) BH89   100168
Ah! what a sound! The infinite
fierce chorus (Longfellow)
Y251; AD360   100169
Ah! whither should I go (Wesley)
H269; I283; AZ1288; BR290
                              100170
Aj, ten silný lev udatný
(Bohemian. 1650) BT211
                              100171
Ajar the temple gates are swing-
ing (Franzén) N402   100172
Al people yt on earth do dwel
(Day's Psalter, 1560) Y296
                              100173
Al verden nu raabe for Herren
med Fryd (Koren) BT44
                              100174
Alas! and did my Saviour bleed
(Watts) G142; H170; I146;
J486; K101; L242; M406; N
111; O318; P184; Q154; R199;
S249; U101; V148; AA214; AE
112; AG95; AH285; AI74; AK
153; AL101; AM195; AO170;
AR167; AS142; AT94,101;
AU112,244; AV109; AW108;
AX116,311; AY249; AZ107;
BA203; BB124; BZ   100175
Alas and did my Saviour bleed,
with refrain: At the cross
(Hudson) U97; AE289; AI74a;
AS142; AT94; AU112; AX311
                              100176
Alas and did my Saviour bleed,

with refrain: He loves me
(---) AX116; AY249   100177
Alas! and did my Saviour bleed,
with refrain: Help me, dear
Saviour (Coffman) BB124
                              100178
Alas, my God! my sins are
great (Rutilius) N411; O523;
Q317; AA421   100179
Alas! what hourly dangers rise
(Steele) V473   100180
All alone, and yet not lonely
(Arnold) AZ253   100181
All are architects of fate (Long-
fellow) AN346; AQ175 100182
All as God wills, who wisely
heeds (Whittier) G340; X438;
Y132; AB209; BF405; BH88;
BX279   100183
All beautiful the march of days
(Wile) R96; S471; Y48; Z588;
AB390; AC326; AD450; AF
456; AG56; AK429; AL580;
AN131; AQ304; AR586; BB94;
BD53; BF645; BK128; BX168;
BZ   100184
All because we do not love them
(Teasley) R Many souls today
                              100185
All bells in paradise (English
trad carol) R Over yonder's a
park X Down in yon forest
                              100186
All blessing, honor, thanks and
praise (Speratus) N342
                              100187
All blessing, honor, thanks and
praise (Speratus) X To us
salvation now is come
                              100188
All creatures of our God and
King (St Francis of Assisi)
F172; G65; R100; W13; X439;
Y307; Z157; AB47; AC45; AD
98; AE9; AF64; AG58; AH190;
AK15; AL29; AN198; AQ23;
AR19; AT3; BC4; BK51; BV
251; BY1; BZ   100189
All depends on our possessing
(Nurnberg G-B., 1676) M280;
Q425; AA363   100190
All' die ihr jetzund leidet (Aus-
bund) BU52   100191

All earth to Him her homage bring
(U. P. Psalter, 1912) R The
ends of all the earth shall hear
100192
All' Ehr' und Lob soll Gottes sein
(Babst. Geistliche lieder.
Leipzig, 1545) BT238 100193
All for Jesus! all for Jesus
(James) AX403; AY108 100194
All glory be to God alone Babst.
(Geistliche lieder 1545) M142;
Q238 100195
All glory be to God most high
(Decius) BX572 X All glory
be to God on high 100196
All glory be to God most high,
and on the earth be peace (Hay)
BE9 100197
All glory be to God on high
(Decius) J132; K160; M141;
N300; O2; P1; Q237; AA261;
AE15; AF2; AI28; AK2; AM92;
AR13; AW521; AZ735; BA648;
BX572 100198
All glory be to thee, most high
(Decius) N300 X All glory be
to God on high 100199
All glory be to thee, O Lord (---)
BRp467 100200
All glory, laud, and honor (St
Theodulph) A62; B143; D90;
E622; F98, 597; G128; I31;
J74; K86; L129; M428; P34;
Q160; R187; S146; T322; U318;
V157; W91; X135; Z221; AB
133; AC116; AD140; AE106;
AF155; AG90; AH281; AK135;
AL81; AM173; AO155; AP252;
AR155; AS115; AT151; AV142;
AW100; AZ849; BA206; BB15;
BF309; BI102; BK134; BL25;
BM47; BN32; BQ26; BR172;
BV166; BY114; BZ 100201
All glory, praise and honor (St
Theodulph) M428 X All glory,
laud, and honor 100202
All glory to God, the Father and
Son (---) Lp744 100203
All glory to the Sovereign Good
(Schütz) AZ738; BA649 100204
All good gifts around us (Claudius)
R We plow the fields 100205
All hail, adored Trinity (Latin,

before 11th c) E633; F617;
BV228 100206
All hail, all hail to the New
(Lathbury) AC534 100207
All hail, dear Conqueror, all
hail! (Faber) BP37 100208
All hail, our church's Elder
dear (Montgomery) AZ878;
BA795 100209
All hail our glorious Saviour
(Seebach) R O Christians
leagued together (Cassady)
100210
All hail the glorious day (Johnson)
BC223 100211
All hail the glorious morn (Pea-
cock) L266 100212
All hail the great Immanuel's
name (Perronet) BI23 X All
hail the power of Jesus' name
100213
All hail, the pageant of the years
(Holmes) Z516; AD364; AN146;
AQ205; BF491 100214
All hail the power of Jesus'
name (Perronet) A355; B192;
D450; E364; F217; G164;
H192; I180; J426; K131; L114;
M184; N153; O6; P7; Q339;
R132; S192; T324; U116; V196;
W139; X440; Y362; Z252; AA
93; AB87; AC135; AD180; AE
129; AF195; AG114; AH198;
AK184; AL46; AM218; AN180;
AO208; AP254; AR101; AS159;
AT133; AU1; AV133; AW3;
AX13; AY1; AZ162; BA90;
BB156; BF327; BI23; BR53;
BV265; BY180; BZ 100215
All hail, thou day of wondrous
grace (Brueckner) M544
100216
All hail! to dear Mary (---) R
'Tis the month of our Mother
100217
All hail to the days that merit
more praise (Durfey) BG5
100218
All hail to the Power who giveth
men might (Dearmer) X441;
Y388 100219
All hail to thee, O blessed morn
(Wallin) J33; M361; N25

  100220

All hail, ye little martyr flowers
  (Prudentius) E34   100221
All hail, ye little martyr flowers
  (Prudentius) X O martyrs
  young and fresh   100222
All hidden lie the future ways
  (Hosmer) AN440; AW299
                                        100223
All his suffering ended (Havergal)
  R Golden harps are sounding
                                        100224
All his work is ended (Havergal)
  R Golden harps are sounding
                                        100225
All honor and praise, dominion
  and might (Santeuil) Y386 X
  Disposer Supreme and judge
                                        100226
All is bright and cheerful round
  us (Neale) W609; AI378
                                        100227
All is o'er: the pain and sorrow
  (Moultrie) AZ594   100228
All labor gained new dignity
  (Oxenham) A510; AK255 100229
All lands and peoples, all the
  earth (Brooke) W231 100230
All lands to God in joyful sounds
  [st. 3: All on the earth shall
  worship thee] (Scottish Psalter,
  1650) AP56   100231

All lands to God, in joyful sounds
  [st. 3: Yea all the earth] (U.P.
  Psalter, 1912) T119; AJ173;
  AM381   100232
And let our bodies part, to differ-
  ent climes (Wesley) AY378
                                        100233
All living souls shall bless thy
  name (Moise) BH55   100234
All mankind fell in Adam's fall
  (Spengler) Q369   100235
All men living are but mortal
  (Albinus) Q601   100236
All men on earth that live (U.P.
  Psalter, 1912) T454; AJ316
                                        100237
All my heart this day rejoices
  (Gerhardt) M353 X All my
  heart this night rejoices
                                        100238

All my heart this night rejoices
  (Gerhardt) A32; B545; D538;
  G91; J26; K22; M353; N35;
  O177; P130; Q77; R172; S125;
  W41; Y344; Z186; AA145;
  AB113; AC85; AD111; AF123;
  AG77; AH262; AI68; AK119;
  AL48; AM150; AN121; AR140;
  AW525; AZ875; BA169; BB110;
  BD224; BF280; BR552; BV92;
  BY88; BZ   100239
All my hope and consolation (St
  Bernard of Clairvaux) AZ910
                                        100240
All my hope on God is founded
  (Neander) W448; X442; Z354;
  AF339; AN219; AQ35; BJ69;
  BY492   100241
All nations, clap your hands
  (U.P. Psalter, 1912) T88;
  AJ130   100242
All nations whom thou mad'st
  shall come (Scottish Psalter,
  1650) AP71   100243
All nature's works His praise
  declare (Ware) G552; R23;
  S478; AD10; AE16; AK360;
  AN454; AR12; BX500; BZ
                                        100244
All of seeing, all of hearing
  "M.J.", Father BN143
                                        100245
All on the altar, dear Jesus
  (McKinney) AU83   100246
All people of the earth (McWhood)
  G508   100247
All people that dwell on the
  earth (U.P. Psalter, 1912)
  AJ269   100248
All people that on earth do
  dwell, Sing to the Lord (Kethe)
  A278; B249; D470; E365; F
  166; G13; I16; Q14; R24;
  S1; T184; V3; W229; X443;
  Y296; AD4; AF4; AG7; AJ
  268; AK24; AL669; AM1;
  AN496; AO10; AP86; AQ18;
  AR2; AS8; AT13; AU3; AW
  594; AZ302; BA639; BB13;
  BDp. 2; BF174; BJ79; BK61;
  BL79; BV231; BX2; BY2; BZ
                                        100249

All poor men and humble (Welsh trad. carol) BG34; BV94 100250

All power is given unto our Lord (Root) BE10 X A mighty fortress is our God (Luther) 100251

All praise and thanks to God (Rinkart) X406 X Now thank we all our God 100252

All praise be to God, Whom all things obey (Bridges) F566; BJ89 100253

All praise to God who reigns above (Schütz) K285 X Sing praise ... 100254

All praise to Him, who built the hills Bonar) D463 100255

All praise to Him who reigns a above (Clark) AX3; AY10 100256

All praise to Jesus' hallowed name (Latin, 11th c) AA147 100257

All praise to our redeeming Lord (Wesley) G417; I553; AL372; AW322; AX547; AY432; BZ 100258

All praise to St Patrick (Faber) AH140; BO135 100259

All praise to the Father, the Son, and Spirit (---) Lp743 100260

All praise to the Lamb! accepted I am (Wesley) AZ1422 100261

All praise to thee, eternal God (Luther) Q80 X All praise to thee, eternal Lord, clothed in a garb 100262

All praise to thee, eternal Lord, clothed in a garb (Luther) D320; J21; K18; L219; Q80; S119; AG78; AM155; BA50; BR553 100263

All praise to thee, for thou, O King divine (Tucker) A366; AF147; BV253; BY198; BZ 100264

All praise to thee, my God, this night (Ken) A165; B25; D18; E267; F23; G51; I49; J223; K471; L15; M568; N552; O560; Q558; R63; S42; U461; V45; W291; X45; Z148; AA 36; AB30; AD62; AE46; AG32; AI55; AK59; AL544; AM341; AO36; AP673; AQ270; AR49; AS31; AV19; AW33; AZ394; BA778; BB53; BF200; BJ55; BK35; BL72; BR117; BV64; BX131; BY694; BZ 100265

All praise to thee, O Lord (Beadon) O232 Glory to thee, O Lord, who by thy mighty power 100266

All praise to thee we bring (Klein) BH203 100267

All praise to thee, who safe hast kept (Ken) A152; W257; AL529b; AP653b 100268

All prophets hail thee, from of old announcing (St Rabanus Maurus) E208 100269

All-seeing Lord, whose power unknown (Bridges) BJ68 100270

All souls, O Lord, are thine (Sargent) AN431 100271

All that I am I owe to thee (U.P. Psalter, 1912) T276; AJ383; AM34 100272

All that I was, my sin, my guilt (Bonar) K304; L131; N442; O440; Q378; V376; AA308 100273

All that's good and great and true (Thring) AN481; BX 524; BY48 100274

All the bliss which we possess (Zinzendorf, N.L.) AZ1047; BA111 100275

All the gay gems of day (Denisot) BG101 100276

All the happy children, Gladly join our song (Dillingham) AL583; BD43 100277

All the past we leave behind (Whitman) X304; Y164; AB 308; AC211; AD491; AQ211 100278

All the scenes of nature quicken (Smart) X17 100279

All the toil and sorrow done (Stanley) X149; Z251 100280

All the way my Saviour leads me
(Crosby) N464; R365; U211;
V736; Z396; AE207; AG154;
AH375; AI289; AL445; AM505;
AP606; AR434; AS253; AT268;
AU369; AV360; AX466; AZ965;
BB259; BY537; BZ   100281

All the world give praises due
(Held) AZ42; BA146   100282

All the world shall come to serve
thee (Jewish) AH152; BH63
                                  100283

All things are doubly fair
(Gautier) AQ135   100284

All things are thine; no gift have
we (Whittier) A227; B460;
E173; G611; J244; R313; S475;
U383; W254; X189; Z606; AB
328; AC310; AD413; AE349,
464; AF537; AG293; AK508;
AL207; AN460; AP699; AR522;
AS440; AT403; AU493; AX643;
BA324; BB483; BV658; BX495;
BZ   100285

All things bright and beautiful
(Alexander) A311; B358; E587;
F442; G447; K554; R456; W18;
X444; AE429; AF478; AL582;
AM636; AP725; AR93; AT8;
AV400; AW410; BB421; BD39;
BH252; BK10; BV233; BY733;
BZ   100286

All things praise thee, Lord most
high (Conder) BY3   100287

All things which live below the
sky (Brailsford) X445;BY49
                                  100288

All this night bright angels sing
(Austin) BR555   X   All this
night shrill chanticleer
                                  100289

All this night shrill chanticleer
(Austin) BG123; BR555
                                  100290

All those who love and obey my
word (McPhail) AX585; AY
307   100291

All through the long bright days
in June (Whittier) BH186
                                  100292

All to Jesus I surrender (Van
DeVenter) AT363; AU82;
BB573   100293

All under the leaves, the leaves
of my life (English trad
carol) BG43   100294

All unseen the Master walketh
(MacKellar) AP237   100295

All who with heart confiding
(U.P. Psalter, 1912) T255;
AJ355   100296

All-wise, All-great whose ancient
plan (Dobson) BH218 100297

All ye a certain cure who seek
(Latin, 18th c) S226   100298

All ye dwellers on earth, when
the Shofar is sounded
(Jewish traditional) BH317
                                  100299

All ye Gentile lands, awake!
(Rist) BR151   100300

All ye saints of light proclaim
("J.V.C." [Crosby?]) AX272
                                  100301

All ye that fear God's holy name
(U.P. Psalter, 1912) R35;
T33; AJ48; AM6   100302

All ye that fear Jehovah's name
(U.P. Psalter, 1912) T33   X
All ye that fear God's holy
name   100303

All ye that pass by, To Jesus
draw nigh! (Wesley) L374;
AZ1419; BY138   100304

All ye who grace inherit (---)
Lp742   100305

All ye who like the birds can
soar (Grundtvig) M636
                                  100306

All ye who love the Lord draw
near! (Tweedy) BF173
                                  100307

All ye who on this earth do
dwell (Gerhardt) Q581
                                  100308

All ye who seek a comfort sure
(Latin, 18th c) E71; F104;
BJ5; BN70; BO18; BQ67;
BV466   100309

All ye who seek for sure relief
(Latin, 18th c) F104 X All
ye who seek a comfort sure
                                  100310

All you that are to mirth inclined
(English carol, 17th c) BG51
                                  100311

All you who seek a comfort sure
(Latin, 18th c) BN70 X All
ye who seek a comfort sure
100312
Alle Menschen müssen sterben
(Albinus) BT601 100313
Allein Gott in der Höh' sei Ehr'
(Decius) BT237; BW521
100314
Allein zu dir, Herr Jesu Christ
(Schneesing) BT319 100315

Note: Alleluia has been taken as
the approved spelling of this
word (any language) for the purpose of the index. 100316

Alleluia! Alleluia! [etc] (Bible.
Revelation) AU477 100317
Alleluia! Alleluia! Earth and
heaven in sweet accord
(U.P. Psalter, 1912) T456;
AJ413 100318
Alleluia! Alleluia! He is coming
again (Crosby) R He is com-
ing, the "Man of Sorrows"
100319
Alleluia! Alleluia! Heart and
voice to heaven raise (Words-
worth, C.) AT114 X Alleluia!
Alleluia! Hearts and voices
heavenward raise 100320
Alleluia! Alleluia! Hearts and
voices heavenward raised
(Wordsworth, C) A92; B520;
D123; E127; F137; G153; J108;
K116; T345; U104; V757; W126;
X150; AE126; AF180; AI87;
AK174; AM204; AO186; AP219;
AT114; AZ960; BA233; BV178
100321
Alleluia! Alleluia! Hearts to
heaven and voices raise
(Wordsworth, C.) T345 X
Alleluia! Alleluia! Hearts and
voices heavenward raise
100322
Alleluia! Alleluia! In His temple
God be praised. (U.P. Psalter.
1912) T295; AJ409; AM9
100323
Alleluia! Alleluia! let the holy
anthems rise (Caswall) AH127;
BM98; BO173 100324

Alleluia, Alleluia. Praise the
Lord with thanksgiving
(Fyleman) R Lift your hidden
faces 100325
Alleluia! alleluia! Shout aloud,
ye sons of men (Greiner)
M446 100326
Alleluia! Alleluia! Ye redeemed
in thanks unite (Pados) BL33
100327
Alleluia! best and sweetest
(Latin, 11th c) AZ1400 100328
Alleluia, Christus lebt! (Garve)
BT188 100329
Alleluia! Fairest morning!
Fairer than our words can
Say (Krause) K439; L40;
AK40 110330
Alleluia! Jesus lives! He is now
the living one (Garve) O326;
Q188 100331
Alleluia! Jesus lives! won the
battle glorious! (Garve) J100
100332
Alleluia! Let praises ring
(Darmstadt G-B., 1698) Q23
100333
Alleluia, lo He wakes (Schmolck)
M449 100334
Alleluia! Lob, Preis und Ehr'
(Darmstadt G-B., 1698) BT23
100335
Alleluia, praise Jehovah, From
the heavens praise (U.P. Bi-
ble songs hymnal, 1927) AM
105 100336
Alleluia, praise Jehovah, O my
soul, Jehovah praise (U.P.
Psalter, 1912) T288; AJ400;
AM53 100337
Alleluia! Praise the Savior, His
the scepter (---) BI4-D
100338
Alleluia! Praise ye God (Westra)
AJ430 100339
Alleluia! Raise, O raise To our
God the song of praise
(Conder) AM49; AP101 100340
Alleluia! sing to Jesus (Dix)
A347; B193; D368; E301; F399;
I176; J417; K127; W138; X260;
AW124; BV383; BY168100341
Alleluia, song of gladness

(Latin, 11th c) A54; B110;
D73; E63; F82; J58; K57;
AO183   100342
Alleluia, song of sweetness
(Latin, 11th c) E63 X Al-
leluia, song of gladness
                         100343
Alleluia, sweetly singing (---)
R Humble praises, holy Jesus
                         100344
Alleluia! Thine the glory; Al-
leluia! Amen! (Mackay) R
We praise thee, O God, for
the Son of thy love   100345
Alleluia 'tis done! I believe in
the Son (Bliss) R 'Tis the
promise   100346
Alleluia to Jesus, who died on
the tree (English trad carol)
R As Jacob with travel was
weary   100347
Alleluia! What a Saviour!
(Chapman) R Jesus! what a
Friend for sinners   100348
Alleluia, what a Saviour! Who
can take a poor lost sinner
(Johnston) R There's a sweet
and blessed story   100349
Alles ist an Gottes Segen
(Nurnberg G-B., 1676) BT425
                         100350
Allez, mon voison, à la crèche
(French trad carol) R Prompte-
ment levez-vous   100351
Alma, Alma, Alma, Redemptoris
Mater (Hermannus Contractus)
BO-298 X Alma Redemptoris
Mater   100352
Alma Redemptoris Mater (Her-
mannus Contractus) BN140;
BO298; BQ202   100353
Almighty Builder, bless we pray
(Church) AE348; AN456; AR524;
BX487   100354
Almighty Father, bless the word
(Hart) D33; O56; Q52; V21;
AS64; BA366   100355
Almighty Father, God of love
Hear from thy throne (Hawkins)
AB379   100356
Almighty Father, God of love
Look down in mercy (Wigles-
worth??) BH6   100357

Almighty Father, hear our cry
(Bickersteth) D307   100358
Almighty Father, hear our
prayer (--- American?) R542;
AE462; AF502; AG331; AH
563; AR651; AT529; BF689
                         100359
Almighty Father, heaven and
earth (Dayman) Q438; AA360;
AI319; AR352; AS355 100360
Almighty Father, Lord most
high (Coles) F405   100361
Almighty Father of all things
that be (Dugmore)
W503; BY626   100362
Almighty Father strong to save
(Missionary service book 1937)
A513; R522   100363
Almighty Father strong to save
(Missionary service book, 1937)
A513 X Eternal Father,
strong to save (Whiting)
                         100364
Almighty Father, who dost give
(Masterman) A530; F583; W
491; AK363; AL389; BY657
                         100365
Almighty Father, who for us thy
Son didst give (Caird) BV591;
BY639   100366
Almighty God, eternal Lord
(Wallin) N167   100367
Almighty God, I call to thee
(Luther) BR360   100368
Almighty God, I humbly ask
(Kuhlmann) M258   100369
Almighty God, in humble prayer
(Montgomery) AZ119; BA591;
BH28; BX355   100370
Almighty God, thy lofty throne
(U.P. Psalter, 1912) T89;
AJ242; AM619   100371
Almighty God, thy word is cast
(Cawood) J196; K432; L313;
M20; N81; O261; Q49; V24;
W295; AA13; AM317; AO239;
AZ163; BV135   100372
Almighty God, thy word is sown
(Cawood) M20 X Almighty
God, thy word is cast 100373
Almighty God, who from the
flood (Latin, 6th or 7th c)
E61   100374

Almighty God, who hearest prayer
(Lucas) BH53   100375
Almighty God, whose only Son
(Baker) D499; AY456   100376
Almighty Lord, before thy throne
(Steele) Q579; AA303   100377
Almighty Lord of earth and
heaven (Denicke) M58 100378
Almighty Lord, whose sovereign
right (Hasse) BA337   100379
Almighty Lord, with one accord
(Stryker) G558; I687; U328;
Y137; AE373; AI368; AK450;
AO488; AR537; AS392; AW390;
BF632   100380
Almighty Sovereign of the skies,
to thee let songs of gladness
rise (Watts or Strong??)
AR593; AS427   100381
"Almost persuaded" now to believe
(Bliss) P251, 256; U154; AH341;
AI191; AT248; AU169; AV335;
AX263; AY506; BB228 100382
Aloft in yonder belfry (Brueckner)
M517   100383
Alone thou goest forth, O Lord
(Abelard) A68; AF159; BV169;
By139; BZ   100384
Alone to God on high be praise
(Decius) BR153   100385
Alone with God, the world for-
bidden (Oatman) R When
storms of life   100386
Alone with thee, my God, in
prayer (Aufranc) BB335
                       100387
Alone with thee, O Lord, when
day is dead (Urseth) P332
                       100388
Along my earthly way (Edmeston)
AZ1337   100389
Als Christus mit sein'r wahren
Lehr (M. Sattlers) BU7 100390
Als man zählt tausend fünf
hundert Jahr (H Buchel) BU29
                       100391
Also hat Gott die Welt geliebt
(German. 1791) BT245
                       100392
Also redt der wahrhaftig Gott
(Ausbund Psalm 50) BU128
                       100393
Altissimo, omnipotente, bon

Signore (St Francis of Assisi)
Y307   110394
Always with us, always with us
(Nevin) L430; AI186; AO367;
AW256   100395
Am I a soldier of the cross
(Watts) A550; B488; D508; G
284; H381; I393; J554; L539;
M247; N454; O490; Q445;
R353; U307; V475; AA378;
AE260; AH295; AI322; AM481;
AO405; AR313; AS329; AT405;
AU176, 395*; AV213; AX425;
AY122,*354*; AZ189; BA451;
BB356; BZ
*with refrain   100396
Am I a soldier of the cross
(Watts) refrain: In His name
I'll bear the cross   (---)
AY354   100397
Am I a soldier of the cross
(Watts) refrain: "And when the
battles over" (Watts) AU395;
AY122   100398
Amazing grace! how sweet the
sound (Newton) G209; H288;
I309; L125; R275; U143;
V244; AE231; AG179; AH335;
AI136; AM402; AR433; AT188;
AU161; AV181; AW463; AX
322; BA423; BB295; BZ
                       100399
Ambrosius Klärich beschrieb
(Ausbund) BU9   100400
America, America. The shouts
of war shall cease (Cross)
AO660; BD127; BF546 100401
America, awake! Behold the
glory of the morning star
(Wilson) BD178   100402
America triumphant! Brave land
of pioneers (Holmes) Y280;
AN372; BD176; BF547 100403
Amid the din of earthly strife
(Hawkes) BX230   100404
Amid the thronging worshipers
(U. P. Psalter, 1912) AJ51
                       100405
Amid the trials which I meet
(Mund) AI288; AS311; AX488;
AY88   100406
Amid the world's deceitful cares
(Gothus) O391   100407

Among His people, God is known
  (U. P. Psalter. 1912) AJ208
                              100408
An alien from God and a stranger
  to grace (Cox) H811   100409
An angel from on high (Pratt)
  BC224   100410
An awe-full mystery is here
  (Loy) Q304; AA437   100411
An endless line of splendor
  (Lindsay) Z534; AD370; BF523
                              100412
An image of that heavenly light
  (Latin, 15th c) E233   100413
An Wasserflüssen Babylon
  (Dachstein) BT142; BW533
                              100414
Ancient of Days, who sittest
  throned in glory (Doane) A274;
  B519; D311; G59; I76; J137;
  M481; O74; R246; S58; U4;
  V84; Y26; Z99; AB16; AC34;
  AD67; AF249; AG46; AH191;
  AK197; AO235; AR14; AS72;
  AV27; BB680; BD28; BF210;
  BZ   100415
And am I born to die (Wesley)
  I590   100416
And are we yet alive (Wesley)
  H428   X   And are we yet to
  live   100417
And are we yet to live (Wesley)
  G402; H428; I560; AX641; AY
  377; BZ   100418
And art thou come with us to
  dwell (Greenwell) S134 100419
And art thou with us, gracious
  Lord (Doddridge) L514
                              100420
And can I yet delay (Wesley) H267;
  I275   100421
And can it be that I should gain
  (Wesley) G229; I310; W110;
  AL276; BV496; BY426; BZ
                              100422
And did those feet in ancient time
  (Blake) E72app. ; F578; W640;
  X446; Y162; AC269; AL522
                              100423
And didst thou, Jesus, condescend
  ("Am-a" 1769) L403   100424
And didst thou love the race that
  loved not thee? (Ingelow) S330;

X447; AL126; BY140   100425
And dost thou say, "Ask what
  thou wilt?" (Newton) AZ333
  X   Lord, dost thou say, "Ask'
                              100426
And have the bright immensities
  (Robbins) A354; AD171;BZ
                              100427
And he walks with me (Miles)
  R   I come to the garden
                              100428
And I couldn't hear nobody pray
  (Negro spiritual) AH607
                              100429
And I? Is there some desert or
  some pathless sea (Hale)
  AC497   100430
And I shall see Him face to face
  (Crosby) R   Some day the sil-
  ver cord will break   100431
And is it so? "A little while,"
  and then the life undying.
  (Songs of Zion, 1864) V659
                              100432
And is it true as I am told
  (Hull) AZ630   100433
And is the time approaching
  (Borthwick) AZ818 X Hasten
  the time appointed   100434
And it holds, my anchor holds
  (Martin) R Though the angry
  surges roll   100435
And let our bodies part (Wesley)
  G403; I227   100436
And let this feeble body frail
  (Wesley) I607; AA521; AY182
                              100437
And must I be to judgment
  brought (Wesley) H491; I600;
  AW501   100438
And must this body die (Watts)
  AA533   100439
And now another day is gone
  (Watts) F36; AX71; AY292;
  AZ88; BA902   100440
And now, beloved Lord, thy soul
  resigning (Alderson) E119;
  F123; W103; AZ1219   100441
And now may the courage of the
  early morning's dawning (---)
  AR677   100442
And now, my soul, another year
  (Browne) I570; AX629; AY246

100443
And now, O Father, mindful of
the love (Bright) A189; B333;
D228; E302; F397; J278; S355;
W320; X261; AD402; AF292;
AH222; AK340; BY307 100444
And now the sun hath sunk to
rest (---) M574   100445
And now the wants are told that
brought (Bright) A488; F32;
W296; X41; AP335   100446
And now this holy day (Harland)
AZ480   100447
And now to God the Father, God
the Son (---) Lp744 100448
And now we must bid one another
farewell (Clausen) O51; P63
100449
And shall we still be slaves
(Doddridge & Watts) L255
100450
And take me as I am (Hamilton)
R O Jesus Lord, to thee I
pray   100451
And that will be glory for me
(Bliss) R I know not the hour
100452
And then the Savior turned
(Petursson) M410   100453
And whate'er the need may be
(Ward) AHp27   100454
And when the battle's over we
shall wear a crown (---) R
Am I a soldier of the cross
(Watts)   100455
And will the great eternal God
(Doddridge) H410; I663 100456
And will the Judge descend
(Doddridge) M322; Q610; AA554;
AZ1289; BA737   100457
And wilt thou pardon Lord, A
sinner such as I (St Joseph the
Hymnographer) K323; M71;
Q322; AA422   100458
Angel of peace, thou hast wander-
ed too long (Holmes) BD184
100459
Angel, roll the rock away
(Scott) M433 X Angels, roll
the rock away   100460
Angel voices, ever singing
(Pott) B461; D304; F246; G15;
H7; I27; J240; K240; N584;

R30; S455; U15; V87; W252;
Y203; Z101; AC228; AD18;
AE12; AG297; AH203; AI21;
AK457; AL202; AM8; AO6;
AP320; AR15; AV46; BA641;
BB19; BF218; BV234; BY4;
BZ   100461
Angel voices, sweetly singing
(Bonar) BB556   100462
Angels and ministers, spirits
of grace (Dearmer) A122;
X238   100463
Angels at the Saviour's birth
(Campbell) BE11   100464
Angels, from the realms of glory
(Montgomery) A28; B80; D60;
F64; G87; H140; I113; J31;
K27; L221; M375; N26; O192;
P127; Q136; R168; S124; T335;
U49; V122; W65; X71; Z192;
AA187; AC88; AD106; AE91;
AF117; AG71; AH246; AI58;
AK104; AL64; AM164; AO128;
AP179; AR139; AS108; AT76;
AU145; AV91; AW81; AX102;
AY242; AZ1386; BA164; BB
113; BD228; BF285; BG119;
BI534; BK147; BR159; BV93;
BY89; BZ   110465
Angels, holy, high and lowly
(Blackie) K280; S76; X448;
AB55; AD96; AF73; BG160;
BX67; BY5   100466
Angels of Jesus, angels of light
(Faber) R Hark, hark my
soul! angelic songs   100467
Angels of mercy, angels of light
(Faber) BI74 X Hark, hark
my soul! angelic songs
100468
Angels roll the rock away
(Scott) B177; D116; H187; M433;
AH303; AI86; AO179; BI105;
BR181   100469
Angels sing his triumph as you
sang his birth (Brooks) R
God hath sent his angels
100470
Angels we have heard on high
(French trad carol) A42; J30;
R158; Z187; AD117; AE89;
AF116; AH256; AK105; AN
175; AQ294; AR138; AT64;

AW82; BD227; BK143; BL9;
BM65; BN12; BO154; BP16;
BQ7   100471
Angels, where'er we go, attend
(Wesley) AZ223   100472
Angelus ad virginem, Subintrans
in conclave (Latin carol, 14th
c) BG52   100473
Angularis fundamentum lapis
Christus missus est (Latin,
7th c.) BT466; BW277 100474
Another day has passed away
(Schuette) M565   100475
Another day is at an end
(Klantendorfer) AZ400 100476
Another day is at its close
(Herzog) N557   100477
Another day is dawning (Havergal)
AU275 X Another year is
dawning   100478
Another day is past and gone
(Coffin) AZ1459   100479
Another day its course hath run
(Pierpont) BX527   100480
Another six days' work is done
(Stennett) H73; I70; L41; V60;
BB456   100481
Another year completed (St Paulin-
us of Nola) E195   100482
Another year is dawning (Haver-
gal) E285; G534; I571; U476;
Z587; AE421; AG291; AH497;
AI348; AK424; AN144; AO574;
AR580; AS432; AT497; AU275;
AV311; AW380; AX631; BD232;
BF642; BK130; BX183 100483
Another year of setting suns
(Chadwick) AC328; AN132; AR581;
AS435; AW381; BD234 100484
Anxious heart, be rid of sadness
(Brorson) P168   100485
Anywhere, dear Saviour, In thy
vineyard wide (Ogden) BB344
                          100486
Anywhere with Jesus I can safely
go (Pounds & Alexander) AI399;
AM680; AS271; AX470; BB589
                          100487
Approach, my soul, the mercy-
seat (Newton) B303; D652; F345;
H48; I285; J369; K321; L410;
N408; O442; Q456; R386; S10
app; U367; V461; W451; AA399;

AL310; AM423; AO311; AP
490; AZ164; BA410; BV1;
BY332   100488
Are thy toils and woes increas-
ing (St Methodius II) AZ431
                          100489
Are ye able, asked the Master
(Marlatt) Y174 X "Are ye
able," said the Master
                          100490
"Are ye able," said the Master
(Marlatt) G268; Y174; Z360;
AC205; AE443; AG189; AR
311; AT351; AU396; AW392;
BZ   100491
Are you adorning the doctrine
(Naylor) AX158   100492
Are you formed a creature new
(Zinzendorf, N. L.) AZ1062
                          100493
Are you ready? Are you ready?
(Thompson) R There's a
great day   100494
Are you tired of the life you're now
living (Keegan) AU357 100495
Are you washed in the blood
(Hoffman) R Have you been
to Jesus   100496
Are you weary, are you heavy-
hearted (Rankin) AU110; AW
476   100497
Are you weary, heavy laden
(---) AX223; AY226   100498
Arglwydd, arwain trwy'r
anialwch (W. Williams) BT
54; BW160   100499
Arise, all souls, arise The
watch is past (Lathbury)
BR186   100500
Arise and be baptized (Bicker-
steth) N229   100501
Arise and shine in splendor
(Opitz) Q126   100502
Arise, arise and shine, On
thee hath dawned (Mesechre)
BE14   100503
Arise, arise, the Master calls
for thee (Merrill) AT423 X
Arise, O youth of Christ
                          100504
Arise, arise, united youth
(Solberg) P371   100505
Arise, arise, ye Christians

(Rist) M329 X Arise, the king-
dom is at hand   100506
Arise, my soul, arise, And with
a cheerful voice (Wesley??)
BR200   100507
Arise, my soul, arise, Shake
off thy guilty fears (Wesley)
G211; H301; I301; K138; L249;
M172; N145; O357; V178; AA
240; AH365; AM223; AO344;
AS205; AX112; AY263; BA91;
BC227; BZ   100508
Arise, my soul, arise! Stretch
forth to things eternal (Kahl)
J180   100509
Arise, my soul, new light re-
ceiving (Achrenius) M309
                         100510
Arise my Spirit, bless the day
(Rist) AZ985   100511
Arise, O Christian soldiers (---)
AO474   100512
Arise, O glorious Sion (Mills)
BC225   100513
Arise, O God, and shine (Hurn)
O124 X Arise, O Lord, and
shine   100514
Arise, O King of grace, arise
(Watts) H407; V65; AO426;
AZ132   100515
Arise, O Lord, and shine (Hurn)
D259; N70; O124; Q642; AI169;
AM386   100516
Arise, O Lord, exalt thy grace
(Zinzendorf, N. L.) BA338
X In these our days exalt thy
grace   100517
Arise, O Lord, our God, arise
(U. P. Psalter. 1912.) R518;
T264; AJ368; AM100   100518
Arise, O youth of God [with re-
frain](Merrill) AT423 X Rise
up, O men of God   100519
Arise, sons of the Kingdom
(Rist) Q69 X Arise, the King-
dom is at hand   100520
Arise, the Kingdom is at hand
(Rist) K15; L213; M329; Q69;
AA142; AE75; AK93   100521
Arise to praise the Lord (Ham-
burg Temple hymnal) BH74
                         100522

Arise ye people, take your
stand (Hay) BE12   100523
Arm of the Lord, awake!
awake! (Shrubsole) B487; D
265; I216; R497; V591; W369;
AM372; AP393   100524
Arm these thy soldiers mighty
Lord (Wordsworth, C) Q332;
AA410; AZ930; BX369 100525
Around my path life's mysteries
(Greg) BX254   100526
Around the throne of God, a
band (Neale) A120; B291;
E243; F448; Q256; X239; BA
37; BV452   100527
Around the throne of God in
heaven (Shepherd) K553; L583;
N653; P362; S450; U326; V
653; W600; AH550; AL615;
AM648; AP790; AW405; AZ169;
BA818; BY608   100528
Around the throne of God, The
host angelic throngs (Ware)
V110   100529
Around the weary world are
gently drawn (Levy) BH17
                         100530
Art thou weary, art thou laden
[troubled; languid] (Neale)
from St Stephen of Mar Saba
A406; B386; D342; E366; F
348; G193; H257; I293; J517;
K72; L357; Q513; R264; S221;
U152; V267; W391; Z286;
AB154; AC151; AD208; AE167;
AG140; AK302; AL471; AM
389; AO249; AP401; AR302;
AT245; AU426; AV157; AW143;
AY446; AZ1140; BA477; BB
341; BF347; BR396-397; BV
467; BY409; BZ   100531
Art thou weary, heavy laden
(Neale) S221 X Art thou
weary, art thou laden 100532
As above the darkest storm-
cloud (Howard) BR271 100533
As after the waterbrooks panteth
(Grundtvig) O453; P250 100534
As birds unto the genial home-
land fly (Levy) BH113 100535
As by one's sin fell all our kin
(Cronenwett) M135   100536

As comes the breath of spring
(Ritchie) AB96; AC65; AL151
100537
As darker, darker fall around
(Longfellow, S. ? ?) W276; AL
564; AP669; BX141; BY687
100538
As each happy Christmas (Hey)
K539; N634   100539
As every day thy mercy spares
(Shrubsole) AZ675   100540
As fades the daylight splendor
(Kockritz) AK52   100541
As fades the glowing orb of day
(St Ambrose) BQ139   100542
As God doth lead me I will go
(Gedicke) O216   100543
As gold by fire is tested (Inge-
mann) BE15   100544
As He heard His waiting people
(McKinney) AU305   100545
As helpless as a child who clings
BR526   100546
As I dream of a city I have not
seen (Tuttle) R I think of a
city I have not seen   100547
As I passed by a riverside
(English trad carol) BG53
100548
As I sat on a sunny bank (English
trad carol) BG3   100549
As it fell out one May morning
(English trad carol) BG56
100550
As it fell out upon one day, Rich
Dives made a feast (English
trad carol) BG57   100551
As Jacob with travel was weary
one day (English trad carol)
BG58   100552
As Joseph was a-walking (English
trad carol) BG66b X Joseph
was an old man   100553
As light, O Christ, thou cam'st
to earth (Russian) AL303
100554
As long as Jesus Lord remains
(Zinzendorf, N. L.) AZ285; BA
272   100555
As men of old their first fruits
brought (Frank v. Christierson)
BZ   100556
As now the sun's declining rays

(Coffin) B30; E265; F29; S
510; W274; BR534   100557
As oft with worn and weary
feet (Edmeston) L234; V139;
AZ669; BA75   100558
As, panting in the sultry
beam (Bowdler) BR287
100559
As pants the hart for cooling
streams (Tate & Brady)
A450; E367; F314; G366;
H332; I316; J388; K257; Q
525; R322; S317; T78; V401;
X449; AD283; AE205; AF390;
AG178; AJ116; AL649; AM
554; AN20; AO302; AP37;
AS209; AW586; AY416; AZ
208; BA517; BH30; BR358;
BT525; BV516; BX234; BY
571; BZ   100560
As pants the hart for streams
of living water (U.P. Psalter,
1912) T77; AJ115   100561
As pants the wearied hart for
cooling springs (Lowth)
B313; D661; F314; BR102
100562
As pilgrims and strangers we
journey through life (Orr)
AX583   100563
As sings the mountains stream
(Seymer) BE16   100564
As sinks beneath the ocean
(Skavlan) P422   100565
As Sion's pilgrims in accord
(Rivers) AY157   100566
As stars come with the night
(Cross) AB309   100567
As swiftly my days go out on
the wing (---) BC5   100568
As the angels sang, we sing
(---) R Clear upon the night-
air sounding   100569
As the dawn was calmly break-
ing (Buzzard) AY492 100570
As the dew from heaven dis-
tilling (Pratt) BC232 100571
As the disciples, when the Son
had left them (Dearmer)
X262   100572
As the hart when noon is burn-
ing (Collier) AI415   100573
As the hart with eager yearning

(Curtis) AK234   100574

As the rose shall blossom here
  (Grundtvig) M602   100575

As the storm retreating, Leaves
  the vales in peace (Williams)
  AN430; BD108; BX145   100576

As the sun doth daily rise (Latin)
  R42; S25; Z114; AF33; AM329;
  AO22; AR41; AX62; AY284;
  BD3   100577

As the sunflower turns in the
  morning (Overby) P54   100578

As the sun's enlivening eye
  (Newton) BX512   100579

As thirsts the hart for cooling
  flood (U. P. Psalter. 1912)
  AJ118   100580

As thirsts the hart for water-
  brooks (U. P. Psalter, 1912)
  AJ114   100581

As thou, O Lord, hast made me
  strong (U. P. Psalter. 1912)
  T27; AJ36   100582

"As thy day, thy strength shall
  be!" (Havergal) AZ45; BA855
                           100583

As torrents in summer, Half-
  dried in their channels
  (Longfellow) Y15; AB305
                           100584

As tranquil streams that meet
  and merge (Ham) AN406;
  AQ253   100585

As Victor in the Strife (Lee)
  BN45   100586

As we begin another week
  (Wandersleben) Q7   100587

As we leave this friendly place
  (Silliman) BK7   100588

As we rode down the steep hillside (Kendon) BG146   100589

As when, in far Samaria (Hodges)
  A187   100590

As when the Hebrew prophet
  raised (Watts) AM422 AP207
                           100591

As when the weary traveller
  gains (Newton) D677; BR342
                           100592

As wide as the skies is thy
  mercy, O God! (Ingemann)
  M147; P292   100593

As with gladness men of old

(Dix) A52; B94; D65; E39; F
  79; G90; H148; J52; K38;
  L226; M374; N60; O219;
  Q127; R174; S135; T336; V
  113; W63; X83; Z196; AA183;
  AB120; AC95; AD125; AE90;
  AF119; AG79; AH271; AK123;
  AL50; AM154; AN153; AO119;
  AP177; AR145; AS111; AT68;
  AV88; AW530; AZ1259; BA
  181; BB112; BD219; BF282;
  BR156; BV126; BY90; BZ
                           100594

As you are, just as you are
  (Hoffman) R Shall I come
                           100595

Ascend, dear Lord! Thy earthly
  toil is done (Hoppe) N152
                           100596

Ascend thy throne almighty Lord
  (Beddome) V593   100597

Ashamed of thee, O dearest
  Lord (How) D598   100598

Ask the Saviour to help you
  (Palmer) R Yield not to
  temptation   100599

Ask ye what great thing I know
  (Schwedler) G147; R371; S312;
  AD149; AE288; AG180; AK
  239; AO172; AR331; AT161;
  AV129; AZ1157; BZ   100600

Asleep in Jesus! blessed sleep
  (Mackay) B413; D244; H487;
  I583; K507; L568; M293; N
  598; O593; P419; Q587; U
  420; V672; AA540; AH538;
  AO565; AP621; AS484; AU165;
  AV299; AW314; AX621; AY179;
  AZ411; BA719; BB489 100601

Assist thy servant, Lord (---)
  AY37   100602

At all times praise the Lord
  (Howson) T298; AD271 100603

At Cana, Lord, thou didst appear
  (Berridge) M261   100604

At eve, when now be breathed
  no more (Darbyshire) X142
                           100605

At even, ere the sun was set
  (Twells) D14 X At even,
  when the sun was set 100606

At even when the sun was set
  (Twells) A168; B399; D14;

E266; F20; G48; I54; J232;
K233; Q557; R55; S43; U468;
W277; X42; AB132; AD135;
AE99; AF55; AG24; AK57; AG
24; AK57; AL541; AM336; AP
676; AR149; AV100; AW37;
BA779; BF205; BR170; BV49;
BY688; BZ   100607

At evening time let there be
light (Montgomery) AO39;
AZ663   100608

At first I prayed for Light
(Cheney) AN275; BB328 100609

At God's right hand in countless
numbers (Montgomery, I.)
AZ997   100610

At home and abroad on life's
battlefields (Smith) AY327
                                   100611

At Jesus' feet our infant sweet
(Loy) M38   100612

At last he's blest who by the
Savious's blood (Bernstein)
AZ464   100613

At length there dawns the glorious
day (David) G469; U335; Y256;
Z511; AB269; AC286; AD343;
AE405; AG251; AK400; AN356;
AR371; BD124; BF497; BZ
                                   100614

At midnight, so the sages tell
(Isaacs) BH175   100615

At our life's last moment fleeting
(Benedictine, "Ultima") BN191
                                   100616

At that first Eucharist before
you died (Turton) BM11 100617

At the cross, at the cross,
Where I first saw the light
(Hudson) U97 X Alas! and did
my Saviour bleed (Watts)
                                   100618

At the cross her station keeping
(Jacopone) A76; B161; D103;
E115; F118; G138; I154; J84;
N104; O320; W99; AD151; AH
113; AK150; AL95; AP197;
AZ643; BA211; BJ1a, 44; BL
21; BN34; BP25; BQ23 100619

At the cross her station keeping
(Jacopone) X138 X In the
place of sorrow, waiting
(Dearmer)   100620

At the golden gate, we will
come (Shacklock) R Would
you know the love   100621

At the Lamb's high feast we
sing (Latin, 4th c) A89; B
178; D118; E128; F139; H435;
J95; AM365; AZ1061; BL28;
BM2   100622

At the name of Jesus (Noel)
A356; B528; D518; E368; F
225; J430; R143; T321; U121;
V200; W178; X392; AF197;
AI99; AL113; AM124; AP259;
BA110; BV254; BY199;BZ
                                   100623

At thy command, our dearest
Lord (Isaacs) V547; AA440
                                   100624

At thy feet, At thy pierced feet
I lie (Holmes) AZ717 100625

At thy feet, O Christ, we lay
(Bright) E256; F6; J203; W
265; X24; BV46; BY671
                                   100626

At thy feet, our God and Father
(Burns) G37; U473; W605;
Z137; AH195; AI347; AK423;
AM610; AP696; AR4; BA176;
BF219; BR72; BY711; BZ
                                   100627

At thy table, Lord of life (---)
BR468   100628

At work beside his father's
bench (Pullen) BK16   100629

Attend, O Saviour, to our
prayer (Gambold) AZ281
                                   100630

Attende, Domine, et miserere
(Latin) BM73; BN29; BQ297
                                   100631

Audi, benigne Conditor (St
Gregory the Great) BN27;
BO286   100632

Audi, Deus me vocantem (Lobwasser. Psalter, 1617) BJ
92 notes   100633

Auf, auf, ihr Reichsgenossen
(Rist) BT69   100634

Auf, auf, mein Herz, mit
Freuden (Gerhardt) BT192
                                   100635

Auf Christi Himmelfahrt allein
(Wegelin) BT216   100636

Auf, ihr Christen, Christi Glieder
  (Falckner) BT472   100637
Auf meinen lieben Gott (Wein-
  gartner) BT526   100638
Auf, Sele, auf und fäume nich!
  (Unparth, G.B.) AY23d
                           100639
Aurinko armas vallolansa (Finnish,
  1836) BT545   100640
Aus dem Himmel ferne, Wo die
  Englein sind (W. Hey) BW433
                           100641
Aus Gnaden soll ich selig werden!
  (Scheidt) BT373   100642
Aus Gnaden wird der Mensch
  gerecht (Unparth, G.B.) AY43d
                           100643
Aus meines Herzens Grunde
  (Nigidius) BT548   100644
Aus tiefer Not schrei' ich zu dir
  (Luther) BT329; BW531
                           100645
Aus tiefer Noth schrey ich zu
  dir, Ach Gott erhör mein
  Rufen Dein Heil'gen Geist fend
  du zu mir (Ausbund. Seven
  Brothers) BU61   100646
Auspicious morning, hail (Smith)
  AZ1231   100647
Author of faith, eternal Word
  (Wesley) I298; AL275; BC228;
  BZ   100648
Author of faith, to thee I cry
  (Wesley) O390   100649
Author of life divine (Wesley)
  E303; F394; J268; W317; X263;
  AL226; AW309; BX484; BZ
                           100650
Author of the whole creation
  (Rist) AZ907; BA781   100651
Ave, ave verum corpus natum
  (Innocent VI, Pope) BQ233
  X Ave verum corpus natum
                           100652
Ave Maria! blessed maid (Keble)
  E216   100653
Ave Maria gratia plena (Latin,
  13th c) BP72; BQ200   100654
Ave Maria! O Virgin and Mother
  (St Patrick's hymnal) BQ74
  X Ave Maria! Thou Virgin
  and Mother   100655
Ave Maria! Thou Virgin and
  Mother (St Patrick's hymnal)

BP77; BQ74   100656
Ave, maris stella, Dei Mater
  (Latin, 9th c) BN127; BO263;
  BQ201   100657
Ave, Regina Caelorum (Latin,12th
  c) BN141; BO299; BQ203
                           100658
Ave, Regina sacratissimi (Litany
  of Loreto) BN156   100659
Ave, Tu Rex Pacis Nobiscum
  esto (Donnelly) BP107
                           100660
Ave verum corpus natum (Inno-
  cent VI, Pope) BN85; BO36;
  BP50; BQ233   100661
Awake, and sing the song (Ham-
  mond) B261; D369; H3; L121;
  V193; AP257; AZ1298; BA108;
  BV255   100662
Awake, arise! lift up thy voice
  (Smart) X151   100663
Awake, awake, awake. Put on
  thy strength (Bible. Isaiah 52.)
  AU473   100664
Awake, awake good people all
  (English trad carol) BG47
                           100665
Awake, awake, O earth (Flem-
  ing) AX120; AY347   100666
Awake, awake, O Sion! Put on
  thy strength Divine (Gough)
  BR210   100667
Awake, awake to love and work
  (Studdert-Kennedy) A156; G455;
  X450; Z323; AD273; AF34; AR
  369; BF392; BZ   100668
Awake, awake, ye drowsy souls
  (English trad carol) BG44
                           100669
Awake, Jerusalem, awake!
  (Wesley) H417; I217; BB293
                           100670
Awake, my heart, and marvel
  at nature's beauty (Gerhardt)
  M635   100671
Awake, my heart, and render
  (Gerhardt) A149   100672
Awake, my heart, with gladness
  (Gerhardt) Q192; AA218
                           100673
Awake, my soul, and with the
  sun (Ken) A151; B2; D2;
  E257; F3; G34; H26; I44; J
  202; K449; L10; M552; N546;

O539; Q536; R50; V33; W256;
X25; AA29; AD37; AE37; AF
32; AI45; AL529; AM331; AN
93; AP653; AQ265; AS24; AV3;
AW25; AZ356; BA765; BB44;
BF178; BJ9,25; BR4; BV34;
37; BX129; BY672; BZ   100674

Awake, my soul, in joyful lays
(Medley) H284; I539; L163;
O432; Q340; U148; V190; AA92;
AI2; AM138; AO404; AP265;
AS15; AT26; AV11; AX17; Ay
28; AZ293; BA478; BB667
                              100675

Awake, my soul, stretch every
nerve (Doddridge) A577; B111;
D503; G359; H385; I396; J552;
K380; L535; N506; R346; S278;
U291; V493; Y165; Z369; AB
241; AC195; AD302; AF362;
AG197; AH436; AI321; AK285;
AM480; AN298; AO401; AQ222;
AR316; AS325; AT309; AU253;
AV201; AZ193; BA450; BB355;
BD90; BF468; BX364; BZ
                              100676

Awake my soul to joyful lays
(Medley) Q340 X Awake my
soul in joyful lays   100677

Awake, my soul, to sound His
praise (Watts) V525   100678

Awake, my tongue, thy tribute
bring (Needham) Z152; AT24
                              100679

Awake, O Church of God, the
night is past (Tiplady) AR492
                              100680

Awake, O Lord, as in the time
of old! (Twells) BY222 100681

Awake! O ye people, the Saviour
is coming (Phelps) BC183
                              100682

Awake, our souls! Away, our
fears! (Watts) I405; V480;
X451; AL413; AN103; AW258;
BV570; BX134; BY572   100683

Awake! The watchman crieth
(Franzén) N395   100684

Awake, thou Spirit bold and daring
(Bogatzky) M112   100685

Awake, thou Spirit of the watchmen (Bogatzky) A255; J255
                              100686

Awake, thou Spirit, who didst
fire the watchmen (Bogatzky)
K213; L305; N380; O116; Q
494; AA481   100687

Awake thou that sleepest, arise
from death's slumber (Landstad) O159]   100688

Awake were they only those shepherds so lonely (Roberts)
BG59   100689

Awake, ye saints, and raise
your eyes (Doddridge) BB
175   100690

Awake, ye saints, awake (Scott)
H186; L48   100691

Awake, ye saints of God, awake
(Snow) BC229   100692

Awaked by Sinai's awful sound
(Occum) V305   100693

Awaked from sleep we fall before
(Greek) F9   100694

Away in a manger, no crib for
his bed (American carol)
A43; G434; K536; N637; P363;
R157; S126; W657; X353; Z
199; AD116; AE435; AF137;
AG76; AH265; AK109; AL598;
AM641; AO630; AP729; AR
137; AS107; AT77; AU314; AV
92; AW414; AY482; BK153;
BV95; BY734; BZ   100695

Away, my needless fears (Wesley) H123   100696

Away, O soul, hoist up the
anchor now (Whitman) AQ78
                              100697

Away with gloom, away with
doubt (Shillito) G158; BY181
                              100698

Away with our fears, Our troubles
and tears (Wesley) BV213;
BY223   100699

Awhile in spirit, Lord to thee
(Thrupp) D80; K79   100700

Ayn Kay-lo-hay-nu (Jewish liturgical) BH275   100701

Ayn ko-mo-cho bo-e-lo-heem
(Jewish Traditional) BH304
                              100702

Ay-yukh-nyehm (Russian trad)
Y313   100703

B

Back of the loaf is the snowy
flour (Babcock) AC532
100704

Back to the cross I go again
(Becker) M186   100705

Backward looking o'er the past
(Chadwick) BD235   100706

Backward we look, O God of all
our days (Freeman) AB397;
AC233; BF653   100707

Baptize us anew, with power from
on high (Ogden) BB525
100708

Baptized into our Saviour's death
(Doddridge) AX165   100709

Baptized into thy name most holy
(Rambach) M539; N59; Q298;
AA400   100710

Baptized into thy name most holy
(Rambach) M539 X I am baptized into thy name 100711

Be firm and be faithful (---) BE18
100712

Be firm, ye sentinels of Truth
(Sargant) BE17   100713

Be joyful in God, all ye lands
of the earth (Montgomery)
L74; BA368   100714

Be joyful, Mary, heavenly Queen
(Latin, 17th c) BM85; BN49
100715

Be known to us in breaking bread
(Montgomery) G408 X Shepherd
of souls refresh and bless
100716

Be like Jesus, this my song
(Rowe) R Earthly pleasures
vainly call me   100717

Be, Lord, the happy guide
(Dearmer) X407   100718

Be merciful, O God of grace
(Conder) AY63   100719

Be merciful to me, O God
(Scottish Psalter, 1650) AP47
100720

Be not dismayed, thou little flock
(Altenberg) K196; N263; O85
100721

Be not dismayed whate'er betide
(Martin) R124; AH381; AM696;
AT274; AV366; AX480; BZ

100722
Be of good cheer, the Master
said (Marlatt) Y195; AC193
100723

Be our Comfort which ne'er
faileth (Gregor) AZ1109
100724

Be present at our table, Lord
(Cennick) G563; W656; AR
551; AS464; AT396; AX650;
AZ308; BA895; BZ   100725

Be present, Holy Trinity
(Latin, ca 10th c) E159
100726

Be present with thy servants,
Lord (Zinzendorf, N. L.)
AZ323; BA534   100727

Be ready, Be ready, Be ready
(Teasley) R Would you flee
100728

Be silent, be silent, A whisper
is heard (Crosby) AR437;
AS43; AU485; AX39; AY448;
BB601   100729

Be still my heart, these anxious
cares (Newton) AZ421; BA
706; BV497   100730

Be still, my soul, for God is
near (Maclagan) J267; K181;
BA292   100731

Be still, my soul: the Lord is
on thy side (Schlegel) G73;
Q651; R374; S281; W556;
AB231; AD80; AE211; AF77;
AG215; AH403; AK87; AM579;
AP512; AR263; AU479; AW54;
BF255; BV520; BZ   100732

Be strong! we are not here to
play (Babcock) G300; I407;
S488; U269; Y185; AB176;
AC182; AD488; AH449; AK
293; AO395; AR304; BF400
100733

Be this henceforth my constant
care (Heermann) AZ1096
100734

Be this our happy destiny (Foster) AZ1100   100735

Be thou exalted, holy Lord (Morgan) BV311   100736

Be thou exalted, O my God
(Watts) BI15   100737

Be thou my Guardian and my

Guide (Williams) E369; F300; X100; BV146   100738
Be thou my helper in the strife (U.P. Psalter, 1912) T59; AJ 92   100739
Be thou my judge, O righteous Lord (U.P. Psalter, 1912) AJ69   100740
Be thou my Vision, O Lord of my heart (Irish ancient) R303; S325; W477; Z321; AC236; AD 307; AE449; AF391; AG174; AL336; AR195; AT62; BF386; BK93; BV571; BY462; BZ 100741
Be thou, O God, exalted high (Tate & Brady) AN497; AO53; AR633; BE1; BR51; BX1 100742
Be thou our Guardian and our guide (Williams) BV146 X Be thou my Guardian   100743
Be tranquil, O my soul! (Hastings) AZ478; BA857   100744
Be true and list the voice within (Colby) BE20   100745
Be with me all my journey (Crosby) U364   100746
Be with me every moment (Crosby) R Be with me all my journey   100747
Be with me, Lord, where'er I go (Cennick) U366; AZ359; BA767   100748
Be with us gracious Lord, today (Bell) BY266   100749
Be ye doers of the Word (Linthicum) R Out of James 100750
Be ye joyful, earth and sky (---) P129   100751
Be ye lamps unto yourselves (Gautama Buddha) AQ110 100752
Be ye strong in the Lord and the power of his might (Whittle) AX448; AY461   100753
Beati mortui in Domino morientes (Breviary) BQ250   100754
Beauteous are the flowers of earth (Dix) I673   100755
Beautiful day of peace and rest (Townsend) R The day dawn is breaking   100756

Beautiful Saviour Münster G-B. 1677 O576 X Fairest Lord Jesus   100757
Beautiful Sion, built above (---) BC78   100758
Beautiful Sion for me (Penrose) BC6   100759
Beautiful Star of Bethlehem, shine on (Boyce) R O, beautiful Star of Bethlehem 100760
Beautiful upon the mountain are the feet of shepherds true (French 1830-50) M93 100761
Beautiful Valley of Eden (Cushing) AU166; AV312; AX678; BB550   100762
Beautiful words, wonderful words (Bliss) R Sing them over again to me   100763
Beauty around us, Glory above (---) AK67   100764
Because I have been given much, I, too, must give (Crowell) AD314; AK259; AR340; BF500 100765
Because I knew not when my life was good (Williams) R274; AB161; BF355   100766
Because thou hast made charity the sign (Mary Francis, Sr.) BN208   100767
Because thy trust is God alone (U.P. Psalter. 1912) T170; AJ249   100768
Because you live again, O Rose (The Abatal, 1532) BN162 100769
Bedenke, Mensch, das Ende (Unparth, G.B.) AY17d 100770
Befiehl du deine Wege (Gerhardt) AW558; BT520; BW558 100771
Before Jehovah's awful throne (Watts) M503 X Before the Lord Jehovah's throne 100772
Before Jehovah's glorious throne (Watts) BA21 X Before the Lord Jehovah's throne 100773
Before my journey is complete (U.P. Psalter, 1912) T188;

AJ274   100774
Before Pilate the Jews me brought
(English trad carol) X Tomorrow
shall be my dancing day
                               100775
Before the cross of Jesus (Blan-
chard) AB141; AF161; AK261;
BF379   100776
Before the day draws near its
ending (Ellerton) R57; S509;
W271; AF508   100777
Before the ending of the day (St
Ambrose) B28; D21; E264;
F16; BR118   100778
Before the Father's awful throne
(Wesley) AZ670   100779
Before the great Three-One
(Jewish Doxology) AZ1192 X
The God of Abraham praise
                               100780
Before the heavens were stretched
abroad (Watts) AZ349 100781
Before the Lord a man is small
(Patton) AQ68   100782
Before the Lord Jehovah's throne
(Watts) A300; B309; D473;
F370; G3; H20; J161; K492;
L68; M503; N290; O14; Q13;
R81; S63; U444; V2; W230;
AA78; AB68; AE54; AF9; AG
47; AK25; AL6; AM62; AO8;
AP87; AR16; AS78; AV33; AW
272; AY413; AZ312; BA21; BB1;
BV236; BW272; BX27; BY6; BZ
                               100783
Before the Lord we bow, The God
who reigns above (Key) J339;
K491; L557; N568; O520; Q575;
AO23   100784
Before the throne of God above
(DeChenez) BV518   100785
Before thee, God, who knowest all
(Landstad) O97; Q318; AM409
                               100786
Before thee, Lord, a people waits
(Presbyterian hymnal, 1874)
T117; AJ168   100787
Before thee, Lord, I bow my
head (Dean) BC231   100788
Before thee we appear, Thou
wilt receive (Foster) AZ549
                               100789
Before thy feet I fall (Ross)

X452; AB41   100790
Before thy people I confess
(U. P. Psalter, 1912) AJ112;
AM565   100791
Before thy throne I now appear
(Hodenberg) AA35   100792
Before thy throne, O God, we
kneel (Carpenter) A499;
AD329; AR256; BF357 100793
Begin, my tongue, some heaven-
ly theme (Watts) I89; P375;
R86; S94; V111; Z153; AB65;
AD7; AH192; AR17; AS12; AT
49; AV35   100794
Begin the day with God (Bonar)
AX61; AY277   100795
Begone, unbelief; for my Saviour
is near (Newton) AZ506; BV
519; BY573   100796
Begone, unbelief: my Saviour is
near (Newton) BV519 X Be-
gone unbelief; for my Saviour
is near   100797
Begone! vain world, with all thy
pleasures (Scheffler) O445
                               100798
Behold a Branch is growing
(Speier Gebetbuch. 1599) K533;
P138; Q645; AK113; AM153
                               100799
Behold a host arrayed in white
(Brorson) M313 X Behold a
host like mountain bright
                               100800
Behold a host like mountain
bright (Brorson) J599; M313;
N207; O492; P434; Q656
                               100801
Behold a humble train (Harland)
D153   100802
Behold a little child (How) A237;
E588; W76; BY116   100803
Behold, a Rose of Judah from
tender branch (Speier Gebet-
buch. 1599) BM78   100804
Behold! a royal army (Crosby)
BC7   100805
Behold a simple tender babe
(Southwell) BG170; BN13
                               100806
Behold a Sower! from afar
(Gladden) A401; G391; S486;
AB292; AK201; AN74; AQ122,

236; BF269; BX444   100807

Behold! a Stranger at the door
(Grigg) G196; H247; I249; L
367; M193; N396; Q650; S225;
U168; V258; AA51; AD202;
AG143; AH326; AL489; AO247;
AP405; AR255; AS194; AV155;
AW141; AZ364; BA397; BB227;
BV469   100808

Behold a Stranger's at the door
(Grigg) V258 X Behold! a
Stranger at the door   100809

Behold, all ye that serve the
Lord (U.P. Book of Psalms.
1871) AP119   100810

Behold! behold He cometh (Latin)
BQ3   100811

Behold, by grace, and grace
alone (Olson) M124; N444
                         100812

Behold, by sovereign grace alone
(Olson) N444 X Behold, by
grace, and grace alone 100813

Behold He comes, thy King most
holy (Webb) AZ701   100814

Behold, how glorious is yon sky
(Ramler)   O252   100815

Behold, how good a thing It is to
dwell in peace (Wesley) Q405
                         100816

Behold, how pleasant and how good
(U.P. Psalter. 1912) T266; AJ
371   100817

Behold, I stand at the door (Bible.
Revelation. 2) AI273   100818

Behold, it is the spring-tide of
the year (Lucas) BH129
                         100819

Behold Me standing at the door
(Crosby) BY410   100820

Behold that star (Talley) Y323;
BK164   100821

Behold the amazing gift of love
(Watts) R120; W483; AL328;
AP469; BV521   100822

Behold the amazing sight (Doddridge) L251   100823

Behold the Bridegroom cometh
(Greek. 8th c) E3; O512 100824

Behold the Bridegroom cometh
(Greek 8th c) X Behold the
Bridegroom draweth nigh
                         100825

Behold the Bridegroom draweth
nigh! (Greek. 8th c) F46
                         100826

Behold! the Christian warrior
stand (Montgomery) I397; BE
326   100827

Behold the eternal King and
Priest (Congregational Ch.
hymnal. 1887) BV369; BY308
                         100828

Behold the glories of the Lamb
(Watts) I167; AY418   100829

Behold the glories of the Lamb
(Watts) X Hark how the adoring hosts above   100830

Behold the great creator makes
(Pestel) E20; F69; X72
                         100831

Behold the great Redeemer die
(Snow) BC230   100832

Behold the heavenly city stands
(Howard) BR219   100833

Behold, the joyful day is nigh
(Wallin) M357; N45   100834

Behold the Lamb of God, O Thou
for sinners (Bridges) A338;
B148; D96; F212; J83; K102;
O265; Q165; S153; AK148;
BB129   100835

Behold the Lamb of God, who
bears (Wesley) BV468
                         100836

Behold the lilies of the field that
bloom around (---) AY361
                         100837

Behold the lilies of the field
They neither toil nor sow
(Caddell) BV495   100838

Behold the man! how heavy lay
(Muenter) M384   100839

Behold, the Master passeth by
(How) D169; U86; V262; BA
396   100840

Behold the morning sun (Watts)
V77   100841

Behold the mountain of the Lord
(Bruce) L354; W365; AL521;
AM272; BC297; BV416; BY
658   100842

Behold the Saviour at the door
(Grigg) BB227 X Behold! a
Stranger at the door   100843

Behold the Saviour of mankind

(Wesley, S.,Sr) G136; H170;
I142; Q176; AA211; AX108;
AY251; BZ   100844
Behold the shining Sabbath sun
(Dennis) H86   100845
Behold the sin-atoning Lamb
(Fawcett) V245   100846
Behold the stone is rolled away
(Whittle) R O, day of awful
story   100847
Behold the sun, that seemed but
now (Wither) X43   100848
Behold the sure foundation-stone
(Watts) L281; O82; Q460;AA
452   100849
Behold the temple of the Lord
(Kelly) BV659   100850
Behold the throne of grace! (New-
ton) H54; V466; AM530; AZ
1302; BA592   100851
Behold, they stand in robes of
white (Brorson) BE19 100852
Behold, thy sons and daughters,
Lord (Pratt) BC24   100853
Behold us, Lord, a little space
(Ellerton) B10; F13; G459;
I394; J213; K429; U286; W242;
X39; AF395; AK228; AL206;
AN107; AO508; AP329; AZ201;
BA594; BF439; BV590; BX164;
BY627; BZ   100854
Behold us, Lord, before thee
met (Bright) E340   100855
Behold we come, dear Lord, to
thee (Austin) AL194; BV66
                            100856
Behold what love, that God should
give (Ryden) M153; N189
                            100857
Behold what love the Father hath
On guilty men bestowed (Bos-
well) AZ111; BA41   100858
Behold what love, yes, love divine
(Warren) AX84   100859
Behold, what wondrous grace
(Watts) U145; V316; AE72;
AK81; AO93   100860
Behold, where in a mortal form
(Enfield) H150; K53; AX169;
AY435; AZ178; BA77   100861
Bei frühem Morgenlicht. (German
c1800.) BW19   100862
Believe it, O sinner, believe it

(Sayford) R Redemption! O
wonderful story   100863
Believe not those who say
(Brontë) X453; AB250; AC
183; AD293; AE253; AN300;
AW210; BD98; BF463; BH231;
BX358   100864
Believing fathers oft have told
(Charteris) J540; W521
                            100865
Believing souls, rejoice and sing
(Swertner) AX1431; BA230
                            100866
Bells in the high tower Ringing
o'er the snow (Box) AQ303
                            100867
Beloved, "It is well!" God's
ways are always right (Doane)
L521; Q519; AA518   100868
Beloved Jesus, what law hast
thou broken (Heermann)
AA198 X O dearest Jesus,
what law   100869
Beloved, let us love: for Love
is God (Bonar) BE21 X
Beloved, let us love: love is
of God   100870
Beloved, let us love: love is of
God (Bonar) S500; W488; AP
569; BE21; BY591   100871
Bend back the lance's point
(Ruskin) AQ207   100872
Bending low in adoration (---) R
Like a strong and raging fire
                            100873
Beneath the amazing gift of love
(Watts) AM442   100874
Beneath the cross of Jesus
(Clephane) A341; B150; E567;
G144; J482; N451; O321; P
180; R190; S162; T344; U95;
V252; W691; Y105; Z235; AB
138; AC120; AD154; AE110;
AF160; AG91; AH290; AI75;
AK161; AL98; AM177; AO163;
AP209; AR165; AS332; AT345;
AU234; AV110; AW112; BA189;
BB280; BF317; BV152; BY427;
BZ   100875
Beneath the forms of outward
rite (Blaisdell) Y87; Z459;
AB327; AE334; AR511; BF
601; BZ   100876

Beneath the shadow of the cross
(Longfellow) AN187; AO481;
AP567; AQ312; AR354; AS141;
AZ227; BX248   100877
Beneath Thy cross I stand (Leh-
mann) M393   100878
Beneath thy shadow hiding (Ran-
kin) AY93   100879
Beneath thy wing, O God, I rest
(Waring) BB82   100880
Beset with snares on every hand
(Doddridge) I425   100881
Beside thy manger here I stand
(Gerhardt) M619   100882
Besprinkle with thy blood my
heart (Hutton) AZ100 100883
Bethany, O peaceful habitation
(Gregor) AZ1008; BA520
                         100884
Bethlehem in land of Judah
(Prudentius) BR154 X Earth has
many a noble city   100885
Bethlehem, of noblest cities
(Prudentius) E40; X84; AW88;
BN25; BO162   100886
Bethlehem, of noblest cities
(Prudentius) X Earth has many
a noble city   100887
Beyond, beyond that [the] bound-
less sea (Conder) X454; BX
158   100888
Beyond the ever-lasting hills
(Ryden) J295   100889
Beyond the smiling and the weep-
ing (Bonar) H502; I627; U
435; V696   100890
Beyond the starry skies (Turner)
BB170   100891
Beyond the sunset's radiant glow
(Pollard) AU88   100892
Beyond the wheeling worlds of
light (Tiplady) AK73   100893
Bid the din of battle cease (Howe)
AB362   100894
Birds are singing, woods are
ringing (Cole) AL587; AP723;
AW409   100895
Bis hieher hat mich Gott gebracht
(Amilie Juliane) BT33 100896
Bless Him, ye angels (U.P.
Psalter.1912) T195 X O come,
my soul, bless thou the Lord
thy maker   100897

Bless me, Lord, and make me
a blessing (Zelley) R I do
not ask to choose   100898
Bless, O Lord, this church of
thine (Mack) AR493 100899
Bless, O Lord, we pray thee
(Collier) AO664   100900
Bless, O Lord, we pray, Thy
congregation (Benade) AZ
1015; BA599   100901
Bless, O my soul! the living
God (Watts) L82; R8; U17;
V95; AY19; AZ362; BA40
                         100902
Bless the four corners of this
house (Guiterman) G433;
Z599; AC527; AD420; AR542;
AW363   100903
Bless the words we here have
spoken (Crosby) R Heavenly
Father, we beseech thee
                         100904
Bless thou the gifts our hands
have brought (Longfellow)
G609; R553; S29app.; U495;
AC340; AD505; AE465; AF538;
AG326; AH568; AK507; AN508;
AR673; AS493; AT533; AU490;
AW611; BF693   100905
Blessed are the heirs of heaven
(Klopstock) O590   100906
Blessed are the sons of God
(Humphreys) Q391; V315;
AA315; AM443; AR332 100907
Blessed are they that have the
faith (Auerbach) BC233
                         100908
Blessed are they that undefiled
(Scottish Psalter, 1650) AP107
                         100909
Blessed art thou, O Lord of all
(---) BH15   100910
Blessed assurance, Jesus is
mine (Crosby) G238; H298;
I548; R139; V731; Z412; AE
208; AG216; AH209; AR436;
AS285; AT269; AU120; AV
359; AW480; AX477; AY207;
BB608; BY493; BZ   100911
Blessed be God! Blessed be His
Holy Name (Latin) BO275;
BP102; BQ147   100912
Blessed be the Lord God of

Israel (Psalter version) AJ
p394 X Now be the God of
Israel blessed (Watts) 100913

Blessed be the name, Blessed
be the name (---) R O for a
thousand tongues (Wesley) R
All praise to Him who reigns
above (Clark) 100914

Blessed be thy name Jesus
Christ! -- the same (Montgomery) AZ538; BR67
100915

Blessed Bible, how I love it
(Palmer) AS183; AX143; AY
194   100916

Blessed, blessed be Jehovah
(Bible. Psalm 106) AP813
100917

Blessed, blessed he who knoweth
(Wallin) N417   100918

Blessed book, precious book
(Williams) R There's a dear
and precious book   100919

Blessed city, heavenly Salem
(Latin, 7th c) A383; B508;
D400; E169; F474,620; J245;
X190; AZ626; BR217; BT466;
BV660   100920

Blessed city, heavenly Salem
(Latin 7th c) X Come thou now
and be among us   100921

Blessed feasts of blessed martyrs
(Latin, 12th c) A135; E184
100922

Blessed Fount of heavenly gladness (Fliedner) N386 100923

Blessed fountain, full of grace
(Kelly) AY283   100924

Blessed Francis, holy father,
now our hearts to thee
(Franciscan manual) BN179;
BQ102   100925

Blessed hour of prayer (Crosby)
R 'Tis the blessed hour of
prayer   100926

Blessed is the man that never
(Gerhardt) O455   100927

Blessed Jesus all our hearts
incline (Pfeil) AZ517 100928

Blessed Jesus, at thy word
We are gathered [general]
(Clausnitzer) G310; K421;
M3; N302; O34; P46; Q16;
AA3; AE32; AF212; AK26;
AM220; AZ591; BA372; BB27;
BR100; BV2   100929

Blessed Jesus, here are we
[Baptism] (Schmolck) A186;
E336; N225; O145; W307;
AA402; AF279; AZ592; BA
282   100930

Blessed Jesu! here we stand
(Schmolck) E336 X Blessed
Jesus, here are we   100931

Blessed Jesus, high in glory
(Macleod) W465   100932

Blessed Jesus, meek and lowly
(Smith, A.R. BB268 100933

Blessed Jesus, we implore thee
(Hartley) AZ1409; BA620
100934

Blessed Jesus, we will love thee
(Smith) R In the early days of
childhood   100935

Blessed Lord, how much I need
thee (Belden) BB578 100936

Blessed Lord, in thee is refuge
(Booth) AI248; AM420
100937

Blessed Lord, what shall we
render (Cennick) BR75B
100938

Blessed Master, I have promised
(Dickinson) G223; S244; AS
443   100939

Blessed night, when Bethlehem's
plain (Bonar) BA51 X
Blessed night, when first that
plain   100940

Blessed night, when first that
plain (Bonar) AZ1126,1127;
BA51; BI81   100941

Blessed night, when first the
plain (Bonar) BI81 X Blessed
night, when first that plain
100942

Blessed, O blessed moment most
holy (Jastrow) BH153,154
100943

Blessed quietness, holy quietness
(Ferguson) R Joys are flowing   100944

Blessed Redeemer! precious
Redeemer (Christiansen) R
Up Calvary's mountain
100945

Blessed Saviour, thee I love
(Duffield) AE206; AO285;
AS292; AU195; AY197; AZ1282;
BA452   100946

Blessed Saviour, thou hast taught
me (Neale) N251 X Blessed
Saviour who hast taught me
                          100947

Blessed Saviour, thou wilt guide
us (Snow) R Truth reflects
upon our senses   100948

Blessed Saviour, we adore thee
(McKinney) AT138   100949

Blessed Saviour, who hast taught
me (Neale) J290; K176; N251;
O109; P109; Q333   100950

Blessed Saviour with love's sacred
fire (Schlicht) AZ516 100951

Blessing and honour and glory and
power (Bible. Revelation 5)
BY305B   100952

Blessing and honor, and glory and
power (Bonar) J166; K295;
L146; N336; P22; R137; S196;
W169; AD178; AK178; AL42; AM
219; AP253; AR103; AZ1155;
BI48   100953

Blessing, honour, thanks and
praise (Wesley) D241   100954

Blest are humble souls that see
(Watts) AI215; AS305   100955

Blest are the moments, doubly
blest (Wordsworth) B9; E263;
J218; X40   100956

Blest are the pure in heart
(Keble) A418; B277; D410;
E370; F335; G369; I360; J394;
K369; L459; N492; O469; R
226; V321; W478; X455; AF
214; AK247; AL325; AP482;
AS313; AW205; AZ1370; BA
621; BR31; BV638; BY463; BZ
                          100957

Blest are the sons of peace
(Watts) V607   100958

Blest are the undefiled in heart
(Watts) L445; AM447   100959

Blest are they, supremely blest
(Wolf [or Wolff]) AZ67; BA
503;   100960

Blest be that sacred covenant-
love (Wesley) AZ224; BA893
                          100961

Blest be the day when I must
roam (Moravian emigrants
hymn) BA938   100962

Blest be the day when moved I
was (Bunyan) X456   100963

Blest be the dear uniting love
(Wesley) G404; I228; V611;
Z482; AX542; BZ   100964

Blest be the everlasting God
(Watts) W137; AL467; AP638;
AW266; BV517   100965

Blest be the Lord! for us he
cares (U. P. Psalter. 1912)
T124; AJ181   100966

Blest be the Lord, by Rock, my
Might (U. P. Psalter. 1912)
T284; AJ392   100967

Blest be the Lord, our Father's
God (U. P. Psalter. 1912)
T452; AJ195, 196   100968

Blest be the tie that binds
(Fawcett) A495; B489; D672;
G416; H429; I556; J543; L284;
M21; N356; P58; Q464; R473;
S343; T380; U373; V608; W
490; Y383; Z476; AA462; AB
324; AC312; AD409; AE340;
AF272; AG237; AH458; AI276;
AK280; AL376; AM285; AN563;
AO420; AP571; AR505; AS67;
AT366; AU239; AV217; AW41;
AX548; AY399; AZ1335; BA
666; BB432; BF490; BK174;
BR502; BY355; BZ   100969

Blest be thy love, dear Lord
(Austin) H341; AA388; BR
330   100970

Blest Christmas morn, though
murky clouds (Eddy) BE23
                          100971

Blest Comforter Divine, whose
rays of heavenly love (Sigourney) V216; BR207   100972

Blest Creator of the light
(Latin) F44   100973

Blest day of God! most calm,
most bright (Mason) D31;
H82; L37; N309   100974

Blest Easter Day, what joy is
thine (Petri) N125   100975

Blest feast of love divine (Denny)
Z457; BA302; BV387; BY329

100976
Blest holder of the heavenly Keys
(Breviary. Venice, 1798) R
Seek ye a Patron to defend
100977
Blest hour, when mortal man re-
tires (Raffles) BB28   100978
Blest is he that never walketh
(Gerhardt) P261   100979
Blest is he who cries to heaven
(Paulsen) M128   100980
Blest is he who loves God's pre-
cepts (U. P. Psalter. 1912)
T1; AJ2   100981
Blest is that man who sets his
soul's desire (Auslander)
AQ229   100982
Blest is the bond of wedded love
(Moise) BH219   100983
Blest is the Faith, divine and
strong (Faber) BQ123 100984
Blest is the home when God is
there (Ware) AR545 X
Happy the home when God is
there   100985
Blest is the man, for-ever blest
(Watts) L421; Q392; AA309
100986
Blest is the man who dies in
peace (Barbauld) BR431 X
How blest the righteous when
he dies   100987
Blest is the man who shuns the
place (Watts) V442   100988
Blest is the man whose softening
heart (Barbauld) V574 100989
Blest Jesus! when my soaring
thoughts (Heginbothom) L437
100990
Blest Jesus, when thy cross I
view (Speece) V192   100991
Blest land of Judea! thrice hal-
lowed in song (Whittier) AC
105; AD134   100992
Blest martyr, let thy Triumph
day (Prudentius) E185 100993
Blest morning, whose first dawn-
ing rays (Watts) W116; AP218
100994
Blest Spirit, one with God above
(St Ambrose) K148   100995
Blest the man that fears Jehovah
(U. P. Psalter. 1912) T258; AI

366; AJ360; AM626   100996
Blest the man who fears Jehovah
(U. P. Book of Psalms. 1871)
AP115   100997
Blest Trinity, from mortal sight
(Santeuil) AZ410   100998
Bliss beyond compare which in
Christ I share (---) AZ534; BA
506   100999
Bliv hos os, Mester, Dagen
helder! (Boye) BT194
101000
Blow, blow, thou winter wind
(Shakespeare) BG171 101001
Blow, golden trumpets, sweet
and clear (Deland) AC134
101002
Blow on, thou Mighty Wind
(Hopkins) BR209   101003
Blow the trumpet, trusty watch-
man (Gilmour) R Watchman,
blow the gospel trumpet
101004
Blow winds of God, and bring
us on our way (Hodge) AN
552   101005
Blow, winds of God, awake and
blow (Whittier) AB74
101006
Blow ye the trumpet, blow!
(Wesley) D330; G189; H229;
I294; L369; V234; AM392;
AO116; AP392; AT250; AV165;
AZ1182; BA398; BZ   101007
Bondage and death the cup con-
tains (Sargent) AO613 101008
Book of books, our people's
strength (Dearmer) A403;
G390; R248; X457; Y337; AC
69; AD196; AF253; AK203;
BY241; BZ   101009
Book of grace and book of glory
(MacKellar) Z439; BY242
101010
Bo-r'-chu es Adonoy (Jewish
traditional) BH268   101011
Boroch atoh Adonoy (Jewish
liturgy) AHp148; BH297
101012
Bo-ruch shaym k'vod mal-chu-
so (Jewish traditional) BH
331   101013
Bound upon th'accursed Tree

34 Hymns and Tunes

(Milman) AZ1078   101014

Boundless glory, Lord, be thine
(Kelly) V389   101015

Bow down in worship now, before the Christ (Glen) BI
50D   101016

Bow down thine ear, Almighty
Lord (Powell) D286; V562;
AA493; BA306; BV409 101017

Bow down thine ear, Lord, hear
thou my cry (Mayer) BH35
101018

Bow down thine ear, O Lord
(U. P. Psalter. 1912) AM75
X Bow down thy ear. . .
101019

Bow down thy ear, O Lord, and
hear (U. P. Psalter, 1912)
AJ233; AM75   101020

Bow down ye followers of the
Lamb (Lauterbach) AZ692
101021

Bowed down beneath a weight of
woe (Kuhlman) M415 101022

Bowed low in supplication (How)
W342   101023

Bowing low, then, offer homage
(Avery) BM33   101024

Braving the wilds all unexplored
(Freeman) S418; AB346
101025

Bread of heaven, on thee we
feed (Conder) A212; B332;
D224; E304; F411; K192; X264;
AE330; AF281; AH505; AR512;
AT395; AU232; AV253; AW311;
BA293; BV370; BY309 101026

Bread of life, Christ by Whom
alone we live (Zinzendorf,
N. L.) AZ719   101027

Bread of the world, in mercy
broken (Heber) A196; B336;
D225; E305; F409; G414; H
442; I238; J279; K194; L332;
R445; S353; V552; W318; X
265; Z453; AD403; AE339; AF
282; AG239; AH502; AK337;
AL224; AM358; AO443; AP358;
AR514; AS460; AT394; AV254;
AW304; BB476; BF603; BJ19;
BR472; BV371; BY310; BZ
101028

Break, day of God, O break

(Burton) G504; AD355; AL
529   101029

Break forth, O beauteous
heavenly light (Rist) A25;
J29; AF118; AN492; AQ297;
BC239; BI90; BL7; BZ
101030

Break forth, O living light of
God (Frank v. Christierson)
BZ   101031

Break, new-born year, on glad-
eyes break! (Gill) I572;
S469   101032

Break thou, O Lord, the Bread
of life to me (Lathbury) BI
66 X Break thou the Bread
of life   101033

Break thou the Bread of life
(Lathbury) G387; H89; I325;
J491; L309; M36; P87; R250;
S216; T405; U381; V553; W
202; Y101; Z461; AB99; AC71;
AD197; AE162; AF254; AG132;
AH236; AK204; AL187; AM
256; AO243; AP291; AR236;
AS182; AT178; AU192; AV81;
AW288; AX144; AY439; BA
367; BB218; BF270; BI66;
BR301; BV303; BY243; BZ
101034

Breaking through the clouds of
darkness (Heywood) BE29
101035

Breast the wave, Christian,
When it is strongest (Stam-
mers) A565; B112; D656; H
354; BR400   101036

Breathe o'er our waiting spirits,
Lord (Slemp) AU286 101037

Breathe on me, Breath of God
(Hatch) A375; B380; F236;
G180; I196; J470; R235; S
213; W194; X458; Y98; AB93;
AC61; AD187; AE143; AF233;
AG123; AK191; AL148; AN59;
AO228; AP270; AR220; AT167;
AV146; AW135; BB679; BF
260; BN121; BV287; BX357;
BY592; BZ   101038

Breathe upon us, Holy Spirit
(Hoffman) AR218; AS169
101039

Brethren, called by one vocation

(Spitta) O407   101040
Brethren, let us join to bless
    (Cennick) BV14   101041
Brethren, we have met to wor-
    ship (Atkins) AT368; AU198;
    AX33   101042
Brethren, while we sojourn here
    (Swain) AZ1065   101043
Brich auf und werde lichte
    (Opitz) BT126   101044
Brief life is here our portion
    (St Bernard of Cluny) A596;
    B69; D406; E371; F275; J527;
    K527; L607; O612; Q448; R430;
    V692; W597; X459; AA557; AL
    463; AO554; AP626; AZ822;
    BA741   101045
Brief our days, but long for sing-
    ing (Patton) AQ28   101046
Bright and glorious is the sky
    (Grundtvig) J57   101047
Bright and joyful is the morn
    (Montgomery) H144; AZ61
                       101048
Bright the vision that delight
    (Mant) E372; F161; X460;
    BV15   101049
Bright was the guiding star that
    led (Auber) AZ173   101050
Brightest and best of the sons
    of the morning (Heber) A46;
    B95; D66; E41; F75; G119;
    H132; I114; J53; K39; L228;
    M377; O224; P151; Q128; R
    175; S136; T337; U62; V114;
    W64; X85; Z202; AA181; AB
    125; AD126; AF126; AG81;
    AH272; AI63; AK121; AL49;
    AM167; AO138; AP178; AR144;
    AS109; AT67; AV94; AW91;
    AX104; AY487; AZ1150; BA183;
    BD212; BF277; BI87; BR152;
    BV125; BY91; BZ   101051
Brightly beams our Father's mercy
    (Bliss) G254; U316; Z313; AC
    253; AE290; AH438; AS351; AT
    300; AU262; AW448; AX193;
    BB628; BC301; BZ   101052
Brightly gleams our banner
    (Potter & How) A559; B529;
    D515; G446; H445; I681; L407;
    S457; U306; V485, 759; W538;
    Z485; AC208; AD482; AH440;

AO398; AP781; AV218; AZ773;
    BA812; BD83; BF621; BR514;
    BV549; BY464   101053
Bring a torch, Jeanette (French
    trad) Y304; AF124   101054
Bring beams of oak, and boulder-
    stone (Johnson) AN459
                       101055
Bring flowers of the fairest (---)
    AH137; BO105   101056
Bring, heavy heart, your grief
    to me (Auerbach) BC349
                       101057
Bring, O morn, thy music
    (Gannett) Y17; AC5; AN8;
    AQ5; BD23; BF229; BX6
                       101058
Bring, O past, your honor
    (Lyttle) AQ254   101059
Bring them in, Bring them in
    (Thomas) R Hark 'tis the
    Shepherd's voice I hear 101060
Bring ye all the tithes into the
    storehouse (Leech) AT404;
    AU393   101061
Bringing in the sheaves (Shaw)
    R Sowing in the morning
                       101062
Bringing our praise, we kneel
    before Thy altar (Mary Francis,
    Sr.) BN203   101063
Broad is the road that leads to
    death (Watts) V447; AY394
                       101064
Brood o'er us with thy sheltering
    wing (Eddy) BE30   101065
B'ro-sh ha-sho-no yi-ko-say-vun
    (Jewish traditional) BH328
                       101066
Brother afar from the Saviour
    today (Berry) AX275 101067
Brother along on the highway of
    life (Henson) AX443   101068
Brother, hast thou wandered far
    (Clarke) AO251; BF341
                       101069
Brother, here's a message I
    give (Garrett) AS308 101070
Brother Man, awake! Strength
    withers, of tomorrow dream-
    ing (Maurer) BF512 101071
Brother, sing your country's
    anthem (Bacon) AN401;

BK109   101072
Brother, thou hast left us lonely
  (---) AY172   101073
Brothers and sisters, we now
  must depart (Larsen) P69
                                   101074
Brothers, joining hand in hand
  (Warner) F294   101075
Build thee more stately mansions,
  O my soul (Holmes) AC498
                                   101076
Builder of mighty worlds on
  worlds (---) AZ215; BA322
                                   101077
Built by Jehovah's hand (Hymns of
  the English Conf. 1880) BR224
                                   101078
Built on a rock the church doth
  stand (Grundtvig) J151; M92;
  O132; P81; Q467; R432; AF
  270   101079
Built on the Rock, the Church
  doth stand (Grundtvig) P81 X
  Built on a Rock   101080
Built on the Rock, without spot or
  wrinkle (Winsett) AX152
                                   101081
Buried beneath the yielding wave
  (Beddome) BB438   101082
Bursting forth, from Pharaoh's
  prison (Cummins) BL26
                                   101083
"But for a moment" -- this val-
  ley of sorrows (Pollard)
  AY450   101084
But for the cockerell calling the
  noon-hour (Fan Cheng-ta)
  AQ322   101085
But God hath promised strength
  for the day (Flint) R God
  hath not promised   101086
But I know whom I have believed
  (Whittle) R I know not why
  God's wondrous grace   101087
But the Lord is mindful (Bible.
  Psalms) AH621   101088
By all whom Thou has made (U.P.
  Psalter. 1912) R117; T159;
  AJ236   101089
By and by, when the morning
  comes (Tindley) R Trials
  dark on every hand   101090
By angels in heaven, of every

degree (---) Lp742   101091
By Babel's riverside we sat in
  tears (U.P. Psalter. 1912)
  T273; AJ380   101092
By Babel's streams we sat and
  wept (U.P. Psalter, 1912)
  T272; AJ379   101093
By Christ redeemed, in Christ
  restored (Rawson) B335;
  D236; H437; I239; W322; AL
  229; AO448; AP361; AS467;
  AW310; AZ12; BA294; BB475;
  BV372; BY311   101094
By cool Siloam's shady rill
  (Heber) A328; B351; D565;
  H451; I678; S349; V650; W309;
  AW400; AI375; AL218; AN438;
  AO431; AP787; AS394; AY363;
  AZ1448; BA838; BB340; BX517
                          101095
By every nation, race and tongue
  (George) BV32   101096
By faith I view my Saviour dy-
  ing (Jukes) AX313   101097
By faith we are divinely sure
  (Brorson) M120   101098
By grace are ye saved through
  faith (Whittle) R In grace the
  holy God   101099
By grace I am an heir of heaven
  (Scheidt) M123; P274; AM584
                          101100
By grace I'm saved, grace free
  and boundless (Scheidt) Q373;
  AA311; AM399   101101
By help of God I fain would tell
  (Luther) BT259   101102
By Jesus' grave on either hand
  (Smith, I.G.) E121; F125;
  W114; AZ5   101103
By law from Sinai's clouded steep
  (Williams) AN129; BF190;
  BX16   101104
By nature deaf to things divine
  (Hoppe) N177   101105
By nature man cannot achieve
  (Denicke) M97   101106
By sin weighed down and sorely
  stricken (Tietze) M68
                          101107
By the blood that flowed from
  thee (Cadell) AO655; BN35;
  BO169; BQ20   101108

By the breadth of the blue that
shines in the silence (Van
Dyke) X18   101109
By the Cross her vigil keeping
(Jacopone) BM80   10110
By the Cross of Jesus standing
(Bonar) W104; AM185; AZ648;
BR178   101111
By the first bright Easter-day
(Cadell) BO172; BQ137 101112
By the gracious saving call
(Pollock) A230; B142b 101113
By the holy hills surrounded
(Spitta) O80   101114
By thy birth and by thy tears
(Grant) G207; I280; BZ
                         101115
By thy birth and by thy tears
(Grant) X Saviour when in
dust to thee   101116
By thy blessed Word obeying
(Warner) AX415   101117
By thy Cross, O Christ, and
passion (Wallin) J381 101118
By weary stages, the old world
ages (Masefield) X86 101119
By what means shall a young
man learn (Scottish Psalter,
1650) AL678; AP107b   101120

C

Call Jehovah thy salvation
(Montgomery) A448; B310;
D415; R123; S292; AM566;
AO360; AP76; AZ941; BA680;
BB257; BE33; BX12   101121
Call the Lord thy sure salvation
(Montgomery) BE33 X Call
Jehovah thy salvation   101122
Call them in! The poor the
wretched (Shipton) D619
                         101123
Called to the feast by the King
are we (Landor) BB537
                         101124
Calling to thee, calling to thee
(Crosby) R Out on the mountain
                         101125
Calling today, calling today
(Crosby) R Jesus is tenderly
calling thee home   101126
Calm me, my God, and keep me

calm (Bonar) U244; AO363;
AZ194; BA513; BB334
                         101127
Calm on the listening ear of
night (Sears) A24; B84; D55;
L217; N38; Z201; AI61; AK
103; AN159; AO124; AV99;
AZ1463; BA53; BD209; BI98;
BX189   101128
Calm soul of all things, make it
mine (Arnold) AQ85 101129
Calmly, calmly lay him down
(Gaskell) AN452; BX474
                         101130
Can a father see his child (Blake)
AQ163   101131
Can a growing child like me
(Dodge) AE431; AH544; AL584;
AM645; AP719; AW435; BK
15   101132
Can a little child like me (Dodge)
AH544 X Can a growing child
like me   101133
Can a mortal flee from sorrow?
(---) AZ598   101134
Can I see another's woe (Blake)
X461   101135
Can men tell that you love
Jesus (Sellers) R Would
men know   101136
Can my soul find rest from sor-
row (---) AY286   101137
Can truth divine fulfillment
fail? (Stockton) H17 101138
Can you count the stars that
brightly (Hey) A245; X462;
BD52   101139
Canst thou count the stars (Hey)
BD52 X Can you count the
stars   101140
Canticle of the sun (St Francis
of Assisi) X All creatures of
our God and King (tr. by
Draper) X Most high, omni-
potent, good Lord (tr. by
Robbins)   101141
Captain of Israel's host, and
Guide (Wesley) AL440; AW168;
BC236; BZ   101142
Captains of the saintly band
(Santeüil) E177; F507 101143
Care for me, O God of grace
(Ludämilia Elisabeth) P302

101144
Carried away to the realms of
light (Jones) R When I have
reached   101145
Carry on! carry on! Fight the
good fight and true (Service)
Y160   101146
Čas radosti, veselosti (Latin.
12th c) BT82   101147
Cast me not in wrath away
(Albinus) M67   101148
Cast thy bread upon the waters
(Hanaford) AZ260   101149
Cast thy burden on the Lord
Only lean upon His word
(Hill. Psalms and hymns.)
H353; I468; S288; U197; V505;
AI243; AM559; AO347; AR314;
AT254; AV234; AZ71; BA700;
BF394;   101150
Cast thy burden upon the Lord
(Bible. Psalms 55,16) AU478;
BB692; BC235   101151
Cast thy care on Jesus (Scott)
AR196   101152
Cast upon the Lord thy care
(Hymns of the English Confer-
ence, 1880) BR270   101153
Chant your songs of glad thanks-
giving (Glenn) BI114   101154
Chariot rode on the mountain top
(Negro spiritual) R Great Day!
great day, the righteous march-
ing   101155
Chaun dong whan lotsan mei chu
(Chinese trad) Y311   101156
Cheer thy chosen witnesses, O
Jesus (Batty) AZ1014 101157
"Cheer up, desponding soul"
(Byrom) AZ475   101158
Cheer up, friends and neighbours
(Dearmer) BG147a X Take
heart, friends and neighbours
101159
Chief of sinners though I be
(McComb [M'Comb]) K330;
L500; M176; N421; Q342; AA
99; AI434; AZ1266; BB238
101160
Chief Shepherd of thy chosen
sheep (Newton) AX635 101161
Child in the manger (MacDonald)
W53; BV96; BY92   101162

Child Jesus comes from heavenly height (Anderson) BR547
101163
Child of a Virgin, Maker of thy
Mother (Latin, 8th c) BN183
101164
Childhood's years are passing
o'er us (Dickson) AP782
101165
Children, come, hither come
(U. P. Board of Publ. 1909) R
Ye children, come, give ear
to me   101166
Children of God, born again of
His Spirit (Brorson) M130
101167
Children of Jerusalem, Place the
royal diadem (---) BI1
101168
Children of Jerusalem Sang the
praise of Jesus' name (Hen-
ley) W658; AL607; AP751;
AW404; AZ1285; BA822; BV
344; BY735   101169
Children of light, arise and
shine! (Denny) AZ640
101170
Children of the heavenly Father
(Berg) J572; N487; P368;
AE256; BZ   101171
Children of the heavenly King
(Cennick) A578; B517; D452;
E373; F295; G326; H352;
I547; K263; L457; N332; O
458; P333; R340; S347; U243;
V504; W574; X463; Z267; AD
229; AG236; AH399; AI334;
AM499; AO541; AP611; AR
315; AV212; AZ75; BA626;
BD20; BJ95; BR434; BV550;
BZ   101172
Chime, happy Christmas bells,
once more (Grundtvig) N31
101173
Choose my path, O blessed
Saviour (Reed) AX493;
AY123   101174
Choose the right, when a choice
is placed before you (Town-
send) BC110   101175
Chosen not for good in me
(McCheyne) V370; AZ1265
101176

Chosen seed and Zion's children
   (Rutström) N267   101177
Christ above all glory seated
   (Latin. 5th c) D371; H189;
   AO197; BV198   101178
Christ alone is our salvation
   (Latin. 7th c) O81   101179
Christ be my leader by night, as
   by day (Dudley-Smith) BV572
                          101180
Christ be with me, Christ within
   me (St Patrick) A268; B525;
   BN61; BY433b   101181
Christ, by heavenly hosts
   adored (Harbaugh) D188; J341;
   K495; Q566; V624; ♪A296; AI
   364; AM623; AO598; AZ57;
   BA873; BI12   101182
Christ comes again with holy
   power (Campbell BE34
                          101183
Christ crucified, my soul, by
   faith (Schmidt) AZ694 101184
Christ, enthroned in highest
   heaven (Latin 13th c) E350
                          101185
Christ, everlasting Source of
   light (Meusslin) AA34 101186
Christ for the whole wide world
   (Allen) AU444   101187
Christ for the world we sing!
   (Wolcott) A537; B486; D580;
   G481; H397; I635; J311; K218;
   L335; P400; R489; S378; T368;
   U404; Y355; Z538; AB368;
   AD385; AE352; AF295; AG266;
   AH463; AK372; AL241; AM371;
   AO517; AP373; AR559; AS378;
   AT458; AU267; AV262; AW327;
   BA539; BB452; BF535; BY364;
   BZ   101188
Christ, from whom all blessings
   flow (Wesley) AZ1060; BV417;
   BY361; BZ   101189
Christ has come for our salvation
   (Dayman) AZ646   101190
Christ has for sin atonement
   made (Hoffman) AE174; AS144;
   AT130; AW473; BB644 101191
Christ hath a garden walled
   around (Watts & Bridges) X
   245; AM273; AP302; BJ96;
                          101192

Christ hath a work for thee to
   do (Sedding) BV35 X A
   work hath Christ for thee to
   do   101193
Christ Himself, my Pride and
   Glory (Olearius) M191;
   Q408   101194
Christ in highest heaven en-
   throned (Santeüil) AZ620
                          101195
Christ in His heavenly garden
   walks all day (Palgrave)
   AD207; AR254   101196
Christ in His word draws near
   (Lynch) AI152; AM261 101197
Christ in the night He was be-
   trayed (---) AY261 X Christ
   on the night He was betrayed
                          101198
Christ is arisen From the
   grave's dark prison (Latin,
   11-12th c) Q187   101199
Christ is coming! let creation
   (MacDuff) I602; V183; W163;
   AL135; AM238; AS164; AW
   127; AZ1388   101200
Christ is gone up; yet ere He
   passed (Neale) E166; F470
                          101201
Christ is knocking at my sad
   heart (Palmer) AS195; BB
   565   101202
Christ is made the sure founda-
   tion (Latin, ca 7th c) A384;
   B457; D483; E170; F620; H406;
   I662; J242; K241; L293; N273;
   O129; P241; Q466; R433; S336;
   T361; U385; V572; W207; X
   190; AA454; AE317; AF263; AG
   232; AK324; AL163; AM268;
   AO415; AP293; AV248,308;
   AW277; AZ625; BA326; BB487;
   BT466; BZ   101203
Christ is now risen again
   (Coverdale) F601   101204
Christ is our corner-stone (Latin
   7th c) B458; D294; F243; L
   282; O130; Q465; S472; X464;
   AA453; AO462; AP303; AS437;
   AW9; AZ1173; BA261; BV456;
   BY267   101205
Christ is our Head, our strength,
   our life (Coffin) BN204

101206
Christ is our Master, Lord, and
  God (Cennick) BA446 X The
  doctrine of our dying Lord
                     101207
Christ is risen! alleluia! (Mon-
  sell) K117; AI85; BY152
                     101208
Christ is risen! Christ is risen!
  (Gurney)   D113; U108; V168;
  X152; Z240   101209
Christ is risen from the dead
  (Becker) M430; N641   101210
Christ is the foundation of the
  house we raise (Monsell) N
  279   101211
Christ is the King! O friends re-
  joice X242 X Christ is the
  King! O friends upraise 101212
Christ is the King! O friends up-
  raise (Bell) A543; X242; BY
  356   101213
Christ is the vine, we branches
  are (Nitschmann) AZ284
                     101214
Christ is the world's redeemer
  (St Columba) R136; W179
                     101215
Christ is the world's true light
  (Briggs) A258; R492; X60;
  AF198; BV418; BY659; BZ
                     101216
Christ ist erstanden Von der
  Marter alle; (Latin 11-12th c.)
  BT187   101217
Christ Jesus lay in death's strong
  bands (Luther) J98; K110;
  O330; Q195; AM207; BY153;
  BZ   101218
Christ Jesus, once to death abased
  (Luther) AZ912   101219
Christ lag in Todesbanden (Luther)
  BT195   101220
Christ leads me through no darker
  rooms (Baxter) A445 101221
Christ must be served indeed
  (Sawson) BF460   101222
Christ, my Rock, my sure De-
  fence (Luise Henriette) AZ588
  X Jesus Christ my sure De-
  fence   101223
Christ, of all my hopes the ground
  (Wardlaw) B219; R314; S316;

X465; AL342; AM437; AP481
                     101224
Christ of holiness the Fountain
  (Craeselius) M199   101225
Christ of the upward way
  (Mathams) R295; S277; AB235;
  AC235; AD305; AE439; AG
  312; AK250; AR278; BF380;
  BY538   101226
Christ on the night He was be-
  trayed (---) AX175; AY261
                     101227
Christ our King to heaven as-
  cendeth (Hopkins) D127
                     101228
Christ our Lord will soon be
  coming (Hayes) AX130
                     101229
Christ our Redeemer died on
  the Cross (Foote) AU70; AX
  307; AY240   101230
Christ shall have dominion
  (U. P. Psalter. 1912) R502;
  T134; AJ200; AM678   101231
Christ the fair glory of the holy
  holy angels (St Rabanus
  Maurus) A123; E242; F564
                     101232
Christ, the glory of the sky
  (Latin, 5th c) BN192   101233
Christ, the good Shepherd,
  God's own Son (Scheffler)
  AZ1424   101234
Christ, the life of all the living
  (Homburg) D361; J79; K98;
  M400; N91; Q151; AA196;
  AW535   101235
Christ the Lord cometh? per-
  chance at the dawn (Wesley,
  E. G.) AX125; AY532 101236
Christ the Lord hath risen
  From his three-day prison
  (Weisse) BQ329   101237
Christ the Lord is my true
  Shepherd (Terry) BN59
                     101238
Christ the Lord is risen again
  (Weisse) D114; E129; F136;
  J107; K114; L268; O334; P
  197; Q190; X153; AA225;
  AF183; AP221; AW544; AZ
  1159; BA231; BV179   101239
Christ the Lord is risen! Now

the hour (Watts) R Now is the
hour of darkness past   101240
Christ the Lord is risen today!
Christians haste your vows
(Wipo??) F131; J99; K112;
M431; N130; Q191; BN40;
BO175; BP38; BQ31; BV183
                              101241
Christ the Lord is risen today.
Sons of men and angels say
(Wesley) A95; B175; D111;
E135; F141; G154; H181; I156;
J91; K111; L261; N132; Q193;
S165; U118; V159; X160; Y331;
Z239; AA221; AB143; AC129;
AD158; AE121; AF182; AG102;
AH298; AI82; AK167; AL104;
AM205; AN192; AO176; AP214;
AR182; AS146; AT115; AU33;
AV120; AX123; AZ46; BA232;
BB134; BC10; BF318; BK135;
BV180; BY154; BZ   101242
Christ the Lord, the Lord most
glorious (Mueller) AZ276;
BA171   101243
Christ the Lord to us is born
(Tranovsky) M359; Q86;
                              101244
Christ the Saviour came from
heaven's glory (McKinney)
AU336   101245
Christ, the transforming Light
(Smith, G) AU418   101246
Christ the word to earth descended
(St Thomas Aquinas) BN93
                              101247
Christ, thou art the sure Founda-
tion (Latin ca 7th c) N273 X
Christ is made the sure Founda-
tion   101248
Christ, thou the champion of the
band we own (Loewenstern)
AA279; AZ529   101249
Christ, thy all-atoning death
(Zinzendorf, N.L.) BA681 X
Rise, exalt our Head and King
(Hehl)   101250
Christ to know is life and peace
(Toplady) AZ1476   101251
Christ to us across the water
(Dearmer) X302b   101252
Christ we do all adore thee
(Dubois) AR634   101253

Christ we praise thee, Christ
we worship thee (Latin) R
O King of Kings in splendor
                              101254
Christ went a building to pre-
pare (---) AX481   101255
Christ who knows all his sheep
(Baxter) X288   101256
Christ who left his home in
glory (Kolb) AY266 101257
Christ, who once amongst us
(Bourne) F447; I683   101258
Christ who welcomed little chil-
dren (Martin) BY284 101259
Christ, whose glory fills the
skies (Wesley) A153; B4;
D312; E258; F7; G32; J208;
K450; L5; N321; O543; P150;
Q359; R47; S26; U455; V30;
W261; X26; AA100; AB197;
AD42; AF43; AG20; AL535;
AM330; AP658; AS23; AT22;
AW26; AZ1271; BA46; BE35;
BR12; BV36; BY673; BZ
                              101260
Christ will gather in His own
(Zinzendorf, N.L.) AZ53
                              101261
Christ will me His aid afford
(Oatman) AS299   101262
Christe, du Beistand deiner
Kreuzgemeine (Löwenstern)
BT258; BW278   101263
Christe, du Lamm Gottes, der
du trägst die Sünd der Welt
(Latin: Agnus Dei) BT147
                              101264
Christe, freundlicher Ritter
(Ausbund) BU78   101265
Christe mein Herr, ich bin ganz
ferr (Ausbund) BU62
                              101266
Christe, qui lux es et dies
(Latin, before 9th c.) BT559
                              101267
Christe thu dich erbarmen
(Ausbund) BU77   101268
Christian children must be holy
(---) L460   101269
Christian, do you see him
(Dearmer) X466   101270
Christian, dost thou see them
(St Andrew of Crete) A556;

B126; D81; E72; F91; G275;
I616; J68; K73; R360; S275;
U305; V474; Y168; AB245;
AC179; AD295; AF364; AG194;
AI323; AK294; AM483; AO390;
AR319; AV194; AZ766; BA570;
BB367; BD79; BF472; BR401;
BV137; BY506; BZ   101271

Christian hearts, in love united
(Zinzendorf, N. L.) AZ942;
BA667   101272

Christian Leaguers, rally at the
Lord's command (Solberg)
P373   101273

Christian, let your burning light
(Coleman) AR435; AS350
                          101274

Christian, rise and act thy creed
(Russell) Y230; Z518; AB260;
AD353; AF416; AN282; AO504;
BF483; BX337   101275

Christian, seek not yet repose
(Elliott B128; E374; F308;
I494; M240; V503; W523; X467;
AB247; AL396; AM471; AP547;
BA571; BB357; BE67; BR349;
BV573; BY507   101276

Christian Soul, the times are
calling (Edwards) AD300
                          101277

Christian, unflinching stand
(Leachman) BV551   101278

Christian, walk carefully, danger
is near (---) AX444   101279

Christian, work for Jesus
(Hasloch) W343; AP585 101280

Christians awake, salute the
happy morn (Byrom) A16; B
76; D56; E21; F61; G93; J19;
K24; Q84; W54; X73; AF127;
AK115; AL67; AP175; AR134;
AW71; AZ1501; BA159; BR
148; BV97; BY93   101281

Christians, come in sweetest
measures (Adam of St Victor)
Q282; AA121   101282

Christians, come, new anthems
raise (St Joseph the Hymnographer) AZ864 X Let us
now our voices raise   101283

Christians, dismiss your fears
(Hart) AZ1494; BA228 101284

Christians, keep your banners

waving (Arends) M244
                          101285

Christians, lo, the star appeareth (Blaisdell) Y220;
AB124; AC90; BD208; BF489
                          101286

Christians, prayer may well
employ you (Arends) O165;
Q444   101287

Christians, rise, put on your
armor (Falckner) M248
                          101288

Christians, sing out with exultation (Pictet) Q100; AZ991
                          101289

Christians, sound the Name that
saved us (Farrell) BM44
                          101290

Christians, to the Paschal Victim (Wipo??) A97; E130;
F138   101291

Christmas brings joy to every
heart (Ingemann) J46
                          101292

Christmas day is come; let's all
prepare (Irish trad carol)
BG6   101293

Christmas is here with joy untold (Ingemann) M617
                          101294

Christ's life our code, His cross
our creed (Copeland) G331;
I138   101295

Christ's love invites us To flee
to Him for rest (Dober)
AZ546   101296

Christ's love produces love; and,
kindled thus (Zinzendorf, N.
L.) AZ463   101297

Christ's loving children, for his
hope abiding (St Gregory the
Great) BJ49   101298

Christum wir sollen loben schon
(Sedulius) BT104   101299

Christus das Lamm auf Erden
kam (H. Betz) BU108
                          101300

Christus der Herr ist gangen
(H. Betz) BU110   101301

Christus, der ist mein Leben
(Vulpius. Ein schön geistliche
G-B. 1609) BT597   101302

Christus factus est pro nobis

(Breviary) BQ193   101303
Christus ist erstanden Von des
   Todes Banden (Latin 11-12th.
   c.) BT190; BW544   101304
Christus vincit! Christus regnat!
   Christus imperat! (Latin, 8th c)
   BN76; BP106; BQ248   101305
Church of God, beloved and chosen
   (Havergal) AZ964   101306
Church of God, thou spotless vir-
   gin (Warner) AX151   101307
Church of God, whose conquering
   banners (Bugbee) AY518
                                    101308
Church of Jesus, sing, Praise the
   Lord and King (Promnitz) AZ
   533   101309
Church of the ever-living God
   (Bonar) BE36   101310
City not made with hands (Pal-
   grave) A491; F259; X615;
   Z478; AB350; AN396; AP305
                                    101311
City of David, Bethlehem (Rose)
   BI84   101312
City of God, how broad and far
   (Johnson) A386; B470; E375;
   F258; G420; I209; J330; R436;
   S338; W209; X468; Y66; Z426;
   AB320; AC267; AD386; AE319;
   AF261; AG229; AK330; AL171;
   AN410; BD191; BE37; BF589;
   BX451; BY255   101313
City of peace, our Mother dear
   (Prid) X393   101314
City strong and mighty (Pendleton)
   BI16-D   101315
Claro paschali gaudio. (Latin.
   4th c.) BW415   101316
Cleanse my heart, O Father,
   cleanse it (---) BR34   101317
Clear is the call that bids us
   come (Bement) BF626 101318
Clear upon the night-air sounding
   (---) BR559   101319
Cling to the Bible, tho' all else
   be taken (Smith, M. J.) AX
   140; AY500   101320
Close by the heedless worker's
   side (Studdert-Kennedy) X469
                                    101321
Close to my Savior, there would
   I be (Mishler) AS219 101322

Close to Thee, close to Thee
   (Crosby) R Thou my ever-
   lasting portion   101323
Closer, my child, to me (War-
   ren) R When I get weary
                                    101324
Closer to thee, my Father, draw
   me (Chapman) BB632
                                    101325
Closer with the cords of love
   (Chapman) R Closer to thee,
   my Father, draw me 101326
Come, all that heavy-laden are
   (Lehr) AZ1089 X My Saviour
   sinners doth receive   101327
Come, all ye faithful (Latin,
   18th c) BI83 X O come, all
   ye faithful   101328
Come, all ye people, bless our
   God (U. P. Psalter, 1912)
   AJ175   101329
Come, all ye people, come away
   (Seltzer) J249   101330
Come all ye Saints and sing his
   praise (---) BC11   101331
Come, all ye saints of God
   (Boden) AZ1240; BA114
                                    101332
Come, all ye Saints who dwell
   on earth (Phelps) BC12
                                    101333
Come, all ye servants of the
   Lord (U. P. Psalter, 1912)
   T267   101334
Come, all ye shepherds, and be
   not afraid (Bohemian trad)
   BD221 X Come, all ye shep-
   herds, ye children of earth
                                    101335
Come, all ye shepherds, ye
   children of earth (Bohemian
   trad) Y308; AD108; AK111;
   AW79; BD221   101336
Come, all ye sons of God who
   have received the priesthood
   (Davenport) BC302   101337
Come, all ye sons of Sion
   (Phelps) BC303   101338
Come, all you faithful Christians
   (English trad carol) BG7
                                    101339
Come all you worthy Christian
   men (English trad carol)

BG60   101340

Come all you worthy gentlemen
(English trad carol) BG8
                                  101341

Come along, come along, is the
call that will win (Willes)
BC19   101342

Come and deck the grave with
flowers (Monsell) AZ241
                                  101343

Come and hear the grand old story
(Bonar) K531   101344

Come, and let us sweetly join
(Wesley) AF525; AZ1056; BZ
                                  101345

Come and rejoice with me
(Charles) BY428   101346

Come, be my heart's beloved
Guest (Mencken) BA295
                                  101347

Come, blessed Saviour! Source
of light (Beddome) BR22 X
Come blessed Spirit! Source of
light   101348

Come blessed Spirit! Source of
light (Beddome) V208; BE240;
BR22   101349

Come, brethren, let us hasten
on (Tersteegen) O451 101350

Come, children, join to sing
(Bateman) W177 X Come
Christians, join to sing 101351

Come, children of tomorrow,
come (Gale) AQ193   101352

Come, children, with singing,
with sweet voices ringing ---
BR549   101353

Come, Christian brethren, ere
we part (White) V22   101354

Come, Christian children, come
(Thrupp) D554   101355

Come, Christians, join to sing
(Bateman) R131; S191; W177;
AL597; AP755; BZ   101356

Come, come, ye Saints, no toil
nor labor fear (Clayton) BC13
                                  101357

Come, dearest Lord, descend and
dwell (Watts) R531; S1 app.;
V5; W297; AM250; AV36; BC
237; BY758   101358

Come down, O Love divine
(Bianco da Siena) A376; B152;

F235; J123; W191; X177; AF
239; BL34; BV214; BY224;
BZ   101359

Come, ever blessed Spirit, come
(Wordsworth) AO222; BA289;
BV362   101360

Come every pious heart, that
loves the Saviour's name
(Stennett) V167   101361

Come, every soul by sin op-
pressed (Stockton) G184;
I261; AE209; AH333; AI190;
AM724; AR244; AS196; AT
235; AU197; AV331; AW457;
AX227; AY102; BB567; BZ
                                  101362

Come, faithful people, come
away (Moultrie) E619; X
136   101363

Come, faithful Shepherd, bind
me (Hutton) AZ811; BA595
                                  101364

Come, Father, Son, and Holy
Ghost (Wesley) I229; AW301;
AZ98; BZ   101365

"Come, follow me," the Saviour
said, Then let us (Nicholson)
BC14   101366

Come, follow me, the Saviour
spake (Scheffler) M232; Q
421; AA334   101367

Come for the feast is spread
(Burton) H438; AI202; AM
391   101368

Come forth, my friend, the
bride to meet (Alkobetz) R
"Observe ye" and "remember"
still   101369

Come forth, O Christian youth
(Jackson) AE448   101370

Come forth, ye men of every
race and nation (Smith, J.H.)
Z487; AR570   101371

Come gentle peace, while
shadows fall (---) BJ81 101372

Come, go with me, beyond the
sea (Wheelock) BC15
                                  101373

Come God Creator, Holy Ghost
(Latin, 11th c) AA249 101374

Come, gracious Lord, descend
and dwell (Watts) V5 X
Come, dearest Lord, descend

and dwell   101375
Come, gracious Spirit, heavenly
Dove, with light and comfort
(Browne) A378; B201; D379;
F232; J127; K150; L174; S209;
V209; W188; AF238; AH229;
AO223; AP283; AR221; AV145;
AX44; AY2; AZ928; BB204;
BE39; BR13a; BV215   101376
Come, hail the cause of Zion's
youth (Kleinman) BC16 101377
Come, heaven-bound pilgrims,
and join in God's praise (Shenk)
AX56; AY323   101378
Come hither, all ye weary ones
(Watts) V260   101379
Come hither, ye children, O come
one and all (Schmidt) AW413
X O come, little children
                         101380
Come hither, ye faithful (Latin,
18th c) D50; K21; L216; M347;
N33; O195; P125; AA159; AZ507;
BA155; BR149   101381
Come, Holy Ghost, come, Lord
our God (Hermannus Contractus)
AZ1033   101382
Come, Holy Ghost, Creator blest
(Latin, 9th c) A218; B375; D380;
O355; P227; Q233; AH128; BM
89; BN119; BO186; BP46 101383
Come, Holy Ghost, Creator, come
From thy bright heavenly
(Latin, 9th c) BQ35   101384
Come, Holy Ghost, God and Lord
(Luther) Q224 X Come, Holy
Spirit, God and Lord X Veni
creator   101385
Come, Holy Ghost, in love
(Latin, 9th c) G17; H215; I184;
K143; L172; O382; Q227; U129;
V210; AL145; AM249; AS170;
AW131; BA252; BY225 101386
Come, Holy Ghost! in us arise
(Gill) AP279   101387
Come Holy Ghost, our hearts
inspire, Let us Thine influence
prove (Wesley) G175; H211;
I181; W196; AL155; AP287;
AZ148; BA132; BV288; BY244;
BZ   101388
Come, Holy Ghost, our souls
inspire and lighten with

(Latin, 9th c) A217; B455;
D289; E153; G636; J117; K
142; R237; W182; X178; AE
148; AF231; AL143; AP267;
AZ373; BA133; BR481*; BV
216; BY226; BZ
*composite   101389
Come Holy Ghost, our souls
inspire, Let us Thine influence prove (Wesley) AZ148
X Come Holy Ghost, our
hearts inspire ...   101390
Come Holy Ghost, send down
those beams (Latin, 9th c)
BO187   101391
Come, Holy Ghost, who ever
one art (St Ambrose) B8;
F11; BN120; BO183   101392
Come, Holy Ghost, with God the
Son (St Ambrose) A160; E
255   101393
Come, Holy Spirit, calm my
mind (Lock Chapel Collection
1803) V211; AY192   101394
Come, Holy Spirit, come! Let
thy bright beams arise
(Hart) D376; H219; K151; L
180; M460; Q225; T355; V214;
W190; AA258; AL146; AM254;
AP281; AZ1329; BA135; BB205;
BV290   101395
Come, Holy Spirit come, O hear
my lowly prayer (Thrupp)
BV289   101396
Come, Holy Spirit, come with
energy divine (Beddome) I
182   101397
Come, Holy Spirit, Dove divine,
Bestow Thy glorious grace
(Hickok) AR222; BF262
                         101398
Come, Holy Spirit, Dove divine,
On these baptismal waters
shine (Judson) AT385; AV
252   101399
Come, Holy Spirit from above,
And from the realms (Latin,
9th c) AZ633   101400
Come, Holy Spirit, from avove
and kindle in our hearts
(Latin, 9th c) N159   101401
Come, Holy Spirit, from on
high (---) BA283   101402

Come, Holy Spirit, God and Lord
(Luther) J122; K146; L442;
M471; N154; O375; Q224; AA
257; AF235; BV217   101403

Come, Holy Spirit, God-head
One (St Ambrose) BM88
                             101404

Come, Holy Spirit, heavenly
Dove, My sinful maladies re-
move (Browne) AP283 X
Come gracious Spirit, heavenly
Dove, with light and comfort
from above   101405

Come, Holy Spirit, heavenly
Dove, with all thy quickening
powers (Watts) A369; B200;
D377; G172; H209; I183; L173;
M461; N161; R239; S206; T354;
U130; V205; AA255; AE145; AF
240; AG128; AI123; AL156; AO
220; AP278; AS168; AT169; AU
268; AV147; AZ142; BA138;
BB207; BR208; BZ   101406

Come, Holy Spirit, raise our
songs (Wesley) H214   101407

Come home, come home, O why
will you longer roam (Frost)
R O soul, in the far-away
country   101408

Come home, come home, Ye who
are weary (Thompson) R
Softly and tenderly   101409

Come home, poor sinner, why
longer roam (Jeffrey) AX232
                             101410

Come, humble sinner, in whose
breast (Jones) H252; I260;
V293; AU454   101411

Come, humble soul, receive the
good (Loy) M45   101412

Come in, O come! The door
stands open now (Moule)
BB336   101413

Come in, Thou blessed, honored
Lord (Proud) BR83   101414

Come in, Thou blessed of the
Lord (Montgomery) H416;
AE341; AZ133   101415

Come Jesus, from the sapphire
throne (Palmer) D297; L299;
Q634; V571; AA455; BA325
                             101416

Come, Jesus, Redeemer, abide

thou with me (Palmer) AZ
497   101417

Come, join the throng, on this
glad day (Fries) BA330
                             101418

Come join, ye saints, with
heart and voice (Medley)
AZ638   101419

Come, kindred, upstand in the
valour of Jesus (Clayton) X
470   101420

Come, Kingdom of our God
(Johns) S404; V604; Y243;
AD331; AE356; AN289; AO
525; AR571; AW269; AZ1375;
BD156; BX392   101421

Come, labor on, Who dares
stand idle (Borthwick) A576;
B497; F339; R287; S366; X
471; AB262; AD317; AF293;
BE41; BV593; BY511   101422

Come, lay his books and papers
by (Greenwood) BC338
                             101423

Come, let our hearts and voices
join (Swain) V379   101424

Come let us adore Him, Come
bow at His feet (Latin, 18th c)
Lp744; BR73   101425

Come let us all unite and sing
(Hurditch) AP717 X Come let
us all unite to sing   101426

Come let us all unite to sing,
God is love (Hurditch)
AE70; AP717; AS85; AW439;
AX81   101427

Come, let us all with one accord
(Chester) D26   101428

Come, let us anew, our journey
pursue (Wesley) G536; I568;
AL573; AZ22; BB369; BC17;
BY712   101429

Come, let us join our cheerful
songs (Watts) D447; E376;
F221; H8; I24; J413; K130;
L151; M414; Q343; V202;
W175; X472; AA102; AL120;
AO210; AR18; AS160; AV144;
AW17; AY13; AZ146; BA115;
BJ10; BV16; BY200   101430

Come, let us join our friends
above (Wesley) F628; G422;
H426; I611; K205; N210; O495

Q478; V615; AL176; AP309;
AW319; AZ143; BA273; BY402;
BZ   101431
Come, let us join our sacred
songs (Watts) AY13 X Come,
let us join our cheerful songs
101432
Come, let us join the Church
above (Riley) E186   101433
Come, let us join with faithful
souls (Tarrant) Y274; AB280;
AC241; AF346; AK390; AN303;
BD144; BF485; BX365   101434
Come, let us join with one ac-
cord (Wesley) H83; I63; U443;
V66; AM323   101435
Come, let us praise our God and
Lord (Montefiore) BH201
101436
Come, let us rise with Christ
our Head (C. Wesley) BZ
101437
Come, let us sing a tender song
(Chadwick) AB405; BF671
101438
Come, let us sing an evening
hymn (Phelps) BC238   101439
Come, let us sing before the
Lord (U. P. Psalter. 1912) T
180; AJ264   101440
Come let us sing in sweet accord
(Stern) BH217   101441
Come, let us sing of a wonderful
love (Walmsley) AL488; AM
669; AP399; BY411   101442
Come let us sing: Praise to our
King (Horne) R Sing we the
King who is coming to reign
101443
Come, let us sing the song of
songs (Montgomery) D448;
V194; AZ334; BA116; BB153;
BV252   101444
Come, let us sing unto the Lord
(Asso. Refd. Presby. Psalter,
1931) AM15   101445
Come, let us to the Lord our
God (Morison [Morrison])
R125; W400; AD217; AI433;
AL269; AM516; AP436; AW146;
BV143; BY429   101446
Come, let us tune our loftiest
song (West) G21; H66; I21;

AT128; BZ   101447
Come, let us use the grace
divine (Wesley) G540; I569
BZ   101448
Come, let us who in Christ
believe (Wesley) I36; AL329;
BZ   101449
Come, let us with our Lord
arise (Wesley) BV69 101450
Come, let us worship and fall
down before Christ (St John
Chrysostom??) BL44 101451
Come, linger here with the
Master (McKinney) AU453
101452
Come, listen to a prophet's
voice (---) BC46   101453
Come, Lord, and tarry not
(Bonar) H203; L345; R233;
S188; U123; V185; AR209;
AV121; AW129; AZ1334; BA
99; BB174   101454
Come, Lord, and warm each
languid heart (Steele) V578
101455
Come, Lord, Thyself, in all Thy
grace (Petrusson) M308
101456
Come, Lord, Thyself with Thine
abounding grace (Petrusson)
P424   101457
Come, lost one, your Saviour is
calling (Shoemaker) AX225;
AY230   101458
Come, love we God! of might is
most the Father (Richard
Shanne ms) BG10   101459
Come, lowly souls that mourn
(Stennett) AZ1336   101460
Come, Master Workman, work
with us (Hingley) Y215
101461
Come, mighty Spirit, penetrate
(Bonar) AN49; BX280 101462
Come, my heart, canst thou not
hear it (Knight) AB110;
BF296   101463
Come, my Redeemer, come
(Reed) AY264   101464
Come, my soul, thou must be
waking (Canitz) A154; B3;
D3; G30; J207; K445; L4;
O547; R44; S487; T302; V37;

Y359; Z134; AB2; AD36; AE39;
AF506; AG19; AH160; AK46;
AM334; AN88; AO18; AP660;
AR43; AV10; AW27; AZ595;
BA769; BD1; BF177; BK39;
BV38; BX150; BY674; BZ
101465

Come, my soul, thy plea prepare
(Newton) BV607 X Come, my
soul, thy suit prepare   101466

Come, my soul, thy suit prepare
(Newton) B304; D651; E377; F
319; H60; I507; K277; L409;
M74; N304; O16; Q459; R529;
S17app.; U357; V467; W450;
X473; AA56; AL347; AM531;
AP497; AZ72; BA596; BB318;
BV607; BY333   101467

Come, my way, my truth, my
life (Herbert) X474; AQ123;
AZ86; BL32   101468

Come now, all people, keep high
mirth (Dearmer) X475 101469

Come, O come in pious lays
(Wither) BX18   101470

Come, O come, thou quickening
Spirit, Thou from ... (Held)
J126; K149; M465; N157; O426;
P231; Q226; AA246; AM247;
AW548; AZ608   101471

Come, O Creator Spirit blest
(Latin, before 10th c) H207;
AM251; AO226; AZ375; BA
134   101472

Come, O Creator Spirit, come
(Latin, before 10th c) E154;
F152; X179; BJ48   101473

Come, O holy Sabbath evening
(Mayer) BH105   101474

Come, O Jesus, and prepare me
(Franzèn) M55; N245 101475

Come, O Lord, like morning
sunlight (Littlefield) G33; AB
44; AC14; AD38; BF223; BK
42   101476

Come, O my soul, on sacred lays
(Blacklock) H108; I23; AV29
101477

Come, O Sabbath day, and bring
(Gottheil) AHp.150; BH118
101478

"Come, O sinner, all is ready!"

(Dahl) N244   101479

Come, O Spirit, seal me thine
(Warner) R Fill me with Thy
Spirit, Lord   101480

Come, O thou all-victorious
Lord (Wesley) I241; BV482
101481

Come, O thou God of grace
(Evans) G550; I661; S483;
AD415; AE347; AR523; AS
438; BF592; BZ   101482

Come, O thou King of Kings
(Pratt) BC20   101483

Come, O thou Traveler unknown
(Wesley) B230; E378; F343;
G311; I511; J471; W416;
X476; AL312; BB243; BX114;
BY767; BZ   101484

Come on, my partners in distress (Wesley) I432 101485

Come! Peace of God, and dwell
again on earth (Rowland)
G510; Z555   101486

Come, praise your Lord and
Saviour (How) D533; W70;
AP748; AZ847; BA814 101487

Come, pure hearts, in sweetest
measure (Latin, 12th c) A134;
B288; D497; F508; AZ642;
BR241   101488

Come, Rain from the heavens
(Stegmann) M473   101489

Come, Redeemer, blessed Jesus
(Wesley) BR160 X Come, thou
long-expected Jesus   101490

Come, rejoice, the King of glory
(Cannon) BC1   101491

Come rejoicing, Faithful men
with rapture singing (Latin,
11th c) or earlier C22
101492

Come rejoicing, Praises voicing,
Christmas day is breaking
(Latin 12th c) Q82   101493

Come, ring out our joy to the
Lord (Ladies of the Grail)
BSp30   101494

Come, risen Lord, and deign to
be our guest (Briggs) A207;
X266; AF286; AW307; BV374;
BY312   101495

Come, sacred Spirit, from above
(Doddridge) V582   101496

Come, said Jesus' sacred voice
(Barbauld) G192; H260; I257;
L364; AO636; AT244; AV158;
BA400; BR391   101497

Come, Saviour, come, and give
thy Spirit course (Bayley) R
O Jesus, Lord and Saviour,
the soul's ...   101498

Come, Saviour dear, with us
abide (Rutström) N298 101499

Come, Saviour Jesus, from above
(Bourignon) I379   101500

Come, says Jesus' sacred voice
(Barbauld) AT244 X Come said
Jesus' sacred voice   101501

Come, see the place where Jesus
lay (Kelly) B174; N126; AZ
632   101502

Come, sing, thou happy church of
God (Zinzendorf, N.L.) AZ736
                         101503

Come, sing to the Lord, His name
to praise (deJong) BC32
                         101504

Come, sing to the Lord of harvest (Monsell) BI113 X Sing
to the Lord of harvest 101505

Come, sing with holy gladness
(St John of Damascus) BD239
X The day of resurrection
                         101506

Come, sing, ye choirs exultant
(Adam of St Victor) A133;
E179; F509   101507

Come, sinners, to the gospel
feast (Wesley) G186; H251;
I256; AZ414; BZ   101508

Come, sound his praise abroad
(Watts) G22; H4; I3; L81; N294;
V106; Z118; AI14; AM102; AO69;
AS77; BA640; BB172; BR82; BX
23; BZ   101509

Come, take by faith the Body of
your Lord (Bangor Antiphoner)
BA296 X Draw nigh and take the
Body   101510

Come, Thou all-transforming
Spirit (Evans) BE42 X Come,
thou soul-transforming Spirit
                         101511

Come, thou almighty King (Whitfield. Hymnbook. 1757) A271;
B209; D388; G2; H15; I2; J136;

K164; L179; M480; N164; O73;
P237; Q239; R244; S52; T296;
U3; V81; Y354; Z122; AA262;
AB13; AC38; AD20; AE154;
AF246; AG12; AH189; AI24;
AK4; AL5; AM89; AN10; AO2;
AQ26; AR21; AS1; AT12;
AU4; AV32; AW8; AX1; AY
27; AZ1234; BA10; BB3; BD
24; BF216; BI39; BK63; BX8;
BZ   101512

Come, thou Almighty Will!
Our fainting bosoms fill
(Hymns of the Spirit. 1864)
AN47; BX9   101513

Come, thou bright and morning-
star (Rosenroth) J212; Q529;
X27; AW554a   101514

Come, thou bright and morning-
star (Rosenroth) X Dayspring
of eternity   101515

Come, thou Desire of all thy
saints (Steele) H8; V413
                         101516

Come, thou everlasting Spirit
(Wesley) AP273; AY16; BY
227   101517

Come, thou Fount of every blessing (Robinson) G23 X Saviour,
Source of every blessing
                         101518

Come, thou glorious day of
promise (Neibaur) BC240
                         101519

Come, thou holy Paraclete
(Latin, 13th c) E155; W186;
X180; AL144; AP266   101520

Come, thou Holy Spirit, come!
(Latin, 9th c) A109; B196;
D378; BO189; BR205; BV225;
BY228   101521

Come, thou long-expected Jesus
(Wesley) A1; B55; D48; F54;
G84; H133; I116; J5; K12;
L404; M340; N22; O202; P120;
R151; S113; T350; U64; V124;
W150; AE76; AF103; AG62;
AK89; AL132; AM145; AO117;
AP248; AR104; AT70; AV93;
AW69; AZ255; BA148; BL2;
BR160; BV86; BY78; BZ
                         101522

Come, thou my Light, that I

may see (Kerr) AR399 101523

Come Thou now and be among
us (Latin, 7th c) K242; L295;
O131   101524

Come thou, O come, sweetest and
kindliest (St Anselm of Canterbury) AB97; BR201   101525

Come, thou precious Ransom,
come (Olearius) Q55; AA134
101526

Come thou Redeemer of the
earth (St Ambrose) E14
101527

Come, thou Saviour of our race
(St Ambrose) N23; O186; P
123   101528

Come, thou soul-transforming
Spirit (Evans) AZ1407; BE42
101529

Come, thou universal Blessing
(Wesley) AZ962   101530

Come, though with purifying fire
(Scudder) Y292   101531

Come to Calvary's holy mountain
(Montgomery) J82; L363; M
405; N106; O399; P253; Q149;
AA212; AZ597; BA193   101532

Come to Jesus, come to Jesus
(---) R Are you weary, heavy
laden   101533

Come to Jesus, ye who labor
(Parker) Z282; AT246; BF346
101534

Come to our dark nature's night
(Rawson) BV286 X Come to
our poor nature's night 101535

Come to our poor nature's night
(Rawson) B203; D135; H208;
V215; AB98; AI118; AK189;
AL161; AM248; AO229; AP271;
AZ1133; BB216; BR202; BV286;
BY229   101536

Come to the church in the wildwood (Pitts) R There's a
church in the valley   101537

Come to the land of peace (Hemans) BE44   101538

Come to the Light, 'tis shining for
thee (Bliss) R The whole world
was lost   101539

Come to the Saviour, make no delay (Root) N647; AI391; AM693;
AP758; AX233   101540

Come to the Saviour now, He
gently calleth thee (Wigner)
G190; R261; S220; T431; U
166; V263; Z278; AG138; AK
463; AM395; AO644; AR245;
AT226   101541

Come to the Saviour, On Him
your burdens roll (McKinney)
R O, come, all ye that labor
101542

Come tonight and do not tarry
(Toews) R Come, ye weary
ones   101543

Come unto Jesus; ye heavy laden
(Huish) BC22   101544

"Come unto me," it is the
Saviour's voice (Norton) AI
194; AS193   101545

Come unto me, when shadows
darkly gather (Esling) G350;
H372; I462; L358; N523; O517;
V765; AO253; AR439; BB323;
BX273   101546

Come unto me, ye weary (Dix)
B387; D437; E379; F350; G
194; I295; L361; O514; P249;
Q276; R268; S222; T432; U
165; V255; W390; Z277; AA
49; AB156; AF315; AH614;
AI204; AK305; AL470; AM405;
AP396; AR246; AT227; AV159;
AW240; AZ844; BA401; BE43;
BF343; BR353; BV470; BY412
101547

Come, we that love the Lord
(Watts) G227; H12; I22; J165;
K308; L455; R408; U208; V526;
W447; Z119; AE282; AH199;
AK30; AL288; AO72; AP444;
AR441; AS287; AT308; AU8;
AV343; AW443; AX29; AY138;
AZ1354; BA369; BB640; BC
25; BY495; BZ   101548

Come, we who love the Lord
(Watts) AK30 X Come, we
that love the Lord   101549

Come with thy sins to the fountain (Crosby) AX231 101550

Come with us, O blessed Jesus
(Hopkins) A211; J283 101551

Come, women, wide proclaim
(Heck) AU214   101552

Come, worship at Immanuel's

feet (Watts) AZ336   101553
Come, ye children of the Lord
(Wallis) BC23   101554
Come, ye disconsolate, where'er
ye languish (Moore & Hastings)
A483; B388; D637; G312; H441;
I526; J569; K412; L366; M27;
N477; O438; P266; Q531; R373;
S293; U229; V428; W688; Z398;
AA512; AD264; AE163; AG134;
AH382; AI293; AK303; AL435;
AM518; AO250; AP532; AR247;
AS198; AT297; AU449; AV280;
AW243; AY350; AZ1152; BA
693; BB223; BC18; BE40; BR
339; BZ   101555
Come ye faithful, raise the
anthem (Hupton) E380; F222;
X477; AZ627; BV257; BY201
101556
Come, ye faithful, raise the
strain (St John of Damascus)
A94; B170; D110; E131; F133;
G151; I163; J106; K108; M445;
N131; O328; P195; Q204; R205;
S168; V767; X144; Z242; AD
162; AE136; AF185; AG101;
AH301; AK169; AM200; AO180;
AR183; AT109; AW113; AZ865;
BB136; BD246; BF319; BR179;
BY155; BZ   101557
Come, ye faithful servants (Levy)
BH101   101558
Come, ye people, raise the an-
them (Hupton) X477 X Come
ye faithful, raise the anthem
101559
Come, ye people, rise and sing
(Alington) R39   101560
Come, ye saints, look here and
wonder (Kelly) BA235 101561
Come, ye sinners, poor and
needy (Hart) G187; H255; I
259; N399; V253; W393; AI195;
AL476; AM393; AP404; AT241;
AU229; AV341; AW459; AX240;
AY229; AZ1408; BA399; BV473;
BZ   101562
Come, ye sinners, poor and
wretched (Hart) V253 X Come,
ye sinners, poor and needy
101563
Come, ye souls by sin afflicted

(Swain) W392; AM390; AP
403; BV471; BY413   101564
Come, ye thankful people, come
(Alford) A137; B421; D193;
E289; F482; G545; H521; I717;
J360; K484; L555; M491; N
574; O532; P243; Q574; R525;
S460; T444; U483; V617; W
619; X9; Z593; AA295; AB
389; AC322; AD447; AE426;
*AF461, 462; AG287; AH493;
AI350; AK434; AL577; AM615;
AN141; AO579; AP691; AQ
278; AR594; AT490; AU136;
AV307; AW377; AZ1050; BA
861; BB496; BC29; BD198;
BF650; BK136; BL55; BR490;
BV648; BX177; BY724; BZ
*words differ, these two poems
101565
Come, ye that fear Jehovah
(U. P. Psalter. 1912) T35;
AJ50; AP18   101566
Come, ye that fear the Lord,
and hear (U. P. Psalter. 1912)
R296; AJ174   101567
Come, ye that love the Lord
(Watts) L455 X Come, we
that love the lord   101568
Come, ye that love the Saviour's
name (Steele) I34; V188;
AM588   101569
Come, ye wanderers, all for-
saken (Pollock) AX222; AY
225   101570
Come, ye weary, heavy laden
(Pollock) R Come, ye wan-
derers   101571
Come, ye weary ones, tonight
(Toews) AX234   101572
Come, ye weary sinners, come
(Wesley) O515; AA58 101573
Come ye yourselves apart and
rest awhile (Bickersteth)
BV375   101574
Come, your hearts and voices
raising (Gerhardt) Q90
101575
Comes any good from Nazareth
(Sangster) Y69; AB152
101576
Cometh sunshine after rain
(Gerhardt) X478   101577

Comfort, comfort ye, my people
(Olearius) J12; K8; M337;
N3; O170; Q61; AA130; AF104;
AI440; AK90; AM148; AR333;
AZ91   101578
Comfort ye, my people, saith
your God (Bayly) R O joyful
hope   101579
Coming home, coming home
(Kirkpatrick) R I've wandered
far   101580
Coming now to thee, O Christ
my Lord (McKinney) AT342
                                    101581
Command thy blessing from above
(Montgomery) W241; AZ305;
BA370; BY357   101582
Commit thou all that grieves thee
(Gerhardt, tr. by Farlander)
A446; M269; P285   101583
Commit thou all thy griefs (Ger-
hardt, tr. by Wesley) I435;
K399; L516; N474; W546; X479;
AK308; AL420; AM560; AO102;
AP516; AW558a; BR316; BV525;
BW558; BX309; BY574   101584
Commit thou every grievance
(Gerhardt) AZ807; BA682
                                    101585
Commit whatever grieves thee
(Gerhardt, tr. by Kelly) Q520;
AA525   101586
Comrades known in marches many
(Halpine) Y148; AC238 101587
Concordi laetitia (Latin, 13th c)
BN151; BO123; BP74; BQ197
                                    101588
Conditor alme siderum (Latin,
9th c) BJ47b   101589
Comfirma hoc Deus (Latin) BQ
245   101590
Conquering kings their titles
take (Breviary, Nevers. 1727)
A324; B91; D322; E37; F191;
J509; AZ69; BV552   101591
Conquering now and still to con-
quer (Crosby) AI330; AM665
                                    101592
Conquering Prince and King of
Glory (Tersteegen) O363; AZ
901; BV199   101593
Conquering Prince and Lord of
Glory (Tersteegen) AZ901 X

Conquering Prince and King of
Glory   101594
Consider well your ways and
lives (Torrence) AQ262
                                    101595
Constantine! Constantine! Look
above the battle scene (Hen-
derson) Y114   101596
Content, O Lord, and free from
fear (Wolcott) AE214 101597
Cor, arca legem continens
(Breviary, Bologna. 1827) BN
66; BQ240   101598
Cor dulce, cor amabile Latin
BN68; BO15   101599
Cor Jesu sacratissium (Litany
of the Sacred Heart) BN67;
BO23; BQ238   101600
Cor Jesu, salus in te speran-
tium (Latin) BQ237   101601
Corde natus ex Parentis
(Prudentius) BT98   101602
Count your blessings (Oatman)
R When upon life's billows
                                    101603
Countless hosts before God's
throne (Gregor) BA746 X
O how excellent and fair
                                    101604
Courage, brother! do not stumble
(MacLeod) G298; I513; W529;
AO402; AP533; BA573; BB
263; BH87; BY563   101605
Courage, my sorely tempted
heart! (Boehmer) AZ512
                                    101606
Courage my soul! While God is
near (---) L512   101607
Courans à la fete, ne différons
pas (French trad carol)
BG154b   101608
Cover with His life, whiter than
snow (Belden) R Look upon
Jesus, sinless is He 191609
Create in this weak form of
mine (Weitzman) BH170
                                    101610
Creation's Lord, we give Thee
thanks (Hyde) A548; Z492;
AB177; AD344; AF303; AL416;
AN311; AQ108,221; BF581;
BX348   101611
Creator alme siderum (Latin,

7th c) BN3; BO285; BP2; BQ
151   101612
Creator of the earth and sky (St
Ambrose) E49; X44   101613
Creator of the starry height
(Latin, 9th c) F45; O174; BP3
                             101614
Creator of the stars of night
(Latin, 9th c) A6; E1; AF113;
BL4; BM97; BZ   101615
Creator of the universe, we lift
our minds (Hughes) BK33
                             101616
Creator of the world, to thee
(Coffin) F83   101617
Creator of the world we pray
(St Ambrose) BM96   101618
Creator Spirit, all divine (Latin,
9th c) BP45   101619
Creator Spirit, by whose aid
(Latin, 9th c) A371; B198; D
381; E156; I194; J124; Q236;
V219; W184; X181; AD183; AN
61; AP268; AZ376; BA140; BL
35; BX72; BY230   101620
Creator, Spirit, heavenly Dove
(Latin, 9th c) M464   101621
Creator Spirit, Lord of grace
(Latin, before 10th c) 101622
BP43
Cross of Christ, O sacred tree
(Taylor) AS137; AX117; AY199
                             101623
Cross of Jesus, cross of sorrow
(Simpson) R196; S155; V754;
AE113; AK163; AO173; AR171;
AW111; BZ   101624
Crown him! crown him! Angels
crown him (Stebbins) AY267 X
Look, ye saints (Kelly)101625
Crown Him the Lord of peace
(Bridges) BT341 X Crown him
with many crowns   101626
Crown him upon the throne
(Dearmer) X480   101627
Crown him with many crowns
(Bridges) A352; B190; D374; E
381; F224; G170; H198; I179;
J431; K134; L153; M452; N341;
P30; Q341; R213; S190; T349;
U115; V195; W136; Y333; Z250;
AA104; AB88; AC136; AD170;
AE132; AF199; AG100; AH328;

AK176; AL115; AM216; AO198;
AP227; AR105; AS157; AT152;
AU18; AV141; AW118; AZ
1492; BA243; BB162; BF325;
BL58; BN75; BQ43; BT341;
BV209; BY182; BZ   101628
Crown His head with endless
blessing (Goode) V199; AM
130; AV127   101629
Crown with thy benediction
(Greenwood) O535   101630
Crushed by my sin, O Lord, to
Thee (Gellert) N237; O102
                             101631
Cry out with joy to the Lord,
all the earth! (Ladies of the
Grail) BSp42   101632

D

Da Jesus an des Kreuzes Stamm
(Böschenstain) BT177 101633
Daily, daily, sing the praises
(Baring-Gould) E568; H515
                             101634
Daily, daily sing to Mary (St
Bernard of Cluny) BN132 X
Daily sing in praise of Mary
                             101635
Daily sing in praise of Mary
(St Bernard of Cluny) BM52;
BN132; BO59; BP79; BQ75
                             101636
Daisies are our silver (Struther)
X354   101637
Dank sei Gott in der Höhe
(Mühlmann) BT544   101638
Dankt dem Herrn! mit frohen
Gaben. (G. N. Fischer) BW
376   101639
Dankt Gott in seinem hochsten
Thron (Ausbund) BU43
                             101640
Dans cette étable (French trad
carol) BG75b   101641
Dare to be a Daniel (Bliss) R
Standing by a purpose true
                             101642
Dare to be brave, dare to be
true (Rooper) AH613; AT411;
AU320; AV401   101643
Dare to do right, dare to be
true (Taylor) AP772 101644

Dark and thorny is the desert
(---) AX449; BY388   101645
Dark hills at evening in the west
(Robinson) AQ273   101646
Dark is the hour when death
prevails (Smith, U.) BB492
                                  101647
Dark the day on Calvary's cross
(Watt) W112; AW538   101648
Dark the night lay, wild and
dreary (Welsh trad carol) BG
9   101649
Darkening night the land doth
cover (St Anatolius) AW32
BJ64   101650
Darkly rose the guilty morning
(Anstice) V155   101651
Darkness o'er the earth is steal-
ing (Landstad) O558   101652
Das alte Jahr vergangen ist
(Steuerlein) BT125   101653
Das ist der Gemeinde Stärke
(Preiswerk) BT461   101654
Das Wort der Wahrheit Jesu
Christ (Ausbund) BU67
                                  101655
Daughter of a mighty Father (---)
BO81   101656
Daughter of God the Father (---)
BO115   101657
Daughter of Zion, awake from thy
sadness (Fitzgerald. Collection,
1830) L353; BB303; BE200;
BI50   101658
Daughter of Zion, from the dust
(Montgomery) H474   101659
Day by Day, Dear Lord, of Thee
three things I pray (St Richard
of Chichester) A429; R541; S
39app.; X399; AG336; AR555
                                  101660
Day by day the manna fell (Con-
der) I438; AN66; AP509; AW
247; AZ44; BA27; BE46; BR
254; BX99   101661
Day by day we magnify thee
(Ellerton) AP716   101662
Day is dawning in the east (Lath-
bury) M637   101663
Day is done, gone the sun, from
the lakes (---) Y399; AC344;
AG339; AH566; BB370   101664
Day is dying in the west (Lath-

bury) G44; I57; J234; L20;
M638; N559; R65; S39; T307;
U463; V54; Y96; Z144; AB23;
AC17; AD47; AE43; AF45;
AG31; AH168; AI53; AK481;
AL562; AM343; AO27; AR50;
AS25; AT29; AU87; AV12;
AW31; AY440; BA782; BB51;
BD13; BF202; BK44; BY689;
BZ   101665
Day of judgment -- day of won-
ders (Newton: Dies irae)
L577; N610; V684; AI98; AM
241; AZ1377; BA738   101666
Day of judgment -- day of won-
ders (Newton) X Day of
wrath, O day of mourning
(Latin, 13th c)   101667
Day of wonder, day of gladness
(Hall) N129   101668
Day of wrath and doom impending
(Latin, 13th c) E351 X Day of
wrath! O day of mourning
                                  101669
Day of wrath! O day of mourning
(Latin, 13th c: Irons tr) A
468; D36; E351; F466; I747;
K515; O601; Q607; AA555;
AZ1513; BA929; BJ1b 101670
Day of wrath, O dreadful day
(Latin, 13th c : Stanley tr)
I599   101671
Day of wrath! that day of mourn-
ing (Latin, 13th c) O601 X
Day of wrath! O day ...
                                  101672
Days and moments quickly flying
(Caswall) E382; V632; W585;
AP609; AZ270; BA742 101673
Dayspring of Eternity, Bright-
ness of the Father's glory
(Rosenroth) N548 X Dayspring
of Eternity, Light from end-
less Light   101674
Dayspring of Eternity, light from
endless Light proceeding
(Rosenroth) K454; M555; N
548; O548; P52; AK47 101675
Dayspring of Eternity, Light of
Light, from God proceeding
(Rosenroth) M555 X Dayspring
of Eternity, Light from end-
less light   101676

Daystar on high, bright harbinger
of gladness (Stainer) F604
                                101677
Dear angel, ever at my side
(Faber) BN163; BO195; BP88;
BQ112   101678
Dear Christians, let us all re-
joice (Luther) M121   101679
Dear Christians, one and all re-
joice (Luther) N433; O526;
Q387; AA310   101680
Dear Crown of all the virgin-
choir (Latin, 8th c) BQ109
                                101681
Dear Father, here thy children
come (Rosewater) BH257
                                101682
Dear Father, keep me through
this day (Briggs) X400
                                101683
Dear Father, loud the ocean rolls
(Gower) Z330   101684
Dear Father-Mother, thou dost
grant (Sargant) BE48   101685
Dear Father, to thy mercy-seat
(Steele) AK229; AO312   101686
Dear Father, who hast made us
all (Knapp) Q299   101687
Dear God, how glorious is thy
name (Snelling) BE45   101688
Dear God, our Father, at Thy
knee confessing   (Bates)
G361; Y144; Z291; AC153; AR
400; BF358   101689
Dear God, the sun whose light is
sweet (Knapp) Y67; AB333;
AN217   101690
Dear Guardian of Mary (Faber)
AH141; BO128   101691
Dear Heart of Jesus, hear! (---)
R O Sacred Heart of Christ
aflame   101692
Dear Jesus, ever at my side
(Faber) D564   101693
Dear Jesus, receive me (Crosby)
R Loving Saviour, hear my
cry   101694
Dear land, of liberty, hope of the
(Richards) AO602   101695
Dear little One how sweet thou
art (Faber) BO155; BQ127
                                101696
Dear Lord and Father of mankind

(Whittier) A435; B120; E382;
F184; G342; H328; I543; J467;
N331; R416; S302; T406; U
242; V410; W245; X481; Y80;
Z411; AB212; AC152; AD279;
AE176; AF341; AG202; AH
400; AK226; AL286; AN250;
AO366; AP437; AQ118; AR334;
AS303; AT335; AU401; AV63;
AW181; BA514; BB116; BD
112; BE49; BF421; BK83;
BV608; BX285; BY50; BZ
                                101697
Dear Lord and Father of us all
(Whittier) BE49 X Dear Lord
and Father of mankind
                                101698
Dear Lord and Master mine
(Gill) AM576   101699
Dear Lord, before we part
(Psalms and hymns, 1858)
BY313   101700
Dear Lord, for all in pain
(Carmichael) BV396   101701
Dear Lord, I come at last
(McManus) AY227   101702
Dear Lord, my soul desireth
(Gambold) AZ569   101703
Dear Lord, to thy true servants
give (Polack) Q482   101704
Dear Lord, today, our child
(Busch) AM353   101705
Dear Lord, who sought at dawn
of day (Farrington) Y108;
AB276; AC112; AR279; BF
307   101706
Dear Maker of the starry skies
(Latin, 7th c) BN4   101707
Dear Master, in whose life I
see (Hunter) G376; S507;
W460; Z318; AF208; BY465;
BZ   101708
Dear Master, what can children
do? (Matheson) W361
                                101709
Dear Redeemer, we would hal-
low (Warner) R By thy
blessed word   101710
Dear refuge of my weary soul
(Steele) H349; L511; V368;
AA502   101711
Dear St Joseph, pure and gentle
(---) BO132   101712

Dear Saviour, bless us ere we
go (Faber) AO45 X O Saviour,
bless us ere we go   101713
Dear Saviour, if these lambs
should stray (Hyde) H453; V
545; AZ358; BA849   101714
Dear Saviour, stretch thy loving
arms (Smyth) BR525   101715
Dear Saviour, we are thine
(Doddridge) V452; AO368
                                           101716
Dear Saviour, we bless thee that
thou wast a child (Cennick)
AZ490   101717
Dear Saviour, we would know thy
love (---) BB147   101718
Dear Saviour, when I think of
thee (Kolb) AY248   101719
Dear Shepherd of thy people hear
(Newton) V569 X Great Shep-
herd of thy people   101720
Dear ties of mutual succor bind
(Bryant) I689   101721
Dear to the heart of the Shepherd
(Wingate) BC26   101722
Dearest children, God is near
you (Walker) BC170   101723
Dearest Jesus, come to me
(Scheffler) AZ37   101724
Dearest Jesus, draw thou near
me (Kingo) O37; P39   101725
Dearest Jesu, we are here,
At thy call [general hymn]
(Clausnitzer) F408; G310
                                           101726
Dearest Jesus, we are here,
Gladly thy command obeying
[Baptism] (Schmolck) Q300
                                           101727
Dearest of all the names above
(Watts) V128   101728
Death, death, thou hast con-
quered me (Sower [Sauer])
AR418   101729
Death in all this world prevaileth
(Albinus) O513   101730
Death shall not destroy my com-
fort (---) AY191   101731
Debilis cessent elementa legis
(Besnault) BT117   101732
Deceit and falsehood I abhor
(U. P. Psalter. 1912) T239;
AJ335   101733

Deck the hall with boughs of
holly (English trad carol)
BG50b   101734
Deck thyself, my soul, with
gladness (Franck) A210;
E306; F393; J262; K182;
L48; N246; O149; P100; Q
305; W324; X267; AA432;
AI426; AK334; AL221; AN
494; AW552; AZ423; BY314;
BZ   101735
Deck thyself with joy and gladness (Franck) J262 X Deck
thyself, my soul, with glad-
ness   101736
Declare, O heavens, the Lord
of space (Edwards) BL76
                                           101737
Deem not that they are blest
alone (Bryant) I456 X O
deem not they are blest alone
                                           101738
Deep and glorious, word vic-
torious (Oldenburg) O251;
P160   101739
Deep and precious, strong and
gracious (Oldenburg) M34
                                           101740
Deep are his wounds, and red
(Johnson) J80   101741
Deep are the wounds which sin
has made (Steele) H223
                                           101742
Deep in the dust before Thy
throne (Watts) L377 101743
Deep river, My home is over
Jordan (Negro traditional)
AR488   101744
Deeper yet, deeper yet, Into
the crimson flood (Oatman)
R In the blood from the cross
                                           101745
Deeply moved and duly heeding
(Zinzendorf, A. N.) AZ429
                                           101746
Defend me, Lord, from shame
(Tate & Brady) AJ82 101747
Defend me, O God, and plead
my cause (Ladies of the
Grail) BSp20   101748
Defend us, Lord, from every
ill (Hay) I403; AV70 101749
Deign this union to approve

(Collyer) AX1268   101750
Delay not, delay not, O sinner,
    draw near (Hastings) L371;
    M24; Q278; U164; V270; AA547;
    AI207   101751
Deliver me from evil, Preserve
    me, Lord (U.P. Psalter, 1912)
    T277; AJ385   101752
Deliver me, my God, from all
    that's now enchanting (Gedicke)
    AZ711   101753
Den store hvide Folk vi se
    (Brorson) BT656   101754
Den Vater woll'n wir loben (G.
    Wagner) BU34   101755
Depth of mercy! can there be
    (Wesley) G200; H265; I267;
    R273; U173; V286; AG146; AI
    216; AK209; AO264; AP434; AS
    199; AT242; AU288; AV164;
    AY216; BB234; BZ   101756
Der Bräut'gam wird bald rugen
    (Walther) BT67   101757
Der Glaub beschutzt mich ganz
    und gar (Ausbund) BU60
                                101758
Der Heiland rufet mir und dir
    (Unparth. G.B.) AY34d 101759
Der herr uns segne und behüt
    (Unparth. G.B.) AY6d
                                101760
Der mange skal komme fra
    Ost og fra Vest (Landstad)
    BT415   101761
Der Tag, der ist so freudenreich
    (Latin 14th c) BT78   101762
Der Winter kalt, rauh ungestalt
    (Ausbund) BU47   101763
Descend, descend, O Sabbath
    Princess (Cohen) BH107
                                101764
Descend to thy Jerusalem, O
    Lord. (Taylor) BX202 X Draw
    night to thy Jerusalem 101765
Desire of every nation (Hoppe)
    N69   101766
Despair not, O heart, in thy sor-
    row (Prudentius) J297; O595;
    P418   101767
Despise not, Lord, my lowly
    penitence (Ha-Levi) BH162
                                101768
Destroy, O Lord, the carnal

mind (Zinzendorf, N.L.)
    AZ921   101769
Deus, tuorum militum (Latin,
    6th c) BN181; BO290 101770
Dha-ke-de hia-u-dha (Omaha
    [Indian] trad) Y314   101771
Decimus grates tibi, summe
    rerum (Melanchthon) BT254
                                101772
Did Christ o'er sinners weep
    (Beddome) I276; U178; V284;
    AY262; AZ1294   101773
Did you pray till the answer
    came (Poole) R Have you
    prayed all night   101774
Didst thou, dear Jesus, pray for
    me (Ryden) M404; N141
                                101775
Didst thou, dear Jesus, suffer
    shame (Maxwell) U182; V438
                                101776
Die Asche will nicht lassen ab
    (Luther) BT259   101777
Die beste Freud aus Gottes
    Wort (Ausbund) BU14 101778
Die ganze welt, Herr Jesu
    Christ (German carol, 1623)
    BG96b   101779
Die güldne Sonne, Voll Freud
    und Wonne (P. Gerhardt)
    BW555   101780
Die helle Sonn' leucht't herfür
    (Herman) BT547   101781
Die Lieb ist kalt jetzt in der
    Welt (L.Schornschlager) BU
    57   101782
Die Nacht ist kommen (Herbert)
    BT556   101783
Die sach' ist dein, Herr Jesu
    Christ (Preiswerk) AW550b;
    BW550   101784
Dies est laetitia, In ortu regali
    (Latin, 14th c) BQ294 101785
Dies irae, dies illa (Latin, 13th
    c) BMp.162; BN243; BOp.258;
    BQ270D; BT607   101786
Dies ist die Nacht, da mir
    erschienen (Nachtenhöfer)
    BT88   101787
Dies sind die heil'gen Zehn
    Gebot (Luther) BT287 101788
Dim mine eyes with many tear-
    drops (Rypins) BH173 101789

Dir, dir Jehova, will ich singen
  (Crasselius) BT21; BW569
                         101790
Dir, Herr, sei dieses Kind em-
  pfohlen (Neander, C.F.) BT
  303   101791
Dismiss me not thy service,
  Lord (Lynch) E555; W354;
  X297; AL381; AP578; BR380;
  BY512   101792
Dismiss us, Lord, with blessing,
  we pray (Froom) BB702
                         101793
Dismiss us with thy blessing,
  Lord! (Hart) L61; U450;
  V20; Z639; AP342; AX80; AY
  411; AZ327   101794
Disposer supreme, and Judge of
  the earth (Santeuil) E178; F
  506; X211; Y386; BJ52; BV
  459   101795
Divinity is round us (Fahs) AQ
  58   101796
Do life's storms above thee roll?
  (Reed) AX516; AY311   101797
Do no sinful action, speak no
  angry word (Alexander) E589;
  F433; W663; AP771   101798
Do not I love thee, O my Lord
  (Doddridge) H329; I338; V378;
  AR106   101799
Do not turn the lambs away
  (Mitchell) R Hark! I hear my
  Saviour say   101800
Do ye, O men, speak righteousness
  (U.P. Psalter. 1912) T107; AJ
  156   101801
Do you ask what most I prize
  (Schwedler) AZ1158; BA480
                         101802
Do you love the world, in its
  pomp and show (Warren) AX
  265   101803
Do you seek for a friend who is
  always the same (Bills) AX
  279   101804
Do what is right; the day-dawn is
  breaking (---) BC27   101805
Does Jesus care when my heart is
  pained (Graeff) AX528; AY
  464   101806
Does the journey seem long
  (Smith, J.F.) BC245   101807

Does thy soul leap up within thee
  (Versteeg) AK139   101808
Dominic, our Lady's champion
  (Lee) BN177   101809
Dona nobis pacem, pacem (---)
  BK34   101810
Done is the work that saves
  (Bonar) AZ1179   101811
Don't forget the Sabbath, The
  Lord our God hath blest
  (Crosby) BB653   101812
Don't let your light burn low
  (Ussery) R O would you be
  a blessing   101813
Don't turn him away (Lillenas)
  R Patiently, tenderly pleading
                         101814
Don't you hear the bells now
  ringing (DeMarbelle) R
  There's a land   101815
Don't you want to go to heaven
  (Negro spiritual) AH597 X
  We are climbing Jacob's lad-
  der   101816
Dormi, Jesu! mater ridet
  (Latin carol) BG175   101817
Dost thou in a manger lie (Mau-
  burn) A29; B550; AZ1087;
  BR142   101818
Dost thou truly seek renown
  (Latin, 14th-15th c) E97
                         101819
Down at the cross where my
  Saviour died (Hoffman) AT
  95; AU185; AV386; AW464;
  AX4   101820
Down by the river's verdant
  side (Bible. Psalm 137) BC
  55   101821
Down from the worlds of radiant
  light (Proud) BR131 101822
Down in the valley where sum-
  mer's laughing beam (Binyon)
  BG161   101823
Down in the valley with my
  Saviour (Cushing) AU118;
  AX412   101824
Down in yon forest there stands
  a hall (English trad carol)
  BG61   101825
Down the dark future, Through
  long generations (Longfellow)
  AC292   101826

Down the mines for buried treas-
ure (Jackson) BY365   101827
Down through the ages vast
(Omaha [Indian] trad) Y314
                                101828
Down to the sacred wave (Smith,
S.F.) AS456; AU282   101829
Down with the rosemary and bays
(Herrick) BG126   101830
Draw, Holy Ghost, thy sevenfold
veil (Keble) D214   101831
Draw me nearer, nearer, blessed
Lord (Crosby) R I am thine,
O Lord   101832
Draw me, O Lord, to thee,
Nearer to thee (Jacobs) N449
X Nearer my God to thee!
Nearer to thee. Through word
and sacrament   101833
Draw near, draw near (McKin-
ney) AU304   101834
Draw near, O Son of God, draw
near (Wesley) H465   101835
Draw nigh and take the Body of
the Lord (Bangor Antiphoner,
ca 690) A202; B330; D220; E
307; F386; J273; K187; L325;
O150; Q307; X268; AA427; AO
442; AY433; BA296; BR475;
BV373   101836
Draw night, draw nigh, Immanuel
(Latin, ca 9th c) AZ677 X
O come, O come, Emmanuel
                                101837
"Draw nigh to God, he will draw
nigh to you." (Tarrant) BX
274   101838
Draw nigh to thy Jerusalem, O
Lord (Taylor) S148; Y246;
AC118; AD142; AF156; BF310;
BV168; BX202   101839
Draw Thou my soul, O Christ
(Larcom) G297; R284; U250;
Y370; Z299; AB264; AC149;
AE273; AF318; AG160; AK206;
AR348; AS242; AT314; BZ
                                101840
Draw us in the Spirit's tether
(Dearmer) X274b   101841
Draw us to thee, For then shall
we (Funcke) M454; Q215; AA
234   101842
Draw us to thee in mind and

heart (Funcke) O58; P215
                                101843
Draw us to thee, Lord Jesus
(Funcke) AZ799; BA519
                                101844
Draw to the cross, which thou
hast blessed (Irons) H173;
Q390; AA321; BY430   101845
Dread Jehovah, God of nations
(Foster) D201; I709; L560;
N576; V625; AZ267   101846
Drei König wandern aus morgen-
land (Cornelius) BG193b
                                101847
Drooping souls, no longer grieve
(Hastings?) AY320   101848
Drop, drop, slow tears (Flet-
cher) A69; E98; X125 101849
Du glaubigs Herz, so benedey
(Walpurg v. Bappenheim)
BU75   101850
Du Lebensbrot, Herr Jesu
Christ (Rist) BT312 101851
Du unbegreislich höchstes Gut
(Unparth.G.B.) AY12d 101852
Durch Gnad so will ich singen
(H. Straub) BU56   101853
Dust to dust, the mortal dies
(U.P. Psalter, 1912) T93;
AJ136   101854
Dwell in me, O blessed Spirit
(Lankton) AI124; AK464; AO
650   101855
Dying with Jesus, by death
reckoned mine (Whittle) AH
401; AI313; AM708; AU58;
BB583   101856

E

Each cooing dove, and sighing
bough (Morris) AU437; BC
38   101857
Each little flower that opens
(Alexander) R All things
bright and beautiful   101858
Each morning brings us fresh
out-poured (Zwick) AF498
                                101859
Early, my God, without delay
(Watts) V8; BB72   101860
Early will I seek Thee, God,
my refuge strong (Salomon

ibn Gabirol) BH18   101861
Earth arrayed in wondrous beauty
    (Silliman) AQ48   101862
Earth below is teeming (Monsell)
    Z596; AZ774   101863
Earth has many a noble city
    (Prudentius) A48; B93; D63;
    F76; J51; BR154; BV127;
    BZ   101864
Earth has nothing sweet or fair
    (Scheffler) AO304; AZ48
                          101865
Earth holds no treasures but
    perish with using (Teddlie)
    AX604   101866
Earth is waking, day is breaking!
    (---) BD150   101867
Earth thou dost visit, watering it
    (Scottish Psalter, 1650) AP55
                          101868
Earth today rejoices and celestial
    voices (Neale) BG141 101869
Earth was waiting, spent and rest-
    less (Smith, W. C.) BY79
                          101870
Earth, with all thy thousand
    voices (Churton) BH64 101871
Earth, with her ten thousand
    flowers (Taylor) BC30 101872
Earthly friends will change and
    falter (Neale) BG135 101873
Earthly joys no longer please us
    (Ford) AZ257   101874
Earthly pleasures vainly call me
    (Rowe) AS236   101875
Earth's mighty Maker, whose
    command (Latin, ca 7th c) E
    59   101876
Easter eggs! Easter eggs! Give
    to him that begs! (Russian trad
    carol) BG94   101877
Easter flowers are blooming bright
    (Nicholson) B558; K548; AC126;
    AD477   101878
Easter morrow stills our sorrow
    (Grundtvig) P196   101879
Eastern monarch, sages three
    (Latin, 15th c) BL16 101880
Ecce iam noctis tenuatur umbra
    (St Gregory the Great) BJ75b
                          101881
Ecce nomen Domini Emmanuel
    (Latin early) BQ157   101882

Ecce panis angelorum (St
    Thomas Aquinas) BN86; BP53;
    BQ231   101883
Ecce Sacérdos magnus (Latin)
    BQ246   101884
E'en in thy childhood, 'mid the
    desert places (Paul the
    Deacon) E224   101885
E'en tho' the clouds sweep fast
    and wild (Kuipers) R In the
    good ship of our Captain
                          101886
Ein' feste Burg ist unser Gott
    (Luther) AD289; BT262;
    BW549   101887
Ein g'fahre Zeit vor nie erhört
    (H. Buchel) BU46   101888
Ein grosse Freud ist ingemein
    (Ausbund) BU18   101889
Ein Kind geborn zu Bethlehem
    (German trad carol) BG85b
                          101890
Ein Kindlein in der Wiegen
    (German trad carol) BG84
                          101891
Ein Lämmlein geht und trägt die
    schuld (Gerhardt) BT142;
    BW533   101892
Ein Liedlein will ich singen
    (Ausbund) BU89   101893
Ein Mägdelein von Gleidern zart
    (Ausbund) BU13   101894
Eins ist not, ach Herr, dies
    eine (Schröder) BT366
                          101895
Eins Morgens früh vor Tage
    (Ausbund) BU66   101896
Einsmals spatziert ich hin und
    her (H. v. Bilach) BU48
                          101897
Eleazer steadfast, strong (Le-
    vinger) R In the candles'
    rays I see   101898
Emmanuel! we sing Thy praise
    (Gerhardt) K26; L140; M331;
    N29; O180; AA161; BA55
                          101899
En clára vox redarguit (Latin,
    5th-6th c) BQ154   101900
En Kelohenu (Jewish) AH151
                          101901
En mitten in des lebens zeyt.
    (Munich. MSS. 15th c.) BT

590   101902
Encamped along the hills of light
  (Yates) AH450; AT256; AV355;
  AX456   101903
Ended His strife, the battle won
  (Latin. 1695) P198 X The
  strife is o'er, the battle done
                        101904
Enduring Soul of all our life
  (Oakley) X482; Y28; AB91;
  AD75; BF378; BX76   101905
England, arise! The long, long
  night is over (Carpenter) X316
                        101906
Engraved as in eternal brass
  (Watts) BV526 X My hiding-
  place, my refuge, tower
                        101907
Enhver som tror og bliver döbt
  (Kingo) BT301   101908
Enkindling Love, eternal Flame
  (Barrows) AB60; BF253
                        101909
Enrich, Lord, heart, mouth,
  hands in me (Herbert) X401;
  AF527   101910
Enslaved by sin and bound in
  chains (Steele) Q141; AA202
                        101911
Enter Thy courts, thou Word of
  life (Bridges) W250; X483;
  BJ98   101912
Enthrone thy God within thy heart
  (Penn) BV618   101913
Enthroned on high, almighty Lord!
  (Haweis) V204; AS167 101914
Equip me for the war (Wesley)
  H391; L536   101915
Ere another day shall close (---)
  BR104   101916
Ere I sleep, for every favor
  (Cennick) S511; W294; AL555;
  AM337; AZ877; BA783; BV48;
  BY690   101917
Ere mountains reared their forms
  sublime (Auber) BB79 101918
Ere space exists, or earth, or
  sky (Jewish trad: Adonoi
  melech) BH159   101919
Ere to the world again we go
  Ellis. (Psalms and hymns.
  1845.) L58   101920
Ere we know our lost condition

(Zinzendorf, N. L.) BA515
                        101921
Ere yet in darkness ends the
  day (St Ambrose) BJ91
                        101922
Ere yet the dawn hath filled the
  sky (Heermann) L2; M437;
  O335   101923
Ere you left your room this
  morning (Kidder) AU335;
  AX361; BC31   101924
Erhalt uns deine Lehre (Gry-
  phius) BT264   101925
Erhalt uns, Herr, bei deinem
  Wort (Luther) BT261
                        101926
Ermuntert euch, ihr Frommen
  (Laurenti) BT72   101927
Erneure mich, o ew'ges Licht
  (Ruopp) BT398   101928
Erstanden, erstanden ist Jesus
  Christ (Walther) BT198
                        101929
Es b'gab sich auf ein Zeite
  (H. Buchel) BU45   101930
Es gibt ein wunderschönes Land
  (Unparth. G. B.) AY16d 101931
Es hatt' ein Mann zween knaben
  (M. Schneider) BU99 101932
Es ist das Heil uns kommen her
  (Speratus) BT377   101933
Es ist ein Reis (Ros') entsprun-
  gen (Speier Gebetbuch. 1599)
  BG76b; BT645   101934
Es ist ein wunder schöne Gab
  (Ausbund Suppl.) BU3 101935
Es ist gewisslich an der Zeit
  (Ringwaldt) BT611   101936
Es ist noch eine Ruh' vorhanden
  (Kunth) BT615   101937
Es ist noch Raum! Sein Haus
  ist noch nicht voll. (German)
  BT509   101938
Es ist vollbracht! Gott Lob, es
  ist vollbracht! (Gryphius)
  BT599   101939
Es kommt ein Schiff geladen
  (German trad carol) BG90b
                        101940
Es war die ganze Welt (Olearius)
  BT272   101941
Es war ein Gottesfüchtiges
  (Ausbund Suppl.) BU5 101942

Es waren auch zween Brüder
gut (Ausbund) BU16   101943
Es woll' uns Gott genädig sein
(Luther) BT500   101944
Established in the highest heavens
(U.P. Psalter, 1912) T182;
AJ279   101945
Eternal and immortal King (Dodd-
ridge) BX26   101946
Eternal Beam of Light divine
(Wesley) AL417; BX241101947
Eternal depth of love divine
(Zinzendorf, N.L.) BB62
                         101948
Eternal Father, God of love
(Beeden) BB31   101949
Eternal Father, strong to save
(Whiting) A512; B415; D306;
E540; F487; G553; J338; K503;
R521; S492; T445; U363; V644;
W626; X336; Z610; AB380;
AD456; AE61; AF429; AH216;
AL452; AM629; AO615; AP709;
AR67; AT61; AV69; AW169;
AZ667; BA890; BF615; BR507;
BV408; BY665; BZ   101950
Eternal Father, thou hast said
(Palmer) BV312   101951
Eternal Father, throned above
(Raffles) Lp.473; AZ920
                         101952
Eternal Father, when to thee
(Ganse) V85; AY414   101953
Eternal Father, who didst all
create (Bridges) X484 101954
Eternal Father, whose great love
(Boreham) BY288   101955
Eternal Glory of the sky (Latin,
6th c) E56   101956
Eternal God, before thy throne we
bend (Ryden) J178   101957
Eternal God, Omnipotent (Rohr)
M599   101958
Eternal God, our Father (Hoppe)
P48   101959
Eternal God! we look to thee
(Merrick) D435; BX235 101960
Eternal God, whose power upholds
(Tweedy) A265; G476; J322;
R485; Z535; AB369; AD358;
AE357; AF294; AG276; AK367;
AR560; BF530; BZ   101961
Eternal God, whose searching eye

doth scan (Poteat) AR572
                         101962
Eternal Light, Divinity (Latin,
18th c) E632   101963
Eternal Light! eternal Light!
(Binney) A478; B241; V739;
W36; AL36; AP155; BB85;
BV4; BY51   101964
Eternal Mind the Potter is
(Dayton) BE51   101965
Eternal Monarch, King most
high (Latin, 5th c) E141
                         101966
Eternal One, thou living God
(Longfellow) AN367; AQ246;
AW369; BD141; BK60; BX
441   101967
Eternal Peace, whose world of
old (Brooke) BX290 101968
Eternal Power, whose high abode
(Watts) E635; F621; H21; I17
                         101969
Eternal Ruler of the ceaseless
round (Chadwick) B491; E384;
J350; S406; U344; W489; X
485; Y213; Z506; AB273;
AD336; AF275; AK411; AL
370; AN349; AP566; AR391;
BF494; BV419; BX443; BY
358   101970
Eternal Son, eternal Love (Wes-
ley) BZ X Spirit of grace,
and health, and power 101971
Eternal Son of God, O Thou
(Latin, 11th c) M514; O128;
AA456   101972
Eternal Source of every joy
(Doddridge) I715; AO61; AS
431; AZ935; BR81; BX171
                         101973
Eternal Source of joys divine
(Steele) AY85   101974
Eternal Source of life and
light, Supremely good (Estlin)
BR37   101975
Eternal Source of light divine
(Wesley) BX241 X Eternal
Beam of Light divine 101976
Eternal Spirit, evermore creating
(Robins) Z161   101977
Eternal Spirit, God of truth
(Cotterill) AI119   101978
Eternal Spirit of the chainless

mind (Byron) AQ167   101979
Eternal Spirit, Source of life
  (Oakley) AB91 X Enduring
  Soul of all our life   101980
Eternal Spirit! we confess (Watts)
  L171; V206   101981
Eternal Sun of Righteousness
  (Wesley) AZ98 X Come,
  Father, Son, and Holy Ghost
    101982
Eternal thanks be thine (Gersdorf)
  AZ781; BA122   101983
Eternity draws near, As time
  moves on (Warren) AX290
    101984
Eternity! eternity! Where will
  you spend eternity? (Hoffman)
  R Where will you spend eter-
  nity   101985
Even me, even me, Let some
  drops (Codner) R Lord, I
  hear of showers of blessing
    101986
Evening and morning, Sunset and
  dawning (Gerhardt) J215; K447;
  P291; AK49; AW555; AZ1514;
  BR266   101987
Evening sun descending (Hoff-
  mann) P70   101988
Evensong is hushed in silence
  (Purchas) E569   101989
Ever are my longing eyes (U.P.
  Psalter, 1912) T43; AJ66
    101990
Ever content with the ways of my
  Father (Kretzmann) M287
    101991
Ever gracious Lord, I fly to the
  haven of thy breast (Wesley)
  BR313   101992
Ever growing, swiftly flowing
  (Jones) R Haste, O haste,
  delightful morning   101993
Ever patient, gentle, meek
  (Elliott) L462; AO305   101994
Everlasting arms of love (Mac-
  duff) V326; AO350; BE53
    101995
Every day, every hour, Let me
  feel Thy cleansing power
  (Crosby) R Saviour, more than
  life to me   101996
Every day will I bless thee ("J.E.

A. ") R My Savior's praises
  will I sing   101997
Every day with Jesus Is sweet-
  er than the day before
  (Loveless) AU325   101998
Every hour, every hour, Blessed
  Lord (Belden) R Blessed
  Lord, how much I need thee
    101999
Every morning mercies new
  (Phillimore) D4; K448; Q
  537; T303; V31; AA28; AI
  46; AM328; AS20; AX57;
  AZ1278; BA770; BF184; BR
  5   102000
Every morning the red sun
  (Alexander) E590; W591;
  AZ727   102001
Every night and every morn
  (Blake) AQ184   102002
Every Sunday evening, To the
  church we go (Shumate)
  AU312   102003
Everything changes (Goethe)
  X486   102004
Every work for Jesus will be
  blest (Kirk) R Hear ye the
  Master's call   102005
Everywhere, everywhere,
  Christmas tonight (Brooks)
  AC452   102006
Ewiger Vater im Himmelreich
  (Ausbund) BU51   102007
Ewiger Vater vom Himmelreich
  (Ausbund) BU36   102008
Exalt the Lord, His praise
  proclaim (U.P. Psalter,
  1912) T270; AJ375; AM12
    102009
Exortum est in love and lysse
  (English trad carol, 1450)
  BG62 X Nowell sing we, both
  all and some   102010
Exsultet orbis gaudiis (Latin,
  10th c) BN180; BO289
    102011
Extended on a cursed tree
  (Gerhardt) H164   102012
Extol the love of Christ, ye
  saints (Coffman) AX173
    102013
Exultet orbis gaudiis (Latin,
  10th c) BO289 X Exsultet

orbis gaudiis   102014

F

Face to face with Christ my
   Saviour (Breck) AH527;
   AT475; AU106; AV390; AX126;
   BB545   102015
Facing a task unfinished (Hough-
   ton) BV313   102016
Fade, fade, each earthly joy;
   Jesus is mine (Bonar, J.C.)
   I529; N601; AS288; AU205;
   AX404; BB277   102017
Fading away like the stars of the
   morning (Bonar) AX584; AY
   530   102018
Fading, still fading, the last
   beam is shining (---) AS32
                                102019
Fahre fort, fahre fort (Schmidt)
   BT479   102020
Fain would my soul with wonder
   trace (Knight) L164   102021
Fair as a beauteous tender flower
   (Robertson) AP206   102022
Fair beyond telling, Lord is thy
   dwelling (Grundtvig) M23
                                102023
Fair is their fame who stand in
   earth's high places (Housman)
   AN427; AQ72   102024
Fair the night in Bethlem land
   (Stubbs) AB117   102025
Fair waved the golden corn (Gur-
   ney) D569; E290; F338; W494;
   X10; AP777; BV649; BY725
                                102026
Fairest Bridegroom mine (Drese)
   M194   102027
Fairest Lord Jesus (Münster,
   1677 & Leipzig, 1842) A346;
   B356; G111; I118; J434; K129;
   L111; M623; N317; O576; P6;
   Q657; R135; S194; U72; V751;
   Y58; Z261; AB84; AC137; AD
   181; AE103; AF227; AG113;
   AH314; AI105; AK182; AM129;
   AN483; AO211; AR100; AT159;
   AU211; AV102; AW97; AX565;
   AZ465; BA119; BB165; BD63;
   BF331; BK21; BY202; BZ
                                102028

Faisons éclater notre joie
   (Pictet) BT100   102029
Faith comes by hearing God's
   record (Erskine)   AZ342
                                102030
Faith grasps the blessing she
   desires (Martineau) BE54
                                102031
Faith, hope, and charity, these
   three (Montgomery) AZ415
                                102032
Faith is a living power from
   heaven (Herbert) I286; O337;
   AX455   102033
Faith is the brightest evidence
   (Watts) AO386   102034
Faith is the victory (Yates) R
   Encamped along the hills of
   light   102035
Faith is wisdom from on high
   (Cronenwett) M126   102036
Faith of our fathers, holy faith
   (Faber) R Faith of our
   fathers! living still   102037
Faith of our fathers! living still
   (Faber) A393; B441; G256;
   I415; J516; M227; N214; P370;
   R348; S267; T381; U210; V
   743; Y109; Z348; AB168; AC
   256; AD387; AE216; AF365;
   AG200; AH142,429; AI237;
   AK282; AL399; AM487; AN
   546; AO607; AP545; AR320;
   AS322; AT252; AU201; AV249;
   AW154; AX434; AZ676; BA
   275; BB349; BD148; BF456;
   BK69; BL87; BO207; BQ121;
   BX401; BY466; BZ   102038
Faith of our fathers! loving still
   (Faber: Catholic variant)
   AH142 X Faith of our fathers!
   living still   102039
Faith of our mothers, living
   still (Patten) AU203   102040
Faith of the larger liberty
   (Silliman) AQ257   102041
Faithful cross! above all other
   (Latin) E737   102042
Faithful Lord, my only joy and
   pleasure (Zinzendorf, N.L.)
   AZ1021   102043
Faithful Shepherd, feed me
   (Pollock) B357; F415   102044

Fang dein Werk mit Jesu an
(Morgen- und Abend-segen.
Waldenburg, 1734) BT540
                          102045
Far and near the fields are teem-
ing (Thompson) AI188; AM
668; AW325; AX210; AY334;
BB448   102046
Far as thy name is known
(Watts) V532   102047
Far away in the depths of my
spirit tonight (Cornell) BB
610   102048
Far be sorrow, tears and sigh-
ing (Latin, 13th c) AZ750
                          102049
Far down the ages now (Bonar)
K204; BA265   102050
Far, far away on Judea's plains
(McFarlane) BC33   102051
Far, far beyond the starry sky
(Toews) AX607   102052
Far from all care we hail the
Sabbath morning (Aufranc)
BB468   102053
Far from my heavenly home
(Lyte) B408; D333; V703;
BJ46   102054
Far from my thoughts, vain
world, begone! (Watts) H74
                          102055
Far from these scenes of night
(Steele) H507   102056
Far in the west the sunset's
golden splendour (Moore)
BY691   102057
Far o'er yon horizon (Alford)
AZ776 X Forward! be our
watchword   102058
Far off I see the goal (Roberts)
R337; S183; W572   102059
Far off, O God, and yet most
near (Barber) AB37; BX508
                          102060
Far out on the desolate billow
(Raymond) AI35   102061
Far round the world Thy children
sing their song (Mathews)
W373; X299; AC8; AL251; BF
622; BY366   102062
Far-shining names from age to
age (Savile) F576   102063
Farewell, all earthly honors

(Bone) BC35   102064
Farewell, dear friends, I bid
you (Teasley) AX617 102065
Farewell, henceforth for ever
(Herberger) AZ797 X Fare-
well I gladly bid thee 102066
Farewell I gladly bid thee
(Herberger) Q407; AA532;
AZ797   102067
Farewell! I say with gladness
(Herberger) AA532 X Fare-
well I gladly bid thee 102068
Farewell, my dear brethren,
the time is at hand (---) AY
407   102069
Farewell, my friends beloved
(Harbottle) BY759   102070
Fast sinks the sun to rest
(Latin, 18th c) F37   102071
Father, again in Jesus' name
we meet (Whitmore) H6;
P37; S48; U447; V15; W243;
AD23; AI23; AK31; AM311;
AO1; AS56; BB26; BR101;
BV3   102072
Father, again to Thee our hearts
we lift (Ellerton: Jewish
variant) BH177 X Saviour
again to thy dear name
                          102073
Father, again to Thy dear name
we raise (Ellerton) AN126 X
Saviour, again to Thy dear
name   102074
Father all-holy, Lord of crea-
tion (Synnestvedt) BI24
                          102075
Father all-seeing, friend of all
creation (Bell) X330; BY666
                          102076
Father Almighty, bless us with
thy blessing (Berwick hymnal,
1886) Y44; Z344; AD216;
AE241; AF333; AH350; AK
227; AN117; AR79; AW59;
BD114; BF366; BK175; BX
160   102077
Father Almighty, darkness now
is deepening (Sigmond) P61
                          102078
Father Almighty, grant us now
thy blessing (Berwick hymnal,
1886) AE241 X Father Al-

mighty, bless us with thy
blessing   102079
Father and Friend! Thy light,
Thy love (Bowring) S89; AN
79; AW63; BX90   102080
Father, as the day I greet (Hess)
BH241   102081
Father, at thy footstool see
(Wesley) BR503   102082
Father, be thy blessing shed
(Gilman) M533; N286; O02
                                                     102083
Father bless these [this] birthday
children [child] (Hess) BHp.
566   102084
Father, bless us as we part
(Edworthy) AK510   102085
Father divine, the deadening
power control (Tuckerman)
BR427   102086
Father eternal, Ruler of creation
(Housman) A532; R486; W645;
X326; Y247; AB365; AC287;
AD362; AF445; AK401; AW354;
BZ   102087
Father, fill us with thy love (---)
R538; S37app   102088
Father from thy throne on high,
Far above (Pollock) BX528 X
Jesus from thy throne on high
                                                     102089
Father, give thy benediction
(Longfellow) G615; R557;
S45app.; Y95; AD511; AF540;
AK509; AR678; BK176; BZ
                                                     102090
Father, God, thy love we praise
(Wesley) AZ1480; BA910
                                                     102091
Father, gracious Father! God of
might and power (Faber) AH
541 X Jesus, gentlest Saviour
                                                     102092
Father, have mercy, Father, have
mercy (---) R Fading, still fad-
ing. The last beam is shining
                                                     102093
Father, hear our prayer, We
ask for Jesus sake (---) AU313
                                                     102094
Father, hear the prayer we offer
(Willis) E385; F182; X487;
AE244; AF368; AN85; BA572;

BD93; BE55; BH42; BV579;
BX122; BY467   102095
Father, hear thy child, In thy
mercy mild (Kretzmann)
M582   102096
Father, hear thy children's
call (Pollock) D529; U179;
AB162; AI223; AO276; AP432;
AR280; AV413; BF360
                                                     102097
Father, hear us as we pray
(MacAlister) S350   102098
Father, here we dedicate
(Tuttiett) AZ728 X Father,
let me dedicate   102099
Father, how wide thy glory
shines (Watts) I79; L130
                                                     102100
Father, I come to thee (Mitchell)
BI22; BR457   102101
Father, I dare believe Thee
merciful and true (Wesley)
H271   102102
Father, I go to Thee! (Mitchell)
BR457 X Father, I come to
thee   102103
Father, I know that all my life
(Waring) I465; L483; O256;
U209; V418; W548; AD259;
AI298; AL432; AM444; AP
572; AV60; AZ732; BA697;
BF451; BX291; BY468
                                                     102104
Father, I long, I faint to see
(Watts) V700   102105
Father, I stretch my hands to
Thee (Wesley) G202; H280;
I277; AI233; AR281; AS200;
AT46; AU274; AV58; AX360;
AY41; BB670; BZ   102106
Father, I yield to thee my life
(Aufranc) BB682   102107
Father, in heaven, hear us to-
day (Ames) U355; Y102;
AC161; AR283; AS54 102108
Father in heaven, in thy love
abounding (Hibbard) BC34
                                                     102109
Father in heaven, Lo, thine
angel chorus (Huffaker) AR
372   102110
Father in heaven, Thy children
hear (Williams) AH617

102111

Father in heaven, we do believe
(Pratt) BC41   102112

Father in heaven, we wait before
Thy face (Phalen) BY344
102113

Father in heaven, who lovest all
(Kipling) A506; B367; G294;
U327; W647; X488; Y178,286;
AC175; AD492; AF392; AL513;
AN482; AS403; AT460; AW401;
BD107, 171; BF484; BV575;
BX539; BY644   102114

Father, in high heaven dwelling
(Rawson) L34; W283; AL549;
AP683; AZ641; BV50; BY692
102115

Father! in my life's young morning (MacKellar) AX562; AY
64   102116

Father, in the morning, Unto
thee I pray (Cummings) AY
69   102117

Father, in thy mysterious pres-
ence kneeling (Johnson) R384;
S256; Z345; AB224; AD211;
AF334; AG223; AH348; AN229;
AO317; AV65; AW188; BF363;
BR26; BX268   102118

Father, in thy presence kneeling
(Pilcher) BY617   102119

Father, in whom we live (Wesley)
L183; M478; Q241; AA270;
BY38; BZ   102120

Father, lead me day by day
(Hopps) G437; R458; S445;
W565; AD213; AE434; AG305;
AK458; AL596; AN479; AO617;
AP788; AR282; AS316; BA824;
BB331; BD106; BX523; BY469
102121

Father, let me dedicate (Tuttiett)
B448; F72; G535; Q118; W606;
AA166; AR582; AS433; AT498;
AZ728; BR501; BV657; BY713
102122

Father, let thy blessing, touch
us and remain (Ogden) BH102
102123

Father, let thy Kingdom come
(Hopps) AN336; BX393; BY
367   102124

Father, let thy smiling face

(Moore) V83   102125

Father, long before creation
(Chinese, ca 1952) R107
102126

Father, loving Father, Hear thy
children call (Gower) Z325
102127

Father, merciful and holy (Rist)
N558; AA31   102128

Father most high, be with us
(Prudentius) F112   102129

Father, most holy, merciful and
loving (Latin, 10th c) BV226
X Father most holy, merciful
and tender   102130

Father most holy, merciful and
tender (Latin, 10th c) E160;
F158; O75; P238; Q240; X
186; BV226   102131

Father, now thy sinful child
(Conder) BA430   102132

Father, O hear us; Saviour,
draw near us (---) AR616;
AW609   102133

Father, O hear us, Seeking now
to praise thee (Walmsley)
BY345   102134

Father of all, from land and
sea (Wordsworth) D495;
I566; S426; W213; AK412;
AO422; AZ9; BA669   102135

Father of all, in every age
(Pope) AQ133 X What con-
science dictates to be done
102136

Father of all, thy care we bless
(Doddridge) I670; N532
102137

Father of all, to thee (Julian)
E386; X252   102138

Father of all, we come to thee
(Blaxill) BY470   102139

Father of all, we lift to thee our
praise (Harvard) AN307
102140

Father of all, whose love pro-
found (Cooper) B206; D139;
E387; F164; J140; K165; L181;
M477; O388; Q242; T317; W5;
AA269; AK196; AL3; AM88;
AP138; AZ311; BA15; BV483;
BY39   102141

Father of eternal grace (Mont-

gomery) AK246; AO380; BA
42   102142
Father of glory, to thy name
(Watts) Q248; AA267   102143
Father of heaven, who hast created
all (Knapp) B342; D206; K173;
AA405   102144
Father of heaven, whose love pro-
found (Cooper) Q242 X Father
of all, whose love profound
                          102145
Father of Jesus, by whose grace
(Moxley) BY268   102146
Father of Jesus Christ, My Lord
(Wesley) G203; H292; I297; AA
219; AZ221   102147
Father of lights, eternal Lord
(Wallin) N222   102148
Father of lights, in whom there
is no shadow (Wilson & Tho-
burn) G592; S7app.; Y21;
AC1; AD69; AR26; BF180;
BK59   102149
Father of lights, we sing thy
name (Doddridge) BX51
                          102150
Father of love and power (Raw-
son) Z146; BY693   102151
Father of love, our Guide and
Friend (Irons) AZ1457 102152
Father of men, in whom are one
(Shuttleworth) E528; G418;
S489; W493; X338; AB315;
AL369; AW388; BY359   102153
Father of mercies, bow thine ear
(Beddome) D287; V565; AS447;
AZ317; BA307; BY346   102154
Father of mercies, condescend
(Morell) AZ204; BA318 102155
Father of mercies, God of love
(Flowerdew) BH185 X Fountain
of mercy, God of love   102156
Father of mercies! in thy word
(Steele) D283; F251; G389;
H92; J256; K172; L308; N218;
O135; P92; Q284; R249; S218;
U142; V70; Z440; AA117; AD195;
AE161; AG130; AH235; AL183;
AM259; AP292; AR235; AS179;
AZ182; BA2; BR234; BV300;
BY245; BZ   102157
Father of mercies, send thy grace
(Doddridge) V573   102158

Father of mercy, Father of love
(Hopps) X Hark, hark, my
soul! Thy Father's voice
                          102159
Father of mercy, Lover of all
children (Moore) A238
                          102160
Father of peace, and God of
love (Doddridge) R328; W481;
AL327; AM98; AP486; BV619;
BY593   102161
Father of spirits, whose divine
control (Prudentius) E352
                          102162
Father, our children keep
(Bonar) W650; AL395 102163
Father! reveal thy son in me
(Montgomery) AZ739 102164
Father, see thy children bending
at thy throne (Jervois) E
308   102165
Father, see thy suppliant children
(Hamburg Temple hymnal)
BH150   102166
Father, Son, and Holy Ghost,
Bless the young before thee
(Döring) O108; P107; AP353
                          102167
Father, Son, and Holy Ghost
In solemn power (Wesley)
AZ1483   102168
Father, Son, and Holy Ghost
One God whom we adore (---)
Lp. 742; AZ1472   102169
Father, Son, and Holy Ghost
One in Three and Three in
One (Wesley) M479; AZ1277
BV628   102170
Father, Son, and Holy Ghost
Three in One; from every
coast (---) Lp. 743   102171
Father, Son, and Holy Spirit
I'm baptized in Thy dear
name (Rambach) K177; O105
                          102172
Father, Son, and Holy Spirit
Thou One in Three (---)
Lp. 743   102173
Father, Son, and Spirit, hear
(Wesley) AO427   102174
Father, source of life and light
(Hendrickson) P49   102175
Father, Supreme, by Whom we

live (Dewart) BA882   102176
Father, the watches of the night
are o'er (Disciples' Hymn
book) R530; S8app.; AN95;
BX41   102177
Father, thou are calling, calling
to us plainly (Blake) AN18;
BX7   102178
Father, thou joy of loving hearts
(St Bernard of (Clairvaux)
BE56 X Jesus, thou Joy of
loving hearts   102179
Father, throned on high (Mont-
gomery) BR67 Blessed by thy
name   102180
Father, throughout the coming
year (Gaskell) BX179 102181
Father, thy children to thee now
raise (Stephens) BC43 102182
"Father, thy will not mine, be
done!" (Montgomery) AZ634
                       102183
Father, thy wonders do not singly
stand (Very) AN41; BX45
                       102184
Father 'tis thine each day to
yield (Osler) AO101   102185
Father, to thee we look in all
our sorrow (Hosmer) E538;
X347; AB207; AF467; AN227;
AR86; AV221; AW249; BE57;
BF407; BH96; BV401; BX272
                       102186
Father to thee we turn away from
sorrow (Hosmer) BE57 X
Father, to thee we look in all
our sorrow   102187
Father, to thy dear name I lift
my voice (Levy) BH85 102188
Father, to us, thy children humbly,
kneeling (Clarke) AD210; AN231;
BF356; BI63; BR458; BX271
                       102189
Father, we come in Jesus' name
(Shoemaker) AX55; AY6
                       102190
Father, we come to thee, No
other help have we (Belden)
BB599   102191
Father, we come, with youth and
vigor pressing (Clayton) A509
                       102192
Father we greet thee, God of love

(Adderley) R285; X269
                       102193
Father, we praise thee, now the
night is over (St Gregory the
Great??) A157; E165; J204;
R43; S24; W263; X28; Z102;
AC26; AD41; AF41; AK44;
AL540; AW24; BY675; BZ
                       102194
Father, we thank thee, Father,
we thank thee (Giffin) BK9
                       102195
Father, we thank thee for the
night (Weston) A240; R467;
X355; AE438; AF479; AL585;
AM659; AP720; AR554; AT
341; AU310; AW423; BK6; BY
736   102196
Father, we thank thee who has
planted (Greek, from the
Didache) A195; AF289; BY
315; BZ   102197
Father, we thy loving children
(Adams) BE58   102198
Father, whate'er of earthly
bliss (Steele) A447; B396;
D670; F180; I523; K406; L473;
O473; U246; V390; AH396;
AM562; AN444; AO345; AS
238; AV57; AW251; AZ120;
BA713; BB333; BI19; BR245;
BX479   102199
Father, who art all alone, Our
helper and our stay (Jones)
G554; W630; Z609; AR264;
BY667   102200
Father, who hast created all
(Knapp) N227   102201
Father, who on man dost [doth]
shower (Dearmer) B506; E
531; N195; O500; W349; X
340; AC171; AE380; BD105
                       102202
Father, who the light this day
(Elliott) O40; Q8; AA123
                       102203
Father, whose hand hath led me
so securely (Spitta) AZ1221;
BT453   102204
Father, whose will is life and
good (Rawnsley) A516; G478;
R309; W353; AC169; AD316;
AL254; AR387; AW326; BY

634; BZ   102205

Fear, my child, thy God and
Lord (Pedersen) O110 102206

Fear not, for God the Father
(Homer) AX464   102207

Fear not! God is thy shield
(Taylor) BR521   102208

Fear not, my soul, alone to stand
(Hunter Clare) BV576 102209

Fear not, O little flock, the foe
(Altenberg) I445; L352; AA276;
AM470; AP530; AZ636; BA267
102210

Fear not, thou faithful Christian
flock (Altenberg) J156; W217;
BJ72   102211

Fears oft affright us (Cleaton) R
O Father, lead us   102212

Feeble, helpless, how shall
I Learn to live (Furness) K56
102213

Feed thy children, God most holy
(Heermann) Q659   102214

Feet of the urgent pioneer
(Patton) AQ232   102215

Felix dies, quam proprio (Besnault) BT115   102216

Fellow Christians, let us gather
(Solberg) M116   102217

Fels des Meils, geöffnet mir
(A.M. Toplady) BW148
102218

Fervent in spirit, serving the
Lord (Kretzmann) M224
102219

Fesans raijouissance (Prost) BG
106b   102220

Fields of corn, give up your ears
(Farjeon) X11; BG158 102221

Fiercè and wild the storm is
raging (Whittle) AU431 102222

Fierce raged the tempest o'er
the deep   (Thring) E541;
F313; I485; O242; W83; X489;
AL75; AO149; AP182; AZ1141;
BA78; BR168; BV553; BY117
102223

Fierce was the billow wild (St
Anatolius) N77 X Fierce was
the wild billow   102224

Fierce was the storm of wind
(Beadon) D71   102225

Fierce was the wild billow (St

Anatolius) B416; E388; F312;
K48; N77; W84; X490; Y77;
AD138; AM513; AZ751; BA76;
BP100; BR343   102226

Fight the good fight with all thy
might (Monsell) A560; B113;
D505; E389; F304; G286; I
409; J557; O258; Q447; R359;
S270; T421; U299; W517; X
491; Y158; Z376; AA376; AB
240; AC207; AD291; AE257;
AF367; AG201; AH453; AK298;
AL400; AM484; AO392; AP
544; AR318; AT406; AU270;
AV200; AZ380; BA574; BD
85; BE59; BF467; BV577;
BY289; BZ   102227

Fight, then, good soldiers, Fight
and be brave (Rooper) R
Dare to be brave   102228

Fill me now, Fill me now
(Stokes) R Hover o'er me
102229

Fill me with thy Spirit, Lord
(Warner) AX137   102230

Fill thou my life, O Lord my
God (Bonar) F373; U267;
X492; AF396; AI277; AL346;
AM495; BK68; BV621; BY
628   102231

Filled full and flushed with
morning (Hooker) Y124
102232

Finita iam sunt praelia (Latin.
publ Cologne 1695) BT210;
BW116   102233

Firm as the mountains around us
(Fox) BC42   102234

Firm this cornerstone be laid
(Moise) BH212   102235

Firmly I believe and truly (Newman) E390; F186   102236

Firmly stand for the right
(Whittle) R Be ye strong
102237

Fit us for thy service, Lord
(Zinzendorf, N.L.) BA542
102238

Flee as a bird to your mountain
(Dana) AI244; BU459; BB232
102239

Fling out the banner! let it float
(Doane) A259; B482; D253;

E546; F268; G502; H473; I639;
J315; L341; R506; S384; U403;
W383; Y269; Z540; AB372; AC
304; AD379; AF296; AG256;
AH465; AI172; AK381; AL245;
AM378; AN405; AO534; AP391;
AS369; AT446; AU152; AV258;
AW331; BA340; BB450; BF
526   102240
Fling wide the gates of righteous-
ness (---) BH132   102241
Fling wide thy gates, O Church
(Kuhlman) M335   102242
Flower in the crannied wall
(Tennyson) Y14; AC436 102243
Flung to the heedless winds
(Luther) I641; M80; Q259;
AZ484   102244
Föhlich pfleg ich zu singen
(Ausbund) BU65   102245
Follow! follow! I would follow
Jesus (Cushing) R Down in
the valley   102246
Follow, I will follow thee, my
Lord (Brown) R Jesus calls
me   102247
"Follow me," the Master said
(Voice of praise, 1887) AP766;
AS333   102248
Follow the path of Jesus (Hymns
and tunes, 1890) AX498; AY305
                                  102249
Follow, we will follow Jesus
(Lindsay) R Walking in the
sunshine   102250
Fools in their heart have said
(U.P. Psalter, 1912) T101;
AJ146   102251
Footprints of Jesus that make the
pathway glow (Slade) R Sweet-
ly, Lord, have we heard
                                  102252
For a season called to part
(Newton) L64; N359   102253
For air and sunshine pure and
sweet (Child songs) BY737
                                  102254
For all the blessings of the year
(Hutchinson) G546; U480; AD
444; AT495; AU301; BD202;
BZ   102255
For all the love that from our
earliest days (Smith) BY7

                                  102256
For all the saints, who from
their labors rest (How)
A126; B295; D176; E641;F527;
G527; H433; I430; J144; K
250; N629; Q463; R425; S429;
T379; U309; V614; W220; X202;
Y345; Z576; AB412; AC330;
AD461; AE309; AF306; AG
284; AH525; AK417; AL174;
AM281; AN428; AO540; AP
310; AQ75; AR419; AV283;
AW317; AZ527; BA740; BB
364; BD248; BF655; BL70;
BR446; BV460; BX463; BY403
BZ   102257
For all the souls who sought
thy way, O Lord (Swayne)
BK76   102258
For all thy care we bless thee
(Doudney) U48   102259
For all thy love and goodness
(How) W610   102260
For all thy saints, a noble
throng (Alexander) D165;
F557; BV445   102261
For all thy saints, O Lord
(Mant) Q468 X For thy dear
saints, O Lord   102262
For all thy saints, who from
their labors rest (How)
AZ527 X For all the saints,
who from   102263
For all who watch tonight
(Coote) BV51   102264
For Autumn's golden days (---)
BD49   102265
For Christ and the Church let
our voices ring (Hewitt)
AR494; AS324; AX153 102266
For Christ our dear Redeemer
(Hewitt) R For Christ and
the Church   102267
For common gifts we bless thee,
Lord (Packard) AN266; AW
176; BX321   102268
Forever at His feet I'll sit
(Hoffman) R I wonder, often
wonder   102269
For ever here my rest shall be
(Wesley) G373; H304; I357;
U180; V449; AM458; AE656;
AS458; AX172; AY258; AZ187;

BA205   102270

For ever settled in the heavens,
Thy word, O Lord (U. P.
Psalter, 1912) T 236; AJ332;
AM54   102271

For ever trusting in the Lord
(U.P. Psalter, 1912) AJ100;
AM569   102272

For ever we would gaze on Thee
(Chatfield) BV258   102273

For-ever with the Lord, Amen
so let it be (Montgomery)
B516; D675; E391; F346; H517;
I625; J590; K520; L604; M310;
N520; O618; Q616; V656; W583;
X195; AA567; AH526; AL462;
AO551; AP629; AV294; AW261;
AZ1303, 1304; BA721; BR430;
BT616; BV428; BX311; BY609
                               102274

"For-ever with the Lord!"
Father if 'tis thy will
(Montgomery) AZ1304 X Forever with the Lord, Amen so
let it be   102275

For flowers that bloom about our
feet (---) AQ30   102276

For garnered fields and meadows
cropped (Leiser) BH182
                               102277

"For God so loved!" O wondrous
theme (Whittle) AI9   102278

For God so loved this sinful
world (Morris) AX476 102279

For great is the Lord, His name
shall endure (Hay) R Lord,
with devotion we pray   102280

For He is so precious to me
(Gabriel) R So precious is
Jesus, my Saviour   102281

For he loves me, yes, He loves
me (Bateman) R I will early
seek the Saviour   102282

For health and strength and daily
food (---) AR552   102283

For help, O whither shall I flee
(Neander) O499   102284

For his mercies aye endure
(Milton) R Let us with a glad-
some mind (Milton) R Praise,
O praise our heavenly King
(Trend) R Praise, O praise
our God the King (Baker)

                               102285

For man's unceasing quest for
God (Pullen) BK32; BY246
                               102286

For many years, O God of grace
(Czamanske) Q639   102287

For me to live is Jesus (Vulpius.
Ein-schön geistliche G-B.1609)
M295; Q597; AA529   102288

For mercies, countless as the
sands (Newton) AQ99 102289

For mercy, courage, kindness,
mirth (Binyon) X493; Y198;
AC165; AQ152   102290

For mother-love and father-care
(---) BH242   102291

For My sake and the Gospel's
go (Bickersteth) W370; AM
377; AP384; BV335   102292

For no sect elect is the soul's
wine poured (Swinburne) AQ
166   102293

For now we stand on Jordan's
strand (Nelson) R My days
are gliding swiftly by 102294

For our devotions, Father, we
invoke Thy Spirit (Naisbitt)
BC107   102295

For our transgressions thou wast
wounded (LaTrobe) AZ996;
BA190   102296

For peace and for plenty
(Sangster) BI112   102297

For soon the reaping time will
come (---) R Though in the outward Church   102298

For sun and moon and stars (---)
1929 BY738   102299

For swinging wind and treetop
birds (Irwin) Y197   102300

For the beauty of the earth
(Pierpoint) A296; B425; E309;
F171; G18; I28; J444; K292;
M588; N338; O529; P245; R2;
S71; U16; W17; X494; Y357;
Z167; AB313; AC46; AD94;
AE14; AF66; AG59; AH206;
AK12; AL15; AN32, 269; AO
65; AP140; AQ12; AR92; AT
153; AU246; AV309; AW51;
AX634; AZ1257; BA642; BB22;
BD40; BF257; BK126; BL78;
BR68; BV18; BX13; BY8; BZ

102301
For the brave of ev'ry race (Briggs) A582; X243; AF308; AN426   102302
For the bread and for the wine (Bonar) AZ24   102303
For the bread, which Thou hast broken (Benson) G412; J282; R449; S359; Z463; AR518; BZ
102304
For the darkness shall turn to dawning (Nichol) R We've a story to tell to the nations
102305
For the deep love that kept us (Burleigh) BF181   102306
For the golden sun and the darting rain (Hess) BH184 102307
For the joy of human love (Pierpoint) AN269 X For the beauty of the earth   102308
For the mercies of the day (Missionary minstrel, 1826) L28   102309
For the might of Thine arm, we bless thee (Horne) G492; W 212; X495; Y334; BC241; BY 256; BZ   102310
For the mountains shall depart and the hills be removed (Jewish Trad: Shofar) BH316
102311
For the strength of the hills we bless thee (Horne) BC241 X For the might of thine arm
102312
For the summer's glowing pageant (Hubbell) AR595   102313
For the year that came from thee (Graham) BK31   102314
For Thee, my God, for Thee alone (Burns) W472   102315
For Thee, O dear, dear country (St Bernard of Cluny) A598; B512; D407; E392; F277; I614; J534; O608; Q614; R429; T436; V691; W598; AP627; AV278; AZ823; BO202; BR438,449
102316
For them whose ways are in the height (Roberts) AL454; AW 166   102317
For those we love within the veil

(Piggott) A222; G425; J598; W218; X289; AD460; AL181; BY610   102318
For those who wrought with loving heart (Allen) AB394; BF447   102319
For thy dear saint, O Lord (Mant) X203 X For Thy dear saints   102320
For thy dear saints, O Lord (Mant) A124; B293; D181; E196; F531; J141; K249; L 298; N206; Q468; V609; X 203; AA289; AN415; AZ1364; BV461; BX461   102321
For thy mercy and thy grace (Downton) B447; D204; E286; F73; K481; L550; M367; O213; Q121; W604; X1; AA168; AK 426; AL570; AM611; AP695; AW528; BA175; BF647; BR 499; BV656; BY714   102322
For thy mercy aye pursuing (Freeman) AB70; BF254
102323
For you I am praying (Clough) R I have a Saviour, He's pleading in glory   102324

NOTE: Other compounds formed with for are filed below as compound words   102325

Forget them not, O Christ, who stand (Sangster) Y117 X O Christ, forget not them who stand   102326
Forgive, O Lord, our severing ways (Whittier) R476; S344; Y263; Z484; AD392; AF262; AN419; BD188; BF587; BX 450   102327
Forgive the things I've said in haste (Williams) AU416
102328
Forgive them, O my Father (Alexander) E112; F114
102329
Forgive us Lord, we turn to Thee (Montefiore) BH163
102330
Forsake me not, my God (Franck) K397; O521 102331
Forsake me not! O Thou, my

Lord, my Light (Hohlfeldt)
BR299   102332

Forsaken once, and thrice denied
(Alexander) B283; E227; F
323   102333

Fortem virili pectore (Antoniano)
BN184   102334

Forth in thy name, O Lord I go
(Wesley) A150; B7; D639;
E259; F336; G290; H390; I400;
J214; K455; N502; W651; X29;
AE35; AF406; AL350; AP661;
AZ402; BA537; BB47; BF441;
BR381; BV604; BY629; BZ
102335

Forth in thy name, O Lord we
go (Wesley) AZ402 X Forth
in thy name, O Lord I go
102336

Forth to the fight he fared
(Oxenham) AC508   102337

Forth to the fight, ye ransomed
(Kirby) BR515   102338

Fortress-Rock, my God, my air!
(Jewish hymn) BH208   102339

Forty days and forty nights
(Smyttan) A55; B123; D79;
E73; F92; N85; W79; X97;
AF148; AK143; AO143; BV141;
BY118;   102340

Forty days of Eastertide (Mason)
B180   102341

Forward! be our watchword,
Steps and voices joined (Al-
ford) A561; B531; D523; E
642; H399; I384; J565; L542;
S369; W579; X394; AB218;
AD227; AH362; AL451; AN334;
AP605; AV220; AZ775-776;
BA575,744; BD143; BF382; BR
508; BX377; BY539   102342

Forward, Christian, forward
(Francis) BB353   102343

Forward, Christian Leaguers
(Solberg) R Christian Leaguers,
rally   102344

Forward through the ages, in un-
broken line (Hosmer) A546;
U374; Y113; Z498; AC263; AD
299; AE313; AF383; AN329;
AQ215; AR502; AT463; AU419;
AW267; BD146; BF515; BK108;
BX378   102345

Founded on thee, our only Lord
(Smith, S.F.) N280; Q637;
S474; AF477; AR525; AS438
102346

Fountain of good, to own thy
love (Doddridge) D269; L
444; W345; AL385; AM282;
AP589; AW218   102347

Fountain of grace, rich, full
and free (Edmeston) U241;
V395; AI257; AM591   102348

Fountain of life and light
(Benade) AZ1162   102349

Fountain of light and living
breath (Quarles) BX115
102350

Fountain of mercy, God of love
(Flowerdew) L554; W617;
AP686; BA862; BH185
102351

Fountain of never-ceasing grace
(Toplady) AM440   102352

Four things a man must learn
to do (Van Dyke) AC485
102353

Free from the law, O happy
condition (Bliss) AI129; AT
199; AU340   102354

Freedom is the finest gold that
the sun strews (Thomas of
Strängnäs, Bp.) AQ170
102355

Frequent the day of God returns
(Browne) V68   102356

Fret not thyself, nor envious be
(U.P. Psalter, 1912) T62;
AJ95   102357

Freudenvoll, freudenvoll walle
ich fort (Unparth.G.B.) AY
47d   102358

Freuet euch, ihr Christen alle!
(Keimann) BT96   102359

Friend after friend departs
(Montgomery) I587; L574;
AZ1225; BA722; BH223
102360

Friend of sinners! Lord of Glory!
(Hall) I130; V181; AZ266
102361

Friend of the home: as when in
Galilee (Lewis) G406; AD
399; AE326; AK333; AR550;
AT376; BF610; BY285 102362

Friend of the weary, O refresh
us (Gotter) K347; N88 102363
Friends of Jesus in their parting
(Schjörring) P66 102364
Frölich pfleg ich zu singen
(Ausbund) BU65 X Fölich phleg
ich 102365
Frölich so will ich singen (S.v.
Bosch) BU70 102366
Fröhlich soll mein Herze springen
(Gerhardt) BT77; BW525
102367
From afar, across the waters
(Rohr) M634 102368
From age to age how grandly
rise (Hosmer) AN423; AQ231;
BX455 102369
From age to age they gather
(Hosmer) Y155; AN566; AO601;
BD149; BF465; BX409 102370
From all that dwell below the
skies (Watts) A277; B250;
D468; F630; G17; H22; J429;
K293; L79; O21; P35; Q15;
R33; S388; V6; W228; X408;
Z104; AA79; AD6; AE5; AF11;
AG4; AH182; AK386; AL16;
AM3; AN498,502; AP104; AQ
13; AR22; AS9; AY18; AZ314;
BA353; BB2; BC52; BDp.1;
BE62; BI37; BJ80; BM104;
BR50; BV31; BX3; BY760;
BZ 102371
From all the dark places, of
earth's needy races (Slade)
G483; I633; AT409; AU125
102372
From all the dark places, of
earth's heathen races (Slade)
AU125 X From all the dark
places, of earth's needy races
102373
From all the fret and fever of
the day (Beardsley) AQ84
102374
From all thy saints in warfare
(Nelson) B267; D174; K251;
N48; O494; P240; AH457; AV
289; AZ802; BA806 102375
From all who dwell below the
skies (Watts) L79 X From
all that dwell 102376
From Bethany, the Master comes

down Mt. Olive's slopes
(Ham) Z222; AN181; AR157
102377
From city and from prairie
(Hale) BX536 102378
From depths of woe I cry to
thee (Luther) Q329 X Out of
the depths I cry to thee
102379
From depths of woe I raise to
thee (Luther) AM461 X Out
of the depths I cry to thee
102380
From distant shores returning
(Barth) M644 102381
From east to west, from shore
to shore (Sedulius) E18; F57;
J20; O291; BY94 102382
From eternity, O God (Neu-
mann) Q411 102383
From every clime and country
(Gaines) Y260 102384
From every stormy wind that
blows (Stowell) A421; B32;
D481; G317; H42; I495; L466;
N437; R419; U365; V458; Z
394; AG210; AH353; AI231;
AL426; AM528; AO319; AP
498; AR262; AS46; AT296;
AU189; AV185; AX369; AZ
418; BA593; BB241; BY334;
BZ 102385
From far away we come to you
(Morris) BG186 102386
From foes that would the land
devour (Heber) E557; AZ
1149 102387
From glory to glory advancing
(Liturgy of St. James) A492;
E310; F417; X496 102388
From glory unto glory (Havergal)
D205; I573; S467; AE422; BD
233; BE65 102389
From God shall naught divide
me (Helmbold) O349; Q393;
AA509 102390
From Greenland's icy mountains
(Heber) A254; B476; D254;
E547; F265; G484; H479; I655;
J310; K220; L338; M100; N
376; O120; P393; Q495; S385;
U405; V586; W371; AA474;
AG265; AH467; AI168; AL256;

AM383; AO528; AP376; AS367;
AT449; AU35; AV269; AW333;
AY329; AZ828; BA341; BB445;
BC40; BF539; BR225   102391
From heart to heart, from creed
to creed (Gannett) AN54; AQ
251; BX79   102392
From heaven above to earth I
come (Luther) M356 X From
heaven high I come to you
102393
From heaven high I come to you
(Luther) A22; J22; M356;
O181; P126; Q85; AA150; AF
121; AI418; AK114; AM166; AW
527a; BK156   102394
From heav'n the Lord with search-
ing eye (U.P. Psalter, 1912)
AM474 X The God who sits
enthroned on high   102395
From heavenly Jerusalem's towers
(Charles) W596   102396
From heaven's height Christ spake
to call (St Peter Damiani)
F540   102397
From heaven's height, Soft, vernal
breezes blow (Philippson) BH
124   102398
From heaven's heights the thunder
peals (Wise) BH142   102399
From homes of quiet peace
(Draper) AC315   102400
From land to land the Christian
goes (Zinzendorf, N.L.) AZ
903; BA724   102401
From lands beyond the waters
wide (Bartholomew) AO515
102402
From lips divine like healing
balm (Burleigh) H366 102403
From many ways and wide apart
(Hosmer) AB318   102404
From my own works at last I
cease (Wesley) AZ408 102405
From north and south and east
and west (Coster) BY369
102406
From ocean unto ocean (Murray)
G486; J340; K494; R509; S390;
U411; Z541; AD371; AG258;
AI357; AK376; AL510; AO531;
AP649; AT450; BA878; BF538
102407

From out of the wood did a
cuckoo fly (Czech carol)
X381; BG103   102408
From out of the cloud of fiery
light (Alexander) F548
102409
From out the depths, I cry, O
Lord, to thee (U.P. Psalter,
1912) T260; AJ362; AM463
102410
From out the depths I cry to
thee (U.P. Psalter, 1912)
AJ364   102411
From out the Rock whence we
were hewn (Cross) AB393
102412
From over hill and plain, There
comes the signal (Cassel)
AT407; AU374   102413
From peaceful slumber waking
(Wallin) M558; N537   102414
From place to place the Christian goes (Zinzendorf, N.L.)
O589   102415
From sense to Soul my pathway
lies before me (Hay) BE64
102416
From Sinai's height a fountain
gushes (Freund) AH148; BH
143   102417
From sinking sand He lifted
me (Homer) R In loving-
kindness Jesus came   102418
From starry heaven descending
(St Alfonso de Ligouri) BN14
102419
From street and square, from
hill and glen (Higginson) Y
233; AN343   102420
From the Cross the blood is falling (Bonar) AZ645   102421
From   the Cross uplifted high
(Haweis) H259; U157; V254
102422
From the depths do I invoke
thee (U.P. Psalter, 1912)
T261; AJ363   102423
From the depths my prayer
ascendeth (U.P. Psalter,
1912) AJ365; AM570 102424
From the depths we cry to thee
(Sr.M. Teresine) BM76
102425

From the doctrines I'll never waver (Neisser) AZ236 102426

From the eastern mountains (Thring) A49; B92; D62; E615; F595; K562; S380; U63; W66; X388; AB123; AC94; AD 127; AH270; AL257; AO139; AP382; AW89; BA186; BF293; BI91; BV128; BY95 102427

From the first man to climb the hill (---) AO64 102428

From the graves remove the dark crosses (Grundtvig) M447 102429

From the Pilgrim's rock-bound coast (Knapp) AD439 102430

From the table now retiring (Rowe) U379; V556; Z468; AH507; BF606 102431

From Thee all skill and science flow (Kingsley) A515; E525; F479; G462; J216; R315; W351; X285; AB353; AD315; AG244; AK395; AL371; AP574; AR284; BF513; BV398; BY635; BZ 102432

From thee, illustrious Teacher Paul (St Peter Damiani) BO217 102433

From these thy children gathered in thy name (Hay) BE66 102434

From thy holy habitation (Simpson) AZ1108; BA796 102435

From yon distant heaven (Hey) AW433 102436

Fryd dig, du Kristi Brud (Danish, ca 1600) BT57 102437

Full in the panting heart of Rome (Wiseman) BO205 102438

Full many shall come from the east and the west (Landstad) J333; O239; P157; Q415 102439

Full of glory, full of wonders (Faber) BL81; BQ40 102440

Full of reverence at thy word (Muenter) M44 102441

Fully surrendered, Lord divine (Morris) AX400 102442

Für Gott den Herren woll'n wir gohn (Ausbund) BU88 102443

G

Gabriel to Mary came (Latin, 14th c) F547 102444

Gabriel's message does away (Piae cantiones, 1582) BG102 102445

Galilee, bright Galilee (Sherwin) AC106; AV402 102446

Gather around the Christmas tree (---) N636 102447

Gather them in from the byways of sin (---) R In from the highways 102448

Gather us in, thou love that fillest all (Matheson) X497; Y261; AB311; AC300; AD377; AN418; AQ249; BF532; BX 449 102449

Gathering buds, gathering buds (Rowe) R Jesus has taken a beautiful bud 102450

Gathering home! Gathering home! (Slade) R Up to the bountiful Giver of life 102451

Gaudeamus igitur (Latin) Y299 102452

Gebor'n ist uns ein Kindelein (German carol, 17th c) BG 97b 102453

Geh, Seele frisch im Glauben fort (Unparth. G. B.) AY7d 102454

Gehe auf, du Trost der Heiden (Fick) BT498 102455

Gelobet sei der Herr (Olearius) BT38 102456

Gelobt sey Gott der Herre (Ausbund) BU90 102457

Gelobt sey Gott im höchsten Thron (H. Betz) BU122 102458

Gelobet seist du, Jesu Christ (Luther) BT80 102459

Gen Himmel aufgefahren ist, Alleluya (German trad carol) BG127b 102460

Gentle Jesus, meek and mild (Wesley) E591; F451; G444; K561; L464; W662; X356; AL 612; AP760; AT510; AV104; AZ38; BA820; BY739 102461

Gentle Jesus, meek and mild

(Wesley) X Lamb of God, I
  look to Thee (Wesley) 102462
Gentle Mary laid her child
  (Cook) A37; G107; R167; S453;
  AD115; AG68; AL57; AM640;
  AT73; BZ   102463
Gentle Peace, from heaven de-
  scended (---) BB511   102464
Gentle Shepherd, thou hast stilled
  (Meinhold) E353; V671; AA537;
  AI333; AO570   102465
Gently, Lord, O gently lead us
  (Hastings) I319; L196; U258;
  V345; AI300; AV54; AY351;
  AZ947; BA701   102466
Gently raise the sacred strain
  (Phelps) BC92   102467
Gethsemane, Gethsemane, I must
  remember thee (Norwegian) R
  The hour in dark Gethsemane
                            102468
Gird on the armor, brave soul,
  today (Perkins) BD80 102469
Gird on thy sword, O man, thy
  strength endue (Bridges) X498;
  AN341; AQ212   102470
Gird thy heavenly armor on
  (Elliott) BE67 X Christian
  seek not yet repose   102471
Gird us, O God, with humble
  might (Foulkes) AC246;
  BH24   102472
Give as the Lord hath prospered
  you (Hartsough) AX647
                            102473
Give ear unto me when I call
  (Scottish Psalter, 1650) AP4
                            102474
Give ear unto my words, O Lord
  (Scottish Psalter, 1650) AP5
                            102475
Give ear, ye children, to my law
  (Belknap) AI370; AN366; BX
  402   102476
Give forth thine earnest cry
  (Hymns of the Spirit, 1864)
  BX391   102477
Give, give with a willing hand
  (Hartsough) R Give as the
  Lord   102478
Give God the Father praise, Give
  glory to the Son (---) AZ1376
                            102479

Give heed, my heart, lift up
  thine eyes (Luther) AD123
  X Ah, dearest Jesus, holy
  Child   102480
Give me a foot-hold on the Rock
  (MacKellar) AX519; AY72
                            102481
Give me a new, a perfect heart
  (Wesley) I366   102482
"Give me, my child," the
  Father saith, "thy heart"
  (Richter) AZ705   102483
Give me, O Christ, the strength
  that is in Thee (Carter) BV
  557; BY564   102484
Give me, O Lord, a heart of
  grace (Gilbert) Y196; AB
  271   102485
Give me, O Lord, a spirit lowly
  (Loy) M257   102486
Give me, O Lord, and under-
  standing heart (Rome) BE69
                            102487
Give me the Bible, Star of glad-
  ness (Owens) AX138; BB655
                            102488
Give me the faith which can
  remove (Wesley) BY347
                            102489
Give me the wings of faith to
  rise (Watts) B301; E197;
  F571; G424; H430; I606; J
  594; V638; X204; AL179;
  AP312; AV279; BV462; BY404;
  BZ   102490
"Give me thy heart," says the
  Father above (Hewitt) AI196;
  AM723; AX260   102491
Give me to know thy will, O God
  (MacKellar) AY41   102492
Give me your whole heart, Love
  and adore me (Bhagavad-
  Gita) AQ134   102493
Give of your best to the Master
  (Grose) AS407; AT353; AU366;
  AV375; AW400   102494
Give peace, O God, the nations
  cry (Norris) A526   102495
Give praise and glory unto God
  (Schuetz) A287   102496
Give praise and thanks unto the
  Lord (Scottish Psalter, 1650)
  AL674; AP95   102497

Give praise to God our King
(Russell) O26; P5   102498
Give thanks and praise to God
above (U.P. Psalter, 1912)
T222; AJ319   102499
Give thanks for the corn and the
wheat (---) AQ21   102500
Give thanks to God, call on His
name (Scottish Psalter, 1650)
AP94   102501
Give thanks to God, for good is
He (Norton) T271; AJ378
                          102502
Give thanks to God; He reigns
above (Watts) BR78   102503
Give thanks to God, His praises
sing (Bible. Psalm 136) BI21
                          102504
Give thanks to God most high
(Watts) L103   102505
Give thanks unto the Lord,
Jehovah (---) AI444; AM512
                          102506
Give thou thy youth to God (Bonar)
AO619   102507
Give thy heart's love and labor
(Gerhardt) AD232   102508
Give to our God immortal praise
(Watts) J441; K307; L70; M
590; O28; P24; AA70; AL39;
AM20; AP121; AW11; AZ304; BA
34; BV235; BX47; BY9 102509
Give to the winds thy fears
(Gerhardt) I437; K400; L484;
R364; S294; U222; V365; Z402;
AB246; AD238; AE213; AF337;
AG221; AL421; AN247; AP517;
AS304; AW246; AZ1495; BA31;
BF408; BX308; BZ   102510
"Give us each day our daily
bread." (Hawkes) BX476
                          102511
"Give us room that we may dwell"
(Kelly) BC256   102512
Give us the wings of faith to rise
(Watts) F571 X Give me the
wings of faith   102513
Give ye to Jehovah, O sons of the
mighty (U.P. Book of Psalms,
1871) AP27   102514
Giver of concord, Prince of Peace
(Wesley) I563   102515
Giving our best to the Saviour

(Toews) R Loyal and true and
faithful   102516
Glad day! Glad day! Is it the
crowning day (Whitcomb) R
Jesus may come today 102517
Glad that I live am I (Reese)
X499; Y191; AC172   102518
Glad tidings to all men, Glad
tidings sing (English trad) R
A child this day is born
                          102519
Glad was my heart to hear
(Montgomery) AP111 102520
Gleaning on the hillside (Thomas)
R 'Tis the harvest time
                          102521
Gloomy night embraced the place
(Crashaw) BG124   102522
Gloria, Gloria! O come let us
join (Russian trad) BK13
                          102523
Gloria, laus et honor (St Theo-
dulph of Orleans) BN31; BQ
168; BT160; BW100   102524
Gloriosi salvatoris Nominis
praeconia (Latin, 15th c.)
BT116   102525
Glorious are the lofty mountains
(Warren) BB96   102526
Glorious, Glorious, Glorious
is thy name (McKinney) R
Blessed Saviour we adore thee
                          102527
Glorious majesty, before thee
(Hedborn) J189; N315 102528
Glorious Mary, Queen and
Giver of the Rosary (Litany
of Loreto) BN156   102529
Glorious Patron! low before thee
kneel thy sons (Sr. Mercedes)
BQ101   102530
Glorious Saint, whose deeds im-
mortal (Driscoll) BN178
                          102531
Glorious things are sung in Sion
(Phelps) BC243   102532
Glorious things are sung in Sion
(Phelps) BC243 X Glorious
things of thee are spoken (New-
ton)   102533
Glorious things of thee are spoken
(Newton) A385; B468; D490;
E393; F257; G382; H402; I210;

80 Hymns and Tunes

J152; K197; L294; M85; N271;
O88; P78; Q469; R434; S339;
T358; U352; V529; W206; X
500; Z431; AA464; AB248; AD
393; AE315; AF267; AG231;
AH518; AI145; AK323; AL166;
AM269; AN393: AO419; AP297;
AR495; AS193; AT381; AV241;
AW274; AX154; AZ937; BA276;
BB304; BC244; BE71; BF583;
BI49; BR214; BV424; BX454;
BY257; BZ   102534
Glorious Virgin, thee we sing
    (Breviary) BO89   102535
Glorious Yuletide, glad bells
    proclaim it (Olson) N43
                          102536
Glory and honour and laud (St
    Theodulph of Orleans) F598
                          102537
Glory and praise and dominion be
    thine (St Theodulph of Orleans)
    E621   102538
Glory and praises ever be (---)
    BRp.467   102539
Glory be to God on high. Alleluia
    (Williams) Z100; AF65 102540
Glory be to God on high, God
    whose glory fills the sky (Wes-
    ley) BE72   102541
Glory be to God the Father,
    Glory be to God the Son
    Dying, risen ... (Wordsworth)
    AZ975   102542
Glory be to God the Father
    Glory be to God the Son
    Glory be to God the Spirit
    (Bonar) D617; J139; K163;
    Lp.744; N666; P236; Q244;
    S60; W7; AA268; AC377; AK
    194; AL2; AO236; AP136; AZ
    1385; BA645   102543
Glory be to Jesus! Let all His
    children say (Ellerton) R
    Again the morn of gladness
                          102544
Glory be to Jesus, who in bitter
    pains (Italian, 18th c) A335;
    B162; D362; E99; F107; J76;
    K90; N639; Q158; AA208; AM
    190; AZ756; BA92; BN73; BO
    28; BQ72; BV154   102545
Glory be to the Father, and to

the Son (Latin, 2d c) A602;
G569; Hp.9; I737; Jp.43; Kp.
10; Lp.45; Mp.8; Np.689;
Op.22; Pp.409; Qp.16; R545;
Ssuppl.93; T458; U488; W708;
Y389; Z612; AAp.2; AB425;
AC335; AD493; AE471; AF511;
AG323; AH574; AI449; AK491;
AMp.xv; AO662; AR636; AS
488; AT524; AU495; AV428;
AW606; AX649; BA943; BB
689; BF680; BZ   102546
Glory eternal be to thee, O God,
    the Father (---) BRp.467
                          102547
Glory flaming in the cloud
    (Pendleton) BI54   102548
Glory! glory! Hallelujah (Howe)
    R Mine eyes have seen the
    glory   102549
Glory, glory! how the angels
    sing (Cushing) R Ring the
    bells of heaven   102550
Glory, Glory! Joy to my heart
    'twill bring (Morris) R
    Jesus is coming to earth
    again   102551
Glory, honor, praise and pure
    oblations (Rutgers) BE73
                          102552
Glory, praise and blessing be,
    Lord, our Savior (---) BI
    20-D; BRp.867   102553
Glory, praise, to thee be given
    (Rist) AZ1083   102554
Glory to God and praise and
    love (Wesley) BT360 X O for
    a thousand tongues to sing
                          102555
Glory to God, Glory to God
    (MacFarlane) R Far, far
    away on Judea's plains
                          102556
Glory to God! Glory to God!
    Glory to God. (Washburne) R
    Softly the night is sleeping
                          102557
Glory to God in the highest
    (Warren) AX103   102558
Glory to God on high (Allen)
    H16; L119; M597; AX15; AZ
    1237; BC44   102559
Glory to God on high (Boden)

BC44 X Glory to God on high
(Allen)   102560
Glory to God the Father (Whittle)
R "For God so loved!" 102561
Glory to God, whose Spirit draws
(Noel) BY290   102562
Glory to God! whose witness-
train (Zinzendorf, N. L.) H386;
V478; AZ96; BA579   102563
Glory to His name (Hoffman) R
Down at the cross   102564
Glory to the blessed Jesus (---)
B347; D537; L144   102565
Glory to the Father give (Mont-
gomery) D547; N640; AZ63;
BA821   102566
Glory to the Father, Who in
Christ Jesus (Gregor) AZ525
102567
Glory to the King of angels
(Bonar) AC337 X Glory be to
God the Father   102568
Glory to Thee, my God, this
night (Ken) M568 X All praise
to Thee, my God, this night
102569
Glory to Thee, O Lord, who be
thy mighty power (Beadon) D
70; N74; O232; AO135; BR164
102570
Glory to thee, O Lord, who from
this world of sin (Toke) D147
102571
Glory to thee, who safe hast
kept (Ken) BJ25 X Awake my
soul, and with the sun 102572
Glucksel' ger Tag, da ich erkor
(Unparth. G.B.) AY39d
102573
Go and let my grave be made
(Arndt) O588   102574
Go and seek the lost and dying
(Hartzler) AE358   102575
Go and tell the sweet old story
(Lyon) AY369   102576
Go as a witness for Jesus (Crosby)
U314   102577
Go bury thy sorrow (Bachelor)
AU293   102578
Go down, Moses (Negro spiritual)
R When Israel was in Egypt's
land   102579
Go, follow the Saviour (Cennick)

AZ1114   102580
Go forth and stand upon the
mount (Sargant) BE74 102581
Go forth in spirit, go To Cal-
vary's holy mount (Gambold)
AZ1292; BA200   102582
Go forth, my heart, and seek
delight (Gerhardt) M645
102583
Go forth, strong word of God
(Cross) AE159   102584
Go forth to life, O child of earth!
(Longfellow) G296; W672;
Z319; AN290; AW211; BD102;
BF631; BX372   102585
Go forth with God! the day is
now (Baron) F500   102586
Go forth, ye hearlds, in my
name (Maxwell) M95; N378
102587
Go forward, Christian soldier
(Tuttiett) A553; B535; D510;
I387; U304; AH432; AO397;
AZ855; BA577; BD81; BR
403   102588
Go, heralds of salvation, forth
(Smith, S. F.) AK352; AO
536   102589
Go joyfully forth To war against
sin (Barth) M541   102590
Go, labor on! spend and be
spent (Bonar) A573; B490;
D584; E556; G292; H378;
I399; M256; N509; P409;
R283; S376; T372; U285;
V497; W356; Z473; AD313;
AE276; AG198; AH412; AK
355; AL384; AM496; AO502;
AP579; AR253; AV206; AW
231; AZ367; BA540; BF434;
BV595; BY513   102591
Go labor on, spend and be spent
(Bonar) X Go labor on, while
it is day (Bonar)   102592
Go, labor on, while it is day
(Bonar) U282; V498; AE276;
AK355; BB441; BF434; BV
595   102593
Go, my soul, go every day
(Worthington) AZ56   102594
Go not far from me, O my
strength (Waring) AZ733
102595

Go not, my soul, in search of
Him (Hosmer) AN58; AQ88;
BF263; BX75   102596

Go out and gather the golden
grain (Chapman) AY337
                                   102597

"Go, preach my gospel," saith
the Lord (Watts) V561; AI
180; AO455; BB440   102598

Go search it out, and bring it
home (Schell) R The ninety-
nine within   102599

Go tell it on the mountain
(Negro Spiritual) AF488; BK
163; BZ   102600

Go, tell, Mary and Martha
(Negro Spiritual) R In-a-this-a
band we have sweet music
                                   102601

Go thou, in life's fair morning
(Bradbury. Oriola, 1860) AZ
846; BA815   102602

Go to dark Gethsemane (Mont-
gomery) A70; B151; D93; E100;
F110; J78; K93; L240; M416;
N102; O304; P170; Q159; R193;
V147; Z227; AA199; AE114;
AF158; AH284; AK144; AL93;
AO159; AP190; AR160; AS134;
AT105; AW107; AZ1250; BA
204; BB122; BR174; BZ
                                   102603

Go to the deeps of God's promise
(Breck) AI241   102604

Go the grave in all thy glorious
prime! (Montgomery) AZ458;
BA725   102605

Go to the lost and dying, brother
(Evilsizer) R Out in the de-
sert   102606

Go to thy rest, fair child
(Sigourney) AX627; AY177;
AZ485   102607

Go when the morning shineth
(Simpson) BR21   102608

Go with Jesus to thy task (Mor-
gen- und Abendsegen. Waldenburg. 1734) M216   102609

Go, ye messengers of glory
(Taylor) BC247   102610

Go, ye messengers of God
(Marsden) I640   102611

God Almighty and all-seeing
(Pierpont) AZ1390   102612

God Almighty, in thy temple
(Baynes) D548; BA825; BY
40   102613

God and Father we adore thee
(Darby & Falconer) W59
                                   102614

God be in my head (Book of
hours. 1490) A466; F332;
R395; X501; AF393; AL364;
AR679; BV623; BY471; BZ
                                   102615

God be merciful to me (U.P.
Psalter, 1912) R282; T97;
AJ140; AM415   102616

God be with thee! Gently o'er
thee (Williams) AN471; BE81;
BX511   102617

God be with you now and ever
(Overby) P76   102618

God be with you till we meet
again (Rankin) A490; E524;
F489; G557; H434; I564; L67;
M650; N364; R78; U449; V26;
W624; X334; Z129; AF61; AG
14; AH177; AI344; AM632;
AN472; AO48; AP701; AR506;
AS63; AT372; AU480; AV235;
AW365; AX654; AY405; BA932;
BB35; BC47; BY761; BZ
                                   102619

God bless America, Land that I
love (Berlin) AH488   102620

God bless and keep thee (De-
Fluiter) BB38   102621

God bless our native land, Firm
may she ever stand (Mahlmann)
A146; B428; G490; H530; I703;
J358; K489; L559; M498; N
566; O519; P411; Q577; R514;
S413; U343; W632; AA305;
AB335; AC283; AD441; AE
395; AH475; AK439; AN385;
AR603; AS384; AV306; AW348;
AZ1232; BA871; BD173; BF
542; BI11; BR494; BX421
                                   102622

God bless our native land, May
heaven's protecting hand
(Hickson) AN386; BB512;
BX423; BY640   102623

God bless the master of this
house (English trad carol)

23; AQ117; AR5; AW2; BC246;
BD15; BH4; BX32   102661
God is in His temple, Let us fall
before Him (Tersteegen) BR
14 X God is in His Temple, O
let us adore   102662
God is in His temple; O let us
adore him (Tersteegen) M9;
BR14   102663
God is in His temple, O let us
adore Him (Tersteegen) X
God Himself is with us 102664
God is in His temple, The al-
mighty Father (Matson) BY
41   102665
God is King forever: let the
nations tremble (U. P. Psalter,
1912) T182; AJ266   102666
God is known among His people
(U. P. Psalter, 1912) T140;
AJ207; AM63   102667
God is known in loving-kindness
(Heermann) BE76   102668
God is love, by him upholden
(Monsell) BX327 X God is
love! The heavens tell it
                         102669
God is love; His mercy brightens
(Bowring) G75; H116; I88; K
297; L102; M156; N295; R103;
S80; U24; V107; W33; Z178;
AA510; AB66; AD81; AE73; AG55;
AK76; AL13; AN83; AO83; AP
156; AR87; AS86; AT50; AV48;
AW55; AX86; AY372; BA643;
BD61; BE79; BF244; BI8; BR
74; BX121; BZ   102670
God is love: his the care
(Dearmer) X502   102671
God is love: let heaven adore Him
(Rees) BY52   102672
God is love! The heavens tell it
(Monsell) BR61; BX327; BZ
                         102673
God is my Light! My soul, do
not despair (Hengstenberg)
AW560   102674
God is my strong salvation (Mont-
gomery) G324; I448; R347;
S92; U216; W527; AD242; AF
373; AL398; AM568; AN257; AP
25; AQ20; BD82; BE77; BF411;
BH95; BR399; BX330; BY575;

BZ   102675
God is near thee, therefore
cheer thee (Curwen. Stand-
ard course. 1860) AP536
                         102676
God is not far from any one of
us (Clark) AE71; AK78
                         102677
God is of mine inheritance
(Scottish Psalter, 1650) AP11
                         102678
God is our refuge and defense
(Montgomery) I97; BE80
                         102679
God is our refuge and our
strength, A helper ever near
us (U. P. Psalter, 1912)
AJ128   12680
God is our refuge and our
strength, In straits a present
aid (Scottish Psalter, 1650)
S91; AL651; AP41; AW588
                         102681
God is our refuge and our
strength, Our everlasting aid
(U. P. Psalter, 1912) R381;
T86; AJ126; AM37   102682
God is our stronghold and our
stay (Wordsworth, E) B214
                         102683
God is the name my soul adores
(Watts) I80   102684
God is the refuge of his saints
(Watts) H411; I218; L481;
P290; V536; AL33; AM292;
AO87; AV68; AW257; BA705;
BB89; BR274   102685
God is with me, gently o'er me
(Williams) BE81 X God be
with thee! Gently o'er thee
                         102686
"God is with us, God is with us"
(Mathams) BY370   102687
God is working his purpose out
(Ainger) A538; B483; E548;
F271; R500; W380; X300; AF
298; AP394; BE82; BV315;
BY371   102688
God Jehovah reigns, His are
all domains (Brondsema)
AJ432   102689
God laid his rocks in courses
(Gannett) AN458; AQ260;

BX491   102690

God! Let the torrents like a shout of nations (Coleridge) AC435   102691

God liveth still! Soul, despair not (Zihn) AA513   102692

God, Lord of Sabaoth, Thou who ordainest (Chorley & Ellerton) Q582 X God the Omnipotent, King who ordainest   102693

God loved our erring mortal race (Olearius) N436   102694

God loved the world of sinners lost (Stockton) AL479; AP425; AX83   102695

God loved the world so that He gave (German, 1791) Q245   102696

God loved us, so he sent his Son (Kimball) BC178   102697

God loveth the righteous, His goodness is sure (U. P. Psalter, 1912) T135; AJ201   102698

God made all His creatures free (Montgomery) BE83   102699

God made me for Himself, to serve Him here (Baker) BV 484   102700

God make my life a shining light (Betham-Edwards) BY741 X God make my life a little light   102701

God make my life a little light (Betham-Edwards) G450; BY 741   102702

God makes a path, provides a guide (Williams) AQ45 102703

God, most mighty, sovereign Lord (Harbaugh) AZ57 X Christ, by heavenly hosts adored   102704

God most truly honored thee (Currie) BN175   102705

God moves in a mysterious way (Cowper) A310; B216; D427; E394; F181; G68; H115; I96; J484; K409; L477; M148; N478; O421; P304; Q514; R112; S103; T395; U221; V92; W31; X503; Y372; Z162; AA524; AB216; AD88; AE58; AF87; AG45; AH 225; AI414; AK75; AL40; AM21; AN244; AO97; AP154; AQ34;

AR78; AS81; AT53; AV55; AW60; AX85; AY84; AZ89; BA709; BB84; BC48; BD50; BE399; BF431; BH83; BK71; BR263; BV403; BX299; BY53; BZ   102706

God, my Father, hear me pray (Holme) D384   102707

God my Father loving me (Briggs) A239; X357; BY742   102708

God, my King, thy might confessing (Mant) A280; B311; D465; V521; AM2; BL98   102709

God, my supporter and my hope (Watts) L519; V339   102710

God of ages, all transcending (Neumann) M7   102711

God of all grace, thy mercy send (Greek) A180; E652   102712

God of all power, and truth, and grace (Wesley) I378; BZ   102713

God of compassion, in mercy befriend us (Moment) R122; S290   102714

God of earth and sea and heaven (Edwards) AF316   102715

God of eternal love (Seaton. Church hymn book, 1855) K265; O69   102716

God of eternity, Lord of the ages (Merrington) W642   102717

God of every land and nation (---) AZ1402   102718

God of grace and God of glory (Fosdick) A524; G279; R358; Z378; AD297; AE246; AF366; AK287; AN345; AQ27; AR321; AT465; BF464; BK77; BY372; BZ   102719

God of grace, O let thy light (Churton) BH75   102720

God of heaven, hear our singing (Havergal) K563 X God in heaven . . .   102721

God of Israel, keep us faithful (Mayer) BH52   102722

God of Israel's faithful three (Wesley) AZ1470   102723

God of our life, through all the
circling years (Kerr) R108;
S88; Z583; AB400; AE62; AF
97; AR68; BF641; BZ   102755

God of our salvation, hear us
(Kelly) L44; V25   102756

God of our saving health and
peace (Milton) AP69   102757

God of our strength, enthroned
above (Crosby) AV25   102758

God of our youth, be with us yet
(Forbush) R God of our boyhood, whom we yield   102759

God of our youth, to whom we yield
(Forbush) Z608 X God of our boyhood, whom we yield   102760

God of peace, in peace preserve us
(Olson) J349   102761

God of pity, God of grace (Morris)
K278; L194; S252; W240; AK223;
AL204; AM466; AP327; BR33;
BY431   102762

God of pity, Lord of grace (Morris)
BR33 X God of pity, God of
grace   102763

God of power, God of right (Bennett) BC36   102764

God of that glorious gift of grace
(Monsell) AZ384   102765

God of the ages, by whose hand
(Burrowes) BZ   102766

God of the changing year (Taylor)
BF644; BX184   102767

God of the circling realms of
light (Lee) AB360; BF569
                             102768

God of the earnest heart (Johnson)
Y225; AN301; AQ224; BD100;
BX344   102769

God of the earth, the sky, the
sea (Longfellow) Y55; Z120;
AB50; AC49; AD29; AF67;
AK68; AN28; AQ43; AR94; AS
92; AW52; BD34; BF234; BK
127; BX49; BZ   102770

God of the fertile fields (Harkness)
AE418   102771

God of the glorious sunshine
(Paxton) AC42; AK69   102772

God of the living, in whose eyes
(Ellerton) A225; B410; K508;
W332; AF468; BX472; BY611
                             102773

God of the morning, at whose

voice (Watts) F8; BR11;
BV39; BX133; BY676   102774

God of the moving years (Morse)
AR72   102775

God of the nations, hear our
call (Campbell) Y276; BD
179   102776

God of the nations, near and far
(Holmes) Z556; AB363; AC
296; AD354; AN399; BD185;
BF564; BH226; BK107; BX
426   102777

God of the nations, who from
dawn of days (Bowie) Y272;
AB270; AC274; AD430; AF432;
AH469; AN377; AR607; BD
164; BF545   102778

God of the nations, who hast led
(Edwards) B442   102779

God of the pastures, hear our
prayer (Hunter-Clare) BV645
                             102780

God of the prophets, bless the
prophets' sons (Wortman)
A220; B451; D280; Q483; R520;
S481; Z472; AA486; AB329;
AD414; AE321; AF470; AK349;
AO450; AR520; BA310; BF
596   102781

God of the shining hosts that
range on high (Rowland) AC
289   102782

God of the Spirit-wind (Marlatt)
AR223   102783

God of the strong, God of the
weak (Gilder) G457; Y217;
Z311; AB257; AC212; AD446;
BDp.58; BF426   102784

God of the universe, to Thee
("O, Miss Mary", 1841)
BB486   102785

God of truth, eternal good
(Brewer) BE85   102786

God of years, thy love hath led
us (Eldridge) AK362 102787

God, omnipotent Creator
(Albert) AZ593   102788

God, our Father, hear us pray
(Malin) BC8   102789

God, our Father, made the daylight (Compton) BK12 102790

God, our Father, we adore thee
(Frazer) AT5   102791

God reigneth, He is clothed with
majesty (Scottish Psalter,
1650) AP80   102792
God rest you merry, gentlemen
(English carol, 18th c) A40;
R166; S131; AD109; AF122; AG
67; AH259; AL66; AM160; AP
731; BG11; BV91; BY96; BZ
102793
God reveals His presence (Ter-
steegen) W234 X God himself
is with us   102794
God righteous judgment executes
(Scottish Psalter, 1650) AP
90b   102795
God save America! New world
of glory (Ballantine) Z547;
AH481; AN374; AO587; AU387;
BF551; BK122   102796
God save our gracious King
(Great Britain. National
Anthem. 17th-18th c) E560;
P417; AN387; BB506; BC115-a;
BX545   102797
God save our gracious Queen
(Great Britain. National anthem.
17th-18th c) F577; J361; W631;
X318; AE392; AL508; AP639;
AQ244; BV664; BY641 102798
God save our native land (Seelye)
M499   102799
God saved His people from dis-
tress (U. P. Psalter, 1912)
AJ180   102800
God sees the little sparrow fall
(Straub) AL588; AM635; AP
721; AW408   102801
God send us men whose aim 'twill
be (Gillman) Z377; AB352;
AC255; AD351; AE398; AF434;
AH460; AN313; AQ217; AR604;
AS388; BF560; BH233; BK125;
BZ   102802
God shall "wipe away all tears"
(Clements) R In the land of
fadeless day   102803
God so loved the world (Bible.
John 3) AU476   102804
God spake, my child, God spake
to thee (Hänel) K551 102805
God speaks to us in bird and
song (Johnson) Z180   102806
God speed the gospel! Father in
pity (Stryker) H477   102807

God supreme! to thee we pray
(Moise) AH155; BH93 102808
God that doest wondrously (Moses
ibn Ezra) BH176   102809
God, that madest earth and
heaven (Heber & Whateley)
A169; B26; D19; E268; F26;
G43; J230; K468; L19; P73;
R58; S41; T308; V39; W293;
X46; Y306; Z143; AA44; AB
29; AC18; AD52; AF58; AG
30; AH167; AI51; AL547; AM
344; AN100; AO43; AP674;
AS33; AT30; AV21; AW35; AZ
1506; BF201; BK48; BR540;
BX152; BZ   102810
God the All-merciful (Chorley)
AB366 X God, the Omnipotent
102811
God, the All-terrible (Chorley)
B435 X God, the Omnipotent
102812
God the Almighty One (Chorley)
AT42 X God the Omnipotent
102813
God the father, be our stay
(German litany, 13-14th c)
Q247; AA271   102814
God the Father, God the Son
(Littledale) B141; D528; E
647, 655   102815
God the Father, God the Son
(Pollock) A229-30-31; B142;
E648, 651; F587   102816
God the Father, God the Son
([Children's litany] Thring)
E654; F590   102817
God the Father, God the Word
(Littledale) E653   102818
God the Father, seen of none
(Littledale) E649   102819
God the Father, Son and Spirit
(Polack) Q640   102820
God, the Hope of those who pray
(Trask) AO657   102821
God, the Lord, a King remaineth
(Keble) R90; S61; AM60;
AP79   102822
God the Lord is King; before him
earth with all (Rawson) AM
43; AP85   102823
God the Omnipotent, King, who
ordainest (Chorley & Eller-
ton) A523; B435; D198; F491;

G505; I707; J354; K497; Q582;
R487; S420; W641; Y264; Z565;
AB366; AC284; AD368; AE404;
AF446; AG281; AI356; AK405;
AL517; AM617; AP650; AR608;
AT42; AV72; AW351; BB78;
BF567; BH265B; BZ   102824

God, though this life is but a
wraith (Untermeyer) AW114
                            102825

God, we thank thee; not in vain
(Dearmer) E353b   102826

God, who are love, the same
both now and ever (Foster)
AZ708   102827

God who created me, Nimble and
light of limb (Beeching) W673;
X504; Y140; AC170; BY11
                            102828

God, who hath made the daisies
(Hood) W81; BY743   102829

God who made the earth, the air,
the sky, the sea (Rhodes) A
248; R466; W20; X358; AC58;
AL595; AM637; AP722; BV237;
BY744   102830

God, who madest earth and
heaven, darkness and light
(Heber & Whately) AA44 X
God that madest earth and
heaven   102831

God who madest earth and heaven,
Father, Son and Holy Ghost
(Albert) J205; K446; M553;
O544; Q549; AA23; AR44; AW
573a; AZ1275; BA771   102832

God, who touchest earth with
beauty (Edgar) R102; Z315; AC
223; AD490; AE451; AG304;
AH397; AR355; AT45; BY472;
BZ   102833

God, whose city's sure foundation
(Alington) F574   102834

God, whose eternal mind (Struther)
X282   102835

God, whose farm is all creation
(Arlott) BY726; BZ   102836

God whose name is Love, happy
children we (Hoatson) A244;
X359   102837

God will I bless all times; His
praise (Scottish Psalter, 1650)
AP32   102838

God will our strength and refuge
prove (U.P. Psalter, 1912)
AJ127   102839

God will take care of you (Martin) R Be not dismayed whate'
er betide   102840

God with us! Oh glorious name!
(Slinn) H149; V127   102841

God's boundless love and arching
sky (Babcock) Y41; AO81
                            102842

God's dear Son without beginning
(English trad carol) BG13
                            102843

God's eternal Word is spoken
(Oldenburg) BE84   102844

God's free mercy streameth
(How) BB5 X Summer suns
are glowing   102845

God's glory is a wondrous thing
(Faber) V477; AB237; AF
369; AN305; BE86; BX301
                            102846

God's law is perfect and converts
the soul (Scottish Psalter, 1650)
AL635; AP15; AW578 102847

God's mercies I will ever sing
(Scottish Psalter, 1650) AP72
                            102848

God's perfect law restores (U.P.
Book of Psalms, 1871) AP
14b   102849

God's trumpet wakes the slumber-
ing world (Longfellow) G262;
Y146; AB255; AC203; AD292;
AN309; AQ213; AW194; BD91;
BF476; BX366   102850

God's way is best; if human wisdom (Naylor) AX389 102851

God's way is the best way
(Leech) AI290   102852

God's word is our great heritage
(Grundtvig) J257; O137; P
91; Q283   102853

Going by, going by (Cooper)
R There are lonely hearts
                            102854

Golden breaks the dawn (Chao)
AF486   102855

Golden harps are sounding
(Havergal) A359; B560; D
545; I175; J115; K549; M457;
P222; S456; V750; W133;

AH307; AM213; AO199; AP736;
AS152; AZ771; BA245; BR195;
BY166   102856
Golden light serene and bright
   (Grundtvig) J210   102857
Gone are those great and good
   (Pierpont) AN364; BX417
                             102858
Gone from my heart the world
   and all its charms (---) AU210
                             102859
Gone the night! The world is
   filled with light (---) R Let
   the whole creation sing 102860
Gone! yes, but for a little while
   (Howard) BR450   102861
Good and pleasant 'tis to see
   (Müller) O397   102862
Good-bye, good-bye, We breathe
   a sigh (Oatman) R These
   scenes so bright   102863
Good-bye mourner, I'm going
   home (Negro spiritual) AH
   598   102864
Good.bye! Our school is over
   (Dearmer) X386g   102865
Good cheer! good cherr! good
   cherr! Let all men know
   (Trench) Y194 X Good cheer!
   Let all men know That all men
   move   102866
Good cheer! Let all men know
   that all men move (Trench)
   X505; Y194   102867
Good cheer! Let all men know
   That all men move (Trench &
   Dearmer) X505 X Let all men
   know that all men love (Trench
   in Julian. Dictionary of hymn-
   ology)   102868
Good Christian men, rejoice and
   sing (Alington) F603; J109;
   S130; W58; X154; AF184; BK
   133; BV181; BY156; BZ
                             102869
Good Christian men, rejoice;
   with heart (Latin carol, 14th c)
   A31; B549; G10; J39; R165;
   Z193; AB118; AD110; AE80; AF
   125; AG70; AH258; AK116;
   AL61; AM159; AN177; AR129;
   AT74; AZ722; BD230; BF278;
   BK159; BV99; BY97; BZ

                             102870
Good day to you all (Dearmer)
   X386a   102871
Good Joseph had a garden
   (Milner-Barry) F438; BV184
                             102872
Good King Wenceslas (Neale)
   AH252; BG136   102873
Good morning to you (---) AU
   308   102874
Good news from heaven the
   angels bring (Luther) K19;
   N27; AZ291; BI86   102875
Good people all, this Christmas-
   time (English trad carol)
   BG14   102876
Good unto all men is the Lord
   (Scottish Psalter, 1650) AL
   689; AP128   102877
Goodly were thy tents, O Israel
   (Wolcott) BX416   102878
Gospel bells, how they ring
   (Martin) R The gospel bells
   are ringing   102879
Gospel of Jesus, Gospel of
   light (Consterdine) R Hark,
   hark my soul! The voice of
   Jesus calling   102880
Gott, der du alles wohl bedacht
   (Unparth. G. B.) AY37d
                             102881
Gott der Vater wohn' uns bei
   (German litany, 13-14th c)
   BT247   102882
Gott des Himmels und der Erden
   (Albert) AW573b; BT549; BW
   573   102883
Gott, du hast in deinem Sohn
   (Neumann) BT411   102884
Gott fähret auf gen Himmel
   (Sacer) BT214   102885
Got Führt ein recht Gericht
   (G. Blaurock) BU5   102886
Gott Heil' ger Geist, hilf uns mit
   Grund (Ringwaldt) BT293
                             102887
Gott ist die Liebe, Lässt mich
   erkösen (Unparth. G. B.) AY
   42d   102888
Gott ist gegenwartig! (Terstee-
   gen) AE4; BT4; BW506
                             102889
Gott ist mein Licht! (Hengsten-

berg) BW560   102890
Gott mit euch, bis wir uns
wiederseh'n (J. E. Rankin) AY
49d   102891
Gott segne Sachsenland (S. A.
Mahlmann) BT577; BW348
102892
Gott sei Dank durch alle Welt
(Held) BT91   102893
Gott sei gelobet und gebenedeiet
(Luther) BT313   102894
Gott Vater, Sohn, Heiliger
Geist (Ausbund) BU68
102895
Gott Zebaoth, der war, und ist
(H. Betz) BU107   102896
Gottes Sohn ist kommen (Horn)
BT74   102897
Grace and peace from God our
blessed Saviour (Swertner)
AZ1002; BA799   102898
Grace and truth shall mark the
way (U. P. Psalter, 1912) R
372; T42; AJ65   102899
Grace, dear Lord, Grace, dear
Lord (Minkler) AX325 102900
Grace for today, O Love divine
(Robertson) BE91   102901
Grace, Grace, God's Grace
(Johnston) R Marvelous grace
of our loving Lord   102902
Grace, grace, Oh, that's a joyful
sound (Gruenbeck) AZ1432
102903
Grace, love, and peace abide,
now with you (Brown) AT539
102904
Grace! 'tis a charming sound
(Doddridge) H238; I288; L126;
Q374; U147; V243; AA328; AM
401; AV163; AX323; AY368;
AZ1351; BA425; BY54;   102905
Gracious Father, guard thy chil-
dren (---) BB663   102906
Gracious Father, hear our prayer
(---) AP807   102907
Gracious God, again is ended
(Neumann) Q560   102908
Gracious God, my heart review
(U. P. Psalter, 1912) T98;
AJ141   102909
Gracious God, we worship thee
(Francis) BV19   102910

Gracious King enthroned above
(Wayland) AI217; AS206
102911
Gracious Lord, our Shepherd
and Salvation (Swertner) AZ
1010; BA798   102912
Gracious Lord, remember David
(U. P. Psalter, 1912) T263;
AJ367   102913
Gracious Saviour, gentle Shepherd, children all are dear
to thee (Leeson) D555; Q627;
U486; V647; W310; AA447;
AI373; AL216; AM354; AP352;
AW298; AZ622; BA827; BY286
102914
Gracious Saviour, gentle Shep-
herd, Little ones are dear to
thee (Leeson) U486 X Gra-
cioud Saviour, gentle Shep-
herd, children all...   102915
Gracious Saviour, gentle Shep-
herd, Our little ones (Lee-
son) AI373 X Gracious Sa-
viour, gentle Shepherd, child-
ren all   102916
Gracious Saviour, thus before
thee (Bateman) AZ272 102917
Gracious Saviour, who didst
honor (Shirreff) AO563;
AR547; AS417; AT503 102918
Gracious Spirit, Dove divine
(Stocker) H222; K154; L175;
M466; N162; O376; P230;
V217; AA253; AE141; AM
245; AP286; BB215; BR204
102919
Gracious Spirit! dwell with me
(Lynch) I195; R241; S214;
W187; X506; Z270; AB92;
AE144; AF245; AK192; AL
152; AR224; AS172; BE88;
BF259; BV295; BY231
102920
Gracious Spirit, Holy Ghost
(Wordsworth A379; B121;
D76; E396; F233; J119; O498;
W484; X507; AL367; AS346;
AW174; AX541; AZ1135; BA
671; BV543; BY232   102921
Gracious Spirit - Love divine
(Stocker) M466 X Gracious
Spirit, Dove divine   102922

Grand Dieu! Que de merveilles
(French trad carol) BG111
                              102923
Grant me strength when skies
are azure (Weitzman) BH48
                              102924
Grant, most gracious Lamb of
God (Scheffler) AZ40; BA453
                              102925
Grant that we ask, Almighty
Lord (---) BRp.467   102926
Grant us, Lord, the grace of
giving (---) AD507; AR674;
AT537; BF695   102927
Grant us, O God, a single aim
(Jones) AB283   102928
Grant us, O our heavenly Father
(Thring) D574   102929
Grant us the will to fashion as
we feel (Drinkwater) Y181;
AC187; AK264; AR412   102930
Grant us thy light, that we may
know (Tuttiett) AE375 X O
grant us light   102931
Grant us Thy peace; for thou alone
canst bend (Masterman) BY660
                              102932
Granted is the Saviour's prayer
(Wesley) AO230   102933
Great and fair is she, our land
(Watson) AH482; AN379; BD
177; BX414   102934
Great Arbiter of human fate
(Moise) BH209   102935
Great art Thou, God! The hosts
of heaven wonder (Pawels)
M152   102936
Great Creator, Lord of all
(Pollock) D546   102937
Great day! Great day! The
righteous marching (Negro
spiritual) AH605   102938
Great Giver of all good, Teach
us to give like Thee (---)
AE367; AR342; AS356   102939
Great God, a blessing from thy
throne (Schuette) M510 102940
Great God! and wilt thou conde-
scend (Taylor) W550   102941
Great God, as seasons disappear
(Butcher) AZ313   102942
Great God, attend, while Zion
sings (Watts) H415; I213; V18;

BC248; BZ   102943
Great God! beneath whose
piercing eye (Roscoe) H520;
I708   102944
Great God, how infinite art
Thou! (Watts) L97; U11;
V91; AM22   102945
Great God in heaven, Who by
my bed (---) BR542   102946
Great God, indulge my humble
claim (Watts) H110; L439;
V337; AY212   102947
Great God, let all our tuneful
powers (Heginbothom) H65
                             102948
Great God of Abraham, hear our
prayer (Cotterill) W366
                             102949
Great God of nations, now to
thee (Woodhull) G509; I706;
AH494; AK437; AO595; AR
609; AW349; AZ307; BA880;
BK119   102950
Great God of wonders! all thy
ways are worthy of thyself
(Davies) AM71; AP161; BY
55   102951
Great God, the followers of thy
Son (Ware) AN21; AW13;
BX25   102952
Great God, the nations of the
earth (Gibbon) I645; V600
                             102953
Great God! Thou dost all nations
rule (Hymns of the English
Conf. 1880) BR495   102954
Great God, To thee my evening
song (Steele) D644; BC59
                             102955
Great God, to what a glorious
height (Watts) L116   102956
Great God, to whom alone be-
long (---) H527   102957
Great God, we give Thee praise
(Hymns of the English Conf.
1880) BR236   102958
Great God, we praise thy gra-
cious care (Cennick) N541 X
We thank thee, Lord, for this
our food   102959
Great God, we sing that guiding
hand (Doddridge) BY715 X
Great God, we sing that mighty

hand   102960
Great God, we sing that mighty
    hand (Doddridge) G539; J533;
    K482; L551; M369; N49; O214;
    Q119; R527; S470; U475; V627;
    W607; Z586; AA167; AD449;
    AF454; AG292; AK425; AM612;
    AO573; AP143; AV310; AW383;
    AZ295; BA177; BF639; BX172;
    BY715; BZ   102961
Great God, what do I see and
    hear (Collyer) B64; D37; E4;
    K514; L580; N611; O604; Q604;
    V687; AA553; AM240; AZ748;
    BA734; BB195; BJ16; BV78
                            102962
Great God! whatever through thy
    church (---) BO209; BQ128
                            102963
Great God who hast delivered us
    (Extrait du Recueil. 1957)
    AF577   102964
Great God who knowest each man's
    need (Tennyson, E) AO44
                            102965
Great High-Priest, we view thee
    stooping (Hart) AZ944; BA
    208   102966
Great is the Lord, and greatly
    He (U.P. Book of Psalms,
    1871) AP42   102967
Great is the Lord our God
    (Watts) K243; L280; M82; Q
    636; V534; AA458; AS189; AZ
    1365   102968
Great is the Lord; 'tis good to
    praise (Snow) BC234   102969
Great is the love that brought me
    (Crosby) AE291   102970
Great is their joy who hide their
    own (Darbyshire) X241 102971
"Great is thy faithfulness," O God
    my Father (Chisholm) Z165;
    AE68; AM27; AR429; AT47;
    BV238; BY576   102972
Great Jehovah! we adore thee
    (---) Lp.744; AZ1394; BA911
                            102973
Great joy and consolation I find
    O Christ, in Thee (Wallin)
    N392   102974
Great King of glory, come (Fran-
    cis) I656; BB485   102975

Great King of heaven, our hearts
    we raise (Thomas) BC53
                            102976
Great King of Kings and Lord of
    Lords (Hacker) BQ336
                            102977
Great King of kings, why dost
    thou stay (Bonar) O605; P
    427   102978
Great King of nations, hear our
    prayer (Gurney) Q583; V626;
    W643; AM621; AO584; AP643
                            102979
Great King of Peace, hear now
    Thy people's cry (Little)
    BL57   102980
Great King of saints, enthroned
    on high (---) AX638   102981
Great Lord of all thy Churches,
    hear (Kingsbury) V580
                            102982
Great Lord of Life who lives in
    me (Sampter) BH243 102983
Great Master, touch us with thy
    skillful hands! (Bonar) Z317;
    AC222; AR401; BK92   102984
Great mover of all hearts, whose
    hand (Coffin) F316   102985
Great Redeemer, we adore thee
    (Harris) AT154; AU362
                            102986
Great Refuge of the weary soul
    (Hymns of the English Conf.
    1880) BR356   102987
Great Ruler of the land and sea
    (Bonar) AP711   102988
Great Saint Joseph, son of
    David (German hymn) BN170;
    BO126; BP90; BQ93   102989
Great Shepherd of the sheep,
    Who all thy flock (Scottish
    Hymnal, 1884) D571 102990
Great Shepherd of thy people,
    hear (Newton) F247; G313;
    V569; W246; AK230; AL203;
    AP316; AW279; AZ149; BA
    332; BB25; BR16; BV6
                            102991
Great Shepherd of thy people,
    here (Newton) BB25 X Great
    Shepherd of thy people, hear
                            102992
Great Shepherd who leadest thy

people in love (U.P. Psalter,
1912) T149; AI263; AJ220
                          102993
Great truths are portions of the
soul of man (Lowell) AB299
                          102994
Great Western Land, whose mighty
breast (Hazard) AN375 102995
Green are the leaves, and sweet
the flowers (Newman) BO110
                          102996
Green grow'th the holly (English
trad carol) BG63   102997
Gross sind die Merck des Herren
(Ausbund) BU19   102998
Gross Unbild thut mich zwingen
(Ausbund) BU117   102999
Grosser Gott, wir loben dich
(Franz) AW519b; BT250; BW
519   103000
Guardian of pure hearts, and
Hearer (Wallin) N313 103001
Guardian of virgins and holy
father, Joseph (Latin prayer,
19th c) BN169   103002
Guds Ord det er vort Arvegods
(Luther) BT283   103003
Guide me, O thou great Jehovah
(Williams) A434; B42; D414;
E397; F296; G301; H114; I91;
J520; K261; L204; M583; N452;
O285; P307; Q54; R339; S104;
T429; U29; V333; W564; X508;
Y366; Z393; AA340; AD220;
AE235; AF93; AG158; AH406;
AI296; AK80; AL441; AM501;
AO326; AP596; AR286; AS246;
AT55; AU181; AV43; AW160;
AX499; AY65; AZ1381; BA694;
BB409; BC56; BE90; BI34; BR
453; BV555; BX325; BY541; BZ
                          103004
Guide me, O thou great Redeemer
(Williams) X508 X Guide me,
O thou great Jehovah 103005
Guide, O Lord, thy chariot now
(Zwingli) AO605   103006
Guide of my spirit on its devious
way (Cross) Y11; AB222
                          103007
Guide us, O thou great Jehovah
(Williams) BC56 X Guide me,
O thou great Jehovah 103008

Guillaume prends ton tambourin
(LaMonnoye) BG82   103009
Gute Nacht, ihr meine Lieben
(Unparth. G. B.) AY18d
                          103010
Guter Hirt, du hast gestillt
(Meinhold) BT595   103011
Gwine to lay down my burden
(Negro spiritual) Y322
                          103012

H

Hab ich das Haupt zum Freunde
(P. Gerhardt) BW236 103013
Had Christ, that once was slain
(Cowley Carol book) R This
joyful Easter-tide   103014
Had God not come, may Israel
say (Luther) O527; AA282
                          103015
Had I the tongues of Greeks and
Jews (Watts) V381   103016
Had not the Lord been Israel's
help (U.P. Psalter, 1912) AJ
352   103017
Had we naught, had we naught;
Naught beyond this life to
hope (Zinzendorf, N. L.) BA
749 X Had we naught, naught
beyond this life   103018
Had we naught, naught beyond
this life to hope (Zinzendorf,
N. L.) AZ720; BA749 103019
Haec dies quam fecit Dominus
(Bible. Psalm 117) BN43
                          103020
Hail! all hail, great Queen of
heaven (Sister of Notre Dame)
BQ78   103021
Hail, all hail, sweet youth
angelic (A Carmelite Nun)
BP97   103022
Hail, all hail, victorious Lord
and Saviour (Hayn) AZ1007
                          103023
Hail, Alpha and Omega, hail
(Cennick) AZ203; BA440
                          103024
Hail, angelic Bread of heaven
(St Thomas Aquinas) BP54
                          103025
Hail Blessed Saint, hail Ursula

(---) R Afar upon a foreign
shore   103026
Hail, blessed Trinity! Low here
we bow (Berry) AS71   103027
Hail bright Archangel, Prince of
heaven (Faber) BO196   103028
Hail! Christ, our Redeemer,
God of glory and might (---)
BP104   103029
Hail, Church of Christ, bought
with His blood (Cennick) AZ
102   103030
Hail! festal day! to endless ages
known (Fortunatus) B168 X
Hail thee, festival day   103031
Hail, foamy ocean star! (Latin)
R Hail, heavenly Queen! Hail,
foamy ocean star!   103032
Hail full of grace and purity!
(Conway) BQ86   103033
Hail, gladdening Light, of his
pure glory poured (Greek, 3d
c) F18; G637; W281; AB20;
AD49; AL552; AP664; BF196;
BR115; BV54; BY695;   103034
Hail Gladdening Light, of his
pure glory poured (Greek, 3d c)
X O Gladsome Light, O Grace
103035
Hail! gladdening Light, of that
pure glory poured (Greek, 3d c)
BR115 X Hail, gladdening
Light, of His pure glory poured
103036
Hail, glorious angels, heirs of
light (Austin) BJ60 X Hail
glorious spirits, heirs of
light   103037
Hail, glorious apostle, Saint
Basil the Great (Dollard)
BN174; BO1a   103038
Hail, glorious Saint Patrick!
dear saint of our Isle! (Sr.
Agnes) BO137; BP92; BQ96
103039
Hail, glorious spirits, heirs of
light (Austin) F626; X205;
BJ60   103040
Hail, Guest! We ask not what
thou art (Guiterman) BK8
103041
Hail, happy day! Thou day of
holy rest (Browne) BB464;

BR97   103042
Hail, harbinger of morn, (St
Bede, the Venerable) E225
103043
Hail, harbinger of morn (St
Bede, the Venerable) X The
great forerunner of the morn
103044
Hail, heavenly Queen! Hail
foamy ocean star. (Latin)
BO57   103045
Hail Him the King of glory
(deFluiter) R Tell it to every
kindred and nation   103046
Hail!holy guide of youthful days
(---) BO139   103047
Hail, Holy, Holy, Holy Lord.
Let powers immortal sing
(Perronet) K132; M455
103048
Hail! Holy, Holy, Holy Lord,
Whom One in Three we know
(Wesley) K162; AZ216
103049
Hail, holy Joseph, hail! Chaste
spouse of Mary (Faber) BN
171; BO131; BQ95   103050
Hail, holy Light! The world re-
joices (Parker) AB8 103051
Hail, holy Queen enthroned above
(Hermannus Contractus) BM
50; BN153; BO75; BP84; BQ
83   103052
Hail, Holy Spirit, bright immor-
tal Dove (Browne) AZ442
103053
Hail, Jesus, hail, do thou, good
Shepherd (St Thomas Aquinas)
R Thee prostrate I adore
103054
Hail, Jesus, hail, Who for my
sake (Italian, 18th c) BN74;
BO27; BQ71   103055
Hail, Jesus! Israel's Hope and
Light (Harbaugh) AO109
103056
Hail! Kingly Jesus, to thy feet
(Thompson) AZ114; BA187
103057
Hail Mary, full of grace (Latin,
13th c) BQ149 X Hail Mary,
hail Mary full of grace
103058

Hail Mary, full of grace, Hail flower of Adam's race (Camm) BN145; BO68   103059

Hail Mary, hail Mary, full of grace (Latin, 13th c) BP72; BQ149   103060

Hail! my ever blessed Jesus (Wingrove) L141; V309 103061

Hail, noble column, speak and tell (Herman) BP29   103062

Hail, O Holy Queen! Hail, O Mother all Merciful (Hermannus Contractus) BP76   103063

Hail, O Mary, full of grace (White) F499   103064

Hail, O Star that pointest (Latin, 9th c) E213   103065

Hail, Ocean's beauteous Star (Latin, 9th c) BO122   103066

Hail our monarch, son of David (Latin) Eapp3   103067

Hail, peaceful day! divinely blest (Smith) BB457   103068

Hail! princess of the host of heaven (Santeuil) F549 103069

Hail, Queen of heaven, hail our Mother compassionate (Hermannus Contractus) BL61   103070

Hail, Queen of heaven, The ocean star (Hermannus Contractus) BN133; BO102; BP81; BQ84   103071

Hail, Queen of the heavens! Hail, Mistress of earth (Hermannus Contractus) BO90   103072

Hail, Rock of ages, pierced for me (Bridges) BQ70 X This is an everlasting home   103073

Hail! sacred day of earthly rest (Thring) D25; H76; W269; AL 192; AP347; BR92; BX105   103074

Hail St Joseph; Spouse of Mary (---) R Dear St Joseph, pure and gentle   103075

Hail! sweetest dearest tie (Sutton) AY409   103076

Hail the blest morn when the great mediator (Heber) AX104 X Brightest and best   103077

Hail the day so rich in cheer (Latin, before 1422) Q78

Hail the day that sees Him rise. Alleluia (Wesley) A104; D 128; E143; F147; I162; J111; L272; N148; Q213; S171; X 172; AA243; AD169; AF205; AH306; AK175; AL114; AP 222; AS154; AW117; AZ47; BA248; BB131; BR192; BV 203; BY167   103079

Hail the day when Jesus rose (Gordon) AB147   103080

Hail the glorious golden city (Adler) Y61; Z488; AB286; AC264; AD426; AF424; AN392; AQ192; BD137; BF510; BH227; BX427   103081

Hail the hero workers (Spencer) AB281; AC190; AN330; BF 436   103082

Hail the Sign, the Sign of Jesus (Baring-Gould) E592 103083

Hail thee, festival day! [Ascension sequence] (Fortunatus) A102; B184; E628; X389   103084

Hail thee, festival day! [Dedication sequence] (Fortunatus) E634; X389   103085

Hail thee, festival day! [Easter sequence] (Fortunatus) A86; B168; E624; X389   103086

Hail thee, festival day! [Whitsunday sequence] (Fortunatus) A107; B195; E630; X389   103087

Hail thee, Saviour and Atoner (Arnold of Louvain) M202   103088

Hail thee! Spirit, Lord eternal (Wallis) A110   103089

Hail, thou bright and sacred morn (Elliott) W266; BT8   103090

Hail, thou everblessed morn (Caswall) R See, amid the winter's snow   103091

Hail, thou King of saints ascending (St Bernard of Clairvaux) AZ434   103092

Hail, thou living Bread from heaven (Latin, 1815) BO54   103093

Hail, thou living Victim blest
(Latin) BO46   103094
Hail, thou long-expected Jesus
(Wesley) AT70 X Come,
thou long-expected Jesus
                              103095
Hail, thou martyr host of heaven
(---) AZ1080   103096
Hail, thou once despised Jesus!
(Bakewell) A357; B191; D365;
G166; H190; I171; J435; K60;
L142; M450; N149; O303; P
221; Q367; R210; U113; V156;
AA242; AE134; AH318; AI
139; AK179; AL117; AM128;
AO200; AP228; AR192; AT149;
AW122; AZ955,970; BA192;
BV259; BY173; BZ   103097
Hail, thou Source of every bless-
ing (Woodd) E616; K41; M371;
N64; Q129; AA182; BV124
                              103098
Hail thou Star of Ocean (Latin,
9th c) BM55; BO76; BQ73
                              103099
Hail, thou who man's Redeemer
art (Latin, 7th c) BP41
                              103100
Hail, thou wondrous Infant
Stranger (Lamb) AZ1401; BA
61   103101
Hail to the brightness of Zion's
glad morning (Hastings) G488;
H478; J319; M99; N381; O112;
P399; R505; S391; T369; U408;
V598; Z523; AC303; AD380;
AG259; AH466; AK378; AM
274; AO519; AR561; AT453;
AU248; AV266; AW332; AZ1151;
BA343; BB302; BC182; BF524;
BI16   103102
Hail to the Lord who comes
(Ellerton) A115; B274; D154;
E209; F544; BL18; BV441
                              103103
Hail to the Lord's Anointed
(Montgomery) A545; B99; D
323; E45; F219; G85; H137;
I650; J328; K42; L147; M325;
N16; O168; Q59; R146; S111;
U400; V584; W154; X87; Y
244; Z257; AA132; AB105;
AC301; AD177; AE77; AF105;

AH315; AK366; AL139; AM224;
AN151; AO513; AP60; AQ282;
AV95; AW65; AZ801; BA184;
BE75; BF337; BR128; BV129;
BX201; BY80; BZ   103104
Hail to the Prince of Life and
Peace (Doddridge) V191
                              103105
Hail to the Prophet ascended
to heaven (Phelps) R Praise
to the man who communed with
Jehovah   103106
Hail to the Sabbath day! (Bul-
finch) H81; I66; AS40; AY
428   103107
Hail to thee, true Body, sprung
(Innocent VI, Pope) BQ51
                              103108
Hail to this holy day (Bulfinch)
AS40 X Hail to the Sabbath
day   103109
Hail, true Body, born of Mary
(Innocent VI, Pope) E311;
F407   103110
Hail, true Body, truly born of
the Virgin Mary mild (Inno-
cent VI, Pope) BP50
                              103111
Hail, true Victim, life and light
(Peckham) BN94   103112
Hail Virgin, dearest Mary, Our
lovely Queen of May (---)
BQ81   103113
Hail we now this happy morn
(Chubb) AN147   103114

NOTE: Hallelujah, as variously
spelled beginning with letter
H, is herein spelled and filed
as Alleluia   103115

Hands that have been handling
(Liturgy of Malabar) F494
                              103116
Happiness, delightful name
(Toplady) AZ1058; BA521
                              103117
Happy are they, they that love
God (Coffin) E398; F261; W
440; X509; AD255; AL290;
AP442; BJ34; BV532; BY496
                              103118
Happy day, happy day, When

Jesus washed ... (Doddridge)
R O happy day, that stays
[fixed] my choice   103119
Happy he that never wanders
(Hamburg Temple hymnal)
BH100   103120
Happy he who walketh ever
(Voorsanger) AH153; BH25
                           103121
Happy race of witnesses (Zinzen-
dorf, N. L.) AZ1036   103122
Happy Saint; in bliss adoring
Jesus, Saviour of mankind
(---) R Holy patron; thee salut-
ing   103123
Happy soul, secure from harm
(Wesley) BR319 X Shepherd,
with thy tenderest love 103124
Happy soul, thy days are ended
(Wesley) AZ243; BA726 103125
Happy the heart where graces
reign (Watts) L454   103126
Happy the home when God is
there (Ware) G428; AE388;
AI366; AL394; AM627; AP708;
AR545; AS415; AT374; AW361;
AX556; BB413; BZ   103127
Happy the man, and happy he
alone (Horace: Dryden para)
AQ185   103128
Happy the man that finds the
grace (Wesley) I372   103129
Happy the man who feareth God
(Luther) AA446   103130
Happy the man who knows His
Master of obey (Upham) BE92
                           103131
Happy the man whose heart can
rest (McKenzie) BE93 103132
Happy the souls to Jesus joined
(Wesley) BZ   103133
Happy we, who, thus united
(Vaughan) BO55; BQ136
                           103134
Happy who in early youth (Ham-
burg Temple hymnal) BH253
                           103135
Hard is not the constant woe
(Fox) AQ129   103136
Hark, a burst of heavenly music
(Meigs) AO134   103137
Hark! a hearld voice is calling
(Latin, 6th c) X61 X Hark!

a thrilling voice   103138
Hark! a hundred notes are swell-
ing (Briggs) X360   103139
Hark! a mystic voice is sound-
ing (Latin, 6th c) BQ1 X
Hark! a thrilling voice
                           103140
Hark! a thrilling voice is sound-
ing (Latin, 6th c) A9; B63;
D41; E5; F47; J1; K3; N12;
O164; Q60; X61; AA133; BO
148; BQ1; BV76   103141
Hark! a voice divides the sky
(Wesley) AA536; AZ1037
                           103142
Hark! a voice in the wilderness
crying (Milligan) AD373 X
There's a voice ...   103143
Hark, a voice saith all are
mortal (Albinus) M305; AA
530   103144
Hark! are they not angels that
gladly are bringing (Willman)
AX91   103145
Hark! from the tomb a doleful
sound (Watts) AY183 103146
Hark, hark my soul! Angelic
songs are swelling (Faber)
A472; B290; D398; E399; F
354; G532; H510; I621; J498;
L587; O607; P347; R426; S
431; T430; U426; V694; W580;
Y343; Z582; AB404; AC329;
AD462; AG282; AH369; AK
420; AL442; AN549; AO546;
AP601; AR421; AS476; AT469;
AU62; AV286; AW260; AZ
1024; BA745; BB375; BD153;
BF385; BI74; BO198; BQ111;
BR447; BX464   103147
Hark, hark, my soul! The Sa-
viour's voice is calling
(Hopps) BR382 X Hark, hark
my soul! Thy Father's voice
                           103148
Hark, hark, my soul! The voice
of Jesus calling (Consterdine)
BV316   103149
Hark, hark, my soul! Thy
Father's voice is calling
(Hopps) AN432; BR382; BX
465;   103150
Hark! hark! The organ loudly

A316; B518; D35   103177

Hark, the voice of children
(Sonnenschein & Wolsee)
BH146   103178

Hark! the voice of Jesus calling,
"Follow me." (Sleight) AX255
                         103179

Hark, the voice of Jesus calling
-- "Who will go?" (March)
G288; H392; I402; J59; N80;
O121; P384; Q496; U283; V501;
AA476; AB348; AH421; AI189;
AK383; AL387; AM691; AP586;
AS379; AT440; AU407; AV268;
AX205; AY332, 335; AZ954;
BA345; BB447   103180

Hark, the voice of Jesus crying
(March) O121 X Hark, the
voice of Jesus calling   103181

Hark! the voice of love and mercy
(Evans) H171; L250; V140;
AI73; AM187; AO167; AZ1399;
BA209; BV172   103182

Hark, the waking up of nations
(Coxe) AV273 X We are living,
we are dwelling   103183

Hark! through the courts of
heaven (Alford) L384   103184

Hark, 'tis the Saviour's voice I
hear (Dobell. Selections, 1806)
M201   103185

Hark! 'Tis the Shepherd's voice
I hear (Thomas) AM684; AT
429; AU266; AX213; BB625
                         103186

Hark, 'Tis the watchman's cry
(The Revivalist, 1859) AZ1248;
BA545; BV85   103187

Hark to the sound, it rings from
sea to sea (Kimball) Y285;
BD168   103188

Hark, what a sound, and too divine for hearing (Myers) R
150; S110; X511; AD103; AL
133; AR211   103189

Hark! what mean those holy voices
(Cawood) B81; D61; H139; I109;
K33; L218; M349; N28; O190;
Q83; U61; V115; AA160; AH
248; AI69; AO123; AS105; AV
96; AX93; AY243; AZ274; BA
165; BI79; BR143   103190

Hark, what music fills the sky

(---) AZ1132   103191

Hark! while infant voices sing
(Henley) R Children of Jerusalem   103192

Har-nee-nu lay-lo-heem (Jewish
traditional) BH308   103193

Hast not thy heart within thee
burned (Bulfinch) AN109
                         103194

Hast thou heard it, O my brother
(Williams) AN476; BD76;
BX540   103195

Hast thou not known, hast thou
not heard (Watts) X512; AF
78; AL414; AM28; AP534;
BV250   103196

Hast to the plow thou put thy
hand (Grundtvig) M259
                         103197

Haste not! haste not! do not
rest! (Goethe) BH43   103198

Haste, O haste, delightful
morning (Jones) BF521
                         103199

Haste thee away, why wilt thou
stay? (Crosby) R Come with
thy sins   103200

Haste, traveler, haste! The
night comes on (Collyer)
I251   103201

Hasten, Lord, the glorious time
(Auber) H475; I637; K227;
L336; M379; V592; AZ1055;
BA346   103202

Hasten, O sinner, to be wise
(Scott) L371 X Hasten, sinner, to be wise   103203

Hasten, sinner to be wise
(Scott) H256; I248; L370; M
26; V269; AA55   103204

Hasten the time appointed (Borthwick) A257; B477; D255; M
101; AN326; AQ209; AZ818;
BD186; BE196; BX430 103205

Hath not thy heart within thee
burned (Bulfinch) BE94; BX
84   103206

Have faith in God, my heart
(Rees) AF361; VV499; BV
577; BZ   103207

"Have faith in God," the Saviour
said (Hewitt) AY359   103208

Have faith in God When your

pathway is lonely (McKinney)
AT253; AU52   103209

Have I done any good in the
world today? (Thompson) BC
58   103210

Have I need of aught, O Saviour
(Davis) BB580   103211

Have mercy, Lord, on me (Tate
& Brady) D351; E74; AP46;
BJ65   103212

Have mercy on me, God, in your
kindness (Ladies of the Grail)
BSp. 22   103213

Have mercy on us, God most high
(Faber) E161; BO7   103214

Have thine own way, Lord (Pollard) R302; Z324; AE270; AH
426; AI280; AM574; AR351;
AS241; AT355; AU254; AV384;
AW217; AX395; BB272; BZ
103215

Have thy affections been nailed
to the cross? (Hoffman) AX274
103216

Have ye heard the invitation
(Hoppe) N192   103217

Have ye not heard, have ye not
known (Bible. Isaiah) R O thou
who spreadest the heaven like
a tent   103218

Have you any room for Jesus
("L.W.M.")AX259   103219

Have you been to Jesus (Hoffman) AT192; AU111; AX276
103220

Have you failed in your plan
(McKinney) AT231; AU397
103221

Have you found rest and peace
within (DeArmond) AX346
103222

Have you prayed all night, Till
the break of day (Poole)
AU121   103223

Have you read the story of the
cross (Dennis) AU283   103224

Have you sought for the sheep
that have wandered (Crosby)
AX198; AY526   103225

Ha-yom t'-am' tsay-nu (Jewish
traditional) BH333   103226

He brought me out of the miry
clay (Gilmour) R My heart

was distressed (Zelley)
103227

He came among us at Christmas-
tide (German carol) R Joseph
dearest, Joseph mine R Long
ago and far away   103228

He comes! He comes with
trumpet sound (Pratt) AX124
103230

He cometh not a King to reign
(Whittier) BD70 X O Lord
and Master of us all X Immortal love forever   103231

He did not die in vain (Hoppe)
M192   103232

He died of a broken heart for
you (Dennis) Have you read
the story   103233

He died! the Great Redeemer
died (Watts) BC263 X He
dies! the Friend of sinners
dies!   103234

He dies! the Friend of sinners
dies! (Watts) I165; AO174;
BC263   103235

He expecteth, He expecteth
(Janvrin) BV318   103236

He has come! the Christ of
God (Bonar) AZ1057 103237

He hides within the lily (Gannett)
AN29; BD47; BX65   103238

He hideth my soul (Crosby) R
A wonderful Saviour is Jesus
my Lord   103239

He is able to deliver thee
(Ogden) R 'Tis the grandest
theme   103240

He is arisen! Glorious word!
(Boye) M440; O329; P194;
Q189   103241

He is coming again (Camp) R
Lift up your heads, Pilgrims
aweary   103242

He is coming, He is coming,
Not as once He came before
(Alexander) H204; V180; AZ
963   103243

He is coming! He is coming! We
hear triumphal shouting (Mac-
Farland) AC464   103244

He is coming, the "Man of Sorrows" (Crosby) AT121
103245

He is gone; a cloud of light
(Stanley) I170; W129; AB150;
BA250   103246

He is gone - beyond the skies
(Stanley) W129 X He is gone;
a cloud of light   103247

He is here, whom seers in old
time (Prudentius) AZ898 X
Of the Father's love begotten
                                   103248

He is risen, he is risen (Alexander) A90; B179; D117; E132;
F143; BC61; BR182   103249

He is waiting to receive (Latta)
R Wanderer in sinful ways
                                   103250

He is watching, He is waiting
(Keegan) R Are you tired
                                   103251

He just put Himself in my place
(---) R Shall I tell you   103252

He keepeth me ever (Latta) AY
316   103253

He knoweth the way that I take
(Hoffman) AX487; AY118
                                   103254

He knoweth thy grief (Reed) AY
317   103255

He knows, He knows just what is
best (Hott) R 'Tis hard to
bear   103256

He knows, He knows the storms
that would my way oppose
(Henry) R I know my heaven-
ly Father knows   103257

He knows the bitter, weary way
(---) AU452   103258

He leadeth me! O blessed thought
(Gilmore) A426; B245; D616;
G242; H130; I489; J478; L544;
M279; N497; P328; R338; S106;
U46; V346; Z405; AD222; AE
292; AF370; AG53; AH405;
AI301; AK466; AL483; AM500;
AN565; AO632; AP519; AR442;
AS251; AT58; AU422; AV59;
AW478; AX495; BA686; BB393;
BD120; BE95; BF415; BZ
                                   103259

He leads us on through childhood's wondering years (Wiley)
BY542 X He leads us on by
paths we did not know   103260

He leads us on by paths we did
not know (Wiley) U30; AI
295; AN240; BX264; BY542
                                   103261

He lives again! Our risen Lord,
today (Fleming) R Awake,
awake O earth   103262

He lives, He lives, Christ Jesus
lives today (Ackley) R I serve
a risen Saviour   103263

He lives! O fainting heart, anew
(Wallin) N136   103264

He lives on high (McKinney) R
Christ the Saviour came
                                   103265

He lives! the great Redeemer
lives (Steele) V177; AO196;
AV116; AY515   103266

He liveth long who liveth well
(Bonar) W522; AL351; AN291;
BF444; BX347   103267

He loves me, He loves me (---)
R Alas! and did my Saviour
bleed (Watts)   103268

He loves me too (Straub) R
God sees the little sparrow
fall   103269

He loveth me, He loveth me
(Hay) AS122   103270

He must reign, Who won the
right (Edwards) BA95
                                   103271

He prayeth best who loveth best
(Coleridge) BB319 X Prayer
is the soul's sincere desire
(Montgomery)   103272

He presses on before the race
(Markham) AQ40   103273

He reigns! the Lord, the Saviour
reigns (Watts) BB179 103274

He sat to watch o'er customs
paid (Bright) E240; F563; X
237; BV450   103275

He seeks His wandering sheep
(Newton) R The Shepherd's
heart   103276

He sent His word, His holy word
BE101   103277

He sleeps in Jesus -- peaceful
rest (Smith) BB494   103278

He smiles within his cradle (German trad carol) BG84 103279

He stood of old, the holy Christ

(Whittier) BE96   103280

He that believes and is baptized
(Kingo) J259; N230; O140;
P94; Q301; AR659   103281

He that confides in his Creator
(Neumark) AZ695   103282

He that dies shall not die lonely
(Morris) AQ80   103283

He that goeth forth with weeping
(Hastings) H466; L548; V500;
AY256; AZ966; BB627; BE97
103284

He that hath God his guardian
made (Tate & Brady) BE99,
100   103285

He that hath made his refuge God
(Watts) V336   103286

He that is down needs fear no
fall (Bunyan) F301; W557;
X513   103287

He wants not friends that hath
thy love (Baxter) R401; F274;
W225; X514; BV430; BY360
103288

He was nailed to the cross for
me (---) R What a wonderful,
wonderful Saviour   103289

He was wounded for our transgressions (Oliver) R Who hath
believed   103290

He waters the hills with rain from
the skies (U.P. Psalter, 1912)
AJ286   103291

He who dwells in the shelter of
the Most High (Ladies of the
Grail) BSp.25   103292

He who has helped me hitherto
(Grundtvig) M291   103293

He who himself and Lord would
know (Martineau) Y56; AN106;
BX87   103294

He who is upright, kind, and
free from error (Horace) Y297
103295

He who made the starry skies
(Chester ms. cal425) BG67
103296

He, who once in righteous vengeance (Breviary. Bologna,
1827) AZ599; BQ18   103297

He who once to die a victim
(Breviary. Cluny. 1686) BM4
X Wondrous gift! The word

103298

He who suns and worlds up-
holdeth (Gill) BF240; BX
326   103299

He who to Jesus manfully bore
witness (Latin, 8th c) F519
103300

He who would be in God confiding (Neumark) AW571a; BR
260   103301

He who would valiant be (Bunyan)
A563; B117; E402; F293; G
265; J563; R345; S276; W576;
X515; Y169; Z364; AB175;
AC204; AD226; AF371; AG
193; AK296; AN213; AQ94;
AR322; BF409; BK79; BV587;
BY561; BZ   103302

He whom joyous shepherds
praised (Latin, 1410) A35
103303

He, whose confession God of old
accepted (Latin, 8th c) E188
103304

He will come, let us watch and
be ready (Belden) R We know
not the hour of the Master's
appearing   103305

He will gather the wheat in His
garner (MacKeever) R When
Jesus shall gather the nations
103306

He will hide me, He will hide
me (Servoss) R When the
storms of life   103307

He will hold me fast (Habershon)
R When I fear my faith will
fail   103308

Head of the Church and Lord of
all (Tritton) BY258   103309

Head of the Church Triumphant
(Wesley) AB85; AP256; AZ
1081   103310

Head of thy Church Triumphant
(Wesley) AP256 X Head of
the Church Triumphant
103311

Heal me, O my Saviour,   heal
(Thring) B137; D356; AZ
1131; BR292   103312

Heal us, Immanuel! Hear our
prayer (Cowper) BY335
103313

Healer Divine, who walkest still
  (Neumann) AK248   103314
Heap high the farmer's wintry
  hoard (Whittier) BK139
                                    103315
Hear, hear, O ye nations, and
  hearing obey (Hosmer) AN398;
  AQ194; AT467; BD182; BF566;
  BX429   103316
Hear, Lord, the voice of my
  complaint (U. P. Psalter, 1912)
  T115; AJ165   103317
Hear my prayer, O hear my
  prayer (Hess) BH168   103318
Hear my prayer, O heavenly
  Father (Parr) L33 X Hear
  our prayer   103319
Hear my words, O gracious Lord
  (U. P. Psalter, 1912) R48
                                    103320
Hear, O hear us heavenly Father
  (Garrett) AS53   103321
Hear, O Lord, our humble sup-
  plication (---) AK504   103322
Hear our entreaties, Lord, and
  show Thy mercy (---) BN29
                                    103323
Hear our prayer, O gracious
  Father (Heywood) BE102
                                    103324
Hear our prayer, O heavenly
  Father (Parr) D647; L33; AZ
  271; BA899   103325
Hear the royal proclamation
  (---) AZ435   103326
Hear then, in love, O Lord, the
  cry (Bonar) R When the
  wear seeking rest   103327
Hear this, all ye people, hear
  (U. P. Psalter, 1912) T92;
  AJ135   103328
Hear thou our hymn, O Lord
  (Asper) BC96   103329
Hear thou our prayer, Lord
  (Huffman) AR658   103330
Hear thy children, gentle Jesus
  (Stanfield) BQ124   103331
Hear thy children, gentlest
  Mother (Stanfield) BQ87
                                    103332
Hear us, Eternal King, Hear thou
  the praise (Davieson) BH136
                                    103333

Hear us, O Lord, from heaven
  (Gill) AL338   103334
Hear us, our Father! We know
  thou wilt hear us (---) Z336
                                    103335
Hear us, Thou that broodest
  (Thring) B524; D133   103336
Hear what God the Lord hath
  spoken (Cowper) I211; AZ
  949; BX447   103337
Hear what the voice from heaven
  proclaims (Watts) E354; I588
                                    103338
Hear ye the Master's call (Kirk)
  AT437; AU343   103339
Hearken, all! what holy singing
  (---) G108   103340
Hearken, O Lord, have mercy
  upon us (Latin) R To Thee,
  Redeemer, King of highest
  heaven   103341
Heart and mind, possessions,
  Lord (Tilak) AF394   103342
Heart of Christ my King! I
  greet thee (Latin, 15th c)
  AZ430   103343
Heart of Jesus! golden chalice
  (Casartelli) BQ62   103344
Heart of Jesus I adore thee
  (---) BQ331   103345
Heart of Mary, Heart all pure
  (---) BM53   103346
Heart of our Lord, O loving
  Heart (Latin) BN69   103347
Heart of the Holy Child, Hide
  me in thee ("M.B.", Sr.)
  BO160   103348
Hearts at Christmas time were
  jolly (Gerhardt) X89   103349
Heaven and earth and sea and
  air (Neander) K290; N330;
  O63; P23; R6; S27; AD99;
  AF75; AK45; AN34; AQ33;
  AW510; BX60   103350
Heaven at last, heaven at last,
  O, the joyful story (Bonar)
  R Angel voices sweetly sing-
  ing   103351
Heaven holds all to me (Teddlie)
  R Earth holds no treasures
                                    103352
Heaven is a holy place (Naylor)
  AX283   103353

Heaven is here, where hymns of
  gladness (Adams) G461; Y221;
  AC240; AN553; AO495; BF504
                            103354
Heavenly Father, bless me now
  (Clark) G304; H58; BZ 103355
Heavenly Father, God of love
  (Wesley) BR18   103356
Heavenly Father, I would pray
  (Kurzenknabe) AO325   103357
Heavenly Father, may thy bless-
  ing (Piggott) X516   103358
Heavenly Father, may thy love
  (Guest) BV340   103359
Heavenly Father, send thy bless-
  ing (Wordsworth) D556; E593;
  H446; K559; O578; U324; V646;
  AI372; BA829   103360
Heavenly Father, thou hast brought
  us (Hawkins) W603   103361
Heavenly Father, to whose eye
  (Conder) AZ64; BA597; BR
  255   103362
Heavenly Father, we beseech
  Thee (Crosby) N360; AI345
                            103363
Heavenly Light, benignly beam-
  ing (Wallin) N325   103364
Heavenly Shepherd, Thee we
  pray (Woodhouse) D290; N287
                            103365
Heavenly Shepherd, true and holy
  (Thrupp. Hymns) BX529 X
  Saviour, like a Shepherd
                            103366
Heavenly Sower, Thou hast
  scattered (Hoppe) N79 103367
Heavenly Spirit, all others
  transcending (Brun) M469;
  O377; P229   103368
Heavenly sunlight, heavenly sun-
  light (Zelley) R Walking in
  sunlight   103369
Heavenward still our pathway
  tends (Schmolck) K516; O507;
  AK421; AZ578; BR444   103370
Heavenward stretch, my soul,
  thy pinions (Schmolck) BR444
  X Heavenward still our path-
  way   103371
Heir of all the ages, I, -- (Door)
  AN347; AQ245   103372
Heir of all the waiting ages

(Ham) AN178; AQ293 103373
Heir of the Kingdom, O why
  dost thou slumber? (---) BB
  185   103374
Heirs of unending life (Onder-
  donk) D502   103375
Helft mir Gott's Güte preisen
  (Eber) BT112   103376
He'll never forget to keep me
  (Graves) R My Father has
  many dear children   103377
Help, Helper, help in fear and
  need (Moller) AA523 103378
Help, Lord Jesus, let thy bless-
  ing (Rist) O210   103379
Help, Lord, the souls which thou
  hast made (Newman) BN186;
  BO142; BQ113   103380
Help me, dear Lord, to love
  thee more (Buchanan) BV596
                            103381
Help me, dear Saviour, thee to
  own (Coffman) R Alas! and
  did my Saviour bleed (Watts)
  R O weary wanderer   103382
Help me, Lord, by thy great
  power (Hovden) M238 103383
Help me to be holy (Gordon)
  AE185   103384
Help us, O Lord, behold, we
  enter (Rist) N58; Q120; AA
  171; BX182   103385
Help us, O Lord, thy yoke to
  wear (Cotterill) I691; AE369
                            103386
Help us, O Lord, to bear the
  cross (Sinclair) BE104
                            103387
Help us to help each other,
  Lord (Wesley) H432; I555;
  X517; AE275; AR374; AS349;
  BE105; BR285   103388
Help us to win them, help us to
  gather (Hott) R In from the
  highway   103389
Her Virgin eyes saw God incar-
  nate born (Ken) E217; F513
                            103390
Heralds of Christ, who bear the
  King's commands (Copenhaver)
  G482; J320; R498; S379; U407;
  Z533; AB377; AC258; AD374;
  AE359; AG264; AK385; AR567;

AT452; BF529; BZ   103391
Here a little child I stand (Her-
rick) X402   103392
Here at thy table, Lord, this
sacred hour (Hoyt) Z451; AO
440; AT392; BF599   103393
Here at thy table, Lord, we
meet (Stennett) L322; N242;
Z455; AS461   103394
Here behold me, as I cast me
(Neander) K273; N352; O276
103395
Here betwixt ass and oxen mild
(French, 13th c) A38 103396
Here from the world we turn
(Crosby) AM345; AP330
103397
Here I can firmly rest (Gerhardt)
AZ1317   103398
Here in our upper room with thee
(Robinson) AE336; AR508
103399
Here in the country's heart (Gale)
X518   103400
Here in the Name of Christ our
Lord (Bruiningk) BA290
103401
Here in this water I do vow thee
(Giles) BY291   103402
Here, in thy Name, eternal God
(Montgomery) K244; L291; M
515; N277; O133; Q635; AA459
103403
Here in thy presence we appear
(Clausnitzer) AZ685   103404
Here let thy people come, dear
Lord (Loveman) BH5   103405
Here, Lord, assembled in Thy
Name (Boaden) AO614 103406
Here, Lord of life and light, to
thee (Bacon) AX637   103407
Here, Lord, we offer thee all
that is fairest (Blunt) W347;
AO500; AP800; BY721 103408
Here, O God, thy healing presence
(Baum) BE109   103409
Here, O my Lord, I see the face
to face (Bonar) A208; B334;
D219; E312; F414; G415; I237;
J275; K183; L329; R442; S352;
T364; U382; V549; W323; X
270; Z458; AD401; AE333; AF
287; AG240; AH510; AK341;

AL220; AM310; AO435; AP
354; AR519; AT391; AW303;
AZ459; BA297; BE108; BF
600; BR477; BV376; BY316;
BZ   103410
Here, O my Lord, I'd see thee
face to face (Bonar) BE108
X Here, O my Lord, I see
thee   103411
Here on the paths of everyday
(Markham) AQ180   103412
Here, Saviour, we would come
(Campbell. Christian hymn
book) Z450   103413
Here we come awassailing
(English trad carol) BG15
103414
Here we come with every burden
(Slemp) R In the quiet hours
of morning   103415
Here we come with gladness
(Johnston) X386b; AW421;
BV345   103416
Here we often are perplexed
(Trabert) N142   103417
Here, where the sun shines
lovingly (Auryansen) AB303
103418
Here, while the cherubim within
the veil (Greek, 6th c) F391
103419
Here's love and grief beyond
degree (Watts) H194 103420
Herr! Dir ist Niemand zu
vergleichen! (J.A. Cramer)
BW518   103421
Herr, es ist von meinem Leben
(Neumann) BT560   103422
Herr, Gott, dich loben alle wir
(Melanchthon) BT254 103423
Herr Gott! dich will ich loben
(G. Blaurock) BU30   103424
Herr Gott, erhalt uns für und
für (Helmbold) BT288 103425
Herr Gott in deinem Reiche
(M. Schneider) BU96 103426
Herr Gott! streit wider meine
Feind (Ausbund. Psalm 35)
BU127   103427
Herr Gott! thu mich erhören
(Ausbund. Psalm 86) BU129
103428
Herr Gott Vater im Himmelreich

(Ausbund) BU63   103429

Herr Gott Vater im Himmelreich
(H. Betz) BU111   103430

Herr Gott Vater in deinem
Thron! (M.Schneider) BU85
                        103431

Herr Gott Vater, von dir allein
(H. Betz) BU112   103432

Herr Gott Vater, wir preisen dich
(Schneegass) BT124   103433

Herr Gott Vater, zu dir ich schrey
(H. Betz) BU81   103434

Herr, ich habe missgehandelt
(Franck) BT326   103435

Herr Jesu Christ, dich zu uns
wend (ascr to Wilhelm II,
Duke) AY2d; BT3   103436

Herr Jesu Christ, du hast
bereit't (Kinner) BT306 103437

Herr Jesu Christe, starker Gott,
(Ausbund) BU73   103438

Herr Jesu, der du selbst (Fischer)
BT485   103439

Herr Jesu, Licht der Heiden
(Franck) BT138   103440

Herr, öffne mir die Herzenstür
(Olearius) BT5   103441

Herr! starker Gott ins Himmels
Thron (Ausbund) BU71 103442

Herr, unser Gott, lass nicht
zuschanden werden (Heermann)
BT269   103443

Herr, wie du willst, so schick's
mit mir (Bienemann) BT406
                        103444

Herre Jesu Krist! Min Frelser
du est (Sthen) BT353   103445

Hers the Kingdom, hers the
scepter (Vere) R Holy Church
now stands   103446

Herzlich lieb hab' ich dich, o
Herr (Schalling) BT429 103447

Herzlich thut mich erfreuen Die
liebe Sommer-Zeit (Ausbund)
BU64   103448

Herzliebster Jesu, was hast du
verbrochen (Heermann) BT143;
BW534   103449

He's coming, coming, coming
soon I know (---) R How sweet
are the tidings that greet
                        103450

He's coming once again (Belden)

BB191   103451

He's risen, He's risen, Christ
Jesus, the Lord (Walther)
Q198   103452

He's the Lily of the Valley
(Fry) R I have found a friend
in Jesus   103453

Heut' fangen wir in Gottes
Nam'n (Wandersleben) BT7
                        103454

Heut Fänget an das neue Jahr
(Unparth. G. B.) AY25d
                        103455

Hibernia's Patron, Saint, all
hail (---) BO136   103456

Hic breve vivitur, hic breve
plangitur (St. Bernard of
Cluny) BT448   103457

Hide me, hide me, O blessed
Saviour, hide me (Crosby) R
Hide me, O my Saviour, hide
                        103458

Hide me, O my Saviour, hide
me (Crosby) V761; AI247;
AW483; AX513; AY71 103459

Hiding in thee (Cushing) R O
safe to the Rock that is higher
than I   103460

High in the heavens, Eternal
God (Watts) G82; H112; O67;
V94; AF82; AM52; AZ926;
BB69; BE111; BV240; BY56
                        103461

High in yonder realm of light
(Raffles) AY155 X High in
yonder realms of light
                        103462

High in yonder realms of light
(Raffles) L584; V714; AY155;
BR442   103463

High let us swell our tuneful
notes (Doddridge) F592; L
227   103464

High o'er the lonely hills,
(Struther) A473; X63; AD102;
AF42; AN96; AQ267 103465

High on his everlasting throne
(Spangenberg) I221; AZ914;
BA546   103466

High on the mountain top a banner (Johnson) BC62   103467

High-Priest before the Father's
face (Zinzendorf, N. L.) AZ

231   103468
High Priest divine, from whom
  alone (Lewis) BY348   103469
High to heaven let song be soar-
  ing (Baum) BE112   103470
High word of God, who once
  didst come (Latin, 10th c)
  E2   103471
Highly favored congregation,
  founded firm on Christ
  (Swertner) AZ900; BA263
                          103472
Highly favored congregation,
  Loved by Jesus and esteemed
  (Benade) BA263 X Highly
  favored congregation (Swertner)
                          103473
Hilf Gott dass ich mög singen
  (Ausbund) BU123   103474
Hilf, Herr Jesu, lass gelingen
  (Rist) BT120   103475
Hills of the north, rejoice (Oak-
  ley) F269; J321; R478; W372;
  Y267; AF106; AL248; BV314;
  BY374   103476
Him on yonder cross I love
  (Rube) AZ1067   103477
Him that cometh unto me (Hewitt)
  R Listen to the blessed invita-
  tion   103478
Himmel, Erde, Luft und Meer.
  (Neander) BW510   103479
Hinunter ist der Sonnenschein
  (Herman) BT563   103480
Hinweg ist mir genommen (Aus-
  bund) AU24   103481
His are the thousand sparkling
  rills (Alexander) A77; B156;
  E117; F120; W101; AM180;
  AP205   103482
His cheering message from the
  grave (Latin, 4th or 5th c)
  E124   103483
His face? I know not whether it
  be fair (Munson) AC506 103484
His flock our Shepherd feeds
  (---) BH111   103485
His Name for ever shall endure
  (Scottish Psalter, 1650) AL658;
  AM7; AW591   103486
His pow'r can make you what
  you ought to be (Nussbaum)
  R Would you live for Jesus

                          103487
His saints shall live, and to the
  King (U. P. Psalter, 1912)
  T133; AJ199   103488
His tender mercies ever sure
  (U. P. Psalter, 1912) R O
  thank the Lord, the Lord of
  love   103489
His trial o'er, and now, beneath
  His own cross (Coffin) O296
                          103490
His was no regal splendor
  (Kramer) AK127   103491
His wide dominion shall extend
  (U. P. Psalter, 1912) AJ194
                          103492
His yoke is easy, His burden
  is light (Warner) R I've
  found my Lord R The Lord is
  my Shepherd (Montgomery)
                          103493
Ho! every one that thirsts draw
  nigh (Wesley, J & C) H249;
  I258; AZ389; BA403   103494
Ho! my comrades, see the sig-
  nal (Bliss) E570; AU303
                          103495
Ho! reapers of life's harvest
  (Woodbury) AO473; BB444
                          103496
Ho! ye that rest beneath the
  Rock (Sears) BR523   103497
Ho! ye that thirst approach the
  spring (Scottish paraphrases,
  1781) AL472; AP402   103498
Ho-du la-do-noy kee tov (Jewish
  traditional) BH302   103499
"Hold fast till I come" (Belden)
  R Sweet promise is given to
  all who believe   103500
Hold o'er thy Church, Lord thy
  protecting hand (Zinzendorf,
  N. L.) AZ521   103501
Hold the fort, for I am coming
  (Bliss) R Ho! my comrades,
  see the signal   103502
Hold the ropes, then, hold them
  bravely (Jackson) R Down
  the mines   103503
Hold thou my hand! So weak I
  am, and helpless (Crosby)
  AP527; AU207; AX469; BY
  578   103504

Hold thou my hands! (Canton) E
403; W555; X519   103505

Hold to God's unchanging hand!
(Wilson) R Time is filled
103506

Hold to the rod, the iron rod
(Townsend) R To Nephi, seer
of olden time   103507

Holiness becomes Thy house,
'Tis thou who dost dwell (Armenian liturgy) BE113 103508

Holy and infinite! viewless!
eternal! (Havergal) AZ1154
103509

Holy and reverend is the name
(Needham) L92; AR24; AS10
103510

Holy, and true, and righteous
Lord (Wesley) I377   103511

Holy as thou, O Lord, is none
(Wesley) BB80   103512

Holy Bible, book divine (Burton)
H90; AI407; AK202; AM674;
AS177; AT179; AU237; AV80;
AX145; AY499; BB219; BE114
103513

Holy Bible, how I love it (Stratton) AX142   103514

Holy Church now stands triumphant
(Vere) BL66; BM94; BN200
103515

Holy day, Jehovah's rest (Belden)
BB654   103516

Holy Father, cheer our way
(Robinson) A275; B16; D9;
E270; F22; I56; K475; W282;
X47; AL553; AP667; AW254;
BR121   103517

Holy Father, great Creator
(Griswold) A267; B210; D386;
L188; BA657   103518

Holy Father, hear my cry (Bonar)
V409; AE153; AZ1068   103519

Holy Father, in thy mercy (Stevenson) A514; E520; F488; J337;
K500; N586; Q643; W629; AM630;
AP713; BA891; BV406; BY668
103520

Holy Father, thou hast given
(Bruce) W204; AC73; BF272
103521

Holy Father, thou hast taught me
(Neale) L189; M366; V344; AA

336; BE115   103522

Holy Father, thou hast taught us
(Neale) M366 X Holy Father,
thou hast taught me   103523

Holy Father! We address thee
(Peters) AZ619   103524

Holy Ghost, come down upon thy
children (Faber) E571
103525

Holy Ghost, dispel our sadness
(Gerhardt) H217; I192; N155;
O381; AL147; AM246; AO233;
AP275; AW134; AZ909; BZ
103526

Holy Ghost, Illuminater (Wordsworth) AZ969 X See the
Conqueror mounts in triumph
103527

Holy Ghost, my conforter (Latin,
9th c) O378; AL160   103528

Holy Ghost, the Infinite (Rawson)
AI118 X Come to our poor
nature's night   103529

Holy Ghost, with light divine
(Reed) H216; I185; K156;
L184; M633; N158; Q234; U
133; V218; AA259; AG127;
AH231; AI122; AN68; AO231;
AS171; AT170; AU204; AV151;
AX134; AY451; BA137; BB206;
BE118; BX98   103530

Holy God, we praise thy name
(Franz) A273; D140; J167;
Q250; AF247; AH145; AW519a;
AX10; BL82; BM91; BN196;
BO3; BP47; BQ39; BZ 103531

Holy God, we show forth here
(Dearmer) E313; X271 103532

Holy habitations, after weary
flight (---) BR448   103533

Holy, Holy, holy, blessed Lord
(Gerok) N337   103534

Holy, Holy, Holy, Blessed
Trinity (---) R Round the
throne of glory   103535

Holy, Holy, Holy is the Lord!
Sing, O ye people (Crosby)
Z97; AH205; AI31; AS11
103536

Holy, holy, holy Lord, Be thy
glorious name adored, Be
thy praise (Smith) BI26
103537

Holy, holy, holy Lord! Be thy
glorious name adored Lord
thy mercies (Williams) L72;
BR69   103538
Holy, Holy, Holy! Lord God Al-
mighty (Heber) A266; B205;
D383; E162; F160; G1; H1;
I78; J131; K158; L177; M140;
N163; O72; P232; Q246; R11;
S57; T316; U1; V88; W1;
X187; Y18; Z107; AA263; AB
17; AC4; AD25; AE155; AF
251; AG1; AH159; AI27; AK1;
AL1; AM87; AN17; AO234;
AP135; AQ4; AR1; AS17; AT
1; AU6; AV1; AW1; AX12; AY
30; AZ780; BA8; BB73; BD22;
BE117; BF186; BI25; BK41;
BL37; BM92; BR44; BV227;
BX5; BY52; BZ   103539
Holy, Holy, Holy, Lord God of
Hosts, eternal King (Words-
worth) A270; B208; D385; I77;
K159; L185; U2; V86; AO237;
AR25; AS69; AZ1258; BA257;
                          103540
Holy, holy, holy, Lord God of
Hosts, Heaven and earth
(Lathbury) R Day is dying in
the West (Lathbury)   103541
Holy, holy, holy Lord God of
Hosts! When heaven and earth
(Montgomery) N165; AK198;
AP137; AZ1064; BA11; BI38
                          103542
Holy, holy, holy, Lord, Thy
disciples Gather in devotion
(Mackaye) Y75; AC107; AD133
                          103543
Holy, holy, holy, O Thou Love
Eternal ("D.S.", 1920) AN503
                          103544
Holy, holy Lord, We with one
accord (Goldsmith) BX324
                          103545
Holy is God! The light and dark-
ness praise Him (Mary Francis,
Sr.) BN207   103546
Holy Jesus, be my light (---)
AO329   103547
Holy Jesus! Fountain streaming
(Crasselius) O279   103548
Holy Jesus! God of love (Parnell)

E314   103549
Holy Lamb, who thee confess
(Wesley) H153; AL343
                          103550
Holy Lord, By thy body given
to death (Swertner) AZ715
                          103551
Holy Lord, Holy Lord, Holy
and Almighty Lord (Gregor)
AK200; AW520   103552
Holy Lord, Holy Lord, Thanks
and praise be ever Thine
(Gregor) BA3 X Holy Lord,
Thanks and praise   103553
Holy Lord, thanks and praise
be ever Thine (Gregor) AZ
713; BA3   103554
Holy Love, from heaven de-
scended (---) BR528 103555
Holy Majesty, before thee
(Hedborn) N315 X Glorious
Majesty, before thee 103556
Holy Mary, Mother mild (---)
BO101   103557
Holy night! peaceful night!
(Mohr) O178; V749; AO132;
AP172; AV87; BI97   103558
Holy offerings, rich and rare
(Monsell) A480; B504; D478;
AO496; AZ871; BR296
                          103559
Holy patron! Thee saluting,
Here we meet (---) BO124
                          103560
Holy Queen we bend before thee
(St Bernard of Cluny) BO56
X Holy Queen we come before
thee   103561
Holy Queen, we come before thee
(St Bernard of Cluny) BN134;
BO56; BP85   103562
Holy, righteous, heavenly King
(Metcalfe) BB70   103563
Holy Saviour, truth Divine
(Longfellow) BR43 X Holy
Spirit, Truth divine 103564
Holy Saviour! we adore thee
(Deck) AZ1411   103565
Holy Spirit, breathe on me
(Hatch & McKinney) AT174;
AU417   103566
Holy Spirit, come and shine
(Latin, 9th c) AZ1124; BO

185   103567
Holy Spirit, come with light
(Grundtvig) M472   103568
Holy Spirit, faithful Guide,
Ever near the Christian's side
(Wells) G243; H213; I193; U
132; V212; Z276; AE150; AG
126; AH227; AO232; AR443;
AS252; AT165; AU245; AV152;
AW137; AX135; AY196; BB211;
BZ   103569
Holy Spirit, Faithful Guide, Lead
us heavenward (---) BB701
103570
Holy Spirit, from on high
(Bathurst) AT171   103571
Holy Spirit, gently come (Latin,
9th c) F614   103572
Holy Spirit, God of love, who
our night dost brighten (Boye)
Q230   103573
Holy Spirit, hear us, Help us
while we sing (Parker) G438;
K550; M632; W189; AL616; AM
638; AP756; BA828; BV292;
BY233   103574
Holy Spirit, hear us on this Sab-
bath day (Mohr) AO225 X
Holy Spirit, hear us on this
sacred day   103575
Holy Spirit, hear us on this sacred
day (Mohr) Q229; AA256; AO
225   103576
Holy Spirit, heavenly Dove (Little-
dale) D524   103577
Holy Spirit, in thy might (Raw-
son) AB98 X Come to our poor
nature's night   103578
Holy Spirit, lamp of light (Raw-
son) BB216 X Come to our
poor nature's night   103579
Holy Spirit, Light divine (Reed)
AN68 X Holy Ghost, with light
divine   103580
Holy Spirit, Lord of glory (Baynes)
D215; N254; BA288   103581
Holy Spirit, Lord of light (Latin,
12th c) K144; AZ1125;
BA136; BN56; BQ34   103582
Holy Spirit, Lord of love (Mac-
lagan) B371; D213; BA291;
BF612   103583
Holy Spirit, make us strong!

(Dearmer) X391   103584
Holy Spirit, Source of gladness
(Gerhardt) K147; AN3; BE
119; BX119   103585
Holy Spirit, Truth divine
(Longfellow) A377; B373;
G173; H220; J130; R240; S
208; T356; W193; X520; Y
100; Z274; AB94; AC60;
AD185; AE151; AF242; AH
232; AK188; AL154; AP284;
AR219; AW136; BF267; BK
98; BM90; BR34; BV293;BY
234; BZ   103586
Holy temples on Mount Zion
(Bennett) BC63   103587
Holy Trinity, thanks and praise
to thee (Nyberg) BA194
X Holy Trinity, we confess
with joy   103588
Holy Trinity, we confess with
joy (Nyberg) AZ537; BA194
103589
Holy Week responsories (Brev-
iary) BQ170 to 181 103590
Home, home, sweet sweet home
[slight variations] R 'Mid
pleasures and palaces (Payne)
R 'Mid scenes of confusion
(Denham)   103591
Home, sweet home! Happy
home, sweet home. ("Louisa
E. ") R I love to think of my
home above   103592
Honor and glory, power and
salvation (Housman) G16;
S42app.; X409   103593
Honor and glory, thanksgiving
and praise (Dayman) AB51
103594
Hope of Israel, Zion's army
(Townsend) BC64   103595
Hope of our hearts, O Lord,
appear (Denny) AZ1444
103596
Hope of the world, Thou Christ
of great compassion (Hark-
ness) J581; R291; AE360;
AF398; AT282; BZ   103597
Hora novissima, tempora pessi-
ma (St Bernard of Cluny)
BT605   103598
Höret, ihr Eltern, Christus

spricht (Helmbold) BT630
                               103599
Hosanna! be the children's song
   (Montgomery) H455; I679;
   AR107; AS401   103600
Hosanna, Hosanna, Hosanna in
   the highest (---) R Gather
   around the Christmas tree
                               103601
Hosanna in the highest! Our eager
   hearts (Lathrop) R O bold, O
   foolish peasants   103602
Hosanna in the highest To our
   exalted Saviour (Wesley) F421
                               103603
Hosanna, loud hosanna (Threlfall)
   G127; K545; Q161; R185; S147;
   W93; AC117; AD478; AE107;
   AG89; AH279; AK136; AL82;
   AP749; AR156; BZ   103604
Hosanna! Music is divine (Smart)
   X521   103605
Hosanna! raise the pealing hymn
   (Havergal) D559; AZ219; BA
   120   103606
Hosanna to our only Lord (---)
   R Jesus, to thee be endless
   praise   103607
Hosanna to the living Lord (Heber)
   A318; B53; D316; F241; J424;
   K425; Q70; S53; V14; AD168; AM
   314; AO63; AR200; AZ392; BA
   373; BF334; BY269   103608
Hosanna to the Prince of grace
   (Watts) AZ177   103609
Hosanna to the royal Son, Of
   David's ancient line (Watts)
   L112   103610
Hosanna we sing, like the children
   dear (Hodges) F453; AP753
                               103611
Hosanna with a cheerful sound
   (Watts) L14   103612
Hostis Herodes impie (Sedulius)
   BT131   103613
Hours and days and years and
   ages (Dutch) AI410   103614
Hover o'er me, Holy Spirit
   (Stokes) AE149; AS173; AX
   136; AY204; BB212   103615
How are thy servants blest, O
   Lord! (Addison) E542; G71;
   I102; L482; X522; AW338; AZ

124; BA550; BZ   103616
How beauteous are their feet
   (Watts) D498; F510; H460;
   L303; N283; O93; Q487;
   V558; AA490; AO454; AP
   370; AY381; BB442; BJ66;
   BR227   103617
How beauteous on the mountains,
   The feet of Him that brings
   (Gough) BE120; BR226
                               103618
How beauteous were the marks
   divine (Coxe) B108; G116;
   I127; L136; AS123; AT84;
   AU298; AV101; AZ340; BA
   80; BE352; BZ   103619
How beautiful heaven must be
   (Bridgewater) R We read
   of a place   103620
How beautiful the sight (Mont-
   gomery) AM283; AP118
                               103621
How beautiful thy temples,
   Lord   (Kooyman) BC65
                               103622
How beautiful to walk in the
   steps (Hewitt) R Trying to
   walk   103623
How beautiful upon the moun-
   tains (Bible. Isaiah 52) R
   Awake, awake   103624
How blessed are the perfect in
   the way (Westra) AJ428
                               103625
How blessed from the bonds of
   sin (Spitta) J60; K258; O254
                               103626
How blessed is the heavenly
   choice (Doddridge) BR462
   X O happy day, that [...] my
   choice   103627
How blessed is the host in
   white (Lee) P432   103628
How blessed is the little flock
   (Holm) M86; O50; P268
                               103629
How blessed is this place, O
   Lord (Ryden) J241; M513;
   N581; BZ   103630
How blest am I, most gracious
   Saviour (Dessler) AZ1088
                               103631
How blest and lovely thy earth-

ly dwellings (Augusta) AZ544;
BA334   103632
How blest are the moments that
Jesus bestows (Ahnfelt. Sanger)
N463   103633
How blest are thy who hear God's
word (Brun) J253; M19; O46;
P59; Q48   103634
How blest are thy who through
the power (Hoppe) N194
                              103635
How blest are they whose hearts
are pure (Bathurst) X523;
AW206; BE121   103636
How blest is he whose trespass
(U.P. Psalter, 1912) R281;
T53; AJ83; AM462   103637
How blest the man that fears the
Lord (U.P. Book of Psalms,
1871) AP100   103638
How blest the man who fears the
Lord. And greatly loves (U.P.
Psalter, 1912) T212; AJ305
                              103639
How blest the man, who fears to
stray. (Kennedy) BH27
                              103640
How blest the man who thoughtfully
(U.P. Psalter, 1912) T75;
AJ113   103641
How blest the perfect in the way
(U.P. Psalter, 1912) T225;
AJ321   103642
How blest the righteous when he
dies (Barbauld) H488; I582;
L567; N597; V669; AO567;
BR431   103643
How blest the sacred tie that
binds (Barbauld) BR504 103644
How blest the tie that binds
(Fawcett) BR502 X Blest be
the tie that binds   103645
How blest was that life once
lived upon earth (Turner)
AI102   103646
How bright appears the Morning
Star (Nicolai) A329; B98; J
404; X90; AB76; AW529; BA
54; BG104; BL13; BR135; BV
130   103647
How bright these glorious spirits
shine (Watts, 1707, in Scottish
Paraphrases, 1781) A127; B

302; E199; F528; W223; X207;
AL180; AM606; AP311; AZ184;
BJ40; BV464; BY405   103648
How brightly beams the Morning
Star (Nicolai) X90 X How
bright appears the Morning
Star   103649
How brightly shines the Morn-
ing Star (Nicolai) AB76 X
How bright appears the Morn-
ing Star   103650
How calm and beautiful the morn
(Hastings) L265; V158; AM
209; AR184; AS147   103651
How calm and how bright is this
holy day (Hoffman) AX66;
AY274   103652
How calmly the evening once
more is descending (Lynch)
BY696   103653
How can a sinner know (Wesley)
G208; H295; I303; BZ
                              103654
How can I cease to pray for
thee? Some where ... (Dorr)
X290   103655
How can I thank thee, Lord
(Denicke) Q417; AA344
                              103656
How can she sing in the dark like
this? (Havergal) BW454
                              103657
How charming is the place
(Stennett) H420; V7   103658
How cheering is the Christian's
hope? (---) BB387   103659
How condescending and how kind
(Watts) L138; V150   103660
How dear to me, O Lord of
Hosts (U.P. Psalter, 1912)
R440; AJ225   103661
How dear to my heart is the
story of old (Yates) AY355
                              103662
How dearly God must love us
(Partridge) BY57   103663
How did my heart rejoice to
hear (Watts) V610   103664
How excellent in all the earth
(Scottish Psalter, 1650)
AP6   103665
How fair the Church of Christ
(Kingo) O406; P79   103666

How far from home? I asked
(Smith) BB665   103667
How far is it to Bethlehem?
(Chesterton) BG142   103668
How firm a foundation, ye saints
of the Lord (Rippon's Selection
of hymns, signed "K") A564;
B212; D636; G315; H374; I461;
J558; K344; L509; M237; N439;
O340; P202; Q427; R369; S283;
T397; U205; V325; Y363; Z406;
AA375; AB174; AC74; AD233;
AE189; AF372; AG212; AH379;
AI156; AK314; AL403; AM80; AO
362; AP531; AR260; AS259; AT
262; AU199; AV228; AW151;
AX146; AY33; AZ501; BA689;
BB255; BC66; BD75; BE123;
BF413; BR248,310; BY579; BZ
                              103669
How gentle God's commands (Dodd-
ridge) G69; H124; I100; R105;
S279; T396; V356; Y384; Z399;
AB208; AD239; AE67; AF76;
AG50; AH226; AM561; AN253:
AO103; AV77; AW56; AX489;
AY401; BB64; BC67; BE124;
BF395; BR123; BX312; BZ
                              103670
How glad I am each Christmas Eve
(Wexelsen) P369 X I am so
glad each Christmas Eve
                              103671
How gladly I my place have taken
(Vig) M138; P280   103672
How glorious is the hour (Bulfinch)
BR289   103673
How glorious is the life above
(Wesley) F420   103674
How glorious is the sacred place
(Watts) V540 X How glorious
Zion's courts appear   103675
How glorious Zion's courts appear
(Watts in Scottish Paraphrases,
1781) S340; V540; AL167; AP
298   103676
How good and pleasant is the sight
(U.P. Psalter, 1912) AJ370
                              103677
How good is the God we adore
(Hart) BV30 X This God is the
God we adore   103678
How good it is for brethren (Wet-

zel) M643; P408   103679
How good it is, how pleasant to
behold (Czerwenka)[Cervenka]
AZ437; BA668   103680
How good it is to thank the
Lord and praise to Thee
Most High (U.P. Psalter,
1912) T171; AJ250; AM535
                        103681
How good it is to thank the
Lord, To praise Thy name
(Weisberg) BH109   103682
How goodly is thy house, O
Lord! (Jacobs) BH1 103683
How great, Almighty, is thy
kindness (Gellert) AW516
                        103684
How great at last my joy will
be (Bonin) AZ905   103685
How great is your name (Ladies
of the Grail) BSp.8 103686
How great the bliss to be a
sheep of Jesus (Rambach)
AZ709; BA499   103687
How great the goodness kept in
store (U.P. Psalter, 1912)
T52; AJ81; AM563   103688
How great the harvest is
(Dearmer) X169; BG152
                        103689
How great the wisdom and the
love (Snow) BC68   103690
How happy are the young who
hear (Bruce) L447; N483;
V233; AL291; AP446; AX503;
AY367; BE215   103691
How happy are these little ones
(---) AY167   103692
How happy are they who Jesus
obey (Wesley) AZ1421 X O
how happy are they who the
Saviour obey   103693
How happy are they, who their
[the] Saviour obey (Wesley)
H294 X O how happy . . .
                        103694
How happy every child of grace
(Wesley) G522; H336; I605;
BZ   103695
How happy is he born and taught
(Wotton) X524; AN294; AQ
99; AW208; BX351   103696
How happy is he born or taught

(Wotton) AN294 X How happy
is he born and taught   103697
How happy is the man who hears
(Bruce) N483 X How happy are
the young who hear   103698
How happy is the pilgrim's lot
(Wesley) I624   103699
How heart-affecting Christ to
see (Cennick) AZ885   103700
How helpless guilty nature lies
(Steele) N412; P252; V220
                            103701
How I love thy law, O Lord (U.
P. Psalter, 1912) R253; T237;
AJ333   103702
How joyful 'tis to sing (Nicholson)
F493   103703
How large the promise, how divine
(Watts) H456; V541   103704
How little our true majesty is
shown (Wheelock) AQ69
                            103705
How long? How long must we wait?
(Glasgow) R Long have we
sought   103706
How long, O Lord, most holy and
true (Widstoe) BC69   103707
How long, O Lord, our Saviour
(Deck) AZ817   103708
How long wilt thou forget me
(Sternhold) T17; AJ22; AM
541   103709
How lost was my condition (New-
ton) AZ813; BA431   103710
How lovely are thy dwellings
fair (Milton) X525; AF274;
AL660; AN19; AP68; AW592; BE
125; BH2,3; BR87; BX113
                            103711
How lovely are thy dwellings,
Lord (Milton) BE125 X How
lovely are thy dwellings fair!
                            103712
How lovely, how divinely sweet
(Steele) L53   103713
How lovely is thy dwelling-place,
O Lord of hosts, to me!
(Scottish Psalter, 1650) G383;
AL659; AP65; BZ   103714
How lovely is thy dwelling place!
Within its courts we turn to
thee (Brightbill) AR3   103715
How lovely, Lord of hosts, to me

(U. P. Psalter, 1912) AJ229
                            103716
How lovely now the Morning Star
(Wiesenmeyer) AA24 X How
lovely shines the Morning Star
                            103717
How lovely shines the Morning
Star, In twilight sky it gleams
afar (Wiesenmeyer) Q546;
AA24   103718
How lovely shines the Morning
Star, The nations see and hail
afar (Nicolai) Q343; AM434;
AZ1097   103719
CAUTION NOTE: Two poems be-
gin (in German) "Wie schön
leuchtet." Tr. as "How lovely
shines". Authors are Gerhardt
and Wiesenmeyer.   103720
How many times, discouraged
(Rexford) AX534; AY91
                            103721
How many were the silent prayers
(---) AY181   103722
How marvellous God's greatness
(Briem) J449   103723
How near to us, O God, thou art
(Hunter. Hymns of faith and
life, 1889) AD90; BF249
                            103724
How needful, strictly to inquire
(Benade) AZ883; BA623
                            103725
How oft, alas! This wretched
heart (Steele) V287; AX339;
AY208   103726
How oft have sin and Satan
strove (Watts) V335   103727
How oft, O Father, my heart is
burning (Overby) P343 103728
How pleasant and how good it is
(U. P. Psalter, 1912) T265;
AJ369; AX546   103729
How pleasant, how divinely fair
(Watts) H414; I215; V19
                            103730
How pleasant thus to dwell below
(---) AY398   103731
How pleased and blest was I
(Watts) BY270   103732
How pleasing is thy voice (Dwight)

AB384   103733

How precious is the book divine
  (Fawcett) H91; I201; N217;
  P93; Q285; U140; V74; AA111;
  AI153; AM265; AO242; AV79;
  AZ170; BA4; BR242   103734
How rich thy bounty, King of kings
  (Doddridge) I224   103735
How sad our state by nature is!
  (Watts) I268; V224; AZ108
                          103736
How shall come the Kingdom holy
  (Savage) AN358; AR573 103737
How shall I follow Him I serve
  (Conder) I339; K55; N94; AZ
  387; BA79; BB519; BY473
                          103738
How shall I meet my Saviour
  (Gerhardt) BA149 X O how
  shall I receive thee   103739
How shall I sing that Majesty
  (Mason) E404; X526; AL32;
  AP150   103740
How shall the young direct their
  way (U.P. Psalter, 1912) R258;
  T226; AJ322; AM264   103741
How shall the young secure their
  hearts (Watts) I204; L315; N
  223; O573; P379; Q286; V76;
  AA112; AO241; AS404   103742
How shall we celebrate thy love
  (Proud) BR239   103743
How shall we stand in that great
  day (Belden) R The judgment
  has set, the books have been
  opened   103744
How short and hasty is our life
  (Watts) L372   103745
How solemn are the words (Mid-
  lane) BA426   103746
How strong and sweet my Father's
  care (---) Z168; AC53; AO96;
  AR81   103747
How sweet and awful is the place
  (Watts) V448; AM271   103748
How sweet and silent is the place
  (Palmer) AB326; AH509; AN
  446; BF602; BX478   103749
How sweet are the tidings that
  greet the pilgrim's ear (---)
  BB669   103750
How sweet, how heavenly is the
  sight (Swain) H425; I554; U372;

V612; Z475; AI275; AO428;
  AW323; AX544; AY358; AZ
  112; BA674; BB431; BE126
                          103751
How sweet the light of Sabbath
  Eve! (Edmeston) BB460 X
  Sweet is the light of Sabbath
                          103752
How sweet the name of Jesus
  sounds (Newton) A455; B
  232; D433; E405; F192; G
  347; H235; I137; J406; K343;
  L165; N54; O417; P278; Q
  364; R130; S310; T424; U75;
  V374; W419; X527; Z264;
  AA96; AB254; AE104; AF
  221; AG185; AH317; AI427;
  AL306; AM544; AO282; AP
  457; AR108; AS286; AT160;
  AU455; AV135; AX14; AY21;
  AZ139; BA65; BB150; BJ50;
  BR163; BV260; BY203; BZ
                          103753
How sweet this bond of perfect-
  ness (Warner) AX550
                          103754
How sweet thy dwellings, Lord,
  how fair (Merrick) AZ683
                          103755
How sweet to leave the world
  awhile (Kelly) AZ391
                          103756
How sweet upon this sacred day
  (Follen) BB458   103757
How sweetly flowed the gospel
  sound (Bowring) H157; I290;
  V136; BE128   103758
How swift the torrent rolls
  (Doddridge) I580   103759
How tedious and tasteless the
  hours (Newton) G349; I538;
  V371; AH368; AI271; AT306;
  AU24; AV180; AZ1508; BB
  660   103760
How to reach the masses, men
  of every birth (Oatman) AU
  60   103761
How vain is all beneath the
  skies (Ford) BB490 103762
How vain the cruel Herod's fear
  (Sedulius) F74   103763
How vast the benefits divine
  (Toplady) AI127; AM95

103764
How vast the treasure we possess!
  (Watts) BY497   103765
How welcome was the call (Baker)
  AO560; AP706; AZ1371; BA846
                            103766
How wondrous and great Thy
  works, God of praise
  (Onderdonk) A260; B254; D467;
  N372; BC146   103767
How wondrous is Thy mercy,
  Lord (Bible. Psalm 36: Danish
  version) BE130   103768
How wondrous is thy world, O
  Lord (Lucas) BH56   103769
Humble praises, holy Jesus (---)
  N643; AI380   103770
Humble thyself and the Lord will
  draw near thee (Oatman) R If
  thou wouldst have   103771
Humbly I adore thee (St Thomas
  Aquinas) A204; BP49   103772
Humbly we adore thee, Christ,
  Redeemer King (St Thomas
  Aquinas) BM10   103773
Humility, thou secret vale (Schell)
  AX431   103774
Hush all ye sounds of war
  (Draper) Z195   103775
Hush! blessed are the dead
  (Bickersteth) AP618; AZ479
                            103776
Hush! dear child, lie still and
  slumber (Watts) BA851 X
  Hush! my dear, lie still
                            103777
Hush! my dear, lie still and
  slumber (Watts) A242; N656;
  X382; BA851; BG130   103778
Hushed was the evening hymn
  (Burns) B359; D568; G451;
  I674; W251; AH364; AI374; AL
  211; AM655; AO626; AP806;
  AW416; BB428; BC252; BD196;
  BK23; BV361; BX518; BY474
                            103779

I

I aint gwine study war no more
  (Negro spiritual) X Gwine to
  lay down my burden   103780
I am a little child, you see

(Zinzendorf, N. L.) BA840
  X Thou, gracious Saviour, for
  my good   103781
I am a part of all that I have
  met (Tennyson) AQ65 103782
I am a poor, way-faring strang-
  er (White spiritual) AU74
                            103783
I am a stranger here, within a
  foreign land (Cassel) AI197;
  AM695; AT433   103784
I am baptized into thy name
  (Rambach) L320; M539; P98
                            103785
I am bought not with riches
  (Kidder) AU337; AX486; AY
  371; BB617   103786
I am bound for the promised
  land (Stennett) AH529 X On
  Jordan's stormy banks 103787
I am coming Lord! Coming now
  to thee (Hartsough) R I Hear
  thy welcome voice   103788
I am coming to the cross (Mc-
  Donald) G246; H272; I351;
  R278; U177; V747; AH339; AP
  430; AR257; AT243; AU260;
  AV173; AX306; BA903; BB600;
  BZ   103789
I am content! My Jesus liveth
  still (Möller) Q196; AA226
                            103790
I am dwelling on the mountain
  (---) AU27; AY353   103791
I am fighting in the army of the
  Lord (Henry) AX180 103792
I am happy today (McConnell)
  AT209   103793
I am in my Father's keeping
  (Morris) R When the early
  morning breaking   103794
I am Jesus' Little lamb (Hayn)
  K556; N650; Q648; AM643;
  AW430   103795
I am looking for the city built of
  God (Hott) AX269; AY146
                            103796
"I am nearing the port" (Dale)
  AY162   103797
I am needy, yet forgiven (Zinzen-
  dorf, C.R.) AZ425   103798
I am not skilled to understand
  (Greenwell) S326; W698; BV

624; BY204   103799

I am not worthy, holy Lord (Baker)
B323; D234; N248; S498; W316;
AD200; AI220; AL223; AP363;
BA298; BV377   103800

I am redeemed but not with silver
(Gray) R Nor silver nor gold
                                    103801

I am resolved no longer to linger
(Hartsough) AT216; AU105;
AX298   103802

I am satisfied with Jesus (Mc-
Kinney) AT436; AU375   103803

I am so glad each Christmas-
Eve (Wexelsen) J45; P369
                                    103804

I am so glad that Jesus loves me
(Oakey) R I am so glad that
our Father in heaven   103805

I am so glad that our Father in
heaven (Oakey) G435; AH543;
AL480; AM647; AP742; AT509;
AU319; AX38; AY484; BB423;
BY498   103806

I am so happy in Christ today
(Oatman) AT194   103807

I am the Lord, O hear my voice
(Scheffler) AW565   103808

I am the vine and ye are the
branches (Shaw) AX414 103809

I am the way, the truth, the life
(Caswall) BE131   103810

I am thine, O Lord, I have heard
thy voice (Crosby) G252; H345;
R320; U217; V734; Z312; AE
191; AG148; AH361; AI272; AL
490; AM713; AO648; AP483;
AR444; AS232; AT349; AU56;
AV368; AW475; AX411; AY473;
BB594; BZ   103811

I am thinking today of that beautiful land (Hewitt) AT470; AY
508; BB626   103812

I am trusting day by day in his
word (Newell) AX460; AY97
                                    103813

I am trusting in my Saviour
(Lyon) AX462; AY94   103814

I am trusting, Lord, in thee
(McDonald) R I am coming to
the cross   103815

I am trusting thee, Lord Jesus
(Havergal) Q428; S287; U176;

V353; W695; AA370; AI242;
AM424; AO352; AP502; AR
265; AS265; AV202; AZ1139;
BA716; BB256; BF351; BV
498; BY432   103816

I am whatever you make me,
nothing more (Lane) AC516
                                    103817

I ask not, Lord, for less to
bear (Smith) BB251   103818

I ask thee for the daily strength
(Waring) BX292   103819

I believe in thee, Lord Jesus
(Wine) AR507   103820

I believe the Bible, it taught me
how to pray (Ufford) AX139
                                    103821

I believe the promises of God
(Smith) R I was wandering
                                    103822

I belong to Jesus (Fraser) AI
253; AM649   103823

I bind my heart this tide (Watt)
R286; S243; Y143; Z302; AB
163; AC121; AE444; AG169;
AK251; AR356   103824

I bind unto myself today (St
Patrick) A268; B525; E212;
F162; W506; X528; BV229;
BY433   103825

I bless the Christ of God
(Bonar) BY434   103826

I bless thee, Father, for the
grace (Aguilar) BH115
                                    103827

I bless thee, Lord, for sorrows sent (Johnson) BX257
X I praise thee, Lord for
blessings sent   103828

I bow in utter need and mortal
weakness (Plummer) BI65
                                    103829

I bow my forehead in the dust
(Whittier) I472; J371; N414;
R109; S282; T398; U31; AB
211; AI218; AK310; AO343
                                    103830

I bow my forehead to the dust
(Whittier) J371 X I bow my
forehead in the dust 103831

I bring my hymn of thankfulness
(Cooke) BX317   103832

I bring my sins to Jesus (Bonar)

AY228 I lay my sins on Jesus
103833

I came defiled and guilty (Teasley)
AX337   103834

I came not hither of my will
(Hosmer) AN252; BX298
103835

I can hear my Saviour calling
(Blandly) AH336; AR248; AS
207; AT361; AU164; AV338;
AW500; AY115   103836

I cannot always trace the way
(Bowring) BE133; BR341; BX
260   103837

I cannot be idle, for Jesus says,
"Go." (Henry) AX190   103838

I cannot find thee! Still on restless pinion (Scudder) Y4; AB
36; AN72; BX108   103839

I cannot put the Presence by
(Kemp) AC139   103840

I cannot tell thee whence it came
(Brown) AS306   103841

I cannot tell why He, whom angels
worship (Fullerton) BV262;
BY183   103842

I cannot think of them as dead
(Hosmer) AN202 X We cannot
think . . .   103843

I cannot think or reason (Wattles)
Y72; AC122   103844

I close my heavy eye (Bonar)
BR336   103845

I come, invited by thy word
(Kingo) M53   103846

I come, O Saviour, to thy table
(Heyder) Q315   103847

I come to the garden alone
(Miles) AH329; AU356; BB606
103848

I come to thee, O blessed Lord
(Landstad) M54; O101; P104;
Q330   103849

I come to thee, O Father (Moser)
BB286   103850

I constant care will take (U. P.
Psalter, 1912) T69; AJ105
103851

I could not do without thee (Havergal) B239; D603; E572; F353;
I353; M162; O472; P276; S311;
U190; V302; AI109; AZ809; BA
485; BV485   103852

I cried to God in my distress
(U. P. Psalter, 1912) T247;
AJ343   103853

I dared not hope that thou wouldst
deisn to come (Hatch) AD
240   103854

I did thee wrong, my God
(Bonar) AZ481   103855

I do not ask, O Lord, that
life may be (Proctor) B385;
D633; I542; S305; U43; Z340;
AD266; AE204; AL431; AP
505; AR402; AW471; BA507;
BF420; BR392   103856

I do not ask to choose my path
(Zelley) AX416   103857

I do not come because my soul
(St John) Q379; AA316
103858

I entered once a home of care
(---) AY110   103859

I fell asleep in Jesus' wounds
(Eber) Q585; AA545 103860

I feel the winds of God today
(Adams) W528; Z301; AW
391   103861

I gave my life for thee (Havergal) M182; Q405; U163; V
748; AE171; AG145; AH287;
AI138; AS244; AT399; AU222;
AV378; AX312; BB230;
103862

I give my heart to thee (Latin,
9th c) BB285; BY435
103863

I give myself to thee (Symons)
BV338   103864

I go to prove my soul (Browning) AC443   103865

I graciously will teach thee
(U. P. Psalter, 1912) T54;
AJ84   103866

I greet thee, who my sure Re-
deemer art (Calvin) R144;
AD77; AF207; AI232; AK277;
AM135; AO609   103867

I have a friend in whom I trust
(Presley) AX538   103868

I have a friend so patient, kind,
forbearing (Rosenius) M626;
N468; P295   103869

I have a Friend so precious
(Lancaster) AO611; AY326;

BB533   103870
I have a home above (Bennett)
L601   103871
I have a mother yonder (Negro
spiritual) AH596   103872
I have a Saviour, He's pleading
in glory (Clough) G237; AE
166; AH435; AS197; AT232;
AU78; AV332; AW460; AX367;
BB575   103873
I have a song I love to sing (Ex-
cell) AT208; AU108; BB638
103874
I have chosen thee, my Saviour
(German) M550   103875
I have decided to follow Jesus
(---) AX304   103876
I have followed Truth and Justice
(U.P. Psalter, 1912) T240;
AJ336   103877
I have found a friend in Jesus
(Fry) AT87; AU363; AW446;
AX25   103878
I have head of a land on the far-
away strand (Moore) AU348
103879
I have heard thy voice, Lord
Jesus (Cherry) P322   103880
I have made my choice to follow
(Leech) AS336; AX181 103881
I have read of a beautiful city
(Atchinson) AU386   103882
I have ridden the wind (Rice)
Y7   103883
I have something I would tell you
(Latta) AX334; AY344 103884
I have work enough to do (Pollard)
BC71   103885
I have yielded myself to thy serv-
ice (Naylor) AX392   103886
I hear a sweet voice ringing clear
(Hood) L502   103887
I hear a voice that comes from
far (Kelly) V275   103888
I hear in the air, 'neath the canopy
blue (Kuipers) AI199   103889
I hear the Saviour say (Hall) Z
284; AM690; AT225; AU258;
AV337; AW462; AX320; AY235;
BB527   103890
I hear the words of love (Bonar)
V396; AZ1487; BV503   103891
I hear thy voice, within the silence

speaking (Ham) AN232; BF
266; BX269   103892
I hear thy welcome voice (Hart-
sough) E573; P262; W689;
AH240; AL481; AM406; AP
435; AR446; AS204; AT224;
AU265; AV170; AX299; BA
908; BB224   103893
I heard a sound of voices (Thring)
A593; B542; D404; I626; J597;
S437; U433; AO552   103894
I heard the bells on Christmas
Day (Longfellow) AB361; AD
124; AH267; AN161; AR133;
AT78; AU148; BC219; BF294;
BX193   103895
I heard the dear Redeemer say
(Warner) AX406   103896
I heard the voice of Jesus say
(Bonar) A424; B242; D673;
E574; F351; G210; H297; I304;
J499; K365; L161; M163; N
432; O395; Q277; R280; S236;
T385; U183; V297; W410; X
529; Y83; Z288; AA46; AB199;
AC147; AD204; AE170; AG
163; AH332; AI203; AK236;
AL271; AM221; AO246; AP
412; AR267; AS302; AT302;
AU163; AV175; AW142; AX
329; AY472; AZ1464; BA505;
BB225; BF344; BJ17; BR393;
BV513; BY436; BZ   103897
I hope for the salvation of the
Lord (Abraham ibn Ezra)
BH92   103898
I hunger and I thirst (Monsell)
B325; D343; F413; L331; V
455; X272; AW308; BA299;
BV378; BY317   103899
I Hus og Hjem, hvor Mand og
Viv (Landstad) BT624 103900
I intend to go through (Buffum)
R My heart is so happy
103901
I joyed when to the house of
God (Scottish Psalter, 1650)
AL682; AP110; AW599 103902
I kneel in spirit at my Saviour's
cross (Cennick) AZ436
103903
I know a flower so fair and fine
(Gruntvig) P380   103904

I know a kingdom without end
(German, 16th c. or earlier)
P117   103905
I know a lovely Angel-game
(Laufenberg) BG145 notes
103906
I know a rose-tree springing
(Speier Gebetbuch, 1599) A17
103907
I know a soul that is steeped in
sin (---) AC467   103908
I know a way beseiged and throng-
ing (Gjertsen) P306   103909
I know, I know, I have another
building R Christ went a build-
ing   103910
I know I love thee better, Lord
(Havergal) AS283; AU94; AX479
103911
I know in my heart what it means
(Teasley) R When I read how
my Saviour   103912
I know in whom I trust (Wallin)
N434   103913
I know my faith is founded (Neu-
meister) Q381   103914
I know my heavenly Father knows
(Henry) BB591   103915
I know no life divided (Spitta)
H317; AV174; BE135   103916
I know not how that Bethlehem's
babe (Farrington) A330; G112;
P206; R224; S181; U204; Z206;
AC143; AF149; AG118; AH321;
AK241; AR270; AT276; AW99;
BF330; BZ   103917
I know not the hour (Bliss) AU
341   103918
I know not what the future hath
(Whittier) A441; G517; H359;
J593; W558; X530; Z571; AC
332; AD465; AF360; AL427;
AN78; AP520; AR422; AW241;
BA707; BF665; BX469   103919
I know not where the road may
lead (Cummins) A432   103920
I know not why God's wondrous
grace (Whittle) AE221; AH385;
AI252; AM712; AR447; AT275;
AW450; AX478; AY459; BY437
103921
I know of a river whose beautiful
stream (---) AX257   103922

I know of a sleep in Jesus'
name (Landstad) J299; M
299; O506; P331; Q592
103923
I know that, He liveth, Redeemer
and Friend (Turner) R How
blest was that life   103924
I know that my Redeemer lives,
and ever prays for me (Wes-
ley) H183; I370; V175; AA
245; AH310; AI254; AM586;
AO214; AS163; AV118
103925
I know that my Redeemer lives;
He lives, and on the earth
(Wesley) BB488   103926
I know that my Redeemer lives;
He lives, who once was dead
(Wesley) Z245   103927
I know that my Redeemer lives,
In this my faith is fast (Ger-
hardt) O332   103928
I know that my Redeemer lives;
O the sweet joy (Medley)
BV185 X I know that my Re-
deemer lives; What joy the
blest   103929
I know that my Redeemer lives;
What comfort this sweet sen-
tence gives (Medley) M438
X I know that my Redeemer
lives! What joy the blest
103930
I know that my Redeemer lives;
What joy the blest (Medley)
G329; H182; I168; J387; K
136; M438; N124; P203; Q
200; AA229; AE120; AR186;
AS151; AZ294, 350; BA236;
BC95; BV185; BY174;BZ
103931
I know that my Redeemer liveth,
and on the earth (Pounds)
Z255; AR448; AT127; AU
413; AW453; AY491 103932
I know that the Lord is almighty
(U.P. Psalter, 1912) T269;
AJ373   103933
I know the Bible was sent from
God (McKinney) AT184
103934
I know whom I believe in
(Arndt) M651   103935

I lay my sins on Jesus (Bonar)
  D605; E575; G230; H246; I488;
  J492; K338; L499; M197; N418;
  O439; P273; Q652; T386; U191;
  V299; W694; AA322; AL486;
  AM430; AO266; AP413; AT210;
  AV166; AW444; AY228; AZ833;
  BA432; BB278   103936
I learned it in the meadow path
  (Larcom) X531; AB310 103937
I leave all things to God's direc-
  tion (Franck) Q529; AA499
                        103938
I leave the burdens of my life
  (Navra) BH221   103939
I leave thee not, thou art my
  Jesus ever (Dessler) AA87
                        103940
I lift mine eyes unto the hills
  (Caddell) BH33   103941
I lift my eyes unto heaven above
  (Runeberg) J396   103942
I lift my heart to Thee, Saviour
  divine (Mudie) H337; L453;
  O398; W427; AI320; AS277;
  AZ444; BA482; BY438   103943
I lift up my eyes to the mountains;
  from whence shall come my
  help? (Ladies of the Grail)
  BSp.40   103944
I little see, I little know (Hosmer)
  I450; BX229   103945
I live, and I know the span of my
  years (Ingemann) M239 103946
I live for those who love me
  (Banks) AS411; AV227 103947
I long for household voices gone
  (Whittier) BX469 X I know not
  what the future hath   103948
I long to behold Him arrayed
  (Wesley) BB200   103949
I look not back; God knows the
  fruitless efforts (---) N431;
  AI235   103950
I look to Jesus, and the face
  (---) L468   103951
I look to thee in every need
  (Longfellow) B397; E406; G
  325; I473; J490; R114; S79;
  X532; AB200; AD237; AF92;
  AN258; AR83; AW244; BE134;
  BF402; BX284; BZ   103952
I love all beauteous things

I love God's tiny creatures
  (Briggs) X361   103954
I love Him, I love Him, Be-
  cause He first loved me
  (---) R Gone from my heart
                        103955
I love the Lord, because He
  heareth me (Collier) AI416
                        103956
I love the Lord, because my
  voice (Scottish Psalter, 1650)
  AL675; AP102; AW597
                        103957
I love the Lord for he has
  heard the cry of my appeal
  (Ladies of the Grail) BSp.
  34   103958
I love the Lord, for my request
  and humble plea (U.P.
  Psalter, 1912) T217; AJ310
                        103959
I love the Lord: he heard my
  cries (Watts) H360; L452;
                        103960
I love the Lord; he heard my
  voice (Proud) BR415
                        103961
I love the Lord! He lent an ear
  (Montgomery) AZ105
                        103962
I love the Lord, his strength is
  mine (U. P. Psalter, 1912)
  R370; AJ34   103963
I love the Lord, the fount of
  grace (Kuipers) AJ426
                        103964
I love the Lord who died for
  me (Cennick) AZ335 103965
I love the Lord who heard my
  cry, and granted my request
  (U. P. Psalter, 1912) T219;
  AJ312   103966
I love the sacred book of God
  (Kelly) BB220   103967
I love the voice Divine that
  speaks (Proud) BR355
                        103968
I love Thee, I love Thee (---)
  AT150; BB343   103969
I love thee, O thou Lord most
  high (Cologne Psalteriolium,
  1710) BN209   103970

(Bridges) AQ137   103953

I love thy Church, O God (Dwight) AN411 X I love thy kingdom, Lord   103971

I love thy Kingdom, Lord (Dwight) A388; B315; D485; G379; H418; I208; J158; K199; L292; M79; N261; O89; P83; Q462; R435; S337; T359; U353; V606; W 210; Y381; Z428; AA468; AB 323; AC311; AD398; AE316; AF269; AG233; AH516; AI146; AK329; AL172; AM280; AN411; AO419; AP300; AR490; AS191; AT382; AU196; AV247; AW275; AX149; AY380; AZ1352; BA331; BF591; BZ   103972

I love thy way of freedom, Lord (Hay) BE136   103973

I love thy Zion, Lord (Dwight) L292; X I love thy Kingdom, Lord   103974

I love to hear the story, how the Lord from heaven came (---) BR545   103975

I love to hear the story which angel voices tell (Miller) E 594; F445; N632; P364; S447; W71; AL69; AO623; AP739; AS402; BA816; BV347; BY119   103976

I love to steal awhile away (Brown) G55; H46; I498; L429; N555; U259; V44; AI226; AR51; AS49; AV18; AX72; AY291; BB317   103977

I love to tell the story (Hankey) G249; H240; I544; J324; P388; R383; S443; U312; V236; Z532; AD253; AF317; AG186; AH346; AI390; AK467; AL504; AM387; AO635; AP592; AR440; AS295; AT141; AU371; AV385; AW493; AX200; AY348; BA906; BB518; BE414; BY415; BZ   103978

I love to think of my home above ("Louisa E") AS478; AX586; AY151   103979

I love to think that Jesus saw (Skemp) AF480   103980

I may not climb the heights which saints (Tiplady) AR431 103981

I must needs go home (Pounds) AT196; AX424   103982

I must tell Jesus all of my trials (Hoffman) AT298; AV347; AX 357; AY449   103983

I name thy hallowed name (Benson) S253; AX63   103984

I near the grave, where'er I go (Brorson) N603   103985

I need no other plea (Elliott) AZ1226   103986

I need not care if days to come be dark or fair (Bradley) BR253   103987

I need thee every hour (Hawks) A438; D602; G232; H55; I506; J479; L401; M629; N462; P 319; R324; S332; T407; U303; V492; W700; Z341; AC150; AD275; AE196; AF342; AG 170; AH322; AK469; AL493; AM710; AO640; AP480; AR 306; AS218; AT334; AU193; AV346; AW187; AX354; AY68; BB258; BC79; BE137; BF364; BY475; BZ   103988

I need thee, Lord (Lear) R The way is dark   103989

I need thee, O I need thee (Lowry) R I need thee every hour (Hawks)   103990

I need thee, precious Jesus (Whitfield) D601; E576; K367; N450; O231; P155; AI221; AL 487; AM419; AO271; AP414; AS216; AT221; AV153; AX338; AY73; AZ836; BA412; BB605; BQ41   103991

I never can forget the day (Van de Venter) AU95   103992

I now have found for hope of heaven (Rothe) AK224   103993

I once was a stranger to grace and to God (McCheyne) V307   103994

I open wide the portals of my heart (Hoppe) M203   103995

I ought to love my Saviour (---) P372   103996

I owe the Lord a morning song (Herr) AX58; AY278 103997

I place myself in Jesus' hands (Spitta) O163   103998

I praise thee, Lord, for blessings sent (Johnson) BE138; BX256   103999

I praise thee, O my God and Father (Mentzer) O10   104000

I praised the earth, in beauty seen (Heber) A306; F173; X 533   104001

I pray thee, dear Lord Jesus (Kingo) Q655   104002

I pray thee, Lord, to guide my ways (Watts) BI4   104003

I rejoiced when I heard them say (Ladies of the Grail) BSp.42   104004

I saw a fair maiden sitten and sing (English trad carol, 15th c) BG182   104005

I saw a mighty angel fly (---) BC255   104006

I saw a way-worn trav'ler (Matthias) AY132   104007

I saw Him in childhood with eyes brightly beaming (Birkedal) P308   104008

I saw One hanging on a tree (Newton) AU410   104009

I saw One weary, sad, and torn (Smith) BB371   104010

I saw the city of the Lord (Tarrant) Y62; AN394; AQ 204; BX428   104011

I saw the cross of Jesus (Whitfield) AT190; AU20   104012

I saw the holy city (Thring) I626 X I heard a sound a voices   104013

I saw three ships come sailing in (English trad carol) BG18   104014

I say to all men, far and near (Hardenburg) AB148; AZ95   104015

I see a Man at God's right hand (Bonar) AZ1435   104016

I see by rays surrounded (St Bernard of Clairvaux) BP71   104017

I see my Jesus crucified (---) BQ24   104018

I see my Saviour languish (Wobeser) AZ792   104019

I see the crowd in Pilate's hall (Bonar) AZ106   104020

I see the wrong that round me lies (Whittier) AN256; BX 253   104021

I see thee standing, Lamb of God (Brorson) M407; P220   104022

I serve a living Saviour (Ackley) AE287; AT279   104023

I shall approach the altar of the Lord (Burke) BL42   104024

I shall be like Him (Spencer) R When I shall reach104025

I shall go out as all men go (Pulsifer) Y130   104026

I shall know Him, I shall know Him (Crosby) R When my life work is ended   104027

I shall not want; in deserts wild (Deems) I436   104028

I shot an arrow into the air (Longfellow) AC503 104029

I sing a song of the saints of God (Scott) A243; AF481; BY259   104030

I sing of a maiden that is makè less (English trad carol, 15th c) BG183   104031

I sing the almighty power of God (Watts) H102; R84; S65; U12; V97; AE56; AF68; AG 37; AI43; AM106; AR95; AW 47; BB93; BD38; BV241; BX 64; BY58; BZ   104032

I sing the birth was born to-night (Jonson) F70; BG168   104033

I sing the mighty power of God (Watts) R84 X I sing the almighty power   104034

I sing the praise of love unbounded (Tersteegen) AK17   104035

I sing to thee with voice and heart (Gerhardt) O384; AI 294   104036

I smite upon my guilty breast (Gregor) AZ688   104037

I sought his love in sun and stars (Clark) Y8; Z385; AC142; AR89   104038

I sought the Lord, and afterward I knew (Holy songs, carols and sacred ballads,

1878) A405; B398; G316; J473;
R402; S324; U193; Z403; AD
281; AF408; AG220; AI133;
AK237; AM397; AR179; BR417;
BY499; BZ   104039

I sought thee round about, O thou
my God (Heywood) X534
104040

I stand all amazed at the love
Jesus offers (Gabriel) BC80
104041

I stand amazed in the presence
(Gabriel) AH304; AT139; AX
24   104042

I stood alone at the bar of God
(Hussey) AU447   104043

I stood at the time-beaten portals
(Teasley) AX296   104044

I surrender all (Van Deventer) R
All to Jesus I surrender
104045

I thank the Lord, my Maker
(MacKellar) AX632; AY302
104046

I thank thee, Lord, for life
(Butcher) AC166; BY500
104047

I thank thee, Lord, for precious
things (Larcom) AN271; BX
320   104048

I thank thee, Lord, for strength
of arm (Davis) S397; Y211;
Z499; AD320; AN279; AR375;
BD135; BF505; BX334   104049

I thank thee, Savior, for the grief
(Loy) M277   104050

I thank thee that how e'er we
climb (Coates) Y154; AB302
104051

I thank thee, uncreated Sun
(Scheffler) I367   104052

"I the good fight have fought."
(Wesley) I391   104053

I think of a city I have not seen
(Tuttle) AY187   104054

I think that I shall never see
(Kilmer) AC437   104055

I think when I read that sweet
story of old (Luke) A246;
B350; D562; E595; G440; H452;
I682; J497; K557; L450; N649;
P359; R460; S442; U325; V645;
W82; Z213; AD475; AE433; AF

483; AH553; AI384; AK460;
AL603; AM650; AO622; AP
738; AR549; AS398; AT506;
AU316; AV86; AW427; AY
342; AZ499; BA832; BB422;
BD64; BR539; BV346; BY
120   104056

I thirst, thou wounded Lamb of
God (Zinzendorf, N. L.) H339;
I335; AO292   104057

I thought upon the days of old
(U. P. Psalter, 1912) T143;
AJ212   104058

I to the hills will lift mine
eyes, From whence doth come
mine aid? (Scottish Psalter,
1650) X410; AF85; AL680;
AP108; BY59   104059

I to the hills will lift my eyes,
O whence shall come my aid
(U. P. Psalter, 1912) R377;
AJ344; BZ   104060

I trusted even when I said
(Ladies of the Grail) BS
p. 36   104061

I vow to thee, my country, all
earthly things above (Spring-
Rice) Y126 X I vow to thee,
my country, all other things
above   104062

I vow to thee, my country, all
other things above (Spring-
Rice) F579; X319; Y126;
AC331; BY642   104063

I wait for thy salvation, Lord
(Watts) V402   104064

I waited for the Lord Most High
(U. P. Psalter, 1912) AJ111;
AM523   104065

I waited for the Lord my God,
and patiently did bear (Scottish Psalter, 1650) AL648;
AP36; AW585; BY501 104066

I waited for the Lord my God,
Yea patiently drew near (U.
P. Psalter, 1912) R413; T72;
AJ108   104067

I walk amidst thy beauty forth
(Gill) AN136; AQ327; BX
166   104068

I walk in danger all the way
(Brorson) O269; P313; Q413
104069

I walk the unfrequented road
(Hosmer) AQ277   104070

I walk with Love along the way
(Ayers) BE139   104071

I wander through the stilly night
(Curtis) BC294   104072

I wandered in the shades of night
(Van Deventer) AU376 104073

Iwwant a principle within (Wesley)
G299; I320; BR291; BZ 104074

I want to be a worker for the
Lord (Baltzell) AX184 104075

I want to be more like Jesus
(Stillman) AS226; AX376
104076

I want to love Him more (Snyder)
R There is a story   104077

I was a wandering sheep (Bonar)
H299; I300; L128; V382; AA
105; AI222; AM396; AV171;
AZ1489; BA454   104078

I was made a Christian (Jones)
K552   104079

I was once far away from the
Saviour (Bobbitt) AX340
104080

I was sinking deep in sin (Rowe)
AH340; AT212; AU352; AX330
104081

I was wandering and weary
(Faber) AL484; AP422 104082

I was wandering in a wilderness of
deep despair and sin (Smith)
AX472; AY124   104083

I will a little pilgrim be (Cennick)
AZ370   104084

I will arise and to my Father go
(Earle) X411   104085

I will be true to Thee, Lord
(Morris) R Fully surrendered,
Lord divine   104086

I will bless thee, said the Saviour
(Kretzmann) M532   104087

I will early seek the Saviour
(Bateman) BB417   104088

I will ever sing thy praises (Gotter)
AK18   104089

I will extol thee, O my God (U.P.
Psalter, 1912) AJ394 104090

I will follow the upward road today (Edgar) AC502   104091

I will follow thee, my Saviour
(Lawson) BB266   104092

I will guide thee, I will guide
thee (Niles) R Precious
promise   104093

I will hasten to Him (Hartsough)
R I am resolved no longer to
linger   104094

I will leave my Jesus never!
(Keimann) O338   104095

I will love thee, all my treasure
(Scheffler) AO293   104096

I will never, never leave thee
(---) BB397   104097

I will never turn back, He's my
light (Grisham) R Once I
wandered   104098

I will not be afraid (Govan)
AE453; AR323   104099

"I will not forget thee" (Gabriel)
R Sweet is the promise
104100

I will press the battle on till
the victory is won (Henry)
R I am fighting   104101

I will rejoice in God, my
Saviour (LaTrobe) AZ1414
104102

I will sing my Maker's praises
(Gerhardt) O436; Q25; AA65
104103

I will sing of Jesus' love
(Belden) BB529   104104

I will sing of my Redeemer
(Bliss) AI10; AM681; AT143;
AU388; AX8   104105

I will sing the wondrous story
(Rowley) W683; AE293; AK
465; AM709; AO651; AT144;
AU377; AV315; BV261; BY
502   104106

I will sing to my Creator (Gerhardt) AZ1082; BA28
104107

I will sing to you a song of that
beautiful land (Gates) G525;
AM729; AS472; AU42; AV399;
AX588; AY164; BB552
104108

I will work, I will pray (Baltzell) R I want to be a worker   104109

I wonder, often wonder (Hoffman) AX30; AY346 104110

I worship thee, Lord Jesus

If God had not been on our side
(Luther) Q267   104149
If God Himself be for me (Ger-
hardt) K335; M274; N473; O272;
P275; Q528; AA526   104150
If God were not upon our side
(Jonas) AA284   104151
If great wonders thou desirest
(Latin) BQ100   104152
If human kindness meets return
(Noel) I236; AZ1451   104153
If I can keep one spirit singing
(Marlatt) AC242 X If I can stop
one heart from breaking (Dick-
inson)   104154
If I can stop one heart from
breaking (Dickinson) Y226;
AC242   104155
If I come to Jesus, He will make
me glad (Crosby) W669; AP
759; BV349   104156
If I walk in the pathway of duty
(Oatman) AX580   104157
If I would be a child of God
(Forney) AX174   104158
If Jesus Christ is a man (Gilder)
AC460   104159
If, now, thou seekest miracles
(Franciscan manual) BN173
                        104160
If, on a quiet sea, toward heaven
(Toplady) G321; H355; I446;
V433; AI335; AV291; BB249;
BZ   104161
If on our daily course, our mind
(Keble) BE140 X Now every
morning is the love   104162
If only I have thee (Hardenberg)
AZ1227   104163
If our all on Christ we venture
(Zinzendorf, N. L.) AZ258
                        104164
If our God had not befriended
(Churton) BH123   104165
If the Lord build not the house
(Baum) BE141   104166
If the Lord does not build the
house (Ladies of the Grail)
BSp. 48   104167
If the world from you withold of
its silver and its gold (Tindley)
AX468   104168
If there be that skills to reckon

(St Thomas à Kempis) E250
                        104169
If there's sunshine in your heart
(Dungan) R You can make the
pathway bright   104170
If thou but suffer God to guide
thee (Neumark) G272; I476;
J568; K398; L485; M285; O
230; P299; Q518; R344; S105;
W541; Z404; AA498; AB225;
AF83; AG156; AI439; AK300;
AL423; AM567; AP500; BA
718; BI46-D; BV523; BY580;
BZ   104171
If thou impart thyself to me
(Wesley) L423   104172
If thou wouldst have the dear
Saviour from heaven (Oatman)
AX430   104173
If thou wouldst life attain (Cas-
wall) AZ1253   104174
If, through unruffled seas,
toward heaven (Toplady) V433
X If, on a quiet sea, toward
heaven   104175
If to Jesus for relief, My soul
hath fled (Newton) AZ1478
                        104176
If we have forgotten the name
of our God (U. P. Psalter,
1912) T83; AJ123*; AM515*
*refrain unusual   104177
If ye would hear the angels
sing (Greenwell) BG134
                        104178
If you are tired of the load of
your sin (Morris) AT230;
AX261   104179
If you could hie to Kolob (Phelps)
BC257   104180
If you from sin are longing to be
free (Jackson) AX256 104181
If you only knew my Saviour
(DeArmond) AU421   104182
Igjennem Nat og Trängsel (Inge-
mann) Y305; BT481   104183
Ihr Christen g'mein, die ihr
seyd rein (H. Betz) BU106
                        104184
Ihr Christen rein, allsammt
gemein (M. Schneider & H.
Betz) BU101   104185
Ihr jungen Helden, aufgewacht

(Unparth. G. B.) AY28d 104186
Ihr Kinder Gottes alle (Ausbund)
BU124   104187
Ihr Kinderlein, kommet, o kommet
doch all'! (Christian Schmidt)
BW413   104188
I'll exchange my cross for a
starry crown (Gabriel) R Just
a few more days   104189
I'll glory in nothing but only in
Jesus (Scheffler) AZ488
104190
I'll go, I'll go, A help to my
Lord to be (Rowe) R My
Saviour needs helpers   104191
I'll go where you want me to go,
dear Lord (Brown) R It may
not be on the mountain's
height   104192
I'll hear what God the Lord will
speak (Scottish Psalter, 1650)
AP70   104193
I'll live for Him who died for
me (Hudson) R My life, my
love, I give to thee   104194
I'll make it my home some day
(Morris) R I've heard of a
beautiful city   104195
I'll of salvation take the cup
(Scottish Psalter, 1650) AL676;
AP103   104196
I'll praise my Maker while I've
breath (Watts) G513; I534;
L91; V516; AA73; AL10; BC
254; BY60; BZ   104197
I'll praise my Maker whilst I've
breath (Watts) AA73 X I'll
praise my Maker while I've
breath   104198
I'll praise my Maker with my
breath (Watts) V516 X I'll
praise my Maker while I've
breath   104199
I'll praise thee with my heart and
tongue (Gerhardt) AZ174; BA
655   104200
I'll sing a hymn to Mary (Wyse)
BN155; BO64   104201
I'll speak the honours of my King
(Watts) V133   104202
I'll thee exalt, my God and King
(---) BI21-D   104203
I'm a little pilgrim, and a stranger

here (Curwen) AP784
104204
I'm a pilgrim, and I'm a
stranger, I can tarry (Dana)
N526; P348; V662; AI314;
BB666; BE415   104205
I'm a pilgrim; I'm a stranger
cast upon the rocky shore
(Petersen) BC261   104206
I'm but a stranger here (Taylor)
M312 X We are but strangers
here   104207
I'm going home, I'm going home
(Hunter) R My heavenly home
is bright and fair   104208
I'm going there to meet (White
spiritual) R I am a poor way-
faring stranger   104209
I'm kneeling at the threshold
aweary, faint, and sore
(Alexander) BR158 104210
I'm not ashamed to own my
Lord (Watts) I441; K180;
L517; R292; T422; V439;
W507; AL349; AM429; AP
560; AW302; AX342; AZ129;
BV501; BY292   104211
I'm pressing on the upward way
(Oatman) AT319; AU269;
AV374; AX382; AY462;
BB631   104212
I'm the child of a King (Buell)
R My Father is rich 104213
I'm trusting to the unseen hand
(Sims) R There is an unseen
hand   104214
Immaculate Mary! Our hearts
are on fire (Parochial Hymn
book) BO-62 X Immaculate
Mary, your praises we sing
104215
Immaculate Mary! Thy praises
we sing (Parochial Hymn
book) BN144 X Immaculate
Mary! Your praises we sing
104216
Immaculate Mary! Your praises
we sing (Parochial Hymn
book, 1897) BM54; BN144;
BO62; BP80   104217
Immanuel see also Emanuel and
Emmanuel   104218
Immanuel! God with us (Kretz-

man) M210   104219
Immanuel! Our God and Lord
(Kretzmann) M525   104220
Immanuel, to thee we sing (Ger-
hardt) M331 X Emmanuel! we
sing thy praise   104221
Immanuel, we sing thy praise
(Gerhardt) O180 X Emmanuel!
we sing thy praise   104222
Immortal babe, who this dear day
(Hall) BG117   104223
Immortal by their deed and word
(Hosmer) AN203; BD67; BX
228   104224
Immortal, invisible, God only
wise (Smith) A301; E407;
F372; G64; J172; R85; S66;
W12; X535; Y23; Z159; AD
73; AF7; AL34; AM35; AN30;
AQ41; AR20; AT43; BL93; BV
242; BX39; BY61; BZ   104225
Immortal Love, for ever full
(Whittier) A360; B404; E408;
F208; G120; H152; I128; J476;
N196; P152; R229; S178; T387;
U84; V135; W141; X536; Y68;
Z254; AB171; AC140; AB250;
AE98; AF230; AG116; AH424;
AI113; AK242; AL123; AN80;
561; AO213; AP183; AQ142;
AR201; AS117; AT277; AV178;
AW173; BA82; BB141; BD70,
72; BE142; BF246; BK91; BR
418; BV537; BX71,217; BY121,
125; BZ   104226
Immortal Love, within whose
rightous will (Brooke) S303;
U240; AB221   104227
Imposture shrinks from light
(Scott) BE143   104228
Improve the shining moments
(Baird) BC73   104229
In a lonely graveyard, many miles
(---) AY504   104230
In a world where sorrow, Ever
will be known (Smith) BC74
                         104231
In age and feebleness extreme
(Wesley) I746   104232
In all my vast concerns with thee
(Watts) V109; BR277   104233
In another land and time (Smith)
X362   104234

In Asia born, from Asia hailed
(Dearmer) X91   104235
In atmosphere of Love divine
("H") BE144   104236
In Bethlehem, 'neath starlit
skies (Stutsman) G103; BZ
                         104237
In Bethlehem, that fair city
(English trad carol, 15th c)
BG120   104238
In boundless mercy, gracious
Lord, appear (Swedenborg)
BR38   104239
In calm and cool and silence
(Niles, from Whittier) BK100
                         104240
In Christ I feel the heart of God
(Larcom) Y66; AB86 104241
In Christ there is no East or
West (Oxenham) A263; G
507; J342; R479; S341; U375;
X537; Y273; Z480; AB357;
AC299; AD378; AE403; AF
414; AG234; AI429; AK406; AL
252; AN413; AR388; AS362; AT
443; AW320; BB436; BF488;
BK112; BL69; BV420; BY661;
BZ   104242
In Christi Wunden schlaf' ich ein
(Eber) BT585   104243
In darkness as in light (Mont-
gomery) BT616 X For-ever
with the Lord   104244
In days of old on Sinai (St Cos-
mas) F559   104245
In days of yore, from Britain's
shore (---) (Canadian national
hymn) P415   104246
In death's strong grasp the
Saviour lay (Luther) M432;
N134; AA224   104247
In dich hab' ich gehoffet, Herr
(Reusner) BT524   104248
In doubt and temptation, I rest,
Lord, in thee (U.P. Psalter,
1912) AJ202   104249
In dulci jubilo (Suso) BG86;
BN15; BT92   104250
In duties and in sufferings, too
(Beddome) AZ121; BA83
                         104251
In every condition, in sickness
and health ("K" in Rippon)

BR421 X In heavenly love abiding 104289

In Jesus' name our work must all be done (Frederiksen) O247 104290

In joyful high and holy lays (Mund) BB650 104291

In Judah's land God is well known (Scottish Psalter, 1650) AP63 104292

In life's earnest morning (Oakley) Y139; Z474; AB314; AC213; AN475; BD197; BF630; BX537 104293

In loud exalted strains (Francis) D482; Q638; AA457; AS442 104294

In love divine all earth-born fear and sorrow (Campbell) BE149 104295

In loving adoration we come to worship thee (Penfield) AH184 104296

In loving-kindness Jesus came (Homer) AI130; AM672; AT 202 104297

In manus tuas, Domini (Latin) BN193 104298

In many a stone-bound city (Sampter) BH180 104299

In memory of the Crucified (Kooyman) BC99 104300

In memory of the Saviour's love (Cotterill) G413; Z462; AE332; AI166; AL225; AR515; AS459; AT393; AX177; AY255; BF598; BZ 104301

In mercy, in goodness, how great is our King (McKenzie) BE150 104302

In mercy, Lord, incline thine ear (Wise) BH211 104303

In mercy, Lord, remember me (Watts) AX71 X And now another day is gone 104304

In mercy, Lord, this grace bestow (Zinzendorf, N.L.) AZ325; BA 538 104305

In mercy, not in wrath (Newton) D352 104306

In my quiet contemplation (Wallin) N498 104307

In numbers, and but these few (Herrick) BG176 104308

In one fraternal bond of love (Montgomery) L283 104309

In one true God we all believe (Tranovsky) Q253 104310

In our dark and doubtful strife (Brooke) BX257 104311

In our day of thanksgiving one psalm let us offer (Draper) F476 104312

In our dear Lord's garden (Armitage) AP744 104313

In our hearts celestial voices (Corelli) AL621; AP809; BB 419 104314

In our work, and in our play, Jesus be thou ever near (Dix) E596; F454 104315

In our work and in our play, Jesus be thou ever near (Piggott) X538 104316

In our work and in our play, Jesus ever with us stay (Wills) G448; AW417 104317

In Oxford town the faggots they piled (---) AC511 104318

In Paradise reposing (Littledale) E355 104319

In peace and joy I now depart (Luther) Q137; AA185 104320

In peace will I lie down to sleep (Scriver) AZ904 104321

In pleasant lands have fallen the lines (Flint) AN370; AW368; BX406 104322

In quiet hours the tranquil soul (Larned) AN267; BX318 104323

In remembrance of thy suffering (Stephens) BC258 104324

In seasons of grief to my God I'll repair (Hunter) AY328 104325

In singing till his heaven fills (Meredith) AQ8 104326

In songs of sublime adoration ("K" in Rippon's Selection, 1787) AI128 104327

In sorrow and affliction (Howard) BR404 104328

In speechless prayer and reverence (Glover) BE151 104329

In spirit I am waiting (Zinzendorf, N. L.) AZ1117 104330

In stable lowly, a little child is born (French trad) BD213 104331

In stature grows the heavenly child (Santeüil) E46; AZ210 104332

In sunny days, when all is bright (Haigh) BY476 104333

In sunshine and in storm, O God (Mayer) BH90 104334

In sweet communion, Lord, with thee (U.P. Psalter, 1912) R 126; T136; AJ203; AM557 104335

In sweet fields of autumn (Madison) AQ276 104336

In tenderness He sought me (Walton) U167; AU65 104337

In tenebris nostrae et densa caligne mentis (Camerarius) BT522 104338

In that beautiful land I'll be (Nicholson) R There's a beautiful land on high 104339

In that poor stable, how charming Jesus lies (French trad carol) BG75 104340

In that sad memorable night (Wesley) AZ653 104341

In the beginning was the word (Longfellow) AR110 104342

In the bleak mid-winter (Rossetti) A44; E25; F67; G104; J36; W 50; X75; AF128; AL56; BG187; BV100; BY99; BZ 104343

In the blood from the cross (Oatman) BB275 104344

In the candles' rays I see (Levinger) BH206 104345

In the Christian's home in glory (Harmer) AU84; AV358; AX 574 104346

In the cross, in the cross, Be my glory (Crosby) R Jesus, keep me near the cross 104347

In the cross of Christ I glory (Bowring) A336; B152; D359; E409; G149; H175; I143; J64; K62; L231; M166; N103; O262; P193; Q354; R195; S154; T343; U94; V143; W113; Y377; Z237; AA95; AB140; AC124; AD157; AE116; AF157; AG94; AH292; AI76; AK164; AL100; AN190; AO165; AP199; AR176; AS 138; AT100; AU180; AV113; AW110; AY188; AZ239; BA 197; BB125; BF316; BV556; BX213; BY141; BZ 104348

In the dark and cloudy day (Rawson) V424 104349

In the day of all days when the world (Latta) AX292; AY 152 104350

In the early days of childhood (Smith) AY486 104351

In the early morning, dark shadows stay (Leyda) S493; AL620 104352

In the field with their flocks abiding (Farrar) I117; W43 104353

In the fullness of thy grace (U.P. Psalter, 1912) AJ10 104354

In the glad time of the harvest (Santee) BB539 104355

In the good ship of our Captain (Kuipers) AI393 104356

In the harvest field there is work to do (Blackall) AU327; AX183; AY528 104357

In the heart of Jesus (Pugh) BB348 104358

In the heavens the Lord Almighty (U.P. Psalter, 1912) AJ282 104359

In the holy Father's keeping (Miller) M585; N140 104360

In the hour of my distress (Herrick) E410 104361

In the hour of trial (Montgomery) A334; B147; D340; G274; H373; I431; J561; K391; L524; M272; N257; O371; P169; Q516; R394; S255; U238; V171; W525; Y104; Z333; AA409; AB 195; AC178; AD148; AE245; AF374; AG151; AH439; AI 286; AK160; AM475; AO407; AP240; AR303; AS321; AT

317; AU467; AV187; AW195;
AY477; AZ764; BA581; BB327;
BF479; BR347; BZ   104362
In the land of fadeless day (Cle-
ments) AI342; AM730; AS470;
BB558   104363
In the land of strangers (Bonar)
AP407   104364
In the Light all light excelling
(Coffin) BO6   104365
In the lonely house of mourning
(Bird) AZ908   104366
In the lonely midnight (Williams)
AC89; AD473; AH251; AN173;
AQ292; BD215; BF287; BX
531   104367
In the Lord's atoning grief (St
Bonaventura) F105   104368
In the midst of earthly life
(Luther) Q590   104369
In the morning I will pray (Fur-
ness) BX126   104370
In the morning, noon, and even-
ing (Wieand) R On the radiant
threshold   104371
In the name of God, the Father
(Hewett) AO418   104372
In the name of Jesus (Noel) W178
X At the name of Jesus 104373
In the Name which earth and
heaven (Ellerton) D292; Q632;
AA451   104374
In the old-time way (McKinney)
R As He heard His waiting
people   104375
In the place of sorrow, waiting
(Dearmer) X138   104376
In the quiet consecration (Coote)
BV379   104377
In the quiet hours of morning
(Slemp) AU107   104378
In the resurrection, In the resur-
rection (Slovak, 1674) Q603
                          104379
In the rifted Rock I'm resting
(James) AX512; AY453 104380
In the secret of His presence
(Goreh) M211   104381
In the shadow of His wings
(Atchinson) AU135   104382
In the silent midnight watches
(Coxe) AX244   104383
In the still air the music lies

unheard (---) U261   104384
In the sun and moon, and stars
(Heber) BB178   104385
In the sweet by and by (Bennett)
R There's a land that is fair-
er than day   104386
In the temple where our fathers
(Söderberg) N349   104387
In the vineyard of our Father
(MacKellar) D577; AZ1412
                          104388
In the warfare that is waging
(Martin) AU358   104389
In thee alone, O Christ, my
Lord (Schneesing) O96; Q
319   104390
In thee I love, and move and
am (Erskine) AZ199 104391
In thee, Lord, have I put my
trust (Reusner) Q524; AA
495   104392
In thee, my God and Saviour,
forevermore the same
(Baum) BE153   104393
In thee, O God, the hosts above
(Palmer) BX240   104394
In thee, O Lord, I out my trust,
I call upon thy name (---)
T51; AJ80   104395
In thee, O Lord, I put my
trust, Shamed let me never
be (U. P. Psalter, 1912) T
130; AJ190   104396
In thee, O Spirit true and tender,
I find my life (Fox) BE154
                          104397
In thee, our Father, are we all
at home (Patterson) AN86
                          104398
In these our days exalt thy
grace (Zinzendorf, N. L.)
AZ1426; BA338   104399
In thine arm I rest me (Franck)
AZ1075   104400
I this lone hour of deep distress
(---) AY180   104401
In this our happy Christmas-
tide (Brorson) O185 104402
In this peaceful house of prayer
(Hymns of the Spirit, 1864)
AN22; BR19; BX338 104403
In this Sacrament, Lord Jesus
(Furniss) BN95; BO40

104404
In this Sacrament, sweet Jesus (Furniss) BO40 X In this Sacrament, Lord Jesus 104405
In this sepulchral Eden (Gregor) AZ1500; BA212 104406
In this stern hour when the spirit falters (Johnson) AQ55 104407
In this world of sin and care (Oatman) AX410; AY66 104408
In this world so full of snares (LaTrobe) AZ587 104409
In this world, the Isle of Dreams (Herrick) X348 104410
In this your month, Creation's Queen ("M.A.", Father) BN146 104411
In those twelve days let us be glad (English trad carol, 1625) R What are they that are but one? 104412
In thy cleft, O Rock of ages (Crosby) L419; AE286; AX 514 104413
In thy dear name and by thy favor (Lutheran. Ohio Synod G.B. 1870) M509 104414
In thy dear wounds I fall asleep (Eber) N596 104415
In thy glorious resurrection (Wordsworth) AZ647 104416
In thy great name, O Lord, we come (Hoskins) L57; AS60 104417
In thy heritage the heathen (U.P. Psalter, 1912) T147; AJ216 104418
In thy holy place we bow (Coffman) AY434 104419
In thy holy temple, O sacred place (McKinney) AU365 104420
In thy love and knowledge, gracious Saviour (Zinzendorf, N.L.) AZ 1004 104421
In thy name, O Lord, assembling (Kelly) K427; L205; N310; V1; AE28 104422
In thy peaceful house of prayer (Hymns of the Spirit, 1864) BR19 X In this peaceful house of prayer 104423
In thy service will I ever (Spitta)

AZ945 104424
In thy wrath and hot displeasure (U.P. Psalter, 1912) T67; AJ102; AM408 104425
In time of tribulation (Montgomery) AZ793 104426
In token that thou shalt not fear (Alford) B344; D209; E337; F424; X250; BV339 104427
In triumph our Redeemer (Geijer) N137 104428
In vain we seek for peace with God (Watts) N420 104429
In vain would boasting reason find (Steele) L311; AA122 104430
In vision to His Saints God spake (U.P. Psalter, 1912) T165; AJ243 104431
In weariness and pain (Wesley) L254; AA504; AZ1311 104432
In yon blessed seats of heaven (---) AZ897 104433
In- a this-a band, we have sweet music (Negro spiritual) AH600 104434
Incline thine ear, O Lord, and show us mercy (Latin) BM 74 104435
Increase my faith, dear Lord, I pray (Van Hoose) AX457 104436
Infant holy, Infant lowly (Polish carol) G105; R164; AE430; BV103; BY100; BZ 104437
Infinite God, to thee we raise (Wesley) I10 104438
Ingrediente Domino in Sanctam (Latin) BQ169 104439
Inspirer and hearer of prayer (Toplady) B34; D643; L32; W560; AZ1512; BV53; BY 570 104440
Instantis adventum Dei (Coffin) BT68 104441
Integer vitae (Horace) Y297 104442
Into my heart, Into my heart (Clarke) AR653; AU321 104443
Into our hands the Gospel is given (Carruth) R Swiftly

we're turning   104444
Into the desert I was led (English
   trad carol) BG71b X Tomor-
   row shall be my dancing day
                         104445
Into the tent where the gipsy boy
   lay (Slade) AU378   104446
Into the tomb of ages past
   (Moise) BH156   104447
Into the woods my Master went
   (Lanier) G132; I745; U99;
   X126; Y84; Z225; AC119; AD
   145; AH277; AR161; AT90;
   AU420; AV114; BB128; BD74
                         104448

Into thy gracious hands I fell
   (Dessler) I305; AZ922   104449
Involata integra et casta es
   Maria (Breviary) BQ208
                         104450
Invited, Lord, by boundless grace
   (Cronenwett) Q308; AA438
                         104451
Is God my strong Salvation! (Ger-
   hardt) AZ798; BA683   104452
Is it nothing to you, all ye that
   pass by? (Faber, Antiphon)
   BV173 X O come and mourn
                         104453
Is my name written there! (Kidder)
   AX486 X I am bought not with
   riches   104454
Is not this the land of Beulah
   (---) R I am dwelling on the
   mountain   104455
Is there a god? The rising sun in
   answer warm (Brethren's Tune
   and hymnbook, 1879) AR77
                         104456
Is there a heart that is waiting?
   (James) AU93   104457
Is there any pleasure, any joy in
   life? (---) AX539   104458
Is this Jesus, then, the Lord
   (Churchman?, 1858) M336
                         104459
Is thy cruse of comfort failing!
   (Charles) AI274; AO472; BE
   360; BR232   104460
Is thy heart right with God (Hoff-
   man) R Have thy affections been
   nailed   104461
Is your all on the altar of sacri-

fice laid? (Hoffman) R You
   have longed for sweet peace
                         104462
Is your life a channel of bless-
   ing? (Smyth) AT438; AU61
                         104463
Isaiah, mighty seer, in days of
   old (Luther) Q249   104464
Israel, Israel, God is calling
   (Smyth) BC81   104465
Ist Gott für mich, so trete
   (Gerhardt) BT528   104466
Iste confessor Dômini (Latin,
   8th c) BN182; BO268
                         104467
It came upon the midnight clear
   (Sears) A19; B79; D59; E26;
   F66; G92; H135; I110; J23;
   K29; L215; N39; P135; R160;
   S127; T338; U58; V116; W
   47; X76; Y245; Z191; AB108;
   AC78; AD107; AE82; AF129;
   AG73; AH245; AK107; AL58;
   AM157; AN162; AO122; AP
   170; AQ287; AR136; AS104;
   AT71; AU141; AV85; AW75;
   AZ1461; BA156; BB99; BC82;
   BD206; BE158; BF289; BK
   146; BR548; BV104; BX191;
   BY101; BZ   104468
It fell upon a summer day
   (Brooke) G443; R461; S444;
   W80; X539; AD476; AG88;
   AL77; BY122   104469
It is a piteous thing to be
   (Hay) AQ154   104470
It is a thing most wonderful
   (How) E597; F435; W436;
   BV350; BY142   104471
"It is finished," all the pain
   (Brooke) AK156   104472
It is finished! Blessed Jesus
   (Maclagan) E120; F124
                         104473
It is finished! Christ hath known
   (Gillett) A78; E118; X139
                         104474
"It is finished." Man of Sor-
   rows (Hedge) G139; AN185;
   BX203   104475
"It is finished," said my
   Saviour (Carnett) AU427
                         104476

"It is finished!" Shall we raise
(A Collection of Psalms and
hymns, 1830) AZ54   104477
It is good to sing thy praises (U.
P. Psalter, 1912) R20; T172;
AJ251   104478
It is my joy in life to find
(Sherman) Y210   104479
It is no earthly summer's ray
(Latin, 6th c) BO141   104480
It is not death to die (Malan)
D419; H498; I585; K504; L561;
O592; Q602; V675; AA533; AO
569; AZ1299; BA723   104481
It is so long a way that I must
go (Luce) AN551   104482
It is something to have wept as
we have wept (Chesterton)
AQ101   104483
It is the day of all the year
(Leonard) BG145   104484
It is the joyful Easter Time
(Milner-Barry) AL618; BY
745   104485
It is well with my soul (Spafford)
R When peace like a river
                        104486
It matters not what be thy lot
(Eddy) BE160   104487
It may be at morn, when the day
is breaking (Turner) AT120;
AU49; AV389; AW455; BB536
                        104488
It may not be on the mountain
height (Brown) BC75 X It
may not be on the mountain's
height   104489
It may not be on the mountain's
height (Brown & Pryor) H398;
EH427; AT425; AV379; AY105;
BC75   104490
It may not be our lot to wield
(Whittier) G291; I398   104491
It must be told (Wight) R 'Tis a
sweet and tender story 104492
It passeth knowledge, that dear
love of Thine (Shekleton) BY
594   104493
It pays to serve Jesus, it pays
every day (Huston) R The serv-
ice of Jesus   104494
It shall be well, let sinners know
(Hoskins) V328   104495

It singeth low in every heart
(Chadwick) G521; Z579;
AB411; AN451; AO543; BF
654; BH220; BX473   104496
It sounds along the ages
(Gannett) AN76; AQ247
                        104497
It swells upon the noonday
breeze (Adams) Y250 104498
It was about the deep of night
(De la Mare) BG163   104499
It was early in the morning
(English trad carol) BG44
X Awake, awake ye drowsy
souls   104500
It was on Christmas Day
And all in the morning (Eng-
lish trad carol) BG17a
                        104501
It was on Holy Wednesday, And
all in the morning (English
trad carol) BG17b   104502
It was the calm and silent night!
(Domett) X77   104503
It will open wide, yes, open
wide (Underwood) R I've
heard them sing again and
again   104504
It's me, it's me, it's me, O
Lord (Negro spiritual) AH
603   104505
I've anchored my soul in the
"Haven of Rest" (Gilmour)
R My soul in sad exile
                        104506
I've brought you here a bunch
of May (English trad carol)
BG48   104507
I've found a friend, O such a
friend (Small) G241; H342;
R220; U188; V763,306; W705;
Z290; AE305; AG162; AH323;
AI108; AK474; AL128; AM
433; AP235; AR449; AT261;
AU28; AV318; AW445; AX
527; BA483; BB531; BF459;
BV626; BY440; BZ   104508
I've found a friend who is all
to me (Scholefield) AT197;
AU339   104509
I've found my Lord and He is
mine (Warner) AX348 104510
I've found the pearl of greatest

price (Mason) L117; AI261;
AM592   104511
I've got a robe, you've got a robe
(Negro spiritual) Y319; AH601
104512
I've heard of a beautiful city above
(Morris) AX605   104513
I've heard them sing again and
again (Underwood) AY154
104514
I've reached the land of joy divine
(Stites) AU114; BB554   104515
I've read of a world of beauty
(Smucker) AY59   104516
I've seen the lightning flashing
(---) AU400   104517
I've surrendered all, I've sur-
rendered all (Oatman) R A
full surrender I have made
104518
I've two little hands to work for
Jesus (Ogden) A$_y$300   104519
I've wandered far away from God
(Kirkpatrick) AI213; AL474;
AP431; AS203; AT237; AX302;
BB560   104520
I've wandered far away o'er
mountains cold (Crosby) R O
hear my cry   104521

J

J'ai oui chanter le rossignol
(French carol, 18th c) BG
140b   104522
Je sais, vierge Marie, Ce que
je dois (French trad carol)
BG162b   104523
Jeg gaar i Fare, hvor jeg gaar
(Brorson) BT413   104524
Jeg kommer her, o söde Gud
(Landstad) BT330   104525
Jeg staar for Gud, som alting
veed (Landstad) BT318 104526
Jeg ved mig en Sovn i Jesu Navn
(Landstad) BT592   104527
Jehova! Jehova! Jehova! Deinem
Namen sie Ehre, Macht, und
Ruhm (Pfeffel) BW507 104528
Jehovah from his throne on high
(U.P. Psalter, 1912) T56;
AJ87; AP30   104529
Jehovah God! Thy gracious power

(Thomson) BR64   104530
Jehovah, God, who dwelt of old
(Amis) I665; N281   104531
Jehovah hear thee in thy grief
(U.P. Psalter, 1912) T30;
AJ43   104532
Jehovah is my light (U.P.
Psalter, 1912) T45; AJ71
104533
Jehovah is our strength (Bar-
nard) L510   104534
Jehovah, Jehovah, Jehovah
Thou art worthy (Pfeffel)
AK494; AW507   104535
Jehovah, Jesus, Lord we own!
(---) BI23-D   104536
Jehovah, let me now adore thee
(Crasselius) O358; Q21; AA
67; AW569   104537
Jehovah, Lord of heaven and
earth (---) BC83   104538
Jehovah, my God, on thy help
I depend (U.P. Psalter, 1912)
T9   104539
Jehovah reigns! He dwells in
light (Watts) V102   104540
Jehovah reigns in majesty
(U.P. Psalter, 1912)
AJ265   104541
Jehovah reigns; let earth be
glad (U.P. Psalter, 1912)
T178; AJ260; AM59
104542
Jehovah reigns supreme! Let
nations tremble now (---)
T183; AJ267   104543
Jehovah sits enthroned in
majesty most bright (U.P.
Psalter, 1912) T173; AJ
252   104544
Jehovah the Lord, our Saviour
and King (McNeely) AT494
104545
Jehovah, thee we glorify (Wallin)
N316   104546
Jehovah to my prayer give ear
(U.P. Psalter, 1912) T103;
AJ148   104547
Jehovah's perfect law (U.P.
Psalter, 1912) AJ38; AM448
104548
Jerusalem, arise, the heavenly
glory view (Proud) BR212

104549
Jerusalem, du hochgebaute Stadt
(Meyfart) BT619   104550
Jerusalem! high tower thy glor-
ious walls (Meyfart) A594; B
543   104551
Jerusalem, Jerusalem! Die du so
hoch gethront (---) AW125b
                              104552
Jerusalem, Jerusalem, thou city
ever blest (Berg) N625 104553
Jerusalem, lift up thy voice
(Wallin) M333; N5   104554
Jerusalem, my happy home
("F.B.P.", based on St.
Augustine) A585; B514; D402;
E638; F282 and 623; H505; I
608; J587; K524; L602; M314;
N623; O609; Q618; V697; W
595; X395; AA558; AF312; AL461;
AP635; AS481; AX610; AY143;
AZ183; BA763; BB309; BJ56;
BQ119; BR445; BT618; BV429
                              104555
Jerusalem on high, My song and
city is (Crossman) E411; F280;
L589; X197; AP633; AZ1189;
BJ43; BV431   104556
Jerusalem, the glorious! The
glory of the elect (St Bernard
of Cluny) V710; AZ825 104557
Jerusalem the golden (St Bernard
of Cluny) A597; B511; D408;
E412; F278; G529; H514; I612;
J584; K528; L585; M306; N622;
O614; P431; Q613; R428; S435;
T435; U432; V690; W599; X198;
Y341; Z569; AA556; AB408; AD
466; AE307; AF309; AG283;
AH523; AI338; AK422; AL463b;
AM604; AN548; AO550; AP628;
AR425; AS469; AT477; AU219;
AV285; AW262; AZ824; BA748;
BB300; BF657; BI18; BO203;
BQ118; BR437; BV432; BX467;
BY406; BZ   104558
Jerusalem, thou city fair and
high (Meyfart) J588; K521;
M315; N626; O610; Q619; AA
559; AZ1224   104559
Jesaia, dem Propheten, das
geschah (Luther) BT249
                              104560

NOTE: Jesu and Jesus are in-
terfiled because usage, even
within a poem, varies in
different anthologies
(hymnals).   104561
Jesus all glorious, Christ all
victorious (Boe) P208
                              104562
Jesus, all hail, who for our
sin (Faber) AZ573   104563
Jesus, all my gladness (Franck)
A453   104564
Jesus, all our ransom paid
(Pollock) X Jesus, in thy
dying woe (VI)   104565
Jesus, all our souls inspire
(Foster) AZ50   104566
Jesus, all thy labor vast
(Pollock) X Jesus, in thy
dying woe (VII)   104567
Jesus and Joseph day after day
(Glover) BY123   104568
Jesus, and shall it ever be
(Grigg) A423; B135; D597;
G258; H335; I443; J514;
K71; L169; M219; N143;
O369; P321; Q346; T428;
U175; V436; AA91; AH367;
AI318; AL353; AM425; AO
378; AP565; AR353; AS279;
AU215; AV125; AW192; AZ
377; BA455; BB152; BY293
                              104569
Jesus, at thy invitation (Rus-
sell) AZ277   104570
Jesu, best and dearest (Franck)
BJ57   104571
Jesus bids us shine with a pure
clear light (Warner) W671;
AH545; AL613; AM653; AP
768; AW420; BY746 104572
Jesus , bless us sensibly
(Gregor) AZ590   104573
Jesus, bless is with thy Spirit
(Toews) AX77   104574
Jesus, Brightness of the Father
(St Rabanus Maurus??)
Q257; AA287   104575
Jesus, by the Holy Spirit
(Zinzendorf, N.L.) AZ263;
BA600   104576
Jesus, call thou me, from the
world to thee (Drese) AZ

511; BA930   104577
Jesus calls me, I must follow
(Brown) AU443   104578
Jesus calls us; o'er the tumult
(Alexander) A566; B268; D
143; E205; F533; G233; I545;
J553; M200; N172; Q270; R
269; S223; T383; U284; V735;
W500; X217; Y106; Z281; AB
159; AC144; AD201; AE164; AF
322; AG144; AH327; AI297; AK
207; AL358; AM491; AO376;
AP553; AR243; AS229; AT360;
AU159; AV188; AW140; AX40;
AY474; AZ269; BA404; BB521;
BF348; BR28; BV442; BY416;
BZ   104579
Jesus came, the heavens adoring
(Thring) D318; Q56; U124; V
184; AA131; AS162; AZ1410;
BA150; BF335; BV84   104580
Jesus, cast a look on me (Ber-
ridge) L463   104581
Jesus Christ as King is reigning
(Hiller) M628   104582
Jesus Christ from death hath
risen (Lindenborn) F605
                              104583
Jesus Christ is made to me
(Jones) AX314   104584
Jesus Christ is passing by(Smith)
D592; AO638   104585
Jesus Christ is ris'n today,
Alleluia! (Latin, 14th c) A85;
B172; D112; E133; F134; G155;
J92; K113; Lp.742; M442; Q
199; R204; S163; T347; V756;
W119; X145; AD159; AF187;
AK166; AL105; AM198; AP215;
AU32; AV115; AW114; AZ80,
87; BA234; BD245; BL30; BN
44; BO180; BQ27; BR190; BV
194; BY157; BZ   104586
Jesus Christ, my heart's true
Captain (Cooke) BY294 104587
Jesus Christ, my Pride and Glory
(Olearius) Q408 X Christ Him-
self my Pride and Glory104588
Jesus Christ my sure Defence
(Luise Henriette) J294; K511;
M444; O509; Q206; AA220;
AK320; AW541; AZ588; BA238
                              104589

Jesus Christ, our blessed
Saviour (Hus??) Q311; AA
441   104590
Jesus Christ, our Lord most
holy (Grodzki) Q169; AM
196   104591
Jesus Christ the King of Ages
("A.E.E.") BM45   104592
Jesus Christ, thou Guiding-
Star (Zinzendorf, N.L.) BA576
X Jesus Christ, thou Leading
Star   104593
Jesus Christ, thou Leading-
Star (Zinzendorf) AZ580;
BA576   104594
Jesus Christus, Gottes Sohn
Mit seiner leiblichen Person
(J. Hus) BU38   104595
Jesus Christus, nostra salus
(Hus??) BT311   104596
Jesus Christus, unser Heiland
(Hus??) BT311   104597
Jesus, come and bless us
(Latta) R Jesus, thou hast
promised   104598
Jesus comes, His conflict over
(Kelly) AZ615   104599
Jesus cometh to fulfill (Peter-
sen) AZ789   104600
Jesu, coróna Virginum (Latin,
8th c) BO269   104601
Jesus, Creator of the world
(Latin, 18th c) BP70; BQ
60   104602
Jesus, day by day Guide us on
our way (Zinzendorf, N.L.)
AZ535 X Jesus, lead the
way   104603
Jesus dear, I come to thee
(Tiffany) AY215   104604
Jesus, dear name! how sweet it
sounds (Watts) AY273
                              104605
Jesu, deine Passion Will ich
jetzt bedenken (Birken) BT
140   104606
Jesu, deine tiefen Wunden
(Heermann) BT144   104607
Jesu Deus, amor meus (Latin)
BQ315   104608
Jesus died for me, all to Him
I owe (Hall) R I hear the
Saviour say   104609

Jesu dulcis memoria (St Bernard of Clairvaux) BJ32b; BM28; BN64; BP22; BQ161; BT350; BW155, 171   104610

Jesus, ever loving Saviour (Holy Family hymns, 1860) BQ135   104611

Jesus! exalted far on high (Cotterill) K87; BA66   104612

Jesus, food of angels, monarch of the heart (St Alfonso M de Liguori) BQ54   104613

Jesus, for thee and thy blessed communion (German, 1712) P315   104614

Jesus, Fountain of my days (Matheson) AD247   104615

Jesus, Friend of little children (Mathams) W667; X363; BB 420; BV357; BY747   104616

Jesus, Friend, so kind and gentle (Gregory) R451; AF277   104617

Jesus, from thy throne on high (Pollock) B368; D526; K569; W469; AP776; BX528   104618

Jesus, from whom all blessings flow (Wesley) I561; AX156; AY62   104619

Jesus, full of all compassion (Turner) L383; V308; BB237   104620

Jesu, geh voran Auf der Lebensbahn (Zinzendorf) AW574b; BT410; BW574   104621

Jesus, gentlest Saviour (Faber) A348; B322; D576; E315; F418; AH541; BN96; BO42; BQ49   104622

Jesus, God of our Salvation (Zinzendorf, E.D.) AZ1106; BA797   104623

Jesus, good above all other (Dearmer) A322; E598; X540; BV263   104624

Jesu, grant me this I pray (Latin, 17th c) E413; F211; L412; BJ24   104625

Jesus, grant that balm and healing (St Bernard of Clairvaux) Q144 X O what precious balm and healing   104626

Jesu, great High-Priest of our profession (Zinzendorf, N.L.) AZ1001; BA89   104627

Jesus, guide our way (Zinzendorf, N.L.) BR387 X Jesus, lead the way   104628

Jesus, hail! enthroned in glory (Bakewell) AZ970 X Hail, Thou once despised Jesus   104629

Jesus' hands were kind hands, doing good to all (Cropper) BV352   104630

Jesus has taken a beautiful bud (Rowe) AX624   104631

Jesus hath procured salvation (Moravian hymn) AZ432   104632

Jesus, hear my humble pleading (Pohjala) J383   104633

Jesus, hear our fervent prayer (Foster) AZ1040   104634

Jesus, hear our humble prayer (Newton) Z640   104635

Jesus, hear our prayer, For thy children care (Zinzendorf, N.L.) AZ542; BA784   104636

Jesus, heed me, lost and dying (Offord) AZ427   104637

Jesus, high in glory (MacKeever) D550; N658; W666; AM661; AP754; BA831; BV353; BY 748   104638

Jesus, highest Heaven's completeness (St Bernard of Clairvaux) BO12   104639

Jesus Himself drew near (Habershon) BV186   104640

Jesus, holy, undefiled (Shapcote) W665; AP803   104641

Jesus, how good the thought of thee (St Bernard of Clairvaux) BN65   104642

Jesus, how sweet the thought of thee (St Bernard of Clairvaux) BJ32   104643

Jesus, I am resting, resting (Pigott) S327; AL505; AM139; AP525; BY582   104644

Jesus, I know, hath died for me (Rothe) K327   104645

Jesus, I live to thee (Harbaugh) B218; D666; G335; H314; K 374; L547; Q591; S246; T414; Z314; AA541; AE271; AK254;

AM438; AO377; AR451; AZ1327;
BA529   104646

Jesus, I long for thy blessed communion (German, 1712) O461
104647

Jesus, I love thee fervently (Seebass) AZ1111   104648

Jesus, I love thy charming name
(Doddridge) H330; V377; AV
140   104649

Jesus, I my cross have taken
(Lyte) B378; D358; G261; H
351; I458; J512; K390; L436;
M271; N446; O408; Q423; R
279; S274; U281; V446; W502;
Z375; AA335; AD258; AE264;
AG192; AH422; AI316; AK249;
AL359; AM593; AO374, 375;
AP558; AR357; AS235; AT387:
AU34; AV176, 215; AX423;
AY112; AZ956; BA457; BB267;
BE166; BR460; BZ   104650

Jesus, I never can forget (Gerhardt) AW533   104651

Jesus, I will follow thee (Glenn)
BB429   104652

Jesus, I will never leave (Kleimann) Q365; AA88   104653

Jesus, I will ponder now (Briken)
Q140; AA192   104654

Jesus, I will trust thee (Walker)
W696; AP511; BV505   104655

Jesus, immortal King, arise!
(Seymour) I632   104656

Jesus, in my walk and living
(Hjertén) N475   104657

Jesus in thee our hopes shall rest
(Hymns of the English Conf.
1880) BR46   104658

Jesus, in thy dying woes
[Seven words: Analytics not
made] (Pollock) A82; B164;
D530; J81; K84; L256; M398;
Q180-186; AB136; AF166; AK
542; AP196; BF313   104659

Jesus, in thy thirst and pain
(Pollock) X Jesus, in thy dying
woes (V)   104660

Jesus, in thy transporting name
(Steele) L157   104661

Jesus included me (Oatman) R
I am so happy   104662

Jesus invites his saints (Watts)

AO447; BB472; BY318
104663

Jesus is all the world to me
(Thompson) AI398; AM664;
AS282; AT155; AX23; BZ
104664

Jesus is coming, is coming
(Gray) R The Saviour who
loves me   104665

Jesus is coming to earth again
(Morris) AT125   104666

Jesus is coming! We know not
how soon (Wesley) R Christ
the Lord cometh   104667

Jesus is God! The glorious
bands (Faber) AZ1434; BO-
9   104668

Jesus is God; the solid earth
(Faber) BO-9 X Jesus is
God! The glorious bands
104669

Jesus is my best of friends
(Arrhenius) BR420   104670

Jesus is my Friend most
precious (Arrhenius) N470
104671

Jesus is my joy, my all
(Fritsch) N491   104672

Jesus is my Light, most fair
(Richter) AZ870   104673

Jesus is now and ever will be
(Oatman) R Christ will me
His aid afford   104674

Jesus is our Shepherd (Stowell)
W552; AP741; BR389 104675

Jesus is passing this way
(James) R Is there a heart
104676

Jesus is pleading, He's interceding (Jeffrey) R Come
home, poor sinner   104677

Jesus is standing at your heart's
door (McKinney) AU101
104678

Jesus is standing in Pilate's
hall (---) AX266   104679

Jesus is tenderly calling thee
home (Crosby) R267; Z280;
AE168; AH330; AI200; AM
697; AT229; AU57; AV334;
AX228; BB569; BY417; BZ
104680

Jesus is the friend you need

(Reynolds) R When the sun
shines bright   104681
Jesu, Jesu, Brunn des Lebens!
(Unparth. G. B.) AY4d 104682
Jesus, Jesus, come to me
(Scheffler) O169; P341; BP58;
BQ131   104683
Jesus, Jesus, how I trust Him
(Stead) R 'Tis so sweet to
trust   104684
Jesus, Jesus, Jesus only(Ludämilia
Elisabeth) M178; O353; P217;
Q348; AA86   104685
Jesus, Jesus, Jesus, Sweetest
name I know (Bridgers) R
There's within my heart104686
Jesus, Jesus, nichts als Jesus
(Ludämilia Elisabeth) BT348
                       104687
Jesus, Jesus, only Jesus
(Ludämilia Elisabeth) O353
X Jesus, Jesus, Jesus only
                       104688
Jesus, Jesus, precious Jesus
(---) R Precious Jesus, O to
love thee   104689
Jesu, joy of man's desiring
(Janus) AR111   104690
Jesus, keep me near the cross
(Crosby) G248; N461; P182;
R376; U218; V732; Z339; AE
172; AH293; AI79; AK462; AL
485; AM704; AO647; AP212;
AR452; AS227; AT97; AU294;
AV350; AW490; AX383; AY470;
BB595; BZ   104691
Jesus, kind above all other (Adam
of St Victor) F456   104692
Jesus, King of Glory (Davison)
B523; D531; L127; N642
                       104693
Jesus, kneel beside me (Cross)
G308; R225; S494; Y107; Z328;
BF345   104694
Jesus knows all about our strug-
gles (Oatman) R There's not a
friend   104695
Jesu, komm doch selbst zu mir
(Scheffler) BT356   104696
Jesus, Lamb of God, for me
(Palmer) V145   104697
Jesus, lead the way (Zinzendorf,
N. L.) A425; B449; D420; E

E206; G336; J532; K260; L533;
M283; N458; O505; Q410; R
334; W567; Z357; AA331; AB
226; AD228; AK284; AL447;
AM504; AP613; AR305; AV
225; AW574a; AX500; AZ535,
541; BA696; BB676; BR387;
BY544   104698
Jesus, lead thou on (Zinzendorf,
N. L.) Q410 X Jesus, lead
the way   104699
Jesus lebt, mit ihm auch ich
(Gellert) BT201; BW543
                       104700
Jesus, let all thy lovers shine
(Wesley) I321   104701
Jesus, let my final rest (Olson)
N605   104702
Jesus, let my soul be fed
(Pedersen) P103   104703
Jesus, let thy pitying eye (Wes-
ley) H264; I491   104704
Jesus, let thy sufferings ease us
(Wesley) AZ872   104705
Jesus, Light, serene, eternal
(Berry) R Lo! a gleam from
yonder heaven   104706
Jesus lives, and Jesus leads
(Hood) AI101; BV264 104707
Jesus lives and so shall I (Gel-
lert) V681; AK168; AM596
                       104708
Jesus lives! no longer now (Gel-
lert) K512; L264; M435; AA
222; AO182; AZ589; BA239;
BR185   104709
Jesus lives! The victory's won
(Gellert) Q201 X Jesus lives!
thy terrors now   104710
Jesus lives! thy terrors now
(Gellert) A88; B176; D122;
E134; F140; O331; Q201var;
V169; W121; X155; AL116;
AM203; AP229; AW543; BV
187; BY158   104711
Jesus, Lord, and precious
Saviour (Arrhenius) J485;
K357; M185; N482; P316
                       104712
Jesus Lord, be thou mine own
(St Alfonso M. de Liguori)
BQ44   104713
Jesus, Lord, hear our prayer

(Ellsworth) R Saviour, hear us, we pray   104714

Jesus, Lord, I ask for mercy (Vaughan) R God of mercy and compassion   104715

Jesus, Lord, most great and glorious (Zinzendorf, N. L.) AZ1101; BA489   104716

Jesus, Lord, of all creation (Wesley) BR24 X Love divine, all loves excelling   104717

Jesus, Lord of life and glory, Bend from heaven, (Cummins) B127; D350; E75; F321; K80; O25; W524; AM472; AP466; AZ1379; BA598; BR286; BV 488   104718

Jesus, Lord of life and glory, Hear thy people's (Petersen) AZ1079; BA935   104719

Jesus, Lord of our salvation (Newman) F573   104720

Jesus, Lord, our captain glorious (Feith) BA912 X Praise the Lord through every nation   104721

Jesus, Lord, Redeemer (Kirkland) W127; AM208; BV55   104722

Jesus, Lord, we look to thee (Wesley) X541; AS449; AW321; BA676; BB68; BV423; BZ   104723

Jesus' love, precious love (Little-wood) R There is no love like the love of Jesus   104724

Jesus' love unbounded (Zinzendorf, N. L.) AZ754; BA624   104725

Jesus, Lover of my soul (Wesley) A415; B223; D335; E414; F193; G338; H348; I463; J393; K371; L122; M204; N419; O244; P 154; Q345; R216; S233; T415; U262; V331; W414; X542; Y 373; Z414; AA107; AB204; AC157; AD212; AE173; AF210; AG153; AH355; AI245; AK316; AL266; AM427; AO336; AP417; AR405; AS212; AT156; AU172; AV233; AW158; AX509; AY314; AZ1044; BA523; BB401; BC84; BF370; BR313*, 323; BV506; BY441; BZ
*   variant   104726

Jesus loves a little child (---) AY370   104727

Jesus loves me, Jesus loves me (Carey) K555; N659; AO620   104728

Jesus loves me! this I know (Warner) L491; R465; W660; AH546; AL623; AM633; AP 746; AT512; AU307; AW428; BA833; BV354; BY749 104729

Jesus loves the little children (Knowlton) AL604; AP743; AU311   104730

Jesus, loving to the end (Pollock) X Jesus, in thy dying woes (III)   104731

Jesus makes my heart rejoice (Hayn) AZ577; BA486 104732

Jesus, Mary, Joseph, help us (Vaughan) R Happy we, who, thus united   104733

Jesus, Master! at thy word (Liebenberg) O413; P209   104734

Jesus, Master, hear me now (Maxwell) U378; V551   104735

Jesus, Master of the feast (Wesley) L327   104736

Jesus, Master, Son of God (Seiss) K238; N390; P385   104737

Jesus, Master, whom I serve (Havergal) BA543 X Jesus, Master, whose I am   104738

Jesus, Master, whose I am (Havergal) J507; K375; O257; U317; V146; W509; AI182; AL379; AM494; AP556; AZ 1270; BA458, 543; BV627;   104739

Jesus may come today (Whitcomb) AM692   104740

Jesus, meek and gentle (Prynne) A358; B361; D567; E415; F194; I685; K567; W462; X543; AL 319; AP491; AZ768; BA637; BR305; BV554   104741

Jesu, meek and lowly (Collins) E416; F213; K74   104742

Jesu, meine Freude (Franck) BT347; BW564   104743

Jesus, meine Zuversicht (Luise

Henriette von Brandenburg)
BT206; BW541   104744

Jesu, meines Lebens Leben
(Homburg) BT151; BW535
   104745

Jesus' mercies never fail (Scheffler) AZ39; BA896   104746

Jesus, merciful and mild (Hastings) D611; AM459   104747

Jesus merciful, Jesus pitying
(Chao) R223   104748

Jesus, mighty King in Zion
(Fellows) BC108   104749

Jesus, my all, to heaven is gone
(Cennick) G199; I306; AW468;
AZ413; BA443   104750

Jesus, my captain, to victory
lead me (Schroeder) M251
   104751

Jesus, my God; behold at length
the time (Chadwick) BO167;
BQ133   104752

Jesus, my great High Priest
(Watts) Q220 X Join all the
glorious names   104753

Jesus, my highest treasure
(Liscovius) BA525   104754

Jesus, my King, thy kind and
gracious scepter (Swertner)
AZ706   104755

Jesus, my Lord! behold at length
(Chadwick) BQ133 X Jesus, my
God; behold at length   104756

Jesus, my Lord, how rich thy
grace (Doddridge) I406; M253;
N505; AZ128; BA563   104757

Jesus my Lord is real to me
(Reynolds) AU346   104758

Jesus, my Lord, my God, my all,
Hear me blest Saviour (Col-
lins) A460; B228; D600; E417;
F202; J504; K351; L155; T425;
W430; Z383; AD246; AL295;
AO297; AP454; AR358; AS129;
AZ668; BA488; BF458; BV535
   104759

Jesus, my Lord, my God, my
all, How can I love thee
(Faber) AH143; BN97; BO43;
BP59; BQ53   104760

Jesus, my Lord, my God, The
God supreme thou art (Wesley)
AZ1353; BA49   104761

Jesus, my Lord, my Life, my
All (Collins) Z383 X Jesus,
my Lord, my God, my all
   104762

Jesus, my Lord, thy nearness
doth impart (Gregor) AZ523
   104763

Jesus, my Lord, to thee I cry
(Hamilton) AU86 X O Jesus,
Lord, to thee I cry   104764

Jesus, my love, my chief delight (Beddome) AO288
   104765

Jesus, my Saviour and my God
(Stennett) L446   104766

Jesus, my Saviour, Brother,
Friend (Wesley) AL322
   104767

Jesus, my Saviour, let me be
(Beddome) AY298   104768

Jesus, my Saviour, look on me
(Elliott) A412; B390; D341;
U236; V487; AM140; AO408;
AZ15; BR304   104769

Jesus my Saviour, Look thou on
me (Lyon) AX522; AY139
   104770

Jesus, my Saviour, my Shepherd
blest (Ingemann) M179
   104771

Jesus, my Saviour, to Bethlehem
came ("A.N.") AU14; AX31
   104772

Jesus, my Savior true, guide
me to thee (Huish) BC85
   104773

Jesus, my Shepherd, let me
share (Harbaugh) AO320
   104774

Jesus, my strength, my hope
(Wesley) A452; B215; D650;
G343; I340; L200; O487; AL
422; AS452; BV522; BX310;
BZ   104775

Jesus, my Truth, my Way (Wesley) I471; K340; Q433; AA
373   104776

Jesus, Name all names above
(St Theoctistus) A342; E418;
J67; K70; N52; O307; X101
   104777

Jesus' name, Jesus' name,
Source of life (LaTrobe)

BA64 X Jesus' name, Source of
life   104778
Jesus, Name of wondrous grace
(Brorson) M188   104779
Jesus! Name of wondrous love
(How) A323; B90; D149; J50;
K35; L159; M180; N51; O211;
P144; Q114; W62; AA178; AP
176; AZ82; BA68   104780
Jesus' name shall ever be (Muh-
lenberg) BT114   104781
Jesus' name, Source of life and
happiness (LaTrobe) AZ718;
BA64   104782
Jesus nimmt die Sünder an
(Neumeister) BT324; BW466
                                104783
"Jesus," O how sweet the name
(Martin) R The name of Jesus
is so sweet   104784
Jesus, O precious name (Hoppe)
N55   104785
Jesus, o'er the grave victorious
(Higbee) AO201   104786
Jesus of Nazareth, Saviour and
King (Dougall) BC86   104787
Jesus, once of humble birth (Pratt)
BC88   104788
"Jesus only!" in the shadow
(Havergal) AZ610; BA70; BR
372   104789
Jesus, our best beloved Friend
(Montgomery) BA541   104790
Jesus, our brother, strong and
good (Davis) BK157   104791
Jesus, our Captain, Hope of our
Salvation (Lowenstern) M161
                                104792
Jesus, our Captain, Hope of our
salvation (Lowenstern) X Lord
of our life, and God of our
salvation   104793
Jesus, our Guardian, Guide, and
Friend (Gerhardt) AZ567
                                104794
Jesu, our hope, our heart's
desire (Latin, 7th c) F146;
BV200   104795
Jesus, our Lord, how rich thy
grace (Doddridge) N505 X
Jesus, my Lord, how rich thy
grace   104796
Jesus, our risen King (Allen)

D367   104797
Jesus, our Saviour, grant us thy
peace (Poppe) AW157a
                                104798
Jesus, our Saviour, only God and
Lord (---) BRp.467   104799
Jesus, our triumphant Head
(Hart) L270   104800
Jesus, our true and only Light
(Heermann) BR40 X O Christ,
our true and only light
                                104801
Jesus, pitying the sighs (Pollock)
X Jesus, in thy dying woes
(II)   104802
Jesus' prayer for all His brethren
(Hay) BE157   104803
Jesus, priceless treasure
(Franck) J575; M213; O351;
P163; Q347; R414; X544;
AA82; AF222; AI428; AK240;
AM550; AW564; BV640; BY
768; BZ   104804
Jésu redémptor ómnium (Latin,
6th c) BP10; BQ155   104805
Jesus, Refuge of the weary
(Savonarola) K92; N95; O264;
Q145; AA210; AD150; AK155;
AO164; AW536a   104806
Jesus reigns, He reigns vic-
torious (---) R Hear the royal
proclamation   104807
Jesu, Rex admirabilis Et Trium-
phator nobilis (St Bernard of
Clairvaux) BT361   104808
Jesus, rule my thoughts and
guide me (---) P365   104809
Jesus, save my dying soul
(Hastings) L379   104810
Jesus, Saviour, come to me!
(Scheffler) M165; Q356; AA
106   104811
Jesus, Saviour ever mild (Little-
dale) W468   104812
Jesus, Savior, hear our cry
(Caddell) R By the blood that
flowed from Thee   104813
Jesus, Savior, Heavenly Father
(Pendleton) BI64   104814
Jesus, Saviour, I implore thee
(Dober) AZ240; BA900
                                104815
Jesus, Saviour, infinite! With

thy blessed inward light (Rawson) BR202 X Come to our poor nature's night 104816

Jesus, Saviour, mighty Lord (---) BI10-D 104817

Jesus, Saviour, pilot me (Hopper) G269; H350; I482; J531; K270; L395; M169; N340; P161; Q 649; R336; S286; T408; U235; V340; W706; Y371; Z409; AB 227; AC160; AD225; AE254; AF213; AG155; AH309; AI302; AK468; AL444; AM497; AO328; AP607; AR288; AS248; AT337; AU158; AV238; AW161; AX501; AY308; BA704; BB398; BC121; BY543; BZ 104818

Jesus, Savior, risen Lord (---) BI22-D 104819

Jesus, Saviour, Son of God (Bonar) K78 104820

Jesus, Savior, thou art mine (Van Andel) AI438 104821

Jesus, Saviour, wondrous mild (Schmolck) M40 104822

Jesus selbst, mein Licht, mein Leben (Olearius) BT408 104823

Jesus shall lead me night and day (Martin) R Where He may lead me I will go 104824

Jesus shall reign where'er the sun (Watts) A542; B480; D261; E420; F220; G479; H195; I631; J307; K219; L344; M106; N368; O117; P164; Q511; R496; S377; T366; U392; V594; W388; X545; Y380; Z527; AA483; AB373; AC305; AD381; AE361; AF202; AG267; AH461; AI167; AK371; AL249; AM374; AO512; AP374; AR563; AS373; AT116; AU150; AV260; AW341; AY426; AZ303; BA94; BE271; BF527; BL59; BR60; BV320; BY184; BZ 104825

Jesus, Shepherd of the sheep (Cook) AA356 104826

Jesus, sinners doth receive (Neumeister) K325; N397; O411; Q324; W394; AA414; AI424; AM 394; BV478 104827

Jesus so lowly, Christ of the earth (Williams) X546 104828

Jesus, Solace of the soul (St Anselm of Lucca) AZ 104829

Jesu, sommo conforto, Tu se' tutto el mio amore (Savonarola) BW536 104830

Jesus, Son of God most high (Pollock) A232; V132; AL 606 104831

Jesus, Son of Mary, Fount of life alone (Swahili hymn) A223; E356; F469 104832

Jesus soon is coming (---) R Long for my Saviour I've been waiting 104833

Jesus, Source of my salvation (Homburg) AZ976; BA196 104834

Jesus spreads His banner o'er us (Park) G411; I235; BR469; BZ 104835

Jesus, stand among us (Pennefather) G593; R222; S13app.; W248; AE457; AK485; AL205; AP323; BV7; BY336; BZ 104836

Jesus, still lead on (Zinzendorf, N.L.) B449 X Jesus, lead the way 104837

Jesus, Sun of gladness (Knak) M198 104838

Jesus, Sun of righteousness (Rosenroth) L166; M564; O22; S30; W262; AL538; AP 659; AR414; AZ1200; BR90 104839

Jesus, tender Saviour, hast thou died for me? (Hodder. New S.S. hymn book 1863) AO618; AZ769; BA826 104840

Jesus, tender Shepherd, hear me (Duncan) A241; B360; D534; E599; G452; J235; K577; N661; S449; V649; W654; X364; AD 480; AH548; AK459; AL622; AM642; AP808; AW425; AZ 273; BB430; BR541; BV348; BY750 104841

Jesus, the all-restoring word (Wesley) I331 104842

Jesus, the calm that fills my breast (North) I549; AE223 104843

Jesus, the Christ of God (Bonar)
AZ1309   104844
Jesus, the conqueror, reigns
(Wesley) I172   104845
Jesus, the Father's only son
(Latin, 6th c) E17   104846
Jesus the Glory of the Holy
Angels (---) BO199   104847
Jesus, the loving Shepherd (Ogden)
BB572   104848
Jesus, the mighty work achieved
(Petursson) M386   104849
Jesus! the Name high over all
(Wesley) G400; H461; I222;
AL111; BV279; BZ   104850
Jesus, the Ransomer of man
(Latin, 6th c) BP11   104851
Jesus, the sinner's Friend, to
thee (Wesley) G201; H274; I
271; AZ403; BZ   104852
Jesus, the truth and power divine
(Wesley) I220   104853
Jesu! -- the very thought is
sweet (St Bernard of Clairvaux?)
E238; F188; O154; W421; X548;
AZ929   104854
Jesus, the very thought of thee
(St Bernard of Clairvaux??)
A462; B316; D434; E419; F189;
G348; H326; I533; J481; K353;
L113; M170; N139; Q350; R401;
S309; T426; U76; V383; W422;
X547; Y358; Z392; AA98; AB
81; AC158; AD251; AE230; AF
225; AG184; AH372; AI112; AK
274; AL298; AM542; AN205;
AO290; AP449; AR109; AS290;
AT135; AU241; AV139; AW155;
AY417; AZ205; BA487; BB158;
BC148; BF340; BJ7; BO13; BQ
17; BR412; BV536; BY205; BZ
                          104855
Jesu, the Virgin's Crown, do
Thou (St Ambrose) E192
                          104856
Jesus, the weary wanderer's rest
(Wesley) BR362   104857
Jesus, these eyes have never seen
(Palmer) F347; H327; I537;
J469; L167; S319; U229; V451;
W418; X550; Z352; AD280; AI
116; AL300; AM545; AO283;
AP451; BA518; BB166; BR414;

BV534; BY206   104858
Jesus, thine all-victorious love
(Wesley) G371; I375; BV
620; BZ   104859
Jesus, thine unbounded love
(Hoppe) M160   104860
Jesus, thou all-redeeming Lord
(Wesley) I263   104861
Jesus, thou art coming (A
Sister of Notre Dame) BN98;
BO51; BQ130   104862
Jesus, thou art mine forever
(Loy) J518; M167; P318; Q
357; AA97   104863
Jesus, thou art my righteousness
(Wesley) K328; L416
                          104864
Jesus, thou art my salvation
(Cennick) AZ876   104865
Jesus, thou art the sinner's
friend (Burnham) U189; V
295; AY45; AZ1455; BA601
                          104866
Jesus, thou divine Companion
(Van Dyke) A511; Y85; AB277;
AC191; AD318; AE415; AF
409; AG243; AK392; AL375;
AO494; AR150; AW372; BA
547; BF442   104867
Jesus, thou hast bought us
(Havergal) AO373 X Who is
on the Lord's side? 104868
Jesus, thou hast promised
That where two or three
(Latta) BB602   104869
Jesus, thou Joy of loving hearts
(St Bernard of Clairvaux??)
A485; B328; D430; F387;
G345; H439; I536; J483; K
354; L330; M171; N241; O419;
R215; S354; T427; U67; V450;
W420; X549; Z419; AB83; AD
404; AE227; AF290; AG206; A
AH506; AI268; AK335; AL297;
AM549; AO436; AP448; AR
202; AT136; AV134; AW171;
BA524; BB154; BE56*; BM
29; BR375, 410; BV380; BY
207; BZ   *much altered
                          104870
Jesus, thou my heart's delight
(Flittner) AA89   104871
Jesus, thou shepherd of the

sheep (Kelly) BR482   104872
Jesus, thou Shepherd of us all
(Hymns of the English Conf.
1880) BR42   104873
Jesus, thou Source of every
good (Ringwaldt) AZ740
                              104874
Jesus, thou source of life, and
light, and love (Hymns of the
English Conf. 1880) BR113
                              104875
Jesus, thou source of life, impart
(Doddridge) AZ687   104876
Jesus, thou who knowest death
(Stockman) BR429   104877
Jesus, thou who once wast dead
(Stockman) AZ860   104878
Jesus, thou wounded Lamb of God
(Zinzendorf, N.L.) K358
                              104879
Jesus, thy blood and righteousness
(Eber & Zinzendorf) G205; H
286; I148; J376; K329; L418;
M177; N426; O415; Q371; U93;
V247; AA326; AL278; AM439;
AO118; AP427; BV504; BY208;
BZ   104880
Jesus, thy boundless love to me
(Gerhardt) B229; D625; G222;
H318; I333; J399; K355; L433;
O347; P212; Q349; R404; S314;
U234; V324; W432; Z380; AA84;
AD262; AG164; AK273; AL296;
AO287; AP453; AR181; AT288;
AV184; AW170; AX42; AZ666;
BA522; BB146; BF461; BZ
                              104881
Jesus, thy church with longing
eyes (Bathurst) H469; K16;
N9; Q64; V186; AA144   104882
Jesus, thy light again I view
(Lange) BA459   104883
Jesus, thy love exceeds by far
(Watts) AZ190   104884
Jesus, thy love unbounded (Bos-
worth's Hymns, 1865) J401;
K363; N489   104885
Jesus, thy memory divine (St
Bernard of Clairvaux) BP23
                              104886
Jesu, thy mercies are untold
(Latin) F201   104887
Jesus, thy name hath power to

bless (Förtsch) N50 104888
Jesus, thy name I love (Deck)
K372; L118; U225; V456;
AM546; AO284; AZ1245;
BA63   104889
Jesus, thy word is my delight
(Hammond) AZ115; BA5
                              104890
Jesus, thyself to us reveal
(Watteville) AZ564; BA632
                              104891
Jesus 'till my latest breath
May I ponder (Moravian) AZ
726   104892
Jesus, to thee be endless praise
(---) BR54   104893
Jesus to thee I now can fly
(Wesley) BB233   104894
Jesus, to thy cross I hasten
(Harbaugh) AO353   104895
Jesus, to thy table led (Baynes)
B327; D222; S361; W314;
AL228; AP362; AZ1130;
BA300; BF597; BR476; BY
319   104896
Jesus took the babes and blessed
them (Loy) J260; M37; N233
                              104897
Jesus took the lambs and
blessed them (Loy) N233 X
Jesus took the babes and
blessed them   104898
Jesus, transporting sound!
(Wesley) AZ1177 X Let
earth and heaven agree
                              104899
Jesus, truest Friend, unite
All the consecrated band
(Zinzendorf, N.L.) K209
                              104900
Jesus, united by thy grace
(Wesley) G419; H427; I557;
AL373; AX549; BZ   104901
Jesus walked this lonesome val-
ley (White spiritual) BK168
                              104902
Jesus, we are far away (Pollock)
S238; W399; AK212   104903
Jesus, we lift ourselves to thee
(Beck) AZ134   104904
Jesus, we look to thee (Wesley)
G25; V453; AZ1323; BY337
BZ   104905

Jesus, we love to meet thee
(Moore) BY271   104906
Jesus, we thus obey (Wesley)
AZ1326; BV381; BY320
104907
Jesus, we want to meet (Olude)
BZ   104908
Jesus wept! those tears are
over (MacDuff) I132; O463;
AY211; AZ596   104909
Jesus! what a Friend for sinners
(Chapman) AM432   104910
Jesus, what offering shall I give
(Lange) AZ674; BY770 104911
Jesus, what precept is like thine
(Livermore) BE163   104912
Jesus, whelmed in fears unknown
(Pollock) X Jesus, in thy dy-
ing woes (IV)   104913
Jesus, when He left the sky
(Rumsey??) AY396   104914
Jesus, when we go to rest
(Lithuanian trad) BN194
104915
Jesus, where'er thy people meet
(Cowper) B459; D296; E422;
F245; G24; I37; S12app; U351;
V570; W247; X551; Z115; AE
26; AF402; AL208; AM309;
AP322; AZ395; BA371; BB515;
BE227; BR15; BV8; BX46; BY
338; BZ   104916
Jesus, while our hearts are bleed-
ing (Hastings) H496; L571;
N599; AX622; AY171   104917
Jesus, who died a world to save
(Hammond) AZ639   104918
Jesus who died, is now Seated
upon His throne (Watts) AZ
1350; BA97   104919
Jesus, who calledst little
ones to thee (Mudie) O572
104920
Jesus, who for my transgression
(Russell) O299   104921
Jesus, who knows full well (New-
ton) V464; AY294; AZ1357
104922
Jesus, who on the cross did die
(Whittle) R Would you lose your
load of sin?   104923
Jesu, who this our Lententide
(Latin) F85   104924

Jesus, who with thee can com-
pare be? (Freylinghausen)
AZ532; BA47   104925
Jesus, whom angel hosts adore
(Bonar) AZ420   104926
Jesus, whom thy church doth
own (Tersteegen) M89
104927
Jesus will I never leave (Kei-
mann) AZ579; BA491 104928
Jesus, with thy church abide
(Pollock) A233; B473; D525;
G380; J153; K207; U350; W
208; AD397; AF301; AI148;
AL168; AM278; AP299; AS
187; AZ1128; BA274; BF593;
BI58; BR221; BY260; BZ
104929
Jesus, with thy death and pas-
sion (German) AZ426 104930
Jezu Kriste, Pane milý
(Grodzki) BT169   104931
Join all the glorious names
(Watts) J412; K44; L158; Q
220; W165; AA244; AF229;
AM222; AO209; AZ1174; BT
220; BV266; BY175   104932
Join, all who love the Saviour's
name (Medley) AE30 104933
Join, all ye ransomed sons of
grace (Wesley) I576   104934
Join, earth and heaven, to
bless the Lord our Righteous-
ness (Wesley) AZ1165
104935
Join in the jubilee (Willes) R
Thanks for the Sabbath School
104936
Join to render thanks and praises
(Foster) AZ1392   104937
Jordanis oras praevia (Coffin)
BT63   104938
Joseph, dearest, Joseph mine
(German carol, 16th c)
A45; BG77; BK155   104939
Joseph lieber, Joseph mein
(German carol, 16th c) BG
77b   104940
Joseph, our certain hope below
(Breviary, 1632) BO127
104941
Joseph, pure spouse of that im-
mortal Bride (Latin, 1670)

BQ94   104942
Joseph was an old man (English
    trad carol) BG66   104943
Joses, the brother of Jesus,
    plodded from day to day
    (Kemps) AC457   104944
Joy and triumph everlastingly
    (Adam of St Victor) A129; E
    200; F523; X291; BJ27   104945
Joy because the circling year
    (Latin) B561; Z447; AD186
                            104946
Joy, behold the Saviour (Whittle)
    R Fierce and wild the storm
                            104947
Joy-bells ringing, children sing-
    ing (Pollard) AP774   104948
Joy cometh in the morning (Wien-
    land) R O weary pilgrim, lift
    your head   104949
Joy dawned again on Easter Day
    (Latin, 4th c) B556; G157;
    AF188; AG104; AW415 104950
Joy fills our inmost hearts today
    (Dix) B552; D539; K534; BR
    141   104951
Joy is a fruit that will not grow
    (Newton) G357; I546   104952
Joy to the world! The Lord is
    come (Watts) A319; B101; D324;
    G89; H141; I107; J15; K34; L
    210; M346; N32; O201; P132;
    R161; S122; T331; U57; V118;
    Y360; Z190; AA158; AB109; AC
    76; AD104; AE83; AF130; AG
    65; AH264; AI60; AK120; AL55;
    AM149; AN163; AO129; AP165;
    AQ299; AR121; AS100; AT65;
    AU137; AV98; AW70; AX92;
    AY189; AZ191; BA160; BB189;
    BC89; BD207; BE164; BF290;
    BI10; BK142; BR140; BX195;
    BZ   104953
Joy to the world, the Lord will
    come (Watts) BC89 X Joy to
    the world, the Lord is come
                            104954
Joy to thee, O Queen of heaven
    (Latin, 14th c) BP33   104955
Joyful, joyful, we adore thee
    (Van Dyke) A281; G12; J438;
    R21; S5; U25; Y49; Z95; AB
    12; AC43; AD9; AE10; AF8;

AG5; AH200; AK21; AN42;
    AO79; AP148; AQ11; AR27;
    AS91; AT44; AV52; AW10;
    BA33; BD29; BF211; BZ
                            104956
Joyful, joyful will the meeting
    be (Root) R Come to the
    Saviour, make no delay
                            104957
Joys are flowing like a river
    (Ferguson) AE294; AI125;
    AU278; AW479; AX131; AY
    466   104958
Jubilate! Jubilate! Jubilate!
    Amen (Moore) R Hark! the
    vesper hymn   104959
Jucundare, plebs fidelis
    (Adam of St. Victor) BT282
                            104960
Judean hills are holy (Stidger)
    AC456   104961
Judge eternal, throned in
    splendor (Holland) A518;
    B432; E423; J343; Q576;
    R517; S417; T448; W636;
    X552; Y277; Z545; AC277;
    AD432; AE397; AF435; AK
    398; AL515; AM620; AN323;
    AP641; AS387; AW345; BV
    662; BX381; BY643; BZ
                            104962
Judge me, God of my salvation
    (U.P. Psalter, 1912) T80;
    AJ120; AM539: AW499
                            104963
Judge me now, my God and
    Saviour (Zinzendorf, N.L.)
    AZ245   104964
Judge me, O God, and plead
    my cause (U.P. Psalter,
    1912) AJ119   104965
Judge me, O Lord, for I have
    walked (Scottish Psalter,
    1650) AP23   104966
Judge my integrity. The
    righteous Judge thou art
    (U.P. Psalter, 1912) T44;
    AJ70   104967
Just a few more days to be
    filled with His praise
    (Gabriel) AX569   104968
Just as I am, thine own to be
    (Hearn) R472; U280; W496;

Y136; Z297; AB160; AC145;
AD486; AE452; AG310; AK
347; AO383; AR344; AS408;
AT249; AU411; AW393; BA837;
BF349; BV630; BY442; BZ
                                    104969

Just as I am, without one plea
(Elliott) A409; B139; D606;
E316; F349; G198; H273; I
272; J370; K337; L494; M132;
N427; O447; P248; Q388; R
272; S230; T388; U174; V296;
W411; X253; Z295; AA318; AD
203; AE265; AF319; AG150;
AH343; AI211; AK214; AL270;
AM431; AO262, 699; AP410;
AR258; AS201; AT240; AU162;
AV169; AW458; AX303; AY213;
AZ1144; BA433; BB222; BV472;
BY443; BZ   104970

Just as seemeth good to thee
(Reed) R Choose my path
                                    104971

Just as Thou art, without one
trace (Cook) N398; V256;
AZ1145   104972

Just lean upon the arms of Jesus
(Lewis) AX471; AY455   104973

Just now, your doubting give o'er
(Morris) R If you are tired
                                    104974

Just outside the door (Rowe) R
O weary soul, the gate is
near   104975

Just over the mountains in the
Promised Land (Whitford arr)
BB642   104976

Just when I need Him, Jesus is
near (Poole) AI110; AS130;
AT267; BB590   104977

K

Kee va-yom ha-zeh y'-cha-payr
(Jewish traditional) BH322
                                    104978

Keep by the mighty hand, O keep
(Bonar) R Great Ruler of the
land and sea   104979

Keep me near thee, blessed Jesus
(Henry) AX506   104980

Keep me, O my blessed Jesus
(Metzler) AY80   104981

Keep me, Saviour, near thy side
(---) BR328   104982

Keep silence, all created things!
(Watts) V112   104983

Keep thou my way, O Lord
(Crosby) AO333   104984

Keep thyself pure! Christ's
soldier, hear (Plumptre) AS
315   104985

Kimi ga yo wa Chi yo mi
(Japanese national anthem)
Y310   104986

Kind and loving to each other
(Henry) R Let us ever love
                       104987

Kind Maker of the world, O
hear (St Gregory the Great)
A56   104988

Kinder, eilt euch zu bekehren
(Unparth. G. B.) AY30d
                       104989

Kinder, lernt die Ordnung fassen
(Unparth. G. B.) AY29d
                       104990

Kindle the taper like the steadfast star (Lazarus) BH204
                       104991

Kindly spring again is here
(Newton) E287; F607; X1
                       104992

King of glory, hear our cry
(Caddell) R By the first
bright Easter-day   104993

King of glory, King of peace
(Herbert) E424; F367; X553;
BJ22; BV539; BY12   104994

King of Glory! Saviour dear
(Mitchell) D549   104995

King of my life I crown thee now
(Hussey) AE295; AF453; AX
111   104996

King of my soul, a crown of
thorns (Neumann) AK154
                       104997

King of saints, to whom the
number (Ellerton) B287;
D168; BV444   104998

King of the City Splendid (Coster)
G473   104999

King Pharim sat a-musing, A-
musing all alone (English trad
carol) BG55(notes)   105000

Kingdom of God! The day how

L

blest (Beach) BX433   105001

Kingdom of light! Whose morning-
star (Miller) I651   105002

Kingdoms and thrones to God belong (Watts) V104; AM67;
AO88   105003

Kirken den er et gammelt Hus
(Grundtvig) BT467   105004

Knock! but O most patient Lord
(Holy songs, carols, and
sacred ballads) BR294   105005

Know, my soul, thy full salvation
(Lyte) AV215 X Jesus, I my
cross have taken   105006

Know, O child, thy full salvation
(Lyte) BE166 X Jesus, I my
cross have taken   105007

Know this, that every soul is
free (Gregg) BC90   105008

Knowledge, they say, drives
wonder from the world (Noyes)
AQ39   105009

Ko-dosh, ko-dosh, ko-dosh
Adonoy (Jewish traditional)
BH285   105010

Kol od balayvoy p'neemo (Imber)
BH266   105011

Komm, du wertes Losegeld
(Olearius) BT55   105012

Komm Gott Vater von Himmeln
(Ausbund) BU37   105013

Komm, Heiliger Geist, Herre
Gott (Luther) BT224   105014

Komm, o komm, du Geist des
Lebens (Held) BT226; BW548
105015

Kommt, Brüder, steht nicht stille
(Unparth. G. B.) AY31d
105016

Kommt und lasst uns Christum
ehren (Gerhardt) BT90
105017

Kreutz, Verfolgung und Trübsal
(Ausbund) BU80   105018

Kürzlich hab ich vorg'nommen
(Ausbund) BU20   105019

Kürzlich vor wenig Tagen (Ausbund Suppl) BU2   105020

Kyrie, God Father in heaven
above (Latin, ca 1100) Q6
105021

Kyrie, Gott Vater in Ewigkeit
(Latin, ca. 1100) BT6   105022

Labor on, labor on. Keep the
bright reward in view (Blackall) R In the harvest field
105023

Laborers of Christ, arise
(Sigourney) V496   105024

Labouruing and heavy laden, Want-
ing help in time of need
(Monsell) D436; O516; BR
308   105025

Lad denne Dag, o Herre Gud
(Brun) BT337   105026

Lady in sorrow, silent thy
womb ("M. J. ", Father) BN
176   105027

Lady of the Visitation (Santeüil)
BN150   105028

Laissez paître vos bêtes (French
carol) R J'ai oui chanter le
rossignol   105029

Lamb of God, all praise to thee
(Gotter) AZ790   105030

Lamb of God beloved (Cook)
AZ755; BA125   105031

Lamb of God, for sinners slain
(Woodford) D543   105032

Lamb of God, I look to thee
(Wesley) A251; D566; E591b;
F451b; I374; X356b   105033

Lamb of God, I look to thee
(Wesley) X Gentle Jesus,
meek and mild   105034

Lamb of God, my Saviour
(Cennick) AZ1076   105035

Lamb of God most holy (Decius)
P99 X Lamb of God pure and
holy   105036

Lamb of God, O Jesus! Thou
who hearest all (St Gelasius'
Sacramentary, 492) M411
105037

Lamb of God, pure and holy
(Decius) M418; P99; Q146;
AW540   105038

Lamb of God, thy precious
blood (Zinzendorf, E. D.) AZ
1049; BA112   105039

Lamb of God, to thee we raise
(Enman) BV446   105040

Lamb of God, we fall before
thee (Hart) L162; Q358; AA

81   105041
Lamb of God, who thee receive
  (Dober) BA435   105042
Lamb of God, whose bleeding love
  (Wesley) AY260 X Lamb of
  God, whose dying love   105043
Lamb of God, whose dying love
  (Wesley) AO437; AY260; AZ
  1468   105044
Lamb, the once Crucified! Lion,
  by triumph surrounded (Heus-
  ser-Schweizer) AZ531   105045
Lament, O man, thy pride of
  life (Bridges) BJ59   105046
Lamp of our feet, our path to
  light (Barton) BI41 X Lamp
  of our feet, whereby we trace
                             105047
Lamp of our feet, whereby we
  trace (Barton) A400; B60;
  D281; H93; I205; N221; O139;
  Q291; R254; U139; V71; W201;
  Z436; AA119; AB101; AC72;
  AD198; AE156; AF256; AG
  133; AH237; AO245; AR242; AS
  178; AV76; BD192; BF271; BI
  41; BV302; BY248; BZ   105048
Land of our birth, we pledge to
  thee (Kipling) Y178, 286 X
  Father in heaven, who lovest
  all   105049
Land of the mountains high (---)
  BC140   105050
Land of the North where battling
  breezes sweep (Ingham) Y284;
  AB339; BF557   105051
Languéntibus in Purgatorio (Latin)
  BQ249   105052
Lapsus est annus: redit annus
  alter (Breviary. Meaux, 1713)
  BW382   105053
Lass mich dein sein und bleiben
  (Selnecker) BT334   105054
Lasset uns mit Jesus ziehen
  (Birken) BT409   105055
Lasst uns alle fröhlich sein
  (Langhans) BT97   105056
Late, late, so late! and dark the
  n ight, and chill (Tennyson)
  I743; AI205   105057
Laud, O Sion, thy salvation (St
  Thomas Aquinas) E317; F622
                             105058

Lauda Sion salvatorem (St
  Thomas Aquinas) BO253
                             105059
Laudate Dominum, laudate
  Dominum omnes gentes (La-
  tin) BQ254   105060
Laudate, laudate, laudate
  Mariam (St Alphonso M. de
  Liguori) R Raise your voices,
  vales and mountains   105061
Launch out into the deep
  (Simpson) R The mercy of
  God   105062
Launch out into the deep And
  brave the stormy sea (Loy)
  M255   105063
L'-cho A-do-noy ha-g'-du-lo
  (Jewish traditional) BH291
                             105064
L'cho do'dee likras kalo
  (Jewish traditional) BH267
                             105065
Le vermeil du soliel (Denisot)
  BG101b   105066
Lead, holy Shepherd, lead us
  (St Clement of Alexandria)
  W569   105067
Lead, kindly Light, amid the
  encircling gloom (Newman)
  A430; B244; D423; E425;
  F298; G514; H347; I460;
  J523; L392; N344; O546; P
  346; R331; S289; T399; U245;
  V419; W568; X554, app. 2;
  Y367; Z578; AB219; AC333;
  AD221; AE202; AF215; AG
  157; AH404; AI299; AK315;
  AL436; AN239; AO327; AP
  600; AR423; AS247; AT60;
  AU238; AV149; AW162; AY
  465; AZ1502; BA685; BB403;
  BC112; BD250; BE169; BF
  414; BJ11; BK89; BL67; BR
  388; BX263; BY545; BZ
                             105068
Lead me gently home, Father
  (Thompson) AU123; AW449
                             105069
Lead me into life eternal
  (Widstoe) BC141   105070
Lead me, Lord, lead me in
  thy righteousness (Concord
  Anthem book, 1925) R539;

AE460; AF524; AG335; AR617;
BZ   105071
Lead me safely on by the narrow
way (Leslie) AX497; AY114
                                       105072
Lead me to some soul today
(Houghton) AU323   105073
Lead me to the living fountain
(Latta) R O I long to see the
beauty   105074
Lead on, lead on, mighty Man of
Galilee (McKinney) R Lead
on, O King of Glory   105075
Lead on, O King eternal (Shurt-
leff) A554; B534; G278; H
375; I408; J550; R332; S371;
T373; U301; Y177; Z363; AB
220; AC199; AD309; AE247;
AF375; AG191; AH445; AK299;
AL402; AM488; AO403; AP540;
AR324; AS255; AT417; AU236;
AV210; AW399; BA578; BB362;
BD87; BF470; BK78; BY375
                                       105076
Lead on, O King of Glory (Mc-
Kinney) AU460   105077
Lead on, O Lord! Above the
New Year's gates (Kretzmann)
M370   105078
Lead on, thou God of Hosts,
lead on (Taylor) U302 105079
Lead them, my God, to thee
(---) BB410   105080
Lead thou me on, and then my
feet (Armstrong) BB406
                                       105081
Lead us, great teacher Paul, in
wisdom's ways (Elpis??)
BQ99   105082
Lead us, heavenly Father, In our
opening way (Herford) V655;
BX521   105083
Lead us, heavenly Father, lead
us (Edmeston) A567; B247;
D421; E426; F311; K274; N
353; O215; R343; S304; T400;
W563; X555; AD223; AE179;
AF344; AK220; AL438; AP597;
AY431; AZ621; BA604; BB87;
BF418; BR302; BV583; BY43
                                       105084
Lead us, heavenly Father, lead
us, Shepherd Kind (Herford)

BX521 X Lead us, heavenly
Father, In our opening way?
                                       105085
Lead us, O Father, in the paths
of peace (Burleigh) A433;
B248; D422; G271; I475; J
472; R341; S262; T409; U41;
W566; X102; Z566; AD230;
AF376; AG159; AL437; AN70;
AO330; AP598; AR291; AW164;
BF416; BY546; BZ   105086
Leader of faithful souls, and
Guide (Wesley) I459; AL439;
BV558   105087
Lean on his arms, trusting in
his love (Lewis) R Just lean
upon   105088
Lean on my ample arm (Curtis)
BC260   105089
Leaning, leaning, leaning on the
everlasting arms (Hoffman)
R What a fellowship   105090
Leaning on Thee, my Guide and
Friend (Elliott) AZ17 105091
Leave God to order all thy
ways (Neumark) AB225 X
If thou but suffer God to guide
thee   105092
Leave starry heaven behind
(Wheelock) AQ70   105093
Leave your burden at the place
of prayer (Lillenas) R When
the clouds   105094
Lebt friedsam, strach Christus
der Herr (Ausbund) BU134
                                       105095
Les anges dans nos compagnes
(French trad) AD117; BG
119b   105096
Lest I forget Gethsemane (Hussey)
R King of my life   105097
Let all exalt Jehovah's goodness
(Westra) AJ427   105098
Let all men living in all lands
(Patton) AQ225   105099
Let all mortal flesh keep silence
(Liturgy of St James, 5th c)
A197; B339; E318; F390; G
594; J281; R148; S112; X273;
AD405; AE459; AF107; AG
337; AK336; AR120; AT80;
BB685; BL52; BY102; BZ
                                       105100

Let all on earth their voices
raise (Latin, 10th c) F504;
G19; I9; AT7; BN180; BZ
                                105101
Let all the earth Jehovah fear
(U. P. Psalter, 1912) AJ86;
AP30   105102
Let all the earth with songs re-
joice (Latin, 10th c) BE168
X Let the round world with
songs rejoice   105103
Let all the multitudes of light
(MacNutt) F150; J113; X156;
BV205   105104
Let all the world in every corner
sing (Herbert) A290; E427;
F375; G8; J418; K287; M600;
R22; S9; W15; X556; AB43;
AD8; AE20; AL38; BV243;
BY13; BZ   105105
Let all together praise our God
(Hermann) BZ   105106
Let all who enter here (---) R
528   105107
Let all who live in freedom
(Patton) AQ171   105108
Let children hear the mighty
deeds (Watts) M56; Q629;
S479; V633; AB325; AM293;
BR497   105109
Let Christian faith and hope
dispel (Logan) AL415; AP
535   105110
Let Christian hearts rejoice to-
day (St Jean de Brébeuf) BN
16   105111
Let Christians all with joyful
mirth (Church-Gallery book)
BG20   105112
Let Christians all with one accord
rejoice (English trad carol,
ca 18th c) BG65   105113
Let dogs delight to bark and bite.
(Watts) BW11   105114
Let each man learn to know him-
self (---) BC91   105115
Let earth and heaven agree (Wes-
ley) H230; I565; AZ1177
                                105116
Let earth's inhabitants rejoice
(Clegg) BC93   105117
Let everlasting glories crown
(Watts) V231; AL185 105118

Let every creature God has
made (Bible. Psalm 148)
BP99   105119
Let every creature hail the
morn (Whittier) BE170
                                105120
Let every creature join (Watts)
L87   105121
Let every ear attend (Watts)
L375 X Let every mortal ear
attend   105122
Let every heart exulting beat
(Breviary, Sarum. 1495)
BR162   105123
Let every lamp be burning bright
(Belden) BB183   105124
Let every mortal ear attend
(Watts) H237; L375; V266
                                105125
Let every tongue thy goodness
speak (Watts) H117   105126
Let folly praise what fancy
loves (Southwell) BL14
                                105127
Let God arise and by His might
(U. P. Psalter, 1912) T123;
AJ179   105128
Let God the Father, and the
Son, and Spirit be adored
(---) AZ140 X Let God the
Father, God the Son, and
Spirit be adored   105129
Let God the Father, God the
Son, and Spirit be adored (---)
AR627; AV409; AZ140 105130
Let hearts and tongues unite
(Newton) AZ1347; BA173
                                105131
Let hearts awaken, now the
night is ended (Latin, 6th c)
F10; BV40   105132
Let heaven highest praises bring
(St Bonaventura) BB297
                                105133
Let Him to whom we now belong
(Wesley) I373   105134
Let Him who would excel
(Confucius) AQ161   105135
Let hymns of joy to grief suc-
ceed (St Ambrose) BM83
                                105136
Let Israel trust in God alone
(Hamburg Temple Hymnal)

BH139   105137
Let love arise and praise him
  (Crum) F627   105138
Let me be thine forever (Sel-
  necker) J506; K271; L435;
  M538; N174; O410; P234;
  Q334; AA408   105139
Let me be with thee, where thou
  art (Elliott) AZ341   105140
Let me but hear my Saviour say
  (Watts) V437   105141
Let me dwell on Golgotha (New-
  ton) AZ52   105142
Let me find a place with that
  happy band (Latta) R In the
  day of all days   105143
Let me go, I cannot stay (Baltzell)
  R On the shore beyond the sea
                               105144
Let me go, let me go, From the
  turmoil (Knak) M642   105145
Let me go where saints are
  going (Hartsough) AX614; AY
  174   105146
Let me go where'er I will (---)
  AC489   105147
Let me with light and truth be
  blest (Tate & Brady) D662
                               105148
Let men their brethren know
  (Clarke) Y257   105149
Let my life be hid in thee (Bull)
  S318; AN223; BX96   105150
Let no hopeless tears be shed
  (Graduel de Paris, 1754) D245
                               105151
Let not such a thought e'er pain
  thee (Gerhardt) AA506 105152
Let not the wise their wisdom
  boast (Wesley) I308   105153
Let not thy hands be slack (Bur-
  row) Y227; AB268; BA548
                               105154
Let not young souls be smothered
  out (Lindsay) AQ150   105155
Let not your heart be faint (La-
  Trobe) AZ1316   105156
Let not your weary heart be
  troubled (Warren) AX533
                               105157
Let, O my Soul, thy God direct
  thee (Neumark) N484   105158
Let others see Jesus in you

(McKinney) R While passing
  thro' this world of sin
                               105159
Let others seek a home below
  (---) BB662   105160
Let our choir new anthems
  raise (St Joseph the Hymnog-
  rapher) E187 X Let us now
  our voices raise   105161
Let party names no more
  (Beddome) AZ1373   105162
Let plenteous grace descend
  on thee (Newton) AR618;
  AS457   105163
Let saints on earth in concert
  sing (Wesley) A397; B299;
  D391; E428; F272; L285;
  W227; X557; BJ41; BV433
                               105164
Let sighing cease and woe
  (Coffin) E27   105165
Let Sion in her beauty rise
  (Partridge) BC262   105166
Let Sion's watchmen all awake
  (Doddridge) G399; H463;
  I223; L306; V560; AE322;
  AX160; BZ   105167
Let songs of praises fill the
  sky (Cotterill) K139; L170;
  M475; Q232; AA254; AZ94;
  BA254   105168
Let the beauty of Jesus
  (Orsborn) AU317   105169
Let the deep organ swell the
  lay (Pise) BO218; BQ105
                               105170
Let the earth exalt the Lord
  (Held) M362 X Let the earth
  now praise the Lord 105171
Let the earth now praise the
  Lord (Held) K32; M362;
  Q91; AA146   105172
Let the loud hosannas ring
  (Sisters of St Joseph,
  Toronto) BO214   105173
Let the lower lights be burning
  (Bliss) R Brightly beams
  our Father's mercy 105174
Let the round world with songs
  rejoice (Latin, 10th c) E176;
  BE168   105175
Let the saints new anthems
  raise (St Joseph the Hymnog-

rapher) AO413 X Let us now
our voices raise   105176
Let the song go round the earth
(Stock) B485; Z531; BV321;
BY376   105177
Let the whole creation cry
(Brooke) J414; S74; X558; Y
45; Z103; AB53; AC44; AF69;
AN35; AQ10; AR28; AW49;
BX61; BY14   105178
Let the whole creation sing,
Joyous carols to our King (---)
BR565   105179
Let the world their virtue boast
(Wesley) AZ1466   105180
Let them praises give Jehovah
(U. P. Bible songs hymnal, 1927)
R Alleluia, praise Jehovah
                           105181
Let them that love Him (---) AZ
1207   105182
"Let there be light," at dawn of
time (Wise) BH141   105183
Let there be light, Lord God of
Hosts (Vories) R480; S402;
U336; Z513; AB358; AC291;
AD339; AE402; AF449; AG255;
AK402; AN397; AQ201; AR393;
AS360; AT444; AW353; BF565;
BH232; BK116; BX434   105184
Let thine example, holy John,
remind us (Paul the Deacon)
E223; X230   105185
Let thoughtless thousands choose
the road (Hoskins) Q608; AA
550   105186
Let thy blood in mercy poured
(Greek) A190; B340; K188;
AM362; AP200; AR516; AS
463   105187
Let thy grace, Lord, make me
lowly (Goode) AY56   105188
Let thy presence go with me
(Zinzendorf, N. L.) AZ1041;
BA311   105189
Let thy Spirit, blessed Saviour
(---) BB207   105190
Let us all in God rejoice
(Langhans) M326; Q97; AA153
                           105191
Let us all press on in the work
of the Lord (Stephens) BC98
                           105192

Let us all with gladsome voice
(Langhans) Q97 X Let us all
in God rejoice   105193
Let us awake our joys (Kings-
bury) AZ1239   105194
Let us be faithful to our passing
hours (Lysaght) AQ83 105195
Let us break bread together, On
our knees (Negro spiritual)
R447; AF288; AR489; BZ
                           105196
Let us choral anthems raise (St
Joseph the Hymnographer) AB
242 X Let us now our voices
raise   105197
Let us employ all notes of joy
(Fox) F423   105198
Let us ever love each other
(Henry) AX543   105199
Let us ever walk with Jesus
(Birken) M220; Q409; AA333
                           105200
Let us go to Galilee (Paulsen)
M630   105201
Let us joyfully give praise to
our God (Chinese trad) Y311
                           105202
Let us keep steadfast guard
(St Gregory the Great) AZ
1345   105203
Let us live, then and be glad
(Latin) Y299   105204
Let us love, and sing, and
wonder (Newton) AM127; AZ
616; BV267   105205
Let us now our voices raise
(St Joseph the Hymnographer)
A136; F518; J546; X215; AB
242; AM284; AO413; AZ864
                           105206
Let us now praise famous men
(Bible. Ecclesiasticus) X432;
AQ230   105207
Let us oft speak kind words to
each other (Townsend) BC94
                           105208
Let us pray for each other
(Kieffer) R There's a city of
light   105209
Let us rejoice, the fight is won
(Dearmer) X157   105210
Let us sing of Easter gladness
(Hill) BE171   ˙105211

Let us sing the King Messiah
  (Ryland) BY377   105212
Let us sing, with one accord
  (Thrupp) AZ1053   105213
Let us thank the Christ for all
  who did their duty (Crum)
  F455   105214
Let us wander where we will
  (Stevenson) AQ60   105215
Let us with a gladsome mind
  (Milton) A308; E532; F377;
  G81; J405; R28; S64; W11;
  X12; Y40; Z181; AC32; AD95;
  AE66; AF70; AG39; AH316;
  AI447; AK77; AL7; AM30; AP
  120; AS82; AW64; BA25; BD25;
  BF220; BH58; BK53; BT570;
  BV20; BX20; BY15; BZ 105216
Let worldly minds the world pur-
  sue (Newton) V444   105217
Licht vom Licht! erleuchte mich
  (Schmolck) BW553   105218
Liebe, die du mich zum Bilde
  (Scheffler) B T397   105219
Liebster Jesu, wir sind hier,
  Dich und dein wort anzuhören
  (Clausnitzer) BT16; BW553
                        105220
Liebster Jesu, wir sind hier,
  Dienem worte nachzuleben
  (Schmolck) AW553b; BT16, 300
                        105221
Life and health are in the name
  (Darbyshire) X286; BV397
                        105222
Life has loveliness to sell (Teas-
  dale) AC227   105223
Life is good, for God contrives it
  (Dearmer) G160; X158; Z248
                        105224
Life is the time to serve the Lord
  (Watts) L359; V658   105225
Life of ages, richly poured
  (Johnson) A373; G405; S95;
  X559; Y190; Z177; AB351; AC
  214; AD330; AF236; AK82; AN
  337; AQ172; BD33; BF427; BX
  394; BY630   105226
Life of all that lives below!
  (Wesley) AN53; AW238; BX
  93   105227
Life on earth is but a vapor
  (Schell) AX579   105228

Life-spring divine and bond of
  all (Latin, 6th c) BJ100
                        105229
Life without Thee would be
  dreary (Henry) R Keep me
  near Thee   105230
Life's day is ended, The battle
  fought and won (Brorson) O
  591   105231
Lift high the cross, the love of
  Christ proclaim (Kitchin) F
  633   105232
Lift high the triumph song to-
  day! (McGregor) G131; AK
  137   105233
Lift Him up, lift Him up. (Oat-
  man) R How to reach 105234
Lift Him up, the risen Saviour
  (Warren) R Lift Him up,
  'tis He that bids you 105235
Lift Him up, 'tis He that bids
  you (Warren) BB520 105236
Lift the strain of high thanks-
  giving (Ellerton) D299; BT632
                        105237
Lift thine eyes, O lift thine
  eyes (Bible. Psalm 121)
  AH620; BC370   105238
Lift thy head, O Zion, weeping
  (Jeszensky) AF377; AK306
                        105239
Lift up, lift up your voices now!
  (Neale) D119; Z241; AB149;
  AE131; AM202   105240
Lift up the banner of salvation
  (Tamminen) M98   105241
Lift up the trumpet, and loud
  let it ring (Strout) BB541
                        105242
Lift up thy light, O man, arise
  and shine (Thaxter) BE172
                        105243
Lift up, ye princes of the sky
  (Aylward) BQ32   105244
Lift up your eyes, ye Christians
  (Solberg) M115   105245
Lift up your heads, eternal gates
  (Tate & Brady) V166 105246
Lift up your heads, Pilgrims
  aweary (Camp) AI97; AM687
                        105247
Lift up your heads, rejoice!
  Redemption draweth nigh

(Lynch) BI109   105248

Lift up your heads, ye gates of brass (Montgomery) E549; F 306; J308; K216; U399; W385; X301; AK368; AL260; AM384; AO514; AP389; BA359; BV319; BY378   105249

Lift up your heads, ye mighty gates (Weissel) A484; B186; D454; G126; J8; K7; M330; N2; O158; Q73; R152; S114; U54; Z224; AA138; AD176; AF114; AG108; AK92; AM146; AN179; AO195; AQ310; AR203; AT247; AW523; AY415; AZ1202; BA 151; BB294; BF321; BR191; BV80; BX200; BY82; BZ   105250

Lift up your heart! lift up your voice X Rejoice the Lord is King X On wings of living light X True lovers of mankind   105251

Lift up your hearts, O King of kings (Masterman) G472; R481; S405; AB278; AC295; AD342; AE379; AG253; AR290; BZ   105252

Lift up your hearts to things above (Wesley) I558   105253

"Lift up your hearts!" We lift them Lord, to thee (Butler) A482; E429; F341; S258; X560; Y176; Z372; AB178; AC3; AD 304; AF352; AK27; AL340; AN226; AR330; BF452; BV 474; BY444   105254

Lift up your hearts, ye people (Parr) AF189   105255

Lift up your voice, ye Christian folk (Lyon) F297   105256

Lift ye the Snow-white Banner (Kirby) R Forth to the fight, ye ransomed   105257

Lift your glad voices in triumph on high (Ware) I159; BR566   105258

Lift your heads, ye friends of Jesus (Wesley) H200   105259

Lift your hidden faces (Fyleman) X1; AQ319; BG156   105260

Light of ages and of nations (Longfellow) AN75; AQ248;

BD183; BX453   105261

Light of Ages, shed my man (Chubb) Y149; AB294; BD140; BF422   105262

Light of conscience, clear and still (Chubb) AB294 X Light of Ages, shed by man 105263

Light of life, so softly shining (Bonar) AP775   105264

Light of life, the great Messiah (---) BR144   105265

Light of light, enlighten me (Schmolck) J186; L45; M4; N346; O33; R73; S21; U439; V32; Z445; AD34; AG17; AK42; AM333; AO15; AP345; AR63; AW553a; BF187; BR91   105266

Light of light, O Sun of heaven (Opitz) N347   105267

Light of light that shineth (Thring) R From the eastern mountains   105268

Light of the anxious heart (St Bernard of Clairvaux??) J475; K46; W249   105269

Light of the Gentile nations (Franck) K51; M378; N65; O203; Q138; AA190   105270

Light of the lonely pilgrim's heart (Denny) F209; H202; W381; AL243; AM232; AO 110; AP250; BA100; BV268   105271

Light of the world, come nigh and bless (Harvey) BA170   105272

Light of the world! for ever ever shining (Bonar) W171; AB75; AL119; BY209 105273

Light of the world, how long the quest (Poteat) Z320 105274

Light of the world, we hail thee (Monsell) G114; R138; S422; T370; U398; Y19; Z208; AB 72; AC9; AD467; AG277; AK 124; AO518; AR112; AT454; BF185; BZ   105275

Light of the world! whose kind and gentle care (Bateman) I505   105276

Light of those whose dreary dwelling (Wesley) B100; D

325; H199; I638; L212; AZ943; BA608   105277

Light, that from the dark abyss (Pirks) L187   105278

Light up this house with glory, Lord (Harris) AD28; BA328; BY272   105279

Lighten the darkness of our life's long night (Owen) E430; X103; AF386   105280

Light's abode, celestial Salem (St Thomas à Kempis) A587; B507; D399; F279; J591; O250; X199; AP632; AZ629; BR216; BV434   105281

Light's glittering morn bedecks the sky (Latin, 4th c) F602; BY159   105282

Like a river glorious (Havergal) W443; AM587; AT294   105283

Like a shepherd, true, Jesus leads (Clements) AY120
                    105284

Like a strong and raging fire (---) AH139   105285

Like as a father pities his child (Belden) BB66   105286

Like as a mother, God comforteth His children (Baum) BE174
                    105287

Like as the hart doth breathe and bray (Tate & Brady) BT525 X As pants the hart for cooling streams   105288

Like Enoch, let me ever walk with Thee (Hoppe) M207   105289

Like Mary at her Saviour's feet (Montgomery) AZ880; BA836
                    105290

Like Noah's weary dove (Muhlenberg) D486; H419   105291

Like pilgrims sailing thro' the night (Harris) AN361; BDp.21; BX407   105292

Like radiant sunshine that comes after rain (Barratt) AT285; AU116   105293

Like shadows gliding o'er the plain (Taylor) BX180   105294

Like sheep we went astray (Watts) V250   105295

Like silver lamps in a distant shrine (Dix) B548   105296

Like Sion's steadfast mount are they (U.P.Psalter, 1912) AJ 354; AM585   105297

Like the deer that yearns for running streams (Ladies of the Grail) BL54; BSp.16
                    105298

Like the eagle, upward, onward (Bonar) V502   105299

Like the golden sun ascending (Kingo) O325; Q207   105300

Like the stars of the morning (Cushing) R When He cometh, when He cometh
                    105301

Like the sunshine after rain (Lillenas) AU361   105302

Listen! the Master beseecheth (Punshon) AL506   105303

Listen to our prayer, O Lord; Hear our humble plea (Indian [Asia] Prayer) BZ   105304

Listen to the blessed invitation (Hewitt) AX252 105305

Listen to the gentle promptings (Montgomery) AX248; AY 373   105306

Listen to the Lambs (Negro spiritual) AH602   105307

Listen to those happy voices (Loy) M351   105308

Little Baby Jesus, born today (Kretzmann) M616 105309

Little children, Lord are we (---) BH249   105310

Little children, praise the Lord (Pollock) AY324   105311

Little children, praise the Saviour (Juvenile harmonist, ca 1837) AP747   105312

Little children, wake and listen (S.P.C.K. Appendix, 1869) W44; AL599; AN158; BD223; BX530   105313

Little David, play on your harp (Negro spiritual) Y317
                    105314

Little drops of water, Little grains of sand (Carney & Dearmer) E600; X365; AP778   105315

Little Jesus, sweetly sleep, do

(Wesley) I579; V664; AZ558;
BA411; BB384   105350
Lo! on the water's brink we stand
(---) BC97   105351
Lo, our Father's tender care
(Gutheim) BH82   105352
Lo, round the throne, a glorious
band (Hill) F525; BJ3   105353
"Lo, she is not dead, but sleep-
ing" (Brooks) AX620   105354
Lo! The Angels' Food is given
(St Thomas Aquinas) E317b;
F622b   105355
Lo! the clouds have burst asunder
(Childs) BI6   105356
Lo, the day of days is here
(Hosmer) AN199; AQ317;
AW545; BD237; BX206   105357
Lo! The day of rest declineth
(Robbins) BX34   105358
Lo, the earth awakes again (Long-
fellow) AQ318 X Lo, the earth
is risen again   105359
Lo, the earth is risen again
(Longfellow) AN200; AQ318;
BD242; BK132; BX210   105360
Lo! the earth rejoices At the
dawn of day (---) BH248
                            105361
Lo, the Easter-tide is here
(Hosmer) AN201   105362
Lo! the heavens are breaking
(---) AW434   105363
Lo, the mighty God appearing
(Goode) BC264   105364
Lo, the pilgrim Magi leave their
royal halls (Coffin) BR158
                            105365
Lo! the stone is rolled away
(Scott) V160   105366
Lo! the voice of Jesus (Evans)
D608   105367
Lo, they come in glad procession
(Glenn) BI104   105368
Lo, upon the altar lies Bread of
heaven from the skies (St
Thomas Aquinas) M52; AA
433   105369
Lo, we tread on holy ground
(Tressel) M507   105370
Lo! what a cloud of witnesses
(Scottish Paraphrases, 1745)
A569; B300; C393; BA808

                            105371
Lo! what a glorious sight ap-
pears To our admiring eyes
(Watts) AM601; AP636
                            105372
Lo, what a pleasing sight
(Watts) L289; AX545; AY116
                            105373
Lo, when the day of rest was
past (Dearmer) X159 105374
Lobe den Herren, den mächtigen
König der Ehren! (Neander)
BW515   105375
Lobe den Herren, O meine Seele
(Herrnschmidt) AW513b; BT
26; BW513   105376
Lobt Gott, ihr Christen all-
zugleich (Herman) BT105
                            105377
Long ago and far away (Horn)
J44   105378
Long ago the lilies faded (Tar-
rant) BD62   105379
Long ago, there was born In the
City of David (Blackmer)
AR127   105380
Long ago, when heathen darkness
(Callin) BY249   105381
Long ago when Jesus walked in
Galilee (Bayly) BY751
                            105382
Long as I live I'll bless thy
name (Watts) AY9; BR496
                            105383
Long did I toil, and knew no
earthly rest (Quarles) E432;
O396; W544; X104; AD263;
AZ703   105384
Long for my Saviour I've been
waiting (---) BB186 105385
Long hast thou stood, O Church
of God (Grundtvig) BE176
                            105386
Long has thou wept and sorrowed
(Heusser-Schweizer) N183;
O465   105387
Long have I sat beneath the
sound (Watts) I281; L388
                            105388
Long have they waited in the far
distant lands (Schell) AX214
                            105389
Long have we sought eternal life

(Glasgow) AU131   105390

Long live the Pope! His praises
sound (Henry) BO206; BQ122
                                              105391

Long upon the mountains, weary
(Smith) BB664   105392

Long years ago o'er Bethlehem's
hills (Brewer) G99; I120
                                              105393

Look down, O Lord, from heaven
behold (Luther) O424; Q260
                                              105394

Look down to us, Saint Joseph
(McNaspy) BL64   105395

Look for the beautiful, look for
the true (Belden) AR309;
AS318   105396

Look for the waymarks (Belden)
BB671   105397

Look from the sphere of endless
day (Bryant) AP385 X Look
from thy sphere   105398

Look from Thy sphere of endless
day (Bryant) D251; H470; I
644; J325; K232; L340; N384;
O115; P389; Q499; W340; AA
479; AD340; AE354; AI175; AK
375; AO537; AP385; BA347; BF
537; BX89; BY645   105399

Look! Look! Look and live (Hull)
R There is life for a look
                                              105400

Look to Jesus Christ thy Saviour
(Franzén) N467   105401

Look to the Lamb of God (Jackson)
R If you from sin   105402

Look up, by failure daunted
(Dearmer) X232   105403

Look up, my soul, to Christ
thy joy (Schade) AZ889; BA
692   105404

Look upon Jesus, sinless is He
(Belden) BB593   105405

Look upon us, blessed Lord
(Clausnitzer) J190; W203
                                              105406

Look with mercy, Lord (Bible.
Joel, 2) BM72   105407

Look, ye saints, the day is breaking (Kelly) BE177   105408

Look, ye saints, the sight is
glorious (Kelly) A105; B185;
D130; G165; H193; I169; J114;

K121; L273; Q222; R133;
S201; U111; V163; W134;
Z256; AD172; AE124; AF
203; AH299; AK180; AL108;
AM217; AO194; AP224; AS
161; AT148; AU425; AW119;
AX121; AY267; AZ1403; BA
247; BV206; BY169; BZ
                                              105409

Looking unto Jesus, in faith I
come (Loes) AU132 105410

Looking upward every day,
Sunshine on our faces
(Butler) U220; W674; AL
326; AP786; BD95; BY477
                                              105411

Lord, a little band and lowly
(Shelly) W661; AP726; AX
564; AY340   105412

Lord, a Saviour's love display-
ing (Hawkins) D258 105413

Lord, accept into thy kingdom
(Gabbott) BC100   105414

Lord, accept our true devotion
(Alldridge) BC101   105415

Love, accept the alms we offer
(Sedgwick) F406   105416

Lord, accept the gifts we offer
(Latin) BM6   105417

Lord, all I am is known to thee
(Watts) H106; L99   105418

Lord, and is thine anger gone
(Wesley) AZ1471   105419

Lord and Master, who hast
called us (Smith) F495;
BV414   105420

Lord and Saviour, true and kind
(Moule) G560   105421

Lord, as a pilgrim on earth I
roam (Malmivaara) J536
                                              105422

Lord, as of old at Pentecost
(Gabriel) AT173   105423

Lord, as this solemn rite we
keep (Kauffman) R We bow
to thee   105424

Lord, as thou wilt, deal thou
with me (Bienemann) Q406;
AA383   105425

Lord, as to thy dear cross we
flee (Gurney) A413; B125;
D346; F334; J455; N170; O
392; S145; U87; W90; Z326;

AD152; AF347; AK222; AL78;
AP510; AZ175; BA81; BF404;
BR354; BV487   105426
Lord, as we thy Name profess
(Parker) G295; AC176; AV207;
BF450   105427
Lord, as we to thy Mercy flee
(Gurney) BR354 X Lord, as to
thy dear cross we flee 105428
Lord, at this closing hour (Fitch)
L63; Z131; AY289; AZ1333;
BB32   105429
Lord! at thy feet we humbly kneel
(Browne) BB236   105430
Lord, at thy table we behold
(Stennett) Z464   105431
Lord, be thy word my rule (Words-
worth) F327; BV299   105432
Lord, before thy Presence come
(Taylor) BX31   105433
Lord, before thy throne we
bend (Bowdler) BR103 105434
Lord, behold us with thy blessing
(Buckoll) E523; F457; W677;
X333   105435
Lord, bestow on us thy blessing
(Swedberg) P65   105436
Lord, bless and pity us... That
all the earth thy way may
know (U.P. Psalter, 1912)
R493; T122; AJ178   105437
Lord bless and pity us... That
the earth thy way, and nations
all may know (Scottish Psalter,
1650) AL657; AP57   105438
Lord, bless thy word to every
heart (Howard) BB700 105439
Lord, cause thy face on us to
shine (Cotterill) M94; AX
640   105440
Lord Christ, reveal thy holy face
(Wilhelm II, duke) AZ321;
BA374   105441
Lord Christ, when first thou
cam'st to men (Bowie) A522;
X562; AD146; AF325; AR366;
BZ   105442
Lord Christ, who on thy heart,
didst bear (Thomas) BY636
                            105443
Lord, dismiss us with thy bless-
ing; Fill our hearts (Fawcett??)
A489; B51; D34; G26; H37; I39;

J191; K431; L66; M16; N
354; O48; P55; Q50; R79;
S54; U448; V27; W299; Z
127; AA17; AD65; AE33;
AF63; AG13; AH176; AI26;
AK35; AL215; AM319; AN
470; AO49; AP340; AR48;
AS62; AT31; AV23; AW45;
AX79; AZ1395; BA378; BB
33; BC105; BF207; BK172;
BV56; BX510; BY762; BZ
                            105444
Lord, dismiss us with thy
blessing, Hope and comfort
(Fawcett??) AN470 X
Lord dismiss us ... Fill our
hearts   105445
Lord, dismiss us with thy bless-
ing, May our praise to thee
(Fawcett??) BK172 X Lord
dismiss us ... Fill our
hearts   105446
Lord, dismiss us with thy
blessing, Thanks for mercies
(Buckoll) F458; W678; X
333b; BR105   105447
Lord, disperse the mists of er-
ror (Aström) N415 105448
Lord, do thou guide me on my
pilgrim way (Lucas) BH22
                            105449
Lord, dost thou say, "Ask what
thou wilt?" (Newton) V460;
AZ333; BV622   105450
Lord, enthroned in heavenly
splendour (Bourne & Dearmer)
E319; F400; X274; AD407;
AF291; AK344; BV382
                            105451
Lord, for ever at thy side
(Montgomery) A451; B306;
D649; L461; V320; AZ1066
                            105452
Lord, for grace we thee en-
treat (Zinzendorf, N.L.)
AZ869   105453
Lord, for the mercies of the
[this] night (Mason) K453;
L7; R533; S9app.; AF501;
AY280   105454
Lord, for thy coming us pre-
pare (Gregor) AZ568; BA
p.149   105455

Lord, for tomorrow and its needs (Mary Xavier, Sr. i.e. Sybil F. Partridge) B36; G314; I 510; U360; Z327; AC317; AE 236; AG222; AH388; AL433; AO315; AP514; AR292; AS 317; AT339; AU259; AV197; BB604; BD110; BN189; BO 194; BQ143   105456

Lord! from far-severed climes we meet (Hay) AV70 X Defend us, Lord   105457

Lord, from the depths to thee, I cried, My voice, Lord, do thou hear (Scottish Psalter, 1650) R277; S240; AL686; AP116   105458

Lord, from whom all blessings flow (Wesley) BY361 X Christ, from whom all blessings flow   105459

Lord, from whose hand we take our charge (Piggott) X346; BY349   105460

Lord, give me light to do thy work (Bonar) AX505; AY75; BR505   105461

Lord, give us a vision of souls gone astray (Davis) AX195   105462

Lord, give us light to do thy work (Bonar) BR505 X Lord, give me light   105463

Lord God almighty, in thy hand (Coster) BY62   105464

Lord God almighty, King of heaven (Kertzmann) M518   105465

Lord God, by whom all change is wrought (Gill) AN359; BX185   105466

Lord, God, from whom all life (Burroughs) X343; AD44; BY 503   105467

Lord God of hosts, by all adored (Gambold) L109; V517; AO52   105468

Lord God of hosts, how lovely (U.P. Book of Psalms, 1871) AK327; AP67   105469

Lord God of hosts, in mercy (U.P. Psalter, 1912) T154; AJ228   105470

Lord God of hosts, uplift thine hand (Ainger) R God of our fathers, unto thee   105471

Lord God of hosts, whose mighty hand (Oxenham) A529; B438; J359; U341; Y288; AH 208; AO591   105472

Lord God of hosts, whose purpose, never swerving (Knapp) R288; S368; Y209; Z497; AB 232; AC247; AD328; AF411; AH514; AK266; AR325; BF570   105473

Lord God of hosts, within whose hand (Housman) E219; X227   105474

Lord God of morning and of night (Palgrave) L1; AF500; AL534; AN89; AZ933; BX130; BY677   105475

Lord God Omnipotent, Lord God alone (Smith) AB54; BX66   105476

Lord God, our Father, thou our chiefest stay (Latin) O43   105477

Lord God, our Salvation (Swertner) AZ1027   105478

Lord God the Holy Ghost (Montgomery) F615; K141; L275; N160; U128; V213; AL158; AP274; AW132; AZ1484; BA 253; BV219; BY235   105479

Lord God, thy praise we sing (Latin, 5th c) AZ1112; BA p.170   105480

Lord God, we all give praise to thee (Melanchthon) M483; Q254; AA286   105481

Lord God, we all to thee give praise (Melanchthon) Q254 X Lord God, we all give praise to thee   105482

Lord God, we worship thee! (Franck) A144; B440; D200; K496; M506; AZ785; BA875   105483

Lord God, who art my Father dear (Mathesius) AA517   105484

Lord God, whose breath the universe controls (Lucas) BH 37   105485

Lord, grant that we e'er pure retain (Melmbold) AA390 105486

Lord, grant thy servants grace (Heermann) AZ786; BA309 105487

Lord, grant us light that we may know (Tuttiett) BA887 X O grant us light, that we may know 105488

Lord, grant us, though deeply abased with shame (Schlicht) AZ494; BA312 105489

Lord, guard and guide the men who fly (Hamilton) Y187; AB 382; AC290; AH478; AN468; BZ 105490

Lord, hear me in distress, Regard my suppliant cry (U.P. Psalter, 1912) T281; AJ389 105491

Lord, hear me when I pray (U.P. Psalter, 1912) AJ72 105492

Lord, hear my prayer, and let my cry (Psalter, 1860 Kennedy) T186; AJ272 105493

Lord, hear my voice, my prayer attend (U.P. Book of Psalms, 1871) AP50 105494

Lord, hear the right, attend my cry (Scottish Psalter, 1650) AJ33; AP12 105495

Lord, hear the right, regard my cry (U.P. Psalter, 1912) T23; AJ31 105496

Lord, hear the voice of my complaint (Agricola) O275; AA365 105497

Lord, help me live from day to day (Meigs) AS338; AU77 105498

Lord, help us ever to retain (Helmbold) Q288 105499

Lord, her watch thy Church is keeping (Downton) B481; D 260; F267; K226; U397; W378; BB437; BY379 105500

Lord, how secure and blest are they (Watts) H285; I439 105501

Lord, how secure my conscience was (Watts) V280 105502

Lord, I am come! Thy promise is my plea (Newton) AZ462 105503

Lord, I am fondly, earnestly longing (Hoffman) AX371; AY339 105504

Lord, I am thine, entirely thine (Davies) G224; H309; I342; U186; V318; AZ381; BA456 105505

Lord, I believe a rest remains (Wesley) I356 105506

"Lord, I believe! help thou mine unbelief," (Gould) BR 332 105507

Lord! I believe, thy power I own (Wreford) U214; V349; AE194; AI234; AM428; AO 356; AR269 105508

Lord, I cannot let thee go (Newton) I514 105509

Lord, I care not for riches (Kidder) AX486 X I am bought not with riches 105510

Lord, I feel a carnal mind (Toplady) AZ1477 105511

Lord, I have made thy word my choice (Watts) V79; BV304 105512

Lord, I have passed another day (Taylor) AZ360 105513

Lord, I hear of showers of blessing (Codner) D589; H 57; I346; L399; N407; O268; U452; V579; W687; AH352; AI265; AL334; AM527; AO634; AP471; AS45; AU297; AV348; AW204; AX41; AY244; AZ 268; BA904; BB208 105514

Lord, I know thy grace is nigh me (Ganse) AO278 105515

Lord, I lift my soul to thee (U. P. Psalter, 1912) AJ64; AM 583 105516

Lord, I thank thee for thy love (Kauffman) R Worthy art thou, Lord divine 105517

Lord, I want to be a Christian in my heart (Negro spiritual) R317; AE454; AF353; AG318; AH608; AR486; BK167; BZ 105518

Lord I was blind: I could not see
(Matson) AL337; BV486; BY
445   105519

Lord, I will praise thy name
(U. P. Psalter, 1912) AJ78
105520

Lord, I would own thy tender care
(Taylor) E601; F443; W655;
BV538   105521

Lord, if at thy command (Wesley)
I648; AA487; AX164   105522

Lord! in love and mercy save us
(Symington) AZ275   105523

Lord, in the fullness of my might
(Gill) AL352; AP563; AW397; BB
BB386; BY446   105524

Lord, in the hollow of thy hand
(Briggs) X337; AN467; BV
407   105525

Lord, in the morning thou shalt
hear (Watts) H28; I41; L8;
S28; V34; AD45; AM332; AO
21; AW20; AY281; BB39; BR9
105526

Lord, in the strength of grace
(Wesley) G217; I352; AL363;
BZ   105527

Lord, in thee am I confiding
(U. P. Psalter, 1912) T68;
AJ103   105528

Lord, in this blest and hallowed
hour (Conder) BY321   105529

Lord, in this sacred hour (Bulfinch) L49; BH112   105530

Lord, in this thy mercy's day
(Williams) A57; B122; D88;
E76; F94; H283; W405; AL274;
AO280; AP428; AZ1128; BA416;
BR293   105531

Lord, in thy kingdom there shall
be (Anstice) AA461   105532

Lord in thy love abide with us
(Latin) BI53-D   105533

Lord, in thy name tny servants
plead (Keble) B183; D189; E140;
F144; J362; W611; X171; BV
646   105534

Lord, in thy name we meet
(Zinzendorf, E.D.) AZ1163;
BA801   105535

Lord in thy presence dread and
sweet (Catholic hymnal, 1860)
B377; E342   105536

Lord, in thy presence here we
meet (---) AS450; AX52;
AY11   105537

Lord, in thy temple we appear
(---) AJp.394   105538

Lord, into thy sacred dwelling
(Berkowitz) BH144   105539

Lord, it belongs not to my
care (Baxter) B392; D665;
E433; F342; G516; H365;
I470; J368; K403; L513; M
304; O502; Q527; V421; W549;
X105; AA496; AL429; AO335;
AP522; AW253; AZ1443; BY
612; BZ   105540

Lord, it is good for us to be
(Stanley) B286; D166; E235;
H159; I131; N204; W88; X
235; AB130; AO151; AZ931;
BA72   105541

Lord Jesus, are we one with
thee (Deck) V298; AZ1446;
BV269   105542

Lord Jesus, bless thy witnesses
(Zinzendorf, N.L.) AZ925
105543

Lord Jesus, blessed Giver
(Wells) AO497   105544

Lord Jesus, by thy death
(Zinzendorf, N.L.) AZ724
105545

Lord Jesus, by thy passion
(Littldale) D635; L236;
O479; P171   105546

Lord Jesus Christ, all praise
to thee (Latin, 11th c) BA
56   105547

Lord Jesus Christ, be present
now (Wilhelm II, duke) J188;
K419; M2; O36; P40; Q3;
AF521; AK28; AM312; BZ
105548

Lord Jesus Christ, be with us
now (Wilhelm II, duke) M2
X Lord Jesus Christ, he
present now   105549

Lord Jesus Christ, I flee to
thee (---) P279   105550

Lord Jesus Christ, I humbly
pray (Pappus) AZ339
105551

Lord Jesus Christ, in thee
alone (Schneesing) N410;

AA413; AZ1032   105552
Lord, Jesus Christ, in thee I
trust eternally (Heermann) AZ
556   105553
Lord Jesus Christ, my life, my
light (Behm) O584; Q148; AA
195   105554
Lord Jesus Christ, my Saviour
blest (Sthen) M284; O278;
P218; Q353   105555
Lord Jesus Christ, of Virgin born
(Luther) M344   105556
Lord Jesus Christ, our Lord most
dear (Laufenberg) E338 X O
Jesus Christ, our Lord most
dear   105557
Lord Jesus Christ, strong hero
thou (Helder) AA230   105558
Lord Jesus Christ, the cause is
thine (Preiswerk) M105
                         105559
Lord Jesus Christ, the Prince of
peace (Ebert) M496   105560
Lord Jesus Christ, the children's
friend (Hoppe) N394   105561
Lord Jesus Christ, the work is
thine (Prieswerk) BV326
                         105562
Lord Jesus Christ, thou hast pre-
pared (Kinner) Q306   105563
Lord Jesus Christ, thou highest
good (Ringwaldt) O98   105564
Lord Jesus Christ, thou living
Bread (Rist) Q312   105565
Lord Jesus Christ, to thee we
pray (Luther) N240   105566
Lord Jesus Christ, to us attend
(---) AA1   105567
Lord Jesus Christ, true man and
God (Eber) K506; N594; O
587; AA527   105568
Lord Jesus Christ, we humbly
pray (Jacobs) J265; K190;
Q314   105569
Lord Jesus Christ, we seek thy
face (Stewart) BV9   105570
Lord Jesus Christ, with us abide
(Selnecker) M187; O427; Q292;
S506; AA110   105571
Lord Jesus, for our call of grace
(Zinzendorf, N. L.) AZ917;
BA802   105572
Lord Jesus, from thy throne

above (Darbyshire) A250
                         105573
Lord Jesus, God and man
(Baker) AZ1369 X O Jesus,
God and man   105574
Lord Jesus, God of heaven
(Hymns of the English Conf.
1880) BR484   105575
Lord Jesus hath a garden full
of flowers gay (Dutch carol,
17th c) BG105   105576
Lord Jesus, I have promised
(Bode) BR384 X O Jesus, I
have promised   105577
Lord Jesus, I long to be per-
fectly whole (Nicholson)
P267; AI282; AO639; AR
445; AS452; AT201; AU9;
AW469; AX407; AY233; BB
592   105578
Lord Jesus, I love thee, I
know thou art mine (London
hymn book, 1864) G234;
BZ   105579
Lord Jesus, I pray, On Earth
while I stay (J. F. Cam-
merhoff) AZ   105580
Lord Jesus, in the days of old
(Noble) AE44; AL554   105581
Lord Jesus, in thy footsteps
(Martin) BY295   105582
Lord Jesus, in thy presence
we are blest (Schlicht) AZ
438   105583
Lord Jesus, Life eternal, be-
fore thy throne I bow
(Hemminki) M64   105584
Lord Jesus, may I constantly
(Watteville) AZ326   105585
Lord Jesus, 'mid thy flock
appear (Swertner) AZ916;
BA174   105586
Lord Jesus, on the holy mount
(Anketell) N205   105587
Lord Jesus, Son of Mary
(Crane) AB114; AC86; BF
298   105588
Lord Jesus, think of me (Syne-
sius of Cyrene) A417; B393;
D614; E77; F200; J365; K
320; O103; Q320; R270; S
239; X106; AF314; AG149;
AL265; AW196; BV138; BY

Lord of all hopefulness, Lord of
all joy (Struther) A363; X565;
AD484; AF217; AR53; BY631
105622

Lord of all majesty and might
(Briggs) A295; X566; AN46;
AQ32   105623

Lord of all power and might
(Stowell) D328; G392; I206;
K221; N211; AZ1243   105624

Lord of all, to thee we raise
(Pierpoint) R For the beauty of
the earth   105625

Lord of all, to whom alone
(Alington) BY447   105626

Lord of beauty, thine the splendour
(Alington) F174   105627

Lord of Creation, bow thine ear,
O Christ, to hear (Latin, before 11th c) E174   105628

Lord of earth, thy forming hand
(Grant) I469   105629

Lord of every land and nation
(Robinson) AO203 X Mighty
God, while angels bless thee
105630

Lord of glory, thou hast bought
us (Alderson) O449; Q442;
AA358; AZ247; BA565   105631

Lord of glory, who hast bought us
(Alderson) Q442 X Lord of glory,
thou hast bought us   105632

Lord of Good Life, the hosts of
the undying ("The inner light")
AD306   105633

Lord of grace and holiness (Benson) AO430   105634

Lord of harvest, send forth
reapers (Thompson) R Far
and near the fields are teeming   105635

Lord of health, thou life within
us (Dearmer) R12; X567;
Y193; AC167   105636

Lord of hosts! to thee we raise
(Montgomery) H422; L296;
AO465; AX644; AZ65   105637

Lord of hosts, whom all adore
(Jewish hymn) BH178   105638

Lord of life and King of glory
(Burke) E530; F498; G426;
K418; W652; AR546; AS418;
AW363; BA852; BY618; BZ

105639

Lord of life and light and blessing (Rohr) M622   105640

Lord of life! now sweetly
slumber (LaTrobe) AZ940;
BA207   105641

Lord of life, of love, of light
(Hall) D301; N580; BA335
105642

Lord of life, who once wast
cradled (Piggott) X342;
BY619   105643

Lord of light, whose Name
outshineth (Lewis) W337;
Y222; Z504; AD324; AK268;
AL377; AP568; AR376; AW
342; BF517; BY380   105644

Lord of loveliness, all beauty,
Bears thy touch (Morse)
AR386   105645

Lord of mercy and of might,
God and Father of us all
(Heber) AZ1274; BA647
105646

Lord of mercy and of might,
Of mankind the life and
light (Heber) B41; D527;
K85; W159; AZ1138; BA
606   105647

Lord of my heart's elation
(Carmen) Y131   105648

Lord of my Life! O, may thy
praise (Steele) L13; AA27
105649

Lord of my life, whose tender
care ⌒ [Omega] Chelsea,
England) Q24; AA18 105650

Lord of nations, bless in kindness (Farrell) BM95
105651

Lord of our highest love
(Tickle) Z466   105652

Lord of our life, and God of
our salvation (Löwenstern)
A395; B469; D496; E435;
F253; J157; K208; M489;
O84; P14; Q258; U348; W
216; X349; Z430; AD389;
AE399; AF379; AI150; AL
165; AM473; AN491; AO414;
AP294; AR326; AV71; AW
278; AZ468; BA270; BB262;
BF588; BI60; BR41; BV405;

BY261   105653
Lord of our life, God whom we
fear (Smith, S. F.) G307; I
503   105654
Lord of spirits, I surrender
(Welhaven) P383   105655
Lord of starry vasts unknown
(Tweedy) BF354   105656
Lord of the Church, we humbly
pray (Osler) D182; J303; K
210; L302; N284; O95; P110;
Q489; S482; AA485; AX159;
BA308   105657
Lord of the endless age! We
raise to thee (McCook) AO608
                               105658
Lord of the harvest, bend thine
ear (Hastings) V559   105659
Lord of the harvest, hear thy
needy servants (Wesley) D185;
H462; K215; L339; N369; P398;
Q488; AA491; AZ1199; BA349;
BV410; BZ   105660
Lord of the Harvest, it is right
and meet (Stone) F378 105661
Lord of the harvest, once again
(Anstice) W615; AZ660 105662
Lord of the harvest, thee we hail
(Gurney) D190; M493; BH188
                               105663
Lord of the hearts of men
(Coffin) D75; AO499   105664
Lord of the home, thine only
Son (Bayly) BY620   105665
Lord of the lands, beneath the
bending skies (Watson) AE391;
AL511; AP648   105666
Lord of the living harvest (Mon-
sell) D285; G401; H458; I219;
J304; K211; N285; O94; Q492;
U387; W335; AL234; AP368;
AR558; BA317; BV324; BY381
                               105667
Lord of the mountain (Navajo
prayer) Yp.439; AC473 105668
Lord of the nations, Father of all
(Pounds) AE406; AR394; AS361
                               105669
Lord of the ocean vast and deep
(Harker) BB97   105670
Lord of the Sabbath and its light
(---) BB455   105671
Lord of the Sabbath hear our vows

(Doddridge) I73 X Lord of
the Sabbath, hear us pray
                               105672
Lord of the Sabbath, hear us
pray (Doddridge) H75; I73;
AM322   105673
Lord of the Strong, when earth
you trod (Hankey) X568;
Y78; AB291; BF300 105674
Lord of the worlds above
(Watts) F248; H421; J238;
K239; L59; N322; Q480;
R14; S50; V16; AA469; AL
198; AM302; AO9; AP66;
AR574; AS190; AZ1168;
BA376; BV559; BY273
                               105675
Lord of the worlds, unseen or
seen (Blakeney) F492
                               105676
Lord of true light, we grate-
fully adore thee (Moxley)
AF471; BY350   105677
Lord, on thee alone I stay me
(---) BR338   105678
Lord, open thou both heart and
ear (Olearius) M10 105679
Lord, open thou my heart to
hear (Olearius) Q5; AA2
                               105680
Lord, our eyes unseal, to our
minds reveal (Russell) AZ
536   105681
Lord, our High-priest and
Saviour (Zinzendorf, N.L.)
AZ571   105682
Lord, our Lord in all the
earth (U.P. Psalter, 1912)
R Lord, our Lord, thy glor-
ious name   105683
Lord, our Lord, thy glorious
name (U.P. Psalter, 1912)
T10; AJ15; AM107   105784
Lord, pour thy Spirit from on
high (Montgomery) A219; B
450; D183; F473; J302; M96;
O90; P111; AA488; AO452;
BR483   105685
Lord, rebuke me not in anger
(U.P. Psalter, 1912) T8;
AJ12   105686
Lord, save thy world (Bayly)
AF452   105687

Lord, send a revival (McKinney)
R Send a revival   105688
Lord, send the old-time power
(Gabriel) R Lord, as of old at
Pentecost   105689
Lord, send thy Spirit from above
(Watts) BR208 X Come Holy
Spirit, heavenly Dove, with all
thy quickening   105690
Lord, send thy word, and let it
fly (Gibbons) L334   105691
Lord, shall thy children come to
thee (Hinds) B376   105692
Lord, speak to me that I may
speak (Havergal) A574; B502;
D586; G460; H389; I410; J538;
K212; P323; R298; S399; T
374; U279; V499; W338; Y216;
Z470; AB266; AC251; AD321;
AE277; AF397; AG248; AH425;
AI187; AK255; AL383; AO476;
AP570; AR532; AS444; AT340;
AV211; AW296; AX161; BA536;
BB407; BD117; BF445; BK84;
BV597; BY514; BZ   105693
Lord, take my heart just as it is
(Stonehouse) AZ214   105694
Lord, teach us how to pray aright
(Montgomery) E78; F317; J452;
K279; N303; O360; P28; AF336;
AZ122; BA607; BV609   105695
Lord, the God of my Salvation
(U. P. Psalter, 1912) T162;
AJ240   105696
Lord, the wind and sea obey thee
(Dearmer) E543   105697
Lord, thee I love with all my
heart (Schalling) Q429; AA366
                          105698
Lord, thee, my God, I'll early
seek (Scottish Psalter, 1650)
AL655; AP52   105699
Lord, thine ancient people see
(Harland) M119; O127; P401;
AO538   105700
Lord, thine appointed servants
bless (---) AO458   105701
Lord, thine fore'er today I vow
to be (Kretzmann) M549
                          105702
Lord, thine humble servants hear
(Jewish liturgy: Yom Kippur)
BH169   105703

Lord, this day thy children
meet (How) H447; W238;
AL617; AP801; AS395; BD
14; BX525   105704
Lord, thou hast been our dwell-
ing place In every genera-
tion (Gill) AM287   105705
Lord, thou hast been our dwell-
ing place Through all the
ages (U. P. Psalter, 1912)
R88; T167; AJ245   105706
Lord, thou hast been thy peo-
ple's rest (Montgomery) AW
568; AZ743   105707
Lord, thou has favor shown thy
land (U. P. Psalter, 1912)
T156; AJ231   105708
Lord, thou hast greatly blessed
our land (U. P. Psalter, 1912)
AJ230   105709
Lord, thou hast known our joy
(Mills) AF472   105710
Lord, thou hast promised grace
for grace (Cox) I347
                          105711
Lord! Thou hast searched and
seen me through (Watts)
V96; AO84; BR278   105712
Lord, thou hast searched me,
and dost know (U. P. Psalter,
hymnal, 1927) S102; T275;
AF576; AJ382; AM33
                          105713
Lord, thou hast taught our
hearts to glow (Palmer)
AO480   105714
Lord, thou hast told us that
there be (Washbourne) X107
                          105715
Lord, thou lovest the cheerful
giver (Murray) AK260; AM
368; AP562; AS354; BF607
                          105716
Lord, thou shalt early hear my
voice (Scottish Psalter, 1650)
AL631; AW576   105717
Lord! Thou Source of all per-
fection (Muenter) N190
                          105718
Lord, thou who gavest me all I
have (Farjeon) X569 105719
Lord, thou wilt hear me when
I pray (Watts) BC265

105720

Lord, through all the generations
(U.P. Psalter, 1912) T166;
AJ244   105721

Lord, through changing days, unchanging (Bowie) AW402; BF
637   105722

Lord through theis Holy Week of
our salvation (Draper) F100;
AF168   105723

Lord, thy children guide and keep
(How) B374; D572; AZ1283;
BB408   105724

Lord, thy death and passion give
(Heermann) K95; N92; AI421
105725

Lord, thy glory fills the heaven
(Mant) O62 X Round the Lord
in glory seated   105726

Lord, thy Kingdom bring triumphant (Bayly) BY382   105727

Lord, thy mercy now entreating
(Sidebotham) W404; AF332;
AK216; AL277; AP429; AW
147   105728

Lord, thy omniscience I adore
(Cronenwett) M155   105729

Lord, thy servants forth are going
(Winks) BY383   105730

Lord, thy word abideth (Baker)
A399; B59; D282; E436; F250;
K168; L312; N224; O140; R252;
V80; W199; X570; AF258; AG
298; AL186; AM266; AP288;
AW292; AZ23; BI42; BJ4; BR
237; BV305; BY250   105731

Lord, thy word hath taught
(Hunter-Clare) BV136 105732

Lord thy word, that sacred
treasure (Zinzendorf, N.L.)
M28   105733

Lord, thy word to me remember
(U.P. Psalter, 1912) T231;
AJ327   105734

Lord, 'tis not that I did choose
thee (Conder) Q37; AA69
105735

Lord to me thy ways make known
(U.P. Psalter, 1912) AJ67
105736

Lord, to our humble prayers attend (Greek liturgy: Great collect) E650; F588   105737

Lord, to thee alone we turn
(Evans) AO654   105738

Lord, to thee I make confession
(Franck) N405; O497; Q326;
AA416; AZ433   105739

Lord, to thee I now surrender
(Rambach) J293   105740

Lord, to thee, in whom is
dwelling (---) BRp.467
105741

Lord, to thee my soul is lifted
(Collier) AI441   105742

Lord, to whom except to thee
(Monsell) K370   105743

Lord, unto thee we look for
salvation (Sellers) AU441
105744

"Lord, we are able." (Marlatt)
R "Are ye able"   105745

Lord, we ask thee, ere we
part (Manwaring) BC119
105746

Lord we beseech thee (Huffman) AR655   105747

Lord, we come before thee now
(Hammond) H59; I35; L197;
P47; Q18; S11app.; U446;
V17; Z116; AA7; AH164;
AI17; AO4; AX53; AY54; BB
30; BC142   105748

Lord, we come with hearts
aflame (Braley) AC250;
BB229   105749

Lord, we confess our numerous
faults (Watts) L417; N409;
Q382; AA307   105750

Lord, we have come to thee
(Sargent) BV631   105751

Lord, we humbly bow before
thee (Thompson) O42
105752

Lord, we thank thee for our
brothers (Powell) AF268
105753

Lord, we thank thee for the
pleasure (Jex-Blake) BY17
105754

Lord, what a change within us
one short hour (Trench) S250;
AB223; AD286; AE237; AR
277; AW183; BF367 105755

Lord, what offering shall we
bring (Taylor) AN281; BH

148; BR47; BX336   105756
Lord, when at thy command
(Wesley) AA487 X Lord, if at
thy command   105757
Lord! when before thy throne we
meet (Nicholas) BR470 105758
Lord! when I all things would
possess (Gill) I343   105759
Lord, when in Simon's house of
yore (Henshaw) V634   105760
Lord, when the wise men came
from far (Godolphin) X571
                         105761
Lord, when thou makest thy
presence felt (Hardenberg)
BR71   105762
Lord, when thy kingdom comes,
remember me (Maclagan) E
113; F116; W98; AK157; AO
259; AZ449   105763
Lord, when we bend before thy
throne (Carlyle) A410; B124;
D354; E79; H52; Q22; U445;
V462; X108; AA6; AO313;
AP328; AZ197; BA602; BF
359; BR280; BV142; BX251
                         105764
Lord, when we have not any light
(Matheson) G453   105765
Lord, while for all mankind we
pray (Wreford) B431; E561;
F581; G499; H531; I701; Q578;
W633; X320; Z544; AA302; AD431;
AH486; AL519; AN390; AO593;
AP645; AZ158; BA870; BB509;
BF562; BX425; BY646; BZ
                         105766
Lord, while I with thee remain
(Loskiel) AZ1039   105767
Lord, who at Cana's wedding
feast (Thrupp) A215; D237;
J301; K414; N527; O536; Q620;
AA443; BA842; BQ150 105768
Lord, who can be with thee com-
pared? (Cramer) AW518
                         105769
Lord, who didst sanctify thyself,
and hast thereby (Foster) AZ
548   105770
Lord, who didst send, by two and
two before thee (Wilson) A575;
X344   105771
Lord, who dost the voices bless

(Williams) AN450; BX489
                         105772
Lord, who fulfillest thus anew
(Mozley) B272   105773
Lord, who hast made me free
(Briggs) X109   105774
Lord, who in thy perfect wisdom
(Rees) BY647   105775
Lord, who left the highest heaven
(Dudley-Smith) BV395 105776
Lord who lovest little children
(Rowland) AH555   105777
Lord, who ordainest for mankind
(Bryant) AN439   105778
Lord, who shall come to thee
(Scrimger) AJ25; AK263; AM
445; AP10   105779
Lord, who shall sit beside thee
(Romanis) E232; X234
                         105780
Lord, who throughout these forty
days (Hernaman) A59; B134;
D78; N84; R181; S144; AF153;
AK141; BA198; BL19; BM75*;
BV144 *major variant 105781
Lord, who thyself hast bidden us
to pray (Briggs) X572
                         105782
Lord, whom winds and seas obey
(Wesley) I103   105783
Lord, whose glory fills the skies
BR12 X Christ whose glory
fills   105784
Lord, whose love through hum-
ble service (Bayly) BZ
                         105785
Lord, wilt thou in this temple
reign (Mudge) AD390 105786
Lord, with devotion we pray
(Hay) AR456; AS13   105787
Lord, with glowing heart I'd
praise thee (Key) A454; B233;
D443; H61; J403; K291; L86;
N296; O15; U315; AI5; AM69;
AO54; AW511; AZ974; BA651;
BB23   105788
Lord, written in rocks and in
woodland (Hess) BH39
                         105789
Lost in the night doth the heathen
yet languish (Finnish) P396
                         105790
Loud let the swelling anthems

rise (Hamburg Temple hymnal)
BH78   105791
Loud lift your voices in triumph
on high (Ware) R Lift your
glad voices in triumph   105792
Lov og Tak og evig Äre (Kingo)
BT401   105793
Love came down at Christmas
(Rossetti) G94; J37; S133;
W52; X92; BV105; BY103;
BZ   105794
Love can tell, and love alone
(Bridges) AQ162   105795
Love consecrates the humblest
act (McManus) AX170; AY268
105796
Love divine, all loves [love] ex-
celling (Wesley) A479; B226;
D432; E437; F205; G372; H322;
I355; J397; K276; L202; M158;
N297; O295; P38; Q351; R399;
S308; T326; U21; V323; W479;
X573; Y356; Z379; AB193; AC
67; AD245; AE188; AF228;
AG176; AH223; AK272; AL330;
AM460; AN50; AO295; AP463;
AR178; AS116; AT2; AU19;
AV183; AW178; AX43; AY15;
AZ948; BA490; BB142; BF256;
BI3; BK52; BR24,29; BV625;
BX118; BY595; BZ   105797
Love divine, all loves excelling
(Wesley) X Come, thou uni-
versal blessing (Wesley)
105798
Love divine, all loves excelling
(Wesley) X Peace of God,
which knows no measure (Book
of hymns, 1846)   105799
Love from God our Lord, Ever
forth has poured (Schjørring)
M278   105800
Love is kind and suffers long
(Wordsworth) Z386; BE173
105801
Love is life's true crown and
glory (Grundtvig) BE178
105802
Love is the theme, love is su-
preme (Fisher) R Of the
themes that men have known
105803
Love lifted me! (Rowe) R I was

sinking deep in sin   105804
Love not the world! Its dazz-
ling show (Flory) AX409;
AY385   105805
Love of God, eternal love
(Wine) AR88   105806
Love of Jesus, all divine
(Bottome) B231; D607
105807
Love of love, and Light of light
(Bridges) AN220; BJ97; BX
110   105808
Love of the Father, love of God
the Son (Latin, 12th c) E
438; F238; J125; X574; BJ
28; BL99   105809
Love one another, -- word of
revelation (Morrison) BE
179   105810
Love, the found of light from
heaven (Grundtvig) O448;
P293   105811
Love the Lord thy God! Love
is staff and rod (Schjørring)
BE180   105812
Love thyself last (Wilcox) AC
239   105813
Love, unto thine own who
camest (Bridges) BJ92
105814
Love, who in the first begin-
ning (Scheffler) AZ605
105815
Loved with everlasting love
(Robinson) W434; BY448
105816
Lovely appear over the moun-
tains (Bible. Isaiah 52)
AH619   105817
Love's redeeming work is done
(Wesley) X160 X Christ the
Lord is risen today   105818
Loving Father, we thy children
(Hackett) BE181   105819
Loving Jesus, gentle Lamb
(Wesley) I374 X Lamb of
God, I look do thee   105820
Loving Saviour, hear my cry
(Crosby) AX249   105821
Loving Shepherd of thy sheep
(Leeson) D552; E602; F444;
W668; X366; AW429; BQ45;
BV337; BY287   105822

Lovingly, tenderly calling to me
(Ogden) R Jesus, the loving
Shepherd   105823

Lovingly the Shepherd, Seeking
the lost (Ukrainian trad.) AL
492   105824

Low at thy pierced feet, Saviour
of all (Stephens) BB239
                             105825

Low in the grave He lay (Lowry)
AE123; AH302; AI81; AM206;
AR185; AS150; AT113; AU127;
AV317; AW452; AX119; AY
265; BY160; BZ   105826

Löwen, lasst euch wieder finden
(German. 1712) BT470
                             105827

Lowly entombed he lay (Hugg)
AY265 X Low in the grave He
lay (Lowry)   105828

Loyal and true and faithful
(Toews) AX447   105829

Lucis creátor optime (St Gregory
the Great) BO283; BQ26
                             105830

Lullay my liking, my dear son
(English trad carol, 15th) R
I saw a fair maiden, sitten and
sing   105831

Lullay, thou little tiny child
(Pageant of the Shearmen) BL
15 X Lully, lulla, thou little
tiny child   105832

Lully, lulla, thou little tiny child
(Pageant of the Shearmen. 15th
c) BG22; BL15   105833

Lully, lulley, lully, lulley,
The falcon hath borne my make
away (English trad. 15th c)
BG61 notes   105834

M

M.I.A. we hail thee (Fox) BC
111   105835

Mache dich, mein Geist, bereit,
(Freystein) BT446   105836

Macht hoch die Tür, die Tor'
macht weit (Weissel) BT73;
BW523   105837

Make lowly wise, we pray no
more (Hosmer) X575; AN274;
AQ188; BF437; BX342 105838

Made of one blood with all on
earth to dwell (Best) AD338
                             105839

Magdalene, thy grief and gladness (Grève) F556   105840

Magdalene, thy grief and gladness (Grève) X Sing we all
the joys and sorrows 105841

Magnify Jehovah's name (Montgomery) D475; BH59 105842

Magnify th' Eternal's name
(Montgomery) BH59 X Magnify
Jehovah's name   105843

Maiden Mother, meek and mild
(Latin, 13th c) BP75 105844

Majestic sweetness sits enthron-
ed (Stennett) A353; B194;
G220; H323; I135; J570; L152;
O66; P8; R142; S197; T327;
U71; V129; Z381; AB82; AE
100; AG111; AH311; AI106;
AK183; AM143; AO202; AR
113; AS126; AT118; AU188;
AV132; AW120; AX18; BA
493; BB159; BZ   105845

Make channels for the streams of
love (Trench) AN276; AQ157;
BD123; BE182; BX340
                             105846

Make haste, O God, to save
(U.P. Psalter, 1912) AJ189
                             105847

Make haste, O man, to do
(Bonar) BE183 X Make haste,
O man, to live   105848

Make haste, O man, to live
(Bonar) I390; U415; V667;
BE183   105849

Make haste, O my God, to
deliver (U.P. Psalter, 1912)
T129; AJ188   105850

Make large our hearts with thine
own love (Goforth) BK101
                             105851

Make me a blessing (Wilson)
R Out on the highways
                             105852

Make me a captive, Lord (Mathe-
son) G367; J508; R308; S
247; W464; X576; AB194;
AE266; AF356; AG314; AI92;
AK243; AL313; AO294; AR359;
BB284; BF454; BV633; BY

478; BZ   105853
Make me a channel of blessing to-
day (Smyth) R Is your life a
channel   105854
Make me, O Lord, an instrument
of thy peace (St Francis of As-
sisi??) BN60   105855
Make my calling and election
(Gregor) AZ977; BA747
                                     105856
Make use of me, my God (Bonar)
AZ1290; BA553   105857
Make we joy now in this feast
(English trad. carol, 15th c)
BG23   105858
Make me merry, both more and
less (English trad carol, ca
1500) BG172   105859
Make wide the door, unbar the
gate! (Weissel) P115   105860
Maker, keeper, Thou, be my
Guardian now (St Ambrose)
AY288   105861
Maker of all things, Lord our
God (Latin) AZ289   105862
Maker of all things, mighty Lord
(Doddridge) L106   105863
Maker of earth and sea and sky
(Lord) W350   105864
Maker of earth, to thee alone
(Coffin) E64   105865
Maker of man, who from thy
throne (Latin, ca 7th c) E62
                                     105866
Maker of stars, Eternal King
(Cross) Y232   105867
Man imperishably stands (Laing)
AQ67   105868
Man is the earth upright and
proud (Patton) AQ62   105869
Man lives not for himself alone
(Shuttleworth) AN510; AQ151
                                     105870
Man of Sorrows, now my soul
(Zinzendorf, C.R.) AK152; AW
537   105871
Man of Sorrows! what a name
(Bliss) AM175 X Man of Sor-
rows! wondrous name   105872
Man of Sorrows! wondrous name
(Bliss) W693; AM175; AP213;
AR166; AS135; AT163; AU257;
AV321; BV159; BY187   105873

Man of Sorrows, wrapt in grief
(Slovak hymal) AL88; BQ19
                                     105874
Man's comradeship is very wide
(Frank) AN403; AQ148
                                     105875
Many and great, O God, are
thy things (Dakota Indian
Hymn) BZ   105876
Many souls today are dying
(Teasley) AX217   105877
Many woes had Christ endured
(Hart) AZ1261   105878
March, march onward, Soldiers
true (Plumptre) BI5 105879
March on, march on to victory
(Moultrie) BI7 X We march,
we march to victory   105880
March on, my soul, with
strength (Wright) W537; BY
716   105881
March on, O soul, with strength
(Coster) G264; R351; S273;
U300; Y110; Z359; AB249;
AC184; AD290; AE251; AF
380; AH446; AK291; AO406;
AR327; AT422; BD84; BF
478; BZ   105882
Marching home, we're marching
home (---) R We are marching
homeward with the blest
                                     105883
Marching on, marching on, For
Christ count everything R
There's a royal banner given
                                     105884
Marching with the heroes
(Tarrant) U298; Y112; Z322;
AC259; AH447; AN480; BD88;
BF625; BX543   105885
Maria die wollt' wandern geh'n
(German trad carol) BG93b
                                     105886
Maria gin'g aus wandern
(German trad carol) BG179b
                                     105887
Maria, mater gratiae (Fortuna-
tus??) BN148; BO84
                                     105888
Marter Gottes, wer kann dein
vergessen (C.R. v. Zinzendorf)
BW537   105889
Martyr of God, whose strength

was steeled (Latin, 10th c) E
180   105890
Marvelous grace of our loving
Lord (Johnston) AE224; AM705;
AR457; AT200; AX321 105891
Mary! how sweetly falls that word
(---) BO92   105892
Mary Immaculate, Mother and
Maid (Currie) BN149   105893
Mary Immaculate, Star of the
morning (Weatherell) BM56
                       105894
Mary the Dawn, Christ the Per-
fect Day (---) BM49   105895
Mary to the Saviour's tomb
(Newton) AY315   105896
Mary, weep not, weep no longer
(Grève) E231   105897
Master and Lord, 'tis good to be
here (Pray) BE185   105898
Master, no offering (Parker) B
500; G464; N662; R299; S407;
U277; Y229; Z303; AB263;
AC252; AD322; AE281; AF
405; AG246; AK396; AN558; AO
493; AR377; AT401; AV214;
BB478; BF502   105899
Master of eager youth (St Clement
of Alexandria) A362   105900
Master, speak! Thy servant
heareth (Havergal) G221; AW
219; AZ609; BA527; BR369;
BV475; BY479; BZ   105901
Master, the tempest is raging
(Baker) AM701; AU471; BB677;
BC106   105902
Master, we thy footsteps follow
(Jackson) BY296   105903
Masters in this hall, Hear ye
news today (Morris) BG137
                       105904
May God be praised henceforth
and blest forever (Luther) O156;
AA431   105905
May God bestow on us His grace
(Luther) O29; Q500; AA480
                       105906
May He, by whose kind care we
meet (Newton) V613   105907
May He who kept us through the
hours of night (Lucas) BH10
                       105908
May Jesus Christ, the spotless

Lamb (Greek) AZ563
                       105909
May Jesus' grace and blessing
(Mathesius) AZ565; BA773
                       105910
May my heart be turned to
pray (---) R There is an
hour of peace and rest
                       105911
May nothing evil cross this door
(Untermeyer) AC530; AQ
159   105912
May the grace of Christ our
Saviour (Newton) A216;
F636; G27; I40; K436; L65;
M14; N362; R76; S495; Z
126; AD512; AE468; AF539;
AG334; AJp.393; AK36; AP
338; AR682; AS68; AT538;
AU497; AW613; AX75; AZ
953; BA913; BV21; BY763;
BZ   105913
May the Lord depend on you
(Martin) R In the warfare
                       105914
May the mind of Christ my
Saviour (Wilkinson) BV634;
BY596   105915
May the stream from Thee,
the Rock, Gracious Jesus
(Swertner) AZ725   105916
May we sow righteous seed for
the reaping (Winsett) R
There is coming a day
                       105917
May we thy precepts, Lord,
fulfill (Osler) M214; Q412;
AA339   105918
May we to thee, our Shepherd
cleave (Horne) AZ682
                       105919
May you who enter here,
Draw near to God (---) S
16app.   105920
Mee Cho-mo-cho bo-ay-leem
A-do-noy (Jewish traditional)
BH270   105921
Meet and right it is to sing
(Wesley) AZ1479 105922
Mein frölich Herz das treibt
mich (Ausbund Suppl.) BU4
                       105923
Mein frölich Herz das treibt

mich an zu singen (Ausbund)
BU133   105924
Mein Gott! das herz ich bringe
dir (Unparth. G. B.) AY13d
                            105925
Mein Gott dich will ich loben
In meiner letzten Stund
(L. Schneider) BU39   105926
Mein Heiland nimmt die Sünder an
(Lehr) BT386   105927
Mein Herz will ich dir schenken
(German. 1653) BT89 105928
Mein Jesu, wie du willt (Schmolck)
BT420; BW250   105929
Mein Muth und Sinn steht mir
dahin (M. Schneider) BU102
                            105930
Mein Schöpfer, steh mir bei
(Rambach) BT335   105931
Meinen Jesum lass' ich nicht
(Keimann) BT365   105932
Men and children everywhere
(Moment) S4; Z96; BZ 105933
Men go out from the places where
they dwelled (Turner) AQ216
                            105934
Men, my brothers, men the
workers (Tennyson) AC522
                            105935
Men of England, who inherit
(Campbell) X321   105936
Men of the Church of the Living
God (Glasgow) U297   105937
Men true of heart and strong in
faith (Boden) BY547   105938
Men who walk in folly's way (U.P.
Psalter, 1912) T205; AJ294
                            105939
Men whose boast it is that ye
(Lowell) X306; AF425; AN318;
AQ173; BD159; BH121; BK104
                            105940
Mensch! wilt du nimmer traurig
seyn (O. Rot) BU58   105941
Merciful Saviour, come and be
my comfort (Ehrenberg-Posse)
N460; P311   105942
Mercy there was great, and grace
was free (Newell) R Years I
spent in vanity   105943
Mercy thou art, Creator, Friend!
(Dearmer) X577   105944
Merkt auf ein Sach und die ist

wahr (Ausbund) BU54
                            105945
Merkt auf, ihr Christen all
geleich (Ausbund) BU114
                            105946
Merkt auf ihr Christen all-
gemein (M. Schneider) BU
103   105947
Merkt auf, ihr Menschenkinder
(Ausbund) BU94   105948
Merkt auf, ihr Völker alle
(Ausbund) BU44   105949
Merkt auf, ihr Völker allge-
mein (M. Schneider) BU82
                            105950
Merkt auf, ihr Völker g'meine
(H. Betz) BU109   105951
Merkt auf, ihr Völker überall
(Ausbund) BU21   105952
Merkt auf mit Fleiss, ein
Himmelspeiss. (H. Betz)
BU92   105953
Merkt auf und nehmt zu Herzen
(Ausbund) BU33   105954
Merry Christmas bells are ring-
ing (---) BI80   105955
Met around the sacred tomb
(Latrobe) AX1249   105956
Mich verlanget zu allen Zeiten
(M. Schneider) BU93
                            105957
Michael, prince of all the angels
(Lee) BN164   105958
'Mid all the traffic of the ways
(Oxenham) G341; S322; U
237; AC159; AD265; AG204;
AK232; BF391; BK88; BZ
                            105959
'Mid pleasures and palaces
though we may roam (Payne)
P349; AS412; BB415; BC185
                            105960
'Mid scenes of confusion and
creature complaints (Denham)
L605; U428; V715; AI339;
AX573; AY393   105961
'Mid the trials we experience
(Foster) AZ979   105962
Mighty God, the First, the Last
(Gaskell) BE186; BX175
                            105963
Mighty God, to thy dear name
be given (Dass) J357
                            105964

Mighty God, we humbly pray (St
Ambrose & N. L. Zinzendorf)
AZ83; BA627   105965
Mighty God, while angels bless
thee (Robinson) H101; I85;
P21; R10; U114; V197; Z160;
AD72; AE60; AG42; AH186;
AM5; AO203; AR76; AT4; AV
50; AW46; BF238; BY210
105966
Mighty King of heaven, Our Re-
deemer, Saviour (Latin) R
Incline thine ear, O Lord, and
show us mercy   105967
Mighty King of righteousness
(Bonar) AZ1127 X Blessed
night, when first that plain
105968
Mighty Lord, extend thy kingdom
(Cottle) N375   105969
Mighty Rock in a weary land
(Charlesworth) R The Lord's
our Rock, in Him we hide
105970
Mighty Rock, whose tow'ring form
(Crosby) Z407; AI249   105971
Mighty Saviour, gracious King
(Osler) AO5   105972
Mighty to save, mighty to save
(Todd) R O who is this that
cometh   105973
Mindful of our human frailty
(U. P. Psalter, 1912) T193;
AJ281   105974
Mine eyes have seen the glory
(Howe) B434; J356; W155; X578;
Y289; AC280; AF443; AH485;
AN567; AO600; AT488; AV301;
BD170; BX410; BZ   105975
Mine eyes look toward the moun-
tains (Bible. Psalm 121:
Swedish version) BE189
105976
Mine eyes unto the mountains
(Olson) J398; N323   105977
Mine hour appointed is at hand
(Herman) AZ746   105978
Mir mit Erbarmung widerfahren
(Tersteegen) AW562b; BW562
105979
Mir nach! spricht Christus, unser
Held (Scheffler) BT421; BW
565   105980

Miserere illi Deus (Latin) BQ
253 X Qui regnas in per-
petum   105981
Mit Angst und Roth ruff ich
dich an (M. Gerfass) BU41
105982
Mit einem zugeneigten G'müth
(Ausbund) BU137   105983
Mit Ernst, o Menschenkinder
(Thilo) BT75   105984
Mit Freuden woll'n wir singen
(Ausbund: Fourteen Author)
BU100   105985
Mit Fried' und Freud' ich
fahr' dahin (Luther) BT
137   105986
Mit Lust so will ich singen
(F. Mantzen) BU6   105987
Mit Lust so will ich singen
Ein schöne Tageweiss
(Ausbund) BU79   105988
Mit Lust und Freud will ich
Gott lobsingen, Dem Vater
gut. (M. Schneider) BU95
105989
Mitten wir im Leben sind
(Luther) BT590   105990
Moment by moment I'm kept
in his love (Whittle) R Dy-
ing with Jesus   105991
More about Jesus I would know
(Hewitt) AH409 X More
about Jesus would I know
105992
More about Jesus would I know
(Hewitt) R316; AE296; AH
409; AI283; AM676; AR455;
AS225; AT321; AV324; AX
373; AY48; BY597   105993
More and more like Jesus
(Stillman) R I want to be
more like Jesus   105994
More holiness give me (Bliss)
U264; V412; AR404; AS222;
AT338; AU217; AX429; AZ
496; BA633; BC114   105995
More light shall break from out
thy word (Cross) AB392;
AD436   105996
More like Jesus would I be
(Crosby) AT316; AV190
105997
More like the Master I would

ever be (Gabriel) AT325
                          105998
More like thee, O Saviour, let
  me be (Davis) AR458; AS223;
  AX375; AY44   105999
More love to thee, O Christ
  (Prentiss) A461; D654; G364;
  H333; I317; J392; L198; N493;
  P310; R397; S315; T410; U
  224; V372; Z390; AD256; AE
  198; AF400; AG168; AH347;
  AI117; AK471; AL498; AM548;
  AO642; AP461; AR407; AS280;
  AT292; AU218; AV195; AW472;
  AX379; BA461; BB385; BF462;
  BZ   106000
More lovely than the noonday rest
  (Farjeon) X579   206001
More than all, one thing my
  heart is craving (Knapp) AZ
  1005   106002
More than shepherd's faithfulness
  (Gregor) AZ585   106003
Morgenglanz der Ewigkeit
  (C.K. von Rosenroth) AW554b;
  BT539; BW554   106004
Morn of joy and morn of praise
  (Sewall) BI103   106005
Morning breaks upon the tomb
  (Collyer) N133; Q203   106006
Morning has broken Like the first
  morning (Farjeon) R464; X30;
  AD469; AF38; AN97; AQ266
                         106007
Morning has come, the table is
  spread (---) AR553   106008
Morning, so fair to see (Silliman)
  AN45; AQ14   106009
Morning Star, O cheering sight!
  (Scheffler) AZ1156; BA59
                         106010
Morn's roseate hues have decked
  (Breviary. Cluny) D120; AZ4;
  BR187   106011
Most ancient of all mysteries
  (Faber) F159; J138; X188
                         106012
Most fervent thanks I render (---)
  M563   106013
Most glorious Lord of life, that
  on this day (Spenser) E283;
  X22; BV73   106014
Most gracious God and Lord

(Zinzendorf, N.L.) AZ782;
  BA122   106015
Most High, omnipotent, good
  Lord (St Francis of Assisi)
  A307   106016
Host Holy Lord and God, Holy,
  Almighty God (Breviary,
  Paris, 1531) AZ1205; BA
  199   106017
Most holy Lord and God of
  heaven (Latin, 4th-5th c)
  E60   106018
Most holy Lord, mankind's
  Creator (Swertner) AZ1415
                         106019
Most holy Mary at thy feet
  (Caswall) R This is the
  image of our Queen   106020
Most perfect is the law of God
  (U.P. Psalter, 1912) R257;
  AF255; AI315; AJ41; AM
  450*   106021
  *refrain is unusual
Most wondrous is of all on
  earth (Grundtvig) P224 X
  O wondrous kingdom here on
  earth   106022
Mother dear, O pray for me
  (---) AH132; BO79   106023
Mother Mary, at thine altar
  (Faber) BO83; BP82 106024
Mother of Christ, Mother of
  Christ, What shall I ask of
  thee? (A Sister of Notre
  Dame) BQ89   106025
Mother of mercy, day by day
  (Faber) BO67; BQ77
                         106026
Motherhood, sublime, eternal
  (Cutler) Z604; AN557; AW
  364   106027
Mount Sion -- where the Lamb
  of God (Swertner) AZ891
                         106028
Mount up with wings as eagles
  (Cross) AB414; BF670
                         106029
Mourn for the thousands slain
  (Brace) H526; I698; AZ1296;
  BB502   106030
Move in our midst, Thou Spirit
  of God (Morse) AR225
                         106031

Much in sorrow, oft in woe (White)
W533 X Oft in danger, oft in
woe   106032
Müde bin ich, geh' zur Ruh'
(Unparth. G. B.) AY46d 106033
Muss es nun seyn gescheiden
(Ausbund) BU136   106034
Must I go and empty-handed
(Luther, C. C.) AT430; AU
296; AX345; AY527   106035
Must Jesus bear the cross alone
(Shepherd) G276; H370; I428;
L525; M394; N472; P314; R290;
U416; V440, 766; Z366; AE219;
AH294; AI317; AO384; AR317;
AS330; AT428; AU153; AV204;
AX426; AY113; AZ93; BA463;
BB274; BZ   106036
Mute are the pleading lips of Him
(Wallin) M424; N120   106037
My all for thee (McKinney) R
All on the altar   106038
My all I to my God commend
(Leon) O481   106039
My All-in-all, my faithful Friend
(Zinzendorf, N. L.) AZ686
                       106040
My bark is wafted to the strand
(Alford) I451   106041
My beautiful home is in heaven
above (Poyry) M303   106042
My blest Redeemer and my Lord
(Watts) BB140 X My dear
Redeemer and my Lord 106043
My case to thee is fully known
(Rose) AZ884   106044
My Church! My Church! My dear
old Church (Lutheran Church.
General Council S.S. Book,
1887) L286; M87; N276; P376
                       106045
My country is the world; My flag
with stars impearled (Whitaker)
Y271; Z514; AC294; AN402;
AQ149; AR610   106046
My country 'tis of thee (Smith,
S. F.) A141; B427; G489; H529;
I702; J360; K490; L556; M505;
N567; P410; R513; S412; T446;
U338; Y293; Z548; AB334; AC279;
AD440; AE393; AF437; AG274;
AH474; AI363; AJp. 393; AK441;
AN384; AO586; AQ242; AR611;

AS383; AT487; AU458; AV302;
AW344; AZ1230; BB510; BC
115; BD172; BF541; BH264;
BI11; BK118; BR493; BX420;
BZ   106047
My country, to thy shore (Wil-
liams) AN382; BDp. 56; BX
418   106048
My course is run. Praise God,
my course is run (Gryphius)
Q599   106049
My crucified Saviour, despised
and contemned (Rutström)
N114   106050
My days are gliding swiftly by
(Nelson) L569; U417; V657;
AS474; AV288; AW503; AX571;
AY89; BR522   106051
My dear Jesus I'll not leave
(Keimann) AA88 X Jesus I
will never leave   106052
My dear Redeemer, and my Lord
(Watts) H155; I140; K52; L
137; N188; U85; V138; Z207;
AD136; AH234; AM171; AO
142; AR151; AS118; AT83;
AZ417; BA84; BB140; BR165;
BY124   106053
My dearest friends, in bonds of
love (---) AX655; AY406
                       106054
My dearest Saviour I would fain
(---) BO20   106055
My drowsy powers, why sleep ye
so? (Watts) L199   106056
My end, Lord, make me know
(U. P. Psalter, 1912) T71;
AJ107   106057
My faith it is an oaken staff
(Lynch) Y138; AC185; AF381;
BK74; BY548   106058
My faith looks up to thee (Palmer)
A449; B211; D345; E439; G213;
H40; I334; J375; K360; L190;
M234; N425; O456; P269; Q
394; R378; S285; T390; U194;
V357; W415; X580; Z355; AA
351; AB172; AC155; AD218;
AE193; AF348; AG211; AH
358; AI238; AK221; AL263;
AM454; AO274; AP419; AR
261; AS270; AT257; AU209;
AV168; AW150; AX453; AY60;

AZ1244; BA429; BB246; BF
369; BR303; BV507; BY549;
BZ   106059
My faith shall be my rock of
might (Abraham ibn Ezra) BH
200   106060
My faith shall triumph O'er the
grave (Watts) AZ1460 106061
My faithful Shepherd is the Lord
(U. P. Psalter, 1912) AJ54
                            106062
My Father bids me come (Wesley)
BR290 X Ah! Whither should I
go   106063
My Father! cheering name!
(Steele) L522; V103; AA519;
AS79   106064
My Father for another night
(Baker) B6; D640; F5; K571;
AP656; BV41   106065
My Father has many dear children
(Graves) AU25   106066
My Father, hear my prayer
(Horder. Book of praise for
children. 1875) K573 106067
My Father is rich in houses and
lands (Buell) AM720; AT270;
AU47; AV342; BB614   106068
My Father, when I come to thee
(Hart) AZ379   106069
My Father's house on high
(Montgomery) M310 X For-
ever with the Lord   106070
My former hopes are fled (Cowper)
H228   106071
My glorious Victor, Prince Divine
(Moule) BB648   106072
My God, accept my heart this day
(Bridges) A404; B372; D429;
E341; F459; I369; J289; K178;
L441; N253; O111; P257; Q336;
S232; U185; X254; AA412; AE
269; AF321; AH351; AK346;
AX166; AZ135; BA460; BL36;
BQ132; BV363   106073
My God and Father, day by day
(Elliott) AM575 X My God,
my Father, while I stray
                            106074
My God and Father, while I stray
(Elliott) U42; X My God, my
Father, while I stray 106075
My God, and is thy table spread

(Doddridge) O153 X My God,
thy table now is spread
                            106076
My God, how endless is thy love
(Watts) L12; S78; V36; AX
45; AY25; BB414; BR250; BV
42   106077
My God! how ought my grateful
heart (---) BO200 X O God!
how ought my grateful heart
                            106078
My God, how wonderful thou art
(Faber) A284; B221; D441;
E441; F169; I86; J181; K303;
L101; N339; O64; P19; W27;
X581; AI413; AL18; AM31;
AO106; AP149; AS84; BA17;
BN197; BO2; BP101; BV10;
BY64;   106079
My God, I am determined (---)
R In every waking moment
                            106080
My God, I am thine, what com-
fort divine (Wesley) AZ1420
                            106081
My God, I believe in thee
(Latin) BQ145   106082
My God, I feel thy wondrous
might (Cary) BX57   106083
My God, I know, I feel thee
mine (Wesley) AY39   106084
My God, I know that I must die
(Schmolck) N593; O586
                            106085
My God, I love thee; not because
(St Francis Xavier??) A456;
D653; E80; F106; G214; H324;
I483; J489; K58; L451; S313;
W433; X110; AD248; AF313;
AL305; AO286; AV137; AZ152;
BA496; BJ2; BO170; BY211
                            106086
My God I rather look to thee
(Scudder) BX470   106087
My God, I thank thee! May no
thought (Norton) BX247
                            106088
My God, I thank thee, who hast
made (Proctor) B384; D624;
G9; I29; J447; R409; S73;
W441; X582; Y204; Z109; AB
213; AC51; AD270; AE19; AF
98; AG183; AH398; AL289;

AN263; AP440; AR31; AV49;
AW177; BA36; BF389; BR423;
BV581; BX316; BY504; BZ
106089

My God, I will extol thee (U.P.
Psalter, 1912) AJ202 X In
doubt and temptation   106090

My God, I will extol thee And
ever bless thy name (U.P.
Psalter, 1912) AJ399   106091

My God, is any hour so sweet
(Elliott) H45; I501; P29; U362;
V465; W449; AI224; AL335;
AM529; AP487; AS48; AV17;
AZ10; BA609; BB325; BR35
106092

My God, it was thy grace
(U.P. Psalter, 1912) AJ79
106093

My God, my Father, blissful name
(Steele) V103 X My Father!
Cheering name   106094

My God! my Father! cheering
name (Steele) AS79 X My Father! Cheering name   106095

My God, my Father, let me rest
(Bickersteth) BV600   106096

My God, my Father, make me
strong (Mann) Q424; X583; AK
208; BE190; BV574; BY480
106097

My God, my Father, while I
stray (Elliott) A420; B391;
D667; E440; F357; G306; H
362; I521 and 736; J465; K
408; L497; O238; Q418; U42;
V435; W539; AA386; AE261;
AL430; AM575; AO346, 702;
AP504; AS237; AU103*; AV
237; AW245; AX390*; AY478;
AZ16; BA695; BR345; BQ332;
BX262 *Refrain   106098

My God! my God! and can it be
(Faber) E101   106099

My God, my God, I cry to thee
(U.P. Psalter, 1912) T32;
AJ47   106100

My God, my God, O why hast
thou ("Joint committee")
AI72   106101

My God, my God, why dost thou
me forsake? (Bridges) AL
635; AP17; BJ77   106102

My God, my King, thy various
praise (Watts) AV42
106103

My God, my life, my love
(Watts) H338   106104

My God, my portion, and my
love (Watts) H340   106105

My God, my strength, my hope
(Wesley) AS452 X Jesus, my
strength, my hope   106106

My God, permit me not to be
(Watts) D353; L434; V445;
BR275   106107

My God! The covenant of thy
love (Doddridge) V329; AO90;
AP507; AZ130   106108

My God, the spring of all my
joys (Watts) H291; I535;
L456; V384; AI260; AL283;
AO92; AS298; AZ109   106109

My God, thy table now is spread
(Doddridge) A203; B329; D
231; E320; F396; H436; O153;
W311; AA429; AE338; AH501;
AL231; AP357; BA301; BR
471; BV390   106110

My God, whose gracious pity
I may claim (Newton) BR
259   106111

My gracious Lord, I own thy
right (Doddridge) G257; H311;
I336; V317; AO388; BB21; BY
515   106112

My griefs of heart abound
(Palmer??) AJ63   106113

My grieving soul revive, O Lord
(U.P. Psalter, 1912) T228;
AJ324   106114

My happy lot is here, The Lamb
to follow (Gregor) AZ471
106115

My heart delights, O Lord, Upon
thy works to ponder (French
hymn) M157   106116

My heart doth overflow (U.P.
Psalter, 1912) T84; AJ124;
AM125   106117

My heart is filled with longing
(Bridges) BJ82   106118

My heart is fixed, O God, A
grateful song I raise
(U.P. Psalter, 1912) T208;
AJ299   106119

My heart is full of Christ, And
  longs (Wesley) H197   106120
My heart is longing to praise my
  Saviour (Eugenie, Princess of
  Sweden) P26   106121
My heart is resting, O my God
  (Waring) B220; R406; S300;
  W446; AD267; AL282; AP441;
  BA530; BB332; BX233; BY505
                            106122
My heart is so happy in Jesus
  my Lord (Buffum) AX305
                            106123
My heart its incense burning
  (Mathesius) O542; P51 106124
My heart lies dead; and no in-
  crease (Herbert) AZ13 106125
My heart looks in faith (Chao)
  AE197   106126
My heart prepare to give account
  (Brorson) M69   106127
My heart was distressed 'neath
  Jehovah's dread frown (Zelley)
  AU50   106128
My heart was glad to hear the
  welcome sound (U.P. Psalter,
  1912) T251; AJ349   106129
My heavenly home is bright and
  fair (Hunter) I628; AU261;
  AX591; AY144   106130
My hiding-place, my refuge tower
  (---) BV526   106131
My hope is built on nothing less
  (Mote) D622; G244; H289;
  I330; J385; K331; L415; M190;
  N424; O236; P283; Q370; R
  368; T391; U219; V354; W697;
  AA306; AE203; AH370; AI141;
  AM582; AP426; AR460; AS274;
  AT283; AU96; AV362; AW487;
  AX482; AY458; BA439; BB581;
  BT370; BV527; BZ   106132
My hope, my all, my Saviour
  thou (---) I444; K366   106133
My hope, my portion, and my
  God (Watts) L388 X Long have
  I sat beneath the sound 106134
My inmost heart now raises
  (Ngidius) N544; Q548; AA22
                            106135
My Jesus, as thou wilt (Schmolck)
  B395; D634; G330; H371; I524;
  J580; K395; L501; M273; N490

O233; P156; Q420; R367; S
  280; T418; U247; V429; Z
  408; AA387; AB241; AG214;
  AH392; AI291; AK313; AM
  572; AO337; AR360; AS234;
  AT251; AU178; AV222; AW250;
  AX391; AY475; AZ486; BA
  687; BB404; BR327; BZ
                            106136
My Jesus, I love thee, I know
  thou art mine (Featherstone)
  H321; P216; R405; U223;
  Z382; AE178; AH297; AI115;
  AM547; AO643; AR462; AS
  275; AT289; AU154; AV323;
  AW216; AX396; AY195; BA
  905; BB276   106137
My Jesus, if the Seraphim
  (Dessler) AZ992   106138
My Jesus, pierced for love of
  me (Paderborn G-B., 1726)
  S513   106139
My latest sun is sinking fast
  (Haskell) AU53; AV313;
  AX575   106140
My life flows on in endless song
  (Lowry) BB265   106141
My life is hid in Jesus (Vulpius.
  Ein schön geistliche G-B.
  Jena, 1609) O583; P420
                            106142
My life, my love I give to thee
  (Hudson) Z293; AH418; AR
  341; AS245; AT359; AU168;
  AX408; AY103   106143
My life, O lord, I give to thee
  (Howard) R Since Jesus gave
  his life   106144
My life was lost in selfishness
  (Shank) AY507   106145
My life's a shade, my days
  Apace to death decline
  (Crossman) BJ73   106146
My Lord calls me (Negro spirit-
  ual) R Steal away   106147
My Lord, how full of sweet con-
  tent (Guyon) G334; I518; L
  467; AZ927   106148
My Lord, I do not ask to stand
  (Richardson) AI367; AR543;
  AS416   106149
My Lord, my God, my only
  King (Proud) BR56   106150

My Lord, my Life, my Love
(Bridges) E442; S328; X584;
BF35; BJ35   106151
My Lord, my love, was crucified
(Mason) AI20; BJ38   106152
My Lord, my Master, at thy feet
adoring (Bridaine) F103; K96;
W95; AL91; AP195; AZ127
                             106153
My Lord, what a morning (Negro
spiritual) BK171 X My Lord,
what a mourning   106154
My Lord, what a mourning (Negro
spiritual) AH599; BK171
                             106155
My Lord, who in the desert fed
(Houghton) BV306   106156
My Maker and my King (Steele)
BB71   106157
My Maker, be thou nigh (Ram-
bach) Q335   106158
My Master was a worker, with
daily work to do (Tarrant)
Z500; AB179; BF435   106159
My Master was so very poor
(Lee) S497; Z216; AC110;
AD129; AR152; BK22   106160
My name's written there (Kidder)
R I am bought not with riches
                             106161
My opening eyes with rapture see
(Hutton) AZ372; BR94   106162
My own dear land (Oxenham) AH
473; AL512; BF552   106163
My people, give ear, attend to
my voice (U.P. Psalter, 1912)
T145; AJ213; AM301   106164
My portion is the Lord; I seek
his favor (Gregor) AZ470;
BA448   106165
My Redeemer knoweth me (Frey-
linghausen G-B.) AZ584
                             106166
My Redeemer, over-whelmed
with grief (Zinzendorf, C.R.)
BA214 X O delightful theme,
past all expression   106167
My righteous God, who oft of old
(U.P. Psalter, 1912) T4; AJ
6   106168
My Saviour, as thou wilt
(Schmolck) BR327 X My Jesus,
as thou wilt   106169

My Saviour guides me day by
day (Bowman) AY127
                             106170
My Saviour, my almighty
Friend (Watts) V189
                             106171
My Saviour needs helpers from
day to day (Rowe) AX211
                             106172
My Saviour, on the word of
truth (Waring) I364 106173
My Saviour sinners doth receive
(Lehr) Q386; AZ1089
                             106174
My Saviour, that I without thee
(Zinzendorf, A.N.) AZ409
                             106175
My Saviour, thou hast offered
rest (Hamilton) BV489
                             106176
My Saviour was betrayed
(Wobeser) BA215   106177
My Saviour, whom absent I
love (Cowper) AZ1510
                             106178
My Saviour's pierced side
(Watts) AZ1301   106179
My Saviour's praises I will
sing ("J.E.A.") AI8; AM703
                             106180
My Shepherd is the Lamb
(Beaumont) AZ1496 106181
My Shepherd is the living Lord
(Rous) BT436 X The Lord's
my Shepherd, I'll not want
(Scottish Psalter, 1650)
                             106182
My Shepherd is the Lord, There
is nothing I shall want
(Ladies of the Grail) BS
p.10   106183
My Shepherd is the Lord who
knows my needs (U.P.
Psalter, 1912) T39; AJ56
                             106184
My Shepherd's mighty aid
(Roberts) AZ1195   106185
My sins and faults of youth,
(U.P. Psalter, 1912) AJ61
                             106186
My sins, my sins, my Saviour
(Monsell) U169; V282; AI
219; AM464; AO265; AV167

AY510   106187
My song forever shall record
(U. P. Psalter, 1912) R516;
T163; AJ241; AM101   106188
My song is love unknown (Cross-
man) F102; J65; X127; AF
169; AL96; BV155; BY143
                              106189
My song shall bless the Lord of
all (Cowper) AZ329   106190
My soul, awake and render
(Gerhardt) AN487; AZ36; BA
775   106191
My soul, be on thy guard (Heath)
A555; B118; D504; G277; H384;
I493; J559; K272; L538; M241;
N455; O485; Q449; R363; U
295; V470; Y378; Z370; AA379;
AD294; AE255; AH451; AI325;
AN299; AO393; AR328; AS327;
AT420; AU247; AV177; AX451;
AY36; AZ1341; BA580; BB358;
BD92; BF477; BX360; BZ
                              106192
My soul before thee prostrate lies
(Richter) I273; AZ405; BA638
                              106193
My soul, bless the Lord! The
Lord is most great (U. P.
Psalter, 1912) T197; AJ285;
AM110   106194
My soul complete in Jesus stands
(Hinsdale) V313   106195
My soul doth magnify the Lord
(Fünf auserlesene geistliche
Lieder, Marburg, 1535)
Q275   106196
My soul doth magnify the Lord
(German, 1535) X Our souls
shall magnify ...   106197
My soul for thy salvation waits
(U. P. Psalter, 1912) T235;
AJ331   106198
My soul glorifies the Lord (Ladies
of the Grail) BSp. 57   106199
My soul has found the sure founda-
tion (Rothe) M131   106200
My soul, how lovely is the place
(Watts) V10   106201
My soul in sad exile (Gilmour)
AS301; AT228; AU79; AV353;
AX524; AY125   106202
My soul in silence waits for God

(U. P. Psalter, 1912) T111;
AJ161; AM571   106203
My soul is grieved because my
foes (U. P. Psalter, 1912)
AJ155   106204
My soul, now bless thy maker
(Graumann) M592; O7; P9;
Q34; AA59   106205
My soul, praise the Lord, O
God, thou art great (Bridges)
BJ63   106206
My soul repeat his praise
(Watts) H113; I94; K306;
L73; M596; N293; V527;
AA77; AP92   106207
My soul, there is a country
(Vaughan, H.) F286; W463;
X585; AN434   106208
My soul, thy great Creator
praise (Watts) V520 106209
My soul, weigh not thy life
(Swain) H383; V488 106210
My soul with expectation doth
depend on God (Scottish
Psalter, 1650) R113; S86;
AL654; AP51   106211
My soul, with joy attend (---)
AY400   106212
My soul with patience waits
(Tate & Brady) A439; B
314; D334   106213
My soul's best Friend, what
joy and blessing (Dessler)
Q362   106214
My span of life will soon be
done (Cowper) I426 106215
My spirit longs for thee
(Byrom) E443; R321; S508;
W456; X111; AL333; AP467;
AZ474; BR325; BY481
                              106216
My spirit looks to God alone
(Watts) L495   106217
My spirit on thy care (Lyte)
B225; D664; K341; L508;
N438; Q435; U213; V343;
AA369; AG213; AO358; AZ
1356; BA715; BB252; BR251
                              106218
My stead fast heart, O God
(U. P. Psalter, 1912)
AJ298   106219
My times are in thy hand: My

God, I wish them there (Lloyd)
G322; I449; K401; L506; N56;
U198; V434; W551; Z395; AL
424; AM577; AO359; AP503;
AU446; AZ1263; BA714; BV508
106220

My truest Friend abides in heaven
(Schmolck) M631   106221

My trust is in the Lord, How say
ye then to me (Psalms in meter, 1905) AM48; AP8 106222

"My yoke," saith Christ, "upon
you take" (Scheffler) AZ617
106223

Mysterious Presence, source of
all (Beach) S101; AD86; AN63;
AQ130; AR226; BX80   106224

N

Naar Synderen ret ser sin Vaade
(Landstad) BT65   106225

Näher, mein Gott zu Dir (Sarah
F. Adams) AY38d   106226

Name of Jesus, softly stealing
(---) N335   106227

Narodil se Kristus Pán, Veselme
se (Tranovsky) BT86   106228

Nations, attend before his throne
(Watts) BX27 X Before the
Lord Jehovah's throne   106229

Nature, with open volume, stands
(Watts) V229; BV156   106230

Naught have I gotten but what I
received (Gray) AI131; AM698
106231

Nay, do not grieve though life be
full of sadness (Naidu) AQ77
106232

Nay, speak no ill; a kindly word
(---) BC116   106233

Near the cross her vigil keeping
(Jacopone) G138 X At the
cross her station keeping
106234

Near the cross was Mary weeping
(Jacopone) N104 X At the
cross her station keeping
106235

Nearer, dear Savior, to thee
(Townsend) BC117   106236

Nearer, ever nearer (Thring)
AZ763 X Saviour, blessed

Saviour   106237

Nearer, my God to thee,
Nearer to thee (Adams) A
465; B222; D344; E444; F
352; G362; H310; I315; J
577; K407; L428; M290; N
448; O466; P336; Q533; R
326; S261; T411; U265;
V408; W475; X586; Y10;
Z329; AA520; AC156; AD
308; AE201; AF351; AG173;
AH359; AI266; AK318; AL
321; AN245; AO296; AP470;
AQ126; AR397; AS210; AT
322; AU206; AV189; AW202;
AX372; AY86; AZ1241; 1242;
BA612; BB382; BC124; BD
109; BE192; BF376; BK86;
BR357, 374; BT533; BX287;
BY598; BZ   106238

Nearer my God to thee! Nearer to thee. Through word
and sacrament (Jacobs)
K336; N449; AA324; AB185;
BT533   106239

Nearer, O God to thee! Hear
thou our prayer (How) AZ
1242 X Nearer, my God, to
Thee (Adams)   106240

Nearer, still nearer, close to
thy heart (Morris) N494;
U266; AI278; AR259; AS221;
AT281; AV376; AX377; AY
310; BB390   106241

"Nearer the cross!" My heart
can say (Crosby) AW491
106242

Nearer the cross of Jesus
(Abbey) AS228   106243

'Neath the old olive trees
(McKinney) R 'Neath the
stars   106244

'Neath the stars of the night
(McKinney) AU398   106245

Ne'er forget God's daily care
(T.C. Chao) BZ   106246

Neighbour, what was the sound,
I pray (French trad carol)
BG88   106247

Nein, nein, das ist kein Sterben (Malan) BT602 106248

Never further than thy cross
(Charles) G146; I144; AH

366; AL97; BV560; BZ   106249

Never grow old, never grow old
  (Moore) R I have heard of a
  land   106250

Never shone a light so fair
  (Crosby) AI64   106251

Never weather-beaten sail more
  willing bent to shore (Campian)
  X587   106252

New every morning is the love
  (Keble) A155; B1; D1; E260;
  F4; G35; I42; J201; K452;
  R45; S31; T304; V35; W259;
  X31; AD40; AE38; AF36; AG
  22; AL530; AN98; AP654; AW
  22; AZ357; BA766; BB42; BE
  140; BF175; BR6; BV43; BX
  135; BY678; BZ   106253

New every morning is thy love
  (Keble) BR6 X New every
  morning is the love   106254

New Russia rise and proudly stand
  (Stevens) Y312   106255

Night, with ebon pinion (Jameson)
  Z226   106256

Night's shadows falling, men to
  rest are calling (Russell) U
  460; V48   106257

No change of time shall ever
  shock (Tate & Brady) D655;
  AA281   106258

No coward soul is mine (Brontë)
  X588   106259

No eye hath seen, nor tongue de-
  clared (Adams) BE188 106260

No farther go tonight, but stay
  (Cennick) AZ570; BA785
                            106261

No form of human framing (Van
  Dyke) G421; AK414; AR204
                            106262

No gospel like this feast (Charles)
  BY322   106263

No human eyes thy face may see
  (Higginson) BX239   106264

No longer forward nor behind
  (Whittier) AN254 X No longer
  forward or behind   106265

No longer forward or behind
  (Whittier) H121; AN254; AQ
  187; BX232   106266

No longer, Lord, despise me
  (Collier) AI435; AM511 106267

No longer, Lord, thy sons
  shall sow (Marlatt) AC132;
  BF324   106268

No longer of him be it said
  (Kilmer) Y88; Z305 106269

No more, my God! I boast no
  more (Watts) V311 106270

No more we'll roam, no more
  we'll stray (Yoder) R Some
  time we all shall understand
                            106271

No mortal eye hath seen that
  land (Toews) AX601 106272

No mortal sense can still or
  stay (Greenwood) BE194
                            106273

No, never alone; no, never
  alone (---) R I've seen the
  lightning; R How many times
  discouraged (Rexford)
                            106274

No, no, it is not dying (Malan)
  L562; AO568   106275

No, not despairingly come I to
  thee (Bonar) G333; H282;
  I453; AM411; AT206; BA414
                            106276

No shadows yonder (Bonar)
  U429; AS480; AV293; BF
  658   106277

No tears in heaven, no sorrows
  given (Arnold) AX600
                            106278

Noblest, truest, oldest, newest
  (Bonar) R Come and hear
  the grand old story 106279

Nobody knows like Jesus
  (Hugg) R When this poor
  heart   106280

Nobody knows the work it makes
  (---) AU40   106281

Nobody knows the trouble I've
  seen (Negro spiritual) Y320;
  AH612; BK169   106282

Nocte surgentes vigilemus
  omnes (St Gregory the Great)
  BJ49b   106283

Noël nouvelet, noël chantons
  ici (French trad carol) BG
  149b   106284

Noiseless the morning flings its
  gold (---) AQ89 X Unheard
  the dews around me fall

106285
Non nobis, Domini, not unto us,
O Lord (Kipling) A503   106286
None but Christ, my Saviour
(Gregor) AZ1077   106287
None can satisfy but Jesus
(Lear) AS294   106288
None e'er shall be ashamed (---)
AZ1118   106289
None from God so distant are
(Zinzendorf, N. L.) AZ582
106290
None God the Father's favor share
(Zinzendorf, N. L.) AZ167
106291
None is like Jeshurun's God (Wes-
ley) BR48   106292
None other Lamb, none other
name (Rossetti) S504; W412;
AL273; AM115; AP418; BV617;
BY769   106293
Nor earth nor hell my soul can
move (Mote) BT370 X My
hope is built on nothing less
106294
Nor silver, nor gold hath ob-
tained (Gray) AM721   106295
Not a thought of earthly things
(Liturgy of St James) F392
106296
Not all the blood of beasts
(Watts) K339; L232; N423;
Q156; U98; V246; AA319;
AM176; AP421; AU332; AX
109; AY22; AZ1293; BA436;
BV157   106297
Not all the outward forms on
earth (Watts) V303   106298
Not alone for mighty empire (Mer-
rill) A145; G543; J345; R512;
S416; Y239; Z597; AB343; AD
434; AE427; AF439; AG273;
AK442; AN373; AQ239; AR612;
AW355; BD160; BF555; BH229;
BK105; BX415; BZ   106299
Not always on the Mount may we
(Hosmer) A571; F561; I477;
J535; X589; AN215; AQ90; AW
98; BD96; BV283; BX222
106300
Not by far-famed deeds alone
(Phillips) F562   106301

Not by the martyr's death alone
(Santeüil) AO387   106302
Not by the mighty hand (Wood-
ford) B109; D72   106303
Not empty worship the benignant
Father requireth (Whittier)
BF507 X O brother man! fold
to thy heart   106304
Not far from the Kingdom of
heaven (Latta) AX262
106305
Not for more beauty would our
eyes entreat thee (Bates)
AC490   106306
Not for our sins alone (Twells)
F324; BV490; BY449 106307
Not given to us from out the
skies (Wendte) AN391; BX
431   106308
Not gold, but only men can
make (---) AN312; AQ98
106309
Not half has ever been told
(Atchinson) R I have read of
a beautiful city   106310
Not haughty is my heart, Not
lofty is my pride (U.P.
Psalter, 1912) T262; AJ
366; AM578   106311
"Not I, but Christ," be honored,
loved ("A.A.F." [Crosby??])
AS233   106312
Not in anger, mighty God
(Albinus) O522; AZ787
106313
Not in dumb resignation we lift
our hands on high (Hay)
G467; Y234; Z368; AB289;
AN317   106314
Not in Jerusalem alone (Mont-
gomery) AZ171   106315
Not in the temples made with
hands (Warner) AX433
106316
Not in vain the distance beacons
(Tennyson) Y265; AC297;
AN353; AQ195   106317
Not long on Hermon's holy
height (Pease) AN211 X Not
long upon the mountain's
height   106318
Not long upon the mountain's

height (Pease) AB131; AN211;
BD132; BX221   106319
Not, Lord, thine ancient works
alone (Gill) BX188; BY65
106320
Not now, but in the coming years
(Cornelius) AH386; AI292;
AV388; AX619; BB495; BC267
106321
Not of the sunlight, Not of the
moonlight (Tennyson) Y153;
AC231   106322
Not one of Adam's race (Ham-
mond) AZ1286; BA438   106323
Not only when ascends the song
(Gill) I520   106324
Not only where God's free winds
blow (Knapp) AN217 X Dear
God, the sun whose light
106325
Not so in haste, my heart!
(Torrey) G323; R382; S501;
U215; V364; AD277; BK96
106326
Not to the strong is the battle
(Crosby) R Conquering now
and still to conquer   106327
Not to the terrors of the Lord
(Watts) D392; Q478; V232;
AA463   106328
Not unto us, O Lord (Bible.
Psalm 115) E626   106329
Not unto us, O Lord of heaven
(Norton) T215; AJ308; AM68
106330
Not what I am, O Lord, but what
thou art (Bonar) W429; AZ451;
BE195; BX282; BY583   106331
Not what my hands have done
(Bonar) N175 X Not what these
hands have done   106332
Not what these hands have done
(Bonar) K332; N175; O414; Q
389; U187; V312; AA320; AI
134; AM403; AP420; AX318;
AZ1324; BA437; BV491; BY
450   106333
Not with a crowd of angels with-
out number (Gosse) X590
106334
Not with our mortal eyes (Watts)
L426   106335
Not worthy, Lord, to gather up

the crumbs (Bickersteth) H
444; J276; K184; O310; U
377; V548; AH503; AI165;
AM356; AP355; AV162; AZ
440   106336
Not worthy, not worthy (Baker)
AI220 X I am not worthy,
Holy Lord   106337
Nothing between my soul and
the Saviour (Tindley) AU66
106338
Nous allons, ma mie (French
trad carol) BG147b 106339
Nous voici dans la ville (French
trad carol) BG91b   106340
Now a new year opens (Clarke)
D541   106341
Now all give thanks to God
(Rinkart) BJ93   106342
Now all is still; Time holds
his breath (Neumann) AK151
106343
Now all the heavenly splendor
(Gerhardt) AQ268   106344
Now all the woods are sleeping
(Gerhardt) BV57 X Now
woods and wolds are sleeping
106345
Now another stage of travel
(Carpenter) BA178   106346
Now April has come, The
country grows sweet here
(Dearmer) BG155   106347
Now are the days fulfilled (Ger-
man, ca 1746) Q99 106348
Now are the days of humblest
prayer (Faber) BO163
106349
Now are the woodlands resting
(Gerhardt) AB21   106350
Now at the Lamb's high royal
feast (Latin, 4th c) BO176;
BQ30   106351
Now at the night's return we
raise (Bright) BV58
106352
Now be the God of Israel
blessed (Watts) AJp.394
106353
Now be the gospel banner In
every land unfurled (Hastings)
N371; AI173; AO521; AZ830;
BA342   106354

Now begin the heavenly theme
(Madan. Collection: Appendix,
1763) L160; V388; AZ77
                              106355
Now bless the God of all
(Abrahams) BH81   106356
Now blessed be Jehovah, God,
The God of Israel (U. P.
Psalter, 1912) T451; AJ197
                              106357
Now blessed be the Lord our
God (Scottish Psalter, 1650)
AM7 X His name for ever
shall endure   106358
Now blessed be thou, Christ
Jesu (Coverdale) BG131
                              106359
Now blessed thou, O Christ our
Lord (---) BI7-D   106360
Now blessing, honor, glory,
praise (Proud) BR213 106361
Now, brothers, lift your voices
(Prost, Fr.) BG106   106362
Now cheer, our hearts this even-
tide (Selnecker) G58; W278;
AF54; AL542; AW557; BJ13
                              106363
Now Christ, the very Son of God
(Selnecker) AA403   106364
Now comes the light for which
our souls have sought (Quin)
AN355   106365
Now do we come, O God to wor-
ship (Knobel) AD411   106366
Now do we pray God, the Holy
Ghost (Luther) AA260 106367
Now every child that dwells on
earth (Farjeon) BG188 106368
Now for each yearning heart (---)
AT527   106369
Now found is the fairest of roses
(Brorson) P153   106370
Now from the altar of my heart
(Mason) A170; B27; D20; I46;
K470; L29; V55; AL565; AX69
                              106371
Now from the altar of our hearts
(Mason) D20 X Now from the
altar of my heart   106372
Now give heart's onward habit
brave intent (Holmes) AQ178
                              106373
Now glad of heart be every one!

(German trad carol, 16th c)
BG95   106374
Now God be with us, for the
night is closing (Herbert) G
49; I58; J225; K459; M571;
N441; O565; Q556; R53; U
459; V47; W279; X48; Z147;
AA38; AF59; AL567; AN116;
AP675; AZ469; BA787; BB55;
BD5; BR112; BX161; BY697
                              106375
Now, gracious Lord, thine arm
reveal (Newton) AX630; AY
247   106376
Now hail we our Redeemer (St
Ambrose) N21; P122 106377
Now hush your cries and shed
no tears (Hermann) AA539
                              106378
Now I have found the firm foun-
dation (Rothe) Q385   106379
Now I have found the ground
wherein (Rothe) I302; K326;
N441; O478; P281; AL272;
AZ659; BA447; BV528; BY
451   106380
Now I have found the sure
foundation (Rothe) AA312
                              106381
Now I recall my childhood when
the sun (Tagore) AQ82
                              106382
Now I resolve with all my heart
(Steele) BX374   106383
Now I'm resting, sweetly rest-
ing (James) R In the rifted
Rock   106384
Now in holy celebration (Latin,
15th c) E228   106385
Now in joy we sing thy praises
(Farrell) BM79   106386
Now in life's breezy morning
(Myers) X591   106387
Now, in parting, Father, bless
us (Bonar) L333; BA914
                              106388
Now in the days of youth
(Mathams) R469; Z300; AB
233; AC146; AE447; AF490;
AG308; AK446; AN474; AR
345; BD118; BF628; BY452
                              106389
Now in the tomb is laid (Colum)

AQ314   106390

Now is Christmas y-come, Father
and Son together in one
(English trad carol, ca 1500)
BG173   106391

Now is the accepted time (Dobell)
V277; AY24   106392

Now is the healing time decreed
(Latin, before 12th c) E67
                              106393

Now is the hour of darkness past
(Watts) BG148   106394

Now is the time approaching
(Borthwick) AN326 X Hasten
the time appointed   106395

Now Israel may say, and that in
truth (U.P. Psalter, 1912)
R357; T254; AJ353; AM514
                              106396

Now Israel may say, and that
truly: -- If that the Lord had
not our cause (Whittingham)
AL683; AP112   106397

Now Israel's hope in triumph ends
(Hedborn) N61   106398

Now it is evening; time to rest
from labour (Herbert) A167
                              106399

Now Jesus at the door is knocking (Landstad) P119   106400

Now join, ye comrades true!
(Dearmer) X592   106401

Now just a word for Jesus
(Crosby) AX197; BB522
                              106402

Now lay we calmly in the grave
(Weisse) O594; Q596; AA538;
BA720   106403

Now let all loudly Sing praise to
God the Lord (Lowenstern)
Q28   106404

Now let every tongue adore thee!
(Nicolai) Y352 X Wake, awake
for night is flying   106405

Now let my soul, eternal King
(Heginbothom) H96   106406

Now let our cheerful eyes survey
(Doddridge) V174   106407

Now let our mourning hearts revive (Doddridge) AY175
                              106408

Now let the children of the saints
(Watts) V542   106409

Now let the earth with joy resound (Latin, 10th c) BQ
110   106410

Now let the vault of heaven resound (Strodach) J103
                              106411

Now let us all arise and sing
(Balch) AS358   106412

Now let us come before Him
(Gerhardt) Q122; AA174
                              106413

Now let us join our hearts and
tongues (Newton) AZ352
                              106414

Now let us praise the Lord
(Rinkart) AZ783 X Now thank
we all our God   106415

Now let us raise our Harvest
song (Woods) AS421   106416

Now let us rejoice in the day of
salvation (Phelps) BC118
                              106417

Now let us see thy beauty,
Lord (Waugh) BY274   106418

Now Lord be with us, for the
night is closing (Herbert)
BR112 X Now God be with
us   106419

Now, Lord, upon thy sea of air
(Anderson) AD455   106420

Now, Lord, who in this vale of
tears (Gregor) AZ892; BA
915   106421

Now may He who from the dead
(Newton) G612; K434; L56;
Q51; S41app.; W300; AA15;
AL316; AM318; AP337; AZ
60; BY764   106422

Now may the light that shone
in Jesus Christ our Lord
(---) S44app.   106423

Now, my soul, thy voice up-
raising (Santeüil. Paris
Breviary) D99; E623; K94;
N113; AZ623   106424

Now, my tongue, the mystery
telling (St Thomas Aquinas)
A199; B338; F383   106425

Now none but Christ can satisfy
("B.E.") R O Christ, in thee
my soul hath found   106426

Now, on land and sea descending
(Longfellow) G45; R67; U462;

Z141; AD48; AE41; AF52; AG
27; AN111; AQ274; AR54; AT
28; AW28; BF192; BX154; BZ
                          106427
Now once again for help that
never faileth (Stillman) A486
J382; AK311   106428
Now once again he heaven turns
(Patton) AQ320   106429
Now our worship sweet is o'er
(Schenck) M15; N357; Q45;
AA10   106430
Now praise we Christ, the Holy
One (Sedulius) Q104; AA148
                          106431
Now praise we great and famous
men (Tarrant) S491; Y335;
Z603; AB396; AD458; AF476;
AN365; BF663; BY648; BZ
                          106432
Now quit your care (Dearmer)
X98; BG144   106433
Now rest beneath night's shadow
[s] (Gerhardt) K469; M572;
O551; Q554; AA33   106434
Now rest in peace, Now rest in
peace (---) AZ1204   106435
Now rest, ye pilgrim host
(Raymond) N579   106436
Now shadows wane and hevy night
departeth (St Gregory the
Great) BJ75   106437
Now sing we a song for the har-
vest (Chadwick) W614; AP690;
AS428; BY727   106438
Now sing we, now rejoice (Latin
carol, 14th c) O199; P134;
Q92   106439
Now sing we of the Paraclete
(Dearmer) R When Christ
blessed His disciples 106440
Now sweeping down the years un-
told (Nourse) BE198   106441
Now thank we all our God (Rink-
art) A276; B422; D466; E533;
F379; G7; H62; I30; J443;
K283; L77; M492; N299; O31;
P242; Q36; R9; S459; T300;
V635; W29; X350; Y303; Z598;
AA64; AB56; AC325; AD12;
AE11; AF29; AG289; AH196;
AI443; AK72; AL19; AM86;
AN262; AO104; AP147; AQ19;

AR601; AT491; AV44; AW514;
AZ783; BA661; BB90; BC
120; BD200; BE199; BF169;
BK62; BL56; BM14; BN198;
BR492; BV22; BX187; BY18;
BZ   106442
Now thank we all our God
(Rinkart) X To Thee eternal
God (Brueckner)   106443
Now that the day hath reached
its close (Herzog) Q561
                          106444
Now that the daylight fills the
sky (Latin, 6th c) A159;
E254; F1; N538; O541; W
258; AL533; AP657; BR8;
BV44   106445
Now that the day-star glimmers
bright (Latin, 6th c) J211;
W260   106446
Now that the sun is beaming
bright (Latin, 6th c) P50
X Now that the sun is gleam-
ing bright   106447
Now that the sun is gleaming
bright (Latin, 6th c) B5;
K451; L3; N547; P50; AZ
226; BR10; BY679   106448
Now the blessèd Dayspring
(Thomson) D157; N200
                          106449
Now the busy week is done
(Jones) E282   106450
Now the day is over (Baring-
Gould) A172; B364; D535;
E603; F431; G53; I59; J231;
K574; L17; M576; N540;
O562; P67; Q654; R51; S
35; T309; U467; V41; W288;
X49; Y94; Z149; AA45; AB
28; AC23; AD59; AE50; AF
51; AG33; AH170; AI379;
AK56; AL545; AM666; AN
128; AO37; AP681; AR52;
AS30; AT35; AU194; AV15;
AW29; AZ767; BA788; BB52;
BC122; BD6; BF198; BK45;
BR519; BV59; BX144; BY
698; BZ   106451
Now the green blade riseth from
the buried green (Crum) BG
149; BZ   106452
Now the holly bears a berry as

white as the milk (English trad
carol) BG35   106453
Now the hour of worship o'er
(Schenck) Q45 X Now our wor-
ship sweet is o'er   106454
Now the joyful bells aringing
(Roberts) BG50   106455
Now the King in thy strength shall
be joyful, O Lord (U.P. Psal-
ter, 1912) T31; AJ45   106456
Now the laborer's task is o'er
(Ellerton) A224; B411; D242;
E358; F467; G526; J296; K509;
S440; V678; W330; AH532;
AL458; AO564; AP616; AW
315; BA731   106457
Now the light has gone away
(Havergal) K472; Q653
                                   106458
Now the morn new light is pour-
ing (Albert) X32; BV47
                                   106459
Now the shades of night are gone
(Occom) L6; M554; O540; Q
538; AA26; AX60; AY282; AZ
78; BA774; BR7   106460
Now the spring has come again
(Piae cantiones, 1582) AD
470; AQ323; BG98   106461
Now the Triune God confessing
(---) AZ242   106462
Now the wings of day are furled
(Brooke) AN118; BD11; BX
146   106463
Now the world is saved from
darkness (Lee) BN161 106464
Now thy earthly work is done
(Dearmer) X292   106465
Now to God, our Strength and
Saviour (U.P. Psalter, 1912)
T150; AJ222   106466
Now to heaven our prayer as-
cending (Hickson) T375; AN
555; AW371; BC171   106467
Now to Him who loved us (War-
ing) W708; AL624; AP812;
AW617   106468
Now to Jesus Christ all glory and
dominion (---) BI24-D
                                   106469
Now to the great and sacred
Three (---) Lp.741   106470
Now to the King of heaven (Dodd-

ridge) W710; AL626; AW615
                                   106471
Now to the Lamb upon the
Throne (Foster) AZ693
                                   106472
Now to the Lord a noble song!
(Watts & Wesley) H23; V
126; AT19; AV30; AZ330
                                   106473
Now to those who search the
deep (Noyes) Y186   106474
Now unto Jehovah, Ye sons of
the mighty (U.P. Psalter,
1912) T49; AJ76; AM36
                                   106475
Now upon the earth descending
(Levy) BH236   106476
Now welcome, Summer, with
thy sunne soft (Chaucer) BG
128   106477
Now we'll sing with one accord
(Phelps) BC132   106478
Now when the dusky shades of
night (St Gregory the Great)
AB5; AN101; AZ1220; BR3;
BX125   106479
Now while the day in trailing
splendor (Hosmer) AN121;
AQ269; BD8; BX149
                                   106480
Now with angels round the
throne (Conder) AZ1256
                                   106481
Now with creation's morning
song (Prudentius) AC10;
AN102; BX137   106482
Now with joyful exultation
(U.P. Psalter, 1912) T175;
AJ255   106383
Now with joyful songs appear
(Swertner) AZ581   106484
Now with the declining sun
(Coffin) AZ73   106485
Now with the rising, golden
dawn (Prudentius) AO24
                                   106486
Now woods and fields are sleep-
ing (Gerhardt) S505 X Now
woods and wolds are sleep-
ing   106487
Now woods and wolds are sleep-
ing (Gerhardt) R66; S505;
BV57   106488

Now yield we thanks and praise
(Robbins) A14   106489
Nowell, Nowell, now sing a
Saviour's birth (English trad
carol) R The Babe in Beth-
lem's manger laid   106490
Nowell! Nowell! Nowell!
Nowell sing we clear (Morris)
R Masters in this hall 106491
Nowell, Nowell, Nowell, sing
we with mirth (English trad)
BG170 X Behold a simple tender
Babe (Southwell)   106492
Nowell sing we, both all and some
(English trad carol, 1450) BG
62   106493
Nu rinder Solen op Af Österlide
(Kingo) BT542   106492
Nu singet und seyt fro (German
trad carol, 14th c) BG86 notes
X In dulci jubilo   106495
Nun bitten wir den Heiligen Geist
(Luther) BT231   106496
Nun bringen wir den Leib zur
Ruh (Unparth. G.B.) AY15d
                 106497
Nun danket all' und bringet Ehr'
Ihr Menschen in der Welt
(Gerhardt) BT581   106498
Nun danket alle Gott (Rinkart)
Y303; BT36; BW514   106499
Nun freut euch, liebe Christen
g'mein (Luther) BT387
                 106500
Nun Gott Lob, es ist vollbracht
(Schenck) BT45   106501
Nun gute Nacht, ihr Liebsten
mein (Unparth G.B.) AY14d
                 106502
Nun heben wir an in Röthen
(Ausbund) BU42   106503
Nun hört, ihr Freund ehrsamen
(Ausbund) BU28   106504
Nun hört mir zu in mein'm
Gedicht (Ausbund) BU72
                 106505
Nun ist die Zeit erfüllt (German,
1746?) BT99   106506
Nun komm, der Heiden Heiland
(St Ambrose) BT95   106507
Nun lasst uns den Leib begraben
(Weisse) BT596   106508
Nun lasst uns gehn und treten

(Gerhardt) BT122   106509
Nun, lob, mein' Seel', den
Herren (Graumann) BT34
                 106510
Nun preiset alle Gottes Barm-
herzigkeit! (Lowenstern) BT
28   106511
Nun ruhen alle wälder (Gerhardt)
AW556b; BT554; BW556
                 106512
Nun sich der Tag geendet hat
(J.F. Herzog) AY21d; BT
561   106513
Nun sich die Nacht geendet hat
(Unparth. G.B.) AY21d
                 106514
Nun singet und seid froh (Suso)
BT92   106515
Nun wolt ich gerne singen
(H. Betz) BU105   106516
Nunc sancte nobis spiritus
(Latin, 4th c) BJ45 note
                 106517

O

NOTE: "O" has been made the
acceptable form for both "O"
and "Oh". Both spellings will
be found in the same hymn, in
different books. Only "O" is
used herein.   106518

O all ye people, bless our God
(U.P. Psalter, 1912) T120;
AJ174   106519
O, alleluia, yes, 'tis heaven
(Butler) R Since Christ my
soul from sin   106520
O Allmächtiger Herre Gott! (Hut)
BU8   106521
O Almighty Giver, bountiful and
free (Monsell) R Earth below
is teeming   106522
O, anywhere my Saviour leads
(Moore) AX461; AY101
                 106523
O, at last I've found my Saviour
(Janus) AZ983   106524
O awake! my slumbering minstrel
(Snow) BC268   106525
O be joyful in the Lord (Beach)
AF26   106526
O be not thou dismayed (Horn)

AZ842; BA269   106527

O, be saved, His grace is free
(Crosby) R Troubled heart,
thy God is calling   106528

O, be still, thou soul of mine
(Ebel) AX394   106529

O be with us, gracious Father
(Rooker) W244   106530

O beautiful for spacious skies
(Bates) G491; J346; M504;
P413; R510; S411; T447;
U339; Y282; Z550; AB337;
AC271; AD438; AE389; AF
440; AG270; AH483; AK443;
AN383; AO592; AQ241; AR613;
AS382; AT489; AU39; AV300;
AW343; BA877; BB503; BC126;
BD175; BF540; BH262; BK121;
BX419; BZ   106531

O beautiful, my country (Hosmer)
X322; Z542; AB344; AC275;
AD433; AH472; AI355; AN388;
AO596; AQ240; AV305; BD174;
BF553; BX424   106532

O, beautiful Star of Bethlehem
(Boyce) AX95   106533

O, behold the Bridegroom cometh
(Oatman) R Time is gliding
                             106534

O Bethlehem, dear Bethlehem
(Hugg) AY245 X Hark the
hearld angels (Wesley) 106535

O Bethlehem of holy worth (Currie) BN18   106536

O Beulah land, Sweet Beulah land
(Stites) R I've reached the
land   106537

O bleeding Head, and wounded (St
Bernard of Clairvaux) AA201
                             106538

O bless our God with one accord
(Lamberts) AI448; AM348
                             106539

O bless the Lord, my Soul! His
grace to thee proclaim (Montgomery) A293; B318; D474;
H68; O65; AE17; AR29; AS5;
BA653; BH62   106540

O bless, the Lord, my Soul!
Let all within me join (Watts)
K299; L71; N291; Q27; V524;
Z105; AA76; AM72; AO86;
AY23; BR45   106541

O bless, thou heavenly Potentiate
(---) AA300   106542

O blessed are those who fear the
Lord (Ladies of the Grail)
BSp. 50   106543

O blessed Babe divine (Burmeister) O222   106544

O blessed by God, Saint Benedict (Schoehbechler) BN172
                             106545

O blessed day of Motherhood
(McGregor) AC318; AH498;
AT504; AU41; BF614
                             106546

O blessed day when first was
poured (Besnault) Q115 X O
happy day when first was
poured   106547

O blessed faith! Its song of cheer
(Hewitt) R "Have faith in
God."   106548

O blessed Father! sent by God
His mercy to dispense
(Faber) BQ108   106549

O blessed Holy Trinity (Behm)
Q541 X O holy blessed Trinity,
Divine eternal unity   106550

O blessed home where man and
wife (Landstad) Q624 X In
house and home where man
and wife   106551

O blessed hour, when evening
comes (Squires) BB60
                             106552

O blessed house, that cheerfully
receiveth (Spitta) K416; M262;
AR541; AS414; AW358; AX558
                             106553

O blessed is the man who stays
(Wallin) N495   106554

O blessed is the man whose sins
(Scottish Psalter, 1650) AL
641; AP28   106555

O blessed life! the heart at
rest (Matson) U414; BX88
                             106556

O Blessed Light from heaven
(Solberg) M205   106557

O Blessed Light! O Trinity!
Thou ever-blessed Unity (St
Ambrose) AO238   106558

O blessed Saint Joseph, how
great was thy worth (Faber)

BQ92   106559

O blessed Saviour, is thy love
(Stennett) AZ150   106560

O blessed Son of God (Crain)
Z520; AE378; AO468; AR368;
AS341; BF487   106561

O blessed souls are they (Watts)
V285   106562

O blessed Sun whose splendor
(Spitta) J573; K362; O437;
P327   106563

O blest communion with the saints
at rest (Roberts) W226 106564

O blest Creator, God most high
(St Ambrose) AO33   106565

O blest Creator of the day (St
Gregory the Great) A163; E51
106566

O blest Creator of the light (St
Gregory the Great) E51 X O
blest Creator of the day; X
Source of Light and Life divine
106567

O, blest memorial of our dying
Lord (St Thomas Aquinas)
BR478 X Thee we adore, O
hidden Saviour   106568

O blest Redeemer, from thy
radiant throne (Hymns of the
English Conf. 1880) BR456
106569

O blest the house, whate'er befall
(Pfeil) M264; N531; O234; P355;
Q625; AA445   106570

O blest the souls that see and hear
(Hosmer) AN404; BX399
106571

O bold, O foolish peasants
(Lathrop) AN183; AQ309; AR
159   106572

O bona patria, lumina sobria (St
Bernard of Cluny) BT614
106573

O bone Jesu! Miserere nobis
(Latin) BQ256   106574

O boundless joy! There is salvation (Hiller) M137   106575

O boundless wisdom, God most
high (Latin, ca 6th c) E58
106576

O bow thine ear, Eternal One
(Pierpont) BB484   106577

O Bread of Heaven! beneath this

veil (St Alphonso M de'
Liguori) BO50   106578

O Bread of Life, for all men
broken (Lew) R450; BZ
106579

O Bread of Life from heaven
(Latin, 1661) D223; J271;
O287; P90; S357; AZ559
106580

O Bread to pilgrims given
(Latin, 1661) K186; L326;
V554   106581

O breath of God, breathe on us
now (Vine) AL150; BV294
106582

O Breath of life, come sweeping through us (Head) BV
298   106583

O breathe on me, thou Breath
of God (Hatch) BN121 X
Breathe on me   106584

O brethren, how this perfect
love (Warner) R How sweet
this bond   106585

O Bride of Christ, rejoice
(Danish, ca 1600) M328; O
161; Q57   106586

O Brightness of the immortal
Father's face (Greek, 3d c)
A173; B12; D6; BL75 106587

O brother, be faithful! Soon
Jesus will come (Smith)
BB173   106588

O brother man, fold to thy
heart thy brother (Whittier)
A493; G466; J539; R474;
S403; W485; X307; Y258;
Z515; AC244; AD337; AE
407; AF410; AG254; AK393;
AL366; AN348; AO469; AQ
144; AR378; AS340; AT447;
AU403; AV275; AW229; BD
125; BE217; BF495, 507;
BK110; BY662; BZ   106589

O brothers, lift your voices
(Bickersteth) B495; D579;
H400; R333; S372; BA549
106590

O Calvary! dark Calvary! (Darwood) R On Calv'ry's brow
106591

O can you sing the new song
of salvation (Traasdal) P15

106592
O can we say we are ready,
brother? (Crosby) R When
Jesus comes to reward His
servants   106593
O Canada! our home and native
land! (Weir) BB508 X O
Canada! our home, our native
land!   106594
O Canada! our home, our native
land! (Weir) Y295; BB508;
BX544   106595
O cease, my wandering soul
(Muhlenberg) V533; AI246;
BR283   106596
O child of lowly manger birth
(Blanchard) AB170 X O Jesus,
youth of Nazareth   106597
O children, hither do ye come
(Scottish Psalter, 1650) AL645;
AP33; AW584   106598
O Christ, behind thy Temple's
veil (Breviary) BO16   106599
O Christ, forget not them who
stand (Sangster) S387; Y117;
Z526; AB371; AC260; AD383;
AK374; BY368   106600
O Christ, in thee my soul hath
found ("B.E.") W699; AL482;
AW451   106601
O Christ, my God, who seest the
unseen (Rossetti) W545
106602
O Christ my Light, my gracious
Saviour (Gerhardt) AZ993
106603
O Christ, of angel legions the
bright crown (Herman) BP105
106604
O Christ, our hope, our heart's
desire (Latin, 8th c) E144;
J400; K128; L271; N144; O373;
P204; AI425; AM120   106605
O Christ our joy, gone up on
high (Latin, 5th c) F611
106606
O Christ, our joy, to whom is
given (Latin, 5th c) Z142
106607
O Christ, our King, Creator,
Lord (St Gregory the Great)
J62; K59; AM134; AZ280
106608

O Christ, our Leader and our
way (Kite) Y340   106609
O Christ, our Lord, who with
thine own hast been (Bourne)
BY323   106610
O Christ, our true and only
Light (Heermann) K47; L
230; M109; N67; O221; P
147; Q512; AA475; AM296;
AO533; AZ298; BA185; BR
40; BV325; BY384   106611
O Christ, the Way, the Truth,
the Life (Squier) Z410;
AC216; BF419   106612
O Christ, thou art our joy
alone (Latin, 5th c) BN52
106613
O Christ, thou bright and
Morning Star, now shed thy
light (German, 1579) K350;
L192   106614
O Christ, thou gift of love di-
vine (Harmer) Z454 106615
O Christ, thou has ascended
(Bickersteth) AZ819; BA
246   106616
O Christ, thou Lamb of God
that takest away the sin of
the world (Latin, 5th c
[Agnus dei]) Q147   106617
O Christ, Thou Lord of worlds,
Thine ear to hear us bow
(Latin) F505   106618
O Christ, thy grace unto us
lend (Wilhelm II, duke) N
305   106619
O Christ, thy guilty people
spare (St Rabanus Maurus)
BN185; BO219   106620
O Christ, thy love unbounded
(Bosworth's hymns, 1865)
N489 X Jesus, thy love un-
bounded   106621
O Christ, to thee we come
(Hartman) AY276   106622
O Christ, we climb the hill with
thee (Morse) AR408 106623
O Christ, what burdens bowed
thy head (Cousin) AP198
106624
O Christ, who art the Light and
Day (Latin, before 9th c)
E81; F95; O557; Q559; BJ6

106625

O Christ who holds the open gate
(Masefield) X593; Y81; AC
234; AD206   106626

O Christ, whom we may love and
know (Cropper) F450; J453
106627

O Christ! with each returning
morn (St Ambrose) AZ348;
BB41   106628

O Christian, awake! 'tis the
Master's command (Crosby)
BB576   106629

O Christian, haste, thy mission
high fulfilling (Thomson) AB367
X O Sion haste. . .   106630

O Christians, leagued together
(Cassaday) J567; K578; L532;
M524   106631

O Christmas tree, O Christmas
tree (German) M618   106632

O Church of freedom, stand
(Domer) N212   106633

O Church of God, divided (Ham)
Z433   106634

O Church of God, our solitude
forsaking (Schloerb) Z432
106635

O Church of God triumphant
(Harlow) AR496   106636

O Church of God, united (Morley)
AE312   106637

O Church, thy strength abide
(Hayn) AZ472   106638

O come, all ye faithful, joyful
and triumphant (Latin, 18th
c (Oakeley tr) A12; B72; D49;
E28; F59, 593; G96; H147; I
125; J42; Q102; R170; S116;
T332; U56; V769; W55; X78;
Y298; Z205; AB106; AC83;
AD120; AE84; AF132; AG69;
AH263; AI67; AK112; AL47;
AM151; AN156; AO127; AP173,
174*; AQ288; AR143; AS110;
AT66; AU143; AV90; AW80;
AX94; BB105; BC129; BD205;
BF291; BI83; BK149; BL11;
BM63; BN11; BO150a; BP13;
BQ4b; BV106; BX533; BY104;
BZ   106639
*tr. by Mercer

O come, all ye faithful, joyfully
triumphant (Latin, 18th c)
(Mercer tr) AP174 X O come,
all ye faithful, joyful and
triumphant   106640

O, come, all ye that labor
(McKinney) AU462   106641

O come, and dwell in me (Wesley) G377; H296; I362; BZ
106642

O, come, and let us all, with
one accord (Hymns of the
Spirit, 1864) BR99   106643

O come and mourn with me a-
while (Faber) A74; B153;
D105; E111; F113; G134; I
152; J86; K105; R192; S159;
W96; X140; Z233; AF164; AH
126; AK146; AL90; AP193; AZ
422; BN37; BO168; BP32; BQ
21; BV173; BY144   106644

O come and sing unto the Lord
(U.P. Psalter, 1912) R29
106645

O come and to Jehovah sing
(U.P. Psalter, 1912) I176;
AJ256   106646

O come, angel band (Haskell)
R My latest sun is sinking
106647

O come before Jehovah! (Kretzmann) M530   106648

O come before the Lord, our
King (U.P. Psalter, 1912) AJ
254   106649

O come, creator Spirit, come
(Latin, 9th c) A108; BQ36;
106650

O come, Divine Messiah (Pellegrin, Abbé) BN7; BO147
106651

O come, if sinner be thy name
(Lehr) O435   106652

O come, Immanuel, our King
(Latin, 9th c) AB103 X O
come, O come, Emmanuel
106653

O come in the might of the Lord
of Light (Moultrie) B17 X
We come in the might. . .
106654

O come let us adore Him (Mar-

tens) R When blossoms flowered
                              106655
O come, let us sing to the Lord
  (Scottish Psalter, 1650) S49;
  AK22; AL666; AM19; AP81
                              106656
O come, little children, O come,
  one and all (Schmidt) M615;
  AW413; BK152; BN19; BQ6
                              106657
O come, loud anthems let us
  sing (Tate & Brady) B308; D472;
  H64; AW18; BO4   106658
O come, my people, to my law
  (U. P. Psalter, 1912) R255;
  AJ215   106659
O come, my soul, bless thou
  the Lord thy Maker (U. P.
  Psalter, 1912) T195; AJ283;
  AM10   106660
O come, O come, Emmanuel
  (Latin, 9th c) A2; B66; D45;
  E8; F49; G83; H131; J2; K1;
  M117; N7; O172; P118; Q62;
  R147; S108; W149; X66; Z182;
  AB103; AC75; AD100; AE78;
  AF110; AG63; AI57; AK88; AL
  137; AM147; AN150; AO107; AP
  241; AQ280; AR214; AW67; AZ
  677; BA106; BB109; BD203;
  BF275; BK140; BL3; BM61;
  BN6; BO149; BQ2; BR136; BV
  83; BY83; BZ   106661
O come, O come, Immanuel (La-
  tin, 9th c) BB109 X O come,
  O come, Emmanuel   106662
O come to the Lord today (War-
  ren) AX288   106663
O come to the merciful Saviour
  who calls you (Faber) P260
                              106664
O come, ye happy children, and
  sings a gladsome lay (French
  trad) BD222   106665
O comfort to the weary? (Hymns
  of the English Conf., 1880 [J.
  Conder?]) BR373   106666
O Comforter, God Holy Spirit
  (Herbert) AZ374   106667
O cor, amoris victima (Latin)
  BO17   106668
O cor Jesu flagrans amor nostri
  (Latin) BQ236   106669

O cor Jesu, fons amoris
  (Latin) BO24   106670
O could I find from day to day
  (Cleveland) L432; V404;
  BB322   106671
O could I speak the matchless
  worth (Medley) B263; G118;
  H343; I540; K309; L148;
  R134; S203; U73; V130; Z
  265; AE297; AG109; AH178;
  AI111; AL43; AM126; AO
  205; AR115; AS114; AT146;
  AU17; AV126; AX7; AY29;
  BB161; BZ   106672
O could our thoughts and wishes
  fly (Steele) BB244   106673
O could we but love that Saviour
  (Boenisch) AZ952; BA497
                              106674
O cross, no stars thy glow
  outshine (Herman) BP31
                              106675
O darkest woe! Ye tears forth
  flow (Rist) J87; M397; O322;
  P185; Q167; AA215   106676
O dass ich tausend Zungen
  hätte (Mentzer) BT30, 243;
  BW509   106677
O daughter of Zion, awake from
  thy sadness (Fitzgerald. Col-
  lection) BE200 X Daughter
  of Zion, Awake. . .   106678
O daughter, take good heed
  (Scottish Psalter, 1650)
  AP40   106679
O daughters blest of Galilee
  (How) AO491   106680
O, David was a shepherd lad
  (Clarke) F449   106681
O day full of grace which we
  behold (Danish, 14th c) O379;
  P226   106682
O, day of awful story (Whittle)
  AU464   106683
O Day of God, draw nigh (Scott)
  A525; AF444; BY187; BZ
                              106684
O day of joy and wonder (Buch-
  anan) BV220   106685
O day of light and gladness
  (Hosmer) AN196; AQ316;
  BD243; BX204   106686
O day of rest and gladness

O fair Creator of the skies
(Latin, 7th c) BP1   106722

O faith of England, taught of old
(Lacey) E544; X246   106723

O faithful cross, O noblest tree
(Fortunatus) BP30   106724

O faithful God, Thanks be to
Thee (Selnecker) M73; Q321;
AA425   106725

O faithful God, we worship Thee
(Selnecker) AA425 X O faithful God, thanks be to thee
                       106726

O Father above us, our Father
in might (Dearmer) X396a
                       106727

O Father, all creating (Ellerton)
B381; E345; O534; Q621; W
326; AL237; AM628; AP705;
AR538; BA845; BV391; BY622
                       106728

O Father almighty, to thee be
addressed (---) Lp. 744; AZ
505   106729

O Father, bless the children
(Ellerton) D208; N231 106730

O Father, by whose sovereign
sway (Alington) F465   106731

O Father, for this little life
(White) F426; BV341   106732

O Father, hear my morning
prayer (Percy) AL536   106733

O Father in heaven, our Father
on earth (Dearmer) X396b
                       106734

O Father, lead us gently by the
hand (Cleator) AX491; AY119
                       106735

O Father, may thy word prevail
(Brorson) O245; P159   106736

O Father, may we bear each
hour (Castellain) BE203
                       106737

O Father mine, whose mercies
never cease (Hoppe) N171
                       106738

O Father of goodness, thou art
in each one (Dearmer) X396c
                       106739

O Father of mercy, be ever
adored (Wesley) AZ500; BA9
                       106740

O Father of wisdom and friend-

ship and peace (Dearmer) X
396d   106741

O Father, thou who givest all
(Holmes) Z600; AC316; AH
552; AN268; BD201; BH250;
BK36; BX132   106742

O Father, thou who hast created
all (Knapp) O143; W308
                       106743

O Father, thy Kingdom is come
upon earth (Berg) BE204
                       106744

O Father, we thank thee for
Jesus thy Son (Sedding) F441
                       106745

O filii et filiae (Tisserand) BM
81; BN41; BO178; BP35; BQ
195; BT208   106746

O fill us with thy spirit ("L.J.
L.") AY329 X From Green-
land's icy mountains (Heber)
                       106747

O fix my heart, my God, my
strength (Hymns of the English
Conf. 1880) BR315   106748

O Food of exiles lowly (Latin,
1661) BN91   106749

O Food of men wayfaring (Latin,
1661) A192; E321; BL49
                       106750

O Food that weary pilgrims love
(Latin, 1661) F389; BO47;
BP57   106751

O Food to pilgrims given (Latin,
1661) BQ57   106752

O for a closer walk with God
(Cowper) A416; B305; D660;
E445; F325; G228; I492; J466;
M217; N456; O501; P317; R
319; S259; U256; V414; W
457; X112; Z310; AD284;
AE195; AF349; AG172; AH
357; AI279; AK319; AL308;
AO299; AP474; AS213; AT
365; AU208; AV191; AW197;
AX378; AY321; BA628; BB
383; BF368; BJ84; BR288;
BV147; BY599; BZ   106753

O for a faith that will not shrink
(Bathurst) G270; H363; I424;
J395; K266; L422; M127; N
443; O243; Q396; U196; V348;
W474; X594; AA354; AE192;

AI239; AL345; AO385; AP513;
AT255; AU277; AV62; AW153;
AX454; AY357; AZ188; BA708;
BB245; BE205; BV502; BX277;
BZ   106754
O for a glance of heavenly day
(Hart) H276; I274   106755
O for a heart of calm repose
(---) G363; I376; AR227
                            106756
O for a heart to love my God
(Wesley) AS214 X O for a
heart to praise my God 106757
O for a heart to praise my God
(Wesley) A414; B260; D439;
E82; F325; G370; H305; I354;
J389; K264; L414; N453; R325;
S260; U257; V403; W467; X113;
AE181; AG177; AL309; AO300;
AP473; AR398; AS214; AX387;
AY7; AZ116; BA630; BB18; BJ
87; BR284; BV544; BY600; BZ
                            106758
O for a principle within (Wesley)
AZ159; BA629   106759
O for a shout of sacred joy
(Watts) V165   106760
O for a thousand tongues to sing
(Wesley) A325; D440; E446;
F196; G162; H300; I1; J428;
K135; L139; M206; O446; P10;
Q360; R141; S199; T328; U68;
V203; W166; X595; Z262; AA
108; AD182; AE8; AF223; AG
112; AH374; AI13; AK181; AL
41; AM133; AO215; AP261;
AR114; AS113; AT129, 140;
AU5, 279; AV128; AW12; AY
50; AZ200; BA121; BB155;
BT360; BV270; BY212; BZ
                            106761
O for a thousand tongues to sings
(with refrain: Blessed be the
name) (Wesley) AT140; AU
279   106762
O for an overcoming faith (Watts)
H494   106763
O for that flame of living fire
(Bathurst) I187; BB210; BX398
                            106764
O for that tenderness of heart
(Wesley) I278   106765
O for the death of those (Max-

well) V676   106766
O for the peace that floweth
as a river (Crewdson) AN
550; AP477   106767
O, form us all while we re-
main (Gregor) BA915 X
Now, Lord, who in this vale
of tears   106768
O Fount of good, to own thy
love (Doddridge) N388
                            106769
O Fount of grace that runneth
o'er (Crewdson) BY339
                            106770
O Fount of truth and mercy
(Nyström) N301   106771
O Fountain eternal of life and
light (Koitsch) AZ777
                            106772
O Friend of sinners, Son of
God (Hoppe) N185   106773
O Friend of souls, how blest
am I (Dessler) AA109
                            106774
O Galilee! sweet Galilee!
Where Jesus loved so much
to be (Morris) R Each coo-
ing dove   106775
O gentle one, we miss thee
here (Warner) R A gentle
hand   106776
O gentle presence, peace and
joy and power (Eddy) BE
207   106777
O gentle Saviour, from thy
throne on high (Birks) AR
683; AS66   106778
O gift of gifts! Oh grace of
faith (Faber) H290; V351;
AO379   106779
O Gift of God, we praise thee
(Uhler) BB149   106780
O give me back my prophet dear
(Taylor) BC137   106781
O, give thanks to Him who
made (Conder) AZ1279; BX
14; BY19   106782
O give thanks to the Lord, for
he is good, for his great
love is without end (Ladies
of the Grail) BSp.54
                            106783
O give the Lord whole-hearted

praise (U. P. Psalter, 1912)
T211; AI12; AJ304   106784

O give the Lord, you sons of
God (Ladies of the Grail) BS
p. 14   106785

O, give us pleasure in the flowers
today (Frost) AQ324   106786

O give us that good part (Schrautenbach) AZ1167   106787

O Giver of delightful fields
(Morse) AR596   106788

O gladsome light, O grace (Greek,
3d c) A176; E269; J220; Q
101; R61; X50; AF49; AL551;
AR55; AW34; BJ88; BY699
106789

O gloriosa virginum (Fortunatus)
BN124; BO266; BQ210 106790

O glorious Head, thou livest now!
(Tersteegen) AZ681   106791

O glorious hope of perfect love!
(Wesley) I365   106792

O glorious King of Martyr hosts
(Latin, ca 6th c) E183 106793

O Glorious Maid, exalted far
(Latin, ca 9th c) E215 106794

O glory hallelujah, hallelujah,
hallelujah (Lowry) R O worship
the Lord   106795

O glory to Jesus! so sweet to
me (Warner) R Not in the
temples   106796

O God, above the drifting years
(Buckham) AB395; AF297; AK
377; AN362; BF536   106797

O God, accept my heart this day
(Bridges) N253; X O God, accept my heart this day 106798

O God, according to thy grace
(U.P. Psalter, 1912) AJ143
106799

O God, all gracious! In thy gift
(Moise) BH45   106800

O God, Almighty Father, creator
òf all things (German hymn)
BM12; BN57   106801

O God, Almighty Father, thou
Majesty divine (German hymn)
BN57 X O God, Almighty Father
creator of all things   106802

O God, arise! and by thy might
(Collier) AI442   106803

O God, be merciful and bless (U.

P. Psalter, 1912) AJ177
106804

O God, be merciful, be merciful to me (U.P. Psalter,
1912) T105; AJ151 106805

O God, be merciful to me, for
men no mercy show (U.P.
Psalter, 1912) AJ153
106806

O God, be merciful to me, My
soul for refuge (U.P. Psalter
1912) T106; AJ154 106807

O God, be thy annointed Son
(U. P. Psalter, 1912) T132;
AJ198   106808

O God, be with us, for the
night is falling (Herbert)
Q556 X Now God be with us,
for the night is closing
106809

O God, before whose altar
(Lyon) F340; BZ   106810

O God, beneath thy guiding
hand (Bacon) A148; G493;
P416; R523; S462; T449;
Y116; Z543; AB391; AC270;
AD435; AE394; AF438; AG
290; AH477; AI362; AK436;
AN369; AO594; AQ235; AR
605; AS386; AW367; BB507;
BD167; BF543; BK120; BX
405; BZ   106811

O God, creation's secret force
(St Ambrose) A162; E262
106812

O God Creator, in whose hand
(Farrington) G555   106813

O God, Eternal Father, from
thy high throne (---) BL80
106814

O God, Eternal God! thy name
(Slemp) AU302   106815

O God, Eternal Source of love
beyond our knowing (Heer-
mann) J460   106816

O God, forsake me not (Franck)
Q402; AA347   106817

O God, from heaven look down
and see (Luther) AA278
106818

O God, give ear unto my cry,
and to my voice attend (U.
P. Psalter, 1912) AJ160

106819

O God, give ear unto my cry;
Unto my prayer attend (Scottish
Psalter, 1650) AL653; AP49

106820

O God, give thou ear to my plea
(U. P. Psalter, 1912) T104;
AJ150   106821

O God, great Father, Lord, and
King (Hoss) I231   106822

O God-head hid devoutly I adore
thee (Latin) BO44   106823

O God, hear thou the nation's
prayer (Maurer) Y275; BF558
106824

O God, how good thou art To all
the pure of heart (U. P. Psalter,
1912) T137; AJ203   106825

O God! how ought my grateful
heart (---) BO200   106826

O God, how wonderful thou art
(Faber) N339 X My God, how
wonderful thou art   106827

O God, I cried, no dark disguise
(Millay) Y166; AC40; AQ57
106828

O God, I love thee; not that my
poor love (Spanish, 17th c)
J489 X My God I love thee
not because (St Francis Xavier)
106829

O God, I thank thee for each
sight (Mason) AB190; AN91;
BD35; BF179; BX38   106830

O God, I thank thee that the
night (Pierpont) BX526 106831

O God, if thy beloved Son (Heermann) M173   106832

O God, in restless living (Fosdick)
AB295; AD276; AR335; BF393;
BK95   106833

O God! in thine autumnal skies
(Brooks) BX169   106834

O God, in this hour of grace
(Boutflower) F460   106835

O God, in whom we live and
move, In whom we draw each
breath (Briggs) X275; AQ24
106836

O God, in whom we live and
move, Thy love is law, Thy
law is love (Longfellow)
Z179; AB186; BF224; BX83

106837

O God, in whose all-searching
eye (Wordsworth) D211;
BT332   106838

O God, in whose great purpose
(Gilkey) Z607; AB317; AD
423; AK454; AR69   106839

O God, mine inmost soul convert (Wesley) BA411 X Lo,
on a narrow neck of land
106840

O God, most holy are thy ways
(U. P. Psalter, 1912) AJ211;
AM41   106841

O God, most merciful and true
(Wesley) I401   106842

O God, my days are dark indeed (Hojer) AA503   106843

O God, my ever constant Friend
(Mayer) BH192   106844

O God, my heart is fixed; 'tis
bent (Tate) AP48   106845

O God, my heavenly King
(Hymns of the English Conf.,
1880) BR329   106846

O God, my strength and fortitude
(Sternhold) AD74; AL634; AM
524; AP13; BR139; BX313
106847

O God, no longer hold thy peace
(U. P. Psalter, 1912) T152;
AJ224; AM57   106848

O God, not only in distress
(Smith) AB214; AD274; AP
528; BF410; BX261   106849

O God, O Spirit, Light of all
that live (Tersteegen) AN69;
BX44   106850

O God of ages, in whose light
(Jarvis) BV60   106851

O God of Bethel, by whose hand
(Doddridge) A497; B446; D417;
E447; F299; H120; J519; K
254; L489; M236; O286; Q434;
R342; S98; T401; U248; V420;
W562; X596; Z174; AA364;
AD89; AF389; AG52; AL446;
AM498; AO99; AP599; AW167;
BA30; BB88; BF225; BV561;
BY550   106852

O God of earth and altar (Chesterton) A521; E562; J344; R511;
S419; W638; X308; Y236; Z546;

AD347; AF436; AG271; AK370;
AN381; AQ238; BK103; BX412;
BZ   106853
O God of God! O Light of Light
(Julian) B251; D455; I15; N71;
O122; Q132; AO206   106854
O God, of good the unfathomed
Sea (Scheffler) AL11   106855
O God of grace, thy mercy send
(Greek: Litany of the Deacons)
F589   106856
O God of heaven and earth, arise
(Doddridge) AZ301   106857
O God of hosts, the mighty Lord
(Tate & Brady) AM303 106858
O God of hosts, with thy strong
hand (---) BI13   106859
O God of Jacob, by whose hand
(Doddridge) Q434 X O God of
Bethel, by whose hand 106860
O God of life, whose power benign
(Russell) D138; AZ6; BA258;
BY44   106861
O God of Light, thy word, a
lamp unfailing (Taylor) J250;
R247; AE160; AT185; BZ
                       106862
O God of love of truth (Kretzman)
M526   106863
O God of love, O King of peace
(Baker) A528; B436; D199;
F490; G511; I705; J352; K499;
N577; O483; S421; W646; Z557;
AE401; AF447; AG279; AK404;
AL523; AM622; AO604; AP652;
AR389; AS364; AW352; BA881;
BF579; BK113; BX432; BY663
                       106864
O God of love, to thee we bow
(Jenkins) W325; AD416; BY623
                       106865
O God of love, whose spirit
wakes (Tweedy) BY66   106866
O God of loveliness, O Lord of
heaven above (St Alfonso M.
de' Liguori) BQ38   106867
O God of mercies, Father mine
(Hoppe) N193   106868
O God of mercy, God of might
(Thring) D271; E448; J316;
K237; L398; N181; O450; P405;
Q439; U33; W487; AA362; AM
366; AP583; AS344; BA566;

BF492   106869
O God of mercy! hearken now
(Clark) B503; D275; N391;
AK388; BD130   106870
O God of nations, God of men
(Schmidt) AO583   106871
O God of nations, hear thy
people's prayer today
(Pyper) BY649   106872
O God of our fathers, we praise
and adore thee (Pruden) AT
500   106873
O God of peace, thee we implore
(Orwig) AE187   106874
O God of truth, O Lord of might
(St Ambrose) A161; E261;
F12; BR13b   106875
O God of truth, whose living
word (Hughes) A547; B498;
E449; F309; W531; X597;
Y145; Z365; AC181; AK364;
AL411; AM468; AN325; AP
548; BF559; BX384; BY517
                       106876
O God of wisdom, life and love
(Brubacher) AX553   106877
O God of wondrous grace and
glory (Reed) J353   106878
O God of youth, whose Spirit in
our hearts is stirring (Burt)
A508; J548; AF491   106879
O God, our dwelling-place
(Wilson) AN43; BD133; BX
281   106880
O God, our Father-Mother,
Love, Purge thou our hearts
(Sinclair) BE206   106881
O God our Father, throned on
high (Coster) W492; BV541
                       106882
O God our Father, who dost
make us one (Jenkins) BY
765   106883
O God our help in ages past
(Watts) A289; B445; D418; E
450; F165; G533; H104; I577;
J168; K505; L518; M145; N57;
O212; P142; Q123; R111; S77;
T168; U19; V90; W601; X598;
Y30; Z585; AA172; AB58; AC
28; AD1; AE65; AF1; AG40;
AH218; AI412; AJ247; AK63;
AL662; AM26; AN145; AO91;

Thy presence (Osler) A198;
B321; D221; F412; J263; K189;
L328; O152; Z452; BR467;
BV384   106916

O God, we have heard and our
fathers have told (U.P. Psalter,
1912) T81; AJ121   106917

O God, we praise thee; and confess (Tate & Brady) H100;
L80; AB45; AF18; AM90
                               106918

O God, we pray for all mankind
(Conover) AT456; AV267; AW
350; AX365   106919

O God, we pray for faithful wills
(Maurer) AB238   106920

O God, we pray thee, bless thy
children (Gordon) AR619; AS
52   106921

O God, what offering shall I
give (Lange) BY770 X Jesus,
what offering   106922

O God, while generations flee
(---) AN371; BX397   106923

O God, who saidst, "Let there
be light" (Miller) N168
                               106924

O God, who to a loyal home
(Fosdick) AE385   106925

O God, who workest hitherto
(Freckleton) AC189 X The
toil of brain, or heart, or hand
                               106926

O God, whom I delight to praise
(U.P. Psalter, 1912) T209;
AJ300   106927

O God, whom we as Father know
(Knapp) M512   106928

O God, whose daylight leadeth
down (MacDonald) AL546
                               106929

O God, whose law from age to
age (Holmes) U20; AH224;
AK79; BF226; BH97   106930

O God, whose love is over all
(Holmes) U22; Z175; AB38;
AD87; AK70; AR96; BF228
                               106931

O God, whose mighty works of
old (Crum) F501   106932

O God, whose presence glows in
all (Frothingham) AN60; BE214;
BX81   106933

O God, whose smile is in the
sky (Holmes) Z163; AN36;
BF222; BX68   106934

O God, whose will is life
(Rawnsley) BZ X Father,
whose will is life   106935

O God, within whose sight
(Oxenham) AE310; AF265;
AR503; BF586   106936

O golden day, so long desired
(Dickinson) BB434;   106937

O Good Saint Anne, we call on
thy name (---) R To kneel at
thine altar   106938

O Gott, du frommer Gott
(Heermann) BT395; BW
566   106939

O Gott, du grosser her der
Welt (Unparth. G.B.) AY5d
                               106940

O Gott Schöpfer, heiliger Geist
(Ausbund) BU50   106941

O Gott Vater ins Himmels
Throne (Ausbund) BU55
                               106942

O Gott Vater, wir loben dich
(L. Clock) AY1d; BU131;
BY362   106943

O gracious Father of mankind
(Tweedy) G305; S85; Y34;
Z338; AB198; AC66; AD215;
AG175; AK235; AR73; BF
371; BK55; BZ   106944

O gracious God, forsake me not
(U.P. Psalter, 1912) R396;
T131; AJ192   106945

O gracious God, in whom I
live (Steele) D338   106946

O gracious God, whose constant
care (Stock) AF492; AK449
                               106947

O gracious Hand that freely
gives (Russell) N186; O422
                               106948

O grant thy servants through
thy grace (Gambold) AX
642; BA316   106949

O grant us light, that we may
know (Tuttiett) R335; S210;
U44; V738; W466; Z298; AD
422; AE375; AG129; AK187;
AW389; BA887; BF429; BY
540   106950

O great Absolver, grant my soul
may wear (Stone) AZ453
                              106951
O great High Priest, forget not
me (Loy) M547   106952
O greatly blessed the people are
(Scottish Psalter, 1650) AL661;
AM38; AP73   106953
O guardian of the Church divine
(Chamberlain) BR481; BV411
                              106954
O Guidet to every child of thine
(St. Clement of Alexandria)
BZ   106955
O happy band of pilgrims (St
Joseph the Hymnographer) B
536; D511; E452; F289; W577;
X599; AL443; AP602; AZ852;
BA509; BB377; BV582; BY551
                              106956
O happy day, that fixed my choice
(Doddridge) G212 X O happy
day, that stays my choice
                              106957
O happy day, that stays my
choice (Doddridge) D218; G212;
H287; I312; L287; N255; O389;
U192; V310; W499; AH345;
AL361; AM589; AO652; AP564;
AS454; AT389; AU461; AV251;
AW465; AX331; AY271; AZ390;
BA464; BB310; BR462; BY297;
BZ   106958
O happy day, when first was
poured (Besnault) E36; Q115;
AA177; BN24   106959
O happy day when we shall stand
(Wexels) J197; O52; P62
                              106960
O happy days, days marked with
perfect blessings (Foster) AZ
710   106961
O happy home! O blest abode!
(Morton) BC133   106962
O happy home, where thou art
loved the dearest (Spitta)
G427; I671; J336; N533;
O537; P351; Q626; R455; U320;
W648; Y382; Z601; AC313; AD
418; AE383; AH500; AK445; AL
393; AM624; AO562; AP707;
AT373; AU445; BB412; BV394;
BY621   106963

O happy homes among the hills
(Stephens) BC337   106964
O happy is that man and blest
(Scottish Psalter, 1650) AP
129   106965
O happy is the man who bears
(Bruce) V233 X How happy
are the young who hear
                              106966
O happy land, whose sons in
youth (U.P. Board of Publ,
1909) T285; AJ393; AM289;
AP126   106967
O happy rest, sweet happy rest
(Crosby) R Will you come
                              106968
O happy time of reaping (---)
AI349; AR591; AS430   106969
O hark! a glorious sound is
heard (Robinson) BC134
                              106970
O haupt voll Blut und Wunden
(Based on St. Bernard of
Clairvaux) BT172; BW539
                              106971
O have you heard the wondrous
story? (German) M611
                              106972
O have you not heard of that
beautiful stream (Hull. The
casket, 1865) AW232a
                              106973
O he who trusts in God's protec-
tion (Neumark) BE216
                              106974
O he who walked with fishermen
(Iris) AC461   106975
O, he whom Jesus loved has
truly spoken (Whittier) BE
217 X O brother man, fold to
thy heart   106976
O Head so full of bruises (St
Bernard of Clairvaux) BA
216 X O Sacred Head. . .
                              106977
O hear my cry, be gracious now
to me (Crosby) AU289
                              106978
O hear my earnest prayer, dear
Lord (Van Hoose) R Increase
my faith   106979
O hear my prayer, Lord (Scottish
Psalter, 1650) AP125 106980

O hear them marching, marching,
the legions of good will (Ham)
Z564   106981

O, hearken when we cry (Faber)
R Now are the days of humblest
prayer   106982

O Heart of God! Our home lies
deep in thee (Stanfield) AW237;
BO22   106983

O Heart of Jesus, Heart of God
(Fullerton) BQ58   106984

O Heart of Jesus, purest Heart
(Latin, 18th c) BP69; BQ64
106985

O heart of Mary, pure and fair
(---) BN154; BO94   106986

O heavenly Beauty, lovelier far
(Peers) X600   106987

O heavenly grace in holy rite
descending (Spencer) A188
106988

O heavenly Jerusalem, of everlasting halls (Latin, 18th c)
A592; B509; D401; E251; F569
106989

O heavens, send your rain upon
us (Bible. Isaiah, 45) BN2
106990

O Heil'ger Geist, kehr bei uns
ein (Schirmer) BT235; BW546
106991

O heilige Dreifaltigkeit, O hochgelobte Einigkeit (Behm) BT
541   106992

O heiliger Geist, O heiliger Gott
(Niedling) BW547   106993

O help us Lord, each hour of
need (Milman) B33; D337; E83;
F320; K404; W455; X114; AP
464; AZ123; BA712   106994

O here, if ever, God of love
(Taylor) BX481   106995

O Herr dich will ich loben (Ausbund) BU12   106996

O herre Gott, dein göttlich Wort
(German. 1527) BT266 106997

O Herr Gott, gross ist die
Roth (Ausbund) BU98   106998

O Herr! nicht stolz ist mein
Herz doch (Ausbund. Psalm
130) BU130   106999

O Herr thu auf die Lefzen mein
(Ausbund Suppl.) BU6 107000

O Herr! um dein Gnad ruff ich
dich an (Ausbund) BU139
107001

O Herre Gott! hilf mir in deinem
Namen (Ausbund. Psalm 54)
BU83   107002

O Herre Gott in deinem Thron
(M. Schneider) BU87
107003

O Herre Gott, in meiner Roth.
(Ausbund) BU49   107004

O Herre Gott mein Roth thu ich
dir klagen (Ausbund) BU115
107005

O Herre Gott vom Himmelreich
(S. Hans & G. v. Ingersheim)
BU59   107006

O hollow, soulless pomp, which
decks (Howard) BR364
107007

O holy, blessed Trinity, Divine
essential Unity (Behm) O545
X O holy, blessed Trinity,
Divine, eternal Unity 107008

O holy, blessed Trinity, Divine,
eternal Unity (Behm) M143;
O545; Q541; AA20   107009

O holy city, seen of John
(Bowie) A494; G474; J332;
R508; S409; U354; Y63; AB
331; AD429; AF420; AG269;
AK397; AL382; AP577; BF
509; BZ   107010

O holy day! O happy day! (Hoffman) R How calm and how
bright   107011

O Holy Father, Holy Son (Kyle)
Lp.743; AZ310   107012

O holy Father, who in tender
love (Bickersteth) AL222
107013

O Holy Ghost, eternal God
(Helder) AA251   107014

O Holy Ghost, on this great
day inspire (Rawlett) AZ
445; BA256   107015

O Holy Ghost, thou Fount of
light (Adam of St Victor)
AZ635   107016

O Holy Ghost, thou gift divine
(Ringwaldt) O380; P225
107017

O Holy Ghost, thou God of peace

BQ328   107055
O, how is the time so urgent
    (Mack) AR428   107056
O how love I thy law (U. P.
    Psalter, 1912) AM450 X Most
    perfect is the law of God
                                         107057
O how lovely, O how sweet
    (Wengel) Z263   107058
O, how lovely was the morning
    (Manwaring) BC136   107059
O how marvelous, O how wonder-
    ful (Gabriel) R I stand amazed
                                         107060
O how praying rests the weary
    (Kidder) R Ere you left your
    room   107061
"O how shall I keep Christmas?"
    (Westall) BR550   107062
O how shall I receive thee (Ger-
    hardt) J11; K6; L258; M324;
    N4; O157; P112; AK100; AZ
    800; BA149; BR137   107063
O how the thought of God attracts
    (Faber) G374; I363   107064
O how wondrous the grace of our
    God (Kennedy) AR430 X We
    are saved by the grace of our
    God   107065
O Hunter blessed, of hearts dis-
    tressed (Herman) BP94
                                         107066
O I long to see the beauty
    (Latta) AS451   107067
O, I long, yes, I long there to
    dwell (Newell) R A city awaits
                                         107068
O, I love to talk with Jesus (---)
    AX366; AY198   107069
O, I love to tell the merits of
    my Saviour (Jones) R There
    is nothing in the world 107070
"O, I will give you glory,"
    said God (Grimes) AC482
                                         107071
O, I can hear you, God (Sarett)
    AC442   107072
"O, I have seen a king's new
    baby" (Colletet) BG108
                                         107073
O ice and snow, O frost and
    cold (---) AC466   107074
O if the Lamb had not been slain

(Cennick) AZ745   107075
O it is hard to work for God
    (Faber) I442; AZ202   107076
O, it is wonderful that he should
    care (Gabriel) R I stand all
    amazed at the love   107077
O it must be the breaking of the
    day (Sederquist) R 'Tis al-
    most time for the Lord to
    come   107078
O Jehovah, hear my words (U.
    P. Board of Publ. 1909) T6;
    AI229; AJ9; AM47   107079
O Jerusalem, look toward the
    East (Latin) E618   107080
O Jesulein Süss, O Jesulein mild
    (Thilo) BG109b   107081

NOTE: "O Jesu" and "O Jesus"
    are interfiled.   107082

O Jesu, blessèd Lord, to thee
    (Kingo) F419; J284; O155;
    P106; Q309   107083
O Jesus, blest is he (Russell)
    O482   107084
O Jesus, blest Redeemer
    (McAfee) R There is a place
    of quiet rest   107085
O Jesus, bruised and wounded
    more (Alexander) AA428
                               107086
O Jesus Christ, all praise to
    thee (Luther) O184   107087
O Jesus Christ, alone to thee
    (---) BI2D   107088
O Jesus Christ, Dein Kripplein ist
    (Gerhardt) BT81   107089
O Jesu Christ, from thee began
    (Latin, 9th c) E69   107090
O Jesus Christ, grow thou in
    me (Lavater) AL331; AO301;
    BV636; BY601   107091
O Jesus Christ, if aught there
    be (Caswall) AZ1456 107092
O Jesu Christ, mein schönstes
    Licht (Gerhardt) BT349; BW
    170   107093
O Jesu Christ, mein's Lebens
    Licht (Behm) BT148 107094
O Jesus Christ, most holy
    (Zinzendorf, N. L.) AZ794
                               107095

O Jesus Christ, our Lord most dear (Laufenburg) A185; E338; F425; K175; R452; S351; W304; AF278; AM355   107096

O Jesus Christ, our only Lord (Sigstedt) BI15-D   107097

O Jesus Christ, Redeemer, Lord (Watts) BI37   107098

O Jesus Christ, remember, When thou shalt come (Caswall) BQ 55   107099

O Jesus Christ, the Holy One (Saxby) AP364   107100

O Jesus Christ, thou Bread of Life (Rist) N249   107101

O Jesus Christ, thy manger is (Gerhardt) Q81   107102

O Jesu Christe, wahres Licht (Heermann) AY3d; BT512   107013

O Jesus crowned with all renown (Benson) A101; B181   107104

O Jesus, crucified for man (How) A333; B52; D5; I326; K69; O475; U255; AG120; BF328   107105

O Jesus, crucified for me, And all whose sins (Sanger) AR 509   107106

O Jesu, der du felig macht (L. Ringmacher) BU74 107107

O Jesu, einig wahres Haupt (Mentzer) BT477   107108

O Jesus, ever present (Tuttiett) W176; BR394   107109

O Jesus, for thy matchless love (Zinzendorf, N. L.) AZ206   107110

O Jesus, full of pardoning grace (Wesley) W409   107111

O Jesu, gid du vilde (Kingo) BT 655   107112

O Jesus, God and Man (Baker) AO17; AZ1369   107113

O Jesus, I have promised (Bode) A570; B379; D615; E577; F331; G226; H316; I350; J515; M527; N259; O372; P108; R307; S268; T376; U253; W508; X255; Y 369; Z308; AB234; AC196; AD 244; AE263; AF218; AG165; AH428; AK271; AL354; AM552; AO389; AP554; AR346; AS455; AT386; AU187; AV193; AW 212; AZ841; BA465; BB288; BF443; BR384; BV365; BY 298; BZ   107114

O Jesus is a Rock (Charlesworth) R The Lord's our Rock   107115

O Jesus, Joy of loving hearts (St Bernard of Clairvaux) N241 X Jesus, thou Joy of loving hearts   107116

O Jesu, King most wonderful (St Bernard of Clairvaux??) E419b; F189b; J468; K352; L115; O292; Q361; W423; X547b; AA90; AL299; AO216; AP450; AZ196; BA109; BR 416; BV542; BY188   107117

O Jesus, King of glory (Behm) M372; P149; Q130; AA179   107118

O Jesus, Lamb of God, thou art (Helder) Q328; AA417   107119

O Jesus, Lamb of God, who art (Helder) AA417 X O Jesus, Lamb of God, thou art   107120

O Jesu! life-spring of the soul (St Rabanus Maurus??) BL 40   107121

O Jesus, Lord and Saviour, I give myself to thee (Chrisholm) R Living for Jesus   107122

O Jesus, Lord and Saviour, the soul's Eternal King (Bayley) BR31   107123

O Jesus! Lord most merciful (Hamilton) B131; D360   107124

O Jesus, Lord, most mighty King (St Bernard of Clairvaux) BO8   107125

O Jesus, Lord of heavenly grace (St Ambrose) K359; O444; AZ932; BV33; BY680 107126

O Jesus, Lord, to thee I cry (Hamilton) P254; AU86   107127

O Jesus, Master, when today (Newhall) G470; U278; Y212; Z517; AB282; AS1913; AT466;

BF493   107128

O Jesus my Lord, For ever
adored (N. L. von Zinzendorf)
AZ20; BA533   107129

O Jesus, my Redeemer (Belden)
BB613   107130

O Jesus, once a Nazareth boy
(---) Y135; Z505; AC174; AE
450; AH275; AR379; AS410;
BF624   107131

O Jesus, our dear Master (Matters) BE221   107132

O Jesus, our Salvation (Hamilton)
N191; O477   107133

O Jesus, Prince of life and truth
(---) Z505 X O Jesus, once a
Nazareth boy   107134

O Jesus, Saviour dear, how shall
thy name be praised (Heermann)
N250   107135

O Jesu, Saviour of the lost
(Bickersteth) D85; L406; V242;
BA441; BR359   107136

O Jesus, Saviour, Source of good
(---) BR473   107137

O Jesus, shall it ever be (Grigg)
N143 X Jesus, and shall it
ever be   107138

O Jesu so meek, O Jesu so kind
(Thilo) J501; AF135   107139

O Jesu, söde Jesu, dig (Kingo)
BT309   107140

O Jesus, Source of calm repose
(Freylinghausen) N486; O467
                               107141

O Jesus, strong and pure and
true (How) W675   107142

O Jesu sweet, O Jesu mild
(Thilo) AF135 X O Jesu so
meek   107143

O Jesus, thou art standing (How)
A407; B132; D357; E578; F355;
G197; H281; I282; J386; K322;
L360; M77; N401; R266; S228;
T382; U170; V300; W397; Y375;
Z279; AB157; AC148; AD205;
AE169; AF329; AG139; AH325;
AK211; AL469; AM414; AO257;
AP395; AR252; AT346; AU242;
AV179; AW144; AZ837; BA406;
BB231; BF342; BR297; BV476;
BY418; BZ   107144

O Jesu, thou the beauty art (St

Bernard of Clairvaux??)
E419c; X547c; BQ15 107145

O Jesu, thou the Virgin's
crown (St Ambrose??) F521
                               107146

O Jesus, thou wast tempted
(Park) BF301   107147

O Jesus, thy boundless love
(Gerhardt) AR181 X Jesus,
thy boundless love   107148

O Jesus Victim-Priest (Udulutsch) BM43   107149

O Jesu, we adore thee, Upon
the cross (Russell) D364;
R200; S156; V153; Z234;
AI422; AK162; AM193; AZ
835; BA500   107150

O Jesus, we adore thee, Who
in thy love (Udulutsch) BM
9   107151

O Jesus, were we through thy
grace (Zinzendorf, N. L.)
AZ1099   107152

O Jesus, when I think of thee
(Bethune) Z218; AO146; AV
143   107153

O Jesus, youth of Nazareth
(Blanchard) Z217; AB170;
AC103; AE440; AR409; BF
299   107154

O, Joseph being an old man
truly (English trad carol)
BG115   107155

O joy, because the circling
year (St Hilary of Poictiers)
F151   107156

O joy of God, that comest in
the morning (Boutflower) F
404   107157

O joyful hope, in weary hearts
awaking (Bayly) BY84
                               107158

O joyful message, sent from
heaven (Hoppe) M338
                               107159

O joyful sound of gospel grace!
(Wesley) I371   107160

O joyous Easter morning, that
saw the Lord of love arisen
(---) AC125; AR187 107161

O kind Creator, bow thine ear.
(St Gregory the Great??)
E66   107162

O let us praise the Christmas
  tree (German) M620   107199
O life that makest all things new
  (Longfellow) X602; AC219; AL
  319; AN416; AQ54; AR530; AS
  391; BD41; BE218; BX375
                              107200
O life that maketh all things new
  (Longfellow) BX375 X O life
  that makest all things new
                              107201
O Light, from age to age the
  same (Hosmer) J247; X192;
  AN464; AQ255; BF594; BX503
                              107202
O Light, O Trinity most blest!
  (St Ambrose) K462; L24
                              107203
O Light of God's most wondrous
  love (Boye) M459; O383
                              107204
O Light of life, O Saviour dear
  (Palgrave) S46   107205
O Light of Light, by love inclined
  (Latin, 10th c) E234   107206
O Light of Light, within us dwell
  (Gladden) AQ122 X Behold a
  Sower!   107207
O Light that knew no dawn (St
  Gregory Nazianzen) W458; AF
  407; AM23   107208
O Light, whose beams illumine
  all (Plumptre) B40; D424; K
  373; R145; S180; W172; AK244;
  AR293; AZ661; BI40   107209
O listen to our wondrous story
  (Gray) AU385   107210
O little Chid of Bethlehem (Mc-
  Kelway) U65   107211
O little flock, fear not the foe
  (Altenburg) Q263   107212
O little one sweet, O little one
  mild (Thilo) BG109   107213
O little town, O little town
  (Scollard) Y325   107214
O little town of Bethlehem (Brooks)
  A21; B78; D58; E15; F65; G
  100; H145; I121; J27; K31; L
  220; M605; N36; O196; P133;
  Q647; R171; S121; T334; U55;
  V741; W48; X79; Y330; Z184;
  AB107; AC82; AD121; AE85;
  AF134; AG64; AH250; AI66;

AK108; AL51; AM152; AN
165; AO125; AP169; AQ286;
AR126; AS103; AT75; AU
144; AV82; AW84; AX97; BA
157; BB104; BC165; BD226;
BE222; BF292; BG138; BK
150; BR557; BV122; BX198;
BY105; BZ   107215
O living Bread from heaven
  (Rist) J285; K193; N236;
  O148; P105; Q316; AA435
                              107216
O living Christ, chief Corner-
  stone (Cunniggim) G547; BZ
                              107217
O Lord, again in thy blest name
  we meet (Whitmore) BR101
  X Father, again in Jesus'
  name we meet   107218
O Lord all glorious, Life of
  life (Harmony in praise,
  1890) Y25; AB68; AC31;
  BR76   107219
O Lord, almighty God, thy
  works (The Whole Book of
  Psalmes) AF473   107220
O Lord almighty, thou whose
  hands (Newbolt) X323; Y238
                              107221
O Lord! and is thy table spread
  (Doddridge) BR471 X My
  God, thy table now is spread
                              107222
O Lord, and Master of us all
  (Whittier) A501; B496; E
  456; W513; X603; AF223;
  AL348; AP184; AR390; BA
  82, 634; BD70; BF332; BV
  272; BX217; BY125   107223
O Lord, be near me when I
  pray (---) BH19   107224
O Lord, be thou my helper true
  (U.P. Psalter, 1912) T16;
  AJ21; AM45   107225
O Lord, be with us when we
  sail (Dayman) D305; K502;
  M266; N587; V643; W625;
  AP710; BA894; BR506; BY
  669   107226
O Lord, by thee delivered (U.
  P. Psalter, 1912) R127; T
  50; AJ77; AM526   107227
O Lord, devoutly I love thee

(Schalling) N465   107228
O Lord divine, we come to pray
(Toews) AX554   107229
O Lord, encouraged by thy grace
(---) BV343   107230
O Lord, give ear when with my
voice (U.P. Psalter, 1912)
T47; AJ74   107231
O Lord, give heed unto our plea
(Swedberg) N348   107232
O Lord, hear thou my calling
(Marot) O218   107233
O Lord, how are my foes in-
creased! (Sternhold) T3; AJ5;
AM469; AP3   107234
O Lord, how boundless is thy
love! (Watts) BR250 X My
God, how endless is thy love
                                    107235
O Lord, how full of sweet content
(Guyon) L467 X My Lord, how
full of sweet   107236
O Lord, how happy should we be
(Anstice) E457; I519; V361; W
543; X604; AL419; AP515; AW
255; BR335; BV510; BY482
                                    107237
O Lord, how joyful 'tis to see
(Coffin) F244; O412   107238
O Lord, how manifold the works
(U.P. Psalter, 1912) T199;
AJ288   107239
O Lord, how shall I meet thee
(Gerhart) Q58; AA136; AM119
                                    107240
O Lord, I am not worthy (---)
AH133; BN100; BO49; BP66;
BQ129   107241
O Lord, I love thee from my
heart (Schalling) AA366 X Lord,
thee I love with all my heart
                                    107242
O Lord, I sing thy praises
(Grant) W570   107243
O Lord, I sing with lips and
heart (Gerhardt) Q569 X O
Lord, I sing with voice and
heart   107244
O Lord, I sing with mouth and
heart (Gerhardt) AA292 X O
Lord, I sing with voice and
heart   107245
O Lord, I sing with voice and

heart (Gerhardt) M495; Q569;
AA292   107246
O Lord, I unto thee do cry
(Scottish Psalter, 1650) AP
124   107247
O Lord, I would delight in thee
(Ryland) AM543; BE224
                                    107248
O Lord, in me fulfill Whatever
is thy will (Claggett) AZ552
                                    107249
O Lord, in me there lieth
nought (Sidney & Pembroke)
X605   107250
O Lord, in this great mystery
(Gannon) BM5   107251
O Lord, it is a blessed thing
(How) BX159   107252
O Lord Jesus, how long (Turner)
R It may be at morn   107253
O Lord Jesus, I adore thee
(Mauburn) F388   107254
O Lord, look down from heaven,
behold (Luther) Q260 X Look
down, O Lord, from heave be-
hold   107255
O Lord, make haste to hear my
cry (U.P. Psalter, 1912) R
392; T278; AJ386   107256
O Lord, may church and home
combine (Buck) BZ   107257
O Lord most high, with all my
heart (U.P. Psalter, 1912)
R388; T13; AJ17; AM44
                                    107258
O Lord, my best desire fulfil
(Cowper) L505; AA389
                                    107259
O Lord, my earnest cry, Thy
listening ear (U.P. Psalter,
1912) T243; AJ339   107260
O Lord, my God, for thy name's
sake (U.P. Psalter, 1912) AJ
301   107261
O Lord, my God, I cry to thee
(Selnecker) O585; Q600; AA
543   107262
O Lord, my God, most earnestly
(U.P. Psalter, 1912) R327;
T114; AJ163   107263
O Lord, my God, my joyful heart
(U.P. Psalter, 1912) AJ234
                                    107264

O Lord, my God, thy holy law
(Hoppe) M57   107265

O Lord, my God, to thee I pray
(Hamburg Temple hymnal)
BH29   107266

O Lord my God! When I in awesome wonder (Boberg) BZ
                                   107267

O Lord, my inmost heart and
thought (U. P. Psalter, 1912)
R129; AI34; AJ384   107268

O Lord, now let thy servant
(Ryden) M18; N590   107269

O Lord! of goodness so amazing
(Spitta) AZ698   107270

O Lord of health and life, What
tongue can tell (Phillimore)
O235; AO150   107271

O Lord of heaven and earth and
sea (Wordsworth) A305; B426;
D477; E521; F480; G541; I692;
J448; K385; L76; N573; O452;
Q443; S398; T319; U481; W19;
AA357; AB388; AC56; AD261;
AK257; AL26; AO105; AP139;
AR597; AS426; AZ7; BA567;
BD131; BF649; BH66; BR487;
BV599; BX331; BY68; BZ
                                   107272

O Lord of hosts, all heaven possessing (Plumptre) E458;
X606   107273

O Lord of hosts! Almighty King
(Holmes) B437; D197; AH193;
AO603   107274

O Lord of Hosts, how lovely the
place where thou dost dwell
(Asso. Reformed Presbyterian
Psalter, 1931) AM305   107275

O Lord of Hosts, how lovely thy
tabernacles are (U. P. Psalter,
1912) T153; AJ227   107276

O Lord of Hosts, in mercy (U.
P. Psalter, 1912) AJ228
                                   107277

O Lord of Hosts, the fight is long
(Armitage) AP591   107278

O Lord of Hosts, to thee I cry
(U. P. Psalter, 1912) T84;
AJ226   107279

O Lord of Hosts, we now invoke
(Dalrymple) BC271   107280

O Lord of Hosts, who didst up-

raise (Benson) E539; AL412
                                   107281

O Lord of Hosts, whose glory
fills (Neale) D291; H412;
I658; L279; N275; Q633; AA
450; AF475; BA323   107282

O Lord of life, and love, and
power (Armitage) U276; W
355; AL386; BY483   107283

O Lord of Life, the Truth, the
Way (---) BI35; BR77 107284

O Lord of life, thy Kingdom is
at hand (Ham) S370; Z491;
AD341; AN332; BB198; BD
154; BF571; BX385   107285

O Lord of life, thy quickening
voice (MacDonald) W264; Z132;
AB3; AC13; AL537; BX140;
BY681   107286

O Lord of life, to thee we lift
(Gladden) R256; AD192; AE157;
AR239; BE226   107287

O Lord of life where'er they be
(Hosmer) J600; W331; Z575;
AD459; AF469; AL459; AN
195; AW316; BF664; BX207;
BY613   107288

O Lord of life, whose power
sustains (Darbyshire) F585;
BY650   107289

O Lord of love, compassionate
(---) Y398   107290

O Lord of love! Shall we not
understand (Burr) Y82
                                   107291

O Lord of love, thou light divine
(---) AT520   107292

O Lord of stars and sunlight
(Holmes) AQ9   107293

O Lord our banner, God of
might (Wordsworth) AP651
                                   107294

O Lord, our Father, shall we be
confounded (Heermann) Q269
                                   107295

O Lord, our Father, thanks to
thee (Schneegass) Q124; AA
170   107296

O Lord, our fathers oft have
told (Tate & Brady) G498;
I700; AS385; BZ   107297

O Lord, our God, accept, we
pray (Schuette) M516 107298

O Lord, our God, Almighty King (Stratton) I664 107299

O Lord our God, arise (Wardlaw) K225; L277; N374; P395; W 376; AM375; AP379; BV331; BY385 107300

O Lord our God, in reverence lowly (Tersteegen) AZ1104 107301

O Lord, our God, in time to be (Whittier) AK413 107302

O Lord, our God, thy mighty hand (Van Dyke) S415; Y281; AB340; AC272; AH479; AO588; BA876; BD166; BF550 107303

O Lord, our God, to thee (Smith) BI11 X My country 'tis of thee 107304

O Lord, our help in ages past (Watts) BI36 X O God, our help 107305

O Lord our King how bright thy fame (Kennedy) BH72 107306

O Lord, our little ones to thee (Whiting) N228; O144; P97 107307

O Lord, our Lord, in all the earth (U.P. Psalter, 1912) R95; AJ14; BZ 107308

O Lord, our strength in weakness (Wordsworth) D278; N258 107309

O Lord, reprieve the lonely state (Currie) BN187 107310

O Lord, stretch forth Thy mighty hand (How) R To Thee our God we fly 107311

O Lord, the Holy Innocents (Alexander) B87; D575 107312

O Lord, thou art my God and King And I will ever bless thy name (U.P. Psalter, 1912) R5; T286 107313

O Lord, thou art my God and King, Thee will I magnify and praise (Craig) AL688; AP127; AW600 107314

O Lord, thou art the way (---) BR459 107315

O Lord, thou hast ascended (U. P. Psalter, 1912) T125; AJ183 107316

O Lord, thou hast me searched and known (Scottish Psalter, 1650) AP123 107317

O Lord, thou Judge of all the earth (U.P. Psalter, 1912) T174; AJ253; AM46 107318

O Lord, thou living Bread from heaven (---) M50 107319

O Lord, thy all discerning eyes (Adams) BH38 107320

O Lord, thy benediction give (Armstrong) AC218 X O Thou, who makest souls to shine 107321

O Lord, thy heavenly grace impart (Smucker) AY104 107322

O Lord, thy judgments give the King (Scottish Psalter, 1650) AP61 107323

O Lord, thy love through heavenly spheres descending (Plummer) BI78 107324

O Lord, thy people gathered here (Roberts) J258; K251; AN441 107325

O Lord, thy perfect righteousness (U.P. Psalter, 1912) T242; AJ338 107326

O Lord, thy work revive (Brown) H382; AZ1322; BA 907 107327

O Lord, to thee I cry (U.P. Psalter, 1912) T48; AJ75; AP26; AX540; AY77 107328

O Lord, to thee I cry (Link) AX540 X O Lord, to thee I cry (U.P. Psalter) 107329

O Lord! to thee who dwellest above (Jacobs) BH196 107330

O Lord, to us assembled here (---) AR6; AS57 107331

O Lord, to us thy mercy show (U.P. Psalter, 1912) T157; AJ232 107332

O Lord, to whom the spirits live (Littledale) A226; E359; F468 107333

O Lord, turn not away thy face (Marckant) E84; F93; O470; S503; W401; X116; AF580; AK213; BA421; BJ33 107334

O Lord, turn not thy face away
(Marckant) O470 X O Lord,
turn not away thy face 107335

O Lord, turn not thy face from
me (Marckant) F93 X O Lord,
turn not away thy face 107336

O Lord, we praise thee, bless
thee, and adore thee (Luther)
Q313 X Praise we the Lord
and bless his name forever
107337

O Lord, we welcome thee (Ziegler)
Q93   107338

O Lord what is man that Thou
takest knowledge (Bible. Psalm
8) BH335   107339

O Lord when condemnation and
guilt oppress my soul (Gosen-
ius) O281   107340

O Lord, when we the path retrace
(Deck) L247   107341

O Lord, where shall I find thee?
(Judah ben Samuel Halevi) BH
21   107342

O Lord, where'er thy people meet
(Cowper) BE227 X Jesus,
where'er thy people meet
107343

O Lord, while we confess the
worth (Peters) AE325; AX168;
AY269   107344

O Lord, who by thy presence hast
made light (Spitta) AZ461
107345

O Lord, who hast my place assigned (Loy) M254   107346

O Lord, who hast this table
spread (Collier) AO439
107347

O Lord, who in thy love divine
(Wordsworth) Q493 Thou who
the night in prayer didst spend
107348

O Lord, who numberest all our
days (Swertner) AZ365; BA848
107349

O Lord, whose bounteous hand
again (---) Q567; AA291
107350

O Lord, with thankful hearts we
meet (---) BA885   107351

O Lord, within my soul (Hoffman)
AX333; AY190   107352

O Love divine, all else transcending (Tersteegen) M225;
AW517a   107353

O Love divine and golden (Monsell) G430; O533; P350; R
454; S485; AO558; AR540;
AS420; AY443; AZ827; BA
844   107354

O Love, divine and tender
(Monsell) AZ827 X O Love,
divine and golden   107355

O Love divine, how sweet thou
art (Wesley) F195; G218;
H344; I368; O459; W428; AL
301; AP452; AZ637; BB148;
BV531; BY772; BZ   107356

O Love divine, of all that is
(Chadwick) AN51; BX294
107357

O Love divine, that dwells
serene (McKenzie) BE228
107358

O Love divine that stooped to
share (Holmes) B400; D627;
G273: H358; I457; R116; T
402; U212; V641; Z353; AD
236; AE212; AH214; AL124;
AN188; AO369; AP232; AR
307; AS125; AW172; AY419;
BB144; BF247; BX243; BZ
107359

O Love divine, what hast thou
done! (Wesley) G137; H174;
I153; AZ662; BB151; BZ
107360

O Love Divine, whose constant
beam (Whittier) AN56; BE
229; BX73   107361

O Love, how deep, how broad,
how high (St Thomas à Kem-
pis) A344; E459; F187; K63;
S139; AF150; AI419; AM121;
AO144; BL90; BP103; BR169;
BY126   107362

O Love! O Life! Our faith and
sight (Whittier) I479; AB166;
AN206; AQ121; BD65; BE
230; BX218   107363

O, love of God, how rich and
pure (Lehman) R The love
of God   107364

O Love of God, how strong and
true (Bonar) I83; X607; AF

99; AI36; AM73; AN84; BB67; BX85; BY69   107365

O Love of God most full (Clute) R118; S84; AK275; AT52; BX 258   107366

O Love, our Mother, ever near (Matters) BE232   107367

O love that casts our fear (Bonar) A457; B235; D431; U23; AP 468; BV540   107368

O Love that lights the eastern sky (Benson) S433   107369

O Love that nothing can efface (Pados) BL46   107370

O Love that will not let me go (Matheson) AY468 X O Love that wilt not let me   107371

O Love that wilt not let me go (Matheson) A458; B236; F359; G318; I481; J402; K348; M208; N521; P288; R400; S307; T403; U26; V367; W424; Y37; Z388; AB181; AC154; AD249; AE262; AF399; AG181; AH221; AK278; AL311; AM594; AN243; AO289; AP465; AR271; AS266; AT290; AU231; AV232; AW175; AY468; BA492; BB145; BD115; BF245; BK90; BR422; BX286; BY20; BZ   107372

O Love, who formest me to wear (Scheffler) E460; F203; K364; O68; Q397; W496; X608; AA348; BJ12   107373

O Love, who madest me to wear (Scheffler) Q397 X O Love who formest me to wear   107374

O Love whose perfect path is known (Key) BE233   107375

O Loving Father, hear thou thy children (West) AR385   107376

O loving Father, to thy care (Alington) F427   107377

O loving Lord, who art for ever seeking (Jenkins) BY602   107378

O Lue fra Guds Kjärlighed (Boye) BT230   107379

O lux beata Trinitas (St Ambrose) BJ86b   107380

O make a joyful noise, ye lands (U.P. Psalter, 1912) AJ270   107381

O, make thy blest abode with me (Schell) R Humility, thou secret vale   107382

O Maker of the mighty deep (Van Dyke) U40; AB205   107383

O Maker of the sea and sky (Burton) B418; Y43; AB381; AC37; AH217   107384

O Maker of the stars of night (Latin, 9th c) BJ47 107385

O Maker of the world, give ear (Latin) F84   107386

O man, do never faint nor fear (English trad carol) R St Stephen was a holy man   107387

O man of God, arise (Fenner) L342   107388

O martyrs young and fresh as flowers (Prudentius) F538   107389

O Mary, dearest Mother (Russell) BO118   107390

O Mary, don't you weep (Negro spiritual) AH606   107391

O Mary, Mother full of grace (Fortunatus??) BN148   107392

O Mary! We crown thee with blossoms (---) R Bring flowers of the fairest   107393

O Master, it is good to be (Stanley) X235 X Lord, it is good for us to be   107394

O Master, let me walk with thee (Gladden) A572; B493; G259; H158; I411; J537; M223; P 324; R304; S364; T412; U271; W339; Y214; Z306; AB258; AC197; AD312; AE280; AF 418; AG245; AH371; AI185; AK205; AL388; AN208; AO 490; AP582; AR367; AS342; AT426; AU202; AV274; AW 223; AY467; AZ385; BA556; BB346; BD68; BE234; BF 375; BK99; BX225; BY518; BZ   107395

O Master, may my days be spent only for thee (Morse)

(Munger) S395   107431

O my Father, thou that dwellest (Snow) BC138   107432

O my Immanuel, my wounded spirit heal (Zinzendorf, N. L.) AZ723   107433

O, my Saviour crucified (Batty) AU448   107434

O my Saviour, I adore thee (French) M196   107435

O my Saviour lifted (How) F360; S161; AL89; AP204; BV477; BY453   107436

O my soul, bless God, the Father (U. P. Book of Psalms, 1871) G80; AF100; AK83; AT51; BZ   107437

O my soul, bless thou Jehovah (U. P. Psalter, 1912) T194; AI352; AJ280; AX2*   107438
*slightly variant text

O my soul, on wings ascending (Wallin) J462   107439

O my soul, what means this sadness (Fawcett) AZ1384 107440

O my soul, why art thou grieving (U. P. Psalter, 1912) R Judge me, God of my salvation   107441

O mystery of love divine (Gill) AA330; AM436   107442

O Name, all other name's above (Hosmer) AN242; BX296   107443

O, Native Land, how fair you seem (Cherryman) Y278; AC281   107444

O North with all thy vales of green (Bryant) A541; B107; E550; AO529; BY386   107445

O, now I see the crimson wave (Palmer) H241; AX308; BB 598   107446

O now is the Time to remember our Creator (Cousin) AP757   107447

O one with God the Father (How) B97; D68; J56; K43; L203; O259; S137; AB73; AZ 805; BA663; BF424; BR367   107448

O Paradise, O Paradise, who doth not crave for rest?

(Faber) A588; B167; D394; H516; I622; J589; L581; N 663; O616; T437; V705; AA 561; AB402; AO545; AP631; AV297; AZ1504; BA753; BF 659; BO204; BQ120; BR426   107449

O Paradise; O Paradise! Who would not win thy rest (Faber) AB402 X O Paradise, O Paradise, who doth not crave for rest? 107450

O, pardon me, Jesus, thy mercy I implore (Chadwick) R Jesus, my God, behold at length   107451

O Paschal feast, what joy is thine (Latin) J102   107452

O Pater sancte, mitis atque pie (Latin, 10th c) BT240   107453

O peace of all the faithful (St Bernard of Cluny) BR 436 X The world is very evil   107454

O peace of the world, O hope in each breast (Tomlinson) BE236   107455

O people blest, whose sons in youth (U. P. Bd. of Publ., 1909) AM289 X O happy land, whose sons in youth 107456

O perfect God, thy love (Greenway) F121; BV174   107457

O perfect life of love (Baker) F122; I155; J89; K103; N118; Q170; W102; AP208; AZ 1366; BA210; BV175 107458

O perfect love, all human thought transcending (Gurney) A214; B382; D238; E346; F 463; G431; I668; J300; K415; N528; O538; P354; Q623; R 453; S484; U484; V636; W 327; X283; AA444; AD417; AE386; AF465; AG296; AK 356; AL238; AM625; AN453; AO561; AP703; AR539; AS 419; AT501; AW312; BA843; BB416; BF613; BI77; BL65; BV393; BX486; BY624; BZ   107459

O pour thy Spirit from on high

(Montgomery) M96 X Lord
pur thy Spirit from on high
107460

O power of love, all else transcending (Tersteegen) AW517
X O love divine, all else transcending   107461

O praise and bless the Lord, my
soul (U.P. Psalter, 1912)
T190, 453; AJ277   107462

O praise Him, Alleluia (St Francis of Assisi) R All creatures
of our God and King   107463

O praise Jehovah! Who reigneth
on earth and in heaven (Neander) AZ530; BA864   107464

O praise our God today, His constant mercy (Baker) AZ1338;
BA569   107465

O praise our great and gracious
Lord (Auber) E461; BE281
107466

O praise the Father, praise the
Son (---) AP810   107467

O praise the Lord, all you nations
(Ladies of the Grail) BSp.19
107468

O praise the Lord, for He is
good, His mercies still endure
(U.P. Psalter, 1912) AJ297;
AM84   107469

O praise the Lord, for He is
good; Let all in heaven above
(U.P. Psalter, 1912) AJ317
107470

O praise the Lord, His deeds
make known (U.P. Psalter,
1912 T200; AJ239   107471

O praise the Lord! His name extol (Olearius) M482   107472

O praise the Lord and sing a
new song (U.P. Psalter, 1912)
AJ407; AM288   107473

O praise ye the Lord! Praise him
in the height (Baker) F376; X
351; BV23   107474

O praise ye the Lord prepare
your glad voice (Tate & Brady)
D471; BI30; BR65   107475

O praise ye the name of Jehovah
(U.P. Psalter, 1912) T268;
AJ373   107476

O precious is the flow (Lowry) R

What can wash away my
stain?   107477

O precious Saviour, heal and
bless (Hoppe) N393 107478

O precious sign and seal of
heavenly union (Plummer)
BI76   107479

O precious thought! Some day
the mist shall vanish (Rosenius) N518   107480

O Prince of Peace, who man
wast born (Lambeth 15th c
ms) BJ23   107481

O prophet souls of all the years
(Hosmer) AN421; AQ233;
BD180; BX457   107482

O pure reformers! not in vain
(Whittier) AN328; BX456
107483

O purest of creatures! Sweet
Mother (Faber) AH135; BN
136; BO58; BQ79   107484

O Queen of peerless majesty
Maria! (Molitor) BN159
107485

O Queen of the Holy Rosary
(Shapcote) BN157; BO91
107486

O quickly come, dread Judge
of all (Tuttiett) D42; E462;
F227; AM243; AP243; AZ
655   107487

O rain depart with blessings
(Solomon ibn Gabirol) BH
128   107488

O, rejoice, ye Christians,
loudly (Keimann) Q96; AA
152   107489

O render thanks to God above
(Tate & Brady) BH194; BI
111   107490

O rest in the Lord, wait patiently for Him (Bible, Psalm 37)
AH618; AR684; AV424; BF
696   107491

O risen Christ, who from thy
throne (Benson) U388; V
566   107492

O risen Lord! O Conquering
King (Böhmer) O336; AZ895;
BV189   107493

O Rock of ages, one Foundation
(Martin) F554; O91; AZ990;

BA264   107494
O Royal Bride, give heed (U. P. Psalter, 1912) T85; AJ125
                                            107495
O Sacrament most holy, O Sacrament divine (---) BQ330
                                            107496
O sacred day, when first was poured (Besnault) AA177
X O happy day, when first
                                            107497
O sacred head . . . (St Bernard of Clairvaux)
NOTE: All variant translations beginning "O Sacred head" are included here.
A75; B158; D102; E102; F111; G141; H176; I151; J88; K99; L243; M383; N116; O315; P 167; Q172; R194; S151; U103; V152; X128; Y350; Z231; AB 135; AD155; AE109; AF170; AG96; AH289; AI420; AK142; AL94; AM178; AN191; AO160; AP194; AQ311; AR168; AS136; AT91; AV107; AW539; AY490; AZ791; BA216-217; BB130; BF 312; BJ62; BL22; BM78; BN 38; BP26; BQ22; BR175; BV 158; BY145; BZ   107498
O Sacred Heart, O Heart of Jesus, hear! (Williams) BN 72; BO21   107499
O Sacred Heart of Christ aflame (---) BN71   107500
O Sacred Heart! Our home lies deep in thee (Stanfield) BO22
X O Heart of God! Our home lies deep   107501
O Sacred Heart with love benign (Latin) A priestly Heart, the Sacred Heart   107502
O sacrum convivium (Breviary, York, 1493) BQ235   107503
O safe to the Rock that is higher than I (Cushing) N600; P298; AE298; AH308; AL497; AM551; AP523; AR450; AS273; AT271; AU129; AV354; AX523; BB586; BY566   107504
O Saint of summer, what can we sing for you (Struther) X236
                                            107505

O Saint Patrick, we proclaim thy heavenly glory (---)
R Hibernia's Patron Saint
                                            107506
O saints of old! Not yours alone (Gill) BX459   107507
O salig den, Guds Ord har hört (Brun) BT48   107508
O salutáris hostia (St Thomas Aquinas) AH114; BM26; BN 78; BO273; BP55; BQ226
                                            107509
O sanctissima, O piissima (Sicilian trad hymn) BN126; BO112; BP86; BQ206
                                            107510
O save me by thy Name (U. P. Psalter, 1912) T102; AJ 147   107511
O Saving Victim, opening wide (St Thomas Aquinas) A209; B331; D227; E330b; F384b; J277; X277; BL53; BP56
                                            107512
O Saviour, bless us ere we go (Faber) A182; B48; D22; E275; F28; H35; J199; K435; N361; O55; V28; W302; AA 12; AF542; AL213; AO45; AP 334; AW44; AZ673; BA617; BN195; BO192; BQ138; BR 116; BY700   107513
O Saviour dear, thy manger drear (Gerhardt) M360
                                            107514
O Saviour, I have naught to plead (Crewdson) S512; W425; AL294; AP456; AS202; BY454   107515
O Saviour Jesu, not alone (Latin, 9th c) E249 107516
O Saviour, joy of loving hearts (St Bernard of Clairvaux) BR410 X Jesus, thou joy of loving hearts   107517
O Saviour of our race (Laurenti) K45; L222; N75; AZ1362; BA 52   107518
O Saviour, precious Saviour (Havergal) A349; B526; D 444; J419; K361; L110; M 209; N522; O204; P4; Q352; S200; U107; AE21; AI104;

AM118; AZ834; BA501; BB164;
BR62; BV273   107519

O Saviour, the truest, the best of
all friends (Koitsch) AZ778
                      107520

O Saviour Victim, opening wide
(St Thomas Aquinas) X277
X O Saving Victim   107521

O Saviour, where shall guilty man
(May) W111; AP202   107522

O Saviour, who for man hast
trod (Coffin) D131   107523

O Saviour, who in love didst
take (Monsell) O288   107524

O say can you see by the dawn's
early light (Key) A142; B429;
P414; Y291; Z651; AB341; AF
496; AH484; AO599; AT486; AU
457; AV303; BA939; BC131; BF
700; BH265   107525

O say, what is truth? (Jaques)
BC143   107526

O scatter seeds of loving deeds
(Pounds) AW498   107527

O scorned and outcast Lord, beneath (Coffin) AZ233   107528

O, see how Jesus trusts Himself
(Faber) AZ1454   107529

O seek that beautiful stream
(Hull. The casket) R O have
you not heard   107530

O seek the Lord today! (Brorson)
M22; P246   107531

O Seele, ich bitte dich komm
(Hull. The casket) R Ich weis
einen strom   107532

O selig Haus, wo man dich auf-
genommen (Spitta) BT626; BW
358   107533

O send thy light forth and thy
truth (Scottish Psalter, 1650)
AL650; AP38; AW587; BY277
                      107534

O set ye open unto me (Scottish
Psalter, 1650) AL677; AP106
                      107535

O, Shadow in a sultry land
(Packard) BX157   107536

O Shepherd of the faithful (Latin)
R O God-head hid devoutly
                      107537

O Shepherd of the nameless fold
(Lathbury) BZ   107538

O Shepherd of the sheep (Coles)
E190   107539

O sing a joyous carol ("M.B."
Sr.) BQ10   107540

O sing a new song to the Lord,
for wonders He hath done
(Scottish Psalter, 1650)
AL668; AP84   107541

O sing a new song to the Lord,
Sing all the earth and bless
His name (U.P. Psalter,
1912) AJ258   107542

O sing a new song to the Lord,
Sing all the earth to God
(Scottish Psalter, 1650) R37;
S68; AJ257; AL667; AP82
                      107543

O sing a song of Bethlehem
(Benson) R177; S138; W74;
AE101; AL71; AP733; AW92
                      107544

O sing all ye lands with a
jubilant voice (Vilhelm) J
423   107545

O sing the great Apostle (Latin,
17th c) BO216   107546

O, sing to me of heaven (Dana)
AX612; AY137   107547

O sing to the Lord now, his
greatness (Dearmer) X609
                      107548

O sing to the Lord, whose
bountiful hand (Littledale)
E291   107549

O sing with exultation (Arrebo)
O341; Q217   107550

O sing with loud and joyful
song (Blake) AN420; BX445
                      107551

O sing ye Hallelujah! 'Tis
good our God to praise
(U.P. Psalter, 1912) T290;
AJ402   107552

O sinner, for a little space
(Latin, 17th c) O309
                      107553

O sinner, lift the eye of faith
(Latin, 17th c) AZ741 X
O sinner, raise the eye of
faith   107554

O sinner, raise the eye of
faith (Latin, 17th c) E103;
AZ741   107555

O Spirit from on high, Thou comforter divine (Greek Pentecostarion, 8th c) BV218   107587

O Spirit of grace, thy kindness we trace (Moravian) AZ21; BA139   107588

O Spirit of Life, O Spirit of God (Niedling) K145; AR230; AW547   107589

O Spirit of the living God! In all the fullness of thy grace (Montgomery) O125 X O Spirit of the living God! In all thy plenitude of grace   107590

O Spirit of the living God! In all thy plenitude of grace (Montgomery) A256; B475; D288; H464; I188; J306; K222; O125; Q504; R242; S207; V537; W386; AA473; AD190; AF299; AL239; AM253; AO224; AP371; AW330; AZ401; BA350; BI51; BV328; BY387   107591

O Spirit of the living God, Thou Light and Fire Divine (Tweedy) G182; Z273; AK190; AR231; BZ   107592

O Spirit, source of light (Beddome) BE240 X Come, blessed Spirit, source of light   107593

O Splendor of God's glory bright (St Ambrose) A158; E52; F2; G38, 638; J206; Q550; R46; S32; X33; AB1; AC11; AD39; AF39; AH623; AK48; AM56; AR364; BF182; BJ29; BY21; BZ   107594

O, spread the message far and wide (Buzzard) R As the dawn was calmly breaking   107595

O, spread the tidings round (Bottome) AX132; AY206; BB526   107596

O stand beside us, Protect and guide us (Molitar) R O Queen of peerless majesty   107597

O star of truth, down shining (Savage) Y152; AC200; AN246; AQ115; AR294; BD111   107598

O star of wonder, star of night (Hopkins) R We three kings of orient are   107599

O still in accents sweet and strong (Longfellow) G289; H388; I395; AB378; AE323; AN449; AO459; AW294; BA551; BE242; BX490   107600

O Stranger, with no place to lay thy head (Brown) AB192   107601

O Strength and Stay upholding all creation (St Ambrose??) E271; F17; J219; K456; AN435; AP662; AZ1218; BX124   107602

O, such wonderful love (McHose) R O, the great love   107603

O sweet and tender as the dawn (Stone) BE243   107604

O sweet Infant Jesus, we hail thee (A Carmelite Nun) BQ333   107605

O sweeter than the marriage-feast (Coleridge) X613   107606

O take my hand, dear Father (Hausmann) J292; M548; P312; AR299; AW561a   107607

O teach thou us to count our days (U. P. Psalter, 1912) AJ246   107608

O tell me no more of this world's vain store (Gambold) AZ1418; BA469   107609

O, tell me, thou life and delight of my soul (Hastings) BB400   107610

O, tell what He's done for you (DeArmond) R Have you found rest?   107611

O tender and sweet was the Father's voice (Bradford) BB570   107612

O tender, loving Shepherd, We long to follow thee (Root) BE245   107613

O thank the Lord, the Lord of love (U. P. Psalter, 1912) AI377; AJ377   107614

O, that beautiful, beautiful land (Brenneman) R There's a beautiful, beautiful land   107615

O, that I as right and true might
be ("A Calendar of country
song") AC479   107616
O that I could repent (Wesley)
I264   107617
O that I had a thousand voices
(Mentzer) A302; Q30, 243; AA
62; AM11; AW509   107618
O, that I had wings of angels
(Baring-Gould) R Daily, daily,
sing the praises   107619
O that I knew the secret place
(Watts) V411   107620
O, that last great day is coming
soon (Warner) R The earth
shall melt   107621
O that men to the Lord would give
(Scottish Psalter, 1650) AP97
                            107622
O that my load of sin were gone
(Wesley) H224; I381   107623
O, that the Comforter would
come (Wesley) AZ665 107624
O that the Lord would guide my
ways (Watts) K275; L425; N
180; O425; P320; Q416; V73;
AA342; AZ113; BA631; BR300
                            107625
O that the Lord's salvation (Lyte)
D266; K229; M118; N383; P
402; W368; AP375; AZ803
                            107626
O that thou wouldst rend the
heavens (Tranovsky) M332
                            107627
O that thy fire now soon were
kindled (German) M110
                            107628
O that we all could quite fulfill
(Mueller) BA670   107629
O that we with gladness of spirit
for ever (Gregor) AZ492
                            107630
O that will be glory for me,
glory for me (Gabriel) R When
all my labors and trials are
o'er   107631
O! that will be joyful, joyful
(---) R How pleasant thus to
dwell   107632
O the agonizing prayer (MacKeller)
AX179; AY254   107633
O the beautiful garden of prayer

(Schroll) There's a garden
                            107634
O the beautiful old story! (Al-
cott) BX532   107635
O, the best Friend of all is
the "Mighty to save" (Bills)
R Do you seek for a friend
                            107636
O, the best friend to have is
Jesus (Bilhorn) BB528
                            107637
O the bitter shame and sorrow
(Monod) D612; G215; I380;
AK215; AL323; AP478; AR
463; AS281; BA427; BV637;
BY603   107638
O, the bliss of loves ones rest-
ing (Coffman) AY130
                            107639
O, the clanging bells of time
(Gates) BE418   107640
O, the cleft of the Rock
(Good) R There's a cleft in
the Rock   107641
O, the crowning day is coming
(Whittle) R Our Lord is now
rejected   107642
O the deep, deep love of Jesus
(Francis) AM453   107643
O, the delights, the heavenly
joys (Watts) L156; BA45
                            107644
O the depth of love divine (C.
Wesley) BZ   107645
O, the glory gates are ever
open (Hott) R I am looking
for the city   107646
O the golden glowing morning
(LeJeune) Y348   107647
O, the great love the dear
Saviour has shown (McHose)
AX88; AY200   107648
O, the height and depth of
mercy (Crosby) R Take
the world   107649
O the kind words we give
(Townsend) R Let us oft
speak kind words   107650
O the land of cloudless day
(Alwood) R O they tell me
of a home   107651
O, the peace that Jesus gives
(Lillenas) R Like the sun-

shine   107652

O the sunlight! beautiful sunlight!
(Haughey) R There is sunlight
on the hilltop   107653

O, the sweet wonders of that
cross (Watts) L168   107654

O the unsearchable riches of
Christ! (Crosby) AW454; AX
20   107655

O then, sail on, thou ship of
state (Longfellow) Y290
                                   107656

O then to the Rock let me fly
(Johnson) R O sometime s the
shadows are deep   107657

O, there's a sight that rends my
heart (Gregor) AZ690 107658

O, there's sunshine (Hewitt) R
There is sunshine   107659

O they tell me of a home far beyond the skies (Alwood) AH
539; AT484; AU81; AX608;
AY150   107660

O think of the home over there
(Huntington) AT480; AU43; AV
393; AX592   107661

O thou, at whose divine command
(Alford) BR243   107662

O thou, before the world began
(Wesley) D229; F395; BC274
                                   107663

O thou, before whose Presence
(Stone) D585; H525; O283;
P412; W348; AE410; AP584;
AZ839; BA561   107664

O thou best Gift of Heaven
(Nicholls) K381; N504   107665

O thou blest Immanuel (---) M
235   107666

O thou by long experience tried
(Guyon) AP524   107667

O, thou by whom we come to God
(Montgomery) AF336 X Lord,
teach us how to pray aright
                                   107668

O thou essential Word, God from
Eternity (Laurenti) BR161
                                   107669

O thou Eternal Christ of God
(Laufer) G130; BZ   107670

O thou eternal King most high
(Latin, 5th c) F145; BN53;
BO182   107671

O thou Eternal Source of Life
(Schloerb) AD327   107672

O Thou, from whom all good-
ness flows (Haweis) B401;
D663; E85; F117; H367;
K394; L396; M288; Q515;
V640; X117; AA497; AM457;
AO409; AP484; AR197; BA
589; BJ53; BR321   107673

O thou God of all along desirous
roaming (Brooke) Y133
                                   107674

O thou God of my salvation
(Olivers) H18; I25; AT164
                                   107675

O thou God of our salvation
(Clemens) AZ1102   107676

O thou great Friend to all the
sons of men (Parker) S174;
U83; Y219; Z347; AB78; AC
141; AD335; AF219; AN209;
AQ120; AR205; AW224; AZ
454; BD71; BF425; BR395;
BX216   107677

O thou great Shepherd of thy
chosen race (U.P. Psalter,
1912) T148; AJ218   107678

O thou Holy Trinity! Undivided
Unity! (---) R O God,
Eternal Father From thy high
throne   107679

O thou immortal holy Light
(Carolla hymnorum. Cologne
1806) BN58; BO5   107680

O thou Immortal Light Divine
(Corolla hymnorum, Cologne,
1806) BO5 X O thou Im-
mortal holy Light   107681

O Thou in all thy might so far
(Hosmer) A444; E463; I484;
J480; R219; S176; U9; X614;
Y5; AB169; AD84; AG115;
AN241; BF236; BX295; BZ
                                   107682

O Thou in lonely vigil led
(Hosmer) AN171; BD139;
BX439   107683

O Thou, in whom alone is found
(Ware) D293   107684

O Thou, in whom thy saints repose (Ellerton) B462; D302;
N585   107685

O Thou in whom we live and

move (Longfellow) BX83 X O
God, in whom we live   107686

O Thou, in whose presence, my
soul takes delight (Swain) G346;
I530; AR199; AW470; BB160;
BC195; BZ   107687

O Thou, Jehovah, Sovereign in
battle (Bridgman) Y121 107688

O Thou joyful, O thou wonderful
(Falk) AK117   107689

O thou kind and gracious Father
(Denney) BC276   107690

O thou Love unbounded Grant to
eyes enshrouded (Rambach)
Q42   107691

O thou, my Judge and King (Watt)
W402   107692

O thou, my light, my life, my
joy (Montgomery) V623 107693

O thou my soul, bless God the
Lord (Scottish Psalter, 1650)
R121; S16; AL671; AM97; AP
90; AW596; BY70   107694

O thou, my soul, forget no more
(Krishna Pal: Marshman tr)
AV255; BY213   107695

O thou not made with hands (Palgrave) F259 X City not made
with hands   107696

O thou, our God and Father (How)
BR367 X O one with God the
Father   107697

O thou pure light of souls that
love (Latin, 7th-8th c) BQ33
                       107698

O thou Rock of our salvation
(Townsend) BC130   107699

O thou sweetest source of gladness (Gerhardt) AD78 107700

O thou that art the Might One
(Scottish Psalter, 1650) AP39
                       107701

O thou that hearest prayer (---)
AF526   107702

O Thou that hearest the prayer
of faith (Toplady) L496; V301
                       107703

O Thou that hear'st when sinners
cry (Watts) D86; K318; L380;
O99; Q325; AA419; AM413
                       107704

O thou that movest all, O Power
(Duclaux) X616   107705

O Thou that rulest earth, and
sky and sea (Neumark) BI
18D   107706

O Thou, the contrite sinners
Friend (Elliott) C84; H266;
K392; L393; U119; V173; AO
351; AZ1147; BA610   107707

O thou the Eternal Son of God
(Dix) AM191   107708

O, thou the great eternal One
(Byler) AY427   107709

O Thou, through suffering perfect made (How) D272; AK
132; AO145; BV400   107710

O Thou, to whom all creatures
bow (Tate & Brady) V99
                       107711

O Thou to whom, in ancient time
(Pierpont) I12; AN15; BX
438   107712

O Thou to whom in prayer and
praise (Church) BX488
                       107713

O Thou, to whom the fathers
built (Eliot) AQ116   107714

O Thou to whose all searching
sight (Zinzendorf, N. L.) A
411; B119; D339; G360; H308;
I359; K267; O246; V507; AD
310; AF324; AL317; AM525;
AO306; BA619; BB330; BR
361; BZ   107715

O thou true Life of all that live
(St Ambrose??) BR13c
                       107716

O thou who are my King
(Badger) BX359   107717

O Thou, who art of all that is
(Hosmer) AN270; BX293
                       107718

O thou who art the Shepherd
(Shackford) BZ   107719

O Thou, who at thy Eucharist
didst pray (Turton) E324 X
Thou, who at thy first Eucharist didst pray   107720

O Thou, who by a star didst
guide (Neale) J54; K40; AO
334; AZ179; BA182   107721

O Thou who camest from above
(Wesley) A463; E343; F329;
G344; I313; W471; X256; AL
344; AP492; BJ90; BV366; BY

519; BZ   107722

O Thou who didst prepare (Tonna)
AZ1196   107723

O Thou, who didst the temple fill
(Congregational collection) AZ
412   107724

O Thou, who didst with love untold (Toke) B269; D144; E206;
BV458   107725

O Thou who dost accord us (Latin, ca 6th c) E86; O356
107726

O Thou who dost direct my feet
(Houghton) BV580   107727

O Thou who dost to man accord
(Latin, ca 6th c) BV145
107728

O Thou who driest the mourner's
tear (Moore) H368; I522; BT
531   107729

O Thou who gavest power to love
(Creighton) E347; F464; X
284   107730

O Thou, who gavest thy servant
grace (Heber) B86; D146
107731

O Thou, who givest all their food
(Conder) AZ1439; BA863
107732

O Thou, who hast at thy command
(Cotterill) D428; I341; AN295;
BX345   107733

O Thou who hast in every age
(Dewart) BA883   107734

O Thou who hast redeemed of old
(Wesley) BY455   107735

O Thou who hast thy servants
taught (Alford) N488; BX514
107736

O Thou who hearest every heart-
felt prayer (---) R532; S21app.;
U491; AG333; AK503; AR615;
BB684   107737

O Thou who hearest prayer
(Edwards) AZ1198; BA613
107738

O Thou who in Jordan didst bow
(Bethune) AT388; AV250
107739

O Thou, who in that last sad
night (Zinzendorf, N.L.) BA
271   107740

O Thou, who lovest to send relief

(Neale) AZ207; BA859
107741

O Thou, who madest land and
sea (Thring) D276   107742

O Thou who makest souls to
shine (Armstrong) B454;
F471; R305; S480; W334;
AC218; AE372; AK353; AO
423; AP366; AR529; AS393;
BV412   107743

O Thou, who on earth didst
children receive (Cennick)
AZ489   107744

O Thou who once in Galilee
(Hoppe) M586   107745

O Thou Who sealest up the
past (Cole) AB399   107746

O Thou who sendest sun and
rain (---) BR230   107747

O Thou who spreadest the
heaven like a tent (Bible.
Isaiah: Dutch) BE246
107748

O Thou who the Shepherd of
Israel art (Asso. Refd.
Presby. Psalter 1931) AM
279   107749

O Thou, who through this holy
week (Neale) A73; D92; E
109; K89; N99; AF154; AO
157; BA218   107750

O Thou who turnest into morning (Loring) BX148 107751

O Thou who wouldst not have
(Wesley) L382; AA338
107752

O Thou, whom all thy saints
adore (Wesley) H24; I13
107753

O Thou, whom neither time nor
space (Smith) BV655
107754

O Thou whom we adore (Wesley)
AZ1493   107755

O Thou whose all-redeeming
might (Latin, 8th c) E189
107756

O Thou, whose bounty fills my
cup (Crewdson) I531; U77;
AI353   107757

O Thou whose feet have climbed
life's hill (Benson) A507;
B365; G559; J454; K214; Q

486; R468; S490; U329; Y342;
AD421; AE371; AG315; AK451;
AO489; AR531; AS390; BD193;
BF638   107758

O Thou whose glory shone like
fire (Warburton) S477; AC309;
AD394   107759

O Thou whose goodness words can
ne'er express (Gregor) AZ518
                        107760

O Thou whose gracious presence
blest (Benson) AC314; AD419;
AE382; AK444; AR544; AT375
                        107761

O Thou whose gracious presence
shone (Ham) AN448; AQ125;
BX482   107762

O Thou, whose hand hath brought
us (Goadby) G551; S473; AD
410; AK359; AR526; AT379;
BF595; BX492; BY278   107763

O Thou, whose human life for us
(Gregor) BA87   107764

O Thou, whose infant feet were
found (Heber) N66   107765

O Thou whose love has brought
us here (Robinson) BY717
                        107766

O Thou, whose mercy found me
(Monsell) W426   107767

O Thou, whose mercy guides my
way (Edmeston) AZ229
                        107768

O Thou, whose own vast temple
stands (Bryant) U384 X Thou,
whose unmeasured temple
stands   107769

O Thou whose perfect goodness
crowns (Chadwick) AN463; BX
507   107770

O Thou whose power o'er moving
worlds presides (Boethius) AN
67; AQ128; BI69; BX42 107771

O Thou, whose Presence moved
before (Holmes) BH216
                        107772

O Thou whose Spirit witness
bears (Hosmer) AN52; AQ74;
BX69   107773

O Thou, whose tender mercy
hears (Steele) H279; V291
                        107774

O Thou with whom in sweet content (Foote) AN259; BX289
                        107775

O Thou within whose sure control (Munro) AL453 107776

O tidings of comfort and joy
(English carol, 18th c) R
God rest you merry 107777

O timely happy, timely wise
(Keble) W259 X New every
morning is thy love 107778

O, 'tis grace, 'tis wonderful
grace (---) R Saved by grace
                        107779

O, to be there, where the songs
of glory ("A.H.A.") AX349;
AY239   107780

O, to have no Christ, no
Saviour (Cushing) AX226;
AY221   107781

O, to reflect His grace (Smith)
R Christ the transforming
Light   107782

O touch mine eyes, that I may
see (Walton) BY604 107783

O, touch the hem (Root) R
She only touched the hem
                        107784

O Traurigkeit, O Herzeleid!
(Rist) BT167   107785

O Trinity, most blessed Light
(St Ambrose) Q564 X O
Trinity of blessed Light
                        107786

O Trinity, O blessed Light
(St Ambrose) W4 X O
Trinity of blessed Light
                        107787

O Trinity of blessed Light (St
Ambrose??) A171; B11; E
164; F15; J133; Q564; R245;
S59; W4; X51; AL4; AM339;
BJ86   107788

O troubled heart, there is a
home (Bellamy) AU440
                        107789

O troubled Sea of Galilee (Wilson) BX266   107790

O true Bread (St Thomas Aquinas) F622c X Very Bread,
Good Shepherd   107791

O truly is the nation blest
(U.P. Psalter, 1912) AP30
X Jehovah from His throne

on high X Let all the earth
Jehovah fear   107792
O, trust ye in the Lord forever
(Lathbury) H528   107793
O turn, great Ruler of the skies
(Merrick) L381   107794
O turn to Jesus, Mother! turn
and call Him (Faber) BO143;
BQ115   107795
O turn ye, O turn ye (Hopkins)
AI192; AZ508   107796
O 'twas a joyful sound to hear
(Tate & Brady) A390; B307;
D493; S19; AD33; AM277; BX
19   107797
O, 'twas love, love, love that
moved (Gilmour) R When out
in sin   107798
O valiant hearts, who to your
glory came (Arkwright) A531;
F584; G495; X293; Y123; AL
525   107799
O Vaterherz, das Erd' und
Himmel schuf (Knapp) BT299
                              107800
O very God of very God (Neale)
A442; B102; D326; K11; N11
                              107801
O Virgin all lovely, O Mother all
gracious (DeDorz) BN160
                              107802
O, vision bright! The land of
light (Faber) BO116   107803
O wait, meekly wait, and murmur
not (Bellamy) R O troubled
heart R The home where
changes never come   107804
O walk with God along the road
(Gill) BE247; BX353   107805
O walk with God, and thou shalt
find (Coxe) BY553   107806
O walk with Jesus, wouldst thou
know (Hood) BV635   107807
O watch and pray, my soul, the
way (Brorson) M387; O430;
P186   107808
O, we see the gleams of the
golden morning (Graham) R
The golden morning is fast ap-
proaching   107809
O weary pilgrim, lift your head
(Wienland) BE425   107810
O weary soul, the gate is near

BB562   107811
O weary wanderer, come home
(Coffman) AX239; AY222
                               107812
O welcome in our midst
(Dearmer) X335   107813
O welt, sieh hier dein Leben
(Gerhardt) BT171   107814
O, what a change (Habershon)
R Soon will our Saviour from
Heaven appear   107815
O what amazing words of grace
(Medley) H233; I292 107816
O what an act of majesty
(Gregor) AZ689   107817
O what can little hands do?
(Hinsdale) W670; AP780;
BY752   107818
O what could my Jesus do more
(---) AH144; BO53   107819
O what happiness divine (Hayn)
AZ789   107820
O what if we are Christ's
(Baker) D390; K388; AP501;
BA809   107821
O what joy, O what joy
awaiteth me (Gregor) AZ
716   107822
O what praise in highest strain
(Gregor) AZ868   107823
O what praises shall we render
(Burton) N645   107824
O what precious balm and heal-
ing (St Bernard of Clairvaux)
O297; P181; Q144; AA194
                               107825
O what shall I do My Saviour
to praise (Wesley) AZ1423
                               107826
O what songs of the heart
(Townsend) BC87   107827
O, what tender, tender mercy
(Gardiner) R When I see the
way   107828
O what the joy and the glory
must be (Abelard) V709 X
O what their joy and their
glory must be   107829
O what their joy and their glory
must be (Abelard) A589;
B544; D397; E281; J596; R
424; S430; V709; W224; X
200; AF310; AL173; BB202;

BL85   107830

O, when I think of that heavenly
home (Kolb) AX595; AY136
                              107831
O, when shall I see Jesus (---)
AY402   107832
O, when we see God's mercy
(Burnett) BE249   107833
O where are kings and empires
now (Coxe) A382; B471; G384;
H408; I214; J154; K203; L288;
N270; R431; S334; T362; U349;
V539; Z427; AB319; AD395;
AE343; AF264; AG230; AI430;
AK326; AO425; AR497; AS186;
AT383; AV242; AW276; AY429;
AZ127; BA268; BB435; BF582;
BZ   107834
O where are the reapers that
garner in (Rexford) AP588;
AU430; AX216; BB620   107835
O where is he that trod the sea
(Lynch) H154   107836
O where is the home of the soul to
be found? (Joergen) M641
                              107837
O where shall I be when the last
trumpet sounds? (---) R When
judgment day is drawing nigh
                              107838
O where shall rest be found
(Montgomery) D513; H227;
I250; L599; V221; AZ1343; BA
405; BR282   107839
O wherefore do the nations rage
(U.P. Psalter, 1912) T2;
AJ4; AM227   107840
O wherefore hast thou cast me
off (U.P. Psalter, 1912) T
138; AJ205   107841
O who, in such a world as this
(Montgomery) BB381   107842
O who is this that cometh (Todd)
BB636   107843
O who like Thee, so calm, so
bright (Coxe) D314; O225; U
70   107844
O who shall roll away the stone
(Ham) A84   107845
O why not tonight (Reed) R O do
not let the Word depart
                              107846
O, why should I be idle (Jeffrey)

AX207   107847
O, why should you wander in
darkness (Shoemaker) R
Come, lost one   107848
O! wie ist die Zeit so wichtig
(Mack) AR428   107849
O wie selig seid ihr doch, ihr
Frommen (Dach) BT589
                              107850
O wie selig sind die (Unparth.
G.B.) AY40d   107851
O Will of God beneath our life
(Gordon) G78   107852
O with due reverence let us all
(Tate & Brady) D479
                              107853
O with thy tender mercies,
Lord (Scottish Psalter, 1650)
AL663; AP75   107854
O wonderful prayer that Jesus
prayed (Giffe) AS131
                              107855
O wonderful word of salvation
(Hartsough) AS175   107856
O wonderful words of the gospel
(Crosby) P258   107857
O wondrous Conqueror and
great (Homburg) O366
                              107858
O wondrous Kingdom here on
earth (Gruhdtvig) M81; P
224   107859
O, wondrous Name, by prophets
heard (Crosby) BR527
                              107860
O wondrous type! O vision fair
(Latin, 15th c) A119; B285;
D167; F558; J147; N203;
O253; R182; S142; W89; AO
152; AZ319; BA71; BV274
                              107861
O, wondrously sweet is the
story (Hoffman) AX32; AY
517   107862
O word immortal of eternal God
(Justinian, Emperor) E325
                              107863
O Word of God above (Guiet)
E171; F475;   107864
O Word of God incarnate (How)
A402; B58; D284; G386; H87;
I200; J252; K169; L314; N216;
O134; P89; Q294; R251; S215;

U134; V78; W198; Y364; Z434;
AA113; AB100; AC68; AD193;
AE158; AF252; AG131; AH233;
AI151; AK199; AL182; AM267;
AO240; AP289; AR240; AT183;
AU75; AV75; AW289; AX90;
AZ804; BA7; BB217; BE251;
BF274; BI44; BR233; BV307;
BY251; BZ   107865

O Word of God, most holy (How)
BE251 X O Word of God incarnate   107866

O word of pity, for our pardon
pleading (Greenaway) F115;
W97; AF173; BV176   107867

O Word, that goest forth on high
(Latin, ca 7th c) A8   107868

O world, behold! upon the tree
(Gerhardt) O317; AZ576
                             107869

O world invisible, we view thee
(Thompson) X617; Y192
                             107870

O world, see here suspended
(Gerhardt) M427; P179 107871

O worship the King, all glorious
above (Grant) A288; B255; D
459; E466; F167; G4; H13; I
106; J163; K294; L75; N333;
O60; Q17; R26; S2; T297; U7;
V13; W9; X618; Y59; Z94; AB
14; AC36; AD2; AE2; AF6; AG
6; AH187; AI11; AK10; AL21;
AM13; AN6; AO58; AP93; AQ25;
AR33; AS2; AT20; AU2; AV34;
AW7; AX9; AY423; BA20; BB
75; BD27; BF167; BH60; BK65;
BR408; BV248; BX10; BY22;
BZ   107872

O worship the Lord in the beauty
of holiness, Bow down before
Him (Monsell) E42; F77; S7;
U5; X93; Z106; AC12; AD27;
AF31; AL201; AP314; AR39;
AZ1153; BB6; BF217; BV11;
BY35   107873

O worship the Lord in the beauty
of holiness, in the beauty of
holiness, in the beauty of holiness (Lowry) AR432; AS4
                             107874

O would, my God, that I could
praise thee (Mentzer) N178; O

443; AZ697   107875

O would you be a blessing true
(Ussery) AX436   107876

O ye heavens, bend and see
("H. 1708") K537   107877

O ye His angels, that excel
strength (Scottish Psalter,
1650) AL673   107878

O ye mountains high, where the
clear blue sky (Penrose)
BC145   107879

O ye who dare go forth with
God (Bowie) BD161 107880

O ye who taste that love is
sweet (Rossetti) W358; AC
248; AN414; AQ141   107881

O yes, He cares for me (Presley) R I have a friend
                             107882

O, yes, He cares, I know He
cares (Graeff) R Does Jesus
care   107883

O yet we trust that somehow
good (Tennyson) AN237
                             107884

O young and fearless Prophet
(Harlow) G266; Z362; AB
288; AD325; AK391; AR
148; BF516; BK19; BZ
                             107885

O young mariner, you from the
haven (Tennyson) AC231
X Not of the sunlight
                             107886

O Zion, haste, thy mission
(Thomson) G475 X O Sion,
haste, thy mission   107887

Obedient they but to a dream
(Dillon) AQ228   107888

Obgleich die harf, ist gut und
scharf (S. Franck) BU1
                             107889

Object of my first desire (Toplady) AZ1048   107890

"Observe ye" and "remember"
still (Alkabetz) BH108
                             107891

Ocean Star, we greet you
(Latin, 9th c) BN129
                             107892

O'er all the land have the
signs now appeared (Gage)
BB544   107893

O'er all the way green palms and
blossoms gay (Faure?) AH622
107894
O'er continent and ocean (Holmes)
AN400; AQ227   107895
O'er eras past I've pondered
(Zinzendorf, C.R.) AZ560
107896
O'er field and forest stealing
(Gerhardt) AL548   107897
O'er Jerusalem Thou weepest
(Hoppe) N176; Q419   107898
O'er the distant mountains break-
ing (Monsell) D46; N187; O510;
Q606; S189; AA548; AK98; AQ
111; AZ1398   107899
O'er the gloomy hills of darkness
(Williams) H476; Q505; U401;
V589; W387; AL247; AM373;
AP380; AZ1404; BC127; BY
388   107900
O'er the realms of pagan darkness
(Cotterill) AZ1405; BA352
107901
O'er the silent waters, Thro' the
depths of night (---) BI72
107902
O'er the trackless ocean guided
(Adams) AL449; AW165
107903
O'er those gloomy hills of dark-
ness (Williams) W387 X O'er
the gloomy hills of darkness
107904
O'er waiting harp-strings of the
mind (Eddy) BE253   107905
O'erwhelmed in depths of woe
(Breviary, Bologne, 1827)
BQ25   107906
Of all the myriad moods of mind
(Lowell) AB306; BF373
107907
Of all the thoughts of God that are
(Browning) I541; BH224
107908
Of all things beautiful and good
(Markham) AC521   107909
Of him who did salvation bring
(St Bernard of Clairvaux??)
G188; H231; I289   107910
Of His love I shall ever sing
(Fisher) R There's a glad new
song   107911

Of mercy and of judgment
(U.P. Book of Psalms,
1871) AP88   107912
Of mercy and of justice, My
thankful song shall be (U.P.
Psalter, 1912) T185; AJ271
107913
Of my life the life, O Jesu
(Homburg) O319   107914
Of omnipresent grace I sing
(Cronenwett) M150   107915
Of one blood hath God created
(Robins) Z510   107916
Of Sion's honor angels sing
(Cronenwett) M91   107917
Of stones full previous are thy
towers (Prid) X393b 107918
Of that branch in ancient Gar-
den (Cummins) BL24
107919
Of the Father's heart begotten
(Prudentius) X387 X Of the
Father's love begotten
107920
Of the Father's love begotten
(Prudentius) A20; B74; D52;
E613; F58 and 591; J17; K
20; Q98; R7; W60; X387; AF
111; AK13; AL52; AM122;
AP166; AR116; AZ898-899;
BL5; BM46; BV109; BY85;
BZ   107921
Of the glorious Body telling (St
Thomas Aquinas) E326
107922
Of the themes that men have
known (Fisher) AT293
107923
Of Thy love some gracious
token (Kelly) W298; AL212
107924
Oft, as we run the weary way
(Brooke) AB256; BX186
107925
Oft in danger, oft in woe
(White & Fuller-Maitland)
A558; B116; D506; E467;
F291; I412; L546; M268; T
392; V489; W533; X619; AA
500; AL406; AM479; AO411;
AP537; BA584; BR398; BV
584   107926
Oft in sorrow, oft in woe

107927
Oft to every man and nation
(Lowell) BE258 X Once to
every man and nation   107928
Oft when the waves of passion rise
(Wesley) AZ631   107929
Often weary and worn on the path-
way (Cosner) AX531; AY149
107930
NOTE: "Oh" has been eliminated
as an entry word, See "O".
107931
O-lay-nu l'-sha bay-ach (Jewish
traditional) BH329   107932
Om Salighed og Gläde (Arrebo)
BT217   107933
Omnis mundus jucundetur nato
Salvatori (Latin, 12th c) BT
82   107934
On a hill far away (Bennard)
AE186; AH296; AT93; AU71;
AV369; AX105; BB533; BZ
107935
On Calvary's brow my Savior
died (Darwood) AI78; AU439
107936
On Calvary's height the Roman
spear (Dollard) BO19   107937
On Christ, by faith, I would live
(Hoskins) M218 X On Christ,
by faith, my soul would live
107938
On Christ, by faith, my soul
would live (Hoskins) L440;
M218   107939
On Christ, the solid rock, I stand
(Mote) R My hope is built
107940
On Christmas Eve the bells were
rung (Scott) BG189   107941
On Christmas night all Christians
sing (English trad carol) BG
24; BV114   107942
On Christ's ascension I now build
(Wegelin) Q216   107943
On desert sands the vision comes
(White) Y6   107944
On eyes that watch through sor-
row's night (Hosmer) BX211
107945
On God alone my soul resides
(U.P. Psalter, 1912) AJ149
107946

On hills and vales of heaven
(Rowell) BB98   107947
On Jordan's bank the Baptist's
cry (Coffin) A10; B282; D
44; E9; F50; J4; K2; L208;
N13; O176; Q63; W78; X67;
AF115; AK95; AZ318; BA
152; BL1; BM59; BN1; BV
79; BY86   107948
On Jordan's banks the Herald's
cry (Coffin) O176 X On
Jordan's bank the Baptist's
cry   107949
On Jordan's stormy bank I
stand (Stennett) G523; H
509; I617; L596; V702; AH
529; AT478, 479; AU249;
AV282; AX567; AY142; BB
553; BR428; BZ   107950
On Mary, virgin undefiled (---)
O290   107951
On mighty wings rush swiftly
by, The hours, the days,
the year (Hamburg Temple
hymnal) BH161   107952
On mountains and in valleys
(---) BR371   107953
On my heart imprint thine image
(Kingo) O298; Q179 107954
On our way rejoicing (Monsell)
A568; B432; D522; J195; P
382; R80; S56; Z417; AD483;
AG15; AH213; AO361; AZ
757; BA510; BD18; BF617;
BR511   107955
On the Cross is One uplifted
(Collier) AO171   107956
On the good and faithful (U.P.
Psalter, 1912) R52; T5;
AJ7   107957
On the happy, golden shore
(Blair) AX603   107958
On the moorland of life God's
Shepherd is seen (Crum)
X220   107959
On the mountain top appearing
(Kelly) AW336 X On the
mountain's top   107960
On the mountain's top appearing
(Kelly) H404; I647; N269;
U396; V590; AV245; AW336;
AY241; BC273   107961

On the radiant threshold Of this
dawning day (Wieand) AR65;
AS18   107962
On the resurrection morning
(Baring-Gould) D243; E136;
AP617; BV404   107963
On the shore beyond the sea
(Baltzell) BB657   107964
On the wood His arms are
stretched (Latin, 12th c) BP28
                           107965
On Thee, our Guardian, God, we
call (Davies) AZ300   107966
On this day earth shall ring
(Piae Cantiones, 1582) AF136;
BI85   107967
On this day everywhere (Piae
Cantiones, 1582) AQ296
                           107968
On this day, O beautiful Mother
(---) AH134; BO114   107969
On this day, the first of days
(Breviary, Carcassonne, 1745)
B47; F39; AA126; BL41; BN202;
BV70   107970
On this glad day we dedicate
(Lathrop) AR527   107971
On this stone now laid with prayer
(Pierpont) G548; H423; I657;
N274; AR528; BZ   107972
On thy Church, O Power Divine
(Auber) AZ1276   107973
On thy ransomed congregation
(Foster) AZ251; BA280
                           107974
On to victory (Cassell) R From
over hill and plain   107975
On what has now been sown Thy
blessing, Lord, bestow (New-
ton) J193; K430; N355; Q46;
AA11; AZ1169; BT46   107976
On wings of living light (How)
B559; S170; Z243; AC131;
AK171; BB133; BY161   107977
Once again, dear Lord, we pray
(Willcox) W374; AL619   107978
Once again, O blessed time
(Bright) AZ863; BR556   107979
Once again to its close (Drury)
AR583   107980

Once again we come to the
house of God (Naylor) AX
51   107981

Once for all, O Christian re-
ceive it (Bliss) R Free from
the law   107982
Once He came in blessing
(Horn) K10; N10; Q74; AA
143; AZ550; BA154   107983
Once I thought my mountain
strong (Newton) V484
                           107984
Once I wandered in darkness
unsaved (Grisham) AX439
                           107985
Once in Jerusalem of old
(Williamson) BB473   107986
Once in royal David's city
(Alexander) A236; B349;
D540; E605; F432; G442;
J41; K535; M608; N633;
R462; S454; W69; X368;
AD474; AG302; AH242; AI
382; AL70; AM639; AO133;
AP727; AR125; AV84; AW
412; AZ612; BA158; BB424;
BF284; BR558; BV107; BY
106   107987
Once Mary would go wandering
(German trad carol) BG93
                           107988
Once more before we part
(Hart) AX78; AY397; AZ
1331; BA379   107989
Once more, my soul, the ris-
ing day (Watts) AY279
                           107990
Once more, O Lord, do I
awaken (Weitzman) BH7
                           107991
Once more, O Lord, thy sign
shall be (Doane) D38
                           107992
Once more the liberal year
laughs out (Whittier) AC324;
AN137; AQ275; BF651; BH
181   107993
Once more we come before
our God (Hart) I33; AR7;
AS55; AY8   107994
Once, only once, and once for
all (Bright) E327; F398
                           107995
Once pledged by the cross, as
children of God (Bode)
F462   107996

Once to every man and nation
(Lowell) A519; B433; E563;
G263; J547; R361; S373; X
309; Y240; Z558; AB285; AC
220; AD349; AE376; AF441; AG
249; AH410; AK399; AL410; AN
319; AQ168, 220; AR569; AT
418; AW346; BB513; BD163; BE
258; BF480; BK82; BZ   107997
One cup of healing oil and wine
(Drummond) BE259   107998
One day when heaven was filled
with his praises (Chapman)
AM689; AT85; AX309   107999
One gift, my God, I seek (Torrey)
BX103   108000
One God! One Lord! One mighty
King (Moise) BH140   108001
One holy Church of God appears
(Longfellow) S335; Z424; AE
311; AF266; AK325; AN407;
AQ261; AR498; BD189; BE261;
BF590; BX452; BZ   108002
One is kind above all others
(Nunn) AL473; AP737; AW447
108003
One is our God and Father
(Ingemann) O468   108004
One Lord there is, call lords
above (Rands) Y24; AN293;
BX435   108005
One more day's work for Jesus
(Warner) I419; AS27; AU55;
AV387; BB622   108006
One prayer I have, -- all prayers
in one (Montgomery) AN236;
AZ160; BX278   108007
One precious boon, O Lord, I
seek (Fitch) BB338   108008
One radiant morn the mists will
all surrender (Wexels) P337
108009
One resolve, one resolve, you
who falter and fear (Urseth)
P247   108010
One sole baptismal sign (Robinson)
B463; H421; I559; K206; AL169;
AP304; AZ1187   108011
One sweetly solemn thought (Cary)
B407; D676; G515; H497; I620;
L563; O289; P338; T441; U425;
V660, 762; AA531; AH533; AO
548; 704; AP615; AR416; AS

473; AU183; AV392; AW264;
AX611; AZ476; BA727; BB
352; BC272   108012
One there is, above all others
(Newton) H334; I174; J456;
K389; L133; N430; U227;
V375; W145; AL121; AM142
AO291; AP234; AV136; AY
26; AZ601; BA495; BY214
108013
One there is who loves thee
(Ayres) AP406   108014
One thing I of the Lord desire
(Smith) W461; AL324; AP
489; AU408; BB634   108015
One thing needful! This one
treasure (Schroeder) O227
108016
One thing only, Lord, is need-
ful (Schroeder) M222
108017
One thing's needful; Lord this
treasure (Schroeder) Q366;
AA83; AZ989   108018
One thing's needful! then Lord
Jesus (Schroeder) AA83 X
One thing's needful; Lord,
this treasure   108019
One thought I have, my ample
creed (Hosmer) AN77; AQ
50; AW248; BE260; BX74
108020
One Thy Light, the Temple fill-
ing (Keble) Q641   108021
One view, Lord Jesus, of thy
passion (Bossart) AZ995;
BA191   108022
One who us all unfit to count
(Tilak) J384; S234; W406;
AF330; AL279; BY456
108023
One world this, for all its sor-
row (Silliman) AQ145
108024
Only a sinner saved by grace
(Gray) R Naught have I
gotten   108025
Only a step to Jesus (Crosby)
AU432; AX254; AY503
108026
Only-begotten, Word of God
eternal (Latin, ca 9th c)
A228; E636; AL197   108027

Only believe, only believe
(Rader) AU318   108028
Only God can bring us gladness
(Wallin) BE263   108029
Only one prayer today (Dix) D594;
AZ1287; BA202   108030
Only remembered, only remember-
ed (Bonar) R Fading away like
the stars   108031
Only sleeping, sweetly sleeping
(Brooks) R "Lo, she is not
dead"   108032
Only thine, only thine (Warner)
R I heard the dear Redeemer
say   108033
Only thy tender love, Saviour
divine (Crosby) U226   108034
Only to follow Thee (Crosby) R
Only thy tender love   108035
Only trust Him, and be still
(Pierson) R Open wide thy
heart   108036
Only trust Him, only trust Him
(Stockton) R Come, every soul
by sin oppressed   108037
O-no A-do-noy, ka-per no
(Jewish traditional) BH330
          108038
Onward, brothers, march still
onward (Ellis) AN351; BH230
          108039
Onward, children onward, Fear-
less, firm and true (Sonnen-
schein) R Hark the voice of
children   108040
Onward, Christian soldiers (Bar-
ing-Gould) A557; B530; D516;
E643; F629; G280; H393; I383;
J560; K379; L541; M242; N589;
P374; Q658; R350; S365; T377;
U294; V483; W535; X397; Y172;
Z482; AB254; AC209; AD298;
AE250; AF382; AG199; AH442;
AI327; AK292; AL401; AM490;
AN331; AO391; AP538; AT412;
AU46; AV209; AW225; AX196;
AZ772; BA582; BB360; BC128;
BD145; BE264; BF471; BR512;
BV562; BX542; BY520; BZ
          108041
Onward, Christian! though the
region (Johnson) D620; AN216;
BE265; BF449; BX214   108042

Onward march, all-conquering
Jesus (Williams) W384
          108043
Onward, Onward, tho' the re-
gion (Johnson) AN216 X On-
ward, Christian! though the
region   108044
Onward, then, and fear not
(Havergal) R Standing at the
portal   108045
Open, Lord, my inward ear
(Wesley) BV639; BX63
          108046
Open my eyes, that I may see
(Scott) R390; AE200; AG
227; AI158; AR295; AS257;
AT312; AU351; BZ   108047
Open now thy gates of beauty
(Schmolck) J187; K420; M1;
N306; O35; P45; Q1; R40;
Z121; AA5; AF503; AK23;
AM304; AW505; AZ606; BA
381; BZ   108048
Open our eyes, thy glory be-
holding (Sellers) R Lord un-
to thee   108049
Open the wells of grace and
salvation (Hoffman) R Lord,
I am fondly   108050
Open wide thy heart today
(Pierson) AX251; AY505
          108051
Oppressed by sin, O Lord, to
Thee (Gellert) O102 X
Crushed by my sin, O Lord
to Thee   108052
Orémus pro pontifice nostro
(Latin) BN201; BQ247
          108053
Os er idag en Frelser föd
(Boye) BT79   108054
Our babies' names are on the
roll (Dearmer) X386e
          108055
Our baptism first declares
(Hart) AZ1313   108056
Our blessed bond of union
(Murray) AP296   108057
Our blessed Saviour seven times
spoke (Boschenstain) Q177;
AA207   108058
Our blest Redeemer, ere He
breathed (Auber) A368; B

199; D375; E157; F230; G177;
H218; I189; K157; S205; T353;
U131; W180; X182; AD188; AG
124; AH228; AL162; AO227; AP
272; AW138; AZ1142; BA141;
BB214; BF261; BR203; BV223;
BY236   108059
Our children, gracious Lord and
God (Swertner) AZ918; BA
847   108060
Our children, Lord, in faith and
prayer (Haweis) U485; W306;
AI371; AM351; AP350; BV342
                               108061
Our Church proclaims God's love
and care (Niedermeyer) Z425
                               108062
Our country is Immanuel's ground
(Barbauld) L239   108063
Our country's voice is pleading
(Anderson) H480; N382; P390;
U410; AA472; AE362; AO530;
AZ832; BA355   108064
One day of praise is done (Eller-
ton) A175; B49; D23; E38;
W290; AP682; AY436; AZ1359;
BA388; BB58; BF208   108065
One day of praise is ended
(Tymms) BY701   108066
Our faith is in the Christ who
walks with men today (Clark)
Z351; AB167; AH320; BF329
                               108067
Our Father, by whose name
(Tucker) A504; AF466   108068
Our Father, by whose servants
(Briggs) A505; J248; X194;
Y336; BY279   108069
Our Father, for our daily bread
(Briggs) X403   108070
Our Father, God of life and light
("M.L.B.") BX136   108071
Our Father God! not face to face
(Chapin) BX224   108072
Our Father God, thy name we
praise (Clock) BY362   108073
Our Father, God, whose mercies
still abide (Williams) Y397
                               108074
Our Father, hear our longing
prayer (MacDonald) AZ220
                               108075
Our Father hears us when we

pray (Burton) BV610 108076
Our Father in heaven, we hal-
low thy name (Hale) AT343;
AV24; AX652   108077
Our Father, merciful and good
(Petri) N166   108078
Our Father, our King (Jewish
traditional) BH309   108079
Our Father, thou in heaven
above (Luther) O359; Q458;
AA396; AI437; AZ651
                               108080
Our Father, throned in heaven
above (Guthrie) O4   108081
Our Father! through the com-
ing year (Gaskell) U474;
V628; AZ154   108082
Our Father thy dear Name doth
show (Richards) A533; B
499; W486; Z522; BD126;
BF496   108083
Our Father, unto Thee We now
on bended knee (Russell)
AN11   108084
Our Father, we adore Thee
(Bowers) BR27   108085
Our Father, we beseech thy
grace (Goldstein) BH145
                               108086
Our Father, while our hearts
unlearn (Holmes) X620; AN
235; BX212   108087
Our fathers' God, from out
whose hand (Whittier) Y339;
AB345; AH471; BD162; BF
556; BK124   108088
Our Father's God! to thee
(Smith) D196   108089
Our Fathers' God, to Thee we
raise (Copeland) G494; I
713; AH207   108090
Our Father's home eternal
(St Thomas à Kempis??)
E252; F625   108091
Our fathers in the olden days
(Bevier) AO658   108092
Our Father's wondrous works
we see (Brooks) AX16
                               108093
Our fortress strong art thou,
O Lord (Goulston) BH165
                               108094
Our friend, our brother, and

our lord (Whittier) AQ121 X
O Love! O Life! Our faith and
sight   108095

Our friends on earth we meet
with pleasure (Chapman) AX
656 X With friends on earth
                             108096

Our glowing praise to thee
(Morgan) AD443   108097

Our God, He is a God of might
(Perkins) AI411 X Thou art, O
God, the God of might 108098

Our God is all-in-all (Seal) BE
267   108099

Our God is good: in earth and sky
(Gurney) BX86   108100

Our God is love; and all his saints
(Cotterill) I552; J457; N500;
AO82; BE266   108101

Our God is Love, and all His
sons (Cotterill) BE266 X Our
God is love, and all his saints
                             108102

Our God is Love, unchanging
Love (Root) BE269   108103

Our God is truth, most faithful
is His word (Herrnschmidt)
AZ704   108104

Our God leads onward (Butler-
Thwing) Y150   108105

Our God, our God, Thou shinest
here (Gill) AN9; AQ36; BD30;
BX29; BY262   108106

Our God, our help in ages past
(Watts) L518 X O God, our
help in ages past   108107

Our God shall reign where'er the
sun (Watts) BE271 X Jesus
shall reign where'er the sun
                             108108

Our God so loved the world that
He (Olearius) AA327   108109

Our God, to whom we turn
(Grubb) A283; J171; R128;
X621; AF86; AK64; AN490;
AR84   108110

Our God, we raise to thee (Snow)
BC144a   108111

Our God, we thank thee, who
hast made (Proctor) AB213 X
My God, I thank thee, who
hast made   108112

Our heavenly Father calls (Dodd-

ridge) AO444; AZ1310; BA
528   108113

Our heavenly Father hear
(Montgomery) L191; M63;
Q455; AA397; AZ1319; BA
614   108114

Our heavenly Father, Source of
love (Wesley) AZ217; BA14
                        108115

Our highest joys succeed our
griefs (---) I474   108116

Our hymns are sung, our
prayers are said (Hawkes)
BX509   108117

Our Jesus is the Rock where
we safely rest (Jones) R
We have a Rock   108118

Our life is ever on the wing
(Watts) AY134   108119

Our life is hid with Christ
(Bonar) AZ1325   108120

Our Lord and God, O bless this
day (Brun) M537; O106; Q
337   108121

Our Lord Christ hath risen!
(Plunkett) W125; AD163;
AT112; AZ779   108122

Our Lord, his Passion ended
(Burkitt) F155; X183; AW
572; BV224; BY237   108123

Our Lord is now rejected
(Whittle) AU48; AV391; BY
189   108124

Our Lord is risen from the
dead, And rays of glory
crown his head (Boye) J101
                        108125

Our Lord is risen from the
dead, Our Jesus has gone
up on high (Wesley) L269
X Our Lord is risen from
the dead, Our Jesus is gone
up on high   108126

Our Lord is risen from the
dead, Our Jesus is gone up
on high (Wesley, J. & C.)
B187; D132; F609; H180;
I158; L269; W128; AA232;
AO193; AZ934; BB132
                        108127

Our Lord the path of suffering
trod (Santeüil) F517 108128

Our lot is fallen in pleasant

places (Spitta) AZ699   108129

Our loved Dominion bless (Murray: Canadian national anthem) AL509; AP640   108130

Our mountain home so dear (Wells) BC144   108131

Our pious fathers built their shrine (Mendes) BH215
108132

Our Redeemer rose victorious (Gregor) AZ1387   108133

Our rest will soon be given (Leatherman) R Some days are dark   108134

Our Saviour in his earthly life (Van Pelt) AX148; AY391
108135

Our Saviour to the Jordan came (Luther) M42   108136

Our Shepherd is the Lord (Hamburg Temple hymnal) AR272; BH84   108137

Our sins, our sorrows, Lord, were laid on thee (Eddis) N121; AK159; AO169; AZ448 108138

Our souls shall magnify the Lord (---) AJp. 394   108139

Our souls with inmost shame (Allen) AZ1164   108140

Our table now with food is spread (Kingo) N542; O569; P352
108141

Our thanks and praise to Thee be given (Melanchthon) O24
108142

Our thought of Thee is glad with hope (Whittier) G506; I712; AB336; BF544   108143

Our thoughts go round the world (Moore) BK14   108144

Our times are in thy hand (Lloyd) L506 X My times are in thy hand   108145

Our wilful hearts have gone astray (Benson) Y42   108146

Ours be the poems of all tongues (Patton) AQ138   108147

Out from the camp-fire's red glowing (French) BB501
108148

Out in the darkness of sorrow and sin (McKinney) AU442 108149

Out in the desert the lost are

straying (Evilsizer) AX219; AY224   108150

Out in the desert they wander (Wingate) R Dear to the heart of the Shepherd
108151

Out of James one twenty-two (Linthicum) AU326 108152

Out of my bondage, sorrow, and night (Sleeper) AE177; AH342; AI210; AM715; AR459; AT233; AV340; AX300
108153

Out of my need, you come to me, O Father (Sangster) AB312; AC445   108154

Out of our suffering, out of our sadness (Polish trad) Y309
108155

Out of the dark the circling sphere (Longfellow) AN99; AQ208; BD152; BX237
108156

Out of the deep I call (Baker) D349; F322; K315; Q327; AA423; AM412; BR352
108157

Out of the deep I cry to thee (Luther) AZ742 X Out of the depths I cry to thee 108158

Out of the depths I cry to Thee (Luther) J372; K317; L391; M65; N406; O273; Q329; W407; AA415; AK210; AM461; AW531; AZ742; BA413; BY457; BZ   108159

Out of the depths I cry to you, O Lord (Ladies of the Grail) BL20; BSp. 52   108160

Out of the depths, O Lord, I cry to thee (Lucas) BH164
108161

Out of the depths of woe (Montgomery) AZ1291   108162

Out of the depths to Thee I cry (Marcy) I427   108163

Out of the depths to Thee, O Lord, I cry (Bible, Psalm 129) BN188; BP96; BQ117
108164

Out of the gloom and darkness (Shank) R My life was lost
108165

Out of the night that covers me
(Henley) Y188   108166
Out of the orient crystal skies
(English trad carol, 17th c)
BG121   108167
Out of your sleep arise and wake
(English trad carol, 15th c)
BG177   108168
Out on an ocean all boundless we
ride (Unitarian Collection)
BB661; BR517   108169
Out on life's dark heaving ocean
(Dewart) AP508   108170
Out on the highways and byways
of life (Wilson) AT431; AU130
                             108171
Out on the mountain, sad and
forsaken (Crosby) AI201
                             108172
Out on this dark world (Warren)
AX502   108173
Outside the Holy City unnumbered
footsteps throng (Gilkey) AD141;
AH280; AK134; AR169; BF311
                             108174
Over Kedron Jesus treadeth
(Kingo) N101; O302   108175
Over the land in glory (Hosmer)
BD247   108176
"Over the line," hear the sweet
refrain (Bradford) R O tender
and sweet was the Father's
voice   108177
Over the ocean wave, far, far
away (Haskell) AX215; AY35
                             108178
Over there, over there, O think
of the home (Huntington) R O
think of the home   108179
Over yonder's a park which is
newly begun (English trad carol)
BG184   108180
Own thy congregation, O thou
slaughtered Lamb (Zinzendorf)
AZ758; BA805   108181

P

Palms of glory, raiment bright
(Montgomery) E201; F530; L
582; AZ74   108182
Pange lingua gloriosi (St Thomas
Aquinas) BN106; BO254; BQ

241   108183
Panis angelicus (St Thomas
Aquinas) AH130; BN92; BO
33; BP51; BQ230   108184
Parce Domine, parce populo
tuo (Bible, Joel 2) BM71;
BN30; BO164; BQ239
                             108185
Pardoned through redeeming
grace (Osler) L319; AO382;
BA287   108186
Part in Peace! Christ's life
was peace (Adams) R543;
W303; AP339   108187
Part in peace! Is day before
us? (Adams) AD63; AO50;
BF209   108188
Partners of a glorious hope
(Wesley) BE273   108189
Pass me not , O gentle Saviour
(Crosby) G231; H43; I329;
J461; N416; P13; U252; V
760; AE175; AH338; AI212;
AL503; AM707; AO645; AP
495; AR464; AT219; AU230;
AV349; AW474; AX380; AY
457; BA615; BB559; BZ
                             108190
Pass on the torch, pass on the
flame (Cross) Y156; AB293;
AC229   108191
Past are the cross, the scourge,
the thorn (Jewitt) AN194; AQ
315; BD240; BX208   108192
Patapan, patapan, patapan (La-
Monnoye) R Willie, take your
little drum   108193
Patiently, tenderly pleading
(Lillenas) AU433   108194
Patrick, Thee addressing (Lee)
BN166   108195
Paul the preacher, Paul the
poet (Sayle) F542   108196
Peace, be to this congregation
(Wesley) AN24 X Peace be
to this habitation   108197
Peace be to this habitation (Wes-
ley) M263; AN24; AZ938;
BA382; BE276; BI75; BR108;
BX33   108198
Peace be to thy ever dwelling
(Pohlman) O47; AZ1085
                             108199

Peace in our time, O Lord (Oxenham) A527; AE411; AW357; BK
114   108200

Peace is the mind's old wilderness cut down (Holmes) AQ179
                              108201

Peace of God, which knows no
measure (Book of hymns: Unitarian 1846) BR206   108202

Peace on earth, Heaven is pro-
claiming (Lamb) AZ1396; BA
62   108203

Peace, peace, glorious peace
(Teasley) R I came defiled
                              108204

Peace, peace on earth, good will
to men ("H. L. W. ") R So sweet
and clear   108205

Peace, peace, sweet peace (Bilhorn) R There comes to my
heart one sweet strain 108206

Peace! Peace! wonderful peace
(Cornell) R Far away in the
depths of my spirit tonight
                              108207

Peace, perfect peace have they
who trust in God (Wine) AS
307   108208

Peace, perfect peace, in this
dark world of sin (Bickersteth)
A436; B405; D674; E468; F358;
G354; I528; J571; K413; L465;
R420; S301; T420; U231; V391;
W444; AD268; AE229; AG205;
AK245; AL285; AM590; AO364;
AP438; AR337; AS309; AV298;
AW256; AZ1; BA690; BB311;
BF387; BR409; BV422; BY584;
BZ   108209

Peace! perfect peace! the gift
of God within (Hawkes) BX275
                              108210

Peace that passeth understanding
(Montgomery) AZ982   108211

Peace through the cross shall
come (Pounds) AS366 108212

Peace to soothe our bitter woe
(Grundtvig) J200; O49; P210
                              108213

Peace, troubled soul, thou need'st
not fear (Pocket hymn book,
1786) H127   108214

Peacefully lay her down to rest

(---) AX618; AY169   108215

Peacefully round us the shadows
are falling (Blatchford) AB
32; AC21; AE45; AL558; AR
57   108216

Peal out the watchword (Havergal) R True-hearted, whole-
hearted   108217

People, look East, the time is
near (Farjeon) AQ281; BG133
                              108218

People of the living God (Montgomery) V441; AX155; AZ
85   108219

Personent hodie voces puerulae
(Piae cantiones) BG78
                              108220

Peter, faithless, thrice denies
(---) AZ862   108221

Pie Jesu Domine (Henry) R
Unto him, for whom, this
day   108222

Pie Jesu Domine, dona eis
requiem (Latin) BO212;
BQ251   108223

Pilgrim on earth, home and
heaven are within thee ("P.
M. ") BE278   108224

Pilgrims, on! The day is dawning (---) BB373   108225

Pity them, pity them, Christians at home (Haskell) R
Over the ocean wave 108226

Place your hand in the nail-
scarred hand (McKinney) R
Have you failed   108227

Planted in Christ, the living
Vine (Smith) AO449 108228

Pleasant are thy courts above
(Lyte) A392; B467; D489;
E469; F240; J184; K422;
N326; O32; R441; V12; W
235; AL200; AO3; AP317;
AZ1045; BA333; BR309;
BV563; BY280   108229

Pleasure it is to hear (Cornish)
AQ325; BG129   108230

Pledging our lives and our
strength to the cause
(Mayer) BH149   108231

Plunged in a gulf of dark
despair (Watts) H225; I242;
V222   108232

Ponder thou the cross all holy
(Washburne) AZ644   108233
Poor soul, the centre of my sin-
ful earth (Shakespeare) X622
                          108234
Popule meus quid feci tibi?
(Breviary) BQ192   108235
Portal of the world's salvation
(Latin, 15th c) E229   108236
Pour down thy Spirit from above
(Romanis) BY521 X Pour forth
thy Spirit   108237
Pour forth thy Spirit from above
(Romanis) BV427; BY521
                          108238
Pour out thy Spirit from on high
(Montgomery) Q490; W333;
X298; AE345; AK351; AL236;
AP367; AR521; AS446; AW295;
AX636; AY437; AZ351; BA315;
BV413; BY351; BZ   108239
Pour thy blessings, Lord, like
showers (Kimball) I693 108240
Praise and honor to the Father
(Kretzmann) Lp.743; M519
                          108241
Praise be to the Father, to the
Son, and Holy Spirit (---) R
Praise ye the Father   108242
Praise for every scene distress-
ing (West) AZ939; BA123
                          108243
Praise God for ever, Boundless
is His favor (Augusta) AZ
1206   108244
Praise God from whom all blessings
flow (Ken) A139; B25; D192;
E257; F23; G616; Hp.9; I718;
J602; K449; L15; M568; N664;
O655-5; P36; Q644; R544; S
suppl.94; T457; U487; W709;
X413; Y387; Z611; AA578;
AB11; AC334; AD5; AE473;
AF514; AG324; AH570; AI448;
AL625; AMp.16; AN499; AP
816; AR632; AS497; AT514;
AU481; AV408; AW618; AX11;
AY410; AZ309; BA916; BB683;
BC214; BF174; BL79; BM93;
BRp.467; BV64; BY694; BZ
                          108245
Praise God the Lord, ye sons of
men (Hermann) Q105; AA157
                          108246
Praise God, the Love we all
may share (Lyttle) AN500;
AQ37   108247
Praise God, this hour of sorrow
(Heermann) O600; P425
                          108248
Praise God, ye servants of the
Lord (U.P. Psalter, 1912)
R19; T213; AJ306   108249
Praise Him, praise Him, all
his children praise Him
(Dearmer) X386f; AE437;
AL594; AR465; AT511; AU
306; AW426; BK2; BY753
                          108250
Praise Him, praise Him, all
ye little children (Dearmer)
EA437 X Praise Him, praise
Him, all his children praise
Him   108251
Praise Him! praise Him!
Jesus our blessed Redeemer
(Crosby) AH313; AM683; AS
112; AT137; AU355; AV326;
AW438; BB645; BY215
                          108252
Praise, honor, majesty For
Thy great victory (---) AZ
1113   108253
Praise Jehovah, all ye nations
(U.P. Book of Psalms,
1871) AJ315; AM29; AP105
                          108254
Praise Jehovah for His love
(U.P. Psalter, 1912) AJ376
                          108255
Praise, Lord, for thee in Zion
waits (Lyte) L54; U478; V
618; AM114; AV67; BI117
                          108256
Praise, my soul, the King of
heaven (Lyte) A282; B258;
D458; E470; F365; G77; H
17; J160; K289; N327; O9;
P2; R31; S14; U6; V513; W
21; X623; Z259; AD21; AE
22; AF16; AG8; AI3; AK3;
AL17; AM70; AP91; AR34;
AS7; AT18; AV31; AY424;
BA652; BE280; BF213; BL
83; BR55; BV247; BY23;
BZ   108257

Praise now creative Mind (Mc-
Kenzie) BE275   108258
Praise now your God, all ye
peoples (Brucker) BL43
                                 108259
Praise, O my heart, to you (Tor-
rence) AQ2   108260
Praise, O my heart, with praise
from depth and height (Tor-
rence) AQ3   108261
Praise, O praise our God and
King (Baker) F481; K487;
Q570; S463; W620; AA297;
AF463; AY438; BA866; BB10;
BR486; BV650   108262
Praise, O praise our God and
King (Baker) X Let us with
a gladsome mind (Milton)
                                 108263
Praise, O praise our heavenly
King (Trend) BR485 108264
Praise, O praise the Lord of the
harvest (Hamilton) BV651;
BY728   108265
Praise, O Sion, praise thy
Master (St Thomas Aquinas)
F622 X Laud, O Sion, thy sal-
vation   108266
Praise our Father for this Sunday
(Chao) R75   108267
Praise our glorious King and Lord
(Thompson) Lp.742; AZ1054;
BA917   108268
Praise our God above (Chao) AF
487   108269
Praise our great and gracious
Lord (Auber) BE281 X O
praise our great and gracious
Lord   108270
Praise the Almighty, my soul
adore Him (Herrnschmidt) Q26
                                 108271
Praise the Father, earth and
heaven (---) Lp.743; AZ262
                                 108272
Praise the Father throned in
heaven (---) Lp.744   108273
Praise the God of all creation
(Conder) Lp.743; N669; AZ
254, 973; BA919   108274
Praise the God of our salvation
(Conder) AZ254 X Praise the
God of all creation   108275

Praise the Lord; bounteously
He deals with thee (Foster)
AZ714; BA262   108276
Praise the Lord, each tribe
and nation (Franck) N289
                                 108277
Praise the Lord, for He is
good (U.P. Psalter, 1912)
R115; T203; AJ292
                                 108278
Praise the Lord! from the
deeds of martyrs bold (---)
AZ721   108279
Praise the Lord, His glories
show (Lyte) R4; S12; W16;
Z112; AD14; AE23; AF19;
AL24; AP134; AR35; AZ68;
BA659; BB16   108280
Praise the Lord in heavenly
places (U.P. Psalter, 1912)
AJ405   108281
Praise the Lord of heaven;
praise Him in the height
(Browne) E534; F381; J427;
K288; M639; N652; X414;
AN4; AP132; BM13   108282
Praise the Lord! one accord,
sound throughout (Stein)
BH130   108283
Praise the Lord, praise the
Lord (Crosby) R To God be
the glory   108284
Praise the Lord; Praise the
Lord Bounteously He deals
with thee (Foster) BA262
X Praise the Lord, bounteous-
ly He deals   108285
Praise the Lord that He has
built (Aaberg) M88 108286
Praise the Lord through every
nation (Feith) A351; B262;
O364; AZ1107; BA912; BR
351; BV275   108287
Praise the Lord who reigns
above (Wesley) AD15; BZ
                                 108288
Praise the Lord with heart and
voice (Cannon) BC149
                                 108289
Praise the Lord with hearts and
voices (Rist) AZ1084
                                 108290
Praise the Lord! ye heavens,

adore Him (Foundling Hospital Coll. 1796) E535; F368; G11; H19; J407; K300; L84; N292; O12; R3; S10; U10; V515; W 35; X624; Z110; AB39; AC30; AD16; AE13; AF13; AG2; AL 31; AM16; AN2; AO57; AP133; AR36; AT9; AV38; AW16; BA 18; BE282; BF214; BI29; BK 50; BR59, 70; BV29; BX11; BY24; BZ   108291

Praise the Name of God most high (---) Lp. 742; AZ1255; BA920   108292

Praise the Rock of our salvation (Webb) O77; BR220   108293

Praise the Saviour, all ye nations (Francis) I649   108294

Praise the Saviour, now and ever (Fortunatus) J104; N135; P200; AI423; AM174   108295

Praise the Saviour, we who know Him (Kelly) AZ428   108296

Praise thou the Lord, O my soul, sing praises (Herrnschmidt) AF17; AK6; AW513a   108297

Praise to God, almighty Maker (Robinson) BY299   108298

Praise to God and thanks we bring (Gannett) AH492 X Praise to God, your praises bring   108299

Praise to God, immortal praise (Barbauld) A140; B420; D192; F485; H519; K485; L553; N572; Q572; U479; Z595; AA298; AE424; AF464; AH490; AK435; AM112; AN143; AO581; AR598; AS424; AT14; AU251; AX633; AY20; AZ43; BA865; BD26; BF652; BK138; BR488; BX176   108300

Praise to God in the highest! Bless us, O Father (Russian trad. 1815) BG107   108301

Praise to God, the great Creator (Fawcett) AZ248   108302

Praise to God who reigns above (Benson) F565   108303

Praise to God, your praises bring (Gannett) AF458; AH492; AN140; AQ308; BD199; BX178   108304

Praise to Mary, endless praise

(St Alfonso M de' Liguori) R Uplift the voice and sing   108305

Praise to our God, who with love never swerving (Gray) W676   108306

Praise to our God, whose bounteous hand (Ellerton) W634   108307

Praise to the Father, the glorious King of creation (Neander) O387; P233   108308

Praise to the heavenly Wisdom (Ellerton) B275; D155   108309

Praise to the Holiest in the height (Newman) A343; B 259; D453; F185; J411; S 40app.; W32; X625; AF497; AL14; AP153; BA43; BL88; BN199; BO1; BQ142; BV160; BY216   108310

Praise to the living God (Jewish doxology) A286; Y300; Z124; AN1; AQ6; BH54; BX17; BZ   108311

Praise to the Lord! He is King over all creation (Neander) AO66 X Praise to the Lord, the Almighty   108312

Praise to the Lord, the Almighty (Neander) A279; E536; F382; G60; J408; K286; M490; N324; O5; P3; Q39; R1; S6; W22; X626; Z98; AA63; AB 40; AC35; AD13; AE1; AF15; AG3; AI1; AK8; AL9; AM50; AN7; AO66; AQ7; AR37; AT 6; AW515; BB12; BC150; BF172; BK49; BL84; BM1; BN62; BV246; BY25; BZ   108313

Praise to the man, who communed with Jehovah (Phelps) BC147   108314

Praise to Thee and adoration (Kingo) J194; O53; Q401   108315

Praise to Thee, O God, for cities (Schloerb) AE414   108316

Praise to Thee, O Lord, we render (---) AZ1389; BA644

108317
Praise to Thee, thou great
    Creator (Fawcett) V514; AZ246
                                    108318
Praise waits for thee in Zion;
    All men shall worship there
    (U.P. Psalter, 1912) T116;
    AJ170; AM306   108319
Praise waits for thee in Zion,
    Lord; To thee vows shall be
    paid (Scottish Psalter, 1650)
    AL656; AP54; AW590   108320
Praise waits in Zion Lord, for
    thee, And unto thee shall vows
    be paid (U.P. Psalter, 1912)
    AJ166   108321
Praise waits in Zion, Lord, for
    thee, There we will pay our
    vow (U.P. Psalter, 1912)
    AJ172   108322
Praise we Christ, the King, the
    Strength of all (---) BQ335
                                    108323
Praise we God the Father's name
    (Alington) BY45   108324
Praise we now the God of heaven
    (Moxley) BY729   108325
Praise we our God upon His throne
    (Weisse) BN51   108326
Praise we our God with joy
    (Grignon) BQ141   108327
Praise we the Lord and bless
    His name forever (Luther) M46;
    Q313   108328
Praise we the Lord, for His
    mercy endureth forever (Neander)
    BE283   108329
Praise we the Lord this day
    (Murray's Hymnal, 1852) A118;
    B276; D158; F546; Q274; BV
    438   108330
Praise we the Lord, who made all
    beauty (Wilson) X627; AC224;
    BG164   108331
Praise ye Jehovah! praise the
    Lord most holy (Campbell) I20;
    O23; W34; AP157; AZ1223; BA
    654   108332
Praise ye our Father for His lov-
    ing kindness (Charles) BI20
    X Praise ye the Father 108333
Praise ye, praise ye the Lord,
    All creation in accord (Lyon)

AQ31   108334
Praise ye, praise ye the Lord,
    In yonder heavenly height
    (U.P. Psalter, 1912) R98;
    T292; AJ404; AM108
                                    108335
Praise ye the Father for his
    loving kindness (Charles)
    J421; P17; AK14; AO76;
    BB9; BI20   108336
Praise ye the Father! Let every
    heart give thanks to Him
    (---) AU472   108337
Praise ye the Lord; all nature
    join (Watts) V522   108338
Praise ye the Lord among His
    saints (U.P. Psalter, 1912)
    T293; AJ406   108339
Praise ye the Lord, for He is
    good (Norton) T201; AJ290
                                    108340
Praise ye the Lord! for it is
    good His mighty acts to
    magnify (Moise) AH156; BH
    65   108341
Praise ye the Lord; for it is
    good. Praise to our God to
    sing (Scottish Psalter,
    1650) AL690; AP130 108342
Praise ye the Lord, for it is
    good to sing unto our God
    (U.P. Psalter, 1912) R36;
    T291; AJ403   108343
Praise ye the Lord, His praise
    proclaim (U.P. Psalter, 1912)
    T289; AJ401   108344
Praise ye the Lord, His saints
    Who throng His courts
    (U.P. Psalter, 1912) AJ412
                                    108345
Praise ye the Lord! My heart
    shall join (Watts) BC277
                                    108346
Praise ye the Lord! Praise ye
    the Lord most holy (Camp-
    bell) BI45   108347
Praise ye the Lord; Praise ye
    the Lord; Praise ye [4 times]
    (Bible) AU474   108348
Praise ye the Lord, the Almighty
    (Neander) R1 X Praise to the
    Lord   108349
Praise ye the Lord! 'tis good to

raise (Watts) BB14   108350
Praise ye the Lord; with my
whole heart (Scottish Psalter,
1650) AP99   108351
Praise ye the Lord, ye Gentiles
all (Vulpius. Ein schöngeistliche
G.B. 1609) M113   108352
Praise ye the Lord, he hosts
above (U.P. Psalter, 1912)
T455; AJ411   108353
Praise ye the Lord, ye saints be-
low (U.P. Psalter, 1912) AJ
412   108354
Praise ye the Lord, ye immortal
choirs (Watts) H107   108355
Praise ye the Lord, ye servants
of the Lord (Apostolic constitu-
tions, 3d c) J601   108356
Praises, thanks, and adoration
(Swertner) AZ1105; BA918
                     108357
Praises to Him whose love has
given (Bonar) AZ393   108358
Pray for the dead! at noon and
eve (---) BO144   108359
Pray, pray in the old-time way
(Brown) AX359   108360
Pray that Jerusalem may have
(Scottish Psalter, 1650) X628
                     108361
Pray when the morn is breaking
(Simpson) E473; X629; AW180
                     108362
Pray when the morn unveileth
(Moise) BH8   108363
Pray, without ceasing, pray
(Wesley) H53; AZ1321 108364
Prayer is appointed to convey
(Hart) I502   108365
Prayer is the heart's sincere
desire (Montgomery) BE284
X Prayer is the soul's sincere
                     108366
Prayer is the soul's sincere
desire (Montgomery) A419;
E474; G303; H47; I497; J458;
M62; N307; O361; P18; Q454;
R391; U358; V463; X630; Z335;
AA398; AE239; AG225; AH354;
AI227; AN234; AO314; AP493;
AQ91; AR285; AS47; AT336;
AU264; AV182; AW184; AX355;
AY46; AZ157; BA603; BB319*

BC220; BE284; BF362; BV
611; BX276; BY340; BZ
                     108367
*with Coleridge Refrain: "He
prayeth best"
Prayer is the soul's sincere
desire (Montgomery) with
ref. He prayeth best (Cole-
ridge) BB319   108368
Prayer to a heart of lowly dove
(Tilak) BY341   108369
Prayer with our waking thought
ascends (Brewer) BE287
                     108370
Previous Bible; what a treasure
(Newton) AZ614   108371
Precious child, so sweetly
sleeping (Hoppe) N42; P137
                     108372
Precious Jesus, O to love thee
(---) AS208   108373
Precious memories, unseen
angels (Wright) AX559
                     108374
Precious, more precious (Cros-
by) R O, the unsearchable
                     108375
Precious Name, O how sweet
(Baxter) R Take the Name
of Jesus with you   108376
Precious, precious blood of
Jesus (Havergal) H245; L
420   108377
Precious promise God hath
given (Niles) AU90; AV356;
AX492   108378
Precious Savior, dear Redeemer
(Palmer) BC109   108379
Precious word from God in
heaven (Schmolck) M32
                     108380
Preist Gott, der allen Segen
Gibt! (Thomas Ken) AY50d
                     108381
Prepare the way, O Zion!
(Franzén) J9; M601; N1
                     108382
Prepare your lamps, stand
ready (Laurenti) AZ1116 X
Rejoice, rejoice believers
                     108383
Present with the two or three
(Freer) W452; BV613

108384

Present your bodies to the Lord
(Barton) AZ1429; BA467
108385

Preserve in fullest measure
(Gryphius) M31   108386

Preserve thy word, O Saviour
(Gryphius) Q264   108387

Press on, dear traveler, press
thou on (Bell) BE288   108388

Press on, press on, ye sons of
light (Gaskell) U293; Y151;
AN315; BD151; BE290; BF636;
BX370   108389

Primo dierum omnium (St Gregory
the Great) BJ31b   108390

Prince of Peace, control my will
(Dana) D613; G216; I337; L
472; V415; AX421; BB117
108391

Print thine image pure and holy
(Kingo) J71   108392

Proclaim the tidings near and far
(Smith) AR188; AS148   108393

Promptement levez-vous, mon
voison (French trad carol)
BG166b   108394

Prophets, teachers, true record-
ers (Dearmer) X212   108395

Prostrate, dear Jesus, at thy
feet (Stennett) V292   108396

Protect and save me, O my God
(U.P. Psalter, 1912) T108;
AJ157   108397

Publish glad tidings (Thomson) R
O Sion haste, thy mission high
fulfilling   108398

Puer natus in Bethlehem (Latin,
14th c) BM66; BN8   108399

Puer nobis nascitur (Latin carol,
15th c) BG92; BQ159   108400

Pure and free from all corrup-
tion (Horn) AE180   108401

Purer in heart, O God, help me
to be (Davison [or Davidson])
Z343; AR410; AS312; AT369;
AU272; AX386; AY67   108402

Purer yet and purer, I would be
in mind (Goethe) U260; V406;
AE184; AH361; AK447; AO298;
AR310; AS314; AV192; BB388;
BD103   108403

Put down your feet and you shall

feel (Wheelock) AQ156
108404

Put forth, O God, thy Spirit's
might (Robbins) A380; J243;
R477; AD396; AE318; AR
500   108405

Put on the armor of our God
(---) AI324   108406

Put on the whole armour of
pure consecration (Baum)
BE292   108407

Put thou thy trust in God (Gerhardt) F310; J579; W547
108408

Put thou thy trust in God (Gerhardt) X Commit thou all
that grieves   108409

Put your shoulder to the wheel
(Thompson) R The world has
need of willing men 108410

Q

Quae est ista (Latin) BQ222
108411

Queen and Mother, many hearts
cast themselves (---) BO107
108412

Queen of the Rosary, Virgin
thou fairest (---) BP83
108413

Queen, when the earth was first
hurled into space (Latin,
20th c) BN147   108414

Quelle est cetter odeur agréable
(French trad carol) BG164b
108415

Quem pastores laudavere (Latin,
1410) BG79   108416

Quest of the ages, goal of men
(Patton) AQ203   108417

Qui creavit coelum. Lully, lully,
lu (English trad carol, 1425)
BG67 X He who made the
starry skies   108418

Qui regnas in perpetum (Latin)
BQ253   108419

Quick sympathy, hands that
brought health (Dearmer)
X341   108420

Quiet, Lord, my froward heart
(Newton) U39; V392; AO616;
AP499; AZ1263; BE291; BR

256   108421
Quittez, pasteurs, vos brebis
(French trad carol) BG144b
                               108422
Quoi, ma voisine, est-tu fâchée?
(Colletet) BG108b   108423

R

Raise the standard high, Sound
the gathering cry (Belden) BB
500   108424
Raise your voices to the Lord
(Stephens) BC154   108425
Raise your voices, vales and
mountains (St Alfonso M de
Liguori) BO70; BQ90   108426
Raised between the earth and
heaven (Smith) D303; N583
                               108427
Rank by rank again we stand
(Skrine) AN465; AQ258 108428
Reach out thy scepter, King of
love (Zinzendorf, E.D.) AZ
678; BA544   108429
Ready to go, ready to stay (---)
R Ready to suffer grief or
pain   108430
Ready to suffer grief or pain
(---) AT439; AU300; AX401
                               108431
Rebels, who had dared to show
(U.P. Psalter, 1912) T204
                               108432
Receive, O Lord, in heaven above
(St Ephraim the Syrian) E194
                               108433
Rede, liebster Jesu, rede (Anna
Sophia, of Hesse-Darmstadt)
BT296   108434
Redeemed from guilt, redeemed
from fears (Lyte) AO307
                               108435
Redeemed, how I love to proclaim
it (Crosby) AT203; AU92;
AX316; BB635   108436
"Redeemed! redeemed!" O, sing
the joyful strain (Whittle) AY
514   108437
Redeemed, restored, forgiven
(Baker) O404; P282; Q32
                               108438
Redeemer of Israel, Our only de-

light (Swain) BC195 X O
Thou, in whose Presence
                               108439
Redeemer of mankind, God of
all grace (Meyer) AZ519
                               108440
Redemption! O wonderful story
(Sayford) AX315   108441
Regard my grief and rescue me
(U.P. Psalter, 1912) T244;
AJ340   108442
Reges de Saba veniunt (Latin,
14th c) BM67   108443
Regína caeli, jubila (Latin,
17th c) BN48; BQ207
                               108444
Regina caeli Laetáre (Latin,
14th c) BM86; BN47; BO
300; BP33; BQ204   108445
Regnum mundi (Breviary) BQ
217   108446
Rejoice, all ye believers
(Laurenti) U120 X Rejoice,
rejoice believers   108447
Rejoice and be glad! He lives
who was slain (Dearmer)
X161   108448
Rejoice and be glad! The Re-
deemer hath come (Bonar)
BY170   108449
Rejoice and be merry in songs
and in mirth (Church-Gal-
lery Book) BG25   108450
Rejoice and be merry, set sor-
row aside (English trad carol)
R A virgin most pure, as the
prophets   108451
Rejoice, and offer thanks to
God (Mayer) BH259 108452
Rejoice, believer, in the Lord
(Newton) BV529; BY567
                               108453
Rejoice in love we know and
share (Lyttle) AQ42
                               108454
Rejoice, my heart, be glad and
sing (Gerhardt) Q535
                               108455
Rejoice, O land, in God thy
might (Bridges) A520; E
475; F582; X631; AF430;
AN389; BJ54; BV663; BY
651   108456

Rejoice, O people, in the mount-
ing years (Bayley) AF304;
BY389   108457
Rejoice, our nature Christ as-
sumes (St Ambrose) AZ292;
BA60   108458
Rejoice, rejoice, believers
(Laurenti) A4; B61; D43; H
206; K13; L207; M341; N17;
O602; P113; Q72; R231; S
115; U120; V179; AE138; AK99;
AM233; AO112; AR215; AS166;
AZ810, 1116; BA102   108459
Rejoice, rejoice this happy morn
(Boye) J32; O183; P139; Q79;
AI417   108460
Rejoice, rejoice, ye Christians
(Madegburg, Geistliche lieder.
1540) K30; N24; O197   108461
Rejoice, the Lord is King (Wes-
ley) A350; B521; D457; E476;
F216; G171; H185; I178; J436;
K126; L124; O348; R140; S193;
V201; W135; X632; Y346; Z260;
AD179; AE24; AF204; AG110;
AI90; AL112; AM226; AO70;
AP223; AS156; AT108; AW121;
AZ1183; BA251; BC151; BD121;
BR193; BV210; BY190; BZ
                        108462
Rejoice! The year upon its way
(St Hilary) E151; BY238
                        108463
Rejoice today with one accord
(Baker) E537; O17; AZ1030;
BR489; BV25; BX315   108464
Rejoice, ye dead, where'er your
spirits dwell (Bridges) X208
                        108465
Rejoice, ye people, homage give
(U. P. Psalter, 1912) AJ129;
AM61   108466
Rejoice, ye pure in heart
(Plumptre) A579; B537; D520;
E644; F635; G358; I421; J555;
N588; R407; S297; Y199; Z418;
AB19; AC27; AD272; AE7; AF
345; AG209; AH183; AK7; AM502;
AN13; AO62; AP608; AR336;
AT17; AU285; AV47; AW156;
BA124; BB17; BD119; BF170;
BK66; BZ   108467
Rejoice, ye Saints of latter days

(Gabbott) BC207   108468
Rejoice, ye sons of men (How)
D152   108469
Rejoice, ye sons of men alway!
(Freund) AA151   108470
Religion is the chief concern
(Fawcett) I314; V227
                        108471
Remember all God's children
(Dearmer) AW436 X Re-
member all the people
                        108472
Remember all the people
(Dearmer) A262; J317; R495;
X369; Z528; AE363; AF484;
AW436; BW436; BY390
                        108473
Remember Him, the Only One
(Lazarus) BH44   108474
Remember, holy Mary, 'Twas
never heard or known (---)
BQ85   108475
Remember, Lord, thy works of
old (Baker) AI359   108476
"Remember me," the Master
said (Frothingham) AH508;
AN443; AQ165; BX477
                        108477
Remember not, O God, the
sins of long ago (U.P.
Psalter, 1912) AJ217; AM
417   108478
Remember, O thou man, O thou
man, O thou man (Ravens-
croft. Melismata) BG42
                        108479
Remember thy Creator now
(Burton) V648; AS405; AZ
161; BA839   108480
Remember thy Creator, while
thou art (Buerge) AX560
                        108481
Remember us poor Mayers all
(English trad carol) BG49
                        108482
Renew me, O Eternal Light
(Ruopp) Q398; AA350
                        108483
Repent, the kingdom draweth
nigh (Hoppe) N15; P116
                        108484
Rerum Deus tenax bigor (Latin,
6th c) BJ100b   108485

Rescue the perishing, care for
the dying (Crosby) G250; H
395; I697; V770; W681; AG
142: AH417; AL499; AO649;
AP594; AR466; AS377; AT207;
AU80; AV329; AW497; AX194;
AY523; BB623; BY522; BZ
                                108486

Résonet in laudibus (Latin, 14th
c) BN9; BP20; BQ156   108487

Rest for the toiling hand (Bonar)
AZ1344   108488

Rest from thy labor, rest (Montgomery) AZ1300   108489

Rest in the Lord and be thou
still (U.P. Psalter, 1912) AJ
96   108490

Rest in the Lord, my soul (Babcock) BH91   108491

Rest of the weary, joy of the
sad (Monsell) E579; W174;
AL130; AP233; BR320; BY217
                                108492

Rest of the weary! Thou thyself
art resting now (Franck) K107
                                108493

Rest remaineth, O, so sweet
(Hymns of the English Conf.
1880) BR334   108494

Rest, rest for the weary soul
(Naisbitt) BC278   108495

Resting among the cattle mild
(---) BP17   108496

Resting from His work today
(Whytehead) B165; D107; F127;
AO175; AZ1254; BA220 108497

Resting in the silent grave
(LaTrobe) AZ1063   108498

Rett, o Herr Jesu, rett dein'
Ehr' (Heerman) BT265
                                108499

Return, dear Lord, to those who
look (Van Dyke) AB146; BF
333   108500

Return, my roving heart, return
(Doddridge) BR276   108501

Return, O wanderer, return
(Collyer) G195; H253; I255;
L365; Q280; V259; AI193; AO
248; BB221   108502

Return! Return! O wanderer, now
return (Collyer) AI193 X Return, O wanderer, return

                                108503
Reveal thy truth, O Lord
(Hawkes) AN335; BX389
                                108504
Revealing Word, thy light por-
trays (Turner) AT177 108505
Reverently and meekly now
(Townsend) BC280   108506
Revive thy work, O Lord (Mid-
lane) B452; D618; F362; V
583; W679; AM297; AP326;
BV139; BY391   108507
Rex summae majestátis (Man-
uale Cantus sancti. Ratis-
bon, 19th c) BN205 108508
Rich in mercy, Jesus reigns
(Woodworth) BR211 108509
No entries 108510 - 108609
Ride on! ride on in majesty
(Milman) A64; B145; D91;
E620; F99; G125; H162;
I150; J73; K88; L259; M
429; N98; O293; Q162; R188;
S150; T340; W92; X137; Y
349; Z223; AB134; AC115;
AD143; AE105; AF175; AH
282; AI71; AK133; AL85; AM
172; AN182; AO154; AP189;
AR158; AT102; AV103; AW
101; AZ344; BA219; BB127;
BF308; BI101; BR173; BV
167; BX199; BY128; BZ
                     108610
Ride on, ride on, O Saviour-
King (Solberg) P187 108611
Ride on triumphantly! Behold
we lay (Taylor) F599
                     108612
Ring, O ring, ye Christmas
bells (Ham) AN169 108613
Ring, O ye bells, O ring out
ere the daylight advances
(Grundtvig) P124   108614
Ring out, O bell, thy welcome
sound (Bruce) AO466
                     108615
Ring out the old, ring in the
new (Tennyson) R526 X
Ring out, wild bells, to the
wild sky   108616
Ring out, wild bells, to the
wild sky (Tennyson) B444;
G537; R526; S466; U472; X

633; Y324; Z589; AB398; AC
327; AD448; AE423; AF453;
AH495, 496; AK428; AN149;
AO575; AQ305; AR585; AS436;
AT496; AW379; BB514; BC279;
BF646   108617

Ring out, wild bells, to the wild
wild sky (Tennyson) G537 X
Ring out, wild bells, to the
wild sky   108618
Ring out, ye crystal spheres
(Milton) W61; X634   108619
Ring the bells of heaven (Cushing)
AU124   108620
Ringe recht, wenn Gottes Gnade
(Winckler) AY10d; BW563
                                   108621
Rise again, ye lion-hearted (Ger-
man, 1712) Q470   108622
Rise, arise! Rise, arise! Zion
rise to greet thy King (Hoppe)
N6   108623
Rise, children of the kingdom
(Rist) O162   108624
Rise, crowned with light, imperial
Salem rise (Pope) A389; B466;
D487; H484; Q503; S346; U347;
V596; Z477; AA478; AD369;
AI147; AZ455; BA277; BI46; BR
215; BT503   108625
Rise, exalt our Head and King
(Hehl) AZ1034; BA113, 681
                                   108626
Rise, glorious conqueror, rise
(Bridges) I161; AE135; AH305;
AZ1236; BR197   108627
Rise, God! Judge thou the earth
in might (Milton) AN344; BX
383   108628
Rise, help and redeem us (U.P.
Psalter, 1912) AM515 X If we
have forgotten the name of our
God   108629
Rise, Hero bold, from Golgotha!
(Ewald) M246   108630
Rise in the strength of God
(Greenaway) F302   108631
Rise, my soul, adore thy Maker
(Cennick) AZ873; BA772; BV
45; BY682   108632
Rise, my soul, and stretch thy
wings (Seagrave) B114; D512;
G524; H512; I623; L438; N514;

O409; R330; S264; V688; Z
573; AB196; AD303; AG122;
AH363; AN62; AT122; AV
240; AW200; AZ1473; BA
754; BB668; BF381; BR424;
BX322; BZ   108633
Rise, my soul, to watch and
pray (Freystein) M243;
Q446; AA381; AM476 108634
Rise, O Lord, lift up thine
hand (Synnestvedt) BI8-D
                                   108635
Rise, O my soul, pursue the
path (Needham) I404; M
230   108636
Rise, O Salem, rise and shine
(Rist) N68; O223   108637
Rise, thou Light of Gentile
nations (Fick) Q498 108638
Rise, to arms, with prayer
employ you (Arends) Q444
X Christians, prayer may
well   108639
Rise to greet the sun (Chao)
BZ   108640
Rise to the cry of battle
(Greenaway) F497   108641
Rise up, O men of God!
(Merrill) A535; B492; G267;
J541; R352; S401; U274; W
344; X635; Y224; Z374; AB
279; AC254; AD332; AE252;
AF300; AG252; AH459; AK
389; AL378; AN302; AO467;
AP587; AQ218; AR329; AS
363; AT423, 445; AU91, 186;
AW230; BA559; BC332; BD
122; BF482; BK115; BX362;
BY523; BZ   108642
Rise up, O world, the light is
on the hill (Stidger) AE351
                                   108643
Rise up, rise up; you merry
men all (English trad carol)
BG55   108644
Rise ye children of salvation
(Falckner) J556; K202;
O87; Q472   108645
Rock of ages, cleft for me
(Toplady) A471; B217; D336;
E477; F210; G204; H244;
I279; J379; K333; L402; M
181; N422; O27; P284; Q376;

R271; S237; T393; U100; V249;
W413; X636; Y374; Z294; AA
325; AB165; AD209; AE284;
AF358; AG147; AH356; AI137;
AK217; AL267; AM421; AO260;
AP416; AR180; AS211; AT103;
AU171; AV236; AW148; AX521;
AY312; AZ1280; BA434; BB
474; BC382; BE293*; BF353;
BV492; BY458; BZ   108646
*deliberate variant

Rock of ages, let our song
(Stein) AH150; AQ279; BH207
                          108647

Rock of ages, Truth divine (Root)
BE293 X Rock of ages, cleft
for me (Toplady)   108648

Roll on, thou mighty ocean
(Edmeston) AS381; AZ831
                          108649

Roll on, ye stars, exult in youthful prime (Darwin) AQ52
                          108650

Roll out, O song, to God (Sewall)
BI71; BR157   108651

Room for Jesus, King of glory
("L.W.M.") R Have you any
room   108652

Rorate caeli desuper, et nubes
pluant (Bible. Isaiah 45) BN2;
BO146; BP7; BQ291   108653

Rorate caeli de super! Heavens
distill (Dunbar) BG125   108654

Round me falls the night
(Romanis) E272; F35; J237;
K457; Q562; S502; X52; AL563;
BV61   108655

Round Tabor heavenly glories
shone (Zinzendorf, N.L.)
AZ288   108656

Round the earth a message runs
(Struther) X162   108657

Round the Lord in glory seated
(Mant) A269; B207; D387;
J177; K161; O62; S15; U13; V
11; W2; Z156; AD17; AI6, 30;
AM42; AO55; AS6; BA650; BB
74; BI3-D; BY26   108658

Round the throne of glory (---)
AI29   108659

Rouse, then soldiers! Rally
round the standard (Sherwin)
R Sound the battle cry   108660

Rouse, ye Christian workers,
be ye up (MacKay) AX186;
AY529   108661

Rouse ye, rouse ye, face the
foe (Baum) R Rouse ye,
soldiers of the cross
                          108662

Rouse ye, soldiers of the cross
(Baum) BE296   108663

Ruler of the hosts of light
(Breviary. Cluny. 1686)
BR199   108664

Run scheiden wir, ihr herzens-
freund (Unparth.G.B.) AY
36d   108665

Rüstet euch, ihr Christenleute!
(Arends) BT444   108666

S

Sacred Heart in accents burning (Donnelly) BQ66
                          108667

Sacred Heart of Jesus, fount
of love and mercy (---) BQ
59   108668

Sacred Name of Jesus, so
great and holy (Hayn) AZ
526   108669

Sacred the place of prayer and
song (Stephens) BC281
                          108670

Sacris solemniis juncta sint
gaudia (St Thomas Aquinas)
BQ230   108671

Safe home, safe home in port
(St Joseph the Hymnographer)
H501; AB406; AH536; AO556;
AZ1190; BR441   108672

Safe in the arms of Jesus
(Crosby) E580; N608; U207;
V347; W707; AI311; AL507;
AM608; AO637; AP791; AS
483; AU353; AV357; AW313;
AX529; AY173; BB615
                          108673

Safe upon the billowy deep
(Coppée) B417; D309
                          108674

Safe within the arms of Jesus
(Robinson) AY96   108675

Safely, safely gathered in
(Dobree) D246; N607; W328;

BA728   108676

Safely through another week
(Newton) B46; G393; H80;
I69; J185; K428; L38; M6; N
308; O38; Q11; R74; T299; U
437; V59; Z448; AA125; AE
53; AG35; AH161; AI16; AK39;
AL190; AM320; AO12; AP346;
AS37; AT37; AU10; AV9; AW
284; AX64; AY275; AZ1284; BA
385; BB462; BZ   108677

Saint Anthony, we turn to thee
(---) BO140   108678

Saint Joseph, God has chosen you
(Donohue) BM58   108679

Saint Joseph, pride of heaven's
court (Herman) BP91   108680

Saint Mary goes a-seeking (German trad carol) BG179 108681

Saint of God, elect and precious
(Latin, 11th c) E31   108682

Saint of the Sacred Heart, Sweet
teacher of the Word (Faber)
BQ103   108683

St Patrick's Breastplate (St Patrick)
X I bind unto myself today
                                 108684

Saint Stephen was a holy man
(English trad carol) BG26
                                 108685

Saints of God! Lo, Jesu's people
(Riley) E239   108686

Saints of God! the dawn is bright-
ening (Maxwell) D250; P386;
Q502; AA470; AO510; AZ1393;
BA357   108687

Salútis humánae sátor (Latin,
7th c) BP40   108688

Salvation and immortal praise
(Watts) AL629; AP814   108689

Salvation is forever nigh (Watts)
V237   108690

Salvation! O the joyful sound
(Watts) H239; I287; L132; V
235; AY12   108691

Salvation unto us has come
(Speratus) Q377 X To us salvation now is come   108692

Salve, Mater, misericordiae
(Carmelite hymn) BM48; BN
125; BP73; BQ209   108693

Salve, Pater, salvatóris (Latin,
1874) BN167   108694

Salve Regina coelitum (Hermannus Contractus??) BQ
211   108695

Salve, Regina, Mater misericordiae (Hermannus Contractus??) BN142; BO301; BP76;
BQ205   108696

Sancte, venite, corpus Christi
sumite (Bangor Antiphoner,
ca 680) BT307   108697

Sanctify me wholly, Soul of
Christ adored (Latin, 14th c)
BN101   108698

Save me, O God, because the
floods (U.P. Psalter, 1912)
T127; AJ184   108699

Save us waking, O Lord (---)
AR556   108700

Saved by grace, I live to tell
(---) AX324; AY234   108701

Saved by His power divine
(Scholerfield) I've found a
friend   108702

Saved to the uttermost; I am
the Lord's (Kirkpatrick)
AU51   108703

NOTE: "Savior" and "Saviour"
are spelled as in the hymns,
but filed as "Savior"
                                 108704

Saviour, again to thy dear
Name we raise (Ellerton)
A487; B50; D32; E273;
F31; G29; H31; I38; J198;
K437; L62; M17; N363; O
54; P60; Q47; R77; S55; T
301; U451; V23; W301; X53;
Y97; Z128; AA16; AB34; AC
24; AD64; AE34; AF60; AG
16; AH175; AI22; AK32; AL
214; AM316; AN126; AO42;
AP333; AR62; AS61; AT27;
AU252; AV22; AW43; AX74;
AZ439; BA390; BB34; BD21;
BF206; BH177; BK173; BR
109; BV63; BX162; BY702;
BZ   108705

Saviour, all my sins confessing
(Haweis) AA14   108706

Saviour and Regenerator (Cennick) BR75a   108707

Saviour, bless thy word to all

(Breay) AY408   108708
Saviour, blessed Saviour, Listen
while we sing (Thring) A580;
B527; D519; E645; I344; J425;
K564; S202; U74; V405; W476;
Z269; AL315; AM452; AO67;
AP488; AZ761, 763; BA466,
468; BB287; BR510; BY459
                                     108709
Saviour, breathe an evening bless-
ing (Edmeston) A178; B24; D
17; G50; H32; I55; J221; K
467; L22; M577; N554; O559;
P72; Q565; R54; S47; T310;
U469; V40; W285; X54; AA37;
AD55; AE49; AG29; AH173;
AI48; AK60; AL559; AM340;
AO30; AP684; AR58; AS28;
AT34; AU221; AV20; AW38;
AX70; AY285; AZ237; BA790;
BB49; BF197; BI73; BR120;
BZ   108710
Saviour, coming to thee (Warren)
AX301   108711
Saviour eternal! Health and life
of the world unfailing (Latin,
before 11th c) E10   108712
Saviour, for the little one (Thom-
son) D247; N609   108713
Saviour, hear us, we pray (Ells-
worth) G600; AX59   108714
Saviour, I follow on, Guided by
Thee (Robinson) Q422; U202;
V358; AA337; BR386   108715
Saviour, I look to Thee (Hastings)
V355   108716
Savior, I would live for Thee
(Schroll) AS348   108717
Saviour, keep us close to Thee
(Lyon) AY76   108718
Saviour, lead me, lest I stray
(Davis) AH407; AR467; AU104;
AV370; AW502; AY121   108719
Saviour, let thy sanction rest
(Raffles) N529   108720
Saviour, like a shepherd lead us
(Thrupp. Hymns for the young.
1836) A247; B355; D573; G337;
H449; I677; J524; K565; L201;
M624; N644; O571; P361; R380;
S458; U323; V332; W554; Z401;
AD479; AE234; AF327; AG218;
AH402; AI397; AK461; AL434;

AM644; AO621; AP745; AR
296; AS250; AT344; AU13;
AV377; AW395; AX496; AY
128; AZ1413; BA834; BB
394; BF623; BR298; BX529;
BZ   108721
Saviour, more than life to me
(Crosby) G236; H346; I490;
V733; Z397; AH383; AT326;
AU213; AV344; AX422; BZ
                                     108722
Saviour, now the day is ending
(Doudney) J229; K438; L36;
O59; AH172; AL560; AP331;
AZ613; BA791; BR111
                                     108723
Saviour, now with contrite
hearts (Hammer) BA786
                                     108724
Saviour, O Saviour dear
(Evilsizer) R Saviour, we
come to Thee   108725
Savior of my soul, Let me
choose thy goal (Naas) AR
361   108726
Saviour of sinners, now revive
us (Gotter) O171   108727
Saviour of the heathen, come
(St Ambrose) AA141 X
Saviour of the nations, come
                                     108728
Saviour of the nations, come
(St Ambrose) Q95; AA141;
AM165; BP6   108729
Saviour of thy chosen race
(LaTrobe) AZ1251; BA417;
                                     108730
Saviour, quicken many nations
(Coxe) BY392 X Saviour,
sprinkle many nations
                                     108731
Savior, Redeemer, God of Love
(Rose) BI70   108732
Savior, Redeemer of my soul
(Whitney) BC155   108733
Saviour, Saviour, hear my
humble cry (Crosby) R Pass
me not, O gentle Saviour
                                     108734
Saviour, send a blessing to us
(Kelly) AZ1406   108735
Saviour, shed an evening bless-
ing (Edmeston) W54 X

Saviour, breathe an evening
blessing   108736
Saviour, source of every blessing
(Robinson) B243; D442; G23;
H5; I19; K298; L88; N320; P31;
R379; S235; U368; V511; W435;
Z111; AE220; AG9; AH181; AI
4; AK476; AL304; AM400; AO
273; AP447; AR438; AS14; AT
313; AU190; AV223; AW189;
AX35; AY14; AZ961; BA479;
BB291; BC70; BR246; BV17;
BY494; BZ   108737
Saviour, sprinkle many nations
(Coxe) B478; D257; E551; J312;
K223; L337; M103; N365; O114;
Q510; W382; AA477; AL242;
AO520; AP378; AZ972; BA365;
BY392   108738
Saviour, teach me, day by day
(Leeson) A428; B354; D563;
G449; H448; I676; J528; K568;
M159; N654; R457; S452; U322;
W437; X370; Z389; AD481; AE
436; AG299; AH551; AL611;
AM654; AP767; AR403; AS276;
AT291; AV196; AW424; AX418;
AY53; BV545; BY484; BZ
                                108739
Saviour, thee my heart I tender
(Burton) J549; P377; W495;
AL355; AP762; AS406; AW394;
BB427   108740
Saviour, thy dying love Thou
gavest me (Phelps) G219;
H319; I349; J463; L529; N499;
P325; Q403; R311; S396; T378;
U273; V398; Z387; AA353; AD
257; AE215; AF331; AG171;
AH423; AK470; AL478; AM538;
AO641; AP746; AR347; AS278;
AT400; AU149; AV380; AW220;
BA470; BB283; BF453; BV594;
BY485; BZ   108741
Saviour, thy love hath guided
(Mumford) BA804   108742
Saviour, to thee I come (Hott)
AY237   108743
Saviour, visit thy plantation
(Newton) V577; AO429 108744
Saviour, we come to thee (Evil-
sizer) AX34; AY210   108745
Saviour, when in dust to thee

(Grant) A332; B130; D89;
E87; F86; H268; I500; J72;
K82; L235; M408; N96; O
305; Q166; V457; AA213; AK
219; AO270; AP238; AV111;
AW145; AZ1070; BA422; BW
145   108746
Saviour, when night involves
the skies (Gisborne) A469;
B39; D641   108747
Saviour, when we call, O hear
us (Kelly) O271; P177
                                108748
Saviour, while my heart is ten-
der (Burton) P377 X Saviour,
thee my heart I tender
                                108749
Saviour, who didst come to give
(Bartlett) D226   108750
Saviour, who didst healing give
(Rawnsley) E247; F567
                                108751
Saviour, who exalted high (Mant)
BY176 X Son of man, to thee
I cry   108752
Saviour, who thy flock art feed-
ing (Muhlenberg) B343; D207;
H450; J261; K174; L316; M
522; N646; O146; P96; Q631;
S348; V544; AA449; AE328;
AG238; AI161; AO433; AP351;
AZ264; BA823; BF611; BR452
                                108753
Saviour, who thy life didst give
(Lockwood) AB374   108754
Saviour, whom I fain would
love (Toplady) D355   108755
Saviour, whose love is like the
sun (Robbins) AD46; AR338
                                108756
Saw ye my Saviour? Heard ye the
glad sound? (Eddy) BE298
                                108757
Saw ye my Saviour, Saw ye my
Saviour, Saw ye my Saviour
(---) AY253   108758
Saw ye never, in the twilight
(Alexander) A50; B553; D
542; AH274   108759
Say not, "The struggle nought
availeth" (Clough) W536;
X637; Y125; AB301; AN306;
AQ97   108760

Say not they die, those martyr souls (Quin) AN429; AQ76　　108761

Say, sinner! hath a voice within (Hyde) U158; V276　　108762

Scattering precious seed by the wayside (Ogden) AU399; AY 325　　108763

Scattering sunshine all along our way (Smith) R In a world where sorrow Ever will be known　　108764

Schenk mir ein sanft, zerbrochnes herz (Unparth. G.B.) AY44d　　108765

Schier in allen G'schichten g' schreiben staht (Ausbund) BU 3　　108766

Schmücke dich, o liebe Seele (Franck) BT305; BW552　　108767

Schönster Herr Jesu, Herrscher aller Herren (Münster Gesangbuch. 1677) BT657; BW97　　108768

School thy feelings, O my brother (Penrose) BC340　　108769

Science, the angel with the flaming sword (Lynch) BE297　　108770

Scorn not the slightest word or deed (Adams. Hymns for Christian devotion. 1846) U334; V494; AN286; BX341　　108771

Seal my heart with thine impressure (Kingo) P64　　108772

Seal us, O Holy Spirit (Meredith) R238; U287; V742; AT175; AU331　　108773

Seal us, seal us, Seal us just now (Meredith) R Seal us, O Holy Spirit　　108774

Search me, God, and know my heart (Wendell) J378; N496　　108775

Search me, O God, and know my heart (Taylor) AZ165　108776

Search me, O God, my actions try (Bottome) BV148　198777

Search me, O Lord, and try this heart of mine (Crosby) AE233; AR297; AS224　　108778

Searcher of hearts, from mine

erase (Morris) AI354; AM 455; AR289; AS74　　108779

See, amid the winter's snow (Caswall) K532; W51; AM 158; BG190; BO153; BQ5; BV119; BY107　　108780

See, Father, thy beloved Son (Jervois) E328　　108781

See from the rock the waters bursting (Hayn) AZ998　　108782

See Him in raiment rent (Monro) E656 X In His own raiment clad　　108783

See him in the garden lone (Sanders) AR162; AS133　　108784

See how great a flame aspires (Wesley) G500; I643; AL246; AW339; BZ　　108785

See how the rising sun (Scott) L11　　108786

See! in yonder manger low (Caswall) W51 X See amid the winter's snow　　108787

See Israel's gentle Shepherd stand [s] (Doddridge) G 407; H454; I230; M523; N 534; U321; V543; AE329; AL219; AM350; AO432; AP 349; AZ225; BA286; BB411; BR451; BT302; BZ　　108788

See Jesus seated 'midst His own (LaTrobe) AZ894　　108789

See, my soul, God ever blest (Hammond) AZ51; BA153　　108790

See, O God, we children come (Philipson) BH147　108791

See the Conqueror mounts in triumph (Wordsworth) A103; B522; D126; E145; F148; J 112; K120; N147; P223; Q 218; S173; V170; X173; AA 231; AE137; AI89; AM211; AO190; AP226; AZ968-969; BA242; BR189; BV208; BY 171　　108792

See the destined day arise! (Fortunatus) A67; B146; D 97; E110; F101　108793

See the leaves around us falling (Horne) BB491   108794

See the Lord, thy Keeper, stand
   (Wesley) BX323   108795

See the mighty angel flying
   (Thompson) BC342   108796

See the morning sun ascending
   (Parkin) BZ   108797

See the righteous marching on
   (Rivers) R As Sion's pilgrims
   in accord   108798

See the shining dewdrops (Major.
   Book of praise) AL591; AP724;
   AW407   108799

See what a living stone (Watts)
   1869   L 123   108800

See, world, thy life assailed
   (Gerhardt) AA205   108801

See not afar for beauty   (Savage)
   Y12; AB296; AC225; AN40;
   AQ174; BF384   108802

Seek where ye may to find a way
   (Weissel) Q383   108803

Seek ye a Patron to defend your
   cause (Breviary, Venice, 1798)
   BQ98   108804

Seek ye first, not earthly pleasure
   (Taylor) BV629   108805

"Seek ye first the Kingdom"
   (Elliott) BY554   108806

Seek ye who will some other way
   (Weissel) M536   108807

Seele, du musst munter werden!
   (Canitz) BW27   108808

Seems it in my anguish lone
   (Tietze) AA516   108809

Segne, Herr, mit deinem Geiste
   (Lieder-Perlen. Concordia Publ.
   19th c) BT419   108810

Sei Lob und Ehr' dem höchsten
   Gut (Schütz) BT19; BW512
                          108811

Seliger Friede, Köstliche Gab'
   (Poppe) AW157b; BW157
                          108812

Send a great revival in my soul
   R Coming now to thee   108813

Send a revival, O Christ, my
   Lord (McKinney) AT333
                          108814

Send down thy truth, O God (Sill)
   G181; Y242; Z271; AB182; AC
   268; AD333; AF237; AN288;
   AQ124; AR301; BD113; BF430;

BX390   108815

Send forth, O God, thy light
   and truth (Adams) Y33;
   AD11   108816

Send forth the gospel! Let it
   run (Fox) BV329; BY393
                          108817

Send me light! Send me light
   (Bonar) R Lord, give me
   light   108818

Send, O God, a gentle shower
   (Kramer) AA248   108819

Send, O Lord, thy Holy Spirit
   (Lieder-Perlen. Concordia,
   19th c) M534; Q491 108820

Send out thy light and thy truth
   (Bible. Psalm 43) Z624;
   AB416; AH556; AI25; AR631;
   BF674   108821

Send out thy light and truth, O
   God (Montgomery) AZ1029;
   BA348   108822

Send the light! the blessed gospel light (Gabriel) R There's
   a call comes ringing 108823

Send thou, O Lord, to every
   place (Gates) Q506; S383;
   U402; AA484; AK379; AM379;
   AP365; BV322; BY352 108824

Serene I fold my hands and
   wait (Burroughs) AQ186
                          108825

Serene will be our days and
   bright (Wordsworth) AQ158
                          108826

Servant of all, to toil for man
   (Wesley) BY632; BZ
                          108827

Servant of God, remember
   (Prudentius) E104   108828

"Servant of God, well done!
   Rest from thy loved employ"
   (Montgomery) I597; V670;
   AZ1339; BA314; BR379
                          108829

Servant of God, well done! Thy
   glorious warfare's past
   (Wesley) G518; H500; I593;
   AV295; BZ   108830

Servants of God, in joyful lays
   (Montgomery) H27   108831

Servants of God, or sons
   (Arnold) X213   108832

bringing (Latin, 1410) BV111
                                108869
Shepherds, in the field abiding
(Woodward) F594; BP19
                                108870
Shepherds left their flocks astray-
ing (Latin, 1410) BG79
                                108871
Shepherds now go we to yon fair
Bethlehem town (Dickinson)
BK148   108872
Shepherds, shake off your drowsy
sleep (French trad) BD225;
BG133b   108873
Shew me thy ways, O Lord (Scot-
tish Psalter, 1650) AL639; AW
581   108874
Shine forth, O Sun of boundless
love (Browne) BR13a X Come
gracious Spirit, heavenly Dove
                                108875
Shine in me, yes, shine in me
(Oatman) R In this world of
sin and care   108876
Shine in my heart, Lord Jesus
(Griffith) AX385; AY81
                                108877
Shine, mighty God, on Sion shine
(Watts) V619   108878
Shine on our souls, eternal God!
(Doddridge) L193; N471
                                108879
Shine on, thou Star of Bethlehem
(Becker) M607   108880
Shine thou upon us, Lord (Eller-
ton) D587; K386; AL235; AM
631; AO451; AP369; AR533;
AS389; AW293; BA888; BY353
                                108881
Shi-vee-see A-do-noy l'neg-dee
(Jewish traditional) BH336
                                108882
Sh'ma Yisroayl! A-do-noy E-lo-
hay-nu (Jewish traditional)
BH269   108883
Sholom alaychem mal achay
(Jewish liturgy) AH146; BH
278   108884
Should our minds to earthly objects
cleaving (Foster) AZ1019; BA
625   108885
Should we meet no more till the
judgment (Teasley) AX657

                                108886
Shout for joy, ye hosts of angels
(Childs) R Lo! the clouds
have burst asunder   108887
Shout, for the blessed Jesus
reigns (Beddome) AI171; AM
298; AO207   108888
Shout, O earth! from silence
waking (Havergal) AZ618
                                108889
Shout the glad tidings, exultingly
sing (Muhlenberg) A15; B75;
D53; I119; L349; O200; V120;
AV97; BA145; BI100; BR150
                                108890
Show me myself, O holy Lord
(Plymouth hymnal, 1893)
BY773   108891
Show me thy ways, O Lord
(Scottish Psalter, 1650)
AW581 X Shew me thy ways,
O Lord   108892
Show pity, Lord, O lord, for-
give (Watts) H277; I270;
L378; U172; V288; AO269;
AZ378; BA415; BB240 108893
Show us thy way, O God (Holmes)
AN437   108894
Showers of blessing (Whittle)
R There shall be showers of
blessing   108895
Shun, my heart, the thought for-
ever (Gerhardt) N400
                                108896
Sieh! wie sein ist und lieblich
schon (Ausbund. Psalm 133)
BU84   108897
Silent night, holy night (Mohr)
A33; B546; G106; I123; J16;
K530; M603; 604; N46; P140;
Q646; R154; S132; T339; U60;
W49; Y302; Z188; AB116; AC
81; AD119; AE92; AF138; AG
74; AH125, 247; AI381; AK101;
AL53; AM161; AN166, 167; AQ
289; AR135; AS102; AT72; AU
146; AW83; AX100; AY488;
AZ1516; BA168; BB102; BC
160; BD218; BF288; BK151;
BL12; BN20; BO151; BP9;
BQ11; BV113; BX534; BY108;
BZ   108898
Silent night! holy night! Golden

stars shed their light (Mohr)
M604 X Silent night, holy
night   108899
Silent night, holy night! Through
the darkness beams a light
(Mohr) P140 X Silent night,
holy night   108900
Silent night, holy night! Bethlehem
sleeps, yet what light (Mohr)
AH125 X Silent night, holy
night   108901
Silent night, holy night [etc]
(Mohr) X Holy night, peace-
ful night   108902
Silent night! Peaceful night
(Mohr) AI381 X Silent night,
holy night   108903
Silently, silently, they pass away
(---) AX616; AY186   108904
Silently the shades of evening
(Coxe) I52   108905
Simply trusting every day (Stites)
AM682; AP521; AT259; AU328;
AX459   108906
Sin can never enter there (Naylor)
R Heaven is a holy place
                                   108907
Sin has a thousand treacherous
arts (Watts) V225   108908
Sin, like a venomous disease
(Watts) V223   108909
Since Christ has gone to heaven,
His home (Wegelin) AA236
                                   108910
Since Christ my soul from sin
set free (Butler) AX335
                                   108911
Since I have been redeemed
(Excell) R I have a song
                                   108912
Since I have felt the sense of
death (Lyman) AQ81   108913
Since Jesus came into my heart
(McDaniel) R What a wonder-
ful change   108914
Since Jesus freely did appear
(Berridge) I667; AX551; AY295;
AZ168   108915
Since Jesus gave His life for me
(Howard) AX398   108916
Since Jesus is my Friend (Ger-
hardt) J477; K342; L504; R218;
S299; U233; V387; Y202; AD

269; AG207; AW236; AZ1318;
BR257   108917
Since now the day has reached
its close (Herzog) AA30
                                   108918
Since o'er thy footstool here
below (Muhlenberg) AR97;
AS89   108919
Since to the Holiest none may
enter in (Stoney) BB139
                                   108920
Since we can't doubt God's
equal love (Ken) AZ1440
                                   108921
Since we, though unworthy
(Foster) AZ752; BA616
                                   108922
Since what we choose is what
we are (Hyde) AQ108 X
Creation's Lord, we give
thee thanks   108923
Since with my God with perfect
heart (U.P. Psalter, 1912)
AJ35   108924
Since without Thee we do no
good (Browning) I504
                                   108925
Sinful, sighing to be blest
(Monsell) B140; D347; E88;
F87; BV150   108926
Sinful world, behold the anguish
(Quirsfeld) N112   108927
Sing a new song to Jehovah
(U.P. Psalter, 1912) T179;
AJ261   108928
Sing about Jesus who died to
save (Warren) AX5   108929
Sing, all good people gathered
(French trad carol) X193;
BG111   108930
Sing all ye Christian people
(Struther) X163; AD165
                                   108931
Sing alleluia, Christ doth live
(Gregor) AZ1433; BA240
                                   108932
Sing Alleluia forth in duteous
praise (Mozarabic Rite,
5th-8th c) A583; B265; D
462; F283; V616; X247;
AB89; AD174; BL77; BY27
                                   108933
Sing Alleluia forth in loyal

praise (Mozarabic rite, 5th-
8th c) [Note: Great variation
in these two cited versions]
X247, AD174 X Sing alleluia
forth in duteous praise 108934
Sing alleluia, honor, praise (---)
AZ1098   108935
Sing alleluia, praise the Lord
(Swertner) AZ893; BA755
                                108936
Sing aloud on this day! Children
all (Piae cantiones. 1582)
BG78b   108937
Sing, brothers, sing and praise
your King (Alington) X164;
app. 1   108938
Song forth His high eternal name
(Longfellow) AB59; AN308; BF
248; BX28   108939
Sing forth with gladsome voice
(Latin carol, 14th c) M613
                                108940
Sing glory, glory, glory, alleluia
(Smith) R Proclaim the tidings
near and far   108941
Sing, good company, frank and
free (Flemish trad carol)
BG110   108942
Sing it o'er and o'er again (Neu-
meister) R Sinners Jesus will
receive   108943
Sing loud alleluia in jubilant
chorus (Agricola) O19 108944
Sing lullaby! Lullaby baby, now
reclining (Baring-Gould) BV
115   108945
Sing, men and angels, sing
(Masefield) A475; G152; J97;
X165   108946
Sing, my soul, his wondrous love
(Collection. Baltimore, 1800)
A294; B257; D438   108947
Sing, my soul, to God who made
thee (Gerhardt) AK16   108948
Sing, my tongue, the glorious bat-
tle (Fortunatus) A66; D98;
E95; F97; J61; M402; W108;
X129; AM194; BV161; BY146
                                108949
Sing, my tongue, the Mystery
holy, of the Body of my Lord
(St Thomas Aquinas) BN102
                                108950

Sing, my tongue, the Saviour's
battle (Fortunatus) M402
X Sing, my tongue, the
glorious battle   108951
Sing my tongue, the Savior's
glory, Of His cross (St
Thomas Aquinas) BL51;
BM36; BO48; BQ52; BY326
                        108952
Sing Noel, sing noel, and merry
be alway (Raymond) R
There dwelt in old Judea
                        108953
Sing, O my lips, and loudly
proclaim (---) R Mary! how
sweetly falls that word
                        108954
Sing, O! sing of my Redeemer
(Bliss) R I will sing
                        108955
Sing, O sing, this blessed
morn (Wordsworth) A26;
B77; D57; U53; BV116
                        108956
Sing, O ye ransomed of the
Lord (Doddridge) H387
                        108957
Sing of Jesus, sing forever
(Kelly) AO73   108958
Sing of Mary, pure and lowly
(---) A117; BL63   108959
Sing of Mary, pure and lowly
(---) X Sing the Holy
Family's praises (Vaughan)
                        108960
Sing praise to God who reigns
above (Schütz) E478; F366;
G355; J422; K285; L85; M
594; N288; O3; Q19; R15;
AB57; AF20; AM4; AW512;
BV565; BY28; BZ   108961
Sing praise to God who spoke
through man (Dearner)
A299; X640   108962
Sing praises unto God on high
(LaTrobe) AZ737   108963
Sing, sing, ye angel bands
(Faber) BO66   108964
Sing the Holy Family's praises
(Vaughan) BN122   108965
Sing the Holy Family's praises
(Vaughan) X Sing of Mary
(---)   108966

Sing the wondrous love of Jesus
(Hewitt) AT483; AU281
               108967
Sing them over again to me
(Bliss) H88; R265; Z442; AE
306; AG141; AH241; AI406;
AM722; AP761; AS184; AT181;
AU233; AV314; AW494; AX36;
BB574; BZ   108968
Sing to the great Jehovah's praise
(Wesley) G538; H523; I575;
Z590; AL572; BZ   108969
Sing to the Lord a joyful song
(Monsell) W23; AB18; BF215;
BY29   108970
Sing to the Lord most high
(Dwight) AZ1178; BA26 108971
Sing to the Lord of harvest
(Monsell) N571; O530; U482; AE
428; AL578; AP692; AZ851; BA
868; BG159; BI113; BY730
            108972
Sing to the Lord, sing His praise,
all ye peoples (U.P. Psalter,
1912) T177; AJ259; AM65
            108973
Sing to the Lord the children's
hymn (Hawker) E606; F446;
J335; X371   108974
Sing to the Lord, who loud pro-
claims (Doddridge) L107
            108975
Sing to the Lord with joyful voice
(Watts) BW272 X Before the
Lord Jehovah's throne
            108976
Sing to the Sovereign of the skies
(Hamburg Temple hymnal)
BH67   108977
Sing we a song of the Saviour
(Bennett) AY485   108978
Sing we all the joys and sorrows
(Grève) E230   108979
Sing we now at parting (Manwaring)
BC161   108980
Sing we the King who is coming
to reign (Horne) BY191
            108981
Sing we the praises of the great
forerunner (Paul the Deacon)
F551   108982
Sing we the song of those who
stand (Montgomery) AZ141;

BA383   108983
Sing we to our God above (Latin)
14th c) AZ80 X Jesus
Christ is risen today 108984
Sing we triumphant hymns of
praise (St Bede, the Ven-
erable) E146; BM84; BP42
            108985
Sing with all the sons of glory
(Irons) D124; G150; I160;
AK177; AO188; AS149; BR
188; BZ   108986
Sing with awe in strains har-
monious (Gregor) AZ978;
BA222   108987
Sing with humble hearts your
praises (Mueller) BA123
            108988
Sing with joy the Saviour's
glory (St Thomas Aquinas)
BM36 X Sing my tongue,
the Savior's glory 108989
Sing ye faithful, Sing with glad-
ness! (Ellerton) D517
            108990
Sing, ye joyous children, sing,
Glorious is the Christ
(Dunn) BE310   108991
Singers, sing! The hoary world
(Wightman) Y183 108992
Singing for Jesus, our Saviour
and King (Havergal) N657
            108993
Sink not yet, my soul, to
slumber (Rist) AA31 X
Father, merciful and holy
            108994
Sinner, art thou still secure
(Newton) V268   108995
Sinner, hear the Saviour's call
(Newton) AZ1467 108996
Sinners, behold that downward
road (Dobell. A new selec-
tion, 1806) AI208 108997
Sinners, behold the Lamb of
God (Hoskins) V248
            108998
Sinners, come, the Saviour see
(Zinzendorf, N.L.) AZ1043
            108999
Sinners, hear the joyful news
(Dutton) AZ1475 109000
Sinners Jesus will receive

(Neumeister) (Bevan tr)   J377;
S227; AL477; AT195; AU113;
AV330; AW466; AX264
                                109001
Sinners Jesus will receive (Neu-
meister: Bevan tr) J377 X
Jesus sinners doth receive
(Neumeister)   109002
Sinners may to Christ draw near
(Neumeister) M125   109003
Sinners, the voice of God regard
(Fawcett) H254; I246   109004
Sinners, turn: why will ye die
(Wesley) G191; H261; I247;
L373; U155; V272; AA48; AZ
1046; BA408; BZ   109005
Sinners, will ye scorn the mes-
sage (Allen) V279   109006
Sion, founded on the mountains
(U.P. Psalter, 1912) AJ237;
AM369   109007
Sion mourns in fear and anguish
(Heermann) Q268; AA505
                                109008
Sion, on the holy hills (U.P.
Psalter, 1912) T161; AJ239
                                109009
Sion, praise thy Saviour, singing
(St Thomas Aquinas) A193
                                109010
Sion, rise, Sion, rest. Sion,
wake, arise, and shine (Schmidt)
Q479   109011
Sion, Sion, lovely Sion (---)
R Beautiful Sion, built above
                                109012
Sion stands with hills surrounded
(Kelly) H403; I212; K200; L290;
M83; N262; O83; Q474; U346;
V538; AA465; AI149; AM275;
AR499; AS188; AT378; AU364;
AV246; AZ1391; BA266; BC
212   109013
Sion, the marvelous story be tell-
ing (Muhlenberg) R Shout
the glad tidings   109014
Sion, to thy Saviour singing (St
Thomas Aquinas) O311; P172;
AM360; AZ649; BR464 109015
Sion's daughters! Sons of Jeru-
salem! (Adam of St Victor??)
E172   109016
Sion's King shall reign victorious

(Kelly) AL255; AP381
                                109017
Sister, thou wast mild and
lovely (Smith) AX628; AY
170; BC381   109018
Sit down beneath His shadow
(Havergal) AZ30; BV385
                                109019
Sitting at the feet of Jesus, O
what words I hear ("J.H.")
AX413; AY107; BB618
                                109020
Sitting at the feet of Jesus,
Watching, waiting (Minter)
AX47   109021
Skriv dig, Jesu, paa mit Hjerte
(Kingo) BT179   109022
S'-lach no la-a-von ho-om
(Jewish traditional) BH320
                                109023
Slain for my soul, for all my
sins defamed (Young) BP
27   109024
Sleep, baby sleep! Thy mother
watch doth keep (Buermeyer)
K570; AW431   109025
Sleep, comrades, sleep, sleep
and rest! (Longfellow)
AH476   109026
Sleep, holy Babe, upon thy
mother's breast (Caswall)
BN21; BO152; BQ14 109027
Sleep, my little Jesus (Gan-
nett) AH268   109028
Sleep on, beloved, sleep, and
take thy rest (Doudney) H
486; AP620   109029
Sleep, sweet babe! My cares
beguiling (Coleridge) BG
175b   109030
Sleep thy last sleep Free from
care and sorrow (Dayman)
N595; O598; V679; Z580;
AZ1503; BA729   109031
Sleepers, wake, a voice is
calling (Nicolai) BR132
                                109032
Sleepers, wake! the watch-cry
pealeth (Nicolai) F55; BV
77   109033
Sleepers, wake! the watch-cry
pealeth (Nicolai) X Wake,
awake! for night is flying

109034
Slow comes the evening o'er
the hill (Brooke) AN105 X
The morning walks upon the
earth   109035
Slowly, by thy hand unfurled
(Furness) Y89; AB22; AC217;
AD53; AN114; BD12; BF195;
BX128   109036
Slowly sinks the setting sun
(Lacy) V50   109037
Slowly, slowly darkening (Greg)
I464   109038
Slumber, O slumber, dear Jesus
my treasure (Polish trad
carol) BN22   109039
Smiling skies will bend above us
(Rowe) AU429   109040
Smite us not in anger, Lord
(Albinus) K313; P264 109041
So brightly burns Love's holy
glow (Key) BE311   109042
So fades the lovely, blooming
flower (Steele) M297
109043
So gehst du nun mein Jesu,
hin, (Nachtenhöfer) BT150
109044
So God send you all much joy
(English trad carol) R
Awake, awake, ye drowsy
souls   109045
So here hath been dawning
(Carlyle) S451; X34 109046
So I'll cherish the old rugged
cross (Bennard) R On a
hill far away   109047
So let our lips and lives express
(Watts) L526; N459; R289;
U313; V322; AO503; AT323;
AX388; AY17; BE386 109048
So lowly doth the Saviour ride
(Pennewell) BZ   109049
So merket auf ihr Christenleut
(Bible. Maccabees) BU4
109050
So nimm denn meine Hände
(Hausmann) AW561b; BW561
109051
So precious is Jesus, my Saviour
(Gabriel) AE285; AT304
109052
So rest, my Rock (Franck) AA

216   109053
So sweet and clear, so sweet
and clear ("H. L. W. ") BI
89   109054
So wahr ich leb' spricht Gott
der Herr (Herman) BT331
109055
So wash me, Thou, without,
within (Smith) R One thing
I of the Lord   109056
So we lift our hands and sing
out thy praise (Dearmer)
X396e   109057
So will ichs aber haben an
(Bosch) BU69   109058
Soft as the voice of an angel
(Hawthorne) AU466   109059
Softly and tenderly Jesus is
calling (Thompson) G239;
H262; J578; V753; Z283;
AE165; AG135; AH331; AL
494; AM694; AP409; AR250;
AT236; AU100; AV339; AW
456; AX221; AY502; BB563
109060
Softly beams the sacred dawning
(Jacques) BC284   109061
Softly fades the twilight ray
(Smith) G398; H85; I74; L30;
U466; V62   109062
Softly I closed the Book as in
a dream (Garrison) AC450
109063
Softly now the day is ending
(Kingo) M570   109064
Softly now the light of day
(Doane) A177; B19; D13; G
47; H30; I53; K465; L25; M
573; N539; O561; P71; R60;
S34; T311; U458; V49; Z145;
AB26; AD54; AE48; AG25;
AH171; AI56; AK53; AM347;
AN113; AO40; AP677; AR59;
AS29; AT33; AU225; AV14;
AW36; AZ70; BA789; BB48;
BC162; BD9; BK46; BX127;
BZ   109065
Softly the night is sleeping
(Washburne) AZ859; BA57
109066
Softly the silent night falleth
from God (Blatchford)
AO38; BX151   109067

Soldier, go! Thy vow is spoken
(Page) BY300   109068
Soldiers of Christ, arise (Wes-
ley) A552; B346; D509; E479;
F303; G282; H380; I382; J564;
K384; L534; M245; N508; O489;
Q450; R362; S269; U296; V490;
W534; X641; Y171; AA380;
AD287; AE248; AF384; AG187;
AH441; AK289; AL404; AM
482; AO412; AP546; AT416;
AW198; AZ1498; BA583; BB
366; BE312; BF481; BV585;
BY508; BZ   109069
Soldiers of progress, manful and
true (Perkins) R Gird on the
armor, brave soul, today
                     109070
Soldiers of the cross, arise!
Gird you [ye] with your ar-
mour (How) B115; D581; F
305; Q501; V602; W341; X
642; AA482; AB354; AL407;
AP549; BA560; BF506; BV
601; BY524   109071
Soldiers of the cross, arise!
Lo! your Leader from the
skies (Waterbury) G281;
I385   109072
Soldiers, true and faithful
(Wiglesworth) AO397 109073
Soldiers, who are Christ's below
(Breviary. Bourges, 1734)
E480; F524; BV435   109074
Soldiers who to Christ belong
(Breviary. Bourges, 1734)
AM485   109075
Sollt' ich meinem Gott nicht
singen? (Gerhardt) BT25
                     109076
Som den gyldne Sol frembryder
(Kingo) BT207   109077
Somebody follows you (Henson)
R Brother along on the high-
way   109078
Somebody needs your love
(McKinney) R Out in the
darkness   109079
Some day, I know, the mist that
life is veiling (Wexels) M640
                     109080
Some day the silver cord will
break (Crosby) AH455; AI135;

AM726; AV395; AY494; BB
630   109081
Some day these conflicts will
be o'er (Hoffman) AX536;
AY140   109082
Some day you'll stand at the
bar on high (Teddlie) AX
295   109083
Some days are dark and dreary
(Leatherman) AX598; AY158
                     109084
Some near, near day (Hoff-
man) R Some day these
conflicts   109085
Some of these mornings bright
and fair (Negro spiritual)
R O Mary, don't you weep
                     109086
Some-one will enter the pearly
gate (McGranahan) AX291;
BB568   109087
Some soul for thee (Weaver)
R Lord, lay some soul upon
my heart   109088
Some sweet day when life is
o'er (Chord) AS479; AX
623; AY498   109089
Something every heart is loving
(Tersteegen) AZ950 109090
Some time we all shall under-
stand (Yoder) AX570; AY
345   109091
Sometimes a light surprises
(Cowper) A443; F176; G351;
I454; J495; L458; R418; S
296; U45; V385; W439; X643;
Z581; AB201; AD231; AG208;
AL287; AM520; AO332; AP
445; AZ843; BA684; BB254;
BE313; BF417; BR20; BV530;
BY585; BZ   109092
Son of a Virgin, maker of thy
Mother (Latin, 8th c) E
191   109093
Son of God, eternal Saviour
(Lowry) A500; E529; F207;
J542; S393; W359; X339; Z
502; AD323; AE199; AF413;
AR411; BF514; BY652
                     109094
Son of God! to Thee I cry
(Mant) BA605 X Son of
man, to thee I cry   109095

Son of Man, to Thee I cry
(Mant) K83; AP479; AZ1269;
BA605; BY176   109096
Son of the carpenter, receive
(Wesley) BY632 X Servant of
all, to toil for man   109097
Son of the Lord most high
(Briggs) BY129   109098
Songs of immortal praise belong
(Watts) M154; AA61   109099
Songs of praise exultant sing (---)
BI11-D   109100
Songs of praise the angels sang
(Montgomery) A292; B256; D
476; E481; F369; H10; J432;
K311; L178; M589; Q35; S11;
V512; W38; X644; AA68; AO
78; AP159; AZ49; BA660; BV
26   109101
Songs of thankfulness and praise
(Wordsworth) A53; B96; D67;
E47; F81; J55; K37; L149;
N76; Q134; AA184; BM70; BV
131   109102
Sons of labor, dear to Jesus
(Hole) AO506   109103
Sons of men, behold from far
(Wesley) BI92   109104
Sons of Michael, he approaches
(Harrison) BC163   109105
Soon as the morn with roses
(Haweis) M560   109106
Soon falls the evening twilight
(Metzler) AY74   109107
Soon may the last glad song arise
(Vokes) A539; B484; H471;
I630; V603; BB201   109108
Soon trials and conflicts of life
will be o'er (Doughty) AX594;
AY160   109109
Soon will our Savior from heaven
appear (Habershon) AI95
                          109110
Soon will the heavenly Bridegroom
come (Walther) O511   109111
Soon with angels I'll be marching
(---) R Death shall not destroy
my comfort   109112
Sooner or later; yet at last
(Rossetti) S439; W586   109113
Soul, adorn thyself with gladness
(Franck) Q305 X Deck thyself,
my soul   109114

Soul of Jesus, make me whole
(Latin, 14th c) E89
                          109115
Soul of mine, to God awaking
(Rist) M579   109116
Soul of my Saviour, sanctify
my breast (Latin, 14th c)
BN103; BO29; BP68; BQ
47   109117
Soul, what return has God, thy
Saviour (Lochner) Q404;
AA345   109118
Souls in heathen darkness lying
(Alexander) D256; M114; AZ
1397; BA364   109119
Souls of men! why will ye
scatter (Faber) U146 X
There's a wideness in God's
mercy   109120
Souls of the Righteous in the
hand of God (Bible. Wisdom
3) Y127; AB407   109121
Sound aloud Jehovah's praises
(Martin) D142; F616
                          109122
Sound forth the tidings, long,
loud, and clear (Gage) R
O'er all the land have the
signs now appeared 109123
Sound over all waters, reach
out from all lands (Whittier)
X327; ÞD359; AK408; AQ202;
BI99   109124
Sound the battle cry, See! the
foe is nigh (Sherwin) AH
454; AI326; AM686; BB499;
BY525   109125
Sound the chorus loud and clear
(Whittle) R Who came down
from heaven to earth
                          109126
Sound the loud anthem, to hail
the blest morning (---) BR
146   109127
Sound the loud timbrel o'er
Egypt's dark sea! (Moore)
BH131   109128
Sounds of joy have put to flight
(Latin, 13th c) BN152
                          109129
Source of light and life divine
(St Gregory the Great) K
466   109130

Sovereign and transforming grace
  (Hedge) AN25; AQ127; BX30
                                    109131
Sovereign of worlds, display thy
  power (Draper) V597 109132
Sovereign Ruler of the skies
  (Ryland) D669   109133
Sow in the morn thy seed (Mont-
  gomery) H377; I389; L549;
  U275; V495; AM299; AN248;
  AW1360; BA558; BE314; BV
  598; BX307; BY526   109134
Sow the seed beside all waters
  (Murray) AP388   109135
Sowing in the morning, Sowing
  at the noontide (Ogden) R
  Scattering precious seed
                                    109136
Sowing in the morning, Sowing
  seeds of kindness (Shaw)
  Z416; AH416; AP590; AT432;
  AU359; AX187; BB621 109137
Sowing the seed by the daylight
  fair (Oakey) AU404   109138
Sown in the darkness or sown in
  the light (Oakey) R Sowing
  the seed   109139
Spare your people, Lord (Bible.
  Joel, 2) BN30   109140
Speak gently, it is better far
  (Bates) BE315   109141
Speak gently to the erring ones
  (Lee) AX162; AY364 109142
Speak, I pray thee, gentle Jesus
  (Williams) W445; AL495
                                    109143
Speak, Lord, in the stillness
  (Crawford) BB329; BV309
                                    109144
Speak, O Lord, thy servant
  heareth (Anna Sophia of Hesse-
  Darmstadt) M381; O260; Q
  296   109145
Speak to my heart, Lord Jesus
  (Routh) AT331; AU415
                                    109146
Speak to us, Lord, thyself re-
  veal (Wesley) BY486 X Talk
  with us, Lord, thyself reveal
                                    109147
Speed away, speed away on your
  mission of light (Crosby)
  AR472; AS380   109148

Speed away! speed away! Take
  the gospel of light (Hackle-
  man) AX208; AY331
                                    109149
Speed thy servants, Saviour,
  speed them (Kelly) D264;
  K231; N373; P397; U394;
  AI177; AM382; AO527; AP
  387; AZ1382; BA356 109150
Speis uns, O Gott, deine Kinder
  (Heermann) BT659   109151
Spirit blest, who art adored
  (Littledale) A234; B204;
  AI121   109152
Spirit divine, attend our prayers
  [prayer] (Reed) A370; B202;
  D382; F239; H210; I190; M
  463; R243; S212; U127; W
  183; Z275; AD189; AE142;
  AF241; AL153; AN55; AO221;
  AP282; AR234; AT171; AW
  139; AZ212; BA329; BB213;
  BF258; BV297; BX77; BY
  239; BZ   109153
Spirit Divine, Creator, come
  Dwell in our kindred souls
  (Latin, 9th c) U126
                                    109154
Spirit of faith, come down
  (Wesley) G183; H212; I191;
  AZ1348; BA143; BZ 109155
Spirit of God, descend upon my
  heart (Croly) G179; H221;
  I197; J129; L394; R236; S204;
  T357; U125; V417; W195;
  Y99; Z272; AB95; AC62; AD
  184; AE147; AF232; AG125;
  AH230; AI120; AK193; AL157;
  AN48; AO219; AP276; AR232;
  AS174; AT166; AV150; AW
  133; AZ443; BA144; BF265;
  BK85; BX107; BY240; BZ
                                    109156
Spirit of God, dwell thou within
  my heart (Croly) AI120 X
  Spirit of God, descend upon
  my heart   109157
Spirit of God, for every Good
  (Warmingham) AC64
                                    109158
Spirit of God, in thunder speak
  (Chadwick) AN322; BX379
                                    109159

Spirit of God, that moved of old
(Alexander) W185; AM255;
AP269   109160

Spirit of grace, and health and
power (Wesley) BX349; BZ
                              109161

Spirit of grace and union (Adam
of St Victor) BQ37   109162

Spirit of Grace, thou Light of
life (Tersteegen) W192
                              109163

Spirit of holiness, descend
(Smith) AE152; AV148   109164

Spirit of holiness, do thou
(Holroyd) BV296   109165

Spirit of Jesus, who didst move
(Phillips) F511   109166

Spirit of life, in this new dawn
(Marlatt) G178; Y22; AC63;
AE146; AR233; BK43; BZ
                              109167

Spirit of mercy, truth, and love
(Foundling Hospital Coll. 1774)
A111; B197; D136; E631; F153;
J118; K140; M470; X184; AA
250; AZ416; BA255; BV222
                              109168

Spirit of peace, and holiness!
(Smith) AZ419; BA321 109169

Spirit of power, and truth, and
love (Alexander) BX319
                              109170

Spirit of the living God, Fall
afresh on me (Iverson) AR656;
AT523; AU329   109171

Spirit of the living God, Fall
fresh on me (Iverson) AT523
X Spirit of the living God,
Fall afresh on me   109172

Spirit of truth, come down (Wesley)
AZ1348 X Spirit of faith, come
down   109173

Spirit of truth, of life, of power
(Westwood) AN507; AQ146
                              109174

Spirit of truth on this thy day
(Heber) L274   109175

Spirit of truth, we call (White)
D300; N572   109176

Spirit of truth, who makest bright
(Gill) AN57; BX82   109177

Spirit of wisdom, turn our eyes
(Catholic hymnal, 1860) O354

                              109178
Spirit so holy, Spirit of love
(Whittle) AX133; AY203
                              109179

Spirit strength of all the weak
(Pollock) AL159; AM244;
AP280   109180

Splendid are the heavens high
(Grundtvig) M606   109181

Splendor of the morning sunlight
(Adler) BH9   109182

Splendor Paternae gloriae (St
Ambrose) BJ29b   109183

Splendours three, from God proceeding (Goethe) R Every-
thing changes   109184

Spouse of Christ, in arms con-
tending (Contes) E253
                              109185

Spread, O spread, thou mighty
Word! (Bahnmaier) A253;
E552; J323; K166; M107;
O119; Q507; X645; AW551;
BV327; BY394   109186

Spread, still spread, thou
mighty Word (Bahnmaier)
X645 X Spread, O spread,
thou mighty Word   109187

Spread the table of the Lord
(Gregory) BY327   109188

Spring bursts today, for Christ
is risen (Rossetti) X5
                              109189

Spring has now unwrapped the
flowers (Piae cantiones, 1582)
X4; AN135; AQ321; BG99; BK
131; BZ   109190

Springs and streams no longer
bless (U.P. Psalter, 1912)
T107; AJ296   109191

Stabat Mater dolorosa (Jacopone) BN33; BO262; BP24;
BQ162   109192

Stalwart as pillars bearing high
their burden (Phillips) F520
                              109193

Stand fast for Christ thy Saviour
(Mathams) U311; AC180;
BF455   109194

Stand fast, my soul, stand fast
(Brorson) M249   109195

Stand like the brave (Crosby)
R O Christian, awake! 'tis

the Master's command 109196
Stand, soldier of the cross
(Bickersteth) D210; I413; AA
407; BA285; BY301   109197
"Stand still and see!" Yea, see,
today (Fox) BB337   109198
Stand the omnipotent decree!
(Wesley) I598   109199
Stand up and bless the Lord (Mont-
gomery) F374; G39; H2; V9;
W233; AF25; AL210; AM14; AP
318; AT16; AV28; AZ1306; BA
389; BV27; BX22; BY363; BZ
                           109200
Stand up, my soul, shake off thy
fears (Watts) V479; AM478;
AV199; AZ398; BA587   109201
Stand up, stand up for Jesus
(Duffield) A562; B538; D582;
E581; F307; G283; H379; I386;
J551; L531; M250; N447; Q451;
R349; S265; U288; V486; W532;
X646; Y170; Z371; AA377; AB
253; AC201; AD288; AE217;
AF385; AG188; AH443; AI329;
AK290; AL405; AM477; AO394;
AP541; AR468; AS323; AT415;
AU31; AV205; AW193; AX437;
AY303; AZ854; BA585; BB354;
BF473; BV586; BY556; BZ
                           109202
Standing at the portal of the open-
ing year (Havergal) M621;
S468; U471; Z584; AI346; AK
427; AL571; AP697; AR584;
AS434; AZ762; BA179; BF640;
                           109203
Standing by a purpose true (Bliss)
AM660; AP773; AU322; AX563;
BB497   109204
Standing forth on life's rough way
(Bryant) BY342   109205
Standing in the market-place
(Jackson) AL608   109206
Standing on the promises (Carter)
AH391; AT266; AU115; AX474;
BZ   109207
Star of Jacob, ever beaming
(Breviary, Lisbon, 1786) BO
95   109208
Star of our hope! He'll soon ap-
pear (---) BB188   109209
Star of peace to wanderers weary

(Simpson) W627; AL455; AP
712   109210
Star of the East, O Bethlehem
Star (Cooper) AX96 109211
Star, Star, beautiful Star
(Raymond) R There's a
beautiful Star   109212
Star whose light shines o'er me
(Krummacher) BY218
                           109213
Stars of glory shine more
brightly (Husenbeth) BO156;
BQ9   109214
Stars of morning, shout for joy
(---) BC164   109215
Stars of the morning, so glor-
iously bright (St Joseph the
Hymnographer) A121; B289;
D170; E245; F288; F148; K
252; M485; N208; Q255; AA
285   109216
Stay, Master, stay upon this
heavenly hill (Greg) G122
                           109217
Stay, thou insulted Spirit,
stay (Wesley) H278; I269;
V207   109218
Stay with us, Lord, the day
is dying (Boye) P201
                           109219
Stayed upon Jehovah, Hearts
are fully blest (Havergal)
R Like a river glorious
                           109220
Steal away, steal away, steal
away to Jesus (Negro spirit-
ual) Y316; AG315; AH604;
AR487; BK166   109221
Step by step, Ho-yo heave!
(Russian trad) Y313
                           109222
Stern daughter of the Voice of
God (Wordsworth) X647
                           109223
Still nigh me, O my Saviour,
stand (Wesley) F90; BV149
                           109224
Still on the homeward journey
(Borthwick) W602; AP700
                           109225
Still on thy loving heart let me
repose (Spitta) AZ1025
                           109226

Still, still with thee, my God
(Burns) BR124 X Still with
thee, O my God   109227

Still, still with thee, when pur-
ple morning breaketh (Stowe)
G40; I43; J496; O549; P335;
S107; T305; U454; Y20; Z136;
AB7; AC6; AD26; AF37; AG18;
AH210; AK50; AL539; AN104;
AO20; AR45; AS22; AT25; AV
4; AW23; BA776; BB326; BE
317; BF227; BK40; BR407; BX
123; BY683; BZ   109228

Still the night, holy the night
(Mohr) W49, BY108 X
Silent night, holy night
                       109229

Still will we trust, though earth
seem dark and dreary
(Burleigh) E482; I486; T394;
V360; AL418   109230

Still with thee, O my God
(Burns) H51; I525; S100; AP
472; BA622; BB315; BR124;
BX102; BY774   109231

Stille, mein Wille! Dein Jesus
hilft siegen (Schlegel) BT651;
BW54   109232

Stille nacht, heilige nacht (Mohr)
Y302; AD119; AF139; AK101b;
AW83; BT646   109233

Storms of trouble may assail us
(Herrnschmidt) AZ238; BA699
                       109234

Strait is the gate to all that
come (Berg) M296; N631;
O423   109235

Strait is the gate to heaven above
(Berg) O423 X Strait is the
gate to all that come   109236

Strengthen for service, Lord,
the hands (Liturgy of Malabar,
Syriac) A201; E329; J286;
X278; BV386; BY328   109237

Stretched on the cross, the
Saviour dies (Steele) V141
                       109238

"Stricken, smitten, and afflicted"
(Kelly) L237; M399; N117;
O316; P190; Q153; AA209;
AM192   109239

Strike up, O harp and psaltery
(Wallin) N345   109240

Strive aright when God doth call
thee (Winckler) O255; AW
563   109241

Striving onward, pressing forward (---) AX435   109242

Strong Captain, in thy holy
ranks (Crum) F461   109243

Strong of body, high of spirit
(Felton) Y163; AC163; BF
627   109244

Strong, righteous Man of Galilee
(Farrington) AD487; AR396;
BF629   109245

Strong Son of God, immortal
Love (Tennyson) A365; E
483; G206; I139; R228; S
175; W142; X648; Y70; Z349;
AB173; AC215; AD235; AF
357; AG117; AK225; AL428;
AN204; AP264; AR117; AS
264; AV124; AW149; BA
884; BF428; BK70; BZ
                       109246

S'u sh'-o-reem ro-shay-chem
(Jewish traditional) BH288
                       109247

Sub tuum praesidium (Latin)
BO78; BQ213   109248

Such love cannot be fathomed
(Warren) R Behold what
love   109249

Such love, such wondrous love
(Bishop) R That God should
love   109250

Such pity as a father hath
(Scottish Psalter, 1650) AL
672; AP90C   109251

Such', wer da will, Ein ander
Ziel (Weissel) BT383
                       109252

Suffer the children to come to
me (Grundtvig) BE318
                       109253

Suffering Saviour, Lamb of God
(Hart) AZ31   109254

Suffering Son of Man, be near
me (Wesley) K81; N93
                       109255

Summer ended, harvest o'er
(Phillimore) AF579   109256

Summer suns are glowing (How)
P381; U249; V654; W613; X7;
AB386; AL575; AN139; AO

577; AP688; AR587; AV51; AW
386; BA511; BB5; BD44; BF
643; BH155; BR405; BV647;
BX520; BY722   109257

Sun of my soul, thou Saviour dear
(Keble) A166; B20; D11; E274;
F24; G56; H33; I47; J226; K
463; L21; M566; N563; O566;
P77; Q551; R56; S37; T312;
U457; V46; W292; X55; Y93;
Z150; AA42; AB25; AC22; AD
57; AE44; AF50; AG28; AH174;
AI50; AK55; AL556; AM346;
AN108; AO31; AP666; AR56;
AS34; AT15; AU177; AV239;
AW30; AX68; AY129; AZ355;
BA780; BB321; BF194; BJ85;
BL73; BR125; BT551; BV62;
BX139; BY703; BZ   109258

Sun of our life, thy quickening ray
(Holmes) BE319 X Lord of all
being, throned afar   109259

Sunk is the sun's last beam of
light (Hermann) K477; N553
109260

Sunlight, sunlight in my soul today (Van Deventer) R I wandered in the shades   109261

Sunset and evening star (Tennyson) B412; G368; H499; I744;
N591; S438; U419; W588; X649;
Y129; Z574; AB413; AC536; AD
464; AH537; AL457; AO566; AP
614; AR427; AV290; AW265;
AY497; BB678; BF669   109262

Sunset to sunrise changes now
(St Clement of Alexandria)
A81; AF165   109263

Supernae matris gaudia (Adam of
St Victor) BJ 27 notes
109264

Suppliant, lo! Thy children bend
(Gray) BR107   109265

Supreme and universal Light!
(Moore) AN292; BX350
109266

Supreme in wisdom as in power
(Watts) V506; BE320   109267

Surely Christ thy griefs has
borne (Toplady) AO255 X
Weary sinner keep thine eyes
109268

Surely Christ thy griefs hath

borne (Toplady) AZ1262 X
Weary sinner keep thine eyes
109269

Surrounded by unnumbered foes
(Massey) BX368   109270

Suscipe Domine, universam
libertatem meam (Latin)
BQ218   109271

Sweet Agnes, holy child, all
purity (Sister of Notre Dame)
BQ106   109272

Sweet and clear those angel
voices (Meigs) R Hark, a
burst of heavenly music
109273

Sweet are the promises, kind is
the word (Ogden) AR470;
AW481; AX494   109274

Sweet baby, sleep! What ails
my dear? (Wither) BG185
109275

Sweet be thy rest, and peaceful
thy sleeping (Belden) BB
493   109276

Sweet day, so cool, so calm,
so bright (Herbert) X650
109277

Sweet dreams form a shade
(Blake) BG196   109278

Sweet feast of love divine
(Denny) BA302 X Blest
feast of love divine 109279

Sweet flowerets of the martyr
band (Prudentius) Q273
109280

Sweet Gabriel, O blessed youth
(Herman) BP98   109281

Sweet hour of holy, thoughtful
prayer (Gilman) BE322
109282

Sweet hour of prayer (Walford)
G302; H39; I516; N350; P11;
R398; U359; Z337; AE232;
AH349; AI228; AK475; AM
534; AN564; AO316; AR471;
AS44; AT327; AU263; AV186;
AW182; AX353; AY32; AZ923;
BB316; BC166; BR524; BZ
109283

Sweet hymns and songs will I
recite (Jewish trad., 13th
c) BH23   109284

Sweet Infancy! O heavenly fire

(Traherne) X651   109285

Sweet is the breath of morning
air (Smith) AL532   109286

Sweet is the hour when thus we
meet (Stephens) BC12ra
109287

Sweet is the light of Sabbath eve
(Edmeston) H72; BB460
109288

Sweet is the memory of thy grace
(Watts) V620   109289

Sweet is the peace the gospel
brings (Morton) BC191
109290

Sweet is the prayer whose holy
stream (---) H44   109291

Sweet is the promise -- "I will
not forget thee" (Gabriel) AT
278; AU438   109292

Sweet is the solemn voice that
calls (Lyte) W239; AP321
109293

Sweet is the sunlight after rain
(Punshon) AL195   109294

Sweet is the time of spring
(Lloyd) H457   109295

Sweet is the work, my God, my
King (Watts) B44; H71; I
71; J183; K444; S22; V523;
AO16; AV45; AZ396; BA393;
BB46; BC168; BV71; BY281
109296

Sweet is thy mercy, Lord (Monsell) H50; S251; AG226; AO
309   109297

Sweet promise is given to all
who believe (Belden) BB548
109298

Sweet Sabbath! day of sacred joy
(Maurice) BH116   109299

Sweet Sacrament divine! Hid in
thine earthly home (Stanfield)
BO38   109300

Sweet Sacrament, we thee adore
(Faber) R Jesus, my Lord,
my God, my All, How can I
love   109301

Sweet Saviour, bless us ere we
go (Faber) O55 X O Saviour
bless us ere we go   109302

Sweet the lesson Jesus taught
(Leeson) AP764   109303

Sweet the moments, rich in blessing (Shirley) A72; B157;
D104; E105; G143; H168;
J63; K61; L248; M423; N109;
O323; P191; Q155; U102; V
555; AE117; AI80; AL99; AM
189; AO168; AP210; AR170;
AS140; AV112; AX178; AY
250; AZ252; BA131   109304

Sweet the time, exceeding sweet
(Burder) L51; BB516
109305

Sweet was the song the Virgin
sang (Ballet) BG30 109306

Sweet was the time when first
I felt (Newton) AY366
109307

Sweetened by the cross (Garrett) R Brother, here's a
message   109308

Sweeter sounds than music knows
(Newton) W170; AP263; AZ
81   109309

Sweetest note in seraph song
(Hunter) R The Great Phy-
sician now is near   109310

Sweetly, Lord, have we heard
(Slade) AS347; AT362; AU
228; AX508   109311

Sweetly the holy hymn (Spurgeon)
BB40; BY684   109312

Sweetly the tones are falling
(Slade) R Who at my door
109313

Swell the anthem, raise the
song (Strong) I711; Q584;
V622; AA299; AZ1052; BA
879   109314

Swiftly we're turning life's daily
pages (Carruth) AX209
109315

Swing low, sweet chariot (Negro
spiritual) Y321; AH610
109316

T

Take comfort, Christians, when
your friends (Scottish Paraphrases, 1781) AP622
109317

Take courage, Saints, and faint
not by the way (Crystal) BC
167   109317

Take heart, friends and neigh-
bours (Dearmer) X166; BG
147a   109318
Take heart, the journey's ended
(French trad carol, 15th c)
BG91   109319
Take me, O my Father, take
me (Palmer) U251; V399;
AM410; AO279; AZ967; BA
418; BF350   109320
Take my hand and lead me,
Father (Flory) AR298; AS
254   109321
Take my heart, O Father! take it
(---) AR362; AV161; AW441;
AX405; AY61   109322
Take my heart, O Jesus (Paul-
sen) M627   109323
Take my life, and let it be
(Havergal) A408; E582; F361;
G225; H302; I348; J510; K382;
L408; M226; N655; P406; Q
400; R310; S242; T423; U268;
V319; W512; X257; Y142; Z
296; AA355; AC198; AD260;
AE267; AF404; AG166; AH
413; AI230; AK253; AL356;
AM492; AN277; AO492; AP552;
AR349; AS230; AT356; AU174;
AV327; AW215; AX397; AY
223; AZ1071; BA471; BB273;
BD116; BE324; BF446; BK97;
BV641; BX332; BY527; BZ
                              109324
Take, my soul, thy full salvation
(Lyte) AO375 X Jesus, I my
cross have taken   109325
Take, O take me, holy Father
(Schmidt) AO275   109326
Take the Name of Jesus with
you (Baxter) G253; I508; N260;
R411; AG152; AH430; AI100;
AS297; AT305; AU424; AV320;
AW485; AX27; AY460; BB523;
BZ   109327
Take the world, but give me
Jesus (Crosby) AX270; BB
596   109328
Take thou my hand and lead me
(Hausmann) AK312; AX504
                              109329
Take thou my hand, O Father
(Hausmann) AR299 X O take

my hand, dear Father
                              109330
Take thou my heart, I would be
thine alone (Gabriel) R
More like the Master
                              109331
Take thou my life, dear Lord
(Lehmann) M231   109332
Take thou our minds, dear
Lord, we humbly pray
(Foulkes) R306; S245; AB
164; AE374; AG311; AK252;
AR535; BF352   109333
Take thou the heart I cannot
give (Lathbury) BR306
                              109334
Take time to be holy (Long-
staff) G251; H320; R300; Z
346; AE182; AH395; AI284;
AL500; AM706; AR469; AS
50; AT367; AU291; AX428;
AY111; BB603; BY509; BZ
                              109335
Take unto you the boughs of
goodly trees (Lucas) AH149;
BH187   109336
"Take up thy cross and follow
me" (McKinney) AT347;
AU99   109337
Take up thy cross, the Saviour
said (Everest) E484; F333;
G260; I433; O394; R293; U
270; W501; X119; Z285; AL
360; AM507; AO371; AP559;
AR249; AS331; AZ345; BA
588; BE325; BV589; BY510;
BZ   109338
Take us on the Quest of Beauty
(Stock) AR415   109339
Take your burden to the Lord
and leave it there (Tindley)
R If the world from you
                              109340
Talk with us, Lord, thyself re-
veal (Wesley) G309; I499;
AL314; BY486; BZ   109341
Tantum ergo Sacramentum
(St Thomas Aquinas) AH114b;
BM7; BN107; BO274; BP62;
BQ241, 242   109342
Tarry with me, O my Saviour
(Smith) B31; D642; U420;
V639; AO46; AY290 109343

Tausend-tausendmal sei dir
(Homburg) R Jesu, meines
Lebens Leben   109344
Te, Joseph, celebrent agmina
caelitum (Breviary, 1670)
BN168; BO267   109345
Te, lucis ante terminum (St
Ambrose) BJ91b; BQ261
                          109346
Teach me, Lord, the love that
lives (Schroll) R Saviour, I
would live for thee   109347
Teach me, my God and King
(Herbert) A476; E485; F337;
G320; H315; I417; J451; K262;
L413; N503; W511; X652; AF
401; AM555; AN284; AO501;
AW226; AZ1342; BA552; BF448;
BV603; BX343; BY487   109348
Teach me, O Lord, the perfect
way (Scottish Psalter, 1650)
AL679; AP107c   109349
Teach me, O Lord, thy holy way
(Matson) T413; AK262; AM456;
AR300   109350
Teach me, O Lord, thy way of
truth (U. P. Psalter, 1912)
T229; AJ325; AM451   109351
Teach me, O Lord, to follow Him
who trod (Lambert) W510
                          109352
Teach me the measure of my days
(Watts) V663; AX420; AY166
                          109353
Teach me thy way, O Lord (Ram-
sey) BV642   109354
Teach me thy will, O Lord
(Grimes) AX566   109355
Teach me to do the thing that
pleaseth thee (Monsell) AZ460;
BA476; BR376   109356
Teach me to pray, Lord, teach me
to pray (Reitz) AT330 109357
Teach me yet more of thy blest
ways (Hutton) AZ136; BA502
                          109358
Teach ye, O Lord, true brother-
hood (Savage) U370; BF486
                          109359
Teach us what thy love has borne
(Pollock) A231; B142c
                          109360
Tell how He pities the erring

(Crosby) R Go as a witness
                          109361
Tell it again! Tell it again!
(Slade) R Into the tent
                          109362
Tell it o'er and keep on telling
(Lyon) R Go and tell the
sweet old story   109363
Tell it out among the heathen
that the Lord is King (Haver-
gal) I634; AI170   109364
Tell it out among the nations
(Havergal) AI170 X Tell it
out among the heathen
                          109365
Tell it to every kindred and
nation (de Fluiter) BB543
                          109366
Tell it to Jesus, Tell it to
Jesus (Rankin) R Are you
weary   109367
Tell me, my Saviour, where
thou dost feed thy flock
(Robinson) AO627   109368
Tell me the old, old story
(Hankey) E583; N351; R403;
U144; V239; W682; Z438;
AH344; AL496; AM521; AO
633; AP433; AS181; AT222;
AU370; AV345; AW495; AX
280; AY521; AZ806; BA420;
BB524; BV481; BY420
                          109369
Tell me the stories of Jesus I
love to hear (Parker) G441
R459; Z214; AE432; AG303;
AH540; AL605; AP763; AR
474; AA400; AT505; AV405;
AW419; BV356; BY130; BZ
                          109370
Tell me the story of Jesus
(Crosby) AH276; AM685;
AT211; AU367; AX317; BB
534   109371
Tell me, whom my soul doth
love (Wolcott) AZ32
                          109372
Tell out, my soul, the great-
ness of the Lord (Dudley-
Smith) BV439   109373
Tell the blessed tidings (Miller)
G445; I652   109374
Tell us now, O Death, where is

thy sting? (Hanrahan) BN50
109375

Temper my spirit, O Lord
(Untermeyer) Y182; AC173;
AG307; AR657   109376

Ten thousand martyrs died for
Israel's cause (Meyerhardt)
BH135   109377

Ten thousand times ten thousand
(Alford) A590; B541; D396;
E486; F284; G531; I618; J595;
K519; L351; M318; N617; O617;
Q476; R427; S427; T352; U430;
V706; W221; Z568; AA288; AB
415; AD457; AE308; AF311;
AG285; AH524; AI341; AK416;
AL175; AM234; AN547; AO553;
AP308; AR426; AT476; AV292;
AZ848; BA756; BB306; BD249;
BF662; BR440; BV437; BX462;
BY407   109378

Tender Shepherd, thou hast stilled
(Meinhold) B414; D248; L570;
O599; P423; Q595; AZ586
109379

Tent-like this day the King stretched out the sky (Kalir) BH160
109380

Thank and praise Jehovah's name
(Montgomery) L95; V528; AE
18; AP96; BA16   109381

Thank God for the things of the
spirit (Malloch) AC488
109382

Thank God! My Jesus cleanseth
me (Olearius) AA189 109383

Thank the Lord! With bounteous
measure (Fischer) AW376
109384

Thank we now the Lord of heaven
(Hawkes) AN172; AQ290; BX
197   109385

Thank you for the world so sweet
(Leatham) X404; BY754
109386

Thanks and praise, Jesus, unto
thee are due (Moravian) AZ712
109387

Thanks be to God for His wonderful love (Emerson) AO64
109388

Thanks for the Sabbath School
(Willes) BC177   109389

Thanks to the Man of sorrows
be (Watteville) AZ684
109390

Thanksgiving, honor, praise
and might (Arnold) AZ691
109391

That awful day will surely
come (Watts) H492; V682
109392

That cause can neither be lost
nor stayed (Ostergaard)
Z493; AE377; AR534; BK28
109393

That day of wrath, that dreadful day (Latin 13th c Scott
tr) E487; F228; H493; I603;
J298; L578; M323; N613;
O606; Q612; V683; W161;
AA551; AL142; AM242; AP
247; BA736; BJ36   109394

That doleful night before His
death (Hart) AX171 X That
solemn night   109395

That Easter Day with joy was
bright (Latin, 5th c) A98;
J94; AO178   109396

That Easter-tide with joy was
bright (Latin, 5th c) AO178
X That Easter Day with joy
was bright   109397

That God should love a sinner
such as I (Bishop) AX87
109398

That man a godly life might live
(Luther) Q287; AA391
109399

That man hath perfect blessed-
ness (Scottish Psalter, 1650)
AL630; AP1; AW575 109400

That man is blest who, fearing
God (U. P. Psalter, 1912)
AJ1; AM446   109401

That mystic word of thine, O
sovereign Lord (Stowe) BY
775 X Abide in me, O Lord
109402

That our Lord's views with us
may be attained (Zinzendorf,
N. L.) AZ522   109403

That solemn night before His
death (Hart) AE331; AX171;
AY257   109404

That we our will to Him might

yield (Luther) M59   109405

The abyss of many a former sin
(St Joseph the Hymnographer)
O400; AA420   109406

The advent of our God (Coffin)
E11; F48; J3; K4; Q68; X68;
AA137; BR130; BV88   109407

The advent of our King (Coffin)
F48 X The advent of our God
109408

The ages one great minster seem
(Lowell) AM417; BX448
109409

The amplitude of space comes
down to your own door (Wheelock) AQ182   109410

The ancient law departs (Besnault)
A113; B88; D148; F539; Q117;
AA176; AZ1320   109411

The angel Gabriel from God
Was sent to Galilee (English
trad carol) BG37   109412

The angel sped on wings of light
(How) D156   109413

The art, the science, and the
lore (Trapp) AQ250   109414

The atoning work is done (Kelly)
L143; AA241; AZ1188 109415

The Babe in Bethlem's manger
laid (English trad carol)
BG69   109416

The beam that shines from Zion
hill (Bruce) AP383   109417

The beauteous day now closeth
(Gerhardt) AD60 X The
duteous day now closeth
109418

The best friend to have is Jesus
(Bilhorn) R O, the best friend
to have is Jesus   109419

The bird let loose in eastern
skies (Moore) BR530
109420

The blasts of winter are fierce
and cold (---) AC454
109421

The blessings of the earth and
sky (Patton) AQ256   109422

The bliss for which our spirits
pine (Hayne) AB410; BF667
109423

The boar's head in hand bear I
(Queen's College, Oxford,

1812) BG19   109424

The body, Lord, is ours to
keep (Stock) AC164 109425

The bread of life, for all men
broken (Lew) BZ X O Bread
of life   109426

The bread that bringeth strength
I want to give (Fitch) Y231;
AE279; AR380; AS357
109427

The bread that giveth strength
(Fitch) AE279 X The bread
that bringeth strength
109428

The breaking waves dashed high
(Hemans) BX546   109429

The Bridegroom comes; Bride
of the Lamb, awake (Bonar)
BR222   109430

The Bridegroom soon will call
us (Walther) M339; Q67;
AA134; AX128   109431

The builders, toiling through the
days (Ham) AN455 109432

The call to arms is sounding
(Hernaman) AZ845 109433

The chariot! the chariot! its
wheels rool on fire (Mil-
man) BT162   109434

The Child of humble Virgin
born (Schneegass) M352
109435

The Child sweetly rests (Cennick) AZ1417   109436

The children of the Hebrews,
carrying palms and olive
branches (Bible. Psalm 122)
E617   109437

The chimes of the Sabbath reḛ-
cho abroad (Overby) P42
109438

The chosen three, on mountain
height (Ela) I129 109439

The Christ- child lay on Mary's
lap (Chesterton) BG143
109440

The Christ will our Pilot be
(DeArmond) R We sail along
109441

The Christian warrior, see him
stand (Montgomery) BE326
X Behold! The Christian
warrior stand   109442

The Church above forever rings
(Latin, 7th c) M511   109443

The Church has one foundation
(Stone) BB443 X The Church's
one foundation   109444

The Church has waited long (Bonar)
AZ1485; BA101; BB177 109445

The Church of Christ, that He
hath hallowed here (Spangenberg) AZ524; BA279   109446

The Church of God a Kingdom is
(Muirhead) A387; E488; F254;
X248; BJ61   109447

The Church of God is stablished
(Thayer) AB322; BF585
                                   109448

The Church on earth, in humble
strain (Scheffler) AZ988 X
Thy majesty, how vast it is
                                   109449

The Church triumphant in thy love
(Wesley) E639   109450

The Church's one foundation
(Stone) A396; B464; D491; E
489; G381; H401; I207;
J149; K198; L278; M78; N264;
O78; P80; Q473; R437; S333;
T360; U345; V531; W205; X249;
Y347; Z423; AA466; AB321; AC
308; AD391; AE314; AF260;
AG228; AH511; AI144; AK322;
AL164; AM270; AO416; AP295;
AR491; AS185; AT380; AU406;
AV244; AW273; AZ814; BA260;
BB433; BF584; BL96; BR223;
BV425; BY263; BZ   109451

The city, Lord, where thy dear
life (Dudley) AD428; AR365;
BF561   109452

The cleansing stream I see, I
see! (Palmer) R O, now I see
the crimson wave   109453

The clouds hang thick o'er Israel's
camp (Drane) BO111   109454

The Comforter has come (Bottome)
R O, spread the tidings round
                                   109455

The coming King is at the door
(Belden) BB546   109456

The corn is ripe for reaping (---)
AO578   109457

The crest and crowning of all good
(Markham) Y259; AN350; AQ

143   109458

The cross is not greater than
His grace (Booth) R The
cross that He gave   109459

The cross is on our brown
(Dix) B369; D212   109460

The cross it standeth fast,
Hallelujah (Bonar) AU470
                                   109461

The cross, like pilgrim war-
riors, we follow (Gosse)
X590b   109462

The cross that He gave may be
heavy (Booth) AU372; AX
427; AY463   109463

The cross, the cross, O, that's
my gain (Taylor) AZ279
                                   109464

The dark night is ending (Whittier) R Sound over all
waters   109465

The darkness now is over
(Brock. The Children's hymn
book, 1881) W270   109466

The dawn is sprinkling in the
east (Latin, before 8th c)
E57   109467

The dawn of God's dear Sabbath
(Cross) I72; AL191; AR66;
AS39; AW283; BB467; BR84
                                   109468

The dawn of God's own Sabbath
(Cross) BR84 X The dawn
of God's dear Sabbath
                                   109469

The dawn was purpling o'er the
sky (Latin, 4th c) BO174
                                   109470

The dawn-wind now is waking
(Dearmer) BG157   109471

The day dawn is breaking
(Townsend) BC179   109472

The day departs; Our souls and
hearts (Freylinghausen) BY
704   109473

The day departs, yet thou art
near (Franzén) M575; N564
                                   109474

The day draws on with golden
light (Latin, 4th-5th c) E
123   109475

The day is done, the night draws
nigh (Weitzman) BH12

109476
The day is fast declining (Himmerich) P75   109477
The day is gently sinking to a close (Wordsworth) B13; D7; H36; I61; K461; L27; AO28; AV16; AZ702; BR127   109478
The day is past and gone (Leland) B21; D645; L31; V53; AA41; AO51; AY287   109479
The day is past and over (St Anatolius) A184; B23; D16; E276; F21; G52; J224; K458; L18; O555; Q555; S44; U465; V43; W287; AD50; AI54; AL 557; AM342; AN124; AO35; AP 670; AZ29; BA794; BF203; BV65; BX153; BY705; BZ
109480
The day is past; the shadows round are falling (Burton) AC19   109481
The day is slowly wending (Rowland) G57; BZ   109482
The day is surely drawing near (Ringwaldt) M321; N614; P 428; Q611; AA552   109483
The day is surely drawing near (Ringwaldt) X Dies irae (Latin, 13th c)   109484
The day, O Lord, is spent (Neale) K473; L23; AZ1315
109485
The day of resurrection (St John of Damascus) A96; B171; D 115; E137; F132; G159; H177; I164; J105; K115; L263; M441; N128; O327; Q205; R208; S166; T348; U106; W123; X146; Y301; Z247; AB144; AC127; AD160; AE125; AF192; AG99; AH300; AI83; AK165; AL103; AM197; AO184; AP220; AR189; AT111; AW115; AZ816; BA229; BB135; BD238, 239; BF322; BL29; BP 34; BR180; BV190; BY162; BZ
109486
The day of the Lord is at hand, at hand (Kingsley) X310; AF 417   109487
The day of wrath, that dreadful day (Latin 13th c Scott tr) L578 X That day of wrath,

that dreadful day   109488
The day thou gavest, Lord, is ended (Ellerton) A179; B 29; E277; F33; G54; I60; J 227; R59; S45; T313; U464; W289; X56; Z140; AB33; AD 58; AE47; AF47; AG26; AK 54; AL568; AM338; AN120; AO32; AP671; AR60; BA395; BB57; BD10; BF191; BK47; BV52; BX147; BY706; BZ
109489
The day will bring some lovely thing (Crowell) AC430
109490
The daylight fades, the evening shades are gathering (Summers) K576   109491
The days that were, the days that are (Lewis) BY557
109492
The death of Jesus Christ, our Lord (Spegel) N234; Q163; AA434   109493
The doctrine of our dying Lord (Cennick) AZ652; BA446
109494
The duteous day now closeth (Gerhardt) A181; E278; F34; J228; N560; W284; X57; AD 60; AF53; AK58; AN112; AP 668; AW556a; BJ83; BY707
109495
The dying robber raised his aching brow (Lacey) E114
109496
The earth and the fullness with which it is stored (U.P. Psalter, 1912) T40; AJ57
109497
The earth is home and all abundant (Patton) AQ56
109498
The earth is hushed in silence (---) U441; AC7   109499
The earth, O Lord, is one great field (Neale) E168; F472
109500
The earth, O Lord, is one wide field (Neale) F472 X The earth, O Lord, is one great field   109501
The earth shall melt with fer-

vent heat (Warner) AX287
                              109502
The earth with all that dwells
   therein (U. P. Psalter, 1912)
   R38; AJ59; AM66   109503
The ends of all the earth shall,
   hear (U. P. Psalter, 1912) R
   501; T34; AI178; AJ49; AM295
                              109504
The eternal gates lift up their
   heads (Alexander) D129; X174;
   AZ97   109505
The eternal gifts of Christ the
   King! (St Ambrose) A132; E
   175; F503   109506
The evning winds begin to blow
   (Long) BX143   109507
The evntide falls gently now
   (Brooks) AX110   109508
The ever-changing seasons (How)
   BX173   109509
The eye can naught but water see
   (Luther) AZ1031   109510
The fading day adorns the west
   (Steingrimur) J236   109511
The fast, as taught in holy lore
   (Latin, 6th c) E65   109512
The Father and the Son and Spirit
   we adore (---) AZ1328
                              109513
The fathers built this city (Tar-
   rant) S408; Z503; AB330;
   AC266; AD425; AN395; BD138;
   BF508; BX538   109514
The fields are all white, and the
   reapers are few (Barrett.
   Book of praise for children,
   1881) W362; BV360   109515
The fight is on, the trumpet sound
   (Morris) AH448; AU402
                              109516
The first fruits of the land we
   bring (Pendleton) BI110
                              109517
The first good joy that Mary had
   (English trad carol, 15th c)
   BG70   109518
The first Nowell [Noel] the angel
   did say (English carol) A30;
   B551; G97; J40; R156;
   S129; W45; X384; Y328;
   Z197; AB119; AC79; AD114;
   AE86; AF141; AG72; AH

124; AK118; AL65; AN174;
AP730; AQ285; AR132; AT
63; AU140; AW76; BB108;
BC39; BD231; BF281; BG27;
BI82; BK160; BL8; BN23;
BO159; BP15; BV117; BX
535; BY109; BZ   109519
The generations as they rise
   (Russell) AQ104   109520
The gloomy night will soon be
   past (Tregelles) AZ1143
                              109521
The glorious gates of righteous-
   ness (U. P. Psalter, 1912)
   R71; T224; AJ318   109522
The glorious gospel light has
   shone (Johnson) BC45
                              109523
The glorious universe around
   (Montgomery) AZ147; BA
   675   109524
The glory of the Lord, The
   heavens declare (U. P. Book
   of Psalms, 1871) AP14a
                              109525
The glory of the spring how
   sweet (Gill) P228; W608;
   AE420; AI42; AK430; AL
   574; AN134; AO576; AP687;
   AW385; BB95; BD42; BX
   165; BY720   109526
The glory of these forty days
   (Latin, 6th c) A61; E68
                              109527
The God of Abraham praise
   (Jewish doxology) A285; B
   253; D460; E646; F631; G5;
   H14; I4; J410; K284; Q40;
   R89; S8; V89; W571; X398;
   AD70; AF14; AG38; AK61;
   AL25; AM32; AP144; AR38;
   AW14; AZ1192; BA19; BB76;
   BF212; BI5-D; BK58; BL97;
   BV249; BY30; BZ   109528
The God of harvest praise
   (Montgomery) AO582; AS422;
   AY58; AZ1233; BA867; BI116
                              109529
The God of love my Shepherd is,
   And he that doth me feed
   (Herbert) E93; F178; X
   653; BJ26   109530
The God of love my Shepherd

is, My gracious constant guide
(Rawson) D413   109531
The God of mercy be adored
(Watts) L p. 741; AZ1437
                        109532
The God of mercy warns us all
(Heber) AO479   109533
The God of the ages your refuge
(Kretzmann) M543   109534
The God that to the fathers re-
vealed His holy will (Savage)
BD147; BH234   109535
The God who made both heaven
and earth (---) BE327
                        109536
The God who sits enthroned on
high (U. P. Psalter, 1912)
T18; AJ23; AM474   109537
The God, whom earth, and
sea, and sky (Fortunatus)
E214; F512; BL62; BV440
                        109538
The gold and silver are the
Lord's (---) AZ388   109539
The golden gates are lifted up
(Alexander) F439; H184;
W130; AM214; AO192; BV
203   109540
The golden morning is fast ap-
proaching (Graham) BB547
                        109541
The good man's steps are led
aright (U. P. Psalter, 1912)
T64; AJ98   109542
The gospel bells are ringing
(Martin) BY421   109543
The Gospel shows the Father's
grace (Loy) M35; Q297; AA
116   109544
The grace of our Lord Jesus
Christ, The love of God so
highly prized (Watteville)
AZ286; BA922   109545
The grave itself a garden is
(Wordsworth) B166; D108
                        109546
The gray hillstaught me patience
(Cross) Y161; AC186 109547
The great Creator of the worlds
(Epistle to Diognetus) A298
                        109548
The great forerunner of the
morn (St Bede, the Venerable)

F553   109549
The great God of heaven is
come down to earth (Bram-
ley) E29   109550
The great Physician now is
near (Hunter) P271; AH334;
AI389; AP752; AS128; AT
86; AU226; AX535; BB530
                        109551
The great Redeemer we adore
(Stennett) AS453   109552
The greatness of God in his
love has been shown (Dear-
mer) X94; BG139   109553
The half has never yet been
told (Havergal) R I know I
love thee better   109554
The hand that was nailed to the
cross (Pierson) AX106; AY
512   109555
The happy Christmas comes
once more (Grundtvig) J28;
K23; M358; O193; AW411
                        109556
The happy day has rolled on
(Dibble) BC250   109557
The happy morn is come!
(Haweis) L260; AZ1176
                        109558
The happy sunshine now is gone
(Hermann) AA32; BR119
                        109559
The harp at nature's advent
strung (Whittier) Y47; AB
49; AD32; AN38; AQ93; BX
58   109560
The head that once was crowned
with thorns (Kelly) A106;
B188; D372; E147; F218;
G163; H191; I173; J439; L145;
M456; N150; O365; P211; Q
219; R211; S195; T330; U109;
V162; W131; X175; AA237;
AE122; AF200; AG107; AL
118; AM215; AO191; AP225;
AR193; AS155; AT117; AV
117; BA249; BJ15; BV207;
BY192; BZ   109561
The heaven of heavens cannot
contain (Drennan) F619
                        109562
The heavenly child in stature
grows (Santeuil) F78; BV

132   109563

The heavenly King must come
   (Martin) N201   109564
The heavenly word, proceeding
   forth (St Thomas Aquinas) X
   F384 The word of God proceed-
   ing forth   109565
The heavens are declaring the
   Lord's endless glory (---)
   AH179   109566
The heavens are thine, Thou King
   of Kings, Their glory shines
   for Thee (Plummer) BI6-D
                           109567
The heavens are thine, Thou King
   of Kings, Their glory thine
   (Odhner) BI12-D   109568
The heavens cannot thee embrace
   (Brueckner) M520   109569
The heavens declare His glory
   (Conder) BD37   109570
The heavens declare the glory
   Of Him who made all things
   (Root) BE329; BK57   109571
The heavens declare thy glory
   The firmament thy power
   (Birks) O8; Y50; AC41; AI
   39; AK71; AS90   109572
The heavens declare thy glory,
   Lord (Watts) F252; H95; I202;
   R259; S217; U141; V230; Z441;
   AA114; AD194; AF257; AG263;
   AL28; AM263; AO95; AR32;
   AT187; AV73; AW291; BF268;
   BV308; BZ   109573
The heavens in their splendor
   declare (Collier) AI40 X The
   law that the Lord has ordained
                           109574
The heavens, O God, thy glory
   tell (Kennedy) BH57   109575
The heavens resound with His
   praises eternal (Hofer) AH616
                           109576
The hidden years at Nazareth
   (Cross) Y73; AB126; AC97;
   BB114; BK17   109577
The highest and the holiest place
   (Alford) E210; F545; BV451
                           109578
The holly and the ivy When they
   are both full grown (English
   trad carol) BG38; BV108

                    109579

The holly's up, the house is all
   bright (Cornelius) BG191
                           109580
The holy angels, When they to
   Christ draw near (Zinzen-
   dorf, N.L.) AZ545
                           109581
The holy Child Jesus (Cennick)
   AZ1115   109582
The Holy Ghost is here (Spur-
   geon) AT168; AZ1367
                           109583
The Holy Son of God most high
   (More) J34; X80   109584
The Holy Supper is kept indeed
   (Lowell) AC500   109585
The home where changes never
   come (Bellamy) BB616
                           109586
The Homeland, O the Homeland
   (Haweis) G530; I615; M307;
   T438; V693; AA562; AH520;
   AV284; BA757; BB639; BF
   660   109587
The hour in dark Gethsemane
   (Norwegian) P175   109588
The hours' decline and setting
   sun (Herman) AZ399
                           109589
The hours of day are over
   (Ellerton) K575; L26; O567
                           109590
The hymn for conquering mar-
   tyrs raise (St Bede, the
   Venerable) E35   109591
The joyous life that year by
   year (How) AH519 109592
The judgment has set, the books
   have been opened (Belden)
   BB482   109593
The King, O God, his heart to
   thee upraiseth (Bridges)
   E564; F580; X324; AL518;
   BJ74   109594
The King of Glory standeth
   (DeChenez) R410; S298; W
   396   109595
The King of heaven His table
   spreads (Doddridge) G409;
   I233; BZ   109596
The King of love my shepherd
   is (Baker) A345; B326; D

(St Anatolius) E32   109628
The Lord ascendeth up on high,
Decked with resplendent
wounds (Hart) AZ156
                                    109629
The Lord ascendeth up on high,
The Lord hath triumphed
(Russell) E148; O362; R212;
S172; W132; BV211; BY177
                                    109630
The Lord at first did Adam
make (English trad carol)
BG1   109631
The Lord be praised! I'm home-
ward bound (Larsen) M311
                                    109632
The Lord be with me everywhere
(Hammond) AZ561   109633
The Lord be with us as each day
(Ellerton) G28; Z125; AE36;
AK33; AN473; AO47; AP336;
AR61; AS65; AW42; AX76; BA
384; BB37; BC28; BD19; BX
515   109634
The Lord be with us as we bend
(Ellerton) AK33 X The Lord
be with us as each day
                                    109635
The Lord be with us as we walk
(Ellerton) BC28 X The Lord
be with us as each day
                                    109636
The Lord bless and keep thee in
His power (Gregor) AZ1020;
BA923   109637
The Lord bless thee and keep
thee (Bible. Numbers) AU498
X The Lord bless you
                                    109638
The Lord bless you and keep
you (Bible. Numbers) G614;
I748; AC25; AE474; AG340;
AU498; AW614; BB695; BF
698; BY305a   109639
The Lord descended from above
(Sternhold) BR139 X O God,
my strength and fortitude
                                    109640
The Lord doth reign and clothed
is He (Scottish Psalter, 1650)
AL665; AW593   109641
The Lord for ever doth endure
(Scottish Psalter, 1650) AL

632   109642
The Lord for ever sits as King
(Scottish Psalter, 1650) AP7
                                    109643
The Lord God Jesus Christ
doth reign (Bostock) BI53
                                    109644
The Lord has heard and an-
swered prayer (U.P. Psalter,
1912) AM25 X Thou, O
Jehovah, shalt endure
                                    109645
The Lord hath helped me hither-
to (Amilie Juliane) M529;
Q33; AA80   109646
The Lord hath reigned, and
reigns: let earth (Keble)
AP83   109647
The Lord hath said, "Seek ye
my face" (Sadler) BX245
                                    109648
The Lord hath yet more light
and truth (Rawson) R We
limit not the truth of God
                                    109649
The Lord Himself gave forth
the word (Zinzendorf, N.L.)
AZ679   109650
The Lord I will at all times
bless, In praise my mouth
employ (U.P. Psalter, 1912)
AJ88   109651
The Lord I will at all times
bless, My mouth his praises
(U.P. Psalter, 1912) R412;
T57; AJ90   109652
The Lord imparted from above
(Snow) BC298   109653
The Lord, in his righteousness,
judges the people (Annin)
Y27; AN327; BI14   109654
The Lord in Sion reigneth
(Crosby) BB7   109655
The Lord into His Father's
hands (Petursson) M390
                                    109656
The Lord is come! On Syrian
soil (Stanley) A327; E48;
X95; AB129; AK125; BF339;
BX196   109657
The Lord is coming! let this be
(---) BB187   109658
The Lord is great; with worthy

praise (U.P. Psalter, 1912)
T89; AJ131   109659
The Lord is in his holy place,
In all things near and far
(Gannett) X655; AD31; AN73;
BD31; BX111   109660
The Lord is in his holy place,
Let all the earth be still
(Grundtvig) BE332   109661
The Lord is King! I own His
power (Terry) BY488 109662
The Lord is King! lift up thy
voice (Conder) F175; I90;
L98; M144; R83; W25; AL8;
AM58; AP162; AY422; BA24;
BV239; BY194   109663
The Lord is King: -- upon His
throne (Montgomery) AZ734;
BA23   109664
The Lord is king, with majesty
enrobed (Ladies of the Grail)
BSp28   109665
The Lord is my light; then why
should I fear (Nicholson) BB
577; BC103   109666
The Lord is my Shepherd, I
shall not want (with refrain:
His yoke is easy by Hudson)
AX473   109667
The Lord is my Shepherd, I shall
not want (Scottish Psalter,
1650) AX473 X The Lord's
my Shepherd, I'll not want
                                109668
The Lord is my Shepherd, no
want shall I know (Montgomery)
I104; V509; Y365; Z170; AC57;
AD234; AH212; AI304; AM663;
AN261; AO321; AS260; AT57;
AU22; AV66; AW62; AZ499;
BA691; BB405; BC104; BD56;
BF242; BI2; BR267; BX305
                                109669
The Lord is near! Why should
we fear? (Kretzmann) M334
                                109670
The Lord is rich and merciful
(Lynch) S82; W398; AB158;
AF328; AM519; BY422
                                109671
The Lord is risen again, Ye
heavens, exultant sing
(Sigstedt) BI107   109672

The Lord is risen indeed
(Kelly) E627; F142; H188;
I157; W120; BV188   109673
The Lord is strong to help the
weak (U.P. Psalter, 1912)
T287; AJ396   109674
The Lord Jehovah lives, and
blessed be my Rock! (Hast-
ings) L486   109675
The Lord Jehovah reigns
(Watts) G63; I81; V101;
BB11; BZ   109676
The Lord my faithful Shepherd
is (Arrebo) O345   109677
The Lord, my God, be praised
(Olearius) Q38; AA272
                                109678
The Lord my pasture shall pre-
pare (Addison) B317; D659;
E491; F179; M149; Q368; X
656; AA85; BC113; BR252
                                109679
The Lord my pasture will pre-
pare (Addison) BC113 X
The Lord my pasture shall
prepare   109680
The Lord my Shepherd holds
me (U.P. Psalter, 1912)
T38; AJ55   109681
The Lord my Shepherd is
(Watts) J526; K255; N480;
O346; Q426; V342; AA374;
AK307; AO322; AS261; AY
117; BR258   109682
The Lord my Shepherd is and
Guide (Meusslin) AZ744
                                109683
The Lord, my Shepherd still has
been (Lucas) BH86 109684
The Lord of all, who reigns
supreme (Jewish trad) BH76,
276   109685
The Lord of earth and sky
(Wesley) AZ1171   109686
The Lord of glory is my light
(Watts) AO74; AX490; AY
92   109687
The Lord of heaven confess
(Wither) X657; AP131
                                109688
The Lord of life is risen
(Lange) AK172; AO189; AZ
730; BT566   109689

The man of life upright (Campian)
AQ107   109721
The man that fears the Lord
(U.P. Psalter, 1912) AJ62
109722
The man who once has found
abode (U.P. Book of Psalms,
1871) G74; T169; AF91; AJ
248; AM74; AP77; BZ   109723
The maple leaf our emblem dear
(---) R In days of yore, from
Britain's shore   109724
The mass of unborn matter knew
Thee (Duclaux) X616b 109725
The Master comes! He calls for
thee (Crawford) BV332
109726
The Master hath come, and He
calls us (Doudney) AT427
109727
The men of the Church for the
Master (Cooper) M528 109728
The mercies of my God and King
(Lyte) AZ1438   109729
The mercy of God is an ocean
divine (Simpson) AU45
109730
The merits of the saints (Latin,
8th c) E182   109731
The mighty God, Jehovah, speaks
(U.P. Psalter, 1912) T94;
AJ137   109732
The mighty God, the Lord, Has
spoken unto all (U.P. Psalter,
1912) T96; AJ139   109733
The mighty God, the Lord, Hath
spoken unto all (Scottish
Psalter, 1650) AM239; AP44
109734
The moon shines bright, and the
stars give a light (English
trad carol) BG46   109735
The more thou puttest in the Lord
thy trust (Howard) BR331
109736
The morning breaks; the shadows
flee (Pratt) BC269   109737
The morning bright, with rosy
light (Summers) K572; W653;
AO629; AP804   109738
The morning hangs a signal
(Gannett) AN90; AQ1   109739
The morning kindles all the sky

(Latin, 4th c) AZ1445
109740
The morning light is breaking
(Smith) A264; B479; D252;
G487; H482; I653; J313; K
230; L347; M104; N366;
O113; P391; Q497; R499;
S389; U406; V587; Z524;
AA471; AB375; AD376; AE
364; AF305; AG260; AH468;
AK384; AL262; AN409; AO
511; AP386; AT448; AU12;
AV271; AW324; AZ856; BA
354; BB453; BE335; BF531;
BX329   109741
The morning Star upon us
gleams (Nicolai) O220; P
146   109742
The morning sun illumes the
skies (Hermann) M559
109743
The morning sun is brightly
beaming (Finnish, 1836)
Q545   109744
The morning walks upon the
earth (Brooke) Y54; AB6;
AN105; BD2; BX55
109745
The mouth of fools doth God
confess (Luther) AA277
109746
The mystery hidden from the
eyes (Gerhardt) AA264
109747
The Name of Jesus is so sweet
(Martin) AM711; AU102; BB
643   109748
The new-born Child this early
morn (Schneegass) AA169
109749
The new-born King who comes
today (---) K538; N40
109750
The new church year again is
come (Olearius) M342
109751
The night has a thousand eyes
(Bourdillon) AQ164 109752
The night is come like to the
day (Browne) X58 109753
The night is come wherein at
last we rest (Herbert) AZ
528   109754

The night is ended and the morning nears (Tennyson, F) X328; AD365   109755

The night was dark and stormy (Eliot) BD216   109756

The nighty-nine within the fold (Schell) AX202   109757

The ocean hath no danger (Thring) K501   109758

The offering on the altar burned (U.P. Psalter, 1912) T73 AJ109   109759

The offerings to thy throne which rise (Bowring) BX499 109760

The old year now away is fled (New Christmas carols, 1642) BG28   109761

The old year now hath passed away (Steuerlein. Seiben und zwantzig...) M368; O207; P 145; Q125; AA173   109762

The old year's long campaign is o'er (Stone) BY718   109763

The one thing needful, that good part (Ingham) AZ353; BA444 109764

The only Son from heaven (Cruciger) O167; P114 109765

The parson knew that he had lost the eyes (Jean Ingelow) BW 144   109766

The passion theme pursuing (Zinzendorf, C.R.) AZ796 109767

The past is dark with sin and shame (Higginson) AN321; BX380   109768

The past yet lives in all its truth, O God! (Appleton) BX442 109769

The peace of God protects our hearts (Grundtvig) M134 109770

The peace which God alone reveals (Newton) AZ924   109771

The people of the earth go down (MacLeish) AQ112   109772

The people that in darkness sat (Morison) F80; Q106; AM123; BR155; BV133; BZ   109773

The perfect world, by Adam trod (Willis) I660   109774

The pity of the Lord To those that fear His name (Watts) V 661   109775

The praises of that Saint we sing (Antoniano) E193; BN 184   109776

The praises of thy wonders, Lord (Scottish Psalter, 1650) AM38 X O greatly blessed the people are   109777

The praying spirit breathe (Wesley) H56   109778

The Prince of Peace His banner spreads (Fosdick) Z553; AB356; AD357; AK409; BF 576   109779

The Queen, O God (Bridges) AL518 X The King, O God 109780

The race that long in darkness sat (Morison) E43; N41; R153; X96; AL60; AP167; BJ71; BY110   109781

The radiant morn hath passed away (Thring) B14; D8; E279; F19; G41; J222; K460; N561; O553; P334; S38; V51; W279; AL566; AP679; AT32; AZ11; BY708   109782

The radiant morn shines in the skies (Hermann) Q547 109783

The reproach of Christ is glorious (Gotter) AZ234 109784

The restless day now closeth (Gerhardt) N560 X The duteous day now closeth 109785

The riches of God are eternal (Wine) AR475   109786

The righteous ones shall be forever blest (Thai Christian's paraphrase) BZ   109787

The river of death has brimmed his banks (Newboldt) Y159 109788

The roseate hues of early dawn (Alexander) D409; E493; N 513; AZ1465   109789

The royal banner is unfurled (Fortunatus) AZ180 X The royal banners forward go 109790

The royal banners forward go
(Fortunatus) A63; B144; D94;
E94; F96; H166; J75; K91; Q
168; X130; AZ180, 324; BY
147   109791

The royal standard forward goes
(Fortunatus) K91 X The royal
banners forward go   109792

The Sabbath day has reached its
close (Elliott) BB61   109793

The Sabbath day was by (Robbins)
A100   109794

The Sabbath light is burning
bright (Sampter) BH106
                           109795

The saint who enters heaven
(Heatwole) AX432; AY165
                           109796

The Saint who first found grace
to pen (Housman) E220; X
228   109797

The saints of God! Their conflict
past (Maclagan) A128; B294;
D175; F572; J145; K247; T439;
W219; AO539; AP306; BA764;
BL71   109798

The saints on earth and those
above Q478 X Not to the terrors of the Lord (Watts) X
Come, let us join our friends
above (Wesley)   109799

The saints who toiled from place
to place (Frere) F522 109800

The sands have been washed in
the footprints (---) AU26
                           109801

The sands of time are sinking
(Cousins) O597; S434; T440;
U418; V677; W581; AH521; AI
336; AL465; AM599; AO544; AP
612; BA758; BY776   109802

The Saviour calls; let every ear
(Steele) L356; Q281; V278;
AA47; BY423   109803

The Saviour died, but rose again
(Church of Scotland, 1745) BV
276   109804

The Saviour in Gethsemane Bows
low in bitter agony (Petursson)
M422   109805

The Saviour is risen, Light bursts
from the tomb (Franzén) M443;
N123   109806

The Saviour kindly calls (Doddridge) L321; Q302; AA406
                           109807

The Saviour lives, no more to
die (Medley) AZ294 X I
know that my Redeemer lives
what joy [comfort]   109808

The Saviour! O what endless
charms (Steele) H234; U69;
V131; AO357; AY51; AZ1436
                           109809

The Savior reigns, The Lord
most high (Plummer) BI27d
                           109810

The Saviour who loves me
(Gray) AU44   109811

The Saviour's blood and righteousness (Eber & Zinzen-
dorf) AZ278; BA445
                           109812

The Saviour's precious blood
(Korean hymn) BY664)109813

The sea withdraws and fetters
break (Franciscan manual)
R If, now, thou seekest
miracles   109814

The seasons are fixed by wisdom divine (U.P. Psalter,
1912) T198; AJ286   109815

The Seer, the Seer, Joseph,
the Seer! (Taylor) BC296
                           109816

The sepulcher is holding (St
Cosmas) AZ27; BA213
                           109817

The Seraphim of God Exalt
their voices (Gregor) AZ
1119   109818

The service of Jesus true
pleasure affords (Huston)
AU414   109819

The shadows lengthen, Lord,
with me abide (---) BB698
                           109820

The shadows of the evening
hours (Proctor) B22; D15;
G46; I62; S36; T314; U456;
V38; Z142; AB24; AD51; AH
165; AL543; AN122; AO26; AP
678; AS26; AV13; AZ1458; BA
793; BB54; BF204; BX156
                           109821

The shepherds had an angel

(Rossetti) G436; S448; X372;
AH547; AL601; AP732   109822

The Shepherd's heart is saddened
(Newton) AX267; AY219
109823

The ships glide in at the harbor's
mouth (Sangster) U333; AC
226; AL592   109824

The sky can still remember
(Brooks) S123; AB112   109825

The sky has gathered the flowers
of sunset (Torrence) AQ197
109826

The snow in the street and the
wind in the door (Morris) R
From far away we come to you
109827

The snow lay on the ground
(Sedulius of Liege) A41; BQ8
109828

The snow lies thick upon the earth
(Image) BG192   109829

The soldiers led the Saviour out
(Petursson) M391   109830

The solemn moment is impending
(Amilie Juliane) AZ696; BA
733   109831

The solemn season calls us now
(Breviary, Paris, 1736) AO
267   109832

The Son of Consolation (Coote)
B281; D162; E222; BV443
109833

The Son of God goes forth for
Peace (Allen) Z559   109834

The Son of God goes forth to war
(Heber) A549; B85; D507; E202;
F529; G285; H394; I416; J562;
K383; L530; M382; O491; Q452;
R354; S271; U290; V491; W530;
X216; Y118; Z358; AB251; AC
262; AD296; AE249; AF388; AG
196; AH444; AK288; AL409; AM
489; AO396; AP543; AT414; AU21;
AV198; AZ1427; BA586; BB361;
BF469; BR402; BV457; BY558;
BZ   109835

The Son of God, the Prince of
Peace (Maurer) AB252
109836

The Son of Man goes forth to war
(Heber) BR402 X The Son of
God goes forth to war   109837

The Son of Man goes forth today (Barstow) AK267
109838

The soul wherein God dwells
(Scheffler) AQ92   109839

The Sower goeth forth to sow
(Hoppe) N82   109840

The sower went forth sowing
(Bourne) F486; BV652
109841

The spacious firmament on
high (Addison) A309; B252;
D464; E297; F170; G66; H
111; I84; J442; R97; S69; U
8; V100; W10; X659; Z164;
AB48; AC47; AD97; AF72;
AG57; AH188; AI41; AK66;
AL27; AM103; AN33; AO59;
AP142; AQ47; AR98; AS88;
AT10; AV53; AW50; BA32;
BB91; BD36; BF230; BK129;
BV232; BX52; BY74; BZ
109842

The spacious firmament on high
(Addison) X occasionally includes The starry firmament
on high (Grant)   109843

The spacious heavens declare
(U. P. Psalter, 1912) T28;
AJ37   109844

The Spirit and the Bride (---)
BA104   109845

The Spirit breathes upon the
word (Cowper) H94 X A
glory gilds the sacred page
109846

The Spirit, in our hearts
(Onderdonk) D596; K319;
L362; M25; O486; V265;
AZ1330   109847

The Spirit of God like a fire is
burning (Phelps) BC213
109848

The Spirit of the Lord revealed
(Briggs) J251; X660; Z437;
AD199; AW570; AX147
109849

The Spirit's fruits are peace
and love (Cronenwett) M228
109850

The spirits of the just (Hart)
AZ1486   109851

The splendours of thy glory,

Lord (Coffin) X35   109852
The spring again is here (Benson) AC319   109853
The springs of salvation from Christ the Rock bursting (Foster) AZ1090; BA363   109854
The stable was old and rude and bare (Wagner) BK158   109855
The star proclaims the King is here (Sedulius) Q131; AA180   109856
The starry firmament on high (Grant) I203; BE336   109857
The stars shall light your journey (Kendon) R What songs are these   109858
The stars they sing together (Cross) Y64   109859
The stars were silent and the hills stood dark against the sky (Royce) AW77   109860
The steps of those whom He approves (U. P. Psalter, 1912) R422; T66; AJ101   109861
The storm-god of stern Sinai's hill (Farrington) AD356   109862
The story grows sweeter and sweeter (Hoffman) R O, wondrously sweet   109863
The story that never grows old (Yates) R How dear to my heart   109864
The strain upraise of joy and praise ((St Notker) D461; E 494; W14; AP151   109865
The strife is o'er, the battle done (Latin, 1695) A91; B173; D121; E625; F135; G156; J90; K109; M434; O324; P198; Q210; R203; S164; T346; U105; V737; W122; X147; Z238; AB142; AC133; AD167; AE128; AF181; AG103; AH312; AI84; AK173; AL109; AM201; AO177; AP216; AR190; AT107; AW116; BA237; BF323; BP39; BR183; BV192; BY163; BZ   109866
The summer days are come again (Longfellow) E288; W612; X8; AC321; AD452; AF457; AK431; AL576; AN138; AQ326; BD46; BX167   109867

The sun arises now in light and glory (Kingo) M562; Q542   109868
The sun ascending, To us is lending (Gerhardt) M557   109869
The sun declines; o'er land and sea (Walmsley) K464; S40; W273; AP672   109870
The sun goes down, the shadows rise (Jewish) BH179   109871
The sun has gone down (Bruun) O554; P74   109872
The sun in splendor rose (Currie) BN46   109873
The sun is on the land and sea (Benson) S29; AI44; AK195; BB45   109874
The sun is sinking fast (Latin, 1805) A183; B17; D10; E280; F30; K474; O564; W272; AL569; AP680; BY709   109875
The sun is sinking in the west (Bersagel) P68   109876
The sun rolls down The distant west (---) BB59   109877
The sun shines in splendor (---) BK1   109878
The sun's bright rays are lost in sight (Hermann) M578   109879
The sun's last beam of light is gone (Hermann) Q563   109880
The sweet June days are come again (Longfellow) AQ326 X The summer days are come   109881
The tempter to my soul hath said (Montgomery) BB253   109882
The tender love a father has (U. P. Psalter, 1912) T191; AJ278; AM85   109883
The tenor of the gospel word (Heatwole) AY297   109884
The things of the earth in the earth let us lay (St Joseph the Hymnographer) L572;

N606   109885
The thought of Jesus, O how sweet
(St Bernard of Clairvaux) P
101   109886
The time for toil is past (Akers)
AX581; AY131   109887
The time is far spent, there is
little remaining (Snow) BC184
109888
The time is near when Zion's
sons (Cottrell) BB307
109889
The time of the harvest is nigh
(Evilsizer) AX204; AY333
109890
The time shall come when, free
as seas of wind (Pope) AQ199
109891
The toil of brain, or heart or
hand (Freckelton) I414; AC189;
AS240; BF440; BX227 109892
The touch of human hands (Clark)
Y207; AC237   109893
The trepass of the wicked man
(U.P. Psalter, 1912) T60; AJ
94   109894
The tribute of our thanks we
bring (Fischer) M395 109895
The true Messiah now appears
(Watts) V134   109896
The trumpet call of duty (Miles)
BD94   109897
The trumpet is sounding, we're
off to the fray (Smith) R At
home and abroad   109898
The turf shall be my fragrant
shrine (Moore) Y53   109899
The twilight falls the night is
near (Cheevers. Commonplace
book; 1831) AI52   109900
The twilight shadows round me
fall (Ryden) J233; M569; N556
109901
The unbounded love of my Creator
(Zinzendorf, N.L.) AZ1009
109902
The uplifted eye and bended knee
(Scott) BX352 X The lifted
eye and bended knee   109903
The very Angels' Bread Doth food
to man afford (St Thomas
Aquinas) BQ46   109904
The voice of free grace cries,

"Escape to the Mountain!"
(Burdsall) L368; AZ504
109905
The voice of God again is
heard (Stephens) BC289
109906
The voice of God is calling
(Holmes) G454; P407; Y235;
Z490; AB284; AF426; AK387;
AN316; AQ214; AR251; BD
158; BF499; BH238; BX541
BZ   109907
The voice that breathed o'er
Eden (Keble) B383; D240;
E348; N530; Q622; AA442;
AO559; AP704; AT502
109908
The Wallapai, the Navaho
(Brink) AI174   109909
The wanderer no more will
roam (Walker) AZ1148
109910
The war in which the soldier
fights (---) AY387
109911
The water's going out to sea
(Masefield) AC468 109912
The way is dark, I dare not go
alone (Lear) AS217 109913
The way is long and dreary
(Proctor) O267   109914
The way of the cross leads
home (Pounds) R I must
needs go home by way of
the cross   109915
The way that I take He knoweth
(Hoffman) R He knoweth the
way   109916
The way that unto Jesus leads
(Kingo) P121   109917
The way, we know, is rough and
weary! (Howard) BR536
109918
The whole bright world rejoices
now (German carol. 1623)
X167; AF194; BG96 109919
The whole wide world for Jesus,
This shall our watchword be
(Johnson) AE355; AO524;
AS368; AV270; AW340; BY395
109920
The whole wide world for Jesus
Once more, before we part

(Johnson??) AV270 X The
whole wide world for Jesus,
This shall our watchword be
                           109921
The whole world was lost in the
darkness of sin (Bliss) AE
301; AI392; AM679; AR473;
AT88; AU330; AW467; AX273
                           109922
The wicked watching for their
prey (U.P. Psalter, 1912)
T65; AJ99   109923
The will of God is always best
(Albrecht v. Brandenburg)
Q517   109924
The winds and the waves shall
obey thy will (Baker) R
Master, the tempest   109925
The winged herald of the day
(Prudentius) E53   109926
The winter night was dark and
still (Benson) AC80; AD122
                           109927
The winter's sleep was long and
deep (Dearmer) E221; X229
                           109928
The wintry day, descending to its
close (Whitney) BC292
                           109929
The wise may bring their learn-
ing (Barrett. Book of praise
for children, 1881) G439; J
545; P357; W363; X373; Z316;
AH273; AL590; AM657; AP779;
AT513; AW418; BF616; BG121b
BH246; BV351; BY528   109930
The wise men from the East
adored (Greek) AZ562 109931
The wonderful! The Counsellor!
(Crosby) R O, wondrous
Name, by prophets heard
                           109932
The wonders of redeeming love
(Cottrell) BB143   109933
The Word, descending from above
(St Thomas Aquinas) BQ50
                           109934
The Word of God, proceeding
forth (St Thomas Aquinas)
E330; F384   109935
The Word of God which ne'er
shall cease (Moravian) AZ315;
BA1   109936

The Word, whose word can
make me whole (Govan)
BB203   109937
The work is thine, O Christ
our Lord (Preiswerk) AK
269; AR562; AW550a
                           109938
The works, O Lord, our hands
have wrought (Wilson) BX
501   109939
The world has need of willing
men (Thompson) BC206
                           109940
The world in condemnation lay
(Montgomery) AZ986
                           109941
The world is glad, the world
is bright (Howe) AR588
                           109942
The world is very evil (St
Bernard of Cluny) A595; B
68; D405; E495; F276; J596;
K526; Q605; V689; AZ812;
BA750; BR436   109943
The world itself is blithe and
gay (---) AD166   109944
The world itself keeps Easter
Day (Neale) AH304; BG150
                           109945
The world looks very beautiful
(Warner) W575; AP765; BV
359   109946
The world of sinners know not
God (Naylor) AX442 109947
The world stands out on either
side (Millay) AQ57 X O
God, I cried   109948
The world's astir! The clouds
of storm (North) G562;
AR536   109949
The world's great age begins
anew (Shelley) X311
                           109950
The worst of evils we can name
(Worgan) AZ1430   109951
The year begins with Thee
(Keble) AA175   109952
The year is gone beyond recall
(Breviary, Meaux, 1713)
AW382; BW382   109953
The year is swiftly waning
(How) E294; W621; X15;
AW387   109954

The year of jubilee has come
(Wesley) R Blow ye the trum-
pet, blow   109955
The year's at the spring (Brown-
ing) X6; Y57; AC431   109956
The Yigdal (Daniel ben Judah)
X Praise to the living God
(Jewish doxology   109957
The young child, Christ, is
straight and wise (Sandberg)
AC455   109958
Thee, Father, Spirit, Son, We
joyfully adore (---) Lp.741
                         109959
Thee God we praise, Thy holy
name we bless (Latin, 5th c:
Te Deum) P12 X Thee God
we praise, Thy name we bless
                         109960
Thee God we praise, Thy name
we bless (Latin, 5th c: Te
Deum) O1; P12, 16   109961
Thee, God's Anointed, hail we
our King (Hacker) R Great
King of Kings and Lord of
Lords   109962
Thee, holy Father, we adore
(Laufer) S13   109963
Thee, living Christ, our eyes be-
hold (Morgan) F422   109964
Thee, Lord, before the close of
day (St Ambrose) BL74
                         109965
Thee, O Christ, the Father's
splendour (St Rabanus Maurus)
E241   109966
Thee prostrate I adore, the
Deity that lies (St Thomas
Aquinas) BQ48   109967
Thee we address in humble prayer
(Wesley) AZ117; BA898
                         109968
Thee we adore, eternal Lord, We
praise thy name with one ac-
cord (Latin, 5th c: Te Deum)
J415; K281; L94; M598; N319;
AA66; AI19; AM18; BA22
                         109969
Thee we adore, O hidden Saviour,
Thee (St Thomas Aquinas)
E331; F385; J272; W319; X
279; BR478; BY330   109970
Thee we praise, eternal Lord

(Latin, 6th c) BR80 109971
Thee will I love, my God and
King (Bridges) X661; BJ
99; BY75   109972
Thee will I love, my strength,
my tower (Scheffler) J505;
K301; M233; N469; O474;
P309; Q399; W431; AA349;
AK276; AL293; AP455; AR
118; AZ672; BA494; BV547
                         109973
Their God and Saviour they for-
got (U.P. Psalter, 1912)
T202; AJ291   109974
Then away, haste away (Baird)
R When the rosy light of
morning   109975
Then away to the work I will
go (Henry) R I cannot be
idle   109976
Then come, wanderer, come
(Pratt) R Afar on the
mountain   109977
Then day by day along your
way (Pounds) R O scatter
seeds   109978
Then drink to the holly berry
(English trad) BG189 R On
Christmas Eve the bells
were rung (Scott)   109979
Then let men and Angels praise
thee (Sister of Notre Dame)
R Hail! All hail, great
Queen of heaven   109980
Then let us adore, His heart
that loves (Dollard) R On
Calvary's height the Roman
spear   109981
Then Mary took her young Son
(English trad carol) X
Joseph was an old man
                         109982
Then sings my soul, my Saviour
God to thee (Boberg) R O
Lord my God! When I in
awesome wonder   109983
Then trim your lamps, my
brethren dear (Belden) R
Let every lamp be burning
bright   109984
Then trust Him in shine and
shade (Homer) R Fear not,
for God   109985

Then, O my Lord prepare my
soul (Bonar) R A few more
years shall roll   109986
Then praises bring our Lord and
King (Woods) R Now let us
raise   109987
Then sing you all, both great
and small (English trad carol)
R When righteous Joseph wed-
ded was   109988
Then stand! stand firm! defy the
foe! (---) R Put on the armor
                          109989
Then trust in God thro' all thy
days (Cornelius) R Not now,
but in the coming Years
                          109990
Then wake up, and do something
more (Thompson) R Have I
done any good   109991
Then welcome each rebuff
(Browning) X662   109992
Then we'll be happy with Christ
(Jacobs) R When the trump
shall sound   109993
Then why will ye die? (Penn)
R There is a Rock   109994
Then work, brothers, work, let
us slumber no more (Punshon)
R Listen! The Master.
                          109995
Theories, which thousands cherish,
Pass like clouds (Waterston)
BE337   109996
There are a myriad means, O
Lord (Dearmer) X663; Y2
                          109997
There are ooming changes great
(Matheson) BF575   109998
There are hearts that never falter
(---) AS335   109999
There are lonely hearts to cherish
(Cooper) AU394; AX182
                          110000
There are loved ones in the glory
(Habershon) AX613   110001
There are none friendless, none
afraid (McKenzie) BE339
                          110002
There came a little Child to earth
(Elliott) K540; W68; AP728
                          110003
There came three kings, ere break

of day (Moultrie) K543;
AO137   110004
There comes a ship asailing
(German trad carol, 1470-
80) BG90   110005
There comes to my heart one
sweet strain (Bilhorn) U230;
AE300; AI256; AR476; AT
299; AU381; AX336; BB609
                          110006
There dwelt in old Judea (Ray-
mond) AH249   110007
There is a Balm in Gilead
(Negro Spiritual) BZ
                          110008
There is a better world, they
say (Lyth) AP793   110009
There is a blessed home
(Baker) A591; B515; D679;
E496; O615; V713; W594;
AP630; AZ482; BA759
                          110010
There is a blessed hope (---)
BB379   110011
There is a blessed power, that
shields us from all woe
(Aaberg) M129   110012
There is a book that all may
read (Keble) Z435 X There
is a book, who runs may
read   110013
There is a book who runs may
read (Keble) E497; F168;
W8; X664; Z435; AB46;
AN39; AZ118; BB92; BF239;
BR368; BV134; BX59; BY76;
                          110014
There is a calm for those who
weep (---) AY176   110015
There is a city bright (Deck)
W480; AM662; AP792; BV493
                          110016
There is a dear and hallowed
spot ("Anne") L246 110017
There is a flower springing
(Speier Gebetbuch, 1599)
BG76   110018
There is a fountain filled with
blood (Cowper) D593; E332;
G140; H232; I291; J373; K77;
L238; N97; O314; P277;
Q157; R276; S241; U150; V
251; W692; AA200; AE183;

AG98; AH286; AI140; AL491;
AM188; AO272; AP203; AR
477; AT92; AU37; AV154; AW
492; AX118; AY236; AZ92; BA
201; BB163; BV509; BY148;
BZ   110019
There is a gate that stands ajar
(Baxter) N616; P263; AI408;
AX250; BB561   110020
There is a gentle Gardener
Who owns a garden fair
(German) M625   110021
There is a God who reigns
above (Watts) V685   110022
There is a green hill far away
(Alexander) A65; B159; D544;
E106; F214; G135; H242; J77;
K544; M419; N108; P174; R
202; S157; U91; V752, 149;
W105; X131; Z230; AB139;
AD153; AE111; AF171; AG92;
AH288; AK149, 479*; AL87;
AM184; AO162; AP734; AR172;
AS145; AT98; AU98*; AV106*;
AW104; AZ1449; BA226; BB
126; BC201; BF314; BV163;
BY149; BZ   110023
*Ref. attached
There is a happy land, Far, far
away (Young) E608; W587;
AP795; AS471; AZ1247; BB
301   110024
There is a holy sacrifice (Elliott)
W408; AP424; AZ18; BA428
                            110025
There is a house not made with
hands (Watts) L448; AZ155
                            110026
There is a joy the heart can feel
(Loveman) BH79   110027
There is a land immortal (Mac-
Kellar) L603   110028
There is a land mine eye hath
seen (Robins) H504   110029
There is a land of corn and wine
(Stites) BB554 X I've reached
the land of joy   110030
There is a land of pure delight
(Watts) A586; B513; D678;
E498; F285; G528; H508; I
604; J583; K518; L586; M298;
N620; O611; U423; V699; W
592; X201; AA560; AG286; AH

528; AI340; AL464; AM597;
AO549; AP634; AU216; AV
281; AX596; AY141; AZ176;
BA760; BB299; BR435; BV436;
BX468; BY614   110031
There is a land whose sunny
vales (Huish) BC72 110032
There is a mystic tie that joins
(Meyerhardt) BH137 110033
There is a name I love to hear
(Whitfield) P143; AI387;
AT131; AU283; AW496; AX
46; AY47; BB171; BV548
                            110034
There is a place of quiet rest
(McAfee) R318; AE225;
AR478; AT301; AU273; AW
239; AX50; BB681   110035
There is a road, though nar-
row and obscure (Aufranc)
BB374   110036
There is a Rock in a weary
land (Penn) AU23   110037
There is a safe and secret
place (Lyte) O70; U35;
V341; AE228; AO354; AZ
211; BB399   110038
There is a sea of mercy (Sol-
berg) P255   110039
There is a spot to me more
dear (Hunter) AX327; AY318
                            110040
There is a story ever new
(Snyder) AX374; AY202
                            110041
There is a stream whose
waters rise (Neale) BR439
                            110042
There is a voice of sovereign
grace (Watts) L405 110043
There is an arm that never
tires (Burton) AS268
                            110044
There is an everlasting home
(Bridges) BQ69, 70
                            110045
There is an eye that never
sleeps (Wallace) P25; AE
242; BH68; BV615   110046
There is an hour of hallowed
peace (Tappan) M282 X
There is an hour of hallowed
rest   110047

There is an hour of hallowed rest
(Tappan) L590; M282   110048
There is an hour of peace and
rest, Unmarred by (---)
BC172   110049
There is an hour of peaceful rest
To mourning wanderers
(Tappan) H503; I609; L592;
Q617; V704; AA564; AO55;
AY133   110050
There is an unseen hand to me
(Sims) AX467   110051
There is beauty all around
(McNaughton) AE384; AS413;
AW360; AX555; AY444; BC169
                               110052
There is coming a day when to
judgment we'll go (Winsett)
AX297   110053
There is life for a look at the
Crucified One (Hull) AX328
                               110054
There is never a day so dreary
(Russell) AT142; AU69; AV367
                               110055
There is no love like the love of
Jesus (Littlewood) BY424
                               110056
There is no name so sweet on
earth (Bethune) AI388; AM652;
AO624; AS397; AV138; AW440;
AX22   110057
There is no night in heaven
(Knollis) K522; W590; AM598;
AP624   110058
There is no other hope (Hoffman)
R O Lord, within my soul
                               110059
There is no other name than thine
(---) AZ371; BA69   110060
There is no sorrow, Lord, too
light (Crewdson) S295; W148;
X665; Z342; AL127; AM517;
AP239; AW259; AZ228; BV614
                               110061
There is no unbelief; who ever
plants a seed (Case) AC486
                               110062
There is not a friend like Jesus
(Hendricks) AX526   110064
There is nothing in the world like
Jesus (Jones) AX271   110065
There is one way, and only one

(Alexander) D160   110066
There is One whom I love
(Payn) AI267   110067
There is pow'r, pow'r, wonder-
working pow'r (Jones) R
Would you be free   110068
There is rest by and by
(Cosner) R Often weary
                               110069
There is rest for the weary
(Harmer) R In the Christian's
home   110070
There is rest, sweet rest, at
the Master's feet (Hewitt)
AU109   110071
There is sunlight on the hilltop
(Haughey) BB612   110072
There is sunshine in my soul
(Hewitt) AT273; BB607;
BC174   110073
There is sweet rest for feet
now weary (Belden) BB380
                               110074
There is sweet rest in heaven
(Bone) R Farewell, all earth-
ly honors   110075
There is sweet rest in heaven
(Metzler) R When trials and
temptations   110076
There is within this heart of
mine (Walther) AA460
                               110077
There lives a God! Each finite
creature (Hamburg Temple
hymnal) BH61   110078
There lives a voice within me
(Massey) BB281   110079
There many shall come from the
east and the west (Landstad)
O239 X Full many shall
come   110080
There shall be no night in heaven
(Hostetler) R Shadows never
darken heaven   110081
There shall be showers of bless-
ing (Whittle) AH389; AI262;
AM716; AT264; AU97; AX37;
BB652   110082
There still is room! His house
is not yet filled (German)
Q509   110083
There was a star in David's
land (English trad carol)

BG54   110084
There was a time when children
sang (Taylor) I684   110085
There was One who was willing
to die (Breck) AU345; BB123
                                    110086
There were ninety and nine that
safely lay (Clephane) E584;
F247; W685; AH373; AI181;
AL475; AM137; AP408; AU36;
AY501; BB673; BR532; BY425
                                    110087
There were three lights that night
(Turner) AD113   110088
Therefore we, before him bending
(St Thomas Aquinas) A200; B
338b; E326b; F383b; X280
                                    110089
There'll be no shadows in heaven
(Cook) AX606   110090
There'll be no sorrow there
(Dana) R O sing to me
                                    110091
There's a beautiful, beautiful land
(Brenneman) AX589; AY135
                                    110092
There's a beautiful land on high
(Nicholson) AY159   110093
There's a beautiful star, a beauti-
ful star (Raymond) AC93
                                    110094
There's a blessing in prayer
(Hewitt) R There is rest,
sweet rest   110095
There's a breathless hush in the
close tonight (Newbolt) Yp423
                                    110096
There's a call comes ringing o'er
the restless wave (Gabriel)
AT457; AU117; AV381; AX212;
AY330   110097
There's a church in the valley
(Pitts) AG295; AH515 110098
There's a city of light 'mid the
stars (Kieffer) AX370; AY
153   110099
There's a cleft in the Rock of
Ages (Good) AX511; AY447
                                    110100
There's a dear and precious book
(Williams) AH239; AU380
                                    110101
There's a deep settled peace in my

soul (Brown) R I cannot tell
thee whence it came 110102
There's a fountain free, 'tis
for you and me (Slade) AX
230   110103
There's a Friend for little chil-
dren (Midlane) B363; D553;
E607; F452; I680; J592; K
558; P360; W593; AH542;
AO625; AP789; AS396; BA
813; BV358; BY615   110104
There's a garden where Jesus
is waiting (Schroll) AU342;
AX362   110105
There's a glad new song ring-
ing (Fisher) AT311 110106
There's a God who's standing at
heaven's door (Ellis) AX
282   110107
There's a great day coming
(Thompson) AU333   110108
There's a Kingdom fair and
gently looming (Overby)
P205   110109
There's a land beyond the
river (DeMarbelle) AU360
                                    110110
There's a land that is fairer
than day (Bennett) N621;
U424; AH535; AT471; AU344;
AV396; AW504; AX587; BB
551   110111
There's a light upon the moun-
tains (Burton) G123; Y248;
Z249; AB155; AC285; AR216;
AT124; BF338   110112
There's a Rose that is bloom-
ing for you, friend (Palmer)
AR479   110113
There's a royal banner given
(Whittle) AT408; AU59
                                    110114
There's a song in the air!
There's a star in the sky
(Holland) G98; I112; R155;
Z198; AC84; AD118; AE87;
AH257; AI65; AR131; AT69;
BB106; BZ   110115
There's a Stranger at the door
(Atchinson) AH337; AU29;
AX246; BB566   110116
There's a sweet and blessed
story (Johnston) AU382

110117
There's a voice in the wilderness crying (Milligan) G503; AD 373; AK94; AL244; BZ 110118
There's a way that is free from sin (Brooks) AX363   110119
There's a wideness in God's mercy (Faber) A304; B240; E499; F364; G76; H243; I98; J493; K257; L89; N435; P259; R110; S93; T320; U18, 146; V240; W395; X666; Y39; Z172; AB71; AC55; AD82; AE74; AF 101; AG54; AH180; AI37; AK85; AL468; AN556; AO256; AP397; AQ44; AR91; AS87; AT48; AU 182; AV64; AW58; AZ250, 959; BA407; BB65; BD58; BE340; BF250; BK67; BV480; BW58; BY419; BZ   110120
There's but a small beginning made (Stach) AZ283; BA358
110211
There's heaven above, and night by night (Browning) X667
110122
There's no other name like Jesus (Belden) BB517   110123
There's not a bird with lonely nest (Noel) L487; AB69; AC52; AS 98   110124
There's not a friend like the lowly Jesus (Oatman) AI396; AY352   110125
There's sunshine in my soul (Hewitt) BB607 X There is sunshine   110126
There's within my heart a melody (Bridgers) AT307; AU391
110127
There's work for the hand and there's work for the heart (---) AX192; AY520   110128
These are the gifts I ask of Thee (Van Dyke) Y206; AC472
110129
These scenes, so bright, now take their flight (Oatman) AY404
110130
These things shall be: a loftier race (Symonds) G512; S423; W639; X312; Y189; Z507; AB 355; AC293; AD363; AE400;

AF450; AG278; AK407; AL 514; AN360; AQ190; AR576; BD181; BF563; BH237; BK 106; BX408; BY196; BZ
110131
They all were looking for a king (MacDonald) X668   110132
They are all gone into the world of light (Vaughan, the Silurist) X294   110133
They are nailed to the cross (Breck) BB123 X There was one who was willing
110134
They brought their gifts to Jesus (Rexford) BB658
110135
They cast their nets in Galilee (Percy) A437; R421; AF 340; AQ111   110136
They come from the east and west (Landstad??) BB453
110137
They come from the thorny path (Landstad??) R They come from the east and west
110138
They come, God's messengers of love (Campbell) E246; F287; K253; L566   110139
They in the Lord that firmly trust (Scottish Psalter, 1650) AL684; AP113 110140
They sailed! They sailed! Then spake the mate (Miller) AC510   110141
They saw the light shine out afar (Dearmer) BG165
110142
They that traffic on the sea (U.P. Psalter, 1912) T206; AJ295   110143
They the builders of the nation (Alldredge) BC173 110144
They to my precepts are always true (McPhail) R All those who love   110145
They were nailed to the cross (Breck) R There was One
110146
They who hunger after Christ, are fed (Foster) AZ514
110147

They who Jesus' followers are
(Gambold) BA677   110148
They who know our Lord indeed
(Gambold) BA504   110149
They who on the Lord rely
(Auber. Spirit of the Psalms.
1829) BR261   110150
They who seek the throne of grace
(Holden) I515; U361; V468;
AE240; AK233; AO310; AR71;
AY341; AZ66; BE341; BF374
                       110151
They who tread the path of labour
(Van Dyke) Z496; AD319
                       110152
They whose course on earth is
o'er (Neale) E500; F273; X
295   110153
Thine advent, Lord, we hail
(Odhner) BI55   110154
Thine agony, O Lord, is o'er
(Wallin) N119   110155
Thine are all the gifts, O God
(Whittier) X331; AO505; AP
575   110156
Thine arm, O Christ, in days of
old (Plumptre) BY637 X
Thine arm, O Lord   110157
Thine arm, O Lord, in days of
old (Plumptre) A517; D273;
E526; F478; J324; K236; N
385; R179; W86; X287; AC111;
AD137; AE102; AI70; AL76;
AO147; AP186; AR153; AS119;
AW95; AZ1441; BA860; BV399;
BY637   110158
Thine be the glory (Budry) BV193
X Thine is the glory   110159
Thine earthly Sabbaths, Lord, we
love (Doddridge) L594; V57
                       110160
Thine for ever [forever] ! God
of love (Maude) A427; B370;
D216; E344; F330; H303; J511;
K179; M546; N252; O107; Q338;
S248; W504; X258; AA411; AK
348; AL357; AO348; AP555; BA
472; BB282; BR463; BV364;
BY586   110161
Thine for ever! Thine for ever
(Wordsworth) BR461   110162
Thine for service when the days
are drear (Leech) R I have

made my choice to follow
                       110163
Thine holy day's returning
(Palmer) L43; BR85
                       110164
Thine honor rescue, Christ our
Lord (Heermann) AA275
X Thine honor save, O Christ
                       110165
Thine honor save, O Christ,
our Lord! (Heermann) Q
265; AA275   110166
Thine is the glory, Risen,
conquering Son (Budry) J566;
R209; Z244; AE127; AF193;
AR194; BV193; BY164; BZ
                       110167
Thine is the glory, Thine O
Lord the praise (Woods)
BK30   110168
Thine is the power, Lord,
humbly we crave (Sangster)
AO303   110169
Thine, O Jesus, now and ever
(Oldenburg) P305   110170
Thine own, O loving Saviour
(Franzén) J264; N235
                       110171
Think gently of the erring one
(Carney) I699; AE381; BH
239   110172
Think not when you gather to
Zion (Snow) BC21   110173
Think on our brethren, Lord
(---) AZ551   110174
Think on thy way, O thou
storm-laden child (Scholfield)
AI206   110175
Thirsting for a living spring
(Appleton) AB184; AN221;
BX92   110176
Thirsting for the living Fountain,
Streaming from (Hungarian
Mass-song, 1855) BL45
                       110177
Thirty years among us dwelling
(Fortunatus) E96   110178
This body in the grave we lay
Q596 X Now lay we calmly
in the grave   110179
This child was born to men of
God (German carol, 17th c)
BG97   110180

This child we consecrate to thee
(Neander) AO434 X This child
we dedicate   110181
This child we dedicate to thee
(Neander) I232; Q303; AA404;
AE327; AK331; AO434; BH240
110182
This day at thy creating word
(How) Q12 X This day the
light of heavenly birth 110183
This day in thy dear name we
meet (Daries) AK41   110184
This day is holy to the Lord
(Foster) AZ887; BA386
110185
This day the first of days was
made (St Gregory the Great??)
E50; BJ31   110186
This day the light of heavenly
birth (How) K440; L42; Q12;
V58; AA127; AM324   110187
This endris night (English trad
carol, 15th c) BG39   110188
This Feast of the Law all your
gladness display (Jewish hymn)
BH199   110189
This God is the God we adore
(Hart) H129; BV30   110190
This house we dedicate to thee
(Naisbett) BC176   110191
This is my body, which is given
for you (Ford) AO441 110192
This is my Father's world
(Babcock) G72; J487; R101;
S70; U332; Y51; Z171; AB64;
AC39; AD93; AE55; AF485;
AG60; AH202; AI32; AK65;
AL589; AM109; AR99; AS94;
AT59; AV406; AW48; BB646;
BF399; BK26; BZ   110193
This is my prayer! Give me the
strength lightly to bear my
joys and sorrows (Tagore) AC
477   110194
This is my song, O God of all the
nations (Stone) BK37; BZ
110195
This is my story, this is my
song (Crosby) R Blessed as-
surance   110196
This is not my place of resting
(Bonar) V701; AX582 110197
This is the charge I keep as mine

(Hill) AQ147   110198
This is the day of light (Ellerton) B45; D28; F42; G397;
H79; K442; R72; S20; W
267; Z446; AB10; AD35; AE
51; AK37; AL189; AM327;
AP343; AR42; AS41; AW287;
AZ1355; BB461; BF189; BR
93; BV68; BY282   110199
This is the day of rest (Eller-
ton) BB461 X This is the
day of light   110200
This is the day that our Father
hath given (Grundtvig) M12
110201
This is the day the Lord hath
made; Be glad, give thanks
(Randall) BE342   110202
This is the day the Lord hath
made. He calls the hours
his own (Watts) F43; H178;
K443; L46; Q10; R69; S23;
U436; V67; X23; AA129;
AF504; AG34; AM326; AT39;
AU280; AV7; AX122; AY
356; AZ131; BA392; BV74;
BZ   110203
This is the day we celebrate
(Schuette) M649   110204
This is the day where-on the
Lord's true witness
(Latin, 8th c) BN182
110205
This is the hour of banquet and
of song (Bonar) A206
110206
This is the hour of banquet and
of song (Bonar) X Here,
O my Lord, I see thee face
to face   110207
This is the image of our Queen
(Caswall) BO77; BQ82
110208
This is the image of the Queen
(Caswall) BQ82 X This is
the image of our Queen
110209
This is the message that I
bring (Cassel) R I am a
stranger here   110210
This is the truth sent from
above (English trad carol)
BG68   110211

This joyful Eastertide, Away with
sin and sorrow (Cowley Carol
Book, 1902) AL110; BN45;
BV197   110212
This new Christmas carol Let us
cheerfully sing (English trad
carol) BG29   110213
This night a wondrous revelation
(Nachtenhöfer) M345; Q88
                         110214
This night, O Lord, we bless
thee (Burns) AM349   110215
This rite our blest Redeemer
gave (Phelps) AT384   110216
This sanctuary of my soul
(Sorley) Y141   110217
This ship, we now commend to
thee (Fergusson) AZ338
                         110218
This solemn hour O let us be
(Erikson) M580; N578   110219
This stone to thee in faith we lay
(Montgomery) W253; AX646;
AZ306   110220
This, this is Christ the King
(Dix) R What child is this,
who laid to rest   110221
This thought shall have our whole
allegiance (Goethe) AQ176
                         110222
This was the song the angels
sang (Stephens) BC359 110223
Those eternal bowers Man hath
never trod (St John of Damas-
cus??) A581; B540; D395; AL
460   110224
Those who love and those who
labour (Dearmer) X669; AF403
                         110225
Thou art coming, O my Saviour
(Havergal) B67; D317; L579;
S186; W157; AM235; AO113;
AP245; AW126; AZ1203; BB196;
BV87   110226
Thou art gone up on high (Toke)
B189; D373; E149; F149; K
123; O368; AP230; AZ1497;
BA244; BR198   110227
Thou art my God, O God of grace
(U.P. Psalter, 1912) T113;
AJ164   110228
Thou art my hiding-place, O Lord
(Raffles) B403; K396; L492; AM

553; AZ1442   110229
Thou art my life; if thou but
turn away (Quarles) X670
                         110230
Thou art my portion, Lord
(U.P. Psalter, 1912) T232;
AJ328   110231
Thou art my Shepherd, caring
in every need (Thalheimer &
Haycraft) AC54; AI303
                         110232
Thou art, O Christ, the light
and life (Rominger) BB389
                         110233
Thou art, O God, the God of
might (Perkins) S67; AI411
                         110234
Thou art, O God, the life and
light (Moore) E298; X20;
AB52; AN31; BX40   110235
Thou art our comfort, blessed
Jesus (Tranecker) AZ999
                         110236
Thou art the Christ, O Lord
(How) D164; F555; BV454
                         110237
Thou art the everlasting Word
(Conder) BY219   110238
Thou art the mighty King of
Kings (Hymns of the English
Conf. 1880) BR66   110239
Thou art the way: by thee alone
(Doane) BR390 X Thou art
the way, to thee alone
                         110240
Thou art the Way, the Truth,
the Life from heaven
(Krummacher) N428; P214
                         110241
Thou art the Way, to thee alone
(Doane) A361; B279; D425;
F199; G332; H151; I133; J
390; K368; L120; M164; N
429; O339; Q355; R221; S
254; U81; V137; W173; AA
94; AG167; AK238; AL339;
AM116; AO217; AP185; AR
177; AS121; AV172; AW185;
AX341; AY209; AZ181; BA85;
BE343; BR390; BV455; BY
220; BZ   110242
Thou by heavenly hosts adored
(Harbaugh) K495 X Christ

by heavenly hosts adored
110243
Thou camest down from heaven
on high (Hoppe) N87   110244
Thou city of the angels, thou
city of the Lord (St Bernard of
Cluny) BR438 X For thee, O
dear, dear country   110245
Thou dear Redeemer, dying
Lamb (Cennick) I532; AZ1450
110246
Thou delightest, O Lord, when
thy children draw near (Wells)
U37; AI18   110247
Thou didst leave thy throne and
thy kingly crown (Elliott) A321;
B83; D319; E585; F363; G95;
H146; I122; J433; K541; N47;
R184; S231; U79; W67; Z292;
AB115; AC101; AD131; AE94;
AF326; AG84; AH254; AK126;
AL68; AM170; AO130; AP180;
AR142; AT82; AU138; AV123;
AX99; BA88; BB103; BF304;
BV277; BY111   110248
Thou didst live to God alone
(Wesley) E591c; F451c 110249
Thou didst teach the thronging
people (Ninde) AK129 X Thou
who taught   110250
Thou dost not weep to weep alone
(Snow) BC181   110251
Thou dost reign on high (Elliott)
AM170 X Thou didst leave thy
throne   110252
Thou, earth, art ours, and ours
to keep (Howitt) AN44; AQ307
110253
Thou ever-present Perfect Friend
(Newman) BH41   110254
Thou fairest Child Divine
(Tersteegen) AZ1491   110255
Thou Father of us all (Clark)
AR577   110256
Thou glorious God, before whose
face (Chadwick) AL37; AN462;
BX437   110257
Thou, God, all glory, honour,
power (Tate & Brady) D456
110258
Thou God of all, whose spirit
moves (Holmes) Z554; AF419
110259

Thou God, whose living voice
was heard (Holmes) Y254
110260
Thou goest to Jerusalem
(Hoppe) N83   110261
Thou Grace divine, encircling
all (Scudder) AD83; AN224;
AW57; BF251; BX116
110262
Thou gracious God, whose
mercy lends (Holmes) F502;
G432; I669; W649; Z602; AE
387; AL392; AN264; AP702;
AW359; AX557; BX496
110263
Thou gracious Power, whose
mercy lends (Holmes) W649
X Thou gracious God, whose
mercy lends   110264
Thou, gracious Saviour, for
my good (Zinzendorf, N.L.)
AZ218; BA840   110265
Thou great mysterious God un-
known (Wesley) I318 110266
Thou hallowed chosen dawn of
praise (St John of Damascus)
X168 X Thou hallowed chosen
morn of praise   110267
Thou hallowed chosen morn of
praise (St John of Damascus)
A93; E138; X168   110268
Thou hast canceled my trans-
gression (Rist) AZ980
110269
Thou hast indeed made manifest
(Hoppe) N73   110270
Thou hast no shore, fair ocean
(St Bernard of Cluny) X
459b   110271
Thou hast, O Lord, most glor-
ious (Scottish Psalter, 1650)
AP59   110272
Thou hast said, exalted Jesus
(Giles) AT390   110273
Thou hidden Love of God, whose
height (Tersteegen) A464;
B227; D658; G375; I345; J
391; K346; N485; O476; W
459; X671; AK321; AL307;
AN82; AP462; BR317; BV
494; BX288; BY460; BZ
110274
Thou hidden Source of calm re-

pose (Wesley) G339; I466; R
423; AG203; AL284; AM426; AZ
664; BB169; BR318; BX306; BY
587; BZ   110275
Thou hidden Source of calm re-
pose (Wesley) X Thou hidden
Love of God, whose height
(Tersteegen)   110276
Thou holy Church, God's city
shine (Landstad) O79   110277
Thou, Jehovah, art my Shepherd
(U. P. Psalter, 1912) T36;
AJ52   110278
Thou, Jesus, art our King
(Scheffler) AZ1160; BA127
                       110279
Thou, Jesus! art the way (Hymns
of the English conf. 1880) BR
30   110280
Thou Judge by whom each Empire
fell (Dearmer) X672; AF442;
AR614   110281
Thou judge of quick and dead
(Wesley) L576; AP244   110282
Thou knowest, Lord, the weari-
ness and sorrow (Borthwick)
B402; D630; O556; AZ1201;
BR348   110283
Thou knowest, Lord! Thou knowest
my life's deep story (Hawkes)
BX267   110284
Thou knowest my tongue, O God
(Solomon ibn Gabirol) BH31
                       110285
Thou Lamb of God, Thou Prince
of Peace (Richter) BR351
                       110286
Thou Life within my life, than
self more near (Scudder) S320
AD282; AN81; BF383; BX106
                       110287
Thou Light of Gentile nations
(Franck) Q138 X Light of the
Gentile nations   110288
Thou little flock, be not afraid
(Altenburg) M90   110289
Thou living light of pentecostal
glory (Goodenough) BE345
                       110290
Thou long disowned, reviled, op-
pressed (Scudder) X673; BX
78   110291
Thou, Lord, art Love (Burns)

AI38   110292
Thou, Lord, by strictest search
hast known (Tate) AP122;
BR279   110293
Thou, Lord, hast dealt well
with thy servant (U. P.
Psalter, 1912) T233; AJ329
                       110294
Thou, Lord, has forsaken, to
shame brought our boasts
(U. P. Psalter, 1912) T82;
AJ122   110295
Thou, Lord, hast given thyself
for our healing (Browne)
BY396   110296
Thou, Lord, hast power to heal
(Greek: Paracletice) E349
                       110297
Thou, Lord, must for thy sake
forgive (Wesley) AZ101
                       110298
Thou Lord of all above (Bed-
dome) L387; AO268 110299
Thou Lord of Hosts, whose
guiding hand (Frothingham)
J305; AN310; BD77; BX376
                       110300
Thou Lord of life and death
(Hoppe) N197   110301
Thou Lord of life, our saving
health (Longfellow) Y218;
Z309; AB261; AN469; AR
363; BX255   110302
Thou Lord of light, across the
years (North) AC257; AK
365   110303
Thou lovely source of true de-
light (Steele) U136; V72;
AO212   110304
Thou loving Saviour of mankind
(St Gregory the Great) AO
158   110305
Thou mighty God who didst of
old (Chadwick) AN422; BX
440   110306
Thou must be true thyself
(Bonar) AS445   110307
Thou must increase, Lord, and
I must decrease; yes, I
offer (Jensen) M212 110308
Thou my everlasting portion
(Crosby) G235; I332; Z413;
AE299; AH324; AI269; AR

ion me (U.P. Psalter, 1912)
T234; AJ330   110347
Thou who didst on Calvary bleed
(Burns) W690; AZ1136 110348
Thou who didst stoop below
(Miles) W147   110349
Thou who dost rule on high
(Littlewood) BY670   110350
Thou who hast called us by thy
word (Bode) AO261   110351
Thou who hast in Zion laid
(Bulmer) AZ1482   110352
Thou who hast known the care-
worn breast (Rawson) AP665
                        110353
Thou who, hero-like hast striven
(Drane) BO138   110354
Thou, who on that wondrous
journey (Alford) D77; AO471
                        110355
Thou who once on mother's knee
(Palgrave) X374; AP740; BY
756   110356
Tho who rollest the year around
(Palmer) Q111; U477; V630;
AA165; AO572   110357
Thou, who sentest thine apostles
(Ellerton) D173; E248; F568
                        110358
Thou who taught the thronging
people (Ninde) AC113; AK129
                        110359
Thou who the night in prayer
(Wordsworth) D184; N282; Q
493; AA492; BT493   110360
Thou who thyself didst sanctify
(Rawson) AW297   110361
Thou who wast a child on earth
(Doddridge) M521   110362
Thou who wast rich beyond all
splendour (Houghton) BV101
                        110363
Thou, whom shepherds worshipped,
hearing (Latin, 1410) F596
                        110364
Thou, whose almighty word
(Marriott) A272; B104; D327;
F266; G477; I629; J309; K217;
L182; M111; N370; O123; Q508;
S392; V82; W364; X303; Z536;
AD384; AI176; AL240; AM376;
AO522; AP372; AR566; AS371;
AT461; AV259; AZ1235; BA13;

BB451; BE346; BV333; BY46;
BZ   110365
Thou whose birth on earth,
Angels sang to men (Swin-
burne) X81   110366
Thou, whose coming seers and
sages (Spitta) O191 110367
Thou, whose glad summer
yields (Johnson) BX460
                        110368
Thou whose love brought us to
birth (Foote) AN193
                        110369
Thou whose name is called
Jesus (Pigott) BV278
                        110370
Thou whose spirit dwells in all
(Chadwick) AN65; BX95
                        110371
Thou, whose unmeasured temple
stands (Bryant) G549; I659;
J246; L300; N278; S476; U
384; V568; Z605; AC525;
AD412; AE346; AG294; AK
357; AN461; AO463; AP698;
AS441; AX645; BA327; BX
498   110372
Thou Wind of God, whose com-
ing stirred (Crum) F440
                        110373
Thou, with thy counsel, while I
live (Scottish Psalter, 1650)
AP62   110374
Though all my foes combine
(---) BR311   110375
Though angels bright escape
our sight (Loy) M484
                        110376
Though but a little child I am
(Cennick) AZ328   110377
Though by nature I'm defiled
(Gregor) AZ1086   110378
Though deepening trials throng
your way (Snow) BC285
                        110379
Though faint, yet pursuing
(Darby) D628; U47; V508;
AI305; AO323; AY309; AZ502;
BR383   110380
Though Fatherland be vast and
fair (Cross) Y119; AB364;
BF568   110381
Though I am poor and sorrow-

ful (U. P. Psalter, 1912)
T126; AJ187   110382
Though I speak with angel tongues
(Lange) AO370; AZ1272
                       110383
Though I'm in body full of pain
(Cennick) AZ343   110384
Though in midst of life we be
(Latin, 12th c) O240   110385
Though in the outward Church be-
low (---) BC102   110386
Though lowly here our lot may
be (Gaskell) AW374 X Though
lowly here our work may be
                       110387
Though lowly here our work may
be (Gaskell) W515; X676; AB
272; AW374; BD99   110388
Though man, the fiery element,
sinks like fire (Holmes) AQ
61   110389
Though mighty foes assail me,
Lord (U. P. Psalter, 1912)
T245; AJ341   110390
Though mountains may depart
from thee (Lias) BE347
                       110391
Though nature's strength decay
(Jewish doxology) AZ1192 X
The God of Abraham praise
                       110392
Though others may forsake the
Lord (Childress) R Upon the
first day   110393
Though our hearts dwell lovingly
(Sternberg) BH228   110394
Though the angry surges roll
(Martin) AH387; AM717
                       110395
Though the way we journey may
be often drear (Jones) AT474
                       110396
Though troubles assail, and
dangers affright (Newton) I92;
N476; P300; W30; AI306; AM79;
BR244; BY588   110397
Though troubles assail us, and
dangers affright (Newton) N476
X Though troubles assail, and
dangers affright   110398
Though troubles great o'ershadow
me (U. P. Psalter, 1912) AJ
191   110399

Though we all in sinful blind-
ness (Palgrave) N173; O402
                       110400
Though we long, in sin-wrought
blindness (Palgrave) O402
X Though we all in sinful
blindness   110401
Though your sins be as scarlet
(Crosby) U159; AH384; AI198;
AM465; AT213; AU350
                       110402
Thousand times by me be
greeted (St Bernard of Clair-
vaux) AZ906   110403
Thousands, O Lord of hosts,
today (Montgomery) BA858
                       110404
Three in One and One in Three
(Rorison) B38; D389; E501;
F163; AS70; AZ1134; BA259;
BV230; BY47   110405
Three kings are here, both
wealthy and wise (Flemish
trad carol) BG80   110406
Three kings from Persian lands
afar (Cornelius) BG193
                       110407
Three kings in great glory of
horses and men (Image) BG
194   110408
Thrice blest is he to whom is
given (Faber) AB237 X
God's glory is a wondrous
thing   110409
Throned upon the awful [awe-ful]
tree (Ellerton) E116; F119;
K104; Q174; R197; W100;
X141; AF174; AL92; AM183;
AP191; AW109; BV177
                       110410
Through all the changing scenes
of life (Tate) E502; F290;
G14; J420; L475; O454; Q29;
S83; V105; X677; AA75; AF81;
AL643; AM522; AO342; AP
31; AW583; AY365; AZ192;
BA656; BV512; BY589; BZ
                       110411
Through all the long dark night
of years (Massey) X313;
AQ169   110412
Through all the various shifting
scene (Collett) BX244

110413

Through all the years, may
Israel say (U.P. Psalter,
1912) T259; AJ361   110414

Through good report and evil,
Lord (Bonar) K259; L479;
W514; AM503; AZ8; BA475;
BR385   110415

Through Him who all our sickness felt (Wesley) B505; D588
                                110416

Through Jesus' blood and merit
(Dach) Q372; AA323   110417

Through Jesus' bloody merit
(Dach) AA323 X Through
Jesus' blood and merit
                                110418

Through life's long day and
death's dark night (Faber)
R O Saviour bless us 110419

Through love to light! O wonderful the way (Gilder) G599;
S499; AB230; BF196   110420

Through love to light! O wonderful the way (Gilder) BF196
X Hail gladdening light (Greek)
                                110421

Through midnight gloom from
Macedon (Stone) O118; AZ
654   110422

Through north and south and
east and west (Dearmer)
A540; X415; AN506   110423

Through the dark the dreamers
came (Marlatt) Y327; AC91;
AD128   110424

Through the day thy love has
kept us (Kelly) BR110 X
Through the day thy love has
spared us   110425

Through the day thy love has
spared us (Kelly) B15; D646;
E281; F25; K478; L35; M567;
N562; O563; Q553; V52; AA
43; AL561; AO41; AP685;
AZ603; BA792; BR110 110426

Through the day thy love hath
spared us (Kelly) BA792 X
Through the day thy love has
spared us   110427

Through the love of God our
Father (Peters) P296; W702;
AV230; BE350; BF398; BY590

110428

Through the love of God our
Saviour (Peters) W702 X
Through the love of God our
Father   110429

Through the night of doubt and
sorrow (Ingemann) A394;
B539; D521; E503; F292;
H424; I567; J529; K201; L
301; O86; P82; Q481; R475;
S345; W214; X678; Y305;
Z481; AB239; AD219; AF
387; AG235; AH431; AK415;
AL448; AN433; AO653; AP
603; AZ971; BA278; BD142;
BE351; BF661; BV566; BX
446; BY559   110430

Through the night thy angels
kept (Canton) E609; F429;
X375   110431

Through thee as we together
came (---) BR106   110432

Through willing heart and help-
ing hand (Hosmer) AN457;
BX494   110433

Through-out the night, O God
above (Wise) BH244 110434

Throughout these forty days,
O Lord (Hernaman) BM75
X Lord, who throughout
these forty days   110435

Throw away thy rod, Throw
away thy wrath (Herbert)
AP485   110436

Throw out the life-line (Ufford)
AH415; AT217; AU72; AX188;
BB624   110437

Thus angels' Bread is made
the Bread of man (St Thomas
Aquinas) BP52   110438

Thus far the Lord hath [has]
led me on (Watts) I51; V56;
AA39; AO100; BR273 110439

Thus saith the mercy of the
Lord (Watts) AI160 110440

Thus speaks the Lord to
wicked men (U.P. Psalter,
1912) T95; AJ138   110441

Thy beauty, Lord, thou hast revealed (Brightman) Y32
                                110442

Thy blessing, Lord, on all
vacation days (Haley) AD453

110443
The blood, so dear and precious
(Praetorius) AZ795; BA498

110444
Thy blood, thy blood the deed hath
wrought (Gersdorf) AZ230

110445
Thy bounties, gracious Lord
(Scott) Z421   110446
Thy broken body, gracious Lord
(---) BB471   110447
Thy ceaseless, unexhausted love
(Wesley) H236; AL12; BY31

110448
Thy children, Lord, of many
lands and nations (Stevenson)
AB215 X Thy people, Lord,
of many lands and nations

110449
Thy cross, O Jesus, thou didst
bear (Geijer) M385; N105;
P173   110450
Thy faithful servant, Lord, doth
yearn (Solomon ibn Gabirol)
BH167   110451
Thy glory thou didst manifest
(Higbee) AO141   110452
Thy gospel, Jesus, we believe
(---) A249   110453
Thy grace impart! In time to be
(Whittier) Y263 X Forgive, O
Lord, our severing ways

110454
Thy hand, O God, has guided
(Plumptre) E545; F256; J159;
W215; Y268; AC307; BV426;
BY264   110455
Thy heaven, on which 'tis bliss to
look (Moore) X679   110456
Thy holy day's returning (Palmer)
BR85 X Thine holy day's
returning   110457
Thy holy Sabbath, Lord (---)
BB470   110458
Thy kingdom come! O Father
hear our prayer (Seebach)
J318   110549
Thy kingdom come, O God (Hensley)
A544; B105; D329; F262; J329;
V605; W152; Y262; AL140; AN
340; AP251; AW271; AZ483;
BA107; BV334; BX388; BY397

110460

"Thy Kingdom come!" O Lord,
we daily cry (Hawkes) AB
297; AN333; AW356; BX386

110461
Thy kingdom come, O Lord,
wide-circling (Hosmer) A534;
R488; S425; T443; Z562; AD
366; AE365; AF448; AK403;
AL526; AN339; AO486; AQ
210; AR568; AS359; AW270;
BD157; BF580; BX387

110462
Thy kingdom come! on bended
knee (Hosmer) A391; B56;
E504; F263; G463; J331;
R484; S363; T371; U331;
W153; X680; Z539; AD345;
AK369; AL138; AN338; AP
249; AW268; BA360; BB193;
BD155; BX458; BY398

110463
Thy kingdom, Lord, Thy kingdom (Scudder) Y237; AB
287; AD346; AR217; BF573

110464
Thy kingdom, Lord, we long for
(Scudder) AB287 X Thy king-
dom, Lord, Thy kingdom

110465
Thy law is perfect, Lord of
light (Montgomery) AZ125;
BA6   110466
Thy life was given for me
(Havergal) B238; D604; J
513; K67; L233; O431; P329;
R262; S229; U92; V154; Z
289; AA352; AM536; AP550;
AR339; AZ553; BA473; BV
643   110467
Thy little ones, dear Lord, are
we (Brorson) J49; M609;
O179; P366; AI383   110468
Thy love, O gracious Lord and
God (Kingo) O434   110469
Thy love to me, O Christ
(Gates) AS284   110470
Thy loving-kindness, Lord, is
good and free (U.P. Psalter,
1912) R393; T128; AJ187;
AM510   110471
Thy majesty, how vast it is
(Scheffler) AZ987-988; BA
130   110472

Thy mercy and thy truth, O Lord
(U. P. Psalter, 1912) R82;
T61; AJ94; AM55   110473
Thy mercy, Lord, is in the
heavens (Rouse) V98; AL646;
AP34   110474
Thy mercy, Lord, to us dispense
(Luther) AZ1425; BA339
                           110475
Thy might sets fast the mountains
(U. P. Psalter, 1912) R99; T
118; AJ171; AM111; BZ
                           110476
Thy mighty love, O God, con-
straineth me (Crawford) BB63
                           110477
Thy mighty power we sing (Hymns
of the English Conf. 1880) BR
79   110478
Thy palm-trees fed with dew and
sun (Bates) AC114   110479
Thy people, Lord, of many lands
and nations (Stevenson) Y90;
AB215   110480
Thy praise, O Lord, will I pro-
claim (Jewish: "A'ameer")
BH183   110481
Thy oresence, gracious God, af-
ford (Fawcett) AA4; AY3; AZ
316; BA394   110482
Thy promised mercies send to
me (U. P. Psalter, 1912) T
230; AJ326   110483
Thy sacred word, O Lord, of old
(Petri) M488; N215   110484
Thy saints are crowned with glory
great ("F.B.P.") X395c
                           110485
Thy scepter, Jesus, shall extend
(Franzén) N265   110486
Thy seamless robe conceals thee
not (Chadwick) BX112 110487
Thy servant, blest by thee, shall
live (U. P. Psalter, 1912) T
227; AJ323; AM260 110488
Thy soul, O Jesus, hallow me
(Scheffler) M426; AA206
                           110489
Thy spirit, Lord, has stirred our
souls (Kooyman) BC204
                           110490
Thy spirit, O Lord, makes life
to abound (U. P. Psalter, 1912)

AJ287   110491
Thy table I approach (Molanus)
M47; Q310; AA430   110492
Thy temple is not made with
hands (Alexander) D295;
H413   110493
Thy tender mercies, O my Lord
(U. P. Psalter, 1912) T74;
AJ110   110494
Thy vineyards and thy orchards
are ("F.B.P;") X395d
                           110495
Thy voice hath spoken, souls
have heard (Maxwell) BB36
                           110496
Thy walls are made of precious
stones ("F.B.P.") X395b
                           110497
Thy way and all thy sorrows
(Gerhardt) O284   110498
Thy way is in the deep, O
Lord (Martineau) AN186;
AW242; BX250   110499
Thy way is in the sea (Fawcett)
H125; L478; V416   110500
Thy way, not mine, O Lord
(Bonar) B394; D632; E505;
F356; I527; K393; L503; Q
532; U38; V430; W553; AA
384; AE268; AL425; AM573;
AO339; AP506; AS243; AW
252; AZ473; BA688; BB396;
BF406; BR324; BV644
                           110501
Thy way, O God, is in the sea
(Fawcett) L478 X Thy way
is in the sea   110502
Thy ways, O Lord! with wise
design (Serle) L476; Q530;
AA514   110503
Thy will, almighty Father,
Thine and thine alone ("H")
BE349   110504
"Thy will be done!" In devious
ways (Bowring) AO700; BI
57   110505
Thy will be done in me
(McKinney) AU103, AX390
X My God, my Father (El-
liott)   110506
Thy will, O Lord, not mine
(Daniels) BR307   110507
Thy wondrous testimonies,

Lord, my soul will keep
(U. P. Psalter, 1912) T241; AJ
337   110508
Thy word is a lamp to my feet
(Sellers) AI155; AM671; AT
180; AU389; AV372; AX141
                        110509
Thy word is like a garden, Lord
(Hodder) P88; S219; AC70;
AD191; AI159; AM257; AR241;
AT182; AW290; BF273; BK24;
BY253   110510
Thy word is to my feet a lamp
(Tate & Brady) BH36   110511
Thy word, O God, declareth
(Walther) J585; K523   110512
Thy word, O Lord, like gentle
dews (Garve) J254; K171;
N219; O136; P84; AI154; BR
240   110513
Thy word sheds light upon my
path (U.P. Psalter, 1912)
T238; AJ334   110514
Thy works, how beauteous, how
divine (Coxe) BE352 X How
beauteous were the marks
divine   110515
Thy works, not mine, O Christ
(Bonar) K68; N89; Q380;
AA329; AM441; AZ1186
                        110516
Tibi, Christe, splendor Patris
(St Rabanus Maurus) BT257
                        110517
Tidings true there be come new
(English trad carol, 15th c)
BG36   110518
"Till he come!" O, let the words
(Bickersteth) H440; I240; T
365; V550; W321; AI162; AM357;
AP359; AS462; AV257; AZ1252;
BA305; BV388   110519
Till permitted hence to go
(Gregor) AZ35   110520
Till we meet, till we meet (Ran-
kin) R God be with you
                        110521
Time is filled with swift transition
(Wilson) AX446   110522
Time is gliding like the shuttle of
the weaver (Oatman) AX127
                        110523
'Tis a pleasant thing to see (Lyte)

AZ1281; BA665   110524
'Tis a point I long to know
(Newton) V481   110525
'Tis a sweet and tender story
(Wight) AY522   110526
'Tis almost time for the Lord
to come (Sederquist) BB
182   110527
'Tis by the faith of joys to
come (Watts) L507; V363;
BB242   110528
'Tis by thy strength the moun-
tains stand (Watts) V621
                        110529
'Tis faith supports my feeble
soul (Beddome) V350
                        110530
" 'Tis finished!" Jesus cries,
He bows his head and dies
(Foster) AZ547   110531
'Tis finished now, Redemption's
finished now (Gregor) AZ
1228   110532
" 'Tis finished!" so the Saviour
cried   (Stennett) H160; I149;
M421; N110; P189; U10; V
144; BB535   110533
'Tis finished! the Messiah dies
(Wesley) H165; BZ   110534
'Tis from the mercy of our
God (Watts) AP163   110535
'Tis God the Spirit leads (Bed-
dome) BE354   110536
'Tis gone, that bright and
orbéd blaze (Keble) AN108
X Sun of my soul   110537
'Tis good, Lord, to be here!
(Robinson) E236; F560; K49;
Q135; BV256; BY131
                        110538
'Tis hard to bear the heavy
load (Hott) AY322   110539
'Tis midnight; and on Olive's
brow (Tappan) G133; H163;
I147; L241; N100; R189;
T341; U96; V151; Z232;
AD144; AE118; AF178; AG92;
AH283; AK145; AM182; AO
161; AR163; AS132; AT104;
AU295; AV105; AW103; AX
114; AY360; BA223; BB121;
BZ   110540
'Tis midnight and the Saviour

calls (Buerge) AX242 110541
'Tis my happiness below (Cow-
    per) V422; BB248   110542
'Tis not that I did choose thee
    (Conder) U156; V241; AI126;
    AM96; AZ840; BT37   110543
'Tis not the large, the huge, the
    vast (Cronbach) BH235
                                    110544
'Tis not with eyes of flesh we
    see (Garber) AR275   110545
'Tis religion that can give
    (Masters) AS296   110546
'Tis so sweet to trust in Jesus
    (Stead) AE302; AI236; AM699;
    AR276; AS272; AT258; AU284;
    AV322; AW488; AX458; AY98;
    BB588; BZ   110547
'Tis sure that awful time will
    come (Ringwaldt) AZ747;
    BA735   110548
'Tis sweet to sing the match-
    less love (Manwaring) BC187
                                    110549
'Tis the blessed hour of prayer
    (Crosby) Z332; AE238; AP
    496; AR481; AS42; AT329;
    AU156; AX352; AY430; BB
    324   110550
'Tis the day of Resurrection
    (St John of Damascus) BP34
    X The day of Resurrection
                                    110551
'Tis the grandest theme thro' the
    ages rung (Ogden) AT198
                                    110552
'Tis the harvest time, 'tis the
    harvest time (Thomas) AX206;
    AY336   110553
'Tis the Lord! O wondrous story
    (Hanby) R Who is He in
    yonder stall?   110554
'Tis the month of our Mother
    (---) AH136; BN61   110555
'Tis the most blest and needful
    part (Zinzendorf, C.R.) AZ
    879; BA532   110556
'Tis the promise of God full
    salvation to give (Bliss) AV
    156; AW442   110557
'Tis thine alone, Almighty Name
    (Hatfield) AZ213   110558
'Tis true, O, yes, 'tis true

(Morris) R For God so
    loved   110559
'Tis winter now; the fallen
    snow (Longfellow) E295;
    W623; X16; AF455; AL581;
    AN133; AP693; AQ301;
    AW384; BD54; BH198; BX
    170; BY723   110560
To all the nations, Lord (Tip-
    lady) Z552   110561
To avert from men God's
    wrath (Hus) AZ1260; BA
    304   110562
To be alive in such an age!
    (Morgan) AC518   110563
To Bethel came the patriarch
    (Mendes) BH49   110564
To bless the earth God sendeth
    (U.P. Psalter, 1912) BZ
    X Thy might sets fast the
    mountains   110565
To bless thy chosen race (Tate
    & Brady) D500   110566
To Christ, the king of glory
    (---) AZ28   110567
To Christ, the Prince of Peace
    (Latin, 18th c) F198; BQ
    63; BR184   110568
To Christ we homage pay
    (Benade) AZ1166; BA800
                                    110569
To cloisters of the spirit
    (Gannett) AQ260 X God laid
    his rocks in courses 110570
"To Damascus!" Paul had
    shouted (Dearmer) X222
                                    110571
To every man there openeth
    (Oxenham) AC232   110572
To Father, Son, and Holy
    Ghost, Be praise (---)
    Lp741   110573
To Father, Son, and Holy Ghost,
    One God, whom we adore
    (Tate & Brady) G617; Lp741;
    N665; X416; AL629; AO705;
    AZ144; BA925   110574
To Father, Son, and Holy Ghost,
    Our God forever (---)
    Lp743   110575
To Father, Son and Holy Ghost
    The God, whom we adore
    (Tate & Brady) AO705 X

To Father, Son, and Holy
Ghost, One God, whom we
adore   110576

To Father, Son, and Spirit
blest, Supreme o'er (---)
Lp744   110577

To Father, Son and Spirit,
Eternal One in Three (---)
AZ26   110578

To Father, Son, and Spirit, ever
blest (---) AZ446   110579

To Father, Son, and Spirit,
From earth let praise (---)
Lp742   110580

To Father, Son, and Spirit,
God ever Three in One (---)
Lp742   110581

To God be glory, peace on
earth (Tate & Brady. Suppl.
1700) M11; AA74   110582

To God be honor, laud and
praise. (Darmstadt G-B. 1698)
M146   110583

To God be the glory, great
things he hath done (Crosby)
AI142; AM667; AT41; BB647;
BV280; BY32   110584

To God for help will I repair
(U.P. Psalter, 1912) T141;
AJ209   110585

To God I lift mine eyes, From
God is all mine aid (Watts)
L488; AO338   110586

To God I lift mine eyes,
My trust is in His Name
(---) BR32   110587

To God let all the human race
(Melanchthon) AZ346 110588

To God my earnest voice I
raise (U.P. Psalter, 1912)
R387; T279; AJ387; AM509
                         110589

To God on high be thanks and
praise For mercy ceasing
never (Decius) I93; AH624
                         110590

To God on high be thanks and
praise, Who deigns our bonds
(Ball) AN488   110591

To God our Father, Builder and
Creator (Mary Francis, Sr.)
BN210   110592

To God our hearts we lift (Tip-

lady) Z176   110593

To God, our Immanuel, made
flesh as we are (Gregor)
AX491   110594

To God the anthem raising
(Eber) O209; Q112 110595

To God the Ever-glorious (---)
N668   110596

To God, the everlasting, who
abides (Symonds) X681
                         110597

To God the Father, God the
Son (Wilhelm II, Duke)
Lp741, p743; AZ658; BA924
                         110598

To God, the Father of all love
(Schütz) AA60   110599

To God the Father, Son and
ever blessed Spirit (Hatfield)
LP742 X To God the Father,
Son, and Spirit ever blest
                         110600

To God the Father, Son, and
Spirit, ever blest O(Hatfield)
Lp742; AZ1184   110601

To God the Father, Son, and
Spirit, One in Three (Wesley)
Lp741; N667   110602

To God the Father, Son, and
Spirit, The everlasting Three
in One (---) Lp744 110603

To God -- the Father, Son,
and Spirit -- Three in One
(---) Lp742; AZ1246 110604

To God, the Father, Spirit,
Son (---) BR544   110605

To God the Father's throne,
Perpetual honors raise (---)
AZ1307   110606

To God the Father's throne,
Your highest honors raise
(---) Lp741; AZ1185 110607

To God the only wise (Watts)
G618; K305; L93; AL627;
AO71; AP815; AW616; AZ
1297; BA117; BZ   110608

To God we render praise
(Simpson) AZ1123; BA761
                         110609

To God who makes all lovely
things (Crum) X376
                         110610

To God will I direct my prayer

(U. P. Psalter, 1912) AJ210
110611

To God, with heart and cheerful
voice (Wither) X176   110612

To God your every want In in-
stant prayer display (Wesley)
I512   110613

To Him that loved the souls of
men (Watts) AL628; AP811
110614

To Him who children blessed
(Clarke) BF609; BR455
110615

To Him who for our sins was
slain (Russell) D366   110616

To Him who hallows all our days
(Rosser) AT499   110617

To Him who sits upon the throne
(Watts) S35app; W711; AHp26
110618

To hold thy glory, Lord of all
(Williams) BX493   110619

To Jesus Christ be glory given
(Mason) BR49   110620

To Jesus Christ, our only Lord
(---) BI1-7   110621

To Jesus' Heart all burning
(Christie) AH138; BO25; BQ
61   110622

To Jordan came our Lord, the
Christ (Luther) AA401 110623

To kneel at thine altar, in faith
we draw near (---) BO133
110624

To make this earth, our hermitage
(Stevenson) AQ306   110625

To me to live is Christ (Smith)
BY605   110626

To Mercy, Pity, Peace, and Love
(Blake) E506; X682; Y36; AN
285; AQ132   110627

To my heart in that dark lonely
hour (Bobbitt) R I was once
far away   110628

To my humble supplication (Bryan)
E90; R536; X121; AF519
110629

To Nephi, seer of olden time
(Townsend) BC186   110630

To our Redeemer's glorious name
(Steele) D451; L150; M403;
Q363; V380; AA101; AZ145;
BA118   110631

To realms of glory I behold
(Wallin) M458 X To realms
of glory in the skies 110632

To realms of glory in the skies
(Wallin) J116; M458; N146
110633

To render thanks unto the Lord
(Scottish Psalter, 1650) AL
664; AP78   110634

To Shepherds as they watched
by night (Luther) Q103; AA
162   110635

To Sion's hill I lift mine eyes
(Tate & Brady) AO94 X To
Sion's hill I lift my eyes
110636

To Sion's hill I lift my eyes
(Tate & Brady) D648; AO94
110637

To suffer woes which hope thinks
infinite (Shelley) AQ100
110638

To that Lord who unconstrained
(Zinzendorf, N. L. & Anna)
AZ424   110639

To the cross of Christ I'm
clinging (Jackson) AY232
110640

To the God of all creation
(Hull) BH20   110641

To the hills I lift mine eyes
To the everlasting hills
(Wesley) AZ1474; BA702
110642

To the hills I lift mine eyes
To the God eternal (Ber-
sagel) P286   110643

To the hills I lift my eyes;
Whence shall help for me
arise? (Wesley) T248; AJ
345   110644

To the knights in the days of
old (Bryn Mawr College,
1923) Y147; AC230; AG306
110645

To the Lord in the hour of my
distress I call (Ladies of the
Grail) BSp38   110646

To the name of God on high
(Bonar) L186   110647

To the name of our salvation
Laud and honor let us pay
(Latin, 15th c) A326; B89;

D321; E507; F190; G79; K36;
O208; Q116; W164; AZ628;
BA67; BN63; BO14; BQ16;
BV282; BY221   110648
To the name that brings salvation
(Latin 15th c) E507 X To the
name of our salvation 110649
To the name that is salvation
(Latin, 15th c) G79 X To the
name of our salvation 110650
To the name that is salvation
Praise and homage let us pay
(Dearmer) X683; BF237
                       110651
To the name that is salvation
Praise and homage let us pay
(Dearmer) X To the name of
our salvation (Latin, 15th c)
                       110652
To the promised home in glory
(---) AX599; AY384   110653
To the regions beyond I must go
(Simpson) AU76   110654
To the soul that seeks Him
Christ is gracious (Foster)
AZ1017   110655
To the work! to the work!
(Crosby) AT435; AU64; AX185
                       110656
To Thee, above all creatures gaze
(Hamburg Temple hymnal) BH
126   110657
To Thee all praise ascendeth
(Rist) O385; P235   110658
To Thee alone our prayer and
praise ascending (---) BRp467
                       110659
To Thee be glory, honor, praise
(St Theodulph) AZ297   110660
To Thee be praise for ever (---)
AZ829; BRp467   110661
To Thee before the close of day
(St Ambrose) A164; AF507;
BZ   110662
To Thee eternal God, Our fervent
thanks we render (Brueckner)
M531   110663
To Thee, Eternal Soul, be praise
(Gilder) G10; I14; Y111; AB61;
AD19; AN424; BF235; BX436
                       119664
To Thee, God Holy Ghost, we
pray (Zinzendorf) AZ397; BA

142   110665
To Thee I lift my soul, In Thee
my trust repose (U. P.
Psalter, 1912) T41; AJ60
                       110666
To Thee I lift my soul; O
Lord, I trust in Thee
(Scottish Psalter, 1650)
AP22   110667
To Thee I send my cry, Lord
Jesus (Agricola) AZ994
                       110668
To Thee, Lord Christ, all
praise be given (Swertner)
AZ296   110669
To Thee, Lord Jesus, thanks
we give (Vischer) AA193
                       110670
To Thee, most holy Lord
(Oerter) BA362   110671
To Thee, my God and Saviour
(Haweis) V187   110672
To Thee, my heart, eternal
King (Exeter Collection)
Z108   110673
To Thee my heart I offer
(German, 1653) Q89 110674
To Thee, O blessed Saviour
(---) AZ858; BA889
                       110675
To Thee, O Comforter divine
(Havergal) D134; F613;
K152; L276; AM252; AP285
                       110676
To Thee, O dear, dear Saviour
(Monsell) I324; O480; AA
371; AI114; AO308; AP443;
BA484; BB264   110677
To Thee, O Father, lamp of
all the living (Gorell) F428
                       110678
To Thee, O Father, throned on
high (Doane) D239 110679
To Thee, O God in heaven,
This little one we bring
(Clarke) BR454; BX516
                       110680
To Thee, O God, our hearts we
raise (Dixon-Wright) Y134;
BY302   110681
To Thee, O God, we bring our
adoration (Mace) BE356
                       110682

To Thee, O God, we raise (Pier-
son) O44; AZ784   110683
To Thee, O God, we render thanks
That thou to us hast given
(Thring) W200   110684
To Thee, O God, we render thanks
To Thee give thanks sincere
(U.P. Psalter, 1912) T139
AJ206   110685
To Thee, O gracious Lord, we
sing (Phillips) AY40   110686
To Thee, O heavenly Father
(Welch) BY625 X We lift our
hearts, O Father   110687
To Thee, O jesus Christ, we
raise (---) BI29-D   110688
To Thee, O Lord, alone, Whom
heaven (---) BRp467   110689
To Thee, O Lord, be glory given
(---) BI28   110690
To Thee, O Lord, I fly (U.P.
Psalter, 1912) T22; AJ29;
AM581   110691
To Thee, O Lord, I humbly cry
(U.P. Psalter, 1912) T280;
AJ388   110692
To Thee, O Lord, I lift mine
eyes (U.P. Psalter, 1912) AM
540 X To Thee, O Lord, I
lift my eyes   110693
To Thee, O Lord, I lift my eyes
(U.P. Psalter, 1912) T253;
AJ351; AM540   110694
To Thee, O Lord, I yield my
spirit (Senfft von Pilsach)
O581   110695
To Thee, O Lord, my Saviour
(---) BR419   110696
To Thee, O Lord, our hearts we
raise, For all thy works
(Plummer) BI9-D   100697
To Thee, O Lord, our hearts we
raise, In hymns of adoration
(Dix) D191; E292; F484; J445;
K483; N570; O528; Q573; W616;
X13; AA294; AK433; AP689;
AW378; BV653; BY731; BZ
                             110698
To Thee, O Lord, the God of
all (Landstad) J380   110699
To Thee, O Lord, will I sing
praises (Crasselius) M587
                             110700

To Thee, our fathers' God, we
bow (Cronenwett) M260
                             110701
To Thee our God we fly (How)
B182; D187; E565; F606; O
518; Q580; W635; AA304;
AI360; AM618; AP647; AZ
1180; BX413; BY653;   110702
To Thee, our loving Father,
God (---) BE357   110703
To Thee our vows with sweet
accord (Swertner) AZ888;
BA853   110704
To Thee, Redeemer, King of
highest heaven (Latin) F586
                             110705
To Thee, the Lord of all, I'll
humbly sing (Freylinghausen,
G-B. 1714) AZ447   110706
To Thee this temple we devote
(Scott) L297   110707
To Thee we give ourselves to-
day (Gottheil) BH166 110708
To Thee, who makest all
(Dearmer) X417   110709
To Thee whose eye all nature
owns (Hardy) X684   110710
To thine eternal arms, O God
(Higginson) S90; BX246
                             110711
To thy brethren ever be propi-
tious (Swertner) AZ1006
                             110712
To thy house, O Lord, with re-
joicing we come (Naylor) R
Once again we come   110713
To thy pastures, fair and large
(Merrick) AX485; AY83
                             110714
To thy temple I repair (Mont-
gomery) D30; K426; L52;
Q2; V454; AA8; AM313; AP
324; AR8; AS59; BA391;
BR89; BV12   110715
To thy temple we repair (Mont-
gomery) L52 X To thy tem-
ple I repair   110716
To us a child of hope is born
(Morison) H134; U52; V123;
AA155; AM163; AO131; AR123;
AS106; AX101; BB100; BE362
                             110717
To us a child of royal birth

(Wesley) F71; BV120 110718
To us from heaven's lofty
  height (German) M614
                      110719
To us in Bethlehem city
  (Cologne Psalter, 1638) X
  685; BG112   110720
To us is born a blessed child
  (German before 1422) O189
                      110721
To us salvation now is come
  (Speratus) O205; Q377; AA
  314   110722
To worship God in truth (Mayer)
  BH214   110723
To you have I lifted up my eyes
  (Ladies of the Grail) BSp44
                      110724
To you was given, O saint be-
  loved (Merryweather) F537
                      110725
Tobias war ein frommer Mann
  (Ausbund Suppl.) BU1
                      110726
Today be joy in every heart
  (Hosmer) AN157; AW72; BD
  214; BX190   110727
Today beneath benignant skies
  (Wortman) AO461   110728
Today I arise, Invoking the
  Blessed Trinity (St Patrick)
  W505   110729
Today the Saviour calls (Smith)
  V271; W686; AM388; AO646;
  AP398; AY313; AZ1372
                      110730
Today thy mercy calls me
  (Allen) H263 X To-day thy
  mercy calls us   110731
To-day thy mercy calls us
  (Allen) D590; H263; Q279;
  V264; W684; AA50; AP400;
  BA909   110732
Today we celebrate the birth
  (Luther) BA167   110733
Today, while the sun shines,
  work with a will (Douty) BC
  215; BH258   110734
Together, Lord, we come to thee
  (Gilbert) AL318   110735
Toil on a little longer here
  (Smith) BB247   110736
Toiling on, toiling on (Crosby)

R To the work   110737
Tollite hostias, et introite in
  atria ejus (Latin) BQ160
                      110738
Tomorrow, Lord, is thine
  (Doddridge) I253; V668
                      110739
Tomorrow shall be my dancing
  day (English trad carol)
  BG71   110740
Too soon we rise; the symbols
  disappear (Bonar) BR477
  X Here, O my Lord, I see
  thee   110741
Torches, torches, run with
  torches (Spanish trad carol)
  BG81   110742
Tossed upon the raging billow
  (Bethune) V642   110743
Tota pulchra es, Maria
  (Latin, 15th c) BQ212
                      110744
Touch me, Lord Jesus, with
  thy love divine (Creamer)
  AU463   110745
Touch thou mine eyes, -- the
  somber shadows falling
  (Ham) AN230; BX270
                      110746
To-vo, to-vo l'-fo-ne-cho
  (Jewish traditional) BH324
                      110747
Trauren will ich stehen lassen
  (Ausbund) BU17   110748
Tread softly, tread softly, the
  Master is here (Crosby)
  R Be silent, be silent
                      110749
Trembling soul, beset by fears
  (Shepherd) AM670 110750
Trials dark on every hand
  (Tindley) AT473; AU134
                      110751
Triumph all ye cherubim
  (Hermannus Contractus) R
  Hail, holy Queen, enthroned
  above   110752
Triumph, ye heavens! rejoice
  ye with high adoration
  (Tersteegen) N37; O187
                      110753
Triumphant Lord, thy work is
  done (Irons) D370; H196

110754

Triumphant Sion, lift thy head
(Doddridge) A381; B472; D488;
H468; L346; AV243; BI47; BR
218   110755

Triumphantly doth Christ unfurl
(Latin, 20th c) BN77   110756

Triumphs today the Lord of life
(---) BI108   110757

Tröstet, tröstet meine Lieben
(Olearius) BT61   110758

Troubled heart, thy God is calling,
He is drawing (Crosby) AX
241; AY218   110759

Troubled soul, thy God is calling,
Softly calling (Buerge) AX235
                                 110760

Trudge on, singing praise for a
spirit twice gifted (Clayton)
X470b   110761

True Bread of life, in pitying
mercy given (Bonar) AZ441
                                 110762

True-hearted, whole-hearted
(Havergal) G255; H396; I420;
AH456; AS326; AT410; AV383;
BY303; BZ   110763

True Light, that lightest all in
heaven and earth (Thring)
O613   110764

True lovers of mankind (Tweedy)
BF520   110765

True Son of man, thou crown
of human valour (Dearmer)
X230   110766

True, the heart grows rich in
giving (Charles) BE360 X
Is thy cruse of comfort
                                 110767

True to the faith that our parents
have cherished (Stephens) R
Shall the youth of Sion falter
                                 110768

Truly, that eventful day (Gregor)
AZ583   110769

Truly the light is sweet (Peabody)
AQ136   110770

Trumpet of God, sound high
(Brooks) F270   110771

Trust all to God, the Father,
Confide thou in none other
(Gerhardt) BE361   110772

Trust and obey (Sammis) R When

we walk with the Lord
                                 110773

Trust Me, try Me, prove Me
(Leech) R Bring ye all the
tithes   110774

Trust the Eternal when the
shadows gather (McKenzie)
BE359   110775

Trust your hand into His
(Penner) R O soul, you
know   110776

Trusting as the moments fly
(Stites) R Simply trusting
                                 110777

Truth comes alike to all
(Avery) BE355   110778

Truth eternal, truth divine
(Pratt) BC189   110779

Truth is the trial of itself
(Jonson) AQ105   110780

Truth reflects upon our senses
(Snow) BC188   110781

Try us, O God!and search the
ground (Wesley) I555 X
Help us to help each other,
Lord   110782

Trying to walk in the steps of
the Saviour (Hewitt) AX561
                                 110783

Tu, Christe, nostrum gaúdium
(Latin, 5th c) BN52
                                 110784

Tu gloria Jerusalem (Latin)
BQ223   110785

Turn back, O man, forswear
thy foolish ways (Bax)
A536; J348; R490; S424;
X329; Y252; Z567; AB298;
AD361; AE412; AF451; AK
410; AL520; AN342; AQ196;
AR578; BF574; BK102; BL
92; BZ   110786

Turn, Lord, thy wrath away,
in mercy spare us (Thymus)
O104   110787

Turn us again, O God of hosts
(Scottish Psalter, 1650)
AP64   110788

Turn your faces toward the
morning (Pounds) AY469
                                 110789

Turned by thy grace, I look
within (Bradley) D595

110790
Tut mir auf die schöne Pforte
(Schmolck) BT1; BW505
110791
'Twas about the dead of night
(Neale) BG151   110792
'Twas by thy Blood, immortal
Lamb (Watts) F634   110793
'Twas Jesus died on Calvary
(Manwaring) R 'Tis sweet to
sing the matchless love
110794
'Twas like a dream, when by the
Lord (Scottish Psalter, 1650)
BH120   110795
'Twas on that dark, that doleful
night (Watts) O312; Q164; V546;
AA439; AF558   110796
'Twas on that night when doomed
to know (Morison) R448; S360;
W312; AD406; AH504; AL231;
AM359; AP356; AR164; BY331
110797
'Twill all be joy up in heaven
(Cook) R There'll be no sha-
dows   110798
'Twixt gleams of joy and clouds
of doubt (Shairp) W559; AB
210; AN251; BX236   110799
Two empires by the sea (Hunting-
ton) Z549; VX422   110800
Two little hands are sweetly
folded (Warner) BX625
100801

U

Ubi caritas et amor Deus (Latin:
Mandatum) BM15; BN87
110802
Ultima in mortis hora (Benedictine:
Ultima) BN191   110803
Un flambeau, Jeannette (French
trad.) Y304   110804
Unanswered yet? The prayer your
lips have pleaded (Adams) BC
286   110805
Unbar the door! and let the Lord
Christian (Oxenham) Y253;
Z287   110806
Unchanging God, hear from eter-
nal heaven (Stone) O126; P403
110807

Unchanging God, who livest
(Wilder) F496   110808
Under His wings I am safely
abiding (Cushing) AS263
X Under His wings I'm safely
abiding   110809
Under His wings, I'm safely
abiding (Cushing) P303; AS
263; AX525; BB587   110810
Under His wings, Under His
wings (U.P. Board, 1917)
R Under the care of my God
110811
Under the care of my God, the
Almighty (U.P. Board, 1917)
AI307; AM78   110812
Under the feeble stable light
(Keller) J43   110813
Under the shadows of Calvary
(Minkler) R Grace, dear
Lord   110814
Under the wide and starry sky
(Stevenson) Y128   110815
Une vaine crainte trouble vos
esprits (French trad carol)
BG156b   110816
Ungnad begehr ich nicht von dir
(Ausbund) BU32   110817
Unheard the dews around me fall
(---) AN115; AQ89; AW39;
BX70   110818
Unknown and unrewarded (Dear-
mer) X244   110819
Unless the Lord the house shall
build (U.P. Psalter, 1912)
T257; AJ359; AM291 110820
Unser Vater im Himmelreich,
Dein Nam sei heilig ewiglich
(Betz) BU104   110821
Unshaken as the sacred hill
[hills] (Watts) V338; BB392
110822
Unto a thousand, yea, to eight
thousand ages (Japanese na-
tional anthem) Y310 110823
Unto Caesar let us render
(Cronenwett) M501   110824
Unto God our Saviour, Sing a
joyful song (U.P. Psalter,
1912) T181; AJ262   110825
Unto God, our King, Joy and
strength of Israel (Essenburg)
AJ431   110826

Unto him, for whom this day
(Juste judex ultionis) BQ116
110827
Unto him who hath loved us
(Pierson) R With harps and
with viols   110828
Unto him whose name is holy
(Elliott) AZ874   110829
Unto Jesus' cross I'm now retir-
ing (Zinzendorf, C.R.) AZ
1016   110830
Unto Mary, demon-haunted
(Struther) X233   110831
Unto my Lord Jehovah said,
"At my right hand" (Irish
Psalter, 1898) AM229; AP98
110832
Unto the calmly gathered thought
(Whittier) BK87   110833
Unto the hills around do I lift up
(Campbell) J488; S96; T250;
U201; Z166; AD79; AE64; AG
219; AJ347; AK86; AL681; AM
82; AO331; AP109; AR85; AW
598; BV567   110834
Unto the hills I lift mine eyes,
O whence shall come (U.P.
Psalter, 1912) BZ X I to the
hills will lift my eyes 110835
Unto the hills I lift mine eyes,
Whence comes my help (Lucas)
BH13   110836
Unto the Lord lift thankful voices
(Brondsema) AJ425   110837
Unto the Lord of all creation
(Afzelius) N314   110838
Unto thee, most faithful Saviour
(Gregor) AZ981   110839
Unto Thee my heart is sighing
(Bridges) BJ58   110840
Unto Thee, unto Thee, Precious
Saviour, now I flee (Crosby)
R Mighty Rock, whose tower-
ing form   110841
Unto thy temple, Lord, we come
(Collyer) AE27; AF276; AK328;
AN14; AQ252; AR10; AW282;
BX24   110842
Unto us a boy is born (Latin
carol, 15th c) A34; X385; AF
142; BG92; BV121; BY112
110843
Unumschränkte Liebe (Rambach)

BT42   110844
Unveil mine eyes that of thy law
(Scottish Psalter, 1650) BH
202   110845
Unveil thy bosom, faithful tomb
(Watts) H490; I586   110846
Unworthy to be called thy son
(Furness) BX249   110847
Up and get us gone, to help the
world along (Wilson) R Up,
my neighbour   110848
Up! arouse thee, O beautiful
Sion (Woodmansee) BC283
110849
Up, awake, ye defenders of Zion
(Penrose) BC37   110850
Up Calvary's mountain, one
dreadful morn (Christiansen)
AT106; AU428   110851
Up from the grave He arose
(Lowry) R Low in the grave
He lay   110852
Up, my neighbour, come away
(Wilson) BG166   110853
Up, my soul, gird thee with
power (Freystein) M229
110854
Up now, laggardly lasses
(Spanish trad carol) BG113
110855
Up to the bountiful Giver of life
(Slade) AU128   110856
Up to the hills I lift mine eyes
(Watts) BR265 X Up to the
hills I lift my eyes   110857
Up to the hills I lift my eyes
(Watts) L100; BR265 110858
Up to the throne on high
(Blakeney) F315   110859
Up to those bright and gladsome
hills (Vaughan, the Silurist)
X686   110860
Up, ye Christians, join in sing-
ing (Arnschwanger) BR133
110861
Uplift the song of praise (Hos-
mer) AN378; AW366; BH261;
BX404   110862
Uplift the voice and sing (St
Alphonso M de' Liguori) BO
106   110863
Upon the cross downlying
(Petursson) M389   110864

Upon the cross of Calvary (Raile)
BC221   110865
Upon the cross the robber prayed
(Peturrson) M412; P166
110866
Upon the first day of the week
(Childress) AX67   110867
Upon the gospel's sacred page
(Bowring) I199; AS180; BE
363   110868
Upon the mountain top alone I
stand (Chippewa Indian trad)
Y315   110869
Upon this happy morn (---) AZ
1170   110870
Upward I lift mine eyes (Watts)
AO338 X To God I lift mine
eyes   110871
Upward where the stars are burn-
ing (Bonar) S428; V711; AB
401; AZ650   110872
Urbs Sion aurea, patria lactea
(St Bernard of Cluny) BT
613; BW262   110873
Urged by love, to every nation
(Zinzendorf, N. L.) AZ896
110874
Use me, O my gracious Saviour
(Woodrow) AX419; AY106
110875
Utah, Utah, beautiful beautiful
land (Huish) R There is a land
whose sunny vales   110876

V

Va-a-nach-nu ko-r'eem umishta-
chaveem (Jewish traditional)
BH274   110877
Vain are the hopes the sons of
men (Watts) V314   110878
Vain, delusive world, adieu (Wes-
ley) H306   110879
Vainly, through night's weary
hours (Auber) AZ259; BE364
110880
V'-al ku-lom, E-lo-a (Jewish
traditional) BH325   110881
Valet will ich dir geben (Her-
berger) BT407   110882
Vanish doubt and hesitation
(Schlegel) N440   110883
Vater unser im Himmelreich

(Luther) BT458   110884
Va-y' -da-bayr Mo-she es mo-
a-day (Jewish trad.) BH300
110885
Va-yo-mer A-do-noy (Jewish
traditional) BH321   110886
Veiled in darkness Judah lay
Rights (AN152; AQ284; AW
68   110887
Veni Creator Spiritus (Latin,
9th c) BJ48b; BN118; BO261;
BP44; BQ199; BT233
110888
Veni, Jesu, amor me (Latin)
AH131; BO35   110889
Veni, Redemptor gentium (St
Ambrose) BT95   110890
Veni, Sancte Spiritus (Innocent
III, Pope??) BN55; BO260;
BQ198; BT227; BW131
110891
Veni Sponsa Christi (Breviary)
BQ215   110892
Veni, veni, Emmanuel (Latin,
9th c) BN5; BP5; BQ152;
BT62; BW67   110893
Venite adoremus, Dominum
(Sedulius of Liege) R The
snow lay on the ground
110894
Věříme v všemohoucího (Tranov-
sky) BT253   110895
Very Bread, good Shepherd,
tend us (St Thomas Aquinas)
A194; E317c; J280   110896
Very softly I will walk (Kellogg)
AH554   110897
Verzage nicht, du Häuflein Klein
(Altenburg) BT263   110898
Vexilla Regis pródeunt (Fortuna-
tus) BN28; BO287; BQ182;
BT168   110899
Victim Divine, thy grace we
claim (Wesley) E333; J274
110900
Victimae Paschali laudes im-
molent Christiani (Wipo??)
BN39; BQ196; BT191 110901
Victoria! Victoria! Surrexit
nostra gloria (Latin) BO171
110902
Victory, victory, through him
that redeemed us (Crosby)

R Behold! a royal army
                          110903
Virgin-born, we bow before Thee
  (Heber) E640; F514   110904
Virgin wholly marvellous (St
  Ephraim the Syrian) BO117
                          110905
Virginis proles, opifex que
  Matris (Latin, 8th c) BN
  183   110906
Virtue supreme, thy mighty
  stream (Dearmer) X214
                          110907
Viva! Viva! Gesù! che per mio
  bene (Italian, 18th c) BT158
                          110908
Vivat! vivat! vivat Pastor bonus!
  (Latin) BO210   110909
V'-nis-lach l'-chol a-das b'-nay
  (Jewish traditional) BH319
                          110910
Voison, d'ou venait ce grand bruit
  (French trad carol) BG88b
                          110911
Vom himmel hoch da komm' ich
  her (Luther) AW527b; AY24d;
  BT85; BW527   110912
Vom himmel hoch, o Engel,
  kommt (German trad carol,
  15th c) BG118b   110913
Vom Himmel kam der Angel Schar
  (Luther) BT103   110914
Von Gott will ich nicht lassen
  (Helmbold) BT393   110915
Von Grönlands eis'gen Zinken.
  (R. Heber) BW333   110916
Von Herzen will ich loben (Aus-
  bund) BU120   110917
Von Herzen woll'n wir singen
  (Ausbund) AY35d; BU119
                          110918
Vox clara ecce intonat (Latin,
  6th c) BT60   110919
V'shom'ru V'-nay Yis-ro-ayl es
  ha-shab-bos (Jewish trad)
  BH272   110920
Vzkříšení čekame. (Slovak. 1674)
  BT603   110921

W

Wach auf, du Geist der ersten
  Zeugen (Bogatzky) BT494

                          110922
Wach auf, wach auf, o Men-
  schenkind! Von deinem Schlaf
  stand auf geschwind (Aus-
  bund) BU118   110923
Wachet auf! ruft uns die Stimme
  Der Wächter sehr hoch auf
  der Zinne (Nicolai) BT609;
  BW522   110924
Wacht auf, ihr Brüder werthe
  (Ausbund) BU113   110925
Waft [sic] my sould upon the
  Lord (Lloyd) AI285 X Wait
  my soul upon the Lord
                          110926
Wait, my soul! upon the Lord
  (Lloyd) V423; AI285; AO
  349; BE365   110927
Wait, O my soul, thy Maker's
  will (Beddome) V425
                          110928
Wait on God, and trust Him
  through all thy days (Räder)
  AK478   110929
Waiting and watching, Waiting
  and watching ("S.M.H.")
  R We know not the time when
  He cometh   110930
Wake, arise! a voice appalling
  (Nicolai) N612   110931
Wake, awake for night is flying
  (Nicolai) A3; B62; D40; E
  12; J7; K5; L214; N199; O
  508; P426; Q609; W162; X
  687; Y352; AA549; AB153;
  AD173; AF24, 108; AI446;
  AK96; AL134; AM231; AN
  486; AO115; AP242; AQ17;
  AR207; AW522; AZ1103; BA
  103; BB197; BI17-D, 52; BK
  56   110932
Wake, harp of Sion, wake again
  (Edmeston) D267   110933
Wake, O wake, for night is fly-
  ing (Nicolai) X687 X Wake,
  awake, for night is flying
                          110934
Wake, o wake! with tidings
  thrilling (Nicolai) E12 X
  Wake, awake for night is
  flying   110935
Wake, Spirit, who in times now
  olden (Bogatzky) W377

110936
Wake the song of joy and gladness (Sherwin) BB649   110937
Wake the song of jubilee (Bacon) L350; AZ76   110938
Wake! the welcome day appeareth (Freylinghausen) O160 110939
Waken, Christian children (Hamerton) BR531   110940
Walk daily with your Saviour (Hoffman) AX445; AY127
110941
Walk in the light, and thou shalt own (Barton) BY560 X Walk in the light, so shalt thou know   110942
Walk in the light, so shalt thou know (Barton) G378; I361; J474; L424; W482; Z479; AD224; AH 238; AN562; AR274; AT370; AW209; AX450; AY90; BA635; BB339; BD97; BE367; BF403; BK81; BV447; BX354; BY560; BZ   110943
Walk in the light, so thou shalt know (Barton) BE367 X Walk in the light, so shalt thou know
110944
Walk with the Lord! along the road (Gill) BX353 X O walk with God!   110945
Walking in sunlight all of my journey (Zelley) AU119; AX28; AY471   110946
Walking in the sunshine, beautiful and bright (Lindsay) AX440; AY479   110947
Walking, Saviour, close to Thee (Newell) AY95   110948
Walte, walte nah und fern (Bahnmeier) BT507; BW551 110949
Wanderer in sinful ways (Latta) AX238; AY220   110950
Wann der Herr die G'sägniss Zion (Ausbund. Psalm 126) BU86   110951
Wär' Gott nicht mit uns diese Zeit (Luther) BT267 110952
Wår Herres Jesu Kristi död (Spegel) BT163   110953
Warrior, at thy station stand (Zinzendorf, N. L.) AZ1042; BA554   110954

Warrior, on thy station stand (Zinzendorf, N. L.) BA554
X Warrior, at thy station stand   110955
Warum sollt' ich mich denn grämen? (Gerhardt) BT523
110956
Was ever grief like Thine (Wesley) AZ1488; BJ50
110957
Was frag' ich nach der Welt (Pfefferkorn) BT430 110958
Was gibst du denn, o meine Seele (Lochner) BT404
110959
Was Gott tut, das ist wohlgetan! Es bleibt gerecht sein Wille (Rodigast) BT521; BW567
110960
Was Gott tut, das ist wohl getan! So denken Gottes Kinder (Schmolck) BT571
110961
Was kann ich doch für Dank (Denicke) BT417   110962
Was mein Gott will, das G' scheh' allzeit (Albrecht, von Brandenburg) BT517
110963
Was mich auf diefer Welt betrübt (Unparth. G. B.) AY 8d   110964
Was the trial sore? Temptation sharp? Thank God a second time (Browning) AC474
110965
Was there ever kindest shepherd (Faber T320 X There's a wideness in God's mercy
110966
Was wend wir aber heben an (Ausbund) BU140   110967
Was woll'n wir aber singen (Ausbund) BU26   110968
Wash me, O Lamb of God, wash me from sin (Beegle) AY78
110969
Wassail, wassail, all over the town (English trad carol) (two versions) BG32, 31*110970
*differing texts
Watch and pray, watch and pray (Brooks) R There's a way

that is free   110971
Watch, my soul, and pray (Wal-
  lin) N479   110972
Watch o'er me, O my Saviour
  (Plummer) BI61   110973
Watch, ye saints, with eyelids
  waking (Palmer) BB549
                                     110974
Watchman, blow the gospel trum-
  pet (Gilmour) BB619   110975
Watchman, tell me, does the
  morning (Brewer) AX129; AY
  79; BB180   110976
Watchman, tell us of the night
  (Bowring) A440; B106; D331;
  G485; H483; I636; J525; L355;
  Q71; R149; S109; U393; V585;
  Y249; Z183; AB104; AC298;
  AD101; AE79; AF109; AG61;
  AH244; AK91; AN154; AO526;
  AQ283; AR124; AS99; AT462;
  AV263; AW66; AZ84; BA188;
  BD204; BE368; BF276; BI95;
  BK141; BR229; BX194; BZ
                                     110977
Watchmen on the walls of Zion
  (---) BB184   110978
We all believe in one true God,
  Father, Son, and Holy Ghost
  (Clausnitzer) O76; Q252;
  AA393; AF250; BZ   110979
We all believe in one true God,
  Maker of the earth and heaven
  (Luther) M60; O71; Q251;
  AA394   110980
We are adventurers who come
  (Carmen & Hovey) Y167
                                     110981
We are all blind, until we see
  (Markham) AK103   110982
We are all enlisted till the conflict
  is o'er (---) BC210   110983
We are building in sorrow or joy
  (Sargent) AX199; AY519
                                     110984
We are but little children poor
  (Alexander) E610; W516; AP
  769; BR538   110985
We are but little children weak
  (Alexander) W516 X We are
  but little children poor   110986
We are but strangers here,
  Heaven is our home (Taylor)

L591; M312; N519; O462;
Q660; V712; AA563; AM605;
AS477; AX609; AY147; BB659;
BR432   110987
We are children of one Father
  (Larcom) BX522   110988
We are climbing Jacob's ladder
  (Negro spiritual) Y318;
  AF495; AG319; AH597;
  BK165; BZ   110989
We are come with joy and glad-
  ness (Walmsley) BD48
                                     110990
We are going down the valley,
  one by one (Pounds) AX615;
  AY496   110991
We are hid with Christ forever
  (Mace) BE370   110992
We are little gleaners, Little
  we can do (---) AY481
                                     110993
We are little reapers, toiling
  all the day (---) AY483
                                     110994
We are living, we are dwelling
  (Coxe) R356; S374; U310;
  Z494; AD348; AE259; AF427;
  AG275; AK297; AO482; AT
  421; AV273; BB359; BF519
                                     110995
We are marching homeward
  with the blest (---) AY145
                                     110996
We are nearing home! We are
  nearing home! (Whitford,
  arr) R Just over the moun-
  tains in the Promised Land
                                     110997
We are not here to play, to
  dream (Babcock) U269 X
  Be strong! we are not here
  to play, to dream   110998
We are not left to walk alone
  (Walker) AZ936   110999
We are saved by the grace of
  our God (Kennedy) AI132;
  AR430; AS291   111000
We are soldiers of Christ who
  is mighty to save (Pollock)
  AI328   111001
We are sowing, daily sowing
  (---) BC192   111002
We are standing in the great

dawn of a day (Shepard) AC
520 111003
We are that chosen nation, Lord
(Bible. Joel 2) R Look with
mercy, Lord 111004
We are the Lord's: His all-suffi-
cient merit (Spitta) K410; O
226; Q453; AI255; AP561; AZ
1222 111005
We are Thy people, Thou art our
King (Jewish traditional) BH
326 111006
We are waiting for the morning
(Cushing) R We are watching
we are waiting 111007
We are watching, we are waiting
(Cushing) H205; U391; V601;
AI93 111008
We are weary of life-long toil
(Purchas) R Evensong is hush-
ed in silence 111009
We bear the strain of earthly
care (Davis) G471; R227;
S179; U369; Y86; Z521; AB275;
AC194; AF220; AG119; AK279;
BF336; BX226; BZ 111010
We believe in One true God,
Father, Son and Holy Ghost
(Clausnitzer) BZ X We all
believe 111011
We bid thee welcome in the name
(Montgomery) I226; Q484; AA
489; AE342; AK350; AO460;
BA319 111012
We bless the name of Christ, the
Lord (Coffman) AX167 111013
We bless thee, for thy peace, O
God (Church melodies, 1858)
H361; U232; V393; Y103; AE
226; BF388; BX356; BY489
111014
We bless thee, Jesus Christ our
Lord (Vischer) O308 111015
We bless thee, Lord, for all this
common life (White) Y338;
AC221 111016
We bow before thy throne (Simp-
son) AZ1122; BA44 111017
We bow to thee, O Lord, on high
(Kauffman) AY379 111018
We bring no glittering treasures
(Phillips) AZ857 111019
We build a sanctuary sure (Hum-

bert) AE344 111020
We build an altar here, and
pray (Martin) AC529
111021
We build our school on thee,
O Lord (Meyer) B366; BD
194; BH254 111022
We cannot always trace the way
(Bowring) BX260 X I can-
not always trace 111023
We cannot build alone (Coles)
U386; V567 111024
We cannot kindle when we will
(Arnold) AQ86 111025
We cannot think of them as
dead (Hosmer) G423; AL178;
AN202; AQ73; AW318; BF666;
BX231 111026
We care for our Lord's acres
(Clarke) AR590 111027
We Christians may Rejoice
today When Christ was born
(Füger) Q107; AA156 111028
We Christians should ever con-
sider (Spegel) N445 111029
We come in the might of the
Lord of light (Moultrie) R
We march, we march to vic-
tory 111030
We come, Lord, to thy feet
(Whitmore??) D536; V651
111031
We come, O Christ, to thee
(Clarkson) BV285 111032
We come, O Lord, before thy
throne (Brown) L606
111033
We come unto our father's
God (Gill) A303; B424;
G385; R16; S342; W211; AF
271; AK361; AL170; AN363;
AO610; AP301; AQ15; BX
403; BY265; BZ 111034
We come with songs and glad-
ness (---) BD45 111035
We covenant with hand and
heart (Benade) AZ886; BA
673 111036
We dedicate this temple
(Emurian) R519 111037
We ever pray for thee, our
Prophet dear (Stephen) BC
386 111038

We gather 'round your shrine
today, Salve Regina (---)
BM51   111039
We gather together to ask the
Lord's blessing (Dutch trad.)
A315; G20; R18; Y29; Z117;
AD22; AF21; AG10; AH185;
AM286; AR9; AT492; BB8;
BD17; BF171; BK137; BL91;
BZ   111040
We gather, we gather, dear Jesus,
to bring (Harlingen) N660;
O570; P356   111041
We give immortal praise (Watts)
D141; AO60; AZ1181   111042
We give thee but thine own
(How) A481; B319; D268; E
522; G456; H313; I688; J544;
K387; L543; M252; N182; P
404; Q441; R312; S394; U337;
V575; W346; X332; Y396; Z422;
AA361; AB267; AC339; AD508;
AE368; AF535; AG247; AH411;
AI450; AK258; AL374; AM367;
AN287; AO498; AP576; AQ131;
AR343; AS353; AT402; AU492;
AW213; AX648; AZ1361; BA568;
BB477; BC180; BD129; BF503;
BR231; BV605; BX363; BY530;
BZ   111043
We give thee thanks, O God, this
day (Offord) AR600; AS429
                        111044
We go not on a pilgrimage (Very)
AN265; BX297   111045
We hail thee, Lord, thy Church's
Rock (Zinzendorf, N. L.) N213;
O525   111046
We hail thy Presence glorious
(Parsons) F403   111047
We have a King who came to earth
(Cropper) F434; BY531 111048
We have a Rock, a safe retreat
(Jones) AM319   111049
We have a sure, prophetic word
(Cronenwett) M30; P85; Q290;
AA120   111050
We have an anchor (Owens) R
Will your anchor hold 111051
We have heard a joyful sound
(Owens) W680 X We have
heard the joyful sound 111052
We have heard from the bright,

the holy, land (Hyde) BB
305   111053
We have heard the joyful sound
(Owens) R503; W680; Z537;
AH408; AI103; AL259; AM370;
AP798; AR480; AS293; AT
191; AU15; AW334; AX201;
AY231; BB637; BV330; BY
399;   111054
We have not known thee as we
ought (Pollock) AM418; BB
350; BY606   111055
We have not wings, we cannot
soar (Longfellow) AN560
                        111056
We hear the call of Israel's
children (Rosewater) BH256
                        111057
We honor those whose work
began (Horton) BX504
                        111058
We hope in thee, O God
(Hearn) G365; I328 111059
We in one covenant are joined
(Swertner) AZ881; BA672
                        111060
We join to pray, with wishes
kind (Gaskell) AX552; AY
296   111061
We join with all, in every place
(Coster) AO446   111062
We journey through a vale of
tears (Barton) I447; L498
                        111063
There is none other name than
thine (---) BA69 X There
is no other name   110063
We journey with a multitude
(Patton) AQ66   110064
We knelt before Kings; we bent
before lords (Merrill) BF498
                        111065
We know, by faith we know
(Wesley) H506   111066
We know not a voice of that
river (Rossetti) S432
                        111067
We know not the hour of the
Master's appearing (Belden)
BB540   111068
We know not the time when he
cometh ("S. M. H.") BB542
                        111069

We know the paths where-in our feet should press (Drinkwater) AC187 X Grant us the will
111070

We know thee who thou art (Bright) AZ1374
111071

We leave thy house but leave not thee (Tiplady) Z130
111072

We lift our hearts in praise, O God of Life, to thee (Morrison) BE371
111073

We lift our hearts in thanks to-day (Chubb) AN12
111074

We lift our hearts, O Father (Welch) BV392; BY625 111075

We lift our hearts to thee (Wesley, J & C) G36; I45; L9; AA25; AO75; BZ
111076

We limit not the truth of God (Rawson) AF259; BY254
111077

We love the place, O God (Bullock) A398; B465; D484; E508; F242; J239; O41; W236; X688; AL199; AP325; AW281; AZ477; BC203; BR23,95; BV13; BY 283
111078

We love the venerable house (Emerson) AN466; AO464; AP319; BX502
111079

We love thee, Lord, yet not alone (Elliott) AZ1447
111080

We love thy house, O God (Bullock) BC203 X We love the place, O God
111081

We love to sing around the king (Bethune) R There is no name
111082

We march, we march to victory (Moultrie) B533; D514; I418; L537; AH437; AO400; AP539; AV216; BA937; BD89; BF466; BI7; BR509
111083

We may not climb the heavenly steeps (Whittier) X Immortal love, forever full
111084

We meet again in gladness (---) BH255
111085

We meet again in Sabbath School (Manwaring) BC193
111086

We meet, as in that upper room they met (Briggs) AR513
111087

We men of earth have here the stuff (Markham) AC535
111088

We met them on the common way (Cardoza) AD311; AQ 237
111089

We mix from many lands (Swinburne) Z509
111090

We move in faith to unseen goals (Quin) AN357; AQ200 111091

We need not climb the heavenly steeps (Whittier) N196 X Immortal love forever full
111092

We nned not soar above the skies (Stockton) H103
111093

We now have met to worship thee (Shoemaker) AX54; AY5
111094

We now implore God, the Holy Ghost (Luther) M474; Q231
111095

We now return, each to his tent (Hartley) AZ882; BA387
111096

We, O Jesus, claim thy special care (Allen) AZ513
111097

We owe the Lord an evening song (Loewen) AX73 111098

We plough the fields and scatter (Claudius) X We plow the fields
111099

We plow the fields and scatter (Claudius) A138; B423; E293; F483; G544; I716; J364; K486; N569; P244; R524; S464; W 618; X14; Y46; Z594; AB387; AC323; AD445; AE417; AF460; AG288; AH489; AI351; AK432; AL579; AM614; AN142; AO580; AP141; AR592; AS425; AT493; AW375; AZ850; BA869; BD51; BF648; BH195; BR491; BV654; BX174; BY732; BZ
111100

We praise and bless thee, gracious Lord (Spitta) O386; BA424; BY607
111101

We praise thee, God, for harvests earned (Adams) Y157; AC206; AD301; AN314; AQ219; BD86; BX371
111102

We praise thee, Lord, for all the martyred throng (Heber)

F532   111103
We praise thee, Lord, for hours
  of bliss (Hopps) I550   111104
We praise thee, Lord, with
  earliest morning ray (Franck)
  AF502; AN94; BX43   111105
We praise thee, O God! For the
  days of our youth (Kuipers)
  AI376 X We praise thee, O
  God! for the Son of thy love
  (Mackay)   111106
We praise thee, O God! for the
  Son of thy love (Mackay &
  Kuiper) U27; AI376; AM634;
  AP718; AS16; AT205; AU155;
  AV328; AW437; AX417; AY420
                          111107
We praise thee, O God, our Lord
  and our King! (Schmidt) AI361
  AO597   111108
We praise thee, O God, our Re-
  deemer, Creator (Dutch hymn,
  1626) J450; P20; Q568; R17;
  S461; AB63; AC29; AD76; AE25;
  AF21; AH204; AI7; AK19; AM
  83; AO80; AT11; AW15; BF252
                          111109
We praise thy grace, O Saviour
  (How) B278; D159; BV449
                          111110
We praise thy name, all-holy Lord
  (Newell) E211; F575; X225
                          111111
We praise thy name, O Lord most
  high (---) B284   111112
We praise, we worship thee, O
  God (Gell's Psalms and hymns,
  1815) W3; BY33   111113
We pray no more, made lowly
  wise (Hosmer) AN274 X Made
  lowly wise, we pray   111114
We pray thee, heavenly Father
  (Coles) E334; F401; BV389
                          111115
We pray thee, Jesus, who didst
  first (Phillimore) AS448; BA320
                          111116
We pray thee, wounded Lamb of
  God (Zinzendorf, N. L.) AZ
  404; BA474   111117
We read of a place called heaven
  (Bridgewater) AX590   111118
We rear not a temple, like Ju-

dah's of old (Ware) I666
                          111119
We rest on thee, our shield
  and our defender (Cherry)
  BV569   111120
We sail along toward the har-
  bor light (DeArmond) AU
  299   111121
We saw not, when thou camest
  to die (Dearmer) X689b
                          111122
We saw thee not when, far
  away (Dearmer) X689a
                          111123
We saw thee not when thou
  didst come (Richter) E509;
  P162; W72; AP262; AS124;
  BR167; BV514; BY132
                          111124
We search the world for truth
  (Whittier) AC449   111125
We see him come, and know
  him ours (Herrick) R What
  sweeter music can we bring
                          111126
We see not, know not; all our
  way (Whittier) AB203
                          111127
We shall build on! (Studdert-
  Kennedy) AC483   111128
We shall know as we are known
  (Herbert) R When the mists
                          111129
We shall reach the river side
  (French) AU271   111130
We shall see the King some
  day (Jones) R Though the
  way we journey   111131
We shall sleep, but not forever
  (Kidder) N604; AY185
                          111132
We sing a song and then we
  part (Tilton) AZ1515
                          111133
We sing his love who once was
  slain (Hill) AO542   111134
We sing, Immanuel, thy praise
  (Gerhardt) Q108   111135
We sing now together our song
  of thanks giving (Buehrer)
  AQ22   111136
We sing of God, the mighty
  source (Smart) A314; X690

111137
We sing of golden mornings
(Emerson) AQ40   111138
We sing the almighty power of
God (Watts) L104; Q43; AA
293   111139
We sing the glorious conquest
(Ellerton) A114; B271; D150;
E207; F541; AM404; BV453
111140
We sing the praise of him who
died (Kelly) A340; B160; D100;
E510; F215; H161; J494; K66;
O483; Q178; W109; X132; AL
102; AP211; AZ347; BA195;
BB296; BV162; BY150   111141
We sing the rapture of the breath
(Meredith) AQ139   111142
We sing to thee, Immanuel (Ger-
hardt) AZ320   111143
We speak of the realms of the
blest (Mills) L600; N619;
AZ1507; BB199   111144
We stand in deep repentance
(Palmer) O100; AI432; BB235
111145
We thank thee and we bless thee
(Dunn) BE374   111146
We thank thee, heavenly Father,
for thy correcting rod (Whitney)
BE376   111147
We thank thee, Jesus, dearest
Friend (Praetorius. Musae
sioniae 1607) Q223; AA239
111148
We thank thee, Lord, for eyes to
see (Perkins) BK27   111149
We thank thee, Lord, for sending
us (Curry) BL68   111150
We thank thee, Lord, for this
fair earth (Cotton) AE425;
AS97; BF233; BH193   111151
We thank thee, Lord, for this our
food (Cennick) G564; N541;
O568; P352; X691; AX651; BZ
111152
We thank thee Lord, for this our
food (two versions) (Cennick)
BZ   111153
We thank thee, Lord, for using
us (Bonar) AO487; BY354
111154
We thank thee, Lord, thy paths of

service lead (Laufer) G458;
R294; S367; Y223; Z495;
AC249; AF421; AK265; AR
383; BF501; BZ   111155
We thank thee, loving Father
(---) X405   111156
We thank thee, O God, for a
prophet (Fowler) BC196
111157
We thank thee, O our Father
(---) AL586; AS95; AW422
111158
We thank you, Lord of Heaven
(Struther) A313; X692;
AN477; AQ29; BY34
111159
We three kings of orient are
(Hopkins) A51; B554; G102;
R176; Z204; AB122; AC96;
AF143; AG82; AH269; AN
176; AO136; AQ300; AR141;
AU139; AW90; BB107; BD229;
BG195; BI88; BK161; BL17;
BZ   111160
We, thy children, join the
chorus (Cole) R Birds are
singing   111161
We turn to thee, O Lord, and
sing in sweet accord (Hill)
BE378   111162
We walk by faith, and not by
sight (Alford) B270; D426;
AW152; BA710   111163
We welcome thee in Jesus'
name (Palmer) L307
111164
We who here together are as-
sembled (Zinzendorf, C.R.)
AZ1011   111165
We, who would lead thy flock,
must be (Symons) BV415
111166
We will carol joyfully (---)
K547   111167
We will give, we will pray
(Allen) R Christ for the
whole wide world   111168
We will rest in the fair and
happy land (unusual refrain)
(Stennett) AT478 X On Jor-
dan's stormy bank   111169
We wish you many happy re-
turns of the day (Dearmer)

X386a   111170
We worship thee, almighty Lord
   (Wallin) J174; R25; S17; AF
   28   111171
We worship thee, we bless thee
   (Havergal) R O Saviour,
   precious Saviour   111172
We would be building, temples
   still undone (Deitz) R470;
   Z489; AE441; AF494; AG313;
   AK452; AR384; BK117 111173
We would extol thee, everblessed
   Lord (Grieve) F380; BV28
                              111174
We would see Jesus; for the
   shadows lengthen (Warner)
   B406; D629; I323; N524; O294;
   P342; S263; U412; V665; Z400;
   AB229; AH393; AR413; AS215;
   AT324; AU220; AV219; AW201;
   AY476; AZ1216; BA531; BB
   29   111175
We would see Jesus; lo! his star
   is shining (Park) G113; R183;
   U51; Y71; Z209; AB127; AC
   100; AD471; AE95; AF152; AG
   85; AK456; AL602; AR146; AT
   89; BF305; BK18; BZ 111176
We would see Jesus, Mary's Son
   most holy (Park) AB127 X
   We would see Jesus; lo! His
   star is shining   111177
We would see Jesus, on the
   mountain teaching (Park) BK18
   X We would see Jesus, Lo! his
   star   111178
Wearily at daylight's close (---)
   BR543   111179
Weary of earth, and laden with
   my sin (Stone) A58; B129;
   D82; E91; I284; J366; K324;
   L389; N404; O484; U181; V
   283; AL268; AM467; AO258;
   AP411; AV160; AZ450; BA409;
   BB289; BR295   111180
Weary of self, and laden with my
   sin (Stone) B129 X Weary of
   earth, and laden   111181
Weary of wandering from my God
   (Wesley) B136; D83; AL264;
   AP415   111182
Weary sinner, keep thine eyes
   (Toplady) L252; AO255; AZ

1262   111183
Weary soul by sin oppressed
   (Grimes) AS51   111184
Weary souls that wander wise
   (Wesley) H258; I262 111185
Weep not for a brother deceas-
   ed (Wesley) I594   111186
Weep not for Him who onward
   bears (Pollock) W94
                              111187
Weep, Sion, weep, in death's
   deep sleep (LaTrobe) AZ510
                              111188
Weeping endures but for a
   night (Smith) BB312 111189
Weighed in the balance of jus-
   tice true (Warren) AX294
                              111190
Weil ich Jesus Schäflein bin
   (Hayn) BT648; BW430
                              111191
Weil nun die Zeit vorhanden ist
   (Ausbund) BU135 111192
Welcome among thy flock of
   grace (Zinzendorf, N. L.)
   AZ913; BA803   111193
Welcome be thou, heaven-king
   (English trad carol, 15th c)
   BG174   111194
Welcome, blessed Heavenly
   Stranger (Smart) AZ244
                              111195
Welcome, day of sweet repose
   (Evans) BB469   111196
Welcome, day of the Lord
   (Dearmer) G395; X390
                              111197
Welcome, delightful morn,
   Thou day of sacred rest (Hay-
   ward) G394; H77; I67; L47;
   U442; V61; Z444; AA124; AM
   325; AT21; AU175; AV5; AZ
   1172; BB465   111198
Welcome, happy morning! age
   to age shall say (Fortunatus)
   A87; B169; D109; G161; I
   166; J93; K118; N122; Q202;
   R207; S169; V764; W115; Y
   332; Z246; AB145; AC130;
   AD161; AE133; AI88; AK170;
   AL107; AM199; AO181; AP
   217; AR191; AT110; AV119;
   AZ770; BA241; BD236; BF

320; BR513; BV195; BY165;
BZ   111199
Welcome, morning, bright and
blue (Tarrant) Y200; AC168
                             111200
Welcome, morning of joy, glad
feast (Ascentiontide) (Fortuna-
tus) F608   111201
Welcome, morning of joy, glad
feast (Dedication) (Fortunatus)
F618   111202
Welcome, morning of joy, glad
feast (Easter) (Fortunatus) F
600   111203
Welcome, morning of joy, glad
feast (Whitsunday) (Fortunatus)
F612   111204
Welcome, sweet day of rest
(Watts) D27; H78; I64; L39;
V63; AO14; AY376; AZ1332;
BR96   111205
Welcome, thou victor in the strife
(Schmolck) K119; M436; N127;
AA228; AW542   111206
Welcome to earth, thou noble
guest (Luther) L223   111207
Welcome to earth, thou noble
guest (Luther) L223 X From
heaven high   111208
Welcome, wanderer, welcome
(Bonar) R In the land of
strangers   111209
Welcome, welcome, day of rest
(---) AY272; BB459   111210
Welcome, welcome, ever welcome
(Crosby) R Don't forget the Sab-
bath   111211
Welcome, welcome, Sabbath morn-
ing (Baird) BC190   111212
Welcome Yule, thou merry man
(English trad carol) BG174 X
Welcome be thou, heaven-king
                             111213
Well for him who, all things los-
ing (---) BE379   111214
We'll be gathered home to Zion
(Hayes) R Christ our Lord will
soon be coming   111215
We'll build on the Rock, the living
Rock (Belden) BB579   111216
We'll never say good-by in heaven
(Chapman) R With friends on
earth we meet   111217

We'll sing all hail to Jesus'
name (Alldridge) BC218
                             11218
We'll sing and we'll shout
(Phelps) R The Spirit of
God like a fire is burning
                             111219
We'll sing the songs of Sion
(Mills) BC205   111220
We'll to God's tabernacles
go, and at his footstool bow
(Scottish Psalter, 1650)
AL687; AP117   111221
We'll walk in the light, beauti-
ful light ("J. V. C. ")
[Crosby??] R All ye saints
of light   111222
We'll work till Jesus comes
(---) R Let others seek a
home below   111223
We'll work till Jesus comes
(---) R O land of rest (Mills)
                             111224
Wenn dein herzliebster Sohn, o
Gott (Heermann) BT375
                             111225
Wenn mein Stündlein vorhanden
ist (Herman) BT594
                             111226
Wenn meine Sünd' mich kränken
(Gesenius) BT152   111227
Wenn wir in höchsten Nöten sein
(Eber) BT522   111228
Wenn's doch alle Seelen wussten
(Unparth. G. B.) AY45d
                             111229
Wer Christo jetzt will folgen
nach (J. Wagner) BU11
                             111230
Wer Gott vertraut, hat wohl
gebaut (Magdeburg) BT437
                             111231
Wer nur den lieben Gott lässt
walten (Neumark) AW571b;
BT518; BW571   111232
Wer weiss, wie nahe mir mein
Ende! (Ämilie Juliane, coun-
tess) BT598   111233
Wer will mit uns nach Zion
gehn (Unparth. G. B.) AY32d
                             111234
Were you there when they
crucified my Lord (Negro

spiritual) A80; J500; R201;
AE455; AF179; AG317; AH609;
AR173; BK170; BL23; BZ
111235

We're bound for the land of the
pure and the holy (---) BB368
111236
We're going home, no more to
roam (Griswold) AX593
111237
We're marching on to glory
(Chamberlain) BC194   111238
We're marching to Zion (Watts)
R Come we that love the
Lord   111239
We're nearing the shore of that
beautiful land   (Doughty) R
Soon trials and conflicts of life
111240
We're not ashamed to own our
Lord (Phelps) BC266   111241
We're not ashamed to own our
Lord (Phelps) X I'm not a-
shamed to own my Lord
(Watts)   111242
We've a story to tell to the nations
(Nichol) G501; R504; U389;
V740; Z532; AC302; AE353;
AG261; AH464; AP797; AR564;
AS370; AT455; AU379; AV261;
AW335; BF525; BY400; BZ
111243
"We've no abiding city here"
(Kelly) L597; AY390; BB308
111244
What a fellowship, what a joy
divine (Hoffman) AH390; AI
401; AM718; AT371; AU276;
AW489; AX49; BB611   111245
What a friend we have in Jesus
(Scriven) A422; G240; H38;
I551; J459; L427; M581; N343;
O488; P33; Q457; R385; S257;
U356; V469; W701; Z331; AA
395; AD214; AE303; AF335;
AG224; AH319; AI107; AK472;
AL502; AM533; AO318; AP
494; AR483; AS127; AT328;
AU160; AV319; AW186; AX
350; AY55; AZ957; BA618;
BB320; BF372; BV612; BY
343; BZ   111246

What a mighty God we serve
(Brooks) R Our Father's
wondrous works   111247
What a sea of tears and sorrows
(Breviary, 1746) BQ146
111248
What a wonderful change in my
life (McDaniel) AT310
111249
What a wonderful Saviour (Hoffman) R Christ has for sin
111250
What a wonderful, wonderful
Saviour (---) AX107 111251
What affords the Christian warrior vigor (Zinzendorf, N. L.)
AZ1022   111252
What are these in bright array
(Montgomery) K246 X Who
are these in bright array
111253
What are these that glow from
afar (Rossetti) E203; X209
111254
What are they that are but
one? (English trad carol,
1625) BG64   111255
What are those soul-reviving
strains (Montgomery) AZ
332; BA224   111256
What beauteous sun-surpassing
star (Coffin) BO161
111257
What brightness dawned in
resurrection (McKenzie) BE
381   111258
What brought us together, what
joined our hearts? (Schlicht)
AZ493; BA678   111259
What can I give to Jesus (---)
AT508   111260
What can wash away my sin
(Lowry) AM677 X What can
wash away my stain 111261
What can wash away my stain
(Lowry) AI395; AM677; AT
204; AU456; AX115; AY511
111262
What can we offer thee, O
Lord (Spangenberg) BA546
X High on his everlasting
throne   111263
What cheering words are these

(Kent) K411; L470; N481;
AZ1349   111264
What child is this, who, laid to
rest (Dix) A36; G109; R159;
Z200; AB121; AF140; AG300;
AH255; AW78; BD220; BF295;
BK162; BZ   111265
What conscience dictates to be
done (Pope) X693; AQ133
                            111266
What contradictions meet In
minister's employ (Newton)
BT46 X On what has now been
sown   111267
What do I owe! Nay, Lord what
do I not? (Oxenham) BY490
                            111268
What doth the Lord require of thee
(Cross) AD326   111269
What else is wisdom. What else
man's endeavor (Euripides)
AQ109   111270
What equal honors shall we bring
(Watts) AV131   111271
What glorious scenes mine eyes
behold (---) BC197   111272
What glory gilds the sacred page
(Cowper) BR235 X A glory gilds
the sacred page   111273
What God ordains is always good
(Rodigast) M281 X Whate'er
my God ordains is right
                            111274
What good news the angels bring
(Hammond) AZ62; BA162
                            111275
What grace, O Lord, and beauty
shone (Denny) G115; I126; R
180; S143; W87; Z219; AE97;
AG87; AL79; AO148; AP187; AS
120; BR171; BZ   111276
What happiness can equal mine
(Faber) BN104; BO39; BP67
                            111277
What happiness, what joy and
happiness (Gregor) AZ1229
                            111278
What has drawn us thus apart
(Chadwick) AN222; BX97
                            111279
What heroes thou hast bred
(Menzies) X325   111280
What is it that makes us stand

fast in one spirit (Schlicht)
AZ1091   111281
What is our calling's glorious
hope (Wesley) I358   111282
What is the thing of greatest
price (Montgomery) I243;
U149   111283
What is the world to me
(Pfefferkorn) M195; Q430;
AA385   111284
What is this life if, full of
care (Davies) AQ183
                            111285
What is thy birthright, Man
(Seal) BE382   111286
What joy to reach the harbor
(Brorson) P330   111287
What joy, to think of that vast
host (Wexels) BY408
                            111288
What laws, my blessed Saviour,
hast thou broken (Heermann)
AZ466   111289
What lovely Infant can this be
(---) BO157   111290
What makes a city great and
strong (---) AQ102   111291
"What means this glory round
our feet" (Lowell) AN160;
BX192   111292
What mercy and divine com-
passion (Tersteegen) AW
562a   111293
What mortal tongue can sing
your praise (Santeüil) BN
158; BO82   111294
What, my soul, should bow thee
down (Cennick) AZ33
                            111295
What offering shall I bring to
thee (Toeltschig) AZ919;
BA58   111296
What our Father does is well
(Schmolck) K488; L480;
M497; N466; O531; P301;
Q571; AA301; AZ1267
                            111297
What praise to thee, my Saviour
(Gambold) AZ566; BA897
                            111298
What purpose burns within our
hearts (Savage) BY532
                            111299

What secret hand, at morning
light (Montgomery) BA768
                              111300
What secret place, what distant
star (Gill) BX91   111301
What service shall we render
(Dodgshun) W644   111302
What shall I do, my God, to
love (Wesley) H293; AP459;
BZ   111303
What shall I do, my Lord, my
God (Larcom) AB191
                              111304
What shall I render to my God
For all His gifts to me
(Mason) K302; L83; N334
                              111305
What shall I render to my God
For all His kindness shown
(Watts) V519; AM537; AR350;
AS352   111306
What shall I render to my God
For all his mercy's store
(Wesley) BZ   111307
What shall I render to the Lord,
For all his benefits to me
(U.P. Psalter, 1912) T218;
AJ311   111308
What shall I render to the Lord,
What shall my offering be
(U.P. Psalter, 1912) R32;
T220; AJ313   111309
What shall I render unto thee
O Lord, For all the gifts
(Van Rensselaer) AH129
                              111310
What sinners value, I resign
(Watts) L575; V680; AZ383
                              111311
What songs are these, faint heard
and far (Kendon) BG140
                              111312
What Star is this, so radiant,
More lovely than the Sun
(Coffin) BN26   111313
What star is this, with beams
so bright (Coffin) A47; E44;
AF144; AW87; BJ8   111314
What sweet of life endureth (St
John of Damascus) E360
                              111315
What sweeter music can we
bring (Herrick) BG122

                              111316
What thanks and praise to thee
we own (Maclagan) D172;
BV448   111317
What thou wilt, O Father, give
(Whittier) AN278; BX333
                              111318
What though I cannot break my
chain (Toplady) AM398
                              111319
What though the arm of con-
quering death (Doddridge)
I592   111320
What tidings bringest thou,
messenger (English trad car-
ol, 15th c) R A babe is
born of high nature   111321
What time I am afraid (U.P.
Psalter, 1912) AJ152; AM
564   111322
What tongue can tell thy good-
ness, Lord (---) BI19-D
                              111323
What various hindrances we
meet (Cowper) H41; I496;
V459; AZ407; BV616
                              111324
What voice salutes the startled
ear (Naisbitt) BC275
                              111325
What wait I for but thee (U.P.
Psalter, 1912) T70; AJ106
                              111326
What was witnessed in the
heavens (Davis) BC299
                              111327
What wealth of joy thy presence
lendeth (Dessler) M267
                              111328
What will it be? What will it
be? (Teddlie) R Some day
you'll stand at the bar on
high   111329
What will you do with Jesus
(---) R Jesus is standing at
your heart's door (McKinney)
R Jesus is standing in Pilate's
hall (---)   111330
What within me and without
(Francke) BR366   111331
What wondrous love is this, O
my soul, O my soul (Negro
spiritual) BZ   111332

What would you give in exchange
(Berry) R Brother afar from
the Saviour   111333
What, ye ask me, is my prize
(Schwedler) S331; AM435
                           111334
Whate'er God will, let that be
done (Albrecht of Brandenburg
- Culmbach) AA494   111335
Whate'er I am, whate'er I do
(Zinzendorf, N. L.) AZ680
                           111336
Whate'er my God ordains is right
(Rodigast) D668; I487; J582;
K402; M281; O370; Q521; R
366; S291; W540; AF96; AK
309; AM94; AW567; BA703;
BR272; BV515   111337
Whate'er our God ordains is
right (Rodigast) J582 X
Whate'er my God ordains
                           111338
Whatever dims thy sense of truth
(Hale) BE383   111339
Whatever God ordains is right
(Rodigast) AA507 X Whate'er
my God ordains ...   111340
When a deed is done for freedom
(Lowell) AQ168 X Once to
every man and nation   111341
When a knight won his spurs
(Struther) X377   111342
When adverse winds and waves
arise (Sigourney) AZ657
                           111343
When afflictions sore oppress you
(Olearius) O277   111344
When all my labors and trials
are o'er (Gabriel) AT485;
BB641   111345
When all the world was cursed
(Olearius) Q272   111346
When all thy mercies, gracious
Lord (Addison) BR249 X
When all thy mercies, O my
God   111347
When all thy mercies, O my God
(Addison) A297; B237; D657;
E511; F177; G542; H67; I105;
J440; K296; L108; M591; N328;
O20; Q31; R119; S81; U36; V
518; W26; X694; AA72; AF94;
AG48; AH220; AK84; AL23; AM

51; AN225; AO98; AP145;
AR82; AS83; AV56; AZ186;
BA35; BR249; BV568; BX
117; BY77; BZ   111348
When along life's thorny road
(Deck) O503; AZ1069
                           111349
When at thy footstool, Lord,
I bend (Lyte) D591   111350
When blooming youth is snatched
away (---) AY178   111351
When blossoms flowered 'mid
the snows (Martens) BQ
126   111352
When by fear my heart is
daunted (Dearmer) G319; X
695   111353
When Caesar Augustus had
raised a taxation (English
trad carol) BG114   111354
When came in flesh the incar-
nate word (Anstice) E13;
F56; BV75   111355
When children, blest by Jesus
(Rothe) AZ572; BA730
                           111356
When Christ at evening hour
(Jenkins) BV196   111357
When Christ beheld, in sinful
night (---) AY442   111358
When Christ blessed his
disciples (Dearmer) BG153
                           111359
When Christ had shown God's
dawning Reign (Dearmer)
X185   111360
When Christ, our Lord and
Saviour, dwelleth (Swertner)
AZ1416   111361
When Christ our Lord had
passed once more (Latin,
4th c) E150   111362
When Christ, our Saviour, did
ascend (Cennick) AZ575
                           111363
When Christ was born in
Bethlehem, Fair peace of
earth (Housman) A112; E
611; X221   111364
When Christ was born in Bethle-
hem, 'Twas night, but seem-
ed the noon (Longfellow)
BC295   111365

When Christ was born of Mary
free (English trad. carol,
15th c) B547; BG178; BR560;
BV118   111366
When Christ was born to set us
free (English trad carol, 15th
c) BP18   111367
When Christmas morn is dawning
(Ehrenborg-Posse) J35; M610;
N635   111368
When cold our hearts and far from
thee (Monsell) M584   111369
When courage fails and faith burns
low (Hosmer) Z356; AB228;
AN238; AQ95; AW191; BF432
                                 111370
When dark and drear the skies
appear (Woodmansee) BC293
                                 111371
When darkness gathers round thy
way (Smith) BB314   111372
When day's shadows lengthen
(Lee) BQ140; BR114   111373
When doomed to death, the Apostle
lay (Bryant) D279   111374
When downward to the darksome
tomb (Palmer) BA732 111375
When first the glorious light of
truth (Clayton) BC198 111376
When from Egypt's house of
bondage (Threlfall) W573;
AP785   111377
When from the city of our God
(Wordsworth) AO478   111378
When from the East the wise
men came (Hopkins) D64
                                 111379
When gathering clouds around
I view (Grant) I134; V637;
AI287; AO410; AZ656; BR
333   111380
When God is seen with men to
dwell (Ballou) BE384   111381
When God of old came down from
heaven (Keble) E158; F154;
W181; AP277; AZ110   111382
When great Saint Patrick raised
the cross (---) BN165 111383
When He cometh, when He
cometh (Cushing) N651; W158;
AL614; AM651; AP794; AU315;
AW432; BB418; BV355   111384
When here, O Lord, we seek thy

face (Montgomery) AX646
X This stone to thee 111385
When his salvation bringing
(King) D558; F437; G129;
K546; L257; N638; O577;
P358; R186; S149; AE108;
AH278; AI386; AK138; AL
83; AM646; AO156; AP750;
AR175; AZ826; BA817; BF
620; BR537   111386
When I by faith my Saviour
see (Newton) AZ361
                                 111387
When I can read my title
clear (Watts) H369; I440;
L469; N618; U427; V698;
AA368; AI337; AT468; AU
16; AV287; AY362   111388
When I fall on my knees
(Negro spiritual) R Let us
break bread together
                                 111389
When I fear my faith will fail
(Habershon) AI310   111390
When I get weary with toils of
the day (Warren) AX532
                                 111391
When I have reached earth's
borderland (Jones) AX537
                                 111392
When I read how my Saviour
was nailed to the cross
(Teasley) AX347   111393
When I see the blood (Foote)
R Christ our Redeemer died
on the cross   111394
When I see the way my Saviour
leads me (Gardiner) AX26
                                 111395
When I shall reach the more
excellent glory (Spencer)
AX568   111396
When I shall wake in that fair
morn of morns (Bonar)
H331   111397
When I survey the wondrous
cross (Watts) A337; B154;
D101; E107; F108; G148;
H169; I141; J503; K97; L245;
M420; N107; O306; P178;
Q175; R198; S152; T342; U
88; V142; W106; X133; Y
376; Z228; AA204; AB137;

now descended (Gryphius)
BJ37   111431
When marshalled on the nightly
plain (White) H143; I124; V125;
BI93   111432
When Mary brought her treasure
(Struther) X223   111433
When Mary, immaculate, tender
and mild (Currie) BN138
111434
When morning fills the skies
(German, ca 1800) BN190
111435
When morning gilds the skies
(German, ca 1800) A367; B37;
D445; E512; F223; G31; H29;
I32; J416; K310; M556; R41;
S3; T323; V29; W167; Y201;
Z135; AB77; AC2; AD43; AE40;
AF35; AG21; AH158; AK43; AL
45; AM131; AN92; AO19; AP255;
AR46; AS19; AT23; AU7; AV2;
AW19; AZ554; BA128; BB43;
BD4; BF176; BJ67; BK38; BO
10; BQ42; BR1; BV271; BY
685; BZ   111436
When morning lights the eastern
skies (U. P. Psalter, 1912)
R49; T283; AJ391   111437
When mothers of Salem (Hutchings)
S446; W659; AL609; AP796;
BY401   111438
When musing sorrow weeps the
past (Noel) I455   111439
When my last hour is close at
hand (Hermann) O582; Q594;
AA528   111440
When my life-work is ended and
I cross the swelling tide (Crosby)
AT472; AV397; AX572; AY495
111441
When my lips can frame no sound
(Comenius) BA854   111442
When my love to Christ grows
weak (Wreford) BA227 X When
my love to God grows weak
111443
When my love to God grows weak
(Wreford) U89; X134; AF162;
AN189; AQ313; AW102; BA227;
BV165   111444
When, my Saviour, shall I be
(Wesley) BB250   111445

When o'er my sins I sorrow
(Gesenius) Q152; AA197
111446
When on my day of life the night
is falling (Whittier) G519;
I589; W589; X697; AB403;
AD463; AK419; AL456; AN
436; AP625; BF668; BR425;
BX471; BY777   111447
When on Sinai's top I see
(Montgomery) AZ55 111448
When our heads are bowed with
woe (Milman) A79; B409;
D348; E513; K76; O464; W
329; AL131; BA664; BR346;
BT162   111449
When out in sin and darkness
lost (Gilmour) AX89; AY
201   111450
When, overwhelmed with grief
(Watts) BR281   111451
When peace, like a river, at-
tendeth my way (Spafford)
L493; N525; P213; AE190;
AH394; AI258; AM580; AR
484; AS310; AT265; AU73;
AV363; AW484; AX484; AY
452; BB313   111452
When righteous Joseph wedded
was (English trad carol)
BG41   111453
When rising from the bed of
death (Addison) E92; L390
111454
When Rome had shrouded earth
in night (Luther) AA283
111455
When shadows gather on our way
(Hosmer) S323; AN125; BX
104   111456
When shall thine hour, , dear
Jesus come (Zinzendorf, N.
L.) AZ282   111457
When shall we meet again ?
Meet ne'er to serve?
(Watts & Smith) L598; AY
301   111458
When shepherds watched their
flocks by night, In Bethle-
hem's fields so still (Westall)
BR561   111459
When simplicity we cherish
(Spangenberg) AZ235; BA636

111460
When sinners see their lost con-
dition (Landstad) M343; O173;
P270; Q65   111461
When sins and fears prevailing
rise (Steele) V359   111462
When Sion in her low estate
(U.P. Psalter, 1912) T256;
AI264; AJ357   111463
When Sion's bondage God turned
back (Scottish Psalter, 1650)
AL685; AP114   111464
When sorrow and remorse
(Gesenius) K75   111465
When spring unlocks the flowers
to paint the laughing soil
(Heber) E299; X21; Z592;
AD451   111466
When Stephen, full of power and
grace (Struther) X219; AF493;
AN425; AQ155   111467
When storms of life are round
me beating (Oatman) AX358
111468
When streaming from the eastern
skies (Shrubsole) D638; N549;
O550; Q543; AA19; AI47; AZ
671   111469
When sun rays crown thy pine
clad hills (Boyle) AL524
111470
When the blind suppliant in the
way (Bryant) H156   111471
When the book of life is opened
(Snyder) R When your toils
111472
When the clouds are hanging low
(Lillenas) AU334; AX364
111473
When the corn is planted In the
dark deep bed (---) BY757
111474
When the day of toil is done
(Ellerton) W584; AA546; AL466;
AO29; AP619; AZ1137   111475
When the early morning breaking
(Morris) AI308   111476
When the gladsome day declineth
(Savage) AN123; AQ272
111477
When the golden evening gathered
On the shore of Galilee (Daw-
son) Y76; Z212; AC108; AK

130; AR154   111478
When the great sun sinks to his
rest (Babcock) S72 111479
When the heart is sad within
(Milman) BR346 X When
our heads are bowed 111480
When the herds were watching
(Canton) X379   111481
When the King comes in,
brother (Landor) R Called
to the feast by the King are
we   111482
When the light of day is waning
(Geldart) BX155   111483
When the Lord of Love was
here (Brooke) S141; U78;
W85; Z215; AB128; AC104;
AL80; AN207; BB115; BD66;
BF306; BX215; BY133
111484
When the Lord turned the cap-
tivity of Sion (Ladies of the
Grail) BSp46   111485
When the mists have rolled in
splendor (Herbert) AU354
111486
When the night is still and far
(Gannett) Y13   111487
When the paschal evening fell
(Stanley) BV170; BX485
111488
When the roll is called up
yonder (Black) R When the
trumpet of the Lord 111489
When the rosy light of morn-
ing (Baird) BC200 111490
When the Sabbath, peace-invit-
ing (Jastrow) BH114
111491
When the stars at set of sun
(---) BH245   111492
When the storms of life are rag-
ing, Stand by me (Tindley)
AU30; BZ   111493
When the storms of life are
raging, Tempests wild on
land and sea (Servoss) AU
409   111494
When the sun had sunk to rest
(French) BF279   111495
When the sun shines bright and
your heart is light (Reynolds)
AT214; AV352   111496

When the trump shall sound and
time (Jacobs) AY383   111497
When the trump shall sound
(Jacobs) X When the trumpet
of the Lord (Black)   111498
When the trumpet of the Lord
shall sound (Black) AH530;
AM727; AT482; AX577   111499
When the trumpet of the Lord
(Black) X When the trump shall
sound (Jacobs)   111500
When the unquiet hours depart
(Russell i.e. "A.E.") X122
111501
When the weary seeking rest
(Bonar) D609; I509; V758;
W255; AB180; AK231; AL332;
AM532; AP236; AW203; AZ
1505; BA611; BF365; BR25
111502
When the world around us throws
(Williams) AN233; BF361;
BX259   111503
When there is peace, Where
praise hath been (Davis) BH
16   111504
When they bereaved his life so
good (English trad carol) G72
X When Jesus Christ was
twelve years old   111505
When this passing world is done
(McCheyne) W582; AL302; AM
600; AP460; AZ1264; BY616
111506
When this poor heart is burdened
with grief (Hugg) AY375
111507
When this song of praise shall
cease (Bryant) AR47; BH103
111508
When Thou, my righteous Judge,
shalt come (Huntingdom) H495;
U422; V686; AI96; BB190
111509
When through the sail the wild
tempest is streaming (Heber)
N78; BR363   111510
When through the whirl of wheels,
and engines humming (Studdert-
Kennedy) X698; Y184; AC192;
AD350; AF422; BF511   111511
When thy heart with joy o'er flowing (Williams) U371; Z508; AC

245; AE278; AH513; AN280;
AO470; AQ226; AR373; AS345;
AW227; BD134; BF608; BH
197; BK111; BX335   111512
When thy soldiers take their
swords (Owen) AK345; AM
486; AO372; AP557; BX367
111513
When time seems short and
death is near (Bethune)
I296; BW440   111514
When trials and temptations
around thee (Metzler) AX
530; AY386   111515
When upon life's billows you
are tempest-tossed (Oatman)
AT318; BC202   111516
When upon the raging waters
(Kretzman) M174   111517
When very early in the dawn
(Synnestvedt) BI106
111518
When vesper bells are calling
(Franzén) N565   111519
When virgin morn doth call
thee to arise (Herrick) X
36   111520
When warmer suns and bluer
skies (---) BH134   111521
When waves of trouble round
me swell (Elliott) AO355
111522
When we all get to heaven
(Hewitt) R Sing the wondrous
love of Jesus   111523
When we devote our youth to
God (Watts) AZ166   111524
When we have ended searching
(Patton) AQ181   111525
When we hear the music ring-
ing (---) AY156   111526
When we walk with the Lord
(Sammis) AE210; AH420;
AI400; AM700; AR485; AS
269; AT260; AU390; AV373;
AW486; AX465; AY454;
BB582; BY491; BZ   111527
When wilt thou save the people
(Elliott) A496; B501; E566;
S375; X314; Y241; Z563; AB
290; AC288; AD352; AG280;
AL527; AN324; AO483; AP
642; AR90; AV229; BB675;

BD165; BF577; BX382; BY654
111528

When winds are raging o'er the upper ocean (Stowe) P297; AB217; AN228; BF390; BX265;
111529

When wounded sore the stricken soul [heart] (Alexander) B138; F88; H226; L520; BV140
111530

When your toils below are ended (Snyder) AX293; AY389
111531

When came the armies of the sky (---) BB378   111532

Whence these sounds symphonious (Kelly) AZ759   111533

When-e'er I think of her so dear (Van de Venter) R I never can forget   111534

When e'er we contemplate the grace (Gregor) O344; AZ902
111535

Whenever war, with its red woes (Finley) Y228   111536

Where ancient forests widely spread (Norton) AN27; BX 35   111537

Where are the reapers? O who will come (Rexford) R O where are the reapers   111538

Where are you going, Greatheart? (Oxenham) AC499   111539

Where could I go, O where could I go (Coats) R Living below in this old sinful world
111540

Where cross the crowded ways of life (North) A498; B494; G465; I423; J351; K235; N387; P387; R507; S410; T442; U330; Y60; Z519; AB332; AC265; AD427; AE413; AF423; AG268; AH512; AI179; AK394; AL380; AN218; AO475; AP581; AQ189; AR198; AS339; AT464; AU405; AV276; AW222; BA555; BD136; BF522; BK80; BX223; BY533; BZ
111541

Where for safety shall I fly? (Hymns of the English conf. 1880) BR350   111542

Where He leads I'll follow (Ogden)

R Sweet are the promises
111543

Where He leads me I will follow (Blandly) R I can hear my Saviour calling   111544

Where He may lead me I will go (Martin) AS249; AX507
111545

Where high the heavenly temple stands (Bruce) F204; K137; R389; V172; W140; AL122; AP231; AZ354; BA96; BB137; BV212; BY178   111546

Where is death's sting? We were not born to die (Bradby) A470; X296   111547

Where is he that came to save (Beach) BX209   111548

Where is my wandering boy (Lowry) AU89   111549

Where is our holy Church (Wilson) AN412; AQ259
111550

Where is the Friend for whom I'm ever yearning (Wallin) N517; S329   111551

Where is the true man's fatherland? (Lowell) AB359; BF 578   111552

Where is thy Lord, my soul? (Lynch) X699; Y16; AB188; BX100   111553

Where is thy hope, poor sinner (Warren) AX289
111554

Where is your God? they say (Martineau) Y3; AB35; AD 92; AN71; AQ87; BX109
111555

Where Judah's faithful sons are found (Mayer) BH210
111556

Where lies our path? We seek to know (North) AB316
111557

Where loyal hearts and true (Faber) R O paradise, O paradise   111558

Where, O God eternal, where art thou? (Kálmán) AK62
111559

Where restless crowds are thronging (Clark) J355;

BY655   111560
Where shall my wondering soul
   begin? (Wesley) BZ   111561
Where the angel-hosts adore thee
   (Santeüil) D171; N318; BA38
                               111562
Where the great ships, passing
   (Rowland) G556; AB383
                               111563
Where the mourner, weeping
   (Oswald) BR340 X O let him
   whose sorrow   111564
Where the olive grove stood
   darkly (Tiplady) Z229 111565
"Where two or three, with sweet
   accord" (Stennett) AY193;
   AZ406   111566
Where will I go? (Warren) R
   Eternity draws near   111567
Where will you spend eternity
   (Hoffman) AU290; AX268; AY
   531   111568
Where wilt thou go, since night
   draws near (Homburg) M451;
   Q197; AA227   111569
Where winds the road o'er hill and
   dale (Mather) Z420; AR382
                               111570
Where'er have trod thy sacred
   feet (---) D315   111571
Where'er his creatures gather
   (U.P. Psalter, 1912) T151;
   AJ223   111572
Where'er I go, whate'er my task
   (Flemming) AA372   111573
Where-fore do the nations rage
   (Grant) AJ3   111574
Wherefore, O Father, we thy
   humble servants, Here bring
   before thee (Jervois) A205;
   E335; F416   111575
Wherefore, O Father, we thy
   humble servants Offer our
   praises (Dearmer) X281; AK
   342; BV368   111576
Wherefore weep we over Jesus
   (Spitta) AZ958   111577
Wherever he leads I'll go (Mc-
   Kinney) R Take up thy cross
                               111578
Wherever men adore thee (Van
   Dyke) AK414 X No form of
   human framing   111579

Wherever through the ages rise
   (Whittier) AN442; BX483
                               111580
Wherewith, O Lord, shall I
   draw near (Wesley) I244
                               111581
Whether day my spirit's yearn-
   ing (Goethe) AQ63   111582
Whether the end of earthly life
   (Zinzendorf, N.L.) BA711
                               111583
While filled with sadness and
   dismay (Newton) V581
                               111584
While humble shepherds watched
   their flocks (Tate) W42 X
   While shepherds watched their
   flocks   111585
While in sweet communion feed-
   ing (Denny) Z460; AI163;
   AS465   111586
While Jesus whispers to you
   (Witter) AU212; AX229;
   BB564   111587
While life prolongs its precious
   light (Dwight) H248; I254;
   V273   111588
While my Redeemer's near
   (Steele) BR262   111589
While o'er the deep thy servants
   sail (Burgess) D308
                               111590
While of these emblems we par-
   take (Nicholson) BC217
                               111591
While passing thro' this world
   of sin (McKinney) AT348;
   AU423   111592
While shepherds kept their
   watching (Negro spiritual) R
   Go tell it on the mountains
                               111593
While shepherds watched their
   flocks by night (Tate) A13;
   B71; D54; E30; F62; G88;
   H136; I115; J24; K28; L225;
   M350; N44; O188; P131; Q
   109; R169; S120; U50; V117;
   W42; X82; Z185; AD112; AE
   88; AF146; AG80; AH260; AI
   62; AK106; AL62; AM156;
   AN155; AO120; AP168; AQ
   295; AR130; AT79; AU147;

AV89; AW73; AX98; AY489;
AZ1462; BA161; BB101; BC222;
BD210; BF283; BG33; BJ39;
BK145; BR551; BV123; BY113;
BZ   111594
While sinks our land to realms
of night (Pattinson) BX142
                            111595
While successive years are wast-
ing (Okely) AZ1383   111596
While the pilgrim travels (Zinzen-
dorf, N. L.) AZ753; BA39
                            111597
While the sun is shining (Stowell)
N507; AI183   111598
While the years of eternity roll
(Gates) R I will sing to you
a song   111599
While thee I seek protecting
Power (Williams) B35; D671;
H122; I517; L474; V426; Z334;
AE243; AN255; AO89; AV41;
AW199; AY43; AZ1452; BA901;
BR247; BX304   111600
While thou, O my God, art my
help and defender (Young) BE
389; BR312   111601
While we lowly bow before thee
(Colesworthy) L206;   111602
While we pray and while we plead
(Whittle) AT218; AV333; AX236
                            111603
While we take our seat (Zinzen-
dorf, N. L.) AZ540   111604
While with ceaseless course the
sun (Newton) H522; I574; L552;
N53; Q113; V629; AA163; AM
613; AZ1073; BA180; BR500
                            111605
While yet the earth midst chaos
whirled (Rypins) BH99 111606
While yet the morn is breaking
(Mühlmann) M551; N543; Q544;
AA21   111607
Whisper a prayer, whisper a
prayer (McKinney) R Come lin-
ger here   111608
Whispering hope (Hawthorne) R
Soft as the voice of an angel
                            111609
Whiter than snow, yes, whiter
than snow (Nicholson) R Lord
Jesus, I long to be perfectly

whole   111610
Whither pilgrims, are you go-
ing (Golden chain, 1861)
[Crosby?] W578; AP783
                            111611
Whither thus in holy rapture
(Santeüil) BO96; BQ80
                            111612
Who are these arrayed in white
(Wesley) I619   111613
Who are these in bright array
(Montgomery) B298; D180;
K246; L595; N209; AO557;
AZ1059; BA752; BR443
                            111614
Who are these like stars appear-
ing (Schenck) A130; B296;
D178; E204; F570; K245; N630;
O493; W222; X210; AM602;
AZ607; BA810; BV465
                            111615
Who at my door is standing
(Slade) AX245; AY374
                            111616
Who came down from heaven to
earth (Whittle) AI385
                            111617
Who dares to bind to his dull
sense (Rawson) AN368; BX
400   111618
Who dreads, yet undismayed
(Darbyshire) F534; X218
                            111619
Who fathoms the eternal
thought (Whittier) W558 X
I know not what the future
hath   111620
Who goes there, in the night
(Clark) Y122; AC261
                            111621
Who has seen the wind (Rosset-
ti) X386d   111622
Who hath believed after hear-
ing the message (Oliver)
AM673   111623
Who is he, in yonder stall
(Hanby) E612; K560; W77;
AE96; AL72; AP735; AW96;
BV284; BY134   111624
Who is he whom crowds ac-
claim (Dearmer) X700b
                            111625
Who is like thee, O universal

Lord (Gutheim) BH69 111626
Who is on the Lord's side (Haver-
gal) R355; S272; U292; V752;
W519; Z367; AB349; AC202;
AE272; AG190; AH434; AI331;
AK286; AL365; AM493; AO373;
AP551; AT413; AU63; AV208;
AW190; BF475; BV592; BY534
111627
Who is she that stands triumphant
(Vere) BM94 X Holy Church
now stands   111628
Who is the man that shall ascend
(Scottish Psalter, 1650) AP
20   111629
Who is the patriot? He who lights
(Knowles) AQ243   111630
Who is there like thee, Jesus,
unto me? (Freylinghausen)
O30; AO381; AZ543   111631
Who is there that singeth so,
Nowell? (Smart) BG21
111632
Who is this so weak and helpless
(How) E514; L211; W73; AL74;
AM169; AP260   111633
Who is this that comes from
Edom (Kelly) D449; Q209;
AA223; AM228; AZ604 111634
Who is this that comes in glory
(Wordsworth) BR189 X See the
Conqueror mounts in triumph
111635
Who is this, with garments dyed
(Dayman) AZ557   111636
Who is this with garments gory
(Coxe) E108   111637
Who is thy neighbor? He whom
thou (Cutter) I690; AW228;
BX339   111638
Who knows how near my end may
be? (Amilie Juliana) L564;
M301; O579; Q598; AA544
111639
Who knows how near my life's
expended (Amilie Juliana)
O579 X Who knows how near
my end   111640
Who knows how soon my days are
ended (Amilie Juliana) M301 X
Who knows how near my end
111640a
Who knows when death may over-

take me (Amilie Juliana) Q598
X Who knows how near my
end   111641
Who made ocean, earth, and
sky (Compton) BK4 111642
Who, O Lord, shall dwell with
thee (U. P. Psalter, 1912)
AJ26   111643
Who, O Lord, with thee abiding
(U. P. Psalter, 1912) T19;
AJ24   111644
Who overcometh shall abide
forever (Moravian) AZ1023
111645
Who pits his trust in God most
just (Magdeburg) AA511;
AZ1093; BA698   111646
Who saved us from eternal loss
(Gray) R O Listen to our
wondrous story   111647
Who shall open for us the por-
tals (Peter) M364   111648
Who shall all the Lord's elect
condemn (Watts) AA313
111649
Who taught the bird to build
her nest (---) BH247
111650
Who thou art I know not
(Kemp) AQ46   111651
Who trusts in God, a strong
abode (Magdeburg) K334;
N86; O282; Q437; R375; U
199; AB244; AF354; AM558;
BF397   111652
Who will build the world anew
(Clark) AE408; AR579
111653
Who will join the throng to
heaven (Brorson) M70
111654
Who will now indict me (Franck)
P272   111655
Who within that stable cries
(Dearmer) X700a   111656
Who would true valor see
(Bunyan) F293 X He who
would valiant be   111657
Whole-hearted thanksgiving to
thee will I bring (U. P. Psal-
ter, 1912) T12; AJ16
111658
Who'll be the next to follow

Jesus (Hawks) AX258   111659

Whom have we, Lord, in heaven
but thee, and whom on earth
besides (Birks or Auber)
(identification not possible)
BR269   111660

Whom oceans part, O Lord, unite
(Lewis) W628; Z525; AD454;
AE366; AR504; BY656   111661

Who's on the Lord's side? Who?
(Cornaby) BC175   111662

Whose works, O Lord, like thine
can be (Lucas) BH222 111623

Whose in God alone confideth
(Neumark) BR260 X He who
would be in God confiding
                         111664

"Whosoever hearteh," shout
(Bliss) AT238; AU126; AX
220; BB571   111665

"Whosoever" surely meaneth me
(McConnell) R I am happy today   111666

Why art thou cast down my soul?
(Schmolck) O237; P294
                         111667

Why art thou cast down my soul,
why disquieted in me? (Hamburg Temple hymnal) BH171
                         111668

Why art thou heavey-hearted
(Gerhardt) M270   111669

Why art thou sorrowful, servant
of God (Faber) BQ144
                         111670

Why do the heathen rage (Kennedy) O217   111671

Why do we mourn departing
friends (Watts) I595; L573;
Q593; V673; AA542; AY168;
AZ104   111672

Why do you wait, dear brother
(Root) AT220; AU170; AX243
                         111673

Why dost thou stand afar (U. P.
Psalter, 1912) AJ19; AM508
                         111674

Why, impious Herod, shouldst
thou fear (Sedulius) E38
                         111675

Why is thy faith in God's great
love so small (Sherwin) BE
390   111676

Why, my soul, thus trembling
ever (Gerhardt) O342
                         111677

Why not now? (Whittle) R
While we pray and while we
plead   111678

Why not? why not? Why not
come to Him now? (Root)
R Why do you wait   111679

Why rage the heather? and vain
things (Scottish Psalter,
1650) AP2   111680

Why search the future and the
past (Barlow) BE391
                         111681

Why should cross and trial
grieve me (Gerhardt) Q523
AA501; AM506   111682

Why should I fear the darkest
hour (Newton) AP529; BV
578   111683

Why should I feel discouraged
(Martin) AI312; AM725
                         111684

Why should I repine in sadness
(Gerhardt) M275   111685

Why should our tears in sorrow
flow (Bathurst) I591
                         111686

Why should sorrow ever grieve
me (Gerhardt) AA501 X Why
should cross and trial 111687

Why should the children of a
king (Watts) I299; V304;
AZ198   111688

Why should we start and fear to
die (Watts) H489; I581; AZ
366   111689

Why sleep ye, my brethren?
Come, let us arise (Hopkins)
AY57   111690

Why standest thou afar, O
Lord (U. P. Psalter, 1912)
T14; AJ18   111691

Why this tumult among nations
(Ladies of the Grail) BSp6
                         111692

Why those fears? Behold, 'tis
Jesus (Kelly) O241 111693

Why will ye waste on trifling
cares (Doddridge) U160;
V274; AZ386   111694

Wide open are thy hands (St

(Ausbund) BU35 111732
Wir glauben all an einen Gott,
Und lieben ihn (Athanasian
Creed) BU2 111733
Wir glauben all'an einen Gott
Vater, Sohn und Heil'gen
Geist. (Clausnitzer) BT252
111734
Wir pflügen und wir streuen.
(M. Claudius) BW375 111735
Wir sind des Herrn, wir leben
oder sterben (Spitta) BT453
111736
Wir singen dir, Immanuel (Ger-
hardt) BT108 111737
Wir treten zum Beten vor Gott
den Herren (Dutch traditional)
BT568 111738
Wir warten dein, O Gottes Sohn
(P. F. Hiller) BW524 111739
Wir werfen uns danieder (Un-
parth. G. B.) AY33d
111740
Wir wollen alle frölich sein
(German trad carol, 16th c)
BG95b 111741
Wir zieh'n nach dem verheiss'-
nen Land (Unparth. G. B.) AY
41d 111742
Wisdom and power to Christ be-
long (Wesley) AZ890; BA926
111743
Wisdom hath treasures greater
far (Bruce) AN273; AQ96
111744
Wisdom, righteousness and
power (Jones) R Jesus Christ
is made to me 111745
Wise men seeking Jesus, travel-
ed from a far (East) Z203;
AD472; AL600; BF618; BY135
111746
With all my heart I love thee,
Lord (Schalling) O393 111747
With all my heart will I record
(Westra) AJ429 111748
With all my powers of heart and
tongue (Watts) H63; BC216
111749
With all the power of heart and
tongue (Watts) BC216 X With
all my powers of heart and
tongue 111750

With all the powers my poor
heart hath (St Thomas
Aquinas) K185 111751
With awe, and deeply bowed
(Moravian) AZ1121 111752
With broken heart and contrite
sigh (Elven) A60; B133;
D87; H275; J367; K316; L376;
M 72; N184; O441; Q323; U
171; V281; AA418; AI214; AM
416; AO263; BA419 111753
With Christ we share a mystic
grave (Neale) E339 111754
With deep humility, O Lord
(Trabert) N247 111755
With deeply humbled hearts we
make confession (Simpson)
AZ467 111756
With eternal day before us
(Rowe) R Smiling skies will
bend above us 111757
With firm resolve I held my
peace (U. P. Psalter, 1912)
AJ104 111758
With friends on earth we meet
in gladness (Chapman) AU412;
AX656; AY184 111759
With gladness we hail this
blessed day (Grundtvig) M
348 111760
With gladsome feet we press
(Singleton) AZ1194; BR516
111761
With gladsome hearts we come
(MacLeod) D532 111762
With glorious clouds encom-
passed round (Wesley) I327
111763
With glory clad, with strength
arrayed (Tate) AM64; AN489;
BX53 111764
With God and his mercy, his
Spirit, and word (Rosenius)
N272; P43 111765
With God in grace I'm dwelling
(Hauge) P326 111766
With golden splendour and with
roseate hues of morn
(Elpis??) E226 111767
With grateful heart my thanks I
bring (U. P. Psalter, 1912)
T274; AJ381; AM76 111768
With happy voices ringing

(Tarrant) R463; S441; Z113;
AC320; AD468; AE31; AG301;
AH201; AK455; AN478; AR11;
AS93; AT507; AV407; BD16;
BF619; BX519   111769
With happy voices singing (Tar-
rant) S441 X With happy
voices ringing   111770
With harps and with viols (Pier-
son) AM714   111771
With heart and hand you now we
own (Gregor) AX287   111772
With hearts and with voices, O
praise ye the Lord (Herrns-
schmidt) AZ495   111773
With heavenly power, O Lord, de-
fend (Hill) V563   111774
With holy joy my heart doth
beat (Hedborn) N243   111775
With humble prayer, O, may I
read (---) AZ322   111776
With Jesus for hero, for teacher
and friend (Dearmer) X69
                              111777
With joy and gladness in my soul
(U. F. Psalter, 1912) AJ348
                              111778
With joy I heard my friends
exclaim (U. P. Psalter, 1912)
R439; T252; AJ350   111779
With joy we claim the growing
light (Longfellow) AQ246 X
Eternal One, thou living God
                              111780
With joy we hail the sacred day
(Auber) D29; H84; I65; V69;
AA128; AT38; AV6   111781
With joy we meditate the grace
(Watts) L135; V176; AL125;
BA98; BV281; BY179   111782
With joyful heart your praises
bring (Günther) O13   111783
With joyfulness and longing
(Ellis) BA336   111784
With love and peace and joy
supreme (Nourse) BE392
                              111785
With loving hearts and hands we
rear (Ames) BX497   111786
With mercy heart let all rejoice
in one (Piae Cantiones) BG83
                              111787
With new life endowed by Christ

our Saviour (Zinzendorf, N.
L.) AZ1003   111788
With one consent let all the
earth (Tate & Brady) D469
                              111789
With praise, O God, we wor-
ship thee (Froom) BB697
                              111790
With reverence let the saints
appear (Watts) V108; BB4
                              111791
With silence only as their
benediction (Whittier) AP
623   111792
With solemn joy we come, dear
Lord (Ryden) J291; M542;
N256   111793
With songs and honors sound-
ing loud (Watts) H518; S
75; AB385; AF459; AH491;
AM113; BI115; BR63; BX56
                              111794
With tearful eyes I look around
(Elliott) D631; V294; AY
395   111795
With tears of anguish I lament
(Stennett) L386; V476
                              111796
With tender greeting, Lo, thy
children meeting (---) BP
93   111797
With thankful hearts, O Lord,
we come (Mohler) AR599,
AS423   111798
With thankful hearts we meet,
O Lord (Peters) AY4
                              111799
With thankful voice praise ye
the Lord (U. P. Psalter,
1912) T221; AJ314   111800
With the Lord begin thy task
(Morgen-und Abendsegen.
Waldenburg, 1734) Q540
                              111801
With the Lord thy task begin
(Hohlfeldt) M646   111802
With the sweet word of peace
(Watson) B419; AO509;
AZ1197; BA892   111803
With the voice of sweet song
(Mayer) BH70   111804
With Thee, O Lord, alone to
go (Kretzmann) M535

111805
With thine own pity, Saviour, see
(Palmer) AE320; BZ   111806
With thy presence, Lord, our
Head and Saviour (Gregor)
AZ1013; BA927   111807
With trembling awe the chosen
three (How) O249   111808
With willing hearts we tread
(Smith) BB439   111809
With wonderful deathless ditties
(O'Shaughnessy) X315   111810
With wondering awe the wise men
saw (---) BC209   111811
Withhold not, Lord, the help I
crave (Spitta) O428   111812
Within the Father's house (Wood-
ford) D69; N72; O228; Q133;
AK128; AO153; BA73   111813
Within the maddening maze of
things (Whittier) AF360 X
I know not what the future
hath   111814
"Within the veil!" Be this be-
loved (Allen) BB138   111815
Within this temple, reared of old
(Blatchford) BX506   111816
Within thy house, O Lord, our
God (Hymns adapted to the
public worship, 1828) AS58
111817
Within thy tabernacle, Lord, be
with us through this day (Hymns
of the English Conf. 1880)
BR88   111818
Within thy tabernacle, Lord, Who
shall abide (Scottish Psalter,
1650) AL633; AP9; AW577
111819
Within thy temple, Lord, In that
most holy place (U.P. Psalter,
1912) AJ134   111820
Within thy temple, Lord, We on
thy mercies dwell (U.P. Book
of Psalms, 1871) AM307; AP
43   111821
Within thy temple, Lord, We think
on mercies past (U.P. Psalter,
1912) T90; AJ133   111822
Within thy temple's sacred courts
(U.P. Psalter, 1912) R438;
AJ132   111823

Without spot and blameless,
O Saviour (Warren) AX150
111824
Witness, ye men and angels,
now (Beddome) D217; AO
457; AY270; AZ151; BA462;
BY304   111825
Wo ist Jesus, mein Berlangen
(Unparth. G.B.) AY11d
111826
Wo kommt das her, o Jesu
Christ (Ausbund) BU125
111827
Wo soll ich mich hin kehren
(Ausbund) BU76   111828
Wo willst du him, weil's Abend
ist (Homburg) BT197
111829
Woe unto him that has not
known the woe of man
(Binyon) AQ153   111830
Wohl einem Haus, da Jesus
Christ (Pfeil) BT625
111831
Wohlauf, mein Herze, sing und
spring (Gerhardt) BT535
111832
Wohlauf, Wohlauf, du Gottes
G'mein (M. Schneider)
BU97   111833
Wollt ihr hören, was ist
geschehn (T. Drucker) BU
23   111834
Wonderful grace of Jesus
(Lillenas) AM702   111835
Wonderful Jesus! glorious friend
(Rowe) AX21   111836
Wonderful love! Wonderful love
(Mund) R In Joyful high and
holy lays   111837
Wonderful peace, beautiful
peace (Barratt) R Like
radiant sunshine   111838
Wonderful Saviour, Redeemer
(Jacobs) AY392   111839
Wonderful story of love (Driver)
AU349; AX281   111840
Wonderful the matchless grace
of Jesus (Lillenas) R Won-
derful grace of Jesus111841
Wonderful, wonderful Jesus
(Russell) R There is never

a day so dreary   111842
Wonders still the world shall wit-
  ness (Trapp) AN352; AQ191
                          111843
Wondrous gift! The word who
  fashioned (Breviary, Cluny,
  1686) BM3-4   111844
Wondrous King, all-glorious
  (Neander) Q41; AM132 111845
Wondrous love that cannot falter
  (The Association of Perpetual
  Adoration) BQ56   111846
Wonn lächelt überall (Unparth.
  G.B.) AY48d   111847
Word of God, across the ages
  (Blanchard) AT176   111848
Word of God to earth descending
  (St Thomas Aquinas) BO41
                          111849
Word of Life, most pure, most
  strong (Bahmaier) AW329; BE
  394   111850
Word supreme, before creation
  (Keble) E33; F536; Q271
                          111851
Work, for the night is coming
  (Coghill) D583; G293; H376;
  I422; L540; M647; R297; W357;
  AH414; AK477; AL390; AM728;
  AO507; AP595; AS334; AT424;
  AU243; AV272; AW221; AX189;
  AZ853; BA562; BB446 111852
Work is sweet, for God has blest
  (Thring) E516; BF433 111853
Work while it is today (Montgomery)
  AZ1346; BA74; BB347 111854
Workers on a building rare
  (Coats) AX191   111855
Working, O Christ, with thee
  (Ogden) BB345   111856
Working together, wary and
  strong (Dearmer) X345
                          111857
Workman of God! O lose not heart
  (Faber) I392; W520; Y173; AL
  408; BB443; BF474; BX300;
  BY535   111858
Worship, glory, praise and
  honour (Wood) BV661 111859
Worship, honour, glory, blessing
  (Osler) F632; X418; 624b
                          111860

Worship the Lord in the beauty
  of holiness (Monsell) U5 X
  O worship the Lord 111861
Worthy art thou, Lord divine
  (Kauffman) AX6   111862
Worthy, O Lamb of God, art
  thou (Conder) R Thou art
  the everlasting Word
                          111863
Worthy, O Lord, art thou
  (Wesley) AZ1161; BA126
                          111864
Worthy, worthy is the Lamb
  (---) BB168   111865
Would men know you've been
  with Jesus (Sellers) AX438
                          111866
Would you be free from the bur-
  den of sin (Jones) AT193
  X Would you be free from
  the guilt   111867
Would you be free from the
  guilt of your sin (Jones)
  AI394; AT193; AX278
                          111868
Would you be free from your
  burden of sin (Jones) AX
  278 X Would you be free
  from the guilt   111869
Would you flee from sin and
  serve the Lord (Teasley)
  AX285   111870
Would you know the love of
  Jesus (Shacklock) AX351;
  AY52   111871
Would you live for Jesus and be
  always pure (Nussbaum) AS
  239; AT239; AU122; AX277
                          111872
Would you lose your load of
  sin (Whittle) AI402
                          111873
Would you win a Saviour's bless-
  ing (Crosby) BB479 111874
Wouldst bring a gift to Jesus
  (Rexford) R They brought
  their gifts to Jesus 111875
Wunderbarer König (Neander)
  BT41   111876

Y

Ya-a-leh ta-cha-nu-nay-nu
(Jewish traditional) BH323
111877

Ye angels round the throne
(---) AZ1308   111878

Ye angels who stand round the
throne (DeFleury) V708; AZ
1511   111879

Ye are the light of the world
(Craig) AX157; AY382
111880

Ye baptized people, one and all
(German) M41   111881

Ye bottomless depths of God's
infinite love (Zinzendorf, N.
L.) AZ1092   111882

Ye children, come, give ear to
me (U. P. Board of Publ.,
1909) AI405; AJ89; AM656
111883

Ye children of our God (Pratt)
BC288   111884

Ye choirs of new Jerusalem (St
Fulbert of Chartres) E122;
139; F128; V161; AZ185; BV
191   111885

Ye chosen twelve, to you are
given (Pratt) BC211   111886

Ye Christian heralds, go, pro-
claim (Draper) A221; B453;
D263; H459; R494; S381; U390;
V595; AB370; AD383; AG262;
AM380; AO453; AP565; AS374;
AT459; AU235; AV265; AW337;
BA361; BF528   111887

Ye Christians, sing a joyful lay
(Hermann) M355   111888

Ye Christians, tune your noblest
strains (Hymns of the English
Conf. 1880) BR196   111889

Ye clouds and darkness, hosts of
night (Prudentius) E54; X37
111890

Ye elders of Israel, come join
now with me (Wheelock) BC344
111891

Ye fair green hills of Galilee
(Conder) G124; W75; AC102;
AD130; AG83; AL84; AW94
111892

Ye faithful, with gladness
(Latin, 18th c) BQ4a
111893

Ye gates, lift up your heads
on high (Scottish Psalter,
1650) AL638; AP21; AW
580; BY172   111894

Ye gates, lift your heads, the
glad summons obey (U. P.
Psalter, 1912) AJ58
111895

Ye gates of peace and joy untold (U. P. Psalter, 1912)
T223; AJ320   111896

Ye heavens on high, praise ye
the Lord. Angelic hosts to
him accord (Grieve) AL691
111897

Ye holy angels bright (Baxter
& Gurney) A600; B264;
E517; F371; J409; W39;
X701; AB67; AF23; AM17;
AN5; AP158; BV24; BX62;
BY36   111898

Ye humble souls, approach
your God (Steele) L90
111899

Ye lands to the Lord make a
jubilant noise (Koren) O11;
P27; Q44   111900

Ye men and angels! witness
now (Beddome) AY270 X
Witness, ye men and angels;
now   111901

Ye men of Christ awake
(Schmidt) AI184; AO477
111902

Ye messengers of Christ
(Vokes) BE396; BL86
111903

Ye must be born again
(Sleeper) R A ruler once
came   111904

Ye nations round the earth!
rejoice (Watts) V4; AX19
111905

Ye parents, hear what Jesus
taught (Helmbold) Q630
111906

Ye righteous in the Lord rejoice (Hopkins) T55; AJ85;
AL642; AM40; AP29 111907

Ye saints, proclaim abroad
(Ryland) L134; M401; AO68;
111908

Ye servants of God, your Master
proclaim (Wesley) F226; G
169; H11; I11; J446; P32; R
27; S198; U110; V198; W168; Y
385; Z258; AB15; AD3; AE3; AF
206; AG106; AH194; AK11; AL
44; AM136; AO56; AP258; AR
119; AS3; AT147; AV325; AW
6; AZ503; BA129; BB342; BF
168; BV336; BY37; BZ 111909

Ye servants of the Lord (Doddridge) B456; D186; E518; F
229; H467; I429; L545;
O429; V471; W156; X702; AA
382; AL141; AO456; AP580;
AW128; AZ1314; BA557; BB351;
BE398; BV606; BX361; BY
197   111910

Ye shepherd plains of Bethlehem
(Crane) AN168; AQ291
111911

Ye simple souls that stray
(Wesley) BC290   111912

Ye sons and daughters of the
King (Tisserand) E626; Q208;
X143   111913

Ye sons and daughters of the Lord
(Tisserand) BM82; BO177; BP
36; BQ28;   111914

Ye sons of earth, prepare the
plough (Cowper) BV479
111915

Ye sons of men, O hearken
(Thilo) Q75   111916

Ye souls of the faithful! Who
sleep in the Lord (Naketenus.
Coeleste palmetum. 1669)
BO145; BP95; BQ114
111917

Ye that do the Master's will
(Wesley) BJ94   111918

Ye that have spent the silent
night in sleep (Gascoigne) AL
531 X You that have spent
111919

Ye that know the Lord is gracious
(Alington) F260; BV588
111920

Ye timid saints, fresh courage
take (Cowper) BE399 X God

moves in a mysterious way
111921

Ye tribes of Adam, join
(Watts) V510   111922

Ye watchers and ye holy ones
(Riley) A599; B266; E519;
F6; J437; Q475; R34; AD66;
AE29; AF30; AK9; BB77;
BL27; BZ   111923

Ye who are banded as com-
rades and brothers (Lowry)
BY536   111924

Ye who are called to labor
(Page) BC345   111925

Ye who called to Christ's service are (Schlicht) AZ515;
BA313   111926

Ye who called, ye who called
to Christ's service are
(Schlicht) BA313 X Ye who
called to Christ's   111927

Ye who his temple throng,
Jehovah's praise prolong
(U. P. Psalter, 1912) T294;
AJ408   111928

Ye who own the faith of Jesus
(Coles) E218   111929

Ye who rose to meet the Lord
(---) BB181   111930

Ye who the name of Jesus bear
(Scottish Paraphrases, 1781)
AL73; AP188   111931

Ye wretched, hungry, starving
poor (Steele) V261 111932

Yea, as I live, Jehovah saith
(Heermann) O401; Q331;
AA426   111933

Yea, I will extol thee (Montgomery) AZ760   111934

Yea, o'er me soared the eternal sky (Larcom) Y205
111935

Years are coming -- speed
them onward (Ballou) AN
554; AQ198   111936

Years I spent in vanity and
pride (Newell) AT96; AX332;
AY513   111937

Yes, for me, for me he careth
(Bonar) U200; V352; AI251;
AM688; AY99; AZ946
111938

Yes, he is risen who is the

first and last (Bonar) AZ456
111939
Yes, he knows the way is dreary
(Havergal) AX611; BR370
111940
Yes, heaven is the prize
(Vaughan) BO201   111941
Yes, I do feel, my God, that I
am thine (Monsell) AZ452
111942
Yes, I'll sing the wondrous story
(Rowley) R I will sing the
wondrous story   111943
Yes, Jesus loves me (Warner)
R Jesus loves me, this I know
111944
Yes, Lord, we thank thee for this
day (Loewen) R We owe the
Lord   111945
Yes, my heart says amen (Naylor)
R I Have yielded myself to thy
service   111946
Yes, others, Lord, yes others
(Meigs) R Lord, help me to
live   111947
Yes, since God himself hath said
it (Newton) AZ602   111948
Yes, sleeping on guard (French)
R Out from the camp fire's
red glowing   111949
Yes, the redeemer rose (Dodd-
ridge) L267; AO185   111950
Yes, there is rest over Jordan's
waters (---) R To the pro-
mised home in glory   111951
Yes, there remaineth still a rest
(Kunth) AA566   111952
Yes, we'll gather at the river
(Lowry) R Shall we gather at
the river   111953
Yesterday with exultation (Adam
of St Victor) F535   111954
Yet when the splendor of the
earth (MacLeish) AQ115
111955
Yield not to temptation (Palmer)
N648; U161; W704; AE258;
AG195; AH452; AI404; AM658;
AO631; AP770; AS320; AT364;
AU338; AV371; AW477; AX441;
AY445; BA835; BB498; BY569
111956

Yigdal Elohim chayveyish
tabbach (Jewish doxology)
Y300; AHp152; BH277
111957
Yim-loch A-do-noy l'olom
(Jewish traditional) BH287
111958
You can make the pathway
bright (Dungan) BC208
111959
You can't do wrong and get
by (Ellis) R There's a God
who's standing   111960
You have longed for sweet
peace (Hoffman) AT350;
AU54; AX402   111961
You that have faith to look with
fearless eyes (Seaman) AQ
206   111962
You that have spent the silent
night in sleep (Gascoigne)
X38; AF505; AL531; AN485;
AP655; AQ264   111963
Young and radiant, he is stand-
ing (Cross) AC99   111964
Your goal was not some island
of the blessed (Clark) AC
509   111965
Your harps, ye trembling
saints (Toplady) V369;
W561   111966
Your little flame of life we
guard (Sassoon) AQ263
111967
Youth of the world, unite
(Davies) AC480   111968
Y'-vo-re-ch'-cho A-do-noy
(Jewish traditional) BH301
111969

Z

Zeal of the lord, for ever
burning (Dearmer) X703
111970
Zeuch ein zu meinen Toren
(Gerhardt) BT228   111971
Zeuch uns nach dir (Funcke)
BT215   111972

NOTE: "Zion" in English texts
is spelled "Sion" in this in-

Anonymous

Anonymous hymns

NOTE: Satisfactory sources could not be identified for these first lines.

A glorious day is dawning
A holy stillness, breathing
A shepherd band their flocks
Afar upon a foreign shore;
   R103026 Hail Blessed Saint
All glory be to thee, O Lord
All glory to God, the Father
All praise to the Father
All ye who grace inherit
Alleluia! Praise the Savior
Almighty Father, hear
And now may the courage
And now the sun hath sunk
And now to God the Father
Are you weary, heavy laden;
   R101533 Come to Jesus, come
Arise, O Christian soldiers
As swiftly my days go out
Assist thy servant, Lord
At thy table, Lord of life
Be firm and be faithful
Be ye joyful, earth and sky
Beautiful Sion, built above;
   R109012 Sion, Sion, lovely
Beauty around us, glory above
Behold the lilies of the field
Blessed art thou, O Lord
Bliss beyond compare
Bring flowers of the fairest;
   R107393 O Mary! We crown thee
Brother, thou hast left us
Builder of mighty worlds
By angels in heaven
Can a mortal flee from sorrow
Can my soul find rest
Children of Jerusalem

Christ on the night He was;
   X101198 Christ in the night
Christ went a building; R103910
   I know, I know
Christian children must be
Christian, walk carefully
Cleanse my heart, O Father
Clear upon the night-air;
   R100569 As the angels sang
Come all ye Saints and sing
Come, children, with singing
Come gentle peace
Come, Holy Spirit, from
Come, listen to a prophet's
Courage my soul! While God is
Dark and thorny is the desert
Daughter of a mighty Father
Daughter of God the Father
Day is done, gone the sun
Dear St Joseph, pure;
   R103075 Hail St Joseph
Dear Saviour, we would know
Death shall not destroy;
   R109112 Soon with angels
Do what is right; the day-dawn
Dona nobis pacem, pacem
Earth is waking, day is
Ere another day shall close
Fading, still fading, The last;
   R102093 Father, have mercy
Farewell, my dear brethren
Father, fill us with thy love
Father, hear our prayer
Father, O hear us; Saviour
Father, Son, and Holy Ghost
Father, Son, and Holy Ghost, Three in One; from every coast
Father, Son, and Holy Spirit, Thou One in Three
Fling wide the gates
For Autumn's golden days
For flowers that bloom about
For health and strength
For Mother-love and Father-care

For sun and moon and stars
From the first man to climb
Gather around the Christmas;
R103601 Hosanna, Hosanna
Gentle Peace, from heaven
Give God the Father praise
Give thanks for the corn
Give thanks unto the Lord
Glory and praises ever be
Glory eternal be to thee
Glory, praise and blessing be
Glory to the blessed Jesus
God incarnate, veil thy
God is great, God is good
God of every land and nation
God of my heart! Its earliest
Gone from my heart, the world;
R103955 I love Him
Good morning to you
Gracious Father, guard
Gracious Father, hear our
Grant that we ask, Almighty
Grant us, Lord, the grace
Great Giver of all good
Great God in heaven, who by
Great God, to whom alone
Great God! whatever through
Great Jehovah! we adore thee
Great King of saints, enthroned
Hail! Christ, our Redeemer
Hail! holy guide of youthful
Hail, thou martyr host
Hail Virgin, dearest Mary!
Hark! hark! The organ loudly
Hark, listen to the trumpeters
Hark! the skies with music
Hark, what music fills
He knows the bitter weary way
Hear, O Lord, our humble
Hear our entreaties, Lord
Hear the royal proclamation;
R104807 Jesus reigns, He
Hear us, our Father! We know
Heart of Jesus I adore thee
Heart of Mary, heart all pure
Heir of the kingdom, O why
Hibernia's Patron Saint, all;
R107506 O St Patrick, we
His flock our Shepherd feeds
Holy habitations, after weary
Holy Jesus, be my light
Holy Love, from heaven
Holy Mary, mother mild;

R106720 O exult ye cherubim
Holy patron! thee saluting;
R103123 Happy Saint; in bliss
Holy Spirit, faithful guide
How cheering is the christian's
How happy are these little ones
How many were the silent
How pleasant thus to dwell;
R107632 O! that will be
How strong and sweet
How sweet are the tidings;
R103450 He's coming, coming
Humble praises, holy Jesus;
R100344 Alleluia, sweetly
I am dwelling on the mountain;
R104455 Is not this the land
I entered once a home of care
I have decided to follow
I know a soul that is steeped
I know of a river;
R107556 O sinner, we pray
I look not back; God knows
I look to Jesus, and the face
I love thee, I love thee
I love to hear the story
I ought to love my Saviour
I saw a mighty angel fly
I see my Jesus crucified
I will never, never leave
I'll thee exalt, my God
In a lonely graveyard
In days of yore, from Britain's;
R109724 The maple leaf
In every waking moment;
R106080 My God, I am de-
termined
In from the highways;
R102448 Gather them in
In Oxford Town the faggots
In the still air the music
In this lone hour of deep
In yon blessed seats of heaven
Is there any pleasure, any joy
I've seen the lightning;
R106274 No, never alone
Jehovah, Jesus, Lord we own
Jehovah, Lord of heaven
Jerusalem, Jerusalem! Die du
so
Jesus is standing in Pilate's;
R111330 What will you do
Jesus loves a little child
Jesus, our Saviour, only God

Jesus, rule my thoughts
Jesus, Savior, mighty Lord
Jesus, Savior, risen Lord
Jesus the glory of the holy
Jesus, to thee be endless;
   R103607 Hosanna to our only
Keep me, Saviour, near
Land of the mountains high
Lead them, my God, to thee
Let all who enter here
Let each man learn to know
Let God the Father, God the
   Son; X105129 Let God the
   Father, and the
Let me go where'er I will
Let others seek a home below;
   R111223 We'll work till
Let the whole creation sing;
   R102860 Gone the night
Let them that love Him
Let thy Spirit, blessed
Light of life, the great
Like a strong and raging fire;
   R100873 Bending low
Little children, Lord, are we
Lo! on the water's brink we
Lo! the earth rejoices at the
Lo! the heavens are breaking
Long for my Saviour I've been;
   R104833 Jesus soon is coming
Lord in thy presence here we
Lord in thy temple we appear
Lord Jesus Christ, I flee
Lord Jesus Christ, to us
Lord, let us now depart in
Lord of the Sabbath and its
Lord, on thee alone I stay me
Lord, thine appointed servants
Lord, to thee, in whom is
Mary! how sweetly falls that;
   R108954 Sing, O my lips
Mary the Dawn, Christ the
May you who enter here
Merry Christmas bells are
Morning has come,the table
Most fervent thanks I render
Mother dear, O pray for me
My dearest friends, in bonds
My dearest Saviour I would
My hope, my all, my Saviour
My hiding place, my refuge;
   X101907 Engraved as in etern-
   al (Watts)

My soul with joy attend
Name of Jesus, softly stealing
Nay, speak no ill; a kindly
Nobody knows of the work
None é er shall be ashamed
Not gold, but only men can
Now blessed thou, O Christ
Now for each yearning heart
Now may the light that shone
Now rest in peace, now rest
Now to the great and sacred
Now the triune God Confessing
Now to Jesus Christ all glory
O bless, thou heavenly Potentate
O Father Almighty, to thee be
O for a heart of calm repose
O God, Eternal Father, from;
   R107679 O thou Holy Trinity
O God! how ought my grateful;
   X106078 My God! how
   ought
O God of Hosts, with thy
O God, while generations flee
O happy time of reaping
O heart of Mary, pure and fair
O holy joy that raises
O, I love to talk with Jesus
O ice and snow, O frost
O Jesus Christ, alone to thee
O Jesus, once a Nazareth boy
   X107134 O Jesus, Prince of
O Jesus, Saviour, Source of
O joyous Easter morning
O Lord, be near me when I
   pray
O Lord, encouraged by thy grace
O Lord, I am not worthy
O Lord of Life, the Truth
O Lord of love, compassionate
O Lord of love, Thou light
O Lord, thou art the way
O Lord, thou living Bread
O Lord, to us assembled here
O Lord, whose bounteous hand
O Lord, with thankful hearts
O Mother! most afflicted
O praise the Father, praise
O Sacrament most holy
O Sacred Heart of Christ;
   R101692 Dear Heart of
   Jesus
O thou blest Immanuel
O thou that hearest prayer

O thou who hearest every
O thou who sendest sun and rain
O what could my Jesus do more
O, when shall I see Jesus
O'er the silent waters
On Mary, Virgin undefiled
On this day, O beautiful
On mountains and in valleys
Our highest joys succeed our
Our souls shall magnify;
    X106197 My soul doth magnify
Peacefully lay her down
Peter, faithless, thrice denies
Pilgrims, on! The day is
Praise, honor, majesty, For thy
Praise the Father throned
Praise the Father, earth and
Praise the Lord! From the
    deeds
Praise the name of God most
Praise to thee, O Lord, we
Praise we Christ; the King
Praise ye the Father! Let;
    R108242 Praise be to the
    Father
Pray for the dead! at noon
Precious Jesus, O to love;
    R104689 Jesus, Jesus,
    precious
Put on the armor of our God;
    R109989 Then stand! stand
Queen and Mother, many hearts
Queen of the Rosary, Virgin
Ready to suffer grief or pain
    R108430 Ready to go
Resting among the cattle mild
Remember, holy Mary, 'Twas
Round the throne of glory;
    R103535 Holy, Holy, Holy
Sacred Heart of Jesus, fount
St Anthony, we turn to thee
Save us waking, O Lord
Saved by grace, I live to tell;
    R107779 O, 'tis grace
Saw ye my Saviour
Shall I tell you what brought;
    R103252 He just put Himself
Silently, silently they pass
Sing alleluia, honor, praise
Sing of Mary, pure and lowly;
    X108966 Sing the Holy Fam-
    ily's (Vaughan)
Songs of praise exultant sing

Sound the loud anthem, to hail
Star of our hope! He'll soon
Stars of morning, shout
Striving onward, pressing
Sweet is the prayer whose holy
Take my heart, O Father! take
The blasts of winter are fierce
The corn is ripe for reaping
The earth is hushed in silence
The Father and the Son
The God who made both heaven
The gold and silver are the
The heavens are declaring
The Lord is coming! let this
The Lord is my Shepherd, I
The new-born King who comes
The sands have been washed in
The shadows lengthen, Lord
The Spirit and the Bride
The sun rolls down the distant
The war in which the soldier
The sun shines in splendor
The world itself is blithe
Thee, Father, Spirit, Son we
There are hearts that never
There is a blessed hope
There is a calm for those who
There is an hour of peace;
    R105911 May my heart be
There is no other Name than;
    X110063 There is none other
There's work for the hand
Think on our brethren Lord
Thou warrior angel of the Lord
Thou who a tender Father art
Though all my foes combine
Though in the outward Church;
    R102298 For soon the reaping
Through thee as we together
Thy broken body, gracious Lord
Thy Gospel, Jesus, we believe
Thy holy Sabbath, Lord
'Tis the month of our Mother;
    R100217 All hail! to dear
    Mary
To Christ, the King of glory
To Father, Son, and Holy Ghost
    Be praise
To Father, Son, and Holy Ghost
    Our God forever
To Father, Son and Spirit
To Father, Son, and Spirit blest,
    Supreme o'er

To Father, Son, and Spirit, ever
blest
To Father, Son, and Spirit
From earth let praise
To Father, Son, and Spirit
God ever Three in One
To God I lift mine eyes
To God the Ever-glorious
To God the Father, Son, and
Spirit, the everlasting
To God -- the Father, Son,
and Spirit -- Three in
To God, the Father, Spirit, Son
To God the Father's throne
Perpetual honors raise
To God the Father's throne
Your highest honors raise
To Jesus Christ, our only Lord
To kneel at thine altar, in;
R106938 O Good St Anne, we
To the promised home in glory;
R111951 Yes, there is rest
To thee alone our prayer
To thee be praise for ever
To thee, O blessed Saviour
To thee, O Jesus Christ, we
To thee, O Lord, alone
To thee, O Lord, be glory
To thee, O Lord, my Saviour
To thee, our loving Father
Triumphs today the Lord of life
Unheard the dews around me;
X106285 Noiseless the morning
Upon this happy morn
Watchmen on the walls of Zion
We are all enlisted till the
We are little gleaners
We are little reapers
We are marching with the blest
R105883 Marching home, we're
We are sowing, daily sowing
We come with songs of gladness
We gather 'round your shrine
We meet again in gladness
We praise thy name, O Lord
We thank thee, loving Father
We thank thee, O our Father
We will carol joyfully
Wearily at daylight's close
Welcome, welcome, day of rest
Well for him who, all things
We're bound for the land
What a wonderful, wonderful;

R103289 He was nailed
What can I give to Jesus
What glorious scenes mine
eyes
What lovely Infant can this be
What makes a city great
What tongue can tell thy
When blooming youth is snatched
When Christ beheld, in sinful
When great St Patrick raised
When judgment day is drawing
R107838 O where shall I
be
When the corn is planted
When the stars at set of sun
When warmer suns and bluer
When we hear the music ring-
ing
Whence came the armies of the
Where'er have trod Thy sacred
Who taught the bird to build
With humble prayer, O, may I
With tender greeting, Lo, thy
With wondering awe The wise-
men
Worthy, worthy is the Lamb
Ye angels round the throne
Ye who rose to meet the Lord

A

A.A.F. [Crosby??]
Not I, but Christ, be honor-
ed
A.E. pseud see
Russell, George William
A.E.E.
Jesus Christ the King of ages
A.H.A.
O, to be there, where the
songs
A.N.
Jesus, my Saviour, to Bethle-
hem
Aaberg, J.C.
Praise the Lord that He has
There is a blessed power
The Abatal, 1532
Because you live again, O
Rose
Abbey, Charlotte
Nearer the cross of Jesus
Abelard, Peter, 1079-1142

Alone thou goest forth, O Lord
O what their joy and their;
X107829 O what the joy
Abraham ibn Ezra
I hope for the salvation
My faith shall be my rock
Abrahams, Israel
How bless the God of all
Achrenius, Antti
Arise, my soul, new light
Ackley, A. H., 1887-
I serve a risen Saviour;
R103263 He lives, He lives
Adam of St Victor, 12th c
Christians, come, in sweetest
Come sing, ye choirs exultant
Jesus, kind above all others
Joy and triumph everlasting
Jucundare, plebs fidelis
O Holy Ghost, thou Fount of
Sion's daughters! Sons of
Spirit of grace and union
Supernae matris gaudia
Yesterday with exultation
Adam, A.
O holy night; the stars are
Adams. Hymns for Christian
devotion, 1846
Scorn not the slightest word
Adams, Elizabeth C
Father, we thy loving children
God giveth light to all who
No eye hath seen, nor tongue
Adams, Jessie, 1863-1954
I feel the winds of God
Adams, John Coleman, 1849-
It swells upon the noon-day
We praise thee, God, for
Adams, John Greenleaf, 1810-87
Heaven is here, where hymns
Adams, John Quincy, 1767-1848
O Lord, thy all discerning
Send forth, O Lord, thy light
Adams, Ophelia G
Unransomed yet? The prayer
Adams, Sarah Flower, 1805-48
Näher, mein Gott zu Dir
Nearer, my God, to thee;
X106240 Nearer, O God to
thee (How)
Part in peace: Christ's life
Part in peace! Is day before

Adams, William Henry, 1864-1932
O'er the trackless ocean
Adderley, James G., 1861-1942
Father, we greet thee, God
of
Addison, Joseph, 1672-1719
How are thy servants blest
The Lord my pasture shall;
X109680 The Lord...will
The spacious firmament on
high; X109857 The starry
firmament (Grant)
When all thy mercies, O my
God; X111347 When all...
gracious
When rising from the bed
of
Adler, Felix, 1851-1933
Hail the glorious Golden City
Splendor of the morning
Afzelius, Arvid August, 1785-
1871
Unto the Lord of all creation
Agnes, of County Cork, Sr.
Hail, glorious St Patrick
Agricola, Johannes, 1492-1566
Lord, hear the voice of my
Sing aloud alleluia in jubilant
To thee I send my cry, Lord
Aguilar, Grace
Ah, well it is that God should
I bless thee, Father, for
Ahnfelt, Oskar Sanger, 1813-62
How blest are the moments
Ainger, Arthur Campbell, 1841-
1919
God is working his purpose
God of our fathers, unto thee;
R105471 Lord God of hosts
Akers, Elizabeth
The time for toil is past
Albert, Heinrich, 1604-51
God, omnipotent creator
God who madest earth and
heaven
Gott des Himmels und der
Erden 1644
Now the morn new light is
Albinus, Johann Georg, 1624-79
All men living are but mortal
Alle Menschen müssen sterben
1652

Cast me not in wrath away
Death in all this world
Hark, a voice saith, all are
Not in anger, mighty God
Smite us not in anger, Lord
Albrecht von Brandenburg-Culm-
bach, 1522-57
  The will of God is always
  Was mein Gott will, das g'
  scheh' allzeit 1554
  Whate'er God will, let that
Alcott, Louisa May, 1833-88
  A little kingdom I possess
  O the beautiful old story!
Alderson, Eliza Sibbald Dykes
1818-88
  And now, beloved Lord, thy
  Lord of glory, thou has bought;
   X105632 Lord of glory, who
Alexander, Cecil Frances, 1823-
95
  All things bright and; X101858
   Each little flower
  Do not sinful action, Speak
  Every morning the red sun
  For all thy saints, a noble
  Forgive them, O my Father
  Forsaken once, and thrice
  From out the cloud of fiery
  He is coming, he is coming
  He is risen, he is risen
  His are the thousand sparkling
  Jesus call us; o'er the tumult
  O Jesus, bruised and wounded
  O Lord, the Holy Innocents
  Once in royal David's city
  Saw you never, in the twilight
  Souls in heathen darkness
  Spirit of God, that moved
  The eternal gates lift up
  The golden gates are lifted
  The roseate hues of early
  There is a green hill; R106699
   O dearly, dearly
  There is one way, and only one
  Thou Power and Peace, in whom
  Thy temple is not made
  We are but little children;
   X110986 We are ... weak
  When wounded sore the stricken
Alexander, William Lindsay,
1808-84
  I'm kneeling at the threshold

Spirit of power, and truth
Alford, Henry, 1810-71
  Come, ye thankful people,
   come
  Forward! be our watchword;
   X102058 Far o'er yon
   horizon
  Hark! through the courts
  In token that thou shalt not
  My bark is wafted to the
   strand
  O thou, at whose divine com-
   mand
  O thou, who hast thy servants
  Ten thousand times ten thou-
   sand
  The highest and the holiest
  Thou who on that wondrous
  We walk by faith, and not by
  When in the Lord Jehovah's
Alfred, Lord Tennyson see
  Tennyson, Alfred
Alington, Cyril Argentine,
1872-1955
  Come, ye people, rise and
   sing
  God, whose city's sure
   foundation
  Good Christian men, rejoice
  Lord of all, to whom alone
  Lord of beauty, thine the
  O Father, by whose sovereign
  O loving Father, to thy care
  Praise we God the Father's
   name
  Sing, brothers, sing and
   praise
  Ye that know the Lord is
Alkabetz, Solomon
  "Observe ye" and "remem-
   ber"; R101369 Come
   forth, my friend
Alldredge, Ida R.
  They the builders of the na-
   tion
Alldridge, R
  Lord, accept our true
  We'll sing all hail to Jesus'
Allen, Ernest Bourner
  The Son of God goes forth
   for peace
Allen, Freda Hanbury
  "Within the veil!" Be this,

Allen, Hattie Bell
  Christ for the whole wide;
    R111168 We will give
Allen, James, 1734-1804
  Glory to God on high, Let;
    X102560 Glory to God on
    high (Boden)
  Jesus, our risen King
  Our souls with inmost shame
  Sweet the moments see Walter
    Shirley
  We, O Jesus, claim thy special
Allen, Jonathan??
  Sinners, will ye scorn
Allen, Lillian Manker
  For those who wrought
Allen, Oswald
  Today thy mercy calls us;
    X110731 Today ... calls
    me
Allon. Children's worship, 1878
  Hark, hark, my soul!
Alstyne, Frances Van see
    Crosby, Fanny
Altenberg, Johann Michael, 1584-
  1640
  Be not dismayed, thou little
  Fear not, O little flock, the
  Fear not, thou faithful
  O little flock, fear not
  Thou little flock, be not
  Verzage nicht, du häuflein
Alwood, J. K.
  O they tell me of a home far;
    R107651 O the land of cloud-
    less
"Am-a". 1769
  And didst thou, Jesus, condes-
    cend
American carol
  Away in a manger, no crib
American folk hymn
  Note: In hymnal BZ all Negro
  Spirituals are cited as above.
  Within this index see Negro
  spirituals
Ames, Charles Gordon, 1828-1912
  Father in heaven, hear us
  With loving hearts and hands
Amilie Juliana, Countess of
  Schwarzburg-Rudelstadt, 1637-
  1706
  Bis hieher hat mich Gott

The Lord hath helped me
The solemn moment is im-
  pending
Wer weiss, wie nahe mir
  mein Ende! 1688
Who knows how near my end
  may; X111640 Who ... my
  life's ; X111640A Who
  knows how soon; X111641
  Who knows when death
Amis, Lewis R., 1856-1904
  Jehovah, God, who dwelt of
Andersdatter, Elle, ca 1600-
  1650
  In hope my soul, redeemed
    to
Andersen, Hans Christian, 1805-
  75
  Child Jesus comes from
Anderson, Maria Frances,
  1819-
  Our country's voice
Anderson, Mary Louisa
  Now, Lord, upon thy sea
    of air
Andrew, Father see
  Hardy, H. E. (Father Andrew)
  1869-1946
Angelus Silesius see Scheffler,
  Johann, 1624-77
Anketell, John, 1835-1905
  Lord Jesus, on the holy
    mount
Anna Sophia, Countess of
  Hesse-Darmstadt, 1638-83
  Rede, liebster Jesu, rede
  Speak, O Lord, thy servant
"Anne" (perhaps Anne Taylor,
  1782-1866)
  There is a dear and hallowed
Annin, Katharine Huntington,
  1893-
  The Lord, in his righteous-
    ness
Anstice, Joseph, 1808-36
  Darkly rose the guilty morn-
    ing
  Lord, in thy kingdom there
  Lord of the harvest, once
  O Lord, how happy should
    we be
  When came in flesh the in-
    carnate

Anstruther, Joyce, see Struther,
Jan pseud, 1901-53
Antoniano, Silvio, 1540-1603
Fortem virili pectore
The praises of that Saint we
Apostolic Constitutions. 3d c.
Praise ye the Lord, ye servants
Appleton, Francis Parker, 1822-
1903
The past yet lives in all its
Thirsting for a living fountain
Arends, William Erasmus, 1677-
1721
Christians, keep your banners
Christians, prayer may well;
X108639 Rise, to arms
Rüstet euch, ihr Christenleute
1714
Arkwright, John Stanhope
O valiant hearts, who to your
Arlott, John, 1914-
God, whose farm is all crea-
tion
Armenian liturgy.
Holiness becomes thy house
Armitage, Ella Sophia, 1841-
In our dear Lord's garden
O Lord of hosts, the fight
is
O Lord of life, and love, and
Armstrong, Harry
Lead thou me on, and then
my
Armstrong, John, 1813-56
O thou, who makest souls to;
X107321 O Lord, thy bene-
diction
Arndt, Ernst Moritz, 1769-1860
Go and let my grave be made
I know whom I believe in
Arnold, of Louvain
Hail thee, Saviour and Atoner
Arnold, Gottfried, 1666-1714
All alone, and yet not lonely
Thanksgiving, honor, praise
Arnold, Matthew, 1822-88
Calm soul of all things, make
Servants of God, or sons
We cannot kindle when we will
Arnold, Robert S.
No tears in heaven, no sorrows
Arnschwanger, Johann Christoph
1625-96

Up, ye Christians, join in
Arrebo, Anders C., 17th c
O sing with exultation
Om salighed og gläde
The Lord my faithful shep-
herd
Arrhenius, Jacob, 1642-1725
Jesus is my best of friends
Jesus is my Friend most
precious
Jesus, Lord and precious
Asper, Frank Wilson, 1892-
Hear thou our hymn, O Lord
Associate Reformed Presbyter-
ian Psalter, 1931.
Come, let us sing unto the
Lord
O Lord of hosts, how lovely
O thou who the Shepherd of
Israel
The Association of Perpetual
Adoration.
Wondrous love that cannot
Aström, Johan, 1767-1844
Lord, disperse the mists
Atchinson, Jonathan Bush,
1740-
I have read of a beautiful
city; R106310 Not half has
ever
In the shadow of his wings
There's a Stranger at the
door
Athanasian Creed.
Wir glauben all an einen
Gott, Und lieben ihn
1564
Atkins, George
Brethren, we have met to
worship
Auber, Harriet, 1773-1862
Bright was the guiding star
Ere mountains reared their
Hasten, Lord, the glorious
time
O God, our strength, to thee
O praise our great and gra-
cious; X108270 Praise our
great
On thy church, O Power
Divine
Our blest Redeemer, ere he
They who on the Lord rely

(authorship in doubt)
Vainly, through night's weary
Whom have we Lord in heaven
(authorship in doubt)
With joy we hail the sacred
Auerbach, Herbert
    Blessed are they that have
    Bring, heavy heart, your grief
Aufranc, D. A. R.
    Alone with thee, my God
    Far from all care we hail
    Father, I yield to Thee my life
    There is a road, though nar-
        row
Augusta, Johann, ca 1500-1572
    How blest and lovely thy
    Praise God for ever! Bound-
        less
Auryansen, Lucia Trevitt
    Here, where the sun shines
Ausbund
    Note: Cited as item BU within
    this index, it is the oldest
    Protestant hymnal which has
    been in constant use.
    Ach fröhlich will ich singen
    Ach Gott vom Himmelreiche!
    All' die ihr Jetzund leidet
    Ambrosius klärlich beschrieb
    Christe, freundlicher Ritter,
        1564
    Christe mein Herr, ich bin
        ganz ferr
    Christe thu dich erbarmen
        1564
    Dankt Gott in seinem hochsten
        Thron. 1522
    Das Wort der Wahrheit Jesu
        Christ 1564
    Der Glaub beschützt mich ganz
        und gar
    Der Winter kalt, rauh unge-
        stalt.
    Die beste Freud aus Gottes
        Wort. 1553
    Ein Grosse Freud ist inge-
        mein. 1564
    Ein Liedlein will ich singen.
        1564
    Ein Magdelein von Gleidern
        zart. 1564
    Eins Morgens früh vor Tage
        1564

Es waren auch zween Brüder
    gut 1564
Ewiger Vater im Himmel-
    reich 1564
Ewiger Vater vom Himmel-
    reich. 1529
Föhlich pfleg ich zu singen;
    X102365 Frölich pfleg ich
    zu
Für Gott den Herren woll'n
    wir gohn 1564
Gelobt sey Gott der Herre.
    1564
Gott Vater, Sohn, Heiliger
    Geist. 1564
Gross sind die Merck des
    Herren. 1552
Gross Unbild thut mich
    zwingen. 1510
Herr Gott Vater im Himmel-
    reich
Herr Jesu Christe, Starker
    Gott. 1564
Herr! starker Gott ins Him-
    mels Thron. 1564
Herzlich thut mich erfreuen
    Die liebe Sommer-Zeit
Hilf Gott das ich mög singen.
    1564
Hinweg ist mir genommen
Ich weiss, wer Gottes Wort
    bekennt 1564
Ich will von ganzem Herzen
    mein 1564
Ihr Kinder Gottes alle.
    1564
In Gottes Namen heb'n wir
    an. 1564
Komm Gott Vater von
    Himmeln. 1564
Kreutz, Verfolgung und
    Trübsal 1564
Kurzlich hab ich vorg'nom-
    men. 1529
Lebt friedsam, sprach
    Christus der Herr. 1564
Mein fröhlich Herz das
    treibt mich an zu singen.
    1564
Merkt auf ein Sach und die
    ist wahr. 1564
Merkt auf, ihr Christen all
    gleich. 1564

Merkt auf, ihr Menschenkin-
der. 1564
Merkt auf, ihr Völker alle
1557
Merkt auf, ihr Volker
überall
Merkt auf und nehmt zu
Herzen. 1564
Mit einem zugeneigten G'müth.
1564
Mit Lust so will ich singen
Ein schöne Tageweiss. 1564
Muss es nun seyn gescheiden.
1564
Nun heben wir an in Nöthen
Nun hört, ihr Freund ehrsa-
men. 1570
Nun Hört mir zu in mein'm
Gedicht. 1564
O Gott Schöpfer, heiliger Geist.
1564
O Gott Vater ins Himmels
Throne. 1564
O Herr dich will ich loben.
1550
O Herr! um dein Gnad ruff ich
dich an. 1564
O Herre Gott, gross ist die
Roth. 1564
O Herre Gott, in meiner
Roth. 1564
O Herre Gott mein Roth thu
ich der Klagen 1564
O Menschenkind, vernimm mich
wohl. 1564
Schier in allen G'schichten
g'schrieben staht
Trauren will ich stehen lassen
1564
Ungnad begehr ich nicht von
dir. 1527
Von Herzen will ich loben.
1564
Von Herzen woll'n wir singen.
1564
Wach auf, wach auf, O Men-
schenkind! Von deinem
Schlaf stand auf geschwind.
1564
Wacht auf, ihr Brüder werthe.
1564
Was wend wir aber heben an
1564

Was Woll'n wir aber singen
Weil nun die Zeit vorhanden
ist. 1564
Wir bitten dich, ewiger Gott.
1528
Wir danken Gott von Herzen
1530
Wo kommt das her, o Jesu
Christ. 1564
Wo soll ich mich hin kehren
1564
Zu Lob Gott Vater, Sohne
1559
Zu sing'n hab ich im Sinn:,:
1564
Zu singen will ich heben an
1564
Ausbund (Fourteen authors)
Mit Freuden woll'n wir
singen. 1564
Ausbund (Seven Brothers)
Aus tiefer Noth schrey ich
zu dir, Ach Gott erhör
mein Rufen, Dein Heil'
gen Geist fend du zu
mir. 1564
Ausbund. Psalm 34.
Ich will loben den
Herren. 1564
Ausbund. Psalm 35.
Herr Gott! streit wider
meine Feind. 1564
Ausbund. Psalm 50.
Also redt der wahrhaftig
Gott. 1564
Ausbund. Psalm 54.
O Herre Gott! hilf mir in
deinem Namen. 1564
Ausbund. Psalm 86
Herr Gott! thu mich
erhören. 1564
Ausbund. Psalm 126
Wann der Herr die
G'sangniss Zion. 1564
Ausbund. Psalm 130
O Herr! nicht stolz ist
mein Herz doch. 1564
Ausbund. Psalm 133
Sieh! wie sein ist und
lieblich schon. 1564
Ausbund. Suppl.
Es ist eind wunder schöne
Es war ein Gottesfürchtiges

Kürzlich vor wenig Tagen
Mein fröhlich
    Herz das treibt mich
O Herr thu auf die Lefzen
    mein
Tobias war ein frommer Mann

NOTE: Identified authors represented in Ausbund are:

Athanasian Creed.
Bappenheim, W.
Betz, H.
Bible, Maccabees.
Bilach, H. v.
Blaurock, G.
Bosch, S. v.
Büchel, H.
Clock, L.
Drucker, T.
Franck, S.
Gerfass, M.
Hans, S.
Hus, John
Hut, H.
Koch, H.
Landis, H.
Mantzen, F.
Ringmacher, L.
Rogel, H.
Rot, O.
Sattlers, M.
Schneider, L.
Schneider, M.
Schornschlager, L.
Straub, H.
Wagner, G.

Auslander, Joseph, 1897-
    Blest is that man who sets his
Austin, John, 1613-69
    Behold we come, dear Lord
    Blest be thy love, dear Lord
    Hark, my soul, how every
        thing
    Hail, glorious spirits, heirs;
        X103037 Hail, glorious
        angels
Austin, William, 1587-1633
    All this night shrill chanti-
        cleer; X100289 All this
        night bright
Avery, Benedict

Bowing low, then offer homage
Avery, Samuel J.
    Truth comes alike to all
Ayers, Minny M. H.
    I walk with love along the way
Aylward, James Ambrose, 1813-
72
    Lift up, ye princes of the sky
Ayres, H. C., ca 1894-
    One there is who loves thee

B

"B. E.
    O Christ, in thee my soul
        hath; R106426 Now none but
        Christ
Babcock, Maltbie Davenport,
1858-1901
    Back of the loaf is the snowy
    Be strong! We are not here;
        X110998 We are not here
    God's boundless love and
    Rest in the Lord, my soul
    This is my Father's world
    When the great sun sinks to
Babst. Geistliche lieder. Leipzig,
1545
    All' Ehr' und Lob soll Gottes
    All glory be to God alone
Bachelor, Mary A
    Go bury thy sorrow
Bacon, Josephine Daskam, 1876-
    Brother, sing your country's
Bacon, Leonard, 1802-81
    Here, Lord of life and light
    O God, beneath thy guiding
    Wake the song of Jubilee!
Badger, George Henry, 1859-
    O thou who art my king
Bahnmaier, Jonathan Friedrich,
1774-1841
    Spread, O spread, thou mighty
        X109187 Spread, still spread
    Walte, walte nah und fern
        1827
    Word of life, most pure,
        most
Baird, R. B.
    Improve the shining moments
    Welcome, welcome, Sabbath
    When the rosy light of morn-
        ing; R109975 Then away,

haste
Baker, Henry Williams, 1821-77
  Almighty God, whose only Son
  God made me for Himself, to
  How welcome was the call
  I am not worthy, holy Lord;
    R106337 Not worthy, not
  Lord, thy word abideth
  My Father, for another night
  O God of love, O King of peace
  O Holy Ghost, thy people bless
  O Jesus, God and man; X105574
    Lord Jesus, God
  O perfect life of love
  O praise our God today
  O what if we are Christ's
  Out of the deep I call
  Praise, O praise our God;
    R102285 For his mercies
    aye
  Redeemed, restored, forgiven
  Rejoice today with one accord
  Remember, Lord, thy works
  Shall we not love thee
  The King of love my shepherd
  There is a blessed home
Baker, Mary A.
  Master, the tempest is raging;
    R109925 The winds and the
    waves
Bakewell, John, 1721-1819
  Hail, thou once despised Jesus;
    X104629 Jesus, hail!
Balch, Emily Greene
  Now let us all arise and sing
Balfern, William Poole, 1818-87
  O Lamb of God most lowly
Ball, William, 1784-1869
  To God on high be thanks
Ballantine, William G., 1848-
1937
  God save America! new world
Ballet, William, 17th c
  Sweet was the song the Virgin
Ballou, Adin, 1803-90
  Years are coming -- speed
Ballou, Hosea, 1771-1852
  When God is seen with me to
Baltzell, I.
  On the shore beyond the sea;
    R105444 Let me go, I can-
    not
Baltzell, L.

I want to be a worker for
  the; R104109 I will work,
  I will
Bangor Antiphoner, ca 690
  Draw nigh and take the
    Body; X101510 Come,
    take by faith
  Sancti, venite, corpus Chris-
    ti sumite
Banks, George Linnaeus, 1821-
81
  I live for those who love me
Bappenheim, Walpurg von
  Du glaubigs Herz, so bene-
    dey. 1564
Barbauld, Anna Laetitia, 1743-
1825
  Blest is the man whose
  Come, said Jesus' sacred
    voice; X101501 Come,
    says Jesus'
  How blest the righteous
    when; X100987 Blest is
    the man
  How blest the sacred tie
  Our country is Immanuel's
  Praise to God, immortal
    praise
Barber, Henry Hervey, 1835-
  Far off, O God, and yet
    most
Baring-Gould, Sabine, 1834-
1924
  Daily, daily sing the praises;
    R107619 O, that I had
    wings
  Hail the Sign, the Sign of
    Jesus
  Now the day is over
  On the resurrection morn-
    ing
  Onward, Christian soldiers
  Sing lullaby! Lullaby baby!
Barlow, Charles H.
  Why search the future and
Barnard, S., 18th c
  Jehovah is our strength
Baron, Barclay, 1884-
  Go forth with God! the day
Barratt, Alfred, 1879-
  Like radiant sunshine that;
    R111838 Wonderful peace
Barrett. Book of praise for

children, 1881
   The fields are all white
   The wise may bring their
Barrows, Samuel J.
   Enkindling Love, eternal Flame
Barstow, H. H.
   The Son of Man goes forth
Barth, Christian Gottlob, 1799-
1862
   From distant shores returning
   Go joyfully forth, To war
Bartholomew, Julia H.
   From lands beyond the waters
Bartlett, Franklin Weston, 1843-
   O God Supreme, who dost
   Saviour, who didst come to
Barton, Bernard D., 1784-1849
   Lamp of our feet, whereby we;
      X105047 Lamp ... our path
      to
   Walk in the light! so shalt;
      X110942 Walk ... and thou;
      X110944 Walk ... so thou
   We journey through a vale
Barton, William, 1603-78
   Present your bodies to the
   Lord
Bateman, Christian Henry, 1813-
89
   Come, Christians, join to sing;
      X101351 Come, children,
      join
Bateman, Henry, 1802-72
   Gracious Saviour, thus before
   Light of the world! whose kind
Bateman, Mrs. L. M. B.
   I will early seek the Saviour;
      R102282 For He loves me,
      yes
Bates, David, 1810-70
   Speak gently, it is better far
Bates, Katharine Lee, 1859-1929
   A little Child, a Joy-of heart
   Dear God our Father, at thy
   Not for more beauty would our
   O beautiful for spacious skies
   The Kings of the East are
   The palm-trees fed with dew
Bathurst, William Hiley, 1796-
1877
   Hark, the distant isles
   Holy Spirit, from on high
   How blest are they whose hearts

Jesus, thy church, with long-
   ing
O for a faith that will not
O for that flame of living
Why should our tears in sor-
   row
Batty, Charles
   O, my Saviour crucified
Batty, Christopher, 1715-97
   Cheer thy chosen witnesses
Baum, Maria Louise
   Here, O God, thy healing
   High to heaven let song be
   If the Lord build not the
   In thee, my God and Saviour
   Like as a Mother, God com-
      forteth
   Put on the whole armor of
   pure
   Rouse ye, soldiers of the
      cross; R108662 Rouse ye,
      rouse ye
Bax, Clifford, 1886-
   Turn back, O man, forswear
Baxter, Lydia, 1809-74
   Take the name of Jesus;
      R108376 Precious Name,
      O how
   There is a gate that stands;
      R106704 O depth of mercy
Baxter, Richard, 1615-91
   Christ leads me through no
   Christ who knows all his
      sheep
   He wants not friends that
      hath
   Lord, it belongs not to my
   Ye holy angels bright
The Bay Psalm book see The
   Whole Booke of Psalmes,
   1647
Bayley, Jonathan
   O Jesus, Lord, and Saviour;
      R101498 Come, Saviour,
      come
Bayly, Albert F., 1901-
   Long ago when Jesus, walk-
      ed
   Lord of the home, thine only
   Lord, save thy world; in bit-
      ter
   Lord, thy kingdom bring
   Lord, whose love through

humble service c1961
O joyful hope, in weary hearts;
R101579 Comfort ye, my
people
Rejoice, O people, in the
mounting
Baynes, Robert Hall, 1831-95
God Almighty, in thy temple
Holy Spirit, Lord of glory
Jesus, to thy table led
Beach, Curtis, 1914-
O be joyful in the Lord
O how glorious, full of wonder
Beach, Seth Curtis, 1837-1932
Kingdom of God! the day how
Mysterious Presence, source
Thou One in all, thou All in
Where is he that came to save
Beadon, Hyde Wyndham, 1812-
Fierce was the storm of wind
Glory to thee, O Lord, who by;
X100266 All praise to thee
Beaumont, John, 1582-1628
My Shepherd is the Lamb
Beardsley, Monroe, 1915-
From all the fret and fever
Beck, Thomas, late 18th c
Jesus, we lift ourselves
Becker, Henry Albert
Back to the cross I go again
Christ is risen from the dead
Shine on, thou Star of Bethle-
hem
Beddome, Benjamin, 1717-95
Ascend thy throne, Almighty
Buried beneath the yielding
Come, blessed Spirit! source;
X101348 Come, blessed
Saviour; X107593 O Spirit,
source
Come, Holy Spirit, come, with
Did Christ o'er sinners weep
Father of mercies, bow thine
God, in the gospel of his Son
If Christ is mine, then all is
In duties and in sufferings
Jesus, my love, my chief
Jesus, my Saviour, let me be
Let party names no more
Shout for the blessed Jesus
Thou Lord of all above
'Tis faith supports my feeble
'Tis God the Spirit leads

Wait, O my soul, the Maker's
When Israel through the
desert
Witness, ye men and angels;
X111901 Ye men and
angels
Beeching, Henry Charles, 1859-
1919
God who created me
Beegle, H. B.
Wash me, O Lamb of God,
wash
Berry, Adaline Hohf, 1859-
1929
Hail, blessed Trinity, Low
Lo, a gleam from yonder
heaven; R104706 Jesus,
Light, serene
Behm, Martin, 1557-1662
Lord Jesus Christ, my life
O heilige Dreifaltigkeit, O
hochgelobte Einigkeit.1593
O holy, blessed Trinity,
divine; X106550 O blessed
Holy; X107008 O holy ...
essential
O Jesu Christ, mein's leb-
ens
O Jesus, King of glory
O König aller ehren
Belden, F. E., 19th c
Blessed Lord, how much I
need; R101999 Every hour
Eternal Father, God of love
Father, we come to thee
He's coming once again
Holy day, Jehovah's rest
I will sing of Jesus' love
I would be, dear Saviour
If any little word of mine;
R102642 God help me
speak
Let every lamp be burning;
R109984 Then trim your
lamps
Like as a father pities his
Look for the beautiful, look
Look for the waymarks
Look upon Jesus, sinless is
He; R101609 Cover with
His life
O Jesus, my Redeemer
Raise the standard high

Shepherd divine, thou leadest
Sweet be thy rest, and peaceful
Sweet promise is given to all;
    R103500 "Hold fast till I"
The coming King is at the door
The judgment has set, the
    books; R103744 How shall
    we stand
There is sweet rest for feet
There's no other name like
We know not the hour; R103305
    He will come, let us
We'll build on the Rock
Belknap, Jeremy, late 18th c arr
Give ear, ye children to my
Bell, Charles Dent, 1818-98
Be with us, gracious Lord
Bell, George Kennedy Allen
Christ is the King! O friends;
    X101212 Christ ... friends
    rejoice
Bell, M. Bettie
Press on, dear traveller,
    press
Bell, Maud, 1868-1957
Father all-seeing, friend of
Bell, Maurice Frederick, 1862-
1947
O dearest Lord, accept today
O dearest Lord, by all adored
Bellamy, W.H.
O troubled heart, there is;
    X107804 O wait, meekly wait
The home where changes never;
    X107804 O wait, meekly
    wait
Bement, Howard, 1875-1936
Clear is the call that bids
Benade, Samuel T., 1746-1830
Bless, O Lord, we pray, thy
Fountain of life and light
How needful, strictly to
To Christ we homage pay
We covenant with hand and
    heart
Benedictine "Ultima"
At our life's last moment
Ultima in mortis hora
Bennard, George
On a hill far away; R109047
So I'll cherish

Bennett, Archibald F
Holy temples on Mt Zion
Bennett, Henry, 1813-68
I have a home above
Bennett, Sanford Fillmore,
1836-1898
Sing we a song of the Saviour
There's a land that is fairer;
    R104386 In the sweet by
    and
Bennett, Wallace F.
God of power, God of right
Benson, Arthur Christopher,
1862-
Lord of grace and holiness
O Lord of hosts, who didst
The spring again is here
Benson, Edward White, 1829-
96
O Jesus, crowned with all
Benson, Louis Fitzgerald, 1855-
1930
A King might miss the guiding
For the bread, which thou
    hast
I name thy hallowed name
O Love that lights the
    eastern
O risen Christ, who from
    thy
O sing a song of Bethlehem
O Thou whose feet have
    climbed
O Thou whose gracious
    presence
Our wilful hearts have gone
The lamps of heaven
The light of God is falling
The sun is on the land
The winter night was dark
Benson, Richard Meux, 1824-
1915
Praise to God who reigns
Berg, Carolina Vilhelmina
Sandell, 1832-1903
Children of the heavenly
Jerusalem, Jerusalem, thou
O Father, thy kingdom is
    come
Strait is the gate to all;
    X109236 Strait ... to

heaven
Berkowitz, Henry
    Lord, into thy sacred dwelling
Berlin, Irving, 1889-
    God bless America
Bernstein, Christian Andreas,
1672?-1699
    At last he's blest who by
Berridge, John, 1716-93
    At Cana, Lord, thou didst
    Jesus, cast a look on me
    Since Jesus freely did appear
Berry, F. J.
    Brother afar from the Saviour;
        R111333 What would you
        give
Bersagel, Andreas
    The sun is sinking in the west
    To the hills I lift mine eyes
Berwick hymnal, 1886
    Father Almighty, bless us;
        X102079 Father Almighty,
        grant
Besnault, Sebastian, Abbe, ca
ca1660-1724
    Debilis cessent elementa legis
    Felix dies, quam proprio
    O happy day, when first was;
        X106547 O blessed day;
        X107497 O sacred day, when
    The ancient law departs
Best, Nolan R.
    Made of one blood with all
Betham-Edwards, Matilda B.,
1836-1919
    God make my life a little;
        X102701 God ... a shining
Bethune, George Washington,
1805-62
    O Jesus, when I think of thee
    O thou who in Jordan didst
    There is no name so sweet;
        R111082 We love to sing
    Tossed upon the raging
    When time seems short and
Betz, Hans
    Christus das Lamm auf
        Erden kam. 1564
    Christus der Herr ist gangen.
        1564
    Gelobt sey Gott im höchsten
        Thron. 1564
    Gott Zebaoth, der war, und

ist
Herr Gott Vater im Himmel-
    reich. 1564
Herr Gott Vater, von dir
    allein. 1564
Herr Gott Vater, zu dir ich
    schrey. 1564
Ihr Christen g'mein, die
    ihr seyd rein. 1564
Merkt auf, ihr Völker g'
    meine. 1564
Merkt auf mit Fleiss, ein
    Himmelspeiss. 1564
Nun wolt ich gerne singen.
    1564
Unser Vater im Himmelreich,
    Dein Nam sei heilig ewig-
    lich. 1564
Bevier, Louis
    Our fathers in the olden
Bhagavad-Gita
    Give me your whole heart
Bianco da Siena, d 1434
    Come down, O Love divine
Bible.

NOTE: First lines of hymns
are listed alphabetically,
followed by citation when it
is known.

Alleluia, alleluia: i. e.
    Hallelujah Chorus (Revela-
    tion)
Awake, Awake, Awake, Put
    on thy strength (Isaiah 52);
    R103624 How beautiful
    upon
Behold I stand at the door
    (Revelation 3)
Blessed, blessed, be Jehovah
    (Psalm 106)
Blessing and honour and glory
    (Revelation 5)
But the Lord is mindful
    (Psalms)
Cast thy burden upon the
    Lord (Psalm 55 or 16)
Down by the river's verdant
    (Psalm 137)
Give thanks to God
    (Psalm 136)
God so loved the world

(John 3)
Haec dies quam fecit Dominus
  (Psalm 117)
How wondrous is thy mercy
  (Psalm 36: Danish)
Let every creature God has
  (Psalm 148)
Let us now praise famous men
  (Ecclesiasticus 44)
Lift thine eyes, O lift
  (Psalm 121)
Look with mercy, Lord
  (Joel 2): R111004 We are
  that chosen
Lovely appear over the moun-
  tain (Isaiah 52)
Mine eyes look toward the
  mountains (Psalm 121:
  Swedish)
Not unto us, O Lord
  (Psalm 115)
O heavens, send your rain
  (Isaiah 45)
O Lord, what is man that Thou
  takest knowledge (Psalm 8)
O rest in the Lord, wait
  (Psalm 37)
O thou who spreadest the
  heaven (Isaiah: Dutch tr);
  R103218 Have ye not heard
Out of the depths to thee
  (Psalm 129)
Parce Domini, parce populo
  (Joel 2)
Praise ye the Lord
Rorate caeli desuper (Isaiah
  45)
Send out thy light and thy
  truth (Psalm 43)
So merket auf ihr Christen-
  leut. (Maccabees)
Souls of the righteous
  (Wisdom 3)
Spare your people, Lord
  (Joel 2)
The children of the Hebrews
  (Psalm 122)
The Lord bless you and keep
  (Numbers); X109638 The
  Lord bless thee
Bickersteth, Edward Henry,
  1825-1906
  Almighty Father, hear our

Arise and be baptized
Come ye yourselves apart
For My sake and the Gospel's
Hush! blessed are the dead
My God, my Father, let me
  rest
Not worthy, Lord, to gather
O brothers, lift your voices
O Christ, thou hast ascend-
  ed
O God, the Rock of Ages
O holy Father, who in ten-
  der
O Jesu, Saviour of the lost
Peace, perfect peace, in
  this
Stand, soldier of the cross
"Till he come!" oh, let the
Bienemann, Kaspar, 1540-91
  Lord, as thou wilt, deal thou
Bilach, Hanslein von
  Einsmals spatziert ich hin
  und her
Bilhorn, Peter P., 1861-1936
  O, the best friend to have;
  R109419 The best friend
  to
There comes to my heart
  one; R108206 Peace,
  peace, sweet
Bills, G.M.
  Do you seek for a friend;
  R107636 O, the best
  Friend
Binney, Thomas, 1798-1874
  Eternal Light! eternal Light!
Binyon, Laurence, 1869-1943
  Down in the valley where
  For mercy, courage, kind-
  ness
  Woe unto him that has not
Bird, Thomas, 1780?-1828
  In the lonely house of mourn-
  ing
Birkedal, Wilhelm, 1809-92
  I saw Him in childhood with
Birken, Sigismund von, 1626-
  81
  Jesu, deine Passion will ich
  Jesus, I will ponder now
  Lasset uns mit Jesus ziehen
  1653
  Let us ever walk with Jesus

Birks, Thomas Rawson, 1810-83
O gentle Savior, from thy
O King of mercy, from thy throne
The heavens declare thy glory
Whom have we Lord in heaven (authorship in doubt)
Bishop, C.
That God should love a sinner; R109250 Such love, such
Black, James M.
When the trumpet of the Lord; R111489 When the roll is; X111498 When the trump shall (Jacobs)
Blackall, Christopher Ruby, 1830-
In the harvest field there is; R105023 Labor on, labor on
Blackie, John Stuart, 1809-95
Angels, holy, high and lowly
Blacklock, Thomas, 1721-91
Come, O my soul, in sacred
Blackmer, P.W.
Long ago, there was born
Blair, H.E.
On the happy, golden shore
Blaisdell, James Arnold, 1867-
Beneath the forms of outward
Christians, lo, the star
Blake, James Vila, 1842-1920
Father, thou art calling
O sing with loud and joyful
Blake, William, 1757-1827
And did those feet in ancient
Can a father see his child
Can I see another's woe
Every night and every morn
Sweet dreams form a shade
To Mercy, Pity, Peace and Love
Blakeney, E.H.
Lord of the worlds, unseen
Up to the throne on high
Blanchard, Ferdinand Q., 1876-
Before the cross of Jesus
O Jesus, youth of Nazareth; X106597 O child of lowly
Word of God, across the ages
Bland Tucker, Francis, 1895-
see Tucker, Francis B.
Blandy [Blandy], E.W.

I can hear my Saviour calling; R111544 Where He leads me
Blatchford, Ambrose Nichols, 1842-1924
A gladsome hymn of praise; R104276 In him rejoice with
Peacefully round us the shadows
Softly the silent night
Within this temple, reared
Blaurock, Georg
Gott führt ein recht Gericht. 1564
Herr Gott! dich will ich loben. 1528
Blaxill, E. Alex, 1873-1953
Father of all, we come to
Blenkhorn, Ada
In hymns of praise your voices
Bliss, Philipp, 1838-76
(sometimes written as Bliss, Philip Paul)
"Almost persuaded" now to
Brightly beams our Father's R105174 Let the lower lights
Free from the law, O happy; R107982 Once for all
God is always near me
Ho! my comrades, see the signal; R103502 Hold the fort
I know not the hour; R100452 And that will be
I will sing of my Redeemer; R108955 Sing, O! sing
Man of sorrows! wondrous Name; X105872 Man of Sorrows! what
More holiness give me
Sing them over again to me; R100763 Beautiful words
Standing by a purpose true; R101642 Dare to be a Daniel
The whole world was lost; R101539 Come to the Light
'Tis the promise of God; R100346 Alleluia 'tis done

"Who-so-ever heareth," shout
Blough, J.M., 1876-
   O Holy Spirit, come to me
Blunt, Abel Gerald Wilson, 1827-
1902
   Here, Lord, we offer thee all
Boaden, Edward, 1827-
   Here, Lord, assembled in thy
Bobbitt, J.P.
   I was once far away from;
      R110628 To my heart in
      that
Boberg, Carl
   O Lord my God! When I in;
      R109983 Then sings my soul
Bode, Alice M., ca 1850-
   Once pledged by the cross
Bode, John Ernest, 1816-74
   O Jesus, I have promised;
      X105577 Lord Jesus, I have
   Thou who hast called us
Boden, J. Waugh, 1855-1943
   Men true of heart and strong
Boden, James, 1757-1841
   Come, all ye saints of God
Boe, V.E., 1872-
   Jesus all glorious, Christ all
Boehmer, Justus Henning, 1674-
1749
   Courage, my sorely tempted
Boehnisch, Frederick, 1710-63
   O could we but love that
Boethius, Anicius, M.S., 480-
524
   O thou whose power o'er mov-
   ing
Bogatzky, Karl Heinrich von,
1690-1774
   Awake, thou Spirit bold
   Awake, thou Spirit of the
   Awake, thou Spirit, who didst
   Wach auf, du Geist der ersten
      Zeugen 1750
   Wake, Spirit, who in times
Bohemian traditional, etc.
   Aj, ten silný lev udatný (1650)
   Come all ye shepherds; X101335
      Come ... and be not
   Lo, Judah's Lion wins (1650)
Bohemian Brethren see Moravian
Böhmer, Justus Henning, 1674-
1749

O risen Lord! O conquering
Bonar, Horatius, 1808-89
   A few more years shall roll;
      R109986 Then, O my Lord
   A sinful man am I
   All praise to Him, who built
   All that I was, my sin, my
   Angel voices, sweetly sing-
      ing; R103351 Heaven at
      last
   Begin the day with God
   Beloved, let us love; love is
      X100870 Beloved ... love
      is
   Beyond the smiling and the
   Blessed night, when first;
      X100940 Blessed ... when
   Bethlehem's; X100942
      Blessed ... first the;
      X105968 Mighty King of
      righteousness
   Blessing and honor, and
      glory
   By the cross of Jesus
   Calm me, my God, and
      keep me
   Church of the ever-living
      God
   Come and hear the grand
      old; R106279 Noblest,
      truest
   Come, Lord, and tarry not
   Come, mighty Spirit, pene-
      trate
   Done is the work that saves
   Fading away like the stars;
      R108031 Only remember-
      ed
   Far down the ages now
   Father, our children keep
   For the bread and for the
      wine
   From the cross the blood is
   Give thou thy youth to God
   Glory be to God the Father;
      X102568 Glory to the
      King
   Go, labor on! spend and be
   Go, labor on, while it is day;
      X102592 Go ... spend and
      be
   Great King of kings, why

dost
Great master, touch us with
Great Ruler of the land and;
  R104979 Keep by the mighty
He has come! the Christ of
  God
He liveth long, who liveth
Here, O my Lord, I see thee;
  X103411 Here ... I'd see;
  X110207 This is the hour;
  X110714 Too soon we rise
Holy Father, hear my cry
I bless the Christ of God
I close my heavy eye
I did thee wrong, my God
I hear the words of love
I heard the voice of Jesus
I lay my sins on Jesus;
  X103833 I bring my sins
I see a man at God's right
I see the crowd in Pilate's
I was a wandering sheep
In the land of strangers;
  R111209 Welcome, wanderer
Jesus, Saviour, Son of God
Jesus, the Christ of God
Jesus, whom angel hosts adore
Light of life, so softly
Light of the world! for ever
Like the eagle, upward, on-
  ward
Lo! God, our God, has come
Lord, give me light to do;
  X105463 Lord, give us light;
  R108818 Send me light
Make haste, O man, to live;
  X105848 Make haste ... to
  do
Make use of me, My God
No, not despairingly Come I
  to
No shadows yonder
Not what I am, O Lord
Not what these hands have done;
  X106332 Not what my hands
Now, in parting, Father bless
O everlasting Light! Shine;
  X106717 O ... Giver of
  dawn
O Love of God, how strong
O love that casts out fear
Our life is hid with Christ
Praises to Him whose love has

Rejoice and be glad!
Rest for the toiling hand
The Bridegroom comes;
  Bride of
The church has waited long
The cross it standeth fast
This is not my place of rest-
  ing
This is the hour of banquet
Thou must be true thyself
Through good report and
  evil
Thy way, not mine, O Lord
Thy works, not mine, O
  Christ
To the name of God on high
True Bread of life, in pity-
  ing
Upward where the stars are
We thank thee, Lord, for
When I shall wake in that
When the weary, seeking
  rest; R103327 Hear then,
  in love
Yes, for me, for me He
  careth
Yes, He is risen who is
Bonar, Jane Catharine, 1821-84
  Fade, fade, each earthly joy
Bone, Mary W.
  Farewell, all earthly honors;
  R110075 There is sweet
  rest
Bonin, Ulrich Bogislaw von,
1682-1752
  How great at last my joy
Bonn Gesangbuch, 1561
  In God's name let us on our
Book of hours (French) 1490
  God be in my head, and in
  my
Book of hymns (Unitarian) 1846
  Peace of God, which knows
  no; X105799 Love divine
  (Wesley)
The Book of praise for children
  see Barrett, G.S. The Book
  of praise, 1881
Booth, Ballington, 1859-1940
  The cross that He gave may
  be; R109459 The cross is
  not
Booth, Herbert

Blessed Lord, in Thee is
  refuge
Boreham, F.W., 1871-1959
  Eternal Father, whose great
Borthwick, Jane Laurie, 1813-
97
  Come, labor on, who dares
  Hasten the time appointed;
    X100434 And is the time;
    X106395 Now is the time
  Still on the homeward journey
  Thou knowest, Lord, the
    weariness
Bosch, Sigmund von
  Fröhlich so will ich singen
  So will ichs aber heben an
    1564
Böschenstein, Johann, 1472-1540
  Da Jesus an des Kreuzes
    Stamm
  Our blessed Saviour seven;
    X108841 Seven times our
    blessed
Bossart, John Jacob, 1721-89
  One view, Lord Jesus, of thy
Bostock, Edward C., arr
  The Lord God Jesus Christ
Boswell, Robert, 1746-1804
  Behold what love the Father
Bosworth's Hymns, 1865
  Jesus, thy love unbounded;
    X106621 O Christ, thy love
Bottome, Francis, 1823-94
  Love of Jesus, all divine
  O, spread the tidings round;
    R109455 The Comforter has
  Search me, O God, my actions
Bourdillon, Francis William,
  1852-1921
  The night has a thousand eyes
Bourgignon, Antoinette, 1616-80
  Come, Saviour Jesus, from
    above
Bourne, George Hugh, 1840-1925
  Lord, enthroned in heavenly
  O Christ, our Lord, who with
Bourne, William St Hill, 1846-
1929
  Christ, who once amongst us
  The Sower went forth sowing
Boutflower, C.H., 1863-1942
  O God, in this thine hour
  O joy of God, that comest

Bowdler, John, 1783-1815
  As, panting in the sultry
  Lord, before thy throne we
  To God I lift mine eyes
Bowers, J.E.
  Our Father, we adore thee
Bowie, Walter Russell, 1882-
  God of the nations, who
    from
  Lord Christ, when first thou
  Lord, through changing days
  O holy city, seen of John
  O ye who dare go forth with
Bowman, J.M.
  My Saviour guides me day
    by
Bowring, John, 1792-1872
  Father and Friend! Thy light
  God is love; his mercy
  How sweetly flowed the gos-
    pel
  I cannot always trace the
    way; X111023 We cannot
    always
  In the cross of Christ, I
    glory
  The offerings to thy throne
  "Thy will be done!" In
    devious
  Upon the gospel's sacred
    page
  Watchman, tell us of the
    night
Box, Howard, 1926-
  Bells in the high tower
Boyce, R. Fisher
  O, beautiful Star of Bethle-
    hem; R100760 Beautiful
    Star of
Boye, Birgitte Cathrine, 1742-
1824
  He is arisen! Glorious word
  Holy Spirit, God of Love
  O Light of God's most won-
    drous
  O Lue fra Guds Kjärlighed
  Os er idag en Frelser föd
  Our Lord is risen from the
  Rejoice, rejoice this happy
Boye, Caspar Johannes, 1791-
1853
  Abide with us, the day is
  Bliv hos os, Mester, Dagen

Stay with us Lord, the day
Boyle, Cavendish, 1849-1916
 When sun rays crown thy pine-
  clad
Brace, Seth Collins, 1811-
 Mourn for the thousands slain
Bradbury. Oriola, 1860
 Go thou, in life's fair morning
Bradby, Godfrey Fox
 Where is death's sting? We
Brady, Nicholas, 1659-1726, see
 Tate, Nahum 1652-1715 &
Brady, Nicholas, 1659-1726
Bradford, Mrs. N. K.
 O tender and sweet was;
  R108177 "Over the line"
Bradley, E. A.
 Turned by thy grace, I look
Bradley, Mary
 I need not care If days to
Brailsford, Edward John, 1841-
1921
 All things which live below
Braley, Berton, 1882-
 Lord, we come with hearts
Bramley, Henry Ramsden, 1833-
1917
 The great God of heaven is
Breay, John George, 1796-1839
 Saviour, bless thy word to all
Breck, Mrs. Frank A., 1855-
1934
   Face to face with Christ
   Go to the deeps of God's
   There was One who was will-
    ing; R110134 They are nail-
    ed; R110146 They were
    nailed
Brenneman, H. B.
   There's a beautiful, beautiful;
    R107615 O, that beautiful
Brethren's Tune and hymn book.
 1879
   Is there a God? The rising
    sun
Breviary.

NOTE: First lines of hymns are
listed alphabetically, followed
by place and date of publication when known.

Adoremus te Christe, et
 benedicimus tibi
Beati mortui in Domino
Christi factus est pro nobis
Conquering kings their titles
 take (Nevers, 1727)
Cor, arca legem contenens
 (Bologna, 1827)
Glorious Virgin, thee we
 sing
He, who once in righteous
 vengeance (Bologna, 1827)
Holy Week Responsories
Inviolata integra et casta
Joseph our certain hope
 (1632)
Lapsus est annus: redit annus
 (Meaux, 1713)
Let every heart exulting beat
 (Sarum, 1495)
Morn's roseate hues have
 decked (Cluny, 1686)
Most holy Lord and God
 (Paris, 1531)
O Christ, behind the tem-
 ple's
O let the heart beat high
 (Sarum, 1495)
O sacrum convivium (York,
 1493)
O'erwhelmed in depths of
 woe (Bologna, 1827)
On this day, the first of days
 (Carcassonne, 1745)
Popule meus quid feci tibi
Regnum mundi
Ruler of the hosts of light
 (Cluny, 1686)
Seek ye a patron to defend
 (Venice, 1798); R100977
 Blest holder of ... the
 keys
Seven Last Words on the
 Cross
Soldiers, who are Christ's
 below (Bourges, 1734)
Soldiers who to Christ be-
 long (Bourges, 1734)
Star of Jacob, ever beaming
 (Lisbon, 1786)
Te, Joseph, celebrent
 (1670)

The solemn season calls us
now (Paris, 1736)
The year is gone beyond re-
call (Paris, 1713)
Veni Sponsa Christi
What a sea of tears (1746)
Wondrous gift! The word who
fashioned (Cluny, 1686);
X103298 He who once to
die

Brewer, Edith Gaddis
God of truth, eternal good
Prayer with our waking thought

Brewer, Leigh Richmond, 1839-
1916
Long years ago o'er Bethlehem's

Brewer, Sidney S.
Watchman, tell me, does

Bridaine, Jacques, 1701-67
My Lord, my Master, at thy
feet

Bridgers, Luther B., 1884-1948
There's within my heart;
R104686 Jesus, Jesus,
Jesus

Bridges, Matthew, 1800-94
Behold the Lamb of God
Crown Him with many crowns;
X101626 Crown Him the
Lord
My God, accept my heart;
X106798 O God, accept my
Rise, glorious Conqueror,
rise
There is an everlasting home;
X103073 Hail, Rock of ages

Bridges, Robert Seymour, 1844-
1930
All praise be to God
All-seeing Lord, whose power
Enter thy courts, thou Word
Eternal Father, who didst all
Gird on thy sword, O man
I love all beauteous things
Lament, O man, thy pride
Love can tell, and love alone
Love of love, and Light of
light
Love, unto Thine own who
My God, my God, why dost
thou
My heart is filled with long-
ing

My Lord, my Life, my Love
My soul, praise the Lord
Rejoice, O land, in God
Rejoice, ye dead! Where'er
The King [The Queen], O
God, his [her] heart to
thee
Thee will I love, my God
Unto thee my heart is sigh-
ing
When Jesus to our rescue
drew

Bridgewater, A. S.
We read of a place called;
R103620 How beautiful
heaven

Bridgman, Amy Sherman
O Thou, Jehovah, Sovereign

Briem, Valdimer, 1848-1930
How marvellous God's great-
ness
Lord, let thy Spirit, from

Briggs, George Wallace, 1875-
1959
Christ is the world's true
Come, risen Lord, and deign
Dear Father, keep me
through
For the brave of every race
God hath spoken -- by His
God my Father, loving me
Hark! a hundred notes are
I love God's tiny creatures
Lord, in the hollow of thy
Lord of all majesty and
might
Lord, who hast made me
free
Lord, who thyself hast bid-
den
O God, in whom we live and
Our Father, by whose ser-
vants
Our Father, for our daily
She who stood beside the
cross
Shall God not share His chil-
dren's
Son of the Lord most high
The Spirit of the Lord re-
vealed
We meet, as in that upper
room

Briggs, LeBaron Russell, 1855-
1934
    God of our fathers, who hast
Bright, William, 1824-1901
    And now, O Father, mindful
    And now the wants are told
    At thy feet, O Christ, we lay
    Behold us, Lord, before Thee
    He sat to watch o'er customs
    Now at the night's return we
    Once again, O blessèd time
    Once, only once, and once for
    We know thee who thou art
Brightbill, Alvin Franz, 1903-
    How lovely is thy dwelling
Brightman, Edgar Sheffield
    Thy beauty, Lord, thou hast
Brink, L. P.
    The Wallapai, the Navaho
Brock, Mrs. Carey. The Chil-
dren's hymn book, 1881
    The darkness now is over
Brondsema, S. G.
    God Jehovah reigns, His are
    Unto the Lord lift thankful
Brontë, Anne, 1820-49
    Believe not those who say
Brontë, Emily, 1818-48
    No coward soul is mine
Brooke, Rupert, 1887-1915
    O thou God of all long desir-
ous
Brooke, Stopford Augustus,
1832-1916
    All lands and peoples, all
    Eternal Peace, whose word
of
    Immortal Love, within whose
    In our dark and doubtful
    It fell upon a summer day
    "It is finished," all the
pain
    Let the whole creation cry
    Now the wings of day are
    Oft, as we run the weary way
    The morning walks upon;
        X109035 Slow comes the even-
ing
    When the Lord of Love was
here
Brooks, Charles Timothy, 1813-
83
    God bless our native land see

    Mahlmann, S. A.
    O God! in Thine autumnal
Brooks, Clara M.
    "Lo, she is not dead; but--"
        R108032 Only sleeping,
sweetly
    Our Father's wondrous works;
        R111247 What a mighty
God we
    The eventide falls gently
    There's a way that is free;
        R110971 Watch and pray
Brooks, Phillips, 1835-93
    Everywhere, everywhere
    God hath sent his angels;
        R100470 Angels sing his
    O Little town of Bethlehem
    The sky can still remember
Brorson, Hans Adolf, 1694-1764
    Anxious heart be rid of sad-
ness
    Behold a host like mountain;
        X100800 Behold ... ar-
rayed
    Behold, they stand in robes
    By faith we are divinely sure
    Children of God, born again
    I near the grave where'er I
go
    I see thee standing, Lamb
    I walk in danger all the way
    In this our happy Christmas-
tide
    Jeg gaar i Fare, hvor jeg
gaar 1734
    Jesus, name of wondrous
grace
    Life's day is ended, the battle
    My heart, prepare to give
    Now found is the fairest of
    O Father, may thy word pre-
vail
    O seek the Lord today
    O watch and pray, my soul
    Stand fast, my soul, stand
fast
    Thy little ones, dear Lord
    What joy to reach the harbor
    Who will join the throng
Brown, Ann, 1908-
    Grace, love, and peace abide
Brown, Elmer Elsworth
    O Stranger, with no place

Brown, Howard I.
  Jesus calls me, I must follow;
    R102247 Follow, I will fol-
    low
Brown, J.A.
  Pray, pray in the old-time
Brown, J.S.
  I cannot tell thee whence;
    R110102 There's a deep
Brown, Kathryn Wright, 1910-
  O Master of all grace
Brown, Mary and C.E. Pryor
  It may not be on the mountain's
    R104192 I'll go where you;
    X104489 It may not be on ...
    mountain
Brown, Phoebe Hinsdale, 1783-
1861
  I love to steal awhile away
  O Lord, thy work revive
  We come, O Lord, before thy
Brown-Borthwick, Robert, 1840-94
  O Holy Jesu, Prince of Peace
Browne, R.D., 1905-
  Thou, Lord, hast given Thyself
Browne, Simon, ca 1680-1732
  And now, my soul, another
  Come, gracious Spirit, heaven-
    ly; X101405 Come, Holy
    Spirit; X108875 Shine forth,
    O Sun
  Frequent the day of God
  Hail, happy day! Thou day of
  Hail, Holy Spirit, bright
  Lord! at thy feet we humbly
Browne, Sir Thomas, 1605-82
  The night is come like to
Browne, Thomas Briarly, 1805-
74
  Praise the Lord of heaven
Browning, Elizabeth Barrett,
1809-61
  Of all the thoughts of God
  Since without thee we do no
Browning, Robert, 1812-89
  I go to prove my soul
  The year's at the spring
  Then welcome each rebuff
  There's heaven above, and
    night
  Was the trial sore? Temptation
Brubacher, Menno M.
  O God of wisdom, life and love

Bruce, Michael, 1746-1767
  Behold, the mountain of the
    Lord
  How happy are the young;
    X103698 How happy is the
    man; X106966 O happy is
    the man
  The beam that shines
  Wisdom hath treasure greater
Bruce, William, 1812-82
  Holy Father, thou hast given
Bruce, William Patterson
  Ring out, O bell, thy wel-
    come
Brucker, H.F.
  Accept from human hands
  Accept this host, O God
  Praise now your God, all ye
Brueckner, Hermann, 1866-
1942
  All hail, thou day of wond-
    rous
  Aloft in yonder belfry
  The heavens cannot thee
    embrace
  To thee eternal God, our
    fervent (Rinkart); X106443
    Now thank we all our
Bruinengk, Heinrich von,
1738-85
  Here in the name of Christ
Brun, Johan Nordahl, 1745-1816
  Heavenly Spirit, all others
  How blest are they who hear
  In heaven is joy and glad-
    ness
  Lad denne Dag, o Herre Gud
    1786
  O salig den, Guds Ord har
  Our Lord and God, O
    bless
Bruun, Samuel O., d 1694
  The sun has gone down
Bryan, Joseph
  To my humble supplication
Bryant, William, 1850-1913
  Standing forth on life's
Bryant, William Cullen,
1794-1878
  Dear ties of mutual succor
  Lo! in the clouds of heaven
  Look from thyssphere;
    X105398 Look from the

sphere
Lord, who ordainest
O deem not they are blest;
  X101738 Deem not that they
O North, with all thy vales
Thou, whose unmeasured temple; X107769 O Thou, whose own
When, doomed to death, the
When the blind suppliant
When this song of praise
Bryn Mawr College, 1923.
  To the knights in the days
Buchanan, Violet Nita, 1891-
  Help me, dear Lord, to love
  O day of joy and wonder
Büchel, Hans
  Als man zählt tausend fünf hundert Jahr. 1557
  Ein g'fahre Zeit vor nie erhört.
  Es b'gab sich auf ein Zeite. 1564
Buck, Carlton C., d 1961
  O Lord, may church and home combine c1961
Buckham, John Wright
  O God, above the drifting
Buckholl, Henry James, 1803-71
  Lord, behold us with thy
  Lord, dismiss us with thy
Buddha, The Lord Gautama see Gautama Buddha, 5th c B.C.
Budry, Edmond, 1854-1932
  Thine is the glory, risen;
  X110159 Thine be the glory
Buehrer, Edwin T., 1894-
  We sing now together our song
Buell, Harriet E., 1834-1910
  My Father is rich in houses;
  R104213 I'm the child of a King
Buerge, C. G.
  Remember thy Creator, while
  'Tis midnight and the Saviour
  Troubled soul, thy God is
Buermeyer, Ferdinand F.
  Sleep, baby, sleep! Thy mother
Buffum, Herbert
  My heart is so happy in Jesus;
  R103901 I intend to go
Bugbee, Emily
  Church of God, whose conquer-

ing
Bulfinch, Stephen Greenleaf, 1809-70
  Hail to the Sabbath day;
  X103109 Hail to this holy
  Hath not thy heart within
  How glorious is the hour
  Lord, in this sacred hour
Bull, John, 1777-1871
  Let my life be hid in thee
Bullock, William, 1798-1874
  We love the place, O God;
  X111081 We love thy house
Bulmer, Agnes Collinson, 1775-1837
  Thou who hast in Zion laid
Bunyan, John, 1628-88
  Blest be the day when moved
  He that is down needs fear no
  He who would valiant be;
  X111657 Who would true valor
Burder, George, 1752-1832
  Sweet the time, exceeding
Burdsall, Richard, 1735-1824
  The voice of free grace cries
Burgess, George, 1809-66
  While o'er the deep thy servants
Burgess, Walter H.
  Again as daylight fades
Burke, Christian, 1859-1944
  Lord of life and King of glory
Burke, Herbert C.
  I shall approach the altar
Burkitt, Francis Crawford, 1864-1933
  Our Lord, his Passion ended
Burleigh, William Henry, 1812-71
  Abide not in the realm
  For the deep love that kept
  From lips divine, like healing
  Lead us, O Father, in the
  O, deem not that earth's
  Still will we trust though
Burmeister, Franz Joachim, d1672
  O blessed Babe divine
Burnett, Vivian

O, when we see God's mercy
Burnham, Richard, 1749-1810
   Jesus, thou art the sinner's
Burns, James Drummond, 1823-
64
   As helpless as a child
   At thy feet, our God and
   For thee, my God, for thee
   Hushed was the evening hymn
   Still with thee, O my God;
      X109227 Still, still with thee
   This night, O Lord, we bless
   Thou, Lord, art love
   Thou who didst on Calvary
Burntvedt, T.O.
   God is faithful, He will never
Burr, Amelia Josephine, 1878-
   O Lord of Love! shall we not
Burroughs, E.A., 1882-1934
   Lord God, from whom all life
Burroughs, John, 1837-1921
   Serene I fold my hands
Burrow, S.E.
   Let not thy hands be slack
Burrowes, Elizabeth
   God of the ages, by whose
      hand ca.1863
Burt, Bates Gilbert, 1878-1948
   O God of youth, whose Spirit
Burton, Henry, 1840-1930
   Break, day of God, O break
   Come for the feast is spread
   O King of kings, O Lord
   O Maker of the sea and sky
   There is an arm that never
   The day is past; the shadows
   There's a light upon
Burton, John, 1773-1822
   Holy Bible, book divine
Burton, John, 1803-77
   O what praises shall we render
   Our Father hears us when we
   Remember thy Creator now
   Saviour, thee my heart I;
      X108749 Saviour, while my
Busch, Calvin A.
   Dear Lord, today, our child
Butcher, Edmund, 1757-1822
   Great God, as seasons
Butcher, John Williams, 1857-
1937
   I thank thee, Lord, for life
Butler, C.J.

Since Christ my soul from
   sin; R106520 O alleluia,
   yes, 'tis
Butler, Henry Montagu, 1833-
1918
   "Lift up your hearts!" We
   lift
   O merciful and holy
Butler, Mary
   Looking upward every day
Butler-Thwing, Francis W.
   Our God leads onward
Buzzard, Rufus
   As the dawn was calmly;
      R107595 O, spread the
      message
Byler, Elsie
   O, thou the great eternal
   One
Byrom, John, 1690-1763
   "Cheer up, desponding soul."
   Christians, awake, salute
   My spirit longs for thee
Byron, George Gordon, Lord
Byron, 1788-1824
   Eternal spirit of the chain-
   less

C

Caddell, Cecilia Mary, 1813-77
   Behold the lilies of the field
   By the blood that flowed;
      R104813 Jesus, Savior,
      hear
   By the first bright Easter;
      R104993 King of glory,
      hear
   I lift mine eyes unto the hills
Caird, George Bradford, 1917-
   Almighty, Father, who for
   us
Calabrian Shepherds hymn:
   As darker, darker see
   Longfellow, Samuel (possible
   translator)
A Calendar of country song
   O that I as right and true
Callin, R.W., 1886-1951
   Long ago, when heathen dark-
   ness
Calvin, John, 1509-64
   I greet thee, who my sure

Camerarius, Joachim, 1500-74
    In tenebris nostrae et densa
        caligne mentis 15thc.
    When in the hour of utmost
Camm, Bede, O.S.B.
    Hail Mary, full of grace
Cammerhof, Johann Friedrich,
1721-51
    Lord Jesus, I pray, on earth
Camp, Mabel Johnston
    Lift up your heads, Pilgrims;
    R103242 He is coming again
Campbell, A. Christian hymn
    book.
    Here, Saviour, we would
        come
Campbell, J. Comprehensive
    hymnbook, 1837
    A glory in the word we find
Campbell, John, 1845-1914
    Unto the hills around do I
Campbell, Margaret C., d1841
    Praise ye Jehovah! praise
Campbell, Margaret C.
    Praise ye the Lord! Praise
        ye
Campbell, Marion Susan
    Angels at the Saviour's birth
    Christ comes again with holy
Campbell, Robert, 1814-68
    They come, God's messengers
Campbell, Susan F.
    In Love divine all earth-born
Campbell, Thomas, 1777-1844
    Men of England, who inherit
Campbell, Vera
    God of the nations, hear our
Campian, Thomas, 1567-1620
    Never weather-beaten sail
    Sing a song of joy, praise
    The man of life upright
Canadian national anthems, etc.
    see ---. In days of yore;
    Murray. Our loved Dominion;
    Weir. O Canada
Canitz, Friedrich Rudolph
    Ludwig von, 1654-99
    Come, my soul, thou must be
    Seele, du musst munter wer-
        den!
Cannon, Tracy Y.
    Come, rejoice, the King of
    Praise the Lord with heart

Canton, William, 1845-1926
    Hold thou my hands!
    Through the night thy angels
    When the herds were watch-
        ing
Cardoza, Elizabeth C.
    We met them on the common
        way
Carey, William
    Jesus loves me, Jesus loves
        me
Carlyle, Joseph Dacre, 1758-
1804
    Lord, when we bend before
        thy
Carlyle, Thomas, 1795-1881
    So here hath been dawning
Carmelite hymn.
    Salve, mater misericordiae
A Carmelite Nun.
    Hail, all hail, sweet youth
    O sweet Infant Jesus, we hail
Carmen, Bliss, 1861-
    Lord of my heart's elation
    We are adventurers who come
        (with R. Hovey)
Carmichael, Amy Wilson,
1867-1951
    Dear Lord, for all in pain
Carnett, Ellis L.
    "It is finished," said
Carney, Julia A., 1823-
    Little drops of water, little
    Think gently of the erring
Carols will be found under head-
    ings such as: English tradi-
    tional; German traditional;
    Traditional; etc.
Carpenter, Edward, 1844-1929
    England, arise! The long,
        long
Carpenter, William Boyd, 1841-
1918
    Before thy throne, O God, we
    Now another stage of travel
Carruth, Mrs. Roy
    Swiftly we're turning life's;
    R104444 Into our hands
Carruth, William H., 1859-
    A haze on the far horizon
Carter, Henry Child, 1875-1954
    Give me, O Christ, the
        strength

Carter, R. Kelso,
  Standing on the promises
Cary, Phoebe, 1824-71
  One sweetly solemn thought
Cary, Alice, 1820-71
  My God, I feel thy wondrous
Casartelli, Bishop.
  Heart of Jesus! golden chalice
Case, Elizabeth York
  There is no unbelief; whoever
Cassaday, Lillian Weaver, 1861-
1914
  O Christians, leagued together;
    R100210 All hail our glor-
    ious
Cassel, E. Taylor, 1849-1930
  From over hill and plain;
    R107975 On to victory
  I am a stranger here, within;
    R110210 This is the message
Castellain, Lewie Prittie
  O Father, may we bear each
Caswall, Edward, 1814-78
  Alleluia! alleluia! Let the
    holy anthem
  Days and moments quickly
  If thou wouldst life attain
  O Jesus Christ, if aught there
  O Jesus Christ, remember
  See, amid the winter's snow;
    R103091 Hail, thou ever-
    blessed; X108787 See! in
    yonder manger
  Sleep, holy Babe, upon thy
  This is the image of our;
    R106020 Most holy Mary;
    X110209 This is the image
Caswall, Miss L.T.
  I am the way, the truth, the
Catholic hymnal, 1860
  Lord, in thy presence dread
  Spirit of wisdom, turn our
Cawood, John, 1775-1852
  Almighty God, thy word is;
    X100373 Almighty God ...
    sown
  Hark! what mean those holy
Cennick, John, 1718-55
  Be present at our table, Lord
  Be with me, Lord, Where'er I
  Blessed Lord, what shall we
  Brethren, let us join to bless
  Children of the heavenly King

Dear Saviour, we bless thee
Ere I sleep, for every favor
Go, follow the Saviour
Hail, Alpha and Omega, hail
Hail, Church of Christ,
  bought
How heart-affecting Christ to
I kneel in spirit at my Saviour's
I love the Lord who died for
I will a little pilgrim be
Jesus, my all, to heaven is
Jesus, thou art my salvation
Lamb of God, my Saviour
Lo! He comes with clouds;
  X105339 Lo, He cometh
No farther go tonight, but
O if the Lamb had not been
O Thou, who on earth didst
Rise, my soul, adore thy
Saviour and Regenerator
The child sweetly rests
The doctrine of our dying;
  X101207 Christ is our
  Master
The holy Child Jesus
Thou dear Redeemer, dying
Though but a little child, I
Though I'm in body full of
We thank thee, Lord, for this;
  X102959 Great God, we
  praise; X111153 We thank
  thee Lord
What, my soul, should bow
When Christ, our Saviour,
  did
Červenka, Matthias see Czer-
  wenka, Matthias
Chadwick, James, 1813-82
  Jesus, my God, behold at;
    X104756 Jesus, my Lord;
    R107451 O, pardon me,
    Jesus
Chadwick, John White, 1840-1904
  Another year of setting suns
  Backward looking o'er the
    past
  Come, let us sing a tender
  Eternal Ruler of the cease-
    less
  It singeth low in every heart
  Now sing we a song for the
  O Love divine, of all that is
  O thou whose perfect goodness

Spirit of God, in thunder
Thou glorious God, before
Thou mighty God, who didst of
Thou whose spirit dwells in
Thy seamless robe conceals
What has drawn us thus apart
Chamberlain, John M.
We're marching on to glory
Chamberlain, Thomas, 1810-92
O guardian of the Church
Chandler, John, 1806-76
Above the clear blue sky
Chao, Tzu Ch'en, 1888-
Golden breaks the dawn
Jesus merciful, Jesus pitying
My hearts looks in faith
Ne'er forget God's daily care
Praise our father for this
Praise our God above
Rise to greet the sun
Chapin, Edwin Hubbell, 1814-
80
Our Father God! Not face to
Chapman, Mrs. E.W.
Closer to thee, my Father;
R101326 Closer with the
cords
Go out and gather the golden
With friends on earth we meet;
X108096 Our friends on
earth; R111217 We'll never
say
Chapman, J. Wilbur, 1859-1918
Jesus! what a Friend for;
R100348 Alleluia! what a
One day when heaven was filled;
R105326 Living, He loved
me
Charles, David, 1762-1834
From heavenly Jerusalem's
Charles, Elizabeth Rundle,
1828-96
Come and rejoice with me
Is thy cruse of comfort;
X110767 True, the heart
Never further than thy cross
No Gospel like this feast
Praise ye the Father for his;
X108333 Praise ye our
Father
Charlesworth, Vernon J., 1939-
The Lord's our Rock, in Him;
R105970 Mighty Rock in a

R107115 O Jesus is a
Rock
Charteris, Archibald Hamilton,
1835-1908
Believing fathers oft have
Chatfield, Allen William, 1808-
96
For ever we would gaze on
thee
Chaucer, Geoffrey, 1340?-1400
Now welcome, Summer, with
Cheevers, Commonplace book of
American poetry, 1831
The twilight falls, the night
Cheney, Ednah Dow, 1824-1904
At first I prayed for Light
Cherry, Edith Gilling, 1872-97
I have heard thy voice, Lord
We rest on thee, our shield
Cherryman, Myrtle Koon.
O, Native Land, how fair
Chester, Henrietta Mary, 19th c
Come, let us all with one
Chester ms., ca 1425
He who made the starry skies;
X108418 Qui creavit,
coelum
Chesterton, Frances, d 1938
How far is it to Bethlehem?
Chesterton, Gilbert Keith,
1874-1936
It is something to have wept
O God of earth and altar
The Christ-child lay on
Mary's
Child songs.
For air and sunshine pure
Childress, J.H.
Upon the first day of the week;
R110393 Though others may
Childs, R.W.
Lo! the clouds have burst;
R108887 Shout for joy, ye
Chinese (authorship unknown)
Chaun dong whan lo tsan mei;
R102656 God is forever
Father, long before creation
Let us joyfully give praise
Chippewa (Indians) traditional
Upon the mountain top alone
Chisholm, Thomas O., 1866-
1960
"Great is thy faithfulness"

Living for Jesus, a life that;
  R107122 O Jesus, Lord
Chord, S. H.
  Some sweet day when life is
Chorley, Henry Fothergill, 1808-
72
  God the Omnipotent! King,
    who; X102693 God, Lord of
    Sabaoth; X102811 God the
    All-merciful; X102812 God
    the All-terrible; X102813
    God the Almighty One
Christiansen, Avis Burgeson,
1895-
  Up Calvary's mountain one;
    R100945 Blessed Redeemer
Christie, A. J.
  To Jesus' Heart all burning
Christierson, Frank von, 1900
  As men of old their first fruits
    brought
  Break forth, O living light of
    God.
Chubb, Percival, 1860-
  Hail we now this happy morn
  Light of Ages, shed by man;
    X105263 Light of conscience
  We lift our hearts in thanks
Church, Edward Alonzo, 1844-
1929
  Almighty Builder, bless, we
  O thou to whom in prayer
    and
Church-Gallery book, Dorset
  Let Christians all with joyful
  Rejoice and be merry in songs
Church melodies, 1858
  We bless thee for thy peace
Church of Scotland, 1745
  The Saviour died, but rose
The Churchman (?), 1858
  Is this Jesus, then the Lord
Churton, Edward, 1800-74
  God of grace, O let thy light
  Earth, with all thy thousand
  If our God had not befriended
Claggett, Martha, 1692-1773
  O Lord, in me fulfill whatever
Clare, John, 1793-1864
  A Stranger once did bless
Clare, Thomas Charles Hunter,
  1910- see Hunter-Clare,
    T. C., 1910-

Clark, Alexander, 1835-79
  Heavenly Father, bless me
Clark, Emily V.
  O God of mercy! hearken now
Clark, Thomas Curtis, 1877-
1953
  God is not far from any one
    of
  I sought his love in sun and
  Our faith is in the Christ
    who
  The touch of human hands
  Thou Father of us all
  Where restless crowds are
  Who goes there, in the
    night
  Who will build the world
    anew
  Your goal was not some
    island
Clark, W. H.
  All praise to Him who reigns;
    R100914 Blessed be the
    name
Clarke, C. Erskine, 1871-1926
  O, David was a shepherd lad
Clarke, Dumont, 1883-
  We care for our Lord's
    acres
Clarke, Harry D., 1888-
  Into my heart, into my heart
Clarke, James Freeman, 1810-
88
  Brother, hast thou wandered
  Father, to us thy children
  To Him who children blessed
  To thee, O God in heaven,
    this
Clarke, Samuel Childs, 1821-
1903
  Now a new year opens
Clarke, William Newton
  Let men their brethren know
Clarkson, Edith Margaret, 1915-
  We come, O Christ, to thee
Claudius, Matthias, 1740-1815
  We plow the fields, and
    scatter; R100205 All good
    gifts; X111099 We plough
    the fields
  Wir pflügen und wir streuen
Clausen, Martha
  And now we must bid one

Clausnitzer, Tobias, 1619-81
　Dearest Jesu, we are here
　(see also the easily confused:
　Schmolck. Blessed Jesus,
　here are we)
　Here in thy presence we ap-
　　pear
　Liebster Jesu, wir sind hier
　Look upon us, blessed Lord
　We all believe in one True
　　God; X111011 We believe
　　in One
　Wir glauben all' an einen
Clayton, Edith
　Father, we come, with youth
Clayton, P.B.
　Come, kindred, upstand in the
　Trudge on, singing praise for
Clayton, William
　Come, come, ye Saints, no
　　toil
　When first the glorious light
Cleator, Alice Jean
　O Father, lead us gently by;
　　R102212 Fears oft affright
Clegg, William
　Let earth's inhabitants rejoice
Clemens, Christian Gottfried,
　ca 1750-1825
　O thou God of our salvation
Clements, John R.
　In the land of fadeless day;
　　R102803 God shall "wipe
　　away"
　Like a shepherd, tender, true
Clephane, Elizabeth Cecilia,
　1830-69
　Beneath the cross of Jesus
　There were ninety and nine
Cleveland, Benjamin, 1733-1811
　O, could I find, from day to
Clock, Leenaert
　O Gott Vater, wir loben dich.
　　1625
　Our Father God, thy name we
Clough, Arthur Hugh, 1819-61
　Say not, "The struggle naught"
Clough, Samuel O'Maley
　I have a Saviour, He's plead-
　　ing; R102324 For you I am
　　praying
Clute, Oscar, 1837-1901
　O Love of God most full

Coates, Florence Earle, 1850-
　I thank thee that how-e'er we
Coates, J.B.
　Living below in this old;
　　R111540 Where could I go
　Workers on a building rare
Coblentz, Stanton A.
　I would not reach the moun-
　　tain's
Cockburn-Campbell, Margaret
　see Campbell, Margaret C.
　1808-41
Codner, Eliza.
　Lord, I hear of showers of;
　　R101986 Even me, even
　　me, Let
Coffin, Charles, 1676-1749
　Another day is past and gone
　As now the sun's declining
　Christ is our Head, our
　　Strength
　Creator of the world, to thee
　God from on high hath heard
　Great mover of all hearts
　Happy are they, they that
　　love
　His trial o'er, and now be-
　　neath
　In the Light all light
　Instantis adventum Dei
　Jordanis oras praevia
　Let sighing cease and woe
　Lo, from the desert homes
　Lo, the pilgrim Magi leave
　Lord of the hearts of men
　Maker of earth, to thee alone
　Now with the declining sun
　O Holy Spirit, Lord of grace
　O Lord, how joyful 'tis to
　　see
　O Saviour, who for man hast
　O scorned and outcast Lord
　On Jordan's bank the Baptist's
　　X107949 On Jordan's ...
　　the Herald's
　The advent of our God;
　　X109408 The advent ...
　　King
　The splendours of thy glory
　What beauteous sun-surpass-
　　ing
　What star is this, so radiant
　What star is this, with beams

Coffman, J. S.
  O, the bliss of loved ones
  O weary wanderer, come home;
    R103382 Help me, dear
    Saviour
Coffman, S. F.
  Extol the love of Christ
  In thy holy place we bow
  We bless the name of Christ
Coffman, see also Kauffman
Coghill, Anna Louisa (Walker),
1836-1907
  Work, for the night is coming
Cohen, Aaron
  Descend, descend, O Sabbath
Colby, Kate L.
  Be true and list the voice
Cole, L. F.
  Birds are singing, woods are;
    R111161 We, thy children,
    join
Cole, Samuel Valentine, 1851-
  O thou who sealest up the past
Coleman, E. G., 1872-
  Christian, let your burning
Coleridge, Samuel Taylor, 1772-
1834
  God! Let the torrents like a
  He prayeth best who loveth
  O sweeter than the marriage-
    feast
  Sleep, sweet babe! My cares
Coles, Abraham
  We cannot build alone
Coles, Vincent Stuckey Stratton,
1845-1929
  Almighty Father, Lord most
    high
  O Shepherd of the sheep
  We pray thee, heavenly Father,
  Ye who own the faith of Jesus
Colesworthy, Daniel C., 1810-
93
  While we lowly bow before
    thee
Collection. Baltimore, 1800
  Sing, my soul, his wondrous
A Collection of Psalms and hymns
  for St Mary's and St Giles.
  Reading, 1830
  "It is finished!" Shall we
Colletet, Francois
  "O, I have seen a king's new"

"Quoi, ma voisine, est-tu"
Collier, Edward Augustus, late
19th c
  As the hart when noon is
  Bless, O Lord, we pray thee
  I love the Lord, because
  Lord, to thee my soul is
  No longer, Lord, despise me
  O God, arise! and by thy
    might
  O Lord, who hast the table
  On the cross is One uplifted
  The law that the Lord has;
    X109574 The heavens in
    their
Collins, Henry, 1827-1919
  Jesu, meek and lowly
  Jesus, my Lord, my God,
    my All; X104762 Jesus,
    my Lord, my Life
Collyer, Robert, 1823-
  Unto thy temple, Lord, we
    come
Collyer, William Bengo, 1782-
1854
  Deign this union to approve
  Great God, what do I see and
  Haste, traveler, haste! the
  Morning breaks upon the tomb
  Return, O wanderer, return;
    X108503 Return! Return! O
Cologne Psalter, 1638
  To us in Bethlehem city
  Zu Bethlehem geboren
Cologne Psalteriolium, 1710
  I love thee, O thou Lord most
Colum, Padraic, 1881-
  Now in the tomb is laid
Comenius, John Amos, 1592-
1670
  When my lips can frame no
Compton, Richard
  God, our Father, made the
  Who made ocean, earth, and
    sky
Concord Anthem book, 1925
  Lead me, Lord, lead me in
    thy
Conder, Eustace Rogers, 1820-
92
  Ye fair green hills of Galilee
Conder, George William, 1821-
74

All things praise thee, Lord
Conder, Josiah, 1789-1855
  Alleluia! Raise, O raise
  Be merciful, O God of grace
  Beyond, beyond that boundless
  Bread of heaven, on thee we
  Day by day the manna fell
  Father, now thy sinful child
  Heavenly Father, to whose
    eye
  How shall I follow Him I
    serve
  Lord, in this blest and hallow-
    ed
  Lord, 'tis not that I did
  Now with angels round
  O Comfort to the weary see
  Hymns of the English Conf.
  O give thanks to Him who
    made
  O thou, who givest all our
  Praise the God of all creation:
    X108275 Praise ... our
    salvation
  The heavens declare His glory
  The Lord is King! lift up thy
  Thou art the everlasting Word;
    R111863 Worthy, O Lamb
  'Tis not that I did choose
    thee
Confucius, 551-497, B.C.
  Let him who would excel
Congregational Church Hymnal.
  1887
  Behold the eternal King and
Congregational Collection
  O thou, who didst the temple
Conover, Howard J., 1850-1922
  O God, we pray for all man-
    kind
Consterdine, James, 1852-1925
  Hark, hark my soul! The
    voice; R102880 Gospel of
    Jesus
Contes, Jean-Baptiste de, 1601-
  79
  Spouse of Christ, in arms
Conway, John Placid, 1855-
  Hail full of grace and purity
Cook, Henry, 1788-1868
  Jesus, Shepherd of the sheep
Cook, J., 1736-61
  Lamb of God beloved

Cook, John T.
  There'll be no shadows;
    R110798 'Twill all be joy
Cook, Russell Sturgis, 1811-64
  Just as thou art, without one
Cooke, Greville, 1894-
  Jesus Christ, my heart's
    true
Cooke, Rose Terry, 1827-92
  I bring my hymn of thankful-
    ness
Cooke, William, 1821-94
  In exile here we wander
Cook, Joseph Simpson
  Gentle Mary laid her child
Cooper, Arthur Eugene, 1872-
  1944
  The men of the Church
Cooper, Edward, 1770-1833
  Father of all, whose love;
    X102145 Father of heaven
Cooper, George, 1840-
  Star of the East, O Bethle-
    hem
  There are lonely hearts to;
    R102854 Going by, going
    by
Coote, Constance, 1844-1936
  For all who watch tonight
  In the quiet consecration
Coote, Maude Oswell, 1852-
  1935
  The son of consolation
Copeland, Benjamin, 1855-
  Christ's life our code, His
  Our fathers' God, to thee we
Copenhaver, Laura Scherer,
  1868-1940
  Heralds of Christ, who bear
Coppée, Henry
  Safe upon the billowy deep
Corelli, Marie
  In our hearts celestial voices
Cornaby, H.
  Who's on the Lord's side?
    Who?
Cornelius, Carl A. Peter, 1824-
  74
  Drei König wandern aus
  The holly's up, the house is
  Three kings from Persian
    lands
  Wie schön geschmuckt der

Cornelius, Maxwell N.
  Not now, but in the coming;
    R109990 Then trust in God
Cornell, W. D.
  Far away in the depths of my;
    R108207 Peace! peace!
Cornish, William, d 1523
  Pleasure it is To hear
Corolla Hymnorum, Cologne,
  1806
  O thou immortal, holy Light ;
    X107861 O ... Light Divine
Cosner, W. F.
  Often weary and worn on the;
    R110067 There is rest by
    and
Coster, George Thomas, 1835-
  1912
  From north and south and
    east
  King of the City Splendid
  Lord God Almighty, in thy
    hand
Collett, Samuel, 18th c
  Through all the various shifting
  March on, O soul, with strength
  O God, our Father, throned
  We join with all, in every
Cotterill, Jane Boak, 1790-1825
  O Thou, who hast at thy com-
    mand
Cotterill, Thomas, 1779-1823
  Eternal Spirit, God of truth
  Great God of Abraham, hear
  Help us, O Lord, thy yoke
  In memory of the Saviour's
  Jesus! exalted far on high
  Let songs of praises fill
  Lord, cause thy face on us
  O'er the realms of pagan
  Our God is love; and all his;
    X108102 Our God ... his
    sons
Cottle, Joseph, 1770-1853
  Mighty Lord, extend thy king-
    dom
Cotton, George Edward Lynch,
  1813-66
  We thank thee, Lord, for this
Cottrell, R. F.
  O solemn thought! and can it
    be
  The time is near when Zion's

The wonders of redeeming
  love
Cousin, Anne Ross, 1824-1906
  O Christ, when burden bowed
  O now is the time to remem-
    ber
  The sands of time are sink-
    ing
Coverdale, Miles, 1487-1569
  Christ is now risen again
  Now blessed be thou, Christ
Cowley Carol book, 1902
  This joyful Eastertide;
    R103014 Had Christ, that
    once; R104147 If Christ
    who once
Cowper, Frances Maria Madan,
  1727-97
  My span of life will soon be
Cowper, William, 1731-1800
  A glory gilds the sacred
    page; X111273 What glory
    gilds; X109846 The Spirit
    breathes
  God moves in a mysterious
    way; X111921 Ye timid
    saints
  God of my life, to thee I
    call; X102737 God ... on
    thee
  Hark, my soul! it is the Lord
  Heal us, Immanuel! Hear our
  Hear what God the Lord hath
  In thy holy contemplation
  Jesus, where'er thy people;
    X107343 O Lord, where'
    er thy
  My former hopes are fled
  My Saviour, whom absent I
    love
  My song shall bless the Lord
  O for a closer walk with
    God
  O Lord, my best desire fulfil
  Sometimes a light surprises
  There is a fountain filled
  'Tis my happiness below
  What various hindrances we
  Ye sons of earth, prepare
    the
Cox, Christopher Christian,
  1816-82
  Silently the shades of evening

Cox, Luther J.
  An alien from God and a
Cox, Samuel K.
  Lord, thou hast promised
    grace
Coxe, Arthur Cleveland, 1818-96
  How beauteous were the marks;
    X110515 Thy works, how
    beauteous
  In the silent midnight
  O walk with God, and thou
  O where are kings and empires
  O who like thee so calm so
  Saviour, sprinkle many nations;
    X108731 Saviour, quicken
  We are living, we are dwelling;
    R103183 Hark, the waking
    up
  Who is this with garments
Craig, John, 1512-1600
  O Lord, thou art my God
Craig, R.J.
  Ye are the light of the world
Crain, Harry L.
  O blessed Son of God
Cramer, Johann Andreas, 1723-
  88
    Herr! Dir ist Niemand zu ver-
      gleichen!
    Lord, who can be with thee
Crane, William Merriam, 1880-
  Lord Jesus, Son of Mary
  Ye shepherds plains of Bethle-
    hem
Crashaw, Richard, 1613?-49
  Gloomy night embraced
Crasselius, Bartholomäus, 1667-
  1724
    Christ of holiness, the Fountain
    Dir, dir Jehova, will ich
    Holy Jesus! Fountain streaming
    Jehovah, let me now adore
    To thee, O Lord, will I sing
Crawford, Emily May Grimes,
  1864-1927
    Speak, Lord in the stillness
    The Master comes! He calls
    Thy mighty love, O God
Creamer, Louise
  Touch me, Lord Jesus, with
Creighton, Mandell, 1843-1901
  O thou who gavest power to
    love

Crewdson, Jane Fox, 1809-63
  O for the peace that floweth
  O Fount of grace, that run-
    neth
  O Saviour, I have naught to
  O thou, whose bounty fills
    my
  There is no sorrow, Lord,
    too
Croatian traditional
  Hark, the angel voices sing-
    ing
Croly, George, 1780-1860
  Spirit of God, descend upon;
    X109157 Spirit ... dwell
    thou
Cronbach, Abraham
  'Tis not the large, the huge
Cronenwett, Emanuel, 1841-
  1931
    As by one's sin fell all
    Faith is wisdom from on
      high
    Invited, Lord, by boundless
    Lo, in Sion a foundation
    Lord, thy omniscience I
      adore
    Of omnipresent grace I sing
    Of Sion's honor, angels sing
    The Spirit's fruits are peace
    To thee, our Fathers' God
      we
    Unto Caesar let us render
    We have a sure prophetic
      Word
Cropper, Margaret Beatrice,
  1886-
    Jesus' hands were kind hands
    O Christ, whom we may love
    We have a King who came to
Crosby, Fanny, 1820-1915
NOTE: American books use this
    form of her name; British
    books use: Van Alystyne.
    She used many pseudonyms
    which are identified in Jul-
    ian's Dictionary. Others
    presumed are: A.A.F.,
    J.V.C., and Sallie Martin.

    A wonderful Saviour is Jesus;
      R103239 He hideth my soul
    A year of precious blessings

All the way my Saviour leads
Be silent, be silent;
    R110749 Tread softly, tread
Be with me all my journey;
    R100747 Be with me every
Behold! a royal army; R110903
    Victory, victory
Behold me standing at the door
Blessed assurance, Jesus is;
    R110196 This is my story
Come with thy sins; R103200
    Haste thee away, why
Conquering now, and still;
    R106327 Not to the strong
Don't forget the Sabbath;
    R111211 Welcome, welcome,
Go as a witness for Jesus;
    R109361 Tell how He pities
God of our strength enthroned
Great is the love that brought
Have you sought for the sheep
He is coming, the Man of Sor-
    rows; R100319 Alleluia!
    Alleluia
Heavenly Father, we beseech;
    R100904 Bless the words we
Here from the world we turn
Hide me, O my Saviour, hide;
    R103458 Hide me, hide me
Hold thou my hand! so weak
Holy, holy, holy is the Lord
I am thine, O Lord; R101832
    Draw me nearer
If I come to Jesus, He will
In thy cleft, O Rock of ages
Jesus is tenderly calling;
    R101126 Calling today
Jesus, keep me near the cross;
    R104347 In the cross
Keep Thou my way, O Lord
Loving Saviour, hear my cry;
    R101694 Dear Jesus, receive
Mighty Rock, whose towering;
    R110841 Unto Thee, unto
    Thee
More like Jesus would I be
"Nearer the cross!" My heart
Never shone a light so fair
Now just a word for Jesus
O Christian, awake! 'tis the;
    R109196 Stand like the brave
O hear my cry, be gracious
    now; R104521 I've wandered

far
O the unsearchable riches;
    R108375 Precious, more
    precious
O wonderful words
O, wondrous name, by proph-
    ets; R109932 The wonder-
    ful!
Only a step to Jesus
Only thy tender love,
    Saviour; R108035 Only to
    follow Thee
Out on the mountain, sad;
    R101125 Calling to thee
Pass me not, O gentle
    Saviour; R108734 Saviour,
    Saviour,
Praise Him, praise him!
    Jesus
Redeemed, how I love to
Rescue the perishing
Safe in the arms of Jesus
Saviour, more than life;
    R101996 Every day, every
    hour
Search me, O Lord, and try
Some day the silver cord;
    R100431 And I shall see
    Him
Speed away, speed away on
    your
Take the world, but give me;
    R107649 O, the height
Tell me the story of Jesus
The Lord in Sion reigneth
The Lord's our Rock (see
    also Charlesworth, V.J.)
Thou my everlasting portion;
    R101323 Close to Thee
Though your sins be as
    scarlet
'Tis the blessed hour of
    prayer; R100926 Blessed
    hour
To God be the glory; R108284
    Praise the Lord
To the work! to the work;
    R110737 Toiling on, toil-
    ing
Troubled heart, thy God is;
    R106528 O, be saved, His
When Jesus comes to reward;
    R106593 O can we say we

are
When my life-work is ended;
  R104027 I shall know Him
Whither, pilgrims, are you
  going (in Golden chain, 1861:
  presumed author)
Will you come, will you come;
  R106968 O happy rest,
  sweet
Would you win a Saviour's
Cross, Ada Cambridge, 1844-
  The dawn of God's dear Sab-
  bath; X109469 The dawn ...
  own
Cross, Allen Eastman, 1864-
  America, America, the shouts
  As stars come with the night
  From out the Rock whence we
  Guide of my spirit on its
  Jesus, kneel beside me
  Maker of stars, Eternal King
  More light shall break
  Mount up with wings as
  eagles
  Pass on the torch, pass on
  The gray hills taught me
  The hidden years at Nazareth
  The stars they sing together
  Thou Fatherland be vast and
  What doth the Lord require
  Wild roars the blast, the
  storm
  Young and radiant, he is
Cross, Frank
  Go forth, strong word of God
Crossman, Samuel, 1624-83
  Jerusalem on high, My song
  My life's a shade, my days
  My song is love unknown
Croswell, William, 1804-51
  Lord, lead the way; X105607
  Lord ... my Saviour;
  X105608 Lord ... our Saviour
Crowell, Grace Noll, 1877-
  Because I have been given
  The day will bring some
Cruciger, Elisabeth Meseritz,
  d 1535
  The only son from heaven
Crum, J.M.C., 1872-
  Let love arise and praise him
  Let us thank the Christ for
  Now the green blade riseth

O God, whose mighty works
  On the moorland of life
  Strong Captain, in thy holy
  Thou Wind of God, whose
  coming
  To God who makes all lovely
Crystal, James
  Take courage, Saints, and
Cummings, A.
  Father, in the morning,
  unto
Cummins, Evelyn Atwater
  I know not where the road
Cummins, James John, 1795-
  1867
  Jesus, Lord of life and glory
  Shall hymns of grateful love
Cumins, Patrick
  Bursting forth from Pharaoh's
  Of that branch in ancient
Cuninggim, Maud M., 1874-
  O living Christ, chief Corner
Currie, Edward C.
  God most truly honored thee
  Mary Immaculate, Mother
  O Bethlehem of holy worth
  O Lord, reprieve the lonely
  The sun in splendor rose
  When Mary, immaculate,
  tender
Curry, R. Donald
  We thank thee Lord for send-
  ing
Curtis, Christine
  As the hart with eager
Curtis, Theodore E.
  Again, our dear redeeming
  Lord
  I wander through the stilly
  Lean on my ample arm
Curwen, John. Standard course,
  1860
  God is near thee, therefore
Curwen, John, 1817-80
  I'm a little pilgrim, and a
Cushing, William Orcutt, 1823-
  Beautiful valley of Eden
  Down in the valley with my;
  R102246 Follow! follow! I
  O safe to the Rock that is;
  R103460 Hiding in thee
  O, to have no Christ
  Ring the bells of heaven;

R102550 Glory, glory! how
Under His wings, I'm safely;
    X110809 Under ... I am
    safely
We are watching, we are wait-
    ing; R111007 We are wait-
    ing
When He cometh, when He;
    R105301 Like the stars
Cutler, J.S.
    Motherhood, sublime, eternal
Cutter, William F., 1801-67
    She loved her Saviour, and to
    Who is thy neighbor? He
    whom
Czamanske, William Martin,
    1873-
    For many years, O God of
Czech traditional.
    From out of a wood did a
    cuckoo
    Little Jesus, sweetly sleep
Czerwenka, Matthias, 1521-69
    How good it is, how pleasant

D

"D.S., 1920"
    Holy, holy, holy, O thou love
Dach, Simon, 1605-59
    Ich bin bei Gott in Gnaden
    1651
    O how blest are ye whose toils
    O wie selig seid ihr doch, ihr
    Frommen 1635
    Through Jesus' blood and merit;
    X110418 Through ... bloody
Dachstein, Wolfgang, 16th c
    An wasserflüssen Babylon
Dahl, Christopher [Kristoffer]
    1758-1809
    Come, O sinner, all is ready
Dakota (Indians) hymn
    Many and great, O God, are thy
    things
Dale, W.T.
    "I am nearing the port"
Dalrymple, A.
    O Lord of hosts, we now
Damrosch, Frank, jr
    God, deigning man to be
Dana, Mary Stanley Bunce
    Shindler, 1810-
    Flee as a bird to your mountain

I'm a pilgrim, and I'm a
O, sing to me of heaven;
    R110091 There'll be no
    Prince of Peace, control
Daniel ben Judah, 14th c. "The
    Yigdal": see Jewish doxology
Daniels, E.D.
    Thy will, O Lord, not
    mine
Danish traditional
    Fryd dig, du Kristi Brud
    (ca 1600)
    In God, my Saviour, I put
    my (1600)
    In Jesus I find rest and
    peace (1740)
    O Bride of Christ, arise
    (ca 1600)
    O day full of grace, which
    we (14th c)
Darby, John Nelson, 1800-82
    God and Father we adore
    thee
    O eyes that are weary
    Though faint, yet pursuing
Darbyshire, John Russell,
    1880-1948
    At eve, when now he
    breathed
    Great is their joy who hide
    Life and health are in the
    Lord Jesus, from thy throne
    O Lord of Life, whose
    power
    Who dreads, yet undismayed
Daries, Frederick R.
    This day in thy dear name
    we
Darmstadt. Gesangbuch, 1698
    Alleluia! Let praises ring
    Alleluia! Lob, Preis und
    Ehr'
    To God be honor, laud
Darwin, Erasmus, 1731-1802
    Roll on, ye stars, exult in
Darwood, W. M'K.
    On Calvary's brow my
    Saviour; R106591 O Cal-
    vary! dark
Dass, Petter, 1647-1707
    Mighty God, to thy dear
    Name
Davenport, T.

Come, all ye sons of God,
who
Davies, Mary Carolyn
Youth of the world, unite
Davies, Samuel, 1723-61
Great God of wonders! all thy
Lord, I am thine, entirely
On thee, our Guardian, God,
we
Davies, William Henry, 1871-
1940
What is this life, if full of
Davieson, Eve
Hear us, Eternal King, hear
Davis, Corie F.
Have I need of aught, O
Davis, Frank M., 1839-96
More like thee, O Saviour, let
Saviour, lead me, lest I stray
Davis, John S.
What was witnessed in the
Davis, O.S. (c1947)
Lord, give us a vision
Davis, Ozora Stearns, 1866-1931
At length there dawns
O holy Spirit, gracious gift
We bear the strain of earthly
Davis, Robert, 1881-1950
I thank thee, Lord, for
Jesus, our brother, strong
Davis, T.A.
When there is peace, where
Davison [Davidson], Anna L.
Purer in heart, O God, help
Davison, W. Hope, 1827-94
Jesus, King of glory 1928
Dawson, William James, 1854-
Chri st must be served indeed
When the golden evening
Day's Psalter, 1561
Al people yt on earth do dwel
Day, George E.
O Master of the callous hand
Dayan, Daniel ben Judah.
The Yigdal see Jewish doxology
Dayman, Edward Arthur, 1807-90
Almighty Father, heaven and
Christ has come for our
Honor and glory, thanksgiving
O Lord, be with is, when we
Sleep thy last sleep, free
"Who is this, with garments"
Dayton, Mary Alice

Eternal mind the Potter is
Dean, Joseph H.
Before Thee, Lord, I bow
my
Dearmer, Geoffrey, 1893-
Those who love and those
who
"To Damascus!" Paul had
When Judas did his Lord
reject
Dearmer, Percy, 1867-1936
NOTE: A letter dated 28/4/64
from Oxford Univ. Pr. to
the author listed the initials
used as pseudonyms by
Percy Dearmer. Frequently
they are initials of hymnals
in which his poems first ap-
peared, Here they are:
A. F., A.G., B.R., E.H.,
N.B. L., O.B.C., O.B.C.V.,
S.P., S.P.B.G., S.P.V.,
S. T., T.S.N. As the books
are being reprinted, Oxford
Univ. Pr. is replacing these
initials with the author's
name.

A brighter dawn is breaking
Ah! think not, "The Lord
... "
All hail to the Power who
Angels and ministers, spirits
As the disciples, when the
Be, Lord, the happy guide
Books of books, our people's
Christ to us across the water
Christian, do you see him
Come now, all people, keep
Crown him upon the throne
Draw us in the Spirit's
tether
Father, who on man dost
God is love; his the care
God, we thank thee; not in
Good-bye! Our school is
over
Good day to you all
Holy God, we show forth
here
Holy Spirit, make us strong
How great the harvest is
In Asia born, from Asia

hailed
In God rejoice! his good
In the place of sorrow, wait-
  ing; X100620 At the cross
  her
Jesus, good above all others
Let us rejoice, the fight is
Life is good, for God contrives
Lo, in the wilderness a voice
Lo, when the day of rest was
Look up, by failure daunted
Lord of health, thou life
Lord, the wind and sea obey
Mercy thou art, Creator,
  Friend
Now April has come
Now join, ye comrades true
Now quit your care
Now thy earthly work is done;
  R105321 Live in peace,
  where
O dear and lovely Brother
O Father above us, our father
O Father in heaven, our father
O Father of goodness, thou
  art
O Father of wisdom and friend-
  ship
O Holy Spirit, God, all
O sing to the Lord now, his
O welcome in our midst
Our babies' names on the
Praise him, praise him, all;
  X108251 Praise ... all ye
Prophets, teachers, true
Quick sympathy, hands that
Rejoice and be glad! he lives
Remember all the people;
  X108472 Remember all God's
Servants of the great
Sing praise to God who spoke
So we lift up our hands and
Take heart, friends; X101159
  Cheer up, friends
The dawn-wind now is waking
The greatness of God in his
The winter's sleep was long
There are a myriad means
They saw the lights shine out
Thou Judge by whom each Em-
  pire
Thou true Vine, that heals
Through north and south and

To the name that is salvation
To thee, who makest all
True Son of Man, thou crown
Unknown and unrewarded
Virtue supreme, thy mighty
We saw not, when thou cam'st
We saw thee not when, far
We wish you many happy re-
  turns
Welcome, day of the Lord
When by fear my heart is
When Christ blessed his;
  R106440 Now sing we of
When Christ had shown God's
Wherefore, O Father, we thy
Who is he whom crowds ac-
  claim
Who within that stable cries
Winds of God unfailing
Winter creeps, Nature sleeps
With Jesus for hero, for
Working together, wary and
Zeal of the Lord, for ever
De Armond, Lizzie
  Have you found rest and
    peace; R107611 O, tell
    what He's
  If you only knew my Saviour
  We sail along toward the;
    R109441 The Christ will
    our
DeChenez, Charitié Lees
  Bancroft, 1841-1923
  Before the throne of God
  The King of glory standeth
Decius, Nikolaus [Nicolaus]
  d 1541
  All glory be to God on high;
    X100196 All glory ... most
    X100199 All glory be to
    thee
  Allein Gott in der Höh sei
  Alone to God on high be
    praise
  Lamb of God, pure and holy;
    X105036 Lamb of God most
    holy
  O Lamb of God, most holy
  O Lamb of God, unspotted
  O, Lamb of God, who, bleed-
    ing
  O Lamm Gottes, unschuldig
  To God on high be thanks

Dietrick, Emma G.
  Abide with me, I need thee
Dillon, George, 1906-
  Obedient they but to a dream
Dillingham, Frances Bent
  All the happy children Gladly
Disciples Hymn book.
  Father, the watches of the
Dix, William Chatterton, 1837-
98
  Alleluia! sing to Jesus
  As with gladness men of old
  Beauteous are the flowers
  Come unto me, ye weary
  In our work, and in our play
  Joy fills our inmost hearts
  Like silver lamps in a distant
  O thou the Eternal Son of God
  Only one prayer today
  The cross is on our brow
  To thee, O Lord, our hearts
  What child is this, who, laid;
    R110221 This, this is Christ
Dixon-Wright, Henry Dixon, 1870-
1916
  To thee, O God, our hearts
Doane, George Washington, 1799-
1859
  Beloved, "It is well!" God's
  Fling out the banner! let it
  Once more, O Lord, thy sign
  Softly now the light of day
  Thou art the way, to thee;
    X110240 Thou ... by thee
Doane, William Croswell, 1832-
1913
  Ancient of Days, who sittest
  To thee, O Father, throned on
Dobell, John. A new selection,
  1806
  Hark, 'tis the Saviour's
  Now is the accepted time
  Sinners, behold that downward
Dober, Anna Schindler, 1713-39
  Lamb of God, who thee receive
Dober, Leonhard, 1706-66
  Christ's love invites us
Dober, Martin, 1703-48
  Jesus, Saviour, I implore
Dobree, Henrietta Octavia deLisle,
1831-94
  Safely, safely gathered in
Dobson, Austin

All-wise, All-great whose
Doddridge, Philip, 1702-51
  And art thou with us, gra-
    cious
  And shall we still be slaves
    (with Watts)
  And will the great eternal
    God
  And will the Judge descend
  Awake, my soul, stretch
    every
  Awake, ye saints, and raise
  Baptized into our Saviour's
  Behold the amazing sight
  Beset with snares on every
  Come, sacred Spirit, from
    above
  Dear Saviour, we are thine
  Do not I love thee, O my
    Lord
  Eternal and immortal King
  Eternal source of every joy
  Father of all, thy care we
  Father of lights, we sing thy
  Father of mercies, send thy
  Father of peace, and God of
  Fountain of good, to own thy
  God of my life, through all
  Grace! 'tis a charming sound
  Great God, we sing that
    mighty; X102960 Great
    God ... guiding
  Hail to the Prince of Life
  Hark! the glad sound! The
  High let us swell our tune-
    ful
  How gentle God's commands
  How rich thy bounty, King of
  How swift the torrent rolls
  Jesus, I love thy charming
  Jesus, my Lord, how rich
    thy; X104796 Jesus, our
    Lord, how
  Jesus, thou Source of life
  Let Sion's watchmen all
    awake
  Lord, let thy goodness lead
  Lord of the Sabbath, hear
    us; X105672 Lord ... hear
    our vows
  Maker of all things, mighty
  My God! the covenant of thy
  My God, thy table now is;

X106076 My God, and is thy; X107222 O Lord! and is thy
My gracious Lord, I own thy
Now let our cheerful eyes
Now let our mourning hearts
Now to the King of heaven (with Watts)
O Fount of good, to own thy
O God of Bethel, by whose hand; X106860 O God of Jacob
O God of heaven and earth
O happy day, that stays my; R103119 Happy day, happy day; X103627 How blessed is the; X106957 O happy day, that
Our heavenly Father calls
Return, my roving heart, return
See Israel's gentle Shepherd; X105347 Lo, Israel's gentle
Shine on our souls, eternal
Sing, O ye ransomed of the
Sing to the Lord, who loud
The King of heaven his table
The Saviour kindly calls
Thine earthly sabbaths, Lord
Thou who wast a child on earth
Tomorrow, Lord, is thine
Triumphant Sion, lift thy
What though the arm of conquering
Why will ye waste on trifling
Ye servants of the Lord
Yes, the Redeemer rose

Dodge, Mary Mapes, 1831-1905
Can a growing child like me X101133 Can a little child

Dodgshun, Ernest, 1876-1944
What service shall we render

Dollard, James B. d 1946
Hail, glorious apostle, St Basil
On Calvary's height the Roman; R109981 Then let us adore

Domer, Harry Tennyson, 1877-
O Church of freedom stand

Domett, Alfred, 1811-87
It was the calm and silent

Donne, John, 1573-1631
Wilt thou forgive that sin, by

X111717 Wilt thou ... where I

Donnelly, Eleanor C.
Sacred Heart in accents

Donnelly, F.P.
Ave, tu Rex Pácis nobiscum

Donohue, James J.
St Joseph God has chosen you

Döring, Carl August, 1783-1844
Father, Son, and Holy Ghost

Dorr, Julia Caroline Ripley, 1825-1913
Heir of all the ages, I
How can I cease to pray for

Doudney, Sarah, 1843-1926
For all thy care we bless
Saviour, now the day is
Sleep on, beloved, sleep
The Master hath come, and He

Dougall, Hugh W.
Jesus of Nazareth, Saviour and

Doughty, A.S.
Soon trials and conflicts of; R111240 We're nearing

Doughty, Nicholas
Today, while the sun shines

Downton, Henry, 1818-85
For thy mercy and thy grace
Lord, her watch, thy church

Drane, Augusta Theodosia, 1823-94
The clouds hang thick
Thou who, hero-like, hast

Draper, Bourne Hall, 1775-1843
Sovereign of worlds, display
Ye Christian heralds, go

Draper, William Henry, 1855-1933
All creatures of our God (see St Francis of Assisi)
From homes of quiet peace
Hush, all ye sounds of war
In our day of Thanksgiving
Lord, through this Holy Week

Drennan, William, 1754-1820
The heaven of heavens cannot

Drese, Adam, 1620-1701
Fairest Bridegroom mind
Jesus, call thou me, from the

Drinkwater, John, 1882-1937

A shining city, one happy
Grant us the will to fashion;
  X111070 We know the paths
Driscoll, John, d 1940
  Glorious Saint whose deeds
  The living God my Shepherd is
Driver, J.M.
  Wonderful story of love
Drucker, Thomas
  Wollt ihr hören, was ist
    geschen, 1557
Drummond, William Hamilton,
  1772-1856
  One cup of healing oil
Drury, Miriam
  Once again to its close
Dubois, Theodore, 1837-1924
  Christ, we do all adore thee
Duclaux, Mme (nee A. Mary F.
  Robinson) 1857-1944
  O thou that movest all
  The mass of unborn matter
    knew
Dudley, William Ewart, 1887-
  The city, Lord, where thy
Dudley-Smith, Timothy, 1926-
  Christ be my leader by night
  Lord, who left the highest
  Tell out, my soul, the great-
    ness
Duffield, George, jr., 1818-88
  Blessed Saviour, thee I love
  Stand up, stand up, for Jesus
Duffield, Samuel Willoughby,
  1843-87
  O, land relieved from sorrow
Dugmore, Ernest Edward, 1843-
  1925
  Almighty Father of all things
Dunbar, William, ca 1465-1530
  Rorate coeli de super
Duncan, Mary Lundie, 1814-40
  Jesus, tender Shepherd, hear
Dungan, Helen
  You can make the pathway;
    R104170 If there's sunshine
Dunham, Barrows, 1905-
  Winter is a cold thing
Dunkerley, William Arthur,
  1852-1941, see Oxenham,
  John, 1852-1941
Dunn, John Randall
  Sing, ye joyous children, sing

We thank thee and we bless
Durfey, Tom, 1653-1723
  All hail to the days that
Dutch traditional
  A message came to a maiden
    (1928)
  Hours and days and years
  Lord Jesus hath a garden
    (17th c)
  O Sion's daughter, where art
  We gather together to ask
    (1625)
  We praise thee, O God, our
  Wilt heden nu treden voor
    God den Heere 16th c
  Wir treten zum Beten vor
    Gott den Herren tr. by
    Budde, 1897
Dutton, Thomas
  Sinners, hear the joyful news
Dwight, Timothy, 1752-1817
  How pleasing is thy voice
  I love thy kingdom, Lord;
    X103971 I love thy Church;
    X103974 I love thy Zion
  Shall man, O God of light
  Sing to the Lord most high
  While life prolongs its

                        E

Earle, J.C., 1821-99
  I will arise and to my Father
East, James T., 1860-1937
  Wise men seeking Jesus
Eastburn, James Wallis, 1797-
  1819
  O Holy, Holy, Holy Lord
Ebel, William
  O, be still, thou soul of
    mine
Eber, Paul, 1511-69
  Helft mir Gott's Güte preisen
  I fall asleep in Jesus'
  In Christi Wunden schlaf' ich
    ein 1638
  In thy dear wounds I fall
  Jesus thy blood and righteous-
    ness (with Zinzendorf)
  Lord Jesus Christ, true man
  The Saviour's blood and (with
    Zinzendorf)
  To God the anthem raising

Wenn wir in höchsten Nöten
sein 1547
When in the hour of utmost
need see Camerarius. When
in the hour.
Lord Jesus Christ, the Prince

Eddis, Edward Wilton, 1825-
1905
Our sins, our sorrows, Lord
Thou standest at the altar

Eddy, Mary Baker, 1821-1910
Blest Christmas morn, though
Brood o'er us with thy shelter-
ing
It matters not what be thy lot
O gentle presence, peace and
O'er waiting harp-strings
Saw ye my Saviour? Heard
ye
Shepherd, show me how to go

Edgar, Mary S., 1889-
God, who touchest earth with
I will follow the upward road

Edmeston, James, 1791-1867
Along my earthly way
As oft with worn and weary
Fountain of grace, rich, full
Lead us, heavenly Father
lead
Little travelers Zionward
O thou, whose mercy guides
my
Roll, on thou mighty ocean
Saviour, breathe an evening;
X108736 Saviour, shed an
Sweet is the light of Sabbath;
X103752 How sweet the
light
Wake, harp of Sion, wake

Edwards, Annie, 1832-
He must reign, who won the

Edwards, Frank, 1898-
God of earth and sea

Edwards, Frederick
God of the nations, who hast

Edwards, Louise Betts
Christian Soul, the times are

Edwards, Robert Lansing
Declare, O heavens, the Lord

Edwards, William, 1798-1879
O thou who hearest prayer

Edworthy, Z. B.
Father, bless us as we part

Ehrenberg-Posse, Katarina
Elizabeth, 1818-80
Merciful Saviour, come and
be
When Christmas morn is
dawning (arr.)

Ela, David Hough, 1831-
The chosen three, on mountain

Eldridge, Jay Glover
God of years, thy love hath

Eliot, Frederick May, 1890-
1958
O thou, to whom the fathers
The night was dark and
stormy

Ellerton, John, 1823-93
Again the morn of gladness;
R102544 Glory be to Jesus
Before the day draws near
its
Behold us, Lord, a little
space
Day by day we magnify thee
God of the living, in whose
Hail to the Lord who comes
In the name which earth
King of saints, to whom the
Lift the strain of High
Now the laborer's task is
o'er
O Father, all creating
O Father, bless the children
O Son of God, our Captain
O thou in whom thy saints
Our day of praise is done
Praise to our God, whose
Praise to the heavenly wis-
dom
Saviour, again to thy dear;
X102073 Father, again to
Thee; X102074 Father,
again to thy
Shine thou upon us, Lord
Sing ye faithful, sing with
The day thou gavest, Lord
The hours of day are over
The Lord be with us as each;
X109635 The Lord ... bend
X109636 The Lord ... walk
This is the day of light;
X110200 This ... day of
rest

Thou, who sentest thine
Throned upon the awful Tree
We sing the glorious conquest
When the day of toil is done
Elliott, Charlotte, 1789-1871
  Christian, seek not yet;
    X102471 Gird thy heavenly
  Ever patient, gentle meek
  God of my life, thy boundless
  Jesus, my Saviour, look on
    me
  Just as I am, without one
  I need no other plea
  Leaning on thee, my Guide
  Let me be with thee, where
  My God, is any hour so sweet
  My God, my Father, while I;
    X106074 My God and Father,
    day by; X106075 My God
    and Father, while I; R
    110506 Thy will be done
  O Holy Saviour, Friend un-
    seen
  O thou, the contrite sinners'
  The Sabbath day has reached
  There is a holy sacrifice
  When waves of trouble round
  Wie ich bin, komm' ich zu
    dir--
  With tearful eyes I look
Elliott, Ebenezer, 1781-1849
  When wilt thou save the people
Elliott, Emily Elizabeth
 Steele, 1836-97
  There came a little child
  Thou didst leave thy throne;
    X110252 Thou dost reign
  Unto Him whose name is holy
Elliott, Julia Anne, 1809-41
  Father, who the light this
  Hail thou bright and sacred
  We love thee, Lord, yet not
Elliott, Norman, 1893-
  "Seek ye first the kingdom"
Ellis, Frederick, 1835-
  With joyfulness and longing
Ellis, G.E. Psalms and hymns.
 Boston, 1845
  Ere to the world again we go
Ellis, Henry Havelock, 1859-
 1939
  Onward brothers, march still
Ellis, Lethal A.

There's a God who's standing;
  R111960 You can't do
  wrong
Ellsworth, W.W.
  Saviour, hear us, we pray;
    R104714 Jesus, Lord,
    hear
Elpis, ca 500
  Lead us, great teacher Paul
  With golden splendour and
    with
Elven, Cornelius, 1797-1873
  With broken heart and con-
    trite
Emerson, George D.
  Thanks be to God for his
Emerson, Ralph Waldo, 1803-
 82
  We love the venerable house
  We sing of golden mornings
Emilie Juliana, countess ...
 see Amilie Juliane, countess
  ... 1637-1706
Emrick, Ernestine Hoff, 1918-
  O master of all, come we to
Emurian, Ernest K., 1912-
  We dedicate this temple
Enfield, William, 1741-97
  Behold, where in a mortal
    form
English traditional, etc.
  A babe is born all of a may
    (15th c)
  A babe is born of high nature
    (15th c) R111321 What tidings
  A child this day is born;
    R102519 Glad tidings to all
  A virgin most pure, as the
    X100076 A virgin ... did
    tell; R108451 Rejoice and
    be merry
  About the field they piped
    (ca 1450)
  Adam lay abounden, Bounden
    in (15th c)
  All under the leaves, the
  All you that are to mirth
    (17th c)
  As I passed by a riverside
    (13th-14th c)
  As I sat on a sunny bank
  As it fell out one May
    morning

As it fell out upon one day
As Jacob with travel was
  weary; R100347 Alleluia to
  Jesus
Awake, awake, good people
  all
Awake, awake, ye drowsy
  souls; X102625 God bless
  the ruler; X104500 It was
  early in the; R109045 So
  God send you all
Come all ye faithful Christians
Come all you worthy Christian
  men
Come all you worthy gentlemen
Deck the hall with boughs
Down in yon forest there stands;
  R100186 All bells in para-
  dise
God bless the master of this
God rest you merry (18th c);
  R107777 O Tidings of com-
  fort
God's dear Son without
Good people all, this Christmas
Green grow'th the holly
Here we come awassailing
I saw a fair maiden (15th c);
  R105831 Lullay my liking
I saw three ships come sail-
  ing
I sing of a maiden that is
  makèless (15th c)
In Bethlehem, that fair city
  (15th c)
It was on Christmas day
It was on Holy Wednesday
I've brought you here a bunch
Joseph was an old man;
  X100553 As Joseph was
  a-walking; X109982 Then
  Mary took her; X102010
  Exortum est in love
King Pharim sat a-musing
Let Christians all with one
  (18th c?)
Lully, lulley, lully, lulley
Make we joy now in this feast
  (15th c)
Make we merry, both more and
  (ca 1500)
Now is Christmas y-come
Now the holly bears a berry

Nowell sing we, both all
  (ca 1450)
O, Joseph being an old man
O mortal man, remember
  well
On Christmas night all
Out of the orient crystal
  (17th c)
Out of your sleep arise and
  (15th c)
Over yonder's a park which;
  R100186 All bells in
  paradise
Remember us poor Mayers
  all
Rise up, rise up, you merry
St Stephen was a holy man;
  R107387 O man, do never
The angel Gabriel from God
The Babe in Bethlem's man-
  ger; R106490 Nowell,
  Nowell, now sing
The first good joy that Mary
  (15th c)
The first nowell the angel
  did
The holly and the ivy
The Lord at first did Adam
The moon shines bright, and
There was a star in David's
  (13th-14th c)
This endris night (15th c)
This is the truth sent from
This new Christmas carol
Tidings true there come
  new (15th c)
Tomorrow shall be my danc-
  ing X100775 Before Pilate;
  X104445 Into the desert
Wassail, wassail, all over
Welcome be thou, heaven-
  king (15th c); X111213
  Welcome Yule, thou
What are they that are but
  one (1625, or earlier);
  R104412 In those twelve
  days
When Caesar Augustus had
  raised
When Christ was born of
  Mary (ca 1456); R104257
  In excelsis gloria
When Christ was born to set

(15th c)
When Jesus Christ was twelve;
   X111505 When they be-
   reaved
When righteous Joseph wedded;
   R109988 Then sing you all
Enman, William Edgar, 1869-
1950
   Lamb of God, to thee we
Epistle to Diognetus, ca 150
   The great Creator of the
Erfurt Enchiridion, 1527
   O God, our Lord, thy holy
   Word
Erikson, Gustaf
   This solemn hour O let us be
Erskine, Ralph, 1685-1752
   Faith comes by hearing God's
   In thee I live, and move
Esling, Catherine H., 1812-97
   Come unto Me, when shadows
Essenburg, B.
   Unto God, our King, joy and
Estlin, John Prior, 1747-1817
   Eternal Source of life
Eugenie, princess of Sweden
   My heart is longing to praise
Euripides. The Bacchae, ca 407
B.C.
   What else is wisdom? What
   else
Evangelical Theological Seminary.
   Class of 1900
   Servants of the Christ your
Evans, Albert Eubule, d1896
   Lo! the voice of Jesus
   Lord, to thee alone we turn
Evans, I.H.
   Welcome, day of sweet repose
Evans, Jonathan, 1748 or 49-
1809
   Come, thou soul-transforming;
   X101511 Come, thou all-
   transforming
   Hark! the voice of love and
Evans, William Edwin, 1851-
   Come, O thou God of grace
Everest, Charles William 1814-
77
   Take up thy cross, the
   Saviour
Evilsizer, Mrs. L.M.
   Out in the desert the lost;

   R102606 Go to the lost
Saviour, we come to thee;
   R108725 Saviour, O
   Saviour
Evilsizer, R.A.
   The time of the harvest;
   R109604 The laborers
   are few
Ewald, Johannes
   Rise, hero bold, from
   Golgotha
Excell, Edwin O., 1851-1921
   I have a song I love to sing;
   R108912 Since I have
   been
Exeter Collection
   To thee, my heart, eternal
Extrait du Recuiel Louange
et Prière. 4th ed., 1957
   Great God who hast deliver-
   ed

                          F

F.B.P., ca 16th c.
NOTE: An unidentified poet's
   version of St Augustine

   Jerusalem, my happy home
   O mother dear, Jerusalem
   Thy saints are crowned with
   Thy vineyards and thy or-
   chards
   Thy walls are made of
   precious
Faber, Frederick William,
1814-63
   All hail, dear Conqueror,
   all
   All praise to St Patrick
   Blest is the faith, divine;
   R107563 O, Sion's songs
   are
   Dear angel, ever at my side
   Dear Guardian of Mary
   Dear Jesus, ever at my
   side
   Dear little One how sweet
   Faith of our fathers! living;
   R102037 Faith ... holy
   faith; X102039 Faith ...
   (Catholic variant)
   Full of glory, full of wonders

God's glory is a wondrous;
  X110409 Thrice blest is he
Hail bright Archangel, Prince
Hail, holy Joseph, hail!
  Chaste
Hark, hark my soul! angelic;
  R100467 Angels of Jesus;
  R100468 Angels of mercy
Have mercy on us, God most
Holy Ghost, come down upon
I was wandering and weary
I worship thee, most gracious;
  X104114 I worship thee,
  sweet
Jesus, all hail, Who for our;
  X102092 Father, gracious
Jesus, gentlest Saviour, God
Jesus is God! the glorious;
  X104669 Jesus ... the
  solid
Jesus my Lord, my God, my
  all; R109301 Sweet Sacra-
  ment
Most ancient of all mysteries
Mother Mary, at thy altar
Mother of mercy, day by day
My God, how wonderful thou;
  X106827 O God, how wonder-
ful
My God! my God! and can it
  be; R106982 O hearken when
  we
Now are the days of humblest
O blessed Father! sent by God
O blessed St Joseph, how
O come and mourn with me;
  X104453 Is it nothing to you
O come to the merciful Saviour
O, gift of gifts! O, grace of
O God, thy power is wonderful
O how the thought of God
O it is hard to work for God
O Paradise, O Paradise, who;
  X107450 O Paradies ...
  would not win; R111558
  Where loyal hearts
O purest of creatures! Sweet
O Saviour, bless us ere we
  go; X101713 Dear Saviour,
  bless; X109302 Sweet Sa-
  viour, bless; R110419 Through
  life's long
O, see how Jesus trusts himself

O turn to Jesus, Mother!
  turn
O, vision bright! the land of
Saint of the Sacred Heart
Sing, sing, ye Angel Bands
There's a wideness in God's;
  X109120 Souls of men!
  Why; X110966 Was there
  ever
What happiness can equal
  mine
Why art thou sorrowful
Workman of God! O lose not

Fahs, Sophia Lyon, 1876-
  Divinity is round us

Falckner, Justus, 1672-1723
  Auf, ihr Christen, Christi
    Glieder   1697
  Christians, rise, put on your
  Rise, ye children of salvation

Falconer, Hugh, 1859-1931
  God and Father <u>see</u> Darby,
  J. N.

Falk, Johannes Daniel, 1768-
1826
  O thou joyful, O thou wonderful

Fan Cheng-ta, ca 1186
  But for the cockerel calling

Farjeon, Eleanor, 1881-
  Fields of corn, give up your
  Lord, thou who gavest me all
  More lovely than the noon-
    day
  Morning has broken Like the
  Now every child that dwells
  People look East The time is

Farningham, Marianne, pseud.
  see Hearn, Marianne, 1834-
  1909

Farrar, Frederick William, 1831-
1903
  In the field with their flocks

Farrell, Melvin
  Christians, sound the name
  Lord of nations, bless in
  Now in joy we sing thy
    praises

Farrington, Harry Webb, 1880-
1931
  Dear Lord, who sought at
    dawn
  I know not how that Bethle-

hem's
O God Creator, in whose hand
Strong, righteous Man of
The storm-god of stern
  Sinai's
Faure, Jean Baptiste
  O'er all the way green palms
Fawcett, John, 1739-1817
  Behold the sin atoning Lamb
  Blest be the tie that binds;
    X103645 How blest the tie
  How precious is the book
  Lord, dismiss us with thy;
    X105445 Lord, dismiss ...
    Hope and comfort; X105446
    Lord, dismiss ... My our
    praise
  O my soul, what means this
  Praise to God, the great
  Praise to thee, thou great
  Religion is the chief concern
  Sinners, the voice of God
  Thy presence, gracious God
  Thy way is in the sea; X110502
  Thy way, O God, is
Featherstone, William R., 1842-
78
  My Jesus, I love thee, I know
Feith, Rhijnvis
  Praise the Lord through every;
    X104721 Jesus, Lord, our
Fellows, John, d 1785
  Jesus, mighty King in Zion
Felton, Richard
  Strong of body, high of spirit
Fenner, Harlan K.
  O man of God, arise
Ferguson, Mrs. Manie Payne
  Joys are flowing like ariver;
    R100944 Blessed quietness
Ferguson, Robert
  This ship we now commend
Fick, Herman, 1822-85
  Gehe auf, du Trost der Heiden
    1917
  Rise, thou Light of gentile
Fillmore, Charles M.
  Abide in me, the true and
Fillmore-Bennett, S., see
  Bennett, S. Fillmore
Finley, John
  When-ever war, with its
    red

Finnish traditional, etc
  Aurinko armas vallolansa
    (1836)
  Lost in the night
  The morning sun is brightly
    (1836)
Fischer, Christoph, 1520-97
  Lord Jesus, we give thanks
  The tribute of our thanks
    we
  Wir danken dir, Herr Jesu
Fischer, Eberhard Ludwig,
1695-1773
  Herr Jesu, der du selbst
    1741
  Lord Jesus, who art come
Fischer, Gottlob Nath., 1748-
1800
  Dankt dem Herrn! mit fro-
    hen Gaben
  Thank the Lord! With bounteous
Fisher, Albert C., 1886-1946
  Of the themes that men have;
    R105803 Love is the theme
  There's a glad new song;
    R107911 Of His love I shall
Fitch, Charles
  One precious boon, O Lord
Fitch, Eleazar Thompson,
1791-1871
  Lord, at this closing hour
Fitch, W.R.
  The bread that bringeth
    strength; X109428 The
    bread ... giveth
Fitzgerald. Collection, 1830
  Daughter of Zion, awake from;
    X106678 O daughter of
    Zion
Fleming, Lucy Randolph
  Awake, awake, O earth;
    R103262 He lives again!
    Our
Flemish traditional, etc.
  A little child on the earth
  Sing, good company, frank
  Three kings are here, both
Flemming, Paul, 1609-40
  Where'er I go, whate'er my
Fletcher, Frank, 1870-1954
  O Son of Man, our hero
    strong
Fletcher, Phineas, 1582-1650

Drop, drop, slow tears
Fliedner, Theodor, 1800-64
Blessed Fount of heavenly
Flint, Annie Johnson
God hath not promised skies;
R101086 But God hath
promised
Flint, James, 1779-1855
In pleasant lands have fallen
Flittner, Johann, 1618-78
Jesus, thou my heart's delight
Flory, Gertrude A.
Love not the world! Its
Take my hand and lead me
Flowerdew, Alice, 1759-1830
Fountain of mercy, God of;
X102156 Father of mercies
Follen, Eliza Lee (Cabot), 1787-1860
How sweet upon this sacred
The Lord -- the Lord of glory
Foote, Henry Wilder, 1838-89
O thou with whom in sweet
Foote, Henry Wilder, II, 1875-1964
Thou whose love brought us
Foote, John G., ??
Christ our Redeemer died;
R111394 When I see the blood
Forbush, William Bryon, 1868-1928
God of our boyhood, whom we;
R102759 God of our youth,
be; X102760 God of our
youth, to
Ford, Charles Lawrence, 1830-
Earthly joys no longer please
"This is my body, which is"
Ford, David E.
How vain is all beneath
Forney, Lydia A.
If I would be a child of God
Förtsch, Basilius, d 1619
Jesus, thy name hath power
Fortunatus, Venantius Honorius
Clementianus, 530-609
Hail thee, festival day: Se-
quences for Easter, Ascen-
ciontide, Whitsunday
Dedication
[But NOTE: First couplet is
from Fortunatus. Balance
is later writing.] X103031

Hail! festal day
Maria, Mater gratiae
O faithful cross, O noblest
O gloriosa virginium
O Mary, Mother full of grace
Praise the Saviour, now and
See the destined day arise
Sing, my tongue, the glorious
X108951 Sing ... the
Saviour's
The God whom earth, and sea,
The Lord whom earth, and
stars; X109707 The Lord
... and air
The royal banners forward go;
X109790 The royal banner
is; X109792 The royal stan-
dard
Thirty years among us dwell-
ing
Vexilla regis prodeunt
Welcome, morning of joy
"Welcome, happy morning!"
Fosdick, Harry Emerson, 1878-
God of grace and God of
glory
O God, in restless living
O God, who to a loyal home
The Prince of Peace, his
Foster, Catherine, i. e. "C. F.",
pseud.
Dread Jehovah! God of nations
Foster, Mrs. D.
'Mid the trials we experience
Foster, Frederick William,
1760-1835
Be this our happy destiny
Before thee we appear, thou
God, who art love, the same
In humble, grateful lays
Jesus, all our souls inspire
Jesus, hear our fervent
Join to render thanks and
Lord, who didst sancify thy-
self
Now to the Lamb upon the
throne
O happy days, days marked
On thy ransomed congregation
Praise the Lord; bounteously;
X108285 Praise the Lord;
Praise the
Should our minds to earthly

Look to Jesus Christ thy
Prepare the way, O Zion
The day departs, yet thou art
The little while I linger
The Saviour is risen
Thine own, O loving Saviour
Thy scepter, Jesus, shall
When vesper bells are calling
Fraser, M.
  I belong to Jesus
  Willing to own thee Master
Frazer, George W., 1830-96
  God, our Father, we adore
Freckelton, Thomas Wesley, 1827-
1903
  The toil of brain, or heart;
    X106926 O God, who workest
Freeman, Robert
  Backward we look, O God
  Braving the wilds all
  For thy mercy aye pursuing
Freer, Frances, 1801-91
  Present with the two or three
French, Arthur W.
  Out from the camp-fire's red;
    R111949 Yes, sleeping on
  We shall reach the river side
French traditional, etc.
  Angels we have heard on high
  Beautiful upon the mountain
    (1830-1850)
  Bring a torch, Jeannette
  Courons à fete, ne différons
  Dans cette étable
  Grand Dieu, Que de merveilles
  Hearken all! what holy singing
  Here, betwixt ass and oxen mild
    (13th c)
  In stable lowly
  In that poor stable
  J'ai ouï chanter le rossignol
    (18th c); R105029 Laissez
    paitre vos
  Je sais, vierge Marie, Ce que
  Les anges dans nos compagnes
  My heart delights, O Lord
  Neighbour, what was the sound
  Noël nouvelet, Noël chantons
  O come, ye happy children
  Nous allons, ma mie
  Nous voici dans la ville
  O leave your sheep, your lambs
  O my Saviour, I adore thee

  Promptement levez-vous;
    R100351 Allex, mon voi-
    son
  Quelle est cette odeur
  Quittez, pasteurs, vos bre-
    bis
  Shepherds, shake off
  Sing, all good people
  Take heart, the journey's
    (15th c)
  Un flambeau Jeannette
  Une vaine crainte trouble
    vos
  Voison, d'ou venait ce grand
  When the sun had sunk to
    rest
Frere, W.H., 1863-1938
  The saints who toiled
Freund, Cornelius
  Rejoice, ye sons of men
    alway
Freund, Jacob
  From Sinai's height a foun-
    tain
Freylinghausen, Johann Anastas-
ius, 1670-1739
  Jesus, who with thee
  O Jesus, source of calm
    repose
  The day departs; Our souls
  Wake! the welcome day ap-
    peareth
  Who is there like thee
Freylinghausen. Geist-reiches
Gesang-buch. 1714
  My Redeemer knoweth me
  To thee, the Lord of all
Freystein, Johann Burkhard,
1671-1718
  Mache dich, mein Geist,
    bereit 1697
  Rise, my soul, to watch
  Up, my soul, gird thee
Fries, Henry E., 1857-
  Come, join the throng, on
Fritsch, Ahasuerus, 1629-1701
  Jesus is my joy, my all
Froom, L. E.
  Dismiss us, Lord, with
    blessing
  With praise, O God
Frost, Mabel
  O soul in the far-away;

R101408 Come home, come
home
Frost, Robert Lee, 1875-1963
O, give us pleasure in
Frothingham, Nathaniel Langdon,
1793-1870
O God, whose presence glows
"Remember me," the Master
said
Frothingham, Octavius Brooks,
1822-95
Thou Lord of Hosts, whose
Fry, Charles W., 1837-82
I have found a friend in Jesus;
R103543 He's the Lily of the
Füger, Caspar, 16th c
We Christians may Rejoice
today
Wir Christen leut' Hab'n
Fullerton, Georgiana Charlotte,
Lady, 1812-85
O Heart of Jesus, Heart of
God
Fullerton, William Young, 1857-
1932
I cannot tell why He, whom
Funcke, Friedrich, 1642-99
Draw us to thee, for then
Draw us to thee in mind
Draw us to thee, Lord Jesus
Zeuch uns nach dir
Fünf auserlesene geistliche
Lieder, Marburg, 1535
My soul doth magnify the Lord
Furness, William Henry, 1802-
96
Feeble, helpless, how shall I
In the morning I will pray
Slowly, by thy hand unfurled
Unworthy to be called thy son
Furniss, John J., d 1865
In this Sacrament, Lord Jesus;
X104405 In this Sacrament,
sweet
Fyleman, Rose, 1877-1957
Lift your hidden faces; R100325
Alleluia, Alleluia

G

"G.M.J.", presumed pseud. of
James McGranaham.
Someone will enter the pearly

Gabbott, Mabel Jones
In humility, our Saviour
Lord, accept into thy King-
dom
Rejoice, ye Saints of Latter
Days
Gabirol, Solomon ibn see
Solomon ibn Gabirol
Gabriel, Charles H., 1856-
1932
I stand all amazed at the
love; R107077 O, it is
wonderful
I stand amazed in the pre-
sence; R107060 O how
marvelous
Just a few more days;
R104189 I'll exchange my
Lord, as of old at Pentecost;
R105689 Lord, send the
old-time
More like the Master I would;
R109331 Take thou my
heart
So precious is Jesus, my;
R102281 For He is so
precious
Sweet is the promise; R104100
"I will not forget"
There's a call comes ringing;
R108823 Send the light
When all my labors and trials;
R107631 O that will be glory
Gage, W.C.
O'er all the land have;
R109123 Send forth the
tidings
Gaines, Samuel Richards
From every clime and country
Gale, Norman, 1862-1948
Here in the country's heart
Gale, Zona, 1874-1938
Come, children of tomorrow
Gambold, John, 1711-71
Attend, O Saviour, to our
Dear Lord, my soul desireth
Go forth in spirit, go
Lord God of hosts, by all
O grant thy servants, through
O tell me no more Of this
They who Jesus' followers
are
They who know the Lord indeed

What praise to thee, my Sa-
viour
Gannett, William Channing, 1840-
1923
  Bring, O morn, thy music
  From heart to heart, from
  God laid his rocks in courses;
    X110570 To cloisters of
  He hides within the lily
  It sounds along the ages
  Praise to God, your praises;
    X108299 Praise ... and
    thanks
  Sleep, my little Jesus
  The Lord is in his holy place
  The morning hangs a signal
  When the night is stall and
Gannon, Michael
  O Lord, in this great mystery
Ganse, Hervey Doddridge, 1822-
91
  Eternal Father, when to thee
  Lord, I know thy grace is
  nigh
Garber, Ora W., 1903-
  'Tis not with eyes of flesh
Gardiner, William Henry
  When I see the way my Sa-
  viour; R107828 O, what
  tender, tender
Garrett, Marguerite Bixler
  Brother, here's a message;
    R109308 Sweetened by the
    cross
  Hear, O hear us, Heavenly
Garrison, Winfred Ernest, 1874-
  God of our fathers, the
  Softly I closed the Book as
  in
Garve, Carl Bernhard, 1763-
1841
  Alleluia, Christus lebt
  Alleluia! Jesus lives! He is
  Alleluia! Jesus lives! Won
  Thy word, O Lord, like gentle
Gascoigne, George, ca1525-77
  You that have spent the silent;
    X111919 Ye that have spent
Gaskell, William, 1805-44
  Calmly, calmly lay him down
  Father, throughout the coming
  Mighty God, the First, the
  Last

Our Father! through the com-
ing
Press on, press on, ye sons
Though lowly here our work;
  X110387 Though lowly ...
  lot
We join to pray, with wishes
Gates, Ellen Huntington, 1835-
1920
  I will sing you a song of
  that; R111599 While the
  years
  O, the clanging bells of
  time
Gates, Mary Cornelia, mid
19th c
  Send thou, O Lord, to every
  Thy love to me, O Christ
Gautama Buddha, 5th c B.C.
  Be ye lamps unto yourselves
Gautier, Théophile, 1811-72
  All things are doubly fair
Gedicke, Lampertus, 1683-1735
  As God doth lead me, I will
  go
  Deliver me, my God, from
  all
Geijer, Erick Gustaf
  In triumph our Redeemer
  Thy cross, O Jesus, thou
  didst
Geldart, Edmund Martin
  When the light of day
Gellert, Christian Fürchtegott
1715-69
  Crushed by my sin, O Lord;
    X108052 Oppressed by sin
  How great, Almighty, is thy
  Jesus lebt, mit ihm auch ich
  Jesus lives and so shall I
  Jesus lives! no longer now
  Jesus lives! Thy terrors
  now; X104710 Jesus ...
  victory's
  Wie gross ist des Allmächt'
  gen Güte!
Gell's Psalms and hymns, 1815
  We praise, we worship thee
George, Hereford Brooke, 1838-
1910
  By every nation, race
Gerfass, Mattheiss.
  Mit Angst und Roth ruff

ich dich an. 1566
Gerhardt, Paulus, 1607-76
  A Lamb goes forth our griefs
  A Lamb goes uncomplaining
  A pilgrim and a stranger
  All my heart this night;
    X100238 All ... this day
  All ye who on this earth
  Auf, auf, mein Herz, mit
  Awake, my heart, and marvel
  Awake, my heart, and render
  Awake, my heart, with glad-
    ness
  Befiehl du deine Wege 1656
  Beside thy manger here I
  Blessed is the man that
  Blest is he that never
  Come, your hearts and voices
  Cometh sunshine after rain
  Commit thou all that grieves;
    X108409 Put thou thy trust
  Commit thou all thy griefs
  Commit thou every grievance
  Commit whatever grieves thee
  Die güldne Sonne, Voll Freud'
    und Wonne
  Ein Lämmlein geht und trägt
  Emmanuel! we sing thy praise;
    X104221 Immanuel, to thee
    we; X104222 Immanuel, we
    sing
  Evening and morning, Sunset
  Extended on a cursed tree
  Frohlich soll mein Herze
  Give thy heart's love
  Give to the winds thy fears
  Go forth my heart and seek
  Hab ich das Haupt zum Freunde
  Hearts at Christmas time
  Here I can firmly rest
  Holy Ghost, dispel our sad-
    ness
  Holy Spirit, Source of gladness
  I know that my Redeemer lives
  I sing to thee with voice
  I will sing to my creator
  I will sing my Maker praises
  Ich bin ein Gast auf Erden
    1666
  Ich singe dir mit Herz und Mund
    1653
  If God be on my side
  If God himself be for me

I'll praise thee with my
  heart
Is God my strong Salvation
Ist Gott für mich, so trete
  1656
Jesus, I never can forget
Jesus, our Guardian, Guide
Jesus, thy boundless love;
  X107148 O Jesus, thy
  boundless
Kommt und lasst uns Chris-
  tum
Let not such a thought
My soul, awake and render
Now all the heavenly splen-
  dor
Now are the woodlands rest-
  ing
Now let us come before Him
Now rest beneath night's
Now woods and wolds;
  X106345 Now all the woods;
  X106487 Now woods and
  fields
Nun danket all' und bringet
  Ehr', Ihr Menschen in der
  Welt 1648
Nun lasst uns gehn und tre-
  ten
Nun ruhen alle wälder
O Christ my Light, my
  gracious
O draw me, Saviour, after
  thee
O Du allersüsste Freude
O enter, Lord, thy temple
O how shall I receive thee;
  X103739 How shall I meet
  my
O Jesu Christ, dein Kripplein
O Jesus Christ, mein schön-
  stes Licht 1653
O Jesus Christ, thy manger
  is
O Lord, how shall I meet
  thee
O Lord, I sing with voice;
  X107244 O Lord ... lips
  and; X107245 O Lord...
  mouth and
O sacred head, sore wounded
(based on St Bernard of
Clairvaux)

O Saviour dear, thy manger
O thou sweetest source
O welt, sieh hier dein leben
O world, behold! Upon the tree
O world, see here suspended
O'er field and forest stealing
Put thou thy trust in God
Rejoice, my heart, be glad
See, world, thy Life assailed
Shun, my heart, the thought
Since Jesus is my Friend
Sing, my soul, to God who made
Sollt' ich meinem Gott nicht
The duteous day now closeth;
  X109418 The beauteous day;
  X109785 The restless day
The mystery hidden from
The sun ascending, To us is
Thy way and all thy sorrows
Trust all to God, the Father
Warum sollt' ich mich denn grämen? 1653
We sing, Immanuel, thy praise
We sing to thee, Immanuel
Why art thou heavy-hearted
Why, my soul, thus trembling
Why should cross and trial;
  X111687 Why should sorrow
Why should I repine in sadness
Wie soll ich dich empfangen
Wir singen dir, Immanuel
Wohlauf, mein Herze, sing und spring 1653
Zeuch ein zu meinen Toren
German traditional, etc.
A babe is born in Bethlehem
A babe lies in the cradle
A boy was born in Bethlehem
A little child there is y-born (15th c)
Also hat Gott die welt geliebt (1791)
Bei frühem Morgenlicht (ca 1800)
Die ganze welt, Herr Jesu (1623)
Ein Kind geborn zu Bethlehem
Ein Kindlein in der Wiegen (1649)
Es ist noch Raum (19th c)
Es kommt ein Schiff geladen

(1470-80)
Gebor'n ist uns ein Kinde-lein (17th c)
Gen Himmel aufgefahren ist (17th c)
God loved the world (1791)
God the Father, be our Stay (13-14th c)
Gott der Vater wohn' uns bei (13-14th c)
He smiles within His cradle (1649)
I have chosen thee, my Sa-vior
I know a Kingdom without end (16th c or earlier)
Jesus, I long for thy bless-ed (1712)
Jesus, for thee and thy blessed (1712)
Jesus, with thy death
Joseph dearest, Joseph mine (16th c); R103228 He came among us
Joseph lieber, Joseph mein (16th c)
Löwen, lasst euch wieder (1712)
Maria die wollt' wandern
Maria ging aus wandern
Mein Herz will ich dir schenken (1653)
Now are the days fulfilled (1746 or earlier)
Now glad of heart (16th c)
Nun ist die zeit erfüllt (1746 or earlier)
O Christ thou bright (1579)
O Christmas tree, O Christ-mas
O God, Almighty Father, Creator; X106802 O God ... thou Majesty
O have you heard the won-drous
O Herre Gott, dein göttlich (1527)
O let us praise the Christ-mas tree
O that thy fire now soon
Once Mary would go wander-ing
Rise again, ye lion-hearted

(1712)
St Mary goes aseeking
The whole bright world (1623)
There comes a ship asailing
   (ms. 1470-80)
There is a gentle Gardener
There still is room!
This child was born to men
   (17th c)
To thee my heart I offer
   (1653)
To us from heaven's lofty
To us is born a blessed
   (before 1422)
Vom Himmel hoch, o Engel
   (before 1422)
When morning fills the skies
   (ca 1800)
When morning gilds the skies
   (ca 1800)
Wir wollen alle frölich sein
   (16th c)
Ye baptized people, one and
Gerok, Friedrich Karl von,
1815-90
   Holy, holy, holy, blessed
   Lord
Gersdorf, Abraham von, 1704-
84
   Eternal thanks be thine
   Thy blood, thy blood the deed
Gesenius, Justus, 1601-73
   O Lord when condemnation
   Wenn meine Sünd' mich
      Kränken
   When o'er my sins I sorrow
   When sorrow and remorse
      (with David Denicke)
Gibbons, Thomas, 1720-85
   Great God, the nations of
   Lord, send thy word, and let
   When Jesus dwelt in mortal
Giffe, William T.
   O wonderful prayer that Jesus
Giffin, Clare
   Father, we thank thee, Father
Gilbert, Ann Taylor, 1782-1866
   see Taylor, Ann. (This order
   retained to keep Ann and Jane
   Taylor together)
Gilbert, Edwin, 1859-
   Together, Lord, we come
Gilbert, Rosa Mulholland, d 1921

Give me, O Lord, a heart
Gilder, Richard Watson, 1844-
1909
   God of the strong, God of the
   If Jesus Christ is a man
   Through love to light! O
   To thee, Eternal Soul, be
Giles, John Eustace, 1805-75
   Thou hast said, exalted Jesus
Giles, John Philip, 1905-
   Here in this water I do vow
Gilkey, James Gordon, 1899-
   O God, in whose great pur-
   pose
   Outside the Holy City
Gill, Thomas Hornblower, 1819-
1906
   Break, new-born year, on
   glad
   Come, Holy Ghost! in us
   arise
   Dear Lord and Master mine
   He who suns and worlds
   I walk amidst thy beauty
   forth
   Lord, God, by whom all
   change
   Lord, in the fullness of my
   Lord, thou hast been our
   Lord! when I all things
   would
   Not, Lord, thine ancient
   works
   Not only when ascends the
   song
   O mean may seem this house
   O mystery of love divine
   O saints of old! not yours
   O walk with God along the
   road; X110945 Walk with
   the Lord
   Our God, our God, thou
   shinest
   Spirit of Truth, who makest
   The glory of the spring
   We come unto our fathers'
   God
   What secret place, what dis-
   tant
Gill, William Henry, 1839-1923
   Hear us, O Lord, from
   heaven
Gillett, George Gabriel Scott,

1873-
It is finished! Christ hath
Gillman, Frederick John, 1866-
1949
God send us men whose aim
Gilman, Caroline, 1794-1888
Sweet hour of holy, thoughtful
Gilman, Samuel, 1791-1858
Father, be thy blessing shed
Gilmore, Joseph Henry, 1834-
1918
He leadeth me! O blessed
Gilmour, H. L.
My soul in sad exile; R104506
I've anchored my
Watchman, blow the gospel;
R101004 Blow the trumpet
When out in sin and darkness;
R107798 O, 'twas love, love
Gisborne, Thomas, ca 1760-
Saviour, when night involves
Gjertsen, M. Falk, 1847-1913
I know a way besieged
Gladden, Washington, 1836-1918
Behold a sower! from afar;
X107207 O Light of Light
O Lord of life, to thee we
O Master, let me walk with
Gladstone, William Ewart,
1809-98
O lead my blindness by the
Glasgow, Samuel M.
Long have we sought eternal;
R103706 How long? How
long
Men of the Church of the
Glenn, Creda
Bow down in worship now
Chant your songs of glad
Lo, they come in glad
O Lamb of God, have mercy
Glenn, Grace
Jesus, I will follow thee
Glover, Ellen J.
In speechless prayer
Glover, Terrot Reaveley, 1869-
1943
Jesus and Joseph day after
Goadby, Frederick William,
1845-80
O thou, whose hand hath
Godolphin, Sidney, 1610-43
Lord, when the wise men

came
Goethe, Johann Wolfgang von,
1749-1832
Everything changes; R109184
Splendours three
Haste not! haste not! do not
Purer yet and purer
This thought shall have our
Whether day my spirit's
Goforth, Caroline
Make large our hearts
Golden chain, 1861 [Crosby?]
Whither, pilgrim, are you
Goldsmith, Peter Hair, 1865-
Holy, holy Lord, we with
one
Goldstein, Ida
Our Father, we beseech thy
Good, S. E.
There's a cleft in the Rock;
R107641 O, the cleft
Goode, William, 1762-1816
Crown His head with endless
Let thy grace, Lord, make
me
Lo, the mighty God appear-
ing
Goodenough, Lucy M.
Thou living light of pente-
costal
Gordon, Adoniram Judson,
1836-95
Help me to be holy
Gordon, Anna A.
O God, we pray thee, bless
Gordon, George A., 1853-1929
Hail the day when Jesus
rose
O Will of God beneath our
life
Goreh, Ellen Lakshmi, 1853-
In the secret of His presence
Gorell, Ronald, 1884-
To thee, O Father, lamp of
all
Gosse, Edmund, 1849-1928
Not with a choir of angels
The cross, like pilgrim
Gostick, Joseph, d 1887
The light pours down
Gothus, L. P.
Amid the world's deceitful
cares

Gotter, Ludwig Andreas, 1661-
1735
  Friend of the weary, O re-
    fresh
  I will ever sing thy praises
  Lamb of God, all praise
  Saviour of sinners, now
  The reproach of Christ is
Gottheil, Gustav, 1827-1903
  Come, O Sabbath day and bring
  To thee we give ourselves
Gough, Benjamin, 1805-77
  Awake, awake, O Sion
  How beauteous on the moun-
    tains
Gould, Edwin
  "Lord, I believe: help thou"
Goulston, Mrs.
  Our fortress strong art thou
Govan, G.E.M.
  I will not be afraid
Govan, W.J.
  The Word, whose word can
    make
Gower, Jean Milne, 1867-
  Dear Father, loud the ocean
  Father, loving Father, hear
Graduel de Paris, 1754
  Let no helpless tears be shed
Graeff, Frank E.
  Does Jesus care when my
    heart; R107883 O, yes, He
    cares
Graham, Abbie
  For the year that came from
Graham, S.J.
  The golden morning is fast;
    R107809 O, we see the
    gleams
Gramann, Johann, see Grau-
    mann, Johann
Grant, Peter, 1783-1867
  O Lord, I sing thy praises
Grant, Robert, 1785-1838
  Lord of earth, thy forming
  O worship the King
  Saviour, when in dust to thee;
    X101116 By thy birth and
    by
  The starry firmament on high;
    X109843 The spacious
    firmament

When gathering clouds around
Where-fore do the nations
  rage
Graumann, Johann, 1487-1541
  My soul, now bless thy
    Maker
  Nun lob, mein' Seel', den
Graves, F.A.
  My Father has many dear;
    R103377 He'll never forget
Gray, Herbert Branston, 1851-
1929
  Praise to our God, who with
Gray, James M., 1851-1935
  Naught have I gotten but what;
    R108025 Only a sinner
    saved
  Nor silver nor gold hath;
    R103801 I am redeemed
    but
  O listen to our wondrous;
    R111647 Who saved us from
  The Saviour who loves me;
    R104665 Jesus is coming
Gray, Thomas, jr., 1803-49
  Suppliant, lo! Thy children
Gt. Brit. National anthem.
17-18th c.
  God save our gracious King
  God save our gracious Queen
Greek traditional, etc. (chiefly
from service and liturgical
books)
  Awaked from sleep, we fall
    (4th c)
  Behold the Bridegroom cometh
    (8th c)
  Behold the Bridegroom
    draweth (8th c); X100825
    Behold ... cometh
  God of all grace, thy mercy
  Hail, gladdening Light (3d c)
    X110421 Through love to
    light (Gilder); X103036
    Hail! ... of that pure
  Here, while the cherubim
    (6th c)
  Let thy Blood in mercy pour-
    ed
  Lord, to our humble prayers
  May Jesus Christ, the spot-
    less

O Brightness of the immortal
(3d c)
O gladsome light (3d c);
X103035 Hail Gladdening
Light
O God of grace, thy mercy
O King enthroned on high
(Pentecostarian   8th c)
O Spirit from on high (Pente-
costarian, 8th c)
The King shall come when
(Hymns of the Russian
Church)
The wise men from the East
Thou, Lord, hast power to
heal (Paracletice)
Greenaway, Ada Rundall, 1861-
1937
O perfect God, thy love
O word of pity, for our pardon
Rise in the strength of God
Rise to the cry of battle
Greenwell, Dora, 1821-82
And art thou come with us
I am not skilled to under-
stand
If ye would hear the angels
Greenwood, Annie Pike
Come, lay his books and papers
Greenwood, John Brooke, 1828-
Crown with thy benediction
Greenwood, Samuel
No mortal sense can still or
Greg, Samuel, 1807-77
Around my path life's
Slowly, slowly darkening
Stay, Master, stay upon this
Gregg, William C.
Know this, that every soul is
Gregor, Christian, 1723-1801
Be our Comfort, which ne'er
Bethany, O peaceful habitation
Glory to the Father, Who in
Holy Lord, Holy Lord, Holy
and
Holy Lord, thanks and praise;
X103553 Holy Lord, Holy
Lord
I smite upon my guilty breast
In this sepulchral Eden
Jesus, bless us sensibly
Jesus, my Lord, thy nearness
Lord, for thy coming us

Make my calling and election
More than shepherd's
My happy lot is here
My portion is the Lord
None but Christ my Saviour
Now, Lord, who in this vale;
X106768 O, form us all
while
O Eternal Word, Jesus
Christ, our Lord (Author-
ship very complicated: cf
Julian 377)
O how excellent and fair;
X101604 Countless hosts
O that we with gladness
O, there's a sight that
rends
O Thou, whose goodness
words
O Thou, whose human life
O what an act of majesty
O what joy, O what joy
awaiteth
O what praise in highest
strain
Our Redeemer rose victor-
ious
Sing alleluia, Christ doth
Sing with awe in strains
The Lord bless and keep thee
The seraphim of God exalt
Though by nature I'm defiled
Till permitted hence to go
'Tis finished now, redemp-
tion's
To God, our Immanuel,
made
Truly, that eventful day
Unto thee, most faithful
What happiness, what joy
and
Whene'er we contemplate;
X106688 O days of perfect
With heart and hand you now
With thy presence, Lord,
our
Gregory, G.O., 1881-
Spread the table of the Lord
Gregory, Philip E., 1886-
Jesus, Friend, so kind and
Greiner, Minnie A.
Alleluia! Alleluia! Shout aloud
Grève, Philippe de, d 1236

Guest, Benjamin, 1788-1869
  Heavenly Father, may thy love
Guiet, Charles, 1601-64
  O Word of God above
Guiney, Louise Imogen, 1861-
1920
  The little cares that fretted
Guiterman, Arthur, 1871-1943
  Bless the four corners of
  Hail Guest! We ask not what
Gunther, Cyriacus, 1649-1704
  With joyful heart your praises
Gurney, Archer Thompson, 1820-
87
  Christ is risen! Christ is
Gurney, Dorothy Frances
  (Bloomfield), 1858-1932
  O perfect love, all human
Gurney, John Hampden, 1802-
62
  Fair waved the golden corn
  Great King of nations, hear
  Lord, as to thy dear cross;
    X105428 Lord, as we to
    thy
  Lord of the harvest, thee we
  Our God is good! in earth and
Gustavus Adolphus, King of
Sweden, see Altenburg,
  Fear not, O little flock
Gutheim, James K.
  Lo, our Father's tender care
  Who is like Thee, O universal
Guthrie, John, 1814-78
  Our Father, throned in heaven
Guyon, Mme., i.e. Jeanne Marie
Bouvièrs de la Mothe, 1648-
1717
  I would love thee, God and
  My Lord, how full of sweet;
    X107236 O Lord, how full
  O thou, by long experience

H

"H"
  In atmosphere of Love divine
  O ye heavens, bend and see
    (1708)
  Thy will, almighty Father
"H. L. W."
  So sweet and clear, so sweet;
    R108205 Peace, peace on

earth
Habershon, Ada Ruth, 1861-1918
  Jesus Himself drew near
  Soon will our Saviour from;
    R107815 O, what a change
  There are loved ones in the;
    R111707 Will the circle
  When I fear my faith will
    fail; R103308 He will hold
    me fast
Hacker, J. G.
  Great King of Kings and Lord;
    R109962 Thee, God's
    Anointed
Hackett, Rosemary B.
  Loving Father, we thy chil-
    dren
Hackleman, W. E. M.
  Speed away! Speed away!
    Take
Haigh, Emily Waddington
  In sunny days, when all is
Hale, Edward Everett, 1822-
1909
  And I? Is there some desert
  From city and from prairie
Hale, Mary Whitwell, 1810-62
  Whatever dims thy sense of
    truth
Hale, Sarah Josepha, 1795-
1879
  Our Father in heaven
Ha-Levi, Jehudah
  Despise not, Lord, my lowly
Haley, Molly Anderson
  Thy blessing, Lord, on all
Hall, Benjamin H.
  Day of wonder, day of glad-
    ness
  Lord of life, of love, of
    light
Hall, Christopher Newman,
1816-1902
  Friend of sinners! Lord of
Hall, Elvina M., 1818-89
  I hear the Saviour say;
    R104609 Jesus died for
    me
Hall, Joseph, 1574-1656
  Immortal babe, who this dear
Halpine, Charles Graham, 1829-
68
  Comrades known in marches

Ham, Marion Franklin, 1867-1956
  As tranquil streams that meet
  From Bethany, the Master
    comes
  Heir of all the waiting ages
  I hear thy voice, within the
  O Church of God, divided
  O, hear them marching,
    marching
  O Lord of life, thy kingdom
  O thou whose gracious presence
  O who shall roll away the
    stone
  Ring, O ring, ye Christmas
  The builders, toiling through
  Touch thou mine eyes
Hamburg Temple Hymnal
  Arise to praise the Lord
  Father, see thy suppliant
  Happy he that never wanders
  Happy who in early youth
  Let Israel trust in God alone
  Loud let the swelling anthems
  O Lord, my God, to thee I
    pray
  On mighty wings rush swiftly
  Our Shepherd is the Lord
  Sing to the Sovereign
  There lives a God! Each
    finite
  To thee, above all creatures'
  Why art thou cast down my
    soul
Hamerton, Samuel Collingwood,
  1833-72
  Waken, Christian children
Hamilton, Eliza H., fl. ca.
  1888
  My Saviour, thou hast
  O Jesus, Lord, to thee I cry;
    R100451 And take me as I
    am; X104764 Jesus, my
    Lord, to
Hamilton, James, 1819-96
  Across the sky the shades
  O Jesus! Lord most merciful
  O Jesus, our Salvation
  Praise, O praise the Lord
Hamilton, Mary C.D.
  Lord, guard and guide the
    men
Hammer, John Beck, 1856-80
  Saviour, now with contrite

Hammond, William, 1719-83
  A stranger and a pilgrim
  Awake, and sing the song
  Jesus, thy word is my de-
    light
  Jesus, who died a world
  Lord, we come before thee
    now
  Not one of Adam's race
  See, my soul, God ever
    blest
  The Lord be with me every-
    where
  What good news the angels
Hanaford, Phoebe A., 1829-
  Cast thy bread upon the
    waters
Hanby, Benjamin Russell,
  1833-67
  Who is he, in yonder stall;
    R110554 'Tis the Lord!
    O
Hänel
  God spake, my child, God
    spake
Hankey, Donald, 1884-1916
  Lord of the strong, when
    earth
Hankey, Arabella Katherine,
  1834-1911
  Advent tells us Christ is near
  I love to tell the story
  Tell me the old, old story
Hanrahan, T. James
  Tell us now, O Death, where
Hans, Schmit, & Georg v.
  Ingersheim
  O Herre Gott vom Himmel-
    reich. 1564
Harbaugh, John Henry, 1817-
  67
  Christ by heavenly hosts;
    X102704 God, most mighty;
    X110243 Thou by heavenly
  Hail, Jesus! Israel's Hope
    and
  Jesus, I live to thee
  Jesus, my Shepherd, let me
  Jesus, to thy cross I hasten
Harbottle, Joseph, 1798-1864
  Farewell, my friends beloved
Hardenberg, Georg Friedrich
  Philipp von, 1772-1801

I say to all men, far and near
If only I have thee
Lord, when thou makest thy
Hardy, Henry Ernest, i.e.
 Father Andrew, 1869-1946
O dearest Lord, thy sacred
Hardy, Thomas, 1840-1928
To thee whose eye all nature
Harker, A.
Lord of the ocean vast and
Harkness, Georgia, 1891-
God of the fertile fields
Hope of the world, thou Christ
Harland, Edward, 1810-90
And now this holy day
Behold, a humble train
Lord, thine ancient people
  see
Harlingen, J. N. van
We gather, we gather, dear
Harlow, S. Ralph, 1885-
O Church of God triumphant
O young and fearless Prophet
Harmer, Charles H., 1865-
O Christ, thou Gift of love
Harmer, Samuel Young, 1809-
In the Christian's home;
  R110070 There is rest
Harmony in praise, 1890
O Lord, all glorious, Life
Harris, Florence, 1891-1933
Like pilgrims sailing
Harris, John, 1802-56
Light up this house with glory
Harris, John Roy, 1891-
Great Redeemer, we adore
  thee
Harris, Thomas Lake, 1823-1906
O Earth! thy past is crowned
Harrison, Edward L. T.
Sons of Michael, he approaches
Hart, Joseph, 1712-68
Almighty Father, bless the
Christians, dismiss your fear
Come, Holy Spirit, come
Come, ye sinners, poor and
  needy; X101563 Come ...
  poor and wretched
Dismiss us with thy blessing
Great High-Priest, we view
Jesus, our triumphant Head
Lamb of God, we fall before
Many woes had Christ endured

O for a glance of heavenly
Once more before we part
Once more we come before
  our
Our baptism first declares
Prayer is appointed to convey
Suffering Saviour, Lamb of
  God
That solemn night before;
  X109395 That doleful night
The Lord ascendeth up on
  high
The spirits of the just
This God is the God we adore;
  X103678 How good is the
  God
Hart, Oliver, 1723-95
My Father, when I come to
  thee
Hartley, John, 1762-1811
Blessed Jesus, we implore
  thee
We now return, each to his
  tent
Hartman, George
O Christ, to thee we come
Hartsough, Lewis, 1828-1919
I hear thy welcome voice;
  R103788 I am coming Lord
Let me go where saints are
Hartsough, Palmer, 1844-1932
Give as the Lord hath pros-
  pered; R102478 Give, give
  with
I am resolved no longer to;
  R104094 I will hasten
O wonderful word of salvation
Hartzler, Henry B.
Go and seek the lost and dy-
  ing
Harvard, Lionel deJersey, 1893-
1916
Father of all, we lift to thee
Harvey, Charles E. W., 1846-
1922
Light of the world, come
  nigh
Haskell, Jefferson, 1807-
My latest sin is sinking fast;
  R106647 O come, angel
  band
Haskell, Julia Sampson
Over the ocean wave, far,

viour
Thy life was given for me
To thee, O Comforter divine
True-hearted, whole-hearted;
  R108217 Peal out
Who is on the Lord's side;
  X104868 Jesus, thou hast
Yes, He knows the way
Havergal, William Henry, 1793-
1870
  Hosanna! raise the pealing
  Shout, O Earth! from silence
Haweis, Hugh R., 1838-1901
  The homeland, O the homeland
Haweis, Thomas, 1732-1820
  Enthroned on high, almighty
  From the cross uplifted high
  O thou, from whom all good-
    ness
  Our children, Lord, in faith
  Saviour, all my sins
  Soon as the morn with roses
  The happy morn is come
  To thee, my God and Saviour
Hawkes, Henry Warburton, 1843-
1917
  Amid the din of earthly
  "Give us each day our daily"
  Our humns are sung, our
  Peace! perfect peace! the gift
  Reveal thy truth, O Lord
  Thank we now the Lord
  Thou knowest, Lord! Thou
  "Thy kingdom come!" O Lord
Hawkes, Robert Stephen, of
Morwenstow, 1804-75
  Sing to the Lord the children's
Hawkins, Ernest, 1802-66
  Lord, a Saviour's love
Hawkins, Hester Perriam, 1846-
1928
  Almighty Father, God of love
  Heavenly Father, thou hast
Hawks, Annie Sherwood, 1835-
72
  I need thee every hour;
    R103990 I need thee (Lowry)
  Who'll be the next to follow
Hawthorne, Alice[pseud] 1827-1902
  Soft as the voice of an angel;
    R111609 Whispering hope
Hay, Edyth Hillery, d 1943
  He loveth me, He loveth me

Lord, with devotion we pray;
  R102280 For great is the
    Lord
Hay, John, 1838-1905
  Defend us, Lord, from
    every; X105457 Lord!
  from far-severed
  Not in dumb resignation
Hay, Sara Henderson, 1906-
  (Mrs. N. Lopatnikoff)
  It is a piteous thing to be
Hay, Violet, fl. ca. 1931
  All glory be to God most
    high
  Arise ye people, take your
  From sense to soul my path-
    way
  From these thy children
  I love thy way of freedom
  Jesus' prayer for all his
  Lo, He sent His word and
    healed
Hayes, Oleta
  Christ our Lord will soon
    be; R111215 We'll be
    gathered
Hayn, Henriette Luise von,
1724-82
  Hail, all hail, victorious
  I am Jesus' little lamb
  Jesus makes my heart re-
    joice
  O Church, thy strength abide
  O what happiness divine
  Sacred name of Jesus, so
  See from the rock the
    waters
  Weil ich Jesu Schäflein bin
    1778
Hayne, Paul Hamilton, 1831-
86
  The bliss for which our
    spirits
Hayward, Thomas
  Welcome, delightful morn
Hazard, Caroline, 1856-
  Great western land, whose
Head, Bessie Porter, 1850-
1936
  O Breath of life, come
Hearn, Marianne Farningham,
1834-1909
  Just as I am, thine own to

We hope in thee, O God
Heath, George, 1750-1822
  My soul, be on thy guard
Heatwole, L. J.
  The saint who enters heaven
  The tenor of the gospel word
Heber, Reginald, 1783-1826
  Bread of the world, in mercy
  Brightest and best; X103077
    Hail the blest
  By cool Siloam's shady rill
  From foes that would the land
  From Greenland's icy moun-
    tains; R106747 O fill us
    (L. J. L.)
  God, that madest earth;
    X102831 God, who madest
  Holy, Holy, Holy, Lord God
  Hosanna to the living Lord
  I praised the earth, in beauty
  In the sun, and moon, and
    stars
  Lord of mercy and of might,
    God and Father of us all
  Lord of mercy and of might,
    Of mankind the Life
  O God the Son eternal
  O, most merciful! O most
  O thou, who gavest thy servant
  O thou, whose infant feet
  Spirit of truth, on this
  The God of glory warns us all
  The Lord of might, from
    Sinai's
  The Son of God goes forth;
    X109837 The Son of Man
    goes
  Virgin-born, we bow
  Von Grönlands eis'gen Zinken
  We praise thee, Lord, for all
  When spring unlocks
  When through the torn sail
Hebrew traditional, etc.
  see Jewish traditional, etc.
Heck, Fannie E. S.
  Come, women, wide proclaim
Hedborn, Samuel Johan, 1783-
1849
  Glorious Majesty, before thee;
    Z103556 Holy Majesty, be-
    fore
  Now Israel's hope in triumph
  With holy joy my heart

Hedge, Frederick Henry, 1805-
90
  "It is finished!" Man of
  Sovereign and transforming
Heermann, Johann, 1585-1647
  Ah, holy Jesus; X100162
    Ah, dearest Jesus
  Ah! Lord our God, let them
  Be this henceforth my cons-
    tant
  Ere yet the dawn hath filled
  Feed thy children, God most
  God is known in loving-kind-
    ness
  Herr, unser Gott, lass nicht
  Herzliebster Jesu, was hast
  Jesu, deine tiefen Wunden
  Lord, grant thy servants
  Lord, Jesus Christ, in thee
  Lord, thy death and passion
  O Christ, our true and only;
    X104801 Jesus, our true
    and
  O dearest Jesus, what law;
    X100869 Beloved Jesus,
    what
  O God, eternal source
  O God, if thy beloved Son
  O God, thou faithful God
  O Gott, du frommer Gott
    1630
  O Jesu Christe, wahres Licht
    1630
  O Jesus, Saviour dear
  O Lord, our Father shall we
  Praise God, this hour
  Rett, o Herr Jesu, rett
  Sion mourns in fear
  Speis uns, o Gott, deine
    Kinder 1656
  Thine honor save, O Christ;
    X110165 Thine honor
    rescue
  Wenn dein herzliebster Sohn,
    o Gott 1630
  What laws, my blessed Sa-
    viour
  Yea, as I love, Jehovah saith
  Zion klagt mit Angst
Heginbothom, Ottiwell, 1744-68
  Blest Jesus! when my soar-
    ing
  Great God, let all our tune-

forth; X102068 Farewell!
I say with
Valet will ich dir geben 1613
Herbert, Annie
When the mists have rolled;
  R111129 We shall know as
  we
Herbert, George, 1593-1633
  Come, my way, my truth
  Enrich, Lord, heart, mouth
  King of glory, King of peace
  Let all the world in every
  My heart lies dead
  Sweet day, so cool, so calm
  Teach me, my God and King
  The God of love my shepherd
  Throw away thy rod, Throw
    away
Herbert, Petrus, d 1571
  Die Nacht ist kommen
  Faith is a living power
  Now it is evening; time to;
    X106419 Now Lord be with
    us; X106809 O God, be with
    us
  O comforter, God Holy Ghost
  O, exalt and praise the Lord
  The night is come wherein
Herford, Brooke, 1830-1902
  Lead us, heavenly Father;
    X105085 Lead us ... Shep-
    herd Kind
Herman, Norbert, 20th c
  Hail, noble Column, speak
  O Christ, of angel legions
  O Cross, no stars thy glow
  O Hunter blessed, of hearts
  St Joseph, pride of heaven's
  Sweet Gabriel, O blessed
Herman, Nicolaus (or Hermann,
  Nikolaus), ca 1480-1561
  Die helle Sonn' leucht't
  Let all together praise our God
  Lobt Gott, ihr Christen
  Mine hour appointed is at hand
  Hinunter ist der Sonnenschein
    1560
  Now hush your cries and shed
  Praise God the Lord, ye sons
  So wahr ich leb' spricht Gott
    der Herr 1560
  Sunk is the sun's last beam
  The happy sunshine now is gone

The hours' decline and
  setting
The morning sun illumes
The radiant sun shines
The sun's bright rays are
The sun's last beam of
  light
Wenn mein Stündlein vorhan-
  den ist 1562
When my last hour is close
Ye Christians, sing a joyful
Hermannus Contractus, d 1054
  (ascribed to)
  Alma redemptoris Mater;
    X100352 Alma, Alma,
    Alma
  Come, Holy Ghost, come,
    Lord
  Hail holy Queen enthroned;
    R110752 Triumph all ye
  Hail, O Holy Queen! Hail
  Hail, Queen of the Heavens!
    Hail, Mistress
  Hail, Queen of heaven, hail
    our Mother
  Hail, Queen of heaven, the
    Ocean Star
  Salve Regina coelitum
  Salve Regina, Mater miseri-
    coridae
Hernaman, Claudia Frances,
  1838-98
  Lord, who throughout these
    forty; X110435 Throughout
    these
  The call to arms is sound-
    ing
Herr, Amos
  I owe the Lord a morning
    song
Herrick, Robert, 1591-1674
  Down with the rosemary
    and bays
  Here a little child I stand
  In the hour of my distress
  In numbers, and but these
    few
  In this world, the Isle of
  What sweeter music can we;
    R111126 We see him come
  When virgin morn doth call
Herrnschmidt, Johann Daniel,
  1675-1723

Lobe den Herren, O meine
Our God is truth, most faith-
ful
Praise the Almighty, my soul
Praise thou the Lord, O my
Storms of trouble may assail
With hearts and with voices
Hertzog (or Herzog), Johann
Friedrich, 1647-99
And now another day is gone
see Isaac Watts, And now
Another day is at its close
Now that the day hath reached
Nun sich der Tag geendet hat
1670
Since now the day has reached
Hess, Isabella R., 20th c
A week within the sukko green
Father, as the day I greet
Father bless these [this] birth-
day children [child]
For the golden sun
Hear my prayer, O hear my
Lord, written in rocks
Hester, James McNaughton, 1924-
O Mother dear, this day in
May
Heusser-Schweizer, Meta, 1797-
1876
Lamb, the once Crucified!
Lion
Long hast thou wept
Hewett, John William, 1824-86
In the name of God, the Father
Hewitt, Eliza E., 1851-1920
For Christ and the church let;
R102267 For Christ our
dear
"Give me thy heart," says
"Have faith in God," the Sa-
viour; R106548 O blessed
faith
I am thinking today; R111708
Will there be any
Listen to the blessed; R103478
Him that cometh unto
More about Jesus would I
know; X105992 More ... I
would know
Sing the wondrous love of;
R111523 When we all get to
There is rest, sweet rest;
R110095 There's a blessing

There is sunshine in my
soul; R107659 O, there's
sunshine; X110126 There's
sunshine in
Trying to walk in the steps;
R103623 How beautiful to
walk
Hay, Johann Wilhelm, 1789-
1854
As each happy Christmas
Hey, Wilhelm, 1789-1854
Aus dem Himmel ferne, Wo
die Englein sind
Can you count the stars;
X101140 Canst thou count
From yon distant heaven
Heyder, Friedrich Christian,
1677-1754
I come, O Saviour, to thy
table
Ich komm' zu deinem Abend-
mahle 1710
Heywood, Florence L.
Breaking through the clouds
Hear our prayer, O gracious
Heywood, Thomas, 1574?-1641
I sought Thee round about
Hibbard, Agnus S.
Father in heaven, in thy
love
Hickok, Francis Marion, 1844-
1916
Come, Holy Spirit, Dove
divine
Hickson, William Edward,
1803-70
God bless our native land
Now to heaven our prayer
Higbee, E.E., 1830-99
Jesus, o'er the grave
Thy glory thou didst mani-
fest
Higginson, Thomas Wentworth,
1823-1911
From street and square,
from
No human eyes thy face
may see
The past is dark with sin
To thine eternal arms, O
God
Hill, Frances Thompson
Let us sing of Easter glad-

O God, my days are dark in-
deed
Holden, Oliver, 1765-1844
They who seek the throne
Hole, Samuel Reynolds, 1819-
1904
Sons of labor, dear to Jesus
Holland, Henry Scott, 1847-1918
Judge eternal, throned in
Holland, Josiah Gilbert, 1819-81
There's a song in the air
Holling, T. Ernest, 1867-
O Holy Spirit, Comforter
Holm, Nils J., 1778-1845
How blessed is the little
Holme, James, 1801-82
God, my Father, hear me
pray
Holmes, John, 1904-62
Now give heart's onward
habit
O Lord of stars and sunlight
Peace is the mind's old
Though man, the fiery element
Holmes, John B., 1767-1843
At thy feet, at thy pierced
Holmes, John Haynes, 1879-
All hail, the pageant of
America triumphant! Brave
land
God of the nations, near
O Father, thou who givest all
O God, whose law from age to
O God, whose love is over all
O God, whose smile is in the
sky
O thou, whose Presence moved
O'er continent and ocean
Show us thy way, O God
The voice of God is calling
Thou God of all, whose Spirit
Thou God, whose living voice
Holmes, Oliver Wendell, 1809-
94
Angel of peace, thou hast
Build thee more stately
Lord of all being, throned;
X109259 Sun of our life,
thy
O Lord of hosts! Almighty
King
O Love divine, that stooped
Our Father, while our hearts

Thou gracious God, whose
mercy; X110264 Thou
gracious Power
Holroyd, James, 1850-1933
Spirit of holiness, do thou
Holy Family Hymns, 1860
Jesus, ever loving Saviour
Holy songs, carols, and
sacred ballads, 1878
I sought the Lord, and
afterward
Knock! but O most patient
Homburg, Ernst Christoph,
1605-81
Christ, the life of all
Jesus, meines Lebens Leben;
R109344 Tausend-tausend-
mal
Jesus, source of my salva-
tion
O wondrous Conqueror
Of my life the life, O Jesus
Where wilt thou go, since
night
Wo willst du hin, weil's
Homer, Charlotte G.
Fear not, for God the
Father; R109985 Then
trust Him in
In loving kindness Jesus
came; R102418 From
sinking sand
Hood, Edwin Paxton, 1820-
85
God, who hath made the
daisies
I hear a sweet voice ringing
Jesus lives, and Jesus leads
O walk with Jesus wouldst
Hooker, Brian, 1880-
Filled full and flushed
Hopkins, John, 16th c
Ye righteous in the Lord
Hopkins, John Henry, 1820-91
Blow on, thou mighty wind
Christ our King to heaven
Come with us, O blessed
Jesus
God of our fathers, bless
We three kings of Orient
are; R107599 O star of
wonder
When from the East the wise

men
Hopkins, Josiah, 1786-1862
    O turn ye, O turn ye, for why
    Why sleep ye, my brethren
Hoppe, Anna Bernardine Dorothy
1889-1941
    Ascend, dear Lord! Thy earth-
        ly
    By nature deaf to things divine
    Desire of every nation
    Eternal God, our Father
    Have ye heard the invitation
    He did not die in vain
    Heavenly Sower, thou hast
    How blest are they who through
    I open wide the portals
    Jesus, O precious name
    Jesus, thine unbounded love
    Like Enoch, let me ever walk
    Lord Jesus Christ, the child-
        ren's
    O dear Redeemer, crucified
    O Father mine, whose mercies
    O Friend of sinners, Son
    O God of mercies, Father
        mine
    O joyful message, sent from
    O Lord, my God, thy holy law
    O precious Saviour, heal
    O thou who once in Galilee
    O'er Jerusalem thou weepest
    Precious child, so sweetly
    "Repent, the kingdom draweth"
    Rise, arise! Rise, arise!
        Zion
    The Sower goeth forth to sow
    Thou camest down from heaven
    Thou goest to Jerusalem
    Thou hast indeed made manifest
    Thou Lord of life and death
    Thou virgin-born incarnate
Hopper, Edward, 1818-88
    Jesus, Saviour, pilot me
Hopps, John Page, 1834-1911
    Father, lead me day by day
    Father, let thy Kingdom come
    God of our fathers, hear
    Hark, hark, my soul! Thy
        Father's voice; R102159
        Father of mercy; X103148
        Hark ... The Saviour's
    We praise thee, Lord, for
        hours

Horace, i.e. Quintus Horatius
Flaccus, 65 to 8, B.C.
    Happy the man, and happy
        he
    He who is upright, kind
    Integer vitae
Horder. Book of praise for
children, 1875
    My father, hear my prayer
Horn, Edward Traill, III,
1909-
    Long ago and far away;
        R103228 He came among
        us
Horn, Johann, i.e. Johann Roh,
d 1547
    Gottes Sohn ist kommen
    O be not thou dismayed
    Once He came in blessing
Horn, William W., 1773-1826
    Pure and free from all
Horne, Charles Silvester,
1869-1914
    For the might of thine arm;
        X102313 For the strength
    Sing we the King who is com-
        ing; R101443 Come let us
        sing
Horne, George, 1730-92
    See the leaves around us
Horne, William, 1716-
    May we to thee, our Shep-
        herd
Horton, Edward Augustus, 1843-
    We honor those whose work
Hoskins, Joseph, 1745-88
    In thy great name, O Lord
    It shall be well, let sinners
    Let thoughtless thousands
    On Christ, by faith, my soul;
        X107938 On Christ ...
        I would
    Sinners, behold the Lamb of
        God
Hosmer, Frederick Lucian,
1840-1929
    All hidden lie the future
    Father, to thee we look in
        all; X102187 Father ...
        turn away
    Forward through the ages
    From age to age how grand-
        ly

From age to age they gather
From many ways and wide a-
part
Go not, my soul, in search
Hear, hear, O ye nations
I came not hither of my will
I little see, I little know
I walk the unfrequented road
Immortal by their deed
Lo, the day of days is here
Lo, the Easter-tide is here
Made lowly wise, we pray no;
    X111114 We pray no more
Not always on the mount may
we
Now while the day in trailing
O beautiful, my country
O blest the souls that see
O day of light and gladness
O Light, from age to age
O Lord of life, where'er they
O Name, all other names
above
O prophet souls of all the
years
O thou in all thy might so far
O thou in lonely vigil led
O thou, who art of all that is
O thou, whose Spirit witness
On eyes that watch through
One thought I have, my ample
Over the land in glory
Through willing heart and
Thy kingdom come! on bended
Thy kingdom come, O Lord
Today be joy in every heart
Uplift the song of praise
We cannot think of them;
    X103843 I cannot think
When courage fails and faith
When shadows gather on our
way
Hoss, Elijah Embree, 1849-
O God, great Father, Lord
Hostetler, C. K.
Shadows never darken heaven;
    R110081 There shall be no
Hostetter, P.
A servant of God, the apostle
Hott, George P.
I am looking for the city;
    R107646 O, the glory gates
In from the highway, in from;

R103389 Help us to win
them
Saviour, to thee I come
'Tis hard to bear the heavy;
    R103256 He knows, He
knows
Houghton, Frank, 1894-
Facing a task unfinished
My Lord, who in the desert
fed
O thou who dost direct my
feet
Thou who wast rich beyond
Houghton, Will H.
Lead me to some soul to-
day
Housman, Laurence, 1865-
1959
Fair is their fame who
stand
Father eternal, Ruler of
Honor and glory, power and
Lord God of Hosts, within
The maker of the sun and
moon
The Saint who first found
When Christ was born in
Hovden, A.
Help me, Lord, by thy great
Hovey, Richard, 1864-1900
See Carmen, Bliss. We are
adventurers
How, William Walsham, 1823-
97
Ashamed of thee, O dearest
Lord
Behold a little child
Behold, the Master passeth
by
Bowed low in supplication
Come, praise your Lord
For all the saints, who from;
    X102263 For all thy saints
For all thy love and good-
ness
It is a thing most wonderful
Jesus! Name of wondrous
love
Lord Jesus, when we stand
afar
Lord, this day thy children
Lord, thy children guide
O daughters blest of Galilee

O holy Lord, content to fill
O Jesus, crucified for man
O Jesus, strong and pure
O King of Kings, whose reign
O Lord, it is a blessed thing
O my Saviour lifted
O one with God the Father;
   X107697 O thou, our God
   and
O Jesus, thou art standing
O thou, through suffering
O Word of God incarnate;
   X107866 O Word ... most
   holy
On wings of living light;
   X105251 Lift up your heart
Rejoice, ye sons of men
Soldiers of the cross, arise
Summer suns are glowing;
   X102845 God's free mercy
The angel sped on wings
The ever-changing seasons
The joyous life that year by
The year is swiftly waning
This day the light of heaven-
   ly; X110183 This day at
   thy
Thou art the Christ, O Lord
To thee our God, we fly;
   R107311 O Lord, stretch
We give thee but thine own
We praise thy grace, O Sa-
   viour
Who is this so weak and help-
   less
Winter reigneth o'er the land
With trembling awe the chosen
Howard, D. H.
  As above the darkest storm-
   cloud
  Behold the heavenly city
  Gone! yes, but for a little
  In sorrow and affliction
  O hollow, soulless pomp
  The more thou puttest in
  The way, we know, is rough
Howard, Mildred E.
  Since Jesus gave his life;
   R106144 My life, O Lord
Howard, Pearl Waggoner
  Lord, bless thy word to every
Howard, W. James

O King of nations, Splendor
Howe, Julia Ward, 1819-1910
  Bid the din of battle cease
  Mine eyes have seen the
   glory; X102549 Glory,
   glory!
  The world is glad, the
   world
Howitt, Mary Botham, ca
  1804-88
  Thou, earth, art ours
Howson, John Saul, 1816-85
  At all times praise the
   Lord
Hoyt, May P.
  Here at thy table, Lord
Hubbell, Susan S.
  For the summer's glowing
Huckel, Oliver, 1864-
  O Mind of God, broad as
Hudson, Ralph E., 1843-1901
  At the cross, at the cross
   <u>see</u> Watts. Alas and did
   <u>my</u> Saviour bleed
  My life, my love I give;
   R104194 I'll live for Him
Huffaker, Perry L., 1902-
  Father in heaven, lo, thine
Huffman, Nelson T., 1901-
  Hear thou our prayer, Lord
  Lord, we beseech thee
Hugg, George C.
  When this poor heart is
   burdened; R106280 Nobody
   knows like
Hughes, J. Donald
  Creator of the universe
Hughes, Thomas, 1823-96
  O God of truth, whose living
Huish, O. P.
  Come unto Jesus; ye heavy
   laden
  Jesus, my Savior true
  There is a land whose sunny;
   R110876 Utah, Utah, beau-
   tiful
Hull, Amelia Matilda, ca 1825-
  82
  And is it true as I am told
  There is life for a look;
   R105400 Look! Look!
   look

Hull, A. The casket, 1865
Ich weiss einen Strom;
R107532 O Seele, ich bitte
O have you not heard of that;
R107530 O seek that beautiful
Hull, William Winstanley, 1794-1873
To the God of all creation
Humbert, Harold
We build a sanctuary sure
Humphreys, Joseph, 1720-
Blessed are the sons of God
Hungarian Mass-song
O Most Holy, One and only
God   (1797)
Thirsting for the living (1855)
Hunter, J. Hymns of faith and life, 1889
How near to us, O God
Hunter, John, 1848-1917
Dear Master, in whose life
Hunter, William, 1811-77
In seasons of grief to my God
My heavenly home is bright;
R104208 I'm going home
The Great Physician now;
R109310 Sweetest note
There is a spot to me more
Hunter-Clare, Thomas Charles, 1910-
Fear not, my soul, alone to
God of the pastures, hear our
Lord, thy word hath taught
Huntingdon, Selina, countess, 1707-91
When thou, my righteous Judge
Huntington, DeWitt C., 1830-1912
O think of the home over there;
R108179 Over there, over
Huntington, George
Two empires by the sea
Hupton, Job, 1762-1849
Come ye faithful, raise;
X101559 Come, ye people
Hurditch, Charles Russell, 1839-
Come let us all unite to sing;
X101426 Come ... unite and
Hurn, William, 1754-1829
Arise, O Lord, and shine;
X100514 Arise, O God,

and
Hus [Huss], John [Jean], 1373-1415 (authorship in some doubt)
Jesus Christ, our blessed
Jesus Christus, Gottes Sohn. 1415
Jesus Christus, nostra salus
Jesus Christus, unser Heiland
To avert from men God's wrath
NOTE: This is the oldest known Moravian hymn, ca 1400
Husenbeth, Frederic Charles, 1796-1872
Stars of glory shine
Hussey, Jennie E., 1874-
I stood alone at the bar of God
King of my life, I crown thee;
R105097 Lest I forget
Huston, Frank C.
The service of Jesus true;
R104494 It pays to serve
Hut, Hans.
O Allmächtiger Here Gott! 1564
Hutchings, William Medlen, 1827-76
When mothers of Salem
Hutchinson, Albert H.
For all the blessings of the
Hutton, James, 1715-95
Besprinkle with thy blood my
Come, faithful Shepherd, bind
My opening eyes with rapture
Teach me yet more of thy blest
Hyde, Abigail Bradley, 1799-1872
Dear Saviour, if these lambs
Say, sinner! Hath a voice
Hyde, W. H.
We have heard from the bright
Hyde, William DeWitt, 1858-1917
Creation's Lord, we give thee;
X108923 Since what we choose
Hymns adapted to the public

worship of the Christian Church.
Princeton, 1828
   Within thy house, O Lord
Hymns and Tunes, 1890
   Follow the path of Jesus
Hymns of the English Conference
[Swedenborgian] 1880
   Built by Jehovah's hand
   Cast upon the Lord thy care
   Great God! thou dost all
   Great God, we give thee praise
   Great refuge of the weary soul
   Jesus, in thee our hopes
   Jesus, thou Shepherd of us all
   Jesus, thou source of life
   Lord Jesus, God of heaven
   O blest Redeemer, from thy
   O comfort to the weary
   O fix my heart, my God
   O God, my heavenly King
   O King of Kings, beneath
   Rest remaineth, O, so sweet
   The Lord our Saviour is the
     way
   Thou art the mighty King
   Thou, Jesus, art the way
   Thy mighty power we sing
   Where for safety shall I fly
   Within thy tabernacles, Lord
   Ye Christians, tune your
Hymns of the Spirit, 1864
   Come thou Almighty Will
   Give forth thine earnest cry
   God is in His holy temple
   In this peaceful house;
     X104423 In thy peaceful
   O, come, and let us all, with

I

Image, Selwyn
   The snow lies thick upon
   Three kings in great glory
Imber, N. H.
   Kol od balayvov p'neemo
Indian (Asia) Prayer
   Listen to our prayer, O Lord
Indians (American) traditional
   see Chippewa, Dakota, Omaha
Ingelow, Jean, 1820-97
   And didst thou love the race
   The parson knew that he had
Ingemann, Bernhardt Severin,

1789-1862
   As gold by fire is tested
   As wide as the skies
   Christmas brings joy
   Christmas is here with joy
   I live, and I know the span
   Igjennem Nat og Trängsel
     1825
   Jesus, my Saviour, my
     Shepherd
   One is our God and Father
   Through the night of doubt
Ingham, Benjamin, 1712-72
   The one thing needful
Ingham, John Hall
   Land of the North, where
"The Inner Light"
   Lord of Good Life, the
     hosts
Innocent III, Pope, 1161-1216
   Veni, Sancte Spiritus BUT
   NOTE: Most translations of
     this hymn are filed within
     "Latin, 12th c" sequence
Innocent VI, Pope, d 1362
   Ave verum Corpus natum;
     X100652 Ave, ave verum
     corpus
   Hail to thee, true Body,
     sprung
   Hail, true Body, born of
     Mary
   Hail, true Body, truly born
Iris, Scharmel
   O, he who walked with
     fishermen
Irish traditional, etc.
   Christmas day is come; let's
     (17th c)
   Be thou my Vision O lord
     (ancient)
Irish Psalter, 1898
   Unto my Lord Jehovah said
Irons, Genevieve Mary, 1855-
1928
   Drawn to the cross, which
     thou
Irons, William Josiah, 1812-
83
   Father of love, our Guide
   Sing with all the sons
   Triumphant Lord, thy work
Irwin, Samuel Wesley, 1875-

For swinging wind, and tree-
top birds
Isaacs, A.S., 1851-1920
A noble life, a simple faith
At midnight, so the sages
Italian traditional, etc.
Glory be to Jesus, who in
(18th c)
Hail, Jesus, hail, who for
my (18th c)
Viva! Viva! Gesù! che per
mio (18th c)
Iverson, Daniel
Spirit of the living God;
X109172 Spirit ... fall fresh

J

NOTE: Words, such as Iam,
Iesù, etc., are herein spelled
Iam, Jam, Jesù, etc., and
are filed accordingly.
Jesu and Jesus are always
interfiled.

"J.E.A."
My Savior's praises I will;
R101997 Every day will I
"J.H."
Sitting at the feet of Jesus
"J.V.C." [Crosby?]
All ye saints of light; R111222
We'll walk in
Jackson, F.A., 1867-1942
Down the mines for buried;
R103503 Hold the ropes,
then
Master, we thy footsteps
Jackson, Frederick
Standing in the market-place
Jackson, H.G.
If you from sin are longing;
R105402 Look to the Lamb
Jackson, Mary E.
Come forth, O Christian youth
Jackson, W.P.
To the cross of Christ I'm
Jacobs, George
O Lord! to thee who dwellest
Jacobs, Henry Eyster, 1844-
1932
Lord Jesus Christ, we humbly
Nearer my God to thee ...

Through word and sacra-
ment; X101833 Draw me,
O Lord
Jacobs, Henry S.
How goodly is thy house
Jacobs, W.K.
When the trump shall sound;
R109993 Then we'll be
happy; X111500 When the
trumpet (Black)
Wonderful Saviour, Redeemer
Jacopone, i.e. Jacopone di
Benedetti of Todi, d 1306
At the cross her station;
X106234 Near the cross
her; X106235 Near the
cross was
By the cross her vigil
Stabat Mater dolorosa
Jahn, Martin, ca 1620-ca 82
see Janus, Martin
James, Annie L.
Is there a heart that is;
R104676 Jesus is passing
James, Mary D.
All for Jesus! All for Jesus!
In the rifted Rock I'm;
R106384 Now I'm resting
Jameson, Love H., 1811-92
Night, with ebon pinion
Janus, Martin, ca 1620-ca 82
Jesu, joy of man's desiring
O, at last I've found
Janvrin, Alice Jan, 1846-1908
He expecteth, He expecteth
Japanese national anthem
Kimi ga yo wa chi yo
Unto a thousand, yea
Jaques, John
O say, what is truth
Softly beams the sacred
Jarvis, Mary, 1853-1929
O God of ages in whose light
Jastrow, Marcus Mordecai,
1829-1903
Blessed, O blessed, moment
When the Sabbath peace-invit-
ing
Jeffrey, H.R.
Come home, poor sinner, why;
R104677 Jesus is pleading
O, why should I be idle;
R109603 The laborers are

Ya-a-leh ta-cha-nu-nay-nu
Yigdal Eloheem chai (Doxology)
Yim-loch A-do-noy l'olom
Y'-vo-re-ch'-cho A-do-noy
Zoch-ray-nu la-cha-yeem
Jewitt, Alfred Charles, 1845-
1925
Past are the cross, the scourge
Jex-Blake,Thomas William, 1832-
1915
Lord we thank thee for
Joergen, L.
O where is the home of the
soul
"John", pseud, see Foote, John
G., supposed author
John, Duke of Argyll, see Camp-
bell, John, Duke of Argyll,
1845-1914
Johns, John, 1801-47
Come, Kingdom of our God
Johnson, Catherine H., 1835-
The whole wide world for Jesus;
X109921 The whole ... once
more before we
Johnson, Erastus, 1826-1909
O sometimes the shadows are;
R107657 O then to the Rock
Johnson, Henry Harrold, 1869-
Bring beams of oak
Johnson, Joseph, 1848-1926
God speaks to us in bird
Johnson, Joel H.
All hail the glorious day
High on the mountain top
The glorious gospel light
Johnson, Josephine, 1890-
In this stern hour
Johnson, Samuel, 1822-82
City of God, how broad
Father, in thy mysterious
God of the earnest heart
I praise thee, Lord, for;
X103828 I bless thee, Lord
Life of ages, richly poured
Onward, Christian! though;
X108044 Onward, Onward,
tho'
Thou, whose glad summer
yields
Johnson, William, 1906-
Deep are his wounds, and
red

Johnson, Julia Harriette, 1849-
1919
Here we come with gladness
Marvelous grace of our lov-
ing; R102902 Grace,
Grace, God's
There's a sweet and blessed;
R100349 Alleluia, what a
"Joint Committee".
My God, my God, O why
hast
Jonae, Laurentius, d 1597
A Star is moving through
Jonas, Justus, 1493-1555
If God were not upon our
side (Ps. 124, tr. by
Winkworth)
Jones, Charles P.
Jesus Christ is made to me;
R111745 Wisdom, righteous-
ness
There is nothing in the world;
R107070 O, I love to tell
Jones, Edith, 1849-1929
Father, who art alone
Jones, Edmund, 1722-65
Come, humble sinner, in
whose
Jones, Harriet E.
We have a Rock, a safe;
R108118 Our Jesus is the
Rock
Jones, John Samuel, 1831-
I was made a Christian
Now the busy week is done
Jones, Lewis E., 1865-1936
Though the way we journey;
R111131 We shall see the
King
When I have reached earth's
R101145 Carried away to
Would you be free from the;
R110068 There is pow'r;
X111867 Would you be
free from the burden;
X111869 Would you be
free from your burden
Jones, R. Lawrence
Grant us, O God, a single
aim
Jones, Samuel M.
Haste, O haste, delightful;
R101993 Ever growing,

swiftly
Jonson, Ben, 1573-1637
    I sing the birth was born
    Truth is the trial of itself
Joseph of the Studium, d 883
    see St Joseph, the hymno-
    grapher, d 883
Judah ben Samuel Halevi
    O Lord, where shall I find
Judson, Adoniram, 1788-1850
    Come, Holy Spirit, Dove
    divine
Jukes, Richard
    By faith I view my Saviour
Julian, John, 1839-1919
    Father of all, to thee
    Hark! the voice eternal
    O God of God! O Light of
    Light
Justinian, Emperor, 483-565
    O Word immortal of eternal
    God
Juvenile Harmonist, 1837
    Little children praise

                    K

"K", in Rippon. Selection of
    hymns, 1787
    How firm a foundation, ye;
        X104252 In every condition
    In songs of sublime adoration
Kahl, Johan, 1721-46
    Arise, my soul, arise!
    Stretch
Kalir, Eleazer
    Tent-like this day the King
Kálmán, Farkas
    Where, O God eternal, where
Kauffman, Daniel
    We bow to thee, O Lord, on
        high; R105424 Lord, as this
        solemn
Kauffman, Frieda
    Worthy art thou, Lord divine;
        R105517 Lord, I thank thee
Kauffman, see also Coffman
Keats, John, 1795-1821
    A thing of beauty is a joy
Keble, John, 1792-1866
    Ave Maria! blessed Maid
    Blest are the pure in heart
    Draw, Holy Ghost, thy seven-

fold
    God, the Lord, a King re-
    maineth
    Lord, in thy Name thy ser-
    vants
    New every morning is thy
        love; X104162 If on our
        daily; X106254 New ... is
        thy love; X107778 O timely
        happy
    One thy Light, the temple
    Sun of my soul, thou Saviour;
        X110537 'Tis gone, that
    The Lord hath reigned, and
    The voice that breathed o'er
    The year begins with thee
    There is a book who runs may;
        X110013 There is ... that
        all
    When God of old came down
    Word supreme, before crea-
    tion
Keegan, G. Kearnie
    Are you tired of the life;
        R103251 He is watching
Keimann, Christian, 1607-62
    Freuet euch, ihr Christen
    I will leave my Saviour never
    Jesus I will never leave;
        X106052 My dear Jesus
        I'll
    Jesus will I never leave
    Meinen Jesum lass' ich nicht
    1658
    O, rejoice, ye Christians
Keller, Arnold Frederick, 1890-
    Under the feeble stable light
Kellogg, Caroline
    Very softly I will walk
Kelly, Claire B.
    O Holy Spirit, lead us
Kelly, Thomas, 1769-1854
    Behold the temple of the Lord
    Blessed fountain, full of
    grace
    Boundless glory, Lord, be
    thine
    Come, see the place where
    Jesus
    Come, ye saints, look here
    "Give us room that we may"
    God of our salvation, hear
    us

Hark, ten thousand harps and
Hark! ten thousand voices
Hark! that shout of rapture
How sweet to leave the world
I hear a voice that comes
I love the sacred book of God
In thy name, O Lord, assemb-
    ling
Jesus comes, his conflict over
Jesus, thou Shepherd of the
Look, ye saints, the day;
    R101625 Crown him! Crown
    him (Stebbins)
Look, ye saints, the sight
On the mountain's top; X107960
On the mountain top
Of thy love some gracious
Praise the Saviour, we who
    know
Saviour, send a blessing
Saviour, when we call, O hear
Sing of Jesus, sing forever
Sion stands with hills
Sion's King shall reign
Speed thy servants, Saviour
"Stricken, smitten, and"
The atoning work is done
The head that once was crown-
    ed
The Lord is risen indeed
Through the day thy love has;
    X110425 Through ... kept
    us; X110427 Through ...
    hath spared
We sing the praise of him
"We've no abiding city here"
Whence these sounds symphon-
    ious
Who is this that comes from
Why those fears! Behold, 'tis
Kemp, Harry, 1883-1960
    I cannot put the Presence by
    Joses, the brother of Jesus
    Who thou art I know not
Ken, Thomas, 1637-1711
    All praise to thee, my God;
        X102569 Glory to Thee,
        my
    All praise to thee, who safe
    Awake, my soul, and with;
        X102572 Glory to thee,
        who
    Her Virgin eyes saw God

Praise God, from whom all
Preist Gott, der allen Segen
    Gibt!
Since we can't doubt God's
Kendon, Frank, 1893-
    As we rode down the steep
    What songs are these, faint;
        R109858 The stars shall
Kennedy, Benjamin Hall, 1804-
89
    How blest the man, who fears
    O Lord our King how bright
        thy
    The heavens, O God, thy
        glory
    Why do the heathen rage
Kennedy, Gerald, 1907-
    God of love and God of
        power
Kennedy, Mrs. W. J.
    We are saved by the grace;
        R107046 O how deep are
        the; X107065 O how won-
        drous
Kent, John, 1766-1843
    What cheering words are
        these
Kerr, Hugh Thomson, 1872-
1950
    Come thou my Light, that I
        may
    God of our life, through all
Kethe, William, d ca 1593
    All people that on earth
Key, Francis Scott, 1779-1843
    Before the Lord we bow
    Lord, with glowing heart
    O say can you see by the
        dawn's
Key, Robert Ellis
    O Love whose perfect path
    So brightly burns Love's
        holy
Kidder, Mary Ann, 1820-1905
    Ere you left your room this;
        R107061 O how praying
        rests
    I am bought not with riches;
        X104454 Is my name
        written; X105510 Lord, I
        care not; R106161 My
        name's written
    We shall sleep, but not

Kieffer, A.A.
There's a city of light 'mid;
R105209 Let us pray
Killinghall, John, d 1740
In every trouble, sharp and
Kilmer, Joyce, 1886-1918
I think that I shall never
No longer of him be it said
Kimball, Edward P.
God loves us, so he sent
Kimball, Marriet McEwan, 1834-1905
Pour thy blessings, Lord
Kimball, Rosamond
Hark to the sound; it rings
King, John, 1789-1858
When his salvation bringing
Kingo, Thomas Hansen, 1634-1703
Dearest Jesus, draw thou
Enhver som tror og bliver
döbt 1689
He that believes and is
How fair the church of Christ
I come, invited by thy Word
I pray thee, dear Lord Jesus
Like the golden sun ascending
Lov og Tak og evig Äre 1689
Nu rinder Solen op Af Öster-lide 1699
O dearest Lord, receive from
O Jesu, blessed Lord, to thee
O Jesu, gid du vilde
1699
O Jesu, söde Jesu, dig 1689
On my heart imprint thine
Our table now with food
Over Kedron Jesus treadeth
Praise to thee and adoration
Print thine image pure and
Seal my heart with thine
Skriv dig, Jesu, paa mit
Softly now the day is ending
Som den gyldne Sol frembryder
The kingdom Satan founded
The sun arises now in light
The way that unto Jesus leads
Thy love, O gracious Lord
Kingsbury, William, 1744-1818
Great Lord of all thy churches
Let us awake our joys
Kingsley, Charles, 1819-75
From thee all skill and

The day of the Lord is at
Kinner, Samuel, 1603-68
Herr Jesu Christ, du hast
bereit't 1638
Lord Jesus Christ, thou hast
Lord Jesus, thou art truly
Kipling, Rudyard, 1865-1936
Father in heaven, who
lovest; X105049 Land of
our birth
God of our fathers, known
of
Non nobis, Domine! Not un-
to
Kirby, W. H.
Forth to the fight, ye;
R105257 Lift ye the
Snow-white
Kirk, S.C.
Hear ye the Master's call;
R102005 Every work for
Jesus
Kirkland, Patrick Miller,
1857-1943
Jesus, Lord, Redeemer
Kirkpatrick, William J.
I've wandered far away from;
R101580 Coming home,
coming
Saved to the uttermost
Kitchin, G.W., 1827-1912
Lift high the cross, the
love
Kite, Florence Lauer
O Christ, our leader and
our
Klantendorfer, Paulus, d 1566
Another day is at an end
Klein, Max D.
All praise to thee we bring
Kleinman, Bertha A.
Come, hail the cause of
Zion's
Klopstock, Friedrich Gottlieb,
1724-1803
Blessed are the heirs of
heaven
Knak, Gustav Friedrich Ludwig,
1806-78
Jesus, Sun of gladness
Let me go, let me go,
from
Knapp, Albert, 1798-1864

Dear Father, who hast made
Father of heaven, who hast
Father, who hast created all
More than all, one thing my
O Father, thou who hast
O God, whom we as Father
O Vaterherz, das Erd' und
Knapp, Edward Everett
From the Pilgrims' rock-
bound
Knapp, Shepherd, 1873-1946
Dear God, the sun whose;
X106325 Not only where
God's
Lord God of Hosts, whose
Knight, Joel Abel
Fain would my soul with
Knight, William Allen
Come, my heart, canst thou
Knobel, Elizabeth
Now do we come, O God, to
Knollis, Francis Minden, 1815-
63
There is no night in heaven
Knorr, Christian, Baron von
Rosenroth, 1636-89 see
Rosenroth, Christian Knorr
von, 1636-89
Knowles, Frederick Lawrence,
1869-1905
Who is the patriot? He who
Knowles, James Davis, 1798-
1838
O God, though countless worlds
Knowlton, Miss H.O.
Jesus loves the little children
Koch, Hans, & Leonhard Meister
Ach Gott Vater im Höchsten
Thron. 1524
Kockritz, Ewald, 1876-1931
As fades the daylight splendor
Koitsch, Christian Jacob, 1671-
1734
O Fountain eternal of life
O Saviour, the truest, the
best
Kolb, A.B.
Christ who left his home in
Dear Saviour, when I think of
Kolb, A.C.
O, when I think of that
Kooyman, Frank I.
How beautiful thy temples,

Lord
In memory of the crucified
Thy spirit, Lord, has
stirred
When in the wondrous
realms
Korean hymn
The Saviour's precious blood
Koren, Ulrik Vilhelm, 1826-
1910
Al verden nu raabe for
Herren
Ye lands to the Lord make
a
Kramer, Edgar Daniel
His was no regal splendor
Kramer, Maritius
Send, O God, a gentle
shower
Krause, Jonathan, 1701-62
Alleluia! Fairest morning!
Kretzmann, Paul Edward,
1883-
Ever content with the ways
of
Father, hear thy child
Fervent in spirit, serving
I will bless thee, said the
Immanuel! God with us!
Immanuel! Our God and
Lord
Lead, O Lord! above the
Little Baby Jesus, born to-
day
Lord God Almighty, King of
Lord, thine fore'er today I
O come before Jehovah
O God of love and truth
O mighty God of earth and
Praise and honor to the
Father
The God of the ages your
refuge
The Lord is near! why
should
When upon the raging waters
With thee, O Lord, alone
to go
Krishna Pal, ca 1764-1822
O thou, my soul, forget no
Krummacher, Cornelius, 1824-
84
Star whose light shines o'er

Krummacher, Friedrich Adolf,
1767-1845
  Thou art the Way, the Truth
Kuhlmann, J. H.
  Almighty God, I humbly ask
  Bowed down beneath a weight
  Fling wide thy gates, O church
  God of nations, throned above
  Hark! the King of heaven is
Kuipers, William
  I hear in the air, 'neath the
  I love the Lord, the fount of
  In the good ship of our captain;
    R101886 E'en tho' the clouds
Kunth, Johann Sigismund, 1700-
  79
  A rest remaineth for the weary
  Es is t noch eine Ruh' vor-
    handen 1730
  Yes, there remaineth still
Kurzenknabe, J. H.
  Heavenly Father, I would pray
Kyle, R. W.
  O Holy Father, Holy Son

L

"L. W. M. "
  Have you any room for Jesus;
    R108652 Room for Jesus
Lacey, Thomas Alexander, 1853-
1931
  O faith of England, taught of
  The dying robber raised his
Lacy, William S., d ca 1900
  Slowly sinks the setting sun
Ladies of the Grail, England
  Come ring out our joy
  Cry out with joy to the Lord
  Defend me, O God, and plead
  Have mercy on me, God, in
  He who dwells in the shelter
  How great is your name
  I lift up my eyes to the moun-
    tains
  I love the Lord for he has
  I rejoiced when I heard them
  I trusted even when I said
  If the Lord does not build
  Like the deer that yearns
  My shepherd is the Lord
  My soul glorifies the Lord
  O blessed are those who fear
  O give thanks to the Lord

O give the Lord, you sons
O praise the Lord, all you
Out of the depths I cry
The Lord is king, , with maj-
  esty
The Lord's is the earth and
To the Lord in the hour of
To you have I lifted up my
When the Lord turned the
Why this tumult among na-
  tions
"A Lady", in Sacred melodies,
1840-41
  O speed thee, Christian, on
Laing, Dilys Bennett, 1906-
60
  Man imperishably stands
Lamb, Thomas, 1758-
  Hail, thou wondrous Infant
  Peace on earth, heaven is
Lambert, N.
  Teach me, O Lord, to fol-
    low
Lamberts, L. J.
  O bless our God with one
Lambeth Palace. 15th c ms
  O Prince of Peace, who man
LaMonnoye, Bernard de, 1641-
1728
  Guillaume prends ton tam-
    bourin
  Willie take your little drum;
    R108193 Patapan
Lamp, M. Willard, 1883-
  God of our history, our
    fathers
Lancaster, Mary Ann Elizabeth
(Shorey), 1851-
  I have a Friend so precious
Landis, Hans
  Ich hab ein schön neu Lied
    gemach. 1614
Landor, J. E.
  Called to the feast by the
    King; R111482 When the
    King comes
Landstad, Magnus Brostrup,
1802-80
  A slumber I know in Jesus'
  Awake thou that sleepest
  Before thee, God, who
    knowest
  Darkness o'er the earth is

Der mange skal komme fra
Öst og fra Vest. 1861
Full many shall come from
the; X105349 Lo, many shall
come; X110080 There many
shall
I come to thee, O blessed Lord
I hus og Hjem, hvor Mand og
Viv. 1861
I know of a sleep in Jesus'
In house and home where man;
X106551 O blessed home
Jeg kommer her, o söse Gud.
1863
Jeg staar for Gud, som Alting
veed. 1861
Jeg ved mig en Sovn i Jesu
Navn. 1861
Naar Synderen ret Ser sin
Now Jesus at the door is
They come from the east and
(authorship uncertain);
R110138 They come from
the thorny path
Thou holy Church, God's city
To thee, O Lord, the God of
When sinners see their lost
Lane, Franklin K.
I am whatever you make me
Lange, Ernst, 1650-1727
Though I speak with angel
Lange, Joachim, 1670-1742
Jesus, thy light again I view
Jesus, what offering shall;
X106922 O God, what offer-
ing
Lange, Johann Peter, 1802-44
The Lord of life is risen
Langhans, Urban, fl 1540-62
Lasst uns alle frölich sein
Let us all in God rejoice;
X105193 Let us all with
Larned, Augusta, 1835-
In quiet hours the tranquil
Lanier, Sidney, 1842-81
Into the woods my Master
went
Lankton, Martha J.
Dwell in me, O blessed Spirit
Larcom, Lucy, 1826-93
Draw thou my soul, O Christ
I learned it in the meadow
I thank thee, Lord for prec-

ious
In Christ I feel the heart
O God, thy world is sweet
We are children of one
Father
What shall I do, my Lord
Yea, o'er me soared the
eternal
Larsen, Jens
Brothers and sisters, we
now
The Lord be praised! I'm
Lathbury, Mary Ann, 1841-
1913
All hail, all hail to the New
Arise, all souls, arise!
Break thou the Bread of life;
X101033 Break thou, O
Lord
Day is dawning in the east
Day is dying in the west;
R103541 Holy, holy,
holy
O Shepherd of the nameless
fold
O, trust ye in the Lord
Take thou the heart I can-
not
Lathrop, John Howland, 1880-
O bold O foolish peasants;
R103602 Hosanna in the
Lathrop, Theodore B., 1881-
On this glad day we dedicate
Latin traditional, etc.
NOTE: Hymns within this sec-
tion were either published
anonymously or have had
such a long acceptance with-
in the office hymns and the
liturgy of the Church that
the author was forgotten
centuries ago. Other hymns,
of known source, are cited
under that source. Translators have not been recog-
nized.

A child is born in Bethlehem
(14th c carol)
A messenger within the grave
(4th-5th c)
A priestly Heart the Sacred
Heart; R107502 O Sacred

with
Ad coenam Agni providi
Ad regias Agni dapes (4th c)
Adeste, fideles (18th c);
    X100134 Adeste fideles
    (English text)
Adoremus te, panem coelitum
All hail, adorèd Trinity (be-
    for 11th c)
All praise to Jesus' hallowed
    (11th c)
All ye a certain cure (18th c)
All ye who seek a comfort
    sure (18th c); X100310 All
    ye ... sure relief; X100312
    All you who seek
Alleluia! best and sweetest
    (11th c)
Alleluia, song of gladness
    (11th c); X100343 Alleluia
    ... sweetness
Almighty God, who from the
    flood (6th-7th c)
An image of that heavenly light
    (15th c)
Angelus ad virginem (14th c)
As the sun doth daily rise
At the Lamb's high feast
    (4th c)
Attende, Domine, et miserere
    X100131 Ad te Rex summe
Ave Maria gratia plena (13th
    c)
Ave, Maris stella, Dei Mater
    (9th c)
Ave, Regina caelorum (12th c)
Be joyful, Mary, Heavenly
    (17th c)
Be present, Holy Trinity (ca
    10th c)
Behold! behold He cometh
Blessed be God! Blessed be
Blessed City, heavenly Salem
    (7th c)
Blessed feasts of blessed
    martyrs (12th c)
Blest creator of the light
Cas radosti, veselosti (12th c)
Child of a Virgin, Maker (8th
    c)
Christ above all glory (5th c)
Christ alone is our salvation
    (7th c)

Christ, enthroned in highest
    (13th c)
Christ is arisen From the
    grave's (11th-12th c)
Christ is made the sure
    (7th c); X101248 Christ,
    thou art
Christ is our corner-stone
    (7th c)
Christ ist erstanden (11th-
    12th c)
Christ the glory of the sky
    (5th c)
Christe, du Lamm Gottes (5th
    c)
Christe, qui lux es et dies
    (before 9th c)
Christus ist erstanden
    (11th-12th c)
Christus vincit! (8th c)
Claro paschali gaudio (4th c)
Come God Creator, Holy
    Ghost (11th c)
Come hither, ye faithful
    (18th c)
Come, Holy Ghost, Creator
    blest (9th c)
Come, Holy Ghost, Creator
    come (9th c)
Come, Holy Ghost, in love
    (9th c)
Come, Holy Ghost, our souls
    (9th c)
Come Holy Ghost, send down
    (9th c)
Come, Holy Spirit from above
    And from the realms
    (9th c)
Come Holy Spirit, from above
    And kindle in our breasts
    (9th c)
Come let us adore Him (18th
    c)
Come, O Creator Spirit blest
    (9th c)
Come, O Creator Spirit,
    come (9th c)
Come, pure hearts, in sweet-
    est (12th c)
Come rejoicing, Faithful
    men (11th c or earlier)
Come rejoicing, Praises voic-
    ing

Come, thou Holy Paraclete
(13th c)

Come, thou Holy Spirit, come
(9th c)

Come thou now and be among
us (7th c); X100921 Blessed
city

Concordi laetitia (13th c)

Conditer alme siderum (9th c)

Cor dulce, cor amabile

Cor Jesu, salus in te

Confirma hoc Deus

Creator alme siderum (7th c)

Creator of the starry height
(9th c)

Creator of the stars of night
(9th c)

Creator Spirit, all divine (9th
c)

Creator Spirit, by whose aid
(9th c)

Creator, Spirit, heavenly Dove
(9th c)

Creator Spirit, Lord of Grace
(before 10th c)

Day of wrath! O day (13th c,
perhaps by Thomas Celano)
X101667 Day of judgment
(Newton); X101669 Day ...
doom impending; X101672
Day ... that day of

Day of wrath, O dreadful (13th
c, Perhaps by Thomas
Celano)

Dear crown of all the Virgin-
choir (8th c)

Dear Maker of the starry skies
(7th c)

Der Tag, der ist so freudenreich (14th c)

Deus, tuorum militum (6th c)

Dies est laetitia (14th c)

Dies irae, dies illa (13th c,
perhaps by Thomas Celano)
X109484 The day is surely
(Ringwaldt)

Dormi Jesu! Mater ridet

Dost thou truly seek renown
(14th-15th c)

Earth's mighty Maker, whose
(7th c)

Eastern monarchs, Sages three
(15th c)

Ecce nomen Domini Emmanuel
(very early)

Ecce sacérdos magnus

En clára vox redarguit (5th-
6th c)

Eternal glory of the sky (6th
c)

Eternal Light, Divinity (18th
c)

Eternal Monarch, King most
high (5th c)

Eternal Son of God, O Thou
(11th c)

Exsultet orbis gaudiis (10th
c); X102014 Exultet orbis

Faithful cross! above all
others

Far be sorrow, tears and
sighing (13th c)

Fast sinks the sun to rest
(18th c)

Father, most holy, merciful
(ca 10th c); X102130
Father ... and tender

Finita iam sunt praelia
(publ. Cologne, 1695)

Gabriel to Mary came (14th
c)

Gaudeamus igitur

Gloriosi salvatoris (15th c)

Glory be to the Father, and
to the Son (2d c)

Good Christian men, rejoice
(14th c)

Guardian of virgins (19th c)

Hail, heavenly Queen! Hail;
R103032 Hail, foamy ocean

Hail Mary, hail Mary, full of;
(13th c); X103058 Hail
Mary, full of

Hail, O Star that pointest
(9th c)

Hail Ocean's beauteous Star
(9th c)

Hail, our monarch, son of
David

Hail the day so rich in cheer
(before 1422)

Hail, thou living Bread
(1815)

Hail thou living Victim blest

Hail thou Star of ocean (9th
c)

Hail, thou who man's Redeemer
   (7th c)
Hark! a thrilling voice (ca
   6th c); X103138 Hark! a
   herald voice; X103140 Hark!
   a mystic voice
Hark! the herald host (11th c)
Hark the hosts of heaven (11th
   c)
He who to Jesus manfully bore
   (8th c)
He whom joyous shepherds
   (1410)
He, whose confession God of
   old (8th c)
Heart of Christ my King (15th
   c)
Heart of our Lord, O loving
High Word of God, who once
   (10th c)
His cheering message from
   (4th-5th c)
Holy Ghost, my comforter
   (9th c)
Holy Spirit, come and shine
   (9th c)
Holy Spirit, gently come
   (9th c)
Holy Spirit, Lord of Light
   (12th c)
I give my heart to thee (9th c)
If great wonders thou desirest
Incline thine ear, O Lord;
   R105967 Mighty King of
   heaven
Ingrediente Domino in sanctam
Iste conféssor Dómini (8th c)
It is no earthly summer's ray
   (6th c)
Jesus Christ is risen today.
   Alleluia (14thc); X108984
   Sing we to our God
Jesu, coróna Virginum (8th c)
Jesus, creator of the world
   (18th c)
Jesu Deus, amor meus
Jesu, grant me this, I pray
   (17th c)
Jesu, our hope, our heart's
   (7th c)
Jésu redémptor ómnium (6th c)
Jesu, the Father's only son
   (6th c)

Jesus, the Ransomer of man
   (6th c)
Jesu, thy mercies are un-
   told
Jesu, who this our Lenten-
   tide
Joseph, pure spouse (1670)
Joy because the circling
   year
Joy dawned again on Easter
   Day (4th c)
Joy to thee, O Queen of
   heaven (14thc)
Kyrie. God Father in heaven
   (ca 1100)
Kyrie, Gott Vater in Ewig-
   keit (ca 1100)
Latin Breviary see Breviary
Laudate Dominum, laudate
Languéntibus in Purgatorio
Let all on earth their voices
   (10th c)
Let hearts awaken, now the
   night (6th c)
Let the round world with
   songs (ca 10th c); X105103
   Let all the earth
Let us live, then, and be
   glad
Life-spring divine and bond
   (6th c)
Light's glittering morn (4th
   c)
Lord, accept the gifts we
   offer
Lord God, our Father, thou
Lord God, thy praise we sing
   (5th c)
Lord in thy Love abide with
Lord Jesus Christ, all
   praise (11th c)
Lord Jesus, who our souls to
   save (14th c)
Lord of Creation, bow thine
   (11th c)
Love of the Father, love of
   God (12th c)
Maiden Mother, meek and
   mild (13th c)
Maker of all things, Lord
Maker of man, who from thy
   (7th c)
Martyr of God, whose strength

(10th c)

Most holy Lord and God (4th-5th c)

My God, I believe in thee

Now at the Lamb's high royal (4th c)

Now in holy celebration (15th c)

Now is the healing time (before 12th c)

Now let the earth with joy (10th c)

Now sing we, now rejoice (14th c)

Now that the daylight fills (6th c)

Now that the day-star glimmers (6th c)

Now that the sun is gleaming (6th c); X106447 Now that ... beaming

Nunc sancte nobis spiritus (4th c)

O bone Jesu! Miserere nobis

O Boundless Wisdom, God most (6th c)

O bread of Life from heaven (1661)

O bread to pilgrims given (1661)

O Christ, our hope, our heart's (8th c)

O Christ our joy, gone up on high (5th c)

O Christ, our joy, to whom (5th c)

O Christ, thou art our joy (5th c)

O Christ, thou Lamb of God (5th c)

O Christ, thou Lord of worlds

O Christ, who art the Light (before 9th c)

O come, all ye faithful (18th c); X100134 Adeste fideles (English text) ; X101328 Come, all ye; X106640 O come ... joyfully

O come, Creator Spirit, come (9th c)

O come, O come, Emmanuel (ca 9th c); X106653 O come, Immanuel; X106662 O come,

O come, Immanuel; X101837 Draw nigh, draw nigh

O cor, amoris victima

O cor Jesu flagrans amore

O cor Jesu, fons amoris

O Emmanuel, Rex et legifer (early)

O esca viatorum, O panis (1661)

O fair Creator of the skies (7th c)

O food of exiles lowly (1661)

O Food of men wayfaring (1661)

O Food that weary pilgrims (1661)

O Food to pilgrims given (1661)

O glorious King of martyr-hosts (ca 6th c)

O glorious Maid, exalted far (ca 9th c)

O God-head hid devoutly; R107537 O Shepherd of

O God the Father, draw thou

O God, thy soldiers' crown (6th c); X106909 O God ... faithful Lord; X106910 O God ... great reward

O Heart of Jesus, purest heart (18th c)

O heavenly Jerusalem (18th c)

O Holy Spirit, Lord of life (4th c)

O Jerusalem, look toward the East

O Jesu Christ, from Thee began (9th c)

O King most high of earth (17th c)

O King of Kings in splendor; R101254 Christ we praise

O Lamb of God, that takest (5th c)

O Light of Light, by love (10th c)

O Maker of the stars of night (9th c)

O Maker of the world, give ear

O Paschal feast, what joy

O Pater sancte, mitis atque (10th c)

O Saviour Jesu, not alone (9th c)

O sing the great Apostle (17th c)

O sinner, for a little space (17th c)

O sinner, raise the eye (17th c); X107554 O sinner, lift

O thou eternal King most high (5th c)

O thou pure light of souls (7th-8th c)

O thou, who dost accord us (6th c)

O thou who dost to man accord (6th c)

O thou, whose all-redeeming (8th c)

O wondrous type! O vision (15th c)

O word, that goest forth (ca 7th c)

Ocean star, we greet you (9th c)

Omnis mundus jucundetur nato (12th c)

On the wood His arms (12th c)

Only-begotten, Word of God (ca 9th c)

Orémus pro Pontifice nostro

Pie Jesu Dómine, dona eis

Portal of the world's salvation (15th c)

Puer natus in Bethlehem (14th c)

Puer nobis nascitur (15th c)

Quae est ista

Queen, when the earth was first hurled (20th c; 1955)

Quem pastores laudavere (1410)

Qui regnas in perpetuum; R105981 Miserere illi

Reges de Saba veniunt (14th c)

Regina caeli, jubila (17th c)

Regina caeli laetáre (14th c)

Rerum Deus tenax bigor (6th c)

Résonet in laudibus (14th c)

Saint of God, elect and precious (11th c)

Salútis humánae sátor (7th c)

Salve, pater Salvatoris (1874)

Sanctify me wholly, Soul of Christ (14th c)

Saviour eternal! health and life (before 11th c)

Shepherds came, their praises (1410)

Shepherds left their flocks (1410

Sing forth with gladsome (14th c)

Son of a Virgin, Maker of (8th c)

Soul of Jesus, make me whole (14th c)

Soul of my Saviour, sanctify my breast (14th c)

Sounds of joy have put to flight (13th c)

Spirit divine, Creator, come (9th c)

Sub tuum praesidium

Suscipe Domine universam

That day of wrath, that dreadful (13th c: Thomas of Celano); X109488 The day of wrath (Scott tr.)

That Easter Day with joy (5th c); X109397 That Easter-tide

The church above forever rings (7th c)

The dawn is sprinkling in the east (before 8th c)

The dawn was purpling o'er the sky (4th c)

The day draws on with golden (4th or 5th c)

The fast, as taught by holy (6th c)

The glory of these forty days (6th c)

The Lamb's high banquet doth invite (7th c)

The Lamb's high banquet we await (7th c); X109605 The Lamb's ... called to

The merits of the saints (8th c)

The morning kindles all the

sky (4th c)
The strife is o'er (publ.
Cologne, 1695); X101904
Ended His strife
The sun is sinking fast (1805)
Thee God we praise, Thy
name (5th c); X109960 Thee
God ... holy name we
Thee we adore, eternal Lord
(5th c)
Thee we praise, eternal Lord
(5th c)
This is the day where-on (8th
c)
Thou that art so fair (13th c)
Thou whom shepherds wor-
shipped (1410)
Though in midst of life we be
(12th c)
To Christ, the Prince of Peace
(18th c)
To the Name of our salvation
(15th c); X110649 To ...
that brings; X110650 To ...
that is; X110652 To the
name that is (Dearmer)
To Thee, Redeemer, King;
R103341 Hearken, O Lord
Tollite hostias, et introite
Tota pulchra es, Maria (15th
c)
Triumphantly doth Christ
(20th c: 1925)
Tu, Christe, nostrum gaudium
(5th c)
Tu gloria Jerusalem
Ubi caritas et amor Deus
Unto us a boy is born (15th c)
Veni creator spiritus (9th c)
X101385 Come, Holy Ghost
Veni, Jesu, amor mi
Veni, veni, Emmanuel (9th c)
Victoria! Victoria! Surrexit
Virginis proles, opifexque
(8th c)
Vivat! vivat! Vivat Pastor
Vox clara ecce intonat (6th c)
When Christ our Lord had
passed (4th c)
Ye faithful, with gladness
(18th c); X100134 Adeste
fideles (English text)

LaTrobe, Benjamin, 1725-86
I will rejoice in God
In this world so full of snares
Jesus' name, Source of life;
X104778 Jesus' name,
Jesus' name
O, how blessed is the station
LaTrobe, Christian Ignatius,
1758-1836
For our transgressions Thou
Let not your heart be faint
Lord of life! now sweetly
Met around the sacred tomb
Resting in the silent grave
Saviour of thy chosen race
See Jesus seated 'midst His
Sing praises unto God on
high
Weep, Sion, weep, in death's
Latta, Eden Reeder, 1839-
He keepeth me ever
I have something I would tell
In the day of all days;
R105143 Let me find a
place
Jesus, thou hast promised;
R104598 Jesus, come and
Not far from the Kingdom
O I long to see the beauty;
R105074 Lead me to the
Wanderer in sinful ways;
R103250 He is waiting
Laufenberg, Heinrich von, d
ca 1458
I know a lovely angel-game
Ich weiss ein lieblich
O Jesus Christ, our Lord
most; X105557 Lord Jesus
Christ
Laufer, Calvin W., 1874-1938
O Master of the loving heart
O thou eternal Christ of God
Thee, holy Father, we adore
We thank thee, Lord, thy
paths
Laurenti, Laurentius, 1660-1722
Ermuntert euch, ihr From-
men
O Saviour of our race
O thou essential Word, God
Rejoice, rejoice believers;
X108383 Prepare your

lamps; X108447 Rejoice, all
ye
Laurinus, Laurentius Laurentii,
1573-1655
In heaven above, in heaven
Lauterbach, Johann Michael,
1716-87
Bow down ye followers of the
Lavater, Johann Caspar, 1741-
1801
O Jesus Christ, grow thou
in
Lawson, James
I will follow thee, my Saviour
Lazarus, Emma, 1849-87
Kindle the taper
Remember Him, the Only One
Leachman, Edgecombe Walter,
1870-1945
Christian, unflinching stand
Lear, John W., 1870-
None can satisfy but Jesus
The way is dark, I dare not
go; R103989 I need thee,
Lord
Leatham, Edith Rutter, 1870-39
Thank you for the world so
Leatherman, Sarah C.
Some days are dark and dreary;
R108134 Our rest will soon
LeDorz, F.
O Virgin all lovely, O Mother
Lee, Frederick George, 1832-
When day's shadows lengthen
Speak gently to the erring
Lee, Harry, 1877-1942
My Master was so very poor
Lee, M. Owen
As Victor in the strife
Dominic, our Lady's champion
Michael, prince of all
Now the world is saved
Patrick, thee addressing
Lee, Olav, 1859-
How blessed is the host in
white
Lee, William Arthur
God of the circling realms
Leech, Lida Shivers, 1873-
Bring ye all the tithes;
R110774 Trust Me, try Me
God's way is the best way
I have made my choice;

R110163 Thine for service
Leeson, Jane Elizabeth, 1807-
82
Gracious Saviour, gentle
Shepherd; X102915 Gra-
cious ... Little ones are;
X102916 Gracious ... Our
little ones
Loving Shepherd of thy sheep
Saviour, teach me, day by
day
Sweet the lesson Jesus
taught
Lehman, F.M.
The love of God is greater;
R107364 O, love of God
Lehmann, W.H.
Beneath thy cross I stand
Take thou my life, dear
Lord
Lehr, Leopold Franz Fried-
rich, 1709-44
Mein Heiland nimmt die
Sünder an. 1732
My Saviour sinners doth;
X101327 Come, all that
O come, if sinner be thy
Leiser, Joseph
For garnered fields
LeJeune, George Fitz-Curwood,
1842-1904
O the golden glowing morn-
ing
Leland, John, 1754-1841
Lord, keep us safe this
night
The day is past and gone
O, when shall I see Jesus
(authorship in doubt)
Leon, Johannes, d 1597
My all I to my God com-
mend
O God, thou righteous
Leonard, George Hare
It is the day of all the year
Leonard, Julia
Little stars are shining
Leslie, J.H.
Lead me safely on the narrow
Levinger, Elma Ehrlich
In the candles' rays I see;
R101898 Eleazer stead-
fast

Levy, David
  Around the weary world
  As birds unto the genial
  Now upon the earth descend-
    ing
Levy, J. Leonard
  Come, ye faithful servants
  Father, to thy dear name
Lew, Timothy T'ingfang (i. e.
  Liu T'ing-fang) 1892-1947
  O Bread of Life, for all men;
    X109426 The bread of life
Lewis, Edgar
  Just lean upon the arms;
    R105088 Lean on his arms
Lewis, Howell Elvet, 1860-1953
  Friend of the home: as when
  High Priest divine, from
    whom
  Lord of light, whose Name
  The days that were, the days
  The light of the morning
  Whom oceans part, O Lord,
    unite
Leyda, Ida F.
  In the early morning dark
Liander, C. G.
  A way to Calvary leadeth
Lias, Una R.
  Though mountains may depart
Liebenberg, M. F.
  Jesus, Master! at thy word
Lieder-Perlen. Concordia, 19th c
  Segne, Herr, mit deinem
    Geiste
  Send, O Lord, thy Holy Spirit
Lillenas, Haldor, 1885-
  Like the sunshine after rain;
    R107652 O, the peace
  Patiently, tenderly pleading;
    R101814 Don't turn him
    away
  Wonderful grace of Jesus;
    R111841 Wonderful the match-
    less
Lillenas, Bertha Mae
  When the clouds are hanging
    low; R105094 Leave your
    burden
Lindborn, Heinrich, 1712-50
  Jesus Christ from death hath
Lindsay, Vachel, 1879-1930
  An endless line of splendor

  Let not young souls be
Lindsay, W. Robert
  Walking in the sunshine;
    R102250 Follow, we will
Linn, Fay
  O May we be still and seek
Linthicum, Blanche
  Out of James one twenty-two;
    R100751 Be ye doers
Liscovius, Salomo, 1640-89
  Jesus, my highest treasure
Litany of Loreto
  Ave, Regina sacratissimi
  Glorious Mary, Queen and
    Giver
Litany of the Sacred Heart
  Cor Jesu sacratissium
Lithuanian traditional, etc.
  Jesus, when we go to rest
Little, Velma G.
  Great King of Peace, hear
    now
Littledale, Richard Frederick,
  1833-90
  God the Father, God the Son
  God the Father, God the
    Word
  God the Father, seen of
    none
  Holy Spirit, heavenly Dove
  I worship thee, Lord Jesus
  In paradise reposing
  Jesus, Saviour ever mild
  Lord Jesus, by thy passion
  O Lord, to whom the spirits;
    R107179 O Lamb of God
  O sing to the Lord, whose
  Spirit blest, who art adored
Littlefield, Milton Smith,
  1864-1934
  Come, O Lord, like morn-
    ing
  O Son of man, thou madest
Littlewood, R. W., 1908-
  Thou who dost rule on high
Littlewood, William Edensor,
  1831-86
  There is no love like the
    love; R104724 Jesus' love
Liturgy of Malabar
  Hands that have been handling
  Strengthen for service,
    Lord

Liturgy of St James, 5th c
    From glory to glory advancing
    Let all mortal flesh keep
    Not a thought of earthly
Livermore, Abiel Abbot, 1811-
92
    A holy air is breathing round
Livermore, Mary A., 1820-1905
    Jesus, what precept is like
Lloyd, William Freeman, 1791-
1853
    My times are in thy hand;
        X108145 Our times are in
        thy
    Sweet is the time of spring
    Wait, my soul! upon the Lord;
        X110926 Waft [sic] my soul
Lobwasser, Ambrosius. Psalter,
1617
    Audi, Deus me vacantem
Lochner, Karl Friedrich, 1634-
97
    Soul, what return has God
    Was gibst du denn, o meine
Lock Chapel Collection, 1803
    Come Holy Spirit, calm my
    mind
Lockwood, Amelia DeF.
    Saviour, who thy life didst
Loehe, Wilhelm, d 1872
    O Son of God, in coeternal
Loes, Harry Dixon
    Looking unto Jesus, in faith
Loewen, Lois
    We owe the Lord an evening
        song; R111945 Yes, Lord,
        we thank
Logan, John, 1748-88
    Let Christian faith and hope
        (authorship disputed)
London Hymn book, 1864
    Lord Jesus, I love thee, I
    know
Long, John Davis, 1838-
    The evening winds begin
Longfellow, Henry Wadsworth,
1807-82
    Ah! what a sound! The in-
    finite
    All are architects of fate
    As torrents in summer
    Down the dark future
    I heard the bells on Christmas

I shot an arrow into the air
O then, sail on, thou ship
Sleep, comrades, sleep,
    sleep
We have not wings, we can-
    not
When Christ was born
Longfellow, Samuel, 1819-92
    A voice by Jordan's shore
    Again, as evening's shadow
    Bless thou the gifts our
    hands
    As darker, darker fall
    around
    Beneath the shadow of the
    cross
    Eternal One, thou living
    God; X111780 With joy
    we claim
    Father, give thy benediction
    Go forth to life, O child
    God of the earth, the sky
    God's trumpet wakes
    Holy Spirit, Truth divine;
        X103564 Holy Saviour,
        truth
    I look to thee in every need
    In the beginning was the
    Word
    Light of ages and of nations
    Lo, the earth is risen again;
        X105359 Lo ... awakes
        again
    Now, on land and sea de-
    scending
    O God, in whom we live;
        X107686 O Thou in whom
    O God, thou Giver of all
    good. 1864
    O life that makest all things;
        X107201 O life that maketh
    O still in accents sweet
    One holy Church of God
    Out of the dark the circling
    Sing forth His high eternal
    The loving friend to all
    The summer days are come;
        X109881 The sweet June
    days
    Thou Lord of life, our sav-
    ing
    'Tis winter now
Longstaff, William D., 1822-94

Take time to be holy
Lopatnikoff, Sara Henderson Hay
(i.e., Mrs. Nikolai Lopatnikoff)
1906- <u>see</u> Hay, Sara Henderson,
1906-
Lord, Emily Bryant, 1839-86
   Maker of earth and sea
Lorenz, S.E. (i.e. presumed
identification of "S.E.L."
signature)
   Ready to suffer grief
Loring, Louisa Putnam, 1854-
   O thou who turnest into
Loskiel, George Henry, 1740-
1813
   Lord, while I with thee
"Louisa E."
   I love to think of my home;
      R103592 Home, sweet home
Louise Henriette von Brandenburg
   see Luise Henriette ...
Loveless, Robert C.
   Every day with Jesus
Loveman, Robert
   Here let thy people come
   There is a joy the heart can
Lowell, James Russell, 1819-91
   Great truths are portions
   Men whose boast it is that ye
   Of all the myriad moods
   Once to every man and nation;
      X107928 Oft to every man;
      X111341 When a deed is done
   The ages one great minster
   The Holy Supper is kept
   "What means this glory"
   Where is the true man's
Löwenstern, Matthäus Apelles
von, 1594-1648
   Christe, du Beistand deiner
   Christ, thou the champion
   Jesus, our Captain, hope
   Lord of our life, and God;
      X104793 Jesus, our Captain
   Now let all loudly sing praise
   Nun preiset alle Gottes
Lowry, Robert, 1826-99
   I need thee, O I need thee
      (refrain only)
   Low in the grave He lay;
      X105828 Lowly entombed;
      R110852 Up from the grave

My life flows on in endless
O worship the Lord in the
   beauty; R106795 O glory
   hallelujah
Shall we gather at the river;
   R111953 Yes, we'll gather
What can wash away my
   stain; R107477 O precious
   is; X111261 What ... my
   sin
Where is my wandering boy
Lowry, Somerset Corry, 1855-
1932
   Son of God, eternal Saviour
   Ye who are banded as com-
   rades
Loy, Matthias, 1828-1915
   An awe-full mystery is here
   At Jesus' feet our infant
   Come, humble soul, receive
   Give me, O Lord, a spirit
   I thank thee, Saviour, for
   Jesus, thou art mine for-
   ever
   Jesus took the babes;
      X104898 Jesus ... the
      lambs
   Launch out into the deep
   Listen to those happy voices
   Lord Jesus, though but two
   or
   O Great High Priest, forget
   O Lord, who hast my place
   The Gospel shows the
      Father's
   The Law of God is good
   Though angels bright escape
Lucas, Alice, 20th c
   Almighty God, who hearest
   Behold, it is the spring-
   tide
   How wondrous is thy world
   Lord, do thou guide me
   Lord God, whose breath
   May He who kept us through
   Out of the depths, O Lord
   "Take unto you the boughs"
   The Lord, my Shepherd still
   Unto the hills I lift mine
   Whose works, O Lord, like
Luce, Charles M.
   It is so long a way

Ludämilia Elisabeth of Schwarz-
burg-Rudelstadt, 1640-72
  Care for me, O God of grace
  Jesus, Jesus, Jesus only;
    X104688 Jesus, Jesus,
    only
  Jesus, Jesus, nichts als
    Jesus. 1687
Luise Henriette von Branden-
burg, 1627-67
  Jesus Christ, my sure Defence;
    X101223 Christ, my Rock
  Jesus, meine zuversicht
Luke, Jemima, 1813-1906
  I think when I read that sweet
Luther, Charles C., 1847-1924
  Must I go, and empty-handed
Luther, Martin, 1483-1546
  A mighty fortress is our God;
    X100047 A mighty ... our
    Lord; X100048 A mighty
    stronghold; X100251 All
    power is given (Root)
  A safe stronghold our God is
  A tower of strength our God
  Ach Gott vom Himmel seih
  Ah, dearest Jesus, holy child;
    X102480 Give heed, my
    heart
  All praise to thee, eternal
    (from an ancient requiem, to
    which stanzas are added)
    X100262 All praise ... God
  Almighty God, I call to thee
  Aus tiefer Not schrei' ich zu
    dir. 1523
  By help of God I fain would
  Christ Jesus lay in death's
  Christ Jesus, once to death
  Christ lag in Todesbanden
  Come, Holy Spirit, God;
    X101385 Come, Holy Ghost
  Dear Christians, let us all
  Dear Christians, one and all
  Die Asche will nicht lassen
  Dies sind die heil'gen zehn
  Ein' feste Burg
  Erhalt uns, Herr, bei,
    deinem
  Es woll' uns Gott genädig sein.
    1525
  Flung to the heedless winds
  From heaven high I come;

    X100161 Ah, dearest
    Jesus; X102393 From
    heaven above to; X111208
    Welcome to earth
  Gelobet seist du, Jesu Christ
  Good news from heaven
  Gott sei gelobet und geben-
    ediet. 1524
  Guds Ord det er vort
    Arvegods
  Had God not come, may
    Israel
  Happy the man who feareth
  If God had not been on our
  In death's strong grasps
  In peace and joy I now de-
    part
  In the midst of earthly life
  Isaiah, mighty seer, in days
  Jesaia, dem Propheten, das
  Komm, Heiliger Geist, Herre
  Lo! Christ is risen from
    the
  Look down, O Lord, from
    heaven; X107255 O Lord,
    look down
  Lord Jesus Christ, of Vir-
    gin
  Lord Jesus Christ, to thee
  Lord, keep us in thy Word
  Lord, keep us steadfast
  May God be praised hence-
    forth
  May God bestow on us His
    grace
  Mit Fried' und Freud' ich
  Mitten wir im Leben sind.
    1524
  Now do we pray God, the
    Holy
  Now let us all right merry
  Nun bitten wir den Heiligen
  Nun freut euch, liebe Chris-
    ten g'mein. 1523
  O God, from Heaven look
    down
  O Holy Ghost, to thee we
    pray
  O Holy spirit, come, we
    pray
  O Jesus Christ, all praise
  O my dear heart, young
    Jesus

Our Father, thou in heaven
Our Saviour to the Jordan
Out of the depths I cry;
    X102379 From ... I cry to;
    X102380 From ... I raise
    to; X108158 Out of the deep
    I
Praise we the Lord and bless;
    X107337 O Lord, we praise
That we our will to Him
    might
That man a godly life
The eye can naught but water
The mouth of fools doth God
Thy mercy, Lord, to us
To Jordan came our Lord
To shepherds as they watched
Today we celebrate the birth
Vater unser im Himmelreich.
    1539
Vom Himmel hoch da Komm'
    ich
Vom Himmel kam der Angel
    Schar
Wär Gott nicht mit uns diese
We all believe in one true
    God
We now implore God the Holy
Welcome to earth, thou
When Rome had shrouded earth
Wilt thou, O man, live happily
Lutheran Church, General Council.
  S.S. Book, 1887
    My Church! My Church! My
        dear
Lutheran Church, Ohio Synod.
  Gesangbuch, 1870
    In thy dear name and by thy
Lyman, Helen Hoyt, 1887-
    Since I have felt the sense
Lynch, Roberta B.
    Science the angel with the
        flaming
Lynch, Thomas Toke, 1817-71
    A thousand years have come
    Christ in His word draws near
    Dismiss me not thy service
    Gracious Spirit! dwell with
    How calmly the evening
    Lift up your heads, rejoice!
    My faith it is an oaken staff
    O where is he that trod
    The Lord is rich and merciful

Where is thy God, my soul
Lyon, Carrie Ward, 1879-
    Praise ye, praise ye the
        Lord
Lyon, George W.
    Go and tell the sweet old;
        R109363 Tell it o'er and
    I am trusting in my Saviour
    Jesus my Saviour, look on
        me
    Saviour, keep us close
Lyon, P.H.B., 1893-
    Lift up your voice, ye
        Christian
    O God, before whose altar
Lysaght, S.R., 1870-1941
    Let us be faithful to our
Lyte, Henry Francis, 1793-
1847
    Abide with me: fast falls;
        X100097 Abide ... fast
        breaks the morning
        (Woods)
    Far from my heavenly home
    God of mercy, God of grace
    Jesus, I my cross have
        taken; X105006 Know, my
        soul, thy; X105007 Know,
        O child, thy; X109325
        Take, my soul, thy
    My spirit on thy care
    O that the Lord's salvation
    Pleasant are thy courts
    Praise, Lord, for thee in
    Praise, my soul, the King
    Praise the Lord, His glories
    Redeemed from Guilt, re-
        deemed
    Sweet is the solemn voice
    The mercies of my God
    There is a safe and secret
    'Tis a pleasant thing to see
    When at thy footstool, Lord
Lyth, John, 1821-86
    There is a better world,
        they
Lyttle, Charles H., 1884-
    Bring, O Past, your honor
    Praise God, the Love we
        all
    Rejoice in love we know

M

"M.A.", Fr., O.C.S.O.
  In this your month, Creation's
M A L [pseud presumed to be
    Lathbury, Mary Ann. See her
    Take thou the heart
"M.B.", Sr.
  Heart of the Holy Child
  O sing a joyous carol
"M.J.", Fr., O.C.S.O.
  All of seeing, all of hearing
  Lady in sorrow, silent
"M.L.B."
  Our Father, God of life
NOTE ON FILING ORDER: Mac,
  Mc, and M' are interfiled as
  though spelled Mac

McAfee, Cleland B., 1866-1944
  There is a place of quiet rest;
    R107085 O Jesus, blest
MacAlister, Edith F.B.
  Father, hear us as we pray
McCheyne, Robert Murray, 1813-
43
  Chosen not for good in me
  I once was a stranger to
    grace
  When this passing world is
McComb (or M'Comb), William,
1793-
  Chief of sinners though I be
McConnell, J. Edwin, 1892-1954
  I am happy today; R111666
    "Whosoever" surely
McCook, Henry C.
  Lord of the endless age! We
    raise
McCrae, John, 1872-1918
  In Flanders' fields
McDaniel, Rufus H., 1850-1940
  What a wonderful change in my;
    R108914 Since Jesus came
    into
MacDonald, George, 1824-1905
  O God, whose daylight leadeth
  O Lord of life, thy quickening
  Our Father, hear our longing
  They all were looking for
MacDonald, Mary, 1789-1872
  Child in the manger
McDonald, William, 1820-1901
  I am coming to the cross;
    R103815 I am trusting, Lord

Macduff, John Ross, 1818-95
  Christ is coming! let crea-
    tion
  Everlasting arms of love
  Jesus wept! those tears are
Mace, Nellie B.
  To thee, O God, we bring
  We are hid with Christ
McFadyen, Henry Richard,
1877-
  The lone, wild fowl
MacFarland, John T.
  He is coming! He is com-
    ing!
MacFarlane, J.
  Far, far away on Judea's;
    R102556 Glory to God
McFayden, Henry R., see
  McFadyen, Henry Richard,
  1877-
McGranahan, James (i.e.,
  G.M.J.)
  Someone will enter the pear-
    ly
McGregor, Ernest F., 1879-
  Lift high the triumph song
  O blessed day of Mother-
    hood
McHose, Irvine N.
  O, the great love the dear
    Saviour; R107603 O,
    such wonderful
Mackay, J.B.
  Rouse, ye Christian workers;
    R111722 Winning souls,
    winning
Mackay, Margaret, 1802-87
  Asleep in Jesus! blessed
Mackay, William Paton, 1839-
85
  We praise thee, O God! for;
    X111106 We praise ... the
    Son (Kuipers); R100345
    Alleluia! Thine the
MacKaye, Percy, 1875-1956
  Holy, holy, holy, Lord thy
MacKeever, Harriet Burns,
1807-87
  Jesus, high in glory
  When Jesus shall gather;
    R103306 He will gather

Mack, Alexander, sr., 1679-
1735
   O how is the time so urgent
   O! wie ist die Zeit so wich-
      tig
Mack, Alexander, jr., 1712-
1803
   Bless, O Lord, this church
MacKellar, Thomas, 1812-99
   All unseen the Master walketh
   Book of grace and book of
   Father! in my life's young
   Give me a foot-hold on
   Give me to know thy will
   I thank the Lord, my Maker
   In the vineyard of our Father
   O the agonizing prayer
   There is a land immortal
McKelway, A.J.
   O little Child of Bethlehem
McKenzie, William P.
   Happy the man whose heart
   In mercy, in goodness, how
   O Love divine, that dwells
   Praise now Creative Mind
   There are none friendless
   Trust the Eternal when
   What brightness dawned
McKinney, B.B., 1886-1952
   All on the altar dear Jesus;
      R106038 My all for thee
   As He heard his waiting;
      R104375 In the old-time way
   Blessed Saviour, we adore;
      R102527 Glorious, Glorious
   Christ the Saviour came;
      R103265 He lives on high
   Come, linger here with; R111608
   Whisper a prayer
   Coming now to thee, O Christ;
      R108813 Send a great revival
   Draw near, draw near
   God give us Christian homes
   Have faith in God when your
   Have you failed in your plan;
      R108227 Place your hand
   Holy Spirit, breath on me
      (cf: Hatch, Breath on me)
   I am satisfied with Jesus
   I know the Bible was sent
   In thy holy temple
   Jesus is standing at your
      heart's; R111330 What will

   you do
Lead on, O King of glory;
   R105075 Lead on, lead on
'Neath the stars of the
   night; R106244 'Neath
   the old olive
O, come, all ye that labor;
   R101542 Come to the Sa-
   viour
Out in the darkness of sor-
   row; R109079 Somebody
   needs
Send a revival, O Christ;
   R105688 Lord, send a
   revival
Serve the Lord with glad-
   ness
"Take up thy cross and
   follow"; R111578 Where-
   ever he leads
While passing thro' this
   world; R105159 Let
   others see Jesus
Maclagan, William Dalrymple,
1826-1910
   Be still, my soul, for God
   Holy Spirit, Lord of love
   It is finished! Blessèd Jesus
   Lord, when thy kingdom
      comes
   The saints of God! their
   What thanks and praise to
      thee
MacLeish, Archibald, 1892-
   The people of the earth
   Yet when the splendor of
MacLeod, John, 1840-98
   Blessèd Jesus, high in glory
MacLeod, Norman, 1812-72
   Courage, brother! do not
   With gladsome hearts we
      come
McManus, S.B.
   Dear Lord, I come at last
   I would that I might walk
   Love consecrates the hum-
      blest
McNaspy, Clement
   Look down to us, St Joseph
McNaughton, J.H.
   There is beauty all around
McNeely, Edwin, 1891-
   Jehovah the Lord, Our Sa-

viour
MacNutt, Frederick Brodie,
  1873-1949
  Let all the multitudes of light
McPhail, John
  All those who love and obey;
    R110145 They to my pre-
    cepts
McWhood, Leonard Beecher,
  1870-
  All people of the earth
Madan. Collection: Appendix
  1763
  Now begin the heavenly theme
Madison, Elizabeth Syle, 1883-
  In sweet fields of autumn
Magdeburg, Joachim, 1525-1583
  or later
  Wer Gott vertraut, hat wohl
    gebaut. 1572
  Who puts his trust in God
  Who trusts in God, a strong
Magdeburg, Geistliche lieder,
  1540
  Rejoice, rejoice ye Christians
Mahlmann, Siegfried August,
  1771-1826
  God bless our native land
  Gott segne Sachsenland
Major. Book of praise for home
and school, 1869
  See the shining dew drops
Malan, Henri Abraham César,
  1787-1864
  It is not death to die
  Nein, nein, das ist kein
  No, no, it is not dying
Malin, Annie
  God, our Father, hear us
Malloch, Douglas
  Thank God for the things
Malmivaara, Wilhelmi, 1854-
  1922
  Lord, as a pilgrim on earth
Mann, Frederick, 1846-1928
  My God, my Father, make me
Mant, Richard, 1776-1848
  Bright the vision that delighted
  For thy dear saints; X102262
    For all thy saints; X102320
    For thy dear saint
  God, my King, thy might
  Round the Lord in glory;

X105726 Lord, thy glory
  fills
Son of man, to thee I cry;
  X108752 Saviour, who
  exalted; X109095 Son of
  God! to Thee
Mantzen, Felix
  Mit Lust so will ich singen.
    1526
Manuale cantus sancti. Ratis-
bon, 19th c
  O King of might and splen-
    dor
  Rex summae majestatis
Manwaring, George
  Lord, we ask thee, ere we
  O, how lovely was the
    morning
  Sing we now at parting
  'Tis sweet to sing; R110794
  'Twas Jesus died
  We meet again in Sabbath
March, Daniel, 1816-1909
  Hark, the voice of Jesus;
    X103181 Hark ... Jesus
    crying
Marckant, John, 16th c
  O Lord, turn not away thy
    face; X107335 O Lord
    ... thy face away;
    X107336 O Lord... thy
    face from me
Marcy, Elizabeth Eunice,
  1822-
  Out of the depths to thee I
Markant, John, see Marckant,
  John
Markham, Edwin, 1852-1940
  He pressed on before
  Here on the paths of every-
    day
  Of all things beautiful
  The crest and crowning
  We are all blind, until we
  We men of earth have here
Marks, Josephine Preston
  Peabody (Mrs. L.S. Marks)
  see Peabody, Josephine
  Preston
Marlatt, Earl Bowman, 1892-
  Angels we have heard
    (French carol arr)
  "Are ye able"; X100490

Are ye able, asked;
R105745 "Lord, we are
able"
Be of good cheer
God of the Spirit-Wind
If I can keep one spirit
No longer, Lord, thy sons
Spirit of Life, in this new
Through the night the dream-
ers
Marot, Clement, ca 1497-1544
O Lord, hear thou my calling
Marquis, Don, 1878-1937
A fierce unrest seethes
Marriot, John, 1780-1825
Thou, whose almighty word
Marsden, Joshua, 1777-1837
Go, ye messengers of God
Marshall, Louis
A new shrine stands
Martens, Frederick H.
When blossoms flowered 'mid;
R106655 O come let us
adore
Martin, Civilla D., 1868-1948
Be not dismayed whate'er;
R102840 God will take care
Why should I feel discouraged
Martin, Henry Arthur, 1831-
1911
O Rock of ages, one Founda-
tion
Sound aloud Jehovah's praises
The heavenly King must come
Martin, Hugh, 1890-
Christ who welcomed little
Lord, Jesus, in thy footsteps
Martin, John
We build an altar here
Martin, Sallie (presumed pseud.
of Fanny Crosby)
Conquering now and still to
Martin, Samuel Wesley, 1839-
The gospel bells are ringing;
R102879 Gospel bells, how
Martin, W.C.
In the warfare that is; R105914
May the Lord depend
The name of Jesus is so sweet;
R104784 "Jesus," O how
sweet
Though the angry surges roll
(arr); R100435 And it holds,

my anchor
Where He may lead me I
will; R104824 Jesus shall
lead me
Martineau, Harriet, 1802-76
Faith grasps the blessing
Martineau, James, 1805-1900
A voice upon the midnight
air
He who himself and God
Thy way is in the deep
Where is your God? they
say
Mary Francis, Sr.
Accept, kind Father, bread
and
Because thou hast made
charity
Bringing our praise, we
kneel
Holy is God! the light
To God our Father, Builder
Mary Teresine, Sr.
From the depths we cry
Mary Xavier, Sr. (secular
name: Sybil F. Partridge)
Lord, for tomorrow and its
Masefield, John, 1878-
By weary stages, the old
world
O Christ who holds the open
Sing, men and angels, sing
The water's going out to sea
Mason, Caroline Atherton,
1823-90
O God, I thank thee for each
Mason, Jackson, 1833-89
Forty days of Eastertide
Mason, John, ca 1645-94
Blest day of God! most calm
How shall I sing that majesty
I've found the pearl
Lord, for the mercies of
My Lord, my love, was
crucified
Now from the altar of my
heart; X106372 Now ...
of our hearts
Thou wast, O God, and thou
What shall I render to my
God
Mason, William, 1725-97
Again returns the day of

holy; X100153 Again the day
returns
To Jesus Christ be glory
Massey, Gerald, 1828-1907
Surrounded by unnumbered foes
There lives a voice within
me
Through all the long dark
Masterman, John Howard Bar-
tram, 1867-1933
Almighty Father, who dost
Grant us thy peace; for thou
Lift up our hearts, O King
Masters, Mary
'Tis religion that can give
Mathams, Walter John, 1853-
1931
Christ of the upward way
"God is with us, God is with"
Jesus, Friend of little
Now in the days of youth
Stand fast for Christ
Mather, Howard E.
Where winds the road
Mathesius, Johannes, 1504-65
Lord God, who art my Father
My Jesus' grace and blessing
My heart its incense burning
Matheson, Annie, 1853-1924
Dear Master, what can chil-
dren
Lord, when we have not any
Matheson, George, 1842-1906
Gather us in, thou love
Jesus, Fountain of my days
Make me a captive, Lord
O Love that wilt not let me
go; X107371 O Love that
will not
There are coming changes
Mathews, Basil Joseph, 1879-
1951
Far round the world thy
Matson, William Tidd, 1833-99
God is in His temple
Lord, I was blind; I could not
O blessed life! The heart at
Teach me, O Lord, thy holy
Matters, Margaret Glenn
O Jesus, our dear Master
O Love, our Mother, ever
near

Matthias, John B.
I saw a way-worn traveler
Mauburn, Jean (John), d 1503
Dost thou in a manger lie
O Lord Jesus, I adore thee
Maude, Mary Fawler, 1819-87
Thine for ever! God of love
Maurer, Irving, 1878-
O God, hear thou the na-
tion's
O God, we pray for faithful
Maurer, Oscar E., 1878-
Brother man, awake!
Strength
The Son of God, the Prince
(with Marion Maurer)
Maurice, Bertha Helena
Sweet Sabbath! day of
sacred
Maurice, May
Thou spotless Lamb of God
Maxwell, James, 1720-1800
Didst thou, dear Jesus,
suffer
Go forth, ye heralds, in
my
Maxwell, Mary E.
Thy voice hath spoken, souls
Maxwell, Mary Hamlin, 1814-
53
Saints of God! the dawn
Maxwell, William
Jesus, Master, hear me now
O for the death of those
May, Caroline Elizabeth, 1808-
73
O Saviour, where shall guilty
Mayer, Harry H.
Bow down thine ear, Lord
Come, O holy Sabbath even-
ing
God of Israel, keep us
In sunshine and in storm
O God, my ever constant
Pledging our lives and our
Rejoice, and offer thanks
To worship God in truth
Where Judah's faithful sons
With the voice of sweet
song
Medley, Samuel, 1738-39
Awake, my soul, in joyful;

X100677 Awake ... to joy-
ful
Come join, ye saints, with
I know that my Redeemer
lives; X103929 I know ...
O the sweet joy; X103930
I know ... comfort; X109808
The Saviour lives
Join, all who love the Saviour's
O could I speak the matchless
O what amazing words of grace
Meigs, Charles D.
Lord, help me to live; R111947
Yes, others, Lord
Meigs, Mrs. M. N.
Hark, a burst of heavenly;
R109273 Sweet and clear
Meinhold, Johann Wilhelm, 1797-
1851
Gentle Shepherd, thou hast
Guter Hirt, du hast gestillt.
1835
Tender Shepherd, thou hast
Meir b. Baruch of Rothenburg
Lo, as the potter molds
Meisser, Leonhard
Winter reigns o'er many
Melanchthon, Philip, 1497-1560
Dicimus grates tibi, summe
Herr Gott, dich loben alle
Lord God, we all give praise;
X105482 Lord ... all to
thee
Our thanks and praise to thee
To God let all the human
race
Melmbold, Ludwig
Lord, grant that we e'er pure
Mencken, Lueder, 1658-1726
Come, be my heart's beloved
Mendes, Fred de Sola
Our pious fathers built their
To Bethel came the patriarch
Mentzer, Johann, 1658-1734
I praise thee, O my God
Lord Jesus, thou the Church's
O dass ich tausend Zungen
O Jesu, einig wahres Haupt.
1726
O that I had a thousand voices
O would, my God, that I could
Menzies, G. K., 1869-1954
What heroes thou hast bred

Mercedes, Sr.
Glorious Patron! Low before
Meredith, George, 1828-1909
In singing till his heaven
We sing the rapture
Meredith, Isaac H., 1872-
Seal us, O Holy Spirit;
R108774 Seal us, seal us
Merrick, James, 1720-69
Eternal God! we look to thee
How sweet thy dwellings,
Lord
O turn, great Ruler of the
skies
To thy pastures, fair
Merrill, William Pierson,
1867-1954
Not alone for mighty empire
Rise up, O men of God;
R100504 Arise, arise;
X100519 Arise, O youth
We knelt before kings, we
bent
Merrington, Ernest Northcroft,
1876-1953
God of eternity, Lord of
Merryweather, F. B., 1883-
To you was given, O saint
Mesechre, Mary I.
Arise, arise and shine
Metcalfe, L. C.
Holy, righteous, heavenly King
Metrical version of Psalms,
1909 see U. P. Board of Publi-
cation, 1909
Metzler, A.
Keep me, O my blessed Jesus
Soon falls the evening's
When trials and temptations;
R110076 There is sweet
rest
Meusslin, Wolfgang, 1497-1563
Christ, everlasting Source
The Lord my Shepherd is
Meyer, Sebastian W.
We build our school on thee
Meyer, Simon, ca 1720-60
Redeemer of mankind, God of
Meyerhardt, Max
Ten thousand martyrs died
There is a mystic tie
When Israel to the wilder-
ness

Meyfart, Johan Matthaeur, 1590-1642
  Jerusalem, du hochgebaute Stadt
  Jerusalem! high tower thy
  Jerusalem, thou city fair
Midlane, Albert, 1825-1909
  How solemn are the words
  Revive thy work, O Lord
  There's a Friend for little
Miles, Alfred H.
  The trumpet call of duty
Miles, C. Austin
  I come to the garden alone;
    R100428 And He walks with
    me
Miles, Sarah Elizabeth, 1807-77
  Thou who didst stoop below
Millay, Edna St Vincent, 1892-
1950
  O God, I cried, no dark;
    X109948 The world stands
    out
Miller, Emily Huntingdon, 1833-
1913
  I love to hear the story
  Kingdom of light! whose
  Tell the blessed tidings
Miller, Joaquin, 1839-1913
  They sailed! they sailed!
Miller, John, see Mueller,
  John
Miller, Samuel Martin, 1890-
  In the holy Father's keeping
  O God, who saidst, "Let there"
  When Jesus comes in glory
Milligan, James L., 1876-
  There's a voice in the wilder-
    ness; X103143 Hark! a
    voice
Mills, Charles S., 1861-1942
  Lord, thou hast known our joy
Mills, Elizabeth, 1805-29
  O land of rest for thee;
    R111224 We'll work till
  We speak of the realms
Mills, William G.
  Arise, O glorious Sion
  We'll sing the songs
Milman, Henry Hart, 1791-1868
  Bound upon th'accursed tree
  O help us Lord; each hour
  Ride on! ride on in majesty
  The chariot! the chariot!
    its wheels

When our heads are bowed;
    X111480 When the heart
    is
Milner-Barry, Alda M., 1875-
1940
  Good Joseph had a garden
  It is the joyful Easter
Milton, John, 1608-74
  God of our saving health
  How lovely are thy dwell-
    ings; X103712 How ...
    dwellings, Lord
  Let us with a gladsome
    mind; X108263 Praise,
    O praise (Baker); R102285
    For his mercies aye
  Ring out, ye crystal spheres
  Rise, God! judge thou the
  The Lord will come and not
    be
Minkler, Ross H.
  Grace, dear Lord, grace;
    R110814 Under the sha-
    dows
Minter, K.C.
  Sitting at the feet of Jesus
Mishler, Roy S.
  Close to my Savior, there
Missionary minstrel, 1826
  For the mercies of the day
Mitchell, E. Craige
  Father, I come to thee;
    X102103 Father, I go to
Mitchell, Elizabeth Harcourt,
1833-
  King of glory! Saviour dear
Mitchell, I.L.
  Hark! I hear my Saviour
    say; R101800 Do not turn
    the lambs
Mohler, J.S.
  With thankful hearts, O Lord
Mohr, Joseph, 1792-1848
  Holy night! peaceful night;
    X108902 Silent night,
    holy
  Holy Spirit, hear us;
    X103575 Holy Spirit,
    hear us
  Silent night, holy night;
    X108901 Silent ... yet
    while; X108899 Silent ...
    golden; X108900 Silent

... through; X108903 Silent
... peaceful; X109229 Still
the night
Stille nacht, heilige nacht
Moise, Penina, late 19th c
All living souls shall bless
Blest is the bond of wedded
Firm this corner-stone be
God supreme! to thee we
pray (with Edward Calish)
Great Arbiter of human fate
In God the holy, wise and just
Into the tomb of ages past
O God, all gracious! In thy
One God! One Lord! One
mighty
Praise ye the Lord! for it is
Pray when the morn unveileth
Molanus, Gerhard Walther, 1633-
1722
Ich trete frisch
Thy table I approach
Molitor, Wilhelm
O Queen of peerless majesty;
R107597 O stand beside us
Möller, Johann J.
I am content! My Jesus liveth
Ich hab g'nug: mein Jesus
Moller, Martin, 1547-1606
Help, Helper, help in fear
Moment, John James, 1875-
God of compassion, in mercy
Men and children everywhere
Monod, Theodore, 1836-1921
O the bitter shame and sorrow
Monro, Edward, 1815-66
In his own raiment clad;
X108783 See Him in raiment
Monsell, John Samuel Bewley,
1811-75
Christ is risen! Alleluia
Christ is the foundation
Come and deck the grave
Earth below is teeming; R106522
O Almighty Giver
Fight the good fight with all
God is love! the heavens tell;
X102669 God ... by Him
upholden
God of that glorious gift
Holy offerings, rich and rare
I hunger and I thirst
Labouring and heavy laden

Light of the world, we hail
Lord of the living harvest
Lord, to whom except to
thee
My sins, my sins, my Sa-
viour
O Love divine and golden;
X107355 O Love ... and
tender
O Saviour, who in love didst
O thou, whose mercy found
me
O worship the Lord in the;
X111861 Worship the Lord
in
O'er the distant mountains
On our way rejoicing
Rest of the weary, Joy of
Sinful, sighing to be blest
Sing to the Lord a joyful
song
Sing to the Lord of harvest;
X101505 Come, sing to
the Lord
Sweet is thy mercy, Lord
Teach me to do the thing
that
To thee, O dear, dear Sa-
viour
When cold our hearts and
far
Yes, I do feel, my God,
that I
Montefiore, Florence
Come, let us praise our
God
Forgive us Lord, we turn to
Montgomery, Ignatius, 1776-
1841
At God's right hand in
Montgomery, James, 1771-1854
A poor wayfaring Man of
grief
According to thy gracious
Almighty God, in humble
Angels from the realms of
At evening time, let there
be
All hail, our church's Elder
Be joyful in God, all ye
Behold! the Christian warrior;
X109442 The Christian
warrior

Blessed be thy name Jesus;
    X102180 Father, throned on
Bright and joyful is the morn
Call Jehovah thy salvation;
    X101122 Call the Lord thy
    sure; X102275 "For-ever"
    ... Father; X104244 In
    darkness as in light; X106070
    My Father's house
Come in, thou blessed of the
Come let us sing the song
Come to Calvary's holy
Command thy blessing from
Daughter of Zion, from the
Faith, hope, and charity
Father of eternal grace
Father! reveal thy Son in me
"Father, thy will, not mine"
For ever with the Lord
Friend after friend departs
Glad was my heart to hear
Glory to the Father give
Go to dark Gethsemane
Go to the grave in all thy
God is in his holy temple
God is my strong salvation
God is our refuge and defense
God made all His creatures
    free
Hail to the Lord's Anointed;
    X102629 God comes, with
Hark! the song of jubilee
Here, in thy name, eternal
Holy, holy, holy Lord God of
Hosanna! be the children's
How beautiful the sight of
I love the Lord! He lent an
In one fraternal bond of love
In the hour of trial
In time of tribulation
Jesus, our best beloved Friend
Lift up your heads, ye gates
Like Mary at her Saviour's
Listen to the gentle promptings
Lord, for ever at thy side
Lord God the Holy Ghost
Lord, let me know my end
Lord of hosts! to thee we
Lord, pour thy Spirit from on;
    X107460 O pour thy Spirit
Lord, teach us how to pray;
    X107668 O, thou by whom
    we

Lord, thou hast been thy
    people's
Magnify Jehovah's name;
    X105843 Magnify th'
    Eternal's
Not in Jerusalem alone
O bless the Lord, my soul!
O God, thou art my God
O Spirit of the living God;
    X107590 O ... the full-
    ness
O thou, my light, my life
O where shall rest be found
O who, in such a world as
One prayer I have -- all
Our heavenly Father, hear
Out of the depths of woe
Palms of glory, raiment
Peace that passeth under-
    standing
People of the living God
Pour out thy Spirit from on
Prayer is the soul's sincere;
    R103272 He prayeth best
    (Coleridge); X108366
    Prayer ... heart's
Rest from thy labor, rest;
    X100716 Be known to us
Send out thy light and truth
"Servant of God, well done"
Servants of God, in joyful
Shepherd of souls, refresh
Sing we the song of those
Songs of praise the angels
Sow in the morn thy seed
Thank and praise Jehovah's
The glorious universe
    around
The God of harvest praise
The Lord is King: -- upon
The Lord is my Shepherd,
    no want; R103493 His
    yoke is easy
The Lord will grace and
The tempter to my soul hath
The world in condemnation
    lay
This stone to thee in faith;
    X111385 When here, O
    Lord
Thousands, O Lord of hosts
Thy law is perfect, Lord of
To thy temple I repair;

X110716 To thy temple we
We bid thee welcome
What are those soul-reviving
What is the thing of greatest
What secret hand, at morning
When Jesus left his Father's;
X111419 When ... into
Salem
When like a stranger on our
When on Sinai's top I see
Who are these in bright ar-
ray; X111253 What are these
in
Work while it is today
Yea, I will extol thee

Moore, C. L.
O, anywhere my Saviour leads

Moore, Francis John
Father of mercy, Lover of all

Moore, Henry, 1732-1802
Supreme and universal Light

Moore, James C., 1888-
I have heard of a land;
R106250 Never grow old
Thou, O Christ of Calvary

Moore, Jessie Eleanor
Our thoughts go round the

Moore, Leslie, H., 1909-
Far in the West the sunset's
Jesus, we love to meet thee

Moore, Thomas, 1779-1852
Come, ye disconsolate
Hark! the vesper hymn;
X104959 Jubilate! Jubilate!
O thou who driest the mourner's
Sound the loud timbrel o'er
The bird let loose in eastern
The turf shall be my fragrant
Thou art, O God, the life
Thy heaven, on which 'tis

Moore, Thomas Vernon, 1818-71
Father, let thy smiling face

Moravian traditional, etc.

NOTE: Entry terms Unitas Fratrum
and Bohemian Brethren are not
used herein. However Bohemian
traditional, Czeck traditional
are used. They include some
secular (folk) items, whereas
Moravian is religious only.

Jesus hath procured salvation
Jesus, 'till my latest breath

O Spirit, of grace, thy
kindness
Thanks and praise, Jesus
The word of God which
ne'er
Who overcometh shall
abide
With awe, and deeply bowed

Moravian Emigrants hymn
Blest be the day when I
must

Mordecai b. Sabbatai
The lifting of my hands,
accept

More, Henry, 1614-87
God is ascended up on high
The holy Son of God most
high

Morell, Thomas, 1781-1840
Father of mercies, con-
descend

Morgan, Angela
Our glowing praise to thee
To be alive in such an age

Morgan, Edmund Robert, 1888-
Be thou exalted, holy Lord
Thee, living Christ, our
eyes

Morgen- und Abendsegen.
Waldenburg, 1734.
Fang dein Wek mit Jesu an
Go with Jesus to thy task
With the Lord begin thy task

Morison [Morrison] John, 1750-
98
Come, let us to the Lord
The people that in darkness
The race that long in dark-
ness
To us a Child of hope is
born
'Twas on that night when
doomed

Morley, Frederick B.
O Church of God, united

Morris, Mrs. C. H., 1862-1929
For God so loved this sinful;
R110559 'Tis true, O,
yes
Fully surrendered, Lord
divine; R104086 I will
be true
If you are tired of the load;

R104974 Just now, your
I've heard of a beautiful city;
    R104195 I'll make it my
    home
Jesus is coming to earth again;
    R102551 Glory, Glory! Joy
    to
Nearer, still nearer, close
    to
The fight is on, the trumpet
When the early morning;
    R103794 I am in my
    Father's
Morris, Eliza Fanny, 1821-74
    God of pity, God of grace;
    X102763 God of pity, Lord
    of
Morris, George Perkins, 1802-
64
    Searcher of hearts, from mine
Morris, Robert, 1818-
    Each cooing dove, and sighing;
    R106775 O Galilee! sweet
Morris, William, 1834-96
    From far away we come to
    you; R109827 The snow in
    the street
    He that dies shall not die
    Masters in this hall; R106491
    Nowell! Nowell! Nowell
Morrison [Morison] John, 1749-
1798
    see Morison, John, 1749-98
Morrison, Margaret
    Love one another, word of
    We lift our hearts in praise
Morse, Kenneth I., 1913-
    God of the moving years
    Lord of loveliness, all beauty
    Move in our midst, thou Spirit
    O Christ, we climb the hill
    O Giver of delightful fields
    O Master, may my days be
    spent
Morton, Mary Ann
    O happy home! O blest abode
    Sweet is the peace the gospel
Moser, Jessie F.
    I come to thee, O Father
Moses, Isaac S.
    O holy Sabbath-day, draw
    near

Moses ibn Ezra
    God that doest wondrously
    Thou, O Almighty, knowest
    all
Mote, Edward, 1797-1874
    My hope is built on nothing;
    X106294 Nor earth nor
    hell; R107940 On Christ,
    the solid
Moule, Handley Carr Glyn,
1841-1920
    Come in, O come! The
    door
    Lord and Saviour, true
    My glorious Victor, Prince
Moultrie, Gerard, 1829-85
    Come, faithful people, come
    There came three kings ere
    We march, we march to
    victory; X106654 O come
    in the might; X105880
    March on, march on;
    X111030 We come in the
    might
Moultrie, John, 1799-1874
    All is o'er: the pain
Moxley, Henry R., 1881-
    Father of Jesus, by whose
    Lord of true light, we
    Praise we now the God of
Mozarabic rite, 5th-8th c
    Sing Alleluia forth in duteous;
    X108934 Sing ... loyal
    praise
Mozley, Henry Williams, 1842-
    Lord, who fulfillest thus
Mudge, E. Leigh
    Lord, wilt thou in this tem-
    ple
Mudie, Charles Edward, 1818-
    I lift my heart to thee
    Jesus, who called'st little
Mueller, John, 1756-90
    Christ the Lord, the Lord
    most
    O that we all could quite
    Sing, with humble hearts
Muenter, Balthasar, 1735-93
    Behold the man! how heavy
    Full of reverence at thy
    word
    Lord! thou Source of all

Muhlenberg, William Augustus,
1796-1877
I would not live alway; I ask
Jesus' name shall ever be
Like Noah's weary dove
O cease, my wandering soul
Saviour, who thy flock
Shout the glad tidings;
 X109014 Sion, the marve-
lous
Since o'er thy footstool here
Mühlmann, Johannes, 1573-1613
Dank sei Gott in her Höhe
While yet the morn is break-
ing
Muirhead, Lionel B.C.L., 1845-
1925
The Church of God a kingdom
is
Müller, Michael, 1673-1704
Good and pleasant 'tis to see
Mumford, Alfred H., 1864-
Saviour, thy love hath guided
Mund, E.D.
Amid the trials which I meet;
 R110332 Thou thinkest,
Lord
In joyful high and holy days;
 R111837 Wonderful love
Munger, Harriet Osgood
O my Father, I would know
Munich. Mss. 15th c
In mitten in des lebens zeyt
Munro, Kathryn
O thou within whose sure
Munson, Ida Norton
His face? I know not whether
Münster Gesangbuch. 1677
Fairest Lord Jesus; X100757
Beautiful Saviour
Schönster Herr Jesu
Murray, Robert, 1832-1909
From ocean unto ocean
Our blessèd bond of union
Our loved Dominion bless
Sow the seed beside all waters
Murray, Robert D.
Lord, thou lovest the cheerful
Murray's Hymnal, 1852
Praise we the Lord this day
Myers, Ernest, 1844-1921
Now in life's breezy morning
Myers, Frederick William Henry

1843-1901
Hark, what a sound, and too
divine

N

Nachtenhöfer, Caspar Freid-
rich, 1624-85
Dies ist die Nacht, da mir
Lord Jesus, thou art going
So gehst du nun mein Jesu,
hin
This night a wondrous reve-
lation
Naidu, Sarojini, 1879-1949
Nay, do not grieve though
life
Naisbitt, Henry W.
For our devotions, Father
Rest, rest for the weary
soul
This house we dedicate
What voice salutes the start-
led
Nakatenus, W. Coeleste palma-
tum, 1669
Ye souls of the faithful! Who
Narayan Vaman Tilak, 1862-
1919 see Tilak, Narayan
Vaman, 1862-1919
Nass, John, 1670-1741
Savior of my soul, Let me
Nathan, El. pseud see Whittle,
Daniel W.
National anthems, hymns, etc.
see these entry words:

  Canadian
  Great Britain
  Japanese
  Newfoundland
  U.S.A.
Navajo (Indians) Prayer
Lord of the mountain
Navra, Sophia
I leave the burdens of my
life
Naylor, C.W.
Are you adorning the doctrine
God's way is best
Heaven is a holy place;
 R108907 Sin can never
enter

I have yielded myself; R111946
 Yes, my heart says
Once again we come to the
 house; R110713 To thy
 house, O Lord
Shall I be ashamed of my
 Saviour
The world of sinners; R100021
 A gospel others
Neale, John Mason, 1818-66
 A time to watch, a time
 All is bright and cheerful
 Around the throne of God
 Art thou weary, art thou laden;
  X100532 Art ... heavy laden
 Blessed Saviour, who hast;
  X100947 Blessed ... thou
  hast
 Christ is gone up; yet ere
 Earth today rejoices
 Earthly friends will change
 Good King Wenceslas
 Holy Father, thou hast taught;
  X103523 Holy ... taught us
 Lift up, lift up your voices
 O Lord of hosts, whose glory
 O thou, who by a star did'st
 O thou, who lov'st to send
 O thou, who through this holy
 O very God of very God
 The day, O Lord, is spent
 The earth, O Lord, is one
  great; X109501 The earth
  ... one wide
 The world itself keeps Easter
 There is a stream whose
 They whose course on earth
 'Twas about the dead of night
 With Christ we share a mystic
Neander, Christoph Friedrich,
1724-1802
 Dir, Herr, sei dieses Kind
 This child we dedicate;
  X110181 This .. consecrate
Neander, Joachim, 1650-80
 All my hope on God is founded
 For help, O whither shall I
 Heaven and earth, and sea
 Here behold me, as I cast me
 Himmel, Erde, Luft und Meer
 Lobe den Herren, den mächti-
  gen König
 O praise Jehovah! who reigneth

Praise to the Father, the
Praise to the Lord, the Al-
 mighty; X108312 Praise
 ... He is King; X108349
 Praise ye the Lord
Praise we the Lord, for His
 Wondrous King, all-glorious
Wunderbarer König
Needham, John, d 1787
 Awake, my tongue, thy tri-
  bute
 Holy and reverend is the
  name
 Rise, O my soul, pursue the
Neele, Henry, 1798-1828
 God of mercy, throned on
  high
Negro Spirituals
NOTE: Instead of this classifica-
 tion, hymnal BZ uses the
 term American folk hymn.
 This permits a blend with
 White Spirituals, and other
 melodies, which have long
 been especially known through
 such books as Sacred harp.

And I couldn't hear nobody
Deep river, my home is over
Go tell it on the mountain;
 R111400 When I was a sin-
 ner; R111593 While shep-
 herds kept
Good-bye, mourner, I'm going
Great day! Great day, the;
 R101155 Chariot rode on
 the
Gwine to lay down my bur-
 den; X103780 I aint gwine
 study
I have a mother yonder
In-a this-a band we have;
 R102601 Go, tell, Mary
 and
It's me, it's me, it's me
I've got a robe
Let us break bread together;
 R111389 When I fall on my
Listen to the Lambs
Little David, play on your
Lord, I want to be a Chris-
 tian
My Lord, what a mourning;

X106154 My Lord ... morning

No-body knows the trouble

O Mary, don't you weep;
R109086 Some of these mornings

Steal away, steal away;
R106147 My Lord calls me

Swing low, sweet chariot

There is a Balm in Gilead

We are climbing Jacob's ladder; X101816 Don't you want to go

Were you there when they crucified

What wondrous love is this

When Israel was in Egypt's land; R102579 Go down, Moses

Neibaur, Alex

Come, thou glorious day

Neisser, Friedrich Wenzel, 1716-77

From the doctrines, I'll never

Nelson, David, 1793-1844

My days are gliding swiftly;
R102294 For now we stand

Nelson, Horatio, Earl, 1823-1913

As the sun doth daily rise

From all thy saints in warfare

Netherlands see Dutch

Neumann, Caspar, 1648-1715

From eternity, O God

God from all eternity

God of Ages, all transcending

Gott, du hast in deinem Sohn

Gracious God, again is ended

Herr, es ist von meinem Leben

Neumann, G. J.

Again, O Lord and Saviour

Healer Divine, who walkest

King of my soul, a crown

Now all is still; Time holds

Neumark, Georg Christian, 1621-81

He that confides in his

He who would be in God: X111664

Whoso in God alone

If thou but suffer God; X105092

Leave God to order

Let, O my soul thy God direct

O he who trusts in God's

O thou that rulest earth

Wer nur den lieben Gott Lässt

Neumeister, Erdmann, 1671-1756

I know my faith is founded

Ich weiss, an wen ich gläube. 1718

Jesus nimmt die Sünder an. 1718

"Jesus, sinners doth receive"; X109002 Sinners Jesus will

Sinners Jesus will receive;
R108943 Sing it o'er

Sinners may to Christ draw

Nevill, E. Mildred, 1889-

God is good; we come before

Nevin, Edwin Henry, 1814-89

Always with us, always with

New Christmas carols, 1642

The old year now away is

New Church (English Conference) hymnal see Hymns of the English Conference, 1880

New Churchman.

O Sion rise in glory

Newbolt, Henry, 1862-1938

O Lord almighty, thou whose

The river of Death has

There's a breathless hush

Newell, Ebenezer Josiah, 1853-1916

We praise thy name, all-holy

Newell, Laura E.

A city awaits us we soon;
R107068 O, I long, yes

I am trusting day by day

Walking, Saviour, close to

Newell, William R., 1868-

Years I spent in vanity;
R105493 Mercy there was great

Newfoundland National anthem see Boyle, Cavendish. When sun rays crown

Newhall, Charles S., 1842-

O Jesus, Master, when today

Sterne, pseud) 1862-1928
  We've a story to tell;
    R102305 For the darkness
Nicholas, Tressilian George,
1822-91
  Lord! when before thy throne
Nicholls.
  O thou best Gift of heaven
Nicholson, James, 19th c
  Lord Jesus, I long to be;
    R111610 Whiter than snow
  The Lord is my light
  There's a beautiful land;
    R104339 In that beautiful
Nicholson, John
  "Come, follow me," the Sa-
    vior
  While of these emblems we
Nicholson, Mary Ann
  Easter flowers are blooming
Nicholson, Sidney Hugo, 1875-
1947
  How joyful 'tis to sing
Nicolai, Philip, 1556-1608
  How bright appears; X103649
    How brightly beams; X103650
    How brightly shines
  How lovely shines
  O Morning Star so pure;
    X107414 O Morning Star,
    how; X107415 O Morning
    Star, so fair
  Sleepers, wake, a voice
  Sleepers, wake, the watch-cry
  The morning Star upon us
  Wachet auf! ruft uns die Stimme
  Wake, arise! a voice appalling
  Wake, awake, for night;
    X106405 Now let every ton-
    gue; X109034 Sleepers, wake;
    X110934 Wake, O wake, for;
    X110935 Wake, O wake! with
  Wie schön leuchtet
Niedermeyer, Mabel, 1899-
  Our church proclaims God's
Niedling, Johann, 17th c
  O Heiliger Geist
  O Spirit of Life, O Spirit
Nigidius, Georg, 1525-88
  Aus meines Herzens Grunde
  My inmost heart now raises
Niles, John Jacob
  In calm and cool and silence

(from Whittier)
Niles, Nathaniel, 1835-
  Precious promise God hath;
    R104093 I will guide thee
Ninde, Henry S.
  Thou who taught the throng-
    ing; X110250 Thou didst
    teach
Nitschman, Anna see Zinzen-
  dorf, Anna Nitschman,
  1715-60
Nitschmann, John, 1712-83
  Christ is the Vine, we
    branches
Noble, James Ashcroft, 1844-
96
  Lord Jesus, in the days of
    old
Noel, Baptist Wriothesley,
1799-1873
  Glory to God, whose Spirit
  There's not a bird with
Noel, Caroline Maria, 1817-
77
  At the Name of Jesus, every;
    X104373 In the name of
    Jesus
Noel, Gerard Thomas, 1782-
1851
  If human kindness meets
  When musing sorrow weeps
Norris, John W.
  Give peace, O God, the na-
    tions
North, Frank Mason, 1850-
1935
  Jesus, the calm that fills
  O Master of the waking
    world
  The world's astir! the
    clouds
  Thou Lord of light, across
  Where cross the crowded
    ways
  Where lies our path? We
    seek
Norton, Andrews, 1786-1853
  My God, I thank thee!
  My no
  Where ancient forests widely
Norton, Nathanael
  "Come unto me," it is the
Norton, Thomas, ca 1532-

Ogden, Althea A.
　Father, let thy blessing touch
Ogden, William A., 1841-97
　Anywhere, dear Saviour, in thy
　Baptize us anew with power
　I've two little hands to work
　Jesus, the loving Shepherd;
　　R105823 Lovingly, tenderly
　Scattering precious seed by;
　　R109136 Sowing in the
　　morning
　Sweet are the promises;
　　R111543 Where He leads
　　I'll
　'Tis the grandest theme thro';
　　R103240 He is able to
　　deliver
　Working, O Christ, with thee
Okely, William, 1762-1824
　While successive years are
Ola Olude, A.T. see Olude,
　A.T. Ola
Oldenburg, Theodor V., 1805-
42
　Deep and glorious, word
　Deep and precious, strong
　God's eternal word is spoken
　Thine, O Jesus, now and ever
Olearius, Johannes, 1611-84
　Ach, wie gross ist deine
　　Gnade
　Again is come the new Church-
　　year
　Christ Himself, my Pride and;
　　X104588 Jesus Christ, my
　　Pride
　Comfort, comfort ye, my
　　people
　Gelobet sei der Herr
　God loved our erring mortal
　Herr, öffne mir die Herzens-
　　tur
　Jesus selbst, mein Licht,
　　mein
　Lord, open thou both heart
　Lord, open thou my heart to
　O, how great is thy compassion
　O praise the Lord! His name
　Our God so loved the world
　Thank God! My Jesus cleanseth
　The Lord, my God, be praised
　The new Church year again is
　Tröstet, tröstet meine Lieben

　When afflictions sore oppress
Olearius, Johann Gottfried,
1635-1711
　Come, thou precious Ran-
　　som
　Es war die ganze Welt
　Komm, du wertes Lose-
　　geld
　When all the world was
　　cursed
Olinger, Mrs. W.H.
　I would not have my way
Oliver, Richard J.
　Who hath believed after;
　　R103290 He was wounded
Olivers, Thomas, 1725-99
　O thou God of my salvation
　The God of Abraham praise;
　　see Jewish doxology ...
Olson, Ernst William, 1870-
　Behold, by grace, and
　　grace; X100813 Behold,
　　by sovereign
　Glorious Yule-tide, glad
　　bells
　God of peace, in peace pre-
　　serve
　Jesus, let my final rest
　Mine eyes unto the mountains
Olude, A.T. Ola
　Jesus, we want to meet
Omaha (Indians) traditional
　Dha-ke-de hia-u-dha
　Down through the ages
♪ [Omega]. Chelsea, 1838
　Lord of my life, whose ten-
　　der
Onderdonk, Henry Ustic, 1789-
1856
　Heirs of unending life
　How wondrous and great
　The Spirit, in our hearts
　When Lord, to this our wes-
　　tern
Opitz, Martin, 1597-1639
　Arise and shine in splendor
　Brich auf und werde lichte
　Light of light, O Sun
　O Sion, rise and brighten
Orr, C.E.
　As pilgrims and strangers
Orsborn, Albert
　Let the beauty of Jesus

Orthodox Eastern Church.
   Liturgy and ritual see Greek
   traditional -- which is chiefly
   liturgical text
Orwig, Aaron W.
   O God of peace, thee we
O'Shaughnessy, Arthur, 1844-81
   With wonderful deathless
Osler, Edward, 1798-1863
   Father, 'tis thine each day
   Lord of the church, we pray
   May we thy precepts, Lord
   Mighty Saviour, gracious King
   O God, unseen but ever near,
      Our blesséd rest (with S.
      Longfellow)
   O God, unseen yet ever near,
      Thy presence may we feel
   Pardoned through redeeming
   Worship, honour, glory
Ostergaard, Christian
   That cause can neither be lost
Oswald, Heinrich Siegmund, 1751-
1834
   O let him whose sorrow; X111-
     564 Where the mourner
Overby, Oscar R., 1892-
   As the sunflower turns
   God be with you now and ever
   How oft, O Father, my heart
   I would gather treasures
   The chimes of the sabbath
   There's a Kingdom fair
Owen, Frances Mary, 1842-83
   Lighten the darkness of our
   When thy soldiers take their
Owens, Priscilla Jane, 1829-
1907
   Give me the Bible, Star of
   We have heard the joyful sound;
     X111052 We ... heard a joy-
     ful
   Will your anchor hold; R111051
     We have an anchor
Oxenham, John, 1852-1941
   All labor gained new dignity
   Forth to the fight he fared
   In Christ there is no East
   Lord God of hosts, whose
   'Mid all the traffic of the ways
   My own dear land
   O God, within whose sight
   Peace in our time, O Lord

To every man there openeth
Unbar the door! and let
What do I owe? Nay Lord
Where are you going, Great-
   heart

P

"P.M."
   Pilgrim on earth, home and
Packard, Charlotte Mellen,
1839-1923
   For common gifts we bless
     thee
   O Shadow in a sultry land
Paderborn Gesangbuch, 1726
   My Jesus, pierced for love
     of
Pados, Virginia Bogdan
   Alleluia! Alleluia! Ye re-
     deemed
   O Love that nothing can ef-
     face
Page, Mary Judd
   Ye who are called to labor
Page, T.E., 1850-1936
   Soldier, go! Thy vow is
Pageant of the Shearmen and
   Tailors, 15th c
   Lully, lulla, thou little tiny;
     X105832 Lullay, thou little;
     X107564 O sisters too,
     how
Palgrave, Francis Turner,
1824-97
   Christ in his heavenly gar-
     den
   City not made with hands;
     X107696 O thou not made
     with
   Lord God of morning and of
     night
   O Light of life, O Saviour
   Thou say'st, "Take up thy"
   Thou who once on mother's;
     X110331 Thou that once,
     on
   Though we all in sinful;
     X110401 Though we long,
     in
Palmer, Alice Freeman, 1855-
1902
   How sweet and silent is

Palmer, Horatio Richmond, 1834-
1907
  Christ is knocking at my sad
  My griefs of heart abound
  Precious Saviour, dear
  There's a Rose that is
  Yield not to temptation;
    R100599 Ask the Saviour
Palmer, Phoebe
  Blessed Bible, how I love it
  O, now I see the crimson wave;
    R109453 The cleansing
    stream
  Watch, ye saints, with eyelids;
    R105337 Lo! He comes, Lo!
Palmer, Ray, 1808-87
  Come Jesus, from the sapphire
  Come, Jesus, Redeemer, abide
  Eternal Father, thou hast said
  In thee, O God, the hosts
  Jesus, Lamb of God, for me
  Jesus, these eyes have never
  Lord, my weak thought in vain
  Lord, thou hast taught our
  My faith looks up to thee
  Take me, O my Father, take
    me
  Thine holy day's returning;
    X110457 Thy holy day's
  Thou who rollest the year
  We stand in deep repentance
  We welcome thee in Jesus'
  When downward to the darksome
  With thine own pity, Saviour
Pappus, Johann, 1549-1610
  Lord Jesus Christ, I humbly
Park, J. Edgar, 1879-
  O Jesus, thou wast tempted
  We would see Jesus; X111177
    We would ... Mary's; X111178
    We would ... on the mountain
Park, Roswell, 1807-69
  Jesus spreads His banner o'er
Parker, Edwin Pond, 1836-1925
  Come to Jesus, ye who labor
  Hail, holy Light! the world
  Lord, as we thy name profess
  Master, no offering
Parker, Theodore, 1810-60
  O thou great Friend to all
Parker, William Henry, 1845-
1929
  Holy Spirit, hear us

  Tell me the stories of Jesus
Parkin, Charles C., d 1953
  See the morning sun ascend-
  ing
Parnell, Thomas, 1679-1717
  Holy Jesus! God of love
Parochial Hymn book, 1897
  Immaculate Mary, your
    praises; X104215 Imma-
    culate ... Our hearts;
    X104216 Immaculate ...
    Thy praises
Parr, Harriet, 1828-1900
  Hear our prayer, O heaven-
    ly; X103319 Hear my
    prayer
Parr, Leonard A., 1880-
  Lift up your hearts, ye
    people
Parsons, Charles
  O do not bar your mind
Parsons, R.G., 1882-1948
  We hail thy Presence glor-
    ious
Partridge, Edward
  Let Sion in her beauty rise
Partridge, Samuel William,
1810-1903
  How dearly God must love
    us
Partridge, Sybil F. (Lord, for
  tomorrow) see Mary Xavier,
  Sr.
Patton, A.B.
  Faith of our mothers, living
Patterson, Adoniram Judson,
1827-1909
  In thee, our Father, are we
    all
Pattinson, Janet Steel, 1848-
  While sinks our land to
    realms
Patton, Kenneth L., 1911-
  Before the stars a man is
  Brief our days, but long for
  Feet of the urgent pioneer
  Let all men living in all lands
  Let all who live in freedom
  Man is the earth upright
  Now once again the heaven
  Ours be the poems of all
  Quest of the ages, goal of
    men

The blessings of the earth
The earth is home and all
We journey with a multitude
When we have ended search-
ing
Paul the Deacon, 8th c
E'en in thy childhood, 'mid
Let thine example, holy John
Sing we the praises of the
great
Paulsen, P.C.
Blest is he who cries to
Let us go to Galilee
Take my heart, O Jesus
Pawels, E.
Great art thou, God!
Paxton, Thomas
God of the glorious sunshine
Payn, A.A.
There is One whom I love
Payne, John Howard, 1792-
1852
'Mid pleasures and palaces;
    R103591 Home, home, sweet
Peabody, Josephine Preston
(Mrs. L.S. Marks), 1874-1922
Truly the light is sweet
Pease, Theodore Claudius, 1853-
Not long upon the mountain's;
    X106318 Not long on Her-
mon's
Peckham, John, d 1294
Hail, true Victim, life
Pedersen, Bertel
Fear, my child, thy God
Jesus, let my soul be fed
Peers, E. Allison, 1890-1952
O heavenly Beauty, lovlier far
Pellegrin, Abbé, d 1745
O come, divine Messiah
Pembroke, Lady Mary Sidney
see Sidney, Sir Philip.
O Lord, in me there lieth
Pendleton, Eo.
The first fruits of the land
Pendleton, W.F.
City strong and mighty
Glory flaming in the cloud
Jesus, Saviour, heavenly
Penfield, Thornton B., 1867-
In loving adoration
Penn, W.E.
There is a Rock in a weary;

R109994   Then why will ye
die
Penn, William Joseph, 1875-
1956
Enthrone thy God within thy
Pennefather, William, 1816-73
Jesus, stand among us
Penner, Edwin
O soul, you know the pre-
sent; R110776 Trust
your hand into
Pennewell, Almer T., 1876-
So lowly doth the Saviour
ride
Penrose, Charles W.
Beautiful Sion for me
God of our fathers, we come
O ye mountains high, where
School thy feelings, O my
Up, awake, ye defenders of
Penstone, Maria M., 1859-
1910
God has given us a book full
When lamps are lighted
Percy, Frances A.
O Father, hear my morning
Percy, William Alexander
They cast their nets in
Galilee
Perkins, Emily S.
Thou art, O God, the God;
    X108098 Our God, He is
a God
Perkins, H.S.
Gird on the armor, brave
soul; R109070 Soldiers
of progress
Perkins, Jeanette E.
We thank thee, Lord, for
eyes
Perpetual Adoration, Asso.
of see The Association of
Perpetual Adoration
Perronet, Edward, 1726-92
All hail the power of Jesus';
    X100213 All hail the
great Immanuel's
Hail, Holy, Holy, Holy,
Lord
Pestel, Thomas, 1584-1659
Behold the great Creator
Peter, P.A.
Who shall ope for us

Peters, Mary Bowly, 1813-56
   Holy Father! we address thee
   O Lord, while we confess
   Through the love of God;
      X110429 Through ... our
      Saviour
   With thankful hearts we meet
Petersen, H. H.
   I'm a pilgrim; I'm a stranger
Petersen, Johann Wilhelm,
   1649-1727
   Jesus cometh to fulfill
   Jesus, Lord of life and glory
Petri, Olavus, 1497-1552
   Blest Easter Day, what joy
   Our Father, merciful and good
   Thy sacred Word, O lord, of
Petursson, Hallgrim, 1614-74
   And then the Savior turned
   Come, Lord, Thyself, in all
   Come, Lord, Thyself with
      thine
   Jesus, the mighty work
   The Lord into his Father's
   The Savior in Gethsemane
   The soldiers led the Savior
   Upon the cross down-lying
   Upon the cross the robber
Pfeffel, Gottlieb Konrad, 1736-
   1809
   Jehova! Jehova! Jehova!
      Deinem Namen sei Ehre
   Jehovah, Jehovah, Jehovah,
      Thou art worthy
Pfefferkorn, Georg Michael, 1645-
   1732
   Was frag' ich nach der Welt
   What is the world to me
Pfeil, Christoph Carl Ludwig
   von, 1712-84
   Blessèd Jesus all our hearts
   O blest the house, whate'er
   Wohl einem Haus, da Jesus
Phalen, Frank
   Father in heaven, we wait
Phelps, Sylvanus Dryden, 1816-
   95
   Saviour, thy dying love
   This rite our blest Redeemer
Phelps, William W.
   Awake! O ye people, The Sa-
      vior

Come, all ye Saints who
   dwell
Come, all ye sons of Sion
Come, let us sing an even-
   ing
Gently raise the sacred strain
Glorious things are sung
If you would hie to Kolob
Now let us rejoice, in the
   day
Now we'll sing with one ac-
   cord
O God, the Eternal Father
Praise to the man who com-
   muned; R103106 Hail to
   the Prophet
The Spirit of God like a
   fire; R111219 We'll sing
   and we'll
We're not ashamed to own
Phelps, William W. see para-
   phrases of; Watts, I'm not
   ashamed Newton, Glorious
   things
Philippson, L.
   From heaven's height, Soft,
      vernal
Philipson, David
   See, O God, we children
      come
Phillimore, Greville, 1821-84
   Every morning mercies new
   O Lord of health and life
   Summer ended, harvest o'er
   We pray thee, Jesus, who
      didst
Phillips, Charles Stanley,
   1883-1949
   Not by far-famed deeds
      alone
   Spirit of Jesus, who didst
   Stalwart as pillars bearing
Phillips, D. C.
   To thee, O gracious Lord,
      we
Phillips, Harriet Cecilia,
   1806-84
   We bring no glittering
Piae cantiones, 1582
   Gabriel's message does away
   Now the spring has come
      again

Polish traditional, etc.
  Infant holy, Infant lowly
  Out of our suffering, out of
  Slumber, O slumber, dear
    Jesus
Pollard, Adelaide Addison, 1862-
1934
  "But for a moment" -- this
  Have thine own way, Lord
Pollard, Josephine, ca 1840-
  Beyond the sunset's radiant
  I have work enough to do
  Joy-bells ringing, children
Pollock, Charles Edward
  Come, ye wanderers, all (arr);
    R101571 Come, ye weary,
    heavy
  Little children, praise the
Pollock, Thomas Benson, 1836-
96
  By the gracious saving call
  Faithful shepherd, feed me
  Father, hear thy children's
  God the Father, God the Son
  Great Creator, Lord of all
  Jesus, from thy throne on
    high; X102089 Father from
    thy throne
  Jesus, in thy dying woes;
    X104565 Jesus, all our ran-
    som; X104567 Jesus, all
    thy labor; X104660 Jesus,
    in thy thirst; X104731 Jesus,
    loving to the; X104802 Jesus,
    pitying the; X104913 Jesus,
    whelmed in
  Jesus, Son of God most high
  Jesus, we are far away
  Jesus, with thy church abide
  Spirit, Strength of all
  Teach us what thy love has
  We are soldiers of Christ
  We have not known thee as we
  Weep not for Him who onward
Poole, William C., 1875-1949
  Have you prayed all night;
    R101774 Did you pray till
  Just when I need Him, Jesus
Pope [The Holy Father] see
  the given name used during
  incumbency
Pope, Alexander, 1688-1744
  A herald voice the lonely

Rise, crowned with light
The time shall come when,
  free
What conscience dictates;
  X102136 Father of all, in
Poppe, Erhard Christoph,
1804-78
  Jesus, our Savior, grant us
  Seliger Friede, Köstliche
Posse, Katarina Elisabet see
  Ehrenberg-Posse, Katarina
  Elizabeth, 1818-80
Poteat, Edwin McNeill, 1892-
1955
  Eternal God, whose search-
    ing
  Light of the world, how long
Pott, Francis, 1832-1909
  Angel voices, ever singing
Potter, Thomas Joseph, 1827-
73
  Brightly gleams our banner
Pounds, Jessie H. Brown,
1861-1921
  Anywhere with Jesus I can
    (with Mrs. C.M. Alexan-
    der)
  I know that my Redeemer
    liveth
  I must needs go home;
    R109915 The way of the
    cross
  Lord of the nations, Father
  O scatter the seeds;
    R109978 Then day by day
  Peace through the cross
  Turn your faces toward
  We are going down the valley
Powell, Roger K., 1914-
  Lord, we thank thee for our
Powell, Thomas Edward,
1823-1901
  Bow down thine ear, Al-
    mighty
Poyry, Edla
  My beautiful home is in
    heaven
Praetorius. Musae sioniae,
1607
  We thank thee, Jesus
  Wir danken dir, Herr Jesu
Praetorius, Johann, 1738-82
  Thy blood, so dear and

Pratt, O. A.
    Afar on the mountain; R109977
        Then come, wanderer
    He comes! He comes with
Pratt, Parley P.
    An angel from on high;
        R105343 "Lo, in Cumorah's"
    As the dew from heaven
    Behold thy sons and daughters
    Come, O thou King of Kings
    Father in heaven, we do
    Jesus, once of humble birth
    The morning breaks, the sha-
        dows
    Truth eternal, truth divine
    Ye children of our God
    Ye chosen Twelve, to you
Pray, Benjamin S.
    Master and Lord, 'tis good to
Preiswerk, Samuel, 1799-1871
    Das ist der Gemeinde Stärke
    Die sach' ist Dein, Herr Jesu
    Hark! the church proclaims
    Lord Jesus Christ, the cause
    Lord Jesus Christ, the work
    The work is thine, O Christ
Prentiss, Elizabeth, 1818-78
    More love to thee, O Christ
Presbyterian hymnal. Phila.,
1874
    Before thee, Lord, a people
Presbyterian sources see also
    United Presbyterian ...
    written as U.P. ...
Presley, L. G.
    I have a friend in whom I;
        R107882 O yes, He cares
        for
Price, Mrs.
    Above the trembling elements
Prid, William, 16th c
    City of Peace, our mother;
        X107425 O mother dear
        (F. B. P.)
    O mother dear, Jerusalem
    Of stones full precious are
Prid, William, see also F. B. C.
    Jerusalem ...
Proctor, Adelaide Anne, 1825-64
    I do not ask, O Lord, that
    My God, I thank thee, who
        hast; X108112 Our God,

    we thank
    The shadows of the evening
    The way is long and dreary
Promnitz, Balthasar Friedrich
von, 1711-44
    Church of Jesus, sing
Proprium Officiorum. Prague,
1720
    God in whom all graces
        dwell
Prost, Christen, d 1676
    Fesans raijouissance
    Now, brothers, lift your
Proud, Joseph, 1745-1826
    Come in, thou blessed hon-
        ored
    Down from the worlds of
    How shall we celebrate thy
    I love the Lord; He heard
        my
    I love the voice divine that
    Jerusalem, arise, the
        heavenly
    My Lord, my God, my only
        King
    Now blessing, honor, glory
Pruden, Edward Hughes, 1903-
    O God of our fathers, we
        praise
Prudentius, Aurelius Clemens,
348-413
    All hail, ye little martyr
    Bethlehem, of noblest cities
    Blest martyr, let thy
        triumph
    Corde natus ex parentis
    Despair not, O heart, in
        thy
    Earth has many a noble city;
        X100885 Bethlehem in land
        of; X100887 Bethlehem, of
        noblest
    Father most high, be with
        us
    Father of spirits, whose
    Lo! golden light rekindles
    Now with creation's morning
    Now with the rising golden
    O martyrs young and fresh;
        X100222 All hail, ye little
    Of the Father's love begot-
        ten; X107920 Of ...

heart begotten; X103248
He is here, whom
Servant of God, remember
Sweet flowrets of the martyr
The wingèd herald of the day
Ye clouds and darkness, hosts
Prynne, George Rundle, 1818-1903
Jesus, meek and gentle
Psalms and hymns, 1858
Dear Lord, before we part
Psalms in meter, 1905
My trust is in the Lord
Psalter. New version see Tate & Brady
Psalter, 1860 (Kennedy)
Lord, hear my prayer, and let
Psalter, 1912 see U.P. Psalter, 1912 (i.e. United Presbyterian Psalter, 1912
Pugh, Alice
In the heart of Jesus
Pullen, Alice M., 1889-
At work beside his father's
For man's increasing quest
Thou perfect Hero-Knight
Pulsifer, Harold Trowbridge, 1886-
I shall go out as all men go
Punshon, William Morley, 1824-81
Listen! the Master beseecheth; R109995 Then work, brothers
Sweet is the sunlight after
Purchas, John, 1823-72
Evensong is hushed in silence; R111009 We are weary
Pye, Henry John, 1825-1903
In His temple now behold Him
Pyper, F.R., 1859-1915
O God of nations, hear thy

Q

Quarles, Francis, 1592-1644
Thou art my life; if thou but
Quarles, John, 1624-65
Fountain of light, and living
Long did I toil, and knew (with H.F. Lyte)
O King of kings, before whose
Queen's College, Oxford, 1812

The boar's head in hand
Quin, Malcolm, 1855-
Now comes the light for which
Say not they die, those martyr
We move in faith to unseen
Quirsfeld, Johann, 1642-86
Sinful world, behold
Plechtchéev
When Jesus Christ was yet a child

R

Rabanus Maurus see St Rabanus Maurus
Räder, Friedrich
Wait on God, and trust Him
Rader, Paul
Only believe, only believe
Radford, Benjamin J., 1838-1933
In homes where pride
Raffles, Thomas, 1788-1863
Blest hour, when mortal man
Eternal Father, throned above
Hark, ten thousand thousand
High in yonder realms of light; X103462 High ... realm of
Lord, like the publican
Saviour, let thy sanctions
Thou art my hiding-place
Raile, Vilate
Upon the cross of Calvary
Rambach, Johann Jakob, 1693-1735
A year again is now descending
Baptized into thy name most
Father, Son, and Holy Spirit
How great the bliss to be
I am baptized into thy name; X100711 Baptized into thy
Ich bin getauft auf deinen
Lord Jesus, who before thy
Lord, to thee I now surrender
Mein Schöpfer, steh mir bei
My Maker, be thou nigh
O thou Love unbounded,

grant
Unumschränkte Liebe
Ramler, Karl Wilhelm, 1725-98
  Behold, how glorious is yon
Ramsey, Benjamin Mansell, 1849-
1923
  Teach me thy way, O Lord
Randall, Laura Lee
  This is the day, the Lord hath
Rands, William B., 1827-82
  One Lord there is, all lords
Rankin, Jeremiah Eames, 1828-
1904
  Are you weary, are you heavy-
    hearted; R109637 Tell it to
    Jesus
  Beneath thy shadow hiding
  God be with you till we meet;
    R110521 Till we meet
  Gott mit euch, bis wir uns
    wiederseh'n
  Shepherd of one fold is He
Ravenscroft, Thomas. <u>Melismata,</u>
1611
  Remember, O thou man, O
    thou
Rawlett, John, 1642-87
  O Holy Ghost, on this great
Rawnsley, Hardwicke Drummond,
1851-1920
  Father, whose will is life;
    X106935 O God, whose will
    is
  Lord Jesus, who at Lazarus'
  Saviour, who didst healing
Rawson, George, 1807-89
  By Christ redeemed, by Christ
  Come to our poor nature's;
    X101535 Come ... dark na-
    ture's; X103529 Holy Ghost,
    the Infinite; X103578 Holy
    Spirit, in thy; X103579
    Holy Spirit, lamp of;
    X104816 Jesus, Saviour,
    infinite
  Father, in high heaven
  Father of love and power
  God the Lord is King; before
  In the dark and cloudy day
  The God of love my Shepherd
  Thou who hast known
  Thou who thyself didst sanctify
  We limit not the truth; R109649

The Lord hath yet
Who dares to bind to his dull
Raymond, Rossiter Worthing-
ton, 1840-1918
  Far out on the desolate
  Now rest, ye pilgrim host
  There dwelt in old Judea
    R108953 Sing Noel, sing
    Noel
  There's a beautiful star;
    R109212 Star, Star,
    beautiful
Reed, Andrew, 1787-1862
  Come, my Redeemer, come
  Holy Ghost, with light di-
    vine; X103580 Holy Spirit,
    Light
  Spirit divine, attend our
Reed, Eliza, 1794-1867
  O do not let the Word de-
    part; R107846 O why
    not tonight
Reed, Ida L.
  Choose my path, O blessed;
    R104971 Just as seemeth
    good
  Do life's storms above thee
  He knoweth thy grief
Reed, Luther D., 1873-
  O God of wondrous grace
Rees, Bryn Austin, 1911-
  Have faith in God, my
    heart
Rees, Timothy, 1874-1939
  God is love: let heaven
    adore
  Lord, who in thy perfect
Reese, Lizette Woodworth,
1856-1935
  Glad that I live am I
Reformed Presbyterian Church.
Book of Psalms, 1940
  O God, thy judgments give
Reitz, Albert S., 1879-
  Teach me to pray, Lord,
    teach; R105327 Living
    in Thee, Lord
Reusner, Adam, 1496-ca 1575
  In dich hab' ich gehoffet
  In thee, Lord, have I put
    my
The Revival, 1859
  Hark, 'tis the watchman's

cry

Rexford, Eben Eugene, 1848-
How many times, discouraged;
R103721 No, never alone
O where are the reapers;
R111538 Where are the
reapers
They brought their gifts;
R111875 Wouldst bring a gift

Reynolds, Isham E., 1879-1949
Jesus my Lord is real to me
When the sun shines bright;
R104681 Jesus is the friend

Rhodes, Sarah Betts, 1829-1904
God who made the earth

Rice, Cale Young, 1872-1943
I have ridden the wind

Rice, Caroline Laura, 1819-
Wilt thou hear the voice of

Richard Rolle of Hampole, d
1349
Lord Jesus, when I think of

Richards, Charles Herbert
Dear land of liberty, Hope of
Our Father, thy dear Name

Richards, Laura E., 1850-
1943
The little flowers came

Richardson, Norman E.
My Lord, I do not ask to
stand

Richter, Anne Rigby, d 1857
We saw thee not when thou

Richter, Christian Frederick,
1676-1711
"Give me, my child," the
Father
Jesus is my Light most fair
My soul before thee prostrate
Thou Lamb of God, thou Prince

Rights, Douglas LeTell, 1891-
Veiled in darkness Judah lay

Riley, John Athelstan Laurie,
1858-1945
Come, let us join the church
Saints of God! Lo, Jesus'
Ye watchers and ye holy ones

Ringmacher, Lorentz
O Jesu, der du felig mach.
1564

Ringwaldt, Bartholomäus, 1532-
99
Es ist gewisslich an der Zeit

Gott Heil'ger Geist, hilf uns
Jesus, thou Source of every
Lord Jesus Christ, thou
highest
O Holy Ghost, thou gift
O Holy Spirit, grant us
grace
The day is surely drawing
near (Dies irae)
'Tis sure that awful time
will

Rinkart, Martin, 1586-1649
Now all give thanks to God
Now thank we all our God;
R100252 All praise and
thanks; X106415 Now let
us praise
Nun danket Alle Gott

Rippon, John. Selection of
hymns, 1787 "K" in Rippon,
see "K"

Rist, Johann, 1607-67
All ye Gentile lands, awake
Arise my spirit, bless
Arise, the kingdom is at
hand; X100506 Arise,
arise, ye; X100520 Arise,
sons of the
Auf, auf, ihr Reichsgenos-
sen
Author of the whole creation
Break forth, O beauteous
Du Lebensbrot, Herr Jesu
Father, merciful and holy;
X108994 Sink not yet, my
soul
Glory, praise, to thee be
Help, Lord Jesus, let thy
Help us, O Lord, behold,
we
Hilf, Herr Jesu, lass gelin-
gen
Lord Jesus Christ, thou liv-
ing
O darkest woe! Ye tears
forth
O Jesus Christ, thou Bread
of
O living Bread from heaven
O sorrow deep! Who would
not
Praise the Lord with hearts
Rise, O Salem, rise and

shine
Rise, children of the Kingdom
Soul of mine, to God awaking
Thou hast canceled my
To thee all praise ascendeth
Wie wohl hast du gelabet
Ritchie, David Lake
  As comes the breath of spring
Rivers, W. P.
  As Sion's pilgrims in accord
    R108798 See the righteous
Robbins, Chandler, 1810-82
  Lo! the day of rest declineth
Robbins, Howard Chandler, 1876-
1952
  And have the bright immensities
  Now yield we thanks and praise
  Put forth, O God, thy Spirit's
  Saviour, whose love is like
  The Sabbath day was by
Roberts, Daniel Crane, 1841-
1907
  God of our fathers, whose
Roberts, John, 1731-1806
  O blest Communion with the
Roberts, Katherine Emily, 1877-
  Awake were they only, those
  Now the joyful bells aringing
  O Lord, thy people gathered
Roberts, Richard, 1874-
  For them whose ways are in
    the air
Roberts Robert Rowland, 1865-
1945
  Far off I see the goal
Roberts, Thomas
  My Shepherd's mighty aid
Robertson, Nemi
  Grace for today, O Love divine
Robertson, William, d 1745
  Fair as a beauteous tender
Robertson, William, 1820-64
  A little child the Saviour
Robilliard, H. W.
  God of love, our Father, Sa-
    viour
Robins, Gurdon, 1813-
  There is a land mine eye hath
Robins, Henry B.
  Eternal Spirit, evermore
  Of one blood hath God created
Robinson, Charles Seymour, 1829-
99

Saviour, I follow on
Tell me, my Saviour, where
Robinson, Edith
  Safe within the arms of
    Jesus
Robinson, Edwin Arlington,
1869-1935
  Dark hills at evening
Robinson, George
  One sole baptismal sign
Robinson, George Wade, 1838-
77
  Loved with everlasting love
Robinson, H. Wheeler, 1872-
1945
  O thou whose love has
    brought
Robinson, Joseph Armitage,
1858-1933
  'Tis good, Lord, to be
    here!
Robinson, Paul M., 1914-
  Here in our upper room
    with
Robinson, Richard Hayes, 1842-
92
  Holy Father, cheer our way
Robinson, Robert, 1735-90
  Mighty God, while angels
    bless; X105630 Lord of
    every land
  Saviour, source of every;
    X101518 Come, thou
    Fount
Robinson, W. O.
  O hark! A glorious sound
Robinson, William, 1888-
  Praise to God, almighty
Rodigast, Samuel, 1649-1708
  Was Gott tut, das ist wohl-
    getan!
  Whate'er my God ordains is;
    X111274 What God ordains;
    X111338 Whate'er our God;
    X111340 Whatever God
    ordains
Rogel, Hans
  Ach Gott! verleih mir dein
    Genad. 1539
Roh, Johann, 16th c see Horn,
John, 16th c
Rohr, A. F.
  Eternal God, omnipotent

From afar, across the waters
Living Fountain, freely
Lord of life and light
Romanis, William, 1824-99
  Lord, who shall sit beside
  Pour forth thy spirit from;
    X108237 Pour down thy
    Spirit
  Round me falls the night
Rome, James J.
  Give me, O Lord, an under-
    standing
Rominger, Charles H.
  Thou art, O Christ, the light
Rooker, Alfred, 1814-75
  O be with us, gracious Father
Rooper, W. J.
  Dare to be brave, dare to be;
    R102228 Fight, then, good
Root, Frederic W.
  All power is given unto
    see Luther. A mighty . . .
  O tender, loving Shepherd
  Our God is love, unchanging
  Rock of ages, Truth divine
    see Toplady. Rock of ages
  The heavens declare the glory
Root, George Frederick, 1820-
95
  Come to the Saviour, make no;
    R104957 Joyful, joyful, will
  She only touched the hem;
    R107784 O, touch the hem
  Why do you wait, dear brother;
    R111679 Why not? why not?
Rorison, Gilbert, 1821-69
  Three in One, and One in
    Three
Roscoe, William, 1753-1831
  Great God! beneath whose
Rose, D. F.
  City of David, Bethlehem
  Saviour, Redeemer, God of
    Love
Rose, Elizabeth Dorothy
  My case to thee is fully
    known
Rosenius, Agata, 19th c
  Abode of peace, my Father's
Rosenius, Carl Olof, 1816-68
  I have a friend, so patient
  O precious thought! Some day
  With God and His mercy, His

Rosenroth, Christian Knorr
von, 1636-89
  Come, thou bright and
    morning-star
  Dayspring of eternity, Light;
    X101515 Come, thou
    bright; X101674 Day-
    spring ... Brightness of
    the Father's; X101676
    Dayspring ... Light of
    Light
  Jesus, Sun of righteousness
  Morgenglanz der Ewigkeit
Rosewater, Adeline R.
  Dear Father, here thy chil-
    dren
  We hear the call of Israel's
Ross, Ronald, 1857-1932
  Before thy feet I fall
Rosser, John L., 1875-
  To Him who hallows all our
    days
Rossetti, Christina Georgina,
1830-94
  In the bleak midwinter
  Love came down at Christ-
    mas
  None other Lamb, none
    other
  O Christ, my God, who
    seest
  O ye who taste that love is
  Service and strength, God's
  Sooner or later: yet at last
  Spring bursts today, For
    Christ
  The shepherds had an angel
  We know not a voice of that
  What are these that glow
  Who has seen the wind?
Rot, Othmar
  Mensch! wilt du nimmer
    traurig seyn. 1564
Rothe, Johann Andreas, 1688-
1758
  Jesus, I know, hath died for
  I now have found for hope
  Ich habe nun den Grund
  My soul has found the sure
  Now I have found the ground
  Now I have found the sure
  Now I have found the firm
  When children, blest by

Jesus
Rouse, Francis, 1579-1659
  Thy mercy, Lord, is in the
    heavens
Routh, Gene
  Speak to my heart, Lord Jesus
Rowe, Ed. M.
  O sons of Sion, hear the voice
Rowe, James
  Earthly pleasures vainly call;
    R100717 Be like Jesus,
    this
  I was sinking deep in sin;
    R105804 Love lifted me
  Jesus has taken a beautiful;
    R102450 Gathering buds
  My Saviour needs helpers;
    R104191 I'll go, I'll go
  O weary soul, the gate is
    near; R104975 Just outside
    the door
  Smiling skies will bend above;
    R111757 With eternal day
  Wonderful Jesus! glorious
Rowe, John, 1764-1833
  From the table now retiring
Rowell, Eugene
  On hills and vales of heaven
Rowland, May, 1870-
  Come! Peace of God, and
    dwell
  God of the shining hosts that
  The day is slowly wending
  Where the great ships, pass-
    ing
Rowland, Mira
  Lord who lovest little children
Rowley, Francis Harold, 1854-
1952
  I will sing the wondrous;
    R111943 Yes, I'll sing
Royce, E.
  The stars were silent and the
    hills
Rube, Johann Christoph, 1665-1746
  Him on yonder cross I love
Rumsey, Mrs. Mary
  Jesus when He left the sky;
    (authorship disputed)
Runeberg, Johan Ludvig, 1804-
77
  I lift my eyes unto heaven
Ruopp, Johann Friedrich, d 1708

Erneure mich, o ew'ges
  Licht
  Renew me, O eternal Light
Ruskin, John, 1819-1900
  Bend back the lance's point
Russell, Anna B., 1862-1954
  There is never a day so
    dreary; R111842 Wonder-
    ful, wonderful
Russell, Arthur Tozer, 1806-
74
  Give praise to God our King
  Jesus, at thine invitation
  Jesus, who for my trans-
    gression
  Lord, our eyes unseal
  Night's shadows falling
  O God of life, whose power
  O gracious Hand that freely
  O Jesu, we adore thee
  O Jesus, blest is he
  The Lord ascendeth up on
    high
  To Him who for our sins
    was
Russell, Byron G., 1850-
  Our Father, unto thee, we
    now
Russell, Francis Albert Rollo,
1849-1914
  Christian, rise, and act thy
Russell, George William, i.e.
"A.E.", 1867-1935
  The generations as they rise
  When the unquiet hours de-
    part
Russell, Matthew, 1834-
  A message from the Sacred
    Heart
  O Mary, dearest Mother
Russian traditional, etc.
  As light, O Christ, thou
  Ay-yukh-nyehm
  Easter eggs! Easter eggs!
    Give to
  Gloria, gloria! O come let
    us
  Praise to God in the highest
  Step by step (Volga boatmen)
Rutgers, Abraham, 1751-1809
  Glory, honor, praise and
    pure
Rutilius, Martin, 1550-1618

Ach Gott und Herr, Wie gross
Alas, my God! my sins are
Rutström, Andreas Carl, 1721-
72

Chosen seed of Zion's children
Come, Saviour dear, with us
My crucified Saviour, despised
Ryden, Ernest Edwin, 1886-
Behold what love, that God
Beyond the everlasting hills
Eternal God, before thy throne
Didst thou, dear Jesus, pray
How blessed is this place
O blessed is the man who
stays see Wallin, O blessed
is the man . . .
O Lord, now let thy servant
The twilight shadows round me
With solemn joy we come
Ryland, John, 1753-1825
Let us sing the King Messiah
O Lord, I would delight in
Sovereign Ruler of the skies
Ye saints, proclaim abroad
Rypins, Mrs. Isaac L.
Dim mine eyes with many
While yet the earth midst

S

"S.E.L." presumed to be
Lorenz, E.S.
"S.M.H."
We know not the time when
He; R110930 Waiting and
watching
"S.N.D." i.e. Sister of Notre
Dame, identified as Mary
Xavier, Sr., whose secular
name is Sybil Partridge. (There
may, however be another per-
son who has used these initials.
No universal decision is made
herein.)

Sacer, Gottfried Wilhelm, 1635-
99
Gott, fähret auf gen Himmel
Lo, God to heaven ascendeth
Sadler, Thomas, 1822-91
The Lord hath said, "Seek ye"
Saint . . .
NOTE: Abbreviation St is used
for canonized authors, whether

men or women. Persons
better known under other
form of name are usually
granted the alternative.
Secular surnames beginning
with St follow (the number
is small).
St Alfonso de Ligouri, C.SS.
R., 1696-1787
From starry heaven de-
scending
Jesus, food of angels
Jesus Lord, be thou mine
own
O Bread of Heaven! beneath
O God of loveliness, O
Lord
O Mother blest, whom God
Raise your voices vales and;
R105061 Laudate, laudate
Uplift the voice and sing;
R108305 Praise to Mary
St Amandus, 1300-1365/6 see
Suso, Henry
St Ambrose, 340-397
As fades the glowing orb
Before the ending of the day
Blest Spirit, one with God
Come, Holy Ghost, with God
Come, Holy Ghost, who
ever One
Come, Holy Spirit, God-
head
Come, thou Saviour of our
race
Come thou Redeemer of the
earth
Creator of the earth and
sky
Creator of the world, we
pray
Ere yet in darkness ends
Jesus, the Virgin's crown,
do
Let hymns of joy to grief
Maker, keeper, thou, Be my
Mighty God, we humbly
pray
NOTE: This 4-line stanza
precedes several Zinzendorf
hymns.

Now hail we our Redeemer

Nun Komm, der Heiden Heiland
O blessed Light! O trinity
O blest Creator, God most
    high
O Christ! with each returning
O God, creation's secret force
O God of truth, O Lord of
    might
O God, the world's sustaining
O Jesus, Lord of heavenly
O Jesu, thou the virgin's
O light, O Trinity most blest
O lux beata trinitas
O Splendor of God's glory
O Strength and Stay upholding
O thou true Life of all that
O Trinity of blessed light;
    X107786 O Trinity, most;
    X107787 O Trinity, O blessed
Rejoice, our nature Christ
Saviour of the nations, come;
    X108728 Saviour of the
    heathen
Splendor paternae gloriae
Te deum, see Latin, 5th c
Te, lucis ante terminum
The eternal gifts of Christ
Thee, Lord, before the close
Thou who art Three in Unity
To thee before the close of day
Veni, Redemptor gentium
St Anatolius, late 6th c
    A great and mighty wonder
    Darkening night the land doth
    Fierce was the wild billow;
        X102224 Fierce ... billow
        wild
    The day is past and over
    The Lord and King of all
St Andrew of Crete, 660-732
    Christian, dost thou see them
        (ascribed to)
St Anselm of Canterbury, 1033-
1109
    Come thou, O come: Sweetest
Ah, holy Jesu, see Heermann
St Anselm of Lucca
    Jesus, solace of the soul
St Augustine, see "F.B.P.",
    the Jerusalem hymns
St Bede, the Venerable, 673-735
    A hymn of glory let us sing
    Hail, harbinger of morn

Sing we triumphant hymns
The great forerunner of the
    morn; X103044 Hail,
    harbinger
The hymn for conquering
St Bernard of Clairvaux, 1091-
1153
    All my hope and consolation
    Hail, thou King of saints
    I see by rays surrounded
    Jesu dulcis memoria
    Jesus, highest heaven's
    Jesus, how good the thought
    Jesus, how sweet the thought
    Jesu, Rex admirabilis
    Jesu! the very thought is
        sweet
    Jesus, the very thought of
        thee
    Jesus, thou Joy of loving;
        X102179 Father, thou joy;
        X107116 O Jesus, Joy of
        X107517 O Saviour, joy of
    Jesus thy memory divine
    Light of the anxious heart
    O bleeding Head, and wound-
        ed
    O Haupt voll Blut und Wun-
        den
    O Jesu, King most wonderful
    O Jesus, Lord, most mighty
    O Jesu, thou the beauty
        art
    O sacred head ... X106977
        O Head so full
    O what precious balm;
        X104626 Jesus, grant that
    Of Him who did salvation
    The thought of Jesus, O how
    Thousand times by me be
        greeted
    Wide open are thy hands;
        X111696 Wide ... thy
        loving
St Bernard of Cluny, 12th c
    Brief life is here our portion
    Daily sing in praise of Mary;
        X101635 Daily, daily sing
        to
    For thee, O dear, dear
        country; X110245 Thou
        city of the angels
    Hic breve vivitur, hic breve

Holy Queen, we come before;
   X103561 Holy Queen we
   bend
Hora novissima, tempora
Jerusalem, the glorious
Jerusalem the golden
O bona patria, lumina sobria
The world is very evil;
   X107454 O peace of all
Thou hast no shore, fair ocean
Urbs Sion aurea, patria
St Bonaventura, 1221-74
   In the Lord's atoning grief
   Let heaven highest praises
St Clement of Alexandria, ca
170-220
   Lead, holy Shepherd, lead us
   Master of eager youth
   O Guide to every child
   Shepherd of tender youth;
      X108861 Shepherd of eager
   Sunset to sunrise changes
St Columba, 521-597
   Christ is the world's Redeemer
   O God, thou art the Father
St Cosmas, d ca 760
   In days of old on Sinai
   The sepulcher is holding
St Ephraim the Syrian, ca 307-
373
   Receive, O Lord, in heaven
   Virgin wholly marvellous
St Francis of Assisi, 1181-
1226
   All creatures of our God;
      R107463 O praise Him,
   Alleluia; X101141 Canticle
      of the sun
   Altissimo, omnipotente, bon
   Make me, O Lord, an instru-
      ment
   Most high, omnipotent, good;
      X101141 Canticle of the sun
   O most high, almighty, good
St Francis Xavier, 1506-52
   My God, I love thee not be-
      cause; X106829 O God, I
      love thee (Spanish, 17th c)
   O Deus, ego amo te
   O God, thou art the object
St Fulbert of Chartres, ca 1000
   Ye choirs of new Jerusalem
St Gelasius. Sacramentary, 492

Lamb of God, O Jesus (Ag-
   nus dei)
St Germanus, ca 634-734
   A great and mighty wonder
St Gregory the Great, 540-
604
   Audi, benigne conditor
   Christ's loving children
   Ecce iam noctis tenuatur
   Father we praise thee, Now
      the night
   Kind Maker of the world
   Let us keep steadfast guard
   Lucis créator óptime
   Nocte surgentes vigilemus
   Now shadows wane, now hevy
      night
   Now, when the dusky shades
   O blest, Creator of the day;
      X106567 O blest ... of
      the light
   O Christ, our King, Creator
   O kind Creator, bow thine
      ear
   O merciful Redeemer, hear
   Primo dierum omnium
   Source of light and life;
      X106567 O blest Creator
   This day the first of days
   Thou loving Saviour of man-
      kind
St Gregory Nazianzen, 325-
390
   O light that knew no dawn
St Hilary of Poictiers, dd368
   Again the slowly circling
      year
   O joy, because the circling
   Rejoice, the year upon its
      way
St Jean de Brebeuf, d 1649
   Let Christian hearts rejoice
St John Chrysostom, 347-407
   Come, let us worship and
      fall
St John of Damascus, 8th c
   Come ye faithful, raise
   The day of resurrection;
      X101506 Come, sing with
      holy; X110551 "Tis the
      day
   Those eternal bowers
   Thou hallowed chosen morn;

Tantum ergo Sacramentum
The very Angels' Bread
The Word, descending from
above
The Word of God, proceeding;
    X109565 The heavenly word
Thee prostrate I adore;
    R103054 Hail, Jesus, hail
Thee we adore, O hidden Sa-
    viour; X106568 O, blest
    memorial
Therefore we, before him
Thus angels' Bread is made
Very Bread, good Shepherd;
    X107791 O true Bread
With all the powers my poor
Word of God to earth descend-
    ing
Saint (secular names)
NOTE: Only secular names begin-
    ning St follow. Religious names
    are above.

St John, Frank B.
    I do not come because my soul
St Patrick's hymnal, 1862
    Ave Maria! Thou Virgin;
        X100655 Ave Maria! O Vir-
        gin
Sammis, James H., d 1919
    When we walk with the Lord;
        R110773 Trust and obey
Sampter, Jessie E.
    Great Lord of Life who lives
    In many a stone-bound city
    The Sabbath light is burning
Sandburg, Carl, 1878-
    The young child, Christ, is
Sanders, H.
    See Him in the garden lone
Sandys, George, 1577-1643
    Thou who art enthroned above
Sanger, Florence Ziegler, 1906-
    O Jesus, crucified for me
Sangster, Margaret E., (Mrs.
 Gerrit van Deth), 1838-1912
    Comes any good from Nazareth
    For peace and for plenty
    O Christ, forget not them;
        X102326 Forget them not
    Out of my need, you come to
    me
    The ships glide in at the har-

bor's
    Thine is the power, Lord
Santee, L. D.
    In the glad time of the
    harvest
Santeüil, Claude de, 1628-84
    Blest Trinity, from mortal
    Now, my soul, thy voice
Santeüil, Jean-Baptist de,
 1630-97
    All honor and praise,
    dominion
    Captains of the saintly band
    Christ in the highest heaven
    Disposer supreme, and Judge;
        X100226 All honor and
        praise
    Hail! princes of the host
    In stature grows the heaven-
    ly
    Lady of the visitation
    Not by the martyr's death
    alone
    O Sion, open wide the gates
    Our Lord the path of suffering
    The heavenly Child in stature
    What mortal tongue can sing
    Where the angel-hosts adore
    Whither thus in holy rap-
    ture
Sarett, Lew, 1888-
    God is at the anvil, beating
    O, I can hear you God
Sargant, Edmund Beale
    Be firm, ye sentinels of
    Truth
    Dear Father-Mother, thou
    dost
    Go forth and stand upon
Sargent, Edward Hewlett Glad-
 stone, 1887-
    Lord, we have come to thee
Sargent, Epes, 1813-80
    All souls, O Lord, are thine
Sargent, Lucius Manlius, 1788-
 1867
    Bondage and death the cup
Sargent, N. B.
    We are building in sorrow
Sassoon, Siegfried, 1886-
    Your little flame of life
Sattlers, Michael
    Als Christus mit sein'r

ca 35
O Heil'ger Geist, kehr bei
O Holy Spirit, enter in
Schjörring, Jens N. L. , 1829-
1900
Friends of Jesus in their part-
ing
Love from God our Lord
Love the Lord thy God; Love
is
Schlegel, Johann Adolf, 1721-93
Vanish doubt and hesitation
Schlegel, Katharina Amalia
Dorothea von, 1697-
Be still, my soul: The Lord
is
Stille, mein Wille! Dein Jesus
Schlicht, Ludolf Ernst, 1714-69
Blessèd Saviour with love's
Lord, grant us, though deeply
Lord Jesus, in thy presence
What brought us together, what
What is it that makes us stand
Ye who callèd to Christ's;
X111927 Ye who callèd, ye
who
Schloerb, Rolland W. , 1893-
O Church of God, our solitude
O God, thy summons still is
O thou Eternal Source of Life
Praise to thee, O God, for
Schmidt, Ambrose M.
O God of nations, God of men
Take, O take me, holy Father
We praise thee, O God, our
Lord
Ye men of Christ awake
Schmidt, Christian von, 1768-
1854
Ihr Kinderlein, kommet
O come, little children, O
come; X106690 O dear
little children; X101380
Come hither, ye children
Schmidt, Johann Eusebius, 1670-
1745
Christ crucified, my soul, by
Fahre fort, fahre fort
Sion, rise, Sion, rise, Sion,
wake, arise
Schmolck, Benjamin, 1672-1737
Alleluia, lo, He wakes
Blessed Jesus, here are we;

X100931 Blessed Jesu!
here we stand
Blessed Jesus, we are here
[Baptism]
Heavenward still our path-
way; X103371 Heaven-
ward stretch
Jesus, Saviour, wondrous
mild
Lich vom Licht! erleuchte
Liebster Jesu, wir sind hier
Light of light, enlighten me
Mein Jesu, wie du willt
My God, I know that I must
My Jesus, as thou wilt;
X106169 My Saviour, as
thou
My truest Friend abides
O how holy is this place
Open now thy gates of beauty
Precious word from God in
Tut mir auf die schöne
Pforte
Was Gott tut, das ist wohl
Welcome, thou Victor in the
strife
What our Father does is
well
Why art thou cast down
Willkommen, Held im
Streite
Schneegass, Cyriacus, 1546-
97
Herr Gott Vater, wir preisen
O Lord, our Father, thanks
to
The child of humble Virgin
The new-born Child this
early
Schneesing, Johannes, d 1567
Allein zu dir, Herr Jesu
Christ
In thee alone, O Christ
Lord Jesus Christ, in thee
Schneider, Leopold
Mein Gott dich will ich
loben. 1528
Schneider, Michael
Es hatt' ein Mann zween
Knaben. 1564
Herr Gott in deinem Reiche.
1564
Herr Gott Vater in deinem

Thron! 1564
Ihr Christen rein, allkammt
(with Hans Betz) 1564
Mein Muth und Sinn steht mer
dahin. 1564
Merkt auf ihr Christen allge-
mein. 1564
Merkt auf, ihr Völker allge-
mein. 1564
Mich verlanget zu allen
Zeiten. 1564
Mit Lust und Freud will ich
Gott lobsingen, Dem Vater
gut. 1564
O Herre Gott in deinem Thron.
1564
Wohlauf, Wohlauf, du Gottes
G'mein. 1564
Schoenbechler, Roger
O blessed by God, St Bene-
dict
Scholefield, Jack P., 1882-
I've found a friend who is all;
R108702 Saved by His power
Think on thy way, O thou
storm-driven
Schornschlager, Leopold
Die Lieb ist kalt jetzt in der
Welt. 1564
Schrautenbach, Ludwig Karl, von
1726-83
O give us that good part
Schröder, Johann Heinrich, 1667-
99
Eins ist not, ach Herr, dies
Jesus, my captain, to victory
One thing needful! This one
One thing only, Lord, is
One thing's needful; Lord this;
X108019 One ... then Lord
Schroeder, Martin, 1888-
God calls to man, His acres to
Schroll, Eleanor Allen
Savior, I would live for thee;
R109347 Teach me, Lord
There's a garden where Jesus;
R107634 O the beautiful
Schuette, Conrad Herman Louis,
1843-
Another day has passed away
Great God, a blessing from
O Lord, our God, accept, we
pray

Schuette, Walter E.
This is the day we celebrate
Schütz, Johann Jakob, 1640-90
All glory to the Sovereign
Give praise and glory unto
Sei Lob und Ehr' dem
höchsten
Sing praise to God who reigns;
X100254 All praise to God
To God, the Father of all
love
Schwedler, Johann Christoph,
1672-1730
Ask ye what great thing I
know
Do you ask what most I prize
What, ye ask me, is my
prize
Scollard, Clinton, 1860-
O little town, O little town
Scott, Clara H., 1841-97
Open my eyes, that I may
see
Scott, Elizabeth, 1708-76
Awake, ye saints, awake
See how the rising sun
Thy bounties, gracious Lord
Scott, Frederick G.
Cast thy care on Jesus
Scott, Jacob Richardson, 1815-
61
To thee this temple we de-
vote
Scott, Lesbia
I sing a song of the saints
Scott, Robert B.Y., 1899-
O day of God, draw nigh
Scott, Thomas, 1705-75
Angels, roll the rock away
(with Thomas Gibbons);
X100460 Angel, roll the
rock
Hasten, sinner, to be wise;
X103203 Hasten, O sinner,
to
Imposture shrinks from light
Lo! the stone is rolled away
The lifted eye and bended
knee; X109903 The uplift-
ed eye
Scott, Sir Walter, 1771-1832
On Christmas Eve the bells;
X109979 Then drink (Engl.

trad)
That day of wrath (Dies irae)
see Latin, 13th c
When Israel of the Lord
Scott, William, tr. see Korean
hymn: The Saviour's precious
blood
Scottish hymnal, 1884
Great Shepherd of the sheep
Scottish paraphrases, 1745
Lo! what a cloud of witnesses
O let triumphant faith dispel
Scottish paraphrases, 1781
Ho! ye that thirst, approach
Take comfort, Christians,
when
Ye who the Name of Jesus
bear
Scottish Psalter, 1650

NOTE: Following the first line,
the Psalm number is given
parenthetically. Sixty-eight
Psalms are included, fifteen
of them several times.

After thy loving-kindness (Ps
51)
All lands to God, in joyful
(Ps 66)
All nations whom thou mad'st
(Ps 86)
Be merciful to me, O God
(Ps 57)
Blessed are they that undefiled
(Ps 119)
By what means shall a young
man (Ps 119)
Earth thou dost visit (Ps 65)
Give ear unto me when I call
(Ps 4)
Give ear unto my words (Ps
5)
Give praise and thanks unto
(Ps 106)
Give thanks to God, call on
(Ps 105)
God is of mine inheritance (Ps
16)
God is our refuge and our
strength (Ps 46)
God reigneth, He is clothed
(Ps 93)

God righteous judgement
executes (Ps 103)
God will I bless all times
(Ps 32)
God's law is perfect (Ps
19)
God's mercies I will ever
sing (Ps 89)
Good unto all men is the
Lord (Ps 145)
His name for ever shall en-
dure (Ps 72); X106358
Now blessed be
How excellent in all the
earth (Ps 8)
How lovely is thy dwelling
(Ps 84)
I joyed when to the house
(Ps 122)
I love the Lord, because
(Ps 116)
I to the hills will lift mine
(Ps 121)
I waited for the Lord my
God (Ps 40)
I'll hear what God the Lord
(Ps 85)
I'll of salvation take the cup
(Ps 116)
In Judah's land God is well
known (Ps 76)
Judge me, O Lord, for I
have walked (Ps 26)
Lord bless and pity us (Ps
67)
Lord from the depths to thee
(Ps 130)
Lord, hear the right, attend
(Ps 17)
Lord, thee, my God, I'll
early seek (Ps 63)
Lord, thou shalt early hear
(Ps 5)
My soul with expectation doth
(Ps 62)
O blessed is the man whose
(Ps 32)
O children, hither do ye
come (Ps 34)
O come, let us sing to the
Lord (Ps 95)
O daughter, take good heed
(Ps 45)

O God, give ear unto my cry
(Ps 61)

O greatly blessed the people
(Ps 89); X109777 The
praises of thy

O happy is that man and blest
(Ps 146)

O hear my prayer, Lord (Ps
148)

O Lord, I unto thee do cry
(Ps 141)

O Lord, thou hast me searched
(Ps 139)

O Lord, thy judgments give
(Ps 72)

O send thy light forth (Ps
43)

O set ye open unto me (Ps
118)

O sing a new song to the Lord,
For wonders He hath done
(Ps 98)

O sing a new song to the Lord,
Sing all the earth to God
(Ps 96)

O that men to the Lord would
(Ps 107)

O thou my soul, bless God the
Lord (Ps 103)

O thou that art the mighty one
(Ps 45)

O with thy tender mercies (Ps
90)

O ye His angels, that excel
(Ps 103)

Praise waits for thee in Zion
(Ps 65)

Praise ye the Lord: for it is
good (Ps 147)

Praise ye the Lord: with my
whole heart (Ps 111)

Pray that Jerusalem may have
(Ps 122, 133, 116)

Set thou thy trust upon the
Lord (Ps 37)

Shew me thy ways, O Lord
(Ps 25); X108892 Show me
thy ways

Such pity as a father hath
(Ps 103)

Teach me, O Lord, the perfect
(Ps 119)

That man hath perfect blessed-
ness (Ps 1)

The Lord doth reign, and
clothed (Ps 93)

The Lord for ever doth endure (Ps 9)

The Lord for ever sits as
King (Ps 9)

The Lord prepared hath
his throne (Ps 103)

The Lord will I at all times
(Ps 34)

The Lord's my light and
saving (Ps 27)

The Lord's my shepherd,
I'll not want (Ps 23);
X106182 My Shepherd
is (Rous); X109668 The
Lord is my

The mighty God, the Lord
(Ps 50)

They in the Lord that firmly (Ps 125)

Thou hast, O Lord, most
glorious (Ps 68)

Thou my sure portion art
alone (Ps 119)

Thou shalt arise, and mercy
(Ps 102)

Thou, with thy counsel,
while (Ps 73)

To render thanks unto the
Lord (Ps 92)

To thee I lift my soul
(Ps 25)

Turn us again, O God of
hosts (Ps 80)

'Twas like a dream, when
by (Ps 126)

Unveil mine eyes that by
thy law (Ps 119)

We'll to God's tabernacles
(Ps 132)

When Sion's bondage God
turned (Ps 126)

Who is the man that shall
ascend (Ps 24)

Why rage the heathen? and
vain (Ps 2)

Within thy tabernacle Lord
(Ps 15)

Ye gates, lift up your heads
(Ps 24)

Scrimger, John, 1849-1915

Lord, who shall come to Thee
Scriven, Joseph, 1820-86
 What a friend we have
Scriver, Christian, 1629-93
 In peace will I lie down
Scudder, Eliza, 1821-96
 Come, though with purifying
 I cannot find thee! Still on
 My God I rather look to thee
 Thou Grace divine, encircling
 Thou Life within my life
Scudder, Vida Dutton, 1861-
 Thy kingdom Lord, thy king-
     dom; X110465 Thy kingdom,
     Lord, we
Seagrave, Robert, 1693-1759
 Rise my soul, and stretch thy
Seal, Emily F.
 Our God is All-in-all
 What is thy birthright, man
Seaman, Owen, 1861-1936
 You that have faith to look
Sears, Edmund Hamilton, 1810-
76
 Calm on the listening ear
 Ho! ye that rest beneath
 It came upon the midnight
     clear
Seaton. Church hymn book, 1855
 God of eternal love
Sedding, Edward Douglas, 1884-
 A work hath Christ for thee;
     X101193 Christ hath a work
 O Father, we thank thee for
Sederquist, G. W.
 'Tis almost time for the Lord;
     R107078 O it must be the
     breaking
Sedgwick, S. N., 1872-1941
 Lord, accept the alms we offer
Sedulius of Liege, 15th c
 The snow lay on the ground;
     R110894 Venite adoremus
Sedulius, Coelius, ca 450
 A solis ortus cardine
 Christum wir sollen loben
 From east to west, from
     shore
 Hostis Herodes impie
 How vain the cruel Herod's
     fear
 Now praise we Christ
 The star proclaims the King

Why, impious Herod,
     shouldst
Seebach, Margaret Reynolds,
 1875-1948
 Thy Kingdom come! O
 Father hear
Seebass, Friedrich Wilhelm, d
 1758
 Jesus, I love thee fervently
Seelye, J. H.
 God save our native land
Seiss, Joseph Augustus, 1823-
 1904
 Jesus, Master, Son of God
Sellers, Ernest O.
 Lord, unto Thee we look;
     R108049 Open our eyes,
     thy
 Thy Word is a lamp to my
     feet
 Would men know you've been;
     R101136 Can men tell
     that you
Selnecker, Nicolaus, 1528-92
 Abide with us, O Saviour
     dear
 Ach bleit bei uns, Herr
     Jesu
 Lass mich dein sein und
     bleiben
 Let me be thine for ever
 Lord Jesus Christ, with us
 Lord Jesus, with thy chil-
     dren
 Now cheer our hearts this
 Now Christ, the very Son
     of God
 O faithful God, thanks be;
     X106726 O ... we wor-
     ship Thee
 O Lord, my God, I cry to
     thee
 Wir danken dir, o treuer
     Gott
Seltzer, George Rise, 1902-
 Come, all ye people, come
Senfft von Pilsach, L. R.
 To thee, O Lord, I yield
     my
Serle, Ambrose, 1742-1812
 Thy ways, O Lord! with
     wise
Service, Robert William,

1874-1958
  Carry on! carry on! Fight the
    good fight
Servoss, Miss M.E.
  When the storms of life;
    R103307 He will hide me
Sewall, Frank
  Morn of joy and morn of
  Roll out, O song, to God
Seymer, Violet Ker
  As sings the mountain stream
  In God I find a precious gift
Seymour, Aaron Crossley Hobart,
  1789-1870
  Jesus, immortal King, arise!
Shackford, John W., 1878-
  O thou who art the Shepherd
Shacklock, Mrs. C.L.
  Would you know the love;
    R100621 At the golden gate
Shairp, John Campbell, 1819-
  85
  'Twixt gleams of joy
Shakespeare, William, 1564-1616
  Blow, blow, thou winter
    wind
  Poor Soul, the centre of my
    sinful earth
Shank, J.W.
  My life was lost in selfish-
    ness; R108165 Out of the
    gloom and
Shanne, Richard. ms. 1611
  Come, love we God, of might
Shapcote, Emily Mary, 1829-
  1909
  Jesus, holy, undefiled
  O Queen of the Holy Rosary
Shaw, Knowles, 1834-78
  I am the vine and ye are
  Sowing in the morning, sow-
    ing; R101062 Bringing in
    the sheaves
Shekleton, Mary, 1827-83
  It passeth knowledge, that
Shelley, Percy Bysshe, 1792-
  1822
  The world's great age begins
  To suffer woes which hope
Shelly, Martha Evans Jackson,
  1812-1901
  Lord, a little band and lowly
Shenk, J.M.

Come, heaven-bound pilgrims
Shepard, Odell
  We are standing in the great
Shepcote, Mrs. "E", see Shap-
  cote, Emily Mary, 1829-
  1909
Sheperd, Anne Houlditch, 1809-
  57
  Around the throne of God in
    heaven
Shepherd, Fred S.
  Trembling soul beset by fears
Shepherd, Thomas, 1665- 1739
  Must Jesus bear the cross
Sherman, Frank Dempster,
  1860-1916
  It is my joy in life
Sherman, H.H.
  Serving the Lord with glad-
    ness
Sherwin, William Fisk, 1826-88
  Galilee, bright Galilee
  Sound the battle cry; R108660
    Rouse, then, soldiers
  Wake the song of joy
  Why is thy faith in God's
Shillito, Edward, 1872-1948
  Away with gloom, away with
Shindler, Mary S.B., see
  Dana, Mary S.B.S.
Shipton, Anna, ca 1815-1901
  Call them in! the poor
Shirley, Walter, 1725-86
  Sweet the moments, rich
Shirreff, E.L.
  Gracious Saviour, who didst
Shoemaker, J.S.
  Come, lost one, your Saviour;
    R107848 O, why should you
  Father, we come in Jesus'
    name
  We now have met to worship
Shrubsole, William, 1759-1829
  Arm of the Lord, awake!
    awake
  As every day thy mercy spares
  When, streaming from the
    eastern
Shumate, Aurora M.
  Every Sunday evening, To the
Shurtleff, Ernest Warburton,
  1862-1917
  Lead on, O King eternal

Shuttleworth, Henry Cary, 1850-
1900
　Father of men, in whom
　Man lives not for himself
Sidebotham, Mary Anne, 1833-
1913
　Lord, thy mercy now entreat-
　　ing
Sicilian traditional, etc.
　O most holy One, O most lowly
　O sanctissima, O piissima
Sidney, Sir Philip, 1554-86
and Mary Sidney (his sister),
i.e. Lady Mary Pembroke,
1561-1621
　O Lord in me there lieth
Sigmond, Sven O, 1872-
　Father Almighty, darkness now
Sigourney, Lydia Huntley,
1793-1865
　Blest Comforter Divine, whose
　Go to thy rest, fair child
　Laborers of Christ, arise
　When adverse winds and waves
Sigstedt, Cyriel O.
　O Jesus Christ, our only Lord
　The Lord is risen again! Ye
Sill, Edward Rowland, 1841-87
　Send down thy truth, O God
Silliman, Vincent Brown, 1894-
　As we leave this friendly
　Earth arrayed in wondrous
　Faith of the larger liberty
　Morning, so fair to see
　One world this, for all its
Silver, Rabbi Abba Hillel, 1893-
　God built him a continent
Simonsson, Thomas, Bp. of
Strängnos, Sweden, see
　Thomas, Bishop . . . d 1443
Simpson, A.B.
　The mercy of God is an ocean;
　　R105062 Launch out
Simpson, Jane Cross Bell, 1811-
86
　Go when the morning shineth
　Pray when the morn is break-
　　ing
　Star of peace to wanderers
Simpson, Margaret M.
　To the regions beyond I must
Simpson, Robert, 1771-1843
　From thy holy habitation

　To God we render praise
　We bow before thy throne
　With deeply humbled hearts
Simpson, William James Spar-
row, 1860-1952
　Cross of Jesus, cross of
Sims, A.J.
　There is an unseen hand;
　　R104214 I'm trusting
Sinclair, Duncan
　Help us, O Lord, to bear
　O God, our Father-Mother,
　　Love
Singleton, Robert Corbet,
1810-81
　With gladsome feet we press
Sister of Notre Dame
　Hail! all hail, great Queen;
　　R109980 Then let men and
　　Angels
　Jesus, thou art coming
　Little King, so fair and
　　sweet
　Lord for tomorrow see Mary
　　Xavier, Sr., born Sybil F.
　　Partridge
　Mother of Christ, Mother of
　Sweet Agnes, holy child, all
Sisters of St. Joseph, Toronto
　Let the loud hosannas ring
Skavlan, Sigvald
　As sinks beneath the ocean
Skemp, Ada, 1851-1927
　I love to think that Jesus
Skrine, John Huntley, 1848-
1923
　Rank on rank again we stand
Slade, Mariana B. (perhaps:
Mary B.C. Slade, 1826-82)
　Up to the bountiful Giver;
　　R102451 Gathering home
Slade, Mary B.C., 1826-82
　From all the dark places;
　　X102373 From ... needy
　　races; R109600 The king-
　　dom is coming
　Into the tent where the gipsy;
　　R109362 Tell it again
　Sweetly, Lord, have we heard;
　　R102252 Footprints of
　　Jesus
　There's a fountain free;
　　R111709 Will you come to

the
Who at my door is standing;
  R109313 Sweetly the tones
Sleeper, William T., 1819-1904
  A ruler once came to Jesus;
    R111904 Ye must be born
  Out of my bondage, sorrow
Sleight, M. B.
  Hark! the voice of Jesus
Slemp, John C.
  Breathe o'er our waiting
  In the quiet hours of morning;
    R103415 Here we come
  O God, Eternal God! Thy
    name
Slinn, Sarah
  God with us! O, glorious name
Slovak traditional, etc.
  In the resurrection
  Man of sorrows, wrapt in grief
  Vzkříšeni čekáme
Small, James Grindly, 1817-88
  I've found a friend, O such
Smart, Christopher, 1722-71
  All the scenes of nature
  Awake, arise! lift up thy
  Hosanna! music is divine
  We sing of God, the mighty
  Welcome, blessed Heavenly
Smart, Richard, 15th c
  Who is there that singeth so
Smith, Annie R.
  Blessed Jesus, meek and lowly
  Hail, peaceful day! divinely
  He sleeps in Jesus -- peaceful
  How far from home? I asked
  I ask not, Lord, for less
  I saw one weary, sad, and
  Long upon the mountains
  Toil on a little longer here
  Weeping endures but for a night
  When darkness gathers round
Smith, Caroline Louisa Sprague,
  1827-86
  Tarry with me, O my Saviour
Smith, Eleanor, 1858-1942
  In another land and time
Smith, Florence Margaret, 1886-
  1958
  Lord and Master, who hast
Smith, Frederic, 1849-
  O God, not only in distress

Smith, Fronia Savage
  Proclaim the tidings near;
    R108941 Sing glory, glory
Smith, G. N.
  Holy, holy, holy Lord
Smith, Gipsy [pseud] see Smith,
  Rodney, 1860 -- [i.e. Gipsy
  Smith]
Smith, Horace, 1836-1922
  O thou whom neither time
Smith, Horace, 1839-
  Sweet is the breath of morn-
    ing
Smith, Isaac Gregory, 1826-1920
  By Jesus' grave on either
    hand
Smith, J. B.
  At home and abroad, on life's;
    R109898 The trumpet is
    sounding
  In the early days of child-
    hood; R100935 Blessed
    Jesus, we
Smith, Jay Holmes
  Come forth, ye men of every
Smith, Joseph Denham, ca 1816-
  Jesus Christ is passing by
Smith, Joseph Fielding
  Does the journey seem long
Smith, L. J. Egerton, 1879-
  1958
  For all the love that from
Smith, Lanta Wilson
  I was wandering in a wilder-
    ness; R103822 I believe
    the promises
  In a world where sorrow;
    R108764 Scattering sun-
    shine
Smith, M. J.
  Cling to the Bible
Smith, Robert Archibald.
  Sacred harmony, 1828
  Lord, let thy mercy now
Smith, Rodney, 1860-
  [i.e. Gipsy Smith]
  Christ the transforming Light;
    R107782 O, to reflect His
Smith, Samuel Francis, 1808-
  95
  Auspicious morning, hail
  Down to the sacred wave

Founded on thee, our only
Go, heralds of salvation
Lord of our life, God whom
My country, 'tis of thee;
    X107304 O Lord, our God,
    to
Our Father's God! to thee
Planted in Christ, the living
Sister, thou wast mild
Softly fades the twilight
Spirit of holiness, descend
Spirit of peace and holiness
The morning light is breaking
Today the Saviour calls
When shall we meet again (with
    A.A. Watts)
With willing hearts we tread
Smith, Uriah
    O brother, be faithful! Soon
Dark is the hour when death
Smith, Walter Chalmers, 1824-
1908
    Earth was waiting, spent
    Immortal, invisible, God only
    Lord God omnipotent, Lord
    God
    One thing I of the Lord;
        R109056 So wash me, Thou
    To me to live is Christ
Smith, Wharton Buchanan, 1848-
    Raised between the earth and
Smucker, S.J.
    I've read of a world
    O Lord, thy heavenly grace
Smyth, Clifford
    Dear Saviour, stretch thy
Smyth, Harper G., 1873-1945
    Is your life a channel;
        R105854 Make me a channel
Smyth, Richard
    Israel, Israel, God is
Smyttan, George Hunt, 1822-70
    Forty days and forty nights
Snelling, J. Palmer
    Dear God, how glorious is
Snow, B.
    Our God, we raise to thee
Snow, Eliza R.
    Again we meet around
    Awake, ye Saints of God
    Behold the great Redeemer die
    Great is the Lord; 'tis good
    How great the wisdom

O awake! My slumbering
O my Father, thou that
    dwellest
The Lord imparted from
    above
The time is far spent
Think not when you gather
Thou dost not weep to weep
Though deepening trials
Truth reflects upon our;
    R100948 Blessed Saviour,
    thou
Snyder, F.L.
    There is a story ever new;
        R104077 I want to love
        him
    When your toils below are;
        R111472 When the book
        of life
S.P.C.K. Appendix, 1869
    Little children, wake and
Söderberg, Erik Natanael,
1869-
    In the temple where our
Sola Mendes, Fred de see
    Mendes, Fred de Sola
Solberg, C.K., 1872-
    Arise, arise, united youth
    Christian Leaguers, rally;
        R102344 Forward, Chris-
        tian Leaguers
    Fellow Christians, let us
    Lift up your eyes, ye Chris-
    tians
    O Blessed Light from heaven
    Ride on, ride on, O Sa-
    viour-King
    There is a sea of mercy
Solomon ibn Gabirol
    Early will I seek thee, God
    O rain depart with blessings
    Thou knowest my tongue
    Thy faithful servant, Lord
Songs of Zion, 1864
    And is it so?"A little while"
Sonnenschein, S.H.
    Hark, the voice of children;
        R108040 Onward, children
Sorley, Charles Hamilton d
1915
    This sanctuary of my soul
Southwell, Robert, ca 1561-
94

Behold a simple tender babe;
R106492 Nowell, Nowell,
Nowell (English trad)
Let folly praise what fancy
Sower, Christopher, jr., 1721-
84
Death, death, thou hast
Spafford, Horatio Gates, 1828-
88
When peace, like a river;
R104486 It is well with my
Spangenberg, Augustus Gottlieb,
1704-92
High on his everlasting throne;
X111263 What can we offer
The church of Christ, that He
When simplicity we cherish
Spanish traditional, etc.
Torches, torches, run with
Up now, laggardly lasses
Speece, Conrad, 1776-1836
Blest Jesus, when thy cross
Spegel, Haquin, 1645-1714
The death of Jesus Christ
War Herres Jesu Kristi död
We Christians should ever
Speier Gebetbuch, 1599
Behold a Rose of Judah
Es ist ein Reis (Ros')
I know a rose-tree springing
Lo, how a Rose e'er blooming
There is a flower springing
Spencer, Anna Garlin
Hail the Hero workers
Spencer, Robert Nelson
Eternal Father, strong to save
see Whiting, William
O heavenly grace in holy rite
Spencer, W.A.
When I shall reach the more;
R104025 I shall be like Him
Spengler, Lazarus, 1479-1534
All mankind fell in Adam's
Spenser, Edmund, 1553-99
Most glorious Lord of life
Speratus, Paul, 1484-1551
All blessing, honor, thanks
Es ist das Heil uns kommen
To us salvation now is come;
X100188 All blessing, hon-
or; X108692 Salvation unto
us has
Spitta, Karl Johann Philipp, 1801-

59
Ah, this heart is void
Brethren, called by one
By the holy hills surround-
ed
Father, whose hands hath
led
How blessed from the bonds
I know no life divided
I place myself in Jesus'
hands
In thy service will I ever
O blessed house, that
O blessed Sun whose splen-
dor
O happy home, where thou
art
O Lord! of goodness so
O Lord, who by thy pres-
ence
O selig Haus, wo man dich
Our lot is fallen in pleasant
Still on thy loving heart let
Thou, whose coming seers
We are the Lord's: His all-
sufficient
We praise and bless thee
Wherefore weep we over
Jesus
Wir sind des Herrn, wir
leben
Withhold not, Lord the help
Spring-Rice, Cecil, 1859-1918
I vow to thee, my country;
X104062 I vow ... all
earthly
Spurgeon, Charles Haddon,
1834-92
Sweetly the holy hymn
The Holy Ghost is here
Squier, George L.
O Christ, the Way, the
Truth
Squires, N.J.
O blessed hour, when even-
ing
St, see above as if spelled
Saint
Stach, Matthew, 1711-87
There's but a small begin-
ning
Stainer, J R.L., 1866-1939
Daystar on high, bright

On Jordan's stormy banks I;
  R103787 I am bound for the;
  R111169 We will rest in the
Prostrate, dear Jesus, at thy
Thou Sun of love, whose
" 'Tis finished!" So the Saviour
Where two or three with sweet
With tears of anguish I lament
Stephens, Evan
  Father, thy children to thee
  In remembrance of thy suffer-
    ing
  Let us all press on
  O happy homes among the hills
  O home beloved, where'er
  Raise your voices to the Lord
  Sacred the place of prayer
  Shall the youth of Sion; R110768
  True to the faith
  Sweet is the hour when thus
  The voice of God again is
  This was the song the angels
  We ever pray for thee
Stephens, James, 1882-1950
  Little things that run
  Low at thy pierced feet
Stephenson, Isabella S., 1843-90
  see Stevenson, Isabel S., 1843-
  90
Sterling, John, 1806-44
  O Source divine, and life
Stern, Louis
  Come let us sing in sweet
Sternberg, Sadye
  Though our hearts dwell
Sternhold, Thomas, d 1549
  How long wilt thou forget me
  O God, my strength; X109640
  The Lord descended
  O Lord, how are my foes
Steuerlein, Johann. Sieben und
  zwantzig newe geistliche
  Gesange. Erfurt, 1588
  Das alte Jahr vergangen ist
  The old year now hath passed
Stevens, David
  New Russia, rise and proudly
Stevenson, Isabel Stephana, 1843-
  90
  Holy Father, in thy mercy
Stevenson, Robert Louis, 1850-
  94
  Let us wander where we will

Thy people, Lord, of many;
  X110449 Thy children,
  Lord
To make this earth, our
  hermitage
Under the wide and starry
  sky
Stewart, Alexander, 1843-1923
  Lord Jesus Christ, we seek
Sthen, Hans Christenson, 16th
  c
  Herre Jesu Krist! Min
    Freiser
  I know a Kingdom without
    end
  Lord Jesus Christ, my Sa-
    viour
Stidger, William L.
  Judean hills are holy
  Rise up, O world, the light
Stiles, E.P., see Stites,
  E.P. [printing error]
Stillman, J.M.
  I want to be more like Jesus;
    R105994 More and more
    like
Stillman, Mildred Whitney,
  1890-
  Now once again for help that
Stites, Edgar Page
  I've reached the land of joy;
    R106537 O Beulah land;
    X110030 There is a land
  Simply trusting every day;
    R110777 Trusting as the
    moments
Stock, Eleanor B.
  Take us on the Quest of
    Beauty
  The body, Lord, is ours
Stock, Harry T., 1891-1958
  O gracious God, whose con-
    stant
Stock, Sarah Geraldina, 1838-
  98
  Let the song go round
  O Master! when thou callest
Stocker, John
  Gracious Spirit, Dove divine;
    X102922 Gracious ... Love
    divine
Stocking, Jay T., 1870-1936
  O Master Workman of the

race
Stockman, Paul, 1602-36
  Jesus, thou who knowest death
  Jesus, thou who once wast
    dead
Stockton, John Hart, 1813-77
  Come, every soul by sin;
    R108037 Only trust Him
Stockton, Martha, 1821-85
  God loved the world of sin-
    ners
Stockton, Thomas H., 1808-68
  Can truth divine fulfillment
Stokes, E. H.
  Hover o'er me, Holy Spirit;
    R102229 Fill me now
Stone, Ella A.
  O sweet and tender as the
    dawn
Stone, Lloyd
  This is my song, O God of
    all
Stone, Samuel John, 1839-1900
  Lord of the Harvest, it is
  O great Absolver, grant my
  O thou, before whose Presence
  The Church's one foundation;
    X109444 The Church has one
  The old year's long campaign
  Through midnight gloom
  Unchanging God, hear from
  Weary of earth, and laden
    with; X111181 Weary of
    self
Stonehouse, Maria Th., 1722-51
  Lord, take my heart just as
    it
Stoney, C. Butler
  Since to the Holiest none may
Stowe, Harriet Beecher, 1812-96
  Abide in me, O Lord, and I
    in; X100093 Abide ... o'er
    shadow; X109402 That mys-
    tic word
  Still, still with thee, when
  When winds are raging o'er
Stowell, Hugh, 1799-1865
  From every stormy wind that
  Jesus is our Shepherd
  Lord of all power and might
Stowell, Thomas Alfred, 1831-
  While the sun is shining
Stratton, Mrs. F. K.

O Lord, our God, Almighty
  King
Stratton, Maggie
  Holy Bible, how I love it
Straub, Hans
  Durch Gnad so will ich
    singen. 1564
Straub, Maria, 1838-98
  God sees the little sparrow;
    R103269 He loves me too
Strauss, Victor Friedrich von
  1809-99
  Thou, sore opprest, the
    sabbath
Strodach, Paul Zeller, 1876-
  1947
  God of our life, all-glorious
  Now let the vault of heaven
Strong, Nathan
  Almighty Sovereign of the
    skies, see Watts, Isaac
    Almighty Sovereign ...
  Swell the anthem, raise the
Strout, Jessie E.
  Lift up the trumpet, and
Struther, Jan, 1901-53
  Daisies are our silver
  God, whose eternal mind
  High o'er the lonely hills
  Lord of all hopefulness
  O Saint of summer, what
    can
  Round the earth a message
  Sing, all ye Christian people
  Unto Mary, demon-haunted
  We thank you, Lord of
    heaven
  When a knight won his spurs
  When Mary brought her
    treasure
  When Stephen full of power
Stryker, Melanchthon Woolsey,
  1851-1929
  Almighty, Lord, with one
    accord
  God speed the gospel! O
    Father
Stubbs, Charles William, 1845-
  Fair the night in Bethlem
    land
Studdert-Kennedy, Geoffrey
  Anketell, 1883-1929
  Awake, awake to love and

work
Close by the heedless worker's
We shall build on!
When through the whirl
Stutsman, Grace M.
  In Bethlehem 'neath starlit
Stuttle, Mrs. L. D. Avery
  O let me walk with thee, my
Summers, Thomas Osmund, 1812
-82
  The daylight fades, the evening
  The morning bright, with rosy
Suso, Henry, 1300-66
  In dulci jubilo; X106495
    Nu singet und seyt
    Nun singet und seid froh
Sutton, Amos, 1802-54
  Hail! sweetest, dearest tie
Swahili hymn
  Jesus, Son of Mary, Fount of
Swain, Joseph, 1761-96
  Brethren, while we sojourn
  Come, let our hears and
    voices
  Come, ye souls by sin afflicted
  How sweet, how heavenly is
  O Thou, in whose presence my;
    X108439 Redeemer of Israel
Swain, Leonard, 1821-69
  My soul, weigh not thy life
Swayne, Amelia W.
  For all the souls who sought
Swedberg, Jesper, 1653-1735
  Lord, bestow on us thy bless-
    ing
  O Lord, give heed unto our
Swedenborg, Emanuel, 1688-
1772
  in boundless mercy, gracious
Swertner, John, 1746-1813
  Believing souls, rejoice and
  Grace and peace from God our
  Gracious Lord, our Shepherd
  Highly favored congregation;
    X103473 Highly favored
    (Benade)
  Holy Lord, by thy body given
  Jesus, my King, thy kind and
  Lord God, our Salvation
  Lord Jesus, 'mid thy flock
  May the stream from thee
  Most holy Lord, mankind's
  My Sion where the Lamb of

God
  Now with joyful songs ap-
    pear
  O Lord, who numberest all
    our
  Our children, gracious Lord
  Praises, thanks, and adora-
    tion
  Sing alleluia, praise the
    Lord
  To thee, Lord Christ, all
    praise
  To thee our vows with sweet
  To thy brethren ever be
  We in one covenant are
    joined
  When Christ, our Lord
Swinburne, Algernon Charles,
1837-1909
  For no sect elect
  Thou whose birth on earth
  We mix from many lands
Switton, Florence
  A message sweet the breezes
Symington, Andrew James,
1829-
  Lord! in love and mercy
    save
Symonds, John Addington,
1840-93
  These things shall be
  To God, the everlasting,
    who
Symons, Emily, 1842-1924
  I give myself to thee
  We, who would lead thy
    flock
Synesius of Cyrene, ca 375-
430
  Lord Jesus, think on me
Synnestvedt, Elsa
  Father all-holy, Lord of
  Rise, O Lord, lift up thine
  When very early in the
    dawn

T

Tagore, Rabindranath, 1861-
1941
  Now I recall my childhood
  The light, my light, world-
    filling light,

This is my prayer: Give me
Tailour, F. Robert. Fiftie select
Psalms, 1615 see Bridges,
Robert.
  The King, O God, his heart
Talley, Thomas
  Behold that star
Tamminen, K. V.
  Lift up the banner of salvation
Tappan, William Bingham, 1794-
1849
  There is an hour of hallowed;
    X110047 There ... Peace
  There is an hour of peaceful
  'Tis midnight; and on Olive's
Tarrant, William George, 1853-
1928
  Come, let us join with faithful
  "Draw nigh to God, he will"
  I saw the city of the Lord;
    X100070 A temple of the
    Lord
  Long ago the lilies faded
  Marching with the heroes
  My Master was a worker
  Now praise we great and famous
  The fathers built this city
  The Light along the ages
  With happy voices ringing;
    X111770 With ... voices
    singing
  Welcome, morning, bright and
Tate, Nahum, 1652-1715, &
Brady, Nicholas, 1659-1726 us-
usually cited as Tate and Brady
  As pants the hart for cooling;
    X105288 Like as the hart
  Be thou, O God! exalted high
  Defend me, Lord, from shame
  Give ear ye children (with
    Watts), see Belknap, Jeremy.
    Give ear ye children
  Have mercy, Lord, on me
  He that hath God his guardian
  Let me with light and truth
  Lift up your heads, eternal
  My soul with patience waits
  No change of time shall ever
  O come, loud anthems let us
  O God, my heart is fixed
  O God of hosts, the mighty
  O God, we praise thee, and
    (Te Deum)

O Lord, our fathers oft have
O praise ye the Lord
O render thanks to God
  above
O thou, to whom all crea-
  tures
O 'twas a joyful sound to
  hear
O with due reverence let us
Thou, God, all glory, honor
Thou, Lord, by strictest
Through all the changing
  scenes
Thy word is to my feet a
  lamp
To bless thy chosen race
To Father, Son and Holy
  Ghost; X110576 To ...
  The God, whom
To God be glory, peace on
To Sion's hill I lift my eyes;
  X110636 To ... lift mine
  eyes
While shepherd's watched;
  X111585 While humble
  shepherds
With glory clad, with strength
With one consent let all
Taylor, Ann, i. e. Ann Taylor
Gilbert, 1782-1866
  Great God! and wilt thou
    (with Jane Taylor)
  Lord, I have passed another
  There is a dear and hallow-
    ed (authorship questioned)
Taylor, C. T.
  Cross of Christ, O sacred
    tree
Taylor, Clare, d 1778
  Lord, my times are in thy
    hand
  The cross, the cross, O
    that's
Taylor, E. G.
  Fear not! God is thy shield
Taylor, Emily, 1795-1872
  God of the changing year
  O here, If ever, God of love
Taylor, George Lansing, 1835-
  Dare to do right
Taylor, Georgiana Mary, 1848-
1915
  Seek ye first, not earthly

Mir ist Erbarmung widerfahren
O glorious Head, thou livest
O God, O Spirit, Light of all
O Lamb of God, who wast for
O Lord our God, in reverence
O Love divine, all else;
  X107461 O power of love
Something every heart is
Spirit of Grace, thou Light
Thou fairest Child divine
Thou hidden love of God,
  whose; X110276 Thou hidden
  Source (Wesley)
Triumph, ye heavens! rejoice
What mercy and divine compas-
  sion
Thai Christian
The righteous ones shall be
Thalheimer, Elsie, & Margaret
Scott Haycroft
Thou art my Shepherd
Thaxter, Celia, 1836-94
Lift up thy light, O man
Thayer, Lucius H.
The Church of God is stablish-
  ed
Thilo, Valentin, 1607-62
Mit Ernst, o Menschenkinder
O Jesulein süss, o Jesulein
O Jesu so meek, O Jesu so;
  X107143 O Jesu sweet, O
  Jesu
O little one sweet, O little
Ye sons of men, O hearken
Thoburn, Helen, 1885-1932
Father of lights, in whom
  see Elizabeth Wilson
Thomas, Bp. of Strängnas,
Sweden, d 1443
Freedom is the finest gold
Thomas of Celano, 13th c may
  have been the author of Dies
  Irae; but see Latin, 13th c
Thomas, Alexcenah
Hark, 'tis the Shepherd's;
  R101060 Bring them in
'Tis the harvest time;
  R102521 Gleaning on the
  hillside
Thomas, Carrie S.
Great King of heaven, our
Thomas, H. Arnold, 1848-1924
Lord Christ, who on thy heart

Thompson, Alexander Ramsay,
1812-95
Hail! kingly Jesus, to thy
  Praise our glorious King
Thompson, Francis, 1859-
1907
O world invisible, we view
Thompson, Henry
Lord, we humbly bow before
Thompson, J. O.
Far and near the fields are:
  R105635 Lord of harvest,
  send
Thompson, Robert B.
See, the mighty angel flying
Thompson, Will Lamartine,
1847-1909
Have I done any good in the;
  R109991 Then wake up,
  and do
Jesus is all the world to
  me
Lead me gently home,
  Father
Softly and tenderly Jesus is;
  R101409 Come home, come
  home
The world has need of will-
  ing; R108410 Put your
  shoulder
There's a great day coming;
  R100494 Are you ready
Thomson, John, 1783-1818
Jehovah God! Thy gracious
Thomson, Mary Ann, 1834-
1923
Now the blessèd Dayspring
O King of saints, we give
  thee
O Sion, haste, thy mission;
  X106630 O Christian,
  haste; X107887 O, Zion,
  haste; R108398 Publish
  glad tidings
Saviour, for the little one
Thorsteinsson, Steingrimur,
d 1913
The fading day adorns the
Threlfall, Jeannette, 1821-80
Hosanna, loud hosanna
When from Egypt's house of
Thring, Godfrey, 1823-1903
All that's good and great

Fierce raged the tempest
From the eastern mountains;
R105268 Light of light
God the Father, God the son
(Children's litany)
Grant us, O our heavenly
Father
Hail! sacred day of earthly
Heal me, O my Saviour, heal
Hear us, thou that broodest
I heard a sound of voices;
X104013 I saw the holy city
Jesus came, the heavens
O God of mercy, God of might
O mighty God, Creator, King
O thou, who madest land and
Saviour, blessed Saviour, lis-
ten; X106237 Nearer, ever
nearer
The ocean hath no danger
The radiant morn hath passed
Thou to whom the sick and
To thee, O God, we render
True Light, that lightest
Work is sweet, for God has
Thrupp, Adelaide
Lord, who at Cana's wedding
Thrupp, Dorothy Ann, 1779-1847
Come, Christian children,
come
Come, Holy Spirit, come
Let us sing, with one accord
Thrupp, Dorothy Ann. Hymns for
the young, 1836
Saviour, like a shepherd lead;
X103366 Heavenly Shepherd
Thrupp, Joseph Francis, 1827-
67
Awhile in spirit, Lord, to
O Son of man, thyself once
Thymus, G.
Turn, Lord, thy wrath away
Tickle, G.Y.
Lord of our highest love
Tietze, Christoph, 1641-1703
By sin weighed down
Seems it in my anguish lone
Tiffany, Emma A.
Jesus dear, I come to thee
Tilak, Narayan Vaman, 1862-
1919
Heart and mind, possessions
One who is all unfit to count

Prayer to a heart of lowly
Tillett, Wilbur Fisk, 1854-
1936
O Son of God incarnate
Tilton, Theodore, 1835-
We sing a song and then we
Timm, H.A.
Abide with me, my Saviour
Tindley, Charles A., 1856-
1937
If the world from you;
R109340 Take your bur-
den
Nothing between my soul and
Trials dark on every hand;
R101090 By and by, when
the morning
When the storms of life
Tiplady, Thomas, 1882-
Above the hills of time
Awake, O church of God
Beyond the wheeling worlds
I may not climb the heights
O men of God, go forth
To all the nations, Lord
To God our hearts we lift
We leave thy house but
leave not
Where the olive grove stood
Tisserand, Jean, 15th c
O filii et filiae
O sons and daughters let us
Ye sons and daughters of
the King; X107579 O
sons and daughters
Ye sons and daughters of the
Lord
Titius, Christophe, 1641-
1703   see Tietze, Christophe
Todd, R.W.
O who is this that cometh;
R105973 Mighty to save
Toeltschig, Johann, 1703-64
What offering shall I bring
Toews, Jacob D.
Come, ye weary ones,
come; R101543 Come to-
night
Far, far beyond the starry
Jesus, bless us with thy
Loyal and true and faithful;
R102516 Giving our best
No mortal eye hath seen

O Lord divine, we come to
When Jesus on the mountain
Toke, Emma Leslie, 1812-72
   Glory to thee, O Lord, who
   O thou, who didst with love
   Thou art gone up on high
Tomlinson, Irving C.
   A Voice from heaven we have
   O peace of the world, O hope
Tonna, Charlotte Elizabeth Brown,
1790-1846
   O thou who didst prepare
Toplady, Augustus Montague,
1740-78
   A debtor to mercy alone
   Christ to know is life
   Fels des Heils, geöffnet mir
   Fountain of never-ceasing
   Happiness, delightful name
   How vast the benefits divine
   If, on a quiet sea; X104175
   If, through unruffled
   Inspirer and hearer of prayer;
     X100066 A sovereign Pro-
     tector
   Lord, I feel a carnal mind
   O thou that hearest the prayer
   Object of my first desire
   Rock of ages, cleft for me;
     X108648 Rock ... Truth di-
     vine (Root)
   Saviour, whom I fain would
   Weary sinner, keep thine eyes;
     X109268 Surely Christ thy
     ... has; X109269 Surely
     Christ thy ... hath
   What though I cannot break
   Your harps, ye trembling
Torrence, Ridgely 1875-1951
   Consider well your ways
   Praise, O my heart, to you
   Praise, O my heart, with
     praise
   The sky has gathered
Torrey, Bradford, 1843-1912
   Not so in haste, my heart!
   One gift, my God, I seek
Townsend, Joseph L.
   Choose the right, when a
     choice
   Hope of Israel, Zion's army
   Let us oft speak kind words;
     R107650 O the kind words

Nearer, dear Saviour, to
   thee
O holy words of truth and
   love
O thou Rock of our Salvation
O what songs of the heart
Reverently and meekly now
The day dawn is breaking;
   R100756 Beautiful day
To Nephi, seer of olden
   time; R103507 Hold to
   the rod
Traasdal, J.
   O can you sing the new song
Trabert, George Henry
   Here we often are perplexed
   With deep humility, O Lord
Traherne, Thomas, 1637-73
   Sweet Infancy! O heavenly
Tranecker, G., 1717-1802
   Thou art our Comfort,
     blessèd
Tranoscius, Georgius, 1591-
1637 see Tranovsky, Juraj,
1591-1637
Tranovsky, Juraj, 1591-1637
   Christ the Lord to us is
     born
   In one true God we all be-
     lieve
   Narodil se Kristus Pán
   O that thou woulds't rend
   Věříme v všemohouciho
Trapp, Jacob, 1899-
   The art, the science, and
   Wonders still the world
     shall
Trask, Harold
   God, the Hope of those who
Tregelles, Samuel Prideaux,
1813-75
   The gloomy night will soon
Trench, Richard Chevenix,
1807-86
   Good cheer! Let all men
     know that all; R102866
     Good cheer! good cheer!
     good cheer
   Lord, what a change within
   Make channels for the
     streams
Trend, Henry, 1804-69
   Praise, O praise our heaven-

ly; R102285 For his mercies
aye
Tressel, W. E.
  Lo, we tread on holy ground
Tribbechovius, J., 1678-1712
  Thou, our Light, our Guiding-
    star
Tritton, Joseph, 1819-87
  Head of the Church and Lord
Tucker, Francis Bland, 1895-
  All praise to thee, for thou
  Our Father, by whose name
Tuckerman, Joseph
  Father divine, the deadening
Turner, Daniel, 1710-98
  Beyond the starry skies
  Jesus, full of all compassion
Turner, H. L.
  It may be at morn, when the;
    R107253 O Lord Jesus, how
Turner, M. Elmore, 1906-
  Revealing word, thy light
Turner, Nancy Byrd, 1880-
  Men go out from places
  O Son of man, who walked
  There were three lights that
Turner, Mrs. R. N.
  How blest was that life;
    R103924 I know that He
    liveth
Turner, Rosa M.
  O dreamer, leave thy dreams
Turton, William Harry, 1856-
1938
  At that first Eucharist
  Thou, who at thy first Euchar-
    ist; X107720 O Thou, who
    at thy
Tuttiett, Laurence, 1825-97
  Father, let me dedicate;
    X102099 Father, here we
  Go forward, Christian soldier
  O Grant us light, that we;
    X102931 Grant us thy light;
    X105488 Lord, grant us
    light
  O Jesus, ever present
  O quickly come, dread Judge
Tuttle, Emma
  I think of a city; R100547 As
    I dream of a city
Tweedy, Henry Hallam, 1868-
1953

All ye who love the Lord
Eternal God, whose power
Lord of starry vasts un-
  known
O God of love, whose spirit
O gracious Father of man-
  kind
O Holy Spirit, making whole
O Spirit of the living God
True lovers of mankind;
  X105251 Lift up your
  heart
Twells, Henry, 1823-1900
  At even, when the sun was
    set; X100606 At even,
    ere the sun
  Awake, O Lord, as in the
    time
  Not for our sins alone
Tymms, Thomas Vincent,
1842-1921
  Our day of praise is ended

U

U. P. Psalter, see below as
  if spelled United Presby-
  terian Psalter (or alternate
  specific name)
Udulutsch, Irvin
  O Jesus Victim-Priest
  O Jesus, we adore thee
Ufford, Edwin S.
  I believe the Bible
  Throw out the life-line
Uhler, Grace Elma
  O Gift of God, we praise
Ukranian traditional, etc.
  Lovingly the Shepherd
Underwood, Lizzie
  I've heard them sing again;
    R104504 It will open wide
Unitarian collection
  Out on an ocean all bound-
  less
United Presbyterian sources
  which follow are cited as
  U. P. followed by the dis-
  tinctive term. The order is
  chronoligical, beginning with
  1871
U. P. Book of Psalms, 1871
NOTE: Following the first

line, the Psalm number is given parenthetically. Eleven Psalms are represented.

Behold all ye that serve (Ps 134)

Blest the man who fears Jehovah (Ps 128)

Give ye to Jehovah, O sons (Ps 29)

God's perfect law restores (Ps 19b)

Great is the Lord, and greatly (Ps 48)

How blest the man that fears (Ps 112)

Lord God of hosts, how lovely (Ps 134)

Lord, hear my voice, my prayer (Ps 61)

O my soul, bless God, the Father (Ps 103)

Of mercy and of judgement (Ps 101)

Praise Jehovah, all ye nations (Ps 117)

The glory of the Lord (Ps 19a)

The Lord thee hear in time of grief (Ps 20)

The man who once has found (Ps 91)

Within thy temple, Lord (Ps 48)

U. P. Board of Publication, 1909

O happy land, whose sons (Ps 144); X107456 O people blest

O Jehovah, hear my words (Ps 5)

Ye children come, give ear (Ps 34); R101166 Children, come, hither

U. P. Psalter, 1912

NOTE: Following the first line, the Psalm number is given parenthetically. All Psalms are represented, except #3 and #13, both of which are credited to Sternhold.

A little that the righteous (Ps 37)

All lands, to God, in joyful sounds (Ps 66)

All men on earth that live (Ps 117)

All nations clap your hands (Ps 47)

All people that dwell on the earth (Ps 100)

All that I am I owe to thee (Ps 139)

All who with heart confiding (Ps 125)

All ye that fear God's holy name (Ps 22); X100303 All ye ... Jehovah's

All ye that fear Jehovah's name (Ps 22)

Alleluia! Alleluia! Earth and heaven in sweet (Ps 150)

Alleluia! Alleluia! In his temple God be praised (Ps 150)

Alleluia, praise Jehovah (Ps 146)

Almighty God, thy lofty throne (Ps 89)

Amid the thronging worshipers (Ps 22)

Among His people, God is known (Ps 76)

Arise, O Lord, our God, arise (Ps 132)

As pants the hart for streams (Ps 42)

As thirsts the hart for cooling (Ps 42)

As thirsts the hart for waterbrooks (Ps 42)

As thou, O Lord, hast made (Ps 18)

Be thou my helper in the strife (Ps 35)

Be thou my judge, O righteous Lord (Ps 26)

Because thy trust is God alone (Ps 91)

Before my journey is complete (Ps 102)

Before thy people I confess (Ps 40)

Behold, how pleasant and how good (Ps 133)

Blest be the Lord! for us He
cares (Ps 68)

Blest be the Lord, my rock
(Ps 144)

Blest be the Lord, our fathers'
God (Ps 72); X100112
Abundant fields

Blest is he who loves God's
(Ps 1)

Blest the man that fears
Jehovah (Ps 128)

Bow down thy ear, O Lord
(Ps 86); X101019 Bow down
thine ear

By all whom thou hast made
(Ps 86)

By Babel's riverside we sat
(Ps 137)

By Babel's streams we sat
(Ps 137)

Christ shall have dominion
(Ps 72)

Come, all ye people, bless
(Ps 66)

Come, all ye servants of the
Lord (Ps 134)

Come, let us sing before the
Lord (Ps 98)

Come, ye that fear Jehovah
(Ps 22)

Come, ye that fear the Lord
(Ps 66)

Deceit and falsehood I abhore
(Ps 119)

Deliver me from evil, preserve me, Lord (Ps 140)

Do ye, O men, speak righteousness (Ps 58)

Dust to dust, the mortal dies
(Ps 49)

Established in the highest
heavens (Ps 103)

Ever are my longing eyes
(Ps 25)

Exalt the Lord, His praise
(Ps 135)

Fools in their heart have said
(Ps 53)

For ever settled in the heavens
(Ps 119)

For ever trusting in the Lord
(Ps 37)

Fret not thyself, nor envious

(Ps 37)

From out the depths I cry,
O Lord (Ps 130)

From out the depths I cry
to thee (Ps 130)

From the depths do I invoke
(Ps 130)

From the depths my prayer
(Ps 130)

Give thanks and praise to
God (Ps 118)

God be merciful to me (Ps
51)

God guards the good with
watchful eye (Ps 34)

God is King forever: let the
nations (Ps 99)

God is known among his
people (Ps 76)

God is our refuge and our
strength, A helper ever
(Ps 46)

God is our refuge and our
strength, our everpresent
(Ps 46)

God loveth the righteous
(Ps 73)

God saved his people from
distress (Ps 68)

God will our strength and
refuge (Ps 46)

Grace and truth shall mark
(Ps 25)

Gracious God, my heart
renew (Ps 51)

Gracious Lord, remember
David (Ps 132)

Great Shepherd who leadest
(Ps 80)

Had not the Lord been
Israel's (Ps 124)

He waters the hills with
rain (Ps 104)

Hear, Lord, the voice of
my complaint (Ps 64)

Hear my words, O gracious
Lord (Ps 5)

Hear this, all ye people
(Ps 49)

His saints shall live, and to
(Ps 72)

His wide dominion shall extend (Ps 72)

Judge my integrity, the righteous judge (Ps 26)

Let all the earth Jehovah fear
(Ps 33); X107792 O truly
is the nation

Let God arise, and by His
might (Ps 68)

Like Sion's steadfast mount
(Ps 125)

Lord, bless and pity us (Ps
67)

Lord God of hosts, in mercy
(Ps 84)

Lord, hear me in distress (Ps
143)

Lord, hear me when I pray
(Ps 27)

Lord, hear the right, regard
(Ps 17)

Lord, I lift my soul to thee
(Ps 25)

Lord, I will praise thy name
(Ps 30)

Lord, in thee am I confiding
(Ps 38)

Lord, my petition heed (Ps
86)

Lord, our Lord, thy glorious
name (Ps 8); R105683 Lord
... in all the earth

Lord, rebuke me not in anger
(Ps 6)

Lord, the God of my salvation
(Ps 88)

Lord, thou hast been our dwelling place (Ps 90)

Lord, thou hast favor shown
(Ps 85)

Lord, thou hast greatly blessed
(Ps 85)

Lord, through all the generations (Ps 90)

Lord, thy word to me remember (Ps 119)

Lord, to me thy ways make
known (Ps 25)

Make haste, O God, to save
(Ps 70)

Make haste, O my God, to
deliver (Ps 70)

Men who walk in folly's way
(Ps 107)

Mindful of our human frailty

(Ps 103)

Most perfect is the law of
God (Ps 19); R107057
O how love I thy law

My end, Lord, make me
know (Ps 39)

My faithful Shepherd is the
Lord (Ps 23)

My God, I will extol thee
(Ps 145)

My God, it was thy grace
(Ps 30)

My God, my God, I cry to
thee (Ps 22)

My grieving soul revive
(Ps 119)

My heart doth overflow
(Ps 45)

My heart is fixed, O God
(Ps 108)

My heart was glad to hear
(Ps 122)

My people, give ear, attend
(Ps 78)

My righteous God, who oft
(Ps 4)

My Shepherd is the Lord
who knows my needs
(Ps 23)

My sins and faults of youth
(Ps 25)

My song forever shall record (Ps 89)

My soul, bless the Lord!
The Lord is (Ps 104)

My soul for thy salvation
(Ps 119)

My soul in silence waits for
God (Ps 62)

My soul is grieved because
(Ps 57)

My steadfast heart, O God
(Ps 108)

Not haughty is my heart
(Ps 131)

Now blessed be Jehovah,
God (Ps 72)

Now Israel may say, and
that in truth (Ps 124)

Now the King in thy strength
(Ps 21)

Now to God, our Strength
and Saviour (Ps 81)

Now unto Jehovah ye sons of
(Ps 29)

Now with joyful exultation
(Ps 95)

O all ye peoples, bless our
God (Ps 66)

O come and sing unto the
Lord (Ps 95)

O come and to Jehovah sing
(Ps 95)

O come before the Lord, our
King (Ps 95)

O come, my people, to my
law (Ps 78)

O come, my soul, bless thou
(Ps 103); R100897 Bless
Him, ye angels

O give the Lord whole-hearted
(Ps 111)

O God, according to thy grace
(Ps 51)

O God, be merciful and bless
(Ps 67)

O God, be merciful, Be merciful to me (Ps 56)

O God, be merciful to me,
For men (Ps 56)

O God, be merciful to me,
My soul for refuge (Ps 57)

O God, be thy anointed Son
(Ps 72)

O God, give thou ear to my
plea (Ps 55)

O God, how good thou art
(Ps 73)

O God, give ear unto my cry
(Ps 61)

O God, most holy are thy
ways (Ps 77)

O God, no longer hold thy
peace (Ps 83)

O God, preserve me, for in
thee (Ps 16)

O God, regard my humble plea
(Ps 61)

O God, the God that saveth me
(Ps 51)

O God, thou hast rejected us
(Ps 60)

O God, to thy anointed King
(Ps 72)

O God, to us show mercy
(Ps 67)

O God, we have heard and
our (Ps 44)

O God, whom I delight to
praise (Ps 109)

O Gracious God, forsake me
not (Ps 71)

O let my supplicating cry
(Ps 119)

O Lord, be thou my helper
true (Ps 12)

O Lord, by thee delivered
(Ps 30)

O Lord, give ear when with
my voice (Ps 27)

O Lord, how manifold the
works (Ps 104)

O Lord, make haste to hear
(Ps 141)

O Lord, most high, with all
my heart (Ps 9)

O Lord, my earnest cry,
thy listening (Ps 119)

O Lord, my God, for thy
name's (Ps 109)

O Lord, my God, my joyful
(Ps 86)

O Lord, my God, most
earnestly (Ps 63)

O Lord, my inmost heart
(Ps 139)

O Lord of hosts, how lovely
(Ps 84)

O Lord of hosts, in mercy
(Ps 84)

O Lord of hosts, to thee
I cry (Ps 84)

O Lord, our Lord, in all
the earth (Ps 8)

O Lord, thou art my God
and King (John Craig may
be author. See Julian p
1022b) (Ps 145)

O Lord, thou hast ascended
(Ps 68)

O Lord, thou Judge of all
(Ps 94)

O Lord, thy perfect righteousness (Ps 119)

O Lord, to thee I cry (Ps
28); X107239 O Lord
(close variant)

O Lord, to us thy mercy
show (Ps 85)

O make a joyful noise, ye lands (Ps 100)

O mighty man, why wilt thou (Ps 52)

O my soul bless thou Jehovah (Ps 103)

O praise and bless the Lord (Ps 107)

O Praise the Lord, for he is good, His mercies still (Ps 107)

O praise the Lord, for he is good, Let all in heaven (Ps 118)

O praise the Lord, his deeds (Ps 105)

O praise ye the Lord, and sing (Ps 149)

O praise ye the name of Jehovah (Ps 135)

O Royal Bride, give heed (Ps 45)

O save me by thy name (Ps 54)

O sing a new song to the Lord (Ps 96)

O sing ye Alleluia! 'Tis good (Ps 147)

O Sion, 'tis thy God's command (Ps 68)

O teach thou us to count our days (Ps 90)

O thank the Lord, the Lord of love (Ps 136); R103489 His tender mercies

O thou great Shepherd of thy chosen race (Ps 80)

O wherefore do the nations (Ps 2)

O wherefore hast thou cast (Ps 74)

Of mercy and of justice (Ps 101)

On God alone my soul relies (Ps 55)

On the good and faithful (Ps 4)

Praise God, ye servants of the Lord (Ps 113)

Praise Jehovah for his love (Ps 136)

Praise the Lord, for He is good (Ps 107)

Praise the Lord in heavenly places (Ps 148)

Praise waits for thee in Sion (Ps 65)

Praise waits in Sion, Lord, for thee, And unto thee (Ps 65)

Praise waits in Sion, Lord, for thee, There we will (Ps 65)

Praise ye, praise ye the Lord (Ps 148)

Praise ye the Lord among His (Ps 149)

Praise ye the Lord, for it is good (Ps 147)

Praise ye the Lord, His praise proclaim (Ps 146)

Praise ye the Lord, His saints who throng (Ps 150)

Praise ye the Lord, ye hosts (Ps 150)

Praise ye the Lord, ye saints (Ps 150)

Protect and save me, O my God (Ps 59)

Rebels, who had dared to show (Ps 107)

Regard my grief and rescue me (Ps 119)

Rejoice, ye people, homage (Ps 47)

Remember not, O God, the sins (Ps 79)

Rest in the Lord and be thou (Ps 37)

Save me, O God, because the floods (Ps 69)

Since with my God with perfect heart (Ps 18)

Sing a new song to Jehovah (Ps 98)

Sing to the Lord, sing His praise (Ps 96)

Sion founded on the mountain (Ps 87)

Sion, on the holy hills (Ps 87)

Springs and streams no longer (Ps 107)

Teach me, O Lord, thy way of truth (Ps 119)

That man is blest who, fear-

Thy Spirit, O Lord, makes
life (Ps 104)

Thy tender mercies, O my
Lord (Ps 40)

Thy wondrous testimonies, Lord
(Ps 119)

Thy word sheds light upon my
(Ps 119)

To God for help will I repair
(Ps 77)

To God my earnest voice I
raise (Ps 142)

To God will I direct my prayer
(Ps 77)

To thee I lift my soul (Ps 25)

To thee, O God, we render
thanks (Ps 75)

To thee, O Lord, I fly (Ps
16)

To thee, O Lord, I humbly
cry (Ps 142)

To thee, O Lord, I lift my
eyes (Ps 123); X110693 To
thee ... mine eyes

Unless the Lord the house
(Ps 127)

Unto God our Saviour, Sing a
(Ps 98)

What shall I render to the
Lord, For all his benefits
(Ps 116)

What shall I render to the
Lord, What shall my offering (Ps 116)

What time I am afraid (Ps 56)

What wait I for but thee?
(Ps 39)

When in his might the Lord
(Ps 126)

When in the night I meditate
(Ps 16)

When Israel out of Egypt went
(Ps 114)

When morning lights the eastern
skies (Ps 143)

When Sion in her low estate
(Ps 126)

Where'er his creatures gather
(Ps 82)

Who, O Lord, shall dwell with
thee (Ps 15)

Who, O Lord, with thee abiding
(Ps 15)

Whole-hearted thanksgiving
to thee (Ps 9)

Why dost thou stand afar
(Ps 10)

Why standest thou afar, O
Lord (Ps 10)

With firm resolve I held my
peace (Ps 39)

With grateful heart my
thanks (Ps 138)

With joy and gladness in my
soul (Ps 122)

With joy I heard my friends
(Ps 122)

With thankful voice praise
ye (Ps 117)

Within thy temple, Lord,
In that (Ps 48)

Within thy temple, Lord,
We think (Ps 48)

Within thy temple's sacred
courts (Ps 48)

Ye gates lift your heads
(Ps 24)

Ye gates of peace and joy
(Ps 118)

Ye who his temple throng
(Ps 149)

U. P. Board of Publication,
1917

Under the care of my God
(Ps 91); R110811 Under
His wings

U. P. Bible songs hymnal, 1927

Alleluia, praise Jehovah
(Ps 148); R105181 Let
them praises give

U. P. Psalter hymnal, 1927

Lord, thou hast searched
me (Ps 139)

U.S.A. National anthems, etc.
see Smith, S. F. My country;
Key, F.S. O say, can

Unpartheyisches Gesangbuch.
(Mennonite) 1804

Auf, Seele, auf und säume
nicht

Aus Gnaden wird der Mensch
gerecht

Bedenke, Mensch, das Ende

Der Heiland rufet mir und
dir

Der herr uns segne und

In my quiet contemplation
Jehovah, thee we glorify
Jerusalem, lift up thy voice
Mute are the pleading lips;
  (paraphrase by E.E.Ryden)
O blessed is the man who
  stays
O let the children come to
  me
O my soul, on wings ascend-
  ing
Only God can bring us glad-
  ness
Strike up, O harp and psaltery
Thine agony, O Lord, is o'er
To realms of glory in the
  skies; X110632 To realms
  ... I behold
Watch, my soul, and pray
We worship thee, almighty
  Lord
Where is the Friend for whom
Wallis, James H.
  Come, ye children of the Lord
Wallis, Sydney James
  Hail thee! Spirit, Lord eternal
Walmsley, Douglas, 1848-1940
  Father, O hear us, seeking
Walmsley, Robert, 1831-1905
  Come, let us sing of a wonder-
  ful
  The sun declines; o'er land
  We are come with joy
Walter, Howard Arnold, 1883-
1918
  I would be true, for there are
  those
Walther, B.
  There is within this heart
Walther, Carl Ferdinand Wilhelm,
1811-87
  Erstanden, erstanden ist Jesus
  Christ
  He's risen, He's risen, Christ
Walther, Johann, 1496-1570
  Der Bräut'gam wird bald rufen
  Soon will the heavenly Bride-
  groom
  The Bridegroom soon will call
  Thy word, O God, declareth
Walton, W. Spencer, 1850-1906
  In tenderness He sought me
  O touch mine eyes, that I may

Wandersleben, Martin, 1608-
68
  As we begin another week
  Heut' fangen wir in Gottes
Warburton, George Augustus,
1859-
  O thou whose glory shone
Ward, J.W.G.
  And whate'er the need may
  be
Wardlaw, Ralph, 1779-1853
  Christ of all my hopes
  O Lord our God, arise
Ware, Henry (the younger)
1794-1843
  All nature's works His
  praise
  Around the throne of God
  Great God, the followers
  Happy the home when God
  is; X100985 Blest is the
  home
  Lift your glad voices;
  R105792 Loud lift your
  voices
  O thou, in whom alone is
  We rear not a temple, like
Waring, Anna Laetitia, 1820-
1910
  Beneath thy wing, O God, I
  rest
  Father, I know that all my
  life
  Go not far from me, O my
  I ask thee for the daily
  In heavenly love abiding;
  X104289 In Jesus' love
  My heart is resting
  My Saviour, on the word of
  truth
Waring, Samuel Miller, 1792-
1827
  Now to him who loved us
Warmingham, Osbert Wright-
man, ca 1890-
  Spirit of God, for every
  Good
Warner, Anna Bartlett, 1821-
1915
  Jesus loves me! this I know
  One more day's work for
  Jesus
  The world looks very beauti-

ful
We would see Jesus; for the
shadows
Warner, D.S.
A gentle hand unseen by us;
R106776 O gentle one, we
By thy blessed word obeying;
R101710 Dear Redeemer,
we
Church of God, thou spotless
Fill me with thy spirit, Lord;
R101480 Come, O Spirit,
seal
How sweet this bond; R106585
O brethren, how this
I heard the dear Redeemer
say; R108033 Only thine,
only thine
I've found my Lord and He is
R103493 His yoke is easy
Not in the temples made with;
R106796 O glory to Jesus
The earth shall melt with
fervent; R107621 O, that
last great
Two little hands are sweetly
Warner, John Allan, 1851-1928
Brothers, joining hand
Warner, Susan, 1819-85
Jesus bids us shine; R111944
Yes, Jesus loves me
Warren, Arthur
Glorious are the lofty
Warren, B.E.
Behold, what love, yes;
R109249 Such love cannot be
Do you love the world
Eternity draws near, as time;
R111567 Where will I go
Glory to God in the highest
I would be closer my Saviour
Let not your weary heart
O come to the Lord today
Out on this dark world
Saviour, coming to thee
Sing about Jesus who died
Weighed in the balance
When I get weary with toils;
R101324 Closer, my child
Where is thy hope, poor sin-
ner
Without spot and blameless
Warren, May E.

Lift Him up, 'tis He that
bids; R105235 Lift Him
up, the risen
Warren, William Fairfield,
1833-1929
I worship thee, O Holy Ghost
Washbourne, Thomas, 1606-87
Lord, thou hast told us that
Washburne, Edward Abiel,
1819-81
Ponder now the Cross, all
holy
Softly the night is sleeping;
R102557 Glory to God
Waterbury, Jared Bell, 1799-
1876
Soldiers of the cross, arise
Waterston, Robert Cassie,
1812-93
Theories, which thousands
cherish
Watson, Albert Durant, 1859-
1926
Lord of the lands, beneath
Watson, George, 1816-98
With the sweet word of peace
Watson, William, 1858-1935
Great and fair is she, our
land
Watt, Lauchlan MacLean, 1867-
1957
Dark the day on Calvary's
I bind my heart this tide
O thou, my Judge and King
Watteville, Johannes de, 1718-
88
Jesus, thyself to us reveal
Lord Jesus, may I constant-
ly
Lord Jesus, with thy presence
Thanks to the Man of Sorrows
The grace of our Lord Jesus
Wattles, Willard Austin, 1888-
1950
"Against my second coming"
I cannot think or reason
Watts, Alaric Alexander, 1797-
1864
When shall we meet again
Watts, Isaac, 1674-1748
A broken heart, my God
Above the heavens, eternal
Ah, how shall fallen men

Alas! and did my Saviour;
  R103268 He loves me;
  R103382 Help me, dear
  Saviour (Coffman); R100618
  At the cross, at the (Hudson)
Almighty sovereign of the skies
Am I a soldier of the cross;
  R100455 And when the battle's; R104278 In His name
  I'll
And must this body die
And now another day is gone;
  X104304 In mercy, Lord
Arise, O King of grace
As when the Hebrew prophet
At thy command, our dearest
Awake, my soul, to sound His
Awake, our souls! away, our
Be thou exalted, O my God
Before the heavens were
Before the Lord Jehovah's;
  X100772 Before Jehovah's
  awful; X100773 Before Jehovah's glorious; X106229
  Nations, attend before;
  X108976 Sing to the Lord
Begin, my tongue, some
Behold the amazing gift of
  love
Behold the glories of the Lamb
Behold the morning sun
Behold the sure foundationstone
Behold, what wondrous grace
Beneath th'amazing gift of love
Bless, O my soul! the living
Blest are the humble souls
Blest are the sons of peace
Blest are the undefiled
Blest be the everlasting God
Blest is the man, for ever
  blest
Blest is the man who shuns
Blest morning, whose first
Broad is the road that leads
Christ hath a garden, walled
  (paraphrase by Bridges)
Come, dearest Lord, descend;
  X101375 Come, gracious
  Lord
Come hither, all ye weary
Come, Holy Spirit, heavenly;

X105690 Lord, send thy
  Spirit
Come, let us join our cheerful; X101432 Come ...
  sacred songs
Come, sound his praise
  abroad
Come, we [ye] that love;
  X101549 Come we who
  love; X101568 Come, ye
  that love; R111239 We're
  marching to
Come, worship at Immanuel's
Dearest of all names above
Deep in the dust before thy
Early, my God, without
  delay
Eternal power, whose high
Eternal Spirit! we confess
Faith is the brightest evidence
Far as thy name is known
Far from my thoughts, vain
Father, how wide thy glory
Father, I long, I faint to
  see
Father of glory, to thy name
From all that dwell below;
  X102376 From all who
  dwell
Give me the wings of faith;
  X102513 Give us the
  wings
Give thanks to God; He
  reigns
Give thanks to God most high
Give to our God immortal
"Go, preach my gospel, "
  saith
God in his earthly temple
God is the name my soul
  adores
God is the refuge of his
  saints
God, my supporter and my
  hope
God of the morning, at whose
Great God, attend, while
Great God, how infinite art
Great God, indulge my
  humble
Great God! to what a glorious

Great is the Lord our God
Had I the tongues of Greeks
Happy the heart where graces
Hark! from the tomb a dole-
ful
Hark, how the adoring hosts;
  X100830 Behold the glories
Hast thou not known, hast thou
He dies! the Friend of sinners;
  X103234 He died! the Great
He reigns! The Lord, the Sa-
viour
He that hath made his refuge
Hear what the voice from
heaven
Here's love and grief beyond
High in the heavens, Eternal
Hosanna to the Prince of grace
Hosanna to the Royal Son
Hosanna with a cheerful
How beauteous are their feet
How bright these glorious
spirits
How condescending and how kind
How did my heart rejoice
How glorious Zion's courts;
  X103675 How glorious is the
sacred
How large the promise, how
divine
How oft have sin and Satan
How pleasant, how divinely
How pleased and blest was I
How sad our state by nature is
How shall the young secure
How short and hasty is our
life
How sweet and awful is the
place
How vast the treasure we
Hush! my dear, lie still and
slumber; X103777 Hush! dear
child, lie
I love the Lord: he heard my
I pray thee, Lord, to guide
I sing the almighty power of;
  Z104034 I sing the mighty
I wait for thy salvation, Lord
I'll praise my Maker while
I've; X104198 I'll praise
... whilst; X104199 I'll
praise ... with
I'll speak the honours of my

King
I'm not ashamed to own my
  Lord; X111242 We're not
ashamed (Phelps)
In all my vast concern with
In vain we seek for peace
Jehovah reigns! He dwells
in
Jesus, dear name! how
sweet it
Jesus invites his saints
Jesus shall reign where'er;
  X108108 Our God shall
reign
Jesus, thy love exceeds by
far
Jesus who died, is now
seated
Join all the glorious names;
  X104753 Jesus, my great
High
Joy to the world! the Lord
is; X104954 Joy ... the
Lord will
Keep silence, all created
Kingdoms and thrones to
God
Let children hear the mighty
Let dogs delight to bark
Let everlasting glories
crown
Let every creature join
Let every mortal ear at-
tend; X105122 Let every
ear attend
Let every tongue thy good-
ness
Let me but hear my Saviour
say
Life is the time to serve
Like sheep we went astray
Lo! what a glorious sight
Lo, what a pleasing sight
Long as I live I'll bless
thy
Long have I sat beneath the
sound; X106134 My hope,
my portion
Lord, all I am is known
Lord, how secure and blest
Lord, how secure my con-
science
Lord, I have made thy word

That awful day will surely
The God of mercy be adored
The Law commands and makes
    us
The Lord Jehovah reigns
The Lord my Shepherd is
The Lord of glory is my light
The man is ever blessed
The pity of the Lord, to those
The true Messiah now appears
There is a God who reigns
There is a house not made
There is a land of pure de-
    light
There is a voice of sovereign
This is the day the Lord hath
Thus far the Lord hath led me
Thus saith the mercy of the
    Lord
'Tis by the faith of joys
'Tis by thy strength the
    mountains
'Tis from the mercy of our
    God
To God I lift mine eyes;
    X110871 Upward I lift mine
To God the only wise
To Him that loved the souls
To Him who sits upon the
    throne
'Twas by thy blood, immortal
'Twas on that dark, that dole-
    ful
Unshaken as the sacred hill
Unveil thy bosom, faithful
    tomb
Up to the hills I lift my eyes;
    X110857 Up ... lift mine
    eyes
Vain are the hopes the sons
We give immortal praise
We sing the almighty power
Welcome, sweet day of rest
What equal honors shall we
What shall I render to my God
What sinners value, I resign
When I can read my title
When I survey the wondrous
When overwhelmed with grief
When we devote our youth
Who shall the Lord's elect
Why do we mourn departing
    friends

Why should the children
Why should we start and
    fear
With all my powers of heart;
    X111750 With all the
    power
With joy we meditate the
    grace
With reverence let the saints
With songs and honors sound-
    ing
Ye nations round the earth!
    rejoice
Ye tribes of Adam, join
Waugh, Benjamin, 1839-1908
    Now let us see thy beauty
Wayland, John W.
    Gracious King enthroned
        above
Weatherell, F.
    Mary Immaculate, Star of
        the morning
Weaver, Mack
    Lord, lay some soul upon
        my; R109088 Some soul
        for thee
Webb, Benjamin, 1820-85
    Behold, He comes, thy King
    Praise the Rock of our sal-
        vation
Wegelin, Josua, 1604-40
    Auf Christi Himmelfahrt
        allein
    On Christ's ascension I now
    Since Christ has gone to
Weingartner, Sigismund
    Auf meinen lieben Gott
    In God, my faithful God
Weir, Robert Stanley, 1856-
    O Canada! Our home, our
        native; X106594 O Canada!
        our home and
Weisberg, Florence
    How good it is to thank
Weisse, Michael, ca 1480-
1534 (various spellings: Weys,
Weyss, etc.)
    Christ the Lord hath risen
    Christ the Lord is risen
        again
    Now lay we calmly in the
        grave; X110179 This
        body in the grave

Nun lasst uns den Leib be-
graben
Praise we our God upon his
throne
Weissel, Georg, 1590-1635
Lift up your heads, ye mighty
Macht hoch die Tür
Make wide the door, unbar
O death, where is thy cruel
Seek where ye may to find a
way
Seek ye who will some other
Such', wer da will, Ein ander
Weitzman, Lily
Create in this weak form
Grant me strength when skies
Once more, O Lord, do I
awaken
The day is done, the night
Welch, Edward Ashurst, 1860-1932
Thou, who didst call thy saints
We lift our hearts, O Father;
X110687 To Thee, O heaven-
ly
Wellhaven, Johan S.C., 1807-73
Lord of spirits, I surrender
Wells, Amos R., 1862-1933
God help our country to be
Lord Jesus, blessed Giver
Thou delightest, O Lord, when
Wells, Emmeline B.
Our mountain home so dear
Wells, Marcus B., 1815-95
Holy Spirit, faithful Guide
Welsh traditional, etc.
All poor men and humble
Dark the night lay, wild and
Wendell, Claus August, 1866-
1950
Search me, God, and know my
Wendte, Charles William, 1844-
1931
Not given to us from out the
skies
Wengel, Paul, 1892-
In his love abiding, wait on
O how lovely, O how sweet
Wesley, Charles, 1707-88
A charge to keep I have
A thousand oracles divine
Ah! whither should I go;
X106063 My Father bids
me

All praise to our redeeming
All praise to the Lamb!
All ye that pass by, to
Jesus
And am I born to die
And are we yet to live;
X100417 And are we yet
alive
And can I yet delay
And can it be that I should
And let our bodies part
And let this feeble body fail
And must I be to judgment
Angels, where'er we go, at-
tend
Arise, my soul, arise, And
with a cheerful voice
Arise, my soul, arise,
Shake off thy guilty fears
Author of faith, eternal Word
Author of faith, to thee
Author of life divine
Awake, Jerusalem, awake
Away, my needless fears
Away with our fears, our
troubles
Before the Father's awful
Behold, how good a thing
Behold the Lamb of God, who
Blessing, honour, thanks and
Blest be that sacred covenant-
love
Blest be the dear uniting love
Blow ye the trumpet, blow;
R109955 The year of
jubilee
Captain of Israel's host
Christ, from whom all bless-
ings; X105459 Lord,
from whom all
Christ the Lord is risen
today; X105818 Love's
redeeming
Christ, whose glory fills the
skies; X105784 Lord,
whose glory
Come, Father, Son, and
Holy Ghost; X101982
Eternal Sun of Righteous-
ness
Come Holy Ghost, our
hearts; X101390 Come
... our

souls
Come, Holy Spirit, raise our
    songs
Come, let us anew our journey
Come, let us join our friends;
    X109799 The saints on earth
Come, let us join with one
Come, and let us sweetly join
Come, let us rise with Christ
Come, let us use the grace
Come, let us who in Christ
Come, let us with our Lord
Come, O thou all-victorious
    Lord
Come, O thou Traveler un-
    known
Come, on my partners in dis-
    tress
Come, sinners, to the gospel
Come, thou everlasting Spirit
Come, thou long-expected
    Jesus; X101490 Come,
    Redeemer, blessed; X103095
    Hail, thou long-expected
Come, thou universal Blessing;
    X105798 Love divine, all
    loves
Come, ye weary sinners, come
Depth of mercy! can there be
Draw near, O Son of God
Equip me for the war
Eternal Beam of Light divine;
    X101976 Eternal Source
Ever gracious Lord, I fly
Father, at thy footstool see
Father, God, thy love we
Father, I dare believe thee
Father, I stretch my hands to
Father, in whom we live
Father of Jesus Christ, my
Father, Son, and Holy Ghost;
    In solemn power
Father, Son, and Holy Ghost,
    One in three
Father, Son, and Spirit, hear
For ever here my rest shall
Forth in thy Name, O Lord I
    go; X102336 Forth ... we
    go
From my own works at last
Gentle Jesus, meek and mild;
    X105304 Lamb of God, I
    look

Give me a new, a perfect
    heart
Give me the faith which can
Giver of concord, Prince
Glory be to God on high
    (Gloria in excelsis, para-
    phrased)
God is gone up on high
God of all power, and truth
God of Israel's faithful
God of love, that hearest;
    X102727 God of love, who
God of my life, whose gra-
    cious
God of my salvation, hear
Granted is the Saviour's
    prayer
Hail! Holy, Holy, Holy
    Lord
Hail the day that sees him
Happy soul, thy days are
Happy the man that finds
Happy the souls to Jesus
    joined
Hark! a voice divides
Hark! the herald angels
    sing; R106535 O Bethle-
    hem, dear; X103153 Hark,
    how all the welkin
Head of the Church trium-
    phant; X103311 Head of
    thy Church
Heavenly Father, God of
    love
Help us to help each other;
    X110782 Try us, O God!
    and
Holy, and true, and right-
    eous
Holy as thou, O Lord, is
    none
Holy Lamb, who thee con-
    fess
Hosanna in the highest
How can a sinner know
How glorious is the life
How happy every child of
    grace
I know that my Redeemer
    lives, And ever prays
    for me
I know that my Redeemer
    lives; He lives, and on

the earth
I know that my Redeemer
lives; He lives, who once
was dead
I long to behold him arrayed
"I the good fight have fought"
I want a principle within
If thou impart thyself to me
In age and feebleness extreme
In that sad memorable night
In weariness and pain
Infinite God, to thee we raise
Jesus, from whom all bless-
ings
Jesus, let all thy lovers
Jesus, let thy pitying eye
Jesus, let thy sufferings
Jesus, Lord, we look to thee
Jesus, Lover of my soul
Jesus, Master of the feast
Jesus, my Lord, my God
Jesus, my Saviour, Brother
Jesus, my strength, my hope;
   X106106 My God, my
   strength
Jesus, my truth, my way
Jesus, the all-restoring Word
Jesus, the conqueror, reigns
Jesus! the Name high over all
Jesus, the sinner's Friend
Jesus, the truth and power
Jesus, the weary wanderer's
Jesus, thine all-victorious
Jesus, thou all-redeeming Lord
Jesus, thou art my righteous-
ness
Jesus, to thee I now can fly
Jesus, united by thy grace
Jesus, we look to thee
Jesus, we thus obey
Join, all ye ransomed sons
Join, earth and heaven
Lamb of God, I look to thee;
   X102462 Gentle Jesus, meek;
   X105820 Loving Jesus, gen-
   tle
Lamb of God, whose dying
   love; X105043 Lamb ...
   bleeding love
Leader of faithful souls
Let earth and heaven agree;
   X104899 Jesus, transporting
Let him to whom we now belong

Let not the wise their wis-
dom
Let saints on earth in con-
cert
Let the world their virtue
Life of all that lives below
Lift up your hearts to things
Lift your heads, ye friends
Light of those whose dreary
Lo! for us the wilds are
glad
Lo! He comes with clouds
descending (a very com-
plicated text) see Cen-
nick, Charles. Lo! He
comes . . .
Lo! I come with joy to do
Lo! on a narrow neck of
land; X106840 O God,
mine inmost
Lord, and is thine anger
Lord, I believe a rest re-
mains
Lord, if at thy command;
   X105757 Lord, when at
   thy
Lord, in the strength of
grace
Lord of the harvest, hear
thy
Lord, whom winds and seas
Love divine, all loves excel-
ling; X104717 Jesus,
Lord, of all
Meet and right it is to sing
My God, I am thine; what
comfort
My God, I know, I feel thee
My heart is full of Christ
None is like Jeshurun's God
O come, and dwell in me
O Father of mercy, be ever
adored
O for a heart to praise my;
   X106757 O ... to love
   my God
O for a principle within
O for a thousand tongues;
   R100914 Blessed be the
   name; X102555 Glory to
   God and praise
O for that tenderness of
heart

O glorious hope of perfect
O God, most merciful and
    true
O how happy are they who the;
    X103693 How happy are they
    who Jesus; X103694 How
    happy are they, who their
    [the] X107052 O how ...
    their Saviour
O Jesus, full of pardoning
O joyful sound of gospel grace
O Lamb of God, for sinners
O Love divine, what hast
O Son of God and man, receive
O that I could repent
O that my load of sin were
O, that the Comforter would
O the depth of love divine
O thou, before the world be-
    gan
O thou who camest from above
O thou who hast redeemed of
    old
O thou who wouldst not have
O thou, whom all thy saints
O thou whom we adore
O what shall I do, my Saviour
Oft when the waves of passion
Open, Lord, my inward ear
Our heavenly Father, Source
Partners of a glorious hope
Peace be to this habitation;
    X108197 Peace ... congre-
    gation
Praise the Lord who reigns
Pray, without ceasing, pray
Rejoice, the Lord is King!;
    X105251 Lift up your heart
See how great a flame aspires
See the Lord, thy Keeper,
    stand
Servant of all, to toil; X109097
    Son of the carpenter
Servant of God, well done
Shepherd divine, our wants
Shepherd of souls, with pitying
    eye
Shepherd, with thy tenderest;
    X103124 Happy soul, secure
Sing to the great Jehovah's
Sinners, turn: why will ye die
Soldiers of Christ, arise
Sons of men, behold from far

Spirit of faith, come down;
    X109173 Spirit of truth
Spirit of grace and health;
    X101971 Eternal Son,
    eternal Love
Stand the omnipotent decree
Stay, thou insulted Spirit
Still nigh me, O my Saviour
Suffering Son of Man, be
    near
Talk with us, Lord, thyself;
    X109147 Speak to us,
    Lord
The Church triumphant in
    thy
The Lord of earth and sky
The praying spirit breathe
Thee we address in humble
    prayer
Thou didst live to God alone
Thou great mysterious God
Thou hidden Source of calm
Thou Judge of quick and
    dead
Thou, Lord, must for thy
    sake
Thou Son of God, whose
    flaming
Thou very present Aid
Through Him who all our
    sickness
Thy ceaseless, unexhausted
'Tis finished! the Messiah
To God your every want
To the hills I lift mine
    eyes, To the everlasting
    hills
To the hills I life my eyes:
    Whence shall help for me
To us a Child of royal birth
Vain, delusive world, adieu
Victim Divine, thy grace we
Was ever grief like thine
We know, by faith we know
Weary of wandering from my
Weary souls that wander wide
Weep not for a brother de-
    ceased
What is our calling's glorious
What shall I do, my God
What shall I render to my
    God
When, my Saviour, shall I be

White spiritual
  I am a poor wayfaring;
    R104209 I'm going there to
    meet
  Jesus walked this lonesome
Whitfield, Frederick, 1829-1904
  I need thee, precious Jesus
  I saw the cross of Jesus
  There is a name I love to
    hear; R107054 O, how I
    love Jesus
Whitfield, George
  Hymnbook, 1757
    Come thou almighty King
Whitford, C. P.
  Just over the mountains in;
    R110997 We are nearing
    home
Whiting, William, 1826-78
  Eternal Father, strong to
    save; X100364 Almighty
    Father (Missionary service
    book)
O Lord, our little ones to thee
Whitman, Walt, 1819-92
  All the past we leave behind
  Away, O soul, hoist up the
    anchor
Whitmore, Lucy Elizabeth
Georgiana, 1792-1840
  Father, again in Jesus' name;
    X107218 O Lord, again in
    thy
  We come, Lord, to thy feet
Whitney, M. Fannie
  We thank thee, heavenly Father
Whitney, Orson F.
  Saviour, Redeemer of my soul
  The wintry day descending
Whittier, John Greenleaf, 1807-
92
  All as God wills, who wisely
  All things are thine; no gifts
  All through the long bright
  Blest land of Judea! Thrice
  Blow, winds of God, awake
  Dear Lord and Father of man-
    kind; X101698 Dear Lord
    ... of us
  In calm and cool and silence
    see Niles, John Jacob
  Forgive, O Lord, our sever-
    ing; X110454 Thy grace

impart
He stood of old, the holy
Heap high the farmer's wintry
I bow my forehead in the
  dust; X103831 I bow
  my forehead to
I know not what the future;
  X103948 I long for household; X111405 When in
  the maddening; X111814
  Within the maddening;
  X111620 Who fathoms the
  eternal
I see the wrong that round
  me
Immortal Love, for ever
  full; X103231 He cometh
  not a King; X111084 We
  may not climb; X111092
  We need not climb
It may not be our lot to
  wield
Let every creature hail
No longer forward or be-
  hind; X106265 No ...
  nor behind
O brother man, fold to thy;
  X106304 Not empty wor-
  ship; X106976 O, he
  whom Jesus
O Lord, and Master of us
  all; X103231 He cometh
  not a King
O Lord our God, in time to
  be
O Love Divine, whose con-
  stant
O Love! O Life! our faith
  and; X108095 Our friend,
  our brother
O pure reformers! not in
  vain
O sometimes gleams upon
  our; X107566 O some-
  times gleams upon my
Once more the liberal year
Our thought of thee is glad
Our fathers' God, from out
Sound over all waters, reach;
  X109465 The dark night
The harp at nature's advent
Thine are all the gifts, O

God
Unto the calmly gathered
We search the world for
   truth
We see not, know not; all our
What thou wilt, O Father, give
When on my day of life the
   night
Wherever through the ages
   rise
With silence only as their
   benediction
Whittingham,   William. d 1579
Now Israel may say, and that
   truly:- If that the Lord
Whittle, Daniel W. , 1840-1901
Be ye strong in the Lord;
   R102237 Firmly stand
Dying with Jesus, by death;
   R105991 Moment by moment
Fierce and wild the storm (by
   W. W. D. , Pseud) ; R104947
   Joy, behold the Saviour
"For God so loved!" O won-
   drous; R102561 Glory to
   God
I know not why God's wondrous;
   R101087 But I know whom I
In grace the holy God did full;
   R101099 By grace are ye
   saved
O, day of awful story; R100847
   Behold the stone
Our Lord is now rejected;
   R107642 O, the crowning
   day
"Redeemed! redeemed!" O,
   sing
Spirit so holy, Spirit of love
There shall be showers of
   blessing; R108895 Showers
   of blessing
There's a royal banner given;
   R105884 Marching on
While we pray and while we;
   R111678 Why not now
Who came down from heaven
   to; R109126 Sound the
   chorus
Would you lose your load of sin;
   R104923 Jesus, who on the
   cross
The Whole Booke of Psalmes, 1647,

i. e. The Bay Psalm Book
   O Lord, Almighty God, Thy
      works
Whytehead, Thomas, 1815-43
   Resting from his work today
Widstoe, John A.
   How long, O Lord, most
      holy
   Lead me into life eternal
Wieand, Albert Cassel, 1871-
   On the radiant threshold;
      R104371 In the morning,
      noon
Wienland, M. M.
   O weary pilgrim, lift your
      head; R104949 Joy
      cometh in the morning
Wiesenmeyer, Burkhard, d
   before 1691
   How lovely shines the morn-
      ing star; X103717 How
      lovely now the
Wight, Almeda E.
   'Tis a sweet and tender
      story; R104492 It must
      be told
Wightman, Richard
   Singers, sing! The hoary
      world
Wiglesworth, Esther, 1827-
   1904
   Almighty Father, God of
      love (authorship uncertain)
   Soldiers, true and faithful
Wigner, John Murch, 1844-
   Come to the Saviour now
Wilcox, Ella Wheeler, 1855-
   1919
   Love thyself last
Wilder, H. C. , 1860-1948
   Unchanging God, who livest
Wile, Frances Whitmarsh, 1878-
   1939
   All beautiful the march of
      days
Wiley, Hiram Ozias, 1831-73
   He leads us on by paths we;
      X103260 He leads ...
      through childhood's
Wilhelm II, duke of Saxe-Wei-
   mar, 1598-1662
   Herr Jesu Christ, dich zu
      uns

Lord Christ, reveal thy holy
  face
Lord Jesus Christ, be present;
  X105549 Lord .. be with us
O Christ, thy grace unto us
To God, the Father, God the
  Son
Wilkinson, Katie Barclay, 1859-
1928
  May the mind of Christ my
Willcox, Mary Jane, 1835-1919
  Once again, dear Lord, we
Willes, William
  Come along, come along, is the
    call
  Thanks for the Sabbath School;
    R104936 Join in the jubilee
Williams, Benjamin, 1725-95
  Holy, holy, holy Lord!
Williams, Corinne
  Forgive the things I've said
Williams, Edith
  Jesus so lowly, Child of the
    earth
Williams, Helen Maria, 1762-
1827
  While thee I seek, protecting
Williams, Irena F.
  Our Father, God, whose
    mercies
Williams, Isaac, 1802-65
  Be thou my Guardian; X100743
    Be thou our Guardian
  Lord, in this thy mercy's
    day
  O Holy Ghost, thou God of
    Peace
Williams, Isabel, d 1911
  O Sacred Heart, O Heart of
    Jesus, hear
Williams, M. B.
  There's a dear and precious
    Book; R100919 Blessed
    book, precious
Williams, Roger, ca 1604-83
  God makes a path, provides a
Williams, Sarah, 1838-68
  Because I knew not when my
    life
Williams, Theodore Chickering
1855-1915
  As the storm retreating
  By law from Sinai's clouded

Glory be to God on high
God be with thee! Gently;
  X102686 God is with me
Hast thou heard it, O my
  brother
In the lonely midnight
Lord, who dost the voices
  bless
My Country, to thy shore
Thou rulest, Lord, the
  lights
To hold thy glory, Lord of
  all
When the world around us
  throws
When thy heart with joy
Williams, Thomas
  Father in heaven, thy chil-
    dren
Williams, William, 1717-91
  Arglwydd, arwain trwy'r
    anialwch
  Guide me, O thou great
    Jehovah; X103005 Guide
    ... great Redeemer;
    X103008 Guide us, O
    thou
  O'er the gloomy hills;
    X107904 O'er those
    gloomy
  Onward march, all-conquer-
    ing
  Speak, I pray thee, gentle
    Jesus
Williamson, T. R.
  Once in Jerusalem of old
Willis, Love Maria Whitcomb,
1824-1908
  Father, hear the prayer we
Willis, Nathaniel Parker,
1807-67
  The perfect world, by Adam
Willman, F. A.
  Hark! Are they not angels
Wills, Whitfield Glanville,
1841-91
  In our work and in our play
Wilson, Edwin Henry, 1898-
  Where is our holy church
Wilson, Elizabeth, 1867- and
Helen Thoburn, 1885-1932
  Father of lights, in whom
Wilson, Ira B., 1880-1950

Out on the highways and by-
ways; R105852 Make me a
blessing
Wilson, Jennie
Time is filled with swift
transition; R103506 Hold to
God's unchanging
Wilson, Lewis Gilbert, 1858-
1928
America, awake! Behold the
glory
O God, our dwelling-place
O troubled sea of Galilee
The works, O Lord, our
hands
Wilson, Sarah Josselyn, 1893-
The land we love is calling
Wilson, Stewart, 1889-
In every town and village
Lord, who didst send by two
Praise we the Lord, who
made
Up, my neighbour, come away;
R110848 Up and get us gone
When Jesus was a baby
Winchester, Caleb Thomas, 1847-
1920
The Lord our God alone is
Winckler, Johann Joseph, 1670-
1722
Ringe recht, wenn Gottes Gnade
Shall I, for fear of feeble man
Strive aright when God doth
Wine, Mary Stoner, 1885-
I believe in thee, Lord Jesus
Love of God, eternal love
Peace, perfect peace have they
The riches of God are eternal
Wingate, Mary B.
Dear to the heart of the Shep-
herd; R108151 Out in the
desert
Wingrove, John, 1720-93
Hail! my ever blessed Jesus
Winks, William Edward, 1842-
1926
Lord, thy servants forth are
Winsett, R. E.
Built on the Rock, without spot
There is coming a day when to;
R105917 May we sow right-
eous
Wipo of Burgundy, d ca 1048

Christ the Lord is risen
today, Christians haste
Christians, to the Paschal
Victim
Victimae Paschali laudes
Wise, Isaac Mayer, 1819-1900
From heaven's heights the
thunder
In mercy, Lord, incline
thine
"Let there be light", at
dawn
Wise, Isidore
Through-out the night, O
God
Wiseman, Nicholas Patrick
Stephen, 1802-65
Full in the panting heart of
Rome
Wither, George, 1588-1667
Behold the sun, that seemed
Come, O come in pious lays
The Lord of Heaven confess
Sweet baby, sleep! What
ails
To God, with heart and
cheerful
Witter, W. E.
While Jesus whispers to you
Wobeser, Ernst Wilhelm von,
1727-95
I see my Saviour languish
My Saviour was betrayed
Wolcott, Samuel, 1813-86
Christ for the world we
sing
Content, O Lord, and free
Goodly were thy tents
Tell me, whom my soul doth
love
Wolf [Wolff], Jakob Gabriel,
1684-1754
Blest are they, supremely
Wolfe, Aaron Roberts, 1821-
1902
A parting hymn we sing
Wood, Maurice Arthur Ponsonby,
1916-
Worship, glory, praise and
honour
Woodbury, Isaac B.
Ho! reapers of life's har-
vest

Wood, Basil, 1760-1831
   Hail, thou Source of every
Woodford, James Russell, 1820-
85
   Lamb of God, for sinners
      slain
   Not by thy mighty Hand
   Within the Father's house
Woodhouse, Charles Goddard
1835-76
   Heavenly Shepherd, thee we
      pray (rewritten by G. Thring)
Woodhull, Alfred Alexander,
1810-36
   Great God of nations, now
Woodmansee, Emily H.
   Up! arouse thee, O beautiful
   When dark and drear the skies
Woodrow, Fred
   Use me, O my gracious Sa-
      viour
Woods, Amy S.
   Now let us raise our Harvest
      song; R109987 Then praises
      bring
Woods, Bertha H.
   Abide with me;fast breaks the
      morning light see Lyte, H. F.
   Abide with me
Woods, Isabel
   Thine is the glory, thine
Woodward, George Ratcliffe,
1849-1934
   Shepherds, in the field abiding
Woodworth, Samuel
   Rich in mercy, Jesus reigns
Wordsworth, Christopher, 1807-
85
   Alleluia! Alleluia! Hearts and
      voices; X100320 Alleluia!
      ... voices heavenward
      raise; X100322 Alleluia!
      ... to heaven and voices
   Arm these thy soldiers
   Come, ever blessed Spirit
   Father, of all, from land
   Glory be to God the Father
   Gracious Spirit, Holy Ghost
   Hark! the sound of holy voices
   Heavenly Father, send thy
      blessing
   Holy, holy, Holy, Lord God
   In thy glorious resurrection

   Lord, be thy word my rule
   Love is kind and suffers long
   O day of rest and gladness
   O God, in whose all-search-
      ing eye
   O Lord of heaven and earth
   O Lord, our strength in weak-
      ness
   See the Conqueror mounts in
      triumph; X103527 Holy
      Ghost, Illuminator; X111635
      Who is this that
   Sing, O sing, this blessed
      morn
   Songs of thankfulness
   The day is gently sinking
   The grave itself a garden is
   Thine for ever! Thine for
      ever
   Thou, who the night in
      prayer; X107348 O Lord,
      who in thy
   When from the city of our
      God
Wordsworth, Elizabeth, 1840-
   God is our stronghold and our
      stay
   O Lord our Banner, God of
      might
Wordsworth, William 1770-1850
   Blest are the moments,
      doubly
   Serene will be our days
   Stern daughter of the Voice
      of God
Worgan, Ann
   The worst of evils we can
Worthington, John, 1725-90
   Go, my soul, go every day
Wortman, Denis, 1835-1922
   God of the prophets, bless
   Today beneath benignant skies
Wotton, Henry, 1568-1639
   How happy is he born and
      taught; X103697 How
      happy ... born or taught
Wreford, John Reynell, 1800-81
   Lord! I believe; thy power
   Lord, while for all mankind
   When my love to God grows
      weak; X111443 When ...
      to Christ
Wright, J.B.F.

PART TWO: THE TUNES

Index III

Tune Names and Variants, with Citations

SDDRRMSDT] BK14   73
Abends (Oakeley) [SDTLLFMR,
RMFSDTLS, T] A120; B291;
C400; D33b; F24a; G42; I48;
J334; K417; O258; Q280; R
62; S46; T58a; V437; W292a;
AB328; AC218; AD86; AE223;
AJ91a; AL556c; AP666a; AR
529; AS393; BA415; BB56;
BE133; BF179; BV62; BY703;
BZ   74
Aber (Monk) [DTLSFM, MSF
MRM, MMMF#] I155; O103;
AZ582-S; BA210   75
Aberavon (Davis) [SFMRFM,
SFMRRD, TDTD] D187b   76
Aberdeen (Chalmers' Collec-
tion) [DRMSDRTD, MRSFMR, DR]
E561; F581; R328; W481b;
X320; AL327; AN303; AP38;
AW596; BY550b   77
Aberdour (Essex) [SDSSLSM,
FMDRMD, DFF] K545   78
Abergele (Lloyd) [SLTDDMRD,
DTDRRM, MM] G328; W183;
Z599; AL300; AM351; BY
203b   79
Aberystwyth (Ouseley) [MRDTTL,
TDMMRM, MSMR] M221; Q591;
V676; AA533   80
Aberystwyth (Parry) [LLTDRMD
TL, DTLS#LT] A415a; B130b;
C130b; E87; F86; G338c; J
393a; K371b; R216a; S233c;
T417; W414; X542; Y249; Z415;
AB104; AC298a; AD101; AF
109; AG61b; AK317; AL88; AM
427; AP238; AR406; AT158;
BA408; BF276; BK141; BV
506b; BY441b; BZ   81
Abglanz aller majestaet (Lüne-
burg G-B. 1686) X Meinhold
                         82
Abide among us (Lindeman) X
O lad din Aand nu med os
voere   83
Abide in grace (Vulpius) X
Cana   84
Abide in me (Fillmore) [MD
RMSLDTLS, RTDRRM] AY87
                         85
Abide with me (Monk) X
Eventide   86

Abide with me, I need thee
(Pollock) [MMFSSLSF#SM,
DTLSMR] AX368; AY70
                         87
Abide with me; 'tis eventide
(Millard) [MMMSMMRR,
RFFFFM, MM] BC2   88
-----. R [STTLSLSS, MSRF
FM, SD]   89
Abiding (Mendelssohn) X
Heavenly love   90
Abiding grace (Camp) [DFM
RDDTDR, DMSLF#S, R]
I504   91
Abingdon (Routley) [MFSLSDR
S, SFMFMSDL] BV558; BY
230   92
Abinger (Williams) [DMFSML
S, SLTDTLLSF] X319b   93
Above the heavens, eternal
God (Schumann) X Canon-
bury   94
Abridge (I. Smith) [DSDDTLSF
MMR, MLSSF#] E369; F300;
K443; L130; R413; T152; V
103; W483b; X100; AJ172;
AL156a; AP32; AW266; AZ
14-L; BA383; BE333; BV146;
BY600b   95
Abschied (Müller) [SF#SLRFT
D, SF#STLSFM] AM39   96
Acadia (Morson) [MMMMMS
FMRRD, SSSFM] Z515; AO
469; AR378; AS340   97
Accept, kind Father (Kelly)
[MLLSSFMRDRM, MF#S#LT]
BN206   98
-----. R [DRDRMFFFSFM,
MF#S#LL]   99
According to thy gracious word
(Wilson) X Martyrdom   100
Accrington (Sewall) [MLSMRD
RM, SDT, DLS, MM] BR75
                        101
Ach, alles was himmel und
erde (Darmstaedt G-B) X
Gregor's 39th metre - B
                        102
Ach bleib bei uns (Calvisius)
X Calvisius   103
Ach bleib mit deiner gnade
(Vulpius) X Cana   104
Ach Gott und Herr (As hymno-

dus sacer, 1625) [DTLSSLT
D, RDTLTLLS,] D197a; E329;
F588; J286; M454; N411; O58;
Q215; S326; W698; X278; AA
234; AF476; AN365; AQ169;
BA323; BE393; BV386; BX572;
BY204a; BZ   105
-----. V [DTLSSLTD, RDTLT
DLS,] E329   105a
-----. V [DTLSSLTD, DRTDTLS,
D] N411   106
-----. V [DTLSSLTD, RDTLTLS,
D] Q215   106a
Ach Gott, verlass mich nicht
  (Neu ordentlich G-B. Hanover,
  1646) X Steadfast   107
Ach Gott, verlass mich nicht
  (Meiningen G-B. 1693) X
  O Gott, du frommer Gott   108
Ach Gott vom himmel (Erfurt
  G-B. 1524) [TDTLMRDT,
  RDTLRDTL,] O424; Q260;
  AA278   109
-----. V [MFMRLLFM, MFM
  RSFMR] Q260   110
Ach Gott vom himmelreiche
  (Praetorius) X Praetorius II
                              111
Ach Gott! was hat vor herrlichkeit
  (Grimm's Choral buch. 1755)
  X Gregor's 172nd metre   112
Ach Gott, wie (As hymodus
  sacer) X Breslau   113
Ach Herr (Praetorius) [MRMFS
  MRD, MRMFSMRD,] F70   114
Ach Herr, wo sind nun meine
  vor'gen kroefte (Grimm's
  Choral buch) X Grimm's
  552nd metre   115
Ach Jesu, dessen treu (Lüneburg
  G-B. 1648) [MLSLTD, RMT
  DLSM, MLS] N434   116
Ach! Wan doch Jesu, liebster
  mein (Spee. Trutz nachtigall,
  1649) X Nachtigall   117
Ach, wann werd ich dahin kom-
  men (Witt) [DTLTDRM, MF
  SFMRDLT] AA58; AN114;
  AQ163   118
Ach, was soll ich sünder machen
  (Flittner) X Flittner   119
Ach wie sehnlich wart ich
  (Briegel) [MMLFMMRM, S#

LDDTD, TD] AA210   120
Achill (Wesley) [MFMRDFML,
  TDRDTD, SM] BA424   121
Achnasheen (Lloyd) [SLSMRD
  RFM, MRDTLTD] S432
                            122
Ack, bliv hos oss (Swedish
  Koralbok. 1697) X Pax
                            123
Ack, saliga stunder (Ahnfelt)
  [SSDMSDDTLTD, DDTLS]
  N272; P43   124
Ackley (Ackley) X He lives
                            125
Ad astra (Ley) [SSSDTLSM,
  FSLSMDRR] F492   126
Ad cenam agni providi (Sarum
  plainsong M 8) [SDLSDTD
  RDTL, LLSMF] E125; F
  129a; BJ30   127
Ad perennis (French church
  mel) [LTDRMLRT, DDRM
  FFM,] A587b; E350; W524b;
  X274b   128
-----. V [LLDRMLRT, DDRM
  FFM,] E350   129
Ad sacratissimum cor Jesu
  (Piel) [DRMMFMMR, RM
  FFFFFM,] BO24   130
Adam lay ybounden (Warlock)
  [LDTLMM, LDTLM, FMMRD,]
  BG180   131
Adam's song (Sanders) [SSSS
  FMR, DRRM, SSSSF] AQ2
                            132
Addeer hu (Jewish trad)
  [MSSMSS, LTDTLLS, SDD]
  AH147; BH125   133
Addison (Emerson) [MMMFM
  R#M, DTLLSSMR, M] L516;
  V670   134
-----. V [MMMFMRM, DTLL
  SSMR, M] V670   135
Addison's (Sheeles) [DMMRS
  FMRDR, SDRMR] B252; E
  297; F170; X659; AQ116;
  BV217   136
Adelaide (Stebbins) [MRMFMD
  TDR, RD#RMR, RD] R302;
  Z324; AE270; AH426; AI280;
  AM574; AR351; AS241; AT
  355; AU254; AV384; AW217;
  AX395; BB272; BZ   137

Ades domine (---) [DDRMFM, SFMRFM, MMF#S] BR114 138

Ades Pater supreme (Melodiae Prudentianae) [MSLTDTL, RD LSLFM, SS] F112 139

Adeste fideles (Wade's Cantus diversi) [DDSDRS, MRMFMRD, DTL] A12; B72; C72; D49; E28; F59; G96; H147; I125; J42; K21; L216; M237; N33; O195; P125; Q102; R170; S 116; T40; U56; V325a; W55; X78; Y298; Z205; AA159; AB 106; AC74; AD120; AE84; AF 132; AG69; AH123; AI67; AJ 57; AK112; AL47; AM36; AN 156; AO127; AP27; AQ288; AR143; AS110; AT66; AU143; AV90; AW80; AX94; AZ39-F; BA155; BB105; BC129; BD56; BE123; BF291; BI83; BK149; BL11; BM63; BN10; BO150, 150a; BP13; BQ4, 158; BR 73; BV106; BX305; BY104; BZ 140

-----. V [DSDRS, MRMFMR, DTLDR] BO150a 141

-----. V [DDSDRTS, MRMFMR, DDT] BQ158 142

Adesto sancta trinitas (Chartres Antiphoner. 1784) [DDSDDRRD, DFFMMRDS,] E159b; R245b; S59; X51b 143

Adesto sancta trinitas (Plain-song M 3) [MRSLDDDTLSLS FM, FF] E159 144

Adjutor (Lewars) [SSLFMR, DMR T, DSLFMR,] K48 145

Admah (Mason) [DDTDRMFMR DTD, MFSL] H197 146

Adon olam (Jewish trad) [MLT DLTS#L, MLTDMRDT] BH157, 311 147

Adon olom (Gerovitch) [MMFM RDTL, MMTLSF#SL] AH154; BH276 148

Adonoy adonoy (Gerovitch) [MD TL, LLS#LT, D#RRD#L, LM] BH313 149

Adonoy hy ho-eloheem (Jewish trad) [DRMRMLLLL, MR SDSSF] BH340 150

Adonoy mo odom (Halpern) [LLDRTMLRRRMR, MMMR] BH334 151

Adonoy yimloch (Binder) [SLTDS, DTLSSFMFR, MF] BH294 152

Adoramus (Spencer-Palmer) [SDTLSMDF, FMFSLTDT,] BV30 153

Adoramus te, panem (Catholic) [SSFMSLSFMR, SSFMSL] BQ232 154

Adoration (Elvey) [MMSSDDS S, LLSDFMMR,] D123b; J 177a; K161 155

Adoration (Hanby) [SSSSSSL, LLSSDDR, DR] K560; W77; AE96; AP735; AW96 156

-----. R [DRMMFMMR, TDR RMRRD] 157

Adoration (Havergal) X St John 158

Adoration (Haydn) X O come, loud anthems ... 159

Adoration (Stewart) [SF#SM R#MDTLS, LTDSMD] H24 160

Adoration (Torrance) [SSDTDF RM, MMTLTSSS] O98 161

Adoration (Tufts) [DDDMRDR M, MMMLSF#S, S] BX61 162

Adoration (Woodman) [DSLTLS SDRMMR, RMRD] BF181 163

Adoro (Barnby) X St Chrysos-tom 164

Adoro te (Barnby) X St Chrysostom 165

Adoro te devote (Benedictine Plainsong M 5) [DMSSSLS FMRDD, DMS] A204; E331; F385a; J272; K183a; W319; X279; AD472; AF557; AL 214b; AN173; AQ128; BL50; BM10; BN88; BO32; BP48; BQ227a; BR331; BY330a 166

-----. V [DMSSLSFMRDD, DMSSL] K183a 167

-----. V [FLDDDRD, L#LS FF, FLDD] BL50 168

Adoro te devote (Gounod) X

Alene Gud i Himmerig (Plainsong. 1539) X To God on
high   249

Alene til dig, Herre Jesus Krist
(Nürnberg, 1541) X Allein zu
dir, Herr Jesu Christ   250

Aletheia (Hall) [MLTS#S#F#S#,
LTDT, TLSS] B416b   251

Aletta (Bradbury) [MSDRRRDR
M, MSDRRRM] G146; H303;
I144; L252; T237; V441; AE
330; AH366; AI407; AJ333; AM
674; AO230; AS177; AT179;
AU237; AV80; AW311; AX421;
BB234   252

Alexander (Everest) [MMR#MD
DDRMF, FFMFRR] L421   253

Alexander (Gibson) [MR#MFD#
MR, DTRSFM, MF#M] Y152
                                        254

Alexander (Smart) [SMDLRDTD,
FMRSDTLS,] V536   255

Alexandria (Arnold) [MMRMSF
MRD, MRMSFMR,] D660a;
L57; T139b; V73; AJ89; AO
300; AS343   256

-----. V [DMRMSMFMRD, MR
MSFM] AO300   257

Alford (Dykes) [MFFDRMD,
MSMDRD, MR] A590; B541;
C541; D396; F284; G421; I618;
J595b; K519; L351; M318; N617;
O617; Q476; R427; S427; T352;
U311; V706; W221b; Z568; AA
288; AB415; AC266; AD141;
AE308; AF311; AG285; AH280;
AK414; AL175; AM234; AN547;
AO553; AP308; AR69; AT476;
AV292; BA756; BB306; BD138;
BE65; BF311; BR440; BV437;
BX462; BY407   258

Alfreton (New version Supple-
ment. 1708) [DMFRMDRT,
RMF#SRMRD] E240; F95b;
X189b   259

Algiers (Herbert) [DDTLTRDS,
DMRLRR, DD] AJ223   260

Alice (Roberts) [LMRDTLTLS#,
RDFMMRM,] W404; AM408
                                        261

Alida (American trad) [SDDMR
DLLDT, LSSSDM] G522; H336;
BB473   262

Aline (Bergquist) [MRDTDRM
FMMR, FMRD#R] J336;
N533   263

All and some (English trad,
ca 1450) [LLLMMSFM, M
MMRRRDTL.] BG62   264

-----. R [MMMSFMRD, SS
SSLMFRD,]   265

All as God wills (Barnby) X
Holy Trinity   266

All because we do not love
them (Teasley) [DRMSS
FMD, DMRFMRM, D] AX217
                                        267

-----. [MFSMDLSM, DRMSFMR,
D]   268

All bells in Paradise (Shaw)
[LTDTLS, MMF#LS#L, SSLS]
BG184   269

All creatures of our God
(Cologne G-B) X Vigiles et
sancti   270

All' ehr' und lob (Kirchen
G.-B. Strassbourg. 1541)
[DDRMDFFM, RMFSMFRD,]
Q236   271

All for Jesus (Lough) [MFSL
SMMR, RMFLSFM, M] AX
403; AY108   272

All for Jesus (Stainer) X
Oxford   273

All glory be to God most high
(As hymnodus sacer. 1625)
X Ach Gott und Herr   274

All glory be to thee (Plainsong. 1539) X To God on
high   275

All glory, laud (Lindeman)
[DDRMDSS, LSMDMR, SFM]
P34   276

All glory, praise [laud] and
honor (Teschner) X St
Theodulph   277

All hail, dear conqueror
(Bragers) [SDTRDTLS, SR
MFMRDR,] BP37   278

All hail the glorious day
(Stephens) [MFSDTLSFMFS,
LSMRM] BC223   279

All hail the great Immanuel's
name (Holden) X Corona-
tion   280

All hail the power (Holden) X

312
All things bright (Monk) X All
   things bright and beautiful
                      313
All things bright (Ouseley) [DD
   MFSLS, SDMSFMR, FF] W18b;
   BY472a   314
All things bright (Spohr) X
   Gerald   315
All things bright and beautiful
   (Danish trad) [SDDRRMRD, RM
   SRMD, SD] AM636   316
-----. R [MSLSMFMR, MFSFRM,
   SD]   317
All things bright and beautiful
   (Monk) [DMFLSMD, MRTTLS,
   DMF] F442; K554; AP724;
   BY733a   318
-----. R [LSDDTDD, LSDDTD,
   D#RM]   319
All things bright and beautiful
   (Shelley) [DRMDRRD, DDRMDRS,
   RM] BH252   320
All this night (Maker) [DRMMFS
   LSR, MMR, DDT, R] D538b;
   BY88a   321
All this night (Sullivan) [DRM
   FSLS, DRMFSLS, SS] BR555
                      322
All through the night (Welsh trad)
   X Ar hyd y nos   323
All to Christ I owe (Grape)
   [DMSLSMD, DRRDRM, DMS]
   Z284; AM690; AT225; AU258;
   AV337; AW462; AX320; AY
   235; BB527   324
-----. R [SLSMD, SLSMR, SL
   SMDT]   325
All waters (Shaw) [SFMRDSDRM
   RD, SFMRD] X327   326
-----. R [TSFR#RR#FR#RDS,
   SLDRM]   327
All wise, All great (Singer)
   [SLSSDDTT, SLSSRRDD,]
   BH218   328
All ye dwellers (Jewish trad)
   [SSDDDD, DDMMDSR, R#T, S]
   BH317   329
All ye who seek (Montani) [MM
   DRMFMRD, SSMFSLR,] BQ67
                      330
All ye who seek (Tozer) X
   Jazer   331

All ye who seek (Lee) [SSS
   LSFSM, DRMFFM, SL] BN
   70   332
Alla trinita beata (Laudi spirit-
   uali) X Alta trinita beata
                      333
Alle deine gaben (Gregor)
   X Gregor's 7th metre
                      334
Alle jahre wieder (Rinck)
   [MMSSFR, DRMFR, FFMML]
   K539; N634   335
Alle menschen (Hintze) X
   Salzburg   336
Alle menschen müssen sterben
   (Weimar G-B. 1681) X
   Jesu, meines lebens leben
                      337
Alle vögel (German) X Jesus
   lives, and Jesus leads
                      338
Allegiance (Sampaix) [SMDL
   SMFMDRD, SMDDT] H396
                      339
-----. R [MFSLTLSFMFSFF,
   MFS]   340
Allein Gott in der höh sei ehr
   (Plainsong) X To God on
   high   341
Allein zu dir, Herr Jesu Christ
   (Nürnberg, 1541) [DSLDM
   RRD, MDLRDTTL,] N410;
   O96; Q319; AA413; AZ202-a
                      342
-----. V [DSLDMRRD, MRDT
   DTL, D] O96   343
-----. V [DSLDMRDTD, MRD
   TSLR] Q319   344
-----. V [DSLTDRMRRD, SL
   TDRT] AZ202-a   345

Alleluia
   NOTE: Other spellings of this
word are not used herein, no
matter the language.

Alleluia (Lowe) X Praise
                      346
Alleluia (Wesley) [DDTDLSLT,
   DRMSLLS, S] A281; B193;
   C193b; D368a; F399a; J417;
   K127; S10a; W138; AB39;
   AL377; AP148; BE171; BI

3-D; BV383b; BY168   347
Alleluia! Alleluia! (Catholic)
[MFSSMRDDTLSRSFM,M]
AH127; BO173   348
(H) Alleluia chorus (Handel)
[DSLS,DSLS,DDDD,DDDD]
AU477   349
Alleluia, Christ is risen (Kestel)
[SDMFRMDS,SDMSMRM,S]
BL26   350
Alleluia, dulce carmen (Essay
on the Church plain chant. 1782)
X Dulce carmen   351
Alleluia, dulce carmen (LaFeilleé.
Methode. 1808) [MMRFRDRF
FRM,RFLSF] F82a   352
Alleluiah for the cross (McGrana-
han) [SDTDRMFS,DRDTRMR
D,] AU470   353
Alleluia! Gott zu loben (Baessler)
[SDRMLSSFM,RMFSMRD,]
AA223   354
Alleluia, Jesus lives (Wonnber-
ger) [DSMDSTD,RRMMF#MF#
SR,] M449   355
Alleluia, let the holy anthem
rise (Terry) X Holy church
356
Alleluia perenne (Monk) [SMMM
FSDLDS,SLSTD] B265a; C265;
D262b; V616; AB89   357
Alleluia piis edite (Hodges) [DF
MRDDDRMR,RSFMS] B265b
358
Alleluia! Praise the Savior (Sulli-
van) X Lux eoi   359
Alleluia! Sing to Jesus (French
Paroissien mel) X Daily,
daily   360
Alleluia song (Hungarian trad)
[SFMFSMRD,RMFFMLS,S]
BL33   361
Alleluia, 'tis done (Husband) X
We praise thee, O God 362
Alleluia, what a Saviour (Bliss)
X Man of sorrows   363
Alleluias. (Cologne G-B. 1623)
X Vigiles et sancti   364
Alleman (Alleman) [SSSSF#SM,S
LLLDS,SSM] L528   365
-----. R [SRRRMD,SLTDRM,
MMMM]   366
Allen (Allen) X Joyful song 367

Allen (Prout) [DMFSLS,MRD
DTL,LSDD] BA867   368
Allerton (Mann) [SDDTLSLS,
DRMSFMR,S] D435   369
Alles ist an Gottes segen
(Koenig) X Evangelists
370
Allgüter, mein preisgesang
(Weimar) [SMRDDRMFSM,
SLSFMR] F611; J303; W
428a; X521; AL301a; BY482;
BZ   371
Allhallows (Brown) X All hal-
lows   372
Allington (Hopkins) [MRDFFM,
MSMDRT,RFMR] C49a; D
23a; F38   373
Alma (Brackett) [SMSLDRMSL
D,RMMSRM] BE154   374
Alma (Webbe) X Consolation
375
Alma mater (Hendrickson)
[SSMFMRRD,SSMF#SLLS,]
P49   376
Alma mater (Redhead) [SMDM
RD,MRSSF#S,MFFM] D71b
377
Alma redemptoris mater
(Gounod) [SSSDRMFMRMM,
SMMMS] BQ202   378
Alma redemptoris mater (Plain-
song M 5) [DMFSLS,SSL
TDSMMMF] BN140; BQ277
379
Alma redemptoris [mater]
(Webbe) X Consolation 380
Almighty Father (Mendelssohn)
X Almighty Father, hear
381
Almighty Father (Schalit)
[LLSLDMRDRDT,DLLLT]
BH6   382
Almighty Father, hear (Lys-
berg) [SDRMMSFDRM,MM
RRRD] AV418   383
Almighty Father, hear (Men-
delssohn) [SLRDT,DFFFMM
RLTDD] R542; Sap19; AE
462; AH563; AR651; AT529;
AU488; AV415; BB687; BF
689; BY305-C   384
-----. V [SLRDT,TDFFF,
FMMRLT] Sap.19   385

Almighty Father, hear (Mendelssohn) X Intercession (Callcott) 386

Almighty God (Lewandowski) [DTLSFMFS, LSFMRMFM,] BH53 387

Almost (Bliss) X Almost persuaded 388

Almost persuaded (Bliss) [MF FMD, DRRM, MFFMD, RM] P256; U154; AH341; AI191; AT248; AU169; AV335; AX263; AY506; BB228 389

Almsgiving (Dykes) [MMRDSDR M, SDMSFM] A305; B426; C 426a; D477a; F480; H45; I501; J448a; K385; L76; N573; P427; S398; T319; U362; V465; W19b; AA357; AB338; AC56; AD261; AI225; AK257; AL26b; AM575; AO105; AP139; AS48; AV17; AZ3-C; BA475; BB325; BD131; BE190; BF649; BR35; BV599b; BX262a; BY68 390

Almsgiving (Wesley) [SMDSFMMR DFMLSDFM] F204; I401 391

Aloha (Hawaiian trad) X He lives on high 392

Alone with God (Kirkpatrick) [SDDDDMDMS, LSSSSMD] AX 358 393

-----. R [MMFSSLLSM, MRMF RMF] 394

Alone with thee (Conradi) [DMM FFMRSFM, MMMMRD] P332 395

Alpha (Leslie) [SSSF#SLS, SS DRLT, DDD] D583b 396

Alphege (Gauntlett) X St Alphege 397

Alsace (Beethoven) [SDRMMM FMR, SFMRMTLS] C460; H166; I518; AA332; AB358; AM52; BE422 398

-----. V [SDRMMMFMR, SFMR MTDLS] I518 399

Alston (Burleigh) [MFSLSFMM R, DRMSSLS] AP727b 400

Alstone (Willing) [SSLSDMRD, RMFSLSM] B87; C87; D575a; F435; I203; J4; K2; L208; M 515; O176; T123; W516; Y69; AB410; AJ179; AK332; AP769;

AS453; AW300; BA37; BD35; BF232; BR381; BX192; 401

Alta trinita beata (Laudi spirituali. Florence) [DDRMRD FMRMM, RMFMM] A135; E184; G615; R557; Sap.45; X669; AD511; AF403; AN3; AP338; AR678; BQ240; BZ 402

Altenburg (German trad) [SM MFMRDTDR, SFFSFM] M645 403

Althorp (Green. Psalmody. 1744) [SDRMRDFMR, RSFM RDR] F249 404

Althorp (Lomas) [DRMFMRRD, MFSDTLS, S] AO256 405

Altid frejdig naar du gaar (Weyse) X Cheerfulness 406

Alvan (Mason) [SMMDRDRDM S, SMMDRD] L205; V279 407

Alverstoke (Barnby) X Caritas 408

Alverstroke (Barnby) X Caritas 409

Alveston (Harwood) [SDTLTD RRSSSMFMFS] W380 410

Am I a soldier (Sankey) [DM MFMFLS, MSDTLS, FM] AI 322a 411

-----. R [SDTSLTD, TDRDTLS, FM] 412

Am I a soldier of the cross (Arne) X Arlington 413

Amadeus (Warner) [MRLTDRMF, MRSMDDTD] AZ606-A 414

Amara (Perkins) DRMMSFMR R, RMFFLSF] T80; AJ120; AW499 415

-----. R [SSLLFSLSM, SFM RRRD] 416

Amazing grace (American trad) [SDMDMRDLS, SDMDMRS,] G209; R275b; AH335; AM402; AR433; AT188; AU161; AW 463; AX108; AY251, 257; BZ 417

-----. V [SLDMDMRDLS, SLD MDM] AX108 418

-----. V [SLDMDMRDLSS, SLDMD] AY257 419

Amberg (Church of Scotland
Hymn tune book.) [MFSLSDRTD,
DTLRDTL] W449; AK255
420

Ambleside (Lowe) [MRDLTDRD,
DDRRM, MSS] C523a; D531a;
BR405   421

Ambrose (Ambrose) [SSSSSS,
LLLSMR, MMFF#] B407; C407;
G515; H497; L563; O289; P338;
T70; U425; AA531; AH533; AJ
106; AO548; AR416; AS473; AW
264; BA727; BB352; BC272
422

-----. V [SSSSSSSLLSMR, MM
FF#] L563   423

Amelia (Bradbury) [SDDMMS,
MRDMRD, SDDM] T292; AJ
404   424

Amen Court (Bower) [DRMFM
S, MRDRLS, SLDR] F237; BV
218   425

Amen, Jesus han skal raade
(Berggren) [SMRRMFFM, DTLR
SFM, L] G221; J456b; K389a;
N430; O35; P45; AW219; BZ
426

Amen sjunge hvarje tunga (Berggren) X Amen, Jesus han
skal raade   427

America* (Thesaurus musicus,
1740) [DDRTDR, MMFMRDRD]
A141; B427; C427; D196; E
560; F577; G489; H529; I702;
J358; K489; L556; M498; N
566; O519; P410; Q577; R513;
S412; T446; U338; V652; W631;
X318; Y293; Z548; AA305; AB
334; AC279; AD440; AE392;
AF437; AG274; AH474; AI363;
AK439; AL508; AN384; AO585;
AP639; AQ242; AR611; AS383;
AT487; AU458; AV302; AW344;
AZ579-a; BA872; BB506; BC
115; BD172; BF541; BH264;
BI11; BK118; BR493; BX420;
BY641; BZ   428
* British texts call it "National
anthem"

America (Thesaurus musicus,
1740) X Remember (Ravens-
croft. Melismata)   429

America befriend (Merrill) [SS

MLMSFM, DRMFLS, DT]
S415; AB340; AC272; AH
479; AO588; BF550   430

America, the beautiful (Brown)
[MMRRLLSS, DTLFLS, FM]
AO592   431

American hymn (Keller) [SD
RMSSSLSFM, RRMFS] J166;
K295; L146; P22; AO602;
BD184   432

Americus (Gabriel) [SSLSM
MFM, MFSLSFMR,] T113;
AJ164   433

Ames (Neukomm) [SSDTDRT
D, MRTDLSF#S,] M30; R
412; T57; AJ90; AN237
434

Amesbury (Burnap) [SSLTD
DLT, DD#MRSM, MM] N414;
R178; U31; Z210; AB210;
AC98; AE385; AG86; AI218;
AR222; AT441; BA530; BF
262   435

Amherst (Billings) [DMSFMR
D, SDSLSFMR, S] AQ31
436

Amicus (Swedish trad) [SSDD
DDDMDDT, DTLSF] M626;
N468   437

Amid the trials (Lorenz) [SS
MMDRDTT, SSFFRMR] AI288;
AS311; AX488; AY88   438

-----. R [SSMSLR, FFRFSM,
SSMM,]   439

Amnos (Benbow) [DRMSSFMR,
RMFMRDRD,] K188   440

Amor Dei (Kirchen gesang.
Bremen, 1707) [DSFMMRRD,
RMF#SSSF#S,] W425;
AN459   441

Amsterdam (Nares) [DSDRM
RMF, SLSFMR, DS] B114a;
C114a; D512a; G524; H512;
I623; L438; N514; R330; S
264; V688; X286; Z573; AB
196; AD15; AG122; AH363;
AN62; AT122; AV240; AW200;
AZ56-a, 591-d; BA313, 702;
BB668; BE296; BF381; BR
500a; BX322; BZ   442

-----. V [DSDRMRMFSSSFM
R, DS] AZ56-a   442a

-----. V [DSDRMRMF, SFM

-----. V [DMDRMFRD, DMF#
SRSF#S,] AA286   481
-----. V [DDDRMFRM, DMF
SRSF#S] AN26   482
Angels' song (Mendelssohn)
[FMRDDTLS, LFSMSFMR,]
BE342   483
Angel's story (Mann) X Water-
mouth   484
Angels we have heard (French
carol) X Gloria   485
Angels we have heard (Montani)
[SSDSFML, RRSFMRM, SS]
BQ7   486
Angelus (German chorale) [MS
FRMDRR, SSDTLLS, S] AO293
                    487
Angelus (Joseph) [DDRMF#SS
F#S, SLTDTLLS,] A168; B
399; C399; D14; E266; F20;
I313; J232; K79; Q115; R55;
S43; T30b; U468; V313; W
277; X42b; Z602; AA177; AB
132; AD135; AE99; AF55; AG
24; AJ234b; AK57; AL392b;
AM88; AN211; AP348a; AR
149; AV100; AW37; AZ22-N;
BA69; BB296; BD96; BE214;
BF205; BO176; BP70; BR170;
BV49b; BX180; BY688   488
Angelus (Rider) [DDDDDD, SSS
SSS#LT, DL] D535b   489
Angelus ad Virginem (Dublin
Troper) [SMSSFMR, RMDFR
MDD, S] F547; BG52   490
-----. V [SMSSFMR, RMDRD
TDD, S] BG52   491
Angers (Croft. Collection) X
Iste confessor   492
Anglia (Lyra Davidica) X Easter
hymn   493
Anglorum apostolus (Murray)
[DMFSLSFMRM, SLTDTL]
BY39b   494
Angmering (Parry) [MDMLSFM
R, MF#SLTLS, S] F251   495
Anima Christi (English trad)
[MLLSLSFM, SFMRDTL,]
A582; E89   496
Animae hominum (Blanchet)
[SLDTSLDT, SLTDRRR, F]
BV480b; BY419b   497
Annapolis (---) [MMDFMMR,

RD#RMRD, MMD] D603b
                    498
Annetta (Kirkpatrick) [SDTD
STLS, FMLSDFMR,] AJ85
                    499
Annisquam (Noble) [RMMRDRM
FS, RMMLLSF] AK73   500
Anniversary (Sankey) [DRMSTL
SM, DRMFRDD, D] BB480
                    501
Anniversary song (Sherwin)
[MRDSLFMRD, TDRRMRR,]
BB649   502
-----. R [TDRDRMMFFFLSM,
DRM]   503
Annue Christe (Paris Antiphon-
er. 1681) [DDRMMMRMFMR
DD, MMF] E174b; F505; V
713; W594; X688; AD367; AP
630; BV591a; BY639   504
-----. V [DDRMMMRMFMRD
D, DMF] AD367   505
Annue Christi, saeculorum
Domini (Plainsong. M 1)
[RLLTSLTDTL, RDTLSD]
E174   506
Annunciation (Barry) [SSLFMM,
DTSLSS, SRMF] F546   507
Annunciation (Dutch trad. 1896)
[SSDDRMFMRDT, SSLMF] A
317; X226; BG100   508
Another day is dawning (McKin-
ney) [SSFMRDS, SLDRDS, SS
F] AU275   509
-----. R [SSRRMR, SSMMFM,
SDDM]   510
Another year is dawning (Wes-
ley) X Aurelia   511
Anthes (Anthes) [SDTDRMD, DL
FMRD, SDT] Q276   512
Antioch (Handel) [DTLSFMR
D, SLLTTD, DD] C101c; G89;
H141; I107b; J15; K34; L210;
M346; N32; O201; P132; Q87;
R161; S122; T331; U57; V
118b; Y360; Z190; AB109;
AC76; AD104; AE83; AF130;
AG65; AH264; AI60; AK120;
AL55; AM149; AN163; AO
129; AQ299; AR121; AS100;
AT65; AU137; AV98; AW70;
AX92; AY189; BA160; BB189;
BC89; BD207; BE417; BF290;

BI10; BK142; BX195; BZ   513
Antiphoner (Paris. Gradual. 1685)
    [DRMFMDRD, MSLSMFS, S]
    F590; BV19   514
Anton (Gersbach) [SSMFSL, LSD
    MRD, DTLT] T243; AJ339
                                  515
Antwerp (Smallwood) [SSSDDRMF
    M, RRRMF#SL] BV235; BY
    29   516
Anvern (Mason) [SSDMDRTD, D
    DMSMFRM,] L340; T13; V60;
    AJ17a; AO424; AV243; BB307
                                  517
Anxious heart (Norwegian folk)
    [MTDLLFMD, MTDLTSL, M]
    P168   518
Anywhere (Towner) [SSLLSMDRM
    FS, FMRMF] AI399; AM680;
    AS271; AX470; BB589   519
-----. R [RMFMFS, LLSF#S, DD
    DST]   520
Anywhere, dear Saviour (Ogden)
    [MRDSLD, RRMDR, MRDSL]
    BB344   521
Anywhere with Jesus (Towner)
    X Anywhere   522
Apolutrosis (Bach) [MFMRRSFM
    RD, RRDTLS] AA405   523
Appeal (Tomissön. Psalmebog,
    1569) X Franzen   524
Appleton (Boyce) [SSSSSDRM, SSS
    DTLLS,] M201; T223b; AJ
    320; AO423   525
April (Welsh carol) [DMFSD,
    DMRDRD, TDSLS] BG155 526
Ar det ringa kall (English trad)
    [MRDDRFMR, SDTTDMRR#,]
    N28   527
Ar hyd y nos (Welsh trad)
    [DTLDRDTS, LTTD, DTL] A
    169a; E268; F26a; G43; J230;
    P73; R58; S41; T308; X46; Y
    306; Z143; AB29; AC18; AD52;
    AF58; AG30; AH167; AI51; AL
    547b; AN100; AO43b; AS33;
    AT30; AV230; AW35; BE350;
    BF201; BK48; BY590b; BZ
                                  528
Ara (Matthison-Hansen) [DTLSFM
    RDRM, RMF#SLT] M12   529
Arabia (Wilson) [SDRMFLSFM,
    SLSFMMR,] X454; Z591 530

Arator (Schulz) X Claudius
                                  531
Arcadelt (Arcadelt) [MRMDR
    MM, SSSFMR, MRM] O94; AP
    160; BP87; BQ200b   532
Arcadia (Hastings) [SSSDDRM
    D, SLFDLS, SS] L513   533
Arden (Thalben-Ball) [DMDSM
    FMRM, LRMDTLT,] BV268;
    BY304   534
Ardgowan (Finlay) [SRMLSL
    DRSM, SLMMRD] F33a   535
Ardudwy (Roberts) [MMMRDRD
    L, SSSF#MR#M, L] W108b;
    X695; AM43; AN471; BY146b
                                  536
Ardwick (Gauntlett) [SMDLS,
    DDTRRD, MSFMR,] BV213;
    BY223   537
"Are ye able" (Mason) X Bea-
    con Hill   538
Are you adorning the doctrine
    (Byers) [SMRMDRDS, SDDDR
    DRM,] AX158   539
Are you washed in the blood?
    (Hoffman) X Washed in the
    blood   540
Arfon (major: Welsh hymn)
    [SDDTLSDRM, FMRDMRD]
    BZ   541
Arfon (minor: Welsh hymn)
    [MLLS#F#MLTD, RDTLDTL]
    E116; R197; W100; X141;
    AF174; AM183; BV370; BY
    616; BZ   542
Argyle (Ewing) X Ewing 543
Argyle (Turpin) [MSMRDMRD,
    FMLSFMR, R] D159   544
Ariel (Mozart) [SSMMMDDDT
    DMMR, RMF] C263a; G19;
    H343; I9; L148; R134; S203;
    T52; U73; V130; Z265; AE
    297; AG109; AH178; AI111;
    AJ81; AL43; AM126; AO205;
    AR115; AS114; AT7; AU17;
    AV126; AX7; AY29; BB161;
    BZ   545
-----. V [SSMMMDDTRFFM,
    SSDT] BC102   546
Arimathea (Roper) [MMFMFLLS,
    DMMRDRSS] C177; D116a;
    AH303   547
Arimathaea (Wurzburger G-B

1628) X O traurigkeit   548
Arise (American trad) [LDLSL
  DDLSM, SSLSLD] AT241: AU
  229; AV341   549
Arise, my soul, arise (Care-
  less) [DMSLSLTD, DDTLLSFF]
  BC227   550
Arise, my soul arise (Edson)
  X Lenox   551
Arise, O glorious Sion (Care-
  less) [SDSMDFM, MMRRDT,
  SDS] BC225   552
Arise, O Lord (Whittington)
  [SDTLRSFM, MMF#SLLS, L]
  BI51   553
Arise, O youth of God (McKin-
  ney) X Leavell   554
Arise to praise the Lord (Binder)
  [MFSMFRD, MFSMDLS, MF]
  BH74   555
Arizona (Earnshaw) [MMMMMSF
  M, DDTDRMRD] R87; Y276;
  AC59; AE366; AL20b; AP152b;
  BY532   556
Arles (Gabriel) [SDDDDSDMMM
  MD, MSSS] T49; AJ76   557
Arlington (Arne) [DMMMRDDD,
  RMSFMR, F] A325b; B270;
  C237a; D426; G270; H151;
  I354b; J554; L46; M230; N454;
  P278; R69; S23; U143; V233;
  Z435; AE231; AG34; AH295; AI
  136; AL349b; AM116; AN55b;
  AO241; AP33b; AR177; AS121;
  AT39; AU176; AV7; AW152;
  AX55; AY356; AZ14-S; BA392;
  BB355; BE372; BR238; BX78;
  BZ   558
Armageddon (German mel.)
  [SSMRDS, LLDDS, S#S#LDM]
  C523b; R355; S272; U292; V752;
  W519; Z367; AB349; AC202;
  AE272; AG190; AH434; AI331;
  AK286; AL365; AM493; AO373;
  AP551; AT413; AU63; AV208;
  AW190; BF475; BY534;   559
-----. R [DSMDLS, DRMFS,
  DDDDM]   560
Armagh (Turle) [SMFRDDFLS,
  DDTLMLS#] V292; AB378
                             561
Armenia (Pond) [DDTDRRRDRM,
  RMRDTD] G417; H427; I553;

L437; V134; AO409; AW322;
  AX160; BZ   562
Armenian hymn (Armenian
  liturgy) [SLSFMRD, MFSMS
  FMRM] BE113   563
Armes (Armes) [SMRDDLLS,
  SDLTLSLM] A539a; B480;
  F220b; W647a; AP374a; BE
  259; BV156b; BY184a   564
Armonia biblica (Pisani) [SL
  DRMSLS, MRDDRTL, S] AC
  240   565
Arms of Jesus (Doane) [MRD
  SDMFM, SLSMDR, MR] E
  580; N608; U207; V347; W
  707; AI311; AL507; AM608;
  AO637; AP791; AS483; AU
  353; AV357; AW313; AX529;
  AY173; BB615   566
-----. R [RRMRRRS, F#F#
  F#MRRS, RR]   567
Armstrong (Armstrong arr)
  [MMFSSF#RFFMD, MRDMR]
  AO546b   568
-----. R [SLSF#RFSFM, MF
  MRLRR]   569
Armstrong (Chadwick) [MMM
  RLTRDS, MMRSMRD] U78;
  AB128; AC104; BB115; BD
  66; BF306; BX215   570
-----. V [MMMRLTRD, MM
  RSMRDT] AB128   571
Armstrong (Richards) [MFSS
  LSSM, MMSRD#RM, M] J
  493b; K256; L89a; T166;
  U200; Z172; AI80; AJ244;
  AM688; AR595   572
Arncliffe (Statham) [DDMSDT
  LSLRS, FLSFM] F381   573
Arnheim (Ahle) X Liebster
  Jesu   574
Arnold (Arnold) [SSMSFRFM
  F, MR, RMFSL] AL645; AM
  276; AP33a; AW584   575
Arnold (Johnson) [MRMFMRM
  D, DTDMRR, RM] N505
                             576
Arnold (Murrill) [SMDLSSLT,
  TDRMLR, RF] BV608b   577
Arnsberg (Neander) [MMMM
  RR, DDDDTT, LLSD] J164;
  K424; M9; Q4; R13; S51;
  W234; Z123; AD24; AE4;

AF3; AG11; AK29; AL196; AM
132; AP315; AW506; AZ195-A;
BA375; BR12; BY41; BZ   578
-----. V [MMMMRR,DDDDTT,
LLLL] Q4   579
-----. V [MMMFMRR,DDDRDT
T, LL] AZ195-A   580
Arnstadt (Drese) X Rochelle
                          581
Around the weary world (Norden)
[MMMSSFFMDR,R#MSDDT]
BH17   582
Art (Clarke) [SLSMFS,SL#DL
SF,LS,SR] AQ135   583
Art thou weary (Bullinger) X
Geneva   584
Art thou weary? (Warner)
[SLSDDRDT,DRMRR,MFS]
AZ269-F   585
Artavia (Hopkins) [SSDDTLSDR
M,SSFFMRD] A405; B398;
C398; AB161; AD281; AK237;
AL126; AM397b; BF355; BY
140b   586
Arthur's seat (Goss) [SDDTLS,
LTDRMRDR,SM] A237; G264;
L87; R351; S273; U300; Y110;
Z359; AB249; AC184; AD290;
AE24; AF380; AH446; AI259;
AJ37; AK291; AM226; AO60;
AR327; AT422; AW121; BA26;
BD84; BF478; BZ   587
Arundel (Dykes) [SDTDRMMR,
MLTDLLS,M] D125a; J407;
K300; M577; O164; W495a 588
As after the water-brooks (Linde-
man) X Som torstige hjort
                          589
As fades the glowing orb (Webbe)
X Melcombe   590
As God wills (Levenson) [MRD
TDRMR,DTLSLTDT,] BH90
                          591
As pants the hart (Kaiser) [SD
DRRMDLS,STDTLS,S] BH40
                          592
As sinks beneath the ocean
(Christiansen) [LSMRSSF,DTLS
FM,MMM] P422   593
As swiftly my days (---) [DMRD
RRRDRM,MMRMFM] BC5
                          594
-----. R [RDDRMDRRMF,FM

RDRM]   595
As the dawn was breaking (Buz-
zard) [SSLSF#SMM,MMRR
DRM,M] AY492   596
-----. R [SSSSMRDS,RMFR
MFM,M]   597
As the dew from heaven
(Daynes) [SLTDDTSLTRRD,
LTDM] BC232   598
As the hart (Bourjeois) X
Bourgeois   599
As the sun doth daily rise
(Parish choir) X Innocents
                          600
As wide as the skies (---)
[SMRMDTDRDLS,SDDDD]
P292   601
Asaph (Stubbs) [MMMRDL,SSL
SS,SSSF] B527a; AO67 602
Asa's death (Grieg) [MLT,
MLT,DTLTDRDT,ML] Y122;
AC261   603
Asbury (Harrington) [MRD
SRDRMRD,FMRDTD] I143a
                          604
Ascalon (Silesian mel) X St
Elizabeth   605
Ascending King (Bourgeois)
[SMDRM,FMRRD,SSLTD,S]
AJ418   606
Ascending song (Walthall)
[MMMMFSSS,SLTDRDT,T]
I520   607
Ascendit (Morice) [SDSMRDRF
M,SDTDFLS,] X676   608
Ascendit Deus (Schicht) [SLT
DTDRM,MSFMDFMR,] J156b;
R212; S172; W132; BY177a
                          609
Ascension (Bancroft) [SFMDR
MRDRS,LTDRMF] AK94
                          610
Ascension (Gauntlett) X As-
cension tide   611
Ascension (Monk) [MSDDRFM,
MSDRD,MSDDR] A104a;
D128a; F147a; J111; S171;
AD169; AH306; AK175; AL
104; BR192; BV203; BY167a
                          612
Ascension, No. 1 (Monk) X
Ascension   613
Ascension, No. 2 (Gauntlett)

X Ascension tide   614
Ascension tide (Gauntlett) [SM
MRDS, SFFMRM, MRMR] O
368; AB233; BR200   615
-----. V [MMMRDS, SFFMRM,
MRMR] AB233   616
Ascham (Carter) X Slingsby
                           617
Ascription (Emerson) [SSMD
LSMS, SDDMDR, RM] T103;
AJ149   618
Ase's death (Grieg) X Asa's
death   619
Ash grove (English trad) X
A virgin unspotted   620
Ashbourne Road (Morgan) [DRR
DDFMRM, SF#SLTMS] BY246
                           621
Ashburn (Hildebrand) [LLLTD
TL, LTDMRDT, DT] AY341
                           622
Ashburton (Jackson) [MMMRM
FFF, FFFMRSSS,] BR256 623
Ashburton (Wesley, S.S.) [MM
FMRLLS#, LSFMLTDT] W392
                           624
Ashford (Thiman) [MRDRTDTLT,
S#LTDRDS,] BV636; BY741b
                           625
Ashland (Smith) [MMSFMDRMS
FM, MMRMR] AC105   626
Ashray yod'ay (Jewish trad)
[SDDRMSMDMR, MSSLSM] BH
315   627
Ashville (Everett) [SSSSSDRM,
LLLDLS, SS] AS450   628
Ashwell (Mason) [MMMMMFMR,
SF#SMLSF#S,] L61; T259;
AJ361   629
Askenazi tune (Lyra Anglo-
Judaica) [LLLDTLTM, LLLD
TLS#, S#] BH214   630
Asleep in Jesus (Bradbury) X
Rest   631
Asleep in Jesus (Bull) [MMLSS
FMRDLT, MMLSS] P421   632
Asleep in Jesus (Wolle) [MMR#
MFMMRD, DLSFSMR#] BA936
                           633
Aspinwall (Gabriel) [SDDDDSMRD
S, SRRRRD] T198; AJ287 634
Aspiration (Barnby) X St Syl-
vester   635

Aspiration (German trad)
X Mendon   636
Aspiration (Mendelssohn) [M
MRDFMRDTDMR, RRRM]
D661a; F463   637
-----. V [MRDSFMRDTDMR,
RRMF] F463 V Brightest
and best G40   638
Aspiration (Thompson) [SMS
DRM, SLSMDR, RSF#L] AZ
341-C   639
Aspurg (Frech) X Wittenberg
                           640
Assisi (Smith) [DDDRDTTL,
LDRMMR] A307   641
Assiut (Stebbins) [DMMFSDR
DT, DRRMFSL] T104b; AJ
150   642
Assurance (Knapp) [MRDSSFS
LS, SMSDTTL] G238; H298;
I548; R139; V731; Z412; AE
208; AG216; AH209; AR436;
AS285; AT269; AU120; AV
359; AW480; AX477; AY207;
BB608; BY493; BZ   643
-----. R [SSSDSLLLS, SSS
LDTT]   644
Aston (Heywood) [DTLLS#S,
SSMRTD, DTLS] BR352
                           645
Astra matutina (Thorne) [MM
FSFMLSFM, SSLTLS] D170b
                           646
At Calvary (Towner) X Cal-
vary   647
At midnight, so the sages tell
(Handel) X Christmas 648
At sunset (Boe) [SDMRDFLS,
STDRRMFM,] P68   649
At the cross (Hudson) [DMR
DMSFM, SLSFMR, RM] U97;
AE289; AI74a; AS142; AT94;
AU112; AX311   650
-----. R [DRMMMM, FMM
RRDR, RMF]   651
At the golden gate of prayer
(Showalter) [MRDMLDSD,
RMRTDRM, M] AX351; AY
52   652
-----. R [DRMDLS, DDRRDR
M, DRM]   653
At the Lamb's high feast
(Hintze) X Salzburg 654

At the Saviour's right hand
(Holsinger) [DRMR#MDRMFM
FR,MFSL] AX292; AY152
655
-----. R [SDTLSMSFMR,MSDT
LS,] 656
At thy feet (Smart) X Bethany
657
Athanasius (Hopkins) X St
Athanasius 658
Athens (Giardini) [DSFMRDRD,
SLTDSFFM,] M87; N276 659
Athens (Greek mel) X Luke 660
Athens (Piae Cantiones) [MMR
MDTL, LDRMSMM, MM] BG
151 661
Athlone (Quaile) [SSFFMSSDD
RDDT,TDT] S446; W659 662
Athol (Harrison) X Cambridge
663
Atkey (Dyson) [MMSDDRFM,
DLFSLSMR,] BE157 664
Atonement (---) [DRMFSSLRDT
LS,DTDR] AY253 665
Attende (Plainsong M 5) [DMSSS
DTSLS,DSRFSM] E736; F586;
BM73; BN29; BQ279 666
Attende, Domini (Plainsong. M 5)
X Attende 667
Attercliffe (Mather) X Medfield
668
Attolle paulum (Plainsong. 1539)
X To God on high 669
Attwood (Attwood) [SSDTLSMD
RM,MRSLT] A371; B198b;
D289a; E156; J124a; W184; X
181; BY226b 670
Au clair de la lune (French trad)
[DDDRMR,DMRRD,DDDRM]
BV352 671
Au fort de ma détresse (Gene-
van Psalter) [MLTDTLS,DL
TDRM,MRM] E252; X244 672
Auburndale (Parker) [SDDDTT,
DRRRSM,MMM] B458; C458;
D294a 673
Auch jetzt macht Gott (Koch.
Choralbuch. 1816) [SLSFMFMRD,
RMF#SSF#S,] E550; AR213;
BE74 674
Auchincairn (Scott) [SMLSMFF
RSFM,SLDSD] AP157c 675
Auctor omnium bonorum (König)

X Evangelists 676
Auctor vitae (Davies) [DMS
SLL,MRMFMM,DMSS] W
317 677
Auctoritate saeculi (Poitiers
Antiphoner, 1746) [MLDTLT
LSL, LDRMDRR] E176b; F
387a; J155a; X67; AN218
678
Audi, benigni conditor (Plain-
song, M 2) [RDRFMFRM
MRDRR, FMF] E66; F84a;
BN27 679
Audi, benigni conditor (Plain-
song, M 3) [LSLDTLSL,D
RDTLSLL,] BM77 680
Audite audientes me (Sullivan)
[MMMRMFFM,MLMDTL,
MM] D673b; T155; AJ226;
BB319; BR277; BX230 681
Audley (The Hallelujah, 1849)
X Malvern 682
Auf, auf, mein herz (Crueger)
[SMSFMRD,SLTDTLT, LS]
Q192; AA218 683
Auf, auf, weil der tag erschien-
en (Fabricius) X Gregor's
133rd metre - B 684
Auf, auf, weil der tag erschien-
en (Filitz) X Mannheim
685
Auf meinen lieben Gott (Regnart)
X Gottingen 686
Auf, seele, sei geruest't
(Darmstadt G-B) X Darm-
stadt 687
Aughton (Bradbury) [SMRDS
LFF, LSMMRDM] A426; B
245; C245; D616a; G242; H
130; I489; J478; L544; N497;
P328; R338; S106; U46; V
346; Z405; AD222; AE292;
AF370; AG53; AH405; AI301;
AK466; AL483; AM500; AN
565; AO632; AP519; AR442;
AS251; AT58; AU422; AV59;
AW478; AX495; BA686; BB393;
BD120; BE95; BF415; BI6-D;
BZ 688
-----. R [SSDTRDTLS, LSM
MRD] 689
Augsburg (Ahle) [DRRM,SDD
RRM,RMSSF#S,] M370;

AW560   690

Augsburg (Neumark) X Neumark
691

Augusta (Bohemian Br.) [MS
SFMRDSLMSFM, SLT] AZ
69-A; BA334   692

Augustana (Norrbom) [MMMSTD
FMR, FFFMSSF#] M575; N
564   693

Augustine (Abelard) X Gildas
694

Auld lang syne (Shield) [SDDD
MRDR, MDDMSL, LS] G521;
T144; AJ212b; AY409   695

Aurelia (Wesley) [MMMFMMR,
DDLSFM, FSD] A396; B464;
C464; D491; E489; F255; G
324; H70; I207; J149; K42;
L203; M78; N16; O61; P44;
Q473; R437; S333; T121; U
191; V531; W205; X249b; Y347;
Z423; AA466; AB321; AC308;
AD391; AF260; AG228; AH497;
AI144; AJ176; AK322; AL35;
AM224; AN130; AO240; AP
295; AR66; AS39; AT210; AU
406; AV153; AW273; AX631;
AZ151-L; BA260; BB279; BD
244; BE75; BF584; BK130;
BL96; BR223; BV425; BX15;
BY263; BZ   696

Aurora (Benson) [SLTDMSFM,
MMRDMRD, S] BY422   697

Aurora lucis rutilat Pt I (Sarum
Antiphonal M 8) [SSLTDTLS,
DDDTSLDD] E123I; J94b;
X148   698

Aurora lucis rutilat Pt II (Plainsong. M 4) [FFFMRMSLFM,
SLSLDD] E123II   699

Aus dem himmel ferne (Gesangbuch mit noten) [DDMMSM, FFM
RMR, RMFM] AW421   700

Aus der tiefe (Herbst) X Heinlein   701

Aus gnaden soll ich (Knecht) X
Salvation by grace   702

Aus meines herzens grunde (Wolder. Catholic G-B. 1598).
X Wolder   703

Aus tiefer not (Bierman) [MS
FMRDTD, SDTLSFMF] AW532
704

Aus tiefer not (Teutsch. Kirchenampt. 1525) [DTDRRDRM,
FMRDTDRD,] J372; K317;
L391; M384; O380; P225; Q
312; AA383; AK210; AW531
705

-----. V [DTDRRDRM, FMRD
DRD, D] L391]   706

Aus tiefer not [noth] schrei
ich zu dir (Walther) X De
profundis   707

Austin (Bristol tune book. 1876)
X St Austin   708

Austin (Sewall) [MMLDTL, LSL
FFFM, MMS] BR330   709

Austria (Haydn) [DRMRFMRTD,
LSFMRMD] A385; B468; C
468; D299b; E393; F368; G
382; H193; I210; J152b; K
197b; L588; O12; P21; R434;
S339; T179; U352; V529; W
206; X500; Y61; Z431; AB
248; AC264; AD348; AE137;
AF267; AG231; AH518; AI
145; AJ261; AK323; AL31;
AM269; AN75; AO360; AP133;
AQ248; AR495; AS192; AT176;
AV127; AW274; BA276; BB
304; BD183; BE71; BF519;
BI29; BK50; BR72; BV29; BX
416; BY24a; BZ   710

Austrian hymn (Haydn) X
Austria   711

Author of faith, Eternal Word
(Careless) [SLTRDMFSFM,
SDMLRF] BC228   712

Author of life (Powell) [LLTDR
M, SFMRRM, SMSL] BZ 713

Author of life (Stainer) [DRM
FLS, MMRLTDT, RM F] F394b;
BV361a   714

Autumn (Barthélémon) [DRM
RDLSM, DRMRMSR,] B42b;
C42b; D414b; G166; H101; I
171; L196; M366; N129; R10;
S292; T194; U113; V197; Z
160; AA335; AB110; AD323;
AE60; AG42; AH318; AI139;
AJ280; ALSuppl.; AM566; AN
23b; AO326; AP388; AR192;
AT4; AV50; AW2; BA565;
BB268; BF238; BR143; BX

118b; BZ   715
Autumn, No. 2 (Iliffe) [MMFS
   LSRM, SSRMF#S, SD] BR480b
                                  716
Avalon (Doane arr) [SDSLSSM,
   SLSDMS, SDS] AJ78   717
Avanti (Loy) [SSLDRSDDTLS,
   SLTDR] BD146   718
Ave (Hoffman) [DSMRDTTL, R
   LFMRDDT,] M202   719
Ave Maria (Arcadelt) X Arca-
   delt   720
Ave Maria (Bottazzo) [SDSSSDLTR
   DT, TF#MMD] BQ313   721
Ave Maria (Franck) [MSFRT, D
   MMRDT, MDRML] BQ200c 722
Ave Maria (Plainsong. M 1)
   [DSLLMFM, MRDRMM, MRD]
   BN123; BP72; BQ200a   723
Ave Maria klare (Psalteriolum
   harmonicum) [DTSLTDD, MRT
   DLS, SSS] X223   724
Ave Maria! O maiden, O mother
   (Slovak hymnal) [SSSFMMDDT
   TL, FFFMR] BQ74   725
-----. R [RMMFFFMRMFMR,
   MFFS]   726
Ave Maria! Thou Virgin and
   mother (Tozer) [SLSDTLSMF
   SMR, DRDS] BP77   727
Ave Maris stella (Balthasar)
   [MRDMMSFM, RMDMSLS, M]
   BQ201b   728
Ave, Maris stella (Est) X
   Winchester old   729
Ave, Maris stella (Ett) X St
   Martin   730
Ave Maris stella (Grieg) [MRD
   RMSS, MRDRMSS, S#F#] BQ
   201d   731
Ave, Maris stella (Italian mel)
   [SSSSFMFSM, RLSSF#S, D]
   BO264   732
Ave Maris stella (Mohr) [MMSD
   RM, RMFFMR, DDLR] BQ201c
                                  733
Ave, Maris stella (Plainsong M 1)
   [RLLTSLTRDTLSL, LLR] E213;
   BN127; BQ201a   734
-----. V [RLTSLTRDTLSL, LLR
   M] BN127   735
Ave Maris stella (St Peter Dami-
   an) [DDRRMRR, FFMRDTD,

MR] BQ314   736
Ave, Maris stella (Arundel
   hymns) [DDRMRD, MRMFS
   LS, SSL] E213b; O140; AL
   186b; AP288b   737
Ave radix (Sens processional)
   [DSMFSLS, DLTDTLS, MF]
   F213a   738
Ave, Regina (---) [SFMRDTD,
   DLTDTLSFM,] BO299 739
Ave, Regina caelorum (Plain-
   song. M 6) [DTLSLDRD, M
   SFRMRDM] BN141; BQ278
                                  740
-----. V [FMRDRFSF, LDL#
   SLSFL] BQ278   741
Ave, Regina coelorum (Mon-
   tani) [SSSL#L#LSFSS, DSM
   SFM] BQ203   742
Ave, tu Rex pacis (Bragers)
   [MRDRDLDDRD, DTLTLS]
   BP107   743
Ave verum (Rouen mel. M 6)
   [DRMDRRDFMRMM, RDTD]
   E311; F407a; BN85; BP50;
   BQ233e   744
-----. V [DRMDRDFMRM,
   RDTDRM] F407a   745
Ave verum corpus (Gounod)
   [MTRDTLSLLSFM, DDTR]
   BQ233a   746
Ave verum corpus (Guilmant)
   [SF#LSDTDRFFM, DLRDT]
   BQ233d   747
Ave, verum corpus (Mozart)
   [SDMSF#F, FLSFFMM, RR
   M] BO36; BQ233c   748
Ave verum corpus (Saint Saëns)
   [DRMFMMRDRD, MFSLSS]
   BQ233b   749
Ave virgo (Horne) X Gaudeamus
   pariter   750
Ave virgo virginum (Horne)
   X Gaudeamus pariter 751
Ave virgo virginum (Leisen-
   tritt. G-B. 1584) [DDSSDR
   M, LSFMRD, DDS] E131; X
   144; AF186; BN94; BQ136;
   BY155   752
-----. V [DDSSDRMM, LSFM
   RRD, D] BQ136   752a
Ave vivens Hostia (Leisentritt
   G-B. 1584) X Ave virgo

virginum   752b

Aviemore (Hickman) [SDMMRD,
DMSSFM, RRF#S,] R117; T
159   753

Avis (Hartmann) [DDDMRDTRD,
DLDLDSF] M636   754

Avison (Avison) [SLSLSDRMF
MRMFS, LSL] A15; B75; C75;
D53; I119; L349; V120; AV97;
BA145; BI100   755

-----. V [SLSLSDRMFS, SSLS
LS] BI100   756

Avon (Wilson) X Martyrdom
                            757

Avondale (Booth) [SMRFMRDTL
S, SSDTDL] V393   758

Avondale (Gabriel) [MMDFMMR
D, DDDFDM, MS] T191; AI
209; AJ278; AM85   759

Avondale (Shepherd) [DRMSLD
TD, SDTLSDMD] BY82   760

Awake, arise (Nicolai) X
Sleepers, wake   761

Awake, my soul (Handel) X
Christmas   762

Awake, my soul, in joyful lays
(Caldwell) X Loving kindness
                            763

Awake, O earth (Showalter)
[SDRMRD, SLDTLS, SLTD]
AX120; AY347   764

-----. R [MFFM, MRLTDR,
SDRMFS,]   765

Awake! O ye people (Mitton)
[SSDMFMMRMFSFM, DDT]
BC183   766

Awake, put on thy strength
(McKinney) [SDDMMSFMRDFM
RD, SL] AU473   767

Awake, ye saints of God
(Stephens) [SDSLRDTTD, SF#
SLDTT] BC229   768

Away in a manger (American, 19th
c) X Müller   769

Away in a manger (Spilman)
[SDDMRDDSLDLS, SDDR] AS
107; AY482   770

Axson (Campbell) [MSDTLSFM,
RDMLSFMR] V664   771

Ayl nora aleelah (Jewish trad)
[MMRDRSM, MMRDRSM, MM]
BH176   772

Aylesbury (Camp) [SMRDTLS, SD

DDRMR, FM] T69; AJ105;
AM48   773

Aylesbury (Chetham. Psalms.)
[LMRDTL, MSFMRM, DTLM]
F236; R118; W194b; X120a;
AL148a; AZ582-A; BA202; BV
491; BY187b   774

Ayn kay-lo-hay-nu (Freudenthal)
X En kelohenu   775

Ayn kay-lo-hay-nu (Lewandowski) [DSDMRD, SMSFMR, DL
DM] BH275   776

Ayn komocho (Binder) [MML
LLLLLLS#LDT, MMM] BH
304   777

Aynhoe (Nares) [DTLSLTD,
TRTDTLS, SD] O489; Q450;
V364; BB32; BE16   778

-----. V [DDLSTD, RRTDLS,
SDRM] Q450   779

-----. V [DDTLSLTD, TRTDT
LS, S] BB32   780

Ayrshire (Finlay) [SSMSLSLD
D, RMRRDLS,] BZ   781

Aysgarth (Cobb) [DDDRMFS
L, TDRSSFR, R] D318c   782

Az yasheer (Jewish trad)
[DRMRMFM, RMFSMFR,
RR] BH62, 121   783

Azmon (Gläzer) [SDDRRMRD,
RMMFMR, SS] G162; H300b;
I1; J428b; L125; O386; P18;
Q281; R141; S179; T219; U
68; V162; Z262; AA47; AD
182; AE8; AF223; AG107;
AH374; AI13; AJ312; AL
352b; AM133; AO282; AP
804; AR114; AS113; AT117;
AU5; AV117; AW12; AX360;
AY41; BA115; BB438; BE
320; BZ   784

Azmon new (Gläzer) X Azmon
                            785

                B

Babylon's streams (Campian)
[LDRMMRDT, TDRMMRRD,]
A60; E487; F228; L378; W
366; X124; AN184; AP247;
AZ22-M; BE353; BJ36 786

Baca (Bradbury) [MMMMDDDR,
RRMFFMRM,] L367; M193;
T76; AI268; AJ114; AM549b;
AO287; AX44; AY2   787
Baca (Havergal) X Haver   788
Badea (German mel) [SSMDR
M,SFMRRD,SSLF] L134; T44b;
AJ146; AZ582-T; BA621; BB
470; BR82   789
Baden (Gastorius) X Was Gott
tut   790
Baginton (Gooch) [DMRDLSFM,
MRDRMR,DT] W246b   791
Bairn (Danish folk mel) [DDR
MRDSSS,RRMFRSF] BE318
792
Baker Chapel (Sampaix) [SSFM
MMMRD,SLTDFMR,] H375
793
Bala Cynwyd (Barnes) [DDDRM
FMRM,MMMF#SLS] AD439
794
Balcom (Aylward) [DMSSFMRD,
RMF#STTLS] O412   795
Baldwin (Silcher) X Lorelei 796
Balerma (Barthélémon) X Bal-
lerma   797
Balfern (---) [SF#SLSSM,RD#RF
LLS,DT] M392   798
Balfour (Knowles) [DSSDMRLS,
SRMFRD,] A312b; E186; X
620   799
Ballards Lane (Hawkins) [LTDT
LLS#LT,DRDT,LTL] BV45
800
Balle (Balle) X Emmanuel   801
Ballerma (Barthélémon) [DMR
DLSLD,DMRMSMMR,] A127;
E199; H120; I242; J289; L164;
R386; S226; T126a; U367; V293;
W313b; X207; AD217; AE275;
AJ186; AL180; AM77b; AN224a;
AO90; AP36; AR374; AS214;
AT169; AU208; AV147; AX177;
AW57; AY255; BB221; BE126;
BR288; BV420; BZ   802
-----. V [DMRDLSLD, RMRMSM
R,R] AS214   803
Balm in Gilead (Negro spiritual)
[MRMRDSDRM,DMMFMRF,]
BZ   804
-----. R [DMDMMFS, FMMSMR,
DMD   805

Baltimore (Schumacher) [SS
DTLTDS,DRMDFMR,S] Q
481   806
Balty (Thommen's Christen-
schatz.) X Batty   807
Balulalow (Warlock) [DRMFLS
FM,SLDTTLLS,] BG181
808
Bamberg (--- 17th c) [SMFS
DSLTDT,SLTDTL] X6 809
Bamberg (Meiningen G-B.) X
St Leonard   810
Bangor (Tans'ur) [MDTLMLS
FM,MMSF#MR#M,] A68;
B102; E300; F345; W313a;
X259; AF149; AL660b; AN
51; AP68b; BE348; BV1; BY
139a   811
-----. V [MDTLMLSFM,MM
F#SF#MR#] BY139a   812
Bankfield (Harrison) [DMSD
RTD,MRSTLS,SSF] D27b;
H54; V63   813
-----. V [DMSDRTD,MRSS
F#S,SSF] H54   813a
Banner (Lissant) [SDMSMMRD
RM,FMRSDM] D253a   814
Baptism (Lutkin) [MMMLSTDR,
SMDDLLTS] I231   815
Baptiste (Calkin) X Welcome,
happy morning   816
Baptize us anew (Ogden) [MR
DDD,SLDDD,LSDRMM] BB
525   817
-----. R [MFFFLDRMMMM,
MFSMD]   818
Baptized into our Saviour's
death (Havergal) X Evan
819
Baptizien (German trad) [RF
SLSDTL,SDTLSFMR,] M42
820
Barby (Tans'ur) [DMMRMRDT
D,MSFMRDM] V223; AL
349a; AM585; AO220; AP15;
AW578   821
-----. V [DMMRMDTD,MS
FMDMR,S] AM585   822
Barmouth (Macfarren) [DRMM
MFS,LTDTLTS,SS] J203b;
W265   823
Barnabas (Goudimel) X
Gregor's 205th metre 824

Barnard (Barnard) **X** Give of
   your best   825
Barnby I (Barnby) [DDTLTS,
   SDTDR, RMF#LS] D50   826
Barnby II (Barnby) [DRMFLSFM,
   SLTDLS, SL] I87; AZ14-Ee;
   BA656   827
Barnby III (Barnby) [LLDTLS#T
   L, DDMRDTTD,] V155; BR178
                                             828
Barnby (Barnby) **X** Just as I am
                                             829
Barnby (Barnby) **X** Merrial 830
Barnby (Barnby) **X** St Andrew
                                             831
Barnby (Barnby) **X** Sarum 832
Barnby (Barnby) **X** Stand up
                                             833
Barnby's Hymnary, Tune 53
   (Stainer) **X** Laus matutina
                                             834
Barnby's hymnary, Tune 59
   (Stainer) **X** Lux prima   835
Barnby's hymnary, Tune 91
   (Barnby) **X** Kirkdale   836
Barnby's hymnary, Tune 101
   (Barnby) [SSSDDDRMRD, MMM
   RTS] AZ298-C   837
Barnby's hymnary, Tune 140
   (Smart) [SMLSLTDS, MFSDTL
   RT,] AZ95-D   838
Barnby's hymnary, Tune 148
   (Gounod) **X** Lux prima   839
Barnby's hymnary, Tune 154
   (Goss) **X** St Casimer   840
Barnby's hymnary, Tune 222
   (Sullivan) **X** Lacrymae   841
Barnby's hymnary, Tune 224
   (Langran) **X** Langran   842
Barnby's hymnary, Tune 225
   (Sullivan) **X** Lux mundi   843
Barnby's hymnary, Tune 237
   (Barnby) **X** St Andrew   844
Barnby's hymnary, Tune 285
   (Sullivan) **X** St Kevin   845
Barnby's hymnary, Tune 291
   (Smart) [MMRMFLLS, DSMFS
   DMR,] AZ95-E   846
Barnby's hymnary, Tune 474
   (Smart) **X** Sion   847
Barnby's hymnary, Tune 475
   (Smart) [SSSLSS, LTMD, DD
   TLS] AZ141-K   848

Barnby's hymnary, Tune 525
   (Winn) [SLTDRM, SFMRDT,
   TDRM] K332; N293   849
Barnby's hymnary, Tune 590
   (Barnby) **X** Edinburgh 850
Barnby's hymnary, Tune 633
   (Barnby) **X** Nightfall 851
Barnekow I (Barnekow) [MM
   SLSMMS, DDDFMMR, R] J
   210   852
Barnekow II (Barnekow) [MS
   FMDRMD, RMFLSDMR,]
   M134   853
Barnekow III (Barnekow) [MM
   MSFMRMD, DLSFMRD]
   M179   854
Barnet (Jesson) [SDRMSL, SM
   DRMS, SLMM] F223a 855
Barnett (Campbell) [MMRLTD
   RD, DDRMFFFM,] V708
                                            856
Barony (Sullivan) **X** Courage,
   brother   857
Barre (Clark) [MMFSDTLL,
   LSDTLS, FM] T201; AJ290
                                            858
Bartholdy (Mendelssohn) **X**
   Selwyn   859
Bartimaeus (Pilsbury. U. S.
   Sacred harm. 1799) V308;
   AQ44; BZ   860
-----. V [DRMRMSMRD,
   SLTDLSM] BZ   860a
Bartley (Hastings) [MMMRDD
   D, DRRMMR, MMM] L327
                                            861
Barton (---) [SSSDSLSS, DRM
   FMRM, S] I205; AL153b;
   BY239   862
Barton (Knecht) **X** Knecht
                                            863
Bassett (Stair) [SDTDLSRM,
   DLDFMRM, D] Y86; AC169
                                            864
Bath (Cooke) [MMMRFM, MM
   MFRM, MMMF#] I587 865
Bath (Sewall) [MDRMRMSFM
   RD, MMF#SF#] BR41 866
Battell Chapel (Jepson) [SDS
   LTDRSM, MMMF#S#LTD,]
   Y151; BF636   867
Battenberg (Henry, Prince of
   Battenberg) [DDMMMRD,

DDFFLLS,SR] AO430   868
Battishill (Battishill) [SMRDRRM,
   FMLSFMR,SM] W668; X538;
   BY754   869
Battle (Lawes) [DDTLTS#TDR
   M,MRMDRT] E432; X290; AN
   95   870
Battle cry (Gray) [LLLDDTL,
   DSLSFM,SDD] F497   871
Battle cry (Sherwin) [SSMFSLF
   MRD,RMRTSL] AH454; AI326;
   AM686; BB499; BY525   872
-----. R [MDMDRD#RFMD,MT
   DLRD]   873
Battle hymn (Steffe) [SSSSFMSDR
   MMMRD,D] B434; C434; J356;
   Y289; AC280; AF443; AH485;
   AN566; AO600; AT488; AV301;
   BD170; BX410; BZ   874
-----. R [SFMSDRMD,LTDTDLS]
                                                875
Battle hymn of the Republic
   (Steffe) X Battle hymn   876
Battle hymn (---) X When the
   battle's over   877
Battle song (Shaw) [MLSLTDRMS
   TLLSL,MS] W155b; X578; Y
   155   878
Batty (Thommen's Christen-
   Schatz) [DRMRMFSM,LSFM
   RRMS] A72; B100; C157; D
   104; E105; F124a; J63b; K61;
   L560; M14; N109; O146; P318;
   Q155; AA449; AF332; AK216;
   AL99; AN85; AP115; AW147;
   AZ16-A; BA263; BN93   879
-----. V [DRMDRMFSM,LSSM
   FFM,] AW147   880
-----. V [DRMRMSFM,LSFMR
   RM,S] BN93   881
Bavaria (Gale) [MMMRSFM,LR
   MFM,RRSL] D518a   882
Bavaria (Thommen's Christen-
   Schatz) X Cassel   883
Baxter (Burnap) [DMRFMLS,
   DTLSFM,MMM] V430; AO451;
   BA888; BF406   884
Bayeaux (Huet) X Diva servatrix
                                                885
Baynard (Booth) [SSLSSDRM,M
   MRDLSFM,] D622b   886
Be not afraid (Temple Star) [SM
   MRMFM,RDDRRM,SMM] AX

530; AY386   887
-----. R [DRMMMS,FMRRR
   MF,MRD]   888
Be not dismayed (German trad
   15th c) X Kommt her zu
   mir   889
Be present at our table, Lord
   (Mason) X Rockingham   890
Be ready when He comes
   (Teasley) [DRMMMFMRD,
   DRRDRM,D] AX285   891
Be silent (Doane) [SSMDDS,
   MSSSS,SLDDD] AR437; AS
   43; AU485; AX39; AY448;
   BB601   892
Be strong (Eaton) [SD,MRD
   TLSSF#LS,STMR] AB176b
                                                893
Be strong, O men (Fillmore)
   [SLTDDDTDRM,LTD#RRR]
   U269; Y185   894
Be thou exalted (Geistliche
   lieder. 1535) X Wo Gott
   zum haus   895
Be thou faithful (Hughes) [MS
   DSDRM,DRMFMRDMR] BY
   305c   896
Be thou faithful (Mendelssohn)
   X Almighty Father, hear
                                                897
Be Thou King (Sisters of St
   Joseph, Toronto) [DDMM
   SSS,RRFFLLL,SM] BO214
                                                898
-----. R [SLSFMRD,FMRDT
   LS,SD]   899
Be Thou our guide (Holsinger)
   [SDMDLSDMRFM,MMFML]
   AR65   900
-----. R [TDRRDRMMMMF
   MR,MFS]   901
Be with me (Ackley) [SLTDRD
   TRSM,SLTDRD] U364   902
-----. R [MR#MFMMR,RD#
   RMRD,DTD]   903
Be ye doers of the word (Mc-
   Kinney) [SDMMR#MD,TDRM
   RDL,DL] AU326   904
-----. R [MFMRRRR,RMRD
   DDD,DT]   905
Be ye joyful (Bohemian trad)
   [DRMFSSS,FSLS,SSFFM]
   P129; Q86   906

-----.- V [DRMF#SLS, F#SLS, SSFFM] Q86 907

Be ye strong in the Lord (Sankey) [SSDDDTSSFFFFM, SSL] AX448; AY461 908

-----. R [SLSSLS, DDLSFMRD R, S] 909

Beachley (Cottman) [MRDSTLS, LSLDRR, MRD] AS333 910

Beacon Hill (Mason) [SSSMDTTL, FFFRTLS, S] G268; Y174; Z 360; AC205; AE443; AG189; AR311; AT351; AU396; AW392; BZ 911

-----. R [MMMMM, MFDRM, SLTDMR] 912

Bealoth. (Mason. Sacred harp. 1843) [MMMMRD, DRRRMRD, SMM] G183; I191; Z428; AI 146; AR490; AS191; AX149; AY 380; BZ 913

-----. V [SMMMRD, DRRRMRD, SMM] I191 914

Beata (Stotzel. Choralbuch. 1744) X O wie selig seid ihr doch 915

Beata nobis gaudia (Plainsong M 1) X Veni, Redemptor gentium 916

Beata nobis gaudia (Psalterium chorale. Constance) [SMDRM FMRDLTD, DMFS] E185; F391; X44b 917

Beati (Stainer) [MMRDSSFM, SDT LSRD] A128b; B198; C198; D 175a; F572; I459; K247; L320; O476; Q370; T439; W219b; AA 306; AO539; AP306; BA764; BB 247; BE427; BX40; BY460a 918

Beatitudo (Dykes) [DRMSMDFM, LTDMRR, R] A416b; B27; C35a; D391; F528; G419; H122; I79; J213; K87; L101; M253; N57; Q360; R249; S218; T192; U256; V66; W592b; Y103; Z334; AA 108; AB169; AC216; AD195; AE 36; AF350; AG130; AH357; AI 279; AJ195; AK319; AL179b; AM 259; AN236b; AO89; AP312; AR 61; AS65; AW42; AY416; BA2; BB18; BE284; BF368; BR445a;

BV297a; BX74; BY405 919

Beatrice (Coe) [MMSMRMF FM, DLSMRMF#] N335 920

Beatus (Dunhill) [SLTLSFM RM, FSMRMDT] E650 921

Beaufort (Wild) [MR#MFMMR D, SF#STLS, SS] D15b; AB 307 922

Beaumaris (Gauntlett) [SLSS TDDRML, LL#L#LD#R] BR 479 923

Beaumont (Strom) [SDDRRMD, FMDDTD, MRR] N382 924

Beauteous day (Root) [MRR DDTTL, FMMRDRM, M] H205; U391; V601; AI93 925

-----. Beauteous day (Root) R [SSLSMMSM, DDRRMSMR,] 926

Beautiful homeland (Holsinger) [SSLSSSMDMSRD, MFFFL] AY403 927

-----. R [SSSRRRMFM, MMM RRLT] 928

Beautiful land on high (Haven) [MFSF#SMRD, MFSF#SSF# S,] AY159 929

Beautiful river (Lowry) [MMM RMFSM, FFFSFMRS,] AH534; AI409; AP637; AT481; AU 434; AV394; AX597; BB555 930

-----. R [LLDTDLSM, MFMFM FMF] 931

Beautiful Sion, built above (Fones) [DDDDSDMRD, MMM MDMS] BC78 932

Beautiful Sion for me (Thomas) [SLSMFSL, TDRFMFLS, S] BC6 933

Beautiful star (Schilling) [SS SLTDRMFMR#M, D#MRL] AC93 934

-----. R [SLLSF#S, SRSDRM, MFDR] 935

Beautiful star of Bethlehem (Boyce) [SDRMSSSMD, MRD LDDL] AX95 936

Beautiful valley of Eden (Sherwin) X Kelley 937

Beauty of holiness (Lowry)

[SSMDSSSSMDMRRRMF] AR
432; AS4   938
-----. R [TDDTLSM, SSSFR,
LLLS]   939
Because you live again (French
trad) [LMRDLDRM, MLSFMR
MR] BN162; BY126   940
Bechler (Bechler) [SDDRRMFSF
MMRRD, SD] AZ159-D; BA
755   941
Beck (Beck) X Just as I am
                                        942
Beddome (Statham) X Thanksgiv-
ing   943
Bede (Handel) [DTDSFMRDTDRD
T, DTD] F75a; W676   944
Bedford (Bishop) X Leicester
                                        945
Bedford (Wheall) [SMDLSFMR,
SDTLLS, M] A116; B10; C321;
D221a; E83; F320; K404; Q284;
S75; W242; X114; AA117; AL73;
AP5; AZ14-C; BA132; BR87;
BY306   946
Beecher (Zundel) [SSLSMRMRD,
TLDLSF] A304; B240; C240;
G372; H190; I355b; J312; K
276b; L202; M116; N149; P38;
R399; S308a; T175; U21; V323;
Y356; Z379; AB193; AC67; AD
245; AE188; AF228; AG176; AH
223; AJ255; AK272; AL449; AM
368; AN50b; AO295b; AP562;
AR178; AS116; AT2; AU19; AV
183; AW165; AX43; AY516; BA
490; BB142; BD58; BE276; BF
256; BK52; BX532; BZ   947
Beechmont (Burrowes) [SSMDLD
SD, RMRDRMR, S] C81   948
Beechwood (Booth) [MRDRTSDDR
RM, MSMDT] W20; AC58
                                        949
Beecroft (Mallary) [MMMRSLTD
S, DTLLRDT,] H424   950
Beeding (Thiman) [MSDRMRD,
RFMLSF#S, RD] BV573b 951
Beeforth (Mann) [MMMFFLFM,
MLLDLS, SM] O395   952
Beethoven (Beethoven) [MMFSSF
M, RDDRMMRR, MM] B114b;
C114b; D512b; G12; I160; R
21; S5; U25; Y49; Z95; AB12;
AC43; AD9; AE10; AF8; AG

5; AH200; AK21; AN42; AO
79; AQ11; AR27; AS91; AT
44; AV52; AW10; BA33; BB
29; BE58; BF211; BH230;
BI34; BK109; BR188; BX63;
BZ   953
Beethoven (Mason arr) [MFS
LSFMR, MFSLDTLS,] AO
542   954
Befiehl du deine wege (German
trad) X Commit thy way
                                        955
Befiehl du deine wege (Ros-
tocker G-B) X Gregor's
151st metre-H   955
Before the Menorah (Binder)
[DSDSLTD, RRMDMF#S, RL]
BH206   957
Before Thee, Lord, I bow my
head (Dean) [SLTDMDLT,
STDRFMRM,] BC231   958
Begin the day with God (Read)
X Lisbon   959
Behold a branch (Geistliche K-
G. Cologne 1599) X Rosa
mystica   960
Behold a host (Norwegian trad)
[DMSSLSMDMSR, RMFRD]
J599; M313; N207; O492b;
P434; Q656; BE19   961
Behold, a rose (Geistliche K-
G. Cologne. 1599) X Rosa
mystica   962
Behold! a royal army (Geibel)
[SDTDRTS, SDTDRM, MRM]
BC7   963
-----. R [SSSSSS, SSMRDT
LS, SS]   964
Behold a simple, tender Babe
(Monaghan) [MLTDTLSLM,
MLLSFM, M] BN13   965
Behold! behold He cometh
(Webbe) [SMMMMMRR, RMR
DTD, LF] BQ3   966
Behold, I stand at the door
(Gabriel) [DMMMR#MFFM,
MMRDTRD,] AI273   967
Behold it is the springtime
of the year (---) [MSMDRM
FMLSLS, SDTL] BH129
                                        968
Behold me standing (Knapp)
[SSDTDRLR, DTDRD#RMD,]

BY410 969

-----. R [STDRD#RMDS, DM FSMRD] 970

Behold the great Redeemer die (Careless) [MMMLLSFM, S SSLDTLS,] BC230 971

Behold, the mountain of the Lord (Daynes) [SDMFSDRMMRD, DLSFM] BC297 972

Behold the Saviour of mankind (American trad) X Amazing grace 973

Behold the star (Negro spiritual) [MMSRD, FFLRDSL, MMSRD,] Y323; BK164 974

-----. R [DDDSLMMRD, MM RDLDR] 975

Behold thy sons and daughters (Schreiner) [SDDRRMRDR, RMSFMMR,] BC24 976

Behold what love (Teasley) [MS LSMMFM, MSLSMR, MS] AX 84 977

-----. R [SLLLLLS, MSLSMR, MSS] 978

Behold, where, in a mortal form (Arne) X Arlington 979

Belden (Belden) [SLSMRDRMRD, DTLSFM] AR309; AS318 980

Belfry praise (Matthews) [DTLSFM RD, DTLTLS, DL] F496 981

Belgrave (Horsley) [DMSDMFSLR, SFMF#SLT] E511; F479; J 440a; W26; X694; AN225; BY 567 982

-----. V [SMSDMFSLR, SMF# STLS] F479 983

-----. V [SMSDMFSLR, SFM F#SLT] X694 984

Belhaven (Pritchard) [DRRMMFF MRDS, SLTDS] W34; BE356 985

Belief (American trad) X Camp-meeting 986

Believe me if all those endear-ing (Irish trad) X Sweet story 987

Believe not those (Alman) [RR RMFM, DDDRMR, RRMF] BH 231 988

Bell carol (French trad) [MLT DRMRD, LTDT, MLTD] BG162 989

Belleville (Jones) [DMMFRD DL, LSRM, SLTR] C36a; U360; AC317; AP514b; BO 194 990

Belleville (Lutkin) [SSSSSLSS, SSMRDDTT,] I347 991

Bellwoods (Hopkirk) [DTLSML, SMRDRM, MF#S#] A525; BY187a 992

Belmont (Gardiner's Sacred mel. 1812) [SMRDTTLDS, SSFMMR] A328; B166; C27; D20; F189b; G28; H82; I36; L92; N81; P50; Q436; R104C; T73; U34; V69; W309; Z125; AA367; AB327; AE269; AG49; AI38; AJ109; AK395; AL269b; AM265; AN251b; AO47; AP 436; AR78; AS79; AV56; AW 197; BA4; BB295; BF359; BH202; BO8; BR269; BV342; BY339 993

Beloit (Reissiger) [SSLTDRM MFD#R, SSLTD] G470; I145; Z179; AC316; AI367; AJ377; AM46; AR543; AS416 994

Beloved (Lewis) [DDRMFSLS FMRRD, SDD] G346; I530; AR199; AW470; BB160; BC 195; BZ 995

-----. V [DDRMFSLFMRRD, SDDR] AW470 996

Belsize (Elliott) [MSDMRD, DMLDTL, MRRS] D187a; V 510; AA304 997

Belsize (Shaw) [MSFMLR, RFMRS, DDRMM] E415; X543 998

Belstead (Taylor) [MDRMSD, TLSDMR, SMSL] F315 999

Bemerton (Filitz) X Caswall 1000

Bemerton (Greatorex) [MRD TLSDD, DMRDFMRD] U136; V99; AO148; BR264 1001

Bemotzoay (Jewish trad) [LT DTDLMM, LTDTDRM, M] BH 173 1002

Ben Avon (Stebbins) [SSFM RDTD, SDTLSMDR] AJ269 1003

Ben Jonson's carol (Boughton) [LRDLSFSLR, LRDLSFS]

BG168   1004
Ben Rhydding (Reinagle) [DMFS
LTD, TLMSF#M, MFR] D69b;
I94; N423; V524; AA319; BA
73   1005
Beneath the cross (Sankey) [SS
SF#SDS, MSSFRM, SSS] Eap. 22
                              1006
Beneath thy shadow hiding (Ten-
ney) [DRMMMR#MSS, SDDRD
RM,] AY93   1007
-----. R [SSFMMRDMR, SSFMM
RD]   1008
Benedic anima mea (Goss) X
Lauda anima   1009
Benediction (---) [MMMSFMDRM
RD, MSLS, D] AP623   1010
Benediction (Barraclough) [MMM
MMMDRMSFM, FFFF] Sapp44
                              1011
Benediction (Brunk) [SSSSLSDRM,
MMRLT, SS] AY412   1012
Benediction (Froom) [MR#MFM
SSSS, RD#RMRDM] BB702
                              1013
Benediction (Hopkins) X Ellers
                              1014
Benediction (Ledington) [MMMM
MMRS, DFMRRR, MM] BB700
                              1015
Benediction (Lutkin) X The Lord
bless you   1016
Benediction (McKinney) X Bryson
City   1017
Benediction (Mann) X Orient
morning   1018
Benevento (Webbe) [DDDDMRD,
RRRRFMR, MM] E469; H522;
I574; L552; M108; U155; V272;
X256; AL246; AM613; AN140;
AW339; AZ205-M; BE72   1019
Benevolence (Greenwood) [DTDLS
DRD, TDRRR, R#RR#] BE309
                              1020
Benison (---) [MMRDMSFM, MF
FMRD#RM] BR191   1021
Benison (Hullah) [MRMRLSMS,
MRMRLSMS,] H131   1022
Benjamin (Chitty) [DMRRFFMM,
RMRRMR, SF] AZ590-G   1023
Benson (Kingham) [SSLDDTLS,
SLRDTD, MM] B483a; C483;
Eap63; F271; AP394; BV315a;

BY371   1024
Bentley (Hullah) [MRMFLLS,
DTSFLS, MM] B224; C381;
D437b; I454; J495a; L361;
R268; S284b; U45; V255a;
W439; Z581; AB201; AD231;
AG208; AH377; AL287; AM
520; AO332; AP445; BA401;
BE251; BF412; BY251   1025
Benton Harbor (Hoffman) X
Hoffman   1026
Bera (Gould) [MMRDSSRMFM,
DDLSMR] G196; H250; I
249; L523b; S225; T89; U
158; V276; AG143; AH326;
AI319; AJ104; AM525; AO
247; AR255; AS194; AV36;
AW141; BB330; BE99   1027
-----. V [MMRDSSRMFM,
MMRDSS] BE99   1028
Bereden (Swedish mel. 16th c)
X Messiah   1029
Bereden väg för herran (Swe-
dish mel. 16th c) X Mes-
siah   1030
Berggren I (Berggren) [SFMM
R, RLLSFFM, MRDD] J128;
M640; P297; BE209   1031
-----. V [SFMRRLLSFFM,
MRDDT] M640   1032
Berggren II (Berggren) [SST
DRMFFM, MFSRMFR] M69
                              1033
Berkshire (Stark) [MFLSSDM
MR, RMFLSFS] AR47; BH103
                              1034
Berkshire (Wesley, C., the
younger) [SDMLFMRDR, SDM
RSLT] BV240   1035
Berlin (Bourgeois) X Bourgeois
                              1036
Berlin (Crueger) X Ratisbon
                              1037
Berlin (Mendelssohn) X Bright-
est and best   1038
Bernard (---) [DDTDLLLS,
SLTDMR, SS] D537; L144
                              1039
Berne (Beery) [DMDMDSSM,
DRRRFM, DM] AI260; AS
298   1040
Berno (Mann) [SMRDDTLS,
FMFSLR, SM] J182a; W268;

Bevan (Goss) [DDRMFS, SSSFMR,
RMF] B463; D152; M172; O
357; Q220; W635; AM222
                                              1076
Beverly (Baermann) [DMSLTDLS,
DRMF#SLS, S] BX158   1077
Beverly (Monk) [SSDSFMRD, SF
MMRDS,] B67; C67a; D317a;
W157; AM235; AO113; AP245;
AW126; BB196; BV87   1078
Bewdley (Ouseley) [SSLRTDR, MS
RSLTS, LL] F295   1079
Beweley (Taylor) [LSMRDRM,
DTSLMFS, SL#] BV299; BY
481a   1080
Bexfield (--) [SMMSSFF, STRFM,
SMMS] AP575   1081
Beyond (Harrington) [SSS#LTD
RMF, MDRM, SSS#] I627   1082
-----. R [DDRMSFM, DDRMRD.]
                                              1083
Beyond the sunset (Perkins)
[DRMMMRMFLS, MRMFFM]
AU88   1084
-----. R [SLTDDTLS, MRMFFM
RM,]   1085
Bickersteth (Caldbeck) X Pax
tecum   1086
Bid them look to Christ (Perry)
[DDRMMFSLSM, DTDRMS]
AX219; AY224   1087
-----. R [SSF#SMRDMFM, SLS
MDM]   1088
Billesley (Mullinar) [DRFSLMRM
DS, MSRFMD] X497   1089
Billing (Terry) X Newman   1090
Bilsdale (Slater) [SDDFMRDTD,
RMDSLS, S] X361; BY115 1091
Binchester (Croft) [MRDTSFMR,
RMSSF#S, RR] E398; F261;
W440; X509; AD255; AL290;
AP442; BJ34; BV250b; BY496
                                              1092
Bingham (---) [SDDRMSLLTD,
MRTSDM] T3; AI34; AJ384a
                                              1093
Binghampton (Alexander) [MMMM
SMSM, MRRRMFM, M] Y400
                                              1094
Binghamton (Sumner) X The child
of a King   1095
Binney's (Thiman) [LMMMDFMRM,
RDTLTS#, S#] BV4a   1096

Binti hamari (India mel)
[LTRRTRMFM, MLSLM, DD]
BZ   1097
Binyon (Sanders) [LLLTLTDM
MRDT, DDRM] AQ153   1098
Birchington (Butcher) [DRMF
SLTD, RMDLDT, LS] C346b
                                              1099
Birds are singing (Hymns for
children) [SF#SMMR#MD,
RMRTDRM, S] AL587; AP
723; AW409   1100
-----. R [FRTSDMSM, FFF
MMMRD]   1101
Birdstown (Gabriel) [SDDDRM
DL, RDDTTDD, S] AJ302
                                              1102
Birkdale (Barnby) X Diadema
                                              1103
Birkdale (Hiles) [MRDMFLDD,
DTLL, SFMF] O547   1104
Birling (---) [MRDDTLSFMR,
MRDMRD] C20b; E274;
X55; BE91; BV245; BY521
                                              1105
Birmingham (Cunningham's
Selection of Psalm tunes)
[DMDSMLSLTD, SLSFMR]
A531a; E429; X266; AD430;
AR513; AW307; BY626 1106
Birmingham (Mendelssohn)
[DDRMLLSFM, MSSFRD, D]
AR626; AU478; BB692; BC
235   1107
Birthday (Shaw) [SLSLTDM
LSRMD, SLSL] X386c   1108
Bis willkommen (Kittel) [DM
SDTDRR, DMRTLLS, D]
Q576; AA186   1109
-----. V [DMFSDTDRR, DM
RDTLLS] AA186   1110
Bishop (Bishop) X Illsley
                                              1111
Bishop (Holbrook) [MMMSMDR
M, MMMRDLRR,] T229; AJ
325; AM451   1112
Bishopgarth (Sullivan) [SMMM
MFMR, RSLMRDRD] J445;
K334a; R375; T266; U199;
W370; AB244; AF355; AJ
371; AK433; AM377; AP384;
BF373; BY302   1113
Bishopthorpe (Clarke) [SFMR

DTLFMDTD, RMFS] A360a;
B351; E408; F208; J476a; W
137; X536; AB303; AF274;
AL664; AN132; AP78; BE142;
BJ5; BV517; BY121   1114
-----. V [SMRDTLFMDTD, RM
FSS] BJ5a   1115
Bishopthorpe (Parry) [MSDMFS
LR, FMRLDRT, S] D41b   1116
Bist willkommen, liebster freund
(Grimm. Choral buch) X
Tabor   1117
Bithynia (Essay on the church
plain chant) X Dulce carmen
                            1118
Blackbourne (Harrison. Sacred
harmony) [LMRDRDTL, LLTD
RM, SD] E456; W531a; X575
                            1119
Blackburn (Aitken) [MRDFMMRD
RM, SFMMRR] L523a; T18; AJ
23a; BB82   1120
Blackie (Ouseley) [SSLL, TTDS,
MMRSDRT, T] K280   1121
Blaencefn (Thomas) [DMRDSLTD
RMR, DMLTD] W387b; X222
                            1122
Blaenhafren (Welsh trad) [LLSF
MDTLTLS#, LLS#LT] R356;
S374; Z494; AF427; AM539
                            1123
Blaenwern (Rowlands) [SSLLS
DMMR, DTLSSTL] BV612; BY
595b   1124
Blairgowrie (Dykes) [MRMFLSM,
MSMDRM, MRM] D240c; G266;
H263; I219; R454; S485; T290;
U169; V302; Z362; AB42; AD
325; AH211; AI109; AJ402; AO
497; AR148; AS420; AT502; AY
443; BA844; BF516; BZ   1125
Blairgowrie (Thompson) [MS
FMSMRD, RMSDLSFM,] G158;
BY181   1126
Blake's cradle song (Williams)
[MSRMD, MRMSLSMS, TTL]
BG196   1127
Blencathra (Somervell) [SLDRMF
R, MDLSFS, SLDR] A546; X394
                            1128
-----. R [SLSDTLS, DLTDFR,
MD]   1129
Blenden (Kettle) [MFMRLTTD, M

MMMFR, MF] AB211; BR393
a   1130
Blendon (Giardini) [DMFSSDT
LS, SLDLSFM] L70; AA281
                            1131
Bless Jehovah (Vail) X Close
to Thee   1132
Bless the words (Pollock)
[MSSMDMMR, RMFRSFM, M]
AX77; AY61   1133
Blessed are they that have the
faith (Lund) [SMR#MFRD#R,
SRD#RMDRM] BC233 1134
-----. R [SLRSDFTM, MMTD
DRMR,]   1135
Blessed assurance (Knapp) X
Assurance   1136
Blessed be the name (Havergal)
X Evan   1137
Blessed be the name (Hudson)
X Blessed name   1138
Blessed Bible (Landis) [SMD
TLSLSSM, SRMFLS] AX143;
AY194   1139
Blessed Bible, how I love it
(Beery) [SSDDMRDL, LLSD
MMR, S] AS183   1140
Blessed, blessed (Binder)
[MFFMSD, TLDLLS, MFFF]
BH153   1141
Blessed communion (Schör-
ring Koralbog. 1781) X Con-
tentment   1142
Blessed Francis holy father
(Slovak hymn) [MFSDTDRS,
LTDFMRM, M] BQ102 1143
Blessed Francis holy father
(Theophane) [SLTDDRRMD,
DRMFMRD] BN179   1144
Blessed home (Stainer) [MR
LTSD, MRLTSD, DTLT]
B394; C394; D632b; I527;
K386; O615; AZ38-D; BA
31   1145
Blessed hope (Alexis) [SSDST
LS, RRDLSF#S, TT] N609
                            1146
Blessed host (Norwegian trad)
[STRTDRMFSMDT, SDRM]
P432   1147
Blessed host (Norwegian trad)
X Behold a host (Norwegian)
                            1148

Blessed hour (Doane) X Doane
II   1149
Blessed Jesus, at thy word
(Ahle) X Liebster Jesu   1150
Blessed light (Russian mel)
[LDMRMFMRDT, TDRTMD]
AL303   1151
Blessed Lord, how much I need
thee (Belden) [MRDSLDLS, TD
RRDRM, M] BB578   1152
-----. R [SFMRDDL, DLSDMDM
R, S]   1153
Blessed Lord, in thee (Owen)
X Bryn Calfaria   1154
Blessed morn (Roper) [SSMRRDL
S, SSTLSLSF#] C77b; D57b;
U53   1155
Blessed name (Bradbury) X
There is no name   1156
Blessed name (Hudson) [SSDM
DRDDLS, SSDRMF] AT140; AU
279; AX3   1157
Blessed night, when first the
plain (M. B. F.) X Melford
                                       1158
Blessed, O blessed (Kaiser)
[MFMMRD, SLSSFM, RMFF]
BH154   1159
Blessed quietness (Marshall) X
Marshall   1160
Blessed Redeemer (Loes) X
Redeemer   1161
Blessin (Blessin) [SDRMSSDFM
R, FMTDDR] M183   1162
Blessing and honour (Bach, School
of) [DTTDSSLSFM, LS#S#LMM]
BY305-B   1163
Blessing and honor (Parker) X
Pro patria   1164
Blessings (Excell) [MMMFSSS
MFMF, RMFST] AT318; BC
202   1165
----. R [SSDSSMFFF, FFTLS
FM]   1166
Blessings over Chanukkoh lights
(Jewish trad) [SDRMRDD, DR
MMSFMMR,] BH297   1167
Blessings over the Lulav (Jewish
trad) X Kiddush   1168
Blest be the dear uniting
love (Chetham. Psalmody.
1718) X Marlow   1169
Blest be the tie (Naegeli) X

Dennis   1170
Blest is the bond (Heller)
[SF#FMRDTL#L, LLS#SFM
R] BH219   1171
Blest is the Faith (Montani)
[DMSSSLFLD, LSMRDML]
BQ123   1172
-----. R [DDDSFMDLFS, SL
LLFL]   1173
Blest moments (Baxter) [DDR
MMRRM, SFRMMDRM,]
J217b   1174
Bletchley (Bedford) [DMMMF
SSDRM, SLTDDD] BY594a
                                       1175
Bliss (Bliss) [SSFMMRMFLS
FM, SDTL] L493; N525;
P213; AE190; AH394; AI
128; AM580; AR484; AS310;
AT265; AU73; AV363; AW
484; AX484; AY452; BB313
                                       1176
-----. R [SSSSSS, MSLLDDTDD]
                                       1177
Bliv med din store naade (Vul-
pius] X Cana   1178
Blodyn (Roberts) [MRDSFMM
RDDT, RMRDS] W347   1179
Blomstertid (Swedish Koralbok.
1697) J449; N543   1180
Bloomfield chant (Bradbury)
[SSSDDDRM, MMMMMMF#S,]
T214; AJ307   1181
Blow (Blow) X St Agnes   1182
Blumenthal (Blumenthal) [MM
MMSFM, DDRRFMR, MM] I
500b; V457; AJ275; AO427;
BA11; BH43; BR103   1183
Boardman (Devereaux) [DSFM
RDDTLS, SSDDMR] H327;
I129; L310; N334; R38; T
200; AJ289a; AO267; BF590;
BR314   1184
Boar's head carol (English trad)
[SDDDTDS, MFFLFSSD, S]
BG19   1185
-----. R [DDTTDDS, FFLLS
SD.]   1186
Bod Alwyn (Jenkins) [MMMFR
M, DDDRLT, DDDR] BY318
                                       1187
Bodley (Horsley) [DMRDDLRF
M, MDTLSTL] BV440 1188

Bodlondeb (Arthur) [SMDRMLS
DRDT, MR#TTF#] W427;
BY438b   1189
Bodmin (Scott-Gatty) [MRDTLS
LFM, MFSLLLT] BV486; BY
213   1190
Bohemia (Bohemian Br. G-B.)
X O mensch sieh   1191
Bohemia (German trad) [SS
SSLS, DDTLS, SSSSL] J425;
K552   1192
Bohemia (Thommen. Christen-
schatz. 1745) X Cassel   1193
Bohemia #11 (Thommen. Chris-
ten-schatz. 1745) X Cassel
                          1194
Bohemian Brethren (Bohemian
Brethren) [DMFSDTLS, LSF
MRMFRD,] A522; E604; F
423; G355; R15; Sap. 34; X214;
Z637; AB57; AD146; AF20; AN
363; AQ15; AR366, 675; AW
512; BC158; BV565; BY362;
BZ   1195
-----. V [DMFS, DTLSDTLS,
SDRM] Sap. 34   1196
Bohemian hymn (Bohemian
Brethren) X Far off lands
                          1197
Böjd under korset (Blomqvist)
[LLMTDTLS#L, DDRMDRL]
N576   1198
Bolton (Bolton) [MMMFFFFMF
SS, LLSMM] BB271   1199
Bona patria (Sacred hymns and
tunes. Bristol. 1876) [DMSLSF
M, MRFMDR, DMS] Q614   1200
Bonar (Calkin) X Civitas dei
                          1201
Bonar (Mason) [DMMRMF, MRR
DRM, DMMR] L195; BB372
                          1202
Bonaventura (Gower) [MMRRLL
SS, MMRRDMRR,] BB297 1203
Bone pastor (Dykes) X Faith
                          1204
Bone pastor (Plainsong sequence.
M 7) [SSLSTDRMR, MFMRMT
L] A194a; E317c; BQ231b 1205
Bone pastor (Polleri) X Ecce
panis angelorum   1206
Bonifacio (Evans) [DMLSMDRM
DL, TDLM, DM] W568a   1207

Bonn (Beethoven) X Alsace
                          1208
Bonn (Rosenmüller) X Nassau
                          1209
Bonn (Ebeling) X Ebeling I
                          1210
Bonn (Freylinghausen's G-B)
X Festus   1211
Bonn (Gardiner's Sacred melo-
dies) X Gardiner   1212
Bonnie Doon (Scottish trad) X
Candler   1213
Bont-newydd (Roberts) [MRM
SMRDFMR, MFMSMR] W
243a; BY583   1214
Book divine (Schnyder) X
Horton   1215
Booker (Ruebush) [SMFSMRD
L, DSDMDR, RM] AY270 1216
Bor'chu (Jewish trad) [SLSMFS,
LSSLTTDS, DM] BH305
                          1217
Bor'chu (Sulzer) [SSDRDRM,
LTDRD, SDDD] BH268, 279
                          1218
-----. V [LLMMRDR, LLDRTL,
LLL] BH279   1219
Born again (Stebbins) [DMM
MMFSLSF#S, SSFMR] AT215;
AU68; AW461; AX326; AY
509   1220
-----. [SSSMFSL, LLLRMFS,
FM]   1221
Bortniansky (Bortniansky) X
St Petersburg   1222
Bortniansky (Bortniansky) X
Vesper hymn   1223
Boruch shaym I (Jewish trad)
[SDDDTDFMMRDTLS#, SM]
BH331, 332   1224
-----. V [SDDDDDTDFMMRDT
LS#] BH332   1225
Boruch shaym II (Jewish trad)
[LLSFMMR, LRDTLLS#, LT]
BH339   1226
Boruch shaym (Sulzer) X Sh'ma
Yisroayl II   1227
Bossiney (Holst) [DSLDFMRM
RD, SFMMRM] E571   1228
-----. R [RSF#MDLRDT, MM
RRDRM]   1229
Bost (Bost) [DMDSDMFSM,
DSMDRMF] M84   1230

Boston (Burnap) [MMR#MDML
S,SLDMRDR,M] L505; T
139a; AJ206   1231

Boston (Plainsong M 1: arr by
Mason) X Hamburg   1232

Boston (Siedhoff) [DMFSLDRM,
RDTLTS,DS] BE429   1233

Boughs (Jewish trad) [MMMMM
RDTLDRM,MMMM] AH149;
BH187   1234

Bound Brook (Hymns and tunes.
1890) X Follow the path of
Jesus   1235

Boundary (Shaw) [DRMLF#S,
RSMMFF,LSDR] E99   1236

Bounding heart (Brightbill)
[MFSLLTDRTS,LDLSMR]
AR330   1237

Boundless mercy (Union harmony.
1793) [DDRRMSMR,DDMMR
D,DD] R39; AY320   1238

Bourbon (Hesperian harp. 1848)
[MLLDRDLSL,LLLDLDRM,]
AF558   1239

Bourdillon (Gibbons) [DMRDSMF
FS,FMR,RDTL] AQ164   1240

Bourgeois (Bourgeois) [DRMRD
TLS,DRMFMRD] A129; E200;
J12; K8; M337; N347; O53;
P64; Q61; S227; W359; X291;
AA130; AD78; AF104; AI415;
AJ416; AK234; AL147; AM148;
AO197; AP275; AR333; AZ165-
a; BA781; BI104; BJ27; BR
338; BV199   1241

Bourne (Currier) [LTDMMRDTL,
LTDTLS#] A263b   1242

Bournemouth (Parry) [MFSRFM,
RMDLT,TTDMR] F418   1243

Bouwerie (Goldsworthy) [SDRTDR
MFMR,MRDTL] A330   1244

Bovina (Tate) [DDMRDRMSFM,
SDLSMR,] AJ51   1245

Bow Brickhill (Nicholson) [DTLD
SLMFRD,DFMLSD] F215; BV162
a; BY357   1246

Bow Church (Bullivant) [DRMSD,
DRMSD,RMFLSF] F206   1247

Bow down in worship (Purcell)
[DTDRRLTDRM,MRDT,SR]
BI50-D   1248

Bow down thine ear (Poteat)
[SDRMFSSLTD,SLTSLF] AR652

1249
Bow down thine ear, Lord
(Beimel) [DTLSLMRDT,DRM
FMRD] BH35   1250

Bowden (Wesley, S.S.) [SMF
MRD,MSDTLS,SLSF]   W518
                              1251

Bowen (Haydn) [DTDRDTRFM
MR,MRMDT] AA450; AJ131;
AN91; BE185; BI570; BR
196   1252

-----. V [DTDRDTFMMR,
MRMDTT] AJ131   1253

Bowring (---) [SLSMDTLTDS,
SDMRST] AV48   1254

Boxted (R.E.) [MRLDTL,TD
TLSM,MSLD] AN300b
                              1255

Boyce (Boyce) [MDSDRFM,
LSTDFMR,MD] E201; F
186; G560; L461b; W435a;
X375; AP397a; AZ16-H; BR
232; BV198   1256

-----. V [MDSDRMFFM,
LSTDFMM] F186   1257

-----. B [MDSMRFM, LSTDF
MR,MD] L461b   1258

Boyce (Boyce) X Kingsland
                              1259

Boye (Hohenfurth ms. 1410)
X Dies est laetitiae   1260

Boylston (Mason) [SMFSLS,
DDTLLS,SM] A495a; B489;
C489; D672; G287; H227;
I275; L527; M47; N501;
O486; Q225; R301; S343;
T96; U178; V312; Y383;
Z131; AA462; AB324; AC
312; AD408; AE274; AF
273; AG161; AH419; AJ139;
AK280; AM285a; AO445; AP
482b; AR312; AS328; AT168;
AU157; AW214; AX109; AY
22; AZ582-N; BA74; BB205;
BF490a; BX516; BZ   1261

Boynton (Malan) [SDRDTSRMR
D,MFLLDT] L478; AJ352
                              1262

Bracondale (Booth) [MFMSS
LSD,DTLSLFM,M] I209;
Y28; AD75   1263

Bradbury (---) [MMMSSM,MR
MFSM,MMMS] AJ389b

1264
Bradbury (Bradbury) X Pleasant
  pastures   1265
Bradbury (Bradbury) X Rest
                                    1266
Braden (Bradbury) [SMDSLTD,
  SFFMDR, SMR#] H271; L522
                                    1267
Bradfield (Calkin) [SDMSSDRM,
  FSDLLS, TM] V482; AA452;
  AB3; BV258   1268
Bradford (Handel) X Messiah
                                    1269
Bradford (Haydn) [SDTRDMRD,
  DRMFRDT, S] D579b; AS411;
  AV227; BA549   1270
Brady (Spohr) X Gerald   1271
Brahms (Brahms) [SDTDLSDRM
  RMDR, SDT] Y23; AR30   1272
Braint (Welsh trad) [LM, MSF#
  MRDLM, MF#LMRD] W226;
  X505a   1273
Bramley (English trad) [DDSS
  FMMMR, DRMRD, DD] X94;
  BG139   1274
Brandenberg (Crueger. Praxis
  pietatis melica) X Ratisbon
                                    1275
Brandenburg (German trad) X
  Mendon   1276
Branksome (Thorn) [SLSMDRM,
  FSMRDRT, DT] BY431a   1277
Branson (Miller) [MMSLSDRM,
  MS#LTDL, DT] BB236   1278
Brasted (Weimar) [DSLTDRMR
  D, MRDTLLS,] A578a; B304;
  C304; D452b; L457; AA56; AN
  201   1279
Brattle Street (Pleyel) [SSDSMFFR,
  RDRMDSMM] C35b; D671b; V
  426; AN569; AV41; AW199;
  BR247; BX304   1280
Braun (Braun) [MMMRRD, SSMLT
  D, DDRM,] T329; X662; AJ316;
  AM117; AO628   1281
Bread of heaven (Dykes) X Dies
  dominica   1282
Bread of heaven (MacLagan) [SF
  MMRDRM, FSFMMRR,] A212;
  B332; C374; D224b; Eap.43; F
  411b; J377; M521; O257; T365;
  AB92; BA293   1283
Bread of life (Sherwin) [MDMSLS,

MDMR, MDMSLS] G387; H
  89; I325; J491; L309; M36;
  P87; R250; S216; T405; U
  381; V553; Y101; Z451; AB
  99; AC71; AD197; AE162;
  AF254; AG132; AH236; AK
  204; AL187; AM256; AO243;
  AP291b; AR236; AS182; AT
  178; AU192; AV81; AW288;
  AX144; AY439; BA367; BB
  218; BF270; BR301; BV
  303b; BZ   1284
Bread of life (Warren) [SLL
  SDTDR, SDDFMMR, R] S357
                                    1285
Break, day of God (Armistead)
  X Pro patria   1286
Break forth, O beauteous
  heavenly light (Schop) X
  Schop   1287
Break thou, O Lord, the bread
  (Vulpius) X Der tag bricht
  an   1288
Break thou the bread of life
  (Sherwin) X Bread of life
                                    1289
Breathe o'er our waiting Spirits
  (McKinney) [DDDTTLDLS,
  MMMRDR, F] AU286   1290
Breathe on me (McKinney) X
  Truett   1291
Breathe upon us, Holy Spirit
  (Showalter) X Showalter
                                    1292
Brecknock (Wesley) [MDTLS#L
  DTL, FMRD#RRD] F468
                                    1293
Brecon (Heins) [DDDRMSFF,
  MMMRDT, TD] U127; AJ80;
  AO221; AT172; AW139; BF
  258   1294
Bremen (Hastings) [SDDMRDRR
  F, RMMSFML] L352; T16;
  AJ21; AX159   1295
-----. V [DDDMRDRRF, RM
  MSFML] T16   1296
Bremen (Neumark) X Neumark
                                    1297
Bremen (Storl's Wurtemberg G-
  B.) [DRMLSFMM, SSFRRD,
  DR] E195; X255b   1298
Bremen (Vulpius) X Cana
                                    1299

Brent (Weeks) [SDSDSLTD, RM
MRDT, TD] AO192   1300
Breslau (As hymnodus sacer.
Leipzig) [DDDLDRTL, LTDRS
LTS] A6b; B108; C108; 328;
D100; E484; F333; J374; K64;
L259b, 418; M5; N15; O221;
Q7; R293; W501b; X132; AA
350; AF67; AL360a; AM296;
AN321a; BA619; BR169a; BV
162b; BX380; BY136   1301
-----. V [DDDLDRTL, LTDRST
LS,] L418   1301a
-----. V [DDDLTDRDTL, LTD
RSL] C328   1302
-----. [DDDLTDRTL, LTDRDT
D] M5   1303
-----. V [DDDLDRTL, TDRDS
TLS,] BZ   1304
Brethren, we have met to wor-
ship (Moore) X Holy manna
1305
Brich durch mein angefachtnes
herz (Gregor. Chorale book)
X Gregor's 54th metre   1306
Bridgewater (Edson) [DMDRRDT
L, MRDFMRDM] AQ232   1307
Bridgewater (English trad) [M
MRDLS, RDRM, MRDLSF]   E
656   1308
Bridgewater (Fisher) [SDMFLSF
MF#F#S, SSSS#] AR304
1309
Brief life is here our portion
(Wesley) [DRMFMMR, MRD
RMRD, MS] O612   1310
Brierly (Hart) [MRDSFMMRDR,
MRDSFM] D33a   1311
Briesen (Freylinghausen) [MDSL
SFMD, LRTLSF#, SL] AZ157-
B; BA169   1312
Briggs (Tarbutton) [SLSDDTDR,
RMRDMRTD,] T14a; AJ18
1313
Brightest and best (Mendelssohn)
[MRDSFFMRDTDMR, RRM]
D66a; G40; H6; I43; N523;
P342; R455; S107; T79; U412;
V15; Y144; Z136; AB229; AC
6a; AD26; AF37; AG18; AH
210; AJ117; AL539; AM356; AN
104; AO435; AP477; AR45; AS
22; AT25; AU220; AV4; AW23;

AY476; BA531; BE174; BF
266; BH96; BI87; BK40; BX
271; BZ   1314
Brightest and best (Thrupp) X
Epiphany hymn   1316
Brightly beams (Bliss) X
Lower lights   1317
Brightly gleams (Storer) [SDT
RRD, SSSFMR, RFMR] D515c
1318
-----. R [DDDTLTRD, FMRD
TLS, S]   1319
Bring a torch (French trad) X
Un flambeau   1320
Bring flowers of the fairest
(Catholic) X Flowers of the
fairest   1321
Bring, heavy heart, your grief
(Lund) [SMRDRDTT, SFMRS
DRM,] BC349   1322
Bring them in (Ogden) [SSLSM
MRR, SSLSRRDD,] AM684;
AT429; AU266; AX213; BB625
1323
-----. R [MSMRLR, MMMRD
MRRR, M]   1324
Bringing home our sheaves
(Rupp) [DDDRMRMRDLS, DD
RMFM] AX581; AY131
1325
Bringing in the sheaves (Minor)
[SSSLSM, DDDRDL, SSSL]
Z416; AH416; AP590; AT432;
AU359; AX187; BB621 1326
-----. R [MSSLS, LDDLS, SS
DRMD]   1327
Bringing our praise (Francis)
[DTRDRMMRFMM, SMRLS]
BN203   1328
Bristol (Hodges) [SDMLFMRD,
SMRDTLS, MF] B54; C54a;
D47a; BE347   1329
Bristol (Ravenscroft's Psalter)
[SFRMDRRD, FMRRD#R, RM]
A7; E6; F53; W260; X62;
AP279; BJ50; BR131; BV74;
BY81a   1330
Bristol (Wesley) [MMFMRDFM
RM, SDTLSF#] W472 1331
Bristol, No. 1 (Ravenscroft's
Psalter) X Bristol   1332
Broadbent (Sheldon) [LSLTDR
D, LSLFRM, LSL] BV152

1333
Broadlands (Lausanne Choral
buch) [SMLSFMMFLSMR,
SSSL] D277a 1334
Broadwalk (Ashfield) [SMRDSLD
MRMD, LDRMS] BV125b
1335
Broadway (Showalter) [SMRDDRR
SSF, FMRSMD] AR291 1336
Broadwood (Strover) [SMFSSLTD
TLS, DRMFS] BV368 1337
Brockham (Clark) [SDRMTDRT,
RFFMDMF#S,] E220; F45b;
W3; X228; AN133; BB132; BE
235; BJ9; BY533 1338
Brocklesbury (Barnard) [MRDSTLL
S, DDMMRMR,] A241b; B360;
C343; D207a; J261; K174; L
212; M167; N295; O323; P96;
S348; T350b; U469; V642; AD
480; AG238; AH548; AI161;
AJ400; AM642; AO433; AP762;
BA608; BB427; BF611 1339
Brocklesby (Barnard) X Brock-
lesbury 1340
Bromham (Matthews) [DTLSDMR
DRM, MRDSMD] M224; N657
1341
Bromley (Clark) [DMFRDMSSL
SFFM, DFM] A163b; B11b;
AB167; AL231; AP357; BE388;
BJ6 1342
Bromley Common (Shaw) [MMF#
F#SRSLLTS, LLDTL] X187b;
Y75; AN18 1343
Brompton (Schachner) [MFLSDTR
S, LSMDDSFM] BR19 1344
Bromsgrove (Psalmodia evangeli-
ca 1789) [DDSLSLTDFMRDT
D̄, DR] E144; W381; X23; BE
106 1345
-----. V [DDSLTDFMRDTDRM
DT] W381 1346
-----. V [DDSLTDFMRDTD,
DRMD] BE106 1347
Brookend (Holst) [DRSDRML,
SMRDRML, SL] X348 1348
Brookfield (Southgate) [SMMMRLT
DRD, DFMRDT] D308; G121;
H335; I70; N143; T241; V136;
Z217; AB183; AC188; AE387;
AG120; AI359; AJ337; AK270;
AM73; AP564a; AR381; AS123;

AW373; AY515; BA96; BB426;
BF328; BY142b 1349
Brooklyn (Kasschau) [MMRDDR
RS, SDRMFLS, S] AD428
1350
Brooklyn (Zundel) [SDDMSD, S
DSDRM, MRTD] U386; V567
1351
Broome (Dawes) [MMRDSFM
MRMRD, DRMF#] BY696
1352
Brorson (Berggren) [SLTDDRR
MD, FMRMRDL] M70 1353
Brother, here's a message (Gar-
rett) [SSMSDSMSSFFM, SSM
S] AS308 1354
-----. R [SSSSS, LSFMLS, DDS
L#L] 1355
Brother James' air (Bain) X
Marosa 1356
Brotherhood (Reay) [SMDTDMR
D, SFMLRR, RR] AB269
1357
Brotherland (Horner) [SLSMRD
ST, LSMSFM, MS] AB364
1358
Broughton (Hastings) [SSSFMM
R, FFFMRM, SSS] C395; AL
235; AP506b; AW293 1359
Brown (Bradbury) [SDRMDLTD,
LSSDMR, SM] H184; L469;
U259; V44; Z475; AE181; AI
275; AR82; AS83; AT38; AV
6; AX71; AY292; BA121; BB
317 1360
Brown (Brown) X St Anatolius
1361
Browne (Browne) [SDDTTD, SF
MFSLR, RMM] BX546 1362
Brownell (Haydn) [SMSDDTR
SRFFM, SDMS] D638; N549;
O550; AB52; BR333 1363
Browning (Branscombe) [MDRM
FSLS, SDRMFS, LS] Y57
1364
Browning (Burnap) [SMMFMR
MD, TLRTLTD, S] L3; AN
235b 1365
Brownwell (Haydn) X Brownell
1366
Brunswick (Handel) [DMFSDL#
LS, LRMFFSLS] E555; X297
1367

Bryan (Bryan) [MMRMFTD, DT
  DRSSF#S, S] L599; AP22b;
  BR207   1368
Bryant (Alcock) [SSDRMMRR,
  RTDMRD, M] B107; C107; W
  685b; AB205   1369
Bryd frem, mit hjertes trang
  at lindre (Lindeman) [SLDSL
  FSMR, MSF#STDL] K347; O171
                                   1370
Bryn Calfaria (Owen) [MMLTDD
  DT, DDMRDTTL,] E319; J114b;
  R90; X274a; AD407; AF291;
  AI248; AK344; AM187; BV473;
  BZ   1371
-----. V [MMLTDDDT, DRMRD
  TTL,] AD407   1372
Brynhyfryd (Williams) [DMRDT
  DRMDR, DRMLRD] X241; BY
  648   1373
Brynland (Spencer-Palmer) [DSL
  MRMFSSDTL, LRRF] BV581b
                                   1374
Brynteg (Lloyd) [LDRMLTDTL,
  DRMFMMR] W623a; AM59
                                   1375
Bryntirion (Lutteroth) [MFSS
  LLSM, MRDDRRM, M] E248;
  W310   1376
Bryson City (McKinney) [MFMD
  SLSM, DDRFMRM, M] AT540;
  AU497   1377
Bucer (Mason & Webb's Cantica
  laudis) X Heath   1378
Buckland (Haynes) [SMRDRRM,
  SDTSSF#S, D] A428; B354;
  D552a; Eap. 67; F444; Q51;
  W193; AA15; AF236; AH551;
  AL154a; BD140; BV141c; BY
  118b   1379
Bucklebury (Harmonia perfecta.
  1730) [DSDTSLSFM, MMRMF
  SS] X189   1380
Buddugoliaeth (Hughes) [MMRDT
  RRDTL, TDRMMR] BY455a
                                   1381
Bude (Wesley, S.S.) [DMRDDFM
  MR, SDRFMRD,] W515; AP
  287a   1382
Budleigh (Mudie) [MMMFMMRDR
  MM, MMMFM] H337; L453;
  AS277; BA482   1383
Buffham (Hopkins) [DRMMRDFF

  FMRDLS, DD] F455   1384
Bugail Israel (Price) [MFSSLS
  SF, MRSRMRR, S] W465
                                   1385
Builders Porter) [DMFSDL, SM
  SSF#M, MF#ST] Y65 1386
Building for eternity (Coats)
  [MMSMFLS, SSMDRMR, MM]
  AX191   1387
Building for eternity (Sargent)
  [DRMMMMMRD, MFSSSLL]
  AX199; AY519   1388
-----. R [MFSMMSD, DRRRR
  MFM, D]   1389
Built on the Rock (Lindeman)
  X Kirken   1390
Bullinger (Bullinger) X Geneva
                                   1391
Bulstrode (Sharpe) [SDRMSFMR,
  MDTDRTS, S] X367   1392
Bunessan (Gaelic trad) [DMSD
  R, TLSLS, DRMSL, S] R464;
  W53; X30; AD469; AF38;
  AN97; AQ266; BV96; BY92
                                   1393
Bunyan (English trad) [DDRM
  FS, FMRDTD, RMDF] BY759
                                   1394
Bunyan (Mendelssohn) X Stuke-
  ley   1395
Bunyan (Thommen. Christen-
  schatz) [DSLSFM, DRMRD,
  RRMRD] F293; BV551
                                   1396
Bunyan (Thommen. Christen-
  schatz) X Gregor's 37th me-
  tre (Herrnhut ms)   1396a
Burber (Tenney) X Go to thy
  rest, fair child   1397
Burford (Purcell) [LLTDRMR
  DT, S#LTDRMM] A410a; B
  385b; E447; F117; K321; Q
  454; V376; W274b; X596; AA
  303; AL79b; AN236a; AP187;
  AW228; AZ14-D; BA858; BE
  321; BY211a   1398
Burg (Perkins) [DDRRMFMRM,
  MFSLTDD,] S67; AI411
                                   1399
Burke (Burke) [DMMFLSM, RD
  DRMR, RMM] AE21   1400
-----. R [TDSMDLL, LLLTDTL,
  SD]   1401

Burleigh (Barnby) [DSMRDFFSL
S, FMF#SRR] G271; I475
1402
Burleigh (Weekes) [MDDTDMS,
LSDSFMSFM] AB22   1403
Burlington (Burrowes) [DRMFM
RLSDR, SF#STLS] D429; G
388; I198; M456; V620; AR
238; AT186; AV79   1404
Burning light (Coleman) [DDD
SDRM, LSFMRDR, DD] AR435
1405
-----. R [SSSSSMLSFMR, FF
FFF]   1406
Burnley (Barnby) X Diadema
1407
Burton (Woodbury) [SDDDDRTD,
RMMMDTLS,] BB24   1408
Burwell (Herbert) [SMRDDLLLS,
LFRSDRF] D190; AW363; BO50;
BY700b   1409
-----. V [SMRDDLLLS, LFRSDR
M] AW363   1409a
Bushmead (Taylor) [MFLSDRFM,
MTDFMR, MF] BV318   1410
"But for a moment" (Stebbins)
[MR#MSDMMR#MFT, RD#R
SR] AY450   1411
-----. R [SF#SLSMR#MFM,
MRLDTD]   1412
But the Lord (St Paul) (Mendels-
sohn) [SLSSF#LDDDT, SDMSFM]
AH621; AR685   1413
Butler (English trad) [DDMSFLM
FSMR, MFSLS] X378   1414
By and by (Tindley) [DRMMMMM,
RMRDDLD, DR] AT473; AU134
1415
-----. R [SLMDRDDLD, SLM
DRRR]   1416
By grace are ye saved (McGrana-
han) [SSSLTD, DDDTLS, S#
LLL] AU469   1417
-----. R [SSMFSLS, DTLTLS, S
LL]   1418
By the blood that flowed (Montani)
[MMRMDDTD, LLSLTTT, T]
BQ20   1419
-----. R [SLDTSFS, SS#DL#SFS,
SL]   1420
By the blood that flowed (Richard-
son) X Tichfield   1421

By the cross (Mainz G-B. 1661)
X Mainz   1422
By the first bright Easter Day
(Mendelssohn) X Mendels-
sohn   1423
By the first bright Easter Day
(Slovak hymnal) [DRMMFM
MR, MRDTDRMR] BQ137
1424
Byfield (Hastings) [MMMMMFF
M, RDDRMR, RR] M62; V
462; AH354; AO314; BF362
1425
Byrd (Peery) [SDDDDTLS, SD
LSF#S, SS#] G555; J519a
1426
Byzantium (Jackson) X Jack-
son   1427

C

Caddo (Bradbury) [SDMSMR
DMRD, DTLDRD] H235; L
444; R82; T61; AJ94; AM
55   1428
Caergybi (Roberts) [LLTDD
TLT, TDRMMMRM,] K237;
BY430   1429
Caerlleon (Welsh hymn mel)
[LSFMRDRMDT, LSFMRD]
E334; X193a   1430
Caersalem (Edwards) [DSDM
DMSFMRD, MRDFM] E397;
W564b; X508; AL441b; AM
369; AP404; BB409; BY388
1431
Cairnbrook (Prout) [MMSFMR
DT, DDTDMR, MM] D77;
F488; J337; K500; N586;
AK129; AM630; AO471;
AP713a; BV498; BY668a
1432
Caithness (Scottish Psalter,
1635) [DMFSDTDR, MFSLLS,
S] A353; E445; F325; J384b;
M217; O501; P317; W481a;
X112; AF349; AN19; AP459;
AQ74; BE215; BV147b; BY
593; BZ   1433
Calcutta (Heber) [DRMMMMD,
DRRTTD, DR] E547; L499;

Cambridge 1472

Camden (Calkin) X Waltham 1473

Cameronian midnight hymn (Scottish hymn mel) [SDMRDSL DR, MFSRFMR] E401; J147b; X514 1474

Camp (Lutkin) [SDRMDFFM, M LRSDTLS,] I686 1475

Campfields (Monk) [MRMFMRMF, RSSSFM, MF#] W245; BE104 1476

Campian (Campian) [LMDTLLT, DSMDRRD, R] A459; AN452; AQ313 1477

Campian 2 (Campian) [DTLSF#S, SFFMMF#, SSSL] AQ107 1478

Campmeeting (American trad) [DTRRRDMM, MRMFLS, MS] G303; T75; U180; V449; AI 160; AJ69; AM458; AR281; AT 336; AW99; AX355, 490; AY 45; BB670; BZ 1479

Campmeeting (American trad) X X The Lord of glory (refrain: Mosley) 1479a

Can a little child (Bassford) X Thanksgiving 1480

Cana (---) [MMMMMR, RDDDDT, TLLL] AJ151 1481

Cana (Mozart) [SSDTDRMSFMR, TRDLR] D662; I80; AR3; BE 93; BH1; BR71 1482

-----. V [SDTDRMSFMR, TRD LRM] BE93 1483

Cana (Vulpius) [DMRMFSM, LSFMRM, SLT] A252; B383; D511b; E232; F114a; G534; J192; K433; L60; M13, 164; N183; O57, 144; P57; Q53; R347; S92; V411; W368; X 585; Y292; Z365; AA9; AD248; AF373; AK34; AL398; AM568; AN274; AP25; AQ188; AW559; AZ8-A; BA590; BB377; BM58; BR249; BV385; BX341; BY575; BZ 1484

-----. V [DMRMLSFM, LSFM RM, DS] M164 1485

-----. V [DMRMFSFM, LSFMR M, SL] V411 1486

-----. V [DMRMFSSM, LSFM RM, SL] Y292 1487

-----. V [DMRMLSFM, LSF MRM, SL] AZ8-A 1488

-----. V [DRMRMLSFM, LS FMRM, S] BR249 1489

Canaan (Bailey) [SDDRRML S, MFSMFRDD,] AL593; AW 403 1490

-----. R [MFSSSLSFFF, SMD SMM] 1491

Canaan (Baker) [DSMDRTLS, SDDRRM, SF] AA155 1492

Canaan (Rupp) X Jerusalem, my happy home 1493

Candlemas Eve (Church Gallery book) [SDDMDLTD, MS FMRDR, M] BG126 1494

Candler (Scottish trad) [SDD RDRMSMRD, RMRDD] G311; BZ 1495

Cannock (Stanton) [MDRSDFM RM, MRDRSLS] R359b; BV 329; BY470 1496

Cannons (Handel) X Canons 1497

Canon (Tallis) X Tallis' canon 1498

Canon VIII (Ryley) [MLSDD RFM, MFRSDRLT,] F244 1499

Canonbury (Schumann) [SMM MFMRDRM, SLTDRT] B44; C7; D499; G116; H389; I42; J538; K18; L230a; M559; N502; O24; P323; R298; S78; T217; U279; V5; Y216; Z133; AB4; AC251; AD321; AE277; AF46; AG248; AH 425; AI45; AJ310; AK256; ALsuppl; AM93; AN508; AO44; AP661; AR40; AS21; AT84; AU298; AV101; AW 296; AY456; BA50; BB407; BD69; BE322; BF183; BH2; BI43; BK70; BR6; BZ 1500

-----. V [SMMMFRDRM, SLTD RTL] L230a 1501

Canons (Handel) [LMS#LTDRT, DSTDRMFR] E66b; F84b; R392; S421a; X337a; Y188;

Angels of Jesus   1537
Carmen naturae (Donizetti) X
Savery   1538
Carmichael (Spencer-Palmer)
[MMLRDTTL, LTDRFM,
MF#] BV326b   1539
Carnarvon (Martin) [SFMRFMRD,
TLSLDTD, S] Y62   1540
Carne (Joseph) X Keine schönheit
hat die welt   1541
Carol (---) [MMMRDSFMR, DR
MLSF#S,] BR145   1542
Carol (Corner. 1649) X Corner
                         1543
Carol (Willis) [SMRRDLSLS, SL
TDDRMR,] A13b; B79; C79;
D59a; G92; H135; I110; J23;
K29b; L215; N39; P135; R160;
S127; T338; U58; V116; Y245;
Z191; AB108; AC78; AD107;
AE82; AF129; AG73; AH245;
AI159; AK107; AL58b; AM157;
AN162; AO122; AP170b; AO
287; AR136; AS104; AT71; AU
141; AV85; AW75; AX98; AY
489; BA156; BB99; BC82; BD
206; BF289; BK146; BR548b;
BX191b; BZ   1544
-----. V [SMTRDLSLS, SLTDDR
M] L215   1545
Carol melody, 14th c. (Hohenfurth
ms.) X Quem pastores   1546
Carol of beauty (French carol)
X Fragrance   1547
Carol of service (French trad)
[MLLSLSFM, MLSLSFM, S]
BG166   1548
-----. R [LTDRMLLS#LTL, LTD
RM]   1549
Carol of the advent (French trad)
X Besançon carol   1550
Carol of the kingdom (Manx
carol) [MLTDRDL, MMRDTL,
MLT] BG167   1551
Carolina (Johnson) [MRLSMDRM,
MMLSF#S, FM] N210; AI436
                         1552
Carr (Monk) X St Ethelwald
                         1553
Carrick (Finlay) [MDRDTSL, LD
TRDM, MDR] BV639   1554
Carrington (Pollock) X Bless the
words   1555

Carrow (Sullivan) [MMMMRD
DF, MRDT, SSSS] B384;
D624a; BX316   1556
Carry on (Conant) [MMR, MMR,
DTDRRM, DMDM] Y160
                         1557
Carson (Meredith) X Meredith
                         1558
Carter (Carter) X Slingsby
                         1559
Carter (Updegraff) [SSLDTS,
SSLDT, DDTDM] AJ202
                         1560
-----. R [SSRRMRDM, MRRM
RR, SS]   1561
Carthage (Root arr) [SLSSMD
DTLSLS, FSFM] H189
                         1562
Cary (Tourjée) [MSSDRM, MR
MFFM, MMSS] I620; AV392
                         1563
Caryl (Lutkin) [SSSSSSLS, M
F#STLSFM,] I583b   1564
Caskey (Perkins) [SMRDLSD,
DRRDRM, SMR] H325; L
603   1565
Cassel (Cassel) X The King's
business   1566
Cassel (Thommen. Christen-
schatz.) [DRMSFMR, MR
DRDTD, TD] F119; J69; K
92a; L162; M28, 39; N92;
Q37; V511a; W187; AI410;
AL152; AO200; AP479; AW
536; AX449; AY388; AZ167-
A; BA192; BR460a; BY309a
                         1567
-----. V [DRMSFMRR, MRDRD
TD, T] V511   1568
-----. V [DRMSFMRR, MRD
MRTD, D] AO200   1569
Cassidy (Main) [MSTDLSFMR
M, SDMFSL] U83; Y219
                         1570
Cast thy burden on the Lord
(Mendelssohn) X Birmingham
                         1571
Castle Rising (Hervey) [MFM
RLDTLT, TDDRRM, M] D409b;
O66   1572
Castleford (Sacred harmony.
Leeds. 1720) [DMRDLSFM,
MSDTLS, SMD] W197; BV

646   1573
Caswall (Filitz) [MMRRDT, DDR
RM, SSFFMR,] A335; B162;
C162b; D362b; E315b; F107;
J76; K90; N639; Q158; R222;
Sap. 13; W542; Y107; AA208;
AE457; AK485; AL205; AM190;
AP323; BA92; BN73; BO28;
BR337; BV154; BY771   1574
Caswell Bay (Havergal) [SMRDD
TLS, FMFSLRRR,] D586b
                             1575
Cathcart (Bell) [SDRMMMML,
SMRDDDTL,] E546; M383;
Y232   1576
Catherine (Clark) [SSSSSLSD, D
TDRRDRM,] T59; AJ92   1577
Caton (Miller) X Rockingham
                             1578
Cavell (Fowles) [SMSTLSDM, R
TRFMRM, F] Y119; AC111
                             1579
Cecil (Hall) [DSTLSSMRDR, SD
MFLS] B75b   1580
Cecile (Johnson) [DMMR#MFF
M, DMRDTD, MR] J233; M569;
N556   1581
Cecilia (Dykes) X Domines regit
me   1582
Cecilia (Hayne) X St Cecilia
                             1583
Celeste (Swedish Koralbok, 1697)
X Laurinus   1584
Celestia (Danish trad) [DRMFSD
S, LSFMSSR, RM] J57; M606;
O148   1585
Celestial voices (Lloyd) [MMRM
FML, TDMR, MMFSS] S493;
AL621; BB419   1586
Cennick (Hutton. Tunes for the
hymns) [SFMRD, SRRDT, SDTL
SM] AZ587-A   1587
Ceres (English trad) [SMMRDR
D, DSSLLR, RMM] BY725
                             1588
Chadwick (Webster) [DRMFMLSS
FM, MFSLSD] BX443   1589
Chalice (Branscombe) [SDFFM
RD, SDFFMRD, RR] Y147; AC
230a   1590
-----. R [SLDTLSM, SLDTLSM,
RM]   1591
Chalvey (Hayne) [SLSSRF, MMR

RLT, RSF#] A452; B443;
C189; D203a; I340a; K480;
N579; V631; AP230; BA265
                             1592
Chamber music (Bach) [SDR
MR, SRMFM, SSSSFM] BK9
                             1593
Chamouni (Lomas) X Althorp
                             1594
Chant (Boyce) [DDDDDSFM, M
RSSF#S, SS] AP61b   1595
Chant (Dupuis) [DDDDDTDL,
FMRDTDR, R] AP107d
                             1596
Chant (Mornington) [SSSSSS
FM, SLTTLS, DD] AP65c
                             1597
Chant (Hayes) [MMMMMMRD;
FFMRDT, SS] AP11b   1598
Chant (Jacobs) X Hope   1599
Chant (Norris) [DDDDDMSD,
DLTDFMR, R] AP41c   1600
Chant (Randall) X Randall
                             1601
Chant: Troyte, No. 1 (Troyte)
X Troyte, No 1   1602
Chant: Troyte, No. 2 (Troyte)
X Troyte, No. 2   1603
Chant your songs (Gluck) [MS
DDRRFMRR, DTLSLS] BI
114   1604
Chanticleer (English trad)
[DDMSLSLTD, MFSDRMR,]
BG123   1605
Chapel (Wesley's Foundery Col-
lection. 1742) X Savannah
                             1606
Chapel Royal (Boyce) [DDD
RMFRM, DMSLSFMR,] F316;
AL301b   1607
Chapin (Dykes) X Esca via-
torum   1608
Chapman (Marsh) X One day
                             1609
Charing (Russell) [DRMRMSL
S, DLSMLFMR,] E531; X
340   1610
Charity (Jaehnigen) [DRMRS,
FSMDR, RSSF#MR] BE180
                             1611
Charity (Lutkin) [MFMSMDLS
M, MRMRLS, M] Y226; AC
242   1612

Charity (Stainer) [DFMRDRS, LT
DLRDDT, D] B121; C38; D
76a; F233; V424; W484a; BA
671; BV543; BY232b   1613

Charleston (Pilsbury. U.S. Sacred
harmony, 1799) X Bartimaeus
                                        1614

Charlestown (Pilsbury. U.S.
Sacred harm. 1799) X Barti-
maeus   1616

Charlotte (Biggs) [SMFSSLMS,
FRFMDR] A215   1617

Charlotte (Maclean) [MMRDRM,
MLLSFM, SSDT] V429a   1618

Charterhouse (Evans) [SDRMDF
MRMDL, DTLSS] A188; R217;
S177; W146; X283; AB80; AD
139; BE345; BY350   1619

Chartres (French, 15th c)
[LLMMTDRR, LLDRTDL,]
A50a; W44; AL599; AN158;
BG91   1620

-----. V [LLMMTDRR, LTDRTD
L, L] AN158   1621

-----. V [LMMTDRR, LDRTDL,
LMM] BG91   1622

Chatham (Weber) X Seymour
                                        1623

Chautauqua (Sherwin) [DDDLSF#
S, DDDLSF#S, TT] G44; I57;
J234; L20; M637; N559; R65;
S39; T10; U463; V54; Y96; Z
144; AB23; AC17; AD47; AE43;
AF45; AG31; AH168; AI53; AK
481; AL562; AM343; AO27; AR
50; AS25; AT29; AU87; AV12;
AW31; AY440; BA782; BB51;
BD13; BF202; BK44; BY689;
BZ   1624

-----. R [DSDSMD, SFRD, DTD
LSD]   1625

Chebar (Smart) [SMDFMLS, DF
FMRM, SMD] W198; BB363
                                        1626

Cheerful (Shaw) [DDDRDTSLT
D, MRTDTL] E376; J413b;
X472; Y195   1627

Cheerfulness (Weyse) [SSFMRFM,
SLTDTLLS, R] BE141   1628

Chelmsford (Chapin) X Melody
                                        1629

Chelsea (Hutton. Tunes for the
hymns) [DDTDRMMR, DFMRRD,

DM] AZ590-F   1630

Chelsea (Ireland) [SMFSSDLS,
MRMLSRR, S] X164   1631

Chelsea Square (Robbins) [SM
RDSDTLS, MLSFMR,] A380;
J243a   1632

Chenies (Matthews) [SSMMRD
S, SLDDTD, SSM] D252b; K
169; L147; M563; R251; S
123; T151; U134; V78; W
470a; Y50; Z211; AB330;
AC41; AG131; AI151; AL83;
AP289; AS90; BB290; BO118;
BR502b   1633

Cherith (Spohr) X Spohr   1634

Cherry tree (English trad)
[SDTLSDR, MFSFMRDTL,]
E285; W463; X599; BG66a;
BV582b; BY551b   1635

Cherry tree carol (English
trad) X Cherry tree   1636

Cherubic hymn (Bortniansky)
X St Petersburg   1637

Cherubic hymn (Psalterium
chorale. Constance) X
Beata nobis gaudia   1638

Cheshire (Est. Whole book of
Psalms) [LLTDDTTL, LDD
RSM, MM] E109; F342; J
368; K89; S503; W457a; X
105; AP181a; AR670; BE
286; BJ87   1639

-----. V [LLLTDTTL, LDD
DRRSM,] AR670   1640

Cheshire tune (Est. Whole book
of Psalms) X Cheshire
                                        1641

Chester (Chester) [SSSLTDTT
L, LLLTD#R] A566a   1642

Chester (Dykes) X St Bees
                                        1643

Chester ("Oratory hymns")
[MMR#MFMMRR, MDDRR
M, M] C403; L247; M482
                                        1644

Chesterfield (Haweis) X Richmond   1645

Chesterton (Beaumont) [SLDT
MR, TDMRLS, SDTL] BY
250b   1646

Chichester (Whitehead) [MM
L, LF#S#LMRRT, MLT] A
429a   1647

1684
Choose the right (Tuckett) [MF
SSSLDTLSM, RMFST] BC110
1685
-----. R [LTDTLS, RRMFLSFM
FS,]   1686
Chope (Chope's carols) [SSSLT
DMFSRS, LTLSL] I117   1687
-----. R [R#MMMMMSR, MFMF
LFMR,]   1688
Chopin (Woodbury) [SSSDSMRD,
MDMSMDMR,] R29b; T176;
AJ256; AO108; AS58; BB339
1689
-----. V [SSSDDMRD, MDMSM
DMR,] AS58   1690
Choral (Vulpius) X Weimar
1691
Chorley (Reay) [SMSDMFSLS, SR
SMF#SR] M258; O354   1692
Chorus angelorum (Somervell)
X Somervell   1693
Chorus novae Jerusalem (Sarum
plainsong, M 3) [MFSFMRMMR
DRFRMFM,] B556b; E122
1694
Christ arose (Lowry) [SSLLSS,
SFLLS, LTDDS] AE123; AH
302; AI81; AM206; AR185;
AS150; AT113; AU127; AV317;
AW452; AX119; BY160; BZ
1695
-----. R [DDDMSSD, DRMDRD
TLS,]   1696
Christ by heavenly hosts (Wil-
liams) X Gloucester   1697
Christ Church (Steggall) X
Christchurch   1698
Christ, der du bist der helle
tag (Bohemian Br.) X
Gregor's 54th metre   1699
Christ for the whole wide world
(McKinney) [SDTDRM, MFFDR
M, MMRR] AU444   1700
-----. R [SDMRMD, TDRRR
SFM, MF]   1701
Christ has for sin (Hoffman)
X Hoffman   1702
Christ in His word draws near
(Bunnett) X Kirby Bedon
1703
Christ in the night He was be-
trayed (Mason) X Hebron

1704
Christ is all (Williams) [DMM
MRDDD, MSSSSLLS,] AY
110   1705
Christ is born in Bethlehem
(Hugg) [DDDSMFSLS, MMM
MMMF] AY246   1706
-----. R [SDSDRMRD, FFF
DRM, MF]   1707
Christ is knocking (Palmer)
[MMMRDSSM, RRDRM, MMM]
AS195; BB565   1708
Christ is my life (Vulpius) X
Cana   1709
Christ is our Head (La scala
santa) X Coleraine   1710
Christ is risen (Kolb) [SMD
STLSLSM, LSSFMR] AY266
1711
Christ ist erstanden (Latin.
12th c) [MMRMSLM, MRM
DTDLL, R] E134; F601;
J107; K114a; M439; Q187,
190; W121a; X155a, 162;
AA225; AF183; AL116b;
AW543; BG148; BQ329
1712
-----. R [MRDRFM, SMSMR
D, MDLT]   1713
-----. V [LSLDRL, LSLFM
FR, MMR] M439   1714
-----. V [LLSLDRL, LSLF
MFR, SS] Q190   1715
-----. V [DDDTDRMD, SDDD
TLSF] X162   1716
-----. V [MMRMSLM, MRMD
TDL, RR] BQ329   1717
Christ lag in todesbanden
(Latin. 12th c. [Bach arr])
[MR#MF#SLSF#M, MDRMRD
T] J98b; O330; AA224; BZ
1718
-----. V [MRMSLSF#M, MD
RMRDTL,] O330   1719
Christ lag in todesbanden (La-
tin. 12th c) X Christ ist
erstanden (Latin. 12th c)
X Victimae paschali (Plain-
song sequence M 1 ascribed
to Wipo)   1720
Christ lag in todesbanden
(Latin. 12th c.: minor)
[LSLDRDTL, LFSLSFMR]

J98a; K110; M432; Q195; AM
207; AZ154-a; BY153   1721
Christ, my life! (Pincott) [MF
F#SMRMFRDT, RMRSL]
BB139   1722
Christ receiveth sinful men
(McGranahan) X Neumeister
1723
Christ returneth (McGranahan)
[DMRDSLSMRDMR, RMMS]
AT120; AU49; AV389; AW455;
BB536   1724
-----. R [SMMFSLLD, DDD
TLS, TT]   1725
Christ, the glory of the sky
(Scheffler's Heilige seelenlust)
X Culbach   1726
Christ the King (English trad)
X Greensleeves   1727
Christ the Lord cometh (Bentley)
[SF#SLSMSFMR, FMFRMF]
AX125; AY532   1728
-----. R [RRRFFFMMLS,
DDDDTL]   1729
Christ the Lord hath risen (Latin.
12th c) X Christ ist erstanden
1730
Christ the Lord is my true Shep-
herd (Currie) [DSLTDMRD, F
MRMDRM, M] BN59   1731
Christ the Lord is my true Shep-
herd (Terry) [SSLSSDRD, SM
MRDRM, M] BO11   1732
Christ the Lord is risen (Allge-
meinisches Katholisches G-B.
1774) X Te Deum   1733
Christ, the Lord, is risen today
(---) [SDLRDTD, DMRDTLS,
DL#] BN40; BO175   1734
Christ the Lord is risen today
(Bragers) [SMLSLTD, DTDSLL
S, FF] BP38   1735
Christ the Lord is risen today
(Strattner) X Posen   1736
Christ the Lord is risen today
(Lyra davidica) X Easter
hymn   1737
Christ the Lord is risen today
(Montani) [SSDSSFFM, RMFS
MRDR,] BQ31   1738
Christ unser herr zum Jordan kam
(Walther. G-B) [RFSLSDTL, L
DTLSFMR] AA401; AZ201-A

1739
-----. V [RFSLTDTL, S#D
TLSFMR,] AZ201-A   1740
Christ, we do all adore (Du-
bois) [DDDTTLS, LLLDDDD
TD,] AR634   1741
Christ will me his aid (Ent-
wisle) [DDMLSMD, DRMR
RMFM, M] AS299   1742
-----. R [RMFMRMFLS,
LTDTLSM]   1743
Christbaum (Cornelius) X The
Christmas tree   1744
Christchurch (Ouseley) [DDM
SLSMR, SSFMLF#F#M,] E
460   1745
Christchurch (Steggall) [DM
SDRS, DLSSFM, RMSL] B182;
D259; E411; F280; I178; W
537; X197b; AL528; AP633a;
AZ342-I; BR193; BV202; BX
62; BY716   1746
Christe, der du bist tag und
licht (Plainsong, ca 600)
X Christe, qui lux es it
dies   1747
Christe du beistand (Loewen-
stern) [LLTDTMF#SLFM,
SF#MRR] E160; X349a
1748
Christe, du lamm gottes (Bu-
genhagen liturgy. 1528) X
Agnus dei   1749
Christe fons jugis (Rouen church
mel) [MMRMDMFSMFM,
MRMDT] E335; F416; X281;
AB215; AK342; AL456a; AN
436; AP625a   1750
Christe, qui lux es et dies
(Plainsong, ca 600) [RFRD#
RMFMR, FFFFDRF] Q559;
AA34; AZ22-D   1751
-----. V [LDTLS#LTDTL,
DDDDSD] AZ220-D   1752
Christe qui lux es et dies
(Plainsong, M 2) [MMRDRM
FRR, RRFMDRF] Eap.1;
F95a   1753
Christe Redemptor (Sarum
Plainsong, M 1) [DRMSS
FMRFMRDR, DM] A485b;
B328b; E17; F188a; J483a;
W421; X549a; AL297c; BJ

32; BP10; BQ155a   1754
-----.   V [DRMSSFMRMFMR,
DMSL] BP10   1755
Christe, redemptor omnium
(Sarum Plainsong, M 1) X
Christe redemptor   1756
Christe sanctorum (Paris Anti-
phoner. 1681) [SMFMRD,MFSS
LS,SLTD] A157b; E165b; F
10b; J134; R43; S24; W263;
X48b;   Z102; AC26; AD41; AF
41; AK44; AL567b; AN116; AW
24; BV40; BY675; BZ   1757
Christe sanctorum (Sarum plain-
song, M 1) [LSLSFMFRDSS
FSLL] A123a; E242   1758
Christe, sanctorum decus ange-
lorum (Plainsong, M 8) [DRF
MFSSSSSLDTLS, D] F564a
                          1759
Christe, wahres seelenlich
(Freylinghausen G-B. 1704)
[DDRMMLLS#LMFMRRD,D]
K82b; M408; Q113   1760
-----.   V [DDMMLLS#, LMFM
RRD,DD] Q113   1761
Christi blut (As hymnodus sacer.
Leipzig) X Breslau   1762
Christi mutter stund von [mit]
schmerzen (Corner. G-B.)
[SSLSFMSM, SFMMFMRR,]
E115b; G139; X138b; AN185b;
AP197   1763
Christian home (McKinney) [MR#
MFTD, MMMSFMRMF, F] AT
377   1764
Christian soldier (Hugg) [MMMM
RRDD, DRRRDRM, M] AY387
                          1765
Christian soldiers (Fuller) [SLT
DMRDS, TD#R#MSF#MS] C
530b; D516c   1766
Christian, walk carefully (Steb-
bins) [SDMMRDRDTD, SDM
SFM] AX444   1767
Christians, awake (Fuller) [MD
LSSLTDRM, DFMRDT] D56b;
Y213   1768
Christine (Kroeger) [MFSSDLSM
S, SLLRDTL] AJ250   1769
Christmas (Gilchrist) [DRMSLTD
SM, SDDRDM, D] BR548a   1770
Christmas (Handel) [MFSDTLS

DRM,MFSSSF] A577; B111;
C111; D503; G88; H84; I115;
J552; K380; L112; N20; R
169; S120; T293; U291; V493;
Y165; Z185; AA378; AB241;
AC195; AD112; AE88; AF362;
AG80; AH260; AI321; AJ406;
AK106; AM156; AN155a; AO
401; AQ223; AR130; AS325;
AT79; AU147; AV89; AW73;
AZ14-Y; BA161; BB100; BD
90; BE362; BF283; BH175; BK
145; BR435; BX364; BZ
                          1771
Christmas (Handel) X Innocents
(Parish choir)   1772
Christmas (Mendelssohn) X
Mendelssohn   1773
Christmas brings joy (Weyse)
[MDMSMDRM, DLLSFMRS,]
J46; M617   1774
Christmas carol (Davies) [MR
MDMRMD, MLSMRDM, M]
J27b; W48a; X79b; AC80;
AD122; BE223; BV122; BY
105a   1775
Christmas dawn (German trad)
[SMMRMDS, SSSLSM, DLL]
J35; W610, 643; N635; AW
436   1776
-----.   V [SMMRMDS, SSSFSM,
DLL] M643   1776a
Christmas Eve I (English carol)
[MF#SF#MRDFMR, DTLMML,]
BG1a   1777
-----.   R [TDTDRMRDT, SDD
SRM, L]   1778
Christmas Eve II (English carol)
[LMMRDTMLSS, LTTDRF]
BG1b   1779
-----.   R [MLTDRMRDT, TDTL
TDR]   1780
Christmas Eve (Knudsen) [SDD
MRDTDR, SRMFMRM,] J45;
P369   1781
Christmas hymn (Wainwright) X
Yorkshire   1782
Christmas joy (Crueger) [DRM
SFMRD, FMR, MF#S, FS] M
353; Q77; AA145   1783
Christmas morn (Conant) [MFMS
TDRM, SLSFMR, RM] BE24
                          1784

Christmas morn (Freylinghausen.
Geistliche G-B. 1704) X
Mocht hoch die tür   1785
Christmas morn (Hopkins) [DMM
MRMSM, DRRRDRM, D] J545;
W363   1786
Christmas song (Harrington) [SL
SDLT, SSSDMS, SLSD] G98;
I112b; R155; Z198; AC84; AD
118; AE87; AR131; AT69; BB
106; BZ   1787
Christopher (Maker) X St Chris-
topher   1788
Christopher (Peter) [LTDRMFS#,
LTDDRRD, LT] E304; X636a
                            1789
Christopher Sower (Gottshall)
[MFMMMMR, RDDTTL, LMM]
AR418   1790
Christ's return (Hayes) [MR#M
DMSLS, MRDDRMR, M] AX
130   1791
-----. R [MSLDTLLS, MRDDLL
S, M]   1792
Christum wir sollen loben schön
(Geistliche lieder. W'burg.)
[RFSLRSFM, SLDDTLTD,]
J20b; Q104; AA148   1793
Christum wir sollen loben schön.
(German trad) X Cyriacus
                            1794
Christus der ist mein leben
(Vulpius) X Cana   1795
Christus ist auferstanden
(Cologne G-B. 1623) X
Cologne   1796
Christus ist erstanden (Latin. 12th
c) X Christ ist erstanden
                            1797
Christus Rex (Putnam) [DSLM
FSTD, FMRDRTLS,] C145c
                            1798
Christus Rex (Williams) [DMSDT
LSLLS, SFMLS] A543   1799
Christus urunknak (Hungarian
carol) [RRRLLSSLSFM, LLT
SD,] AQ303   1800
Christus vincit (Ambrosian:
ancient) [LLSLL, TLSLL, LSL
MM, S] BP106   1801
Christus vincit (French trad)
[MFMRRMM, MFMRRMM, MF]
BQ248   1802

Christus vincit (Italian Asso. of
St. Cecilia) [MMSSDDMM,
LRSDFMRD.] BQ310   1803
Chrysostom (Barnby) X St
Chrysostom   1804
Church (Holbrook) [SSMDRSRM
RD, MSMFRD] L239; T242;
AJ338   1805
Church (Lindeman) X Kirken
                           1806
Church of God (Rogers) [MR
DDDDDD, TDRRMMR, M] AX
151   1807
Church of God, awake (O'Kane)
[SLSF#SSMRD, LS#LTDTL]
AY518   1808
-----. R [DRMFMRD, TDRDF
MR, DR]   1809
Church triumphant (Elliott) X
Triumphant   1810
Church vigilant (Ziegler) [DM
FSSLDDS, MSLSFMR#] AC
224   1811
City bright (Tyler) [MSFMRD,
RMSFMR, MMFS] W480;
AM662; AP792; BV493   1812
City of David, Bethlehem
(French carol) [DDTLSDRM,
SSFMRDRD] BI84   1813
City of light (Coster) [SMSDR
M, MSFDFM, MSS] G473
                           1814
City Road (Lutkin) [DDRDRM,
MSFMFS, SS#LL] I311   1815
City strong and mighty (Whitting-
ton) [DDDSDD, RRRLRR,
MMMF#] BI16-D   1816
Civitas dei (Caldicott) [SLDFM
MR, MDTDRT, DRM] AB289;
BF508   1817
Civitas dei (Calkin) [SSDDTLT
LS, SSDDDTD] N104; S428;
V711; AB401; BR464a   1818
Claflin (Kotzschmar) [SDRMRR
SM, SDRMRRM, M] AS95
                           1819
Clairvaux (Loyd) [SFMRDTDR, M
LDTRS, SL] AL565   1820
Clairvaux (Polack) [MRDSMFM
RM, MMMF#F#S, S] Q350;
AA98   1821
Clare Market (Palmer) [MRDT
LLSDRDT, SMDTM] AO500

1822
Clarence (Sullivan) [LLLTDTL,
TTTDRDT, D] B140; D347;
W622; BR7 1823

Claribel (Mitchell) [SSSMMRD
SLTT, SSSFF] AN550 1824

Clarion (Rembault) [DSDMDTLS,
SLTDTDMR] D111a 1825

Clark (Main) [SMSDSLSS, DTST
LS, SR] L170b 1826

Clarke's (Clarke) [SSLSSDMMR
DRMS, SSM] L368 1827

Clarksville (Bradbury) [SSFMFS,
LSFMRMFM, SS] AJ79 1828

Claro paschali gaudio (Plainsong,
M 8) X Aurora lucis rutilat
1829

Clarum decus jejunii (Plainsong,
M 2) [DRRRFDRFFMRMM,
SFM] E68 1830

Claudius (Fink) X Bethlehem
1831

Claudius (Mann) [DDTLMMRD,
LTDTLS#, S#L] I595 1833

Claudius (Schulz) [SDDSSMD,
SFMRDS, DT] A138; B423;
C423; E293; F483; J364; K
486; N638; R524; S464; W237;
X14; Y46; Z594; AB387; AC
323; AD445; AE417; AF460;
AG288; AH489; AI351; AK432;
AL193; AM614; AN142; AO580;
AP141; AR592; AW375; BA869;
BD51; BF548; BV654; BX174;
BY732; BZ 1834

-----. [DDDDRR, RMSFMR,]
1835

Clausnitzer (Darmstadt G-B.
1699) [MMSFMRRM, RMFM
RRD, M] M61; O76; Q252;
AA393; AF250 1836

Cleansing (Doane) [SSSMFSLS, S
DTDTLS, S] U159; AH384;
AI198; AM465; AT213; AU350
1837

Cleansing fountain (American
trad) [DMSLSDDLS, DMSSLS
M] G140; I291a; R276; T112;
U151; V251b; AE183; AG98;
AI140; AJ162; AM188; AR477;
AT92; AU37; AV154; AW492; AX
118; AY236; BB163; BZ 1838

Cleansing wave (Knapp) [DM

SMDLDD, LLSSMR, DM] H
241; AX308; BB598 1839

-----. R [SLLLDDSS, MRMF
LLSS,] 1840

Clearway (Baker) X St Timothy
1841

Clemm (Clemm) [MMMRDDD
RDL, SSDDMR] AI188; AM668;
AW325; AX210; AY334; BB
448 1842

-----. [SMSMFFFMR, MMFSS
LS] 1843

Clevedon (Wesley, S.S.) [MD
STDTLLS, FMRDRMR] AP
684a 1844

Cleveland (Burnap) [MRDSLT,
RD#RMRD, MRDS] AA369
1845

Clewer (Filitz) [DDRMFM, SSF
MR, SMLS] B357; E455; AL
545b; AP518 1846

Cliff Town (Routley) [MRD
RSLSDRM, MRDSMR] AQ83;
BV168 1847

Clifton (Burnap) [SLTDRDTRL,
LS, DDDDM] AB217; BF390
1848

Clifton (Clifton) [DMRDTDRM
F, RSMF#SLT] W418b; BV135
1849

Clifton (Jordan) X Rhodes
1850

Clifton (Monk) [SSDMMRD, MM
LSFMR, MM] C312; D332;
L176; W266 1851

Cliftonville (Maker) [MSSSLTD
SS, MSFMRM, M] AP765
1852

Cling to the Bible (Murray)
[DDDDTLSLMSF, RRRRD]
AX140; AY500 1853

-----. R [DDRMDRRMFR,
MMFSSF] 1854

Clinging (Torrance) X Moredun
1855

Clinton (Holbrook) [MMRDSDRM,
MFFMSR, MM] T109; AJ14
1856

Cloisters (Barnby) [MMMMM
SFMRRM, MMMM] A395;
B469; C469; D496; F253b;
J157; K208; M489; U348;
W216a; Z430; AD389; AF

371; AM473; AO414; AR326;
AV71; BA270; BB262; BF588;
BI60; BV405b   1857
Clolata (Palmer) [DDDDMRDD,
FFFFMMRD] D595b; I251;
T26; AJ35; AK473; AO254
                       1858
Clonmel (Irish trad) [SDRDTLS
SLS, FMDMRD] AT182; BE136;
BY743; BZ   1859
Close to my Savior (Mishler)
[MFMMRFSFM, SLSSMMR]
AS219   1860
-----. R [RMFMSFSFM, LFLSM,
SF]   1861
Close to Thee (Vail) [SDMDTRD
S, DMSMDMR, S] G235; I332;
T19; Z413; AE299; AH324; AI
269; AJ24; AR482; AS220; AT
354; AU223; AV382; AX2; BZ
                       1862
-----. R [TDRFTD, MFSSMR,
SDMM]   1863
-----. R [TDRRFTDD, MFSSS
MR, S] AX2   1864
Closer cling to Jesus (Hugg)
[MFMRDTLS, SDMSLSR, M]
AX516; AY311   1865
Closer to Thee, my Father (Ten-
ney) [DDRMMFFMD, DLLD
LS, T] BB632   1866
-----. R [SSLLLLL, SMRRMMF,
MD]   1867
Clovelly (Parker) [LSLMRDTL,
TDRMF#F#S, S] AN187; BX
248   1868
Cluff (Sankey) X I am praying
for you   1869
Clymer (Root) [DMRDTDRD,
DDTLSMDR,] L232   1870
Cobb (Cobb) [DRMMMFMRD,
MFSSSL] A134; B288; D497b;
L34; AM361   1871
Cobbold ("S.M.W.V.R.": Shaw &
Williams) [DDSDRMDM, FSLF
MRD, D] Xapp. 1   1872
Cobern (Gauntlett) [SMDLSSMD
LS, DFFRSM] I92; W168b;
Y388; AJ407; ALsuppl; AM110;
AP93c; AZ39-E; BR244; BV519
                       1873
-----. V [SMDLSSSMDLS, DFF
RS] AZ39-E   1874

Cobham (Finlay) [DSMSLS,
FMSFM, STLSD] BV592b
                       1875
Coblentz (Bourgeois) X Bour-
geois   1876
Coburg (Enckhausen) X
Schönste sonne   1877
Cochran (Burnap) [MRMSLTT
LSM, MRLR, MT] I505 1878
Coelestis aula (Whitney) [DD
SLMSDR, MSDTLTLS] D387b
                       1879
Coeli (Stewart) X Coeli enar-
rant   1880
Coeli enarrant (Stewart) [DM
FSLLS, DRRMFM, MRS]
W335; AB179   1881
Coelites plaudant (Rouen mel.,
17th c) [DSLSFMLTSDDTD,
DRR] A123b; E242b; F564b;
G16; Sap.42; X262a; AL540;
BY345   1882
Coena Domini (Sullivan) [MRD
FMRMDRTDFMRLS] C330b;
D220b; J273; K187; L325;
W453; AO442; AR683; AS66;
AZ1-C; BA296; BR474; BY
323   1883
Colchester (Tans'ur. Compleat
melody) [DDTLSFMRDS, SLT
DRT] AA129; AB237; AN
134; AP51; AQ327; BE182;
BX165   1884
Colchester (Wesley, S.S.)
[MSDFRDTD, SDTLRSFM]
F90; N441; O347; W332; BV
332b; BY349   1885
Cole (Munson) [LSLTL, DLTR
M, SRMRR, T] AQ134 1886
Colebrooke (Smart) [MFMRLS
FM, MSRMTDRT,] AZ92-D
                       1887
Coleman (McKinney) [SMFSD
TLL, LSF#SMRR, S] AT348;
AU423   1888
-----. R [SMRDMRDT, SFMR
FMRD,]   1889
Coleraine (La scala santa. 1681)
[DSSLDDTD, MLLRTLLS,]
E333; BN204   1890
Coleshill (Barton. Psalms)
[LLSDSLLM, DMRDSD, DM]
E492; W31a; X658; AL671b;

AP90b   1891
Collaudemus (French carol)
[DRDTDRRMD, MFSFMRD]
E229b; W554   1892
College (March) [DMSSLMSF, M
RDRM, MFS] AC113   1893
College cross (Grundy) [MRDT
LS, LTTD, MRDRTS,] BV85
                             1894
Collegedale (Miller) [MMMSFM
RMD, MFSLL#LS,] BB147
                             1895
Collingwood (Bate) [DSMRSDRM
FSFFMRDF] F180   1896
Cologne (Cologne G-B. 1623)
[DLSDMRD, DLSDMRD, SL]
X163; AD165   1897
Columba (Irish trad) X St Co-
lumba   1898
Columbia (Blanton) [SDSDMS, FM
MRDRD, SDS] R98; AM108
                             1899
Columbia (Jackson) [DTLSMS,
DTLSMS, F#TLS,] AB335
                             1900
Columbia (Löhr) X St Frances
                             1901
Columbia College (Warren) [DD
DTLTLS, DRMSFMRD] S487
                             1902
Columbia the gem of the ocean
(Becket) X Red, white and
blue   1903
Colwinstone (Lloyd) [MTDFMRR
R, MFLMSRDR,] W408 1904
Colwyn Bay (Linekar) [DMRR
FMRD, MSSLSMF#S,] AM45;
AP452   1905
Colyton (Monk) [MSLTDD, TLS
FMMMFMM] W66   1906
Comavon (James) X Cwmafon
                             1907
Combe Martin (Harwood) [MR
SDTDT, DLSFSMR, S] A174
                             1908
Come (Garrett) X Forgiveness
                             1909
Come, all ye faithful (Wade's
Cantus diversi) X Adeste
fideles   1910
Come all ye saints (Wheelwright)
[SMMRDLSSFM, SLTDRM] BC
11   1911

Come, all ye saints who dwell
(---) [SSSSSSDT, TDLSFM,
MM] BC12   1912
Come, all ye sons of God
(Huish) [SDDMFS, SLLLLS
M, SDD] BC302   1913
Come, all ye sons of Zion
(Tullidge) [SDMFLSM, MF
SSLFS, SD] BC303   1914
Come along, come along
(Smyth) [SSSMRDTLSLTD,
SDDD] BC19   1915
-----. R [SFMMRDDTRDTL,
FMRR]   1916
Come and hear the grand old
story (Ohl) [SDDTSRRD,
SMMRRLR, S] K531   1917
-----. R [MMFMRLTL, SLTD
RMSF,]   1918
Come children (Sewall) [SMS
SLMMFLLTS, SMMM] BR
549   1919
Come closer to me (Warren)
[MMMMMMMRDR, RRRRRR]
AX532   1920
-----. R [MMMFMMD, RRR
MRDS, MM]   1921
Come, come ye saints (English
trad) [DDRMDTDRMF, MDR,
DTD,] BC13   1922
Come dearest Lord (Stephens)
[MDFMRDMRDTDRMRDM,]
BC237   1923
Come, every soul (Stockton)
X Stockton   1924
Come, faithful people (Bicknell)
[MSF#SMLSF#M, MDTLRLT]
E619; X136   1925
Come, follow me (McBurney)
[MDFMSDTLS, SLMFFFS]
BC14   1926
Come, go with me, beyond the
sea (--- arr by Griggs)
[SDRMSDRM, MRDMRD, SD]
BC15   1927
Come, gracious Spirit, heaven-
ly dove (Bradbury) X Baca
                             1928
Come, great deliverer (Doane)
[SFMSDDRDTLL, STDTD]
AU289   1929
-----. R [DTLTDRTLSD,
DDTDRM]   1930

Come, hail the cause (German
trad) X Evergreen   1931
Come, heaven-bound pilgrim
(Shenk) [SSFMLSMFMRDS, SDD
R] AX56; AY323   1932
Come, Holy Ghost (Gibbons) X
Angel's song   1933
Come, Holy Ghost (Hopkins)
[SSSSSLSFS, SLLL#L#] A217b;
B455; C455; D289c   1934
Come Holy Ghost (Sarum plainsong,
M 8) X Veni creator   1935
Come, Holy Ghost, creator blest
(Lambillotte) X Veni, creator
spiritus   1936
Come, Holy Ghost, in love
(Beery) [SSMDRM, SDSLFM,
SFMR,] AS170   1937
Come, Holy Ghost, send down
(---) [SLTDDDDD, SDRMMMR
M] BO187   1938
-----. R [SMDDDDTDRD, SSS
MDD]   1939
-----. [MMMRMRDTLTDR,
MMMR]   1940
Come, Holy Ghost, who ever one
(Pieraccini) X Santa Trinita
1941
Come home (McKinney) [SSF#
SMRDLD, LSDDDRM] AU436
1942
-----. R [SMRD, DLTDRDS, SMDF,
L]   1943
Come home, poor sinner (Jeffrey)
[MRDLD, RDRM, MRDLD, RD]
AX232   1944
-----. R [SSMFL, SSMMR, SSM
FL, S]   1945
Come, humble sinner (---) [LTDL
SMS#LLTD, RMMRD] AU454
1946
Come, just as you are (Showalter)
[MMMMFFM, DDDDRRM, MF]
AX247; AY214   1947
-----. R [SSDDTLS, SSLLSF#S,
SS]   1948
Come, lay his books and papers
by (Edwards) [SDDDDDDD, M
RDMRD, SF] BC338   1949
Come, let us anew (---) [SFM
MRDRMMF#S, SLSF#S,] BB
369   1950
Come, let us anew (Lucas) X

Lucas   1951
Come, let us praise (Grimm)
[SDRMDFMRD, SLSLLTL]
BH201   1952
Come, let us sing an evening
hymn (Cannon) [MSDR
DMFMRRD, FFMSF] BC238
1953
Come, let us sing in sweet ac-
cord (Grauman) [SDDTTLT
S, SSLTDSFM] BH217
1954
Come, let us worship (Russian
mel., 19th c) [MRMFMSFM
RRDTD, DTL] BL44 1955
Come, listen to a prophet's
voice (Daynes) [DMSSF#SLSD
MM, MFSSF] BC46 1956
Come, lost one (Shoemaker)
[DMSSSMRDFF, LSFMMR]
AX225; AY230   1957
-----. R [SLLLDTLLS,
MFMFSSR]   1958
Come, love we God (Shann ms.)
[DSSSSLFS, SL#L#LFSLS]
BG10   1959
Come, my way (La Montaine)
[LLMMF#F#L, LLMMF#F#
L, LL] BL32   1960
Come, O Lord, Jesus (Polish
folk song) [SFMMMMMRM
SF, FFMRR] P311   1961
Come, O Sabbath day (Binder)
X Sabbath hymn   1962
Come, O thou King of Kings
(---) [SMFMRDTD, SLTD
TDLS,] BC20   1963
Come, rejoice (Cannon) [SSDD
RDRMD, FFMDR, SS] BC1
1964
Come, ring out your joy
(Gelineau) [FFLD, DDRD, DLT
L, LSLF, RFSF, FL#S] BSp.
30   1965
Come, Saviour, come (Work)
[MMRDMSDDTL, SSLSMD]
BB544   1966
-----. R [RRDTR, DMRD,
LLTDTLS]   1967
Come, sing to the Lord (de
Jong) [DMDRMSFMRD,
DLFLSM] BC32   1968
Come, sing to the Lord (Gei-

bel) X Trumpet call   1969

Come, sinner, come (Palmer)
[MDRMFLMR, DRDRM, MDR]
AU212; AX229; BB564   1970

Come, thou fount (Wyeth) X
Nettleton   1971

Come, thou glorious day (Smyth)
[MSDMRMFFM, RDDTLST] BC
240   1972

Come, thou Holy Spirit, come
(Webbe) X Veni sancte spiritus
1973

Come, Thou, O come (---)
[MFLS, SDTTLL, SMFMRD]
BR201   1974

Come, thou quickening Spirit
(Meiningen G-B) X St Leonard
1975

Come to Jesus (Pollock) [MFSS
SDDL, LLSLSFM, M] AX223;
AY226   1976

-----. R [TDRRDRMD, SSLDTL
S, M]   1977

Come to me (Brunk) [SMRDDSF
M, SLDSDLRR,] AY395   1978

Come to the fountain (Stebbins)
[SMFSMRDS, DTDRFMR, S]
AX231   1979

-----. R [FFFFMMMM, LLLS
FMRF#]   1980

Come to the Saviour (Maker) X
Invitation   1981

Come to the Saviour (Root) [SL
SMSDRDL, TTDRMDT] N647;
AI391; AM693; AP758; AX233
1982

-----. R [MMFMMRRLR, RRM
RRDD]   1983

Come unto Him and rest (Verdi)
[SSF#SLSMFM, SSF#SLSM]
AU462   1984

Come unto Jesus (Huish) [MF
MLS, SMTRD, LLLSDT] BC22
1985

Come unto Me (Dykes) [DDDLT
DD, RMDRDD, MMM] B387a;
C387a; D437a; F350; T433;
V255b; W390a; AB156; AL470;
AP396; BF343; BY412   1986

Come unto me (Handel) X
Messiah   1987

Come unto Me (Stebbins) [MDRM
MFFFFM, SLSMDD] AI194;

AS193   1988

-----. R [MRMS, SLSD, DTLS
MFFF]   1989

Come, we that love the Lord
(Lowry) [DMDSLTD, RMDSF
MR, RM] AS287; AT308; AU
8; AV343; AW443; AX29; BB
640   1990

-----. R [MSMMMD, MRDSFM
RS, FM]   1991

Come, we that love the Lord
(Williams) X St Thomas
1992

Come, ye disconsolate (Webbe)
X Consolation   1993

Come, ye faithful servants
(Levenson) [MRDTTLD, MR
DTL, MSFM] BH101   1994

Come, ye sinners (Ingalls) X
Invitation   1995

Come, ye sinners (Rousseau)
X Greenville   1996

Come, ye thankful people (Elvey)
X St George's Windsor
1997

Come, ye wanderers (Pollock)
[MFSDMRDDL, DTLSDRM]
AX222; AY225   1998

-----. R [TDRRRDRMD, RM
RDTLS,]   1999

Come, ye weary ones, tonight
(Toews) [MFSSLSM, RDRD
LDS, MF] AX234   2000

Comfort (---) [SLSSMFRSFFM,
SLSSM] AN570; AW229
2001

Comfort (English mel) [MM
MRMFF#S, RRRDRMD, M]
AJ9; BR442   2002

Comfort (Garratt) [MRDSFMR
DRRM, MFSLT] W681   2003

-----. R [SLSDTL, SFMMRD,
DRDS]   2004

Comfort (Rich) [SMRTDDTT, L
SDRMMRR,] BE424   2005

Comfort ye (Genevan Psalter.
1551) X Donne secours
2006

Comforter divine (Reay) [MMM
MMRRS, SSSSSLLT,] D134b
2007

Coming home (Kirkpatrick) X
Lord, I'm coming home

MSMRDM, SDD] AQ40; BZ
2043
-----. V [DDDMSLS, SMMRD
M, DDD] BZ   2044
Comrade heart (Hyatt) [DRMD
RMSSF, LLLSRM, F#] Y207;
AC237   2045
Comrades of the cross (Barnes)
[MFSMRMM, MFSMRM, MF#
S] Y72; AC122   2046
Concord (---) [MMMR#MSRR,
RRRD#RFM, M] C505   2047
Concord (Johnson) [DDRMFMM,
RMRDD, RRFF] BE306   2048
Concordi laetita (Corbeil) X
Orientis partibus   2049
Conditor alme (Sarum antiphonal,
M 4) [MDMSLLFS, SLFSFM
RM] A6a; E1; F45a; J147a;
R245a; X51a; AF113; BJ47;
BL4; BM96; BN3; BO283; BP
2; BZ   2050
-----. V [MDMSSLFS, SLFSFM
RM,] BN3   2051
Conditor alme siderum (Sarum
antiphonale, M 4) X Conditor
alme   2052
Confession (Moravian) X Gregor's
39th metre   2053
Confession (Walther) [LMRMTD
TL, MMLSF#MSF#] M60;
O71; Q251b; AA394   2054
-----. V [LMRMTDTRDTLS#
L, MMF] Q251b   2055
-----. V [RLSLMFMSFMRD#
R, LLR] Q251b   2056
Confidence (Barnby) X Kirkdale
2057
Confidence (Chamberlain) [SM
LSSLDD, SFMLSSMR] V256
2058
Confidence (Crueger. Praxis
pietatis melica) X Ratisbon
2059
Confidence (Moore) [MMRDML
RDTD, MRRRSR] I286   2060
Confirmation (Hayden) X Father,
I come to thee   2061
Confirmation (Rosenmüller) X
Nassau   2062
Congaudeat (Piae cantiones)
[RRMFMR, DRL, LSFF#FMF]
BG83   2063

-----. V [LLTDTLSLM, MRM
FMRMD,] BG83   2064
Congleton (Wise) [LDTDLS#L
SFM, SSMLTD] E312; W98;
X622; AQ69   2065
Congregation (Zinck) [SMD
SSDDT, SDMFMRD, S] BE130
2066
Conisborough (Sanderson) [MF
SLDTLDLLS, SLMSF] Z317;
AC222; AR401; BK92
2067
Coniston (Barnby) X Holy Trin-
ity   2068
Conjugal love (Gould) [DMF
RSSFM, MRDFMR, RM] BR
480a   2069
Conjugial love (?) (Gould)
X Conjugal love (Gould)
2070
Conquering love (Willcocks)
[LLTDRMDR, LDMF#RMM,
M] BV205b   2071
Conquering now (Sweney) X
Victory through grace 2072
Conqueror (Freylinghausen G-
B. 1704) [DRMRMF#SS, D
DTLTLLS,] J435b; M450;
O15; P120; Q129; AA182
2073
-----. V [DRMRMF#SS, DDTD
TLS, D] Q129   2074
Conqueror (Hemy) [DSLSMRD
S, LLFMRMR, D] D126b; H
204; U310; BD160   2075
Conquest (Barrows) [SDLSMD
RM, SLTDRT, DS] A541; BY
219b   2076
Conquest (BridgeP [SLTDMSF,
MRMFFM, SLT] BF585 2077
Conquest (Croft) X Hanover
2078
Conquest (Stainer) [SDTLTDS,
LSMSFM, F#SS] D278a; I448
2079
Conquest (Thommen. Christen-
schatz) X Cassel   2080
Consecration (---) [MDSDLDSD,
MDSDRRRR#] I348a; U268
2081
No entry   2082

Consecration (Byers) [SSSMSDDT
T, DRSSLTD,] AX398   2083
-----. R [SMMMRDRLS, SRRR
MRD,]   2084
Consecration (Brown) [MMMSS
LLFLD, DTLSMS] U261 2085
Consecration (Havergal) [DRM
LSFM, MFSDTLS, ST] F361;
H302; J520; K382; M226; P
406; Q400; W512b; AA355
2086
-----. V [DRMLSFM, MF#SD
TLS, ST] H302   2087
Consecration (Lowry) X Some-
thing for Jesus   2088
Consecration (Malan) X Hendon
2089
Consecration (Morse) [DDRFM
RDR, MLTDRMF] A458a 2090
Consecration (Rounsefell) X
I'll go where you want me to
go   2091
Consecration hymn (Steinel)
[DRMFMLS, SDMTLS, FMF]
BB286   2092
Consecration to Our Lady (Ro-
man hymnal) [MMMSSDD, DF
FFSFM, MM] BO115   2093
-----. R [MMF#SF#T, TDDTLSS
FMM]   2094
Consolation (Beethoven) X Em-
manuel   2095
Consolation (Grimm. Choral
buch) [LTDMRDT, SDRMFFM,
LT] AZ581-F   2096
Consolation (Lindeman) X Holy
mountain   2097
Consolation (Mendelssohn) X
Brightest and best   2098
Consolation (Webbe) [SMDLSS,
FSLTDS, MMMFF] A483; B
388; C388; D637; G312; H441;
I526; J569; K412; L366; M27;
N477; O438; P266; Q531; R373;
S293; U229; V428; W688; Z398;
AA512; AD264; AE163; AG134;
AH382; AI293; AK303; AL435;
AM518; AO250; AP532; AR247;
AS198; AT297; AU449; AV280;
AW243; AY350; BA693; BB223;
BC18; BE40; BO298; BQ117;
BR339; BZ   2099
----- . V [SMDLS, FMFSLTDSS,

MM] BO298   2100
Consolation (Wyeth ...) X
Morning song   2101
Consolator (Arundel hymns)
X Ave, Maris stella 2102
Consolator (Bradshaw) [MSF
MMMRMFDT, RDTDM] BR
348   2103
Consolator (Falconer) [SSDTD
RM, MMSMRDR, MM] D135b
2104
Consolator (Webbe) X Con-
solation   2105
Constance (Doane) [SSDS
MFSRFM, SMRDTS] AV54
2106
Constance (Gauntlett) [SLTDR
MFR, SFMRMRRD,] K106
2107
Constance (Sewall) [MMMSS
M, MMMDRM, MMMF#] BR
324   2108
Constance (Sullivan) [MMMFR
SLS, FMMFRRD, M] H342;
K334b; R220; T271; U188;
AB396; AG162; AJ378; AK
474; AL128; AM433; AP235;
BA337; BF459; BY440b
2109
Constancy (Mendelssohn) [MF
SLSMRFM, SMRDDDT] BE
229   2110
Constantia (Morris) [LLSFM
RMFSLTT, DDTL] X501a
2111
Contemplation (Beethoven)
X Emmanuel   2112
Contemplation (Mendelssohn)
X Trust   2113
Contemplation (Ouseley) [MS
RMSFMRD, MLSMFR, M] F
177; BV489; BY77b   2114
Contentment (Schörring. Koral-
bog. 1781) [DRMMRSLSLS
FM, RMFM] M287; O377;
P229   2115
Contrast (Edson) [DDSDMDMS,
FMFSSFMR,] G349; I538;
V371; AH368; AI271; AT306;
AU24; AV180; BB199 2116
-----. V [DDSDMDMS, FMS
MRDRD,] AH368   2117
Contrition (Bourgeois) X Du

X Eastertime   2156
Cornwall (Wesley) [MSMRDDTL
S,MRDFMLS] F195; BV531b;
BY65   2157
Corona (Stewart) [DSSLSFS,
DFSMFR,RMD] E381b; F224a;
BY452   2158
Coronae (Monk) [MMSSDDMM,
LTDRMSR,M] A105; B185; C
185a; D130; H200; K121; N
375; Q222; R133; S201a; T36;
U111; V163; AE28; AF203; AH
299; AI98; AJ52; AK180; AM
217; AO194; AS161; AW119
                                2159
Coronation (Holden) [SDDDMMRD
R,MRDMRD,R] A355a; B192;
C192a; D450a; H192; I180; J
426b; K131c; L114a; M184;
N153; O6; P7; Q339; R132a;
S192a; T325; U116; V196a; Y
362; Z252; AA93; AB87a; AC
135b; AD180a; AE130; AF195;
AG114; AH197; AJ197; AK184;
AL46b; AM218a; AN9; AO208a;
AP254c; AQ36; AR101; AS159;
AT132; AU1; AV133; AW4; AX
13; AY1; AZ14-R; BA90a; BB
156; BC83; BD30; BE86; BF
327a; BI23; BR53b; BX29; BZ
                                2160
Coronet (Hews) [MRMDRFMMR,
MRMDFMR] AO367   2161
Corpus domini (Malet) [LLLLLLL
S#F#S#L,DDDDD] Eap.47
                                2162
Corwin (Lerman) [SDSMDSMD,
DFMRDT,SD] G262   2163
Costa (Costa) [DSSMDDFMR#
M,RLTDDM] AB51; AR412
                                2164
-----.   V [DSSMDFFMR#M,R
LTDMS] AR412   2165
Cotham (Jenkins) [DDTLTDRS,SM
RD,DDTL] BV80b   2166
Cöthen (Bach) [MRDRSDMRDT
S,LSFMR] X150a   2167
Cottingham (Pullen) [SSMDRMFL
S,SDTLSMR] BK32   2168
Cottman (Cottman) X Morn of
gladness   2169
Country lanes (Vibbard) [MMM
RLSLF,FMMDLS,SM] Y191;

AC172   2170
Courage (Hume) X Dare to be
brave   2171
Courage (LaTrobe) [DSDTLS,
SFMRMFM,DMF#] AZ
595-B   2172
Courage (Parker) [SMDLLLT
DRS,SMDLL] B113b; C113a;
D505a; S270b; AB240a; AK
298; BF467a   2173
Courage (Wales. Univ. Student
hymnal) [MSLSMRDMM,S
MSLSDM] BE380   2174
Courage, brother (Sullivan)
[SSDDDTLTDS, LTDRMS]
G298; I513; AO402; BA573;
BB263; BF627   2175
Courons a la fete (French
trad) X The Spirit   2176
Courtland (Methfessel) [SDS
DRMRD,MRDTLS,SD] M475
                                2177
Coutances (Rouen Antiphoner.
1728) X Because you live
again   2178
Covenant (German trad) X
Gregor's 185th metre-A
                                2179
Covenant (Stainer) [SDMRD
S,FMDRTD,MRS] A285b;
B253b; C253b; D460b; K
284b; BF460   2180
Covenant hymn (Canning) [DD
MSSLSFS,DSFMRRM,] BZ
                                2181
Covenanters (Scottish trad)
[SDDDRMDLLLS,MSDDM]
R153; AT468; AU16; AV
287; BZ   2182
-----.   V [SDDDRMDLLLS,
MSSLD] AT468   2182a
Coventry (Cuzens) [SSDDTD
LSFFM,SSSLS] H349; L170a;
V76; AO97; BB244; BE327
                                2183
Coventry (Howard) [LMTDRDT
L,DRMFMRM,M] AN328;
BX313   2184
Coventry carol (English carol,
1591) [LLS#LDTTLS#,LTD
RTL,M] BG22; BL15   2185
Cover with His life (Belden)
[MMR#MDSSF#SM,MMR#

MDR] BB593 2186

-----. R [TLSDSLLLLS, F#M RD#F#F] 2187

Coverdale's carol (English trad) [MLTDRTLTLSM, MMRTL] BG131 2188

Covert (Tochter Sion. Cologne, 1741) X St Bernard 2189

Cowley (Vale) [DSFMRDRD, DSF#MRSL] A110 2190

Cowper (Mason) [MFSLSMDLS, DRMFMMR,] H232; I291a; L238; M135; N97; Q157b; S 241; T138; U150; V251a; AA 200; AH286; AJ205; AO272a; BA201 2191

Crackington (Sheldon) [MDRM SDTLSLM, F#SLTL] BV316 2192

-----. R [RRDRSFSLS, DLTDD SL] 2193

Cradle hymn (Harmonia sacra, 1753) [MS#LTDTLS#LT, LTDR M] A242 2194

Cradle song (Kirkpatrick) [SDD RMDD, MFSSLF, RMF] A43; S126; W657; X353; AL598; AO630; AP729; AQ276; BK 154; BV95b; BY734a 2195

Craig (Maclean) [DDTLSDDDT LS, LTDRM] V386 2196

Cranham (Holst) [MFSMRD, RMRLR, MFSM] A44; E25; F67; G104; J36; W50; X75; AF128; AL56; BG187; BV100; BY99; BZ 2197

Crasselius (Bach) [SDMRMDLFF SDFRRD, R] X93a 2198

Crasselius (Wittwe. Hamburger Musikalisches handbuch. 1690) [SDSLLSFMD, RMF#SLTD] A255; J255; M98; Q21; AA67; AW569; AZ106-B, 110-A 2199

----. V [SDSLLSFMRD, RMF# SLT] M98 2200

-----. V [SDSLLSLSFMRD, RMF#S] AW569 2200a

-----. V [SDSLLSFMRD, RMMR SL] AZ106-B 2200b

Crasselius (Wittwe. Hamburger Musikalisches handbuch. 1690) X Winchester New (Wittwe.

Hamburger ...) X Wer weiss, wie nahe (Bronner. Choral-buch. 1715) 2201

Create in me (Reynolds) [LLL DTLR, DTTSSLTDR] AT518 2202

Create in this weak form of mine (---) [MRDSLDTT, FM RDRM, MM] BH170 2203

Creation (Haydn) [SDDRRMDL RDT, SLTDR] A309; C252; D464; G66; H111; I84; J442; M493; R97; S69; T270; U8; V100; Z164; AA114; AB48; AC47; AD97; AF72; AG57; AH188; AI41; AJ375; AK66; AL27; AM12; AN33; AO59; AP142; AQ47; AR98; AS88; AT10; AV53; AW50; AY422; BA32; BB91; BD36; BE170; BF230; BI31; BK129; BR 219; BX52; BZ 2204

-----. V [DDRRMDLRDT, TDRMFM] BI31 2205

Creator, alme siderum (Sarum antiphonale) X Conditor alme 2206

Creator alme siderum (Ther- mignon) [DTLSLLSFM, SLTD MRL] BQ151, 309 2207

Creator Spirit, Lord of grace (Bragers) [DDRMDRDT, R RTDRDTL,] BP43 2208

Crediton (Clark) [SDTDSLSF, MSLTDFMR] E206; J54a; W40; X35; AM98; AN238; AP39; BV458 2209

Credo (Stainer) [MMMMLS# LM, RDMSFMRD,] B462; W72; AP262; BV514; BX368; BY132 2210

Creevelea (Davis) [MSFMSFF M, MFSLFMR, R] Y34 2211

Cressbrook (Jackson) [DDD SLTD, RRRMFMR, MM] AO 504 2212

Crete (Dykes) X St Andrew of Crete 2213

Crieff (Finlay) [MSLDTL, SM RF, LRDTLD,] BV303a 2214

Crigglestone (Grundy) [MLTD

MRDL#, LDTLTM, ML] BV509
                                   2215
Crimea (Harris) [MMMFMRMD,
    MMMSF#MF#S,] I124   2216
Crimond (Irvine) [SMFRSFRDT
    D, MMRRF#F#] J522; R104b;
    AF84; AL663b; AM77c; BV
    511a; BY73   2217
Crimson (Doane) X Cleansing
                                   2218
Crispinian (Ivimey) [DDDTSLLS,
    MDRMFSFM] BE56   2219
Croatia (Croatian carol) [DRM
    RMFMDRS, DRMRMF] AK110
                                   2220
Croft (Croft) X Crofts 136th
                                   2221
Croft (Croft) X Hanover   2222
Crofton (Crofton) [SDTLLLFM
    RDT, DD#D#RR] U320; AM624;
    AS414   2223
Croft's (Croft) X Crofts 136th
                                   2224
Croft's 136th (Croft) [SDTDSL,
    SMFSMRDD, MF#] D565;
    F248; J238a; L158; Q580; W
    39; X657; AA124; AF229; AP
    14a; AZ342-F; BJ43; BV196b;
    BY175a   2225
-----. V [SDTDSL, SMSRRD,
    MF#RS] AA124   2226
Croft's 148th (Croft) X Croft's
    136th   2227
Cromer (Lloyd) [SDMLFRDTD,
    RMSDFMR] E237; J62a; X531;
    BV252; BY384   2228
Crosby (Doane) X I am thine
                                   2229
Cross and crown (Booth) [MSLTDT
    LM, LSDFMRM, S] Y256
                                   2230
Cross and crown (Houseley) [SS
    LLDDTT, LSRRR#M, MM] V766
                                   2231
Cross-bearer (Nachtenhöfer) [MM
    MRRDDT, TDRMFRD, M] M385;
    N105; P173; Q150   2232
Cross of Christ (Breedlove)
    [LDMTRTLLSM, SLTRMT]
    AQ68   2233
Cross of Christ, O sacred tree
    (Grove) [MSDSLDS, MRDTDM
    R, MS] AX117; AY199   2234

Cross of Christ, O sacred
    tree (Holsinger) [SSSSLM
    S, SDTRLTD, SS] AS137
                                   2235
Cross of Jesus (Stainer) X
    Crucifixion   2236
Crossing the bar (Barnby) [M
    MMSSD, DFFLLR, RMFS]
    B412; C412; G368; I744;
    N591; S438; W588; Z574;
    AB413; AD464; AH537; AO
    566; AP614; AR427; AV290;
    AW265; BB678; BF669
                                   2237
Crossing the bar (Maker) [MR
    RDSS, SSFDRM, MMMS] Y129
                                   2238
Crossing the bar (Root) X
    Rialto   2239
Crossing the bar (Worden)
    [MDRFFM, RDMSFM, MLSF]
    AY497   2240
Crossings (Gibbs) [DMRTSLLS,
    DDRMSDRS,] X661b   2241
Crowle (Green. Book of psalmody.
    1724) [LMRDTDTLS#L; DT
    LTDR] E463; N248; W94; X
    482; AL310b; AP490a   2242
Crown Him (---) X Hark!
    What mean those holy voices
    (---)   2243
Crown Him (Hughes) X Cwm
    Rhondda   2244
Crown Him (Monk) X Coronae
                                   2245
Crown Him (Montani) [DMM
    LRDT, TDRMDMR, RM] BQ
    43   2246
Crown Him (Terry) [SFMR
    RD, MRSSF#S, DLTS] BN75
                                   2247
Crowned or crucified? [SMMRR
    DFM, MFSDDRMM,] AU447
                                   2248
Croydon (Foss) [DSLSFMRM,
    FSLTDRT, M] X170b; BY
    671   2249
Croyland (LaTrobe) X LaTrobe
                                   2250
Croyland (Statham) X Thanks-
    giving   2251
Crucifer (Irons) [SMMTDDT,
    DLLFLS, SSS] D582b 2252

-----. R [SSSDLLS, SRD#RR#
M, DDD] 2253

Crucifer (Mozart) X Ellesdie
2254

Crucifer (Nicholson) [SDSFSMFS
LR, RMSDLS] F633 2255

Crucifer (Smart) X Bethany
2256

Crucifix (Heber) X Calcutta
2257

Crucifixion (Schumann G-B. 1539)
X Old 112th 2258

Crucifixion (Stainer) [MDSSSDDT,
DMLTDFMM] B152a; C152b;
D201b; E54; I98; J64b; K62a;
N435; R196; S155; V555; Y39;
AD81; AE113; AK163; AM189;
AO173; AP199a; AR171; AW111;
BE102; BV86; BY227 2259

Crucifixion (Zinck. Koralbog.
1801) X Naglet til et kors paa
Jorden 2260

Crucis (Garrett) [SLDDTD, TDM
MR#M, SFMR] N75 2261

Crucis milites (Foster) [SMRD
FLS, DSLSMRDR, R] D581a;
F305; BV435; BY524b 2262

Crucis umbra (Barnby) [SDDTT
LL, LLMRDT, TDR] B150;
C150 2263

Crucis victoria (Foster) [DMF
SMFSL, SSLFMR, RM] F306;
BV319b; BY378 2264

Crudwell (Stanton) [SDRMRDFSL
SM, RMF#SL] BY396b 2265

Crueger (Crueger) [SLSFMRM,
MDDRSM, SLS] D323b; E45;
F219; J495b; K526; W154; X
87; AL139; AN76; BN71; BO19;
BV129; BY80 2266

-----. V [SLSFMRRM, MDDRSM,
SL] BN71 2267

Crueger (Crueger) X Graefenberg
2268

Crueger (Crueger) X St Nicholas
2269

Crueger (Crueger) X Nun danket
2270

Crugybar (Welsh hymn mel)
[DMMMMSMDR, DSLSLSM]
W596; X609; AD334; BY193
2271

-----. V [DMMMMSMDR, DMSL

SLS] AD334 2272

Crusader (Whitney) [SDSLTDRM,
SSMRDL, LR] B85a; C85b;
D507d; S271b; Y274; AC241;
BD161; BF485 2273

Crusader's hymn (Silesian folk)
X St Elizabeth 2274

Crux (Lewis) [DRMMRDMMR
R, RMFSMD,] C163a; D
106a 2275

Crux beata (Miller) X Rockingham 2276

Crux Christi (Mann) X
Watermouth 2277

Crux crudelis (Peace) [MMM
MSSFF, FMMMDMRR,] D
575b 2278

Crux salutifera (Stainer) [RD
TLLS#L, FMRDTDLM, M]
O305 2279

Cry out with joy (Gelineau)
X The Lord is King 2280

Cuddesdon (Ferguson) [SLT
DFF, MDDRM, SLTDF]
W178a; BV128b; BY199a
2281

-----. V [SLTDFF, MRDRM,
SLTDM] BV128b 2282

Culbach (Scheffler's Heilige
seelenlust) [DMSSFSM, DD
TTLLS, ST] A373; D30b;
E286; F73; K481; Q121; W
38b; X1; AA536; AN479; AW
528; BN192; BO117; BV417;
BY327 2283

Culford (Hopkins) [MMSSDDS,
LLSLFMM, MM] G500; I640;
W512a; AZ205-L; BA751; BI
5 2284

-----. V [MMSSDDS, LLSLF
FM, MM] BI-5 2285

Cullingworth (Moss) [MFLSDD
DFMMR, MF#RST] AB207
2286

Culross (Scottish Psalter 1634)
[MLDTLSLT, MLSLTD, LD]
E525b; W353a; X530 2287

-----. V [MLDTLS#LT, ML
S#LTD, SD] W353a 2288

Cultor dei, memento (Plainsong, M 8) [DDDTLTDL, D
DDTSTSL] Eapp. 2 2289

Cumnor (Williams) [LDRMLS,

SMRDRTL, DRM] X213
                                    2290

D

Cumulus (Nicholson) [DTLDTLL
S#, LTDDRMFM] F622   2291

Cura dei (Barrowes) [DRMFS,
LRMFSM, MDTLSF,] A248;
R466   2292

Curfew (Maker) [MMMMRMFFFF
MR, SSLT] Z336; AB32; AC21;
AE45; AR57   2293

Cushman (Turner) [MFSLS, SLT
DMR, DDTLL] G113; R183;
U51; Y71; Z209; AB127; AC
100; AD471; AE95; AF152;
AG85; AK456; AL602; AR146;
AT89; BF305; BK18; BZ
                                    2294

Cutler (Cutler) X All saints new
                                    2295

Cutting (Sherwin) [MRDSLS,
MRDTDR, MLF#S,] J311a;
AI176; AJ298; AK372; AO517;
AT458; AU367; AV262   2296

Cuttle Mills (Griffith) [MMRMFLS
F, MDLFR, SDT] E366; W667;
BV651a;   2297

Cuyler (Brewer) [SDMRDMSR,
RLSMMDRR,] V249a   2298

Cwm Rhondda (Hughes) [SLSD
DTDRMR, MDLFMR] F296b;
G165; J520a; R339a; S104b;
Z256; AD220; AE246; AF93;
AG158a; AK80; AL441a; AM
501; AQ27; AR287; AT55; AU
425; BC56; BK77; BV555b; BY
541; BZ   2299

------. V [SLSDDTDRMR,
MFSFRD] AU425   2300

Cwmafon (James) [LDRMRFMRD,
MRDTMRT] R540; S496; Y92;
AD56   2301

Cwmdu (Evans) [MMMMLDDT, T
DL, SLF, ML] S511b; W294b
                                    2302

Cyprus (Mason) [DDDDDRTD, R
RRRMDTLS,] AP265   2303

Cyprus (Mendelssohn) [DDMMSF
M, MMFLDDD, RM] AB294; AO
304; BF422; BR350   2304

Cyriacus (German trad. 15th c)
[DSSLSFRM, SSSSMFRD,] M352;
AA169   2305

Da Christus geboren war
(Doles) X Lichfield   2306

Da Jesus an des kreuzes
(Babst. G-B. 1545)
[TDTLTRDT, TDTDLLFM,]
Q177; AA207   2307

Da zu dir der heiland kam
(Wagner) [DSLTDRMFM, SD
TTDTL] E313; X271 2308

Dabney (Maclean) [MMMSFM
RD, RMFSDTLS,] V361
                                    2309

Daily, daily (French Parois-
sien mel) [SSDDMDRR, F
LSMFRD, S] E568; AW124;
BO59   2310

------. R [MFSMSSFR, FF
MDMMR, S]   2311

Daily, daily (Hemy) X Conqueror   2312

Daily, daily, sing to Mary
(Catholic) [SMFSDDTLTDS,
FSFMM] BO60   2313

------. R [LLSMRMFSFM,
LTDMSF]   2314

Daily, daily sing to Mary
(French Paroissien mel.)
X Daily, daily   2315

Daily, daily sing to Mary
(Montani) [DDDTLTLS, M
MMRDRT, D] BQ76   2316

Daily, daily sing to Mary
(Piel) [SSDTLSSFM, LDM
RDTL] BP79   2317

Daily, sing in praise of Mary
(Trier G-B.) X Sunrise
                                    2318

Dakota hymn (Dakota Indian
hymn) [LLLMFMMRD, RR
TLTL, L] BZ   2319

Dalalin (Russian trad) X
Easter eggs   2320

Dalarne (Swedish trad) [MLL
LLTDDTLT, RMFMR] M303
                                    2321

Dalehurst (Cottman) [MRDFM
MRD, DRMFFF, RM] C166a;
D108a; H253; I278; J593b;
L441; R319a; S143; T24b;
U370; V298; Y137; Z219;
AA359; AB209; AD431; AE

97; AG87; AH486; AJ5; AL385b; AM360; AN276b; AO277; AP 183a; AR197; AS392; AW218; BA81; BE410; BF486; BR418; BX142   2322

Dalkeith (Hewlett) [SMRDDRM SFM, MMMDDT] D422a; Eap. 25; O235; W429; AB296; AL 268; AP411a; BE297; BI78; BX386   2323

Dallam (Hungarian folk song) [SLTDLS, SDLSFM, LSFM] AN92b   2324

Dallas (Cherubini) [SLSTDLSFF M, SLSTDS] V415; AJ68; BR 328   2325

Dalliba (Bradbury) [DDDDDRRM, MMMSMRRR] AO107b   2326

Damascus (---) [MMMMMRDR, MMMLSSF#S,] AP348b   2327

Dana (Berggren) X Amen, Jesus han skal raade Sardis   2328

Danbury (Gibbs) [MMSLMDD RMS, DDTDS, L] X81   2329

Danby (English trad) [SDTDSL#L S, SDTDRMFMR,] E295; W 623b; X16; AF455; AN291a; AQ90; BY331   2330

Dane (Beethoven) X Sardis   2331

Daniel (Bliss) [MMRDSDD, RM RSM, FFFF] AM660; AP773; AU322; AX563; BB497   2332

Daniel (Irish trad) [DRMFMRDD, SLTDTLSS,] E246; X376; BV 407; BY488   2333

Daniel's band (Bliss) X Daniel   2334

Dank sei Gott [in der höhe] (Gesius) X Commemoration   2335

Danket dem herrn (Bohemian Br.) X Saelir   2336

Dans cette etable (French trad) X Old French noël   2337

Dantzig (Filitz) X Capetown   2338

Dare to be a Daniel (Bliss) X Daniel   2339

Dare to be brave (Hume) [MMM FTLTD, RMFSMRDT] AH613; AT411; AU320; AV401   2340

Dare to do right (Bradbury)

[MRMDMRMS, LSFMRDTD] AP772   2341

-----. R [SDTLTD, LSTLTD, DDTL]   2342

Dark and thorny (Thommen. Christen-schatz) X Cassel   2343

Dark the night (Jones, O.) [LTDMMRDDT, LTDRMRD] BG9   2344

Darkness to dawning (Nichol) X Message   2345

Darmstadt (Darmstadt G-B.) [MDLMRM, TDRDTL, LM F#S] AZ71-A   2346

Darmstadt (Fritsch) [SMRDS SL, LRRSFMRD] A14; J171; Q99; R128; X621; AA385; AB35; AF198; AN71; AQ87; AR84; AW566   2347

-----. V [SMDSSL, LRRSFM RD, SL] Q99   2348

Darmstadt (Maker) [SSSDDD, MFFS, LTDRMM] AB54; BX66   2349

Darmstadt (Meiningen G-B. 1693) X O Gott, du from- mer Gott   2350

Darmstadt (Weimar G-B. 1681) X Jesu, meines lebens leben   2351

Darwall (Darwall) [DMDSMD, TLSFMR, RMDL] A600; B 264; C264; D482b; E517; F371; G171; H185; I26; J 238b; K68; L266; N89; O 130; Q46; R14; S50; V101; W135a; X701; Z260; AA457; AF23; AG110; AL112a; AM 17; AN5; AO9; AP66; AS442; AT108; AW9; AZ342-D; BA 166; BB485; BV24; BX413; BY36; BZ   2352

-----. V [DMDSMD, SLSFMM R, RMD] H185   2353

Darwall's 148th (Darwall) X Darwall (Darwall)   2354

Das alte jahre ist nun dahin (Praetorius) [SDDTDLTD, D RRMRDDT,] AA173   1355

Das herrlich hohe fest (Peter) [DMSLTD, DMDTLT, RRRM] E182b   2356

Das ist meine freude (Freyling-
hausen) [DSMDLTD, MRMLF#
S, RSR] E97   2357
Das ist unbeschreiblich (Herrn-
hut ms.) X Gregor's 141st
metre-A   2358
Das leiden des herrn (German
trad) [LLLMFMMRDT,
RRRRDT] E387; W5a; X119;
AL3b   2359
Das neugeborne (Vulpius) [LLL
MRDMRDT, MMF#SF#M] C494b;
E67b; F395; J274a; W304; X80
b; AF235; AN429; AQ76; BI
47-D; BJ90; BV149   2360
Das neugeborne kindelein (Vul-
pius) X Das neugeborne 2361
Das wahre christenthum (Herrn-
hut ms.) X Gregor's 37th
metre   2362
Das walt' Gott [Vater] (Vetter)
X Vetter   2363
Dauchy (Mendelssohn) [SSF#SL
TDRM, MRMFMRD] AO557
                        2364
Daughter of a mighty Father
(---) [MFSMDLSM, MRMSFM
R, M] BO81   2365
-----. R [SLRMFSM, SLRMFS
M, SS]   2366
Daughter of Zion (---) [DRMMD
DTDRRT, TDRMM] BB303
                        2367
Daughter of Zion (Mason) [MFS
FMRDDRMR, RMFSF] L353
                        2368
-----. R [SLSDTLSLSFM, RMFS
F]   2369
Daughter of Sion (Smart) X
Pilgrims   2370
David (Briggs) [LTDRM, MRDT
LS#S#, LTDT] X501b   2371
David (Dearle) [SDSLSFMFS,
FMDRRD, D] F449; BY483
                        2372
David (Handel) X Thatcher
                        2373
David (Morley) X St Alban's
                        2374
David's harp (---) [MSDTDLRSM,
MMMMRDT] BR56   2375
David's harp (King) [MRDTDRMF
M, RMF#SSSF#S,] A295; B230;

E378; J471; K346; W432;
X476; AP415a; BE100; BY
466   2376
Dawn (Foster) [MSDSMDMR,
DDLSSFMR,] V757   2377
Dawn (Ingham) [MRDRMR, DLS
L, DRMFM] A473; X63; AD
102; AF42; AN96; AQ267;
BY485b   2378
Dawn (Jewish trad) X Rosh
Hashanah I   2379
Dawn (Parker) [SLTDRM, FSF
MRR, RRMF,] L547   2380
Dawn (Stainer) X Laus matu-
tina   2381
Dawn (Wesley) [MSDSLS, MRD
FFMLSFM] Y257   2382
Dawning (Dadman) X Is not
this the land of Beulah
                        2383
Dawning (Sydnor) [SMMRDFF
M, MMRDRM, MS] U65
                        2384
Day (Abbott) [SSDMRMFM,
MFSLSMDM] BB252   2385
Day by day (Carter) X Slings-
by   2386
Day by day (Somervell) X
Stonethwaite   2387
Day of grace (Elliott) [DRRM
FLS, SMMLSF#M, TD] D356b
                        2388
Day of praise (Parker) X
Garden City   2389
Day of praise (Steggall) [SM
DLRT, DLTDFMRM, MM]
D70b; W290; AP682b; BA
388; BV255b   2390
Day of rest (Elliott) [DMSLS
F#SM, RDRMFLR, R] A570
b; B379; C43a; D24a; G352;
I452; K441; M8; S268a; W
508b; Z222; AB234; AD243;
AL188b; AO473; AP344b;
BA380; BE196; BR141; BY
298a   2391
Daymer (Sheldon) [DTSLFSMR,
RFMLS#L, LD] BV134
                        2392
Dayspring (Lloyd) [MFSMDRM
D, RMF#SLT, DS] F434
                        2393
Dayspring (Freylinghausen) X

Gregor's 77th metre   2394
Dayspring (Freylinghausen) X
  Morgenglanz der ewigkeit
                              2395
Daystar (Miller) [SSMMRRD,
  DDDTTL, MMR] N615   2396
Dayton (Showalter) X God moves
  in a mysterious way   2397
Dayton (Wilson) [DTLSDRDRM,
  DFMRMDR] J330b   2398
De boodschap (Dutch trad) X
  Annunciation   2399
De Fleury (Edson) X Contrast
                              2400
De liefde voortgebracht (Oudean.
  Amsterdam Psalter) X Vreu-
  chten   2401
De profundis (English trad)
  [LTDDRRDD, LTDRMFRM]
  E90   2402
De profundis (Walther) [TMTDT
  SLT, TDRDLSFM,] M65; O102;
  Q329; AA415; BY457; BZ
                              2403
-----. V [MLMFMDRM, MFSF
  RDTL,] M65   2404
-----. V [TMTDTLS#LT, TRRDT
  LS] AZ132-E   2405
-----. [TMTDTLSLT, TDRDTLS]
  BY457   2406
De turlu turlutu (French trad)
  X So, Brother   2407
Dear Angel, ever at my side
  (Bragers) [DMMFRDTD, DFSL
  SFMR] BP88   2408
Dear angel! ever at my side
  (Catholic) [SDRMRDTLS, DTD
  RMD, S] BO195   2409
Dear Angel! ever at my side
  (Crookall) [SSSMDTLS, SLTD
  DLFM] BO195a   2410
Dear angel, ever at my side
  (Day's Psalter) X St Flavian
                              2411
Dear Angel! ever at my side
  (Montani) [MMDRMFRDTD, SSM
  FSL] BQ112   2412
Dear crown of all the virgin
  choir (Piel) [MMMSFMRDFFM,
  MFSLR] BQ109   2413
Dear guardian of Mary (Bonitus,
  Brother) [SDTLSMSDRRM, DDT
  LR] AH141; BO128   2414

Dear little One (Walters) [MR
  MSSLFM, MSMDRR, FF] BO
  155   2415
Dear little One! how sweet
  (Montani) [SFMRLSFMDTLS
  LF#S, S] BQ127   2416
Dear Lord, I come (Kolb) [DM
  FMRD, MSLSMR, RRRM]
  AY227   2417
Dear love (Smallman) [SMRDST
  LSDF, LSLTDD] BY594b
                              2418
Dear Maker of the starry skies
  (Piae cantiones, 1582) X
  Ein kind gebor'n   2419
Dear St Joseph, pure (Sisters
  of Notre Dame) [MFSSMDRR,
  FLSDMRD, M] BO132
                              2420
-----. R [RMFFSFMR, MFSL
  SMR, M]   2421
Dear Saviour, when I think of
  thee (Kolb) [SLSFSMFMR,
  STLSLFS] AY248   2422
Dear to the heart (Kirkpatrick)
  [MR#MFMR#MD, DTDRDLS,
  M] BC26   2423
-----. R [DTLDTLTM, DDDRD
  RM, M]   2424
Dearest children God is near
  you (Macfarland) [SMDSMRD
  TL, SMDMMRR,] BC170
                              2425
Dearhurst (Langran) X Deer-
  hurst   2426
Dearmer (Hohenfurth ms.) X
  Quem pastores   2427
Debenham (Redhead) X St Nich-
  olas   2428
Decision (Day) [TMRTRDTLT
  DDRDRM, M] AC232   2429
Decius (Plainsong, 16th c) X
  To God on high   2430
Deck the halls (Welsh trad) X
  Nos galan   2431
Deck thyself (Crueger) X
  Schmuecke dich   2432
Declare, O heavens (Lauben-
  stein) [SDMLRSFM, RMF#
  SLTLS] BL76   2433
Decree (English trad) [MLS#
  LTDMMDT, DLS#LTD] X484;
  BG65a   2434

-----. V [MLS#LTDMMDL,
   MLS#LTD] BG65a   2435
Dedham (Gardiner) [DRRMSFMR,
   RMRDTLS, R] B183b; D189b;
   H388; J428a; K135; L157; V34;
   AA94; AN39; AO210; AR501;
   AW209; AY432; BE105; BR88;
   BX498   2436
Dedicatio anni (Coules) [DRM
   SLLS, DMSMR, DMLS] BR501
                         2437
Dedication (Bentley) [SMRDSSL
   DLS, DTDRMF] AO458   2438
Dedication (Calkin) X Golden corn
                         2439
Dedication (Flittner) X Gregor's
   124th metre   2440
Dedication (Foster) [DRMSSFMF,
   FMRRM, DMS] B448   2441
Dedication (Franz) [MRDFMRDM
   R, SFMRRFM] AR307   2442
Dedication (Gilding) X St Edmund
                         2443
Dedication (Macfarren) [SMFSL
   LL, TLSFM, FLRD] C448; F72b;
   BV657; BY713   2444
Dedication (Sea) X I belong to
   Jesus   2445
Deed (Mason) [MRDTLSDRMR,
   MRDFMR] Y181   2446
Deed (Whitmer) [MRDLTDRMF
   R, MRDLTD] AC187   2447
Deep and glorious (Crueger) X
   St Nicholas   2448
Deep harmony (Parker) [MDMF
   MMMM, MLLSMMRR,] BY281a
                         2449
Deep river (Negro spiritual)
   [MMRDRL, DDDDLSMR, MM]
   AR488   2450
Deeper life (Longacre) [MMFSSLT
   DRDT, TDLSL] G361   2451
Deeper yet (Kirkpatrick) [SSSDD
   D, RRRDRM, SSSD] BB275
                         2452
-----. R [MRDDTL, SSSDMR,
   MRDD]   2453
Deerhurst (Langran) [MSMDTD
   RM, FMRSTLS, M] D292a; E
   ap. 32; F526; J143; K41; M380;
   O121; W2a; AA358; AL177; BB
   237; BE370; BY370   2454
Defend me, O God (Gelineau)

[MLSM, MRM, MTLT, TSM.]
   BSp. 20   2455
Deganwy (Williams) [SMRST
   LDS, DTDRMMR, R] W28;
   BY328a   2456
Deilig er Jorden (Silesian mel)
   X St Elizabeth   2457
Deirdre (Irish trad) [DLDSL
   RDD, DDFMRDM] A268b;
   B525b; C525b; E212b; BN61;
   BY433b   2458
Deirdre (Irish trad) X St
   Patrick (St Patrick) 2459
Delay not (Croft) X Hanover
                         2460
Delhi (Rimbault) [SMDLFM
   RD, MRLSDTLS,] W493a;
   AC248; BY44a   2461
Delight (French) [MFSLSFMF
   SLTDFMRD,] M157   2462
Deliverance (Barnby) X St
   Sylvester   2463
Deliverance (Ogden) [SSDDDD
   RDTT, TDTLLL] AT198
                         2464
-----. R [SSDMRDDTT, TD
   RFMRR]   2465
Deliverance will come (Mat-
   thias) [MRDDDDDD, DRRRR
   M, RM] AY132   2466
Deliverer (---) [MMMMRMSM,
   RRSSFRM, M] AR104; AX
   413; AY107; BB618   2467
Delphine (Danks) [DMRDMRD
   DTLS, SLLLS] T129; AJ188
                         2468
Dem heiligen blute des herrn
   zu gefallen (Schlicht) X
   Gregor's 243rd metre 2469
Demmin (Schop) [DRMDFMR,
   RRMSSF#S, SM] N329 2470
Den blomstertid nu kommer
   (Swedish Koralbok, 1697)
   X Blomstertid   2471
Den des vaters sinn geboren
   (Freylinghausen) [DRMFSS
   MD, LSFMRRD, M] E218
                         2472
Den die Engel droben (Gregor)
   X Gregor's 6th metre
                         2473
Den Herre Krist i dødens baand
   (Latin, 12th c) X Christ lag

in todesbanden 2474
Den signede dag (Weyse) X
Weyse 2475
Den store hvide flok (Lindeman)
[SDDTLSSM, MFFSRMSR,]
O492a 2476
Den store, hvite flokke (Nor-
wegian trad) X Behold a host
2477
Den store mester kommer (Hoff-
man) X Fulfillment 2478
Denbigh (Welsh hymn mel) [LLT
DTL, TDRMRM, MRDT] E439;
W415b; X580; AM376 2479
Denby (Dale) [SLSDRM, MFM
RLT, SLS] B395; J580; M273;
N490; O233; Q259; AB96; AL
151; BD157; BF580 2480
Denfield (Gläzer) X Azmon 2481
Denham (Damon's Psalter, 1579)
X Southwell 2482
Denmark (---) [MFSMM, RDLDD,
TLSDRM] M278; BC145
2483
Dennis (Naegeli) [MMDMRTRD,
DDLDDSDT,] A495b; D502;
G69; H124; I100; J543; L63;
M21; N294; P58; R105; S279;
T41; U373; V608; Y384; Z399;
AB208; AD239; AE67; AF76;
AG50; AH226; AI276; AJ60;
AL376; AM285b; AN563; AO
103; AP571; AR505; AS67; AT
366; AU239; AV77; AW41; AX
489; AY399; BB379; BC67; BE
402; BF395; BK174; BR123;
BX312b; BY355a; BZ 2484
Dennis (Thalben-Ball) [MDRMSLS
MRDM, MFSTL] BE22 2485
Denny (Mason) [MFSSSLTDDD,
LRDTLS,] I126; L423 2486
Dent Dale (English trad) [DDDD
TDR, DRMMFMRDS,] E23; X88
2487
Denver (Houseley) [MMMSMM
RR, RDDFFM, MM] U22; Z175;
AR96 2488
Deo gracias (English trad) X
Agincourt 2489
Deo gratias (Crueger) X Nun
danket 2490
Deo gratias (Ponsonby) [DMMFM
RSSL, SFMFSMR] U333; AC226;

AL592 2491
DePauw (McCutchan) [SMRDD
MSD, DTLSMMDS,] G82;
S423a; AK407 2492
Dependence (Lowry) X Need
2493
Depth of mercy (Beethoven)
[MDRMFLR, RMFSSF#S,
MR] AY216 2494
Der am kreuz (Koenig) [LM
LTDTLS#M, TDRDTTL,]
Q144; AA194 2495
Der Freyschuetz (Weber) X
Jewett 2496
Der Heilige Geist herniederkam
(Schein) [LLLMMFFM, DRM
FMRRD,] AA239 2497
Der lieben Sonne licht und
pracht (Freylinghausen.
Geistriches G-B. 1704) X
Se solens skjøune lys og
pragt 2498
Der mange skal komme (Then
Swenska Psalmboken 1695)
X Stockholm 2499
Der Sabbath ist um's menschen
will'n (German trad) X
Gregor's 159th metre 2500
Der tag bricht an (Vulpius)
[LMMFMRLDTL, LDLMF#S]
E101; X563; BI66 2501
Der tag der ist [so freuden
reich] (Hohenfurth ms. 1410)
X Dies est laetitiae 2502
Der tag mit seinem lichte
(Ebeling) X Shining day
2503
Derbe (Sacred harmony. 1780)
[DRMDSFM, RMFRLSFM, S]
AL573; BY712a 2504
Derry (Dykes) [MMRDLSDR,
RRMFMRD#D#] F323
2505
Derwent (Adcock) [SMLSFM, S
DFMRD, MRSF#] O405
2506
Descend, O sabbath princess
(Nowakowsky) [SSMRDDMS
TLMS, SLFM] BH107
2507
Desire (Geistliche volkslied,
1850) [LTDDRDTT, DTLTL
S#LL] M399; N117; Q153;

AA209; AM192; AO279   2508
Desire (Minor: Geistliche volkslied,
   1850) X Cassel (Major)
                                    2509
Desire (Smart) [DDFMRS, DRR
   M, MMF#SLT,] D654a   2510
Desire (Woodbury) [SDRMDRDTD,
   RMMSMRRR] L575a; AA460
                                    2511
Desiring to love (Handel) [DM
   FSFMRFM, DMFSLTD] AZ
   92-E   2512
Despair not, O heart (Luther.
   Christlich G-B. 1542) X
   Jam moesta   2513
Despise not, Lord (Miller) X
   Sweet Sabbath   2514
Dessau (Ahle) X Liebster Jesu
                                    2515
Dessler (Bach) [DMFSMLSLF
   M, DTLF#SL] X703   2516
Destiny (French trad) [DDDDDR
   RMR, DFFMMMD] Y125
                                    2517
Det kimer nu til julefest (Balle)
   X Emmanuel   2518
Detroit (Fishwick) [DRMDSFM
   RM, MFSMTTD] M616   2519
Detroit (Hastings) [MMFMRM, S
   SLSF#S, SSSL] L251; BR96
                                    2520
Detroit (Suppl. to Kentucky
   harmony, 1820) X Detroy
                                    2521
Detroy (Suppl. to Ky. Harmony,
   1820) [LDRMDRDLS#L, LDR
   MS#L,] AR106; BZ   2522
-----. V [LDRMDRDLSL, LDRM
   SL,] BZ   2523
Detroy (Suppl. to Kentucky Har-
   mony, 1820) X Morning song
   (Wyeth Repository, 1813)
                                    2524
Deus creator omnium (Ambrosian)
   [RFMSSSFM, RMFSRMRD,]
   BJ91   2525
Deus creator omnium (Sarum
   Antiphonal. M 4) [FMSLSFS
   LSFMM, RRLL] E49; X44a
                                    2526
-----. V [FMSLSFSLSFMM,
   RLLL] X44a   2526a
Deus fortis (Norwegian mel) [DR

DSLTDMRD, DRDSLT] J357;
   P205   2527
Deus tuorum militum (Grenoble
   Antiphoner, 1753) [DMSDS
   FMRD, DMDLTDS] A344;
   E181b; F129b; J494a; R83;
   Sap. 29; W356; X633; AD
   448; AE465; AF150; AH568;
   AK438; AL8a; AN149; AP
   152a; AQ305; AR585; BN52;
   BO269; BV35; BY238; BZ
                                    2528
Deus, tuorum militum (Plain-
   song, M 8) X Exultet
   caelum laudibus   2529
Deus vitae (Thurman) [SSMF
   SDDTT, LSLFSM, S] U276
                                    2530
Deus vobiscum (Tomer) X
   God be with you   2531
Deva (Hopkins) [MRMFSS,
   LDTLS, SLSFM] D35a; G
   445; I652; AP697b   2532
Deventer (Tours) [SSDTLSFM,
   SDLRSLTL] I708; V613;
   AB276; AC257   2533
Devereaux (Devereaux) X
   Boardman   2534
Devizes (Tucker) [DDRMFM
   RDTD, RMSFRM] H83; L
   447; N483   2535
Devonshire (English trad:
   Devonshire) [DMMMMMRD,
   RMSSFMR, R] E294; W270;
   X459a   2536
Devonshire (Lampe) X Kent
                                    2537
Devotion (Doane) X More
   love to thee   2538
Devotion (Gower) [SSSF#FM,
   MMDRRM, SSLS] AM536
                                    2539
Devotion (Hall) [SLDLSLDD,
   SDRMDRLD,] AQ183   2540
Devotion (Johnson) [SMRDRD
   TD, MRDTDTLS,] B34; C
   34; D643b; L32; N619   2541
Devotion (Meiningen G-B. 1693)
   X Munich   2542
Dexter Street (Douglas) [SM
   RDMSLSFM, LLSLT] A100
                                    2543
Diadem (Ellor) [SDRMFSDRD

TD, TLSSS] G164c; AM218c;
AO208b; AT134; AU255; AW5;
BZ   2544
-----. R [SFMRFMRDMRDTRD
D, F]   2545
Diadema (Barnby) [MSDTLSMDRRM,
FFMLS] I486; T394; V360;
BX471   2546
Diademata (Barnby) [DTLTTL, S
DTDRSM, MMM] K123; M452
                                  2547
Diademata (Elvey) [DDDMML,
LSDFMR, RMSL] A352; B190;
C190; D374a; F224b; G170;
H198; I179; J431; K134a; L153;
N341; P30; Q341; R213; S190;
T91; U115; V195; W136; Y171;
Z250; AA104; AB88; AC136;
AD170; AE132; AF199; AG100;
AH328; AJ134; AK176; AL115;
AM216; AN248; AO198; AP
227; AR105; AS157; AT152; AU
18; AV141; AW118; AZ595-C;
BA228; BB162; BD118; BE312;
BF325; BK114; BL58; BV209;
BX307; BY182; BZ   2548
Dian (Shaw) [MFSLRMF, FSLS
MDR, MM] E396   2549
Diana (English trad) [DRMDFMR
MFM, SFMR] A585b   2550
Dibden (Jackson) [DMMLSFMF,
MS#LRDT, S#S#] E433; X
254   2551
Dich bit ich, trautes Jesulein
(Helder) [DMDSRFMR, RMD
LSLTD,] AA188   2552
Dich, Jesu, loben vir (Freyling-
hausen) X Gregor's 341st metre
                           2553
Dickinson (Austrian trad) X The
Shepherd   2554
Dickson (Warner) [SSLTDDRM,
MSRMRTDT,] AZ606-C
                           2555
Did you think to pray (Perkins)
[MMFMRDSD, RRFMR, RRR]
AU335; AX361; BC31   2556
-----. R [SSLSF#SDS, MSLSFM
R, M]   2557
Die ganze welt (Cologne G-B) X
Hilariter   2558
Die Gottes seraphin (Eberhard)
X Gregor's 249th metre 2559

Die güldne sonne (Ebeling) X
Philippi   2560
Die helle sonne (Staden)
[DDDLFMRD, SLDSFM, MM]
J6; K9; AW542   2561
Die helle sonn' leucht't (Vul-
pius) [DMFSDTLS, SSF#SL
DTD,] Q547; AA266   2562
Die König (Cornelius) X The
Kings   2563
Die nacht ist kommen (Nigidius)
[DRMFMRRD#RMR, FFFRS]
Q556; X48a   2564
Die sach' ist dein (Haydn, J.
M.) X Salzburg II   2565
Die seele Christi heil'ge mich
(Geistliche gesang. Witten-
burg, 1544) X Rhau[w]
                           2566
Die wanderschaft in dieser
zeit (Herrnhut ms.) X
Gregor's 166th metre   2567
Dies dominica (Dykes) [MSFM
RDD, DTLFLS, MSF] D24c;
F401; K186; V554; BA500;
BV391   2568
Dies est laetitiae (Hohenfurth
ms. 1410) [DDRMFRD, RRLT
DD, DDRM] A29a; C485; M
459; O185; P165; Q78; X11;
AZ215-a; BG158; BQ294
                           2569
-----. V [DDRMFRD, RDLTD
RD, DD] Q78   2570
-----. V [DDDRMFRD, MRR
LTDRD] M459   2571
-----. V [DDRSFMRD, RRLT
DRD, D] AZ215-A   2572
-----. V [DDRMFRD, RRLTD
TD, DD] X11   2573
-----. V [DDRMFSFM, DDTD
LS, DD] BQ294   2574
Dies irae (Dykes) [DTLTDRM
L, FFMLRDTD#,] B65a;
C65; D36; I747; K515
                           2575
Dies irae (Latin mel. ca 1200)
[DRMDFMRD, RRMRDTLS,]
Q607; AA555   2576
Dies irae (Lindeman) [LLD
LTDRMM, DRMRMF#S]
O601   2577
Dies irae (Parry) X Merthyr

SLSMFS,] A20; B74; C74a; D
52a; E613; F58; J17; K20a; Q
98; R7; W60; X387; AF111;
AK13; AL52; AN172; AP166;
AQ290; AR116; BL5; BV109;
BY85a; BZ   2612
-----. V [DDRMFMRD, DMSL
SMR, D] BL5   2613
Dix (Kocher) [DTDRDFFM, LTD
LSSS, D] A52; B94; C94; D65;
E39; F79; G18; H148; I28; J52;
K38; M6; N50; O219; Q127;
R2; S71b; T204; U16; V113;
W63; X83; Y357; Z167; AA
183; AB120; AC46; AD94; AE14;
AF66; AG59; AH206; AI46; AJ
293; AK12; AL15a; AM154;
AN32; AO119; AP58; AQ12;
AR92; AS111; AT14; AU246;
AV88; AW51; AX634; AZ581-
H; BA181; BB22; BD40; BE35;
BF257; BK126; BL78; BR156;
BV126; BX13; BY90; BZ
                             2614
Djupt sjun ker aret i sin gang
(Beethoven) X Emmanuel
                             2615
Do what is right (Kaillmark)
[MRDMRDRDMD, DTLSDM]
BC27   2616
-----. R [SSSLSSSSSLS, SDM
SM]   2617
Do you love the world (Hunter)
[DRMMMDMSSM, DRMMSF]
AX265   2618
-----. R [SSLLFLLSSM, SSFFF
M]   2619
Doane (Calkin) X Waltham 2620
Doane I (Doane) [DRMRDLSD,
DRRRMR, DD] W679b   2621
Doane II (Doane) [DRMR#MFS,
SSDTLS, SSS] Z332; AE238;
AP496; AR481; AS42; AT329;
AU156; AX352; AY430; BB
324   2622
-----. R [MSSSSMSDTLS,
SSLDL]   2623
Dr. Steggall's Tune 172 (Stephens)
[MSDMRMF, LSMDRM, MSD]
AZ591-E   2624
Doers (Costa) X Costa   2625
Does Jesus care (Hall) [SMRDL
LSFM, MRD#RSFM,] AX528;

AY464   2626
-----. R [DTFTRDMS, MRTL
MF#S, T]   2627
Does the journey seem long?
(Pyper) [MFSF#SM, DRMR#
MD, DRMR] BC245   2628
Dolberrow (Stanton) [DSMRDT
DLS, DRMRDTL,] F616
                             2629
Dolce domum (Ambrose) X
Ambrose   2630
Dole (Rees) [MRDTDL, DTM
MR#M, MFMR] W190b 2631
Doles (Doles. Choral-buch)
[SMFSDLSFM, MFMRDFM]
AA400   2632
Dolgelly (Welsh hymn mel)
[LMRDTL, MSF#MR#M, MMR
M] E349; J268b; X263; AL
226b; BX484b   2633
Dolomite chant (Austrian trad)
[MMMFMR, FFFSFM, MMMF]
G323; R382; S501; AD277;
AP618; BK96   2634
Dolut (Meyer) [DTLSDTLS, T
DRMRDRT,] Y339; AC164
                             2635
Dolwyddelan (German, 1693)
[MMLSFM, SRFMRD, MMLS]
BY649   2636
Domenica (Oakeley) X Dominica
                             2637
Domine, clamave (Knecht) [LT
MRDTLS#L, TDDRRM, M]
Q593; AA542   2638
Domine, nobiscum (Barnby)
[MMLSMRDR, MDTLTTS, M]
BR506   2639
Dominic, Our Lady's champion
(Goss) X Lauda anima 2640
Dominica (Oakeley) [SSSDRM,
MRMFRT, SLTD] C45b; D28b;
F42; G397; K442; V496; W
267a; AD35; AL189b; AP343b;
BE92; BV68; BX100   2641
Dominus misericordiae (Stainer)
[MMMMMMMMSSM, MMMMM]
D630b   2642
Dominus regit (Dykes) X Dom-
inus regit me   2643
Dominus regit me (Dykes)
[MSFMMRRD, SSLTDMR,]
A345b; B326; C326a; D412a;

F197; G353; I136; J530a; K
345; L490; M189; O420; R106
a; S99; T404; U80; V334; W
438a; X654b; Y35; Z169; AB
62; AC50; AD252; AE69; AF
79; AG51a; AH219; AK304;
AL280b; AM141; AN87b; AO324;
AP146a; AR600; AS429; AT280;
AV224; AZ15-C; BA295; BB86;
BD59; BE330; BF243; BR411;
BV546b; BX120; BY72a; BZ
                                              2644
Dominus sanctus (Pierre) [DS
LTD, MMFRD, SSMF#S, M] AJ
432   2645
Dominus vobiscum (Somervell)
[DDRMSFMRRM, DDTDLS]
F489   2646
Domus Domini (Jordan) [SMD
LTD, TLLLRT, SDDR] D484a
                                              2647
Dona (Goss) [SDMSFMRD, TL
DTLS, DL] D25b; W200
                                              2648
Dona nobis pacem (---) [DSMRS
FMRDDT, LSFMS] BK34
                                              2649
Dona nobis pacem (Mozart) [MM
MMSFMFMFLFMR, MM] AP
807   2650
Donald (Bergquist) [MDDRMSMR,
DRMSMRR, M] N656   2651
Doncaster (Wesley) [SDMFLS,
SLSTDR, SSDT] A293; D181a;
F310; J3; K4; M335; N72; O
469; W490; AA504; AZ582-I; BA
557; BV525; BY530b   2652
Donne secours (Genevan Psalter,
1551) [MDRMSMDRDTL, MM
RML] E564; F17a; R285; S
386; W360; X324; AD210; AF
334; AL91; AN230; AP157a; AQ
72; BJ74; BY84   2653
Donora (Doane) X Jesus, thy
name I love   2654
Don't forget the Sabbath (Brad-
bury) [DDTLSM, MRMFLLS,
SDD] BB653   2655
-----. R [MMRRDDLL, SMRM
FLS, M]   2656
Don't forget to pray (Perkins) X
Did you think to pray   2657
Don't let your light burn low

(Williams) [SSSSSLTD, LSD
RDRM, S] AX436   2658
-----. R [DMMMDRD, DDD
RDLS, SS]   2659
Don't turn Him away (Lillenas)
[MMMFMRDS, LDDRDLS, T]
AU433   2660
-----. R [MRDRMD, MRDRM
D, LLLR]   2661
Donum Dei (True) [DMMR#MF
M, RSDDTL, LSS] BB149
                                              2662
Donum Dei (Vincent) [MRRR
MFFMRM, MMLSF#M] D228a
                                              2663
Door keeper (Shaw) [DRMM
MRSMD, DRMRDL, M] X196
                                              2664
Dorian mode (Latin, 18th c)
X Christ lag in todes ban-
den   2665
Dorking (English trad) [SDSD
SDRMFS, MFSLSF] X205;
AN157; AW72; BY681 2666
-----. V [SDSDRMFS, MFS
LSFMR] AN157   2667
Dorothea (Johnson) [MFSD
MRDS, LDSDTLS, T] N318
                                              2668
Dorothy (Pratt) [SSSLTDRM,
MRMFSM, DL] AH321; BF
330   2669
Dorothy (Sampaix) [MMRRD
TLS, SSSRSS, MM] H102
                                              2670
Dorrnance (Woodbury) [MM
MDRRMM, SLSMDMR, M]
G143; H32; L133; T193;
U379; V556; Z468; AD512;
AE117; AH507; AJ281; AO
168; AR362; AT538; AV112;
AW441; AX582; BA701; BF
606; BR34   2671
Dort (Mason) [DMDSLS, STS
RMR, DTLS,] H530; I161;
K217; L342; N211; S413;
AC283; AD384; AE135; AH
305; AI369; AO582; AR523;
AS371; AW348; BA871; BB
512; BZ   2672
Doudney (Bonner) [MDSTLSD
RFM, MTRDMM] H486
                                              2673

Dove (Bradbury) X Lottie 2674
Dover (Williams. Psalmody, ca
  1700) X Durham   2675
Doversdale (Stanley) [SDFMRD
  SSLTD, DDDTL] W639; AL391
                          2676
Down Ampney (Williams) [DRM
  SLS, SLSDTLS, S] A376; E152;
  J123; W191; X177; AF239; BL
  34; BV214; BY224   2677
Down by the river's verdant
  side (---) [MFSSSMFSSS,
  MMMMRM] BC55   2678
Down in yon forest (English trad)
  [LTLSLTDTLT, MLTLSL] BG
  61   2679
Downing (Lloyd) [SDDRMRD,
  DRRDTLS, SL] BY574b   2680
Downs (Mason) [DMSLSSFM, S
  LDSF#S, DT] L425; R422;
  T66; V339; AI366; AJ101; AM
  422; AR545; AS415; AV55; BA
  138; BB233   2681
Downshire Hill (Shaw) [SDDDTD
  RMMF, MLSDRF] X328a; AD
  365   2682
Doxford (Terry) [DMFSFMR, DR
  MFMFSLS,] BY364   2683
Doxology (Bourgeois) X Old
  100th   2684
Dransfield (Thalben-Ball) [MR
  MLSDRM, MSDTSLDT] BE26
                        2685
Draw me nearer (Doane) X I
  am thine   2686
Draw near (McKinney) [SDMFS,
  DTDLSS, SLLDS] AU304
                        2687
Draw nigh (Buck) [DRMFRSLSD
  FFM, F#S#TL] E307; BE255
                        2688
Draw us to thee (Norwegian)
  [MMRMLLSM, SFMRDRM, L]
  P215   2689
Dreamers (Daniels) [LMMMFRM,
  SLMDTM, LMM] Y327; AC91;
  AD128   2690
Dresden (Dresden G-B. 1632)
  [DDSSFRM, RRMSLS, SLS]
  M326; Q97; AA153   2691
Dresden (Dresden, 1694) X So
  giebst du   2692
Dresden (Redhead) X Redhead

No. 46   2693
Dresden (Schmidlin) X Swiss
  tune   2694
Dresden (Schulz) X Claudius
                        2695
Drese (Drese) X Rochelle
                        2696
Dretzel I (Dretzel, abr. by
  Monk) [DSSFMRDD, DTLTL
  LS, D] E281; F25; O463;
  BY479b   2697
Dretzel II (Dretzel) [DMDRSF
  MRD, RRRMSSF#] M494;
  Q243; AA62   2698
Drink to me only with thine
  eyes (Melish) X I heard the
  voice of Jesus say   2699
Drumcondra (Wilson) [DRMFS
  MRMD, MFSLL#L#L] X601
                        2700
Du bist ja, Jesu, meine
  freude (Grimm. Choral buch)
  X Old 466th (alt)   2701
Du ewiger abgrund der seligen
  liebe (Freylinghausen) X
  Gregor's 221st metre
                        2702
Du fort de ma detresse
  (Bourgeois) (MLTDTLS, DT
  LDRM, RMF#] O100; AI
  432   2703
-----. V [LRMFMRD, FRM
  FSL, LS#L] AI432   2704
Du friedensfürst, Herr Jesu
  Christ (Gesius) [MDRMSFM,
  SFMRRM, MDR] G52; AN
  124a; BZ   2705
Du lifvets bröd (Sohren) X
  Elbing   2706
Du meine seele singe (Ebeling)
  [DMSDMRR, TDSSFM, DMS]
  J176b; AF189   2707
Du meiner seelen' (Hungarian
  chorale mel 16th c) [MMSF
  RMDR, SSSDTLLS,] AK276;
  AN16; AQ38; AW98   2708
Du, O schönes weltgebaeude
  (Hintze) X Salzburg   2709
Du, O schönes weltegebaudes
  (Crueger) [LMLLTSF#M,
  DMRDTTL, L] O42; AZ
  168-C   2710
Du vaere lovet, Jesus Krist

(Trad. , ca 1400) X Redeemer
2711
Duane Street (Coles) [SDMMDRF
F,RMDTDRSS,] G199; H251;
I306; AM264; AW468; AX156;
AY62; BB371   2712
Düben (Düben) X Jesu   2713
Dublin (---) [LLSDTLS#L,DM
RDTD,DM] AY178   2714
Dublin (Howard) X Smith   2715
Dublin (Lutkin) [DDTTLLS,SL
LSSFFM,D] AC243   2716
Dublin (A collection of hymns...
Dublin, 1749) X Irish   2717
Duke Street (Hatton) [DMFSLTDT
LS,SSSLS] A148; B32; C187;
D132; E167; F268; G17; H22;
I5; J307; K136b; L79; M106;
N368; O28; P24; Q200; R5;
S377; T286; U392; V363; W
517b; X298; Y116; Z152; AA
229; AB373; AC278; AD6;
AE342; AF202; AG267; AH461;
AI167; AJ397; AK350; AL249a;
AM3a; AN14; AO53; AP89; AQ
43; AR22; AS9; AT19; AU150;
AV30; AW341; AY426; AZ22ᵣ
Q; BA34; BB1; BC52; BD34;
BE325; BF527; BK120; BL59;
BR46; BV577b; BX24; BY184b;
BZ   2718
Dulce (Barnby) [MRMFRRD,SF
MF#SF#M,LS] V217   2719
Dulce carmen (Essay on the church
plain chant) [DRMFSFMR,D
DDFMRD,L] A54; B110; C110;
D73a; E63; F82b; G319; J58;
K57; M379; N254; O295; R343;
S304; T361; V513; W563; X
199; Z259; AD223; AE22; AF
344; AK3; AL515b; AN323; AO
111; AP341; AY431; AZ167-G;
BA123; BB87; BE90; BF213;
BQ52; BR55; BV124; BX381;
BY494a; BZ   2720
Dulce domum (Ambrose) X
Ambrose   2721
Dulce nomen (Tours) X Gouda
2722
Dulcetta (Beethoven) [MRDDFM
MR,RRMFLDTM] I88b   2723
Dulcimer (Lewis) X Beloved
2724

Dulcina (English trad) [MFSS
FMRD, LTDDTLS,M] W244
2725
Dulcis Jesu memoria (Ander-
nach, 1608) X Jesu dulcis
memoria   2726
Dulcis memoria (Dykes) X
Faith   2727
Dulwich (McWilliam) [LTDR
MT,RMF#SLM,SF#RT,]
BV507   2728
Dummerston (Herron) [SS
MDSMSLFRM,SDDMR] C220
2729
Dumpton Gap (Grundy) [MLDT
LSFMFS,DRMFSL] BV335
2730
Dunaha (Irish trad) [MMMSS
RMFRM,RDDDDT] W438a
2732
Dunbar (Dunbar) X A few
more years   2733
Dunbar (Dunbar) X I'll live
for Him   2734
Dunblane Cathedral (Barnes)
[DTLSSSDTLS,MMMMLS]
W373; AC8; AD369; AL251
2735
Dundee (Scottish Psalter, 1615)
[DMFSDRMF,MRDDTD,SD]
A397; B269; C269; D417;
E43; F80; G68; H52; I96;
J181; K502; L97; M49; N
242; O64; P19; Q49; R112;
S98; T216a; U11; V91; W
227; X557; Y372; Z162;
AA13; AB102; AD88; AE58;
AF85; AG45; AH225; AI414;
AJ247b; AK75; AL176; AM7;
AN80; AO99; AP108; AQ34;
AR500; AS441; AT398; AW
60; AY49; AZ14-P; BA83;
BB84; BD193; BF225; BI
36; BJ10; BK71; BR155;
BV75b; BX70; BY53; BZ
2736
Dundee (Damon's Booke of
musicke, 1591) X Windsor
(Tye)   2737
Dunelm (Vincent) [MFLSDM
RD,FFMLLSDT] BY540
2738
Dunfermline (Scottish Psalter)

B431; E64; F209; R95; W295; X517; AF395; AL40; AM317; AN203; AP61a; AW575; BB 509; BV304; BX383; BY501; BZ 2739

Dunn Aluinn (Irish trad) [MLL TDL, TTLSL, MMMDR] E356; W525a; X115b 2740

Dunstan (Barnby) X Just as I am 2741

Dunstan (English trad) [MLLD RMRDTL, SSMRMS] E638d; X393b 2742

Durch Adam's fall (German, 1525) [MMRTRDTL, LDRMSF#M, M] O296 2743

Durch Adam's fall ist ganz ver- derbt (German mel) X Gre- gor's 212th metre 2744

Durham (Dykes) X St Agnes 2745

Durham (Ravenscroft's Psalter) [DSMLSMDR, FMSLLS, S] A297; W274a; X525; AL203a; AP107b; AW279 2746

Durham (Williams. Psalmody, ca 1770) [SMFSTD, DTDTLS, MFSL] J564b; K141; L123; M82; Q241; W376; AA270; BR 329; BY428 2747

During (Bradbury) [SSSSSSSSM, DLLDLS, D] L539a 2748

Durrow (Irish trad) [MLTDTLS M, RTLTDRM, M] R93; W454; AF248 2749

Dusseldorf (Havergal) [SDRMFS DT, RSLTDLLS,] V94 2750

Dusseldorf (Mendelssohn) [SMRT DLSM, SDTRDLS, S] BY210b 2751

Dusseldorf (Neander) X Neander 2752

Dutch carol (Dutch carol, 1599) [LDRMSMRD, MSMDRDTL,] BG73 2753

Duties of today (Jewish trad) [SSFMFSD, DTLTD, SSFM] BH258 2754

Dwell in me (Berky) [MFSLSDD T, TDRTLTD, D] AI124; AK 464; AO650 2755

-----. R [DDDDTLSS, SSSSSSS, M] 2756

-----. R [MSLLSFMM, MMR FMRM] 2757

Dwelling place (Mozart) X Cana 2758

Dwight (---) [MMMFFM, MDM SSS, SFMR] L574 2759

Dyb af kjaerlighed (Hartmann) [DDDTLS, MMMRDT, RLLS,] K218a 2760

Dykes (Dykes) X Blairgowrie 2761

Dykes (Dykes) X Mary Magda- lene 2762

Dykes (Dykes) X Nicaea 2763

Dykes (Dykes) X St Oswald I 2764

Dymchurch (Shaw) [DSLSMRDD RDLSF, MFS] X93b 2765

E

Each cooing dove (Palmer) X Memories of Galilee 2766

Eagley (Walch) [SSLTDRMMR D, LLDFLS,] C513b; I406; J440b; M591; T108a; AC189; AJ157; AL243; AM232; AP62; AS240; BA100; BF440 2767

-----. V [SLTDRMMRD, LLD FLS, S] M591 2768

Ealing (Oakeley) [DTDRRDRM, MFMRMDLS,] F387b; BV 380a 2769

Eardisley (English trad) [DRMM RDRMFFMR, DRMF] E601; X393c; BG57 2770

Eardisley (English trad) X Noel 2771

Earl (Turner) [SSDTLS, SLLLL L, LRTL] AB182b 2772

Earlham (Booth) [SMSDML, LS MMRR, RSTT] AA469; AB406; AH536 2773

Early will I seek thee (Sabel) [MMTDLS, DSFMSR, FFD#R] BH18 2774

Earth with all thy thousand voices (Lewandowski) [DRMM FMRDRS, LTDDRD] BH64 2775

Earth, with her ten thousand flowers (Griggs) [SDTSLRTD, RMRDTDL] BC30 2776

Earthly friends (German, 16th c)
[DMSSFLSM, SFMDRD, DM]
BG135   2777

Earthly pleasures (Ackley) [MM
R#R#MMRD, SDRDDT, FF]
AS236   2778

-----. R [MMFMMRL, RRMRR
DS, MS]   2779

East Church (Freeman) [DMM
SFMRLS, SSMDDRR] V435a
2780

East Hill (Bowcher) [MMSSFRD
RFFMM, DDTL] AL201b 2781

East Horndon (English trad) [SD
DDLTDRTLS, SDDDR] E595;
S442a; AP738b; BY120b 2782

East Peckham (Ryley) [SLTDFM
RM, LMRMSFM, M] F319b
2783

Eastbourne (Hardy) [MFMRDRF
M, MFLSMRDR] O459   2784

Easter (Dykes) X Resurrection
2785

Easter (Gilchrist) [SDRMFSM,
RDRMFR, SDR] BR564 2786

Easter (Lyra Davidica) X Easter
hymn   2787

Easter alleluya (Cologne G-B.
1623) X Vigiles et sancti
2788

Easter angels (Parker) X God
hath sent his angels   2789

Easter carol (Foote) [SLSF#SM
SMRDFDM, MRD] BD247
2790

Easter carol (French trad) X
Nous allons   2791

Easter eggs (Russian trad) [RR
RRRR, SSFMRD, MRRM] BG
94   2792

Easter Eve (Krauth) [MMMMMS,
MDDDRM, MLSF] K107 2793

Easter flowers (Custance) [MRD
RMFSLDT, TLFLLS] C558
2794

-----. R [SSMFSLL, LLF#SLTT,
DD]   2795

Easter flowers (Hutchins. S.S.
Hymnal) [SDMDLDSM, SDMDDT
DR,] BR562   2796

Easter flowers (Stebbins) [MM
MDRMSS, LLLLFSLDD,] AC
126   2797

-----. R [LRTLSTMDTL, L
DRFMR]   2798

Easter glory (Lindeman) [DS
MS, FMDR, MSF#STLS, D]
J100; M588; O22; P150; Q8;
AA123   2799

Easter hymn (Lyra Davidica)
[DMSDFLLS, MFSDFMFM
RD] A85; B172; C172; D
112a; E133; F134; G154;
H181; I156a; J92; K113; L
261; M442; O334; P197; Q
199; R204; S163; T347; U
118; V756; W119a; X145,
172; Y331; Z239; AB143;
AC129; AD158; AE121; AF
182; AG102; AH298; AI82;
AK167; AL105; AM198; AN
192; AO176; AP215; AQ318;
AR182; AS146; AT115; AU33;
AV115; AW114; AZ11ᵣW; BA
234; BB134; BC10; BD245;
BE413; BF318; BK135; BL30;
BN44; BR190; BV194; BY
157; BZ   2800

-----. V [DMSDFLS, MFSDM
FRD,] X172   2801

Easter hymn (Monk) [SLDDTLS,
LDRD, SLDDT] D112b; BO
180   2802

Easter morrow (Lindeman) X
Our Lady, Trondhjem
2803

Easter song (Cologne G-B.) X
Vigiles et sancti   2804

Easter song (Russian trad) X
Praise to God   2805

Easter-tide (Oudean. Amsterdam Psalter) X Vreuchten
2806

Easter time (Hancock) [SSS
DTLSMS, MFRRMFM] BY755
2807

Eastergate (Ireland) [MMLLL
TDD, TLRTS#, LLL] E520
2808

Eastern monarchs (Lang) [LL
MMFSM, LLMMFSM, LM]
BL16   2809

Eastertime (English trad) [SD
TDRMFSFMR, MDTDR] AL
618; BG71; BY745   2810

Eastham (Hutton. Tunes for

the hymns) [SDRMFSM,DL
$\overline{\text{SFFM}}$,MRS] BA952   2811
Eastman (Perkins) [SMMRSDDS,
SDDRSM,MR] AB309   2812
Eastnor (King) [MSMDTL,LFMR
DT,RMMS] D300a   2813
Easton (Mozart) [SDTDRMFMR,
RDLRMSTL] H196; T223a;
V427; AJ208   2814
Easton (Nevin) [MMMMRS,DRM
FFM,SDDR] C465b   2815
Eastview (Lee) [MSMDRS,SDR
MFR,RMRM] BV266; BY129b
2816
Eastwell (Oakeley) [DRMFMMM
RDDT,RMF#SD] O224; P151
2817
Eastington (Croft) [DMFRTDRM,
RDTLRT,RS] E639; F201;
X192   2818
Eaton (Chadwick) [MR#MSDRM
RD,LTLRMTL] AC103; AE
440; AR409; BF233   2819
Eaton Square (Fischer) X Hankey
2820
Ebeling I (Ebeling) [DRMRMSLS,
SLF,FSM,MS] A32; B545;
C545; D538c; J26; K22; M275;
N30; O177; P130; Q523; R172;
S125; W41; X89; Z186; AA501;
AB113a; AD111; AF123; AG77;
AI68; AK119; AL48; AM150;
AR140; AW525; AZ157-A; BD
224; BR552; BV92; BY88b; BZ
2821
-----. V [DRMRMSSF#S,SLF,F
SM,D] AW525   2822
-----. V [DRMRMF#SSF#S,SLSF,
FS] AZ157-A   2823
Ebeling II (Ebeling) [DTLTDRRT,
DTRMRRD,D] AA296   2824
Ebeling (Ebeling) X Philippi
2825
Ebeling (Ebeling) X Nicht so
traurig, nicht so sehr   2826
Ebenezer (Williams) [LLTDTLTT
DRDTL,MR] A519; B433; C433;
E108; G263; J547; R361; S373;
W701a; X309; Y240; Z558; AB
285; AC220; AD349; AE376;
AF441; AG249; AI87; AK399;
ALsuppl; AM42; AN319; AP508;
AQ220; AR569; AW346; BB513;

BE258; BF480; BK82; BY
494b; BZ   2827
Ecce agnus (Dresden. Neues
G.B., 1593) [LDDT$\overline{\text{TL}}$,M
$\overline{\text{RRDD}}$T,TDDR] Q165; X638
2828
-----. V [LTDTL,LTDTL,
MRDT,TD] X638   2829
Ecce agnus (Dykes) X St John
2830
Ecce agnus (Trad. mel) [SS
DRTD,DMSFMR,TDMR]
D96b   2831
Ecce agnus (Warren) [MMRDT
L,TDRMFR,MMMM] S153;
AK148   2832
Ecce jam noctis (Sarum plain-
song, M 4) [MFMRMMRDR
MM,MDMS] A71b; B155b;
BJ75   2833
Ecce nomen domine Emmanuel
(Plainsong) [SFMFSFMFS
FS,DRMFS] BQ157   2834
Ecce panis (Dykes) [DDTDF
MMDR,DDTDFMM] J280
2835
Ecce! Panis angelorum (Plain-
song, M 8) [RDRTDTLSFS
S,STRRM] E317b; BP53;
BQ231b   2836
-----. V [RDRTDLFS,STRR
MDRR,] BP53   2837
Ecce panis angelorum (Polleri)
[MFSSLLLS,DRMMFFFM,]
BQ317   2838
Ecce panis angelorum (Portu-
guese mel) [SSDDTRDTLSD
S,DRMR] BQ231a   2839
Ecce tempus idoneum (Plain-
song, M 3) [SLTTLDTLSLT,
STSLM] E67   2840
Eccles (Selby) [LS#LTTD,DTD
RRM,MRSF] F89   2841
Ecclesfield (Scott-Gatty) X
Spirit divine   2842
Ecclesia (---) [MFSDDLSM,
LLSLSSFM] AO186   2843
Ecclesia (Gower) [MLLLLT
DLL,SFMMMMM] Y9; AB
300   2844
Ecclesia (Schafer) [SSSLRMF
FM,MMLSFM,F#] K236
2845

Ecclesia (Terry) X Holy Church
2846
Eden (---) [SSDRMRDL, TDR
MFMR, S] AY130   2847
Eden (Feilden) [SMSDTL, SMD
MF#S, SLDT] F327   2848
Eden (Gregor) [DSLSSFFM, DR
LSFMRR] AZ597-B; BA212
2849
Eden (Havergal) [DMRDTDLS,
LDTLS#L, DD] AM469; AP3;
AY85   2850
Eden (Mason, T.B.) [DMRDDTL
SMRD, SSFMM] C11; D95; AL
275; AP100; BA221; BR230;
BY604   2851
-----. V [MMRDDTLSMRD, SS
FMM] D95   2852
Eden (Sacred hymns and tunes.
Boston, 1850) [DMFSLSM, RM
SLFR, DMF] Q621   2853
Eden (Stainer) X St Giles   2854
Eden, W. (Wesley) [MMRRDD,
DDDM, SSFFMM,] BR386
2855
Edengrove (Smith) [MFSDDTTL,
SFMFSM, MM] B363b; C363a;
D553a; I680; J592; K558; U
387; AH542; AI348   2856
Edgbaston (Tilleard) [MMRDTRF
LLS, SDTLSL] D646a   2857
Edina (Oakeley) [SLTDFM, MSD
RM, RMFSL] A580; B527b;
C527a; D519a; V405; AL315a;
AP488a; BB287; BR510; BY
459   2858
Edinburgh (Barnby) [MMFSDTLS
FFM, MFSLS] B402; C402;
D630a; O556; AZ383-B   2859
Edmeston (Woodbury) [MMSMM
FRM, SDSLSSF#S,] AJ119
2860
Edmund (Dykes) [MMRLSFM,
DTLSMF#S, MM] B231   2861
Edom (Peace) [DTDDDTDD, DMR
DTLS, S] AM228   2862
Edsall (Day) [LLTDTLSLLL, DD
RFM] A207a   2863
Edwards (Kingsley) [DRMMMRM
FS, DSMRDFM] V176   2864
Edwin (Deale) [SDSFSLS, DF
MRDR, SLS] BV139a   2865
Edyfield (Wesley's Foundery col-

lection. 1742) X Savannah
2866
Eeuwig dank en eere (German
trad) X Gregor's 185th
metre - A   2867
Effie (Click) X God is love,
His mercy   2868
Effingham (English) [DSFMM
RDSFMMR, SDTD] H308; L
174; V57   2869
Egbert (Hall) [DLDFMR, DTD
RRRTDRM] B117   2870
Egerton (Thalben-Ball) [DRM
SLSM, FMRDRD, DRM] BE
308   2871
Egham (Turner) [MRDFML,
TDSMFR, RMSF] BA314
2872
Egli (Egli) [SDTDLSFM, MR
RRDTLS,] M35; AA116;
AN264; AW359   2873
Eia, Eia (Nordstern. Fuhrer
...) [SDRMRDTD, DRMSF
MR, S] X685; BG112   2874
Eia, Jesu adorande (Plainsong,
M 3) [FRMFSLSF, SLSFM
RM, M] F388a   2875
Eifionydd (Lloyd) [LLTDTLS#
LTML, S#LTLT] AL74;
AM169; AP260   2876
Eighmey (Pontius) [SDDSMRD
TD, FMRDTLR] I412   2877
Ein' feste burg (Luther) [DD
DSLTDTLS, DTLSLF] A551;
B213; C213; E362; F183;
G67; H405; I101; J150; K195;
L343; M487; N266; O17; P
91; Q262; R91; S266; T87;
U308; V530; W526; X436;
Y351; Z155; AA273; AB243;
AC210; AD289; AE59; AF363;
AG41; AH378; AI309; AJ128;
AK281; AL397; AM81; AN304;
AO606; AP542; AQ16; AR75;
AS258; AT40; AU38; AV37;
AW549; AZ199-A; BA348;
BB261; BC3; BD78; BE10;
BF396; BI-1-D; BK75; BR
365; BV25; BX314; BY562;
BZ   2878
-----. V [DDDSTDTLS, DTLS
LFM] P91   2879
-----. V [DDDSLDTLS, DTLS

LFM] Q262   2880
-----. V [DDDSTDLS, DTLSLF
RD,] BX314   2881
Ein' feste burg ist unser Gott
(Luther) X Ein' feste burg
                         2882
Ein kind gebor'n (Piae cantiones,
1582) [LLLTTDLS, SDMRRDDD,]
E44; S134; X91; BG85, 120;
BN4   2883
-----. V [LLLTTDLS, SDRDTD,
DD] BG85   2884
Ein kindlein in der wiegen
(Corner. 1649) X Corner
                         2885
Ein lamm geht hin (Teutsch kir-
chenampt. Strassburg, 1525)
X Passiontide   2886
Einer, ach nur einer (Gregor.
Choral buch) X Gregor's 208th
metre-C   2887
Einer ist König (Hille) [DSDM
RDMMF#SS, SSSDS] J319b
                         2888
Eins ist not (Bach) X Cöthen
                         2889
Eins ist not (Layriz) [MFSSLT
DD, LSFLSFM, M] Q366; AA83
                         2890
Eins ist noth (Crueger) X Ratis-
bon   2891
Eintracht (German trad) X
Christmas dawn   2892
Eintracht (Mathias) [SSLTDTLDT
LS, SSDRM] AQ46   2893
Eirene (Havergal) [MFRD, DRD
TLSS, DRMSF] D161; O226;
Q453; V765; AI255; AP561;
BR425   2894
Eirene (Taylor) [LDRMMLMRDT
L, DMF#SL] BV405a   2895
Eisenach (Meiningen G.B.) X St
Leonard   2896
Eisenbach (Schein) [DMMSSFM
R, SLTDTL] A93; B86; C133b;
D119b; E138; F187; G344; J
116; M232; N82; O68; Q421;
V237; W241; X168; AA334;
AB68; AF99, 500; AI419; AL
344b; AM474; AN31; AO144;
AQ156; AW508; AZ90-A; BA
140; BE80; BL62; BM88; BN
104; BO141; BV283; BY293;

BZ   2897
-----. V [DRMFSSFMSSLTD
TLL] C133b   2898
-----. V [DMFSSFMR, SLT
DTLLS,] D119b   2899
-----. [DRMFSSFMR, SLTD
TLL] G344   2900
-----. V [DMFSLSFMR, SLT
DTLS,] AZ90-A   2901
Eisleben (German trad) [LS
MFSM, LSMFSM, LS#LT] AZ
519-A; BA199   2902
Eisleben (Wolder. Catechismus
G-B. 1598) X Wolder
                         2903
El Kader (---) [SSSLTD, MRM
FSM, SSSL] BB71   2904
El Nathan (McGranahan) [DM
MFMRDLSS, MSSLSF] AE
221; AH385; AI252; AM712;
AR447; AT275; AW450; AX
478; AY459; BY437   2905
-----. R [DDDDDTLLS, SLSS
FFS]   2906
El paran (Mason) [DRMMFMM
RD, MFSSLSS] L41   2907
Elation (Rossini) [SMMMR#
MSM, MDDRDRR#M] L289
                         2908
Elbe (König. Harmonischer
lieder schatz. 1738) X
Mentzer   2909
Elberfeld (Plainsong. 1539)
X To God on high   2910
Elberton (Harwood) [DMFRS
SFFMR, SLTDSF] F386b
                         2911
Elbing (Sohren) [SDRMLRDT,
SLTDMRD,] A287; N83;
O336; Q306; AA436   2912
-----. V [SDRMLRRT, SLTDM
RD, S] O336   2913
Eldora (Sateren) [SDSLFMRR
D, RMF#SSF#S,] J342a
                         2914
Eleanor (---) [DSLTDRM, FL
SMRDT, DS] D551; BA819
                         2915
Electus (German) [MFSDRMR
SFMRD, MRMF#] M550
                         2916
Elgin (Beery) [LDDRDDT, S#L
TDTRD, LT] AR323   2917

Encamped along the hills of light
(Sankey) X Victory   2985
Endearing young charms (Irish
trad) X Sweet story   2986
Endor (Marsh) [DSSSLLS,DT
DMRD,DSS] AY260   2987
Endsleigh (Ferretti) X Salvatori
2988
Energy (Monk) X St Ethelwald
2989
Engadine (Canzuns spirituaelas.
1765) [MDRTTDMRMM,MRD
MRD] X516b   2990
Engedi (Beethoven) X Salome
2991
Engedi (Wesley) [DRSMRDRDT,
DRSMRDS,] F184b   2992
Engelberg (Stanford) [SDMRSLTD
LS,SSFMR] A366; F527a; AF
147; BV253; BY198   2993
England's Lane (English trad)
[DMRDSMDS,DSRMRTLS]
A26; C425; E309; X494; Y
200; AC168; AL608; BV18;
BY8a   2994
-----. V [DMRDSMDS,DSRM
RDTL] AL608   2995
Enniskerry (Boyle) [LLSLTLDTLL,
LSLTL] X240   2996
Enon (Feilden) [SLSFMM,RMF
FFM,SDTL] D550; BY453a
2997
Enon (Widdeman) X Saviour,
again to thy dear name   2998
Enon's Isle (Woodbury) [SMRDR
DRM,MSFMRDRD,] L431
2999
Enos (Burnap) [SSDRMRL,DT
LTSD,SMR] L562   3000
Entbinde mich, mein Gott (Frey-
linghausen) X Gregor's 118th
metre   3001
Eola (Sellers) X Thy word have
I hid   3002
Ephraim (Leslie) [DSDSDRM,
FRMDTDR,MF] BY367   3003
Epiphany (Filby) [SLSMRDDTLS,
MMFSLT] I159   3004
Epiphany (Hopkins) [MFMRLLRM
FFM,RSF#ML] F75b; AP178
3005
Epiphany II (Hopkins) [SSMFSDD
TLS,SSFMRF] D55b; BX168

3006
Epiphany (Smith) X There
came three kings   3007
Epiphany (Thrupp) X Epi-
phany hymn   3008
Epiphany hymn (Thrupp) [MR
DSLTDTLSFM,RDDF] C
95c; Eap. 9; W64b; AL49a;
AW91; BV125a; BY91a
3009
Epsom (Arnold. Complete
Psalmodist) [DRMRDLTD,
DRMFSMR,R] E506; X682;
AN296; BE3   3010
Epworth (Wesley) [DMSDMRL
SFM,SDTLSF#] W264; X
224; BV204   3011
Epworth (Wesley, S.S.) [SL
SDTLLS,SMRDRMRD,] AP
558   3012
Epworth Church (Copes) [ML
TDTLSTL,TDRMRDL,] BZ
3013
Er ist mein himmel, meine
wonne (Freylinghausen) X
Gregor's 109th metre 3013a
Er wird es thun, der fromme,
treue Gott (Gregor) X
Gregor's 112th metre 3014
Erbarmung (Schicht) X Mir
ist erbarmung widerfahren
3015
Ere you left your room
(Perkins) X Did you think
to pray   3016
Erfreut euch (German mel.,
1536) [DDTDRTLS,RMRD
TLS,D] F625; O259 3017
Erfurt (Ilse) [SLTDRMRD,M
SFMDR,SL] Q232; AA254
3018
Erfurt (Luther) X From heaven
high   3019
Erfurt (Weimar) X Allgütiger,
mein preisgesang   3020
Erfyniad (Welsh hymn mel)
[LDRMRDTLS#L,TDLTMR]
E430; X270; AN341; AQ39
3021
Erhalt uns, herr (Luther) X
Spires   3022
Erie (Converse) [SSLSMDDL,
SDMDSMR,S] A422; G240;

H38; I551; J459; L427; M581;
N343; P33; Q457; R385; S257;
U356; V469; W701; Z331; AA
395; AD214; AE303; AF335;
AG224; AH319; AI107; AK472;
AL502; AM533; AO318; AP494;
AR483; AS127; AT328; AU160;
AV319; AW186; AX350; AY55;
BA618; BB320; BC81; BF372;
BY343a; BZ   3023
Erin (Irish trad) X St Columba
                              3024
Eripe me (Crossley) [MMMRD
MM, MFSRRM, SSS] AR196
                              3025
Erling (Stubbs) X Asaph   3026
Ermuntert euch, ihr frommen
(Freylinghausen) X Gregor's
151st metre-I   3027
Ermuntre dich [mein schwacher
Geist] (Schop) X Schop 3028
Ernan (Mason) [SMFSDDTLTD,
LLLSST] G292; L566; P409;
T246; V582; AD313; AE276;
AH412; AI165; AJ342; AL384b;
AN204b; AO502; AP579; AR
253; AV252; AW231; BA540;
BB60; BR410; BX351   3029
Ernstein (Swift) [SMMRDS, LFF
MR, SDRMF] G438; W189;
AL616; AM638; AP756   3030
Erschienen ist der herrlich tag
(Hermann) [RRRLTDTLS, LTD#
RLDT] F609; Q108; X159;
AA161; BV201   3031
-----. V [LLLMF#SF#MR, MF#
S#LMSF#] X159   3032
Erskine (Gabriel) [SDDTLLSS,
DMRRSM, SD] AJ225   3033
Erskine (Gladstone) [SFMRFM
RD, DRFMLSF#M,] Eap. 34;
W325   3034
Es flog ein kleins waldvöglein
(German trad) X Woodbird
                              3035
Es geh, wies woll (Praetorius)
[LLLDTSLTD, TDRMDRD, L]
O163   3036
Es ist das heil (Etlich Christliche
lider 1524) X Wittenberg
                              3037
Es ist ein born (American trad)
X Campmeeting   3038

Es ist ein ros' entsprungen
(Geistliche K-G. Cologne
1599) X Rosa mystica
                              3039
Es ist genung (Ahle. Geistliche
arien) [DRMF#F#SRRFM,
MFLLS#L,] Q196; AA226
                              3040
-----. V [DRMF#F#SRRFM,
RMSSF#S,] AA226   3041
Es ist gewisslich (Geistliche
lieder. Wittenberg, 1535)
X Luther   3042
Es ist kein tag (Meyer. Geist-
liche seelenfreud) [SDTLSLS
FMRD, MFSSL] E521; F589;
G425; J448b; Q417; W19a;
X289; AL26a; BE191; BV372;
BY62   3043
-----. V [SDLSLFRD, MSSLTD
DT,] Q418   3044
Es ist noch raum (---) [SLSM,
SLLDLS, MRMFSM,] N152
                              3045
Es kam die gnadenvolle (Egli)
X Egli   3046
Es kommt ein schiff (Andernach
G-B. 1608) X Song of the
ship   3047
Es liegt ein schloss (German
trad., 16th c) X Freiburg
                              3048
Es muss die ganze Christen-
schar (Waldis) [MMLDRMRD
TL, MSF#M, LD] AQ325; BG
129   3049
-----. V [MMLDRMRDTL,
MSFM, LD] BG129   3050
Es spricht der unweisen mund
(Walther) [DDTSDRMD, TDR
MFRD, D] AA277   3051
Es woll' uns Gott genädig sein
(Teutsch kirchenampt ...)
N166; Q500; AA480   3052
-----. V [TDTLTRMRDT, RDT
DLS] Q500   3053
Esca viatorum (Dykes) [DMSF
RDRM, DFMLSTDS] B377;
C377; AB256; BO139   3054
-----. V [DMSFRDRM, DFM
LSTDF,] BO139   3054a
Eschol (Garrett) [DMSDMLLS,
DMSDTLLS,] BE111   3055

Eshtemoa (Mason) [MR#MFMLSM
R,MR#MLSSF] L385; U378;
V551   3056
Eskdale (Joseph) [MMMM,MFM
RDTLS#L,LMF] X651   3057
Eskridge (Stebbins) [SMMMRDTD,
SSLTDFMR,] T29; AJ40
                                  3058
Essex (Clark) [DLSMRSFM,SSL
TDRDT,] I162; L95; AO172;
AS154; AV38   3059
Essex (English trad) [MRDSDRM
FR,MFSSMSM] X637b   3060
Essex (Holst) [SLDTSLLL,SMS
MRM,DR] W180a; BY236b
                                  3061
Esslingen (Krieger) X Nun sich
der tag   3062
Esterhazy (Schubert) [SDMLFRD
RM,LSFMRDD] Y205   3063
Et barn er født i Bethlehem
(Lindeman) [SDSLSSFM,MSFM,
MRTS] O194   3064
Et er nødigt (Crueger. Praxis
pietatis melica) X Ratisbon
                                  3065
Et lidet barn saa lystetigt
(Hohenfurth ms. 1410) X Dies
est laetitiae   3066
Et trofast hjerte, Herre min
(Praetorius) X Es geh, wies
woll   3067
Eternal Light (Runkel) [DDTLM
FLS#,S#LFMLT,T] A478
                                  3068
Eternal Light (Willan) [MMRRLL
SS,SDDTSF,MM] AP155
                                  3069
Eternal Source (Holsinger) [SD
RMFRMD,DDMSLSMR,] AS
431   3070
Eternity (Bliss) [MFSSSSS,SF
MMMMM,RD] BE418   3071
Eternity (Gauntlett) [SSDTLS,
SSMFMR,SSDT] V369; BA
405   3072
Eternity (Hutton) [MMRDTLS,SS
LRDT,SSL] W591   3073
Eternity (Schop) [DMFSSLTD,
DMFSSFMR,] M124; N444;
BI15-D   3074
-----. V [DRMFS,SLTDDRMFS
SF] BI15-D   3075

Eternity (Teasley) [MFSSSLS
F#SM,RMFFMF] AX296
                                  3076
Eternity (Wesley, S.S.)
[SLLSDFFM,RDFMLDDT,]
AL204; AM466; AP327
                                  3077
Etherington (Davies) [SSDLS
MFRD,D#RMFSMR,] BE
132   3078
Ethnol (English trad) [SDTLS
LFSM,FSDFMRD,] Y238
                                  3079
Etiam et mihi (Dykes) [MMRM
FFFSM,SLTDDTL] D589b;
O268; V579a; AP471a
                                  3080
Eton (Barnby) [DTLSMRDT,F
MRMRDLT,] I39   3081
Eton College (Barnby) [MRR
DFMMR,SFMRDRT,F] I212;
V27a; BA825   3082
Etona (Goodhart) [MDRMLSM
D,TLTDRMDT,] E559
                                  3083
Eucharist (Brown-Borthwick)
[DMSFMRRM,MDTLSFMR]
D232   3084
Eucharist (Hodges) X Eucharis-
tic hymn   3085
Eucharist (Sewall) [SDRMSF
RD,MMFMDSDR,] BR471
                                  3086
Eucharist (Woodbury) [MMMS
SLSFSM,MRMFMF] G148;
H169; I141; T244; AJ340;
AO288; AS143   3087
-----. V [MMMSSLSF#SM,
MRMFRR] T244   3088
Eucharistic hymn (Hodges)
[SSFMSFMRMFS,SSFMDR]
A196; B336; C336; D225a;
G414; H442; I238; J279;
K194; L332; R445; S353;
V552; Z453; AD403; AE
339; AF283; AG239; AH502;
AM358; AN121; AO443; AR
514; AS460; AT394; AV254;
AW304; BD10; BF603; BZ
                                  3089
Eucharistica (Elliott) [SDRDS
MFM,SMDRMFS,S] D368c
                                  3090

Eucharistica (Stewart) [DMMSD
RMFSFM, MSSTM] BE172
3091
Eucharisticus (Stainer) [MMRM
FR, SDRMF, DLSFF] F418b;
BN96; BO42 3092
-----. V [MMRMFR, DLSFM,
MSDLS] BN96 3093
Euclid (Pfautsch) [LLLMRDTLT
DDRRM, MF] BZ 3094
Euclid (Smyth) [SSDDDTDRL,
LLTTTTL] AT438; AU61
3095
-----. R [SLTDMRDTLT, LTDS
DM] 3096
Eudora (Murray) [MMMFMRMF,
FFFSFMFS,] U480; Z168;
AC53; AI224; AM529; AO96;
AR81 3097
Eudoxia (Baring-Gould) [MMFFS
M, FFMMR, MMR] A172a;
B322; C322; D576b; E315; F
431; G308; K574a; N540a; Q654;
R225; S494; X49; Z328; AF510;
AL545a; AN128a; BV59b; BY
698 3098
Euphemia (Unseld) [MRDSLLSS,
SLTDRMR, M] AJ88 3099
Euroclydon (Noble) [LLLDLL,
LSFL, LLLDTL,] B416; AD
138 3100
Evan (Havergal) [SSDMRDLS,
SSDMDR, FM] C10; H119; I
356; J373; K77; L432; M45;
N180; O111; P25; Q416; R
104a; S97; T37a; U321; V278;
W692; AA342; AB320; AE228;
AH332; AI227; AJ53; AL194b;
AM77a; AN38; AO239; AP49
AR268; AS302; AV76; AW153;
AX52; AY10; BB411; BE357;
BR163; BX58; BZ 3101
-----. V [SDRMRDLS, SDRMDS,
RM] AV76 3102
-----. V [SSDMDDLS, SSDMDR]
AY10 3103
Evan new (Havergal) X Evan
3104
Evangel (Doane) X Tell me the
old, old story 3105
Evangel (Fink) X Bethlehem
3106
Evangel (Hopkins) [DDRMRRMF,

MRDTDLS, D] B127b; D
250b 3107
Evangel (Stainer) [MMFMRM
DD, RMFSMLS, S] C363b;
D553b; F452; W593; X373;
AP789; BA813; BV358; BY
615 3108
Evangelist (Mendelssohn)
[SDTLSFMR, DTDRSSS, S]
G538; Z590; BH3 3109
Evangelists (Koenig) [DDSSFSM
D, MMRRDRTS,] C288;
D497a; F508; M280; Q282;
X212; AA363; AF112; BV50
3110
-----. V [DDSMFSMD, MMR
MDRTS,] M280 3111
Evangelium (Oakeley) [MRTD
MSF, MRSDRT, RMF] D364a
3112
Evans (Steinel) [MLSMRMF,
MMMRDTD, RS] BB469
3113
Evanston (Harrington) [MMRD
RMSS, SFFFMR, FF] G203;
I632 3114
Evarts (Mason) [MFSMLSSM
SFSMFR, MF] J401; K363;
L458; M339; N216; O533;
P350; AX128 3115
Evelyn (Ashford) [DTLTDRD,
FFMRDTLS, S] I515 3116
Evelyn (Sullivan) [MMMMSF
M, RRRRFMR, D] A234b;
B204; C204; AI121 3117
Evelyns (Monk) [MSLSDSFM
RDD, DMF] A356b; B428;
C528; D518b; F225; J430a;
W178b; BV254a; BY199
3118
Even at the door (Belden) [SD
DDRMFS, LMFMRDRM]
BB546 3119
-----. R [MFSDRM, DRM
MMRMFS, S] 3120
Even me (Bradbury) [MFSD
FMMR, RMFRDTD, M] D589a;
H57; I346; L399; N407; U
452; V579b; AH352; AI265;
AL334b; AO634; AP471b;
AS45; AU297; AV348; AW
204; AX41; BA904; BB208
3121

51; AL550; AM335; AN127;
AO25; AP663a; AQ79; AR417;
AS35; AT295; AU179; AV296;
AW40; AX356; AY441; AZ32-K;
BA516; BB50; BC51; BE7; BF
193; BI62; BK72; BR326; BV
500; BX163; BY686; BZ   3157
Eventide (Smart) [MMMMFSLR,
FMRDRM, SD] N170; BA384
3158
Ever faithful (Strattner) X
Posen   3159
Ever faithful (Sullivan) [DDRRMFR,
MRDTLLS, SL] AL7a; BA824;
BR486b   3160
Ever faithful, ever sure (Sullivan)
X Ever faithful   3161
Ever lead me (Warren) [SLSDSD
TLS, SLSDMRD] AX502   3162
Ever will I Pray (Tenney) [MM
RDLS, DRRSM, MMRDL] AY69
3163
Everett (Everett) [MMMMSDRM,
DTLSMR, MM] AR51; AS49
3164
Evergreen (---) [SMRDMRSD, S
MRDMRSD,] N524   3165
-----. R [MFRMFR, MFSDFM
RD.]   3166
Evergreen (German trad) [SDD
DRMMM, MRMFTRD, S] M618;
BC16   3167
Evermore (Gauntlett) [MSRMDRT,
TDFMRRM, S#S#] D216a; V
423; BR463   3168
Eversley (Cottman) [SMSDDTLS,
SDMRDT, RM] BF437   3169
Everton (Smart) [MFSDLTDS,
FSMDRRR, M] B481; C481;
D260; Eap. 27; F207; K226;
W609b; AO506; BE29; BV178b;
BY379   3170
Every day (Doane) X Every day
and hour   3171
Every day (McGranahan) [SSD
MSSFR, FMDTDR, SS] AI8; AM
703   3172
-----. R [MMMTRRD, SSSRFFM,
SS]   3173
Every day and hour (Doane)
[MRDRDLS, SSLDSDMRR]
G236; H346; I490; V733; Z397;
AH383; AT326; AU213; AV344;

AX422; BZ   3174
-----. R [DRMMFS, MRDDR
MR, MRD]   3175
Every morning (Hopkins) X
Kelso   3176
Every morning mercies new
(Hastings) X Toplady 3177
Everyland, No. 1 (Rendle)
[SDRMDMFSL, SFMRM, DM]
G476   3178
Ewhurst (Allen) [MRMDDFFM,
MLLSDMRR,] BV624 3179
Ewing, (Ewing) [DRDFMRD,
MSDTS#L, LS] A597; B511;
C511a; D408a; E412; F278;
G529; H514; I612; J584;
K528; L585; M306; N48;
O480; P431; Q448; R428;
S435a; T38; U432; V690;
W599; X198a; Z569; AA
556; AB408; AD466; AE307;
AF309; AG283; AH523; AI
338; AJ55; AK422; AL463;
AM604; AN144a; AO550a;
AP628; AR425; AS469; AT
477; AU219; AV285; AW262;
AZ151-N; BA748; BB300;
BD57; BE148; BF657a; BI18;
BR437; BV432; BX183; BY
295; BZ   3180
Ex more docti mystico (Plain-
song, M 2) [MSSLLSFSSL,
SMFSFM] E65   3181
Excelsior (Booth) [MFSTDRM,
MTDFMR, MF#S] W674;
AL326; BY477   3182
Excelsior (Mason) X Bethany
3183
Excelsius (Cornell) [DSLTD
RM, RMFMRDDT, D] O409
3184
Exeter (Jackson) [DMSMRDR
MFM, DMSDTL] E528; X
338   3185
Exeter (Mason, H. L.) [MRD
TDRRM, MSMMF#S, MR] R
224; S181; AG118   3186
Exhortation (Hibbard) [DM
SMSMFSFMRD, RMRM] BB
387   3187
Exile (English trad) [FFMFSD
TD, MFSLSFRR,] X573b
3188

SLDLTDTDRD, DRMTDR]
BQ121   3225

---- . [MMMMRD, FMR, MM
MMRDL]   3226

Faith triumphant (James) [DTLL
LSDRM, RMSMRDR] Y268
                                         3227

Faithful (---) [SSLSSDDDTLS, S
LDDD] BB173   3228

Faithful (Bach) [SSMFSDTLS,
SSMFSDT] Y64; AC125; AE
31; AI39; AM104; AR11   3229

Faithful (Scottish trad) [DDD
RMSMSFMRD, DDDR] X282
                                         3230

Faithful guide (Wells) X Holy
Spirit, faithful guide   3231

Faithful legions (Barnes) [MMRS
DLSDFMR, MMRSL#] AD328
                                         3232

Faithfulness (MacFarren) X
Luffenham   3233

Faithfulness (Runyan) [MMMM
RRFFFFM, LTLSF] Z165; AE
68; AM27; AR429; AT47; BV
238; BY576   3234

-----. R [SSRFMM, LLMSFF,
SLTD]   3235

Falan-tidings (Tyrolese trad)
[SDDMDTRTS, LSMFTD, S]
BG121; BV351; BY390   3236

Falckner (Antes) X Hope   3237

Falcon Street (Smith) X Silver
Street   3238

Falconer (Morton) [MMLSMDRM,
MMMMDLMR#] AJ46a   3239

Falfield (Sullivan) [MRDDRMFF,
FFMSSF#S, M] D127; J512b;
K223; AB348   3240

Falkirk (Arne) [DRMFMRDTD,
RMSSFMM] I598   3241

Falkland (Lawes) [SMDFMRRD,
DTSDRMFS] E219; X227; BL
35; BN195   3242

Fall fresh on me (Iverson) X
Spirit of the living God   3243

Falls Creek (McKinney) [SMM
FFSSD, RMMRDR, S] AT347;
AU99   3244

-----. R [SMMMMRD, MSSSMSR,
SM]   3245

Falmouth (Young) [DMSDMMRDT
D, RMSLSF#] BE36   3246

Famous men (Williams) [DRM
SLSMR, MSLDTLSL] X432;
AQ230   3247

Fanad Head (Irish trad) [MLT
DTLTTLSMRMM, ML] X
294   3248

Fang dein werk (Franck) X
Schwing dich   3249

Far and near the fields (Clemm)
X Clemm   3250

Far, far away on Judea's plains
[DDRMMFSSFM, RRMFMS]
BC33   3251

Far, far beyond the starry sky
(Melish) X I heard the voice
of Jesus say   3252

Far Hills (Conant) [SSLLDTLT,
DDFMMRR, R] Y193   3253

Far off lands (Bohemian Br.
mel) [SDSFMRDSS, FMSFR
D] A262; J317; R495; AF
484; AQ247; AR496; BE189;
BZ   3254

Far verden, far vel (Nor-
wegian folk) [MMDTL, MS#L
TDLMS#TL,] O554; P74
                                         3255

Fareham (Goss) X Advent
                                         3256

Farewell (Tomer) X God be
with you   3257

Farewell, all earthly honors
(Bradbury) [DMMRMFM, RD
DRRM, SMM] BC35   3258

-----. R [DRMMMSFMRRMF,
MRDMDDR]   3259

Farley Castle (Lawes) [DMF
SMFSLTD, DTLDSL] E217;
F414; L27; W510; X22; AQ
3; BV73; BY660   3260

-----. V [DMFSMFSLTD,
DTSDSL] L27   3261

Farmborough (Warrell) [LDM
LSMRM, MFSMRDRL,]
E509; X689; BV69   3262

Farmer (Farmer) [DDDMSLS, S
MDTRD, DDD] U409; AH
470; AI349; AO578; AR591;
AS430; BA577; BF554 3263

Farnaby (English trad) [FD
FSLSLS, FDFSLLS,] A231;
E591; X362   3264

Farnboro (Naylor) [MRDLSSF

M, SDTTLS, SF] V133   3265
Farnell (Finlay) [MMSFMRDR
  MM, SLDDTL] BY546   3266
Farnham (English trad) [MLTD
  TLLM, MDDRMRM, D] E525;
  X285   3267
Faroon (Barnby) [DDRMDTLLS
  L, DDR#MSF] BR102   3268
Farrant (Tye) [DDRMRDFR,
  RMF#SSF#S, D] E339; J10;
  K14; Q440; R533; Sap. 9; V
  112; W625; X275; AA524; AD
  32; AF501; AJ158; AL650b;
  AP75; AQ121; AS405; AW587;
  AZ14-U; BA316; BR242; BY
  354   3269
-----. V [DDRMRDFR, RMSSF#
  S, DF] AA524   3270
Fast to thine arm (Lyon) [MR
  DLD, TDRM, MRDLD, TD]
  AX522; AY139   3271
Father all-holy (Gluck) [DDRTD,
  RRMFM, SSLFFS] BI24   3272
Father Almighty, we bow before
  Thee (Handel) X Father, O
  hear us   3273
Father hear (Jewish trad) X
  Eliyahu hanavi   3274
Father, I come to thee (Hayden,
  V.) [DDDTDRD, MMMRMFM,
  RD] BI22; BR457   3275
Father, I stretch my hands to
  thee (Glazer) X Azmon   3276
Father in heaven (Flemming)
  X Flemming   3277
Father in heaven (Handel) [SM
  RDD, DTLSS, LTDRMR] AH617
                          3278
Father in heaven, we do believe
  (Crawford) [MMMMMFMM, R
  DDRR#M, MM] BC41   3279
Father! in life's young morning
  (Brunk) [MSRMDLSD, DDRMM
  RF#S,] AX562; AY64   3280
Father, lead us (Hugg) [DMSDR
  MFMDRD, RRMRT] AX491;
  AY119   3281
-----. R [RRRTLS, FFFFM,
  SSSDR]   3282
Father, let me dedicate (Mac-
  farren) X Dedication   3283
Father, let thy blessing (Miller)
  [SDDTTL, DFFMR, DSFMR]

BH102   3284
Father most holy (Crueger) X
  Herz liebster Jesu   3285
Father, O hear us (Handel)
  [MMMFF, RSFFM, LLTDRS]
  AR616; AV417; AW609
                          3286
Father, see thy suppliant chil-
  dren (Binder) [MMRDFFFR,
  MMRDDF#S, S] BH152 3287
Father, see thy suppliant chil-
  dren (Munn) [MDLDSDRMD,
  MMFMMRL] BH150   3288
Father, see thy suppliant chil-
  dren (Rubin) [MRDSSLSF#
  SM, MF#SLTL] BH151
                          3289
Father, thy children to thee
  now raise (Stephens) [DTLS
  FMRDRM, FFMRMF] BC
  43   3290
Father, to thee we look (Lutkin)
  [SSDMDTLDLLS, SSLSM]
  AV221   3291
Father, to thee we look in all
  our sorrow (Mendelssohn) X
  Brightest and best   3292
Father, to thy dear name
  (Binder) [MFSSF#SRMFFM
  F, DRMM] BH85   3293
Father, to us (Barnby) X
  Sandringham   3294
Father, we come (Arne) X
  Arlington   3295
Father, we come to thee (Bost-
  wick) [SMDTRF, LSFMFS,
  DSMR] BB599   3296
----. R [MMMFFF, SSSL, DT
  LSS#L]   3297
Father, whate'er of earthly
  bliss (Naegeli) X Naomi
                          3298
Fatherland (Edwards) [MMFLL
  S, MRDRM, MMSSS] D420b
                          3299
Fatherland song (Crieg) [DRM
  FSLSD, MF#SDTS, RF] BY
  408a   3300
Fealty (Conant) [MMMMRMF,
  RMFLSFM, MMD] R286; Y
  143; Z302; AC121; AE444;
  AG169; AR356   3301
Fear my child, thy God (Ger-

man, 1544) X Singen wir aus
herzens grund   3302
Fear not (Stebbins) [SDSDRM,
MFMRDR, SDSD] BR521 3303
Federal Street (Oliver) [MMM
FMSSFM, FFFMMF#F#] A423;
B135; C135; D183b; G185; H
158; I271; J514; K52; L137; M
96; N124; O90; P265; Q346;
R518; S90; T264; U175; V436;
Z207; AA91; AD136; AE348;
AF290; AG137; AH234; AI318;
AJ368; AK331; AL489b; AM34;
AN188; AO378; AR353; AS279;
AT83; AV125; AW192; AZ22-Z;
BA84; BB152; BD55; BE352;
BK87; BR36; BX50; BZ   3304
Felix (Mendelssohn) X Brightest
and best   3305
Felix (Mendelssohn) X Selwyn
3306
Felix dies (Plainsong, M 2)
[DDRMRRDT, RTDLSDDD,]
F151a   3307
Fellowship (Lint) [MMSMRMFFM,
SSMFMRM,] AR682; AS68
3308
Fellowship (Wathall) [MMRMMM
RM, MSMF#F#S, ST] I450
3309
Feniton (Nicholson) [DLDRM
SS, LSMDRDLS, D] F392 3310
Feniton Court (Hopkins) [SSDD
MRDT, LTDMSFMM] D421a;
AZ91-F; BA67; BE177   3311
Feodore (Haynes) [SDDDTD, MSS
SF#S, MLSF] AI360   3312
Ferdinand (Marks) [MLSMMRD,
LTDSLTS, ML] K547   3313
Ferguson (Kingsley) [SSMDDTL
S, MFSMFR, MM] G322; I172;
L411; N206; T208; U145; V527;
Z395; AJ299; AM576; AO93
3314
Ferniehurst (Church hymnal)
[DRMFFM, MMMSF#M, MRTD]
I250   3315
Fernshaw (Booth) [SFMRDMRD,
SSDTDR, ML] D31b   3316
Ferree (Price) [MMFSDMRDLS,
FMF#SSR] AE71; AK78 3317
Ferrier (Dykes) [MMMDSLS, SL
TDTLTLS,] D552b; J528;

K568; L584; M159; N654; W
665; AJ135b; AP803; BX126b
3318
Ferry (Green. Psalmody. 1731)
[DTDRSFMR, MFSDFMRD,]
X39; BY634   3319
Fesans raijouissance (French
trad) X So, brother   3320
Festal day (Lewars) [DDRM
DMFS, MDMSMSF#S] J249a
3321
Festal song (Walter) [SDSMSL,
SLTDTLS, RM] A535; B314;
C492; G267a; I413; J541; L
121; R352; S401; U274; Y225;
Z374; AB279; AD332; AE252;
AF300; AG252; AH459; AK
389; AO467; AQ207; AR329;
AS363; BA559; BF463; BV
508; BZ   3322
Festgesang (Mendelssohn) X
Mendelssohn   3323
Festgesang (Wathall) [MMRMFS
DS, MDDRFFM, M] I120a
3324
Festival (Heywood) [DTLSLRM,
DTDRSM, MRM] BR515 3325
Festival carol (Oudean. Amster-
dam Psalter.) X Vreuchten
3326
Festum matris gloriosae (Plain-
song, M 2) [DDRRRDFMRD,
FSLSFS] E228   3327
Festus (Freylinghausen, G-B.
1704) [SDTLSLRFM, MRSMF#
SL] D167b; W170b; AB190;
AQ219; AZ155-A; BA542;
BD138; BV228; BY297   3328
-----. V [DTLSLRFM, RSMF#
SLDT] W170b   3329
Ffigy-sbren (Welsh hymn mel)
[DMMMSFMRRM, DMMMSF]
E324; G406; S320; X560;
AD286; AF219; AL340; AN
226; AW183; BY285   3330
Fiat lux (Dykes) [SDRMRD, SF
MRRM, RTLS,] D328a; I206;
S392; V82; Z536; AO522; AP
372; BA13; BB451   3331
Fiat lux (Hiles) [MSDFSM, DRM
FLR, DDTD,] K143   3332
Fidei defensor (Nevin) [SDDDD
RRR, RSF#FFMRR,] Y120

                                    3333
Fidei unitas (Walther, G-B) X
   Soldau   3334
Fidelis ad mortem (Müller)
   [SMLSFMSFRM, SMLSFM]
   AH142   3335
-----. R [DTLSSLSFM, RRMFM
   RMF]   3336
Fides (Davis) X Goshen   3337
Fides (Scholefield) [DTDRMLSF,
   MMMSFMRM,] D142   3338
Field (Laufer) [SDRMSFMRM
   D, RDRMSL] G458; R294; S
   367; Y223; Z495; AC249; AF
   421; AK265; AR383; BZ   3339
Fierce was the wild billow
   (Cambra) [SDRMRD, LDRD, SDR
   MRD,] BP100   3340
Fifth mode melody (Tallis) [DM
   FSSLFS, FMRM, DMFS] W250;
   X483   3341
Fight of faith (Peace) [DTLSDTL
   S, TDDRRM, MD] BR402a
                                    3342
Filia (Shearer) [MFMLSFFM, S
   LTDTLLS,] J265b   3343
Filius dei (Gaul) [DMFSSLTD,
   RMFSRM, DM] AB158   3344
Fill me now (Sweney) [MMRDS
   LDR, MFSLSMR, M] AE149;
   AS173; AX136; AY204; BB212;
                                    3345
-----. R [SSDLLD, RRDLDLS,
   LLS]   3346
Fill me with thy spirit (Byers)
   [MMMRDRDL, DLSDDTDR,]
   AX137   3347
-----. R [SMDRMDFM, SSSFMM
   DR,]   3348
Fillmore (Belden) [SMDRMFLS,
   DLSMFMR, S] BB447   3349
Fillmore (Fillmore) X Pounds
                                    3350
Fillmore (Ingalls) [DMRDRMRDR,
   MSSSLSM] G229; H159; I310;
   T142; AI287; AJ210; AQ8; BZ
                                    3351
Final rest (Bergquist) [MRDRMFR,
   SSFMRMRR, S] N605   3352
Fine flowers(Scottish trad) [LLLS
   MMLLSM, MDDTDR] AH304
                                    3353
Fingal (Anderson) [MFMRDDTD,

SDDFFM, MD] B404; C404b;
   W141; AJ301; AK33; BE260;
   BY456   3354
Fingal (Irish trad) [MMMMDR
   M, RDLLDRMR, M] R321;
   S508; W456b   3355
Finlandia (Sibelius) [MRMFMR
   MDRRM, MRMFM] G73; P
   12; Q651; R374; S281; W
   556a; Z161; AB231; AD80;
   AE211; AF77; AG215; AH
   403; AK87; AR263; AU479;
   AW54; BF255; BK37; BY683;
   BZ   3356
Finlay (Friedell) [MMSLSLLD
   R, MRMDLSMS,] AF27
                                    3357
Finnart (Finlay) [DMRDSLDRM,
   MSLSDRL] F583; W491a;
   AL581; BV49a; BY657 3358
Finnish song (Suomen Kora-
   alikirja, 1738) [DSDRMRDT
   S, DRMFMRR] J191b   3359
Firenze (Longacre) [SDDRTD
   LS, MFSMSLTS,] AK208
                                    3360
Firm as the mountains around
   us (Durham) [SMSFMRTLS,
   DTDFDM, M] BC42   3361
Firm foundation (Schumacher)
   [SDTDMRDRDTD, RMFSS]
   Q427   3362
Firm this cornerstone be laid
   (Stark) [DTDSTLS, LLSSS
   FM, DD] BH212   3363
Firmament (Davies) [SSSSLT
   DMRD, DDTLSD] W10; BE
   203; BV232b; BY74   3364
Firmament (Root) [MFF#SLT
   DR, DTLSLSFM,] BR76
                                    3365
First Church (Lester) [MMM
   RDSLLS, DRRM, MMM] Y206
                                    3366
First mode melody (Tallis)
   [LLLS#LDTT, TTMMR#M,
   MM] E78; F106a; W433b;
   X625; BJ2   3367
Firth (Firth) [SSMRDTD, SS
   SSLTDT, S] D116c   3368
Fischer (Fischer) X Whiter
   than snow   3369
Fisher (Fisher) [SSDTLSRDT,

SSRTLST] AT293   3370
-----. R [DRDTRMRD, RDLTRD#
RM,]   3371
Fishwick (Fishwick) [MMRSFM
RD, DDRM, MRSF#] M535
                      3372
Fisk (Harrington) [SLSMFMRDR
M, SLSMFM] I185; AJ135a
                      3373
Fitzwilliam (English trad) [DRM
MFFMFM, SFMRDTD] E448;
X539   3374
Flanders (Flemish trad) [LLSM
SFMRMM, LLSMSF] X440; BG
160   3375
-----. R [DDLLMML, DDRRM
ML.]   3376
Flavian (Day's Psalter) X St
Flavian   3377
Flee as a bird (Dana arr) [LM
MMFMMT, LDDRR#MT, L] AI
244; AU459; BB232   3378
-----. V [LMMMFMMRDT, LDD
RR#R#MT, L] BB232   3379
-----. V [LMMMFMMRDT,
LDDRR#R#] BB232   3380
Fleming (Flemming) X Flemm-
ing   3381
Flemish carol (Flemish carol)
X A little child   3382
Flemming (Flemming) [DDDRRM
DDRDT, MMMMR] G327; H266;
I478; J421; M161; N428; O565;
P17; R53; S306; T419; U195;
V48; Y297; Z147; AB189; AD
278; AE241; AF333; AG182;
AH350; AI240; AJ112; AK14;
AL165b; AM179b; AN117; AO
76; AP625b; AR79; AT287; AV
226; AW59; AZ36-E; BA787;
BB9; BC34; BD5; BE179; BF
364; BK175; BR377; BX160;
BY261b; BZ   3383
Flensburg (Spohr) [SMSDDDTLS,
FMFSLR, S] D673b; I465; AB
304; BR140   3384
Fletcher (Gibbons) X Song 46
                      3385
Fling wide the gates (Halevy) X
Min hamaytsar   3386
Flittner (Flittner) [LLDDRRMD,
SSFMRRD, R] M191; Q384;
AA317; AQ170   3387

-----. V [LLDDRRM, MSFMR
RD, RR] AQ170   3388
Flora (Sheldon) [DRSLTDRM,
DFMRLS, SM] BV495 3389
Flow gently sweet Afton (Spil-
man) X Away in a manger
                      3390
Flower (Fillmore) [MRDFFF
MRS, LTDDSMF] AS316;
BB117   3391
Flower of love (Christiansen)
[SMRMFMRDLS, SSFFSM]
P380   3392
Flowers of the fairest (Catholic)
[SDTDMDMRMFTL, MMRL]
AH137; BO105   3393
-----. R [SSF#SLSSSDRM,
MRTSR,]   3394
Foel fras (Harding) [SMRDR
MFRM, SLSSMDM] AR300
                      3395
Folkingham (New version. Sup-
plement. 1708) [MLTDLL
FM, DFMRDRTL,] E558; W
637b; X317; AF431; AN380
                      3396
Follow all the way (Norris)
X Where He leads me
                      3397
Follow, I will follow thee
(Brown) [MMRDTSLD, TSL
FM, MMR] AU443   3398
-----. R [MDSDMLSFT, FM
RD#RR#M,]   3399
Follow me (Garrett) X For-
giveness   3400
Follow me (German trad) X
Jesus lives, and Jesus leads
                      3401
Follow me (Palmer) [MMMMF
MMD, MRRFMM, MM] AX
255   3402
Follow on (Lowry) [SDRMMR
DDDTLS, STTT] AU118; AX
412   3403
-----. R [MSMRD, DRDLLS,
TTTDD]   3404
Follow the gleam (Douglas)
[SSF#SLFM, MMMMRTSRD, S]
AC230b; AG306   3405
-----. R [TL#LFFMSM, MR
SR, RDSD,]   3406
Follow the path of Jesus

(Hymns and tunes. 1790) [DD
RMSMD, RRRRSM, DDR] AX
498; AY305   3407

Folsom (Mozart) [SSSSMSFMF
SFM, DRRM] AV94   3408

Fons sempiternus (Olds) [STLT
SM, FSLSLRMF, SR] AB305
                          3409

Font Hill (Emerson) [SMRDTLSD,
RMRMF#S, SS] L71   3410

Footsteps (Everett) X Sweetly
Lord, have we heard   3411

Footsteps of Jesus (Everett) X
Sweetly Lord, have we heard
                          3412

For all the saints (Barnby) X
Sarum   3413

For Christ and the Church (Kirkpatrick) [SSMFSMRDDD, TL
SSLS] AR494; AS324; AX153
                          3414

------. R [STTLTDS, SLDTLS, SS
D]   3415

For God so loved (McGranahan)
[SDMMRDRFFMRMSSFM]
AI9   3416

------. R [SMFSLSS, SMFSLSS,
SM]   3417

For health and strength (---)
[SSSSFMMMRDDDTD. DD]
AR552   3418

For our devotions, Father
(Fones) [DRRMSFMRFTRD,
RFRM] BC107   3419

For peace and for plenty (Knowlton) [MSMDSS, SDTLS, SSMSL]
BI112   3420

For the beauty of the earth
(Kocher) X Dix   3421

For the mountains (Jewish trad)
[LLMMMRMFM, MMSDRMF]
BH316   3422

For the Sabbath (Ledington)
[MMRFMRDRT, DFMLSF#S]
BB46   3423

For the strength of the hills
(Stephens) [SSDMDSSLS, SFFM
DR, T] BC241   3424

------. R [RRMSSDSLS, DRFM
RD]   3425

For thee, O dear, dear country
(Pierson) [MMFMMMR, DT
LTRD, MMF] BR449b   3426

For thee, O dear, dear country (Sullivan) X Homeland
                          3427

For you and for me (Thompson) X Softly and tenderly
                          3428

Ford (Musgrave) [DRMFLSM,
MSDDRM, MF#F#] D437c
                          3429

Ford Cottage (Maker) [DMSD
DRMFM, SLSFMR, R] G474;
J332   3430

Ford Place (Finlay) [DLSFSL
SM, SFMRMFM, M] BV359
                          3431

Forest (Chapin) [DLSDDMRD,
DMSMDRMR,] H126; L515;
AQ147   3432

------. V [DSLDDMRD, DMSM
DMRD] AQ147   3433

Forest Green (English trad)
[SDDDRMRMFS, MFMDRRD,]
A21a; C78c; E15; F65a; R
96; S471; W612; X79a; Y250;
Z316; AD191; AE344; AF456;
AG56; AK201; AL51a; AN
138; AP169; AQ304; AR586;
AW290; BD46; BE5; BF273;
BG138; BV122a; BY718; BZ
                          3434

Forest Hill Church (Smith,
R. A. L.) [MM, SLTDRMSDR
M, MRRD#] BF400b   3435

Forever here my rest (American trad) X Belief   3436

Forever here my rest (Pollock)
[MFSSLSF#SM, MRDRMFM,]
AX172; AY258   3437

Forgive (McKinney) [SDDDLT
TTDLDS, SDDD] AU416
                          3438

Forgive us, Lord (Jewish trad)
X Yom Kippur mode   3439

Forgiveness (Garrett) [MLSR
MFM, SDTF#SLS, SL#] D592;
V467; BR391; BX30a   3440

Förlossningen är vunnen (Er-
furt Enchiridion, 1524)
[DDMRDTL, MFRMRD, DDM]
N21; O167; P114   3441

Fortem virili pectore (Catholisches G-B. Strassburg
1697) [SDDRRMRMD, MFSS

FMR,] X183; AW572 3442

Fortitude (Filby) [SLSMD, LTD SM, SLSSMD] A565; B112; C112; D656a; H354; BR400 3443

Fortitude (Palmer) X Yield not to temptation 3444

Fortitude (Smith) [MM, RRDFM RDLSFM, MMM] G300; I407; AB176; AC182; AD488; AH449; BF400a; 3445

Fortitude (Young) [MFSLSFMR, DRFM, MF#SL] BE161 3446

Fortitudo (Miller) [SDRMFSSS, MRMFMRDR,] J502a 3447

Fortress (Luther) X Ein' feste burg 3448

Fortress-Rock, my God, my aid (Jewish trad) X Rock of ages 3449

Fortunatus (English trad: old) [LLTDTLMRDT, LLTDTL] E579; W174b; AL130a; AP233a 3450

Fortunatus (Sullivan) [DTDRMFM RDDTD, MFSL] A87; B169; C 169b; D109b; J93; K118; N122; R207; V764; W115; Y332; Z 246; AC130; AD161; AI88; AO 181; AP217; AR191; AV119; BD236; BR513; BY165 3451

Fortune (English trad: old) X Fortunatus 3452

Forward (Edwards) [SDSDDMR, DDTLSSS, SD] D510c 3453

Forward (Smart) X Sion 3454

Foundation (American trad) [SL DLDSD, DMDMS, SLDL] G315b; I461b; R369b; T15; U206; V325b; Z406; AD234; AG212b; AH380; AI306; AJ20; AQ21; AR260; AT 263; AU199; AX146; AY33; BF 242; BZ 3455

-----. V [SDLDSDRMRMS, SD LDS] R369b 3456

-----. V [SLDLDSDDMRMS, SLDL] AQ21 3457

Foundation (Parker) [SDDDDTLS LSFMMR, RL] B212b; D628a 3459

Fount of glory (Landis) X Blessed Bible 3460

Fountain (American trad) X

Cleansing fountain 3461

Fountain of grace (Balle) X Emmanuel 3462

Fountain's Abbey (Slater) [DMRDSLTDRMDLR, LLT] X579 3463

Four seas (Roberts) [LLDT LS, DDLTDR, TDMR] AQ161 3464

Four winds (Foote) [DDRMSM RDLDM, LDTLS] AQ202 3465

Fowler (McCutchan) [MMM SDTDRD, MRSFM, RR] G9b 3466

Fra himlen hoit (Luther) X From heaven high 3467

Fragment (Sarum Gradual, 1527) X The rosy sequence 3468

Fragrance (French carol) [MM RDSDSLMF, SDRMSM] X627; BG164; BV101 3469

Frainsby (Dyson) [MMMMRL DD, SSSTLMSS,] BE39 3470

Frälsta värld! i nadens under (Swedish Koralbok, 1697) [LLMDRDTL, DDTDDRM, L] N101 3471

Frances (McGranahan) [SD RDSMFS, DMFMSLTD,] T55; AJ86; AM40 3472

Franck (Franck) X Schwing dich 3473

Franconia (Ebeling) X Philippi 3474

Franconia (German) [SSFMM R, FFMRM, SSLTD] BR389 3475

Franconia (Koenig) [DRMFSM, SLDFMR, SDTS] A418; B88b; C277; D210; E370; F48b; J 394; K369; N201; O228; Q133; R94; V583; W190a; X455; Z 466; AA406; AF214; AG221; AK247; AL146a; AN253; AP 343a; AW205; BA135; BE44; BR30; BV88; BX312a; BY 463; BZ 3476

Frankfort (Gill) [SMRLTLS, SDLDFLMR, S] D335c; N 165 3477

-----. V [SMRLTSS, SDLD

FLMR,S] N165   3477a
Frankfort (Nicolai) [DSMDSLLS,
SLTDTLLS,] A329; B98; C98;
J33; K153; M146; N25; O183;
P53; Q23; R415; S321; X90;
AA24; AB76; AD285; AF145;
AI417; AK122; AM434; AN493;
AW529; AZ228-a; BA54; BG104;
193; BI19-D; BL13; BR135; BV
130; BZ   3478
-----. V [DSMRDSLLS, SLTDTLL
S.] BI19-D   3479
Frankscot (Barnby) [SSFMRRD,
LLLSFM, DTL] O439; U239;
V397; AG217; BA663   3480
Franzen (Tomissön. Psalmebog.
1569) [DMMFMFSS, SSMFRD;
DM] J264; M545; N235   3481
-----. V [DMMFFSS, SSMFRD,
DMM] N235   3482
Fred til bod (Hartmann) X Peace
of God   3483
Fred til bod (Lindeman) X
Easter glory   3484
Frederick (Kingsley) [SDDRML,
SMRDRM, SDDR] H320; I584a;
L565; T12; V674; AA535; AJ
16   3485
Fredricton (Schuman) [SSDDMM
R, MFRLTD, MRR] Y131
                         3486
Free waters (Everett) [DRMMM
FMRRR, MRDDDT] AX230
                         3487
-----. R [MFSFMRRR, RMFM
RMMM,]   3488
Freedom (Greenwood) [MSLMR,
RFSL#L, TSF#TTD#] BE302
                         3489
Freedom (Shaw) [SDRDMSLSM,
SMDS, SDR] X322a   3490
Freely give (Perkins) [MMMFSLSD,
TLSFM, MMM] BB479   3491
Freeport (---) [SFMFMRDTDM
R, MSFMF] BB464   3492
Freeport (Shoemaker) [SDMDLST
D, DTDFMR, RM] AY6   3493
Freiburg (German trad. 16th c)
[MRDSSLMS, SMMDRRM, D]
J63a; M81; O523; P117   3494
-----. V [MMRDSSLM, SLSMDR
M, M] M81   3494a
-----. V [MMRDSSLM, SSMMDR

M, D] O523   3495
Fremont (Lehmann) [LMRDDT,
DRDTTL, DLSF] M393
                         3496
French (Scottish Psalter. 1615)
X Dundee   3497
French carol (French trad) X
Love is come again   3498
French carol (French trad) X
Picardy   3499
Freshwater (Parry) [MDRMS
D, LSMRMM, MDRM] AL457
                         3500
Freshwater (Statham) [MDM
LSFSM, SLSF#F#M, ML] BA
591   3501
Freu dich sehr (Bourgeois) X
Bourgeois   3502
Freuen wir uns (Bohemian
mel. 1457) [LTDTLSL, DR
MMFMFRM,] E314; X510;
AF579; BV141a   3503
Freuen wir uns all in ein
(Bohemian mel. 1457) X
Freuen wir uns   3504
Freuet euch, ihr christen
(Minor: Hammerschmidt)
[LLSFMMRR, FSLLSSF, M]
Q96; AA152; AZ210-A 3505
-----. [Major) V [MMRDDTL,
DRMMRRD, TD] AZ210-A
                         3506
Freut euch, ihr lieben
(Schröter) [DDDRMFM,
MRDDTD, DDD] Q59; AA132
                         3507
Freylinghausen (Freylinghausen)
X Gregor's 341st metre
                         3508
Freylinghausen (Freylinghausen)
X Macht hoch die tür [thür]
                         3509
Friend (Converse) X Erie
                         3510
Friend (Mendelssohn) [SSS
FMRRD, DRRRDRM, M] P360
                         3511
Friend (Stebbins) [SSMMFM
RR, DTLSLSD, S] G241; V
763; Z290; AE305; AH323;
AI108; AR449; AT261; AU28;
AV318; AW445; AX527; BB
531; BZ   3512

Friend after friend (Grimm)
[DTLDTL, FTRMMM, LTS#L]
BH223   3513
-----. R [DMRDMRD, DLRF
SSS, DR]   3514
Friend of sinners (Crozart)
[SMSDMDLD, SMSDTRR, S]
AI378   3515
Friends of Jesus (Swedish trad)
X Jesus, lat din rädda dufva
                         3516
Friendship (Converse) X Erie
                         3517
Frilford (Ferguson) [MLSMRDR
M, LDTL, MLSM] BV490
                         3518
Frisk op, min sjael (Breitendich.
Koralbog) [SMRDRMFS, MFSLS
F#S, S] O282   3519
Fritwell (Brockless) [SDRMFRSM
L, FSMRDFM] BY368   3520
Froebel (Lewars) [DSLTDFMMR,
MSFRDRM,] K563   3521
Fröhlich soll mein herze (Crueger)
X Christmas joy   3522
Fröhlich soll mein herze springen
(Freylinghausen) X Briesen
                         3523
Frohlock', liebe christenheit
(Grimm. Choral buch) X
Grimm's 265th metre   3524
From all that dwell below the
skies (Hatton) X Duke Street
                         3525
From all that dwell beneath the
skies (Bourgeois) X Old 100th
                         3526
From every stormy wind (Hastings)
X Retreat   3527
From Greenland's icy mountains
(Mason) X Missionary hymn
                         3528
From heaven above (Luther) X
From heaven high   3529
From heaven high (Luther) [DT
LTSLTD, DDSSMFSF] A22; B484;
E17b; F151b; J22; K19; L2; M
51; N27; O133; P106; Q70; R
173; S118; V335; W56; X80a;
AA150; AD123; AF121; AG75; AI
418; AK114; AM166; AN160; AQ
42; AW527; AZ22-B; BA60; BB
201; BE168; BI86; BK156; BV98;

BX53; BY308; BZ   3530
-----. V [DTLTSLTD, DDSSM
SFM,] V335   3531
-----. V [DTLTLSLTD, DD
SSMFS] X80   3532
-----. V [DTLTSLTD, DDSSF
MFS] BB201   3533
From heaven's height (Jacob-
sohn) [SSFM, DLTDLS, MF
MR, SM] BH124   3534
From heaven's heights the
thunder peals (Jewish trad)
X Mee chomocho   3535
From Sinai's height a fountain
gushes (Jewish trad: Akda-
mos mode) X Sinai's height
                         3536
From starry heaven (Italian
carol) [SDTDRMM, RMFSS
FMR, M] BN14   3537
From strength to strength
(Naylor) [DSSSDRM, DDFMR
D, MRDT] J564a; W534b; X
641a; AC146; AD287; AL
404a; BV585b; BY508a 3538
From the depths we cry
(Herbst) X Heinlein   3539
From the eastern mountains
(Sullivan) X St Gertrude
                         3540
From thee, illustrious teacher
Paul (French trad) X The
praises of that saint   3541
Frondeg (Evans) [MLLS#LT
DL, TLSF#M, LTD] W391b
                         3542
Fryd dig, du kristi brud
(Regnart) X Göttingen 3543
Fulbert (Gauntlett) X St Ful-
bert   3544
Fulda (Gardiner's Sacred melo-
dies) X Gardiner   3545
Fulfillment (Hoffman) [SMSD
FMRD, MFSMFLS, L] BE15
                         3546
Full in the panting heart
(Catholic) [DMFSMLTD,
SSLSSMRD] BO205   3547
-----. R [SLDTLSMFLSFM,
DTLS]   3548
Full of glory (Montani) [DM
SSLTDS, LSSFMR, DM] BQ
40   3549

Full of glory (Terry) [DRMSDTL
S, FMRRD, DRM] BL81   3550
Full salvation (Pollock) [MRD
DRRMS, LLSMRDR, M] AY232
3551
Fulton (Bradbury) [MRDLTDSD
MR, MRDLTD] H220   3552
Fulton (Kroeger) [DDTTRRDD, M
FMRDDT, S] AJ396   3553
Für dein empfangen speis und
trank (Praetorius) X Praetor-
ius I   3554
Furry Day carol (English trad)
[DDDRDMFSSLS, LTDSS] BG
49   3555
-----. R [SLLLSFMFSLS, LTD
SS]   3556

G

Gaa nu hen og grav (Swedish)
[SSFMRRD, RRMRMLF#S, D]
O413   3557
Gabriel (Funk) X Bethlehem
3558
Gabriel (Gabriel) X Just when I
need Him   3559
Gabriel (Ouseley) x St Gabriel
3560
Gabriel's message (Piae cantiones.
1582) [LSDRMRM, RMFMMRD,
RM] BG102   3561
Gade (Gade) [LFRMMLLS, DTMSF#
M, LF] M246   3562
Gainsborough (Tans'ur) X St
Martin's   3563
Gairney Bridge (Kroeger) [MR
DFFMRS, SLTDSFMR,] T215;
AJ308; AM68   3564
Gaisberg (Gale) X Galsberg
3564a
Galdan (Danish trad) [MRRDT
DR, FMMRDRM, DD] M630
3565
Galilean (Barnby) [MRMSFRDT,
DLSMRDR, M] Q469; AA476
3566
Galilee (Armes) X Armes   3567
Galilee (Jude) [MSRRRSDD, DD
DLDRM,] A566b; B268b; C
268c; D143; G233; I545a; J553;
M200; N172; R269; S223; T258;
U284; V735; Y106; Z281; AB

159; AC144; AD201; AE164;
AF322; AG144; AH327; AI
297; AJ360; AK207; ALSuppl;
AM491; AO376; AP553a; AR
243; AS229; AT360; AU159;
AV188; AW140; AX40; AY474;
BA404; BB421; BD62; BF348;
BK67; BZ   3568
Galilee (Sherwin) X Sherwin I
3569
Galliard (Dowland) [MRDTLDR,
MSFMRMR, MR] E649; X461;
BE53   3570
Galsberg (i. e. Gaisberg] (Gale)
[SDRMSL, LRMFS, SDRMS]
D515d   3571
Galway (Miller) [DFMMRDTD,
DRMF#SLTL] F328; AP593;
BV602   3572
Gamble (Gamble. Collection)
[SSDRMS, MMRDL, SSDRM]
X379   3573
Gambold (---) [SDDMR, SRRFM,
DMSMFL] AZ587-C; BA469
3574
Ganador (Sanders) [DDRTLSDR
MFMR, DRMD] AQ136   3575
Ganges (American Musical misc.,
1798) [DMMMRSSS, SDSLSL
MR,] T63; V305; AJ97; AP
530   3576
-----. V [DMMMRSSS, SDSLSS
MR,] AP530   3576a
Gannett (Loy) [SLTDRDTTTLS
LS, SLT] AC5; BD23   3577
Garden (English trad) [MMFSM
LSFMR, MFSLT] A202a; X36;
BY475b   3578
Garden City (Parker) [SLDM
RD, SLDMRD, MSRR] A175;
B21; C21b; D23b; G181; S
404; V53; Y242; AC268; AD
331; AR301; BB58; BR208
3579
Gardiner (Gardiner's Sacred
melodies 1815) [SDTDRSL
TD, DTLRTTL] A227; B460;
C86; D146; G260; H75; I339;
J206; K26; L442; N29; O180;
P387; S410; T211; U93; V93;
W109; Y60; Z108; AA115; AB
332; AC10; AD413; AE413; AF423;
AG268; AH512; AI179; AJ304;

AK394; AL8b; AM262; AN102b;
AP16; AR198; AS339; AT403;
AU405; AV45; AW222; AZ22-R;
BA55; BB519; BD141; BE238;
BF224; BK80; BV504; BX137;
BY680; BZ   3580
Garelochside (Finlay)   [SMRDRM
D, RMSDTDL, LR] BV255a
                         3581
Garfirth (Stewart) [DRDFMLS, S
SMDRM, MMD] AB322; BA172
                         3582
Gartan (Irish trad) X Garton
                         3583
Garton (Irish trad) [DRMLSS,
SSSMRMSSSM] G94; J37; W52;
BY103a; BZ   3584
Gastorius (Gastorius) X Was
Gott tut   3585
Gates ajar (Vail) [SSMSDDLS,
MLSMDMR, S] N616; AI408;
AX250; BB561   3586
-----. R [DRD#RMDLD, MSSLS
MDR,]   3587
Gather the golden grain (Davis)
[MFSSSDRMFM, MRRMFL]
AY337   3588
Gather them into the fold (Show-
alter) X In from the highways
                         3589
Gathering buds (Vaughan) [MMM
SMDRDLD, SSSLSM] AX624
                         3590
-----. R [DRMSLSMS, SSSMRDR,
M]   3591
Gathering home (McIntosh) [MMM
MRMSLSM, RFFFSL] AU128
                         3592
-----. R [DMSD, LTDS, SLSSMD
RR]   3593
Gaude, regina gloriae (Bohemian
Br. G-B) [SLSFMFRMFS, LT
DTLS] E55   3594
Gaudeamus igitur (---) [DSS
DLLL, TDRTDMD, DS] Y299
                         3595
Gaudeamus pariter (Horne) [DD
SSDRM, LSFMRD, DD] A94a;
E131; F294; X144; AF186; BN
94; BQ136; BY155; BZ   3596
-----. V [DDSSDRMM, LSFM
RRD, D] BQ136   3596a
Gaudeo (Crueger) X Jesus, all

my gladness   3597
Gaudete (Smith) [MRFMLSFM,
SLTDRS, SF#] C552a; D539;
K534; BR141   3598
-----. R [SSDDTSSRRD, SL
LFMR,]   3599
Gaudia matris (Baker) [SDS
LDRRD, MFFMDRS, F] D
156b   3600
Gaul (Gaul) X Holy City 3601
Gauntlett I (Gauntlett) [MSMR
DDMDLS, SSFMLD] F376b;
X351; BY588b   3602
Gauntlett II (Gauntlett) [SMS
LDS, LDTLS, SLTDR] L541b
                         3603
Gauntlett III (Gauntlett) [SM
DMSL, DFMRRD, RMRM]
AO454   3604
Gauntlett (Gauntlett) X St
George   3605
Gaza (Jewish trad) [LLLLTDR
M, LSFMLLT] A222; C14b;
E279; X650   3606
Gebauer (Gebauer) X Maria,
hun er en jomfru ren
                         3607
Gebor'n ist uns der heil'ge
Christ (Gregor. Choral book)
X Old 271st   3608
Gebor'n ist uns ein kindelein
(Cologne G-B. 1634) X The
secret flower   3609
Geduld, die soll's wir haben
(Gesius) X Commemoration
                         3610
Geer (Greatorex) [SSMDSSSFR
S, SSMDDT] H202; I376; L
511; V477; AN571; AV137;
BA254; BX278b   3611
Geht, erhoeht die majestaet
(Goudimel) X Gregor's 205th
metre   3612
Geibel (Geibel) X Trumpet
call   3613
Gekreuzigter, mein herz sucht
(Freylinghausen) X Gregor's
102d metre   3614
Gelobet seist du (Traditional,
14th c) X Redeemer   3615
Gelobt sei Gott (Vulpius. G-B.
1609) [DTLSSLTD, DDRSDTL
S,] F135a; J109; Q208; W

331; X154; AD459; AF184; AL
109a; BN51; BV192b; BY156a;
BZ   3616
-----. R [DDTDTL, SSF#SFM,
RDTD,]   3617
Gelobt sei Gott, der unsre noth
(Bohemian Br.) X Gregor's
2d metre   3618
Gems of day (Muret) [MFSMFS,
DTLSLSFM, MF] BG101 3619
Gen himmel auf gefahren ist
(German, 16th c) X God is
ascended   3620
Genesis (Garrett) [MMRMFSD,
DLSFSM, MMR] D601b 3621
Geneva (Bullinger) [SLSDMRLTL
S, DDMRLR,] C386b; D342b;
Eap. 18; G223; I293b; L420;
R102; S221a; U152; V267b; Z
282; AC245; AD490; AE278; AG
140a; AH397; AI242; AJ365a;
AL471b; AM389b; AN280a; AO
171; AP401b; AR373; AS265;
AT246; AV202; AW227; AY446;
BA891; BB256; BD134; BF346;
BK111; BX335a; BY432; BZ
                          3622
Geneva (Cole) [DDRMMFSDTD,
LTRDTL] H69; L108; U36;
V518   3623
Geneva (Day) [MDRMLRTDRM,
DLTDLD] A145; J345; R512;
BK105   3624
Geneva (Geneva Psalter. 1551)
[LFFMDRMFMRD, MSLTS] AQ
109   3625
Geneva (Lowden) [MTRDFDMR,
DTSSS, SS#L] Z315; AC223;
AE451; AR355; AT45   3626
Geneva (Wissmer) [DDDRRSFM, M
RDDTD, DD] AK70   3627
Geneva 119 (Bourgeois) X Royal
law   3628
Geneva 124 (Bourgeois) X Old
124th   3629
Geneva 61 (Genevan Psalter,
1562) [LRRDFMRD, FMRD#,
LDLR] BJ92   3630
Genevan 137th (Strassburg
Psalter. 1539) [LDRMMMRM
F#SM, SMRDR] BJ37   3631
Genevan Psalm 12 (Genevan
Psalter. 1551) X Donne se-

cours   3632
Genevan Psalm 22 (Bourgeois)
[DLRDDFFMRD, SDRMMR]
AF408; AL636; AP17; BJ77
                          3633
Genevan Psalm 42 (Bourgeois)
X Bourgeois   3634
Genevan Psalm 86 (Bourgeois)
X Mon Dieu, prête moi l'or-
ielle   3635
Genevan Psalm 110 (Bourgeois)
X L'Omnipotent   3636
Genevan Psalm 118 (Bourgeois)
X Rendez a Dieu   3637
Genevan Psalm 119 (Bourgeois)
X Royal law   3638
Gennesaret (James) [MMRDMS
FM, DTLSLR, RS] Y74 3639
Gentle Jesus (Roe) [MMRMRD
LS, DDFMRR#MM] C361b;
D567b   3640
Gentle Jesus (Shaw) [MFSMFM
R, MFSDMRD, D] A251; E602;
G444; W662a; X356; BY739a
                          3641
Gentle Saviour (Rider) [SSFSM
R, MSSLS, DDTLS] C361a;
D567a   3642
Gently, Lord, Oh gently
(Jacobs) [DRMDFMMD, TDR
D#RR#M, D] AY351   3643
Gently raise the sacred strain
(Griggs) [DSMDSTRFM, SMD
RMSF] BC92   3644
Georgetown (Williams) [SDMFM
RMDLL, TDRMDR,] A437;
R421; AF340; AQ111   3645
Gerald (Spohr) [SSFMDTLL,
LSMSFM, SS] G299; I320; L
475; AE429; AI70; AK480; AO
246; AT8; AV400; BB226; BE
51; BZ   3646
-----. V [SFMDTLL, SMSFM,
SFMD] AE429   3647
Gerar (Mason) [DMDSTD, MMR
SSF#LS, SS] I264; L375; T85;
U98; V246; AJ125; AX545;
AY116   3648
Gerard (Cobb) [SSSDDMD, DR
MFMRD, MS] D590a   3649
Gerard (English trad) X Noel
                          3650
Gerhardt (Magdeburg. Christ-

liche tischgesange. Erfurt,
1572) X Guds Godhed vil vi
prise   3651
Gerhardt (Holbrook) [SMRFMRD,
SFMSRM, SMR] L243b; V153;
AO160   3652
-----. V [SMRFMRD, SFMFSR
M, SM] V153   3653
Gerhardt (Ohl) [MFMMLLS#, S#
LDTS#L, SSD] K517b   3654
Germania (German) [DDRMFS, SLT
DLS, DDRM] D650b   3655
Germany (Beethoven) X Gardiner
(Gardiner's Sacred melodies
1815)   3656
Geronimo (Stanford) [SDTDSFMS,
SDTDSFMS,] F46   3657
Gerontius (Dykes) [MMRDSDMS,
MRSSSS, LRM] A343b; B259;
C259; D234a; F185a; J411; W
32b; AA228; AB59; AL14b;
AP153; BA43; BE408; BF248;
BV160; BX190   3658
Gerrans (Brown) [SLSLTD, SFM
SFMR, SF#M] F9b   3659
Gertrude (Sullivan) X St Ger-
trude   3660
Gesius (Gesius) [DDRMRDTD,
DDDRDTLS#] E417; Q397; X
533; AA348; BI108   3661
Gether (Gether) [SSDDT, SRFF
M, SMDR, SS] M23   3662
Gethsemane (Bliss) X Man of
sorrows   3663
Gethsemane (Brunk) [MRDSLDS,
TDRRMMR, MR] AX179; AY
254   3664
Gethsemane (Carr) X Spanish
chant   3665
Gethsemane (Dykes) X Rock of
ages   3666
Gethsemane (Redhead) X Petra
3667
Gethsemane (Tye) [MMMLLS#
L, LDTLTMLS#, M] F110b;
AL93; AW107; BR174   3668
Gevaert (French noel, 13th c)
[LLTDLMMM, LMMRDRM, L]
A38; BP17   3669
Ghent (Van Damme) X Adoro te,
No. 2   3670
Gibbons (Gibbons) X Angel's song
3671

Gibbons (Gibbons) X Song 13
3672
Gibbons (Gibbons) X Song 46
3673
Gibbons (Gibbons) X Song 67
3674
Giessen (Gauntlett's Comprehen-
sive tune book. 1851) [MM
DSSMDDTLS, FMRDL] W
409; BY347   3675
Gifford (Pritchard) [MDRMSL
DSMRR, MDRMS] W589
3676
Gift of grace (Lindeman) [MD
LLTDDRMD, MFSMDR] P54
3677
Gilbert (Gilbert) X Angelica
3678
Gilberts (Gilbert) X Angelica
3679
Gildas (Abelard) [SDRMRD,
MSSFMR, MDFM] D75; L459a;
AL172b; AP281; BR502a; BY
301   3680
Gilder (Oldberg) [MFSDRMFF
M, SDSLMF#S] I14a   3681
Gilead (Mehul) [SLTDDDDD,
DRRMMDFR,] I202; T180;
AJ264; AO7; BR60   3682
Gillam (Shaw) [LTDRTM, RTD
LTL, LLTD] X649   3683
Gird us, O God (Singer) [LL
LLLDTL, LS#LDMS, FF]
BH24   3684
Give (Grigg) X Grigg   3685
Give me a foothold (Rupp)
[SMRDRDLL, DRDRMR, SM]
AX519; AY72   3686
Give me Jesus (Sweney) [DRM
MRMSF, FMRDRMD, D] AX
270; BB596   3687
-----. R [SSLLFLSM, MMRR
MF#S, D]   3688
Give me the Bible (Lorenz) [MS
DMFMRRMDS, LLTDF] AX
138; BB655   3689
-----. R [SMFSDFMRDLD,
SDRMS]   3690
Give me thy heart (Bourne)
[SDRMMMFDRM, SRMFMF]
AI196; AM723; AX260
3691
-----. R [MSMS, DMDM, L

LLSMDDT]   3692
Give of your best (Barnard) [MM
   MFMRSS, SDRMFMR, M] AS
   407; AT353; AU366; AV375;
   AW400   3693
Give thanks (Simper) [MRDSLR
   DT, TDRMFR, MR] AS425
                                3694
-----. R [SMMFSLSM, RMLS
   F#MF#S,]   3695
Give thanks to God (Plainsong.
   1539) X To God on high 3696
Give to the Lord (Fillmore) [DR
   MFMMRR, SRMFM, DRM] AX
   647   3697
-----. R [SMRDMRR, SRMFFM
   M, SS]   3698
Give us room that we may dwell
   [Shepherd) [MFF#SMSDTLS,
   SRMFMR] BC256   3699
Giver of all (Norden) [SMMM
   RRDD, TLLFMMRR,] BH250
                                3700
Giving (Leech) [DDDDDTDRMS,
   LLLLSM] AT404; AU393
                                3701
-----. R [DSMDSF#SLSMFSL, T
   TD]   3702
Glad tidings (Goss) [DDMSMS
   DDRM, DDDLSD] O200   3703
Gladdening light (Harris) [DDMR
   SSSDRT, SLTDRM] BV54
                                3704
Glade Jul (Grueber) X Holy night
                                3705
Gladje utan Gud ej finnes
   (Düben) X Jesu   3706
Gladness (Barnby) X St Anselm
                                3707
Gladness (Bliss) [SSSSSSSDRM,
   RRRRRD] G435; AH543; AL
   480; AM647; AP742; AT508;
   AU319; AX38; AY484; BB423;
   BY498   3708
-----. R [SSSSMRDLL, SSSRSDR]
                                3709
Gladness (Bohemian trad) [DDRM
   FFMM, RRMMRD, DD] Q82
                                3710
Gladness (Düben) X Jesu   3711
Glan Geirionydd (Welsh hymn
   mel) [LDRMLMRDTL, LDRM
   LS] X592   3712

Glan'rafon (Davies) [DS, LSFM
   RDMR, RMLSFM] X505b
                                3713
Glaser (Glaser) [SMRDMSLS,
   MLSTDMR, R] M259   3714
Glasgow (Moore. Psalm singer's
   ... 1756) [DMRMRDMSLS
   FM, MRFM] R257; W365;
   AL661a; AM272; BV416; BY
   658   3715
Glastonbury (Dykes) [MMRDL
   DS, SSSMRDR, R#R#] D247
                                3716
Gleams of the golden morning
   (Graham) [DRMMMMMMR
   DD, RRMRD,] BB547
                                3717
-----. R [MFSSSSMDDDD,
   RRRDM]   3718
Gleason (Lutkin) [MMMMMRR,
   RSRMFM, MMM] I464b;
                                3719
Glebe Field (Dykes) [DDDRM
   FFM, SMFSLRR, S] C417a;
   D204d; K561; BX209   3720
Glenfinlas (Finlay) [SDRMRDL,
   SDRMS, SLSM] F433a; W663;
   X354; BV59a; BY751; BZ
                                3721
Glenluce (Scottish Psalter, 1635)
   [DMFSLSFM, RMSSF#S, RR]
   X523; AW206   3722
-----. V [MMFSLSFM, RMSS
   F#S, RR] AW206   3723
Glenmont (Harris) [MRDTRD
   TL, RMFLTDRD] BR360
                                3724
Glenn (Rosecrans) [SMFMMR
   R, SRMRRDD, SM] BB429
                                3725
-----. R [SDDTT, SRRDD,
   SMRDT, L]   3726
Glezen (Glezen) [DDRMFMRS,
   SLSMMRDR,] N56   3727
Gloaming (Stainer) [MFRMM
   FRM, DTLR, MFRM] K464;
   W273; BE160   3728
Gloria (French carol mel)
   [MMMSSFM, MRMSMRD, MM]
   A42; F594; G108; J30; R158;
   X71; Z187; AD117; AE89;
   AF116; AH256; AK105; AN
   175; AQ294; AR138; AT64;

AW82; BD227; BF279; BG119;
BK143; BL9; BM65; BN12; BO
154; BP16; BV93; BY89; BZ
 3729
-----. R [SLSFMFSFMRMFMR]
 3730
-----. V [MMRMSSFMD, MMRM
SSF] F594 3731
-----. V [MMMMSSFMD, MMRMM
SS] AN175 3732
Gloria (Pearsall) [SRMFLSFM, R
MF#SLTLS,] E567 3733
Gloria (Pierre) [DMRDMF#S,
DMRDMF#S, ML] AJ430 3734
Gloria dei (Johnson) [DMFMRDR
D, TLLLRDT, D] N141 3735
Gloria in excelsis (Elliott) [DM
RDMSLS, RMRDMSLS,] W231
 3736
Gloria, laus et honor (Plainsong,
M 1) [MRRMRRDRRMRDT,
RRT] BN31 3737
Gloria, laus et honor (Ravanello)
[MMMMSFM, SLTDTSLT, T]
BQ168 3738
Gloria, laus et honor (Sarum
Processional, M 1) [RLL#L
SSLSSFSSLSFMR,] E621;
F598 3739
Gloria patri (Greatorex) X Glory
be to the Father 3740
Gloria patri (Meineke) [DDDDD
RR, RRSRRRMDT] AE471; AK
492; AMp. xv; AR637; AT524;
AU494; AV430; AW607 3741
Glorification (Tscherlitzky) [DS
DDRRM, MRDMR, DSDM] Q118;
AA166 3742
Glorious Mary (Florian) [DRMM
FSLSS, LLDLSSM] BN156
 3743
Glorious name (McKinney) [SSS
MLLSM, DRMSFMRM,] AT138
 3744
-----. R [SFMFSLSFM, FMRM
FSF] 3745
Glorious patron (Browne) [MFSM
DRMD, DTTLLFMR,] BQ101
 3746
Glorious peace (Teasley) [SMM
RMFMD, DRRRRMFM] AX337
 3747
-----. R [MMMRDR, RFFFMR

M, MSM] 3748
Glorious saint whose deeds im-
mortal (Darmstadt G-B) X
All saints 3749
Glorious things (LeJeune)
[MDRMFSLTDT, LSSFMM]
D490b; Y208 3750
Glorious things are sung
(Daynes) [DMSDLF#LS, LSRS
F#FM, D] BC243 3751
Glorious things of thee are
spoken (Conkey) X Rathbun
 3752
Glorious things of thee are
spoken (Hall) X Saviour
breathe an evening blessing
 3753
Glorious things of thee are
spoken (Hanecy) [SDFMRD
TLSD, DDRMRF#] BC244
 3754
Glorious Virgin, thee we sing
(German hymn arr) [DMF
SDDTD, RMRDRF#SS] BO89
 3755
Glory (Harrison) X Cambridge
 3756
Glory (Matthews) X Children's
praises 3757
Glory (Curwen's Tune book.
1842) [DDMFSSLLS, DLR
SSTD,] W600; BY608
 3758
Glory be to Jesus (Filitz) X
Caswall 3759
Glory be to Jesus (Montani)
[LLDMLM, SSRRM, LLDMF]
BQ72 3760
Glory be to the Father (Grea-
torex) [DDDDDDT, DRSSSS
LTL] R546; T458; U488;
Y389; AC335; AE472; AG
323; AHp. 9; AI449; AK493;
AMp. xv; AR637; AS488; AT
525; AU495; AV428; AW606;
BA944; BB689; BF680
 3761
Glory flaming (Whittington)
[DMSSLLM, DDTF#R#D#T,
DM] BI54 3762
Glory gates (Hott) [DRMSS
LSLSMD, DRMSM] AX269;
AY146 3763

-----. R [DSDDSLSLSMD, DR
MSS]   3764
Glory in the highest (Ouseley)
[MDSDLDS, MFSLSDRMR,]
B558; K548   3765
Glory, praise and blessing
(Smith, B. E.) [SMMFSDTLS,
F#F#SLTDT] BI20-D   3766
Glory song (Gabriel) [SDTLSFMS
DM, MRD#MRT] AT485; BB
641; BY191a;   3767
-----. R [MMMMMRMF, FF
FFFSRM,]   3768
Glory to God in the highest
(Stephens) [DTLSLTLS, SML
SFMR, R] BC359   3769
-----. R [SSSFMSFLS, DR#
R#MDR#R#]   3770
Glory to God in the highest
(Warren) [MMFSDLSM, SDTL
RMFL] AX103   3771
-----. R [MMRDMFSD, DDTRM
F#S, F]   3772
Glory to God on high (Giardini)
X Moscow   3773
Glory to his name (Stockton) [M
MRDDTLDS, MMMSSMD] AT
95; AU185; AV386; AW464;
AX4   3774
-----. R [DDDLSLD, MMMDR
MR, MM]   3775
Gloucester (Ravenscroft's Psalter)
[DSMRDFSL, MRMFSM, SM]
W223b; AP698b   3776
Gloucester (Williams) [MR#MS
DLS, DFMLSRFM, R] D611a;
BI12   3777
Gloucestershire wassail (English
trad) [SDDDRMFMRMS, SF
RRR] BG31   3778
Glovernia (Brewer) [DMMMFS
MSLT, SDDTLS] AP569 3779
Glück zu kreuz (Halle, 1697)
X Petersen   3780
Glynthorpe (Shaw) [FSRDLS,
FFMTRRDTLM,] X588   3781
Go as a witness (Ackley) [MM
MMMR#MSS, SF#SMSDT, F] U314
                                        3782
Go bury thy sorrow (Bliss)
[DDTLLSFFLSM, DDTLL]
AU293   3783
Go down Moses (Negro spiritual)

[MDDTTDDL, MMS#S#L, M
DD] AF428; AG611   3784
-----. R [LL, RR, MMRMMRD
L, DLLD]   3785
Go tell it on the mountain
(Negro spiritual) [MMRDLSD,
RRRDRMRMRD,] AK488;
BK163; BZ   3786
-----. R [DMSSLSM, DRRDR
M, DMS]   3787
Go to the deeps (Gabriel)
[SF#SLSDMM, RDFLDTLS,]
AI241   3788
-----. R [DDDDTLSS, MSR
MFSFM,]   3789
Go to thy rest, fair child
(Tenney) [MMMSFM, MRM
FSM, SLSM] AX627; AY
177   3790
Go, ye messengers (Robertson)
[MMMMDFMRMD, RMFSDDM]
BC247   3791
Gobaith (Davies) X Hope
                                        3792
God (Haile) [SMSDDTTD,
MDMLSS, SR] BH68   3793
God be in my head (Davies)
[SSSMR, TLTRTLS, SSSM]
R395; AF543; AL364; AR
679; BV623; BY471; BZ
                                        3794
God be with you (Tomer) [M
MMMMMSRM, LLLLLLL]
G557; H434; I564; L67; M
650; N364; R78; U449; V26;
Z129; AF62; AG14; AH177;
AI344; AM632; AN472b; AO
48; AP701; AR506; AS63;
AT372; AU480; AV235; AW
365; AX654; AY405; BA932;
BB35; BC47; BY761a; BZ
                                        3795
-----. R [MFSDMRDLD,
TLSLSMD]   3796
God bless America (Berlin)
[DTLTLS, RDRM, RMFL,
FM] AH488   3797
God bless our native land
(Mason) X Dort   3798
God cares (Martin) X Martin
                                        3799
"God hath sent his angels"
(Parker) [SMDMSDS, SDMR

D, LMDM] C557; AO187
                            3800
-----. R [SMDRMFSDS, SDM
RD, FF]   3801
God in heaven (Fuller) [MRDSLD
TLLS, DRMFSL] D578   3802
God in nature (Stainer) [SDFFMRS,
SDFFMR, RRS] W18a   3803
God incarnate, veil thy splendor
(Smart) X Bethany   3804
God is ascended (Edmunds) [DM
FSLTDRS, DTLS, LSF] BL38
                            3805
God is ascended (German, 16th c)
[LLRD#RMRDL#L, RFSLTD#]
AD166; BG127   3806
-----. V [LLRD#RMRDTL,
RFSLTD#] BG127   3807
God is good (Bontrager) [SSLS
TLLMS, SDDDTLS] AY427
                            3808
God is great, God is good
(Allgemeines katholisches G-B.
Vienna, 1744) X Te deum
                            3809
God is in his holy temple (Asper)
[MDFMRRDTS, DRMFRDT]
BC246   3810
God is in his holy temple
(Hawkes) [MMRDTDMR, FFMR
DRM, S] BH4   3811
God is love (Bailey) X Praise
him   3812
God is love (Lorenz) [DMFSS
LTD, RTD, DMFSS] AE70;
AW439; AX81   3813
-----. R [SLF, FSM, DDDDDRD
TLS]   3814
God is love (Mendelssohn) X
Trust   3815
God is love, his mercy (Click)
[SSSDRRMS, SSLSDMR, M]
AX86; AY372   3816
God is my strong salvation
(Binder) [DTTDSMRD, MSMD
RR, LR] BH95   3817
God is near thee (Curwen's Stan-
dard course) [SSSMDDDSM
R, RMFMRM] AP536   3818
God is the giver of all (Grau-
man) [MMMSFMLLS, SDSSFM
M] BH66   3819
God knows what is best (Ruebush)

[SSF#SMRDL, DSDDMMRR]
AY322   3820
-----. R [SSDMDRDL, LSDM
DMRR,]   3821
God loved us so he sent his
Son (Schreiner) [DDDDDRFM,
SSSSSDLS,] BC178   3822
God most truly (Daley) [DRM
RDTL, LSLDRTD, DR] BN
175   3823
God moves in a mysterious way
(Binder) [MMDLDTTT, TRM
RDR, MM] BH83   3824
God moves in a mysterious
way (Bradbury) X Harvey's
chant   3825
God moves in a mysterious
way (Showalter) [MFSSSDM
RD, SLDDLS, M] AX85; AY
84   3826
God of grace (Haile) [DRMM
SLTD, TTLLSFM, R] BH75
                            3827
God of hosts (Hopkins) X St
Athanasius   3828
God of Israel (Binder) [SSD
TLSFMRMRDS, SSL] BH52
                            3829
God of love (Hugg) [DRMDT
LTD, MF#STLSF#S] AY
34   3830
God of mercy and compassion
(Montani) [MMFRDTMD,
TLRTLTDM,] BQ134 3831
-----. R [MMMRFMRD, SSS
FLFMR]   3832
God of might (Jewish trad) X
Addeer hu   3833
God of our fathers (Warren)
X National hymn   3834
God of our fathers, known of
old (Robertson) [SSSSLSFS,
SSSLDTLT,] BC77   3835
God of our fathers, known of
old (Woodbury) X Selena
                            3836
God of our fathers, we come
unto thee (Beesley) [MDRMFM
RDTD, MMMSFM] BC50
                            3837
God of our strength (Doane)
X Vision   3838
God of power, God of right

Goeldel (As hymnodus sacer.
1625) X Ach Gott und Herr
3878
Goetchius (Maclean) [MSDFM
R, MSSF#SS, LLSD] V80
3879
Going home (Dvorák) [MSSMRD,
RMSMR, MSSMR] AI267 3880
Going home (Miller) [DMMM
DRMR, DMSSDMRD,] I628;
AU261; AX591; AY144 3881
Golden (English trad) X The
merchants' carol 3883
Golden chain (Barnby) X The
golden chain 3884
Golden corn (Calkin) [MRDDTT,
FMRRDD, DLLL] D569a; I
196; T122b; AJ61 3885
Golden Grove (Cooke) [MFSM
RDMLS, DRMSFMR] F307a
3886
Golden Grove (Littlewood)
[DRMSFFRMFM, MF#SLSF#]
Y338 3887
Golden Hills (Chapin) [DMRDLRR
D, SLSLDLS, S] AY368 3888
Golden mornings (English trad)
[MDTDLSSM, MRMFMRM, M]
BG165 3889
Golden sequence (Langton) X
Veni sancte spiritus (Langton)
3890
Golden sheaves (Basque trad)
[LTDRMRDT, RDLDTSL, L]
BG159 3891
Golden sheaves (Sullivan) [SMS
SFMRD, DRMFLTD, S] D191a;
Eap. 17; F484; N570; O525;
W616; BE392; BV653; BX428;
BY731 3892
Golden trumpets (LWhitmer)
[MSSSLTDR, MSSSLTLS,]
AC134 3893
Golders Green (Fowles) [DTSL
TDRMRDTR, DTSL] BY765
3894
Goldschmidt (Darmstadt G-B)
[LTDTDRMM, LTDTLLS#L, D]
C268b; E382; Q60; X217b;
AA133; AZ16-B 3895
-----. V [LTDTDRMM, LTDTLLS#
L, L] P200 3895a
Golgotha (Harrington) [MMRM, M

RMFFMRM, MRDT] AK151
3896
Gone to bloom above (Teasley)
[SMR#MRDRM, RDDRDLS,
S] AX626 3897
-----. R [MFFDFMR#M, R
DDDRMR, S] 3898
Gonfalon Royal (Buck) [SLD
FMRMDL, LRTSDFM] E
141b; W23; X593; BE271;
BV33b; BY147a 3899
Good-bye (Hugg) [SMMMDDLD,
DTDRRDRM,] AY404
3900
-----. R [MFMFFFMR#M,
MSF#SDMRR,] 3901
Good-bye (Shaw) [SDSFSMM,
MMLS#TL, SDS] X386g
3902
Good bye, mourner (Negro
spiritual) [DMDMDMMMD,
DMDDLDDL] AH598 3903
Good cheer (Perkins) [SDMS
LTD, DRMDFMRTD] Y194
3904
Good King Wencelas (Piae
cantiones, 1582) X Tempus
adest floridum 3905
Good morning to you (---)
[SLSDT, SLSRD, SSMDTL,]
AU308 3906
Good news from heaven
(Luther) X From heaven
high 3907
Good Shepherd (Barnby) [SDS
MRDRMSRM, DFFMR] I104a;
AJ122 3908
Good Shepherd, Rosemont
(Miller) [SMRDMLSM, S
LTDTLS] A378a 3909
Goodwell (Emerson) [SDRMM
SDRMM, RMFMMR] L65
3910
Goodwill (Roberts) [SLSDMM
RDT, D RDTLS, F] AR270
3911
Goodwin (Webb) X Webb 3912
Gopsal (Handel) [SLSMF#S, DF
MRRD, SSML] D457a; E476;
F216; V201; W135b; X632;
BV210; BY190 3913
Gor porten hög (Swedish Koral-
bok, 1697) [LDRMLLS#L,

DRMFMRDT,] N2   3914
Gordon (Barnby) X St Ignatius
                                    3915
Gordon (Gordon) [DMFFMRD
   MRTTD, DMFF] G234; H321;
   P216; R405; T149; U203; Z382;
   AE178; AH297; AI115; AJ211;
   AM547; AO643; AR462; AS275;
   AT289; AU154; AV323; AW216;
   AX396; AY195; BA905; BB276;
   BZ   3916
Gordon (Smart) [SSSDMFLS,
   DRFMRM, SM] J362a; W611;
   BV288   3917
Goring (Thiman) [SMFSLDTD,
   RMSSF#S, SD] BY274   3918
Gorran (Dussek) [DSMTDRMLT
   DR, MLSM, D] C244b   3919
Gorton (Beethoven) [SSSLLS,
   SSSDDR, RMMD] J89; K46;
   N582; T102b; AJ217; AM417;
   AO153; AS36; AV425; BB694
                                    3920
Gorton (Brunk) X Father! in
   life's young morning   3921
Goshen (Davis) [DDTLSM, SMR
   DR, DDTLS] Eap. 70; K564;
   W552; AH541; AP741; BV505
                                    3922
Goshen (Haydn) X St Michel's
                                    3923
Goss (Goss) X St Casimer   3924
Gosterwood (English trad) [DD
   LTDRMD, SFMRDRD, D] E299;
   R410; S298; W70; X21; Y76;
   Z592; AD451; AL576; BE377;
   BV220   3925
-----. V [DDDLTDRMD, SFMRD
   RD,] Y76   3926
Gotha (Knecht) [DDMDMMSM,
   RSMDTDR, D] M400; AK18; AW
   511   3927
Gothenburg (Crueger) X Schmuecke
   dich   3928
Gott der vater wohn' (Walther.
   Geistliche G-B. 1524) [SSLTD
   DT, LDSMFMRD, S] Q247; AA
   271; AN480   3929
-----. V [SSLTDT, DSMFR,
   SSLTD] AN480   3930
Gott des himmels [und der erden]
   (Albert) X Waltham   3931

Gott des himmels und der er-
   den (Meiningen G-B) X St
   Leonard   3932
Gott ein Vater (Silcher) [SL
   SFMR, DRMFMR, MSLS]
   E600; F415; W666; AM661;
   AP585; BV7; BY336a
                                    3934
Gott ist gegenwärtig (Neander)
   X Arnsberg   3935
Gott ist getreu (Ahle) X
   Augsburg   3936
Gott ist mein hort (Egli) [SD
   DTTDRM, MDLRDTLS,]
   AA461   3937
Gott sei dank (Freylinghausen.
   Geistriches G-B.) X Lue-
   beck   3938
Gott sei gelobet (Walther) X
   Walther   3939
Gott sprach zu dir (---) [MM
   FSDTLSFMM, MMLLS] K551
                                    3940
Gott will's machen (Steiner) X
   Steiner   3941
Gott woll'n wir loben (Bohem-
   iam Br.) X Gregor's 520th
   metre   3942
Gottes lamm ruft gnade (Tscher-
   litzky) X Glorification
                                    3943
Gottes sohn ist kommen
   (Weisse) X Ravenshaw
                                    3944
Göttingen (Regnart) [LLMM
   RM, MMRDDT, TDRM] M328;
   N18; O161; Q526; AA508;
   AZ75a   3945
-----. R [MSMMDRR, RMR
   DDTL.]   3946
-----. V [LLTDRM, MMRDR
   T, TDRM] O161   3947
-----. V [LLTDRM, MMRDD
   T, TDRM] Q526   3948
-----. V [LLTDRM, MRRDDT,
   TDRM] AZ75-a   3949
Gottlieb (Maker) X Word of
   life   3950
Gottlob (Wagner. Sammlung ...)
   X Gottlob, es geht nun mehr
   zu ende   3951
Gottlob, es geht nun mehr zu

ende (Wagner. Sammlung ...)
[MDMFMRDR, MMMLTDDT,]
Q163; W271b; X637a; Y111;
AA66; AB8; AD446; AF468;
AN82; BE32; BN97; BY315
                                            3952
-----. V [MDMFMRDRR, MMM
    LTDD] X637   3953
-----. V [MDMFMRMR, MMMLT
    DDT] Y111   3954
-----. V [MDMFMRDR, MLTD
    DT, MD] BE32   3955
Gottschalk (Gottschalk) X Mercy
                                            3956
Gouda (Tours) [SLTDRMRD,
    DDMDFR, SL] I447; BR368
                                            3957
Goudimel (Goudimel) [SLDDTD,
    DLTTLS, SDLT] AA338 3958
-----. V [SLDDTD, DLTDLS,
    SDLT] AJ423   3958a
Goudimel (Goudimel) X Gregor's
    205th metre   3959
Gould (Burnap) [SSMMMSFR,
    FMSDLS, SS] L519   3960
Gould (Gould) X Hymn   3961
Gould (Warren) [DMFSSSLLTDS,
    MRDTS] BR152   3962
Gouldie (Pollock) [DRMRMFSM,
    LSFMRDR, M] AY256   3963
Gounod (Gounod) [SMRDDLSFF
    M, SLTDMR] V344   3964
Gounod (Gounod) X Lux prima
                                            3965
Gounod's Evening hymn (Gounod)
    X Evening hymn   3966
Gower (Gower) X Gower's
    Litany   3967
Gower's Litany (Gower) [MMRM
    SRR, FFMFLSS, SS] AB162;
    AI223; AL159b; AM244; AO276;
    AP280b; AR280; AV413; BF360;
    BK31   3968
Gower's Recessional (Gower)
    X Recessional   3969
Grabesruhe (Rau) [SLTDSMDR
    D, DTLSTLS] AZ89-C; BA70
                                            3970
Grace (American traditional)
    X Amazing grace   3971
Grace (Berggren) [SDDTFLLS,
    MSFSLRDT,] M188   3972
Grace (Nitzsche) [MMR#MLSSF,

MRD#RSFM, S] BA465 3973
Grace (Stenhammer) [MSFM
    RMSF, FLSFMSFM] BE76
                                            3974
Grace (Warren) [DDRRR#R#FR,
    RRMMFFSM,] D595a 3975
Grace after meals (Jewish trad)
    [MMSFMRMF, FFLSFMFS,]
    BH111   3976
Grace Church (Pleyel) [MM
    RDTDRM, SSFMRDTD,] A
    108b; B119; C119; D297a;
    H207; J62b; K59; L181; N126;
    S22; T428b; V247; Y43; Z
    309; AA488; AD310; AF324;
    AK74; AM134; AN64; AO85;
    AR363; BA706; BR40; BX54;
    BY258   3977
Grace Church, cananoque
    (George) [MMRSF#MRM,
    SLTDTLLM,] BZ   3978
Grace dieu (Wesley, S.S.)
    [SDMRSDRRD, SSSDTLF]
    W536   3979
Grace greater than our sin
    (Towner) X Marvelous grace
                                            3980
Grace soit (French trad) [SS
    LTDS, DDRTD, SSLTD] X3;
    AQ319; BG156; BM13   3981
Grace soit rendue (French carol)
    X Grace soit   3982
Grace, 'tis a charming sound
    (Link) [MMFMRMRD, SSLSF
    SFM] AX323; AY77   3983
Graceham (Chitty) [DDRMMRD,
    DRMRDRR, DD] AZ581-K;
    BA434B   3984
Gracias (Beaumont) [SSMRLT,
    SDDDDLS, FMD] BY18a
                                            3985
Gracious Father, O Lord hear
    us (Beethoven) [SSSS, SLSS,
    SSSSSSSL] AU487; AV414
                                            3986
Gracious God whose mercy
    lends (Allgemeines katholisches
    G-B. Vienna, 1774) X Hurs-
    ley   3987
Gracious King, enthroned (Un-
    seld) [MRDSLDS, DRMRR, M
    RDS] AI217; AS206   3988
Graefenberg (Crueger) [DLSD

RMMR, MSFMRD, SM] A370;
E421; F347; G389; J413a; K15;
M11; N127; P8; Q10; R243; S
197a; W351; X38; Z275; AD
189; AE142; AF241; AG229;
AH235; AK183; AL153a; AN
159a; AP4; AQ96; AR234; AS
167; AW242; BE287; BV534;
BY206a; BZ   3989
-----. V [DLSDRMMR, MSFM
RD, SF] AS167   3989a
Grafton (Chants ordinaires ...
Paris) [DRMDMRMFSM, SSFF
MR] E33; F383b; W207; X
129b; BO274c; BV161b; BY326
                              3990
Grafton (Clark) [SSSSFMRD,
RMSLDTLS,] AQ251   3991
Grand Dieu! que de merveilles
(French trad) X The builders
                              3992
Grand Isle (Hopkins) [SDDDMFS
LS, MFSDRM,] A243; AF481;
BY259   3993
Grandpont (Stainer) [MMRDLD,
DTFMMR, SSFM] S500; W488;
BE21   3994
Grange (Brown-Borthwick)
[SSMRDRDT, DDLSFMR, S]
BR70a   3995
Grant me strength (Weinberg)
[MFS#S#S#LTT, DTLS#TS#,
TT] BH48   3996
Grasmere (Barnby) X Edinburgh
                              3997
Grasmere (Freylinghausen) [MM
FSSFFM, MRDRTTDD,] F567
                              3998
Grassmere (Traditional mel)
[DMSSSDLDS, SFM, FMR, D]
L502; AP717   3999
Grateful praises (Kaiser) [SSMD
RMRD, RMSSF#S, RM] BH104
                              4000
Grateful submission (Kolb) [SM
FMSSRM, SSDDRDT, D] AY
379   4001
-----. R [SSSSSSDD, LSMSFMR,
R]   4002
Gratia (Freylinghausen. G-B.
1704) X Luebeck   4003
Gratitude (Bost) [SSDMMSMRF
TD, SSDMM] G460; I410;

L12; V36; AO24   4004
Gratitude (German trad) X
Gregor's 185th metre-A
                              4005
Gratitude (Crueger) X Nun
danket   4006
Gratitude (Dykes) X Beatitudo
                              4007
Gratitude (Herr) X I owe the
Lord a morning song   4008
Gratitude (Wesley, S.S.) [MS
MMRDFMR, RMF#SLTL] C
426b; D477b; W322; AL229a
                              4009
Gratitude (Whitmer) [SLTSSL
TDRM, FMRMRD] AC233;
AD341   4010
Gravity (Mason) X Rockingham
                              4011
Great Arbiter of human fate
(Samuel) [SDTLSFMR,
MFSDRMM, S] BH209   4012
Great day (Negro spiritual)
[SLD, DDSLSSSSLM, MMM]
AH605   4013
Great God, attend (Daynes)
[MFSDRDDTTDRFMRRD,]
BC248   4014
Great God, to thee my evening
song (Kimball) [DMFSLSFMR
D, SLTDDT] BC59   4015
Great God! whatever through
thy church (LaSalle hymnal)
[SDSMSDSM, SDDRMR, RR]
BO209   4016
Great God, whatever through
thy church (Slovak hymnal)
[DDDDMMSSF, MRMFRDT]
BQ128   4017
Great High Priest (Gregor's
Chorale book. 1784) X
Gregor's 12th metre   4018
Great is the Lord; 'Tis good
(Beesley) [DSFMLSFMRD,
SLTDDT] BC234   4019
Great is the love (Kirkpatrick)
[SSSSDTLS, FFFSSM, SSS] AE
291   4020
-----. R [TTTDDRS, DDRRM,
MMMD]   4021
Great is thy faithfulness
(Runyan) X Faithfulness
                              4022

Great King of heaven (Robertson)
[SDMLSSFMLS, SDRTSL] BC
53   4023
Great King of Kings (Kreitmaier)
[DMFSMFLS, SLTDSSFM] BQ
336   4024
-----. R [DTSLSSFMMR, LSM
FMM]   4025
Great King of peace (Roff) [DM
FSMFLSRM, SMRDDL] BL57
                                4026
Great King of saints (Bourgeois)
X Old 100th   4027
Great Physician (Stockton, arr)
[SSMDRMFS, SSDMDRD, S]
P271; AH334; AI389; AM144;
AP752; AS128; AT86; AU226;
AX535; BB530   4028
-----. R [SLTDSTLS, SLTDSTLS,]
                                4029
Great Redeemer! (Conte) X
Redentore   4030
Great St Joseph (Bragers) [MD
SSFMRMD, DRMFRDT] BP90
                                4031
Great St Joseph (Slovak hymn)
[MMLSFMMR, RRMRMFMR,]
BQ93   4032
Great St Joseph (Stein) [DTLS
LRSFMRD, SLF#SL] BN170;
BO126   4033
Great white host (Norwegian trad.,
arr by Grieg) X Behold a
host   4034
Greatorex (Allen) [SLSMDRDLS,
DMSFRDR] T207; AJ296; AO
285   4035
Greek folksong (Greek mel) X
Luke   4036
Greek hymn (Holbrook) [DTLDRD,
MRDMR, DTLDR] C162a; G
275b; I616b   4037
Green are the leaves (Catholic
hymn mel) [SMRDTTLS, SDDMR
DRM,] BO110   4039
Green grow'th the holly (Henry
VIII, King) [MLSMM, MLSM
M, MLLSFM] BG63   4040
Green Hill (Comley) [DMSFMM
RD, DLSSMR, TD] K544b;
P174   4041
Green Hill (Peace) [MMMRDFFM,
RSSFML, LL] I314; O70; U35;

V75; AB82; AE323; AJ224;
AL427; AM498; BA226
                                4042
Green Hill (Stebbins) X The
green hill   4043
Greenland (Haydn) [MSSSS
DM, MRRFFM, RMSS] A4;
B171b; C61; D43a; H206;
I18; M558; N312; R482;
S400; U107; V710; Y280;
Z486; AB284; AD242; AE63;
AF190; AG250; AR395; AS166;
AT111; BA868; BB164; BD
94; BE120; BF411; BQ26;
BX541   4044
-----. V [SSSSSDS, MRRSFM,
RMM] BQ26   4045
Greensleeves (English trad.,
before 1642) [LDRMFMRTS
L, TDLLS#LT] A36; G109;
J48; R159; Y326; Z200; AB
121; AF140; AG300; AH255;
AW78; BD220; BF295; BG
28; BK162; BZ   4046
-----. R [SSF#MRTSL, TD
LLS#LTS]   4047
-----. V [SSFMRTSL, TDLL
S#LTS] Y326   4048
Greenville (Rousseau) [MMRD
DRRMRD, SSFMMR] G187;
H446; I39; L66; N365; V253;
W661; AI195; AL476; AP726;
AT390; AW459; AX240; BC
105; BR78; BY286   4049
-----. V [MMRDDRRMD, SSF
MMR] V253   4050
Greenwell (Leslie) [MDLSMDT
LS, DTDFMMR] BY204b
                                4051
Greenwood (Prout) X Allen
                                4052
Greenwood (Sweetser) [MRDS
LS, TLTDMS, RDRM] G217;
H203; I352; L504; R218; S
299b; T71; U222; V365; Y
202; AA541; AB246; AD269;
AG207; AJ107; AM327; AO569;
AV121; AW236; BA99; BB40;
BR257   4053
Greeting (Shaw) [SDSMF, SDS
MF, SDSMFS] X386a 4054
Greeting (Wathall) [DSFMDS
FM, MLDTMS#F, F] I572

4055
Gregor (Gregor) [MLS#LRDT,
DLRDTTL, ML] AZ581-E
4056
Gregor (Herrnhut ms.) X Gre-
gor's 37th metre   4057
Gregor's 2d metre (Bohemian Br.)
[SLTDRMFS, FMRMRDTD,]
AZ2-A   4058
Gregor's 6th metre (Gregor)
[SDRMFM, SDRMFM, SSFF]
AZ6-B   4059
Gregor's 7th metre (Gregor)
[SDTDRRM, SDTDRRM, SD]
AZ7-B   4060
Gregor's 9th metre (Gregor.
Choral buch) [LDTDLTDR,
MMRDTL, MM] AZ9-a   4061
Gregor's 10th metre (Selnecker)
X Selnecker   4062
Gregor's 12th metre (Gregor.
Choral buch, 1784) [DTDLSFM,
DLRDTLS, DS] AZ11-1; BA453
4063
Gregor's 15th metre (Praetorius)
X Ich dank' dir schon   4064
Gregor's 16th metre (Darmstadt
G-B) X Goldschmidt   4065
Gregor's 20th metre (---) [DM
SMFLSR, MSFRDLTS,] AZ
20-A   4066
Gregor's 22d metre-A (Geistliche
G-B. Wittenberg 1544) X
Rhau[w]   4067
Gregor's 22d metre-C (Crueger)
X Lob sei dem allmachtigen
Gott   4068
Gregor's 22d meter-D (Plainsong,
ca 600) X Christe, qui lux
es et dies   4069
Gregor's 36th metre (Crueger)
X Herzliebster Jesu   4070
Gregor's 37th metre (Herrnhut
ms) [DSLSFM, DRMMRD,
MRMR] AZ37-A; BA448 4071
Gregor's 37th metre (Herrnhut
ms) X Bunyan (Thommen.
Christen-schatz)   4071a
Gregor's 39th metre-A (Moravian)
[DDSMSFMRDTDD, DDSM]
AZ39-A; BA312   4072
Gregor's 39th metre-B (Darm-
stadt G-B) [DMDMSSDDRTD,

DMDMS] AZ39-B   4073
Gregor's 39th metre-C
(Grimm's Chorale book)
[DSSSSLTDDDT, TLLLS]
AZ39-C   4074
Gregor's 45th metre (Wurzber-
ger G-B 1628) X O traureg-
keit   4075
Gregor's 46th metre (Drese)
X Rochelle   4076
Gregor's 54th metre (Bohemian
Br.) [LLTDLTDRM, MMM
SMRR] AZ54-A   4077
Gregor's 54th metre-D (Gregor.
Chorale book) [MRDSLTD,
DTLTLLS, SD] AZ11-Q 4078
Gregor's 56th metre (Nares)
X Amsterdam   4079
Gregor's 58th metre (Walther
G-B.) X Soldau   4080
Gregor's 58th metre, Pt. II
(Walther. G.-B.) X Soldau
Pt. II   4081
Gregor's 61st metre (Stral-
sund G-B) X Praise to the
Lord   4082
Gregor's 70th metre (Lowen-
stern) X Nun preiset alle
4083
Gregor's 74th metre (Gregor)
[LLTDRM, MRRDDT, TDRM
MR] AZ74-B   4084
Gregor's 75th metre (Regnart)
X Göttingen   4085
Gregor's 77th metre (6-line
stanza: Freylinghausen)
[SSDDRRM, RMRDTLS, SS]
AZ77-A; BA46   4086
Gregor's 79th metre (Crueger)
[DSSLTDDTD, DDTLSLL]
AZ79-B   4087
Gregor's 82d metre (Herrnhut
ms.) [SDRMFSFM, SDRMFS
FM,] AZ82-D; BA486
4088
Gregor's 83d metre (Freyling-
hausen. G-B. 1704) X Tu
vins, Jesus   4089
Gregor's 95th metre (Frey-
linghausen) [DDRDFSFMR,
MSLSDTD] AZ95-A   4090
Gregor's 97th metre (Frey-
linghausen. G-B. 1704)

[SDRMFMRD, SDRMFMRD,]
AZ97-A; BA544   4091

Gregor's 99th metre (Gregor)
[MRDLSSFM, SMDRMFMR,]
AZ99-B   4092

Gregor's 101st metre (Darmstadt.
G-B. 1698) [DMF#SSLTD, RMD
TSLDT] AZ101-A   4093

Gregor's 102d metre (Freylinghausen) [MFSMMLTS#, TTT
DTLSS] AZ102-A   4094

Gregor's 106th metre (Wittwe.
Hamburger Musikalisches
handbuch. 1690) X Crasselius
                      4095

Gregor's 107th metre (Gregor)
[MMRDSLSSFM, DFMRDT]
AZ107-C; BA303   4096

Gregor's 109th metre (Freylinghausen) [MMMMRDTLS#LL,
MMMMR] AZ109-C   4097

Gregor's 112th metre (Gregor)
[MSTDDLFMRD, RMMF#F#S]
AZ112-B   4098

Gregor's 114th metre (Richter)
[SSFMSLSDMFSFM, DTL]
AZ114-A   4099

Gregor's 115th metre (Grimm's
Choral buch) [SMLSDTLSFM
RR, SDDT] AZ115-B; BA499
                      4100

Gregor's 118th metre (Freylinghausen) [LMRDTLMLFMRM
DTL, L] AZ118-A   4101

Gregor's 119th metre (Schmidt)
X Fahre fort   4102

Gregor's 124th metre (Flittner)
[MMFSFMRRR, SFMRD, TT]
AZ124-A   4103

Gregor's 126th metre-B (Gregor)
[DDMRFMR, FMDRTD, DDM]
AZ126-B   4104

Gregor's 132nd metre-B (Christliche lieder, 1524) X Nun
freut euch   4105

Gregor's 132d metre-F (Geistliche
lieder. Wittenberg, 1535)
X O Jesu, når jag ... 4106

Gregor's 133d meter-B (Fabricius)
[SLSMFFMM, FMRDDTLS]
AZ133-B   4107

Gregor's 141st metre-A (Herrnhut ms) [DTLSFMM, SDTLS,

DTLS] AZ141-A; BA125
                      4108

Gregor's 151st metre-H (Ros-
tocker G-B. 1659) [SMSD
FMR, RMF#SSF#S, SM] AZ
151-H; BA682   4109

Gregor's 151st metre-I (Freylinghausen) [DMDSRMRD, M
SSSFMR, D] AZ151-I; BA102
                      4110

Gregor's 152d metre-B (Vulpius) X Weimar   4111

Gregor's 155th metre (Freylinghausen G-B.) X Festus
                      4112

Gregor's 156th metre (8-line
stanza: Freylinghausen)
[SSDDRRM, RMRDTLS, SS]
AZ156-A   4113

Gregor's 159th metre (German
trad) [DDSLTDLS, FMSFM
RD, D] AZ159-A; BA532
                      4114

Gregor's 160th metre-B (Gastorius) X Was Gott tut
                      4115

Gregor's 161st metre (Hille)
[SDRMFSFMD, SSFMFMR]
AZ161-A   4116

Gregor's 163d metre (Gregor's
Choral buch) [DSFMDRMFSM,
RSF#SSF#] AZ163-A   4117

Gregor's 166th metre (Herrnhut
ms) [DRMRMFMRDR,
MDRMFM] AZ166-A; BA58
                      4118

Gregor's 167th metre-B (French
trad) [DMRFMRDRF, MLF#
SSF#S,] AZ167-B   4119

Gregor's 167th metre-D (Freylinghausen) [MMMS#LTLS#S#,
TTDLSF#M,] AZ167-D
                      4120

Gregor's 167th metre-E (Darmstadt. G-B. 1698) [LTDMLD
TL, DRMMRRD, L] AZ167-E
                      4121

Gregor's 168th metre-B (German trad) [MMTDRDTL, DDT
LS#LT, M] AZ168-B   4122

Gregor's 168th metre-C (Crueger)
X Du, O schönes welt geb-
audes   4123

4156
Grenoble (Grenoble Antiphoner,
1753) X Deus tuorum militum
4157
Gresham (Shaw) [MRDRMRD,
MFSFMR,M] A593a; W221a;
AD457; AK454   4158
Grey (---) [DDDSDRM,MMLL
SF#S,DD] M240   4159
Greyfriars (Scottish Psalter.
1635) [LDDRRMMFRMM,
SDDRR] W645   4160
Greystone (Waghorne) [DSDRMR
D,DFFMRMFR,D] B358; C358;
Eap.66; AR93; AW410; BK10
4161
-----. R [SSMFSLLS,SDTLM
F#S,S]   4162
-----. V [SDSDRMRD,DFFM
RMFR,] BK10   4163
Grice (McKinney) [SDDDTLSSM,
SDDDTDR] AT184   4164
-----. R [SRDTD,TLLLTDR,
SMR#M]   4165
Grigg (Grigg) [SDMSMRDRM,
RDRMFMR,] L403; T108b;
AJ148; AO426   4166
Grimm's 253d metre (Grimm.
Choral buch) [DMRSSF#S,
DSLSFMR,SM] AZ253-A; BA
136   4167
Grimm's 265th metre (Grimm.
Choral buch) [LTDTLS#L,DR
MFMRM,FM] AZ265-A   4168
Grimm's 315th metre (Grimm.
Choral buch) [MSDDRFM,RS
MDTLS,DD] AZ315-A   4169
Grimm's 349th metre (Grimm.
Choral buch) [DMSSLTD,TR
DTLLS,DM] AZ349-A   4170
Grimm's 480th metre (Grimm.
Choral buch) [DMSSLTDD,M
RDTTLS,F] AZ480-A   4171
Grimm's 552d metre (Grimm.
Choral buch) [LTTDS#LTDR
DTL,TDTD] AZ552-A   4172
Gring (Hollingshead) [MSFMM
RDF,FLSFFMRS,] AO86
4173
Griswold (Griswold) [MMMMSMR
FM,LLLSMSS] BR94   4174
Groeswen (Lloyd) [DSLTDRMD,
FLRDTLS,D] W448b; AL334a

4175
Gröningen (Neander) X Arns-
berg   4176
Groningen (Tours) [MRDLTD
FM,MRSLLS,SL] K378;
M247; V557a   4177
Groombridge (Whitwell) [LD
MRDRDT,LRDTL,LDM] E
592   4178
-----. R [MMRDTDRDL,
MMSMSF#M]   4179
Grosser Gott [wir loben dich]
(Allgemeines katholisches
G-B. Vienna, 1774) X Te
deum   4180
Grostette (Greatorex) [MMM
RDTLS,S#S#S#S#S#LTD]
H471; I139; V186; AS73;
AV124; BA15   4181
Groton (Zeuner) [DDDMDSRM,
LSMFMDS,S] L115   4182
Grüber (Grueber) X Holy
night   4183
Guardian of virgins (Cecilia
Miriam, Sr.) [MRMFFFR
FMRDTL,LTD] BN169
4184
Gud Faders Søn enbaarne
(German Enchiridion, 1524)
X Forlossningen ar vunnen
4185
Gud har af sin . . . (Etlich
christlich lider 1524) X
Wittenberg   4186
Gud skal alting mage (Linde-
man) X Lindeman   4187
Gud var Gud (Lagergren) [DS
DRMFR,DMRTDLS,MM]
K238; M268; N85; AA500
4188
Gud vaere lovet evig nu
(Walther) X Walther   4189
Guds Godhed vil vi prise
(Magdeburg. Christliche
tischgesange. Erfurt. 1572)
[LLTDRTS,SLLTTM,LLT] M
468; O209; Q393; AA5094190
-----. V [RRMFRMD,DRRM
ML,RRM] Q393   4191
-----. V [LLTDLTS,SLLTT
M,LLT] AA509   4192
Guds menighed, syng (Hoff)
X Hoff   4193

Guds Søn er kommen (Etlich
  Christliche lider) X Witten-
  berg   4194
Guernsey (Perkins) [MRDDRD
  TLS, TDRRRDRM,] T161;
  AJ239   4195
Guernsey (Pescott) [DDTDRM,
  MFLSFM, MMTD] AL526 4196
Guidance (Brackett) [DRMLSMR,
  MLSDT, DLSM] BE304   4197
Guidance (Dahle) [DTDRMFRRD,
  SMDFMRL] O216   4198
Guidance (Flotow) [MFLSMDRMD,
  MMSFMDR,] L248; AO532
                                4199
Guide(Wells) X Holy Spirit,
  faithful Guide   4200
Guide me (Viner) X Dismissal
                                4201
Guide me (Warren) [DRMSDTLS
  LSFMMRMR,] Q54; AA340
                                4202
Guide me, O thou great Jehovah
  (Beethoven) X Beethoven
                                4203
Guide me, O thou great Jehovah
  (Hastings) X Sion   4204
Guide us, O thou great Jehovah
  (Hughes) X Cwm rhondda
                                4205
Guidetti (Guidetti) [DDRMDRM
  FMRDD, DMF] A132b; E175b;
  X37a; AD39   4206
Guiding star (Freylinghausen.
  G-B.) X Festus   4207
Guild (Peace) [SSDDTTLL, LSS
  LSS, SS] W521   4208
Guildford (Haynes) [MMFMMRD,
  SSLSSFM, SD] K450   4209
Guildford (Williams) [DDRMSL
  DTSLS, DRMLS] X316   4210
Guildhall (Barnby) X Westcott
                                4211
Gulworthy (Hurst) [SSLDMRRD,
  DDRMFFM, M] K20b   4212
Gun Hill (Shaw) [SLSRRMFMR
  M, MSLSF#S] X486   4213
Gustavus Adolphus (Johnson)
  [SDDDDDS, SLLTRD, MRR]
  N231   4214
Gute bäume bringen (Sohren)
  [LLTDRMM, SMLS#L, LLTD]
  E72; F91b; J68a; X466; BV

137b; BY218b   4215
Gute baume bringen (Sohren)
  X Sohren   4216
Guter hirte [willst du night]
  (Freylinghausen. G-B) X
  Tu vins, Jesus   4217
Gwalchmai (Welsh mel) [MS
  DRMFMR, MFRD, MSDR]
  A95b; E424; F367b; X553;
  Z100; AD14; AF65; AL24;
  AN164; AP134; AR35; BV
  539; BY12   4218
Gwalia (Welsh trad) [MFSFM
  RDRMRM, FMRSF] S186;
  W384; X54; AD150; AL448c
                                4219
Gweedore (Wesley) [MFMRLS,
  DDSMRDD, RML] F394a
                                4220
Gwyneth (Price) [DTLDTLTLL
  S#, S#LTDRM] S512; W411b
  AM431b   4221

H

Habakkuk (Hodges) [SSDDDTLS
  LFM, SLTDR] I368   4222
Haddam (Mason, arr) [SDS
  LTD, SLSFMR, SDSL] H431;
  L486; T28; AJ38; AM448;
  AO209   4223
Haec dies (Willan) [DDDDRMF
  FR, SFMDMRD] BN43 4224
Haf trones lampa färdig
  (Swedish trad) X Vigil
                                4225
Hagerstown (Brunk) [SMDLS
  LTDTMR, RDRMS] AY212
                                4226
Hagerup (Grieg) [MLTDRML
  S#,SDRMFSDT,] Y278; AC
  281; BI13   4227
Hague (Wilms) [SDDDMRDTLS,
  DTDFMR, S] L596; W644;
  AI20; AO612; BR526   4228
Hail, all hail, sweet youth
  (Egbert) [MFSDDTLSM, RLS
  DRMR] BP97   4229
-----. R [SFMRMFSM, SLFRS
  FM, S]   4230
Hail, blessed Trinity (Beery)
  [SSMFSM, DTDR, MSDRMF,]
  AS71   4231

Hail to thee! true Body (Kloss)
[SLTDRMFRDT, RMFSDT]
BQ51   4271
Hail, true Victim (Leisentrit) X
Ave virgo virginum   4272
Hail Virgin, dearest Mary
(Yenn) [SDTDRMR, FMDRRMR,
SR] BQ81   4273
Hakafos melody (Jewish trad)
[SDDRMRDSFMMR, RSSL]
BH199   4274
Hakes (Belden) [MR#MDSLFLLS,
DMSMFM] BB380   4275
Halifax (Handel) [MLLLTDRMM,
RDTLTL] A354b; AF294; BZ
                                    4276
Hall (Laufer) [SMRDRMFSLS,
RDRMFS] R306; S245; AE374;
AK252; AR535   4277
Halle (Algemeines katholisches
G-B. Vienna, 1774) X Te
deum   4278
Halle (Freylinghausen. G-B. 1704)
X Se solens skjønne lys ...
                                    4279
Halle (Plainsong, 1539) X To
God on high   4280
Halle (Schneider) [DDDTLSLTD,
DRDTDTLS,] V359   4281
Halle (The Psalmist, 1830)
[LLTTDDS, LLMMFSSF] A67
                                    4282
Hallel (Jewish trad) [LTDRMM
FMFRM, MDDRR] BH138, 266
                                    4283
-----. V [LTDRMMFMFLM,
RRTDD] BH266   4284
"Hallelujah" in all languages is
spelled and filed as "Alleluia"
                                    4285
Hallett (Shepherd) [SSDSTLS, MFSLS
FMR,S] L185;AO237   4286
Hallon (Schulthes) X Lambeth
                                    4287
Halton Holgate (Boyce) X Boyce
                                    4288
Hambridge (English trad) [MF
MLSMRMD, DTRRMFS,] E355;
X15; BV184   4289
Hamburg (Franck) X Komm,
selle   4290
Hamburg (Plainsong, M 1) [DD
RMRMFMRM, MMMF] A219;

B52b; D5b; G334; H165; I225;
J503a; K69; L168; M58; N
255; O99; P183; Q175a; R
198; S152b; T279; U88; V144;
Y376; Z228; AB137; AC123;
AD156; AE119; AF177; AG
97a; AH291; AI77a; AJ387;
AK158; AL208a; AM186; AN
272; AO248; AP321; AQ146;
AR174; AS331; AT99; AU
191; AV108; AW106; AX113;
AY259; AZ22-P; BA315;
BB220; BD32; BE386; BF315;
BR42; BV173a; BX26; BZ
                                    4291
-----. V [DRMMRMFMRM,
MFFMRR] BV173a   4292
Hamburg (Schop) X Sollt ich
meinem . . .   4293
Hamden (Mason) [SSDRMDR
R, MRDRDTD, S] H201; L
333   4294
Hamilton (Finlay) [SSLDRDRM,
LSDMFMRD] BV12   4295
Hamilton (Swisher) [MMMM
RD, DRMR, MMMMRD,] BD
7   4296
Hamilton (White) [SDMRMFSS
FM, RDMSSD] AQ57   4297
Hammersmith (Gladstone) [MS
MRDLMDTL, RDLFFM,] E
ap. 50; W111; AB333; AL286
a; BE428   4298
Hampden-Sidney (St Alban's
Tune book, 1866) X Leb-
baeus   4299
Hampstead (Davies) [SDMMSF
RMD, DTLDLLT] BE232;
BY20b   4300
Hampstead (Horner) [MMMFL
DTT, LSDRMR, RM] I563
                                    4301
Hampton (Williams. Psalmody)
X Durham   4302
Hampton Lucy (Stanton) [SSDR
MFMRS, DRMSDRD,] BY45
                                    4303
Han lefver! o min ande känn
(Haeffner. Koralbok. 1819)
[MDSMRDTD, DDFRSSF#S,]
N136   4304
Hand in hand (Naff) X We
join to pray   4305

Handel (Handel) [DMSSLTD,
RSMDTLS, SS] N332   4306

Handy (Holbrook) [MMFSDLSM,
MSMRMRMF] T239; AJ335;
AO39   4307
Hanford (Gabriel) [SLSSMSFFM
F, LTLLRS] AT325   4308
-----. R [DTLMSLSLDT, DTL
FSL]   4309
Hanford (Sullivan) [SSSSSFMR,
LLLLLSF] A412; B390; C390a;
D341a; G306; H437; I239; K
259; L497; U42; V487; AE261;
AJ364; AM140; AO408; AS237;
AV237; AW245; AZ3-E; BA12;
BB475; BF410; BR385; BX262b
                      4310
Hankey (Fischer) [SDSSDMRD,
DDLRDLS, S] G249; H240; I
544; J326; P388; R383; S443;
U312; V236; Z532; AD253; AF
317; AG186; AH346; AI390;
AK467; AL504; AM387; AO635;
AP592; AR440; AS295; AT141;
AU371; AV385; AW493; AX200;
BA906; BB518; BE414; BY415;
BZ   4311
-----. R [SSTRMRD, DDFFFFM,
MS]   4312
Hanna (Laufer) [MSRDFFM, SD
FMRRR, MS] S350   4313
Hannah (Fillmore) X Pounds
                      4314
Hanover (Croft) [SDDRMSDRTD,
RMRDTD] A288; B255; C255;
D459; E466; F167; G169; I11;
J163; K294b; M541; O60; Q17;
R27; S2; V198; W9; X618; Y
385; Z258; AA57; AB15; AD2;
AE2; AF206; AG106; AH194;
AK10; AL21a; AM301; AP93a;
AR119; AS3; AW6; AZ39-D;
BA9; BB342; BE236; BF168;
BJ52; BV248; BY22; BZ 4316
-----. V [SDDRMMSDRTD,
RMRDT] AA57   4317
Hansome place (Lowry) X Beauti-
ful river   4318
Happy day (Rimbault) [SDRMSDRM,
MFMRRDMRD,] G212; H287; I312;
L287; U192; V310; AH345; AO

652; AS454; AT389; AU461;
AV251; AW465; AX331; AY
271; BA464; BB310   4319
-----. R [MFSDRM, MFMRD
MRD, SS]   4320
Happy he that never wanders
(Binder) X Happy he who
walketh   4321
Happy he who walketh (Binder)
[LTDLFFFM, LLSFMRDT,]
AH153; BH26   4322
Happy he who walketh ever
(Fabisch) [SSDDRTDS, DRMF
MRDD] BH25   4323
Happy home (Niemeyer) X O
selig haus   4324
Happy home (Bunnett) [MSFM
RDDTDMR, MMMLT] AP707
                      4325
Happy land (Hindu air) [MMRM
SS, MMRD, MMRMSS,] E608;
W587; AP795; AS471; AZ580-
A; BB301   4326
Happy Sion (Woodbury) [SDRM
DLDLS, SDRMDRT] AI149;
AR499; AS188   4327
Happy spirits (Burkett) [MSLS
MDFL, SSLSMDR, M] AY191
                      4328
-----. R [DDRDTLLS, SSDSMDR,
M]   4329
Happy the home when God is
there (Havergal) X Evan
                      4330
Happy, we who thus united
(Herbert) X Holy Queen, we
come   4331
Happy we who thus united (Lei-
sentrit G-B.) X Ave virgo
virginum   4332
Happy who in early youth (Gotts-
chalk) X Mercy   4333
Happy with Christ (Jacobs) [SD
MMFMRDRDL, LSDDM] AY
383   4334
-----. R [MSSLSMF, RFF
SFMRDR]   4335
Hardwick (English trad) [MRR
SMRD, DSSLS[M]FSL] S451;
X34   4336
Hardy Norse men (Norwegian
trad) [SSSSDTLL, LFRDTRD,
S] AW391   4337

Harewood (Wesley, S.S.) [SLTD
RDT, SFMRDMRD, R] B559;
C559; D294b; F243; W458;
X464b; AA453; AF407; AP303;
AZ342-G; BA811; BV456; BY
267   4338
Harington (Harington) [SDTLSFMF
SLLS, SSF#S] E85; X613; AL
659; AP65a; BY607   4339
Hark, a herald voice (Francis)
[MRDTLTDS, SSSMDLS, D]
BO148   4340
Hark, hark my soul (---) [SSFM
MMMRMSF, STRSS] BO198
                                        4341
-----. R [LTDDSFSFM, LTDD
SSS]   4342
Hark, hark, my soul (Hummel)
[SMRD, TLLLLLS, DDTRR]
BI74   4343
Hark! hark! my soul (Montani)
[DSLDRRMDRMFSR, RMD]
BQ111   4344
-----. R [MRDRMS, RDTDRS,
DTLT]   4345
Hark! listen to the trumpeters
(Careless) [SSSSSSSS, SSLTDR
M,S] BC253   4346
Hark! a mystic voice (Montani)
[SSLMMRMM, MMFRDRM, S]
BQ1   4347
Hark! are they not angels ("K")
[SDTDRSSRD#RMD, SMRM]
AX91   4348
Hark ten thousand thousand
voices (Daynes) [DSDSDDTDS,
MMFSLSF] BC249   4349
Hark! the herald angels (Mendels-
sohn) X Mendelssohn   4350
Hark! the herald host (Humper-
dinck) [SLSFMRDL, DRMSDLS,
L] BQ13   4351
Hark, the song of jubilee (Haydn)
X Creation   4352
Hark, the voice of children
(Blunt) X Merrial   4353
Hark! the voice of Jesus calling
(Holsinger) [SLSFMRMS, LLDLS
MR, S] AS379   4354
Hark! the voice of Jesus calling
(Van Arsdale) X Mission song
                                        4355
Hark! the voice of Jesus crying

(Mozart) X Ellesdie   4356
Hark! what mean those holy
voices (---) [MR#MDSF#SM,
RD#RFMRD, M] AX93; AY
267   4357
Hark! what mean those holy
voices (Weber) X Wilmot
                                        4358
Harlech (Welsh trad) [SDTLT
DRM, DFMRDTLT,] K132;
M455; BZ   4359
Harlem (Drese) X Rochelle
                                        4360
Harmony Grove (Oliver) [MM
MMSDRM, MMMMMF#F#S,]
L311; M260; O234; P355;
AA122   4361
Harneenu (Binder) [SDSLSMFS,
LSLTDS, SR] BH308   4362
Harre meine seele (Malan) X
In His love abiding   4363
Harris (Hawley) [DTLSLSM, MF
SLTD, DDT] D284b   4364
Harrogate (Cobb) [DDRMSDLS,
MDMRRD, DD] BY386   4365
Harrowby (Gillespie) [LSLTD
TL, DTLTDRM, FM] BV150
                                        4366
Hart (Stevenson) [DTLTFTLFM,
SSFMRFL] D316b   4367
Hartel (Mason) [DMMMRMFS,
SLSSMFMM,] BB227   4368
Hartford (Dykes) X Blairgowrie
                                        4369
Hartford (Milgrove) X Harts
                                        4370
Hartland (Hopkins) [MDDMS,
LFFLD, DTL, SRM] AP485
                                        4371
Hartmann (Hartmann) [MFSDRM
F, MRSSFMRFM,] M88
                                        4372
Hartmann (Hartmann) X Peace
of God   4373
Harts (Milgrove) [SSDDRRM,
DDFMRDRMR,] E177; F191a;
W11a; X520; AL154b; AP120
b; BV14; BY630a   4374
-----. V [SSDDRRM, DDFMR
DMR, S] AH316   4374a
-----. V [SSDDRRMM, DDFM
RDMR] BO-54   4374b
Hartville (Bixler) [SDRMDDLS,

TTDTLS, SD] AY435   4375
Harvard (Berridge) [MMMFRSDT,
  DSLFFM, RM] U66; Y8; Z385;
  AC142; AR89   4376
Harvard hymn (Paine) [SDLSFMR
  MFLS, RFMLD] B539b; C539b;
  D521b; Y239; AN433; BX415
                          4377
Harvest (Clemm) X Clemm 4378
Harvest (Frost) [DMMLSFSMF
  R, SFMRDM] D262a; F378
                          4379
Harvest (Minor) X Bringing in
  the sheaves   4380
Harvest (Singer) [SDDTLSLLD,
  DRRRDRM,] BH186   4381
Harvest home (Elvey) X St
  George's Windsor   4382
Harvest home (Root) [SDDDDRM
  SLS, DRRRRM] AP588; AU430
  AX216; BB620   4383
-----. R [SSSSSSDRM, MFFFF
  MS]   4384
Harvest Home (Storer) [MRDDTLS
  RM, FSMLFRR,] D191b   4385
Harvest hymn (St Gall G-B., 1863)
  [DSLSMFRM, RMFSFMR, D]
  Q573   4386
Harvest song (Cringan) [SDTDRD
  TDS, MRDTLTD] AP690   4387
Harvest song (Thomas) [LLTDTLS,
  SDMRRM, LLT] BY730   4388
Harvest-tide (Falconer) [SSLSDR
  MMR, DTDRSLF#] T269; AJ373
                          4389
Harvey's chant (Bradbury) [DDDDD
  TDR, RRRRRM, MM] L281; T51;
  AI164; AJ348; AR510; AS466;
  BB4; BC48   4390
Harwell (Mason) [SSDSDMRR,
  SSSDMRD, S] G167; I177; J152a;
  L154; M85; N271; U112; V164b;
  Z268; AA451; AE139; AI30; AM
  225; AO55; AR210; AS158; AT
  70; AU227; AV93; AW123; AY
  425; BC138   4391
Harwich (Crueger) X Nun danket
                          4392
Harwich (Milgrove) [MRDDLSMR
  DDLS, RMFR] X161   4393
Hasidim (Jewish trad) [LMRMDTL,
  LLRSSLM, L] AQ175   4394
Haslemere (Songs and tunes for

education. 1861) [DDMMR,
  RRFFM, MMSSL,] A244;
  X359   4395
Hassler (Hassler) X Passion
  chorale   4396
Hast du denn, Jesu (Stralsund
  G-B. 1665) X Praise to the
  Lord   4397
Hast du Jesus ruf vernommen
  (Sweney) [MMFMRDMD, RS
  FTDRM, M] AW342   4398
Haste not! Haste not! Do not
  rest (Blumenthal) X Blu-
  menthal   4399
Hastings (Hastings) [MFSS
  MRDTLSF, MLSSF] L265; T
  23; V158b; AJ31; AM209;
  AR184; AS147   4400
Hatfield (Gauntlett) [MSLS
  MFMMR, RSLSDTD] D517b;
  AV248   4401
Hatikvo (Jewish trad) X
  Hallel   4402
Hauge (Norwegian trad) [SD
  MSTRDLS, FMDMRDT] J
  146b; P433   4403
Have faith in God (McKinney)
  X Muskogee   4404
Have faith in God (Rosche)
  [MRDSLSDT, FMRLTDRM,]
  AY359   4405
-----. R [DMSSLLMS, SMST
  LLS#S,]   4406
Have I done any good? (Thomp-
  son) [SSDDDDRMRTD, DR
  MRD] BC58   4407
Have mercy on me (Gelineau)
  [LFSM, RFSL, RDRL, LDT
  L,] BSp. 22   4408
Have mercy on us (Haydn)
  [SSDTLSTLS, SSFMRDM]
  BO7   4409
Have Thine own way (Stebbins)
  X Adelaide   4410
Have you any room for Jesus
  (Williams) [SLSDTLLS, FM
  FSLSSM,] AX259   4411
-----. R [RRRRMRDS, LLLLT
  DR, M]   4412
Have you prayed it through
  (Ackley) [DMSSSMSDDD,
  SDTLSF] AU121   4413
-----. R [SF#FFMFSF, SFM

MR#MLS,]   4414
Have you sought? (Sankey) [SD
MMMMMMMFS, SSRMF] AX
198; AY526   4415
Haven (Hastings) [MMRDSFMRM,
MRSLSF#S,] T228; AJ160;
AV279   4416
Haven (Lemare) [MFMRLRMRD,
LTDFMMR] D309b; V83; AH
232   4417
Haven of rest (Moore) X My
soul in sad exile   4418
Haver (Havergal) [SDRMFS, MLS
FSM, SDRM] L233; AZ74-C
4419
Havergal (Barnby) X St Olave
4420
Havergal (Bliss) X I gave my
life for thee   4421
Havewood (Wesley, S.S.) X Hare-
wood   4422
Hawarden (Wesley, S.S.) [SD
TTLS, SDRMRD, SDTT] E496b;
J97; W336; AP369; BY353
4423
Hawes (Wesley arr) X Streatley
4424
Hawkhurst (Gauntlett) [MFMRR
SFM, SF#SLMRDT,] F232;
BV215; BY656   4425
Hawkridge (Wesley) [SLTDMMRD,
FFMRMRR, R] AZ159-C
4426
Haydn (Haydn) [MFRMFSLRDS,
SSSFMM] B3a; C3a; D3a; G
30; J207a; K445; R44; T302;
V37a; Y359; Z134; AB2; AD
36; AE39; AG19; AH160;
AK46; AM334; AO18; AP
660; AR43; AV10; AW27; BF
177; BK39; BZ   4427
-----. V [MFRMFSLRTDS,
SSSFM] G30   4428
Haydn (Haydn) X St Michel's
4429
Haydn (Haydn) X Petition   4430
Haydn (Haydn) X Salzburg II
4431
Haydn, No. 1 (Haydn) X Bowen
4432
Haydn, No. 2 (Gardiner's Sacred
mel. 1812) X Belmont   4433
Haydn's hymn (Haydn) X

Austria   4434
Hayes (Beethoven) X Sardis
4435
Hayn (Herrnhut ms) X Gre-
gor's 82d metre   4437
Hayom t'am'tsaynu (Lewandow-
ski) [LMDDRFTLLS#, LS#,
DS#LR#] BH333   4438
Hazard (MacDougall) [SMMR#
MFT, TFFMRS, SSS#] Y38;
AB202   4439
Hazel (Harewood) [MRDRM
LMRDRM, MRDRM] W330b
4440
-----. R [MRDDFMRDS, DT
LSMFS]   4441
He arose (Hugg) [MRDTFF,
FMRMM, SSLSM] AY265
4442
-----. R [DMRDMFS, SSLL
SMDMR,]   4443
He brought me out (Gilmour)
[DMMMMRDSSSS, SLLLS]
AU50   4444
-----. R [DDDDTLSMS, DD
DDTLT]   4445
He comes (Neff) [SMRDFMDM,
SSRMFMRR,] AX124
4446
He died for me (McKinney)
[SMFMDMR#R, SFFFFM, SM]
AU410   4447
-----. R [MRD#RFMR#M, S
FMRF#LS, F]   4448
He died for thee (Vail) [DMS
MMRRD, FFMMRDR, D] AX
241; AY218   4449
-----. R [LLSMSSM, FFM
MRF#S, DM]   4450
He died of a broken heart
(Dennis) [SDMMDRMFMD,
MMRDTD,] AU383   4451
-----. R [SRRMFMRDRM,
MSFMMR]   4452
He died! The great Redeemer
(Careless) [SSLSMFLSFM,
STLTRD] BC263   4453
He hideth my soul (Kirkpatrick)
[SSFMMRDLLLS, SSFMM]
AE283; AI270; AM675; AS
289; AT272; AX510; BB651
4454
-----. R [STTTTLTDTLS,

SFMFR]   4455
He is coming again (Camp) [SM
    LS, TLSDS, LDLSSLS] AI97;
    AM687   4456
-----. R [SSDTLT, SSRDTD,
    SMRD]   4457
He is not here, but is risen
    (McGranahan) [MMMRDFMR,
    DRRM, MMMR] AU464   4458
-----. R [SSSSSSLTD, LLLL
    LLT]   4459
He is risen (Neander) X Neander
                                 4460
He is so precious (Gabriel) [SM
    MMFMRRDLS, STTTT] AE285;
    AT304   4461
-----. R [MSLTDRDM, SRRRR
    MFM,]   4462
He just put Himself in my place
    (Hammontree) [MFSLTDRDM
    D, DDTDRD] AU384   4463
-----. R [SSDDDTLT, SSRRRDT
    D,]   4464
He keepeth me ever (Rosche)
    [MDRMFM, DRMFM, SRMFL]
    AY316   4465
-----. R [SSSSLS, MMMMFM,
    DMFS]   4466
He keeps me singing (Bridgers)
    X Sweetest Name   4467
He knoweth the way that I take
    (Pollock) [DMMMMRDS, FMM
    MMRDR,] AX487; AY118
                                 4468
-----. R [FMMMMFSLS, MRRRR
    MF]   4469
He knoweth thy grief (Hall) [MM
    R#MFM, RRMRRD, MMR#M]
    AY317   4470
-----. R [SMFSLS, MSFMMR,
    MMR#M]   4471
He leadeth me (Bradbury) X
    Aughton   4472
He leads us on (Webster) [DD
    DMMRRSFM, FMFRML] BX
    264   4473
He lifted me (Gabriel) [SSLLSMM
    F, MMRSRRDD,] AI130; AM
    672; AT202   4474
-----. R [MMMMMSSL, SFFFFF
    MM] AI130   4475
-----. R [SSDMSSTT, STRFLLS
    S, S]   4476

He lives (Ackley) [SSLLDDL,
    FSSLLM, SMM] AE287; AT279
                                 4477
-----. R [SMSMRDDRDLS,
    SSFFL]   4478
He lives on high (Hawaiian trad)
    [SDMRDTDLSS, MRRD#RM]
    AU336   4479
He loves me (---) [SSMDDLD
    D, DMDSMR, SS] AX116; AY
    249   4480
He loveth me (Keeny) [DDRM
    MMFS, SLSMDRMR,] AS122
                                 4481
-----. R [SSDT, RFLS, DMF
    SLSMR,]   4482
He ransomed me (Henderson)
    [MFSSSSLS, MSDDDDRD,]
    AU382   4483
-----. R [TDRRRRRT, LT
    DDDRDS,]   4484
He seeks His wandering sheep
    (Showalter) [SMSFMRL, DT
    LSFM, MSF] AX267; AY219
                                 4485
-----. R [MSSLSM, RDRMF#S,
    SDTL]   4486
He that believes (Etlich Christ-
    liche lider 1524) X Witten-
    berg   4487
He was nailed to the cross
    (Graves) [DRMRDFMMMR,
    TDRRRD] AX107   4488
He was wounded (Oliver) [LM
    MLMMSRRSR, MLTDM] AM
    673   4489
-----. R [MRRDLFMMR, DLT
    SD#RR#]   4490
He who dwells (Gelineau) [TT
    LT, TTSL, DDTD, DDLT,]
    BSp. 25   4491
He who once, in righteous
    vengeance (Mohr) [DSDR
    MSFMR, RMFRDRM,] BQ18
                                 4492
He will gather the wheat (Swen-
    ey) [MFSLSMDMRDL, LSDD
    D] BB538   4493
-----. R [MMFFFFLLSMS, MM
    RSS]   4494
He will hide me (McGranahan)
    [SDRMMFMRMD, SDMSSL]
    AU409   4495

-----. R [LDFLF, SDMSM,
   STRFSF]   4496
He will hold me fast (Harkness)
   [MSMRRSMR, DMDTL, FLS
                                4497
Hear our prayer   (Chopin)
   [SLLSLDTD, RMFMRRD.]
   AT531; AV416   4498
Hear our prayer (Excell) [SL
   LTLSSSM, DLLSSSD] AS487
                                4499
Hear our prayer (Whelpton) [MM
   MMR, FFFFM, MSSSMF,]
   R535; U494; AE461; AH561;
   AI451; AMp.xiv; AR662; AT530;
   AU489; AW604; BB688; BF688
                                4500
Hear thou our hymn (Asper)
   [MLSFSM, SDTLLS, SLTD]
   BC96   4501
Hear thy children (Haydn) [SSDD
   DMSMMR, FFMFRD] BQ87
                                4502
Heart of God (McAfee) X McAfee
                                4503
Heart of Jesus (Forrest) [MMRL
   DT, DDTLS, MMRRS] BB348
                                4504
Heart of Jesus (Montani) [MM
   RMSFMRD, FFMFLSF] BQ331
                                4505
Heart of Jesus! golden chalice
   (Gounod) X Lux prima   4506
Heart of Mary (Herold) [DRM
   DTDR, MSFMRD, DRM] BM53
                                4507
Heart of our Lord (Slovak trad)
   [DRMFMRRD, SMSDTLLS,]
   BN69   4508
Heart of the Holy Child   (Birtch-
   nell) [MRMDLS, DRFS, MRM
   DLS,] BO160   4509
Hearthfire (Barnby) [MMMFFFLS
   FM, DTF#S, SS] AB192   4510
Heart's desire (Cologne G-B. 1623)
   X Hosmer   4511
Heath (Mason & Webb's Cantica
   laudis) [SDSLTD, DFMRDDT, T]
   A555; B118; C21a; D72a; G456;
   H313; I66; J559; L23; N74; O
   65; P398; Q449; R312; S362;
   U215; V77; W561; Z422; AA41;
   AB267; AC339; AD367; AG247;

AH411; AK258; AN363; AO
   17; AR342; AS40; AW213;
   AX648; AY436; BA49; BB
   461; BC180; BD92; BE183;
   BF487; BZ   4512
Heathfield (Perkins) [DMSSS
   DTL, SMMFMR, DM] BR25
                                4513
Heathlands (Smart) [SDTSLL
   S, FRMFSFMR, S] B46; C77a;
   D57a; E395; F264; J444; K
   423; V145; W509; X170a; AB
   313; AL379; AR598; AS96;
   BA543; BR68; BV46; BY231;
                                4514
Heaton Norris (Grimshaw)
   [SDMFSLSFMRM, MSDTDR]
   W499   4515
Heaven (Cook) [DMMMR#MS
   M, DRRRMFM, D]   AX606
                                4516
-----. R [SLLDTLSM, SRSTT
   LS, D]   4517
Heaven (Franck) X Melchior
                                4518
Heaven (Wilson) [SSSDMFSLS
   M, FFFMRM] AT483; AU
   281   4519
-----. R [MSDTLSM, SSDDD
   DDTD]   4520
Heaven at last (Kirkpatrick)
   [SLSMDLSM, DRMFSLSF]
   BB556   4521
-----. R [SMDLDS, MFSLSD
   DTLS]   4522
Heaven holds all to me (Teddlie)
   [MR#MRDRDTLLS, MSLSM]
   AX604   4523
-----. R [MRDSLSD, MSLSM
   DR, MR#]   4524
Heaven is my home (Mason) X
   Oak   4525
Heaven is my home (Sullivan)
   X St Edmund   4526
Heavenly city (Trebel) [SDTLS
   LSRMFSM, SLRD] M316
                                4527
Heavenly father (Kurzenknabe)
   [SSDDRTD, MMFMR, SSMD]
   AO325   4528
Heavenly father (Lowry) [DR
   MDFMMR, TDRDMRD, D]
   N360; AI345   4529

-----. R [SSFMFSMM,MMMTD LR,S] 4530

Heavenly fold (Sherwin) [DRMFM MRD,MDTLS#L,TD] AJ317 4531

Heavenly friend (Silesian trad) [DSSSFMSFMRD,SFMRM] M539 4532

Heavenly guide (Drese) X Rochelle 4533

Heavenly Jerusalem (Franck) X Melchior 4534

Heavenly love (Mendelssohn) [SMDTDMR,DFMLLS,SDS] J573; O343; P199; Z384; AE 222; AR266; AS262; AV231; BB674; BC125; BE376; BO201 4535

Heavenly sunlight (Cook) [SLTDDM RDRS,SLSMDM] AU119; AX28; AY471 4536

-----. R [SSSLFFSLSM,SSSS MM] 4537

Heavenly treasures (Norwegian) [DRMMFMRDS,DRMSSFM] P378 4538

Heavenly voices (Irons) [DMM RRSD,DLLSFM,MMM] D404b 4539

Heavenward (Irish trad) X Clonmel 4540

Hebdomadal (Strong) [DSMDDLLS, SDTSLLS,M] Sap.40; W175 4541

Heber (Barnes) [DDDDDDTD, RRRRDTLS,] BB293 4542

Heber (Hopkins) X Evangel 4543

Heber (Kingsley) [MFSSSMLLL, SMRDLSM] H368; I424; L165; R255; T265b; U75; V374; AA101; AJ215; AO301; AV182 4544

Heber (Mason) X Missionary hymn 4545

Hebron (Barnby) [MDLTDTL,R D#RMFFM,MM] B411b; D242b; K509b 4546

Hebron (Crueger) [LTDTLTS#M, MLRDTTL,L] BY652 4547

Hebron (Mason) [SMSLSLTD,D TRMDTLS,] B459; C292; D 296a; H74; I51; J533; L262; M 94; N49; R289; T32; U172; V20; Z115; AA39; AJ47; AL350b; AN

21; AO100; AS447; AW13; AX175; AY261; BA142; BB 456; BX244; BZ 4548

Heidelberg (Vulpius) X Cana 4549

Heiliger Geist (Corner. Geistliche nachtigall) [LLD MRDTD,MMSMDTD,M] X 391 4550

Heiliger Geist (Crueger) X Holy Ghost 4551

Heil'ger Geist do tröster mein (Grimm. Choral buch) X Grimm's 253d metre 4552

Heiliger Herre Gott (German trad) X Eisleben 4553

Heineken (Heineken) [MMSSS F#S,SSFMDFMR,R] BR18 4554

Heinlein (Herbst) [MMLTDRM, MMSSF#F#M,MM] A55; B123; C123; D79; E92; F92; K78; Q111; V409; W79; X97; AF148; AK143; AL97a; AO 143; BA743; BM76; BR366; BV141b; BY118a; BZ 4555

-----. V [MMLTDRM,MMF# SSF#MM,M] X97 4556

Hela världen fröjdes herren (Swedish Koralbok) X Kalmar 4557

Helder (Helder) X Wohlauf thut nicht verzagen 4558

Helen (Vail) X Close to thee 4559

Helena (Bradbury) [MMMMRD LL,LSDRDRM,M] BA77 4560

Helensburgh (Finlay) [DTLTDR TS,SDTDRMFM] W358 4561

Helfer meiner armen seele (Scheffler. Heilige seelenlust, 1657) X Scheffler 4562

Helft mir Gott's Güte (Figulus) [LLLDDTDR,MDLLS#L,LL] Q112 4563

Helig, helig, helig Herre Gud (Stolpe) [SSLLLLLLS,SSDT LLT] N337 4564

He'll never forget (Graves) [MMFMDRMFM,DRRRDDF] AU25 4565

-----. R [SSSSMSDD, DDSMSDM
R]   4566
Helmsley (Olivers) [DMSDTLSLT
DTLSFM,] A5b; E7; F51; W
160; X65; AP246; BV81; BY185
                                  4567
Help, Lord, the souls (Dutch
trad. , 1500) [LSMLTDDT, MR
DTLT, TD] BN186   4568
Help, Lord, the souls (Gardiner's
Sacred mel.) X Belmont
                                  4569
Help, Lord, the souls (Slovak
hymnal) [MLTDLS#TDR, R#
MTRDTL] BQ113   4570
Help us, O God (Steggall) [DL
LSMRLTDD, DTLMSS] BI43-D
                                  4571
Help us, O God (Weber) [MSS
LSMSFMR, SLTRDL] BI52-D
                                  4572
Helsingfors (Nyberg) [LTDDRDT
L, DRMMLSLM] W402   4573
Hemans (---) [MMFSLS, DRMFM
R, DTLS,] M540; N535   4574
Hemel (Thomas) [MDRMSLTD,
RMSMRD, MD] BY553a   4575
Hemingford (Emerson) [MMMSFMR,
DDRMRD, TTT] L9; AO75
                                  4576
Hendon (Malan) [DDDSDMSFM,
MMMRFRD] C219; G147; H59;
I507; L197; M433; N23; P123;
R310; S312; U272; V17; Z116;
AD260; AE267; AG166; AH413;
AI17; AK239; AM437; AN278;
AO179; AR331; AS230; AT161;
AU184; AV129; AW215; AX53;
AY83; BA480; BB30; BE186;
BI26; BZ   4577
Henham (Shaw) [MRDRMDTLM,
MFSLSMR] X616   4578
Henley (Mason) [SMMMRDDRRM
D, SMMMD] G350b; H372b;
I462; L358; R384; S256; Z345;
AD211; AG223; AH348; AK445;
AO253; AR439; AW188; BB323;
BF363; BR26; BX273   4579
Henllan (Evans) [SSLLSDDT, DRM
DTLS, S] W298; AL212   4580
Henry (Pond) [DDDDTDSLTD,
RRMRDT] L354; N19; T119;
V119; AJ173; AO386   4581

Henryd (Lloyd) [MMMRDMRT,
LDTMRDT, M] W73   4582
Her kommer dine arme smaa
(Schulz) X Paedia   4583
Her vil ties (Hoff) [MMRDTL
TRD, SSFMDTD] O571 4584
Her vil ties (Lindeman) X
Our Lady, Trondhjem   4585
Herald (Shaw) [LLLLLLLT, DD
DL#LSF, M] E205   4586
Herald angels (Dykes) [SSSMSD
MR, DLSSDRR, R] D51b
                                  4587
Herald angels (Mendelssohn) X
Mendelssohn   4588
Herbert (Chope) [MMMMMSF
M, RRRLSSF#S,] AP487;
BR304   4589
Herbert (Hodge) [SLSMRMFM,
SLTLSF#SF#] D613   4590
Herbert (Mason) [DDSLTDRM,
FSRDMR, RR] BB251   4591
Here at thy table (Hall) [MM
FMSDRM, SSLSMRR, R] AS
461   4592
Here behold me (Neander) X
Sieh hier bin ich, Ehren-
könig   4593
Here let thy people (Binder)
[MLTDRMFM, LSMDRM, MS]
BH5   4594
Here, Lord of life and light
(Holsinger) X Wayland
                                  4595
Hereford (Evans) [DRMFSLRS
M, MFMRDMR,] Y335 4596
Hereford (Gauntlett) [SMFSS
DRM, SLSDDT, SM] O495; AB
91; BX167   4597
Hereford (Heins) [SSDDDDTDS
M, DRFFMR] G503; AD373;
AL244; BZ   4598
Hereford (Ouseley) [LLS#LTDR
M, MRDTLS#, TD] F88
                                  4599
Hereford (Wesley) [MMRDRFM
MRDRRM, SS] A463; F329a;
BV366; BY207   4600
Hereford carol (English carol)
[SDRFMDTRD, SFMRDS, S]
BG7   4601
Hermann (Hermann) [DSSSMLS
FM, MFSLLS,] A435a; B270b;

J197; M154,327; O52; P62;
Q105; V90b; X481b; AA157;
AF492; AI425; AJ33b; AK97;
AM123; AN217; AQ118; AZ14-B;
BE101; BI110; BR495; BY408b;
BZ   4602
-----. V [DSSSSLSFM, MFSLLS,
S] M327   4603
-----. V [DSSSSLSM, RMSLF#S,
MS] O52   4604
-----. V [DSSSMLSFM, RMF#
SLLS] V90b   4605
-----. V [DSSSSLSFM, RMF#
SLLS,] AN217   4606
-----. V [DSSSSLSFM, RMF#SS
LS] AZ14-B   4607
-----. V [DSSSSLSM, RMSLLS,
RM] BR495   4608
Hermann (Hermann) X Erscheinen
ist der herrlich tag   4609
Hermann (Strachauer) [DRMDM
FF#, DDTSMF#M, MM] BR214
                                4610
Hermannsburg (Meiningen G-B.)
X St Leonard   4611
Hermas (Havergal) [MMMRDL,
FMRDT, SRMD, R] A568; B532;
C532; D522a; G161; I175; J115;
K549; M457; P222; R80; S56;
V750; W133; AD483; AG15;
AH213; AK170; AL107; AM213;
AO199; AP488b; AS152; AT110;
BA245; BD43; BR195; BV592a;
BY166; BZ   4612

Hermitage (Morris) [LTDTLL,
DDTLSLLM, SL] S133; X92;
BV105a   4613
Hermon (Clark) [MLTDTLTLS#,
TDTDRM, M] AF220; BJ61
                                4614
-----. V [MLTDTLDTLS#, T
DTDRM,] BJ61   4615
Hermon (Gastorius) X Was God
tut?   4616
Hermon (Mason) [SMFSDLDS,
DDDTDRTD,] L477; T283a;
V287; AJ54; AM21; AO459
                                4617
Hernlein [sic] (Herbst) X
Heinlein   4618
Heroes hymn (Minor: Swedish
folk) [LTDMM, LTDMM, FM

RTLL] Y121   4619
-----. (Major) R [DRMSS, DRM
SS, LSSSMD]   4620
Herongate (English trad) [SS
DLSSMRD, SDDMSLS] E597;
W550a; X602; Z216; AD129;
AR152; BV350; BY142a
                                4621
Herr Christ der einig nicht
lassen (German. Enchiri-
dion, 1524) X Förlossningen
är vunnen   4622
Herr, deinen zorn (Crueger)
X Oblation   4623
Herr, dir ist niemand zu
vergleichen (Knecht) [DD
DMDFMRD, MMMRMFM] AW
518   4624
Herr Gott Vater (Besler) [DD
DRRMFS, SSMLTDTL] E
274b; W292b; AL556b   4625
Herr, ich habe missgehandelt
(Crueger) X St Nicholas
                                4626
Herr Jesu Christ dich zu uns
wend (Pensum sacrum.
Goerlitz, 1648) [DMSMRM
F#S, LSFMRDRM] A159b;
E173; G611; J188a; K419;
L230b; M2; N98; O36; P40;
Q3; R555; S475; W254; X40;
Z636; AA1; AE464; AF521;
AK28; AM100; AN489; AT
536; AU493; AZ22-F; BA1;
BZ   4629
-----. V [DMSMRMF#S, LSM
RDDTD,] N98   4630
Herr Jesu Christ, du hast
bereit't (Sohren) X Elbing
                                4631
Herr Jesu Christ, du höchstes
Gut (Sohren) X Elbing
                                4632
Herr Jesu Christ, meines
(As hymnodus sacer. 1625)
X Breslau   4633
Herr Jesu Christ, meines
lebens licht (Nürnberg G-B.
1676) X O Jesus Christ,
meins lebens licht   4634
Herr Jesu Christ, wahr'r
mensch und Gott (Eccard)
[DDDLTDRMRD, MMMLSS]

AA527; AN84   4635
Herr Jesu, ewig's licht (Gregor)
X Gregor's 74th metre   4636
Herr und aeltster deiner kreuz-
gemeine (German trad) X
Gregor's 185th metre-A
                                   4637
Herr und Gott der tag und noechte
(Freylinghausen) X Gregor's
167th metre-D   4638
Herr, wie du willst, so schick's
mit mir (Teutsch kirchen ampt.
Strassburg, 1524 or. 25) X
Aus tiefer not   4639
Herra (Danish hymn) [LLLMFSM
RD, RMMFSM, D] AN122a
                                   4640
Herre Gud Fader, du vor høi'
ste trøst (Tomisson. Psalme-
bog. 1569) [DMDRMRFMRD,
MSMSFM] O43   4641
Herre, jeg har handlet ilde
(Crueger) X St Nicholas
                                   4642
Herre, jeg har handlet ille
(Lindeman) X Repentance
                                   4643
Herre Jesus Krist min frelser
du est (Lindeman) [SDLS, DMRDR,
TRRDTSL] O278; P218; Q353
                                   4644
Herren sig i nad förklarer
(Stenhammer) X Grace   4645
Herrick's carol (Cologne G-B.
1623) [DTLSSLTD, DTLSSLTD,]
BG122   4646
Herrick's ode (Gibbs) [MLMSD
RM, FSMRDTLL, T] BG176
                                   4647
Herrnhut (Gesius) [MLS#LTRDT,
TDRMDRTD,] J376a; M177;
N234; O153; P101; AA434;
AQ189   4648
-----. V [MLSLTDLT, TDRM
DDTD,] N234   4649
-----. V [MLS#LTDLT, TDRMD
DTD,] AA434   4650
Herrnhut (Nicolai) X Sleepers,
wake   4651
Herrnhut (Wesley's Foundery col-
lection) X Savannah   4652
Hershey (Hershey) [SSRDTLSDM,
SSRDTLS] M528   4653

-----. R [SSMMRDTF, MRDD
RR#M, M]   4654
Hervey (Hervey) X Hervey's
litany   4655
Hervey's litany (Hervey) [SL
TDDLT, RFMRDLS, MF]
A233b; B473b; C473b; D89b;
G380; U179; AB136b; AHp.
27; AI148; AL168; AO657;
AP280a; AS187; BF313b;
BX259   4656
Herz und herz vereinst zusam-
men   (French trad) X
Gregor's 167th metre-B
                                   4657
Herzlich lieb hab ich dich, O
Herr (Schmid. Orgelbuch.
Strasburg, 1577) [DTLS
MLLS, DTLSMLLS,] N465;
O393; Q429; AA366; AZ232-
A   4658
-----. V [DTLSFMLLS,
DTLSFML] AA366   4659
-----. V [DTLSMLLS#, DT
LSMLLS#] AZ232-A   4660
Herzlich thut mich erfreuen
(German trad: mediaeval)
[DDDMDSSDTSLSM, DSL]
E284; X249a; AA371   4661
-----. V [DDRMFSSDTSLSM,
DSL] AA371   4662
Herzlich thut mich erfreuen
(Crueger) X St Simon
                                   4663
Herzlich thut mich verlangen
(Hassler) X Passion chorale
                                   4664
Herzliebster Jesu (Crueger)
[LLLSM, LTDDRT, TDRMD,]
A71a; B155; C155; E70; J
85; K100; M413; N115; O75;
P14; Q143; R191; S158; W
216b; X99; AA198; AD147;
AF163; AK147; AM181; AN491;
AW534; AZ36-A; BI67; BJ
42; BV151; BY137; BZ
                                   4665
-----. V [LLLS#F#M, LTD
DRDT, TDR] AN491   4667
-----. V [LLLS#M, LTDDRDT,
TDRM] W216b   4667
He's coming (---) [MFSF#SD
TLSLDRM, MFS] BB669

4668
-----. R [SLFDTLLSSMS, MFSL
S]   4669
He's my friend (Thompson) [MR
DFMMRD, SDDRRM, SS] AI398;
AM664; AS282; AT155; AV351;
AX23; BZ   4670
Heslington (Peel) [SDDTDR, MLL
LRDT, LSD] D632a   4671
Heslington II (Peel) [MFSSSSS
M, DDRMRRD, M] AS396
                                4672
Hesperus (Baker) [MMMSDRRM,
SSSFSMFR] A469; B39; C25b;
D18b; G273; H214; I372; J370a;
K337a; L1; M132; N391; R215;
S89; T278; U44; V311; W501a;
Y22; Z353; AA479; AB173;
AC63; AD404; AE212; AF447;
AG129; AH193; AJ386; AK187;
AL360b; AM507; AN572; AO369;
AP232b; AR389; AS364; AT136;
AV134; AW171; BA79; BE244;
BF247; BK43; BR8; BX88; BY
515; BZ   4673
Heut' ist o mensch (Lowenstern)
X Lowenstern   4674
Heut' triumphiret (Gesius) X
Gesius   4675
Hezekiah (Gibbons) X Song 22
                                4676
Hibernia's patron saint ("B.S.")
[MFSDMSFMRD, MFRFS, M]
BO136   4677
-----. R [DDTLSFMSD, SD
SMDMS]   4678
Hic breve vivitur (Pettet) [MS
DFMRD, MFSLLR, SDM]
F569a   4679
Hickling Broad (Shaw) [DRMDLS
FMFSLRM, DRM] X18   4680
Hide me (Doane) X Hide me, O
my Saviour   4681
Hide me, O my Saviour (Doane)
[MMMRDSLD, SDMRR, MMM]
V761; AI247; AW483; AX513;
AY71   4682
-----. R [MDFLSDRMSSR,
MRDDL]   4683
Hide thou me (Lowry) X Keller
                                4684
Hiding [in Thee] (Sankey) X
O safe to the Rock   4685

Hier legt mein sinn sich vor
dir nieder (Rosenroth) X
Old 29th   4686
Hierapolis (Wesley) [DMRDD
RRM, MRDFMRDT] W239
                                4687
High on the mountaintop (Bees-
ley) [SDDDRM, RMSFMR,
RMRM] BC62   4688
High road (Shaw) [SDDDRDT
LSLT, SDLS, SD] A290a; E
427; R22; X556; AL38
                                4689
Higher ground (Gabriel) [SSD
MMRDL, RDLSDMDR,] AT
319; AU269; AV374; AX382;
AY462; BB631;   4690
-----. R [SDMSSFMF, STR
FFMRM,]   4691
Higher than I (---) [SDDDD
TDRSSS, MMFMR] AY328
                                4692
Highest lauds (LeJeune) [DDD
TTLLS, LTLSLTLS,]   Y348
                                4693
Highland Avenue (Fisher)
[MMMMMDRMM, SSSSSMF#]
AR386   4694
Highwood (Terry) [SLMRTD
LSMDR, MF#LRS] AD103;
BV569; BY127   4695
Hilariter (Cologne. G-B. 1623)
[RFMRLDTL, SSDTLLS#L,]
E164b; X167; AF194; BG96
                                4696
Hilda (Barnby) X St Hilda
                                4697
Hilderstone (Hart) [DMFSLSF
M, DMLRSSF#S,]   F8
                                4698
Hildesheim (Koenig) X Evan-
gelists   4699
Hiles (Hiles) X St Leonard
                                4700
Hilf Gott, dasz mir's gelinge!
(Gregor) X Gregor's 126th
metre   4701
Hill Bourne (Skeffington) [DR
MFLDM, F#SMDRM, MFF]
D43b   4702
Hill Crest (Holst) [RFMRM,
DTDRSRFMRD, T] X86
                                4703

Hillery (Hay) [SSSLLLS,MMMM
SFMR,M] AR456; AS13   4704
-----. R [SDDDDDRDLS,SSRM
FT]   4705
Him that cometh unto Me (Kirk-
patrick) [MMMRDTDLSM,
SSSSDD] AX252   4706
-----. R [MMMRMFS,RRRRDR
M,FF]   4707
Himlens Gud og Jordens Herre
(Meiningen G-B.) X St
Leonard   4708
Himmel (Himmel) [SSLSFSFM,
RRTLSF#S,S] J464; W352
                                          4709
Himmel, erde, luft und meer
(Strattner) X Posen   4710
Hin maeta morgunstunden (Páls-
san) [SLTDLSMSFMRD,SLTD]
AD320; AN279   4711
Hinchman (Burnap) [MDSMFMR,
RDTDRMRD,M] R73; S21;
U439; V32; Z445; AD34b; AG
17; AM333; AO15; AR63; BF
187   4712
Hingham (Holyoke) [DDRMDFMM
R,RMFSLSF] V658   4713
Hinman (Lovelace) [SMDLTD,
SMDLTD,RMF#S,] R471; BZ
                                          4714
Hinton-Martell (Evans) [SLR
SSFM,DRMDRRD,MF#] W321
                                          4715
Hintze (Hintze) X Salzburg
                                          4716
Hir oesi fair (Welsh carol) X
April   4717
His bride (---) [MMRDRSDR
M,MMFMRDT] AY442   4718
His eye is on the sparrow
(Gabriel) [SLSMDRM, FS
LDDS,SFM] AI312; AM715
                                          4719
His forever (Barnby) [SSSDTRD
D,DDFMRSM,M] V306; W705
                                          4720
His tender mercies (McGranahan)
[SSDMMRDS,SDMSSDMR]
AI377   4721
-----. R [SSSSSF#SM,MMMM
R#MD,]   4722
His way with thee (Nusbaum) X
Would you live with Jesus

                                          4723
His yoke is easy (Warren)
[SSSDTLSLSM,SSFFFM]
AX348   4724
-----. R [SSSMFSLLLS,MFR
RMF]   4725
Hitchen carol (English trad)
[TDTLTDRDTLS#MLTDR]
AP168b; BG46a   4726
-----. V [TDTLTDRDTLS#,
MLLTD] BG46a   4727
Hjem jeg laenges (Lindeman)
[LTDLDRMD,MFSMRRD,
M] K81; O316; P190   4728
Hobart (Tucker) [DMSLSS,
SLSDMR,RMSL] T232; AJ
328   4729
Höchster priester (Wesley's
Foundery collection. 1742)
X Savannah   4730
Höchster priester, der du dich
(Gregor. Choral buch, 1784)
X Gregor's 12th metre
                                          4731
Hodges (Hodges) [DMFSLSM,
SFMRSM,MFS] B43a; C43b;
D24b; L257   4732
Hodu and Ono (Halevy) X
Min hamaytsar   4733
Hoff (Hoff) [SSLTDTDMRTD,
TRDLS,] J423; O11; P27;
Q44   4734
Hoffman (Hoffman) [SDDSSTLS,
FFMRDSS,S] AE174; AS144;
AT130; AW473; BB644 4735
-----. R [DRMRDSMDRDRMS,
SSD]   4736
-----. V [SDDSSTLS,FFMR
RMFM] AS144   4737
Hoffman II (Hoffman) [DRM
MMDMFSSSM,DDMR] AT
350; AU54; AX402   4738
-----. R [SSLLLLTLLSMS,
SLLL]   4739
Holborn (Adams) [MSFFMMR,
DTLSSS,SLT] D585a   4740
Holborn (Morley) [DTLSMRD
SFM,LTDMRR] K200; Q
474; AA465   4741
Holborn (Paisiello) X Vigil
                                          4742
Holborn (Thiman) [DDRMDFM
RRD,MMFSML] BY312

4743
Holborn Hill (St Albans Tune book.
1865) [MMMFMMRD, DDDRMF#
F#S,] C133a; D87a; G257;
I199; L376; O115; S160; T174b;
V22; AA419; AB177; AD454;
AJ166; AL318; AM308; AS180;
BA393; BB69; BR278   4744
Holcomb (McKinney) [MMMFF#
SR, DDDFDM, MMM] AT331;
AU415   4745
-----. R [LLLFLSF#SM, RRRF#
MRS,]   4746
Holcombe (Sykes) [MSFMMRRD,
DTLSMLRR,] BA195   4747
Hold fast till I come (Belden)
[SSDRMSLSMR, MFMRMR]
BB548   4748
-----. R [MSSSSSSLSMR, MFF
FF]   4749
Hold oppe, Gud, hos os dit ord
(Luther) X Spires   4750
Hold the fort (Bliss) [SLSMDRDL
SLSMR, SLS] E570; AU303
4751
-----. R [DDDDDSMSLLLDT,
DDD]   4752
Hold thou my hand (Main) [SF#
SLSSMRDDT, RTDRM] AP527;
AU207; AX469   4753
Hold to God's unchanging hand
(Eiland) [DDDSLSLD, MMRDD
MS, S] AX446   4754
Holiness (Bliss) [MMLSF#S,
DDTDMR, MMLS] U264; V412;
AR404; AS222; AT338; AU217;
AX429; BA633; BC114   4755
Holiness (Stebbins) [MMRMFM,
DRDTD, MMRMF] G251; R300;
Z346; AE182; AH395; AI284;
AL500; AM706; AR469; AS50;
AT367; AU291; AX428; AY111;
BB603; BY509a; BZ   4756
Holland (Wilms) X Hague   4757
Holland (Tours) [MRRSMDRM,
MMF#SLTLS,] V499   4758
Holley (Hews) [MR#MDMRMFS
M, SF#SMM] A574b; B502;
C8; D272b; G398; H85; I74;
L25; N396; R372; S209; T43;
U89; V62; W550b; Z470; AA
411; AB261; AD53; AE336; AH
229; AI175; AJ66; AL97b; AN

113; AO4; AP283; AR221;
AS446; AT395; AU232; AV
14; AX161; AY437; BA175;
BB250; BD12; BE419; BF
195; BR204; BX127   4759
Hollingside (Dykes) [MSLSS
FM, DTLSMDR, MS] A408;
B223; C223a; D335a; E414;
F193; G191; H435; I247;
J393b; K371a; L149; O92;
S233b; T416; V331a; W414a;
Y373; AB204; AC157a; AD
212a; AG153b; AL266b; AM
459; AO655; AP417a; AW
159; AZ205-I; BA422a; BB
402; BD199; BF370; BR43,
261; BV506a; BX485; BY
441a   4760
-----. V [MSLSSFM, MMRSS
F#S, MS] BR261   4761
Holly Springs (Maclean) [MM
FLSFFM, MSDLSF#S, M]
V52   4762
Hollywood (Wade) X St Thomas
4763
Holmbush (Richards) [DSMR
DDRTLS, LTDDRR] AK85
4764
Holmes (Holmes) X Eventide
4765
Holmes (Shippen) [MFSLLRS
FM, DTLSFMR,] AD354
4766
Holmfirth (Gill) [MMFSS
LTD, TLSFMMR, M] I611
4767
Holsinger (Holsinger) [DRMSL
FMDRRDRM, MMS] AR265
4768
Holy Bible, book divine (Brad-
bury) X Aletta   4769
Holy Church (Brown) [DMRD
SLS, SMRDMR, SMR] D605;
J304; K211; L26; V299; AB
288; BR84   4770
Holy Church (Terry) [DSDSM
RDR, MFSLTDR, D] BL66;
BM87; BN200; BY365   4771
Holy City (Dale) [SMRRD,
DDLS, SRMRD, DM] AV293
4772
Holy City (Gaul) [SSFMFSM
R, MFFLFM, SF#] D406c;

O608; AT508   4773

Holy City II (Gaul) [MRLTS,D
RRM, LSMFR, RT] U429; BF
658   4774

Holy City (Gaul) X Sanctus
                                4775

Holy comfort (Genge) [LLTDRTD,
LLTDRTM, DD] E410   4776

Holy cross (Brown) [MFMRSD
FMR, STLDF#S, S] W269; BY
773   4777

Holy cross (Wade, arr) [SMRD
STLS, DRSRR#M, SM] G347;
H304; I137; L152; V303; Y47;
Z483; AC328; AE371; AH317;
AJ194; AO311; AP787b; AW
381; BA5   4778

Holy cross (West) [DTLSSLDR,
MRDTDRDT,] C122b; D88b
                                4779

Holy day (Parker) [SSTDRMSFM,
RMMMLSF#] D26   4780

Holy day, Jehovah's rest (Belden)
[MRDDFMR, RRRRRDRM, M]
BB654   4781

-----. R [SMLSFFRSFM, MRDD
FM]   4782

Holy desire (Stebbins) X Adelaide
                                4783

Holy faith (Martin) [MMMSFM
RD, SSSTLSF#S,] Y78; BV535
                                4784

Holy Ghost (Crueger, arr., Voll
standige Psalmen. Bremen,
1639) [LDTD#RDT, DRMFMRD,
MD] A57a; E76; W405a; AL
160b; AP362   4785

-----. V [LDTDRDT, DRMFM
RD, MD] AP362   4786

Holy Ghost, with light divine
(Gottschalk) X Mercy   4787

Holy God, we praise thy name
(Allgemeinisches katholisches
G-B. 1774) X Te deum   4788

Holy guide (Burnap) [SSLTDDT,
LSMMRDT, TM] U38; AJ152;
AM564   4789

Holy Hill (Bourgeois) [DRRDD
FFMR, DRFMRDT] AJ417
                                4790

Holy Hill (Pontius) [DMSSS
DTD, SDTDSFMR] I13   4791

Holy, holy, holy (Dykes) X

Nicaea   4792

Holy, holy, holy Lord (Barnby)
[SSDSLLS, MRDTLLS, SS]
BI38   4793

Holy, holy, holy Lord (Malan)
X Hendon   4794

Holy innocents (Gray) [DRMM
RDTLTDRT, LSS] A112
                                4795

Holy is God (Currie) [MMM
SMFMRDMR, MF#F#SL] BN
207   4796

Holy is the Lord (Bradbury) X
Saboath   4797

Holy Jesus (Lissant) [MRDD
TDRFMR, SMRDTD] D572
                                4798

Holy Lord (Schmidt) X Fahre
fort   4799

Holy Love (Schumann) [DTRD
FMMRR, RRMRTSS,] BR528
                                4800

Holy manger (Keller) [MFM
SDRLR, RMRSSLSM] J43
                                4801

Holy manna (Moore) [SSLDD
RRDMRDL, SSLD] AT368;
AU198; AX33   4802

Holy Mary, mother mild
(Dressler) [DDTDRMRD,
SMDMR, RRD] BO101   4803

-----. R [SSMDRMR, SSMDR
MR, SM]   4804

Holy mountain (Lindeman) [S
MRDDTLTS, SMDRTLS,]
J82; M405; N106; O274; P217;
Q149; AA212   4805

Holy Name (Genevan Psalter,
1562) [SSDRMFS, MSFMDR
D, MR] A323a; W62a   4806

Holy Name (Major reading:
Genevan Psalter, 1562) X
Louez dieu (Minor reading)
                                4806a

Holy night (Grueber) [SLSMSLS
M, RRTDDS, LL] A33; B546;
C546; G106; I123; J16; K530;
M603; N46; O178; P140; Q
646; R154; S132; T339; U60;
V749; W49; Y302; Z188; AB
116; AC81; AD119; AE92;
AF138; AG74; AH125; AI381;
AK101; AL53; AM161; AN166;

AO132; AP172; AQ289; AR135;
AS102; AT72; AU146; AV87; AW
83; AX100; AY488; AZ1516; BA
168; BB102; BC160; BD218;
BF288; BI97; BK151; BL12;
BN20; BO151; BP9; BQ11; BV
113; BX534; BY108; BZ   4807

Holy offerings (Redhead) [MRFM
MRD, SRMSSF#LS,] A480; B504;
C504; D478a; AO496; AZ156-D;
BR296   4808

Holy Offerings (Spinney) [MRR
DDTT, FMMRRDD, DT] D478b
                             4809

Holy Patron! thee saluting (Catholic) [SDDTDLTDS, LSSSFMM]
BO124   4810

-----. R [DTLSSDTLLS, FMM
RDD]   4811

Holy Queen, we bend (Herbert)
X Holy Queen, we come
                             4812

Holy Queen! we bend before thee
(Hurley) [MSDTLSLFS, MSDR
MFM] BP85   4813

Holy Queen, we come (Herbert)
[DSMLSFFM, MFSDFMR, D]
BN134; BO55   4814

Holy quietness (Marshall) X
Marshall   4815

Holy Rood (Brown) [SDRMFS, M
FLRDT, SDTL] AM297; BY282b
                             4816

Holy Sepulchre (Thorne) [DDDD
MSRM, SSSLMSFM] F125;
AZ2-C   4817

Holy Spirit (Campbell) [MMRDD
TT, FFMRRDD, SS] BB701
                             4818

Holy Spirit (LeJeune) [DRMFMRD,
SLTDTTLS, L] B371   4819

Holy Spirit, come and shine
(Catholic) [SDDTLTDRMF#S,
MFRMM] BO185   4820

Holy Spirit, faithful guide (Wells)
[SSDDMRDR, MMSDTDRD,]
G243; H213; I193; L462; N53;
T248; U132; V212; Z276; AE
150; AG126; AH227; AJ345;
AO232; AP346; AR443; AS252;
AT165; AU245; AV152; AW137;
AX135; AY196; BB211; BZ
                             4821

Holy Spirit, lead us (Kelly)
[MFFMDFFFM, LTLSMMR]
AU450   4822

Holy Spirit, Lord of light
(Webbe) X Veni Sancti
Spiritus   4823

Holy Spirit, truth divine
(English trad) X Lew
Trenchard   4824

Holy temples on Mount Zion
(Schreiner) [DMSSLTDS,
LLSDSFMR,] BC63   4825

Holy Trinity (Barnby) [DTLS
F#LLS, FMMMRDT, M] B30;
C30; D270; H210; I299; V
368; AB280; AM517; AN202
b; AO216; AP239; AZ14-
Dd; BA862; BB386; BD234;
BE147; BF513; BH88; BX
228   4826

Holy voices (Geer) [DDDD
RRRR, MRDDLDR, M] D61a
                             4827

Holy war (Booth) [LLLLDTL,
LLSFM, LLLL] C126b; D81b;
K73b; AK295; AO390; BY
506a   4828

Holy Well (English trad)
[SMFMFSDTL, SLRDTD, S]
F277; BG56a   4829

-----. V [SMRMFSDTL, SS
LLRRDTD,] BG56a   4830

Holy Word (Barnby) X St
Sylvester   4831

Holyrood (Stewart) [MFSLTDS,
LLSMRMFFM,] C340
                             4832

Holyrood (Watson) [DMSSLS,
SLDTLS, SSLD] D376; F338;
T355a; W494; AL146b; AP10;
BV649a   4833

Holywell (Joy) [SDTLSFMRD,
MSDTLS, S] V97b   4834

Holywood (Wade) X St Thomas
                             4835

Homburgh (German trad) [DR
MDFMRD, RRMSSF#S, D]
D361   4836

Home I (---) [MDRM, MFFM,
RRMFMFSL,] D676a   4837

Home II (---) [SSMSSMSFRFM,
MMFLS] M641; AI199
                             4838

Home (Bishop) X Home, sweet
   home   4839
Home (Emerson) [DDDRRM, MML
   SMRD, SSM] L601   4840
Home (McNaughton) [SMMRDLD,
   SLSMR, MFSM] AE384; AS413;
   AW360; AX555; AY444; BC169
                                4841
-----. V [SDMRDLD, SLSMR,
   MFSM] AX555   4841a
Home (Mozart) [SDRMFRDRTD,
   MSRTMR] BE34   4842
Home (Stotzel. Choralbuch.
   Stuttgart, 1744) X So fürst
   du doch   4843
Home (Thompson) [SDRMSDRM,
   LSMRDR, MR] G433; AD420
                                4844
Home of the blest (Brenneman)
   X There's a beautiful, beauti-
   ful land   4845
Home of the soul: new (Doughty)
   X Soon trials and conflicts
                                4846
Home of the soul (Phillips)
   [DMSF#SM, SSLTDS, SSF#S]
   G525; AM729; AS472; AU42;
   AV399; BB552   4847
Home of the soul (Pollock) [MF
   SSLSMSDTLS, SDDD] AX588;
   AY164   4848
-----. R [TDRRRRDRM, SSLLL
   DT]   4849
Home over there (O'Kane) [SDD
   DDMRD, TDRRRRFM] AT480;
   AU43; AV393; AX592   4850
-----. R [TDRDRM, MFFFMS
   MR, SF]   4851
Home, sweet home (Bishop)
   [DMFSSMSFMFRM, DMFS]
   H511; L605; P349; U428;
   V715; AI339; AS412; AX573;
   AY393; BB415; BC185   4852
-----. R [SFRDRM, SDTLSMS
   FMF]   4853
-----. V [DRMFFLSMSFM
   FRM, DR] P349   4854
-----. V [DMFLSMSFMFRM,
   DMFL] U428   4855
-----. V [DMFSSMMSFMFRM,
   DDM] BC185   4856
Homeland (Sullivan) [DMMLLSS, FM
   DDTD, DMM] A598b; B281; C281;

D162; G530; I615; J543a; M
307; N450; T436; V691; AA
562; AH520; AV284; BA757;
BD174; BE245; BF553; BO
202; BR449a; BX254   4857
Homeward (Traditional) [DM
   MDMFMRD, MSSFMRR] Y42
                                4858
Homeward bound (---) [MMRDD
   TLDRM, RRRR, MRD] BB661;
   BR517   4859
Homeward bound (---) X No,
   not one (Hugg)   4860
Homines christi (Lowden)
   [SDDDSDRM, SFMRDS, SL]
   AI184; AO477   4861
Hominum amator (Ferguson)
   [MSMDRMM, TDRMLM, MSM]
   E276; BV65a   4862
Honor (---) [SSMRDDT, DR
   D#RR#M, DDS] M428
                                4863
Hope (Antes) [LDTLMFT,
   DRMMRRD, SS] AQ129; AZ
   11-K   4864
Hope (Davies) [DSMDFMMR,
   MDFMRMR] E551; AZ
   167-L; BA242   4865
Hope (Gastorius) X Was Gott
   tut   4866
Hope (Irons) [MMMSTDRM,
   SLSDMLLR,] W522; Y54;
   AB37; AP693   4867
Hope (Jacobs) [MRMS, SSSS
   F#S, MRMD, DD] D676b;
   AP615   4868
Hope (Remsberg) [DRMMMM
   FMR, TDRRMFM] L600
                                4869
Hope of Israel (Clayson) [DD
   DSMFSLSD, RMRSLT] BC64
                                4870
-----. R [DSMSDRM, RRRDR
   MDS, D]   4871
Hopkins (Beethoven) X Alsace
                                4872
Hopkins (Hopkins) X Twilight
                                4873
Hopkins (Monk) [DMSSFMRMF,
   FLFSMDF#] D64   4874
Horbury (Dykes) [DRMSFM, M
   RMFM, MLLSF#] B500; C
   500; E444; F352; X586c;

AC324; AL321a; AP470a; AZ
579-D; BE193   4875
Horeb (Barnby) X Nightfall
                            4876
Horeb (Barnby) X Jordan   4877
Horeb (Polack) [DSLTDMRDT,
LTDRM,MM] AA69   4878
Horeb (Smart) [SSSLLS,MSLDT,
TDLSF#] BY709a   4879
Horsfield (Rusbridge) [SDRMDRM
FRS,MRDLTD] BY542   4880
Hornsey (Wesley, S.S.) [SSDMR
MFS,MRDRSLDT,] Eap.28
                            4881
Horsham (English trad) [MMFS
MRD,MMSSSMRDR,] E344;
R538; S95; X258; AK348   4882
Horsley (Horsley) [DRMFMSFMR,
SMDTLS,] A65a; B159; C159b;
D544; E106; F214; J77b; K544
a; L315b; M419; Q157a; S157b;
V149; W105; X131; Y87; AF171;
AJ384b; AL87; AM191; AP290b;
BB126; BE383; BV163; BY149;
BZ   4883
Horton (Minshall) [MSFMMRD,
FMLSRRR,MM] AB98   4884
Horton (Schnyder) [SDMDDLS,SF
RMDLSTL] H10; I248b; L364;
N158; P385; U357; V468; AA
243; AO231; AT244; AV158;
AX145; AY499; BB219; BR47
                            4885
Hos Gud är idel glädje (Ahnfelt.
Sanger) [SDDDMSM,LSSFRM,
SDD] N632   4886
Hosanna (Campbell) [MFRDRRM
M,MFRDRRMM,] AC114
                            4887
-----. R [SLL,LTT,SSLDMSL,
MFM]   4888
Hosanna (Dykes) [DSFMMRRD,
SSSSLTDRR,] A318; B53; C53;
D316a; J424; K425; S53; V14;
AD168; AM314; AO63; AR200;
BA373; BF334   4889
Hosanna (Dykes) X Hosanna we
sing   4890
Hosanna (Elliott) [DSMFRDTD,
DRMFSLRR,] F241b   4891
Hosanna (Gray) [SDDDTTLL,LFM
RDDTT,] BY269   4892
Hosanna (Kettle) [SDMSDMRD,

DRMF#SRDT] D557   4893
Hosanna in excelsis (Nicholson)
[SDSMFSLT,SLLRDTDR]
F421   4894
Hosanna we sing (Dykes) [MM
DMSSSLTDD,SSDDT] D560;
AP753   4895
Hosmer (Bullard) [MMRDRMR,
MFSFMFS,SS] BD149; BF
465; BX409   4896
Hosmer (Cologne G-B. 1623)
[DDSDRM,SFMRRM,MMMR]
A534; E443; X111; AK263;
AL333; AN335; AP467; AQ92;
AW308; BY481b   4897
Hostis Herodes impie (Plain-
song, M 3) [SSLTDLSFM
RRFMFSS,] E38; F74a
                            4898
Houghton (Gauntlett) X Cobern
                            4899
Houghton (Wesley) X Sebastian
                            4900
Hour of need (Bourgeois) X
Commandments   4901
Hour of prayer (Doane) X
Doane II   4902
Hour of prayer (Hansen) [LM
MMRTDTL,TDDRDRM]
P29; BD74   4903
-----. V [MMMMRTDTL,DD
RDRM,M] BD74   4904
Hover o'er me, Holy Spirit
(Sweney) X Fill me now
                            4905
How beautiful heaven must be
(Bland) [SMMMMRDMD,
MSSSMDM] AX590   4906
-----. V [SDDDMDRD,MSS
SMDMR,]   4907
How beautiful thy temples, Lord
[Cannon] [SMDRMFFM,SL
LSMR,SM] BC65   4908
How blessed is the little flock
(Lindeman) X Ludwig
                            4909
How blest (Kirkpatrick) [SS
LSDDDTLS,SSLTDT] AI102
                            4910
-----. R [SSSSSS,DTDRD,DM
RDD]   4911
How blest are they (Tomissön.
Psalmebog. 1569) X Island

4912
How blest the man (Kinross)
[LDTLS#LMM, F#SMSFM, LD]
BH27   4913
How brightly beams (Nicolai)
X Frankfort   4914
How can I leave thee? (Thuringen
folk song) X Lynde   4915
How fair the Church (Schumann.
G-B. 1539) X Old 112th
4916
How far from home? (---) [DDD
DTLDDM, SSFRLLS] BB665
4917
How firm a foundation (---) [SDDM
SSLSFMSD, SDDD] BC66 4918
How firm a foundation (American
trad) X Foundation   4919
How gentle God's commands
(Naegeli) X Dennis   4920
How gladly (Traditional) [TDMS
SLSDM, SFRTFMR] P280
4921
How good it is to thank the Lord
(Gideon) [MRFLSFMMM, ML
TD#RLT] BH109   4922
How good it is to thank the Lord
(Lewandowski) [MMSDSLDS,
SRMFSLSF] BH110, 267 4923
How goodly is thy house (Mozart)
X Cana   4924
How great is your Name (Gelineau)
[FFLD, DDRD, DLTL, LSLF.]
BSp. 8   4925
-----. R [FDLDRDRFD, LDSF.]
4926
How great the wisdom (McIntyre)
[SMRDDTFFMRM, SLRFS]
BC68   4927
How I Love Jesus (---) X O,
how I love Jesus   4928
How long must we wait? (Caldwell)
[MDRMMFMR#M, MRD#RMRD]
AU131   4929
-----. R [SSL, SSFMF, FFS, FF
MR#M,]   4930
How long, O Lord, most holy
(Gates) [MLTDTMRDD, TMFF
MMR] BC69   4931
How lovely are thy dwellings
(Mendelssohn) X Evangelist
4932
How lovely are thy dwellings

(Schumann) X Canonbury
4933
How marvelous (Gabriel) [SS
MSDRMDDTTTDRD, S] AE
304; AT139; AX24   4934
-----. R]MMRDSSFM, RRR
MFMR, M]   4935
How oft, alas (Pollock) [SM
MMDDDL, SSMMDR, SS] AX
339; AY208   4936
How pleasant and how good
(American trad) X Camp-
meeting   4937
How reads your life-book?
(Byers) [SDDDTLSFM, SLD
TDRD,] AX442   4938
-----. R [SMMMDFMMRR,
SRMFFF]   4939
How sweet, how heavenly
(Bradbury) X Brown   4940
How tedious and tasteless
(Edson) X Contrast   4941
How wondrous (Jewish trad)
X Akdamus   4942
How wondrous and great (Haydn)
X Lyons   4943
Howard (Cuthbert) [MFSLSDLS
FFM, MRSLS] H233; I338;
L390; R121; T190; V280;
AJ277; BB155   4944
Howard (Howard) X Smith
4945
Hoylake (Roberts) [DDRMFM
RL, MR, RSMRDT] W487a
4946
Hoyte (Hoyte) X St Columba
4947
"Hozanna", see "Hosanna" in
all languages   4948
Hsuan P'ing (Confucian temple
chant) [LSMSL, DLSLM, LD
LDR, M] AF487   4949
Hubbard (Chinese folk tune)
[DSLDRM, MSMRDR, RMRD]
R223   4950
Hubert (Darwall) X St Hubert
4951
Huddersfield (Parratt) [MSFM
RMDR, MFSS#LTT, D] Eap.
37; W240; AP667a; BE173;
BY447   4952
Huddersfield (Williams. Psalm-
ody, ca 1770) X Durham

4953
Huddleston (Berridge) [SSLSST
MRDTLS, SSDR] AL603   4954
Hudson (Hudson) X At the cross
4955
Huger (American trad) X
Foundation   4956
Huguenot hymn (Darms) X My
Lord and I   4957
Hull (American Musical misc.,
1798) X Ganges   4958
Humble thyself to walk (Rogers)
[SDRMRDRDLLS, SDMSF]
AX430   4959
-----. R [MMMMMMMRDDT,
SSSSS]   4960
Humility (---) X Deliverer 4961
Humility (Goss) X See, amid the
winter snow   4962
Humility (Hunter) [SDDDRMMM,
SSMDMR, MF] AX431   4963
-----. R [MFSSSMRDDD, MRR
SRM,]   4964
Humility (Mainzer) [DTDRMRD,
RD#RMFMR, MR] AP764
4965
Humility (Tuckerman) [DRMSFM
DRM, SF#SLSMR] D86; T225;
U278; Y212; Z517; AJ321; AS
337; AT466; AV70; BX135
4966
Hummel (Zeuner) [SDDDRMFM,
SFMRDT, TT] I292; Z512; AF
369; AR107; AS401; BB443;
BX211   4967
Hunnys (Seven sobs of a sorrow-
ful soul. 1585) [LDRTDTLS#,
LRDDTD, DR] E79; X108
4968
Huntingdon (Beery) [DRMSDMLD,
DRMDSLR, D] AR298; AS254
4969
Huntingdon II (Beery) [DMDRDDD
TDR, MRMFMM,] AY78
4970
Huntington (Huntington) [SSMR
DDLF#S, SLLLTDR,] L99
4971
Hurdus (Downes) X Solitude
4972
Hurlbut (Bird) [MFMMRDDTD,
MFSSFMM] Y196   4973
Hursley (Allgemeines Katholisches

G. B. Vienna, 1774) [DDD
DTDRMRD, MMMMRM] A166;
B20; C20a; D11a; Eap.39;
F24b; G56; H33; I47; J209;
K463; L21; M525; N563; O
566; P77; Q551; R57; S37;
T132; U457; V46; W292c;
Y93; Z150; AA42; AB25; AC
22; AD57; AE44; AF50; AG
28; AH174; AI50; AJ198; AK
55; AL556a; AM346; AN108;
AO31; AP666b; AR56; AS34;
AT15; AU177; AV239; AW30;
AX68; AY129; AZ22-L; BA
780; BB321; BE227; BF194;
BK54; BL73; BX139; BZ
4974
Hursley (Allgemeines Kathol-
isches G-B. Vienna, 1774)
X Te deum   4975
Hurstmonceaux (Prout) [MR
DS, DRFMRR, SFMMRR]
AB97   4976
Hus (Pensum sacrum) X Herr
Jesu Christ, dich zu uns
wend   4977
Hushed was the evening hymn
(Sullivan) X Samuel 4978
Hussite hymn (Moravian trad)
[LMMRMT, LMMRMT, DTDR]
BE378   4979
Hvad hör jäg? (Schulz) [SDD
MSFMR, MDRDTLS,] N223
4980
Hvad kan os komme til for
Nφd (Geistliche lieder.
Wittenberg, 1535) X Luther
4981
Hvad ljus öfver griften (Jes-
persön. Gradual, 1573)
X Jespersön   4982
Hvad röst, hvad ljuflig röst
jag hör (Ahlstrom) X St
James' Stockholm   4983
Hvo ene lader herren raade
(Neumark) X Neumark
4984
Hvo ved, hvor naer mig er
min ende (Bronner. Choral
buch. 1715) X Wer weiss,
wie nahe   4985
Hvor salig er den lille flok
(Lindeman) X Ludwig 4986

Hyatt (Sweney) [MMSF#FMDDL
  LDS,RSFM] AO142b   4987
Hyfrydol (Prichard) [DRDRM
  FMRDR,SFMMR] A347b; C
  226b; E301; F260; G11; J397a;
  Q423; R123; S113a; W479; X260;
  AB343; AD16; AE13; AF13;
  AG62; AK174; AL117; AM145;
  AN50a; AO651; AP76; AQ192;
  AR36; AT9; AW69; BC49; BE
  175; BF214; BV259; BY173;
  BZ   4988
Hymn (Gould) [SDRMMFRRTD,
  SLSSF#S] H293; I575; AN159b;
  AJ193; BD67; BX189   4989
Hymn for Day of Atonement (Wein-
  berg) [LLLTDRM,MMMRDDT,
  TT] BH169   4990
Hymn for Memorial Day (Fulton)
  [MMMMRSLS, FSFMF#SFM,]
  AH476   4991
Hymn for month of May (Mat-
  thews) X Chenies   4992
Hymn for Tabernacles (Alman)
  [MRDRFMDT, LRMFSM, MM]
  BH185   4993
Hymn for the golden age (Beimel)
  [DRMFLSSFM, RMSMR, DR]
  BH236   4994
Hymn for glory (Garrett) [DDDMRD
  FM, MMMSMRTL] AS153
                            4995
Hymn of glory (Jewish trad) X
  Omnom kayn   4996
Hymn of nations (McWhood) [DM
  SLF#S, DMSLF#S, DTLS,]
  G508   4997
Hymn of praise (Schubert) [SDD
  RDTRRDRM, SMMFM] BK1
                            4998
Hymn of spring (Norden) [SDD
  DDTTLLL,SDDRDR] BH134
                            4999
Hymn of thanksgiving (Hauser)
  [DTDRMFLSFM, MRSSF#M]
  AH129   5000
Hymn of the harvest (Grimm)
  [DSLDRD, MDS, FMRSMRD]
  BH188   5001
Hymn to joy (Beethoven) X Beeth-
  oven   5002
Hymn to mothers (Binder) [SSS
  SSMRD, MSDDTLSL] BH260

                            5003
Hymn to St Joseph (Vulpius)
  X Cana   5004
Hymn to the Cross (Bragers)
  [LDTS#TLDRM, MRTRDLD]
  BP31   5005
Hymn to the Holy Cross (Wilt-
  berger) [SSLSDTLS, LSFMR
  RM,S] BM79   5006
Hymn to the Holy Name (O'
  Connell) [MRDSSSLSRFM,
  MRDLD] BP21   5007
------. R [SMDLLLF#RT,
  TLSDRFM]   5008
Hymn to the sorrowful Mother
  (Walther, G-B. 1524) X
  Venit hora   5009
Hymnus eucharisticus (Rogers)
  [LLTDRMRDTLLS#,S#S#LT]
  E328; W471b; X607a   5010
Hyndland (Finlay) [DTRMRDM,
  SDLSFMSDR,] BV446   5011

                I

I am a stranger (Cassel) X The
  King's business   5012
I am coming, Lord (Hartsough) X
  I hear thy welcome voice
                            5013
I am coming to the cross (Fischer)
  X Coming to the cross   5014
I am not worthy (Converse)
  [SMRDSMRD, DFFLLS, SM]
  AI220   5015
------. R [SSMSLF, LSDRMR,R
  MMF]   5016
I am praying for you (Sankey)
  [SSDMDMMRLTDS, SSDM]
  G237; AE166; AH435; AS
  197; AT232; AU78; AV332;
  AW460; AX367; BB575 5017
------. R [MSSLSM, MMMFM
  R, DDTL]   5018
I am resolved (Fillmore) X
  Resolution   5019
I am so glad (Bliss) X Glad-
  ness   5020
I am the vine (Shaw) [DMSS
  MRDRMD, DMSDSL] AX414
                            5021
------. R [DDDDSLLLSM,
  DDDDSL]   5022
I am Thine (Doane) [MFMRR

RMRDD, DTLLLD] G252; H
345; R320; U217; V734; Z312;
AE191; AG148; AH361; AI272;
AL490; AM713; AO648; AP483;
AR444; AS232; AT349; AU56;
AV368; AW475; AX411; AY473;
BB594; BZ   5023
-----. R [MFSMRDTLS, DTLDM
RD,]   5024
I am Thine, O Lord (Doane) X
I am Thine   5025
I am trusting (Fischer) X Com-
ing to the cross   5026
I am trusting in His word (Moon)
[SSDDMRDRDL, LLSSSDR]
AX460; AY97   5027
-----. R [SSLDTLSM, MFSS
DRMR]   5028
I am trusting in my Saviour
(Mosley) [SSLSMDDT, SLSFTLS,]
AX462; AY94   5029
-----. R [MFMRSRMRD, DDDTD
RM,]   5030
I believe the Bible (Ufford) [MM
MMRDMSSSLS, MMRD] AX139
                            5031
-----. R [DDDDLS, LSMFS,
DDDDL]   5032
I belong to Jesus (Sea) [SMRD
LD, TDRSM, SMRMF] AI253;
AM649   5033
I bless thee, Father, for the
grace (Epstein) [MTDS#LFMR,
LDTLTLS, D] BH115   5034
I bow in utter need (Whttington)
[DTTTDRRRDTL, DFMMR]
BI65   5035
I bring my sins to Jesus (Pol-
lock) [MFSSLDLS, DTDRMR,
RM] AY228   5036
I can hear my Savior calling
(Norris) X Where He leads
me   5037
I cannot be idle ("A. L. B. ")
[SDRMMRDRDLS, SDRMM]
AX190   5038
-----. R [MMSSSLSMS, MSSS
LSM]   5039
I cannot tell thee (Brown) [SDD
DRMMM, FMDTRD, SD] AS
306   5040
-----. R [DDFFFFDRM, MMRRR
F#M]   5041

I come into thy house (Whitting-
ton) [MSMRMDTLSSTDMMR,
S] BI44-D   5042
I come to thee (Hugg) [SDFMM
RR, DDDDRRM, MF] AY215
                            5043
I denne verdens sorger saenkt
(Lindeman) [LDMLSFFM, R
DTLLDDT,] O391   5044
I djupet af mitt jhärta (Ahnfelt)
[SMTDMLS, FMSRSD, MLS]
N516   5045
I do believe (American trad)
X Belief   5046
I gave my life for thee (Bliss)
[SSSMSLDT, LSSFSM, SS]
N512; R262; U163; V748;
Z289; AE171; AG145; AH287;
AI138; AS244; AT399; AU222;
AV378; AX312; BA473 5047
I have a mother over yonder
(Negro spiritual) [DDDLDLL
DL, DDDLSSS] AH596 5048
I have a Savior (Sankey) X I am
praying for you   5049
I have a song (Excell) X
Othello   5050
I have decided to follow Jesus
(Hart) [DDMSSSLSMD, DDDD
DD] AX304   5051
I have made my choice (Leech)
[SSDDDMDSLDS, DRMSS]
AS336; AX181   5052
-----. R [SSLSMSFFF,
FFSFRFM]   5053
I have work enough to do (Kirk-
patrick) [DRMMMMS, MRDMR,
RMFF] BC71   5054
I hear in the air (---) X Home
II   5055
I hear the Saviour say (Grape)
X All to Christ I owe
                            5056
I hear thy welcome voice
(Hartsough) [DMSMRDD, DR
FLSM, SDT] E573; P262; W
689; AH240; AL481; AM406;
AP435; AR446; AS204; AT224;
AU265; AV170; AX299; BA908;
BB224   5057
-----. R [DTLSL, SMRDR,
SLMRDR]   5058
I heard the bells on Christmas

Day (Calkin) X Waltham 5059
I heard the voice of Jesus say
  (Brunk) [SSFMLSFM, DTLSFM,
  SS] AX329; AY472   5060
I heard the voice of Jesus say
  (Melish) [MMMFFSFMRM, FS
  DFMR] AU163; AX607   5061
I himmelen, i himmelen (Linde-
  man) [DMLSMDFM, DLTDMR,
  RR] O263   5062
I himmelen, i himmelen (Swedish
  Koralbok, 1697) X Laurinus
                           5063
I hoppet sig min frälsta själ
  förnöjer (---. 16th c. Northern
  mel) X Sweden   5064
I intend to go through with Him
  (Morris) [MSLSMRDMMFM,
  MSMDT] AX305   5065
I Jesu havn skal al vor gjerning
  ske (Kingo. Gradual. 1699)
  [DTLS#, S#LTDRM, TDLRDT]
  O247   5066
I Jesus söger jeg min fred
  (Lindeman) [MSFMRDRS, SLLSF
  MR, M] O370   5067
I know a kingdom (German trad.
  16th c) X Freiburg   5068
I know a way (Sandström) [SDRM
  MMRDMR, RMRDDR] P306
                           5069
I know God's promise is true
  (Morris) [SSMRDSSMFS, DTL
  FST] AX476   5070
-----. R [SMDTDRD, SMRDDT
  DR, S]   5071
I know I love thee better (Hudson)
  [DMFSSLDD, DDDTLS, DM]
  AS283; AU94; AX479   5072
-----. R [SMDRDDLS, STTLSD,
  SM]   5073
I know in my heart what it means
  (Teasley) [SSDDDDTLSF#LS,
  SSTL] AX347   5074
-----. R [MRRMFMRMS, SLLL
  LTD]   5075
I know that my Redeemer lives
  (Edwards) [SSSTLTLSD, SSST
  LLL] BC95   5076
I know that my Redeemer lives
  (Fillmore) X Pounds   5077
I know whom I have believed
  (McGranahan) X El Nathan

                           5078
I Kristi sar jag somnar in
  (Swedish, 1698) [LDRMT
  DRT, SLTF#SMR#M,] N596
                           5079
I lift mine eyes (Achron)
  [LTLTDRDT, LDTTLSL, L]
  BH33   5080
I lift my eyes (Lagi) [DMR
  DRMFMR, RMFSFMM] J396
                           5081
I lift up my eyes (Gelineau)
  [DDDR, RRM, MMMF, RFM.]
  BSp. 40   5082
I long to be there (Schmucker)
  [SSSSSSDS, SSSSMRDR] AY
  59   5083
I love Him (Foster) [DMFSS
  LDTLS, DMFSSL] AU210
                           5084
I love the Lord (Gelineau)
  [LFSM, FSL, RDRL, LDTDT]
  BSp. 34   5085
I love the Lord (Genevan Psal-
  ter. 1562) X Ainsworth
  97   5086
I love thee (Ingall. Christian
  harmony) [SDDMSSLSMDR
  M, SDDM] AT150; BB343
                           5087
I love thee, O thou Lord
  (Cologne. Symphonia ...
  1695) [SDRMFSDFMR, RM
  FSFM] BN209; BQ316
                           5088
I love thy kingdom, Lord
  (Mason. Sacred harp, 1843)
  X Bealoth   5089
I love to hear the story (Gaunt-
  lett) [MMMMRMFMR, LSFM
  RMF] F445b   5090
-----. R [LTDTLRMFFM,
  MMRDTL]   5091
I love to hear the story (Root)
  X Ellon   5092
I love to steal awhile away
  (Pollock) [MMMSMFMR, RR
  RDRM, SS] AX72; AY291
                           5093
I love to tell the story (Fischer)
  X Hankey   5094
I love to tell the story (Jacobs)
  [DMSSLSSM, SSRMFM, DM]

AY348   5095

I love to think of my home (Pollock) [SSDDDDTRR, RRDMM
DR,]   AS478; AX586; AY151
5096

-----. R [RMD, SSLDS, DMMM
RDR, S]   5097

I must tell Jesus (Hoffman) X
Orwigsburg   5098

I name thy hallowed Name
(Spiess) X Swabia   5099

I need thee [every hour] (Lowry)
X Need   5100

I need thee, precious Jesus
(Showalter) [DRMMFMMR, T
DRFMRD, D] AS216   5101

I need thee, precious Jesus
(Slovak hymn) [MFSSDTLLS,
MSDMRDT,] BQ41   5102

I need thee, precious Jesus
(Webb) X Webb   5103

I owe the Lord a morning song
(Herr) [DDSDRMFMRDTD,
RMRD] AX58; AY278   5104

I praegtige himle (Lindeman)
[DMMFSSSMRDLS, DTMM]
O19   5105

I pray thee, Lord (Mather) X
Medfield   5106

I rejoiced when I heard (Gelineau)
[MLSM, MRM, MTLT, TSMF#
M,] BSp. 42   5107

I remember Calvary (Black)
X Where He may lead me
5108

I saw a mighty angel (Careless)
[SSLTDRMSFRFM, MRLF]
BC255   5109

I saw three ships (English carol)
X Sunny Bank   5110

I see by rays surrounded (Haller)
[DMFSMLS, DTLSRM, RMF]
BP71   5111

I see my Jesus crucified (Montani)
[MLTDDTTS, LFMRMSLT] BQ
24   5112

I see thee standing, Lamb of God
(Danish trad.) X Release
5113

I shall approach the altar (Track)
[MMMSMDDRRM, MDTLSD]
BL42   5114

I shall be like Him (Spencer)

[MMMMRMSSSSM, RRRRD]
AX568   5115

I shall know Him (Sweney)
[DRMMMMMRDMDDLS, SS]
AT472; AV397; AX572; AY
495   5116

-----. R [MMRTLTDS, DRM
MMFMR]   5117

I sing of a maidin (Shaw) [LL
LTDTLSLL, LLTDTL] BG
183   5118

I stand all amazed (Gabriel)
[SSDLSMFSDLTLS, SSR]
BC80   5119

I surrender all (Weeden) X
Surrender   5120

I thank the Lord my Maker
(Webb)   5121

I think when I read (Cornell)
[DRMMMMFMRMRR, RMFS]
BR539   5122

I think when I read (Gifford)
[SMTDRDLSMLS, SLLLR]
U325; AI384b   5123

I think, when I read that sweet
story (Greek mel) X Luke
5124

I trusted even when I said
(Gelineau) X I love the
Lord   5125

I wander through the stilly night
(Dougall) [SSLTDTLS, MFD#
RLSR#M,] BC294   5126

I want to be a Christian
(Negro spiritual) [DDMMSM
RD, DDMSLSM, D] R317;
AF353; AG318; AH608; AR
486; BK167; BZ   5127

-----. V [DDMMSMRD, DDD
MSSLS] AH608   5128

I want to be a worker (Baltzell)
[SDDDRMMRDR, SRRRMF]
AX184   5129

-----. R [SFMSMD, DRMMM
MSMRD]   5130

I want to be more like Jesus
(Stillman) [SSLSDRMFMR,
DTDRMR] AS226; AX376
5131

-----. R [LS#LTDSMS, FMF
MRMFS,]   5132

I want to love Him more
(Smith) [DMRDSLDS, DM

MSSR, DM] AX374; AY202
                                    5133
-----. R [MSSLLS, DMMFMR,
   MSSL]   5134
I was a wandering sheep (Zundel)
   X Lebanon   5135
I was glad when they said (Mc-
   Kinney) [SFMMRDMLS, FM
   RRRMF] AU309   5136
I will arise and go to Jesus
   (American trad) X Arise
                                    5137
I will be true to thee (Morris)
   [MR#MFMMRD, DDDMMR,
   MR#] AX400   5138
-----. R [SSSSLSM, DDDFFM,
   MFM]   5139
I will early seek my Saviour
   (Fillmore) [SMRDMLLS, SFMDL
   TD, S] BB417   5140
-----. R [DDTRRRDM, MMM
   RDLS, S]   5141
I will never turn back (Grisham)
   [DRMMR#MMRD, DMSMR#MM]
   AX439   5142
-----. R [DRMMRD, DRSFFM,
   DRMM]   5143
I will not forget thee (Gabriel)
   X Sweet promise   5144
I will sing (Bilhorn) [MFSSLSDS,
   SSSSLSS, M] AE293; AM709;
   AT144; AU377; AV315   5145
-----. R [SLTDDTLSM, SSSSL
   SS,]   5146
I will sing (McGranahan) X
   My Redeemer   5147
I will sing (Phillips) X Home
   of the soul   5148
I will sing of Jesus' love
   (Belden) [MFSMMRD, RMFL
   LSM, MF] BB529   5149
-----. R [DDDTLSDM, DRMFMM
   RR]   5150
I will sing you a song (Phillips)
   X Home of the soul   5151
I wonder (Pollock) [MFSMFLSM,
   SFMRFM, MF] AX30; AY346
                                    5152
-----. R [SDTLSSFM, SFMRFM,
   SD]   5153
I would be closer to thee (War-
   ren) [SSSDDDDL, LTTTDRM,
   S] AX381   5154

I would be true (Peek) X
   Peek   5155
I would love thee (Hymns and
   tunes. 1890) X May the
   grace of Christ   5156
I would not have my way
   (Byers) [SSF#LSMRDLD,
   LSSDRM] AX393   5157
-----. R [SLLFLDLSMS,
   MMRD#RS]   5158
"Iam" (latin) is written and
   filed as "Jam"   5159
Ibstone (Tiddeman) [DMFSRM,
   SDTLTLS, SSF] F356; I641;
   BV631; BY317b   5160
Iceland (Icelandic mel) [DMM
   SLS, SRRMF#S, LTSD] AN
   247   5161
Ich armer mensch, ich armer
   suender (Wittwe. Hamburger
   Musikalisches handbuch. 1690)
   X Crasselius   5162
Ich blicke nach der hoehe
   (Grimm) X Gregor's 244th
   metre   5163
Ich dank' dir, lieber herre
   (Gerle. Musika teutsch)
   [DDTDRTS, RMRDLS, DDT]
   Q32; AA408   5164
Ich dank' dir schon (Praetor-
   ius) [DDDFRMF#S, SLTD
   TLS, S] Q431; AN394; AQ
   204; AZ15-A   5165
-----. V [DDDFRMF#S, MFS
   LFSF, S] AN394   5166
-----. V [DDDFRMFS, SLTD
   TDLS,] AQ204   5167
Ich fahr dahin (German trad)
   [SDDSFMRD, DTDRSTLS,]
   X667; Y24   5168
Ich halte treulich still (Bach)
   [SMRDSLSS, DRMSFMRD]
   E644; F635; Q532; W547;
   X480; AD271; AF337; BI107;
   BV219; BY435; BZ   5169
-----. V [SMDSLS, SRMFRD,
   RMLF#] Q532   5170
Ich lass dich nicht (Doles)
   [SMRDRMFSLSFM, MMFR,]
   AA87   5171
Ich liebe dich herzlich, O
   Jesu (Grimm's Choral buch)
   X Gregor's 39th metre -

C   5172
Ich ruehme mich einzig (Moravian)
X Gregor's 39th metre   5173
Ich ruf zu dir (Geistliche lieder.
Wittenberg, 1535) X Jeg
raaber, Herr Jesus Krist
5174
Ich seh'in bangen Busz-ideen
(Grimm. Choral buch) X
Saxony   5175
Ich singe dir (Gesangbuch mit
noten. 1890) [DMSDDRDTD,
DRDTLS, R] AR542; AW362
5176
Ich singe dir (Koenig. Harmon-
isches lieder) [SSSSDRTD,
RLTLLS, SD] Q29; AA292
5177
Ich steh an deiner krippe
(Schemelli. G-B. 1736) X
Wonnberger   5178
Ich sterbe täglich (Leipzig ms.)
[DTLSLFSMRD, MRSF#DT]
Q120; AA171   5179
Ich weiss an wen ich glaube
(Gesangbuch mit noten, 1890)
[SDDRRMF, RMFRDTD, SD]
AR246; AW240   5180
Ich weiss ein lieblich engelspiel
(German, 14th c) X Mothering
Sunday   5181
Ich weiss einen strom (Hull.
The Casket) [SDDDDTDRDTD,
DMDDD] AW232; AX257
5182
Ich will dich lieben (Koenig)
[DMSDSLSFM, RMF#SDTL]
J505; K213; M142, 233; N380;
O225; Q399; AA349; AR118
5183
Ich will's wagen (Nares) X
Amsterdam   5184
Idag er naadens tid (Neu ordent-
lich, G-B. Hanover, 1646) X
Steadfast   5185
If any little word of mine
(Hakes) [SMMFFDRM, MRRD
RMS, S] BB629   5186
-----. R [SSSSSFMR, RMMF#F#
SS, S]   5187
If great wonders (Slovak hymn)
[DRMRMFMRR, MFSFMRD,]
BQ100   5188

If I come to Jesus (Doane)
[DSSSLD, TDRMDS, DSSS]
AP759b   5189
-----. R [TTRTDT, LDTLS,
DSSSL]   5190
If I would be a child of God
(Hastings) X Retreat   5191
If, now thou seekest miracles
(Vehe. G-B. 1537) X Wer
da wonet   5192
If our God had not befriended
(Weinberg) [MMTLTDDT, LTD
LTML, S] BH123   5193
If the Lord does not build
(Gelineau) [SSLD, DDDR, DD
DL, LFSL] BSp.48   5194
If thou but suffer God (Neu-
mark) X Neumark   5195
If ye would hear (Souter liede-
kens. 1539) [DDDMMFFS,
DDMMFFSL,] BG134 5196
If you could hie to Kolob
(Daynes) [MFSSF#SLSD,
TLSMSRM,] BC257   5197
If you only knew Him (Moore)
[MFSDMDTL, RDTRLTD,
M] AU421   5198
-----. R [MRDSDSTL, RDTD
RR#M, M]   5199
Ignatius (English trad) [DFM
RDTD, DRMF#STLS, S] AZ
582-O; BA52   5200
Ihr gestirn' (Peter) X Chris-
topher   5201
Ihr kinderlein kommet (Schulz)
X Tekna   5202
Ihr seelen, sinkt, ja sinket
hin (Moravian) X Old 26th
5203
Il buon pastor (Canzuns spirit-
uals, 1765) [SDRMFSFMR
D, SSFMFS] R12; X567;
AC167   5204
Ilfracomb (Schulthes) X Lam-
beth   5205
Ilkley (Dykes) X Calm 5206
I'll go where He sendeth me
(Tinsley) [MSSSMFSLSM,
SLLDTL] AX211   5207
-----. R [SSMDDL, LSSDTLS,
SSM]   5208
I'll go where you want me to
go (Rounsefell) [MMMSMMFF

L, LSFMSMR,] H398; AH427;
AT425; AV379; AY105; BC75
                                    5209
-----. R [SSRRRD#RMDM,
SSRRRD]   5210
I'll live for Him (Dunbar) [SM
MMSMMM, SDMSDRMR,] Z293;
AH418; AS245; AT359; AU168;
AX408; AY103   5211
I'll make it my home (Stafford)
[DMR#MDRMSF#LS, DMR#M
D] AX605   5212
-----. R [MDDDDDD, MSSSSSS,
SL]   5213
I'll praise my Maker (Fones)
[DMFSMDLSFMRD, RMSF]
BC254   5214
I'll sing a hymn (German trad)
X Woodbird   5215
I'll sing a hymn to Mary (Ger-
man trad) [SDDTDRR, SRRDRM,
SMM] BO64   5216
I'll stand by (McGranahan) [SF#
SF#SF#SM, LSFMR, FMF]
AU431   5217
-----. R [SMFSLTDS, LFLDT
LS, D]   5218
I'll Thee exalt (Praetorius) X
Praetorius II   5219
Illa (Mason) [DDDTDMMRD
TD, RRRMD] L53; T252a;
V460; AJ350; AN79b; AO479;
AW63; BX90   5220
Illinois (Spilman) [DRMFSLSMR
MFM, RMSD] I399; AQ59
                                    5221
Illsley (Bishop) [DDSDRMFMRD,
DDSDRM] E62; F1b; J133c;
R335; X610; AB355; AN266;
AW176; BE129; BV58; BY360b
                                    5222
Illuminatio (Elvey) [MMFMMRD,
RLTSDMR, MM] W204; AK
345   5223
Ilona (Lerman) [DRMFMMRSM
RD, DFMLS] G466; AT447;
AV275   5224
Ilsley (Bishop) X Illsley   5225
Ilsley (Ilsley) [MMDDDTLL,
SFMRDTL, L] U146; V240;
BE97   5226
I'm a pilgrim (Italian mel) [DRM
DDDRMSFR, SFMMM] V662;

AI314; BB666; BE415 5227
-----. V [DRMDDRMSFR,
SFRRRR] BE415   5228
I'm a pilgrim (Ahnfelt) X Jag
är främling   5229
I'm a pilgrim, I'm a stranger
(Robertson) [MMMRSLSF,
MSFMRFM, M] BC261
                                    5230
I'm going home (Miller) X
Going home   5231
I'm not ashamed (Arne) X
Arlington   5232
I'm pressing on the upward way
(Gabriel) X Higher ground
                                    5233
Immaculate Mary (Lourdes Pil-
grims hymn) [SDDMDDMRR
MRD, SDDM] BM54; BN144;
BO62; BP80   5234
-----. R [FFMMRRRSD, FFM
MMRM]   5235
Immanuel (---) [MMRDRDLS,
SDRMDR, RM] AS60   5236
Immense caeli conditor (Sarum
plainsong, M 2) [FFSLSSFM,
SMFRDFFF,] E58; X33a
                                    5237
Immortal Babe (German carol)
X Tredeca   5238
Implicit trust (Wathall) [MM
MMMM, MSSSLLSM, MM] I
464a   5239
Improve the shining moments
(Baird) [SDDDRMD, SRRMFM,
SMR] BC73   5240
In-a this-a band (Negro spirit-
ual) [DLSMSSSDTD, DLS
MFF] AH600   5241
-----. R [DMMMRDR, DDRM
MRDD, D]   5242
In a world where sorrow (Ex-
cell) [SSLSTL, SSFFM, SSLS
T] BC74   5243
-----. R [MSSLSMSLTDDT,
FLLT]   5244
In aeternum (Tchaikowsky)
[MMRFMRRDRM, MMLRRS]
Y127   5245
In allen meinen thaten (David-
isches harfen) [MMSFMRD,
RRRMF#SSF#S,] E321
                                    5246

In answer to my prayer (Jewish
trad) X Sheer hasheerem II
                                5247
In Babilone (Dutch trad) [DTL
SDRDRMD, FMRMRDT] A103a;
B191b; C522a; E145; J542; R
110a; S93; X173a; Z502; AD
434; AE76; AF74; AG54a; AK
89; AN352; AQ191; AR612; AW
122; BD48; BE98; BV463; BY
647; BZ   5248
In Bethlemen, that fair city
(Piae cantiones, 1582) X Ein
kind gebor'n   5249
In Christo gelebt (Neander) X
Neander II   5250
In corde meo (Baumbach) [MM
MSFMMMRDTDRMD, D] U493;
AC338; AE463; AH562; AN568;
AR663; AS490; AT532; AV412;
AW608; BB691; BX555   5251
In dark Gethsemane (Hull) [MM
RRFFMM, SSMDMR, MF] P175;
AL101b; AW323; AX239; AY
222   5252
In der wiegen (Corner. Geistliche
nachtigall. 1649) X Corner
                                5253
In dich hab'ich gehoffet
(Sunderreiter. Himmlische
harfen) [DDSSDLTD, DRMFRS
F#S,] Q524; AA494   5254
"In dich hab ich gehofft, Herr"
(Plainsong arr) [LLMTRDTL,
MMF#SF#MF#R] BL47   5255
In dulce jubilo (German mel,
14th c) [DDDMFSLS, SDDMFSL]
A31; B549; C549; G110; J39;
M613; O199; P134; Q92; R165;
S130; W58; Z193; AB118; AD
110; AE80; AF125; AG70; AH258;
AK116; AL61; AM159; AN177;
AR129; AT74; AZ121-A; BD230;
BF278; BG86; BK159; BN15;
BP18; BV99; BY97; BZ   5256
-----. V [DDDMFSLS, DDDM
FSLS] AL61   5257
-----. V [SDDRMFSLS, SDDRM
FS] AZ121-A   5258
In einem kripplein lag ein Kind (Lau-
fenberg) [DTLTDLSS, DTLMSF
MM,] E338   5259
In excelsis gloria (Brown) X

When Christ was born
                                5260
In excelsis gloria (Ouseley)
X Glory in the highest
                                5261
In excelsis gloria (Shaw)
[DMFSLSMD, MFMRDLDR,]
BG178b   5262
-----. R [DRMFMRDRRRSL
L#LS.]   5263
In excelsis gloria (Stokowski)
[LRLLFSLTD, LRLLFSL]
B547b   5264
In from the highways (Showalter)
[SSLSDRMDLS, TTDRMR,]
AS376; AX218; AY338 5265
-----. R [RRMRSLSDRM,
FMMRDR,]   5266
In God, my Saviour (Zinck.
Koralbog, 1801) X Paa Gud
alene   5267
In God, the holy (Shelley)
[SMFFLF#SS, DDLTSLS, S]
BH73   5268
In heaven above (Norwegian trad)
X Hauge   5269
In heaven is joy (Norwegian
trad) [SDMSLSFM, DLRDLT
D, S] P113   5270
In heavenly love abiding (Men-
delssohn) X Heavenly love
                                5271
In His keeping (Morris) [SL
SMRDTS, SLSFMRD, S] AI
308   5272
-----. R [DRMMFMMR, TDR
FMRM, M]   5273
In His kingdom (Norwegian
mel) X Deus fortis   5274
In His love abiding (Malan)
[SSLSMD, RMFS, SSLS
MD] Z391; AK478   5275
In His name (Showalter) [MF
SSLSMSD, SLLDLS, F] AY
354   5276
-----. R [LTDDTLS, FMRLS
FMFS,]   5277
In humility, our Saviour
(Prichard) X Hyfrydol
                                5278
In hymns of praise (Beirly)
[SMDRDTLSLTD, RMFFM]
BC9   5279

-----. R [DTDRTDRM, MRRM
F#S, SD]   5280
In manus tuas (Plainsong, M 6)
[DDDDRRRDRRM, MDRMR]
BN193   5281
In manus tuas (Plainsong, M 6)
[FFFFSLLS, FSLSFRFS] E
739   5282
In manus tuas (Eastertide: Plain-
song, M 6) [FFFSFFFFFMS
L, LLSS] E740   5283
In medio bello (Layard) [SMFS
LSMFSL, SSLTST] C243b 5284
In memoriam (Campbell) [MS
MFMRDRM, FSMLSMD] V545
                                 5285
In memoriam (Maker) [MMRDD
FFM, SSFMDMRD] C335; D236;
AL229b; AO448; AS467; AW
310; BX260   5286
In memoriam (Stainer) X Evangel
                                 5287
In memoriam (Sullivan) [MMMM
RDS, MMMMRDR, SF] B21b
                                 5288
In memory of the Crucified
(Schreiner) [DRMFMRDTD,
MF#SLSF#F#] BC99   5289
In memory of the Saviour's love
(Barthélemon) X Ballerma
                                 5290
In mercy, Lord, incline thine
ear (Binder) [MMRDTRTL, LLL
SFM, RM] BH211   5291
In mercy, Lord, remember me
(Bradbury) X Brown   5292
In morgenrot gekleidet (Beutler)
[MMMFMMRD, SDSFMR, TT]
AA322   5293
In natali domini (Andernach, G-B.,
1608) [LDTLSLTD, DRMFDTL,
T] X478   5294
In palmis (Tours) X Tours
                                 5295
In remembrance of thy suffering
(Stephens) [MSF#LSSDTTL, LRM
SFF] BC258   5296
In tenderness (Gordon) [SSDDRD
T, DRD#RMD, SSM] U167; AU
65   5297
-----. R [SDDRDT, SRRMRD,
MFSM]   5298
In that day (McPhail) [SSSMMRD

LS, SDDMMR, S] AX585; AY
307   5299
-----. R [RRRRDRMSS, LS
MSMRD]   5300
In the cross of Christ (Conkey)
X Rathbun   5301
In the field (Farmer) [MFS
MRDRSLS, DRMMMF] W43
                                 5302
In the garden (Miles) [SSMF
SDRM, RDDDRDLD] AH329;
AU356; BB606   5303
-----. R [MRDDDTLTTT, SS
MMMR]   5304
In the gloaming (Harrison)
[SLSMSFFM, DLDMSFM, S]
AI397b; AS406; BC57 5305
In the good ship (---) [DMSSSLS
M, DSLLLDS, D] AI393
                                 5306
-----. R [RMMMRRDD, DR
RRDRMS,]   5307
In the harvest field (Doane) X
Labor on   5308
In the hour of trial (Lane) X
Penitence   5309
In the land of fadeless day
(Danks) X No night there
                                 5310
In the light all light excelling
(Elgar) [MMSMMRRM, FF
LFMRM, S] BO6   5311
In the lonely midnight (Howard)
X Lonely midnight   5312
In the old-time way (McKinney)
[MFSSLMSS, DTLLDLS, L]
AU305   5313
-----. R [DMSSS, MSDDD,
SSLDTL]   5314
In the rifted rock (Bentley)
[DRMMRDMS, LLSMRDR, D]
AX512; AY453   5315
-----. R [SSDSMMSM, MMR
MFMR, S]   5316
In the shadow of His wings
(Excell) [MFSLSFMMRDRD,
DDTT] AU135   5317
-----. R [MMF, MFS, MSD,
SFMSRSD,]   5318
In the silent midnight watches
(Root) [MMMMMMFM, RRM
RD, MMM] AX244   5319
In the town (French, 15th c)

21; AD60; AF53; AN112; AP668;
AQ268; AW556; BE361; BJ83;
BL49; BN91; BQ57; BY707
                                        5355
-----. V [MDRMFSFM, MFSS
RMRDT] BJ83   5356
Innsbruck (Isaak) X Gregor's
   79th metre (Crueger)   5357
Innsbruck, ich musz dich lassen
   (Isaak) X Innsbruck   5358
Innsbruck new (Isaak) X Inns-
   bruck   5359
Innspruck (Isaak) X Innsbruck
                                        5360
Ins feld geh (Layriz Collection)
   X Layriz   5361
Integer [vitae] (Flemming) X
   Flemming   5362
Intercession (Callcott) [SMMRD
   DD, TDRMR, SMMR] D609b;
   I509; V758; W255; AB180;
   AL332; AM532; AP236; AW
   203; AZ604-A; BA611; BF365
                                        5363
Intercession [refrain] (Callcott)
   X Almighty Father, hear
   (Mendelssohn)   5364
Intercession (Dykes??) [DMRDFM
   RDRTD, TDRM] A333; B52;
   C52a; D5a; I477; K477; L24;
   V562; AB310; AL30; AO145
                                        5365
Intercession (Sankey) X I am
   praying for you   5366
Intercession New (Callcott) X
   Intercession   5367
Intercession Old (Dykes) X Inter-
   cession   5368
Intercessor (Parry) [LSFMMFLDD
   TL, LSFMM] A493; F115; X307;
   AF410; AL341; AQ55; BV176;
   BY662   5369
Into my heart (Clarke) [MMMD,
   MMMD, MSFMRFFM,] AR653;
   AU321   5370
Into our hands (Teddlie) [SDRMDM
   R#MFL, DTLSDM] AX209
                                        5371
-----. R [SSSSMSLSSF, FMFRRS]
                                        5372
Into the tomb of ages (Heller)
   [SMRMMSMRD, DLFMFRM]
   BH156   5373

Into the tomb of ages past
   (Jewish trad) X Adon olom
   II   5374
Into the woods (McKinney)
   [MMMLTDRMFM, DTLTTM,]
   AU420   5375
Into thy hands (Hartog) [SMF
   SSLTDMMR, RMRDR] BH
   14   5376
Invermay (Lamb) [SSMLS, MM
   MRFM, SDTLT] W362 5377
Invitation (Ingalls) [DRMDR
   MRDRMFMR, DTL] H255;
   AY229   5378
Invitation (Hastings) [SMRDSLD
   LS, SLTDRFM] L514   5379
Invitation (LaTrobe) [SMLDSF
   M, RMF#SLLS, SM] AZ591-
   A   5380
Invitation (Maker) [MMMMRR,
   MFFMRM, LLLL] G190; R
   261; S220; T281; U166; V
   263; Z278; AE268; AG138;
   AJ389a; AK463; AM395; AO
   644; AR245; AS359; AT226;
   AW270   5381
Invitation (Root) X Come to
   the Saviour   5382
Invitation (Sophr) X Gerald
                                        5383
Invitation (Wallace) X Serenity
                                        5384
Invocation (Burnap) X Seelye
                                        5385
Invocation [sentence] (Harring-
   ton) X The Lord is in His
   holy temple   5386
Invocation (Landahl) [MDLSS
   DDRRM, MMRDMR] J178
                                        5387
Invocation (Wagner) X Pilgrim
   chorus   5388
Iona (Stainer) [DMSFMRFM,
   RDMRDTD, D] B287; C287;
   D168   5389
Ionia (Belcher) [SDMRDMR,
   RMFFMRM, DT] L51 5390
Ionia (Everett) [MMMMMRM
   FSM, LSFMRD] AS62 5391
Irae (Barnby) [MDTLLLLL, L
   FMRRFFM,] I603   5392
Irby (Gauntlett) [STDDDTDRR
   D, DMSMMR] A236; B349;

D540; E605; F432; G442; J41;
K535; M608; N633; R462; S
454; W69; X368; AA287; AD
474; AG302; AH242; AI382;
AL70; AM639; AO133; AP727a;
AR125; AV84; AW412; AZ89-D;
BA158; BB424; BF284; BR558;
BV107; BY106   5393
Irene (Hopkins) X Ellers   5394
Irene (Scholefield) [SSLSDDT,
RRMFTDR, MM] C203a; D
135a; K85; W584; AL161a;
AM248; AP271; BY229   5395
Iris (French carol) X Gloria
                             5396
Irish (Collection of hymns ...
Dublin, 1749) [DDSDRMFMRM,
SMFSDR] A444; E504; F263;
G14; J331; R29a; S49; V79;
W153; X680; AK22; AL138;
AM19; AP29; AW268; AZ14-
M; BA118; BE145; BV221b;
BY398; BZ   5397
Irish carol (Irish trad) [DDMD
MS, DDDMRDR, SDD] BG6
                             5398
Irish melody (Irish trad) X
Londonderry   5399
Irmer (Haeussler) [DDRMRD,
FLTDD, RDTLD] AK67 5400
Irons (Irons) [SFMRRD, MSL
R, SSMRM] A183; B17; C17a;
D10a; Eap. 42; F30; K474; W
272; AL569; AP680a   5401
Irons (Irons) X Southwell   5402
Irvin (Langden) [SDDTSRD,
RRFMRD#R, DM] L472a
                             5403
Irvine Waterside (Finlay) [SM
RDMFSLS, TDLSFMF] BY265b
                             5404
Irving (Hartshorn) [SFMRMRDM
S, SLSMMRD] T162; AJ240
                             5405
Is it the crowning day (Marsh)
[SLSDRM, SRSM, FSLMRS]
AM692   5406
-----. R [DLTS, FMRMRS,
SDTDRD]   5407
Is my name written there (Davis)
X My name's written there
                             5408
Is not this the land of Beulah

(Dadman) [SDMDRDDL, D
LSSLDD, S] AU27; AX129;
AY79, 353; BB180   5409
-----. V [SDMDRDDL, DLS
SLTD, S] AX129   5409a
-----. V [SDMDRDDL, LLSS
LTD, S] BB180   5409b
Is there any pleasure (Naegeli)
[MFSFMR, DDRSM, LSFMS]
AX539   5410
Is thy heart right with God?
(Hoffman) [SSSMFSLLLD,
MMDRMD,] AX274   5411
-----. R [SSSLLS, DDDDDR,
MMMD]   5412
Is your all on the altar? (Hoff-
man) X Hoffman II   5413
Isca (Wood) [DSFMDMRD,
DLSFMMRD] D239; AO141
                             5414
Ishpeming (Alexis) [SMTRD
TLS, SDDRRM, MM] J301;
N557   5415
Island (Tomissön. Psalmebog,
1569) [LLLDLSFM, DTLSM
FRD,] J253; M19; O46; P
59; Q48   5416
Isleworth (Howard) [MLMFRD
TL, TDRMLSF#] A77; B156;
E557; Q439; S383a; W101;
X253   5417
Israel (Goss) [SDSDRMRD, RM
RMFSFM,] BA236   5418
Israel (Martin) [SSSSFMRD,
LLLLSSFL] W110; AP455
                             5419
Israel, Israel, God is calling
(Converse) X Erie   5420
Israel's song (Levenson) [SM
RDMRDRT, SFMRFM, L] BH
79   5421
Iste confessor (Croft. Collec-
tion) [SDTLSDTDRMM, SSM
FM] E188b; F158b; X231;
AD216; AK227; BV226
                             5422
Iste confessor (Plainsong)
[RDRFFMRMRRDRFF, SF]
BO268   5423
Iste confessor (Plainsong, M 2)
[RFRRDR, FFRMMR, RLL#L]
E188   5424
Iste confessor (Plainsong, M 8:

mediaeval) [SLSMFSSLFLDT
LS, D] A228a   5425
Iste confessor (Poitiers vesper-
ale, 1740) X Rouen I   5426
It came upon the midnight (Willis)
X Carol   5427
It is finished (Carnett) [DRMRM
LSM, SSSFMR#M, M] AU427
                               5428
-----. R [SSSFMR#R#M, DDLDR
DM, M]   5429
"It is finished" (Redhead) X
Redhead, No. 1   5430
It is no earthly summer's ray
(Schein) X Eisenach   5431
It is well (Bliss) X Bliss   5432
It may be at morn (McGranahan)
X Christ returneth   5433
It may not be on the mountain
height (Rounsefell) X I'll go
where you want me   5434
It must be told (Marquis) [DRM
MFMMR, RMFFSFM, D] AY522
                               5435
It pays to serve Jesus (Huston)
[SMR#MMSFMDLS, DDTLT]
AU414   5436
-----. R [MSRMFLTDMLS,
SSRSL]   5437
It singeth low (Grimm) [SDDT
SSLLSM, MTLSLS] BH220
                               5438
Itala (Paris Antiphoner, 1681)
X O quanta qualia   5439
Italian hymn (Giardini) X Mos-
cow   5440
It's me (Negro spiritual) [MM
MMDD, DDDDRRM, MMM] AH
603   5441
-----. R [MMMSMMMDD, DD
DDRRM,]   5442
I've enlisted in the service ("A.
L. B.") [SSDDDRMMRMD, RM
RRR] AX180   5443
-----. R [MMRRRMFSFMRDR
M, DT]   5444
I've found a friend (Stebbins) X
Friend   5445
I've wandered far away (Kirkpatrick)
X Lord, I'm coming home
                               5446
Ives (Beecher. Plymouth collection)

[DRMDMSD, LSMLSMDRM]
E582; X306; AF425   5447
Ivinghoe (Cooke) [SMRSDRD
TS, DRMFSFM] BY294
                               5448
Ivyhatch (Selby) [MFSSSDRMF
M, MMRDTD] F175; BV430
                               5449

J

Jabez (Welsh hymn mel) [LS#
LTDTDT, DRMRDTL, L] W
597   5450
Jackson (Jackson) [SSDTLSFSF
M, MF#SDTL] E210; W507b;
X445; Z132; AL111; AP56;
AQ93; BV276; BY404   5451
-----. V [SSDTLSFSFM,
MSDTLS] Z132   5452
-----. V [SSDLSFSM, MSDTL
S, SM] BY404   5453
Jacobs (Jacobs) X Hope 5454
Jacob's ladder (English trad)
[SDDDMRDRRRFMRDDD]
AD124; AR133; BF294;
BG58   5455
-----. V [SDDDDMRDRRRR
FMRD] BG58   5456
Jacob's ladder (Grauman) [SD
DTLSDRM, FSMLFS, M] BH
49   5457
Jacob's ladder (Negro spiritual)
[MMMMSSSM, RRRRFLLS,]
Y318; AF495; AG319; AH
597; BK165; BZ   5458
Jag är främling (Ahnfelt)
[MRRDSSFFM, DTTLDLS]
N526; P348   5459
Jag gar mot döden, hvar jag
gar (Gotha Cantional. 1726)
[MLTDMMR#M, MRDTDTL,
M] N603   5460
Jag har en vän (Swedish trad)
X Amicus   5461
Jag tror pa Gud, och vet
(German, 1523) [DDDTLDLS,
MSLSDMRD,] O29   5462
Jam Christus astra ascenderat
(Plainsong, M 1) [RRFRR
DFSL, LSDDRDD] E150
                               5463

Jam lucis (Benedictine plainsong,
  M 6) [DDDDDRDD, DDDDTRR]
  A164b; B28b; C28; D21; F11a;
  G58; W258; AD390; AF507;
  BZ   5464
Jam lucis orto sidere (Bendeictine
  plainsong, M 8) [SSLSFSLSL,
  DDDDRD] A159a; E254; F]a
                        5465
Jam moesta (Luther. Christlich
  G-B. 1542) [DFRRMRDRD, D
  RMFSFMR] J297; O595; P153
                        5466
-----. V [DFRRMRDRD, DRMM
  SFM] P153   5467
Jam as moesta quiesce querela
  (Luther. Christlich G-B. 1542)
  X Jam moesta   5468
James Quinter (Frederick) [SS
  SSFMRS, SLLLSS, SS] AR110
                        5469
Jamison (Smart) [SMDMSD,
  LSDSFMR, SML] V321; BY385
                        5470
Janes (Mozart) X Cana   5471
Janet (Stebbins) [SSF#SDRDDT,
  LSTDRMF] T268; AJ374
                        5472
January carol (Piae cantiones,
  1582) [DDRMFMRM, DMRDT
  DLS,] BG141   5473
Jasmine flower (Chinese trad)
  [MMSLDDLSSLS, MMSLS] Y
  197   5474
Jazer (Bradbury) [SSFMMRDDT
  LS, SLTDF] AJ59   5475
Jazer (Tozer) [SSLTDRFFM,
  DDMRDTL] I245; BO18   5476
Je sais, vierge Marie (French
  trad) X Bell carol   5477
Jeg beder dig (German. 1525)
  X Durch Adam's fall   5478
Jeg er rede til at bede (Neander)
  X Sieh hier bin ich, Ehren-
  könig   5479
Jeg har dig hjerteligen kjaer
  (Schmid. Orgelbuch. 1577) X
  Herzlich lieb hab ich dich, o
  Herr   5480
Jeg har min sag til Gud Hjem-
  stilt (Lindeman) [LMMDLLL
  S#, MLSFMRRM] O481   5481

Jeg raaber fast, O Herre
  (Bourgeois) X Du fort de
  ma detresse   5482
Jeg raaber, Herr Jesus Krist
  (Geistliche lieder. Witten-
  burg, 1535) [MDRDLDRM,
  MSMDRFM, M] O275; AA365
                        5483
Jeg ser dig, søde Lam staa
  (Danish trad) X Release
                        5484
Jeg synger Julekind (German,
  14th c) X In dulce jubilo
                        5485
Jeg ved et evigt himmerig
  (German trad. 16th c)
  X Freiburg   5486
Jeg vil din pris unsjunge (Ham-
  burg. Neu Catholisches G-B.
  1598) X Eisleben   5487
Jeg vil mig Herren love (Zinck)
  X Copenhagen   5488
Jehovah (Gerold) [DRMM, MFS
  S, SDSLSFM, R] AK494; AW
  507   5489
Jehovah (Hopkins) [DDDRDDD
  RMFM, MSFMR] O23; BA654;
  BE426   5490
Jehovah, Jesus, Lord (Dixon)
  X Lanesboro   5491
Jehovah, Lord of heaven and
  earth (Holden) X Coronation
                        5492
Jehovah nissi (Crawford) [MS
  FMMMRD, SLTDRMRR,]
  AM470; AP126   5493
Jena (Vulpius) X Das Neuge-
  borne   5494
Jenkins (Miller) [DDRMDS,
  SLSFMR, RMTD] BB170
                        5495
Jericho tune (Handel) X Milites
                        5496
Jersey (Boyce) X Boyce   5497
Jerusalem (Chauvenet Collection)
  [DDDTDR, MRDFMR, RRRM]
  BR212   5498
Jerusalem (Dykes) [SFMRMFR
  D, MFSLLR, SL] F438   5499
Jerusalem (Franck) X Melchior
                        5500
Jerusalem (Haydn, F.J.) X

St Michel's   5501
Jerusalem (Parry) [DMSLDLSFS,
   LSFSMRD] F578; W640; X446;
   Y162; AC269; AL522   5502
Jerusalem (Roper) [DDRMFSLSMS,
   MSMDRM] C510b; D403b; H
   505; L13; AO547b; AZ14-W;
   BA763a   5503
Jerusalem (Spohr) X Gerald
                             5504
Jerusalem (Stainer) X Conquest
                             5505
Jerusalem (Staniforth) [DMMFM
   RMD, LSMMRRSD] B510;
   C510c; D403c; Eap.69; L593b
                             5506
-----. V [SMMFMRMD, LSMMRR,
   SD] C510c   5507
Jerusalem, du Herrens hya stad
   (English) [SMTDDDDRTD, DR
   RRRM,] N626   5508
Jerusalem, du hochgebaute stadt
   (Franck) X Melchior   5509
Jerusalem et Sion filiae
   (Plainsong, M 5) [SDRDFMDR
   DD, MSMDFM] E172   5510
Jerusalem, Jerusalem (Haydn)
   X St Michel's   5511
Jerusalem, my happy home
   (Italian hymn mel) [SDTLS
   LLSFM, MSLTDM] BQ119
                             5512
Jerusalem, my happy home
   (Rupp) [SSFMMMRD, MFM
   RDR, SD] AX610; AY143
                             5513
Jerusalem, the golden (Ewing)
   X Ewing   5514
Jerusalem the golden (Grabow-
   ski) [SMMRDFM, RDDMRDT,
   SR] BQ118   5515
Jerusalem the golden! (Sullivan)
   X Lux mundi   5516
Jervaulx Abbey (Genevan Psalter,
   1562) [DSFMRDRM, MLLSM
   SF] A128a; W219a; AJ421
                             5517
Jesaia, dem propheten (Luther)
   [SSMDMSSLLS, SSFSDF]
   Q249   5518
Jeshurun (Gauntlett) [SDMMMRS,
   SSDDTD, SDM] BR48   5519
Jesmian (Thalben-Ball) [MRD

FMRSLMDRM, RSMD] BY721
                             5520
Jespersön (Jespersön) [DSS
   LTS, SDTLS, MFSSL] M443;
   N123   5521
"Jesu" and "Jesus" are inter-
   filed   5522
Jesu (Düben) [SDTDRSMD, MSD
   TLDR, S] J59; M55; N64;
   BE263   5523
-----. V [SDTDRMFSMD, MF
   SDTD] BE263   5524
Jesus a wedding guest (Good)
   X Since Jesus did appear
                             5525
Jesus all glorious (Boe) [SLS
   MRD, RDRSFM, RMFL]
   P208   5526
Jesus, all my gladness (Crueger)
   [MMRDTL,MF#SMLS#,LTD]
   A453; J575a; M213; Q347;
   R414; X544; AA82; AF222;
   AK240; AW564; AZ208-A;
   BJ57; BV640; BY768; BZ
                             5527
-----. V [MMRDTL, MMF#S#
   LS#, LDTT] J575a   5528
-----. V [MMRDTL, MF#SM
   LS#LDTS#] AZ208-A   5529
-----. V [MMRDTL, MF#S
   SLS#, LTDT] BZ   5530
Jesus allt mitt goda är (Arr-
   henius) [DSLTDRT, DRMSFM
   RR, M] N68   5531
Jesus är min van den bäste
   (Düben) X Jesu   5532
Jesus, be our Guide (Drese)
   X Rochelle   5533
Jesus bids us shine (Excell)
   [DSSSSDRDTT, RSSSSR] AL
   613; AM653; AP768; AW420;
   BY746a   5534
Jesu, bone Pastor (Willcox)
   [MDDTFRRD, SMMRMFMR]
   D573; BR298; BX511   5535
Jesus calls us (Jude) X Galilee
                             5536
Jesus Christ is risen today
   (Monk) X Easter hymn
                             5537
Jesus Christ is risen today
   (Montani) [LLLLDTL, LSFS
   LL, MMM] BQ27   5538

Jesus Christ, my sure defense
(Crueger. Praxis pietatis
melica) X Ratisbon   5539

Jesus Christ, the King of ages
(Goss) X Lauda anima   5540

Jesus Christus blick dich an
(Gregor's choral buch, 1784)
X Gregor's 9th metre   5541

Jesus Christus, unser heiland
(Geistliche lieder. 1535)
[DSMDRMFM, DSMLSFSM,]
Q311; AA441   5542

Jesus, come to me (Sletten)
[LMFMRDT, MLDTS#LT, DD]
P341   5543

Jesus comes (Kirkpatrick) [DD
DRMSLS, RRRMFSLS] BB549
                        5544

-----. R [DRMMRDR, DDDSLS
MS, D]   5545

Jesu corona (Rouen church mel)
[LDRMRMDTL, LSLTLSF#] E65
                        5546

Jesu, corona Virginum (Grenoble
Antiphoner, 1753) X Deus
tuorum militum   5547

Jesus, Creator of the world
(d'Hooghe) [SSSDRMFRD, MF#
F#SMDD] BQ60   5548

Jesu, deine passion (Vulpius) X
Weimar   5549

Jesu, der du meine selle (German trad) X Gregor's 168th
metre-B   5550

Jesu Deus, amor meus (Catholic)
[DDMRRRFM, MMRDTLS, T]
BQ315   5551

Jesu dilectissimi (McCartney)
[MFMRLDT, LSTMRS, SSD] B387
b; C387b; D444a; S311   5552

Jesus, din lhukommelse (Gesius)
X Herrnhut   5553

Jesus, din søde forening et
smage (Schorring. Koralbog,
1781) X Contentment   5554

Jesus, dine dybe vunder
(Bourgeois) X Bourgeois 5555

Jesus! du dig själf uppväkte
(Swedish, 1675) [DSMRDTDD,
MFRSSF#S, D] X325   5556

Jesu, du hoffnung (Joseph) X
Gregor's 298th metre   5557

Jesu, dulcedo cordium (Fisher)

[MR#MLDRDM, MFSLSMD
R,] AR202   5558

Jesu, dulcedo cordium (Poitiers Antiphoner, 1746) X
Auctoritate saeculi   5559

Jesu dulcis memoria (Andernach, 1608) [LSLTTDTLT,
LSLTSLS] A56; E238b; W
420b; X549b   5560

Jesu dulcis memoria (Murphy)
[MTDRMRFMRM, MMMLSF]
BQ296   5561

Jesu dulcis memoria (Antiphonale romanum. M 1) X Exultet cor praecordiis   5562

Jesu dulcis memoria (Sarum
plainsong, M 1) X Christe
redemptor   5563

Jesu dulcis memoria (Schmuck)
[SSLTDLSFM, MMSDTLL]
BQ161b   5564

Jesu dulcis memoria (Vittoria)
[LTLS#LDTLLS#, S#LLSLS]
BQ161a   5565

Jesus er mit haab og trøst
(Crueger. Praxis pietatis
melica) X Ratisbon   5566

Jesus er mit liv i live (Crueger)
X Du, o schönes weltege-
bäude   5567

Jesus, ever loving Saviour
(Schubert) [DSMDFMMR,
MRDRTLS, D] BQ135 5568

Jesus, food of angels (Gounod)
[SSFFMMDRMRDD, SSFF]
BQ54, 227b   5569

-----. V [SSSFFMMDRMRDD,
SSF] BQ227b   5570

Jesus för världen gifvet sitt
lif (Ekström) [DDTMDDT,
LLSMMMRD, D] N421; AI
434   5571

Jesus from whom all blessings
flow (Coles) X Duane Street
                        5572

Jesus, gentlest Saviour (Montani)
[MDSLLS, DLDMR, MDSLL]
BQ49   5573

Jesus, gentlest Saviour (Stainer)
X Eucharisticus   5574

Jesus has died for me ("A. H.
A.") [MMMMRDLDLS,
TTTTLS] AX349; AY239

5575
Jesus, hear (Maasalo) [LMLTD
LTD, RRDTLS#L, L] J383
5576
Jesus, highest heaven's complete-
ness (Dykes) X St Oswald I
5577
Jesus, how good the thought
(Tochter Sion, 1741) X St
Bernard   5578
Jesus, I am resting (Mountain)
X Resting   5579
Jesus, I come (Stebbins) [SF#
SMRDTLS, DTDR, RDR] AE
177; AH342; AI210; AM715;
AR459; AT233; AV340; AX300
5580
Jesus, I my cross (Barnby) X
St Polycarp   5581
Jesus, I my cross have taken
(Mozart) X Ellesdie   5582
Jesus is all the world to me
(Thompson) X He's my friend
5583
Jesus is calling (Stebbins) [SS
SSMFSLTD, DTLT, LS] R267;
Z280; AE168; AH330; AI200;
AM697; AT229; AU57; AV334;
AX228; BB569; BY417; BZ
5584
-----. R [DTLT, RDTD, MRDDT
LSS]   5585
Jesus is coming (Trowbridge)
[SDDDDTLSLSM, RMFMF] AU
44   5586
-----. R [DDDDSDRSRMD,
LTDSD]   5587
Jesus is God (Wurtemberg G-B.)
X Ellacombe   5588
Jesus is passing this way (Doane)
[MR#MFMRDS, DDDDTDR, M]
AU93   5589
-----. R [MFSLLLSM, MFRSSM,
MF]   5590
Jesus is tenderly calling thee
home (Stebbins) X Jesus is
calling   5591
Jesus is the name (Scholfield)
[SMMMSDRM, FMDMRD, SM]
AI387   5592
-----. R [SMDRM, RSMD,
DDDRMMS]   5593
Jesus ist das schönste licht

(Freylinghausen) [MRMFSL
SFFMM, MRDDR] E247
5594
Jesus ist das schoenste licht
(Freylinghausen) X Gregor's
156th metre   5595
Jesu, Jehovah! ich such' und
verlange (Grimm. Choral
buch) X Old 193d   5596
Jesus, Jesus, come to me
(Catholic) [MMRMSFF, FF
MFLSS, DD] BQ131   5597
Jesus, Jesus, come to me
(Marsh) X Martyn   5598
Jesu, Jesu du mein hirt (Hein-
lein) [MMLSFFM, MSF#
MMR#M, MS] E655; F110a;
X506; BE89   5599
Jesus, Jesus, nichts als
Jesus (Bronner. Choral
buch, 1715) [DDSSLTDS,
LSFMRRD, D] Q348; AA
86   5600
Jesu joy of man's desiring
(Schop) [MFSSFMRR, MFS
MRFMR] A211; E418; F275a;
J67b; M381, 534; N3; O37; P
39; Q207; X101; AA31; AI
440; AK90; AQ28; AR111;
AZ165-C; BA665; BI41*
*distinct variant   5601
-----. V [MFSSFMR, MFSF
MRD, MF] E418   5602
-----. V [MFSSFMRR, MFSM
RRD, M] M381   5603
-----. V [MFSSFMRR, MFS
DRRD, M] M534   5604
-----. V [MMFSSFMRR, MF
SMRRD,] AK90   5605
-----. V [MMFSSFMR, MFSM
RRD, R] BA665   5606
-----. V [DDMSSFMR, RMF
RRM, DD] BI41   5607
Jesu, joy of man's desiring
(Schop) X Angelus (German
choral)   5608
Jesus, keep me near the cross
(Doane) X Near the cross
5609
Jesus knows (Hugg) [MMMMR
RDDD, RRRDRMS,] AY375
5610
-----. R [SSSSFMS, LLLSM

MR, MM] 5611
Jesus, kom dog selv til mig
(Lindeman) [DSDDRSM, MS
F#STLLS, F] O169 5612
Jesu, komm doch selbst zu mir
(Wesley's Foundery Collection,
1742) X Savannah 5613
Jesu Kreuz, leiden und pein
(Vulpius) X Weimar 5614
Jesus, lat din rädda dufva
(Swedish trad) [SDMMRDR,
RMFFMRM, S] N262; P66
5615
Jesus leads (Sweney) [MFMR
SRD, DRDTRMRD, M] AY120
5616
Jesu leiden, pein und tod
(Vulpius) X Weimar 5617
Jesus lives, and Jesus leads
(German) [DMSDLDS, FSMDMR,
DMS] AI101; AP766; BV116b
5618
-----. V [DMSDLDLS, FSMDRR
D, S] BV116b 5619
Jesus, Lord and precious Saviour
(Swedish) X Kalmar 5620
Jesus, Lord, be thou mine own
(Perosi) X L'Emmanuello
5621
Jesus, lover of my soul (Barn-
by) X St Polycarp 5622
Jesus, lover of my soul (Hol-
brook) X Refuge 5623
Jesus, lover of my soul (Marsh)
X Martyn 5624
Jesus loves me (Bliss) X Glad-
ness 5625
Jesus loves me (Bradbury) X
Renar 5626
Jesus loves the little children
(Root) [MMMRDLSD, RRMR
DMR, S] AU311 5627
Jesu, magister bone (Dykes)
[MMRLTDD, RMDSFR, MMR]
D363a; O567; V400 5628
Jesu, meine freude (Crueger) X
Jesus, all my gladness 5629
Jesu meine lust und wonne
(Lüneburg G-B. 1686) [MFSLFF
MM, SRDTDR, S] N389 5630
Jesu, meine zuversicht (Crueger.
Praxis pietatis melica. 1653).
X Ratisbon 5631

Jesu meines glaubens zier
(Freylinghausen G-B.) X
Sebastian 5632
Jesu meines herzens freud
(Lüneburg G-B. 1686) [MDS
SFMR, MRRD, TRMMR] AA89
5633
Jesu, meines lebens leben
(Weimar G-B. 1681) [DDTS
LTDD, MSFMRDR, D] J79;
K98; N91; Q151; W379; Z510;
AK155; AL258; AW535; AZ
168-A; BA196 5634
-----. V [DDTSLTDD, MMF
FMMR, D] N91 5635
-----. V [DDTSLTD, MMFFMM
R, MF] W379 5636
-----. V [DDTLSLTDD, MMFF
MMR,] Z510 5637
-----. V [DDTSLTDD, RMFF
MMR, D] AZ168-A 5638
Jesus, mighty King of Sion
(Cannon) [MMFSLLSM, DDT
LSF#S, L] BC108 5639
Jesus, my God; behold (Bry-
daine) [DDRDDRDRRM, DRR
DDR] BO167; BQ133 5640
-----. R [SMRDFM, RMRDRD
T, DRM] 5641
Jesus my life (As hymnodus
sacer, Leipzig) X Breslau
5642
Jesus my Lord is real to me
(Reynolds) [DTDRDSLT, RD#
RMRRDS,] AU346 5643
-----. R [RRRSRMFM, MMMR,
F#MF#S,] 5644
Jesus, my Lord, my God (---)
[SMDDTDRSFFM, MRDFR]
BP59 5645
Jesus, my Lord, my God (Cath
olic) [DMSSSDMLSFR, LSS
MS] AH143; BO43 5646
-----. V [DMSSSDMLSFR,
LSMSF] BO43 5647
Jesus, my Lord, my God
(Montani) [MMRFMRTDRS,
SSFLSF] BQ53 5648
-----. R [RDRMMRMSF, FSL
LSFR] 5649
Jesus, my Lord, my God
(Wagner) X Gottlob, es geht
5650

Jesus, my Saviour true (Huish)
[DRRSF#F, DMRD, DRDSF#F,]
BC85   5651
Jesus nimmt die sünder an
(Neumeister) [MMSRDRMR,
RRMSLSFM,] AM394   5652
Jesus of Nazareth (---) [SLSMD
M, FDRM, MLTDTL,] BC86
                                 5653
Jesus of the manger (Flemish
trad) [MMMRMFRM, RMFFM
RM, M] BG110   5654
Jesus, once of humble birth
(English chorister) [SMSMSFL
R, RMFMRDRM,] BC88   5655
Jesus only (Lindeman) X Holy
mountain   5656
Jesus our Brother (Corbeil) X
Orientis partibus   5657
Jesus paid it all (Grape) X All
to Christ I owe   5658
Jesu pastor (Willcox) X Jesu,
bone Pastor   5659
Jesus, priceless treasure
(Lindeman) X Lindeman)
                                 5660
Jesu, quadragenariae (Plainsong,
M 4) [FMFSLSFRFMFMM,
SLT] E69; F558a; BP40
                                 5661
-----. V [FMFSLSFRFMFSFM,
SL] BP40   5662
Jesu redemptor (Sarum plainsong,
M 1) X Christe redemptor
                                 5663
Jesu redemptor omnium (Taler)
[LLTTTDRM, MRRLLTDD]
BQ155b   5664
Jesu redemptor saeculi (La
Feillée. Méthode du plain
chant) [DRDRMFRM, RMFR
DRFM] Eap.26   5665
Jesus, revealed in me (Young)
[SF#SLFM, SF#STRD, SF#SL]
AU418   5666
-----. R [SFLMRD, D#D#D#RM
F, TDRS]   5667
Jesu, rufe mich (Drese) X
Rochelle   5668
Jesu, salvator saeculi (York
Breviary) [RLLSFMRSLTDTL,
RSL] E249   5669

Jesus saves (Kirkpatrick) X
Salvation   5670
Jesus Saviour, blessed centre
(Mountain) [MRDRMFSM,
MMRDR, MRD] Z229 5671
Jesus, Saviour, heavenly
Father (Costa) [DDDDRDRM
M, FMLSDTD] BI64   5672
Jesus, Saviour, pilot me
(Gould) X Pilot   5673
Jesus, Savior, risen Lord
(Freylinghausen. Geist-
reiches G-B) X Luebeck
                                 5674
Jesus, still lead on (Drese)
X Rochelle   5675
Jesus, Sun of righteousness
(Lindeman) X Easter glory
                                 5676
Jesus the glory (French mel)
[DTDLSDDLMMRD, SLSD]
BO199   5677
Jesus, the Light of the world
(---) [MSSSMRD, MMMLSM
R, MS] AX272   5678
-----. R [SMSSSMSSS,
MSSLSMM]   5679
Jesus the Teacher (Brunk)
[MSFMRDRM, MRRSSF#LS,]
AX148; AY391   5680
Jesus, the very thought of Thee
(---) [DMFSDRRD, SDTLT
LS, R] BQ17   5681
Jesus the very thought of Thee
(Dykes) X St Agnes 5682
Jesus, thou art coming (Bain-
bridge) [DTLMLS, RDTLS,
MTMRR] BO51   5683
Jesus, thou art coming (Schu-
bert) [MMRMFM, RRRMD
R, MMRM] BN98   5684
Jesus, thou art coming (Slovak
hymnal) [SSDTLS, SSFFM,
SLTDD] BQ130   5685
Jesus, thou hast promised
(Perkins) [DSSDLD, TDRSM,
DSSDL] BB602   5686
-----. R [SMMFSFR, MMM
RDR, MMM]   5687
Jesus, thy boundless love
(Bortniansky) X St Peters-
burg   5688

Jesus, thy name I Love (Doane)
[MSFMRD, DFLLSS, SLF#S,]
U225; AJ236   5689

Jesus, united by thy grace (Hastings) X Ortonville   5690

Jesus, when we go to rest
(Lithuanian trad) [MRMFSFM,
SFMFMRMR, M] BN194
                                    5691

Jesus, while our hearts are bleeding (Mason) X Mount Vernon
                                    5692

Jesus will bear me o'er (Nickle)
[MMMMRDFFF, MMMSMDR,]
AX537   5693

-----. R [FFFFFFMMM, MMMS
MR, M]   5694

Jesus with thy Church abide
(Hintze) X Salzburg   5695

Jewels (Root) X When He cometh
                                    5696

Jewett (Weber) [SMDMRFMR,
MDMSSFM, S] G330; H371;
I524; K395; L331; M80; P156;
R367; S280; T282; U247; V429b;
Z408; AA387; AD241; AG214;
AH392; AI291; AJ390; AK313;
AM572; AO337; AR360; AS234;
AT251; AU178; AV222; AW250;
AX391; AY475; AZ38-E; BA687;
BB404   5697

-----. V [SMDRFMR, MDMSSFM,
SL] AV222   5698

Jewish tune (Jewish trad) [DDRM
DSRM, MMSSLFRSM,] BK36
                                    5699

Joachimsthal (Hermann) X Hermann
                                    5700

Joanna (Welsh mel) X St Denio
                                    5701

Job I (English trad) [MFSSLSLTD
TL, SLTSL] BG60a   5702

Job II (English trad) [MLTDMLLL
S, MDRRMF#S] BG60b   5703

Job III (English trad) [SDRTDRM
FR, MFSSFRD,] BG50d   5704

John Nass (Beery) [MMRDRD,
SSFMRM, DDSS] AR361   5705

John Three Sixteen (McKinney)
[MSSLLS, MDDFFM, MRMF]
AU324   5706

Joldwynds (Stanford) [DRFMSD
RTD, MRTLSLT] X56b   5707

Jonathan (Sheldon) [DDDRMD,
DTDRMS, FSLT] BV349
                                    5708

Jones (Jones) [SLSFMSSFF
MF, TL#TLS] AT474 5709

-----. R [MFSLSDT, RMFSL
TS, DR]   5710

Jordan (Barnby) [MSLSMRDRM,
SMF#SLT] A327; B251; D
211; E48; I158; S466; V125;
W128; X95; AB18; AH496;
AK125; AR596; BB514; BF
215; BX196   5711

Jordan's Banks (American
trad) [DRMMMFSFFFM,
RMMMF] AH529; AT479;
AU249; AV282; BB682; BZ
                                    5712

-----. R [DRMMMFSFSFM,
RRMM]   5713

Joseph (Mehul) [SDMRDDTTL
L, RDDTLT] D558; AO156;
                                    5714

Joseph (Price) [MSDSTLSF,
MFSRMFMR] Y221   5715

Joseph and Mary (English trad)
[MLTDMSMRMSL, LTDDT]
BG115   5716

Joseph lieber, Joseph mein
(German carol, 14th c) X
Resonet in laudibus   5717

Joseph, our certain hope (Dykes)
X St Agnes   5718

Joseph, pure spouse (Mattoni)
[SFMSFLLSFFM, SLTDT]
BQ94   5719

Josephine (Kroeger) [MMMRD
SFF, FFFMRLSS,] T62; AJ
95   5720

Joshua (Lutkin) [MMTTTRLD,
LTDRLTDR] I403a   5721

Josie (Kieffer) [DRMSFMR,
RMFRDTD, SS] AY408
                                    5722

Journey's end (Anderson)
[DDDDDDDRDDD#, RFFFD]
G519; AK419   5723

Joy (Beethoven) X Beethoven
                                    5724

Joy (Gadsby) [SLSDMRDT,
LSSLMS, SM] B552; C552b
                                    5725

Joy (Poppen) [MDMRLTRS, S

LSLTDMM] M171   5726
Joy-bells (Tucker) [SSLSF#SD
  SLSF#S,SFFF] AP774   5727
-----. R [SDRM,RDTLSFMS,
  SDRM]   5728
Joy cometh in the morning
  (Lorenz) [DRMSSDLDS,MSLSM
  DM] BE425   5729
-----. R [RMRDRMS,LFLDLSM,
  SL]   5730
Joy of man's desiring (Schop)
  X Jesu joy of man's desiring
                        5731
Joy to the world (Handel) X
  Antioch   5732
Joyful song (Allen) [MSDMRMRDT
  LSD,MSDM] AH313; AM683;
  AS112; AT137; AU355; AV326;
  AW438; BB645; BY215   5733
Joys are flowing (Marshall) X
  Marshall   5734
Joys seven (English trad) [SD
  DDRMRD,DRRTTD,SD] BG70
                        5735
-----. R [DRRRRRMFM,RMM
  MRMF]   5736
Jubilate (Dahle) [DDDLTDRTS,
  RRDTDRM] O358   5737
Jubilate (Farrer) [SDTLSLRSF
  M,F#SSLTLS,] D440   5738
Jubilate (Parker) [SDSMDL,SFM
  FSRM,MMMF#] A350a; B521;
  C521a; J436a; S193b; Y346;
  AC131; AD179; BB133; BC151;
  BD121; BF520   5739
-----. R [SRMFSMFS,LFLRDT]
                        5740
Jubilate (Parry) [DMDSMLM,
  FSMDRM,MSM] BY67   5741
Jubilation (Genevan Psalter) X
  Psalm 138   5742
Jubilee (Mozart) [MMMSDRM,
  FMLSSFFMM] V599   5743
Jubilee (Sullivan) X Bishopgarth
                        5744
Judah (Doty) [SSDLSDMRRD,RM
  SMRD] L575b   5745
Judah's Lion (Bohemian trad)
  [DMSDSLTD,DSLSSFMR] Q211
                        5746
Judas Maccabaeus (Handel) [SM
  FSD,RMFSFMR,MFSL] J566;
  R209; Y285; Z244; AE127; AF

193; AR194; BK30; BV193b;
  BY164; BZ   5747
Jude (Jude) X Galilee   5748
Judea (Arnold) X Alexandria
                        5749
Judea (Dykes) [DMRDDTDFF
  MR,RSFMR] I104b   5750
Judge eternal, throned in splen-
  dor (Smart) X Regent
  Square   5751
Judgment (LaTrobe) [SSDDM
  DRD,MRDTLLS,S] AZ585-A;
  BA364   5752
Judson (Baker) X St Saviour
                        5753
Julian (Maker) [DDDTMLLS,
  DFFMSSF#S,] C251   5754
Julian (Richards) [SDMMRDRM
  FSLS,MMRR] AK293   5755
Julius (Shaw) [MRDRSDTLTS,
  SLTDRM] F584a; BV3
                        5756
Juniata (Beery) [DMSSLSSM,
  DDDRDLS,D] AR454; AS
  256   5757
-----. R [SSSSLSSM,DDDLT
  LS,D]   5758
Juniata (Wood) X St Stephen's
  Church   5759
Just as I am (Barnby) [SLDT
  SDRM,MMMFMRDT,] H173;
  I272a; J316a; L398; N181;
  O450; P405; Q390; R472; T
  389; U280; V296b; Y136; Z
  297; AA321; AB160; AC145;
  AD486; AE452; AG310; AJ
  111; AK347; AM523; AO262
  a; AP410a; AR344; AS408;
  AT249; AU411; AW393; BF
  349; BY442a; BZ   5760
Just as I am (Beck) [MMLSFM
  RD,MSRMMMRD] AZ277-B;
  BA934   5761
Just as I am (Bradbury) X
  Woodworth   5762
Just as seemeth good to thee
  (Hugg) [MFSSLSMS,LLSMM
  RDR,] AX493; AY123 5763
-----. R [RMFFFMRM,SSLL
  SMR,M]   5764
Just for today (Jones) X Belle-
  ville   5765
Just for today (Lee) [SLTDSM

FS, DFMMR, SLT] BN189
                        5766
Just for today (Montani) [MLL
  SDFFM, DDRR, MLLS] BQ143
                        5767
Just for today (Palmer) X Vincent
                        5768
Just outside the door (Ackley)
  [SMR#MRDLS, DTTDRD, SM]
  BB562   5769
-----. R [SFMD#RSMRDD, SDT
  TLS]   5770
Just when I need Him (Gabriel)
  [SSSSMRDRM, FSLDLLS] AI
  110; AS130; AT267; BB590
                        5771
-----. R [LLLLFD, SSSSMS,
  F#MRL]   5772
Jutland (Rung) [DSDRMRDS, LL
  SSDMR, D] M447   5773

K

Kabzeel (Crueger) X Graefenberg
                        5774
Kaerlighen fra Gud (Jaehnigen)
  X Charity   5775
Kalman (Kálmán) [SSLSMRDTD,
  DMRTRDT] AK62   5776
Kalmar (Swedish mel) [DDLLTS
  DD, MFRSSF#S, M] J485; K357;
  N289; P316   5777
Kane (Mason) [SDRMRD, SLTDLS,
  SDRM] J165; K308; N474
                        5778
Kathrine (Gabriel) [SDMMMSFF, F
  RTLTD, SM] AJ116a 5779
Keble (Dykes) [SSLLSDRM, MSF
  MRDRM] D167a; F85; G62; I
  82; V535; AA360; AB149; AO
  152; AS355; BX493; BZ 5780
Keble (Sewall) [MMMMFMRD,
  MMMSMDFM] BR125 5781
Kedron (Dare) [DTLLMMRDT,
  DTLLLTL] A81; AF165; AQ
  114; BZ   5782
Kedron (Spratt) [MMMMRR, FFF
  M, SFMR#MM,] D344b; G333;
  H282; I453; L428b; N449; V408b;
  AM411; AT206; BA414 5783
Kee hinay kachomer I (Jewish
  trad) [MLLMMSLSFM, MSSLTD]
  BH166   5784

Kee hinay kachomer II (Jewish
  trad) [SSLSFMFS, SRDDFF
  MM] BH172   5785
Kee vayom (Lewandowski) [S
  SF#SRSSR#DSR#R#FSR#D,]
  BH322   5786
-----. R [DSLLSSDRRMD,
  DSSLT]   5787
Keep me near thee (Warren)
  [MMRDMSLS, MMRDSMR, M]
  AX506   5788
-----. R [SSSSLLLL, TTTT
  DDD, M]   5789
Keep thou my way (Main)
  [MRDSDT, SDRMRFM, MRD]
  AO333   5790
Keep us close to thee (Show-
  alter) [DRMMFSLS, MRDSS
  LSM] AY76   5791
-----. R [SLSLTDD, LLSSM
  RDR, M]   5792
Keine schönheit hat die welt
  (Joseph: in Scheffler's See-
  lenlust) [MFSFMRRD, MR
  $\overline{MF\#SSF\#S,}$] E586; F429;
  X559; BE366; BY484 5793
Keith (Sanders) [MMLMLDM
  FMRDTL, DRD]   AQ101
                        5794
Keller (Lowry) [SSDMRDSD, R
  DRM, RDDL] L419; AE286;
  AX514   5795
Keller's American hymn (Kel-
  ler) X American hymn
                        5796
Kelley (Sherwin) [SFMMRDLS,
  MRDSMR, SF] AU166; AV
  312; AX578; BB550 5797
-----. R [DDDDTLSM, RMFL
  SMS, D]   5798
Kelso (Hopkins) [DDDFMRD,
  DLSDMRR, DD] D4; K448;
  AD247; AM328; AS20; BA
  770; BF184; BR5   5799
Kemerton (Spohr) X Leyden
                        5800
Kemper (Morse) [DMSSLSFMR,
  MFSDRM] A490   5801
Kendal (Cottman) [MMRDDFD
  M, MDTTLS, SL] AB74
                        5802
Kendal (Somervell) [MRMFRS
  D, FMDRDTD, MLL] A496;

B501; C501; E566; X314; BB
675   5803
Kenosis (Bliss) X I gave my life
for thee   5804
Kensington new (Tilleard) [SDM
RDMSF, MMRLDRD, D] K513;
N8; Y329   5805
-----. V [SSDMRDMSF, MMRLD
RD,] Y329   5806
Kent (Lampe) [SMTDLSFM,
MRSF#SLTL] E347; F71; W
225; X524; BV120; BY178; BZ
                                  5807
Kent (Stanley) [DDLSMRTD,
DRMRTLS, D] AL329   5808
Kerr (Laufer) [MTDFMRLTD
T, DRMLSF] S324; Z403
                                  5809
Kerry (Jowett) [DSDRMFFM,
SDMFSLMR,] W233   5810
Keston (Stainer) X Oxford 5811
Keynsham (Spencer-Palmer)
[MDMLSFMR, RMRSMLMT,]
BV578   5812
Khanta zagun (Basque trad) X
Golden sheaves   5813
Kiddush (Jewish trad) [SDDDD
DD, SSDDDDTDR,] AHp. 148;
BH303   5814
Kidlington (Reinagle) [MRDFRD
TD, MMMF#LSFM,] V102
                                  5815
Kiel (Lutkin) [MMMMFLLS, F
MMMF#LLS,] I140   5816
Kildrostan (Evans) [LLMLTDRD
TDL, MRDTL] W461   5817
Kilgetty (Irish trad) [DSSLTLS
MDRMS, DSSL] BV356; BY
130b   5818
Killin (Gaelic trad) [LDTMDTL,
TDTLDTL, LD] W570   5819
Kilmarnock (Dougall) [DMSLSMMR
D, LSDLSDR] A414; E542; F69;
R125; S28; W400; X522; AD91;
AK230; AL672; AP97; AW338;
BV143; BY423   5820
Kilmorey (Lloyd) [LLTDRMT,
TDTLDT, S#LT] W470b; AL
320b   5821
Kimigayo (Japanese trad) [SLSTR
TL, TRMRMLF#MR,] Y310
                                  5822
Kindle the taper (Binder) [DDDD

SDFMMRRD, MFSM] BH205
                                  5823
Kindle the taper (Singer) [MM
MSSRRRRF, FDRDRM] BH
204   5824
King Edward (Sydenham) [SM
DSRD, DFDMMR, SDSD] C
261a; D369a; Y243; AC183;
AD293   5825
King Herod and the cock (Eng-
lish trad) [MLLDRDLS, MLL
DRD, DR] BG54   5826
King of glory (Parker) [DM
FSDT, LSDFMFM, MRM]
D482a   5827
King of love (Malim) [DFM
RFMRD, MLDFRDT, S] D156a
                                  5828
King of my life (Kirkpatrick)
X Lest I forget   5829
King Olaf (Webbe) [DDTDLS,
LMLS#LT, D#TD#L] Y15
                                  5830
Kingdom (Copes) [SLSDDTLS,
LTDRMRDR,] BZ   5831
Kingdom (German trad. 16th c)
X Freiburg   5832
Kingdom of God (English mel)
[SSDFMR, DDTLS, LLTDR]
BY554   5833
Kingly Vale (Allen) [SMRD
LSLTD, TLSLMRD] BE81;
BY729   5834
Kingo (---) [SSMFRDDFMRM,
MRF#SL] J284   5835
King's College (Mann) [MFST
DD, LSFMR, MFSTD] B524;
C524a; D133b   5836
King's College (Walker) [DT
LSMRRD, SSDLTDRR,] AP
452b   5837
Kings in glory (Shaw) [SDD
RMMRMDLS, RMDLS,] BG
194   5838
King's Land (Lindeman) [SD
LDS, MRSFMRDLLLS,]
M302; P345   5839
King's Langley (English trad)
[MFSSMMFFMR, RMMF
S[S]D] E221; W608; X229;
AX574a; AW385   5840
King's Lynn (English trad)
[MRMLTDRS, FMRDLSL,]

Knocking at the door (Everett)
[MMMMRDDL, SDMSMR, MM]
AX245; AY374   5876
-----. R [LLLLLSM, SLSSMR,
MMM]   5877
Know this, that every soul is
free (Stephens) [SDSLTDRM,
MFMRDTLS,] BC90   5878
Knowhead (Gabriel) [SSSLTLS, SD
DRRM, MFF] AJ356   5879
Knowlton (Harding) [SSLTDRDT,
DDRRFMRM,] AP743   5880
Knowsley (Hopkins) [MRDRMLSSFM,
RMF#SLT] Z460   5881
Knox (Havergal) X Evan   5882
Kocher (Knecht) X Knecht 5883
Kodosh (Sulzer) [SMSFSSSSSM,
RRMFMR] BH285   5884
Koenigsberg (Albert) X Waltham
                         5885
Kol nidre (Jewish trad) [MLS#
MMS#LDLM, LS#LTDT] BH318
                         5886
Kolding (Lutkin) [MMMRDM, RRR
DMT, LLSF] I112c   5887
Kom, du folkefrelser sand
(Walther, G-B. 1524) X Veni,
redemptor   5888
Kom helligaand, Herre Gud
(Erfurt G-B. 1524) X Komm
Heilege Geist, Herre Gott 5889
Komm helligaand, med skaber-
magt (Sarum plainsong, M 8)
X Veni creator   5890
Kom hid til mig, enhver isaer
(German. 15th c) X Kommt
her zu mir   5891
Kom, huldaste forbarmore (Hed-
berg) [DMFSDTLS, MFLSMRD,
D] N298   5892
Komm, Gott schöpfer Heiliger
Geist (Sarum plainsong M 8)
x Veni creator   5893
Komm Heilige Geist, Herre Gott
(Erfurt G-B. 1524) [SLSMSR
MF#S, SLSRFMR] J122a; K146a;
M471; N154; O375; Q224; AA257;
AZ203-A   5894
-----. V [SLSMRMFS, SLSRFMR
D,] N154   5895
-----. V [SLSFMRMF#S, SLSR
FMR] AZ203-A   5896

Komm, o komm, du Geist des
lebens (Meiningen G-B.
1693) X St Leonard   5897
Komm, seele (Franck) [SDSL
SFMM, SFMRRDD, M] E486;
F340; J182b; W176; X255a;
AN316   5898
-----. V [SDSLSFMM,SFMRDD,
MR] AN316   5899
Kommet ihr hirten (Bohemian
trad) [SSMLFSSMLFSMSRMD,]
Y308; AD108; AK111; AW79;
BD221   5900
Kommt her zu mir (German,
15th c) [LLLMRMDT, LDT
DRMRD] J156b; K196; M90;
O85; P110; Q263; AA276
                         5901
-----. V [LLLMRMDT, LDT
DRMRDT,] P110   5902
Kommt, ihr seelen, nehmt zu
herzen (German, Old) X
Stabat mater   5903
Kommt seelen (Bach) X
Rinkart   5904
Korea (Tai Jun Park) [MS
FRDM, SLSMFR, DDSF]
BY664   5905
Koschat (Koschat) X Poland
                         5906
Kozeluch (Kozeluch) [MFS
MDTLSSM, DRMFSS] L28
                         5907
Kremser (Dutch trad) [SSLS
MFSFMRMD, SS] A315; G20;
J450; P20; Q468; R17; S461;
Y27; Z117; AB63; AC29; AD
22; AE25; AF21; AG10; AH
185; AI7; AK19; AM83; AN
327; AO80; AQ22; AR9; AT
11; AW15; BB8; BD17; BE
292; BI14; BK137; BL91;
BZ   5908
Kreuznach (German mel) X
Er freut euch   5909
Kücken (Kücken) [MRDMSLSM,
MRDDRMRD,] L461a; U39;
V392; AC227; AO255;
                         5910
-----. V [MRDMSLSM, MRD
DRMMR] U39   5910a
Kybald Twychen (Harris) [SS

LSLDTD, MMRSLTDT,] F614
5911
Kyrie, Gott Vater (Latin, ca 800)
[SLT, LDDTLLS, LLSFMM]
Q6 5912

L

Laban (Mason) [MFSSSDS, MR
DTLS, MFS] C118; D504b;
G277; H296; I429; K272b; L
538; R363; T122a; U295; V
470; Y378; Z370; AA379; AD294;
AE255; AH451; AI325; AJ178;
AM14; AN299a; AO393; AR328;
AS327; AT397; AU247; AV177;
AX163; AY36; BA580; BB358;
BD113; BF477; BX360; BZ
5913
Labor (Smith) [LDRMMFRM, DM
FSSLF] A510 5914
Labor on (Doane) [DRMMMRDRDL
DLSDDT] AU327; AX183; AY
528 5915
-----. R [DRMRDL, TDRRMDR,
MFS] 5916
Lacrymae (Sullivan) [MMMFSDR
M, SSDTLLS, L] B137; C327;
D222a; H283; W314b; AZ253-C;
BA300; BF597; BR292 5917
Lacy (Campbell) [MSMRMFM,
FSMLFR, SSF] V668 5918
Lady in sorrow (A Monk of Geth-
semani) [DRTDMSSLF#S, MFS
FMR] BN176 5919
Lady of the visitation (Mainz
G-B. 1661) [SFMMFMRR,
MRDRDTL, D] BN150; BO96
5920
Ladywell (Ferguson) [SDRMSFM
R, DRMRDSFM,] F297; W139b;
BV265b; BY180a 5921
Laetabundus (Gatty) [SSSSSMLSF
MRMDRMF] E22b 5922
Laetabundus (Hopkins) [SSLTDLT,
DRMRD, SSLT] D114b 5923
Laetabundus (Plainsong, 11th
c. M 5) [DRDRMD, FSLSFS
LFSF] E22 5924
Lafayette (Herbert) [SSFMMMRD,
DTLDFLS, S] T168a; AJ247a;
AM26b 5925

Lafayette (Stewart) X St
Helen's 5926
Lagergren (Lagergren) X Gud,
var gud 5927
Lahee (Lahee) X Wimbledon
5928
Laissez paitre vos bêtes
(French, ancient) X The
band of children 5929
Lake Enon (Woodbury) [SSMM
RD, SSFFMR, RMSS] G335;
L470; S246a; Z314; AE271;
AK254; AO377; AR451
5930
Lamb of God (Decius) X O
Lamm Gottes 5931
Lambdin (Cassel) [SDDDD,
RMMMMM, SDDD] AT407;
AU374 5932
-----. R [LLLFL, DDDSS,
F#F#F#F#SF#] 5933
Lambeth (Akeroyd) [DMMM
FSSLSF#S, LLSSF] E340;
X346 5934
Lambeth (Schulthes) [MMMFTL
TD, DRMSFMR, M] B279b;
C85d; D346b; H386; I190;
J246; L80; N278; R32; T220;
U81; V137; Y5; Z436; AB
101; AC72; AD84; AE156;
AG115; AH237; AJ313; AM
428; AO146; AP734b; AR
242; AS178; AW185; BA86;
BB213; BF236; BO196; BR
402b; BX477 5935
Lamb's Hill (Lee) [SMFMRD,
SDLSFM, SDTL] AZ71-B
5936
Lambs of Jesus (German) [MF
SDMDLD, FLSDTLS, M] M
39 5937
Lament (Persichetti) [MRR
MRDSRMTLF#, F#SF#M]
AQ314 5938
Lammas (Brown) [MRDDTDSFM
R, RMFTL] A202b; B330;
D220a; O150; BR475 5939
Lamp of our feet (Schop) X
Jesu joy of man's desiring
5940
Lancashire (Smart) [SSMFLS
M, DDFSLR, SSM] A257;

B61; C477; D255; G278; H177;
I387; J550; K13; L129; M101;
N590; Q205; R208; S115; T373;
U120; V179; W123; Y177; Z
247; AB144; AC127; AD160; AE
125; AF192; AG99; AH278; AI
357; AK99; AL182; AM197;
AN196; AO112; AP296; AQ316;
AR215; AS255; AT417; AU236;
AV210; AW115; AZ151-M; BA
229; BB135; BD47; BF297; BI
44; BK78; BR62; BX204; BZ
                                        5941
Lancaster (Howard) [SDRMDFM
R, RMDTLS, SL] J211; K205;
M20; O454; W116; AP99a; AQ
106   5942
Land of our birth (Floyd) [SSSDS
TLS, MDRMDTLS,] C367a; BY
644   5943
Land of our hearts (Lester) [DR
MRDRLSFM, MFLSMM] Y284
                                        5944
Land of rest (American trad)
[SDDRMSDDLS, SDDRM]
A585a; J587a; AF312   5945
Land of rest (Miller) [DRMMMM
SMMR, DRDRRM] AT284; AU167;
AV398; AX203; AY306; BB662
                                        5946
-----. R [SSSLSMR, DMRMSS,
SSS]   5947
-----. V [DRMMMMSMMD, RD
RRMS] BB662   5948
Land of rest (Newman) [SMM
FMRLS, MDDTDR, SM] V615;
AC321   5949
Land of the mountains high
(Stephens) [SDMMR#M, MRFFM,
SDMMR#] BC140   5950
Landskron (Bohemian hymnal,
1531) [SDRDTLSLTD, MSLSMD]
Sap. 38   5951
Lane (Lane) X Penitence   5952
Lanesboro (Dixon) [DSSLTDSFM,
SLFRDTD,] H104; V68; BI23-
D; BR37   5953
-----. V [SDSLTDSFM, SLFRDTD]
BR37   5954
Langa (Soto) [MMFSSSMFSLL,
RRMFF] Eap. 60; Y90; AD463;
BY777   5955
Langdale (Somervell) [MMSDRM

FM, F#SLTLSF, M] E590
                                        5956
Langdon (Campbell) [MRLLS
S, MDDTLS, LRDT] V660
                                        5957
Langdon (Langdon. Divine
harmony) [DDDDD̄D̄RM, MM
M̄RDFMR,] AO306; AP90c;
BA670   5958
Langemarck (Jones) [SSFM
RDTDFMR, FMLF#F#] C491;
AP566   5959
Langford (Langford) [MMR#
MMSFMR#M,SMSFMF] M203;
O484   5960
Langham (Shaw) [MRDTLDRM
DSM, LSMS] A532; R486;
X326; Y247; AD362; AF445;
AK401   5961
Langport (English trad) [MM
MMRD, SSSS, MMMMRD] E
656b   5962
Langran (Langran) [MDRMSF
MMRD, MMRSRF] A58; B
129; C129; D82; F116; G495;
I284; J366; K324a; L389; N
121; R341; S174; T148; U
41; V283; W323; Y11; Z347;
AB311; AD399; AE326; AF
287; AG159; AH510; AI23;
AJ218; AK31; AL220; AM
467; AN40; AO1; AP354;
AR550; AW303; AZ32-F; BA
256; BB289; BD71; BE390;
BF384; BR295; BX41; BZ
                                        5963
Langstaff (Stebbins) X Holiness
                                        5964
Langton (Streatfeild) [MMMSF
M, DDDRFFM, MMM[L345;
BR307   5965
Languentibus in purgatorio
(Plainsong) [LDRDFMRDT
DD, MSLSF] BQ249   5966
Lanherne (Hayman) [MMFSS
DDTLSM, MRDFM] Y209;
AB265; BF507   5967
-----. V [MMFSSSDTLSM,
MRDFM] BF507   5968
Lanier (Hansen) X Hour of
prayer   5969
Lanier (Lutkin) [MMMMRDRL
L, DTLS#L, MM] G132; I745;

U99; Y84; Z225; AC119; AD
145; AH277; AR161; AT90; AV
114; BB128   5970
Lansdowne (Greenwood) [DSFM
RDRLS, LTDRFMS] BE220
5971
Lansing (Gabriel) [SMRDMFSLT
DS, DTSRD] AJ58   5972
Laramie (Bode) [LSMDLDRM,
SDRMRDL, L] A432   5973
Larghetto (Beethoven) X Alsace
5974
Larue (Pleyel) X Seasons 5975
Lassen (Danish mel) [MRMDSDR
M, SFMLSSMR,] M311   5976
Lasset uns mit Jesu ziehen
(Bolze) X Walk with Jesus
5977
Lasst uns alle (Dresden. G-B. ,
1632) X Dresden   5978
Lasst uns erfreuen (Cologne G-B.)
X Vigiles et sancti   5979
Last hope (Gottschalk) X Mercy
5980
Last sleep (Barnby) X Requiem
5981
Lasus (Mann) [SLTDDRMFM,
SFMRMRD] D315; AA70
5982
Latakia (Taylor) [DRMMMMFMM
RDRM, MFS] T31; AJ45; AX
328   5983
Lathbury (Sherwin) X Bread of
life   5984
LaTrobe (LaTrobe) [MMLLTT
D, DLSMRFM, MM] K83; AZ
581-A; BA204   5985
LaTrobe's 121st metre (LaTrobe)
[MDLSFM, LRFDTL, MR#MS]
AZ121-C   5986
LaTrobe's 166th metre (LaTrobe)
[LLTDMRDT, DRFMRDTD,]
AZ166-B   5987
LaTrobe's 578th metre (LaTrobe)
[SFMR, DSDTLS, TDLFMR,]
AZ578-B   5988
LaTrobe's 586th metre (English
trad) [DDDDTLSFMFS, DDLLS]
AZ586-A   5989
Latter day (Beecher. Plymouth
collection) [SLSMDLSM, DLS
MDRM, R] AO482; BB359
5990

Laud (Dykes) [SDDDRMRD,
SFMMRR, RM] D559a; I34;
K131b; L105; V202; AA102
5991
Lauda anima (Andrews) [SM
RDDFLLS, SMSDTLSF#]
AR34   5992
Lauda anima (Goss) [SSSSDTLS,
FMLSMFR] A282; B258;
C258; D421b; E470; F365;
J160a; K289; L273; O129;
R31; S14; W21; X623; AD21;
AF16; AL17; AM63; AP91;
AR76; AS7; AY424; BA652;
BE280; BL83; BM45; BN177;
BV247; BY23; BZ   5993
Lauda, Sion (Catholic) [SDSM
RFMRD, RSRFMSF] BO253
5994
Lauda Sion (Cobb) X Cobb
5995
Lauda Sion (Plainsong sequence,
M 7) [MSLSDTLS, LTSMFMR]
A193a; E317   5996
-----. V [RSLSDTLS, LTSMF
MR] E317   5997
Lauda Sion (Plainsong, M 7)
X Ecce panis angelorum
5998
Lauda Sion salvatorem (Cobb)
X Cobb   5999
Laudate dominum (Gauntlett)
X Cobern   6001
Laudate dominum (Gauntlett)
X Gauntlett I   6002
Laudate dominum (Parry) [SM
DRS, DLSFM, SMRSD, T] F376a;
W168a; AL44; AM288; BV23;
BY37   6003
Laudate dominum (Schubert)
[SDTLSLLS, DMDSMSFM]
BQ254   6004
Laudate dominum (Stralsund
G-B. 1665) X Praise to the
Lord   6005
Laudes domini (Barnby) [MF
SLDTL, SLTDMR, DTD]
A367; B37; C37a; D445a;
F223b; G31; H29; I32; J416;
K310; M556; R41; S3; T323;
U453; V29; W167; Y201; Z
135; AB77; AC2; AD43; AE40;
AF35; AG21; AH158; AK43;

AL45b; AM131; AN92a; AO19;
AP255b; AR46; AS19; AT23;
AU7; AV2; AW21; BA128; BB
43; BD4; BF176; BI116; BK38;
BR2; BV271; BY685a; BZ
6006
Laudon (Thalben-Ball) [DSS
MD, FMRMD, SDMRTL] BE
300   6007
Lauds (Redhead arr) [SLSSDRRD,
SLSSDMRR,] D160b; T14b;
AJ23b; AP653a   6008
Laufer (Perkins) [MMFSDDT,
DRMFFM, MR#M] G468; AB
375   6009
Launch out into the deep (Carter)
[DDMFSSSLDLS, SLLLS]
AU45   6010
-----. R [SDSTLS, SSMDMR,
MRDM]   6011
Lauree (Huffaker) [SSRFMRDTM
RRD, TLMM] AR86   6012
Laurel Hill (---) [MFSMSDDTT,
RMFSLSS] BB72   6013
Laurinus (Swedish Koralbok, 1697)
[LMMRRDDT, LTDRDT, TD]
J146a; M317; N628   6014
Laus deo (Bach) [DSLSFMRDT
DRS, LTDR] F422   6015
Laus deo (Gower) [MMMSSF,
TDDRRM, SSSL] AP633b
6016
Laus deo (Redhead) X Redhead,
No. 46   6017
Laus matutina (Stainer) [MSM
DRMSDTLS, SMRDD] AB5; AZ
552-B; BI45; BR3; BX270
6018
Laus regis (Fischer) [DMDMSD,
SSMFSM, MRSF#] J436b; K126;
L589; AS156   6019
Laus sempiterna (Prout) [SDDDS
DDD, SMFSLMR, S] W211b
6020
Laus sempiterna (Reay) [MMM
SDLS, DFMRD, MMMS] D128b
6021
Laus sempiterna (Scottish Presby-
terian hymnal) [MMMMSDDD,
SMFSLMR, S] AO610b   6022
Laus tibi (German processional)
X Laus tibi Christi   6023
Laus tibi Christi (German proces-

sional) [SSSSLS, FMRRD,
SSSSL] E534; X388; AN430
6024
Lausanne (Lausanne Choral buch)
X Broadlands   6025
Lausanne (Haydn) X Greenland
6026
Lawes' Psalm 47 (Lawes) X
Psalm 47   6027
Lavington (Congregational
Church Music. 1871) [DRMM
FSLSFM, MFSDFM] AP578
6028
Lawes (Lawes) X Psalm 32
6029
Lawson (Lawson) [SSMMRRDD,
LLDDLLS, S] BB266   6030
-----. R [TDRRDRMM, RMFF
MDR, S]   6031
Layriz (Layriz Collection, 1853)
[LDTLDMRM, MDDFMRD#
R] E440; F357   6032
L'cho adonoy (Ephros) [SDDRM
MFSLS, MMMLSF] BH291
6033
L'cho dodee (Lewandowski) X
How good it is to thank the
Lord   6034
Le P'ing (Chinese trad) [DRM
DLSLS, DRMSMS, DR] AF
486; BZ   6035
Le vermeil du soliel (Muret)
X Gems of day   6036
Lea (Summers) [SMDLSDRM,
SMDLLS, RM] M56   6037
Leach (English trad) [DSL
SFMRDFMRDTD, RM] H179
6038
Lead, kindly light (Dykes) X
Lux benigna   6039
Lead me (Davis) X Lead me,
Saviour   6040
Lead me gently home (Thomp-
son) [MFF#SLSMDDTLS,
FSRT] AU123; AW449
6041
-----. R [SMDLSTRSSMDLS
TRS]   6042
Lead me into life eternal
(Schreiner) [DDRSMRDS,
LTDDDTDR,] BC141 6043
Lead me, Lord (Wesley, S.
S.) [MRDFMRDMMR, SMRD

RM] R539; AE460; AF524;
AG335; AR617; AT522; BZ
                              6044
Lead me on (Pollock) [SSDDDD
RMMM, MMRRRM] AX497;
AY114   6045
-----. R [MFSLSM, MFSSSMR,
MFS]   6046
Lead me, Saviour (Davis)
[SMSDTLS, FMRLSFM, SS]
AH407; AR467; AU104; AV
370; AW502; AY121   6047
-----. R [SMDS, MRDLSMRMF,
MMM]   6048
Lead me to Calvary (Kirkpatrick)
X Lest I forget   6049
Lead me to some soul today
(Loveless) [DMMRDFF, LSDM
SRMR, D] AU323   6050
Lead on, lead on (McKinney)
[SSMRDSLS, DRMFRDD, S]
AU460   6051
-----. R [SLSSLS, SSLSDRM, RM
F]   6052
Lead on, thou God of hosts
(Gillis) [MMRDMFMR, LSD
SFM, MR] U302   6053
Lead us, great teacher Paul
(Slovak hymn) [SFFMFSLFM
MR, MRRDD] BQ99   6054
Leaf (---) [SSSSLLSS, DDTLTD,
SM] T130; AJ190   6055
Leamington (Nicholson) [MRD
DDRMSFMR, RRMFM] F385b
                              6056
Lean on His arms (Jones) [SM
MMR#MFMRD, SRRD#RF]
AX471; AY455   6057
-----. R [MMR#MFMRDR, FF
MFSFM]   6058
Lean on my ample arm (Stephens)
[MR#MSFM, TDRS, MR#MS
SS#,] BC260   6059
Leaning on Jesus (Showalter)
[MMMRDRRRDL, SSDTDR]
AH390; AI401; AM718; AT371;
AU276; AW489; AX49; BB611
                              6060
-----. R [MDDL, SDTDRMMR,
MDDL]   6061
Leaning on the everlasting arms
(Showalter) X Leaning on
Jesus   6062

Leave it there (Tindley, arr)
X The roll (Black)   6063
Leave your burden (Lillenas)
[SDMR#MRD, DDRDTLS, SD]
AU334; AX364   6064
Leave your burden at the place
of prayer (Lillenas) X Leave
your burden   6065
Leavell (McKinney) [SDDDMFS,
DTDRTD, SDD] AT423; AU
91   6066
-----. R [SFMFSMRM, DTDR
MRR, S]   6067
Lebanon (Allen) [SLSMDRMRD,
MSMLSSF#] BB21   6068
Lebanon (English) [SSLTDSS,
FMFLSMS, SM] BR498 6069
Lebanon (Zundel) [SDDDTDR,
SRRRDRM, SM] H212; L128;
V382; AI222; AJ82; AM396;
AV171; BA454   6070
Lebbaeus (St Alban's Tune
Book, 1866) [MMMRDDS, DD
RRMMR,] A229; B141; C141;
D528; K84b; L256; M398;
V132; W469; AB136a; AK542;
AP432; BF313a; BR503
                              6071
Ledbury (---) [SDTLSFM, FLS
RFFM, SD] BR33   6072
Lee (McKinney) [SSSLTDS,
LLDTLS, SRR] AT434; AU
347   6073
----. R [SMSDS, LTDDTLS,
FRST]   6074
Lee (Nash) [SSDMDDLSSS,
DSFMSD] AN86   6075
Lee (Swisher) [MSDMLSDMRD,
TDRMFS] BD52   6076
Legion (Brown) [DLSMFRDT,
DSSSFMR, D] D620a   6077
Leicester (Bishop) [MMLS#LR
DTLS#, S#LSFML] E322; J
175; W6; X605; AQ86; BE289;
BJ12   6078
Leicester (Hurst) [SSMRDDRM
FM, SDRMSF] S498; V70;
W316; AL223; AP363a; BA
298   6079
-----. V [SMRDDRMFM, SDRM
SFM] V70   6080
Leigh (Reinagle) [MMRDLSFM,
MSMLSFMR,] AA455 6081

Leighton (Greatorex) [MMRDRM,
SSFMRD,SSLS] C408b; D333b;
H113; I493a; L277b; U128; V
213; AE72; AO68; AW230; BB
174   6082

Leighton (Leighton) [DRMFM
RDRM,MRMF#SRS] E180b;
X245; AL389; AM273; AP302;
BJ96   6083

Leila (McKinney) [SSFMDRMD,
DFFDRM,SS] AT332; AU451
                                   6084

-----. R [DFFLFMMS,MRSF#M
F#S,S]   6085

Leinbach (Leinbach) [DMFSDMR
D,DRMRSLTL] BA931   6086

Leipsic (As hymnodus sacer) X
Breslau   6087

Leipsic (Schein) X Eisenach
                                   6088

Leipzig (Mendelssohn) [SDTDRM
FRSFM,RDDMR] AC290 6089

Leithead (Pritchard) [MFSDDTLS,
MSDRD,MFS] W576b   6090

LeJeune (LeJeune) X Love divine
                                   6091

Leland (Fosbery) [MMMMMS,
SF#FMFR,DDDL] L31   6092

Lella (Pollock) X I love to
steal awhile away   6093

L'Emmanuello (Perosi) [MRSLF
SMR,MSFMRMD,S] B31a;
BQ44   6094

Lemon's Farm (Shaw) [SDRMRS,
SLSLDR,RRRR] X165   6095

Lenoir (Maclean) [DTLSML,LFM
RDT,DDDR] V490   6096

Lenox (Edson) [DDDSLS,SDR
MRD,DMSM] G189; H229; I
294; L249; N70; V234; AH365;
AM223; AO116; AP392; AR
574; AS190; AT250; AV165;
AX112; AY263; BA91; BZ
                                   6097

Leominster (---) [MR#MFMD,
RMFSFM,SF#SL] K168b;
L312   6098

Leominster (Martin) [MMMMM
F,FRRRMR,RMMS] D203b;
E361; G367; I283; J66; M365;
N175; O352; S247b; T22; W
464a; AA487; AB194; AE266;
AH526; AI92; AJ29; AK243;

AL313; AM125; AO294; AR
359; AZ595-B; BA101; BB
284; BF454; BR289;   6099

Leon (Mason) X Denny   6100

Leonard (Hiles) X St Leonard
                                   6101

Leonburg (German) [DMRFM
RRD,MDLRDTLS,] O557
                                   6102

Leoni (Jewish trad) [MLTDR
M,DRMFSM,TDR] A285a;
B253; C253a; D460a; E646;
F631; G5; H14; I4; J410;
K284a; Q40; R89; S8; V89;
W571; X398; Y300; Z124;
AD70; AF14; AG38; AHp.
152; AK61; AL25; AM32;
AN1; AP144; AQ6; AR38;
AW14; AZ345-A; BA19; BB
76; BE371; BF212; BH54,
277; BI5-D; BK58; BL97;
BR311; BV249; BX17; BY
30; BZ   6103

-----. V [MLTDRM,DRMFR
M,TDDD] BH54   6104

-----. V [MLTDRM,DRMFS
M,DDDD] BH277   6105

Les anges dans nos compagnes
(French carol) X Gloria
                                   6106

Les commandemens de Dieu
(Bourgeois) X Command-
ments   6107

Leslie (Campbell) [DMFSS
LLS,SFMRMFM,F#] V158
                                   6108

Lest I forget (Kirkpatrick)
[MMRDDFFM,MRDSMRMM]
AE295; AR453; AX111 6109

-----. R [RRMFLSFM,RRM
FLSFM,]   6110

Lest we forget (Blanchard)
[DTSLMSFM,MMMMMMRL]
U340; V745; Y288; Z560;
AC162; AH208; BB505; BF
633   6111

Let all on earth their voices
(Sheehan) [DDDSSLFS,SDRM
FSFM] BN180   6112

Let Christian hearts (French,
16th c) [MLTDRDTL,SLL
TSL,ML] BN16   6113

Let each man learn (---) [SS

DDRMFM, SMFRSRMR] BC91
6114

Let earth's inhabitants rejoice
(Robertson) [SDMLSFMRM,
SDRTSLS] BC93   6115

Let every creature (Bragers)
[DSFMDFMR, SDRMRDR, D]
BP99   6116

-----. R [SRMFRMSS, DFFMR
DMR]   6117

Let Him in (Excell) [MFSM
DLS, SLS, MFSMDL] AH337;
AU29; AX246; BB566   6118

Let hymns of joy (Cologne G-B.)
X Vigiles et sancti   6119

Let Israel trust in God alone (Lowenberg) [SDTDSMDL, SFMFSRM,
M] BH139   6120

Let Jesus come into your heart
(Morris) X McConnelsville
6121

Let me go (Hartsough) [DMMSDR
MS, LLSMSMR, D] AX614; AY
174   6122

Let not your heart be troubled
(Warren) [SSSF#SLSSD, DRDTL
SF] AX533   6123

-----. R [SFMDDMMR, RMFRRT
DS,]   6124

Let others see Jesus in your
(McKinney) X Coleman   6125

Let Sion in her beauty rise
(Edwards) [DMSDTLSFM, SDD
RR#M, R] BC262   6126

Let the beauty of Jesus (Jones)
[MMMRDMRDSSS, FFFMR]
AU317   6127

Let the deep organ swell (Montani)
[DLLDTLTD, SDRFMRDR,]
BQ105   6128

Let the deep organ swell (Raymond-Barker) [SLDTLSFM, R
MSFMRDT,] BO218   6129

Let the lower lights be burning
(Bliss) X Lower lights 6130

Let the whole creation ring
(Richards) [SLTDSLSD, TLS
MDLS, M] BR565   6131

Let the words of my mouth
(Baumbach) X In corde meo
6132

Let them come to see (Hildebrand) [SLSFMSD, TLSFMLS,

SL] AY370   6133

Let there be light (Mombach)
[SSFMDTLS, LSMFRRM, M]
BH141   6134

Let there be light I (Singer)
[MFSLLRDTDS, SLSFSF]
BH99   6135

Let there be light II (Singer)
[DDDSDMRD, MMMDMSFM,]
BH232   6136

Let the words abide (Dyson)
[DDRMFMRDR.] R547 6137

Let us all press on (Stephens)
[MFSDMSF#SLFMF, FMRT]
BC98   6138

Let us break bread together
(Negro spiritual) X Com-
munion spiritual   6139

Let us oft speak kind words
(Beesley) [SSDDDMRDTL,
LRSTRS] BC94   6140

-----. R [MFSSLSDRMMFM,
SDDM]   6141

Leuchars (Hately) [MMSFMR,
MDDRRM, MFMR] W553;
AP125   6142

Levabo (---) [LLSMDRM, MM
LDT, RDTL] BR340 6143

Lew Trenchard (English trad)
[MFMRMDRM, LLTDTLS#]
A177a; B417; C140; E591b;
X493; BM90   6144

-----. V [DMFMRMDRM, LLT
DTLS#] X493   6145

Lewars (Ohl) [MSDTLSSFM,
RDFMRF#S] K478 6146

Lewes (Randall) [MFRSDRTD,
FMLSFMFM] E250; F64;
W65a; X555a; AL64; AP
179   6147

Lexington (Smart) [DRRSSD,
LRMSFM, MF#SL] V466
6148

Leyden (Spohr) [MMRMFRS,
DTLSSFM, MM] I619; AB
53; BR237   6149

Leyden (Wilms) X Hague
6150

Libera nos (Taylor) [DLTDMLS
MM, SFMRDRR] BY413
6151

Liberation (German trad) [DS
LTDFMMR, MDTLLS, S]

Light (Lindeman) X Kjaerlighet er
lysets kilde   6187
Light divine (Gibbons) X Angel's
song   6188
Light of ages (Lloyd) [MMMMFR
T, DDRMSF#M, LL]   Y149
                                6189
Light of life (Mason) X Star
of peace   6190
Light of light (MacMillan)
[MDRMFMRM, LSTDFMMR,]
AP345   6191
Light of the soul (Freylinghausen
G-B, 1704) X Christe, wahres
seelenlichte   6192
Light of the world (---) [SDRMD
LS, DFMRDR, SDR] AK124;
AO518   6193
Light of the world (Bliss) [SDR
MMRDRDRM, MSSSS]   AE301;
AI392; AM679; AR473; AT88;
AU330; AW467; AX273   6194
-----. R [RRMRSF#MF#S,
RRMRSF#M]   6195
Light of the world (Himmel)
[MDSSSLSSM, SDTLLLR]   I192
                                6196
Light of the world (MacFarren)
[DTLSMDRMFMR, SMRDL]
AB75   6197
Like a river (Mountain) X Remo
                                6198
Like a strong and raging fire
(Root) [SSSSLSSD, SSSSLSR, S]
AH139; AI65b; BC340   6199
-----. V [SSSLSD, SSSLSR, SS
SL] AI65b   6199a
Like as a father (Hakes) [MR#
MFMRMRD, DSMRMRD,]   BB66
                                6200
Like the deer that yearns
(Gelineau) [SSLD, DDR, DDD
L, LRD, SS] BL54; BS p. 16
                                6201
Lilies of the field (Brunk)
[SSFMDRMF, FFFFLSFM,]
AY361   6202
Lille (French trad) [MRDRMFS
LSFM, MRFM, M] AL355;
AP799; AW394   6203
Lille Guds barn (Danish folk mel)
X Bairn   6204
Lily of the valley (Hays) X

Salvationist   6205
Lime Street (Shaw) [DDRTTD,
LDTSM, LLLSL] X85b; BE
279   6206
Limpsfield (Booth) [SSSLRMF
M, DFR, SSSLR] W680; AL
259a; BV330; BY399   6207
Limpsfield (Freeman) [MDRSS
LTDRFF, RMDLS] AD306;
BE210   6208
Lincoln (Paine) [MMFSSLLS,
SDLSRFMR,] AZ277-D
                                6209
Lincoln (Ravenscroft's Psalter)
[DRMRDDTD, DSFFMF, FM]
E140; F144; X171   6210
Lincoln (Vulpius) X Cana
                                6211
Lincoln's Inn (Steggall) [MF
SMFMRM, FSLSMRDR,]
D384   6212
Lind (---) [MMMMMMFM,
RRRRDRM, S] AI163; AS465
                                6213
Lindeman (Lindeman) [MRD
SLS, SFMDMR, MSSF#]   J575b;
O351; P163; AI428; AM550
                                6214
Lindesfarne (Dykes) [SSDSLD
R, MRDMRLTS, S] V169b
                                6215
Lindsey House (Hutton. Tunes
for the hymns) [DMFSDDTD,
MRDTLS, DM] AZ590-A,
BA240   6216
Lingham (Funk) [SDRMFSLSF
MDRTD, MF] AY421   6217
Lingwood (Gibbs) [DDRFMM
FL, SLLTDRM, M] BV662b
                                6218
Linton (Holmes) [MMRRDFFM,
MMSFMR, SS] AP347b
                                6219
Linton (Stanton) [MDFMRSD,
RMSFMR, SSL] BY233
                                6220
Linwood (Rossini) [MDRMSFM
RMD, SDMSLS] I496; AO223;
BE416; BH140   6221
Lisbon (Read) [DLSDRM, MRD
FMR, SDDD] H78; I64; L39;
T173b; V7; AE356; AJ25;
AM445; AO14; AX61; BR17

6222
Lischer (Schneider) [SDRMFLS,
DMSSFSFM, S] G394; H77; I
67; L47; U442; V61b; Z444;
AI90; AM325; AO185; AT21;
AU175; AV5; BB465;   6223
Lisle (Brethren hymnal, 1901)
[DMMRDTLDT, TLTDRM, T]
AQ148   6224
Listen to the gentle promptings
(Weber) X Wilmot   6225
Listen to the lambs (Negro
spiritual) [MRMDLD, MRM
DLD, MRMD] AH602   6226
-----. R [SSSSSMSSS, SSSSTTL]
6227
Litany (---) [SLSMMRD, LLDDFM
R, SL] AL606; AP776   6228
Litany (Brown) [MRDTDFM,
RMDTDRLT, T] E651   6229
Litany (Bunnett) X Agnes 6230
Litany (Carr) X Spanish chant
6231
Litany (Gower) X Gower's
litany   6232
Litany (Hervey) X Hervey's litany
6233
Litany (Monk) [DDTDTLS,DDTD
TLS, MM] J153b; K207   6234
Litany (St Alban's Tune book,
1866) X Lebbaeus   6235
Litany (Scheffler. Heilige seelen-
lust. 1657) X Scheffler 6236
Litany (Scholefield) X Litany,
No. 9   6237
Litany No. 1 (Bunnett) [SSLDFM
MR, SDTDRF#S, S] BR221
6238
Litany, No. 1 (Turpin) [SSLSDMR,
RRMFMRM, SF] D524   6239
Litany, No. 2 (St Alban's Tune
book, 1866) X Lebbaeus
6240
Litany, No. 2 (Turpin) [SSLSDSL,
LLTDTLS, TT] D525   6241
Litany, No. 3 (---) [SSF#SDLS,
DDTDRRR, SS] D526   6242
Litany, No. 4 (Whiting) [DDMSL
LS, MFSLRMFM, M] D527
6243
Litany, No. 5 (Hoyte) X
Lebbaeus (St Alban's Tune
book, 1866)   6244

Litany, No. 6 (Stainer) [MM
MMFRM, MRDTLLT, DT]
C142Ia; D529Ia   6245
Litany, No. 7 (Turpin) X
Turpin's litany   6246
Litany, No. 8 (Turpin) [TT
DMMRM, MRD#RLLL, LL]
C142IIb; D529IIb   6247
Litany, No. 9 (Scholefield)
[MMSMRDR, FFLFMRM, SS]
C142IIIa; D529IIIa; AP196a
6248
Litany, No. 10 (Monk) X
Words on the cross   6249
Litany of the Passion (Dykes)
[MMMMSRR, RRRRFDD, D]
A233a; B142b   6250
Litany of the Passion (Nichol-
son) [MRFMRDR, RMSFMR
RD#, R] F587   6251
Litlington Tower (Barnby)
[DMLSDDRD, FMRDSSF#S,]
L69; AB6   6252
Little Baddow (Gibbs) [MLL
SMFM, MRMDDT, MLL] X
646a   6253
Little brown church (Pitts)
X Wildwood   6254
Little clusters (---) [MFSDM
DDT, RMFTRFFM,] D577;
V332   6255
Little Cornard (Shaw) [LDRM
ML, SMDRML, DTLS] A131;
F269; J321; R478; W372; X
64; AF106; AL248; BV314;
BY374   6256
Little David (Negro spiritual)
[SSMSMDLS, DDMS, SSMS]
Y317   6257
Little flock (German, 15th c)
X Kommt her zu mir
6258
Little flower (Moskowski)
[MMR#R#MMS, SDDRRRSS,
M] Y14   6259
Little hands (Thomson) [DDSS
DR, RMFMFSM, SST] AP
780   6260
Little King, so fair (Slovak)
hymn) [DRMDTLTS, LTDMRD
TD] BQ125   6261
Little ones like me (Holsinger)
[MMMDFMR, RDRDRMD, MM]

RDDDTL, LSSDRR, SS]   BC97
                                6295
Lo, our Father's tender care
   (Rogers) [MMMDSSS, FFFRM
   S, MMM] BH82   6296
Lo! the clouds have burst
   (Cobb) X Moultrie   6297
Lo! the earth rejoices (Binder)
   [DDTDRR, MMRMF, SSFSL]
   BH248   6298
Lo! the heavens are breaking
   (German mel) [MMMFSM,
   FRMMR, MFSMF] AW434
                                6299
Lo! the mighty God (Stephens)
   [SSDRMRDSS, RMFFFFM,]
   BC264   6300
Lo, they come in glad procession
   (Bourgeois) X Bourgeois
                                6301
Lo, what a pleasing sight (Mason)
   X Gerar   6302
Lob sei demm allmächtigen Gott
   (Crueger) [DDRMSFMR, SDTL
   SSF#S,] J102; M513; N73; AZ
   22-C   6303
Lobe den Herren (Stralsund G-B.
   1665) X Praise to the Lord
                                6304
Lobe den Herren, o meine
   (Anhang der Seelen-harpff)
   [DSDDTDRMFFMR, RRMF]
   Q26; AF17; AK6; AW513 6305
Lobet den Herren (Crueger) X
   Oblation   6306
Lobet den Herren, ihr (Vulpius)
   [SSSMRDTDLS, SSMLSF]
   Q19; X475; AM4   6307
Lobet und preiset (German trad)
   [SSSSFMFMRD, MMMMRD]
   BK11   6308
Lobt den Herrn, die morgensonne
   (Evangelisches choralbuch
   Halle, 1829) [DMSDFMRR,
   RMRSTLST] Q461; AA160;
   AN24; AQ63   6309
Lobt Gott (Hermann) X Hermann
                                6310
Lobt Gott (Vulpius) X Lobet
   den Herrn, ihr   6311
Lobt Gott, ihr Christen (Hermann)
   X Hermann   6312

Lodsworth (English trad) [DM
   DFLSMRD, DMDFLSM] E275;
   X336   6313
Lofsongur (Bohemian Br., 1531)
   [MDMSLSF#S, FLFSFMRM,]
   M412   6314
Log College (Warren) [MMRLD
   TRD, MRSLDT, TD] C365; U
   329   6315
Logan (Modern harp) [SMRDDT
   LSDMR, RMRDT] BR291
                                6316
Lohengrin (Wagner) [SSMDM
   DDTL, LLSF#FMR] Y25
                                6317
Lombard Street (Russell) [LD
   MMRDRMRDLL, LDM] A575;
   X698; AF422; AN72; AR400
                                6318
L'Omnipotent (Bourgeois) [LSL
   TDRMRDTL, DTLSL] E538;
   F100; W95; X347; AF467;
   AN232; AQ234   6319
London (Sheeles) X Addison's
                                6320
London new (Scottish Psalter,
   1615) [DSMDSLDT, SDMSR
   D, SD] A310; B216; C216;
   D427; E394; F181; J369;
   N408; W520b; X503; AD89;
   AP34; AZ14-I; BA85; BD50;
   BJ40; BR263; BV319a; BY
   77a   6321
Londonderry (Irish trad) [TD
   RMRMLSMRDL, DMFS] C280
   b; G145; X230; Y79; Z236;
   AB394; AC109; AH473; AL
   512; AN559a; AW396; BE412;
   BF447; BV262; BY183
                                6322
Londonderry air (Irish trad)
   X Londonderry   6323
Lone Acre (Mueller) [MMMMMM
   RM, MLLLTT, ML] AK127
                                6324
Lonely midnight (Howard) [SS
   SLLSFMRD#RS, SSSL] Z203;
   AC89; AH251; BD215; BF287;
   BX531   6325
Lonesome Valley (American
   trad) [LDDMRDLD, DDD
   MMSLS,] BK168   6326

Long have they waited (Warren) [SMFSSSSLDDD, SSSDR] AX 214   6327
-----. R [SSSLSSDDDD, RRRR DD]   6328
Long live the Pope! (Ganss) [SDDDTLTDRM, MFMRDR,] BO206; BQ122   6329
Long Milford (Barnby) [SLRDTD RM, DFFMRDRT] BX507   6330
Long Mynd (Thatcher) [DDRDDTD, LSLSMFS, SL] X465   6331
Longden (Thompson) [SLDLSMRD, MSLSMDR, M] G153   6332
Longfellow (Bullard) [MMRRFF MM, MSMDRM, SS] AJ32 6333
Longstaff (Stebbins) X Holiness   6334
Longwood (Barnby) [MMFSMRDT D, MMF#STL] D422b; J320; S 48; T357a; W566; AD23; AM311; AN69; AO330; AR205; AS174; AT166; AV150; AW164; BF416; BI69; BX44   6335
Lonsdale (Troyte) [DDRMDFMR, RMSFMRDT,] AJ98   6336
Look down on us (Gibson) [SM RDFMRLSSF#, FFSRF] AV 420a   6337
Look for the beautiful (Belden) X Belden   6338
Look for the waymarks (Belden) [DMFSDMRDRM, MLTDDR] BB671   6339
-----. R [SSSSMRDDDRMM, LLTD]   6340
Look to the Lamb of God (Black) [MMFMSDRMFS, SSMDMR,] AX256   6341
-----. R [SSLSDT, RFSTLS, MMFS]   6342
Look up and see (Graun) [SDLS TD, RFMRDTTDD, L] AZ578- A   6343
Looking to Jesus (Keegan) [SSS SSSSLTDS, DTLLL] AU357   6344
-----. R [SSSM, MRDL, DLSSS DRM]   6345
Looking unto Jesus (Loes) [MM R#MSRRDRM, LLS#LDS] AU 132   6346

-----. R [SSF#SLSMSF#F, LLS#LTL]   6347
Lord, a little band (Showalter, arr) X When I see the blood   6348
Lord, accept our true devotion (Daynes) [SLSDTLLS, FMFL SFM, S] BC101   6349
Lord, accept into thy kingdom (Schreiner) [DRMSFMRD, MF#SSLSF#S,] BC100   6350
Lord, be thou with us still (Heller) [SDRMSMSLM, SDRMSMS] BH39   6351
Lord, cause thy face on us to shine (Mason) X Hebron   6352
Lord, dismiss us (Rousseau) X Greenville   6353
Lord, dismiss us (Sicilian mel.) X Sicilian mariners   6354
Lord, do thou guide me (Heller) [SMDTLSTRFM, SLL TLS,] BH22   6355
Lord, for tomorrow (Palmer) X Vincent   6356
Lord, give us a vision (Davis) [DMMMRDMSSLS, SMMMD] AX195   6357
-----. R [SDDDDTLS, DMM DRMR, S]   6358
Lord, I believe (Gould) [MD RMMMMMFS, SFMRFM] BR332   6359
Lord, I hear of showers of blessing (Bradbury) X Even me   6360
Lord, I want to be a Christian (Negro spiritual) X I want to be a Christian   6361
Lord, I'm coming home (Kirkpatrick) [SMMDDLDLS, DD MMR, SM] AI213; AL474; AP431; AS203; AT237; AX 302; BB560   6362
-----. R [MMDDDL, SMMDR, SMMDD]   6363
Lord, in this sacred hour (Shelley) [MSMFMF, RRR DTM, MRDT] BH112 6364
Lord, in thy presence (Havergal) X Evan   6365

Lorica patricii (Irish trad) [MF
 MRSFMRD, MFMRSDT] W505
 6403
-----. R [LDTLLTTDDRDTL
 SL, L]
 6404
Lorraine (Darmstadt G-B. 1698)
 X All saints
 6405
Los Angeles (Smith) [DDMMRD
 SS, FMDDRTLT,] I664b 6406
Lost and found (Tilleard) [SLLSS
 DDT, LLSDSFM, S] M634; O
 338
 6407
Lost forever (Warren) [SSSLSM
 D, DDDRDLS, SS] AX289 6408
Lost in the night (Finnish folk)
 [MMMDTLLLLSMD, RRRSL] P
 396
 6409
Lostwithiel (Turle) [SSSSSSS, SL
 LLTDT, DS] AB85 6410
Lottie (Bradbury) [SSMMRM,
 SSMMRD, SLLD] AY262; BB64
 6411
Loud let the swelling anthems
 rise (Norden) [SDDTTLLS,
 SMRDTL, LF] BH78 6412
Louez dieu (Genevan Psalter,
 1562) [DDFSLL#D, LDL#LFSF,
 LS] E377; X473 6413
Louez dieu (Minor reading: Gene-
 van Psalter, 1562) X Holy
 Name (Major reading) 6414
Loughborough (Briggs) [MSMRLT
 D, RMSLLR, RMF#] X194b;
 Y336 6415
Loughborough College (Briggs)
 [DMSDRTD, MRDTLLS, DM]
 X243; AN426 6416
Louisville (Zundel) [SDMRTD, SL
 DTLS, DTDR] AJ412 6417
Louvan (Taylor) [SSDRMDRDRM,
 MFMRMD] G307; H109; I266;
 J170; L526; S87; T188; U14;
 V208; Y1; Z151; AA235; AB
 187; AC31; AD85; AE57; AF90;
 AG44; AH215; AI33; AJ274;
 AK375; AO320; AR74; AS80;
 AV40; AW53; BB242; BF231;
 BZ 6418
-----. V [SDRMDRDRM, MFM
 RMDM] AD85 6419
Love (Gordon) X Gordon 6420
Love (Richardson) [DMRDFLSF
 M, SF#STLS, S] L156; AO82;

BA66 6421
Love (Young) [SSFFMMRD,
 DRMFLS, FM] BE30 6422
Love at home (McNaughton) X
 Home 6423
Love consecrates the humblest
 act (Showalter) X God
 moves ... 6425
Love divine (Hiller) [MMMRR
 DDT, DRMFMRRD,] AZ96-
 F 6426
Love divine (LeJeune) [DRM
 MFMMR, RMSFRMD,] A479
 b; B226; C226a; D432c; J
 397b; L189; N192; O114; S
 308b; Y85; AB277; AC191;
 AE415; AG243; AK392; AM
 460a; AO164; AR150; BA
 547; BF442 6427
Love divine (Sicilian mel) X
 Sicilian mariners 6428
Love divine (Stainer) [DDDRM
 RDTS, DSSF#SMR,] D207b;
 F205b; V701; BV625a; BX
 118a 6429
Love divine (Zundel) X
 Beecher 6430
Love divine, No. 2 (LeJeune)
 X Love divine 6431
Love each other (Byers) [MM
 DMLSSM, DDRRMFM, M]
 AX543 6432
-----. R [SDTLDLSM, SDT
 RDLS, M] 6433
Love found me (Gilmour) [DM
 SSSSSS, DSS, SLSSS] AX89;
 AY201 6434
Love incarnate (Pettman) [SL
 MRMDS, DRMFSDRMR,]
 BV105b; BY103b 6435
Love is come again (French
 trad) [LMF#RMD, RRMDTL,
 LMF#R] BG149; BN89; BZ
 6436
Love lifted me (Smith) [SLS
 MSLS, SLTDRT, LTL] AH
 340; AT212; AU352; AX
 330 6437
-----. R [MSRD, DMTL, LLTD
 SDD, R] 6438
Love not the world (Holsinger)
 [MRDSMRMD, DDDFFM, MR]
 AX409; AY385 6439

-----. R [RRMFLSFM, DDMSM
R, MR]   6440
Love of God (Beery) [MMMRDRD
T, RRRMDRM, S] AR88   6441
Love of the Father (Edmunds)
[LS#S#LTDTLLS#, LLSFMM]
BL99   6442
Love that will not let me go
(Peace) X St Margaret   6443
Love, the fount of light (Linde-
man) X Kjaerlighed er lysets
kilde   6444
Love unknown (Ireland) [MSLM
RD, RMFSML, LTLS] F192; W76
a; X127a; BV155; BY143a
                              6445
Lovely (Edwards) X Rhosymedre
                              6446
Lovely appear (Gounod) [MMSSLL
DDS, DDLLDS, M] AH619
                              6447
Lover den Herre (Stralsund G-B.,
1665) X Praise to the Lord
                              6448
Love's consecration (Kolb) [SM
FMDDLS, DTDFMR, SM] AY268
                              6449
Love's offering (Parker) [MRDD
TT, DRSM, MRTRDD,] G464;
N662; R299; S407; U277; Y229;
Z303; AB263; AC252; AD322;
AE281; AF405; AG246; AK396;
AN558; AO493; AR377; AT401;
AV214; BB478; BF502   6450
Loving kindness (Caldwell) [SD
DDRMDRRR, MFSFMD] H284;
I539b; L163; U148; V190; AI2;
AM138; AO404; AS15; AT26; AV
11; AX17; AY28; BB667; 6451
-----. V [SDDDMRRR, MFSFM
RDR] V190   6452
Loving Shepherd of thy sheep
(Catholic Hymn tunes, 1849)
X Lugano   6453
Lovingly, tenderly calling
(Ogden) [DRMFLSM, RMFM
RD, DRM] BB572   6454
-----. R [SMMMRDTSSS, SFFF
MR]   6455
Lowe (Lowe) X Praise   6456
Lowell (Bortniansky) X St Peters-
burg   6457
Lowell (Mason) X Diligence

                              6458
Lowell (Nichol) [DSMSDRMF,
SDRMRDT, D] AI189   6459
Löwen, lasst euch wieder-
finden (Klein) [RRFSLTDL,
LTDRDTL, R] Q470   6460
Lowenstern (Lowenstern) [MS
LTDTLRDT, MRDTLS] X
670   6461
Lower lights (Bliss) [SLS
MRDTL, LLRDTDR, S] G254;
U316; Z313; AC253; AE290;
AH438; AI186; AS351; AT
300; AU262; AW448; AX193;
AY525; BB628; BC159; BZ
                        6462
-----. R [DDFFFFFM, MMM
RLRR, S]   6463
Lower Marlwood (Harwood)
[DMSDDRMF, LSFMS, TDR]
BV80a   6464
Lowliness (Hanby) X Adoration
                        6465
Lowrance (Campbell) [MMSFR
M, DDMRTD, MSF#M,] V355
                        6466
Lowry (Lowry) X All the way
                        6467
Lowry (Lowry) X Need   6468
Lowry (Lowry) X Something
for Jesus   6469
Loyal and true (---) [MSLM
RDD, MSLMRDR, MS] AX447
                        6470
-----. R [SLTDTLSM, DFLSM
DS, S]   6471
Loyalty to Christ (Cassel) X
Lambdin   6472
Lubbock (McKinney) [SDMR#
MDMFSSM, DMRRM] AT231;
AU397   6473
-----. R [SSLLLFLS, SSF#
RRMF#S]   6474
Lucas (Lucas) [SDDDDTDRR
RR, SMMDR] I568; BC17
                        6475
Lucas (Wilson) [SSLSDTRD,
MRFMMRL, L] AI85
                        6476
Luccombe (Fuller-Maitland)
[MMFSMRDRMM, SLTDTL]
E641b   6477
Lucerna, laudoniae (Arthur)

[SSMDRML, SDFMDMR, MD]
W17; AL15b   6478
Lucerne (Strassburg Psalter,
    1539) X Psalm 68 (Greiter)
                              6479
Lucerne (Willis) [SSMDTRRD,
    DTTLDLS, S] C93b; N12; AC
    14; AO50; BA643; BF209; BK
    42   6480
Lucia (Donizetti) [SSSDMRDS,
    DTLTDRSM] AI352   6481
Lucile (Gabriel) [DTLSDFMRD,
    DTDFMRR] AJ258   6482
Lucis creator (Angers church
    mel) [LLDLSDRM, RSLSF#M
    RM] E51b; X37b; AN61; AQ
    273   6483
Lucis creator (Sarum plainsong,
    M 4) X Conditor alme   6484
Lucis creator (Sarum plainsong,
    M 8) [SLSFLDDSLSFSS, SR]
    A163a; E51   6485
Lucis creator optime (Plainsong,
    arr. 1539) X To God on high
                              6486
Lucius (Kingsley) [SSMDTTLL,
    LRRSFM, SS] BA840   6487
Luckington (Harwood) [DMSDDRL
    SFM, SLRT, DL] F375; W15a;
    BV243; BY13   6488
Luconer (Coleridge-Taylor)
    [SSLSMMMFMT, DRMTLD]
    Y36   6489
Lucy (Brahms) [MMSMMS, MS
    DTLLS, RMF] G600; AI205;
    AR127; AX59   6490
-----. V [MSMSMSDDTLLS,
    RMFR] AI205   6491
Ludborough (Matthews) [DMFSLS
    FM, MMRDDTLS,] B8; F473;
    W188b   6492
Ludovica (Lindeman) X Easter
    glory   6493
Ludwig (Lindeman) [DSLSFMRM,
    SLDTLS, DS] M86; O50; P268
                              6494
Ludwigsburg (Bourgeois) X
    Bourgeois   6495
Luebeck (Freylinghausen. Geist-
    reiches G-B. 1704) [DMSSLTD,
    TDRTLLS, MF] A253; B47; C
    47; D322b; E552; F39; J323;
    K32; M107; O63; Q2; R6; S27;

V602; W170a; X645; AA106;
AD99; AF75; AI447; AK45;
AL342a; AN222; AW510; AZ
11-B; BA855; BB178; BI22-
D; BL41; BN202; BV70; BX
96; BY234   6496
-----. V [DMFSSLTD, TDR
    DTLSS,] E552   6497
-----. V [DMSSLTD, TRST
    LLS, SD] M107   6498
-----. V [DRMFSSLTD, TDR
    SLTL] R6   6499
-----. V [DMFSSLTD, TRDT
    LLS, D] BI22-D   6500
Luebeck (Darmstadt G-B. 1699)
    [DDTDLTD, MMRSFMRD, D]
    M435; Q55; AA414   6501
Luella (Whitney) [MDSF#SDR
    D#RMDS, MDSF#] AO618
                              6502
Lueneburg (Ebeling) X Ebeling
    II   6503
Luetzen (Hermann) X Hermann
                              6504
Luffenham (Macfarren) [SSS
    LTDRSD, MMRRMFL] K440;
    AC52; AS98   6505
-----. V [SSSLTDRSS, MM
    RRMFL] AC52   6506
Lugano (Catholic Hymn tunes,
    1849) [DDTDLLDD, DTLT
    DRDT] E529; W285a; AL
    559a; AP684c; BQ45   6507
-----. V [DDTDTLLTT,
    DTDLTDR] AL559a   6508
Luise (Crueger) X Ratisbon
                              6509
Luke (Greek folk mel) [DRMM
    MMRMFLSSS, MR] A246;
    B350; C350; D562; G440;
    H452; I682; J497; K557;
    L450; P359; R460; S442b;
    V645; W82; Z213; AD475;
    AE433; AF483; AH553; AK
    460; AM650; AO622; AP738a;
    AR549; AS398; AT506; AV86;
    AW427; BA832a; BB422; BD
    64; BV346; BY120a   6510
-----. V [DRMRMSFMFLSSS,
    MFS] I682   6511
-----. V [DRMRMSFMRLSSS,
    MFS] W82   6512
-----. V [DRMMMMRMFLS

SS, FMR] AT506   6513
Lullaby (Geibel) [MMMRRD,
SSSFM, LLLSS] AH268   6514
Lullay my liking (Holst) [DLT
DLTDRTLS, LTDMR] BG182
                                            6515
-----. R [MMF#STL, RDTL,
LLTDTL]   6516
Lumetto (Arthur) [MDRMLDM
SMS, SSLDMM] W671   6517
Lumina (Sarum plainsong, M 1)
X Splendor paternae   6518
Lundie (Perkins) [SLSMRD, RDR
MS, SLSMR] I529; AS288; AU
205; AX404; BB277   6519
Lüneburg (Ebeling) X Ebeling
                                            6520
Lura (Reynolds) [SSDDDDRMSS,
SFMRDR] AT214; AV352
                                            6521
----. R [SSSLSMF, FFFSFRM,
SS]   6522
Lusatia (Vulpius) [MRDTLTDD,
RMFRMF#S, R] O105   6523
Lute-book lullaby (Ballet) [RRM
FFSFM, LDLL#LSFF,] BG30
                                            6524
Luther (Geistliche lieder. Witten-
berg, 1535) [DDMRDRRM, D
MFSMRD, D] B64; C64, 236a;
D37; E4; F366b; G385; J113;
K514; L580; M173; N265; O18;
P56; Q293; R16; S342; V687;
W211a; X672; AA552; AE15;
AF271; AK361; AL170; AM240;
AP301; AR13, 203, 614; AW521;
AZ132-L; BA734; BB195; BJ
16; BV78; BX181; BY28; BZ
                                            6525
-----. V [DDMRDRRM, DRMFS
FMRD,] AR13   6526
-----. V [DDRMRDRRM, DRMFS
FM] AR203   6527
-----. V [DDMRDRRM, DMFSFM
RD,] AZ132-L   6528
Luther (Hastings) [SSLSFMRD,
MRDFMR, MF] H238; L126
                                            6529
Luther (Luther) X Spires   6530
Luther (Luther) X Ein feste burg
                                            6531
Luther (American, 19th c) X
Müller   6532

Luther League hymn (Haas)
[DMDFRLS, MDDRMR, RMM]
J567; K578; L532; M524
                                            6533
-----. R [SDSMSDD, SLFRDT,
SMT]   6534
Luther Seminary (Dahle) [DTL
SSLTD, DRMFMR, RM] J287;
O361   6535
Luther's chant (Zeuner) [SLTD
LSFM, MRTDRDLT,] AV310;
BX73b   6536
Luther's cradle hymn (Kirk-
patrick) X Cradle song
                                            6537
Luther's hymn (Geistliche
lieder. 1535) X Luther
                                            6538
Luther's hymn (Geistliche
lieder. Wittenberg, 1531) X
Luther (1535)   6539
Luther's hymn (Teutsch kirche-
nampt. Strassburg, 1525)
X Aus tiefer not   6540
Luton (Burder) [SSLSFMRD,
DDTLSFMF] D44b; H27;
I217; M144; T100; V206;
AA144; AJ145; AN15; AO
533   6541
Lutzen (Hermann) X Hermann
                                            6542
Lux aeterna (Gounod) X Radiant
morn   6543
Lux beata (Peace) [SLSSSSS
LTD, TLTS, SL] D423b; S
303; T250; U201; AB221;
AG219; AJ347; AM82; AP
600b   6544
Lux benigna (Dykes) [SDRM
MRDLDLS, DTDR,] A430b;
B244; C244a; D423a; E425;
F298b; G514a; H347; I460;
J523a; L392; N344; O546;
P346; R331; S289; T39; U
240; V419; W568c; X554b;
Y367; Z578; AB219a; AC
333; AD221; AE202; AF215;
AG157; AH404; AI299; AJ56;
AK315; AL436a; AN239; AO
327a; AP600a; AR423; AS
247; AT60; AU238; AV149;
AW162; AY465; AZ601-A;
BA685; BB403; BC112; BD

250; BE169; BF414; BK89;
BR388a; BX263; BZ   6545
Lux coelestis (Basford) [SSSSFM
R#M,DTLSSLDT] T164; AJ
242   6546
Lux dei (Miller) [DDSRSMFR,
SSFMMRLS,] N168   6547
Lux eoi (Sullivan) [SSDSSFFM,
LLSMRDR,S] A92; B520; C
520; D123a; F137; I402; J108;
K116; M174; T345; U104; V
180; W126; AL387; AV268; AZ
167-H; BA233; BE115; BI4-D;
BR189; BV178a; BY17b   6548
Lux fiat (Gounod) X Orient
                          6549
Lux mundi (Sullivan) [MMRDM
RDSR,MDTLMR,S] D357b;
AO341; AZ151-P; BA431; BO
203; BR419   6550
Lux noel (German trad) [SMD
FRSFM,RDSFMMR,S] M620
                          6551
Lux perpetua (Whelan) [DMMMF
S,SFFMMR,RMMM] K522
                          6552
Lux prima (Gounod) [DDDMRDT
DS,MMMSFMR] B425; D312a;
G334; J229; K438; L5; N466;
R47; S26; V375; Z270; AB197;
AD42; AG20; AH172; AL561;
AM247; AO291; AW26; AZ89-E;
BA495; BQ62; BR110; BY214b
                          6553
Lux prima (Macfarren) [MMMMM
RR,FFSRFMM,MF#] AP659
                          6554
Lux prima (Stainer) [DDMSFLDS,
MMRTDDTS] L4; V37b; AZ
86-D; BA769   6555
Lux vera (Gounod) X Lux prima
                          6556
Lux vitae (Barnby) X Barnby
III   6557
Lydbrook (Spencer-Palmer)
[MLDTLLSFFM,DMLSFM]
BV637   6558
Lydia (Phillips) [SSDMRMSDFMR,
SLSFM] L517; BY212b   6559
Lydia (Stebbins) [SLSDRLTLS,
DSFMRSF#] AJ405   6560
Lyle Road (Finlay) [DRFMRD,
MFSLS,SLDTL] BV195   6561

Lymington (Jackson) [SDDRMDS
M,DLLSFM,SD] BY381
                          6562
Lynchburg (Hallstrom) [DRM
DRMDR,MFSLSL,LD] A526b
                          6563
Lynde (Thuringian trad)
[MDLSDRDRMLS,SF#SLF]
AC54; AO627   6564
Lyndhurst (Blunt) X Merrial
                          6565
Lyndhurst (Lane) X Penitence
                          6566
Lyndhurst (Maker) [DRMFMM
RD,D#D#D#RR#M,MR] L
386   6567
Lyne (Magdalen Hospital hymns,
1760) [DRMRDMF#S,SLSFM
FRD,] E296; F454; S445;
W565; X19; AK458; AN68;
AQ152; BD106; BY719   6568
-----. V [DDRMRDMFS,SS
LSFMF] AQ152   6569
Lyngham (Jarman) [DMFSLSFM
FMDRTD,MF] ALSuppl; BY
200b   6570
Lynne (Burt) [DDRMMMRMS
FMRD,MM] A508; J548; AF
491   6571
Lynton (Jamouneau) [MMMRM
SFM,SSS#LMF,TT] AJ391a
                          6572
Lyons (Haydn) [SDDRMDFFM
R,SDDRMF] A260; B254; C
254; D467; F226; G4; H11;
I106; J446; K294a; L75; M
24; N333; P32; R26; S198;
T197; U7; V13; Y59; Z94;
AB14; AC36; AD3; AE3; AF
6; AG6; AH187; AI11; AJ285;
AK11; AM13; AN6; AO56;
AP258; AQ25; AR33; AS2;
AT20; AU2; AV34; AW7; AX
9; AY423; BA20; BB75; BC
146; BD27; BE18; BF167;
BH60; BI30; BK65; BR65;
BX10; BZ   6573
-----. V [SDDRMMDFFMR,
SDDRM] M24   6574
Lyons (Haydn) X O purest of
creatures (Paderborn G-B.
1765)   6576
Lyra (Lyra Davidica, 1708)

X Easter hymn   6577
Lyra (Root) [SFMMMMMRM,
  SMRRDRM,] AP645b   6578
Lystra (Wesley) [SMFMRSDRTD,
  RMFSL] A447   6579
Lyte (Holbrook) [MFLSFM,
  SDMRLTS,SDR] L118; AJ204
  b; AO284   6580
Lyte (Temple star) [MFSLSSMD
  FMMR,MFSL] AY309   6581
Lyte (Wilkes) [DLMFFM,MMM
  LTD,DDDD] B408; C408a;
  D333a; K340; V703   6582
Lytham (Lightwood) [MRDSDDTT,
  LSLTDRM,M] G453   6583
Lytham (Malley) [MR#MFMMMRDR
  M,FSLSMM] AJ253   6584
Lytlington (Nicholson) [MRDM
  SDFMRDRD,SMR] A466; F332b;
  AF393   6585

            M

M.I.A. we hail thee (Robinson)
  [SSLSMT,RDSDT,RRD#RF]
  BC111   6586
-----. R [MSRDDT,FTMRDS,
  SMRD]   6587
Mabon (Murray) X Eudora 6588
Mabyn (Brown) X St Mabyn
                        6589
McAfee (McAfee) [MMR#MM
  FMF,RRRSFM,MM] R318;
  AE225; AR478; AT301; AU
  273; AW239; AX50; BB681
                        6590
-----. R [DLLFLLS,SFMFSM,
  DLL]   6591
Maccabaeus (Handel) X Judas
  Maccabaeus   6592
McCabe (Gabriel) [SSDDDSDRM
  MM,FMRMR] AT457; AU117;
  AV381; AX212; AY330   6593
-----. R [MFSLSFMMM,
  FMRFMRM,]   6594
McCabe (Widdeman) [DRMFMM
  RDRDTD,MFSF] BB120
                        6595
McComb (Sims) [SDRMFMRD,
  SLTDLLS,S] AT384   6596
McConnell (McConnell) [MFSD
  RMFMRLR,DTTLS] AT209
                        6597

-----. R [MSDMRMRDL,
  TDTLSFM]   6598
McConnelsville (Morris) [SS
  SSMSDRMS,DTTTTD] AT230;
  AX261   6599
-----. R [MDLSMLS,MFMR
  LMR,MS]   6600
McDaniel (Gabriel) [MFSLT
  DDRMMFM,RDDL] AT310
                        6601
-----. R [SMMRMDM,RDDL
  DDDS,M]   6602
Macfarren (Macfarren) [MF
  MLSDRM,MRSTLS,SL] M
  565   6603
McGranahan (McGranahan)
  [SSDSMLSS,SDTTLTD,S]
  AT114   6604
Mach hoch die tür (Lemke)
  [SMDDTDRTS,SSLTDLS]
  Q73a   6605
Mache dich, mein geist,
  bereit (Rosenmüller) X
  Nassau   6606
Mach's mit mir Gott (Schein)
  X Eisenach   6607
Macht hoch die tür (Freyling-
  hausen. Geistliche G-B.
  1704) [MSFMRDRMR,SFF
  MRMR] J8b; K7; M330;
  Q73b; X77; AK92; AM146;
  AW523; AZ459-A; BA151
                        6608
-----. V [DSFMRDMR,SFF
  MMRRD,] AK92   6609
Macht hoch die Thür (Stobaeus)
  X Lift up your heads
                        6610
McIntosh (American trad)
  X Amazing grace   6611
Mack (Frederick) [DMSSFF,
  RFLLSS,RSF#S] AR606
                        6612
McKee (Negro mel) [DMSS
  SSLL#L#L,SLDDLSLD,]
  A263a; R479b; AF415
                        6613
Maclagan (Maclagan) X New-
  ington   6614
McPherson (Fisher) [MFSLL
  RMFSS,DRMSMR] AR385
                        6615
Madagascar (Ruud) [DMRM

F#SSF#S,SLSLTDT] J494b
6616
Maddermarket (Shaw) [SMSSDRDT
LTD,RMRDR] X396a   6617
Madison (Willis) [SFMRDTL,
LLTDTLS,SL] AS381   6618
Madison Avenue (Bingham)
[DDLDRMD,RMDMFSM,DT]
AR577   6619
Madrid (Carr) X Spanish chant
6620
Madrid (Matthews) [DTLSFMFS
DDTD,MRDT] BY451   6621
Maelor (Hughes) [LLDFRM,MSM
RDT,TMF#S] BY175b   6622
Maer Down (Sheldon) [SLSFMDR
M,TDRMFTLR,] BV53   6623
Maesgwyn (Edwards) [LMDLRM,
LDTLT,RTDRM] BY506b
6624
Magda (Williams) [SDLSMDRMF
SM,SDLRS] A482b; E273;
F341; W243b; X53; AQ78; BY
344   6625
Magdalen (Stainer) X Beati
6626
Magdalen College (Hayes) [DM
SDLFFM,RMFSLTDR,] A314;
E457; F389a; S482; W543b;
X690; AJ96; AZ92-C; BV531a
6627
Magdalen Tower hymn (Rogers)
X Hymnus eucharisticus
6628
Magdalene (German. 16th c)
[DSSSSLLDTLSFM,MSF] E
392; X591   6629
Magdalena (Stainer) [DFMRDSS,
LSDDRM,F#SD] B239; C239a;
D603a; I200; M162; O203
6630
Magdalena (Spohr) X Spohr
6631
Magdeburg (Bourgeois) X Com-
mandments   6632
Magherafelt (Hogan) [MMRDRM
D,TDRMFLS,TD] AP550
6633
Magi (Lahee) [SDDTDS,FMR
RD,MLLTD] D362a   6634
Magill (Perkins) [DRMDLSDDRDR
MDRMD] L244   6635

Magister (Mason) [DRMDFMMR,
DFMRDTD,D] BY479a
6636
Magnae deus potentiae (Plain-
song, M 2) [RRRMMFRD,
DFSLFFMF] E61   6637
Magnificence (Everett) [SDSM
RDTL,LSSSFM,SD] AR97;
AS89   6638
Magnus (Herbert) [DMMMRDM
SSLS,MRRMF] AJ123; AM515
6639
-----. R [SMRDRD,SLTDS,
DRDLS]   6640
Magyar (Eneke) [LMLTRDTL,
DSDRMRD,L] AF377; AK306
6641
Maidstone (Gilbert) [SLTDRM
FMRM,SFMRM] A392; B467;
C467; D301; Eap.20; F240b;
I469; J184; K422; N326; R441;
V12; W235; AL200a; AO3; AP
317; BA333; BI105; BR309;
BV563a; BX197; BY280;
6642
Mainz (Mainz G-B. 1661) [DR
MRMSFM,MRDTLTLS,] A76a;
B161; C161b; D103c; E115; F
118; G138; J84; W99; X138a;
AD151; AH113; AK150; AL95;
BL21; BM80; BN33; BO262;
BP24; BQ23   6643
-----. V [DRMRMSFM,MRDR
LTLS,] BL21   6644
Mainz (Cologne G-B. 1623) X
Hosmer   6645
Mainzer (Mainzer) [SSSDTLLS,
LFSMDTLS,] B284; C367b;
D279a; K253; V3; W333; AB
395; AL353; AP269b; AS97;
BA767; BX193; BY33; BZ
6646
Mainzer (Mainzer) X Humility
6647
Maitland (---) [MSSLSMDLS,
SLTDMRL] D543   6648
Maitland (Allen) [MFSSDM
RDLD,LSSSDMR,] G276; H225;
I428; L525; M394; N472; R68;
T21; U196; V440; Z366; AE219;
AH294; AI317; AJ28; AO384;
AR317; AS330; AT428; AU153;

AV204; AX426; AY113; BA463;
BB274; BZ   6649
-----. V [MFSSDMRDL, LSSDMR,
M] M394   6650
Majestic sweetness sits enthroned
(Hastings) X Ortonville 6651
Majesty (Neander) X Sieh hier bin
ich, Ehrenkönig   6652
Majesty (Llewellyn) [LLLTLS,
LLLTLS, LTDT] BV5   6653
Majesty (Schicht) [SSDFMRRD,
SLRRMR, SS] BA795   6654
Make me a blessing today (Gil-
mour) [SDDDMDLS, SDDDMR,
SD] AX416   6655
-----. R [SSMDRDLLS, SDDD
MRD]   6656
Make me a blessing (Schuler) X
Schuler   6657
Make me a channel (Smyth) X
Euclid   6658
Make we joy (English carol. 15th
c) [MMMSFMRD, MSMRDTL,
M] BG23   6659
Make we merry (Shaw) [RMFSFM
RD, DRMFSFMR] BG172 6660
Maker (Maker) [SSLSMMSFD#
R, MDDSFM] I89; Z218   6661
Maker (Maker) X St Christopher
6662
Malabar (Williams) [SFMLLSS
D, DTLSMSS,] A201   6663
Maldwyn (Welsh, ca 1600) [MLLT
DDTLTS#L, TDDRT] Q278; X
69   6664
-----. V [MLLTDDTLDTLLS#,
TDD] X69   6665
Mallett (Hall) [MSFMRFFM,
MMRTLSMR,] B236; AB361
6666
Malone (Emerson) [SDDDMFSL,
LLLLLTTD,] T117; AJ168
6667
Malvern (The Hallelujah, 1849)
[SMSDRD, DLDRMR, DTLS,]
J121; V564a; W364b; AL145;
AW131; BY640   6668
-----. V [SMSDRD, DLDRMR,
SSFM] V564a   6668a
Malvern (Mason) [MMMMMMRMF
S, SLLSMF] G24; I37b; M26;
AE26; BB515; BZ   6669
Mamre (Scholinus) [SLSLTDS,

DTRDMR, SMR] W569 6670
Man of sorrows (Bliss) [SSS
MDDT, LLSDTLS, SS] W693;
AM175; AN213; AR166; AS
135; AT163; AU257; AV321;
BV159; BY186   6671
Man of sorrows (Slovak hymn)
[LLS#LTDLT, MMRDTLS#, L]
AM464; AY510; BQ19
6672
-----. V [LLS#LTDT, MMR
DDT, LL] AM464   6672a
Manchester (Rounsefell) X
I'll go where ...   6673
Manchester (Stebbins) [SSFRM
DS, DMRMFRS, SS] Y161; AC
186   6674
Manchester (Wainwright) [DMRD
DLSFM, DSFMLTD] E168;
F472; L356a; V248; X673;
BV281   6675
Manchester new (Wainwright)
X Manchester   6676
Mandor (Emerson) [SMDTLSLS
MMR, MSDLD] L84   6677
Manger (Crueger) [MDDR,
MFFM, SLSMRMSF] M360;
Q81; AA156   6678
Manger (Esmond) [MMFFSRMS,
DDT, LLS, SS] D538a   6679
Manger (Garrett) [MRDMRDT
D, SFMMR#M, MR] BR142
6680
Manger Throne (Steggall)
[DSLSMRMD, RMLSDT, SD]
B548; C548   6681
Manitou (Chippewa Indian mel)
[DDDLLFFFLFFF, LLLL]
Y315   6682
Mann (Mann) [SLSMRD, SMR
DR, RMFLS] M621; AS434
6683
Manna (Barnby) [MRDLSSFM,
MF#SDTLS, F#] BR27
6684
Manna (Gottschalk) X Mercy
6685
Manna (Schicht) [DMDLLRRT,
SDDRRMMR,] F389b 6686
Mannheim (Filitz) [DMSSLSFM,
MFSDMRD, S] A524; E426;
F311; J142; K274; O215;
W564a; X555b; AL216; AP

597; AW298; AZ585-C; BA852; BN111; BR500b; BV583; BY43 6687

Manoah (Rossini) [DRMRDTTLL, RMFMRDDT,] B401; C401; D663b; G378; H67; I105; L138; M277; N303; P375; R86; S94; T235; U69; V24; Z153; AB65; AD7; AE226; AG242; AH192; AJ331; AK213; AM436; AN224b; AO312; AR17; AS12; AT49; AV 35; AY134; BA35; BB25; BE121; BF251; BK81; BR356; BX116; BZ 6688

Manor Street (Shaw) [SDLDSLSF MS, DRMSFM,] X386f 6689

Mansfield (Barnby) [SDTRDM, RDLSSS, SDTR] S170; Z243; AK171 6690

Mansfield (Turpin) [SSSSLDRD, D TLMTDRM,] D243b; AP617 6691

Mansfield Road (Baker) [SMRDM S, SDRDLFRT, SD] BY500 6692

Mant (Morgan) [SDLSDRMFS, LF MRDTD] V11 6693

Mant (Barthélémon) X Autumn 6694

Mantegna (Williams) [MRDRMFM DL#L, MMSFL, M] X126 6695

Maple leaf for ever (Muir) [SM SMDLDS, TDRDTLS, F] P415 6696

-----. R [SMSDSLDS, SSSFMMR, S] 6697

Mar Saba (Barnby) X Hebron 6698

Mara (Wesley, S.S.) [MRFMRS, DRMFMR, SDDT] AZ577-A 6699

Marathon (Williams) [MMRMDLS L, DRMRDLSL,] X302; BV208 6700

Marburg (Crueger) [MMDTRDTL, TDRMFMMR,] AA204 6701

March to victory (Barnby) X To victory 6702

Marchfield (Collier) [SMRDTLTD S, STDRMSF] T234; AJ330; AO439 6703

Marching (Shaw) [MFSSLTDT, D RMRDLS, R] C63b; E503; F182;

J529b; W214b; X678; Y163; AL448a; AN83a; BE364; BV414; BY559 6704

Marching home (Bushey) [DRM MMRDMS, SLDTLS, D] AY 145 6705

Marching to Zion (Lowry) X Come, we that love the Lord 6706

Marcus Whitman (Merrill) [SD RMSLML, LFSLLTST,] S418; AB346 6707

Marenzo (Crueger) X Nun danket 6708

Margaret (Matthews) [DRMM FMRDRM, MFSSM] A321; B83; C83; D319a; E585; F 363; G95; I122; J433; K541; N47; R184; S231; U79; W67; Z292; AB115; AC101; AD131; AE94; AF326; AG84; AH254; AK126; AL68; AM170; AO 130; AP180; AR142; AT82; AU138; AV123; BA88; BB 103; BF304; BV277; BY111 6709

-----. R [SSMFSDDT, LLSDRM RD] 6710

Margaret (Peace) X St Margaret 6711

Margaret (Roberts) [MMM MFMRDRM, SSSSLS] BY775 6712

Margaret Street (Hoyte) [SD LDRMRD, SMDFMRR, R] D99 6713

Margaretting (Brown) [DTLS# LT, LSFM, TTTTR#M,] C416 6714

Marguerite (Walker) X St Marguerite 6715

Maria (Alexis) [MSFMRRD, DT DFMR, RMM] N569 6716

Maria, hun er en Jomfru ren (Gebauer) [MMRDSSFM, MR SDTLS, M] O290 6717

Maria jung und zart (Cologne G-B. 1623) X Hosmer 6718

Maria mater gratia (German, 1669) X Cor dulce, cor amabile 6719

Maria, mater gratia (A Monk

of Gethsemani) [LTDTTLLSM,
LTDTTLL] BN148   6720
Marias Wallfahrt (Brahms) X
The quest   6721
Marias wanderschaft (German trad)
X Mary's wandering   6722
Maribah (Mason) X Meribah
6723
Marietta (White) [SFMRDLS,
MRDFMR, RMF] BB235 6724
Mariners (Rendle) [MRDMSS, LL
MLS, SF#MST] G556; AB383
6725
Mariners (Sicilian mel) X
Sicilian mariners   6726
Marion (Messiter) [DSMRDRM,
MMDRMF#S, S] A579b; B537;
C537; D520a; G358; I421; J555;
N588; R407; S297; Y199; Z418;
AB19; AC27; AD272; AE7; AF
345; AG209; AH183; AK7; AM
502; AN13; AO62; AP608; AR
336; AT17; AU285; AV47; AW
156; BA124; BB17; BD119;
BF170; BK66; BZ   6727
-----. R [SS, SS, SFMRMRD]
6728
Markell (Keiffer) X And now,
my soul, another year   6729
Marken (Tours) X Deventer
6730
Market Street (English) [DMFMR
DTD, SDTLSF#S, S] L339
6731
Marlborough (Sullivan arr) [MM
MMMSLSFFM, MDDTL] AB
312; BR417; BX108   6732
Marlee (Sateren) [LDTLTM, LR
MFMLS#L, LD] J80;   6733
Marlow (Chetham's Psalmody)
[DMMMDSSS, SMDFMR, DM]
A547b; B488; C488; D508;
H365; I8; L106; M57; T371;
U474; V266; AA368; AM481;
AO405; AR7; AS55; AW501;
AX168; AY269; BA451; BB
486; BR239   6734
Marosa (Bain) [DMSDSLDS, FM
DDTD, DM] BK25; BL89
6735
Marshall (Geer) [SSDLDS, MMM
FDRM, SSS] C246b   6736

Marshall (Marshall) [MF
SDDMRDLD, TLSMSDR,] AE
294; AI125; AU278; AW479;
AX131; AY466   6737
-----. R [MFSF#SDTLS#L,
TLSMSD]   6738
-----. R [MFSMS, DTLFL,
DLSMSD] AI125   6739
-----. V [MFSDMRDLD,
TLSMSDR,] AU278   6740
Marter christi (Gnadauer
Choral buch, 1735) [DDTL
RDTDSFMRD, DDT] AK152;
AW537   6741
Martha (Clelland) [DSMRDTLS,
LTDRMF#S, L] AM130
6742
Martha (Hammer) [MDFMMRD,
LLSMRMR, MD] AZ205-S;
BA786   6743
Martham (Maunder) [SSMRD
LLS, SSSLDTLS,] I73; BY
69   6744
Marthina (Marks) [MFF#SD
LSFM, MLTDTLS] AJ249
6745
Martin (Martin) [MFF#SDRM
RD, STLFLSM,] R124; AH
381; AM696; AT274; AV366;
AX480; BZ   6746
-----. R [DTLLSS, STLF,
FLSM, SD]   6747
Martineau (Fairlamb) [SSSSLLS,
SRRRDRM, SS] C534; AC
200; BD81   6748
Martins (Buck) [SLSFSDTLS
MD, RMRMF#] A583; F283;
X247; AD174; BL77; BY27
6749
Marton (Iszlai) [SSFMFSLS, LS
FMRD, SS] AN131   6750
Martyn (Marsh) [MMMDRRR,
MMSFMRD, M] A415c; B
223b; C223b; D335b; G338a;
H348; I463c; J393c; K371c;
L122b; M204; N419; O244a;
P154; Q345; R216b; S233a;
T6; U263; V331c; Y373b;
Z414; AA107; AC157b; AD
212b; AE173; AF210; AG153a;
AH355; AI245b; AJ10; AK316;
ALsuppl; AM427b; AO336a;

AP417b; AR405; AS212; AT156;
AU172; AV233b; AW158; AX
509; AY314; AZ205-K; BA523B;
BB401; BC84; BF370; BP48;
BR323b; BZ   6751
Martyr dei (Plainsong: medieval
M 6) [DDRMMRMRRD, MSSS]
A209a   6752
Martyr dei qui unicum (Hereford
Hymnal) [RMFSFMRMM, MRM
FMSS] E180   6753
Martyrdom (Wilson) [SDLSDRMR
D, MSMDMR,] A410b; B124b;
C124; D85; E367; F299b; G70;
H48; I102; J388; K101; L242;
M406; N111; P184; Q154; R
199; S16b; T37b; U101; V72;
W457b; X449; Z163; AA214; AD
200; AE112; AF285; AG95; AH
285; AI74b; AJ192; AK153; AL
101a; AM195; AN20; AO170;
AP19a; AR167; AT101; AU244;
AV109; AW108; AX69; AY166,
182; AZ14-X; BA203; BB124;
BD185; BE266; BV561a; BY292a;
BZ   6754
-----. V [SDLSDRMRD, MSM
RDMR,] M406   6755
Martyrdom (Wilson) X Liberty
Hall (---)   6756
Martyrs (Scottish Psalter, 1615)
X Plaintive martyrs   6757
Marvelous grace (Towner) [DT
DRDRMRD, TTDRTDD] AE224;
AM705; AR457; AT200; AX321
                          6758
-----. R [MDFM, RRRRMRD
FM, MDF]   6759
Mary (Lewis) [DMRDTD, DRM
FMR, RMFS] AJ30   6760
Mary! How sweetly falls that word
(English hymnal: old) [SMSMR
DTL, DSDDMR, SM] BO92
                          6761
-----. R [RRRRRRRFR, RFR
DDTD]   6762
Mary Immaculate, Mother and
Maid (Kittel) X Quedlinburg
                          6763
Mary Immaculate, Star (Udulutsch)
[DDDRMD, RTDTL, DDDRM]
BM56   6764
Mary Magdalene (Dykes) [DDRM

FM, MMRDT, DDRMF] D
340b; Q516; S255a; W525b;
AJ263; AP240; AV192; BA
662; BB388   6765
Mary the Dawn (Cross) [LL
SL, SLTSL, LSLL, SLT]
BM49   6766
Marylebone (Irish trad) [RM
MMDTLSFM, RMDLTD] X
315a   6767
Marylebone (Parry) [MMRM
DRMDS, FFMLLFM] I746
                          6768
Mary's wandering (German
trad) [MLTDTLTLS, DTM
F#SF#M,] BG93   6769
Maryton (Smith) [MMMFMRR
R, SSFMDDT] A572; B197b;
C493; G178; I232; J537; M
223; N94; P324; R304; S
364; T163; U271; W420a;
Y214; Z307; AB258; AC
197; AD90; AE146; AF418;
AG245; AH371; AI185; AJ
241; AK205; AL297a; AM
101; AN208c; AP448b; AR
233; AS342; AT385; AU
202; AV274; AW223; AY
467; BA443; BB346; BD
68; BE234; BF249; BK99;
BR169b; BV380b; BX225a;
BY63; BZ   6770
Masefield (McCutchan) [SLTD
RD, SLTDRM, TDRM] G
152   6771
Mason (Belden) [MSFMRDRT
D, SLSFMSF] BB31   6772
Mason (Harmonia sacra) [MM
LTS#LTDRTL, MRDTL] X
220   6773
Mason (Mason) X Hebron
                          6774
Mason (Sherwin) [MRDDTT,
DRMSFM, RDLS,] L304;
T158; AJ235; BR58   6775
Mason's Chant (Bradbury)
[SSSSSSSSD, SLLLDS, D]
AJ153   6776
Massachusetts (Davis) [LLM
MRMDR, TDRTLTL, L] BZ
                          6777
Massachusetts (Miller) [MM
MRMFSM, LLLSDSFR,]

BB80   6778

Master, the tempest (Palmer)
X Peace, be still   6779

Masters in the hall (French trad)
[LMMRDR, MRDTDTLS#, LM]
BG137   6780

-----. R [DTLS#LM, DTLS#L,
MSFRM]   6781

Mater (Depew) [MMFSMDRM,
FSDFFM, MM] AC318; AH498;
AT504; AU41; BF614   6782

Mater dolorosa (Corner. G-B.
1625) X Christi Mutter   6783

Mater misericordiae (Scott-
Gatty) X Spirit divine   6784

Materna (Ward) [SSMMSSRR,
MFSLTS, SS] A584b; B510b;
C510a; D403a; G491; H513;
I605; J346; K525; L593a; M
504; N40; P413; R510; S411;
T86; U339; V695; Y282; Z535;
AB337; AC271; AD132; AE357;
AF440; AG270; AH483; AJ126;
AK443; AM37; AN383; AO514;
AQ241; AR613; AS382; AT489;
AU39; AV277; AW343; BA762;
BB265; BC126; BD175; BF496;
BH262; BI115; BK121; BR433;
BX419; BZ   6785

Matheson (Davies) X Hampstead
6786

Mathilda (Strom) [SSSLSFSM,
SFMRDR, RM] N623   6787

Matins (Hodges) [SSSFMRDM, S
DDT, DTLS] C3b; D3b; AN88a;
BD1; BX150a   6788

Matins (Shepherd) [SSDRSM, RDD
RDT, TLSS] BR1   6789

Matthews (McKinney) [MRDRDLS
LD, TTTTDRD] AT333   6790

-----. R [MMRDTDR, FFMRDRM,
SS]   6791

Matthias (Monk) X St Matthias
6792

Mattie (Everett) [MMMSSLSM,
MRMSFM, DS] AR6; AS57;
AX503; AY367   6793

Mauburn (Noble) [MFSFMRM,
DRMFMM,] A29b; B550; C
550   6794

Maud (Scott-Gatty) [MSFMMRD,
RMFMRLS, MS] AO329   6795

Maxon (Glynn) [SLTDML, SM
RDLM, DRM] A475   6796

May (Pollock) X How oft, alas
6797

May carol (English trad) [LL
MRDDRMRT, RDTLSF#]
BG47   6798

May-day garland (English trad)
[DDMSMRTD, DDMSLFM, S]
BH48   6799

May God depend on you? (Wilson) [MFSSDTTL, LDTLSFM,
M] AU358   6800

-----. R [MSDTRDT, STRD#
MRD, DD]   6801

May He who kept us (Rogers)
[MMMFFRRMFM, SSLTSS]
BH10   6802

May Hill (Watson) [MMSMDRM
F, SSTSMF#S, L] BV442b
6803

May song (English trad) [SSM
SSDRM, MRDMRDL, D] G436;
S448; AH547; AL601   6804

May the Christ-life shine in
me (Hugg) [SDMDTDRD, SS
TTLLS, S] AX410; AY66
6805

-----. R [SMRDLSDRM,
SMRDLSD]   6806

May the grace of Christ (Hymns
and tunes, 1890) [DDDSDM
MR, RMFFDRM, D] AX75;
AY82   6807

May the words (Binder) [MR
DRMDSRDTLTDMRR] BH
273   6808

May the words (Jewish trad)
[MMMRDRM, LLLRLRM,
FF] Sap. 18; AR668   6809

May the words (Serbian trad)
[DDDDDDDDDTDLTDLT]
Sap. 20   6810

Mayer (Mayer) [SDTDRMRD,
MRDTLTDT,] M614   6811

Mayfield (Macey) [SDTDSLDS,
MLSSMDMR,] BY476   6812

Mead House (Taylor) [SSDS
DRMD, FMRDTLS, S] BV383
a; BY247   6813

Meadow Cove (Geneva Psalter,
1551) [DRMFMRDDTD, MR

MF#S, L] AQ166   6814
Meadows (White) [SMRDTDRDS,
SLTDRMR,] D511d   6815
Mear (Williams) [DSSMMDMR,
RMDSF#S, SL] C300; D393a;
G617; H226; I592; L573; T216b;
V290; AA354; AJ391b; AO584;
AW299; AY183; BA808; BB39;
BR213; BX112   6816
-----. V [DSSFMMRDRMR,
RMDSM] AY183   6817
Mecklenburg (German) [DDRDMMF
M, SFMRMRRR] BR452c   6818
Med sorgen og klagen hold maade
(Luther. Christliche gesang.
1542) X Jam Moesta   6819
Medfield (Mather) [SDMRFMRD,
TDRTLDTL] L334; X118; AM
38; AO140; BI4   6820
Meditation (Gower) [MMMMMM
DD, DFFMRS, SSS] A65b; B
159b; C159a; G135; J77a; N108;
R202; S157a; T143; U91; AB139;
AD153; AF172; AG93; AH508;
AJ1; AK149; AM184; AO162;
AW104; BC201; BD99; BF314;
BX111; BZ   6821
Meditation (Lewis) X Beloved
6822
Meditation (Perkins) X Lundie
6823
Mee chomocho (Binder) [MS#FM
FS#, S#LTLS#LFS#M,] BH283
6824
Mee chomocho I (Jewish trad)
[SSSLMRDTLS, MRDTLS] BH
142, 295   6825
-----. V [SLMRDTLS, MRDTLS
DD] BH295   6825
Mee chomocho II (Jewish trad)
[LMRMFM, LLD#TD#RD#, S#ML]
BH298   6827
Mee chomocho III (Jewish trad)
[SSLSSMMFFS, SSLSSL] BH307
6828
Mee chomocho (Jewish trad) X
Rock of ages   6829
Mee chomocho (Kaiser) [SDMMRL
DTLS, SDMSFL] BH281   6830
Mee chomocho (Lewandowski)
[MMFMRRDTLS, LLFRDT] BH
270   6831
Meet me there (Kirkpatrick) [DR

MMMMM, DMSSSSS, SS]
AX603   6832
-----. R [SSSLSMD, TLSS
SSLS, S]   6833
Meet Mother in the skies (---)
[MR#MFMDLDDLS, MR#
MFM] AY504   6834
Mehul (Mehul) X Gilead
6835
Mehul (Mehul) X Joseph 6836
Mein G'mut ist mir verwirret
(Hassler) X Passion chor-
ale   6837
Mein heiland (Thommen. Chris-
ten-schatz) [MSSSLMRD, R
MRF#SDT] Q386   6838
Mein heiland nimmt de suender
an (Hille) X Gregor's 217th
metre-B   6839
Mein Jesu, dem die seraphinen
(Dessler) X Gregor's 183d
metre   6840
Mein Jesu, der du vor dem
scheiden (Gregor) X Gre-
gor's 107th metre   6841
Mein leben (Vulpius) X Cana
6842
Mein Salomo, dein freund-
liches regieren (Richter)
X Gregor's 114th metre
6843
Mein Schöpfer, steh mir bei
(Meyer) [DDRMMR, SFM
RRD, DDRM] Q335; AA384;
AQ210   6844
Mein Seel, o Herr, muss loben
dich (Gesius) X Herrnhut
6845
Meine armuth (Freylinghausen)
X Richter   6846
Meine hoffnung (Neander) [L
S#LTDDTM, LSFMRRD, L]
W448a; X442; AF339; AN219;
AQ35; BJ69; BM3; BY492
6847
-----. V [LS#LTDDTM, LSFM
RRM, L] BM3   6847a
Meine liebe lebet noch (Frey-
linghausen) X Jesus ist das
schönste licht   6848
Meinen Jesum lass' ich nicht
(Darmstadt G-B. 1699) X
Luebeck   6849

Meinen Jesum lass ich nicht
(Hammerschmidt) [SSLLTTD,
RRDDTTLS, S] K325; M125;
AA88   6850
Meinen Jesum lass ich nicht (Ulich.
Lüneburg G-B. 1686) [MM
FSRDRMR, RRMFSLS] AK42
                              6851
Meinhold (Lüneburg G-B. 1686)
[MMMSFFM, MMRMFMRD, M]
B414; C414; D248a; J186; K516;
L570; N346; O33; V671; AI333;
AO570; AP200; AR516; AS463;
AZ83-A   6852
-----. V [MMFSSFFM, MMRM
FMRD,] AZ83-A   6853
Meiningen (Meiningen G-B. 1693)
X Munich   6854
Meiringen (Neefe) [SDMSMRFM,
DTLSF#S, SD] J540; K139; U
40; AD364; AO529; BF491; BX
445   6855
Meirionydd (Lloyd) [SFMMRDR
MM, SFMFMRD] A598a; C224;
E473; G194; J355; M319; O504;
R200; S156; W598; X629; Y235;
Z234; AB287; AF426; AI221;
AK305; AM118; AN90; AP627;
AQ1; AT227; AW180; BE313;
BK19; BV389; BY275; BZ
                              6856
Meirionnydd (Lloyd) X Meirionydd
                              6857
Meiromydd (Lloyd) X Meirionydd
                              6858
Meistersinger chorale (Wagner)
X Da zu dir der heiland kam
                              6859
Melanchthon (Meiningen G-B.) X
St Leonard   6860
Melanesia (Smith) [DMFSSLDS,
LSSFMRLT,] D253c   6861
Melchior (Franck) [DSMDMFSLL
S, LSRMF#] A594; B543; C543;
J588; K521; M315; O610; Q619;
AA559; AZ576-A   6862
-----. V [SSMRDMFSLLS, LSR
MF#] M315   6863
-----. V [SMRDMFSLLS, LSRM
F#S] Q619   6864
-----. V [DSMRDMFSLLS, LS
RMF#] AZ576-A   6865
Melchior (Vulpius) X Lobet den

herrn, ihr   6866
Melcombe (Webbe) [SSFMRD
LS, SDTLSSF#S,] A111; B1;
C1; D1; E260; F4; G35; I95;
J201; K232; L82; M150; O
67; Q504; R45; S31; T449b;
V35; W259; X31; AA167; AB
186; AD40; AE38; AF36; AG
22; AK353; AL207; AM121;
AN37; AO84; AP122; AQ158;
AS64; AW22; BA40; BB42;
BD2; BE6; BF175; BN83;
BO5; BQ139; BR126; BV43;
BX239; BY268; BZ   6867
Melford ("M.B.F.") [MMSSF#
SLS, MMMMSFMR,] S361;
BI81   6868
Melita (Dykes) [DMMSSLLS,
SDRTSSF#S,] A512; B415;
C415; D184; E540; F487; G
480; J124b; K331; M190;
R521; S492; T157; U363; V
644; W626; Z610; AA19; AB
380; AD456; AE61; AF429;
AH216; AJ232; AK382; AL
261; AM243; AN574; AO410;
AP709; AR67; AS358; AT61;
AV69; AW169; AZ96-L; BA
890; BE12; BF264; BK124;
BR507; BV408; BX289; BY
288; BZ   6869
Melling (Fawcett) [DSDRMFM
RD, RMDLRDT] E373; W11b;
X463; BV550; BY394   6870
Melmore (Martin) [SSSF#SLS
M, MFMRMFSM,] T256; AI
264; AJ357   6871
Melody (Chapin) [SDRMRDLS,
SDRMF#S, SF] H91; L151;
V473; AY175; BZ   6872
Melody (Praetorius. Musae
sionas. 1610) [DDDSSLTD,
SFSMRR, DD] BK27   6873
Melrose (Maker) [DMSDTLS,
MMRDRMF#S,] Y198; Z377;
AB352; AC165; AD351; AE
398; AF434; AH460; AR604;
AS388; AW384; BA881; BF
560; BK125   6874
Melrose (Scottish Psalter.
1635) [DSMFSFRM, FMDR
MR, SL] E451; X686   6875
Melton (Mason) [DRMFMDMRR

DTD, TDRM] AO441   6876
Memoria (Wesley, S.S.) X
  Gratitude   6877
Memorial (Hodges) [MMFMRM
  RD,MMFMRDT,D] L402b
    6878
Memories of Galilee (Palmer)
  [SDSMSRSF,STSRSDSM,] AU
  437; BC38   6879
-----. R [SDRMSDRM,MRM
  FRMFS,]   6880
Memory (Harmer) [DMMRDTDF,
  SFFMRM,SM] Z454   6881
Mendebas (German trad) X
  Mendebras   6882
Mendebras (German trad) [DRM
  MMRDRDS,DMSSSF] G396; I68;
  L50; R70; S18; T116; U438; Z
  443; AB9b; AD30a; AE52; AG
  36; AH162; AI15; AJ170; AK
  38; AM321; AO13b; AS38; AT
  36; AU11; AV8; AW285; AX65;
  BB463; BR86; BZ   6883
Mendelssohn (Mendelssohn) [SDD
  TDMMR,SSSFMRM,S] A27; B
  73; C73; D51a; E24; F60; G86;
  H138; I111; J25; K25; L224;
  M168; N34; O198; P136; Q94;
  R163; S11; T333; U59; V121;
  W46; X74; Y361; Z189; AA154;
  AB111; AC77; AD105; AE81;
  AF120; AG66; AH253; AI59; AJ3;
  AK102; AL59; AM168; AN169;
  AO126; AP171; AR128; AS101;
  AT81; AU142; AV83; AW85; AZ
  205-R; BA163; BB111; BC60;
  BD211; BE310; BF286; BI94; BK
  144; BL10; BO153a; BR147;
  BV112; BX206; BY98; BZ
    6884
Mendelssohn (Mendelssohn) X
  Brightest and best   6885
Mendelssohn (Mendelssohn) X
  Trust   6886
Mendip (English trad) [SSFMSD
  TL, LSMDDR,DR] E498; W592a;
  X201; AN265; BE87; BY205
    6887
Mendon (German trad) [DTDSDTDR,
  DMDLRDRT] A218; B201; C201;
  D313; G509; H97; I669; J415;
  K142c; L446; M218; N13; Q119;

R370; S474; T25; V522; Y
  189; Z120; AA4; AC293;
  AD29; AE30; AF238; AJ34;
  AK328; AL316; AM64; AN
  290a; AO603; AP337; AR525;
  AS438; AV67; AW211; BA
  350; BB210; BE228   6888
Mendota (---) [SSSMRDLS,
  SSSDTDR,R] AR350; AS352;
  AX162; AY364   6889
-----. V [SSSMRDLLD,
  LSSDTDR,] AY364   6890
Mensch, willt du leben selig
  lich (Walther) [MSSLTDTL,
  TDSLMSFM,] AA392   6891
Mentzer (Koenig's Harmonischer
  lieder schotz) [SMSLSFMRD,
  MRDRMFMR,] A302; K355a;
  L485b; M123; O10; Q30; AA
  311; AM11; AW509   6892
Mer helighet gif mig (Pilgrims-
  harpan) [DDMMSDDTTLS,
  STTTD] N660   6893
Mercersburg (Woodbury) X
  Lake Enon   6894
Merciful Saviour (Traditional)
  [SDMFRDTDRMFSMR,SD]
  P260   6895
Mercy (Gottschalk) [SLSDMMR
  D,DDDTDRMR] C447; G47;
  H216; I53; L184; M546; N
  162; P47; R240; S208; T289;
  U133; V218; Y100; Z274;
  AA259; AB94; AC60; AD185;
  AE141; AF242; AG127; AH
  231; AI122; AJ276; AK188;
  AM245; AN25b; AO380; AP
  286; AR219; AS29; AT170;
  AU204; AV151; AW136; AX
  134; AY451; BA137; BB206;
  BC8; BE46; BF267; BH253;
  BK98; BR270; BX30b; BZ
    6896
-----. V [SLSDMMRD,DTDD
  SMRM] Z274   6897
-----. V [SLSDMMRD,DTD
  DMRMR] BE46   6898
Mercy's free (Auber) [SFMMM
  MMFSLS,SFMRF] AX313
    6899
Meredith (Knecht) X St Hilda
    6900

Meredith (Meredith) [MMMFLSM,
   SRMFMRM, MM] R238; U287;
   V742; AT175; AU331   6901
-----. R [SMDL, SLSMDR, MMM
   MSS]   6902
Meribah (Mason) [DMMMRMFS,
   MLLLSFMR,] B263; C174b;
   H270; I365; K269; L302; M214;
   Q412; R329; T110; U422; V301b;
   AA339; AI96; AJ159; AL301c;
   AM563; AO535; AP50; AW255;
   BB384   6903
Meridian (Sims) [DMMRSDMMR,
   SDSSFMR] AT539   6904
Merlin (Conant) [SSSLM, MMM
   SM, DDDS#D, D] Y153   6905
Merlo (Emerson) [SMMRDRDLS
   M, SFMRMF] L206   6906
Mernle (Symonds) [SMRDRDLS, S
   DSMRS, SM] F445a; BV347
                              6907
-----. R [SFMRMDTL, RSMLS
   F, RM]   6908
Meroe (Bradbury) [DDDTDRDTD,
   DRMMMRD] L169a; T209; AJ
   300   6909
Merrial (Barnby) [SSSSSS, LLS#
   LTLD, DDT] A172b; B364; C
   364a; D535a; G53; I59; J231a;
   K574b; M575; N540b; O562;
   P67; R51; S35; T309; U467;
   V41; Y94; Z149; AA45; AB28;
   AC23; AD59; AE50; AF51; AG
   33; AH170; AJ8; AK56; AL545c;
   AM666; AN128b; AO37; AR52;
   AS30; AT35; AU194; AV15;
   AW29; BA788; BB52; BC122; BD
   6; BF198; BK45; BR519; BX
   144; BZ   6910
Merrial (Blunt) [SLTDDT, SSL
   SS, LTDMM] L17; U260; V406;
   AE184; AH360; AI379; AJ262;
   AK447; AO225; AR310; AS314;
   BA39; BD103; BH146; BI42
                              6911
Merry Christmas (Shaw) [LRTD
   LTSL, DRTDLTSS,] BG189
                              6912
-----. R [RMLLLSML, TMLLSM
   L, T]   6913
Merry Christmas bells (Gilchrist)
   [SMFSFFSDTLSM, SFRS] BI80
                              6914

Merthry Tydvil (Parry) [ML
   S#LMSRM, LTDTMSF#M,]
   X312; AN375; AQ200; BY
   196b   6915
Merton (Barnard) X Brockles-
   bury   6916
Merton (Jewson) [DRMSFMR
   M, MMMFMR, RD] M584
                              6917
Merton (Monk) [DMSSFLLS,
   MF#SSLLS, S] A9; B63; C
   63a; D41a; E5; F47; J1; K
   3; X61; AA14; BE79; BV76;
   BY249   6918
Merton (Oliver) [SLTDRMDD,
   MRDTLS, RD] AO74   6919
Message (Nichol) [DRMMMFM
   R#MD, MFSSLS] G501; R
   504; U389; V740; Z530;
   AC302; AE353; AG261; AH
   464; AP797; AR564; AS370;
   AT455; AU379; AV261; AW
   335; BF525; BY400; BZ
                              6920
-----. R [SSDDDRMMR, RM
   FFFMR]   6921
Messengers (St Alban's Tune
   book) [SDRDTDFSFM, MRT
   DFM] D182; E216   6922
Messiah (Handel) [SDMRDLFM
   FM, SDRTLS] H183; I370;
   L150; M438; V175; Z245;
   AA245; AH310; AI254; AJ
   354a; AM120; AO214; AS
   163; AV118   6923
-----. V [SDMRDLSFMFM,
   SDRTL] L150   6924
Messiah [Come] (Handel) [SS
   FMRDS, TDRMFSS,SS] AH614;
   AI250; AS75; BR353b 6925
-----. V [SSFMRDS, TDRM
   FR, SSF] AS75   6926
Messiah (Herold) [MRDDFMR,
   SLLSMDR, MR] C231; D
   607b; G225; I348b; L408;
   V592; AO654; AY155; BR
   211; BZ   6927
Messiah (Hult) [SSSSDLLS, DD
   TSLSF#M,] N426   6928
Messiah (Swedish. 16th c)
   [DDDDLSS, SLDDTD, DDD]
   J9; M601; N1   6929

Metcalfe (Metcalfe) [MMFSFM
R, SMFFMRS, MM] BB70
                                          6930
Metzler (Redhead) X Metzler's
Redhead, No. 66   6931
Metzler's Redhead No. 66 (Red-
head) [MRDDSLLS, SLTDTL,
LL] Eap. 29; F146; J453; K
128; M288; W423; AP249;
BE367; BV200; BY272a   6932
Meyer (Meyer. Geistliche seelen-
freud. Ulm, 1692) X Es ist
kein tag   6933
Michael (Weisse) [DDDTTDLS,
SLDTLSFM,] E652   6934
Michael, prince (Marsh) [DDD
RMSFMR, DDRFMRM,] BN
164   6935
Michaelmas (Davis) [SSLSDRMFR
TD, MRDRM] BY706b   6936
'Mid pleasures and palaces (Bish-
op) X Home, sweet home
                                          6937
Middlesex (---) [MMRDRMFMR,
RSFMFRD] AL440; AW168
                                          6938
Middleton (Arnold) [DRMMMRRD
RR, DMSMRD] H199; L22;
AO520   6939
Middletown (Winchester) [MMM
FMMRRMRLS, SSST] I451
                                          6940
Midhurst (Gatty) [SSLSSFMRR,
MFSDRRM,] X152   6941
Midian (Allen) [LLTDTLDFMLL,
DDRR#R] BV137a   6942
Midt i livit ere vi (Walther) X
Mitten wir im leben sind
                                          6943
Mid-winter (Holst) X Cranham
                                          6944
Mig hjertelig nu laenges
(Hassler) X Passion chorale
                                          6945
Mig kläd i helig prydnad (Lind-
ström) [SMRDTRL, DDTLSS,
SMR] N311   6946
Migdol (Mason) [SSDLRDTD, M
RMRDTDR] H182; I630; L10;
M95; T289; V19; AJ401; AM
114; AO16; BB154   6947
Mighty rock (O'Kane) [MFSLSDM,
MRDDTLLS, M] Z407; AI249

                                          6948
-----. R [STRFMRD, DRDTL
TSF, M]   6949
Mighty to save (Sanders) [SS
MRTDS, SLDFLS, DDT] BB
636   6950
-----. R [STDR, SDRM, F#F#
F#S, SDMS]   6951
Milan (LaFeille. Methode ...
1782) [DRMRMSFM, MRDTL
RDT] AP813; BR89   6952
-----. V [DRMRMSFM, MRD
TLRT, D] BR89   6952a
Milburn (Price) [DTDFMMRD
R, RSSSFMF,] AK154   6953
Mildred (Johnson) [DMSFMR,
RRSLTLS, F#MS] N229
                                          6954
Miles animosus (Shaw) [SDLR
MDM, SDLRMD, MRS] J551a;
S265b; AL405a   6955
Miles' Lane (Shrubsole) [SDDD
RMRDR, SLSFMRD,] A355b;
B192b; C192b; D450b; E364;
F217; G164b; I167; J426a;
K131a; L114b; R132b; S192b;
T324; U117; V196b; W139a;
X440; Z253; AB87b; AC135a;
AD180b; AE129; AF196; AG
114b; AH198; AI337; AK185;
AL46a; AM218b; AO208a;
AP254a; AR102; AS155; AT
133; AU256; AW3; AZ14-Q;
BA90-B; BB157; BF327B;
BR53a; BV265a; BY180b; BZ
                                          6956
Militant (Barnby) X Sarum
                                          6957
Milites (Handel) [DSDDDDD,
RMDMF#S, DSM] E381; X
343; AD44; BY503   6958
-----. V [DSDDDDD, RMRDM
F#S, SS] BY503   6958a
Milites crucis (Corbeil) X
Orientis partibus   6959
Mill Brow (Routley) [LLDTLS
DR, MMSFR, RRS] BV406b
                                          6960
Mill Lane (St Alban's Tune
book, #10) [DRMFMRLTD,
MFSMDTL] C473a   6961
Millenium (American trad)
[SDDDTLS, SLDTRD, DRM]

Missionary (Mason) X Missionary hymn 6999

Missionary chant (Zeuner) [MM MMDRRT, TDDDDMRM,] A221; B453b; C453; D263; H411; I397; R494; S211; T133a; U285; V104; Y380; Z526; AB370; AD382; AG 198; AI180; AJ199a; AK352; AM 67; AN290b; AO453; AR393; AS 360; AU235; AV131; AW337; BA361; BE218; BF528; BR78; BX35 7000

Missionary hymn (Mason) [DMS SLSM, DTDFMMR, DMS] A254; B476; C476; D254; E577; G401; H479; I655; J310; K220; L338; M100; N367; M120; P357; Q 495; R509; S385; T125; U405; V586; W371a; Z541; AA474; AD371; AG265; AH467; AI168; AJ183; AL256; AM383; AN408a; AO528; AP376; AR558; AS93; AT442; AU35; AV269; AW333; AX90; AY329; AZ151-0; BA341; BB445; BC40; BD187; BE2; BF 301; BR225; BX328a; BY57b 7001

Missionary's farewell (Baltzell) [MFSSDRM, RDLDTDR, MF] BB657 7002

-----. R [RDTLSDMD, FFLDTDR, S] 7003

Misströsta et att Gud är god (Swedish, 1695) [SMRDDTLS, SLMF#SSF#S,] N594; AQ310 7004

Mit freuden zart (Bohemian Br.) X Bohemian Brethren 7004a

Mit fried' und freud' (Walther. Geistliche G-B. 1524) [RLL SRDTL, DLDTL, LDT] Q137; AA 185 7005

Mit haab og Trøst og al Tillid (Tomissön. Psalmebog. 1569) [LLLMLSF#M, MLSFMR#M, L] O428 7006

Mitchell (Mitchell) [SDSTLL, SRF M, SDTLL,] BB239 7007

Mitt hjerta, Jesu! denna dag (Swedish Koralbok, 1884) [SM RDFMRM, SLDDTDD, S] N14 7008

Mitten wir im leben sind (Walther)

[SSLTDDTL, TDRLSFM, S] O240; Q590 7009

Mittit (Malim) X King of love 7010

Mittler, schau auf sie hernieder (Schicht) [SSSDFMMRD, RRMDSFM,] AA290 7011

Mixolydian (Mason) X Boylston 7012

Mizpah (de Fluiter) [SLSMRD RDM, SLL#TSMF#] BB38 7013

Mizpah (Tomer) X God be with you 7014

Moab (Roberts) [LLDTLS, LD DTT, DDLTD] R337; S183; W572 7015

Mobile (Campbell) [MFMRSDRM FRMD, RMFS] V362; AJ201a 7016

Moccas (Reinagle) [DTDRF#S, SLSSFM, MFFM] K504; AZ 582-M 7017

Modena (Woodbury) [SSMMDDL, LSMMDR, SSM] T54; AJ84 7018

Moel Llys (Stock) [DRMSLTD, DDRRD, DRMS] B485; BV321; BY376 7019

Mohler (Showalter) [DDDDRD TD, RRRMDTLS,] AR599; AS 423 7020

Moline (Kirkpatrick) [SSMRR DLSMS, SSRDTF] T199; AI 368; AJ288 7021

Molleson (Fletcher) [SDDDTLS RM, SDRMRDR] G214 7022

Moment by moment (Moody) [SDRMMMFDRM, MRD#RMR] AH401; AI313; AM708; AU58; BB583 7023

-----. R [MFSMRDTDRM, MFSMRD] 7024

Mon Dieu, prête-moi l'orielle (Bourgeois) [LLSLTDTL, LLSLTDTL,] E640; F514; R536; X121; AF519; BJ58 7025

-----. V [LLS#LTDTL, LLS# LTDTL,] BJ58 7026

-----. V [RRDRMFMR, RRD RMFMR] F514 7027

Monica (Foster) [MMSSSFFM,

MMLSSFM, F#] D246   7028

Monk (Monk) [MDRMF#S, SF#
  MR#F#M, MRMF] BX258 7029

Monk (Monk) X Eventide   7030

Monk (Monk) X St Philip   7031

Monk (Monk) X Waltham   7032

Monk Street (Holst) [DRMRDLS
  DRSMFRD, DR] X534   7033

Monkland (Antes) [DMSMFSLTD,
  MMRDTLS,] A308; B175; C
  175b; E532; F377; H144; J405;
  K311; L350; Q570; R28; S64;
  V127; W38a; X12; AA297; AD
  477; AF463; AG39; AL7b; AM
  30; AP120a; BA25; BB10;
  BD25; BK132; BV20; BX20;
  BY15   7034

-----. R [RRDTSDMR, MRDTDD]
                          7035

Monks Gate (English trad) [DRM
  DMFSL, SSDTD, DRM] A362;
  E402; G265; J563a; S276a; W
  576a; X515; AN213; AQ94; BV
  587; BY561   7036

Monk's march (Welsh trad) X
  Ymdaith Mwnge   7037

Monmouth (Davis) [MDLSMRMFM,
  FMFSLST] I534a; BY60a 7038

Monmouth (Geistliche lieder.
  Wittenberg, 1535) X Luther
                          7039

Monod (Vincent) [SLTDRDDT,
  RSSS#LFM, L] D612b; G215;
  AL323; AP478; BA427   7040

Monora (Bradbury) [SSMSDDSD,
  MRDMRD, SS] T115; AJ165
                          7041

Monroe Place (---) [DTLLSS,
  FMRD, SFMMRR,] AA337
                          7042

Monsell (Barnby) X St Andrew
                          7043

Monsell (Sherwin) [DTLSMSLFLL
  SS, DTDR] U5; Z106; AC12;
  AD27b; AF31; AR39; BF217
                          7044

Monsell (Slovak hymn) X Man
  of sorrows   7044a

Monson (Brown) [SSMRDSSFMMR,
  SDRML] V10   7045

Mont Richard (Buck) [MLTDTLSMM,
  MLTDTL] A571a; E633; X148b
                          7046

Montague (Barnes) [MMMMMM
  M, MLLLLL, LSS] W638
                          7047

Monte Cassino (Italian hymn)
  [DSSDRMRD, SRMFMRDD,]
  E150b; AN360a   7048

Montesano (Law) [LS#LMLR
  DTL, LSFMFSD] E122b; X
  491   7049

Montgomery (Champness) [DD
  SLLSFMRDS, SMRDM] E632;
  F549; X612   7050

Montgomery (Hopkins) X Nukapu   7051

Montgomery (Jarvis) X Stanley
                          7052

Montgomery (Woodbury) X
  Nearer home   7053

Montreat (Adams) [STDMRDTL
  SS, TMRDLD] Y397   7054

Montrose (Gilmour. Psalm-
  singer's assistant. 1793) [D
  MSDMRDSD, DDTDTLS,] BV
  241   7055

Montrose (Smyth) [SSLTDM
  DTLSLSRS, SS] BR545   7056

Moody (Towner) X Marvelous
  grace   7057

Moore (Harrington) [MMMM
  MM, MRMFS, SSS#S#L] I685
                          7058

Moore (Moore) [SSSMFLS,
  DDTLSF#S, SS] AT189 7059

Moorehead (Stebbins) [MMM
  RDDTT, DRMFFM, SS] T398;
  AR422   7060

Mooz [t]zur (Jewish trad) X
  Rock of ages   7061

Moravia (West) [DMSDLS, FM
  DMF#S, SRDT] D71a; V343;
  AA388; AZ582-C; BA117;
  BY235   7062

-----. V [DMSDLS, FMDRM
  F#S, SRD] AZ582-C   7063

Moravia (Weisse) X Ravenshaw
                          7064

Moravia (Wolder. Catechismus
  G-B. 1598) X Wolder   7065

Moravian (Emerson) [DMLSM
  MRDRRMFMR, DM] L113
                          7066

More about Jesus (Sweney)
  [SSSSLDDD, RRRRFMMM,]

R316; AE296; AH409; AI283;
AM676; AR455; AS225; AT321;
AV324; AX373; AY48; BY597
7067
-----. R [MSLSDD, RRMFMM,
SSSS] 7068
More holiness give me (Bliss)
X Holiness 7069
More like Jesus (Doane) [MMM
RRDD, RRRDFMR, MM] AT316;
AV190 7070
More like Jesus (Stillman) X
I want to be more like Jesus
7071
More like thee (Showalter) [DM
SLSMRMD, DDRRDRM,] AR
458; AS223; AX375; AY44 7072
-----. R [MFSLSD, DDRRDRM,
DMS] 7073
More love to thee (Doane) [SLS
DRM, MRDR, SLSDRM,] G364;
I317; J392; L198; N493; R397;
S315; T410; U224; Z390; AD
256; AE198; AF400; AG168; AH
347; AI117; AK471; AL498; AM
548; AP461; AR407; AS280; AT
292; AU218; AV195; AW472;
AX379; BA461; BB385; BF462
BZ 7074
More love to thee (Perkins) [MR
MDLS, RDRM, MRMDLS,] P
310; AO642 7075
Morecambe (Atkinson) [MMMFM
LSFFM, DTLSLT] D219b; G
179; H221; J129; L329; N171;
R236; S204; T251; U377; V548;
Y99; Z272; AB95; AC62; AD
184; AE137; AF232; AG125;
AH230; AJ349; AK193; AM310;
AN48b; AO219; AP276; AR232;
AV162; AW133; AY433; BA144;
BB336; BE207; BF265; BK85;
BZ 7076
Moredun (Smart) [MSRMFSLSFM
RD, SFMR] W232; AL201c; AP
314 7077
Moredun (Torrance) [MFMMRDR
FM, SSDDTLS] D610b; Sap. 43;
AA265; AL294; AP365b; AZ
277-A; BA837; BY454 7078
Morewellham (Steggall) X Mor-
wellham 7079
Morgan (Gould) [SSDDMMMMRD,

SLDSLL] BR299 7080
Morgan (Lyra Davidica) X
Easter hymn 7081
Morgenglanz der ewigkeit (Frey-
linghausen) [MRDSLSFM, D
TLTDTLS,] C128b; E374;
J212; K454; M160; O548;
P52; Q539; S30; W262; X27;
AA125; AK47; AL538; AR
414; AW554 7082
-----. V [MDSLFMM, DTLTD
TLS, M] P52 7083
-----. V [MRDSLFMM, DTLT
DTLS,] Q539 7084
-----. V [MDSLSFM, DTLT
DTLS, M] AK47 7085
Morgenglanz der ewigkeit
(Grimm's Choral buch) X
Grimm's 349th metre 7086
Morgenlied (Maker) [DDDSD
RMD, LLSDFMR, R] K117;
BY152 7087
Morgenstern auf finstre nacht
(Freylinghausen) X Gregor's
310th metre 7088
Moriah (Welsh hymn mel)
[MFSLSMD, SSFMLLSMD]
E437; W435b; X573a 7089
Moring (Moring) [MFSDTDM
R, SFFMRDTD] J207b
7090
Morlaix (Knecht) X Knecht
7091
Morley (Morley) X St Alban's
7092
Morley (St Patrick) X St
Patrick 7093
Morn of gladness (Cottman)
[SDTRDFM, MMRRDT, SDT]
B352; C352; U440; V746;
AH163; BD45; BR491 7094
-----. [SMRMRD, DRMFLS, S
SSF] 7095
Morn of joy (Sewall) [SMFRD
MM, SMFRDMM, RS] BI103
7096
-----. R [SMFSLS, FRMSFM,
SMFS] 7097
Morning (Gilbert) [MMTDLS,
LLTDLS, MRSR] D445b 7098
Morning (Haydn) X Haydn
7099
Morning (Monk) X Clifton 7100

Morning (Silcher) [SDRMR,SRM
FM,SSMSFM] K572; AO629
                                    7101
Morning (Wesley) [MRDDTDRMR
D,SFMMRD] W374; AB257;
AL532   7102
Morning has come (---) [SMDSDR
SM,SMDSSRMD.] AR553   7103
Morning hymn (Barthélémon)
[DRMMMFMRRR,SF#SF#M]
A151; B2; C2; D2; E257; F3;
I44; J202; K449; M552; N546; O
539; Q536; R50; V33; W256; X25a;
AA29; AB282; AD37; AE37; AF
32; AL529a; AM331; AN89; AP
653b; AQ265; AS24; AV3; AW25;
BA765; BE384; BF178; BR4;
BV34; BX129; BY672   7104
-----. V [DMMMFMRRR,SF#
SF#MRD] M552   7105
Morning hymn (Boyce) [DMMFM
RRM,DLTDRMFR,] R439; T
252b; AJ199b   7106
Morning light (Webb) X Webb
                                    7107
Morning praise (Geneva Psalter,
1551) X O Seigneur   7108
Morning prayer (Jassinowsky)
[SMMRRDM,RMRRRDDLD,]
BH241   7109
Morning prayer (Leyda) [SSSSDR
M,SSRD,MMSMD] AL620
                                    7110
Morning prayer (Reinecke) [DTD
MRDTD,RMMLFR,RM]
BR542   7111
Morning sacrifice (Störl) X Storl
I   7112
Morning song (Wyeth. Repository.
1813) [MLTDRDTLSM,MLTD
RM,] A156; R508; AF34; AQ
203; BZ   7113
Morning song (Wyeth Repository,
1813) X Detroy (Supplement to
Kentucky Harmony, 1820)
                                    7114
Morning Star (Franck) [SLTDRM
F#S,LSFSM,SFR] M376   7115
Morning Star (Harding) [MRDT
LSSDTDMR,SFM] A46a; B
95b; C95a; D66c; G119; I114;
J53a; K39; L228; M377; N62;
Q128; R175; S136; T337; U62;

V114; Z202; AA181; AB125;
AC239; AD126; AF126; AG
81; AH272; AI63; AK121;
AM167; AO138b; AR144;
AS109; AT67; BA183; BD
212; BZ   7116
Morning Star (Meinecke) [SS
MDDTLLSFM,MMLTD] BR
361   7117
Morning Star (Nicolai) X Frank-
fort   7118
Mornington (Howard) X Lan-
caster   7119
Mornington (Mornington) [SSFM
RD,DTLSLSFM,FF] C314;
D300b; G25; H219; I45; K
520a; L277a; T355b; V214;
AA258; AF401; AJ124; AN
284; AO377; AW226; BE70;
BF448; BX310; BZ   7120
Morris (Barnby) X Just as I
am   7121
Morris (Morris) X Nearer,
still nearer   7122
Morris chant (Bradbury) [MM
MMMMF,FMDLRDT,M]
L274; AJ100   7123
Morrow's Hill (Pollock) [SM
R#MDDRDLS,SSF#SMR]
AY39   7124
Morton (Barnes) [SSSDMRLTD,
DDDDDDT] BB395   7125
Morwellham (Steggall) [MFSL
SMDFM,LTDRMFR,] O256;
S409; U354; W548; Y63; AB
331; AG269; AI298; AK397;
AL382; AM444; AP577; AW
166; BF509; BY468b   7126
Moscow (Calkin) X Elim   7127
Moscow (Giardini) [SMDRTD,
DRMFMR,SMDS,] A271; B
104; C104; D327; E553; F266;
G2; H15; I2; J136; K164; L
179; M480; N164; O73; P237;
Q227; R244; S52; T294; U3;
V81; W364a; X303; Y354;
Z122; AA262; AB13; AC38;
AD20; AE154; AF246; AG12;
AH189; AI24; AJ408; AK4;
AL240; AM89; AN10; AO2;
AP373; AQ26; AR21; AS1;
AT12; AU4; AV32; AW8; AX
1; AY27; AZ579-B; BA10;

BB3; BC44; BD24; BE346; BF
216; BH136; BI39; BK63; BR
79; BV333; BX8; BY46; BZ
7128
-----. V [SMDRDTD, DRMFS
FMR, S] N164   7129
Moscow (Lvov) X Russia   7130
Moseley (Smart) [DRMFLS,
LFSMDR, SMDT] A457; B235;
C325; D343; U23; V455; AB
163; BA299; BE267; BX389
7131
-----. V [DRMFLS, LLFSMDR,
SMD] AB163   7132
Mosley (Showalter) [DMMFFSTD,
RMFSF#S, SL] AR497   7133
Mother dear, O pray for me
(Catholic trad) [MDRDLSMS,
DRRRDRM, S] AH132; BO79
7134
Mother knows (Cassel) [MR#MD
RMFFM, MSRRMFF] AU40
7135
Mother, Mary, at thy altar
(Trier G-B. 1695) X Sunrise
7136
Mother of Christ (Montani) [DD
DDT, FFFFM, SMRDTL,] BQ89
7137
Mother of mercy (Catholic) [MM
MFFSFM, MMMRSF#F#S,]
BO67; BP32   7138
Mother of mercy (Yenn) [SMFSR
MDFMR, RMF#SLT] BQ77
7139
Motherhood (Moore) [MDFMRM
RD, TDRMSFM, M] Z604; AN
557; AW364   7140
Motherhood (White) [MMSFMRRD,
RMFLSFM, M] AO563; AR547;
AS417; AT503   7141
Mothering Sunday (German, 14th
c) [SLTDRLTD, DMFSFSR,
R] BG145   7142
Motherland (Andrews) [DMSLMSM
RM, DMSLMF#S] Y286   7143
Moultrie (Cobb) [SDDTMRRD,
SFMDRMD, S] A125; B207;
C207; D179b; J177b; BF521;
BI6   7144
Mount Airy (Reed) [SDTLSSLSR
FM, RMF#SD] J353   7145
Mount Auburn (Kingsley) [MSMSL

MRD, DTLSMMR, R] T283b;
AJ41   7146
Mount Calvary (Owen) X Bryn
Calfaria   7147
Mount Calvary (Stewart) [MR
DTLLSS, SLTDRR, FM] B272;
C102a; D326; G289; I65; V
541; Y342; BE144; BF404;
BO140; BX276   7148
Mt Elliot (Fishwick) [MFF#SS
L, LDLS, MFMMDT] M549
7149
Mt Ephraim (Milgrove) [DMR
DSFMRD, DTLSRDT] E196;
F531a; W447; X203; BY495b
7150
Mt Holyoke (Wostenholm) [SS
MMRMDS, SSMMRMD, L] G
123; Y248; Z249; AB155;
AC285; AR216; BF338
7151
Mt Olive (Harrison) X Bank-
field   7152
Mount Sion (Parker) [SSSSLTD
MRD, SLLLT] A390; B307;
C307; D493a; S19; AD33; BD
144; BF626; BX19a   7153
Mt Sion (Spielman) [DMSSLTD
D, SSDLSF#S, D] M83   7154
Mount Sion (Sullivan) [MFSL
DTD, SMLLLRR, RM] W582;
AM600; BY19   7155
Mount Vernon (Mason) [MMSM
FLLS, DMMRMFMR,] L571;
M501; T68; AJ103; AO275;
AX622; AY170; BB269
7156
Mt Zion X Mt Sion   7157
Mountain Christians (---)
[SSDDTTDS, SLTDDTD, D]
BY256   7158
Mountain wave (Beethoven)
[MMMMMMMMMM, MMF#SSS]
Y77   7159
Mountain's height (Rounsefell)
X I'll go where you want me
to go   7160
Moville (Irish trad) [LLSLL
TDD, TDRFMRD, R] R136;
W179   7161
Mozart I (Mozart) [MFRDSDRM
FRD, MMMFR] C175a; D111b
7162

Mozart II (Mozart) [DDDTSFF
M, SSMSFRDM] C444; D428;
R388; S242; T27; U472; V231;
Y187; AC327; AD339; AI230;
AJ36; AL356b; AM484; AO
575; AR318; AW329; BA471;
BE47; BF646; BR499; BY527b
7163
-----. V [DDTSFFM, SMSFRDM
RR,] S242   7164
-----. V [DDDTLSFFM, SSMSFR
D] Z376   7165
-----. V [DDTLSFFM, SMSFRD
MR] AI230   7166
-----. V [DDTSFFM, SMSFRDM
R, D] BR499a   7167
Müde bin ich geh zur reh
(Fliedner. Liederbuch. 1842)
X Dijon   7168
Müller (American, 19th c) [SS
FMMRDDTLS, SSLSS] G434;
J47; K536; N637; P363; R157;
Z199; AD116; AE435; AF137;
AG76; AH265; AK109; AM641;
AR137; AT77; AU314; AV92;
AW414; BK153; BZ   7169
Müller (Müller) [SSFMRDRD, R
RMF#SSF#S,] X642; BY448
7170
Mundays (Shaw) [MTRDLSLSFM,
MTRDLS#] X447   7171
Mundi salus affutura (Plainsong,
M. 8) [SSSMFSMR, SLTDTLSF]
E229   7172
Munich (Meiningen G-B. 1693)
[DRMLSFMM, MSFMRRD,]
A114; B58; C58; D150; G386;
H87; I151a; J252; M527; O134;
P89; Q294; R251a; S215; W694;
Y364; Z434; AA113; AB100; AC
68; AD193; AE158; AF252; AH
233; AK193; AM263; AN29; AO
474; AP413; AR240; AT183;
AU75; AV75; AW289; AZ146-C;
BA7; BB217; BD232; BE77; BF
274; BR137; BY701a; BZ
7173
-----. V [DRMLSFMM, MSFRRD,
DR] BR137   7174
Munich (Meiningen G-B. 1693) X
O Gott, du frommer Gott
7175

Munich (Dresden. Neues G-B.
1593) X Ecce Agnus   7176
Munus (Calkin) [MFSDDTD,
LTDSLRR, MF] I438; V622;
Y190   7177
Muriel (Bergquist) [MRDTDR
FM, SLSFMR, MR] N432
7178
Muriel (Gounod) X Lux prima
7179
Muriel (Morley) [SMRDSTL,
STDRSM, MML] U441   7180
Music-makers (Nicholson)
[SLTDFMLR, DTDDRSLS,]
X315b   7181
Muskogee (McKinney) [SMFSLT
DTLLS, SFMRM] AT253; AU
52   7182
-----. R [SLDT, STRD, DTLS,
DDLT]   7183
Must I go, and empty-handed
(Stebbins) X Providence
7184
Must Jesus bear the cross
alone? (Allen) X Maitland
7185
Muswell Hill (English trad)
[SDDMRRFMSDLS, FMFR]
Y138; AC185; AF381; BK
74; BY548   7186
Muswell Hill (Bonner) [DRM
SFLSDT, LSMSFMR,] BK
139   7187
My anchor holds (Towner)
[SSDSMFS, SSLLLLS, SS] AH
387; AM717   7188
-----. R [SSDDDDD, SSRRRRR,
SS]   7189
My beloved (Lewis) X Beloved
7190
My country 'tis of thee
(Thesaurus musicus) X
America   7191
My cross (Norwegian folk)
[LDMRDMMRTD, LTDTLT]
P314   7192
My dancing day (English trad)
X Eastertime   7193
My days are gliding (Root) X
Shining shore   7194
My dearest friends, in bonds
of love (Ingalls) X The mid-

night call   7195
My dearest Saviour (---) [DMSSS
 MDMR, RMFFFLS] BO20 7196
My faith (Levenson) [MMS#S#MR
 MF, MMLLS#FMF] BH221
                                  7197
My faith looks up to thee (Mason)
 X Olivet   7198
My Father knows (Excell) [SDTL
 MSFF, STLSFMFS,] BB591
                                  7199
-----. R [SFRD, STLSFMFS,
 SFRD,]   7200
My Father knows (McKinney) [S
 MMMMFDM, MRMRLTDR,]
 AU452   7201
My God, accept my heart (Montani)
 [MMMFMDLS, DFFMDR, RR]
 BQ132   7202
My God, accept my heart (Walch)
 X Sawley   7203
My God, how endless is thy love
 (Pollock) [SDSLSDMFMRM,
 SDSLS] AX45; AY25   7204
My God! how ought my grateful
 heart (---) X My God, how
 wonderful thou art   7205
My God, how wonderful (Croft)
 X St Anne   7206
My God, howwwonderful (Hassler)
 X Passion chorale   7207
My God, how wonderful thou art
 (---) [SSFMDDSS, SLSFMR, SS]
 BO2   7208
My God, I am determined (---)
 [SDRMSSF, RRRSFM, SDR]
 AX344   7209
-----. R [DLFFSLS, MRRSFM, D
 LF] (---)   7210
My God, I love thee not because
 (Reinagle) X St Peter   7211
My God, my Father (Troyte)
 [DDTDLSFFM, DDTDLSF#]
 BQ332   7212
My God, my Father (Troyte) X
 Troyte, No 1   7213
My heart its incense burning
 (Hamburg. Neu Catholisches
 G-B. 1598) X Eisleben   7214
My heart says Amen (Hunter)
 [SDMMMMRDLD, LLSDRM]
 AX392   7215
-----. R [TDRRRRFMRDS, DR

MMM]   7216
My heavenly home is bright
 and fair (Miller) X Going
 home   7217
My home above (Pollock) X I
 love to think of my home
                                  7218
My hope is built (Bradbury) X
 The solid rock   7219
My Jesus, as thou wilt (Weber)
 X Jewett   7220
My Jesus, I love thee (Gordon)
 X Gordon   7221
My latest sun (Bradbury) [SS
 SSSLDD, LSDMRD, SS] AU53;
 AV313; AX575   7222
-----. R [RRMRD, RRRMRD,
 SDDDR]   7223
My life, my love, I give to
 Thee (Dunbar) X I'll live
 for Him   7224
My Lord and I (Darms) [SD
 SDRMD, LSTRFM, SDS] AO
 611   7225
My Lord and I (Main) [SLSSM
 RD, DDLDRM, SLS] BB532
                                  7226
My Lord and I (Shepard) [MM
 MRDLD, RRRDMR, MMM] AY
 326   7227
My Lord, I'll go (Nafziger)
 [SSSLLDTLS, DMRDRTD,]
 AY507   7228
-----. R [SLTDRDT, TFLTL
 S, SLT]   7229
My Lord, what a morning
 (Negro spiritual) X My
 Lord, what a mourning 7230
My Lord, what a mourning
 (Negro spiritual) [MMRMD
 D, SSMSRRSMFR] AH599;
 BK171   7231
My Master (Day) [MLS#LTS#
 F#M, MDTDRTLS#] AC110;
 BK22   7232
My Master (Harrington) [ML
 SMRDRM, RDRDLDRD,] S
 497   7233
My mother's Bible (Tillman)
 [DDMMMMD, DDDDDLS, SF]
 AH239; AU380   7234
-----. R [SDTSRD, DTLTDM
 RLTD]   7235

My mother's prayer (Weeden)
[MMFSDTDR, FFFTLLSS,]
AU95   7236
-----. R [DDTTLLSS, DDTT
LSF#S,]   7237
My name's written there (Davis)
[SDDRMD, SSLDFM, DRMM]
AU337; AX486; AY371; BB
617   7238
-----. R [DRMMRD, DRMMSR,
MFSS]   7239
-----. V [SSDDRMD, SSLDFM,
DRM] AX486   7240
My prayer (Bliss) X Holiness)
                                              7241
My redeemer (McGranahan) [SD
RMMMRDRR, STRFFF] AI10;
AM681; AT143; AU388; AX8;
BC139, 270   7242
-----. R [DRMFFLDFMM, SD
MRRR]   7243
-----. V [SDRMMMRDRR, SR
MFFF] BC270   7244
My Saviour cares for me (De
Vaughan) [DMMSSMRD, MSLS
MR, DM] AX538   7245
-----. R [SLLFLS, MSLSMR,
DMMS]   7246
My Saviour first of all (Sweney)
X I shall know Him   7247
My Saviour guides me (Bowman)
[SDRMDTRS, SLDFMMRR,]
AY127   7248
-----. R [MSLSDFMR, STRFLS
RR#]   7249
My Saviour's love (Gabriel) X How
marvelous   7250
My Shepherd is the Lord (Gelineau)
[DMSL, LSMRM, MSLD, SLS]
BSp. 10   7251
My song (Hakes) [SMMRDLSD,
RMMSFMR, F] BB613   7252
-----. R [MRRRMFLS, MRRRM
FM, S]   7253
My soul be on thy guard (Mason)
X Laban   7254
My soul in sad exile (Moore)
[SMMMMRDDLDS, SDDDD]
AS301; AT228; AU79; AV353;
AX524; AY125   7255
-----. R [DFFFFFFMMMM,
MDDDD]   7256
My soul, now bless (Lindeman)

X Min sjael, min sjael
lov herren   7257
My testimony (Arterbury) [D
RMMMMDMRD, MFSSSM]
AX340   7258
-----. R [SSLLLFSLSM,
MFSSSM]   7259
Mylor (Stanton) [LTDMRDTT
T, RDRMFMR] BV171   7260

N

Naar mig min synd vil kraenke
(German, 1790) [MLTDLSFM,
SLDRRD, ML] O281   7261
Naar mit øie, traet af møie
(Lindeman) X Holy mountain
                                              7262
Naar synderen ret ser sin
vaade (Meyer) X Rudolstadt
                                              7263
Naar tid og stund den er for-
haand (Wolff) [DSDTDRM
D, MSSMSFM, M] O206; Q
594; AA528; AZ132-K   7264
-----. V [DSLTDRMD, MSS
MSFM, M] Q594   7265
Naar vi i største nøden staa
(Bourgeois) X Commandments
                                              7266
Nachtigall (Spee. Trutz-Nachti-
gal) [MLTDLSFM, SLTDFM
RD,] X313; BV626   7267
Nachtlied (Smart) [MMMFMLS
DRMR, SFMLS] B13; C13a;
D7a; I61; K461; AB230; AV
16; BF196; BR127   7268
Nadolig (Lloyd) [LDMLSFM
RDR, MLSL, LD] W68a
                                              7269
Naglet til et kors paa Jorden
(Zinck. Koralbog, 1801)
[LTDDRRMM, MDTDRDTT,]
O271; P172   7270
Nailed to the cross (Tullar)
[MMMDRMMMFDRM, MMMR]
AU345; BB123   7271
-----. R [SSSF#LS, MMMR#
FM, MMMR]   7272
Nain (Mason) X Today   7273
Name (Chevenix-Trench) [DRM
MMRDRRR, RMFFFM] BB
171   7274

Name of Jesus (Spinney) [MMRF
MRLL, RRD#MRD, SS] D433c
7275
Name of Jesus (Strom) [MMM
RFMRD, SSLSFMR, M] J67a
7276
Nanini (Nanini) [MFMMRRMM,
SSSSSF#SS,] BJ1   7277
Nannie (Pollock) X Thou art the
way   7278
Nannini (Nanini) X Nanini   7279
Nantmel (Williams) [DMLSFM,
SSFMLSSF, MR] BY549b   7280
Naomi (Naegeli) [MMMSFMRMF
M, MLLSF#] A170; B396; C
396; D670a; G202; H44; I277;
J458; L324; N239; O442; T47;
U246; V390; Z310; AE145; AH
396; AI166; AJ74; AL156b; AM
562; AN444; AO345; AP278;
AR515; AS200; AV57; AW251;
BA602; BB322; BI19; BR245; BX
479; BZ   7281
Naphill (Darke) [SDRMFRR, SL
SMRDRD, M] F155; BV224;
BY237   7282
När juldags-morgon glimmer
(German trad) X Christmas
dawn   7283
Nar mit öie (Lindeman) X Holy
mountain   7284
Narenza (Leisentrit. Catholicum
hymnologium. 1584) [DTSLTD,
MRTDLS, SSSL] D185; E518;
J579; K204; O429; W546a; AK
308; AL141b; AP8; BV605;
BY197   7285
Nares (Nares) X Aynhoe   7286
Nashville (Mason, arr) [DMFSS
LLS, SMSDSLLS,] I534b; V516;
BB457   7287
Nassau (Rosenmüller) [MMSSDR
M, LTDMRRD, SR] A95a; B561;
C561; D114a; Eap. 12; F136;
I240; K114b, 313; L268a; M67,
229; O108; P107; Q446; V370;
AA381; AD149; AM476; AP353;
AS462; AW544; AZ149-A; BA
746; BI11-D; BK7; BR181; BV
179; BY167b   7288
-----. V [MMFSSDRM, LTDM
RD, MM] K313   7289
-----. V [MMFSSDRM, LTDMR

RD, M] BI11-D   7289a
-----. V [MFSSDRM, LTDM
RD, MFS] AP353   7290
-----. V [MMSSDRM, LTDM
RRD, MM] AW544   7291
-----. V [MFSSDRM, LTDM
SF#S, MF] BK7   7292
Nathaniel (Sullivan) X St
Nathaniel   7293
National anthem (Smith) [SMD
MSDMRDMF#S, SMRD] A142;
B429; C429; P414; Y291; Z
651; AB341; AF496; AH484;
AO599; AT486; AU457; AV
303; BA939; BC131; BF700;
BH265   7294
National anthem (Thesaurus
musicus. 1740) X America
7295
National hymn (Warren) [DD
RMFMDDTD, MMMSLT] A
143; B430; C430a; G482; I
704; J521; K493; M648; R
498; S379; T450; U342; V
744; Y283; Z533; AB338;
AC273; AD374; AE359; AF
433; AG264; AH480; AI358;
AK385; AM616; AN376; AO
523; AR567; AT54; AU240;
AV26; AW347; BA874; BB504;
BC54; BD169; BF529; BH
263; BK123; BZ   7296
Nativity (Danish trad) [SDSD
RMFMRD, SFM, FMR] M612
7297
Nativity (Lahee) [MMMSSDD
M, RDLLRDT, S] B27b; C101
b; D324b; Eap. 48; F221; I
108; V203; W617; Y32; AO
457; AP165b; BA187; BE164;
BV16; BX19b; BY200a   7298
Nativity (Maker) X All this
night   7299
Nativity (Minke) [SSSMDTLS,
SLLTRR, SS] L220a   7300
Nature (Parry) [DMFSSLFD,
LSMMRDFR,] F173   7301
Nature's praises (Danish trad)
[DRMRDSSS, LTDLRDTL]
P23   7302
Nauford (Sullivan) X Hanford
7303
Navarre (Bourgeois) X Rendez

à Dieu   7304
Navarre (Bourgeois) X Toulon
                                      7305
Nay, speak no ill (---) [MM
   RDTDRMS, MMRDRMF] BC
   116   7306
Nazareth (Harts) [SLTDMSTT, SL
   LFFM, MM] AC97; BB114; BK
   17   7307
Nazareth (Malan) [SDRMSFLLS,
   SDRMSFR] BR167   7308
Nazareth (Perkins) [SSDDRMFS,
   LSMDTDRM] AJ398   7309
Nazareth (Plain song) [DSFMRSL
   S, SDTLSSF#S,] M476   7310
Nazareth (Thalben-Ball) [SLTD
   RMSFMR, MRDLTD] BY123
                                      7311
Nazareth (Webbe) X Melcombe
                                      7312
Neale (Barnby) X Emmaus   7313
Neander (Neander) [DRMDMFS
   S, DTLSMRRD,] A90; B179;
   C179; D117; E241b; F222; J
   187; K202; L40; M1; N306;
   P219; Q1; R40; V538a; W163;
   X477; Z121; AA5; AF503; AK23;
   AL135; AM238; AW127; AZ91-A;
   BA61; BC61; BR182; BV257;
   BY85b; BZ   7314
-----. V [DRMDRMF#SS, DT
   LSDDT] AZ91-A   7315
Neander II (Neander) [SMMRD,
   RMMF#S, SDSFM, S] AZ4-A;
   BA139   7316
Near the cross (Doane) [MFMRD
   LL, SDDMMR, MFM] G248;
   N461; P182; R376; U218; V732;
   Z339; AE172; AH293; AI79;
   AK462; AL485; AM704; AO647;
   AP212; AR452; AS227; AT97; AU
   294; AV350; AW490; AX383;
   AY470; BB595; BZ   7317
-----. R [MSSFLL, SLSMMR,
   MFMR]   7318
Near to the heart of God (McAfee)
   X McAfee   7319
Nearer, dear Savior to thee
   (Clayson) [MDMSMRD, DLFM
   DR, MDM] BC117   7320
Nearer home (Woodbury) [SSS
   MRD, DRRDRM, MFFF] D675b
   Eap. 51; F346; H517; I590; K

520b; L604; V656; W583a;
   AE448; AL462; AP629;
   AW261; AX164; BA721; BY
   609a   7321
Nearer, my God (Mason) X
   Bethany   7322
Nearer, still nearer (Morris)
   [MMMSS, DFFM, LLLSMMM]
   N494; U266; AI278; AR259;
   AS221; AT281; AV376; AX
   377; AY310; BB390   7323
Nearer the cross (Knapp)
   [MRDRMSSS, DSSMMR, MR]
   AW491   7324
Nearer the cross of Jesus
   (Showalter) [MFMRMRDS,
   LTDMMR, MF] AS228   7325
-----. R [FFFLSSMS, MRD
   SMMR, M]   7326
Nearing the port (Pollock) [S
   SSMFSSSLFLS, SSSF] AY
   162   7327
'Neath the old olive trees
   (McKinney) [SSSMFS, DDD
   TLS, SSSR] AU398   7328
-----. R [MMMRDT, FFFM
   R#M, MMRL]   7329
Neckar (German) [MSDDRSFM
   RD, SMLDRM] BR444a
                                    7330
Need (---) [MFMMRRD, DRRF
   FM, MFM] N258   7331
Need (Farjeon) [MFSMDRML,
   DRDMMF#MS,] X569   7332
Need (Lowry) [DMRDTD, DDR
   DLS, SRM] A438a; B131;
   D602; G232; H55; I506; J479;
   L401; M629; N462; P319;
   R324; S332; T407; U303; V
   492; W700; Z341; AC150;
   AD275; AE196; AF342; AG
   170; AH322; AK469; AL493;
   AM710; AO640; AP480; AR
   306; AS218; AT334; AU193;
   AV346; AW187; AX354; AY
   68; BB258; BC79; BE137;
   BF364; BY475a; BZ   7333
-----. R [MMDFMMR, RDM
   RRD, DD]   7334
N'eelah hymn (Jewish trad) X
   Ayl nora allelah   7335
N'eelah melody I (Jewish trad)
   [SSMMDDSLTLSLTLS, S]

BH177   7336
N'eelah melody II (Jewish trad)
  [SLLSSLRRMR, TLTDRT] BH
  179   7337
Neilson (Gower) [SLSMDSF, TD
  DMRDR, SL] U137; AC180
                                             7338
Nenthorn (Hately) [MSLSFM,
  MRDTD, RMF#SL] W475b 7339
Nestling (Winding) X Winding II
                                             7340
Netherlands (Dutch trad) X
  Kremser   7341
Netherlands folksong (Dutch trad)
  X Kremser   7342
Nettleton (Wyeth) [MRDDMSRR,
  MSLSMRD, M] G23; H5; I19;
  L88a; P31; R379; S235; U368;
  V511b; Z111; AE220; AG9;
  AH181; AI4; AK476; AM400;
  AO273; AP447; AR438; AS14;
  AT313; AU190; AV223; AW189;
  AX35; AY14; BA479; BB291;
  BC70; BZ   7343
Neuadd Wen (Evans) [DLMLSFM
  L, TMSF#TDRT,] W393   7344
Neumark (Neumark) [MLTDTLT
  S#M, SSF#MLLS#] E458; G
  272; I476; J568; K398; L485a;
  M68; N484; O230; P141; Q194;
  R344; S105; V139; W541; X
  606; Z404; AA498; AB225; AF
  83; AG156; AI439; AK300; AL
  423; AM567; AP500; AZ106-A;
  BA718; BE216; BH89; BI46-D;
  BL48; BR260; BV523; BX182;
  BY580; BZ   7345
-----. V [MLTDTLTS#M, SSFM
  LLS#] Q194   7346
-----. V [MLTDTLTLS#, SSFM
  LLS#] V139   7347
-----. V [MLTDTLTLS# M, SSF
  MLL] BH89   7348
-----. V [MLTDTLTSM, SSSFM
  LT] BR260   7349
Neumeister (McGranahan) [MFSL
  MLS, SDTLSFM, MF] AT195;
  AU113; AV330; AW466; AX264
                                             7350
-----. R [MFSLDDTLS, SLMSS
  SL]   7351
Never alone (---) [SSSMSDMR#M,
  RD DRDLS,] AU400; AX543; AY

91   7352
-----. R [SMSDMR#MR, DRD
  LS, SSS]   7353
Never shone a light (Lowry)
  [SLSMSLS, MFMDRMD, SL]
  AI64   7354
Nevin (Nevin) [DTLFLS, FMR
  DRSS, DTL] AL112b   7355
New 113th (Hayes) [DTLSDRM
  MRDDT, TDRM] E298; G375;
  W431; X20; BY460   7356
New America (Longacre) [DS
  LSFM, LTDDTD, RMRS,]
  Z514   7357
New Calabar (Farrer) [MRDTT
  LS, DRMFMRDR, S] D651b;
  L463; W238; AD213; AL596;
  AP788; BA596   7358
New England (Noble) [SLDTDRS
  S, MFMRDR] A84   7359
New every morning (Schumann)
  X Canonbury   7360
New Grange (MacAlister) [MR
  DTLLSS, MRDTLS, SD] W
  610   7361
New Haven (Hastings) [DDDMRD,
  RRRFMR, MF#F#S,] L119;
  U129; V210; BA63   7362
New Orleans (Sellers) [SSSSSSS
  SS, SSLLLLL] AT142; AU69
                                             7363
-----. R [MRDSLDDT, TDR
  D#RSTF]   7364
New Prince, new pomp (Ireland,
  J.) [RLTSLTDRDTSL, RRDR]
  BG170   7365
New Russia (Gretchaninoff)
  [SDDDRTDTRL, SDDDRM,]
  Y312   7366
New Sabbath (Phillips) [DSLS
  FMFSDLRDTD, MR] X691
                                             7367
New St Andrew (Gill) X Frank-
  fort   7368
New Ulm (Reuter) [MDLLRDD
  T, DRMFMSMR,] Q50b 7369
New year (Barnby) X St Igna-
  tius   7370
New year (Booth) [MMSLSM, D
  DMFR, MDLSD] D541b
                                             7371
New Year (Mann) X Mann
                                             7372

New York (Noble) [DSSLSFMFS,
SDTLSLT] B437   7373
Newark (---) [SLDDLSMSLD, DR
DMRD,] AY402   7374
Newbold (Kingsley) [SSLSDTRD,
DRMFLSM, S] I24; L217   7375
Newbury (English trad) [DMSS
LFSMRD, MRRMFM] E16; W655;
X395c; BE146; BG46c   7376
-----. V [DMSSFLLSMRD, MR
RMF] BG46c   7377
Newcastle (Everett) [SSLSMDLS,
DRRDTD, RR] AR285; AS47;
AU264   7378
Newcastle (Morley) [DDTTRRDD,
MSFDRM, MM] B120; C241;
V739; W36; Y67; AL36; AP
202; BB85; BE206; BV4b; BY
51a   7379
Newcastle (Sankey) [DMSMDLDSD,
DRMFMR, D] AT121   7380
-----. R [SSRRSSMM, MMRSF#
S, MF]   7381
Newcombe (---) [DDDTMRD, DD
DTTLS, FM] AO305   7382
Newell (Bradbury) [SSMMSSFF,
FFMRMFM, S] AM84   7383
Newell (Swisher) [DMSDMRRD,
RMFSLTLS,] BD237   7384
Newfoundland (Parry) [DMDSFM
RD, SLFDTLS, R] AL524   7385
Newington (Jones) X St Stephen
                       7386
Newington (Maclagan) [MMFRLTD,
RRMRRDT, RM] B180; C180a;
F330; AL357a; AP555; BA472;
BB282; BV364; BY586   7387
Newland (Armstrong) [SDTLSM, F
MRDMR, SDTL] E589; F433b
                       7388
Newland (Gauntlett) [SDMRRM,
MFLSMR, MMRD] B261; D410b;
V396; W102a; BX344b   7389
Newman (Calkin) [SSSLMFFSRM,
DDRM, MS] AB219b   7390
Newman (Terry) [DMSDLSRM, M
LDTLS,] A343a; C70a; BY206b
                       7391
Newnham (Barnby) [MMMMMMM
FMRM, MMMMM] BX267   7392
Newton Ferns (Smith) [SMLFRSM
D, DTLSFRT, M] D465b; W59;
Y148   7393

Niagara (Jackson) [SMSDDRR
M, DTDFMRRR,] AO460;
BY194b   7394
Nicaea (Dykes) [DDMMSS,
LLLSM, SSSSD] A266; B
205; C205; D383; E162; F
160; G1; H1; I78; J131;
K158; L177; M140; N163;
O72; P232; Q246; R11; S57;
T182; U1; V88; W1; X187a;
Y18; Z107; AA263; AB17;
AC4; AD25; AE155; AF251;
AG1; AH159; AI27; AJ266;
AK1; AL1; AM87; AN8; AO
234; AP135; AQ4; AR1; AS
17; AT1; AU6; AV1; AW1;
AX12; AY30; AZ144-C; BA
8; BB73; BD22; BE117; BF
186; BI25; BK41; BL37; BM
92; BR35; BV227; BX5; BY
42; BZ   7395
Nicholls (Pollock) X My God,
how endless is thy love
                       7396
Nicht so traurig (Bach) [DT
LMRDTDRS#, LTDFMR]
E100; F411a; W413c; X264;
AF281; AL267b; AP191; BE
295; BV388; BY309b   7397
Nicht so traurig (Freylinghausen)
X Pressburg   7398
Nicht so traurig, nicht so sehr
(Ebeling) [DRDSDRM, MSF
MRRD, DR] AA28; AN152;
AQ284; AW68   7399
Nicht so traurig, nicht so sehr
(Grimm. Choral buch) X
Consolation   7400
Nicolai (Rosenmüller) X Nas-
sau   7401
Nicolai (Nicolai) X Frankfort
                       7402
Nicolai (Nicolai) X Sleepers,
wake   7403
Nicolaus (Hermann) X Her-
mann   7404
Nielsen (Nielsen) [SSFM
SMTRD, DLFDLSF] M338
                       7405
Nigerian tune (Olude) [SDM
SDMR, DDSLSLDD, M] BZ
                       7406
Nightfall (Barnby) [SFDMRDM

SDDT, LSLSF] G49; I58; J225;
K459; N551; U459; V47; AA38;
AZ36-F; BI20; BR112   7407
-----. V [SFDMRDMSDDTL,
SSSL] BI20   7408
Nightfall (Rau) [SSLSDRMFMR,
MDLSDR] AZ58-D   7409
Nightingale (Staples) [SDTLSM
RDRM, FLSRMS] BY746b   7410
Nil nisi labore (Webster) [DFSM,
SDLFSMDTLS, RT] BY511   7411
Niles (Cooke) [DTLLSDTLS, SF
RDRM, R] D234b   7412
Niles (Niles) [MMMMMMRDTLS,
SDMMR] BK100   7413
Nilus (Gabriel) [MSSSSSSDL,
LSFMSFM] T233; AJ329   7414
Ninety and nine (Bridge) [SLL
DTRDMR, MFSSLSS,] BR533
                             7415
Ninety-third [Psalm] (---) [SLD
LRDLS, SLDLDRMR] AY289
                             7416
Ninety-fifth [Psalm] (Hopkins, arr)
[DDRMFMRD, RMFSF#S, SD]
AY362   7417
Ninth Street (Main) [DRMFRDTD,
RMSDLSF#S,] L54   7418
Nishmas (Alman) [DLSLSLSMS,
SLRRDLD,] BH55   7419
No abiding city here (Brunk)
[SSSF#SLTD, MMMRDTLT,]
AY390   7420
No friend like Jesus (Teasley)
[MMMR#MFSM, FFFMRSM, M]
AX526   7421
-----. R [LLLTDTLSM, FFFM
RSM,]   7422
No hope in Jesus (Lowry) [DRMS
LLSM, DMSRMD, DR] AX226;
AY221   7423
-----. R [SSSSMRRD, SSSMRRD,
D]   7424
No mortal eye hath seen (---)
[SSMMRDLL, DSDDRMR, S]
AX601   7425
No night in heaven (---) [MMM
DRDLSD, SSSSLF#S,] AY161
                             7426
-----. R [SSSSMFSLS, MMMSSF
M]   7427
No night there (Danks) [DRMMFRS,
DRMCRD, DRM] AI342; AM730;

AS470; BB558   7428
-----. R [SSSMLSF, FFFRSF
M, SS]   7429
No, not one (Hugg) [MMRDDT
LDLS, MMRMRD,] AI396;
AY352   7430
-----. R [MSSLSMMRD, MSS
LSMM]   7431
No, not one (Hugg) X Homeward
bound (---)   7432
No room in the Inn (English
trad) [SSSLSMMDFMRD, DM
SS] BG114   7433
No shadows yonder (Kirkpatrick)
[SMRRD, DFLS, DTLLS, DF]
AS480   7434
No tears in heaven (Arnold)
[DDDDDMMMRD, DDDMMR]
AX600   7435
Nobody knows (Negro spiritual)
[MSLDRMMMM, SSLDDLS,]
Y320; BK169   7436
-----. R [MSSSMSSM, SMR,
MSSSM]   7437
Nocte surgentes (Sarum plain-
song, M 6) [RFMRFF, RMD
RFF, FFF] A157a; E165;
F10a; X28a; BJ49   7438
-----. V [LDTLDDLTSLDD,
DDD] X28a   7439
Nocturn (Burstall) [SMRDDD
TLS, SMRDDDT] D11b; AJ
260a   7440
Noel (English mel) [DRMRDRM
FMR, SSMFSLS,] A19a; B
362; C362b; E26; F66; I236;
K29a; L225; S128; W47; X76;
AB390; AE157; AI62; AJ394;
AL58a; AP170a; AR239; AZ
590-I; BA53; BB95; BE373;
BF269; BV104; BY101   7441
Noël nouvelet (French trad)
X Love is come again 7442
Noelsch (Noelsch) [SLSDFM
R, RMLSF#S, SLS] AO568
                             7443
Nomen (Murray) [DMLSMMRD,
SLDDRMR, M] D433b   7444
Nomen Jesu (Corbeil) X Orien-
tis partibus   7445
Nomina (Smart) [DSSMDLLS,
SDDTLS, MF] AZ14-Ff; BA
882   7446

Non nobis, Domini (Plainsong) [TRMRDTLTT, SLTTTTT] E626   7447

Non nobis, Domini (Williams) [LLLLS#L, LLTDRM, DRD] A503   7448

Non-resistance (Heatwole) [SDDD SMSD, SLLLLDLS,] AY297   7449

None but Christ (McGranahan) [SDMMMDMSSS, SMRRDRM,] W699; AL482; AW451   7450

-----. R [SSSSMLSSFM, DRMMM S]   7451

-----. V [SDMMMDMSSS, SM RRRD] AW451   7452

None can satisfy (Showalter) [MF SDTLSM, SLSRSLS, M] AS294   7453

None other Lamb (Ridsdale) [RM MFFSSL, LL#DLSL#LS] W412   7454

Nonington (Grundy) [SLTDSDRM D, MLSMRDL,] BV404   7455

Nor silver nor gold (Towner) [SSMSDSMSFSFR, FFRF] AM721   7456

-----. R [SLTDDTLTF, FFTT LFM,]   7457

Norelius (Johnson) [DMFSLSFMD, SLDSM, FM] N88   7458

Norfolk Park (Coward) [DTLSDMS FM, RLFMRDT,] D519c   7459

Noricum (James) [DDDTLSFM, STDRMSFR,] BY8b   7460

Norman (Doles' Choral buch, 1785) [SDTDRDTD, DMMRDT LL] W529b   7461

Normandy (French trad) [MLL LTDDDTLLSM, MSL] BY734b   7462

Normanton (Vulpius) X Cana   7463

Norris (Norris) X Where He leads me   7464

Norrland (----. 16th c. northern mel) X Sweden   7465

Norse (Lindeman) X Spring of souls   7466

Norse air (Norwegian folk mel) [SSLSDTLL, LFRDTTD, S] BZ   7467

North Coates (Matthews) [SSLLDD, TTDLS, DDMMS] D541a; F360;

K566; S161; W343; AL89; AP204; BA831; BV353; BY 453b   7468

North Petherton (Harris) [SL SDTD, MLTDDT, SLTD] F235   7469

Northampton (King) [MRFM RLT, DSDRMF#S, SF] F369; BV26   7470

Northfield (Ingalls) [DSFMSDM R, RMMRDR, SD] H300; BB 245   7471

Northrepps (Booth) [DDRMLL SF, FMRDRR, RS] D652b; V304; AB228; AJ324; AP 181b   7472

Northrop (Northrop) [DRRM FSFMRD, MRSTLS] Eap. 8; X82b; ALSuppl   7473

Northumberland (Smart) [SS LSMFSDT, LSDFRM, M] W 531b   7474

Northumbria (English trad) [SD TDRFMRD, FFMSRRD,] X 382; BG130   7475

-----. R [MDTDLSSFM, MDT DLSS]   7476

Northumbria (Stanton) [SDDRM FSLSFS, SFRMF] BY389   7477

Norton (Brackett) [SSDDMSLS, MFLDLS, MM] BE254   7478

Norwich (Crespin. Psalms, 1556) [DTLSDMRD, DRM FRM, MR] D38; E404; Q583; W643; X526; Z437; AA521; AD199; AL32; AN58a; AP 122a; AQ88; BJ84   7479

Norwich (Mann) X Lasus 7480

Norwich (Mann) X Watermouth   7481

Norwich (Mason) [LTDTLS#L, DRMRDTD, MM] V268   7482

Norwich (Ravenscroft's Psalter, 1621) [LDRMMFFM, MFDR RD, DM] X577   7483

Norwick (Woods) [SMDLRTS, DLTSMF, SMF#] BY276   7484

Nos Galan (Welsh trad) [SFM RDDRMD, RMFRMRD] BG50   7485

Nostre Dieu (Calvin. Psalter,
1539) [DDDLRLDTL, LTD
RLDTL,] E233b   7486
Not all the blood of beasts
(Mason) X Boylston   7487
Not alone for mighty empire
(Mozart) X Ellesdie   7488
Not dead, but sleeping (Warren)
[SFMSSFFM, MMMRRSS, S]
AX620   7489
-----. R [SSSMMFSLS, SSSRFM
R]   7490
Not far from the kingdom (Tenney)
[SSMFSLLSD, DRRRRDR] AX
262   7491
-----. R [SSMSL, LSSSDRRM,
FMM]   7492
Not half has ever been told
(Presbrey) [MFSF#SLTRDS,
DDDTDR] AU386   7493
Not I, but Christ (Burke) [MRD
FMMRLRDT, SRRSL] AS233
                          7494
Not made with hands (---) [DM
MRDMMR, DSSS, SLSS] AX481
                          7495
,-----. R [DMDS, MSLSMRD, DM
DS, D]   7496
Not now, but in the coming years
(McGranahan) X Some time
we'll understand   7497
Not what these hands have done
(Runyan) [SMDTDRD, MSMRMF
M, SM] AX318   7498
-----. R [MSRSFFM, MMTMRD,
DLL]   7499
Nothing between (Tindley) [MMM
MDRDLLS, DDDDMM] AU66
                          7500
-----. R [DDLSMRDRMD, DDLS
MR]   7501
Nothing but the blood (Lowry)
[DDDRMSM, DDDRMMRD, D]
AI395; AM677; AT204; AU456;
AX115; AY511   7502
-----. R [SMRMSM, RRDRRMS,
SMR]   7503
Nothing like Jesus (Jones) [DRM
MMMMDRD, MFSLSM] AX271
                          7504
-----. R [SSLLLLLDTLLS, MF
SL]   7505

Notting Hill (Purday) [SSLDRM
DL, SLSDMR, SS] H416
                          7506
Nottingham (Clark) X St Mag-
nus   7507
Nottingham (Mozart) X Mozart
II   7508
Nous allons (French carol)
[DMFSLSFMRMFRD, DMF]
E645; X166; BG147   7509
Nous allons, ma mie (French
carol) X Nous allons   7510
Nous voici dans la ville (French,
15th c) X Chartres   7511
Nova vita (Peace) [MMMM
RR, SSSSF#F#, TT] A375b;
B380; C380   7512
Novalis (Mozart) X Cana
                          7513
Novello (Wade) X St Thomas
                          7514
Now are the days (Catholic)
[LDRMMFMD, DTLS#LRMF]
BO163   7515
-----. R [SDRMFMR, MDDR
DT, SDR]   7516
Now at the Lamb's high royal
feast (Joseph) X Angelus
                          7517
Now at the Lamb's high royal
feast (Montani) [LTRDSSFM,
MF#LSDTLS,] BQ30   7518
Now bless the God of all
(Cowen) [SLSMFS, MRDTD
TL, LLR] BH81   7519
Now blessed thou (Bach) [DD
RMFSRMF#S, FMRMFS]
BI7-D   7520
Now for each yearning heart
(Bigelow) [MFMMRR, RMF
MRD, FRRD,] AT527   7521
Now from the altar of my heart
(Wilson) X Martyrdom   7522
Now glad of heart (Bohemian
Br. G-B. 1544) X Betracht'n
wir heut zu dieser frist
                          7523
Now, gracious Lord, thine arm
reveal (Wilson) X Martyrdom
                          7524
Now just a word for Jesus
(Doane) [DMRDDDL, LSMM

RR, FMR] AX197; BB522
7525
-----. R [SDRDLSM, SDTDMMR,
FM]   7526
Now let every tongue adore thee
(Nicolai) X Sleepers wake
7527
Now let the earth with joy
(Spevnicek) [DRRMRSF#MR,
DRRMRSF#] BQ110   7528
Now let us rejoice (---) [MRDM
SLSSDMFLS, SSF] BC118 7529
Now the day is over (Baring-
Gould) X Eudoxia   7530
Now the day is over (Barnby) X
Merrial   7531
Now the shades of night (Fischer)
X Coming to the cross   7532
Now the world is saved from dark-
ness (Hintze) X Salzburg
7533
Now to heaven our prayer (Arndt)
X God speed the right   7534
Now to Jesus Christ (Root) [SS
DDRRMD, MMSSFMR, L] BI24-D
7535
Now we'll sing with one accord
(Daynes) [DMSLTDRM, MFRRR
MD, D] BC132   7536
Nox et tenebrae et nubila (Sarum
plainsong M 1) X Splendor
paternae   7537
Nox praecessit (Calkin) [MMM
DRMMF, RDMSFM, DL] B60;
C60; D281b; H93; I246; S469;
V8; W482; Y66; Z426; AA119;
AC267; AD198; AE388; BA6;
BD97; BE261; BF403; BX353;
BY248   7538
Noyon (Lowden) [SSSFMRD, DT
LSMDR, RR] T92   7539
Nu bede vi den helligaand
(Walther. G-B. 1524) X
Soldau   7540
Nu er frelsens dag oprundet
(Lindeman) [MDSSLTRD, FMR
DTDR, M] O191   7541
Nu fryde sig hver kristen mand
(Christliche lieder. Wittenberg,
1524) X Nu freut euch   7542
Nu hviler mark og enge (Isaak)
X Innsbruck   7543
Nu lader os da grave ned (Her-

mann) [DDDRTDTLS, SDR
MRDT] O594   7544
Nu lukker sig mit oege (Korss-
ing) [SSDDRDT, LLRRFTD,
MM] N504   7545
Nu rinder solen op (Zinck.
Koralbog, 1801) X Zinck
7546
Nu skal du, min sjael (Crueger)
X Schmuecke dich   7547
Nu takker alle Gud (Crueger)
X Nun danket   7548
Nu wol Gott das unser gesang
(Traditional, 16th c) [DSLS
DDRM, MFMRDLTD,] S513
7549
Nukapu (Hopkins) [MFSMDRM
D, LTDDRMFM,] D173; V647
7550
Nun bitten wir den heiligen
Geist (Walther. G-B. 1524)
X Soldau   7551
Nun danket (Crueger) [SSSLLS,
SFMRMRD, SS] A144; B422;
C422; D200; E533; F379;
G7; H62; I30; J443; K283;
L77; M22; N299; O31; Q36;
R9; S459; T300; V635; W29;
X350; Y303; Z173; AA64;
AB56; AC325; AD12; AE11;
AF29; AH196; AI443; AK72;
AL19; AM86; AN262; AO104;
338; AP147; AQ19; AR601;
AT491; AV44; AW514; AZ
146-A; BA122; BB90; BC120;
BD200; BE199; BF169; BI55;
BJ93; BK62; BL56; BM14;
BN198; BR492; BV22; BX187;
BY18b; BZ   7552
-----. V [SSSLLS, MFMRMRD,
SSS] N299   7553
-----. V [SSSLLS, MFMRDTD,
SSS] Q36   7554
-----. V [SSSLLS, SMFMRD,
RRRM] AO338   7555
-----. V [SSSLLS, SFMRSFM
RD, S] AZ146-A   7556
Nun danket all' (Crueger) X
Graefenberg   7557
Nun danket all' und bringet ehr
(Crueger) X Graefenberg
7559
Nun danket all' und bringet ehr

(Störl) X Stoerl I 7560
Nun danket alle Gott (Crueger)
X Nun danket 7561
Nun freut euch (Christliche lieder.
1524) [DDSDFMRD, DRMFMRLT]
E148; F150; M113; O3; Q124;
X640; AA310; AZ132-B 7562
-----. V [DDSDFMRD, DRFMRLT
D] O3 7563
Nun freut euch (Geistliche lieder.
1535) X Luther 7564
Nun freut euch lieben christen
g'mein (Christliche lieder.
1524) X Nun freut euch 7565
Nun komm der heiden heiland
(Walther, G-B. 1524) X Venit
hora 7566
Nun kommt das neue (Darmstadt
G-B) [SSSSSLTD, TDTLTLLS,]
AA140 7569
Nun lasst uns den leib
(Geistliche Gesäng. Witten-
berg, 1544) X Rhau 7570
Nun lasst uns geh'n (Kirchen-und
haus buch. Dresden) [SFMRD
RD, MFSLSFMMR] E104 7571
Nun lasst uns Gott dem herren
(Burgk) X Selnecker (Selnecker)
7572
Nun lob' mein' seel' (Kugelmann.
Concentus novi. 1540) X Tabor
7573
Nun preiset alle (Lowenstern)
[DDRMD, RRMFFF, MMFSR,]
Q28; X236; AZ70-A 7574
-----. V [DDRMD, RRMFMF,
MMFSR] AZ70-A 7575
Nun ruhen alle wälder (Isaak) X
Innsbruck 7576
Nun seht (Bohemian Br.) X
Stettin 7577
Nun sich der tag (Krieger)
[MLTDDRRM, MRMDDT, MD]
C496; Q561; AA30; AZ14-A;
BA859 7578
-----. V [MLTDDRRM, MLDT
LS#, TD] Q561 7579
Nun sich der tag geendet hat (Wil-
liams) X Mear X Nun sich der
tag (Krieger) 7580
Nunc dimittis (Bourgeois) [SLS
FMR, FMDRRD, DS] A176; E
269; J220; Q101; R61; X50;

AF49; AL551; AR55; AW
34; BJ88; BY699 7581
Nunc sancte (Plainsong: early
M 8) [LLLLLLLS, LLLL
SLLL] A160a 7582
Nunc sancte nobis (Latin: old)
[FFSLFSFM, SFFMRFSF,]
BJ45 7583
Nunc, sancte, nobis, spiritus
(Plainsong, M 4) [MMMR
MRDRRMM, FFMRR] E255
7584
Nuremberg (Ahle) X Liebster
Jesu 7585
Nusbaum (Nusbaum) X Would
you live for Jesus 7586
Nutfield (Monk) [MMFSLTDS,
SRSM, MMF] A169b; B26;
C26; D19a; Eap. 15; F26b;
V39; W702; AL547c 7587
Nyberg (Nyberg) [SDMSFM
FS, TLSFMFSF] J145
7588
Nyland (Finnish trad) [SMR
DRDLS, SSLSFM, SM] A431;
J574; R417; S284a; W442;
AD433; AE343; AK301; AL
281; AM306; AN246; AQ115;
AR294; AT303; BV307; BY
581b; BZ 7589

O

O amor quam ecstaticus (Plain-
song M 1) [RLSFMRFSL,
LRDL#LSL] E214b; W143;
X607b; BV580 7590
O amor quam exstaticus X
O amor quam ecstaticus
7591
O anblick der mir's herz
bricht (Gregor) X Gregor's
99th metre 7592
O awake! my slumbering min-
strel (Stephens) [MFSLSSF
MRS, SF#SFFF] BC268
7593
O, be still (Goerz) [DRMRD
LS, SSDDMR, DRM] AX394
7594
O beautiful for spacious skies
(Ward) X Materna 7595
O Bethlehem (Irish trad) [SS

MSMDSD, RMRSMRDR,] BN18
7596
O bless the Lord, my soul (Jewish
trad) X Az yasheer   7597
O blessed are those (Gelineau)
[DDDR, RRM, MMMS, MDR, MM]
BSp. 50   7598
-----. R [DSSSLSMRMDDLLLM.]
7599
O blessed by God (Benedictine trad)
[DRDTLTSD, DRRDRFRM,] BN
172   7600
O blessed day, when first was
poured (Andernach G-B) X
Andernach   7601
O blessed Father! sent (Montani)
[DMFSDRDL, DTDRMFM, D]
BQ108   7602
O blessed St Patrick (Paderborn
G-B. 1765) X O purest of
creatures   7603
O bone patria (Sullivan) X Home-
land   7604
O Bread of heaven (Herbert) X
Burwell   7605
O Bread of life (Isaak) X Inns-
bruck   7606
O breathe on me (Irish trad) X
St Columba   7607
O Brightness (Hume) [SLSLTDTDR
S, SMRDRS,] BL75   7608
O can you sing the new song
(Norwegian trad) [DSDTLFLTD
SFM, DTDR] P15   7609
O Canada (Lavalle) [MSSDRM
FSLR, MF#F#SLT] Y295; AE
391; AL511; AP648; BB508;
BX544   7610
O Christ, behind thy temple's
veil (Gardiner. Sacred melodies)
X Belmont   7611
O Christ, of angel legions
(Bragers) [SLMFSLTDDRD,
RRMDT] BP105   7612
O Christ, thy guilty people spare
(Whitehead) [MFMRMDDTL, T
DRMSFM] BN185; BO219 7613
-----. V [MFMRMDRDTL, TD
RMSF] BO219   7614
O Christe, morgensterne (Gesius)
[DDDDLSRR, RMFRRD, MF] K
350   7615
O Christliche herzen (Portnersches

G-B. 1831) [MLLDTLLDDM
RD, MFMR] BE389   7616
O come, all ye faithful (Wade.
Cantus diversi.) X Adeste
fidele   7617
O come, and mourn (Catholic)
[SDDTDRTS, SDDFMRDR]
AH126; BO168   7618
-----. R [TDRRFMRDR, SRR
FMRD]   7619
O come, and mourn (Catholic)
X Mother of mercy   7620
O come and mourn (Crookall)
[MMRMSFRDRM, MFMFLS]
BO168a   7621
O come and mourn (Montani)
[MMDTLDMSFM, MFRTDR]
BQ21   7622
O come and mourn (Slovak trad)
[LMMTRDTL, LFFMLSF#M,]
BN37   7623
O come, Divine Messiah (French
mel) X The band of children
7624
O come, let us worship (Barnes)
[SLLLRRRSD, DDFFFLS]
Sap. 3   7625
O come, let us worship (Tschai-
kowsky) [LTDLTDL, DDRMR
DT, RR] Sap. 4   7626
O come, loud anthems (Haydn)
[DDSMMRDDTDR, DDSMM]
AW18; BO4; BR287   7627
-----. R [MMRDSFMR, SSLSM
FRD]   7628
-----. V [DDSMMRDDTDR,
DSMMR] BO4   7629
-----. V [DSMMRDDTDR, RD
SMMR] BR287   7630
O come, O come, Immanuel
(Plainsong M 1) X Veni
(Emmanuel)   7631
O cor, amoris victima (Plan-
que) [MMMMRMRD, DMFSM
FFM,] BO17   7632
O cor Jesu (Perosi) [SFMR,
MSSDTLT, DLTSD] BQ236
7633
O, could I speak (Mozart) X
Ariel   7634
O darkest woe (Wurzburg G-B.
1628) X O traurigkeit   7635

O dass ich tausend (Dretzel) X
Dretzel II 7636
O dass ich tausend (Gnadaeur
choralbuch) [DDSLDMRD, RM
F#SDTLS,] AA420; AZ96-E
7637
-----. V [DDSLTDRMR,
RMF#SDTL] AZ96-E 7638
O dass ich tausend zungen hätte
(Gnadaeur choralbuch) X O
dass ich tausend 7639
O dass ich tausend zungen hätte
(Koenig. Harmonischer lieder-
schatz. 1788) X Mentzer
7640
O day full of grace (Weyse) X
Weyse 7641
O day of rest and gladness (Ger-
man trad) X Mendebras 7642
O dear little children (Schulz)
X Tekna 7643
O dearest love divine (Montani)
[MMMMMSF, FRRDRFM, RD]
BQ65 7644
O der alles [hoett' verloren]
(Darmstadt G-B.) X Gold-
schmidt 7645
O Deus, ego amo te (Cologne.
Symphonia ... 1695) X I love
thee, O thou Lord 7646
O du Guds Lam (Söderberg) [SM
RDMLSMDMR, RMRDM] N517
7647
O du hueter Israel (Freylinghausen)
X Festus 7648
O du Liebe (Thommen. Christen-
schatz. Basel, 1745) X Cassel
7649
O du Liebe meiner Liebe
(Darmstadt G-B.) X Gregor's
167th metre-E 7650
O du Liebe meiner Liebe
(Thommen. Christen-schatz.
Basel, 1745) X Cassel 7651
O, du mitt hjartas trangtau
(Haeffner) [SSMFSLSM, SLLTTD,
MR] N371 7652
O du store seierherre (Freyling-
hausen. G-B. 1704) X Con-
queror 7653
O durchbrecher (Freylinghausen)
X Conqueror 7654

O Emmanuel (Plainsong M 2)
[SDTDLTLSLL, TLLTDL]
BQ153 7655
O esca viatorum (Bourgeois)
[LLLSSLDTD, MMSFM]
A192; W543a; AI435; AM
511 7656
-----. V [LLLSLDTD, MMSFM
RRD,] W543a 7657
O esca viatorum (Haydn) [SM
DDLLLS, DTDRFFM, D] BN
90; BO34, 47; BQ42 7658
-----. V [SMDDLLLSS, DTD
RFFM] BO47 7658a
O esca viatorum (Isaak) X
Innsbruck 7659
O everlasting Light (Hallman)
[DDTDRLTD, DFMMRDR, S]
AY349 7660
O Fader var, barmhertig god
(Teutsch kirchenampt. Strass-
burg, 1525) X Es woll' uns
Gott genädig sein 7661
O Fader vor i himmerig
(Schumann. G-B. 1539) X
Old 112th 7662
O fair Creator of the skies
(Bragers) [MDMSSLSFS,
SRFFMMR] BP1 7663
O faithful cross (Catholic) [DD
RMLSFM, MFSMMRDD,]
BP30 7664
O Father, may thy word prevail
(Lindeman) X Ak Fader, lad
dit ord din aand 7665
O filii et filiae (French plain-
song, 15th c: Solesmes ver-
sion M 2) [LDRMRDRDT
L, LDRMR] A99; B555; C555;
E626; F130; J96; R206; S167;
W124; X143; AD164; AF191;
AL106a; AN194; AQ315; BM
81; BN41; BO178; BP35; BQ
28; BR563; BY163b; BZ
7666
-----. R [LLTLS, LDTLM,
TDTL.] 7667
-----. V [LLTLS#, LTDTLTM,
TDRM] X143b 7668
-----. V [LDRMDRDTL, LDR
MDRD] AQ315 7669
O food that weary pilgrims

love (Bragers) [SDSLTDRM,
DRTDRMFS,] BP57   7670

O food that weary pilgrims love
(Haydn) X O esca viatorum
                          7671

O food to pilgrims (Isaak) X
Innsbruck   7672

O for a closer walk with God
(Kingsley) X Elizabethtown
                          7673

O for a faith that will not shrink
(Havergal) X Evan   7674

O for a heart to praise my God
(Showalter) [SLSDSDMR, RMR
DLS, SL] AX387; AY7   7675

O gentle Savior (Sullivan) X
Coena Domini   7676

O give me back my prophet dear
(Careless) [MMRDSSFM, DDL
FMMRR,] BC137   7677

O give thanks (Gelineau) [SLD
DLDR, MRMDRDRT, T] BSp.
54   7678

O give the Lord, you sons of God
(Gelineau) X How great is
your Name   7679

O gloriosa virginum (Jacobsen)
[MRDSFMRD, RRRFRDRM,]
BO266   7680

O gloriosa virginum (Davidisches
harfen, 1744) [SDRMFSRMFM,
RMF#SLS] BQ210a   7681

O gloriosa virginum (La Tombelle)
[LDTDTDRMFM, RDRMRD]
BQ210b   7682

O gloriosa virginum (Plainsong M
2) [LLSMRSLDDTLT, LRRT]
BN124   7683

O God all gracious (---) [SDRMF
SRMFM, RMSSMF#] BH50
                          7684

O God, all gracious (Dunkley)
[DMRDSMDRM, DDTSLTS,]
BH45   7685

O God, almighty Father (Mainz,
G-B. 1833) X O God, eternal
Father   7686

O God eternal (McKinney) [SS
MRRDLLSS, SSFRMR] AU302
                          7687

O God, eternal Father (Mainz
G-B. 1833) [SDTDRMRSLTD
RRD, SD] BL80; BM12; BN57

7688

O God of hosts (Grieg) X
Hagerup   7689

O God of love (The Divine
Companion) [MSFMRMF#
SS, RMRDRT, M] E446; X
595   7690

O God of wisdom (American
trad) X Campmeeting   7691

O God, our help (Croft) X St
Anne   7692

O God, the eternal Father
(Mendelssohn) X Heavenly
love   7693

O God, the refuge (Schumann)
X Canonbury   7694

O God, the Rock of ages
(Achron) [RMRMRRR, RM
RMLL, MSD] BH32   7695

O God thou art (French church
mel., 16th c) [DTLSLSDSF
M, MFMRSL] BL39   7696

O God, thou faithful God
(Meiningen G-B. 1693) X
O Gott, du frommer Gott
                          7697

O God, thy soldiers' faithful
Lord (A Monk of Gethsemani)
[SDDDRMFS, SLLLSFFS,]
BN181   7698

O God, we pray for all mankind
(Hastings) X Ortonville
                          7699

O God, whose law from age to
age (Singer) [FMRRMRDD,
LSFRMFM, F] BH97   7700

O Godhead hid (Terry) [SSFM
RDTLFMR, MSF#MF#] BO
44   7701

O Gott, du frommer Gott
(Fritsch) X Darmstadt
                          7702

O Gott, du frommer Gott
(Meiningen G-B. 1693) [MM
LSFM, MSDRMRD, MML] K
397; M195; N55; O41; P246;
Q395; AA346; AK64; AZ146-C
                          7703

O Gott, du frommer Gott
(Meiningen G-B. 1693) X
Munich   7704

O Gottes Lamm (Mozart) [DM
RDMSFM, DRMFMRM, R]

BQ35 7705

O Gottessohn (Spaeth) [DSFMMFF
SSL, SFMMMM] K529 7706

O grant thy servants through thy
grace (Glazer) X Azmon
7707

O grant us light (Roberts) [MS
FMMRDT, RDTLDTTT,] W466
7708

O grosser Gott (Gesang - und
notenbuch) [SMFSSLTD, TDTL
SLLS,] Q132 7709

O Gud! ditt rike ingen ser (Waldis)
X Waldis 7710

O Gud, du fromme Gud (Meiningen G-B. 1693) X O Gott, du
frommer Gott 7711

O Guds Lam uskyldig (Decius)
X O Lamm Gottes 7712

O happy day (Hermann) X Hermann 7713

O happy home! O blest abode
(Robertson) [SMFSSLFS, SDDD
TLDS,] BC133 7714

O happy home, where thou art
loved (Niemeyer) X O selig
haus 7715

O happy homes among the hills
(Stephens) [MDRMRDRM, DTD
RDTDTSD] BC337 7716

O happy is the man (Everett) X
Mattie 7717

O hark! a glorious band (Asper)
[SDRMFSMD, MLSFMR, SD]
BC134 7718

O haupt voll blut und wunden
(Hassler) X Passion chorale
7719

O heart of God (Stevenson) [SLSS,
MMMFMM, SLTDSF] AW237
7720

O heart of Jesus (---) [DDSLTDR
D, DMRDTDLLS,] BQ64 7721

O heart of Jesus (Montani) [MF
SMDRMD, DTDFMMR, M] BQ58
7722

O heart of Mary (Piel) [SDM
SFMRMRD, MFSMRD] BO94
7723

-----. R [SLMFSFMR, FM
SLTDLS,] 7724

O heart of Mary (Staniforth) [D
MSDSLSFM, SDDDFMR,] BN154

7725

O heilige dreifaltigkeit (Hermann) [DMFSSLLS, SSDTS
LLS,] M59; Q340; AA-20,
120; AM339 7726

-----. V [DDDSSLLS, SSDT
SLLS,] Q340 7727

O Heiliger Geist, O Heiliger
Gott (Scheidt) X O Jesulein
Süss 7728

O helligaand, du skat (Teutsch
kirchenampt. Strassburg,
1524 or 25) X Aus tiefer
not 7729

O Herre Gott (Enchiridion. Erfurt, 1527) [DDLLSDRM, R
SFMRFMR] Q266; AA494
7730

O Herre Gott, in meiner not
(Reiman) [LDTLSDRM,
MMMRMDDT,] AA543 7731

O Herre Gott, in meiner noth
(Gregor) X Old 96th 7732

O Herre Gud, oändelig (Crespin) [DDTLSDRM, DMFSM
FRD,] N167 7733

O hjertens ve (Wurzburger G-
B. 1628) X O traurigkeit
7734

O holy day (Pollock) [SSDRM,
DDRDLS, SSDMS] AX66; AY
274 7735

-----. R [MFSLSM, DRDRM,
SLSML] 7736

O Holy Ghost, thou gift (Teutsch
kirchenampt. Strassburg,
1524-25) X Aus tiefer not
7737

O holy night (Adam) [MMMSS
LLFLDS, SMRDM] AH615;
AU468; AW86 7738

-----. V [MMLSSLLFLDS,
SMRDM] AW86 7739

O holy words of truth and love
(Parry) [SMR#MRDTD, SL
S#LRT, SF] BC135 7740

-----. R [SLSMFLS, DRDLT
RD, DM] 7741

O home beloved, where're I
wander (Parry) [SDDDDRDD
T, DRRRRMR] BC335 7742

O how beautiful the sky (Danish
trad) X Celestia 7743

O how happy are they (---) [SS
SSLDR, MRDLSMS, DR] AY205;
BB292   7744
-----. V [SSSLDR, MDDDLS,
DRMR] BB292   7745
O, how I love Jesus (---) [DM
MMRMDDD, DRRRDRM] AT131;
AU283; AW496; AX46; AY100
7746
-----. R [MMRMDD, RRDRM
SF, MMR]   7747
-----. V [DMMMRRDD, DRRRD
RMS,] AY100   7748
O, how I love Jesus (---) X
O save me at the cross (---)
7749
O how I love thee Jesus (Montani)
[DMFSDLS, SSMRDMRR, R]
BQ328   7750
O how lovely (Milgrove) X
Harts   7751
O, how lovely was the morning
(Smyth) [MFSSSDDT, TDRRR
FFM,]   7752
O Hunter blessed (Bragers) [DM
DSMFSLS, STDRDMR] BP94
7753
O hvor salig er I dog I fromme
(Crueger) [MLSMFMRDRD,
MSF#SLS] O596   7754
O I long to see the beauty
(Showalter) [SDMDRDLD, D
MSDRMR, S] AS451   7755
-----. R [RMFFMRMS, MRD
DDRMR, M]   7756
O, I love to talk with Jesus
(Fischer) [DRMMFMMR, RM
FLSFM, D] AX366; AY198
7757
O ihr ausewoehlten kinder (Hille)
X Gregor's 161st metre   7758
O invidenda martyrum (Dijon
church mel) [SDRMRFMRD,
SLSLTDT] E58   7759
O Jerusalem, du schöne (Störl)
X Storl II   7760
O Jesu (Reimann. Hirschberg G-
B.) [SDRMFSFMR, RMF#SS
F#S,] E406; G325; J490; Q24;
R174; S79; X532; Z499; AB200;
AD237; AF92; AN146; AQ205;
AR83; AW244; BB492; BE311;
BF402; BZ   7761

O Jesu! än de dina (Tomis-
sön. Psalmebog. 1569)
X Franzen   7762
O Jesu Christ (Reinigius)
[LLLSSDRM, MFMRDRRD,]
Eap. 46; F419   7763
O Jesus Christ, alone to thee
(Gastorius) X Was Gott tut
7764
O Jesu Christ, dein kripplein
ist (Crueger) X Manger
7765
O Jesu Christ, du höchstes Gut
(Crueger) [DLSDRMFR, SMD
FMRD, D] N134   7766
O Jesu Christ, meins lebens
licht (Nürnberg G-B. 1676)
[DDRMSDRMR, RMFSMRR]
J376b; K16; N9; O125; Q64;
Z600; AA195; AF208; AN268;
AQ208   7767
O Jesus Christ, our only Lord
(Schop) X Eternity   7768
O Jesus Christ, Redeemer
(Beethoven) X A hymn
anthem   7769
O Jesus Christ, remember
(Montani) [DRMFLLS, SLTD
RDT, TD] BQ55   7770
O Jesu Christe, wahres licht
(Nurnberg G-B. 1676) X O
Jesu Christ, meins lebens
licht   7771
O Jesus, for din pine (Kingo.
Gradual, 1699) [LLTDMTL,
TMRDDT, TMT] O479; P171
7772
O Jesu! life-spring (Peloquin)
[LFMFMRMDR, MSFLSDT]
BL40   7773
O Jesu mi dulcissimi (Clause-
ner. G-B.) [MDLMLSF#M,
DRMFMRDD] E635; X184
7774
O Jesu, när jag hädan skall
(Geistliche lieder. 1535) [D
TLDMRRD, DTLRDTL, D]
N406; AA284; AZ132-F   7775
-----. V [DDLDMRRD, DTLD
RTL, D] AA284   7776
-----. V [DDLTDMRRD, D
TLTDRD] AZ132-F   7777
O Jesus, thou the beauty art

(Montani) [MMRRMRDD,
FFMMFR, SS] BQ15   7778
O Jesus victim-priest (Bach)
X Potsdam   7779
O Jesu, warum legst du mir
(Reimann) X O Jesu   7780
O Jesulein süss (Scheidt) [DDTD
RTDTLS, MRRDRS] F425; J501;
K145; X600; AF135; AR230; AW
547; BG109   7781
-----. V [DDDDR, TDTLS, MRR
DRS] K145   7782
O King of kings (Cologne G-B.
1623) [SSDLTDS, SLLSFM, MFS]
BL60   7783
-----. R [DMRTS, DMRTS, SD
DRRM]   7784
O King of might (Murray) [MLT
DTLSM, MLTDRM, ML] BL100
                                 7785
O King of might and splendor
(Mohr) [MMRSFMRM, MSDRR
D, MM] BN205   7786
O King of nations (Maclean) [SD
TLSLTDRMFRDD, DT] BN99
                                 7787
-----. R [MDLRDT, LSDDRM,
FMRD]   7788
O kom dog hver, som synd har
gjort (Lindeman) [DMSFMLLS,
SFMRRMFM] O435   7789
O lad din aand nu med os vaere
(Lindeman) [SMDMRFMRM, DT
DRSLT] O91; P95   7790
O Lamb of God, have mercy
(Crueger) X Herzliebster Jesu
                                 7791
O Lamm Gottes (Decius) [DM
FSSLS, SDRMFMD, DM] J70;
M418; N90; O147; P99; Q146;
AA203; AK526; AW540; AZ127-A
                                 7792
-----. V [DMFSSLS, SDRMFRD,
DM] N90   7793
-----. V [DMSSSLS, SDRMFMR
D, D] P99   7794
-----. V [DMSSSLSLS, SDRMF
RD,] Q146   7795
-----. V [DMMSSLS, SDRMMFR
D,] AA203   7796
-----. V [DRMFSSLS, SDRMFM
RD,] AW540   7797

O Lamm Gottes unschuldig
(Decius) X O Lamm Gottes
                                 7798
O land of our King (Lindeman)
X King's land   7799
O, land of rest, for thee I sigh
(Miller) X Land of rest
                                 7800
O lead and guide us (Beethoven)
[MRDTTL, TDRMR, SFMRR]
BI59   7801
O leide, leide gern (Gesangbuch
mit noten) [SSMSSFMF, FFM
RLSFM,] AW252   7802
O liebe meiner liebe (Thommen.
Christen-schatz) X Cassel
                                 7803
O Light, whose beams (Barnby)
X St Chrysostom   7804
O little one (Scheidt) X O Jesu-
lein süss   7805
O little town (English trad) X
Forest green   7806
O little town of Bethlehem (Red-
ner) X St Louis   7807
O living Bread (Zinck) X Copen-
hagen   7808
O Lord, be near me (Shelley)
[MMMFTDRM, MSMRMD,
RM] BH19   7809
O Lord, Divine, we come (Hull)
X In dark Gethsemane   7810
O Lord, I am not worthy
(Bragers) [SSSLSFM, RMDFM
R, RFM] BP66   7811
O Lord, I am not worthy
(Catholic trad) [MFSLSDDT,
TDRFLSM, M] AH133; BN
100; BO49   7812
O Lord, I am not worthy
(Montani) [MDRMSDLS, LFS
MSFMR,] BQ129   7813
O Lord, in this great mystery
(Andriessen) [LTDRMRDRT,
LTDTLLS] BM5   7814
O Lord, my God (Sulzer) [ML
MFLSFM, MRDFFF, RM] BH29
                                 7815
O Lord of hosts (Careless)
[SSDMRDDTLS, FMDLSF#]
BC271   7816
O Lord, open thou our eyes

dise 7853
O Paradise! O Paradise (Slovak
hymnal) [DDTTRRDD, MDDFM
R, RR] BQ120 7854
O Pater sancte (Sarum Antiphonal.
Plainsong M 4) [FRMMMMMS
LLSLL#LSS] E160; F158a;
X186a 7855
O perfect love (Barnby) X Sand-
ringham 7856
O perfect love (Smith) [MDMLS
FMRDMR, SLLTD] BI77 7857
O praise the Lord (Gelineau) [MS
LR, LTRDL, LTRDL, RL] BSp.
19 7858
O praise ye the Lord (Haydn)
X Lyons 7859
O precious sign and seal (Hop-
kins) X Ellers 7860
O purest of creatures (Montani)
[MMMMRFTDRMR, RMMMR]
BQ79 7861
O purest of creatures (Paderborn
G-B. 1765) [SDDRMMFLSFMR
D, SDD] AH135; BN136; BO58;
BP92; BQ92; BV336; BY573b
7862
-----. V [SDDRMMFSMRD,
SDDRM] BN136 7863
-----. V [SDDRMMMFSMRD,
SDDR] BP92 7864
O purest of creatures (Paderborn
G-B. 1765) X Lyons (Haydn)
7865
O quanta qualia (Paris Antiphoner.
1681) [DDRMDDFMRRD, SMDF]
A589; B544; C544; D397; E465;
F281; J596b; K184; N208; Q255;
R122; S290; V709; W224; X200;
AD178; AF310; AK178; AL173;
AM219; AP253; AR103; BB202;
BL85; BR98; BY191b 7866
-----. V [DDRMDFFMRRD, SM
DFM] K184 7867
O Queen of peerless majesty
(Benz) [SDSLSDRM, MRM
RD, SDS] BN159 7868
O Queen of the Holy Rosary
(Wurtemberg G-B. 1784) X
Ellacombe 7869
O render thanks (Binder) [SSFM
SLTD, DDTLDTLS,] BH194
7870

O render thanks (Sullivan) X
Valete 7871
O rest in the Lord (Mendel-
ssohn) [DMFRD, DLLTDS, S
SFMF] AH618; AR684; AV
424; BF696 7872
O sacrament most holy (Fulda
mel) [SDMRDLS, SLDRRD,
SDM] BM9 7873
O sacrament most holy (Gounod)
[DTDRMRD, SFMRMFM, M
R#] BQ330 7874
O sacred Heart of Jesus, hear
(Bourgeois) X Old 124th
7875
O Sacred Heart! our home
(Ampleforth) [SMRDDRMFF
M, MFSLDT] BO22 7876
O sacrum convivium (Perosi)
[MFMRRSFM, SLTDTLSF#]
BQ320 7877
O sacrum convivium (Remondi)
[SSSSLLL, LLDLDTTTT]
BQ235 7878
O safe to the Rock (Sankey)
[SSFMMRDDTLTD, DFML]
N600; P298; T135; AE298;
AH308; AJ220; AL497; AM
551; AP523; AR450; AS273;
AT271; AU129; AV354; AX
523; BB586; BY566 7879
-----. R [RRMF, MMFS, SDTL
SMDM] 7880
O sälla land (Ahnfelt) [SSFM
MMFSLSFR, RRDT] N431;
AI235 7881
O salutaris (Duguet) [DMRM
FMRDD, MMRMSF#S] E330b;
AN60; AQ140; BM26; BN82;
82; BO273d; BP61; BQ226b
7882
O salutaris Hostia (Beethoven)
[SMRDFMRDRTD, TDRMF]
BO273c; BR248 7883
-----. V [SMRDFMRDRTD,
TDDRM] BR248 7883a
O salutaris Hostia (Bourgeois)
X Old 100th 7884
O salutaris Hostia (Lee) [LL
TDLDRM, SLSMDRRM,]
BL53 7885
O salutaris Hostia (Montani)

X The Word descending   7886

O salutaris Hostia (Antiphonale
    romanum M 1) X Exultet cor
    praecordiis   7887

O salutaris Hostia (Plainsong M 7)
    [SLSFSLSLTDTLSS, TR]
    BN79   7888

O salutaris Hostia (Plainsong M 8)
    [SSLDTLSFLSLTLSFS,] BN80;
    BQ226c   7889

O salutaris Hostia (Rheinberger)
    [MRMSSFMM, SFMRDTDR,]
    BQ226d   7890

O salutaris Hostia (Webbe) X
    Melcombe   7891

O salutaris Hostia (Werner)
    [SLSDSLLS, SDMRTDTL] AH114;
    BN84; BO273e; BP60; BQ226g
                                     7892

O sanctissima (Sicilian mel) X
    Sicilian mariners   7893

O, save me at the cross (---)
    [SSSMSDDD, RRRDMMM, S]
    AX249   7894

-----. R [MRDLSD, RRDRMD,
    MRDL]   7895

O, save me at the cross (---)
    X O how I love Jesus (---)
                                     7896

O say, can you see! (Smith) X
    National anthem   7897

O say, what is truth (Melling)
    [SMMRDDTLDS, SSDDRM]
    BC143   7898

O Seigneur (Genevan Psalter, 1551)
    [DSSLTDDTLSFS, MMDF] C37b;
    E512; W167; X696; AJ414; AL
    45a; AP255a; AW19; BJ67; BY
    685b   7899

-----. V [DSSLTD, DTLSF#S,
    MMDF] AJ414   7900

O selig haus (Neimeyer) [DMS
    DDTLSFFM, SMSLS] Q626;
    AO562; AW358; AX558   7901

O sing a joyous carol (Geistliche
    kirchengesang. 1599) X Rosa
    mystica   7902

O sing the great apostle (German
    trad) X Woodbird   7903

O, sing to me of heaven (Dunbar)
    X A few more years   7904

O Sion, haste (Storer) [SLDDTLS
    S#LFFM, MRMF] D249b;   7905

-----. R [SLTDRS, LTDR,
    SMTDLS]   7906

O Sion, haste (Walch) X Tid-
    ings   7907

O so bright (Traditional) X
    Grassmere   7908

O sometimes the shadows are
    deep (Fischer) X The Rock
    of refuge   7909

O sons of Sion (Manookin) [SD
    TDLSFMFS, DLTDRD] BC152
                                     7910

O soul Supreme (Binder) [MM
    RDTTL, LFRTLS#, S#LT] BH
    46   7911

O spirit of the living God
    (Est's Psalter) X Old 25th
                                     7912

O store Gud (Swedish folk mel)
    [SSSM, SSSLLFL, LLLSM]
    BZ   7913

-----. R [SSDMRDTDLS,
    DDTR, FL]   7914

O such wonderful love (McHose)
    [SSSLSMRDLD, LSDDMR] AX
    88; AY200   7915

O sueszer Stand, O sel'ges
    leben (Freylinghausen. 1704)
    X Gregor's 184th metre-A
                                     7916

O sweet Infant Jesus (Bansbach)
    [MFSSSLSLSF, FSLLLS]
    BQ333   7917

O take my hand (Silcher) X
    So nimm denn meine Hände
                                     7918

O, the best Friend to have is
    Jesus (Bilhorn) [SDMMR#MF
    LR, DDTDTLS] BB528 7919

-----. R [SSMFSLSF, FFRM
    FSFM,]   7920

O the bitter shame (Mountain)
    [DDDDTDRRD, MMMRRRM]
    AR463; AS281   7921

O the unsearchable riches
    (Sweney) X Unsearchable
    riches   7922

O think of the home over there
    (O'Kane) X Home over there
                                     7923

O thou, before the world began
    (Asper) [MSFMMRMFMRM,
    MMDTT] BC274   7924

O thou eternal King (---) [DMRD
SLTD, MRTDLS, MR] BN53;
BO182 7925

O thou immortal holy Light
(Tallis) X Tallis' Canon 7926

O thou immortal Light divine
(Webbe) X Melcombe 7927

O thou kind and gracious Father
(Careless) [DDRRMDTLS,
SSLTDTL] BC276 7928

O thou pure Light (Slovak hymn)
[MMFSDTDRTDS, LDLSM]
BQ33 7929

O thou that rulest earth (Bourgeois)
X Toulon 7930

O thou Rock of our salvation
(Clayson) [MFSMDLSM, RMFLS
FM, S] BC130 7931

O thou who hearest prayer (Welsh
mel) [LLS#LTD, DTMMR#M,
LLS#L] AF526 7932

O thou whose power o'er moving
worlds (Barnby) X Longwood
7933

O thou, whose presence (Heller)
[MMMSSDDF, FMS#LLSFM,]
BH216 7934

O thou, whose temple stands
(Arne) X Arlington 7935

O traurigkeit (Würzburger G-B.
1628) [MDLT, S#LLS#, MMM
FMRDT] A83; F126; J87;
M387; O322; P185; Q167; AA
215; AZ45-A 7336

-----. V [MDDT, DLLS#, M
MMFMRD, T] O322 7937

-----. V [MDDT, DLLS#, M
MSFMRD, T] AZ45-A 7938

O traurigkeit! O herzeleid!
(Wurzburger G-B. 1628) X O
traurigkeit 7939

O turn to Jesus (Slovak hymn)
[MLTDMRDT, RRRMRDTL,]
BQ115 7940

O turn to Jesus, mother! (---)
[SSSF#SLMSF, FMFLSFM]
BO143 7941

O ursprung des lebens (Selle) X
Zoerbig 7942

O Virgin all lovely (Brun) [LD
DDTL, LDDDTL, LTLS] BN160
7943

-----. R [DRRSF, MRMRD, DRD

TD.] 7944

O, Vision bright (Bowen) [DD
RM, RMFS, SLSMDRMR,]
BO116 7945

O welt, ich muss dich lassen
(Isaak) X Innsbruck 7946

O welt, sieh hier (Friese)
[LFRSFMM, MFFSSLL, LT]
Q171a; AA205 7947

O welt, sieh hier dein leben
(Crueger) X Gregor's 79th
metre 7948

O what a change (Harkness)
[SLDTFFFLTS, MRDSLD]
AI95 7949

-----. R [DTLTLSF#S, MF
SLLLTD] 7950

O what could my Jesus do more
(Sweney) X Story of Jesus
7951

O what precious balm (Bourgeois) X Bourgeois 7952

O what songs of the heart
(Clayson) [SSDDDDMRDLD
S, SSDD] BC87 7953

O, where are the reapers
(Root) X Harvest home
7954

O why not tonight (Bushey) X
Calvin 7955

O wie sehr lieblich! (Bohemian
Br.) X Augusta 7956

O wie selig seid ihr doch
(Stötzel. Choralbuch. 1744)
[DMFSSLSFMSFM, DMFS]
K510; M294; Q589; AA547
7957

O wie selig seid ihr doch ihr
frommen (Crueger) X O
hvor salig er I dog I fromme
7958

O wie selig sind die seelen
(Freylinghausen) X Gregor's
95th metre 7959

O wonderful prayer (Giffe) [SS
MMMRDLRR, TTTTLS] AS
131 7960

O wonderful word of salvation
(Fillmore) [SSFMMRRDDL,
DSSDMMS] AS175 7961

O wonderful words (Swedish trad)
[MLLTDTLTM, MMRRDDL]
P258 7962

O wondrous name (Sankey) [SS
FMDDTL, LSLSMR, SS] BR
527   7963
-----. R [SRTSSMDS, SFMRDDT,
S]   7964
O word of God incarnate (Mason)
X Missionary hymn   7965
O word of God incarnate (Smart)
X Lancashire   7966
O, worship the King (Haydn) X
Lyons   7967
O worship the Lord (Gaul) [SSFM
FMMFSDTTLL, LM] AR630
7968
O worship the Lord (Lowry) X
Beauty of holiness   7969
O ye mountains high (---) X
Denmark   7970
Oak (Mason) [DDRMRD, RDTD,
DDRMRD] L591; AX609; AY
147; BB659   7971
Oak Hill (Kidner) [SSSFMRDRM,
L, SDDMMS,] BV326a   7972
Oakland (Belden) [SDRMDRMF,
FMRDMRTD,] BB441   7973
Oakley (Williams) [LDRMRDRML,
SDRMRDR] X58   7974
-----. R [DRFMRRD#, MM
FMSSF#, SS]   7975
Oakridge Lynch (Shaw) [MRMFM
R, DRMRS, L#LSFM] X518
7976
Oaksville (Zeuner) [DDSMDDDTD
R, RMDRMF#] V380   7977
Obedience (Byers) [DRMSFMMR,
RMFLRFM, D] AX415   7978
-----. R [SSDTFFLS, SSDTTLS,
D]   7979
Oberammergau (Oberammergau)
[MSSDMSSD, SDTLSSF#S] W
92b   7980
Oberlin (Demuth) [SLDDTLSTRTLS,
MRDD] Y20; AC6b; BB326
7981
Obiit (Parratt) [DDRDFMLS, DTL
SFSM, M] BV555a   7982
Oblation (Crueger) [SDTLSMFSS
FM, SLT] A205; E223b; F551b;
J225b; X186b   7983
Oblation (Whitlock) [SLSDRMSRM
RDRL, LRM] BE257   7984
Oblations (Stainer) [DSSLDS, LTDR
MRR, RMT] B215   7985

Ocean Star, we greet you (Ett)
X St Martin   7986
Ockbrook (Hutton. Tunes for
the hymns) [LDLRDFFM,
RLDTTL, MM] AZ590-E
7987
Odumin (Hartmann) X Hart-
mann   7988
O'er the gloomy hills of dark-
ness (Petersen) [MRDSFM
DTLLS, SFMLS] BC127
7989
O'er the silent waters (German
mel) [MMSSDD, LFFSLS, SR
RM] BI72   7990
O'erwhelmed in depths of woe
(Montani) [DDTLTS#, MMRD
RT, TDRM] BQ25   7991
Of all the thoughts of God
(Deutsch) [DMMSFMRMD,
DDTDRMF] BH224   7992
Offertorium (Haydn, J.M.)
[MFSDDTLTDS, SMRMFM]
F176; BV72   7993
Often weary and worn (Pollock)
[DRMMMMMFSSS, SSLL]
AX531; AY149   7994
-----. R [MFSMSD, SSLLL
SSMFS]   7995
Ohne rast und unverweilt
(Knecht) X Vienna   7997
Oikoumenikos (Poteat) [MMM
SSFMMRD, MMMRSD] AR
572   7998
O'Kane (O'Kane) [DMSLSMD
RD, DRRRSFM,] AT478;
AU250; AX567; BB553
7999
-----. R [DRMMMMRMFS,
SSLLLS]   8000
Olaynu (Jewish trad) [SMD
DDTLTLSSSLTD, S] BH329
8001
Old Black Joe (Foster) X I
love him   8002
Old Bohemian carol (Bohemian
trad) X Kommet ihr hirten
8003
Old Commons (Campbell)
[SSSSMDRD, DFSLFR, RR]
BV436a   8004
Old French carol (French trad)
[SDRMFSS, LSMFSD, SDR]

BD222 8005

Old French mel (French carol)
X Gloria 8006

Old French noël (French trad)
[DRMDD, SLLSFM, RMFSS,]
BD213; BG75 8007

Old French melody (Corbeil)
X Orientis partibus 8008

Old German (Harmonia sacra) X
Mason 8009

Old hundred twenty-fourth (Bourgeois) X Old 124th 8010

Old Judea (Jackson) [MLDTS#LM,
FMRDRM, MSR] AH249 8011

-----. R [SDDSMFMRD, DTLLLR
D] 8012

Old martyrs (Scottish Psalter,
1615) X Plaintive martyrs
8013

Old, old story (Doane) X Tell
me the old, old story 8014

Old rugged cross (Bennard) [MF
SF#LSSSLS#TL, LSFM] AE186;
AH296; AT93; AR71; AV369;
AX105; BB533; BZ 8015

-----. R [TDRRRRDTD, DTLLL
DT] 8016

Old-time power (Gabriel) [MR
DDRDTT, SFFFFM, MR] AT173
8017

-----. R [SMMMRRDMDDDLLS,
DD] 8018

Old --- Psalms, etc. by number
follow here 8019

Old First [1st] (Genevan Psalter,
1542) [SLSMSFMFRD, DMFSSL]
AN41 8020

Old 18th (Anglo-Genevan Psalter,
1561) [LLS#LDTTM, MLDTTL,
LL] W586b; X43 8021

Old 22d (Anglo-Genevan Psalter,
1556) [DDRMSFFMDFMRRD,
SL] E163; S85; X176; AF259
8022

Old 23d (Divine musical misc.
1754) [SDSMRDFMMR, MMRM
FM] AL272 8023

Old 25th (Anglo-Genevan Psalter)
[DMRMFS, MMDFRD, MRDS]
B189; E149; F149; W583b;
X195 8024

Old 25th (Est's Psalter, 1592)
[DMRDDFRM, MRDSFFRM,]

BI51 8025

Old 26th (Moravian) [DMFRM
FMRM, SSMRMFM] AZ22-Aa
8026

Old 29th (Rosenroth) [SMFSLS
SFM, SMRMFSM] AZ22-U;
BA289 8027

Old 30th (Est's Psalter, 1592)
[MMR#MLDTL, MSMRDM, M
R] X693 8028

Old 38th (Bourgeois) [DTLT
DRMR, MRDTRRMD] AN88b;
BJ64; BX150b 8029

Old 42d (Bourgeois) X Bourgeois 8030

Old 44th (Anglo Genevan Psalter,
1556) [DDTDLSSD, SFMRRD,
DD] E211; W530b; X655;
AP2 8031

Old 71st (Bourgeois) X Genevan
Psalm 22 8032

Old 72d (Weisse) X Ravenshaw
8033

Old 77th (Este's Whole book of
Psalms, 1592) X Old 120th
8034

Old 77th-A (Freylinghausen)
X Gregor's 77th metre
8035

Old 80th (Scottish Psalter,
1564) X Psalm 80 8036

Old 81st (Old 77th: Day's
Psalter, 1562) [DMFSSLLS
SLTDLT, SD] E461; F529;
W355a; X216 8037

Old 81st (Este's Whole book of
Psalms, 1592) X Old 120th
8038

Old 96th (Gregor) [MDTLLS
FM, SDRMFMRD,] AZ97-B
8039

Old Hundred (Bourgeois) X Old
100th 8040

Old hundred (Bourgeois) X
Tabor (Kugelmann) 8040a

Old 100th (Bourgeois) [DDTLS
DRM, MMMRDFMR,] A139;
B249; C249; D468; E365; F
166; G3; H20; I6; J161; K
492; L68; M10; N275; O1;
P16; Q13; R24; S1; T184;
U487; V1; W229; X443; Y296;
Z104; AA78; AB11; AC334;

AD4; AE5; AF4; AG7; AH182;
AI448; AJ268; AK24; AL6a; AM
1; AN496; AO8; AP86; AQ13;
AR2; AS8; AT13; AU3; AV33;
AW594; AX11; AY410; AZ22-E;
BA21; BB13; BC214; BDp. 1;
BF174; BI29-D; BJ79, 80; BK
61; BL79; BM93; BN81; BO
273b; BR49; BV231; BX1; BY2;
BZ   8041
-----. V [DDTLSDRM, MMMRMFM
R,] BJ80   8043
Old 104th (Ravenscroft's Whole
book of Psalms.) [LDTLMDRF
MR, RMSF#S, D] A260a; E178;
F167a; W30; X211; AL21b; AP
93b; BJ63; BV459; BY573 8044
Old 106th (Gnadaeur choral buch)
X O dass ich tausend   8045
Old 107th (Bourgeois) [LLMLLSS
M, MFMDRD, LL] E493; R230;
S185a; W151; X512; BZ   8046
-----. R [LMF#SLSF#M, LTLMF#
M, MS]   8047
Old 112th (Schumann G-B. 1539)
[MMDRMDTL, MMRSMDRM,]
A147; B410b; C229; E462;
F227; J359a; K506; M390; N
593; O97; P79; Q318; W459a;
X566; AA396; AF44; AI437; AL
22; AM41; AN46; AP243; AQ
32; AZ96-A; BA951; BP103;
BV468a; BY16;   8048
-----. V [MMDRMRDTL, MMRS
MRD] M390   8049
-----. V [MMDRMRDTL, MMF#
SMRD] AZ96-A   8050
Old 113th (Strassburg Psalter)
X Psalm 68 (Greiter)   8051
Old 117th (Genevan Psalter, 1551)
[SDDTSLTD, DTLSFMRD,]
E637; X191   8052
Old 120th (Est's Whole Book of
Psalms) [DMFSLS, SLTDLT,
SDTLS] A115; B274; C274;
E209; F259; Q405; S229; X615;
Z478; AN396; BL18; BV643;
BY449a   8053
Old 124th (Meter: 10 10 10 10 10)
(Bourgeois) [DRMFMRDDTD,
MFSLS] A536; D280a; E114;
F380; J348; Q307; R357; S424;
T254; X329; Y176; Z372; AB298;

AC287; AD361; AE412; AF451;
AJ353; AK410; AL520; AM
514; AN342; AP112; AQ196;
AR578; AW354; BF574; BK
102; BL92; BM11; BN72;
BO21; BV28; BX202; BZ
                                          8054
Old 124th (Bourgeois) X Toulon
                                          8055
Old 127th (Bourgeois) [DFFM
DRMF, FMRDTLSF,] AD183
                                          8056
Old 130th (Strassburg Psalter,
1539) [LRMFMRD, FMRFSL,
SLT] J398; N191   8057
Old 134th (Bourgeois) X St
Michael   8058
Old 136th (Bourgeois) [LTSDT
LSL, MLTLDDTD,] BJ70
                                          8059
Old 136th (Est's Psalter, 1592)
[DSDDTD, LDDLFF, DRTD]
X197a   8060
Old 137th (Crespin. Psalms)
X Norwich   8061
Old 148th (---) [DMSDSFM,
SLLSFMR, SD] BY161   8062
Old 168th (Hintze) X Salzburg
                                          8063
Old 193d (Grimm's Choral
buch) [LDMLMLTMRDTL,
MMMR] AZ298-B   8064
Old 197th (Neander) X Sieh,
hier bin ich, Ehrenkönig
                                          8065
Old 271st (Gregor's Choral buch)
[SDSLFM, SDTTLS, RTSL]
AZ38-A; BA857   8066
Old 466th (Grimm. Choral buch)
[DMSSLSFMRD, RMF#SSL]
AZ185-D (app.)   8067
Old 583d (Hutton. Tunes for the
hymns) [SDRMLSFMRD, MR
DTDR] AZ32-C; BA668
                                          8068
Oldbridge (Quaile) [MMMMDRMD,
SSSFRMDR] Eap. 72; G41;
O605; W213; AQ159; AT495;
AU301; BZ   8069
Olden (Mason) [SDSDDRRM,
MFFMRDMR,] BB535   8070
Oldown (Harwood) [DTDFFFMS,
DMRM, MMRR] W441a; BE

256; BV581a; BY717   8071

Olena (Herbert) [SMRDDTLLS,
SSLTDTD] T104a; AJ39   8072

Oliphant (Baillot) [SSLSMDSLS
M, FSLSTD] U32; V333b; BR
453b   8073

Oliva (Morton) [SSDFMMRD, TLD
FLS, SS] T17; AJ22   8074

Oliva speciosa (Italian) [SMFSD
TLS, LSFMFMRM,] Eap. 49
                        8075

Olivarius (Lutkin) [SSLTDMLSS,
SSDTLLT] I712   8076

Oliver (Oliver) [DMTDFMMRD#
RL, LLLSF] AC221   8077

Oliver (King) [MLTDMRDTL,
S#LDRRM, M] X117   8078

Olive's Brow (Bradbury) [SSS
LLSSS, DDDRMRRD,] G133;
H163; I147; L241; M66; T272a;
U96; V151; Z232; AD144; AE
118; AF178; AG92; AH283;
AJ379; AK132; AL209b; AM182;
AO161; AP332b; AR163; AS132;
AT104; AU295; AV105; AW103;
AX114; AY360; BA223; BB121;
BZ   8079

Olivet (Dykes) [SSDDMS, DFMMR
D, DSSD] D373b   8080

Olivet (Mason) [DMSSFM, RRF
FMR, MRFS,] A449; B211;
C211; D345a; Eap. 58; G176;
I184; J375; K360a; L172; M
234; N212; O456; P269; Q394;
R378; S285; T137; U194; V357;
W415a; Z355; AA351; AB172;
AC155; AD218; AE193; AF348;
AG211; AH358; AI238; AJ204a;
AK221; AL263; AM454; AN11;
AO274; AP419; AR261; AS270;
AT257; AU209; AV168; AW150;
AX453; AY60; BA429; BB246;
BF369; BR303; BY549a; BZ
                        8081

Olivet (Woodbury) X Eucharist
                        8082

Olmutz (Plainsong M 7) [SLSDRD,
DTDLLS, SLSD] C456; D186;
H228; I227; L387; T262a; V277;
AJ366; AM176; AO444; AS304;
AV256; BE404; BF605; BR251;
BX343b   8083

Olney (Gounod) [SSSLMSFF, FTLS

FM, SD] I696   8084

Olney (Mason) [SSFMFS, DTD
FMR, SSFM] L362; V342;
AA382   8085

Olrig Grange (Bridge) [DMDDM
DSFFM, MSSF#MF#] BX39
                        8086

Olwen (Welsh carol) X Poverty
                        8087

Omaha peace song (Omaha
Indian trad) [MRDDLS, MRR
DLSLL, LS] Y314   8088

Ombersley (Gladstone) [MRD
FFFFM, MFSLLRDT,] G205;
J118; W24; Y217; AB83; AC
212; AL20a; AR399; BA658;
BB67; BE243; BV635; BY
393   8089

Omega and alpha (Piae cantiones,
1582) X Puer nobis   8090

Omni dei (Corner. G-B) [DD
RDMSFM, DRMSSF#S, S]
E120; J282; W395b; X217a;
AF539; BY416b   8091

Omnia (Barnby) X Edinburgh
                        8092

Omnipotence (Anderson) [DTD
RDFDRM, MMRDDRD] BB
97   .   8093

Omnom kayn (Jewish trad)
[DDRMFSSLTD, DDTLSR]
BH23   8094

On Jordan's Bank (Vehe. G-B.
1537) [MSSLTDTL, SDRM
RDRT] BM59   8095

On Jordan's Bank (Wittwe.
Musikalisches handbuch.) X
Winchester New   8096

On Jordan's banks (American
trad) X Jordan's Bank 8096a

On Jordan's stormy banks
(O'Kane) X O'Kane   8097

On mighty wings (Jewish trad)
X Oveenu malkaynu   8098

On parting (Jewish trad) X
N'eelah mel I   8099

On the mountain's top appearing
(---) [MMSFRDTDMR, FML
SDR] BC273   8100

On the radiant threshold
(Perkins) [SLTDFF, MRDTM,
RRMRS] AS18   8101

-----. R [SSLSFLTL, SSFMLT,

DF]   8102
On the wood His arms (Traditional:
mediaeval) [MFSSLLS, DTLS,
MFSSL] BP28   8103
On this day earth shall ring
(Piae cantiones, 1582) X
Theodoric   8104
On this day, O beautiful Mother
(Lambillotte) [MRMSSFMFLS,
MRMSSR] AH134; BO114
                                       8105
-----. R [DTLSLSS, DTLSFRM,
SF#]   8105a
On this day, the first of days
(Freylinghausen) X Luebeck
                                       8106
Once again (Dykes) [SF#SMMRD
TL, SLTDTTL] BR556   8107
Once again to its close (Drury)
[DRMDRS, DRMDRS, DDRM]
AR583   8108
Once again we come (Naylor)
[DRMMMRDSSS, LSMMRD]
AX51   8109
-----. R [SSLLLLLSSSS, MRDDS]
                                       8110
Once for all (Bliss) [DMLSMM
RDMR, RD#RFLL] AI129; AT
199; AU340   8111
-----. R [SLTDDDTLLS, SLTDDD]
                                       8112
Once more before we part (Un-
seld) [DDDDRM, MMMSSS,
MMMS] AX78; AY117   8113
Once more, O Lord (Weinberg)
[DDDDDDRRM, DFFMDMF]
BH7   8114
Once more the liberal year (Hel-
ler) [SSSLLDTD, DDDRMFMR]
BH181   8115
One day (Marsh) [SMFSLTDTLS
M, FRMFM] AM689; AT85; AX
309   8116
-----. R [DLDTF, LTLSM,
SFMLLL]   8117
One God! One Lord (Rossini) X
Linwood   8118
One more day's work (Lowry)
[SSSLSDS, DRMDLS, SLS] I419;
AS27; AU55; AV387; BB622
                                       8119
-----. R [SSSLSSD, SSSLSSR,
SM]   8120

One radiant morn (---) X
Taenk, naar engang den
taage (---)   8121
One resolve (Christiansen)
[MMMMMSLSSDDM, MMMR]
P247   8122
One sweetly solemn thought
(Ambrose) X Ambrose   8123
One sweetly solemn thought
(Phillips) [SMDRDLS, SLL
SLSM, SM] V762; AU183;
AX611   8124
-----. R [RMRDS, MFMR,
MRDDTLS]   8125
One thing needful (Crueger)
X Ratisbon   8126
Oneanta (Hall) [MSSDFFMRS,
DTLSLS] A571b; B28; J
535b   8127
Onido (Pleyel) [SSSMFRM,
FSLTDSSFF] L272   8128
Only a sinner (Towner) [SMF
SDTLDLS, FRMTLS] AI131;
AM698   8129
-----. R [SSSLSDRM, MDDR
DDRM,]   8130
Only a step (Doane) [MMMFM
RD, LSDDMR, MMM] AU432;
AX254; AY503   8131
-----. R [LLLDSSSM, MFSM
R, RRR]   8132
Only a step to Jesus (Doane)
X Only a step   8133
Only believe (Rader) [SF#SM
DTDL, SSLSMMMR] AU318
                                       8134
Only remembered (Sankey)
[SF#SDSMSFRFM, LTTDS]
AX584; AY530   8135
-----. R [RRMFF, MMFSS, S
F#SLTD]   8136
Only thee (Blosser) [MFSMLS
F#SM, DRMFMRM] AY197
                                       8137
Only thee (Perkins) [SSSDTDR
D, RMFMR, DRM] BB580
                                       8138
-----. R [SDMDLS, SSSDMDR,
SDM]   8139
Only thine (Byers) [SSDMDLDS,
DRSSDRM, M] AX406   8140
-----. R [SSMMMD, DRSRMF
M, SSM]   8141

Only thy tender care (Ackley)
[SF#LSDM, MFMRL, TLSDR]
U226 8142
-----. R [MDLSF#S, LDFMDS,
MFMR] 8143
Only trust him (Stockton) X
Stockton 8144
Ono adonoy kaper no (Jewish
trad) [DMDDD, LTDTDRD, LLLT]
BH330 8145
Onslow (Batchellor) [SF#SLSM
DLS, SSSLDTD] R467; AE438;
AF479; AL585; AM659; AP720;
AR554; AT341; AU310; AW423;
BK6 8146
Ontario (American mel) [SLSDDDT
LS, STRFRMD] AP492b 8147
Onward (---) [SSSMDDDS, SSLLL
LS, S] BB373 8148
Onward (Barrington) [SSLSMD,
RLTLS, SSLSM] D516b; U374;
AC263; AO391b; AW267; BF
515 8149
Onward (Filby) X Fortitude
8150
Onward (Gauntlett) X University
College 8151
Onward (Roe) [MMRDLS, SMR
DR, MMRDL] K562 8152
Onward brothers, march still on-
ward (Beethoven) X Beethoven
8153
Onward, Christian soldiers (Jude)
[MMMMMRDRM, FMRDR,
MF] AU475 8154
Onward, Christian soldiers (Sulli-
van) X St Gertrude 8155
Op alle som paa Jorden bor
(Hermann) X Hermann 8156
Op, thi dagen nu frembryder
(Lindeman) [DDMRDSLS, DRMM
SFMR,] O160 8157
Open my eyes (Scott) [DTLSLLSS,
RTLSTLSS,] R390; AE200;
AG227; AI158; AR295; AS257;
AT312; AU351; BZ 8158
Open our eyes, thy glory behold-
ing (Sellers) [SDRMMMFMMR,
STRFFL] AU441 8159
-----. R [SF#FMSLSF#SM, FFM
RFS] 8160
Open the wells of salvation (Pol-
lock) [SDRMDRDLSD, DTDRRR]

AX371; AY339 8161
-----. R [SMFSSLSF#S, MM
RDRRR] 8162
Open thou mine eyes (Fill-
more) [DSFMLLTDT, DDDDD
DD] AS495 8163
Open wide thy heart (Owen) [M
MMRDSL, RDTD, RRRRR]
AX251; AY505 8164
-----. R [MMMFMRD, FFF
SFMR, SS] 8165
Opening song (Heller) [SDM
SSLSLS, MRDDRDR] BH
257 8166
Oppidans Mews (Shaw) [SLL#
SLF, RMFSM, TDRMD] X
386b; BV345; BY757 8167
Optatus votis (Plainsong M 4:
Barking hymnal) [MSLLSS
FM, DRFMRFRM] F14
8168
Optimism (Hunnewell) [DDTLS
DRM, DRRRM, DDT] BF575
8169
Ora labora (Noble) [SLSS, DT
LSMLLSFS, M] A576; B497;
C497; R287; S366; AB262;
AD317; AF293 8170
Oremus (Freylinghausen) X
Morgenglanz der ewigkeit
8171
Oremus pro pontifice (Plain-
song M 1) [SLSSDTDRMRD
TDLSS] BN201 8172
Oremus pro pontifice (Schubert)
[MMRDRMMMSFMRDFM, M]
BQ247 8173
Orford (Mason) [MFSLSSMR
MFM, MFSLS] BR504a
8174
Oriel (Bradbury) [MRDSDTDR,
MRDLDDTD,] L468; T186;
AJ272; AO118 8175
Oriel (Ett) [DDDDRMFM,
MMRDTLS, D] A326; B89;
C89; D321a; E228b; F190a;
G79; K36; O131; W164; X
190b; AL163; AP85a; BM31;
BN110; BO14; BR464b; BV
282; BY79 8176
Orient (Gounod) [MMMSMFM
DRRD, SF#SMF#] D66b;
U492; AB416; AH556; AI25;

AR631; AS496; BF674   8177
Orient (Stanford) [SSDTLSFM,
  MMSDMRMD,] BY756   8178
Orient (Steggall) [DRMLSS,DDR
  RM,DMFMR] BR158   8179
Orient morning (Mann) [SDFMRL
  DT,SFMDTLR,S] N233; O241;
  V25   8180
Orientis partibus (Corbeil) [DR
  MDRTD,SSLMFSSM,M] A324;
  B115; C90b; D149b; E129; F524;
  G405; J509; L159; Q193; R457;
  W341; X153; AA221; AB354; AG
  299; AL407; AN25a; AP549; AW
  102; BA68; BD14; BE114; BF
  506; BK157; BN151; BO123;
  BP74; BQ197; BV601b; BY48,
  469; BZ   8181
-----. V [DRMDRTD,SSLMSSM,
  MR] X153   8182
-----. V [DDRMDRTD,DSSLF
  SSM,] BK157   8183
-----. V [DRMDRTDSSLFSSM,
  MR] BQ197   8184
Orison (Custance) [MMMRLSMR
  R#,MMMLDTF#] C16b
                                 8185
Orisons (Evans) [SDMMRS,SDM
  MRS,FMLT] W673   8186
Orisons (Kocher) X Dix   8187
Orisons (Wesley, S.S.) [MMDL,
  LLLLLLL,MMDLL] Y251;
  AD360; AP663b   8188
Ormiston (Spielman) [SDDDRMR
  D,RSSSLTLS,] M331   8189
Orono (Harrington) [MR#MFMSF
  LFM,RDRM,SS] I542   8190
Orpheus (Gluck) [SMFSDDTL,S
  LSFSFMR,] AR620   8191
Ortonville (Hastings) [SDDRRMR
  D,SLLSLS,SD] C194a; D648;
  G220; H94; I135; J570; M296;
  N194; R142; S197b; T327; U71;
  V129; Z381; AE100; AG111;
  AH311; AI43; AL666; AM106;
  AO202; AR108; AS176; AT118;
  AU188; AV62; AW120; AX18;
  AY21; BA493; BB159; BZ
                                 8192
Orwell (Newton) [MSSLMS,SMD
  TDR,MFFM] BY605   8193
Orwigsburg (Hoffman) [DRMSSDR
  MRD,DRMSSD] AT298; AV347;

AX357; AY499   8194
-----. R [DDDDS,DDDDL,
  FSLSSS]   8195
Osborne (Carey) [LLTDFMRDT
  L,MLTDRM,] S319b; X550
                                 8196
Osgood (Mason) [SSLSSTLTD
  SS,MSDLS] AO353   8197
Oslo (Norwegian trad) [LLM
  MRDTLS#, LTDDRR] A596
  a; J586; X232   8198
Oss Kirstna bör tro och besinna
  (Swedish, before 1540) [ML
  LTDDTS#L,TMMRDDT] N445
                                 8199
Ostend (Mason) [SMFSSLSS,
  MRMFSM,SM] T287; AJ297;
  AM230   8200
Ostergaard (Danish folk mel)
  [SMRDTDSRM,TDDFMRR]
  Z493; BK28   8201
Oswald (Dykes) X St Oswald I
                                 8202
Oswald's Tree (Davies) [SS
  LSTLSDTLSM,RDRM]
  F247; BV6   8203
Oswestry (Dykes) [MRMSFMR
  MFMR,FMFLS] BR407
                                 8204
Oswin (Dykes) [DSFMRDRT,
  SDRMFR,SF] V439; AA74
                                 8205
Othello (Excell) [SDRMFSLSF
  M,DMMRDS,] AT208; AU
  108; BB638   8206
-----. R [MFSSMDS,RMFFFF
  F,LT]   8207
Others (Hackleman) [MSLDRD
  LDT,SFFMRDT] AS338
                                 8208
-----. R [SSFLFFM,MMRLF
  LS,SD]   8209
Others (Shields) [SFMMMRMF,
  FTLLTLSS,] AU77   8210
-----. R [MM,MMFF,FFF
  TLS,MMMR]   8211
Otterbourne (Haydn) X Bowen
                                 8212
Ottery St Mary (Ley) [LLLL
  TTDL,DRMRDTT,L] BV379
                                 8213
Otto (English trad) X Comfort
                                 8214

Our best (Tullar) X Tullar 8215
Our brother is born (Fargeon)
[LDTSLDSM, MLFTSD, DT]
BG188 8216
Our Christ (Overby) [DMRDRD
RMSS, MFFMDM] J593a; P206
8217
Our Father (Heys) [DSFMRDRM,
MRDDTD, SD] AJ434 8218
Our Father (Plainsong arr) [MR
MFMRM, MRDRMRD, MR] AW
610 8219
Our Father, our King (Jewish
trad) X Oveenu Malkaynu
8220
Our Father, we beseech thy grace
(Schalit) [LLLLTDTRT, TLT
DRTR] BH145 8221
Our fortress strong (Dunkley)
X O God, all gracious 8222
Our guiding star (Mendelssohn)
X Trust 8223
Our Lady, Trondhjem (Lindeman)
[DSLLFTRD, SMMRMFRM,]
J160b; O9; P2; AA470; BE
291 8224
Our Lord is now rejected (Mc-
Granahan) X The crowning
day 8225
Our mountain home so dear
(Stephens) [MMMSFM, RSF
MFS, LTDT,] BC144 8226
Our Pilot (Wilson) [SLSMRDFFF,
RMFTLS, S] AU299 8227
-----. R [SDTLSLT, FTLSFSM,
MF] 8228
Our pious fathers (Grauman) [ML
DTLS#LTM, MDDRDRM]
BH215 8229
Our prayer (Garrett) [SSDMRDDT,
SSTFMRMD,] AS53 8230
Our Shepherd is the Lord (Lutkin)
X Psalm 23 8231
Our times are in thy hand (Ham-
montree) [MRDLDS, LTDDRD,
MRDF] AU446 8232
Out of my bondage, sorrow and
night (Stebbins) X Jesus I
come 8233
Out of the depths (Bragers) [LL
TDDT, DTLSL, DDRMM] BP96
8234
Out of the depths (Gelineau)

[MMMS, SSMSL, LLLD, DTS]
BL20; BSp. 38 8235
Out of the depths (Ronan)
[SSSLLSSFRM, SDTDRM]
BN188 8236
Out of the depths, O Lord (Bind-
er) [MR#MFMRD, MLS#LM,
MMMR] BH164 8237
Out of the depths, O Lord
(Webbe) X Consolation
8238
Out of your sleep (Shaw) [LR
MDLDRM, LRMDLDRM,] BG
177 8239
Oveenu malkaynu (Jewish trad)
[MLS#LTDTTLLMM, SDSD]
BH161, 309 8240
-----. V [MLS#LTDTTLLM
M, MDSD] BH309 8241
Over Kedron (Lindeman) [MR
DLDTS#M, LTDTMRD, M]
O302 8242
Over the line (Belden) [SSF#
SMRDDDTT, SSSLT] BB570
8243
-----. R [MR#MDSSMR#MD,
RTSRTS] 8244
Over the ocean wave (Bradbury)
[MRDDTLSDMR, MRDDTL]
AX215; AY35 8245
Overberg (Rinck) [MMFSMSFM
RM, MRSMDT] H72; I366;
AI215; AS305 8246
Overdale (Williams) [MFMSM
RDDTD, RMRSFM] Z566
8247
Overlook Park (Mueller) [DDD
RMFRDTD, MMFSSL] AK264
8248
Over X O'er 8249
Ovio (Mason) [SSSMDDDS,
DRMRDMR, R] L548; AY26
8250
-----. V [SSSMDDDS, DDMR
DMR, R] AY26 8250a
Owen (Sweetser) [MMLDTL,
SDSMDRM, MMM] I698
8251
Oxenbridge (Shaw) [SDRMRFM
RDR, RMFSFM] X104 8252
Oxford (Stainer) [MSDTLSSF,
MSDMRDR, R] C100a; D258b;
L231b; AA510; AL13b; AP156;

BF449; BV17; BY141b
8253
Oxford New (Smith, I. Collection)
[DSDTLTDRMRD, MRDTL] F
196a; BV302   8254
Oxnam (McCutchan) [SMRDTD,
SLTDDRT, STL] G267   8255
Ozrem (Woodbury) [MMMSFMRM,
SSDMLSF#S] H457   8256

P

Pa jorden är allting föränderlight
(Mozart) [SSMDDSMSFRM,
SSMDD] N476   8257
Paa Gud alene (Zinck. Koralbog.
1801) [DSFMR, DSSLTD, DSFM
R,] O350; P287   8258
Paa sit kors i Dødens smerte
(Zinck. Koralbog. 1801) [DT
LTDDDT, DTLTDDDT] O311
8259
Pactum (Haas) X Luther League
hymn   8260
Paddington (Wood) [SDLSFM, MRS
SF#S, SDLS] H2   8261
Paddocks (Shaw) [SMFSFMDR,
SMFSFMDT] X402   8262
Paderborn (Katholische kirchen-
gesang) [DDRMFSSS, FMFSF
M, MM] E251; X234   8263
Paderborn (Paderborn G-B. 1765)
X O purest of creatures 8264
Paean (Weber) [SMFSLTDD, LSD
RMRD, S] B267; C267; D174;
K251; AB105; AQ9; BA806
8265
Paedia (Schulz) [DRMMFFMRD,
DMSSLLS] J49; M308; O179;
P366; AI383   8266
Palestine (---) [MMRDDFFM,
MRSSF#S, SM] BR359   8267
Palestrina (Palestrina) X Victory
8268
Palgrave (Blackith) [SDTLSSS,
LLSMFMR, SD] I195; BA417
8269
Palisades (Sowerby) [DLLDRMF
RD, DMMRM] A365   8270
Palm Sunday (Carter) [SDSMRDLS,
SSFMRDTD] AE105   8271
Palm Sunday (Harrington) [MM
RDMRDRDM, MMMR#MS] I684

8272
Palm Sunday (Schulz) X
Claudius   8273
Palm Sunday Anthem (Plain-
song M 1) [RFRRDFSFSLL,
FLDLS] E617   8274
Palmarum (Wolle) [LTDDRMDS
SS, MRDDL] A259a; Y233;
AE35; AZ22-I; BA219   8275
Palmer (---) [SDDMDLLD, LSS
DDR, RM] V476   8276
Palmer (Palmer) X Yield
not to temptation   8277
Palmer (Sweezy) [DDMRDTD,
MMSFMRM, SS] T48; AJ63
8278
Palms of glory (Maclagan)
[SSDRDTD, RMRDTLS, FF]
Eap. 33; F499; K209; AO538;
BE395   8279
Palmyra (Summers) [DRMSFM
RD, SLTDDT, LS] C397; AB
86; BR470; BY218a   8280
Panem vivum (---) [SSFMSSLS
FMMRMMF#F#] BQ319
8281
Pange lingua (Ett) X Oriel
8282
Pange lingua (Sarum plainsong
M 3) [MMMRSSLDDDRDDD
LD] A66; B338; C338b; D98;
E95, 326b; F97a,383a; J61a;
W108a; X129a, 280a; BL51;
BM32; BN106, 107; BO264;
BQ241a, 241b; BV161; BY
146a   8283
-----. V [MMMRSSLTDD, DRD
TLD] E326b   8284
-----. V [LLLSDDRMM, MFS
FFMR] F97a   8285
-----. V [MMFMRSSLDD, DR
DDTL] J61a   8286
Pange lingua gloriosa (Essay on
the church plainchant. 1782)
x Dulce carmen   8287
Panis angelicus (Franck) [MM
RRDD, MMRRDD, LLSF] Y262
8288
Panis angelicus (Lambillotte)
[MMMSFMLSFMMRR, RRR]
AH130; BN92; BO33; BQ
229b   8289
Panis angelicus (Meurers) X

The very Angels' Bread   8290
Panis angelicus (Mohr) [DSDRMR,
FMDRRD, MRMS] BQ230   8291
Panis angelicus (Sarum plainsong
M 7) X Sanctorum meritis
8292
Panis angelicus (Tomadini) [DTDR
RR, MDDDTD, RMRD] BQ318
8293
Panis vitae (Hodges) X Eucharistic
hymn   8294
Panoply of light (Parker) [DSM
SDMRDS, LTDRMRD] BD76
8295
Paraclete (Burnap) [SDMFMRD#
R, STRFFMR#M,] L194; AI118;
AO229; AS346   8296
Paraclete (Erfurt. G-B. 1524) X
Komm Heilige Geist, Herre
Gott   8297
Paraclete (Harker) [MMMR#MS,
DFMMRR, SSST] BB679   8298
Paraclete (Maker) X Maker   8299
Paradise (Barnby) [MFMMMSFF,
MRDRFM, MM] A588; B167;
C167a; D394a; H516; I622b;
J589; L581b; N663; O616; T437;
V705; AA561; AB402; AO545a;
AV297; AZ603-B; BA753; BF
659; BR426   8300
-----. R [SDSTLS, SF#LSF#S,
SDM]   8301
Paradise (Dykes) X Paradise, No.
1   8302
Paradise (Hemy) [SSSDSTLL, FF
MFLSM, S] C167b; BO204 8303
Paradise (Smart) [MSMRDDTT, D
RMFSM, SL] B167b; D394c; L
581a; AL149; AO545b; AP631
8304
Paradise (Weber) X Paean   8305
Paradise No. 1 (Dykes) [MRDRM
RDD, DRDFML, SD] D394b; I
622a; AZ603-A   8306
Paradise, No. 2 (Barnby) X
Paradise   8307
Paran (Neander) X Neander 8308
Parce domini (Day) [SMMSDRRM,
DFFMMR, SM] AO583   8309
Parce, domini (Plainsong M 1)
[MMMRRD, MMMRRDRDTL,]
BM71; BN30; BO164   8310
Park Square (Loomis) [SDRFMLS

MDRM, SDTLS] Y231 8311
Park Street (Venua) [DDDDR
MRDTD, MMMMF#S] B308;
C308a; D472a; H26; I23;
J110; K122; L94; N319; R8;
S63; T33; U17; V95; AB
134; AD68; AE54; AF10;
AG47; AH282; AI19; AJ48;
AK25; AM6; AN313; AO154;
AR16; AS78; AV29; AW272;
AZ22-S; BA880; BB20; BD
139; BE59; BZ   8312
Parker (Harrington) [MRDSLT
L#T, DRD#RR#M, MM] I46
8313
Parker (Parker) [SSSLTDTLS,
LFSMSDT] A63b; B144b;
C144a; D94; J75b   8314
Parker (Parker) X Pro patria
8315
Parker (Parker) X Stella
8316
Parole (Lane) X Penitence
8317
Parousia (Pollock) [MMFSSLLD
LSM, SSLSD] AR212; AS165
8318
Parousia (Stainer) X St Giles
8319
Parratt (Parratt) [SLFMRS,
DTLS, LFMRD] A438b
8320
Parry (Maunder) [MMSSSFM
MR, DDFFMRM,] D548
8321
Parsifal (Wagner) [SDTLSLTL
SF, SLSFSM] E629   8322
Parsons (Hubbard) [SDRDSDR
MRD, MFSMDM] H280
8323
Parting hand (Ingalls) X
The midnight call   8324
Parting hymn (---) [SDDDTDM
DDT, DRRTLT] AY398
8325
Parting hymn (Danish trad)
[SMSLFRFSMDMSR, SMS]
P69   8326
Pascal (Allgemainisches kath-
olisches G-B. Vienna ca
1774) X Te deum   8327
Pascal (Hopkins) X Pascal,
No. 1   8328

Pascal No.1 (Hopkins) [MMM
SDRRM, MMMLMMRR,] AZ
277-C; BA610; BB61; BR406
8329
Paschal (Lindeman) X Our Lady,
Trondhjem   8330
Paschale gaudium (Stainer) [SSM
SDRD, LSDSSFM, SS] I156b
8331
Paskemorgen slukker sorgen
(Lindeman) X Our Lady, Trond-
hjem   8332
Pass me not (Doane) [MRDTDLS
D, RRDRM, MRD] G231; H43;
I329; J461; N416; P13; U252;
V760; AE175; AH338; AI212;
AL503; AM707; AO645; AP495;
AR464; AT219; AU230; AV349;
AW474; AX380; AY457; BA615;
BB559; BZ   8333
-----. R [SMRDL, SDMDR, MR
DTDL]   8334
Pass me not, O gentle Saviour
(Doane) X Pass me not   8335
Passion (Van der Werp) [MMR
DDDTD, LDRMLLS#L,] AI72
8336
Passion chorale (Hassler) [MLSF
MRM, TDDTLTL, ML] A75;
B158; C158a; D102a; E102; F
111; G141; I151b; J88; K99;
L243a; M269; N116; O231; P
155; Q172; R194; S151; V152;
W107; X128; Y350; Z231; AA
201; AB135; AC48; AD155;
AE109; AF170; AG96; AH289;
AI420; AK142; AL94; AM178;
AN191; AO160; AP194; AQ311;
AR168; AT91; AW539; AY490;
AZ151-A; BA215; BB130; BE
252; BF312; BI32; BJ62; BK73;
BL22; BM8; BN38; BP26, 101;
BQ22; BR175; BV158; BX309;
BY145; BZ   8337
-----. V [MLSFMRM, TDDTTL,
MLS] N116   8338
-----. V [MLSFMRM, TDTLS#
L, MLS] AZ151-D   8339
-----. V [MLSFMRRM, TDDTLT
L, M] BI32   8340
-----. V [MLSFMRRM, TDDTTL,
ML] BP101   8340a
Passiontide (Teutsch kirchenampt.

Strassburg, 1525) [SLSM
SFFM, RMFSFMRD,] M396;
Q142; AA191; AW533   8341
-----. V [SLSFMFSFFM,
RMFSFM] AW533   8342
Pastor (Abt) [SSSSDSSS, DRR
LLSFM,] L161   8343
Pastor (Wood) [DSLDFFFM,
RDTMLTS, D] D290   8344
Pastor benignus (Witt) X
Stuttgart   8345
Pastor bonus (Davis) X
Goshen   8346
Pastor bonus (Caldicott) [DD
TLSLTL, SDTLSLTL,] I300;
T298   8347
Pastor bonus (Smyth) [SMR#
MFMDRDRM, SMR#MF] BR
267   8348
Pastor bonus (Stainer) [DDRM
LTD, RFMDMR, DDR] F447;
I683   8349
Pastor pastorum (Silcher)
X Gott ein Vater   8350
Pastor regalis (Bonner) [SF
MMRR, LSRLSSF#, MF#R#]
Y271; AC294   8351
Pastoral (---) [DMMRMRD,
MSSFSFM, MR] D571
8352
Pastoral chant (Cuff) [MSS
S, LSMFFM, MMMF, F#D]
BR532   8353
Pastorale (Naegeli) [SDDRM
FMDRD, SMRDTL] AR588
8354
Patapan (French trad) [LLM
MRMD, TDRT, MDT, TD]
BG82   8355
Pater noster (Buck) [LSDRM
SFM, DRMFRD, DT] BE4
8356
Pater omnipotens (Dickey)
[MMRDRMRMFS, SDTLS]
A530   8357
Pater omnium (Holmes) [DR
MSFRDRM, FMLSDDT] I466;
L234; N469; AB360; AK68;
AL264; AM71; AP415b; AR
256; AS403; BA75; BB146;
BE357; BV547; BY770
8358
-----. R [RTSMMRTSS, SFR

DFMR] 8359
Pathway (Bourgeois) X Lord, to
thee 8360
Patmos (Havergal) X Consecra-
tion 8361
Patmos (Storer) [SSLTDDT,
DRD#RR#M,SM] A593b; D542;
C542a; D404a; I626; J597; S408;
U433; Z503; AD425; AO552
8362
Patmos (Wesley, S.S.) [SMM
MMMMRLL, LSFM, MS] W568b;
AL436b 8363
Patricroft (Heaton) [MR#MFMMRR,
DTDRR#M, MR#] AH509; BF
602 8364
Patten (Lutkin) [SSSDDLLL, L
LLRDDT, S] G558; I687; AK
450; AO488; AW390 8365
Paule, doctor egregie (Plainsong
M 7) [DDDRFMFS, SSSLLSFM]
F145a 8366
Paulina (Donizetti) [SMMMR#MM
DDRM, SMMMM] L471; N606;
T9; AJ13; AO365 8367
Pax (Kilgore) [MTDSLTDMMR,
DLSDDT] J349 8368
Pax (Public School hymn book.
1928) [LTDTLSM, LSFMDRM,]
A224a 8369
Pax (Rendle) [MMMMRDLDRM,
SSSSLT] G510; Z555 8370
Pax (Swedish koralbok. 1697)
[LDTLMRDT, TDTLMMR#M,]
J352a; N110 8371
Pax caelestis (Gould) [SDDTDRM
RD, DMMRMFS] BR536 8372
Pax celeste (Celestial harps. Edin-
burgh, 1824) [DRMFMRRD,
MFSLFR, ST] Q617 8373
Pax dei (Dykes) [DMSSFM, DMR
DDT, DMSD] B313; C313; D32a;
F31b; J489; K58; V417; W301b;
AA427; AB78; AL214c; AO11;
AZ32-G; BA476; BB26; BR395;
BX184; BY330b 8374
Pax dei (Hopkins) X Ellers 8375
Pax orbi (Milligan) [SLSMDR,
RMF#SSFS, SDT] Z552 8376
Pax tecum (Caldbeck) [SSSSSLLL
SS, SDRMRD] A436b; B405; C
405a; D674; F358b; G354; I528;
J571; K413; L465; R420; S301;

T420; U231; V391; W444a;
AD268; AE229; AG205; AK
245; AL285b; AM590; AO364;
AP438a; AR337; AS309; AV
298; AW256; BA690b; BB
311; BF387; BR409; BX274
8377
Pax veritatis (Bornschein)
[MFRSDLSFMR, RMRSLF]
Y253; Z287 8378
Pax veritatis (Parker) [SDTT
LRMF, LSFMSTTT,] B442;
C442 8379
Pax vobiscum (Arthur) [DLD,
SMDR, FMLSFMF#S, F]
R543; W303 8380
Paxtang (Lowry) [DMMSSSLS
M, DDDMMRM] T253; AJ351
8381
Peace (Baermann) [DMSRR
DD#RFM, SDRDTL] BX75b
8382
Peace (Bohemian Br.) X
Saelir 8383
Peace (Chadwick) [SSSDDTD
RMRD, MMMFM] G316; J
473; R274; U193; AG220;
AI133; AM397a; AR179
8384
Peace (Dykes) X Requiescat
8385
Peace (Fesca) [MMMSFMR,
MDDRRRSF#, F] AO102
8386
Peace (Hodges) [DMFRMD,
RMLSF#S, SMSD] D614
8387
Peace (Mozart) X Cana 8388
Peace (The revivalist, 1869)
[SLLDMRDLLL, SLLDLS]
AF578; AQ206 8389
Peace, be still! (Palmer)
[SLSSDMRL, DTLSFSM, S]
AM701; AU471; BB677;
BC106 8390
-----. R [MMMMMMMFFF,
RRM, MMM] 8391
Peace be to this congregation
(Beethoven) [SLSLSSSS, D
DDDDTD, S] BI75 8392
Peace I leave with you (Vassar
College) [SDMRD, SSDMMR
DT, MMM] AK511 8393

Peace makers (German) [MLTD MDTLT, DDRM, DRM] AD356 8394

Peace of God (Hartmann) [MM SLDRM, SMDTDFMR, T] J200; M497; O40; P210; AA71 8395

Peace, perfect peace (Miller) [MR#MSSDDDFM, SLTDSL] AS307 8396

Peace through the cross (Jerusalem's gates reopened) [MRMF MRD, DRRM, RRMRD] AS366 8397

Peace to soothe (Hartmann) X Peace of God 8398

Peacefield (Irish mel) [MMFSMM R, MMMFSRDD, M] A232; B609; X541; BE341; BV545; BY742 8399

Peaceful rest (Emerson) [SSDRM MMRDDT, SSLTD] AY176 8400

Pearsall (Pearsall) [SDTDMLS, SFMRRM, DM] A595; B68; C68; D405; E495; F276; S62a; V689; W396; X198b; AB141; AD346; AK 71; AP18; BN171; BQ95; BV 323a; BY278 8401

Peek (Peek) [MRDSSLTRDDT, FMRTL] Y180; Z361; AB236; AC177; AD489; AE445; AF489; AG309; AH433; AK448; AS319; AT315; AU368; AW207; BB425; BD101; BF457; BK29; BZ 8402

Peel Castle (Manx trad) [SM RDTDDMRDD, DMS] A208b; AC19; AL338 8403

Pekin (German chorale) [MFSD RTD, DRMFFM, MRS] V285 8404

Pelham Street (Covell) [DMRDT LLS, RMDMF#S, SL] AQ24 8405

Pembroke (Foster) [DMRDSSFM RM, MRLSDF] BB36; BY772 8406

Pembroke (Hadley) [LTDRMRDTD T, LTDDRM] X311 8407

Penfield (Pierce) [SDDTLSM, DRMSMRD, SD] AH184 8408

Peniel (Booth) [MMRSSFFM, ML LSMMRR,] C230; D42; AB 345; AH471; AL312b 8409

Peniel (Hastings) [SMRDFM RLTD, MSTLRF#] V384 8410

Peniel (Wesley, S.S.) X Wrestling Jacob 8411

Penitence (Lane) [MMFMLS, DMSRM, MMFM] A334; B 147; C147; D340a; G274; H 373; I431; J561; K391; L524; M272; N257; P169; R52; S 255b; T5; U238; V171; Y104; Z333; AA409; AB195; AC178; AD148; AE245; AF374; AG 151; AH439; AI286; AJ7; AK 160; AM475; AO340; AP406; AR303; AS321; AT317; AU 467; AV187; AW195; AY477; AZ141-E; BA466; BB327; BD108; BF479; BR347; BZ 8412

Penitence (Oakley) [DSMRDDTL S, SLLSTD, M] H264; I491; L397 8413

Penitence (St Alban's tune book, 1866) X Holborn Hill 8414

Penitentia (Dearle) [MMFSDR RMFM, MRDLSS] A208a; B334; C334; D219a; G415; I237; J275; U382; V549; Y 261; AB164; AC300; AD282; AG311; AP355; AR519; AT 391; BE423; BF352; BR259; BZ 8415

Penlan (Jenkins) [MSFMRDT, DRMSFM, MSF] W684; BV 524; BY581a 8416

Pentatone (Davies) [DRMSDLS MM, LSMMRMD,] R109; S282; W446; AD267; BE159 8417

Pentecost (Boyd) [MMMMMRDF, MMMMRRD] A560b; B113; C113b; D505b; F304b; G286; I409; J557; N384; R283; S 270a; T106; U299; W517a; Y158; AB240b; AC207; AD492; AE257; AF367; AG201; AH 453; AJ91b; AK355; AL384a; AM496; AN397b; AO392; AP 544a; AS315; AT406; AU270;

AV200; AW353; BA574; BD85;
BE60; BF434; BK116; BX434;
BZ   8418
Pentecost (Lomas) [MRRMFS, SL
SFSM, STLS,] BY225a   8419
Pentecost (Sewell) [SLSMRMM,
SMFSLDD, MR] BR205   8420
Pentecost (Spielman) [DMSSFM
R, MF#SDTLS, DR] M466   8421
Pentonville (Mason) [SMDRTD,
MRDTLS, RTSD] L255; V250;
AO368   8422
People of the living God (Har-
monia sacra) [MRDDTDR, SF
MRDTD, MR] AX155   8423
Peoria (Bradbury) [SSDMSMSFRS
M, SLFLS] AR24; AS10   8424
Per pacem (Martin) [SDTTLL
MMRD, TTLS, SD] D633a   8425
Percival-Smith (Laufer) [MMDR
MFFM, MLDRMML, M] G130
                            8426
Percivals (---) [MRDSLTD, RM
RDTLS, DD] C354; D563; I676;
AO251; BA676   8427
Perfect love (Barnby) X Sand-
ringham   8428
Perkins (Perkins) [DSDMRD,
SLTDRDT, DMF#] AS422   8429
Perkins (Perkins) X Lundie
                            8430
Perranport (Wilson) [SLTDMSS
S, DMMFS, SLT] F72a   8431
Perry (Sowerby) [DTDRMFSM,
MLSMF#S, FM] BZ   8432
Personent hodie (Piae cantiones.
1582) X Theodoric   8433
Peterboro (Harrison) [DMMFFMRD,
MSSFMR, MR] H292; I404; V98;
AA255; AL572; AO508; BX140
                            8434
Peterborough (Goss) [SSSDSLLS,
SDRMDRDT] H180; M139; N
71; O122; AB393   8435
Peterborough (Harrison) X Peter-
boro   8436
Peterborough Old (Harrison) X
Peterboro   8437
Petersen (Halle, 1697) [SSFMRM
RDRR, MFMLSF] A216; BE103
                            8438
Petersham (Poole) [DMSDLSFM,
MRSLLS, SS] S82; W398; Y73;

AB318; AK409; BX444; BY
254   8439
Peterson (Perkins) [MMFRTL
LS, MMFRTLLS,] BF350
                            8440
Petition (Gower) [MMMRDRM
F, MDRR, SSMF] Z330   8441
Petition (Haydn) [SMRDTTLS,
DFMRDDT, S] G351; H123;
L543; T277; AI104; AJ385;
AO135; AZ582-R; BA714
                            8442
-----. V [SMRDTLS, DFMR
DDT, SM] H123   8443
Petra (Redhead) [DDRMFFM,
DDRMRRD, DMS] A70; B151;
C151; D93; E477; F127; I280;
J78; K93; N102; O27a; P170;
Q159; R193; S214; T97; V147;
W413a; X636b; Z227; AA199;
AE114; AF158; AH284; AJ
140a; AK144; AL92; AM357;
AO159; AP190; AR160; AS
172; AT105; AW109; AZ581-
G; BA220; BB122; BD26; BF
612; BV177; BX367; BY458;
BZ   8444
Petrie (Irish trad) [SDRMFS
FMRDRMFR, SD] X102
                            8445
Petrograd (Tschaikowsky) [DD
DDLTD, RMRDTLTD, S]
Y390   8446
Pevensey (Aufranc) [SLTDMMRD
TRD, MMRDM] BB468   8447
Philadelphia (Bradbury) X
Zephyr   8448
Philadelphia (Wesley arr) [DS
DMRDFMRM, SLSFMR] BY
663   8449
Philippi (Ebeling) [SSLSFM,
SFRMRD, RMF#S,] D367;
J215; K447; M557; P291;
AK49; AN402; AW555; AZ
607-A; BY225b   8450
-----. V [SSLSFM, SFRMR
D, MFSL1 J215   8451
-----. V [SSLSFM, SFRMMR,
DTLS,] AN402   8452
Philippine (Roberts) [MMRDSM
RDRM, SDTLSM] J258; X
251; BE363; BV622; BY174
                            8453

Phoenix (Fowles) X Cavell   8454
Phuvah (Vulpius) X Cana   8455
Picardy (French trad) [LTDRMM
 RMM, MMFSFM] A197; B339;
 C339a; E318; F97b; G594; J
 281; R148; S112; W636; X273;
 AC277; AD405; AE459; AF107;
 AG337; AK336; AL515a; AN178;
 AQ293; AR120; AT80; BB685;
 BL52; BY102; BZ   8456
Picton (Branscombe) [MLTDRM
 LSFM, MDTLSF#] Y272; AC
 118   8457
Pie Jesu (Michel) [MFFMMLS#
 LLS#, MFRTDD] BO212 8458
Pie Jesu (Montani) [MMMRRFFF
 M, SSSFMRD] BQ251   8459
Pie Jesu (Vanden Plas) [LLT
 TDDT, LTDDDTLS#, L] BO213
                         8460
Pierre (Pierre) [DMFSDTDLS,
 SDTLSMD] AJ425   8461
Pietas (---) [SDMSTDRM, F#SL
 TRDTL] D134a   8462
Pilesgrove (Mitchell) [DMSSM
 RDTD, MSFMRDS] H73; L551
                         8463
Pilgrim (Italian mel) X I'm a
 pilgrim   8464
Pilgrim (Mozart) X Ellesdie
                         8465
Pilgrim (Ohl) [SMDTLSMRD,
 LLSMMRM,] J520b; K261 8466
Pilgrim (Sewell) [MMMFRSS,
 MMMFLS, SF#M] BR39 8467
Pilgrim band (Stainer) [MRDSLRT
 S, DTLTDMR, M] W578   8468
-----. R [MRDSLRTS, SF#MRM
 LF#S]   8469
Pilgrim chorus (Wagner) X Pil-
 grim's chorus [sic]   8469a
Pilgrim song (Hagfors) [SDRMDDTD
 R, SRMFRRD] J536   8470
Pilgrim song (Catholic) [MFSDD
 LSM, SLSMFSM, S] P82 8471
Pilgrimage (Barnard) [SLSMMRD,
 LTDSFMR, SL] C348   8472
Pilgrimage (Elvey) [MSDDRMFM,
 FSLDFMR, S] F296; BY40
                         8473
Pilgrimage (Freylinghausen G-B.
 1704) X Se solens skjønne lys
 og pragt   8474

Pilgrimage (Herrnhut ms.) X
 Gregor's 166th metre   8475
Pilgrims (Smart) [MSFMRDR
 MFMR, SDTL] A472; B290;
 C290a; D398a; F354; G532;
 I621a; J498; L587a; P347;
 R426; S431; T196; U434; V
 694a; W580; Y343; Z582; AB
 404a; AC329; AD462; AG282;
 AH369; AJ284; AK420; AL
 442; AN549; AO546a; AP601;
 AR421; AS476; AT469; AU62;
 AV286; AW260; BB376; BD
 153; BF385; BI50; BX464
                         8476
-----. R [RMFS, DLSFM, DT
 LSMD]   8477
-----. V [MSFMMRDRMFM
 R, RSDT] BI50   8478
Pilgrim's chorus (Wagner) [S
 DSMMFSSLSSSF, LRD] Y252;
 AH623; AR619; AS52   8479
Pilgrim's mission (Phillips)
 [DMSLSMRD, RRRRDRM, M]
 AL506   8480
-----. R [DTTTTLTDDDDT,
 DRRR]   8481
Pilgrims of the night (Recueil
 de cantiques) X Swiss
 melody   8482
Pilot (Gould) [MRDTRDLS, F
 MMRDTD, R] G269; H350;
 I482; J531; K270; L240; M
 169; N340; P161; Q649; R
 336; S286; T249; U235; V
 340; Y371; Z409; AB227;
 AC160; AD225; AE254; AF
 213; AG155; AH309; AI302;
 AJ346; AK468; AL444; AM
 497; AO328; AP607; AR288;
 AS248; AT337; AU158; AV
 238; AW161; AX501; AY308;
 BA704; BB398; BC121; BY
 543; BZ   8483
Pimlico Road (Shaw) [SLDSM
 RDRR, MFSLSFM] X617
                         8484
Pine Glen (Huffaker) [MMMMM
 FMRD, SSSSSLS] AR225
                         8485
Pioneer (Ewing) [DMSDDTLS,
 DRMRDTLS,] AR77   8486
Pioneers (Lowens) [MMLLLSL,

RR,SSMLLR,SD] I474   8521
Poacher (Weber) X Jewett   8522
Poland (Koschat) [SMMMMD,
    DMMMF,SFFFF] Y365; Z170;
    AC57; AH212; AI304; AM663;
    AS260; AT57; AU22; AW62;
    BA691; BC104; BI2; BR529
                            8523
-----. R [SDTLSM,MSMFSMDT,
    SD]   8524
Poland (Polish mel) [SSFMMMM
    RMSF,FFMRR] AB224; AD418;
    AL393; AR372; BQ36   8525
-----. V [SSFMMMRMSF,FFM
    RRL] BQ36   8525a
Polish carol (Polish trad) X
    W. Zlobie Lezy   8526
Pollard (Stebbins) X Adelaide
                            8527
Polycarp (Barnby) X St Polycarp
                            8528
Polzeath (Kidner) [MTDMFS,LM
    FSLT,DLSR] BV287b   8529
Pomerania (Wagner. G-B. ms.
    1742) X Wir glauben all' an ein-
    en Gott   8530
Pone luctum (Catholic, 1750)
    [DMRDSDRMD,MFSLSFF] BQ
    78   8531
Pont Neuf (Sanders) [SDSRDR,MF
    MRDRS,SDS] AQ137   8532
Pontiac (Haynes) [MMMFMRLSS,
    MFSLTDS] BB699   8533
Poplar (Strong) [LTDRMLRDT
    SLSL,LSD] F332a   8534
Poppen (Poppen) [SSLSDMRD,
    MRDMMRR,S] M622   8535
Porter (McCutchan) [SMMRDSSL
    DRDTT,DMS] AT521   8536
Porth Kerry (Lloyd) [SDMSLSMD,
    MRRLRR,S] W575   8537
Portland (Taylor) [SSSDSMFS,
    SLDTDRLT,] BV599a; BY480
                            8538
Portsea (Boyce) [LSFMFRMDT,
    LTDRMLT] F124b   8539
Portuguese (Wade. Cantus diver-
    sus) X Adeste fideles   8540
Portuguese hymn (Wade. Cantus
    diversus) X Adeste fideles
                            8541
Posen (Strattner) [DDDDRMFM,S
    SSSLTDT,] D549; M589; R458;

S452; V159; Z177; AB351;
    AD330; AE434; AG305; AM
    654; AN34; AO617; AQ33;
    AR282; AV196; AW424; AX
    123; AZ11-C; BA232; BB331;
    BF423; BR485; BX60   8542
Potsdam (Bach) [DRFMRD,SL
    DTLS,MFLS] B109; C109b;
    Q117; V471; AA175; AF233;
    AL422; AN437; AO228; BE14;
    BM43; BY320   8543
Pounds (Fillmore) [SSMDDTL
    SFM,MRMFRS] Z255; AR
    448; AT127; AU413; AW453;
    AY491   8544
-----. R [SF#SRTLTDSS,
    SF#SRTL]   8545
Pour out thy spirit (Allge-
    meines katholisches G-B.
    Vienna, 1774) X Hursley
                             8546
Poverty (Welsh carol) [SDDR
    DTD,RMMFMR,DMD] BG34;
    BV94   8547
-----. V [SDDRDTD,RMMFM
    R,DRM] BV94   8548
Power in the blood (Jones) X
    There is power . . .   8549
Praeneste (Palestrina) [MMM
    FMRRDDT,SDRMRD] BR
    477   8550
Praetorius I (Praetorius) [DS
    SLSSFM,DRMFFM,MM]
    E549; W130; X174; Y31; AN
    77a; AW248; BI21-D   8551
-----. V [DSSLSSSM,DRMF
    FM,MM] BI21-D   8552
Praetorius (--- 1536, Praetorius
    arr) [SDDRFMRMR,RDDF
    MR,] A133; E179; F509;
    G71; Q67; X146; AA134
                             8553
Praetorius (Geistliche Kirchen-
    gesang Cologne, 1599) X
    Rosa mystica   8554
Prague (Plainsong, ca 600)
    X Christe, qui lux es et
    dies   8555
Prague (Pensum sacrum) X
    Herr Jesu Christ   8556
Praise (Goss) X Lauda anima
                             8557
Praise (Harrington) [DTLLSSL

TDFM, RMFSM] I20   8558
Praise (Hopkins) X Kelso   8559
Praise (Lowe) [DDRRRFFM, MMD
  TLTM, M] K27; AD72; AH186;
  AM5; AO203; BF238; BR61
                                8560
Praise (Sewall) [MMMSSDRM,
  MMMFMRRD,] BR54   8561
Praise (Shaw) [LSLTLDRMRFM
  RLL, MF] E535; X624   8562
Praise (Stralsund G-B. 1665) X
  Praise to the Lord   8563
Praise (Swedish) [DMFSLFFM,
  RDDFMRD, D] J422; N288
                                8564
Praise and prayer (Fisher) [DR
  MFMDRD, MFSLSMF#S,] AR
  493   8565
Praise God from whom (Bourgeois)
  X Old 100th   8566
Praise Him (Bailey) [DDMSLTDL
  SM, DDFMSS,] AE437; AL594;
  AR465; AT511; AU306; AW426;
  BK2; BY753   8567
Praise Him! praise Him (Allen)
  X Joyful song   8568
Praise Jehovah (Stralsund G-B.
  1665) X Praise to the Lord
                                8569
Praise, Lord, for thee in Zion
  waits (Haydn) X Bradford
                                8570
Praise my soul (Goss) X Lauda
  anima   8571
Praise now your God (Kern)
  [LTTDLLRTDLL, DDRMD] BL
  43   8572
Praise the Lord (Bechler) [DSM
  SDRMD, FMRDTDR, M] BA171
                                8573
Praise the Lord (Jewish trad) X
  Addeer hu   8574
Praise the Lord (Pollock) [SSS
  MLSS, FRRLSS, SSS] AY324
                                8575
Praise the Lord (Rolle) [DMS,
  MDRTD, SLTDLLS, M] AZ16-M
                                8576
Praise the Lord in heaven (French
  carol) X Grace soit   8577
Praise the Lord with heart and
  voice (Cannon) [MSDTTLS, MS
  DDTLS, TD] BC149   8578

Praise the Lord! ye heavens
  (Haydn) X Austria   8579
Praise the Saviour (Darm-
  stadt G-B.) X Goldschmidt
                                8580
Praise to God (Russian trad)
  [DSDRMMMFM, RDRMD, R
  M] BG107; BK13   8581
-----. V [DDS, DRM, MMSF
  MRDRMD,] BK13   8582
Praise to God, immortal
  praise (Abbot) X 'Tis re-
  ligion that can give   8583
Praise to the Holiest (Montani)
  [DDDFMDLTD, SDTLTDR,]
  BQ142   8584
Praise to the Holiest (Somer-
  vell) X Somervell   8585
Praise to the Holiest (Tallis)
  X Tallis' Ordinal   8586
Praise to the Lord (Stralsund
  G-B. 1665) [DDSMRDTL
  SLTDRD, DD] A279; E536;
  F382; G60; J408; K286; M
  212; N37; O5; P3; Q39; R1;
  S6; W22; X626; Z98; AA63;
  AB40; AC35; AD13; AE1;
  AF15; AG3; AI1; AK8; AL9;
  AM50; AN7; AO66; AQ7;
  AR37; AT6; AW515; AZ61-
  A; BA864; BB12; BC150;
  BE283; BF172; BK49; BL
  84; BM1; BN62; BV246;
  BY25; BZ   8587
-----. V [DDSMRDTLS, DR
  MRD,] AA63   8588
Praise to the man (---) [DD
  DMDMSDMRDS, FLFM] BC
  147   8589
-----. R [DDDTLSSDDDTLS,
  DDD]   8590
Praise we Christ, the King
  (Michaud) [MMRMFS, SDT
  SLS, SFRM] BQ335   8591
Praise we our God (Montani)
  [LTDRTLS, DRMFMRD, LT]
  BQ141   8592
Praise ye our Father (Barnby)
  X Nightfall   8593
Praise ye the Father (Gounod)
  [SSSDF, FFMRDSFM, MMM]
  AU472   8594
Praise ye the Lord (Isaacs)

[SMFSDTLS, MFMFSMFR,]
AH156; BH65   8595
Praise ye the Lord (Sherwin)
[DDDD, MFFM, SFFMRDLR]
AU474   8596
Praise ye the Lord (Stainer) X
Laus matutina   8597
Praise ye the Lord (Stephens)
[DRMFMRSFM, RRRSRDT]
BC277   8598
Praises (Selby) [SLMSLTDDR,
SMRDTLS] F241a   8599
Praxis pietatis (Stralsund G-B.
1665.) X Praise to the Lord
8600
Pray (Brown) [MMRDRMMD,
DRRRMR, MM] AX359   8601
-----. R [SSLSMD, MRDDDRMR,
SS]   8602
Pray for the dead (---) [LTTD, DD
RM, FMMRDTTL,] BO144
8603
-----. R [MFMR, RSFM, MMFM
RMRD]   8604
Pray when the morn unveileth
(Brandeis) [MRDFMRSMDL,
SDTLSF] BH8   8605
Prayer (---) [SMLSDDTLTDS,
DTLSM] AO317   8606
Prayer (Abbott) X 'Tis religion
that can give   8607
Prayer (Babcock) [SLTDMSFM,
RDDTLS, SS] V463   8608
Prayer (Butcher) [SSMSLLDTL
S, SSSDSM] R126; T136; AJ
203   8609
Prayer (D'Andreiux) [DSDSDRDT
LS, MSMSMF] BH37   8610
Prayer (Dykes) X Almsgiving
8611
Prayer (Greenwood) [MFSLSMRD,
MMFSMRM, M] BE285   8612
Prayer (Marshall) [SFMSMRMMRD
RM, FFFM] L382   8613
Prayer for a holy death (Plain-
song M 1) [SDDMSFMR, SDD
MSFMR] BN191   8614
Prayer for all men (Hastings) X
Ortonville   8615
Prayer for wisdom (Grimm) [SD
DTTLRR, MFMFSRM, M] BH28
8616

Prayer is the soul's desire
(American trad) X Camp-
meeting   8617
Prayer is the soul's sincere
desire (Careless) [DSLSM
SFRD, RMLSF#S, L] BC220
8618
Prayer of St Francis (A Monk
of Gethsemani) [SMFSSSDDR
MFS, SMFS] BN60   8619
Prayers (Milford) [MMSDTL,
SLSMRDRM, MS] X504 8620
Praying for you (Sankey) X I
am praying for you   8621
Precious child (Norwegian trad)
[DRDSDRDS, DMSFMRSF]
P137   8622
Precious Jesus, O to love thee
(Pollock) [MFSMRDLS, SS
DSFMR, M] AS208   8623
-----. R [SSDSMFSM, SDTTLL
S, M]   8624
Precious memories (Wright)
[SSLDDDLS, MRDDDMR, S]
AX559   8625
-----. R [SMSM, MMRD, DDR
DRDMD,]   8626
Precious name (Doane) [SDM
RDRDS, LDTLDLS, S] G253;
I508; N260; R411; AG152;
AH430; AI100; AS297; AT
305; AU424; AV320; AW485;
AX27; AY460; BB523; BZ
8627
-----. R [DTLDLS, DRMSDMR,
MRD]   8628
Precious promise (Bliss) [SL
TDDDRMLL, LTDRRR] AU
90; AV356; AX492   8629
-----. R [SFMMRRMFFM,
MRMSMM]   8630
Precious Savior, dear Redeemer
(Palmer) [MRDDMRDD, SMR
RMFM, M] BC109   8631
Precious to me (Gabriel) X
He is so precious   8632
Preis, lob, ehr', ruhm, dank
(Darmstadt G-B. 1698) X
Gregor's 101st metre   8633
Prentiss (Doane) X More love
to thee   8634
Presbyter (Gautnlett) [SFMRF

MRD, MLSTDFMR,] AB381;
AH217   8635
Presbyter (Wilkinson) [SDDTTLL
S, SMMRRR, MF] U399; Y281
     8636
Prescott (Lutkin) [MRMFMMRR,
LRTLSM, MR] I263   8637
Prescott (Stewart) [SSSLTDSMS,
DDRRFFM,] D449; K133; M196;
N42; O496; AA238; BA93   8638
Presence (Whitlock) [SLSDRMRS
MR, LRMFMD] BE211   8639
Preservation (Störl) X Störl I
     8640
Press on (---) [DDSDRM, DLS
S, RRLRRF] Y227   8641
Pressburg (Freylinghausen) [LS#
LMDTLS#, SLMFSRMR] E358;
W112; X292; AW538   8642
Pressly (Gabriel) [DMMMDLSS,
MSFRRMFM,] T284; AJ370
     8643
Preston (Doane) [SSSDSSFMRM,
SSSDRM] R258; T226; AJ322
     8644
Preston (Maclean) [SSMMMRDDT,
LSSDRDT,] V659   8645
Preston (Miller) [DSDRMDMF,
SLFRDRM, D] BB23   8646
Priestly benediction (Binder) [MM
LTDDRMS, FMRDTL, L] BH301
     8647
Primo dierum omnium (Sarum
plainsong M 4) [RMFSMSFMF,
RMFSMSF] E50; BJ31   8648
Primrose (Chapin) X Melody 8649
Prims (Sheldon) [DRDSMRML, T
DRFMRDR,] BV306   8650
Prince (Hemy) X St Catherine
     8651
Prince of peace (Dykes) [MSMDR
MDL, DSDRMR, MS] D59b 8652
Prince of peace (Maclagan) [SSLS
FMRD, MLDTLS, LM] V421;
BA30   8653
Prince of peace (Smythe) [SDD
RMMFSLS, SFMMRD] BR173b
     8654
Prince of peace, control my
will (Bradbury) X Aletta 8655
Prince Rupert (English march,
1648) [LMLTDRD, TLLS# L, LM]
A316; X397; Y113   8656

-----. R [DSMSDS, DRMFM
R, DSMS]   8657
Princess Eugenie (Norwegian
trad) [MLLS#MMDDTL, TD
LTS#M] P26   8658
Princethorp (Pitts) [MD
FRSFM, RMFMRD, MDF]
D608; N279; T321; V654;
AL113b; AO399; AP132;
AW89; BA110; BN101; BR
389b; BY95   8659
Pro me perforatus (Barnby)
X St Olave   8660
Pro nostris liberis (Lloyd)
[DTSMSLS, SDTLRTSLS,]
W650; AL395   8661
Pro omnibus sanctis (Barnby)
X Sarum   8662
Pro patria (Armistead) [MS
DFMRM, MLRFMRM, MS]
F606b; AD355   8663
Pro patria (Parker) [DRMS
SSSSDTDMR, MMM] B430b;
C430b; D194; S370; AB270;
AC258; BB198; BF571; BX
42   8664
-----. V [DRMSSSDTDMR,
MMMMT] S370   8665
Pro patria (Warren) X Na-
tional hymn   8666
Proclaim the tidings (Mason)
X Sing glory, hallelujah
     8667
Proclamation (Walch) X Tid-
ings   8668
Proclamation (Warner) [SSDS
MFSLLS, SDTSTR] AZ23-C
     8669
Promise (---) [SMLSSMRMS
FFM, SMLS] BB397   8670
Promise (Sanders) [SDRMSL
TDTLS, SDRMS] AN240
     8671
Promised land (American
trad) X Jordan's Banks
[Variants follow:]   8672
-----. V [DRMMDMFSFFFM,
RMMD] AV282   8673
-----. V [DDDDRMRRR, TDD
DRMT,] BB682   8674
-----. V [DRMMDMFSFFSF
M, RMM] BZ   8675
Promises (Carter) [SSSLSFM

Omnipotent   8716
Psalm 118 (Bourgeois) X Rendez
à Dieu   8717
Psalm 119 (Weinberg) [MS#LTRD
TL, LDDRRM, MS] BH191 8718
Psalm 135 (Genevan Psalter, 1562)
X Ministres de l'Eternal 8719
Psalm 136 (Braham. Hebrew melo-
dies) [MSSSMDR, RRMSMDR,
RR] BH58   8720
Psalm 136 (Genevan Psalter) X
Louez Dieu   8721
Psalm 138 (Genevan Psalter)
[DMFSDTLS, SLSMMFMRD]
X661a; AJ429; BJ99; BY75
                          8722
Psalm 146 (Genevan Psalter 1602)
[MFMDRDTL, LDTLLSL, D]
X210b   8723
Psalm of Sion (English trad) X
St Austin   8724
P'u T'o (Chinese mel) [MDDRM
SSLMRD, MDDRM] R75; Y311;
AF71   8725
Puer natus (Piae Cantiones, 1582)
X Ein kind geborn   8726
Puer natus in Bethlehem (Plain-
song M 1) [LDDTDRDT, LDTL,
LDRM] BL6; BM66; BN8
                          8727
-----. V [RFFMFSFMRFMR, RF
SL] BM66   8728
Puer nobis (Piae cantiones, 1582)
[DDRMFMRD, DSSSLTDD] A34,
47; B556; C556; E14; F430; G157;
J94; M395; Q63; R46; S119; X
33d, 385; Y157; AA162; AB152;
AD301; AF39; AG78; AK48; AN
56a; AQ125; AW87; BE323; BG
92; BV121; BY112; BZ   8729
-----. V [DRMFMRD, DSSLTDD,
DR] A34   8730
-----. V [DDRMFMMD, DSLTS
LTD] M395   8731
-----. V [DRMFMRD, SSLTDD,
DRT] BG92   8732
Puer nobis nascitur (Piae can-
tiones, 1582) X Puer nobis
                          8733
Puer nobis nascitur (Scheidemann)
[SMDSLLS, LTDTLS, SMD]
BQ159   8734
Purer in heart (Fillmore) [MFM

MRD, DTLS, RRRMFS,] Z
343; AT369; AU272; AX386;
AY67   8735
Purer in heart (Holsinger)
[MRMDDS, SFMR, MRMDDS,]
AS312   8736
Puritan (Dunham) [DDTLTLSF
M, RDFMLSF#] I713a 8737
Purity (---) [DDMDTRD, MM
SMMRDR, F] AR8; AS59;
AX418; AY53   8738
Purity (Norwegian trad) X
Behold a host   8739
Purleigh (Brown) [DDSLDDTD,
MMDRSDTL,] K210; N185;
O95; V301a; AA485; AJ392;
AP30; BA308; BX188 8740
Purleigh (Calkin) X Golden
corn   8741
Purpose (Davies) X Ainger
                          8742
Purpose (Shaw) [LTDTLSM,
SDTLSL, LTD] A538; E548;
R500; X300; AF298; BV315b
                          8743

Q

Quam dilecta (Jenner) [MFMM
RD, SLMRDR, RMSSL] A398;
B465; C465a; D484b; E508;
F242; J239; K393; W236;
AL199; AP325; AW281; BE
268; BO122; BR23; BV13;
BY283   8744
Quam dilecta (Root) [MMMMM
MMMFM, MSSSSS] N673;
U490; AE456; AG320; AR623;
AT515; AU482; AV411; BB
690   8745
Quebec (Baker) X Hesperus
                          8746
Quedlinburg (Kittel) [DMFSS
DLSFM, RSFMRD] E245;
J596a; X238; BN149 8747
Queen and mother (Catholic)
[SDDTSFFM, SSLSFMMR,]
BO107   8748
Queen of the rosary (Haller)
[SMFSMS, DTLSFM, SLLT]
BP83   8749
Queen, when the earth
(Andrews) [MMRDDMSSFM,

FFMRRF] BN147   8750

Queen's College) (Davenport)
[MMFSDDTLSS, MRRMFS]
AP364   8751

Queenswood (Hann) [LLTDTLFL,
TDRMRS, SL] Y145; AC181
                         8752

Quelle est cette odeur agreable?
(French carol) X Fragrance
                         8753

Quem pastores (Hohenfurth ms.)
[DMSMFSLSR, MFSFM] A35;
B506; C506; E543; F456; N195;
O500; Q90; W349; X540; AC
171; AE380; BD105; BE237;
BG79; BV111; BY617   8754

-----. V [DMSMFSLSR, MSFMRD
L] Q90   8754a

Quem pastores laudavere (Hohenfurth ms) X Quem pastores
                         8755

Quem terra, pontus (Plainsong
M 2) [RRDTDLSDRFFMRM,
SS] E214; F512a   8756

Quest (Spencer-Palmer) [LMFFM
LLS#, LMFFSRFM,] BV629
                         8757

Quest (Poteat) [SLTDDRMFM,
SFMRMDT] Z320   8758

Qui laborat orat (Allen) [DDD
S, SLTRDTDFMM, SF] F339;
BE41   8759

Qui tenet (Barnes) [SDTLSLM
RM, MLSFMLD] Y81; AC234;
AD206   8760

Quietude (Green) X The quiet
hour   8761

Quinquagesima (Jones) [MM
SMDRMR, MSSF#S, LSF]
BY472b   8762

Quinta (Wales. Univ. Students'
hymnal.) [DMSDSM, DSLSFM,
SMRD] W120b   8763

Quittez, pasteurs (French trad)
[SMRDSDRMFSD, SMRDS]
X98; BG144; BV110   8764

-----. V [SMRDSDRMFSS, SM
RDS] BG144   8765

Quoi, ma voisine? (French trad)
X The Kingdom   8766

R

Rabenlei (Rinck) X St Lucian
                         8767

Rachel (Sewall) [DSLSSD, MR
MDDDTLT, D] BR198   8768

Rachie (Roberts) [SDLRDT,
TMDFMR, RSSF] BY539
                         8769

Racine (Diggle) [SMDDSLSFM,
RSDDLT] A529   8770

Racine (Edwards) [SDTLSSDT,
SDTTLLRD] D506b   8771

Racine (Lutkin) [SLSMDDTT,
RRDSMMR, L] I484   8772

Radford (Wesley) [SDRMDFMM
R, RMFSMMR] W289b; AL
568a   8773

Radiance (Smith) [MMMRDSLS,
RMSTLR, R#M] I537   8774

Radiant morn (Freylinghausen)
X Morgenglanz der Ewigkeit
                         8775

Radiant morn (Gounod) [MRM
FSFMRD, SF#SLTLS] I566;
S38; AB214; AT32; BX331b
                         8776

Radlett (Greenwood) [SSFMRM
LSL, TDMSFM, R] BE231
                         8777

Radwell (Chadwyck-Healey)
[RMFSLTDRDTL, FRMFS]
F441   8778

Raglan (Clemens) [MMMMRDTD,
SFMRLDT, F] BA768   8779

Raise your voices to the Lord
(Stephens) [MDSMDRM, FM
RMRDT, FR] BC154   8780

Raise your voices, vales and
mountains (English hymnal:
old) [SSDDRFMM, DMRRT
RDD,] BO70   8781

-----. R [SMMFLS, MSFRFM,
SMMR]   8782

Raise your voices, vales and
mountains (Schulthes) [MMM
RMFMRDDT, DD#RST] BQ
90, 237   8783

-----. V [SMMMRMFMRDDT,
DD#RS] BQ237   8784

Rakem (Woodbury) [MMMSMDR
M, MFMFLSFM,] T95; AJ
138   8785

Raleigh (Prout) [MRMLLS, DTD
 FFM, SDTL] W630; BY667
                                  8786
Ralston (Barnby) X Barnby II
                                  8787
Ramaulx (Selby) [DRMFMRDTDR
 M, RDTLT] B195b   8788
-----. R [MFSLRSSFMF, MRFM
 RD]   8789
Ramoth (Calkin) [SSDDTLS, MM
 SDDRD, SS] D355; W328; AP
 339; AZ205-B; BA521   8790
Ramoth (English trad) [SDDDRMMM,
 RMFSSFMR,] T64; AJ169
                                  8791
Ramoth (Jones) [SMDDTLS, MF
 SLFMRD, S] X464a   8792
Ramwold (Warner) [DTSLFMRD,
 DFMLSDDT,] AF303   8793
Randall (Randall) [SSSDRM, SFM
 MRD, MSSD] M182; AP82b
                                  8794
-----. V [SSSSSDRM, SDTTLS,
 MF] AP82b   8795
Randall (Randall) X Cambridge
                                  8796
Randolph (Williams) [MSLSFMRDD,
 MF#SSLTD] E524; R78a; W624;
 X334; AF61; AN472a; BY761b;
 BZ   8797
Rangoon (Wood) [DMMSSD, SML
 SMFSM, MM] F270   8798
Ransom (Bunnett) [SSMLSSRR,
 MFSLTDSS,] D366; BX186
                                  8799
Raphael (Hopkins) X St Raphael
                                  8800
Raphael (Smith) [DRMFMRDTDR,
 DDDL#LS] BV396   8801
Rapture (Harwood) [DDSLTDRDT
 D, MRDTRM] T65; AJ99 8802
Rapture (Haydn) [MRDDMSFM, R
 MFFRDTD,] C298; D180a
                                  8803
Rapture (Humphreys) [DRMMMSFM
 RRMF, MRDDRMR] G356 8804
Rapture (Scholefield) [SMMMRD
 TRD, TLRFRMR,] AT197; AU339
                                  8805
-----. R [DTLTDR, RDTDRM,
 SMMM]   8806
Rathbon (Crueger) X Ratisbon
                                  8807

Rathbun (Conkey) [SDMDTLSDS,
 SLMRMF#] A336; B152b;
 C152a; D48b; G149; H175;
 I143b; J64a; K62b; L231a;
 M166; N103; O262; P193;
 Q354; R195; S154; T288; U
 64; V143; Y377; Z237; AA
 95; AB140; AC124; AD157;
 AE116; AF157; AG94; AH
 292; AI76; AJ282; AK76;
 AL100b; AN190b; AO165; AP
 199b; AR176; AS138; AT100;
 AU180; AV113; AW110; AY
 188; AB197; BB125; BE379;
 BF316; BI49; BR59; BX213a;
 BZ   8808
Ratisbon (Crueger. Praxis pie-
 tatis melica) [SSLTDDT, LD
 SMFRD, MM] A153, 190; B4,
 340; C4; D224a; E282; F7;
 G32; J294b; K511; L264; M4,
 222; O45, 227; P209; Q20,
 201; S465; V30, 681, 352; W
 394; X24; AA220; AF43; AK
 168; AM362; AN220; AR23;
 AZ83-D, 173-A; BA238; BJ
 97; BR12; BV36; BX110; BY
 673; BZ   8809
-----. R [DRMMMRR, RMFFF
 MM, ML]   8810
-----. V [SMLTDDT, LDSMFM
 RD, S] A190   8811
-----. V [SFMLTDDT, LTDS
 FMFM] E282   8812
-----. V [SMLTDDT, LDLSFM
 RD, S] J294   8813
-----. V [SSLTDDTT, LLSM
 FRD, S] M222   8814
-----. V [SSLTDDDT, LLSFM
 FRM] V352   8815
-----. V [SSLTDDTT, LDSFM
 FRD,] AZ173-A   8816
Rau (Rau) X Grabesruhe   8817
Ravendale (Stokes) [SMRDDTLS,
 SFMSMRDR,] I445; K309
                                  8818
Ravenna (Knecht) X Vienna
                                  8819
Ravensbourne (Maker) [DDD
 RR#MMS, FMDMRR, MF] AB
 146; BF333   8820
Ravenscroft (Ravenscroft. Whole

book of Psalms) X Old 104th
                                    8821
Ravenshaw (Schein) [MSSSFMMR,
    FLRMMR, SF] AZ159-B   8822
Ravenshaw (Weisse. Ave hierar-
    chia, 1531) [DDMFSS, LTDSM
    F#S, FR] A399; B59; D282a;
    E436; F250; K10; N10; Q74;
    W199; X570; AA143; AF258;
    AL186a; AP288a; AW292; AZ581-
    C; BA305; BV305; BY250   8823
-----. V [DDRMF#SLS, LTDSFM
    F#S,] AZ581-C   8824
Ravensworth (Lloyd) [SSSFMSSS,
    SMMRMFSM] AL356a; AP96
                                    8825
Raymond (Noble) [MMMSSLTD,
    LSFM, MMML] B36; C36b
                                    8826
Raynolds (Mendelssohn) X
    Brightest and best   8827
Ready (Tillman) X Tillman   8828
Ready token (Stanton) [MRDSM
    DRMFMR, SMDRS] BY536 8829
Rebecca (Shenk) X Come, heaven-
    bound pilgrims   8830
Recessional (Blanchard) X Lest
    we forget   8831
Recessional (Gower) [DDSDTLM
    S, SDMSMDSR] Y287; Z561;
    AB342; AD442; AO590; BF549
                                    8832
Recessional (Lynes) [SSSLDTLS,
    SSSLDTDR, MDD] C439; Y179
                                    8833
-----. R [SMRDDLSF, FMRD
    TDRD]   8834
Recessional (Noble) [SSSSSSLTD,
    DTLSSMD] B439; C438   8835
Recessional (Wood) [MLLMRMM
    L, TDRMLDTM,] W637a   8836
Rector potens (Plainsong M 2)
    [RDRFSFMR, SSFSFMRD] E261
                                    8837
Rector potens (Sewall) [DRMSDM
    FRRD, MFSLFS] BR13   8838
Red Cross (Lutkin) [SLSDTLSF,
    MRDSFMRF] Y228   8839
Red, white and blue (Becket)
    [SSDDDRSFMD, SLLSFM] BC37
                                    8840
Red Wing Seminary (Dahle) [MFS
    FMRMFM, SMLSFMR,] J185;

O38   8841
Redal (Bradbury) [DMFSSLTD,
    DDDTTDLT,] T156; AJ231
                                    8842
Redcliff (Hopkins) [SDTDSLLS,
    SLTDTRDT,] D120a; BR187
                                    8843
Rede selber uns zu gut (Grimm.
    Choral buch) X Grimm's
    315th metre   8844
Redeemed (Kirkpatrick) [SSSS
    SLTDS, DRRRRDR] AT203;
    AU92; AX316; BB635   8845
-----. R [DFFMDRRRRDRM,
    SLFL]   8846
Redeemed (McGranahan) [MFS
    LS, MFSDTLS, SLSL] AY514
                                    8847
-----. R [SDSDSDTDSL, LR
    LRLR]   8848
Redeemer (Emerson) [SDMRD
    LLS, SSLSDDR, M] T1a; AJ
    2a   8849
Redeemer (Keller) [MMRMDRT
    L, MSLDRM, MM] J480b
                                    8850
Redeemer (Loes) [SSSSMSFMR,
    FFFFRLS] AT106; AU428
                                    8851
-----. R [LLLLFLLLSM, SSS
    SRS]   8852
Redeemer (Traditional, 1400)
    [SSSLSDRD, TRMRDLS, S]
    M344; O184; Q80; AA147
                                    8853
-----. V [SSSLSDRD, DTRM
    RDLS,] O184   8854
Redeemer of Israel (Lewis) X
    Beloved   8855
Redeemer's praise (Richards)
    [MFSSSDDT, RMFFFLLS,]
    AP750   8856
Redeeming love (Fisher) [MRR
    DDRDDTT, FMMRTL] AT311
                                    8857
-----. R [SDMFMRLL, TDRM
    RDSS,]   8858
Redemption (Bilhorn) [SSMDD
    RMSF, FMRDMDR] AX315
                                    8859
-----. R [DLS#LDTLSM, SDT
    LTSL]   8860
Redemption (Cherubini) [MMMM

SSMDFLS,DS] AZ315-B; BA
231   8896
Reitz (Reitz) [MFF#LSDTSF,
RMFTLSR] AT330   8897
-----. R [SLTDSMR#MF, FSLSF
RR#]   8898
Rejoice (Barnby) [SDTDRSLTDS
MRDD,DF] D457b   8899
Rejoice (Freylinghausen) X
Gregor's 151st metre-I   8900
Rejoice, all ye believers (Lauren-
ti) [SDDSSMRD,SFMRDS,TD]
M341   8901
-----. R [DDDDR,RRMMFMR,
RMRM]   8902
Rejoice and be glad (Husband)
X We praise thee, O God
                           8903
Rejoice and offer thanks to God
(Singer) [SDMFSLSS,SLLSLSF
M,] BH259   8904
Rejoice, O people (Thiman) [DT
LSDRMFSM,RMF#SLT]
BV520   8905
Rejoice, the Lord is King (Parker)
X Jubilate   8906
Rejoice, ye saints of latter-days
(Asper) [SDTDRMFS,DLSFMM
DR,] BC207   8907
Rejoicing (Wolder) X Wolder
                           8908
Rejoicing of the law (Jewish trad)
X Simchas torah   8909
Release (Danish trad) [SLSMSS
FR,MDDRSM,SL] J60; M407;
O136; P84; AI154   8910
Reliance (Gower) [SSLSDRM,
SSLSFMF,MM] N142; AI162;
AM486; AO372; AS292   8911
Reliance (Mendelssohn) X Heaven-
ly love   8912
Relief (Fawcett) [MLS#LSMDTL,
DMRDTLT] E497; X614   8913
Remember (Ravenscroft. Melis-
mata) [LLLDTL,SSLTS#M,
LLLD] BG42   8914
Remember Him, the only One
(Henle) [MDLTS#LTRDTL,
DMDLS] BH44   8915
Remember, holy Mary (Slovak
hymn) [MFSDTDLS,MFSDFMR,
M] BQ85   8916
Remember me (Hull) X In dark

Gethsemane   8917
Remember the poor (Irish trad)
[STDDRMRMDTLTS, SLL#]
X310; AF417   8918
Remember thy Creator (---)
[SDDDMSLS, FMDRMD, SD]
AX560   8919
Remembrance (Booth)[SLTDRDT,
DDLFMRM,MS] W682; AL
496b   8920
-----. V [SLTDRDT,DLFMR
M,MSM] AL496b   8921
Remembrance (McCartney) [SD
RDTDRRD,MSFMRDR,] D
233b; T363; AA412   8922
Remembrance (Wesley) [MSMR
DLSFM,SDSLSSF] BE349
                           8923
Remission (Blake) [LLTDMRDT
LSSL,TDRM] F324a   8924
Remo (Mountain) [DDRRMSFF
RRM,DDRRM] T181; W443;
AM587; AT294   8925
-----. R [SSSSLS, FFMMR,
MMRRD]   8926
Remsen (Holbrook) [SMMMRDL
D,FMMMRDRS,] H92; L246;
T20; V225; AJ279; BA564
                           8927
Renar (Bradbury) [SMMRMSS,
LLDLLSS,SM] L491; R465;
W660; AH546; AL623; AM633;
AP746; AT512; AU307; AW
428; BA833; BV354; BY749
                           8928
-----. R [SMSLD, DMDMD,
SMSLD, L]   8929
Renascence (Porter) [SLMM
DTLS,MRMFLSRM,] Y166;
AC40   8930
Rendez à Dieu (Bourgeois) [DL
SDDRFMR, SMMDFMR] A
195; E305; F409a; Q100; W
318; X265; AF282; AI444;
AJ424; AK337; AL224a; AM
512; AN306; AP358a; AQ
269; AW306; BJ19; BV371;
BY310b   8931
Renova (---) [DTRDFM, RRRR
R,DMRSD] M627   8932
Repentance (Lindeman) [MRR
LFMMR,DRMSRMD,M] BE
84   8933

621; AY179; BA719; BB489 8969
Rest (Callcott) X Elim   8970
Rest (Goodrich. Service and
  tune book) [MMMFDRM, MM
  RLTD, DDT] N492   8971
Rest (Maker) [MMMR#MSSF#,
  FMDDRR, MM] A435b; B120b;
  C120; G342; I543; J467; N331;
  R416; S302; T406; U242; V410;
  Y80; Z411; AA564; AB212; AC
  152; AD279; AE176; AF341;
  AG202; AH400; AK226; AL
  286c; AN250; AO366; AP437;
  AQ119; AR334; AS303; AT
  335; AU401; AV63; AW181; BA
  514; BB116; BD112; BE49; BF
  421; BK83; BX285; BY50b;
  BZ   8972
Rest (Redhead) X St Prisca   8973
Rest (Stainer) X Beati   8974
Rest by and by (Pollock) X
  Often weary and worn   8975
Rest for the weary (Dadmun) [M
  FSSLSSD, DRMRDLS, M]
  AU84; AV358; AX574   8976
Rest in the Lord, my soul (Binder)
  [MSFMSDL, LRSFRRM, MM]
  BH91   8977
Rest over Jordan (Holsinger) [DD
  LSDDLS, DDRMRDRS] AX599;
  AY384   8978
-----. R [SLSMMRDDLS, DDRM
  RD]   8979
Rest, rest for the weary soul
  (Careless) [SMDDMRD, LSMM
  RRR, MD] BC278   8980
Resting (Mountain) [SSLSLTTD,
  SSLSTDR, M] S327; AL505;
  AM139; AP525; BY582   8981
Resting-place (Van der Werp)
  [DRMFFMRD, MRDDTD, SS]
  AI431   8982
Resurgam (Adams) [DDRFLSFTT
  LSFSRM, D] D241   8983
Resurgam (Sewall) [MFSSLRDT,
  DSLLLSFF] BR316   8984
Resurgenti nazareno (Bohemian,
  1505) [DDTLSMMR, DRMRM
  FRM,] Q253   8985
Resurrection (Dykes) [MRDSDRM,
  SFMRDTTD,] B177; D116; H
  187   8986
Resurrection (Harmonia sacra,

1753) [MFSSSLTD, DRMFS
  LS] A350b   8987
-----. R [RRMFMMFS, FM
  RDLS]   8988
Resurrection (Neander) X
  Neander   8989
Resurrection (Nevin) [SDSD
  RMM, SFMRDR, SDS] AK
  172; AO189   8990
Resurrection (Slovak, ca 1600)
  [LS#LTDT, DMRDTL, DDT,
  M] Q603   8991
Resurrection hymn (Gauntlett)
  [SLSDDRM, MRDSMRD, MR]
  K112   8992
Resurrection morning (Buck)
  [MRFMRMLL, MRFMRDR, S]
  E136   8993
Resurrection morning (Warren)
  [DRMDLTDR, MFSDTLS,
  D] D243a   8994
Resurrexit (Sullivan) [MMMM
  SSFMR, DDRMFFM, M] D
  113; U108; V168; Z240 8995
Retirement (Harington) X
  Harington   8996
Retreat (Hastings) [MFSSS
  FMLLS, TDRRR] A421; B
  32b; C32; D481; G317; H42;
  I495; L466; M516; N531;
  R419; T247; U365; V458b;
  Z394; AG210; AH353; AI
  231; AJ343; AL426; AM528;
  AO319; AP498; AR262; AS
  46; AT296; AU189; AV185;
  AX167; AY180; BA593; BB
  241; BZ   8997
Return, O wanderer (Root) [DMD
  M, DFFDRM,MRRM,SS] AI193
                                8998
Reunion (Wales. Univ. Students
  hymnal) [DDDRMRDR, MSL
  SFMRD] AN465; AQ258 8999
Reuter (Reuter) [DMRDLSFM,
  MSSFMDR, D] Q283   9000
Revelation (Berggren) X Berg-
  gren I   9001
Revelation (Handel) X Messiah
  [Come unto me]   9002
Reverence (Neander) X Arns-
  berg   9003
Reverently and meekly now
  (Beesley) [MRDDSFMR, DR
  MFRDTD] BC280   9004

Reverently and meekly now
(Marsh) X Martyn   9005
Revive us again (Husband) X We
praise thee, O God   9006
Rex gloriae (Smart) [DSDRMFM
R, SDRMFMR] A103b; B522;
C522b; D126a; E616; F148;
J112; K120; N147; O62; P223;
Q218; V170; X173b; AA231;
AI6; AO190; AP226; BY171
                          9007
Rex gloriose (Andernach G-B.
1608) [DMFSSLTD, SDTLSL]
A8b; E183b; F504; AN102a
                          9008
Rex gloriose martyrum (Ander-
nach G-B. 1608) X Rex
gloriose   9009
Rex regum (Lissant) [SDTDRMRD,
LFMDMR, RS] D110b   9010
Rex regum (Stainer) [MRDDRMFS,
SDDTLS, SS] I607; AB292
                          9011
Rex triumphans (Hill) [MSLLFFS
S, MDTLSLFM] S201b   9012
Reykjavik (Traditional, 15th c)
[RRFMRD#R, RLFSFM, RRF]
M388   9013
Reynolds (Mendelssohn) X
Brightest and best   9014
Reynoldstone (Matthews) [SLS
MRRM, DTLSSF#S, RR] C371;
I599; AL232; AP359   9015
-----. V [MMMSRRM, DTLSSF#
S, RR] I599   9016
Rhau (Geistliche Gesang. Witten-
berg. 1544) [DRDTDRMD, D
RMFMDRM,] M409; Q596;
AA538; AZ22-A; BA445   9017
Rheidol (Roberts) [LS#LTDRTL,
MFMDRDT, L] W687; AM527
                          9018
Rhiw (Wales. Univ. Students'
hymnal) [DMMMRS, DRRRDR
M, MMM] S100; AM555   9019
Rhodes (Jordan) [SSMDTLS, MF
RMFLSSM,] I303; T262b;
V453; AJ19; AM508   9020
-----. V [SMDTLS, MFRMFLSS
M, S] V453   9021
Rhosymedre (Edwards) [SDDRRM,
DFFMRD, SDD] A504; E303;
J65; X127b; AF169   9022

Rhuddlan (Welsh trad) [DDDD
MDRS, TTDDTLS, D] E423;
F556; J343b; R517; S417;
X552; Y277; AE397; AF435;
AK398; AM620; BV662; BY
372b   9023
Rhyddid (Welsh hymn mel)
[DSDMMRDR, DMLSFMRD,]
E222; X643b   9024
Rhyd-y-groes (Edwards) [MM
MLTDTLLS#L, MMF#SL]
BY55b   9025
Rhys (Evans) [DDDDDMRDT
RD, MMMMM] BY578b 9026
Rhys (Thomas) [SLDRMSLDR
M, RRDTLS] G296   9027
Rialto (Root) [DMFSSS, SLTD
DD, DDRM] H499; I157; T
173a; AE378; AJ252; AO468;
AR368; AS341   9028
Riber (Beatson) [MRMDDRMF
SM, SFSMRD] BB63   9029
Richard (Owen) [DLDLSMRDR,
FRMFMRR] E57; X25b
                          9030
Richards (Richards, i.e. Em-
melar) X Armstrong   9031
Richemont (Hervey) [MRDRTD,
FRMDR, MRDRT] D133a
                          9032
Riches of God (Fitzwater) [SD
MRDTDRDS, DRRRRD] AR
475   9033
Riches of grace (Showalter) X
We are saved   9034
Richmond (Everett) [SDDDD
R, MSFMRD, SDDD] G343;
I340b   9035
Richmond (Haweis) [SDMSFM
FRD, MRSDTDLS,] A319;
B101; C101a; D31a; E375;
F258; H407; I63; J330a; K
302; L132; M206; N309; O
446; P10; Q66; R436; S199;
V74; W32a; X468; Z539; AA
139; AD345; AF261; AK181;
AL14a; AN410; AP165a; BE
38; BR234; BV270b; BY255a;
BZ   9036
Richmond Hill (Lloyd) [MFSM
RDSLDLS, SDRMR] BY588a
                          9037
Richter (Freylinghausen) [DR

MFSSLSFMD, FMRR] A154a;
BV38b; BY674   9038

Ridderholm (Swedish Koralbok,
1697) [DRMDMFSM, FSLSSF#
S, D] J104; N135; AI423; AM
174   9039

Ride on, ride on (Dykes) X
St Drostane   9040

Ridgefield (Main) [MTDFMRTD
MR, STD#RMR] AR297; AS
224   9041

Righini (Righini) [DSMRTD,
MDSFRM, SMDR,] G477; I629;
AR566; BR197   9042

Righteous Joseph (English trad)
[DDRMFSFMR, RMFSLS, S]
BG41   9043

Righteous Judge (Goudimel) X
Goudimel   9044

Riley (Shaw) [MDLSDDR, MDLS
DDD, L] A292a; E481; X644;
Y183; BV563b   9045

Rimington (Duckworth) [MRDSM
RRD, MMLSMDFR,] G345;
S32; AL249b; BB14; BY9   9046

Ring out (Shaw) [SDSLSD, RMT
DRMR, RSF] X634   9047

Ring out, wild bells (Gates) [LLT
DMMMFMRM, MRMFM] BC279
                            9048

Ring the bells of heaven (Root)
[SSLSMDRDLTD, TDRDM]
AU124   9049

-----. R [MMSFRTDDM, LLRM
RDT]   9050

Ringe recht (Thommen's Christen-
Schatz 1745) X Batty   9051

Ringland (Naylor) [MDDFMSSS,
SDTDRFTT] D120b   9052

Rinkart (Bach) [SMRDDTLS,
MF#SLRSDT] X60; BV418;
BY659   9053

Ripley (Mason) [DMSMFLSM, S
DFMRRD, D] J403b; K291a;
L141; M103; N251; O109; P
109; AI372; AM53; AR415   9054

Ripon (Haydn) X St Michel's
                            9055

Ripponden (Cocker) [DMSSFMRF,
MRDLSDRM,] BY311   9056

Risby (Rooper) [DDRMRDRMF
S, SLSLSM] X568   9057

Rise, crowned with light (Lvov)
X Russia   9058

Rise, O Lord (Wagner) [DMLL
TDD, DTDSMDRM, M] BI8-D
                            9059

Rise up, O men of God (Asper)
[DMFSLTD, MFMRMF#S,
SS] BC332   9060

Riseholme (Gauntlett) [SSLDD
DRR, DRFFMRRM,] D495a;
AP424b   9061

Risveglio (Loy) [SSSSRD, TLTD
TDFMRD,] BD178   9062

Rittman (Smucker) [SSMMMDD
RDLS, SSDMS] AY104   9063

Rivaulx (Dykes) [SSSSSLLS,
DDLRMFFM,] B206; C206;
D80a; F164b; I244; J140;
K63; O388; T317; V294; W
5b; Y55; AA269; AB27; AJ
17b; AL3a; AN56b; AP138;
BA347; BD201; BE319; BV
483; BX73a; BY39a   9064

Riverdale (Perkins) [SMMRT
SD, DFFMDR, R#MR] Y124
                            9065

Robinson (---) [SDMRTDS, DM
SFRFM, MR] D628b; T83;
V508   9066

Robinson (Belden) [MDSTLR
M, FTRDS, MDST] BB410
                            9067

Robinson (Hastings) [SSSLSM
MR, FFFMRDTD,] T240;
AJ336   9068

Robyn (Cornysshe) [DLTTDTLT,
TTMMRRD, M] X467   9069

Rochelle (Drese) [DDTDR, DRM
RD, MFSFM] A425; B449;
C449; E272; F35; G336; J532;
K260; L533; M194; N458; O
30; Q410; R334; S502; W567;
X52; AA331; AB226; AD228;
AK284; AL447; AO381; AP
613; AR305; AW574; AX500;
AZ46-A; AZ68-A; BA47, 930;
BB676; BR67; BV61; BY544
                            9070

-----. V [DDTDRMFMRD,
MFSFMR] AX500   9071

-----. V [DRMRD, MFMRD, MF
SFMR] AZ46-A   9072

Rochester (Day) [SMSLMS, MRM
FSMRD, DR] AC166   9073
Rochester (Holdroyd) [DDRMDR
TD, MFSLLS, SF] V232; AQ
50   9074
Rochester (Stewart) [DRMFMRD
RM, F#SRDTLS,] W422; X594;
BV296   9075
-----. V [DDRMFMRDRM, F#
SRDTL] W422a   9076
Rock of ages (Dykes) [MMMRDDT,
DMSLSSDMR,] D336; T98; AJ
141; AO260b; BF433   9077
Rock of ages (Hastings) X Top-
lady   9078
Rock of ages (Jewish trad) [DS
DFMRD, SLRFMRD, DS] S4;
Z96; AF26; AH150; AQ179; BE
281; BH207, 208; BZ   9079
-----. V [DSDFMRD, DSLRFM
RD, D] BH208   9080
Rock of refuge (Fischer) X The
Rock of refuge   9081
Rockbridge (Chapin) X Forest
                         9082
Rocking (Czeck mel) [DMSSLL
F#S, LLF#S, FFRM] X383; AF
482; BG87   9083
Rockingham (Mason) [DTDRMSM
R, MRDLSDRD,] G188; H155;
I71; L100; M155; T236; U85;
V138; AA309; AJ332; AO142a;
AS464; AV42; AY192; BB140;
BZ   9084
Rockingham (Miller arr) [DMFR
DMSLS, SDTLSS] A203; B154;
C154; D101; E107; F108; H
110; I17; J503b; K97b; L253;
M420; N241; O306; P178; Q175b;
R387; S152a; T187; V142; W106;
X133; Y41; Z492; AB191; AD
406; AE27; AF357; AG97b; AH
501; AI77b; AJ230; AK262; AL86;
AM44; AN311; AO166; AP192;
AR10; AS118; AW105; AZ22-G;
BA225; BB89; BE188; BF581;
BR176; BV164; BX82; BY151
                         9085
Rockingham [New] (Mason) X
Rockingham   9086
Rockingham Old (Miller) X
Rockingham   9087

Rocklands (Hopkins) [MSFM
RD, DLLSFM, RMMF#] D532a
                         9088
Rockport (Noble) [MLLDTLM
D, LLLDTLS#L,] R146;
AF105; AK366   9089
Rodigast (Gilbert) [SMMMRL
TD, RMFSFMR, S] D668;
I487   9090
Rodman (Mason) [DTLSMSS
FRFFM, DTLS] BB185
                         9091
Rodmell (English trad) [SDT
LRDTLTS, SDMSFM] E611;
X221; BY49   9092
Rodney (Lefebvre) [MRMSMR
M, SDDTLS, MRM] AD470
                         9093
Roepper (Warner) [MSFMRM
RD, RMLSF#TLS,] AZ606-D
                         9094
Rogers (Miller) [SSSDSFM
R, FFFTLSFM,] BB28
                         9095
Roland (Simper) [DRMSLDS,
FLSDFMR, DR] D67b; L595;
Y45; AC44; AW49   9096
Roll call (Black) X The Roll
                         9097
Roll out, O song, to God
(Smyth) [DMSDDD, MSDMM
M, MMMF] BI71; BR157
                         9098
Rolland (Bradbury) [DDDD
RMDL, LSSDRMDR,] T178;
V238; AJ233; AO224   9099
Romberg (Hastings) [DMRDL
SSS, DLRRDTD, D] L7; V
204   9100
Rominger (Skinner) [DRMSFM
MRD#R, LRMFFF] BB389
                         9101
Rondthaler (Peterson) [DMS
SLLS, SSSDTLTLS,] BA491
                         9102
Room for thee (Sankey) [DMS
SSDMMRDTD, DDFS] AX99
                         9103
-----. R [SFMMMRMFL,
LLSSLSF]   9104
Rorate (Scottish trad) [SMR
DDRMSMSL, TDSMF] BG125

9105
Rorate caeli (Lewars) [DSMDDT
D, MRDTLLS, RR] K537   9106
Rorate caeli (Plainsong M 1)
[DRMMLSSFMMR, MFMRD]
E735; BN2; BO146; BP7; BQ
291   9107
-----. V [FSLLRDDL#LLS, LL#
LLS] E735   9108
Rorate coeli (Lewars) X Rorate
caeli   9109
Rosa (Hartmann) [SSMFSMM,
DDMRTD, SSM] M602   9110
Rosa mystica (Geistliche kirchen-
gesang. Cologne, 1599) [SSS
LSSM, FMRDTD, SSS] A17;
B82; C82; E19; F68; J38; K533;
P138; Q76; R162; W81; X70;
Z194; AF131; AK113; AM153;
AQ298; AR122; AW526; BB672;
BD216; BE152; BG76; BM62;
BN17, 48; BQ10; BV90; BY87
                                 9111
-----. V [SSSLSSM, FMRRDDT
D, S] P138   9112
-----. V [SSSLSSSM, MRDRMM,
SS] BN48   9113
Rose Hill (Sweetser) [MMMMFSS
FM, RRRRSTD] L434; T257;
V4; AJ359; AM291   9114
Rose of Sharon (Ledington) [MRD
SLMR, DRMFFM, MRD] BB98
                                 9115
Rose of Sharon (Palmer) [DRM
MMRMRDS, DMSSSS] AR479
                                 9116
-----. R [SSLFLSF#SM, MMRRR
RD]   9117
Roseate hues (Barnby) [SSFMMM
RD, DFFFMRM, M] B181; C181;
D409a; BD124; BE228   9118
Rosedale (Root) [MMMMSMRFR
M, MSFMMR] H41; I596; L365
                                 9119
Rosefield (Malan) [SSDDRDRM,
LDLSDMRT] H258; I262; M
367; T206; V315; AJ295; AM
443; AO77; AR332; AV257;
BB408   9120
Rosenmüller (Hintze) X Salzburg
                                 9121
Rosenmüller (Rosenmüller) [MM
SSFRMR, DDDTDRMR] O408

9122
Rosh Hashanah I (Jewish trad)
[MRMLLDTL, LDTLSF#SL]
BH158   9123
Rosh Hashanah II (Jewish trad)
[MMRMLLLLD, LMRDTL,
M] BH159   9124
Roslyn (Macmillan) [DRMSDL
SR, MMMFMRRS,] AP351
                                 9125
Rosmore (Trembath) [MDSLTD
T, FRTLS, MDSL] C92b;
U63; Y112; Z322; AC94; AH
270; AI346; BA186; BF625
                                 9126
-----. R [SLTDD#RS, SLTD
MRFFM]   9127
Rossetti (Jeater) [SFFMSFFM,
MMSDTLSM] AM115; AP
418   9128
Rosslyn (English trad) [DDRM
DRRR, RRMFTDMS,] G448;
AW417   9129
Rosslyn (Simper) [SSDRMSS,
FMRDRDTL, S] D188b
                                 9130
Roswell (Cottman) X Morn of
gladness   9131
Rothley (Goss) X Dona   9132
Rothwell (Shaw) [LLLSMR,
DTTL, LLLSMR,] C222c;
X586a   9133
Rothwell (Tans'ur) [DMSDS
FMRD, RMF#SSLS] H410;
L269; M502; T165; V177;
AJ243; AV116; BB62
                                 9134
Rotterdam (Tours) [MSDFFM
D, LSDMRD, MSD] B171a;
C171a; D115a; G159; I164;
J56; K43; L263; M441; O
327; S137; T185; U106; V
64a; Y301; Z433; AB9a; AC
15; AI281; AR189; BA246;
BF188   9135
Rouen (Gounod) [MMMFRDT
RD, SSSLFMR] D73b; V182;
BQ146   9136
Rouen (Poitiers Vesperale,
1740) [LMDRMLTDRDTL,
LMDR] A228b; E435; F253
a; X349b; AF378; AL165a;
AM179a; AP201; BY261a

9137
Rouen (Rouen church mel) [LDTL
SLMLL, DRDTLTD] E18b
9138
Rouen (Rouen church mel) X
Christi fons jugis   9139
Rouen (Rouen mel. 17th c) X
Coelites plaudant   9140
Round the throne of glory
(Mortimer) [MMMMSRM, FFT
LS, SSDD] AI29   9141
-----. R [DMSF#SLS, DSTLS,
DMSL]   9142
Rousseau (Rousseau) X Greenville
9143
Routh (McKinney) [MMMM
RDSS, LLLLDRM, M] AT436;
AU375   9144
-----. R [DTTLF, TLLSM, RM
FSLT]   9145
Rowe (Matthews) X Children's
praises   9146
Rowley (---) [DRMRDS, MSFMR
M, SSSM] AS300   9147
Roxbury (Smyth) [MMMMFFFF#,
SSDSMFMR,] BR420   9148
Royal banner (McGranahan) [MFSSS
DMFSLS, DDTRL] AT408; AU
59   9149
-----. R [STRMRD, DFFMRDM
R, SS]   9150
Royal law (Bourgeois) [DRMDMS
SFMR, MDTLSD] AJ428; AQ229
9151
Royal Oak (English trad) [SMS
SFMFL, LTDRTD] A311; E587;
F442; G447; R456; X444; AF
478; AL582; BB421; BV233;
BY733b; BZ   9152
-----. R [SMFMRDTLS, MFLTL]
9153
Royden (Shaw) [RMDRML, DDTDR
S, SSMR] X335   9154
-----. R [MMRD, FMFR, SMLS
MDLT]   9155
Rudolfstadt (German trad) [SMRD
SLSFFM, SLTDTL] AB273
9156
Rudolstadt (Meyer) [DTDRMFMR
D, RMRDTLL] M50; O173;
Q65; AA544   9157
Rugby (Candlyn) [MRMDRM, LTT
DRS, SDTL] Y140; AC170 9158

Rugby (Somervell) [SMRDRT,
DRRMFS, RSMR] BY11
9159
Rugged cross (Bennard) X Old
rugged cross   9160
Ruhe ist das beste gut (Stötzel)
[DSLLSSFM, DRMRRD, DS]
AK231   9161
Ruhetag (Daries) [SMFMRRM
D, SLDTLS, SM] AK41   9162
Ruhe ist des todes schlummer
(Rau) X Grabesruhe   9163
Rung I (Rung) [SFMLSFRDR
M, MRDFRM] M43   9164
Rung II (Rung) [DMDFSLLS,
SRFMDMF, F] M120   9165
Rushford (Ley) [DDRMSDLS,
DDRMSDLT,] A560a; BV
577a; BY289b   9166
Rusper (English trad) [DRM
DSMDMRD, SDDMDL] E379
9167
Russell (Barnes) [SSSLSS
LSM, MMMMMSF] BB494
9168
Russia (Bortniansky) X St
Petersburg   9169
Russia (Lvov) [SLLSMD, DTLS
L, FSSMM] A523; B435; C
435; D487; F491; G505; I
707; J354; K497; N43; R487;
S346; U347; V596; W641; Y
264; Z477; AB366; AC284;
AD368; AE404; AF446; AG
281;   AH481; AI147;
AK405; AL517; AM617; AN
374; AO88; AP650; AR608;
AT42; AU387; AV72; AW351;
AZ32-I; BA277; BB78; BF551;
BH265b; BI46; BK122; BR
215; BX43; BZ   9170
-----. V [SLLSMD, DDDTLS,
LFSM] S346   9171
-----. V [SLLSM, DDTLS, LFS
MMM] BI46   9172
-----. V [SLLSMD, DDTLS, LF
SMM] BR215   9173
Russian anthem (Lvov) X Rus-
sia   9174
Russian Contakion (Kieff mel)
[LS#LDTLS#, DDTLS#LS#LT]
E744   9175
Russian hymn (Lvov) X Russia

9176
Russian vesper (Bortniansky) X
  Vesper hymn   9177
Rustington (Parry) [DDFMRDTS,
  DDLSFSM, R] F292a; Y265;
  BE360; BY380   9178
Ruth (Hartshorn) [SMR#MFMMRD,
  DDTLSMR,] T74; AJ110   9179
Ruth (Smith) [DDDRMS, FFFLD,
  DDTLS] P381; U249; W613; AB
  386; AL575; AO577; AP688; AR
  587; AV51; AW386; BA511; BB
  5; BD44; BF643; BR448b; BX
  520; BY722   9180
Ruth (Webster) [DMMSSDDF, FM
  RDRM, MM] I492a   9181
Rutherford (Urhan) [MMMRRDD,
  DFFMFR, RSS] I614a; O597;
  R281; S434; T53; U418; V677;
  W581; AB295; AD276; AH521;
  AI204; AJ83; AL320a; AM599;
  AO544; AP612; AR335; AV278;
  BA758; BB605; BE151; BF393;
  BK95; BR373a; BY776   9182
Ryburn (Cocker) [DMFSSLSD,
  FFMRDMRD,] BV494; BY324
                                        9183
Ryden (Crueger) X Lob sei
  dem allmächtigen Gott   9184

S

Sa är fulkomnadt (Swedish Koral-
  bok, 1697) X Pax   9185
Saa vil vi nu sige hverandre
  farvel (Lindeman) [DMRDDTLS
  LFM, DTDRR] O51; P63   9186
Sabaoth (Bradbury) [MMMMRDTL
  S, DDRDTRR] Z97; AH205; AI
  31; AS11   9187
Sabaoth (Hopkins) [SDRMRDRMF#
  S, SDRMRD] D195   9188
Sabbata (Hemy) X Siloam   9189
Sabbath (Mason) [DRMMFMR, TD
  RFMRD, DR] C46; G393; H80;
  I69; L38; R74; T299; U437; V
  59a; Z448; AE53; AG35; AH161;
  AI16; ALSuppl; AM320; AO12;
  AS37; AT37; AU10; AV9; AW
  284; AX64; AY275; BB462; BZ
                                        9190
Sabbath bell (Tenny) [SSDMDLTD,
  RRDTLSFM,] T221; AJ314

9191
Sabbath blessing (Binder) [MLL
  DMRDTL, LRMFLSL] BH106
                                        9192
Sabbath chimes (Norwegian
  trad) [SMDRMSLMFRD, DSL
  TD] P42   9193
Sabbath Eve (Jewish trad) X
  Sheer hasheereem I   9194
Sabbath evening (Perkins) [MF
  SDDLSMDRM, MFSFM] T455;
  AJ411   9195
Sabbath hymn (Binder) [MMMM
  RDRM, MLSDRDRM,] AHp.
  150; BH118   9196
Sabbath hymn (Grauman) [SS
  DMRDTDRMFFM, MMR]
  BH113   9197
Sabbath hymn (Nowakowsky)
  [MMTRD, FMTRD, MLMSFM]
  BH108   9198
Sabbath morn (Mason) X Sab-
  bath   9199
Sabbatsdag, hur skön du är
  (Blomqvist) [SMMRRDD, LD
  DLLSS, SF] N640   9200
Sacrament (Gregor) X Gregor's
  107th metre   9201
Sacrament (Hopkins) [MMMSMD
  RFM, LLLSDFM] AP358b;
  AZ184-F; BY310a   9202
Sacramentum unitatis (Lloyd)
  [MRMFRSDDRM, MLLSM]
  A191; B337; C337; D230
                                        9203
Sacred crown (---) [DMRMFSS,
  SFMFSM, DMR] AS136
                                        9204
Sacred Heart! in accents burn-
  ing (Gounod) X Evening hymn
                                        9205
Sacred Heart of Jesus (Slovak
  hymn) [DDTLLS, RTSFFM,
  MSSL] BQ59   9206
Sacred morn (Squires) [MSD
  RMFS, LSFMRLS, SS] AJ
  294   9207
Sacred the place of prayer
  (Stephens) [MMMR#MSFF,
  MRMSFM, SS] BC281   9208
Sacrifice (Bliss) X I gave my
  life for thee   9209
Sacrifice of praise (Genevan

Psalter. 1562) X Ainsworth 97
9210
Sacris solemnis (Mohr) X Panis
angelicus 9211
Sadie (Pollock) X Forever here
my rest 9212
Saelir (Bohemian Br) [LDTDRM,
MRDTT, TMRRD] M410; AZ
1-A 9213
Safe home (Hymns of the Eastern
Church) [SMDFRD, DRRMMF,
RMMM] BR441a 9214
Safe home (Sullivan) [MMSMSS,
RRSRSS, DMMS] H501; AO556;
BR441b 9215
Safe in he arms of Jesus (Doane)
X Arms of Jesus 9216
Safe with Jesus (Gabriel) [MRDR
MDLS, SMMR, FMRM] AY96
9217
-----. R [SSSSLLSM, SMRMR,
MRD] 9218
Safely through another week
(Mason) X Sabbath 9219
Safety (Smith) X Love lifted
me 9220
Saffron Walden (Brown) [MRDSDD
TLS, SFMRTDF] A409a; C156;
E117; F120; W497; AP205; BE
48; BV472; BY442b 9221
Sag was hilft (Speer) X Speer
9222
Sagina (Campbell) [DDRMSFLTR
D, MFRLSD] BY426 9223
SAINT: General note
Many melodies having prefix
Saint are frequently named with-
out prefix. However, the refer-
ences in this file allow for
either designation. 9224
St Aëlred (Dykes) [MMMMMFFM,
LDTLSFFM,] Eap. 62; F313;
I485; O242; W83; AL75; AP182;
AZ270-C; BA78; BR168; BV
553b; BY117 9225
St Agatha (Cramer) [SDDTLTLS,
LTDDRRM, M] BR302b 9226
St Agatha (Southgate) [DRMFM
RM, FFMSSF#S, DR] W690 9227
St Agnes (Blow) [MFMRRRMRD,
DDRMFML] AL270b; AR341;
AS202 9228

-----. V [MFMRRRMRD, DR
MFMLR] AR341 9229
St Agnes (Dykes) [MMMRMFT
D, SSSMRR] A24; B84; C84;
D55a; Eap. 55; F515b; G341;
H47; I33; J256; K172; L167;
M170; N139; O139; Q361;
R239; S206; T354; U76; V
205; W422b; Y358; Z201;
AA90; AB81; AC159; AD251;
AE214; AF225; AG128; AH
372; AI112; AJ344; AK103;
AL298; AM364; AN77b; AO
124; AP449; AR109; AS141;
AT46; AU241; AV58; AW155;
AY417; AZ14-Cc; BA120; BB
158; BC148; BD155; BE37;
BF222; BK88; BO127; BR
300; BX68; BY486; BZ
9230
St Agnes (Langran) X Langran
9231
St Agnes (Statham) X St Joseph
9232
St Agnes School (Jeffery) X
Liddon 9233
St Aidan (Ayres) [MDSMRM,
DMSLS, LDTSR] BV309b
9234
St Aidan (Grey) [MMMFFTRD,
DDTLSMSS] AP529; BY44b
9235
St Aidan (Popple) [SMFSDRD
TL, SLTDLR, M] X331 9236
St Alban (Haydn) [MMRRDS,
SSLLR, FFMMR] D531b;
E643; H399; L127; N642;
V759; Z417; AB281; AE133;
AL571; AM199; AN334; AO
571; AP697a; AR584; AV220;
AZ141-G; BA241; BD18; BF
436; BK108; BR508; BX377
9237
St Alban (St Alban's Tune book,
1865) X Messingers 9238
St Alban (St Alban's Tune book,
1866) X Holborn Hill 9239
St Alban, No. 1 (St Alban's
Tune book, 1866) X Holborn
Hill 9240
St Alban, No. 2 (Haydn) X
St Alban 9241

St Alban's (Haydn) X St Alban
9242

St Alban's (Morley) [MSMRDL,
DTDMS,SS#L] A581; B540;
C527b; D157; J427; K288; M
632; N507; S202; U121; Y139;
Z269; AB314; AC213; AI99; BF
630   9243

St Albans (Steggall) [MDTLDMRT,
DLTS#LFM,M] AZ15-D 9244

St Albinus (Gauntlett) [MDSMLL
S,MRDTLDDS,] A88; B176;
C176; D122; E134b; F140; V
169a; W121b; X155b; AL116a;
AM203; AO182; AP229; BR185;
BV187; BY158   9245

St Alkmund (Dykes) X Interces-
sion   9246

St Alkmund (Parker) [SDTLSFM,
MLSTDR,TDR] D364b; W305
9247

St Alphage (Gauntlett) X St
Alphege   9248

St Alphege (Gauntlett) [DMFSDT
D,DTDFMR,DMF] A596b; B69;
C69; D240a; E348; F275b; J18;
K229; M118; N530; V692; W
597a; X459b; AA442; AB414;
AO554; AP88a; BA741; BF670;
BR436; BV449; BX173; BY439
9249

St Amand (Sewall) [SSLMSLSM,
SSLMSLSM,] BR241   9250

St Ambrose (Gauntlett) [SLDDD
RD,DDTDLLS,SL] W484b 9251

St Ambrose (La Feillée. Methode
du plain chant.) [DDRMFMRD,
SSLSMSFM,] E193; F512b;
AA550; AP332a   9252

St Ambrose (Monk) [DRFMRS,
DDLSFM,LSF#S,] D345b; AA
448; AB479-E   9253

St Ambrose (Sewall) [DMFSDLSS,
SMRMFRDD,] BR544   9254

St Ambrose (Steggall) [DDRM
DDTD,MRTLLS,RF] W276a
9255

St. Ambrose, No. 2 (Monk) X
St Ambrose   9256

St Anatolius (Barnby) [SMRDDDD,
DRMFMRM,MR] D16a   9257

St Anatolius (Brown) [SLSDFMR,
DRMFLS,SL] A184; B23; C23;

D16b; Eap.40; F21; J224;
K458a; L18; O555; Q555;
S44; U465; W287; AD50;
AI54; AL557; AM342; AN
124b; AO35; AP670; BA794;
BF203; BV65b; BX153; BY705
9258

St Anatolius (Dykes) [DTDFMM
R,MLLTDRD,MM] D16c; K
458b; V43   9259

St André (Davies) [MLTDTLT
M,MDRMFMR,D] BE344
9260

St Andrew (Barnby) [MMFSRM,
MMLSF#M,SDTL] B218;
C369; D212; G610; H50; I
276; J451a; K262; M322;
S251; V356; Y396; AB188;
AD508; AE466; AK128; AO
309; AP326; AR676; AT402;
AU492; AZ522-Q; BA97; BD
129; BF503; BX102   9261

St Andrew (Barnby) X Carlton
9262

St Andrew (Tans'ur) X Barby
9263

St Andrew (Thorne) [MMRMFM
LS,DDTLSLS,S] B268; F533;
W500; AP553b; BV442a; BY
416a   9264

St Andrew of Crete (Dykes)
[MMMMMM,MMMMM,LLS
S] A556b; B126; C126a;
D81a; F91a; G275a; I616a;
J68b; K73a; R360; S275; U
305; V474; Y168; AB245; AC
179; AD295; AF364; AG194;
AI323; AK294; AM483; AO
390a; AR319; AV194; AZ
141-F; BA570; BB367; BD79;
BF472; BR401; BV137c; BX
537   9265

-----. R [SDRSMD,MRDLS,
SSDDF]   9266

St Andrews (Barnby) X Carlton
9267

St Anne (Croft) [SMLSDDTD,S
DSLF#S,TD] A289; B85c;
C85c; D392; E450; F165; G
384; I214; J168; K203; L213;
M145; N144; O212; P142;
Q123; R111; S77; T168b;
U19; V90a; W530a; X598;

Y30; Z427; AA172; AB58; AC
28; AD1; AE65; AF1; AG40;
AH218; AI412; AJ309; AK63; AL
409a; AM26a; AN145; AO91;
AP71; AQ51; AR70; AS76; AT
53; AU435; AV39; AW61; AX
639; AY429; AZ14-H; BA29;
BB81; BC123; BD60; BE213;
BF221; BH47; BJ76; BK64; BL
95; BN197; BR496; BV244; BX
396; BY71; BZ   9268
St Ann's (Croft) X St Anne   9269
St Anselm (Barnby) [SSMRMRD,
D#RMFLS, FMM] B43b; C97;
D68b; G544; I72; J585; K523;
L43; AB344; AD30b; AO13a;
AR64; AT493; BE329; BK57;
BR85; BX65   9270
St Anselm (Hayne arr) [DDRMFM
RD, MSLSDTLS] W386   9271
St Ansgar (Strom) [SFMRDTDD,
RRMFSLSFM,] N399   9272
St Anthony chorale (Haydn)
[MFMMFMRD, RMFMMR,
MF] AR392; BZ   9273
-----. V [MFMMFMRD, RMFR
MDMR,] BZ   9274
St Anthony, we turn (Stewart) X
Mount Calvary   9275
St Anthony's choral (Haydn) X St
Anthony chorale   9276
St Apollos (Morgan) [DSLDTLS,
LTDMRDR, MR] W523b; AL
396b   9277
St Asaph (Bambridge) [MMMFSS
SD, DLSLSMR,] A394; B539;
C539a; D521c; G37; J529a; K
197a; M93; R475; S173; Y305;
Z137; AB239; AD219; AE414;
AF387; AG235; AH195; AK268;
AM211; AO653; AP533; AR4;
BA278; BB664; BD142; BE351;
BF219; BZ   9278
St Asaph (Giornovichi) [SDDRRM
SFM, SFFMMR, S] W223; AP
311; BE158   9279
St Asaph (Mann) [SSDTLRDDTLT
DS, MMR] BR312   9280
St Asaph (Shrubsole) X Miles'
Lane   9281
St Athanasius (Hopkins) [SLTDM
RD, FMRDTLS, S] A270; B77;

C208; D385; I77; J135; K159;
N338; S71a; U2; V86; AA99;
AC73; AK39; AO65; BA257;
BB229; BF272   9282
St Audoen (Stewart) [MSFMRD,
DRMFLR, MFML] O89; W
210   9283
St Audrey (Harwood) [DRMRD
DRMRR, MSDMFT] F174;
AP632; BV488   9284
St Audrey (Noble) [DMDMFS,
MLMLTT, TDLT] B253c
                                 9285
St Augustine (Chorale songs for
four voices, 1769) X Gildas
(Abelard)   9286
St Augustine (Goss) [DMSSLS,
SMFMRD, DMSL] O414 9287
St Augustine (Yon) [DTLS#
DTLS#, LTDTLDT, M] AK
215   9288
St Austell (Brown) [SLSFMFM
R, MFMRSLSF#] D216b;
AM313   9289
St Austin (Bristol Tune book,
1876) [MMMRFMRD, RRRLD
TL, M] K94; L577; V140a;
AM241; AP466   9290
St Austin (English trad) [SDRM
DMRD, MFMRD#R, RF] E
638a; X395a; BG132; BV596
                                 9291
St Austin (Lord) [DDTDRDRM,
MSFMMRDR,] BY355b
                                 9292
St Avold (Haydn) [DDMMRRD
D, D#RMFLMR, S] D74; V
264   9293
St Baldred (Bell) [DRMSLDDT,
DTLMSFM, M] D556   9294
St Barbara (Lutkin) [MMM
SRMMSF, MFSSFLL] I456
                                 9295
St Barnabas (---) [DMSTLSD,
SLLLSS, MFF] D373a; BA
244   9296
St Barnabas (Buck) [SLDDTRDT
DLSS, SLDD] BE149   9297
St Bartholomew (Duncalf) [SD
SRSMRDR, SDTLSLS] E81;
W672; X256; BV412b; BY513
                                 9298

St Bartholomew (Smith. Harmoni-
ous companion 1732) [MSMFSL
RD,RSMFRM,SM] BJ26
                                    9299
St Bartholomew's (Williams) [SD
DDDD,RMDLLL,SLTD] AD443
                                    9300
St Basil (German) [MMMMFFM,
LLSSFFM,SS] BR476   9301
St Basil (Martin) X Leominster
                                    9302
St Basil (Willan) [SDRTDRMFR
DD,MRSF#M] AD359; AL34;
BN174; BOp.4   9303
St Bavon (Horsley) [MFRDMSLS,
SLSDMR,R] A387   9304
St Beatrice (Bridge) [MFFLFFM,
RSSTLS,SLL] F486; BV652
                                    9305
St Beatrice (Moulton) [SDRMSSD
RMS,SDMSLL] Y134   9306
St Bede (Dykes) [DSSLTDDM,
LRMFFM,MM] U209; AC139;
AD259; AV60; AZ129-D; BA697;
BF451; BX291   9307
-----. V [DMSSLTDDM, LRMFFM,
M] AZ129-D   9308
St Bees (Dykes) [DDDTLTD,
RRMSLRT,RFM] A294; B90;
C90a; D149a; Eap.52; F344b;
G192; I257; K370; L472b; M
180; N330; R263; S224; T384;
U28; V373; W417a; AA178;
AB176; AG136; AH164; AK253;
AL292b; AM492; AN118b; AO
252; AP284; AZ11-U; BA95;
BB298; BD11; BE273; BF394;
BR413; BV533b; BX146; BY414
                                    9309
St Benedict (Stainer) [SSFMFM
RD, LSFRMFR,S] W437
                                    9310
St Bernard (Gardiner. Sacred mel.)
X Belmont   9311
St Bernard (Monk) [SMSDLSRM,M
RF#SLTDF#] B328; F188b; AB
238; BV33a   9312
St Bernard (Tochter Sion. Cologne.
1741) [SDRMRDFMR,SMLF#F#
S,S] A413; B125; C234; D267;
E71; F104; G332; I133; J371;
K406; Q378; V451; W87; X537;
AA496; AB148; AD152; AF347;

AK222; AL79a; AN73; AP
68a; BA839; BE358; BN65;
BO13; BV140; BY253; BZ
                                    9313
-----. V [DDRMDFMR,SML
F#F#SLT] BN65   9314
St Blane (Scholefield) X Litany
No. 9   9315
St Boniface (Barnby) [MMFS
MRMD,DTLSSLSF#,] I290;
AB405; BF671   9316
St Boniface (Gadsby) [SDMSS
F,MDDTD, LTDF] A561; B
531; C531; D523a   9317
St Boniface (Smart) X Sion
                                    9318
St Botolf (Gower) [MSMMRD
RM,DLSMDRMR,] AM252;
AP285   9319
St Botolph (Slater) [DMDSM
RDTD,RMSLSFS,] E419;
F450; X527a; BV548; BY
557   9320
St Botolph (Smart) X Sion
                                    9321
St Bride (Howard) [LMLDTL,
DSDMRD,MRD] A417; B
246; C246a; D351; E74; F
322; J365b; K315; M71;
O592; Q322; R233; S188;
V221; W403; X699; AA422;
AD238; AE253; AF338; AL
265b; AN59; AP22a; AQ
224; AR209; AW581; AZ
582-B; BJ65; BR281; BV
174; BX344a; BY322; BZ
                                    9322
St Brides (Howard) X St
Bride   9323
St Bride's (Howard) X St
Bride   9324
St Casimer (Goss) [SMFSDD
TT, LSDRMMRR,] B286;
C286; D166; AB130; AO151;
AZ166-F; BA72   9325
St Catherine (Dale) [DMMSS
DT, SLFSMR, RMM] Eap.65;
F355; W348; BV476; BY418
                                    9326
St Catherine (Hemy) [MRDDTD
RLTD,DTLSD] A185; B136;
C227; G256; H318; I194; J
516; K355; L155; M149; N

214; O474; P212; R88; S267; T167; U210; V324; W697; Y109; Z348; AB168; AC49; AD262; AE216; AF365; AG164; AH429; AI237; AJ245; AK282; AL399; AM487; AN546; AO297; AP161; AR94; AS92; AT252; AU201; AV184; AW154; AX434; BA275; BB349; BD148; BF456; BK69; BL87; BR252; BX401; BY606; BZ   9327

-----. R [FFFMMRRM, MRDLD RR]   9328
St Catherine's Court (Strutt) [DR MDRMDRMFSLS, LTD] F476
9329
St Cecilia (Hampton) [SMRDDTL S, TDLRTLLS,] F96b; Q168
9330
St Cecilia (Hayne) [SFMMRD, MRTTLS, RRMF] A544; B105; C105; D329; Eap.64; F262; J 329; R488; S425; V605; W152; AF448; AK403; AL140; AN339; AO486; AP251; AS243; AW271; BA107; BB396; BE382; BV334; BX387; BY317a   9331
St Cecilia (Sewall) [MMMFF RRRM, MMMSSF#F#] BR320
9332
St Cephas (Crosbie) [DDTRDT, RD#RFM, SSLSD] AM124 9333
St Chad (Redhead) [SDTLSMRM, SSDTLLS, S] A454; B233; C 233; D443a; BA651   9334
St Christopher (Maker) [SSSF# LSM, DRMFFM, MD] A339; B 149; C149; D102b; G144; J482; K362; M425; N69; O321; P180; R190; S162; T344; U95; V252; W691; Y105; Z235; AB138; AC120; AD154; AE110; AF160; AG91; AH290; AI75; AK161; AL98; AM177; AO163; AP209; AR165; AS332; AT345; AU234; AV110; AW112; BA189; BB280; BD82; BF317; BR373b; BY427a; BZ   9335
St Chrysostom (Barnby) [MMMM RDRM, SSSSF#MF#] A460; B228; C228; D600; Eap.19; F202; I10; J274b; K351; O

116; T171; V219; W430; Z 383; AB291; AD246; AJ229; AK244; AL295; AM355; AO 446; AP426; AR358; AS129; BA488; BB350; BF253; BI40; BX114; BY611   9336
St Chrysostom (Irons) [MRD DTLSS, MFMMRDTD] D271a
9337
St Chrysostom (Ohl) [MMRD MSFM, SSSRRLS, L] J507; K375   9338
St Clement (Scholefield) [SMFM SMRDRLDT, LSS] A179b; B 29; C29; Eap.16; F33b; G54; I60; J227; R59; S45; T313; U464; W289c; Z140; AB33; AD58; AE47; AF48; AG26; AK54; AL568c; AM338; AO 32; AP671; AR60; BA395; BB57; BD8; BE381; BF191; BK47; BV52b; BX147; BY 706a   9339
St Clement (Steggall) [SLSM RRM, RMLDDTD, MS] D213b
9340
St Clothilde (Franck) [SDMMS, SLSFFM, MMSSD] Y391
9341
St Colomb (Hoyte) X St Columba
9342
St Columba (Hoyte) [DMSDSLS, SDTDRM, MRD] D205b; I 573; K30; S467   9343
St Columba (Irish trad) [DRM FSFSMRD, DRMFSFSL] A345a; C326b; E490; F29; J530b; R106b; S145; W196; X654a; Z326; AF80; AG51b; AL280a; AM271; AN87a; AP 146b; AR80; BE339; BN121; BV546a; BY72b   9344
-----. V [DRMFSFMRD, DRMF SFS] BN121   9345
St Columba (Irons) X Irons
9346
St Columbia (Irons) X Irons
9347
St Constantine (Monk) [MRFM RD, RSF#LS, FMLFM,] A358; B361; Eap.53; F194; K567; W462; AA256; AP491; BR305;

BV477b   9348
St Crispin (Elvey) [MMMSDRRM,
SSSDTLL] A409b; B139; C139a;
D606a; Eap. 36; I258; J325;
N184; Q245; R116; S175; T276;
U86; V96; Y70; Z349; AA326;
AB151; AC33; AD46; AF320;
AG117; AJ383; AK225; AL351;
AO263; AP579a; AR117; AS264;
AW149; BA419; BD136; BF426;
BX223   9349
St Croix (Garrett) [SMSDMMR,
DDTLTD, SMS] K575   9350
St Cross (Dykes) [DDRMLSFM,
MMFSDM] A74; B153; C153;
D105; E111; F113; G134; H164;
I152; J86; K105; M72; N100;
O441; Q164; R192; S159; W96;
X140; Z233; AA439; AF164;
AK146; AL90; AM242; AO174;
AP193; BV173b; BY144   9351
St Cuthbert (Dykes) [DDDRMFF
M, SDMMF#S,] A368; B199;
C199; D375; Eap. 31; F230a;
G177; H76; I189; K157; S205;
T353; U131; W180b; AD188;
AG124; AH228; AL162; AN125;
AO227; AP272; AW138; AZ272-
A; BA141; BB214; BF261; BR
92; BV223b; BX104; BY236a
                              9352
St Cyprian (Chope) [SSLTDS, MD
LRDT, SSFM] C59; D282b;
K168a; N224; R252; AG298;
AM266   9353
St Cyprian (Goss) [SDTLSMFS,
SDRMFSLR,] I594   9354
St Cyril (Bliss) [SDTLSM, FLS
FM, SSDDR] W664   9355
St Darerca (Macalister) [DTSLM
SDRMS, DRMS, SL] S9; W15b
                              9356
St David (Ravenscroft's Psalter)
[DSDMSFMR, DSDFLS, SL] E166;
F470; W31b; X301; AL674; AP
6; BJ60   9357
St David (Thomas) [SSDRDTDMR
DT, DLTDD] AP405a   9358
St David's (Ravenscroft's Psalter)
X St David   9359
St Denio (Welsh mel) [DLFRTSD
MMRD, DLFRTS] A301; E407;
F372; G64; J172; R85; S66; W

12; X535; Z159; AD73; AF7;
AJ201b; AK408; AL403; AM
35; AN30; AQ41; AR20;
AT43; BE150; BL93; BV
242; BY61; BZ   9360
St Denys (Spinney) [DTLSMS
F, RDD#RLS, FMF] B235b;
C235; D431; BR95   9361
St Drostane (Dykes) [SDSDR
MRD, SFMRRRF#S] A64c;
B145; C145a; D91; F99; G
125; I150; J73a; K88; L259
a; M429; O293; R188; S150
a; T340; Z223; AC115; AD
143; AF175; AJ46b; AK133;
AL85b; AM172; AN182b;
AP189a; AR158; AV103; AW
101; BB127; BD73; BF308;
BI101; BR173a; BV167a; BX
199; BY128   9362
St Dunstan (Redhead) X St
Prisca   9363
St Dunstan's (Douglas) [DDS
DRM, FMDMR, DDSDRM,]
A563; B117b; C117; J563;
R345; S276; Y169; Z364;
AB175; AC204; AD226; AF
371; AG193; AK296; AR
322; BF409; BK79; BZ
                            9364
St Eanswyth (Sidebotham)
[SSSDDLS, SSSMMRR, TD]
BA51   9365
St Ebbe (Redhead) [DSSSLS,
MFMRRD, DSSS] AZ342-H
                            9366
St Edith (Knecht) X St Hilda
                            9367
St Edmund (Gilding) [DDMRDT
D, RMSFMR, RRM] E171;
K49; W551b; X120b; BE241
                            9368
-----. V [DDRMRDTD, RMF
SFMMR] BE241   9369
St Edmund (Steggall) [MSRMD
LS, LDRMRRR, MS] B298;
D67; E47; F81; K37; AA
184; BV131   9370
St Edmund (Sullivan) [DDDD
TR, SSLS, SMMMRS,] B222b;
C222b; D344c; G297; I315a;
M312; N77; O462; P251; Q
660; R284; U202; V712; Y

370; Z299; AA563; AB264; AC 149; AE273; AF318; AG160; AK 206; AM605; AN43; AO38; AR 348; AS242; AT314; BA548; BB345; BD109; BR374b; BX151a; BZ   9371

St Edward (Steggall) X St Edmund
                                            9372

St Elizabeth (Silesian mel) [DD DRTD, MMMMFRM, SD] A238; B356b; C356; G111; I118; J 434; K129; L111; M623; N317; O576; P6; Q657; R135a; S194; U72; V751; Y58; Z261; AB84; AC137; AD181; AE103; AF227; AG113a; AH314; AI105; AK182; AM129; AN45; AO211; AQ14; AR100; AT159; AU211; AV102; AW97; AX565; AZ33-C; BA119; BB165; BD63; BE274; BF331; BK21; BQ38; BY270; BZ   9373
-----.   V [DDDRTD, MMMFRM, SDLS] M623   9374

St Elwyn (Hopkins) [SDDTLSLS, FMSLRDT, S] D273; AB38
                                            9375

St Enoch (Gilbert) [SSSSLDSM, MRDRMF#S,] D256   9376

St Enodoc (Lang) [LDTLLRTM, D RMFSM, ML] BV250a   9377

St Erik (Swedish trad) [DSDRMD, TDLLS, SSLTD] J430b   9378

St Etheldreda (Turton) [DDRMRD TD, RMSFMR, MF] F318; J295; K170; O502; W467; AE192; AG 177b; AI413; AM31; AP329; BA 182; BV564b   9379

St Ethelreda (Turton) X St Ethel-dreda   9380

St Ethelwald (Monk) [SFMRMFM, MRSLLS, SLT] C346b; D268b; E479; F303; K272a; M241; Q 374; W534a; X641b; AA361; AB 182a; AL404b; AM595; AP111; BE398; BV585a; BY508b   9381

St Fabian (Barnby) X St Polycarp
                                            9382

St Fidelis (Barnby) X St Boniface
                                            9383

St Finbar (Hemy) X St Catherine
                                            9384

St Flavian (Day's Psalter) [DDT DMRRD, DFMDRM,] A59; B56;

C56a; D78; E161; F159; G 423; J138; K53; N84; Q22; R113; S86; V600; W8; X188; AA463; AD74; AE337; AF153; AI433; AJ185; AK141; AL 178; AM557; AN54; AP47; AW318; BA198; BB193; BL 19; BM75; BN163; BV148; BX76; BY195; BZ   9385

St Frances (Lohr) [DFMRDS FM, MRSLLS, SD] D29a; M122; V227; W90; AM282; AP589; BX226   9386

St Francis (Briggs) [MLLM RDTL, MLLMDRML,] X439
                                            9387

St Francis (Diggs) [MMSSFF M, SSLSMRR, LL] U197
                                            9388

St Francis (Moschetti) [MM SMRMSFMMR, MFSLD] J276   9389

St Francis (Sullivan) [MDR MMMMSFM, RDDRFM,] B 342; C342; D206; K173
                                            9390

St Francis II (Sullivan) [MSF MRDDRFM, MSSFMR] W308
                                            9391

St Francis Xavier (Stainer) X Xavier   9392

St Frideswide (Lloyd) [MRD RMFSM, LLSMFSM, S] D619a
                                            9393

St Fulbert (Gauntlett) [SSDRL SFM, SMSLDT, DS] A456; C302b; D372b; Đ139; F128; J196; K296; V161; W675; X151; AK364; AP282a; AZ 14-V; BA550; BV191; BX355; BY628a   9394

St Gabriel (Braun) X Braun
                                            9395

St Gabriel (Greatorex) [SSMF LSMRDTLS, FMSD] I224
                                            9396

St Gabriel (Ouseley) [MSFM FMRD, DLSFSMF#S,] A180; B14; C14; D8a; F19; J222; K460; N561; O452; V51a; W 279; AD274; AL566; AP424a; BY708   9397

St Gabriel, O blessed youth

(Bragers) [DDTTRRDD,SLLTD
RRR,] BP98   9398
St Gall (St Gall G-B. 1863) [SM
LSMFSFMRD,RMRMS] E292;
X13; AW378   9399
St George (Elvey) X St George's
Windsor   9400
St George (Gauntlett) [MFLSFM,
MRDDTD,SLF#S] A118; B276;
C276; D69a; F63; I390; K387;
V604; W590; AA430; AL420;
AM560; AP516; AS313; BA302;
BE201; BR45; BV157; BY131
                                    9401
St George of Windsor (Elvey) X
St George's Windsor   9402
St George's (Elvey) X St George's
Windsor   9403
St George's Bolton (Walch) [MMR
STRD,SLDTLS,MMR] C131;
D360a; I614b; L607; AE410;
AP368; AV167; BA519; BB467;
BR353a   9404
St George's, Edinburgh (Thomson)
[DDRMFSSS,SFMRDMR,R]
AL638; AP21; AW580; BY172
                                    9405
St George's Windsor (Elvey) [MM
SMDRM,MMSMDRM,MM] A137;
B421; C106a; D118b; E289; F
131b; G545; H481; I636a; J91;
K111; L348; M430; N130; Q71;
R149; S109; T444; U474; V528;
W118; X9; Z593; AA295; AB389;
AC322; AD447; AE79; AG287;
AH482; AI350; AK91; AL250;
AM365; AN141; AO218; AP214;
AQ10; AR594; AT462; AU136;
AV307; AW377; AZ205-F; BA861;
BB496; BC29; BD159; BE369;
BF650; BI95; BK136; BL55;
BR490; BV183; BX18; BY724;
BZ   9406
St Germans (Maker) [DMMMRDS,
FMMMRDDT,D] Z509; AB350
                                    9407
St Gertrude (Sullivan) [SSSSSLS,
RRDRM,DMS] A557; B530;
C530a; D516a; E643a; F629;
G280; H393; I383; J560; K379;
L541a; M242; N589; P373; Q
658; R350; S365; T134; U294;

V483; W535; Y172; Z482; AB
254; AC209; AD299; AE250;
AF382; AG199; AH442; AI
327; AJ200; AK292; AL401;
AM490; AN329; AO391a; AP
538; AQ215; AR502; AT412;
AU46; AW225; AX196; AZ
141-H; BA582; BB360; BC
128; BD145; BE264; BF471;
BI91; BR512; BV562; BX378;
BY520; BZ   9408
-----. R [DDDDDTLTD,RR
RDRM]   9409
St Giles (Bell) [MRDDRM,DTL
LTS,SSFM] J544a; W346;
BR231; BV381   9410
St Giles (Stainer) [MMFSSR
FF,MMRDRM,SD] D635;
AB114; AC86; AO559; BF
298   9411
St Godric (Dykes) [MRDLTD,
RMSFMR,MRSD] C182; D141;
J193; K138; L59; N145; AL
169; AM283; AP118; AZ342-E;
BA376; BX484a; BY653
                                    9412
St Gregory (Knorr. Neuer heli-
con 1684) [SMSLDSFM,SDM
FMRDR,] D199b; E49b; F83
J352b; K482; V192; AL185;
AP654; BA324; BE239; BY
473   9413
St Gregory (Plainsong, Barnby
arr) [DDDRDD,DTDLSS,
DDDR] AB67   9414
St Helen (Hately) [MFFMDTL
SLS,MRRMLS] W556b; AP
512   9415
St Helen (Martin) [DDDMLSMR,
DDLSSLT,S] F400; BV382
                                    9416
St Helen (Stewart) X St Helen's
                                    9417
St Helena (Allen) [SMRRDD,
MDTL,SLTDRM] AM513
                                    9418
St Helena (Milgrove) [DMDRRD,
STSLLS,FMDL] D70a; F475;
K249; M25; AA137   9419
St Helen's (Stewart) [MRFMLS
SF,MRDRM,MMR] S395;
U176; V353; W695; AP502a;

AS443; AZ269-D; BF351   9420
St Hilary (Ganther) [MMSSDRMR,
FMLSFMR, M] J5; K12; M340;
N22; Q640; AA242; BR108
9421
St Hild (Ellis) [MSLTDRM, FLR
DTDR, SF] W159   9422
St Hilda (Barnby) [DDRMLSSF,
MRSMDRM, D] C191; D365;
V156; AM128; AZ167-I; BR
206   9423
St Hilda (Knecht & Husband) [DD
TDRRRD, MMRMFRT, DTD]
A407; B132; C132; D357a; G
197; H281; I282; J386; K322;
L360; M77; N401; R266; S228;
T153; U170; V300; Y375; Z
279; AA435; AB157; AC148;
AD205; AE169; AF329; AG
139; AH325; AJ227; AK211;
AM414; AO257; AR252; AT346;
AU242; AV179; AW144; AZ151-
Q; BA269; BB231; BE221; BF
342; BR297; BX536; BZ   9424
St Hildred (Pearsall) [SFMRDDLS
FM, SDSLLT] C301b   9425
St Hill (Stainer) X Pastor bonus
9426
St Hubert (Darwall) [SSLLSMM
DRM, RMFRMF] D420a; J237;
K457; Z357; AV225; BR387;
BX324   9427
St Hugh (English trad) [DDDLLS
FM, SLLLLS, MF] E606; J335;
W557; X371; BE248   9428
St Hugh (Hopkins) [DDRMDSRM,
MFLSDR, SD] F317; W549a;
AB353; BE303; BR16; BV66;
BX75a; BY325a   9429
St Ignatius (Barnby) [DDRDMFS,
MRDDD, DDRD] W606; AS433;
AT498   9430
St Ignatius (Cooke) [SSDTLDDS,
MMRDTLS, S] C378b; D358c
9431
St Ingrid (Alexis) [SFMFMMRD,
MRDTRDTL] J391a; N485 9432
St Ishmael (Vincent) [SDTLTS,
FMFSLR, RMF#S] BY609b
9433
St Issey (English trad) [DRMRD
LS, DRMRD, TDRM] E388; R
528; Sap. 16; X490   9434

St James (Courteville) [SDRM
DRFM, MLTDLS, RM] A361;
B279; D144; E341; F199;
J247; K279; R221; S254;
W173; X96; Z424; AF266;
AJ341; AK325; AL339; AP
185; AZ14-E; BA607; BR390;
BV445; BY110   9435
St James' Stockholm (Ahl-
ström) [DMSRFMRD, RMR
DTLLS,] J270; N238 9436
St James the Less (Dykes)
X Hollingside   9437
St Jerome (Champneys) [SLS
FMFSRRD, MRMF#SR] B438
9438
St Joan (Coller) [DMSDLS, L
DLSMRM, D] A258; R492
9439
St John (Calkin) X Calkin II
9440
St John (Dykes) [LMRDTL,
LSLFFM, LSLF] B148; C
148; D96a; K102; O265;
BB129   9441
St John (Havergal) [DMMSSD,
DTLSF#S̄, SLTD] Q380; V
167; W710; AA329; AL626;
AM307; AP43; AW615 9442
St John (Turle) X St John's
Westminster   9443
St John (Wade) X St Thomas
9444
St John Baptist (Calkin) X
Bradfield   9445
St John Damascene (Barker)
[SSMFLS, SSFRM, DDTDR]
D395a; AL460   9446
St John Damascene (Brown)
[SLDDDRM, DRMFSS, SLD]
F133; K70   9447
St John's (Havergal) X St
John   9448
St John's College (Garrett)
[SLSDMFML, RSDFMR, MF]
V67   9449
St John's, Highlands ("W. C. B. ")
[MFF#SDDTF, MMMMLLR
R,] D244; R438; T170; AJ
132; AO565b   9450
St John's, Westminster (Turle)
[DTDRMFFM, MRSSF#S, SS]
D233a; G410; I234; AW305

9451
St Joseph (Calkin) [MFMSFMRD,
RMFSDTLS,] W361   9452
St Joseph (Hopkins) [SSSDMRDT,
DRMDLRRS,] B226b   9453
St Joseph (Parry) [MLSMDRMFM
RM,MDTLS] X441   9454
St Joseph (Statham) [MMMMSFM
R,DDRMFRD,M] I132; L363;
AP685   9455
St Joseph, be our guide (Jenkins)
[DRDSLDRMSFMDRF,MR] BL
64   9456
St Joseph, pride of heaven's
court (Bragers) [SMDDTLSDR
M,MFMRRD] BP91   9457
St Jude (Vincent) X Monod   9458
St Katrine (Williamson) [DRMSS
FM,F#STLSF#S,SL] BY260b
9459
St Kentigern (Arthur) [SDRMSLM
S,TDRMDFMR,] W218; AD460
9460
St Kerrian (Dresden mss. 1761
Stainer arr) [DDRMFRM,RR
DSSF#S,RM] D222b; W314
9461
St Keverne (Lang) [MLLLTTDRT
DRMFLS#L,] A492   9462
St Kevin (Patton) [MMFMRLTDR
MR,RMF#SS] AZ596-A; BA
832b   9463
St Kevin (Sullivan) [MMMRDMFS,
DRMFMR,RR] A94b; B170;
C170; D110a; G151; I163; J
106a; K108; M445; N131; R
205; S168; U220; V767; Z242;
AB242; AD162; AE136; AF185;
AG101; AH301; AK169; AM200;
AO180; AR183; AT109; AW113;
AZ152-H; BB136; BD95; BF319;
BR179; BZ   9464
St Kilda (Broomfield) [LLTDMRDT,
DLTDRM,MR] W558   9465
St Lawrence (Hayne) [MMRDTT
LS,SSSFMRDT,] B454; C454;
D169b; F471; AP366; BV412a
9466
St Lawrence (Smith) [DMMFSLM
RD,SLDSFFM] W633   9467
St Lawrence (Steggall) [MSLDSM
MR,DRMLSMR,M] AZ585-F
9468

St Lawrence, Lund (Swedish,
17th c) [SDRMRDTD,MRM
DTLLS,] J302   9469
St Leonard (Meiningen G-B.)
[MRDRSDRDTS,LTDDRS] A
518; B273; C15; D151; E527;
J126; K149; M465; N157; O
59; P231; Q226; X32b; Z545;
AA246; AD432; AL560a; AW
548; AZ89-B; BA288; BN63;
BR444b; BV475; BY638
9470
----. V [MDRSDRTS,LTDDR
SM,M] M465   9471
-----. V [MDRSDRDTS,LTD
DRRM] AZ89-B   9471a
St Leonard (Davis) [DDDRDDT,
LSSDMR,MFS] C536b   9472
St Leonard (Hiles) [DRFMRR
DD,DRRRRR,RM] C22; D
15a; G46; I62; J54b; K40;
N219; S36; T314; U20; V38;
Z142; AB24; AC66; AD51;
AG175; AH165; AJ257; AK79;
AL282; AM553; AN122b; AO
26; AP678; AR73; AS26; AV
13; AZ590-H; BA793; BB54;
BD31; BE224; BF204; BK55;
BR122; BX156   9473
St Leonard (Irons) [SMRDLFMR,
SLDTLSF#S,] Eap.41; W
514   9474
St Leonard (Smart) [SSMLSLT
D,RMDTLS,RT] F443; K
266; N41; W474; BE247; BV
502; BY446   9475
St Leonard's (Barham-Gould)
[MSFMRDDT,DDRMMF#S,D]
BV634; BY596   9476
St Lo (Breton trad) [SDRMDM
RD,RMRDRMLS,] S489; AK
413; AL369; AN510; AW388
9477
St Louis (Redner) [MMMR#MS
FL,RDTDRSM,M] A21b; B
78; C78b; D58b; G100; H145;
I121a; J27a; K31; L220b;
M605; N36; P133; Q647;
R171; S121; T334; U55; V
741; Y330; Z184; AB107;
AC82; AD121; AE85; AF134;
AG64; AH250; AI66; AJ399;

AK108; AL51b; AM152; AN165;
AO125a; AQ286; AR126; AS103;
AT75; AU144; AV82; AW84; AX
97; BA157; BB104; BC165; BD
226; BE222; BF292; BK150;
BX198; BZ   9478
St Lucian (Rinck) [MMRRDS, LT
DMR, MMFMR] J231b; K550;
P70; AP744; AZ141-C; BA637
9479
St Lucy (Poole) [DDRMFMRD,
SSLTDTLS,] AP497   9480
St Luke (---) [SDSLLSMFMRM,
MMFML] M300; O580   9481
St Luke (Clark:Clarke) X Uffing-
ham   9482
St Luke, No 1 (Beethoven) X O
salutaris Hostia   9483
St Luke, No. 2 (Gilmore) [DMM
RDFSFM, MMMR#MF#F#] BR
472   9484
St Luke's (---) X St Luke   9485
St Mabyn (Brown) [MMRDSMMR,
FFMLTDT, R] W395a; AA467;
AL468b; BE337; BY419a   9486
St Mabyn (Humphreys) [SMMMRD
LS, DMRRMR, RF] D240b 9487
St Magnus (Clark) [SDRTSDRM,
RMDMF#S, RM] A106; B188;
C188; D129; E147; F218; G78;
H191; J439; K11; N11; O175;
Q219; R211; S185b; T202; V109;
W131a; X175; AA237; AB347;
AD326; AE122; AF78; AG315;
AH11; AI429; AJ291; AK451;
AL118; AM113; AN251a; AO
191; AP24; AQ98; AT126; AW
582; BA249; BE328; BF638;
BJ21; BR139; BV207; BX236;
BY58b; BZ   9488
-----. V [SDRDTSDRM, RMDR
MF#S,] BJ21b   9489
St Margaret (Dunman) [SDRMSL,
LRMRDT, SMRD] L413   9490
St Margaret (Masser) [MMMSFM
RD, DRMFRSFM,] AP489 9491
St Margaret (Peace) [SSSSLTDDT,
TTTTDR] A458b; C236b; G318;
I481; J402; K348; M208; N521;
P288; R400; S307; T46; U26; V
367; W424b; Y37; Z388; AC154;
AD249; AE262; AF399; AG181;
AH221; AJ73; AK278; AL311;

AM594; AN243; AO289; AP
465; AR271; AS266; AT290;
AU231; AV232; AW175; AY
468; BA492; BB145; BD115;
BE406; BF245; BK90; BR
422; BX286; BY20a; BZ
9492
St Margaret (Statham) [LMM
MMMD, DMMMRR, RFF] F
114b   9493
St Marguerite (Walker) [MD
RDSTLS, SLTDRR, FM] C
56b; D338; I369; U286; V
378; AB166; BA360; BF439;
BR428   9494
St Maria (Haydn) X St Michel's
9495
St Mark (Bell) [MMSFMRD
R, MMRDRRS, M] Eap. 71
9496
St Mark (Crowfoot) [MSLSF
MFRD, RMF#SDTL] F405
9497
St Mark (Elliott) [MLS#LDTL
S#, LSFMLLS#L,] O236
9498
St Mark (Gauntlett) [MSSSFF
FM, MMMMRR, RF] I699;
U232; BA109   9499
St Mark (Mozart) X Mozart II
9500
St Mark (Teschner) X St
Theodulph   9501
St Mark's (Haas) MMMRM
F, LSFM, MMMF#F#S,] K
336   9502
St Martin (Briggs) [MLTDRM
MSFM, RDLT, TD] X572;
AQ58   9503
St Martin (Corbeil) X Orientis
partibus   9504
St Martin (Ett) [SMFMRD,
DMSSLS, LTDT] E416; F
213b; K74; BN129; BO265
9505
St Martin's (Tans'ur) [DDRD
SDRM, MFSFMDR, M] C71c;
D54b; G172; H105; I183; L
193; T227; V117; AD327;
AI370; AJ323; ALsuppl; AM
260; AN366; AO215; AW74;
AY418; AZ14-Aa; BD190;
BR497; BX402; BZ   9506

St Mary (Prys. Psalms, 1621)
[LDTLLSFM, MSDMRD, MS]
E84; F93; O318; W401; X
116; AF497; AL127a; AP206;
AZ14-G; BA421; BJ33; BV144;
BY139b   9507
St Mary Magdalene (Dykes) X
Mary Magdalene   9508
St Mary Magdalene (Jeboult) [DT
DRDTLS#LTM, MLSFM] E112;
W426   9509
St Mary's (Prys) X St Mary
                                    9510
St Matthew (Croft) [SMSDMRDTD,
MRSLSF#S,] A517; C499; E
526; F478; J254a; M186; N385;
O470; R179; W86; X287; AB356;
AD87; AE102; AK190; AL76;
AM57; AN270; AP186; AR153;
AW95; AZ590-B; BA230; BE52;
BV399; BY277a; BZ   9511
St Matthias (Gibbons) X Song 67
                                    9512
St Matthias (Monk) [MRDFMR
MD, MRDRSMF#] A182; B40;
C40; D22; F28; H35; J199; K
175; O55; V28; W302a; AB376;
AL213a; AP268; BA617; BF
533; BV60a; BY700a   9513
St Medan (Monk, arr) [DDTLSLS,
SLSMRMR, DD] B368   9514
St Michael (Bourgeois) [SDMRRM,
SFMRRD, DTLS] A113; B88;
C88; D148; E27; F142; G39;
H81; J141; K215; N438; Q310;
R493; T101; V452; W120a; X
702; AA490; AF237; AJ189;
AL141a; AM72; AN300a; AP
40; AQ259; AT16; AW128; AZ
582-F; BA349; BB270; BD98;
BJ66; BR130; BV188; BY363a;
BZ   9515
St Michael New (Wesley, S.S.)
[MSMDTDRMRD, RMFSSL]
E244   9516
St Michel's (Haydn) [SSFMSFMR,
FMDLRDT, S] G118; I584b; J
322; K414; L371; N625; T82;
U47; V270; AI207; AL531; AM
519; AO321; AR371; AT343; AV
24; AW93; BB405; BE269; BR
383; BY505a; BZ   9517
St Millicent (Sullivan) [MMSFMR

MR, RRFMRDRD] D245a
                                    9518
St Nathaniel (Sullivan) [DSLDD
RRM, RMRMF#S, SS] B220;
V461   9519
St Nicholas (Crueger) [LS#LT
DRTL, DTLTDRM, M] J139;
M34; N405; O251; P160; Q
326; AA416; AF368; AZ91-D
                                    9520
-----. V [LMS#LTDTL, DTLT
DRM, L] N405   9520a
-----. V [LS#LTDRTL, DTLT
DRM, L] O251   9520b
-----. V [LS#LTDDTL, DTLT
DRM, M] AF368   9521
-----. V [LS#STDRDTL, DTL
TDRM,] AZ91-D   9521a
St Nicholas (Ellis) [DTDRMFS
SFMRD, FMRS] F190b
                                    9522
St Nicholas (Havergal) X Eden
                                    9524
St Nicholas (Greene) [LDMLM
FMRDT, DLTDRM,] E265;
S16a; X395d; AD311; AM97;
AP117a; AZ14-Hh; BY277b
                                    9525
-----. V [LDMLMFMRD,
TLTDRM, M] S16a   9526
St Nicholas (Redhead) [SLLSFM
MR, DRMSDLS, S] C55b; O
190; W150; AI69; BA572; BO
95   9527
St Nicholas (Scholefield) [MMM
SMRMFSM, MMLSF] A173;
B12; C12; D6a   9528
St Nicolai (Rosenmüller) X
Nassau   9529
St Nicolas (Nicholson) [MFSRM
FLR, DTLSLFMM,] F576
                                    9530
St Nicolas (Redhead) X St
Nicholas   9531
St Ninian (Dykes) [DDDDDRM
RDTD, MMMF#S] BF277
                                    9532
St Ninian (Monk) [SLSMDRM,
FLSMSFR, MD] K428   9533
St Ninian (Prothero) [DMMSSTL
S, MDDRRM, MS] C239b
                                    9534
Saint of the Sacred Heart

(Montani) [MMMMRD, SDDRM
R, FFFF] BQ103   9535
St Olaf (Dahle) [MMRDMSFMR,
M, MRFMRD,] O143   9536
St Olaf (Haydn) X Petition   9537
St Olaf's sequence (Koralbok for
den Norske Kirke. 1926) [LT
DRDTLDTLSLL, LMS] X59
                              9538
St Olave (Barnby) [DDTLSM,
MMRDTD, DFFM] J513; O431;
P329; U92; V154; AA352   9539
St Olave (Gauntlett) X St George
                              9540
St Olave (Hudson) [DMFSLDTDF
MRM, DMLS] W257; BE140
                              9541
St Oswald I (Dykes, 1857) [SM
LDTLSM, DDRMSLS, S] A434;
B42; C42; D125b; Eap.61; F
292b; I109; V309; W214a; AB
44; AL358b; AM29; AP105;
AZ16-E; BA131; BD61; BE33;
BO12; BV444; BX213b; BY141a
                              9542
St Oswald II (Dykes, 1862) [DS
SSSDTLS, SDDTTLL] K47
                              9543
St Oswin (Dykes) X Oswin   9544
St Osyth (Wood) [SLSM, DRMFM
SM, DLSM,] A509; F550; X511;
BY602   9545
St Pancras (Smart) [DTDSMFMR,
MFSDRSM, M] D318b; K242;
L229; BA150   9546
St Patrick (Gaelic trad) [DDRMM
R, RMFMRD, DMFS] BN166
                              9547
St Patrick (Irish trad) [SDRDDMF
SLSSM, DRDR] AH140   9548
St Patrick (St Patrick) [MLL
SMSMSDMRDDT, TRTS] A268a;
B525; C525; E212; F162; W
506; X528a; BQ97; BV229; BY
433   9549
-----. R [LDRRDRFS, DTLFMM
RD,]   9550
-----. V [MSLLSLDR, SF#MDT
TLS,] X528b   9551
-----. V [MLLLSMSDMRDDT,
TDR] BQ97   9552
St Patrick (St Patrick) X Deirdre
(Irish trad)   9553

St Patrick (Sullivan) [DDD
MSSL, SMRDDTDR, R] AB
150; BA250   9554
St Patrick's Breastplate (St
Patrick) X St Patrick
                              9555
St Paul (Chalmers. Collection,
1749) X Aberdeen   9556
St Paul (Etlich Christliche
lider.) X Wittenberg   9557
St Paul (Goss) X Lauda anima
                              9558
St Paul (Goss) X Tarsus
                              9559
St Paul (Johnson) [SDRMRDLS,
SLTDRMR, M] N189   9560
St Paul's (---) [DMRDLSRM,
MRSF#SLTL] V520   9561
St Paul's (Clarke) X Bishop-
thorpe   9562
St Paul's (Erskine) [SMRMSM
RM, SLTLSMR, D] B31b;
Y222   9563
St Paul's (Stainer) [SSFMFR,
LSFMRM, DTRD] F200; BV
138; BY565b   9564
St Peter (Plainsong arr 1539)
X To God on high   9565
St Peter (Reinagle) [SDTLSS
FM, MRDFMR, MF] A455;
B5; C5; D281a; E405; F13;
G424; H430; I241; J291; K178;
L388; M236; N54; O417; P93;
Q286; R130; S81; T424; U375;
V189; W419; X527b; Y273; Z
264; AA96; AB357; AC299;
AD254; AE56; AF221; AG48;
AI427; AJ27; AK406; AL252;
AM51; AN255; AO101; AP52;
AR387; AS362; AT393; AW
320; AZ14-T; BA65; BB150;
BD19; BE125; BF432; BK
112; BL36; BO170; BV260;
BX232; BY203a; BZ   9566
St Peter's (Ross) X St Peter's
Manchester   9567
St Peter's (Turle) X St Peter's,
Westminster   9568
St Peter's, Manchester (Ross)
[SSSSDDTLT, SDRMDR, D]
J412; K44; L143   9569
St Peter's, Oxford (Reinagle)
X St Peter   9570

St Peter's, Westminster (Turle) [DDDRMFMR, MFSSLLS, M] D318b; S60; AK194; AZ585-G; BA356   9571

St Petersburg (Bortniansky) [SM FSDRDTD, SLDLSM] A499; G 339; H174; I134; J399; L116; M225; N7; O172; P118; Q493; R145; S180; T94; W459b; AA 84; AE148; AG203; AI47; AJ 137; AK17; AL11; AM76, 494; AO591; AP556; AQ56; AR275; AS124; AT177; AW517; AX42; BB153; BC113; BV9, 478; BY 321; BZ   9572

-----. V [MMFSDRDTD, SLDL SMS] L116   9573

-----. V [SSMFSDRDTD, SLDLSM] AL11   9574

-----. V [SMFSDRDTD, LDLSM SF] AP556   9575

St Philip (Barnby) X Sarum   9576

St Philip (Hopkins) [MRMFRM, SLTDLT, TDSL] BA253   9577

St Philip (Monk) [DDRMFMRD, MFSSLSFM,] A57b; B122; C 122a; D88a; Eap.10; F94; O 378; W186; AL160a; AO280; AP428; AZ263-B; BA274; BV 613b; BY319a   9578

St Piran (Hopkins) [SLTDDTR, DD TSM, MRDT] AO505   9579

St Polycarp (Barnby) [LTLS#TD TL, DRMDRMD, D] B378; C 378a; D358a; I463b; V446a; BR323c   9580

St Polycarp (Pleyel) X Grace Church   9581

St Prisca (Redhead) [MMRMFFM, SSDLF#F#S] A79; B146; C146a; D97; E513; F105b; K76; M74; O540; T7; W329; AJ11; AL131; AP434; BA27; BR346; BX257   9582

St Quintin (Parr) [SSFMDDT, DTLSLLS, SS] S243; AK251   9583

St Raphael (Hopkins) [DDTDLTDS, LTDFRDD, D] B127; C127; D 264; E75; F321; K80; M624; N187; O25; V1; W524a; AS164; BA377; BR286   9584

St Regulus (Macmeikan) [MR DSFMRDR, FMLRF#S, S] D670   9585

St Sacrament (Monk) [SFSLSM RDRM, MRDSFM] AB222   9586

St Saviour (Baker) [DDTDLSFM, SLDRRR, SM] C54b; D47b; L209; Q434; V327; AA364; AE420; AL574b; AM162; AP73; BA147; BV472; BY 81b   9587

-----. V [SDTDLSFM, SLDRR R, SM] Q434   9588

St Sebastian (Buck) X Martins   9589

St Sebastian (Cecil) [SLSDTDRD, RMRDTLS, S] D358b   9590

St Sechnall (Irish trad) [SDTL SDSFMFMRDDD, D] F386a; X268   9591

St Sepulchre (Cooper) [DSLS DFSM, SDRMFFFM] E422; F109; BA292; BE331; BY 334   9592

St Serf (Lahee) [SMMDDRRS, LTDDDRMF] D455   9593

St Silas (Lancaster) [MRDFM RDT, TDRMSSF, F] Y154; AD429; AL381; BR380; BY 468a   9594

St Simon (Crueger) [DMMFSSF M, SMMRRD, DM] AZ151-C, 590-C; BA889, 594   9595

-----. V [DMFSSFFM, FM DRRD, DM] AZ590-C   9596

Saint Stephen (English trad) [LS#LMFMRDRMRDR, DRM] BG26   9597

-----. R [S#LTDRMDRDT, TDTDRM,]   9598

St Stephen (Jones) [DSMDRD TDR, MFSDRMRD,] A11; B70; C70b; D29b; E337; F52; H209; I86; J327; K268; L173; R49; S187; V65; W483a; X 250; AA128; AD175; AF201; AK346; AL328; AM236; AN 305; AO92; AP188; AQ261; AR208; AZ14-N; BA332; BB 194; BD123; BE334; BF559; BR284; BV339; BX301; BY 179; BZ   9599

St Victor (Redhead) [SDMDTLS,
SDRMSR, MFM] W342a   9622
St Vigian (Falconer) [MMSFFM,
DTDFMR, RMSS] D604b   9623
St Vincent (Neukomm) [SSF#SM
DRFMRRD, DSFM] A209b;
B331; C331a; D227; I221; J
277b; AO33; BE155; BR127
                                          9624
St Werburgh (Dykes) [DDMSDDL
S, SDSFMRMR] D314a; L91;
AA291   9625
St Wilfred (Hall) [SLTDRFM, RD
LSS, RRSF] B449b   9626
St Winifred (Dykes) [DDDDRM
FSLSM, SSLFS] F103b   9627
St Wystan (Butler) [MRRDFM,
RMRDS, SMDLS] C357a   9628
Saints' days (Smith) X Edengrove
                                          9629
Saints of God (Stainer) X Beati
                                          9630
Saints of God (Sullivan) [MSSSS
DTL, LSFMSRRD,] C462; D175b;
W75; AA481; AC102; BX306
                                          9631
Saints' reward (Hunter) [MMMRM
SLSM, MMMMRDR,] AX579
                                          9632
Salamis (Greek mel) X Luke 9633
Salem (Methfessel's Song book,
1818) [SDTLSSSLSLTDS, SLS]
AL609; AP757; BC184; BY401
                                          9634
-----. V [SDTLSSSLSLTDSS,
SL] BC184   9634a
Salisbury (Barnes) [MMMSDRM,
FFMDDTDR, M] BB216   9635
Salisbury (Hullah arr) [MMSFRL
TD, RRMFMRDR] D667c; O238;
AZ3-D   9636
Salisbury (Ravenscroft's Psalter,
1621) [DRFMSSF#S, MLSFFM,
SM] W296; BY262b   9637
Säll du, som dig at Gud betror
(Waldis) [DSLSDTLS, SLDSMR
D, D] N495   9638
Salome (Beethoven) [SDTDRMRDDT,
MRDTDL] I204; AL564; BY
262b   9639
Salome (Bradbury) [SMSLSDSM, S
FSLSTSR,] AJ254   9640
Salonica (Pollock) [MRDRDLLS,

DRMRFMR, M] T147; AJ
216   9641
Salonica (Scott) [DSLR, DRSR
DLTDMS, SL] X471; BV593
                                          9642
Salus aeterna (Plainsong,
before 11th c M 7) [TRM
TSS, LDTLSTSLS,] E10
                                          9643
Salus mortalium (Gesangbuch.
Erfurt, 1663) [SMDRMFMRD,
SLSFMRD#] F517   9644
Salutas (Silcher) X Lorelei
                                          9645
Salutis humanae sator (Plain-
song M 4 trad) X Jesu,
quadragenariae   9646
Salvation (Etliche Christliche
lieder, 1524) X Wittenberg
                                          9647
Salvation (Kentucky Harmony.
1816) [MDLTS#LLTD, RMD
RDTL] AQ53   9648
Salvation (Kirkpatrick) [SSDSD
RM, SSSMDR, SSD] R503;
Z537; AH408; AI103; AL259b;
AM370; AP798; AR480; AS
293; AT191; AU15; AW334;
AX201; AY231; BB637   9649
Salvation (Weisenthal) [MMMM
SSFMFRFM, DTDS] AS32
                                          9650
Salvation by grace (Knecht)
[SDTRDFRTD, DTLRMDT]
M137; AF499; AM399
                                          9651
-----. V [SDTRDFRTD, DTL
RMTL] AM399   9652
Salvationist (Hays) [MFSSLSS
M, DRDDLS, DR] AT87; AU
363; AW446; AX25   9653
Salvator (Danish) [SMFSLMFS,
LSMFSFM, S] M284   9654
Salvator (Foster) [MRDTLDD,
RRMDFMR, RS] W85; Z215;
BY133   9655
Salvator (Goss) [MDSFMFMR,
DTLFMRD, S] D17b   9656
Salvator amicus (Hirst) [DMS
SLSSM, FMRDRMR, D] D46
                                          9657
Salvator natus (Bohemian trad)
X Be ye joyful   9658

Salvator No. 1 (Sullivan) X
   Lacrymae   9659
Salvatori (Ferretti) [MRDDRRM
   D, DTLRDTD, M] N128; T348;
   AI83; AL191; AO184; AP748;
   AR580; AW283; BA485; BY57a
                                    9660
Salve cordis gaudium (Ahle)
   [MMFSFMRRR, MFMRD, MM]
   F367a   9661
Salve Domini (Watson) [MSSLTD
   S, DDLDRM, SRD#] G114; R138;
   T370; U398; Y19; Z208; AB72;
   AC9; AD467; AG277; AH472;
   AR112; AT454; BD87; BF185
                                    9662
Salve, festa dies (Baden-Powell)
   [DMFSSLTDDT, TTDRDT] B168;
   C168   9663
Salve, festa dies (Sarum proces-
   sional. M 4) [FSMSLFRM, S
   LDLSLSF] E624; F600; X389
                                    9664
Salve festa dies (Williams) [DS
   FMRD, MRDTDRTLS] A86;
   B168; E624b; X390   9665
Salve Jesu (Lewars) [MRMDTL,
   MSFMRD, TDRF] K65   9666
Salve, Mater (Plainsong M 5)
   [DSDDDTLSLS, MMSSFM] BM
   48; BN125; BP73; BQ209
                                    9667
Salve, Pater salvatoris (Andrews)
   [SSSMFMMR, SSSMFMMR]
   BN167   9668
Salve Regina coelitum (Hildesheim,
   1736) X Hail, holy Queen
                                    9669
Salve Regina (Plainsong M 5) [D
   MSLSLDTLSLSS, DSL] BL61;
   BN142; BO301; BP76; BQ280
                                    9670
Salve, Regina (Schubert) [MMFM
   RD, SSSFMRMR, MM] BQ205
                                    9671
Salzburg (Haydn) [DMSSFMMRD,
   DDTDSFM] G383; W562a; Z
   462; AL12b; AP12; AR228; AW
   167; BV615; BY550a; BZ   9672
Salzburg II (Haydn) [SDDDMMR,
   RMFRDTD, SD] L303; M105;
   AK269; AR562; AW550   9673
-----. V [SDDDMMRR, FMFRD

TD, S] M105   9674
Salzburg (Hintze) [SDSLSFM,
   SSFMRRD, SDS] A53; B96;
   C96; D118a; E128; F139;
   J95a; M305; O532; Q601;
   W129; X558; AA513; AF69;
   AL200b; AM623; AN199; AQ
   173; AR428; AW545; AZ205-
   H; BE11; BI58; BK104; BL
   28; BM2; BN161; BO175a;
   BV317; BY14   9675
-----. V [SDSLSFMM, SSFMR
   RD, S] M305   9676
-----. V [DMRD, SSLSFFM,]
   AA513   9677
-----. V [SDSSSFMD, SSFMR
   RD, S] BN161   9678
Samaria (Bullinger) [MFSDLDS
   M, DRMSFMR, M] BA407
                                    9679
Samos (Havergal) [DSMRDLS,
   LDFMRDS, MD] BY507b
                                    9680
Sampford (Ireland) [DTLDSFM,
   MFSLSMR, MF#] F131a;
   BV170   9681
Sampson (Handel) X Samson
                                    9682
Samson (Handel) [DMFSMLTD,
   DSLSMRDT] D131; G472;
   I298; L219; V85; X451; AA
   376; AB61; AL28; AR290;
   AW258; BA224; BB484; BR
   81; BV570; BX86; BY290
                                    9683
-----. V [DMFSMLTD, DSLS
   MDRM] AR290   9684
-----. V [DMFSMLTD, DSLSM
   RDR] BA224   9685
Samuel (Sullivan) [MMSFM
   F, LSF#SDDT, DLS] B359;
   C359; D568; G451; I559; T45;
   W251; Z609; AH364; AI374;
   AJ72; AL211; AM655; AO626;
   AP806; AR264; AW416; BB
   428; BC252; BD196; BK23;
   BV361b; BX518; BY474
                                    9686
San Remo (Barber) [SSLDRFM
   R, DDTDRLS, S] D546   9687
San Vincente (Barnes) [SMDSS
   DRM, DFMRDTDR,] AK248
                                    9688

Sanctissimus (Cooke) [MRMSFM
RMFMRD, DDTL] BY35a
9689
Sanctorum meritis (Sarum plain-
song M 7) [STDRMDR, SLTD
TLSLS,] E182; BP51   9690
Sanctuary (Dickinson) X Agape
9691
Sanctuary (Dykes) [SDMRDLSS, S
SSMRDR, R] B207b; C297a;
D179a; I174; J403a; K248; L
86; V501; AB286; AM607; AO
495; AP307a; BA650; BD137;
BF510; BR271; BX427   9692
Sanctus (Cooper) [MMSSDSFMF
MMR, SSLT] AW601   9693
Sanctus (Gaul) [SLSMFR, MDM
RLR, SLSM] Z615; AG322; BF
682   9694
Sanctus (Richards) [DDTLSLSM,
SSSSLDT, D] S15; W2b; BY26
9695
Sanctus (Wesley, S.) [DD, MM,
LSMFSM, RRSLTL] H99   9696
Sandell (Swedish) [DRMMSMMR,
RMFLSFFM,] J572; N487; P
368; AE256; BZ   9697
Sandford (Stephenson) [SDMMRD,
SFMLRR, MDRT] O232; BR161
9698
Sandon (Purday) [MMMFMMRDR
M, DRTD, M] A430a; F298c;
G514b; J488; O572; R108; S88;
T260; W568d; Z166; AB400;
AD79; AE62; AF97; AJ362;
AK86; AL436c; AM463; AO327b;
AP109; AR68; AW163; BF641;
BL67; BR388b; BY545b; BZ
9699
Sandringham (Barnby) [DMSSSSS
DTTL, RMFSM] A214; B382; C
382; D238; G431; I668; J300;
K415; N528; O538; P354; R453;
S484; T77; U484; V636; W327;
Z291; AA444; AD417; AE386;
AF465; AG296; AJ115; AK50;
AL238; AM625; AN453; AO20;
AP662; AR539; AS419; AT282;
AW312; BA843; BB416; BF358;
BI63; BL65; BX486; BY624;
BZ   9700
Sands (Kirkpatrick) [SDRMRDTD,
SDMSMRDR] AJ246   9701

Sandwith (Micklem) [DMRMFS,
DLSFFM, MF#MF#] BY738
9702
Sandys (English trad) [SSDTSL
T, RDTDTLS, SS] A476; E
485; F337; W511; X652; BE
184; BG2; BR554; BV102;
BY38   9703
Sandys Psalm 8 (Lawes) X
Whitehall   9704
Sanglier (German) [SDMMSSFF,
FMFRDTD, S] BR321   9705
Sankey (Sankey) [SDDRDTLTD
S, SRRMFM] BZ   9706
Sankey (Sankey) X O safe to
the Rock   9707
Sankey (Sankey) X Victory
9708
Sans Day carol (English trad)
[DMSSSFMDMFRTD, DMS]
BG35   9709
-----. R [DMSSLTDDSSSSLT
D, D]   9710
Santa Monica (Noble) [DMRF
MSFM, RDDMRS, S#L] AK
140   9711
Santa Trinita (Pieraccini) [SS
LTDTRDLS, MMRRRD] D379b;
AC37; BA370; BO183; BR15
9712
Santolius (Geistliche volkslied.
1850) X Desire   9713
Santwat (Manx trad) [LLMRDR
MDL, LTDRMDT] X647
9714
Sarah (Gabriel) [SSDMFMRR,
SSTRMD, SS] T230; AI119;
AJ326   9715
Sarah (Thomas) [DMFSMFMR
M, DLTDFMR,] AB369;
AK367; AR560   9716
Sardis (Beethoven) [DTDRMSFM
R, MMMLSF#S,] B700b; C
100b; D325; G27; I40, 131; T
1b; V544; Y220; AB71a; AC
90; AE468; AJ2b; BA38; BE
181; BF489; BH20; BI73;
BR246   9717
-----. V [SDTDRMFR, SSSS
S#LLR,] I131   9717a
Saron (Hughes) [MR#MFDMR
D, DTDFDRM, M] Y132   Y132
9718

Sarratt (Ryley) [MMDFMRSLS,
SLMFSMR] E34; W436a; Y
215; AM556   9719
Sarum (Barnby) [SMFSSLLLLL
S, SDDT] A126b; B295; C295a;
D176; Eap. 23; F527b; G527; H
433; I430; J144b; K250; N629;
R425b; S429a; T379; U309; V
614; Z576; AB412; AC330b; AD
461b; AE309; AF307; AG284a;
AH525; AK417; AL174b; AM281;
AN428b; AO540; AR420; AV283;
AW317; AZ58-E; BA740; BB365;
BD248; BE421; BF655; BR446;
BX463; BZ   9720
Sarum (Hullah) X Salisbury 9721
Sarum New (Lloyd) [SSRDMFLS,
RMSDTLF#R,] BV659   9722
Satis (Whitlock) [DRFFMRLL, S
DTL, MSFF] BE162   9723
Satisfied with Jesus (McKinney)
X Routh   9724
Satterlee (Hopkins) [DMFSSSLTD
R, SMDLTD] H484   9725
Sauveur (Baker) X St Saviour
                              9726
Savannah (Pleyel) [SDRMMMSFM
R, SDRMMM] BR97   9727
Savannah (Wesley's Foundery Coll-
ection. 1742) [SSFMRDRMR,
SSFMRDR] A427; E135; F141;
G295; Q507; R529; S288; W504;
X160; AA26; AF458; AL292a;
AN200; AQ60; AZ11-A; BA42;
BV340; BZ   9728
Save us waking (Plainsong) [DRM
MRMFSFMMRM, MFS] AR556
                              9729
Saved by grace (Stebbins) [MMFM
RSRD, DTDFMRLR,] AH455;
AI135; AM726; AV395; AY494;
BB630   9730
-----. R [MMSSLMSS, SSFFSTLS,]
                              9731
Saved, saved (Scholfield) X Rap-
ture   9732
Saved to the uttermost (Kirk-
patrick) [MMMMRDDTDR, FFFF
MR] AU51   9733
-----. R [SLSMFSMD, RSSF#MF#
S, S]   9734
Savery (Donizetti) [SMMFTRDDT,
LSF#SLSS] L117; AB49; AW

235   9735
-----. V [MFTR, DDTLSF#SL
SSM, S] AW235   9736
Saving health (Etlich Christliche
lider, 1524) X Wittenberg
                              9737
Saviour (Young) [DDTLS, DRMF
MR, SFMLS] BE299   9738
Saviour, again to thy dear name
(Widdeman) [SSDMDRMRM
R, SSDMDM] AX74; AY293
                              9739
Savior, breathe an evening bless-
ing (Beethoven) X Sardis
                              9740
Saviour breathe an evening
blessing (Hall) [SSMFSLSM,
LLLDDLS, S] AX70; AY
285   9741
Saviour, hear us, we pray
(Brahms) X Lucy   9742
Savior, I would live (Fillmore)
[DSFMMRRM, FSLTLS, DS]
AS348   9743
-----. R [SSLLTLS, LLTTDL
R, DT]   9744
Saviour, I'm coming (Warren)
[MDRDLS, RRFRM, MDRDL]
AX301   9745
Saviour, lead me lest I stray
(Davis) X Lead me, Saviour
                              9746
Saviour, like a Shepherd
(Jacobs) [SFMRDLSFMR,
MFSLSL] AY128   9747
Savior, like a Shepherd lead us
(Bradbury) X Pleasant pas-
tures   9748
Saviour, more than life (Doane)
X Every day and hour
                              9749
Saviour of the nations, come
(--- 16th c) [DRFRRDM, F
RDRMDD, RL] BP6   9750
Savior, Redeemer, God of Love
(Palestrina) X Victory
                              9751
Savior, Redeemer of my soul
(Dean) [DMFSSLTD, LRDT
SLF#S,] BC155   9752
Savior, Redeemer of my soul
(Stephens) [MDMFMRTD, R
MRDSDDD,] BC282   9753

-----. R [SMSLSFSM, SDTLTS
F#S]   9754
Savior! teach me (Converse) [S
SSMDLD, SSSMRRR, SS] AS
276   9755
Saviour, teach me day by day
(---) X Purity   9756
Savior, thy dying love (Lowry)
X Something for Jesus   9757
Saviour, we come to thee (Perry)
[MFDMRR, RMTRDD, DTLS]
AX34; AY210   9758
-----. R [SLMSFF, FSRFMM, MF
MR]   9759
Savior, while my heart is tender
(Harrison) X In the gloaming
9760
Savonarola (Benbow) [MLSMRD
RTL, RMLRRMF,] K92b 9761
Savoy Chapel (Calkin) X Calkin
9762
Sawley (Walch) [DTLSMFTLS,
MRDTDL] A462b; B316b; C
316; D92; G374; H211; I363;
J583; K518; S319a; T111; U142;
V295; Z352; AC158; AD280;
AE161; AI116; AJ161; AM545;
AO363; AP106b; AS179; AX166;
BA218; BB37; BD104; BE315;
BF558; BK107; BY741a   9763
-----. V [SDTLSMFTLS, SMRD
TD] BE315   9764
Saxby (Matthews) X Storrs 9765
Saxony (Grimm. Choral buch)
[MDLFMRMDT, DTLS#LRD]
AZ184-B; BA190   9766
Saxony (Hammerschmidt) X
Meinen Jesum lass ich nicht
9767
Saxony (Kirkpatrick) [SSDRMM
FDRM, MMRLTD] AJ212a 9768
Saxony (Oliver) [SSMDRDRMDS,
SSMDRD] AO201   9769
Scarborough (Glynn) [RFLSLDLS,
LFLRDL, S] A298b   9770
Scattering precious seeds (Hugg)
[SSSLSDMRDS, SSSLSD] AU399;
AY325   9771
-----. R [SDSDMRL, TSRFLSM,
SD]   9772
Scepter (Freylinghausen. G-B.
1704) X Gregor's 97th metre
9773

Scheffler (Koenig) X Ich will
dich lieben   9774
Scheffler (Scheffler. Heilige
Seelenlust. 1657) [MRDDRR
M, TDRTLLS, S] A234a; E
648; J153a; W208; AL159a
9775
Schein (Schein) X Eisenach
9776
Schilling (Schilling) [SSF#SLS
DSM, SMRMFML] AO134
9777
Schlaf, Kindlein, schlaf
(Reichardt) [MRRD, DMSSF
FM, DFFRR] K570; AW431;
BN21; BO152a; BQ14   9778
-----. V [MRRD, MSSFFM, M
FFRRS] BN21   9779
Schlaf, liebes Kind (Molthar)
X Gregor's 483d metre
9780
Schmuecke dich (Crueger)
[MRDRMSFM, SMFMRDMR]
A210; E306; F393; J262; K
182; M48; N246; O149; P76;
Q305; W324; X267; AA432;
AI426; AK334; AL221; AN
494; AQ145; AW552; BY314;
BZ   9781
-----. V [MRDRMSFM, SMFM
DMRD,] N246   9782
-----. V [MRDRMFSFM, SM
FMRDR] AN494   9783
-----. V [MRDRMSFM, SSLS
FMRD,] AZ23-A   9784
Schmuecke dich, O liebe seele
(Crueger) X Schmuecke dich
9785
Schönheit (Joseph) X Keine
schönheit hat die welt   9786
Schönste Sonne (Enckhausen)
[DRDRMLS, SFMRDRRD, M]
AA253   9787
Schönster Herr Jesu (Münster
G-B. 1677) X Fairest Lord
Jesus   9788
Schönster Herr Jesu (Silesian
mel) X St Elizabeth   9790
Schönster Immanuel, Herzog
der Frommen (Darmstadt G-
B.) X Gregor's 189th metre
-B   9791
School house (Wood) [MFSDT

LSLDRMR, TDRM] E271; X
344   9792
School thy feelings (Root) X Like
a strong and raging fire   9793
Schop (Schop) [DDRMF#SSF#S,
MFMRMR, D] A25; J29; W492;
AF118; AN492; AQ297; AZ169-A;
BC239; BE13; BI90; BL7; BV
541; BY440a; BZ   9794
-----. V [MRDRMF#SSF#S, MF
MRMRD] AZ169-A   9795
Schop (Schop) X Jesu, joy of
man's desiring   9796
Schörring (Schörring) X Content-
ment   9797
Schroeder (Miller) [DDRMFSL
TD, SDDTSLM] BB79   9798
Schubert (Schubert) [SMMR#R#
MD, DRRFFM, SMM] AM24;
AR251; BR421   9799
Schubert II (Schubert) [SLF#SDR
MMR, DTLSSLS] AO81   9800
Schuler (Schuler) [MR#MSFMRMR
D, FSLDTL] AT431; AU130
                           9801
-----. R [MSMFL, TMRDS, LD
LSMM]   9802
Schulz (Schulz) X Paedia   9803
Schumann (Mason & Webb. Cantica
laudis) X Heath   9804
Schumann (Schumann. G-B. 1539)
X Old 112th   9805
Schwing dich (Franck) [DSDSLSM,
MRMSLS, DSD] F518; M216;
Q540   9806
Schwing dich auf zu deinem Gott
(Crueger) [MMLSLTD, TDRMD
TL, MM] N286   9807
Science (Brackett) [SDLSDRFM,
MRSLDTS, S] BE197   9808
Scientia salutis (Stainer) [DRM
RD, FMRDTRS, SMDL] F604
                           9809
Scotch stilt (Scottish Psalter.
1615) X York   9810
Scotstown (Finlay) [DLSTLSMSF
MRM, MF#LL] BV591b   9811
Scott (Naegeli) [DRMMFMMR,
MRDDRSM, S] AP26   9812
Scott (Scott) X Open my eyes
                           9813
Scudamore (Chope) [DTDSLTD,
RRRDTLS, DR] BA248; BB248

                           9814
Se solens skjønne lys og pragt
(Freylinghausen. G-B. 1704)
[SDMRFMDT, SFMFSMR, S]
O269; P313; Q413; AZ164-A;
BA724   9815
Seabury (Means) [MSSDRMRD,
RMLSSLD] A548   9816
Seal (Russell) [MSDTLS, MRM
FSM, SDTL] D72b   9817
Seal us, O Holy Spirit (Mere-
dith) X Meredith   9818
Search me, O God (Vulpius) X
Das neugeborne   9819
Search me, O Lord (Main) X
Ridgefield   9820
Search the Scriptures (Freyling-
hausen) [S#LTDTLLS#LTD
TDLTD] BI35-D   9821
Seasons (Mendelssohn) X
Heavenly love   9822
Seasons (Pleyel) [SMRDDRM
FM, RMRDRDT] H357; V262;
AO387; BR250   9823
Sebaste (Stainer) [MFSM, LS
DMRR, DDTLSD] F18; G637;
W281; AL552; AP664; BY
695   9824
-----. V [MMMMMMMFSM,
LLLLLL] F18   9825
Sebastian (Bach) X Nicht so
traurig   9826
Sebastian (Freylinghausen G-B.)
[MRFMRMRD, MMRMFFS]
A78; E118; X139   9827
Sebastian (Hodges) [SSSFFMM
R, MFSMRRR, M] B81   9828
Sebastian (Wesley) [MMFMRDTD,
MLSFRDTD,] V550; BE294
                           9829
Sebastian (Wesley, S.S.) X
Almsgiving   9830
Seccomb (Morse) [MMMFMMR
DTRD, MFMLS] BE217
                           9831
Second coming (Morris) [MMM
SSSLMS, SLTDLT, F] AT125
                           9832
-----. R [DTLMSLTRDR,
TRFLLT]   9833
Second mode melody (Tallis)
[LLTDLTTLLSLTTL, LR]
E3; O512   9834

-----. V [LDTDLTTLLSLTTL,
LR] O512   9835
Second Parish (Busch) [SSDDRDT,
DRD#RR#M, SSD] AM353
                      9836
Security (Widéen) [SLSMFMDRD,
MDTMMLS] BE112   9837
Sedgwick (Bristol) [SMMMFSDTL,
SLTDRRM,] J515b   9838
Sedulius (Nürnbergisches G-B.)
[LDRMSDRMR, RMFSMRR] F57a
                      9839
Sedulius (Piae cantiones) X Puer
nobis   9840
See, amid the winter snow (Goss)
[DRDTLSS, DRFMMRR, DR]
K532; W51; AM158; BG190a;
BV119; BY107   9841
-----. R [SSFMRDT, SSFMRDT,
DR]   9842
See! amid the Winter's snow
(---) [DRMFMRD, SLSDLTD,
DR] BO153   9843
-----. R [SSSFMFS, SSSFMFS,
DR] BO153   9844
See, amid the winter's snow
(Catholic) [SFMSDLS, RMLSSFM
R, S] BQ5   9845
-----. R [SLL#SL#LFLLS, SLL#
SL#L]   9846
See! amid the winter's snow
(Mendelssohn) X Mendelssohn
                      9847
See He comes (Young) [MMMDR
MRD, RFFSLLS, M] BP8 9848
See Him in the garden lone
(Showalter) X The garden
                      9849
See, O God, we children come
(---) [LMMMMRDRD, DTLSLLM]
BH147   9850
See, the mighty angel flying!
(Stephens) [SSDTRDTD, TDRR#M
FT, S] BC342   9851
See the shining dewdrops (Kleiner
liederschatz, 1901) [MMRRDS,
DDTDR, FRTSS] AW407   9852
Seeds of promise (Fillmore) [SS
LTDRMDL, RDTLTDT,] AW498
                      9853
-----. R [SSTRFTDMS, SSTRF
SM,]   9854
Seedtime (Wilson) [MRDTTLTDS

SS, DTRDT] U74   9855
Seedtime and harvest (Hunter)
[MSLSMSFMMRD, DFDRM]
AX583   9856
Seek ye a Patron? (Montani)
[MMMSDTDR, RRRFTD,
DD] BQ98   9857
Seek ye the Lord (Laufer)
[SDRSM, LRMLF, MTRDTL]
AE458; AR625   9858
Seeking for me (Hasty) [SFM
MRDRDLL, SDDDRM] AU
14; AX31   9859
-----. R [STRSFMD, STRFL
SM, SF]   9860
Seelenbrautigam (Drese) X
Rochelle   9861
Seelye (Burnap) [SDDTFLLS,
DMMRFMD, S] AO233;
AW134   9862
Sefton (Calkin) [MMRDSSFM,
DTLSF#F#SS,] B366; C
366; D279b; I326; AY415
                      9863
Sefton (Crosbie) [SMDTTLS
D, FMRDTDR, S] W375;
BY210a   9864
Segne uns (Rosenmüller) X
Nassau   9865
Segur (Holbrook) [SMDTRDL
SM, MFSRRSF] L204a; R
339b; U29; V333a; Y366;
AG158b; AI73; AR546 9866
Sei du mir gegrüsset (Enchiri-
dion. Lubeck) [DRMDFM,
RDDTD, MFSML] Q202
                      9867
Seir (Mason) [MFMDRDRD, R
RSTLSLS,] H295; L11
                      9868
Selby (Eyre) [MMMMFSTD,
DLSFMMR, R] F196b
                      9869
Selena (Woodbury) [SSSLSSF#
S, TTDRDDTD,] G137; I153;
T374b; AJ273; AS365; BB
243; BC76; BZ   9870
Seliger friede (Gesangbuch mit
noten) [MR#MFMDTDR,
MR#MFMDT] AW157 9871
Selma (Scottish trad: Isle of
Aaron) [DMRDRMS, SLS
MSLL, LS] E290; S299a;

W249; X10; AG226; AL657;
AP57; BE314; BN46   9872
Selnecker (Selnecker) [DDTLDR
D, DDRTSDT, T] A149; E126;
Q122; X435; AA174; AN487;
AZ10-A; BA775   9873
-----. V [DDTLDTD, DDRTTDT,
TD] Q122   9874
-----. V [DDTLTDRD, DDRTLS
DT] X435   9875
-----. V [DDTLTDRD, DDRTRD
T, T] AZ10-A   9876
Selvin (German trad) [MMRMSFF,
MRMFLSS, DD] G321; I446;
AI335; BB249   9877
Selwood (Staniforth) X Jerusalem
                            9878
Selworthy (Greenwood) [DMLSM
RDRM, SLSF#S, MS] BE28 9879
Selwyn (Mendelssohn) [SDRMR
FMMR, DDDDTRR] D265a; I379;
T272b; V317; AJ154   9880
Semper (Casson) X Semper as-
pectimus   9881
Semper aspectimus (Casson) [S
SFMMMRD, SLTDTLS, L] O
490; BA441   9882
Send me light (Hugg) [SSDMMDL
S, DRRDRM, MS] AX505; AY
75   9883
-----. R [MRDDLS, DRMMRDR,
MFS]   9884
Send the light (Gabriel) X McCabe
                            9885
Sennen (Sherwin) X Chautauqua
                            9886
Sennen Cove (Harris) [SMDFRD
RTD, MRMTDLS,] F528a; BV
655; BY661   9887
Sentinel (Cooke)   [MSDRMRDTL,
LTDTLDR] F308a   9888
Septem verba (Schumacher) [LTD
DRRM, DRMMF#F#S, LS] Q180
                            9889
Septem voces (Hoyte) X Lebbaeus
(St Alban's Tunebook, 1866)
                            9890
Septem voces I (Lewars) [LLDD
RRM, MRFMRRM, MS] K84a1
                            9891
Septem voces II (Lewars) [LMM
RDTL, DSSFMRM, DR] K84a2
                            9892

Septem voces III (Lewars)
[MMSMMRD, MMFSLFFM, M]
K84a3   9893
Septem voces IV (Lewars)
[LDDSLSFM, LDRMRDTD,]
K84a4   9894
Septem voces V (Lewars) [MR
DRMMR, FMRDDRRD, S]
K84a5   9895
Septem voces VI (Lewars)
[DDRDDTD, MRDTLLT, TD]
K84a6   9896
Septem voces VII (Lewars)
[DDDRDTDR, RMDDRMRD,]
K84a7   9897
Septem voces (St Alban's Tune
book, 1866) X Lebbaeus
                            9898
Seraph (Fink) X Bethlehem
                            9899
Seraphim (Alexis) [MRDFM
DMR, SSLSFMR, M] J512a;
N627   9900
Seraphim (Eberhard) X Gre-
gor's 249th metre   9901
Seraphim (Smart) [MRFMLS
FM, DTLSLTLS,] AB55b;
AD96; BX67; BY603   9902
Serenity (Bryan) X Bryan
                            9903
Serenity (Wallace) [MMMFMM
RR, RSRMFM, SS] C404a;
G120; H152; I128; J476b; L
131; N196; P152; R229; S178;
T265a; U9; V135; Y68; Z254;
AB171; AC140; AD250; AE
93; AF230; AG116; AH424;
AI113; AJ369; AK242; AN
561; AO213; AR201; AS84;
AT277; AV178; AW173; BA
82; BB141; BD70; BE23; BF
246; BK91; BZ   9904
-----. V [MMMFMMRR, RS
RMFM, FS] T265a   9905
Sering (Sering) [SMDRDLLSS
D, MRMRRM] M625   9906
Serug (Wesley. European Palm-
ist) [DTDRDTD, MRDFMR,
DTL] AF265; AK5; AL5;
AN364; BE355   9907
Serve the Lord with gladness
(McKinney) X Lee   9908
Service (Nares) X Amsterdam

9909
Service (Webster) [SSMLSSFF,
MMRDRM, SL] I414   9910
Serving the Lord in song (Hilde-
brand) [SLTDRMD, DMLSF#
S, SSS] AY524   9911
-----. R [DDDLLSM, DDDSD
R, RRR]   9912
Sessions (Emerson) [SLSDSLSDRM,
RRMRRM] G224; H157; I342;
L58; T141; U186; V318; AJ209;
AO595; AX455; BB179   9913
Sevenfold Amen (Lutkin) [MSDTL,
DFMR, TMRDMSF] AMp. xvii
9914
Seventh mode melody (Tallis)
[DSRMFS, SLSSF#S, DSRM]
E496   9915
Severn (Howells) [DSFMFSDR,
FMRD, DSFS] X582   9916
Sewell (Sewell) [SMFSDRMR#M,
MRDTDRD] AT194   9917
-----. R [MFMMRL, RMRRDSD,
DDT]   9918
Sewey (Weyse) X Christmas
brings joy   9919
Seymour (Weber) [MRFMLSMR,
MMMMFTD, M] A177b; B19;
C19a; D13; G200; H30; I267;
K465; L30; M573; N379; O561;
P71; R60; S34; T311; U173;
V49; Y89; Z145; AA7; AB26;
AC217; AD54; AE48; AG25;
AH171; AI56; AJ67; AK53;
AM347; AN66; AO40; AP677;
AR59; AS199; AT33; AU225;
AV164; AW36; AY438; AZ11-S;
BA287; BB48; BC162; BD9; BE
365; BF374; BK46; BR107;
BX98; BZ   9920
Shackelford (Cheeswright) [SLS
MDRLL, TLSFFM, SL] U50;
Y48; AB259; AC326; BB94;
BD53; BK128   9921
Shaddick (Burt) [SMRDDRRM,
RMSLLT, S] A419; BZ   9922
Shakespeare's carol I (Arne)
[SFMRDLDDT, DRMFRSF]
BG171a   9923
Shakespeare's carol II (Stevens)
[SDDDRMFMR, TDRMFSL]
BG171b   9924
Shall I be ashamed (Byers) [DM

MR#MSSLSF#S, MMRDR]
AX343   9925
Shall I let Him in (Palmer)
X Christ is knocking   9926
Shall the youth of Sion falter?
(Stephens) [SDMMMRDFM,
MRDDRR#M] BC157   9927
-----. R [MMMMMMFFFFM
R, FFFF]   9928
Shall we gather (Lowry) X
Beautiful river   9929
Shall we know each other there
(Showalter) [SSDDRDRMS,
SLSMMRD] AY150   9930
Shall we meet (Rice) [DRMSLS
SDT, DRRMRDS,] AS482;
AU85; AX602; AY163; BB
557; BC156   9931
-----. R [DMRRFM, MMRMF
MMR, DR]   9932
Shall you? shall I? (McGrana-
han) [MMMMRMDDM, SMLS
SML] AX291; BB568   9933
Shalom (Jewish trad) [LRRM
FRMMFS, SRDL, LR] AQ160
9934
Shamokin (Fischer) X Laus
regis   9935
Shanghai (Chinese mel) [LLDL
SMSDDLSM, SSLS] X17
9936
Shanghai (Chinese mel) X
P'u T'o   9937
Sharon (Boyce) X Boyce   9938
Sharon (Hemy) X Siloam   9939
Sharon (Ouseley) [DDSDFM
RD, MRS#LDTLS,] F617
9940
Shawmut (Mason) [MMMSSM,
LLLLS#L, MMMM] I265
9941
Shawnee (Angell) [MMMMMMM
MMM, MMMMMMM] AT516
9942
Shechem (---) [DMRDMSFM,
DRMFSFMR] H118   9943
Sheen (Holst) [SLDRMDTLS
DFMRDD, D] E310; F417;
X496   9944
Sheer hamaalos (Jewish trad)
[LTDTLLRMFMR, RDMTM]
BH122   9945
Sheer hasheereem I (Jewish

trad) [MSLLSF#SLM,DMSM
RDR] BH105   9946
Sheer hasheerem II (Jewish trad)
[DDMLDSSSM,DDMSFMR]
BH192   9947
Sheffield (English trad) [SDSDR
MR,MFSDMRDTD,] Y244;
Z257; AD177   9948
Sheffield (Mather) X Medfield
9949
Sheffield (Root) [SSSLSSD,DR
RRRDRM,S] AT220; AU170;
AX243   9950
-----. R [MDDLSSTLSSD,MD
DL,S]   9951
Sheldonian (Taylor) [MMSMRD
RMSL,SLTDTL] BY240
9952
Shelter (Ohl) [MMMMMRRS,
SSMRDDF,F] K396   9953
Shelter (Sankey) X O safe to the
Rock   9954
Sheltered Dale (German trad)
[SMMMRMFRT,SDDDTDR,]
G455; Z323; AD273; AR369;
BF392   9955
Sheltering wing (Barnby) X
Westcott   9956
Sheng en (Su Yin-lan) [DDRMDR
MDLL,LDDLDD] R450; BZ
9957
Shepherd (Bradbury) X Pleasant
pastures   9958
Shepherd (Ogden) X Bring them
in   9959
Shepherd (Sullivan) [SSLSMFSF,
RSDTLT,SS] AA560   9960
Shepherd care (Ukranian mel)
[LTDTLTL,DDRMDR,RMF]
AL492   9961
-----. R [MLLTD,TRRRR,
DTLFM,R]   9962
Shepherd true (---) [SFMSDDDT,
RLRFFFM,D] AL484; AP422
9963
Shepherds in the field (French
carol mel) X Gloria 9964
Shepherds in the field abiding
(Traditional) [LTDTLDTLSLM,
LTDTL] BP19   9965
Shepherds left their flocks a-
straying (Hohenfurth ms) X

Quem pastores   9966
Shepherds' pipes (Gay) [MLDT
SLLSM,MLDTSL,M] AF328;
BZ   9967
Shepherds, shake off your
drowsy sleep (French trad)
X Besançon carol   9968
Shepton-Beauchamp (English
trad) [DTTDMRRMR,
RRMRSRM] E389; AP544b
9969
Sherborne (Mendelssohn) X
Cyprus   9970
Shere (Thiman) [DMSDRM,MRS
DTSLS,DF] BV331; BY434
9971
Sherwin I (Sherwin) [DSSDDTT,
RSSRRDD,MS] AC106; AV
402   9972
Sherwin II (Sherwin) [MRDS
DTDRMSFM,DTDR] BB375
9973
-----. R [RMFMSLSMR,SFM
RDTL]   9974
Shield (Barnby) X Kirkdale
9975
Shields (---) [DRMMMRRDM
M,DMSMRD] AY243   9976
Shiloh (Anderson) [MRDTLS#
TL,DTLTDRFM,] W104
9977
Shine in my heart, Lord Jesus
(Kolb) [SLTDTTL,LSSDDR,
SRR] AX385; AY81   9978
Shining day (Ebeling) [SDRMS
RD,SDRMSRD,] A313; X
692; AN477   9979
Shining Shore (Root) [SSDDRM
DR,MDMRDLD,L] L569;
U417; V657; AS474; AV288;
AW503; AX571; AY89; BR
522   9980
-----. R [MSMSLSMR,MSM
LSMR,S]   9981
Ship of State (Kinder) [SDSFM
RDDT,LSLTDRM] Y290
9982
Shipston (English trad) [DMSL
SFMRMD,DMSLSM] E390;
W495b; X364; AD38; AL622a;
AN123; AQ272; BB430; BV
348; BY726   9983

Shirland (Stanley) [DRMFRSTD,
DTRSMLSF#] D501; H56; I512;
L93; V316; AM280b; AW129
9984
Shirleyn (Harper) [SSLTDRDRM,
MFMRMDR,] G112; Z206; BZ
9985
Shiveesee (Sulzer) [LLL, LLL,
LLDDRM, MMDL] BH336
9986
Sh'ma Yisroayl (Binder) [MMMM
MMLMMSFFFDFM,] BH280
9987
Sh'ma Yisroayl I (Jewish trad)
[MDRM, DDFDRMR, DRMRR,]
BH290   9988
Sh'ma Yisroayl II (Jewish trad)
[MMRDTL, MSRRMD, MLRM,]
BH314   9989
Sh'ma Yisroayl III (Jewish trad)
[MMRDTL, MSFMMRMLTD]
BH338   9990
Sh'ma Yisroayl I (Sulzer) [MM
MDS, SDRMRMSM, DDR] BH
269   9991
Sh'ma Yisroayl II (Sulzer) [MM
MMMR#, MMSSSSSF, FF] BH
306   9992
Sh'meenee atseres (Schalit) X
A week within the sukko green
9993
Sh'meenee atseres (Weinberg) X
A week within the sukko green
9994
Shoemaker (Pollock) [MRDSRM
FM, MRDRDTD, R] AY40
9995
Sholom Alaychem (Goldfarb) [MD
TLLS#LTLS#FMMS#S#L] AH146;
BH278   9996
Shoreham (Dykes) [MMMFMRLS,
SDTLSFFM] O553   9997
Shortle (Goodrich) [DMSSLTD
SS, MSLLTDR] I664a; T285;
AJ393; AM289   9998
Should we meet here no more
(Teasley) X The last farewell
9999
Should you feel inclined to censure
(Bliss) X Lower lights 10000
Shout the glad tidings (Avison)
X Avison   10001
Showalter (Showalter) [MMFFMRR

D, MFSSLLS, M] AR218;
AS169   10002
Showalter (Showalter) X Lean-
ing on Jesus   10003
Showers of blessing (McGranahan)
[SSSSLTDS, TTTTDRD, L]
AH389; AI262; AM716; AT
264; AU97; AX37; BB652
10004
-----. R [MR#MDS, MRDRTDR,
MMMR]   10005
Shrewsbury (Hunt) [MSMRDTL
LS, SLTDRR, S] F230b; BV
223a   10006
Sialkot (Stebbins) [SMRDSTL
S, DLTDFMRD,] AJ177
10007
Siberia (German mel) [SFMDR
TDS, LTDLSMR, S] D61b;
AO123   10008
Sicilian hymn (Sicilian mel)
X Sicilian mariners   10009
Sicilian mariners (Sicilian
mel) [SLSFMFSLSFM, SSLT
D] A247; B51; C51; D34;
F410; G26; H37; J191a; K
431; L44; M16; N354; R79;
S54; T456; U448; V27b; Z
127; AA17; AD65; AE33; AF
63; AG13; AH176; AI26; AJ
413; AK35; AL304; AM319;
AN470; AO49; AP782; AR
48; AS140; AT31; AV23; AW
45; AX79; AZ16-L; BA165;
BB33; BE119; BF207; BI3;
BK172; BN126; BO112; BP
86; BQ88; BR120; BX510;
BZ   10010
-----. V [SLSFMSLSFM,
SSLTDT] BP86   10011
Sicilian mariners' hymn (Sicilian
mel) X Sicilian mariners
10012
Sicily (Sicilian mel) X Sicilian
mariners   10013
Sidmouth (Dale) [MLTRDFMM,
RSLSFMDR] BY633   10014
Sidney (Poppen) [SLSMSMFM
DM, RD#RMFS] M446 10015
Sidon (Crotch) [MLSFMLRDT
D, DSFMRM] W549b   10016
Sidwell (Beethoven) [SSSSS#
LSFFM, SSS#LMR] BR265

10017
Sieh hier bin ich, Ehrenkönig
(Neander) [MMLLSSFMD,
SMLSFFM,] K273; M114; N
352; O276; P397; Q56; AA131;
AZ585-H   10018
-----. V [MMLLSSMD, SMLS
FFM, R] P397   10019
-----. V [MMLLSFMD, SMLSFF
M, R] Q56   10020
Sienna (Deane) [SLSDTLS, SS#
S#LFR, MR#M] U123; V185
                                   10021
Silas (Silas) [LRTDTLS#LT
M, LLSSFF] W84   10022
Silcher I (Freylinghausen G-B.,
1704) X Luebeck   10023
Silcher II (Silcher) [MDSSDRMM,
MMF#SSLLS,] AA464   10024
Silcher (Silcher) X So nimm denn
meine hände   10025
Silchester (Malan) [SSMFSLS,
SLDTLSFM, D] AP318   10026
Silchester (Stanton) [MRDRS, DRM
SFM, LSTDR] BY202   10027
Silent (Bixel) [LDLLS#LTS#M
RDTLS#F#S#] AW77   10028
Silent night (Gruber) X Holy
night   10029
Silently bury the dead (Leslie)
X Silently, they pass away
                                   10030
Silently, they pass away (Leslie)
[SMDMDD, DTRD, SMD, MSS]
AX616; AY186   10031
Silesius (Mann) [MRMSFMRD,
RMF#SDTLS,] I367   10032
Silesius (Schein) X Eisenach
                                   10033
Silksworth (Vincent) [DRMDRMFM,
LTDRMF#S, R] Z531   10034
Siloam (Hemy) [SSSDTDRSD, DL
TDMRD] C351; D565; I588;
L83; V623; AO432   10035
Siloam (Horsman) [SLDFMRMR,
RSDDDF, FM] B401b   10036
Siloam (Woodbury) [MFSMLSM
DMR, RMSMRF] H451; I281;
L606; M282; S349; T131; V650;
AD400; AI375; AJ191; AL218;
AN438; AO431; AR618; AS394;
AY363; BA838; BB340; BX517
                                   10037

Silver Street (Smith) [DSS
MSD, MRSDLSF#S,] A552;
B346; C346a; D509a; G22;
H4; I3; K384b; L81; M255;
N508; T88; U147; V106; X
635; Z118; AA328; AI14; AJ
130; AM102; AO69; AS77;
AV28; BA285; BD100; BX
22; BY282a   10038
Silverton (Bradbury) [SDMRDTL
S, SDRMDR, RR] AJ395
                                   10039
Simchas Torah (Jewish trad)
[DSSLSFSMD, DSTDDFM]
BH200   10040
Simcoe (Cringan) [SLTDDLTDF
MR, DRMFM] AP157b
                                   10041
Simeon (Stanley) [SSFMFMRD,
DFMSFTDR,] E320; Sap. 12;
X551; AL514; BV575; BY
196a   10042
Simon (Strover) [DTSLMRDM
SL, RDTLSD] BV193a   10043
Simonside (Harker) [DTRDFM
LS, DDRRR, SFM] BB420
                                   10044
Simplicity (Stainer) [SLSMFS
M, MRDDSFMR, S] F451;
W662b; AP760; BA820   10045
Simpson (Spohr) X Spohr
                                   10046
Sin can never enter there (War-
ren) [SSDDDRMSSLLLTD,
LL] AX283   10047
-----. R [DDDTTRD, MMM
RRFM, SS]   10048
Sinai (Barnby) [SDDTDLLS,
MRRDTLT, S] I600   10049
Sinai's Height (Jewish trad,
"Akdamos mode") [SMDD
DDRDTLL, LLMRL] AH148;
BH143   10050
Since I have been redeemed
(Excell) X Othello   10051
Since Jesus did appear (Good)
[SDMFMRMD, TLLMRR,
SD] AX551; AY295   10052
Since o'er thy footstool
(Everett) X Magnificence
                                   10053
Sine nomine (Williams) [SM
RDSLDRSM, MRRDT] A126a;

C295b; E641; G527; J144a; Q
463; R425a; S429b; W220; X
202; Y345; Z577; AC330a;
AD461a; AF306; AG284b; AK
418; AL174a; AN428a; AP310c;
AQ75; AR419; BB364; BE66;
BK76; BL70; BV460; BY7; BZ
                                    10054
Sing about Jesus (Warren) [SS
SLSSDRM, FMRMDRS] AX5
                                    10055
-----. R [MMMSLSDRM, FMRM
RDT]   10056
Sing aloud on this day (Piae can-
tiones, 1582) X Theodoric
                                    10057
Sing glory, hallelujah (Mason)
[SDTDLSSS, SLLFMMR, R]
AR188; AS148   10058
Sing my tongue (Essay on the
church plain chant. 1782) X
Dulce carmen   10059
Sing my tongue (A Monk of Geth-
semani) [LLDDMFSR, MMDT
LLR, T] BN102   10060
Sing my tongue, the Saviour's
glory (Wade) X St Thomas
                                    10061
Sing praise to Him (Bohemian Br)
X Bohemian Brethren   10062
Sing, sing, ye angel bands
(Catholic) [DMRDLS, SMM
DMMR, RRR] BO66   10063
Sing the Holy Family's praises
(Andachtige ...) X Wurzburg
                                    10064
Sing them over again to me (Bliss)
X Wonderful words   10065
Sing to the Sovereign of the skies
(Levenson) [DSSLMFMRS, SM
SLSFM,] BH67   10066
Sing we now at parting (Beesley)
[MRDSSM, DSLSMR, MRDS]
BC161   10067
Sing we triumphant (Bragers) [S
SMRDSLLS, LTDSLSF] BP42
                                    10068
Sing with joy (Bamberg) [DS
LTDRMD, DLRDTLLS,] BM
36   10069
Singen wir aus herzens grund
(German, 1544) [LDTLS#LT,
TDRMDTL, TD] O110; P103

                                    10070
Singt dem Herrn, nah und fern
(Joseph) X Gregor's 225th
metre   10071
Sinner's friend (Freylinghausen.
G-B. 1704) [DMMRSDFMR,
MSRRMDT] M267; Q362;
AA109; AZ218-A   10072
Sinners Jesus will receive
(McGranahan) X Neumeister
                                    10073
Sinners' Redeemer (Hutton.
Tunes for the hymns) X
Old 583d   10074
Sion (Hastings) [SSSMDSLS,
DDRRDTD, S] H114; I91;
L290; T160; U122; V140b;
Z393; AE235; AH406; AI177;
AJ237; AM275; AO114; AR
286; AS246; AT56; AU181;
AV43; AW336; AX102; AY
211; BA694; BB184   10075
Sion (Mason's Companion) [SF
MRDSLTD, DTLSLSF] X
341   10076
Sion (Morley) X Holborn 10077
Sion (Smart) [SSMRDS, DDRS
M, SSM] A559; B523; C529b;
D523b; J565; L542; S369;
W579; AB218; AD227; AH
362; AZ141-I; BA575; BF382
                                    10078
-----. R [SSMRDS, DFSDL,
LSFS]   10079
Sion quadrata (Docker) [MMSDR
MRD, LTDMRDT, T] BR220
                                    10080
Sion stands with hills sur-
rounded (Hastings) X Sion
                                    10081
Sion stands with hills surrounded
(Smyth) [SLSMFMMRSRD,
LFLSM] BC212   10082
Sion's daughter (Dutch trad)
[SSLSDDTD, DSLSDDTL] BG
                                    10083
Sion's daughters (French) [DRM
DSLSMFS, LTDSLS] Eap. 7
                                    10084
Sion's glad morning (Harmonia
sacra) [SSMSLDRMRDDLS,
SSM] AX104; AY487   10085
Sion's praise (Bourgeois) [MM

MLMFMRD, RMRDTL, M] AJ
419   10086
Sir Christèmas (English carol)
[DDDTLTLSMF#S, DRMRD]
BG21   10087
-----. R [DDTLSS, DRMRDLTD,
SL]   10088
Sister, thou wast mild (Lewis)
[DDTRMLRDT, FMRSMDR]
BC381   10089
Sister, thou wast mild (Mason)
X Mount Vernon   10090
Sitting at the feet of Jesus (---)
X Deliverer   10091
Sitting at the feet of Jesus (Davis)
[MMMMFFMD, DDDDDRM, M]
AX47   10092
-----. R [SSSSLLSM, RRRRDRM,
S]   10093
67th Psalm (Scottish Psalter, 1615)
[SDRRMRMFFS, FMRDTD] E
291; BJ89   10094
Skader, skader nu här alle
(Swedish koralbok. 1697) [TM
S#LTRDT, TDLTS#LT, T]
N112   10095
Skara (Sewall) [MRDFMRDTD
R, MFRSMR] BR38   10096
Skara (Widéen) [LMRDTLDRM,
F#S#LTDTL] J218a   10097
S'lach no (Lewandowski) [DDLTD,
MMRSLTD, DTLT] BH320
                                       10098
Slain for my soul (Young) [DMF#
SDFMMRD, DLTDLR] BP27
                                       10099
Slane (Irish trad) [DDRDLSSLD
DRM, RRR] A122; R303; S325;
W477; X565; Z321; AD307; AE
449; AF217; AG174; AL336; AR53;
AT62; BF386; BV571; BY462;
BZ   10100
-----. V [DDRDLSLDDRM, RRR
RM] R303   10101
-----. V [DDRDLSSLDDRM,
SMRR] AR53   10102
Sleep (Lee) [MR#MFMRMFFM,
LLSMRR] BB491   10103
Sleep, downy sleep (Clark) X
Uffingham   10104
Sleep, holy Babe (---) [MMMS,
MDDRRMD, MMMSM] BO152
                                       10105

Sleep, holy Babe (Reichardt)
X Schlaf, Kindlein, schlaf
                                       10106
Sleep till that morning (Show-
alter) [MR#MDSLDS, DDDDT
DRR] AX618; AY169   10107
-----. R [DTDR, RFFFM,
RDTRD.]   10108
Sleepers, wake (Nicolai) [DM
SSSSLS, SDSDRMRDTLS]
A3; B62; C62; D40a; E12;
F55; J7; K5; L214; M199;
N199; O80; P426; Q444; W
162; X687; Y352; AA549;
AB153; AD173; AF24; AI
446; AK96; AL134; AM231;
AN486; AO115; AP242; AQ
17; AR207; AW522; AZ230-
A; BA103; BB197; BI17-D;
BK56; BR132; BV77   10109
-----. V [DMSSSSLS, SDT
DMRMR] N199   10110
-----. V [DMSSSSLL, SDTD
MRDR] P426   10111
-----. V [DMSSSSLSLS, SDS
DMR] Q444   10112
-----. V [DMF#SSLDTL, SSDT
DMR] AZ230-A   10113
-----. V [DMSSSSLS, SDSDRM
RD] BR132   10114
Sleeping on guard (Davis) [SS
SSMDSM, FFFSFRM, S] BB
501   10115
Slingsby (Carter) [SSSDTLLLR,
TTDRMMR] D574b; I88a; U
24; V649; Z178; AE244; AP
716; BE340; BF244; BR499b
                                       10116
Slingsby (Dykes) X St Bede
                                       10117
Slovakia (Slovak trad) [DDMF#
SLS, F#SLS, SSFFM] M359
                                       10118
Slumber, O slumber (Polish
carol) [MMRMFFMRRFLS,
MMRM] BN22   10119
Smart (Smart) X Eventide
                                       10120
Smart (Smart) X Sion   10121
Smiley (Summers) X Palmyra
                                       10122
Smith (Howard) [MMSFMRDRL
TD, RMF#SD] L271; AL687;

AM571; AP218; BV479   10123
-----. V [MMSFMRDRLTD, RM
F#SR] AL687   10123a
Smithville (---) [SFMRDTDR,
DSSS#LF#S, S] AY99   10124
Smitten Rock (Spencer-Palmer)
[MFLDTL, RDTDLS, SLMF]
BV378   10125
Snow in the street (Williams)
[LDRMLSMR, DFSMRDDF]
BG186   10126
Snowden (Robertson) [MMMMMFFF,
MRRRRSFM,] AJ118   10127
Snowdon (Halstead) [DMFSSDDRD
T, LLSMMR] BB96   10128
So, brother (French trad) [ML
DTRDL, DTLS#TL, MLD] BC
106   10129
So fuehrst du doch recht selig
(Darmstadt G-B.) X Gregor's
192d metre   10130
So fürst du hoch Stötzel. (Choral-
buch. Stuttgart) [SDRMDFM
RMRD, MRDTR] K416; M262
10131
So gehst du nun, mein Jesu, hin
(Nachtenhöfer) X Cross-bearer
10132
So giebst du (Dresden G-B. 1694)
[DMRDMRDDTD, MSFMMD]
E515; X123   10133
So lange Jesus bleibt der Herr
(Gesangbuch mit noten) [SSSSS
LLS, DDDTLSF#S,] AW301
10134
So let our lips and lives confess
(Mason) X Uxbridge   10135
So nimm denn meine hände
(Silcher) [SLSFMMR, MFSM,
SLSFM] J292; M548; P312;
AK312; AR299; AW561; AX504
10136
So sweet and clear (Strachauer)
[SLSDRDTDMDDT, SLSR] BI89
10137
-----. R [SDTR, SRDM, MMMM
RMFR]   10138
So wahr ich leb spricht Gott der
Herr (Schott) [LLTDRMRD,
MSFMRDTL,] AA426   10139
Spode Jesu, vi er her (Ahle)
X Liebster Jesu   10140

Softly and tenderly (Thompson)
[MRDDTDRDLLS, DDDMR]
G239; H262; J578; V753;
Z283; AE165; AG135; AH331;
AL494; AM694; AP409; AR
250; AT236; AU100; AV339;
AW456; AX221; AY502; BB
563   10141
-----. R [SRMDRM, RRRMM
F#SF#F, M]   10142
Softly beams the sacred dawn-
ing (Careless) X O thou
kind and gracious Father
10143
Softly now the light of day
(Weber) X Seymour   10144
Softly the night is sleeping
(Warner) [SF#SDSMFS, MRR
MFSM, S] AZ151-W; BA57
10145
-----. R [RDMS, SMSD, DMD
SMFSL]   10146
Soho I (Barnby) [SSLTDDTDR,
FMSF#MRS,] D554a; G309;
I285; N534; W653; AC13;
AM350   10147
Soho II (Silcher) X Morning
10148
Sohren (Sohren) [LLTDRMM,
MLLS#L, LLT] A556a
10149
Sohren (Sohren) X Gute baume
bringen   10150
Sojourner (Mallary) [DRMFMR
D, RMFSLS, SDD] T50b; AJ
271   10151
Sol justitiae (Margetson) [MM
SFMRD, RRRMF#LS, DT] BR
90   10152
Sol praeceps rapitur (Paris.
Antiphoner, 1681) [MFMRSS
LD, DLDTLSS, L] F37
10153
Soldau (Walther G-B. 1524)
[DRRDLSLD, MSLSMDLD] J236;
M474; O39; Q231; R389; S102;
W140; AA260; AL122b; AM33;
AP269a; AZ58-A, 58-B; BA
279   10154
-----. V [DRRDLSLTD, MSL
SMDL] M474   10155
-----. V [DRRDSLTD, MSLS

MDTL] O39   10156
-----. V [DRRDLSDDTD, MSLSM
D] AZ58-B   10157
-----. V [DRRDLSDDTD, MSLS
MR] AZ58-A   10158
Soldau Pt II (Walther G-B) [MMM
RMRD, RRRMRD, RRR] AZ58-C
10159
Soldiers of Christ (Merrill) [SS
SDSL, LLLRLT, SSSD] S269;
AM482; BA583   10160
Soldiers of the cross (Negro
spiritual) X Jacob's ladder
10161
Solemnis haec festivitas (Paris.
Gradual, 1689) [DMFSSLSFS,
SLTDSMM] E123c; M78; X33b;
AN293; BY21   10162
-----. V [DMFSSLSFS, SLTDSM
F] AN293   10163
Solid Rock (Bradbury) X The
solid Rock   10164
Solitude (Downes) [SF#SMDTLS,
SRMFMRLS,] G612; H153;
I307; L319; N359; Sap. 41; V
320; AA126; BR255   10165
Solitude (Everett) X Everett
10166
Solitude (Showalter) X O for a
heart to praise my God   10167
Soll en nun die gruenen jahre
(Thommen. Christen-schatz)
X Cassel   10168
Soll's sein (Drie schöne neue
geistliche lieder. 1637) [MSFM
RDRT, TDRMFRD, M] E288;
X8; BD38; BE96; BY66   10169
Sollt es gleich bisweilen scheinen
(Fritsch) [MMLLSFM, SLSDDT
D, SM] AA516   10170
Sollt' ich meinem Gott nicht
singen (Schop) [LLMLS#S#LL,
DTLSLF#M, L] Q25; AA65;
AK16; AZ214-A; BA28   10171
-----. V [LDRMLLS#LL, DTLS
FFM,] AK16   10172
-----. V [LTDRMLLS#LL,
DTLSFF] AZ214-A   10173
Solomon (Handel) [DMFSSLLS,
SLSTDR, SL] E80; S313; X110;
AA267; AL346a; BR415; BX56;
BY58a   10174
Solon (American trad) X Amazing

grace   10175
Solothurn (Swiss trad) [DDRM
DSRD, SSLTSDLS,] E243;
F448; R305; S477; W436b;
X239; AB131; AD394; AN
79a; BE385; BV452; BY677
10176
Som hønen klukker mindelig
(Winding) X Winding II
10177
Som torstige hjort (Lindeman)
[DSSFMRDLS, SDDTTLS]
O453; P250   10178
Some day the silver cord will
break (Stebbins) X Saved by
grace   10179
Some near, near day (Pollock)
[SMR#MRDLD, LSSDRM
RD] AX536; AY140   10180
-----. R [DRD#RMDLD, LSS
DRMRD]   10181
Some sweet day (Chord) [MR
DDRRM, SLSMR, MRDD] AS
479; AX623; AY493   10182
-----. R [FFM, SMR, MRD
DRMFMRD,]   10183
Some sweet day (Towner) [DR
MDRMD, DMSMDR, DRM]
AU271   10184
Some time we'll see (King)
[SMMMRDRM, FSLSMMRD]
AX570; AY345   10185
-----. R [MSLSMMRD, DRM
FRMFS,]   10186
Some time we'll understand
(McGranahan) [SMRDMSDT,
TTFLTLSM,] AH386; AI
292; AV388; AX619; BB495;
BC267   10187
-----. R [RRRRRMRS, SRS
F#RDLS,]   10188
Somebody follows you (Henson)
[MMRDMMSSLS, MMRDMR,]
AX443   10189
-----. R [SSLSMS, MMRDMR,
MMRD]   10190
Somebody needs your love
(McKinney) [MR#MSLSDRR#
M, SRMFSF] AU442   10191
-----. R [DMLSF#F, LRMF
SLS, DTR]   10192
Somerset (Barnes) [DDTLLTD
RSS, MMRDMR] AD453

10193
Somerset (Hewlett) [DMSDTLFM,
RDMLTS, LL] G313; AL203b
10194
Somerset carol (English carol)
[DDSSLSMD, TDTMFS, DS]
BG8   10195
Somerset wassail (English trad)
[DDLSFMRDDRMFS, DDL]
BG32   10196
-----. R [SSDRS, SSDRMF,
MFSDL]   10197
Somervell (Somervell) [DRMFM
LSDT, LTDSFMF] F185b; BL
88; BO1; BV270a; BY217b
10198
Something for Jesus (Garrison)
[DRMMMRMSM, MRRRDRM,]
BB658   10199
-----. R [SLLDTLSM, DRRRDR
MS,]   10200
Something for Jesus (Lowry)
[MFMRLR, DTLTDS, MFMR]
G219; H319; I349; J463; L529;
N499; P325; R311; S396; T378;
U273; V398; Z387; AD257; AE
215; AF331; AG171; AH423; AI
202; AK470; AL478; AM391; AO
641; AP476; AR347; AS278; AT
400; AU149; AV380; AW220;
AY237; BA470; BB283; BF453;
BY485a; BZ   10201
-----. V [MFMRLR, DTLTD, MF
MRL] AY237   10201a
Something for Thee (Lowry) X
Something for Jesus   10202
Something I would tell you (Duncan)
[DRMDMSLS, MRDDRMR, D]
AX334; AY344   10203
-----. R [SSMSLSM, DRMDMM
R, D]   10204
Something to do (Ruebuch) [SS
MMMRDRMFL, TLSFF] AX192;
AY520   10205
-----. R [DTDRFMRMDFM,
DDTLS]   10206
Sommerlied (Bonner) [MDTDLL,
FRTDTS, DRMS] AL595; AM
637; AP722; BV237; BY744
10207
Son of man (Coerne) [MMSSLT
LS, MSDTLTS, M] AC99   10208
Sonata (Mozart) [MFMSSRMRFF,

DDRRMS] AW179   10209
Sonata (Mozart) X Stars of
glory   10209a
Song (German) [DMSSSLTDS,
DMSSSMD] AN73   10210
Song 1 (Gibbons) [SSSDRMMRR
D, MMFSSD] A470; E302;
F402; J350; W489; X296;
AD240; AF275; AL370; BV
419; BY358   10211
Song 3 (Gibbons) [MMRMLDTL,
MFMRDT, TD] BJ38 10212
Song 4 (Gibbons) [MLS#LTD
SLFM, MSF#MRD] E113;
X261   10213
Song 5 (Gibbons) [MMMFRM
DT, TDRMLRD#R,] E483;
F164a; X648; AD235; AF509;
AN204a; BJ23   10214
Song 13 (Gibbons) [MFSLRRM,
SLTDLLS, MF] A451; B219;
D204a; E413; F105a; J130;
K156; O515; Q234; W604;
X134; AF162; AL570a; AN22;
AP695a; BJ24; BR199; BV
165; BY333; BZ   10215
-----. V [MFSLRDM, SLTD
LLS, MF] AN22   10216
Song 18 (Gibbons) [MMDRMDT
L, DDRMMMR#M,] E357;
W428b; X604a; BN74
10217
Song 20 (Gibbons) [MMF#S#LT,
LDLSFM, SSF#S] E442; W
546b; X584; BE397; BJ35;
BV503   10218
-----. V [LLTD#RM, RFRD
L#L, DDTD] BJ35   10219
Song 22 (Gibbons) [SSMLSS
FMSR, RMDFRS] A433; D
280b; E438; F238; J125; W
195; X574; AD207; AN48a;
AR254; BE212; BJ28; BV
374   10220
Song 24 (Gibbons) [DDRMM-
RDTTL, MMF#SSF#] E325;
F397a; R530; S488; W545;
X103; AF207; AN70; AQ167;
BE69; BY564   10221
-----. V [FFSLLSFMMR, LLT
DDT] F397a   10222
-----. V [LM, DDRMMRDTTL,
MMF#S] S488   10223

Song 31 (Gibbons) [MLSMSFM,
SMLSF#F#M, SR] BJ94
10224
Song 34 (Gibbons) X Angel's song
10225
Song 46 (Gibbons) [DMDS, DFFF
MR, RTDLS,] A69; E98; F358a;
W444; X125; AL285a; AP438b;
BV373; BY584   10226
Song 46 (Gibbons) X Bourdillon
10227
Song 67 (Gibbons) [DSMFSLLS,
SDLTTL, D] A404; E197; F
325a; R37; S68; W433a; X204;
AB326; AF336; AL667a; AN202a;
AP82a; AQ73; BE262; BJ56;
BV367; BY599   10228
Song of joy (Campian) [SMLRMF
FFSL, LSFSFM] X639   10230
Song of praise (English trad) [M
SMDDRDRM, MSMDDRM] Z447;
AD186; BK12   10231
-----. V [MSMDDRDRMD,
MSMDDR] BK12   10232
Song of Songs (Baden-Powell)
[DTLSMFSLTD, RMRDTL]
D448b   10233
Song of the branches (Kestel) [S
LDTLSLL, SLDRTDTL,] BL24
10234
Song of the crib (German carol,
14th c) X Resonet in laudibus
10235
Song of the dew (Jewish trad) X
Tal   10236
Song of the Nuns of Chester
(Chester ms. ca 1425) [DRM
RDMSL, DTTSLLS, T] BG67
10237
Song of the pilgrims (Alexander)
[SMSMSMRDRMM, SMSMM]
Y133   10238
Song of the Saviour (Gabriel) [SS
LTDRMF, MRDTLTD, S] AY485
10239
Song of the ship (Andernach G-B.
1608) [LLLTTDRM, MRRLTD,
DM] BG90   10240
Song of the Spirit (Dutch trad)
[SDRMRDD, SSMFSL, DTL]
BG153   10241
Song of the Yangtze Boatmen

(Chinese chantey, trad.)
[LDRDLLDRDL, MRDMRD]
AE197   10242
Songs of praise (Rosenmüller)
X Nassau   10243
Sons of light (Lynes) [SMMM
RDTLTL, SMMMRD] U293
10244
Sons of men, behold (Flood)
[DMSDTLS, FMRDFMR, MS]
BI92   10245
Sons of Michael, He approaches
(Thomas) [DRMDRMFMMR,
SFMFRD] BC163   10246
Soon trials and conflicts
(Doughty) [DMMMMRMFF
FF, MRRRR] AX594; AY
160   10247
Sørg, O kjaere Fader, du
(Lindeman) X Spring of
souls   10248
Sorrows (Powell) [MMMMSM,
LSDRM, MMMMS] Z226
10249
Soto (Mason) [SDDDSDRM,
MSMRTLRS,] AJ410 10250
Soul of my Saviour (Bragers)
[DTLLSLTDMR, DTLLSD]
BP68   10251
Soul of my Saviour (Dobici)
[MFMRRRMDRM, SLSFMM]
BQ47   10252
Soul of my Saviour(Maher) [S
DDDTD, DRRM, MRMDT, T]
BN103; BO29   10253
Sound over the waters (Gil-
christ) [MDLDMD, MDLDM,
FRL#RF] BI99   10254
Sound the battle cry (Sherwin)
X Battle cry   10255
Sound the loud timbrel (Wein-
berg) [LMFMDDMRRD,
TLDFML] BH131   10256
South Cerney (Hadow) [MFSS
FMRRM, MRSSLTL] E359;
W496   10257
Southampton (---) [SSDDT, SRM
RD, MSSSFM] U355; Y102;
AC161; AR283; AS54 10258
Southampton (Barnes) [SSS
LSDRMMRMFS, LLL] BB6
10259

Southampton (Croft) [DMRMDRT
D, DSRMF#S, SF] AZ14-F;
BA41   10260
Southgate (Southgate) [DSDRMSF
M, RLTD, DSDR] BY590a
                                  10261
Southill (English trad) [DRM
RDLRMT, RDTDRSM,] E638b;
X395b   10262
Southport (Kingsley) [DRMMM
SLFF, LSRRMFM,] L498; AJ
113   10263
Southport (Lomas) [MMFSMRRM,
SDDTSTLS,] C390b; D341b;
AA386; BR341   10264
Southwark (Tye) [SDRMFSFM,
FMRDDT, RR] W166; AP11a
                                  10265
Southwell (Damon's Psalter, 1579)
[LDDTTL, LDDRRM, MSSF]
D349; E77; F122; J365a; K
75; Q156; R270; S239; W102b;
X106; AA554; AF314; AG149;
AL265a; AM412; AP44; AW196;
AZ582-L; BA737; BJ51; BV175;
BY565a; BZ   10266
Southwell (Irons) [DMMSDDLS, S
DMRRR, SS] A584a; B301; C
514b; D283b; F282; I268; J469;
K524; L602; M314; O609; V55;
W418a; AA558; AL461b; AP635;
BE399; BF388; BR445b; BV300;
BX164; BY76   10267
Southwick (Vincent) [SMRDLLLS,
DTLMTLS, R] AZ480-B   10268
Sovereign grace (Pierre) [DLSDR
MMSFMRD, DLSD] AJ422
                                  10269
Sovereignty (McManiman) [SLTD
FMRD, SFRSSF#LS,] H309
                                  10270
Sowing in the morning (Minor)
X Bringing in the sheaves
                                  10271
Spain (Carr) X Spanish chant
                                  10272
Spain (Dana arr) X Flee as a
bird   10273
Spanish carol (Spanish carol)
[LTDTLSM, SLTLSL, LTD]
BG113   10274
Spanish chant (Carr arr) [DDTD
LDS, MDFRDTD, DD] A332;

B130; C130a; D89a; H268;
I500; J72; K82a; L235; M
431; N96; Q166; R131; S191;
U157; V254; W177; AA213;
AE206; AI182; AJ64; AK198;
AL597; AN281b; AO270; AP
740, 755; AQ127; AR25; AS
69; AT22; AU195; AV111;
AW145; AZ581-M; BA452;
BB238; BC23; BI10-D; BX
336a; BZ   10275
-----. V [DTDLDS, MDFRDT
D, DTD] R131   10276
Spanish hymn (Carr) X Spanish
chant   10277
Spanish melody (Carr) X
Spanish chant   10278
Sparta (Mason) [SSSDDDDR,
RRRMFSMR,] L199   10279
Spazier (Spazier) [SDSMD
SFM, RDSDMR, SR] M544
                                  10280
Speak gently (---) X Mendota
                                  10281
Speak to my heart (McKinney)
X Holcomb   10282
Speed away (Woodbury) [SSS
SSSSSSF#SM, MMMR#]
AR472; AS380; AX208; AY
331   10283
Speer (Speer) [DMRMFS, SFM
R, RRDRMF,] E280   10284
Spencer Lane (Lane) X Peni-
tence   10285
Speranza (Sewall) [SMMRM
FLS, MSMDRMRD] BR439
                                  10286
Speratus (Etlich Christliche
lider) X Wittenberg   10287
Spes mea in deo (Warburton)
[MFRSS#LTDFMR, MMF#SL]
Y12; AB90; AC235; AD305;
BF380   10288
Spes unica (Perry) [MSLSS
DFM, MRFMMRR, M] AA447
                                  10289
Spetisbury (Knapp) [DMFSD,
SLDTD, SFMMDR,] F566
                                  10290
Spicer (Hultman) [MMRDSLM,
MMRDSLF, FR] BB453
                                  10291
Spire (Drese) X Rochelle

10292
Spires (Luther) [LTDTLS#LTD
TL, DRRMDRRM,] A61; E68b;
J155b; L400; M29; N220; O138;
P86; Q5; X277b; AA274; AM91
10293
-----. V [LDLSLDTL, DRRMDRR
M] J155b   10294
-----. V [LDLS#LDTL, DRRMD
RRM] N220   10295
Spirit Divine (Scott-Gatty) [MRM
SLTDR, FMFLTDRM,] U126;
Y175; AC310; AR522   10296
Spirit of grace and union (Montani)
[DDRMDDTD, MMFSMRDR,]
BQ37   10297
Spirit of the living God(Iverson)
[MMMMRMF, MDDRM, MMMM]
AR656; AT523; AU329   10298
-----. V [MMMMRMF, MDRM,
MMMMR] AT523   10299
Spirit so holy (Stebbins) [SMF
SLSMSFMRS, SMFS] AX133;
AY203   10300
Spirit-wind (Frederick) [MFSM
RR, FSLSS, LLLSF] AR223 10301
Spiritus (Walther. G-B. 1524)
X Soldau   10302
Spiritus domini (Wilson) [SDSLDR
DRM, DFFMRDR,] J243b
10303
Spiritus sancti gratia (Triller)
[LLLMMFFM, MTDRMRDTD]
AA32   10304
Spiritus vitae (Hammond) [DTSL
FMRSS, DDRMSMR] BV298
10305
Spitta (Danks) [SDSDMSS, LSMR
MD, SLL] H317; AV174; BR
367   10306
Splendour (Piae cantiones. 1582)
X Puer nobis   10307
Splendor of the morning sunlight
(Tintner) [SSDSMFLS, DRMFLS
FM] BH9   10308
Splendor paternae (Sarum plain-
song M 1) [FFSLL#LSL,
LSDDSLL#] A158a; E52; F2a;
J206a; K359a; X33c; AF40; AQ
110; BJ29   10309
-----. V [DDRMFMRM, MRSSRM
FM] F2a   10310

-----. V [FSLL#LSLL, SDD
SLL#LS] AQ110   10311
Splendor paternae gloriae
(Sarum plainsong M 1) X
Splendor paternae   10312
Spohr (Spohr) [SMMSDMRD,
MLSMFSM, M] B303; C303;
D652a; G363; H332; I309;
L120; N44; Q456; R322; S
317; T78; V401; W451a; AA
399; AB275; AD283; AE205;
AG178; AJ116b; AL649b;
AM554; AN575; AO302; AP
402; AR227; AS120; AV409;
AW586; BA410; BD65; BE230;
BH51; BR358; BX234   10313
-----. V [SMMSDMRD, DLS
MFSM, M] N44   10314
-----. V [DMMSDMRD, DLSM
FSM, M] Q456   10315
Spohr (Sophr) X Gerald
10316
Sponso (Nottingham) [SLDDTD
RD, FFMRDRM, S] AS149
10317
Sponsa Christi quae per orbem
(Plainsong sequence M 1-2)
[RDRFSFMR, LSLFSLL, L]
E253   10318
Sprague Hill (Baumgartner)
[LTDRMLRMFML, LLSSS]
Y52   10319
Spring (Everett) [SLSSDMRD, D
RMSLS, DR] I331   10320
Spring (Shaw) [DRLS, MDRM
DLSLRD, DR] X5   10321
Spring Gardens (---) [MSMDD
RMFM, FSDLTDT,] BB203
10322
Spring has come (Piae cantiones.
1582) X In vernali tempore
10323
Spring of souls (Lindeman) [S
MMRDDF, RRMF#STLS, S]
J106b; O328; P195; AZ205-G
10324
-----. V [SMMRDDF, RRMF#
STLLS,] AZ205-G   10324a
Spring Run (Huffaker) [MMMM
RR, FFFFMM, SSSS] AR72
10325
Spring-tide hour (Barnby) X

Soho   10326
Springfield (Gauntlett) [SFMMRD
  RMFFM, RFMLL] W64a; BP800;
  BY396a   10327
Springfield (Grieg) [DMFSSLLDL
  LS, SMDMS] AC292   10328
Springfield (Minshall) X Coppee
                                    10329
Springhill (Hurndall) [DRFMRDDT,
  DLSDTDR, D] D647b   10330
Springs of salvation (Freyling-
  hausen) X Gregor's 221st
  metre   10331
Springtime (Briggs) [DMSSFLD
  LSMS, DMSSF] X360   10332
Springtime (Keller) [MSMRFMDR,
  DTRDLS, DL] J362b   10333
Sri Lampang (Asian mel) [SS
  SSLDLSMSLD, MRDL] BZ
                                    10334
Stabat mater (Dykes) [DRMDFM
  MRD, DRMDFMM] D103a; AM
  185; AN576; BX203   10335
Stabat mater (German: old)
  [DRMMFSFMM, SSFFMMR]
  AZ95-C; BA211   10336
Stabat mater (Knight) [SSDSMFM
  R, RMRTDRDT,] I154   10337
Stabat mater (Mainz G-B. 1661)
  X Mainz   10338
Stabat mater (Mechlin plainsong
  M 4) [DTDRMRTDT, MMRDT
  SL] A76b; C161a; D103b; E
  115c; BJ44   10339
Stabat mater (Nanini) [DMMRDT
  RD, DTRDDTLS,]   10340
Stabat mater (Tartini) [MMFSLS
  LSLSFM, SFML] BQ162a   10341
Staincliffe (Dixon) [MMR#MF
  MMRD, SSF#SDSS] D172b; L
  169b; V581; AB271; AO34; BA
  80; BB648   10342
Stainer (Stainer) X Beati   10343
Stainer (Stainer) X Evangel
                                    10344
Staines (Attwood) [SSMRDD#RFM
  R, RSFMRD] D588a   10345
Stalham (English trad) [LTDRM
  SMRTL, RMLDRM,] E638c;
  X393a   10346
Stand by me (Tindley) [DRMMM
  RDSLTD, DMSSS] AU30; BZ

                                    10347
-----. V [DRMMMRDS, LDD,
  DMSSS] BZ   10348
Stand firm (Tozer) [SDRDSM
  SD, RMRDMR, SD] AI324   10349
-----. R [MFDMMFDM, MS
  MDRTTL]   10350
Stand like the brave (Bradbury)
  [SSMSDDRMDRM, MRRRS]
  BB576   10351
Stand up (Barnby) [SSSDRMD,
  LSDRTD, DRR] D582c; AB
  317   10352
Stand up (Thalben-Ball) [SD
  DRSMD, LSDDRD, SDD] BV
  586b   10353
Stand up, stand up for Jesus
  (Geibel) X Trumpet call
                                    10354
Stand up, stand up for Jesus
  (Webb) X Webb   10355
Standard (Hakes) [MFSF#SM
  FSLS, MMFMRS] BB500   10356
-----. R [DDFFLFMS, SRRR
  MFM, D]   10357
Standing on the promises
  (Carter) X Promises   10358
Standish (Bower) [LTDTLSLS,
  DRMDRRD, D] F407b   10359
Staniforth (Staniforth) X
  Jerusalem   10360
Stanley (Barnby) [MSMRDRTD,
  SDTLSLF#S,] I170   10361
Stanley (Lutz) [SSDSMMRD, DR
  MFLTRD,] AB129; BF339;
  BR273   10362
Stanley (Mann) [SSSLTDSS,
  DMFMRLRD#] I651   10363
Stanley (Jarvis) [SDSLLSFMR
  DS, SMRDS] AJ286; BY579
                                    10364
Stanstead (Russell) [DTLMMM
  MRDTL, DRMSS] E482; X
  697   10365
Stanton (Hamilton-Gell) [DSM
  FLS, DDDRM, DDTLR] D62b
                                    10366
Star of Jacob (Redhead) X
  St Nicholas   10367
Star of peace (Mason) [DDDD
  RRMR, MMMF#SLT, D]

W627; Z439; AL455; AP712; BY
242   10368
Star of the East (Kennedy) [MR#
MDMFLFM, MR#MDMFM]
AX96   10369
Star-spangled banner (Smith) X
National anthem   10370
Starlight (Hedges) [MFSLFS, MRD
TLT, TRMR] BV540   10371
Stars in my crown (Sweney) [MF
SF#SDMRDTDR, RMFT] AT
470; AY508; BB626   10372
-----. R [MRDRDSMSDDRM,
MFSM]   10373
Stars of glory (Mozart) [MFMSMR
MRFR, DDRRMS] BO156
                            10374
Stars of glory (Mozart) X Sonata
                            10374a
Stars of glory (Janowska) [DRM
DRMRRMRD, TLSFR] BQ9
                            10375
Stars of morning, shout for joy
(Durham) [DMSDDTD, LLLSF
MMRR] BC164   10376
State Street (Woodman) [MMRDLS,
DTDRMR, RMRD] H53; L321;
M310; V284; Y381; Z446; AA
458; AE213; AH517; AM530;
AO499; AS189; AU282; AV291;
AW246; BA592   10377
Statham (Statham) X St Joseph
                            10378
Staunton (Main) [DSDSDRMFMR,
SRTSTL] L460b   10379
Steadfast (Neu ordentlich G-B.
Hanover, 1646) [MLS#LTD, D
RDTLS#F#M, M] A283; O217;
AF86   10380
-----. V [MLS#LTD, DRDTLSF
M, ML] O217   10381
Steal away (Negro spiritual) [DD
DMMM, SSSLRM, DDDL] Y316;
AG316; AH604; AR487; BK166
                            10382
-----. R [LLSLS, MSMSMSM,
DMSS]   10383
Stearndale (Emerson) [DDDDSLLS,
SDMRDTLS,] L104   10384
Stebbins (Stebbins) X Adelaide
                            10385
Stebbins (Stebbins) X Jesus is
calling   10386

Stebbins (Stebbins) X The
Green Hill   10387
Steele (---) [MMMRDDTDR,
DTLSFMR] L166   10388
Stegman (Hartmann) [SSLSFM
RMFSLT, DSSF] M473
                            10389
Steiner (Kolb) X Dear Lord,
I come   10390
Steiner (Steiner) [DMRSSDMR
SS, SFMRMF] A320; E253b;
F364; X487; BE55; BV579a;
BY467b   10391
Stella (Hemy. Easy hymn tunes)
[SSMSSDDTLS, SSFMRM]
C48b; D22b; Eap. 54; F203b;
G124; L567; S314; T146; AB
283; AC83; AJ214; AK273;
AL84; AM426; AO45; AP334
b; AR181; AW94; BB151;
BN133; BO102; BP81; BQ84;
BV468b   10392
-----. V [SSMSSDDTLS, SFM
RMF] BN133   10392a
-----. V [SSMFSLTDTLS, SS
FMR] T146   10393
Stella (Hull. The casket) [MS
SSLSFM, MFMRDR, RR] M
607   10394
-----. R [SMSMMFMRDR,
RRRRMF]   10395
Stella (Parker) [MMMRDTLSS,
MLS, RLS, R] B454b; C545b;
G91; Y344; AB113b; AC85;
AH262; AO121; BB110; BF
280   10396
Stella (Wathall) [SMSLLD, SMS
LLD, DRMM] I112a   10397
Stella maris (Hemy. Easy hymn
tunes) X Stella   10398
Stella orientis (Willan) [MRDF
MRFMLS, DTLSR] AL49b
                            10399
Stephanos (Baker) [MMMRM
SSF, MMRDR, SL] A406;
B386; C386; D342a; F348;
G193; H245; I293a; J517;
K72; L357; Q428; R264a;
S221b; U153; V267a; W391a;
Z286; AA370; AB154; AC151;
AD208; AE167; AG140b; AJ
365b; AK302; AL471a; AM
389a; AO249b; AP401a; AR

DTLLS, SD] A516; F239; M561;
N56; AA27; AN55a; BV297a;
BY560   10434
-----. V [SMSLSFMRM, SDTLLS,
S] AN55a   10435
Störl II (Störl) [SDTLLLRDTS,
DRMFMR] J13; K439; M320;
O166; Q606; V684; AA548; AK
98   10436
-----. V [SDLLLRDTS, DRMFMR
R] Q606   10437
Storm-tossed (Sullivan) [SSSSS
SDSSSSLS, SLL] BR363   10438
Storrington (Thiman) [SSDTSRFM,
DTLRSLS, S] BY704   10439
Storrs (Matthews) [MMMRDDTD,
RRRMSSF#S,] I165; K55; N
394; T280; U414; V321; Y141;
Z306; AA514; AC175; AF392;
AJ388; AK335; AO436; AR461;
AT460; BA556; BB460; BF444;
BY445a   10440
Story of Jesus (Sweney) [MMRD
MFSM, SRMFMRM, M] AH144;
276; AM685; AT211; AU367;
AX317; BB534; BO53   10441
-----. V [SMMMFSLS, MSRM
FMRM] AH144; BO53   10442
Story of love (Root) X Ellon
10443
Story of the cross, Pt. 1 (Brown)
[MMMMFS, DFMR, SSFMRD,]
B163a   10444
-----. V [MDRMFM, DTLS#,LSF
MRD,] B163a   10445
-----. V [DLFFMM, RRFD,
L#LSLDR,] B163a   10446
Stover (Bowman) [MRDFMSLS, R
MFLLSF#S,] AY54   10447
Stow (Mason) [SDDDRM, MRD
FMR, RMRM] L267; AP14b
10448
Stowe (Mason) X Stow   10449
Stowell (Meredith) [DMSDDD, ML
DMMM, DTTM,] G392   10450
Stowey (English trad) [DRMRDLS
FRRRR, DRMR] X377; BG142;
BY509b   10451
Stracathro (Hutcheson) [DMRDRM
DTL, DSMDMRD,] A325a; E
445a; F299a; G340; R327; W451b;
X438; AB272; AD31; AF255; AL
12a; AN52; BE343; BK94; BV

147a; BY70   10452
Straf mich nicht (Rosenmüller)
X Nassau   10453
Strasburg (Teutsch kirchenampt.
Strassburg, 1524 or 25) X
Aus tiefer not   10454
Strassburg (Strassburger Kir-
chen G-B. 1616) [DDDMF
SSS, SLSMFS, SL] X400
10455
Stratford (Dykes) X Jesu,
magister bone   10456
Strattner (Strattner) X Posen
10457
Streatham (Dykes) X Keble
10458
Streatley (Wesley, S. S. arr)
[MRDTDRM, SFMRDTD, RM]
AP552b; BA291   10459
-----. V [MRDTDRM, SFM
RDTRD, M] BA291   10459a
Strength and stay (Dykes)
[MMFSLSMDFMRM, MF#F#
S] B280; C280a; D177; F17b;
J219; K410; Y4; AB232; AC
244; AH514; AN227; AR325;
AU403; AW249; BD125; BE
317; BF356; BK110; BV393;
BX124; BY578a   10460
Stricken, smitten (Lindeman)
X Hjem jeg laenges   10461
Strive aright (Thommen's
Christen-schatz. Basle,
1745) X Batty   10462
Striving, onward, pressing for-
ward (---) [MRRDDMSFFM
M, MRFRD] AX435   10463
Stroudwater (Wilkins Psalmody)
[DSDSMFMRD, DRMFMR, M]
E158; X185; AL632; AP7
10464
Struther (Foote) [SDRMRFMD,
LSMFMRDD] AQ29   10465
Study song (Milgrove) X Harts
10466
Stukeley (Mendelssohn) [MSLS
MDRM, MRSSF#S, SD] BA763b;
BR414   10467
Sturges (Parsons) [LDMRDTLT,
DMRDRM, M] A445   10468
Stuttgart (or Stuttgard, or Stutt-
gardt) (Witt) [SSDDRRMD,
SSLFRSM,] A1; B55; C55a;

D48a; E40; F76; G75; J51; K
297; L404; M156; N386; O516;
Q83; R151b; S113b; T350a; V
124; W113; X84; AB124; AD
507; AE6; AF100; AG55; AK83;
AL13a; AM2; AN23a; AP397b;
AQ117; AR5; AS86; AT50; AW
88; AZ16-F; BA899; BE265;
BF695; BL2; BN25; BO162;
BR154; BV127; BX214; BY78;
BZ   10469
Stuyvesant (Gilbert) [MMRFMRL
T, DRSMRD, MR] AA443 10470
S'u Sh'oreem (Naumburg) [MM
MMDLLMDL, LTDRMF] BH288
                                10471
Suabia (Spiess) X Swabia   10472
Sub tuum praesidium (Haller)
[MLSSDTTTLS#S#, LTDLT]
BQ213a   10473
Sub tuum praesidium (Lambillotte)
[SSDDRRM, DTLSLSFM, S]
BO78   10474
Sub tuum praesidium (Plainsong
M 7) [STDRRTDRMMR, RRD
LD] BQ213b   10475
Submission (Lomas) [DDMSSSDT
LS, TTLS, RS] C385b; D633b
                                10476
Submission (Peace) [DDRMM
RMFFM, RDRM, MF] C385a;
S305; U43; Z340; AD266; AE
204; AL431; AP505; AR402; AW
471; BA507; BF420   10477
Succos (Jewish trad) X The
lulav   10478
Succoth hymn (Jassinowsky) [MM
SMRRDMDTL, LRLMR] BH
182   10479
Such a friend (Stebbins) X
Friend   10480
Such love (Harkness) [SMMDDRDT
LS, SLTDMM] AX87   10481
Such', wer da will (Stobaeus)
[SMFS, DTLS, SMFSMRD, S]
Q383   10482
Sudeley (Stainer) [SMRDSDTL,
SLMFMR, MF] F154a   10483
Suffer the children to come (Og-
den) [DDDDMDL, SSSRDTDR
M] AY343   10484
-----. R [MMSFMRMF, RRFM
RDRM,]   10485

Suffering Savior (Crueger) X
Herz liebster Jesu   10486
Sullivan ("C.A.P." 1855) [SL
SMRDTL, DLSDDTDR,] M89
                                10487
Sullivan (Sullivan) X St Ger-
trude   10488
Sullivan (Sullivan) [SDDDDD
TDRM, DFMRDT,] AH519
                                10489
Summer carol (French trad)
[SDDRTDD, MRFMRD, SDD]
BG157   10490
Summer in winter (Cantiques de
Strasbourg, 1697) [DRMDS
DRMDS, DRMFSD] BG124
                                10491
Summer suns are glowing
(Binder) [SFMSDL, FMDFL
S, SFMS] BH155   10492
Summercourt (English trad)
[DRMSFMRMRDLD, DRMS]
BY94   10493
Summerford (Grimley) [SSDT
DRMFRM, SFMRMR] AB397;
AC274; AH469; BF653
                                10494
Summer time (French carol)
X Grace soit   10495
Sumner (Biggs) [MFM, SFFM
RDRR, RFMR] A429b   10496
Sumus tibi (Button) [SMRDDT,
LFMRS, SDDTM] AL451
                                10497
Sun of grace (Groos) [SMDSL
S, MDTDMR, SMDS] M198
                                10498
Sun of my soul (Allgemeines
katholisches G-B. 1774)
X Hursley   10499
Sun of my soul (Smith) X
Maryton   10500
Sunderland (Smart) X Jamison
                                10501
Sundown (Gower) [SDTTLLTL
MS, SLTLSL] C13b; AB20;
AC231; AD49; AJ219; AO28;
BF494   10502
-----. V [DTTLLTLMSS,
SLTLSL] AC231   10503
Sundridge (Filby) [DSSLSSDS,
MDDRMFLR,] K152   10504
Sunlight (Weeden) [SDDDRMM

M, FSSSLS, SL] AU376   10505
-----. R [DTLSFFFFF, TLSF
MFS]   10506
Sunning Hill (Elvey) [SMTDSLSF
M, SLTDRDT,] D402c   10507
Sunny Bank (English carol) [SD
DDMSMD, DRMRDRTS,] BG3,
18   10508
-----. V [SDDRMSMR, FMDDM
RTS,] BG18   10509
Sunrise (Stainer) X Lux prima
                        10510
Sunrise (Trier G-B. 1695) [MM
RSDRT, DSLTDDTD, T] F6;
BM52; BN132; BQ75   10511
-----. V [MMRSDRTS, DSLTDD
TD,] BM52   10512
Sunrise (Zinck) X Zinck   10513
Sunset (Ambrose) X Ambrose
                        10514
Sunset (Barnby) [MMRRDSFM,
MF#STLSF#M,] D8b; V51b;
BI57   10515
Sunset (Herbert) X Burwell
                        10516
Sunset (Howard) [DRMFMMRDM
SLS, SDDT] AP672   10517
Sunset (Lutz) X Stanley   10518
Sunset (Stocks) [DRMFMRDRS,
DRMFMRD] S509; W271a;
BV52a   10519
Sunset and evening star (Stone)
[DTDRDT, DRMMRDF, RMF]
U419   10520
Sunshine (Sweney) [DRMSLTDR
M, MFMRSRD,] AT273; BB607;
BC174   10521
-----. R [SFMDRDLSM, MFSDM
SF]   10522
Suo-gân (Welsh trad) [DRMRDR,
DRMRMD,] X380   10523
Suomi (Finnish cavalry march)
[SDDTTLDLS, DSDSFMR] G
131   10524
Suomi II (Finish trad) [MLDTS#
L, TDLDMRM, MF#S] J180
                        10525
Suppliant (Stainer) [DSLSDRMD,
RMFMRD#R, R] D274b   10526
Supplication (Monk) [LTDRMLSF,
MMRDTT] A500; B191; J435a;
K60; O264; V399   10527
Supplication (Vincent) [MMRDLTD,

SSFDRM, MRR] D277b; AD
366   10528
Surette (Davis) [SMFSLS, MFR
MRDRD, SS] BZ   10529
Surrender (Stebbins) X Adelaide
                        10530
Surrender (Weeden) [MMFMR
RMR, DDFMRMD, M] AT363;
AU82; BB573   10531
-----. R [DTLSF, TLSFM,
MFLSDT]   10532
Surrexit (Murray) [SMRDMD
RDTL, LSLTDM] BY156b
                        10533
Surrey (Carey) X Carey
                        10534
Surrey (Costellow) [SDTDMLS
FM, MRDSFMM] M369
                        10535
Sursum corda (Handel) X
Solomon   10536
Sursum corda (Lomas) [DDRM
FS, FMRM, SDRMFM,] O398;
R295; S277; AE439; AG312;
AI320; AK250; AR278; BR
336; BY438a   10537
Sursum corda (Smith) [DMSFM
RDRRD, SLTDTL] A482a;
AF286; AQ71; BV376; BY
316   10538
Sursum corda, No. 1 (Sewall)
[MSSLLD, DMRD, DTLSF#S,]
BR186   10539
Sursum corda, No. 2 (Lomas)
X Sursum corda   10540
Sursum voces (Button) [SLDTM
RRD, FMRDTLLS,] BE282
                        10541
Susanni (German trad) [MMRD
SMDRMD, SMSM, DR] BG118
                        10542
Sussex I (English trad) [DSS
FMRMFMR, DRMRMF] B345;
C345; BG45   10543
Sussex II (English trad) [MMM
RDRMRDL, FFMRDM] C311b;
E239; R103; S80; W33; X321;
AL559b; BE338; BV579b; BY
467a   10544
Sussex carol (English carol)
[SSMFSMRDR, TDDRMFM]
BG24a; BV114   10545
Sussex carol (Irish trad) [ML

TDTLSLM, MRDTMLT] BG24b
10546
Sussex mummers carol (English
trad) X Sussex I   10547
Sutherland (Ashford) [DDMRDD
TD, DTDRLDTL,] I377   10548
Sutherland (Bradbury) [SDTDSLLD,
TLSFMRD, S] L103   10549
Sutton Courtenay (Routley) [SL
DTD, RMSF#S, MFSSFM,] BY
712b   10550
Sutton Volence (Russell) [DTDTLL,
SLDTD, DRMRF] E615; X115a
10551
Swabia (Spiess) [SMFRRD, RMF#
SSF#S, SLSL] A375a; B45; C
45a; D28a; H79; I648; Q274;
R72; S20; W478; AA373; AB10;
AE51; AK37; AN287; AQ131;
AR42; AS41; AX63; AZ582-K;
BA613; BF189; BR93; BV51;
BX362; BY329   10552
Swabia No. 1 (Spiess) X Swabia
10553
Swahili (Schulz) [DDTTLS, SDT
DR, MMF#F#S] F469; W476;
AN4; BX521   10554
Swainsthorpe (Booth) [DDMRFFM,
RMSFLS, SDD] D664; AO560
10555
Swanage (Greenwood) [SMRDRSRM
RDRS, SMFM] BE200   10556
Swanmore (Blackall) [MSLMSMDR
M, MLDTRDL] F396a   10557
Swansea (Basque church mel)
[DSMRDRMRDLS, DMSLS] Y
337; AC69   10558
Swanwick (Lucas) [SDDRMDM
RDTD, MFMRD] H9; L192; M
403; T107; V348; AJ156b
10559
Swanwick (Shaw) [LTDRLTLTD,
DTLSMMF#] X546   10560
Sweden (---. 16th c) [LDDRRMM
RDTL, LDDRR] M292; N602;
Q432   10561
Sweden (Hiles) [MMMSDSFM,
MMLF#STLS,] C39; D641;
U351   10562
Swedish litany (Swedish mel.,
1697) [MDTLLS#L, DMRDDTD,]
A82a; J81; AF166   10563
Sweet Agnes, holy child (Slovak

hymn) [SLSMFMRDRM,
FSMR, SL] BQ106   10564
Sweet are the promises (Ogden)
[DMFSSSLFLS, SFFFFM]
AR470; AW481; AX494
10565
-----. R [DDFLSM, SRMFM,
DDFLS]   10566
Sweet be thy rest (Hakes) [M
SF#SM, SLDTLLS, SF#SD,]
BB493   10567
Sweet by and bye [by] (Webster)
[DRMRDRDLS, DRMMMSS]
N621; U424; AH535; AT471;
AU344; AV396; AW504; AX
587; BB551   10568
-----. R [MFSSMR, RMFFF
FMRM, M]   10569
Sweet chariot (Negro spiritual)
[MDMDDLS, DDDDMMSS, L]
Y321; AH610   10570
-----. R [MSDLDDDDDDLS,
DDDD]   10571
Sweet day (Unseld) X Once
more before we part   10572
Sweet home (Bishop) X Home,
sweet home   10573
Sweet hosannas (Handel) [MRD
RMFMMR, SLSMFRM,] AP
747   10574
-----. R [SLSFMFMRMS,
SLSFMF]   10575
Sweet hour (Bradbury) [DMF
SSLTD, LSMMRDRM] G302;
H39; I516; N350; P11; R
398; U359; Z337; AE232;
AH349; AI228; AK475; AM
534; AN564; AO316; AR471;
AS44; AT327; AU263; AV
186; AW182; AX353; BB316;
BC166; BR524; BZ   10576
Sweet hour of prayer (Brad-
bury) X Sweet hour   10577
Sweet hour of prayer (Hall)
[SSSLDTLS, SSSDDTDR,
SSS] AY32   10578
Sweet is the peace the Gospel
brings (Durham) [MMMFM
SRR, MFFMRR, SD] BC191
10579
Sweet is the story (Giffe)
[SSLSMRDDM, SSLSMRD]
AX32; AY517   10580

-----. R [SDDDDTLSM, SDDD
SMR,]   10581
Sweet is the work, my God, my
King (McClellan) [SLTDRMF#
S, SLTDRMDR,] BC168 10582
Sweet peace (Bilhorn) [SMRDMSD
T, SFMRLTLS,] U230; AE300;
AI256; AR476; AT299; AU381;
AX336; BB609   10583
-----. R [MDFMRRRRDLS, S
DDDD]   10584
Sweet peace, the gift of God's
love (Bilhorn) X Sweet peace
                                10585
Sweet promise (Gabriel) [SDRM
MMFRMDS, DRMFS] AT278;
AU438   10586
-----. R [SFMRDRMDLS, STT
RRF]   10587
Sweet rest in heaven (Leather-
man) [DMMR#MSF, RDDRRM,
DMM] AX598; AY158   10588
-----. R [DRRDRMS, MRRDR
M, DMM]   10589
Sweet Sabbath (Miller) [MMMMMM
RMFS, SDTLSS] BH116 10590
Sweet sacrament divine (Stanfield)
[MSFRMD, MLTDRMR, MSF]
BO38   10591
Sweet Saviour, bless us (Catholic)
[SSSDDTDRDDT, SSSRR]
BO192   10592
-----. R [MMMDMMMMF,
FMRDDTT]   10593
Sweet Saviour! Bless us (Herbert)
X Burwell   10594
Sweet Saviour, bless us (Lawes)
X Falkland   10595
Sweet Saviour! bless us (Montani)
[MMRDFMRLSMR, RMRDF]
BQ138   10596
-----. R [FFFFMSDDDT, TT
TTDL]   10597
Sweet story (Gifford) X I think,
when I read   10598
Sweet story (Irish trad) [MRD
RDDMSFLDD, TLSF] N649;
AI384a   10600
Sweet the moments (---) [DDRR
MMRR, MSFMRRD, D] AX178;
AY250   10601
Sweeter sounds (LaTrobe) [SM
LSFMR, MFSFMRD, RM] BA

503   10602
Sweeter than the day before
(Loveless) [SLTDMMMSF#S
F#SF#F, SL] AU325   10603
Sweetest hosannas (Brunk)
[SF#SLSTDRRD, DTDRMR]
AY480   10604
-----. R [DRMFLLTDSD,
DTDRMR]   10605
Sweetest name (Bradbury) X
There is no name   10606
Sweetest name (Bridgers) [M
MR#MFMMRL, TDD#RSFM]
AT307; AU391   10607
-----. R [SLTDFT, SRSR#M,
SLTDR]   10608
Sweetest name (Stockton) X
Great Physician   10609
Sweetly, Lord, have we heard
(Everett) [MMMMRDLLS, S
MDR, MMM] AS347; AT362;
AU228; AX508   10610
-----. R [LFLLSSSLSMR,
MMMMR]   10611
Sweetly resting (Bentley) X
In the rifted rock   10612
Sweney (Sweney) X Fill me
now   10613
Sweney (Sweney) X More about
Jesus   10614
Swiss melody (Recueil de canti-
ques) [MMRMD, SMMMRM
SF, FFM] C290b; E399
                                10615
Swiss tune (Schmidlin) [SMSD
TDRM, SLTDRMFR,] AA73;
AB359; BY60   10616
Switzerland (Schmidlin) X
Swiss tune   10617
Sycamore (Hostetter) [SDSLSDR
MDRD, SLLLD] AY299
                                10618
Sychar (Dykes) X St Oswald I
                                10619
Sykes (Hall) [MFSSSSLLS, SM
MMMFM] AY193   10620
Sylvester (Camp) [DRMFMM
R, RDMSLSELT] I571 10621
Sylvester (Dykes) X St Sylves-
ter   10622
Sympathy (Stockton) X Great
Physician   10623
Symphony (Norwegian trad) X

AQ133; AW326; BA98; BB92;
BJ14; BN199; BV132a; BY332;
BZ   10657
Tallis' Hymn (Tallis) X Tallis'
Canon   10658
Talmar (Woodbury) X Dorrnance
                              10659
Talyllyn (Welsh trad) [SDTLDTLS,
RMDRTD,SD] AK69; BY556b
                              10660
Tana mana dhana (Marathi
trad) [DRMRDRDDLLSSL,MMM]
AF394   10661
Tantum ergo (---) [SFMLSLTDD,
DLSF#SLT] BO274E   10662
Tantum ergo (---) [SSLSFMDLLS,
SSLSFM] BO274g   10663
Tantum ergo (Balthasar) [SLDDR
DTT, LTDRRDD, R] BQ242c
                              10664
Tantum ergo (Beltjens) [MSDLSF
FM, LLSLSFMR] BQ242a
                              10665
Tantum ergo (Essay on the church
plain) X Dulce carmen   10666
Tantum ergo (Dooner) [SLSLDTD
LS, SLMSLTT] BQ326   10667
Tantum ergo (Dubois) [SDMMRR
MFFM, SLTLSM] BQ242i
                              10668
Tantum ergo (Ett) X Oriel 10669
Tantum ergo (Filitz) X Mannheim
                              10670
Tantum ergo [sacramentum]
(Chants ordinaires ... Paris)
X Grafton   10671
Tantum ergo (Miller) [MMMRFFFM
LLSMRDR, M] BO274   10672
Tatum ergo (Mohr) X He who
once in righteous vengeance
                              10673
Tantum ergo I (Montani) [MMM
LTRMM, MSFMRDDT,] BQ242j
                              10674
Tantum ergo II (Montani) [MSL
DTSLS, LTDSFMMR,] BQ323
                              10675
Tantum ergo (Mozarabic plainsong
M 5) [DRMMMRMFMFMRM
RD,] A200c; B338c; BN109;
BP62; BQ325   10676
-----. V [FSLLLSTDLSLSF,
FSL] BQ325   10677

Tantum ergo (Perosi) [SDDLS
FFM, RMSDTLLS,] BQ321
                              10678
Tantum ergo (Plainsong M 5)
[DRRMRDRMSSFM, LSSF]
BN108   10679
Tantum ergo (Ravanello) [MR
MDRDDTD, MF#SLF#F#M,]
BQ242d   10680
Tantum ergo (Rush) [SSSDD
RMM, MFMDRRD, S] BN112;
BO274F   10681
Tantum ergo (Slovak hymn)
[DTDLSMFMRD, MFSRMD]
BQ242g   10682
Tantum ergo (Smit) [DTLSM,
LSFMR, MF#STLS] BQ242E
                              10683
Tantum ergo (Sullivan) [MMM
LTDTLM, DDMRDDT] BQ
324   10684
Tantum ergo (Wade) X St
Thomas   10685
Tantum ergo No. 2 (Palestrina?)
[S#S#LLSSSS, DDDRDDT, T]
E326c; X280b   10686
Tanycastell (Jones) [DDDTTRR
MDFFFMMFM] W502b; AP
228   10687
Tappan (Kingsley) [SSSMRDLS,
SSSFMRDR,] G61; I99; L
448; V702; AO110   10688
Taps (---) [SSDSDMSDMSDM
SDM, D] AC344; AG339; AH
566; BB370   10689
Tarsus (Goss) [SDTDRMFR,
MFSLRMFM,] O467; AB60
                              10690
Task sublime (English trad)
[DRMRDRMFMR, MRDTLS,]
AE311; AR365   10691
Task sublime (English trad)
X Noel   10692
Taylor Hall (Sowerby) [MFSL
SM, RMFSLTS, DT] A527
                              10693
Tchaikowsky's "Legend" (Tchai-
kowsky) X The crown of
roses   10694
Te deum (Allgemeinisches
Katholisches G-B. 1774)
[DDDTDRMRD, MMMRDSM]
A273; J167; L96; Q250; R115;

T203; W413b; AF247; AH145;
AJ292; AK20; AS23; AW519;
AX10; BE88; BL82; BM91;
BN196; BO3; BQ39; BR80;
BZ   10695
-----. V [DDDTDRDRM, MMM
FSSF] J167   10696
-----. V [DDDDRDRD, MMM
FSSFM] L96   10697
-----. V [DMSMRDRD, MMMFS
SFM] R115   10698
Te deum (Allgem. Kath. G-B.
1774) X Hursley X Halle
                                10699
Te deum laudamus (Barnby)
[MDMRDDDFFFFMRS, DD]
AR635; AS494   10700
Te, Joseph, celebrent (Catholic)
[SLDLTDDSLSFMR, SLD]
BO267   10701
Te, Joseph, celebrent (Plainsong
M 1) [RFMFSLRDFMFRDDR,
R] BN168   10702
Te laudant omnia (Swift) [MSDRDT
D, LSTDFMR, MS] BY3   10703
Te lucis (Plainsong arr) [LLLSL
DTL, DRRDRMMM,] BR118
                                10704
Te lucis (Sarum plainsong M 8)
[LDDDDRDT, LLLLTTL] A164a;
E264b; F16   10705
Te lucis ante terminum (Ander-
nach G-B. 1608) [SLMFMRRD,
MFSLLSFM,] E264c   10706
Te lucis ante terminum (Gastor-
ius) X Was Gott tut   10707
Te lucis ante terminum (Plain-
song M 8) [LDLLTDLL, LLTD
TLSL] E264   10708
Teach me, O Lord (Hewlett) [M
MMMRMDLTDR, MFSLS] Sap.
25; AR671   10709
Teach me the measure (Wilson)
X Martyrdom   10710
Teach me thy will, O Lord
(Runyan) [SFMMRD, RMFM,
SFMMRD,] AX566   10711
Teilo Sant (Dobbs) [SMFSLTDTL
S, SDRMLS] BY51b   10712
Tekna (Schulz) [SSMSSMSFRFM,
SSMSS] M615; AW413; BK152;
BN19; BQ6   10713
Tell it again (McIntosh) [MMMM

RDRDLS, SDDDTD] AU378
                                10714
-----. R [FFFR, MMMD,
DDDDTDRM]   10715
Tell it out (Sankey) [SSDTDRM
RMFSMD, MFS] I634; AI
170   10716
Tell it to Jesus (Lorenz)
[DMMRDRDLSD, RRMRS, M]
AU110: AW476   10717
-----. R [RRMRS, MMFMD,
FFFMRD]   10718
Tell me the old, old story
(Doane) [MMFSSLS, SDDD
MF#S, SD] E583; N351; R
403; U144; V239; Z438; AH
344; AL496a; AM521; AO633;
AP433; AS181; AT222; AU
370; AV345; AW495; AX280;
AY521; BA420; BB524; BV
481; BY420   10719
-----. R [MMFSSLS, TTDRR
RD, MM]   10720
Tell me the story (Sweney) X
Story of Jesus   10721
Tell the story (Fischer) X
Hankey   10722
Tell the sweet old story (Show-
alter) [MFSSLSMD, DDDDT
LS, M] AY369   10723
-----. R [DRMMMRDSD, TD
RMRDL]   10724
Tell us now, O Death (Cologne
G-B.) X Vigiles et sancti
                                10725
Tell what He's done for you
(Byers) [SDMMRDTRR, SR
FFMRD] AX346   10726
-----. R [MFSFMFSLS,
RMFMRMF]   10727
Tempest (Huxtable) [DRMFMR,
DTDR, MMMMMT] BR343
                                10728
Tempest (Koenig) [DTLMRDTD
LS#, TTTDRM] F312   10729
Temple (Bartlett) [DMFSFMRM
FM, FSLTLS,] I665   10730
Temple (Davies) [DSSLMS,
STSF#MM, MF] A374; E454
                                10731
Temple (Hopkins) [MMFMM
RRD, LSRM, MMFM] D19b;
K468; L19; W293; AA44;

AO43a; AV21; AZ605-A; BX
152   10732
Temple (Wagner) [SSLDMMRDR
RDSFMFF] Y401   10733
Temple Boro (Pindar) [SDDTDLLS,
MSFRMFM, S] T140; AJ207
                             10734
Temple Bryan (Macalister) [MSL
TDDMMRM, SLTDMR] S330;
W144; BY140a   10735
Tempus adest floridum (Piae can-
tiones. 1582) [DDDRDDS, LS
LTDD, DD] A136; G107; R167;
S453; X4; AD115; AG68; AH
252; AL57; AM640; AN135;
AQ321; AT73; BG99; BK131;
BZ   10736
Ten thousand martyrs (Weinberg)
[LRDTLDLDTL, LDLDLS]
BH135   10737
Ten thousand times ten thousand
(Sankey) [SDDMDSFM, SLTDRDT,
L] AI341   10738
-----. R [SSRDTLSFMD, DDRD
MR]   10739
Tenbury (Nicholson) [SDDTLSM,
SLSMRDD, RM] F627   10740
Tenbury (Ouseley) [DRMFSMS,
LSLFM, DRMF] D656a   10741
Tenbury (Ouseley) X Aberystwyth
                             10742
Tenbury (Statham) [MSMRDDRMS
MR, SLRTL,] X328b   10743
Tender Shepherd (Barnby) [DDTDRM
D, FMRDTLTLS,] D248b
                             10744
Tender thought (Kentucky harmony,
1816) [RMRDLDRMSMR, RMRD
L] AF576   10745
Tenderness (Reinecke) [MFSFM
FLS, MFSDT, TRD] AL604
                             10746
Tenebrae (Redhead) X St Prisca
                             10747
Tent-like this day (Samuel) [MD
TLTDDRRM, LSSDDF] BH160
                             10748
Tenterden (Bullinger) [DMSFMRD
MRD, DMSF#MR#] O396 10749
Ter sanctus (Cruickshank) [MM,
MM, MM, MRDL, RMFSSM]
U489   10750
Ter sanctus (Rostockerhandboken,

1529) [MFMRMDRM, SMD
RMFFM,] J174; N316; R25;
S17; AF28   10751
Terra beata (English trad)
[DRMSMRD, RMFLSMR, LS]
G72; J487; R101; S70; Y51;
Z171; AB64; AC39; AD93;
AE55; AF485; AG60; AH202;
AI32; AK65; AL589; AM109;
AR99; AS94; AT59; AV406;
AW48; BB646; BF399; BK
26; BZ   10752
Terra patris (English trad)
X Terra beata   10753
Teschner (Teschner) X St
Theodulph   10754
Teshiniens (Polish trad) [LT
LS#LTDT, TDRMRDTL,] Q
169; AM196   10755
Tetworth (Garrett) [MLLDTLL
S#, LSSMRRD, M] I380
                             10756
Thacher (Handel) X Thatcher
                             10757
Thalberg (Thalberg) [SSSLF#
SS, MMMSTD, SSS] H176
                             10758
Thanet (Jowett) [MRDDFMMR,
MF#SMF#S, FS] S511a; W
294a; AM337; BV48   10759
Thankful hearts (Rogers) [MM
SSDTT, FFTTRDD, SS] BH
249   10760
Thankfulness (MacFarren) X
Luffenham   10761
Thanks for the Sabbath School
(Murray) [SLSSMRDRDL,
LSDRMR] BC177   10762
-----. R [RRMFFFMMFS,
SSLTLS]   10763
Thanksgiving (Baker) [SDTLLSS,
SLTDMRDT, T] BY34   10764
Thanksgiving (Basswood) [SD
DDDTT, TLTLLSS, SD] AE
431; AH544; AL584; AM645;
AP719; AW435; BK15 10766
-----. R [DSSTL, RLLDT, D
MMMLR]   10767
Thanksgiving (Carter) [SSM
DDDRMFM, MMRDTL] AO
64   10768
Thanksgiving (Crueger) X

Graefenberg   10769

Thanksgiving (Dykes) X Trinity
   College   10770

Thanksgiving (Gilbert) [DTDSLSFM,
   MF#SLTLS, D] B103; C103;
   T11; W389; AA299; AJ15; AM
   107; BA344; BB16   10771

Thanksgiving (Quaile) X Oldbridge
                            10772

Thanksgiving (Schop) X Sollt ich
   meinem Gott   10773

Thanksgiving (Statham) [SSSDFMR
   S, SDLRSLTL] I216; V565; Y
   218; AA437; AB293; AC219;
   AD344; AR530; AS391   10774

Thanksgiving carol (Hohenfurth
   ms.) X Dies est laetitiae
                            10775

Thanksgiving hymn (Balle) X
   Emmanuel   10776

That cause can neither be lost
   (Danish trad) X Ostergaard
                            10777

That doleful night (American trad)
   X Amazing grace   10778

That heavenly home (Kolb) [MR#
   MDSSLTDS, MR#MDTD] AX595;
   AY136   10779

That will be glory for me
   (McGranahan) [SSF#SMRDDTL
   S, SSFMF] AU341   10780

-----. R [SDDDDRML, LRRRR
   DLS,]   10781

Thatcher (Handel) [DMRDSFMR,
   SDRMLTD, D] C225a; D27a;
   H129; I182; J526; K265; L49;
   M401; N374; O346; P395; T84;
   V265; Z457; AA341; AJ62; AO
   359; AY428; BE240; BR32
                            10782

Thaxted (Holst) [MSLDTSDRDT
   LTLSM, M] F579; X379a; BY
   642   10783

The alarm (Beecher. Plymouth
   coll.) X Latter day   10784

The angel Gabriel (English trad)
   [DMSMRDTR, MDLDTL, DM]
   BG37   10785

-----. R [SLTDMRDT, TDTLS
   SM, D]   10786

The armor of light (Lynes) [SSS
   SSLLS, SLTDTLL, T] BX540
                            10787

-----. R [MMMRDTLTLS,
   MMMRDT]   10788

The band of children (French,
   16th c) [SDRMMFM, RDTLD
   TLS, S] BG140; BN7; BO
   147   10789

-----. R [RDTD, RDTD, DFM
   RSFMR,]   10790

The banner of the cross (Mc-
   Granahan) X Royal banner
                            10791

The battle hymn of the republic
   (Steffe) X Battle hymn
                            10792

The beatitudes (Toews) [SFM
   SSSLS, SLTD, DTLL] AX48
                            10793

The beautiful garden of prayer
   (Fillmore) [MFSMSLDLSM,
   DRMDRM] AU342; AX362
                            10794

-----. R [SLTLSFMRDMLS,
   SLTL]   10795

The bell cadence (Tearne)
   [DS, RMFS, SM, SM, SM, SM,
   MD,] AT553   10796

The bellman's song (English
   trad) [SFMRMDRMFLRS,
   SFMF] BG46b   10797

The bellman's song (English
   trad) X Hitchen carol
                            10798

The bellman's song (English
   trad) X Newbury   10799

The best friend of all (Bills)
   [DRMRMDDTLDLS, SSDD]
   AX279   10800

-----. R [SFMMRDDTLDLS,
   SDDD]   10801

The bird let loose ("Franklin
   Square") [SMRDMLSS, MSF
   RMD, SM] BR530   10802

The birds (Czech trad) [SMR
   DDTDRMD, SM, SMRD]
   X381; BG103   10803

The blameless church (Speck)
   [SFMMMMRMFSS, MFSSS]
   AX150   10804

-----. R [MSDDDDTLSM, S
   LLLDT]   10805

The blessed home (Stainer) X
   Blessed home   10806

The blessed name (Barnby)

[DMMRDSLS, SSDTLSM, D]
AP689   10807
The blessed rest (Barnby) [MMM
SSDDRFM, FFMRLS] AP620
                                   10808
The blood of the Lamb (Showalter)
X When I see the blood 10809
The bond of perfectness (Warren)
[SSLSMDRM, SSMDMMR, S]
AX550   10810
-----. R [DTLSSLSD, DRMFS
LS, S]   10811
The bread that giveth strength
(Sullivan) X Livorno   10812
The breaking of the day (Seder-
quist) [SMMMSMFFLD, LSSS
DS] BB182   10813
-----. R [SFMMMMFSLS, FM
RRRM]   10814
The Bridegroom soon will call
us (Mason) X Evarts   10815
The builders (French trad) [SD
DRSFMRDRRMRD, SD] BG111
                                   10816
The call (Williams) [DMSSLSF
S, DMSSLSFS,] AQ123   10817
The call for reapers (Clemm)
X Clemm   10818
The canticle of the Blessed Vir-
gin I (Gelineau) [DDRL, LDLS
L.] BSp. 57   10819
The canticle of the Blessed Vir-
gin II (Gelineau) [SLDLDL, LSL
DLDL, RDT] BSp. 58   10820
The carnal and the crane (English
trad) [MSLLTDMSSM, MLLTDR]
BG53   10821
The cherry tree carol I (English
trad) X Cherry tree   10822
The cherry tree carol II (English
trad) [MDLS#TLM, LLSFLM,
DRD] BG66b   10823
The cherry tree carol III (English
trad) [DMSLTDSM, SLDTLS,
LT] BG66c   10824
The cherry tree carol IV (English
trad) [DDTLDTLS, MFMRFM,
MR] BG66d   10825
The Child Jesus (Scheidt) X O
Jesulein süss   10826
The child of a King (Sumner) [M
SSSMMMMMD, DRRRRM] AM
720; AT270; AU47; AV342;

BB614   10827
-----. R [DMSSSM, MMMMS,
SDTLS]   10828
-----. V [MSF#SMMMR#MD,
DRRRRM] AU47   10829
The children's King (MacLeod)
[SSMRDDT, LSFMRRD, TL]
D532b   10830
The Christian home (McKinney)
[SF#SMMSFDRMR, FM FRS]
AU445   10831
The Christian's Guide (Warren)
[DMMRRMFR, MFSLSMD,
D] AX142   10832
The Christian's passport (Heat-
wole) [MFSMDRM, MFSMF
MR, MF] AX432; AY165
                                   10833
The Christmas manger hymn
(Spilman) X Away in a
manger   10834
The Christmas tree (Cornelius)
[SMDFRSLFM, STDRTSD]
BG191   10835
The Church of the living God
(Winsett) [SSLSDRMMRD,
LTDDRD] AX152   10836
-----. R [SMFSDRMMD, LTD
DRDL]   10837
The church's one foundation
(Wesley) X Aurelia   10838
The city of light (Kieffer) [SD
MDMSLSMDMR, MFSF] AX
370; AY153   10839
-----. R [MFSSLSFMFMR
M, MFSD]   10840
The cleansing wave (Knapp) X
Cleansing wave   10841
The cleft of the rock (Good)
[SSDDDDMDS, SSLLDTL]
AX511; AY447   10842
-----. R [SSSMDS, DTLFM,
SSMSD]   10843
The cleft of the rock (Kirk-
patrick) X He hideth my
soul   10844
The clouds hang thick (Catholic)
[SDSDRMMR, MFRDTD, MR]
BO111   10845
The Comforter has come (Kirk-
patrick) [SSLSMS, DDRDLD,
LSLS] AX132; AY206; BB
526   10846

-----. R [DMRDRM, DDRD
LD, LSLS]   10847
The coming day (Gaines) [SSMFSS
DS, SLSMDR, SS] Y260   10848
The convert (---) [SSRDR, MRD
DLS, DRMRM] H294   10849
The cradle (Corner. 1649) X
Corner   10850
The cross is not greater (Booth)
[SSF# SLMSFR, RMFSTLS] AU
372; AX427; AY463   10851
The crown of roses (Tchaikowsky)
[LLSDRMML, MLSDRMML,]
BG197   10852
The crowning day (McGranahan)
[SSDDRMR, DLDDLS, SSS] AU
48; AV391; BY189   10853
-----. R [DDDFFFFL, LLSSMS
MR]   10854
The cry of Israel (Heller) [MMMM
SMR, RLSS, SDDTM] BH31
                            10855
The cry of Israel (Schalit) [LRD
TLSFS, RRRM, MFFS] BH34
                            10856
The dawn was purpling (Haworth)
[SSSSDTLL, LLLLRDTT,]
BO174   10857
The day dawn is breaking (Clayson)
[SDSSMSSDDRMD, SLLL]
BC179   10858
-----. R [SMSMDRDLS, SMSDDM
R]   10859
The day is done (Levenson) [MM
MRMRRD, RDDTLDTL] BH12
                            10860
The decree (English trad) [DMFS
LSMRFM, DMFSLS] BG65b
                            10861
The decree (English trad) X
Decree   10862
The Divine praises (Bragers) [SL
DD, DDDRMRDD, RRRR] BP
102   10863
The eventide (Warren) [MMFSMFM
R, RRMFMRDM,] AX110
                            10864
The 5th tune (Tallis) [SDRMDFRM
RDTD, SDRM] BJ98   10865
The fight is on (Morris) [SDDD
SLSSSLSS, SRRR] AH448; AU
402   10866
-----. R [SLTDTLMSS, SLTDTL

M]   10867
The first fruits of the land
(Hermann) X Hermann
                            10868
The first noël (English trad)
X The first nowell   10869
The first nowell (English trad)
[MRDRMFSLTDTLS, LT]
A30; B551; C551; G97; J40;
R156; S129; W45; X384; Y
328; Z197; AB119; AC79;
AD114; AE86; AF141; AG
72; AH124; AK118; AL65;
AN174; AP730; AQ285; AR
132; AT63; AU140; AW76;
BB108; BC39; BD231; BF281;
BG27; BI82; BK160; BL8;
BN23; BO159; BP15; BV117;
BX535; BY109; BZ   10870
The five lesser joys (Irish trad)
[LTDDTSLLLTDDRM, MR]
BN138   10871
The fountain (American trad)
X Cleansing fountain 10872
The garden (Showalter) [SSLL
SRD, DDTLLS, MMM] AR162;
AS133   10873
The garden of Jesus (Dutch,
1633) [SDRMFSSSMRRD, SD
RM] BG105   10874
The gate ajar for me (Vail)
X Gates ajar   10875
The glorious gospel light
(Robertson) [SDDDDRTD,
DMRDDT, SS] BC45   10876
The glory song (Gabriel) X
Glory song   10877
The God of harvest praise
(Barnby) X Laudes domini
                            10878
The God that to our fathers
(Isaacs) [LDDTLRD, DTTT
DLS#, MT] BH234   10879
The golden carol (Williams)
[DDTSLSM, DDDTLSLLT] BG
173   10880
-----. V [SDDTSLSM, SDDD
TLSL] BG173   10881
The golden chain (Barnby) [MM
MMMSSS, SDLFLSS, M] AM
287; AO610a; BX403; BY265a
                            10882
The golden harvest (Jeffrey)

[SDDDRMD, DRRDTD, SDD]
AX207   10883
-----. R [MSSSMS, DMMMRM,
SDDD]   10884
The good fight (Barnby) X To
victory   10885
The Good Shepherd (Heinlein) X
Jesu, Jesu du mein hirt
10886
The Good Shepherd (Hunter) [SS
SSDDDMD, MSSSFFM] AX253
10887
-----. R [SDDDDM, MRRRFMR
M, SL]   10888
The gospel bells (Martin) [SDD
DMLS, SSLSDRM, MS] BY421
10889
-----. R [MDSFRS, SSLSDRM,
MSD]   10890
The Great Physician [now is near]
(Stockton) X Great Physician
10891
The great reaping day (Winsett)
[MFSMRDMRDDLS, MFSS]
AX297   10892
-----. R [DDFFFLLLSM, MMR
SSS]   10893
The green hill (Stebbins) [MMM
FMMRD, MSSSFM, MM] T114;
V755; Z230; AE111; AH288;
AI52; AJ163; AK479; AR172;
AS145; AT98; AU98; AV106
10894
-----. R [STLSFMFS, SLLSF#S,
FM]   10895
The hallowed spot (---, arr by
O'Kane) [DDRFDFLS, FLFSFR
D, D] AX327; AY318   10896
The hand that was wounded
(Towner) [SSMFSLMSF#F,
FFRMFT] AX106; AY512
10897
The happy Christmas (Balle) X
Emmanuel   10898
The happy day has rolled on
(Beesley) [SDDDTDLSDTD,
MRTSL] BC250   10899
The happy story hour (Truss)
[SMMRRD, LFFML, TSSFF] AU
312   10900
The haven of rest (Moore) X
My soul in sad exile   10901

The heart's refuge (Doane)
X Arms of Jesus   10902
The heavens (Pond) [SMDDRT
TD, DSMMFRRM] AI40
10903
The heavens are thine (Peruchot)
[MLSDTDRRM, SLTDTLS]
BI12-D   10904
The heavens, O God (Beethoven)
X A hymn anthem   10905
The heavens, O God (Isaacs)
[DMDFRSF#S, DFFMRDRD]
BH57   10906
The hem of His garment (Root)
[SSSSSSF#SLS, MRMSFM,]
AU287   10907
-----. R [SDDTLSLS, SLDSM
R, RM]   10908
The highway (Lutkin) [SSSLTD
S, SSSLTDS, LL] Y13   10909
The holly and the ivy (English
trad) [DDDDLSM, DDDDLS,
SFM] BG38; BV108   10910
The Holy City (Ward) X
Materna   10911
The Holy Well (English trad)
[SDDRMFMRD, MFSSMRD]
BG56b   10912
The Holy Well (English trad)
X Holy Well   10913
The home over there (O'Kane)
X Home over there   10914
The homeland (Stebbins) [SM
MFMMR, DDTDRMM, SM]
T438; BB639   10915
The hundredth Psalm (Bourgeois)
X Old 100th   10916
The Infant King (Basque carol)
[DRTD, RMFSLSFMRM,
DR] BV115   10917
The judgment has set (Belden)
[SSF#SDMMR#MFM, MRD#R
L] BB482   10918
The Kingdom (French trad)
[MLTDTLLSLTL, SLSM, M]
BG108   10919
The Kingdom coming (McIntosh)
[DMMMMD, MSSSSM, SDTL]
G483; I633; AT409; AU125
10920
-----. R [SLLLLTDSSSSM,
SLLL]   10921

The Kingdom is coming (Mc-
Intosh) X The Kingdom coming
10922
The Kings (Cornelius) [SMTRDM
FLSS, SDRMRD] BG193   10923
The King's business (Cassel) [SLD
MMMMRDFFF, FMRF] AI197;
AM695; AT433   10924
-----. R [SSSTTLSD, MRMFSTLS,]
10925
The King's majesty (George) [LD
RFMLDRDTL, LTDM] A64a; J
73b; AF176; BZ   10926
The Lamb of God (English trad)
[MLMRF#MRDLTL, DRMRS]
BG44   10927
-----. R [DRMLSMF#RDRMRD
TL, D]   10928
The last farewell (Teasley) [MF
SSLSMD, SLLTDLS, M] AX617,
657   10929
-----. V [DRMMSMDRMD, SS
LLLR] AX657   10930
The last great day (Warren) [SL
SMDLDD, DRRRRDMS,] AX
287   10931
-----. R [SSLLFLLSSMS, MMR
MF]   10932
The last mile of the way (Marks)
[DRMMMMRDTR, RMFFFF]
AX580   10933
-----. R [MFSSSLSMF, RMFFF
SF]   10934
The last sleep (Barnby) X
Requiem   10935
The lifting of mine hands (Alman)
[DDRDTLTD, DDRDTLTD,]
BH174   10936
The Light of the world [is Jesus]
(Bliss) X Light of the world
10937
The light of the world (Brunk) X
Ye are the light   10938
The Lily of the valley (Hays)
X Salvationist   10939
The long way home (Sullivan)
[DRRMSMR, DRMSDTLS, S]
BR91   10940
The Lord be with us (Arne) X
Arlington   10941
The Lord be with us (Cannon)
[SLDRFMRD, DMFSDR, RM]
BC28   10942

The Lord bless thee (Hughes)
[SLDS, SLDFMRM, DFFRR]
BY305-A   10943
The Lord bless thee (McKin-
ney) [SDDTDRDS, SDDDTT
DR] AT541; AU498   10944
The Lord bless thee (Purcell)
[MMMRDFM, RD#LRRDTLS#]
BY305-A   10945
The Lord bless you (Lutkin)
[SSMDDRFM, SSMSDTLM]
G614; I748; AC25; AE474;
AG340; AT542; AV426; AW
614; BB695; BF698   10946
The Lord God Jesus Christ
(Wagner) [DRR#MRDSMR,
FMRDDRR#] BI53   10947
The Lord imparted from above
(Careless) [SSLTDDTDRMF
M, MSFM] BC298   10948
The Lord in his righteousness
(Dutch trad) X Kremser
10949
The Lord in Zion reigneth
(Danks) [SMDRTDD, MSDT
S#L, SDS] BB7   10950
The Lord is in His holy temple
[DMMMRMFSS, DMMMRDM]
AS485   10951
The Lord is in His holy temple
(Harrington) [SDDDDDMRD
T, SDRMFR] G589; I734; Z
616; AHp. 7; BB703   10952
The Lord is in His holy temple
(Laufer) [SSSLLMFSS,
DRMSMFM] Sap. 5   10953
The Lord is in His holy temple
(Myers) [DDDDLSSSS, SLLL
LTT] AU483   10954
The Lord is King (Gelineau)
[SSLD, DDDL, LLLS.] BSp.
28   10955
The Lord is King (Jewish trad)
X Rosh hashanah II   10956
The Lord is my light (Bischoff)
[SMFMRSRMRD, DDTLSD]
BB577   10957
-----. R [DSMDRSSMDR, MMT
TDM]   10958
The Lord is my light (Sweney)
[SSDRMMSFDRM, MMFLT]
BC103   10959
-----. R [SMRDTDLS, SDMSR

RM, S]   10960
The Lord is my Shepherd (Hudson) [SSLSMDLTDS, SLTDSM]
AX473   10961
The Lord is my Shepherd (Hudson) X His yoke is easy
(Warren)   10962
The Lord is my Shepherd (Koschat)
X Poland   10963
The Lord is our leader (Koschat)
X Poland   10964
The Lord is risen again (Bach)
X Ich halte treulich still
                                10965
The Lord my Shepherd is (Showalter) [DRMSSMRD, RMSLSMR,
M] AS261   10966
The Lord, my Shepherd still has
been (Binder) [MMMRMFML
M, MSFMRDR] BH86   10967
The Lord of all (Jewish trad)
[SDDDMRRR, RMFSLSFM]
BH80   10968
The Lord of all (Sulzer) [SSDTTT
LTD, SLTDRDT] BH76   10969
The Lord of glory (Mosley) [SS
MMDRDLS, SDDMDR, S] AX490;
AY92   10970
-----. R [DTRRRDMM, MRMFLS,
DD]   10971
The Lord of the harvest calls
(Showalter) [SDDDDTLS, MRMF
FMRM,] AX204; AY333 10972
The Lord our God we praise
(Jewish trad) X Leoni 10973
The Lord reigneth (Jewish trad)
X Ashray Yod'ay   10974
The Lord -- The Lord of glory
reigns (Rappaport) [SDSDRMRD,
TLTDRR, SS] BH71   10975
The Lord whom earth (St Gall
Cantarium, 1845) [DMFSSLLS,
SLSFMFMR,] BN137; BO100
                                10976
The Lord's is the earth (Gelineau)
[SSLD, DDDR, DDDL, LLLS,]
BSp. 12   10977
The Lord's prayer (Hays) [SSLLS
DDT, DTDRSM, MF] AJ433
                                10978
The Lord's prayer (Schuman. G-B.
1539) X Old 112th   10979
The Lord's prayer (Toews) [SSM

FSSSLDLS, SSMFS] AX652
                                10980
The love of God (Lehman)
[DDRMSLSSM, SSMRFMR]
AX82   10981
The love of Jesus (Perkins)
[SMMMRMFMRD, RRRRDT,]
BY424   10982
-----. R [FLDMSD, RRRRDT,
SMMM]   10983
The lulav (Jewish trad) [DM
RDRTDRDS, MMSSFM] BH
180   10984
The Magdalen Tower hymn
(Rogers) X Hymnus eucharisticus
                                10985
The Maid of France (French
trad. noël) [LLMLTDTDL
M, DRMFMR] BQ104 10986
-----. R [TTTDTLTDR, DRM
LTDR]   10987
The merchants' carol (English
trad) [MLTDS#LLM, FMRDT
LL, M] BG146   10988
The message (Dutch trad) X
Annunciation   10989
The midnight call (Ingalls) [D
MRDDDRDR, MSMSSMR] AX
248; AY406   10990
The midnight cry (Winsett)
[MFSSSSLSDRMD, DTLL]
AX127   10991
-----. R [DTLTDLLS, DD
RRRRDR]   10992
The miraculous harvest (English
trad) X Capel   10993
The morning breaks; the shadows
flee (Careless) [SSMDTLM
RDT, RTSMRD] BC269
                                10994
The morning star (Hagen)
[SDMDTLTSDR, MF#SMMR]
AZ310-B; BA59   10995
The morning watch (Price)
[SSLDRSSLDMS, RFFMS]
G34; BB44   10996
The mulberry bush (English
carol) X Sunny Bank 10997
The Mystic (Barnes) [SDRMFS,
SDRMFS, SDRM] Y7 10998
The nail-scarred hand (McKinney) X Lubbock   10999
The name of Jesus (Lorenz)

[SDTLMSF#F, TRDTFLSS,]
AM711; AU102; BB643   11000
-----. R [DSLSSFF, RTDTLS
S, MD]   11001
The New Year (Mann) X Valour
                                11002
The ninety and nine (Sankey)
[SSDDDDDTTD, DDMMDD]
E584; G247; W685a; AH373;
AI181; AL475; AM137; AP408;
AU36; AY501; BB673; BY425
                                11003
The ninety-nine (Warren) [DMM
MDRMD, SSSSRMFM,] AX202
                                11004
-----. R [SSSSDTLS, DMMMSF
MR,]   11005
The Old Hundredth (Bourgeois)
X Old 100th   11006
The old rugged cross (Bennard)
X Old rugged cross   11007
The only Son from heaven (Ger-
man Enchiridion, 1524) X
Förlössningen är vunnen
                                11008
The open gate (Hanson) [MSF#S
MDDTDS, SSDMSM] AY154
                                11009
-----. R [SSLFFLSMM, MRR
RRMF#]   11010
The palms (Faure) [SSSMDDTL
DS, RRRRRR] AH622   11011
The peace that Jesus gives
(Lillenas) [MRDDTLS, FSMS
MRR, MR] AU361   11012
-----. R [LSFMFMF, SFMR#
MR#M, DD]   11013
The pilgrim (---) X A few more
years shall roll   11014
The pilgrims' chorus (Wagner) X
Pilgrim chorus   11015
The ploughboy's dream (English
trad) X Forest green   11016
The praise of Christmas (English
trad) [LDTLMLSFMD, DRM
FSF] BG5   11017
The praises of that saint (French
trad) [SDRMMFMRM, MRDTDR
M] BN184; BO217   11018
-----. V [SDRMMFMRM, MR
DTDRD] BO217   11019
The precious name (Doane) X
Precious name   11020

The Prince of Peace (Barker)
[SF#FMRD, MSSLLS, FMMR#]
Z195   11021
The promised land (American
trad) X Promised land
                                11022
The promises of God (Kirk-
patrick) [MFSSSLSFMRDRD
LS, S] AX472; AY124 11023
-----. R [SLSMDDDLS, SLS
MRRR]   11024
The quest (Brahms) [MLDLS
MFS, LSFMRDT, L] BG179
                                11025
The quiet hour (Green) [DDRL
SM, MMF#F#S, DDSS#L] BB
329; BV309a   11026
The radiant morn (Gounod) X
Radiant morn   11027
The regions beyond (Simpson)
[MFSSLSMRDDLS, MFSD]
AU76   11028
-----. R [DRMRDS, TDRDRM,
RDDL]   11029
The righteous marching home
(---) [SLDDDMDLS, SDDDMS,
S] AY157   11030
The river of life (Hull. The
casket) X Ich weiss einen
strom   11031
The Rock of refuge (Fischer)
[SDMDSLDLS, SSDRMFM]
G245; I434; AH376; AT320;
AU133; AX517; BB633; BZ
                                11032
-----. R [DRRRMMMR, RR
MMFSMD]   11033
The Rock that is higher
(Fischer) X The Rock of
refuge   11034
The roll (Black) [DRMMMMM
RDDRDDLS, D] AH530; AM
727; AT482; AX468   11035
-----. R [MFSFMFSM, MMF
MRMFR,]   11036
------. V [DRMMMMMRD
RDDLS, DR] AX468   11037
The rosy sequence (Sarum
Gradual) [SLDTLSMD, DRM
FMRMD] E238c; X548; BE
316   11038
The Sabbath Bride (Jewish trad)
[LMMFMRDRL, LMSFMRD]

BH117   11039

The Sacred Heart (Dykes) [MM
MRMFRMFSM, SSSSD] Eap. 44
11040

The saints of God (Hurd) [MR
DTLTLSD, MRSFMRD] BL71
11041

The salutation carol (English trad.,
15th c) [RRMFSFM, RFMDRM,
LDD] BG36   11042

-----. R [RRFMDMRDTL, LD
DRRM]   11043

The sanctity of sorrow (Spohr)
X Spohr   11044

The Saviour reigns (Smith, B.E.)
[DRRDDFFM, MRDSFM, SD]
BI27-D   11045

The Saviour's work (English trad)
[MLDTS#LDM, DLDTS#M, ML]
BG69   11046

-----. R [MMMFMFSF, MRDTD
RMR,]   11047

The Second tune (Tallis) [LDTL
LLS#L, DTLLS#L, DF] BJ78
11048

The secret flower (Cologne G-B.
1634) [SDRMFSDRMRDRD, DSS]
BG97   11049

The seer, Joseph, the seer
(Neukomm) [SDSMDRSD, SRTD
LTSL] BC296   11050

The seven virgins (English trad)
[LDDTLSTRRML, SLSFRD]
BG43   11051

The sheaves (Minor) X Bringing
in the sheaves   11052

The Sheltering Rock (Penn) [SD
DDMRDLS, DRRRDRM] AU23
11053

-----. R [MDLDSD, DRRMR,
DRMMM]   11054

The Shepherd (Austrian trad)
[DSMDSMSMDRFRD, DSM]
BG161; BK148   11055

The sinner's redemption (English
trad) [LLLTDTLSF#M, MMRDT
L] BG51   11056

The 6th tune (Tallis) [DDDDDRR
M, MRDDTD, DR] BG68   11057

The sleep of the Child Jesus
(French noel, 13th c) X
Gevaert   11058

The snow lay on the ground
(Grieg) [MMFSLSLSM, MDS
MDS, M] BQ8   11059

The snow lies thick (Shaw)
[LDRDLSLL#L, SLDFSMR]
BG192   11060

The Solid Rock (Bradbury)
[SDMSMMRR, MFFFRDTD,]
G244; H289; I330; L415;
R368; T274; U219; AE203;
AH370; AI141; AJ381; AR
460; AS274; AT283; AU96;
AV362; AW487; AX482; AY
458; BA439; BB581; BZ
11061

-----. R [SSSSSLLL, LSMM
DMMR,]   11062

The soul's Bridegroom (Drese)
X Rochelle   11063

The Spirit (French trad) [MF
SLSSDRMRD, MFSLS]
BG154   11064

The Spirit of God like a fire
(---) [SDRRMRDDTLSLS,
FMS] BC213   11065

-----. R [SSMSSMSDMRDT
LSL, T]   11066

The Spirit of the Lord revealeth
(Wolder. Catechismus G-B.
1598) X Wolder   11067

The spiritual sailor (Southern
harmony, 1835) [LMLLTDT,
DLLSFM, MLM] AQ240
11068

The staff of faith (English trad)
X Muswell Hill   11069

The star (German trad) [SDD
RMFRMD, RMFSLFS] BK158
11070

The star-spangled banner
(Smith) X National anthem
11071

The stars watch you (Grauman)
[SMRFMDS, DRMLSFMF, L]
BH245   11072

The story of Jesus (Jutson)
[DRMRMFMRSM, DDLTLS]
BY740   11073

The story that never grows old
(McPhail) [MFSLSMRDRDLS,
DRMR] AY355   11074

-----. R [DDTLDTLSDM, MM
RDMR]   11075

The sun goes down (Jewish trad)
X N'eelah melody II   11076
The sun has gone down (Norwegian
folk mel) X Far verden far
vel   11077
The sun in splendor rose (Scottish
trad) X Selma   11078
The sweet story of old (Engle-
brecht) [SDDDDTDRDTD,
DMRDD] AU316; AY342 11079
The sweetest name (Bradbury)
X There is no name   11080
The temple of God (Warren) [S
SSLSMRD, DRFMRDS, S] AX
433   11081
-----. R [MMRDSD, TTLTDS,
MMRD]   11082
The three traitors (English trad)
[SDRMRDTLTS, RMF#SMD]
BG163   11083
The time is far spent (Methfes-
sel's Song book, 1818) X
Salem   11084
The Torah (Jassinowsky) [SFM
DRMFR, SSLDRMRD] BH203
                              11085
The torch of Israel (Jewish trad)
[MLLLLLLSDTL, LMRDDT]
BH256   11086
The tribes (DeRoo) [SMMMFM
RRR, MRDDRRM] AI174 11087
The Trinity (Giardini) X Moscow
                              11088
The truth from above (English
trad) [MLTDTLSLM, TDDTLSL]
BG68   11089
The unclouded day (Alwood) X
Unclouded day   11090
The Unity's march (Grimm's
Choral buch. 1755) X Gregor's
172d metre   11091
The unseen city (Clark) [SMMM
MMMFMM, MRRRDR] AY187
                              11092
The unseen hand (Sims) [SDD
DRDLS, DMDMDRMR,] AX
467   11093
-----. R [DMSSMMRD, RDLS
DMDR,]   11094
The upper room (McKinney)
[SMLSMRDS, DTLDTLS, S]
AU107   11095
-----. R [SSRRMRDS, SSLDTDR,

S]   11096
The venite (Collection of hymns
and sacred poems. Dublin.
1749) X Irish   11097
The very Angels' Bread (Meur-
ers) [MFLSFM, LTLTDDT,
LSF] BQ46   11098
The Virgin's cradle hymn
(Rubbra) [SLTR, TLMRM
F#, SLTRMR] BG175 11099
The voice of God again is
heard (Stephens) [SMMSM
DRM, RMSDMRS, S] BC289
                              11100
The voice of God is calling
(Levenson) [SSTDRMR, SS
TDMR, SSM] BH238   11101
The way is dark (Hay) [DRM
MMR#MFMR#MD, DDFF]
AS217   11102
-----. R [DLLSSFFM, MRL
SFM, DL]   11103
The way of the cross leads
home (Gabriel) X Way of
the cross   11104
The wayfaring stranger (Amer-
ican trad) [LDRMMRMDL,
LRRRLDR] AU74   11105
The whole wide world (Kirk-
patrick) X Whole wide
world   11106
The whole wide world (Maunder)
[SSSLSSM, MMRMFFM, SS]
AS368; AW340; BY395
                              11107
-----. R [DDMS, DFLD, DTLS
F#LSM,]   11108
The whole wide world (Thomp-
son) [SSLDLDT, TRLTLS,
SSL] AV270   11109
-----. R [MMMMMFF, FFF
FFM, MMM]   11110
The whole world was lost
(Bliss) X Light of the world
                              11111
The wintry day, descending
(Kimball) [SF#STLSFMFM,
MR#MFST] BC292   11112
-----. R [MR#MSFMRD#RS,
SF#SLTR]   11113
The wise may bring their
learning (Rogers) [DDRM
SFF, TTDRSM, DDR] BH246

11114
The wise men (Tours) [SMRD
SMMR, DRMMSF#S,] A50b;
B553; C553; D542; AH274
11115
The Word, descending (Montani)
[MMRDSSFM, MMRDRTLS,]
BQ50   11116
The world has need of willing men
(Thompson) [SMMFMSFM, SLT
DRM, MR] BC206   11117
-----. R [SSDRMFSLMSM, SSDR
M]   11118
The world itself (Piae cantiones.
1582) [DRMMMRDTLS, LMF
SSF] BG150   11119
The world's desire (Negro trad)
[SDDDRMLTD, LSLSLTD,] BG
143   11120
The worth of suffering (Rogers)
[SSSLTDSM, MSSFFM, SL]
BH98   11121
Thee, Lord (Bales) [DDRMFM
RDTD, MMFSMR] BL74 11122
Thee prostrate I adore (Montani)
[SLSDRMR, FMRDRT, SLS]
BQ48   11123
Theoctistus (Calkin) [LTDLMM
M, MMRDTL, LTD] O307
11124
Theodora (Handel) [SDDTLSLR,
MRFMRDS, D] D438b; H423;
L296; V326; BA16; BE324
11125
Theodora (Legge) [DRMFMRM
FM, SSDLSTL] W174a; AL130b;
AP233b; BY217   11126
Theodore (Lutkin) [MMSLTD
MS, FFMRDRLR,] G494; I713b;
AH207; AR408   11127
Theodoret (Ohl) [SLTLSRDS, M
MRSDRT, T] K276a; N377
11128
Theodoric (Piae cantiones. 1582)
[RRLSSL, LLRTDL, SLD, S]
X502; AF136; AQ296; BG78;
BI85   11129
Theodulph (Teschner) X St Theo-
dulph   11130
Theophilus (Ohl) [DMSSLMSS,
MSDDTS#L, L] K389b   11131
There are hearts that never falter
(Pollock) [MRDMSDTL, DLSLS

MR, M] AS335   11132
There came a little child to
earth (Havergal) [SSLTDM
FRM, SFM, SSLT] K540
11133
There came three kings (Smith)
[SSLSSDSLSS, DLTDRF]
K543; AO135   11134
There comes to my heart (Bil-
horn) X Sweet peace
11135
There is a flower (Geistliche
kirchengesang. Cologne,
1599) X Rosa mystica
11136
There is a gate that stands
ajar (Vail) X Gates ajar
11137
There is a green hill (Gower)
X Meditation   11138
There is a green hill (Stebbins)
X The green hill   11139
There is a happy land (Hindu
air) X Happy land   11140
There is a land of pure delight
(Root) X Varina   11141
There is a land where sunny
vales (Huish) [MMFSDTRD,
TTLSRMLS,] BC72   11142
-----. R [DSDSDTDRDLT, TF
STF]   11143
There is a mystic tie (Achron)
[DL#LDDRSS, DFFMMRDR]
BH137   11144
There is a mystic tie (Jewish
trad) X Hallel   11145
There is a place (McAfee) X
McAfee   11146
There is an arm (Showalter)
[MRDSMRDT, LSFFFM, SD]/
AS268   11147
There is an everlasting home
(Mattoni) [DRMRDRRM, MF
MDMSM, M] BQ69   11148
There is an hour of peace
(Peterson) [DRMMMRMFF
F, MFSMRD] BC172   11149
-----. R [SFMSLSF, FMRRS
FM, MF]   11150
There is beauty all around (Mc-
Naughton) X Home   11151
There is life for a look (Taylor)
X Latakia   11152

There is never a day so dreary
(Tours) X Tours   11153
There is no name (Bradbury)
[SDDMDLLD, LSDMDMR, S]
AI388; AM652; AO624; AS397;
AV138; AW440; AX22   11154
-----. R [SLLLLSMS, SLLSMMR,
S]   11155
There is power in the blood
(Jones) [SSSSSSLLLS, DTRD#
R, D] AI394; AT193; AX278
                            11156
-----. R [SDMMRDDLS, TDRDRM,
S]   11157
There is sunlight on the hilltop
(Haughey) [SSMSRMDL, LDSDT
DR, S] BB612   11158
-----. R [MFSMRMRDS, MFSMD
MR,]   11159
There lives a God (Lob) [SLSMD
FMMR, RMRDRMS] BH61
                            11160
There many shall come (Then
Swenska Psalmbok. 1695) X
Stockholm   11161
There shall be showers (McGrana-
han) X Showers of blessing
                            11162
Therefore give us love (Scottish
trad) X Caledonia   11163
There's a beautiful, beautiful
land (Brenneman) [DRMRDRDL
S, DRMSMR, M] AX589; AY135
                            11164
-----. R [SSLSSSMDM, SMM
RDR, S]   11165
There's a great day coming
(Thompson) [SSDDDD, DMM
RD, LSDDD] AU333   11166
-----. R [SSLS, MMFM, DDDDDD
MR]   11167
There's a land (Webster) X Sweet
by and bye   11168
There's a song (New: Martin)
[SSSLTDRMRDLS, SSTL] AI65a
                            11169
There's a song (Root) X Like a
strong and raging fire   11170
There's a stranger at the door
(Excell) X Let Him in   11172
There's no other name like Jesus
(Belden) [SDMR#MSMD, TDR
D#RFM, S] BB517   11173

-----. R [SMMD, TDRD#RLS
M, SMMD,]   11174
There's sunshine in my soul
today (Sweney) X Sunshine
                            11175
Theresa (Sullivan) X St Theresa
                            11176
These things shall be (Levenson)
[SSDMMRFM, MRFMRDTD]
BH237   11177
Thessalonica (German) [SDLS
FM, DRMRRD, MRMR] K400
                            11178
Thetford (Atkinson) [DDDRRM,
SFMMRR, RRLS] BR379
                            11179
Thetford (Aufranc) [MFFMR
DDDFMR, TDRDS] BB374
                            11180
They the builders of the nation
(Durham) [SSLDDRMD, LL
SDDMR, M] BC173   11181
Thine advent Lord (Crueger)
X Nun danket   11182
Thine arm, O Lord (Hassler)
X Passion chorale   11183
Thine for service (Leech) X
I have made my choice
                            11184
Thine forever, God of love
(Pleyel) X Pleyel's hymn
                            11185
Thine house (Barnes) [SMDS
SSLTDR, SMDL, LR] AD411
                            11186
Thine is the glory (Handel) X
Judas Maccabaeus   11187
Thine the glory (Husband) X
We praise thee, O God
                            11188
Think gently of the erring one
(Wurtemberg G-B. 1784) X
Ellacomb   11189
Think not, when you gather
(Tullidge) [SDMLSLSFR, R
MMMMDD] BC21   11190
Think on thy way (Scholfield)
[MDLS, DMSMDT, FRTSSR]
AI206   11191
Third mode melody (Tallis)
[MSSSSLLT, TTTTDT, MT]
A424b; E92; J499a; W559b;
X675; BY505b   11192

Thirsk (Wrigley) [SSDTLSMM,
RDDMRDLS,] D430   11193
Thirsting (Bourgeois) X Bour-
geois   11194
Thirsting for the living fountain
(Hungarian mel) [MMDSLTDDS,
RRDTLSF#] BL45   11195
This child we dedicate (Singer)
[MSMMFSLRR, RFMRMFS]
BH240   11196
This endris nyght (English carol,
15th c) [DMFSSLTLS, SDTLSLF]
E20; G115; R180; W595; X72;
AL194a; AN168; AQ291; BG39;
BV377; BY531   11197
This feast of the Law (Jewish
trad) X Hakafos melody 11198
This house we dedicate (Asper)
[SDRMFMRTD, RMLSF#S, R]
BC176   11199
This is not my place of resting
(Woodbury) X Dorrnance
                               11200
This is the day (A Monk of Gethse-
mani) [DDTDMMRRDTT, LTD
SD] BN182   11201
This is the day the Lord hath
made (Arne) X Arlington
                               11202
This is the image of our Queen
(Catholic) [SLTDSRMD, DTLS
RFM, S] BO77   11203
-----. R [SMLSMDLS, MMM
LS#LT, D]   11204
This is the image of our Queen
(Slovak hymn) [SDDTDRD
RMD, MRMSFM] BQ82   11205
This joyful Eastertide (Oudean.
Amsterdam Psalter) X Vreuch-
ten   11206
This new Christmas carol (Eng-
lish trad) [LDDRMMLTDTTL,
LTDT] BG29   11208
Thomissön (Thomissön) [RRR
DRTDL, FMRD#TDR, R]
M389   11209
Thomisson (Tomissön. (Psalme-
bog, 1569) X Island   11210
Thompson (Thompson) X Softly
and tenderly   11211
Thornbury (Harwood) [SMTDLDT,
RSLFMRM, SM] E545; F256;
J159; W215; X255c; AC307; BE

375; BV426; BY264   11212
Thornes House (Grundy) [MRD
RLS, SDRMFR, TMSF] BV186
                               11213
Thorney Abbey (---) [MMSRR
RMF, FFMRRM, ML] BR315
                               11214
Thou art the way (Pollock)
[MMFSSFMR, RRMFSM, MM]
AX341; AY209   11215
Thou delightest, O Lord (Brown)
[SSSLTDTDFLDM, MMRL]
U37; AI18   11216
Thou dost not weep alone
(Careless) [SDMMRFFLFFM,
MMMDD] BC181   11217
Thou ever present Perfect
Friend (Rinder) [SDDRRMR
D, SLTDTLS, S] BH41 11218
Thou, my everlasting portion
(Vail) X Close to thee
                               11219
Thou spotless Lamb of God
(Kirkpatrick) [DMMMFS, SSM
RDR, DMMM] AX310 11220
Thou that art so fair (Pothier)
[DRMFSLS, DSLSFM, RFM]
BN139; BP78   11221
Thou thinkest, Lord, of me
(Lorenz) X Amid the trials
                               11222
Thou warrior of the Lord
(Catholic) [DMMRMDLS, MR
MFM, MSM] BP89   11223
-----. R [SLTDRMRRRMFSL
S, SF]   11224
Thou who, hero-like (Catholic)
[MFRMDRTD, RLRDDTLS]
BO138   11225
Thou, whose almighty word
(Trebel) [DDRMRD, RRMFM
R, MTLS,] M111   11226
Though deepening trials (Care-
less) [SFMRLSFM, DLSFFM
F#S,] BC285   11227
Though in the outward Church
below (Mozart) X Ariel
                               11228
Though our hearts dwell lov-
ingly (Blumenthal) X Blu-
menthal   11229
Though your sins be as scarlet
(Doane) X Cleansing 11230

Three kings (Flemish trad) [ML
TDRMRFM, MRMDTDL]
BG80   11231
Three kings of orient (Hopkins)
[MRDLTDTL, MRDLTDT]
A51; B554; C554; G102; R
176; Z204; AB122; AC96; AF
143; AG82; AH269; AN176;
AO136; AQ300; AR141; AU
139; AW90; BB107; BD229;
BG195; BI88; BK161; BL17;
BZ   11232
-----. R [TRDDDSDLD, DDD
SDL]   11233
Through the day (Barnby) X
Kirkdale   11234
Throw out the life-line (Ufford)
X Life line   11235
Thule (German folk song) [ML
LMMFD, DRMFRM, MLL] E371
                                        11236
Thuringia (Drese) X Rochelle
                                        11237
Thuringia (German trad) X
Christmas dawn   11238
Thy brother (Heller) [SDDRMFSF
M, MLLRMF, T] BH197
                                        11239
Thy faithful servant, Lord, doth
yearn (Shelley) [MR#TTRDL
L, S#LTDRDRT,] BH167 11240
Thy God reigneth (McGranahan)
[SF#SMFSLTD, DLSS, SF#S]
AM670   11241
Thy great bounty (Byles) [MMM
SSDDMMRFM, MMMF] AD314;
AK259; AR340; BF500   11242
Thy kingdom come (Wennerberg)
[MDTLTMMLSFS, SDTDR]
BE204   11243
Thy life (MacFarren) [DFRM
DL, LSMFRRM, DDD] B238;
C238; D604a   11244
Thy life was given (MacFarren)
X Thy life   11245
Thy little ones (Schulz) X
Paedia   11246
Thy love to me (Avis) [MFMM
RD, RDRR#M, MFMMR] AS284
                                        11247
Thy praise, O Lord (Norden)
[SDDDTLSSS, SMMMFMR] BH
183   11248

Thy spirit, Lord, has stirred
(Schreiner) [MMMMDRRT,
TDRMFMRM,] BC204
                                        11249
Thy testimonies (Whittington)
[SMMMMMSDM, MDDRMDR]
BI38-D   11250
Thy will be done (Barnby) X
Sunset   11251
Thy will be done (McGranahan)
[SMMMRMFMRR, SRRRDR]
AX390; AY478   11252
-----. R [LLLLDMRDR, SMS
FMRDT]   11253
Thy will be done! (McKinney)
[SDDDRMMRR, SRRRMFF]
AU103   11254
-----. R [SLTDSDRDT, SLT
RTRD]   11255
Thy word have I hid (Beale)
[MMMMSFFM, MRRMFFFM,]
AW605   11256
Thy word have I hid (Sellers)
[SDDDMRDS, FMRDRRM, S]
AI155; AM671; AT180; AU
389; AV372; AX141   11257
-----. R [SFMMMMRMF,
FFFFFLS]   11258
Thy word is a lamp to my feet
(Sellers) X Thy word have
I hid   11259
Thy word is to my feet a lamp
(Jassinowsky) [SDDDDTMRD,
DRMFMDR,] BH36   11260
Tibberton (Williams) [DDDMFS,
MLLSRM, MMMM] D374b
                                        11261
Tichfield (Richardson) [MSFM
SDTLS, SDFMMRR,] D188a;
J55; K495; O32; V624; W434;
AP137; BA873; BN35; BO169;
BY361   11262
-----. V [MFMSDTLS, SDFM
MRR, M] BN35   11263
Tideswell (Hopkins) [SMMRDD
FM, DMF#SLRDL,] D84
                                        11264
Tidings (Llewellyn) [SDRMFSM
RDRD, SLTDR] BV439
                                        11265
Tidings (Walch) [DMFSSSDM
RRD, DTLSST] A261; B474;
C474; D249a; G475; I654;

J314; K224; M102; N376; P392;
R491; S382; T195; U395; V768;
Y270; Z529; AB367; AC306; AD
375; AE350; AF302; AG257; AH
462; AJ283; AK380; AL253; AM
10; AO516; AP390; AR557; AS372;
AT451; AU151; AV264; AW328;
BA351; BB449; BF534; BR382;
BZ   11266
-----. R [TLSDL, TLSM, MFMM
RD]   11267
Til fridens hem (Gustaf) [SMRDS,
SMMFMMR, LFD#R] N624
                            11268
Tilak (Bonner) [MFSLFRMFS,
DRMFLTD] BY341   11269
Tillkomme ditt rike (Wennerberg)
X Thy kingdom come   11270
Tillman (Tillman) [MMMMDSS
S, SRMFSM, MM] AT439; AU
300; AX401   11271
-----. R [LLLLSSSS, SRMFSM,
LL]   11272
Tiplady (McCutchan) [SSRRDRM
RD, SSRRDRM,] G404   11273
'Tis midnight (Bradbury) X
Olive's Brow   11274
'Tis not the large, the huge the
vast (Heller) [SSSSSFSLTD,
DTLLSF] BH235   11275
'Tis religion that can give
(Abbot) [SSSMFSM, SSLLSMR,
FF] AS296; AX633; AY20
                            11276
'Tis so sweet (Kirkpatrick) X
Trust in Jesus   11277
'Tis sweet to sing (Asper) [SD
TLSDRDRM, SSFMMR] BC187
                            11278
-----. R [SRDDTRDRM,
DDTLLLTD]   11279
'Tis the blessed hour of prayer
(Doane) X Doane II   11280
'Tis the day of Resurrection
(Bragers) [DMSSLTDS, MRM
DRM, DM] BP34   11281
'Tis the harvest time (Hall)
[SSDMMDDDLL, LSDMFM]
AX206; AY336   11282
-----. R [MRDRDS, MFSMR,
MRDRD]   11283
'Tis the month of our Mother
(French hymnal) [MMMRMSLS,

MRRRRDRM,] AH136; BO
61   11284
-----. R [SSMSMSLSF, FFR
FRFS]   11285
'Tis winter (Heller) [LTLTD
DRDRM, MSFMMR] BH198
                            11286
Tiverton (Grigg) [SDRMRDTL
TD, MRSDTLS,] D382b; L
37; W57; X456; BA329; BY
292b   11287
-----. V [SDRMDTLTD, MRSD
TLS] W57   11288
To Christ, the Prince of Peace
(Montani) [MSDFMR, RMLR
DT, TDDR] BQ63   11289
To God be the glory (Doane)
[SSLTDSDRSRM, MFLFM]
AI142; AM667; AT41; BB
647; BV280; BY32   11290
-----. R [MFSMFS, SMDRM
R, RMF]   11291
To God on high (Plainsong.
1539) [DRMFSFMRM,
MMRMFR] A303; B424;
C424; D303; E103; I93; J
132; K160; M141; N300; O2;
P1; Q33; W407; X561; AA80;
AF2; AH624; AI28; AK2; AM
92; AN488; AW568; AZ132-
A; BA648; BI21; BQ200; BR
153   11292
-----. V [DMFSFMRM, MMR
FRDTD] O2   11293
-----. V [DMFSFMRM, MM
RFMRDT] P1   11294
-----. V [DMFSFMRM, MRM
FMRD#D,] BO260   11295
To God our Father (Becker)
[SSFSDLLSFSD, RRRMF]
BN210   11296
To Jesus' heart all burning
(Catholic trad) [MFSSF#
LSDM, MRMFSSF] AH138;
BO25   11297
-----. R [STTTTDS, SRDTL
SFM, M]   11298
To Jesus' heart, all burning
(Montani) [DSLRFTDM, MSF
MRDR, R] BQ61   11299
-----. R [MMMF#S#LM, DD
DRMF, LMM]   11300
To kneel at thine altar (Lourdes

Pilgrim hymn) X Immaculate
Mary   11301
To Nephi, Seer of olden time
(Clayson) [DSSSFMFS, MRDSF
M, SL] BC186   11302
-----. R [SMFSLSFMRD, SMS
DLS,]   11303
To the God of all creation
(Beethoven) X Sardis   11304
To the Lord in the hour (Gelineau)
X Out of the depths   11305
To the Name that brings salvation
(Meiningen G-B.) X St Leonard
                                11306
To the Name that brings salvation
(Ett) X Oriel   11307
To the Name that brings salvation
(Montani) [SDLRDTDS, LTSFM
LLR,] BQ16   11308
To the work (Doane) X Toiling
on   11309
To Thee, above all creatures'
gaze (Haile) [MRLSMRLS,
MRDTDTLS,] BH126   11310
To Thee, O Jesus Christ
(Bourgeois) X Old 100th
                                11311
To Thee, O Lord (Burney) X
Truro   11312
To Thee, O Lord (Schemelli. G-
B.) [MSFMRRMF#S, RMRDRDT]
BI9-D   11313
To Thee we give ourselves (Jewish
trad) X Kee hinay kachomer
                                11314
To thy pastures, fair and large
(Malan) X Hendon   11315
To us a child of hope (Mason)
X Zerah   11316
To us is born (Hohenfurth ms.)
X Dies est laetitiae   11317
To victory (Barnby) [SSLMSSL
M, MFSLLTDR] B533; C533;
D514; I418; L537; AH437; AO
400; AP539; AV216; BA937; BD
89; BF466; BI7; BR509   11318
-----. R [SSSSSSSSSS, SLLDRM]
                                11319
To You have I lifted (Gelineau)
X I lift up my eyes   11320
Toc H (Shaw) [DTLMRDRM, SLS
MSLSM,] F500   11321
Today (Mason) [SSMMDR, SLF#S,

SSMMSL,] V271; W686; AM
388; AP398; AY313   11322
Today, while the sun shines
(Stephens) [SSDRMDLS#LTL,
RRTDR] BC215   11323
-----. R [DMDMMRDRM, DR
TRMFM]   11324
Toiling on (Doane) [MFSSSS
DRMMMM, RMFF] AT435;
AU64; AX185   11325
-----. R [MFSDMR, RMFSFM,
MFSD]   11326
Tollite hostias (Saint Saëns)
[SSSDSS, LSFMRFMLLS]
BQ160   11327
Tomer (Tomer) X God be with
you   11328
Ton-mân (Evans) [MDRMSMR,
MLS#LTDT, D] A82b; E270;
X47; AD397; AF167   11329
Tonus peregrinus (Pre-reforma-
tion mel) X St Austin
(Bristol Tune book, 1876)
                                11330
Ton-y-botel (Williams) X
Ebenezer   11331
Too late (Lindsay) [MMRMDR
RMRD, SSF#SDR] I743
                                11332
Too late, too late (Brahms)
X Lucy   11333
Toplady (Hastings) [SLSMD
LS, DRMRDTD, T] A471b;
B217b; C217a; D336b; G204;
H244; I279; J379b; K333b;
L402a; M181; N422; O27b;
P284; Q376; R271; S237a;
T393; U100; V249b; Y374a;
Z294; AA325; AB165; AD209;
AE284; AF358; AG147; AH
356; AI137; AJ140b; AK217;
AL267c; AM421a; AO260a;
AR180; AS211; AT103; AU
171; AV236; AW148; AX57;
AY312; AZ581-L; BA434a;
BB474; BC382; BE293; BF
353; BR313; BZ   11334
Torchbearers (Hyatt) [DTLTS
LSL, MFSLDRTS,] Y156;
AC229   11335
Torches (Spanish trad) [DDD
TTTLS, SLTTTLTL] BG81
                                11336

Torgau (Grobe) [MMSFRDMRD,
MRDDDRM] AA482   11337
Torgau (Latin, 12th c) X Christ
lag in todes banden   11338
Toronto (---) [SSDMSLSSM,
MFMMRLS] D589c   11339
Toronto (Hopkins) [MSDMRM
FM, FLSMRDTD] L226; BA
385   11340
Tota pulchra es (Balthasar) [SM
DRM, SLDD, STTSSMM] BQ212
                   11341
Totteridge (Nicholson) [MFSLDR,
SDSLSFS, DRS] F302   11342
Touch me, Lord Jesus (McKinney)
[MRLDT, FFMRM, MMRDSF,]
AU463   11343
-----. R [FFDRMM, RRDRM,
MMRDS]   11344
Touch not the cup (---) X Ye
elders of Israel   11345
Toulon (Meter: 10 10 10 10:
Bourgeois) [DRMFMRDDTD,
MFSLS] A220; B451; C451;
K183b; Q483; R144; S481; Z472;
AA486; AB329; AD77; AE321;
AF432; AK157; AM135; AN67;
AO259; AR520; AV160; BA310;
BD154; BE108; BF545; BI18-D;
BJ20; BR376; BY316   11346
Tourjèe (Tourjèe) X Wellesley
                   11347
Tours (Tours) [MFSDTLSM,
DRMDRMRD,] B495; C495;
D205a; G129; M205; P358; R
186; S111; T35; V187; Z113; AB
112; AC320; AD468; AE77; AG301;
AH201; AJ50; AK138; AM646;
AR175; AT507; AV367; BA817;
BB281; BD16; BF619; BR537;
BX329   11348
Tovo l'fonecho (Jewish trad) [DT
DL, MRRRRRRDRDTL] BH324
                   11349
Town of Bethlehem (Davies) X
Christmas carol   11350
Towner (Towner) [MFMR#MD, RR
DTD, MFMR#M] AE185   11351
Tozer (Tozer) [SLSMMRRD, LDSD
MRR, S] AO278   11352
Trackless ways (Williams) [DDRM
SSFM, SLLLDDTL,] AD455
                   11353

Traeder nu til Herrens Bord
(Rosenmüller) X Nassau
                   11354
Tranmer (Hayes) [DMSFMLS
FM, SLSFMR, R] F168
                   11355
Tranoscius (Slovak trad)
[LLLMSF#M#R, RF#MF#S#
LM, L] M332   11356
Tranquillity (Gregor's Choral
buch) X Old 271st   11357
Transfiguration (Goss) X St
Casimer   11358
Transfiguration (Lutkin) [MM
LLSFSLR, RMSLTS, S] I479
                   11359
Transfiguration (Olsson) [SLT
DMRDTD, SDRMSFM] J316b
                   11360
Transylvania (Hungarian chorale
mel. 16th c) X Du meiner
seelen   11361
Travis Avenue (McKinney) [MF
SLSDDTT, RMFSLTL] AT342
                   11362
-----. R [DDDDDSLDT, RRRRR
ST]   11363
Tread softly (Doane) X Be
silent   11364
Treasure (König. Choralbuch.
1738) X Ich will dich lieben
                   11365
Trebel (Trebel) [SDSMDLRDT,
RMSFRDT] M309   11366
Tredeca (German carol. 13th c)
[DRRDLSTD, DMSLSMDL]
M467; BG117   11367
-----. V [DRRDLSLD, MSL
SMRDL] BG117   11368
Trefaenan (Welsh trad) [SLS
MSLSM, SLSMRDR, S] G160;
X158; Z248   11369
-----. V [SLSMSLSM, DDMDL
TD,] X158   11370
Tregaron (James) [RLSLMFSL,
TDRDTL] A354a   11371
Trentham (Jackson) [MMMFDM,
SFMRMR, MFLS] G180; J470;
N182; R235; S84; T414a; U
213; Z450; AB93; AC61; AD
187; AE143; AF234; AG123;
AK191; AL148b; AM438; AP

270b; AR220; AT52; AV146;
AW135; BF260; BZ   11372

Tres magi de gentibus (Ander-
nach G-B. 1608) [SSMFSSM,
$\overline{SSMFSSM,MM}$] E647; W468;
X305; BY260a   11373

-----. V [SSMFSSM, MSSMFSS
M,M] X305   11374

Treuer heiland (Kocher) X Dix
                          11375

Trewen (Evans) [LDTLS#LTL,
TDTDRDRM,] W560; BY570
                          11376

Trewks (Fischer) [MMRDLS,
RRMFMR,DDDT] L180   11377

Tribute (Hopkins) [DDDFMRD,
DLSDMRRS,D] D140   11378

Trinity (Hermann) X O heilige
dreifaltigkeit   11379

Trinity (Giardini) X Moscow
                          11380

Trinity (Pieraccini) X Santa
Trinita   11381

Trinity (Wesley, S.S.) [MDFR
SM,DDDFFM,DTDR] Y17;
AC107; AD133   11382

-----. V [MDFRSM,DDFFM,R
DDRM] AD133   11383

Trinity College (Dykes) [DMSDSF
SM,RMF#SSTLS,] F57b; J117b;
K235; W339; AA118   11384

Trisagion (Smart) [SSLSMRDRR
M,MRDSF] A121; B289; C289;
D170a; F288; J148; M485; W
169; AA285; AL42   11385

Tristitia (Barnby) X St Chrysostom   11386

Triumph (Cornell) [SDTDSLLRD#
R,RRRMFT] BR150   11387

Triumph (Gauntlett) [DMSSSLS
M,SSDTLLS,M] D321b; J114a;
K50; W134; AD172; AL108; AP
812; AW617; AZ91-E; BA235;
BY221   11388

Triumph No. 2 (Vibbert) [SDTDRM
D,DFFFFM,SDT] U304 11389

Triumphant (Elliott) [SDSMRDLS,
MFSLTDMR] C484; D463a; E
40; I90; L341; R497; T133b;
V191; W25; AJ155; AM58; BE
290; BF631; BR77; BV67; BY
194a   11390

Triumphant Sion (Knapp) X Ware-

ham   11391

Triumphantly doth Christ
(Biggs) [SSFMRMRD,TDRM
FS,SL] BN77   11392

Triumphs today the Lord of
Life (Gesius) X Gesius
                          11393

Troas (Maclagan) [DMFSDTL
S,MFSLSMDR] D229   11394

Troubled soul, thy God is
calling (Davis) X Sitting at
the feet of Jesus   11395

Troyte (Troyte) [MMMMMM
FS,FFFFFMRM,] B391; C
391b; F357b; AO149   11396

Troyte, No. 1 (Troyte) [MMF
S,FMRM,MMRD,RDTD] D
667a; Eap. 59; I736; K408b;
V42b; AL430b; AP504b
                          11397

Troyte, No. 2 (Troyte) [MMR
D,FFMR,SSFM,RRD.] D461;
E494; W14; AL174c; AP151;
BR129   11398

True freedom (Jewish trad) X
Az yasheer   11399

True happiness (Southern harmony) [MSSLDR,MRDLSM
S,RRM] BZ   11400

True-hearted (Booth) [SSLSM
FSDTLS,MRDTT] BY303
                          11401

-----. R [FDRDLLLLTDL,
MRDTR]   11402

True-hearted, whole-hearted
(Stebbins) [DSDMDMSLSF#
SM,FSSL] G255; I420; AH
456; AS326; AT410; AV383;
BZ   11403

-----. R [SF#SLS, MR#MFM,
LSF#SMM]   11404

Truett (McKinney) [MR#MF
DMRD,SF#SLSR,MR#] AT
174; AU417   11405

-----. R [SMFSFDRM, LLS
MF#MF#S,]   11406

Truman (Holbrook) [SMTRDLSM
S,SLRMFLS,] G210b; I304b
                          11407

Trumpet (Pierre) [SSLTD,
DTLSLS,SSLTD,] AJ431
                          11408

Trumpet call (Geibel) [SMMMM

MM, MMDTDFSFF] C538a; G
283; U288; AE218; AI329a; AO
394; AT419; AV365; BA933;
BF473; BI113   11409
-----. R [SMMSF, SRD#RLS,
SLMFF]   11410
Truro (Burney) [DMFSSLTD, SDS
FMRDFM] A484; B187; C308b;
D265; E420; F220a; G126; H
143; I7; J8a; K444; L346; M91;
R152; S114; V126; W369; X
337b; Y115; Z224; AA428; AB
336; AC260; AD363; AE120; AF
82; AG108; AJ129; AK363; AM
61; AN103; AO178; AQ54; AR
186; AS151; AT102; BA177; BB
440; BD77; BE326; BF544; BI
28; BK106; BV39; BX133; BY
645; BZ   11411
Trust (Dykes) X Rock of ages
                                11412
Trust (Kettle) [MMMFMRMFFF
M, RRMFF] AB403; BF668
                                11413
Trust (Mendelssohn) [SSLSDMRD
T, LTDFMRD,] A448; B243; C243
a; D415; G33; G33; L88b; V502;
W382; AA81; AB66; AD324; AN
2; BB257; BD208; BF517; BH87;
BI8; BR160; BX11   11414
Trust (Ohl) [MRDSLS, FMRS, SFM
RDL,] K407a   11415
Trust (Stockton) X Stockton
                                11416
Trust (Torrance) X Moredun
                                11417
Trust and obey (Towner) [DRMM
RDDMSSFM, MMFL] AE210; AH
420; AI400; AM700; AR485; AS
269; AT260; AU390; AV373; AW
486; AX465; AY454; BB582; BY
491; BZ   11418
-----. R [SRSMMMLMSF, FFF
MRM]   11419
Trust him (Gabriel) [SSMRDSS,
DDLFLD, TLS] AX464   11420
-----. R [MRDRMSS, LLLRDT,
LSD]   11421
Trust in Jesus (Kirkpatrick) [MR
DTLDLS, DMSMRDR, M] AE302;
AI236; AM699; AR276; AS272;
AT258; AU284; AV322; AW488;
AX458; AY98; BB588; BZ

                                11422
-----. R [MSSMRDMR, MSS
MRDR, M]   11423
Trust in Jesus (Moore) [SDD
MDLDS, MSLSMMR, S] AX
461; AY101   11424
-----. R [SMLS, SLSMMR, SD
DMDL]   11425
Trust, No. 1 (Mendelssohn)
X Trust   11426
Trust, No. 2 (Wilms) X
Hague   11427
Trust, try, and prove me
(Leech) X Giving   11428
Trust your hand into His
(Penner) [SSLDMSFMRM,
MSLSMR] AX463   11429
-----. R [SSDTLS, SSLSFM,
MFSS]   11430
Trusting (Fischer) X Coming
to the cross   11431
Trusting (Kirkpatrick) X Trust
in Jesus   11432
Trusting in Jesus (Hall) [SD
MRDLS, TDRSLSM, SD] AY
95   11433
-----. R [MD, DL, RSTLSF#S,
SDMRD]   11434
Trusting Jesus (Sankey) [MRFM
MRD, DLDLSDMR, M] AM682;
AP521; AT259; AU328; AX
459   11435
-----. R [SMSMMRR, MTDD
RLT, DD]   11436
Truth (Freylinghausen) [SMF
SLSFM, RRMMRDT, T] AZ82-
C(app)   11437
Truth (Troup) [MRDRMS, FMD
TRD, SFMS] AS445   11438
Truth eternal (Schreiner) [MFS
SDRM, SLTDTLLS, S] BC189
                                11439
Truth reflects upon our senses
(Tillman) [MMMDRMRD, DD
DRDLS, S] BC188   11440
-----. R [FFFFDRMM, SSS
MRDR, M]   11441
Tryggare kan ingen vara
(Swedish) X Sandell   11442
Tryggare kan ingen vara
(Widéen) X Security   11443
Tu, Christe, nostrum gaudium
(Grenoble church mel) X

Deus tuorum militum   11444
Tu vins, Jesus (Freylinghausen.
    G-B. 1704) [LMRDTLS#LL,DD
    RMFMR] AD63; AQ48; AZ83-
    B   11445
-----. V [LMRDTLS#L,DRMFM
    RDD,] AZ83-B   11446
Tubingen (---) [SSDTLSFM,M
    MRSSF#S,S] BR151   11447
Tucker (Abbey) [MMFMMRDR,
    RMFMRDTD,] L508   11448
Tudor (Jewson) [MFMMRDTD,RMTD
    RS,SL] BA563; BY31   11449
Tugwood (Gatty) [SSSSSLLS,SDR
    MSFMR,] E146; BV362   11450
Tullar (Tullar) [SF#FMSD,DTL
    S,STLLSD,] AT437; AU343
                                 11451
-----. R [RD#MRTSDLS,RD#
    MRTSD]   11452
Tunbridge (Clark) [LDTMFRM,
    DMRSLTD,ML] E88; F87; X
    474; BE187; BJ95; BV533a
                                 11453
Tunbridge (Walch) X Tidings
                                 11454
Turin (Giardini) [SSSSLDTLS,
    FMLSSFM] M479   11455
Turle (Turle) X Armagh   11456
Turn your faces toward the morn-
    ing (Fillmore) [DDDRMFSLSM,
    DDDRMF] AY469   11457
-----. R [DDTLSLLSFM,DDTLS
    L]   11458
Turner (---) [DMMFRSSS,MFRFM
    RD,D] ALSuppl   11459
Turpin's Litany (Turpin) [SSLDT
    LS,DDRMFMRM,M] B142a;
    C142IIIb; D529Ib   11460
Tviflan ur min sjal försvinne
    (Wessnitzer) [DRMSFMRD,RRMS
    SF#S,D] N79   11461
'Twas like a dream (Schumann)
    X Canonbury   11462
Twilight (Barnby) X Merrial
                                 11463
Twilight (Hopkins) [MRDTLS,SLD
    S,SLTDRM] C17b; D10b; O564
                                 11464
Twilight (Judefind) [SSDDTTLFTL
    S,SDRMD] H36   11465
Twinkling stars (German trad)
    [DRMMFRLS,MSSFFSF] A245

                                 11466
Two fatherlands (Lester) [SM
    SLDTS, FMDRRM, SFM] Y
    126; AC331   11467
Two little hands (Ogden) [DMM
    RDRMRMS,SSLSMR].AY300
                                 11468
-----. R [MSDFLD,SLSMRRR
    F,MS]   11469
Two little hands (Warren) [MM
    MFMMRDD,DRRSFM,M] AX
    625   11470
Twyford (Blake) [DRFMRDTLS,
    LTDMSMR,] F36; BV482
                                 11471
Tyholland (German trad) [DM
    SLSMFS,DLTDSSFM,] W452a;
    BV613a; BY319b   11472
Tynemouth (Choron) [DDRMF
    SFM, LF#SSF#S,RT] Y2
                                 11473
Tynemouth (Hemy) X St Cath-
    erine   11474
Tyrley, tyrlow (Warlock) [LM
    MRRDDT, TDRMDRTS]
    BG169   11475
Tyrolean cradle song (Tyrolese
    trad) [SDDRMSSFMMRD,
    SDDR] BV95a   11476
Tyrolese (Tyrolese trad) X
    Falan-tidings   11477
Tysk (German mel. sung at
    Tysk Church, Stockholm)
    [DSLSFM,SSLTDT,RSL] A
    477   11478
Tytherton (West) X Moravia
                                 11479

U

Ubi caritas (Plainsong M 6)
    [DDRMMRMFMRMRDDDR]
    BM15; BN87   11480
Uffingham (Clark) [LLSFMTD
    TLS#,MMMRDR] E434; F274;
    Q323; V289; W275a; X564;
    AA418; AF89; AL124a; AM
    416; AP232a; BE94; BJ81;
    BY338   11481
-----. V [LSFMDTLS#,MMRD
    RDTD,] Q323   11482
Ulster (Lowry) X All the way
                                 11483

Ultima (Moffatt) [MDRMDLTD,
RMDDRD, MD] S439; W586a
11484
Ultor omnipotens (Sullivan) [SS
SSSSSDTLL, LSFMR] D198
11485
Un flambeau (French trad) [SDD
TDRMFMR, SDDTDR] Y304;
AF124   11486
Unafraid ("G. E. M. G. ") [SSLSFM,
SSLSFM, MFSL] AE453 11487
Unami (Rau) [MSDTTLLS, DRMF
SMRR] AZ858-I   11488
Unanswered yet? the prayer
(Tillman) [MR#MDMSFDRMM,
MMMFM] BC286   11489
Unclouded day (Alwood) [SSDDDD
DMRDLS, SSDD] AH539; AT484;
AU81; AX608; AY150   11490
-----. R [SLSMDMD, SLSMRDM
MR,]   11491
Unde et memores (Monk) [MMDDR
MMMFS, MRMFF] A189; B333;
C333; D228b; J278; S355; W320;
AD263; AH222; AK340; AL222;
AM579; AR589; BY307   11492
Under his wings (Sankey) [MFF#
SSSSLMSF, RMFLS] AI307;
AM78; AS263; AX525; BB587
11493
-----. R [SMSDTLTD, DSMLSM
MR,]   11494
Underbar en st'jarna blid (Berg-
gren) [MDDTDLS, LTDFM
RDT, M] N52   11495
Undique gloria (Elvey) [SSSDD
RRRRM, DTLS, SL] J418; K287;
M600   11496
Undique gloria (Reay) [SDSSFMDT
LS, FMRM, LR] AB43   11497
Une vaine crainte (French carol)
X Grace soit   11498
Union Square (Dykes) X Blair-
gowrie   11499
Unitas Fratrum (Bohemian Br. ,
1566) [DTLSSDRD, DSLSDT]
A194b   11500
Unity (Mason) [DMMFMM, MRRF
FM, MSSL] L598; AY301 11501
Unity (Warren) [DMMSSLLS,
SRFM, DMMS] AS85   11502
Unity (Woodman) [SDDMSD, DTS
SLS, SSDD] S472   11503

Universal praise (Whinfield)
[DDRMFSSLTDMR, SSF#]
A290e; Eap. 56; AD8   11504
University (Collignon) [SFM
RDDRMSFM, SMDLS] E93;
F178; W498; X653; AL352a;
AP254b; BY212a   11505
University College (Gauntlett)
[MDLSFMR, MDSSSF#S, MR]
A558; B116; C116; D506a;
E467; F291; H90; J50; K35;
L270; T392; V489; W533; X
619; AB184; AK233; AL406;
AM479; AN65; AO411; AP
537; AS449; BA584; BR398;
BV584; BX94; BY524a;
11506
University hymn (Smith) [SSSS
DT, DTLSF#S, FFSM] Y150
11507
Un'saneh tokef (Jewish trad)
[DMDDD, LLLTDRDTDLD]
BH328   11508
Unsearchable riches (Sweney)
[SSSSMSDDDD, RRRDDR]
AW454; AX20   11509
-----. R [RSFMD, MRDTDLS,
MMMM]   11510
Unser Herrscher [unser König]
(Neander) X Neander
11511
Unter lilien jener freuden
(G-B mit noten. 1890) [ML
SSRRSFFM, DTLSF#S] AW
32   11512
Unto him, for whom, this day
(Montani) [MDRMFRM, MSS
FRMMRD] BQ116   11513
Unto the hills (Beimel) [LTT
DLTSL, LTRDTDLT,]   BH13
11514
Unto us a boy is born (Piae
cantiones. 1582) X Puer
nobis   11515
Unveil mine eyes (Gardiner's
Sacred melodies. 1812) X
Belmont   11516
Up! Arouse thee, O beautiful
Zion (Robertson) [MRFMRRM
FSF, MSSDSL] BC283
11517
Up, awake, ye defenders of
Zion (Becket) X Red, white

-----. R [DDDDRMRMDRMRM
FMR]   11553
Valet will dich dir geben (Tesch-
ner) X St Theodulph   11554
Valete (Sullivan) [MMSDMLTD,
DRFMLSF#S,] AA410; BE288;
BI111; BR279   11555
Valiant hearts (Holst) [DFRSMFM
RRD, DFRSD] A531b; X293a
                                    11556
Valley (Knight) [DMFSSDDS, SLS
MFS, DM] F446   11557
Valley Forge (Clarke) [MDTLTS,
LTDRMSF#M, DL] AQ302
                                    11558
Valour (Allen) [DDRMDMLS,
DDRMMSFR,] BE61   11559
Valour (Mann) [DSDRDT, DRM
FMR, MMM] A49; B92; C92a;
D62a; S380; AB123; AD127;
AK427; AO139; BF293   11560
Valor (Irish trad carol) [DMFS
LSMFSFM, SDMFS] E91; X
293b; Y123; BG128   11561
-----. V [DMFSLSMFSFM, DMF
SL] BG128   11561a
Van der Werp (Van der Werp)
[SSLSDSFMRD, MRSSLT] AI
12   11562
Varina (Root) [SSSSDMMM,
SDDDRM, SS] G523; H508; I604;
L586; U184; V297b; AG286; AH
528; AI340; AO549; AU216; AV
281; AX173; AY141; BA760; BB93
                                    11563
Varndean (Routley) [DSMSLLS, M
FSDRM, LMD] BV264   11564
Vater unser [im Himmelreich]
(Schumann. G-B. 1539) X Old
112th   11565
Vaterland, in deinen gauen
(Mendelssohn) X Mendelssohn
                                    11566
Vaudois (Swiss trad) [MFSLTDMLS
M, DTDFMR,] Y334   11567
Vaughan (Hopkins) [LDTLM, RDTL
T, MMFSLT] L374   11568
Va-y'dabayr Moshe (Binder)
[SSDRMFFSSS, SLL#L, SF] BH
300   11569
Vayomer Adonoy (Lewandowski)
[SMMMMS, DTDFMMR, RFF]
BH321   11570

Veni (Elliott) [MFSMDRMFM
R, MMFMRM] D319b   11571
Veni (Stainer) [MMRFRT,
SDRMSR, MMRF] I389; T
359b; AM280a; BV289
                                    11572
Veni, anima mea (Dickey)
[SSDDRMFM, SSSFMRDT]
AF506   11573
Veni Creator (Sarum plainsong
M 8) [SLSFSLSDRDD, DSLD
R] A108a; B375; D289b; E
154; F157; G636; J117a; K
142a; M464; O355; P111; Q
233; R237; W182; X179; AA
249; AF575; AL143; AP267;
AZ22-O; BA133; BJ48; BN
118; BO261; BP44; BQ199b;
BV216; BY226a; BZ   11574
-----. V [SLSFSLSDRRD, DS
LDR] D289b   11575
-----. V [SLSFSDRD, DSTD
RMMR,] M464   11576
-----. V [DRDTDFSF, FDM
FSLLS,] M464   11577
-----. V [SLSFSDRD, DSLTD
RMM] AZ22-O   11578
Veni Creator (Tallis) [LLS#LM
MRM, MF#SLTLSF] E153; X
178   11579
Veni Creator, No. 1 (Attwood)
X Attwood   11580
Veni Creator, No. 2 (Dykes)
[SSMFSLSSS, LMF#SRDT]
F152; K142   11581
Veni Creator, No. 3 (Hopkins)
X Come, Holy Ghost 11582
Veni Creator Spiritus (Polish
mel.) X Poland   11583
Veni, Creator Spiritus (Lambil-
lotte) [SSSDRRRM, MRMSFM
MF] AH128; BM89; BN119;
BO186   11584
Veni Creator Spiritus (Montani)
[LDTSMLLM, MF#SLF#TTS,]
BQ199a   11585
Veni Creator Spiritus (Sarum
plainsong M 8) X Veni
Creator   11586
Veni Creator Spiritus (Ther-
mignon) X Creator alme
siderum   11587
Veni, Domini Jesu (Barnby)

[MMFSMLLSRM, SSDTLT]
H146   11588
-----. F [SSLSFDDS, MMDTD
RMD]   11589
Veni Emmanuel (Gounod) [MSFMD
MRD, STLSMSFM] D45b; AO
107a; BA106   11590
Veni Emmanuel (Plainsong M 1)
[LDMMMRFMRD, RMDLDR]
A2; B66; C66; D45a; E8; F49;
G83; J2; K1; M117; Q62; R147;
S108; W149; X66; Z182; AB103;
AC75; AD100; AE78; AF110;
AG63; AK88; AL137; AM147;
AN150; AP241; AQ280; AR214;
AW67; BB109; BD203; BF275;
BK140; BL3; BM61; BN5; BO
149; BP4; BQ152; BR136b; BV
83; BX200; BY83; BZ   11591
Veni, Immanuel (Plainsong M 1)
X Veni Emmanuel   11592
Veni, Jesu, amor mi (Cherubini)
[MMMMMFRS, DDRRMDSM]
AH131; BO35   11593
Veni lux (Brown) [DMMRDSLLS,
DTLSMSF#] L187   11594
Veni, O Sapientiae (Plainsong)
[MMMMFSFMR, MFMRDRR]
BQ2   11595
Veni, redemptor (Walther G-B.
1524) X Venit hora   11595a
Veni, Redemptor gentium (Plain-
song M 1) [DRRLL#LLLSS
LSSF, LL] E14   11596
Veni Redemptor gentium (Walther
G-B. 1524) X Venit hora
                            11597
Veni Sancte Spiritus (Langton:
Plainsong M 1) [DRMFMRDR,
FSLL#LSFS] A109a; B196a;
E155; X180a; BN55   11598
Veni Sancte Spiritus (Webbe)
[DDDRMRD, RMRSSF#S, LS]
A109b; B196b; C196; D378; E
155; F156; K144; W186b; X180b;
AL144; AP266; BN56; BO189;
BQ34; BV225; BY228   11599
Veni Spiritus (Stainer) [MRDDRM,
LSF#MR#M, MDDT] W194a;
AP270a; BY592a   11600
Veni, veni Emmanuel (Plainsong
M 1) X Veni Emmanuel 11601

Venice (Amps) [SLSFMRMFM,
DDRMFMR] A372; F510;
K45; L222; AP370; BV139b;
BZ   11602
Venice (Haydn) X St Avold
                            11603
Venit hora (Walther, G-B.
1524) [LLSDTLTL, LTDRDR
MD,] C146b; E110; F101;
M52; O186; Q91; W417b; X
295; AA141; AM165; AQ67;
AZ11-D; BA153; BM57
                            11604
-----. V [LLSDTTL, LDRDR
MD, DR] M52   11604a
-----. V [LLSDTLTL, LDRD
RMD, D] Q91   11604b
Venite ad me (Sullivan) [DTRD
FMRD#, RTDLS, DTL] BV
651b   11605
Venite adoremus (Traditional)
[SMRDTD, SFMR, RDTL]
A41   11606
-----. R [MSFRRMSFMF,
FFMR]   11607
Venting (Reynolds) [SSSSMF
SLLLL, RRRRR] AT285; AU
116   11608
-----. R [DTLF, TLSM, RF#
LDTLRS]   11609
Ventnor (Barnby) X Caritas
                            11610
Verbum pacis (Lomas) [MRM
SFM, RDMLTDT, SLT] AO
509; BA892   11611
Verbum pacis (Monk) [MDMS
FM, RDLSF#MF#S, SL] B419
C419; AZ345-B   11612
Verbum supernum (Mechlin.
Antiphonarium romanum. M
8) [SLSLDTLSMFS, STDRD]
E2; F384a; J277a; W188a;
X277a; BY124   11613
Verbum supernum (Sarum plain-
song M 2) [MDMSLTLL, SL
DDTS] A8a; E2   11614
Verbum supernum (Sarum plain-
song M 1) X Vexilla regis
                            11615
Verdi (Belden) [MFSMSDM,
RDLDDLS, MF] BB191
                            11616

Veritas (Burnham) [DDMFSDFRR
D, DDFMRS] U203; AC143
                              11617
Vermont (Floyd) [SSFMRLLSFM,
SDTMF#S] AD19   11618
Vermont (Miller) [LMRMDRDTL,
LLSFFM,] A526a   11619
Vernham Dean (Alleyne) [SMRD
SLTDT, DSLSFMR] F522
                              11620
Vernon (Lacy) [MRDDTLSLTD,
RMRTRD] V50   11621
Vernon (Lowry) X Need   11622
Verona (Deane) [SDDTTLLS, DSF
MMRR, M] BR302a   11623
Veryan (Knight) [DMSLSDTLSMDR
M, DMS] F9a   11624
Vesalius (Perry) [SLSSSLTDMRD
T, RDTD] AC313   11625
Vesper (Acfield) [MMR#MFM,
SDDFM, MMMF#S] BF345
                              11626
Vesper (Ingalls) [DLDLSLTD, D
MSMRDR, S] AY277   11627
Vesper (Mann??) [SMSMSM, MSF
RM, LFFLS] G593   11628
Vesper (Miller) [MMMMFSSFM
R, MDMLSF#] BB59   11629
Vesper (Parkyn) [DMMMRDLLS
FM, MMMLL] BB698   11630
Vesper (Stainer) [MFSLTDSF, MR
DRMFR, M] B16; D9b; F22;
K475; BV286; BY431b   11631
Vesper hymn (Bortiansky) [MS
FSMSRS, MSFRDTD] A178;
B24; C24; D17a; G45; M349;
N643; R67; Y91; Z141; AC16;
AD48; AE41; AF52; AG27; AH
166; AI380; AK60; AM410; AN
111; AQ274; AR54; AT28; AW
28; BF192; BK176; BX154; BZ
                              11632
Vesper hymn (Halstead) [DRMSF
MMRSLTLS, SSD] BB696
                              11633
Vesper hymn (Rendle) [DRMFSM
M, MFSLTDS, SL] G57; BZ
                              11634
Vesperi lux (Dykes) [SLLSDRM,
SRMFMRDDT,] C16a; D9a;
I56; AA546; AO29   11635
Vespers (Brunk) [SDTLSFM, SL
RDLS, SMR] AY287   11636

Vespers (Elliott) [MMMMRDF
FM, SSRMDMS] BR431
                              11637
Vespers (Stewart) [DMSSS
SSL#LS, MDDRMS] AP680b
                              11638
Vetter (Vetter) [DMSSMDRM,
DSSLTDLS,] A160b; E36;
F384b; M143; O545; Q273;
W89; X679; AA300; AF231;
AN291b; BE233; BJ85
                              11639
-----. V [DMSFMDRM, DSS
LDTLS,] AA438   11640
-----. V [DMSSMDRM, DSSLT
DTLS] BJ85   11641
Vetters (Vetter) X Vetter
                              11642
Vexilla regis (Hampton) X St
Cecilia   11643
Vexilla regis (Lewars) [DMF
SLDTD, LLLTRDTL] K91
                              11644
Vexilla regis (Parker) X
Parker   11645
Vexilla regis (Sarum plainsong
M 1) [DRFFMRDRR, MRDT
L,] A63a; B144; E94; F96a;
J75a; X130a; BN28; BP55;
BQ182a   11646
-----. V [DRMFMRDR, RMRDT
L, RR] BN28   11647
Vexilla regis prodeunt (German)
X Cor dulce, cor amabile
                              11648
Vexilla regis prodeunt (Sarum
plainsong M 1) X Vexilla
regis   11649
Vexillum (Smart) [MFSSDS,
MFSRM, DRMSD] C529a; D
515a; I384; W538; AB145;
BD241   11650
-----. R [SSSSDS, MFSRM,
MSDTL]   11651
Vi lofve dig, o store Gud
(Rostockerhandboken. 1529)
X Ter sanctus   11652
Vi tro og trøste paa en Gud
(Walther) X Confession
                              11653
Via bona (Dykes) [SDRDTDR
RM, FFRMRMR] V458a
                              11654

Via dolorosa (Dykes) [DMSSLSM, MMRMFFM, DM] O267   11655

Via dolorosa (Liander) [MLLMR DML, TDMLLT, MD] P176
11656

-----. R [MMLDMRDLT, TTMM DTL,]   11657

Via lucis (Prout) [SFMRDTDLR S, DTRSF#S,] D6b   11658

Via pacis I (Barnby) [DMRDDD, RMSLLS, FMMF] L503; AZ38-C; BA688   11659

Via pacis II (Barnby) [MMMSS F, MRDRRM, MLLS] V16
11660

Viator (---) [DRMMFMLS, FM MSMR, SD] M644   11661

Viborg (Barnekow) [MMSFMLS, S#S#LDRMRD, L] M472   11662

Vicar (Copes) [DMFSLSFMDRM, MFSLS] BZ   11663

Vicaria (Fairlamb) [SMFSSLSF#S M, MRTRDT] N107   11664

Vicenza (La Scala Santa) X Coleraine   11665

Victimi paschali (Wipo. Plain-song sequence M 1) [RDRFSF MR, LSMSFMR,] A97; E130; F138   11666

Victimi paschali (Plainsong, 12th c M 1) [LSLDRDTLMRTRDTL, M] BN39; BQ196   11667

Victimi paschali (Plainsong, 12th c M 1) X Christ ist erstanden X Christ lag in todesbanden
11668

Victor (Darmstadt. G-B) [MRD TLSLTDRD, DRMRD] M251
11669

Victor King (Allgemeinisches Katholisches G-B. 1774) X Te deum   11669a

Victor King (Latin 12th c) X Christ ist erstanden   11670

Victoria (Catholic) [SSFMMRR D, SLTDSLLS,] BO171   11671

-----. R [SRMFMRD, SLTDSM F#S, L]   11672

Victorious (Brahms) X Brahms
11673

Victors (Perkins) [SDRMDLLTD, DTDRDRM,] BD80   11674

-----. R [MMFMDRDRM, MMM RDLS]   11675

Victor's crown (Parker) [SS SSLTDRMD, LTRDLS] B185b; C185b   11676

Victory (Link) [DDDTDR, RRR DRM, MMRD] AY276   11677

Victory (Palestrina) [SSSLSSF MS, MMMMMMR] A91; B173; C173; D121; E625; F135b; G 156; J90; K109; M231var; M434; O324; P198; Q210; R203; S164; T346; U105; V737; W122; X147; Y263; Z238; AA307; AB142; AC 64; AD167; AE128; AF181; AG103; AH312; AI84; AK 173; AL106b; AM201; AN195; AO177; AP107c, 216, 292; AR 190; AS107; AW116; BD188; BF323; BI70; BK133; BL31; BN42; BO177; BP39; BQ29; BR183; BV192a; BX159; BY 163a; BZ   11678

-----. R [MMFMSSLSSDTD]
11679

-----. V [SLSSFMS, MMMM RDR, SS] M231   11680

-----. V [SSSLSFMS, RMMRD R, DR] AA307   11681

Victory (Sankey) [SSDDRDTT, FFRSFM, SS] AH450; AT 256; AV355; AX456   11682

-----. R [SLMSFF, FSRFM M, LLTD]   11683

Victory (Whitehead) [DDDRSM, MMMFMR, SSFM] I391; AV 295   11684

Victory through grace (Sweney) [DMSDSMSDMD, DRMRDT] AI330; AM665; AV361
11685

-----. R [SLTDDTDRS, SSS RMFM,]   11686

Vienna (German trad) X Ich fahr dahin   11687

Vienna (Knecht) [MRDMSFM, LTDRTLS, DT] A239; C115b; D476b; E500; F44; I374; K56; L52; M165; O16; P144; Q18; V319; W450; X357; Z 103; AA433; AF243; AN35; AP176; AQ172; AR28; AZ11-P; BA504; BB131; BE274;

BR254; BV423; BY764　　11688

View me, Lord (Campian) X
Campian　　11689

Vig (---) [DMSDDMRDS, DTLFLLS]
M138　　11690

Viggo (Kalhauge) [DRMDFMMR,
MRRDDRM, D] M178　　11691

Vigil (Paisiello) [SMMRDRD,
MFSMLFR, RM] H355; I625;
L545a; M460; N481; V533;
AM577; AR29; AS5; AW210
　　11692

Vigil (Patton) [MLDDTL, FFFF,
MLDDTL,] AZ580-B; BA545
　　11693

Vigil (Swedish trad) [SDMSSFM,
SLRDTD, SDM] J14; N17
　　11694

Vigil (Thalben-Ball) [DSDRM
FMRDRD, RMDMR] BY300
　　11695

Vigilate (Monk) [MMFMLLS, MM
MMMFR, MM] B128; C128a;
F308b; I494; V503; W523; AB
247; AL396a; AM471; AP547;
BA571; BB357; BE68; BV573a;
BY507a　　11697

Vigiles et sancti (Cologne G-B.)
[DDRMDMFS, DRMDMF] A599;
B266; C266; E519; F172; G6;
J103; Q15; R33; S13; W13; X
157; Y307; Z157; AB47; AC45;
AD66; AE9; AF12; AG4; AH
190; AK9; AL29; AM3b; AN198;
AP121b; AQ23; AR19; AT3; AW
11; BB77; BC4; BF173; BI106;
BK51; BL27; BM83; BN50; BV
32; BY1; BZ　　11698

-----. R [FMRD, FMRD, DTLS,
DT]　　11699

-----. V [DDDRMDMFS, DTLS,
DDD] BN50　　11700

Vigilia (Smyth) X Roll out, O
song, to God　　11701

Vigils (Gardiner's Sacred melodies)
X Belmont　　11702

Village (Stocks) [SFSMRDLSLDLDR
D, SF] W48b; AC87　　11703

Ville de Havre (Bliss) X Bliss
　　11704

Vincent (Palmer) [MMMFMMRD,
DDRM, SSSL] G314; I510; S40;
Z327; AE236; AG222; AH388;

AL433; AO315; AP514a; AR
292; AS317; AT339; AU259;
AV197; BB604; BD110
　　11705

Vincenzo (Sewall) [MRDTLLF#
S, DRMFMMR, M] BR262
　　11706

Vindex (Cutler) X All Saints
New　　11707

Viola (Bradbury) [SDMRDLS,
MSFRDTD, SD] M44; N76
　　11708

Violet (Pollock) [MMMRDRM, SF
MRDR, FMRD] AY294
　　11709

Virgin unspotted II (English trad)
X A Virgin most pure X
Bramley X No room in the
inn　　11710

Virgin most pure (Davies.
Some ancient Christmas
carols) X A virgin most
pure IV (English carol)
　　11711

Virgin wholly marvellous
(Scheffler's Heilige seelenlust) X Culbach　　11712

Virginis proles (Plainsong M
8) [SLSSMFMRRM, DMSLLS]
E191　　11713

Visio Domini (Dykes) [MDRR
D, DRDTDMR, SFMR] B406;
C406; D629; I323; O294;
V665　　11714

Vision (Campbell) [SDRMMM
MRML, LRMFFF] AC236;
BK93　　11715

Vision (Davies) [DRMRMSL
SMDRMFMM, D] W155a
　　11716

Vision (Doane) [MRDSSLDS,
MRDSLSMR,] R501; T34;
AI178; AJ49; AM295; AV25
　　11717

-----. R [SSSSLTDD, DTLS
MDFM]　　11718

Vision (Mason, S) [LSLMRM
LLS, DRMSMRD] E198; X
206　　11719

Visions of Christ (Norwegian
folk) [MSSFFMSDTLLS,
MSSF] P308　　11720

Vita (Berggren) [DMMSDDRTS

FM, MFSSL] M239   11721
Vita (Faning) [MRDSFMRD, DLS
FLM, MS] BE31   11722
Vita (Gauntlett) [MMMRMFMR,
FMRDRMRM] D245b   11723
Vita aeterna (---) [DDTRDTLLS,
MMMRDSF] D124   11724
Vita aeterna (Barnby) [SSSLFSM,
SSSTLS, SSS] AB147   11725
Vita lampada (Candlyn) [MLLTD
RMFM, TDDDRMF] Y159
                               11726
Vittel Woods (Keeler) [SMMMMM
RF, LDTDMRR, S] S433 11727
Viva! viva! Gesu (Filitz) X
Caswall   11728
Vivat! vivat! (Catholic) [DDRR
MSMDDTRTS, DDR] BO210
                               11729
Vivit (Handel) X Messiah 11730
Vladimir (Sewall) [DDDDRMRD,
MMMMMRLD] BR216   11731
V'nislach (Jewish trad) [DDDRMR,
SSMSLSFMFM] BH319   11732
Voice divine (Plainsong M 1:
arr by Mason) X Hamburg
                               11733
Voison, d'où venait? (French trad)
X Waking-time   11734
Vola (Voigtländer) [SFFMDLLS,
MSSFRFFM,] M642   11735
Volga boatman (Russian trad)
[DLRL, DLRL, DFMFMR, DL]
Y313   11736
Voller wunder (Ebeling) [DSLDD
TD, TDRSLTLS, D] E256; J
203a; Q11; W706; X374; AA315;
BV295   11737
-----, V [DSLDDTD, TDRS
LLS, DS] Q11   11738
Vom himmel hoch (Luther) X
From heaven high   11739
Von Gott will ich nicht lassen
(Crueger) [SLSFMRR, MF
MRMD, SLS] AA233   11740
Von Gott will ich nicht lassen
(Madgeburg. Christliche
Tischgesange. Erfurt, 1572)
X Guds Godhed vil vi prise
                               11741
Vox aeterna (Lutkin) [DSDMM
R, FLMRDT, DRMM] D35b
                               11742

Vox aeterna (Parker) [MDSLL
S, SMFMM, MDSLT] B518;
C518a   11743
Vox angelica (Dykes) [DMM
SSLSMDMRD, MMML] B290b;
C290c; D398b; H510; I621b;
L587b; U426; V694b; AB404
b; AZ189-E; BA745; BR447a;
BX465   11744
-----. R [MDMSSSDLS, SSS
SDSS]   11745
Vox angelica (Smart) X Pil-
grims   11746
Vox celestis (Foster) [DLTD
RM, MMMMLS#M, MDL]
Y3; AD92; BX109   11747
Vox dilecti (Dykes) [MMLLT
DDT, TLLLLS#, M] A424a;
B242; C242; D673a; F351;
G210a; H297; I304a; J499b;
K365; M163; Q277; R280;
S236; T385; U183; V297a;
W410; Z288; AA46; AB199;
AC147; AD204; AE170; AG
163; AI203; AJ143; AK236;
AL271a; AM221; AO246a;
AP412a; AR267; AV175; AW
142; AZ590-K; BA505; BB
225; BF344; BR393b; BV
513b; BY436b; BZ   11748
Vox Jesu (Spohr) X Flensburg
                               11749
Vreden di n afvend (Crueger)
X Herzliebster Jesu 11750
Vreuchten (Oudaen. Amsterdam
Psalter 1685) [SDRMFS, SLS
FLSFMRD] X169; AL110;
BG152; BN45; BV197
                               11751
-----. R [DRMFMRMFSLSS
F#S, SF]   11751a
V'shom'ru (Lewandowski) [MS
SSSLL#LFSLSSSSS] BH272
                               11752
Vulpius (Vulpius) X Gelobt sei
Gott   11753
Vulpius (Vulpius) X Cana
                               11754

                W

W. Zlobie Lezy (Polish carol)
[SSDD, TDRRMFSFMRD, S]

G105; R164; AE430; AL63; BV
103; BY100; BZ   11755
Wach auf, mein Geist! erhebe
dich (Schop) X Eternity 11756
Wach auf, mein herz, und singe
(Selnecker) X Selnecker 11757
Wachet auf! (Nicolai) X Sleepers,
wake   11758
Wachet auf, ihr mueden geister
(Grimm. Choral buch) X
Grimm's 480th metre   11759
Wachet doch: erwacht (Crueger.
Praxis pietatis. 1662) [MRDT
MRTL, DDTLS#LT, M] AA163
11760
Wachet, wachet, lieben kinder
(Gregor's Choral buch. 1784)
X Gregor's 163d metre   11761
Wachovia (Chitty) [SFMMR, RR
RMRD, MFMMR,] AZ70-B
11762
Wachterlied (German, 16th c)
[SMSDSDRM, RMFSFMRD,]
X562   11763
Wachuset (Davis) [LMMMTRDLS
L, DRRMSF] BZ   11764
Waddell (Crueger) X Ratisbon
11765
Wainwright (Wainwright) [DDMRL
SFM, SSSDLFF] A240; W473;
X355; AN27; AP53   11766
Wait, and murmur not (Kirk-
patrick) [SSSF#SLSD, MFMRLS
FM,] AU440; BB616   11767
-----. R [SSMSSFFFF, FTLTDS
S]   11768
Wait on God (Malan) X In His love
abiding   11769
Waiting and watching (Pontius)
[SSF#SLSF#SM, DDTDRDL] BB
542   11770
Waits' carol (Stutsman) [SDRMFSS
LLS, MFSMFM] G103; BZ
11771
Wake, arise (Nicolai) X Sleepers,
wake   11772
Wake, awake (Nicolai) X Sleepers,
wake   11773
Wake! awake! (Thorne) [DTDLS
FMS, SLTDTDMR] D40b 11774
Wakeman (Thayer) [MRDSMDRFM
RD, MRDRM] L261b   11775
Waken, Christian children (---)

[SLSFMM, FSFMR, SLSFM]
BR531   11776
Waking-time (French trad)
[DDRMDSSS, FMFSLLSF] BG
88   11777
Walden (Jones) [SSMFSDTTL
S, SSRMFF] AL78; AP19b;
BB260; BV511b   11778
Walder (Walder) [SMRDLSFM,
SDDTLS, TR] Q285; AA111
11779
Waldis (Waldis) [SSSMSLLS,
SMSFMRD, S] M488; N86
11780
Waldrons (Miller) [DMMSDRM
FM, SSSLTDT,] AP130
11781
Walenn (Walenn) [SLTDMRSD,
DRMF#SF#M, T] C339b
11782
Walford (Bradbury) X Sweet
hour   11783
Walford (Thalben-Ball) [MMM
SMDRM, SSSDTLSM] BY443b
11784
Walk daily with your Saviour
(Pollock) [DRMMFMMR, RD
DRRM, DR] AX445; AY126
11785
-----. R [MFSSLLSM, SLLS
F#S, DR]   11786
Walk in the light (Showalter)
[SSLSMMRD, DRRSRM, DM]
AX450; AY90   11787
-----. R [SMDT, FRLS, SMDT,
LSSS]   11788
Walk with Jesus (Bolze) [DRM
FMRR, DRMFMRD, S] M220;
Q409; AA333   11789
Walking in the sunshine (Sankey)
[SF#SLSSMSDRM, LS#LTD]
AX440; AY479   11790
-----. R [MSLTDRDL, SDMM
RDR, M]   11791
Wallace (Baker) [MMMSMRMFS
M, SSF#SDT] T218; AJ311
11792
Wallace (Hamilton) [SMSLDRD,
DTDLSS, SMS] G101; AC92
11793
Wallace (Wallace) [SSMDSMFM
RFLS, SSMD] L572   11794
Wallin (Rostockerhandboken,

1529) X Ter sanctus   11795
Wallog (Davies) [DDLSMRRDR
MLS,SSMM] BE278   11796
Walmisley (Walmisley) [MRDTTL,
DL#LSSF,LTTD] F121   11797
Walsall (Purcell) [LDTLMMRDT
L,DLS#LTD] A501; E13; F56;
N99; R129; S232a; W148; X603;
AD458; AF154; AL348b; AP124a;
AR390; BE17; BV75a; BY687
22798
-----. V [LDTLMMRDTL,DTL
S#LT] AL348b   11799
Waltham (Albert) [DRMFSDTLS,
LTDRMFR] D274a; E132; F
406,636; J205; K446; M553;
O87; Q549; W145; X32a; AA
23; AF323; AK40; AL121; AM
142; AO41; AP234; AR44; AW
370; AZ89-a; BA193; BE166;
BV21,47; BY763   11800
-----. V [DRMSFMDTLS,LTDR
MR] E132   11801
-----. V [DRMSDTLS,LTDRMFR
D,] F636   11802
-----. V [DRMSDTLS,LTDRMR
D,D] M553   11803
-----. V [DRMFSDTLS,LTD
RMRR] AW370   11805
Waltham (Calkin) [DMR#MMFMF,
F#SDTLLSS,] A259b; C285;
D253b; G502; H63; I12; J315;
N509; R506; S384; T174a; U54;
V58; Y269; Z241; AA127; AB
372; AC304; AD379; AE131;
AF296; AG256; AH267; AI172;
AJ127; AK354; AL245; AM202;
AN315b; AO466; AP48; AS369;
AT78; AU148; AV258; AW331;
BA340; BB450; BC219; BD86;
BF526; BI93; BK60; BX370
11806
Waltham (Monk) [MMRMFSM,SSFM
FFM,MF#] F324b; K67; AP
305; AR339; BY449b   11807
-----. V [MMRMFFM,SSFMFSM,
MF#] AR339   11808
Walther (Walther, C) [DDSMMDSSF
MR,RRSF#M] Q198   11809
Walther (Walther) [SSSLSDRDTLS,
LDSFM] M46; O156; Q313; AA
431   11810
Walton (Gardiner's Sacred melo-

dies. X Gardiner   11811
Wansted (German) [DMRSFM
DR,DDTLTDRM] N51
11812
Wär Gott nicht mit uns
(Walther. Geistliche G-B.
Wittenburg, 1524) [RLLMSF
MR,RLTDRDTL,] Q267; AA
282   11813
War no more (Negro spiritual)
[MMMSLDM,MMMMRD,
RRM] Y322   11814
-----. R [MMMMRD,DRMRF
MRD,DR]   11815
Waratah (Cross) [MRDSMSF
M,MTLSSF#SL] I549 11816
Ward (Scottish mel) [SSDTDSL
S,SSSSDRMR] D80b; H65;
I218; L481; M279; T30a; V
336; AB371; AE375; AJ43;
AM292; AN106b; AO87; AV
68; BA307; BB137; BD152;
BE128; BR274; BX84
11817
Wardlaw (Booth) [MSDDRM,
DTLSFM,MMLL] D569b
11818
Ware (Kingsley) [SSSLSDMR,
RDDDMSRS] H112; L487;
T124; V443; AJ181; BB204
11819
Wareham (Knapp) [DDTLSDR
DTD,RMRDTD] A119; B9;
C9; D137; E53; F245; G38;
H95; I215; J127; K66; L279;
N511; O475; Q608; R527;
S470; V18; W253; X631; Z
285; AD449; AF430; AI362;
AK425; AL37; AN63; AO594;
AP143; AQ99; AR226; AT323;
AW208; AY414; AZ22-H; BA
56; BB188; BE391; BF303;
BI47; BR218; BV8; BX80;
BY138; BZ   11820
Warfare (Chadwick) [DDRMFM,
RSDFR,MMMML] D523c
11821
Warfare (Hutton) [DDDTLSS,
LLLTDR,MMM] C357b; AP
771   11822
Waring (Barnby) X Frankscot
11823
Waring (Dykes) X St Bede

11824
Waring (Spohr) X Flensburg

11825
Warner (Bradbury) X Renar

11826
Warner (Rossini) [SSLFMMMFR
D, SDRMMF] H160; L380; M228;
V281   11827
-----. V [DSLFMMMFRD, SDRMM
F] M228   11828
Warner (Warner) X Softly the night
is sleeping   11829
Warren (Campbell) [SMMMMSD
D, MLTDRM, MR] AC332 11830
Warren (Taylor) [SMMMRDRM,
DTLSFMFS] H71   11831
Warren (Warren) X Bread of
life   11832
Warrington (Harrison) [SSFMSD
DRTD, MRRMRD] C480; D251;
E263; F11b; O389; V211; W388;
X25c; AK196; AL33; AM20; AN
57; AO537; AP322; AW257; BA
306; BB187; BE163; BR462; BY
150   11833
Warrior (MacDonald) [SDDDRM
RD, RMSLSFMR] Y146; AB255;
AC203   11834
Warsaw (Clark??) [DSFMDS, M
FSLTDRDDT,] E386; I67; L
510; W165; X252   11835
Warsaw (Polish) [MMMRRDDDT
T, LTDSSF] Y309   11836
Wartburg (Erfurt G-B. 1524) X
Komm, Heiliger Geist, Herre
Gott   11837
Wartburg (Isaak) X Innsbruck
                                11838
Warum sind der Thränen (Schulz)
X Swahili   11839
Warum sollt ich (Ebeling) X
Ebeling I   11840
Warwick (Stanley) [DMSDLSLSM
RD, MSLTD] H28; I41; L8; N
328; V108; W385a; X513; AD45;
AI153; AL537b; AM332; AO21;
AV144; AW20; BY188   11841
-----. V [DMSDLSLSMRD, MSL
DT] N328   11842
-----. V [DMSDLSFLSMRD,
MF#SL] W385a   11843
Warwick (Thalben-Ball) [MRSFM
RDLS, LTDLFMR] BV38 11844

Was frag' ich nach der welt
(Fritsch) X Darmstadt
                                11845
Was fuerrecht du feind Her-
odes (Franck) [DMRDTLSS,
SLTDTRRT,] AA180
                                11846
Was Gott thut das ist wohl-
gethan (Gastorius) X Was
Gott tut   11847
Was Gott tut [thut] (Gastorius)
[SDRMFSFM, LSFMFMRD,]
J582; K402; M281; O603; P
430; Q521; R366; S291; W540;
X403; AA507; AF96; AK309;
AM94; AN44; AQ30; AW524;
AZ160-A; BA703; BI2-D; BQ
261; BR240; BV189   11848
-----. V [SDRMFSFM, LSFM
MRD, S] M281   11849
-----. V [SDRMLSFM, LSFM
FMRD,] O603   11850
-----. V [SDRMFSSM, LSFM
MRD, S] AM94   11851
-----. V [SDRMFSFM, LSFM
MRRD,] AQ30   11852
-----. V [SDRMLSFM, LSFM
FSRD,] BI2-D   11853
-----. V [SDRMLSFM, LSMRRD,
SD] BR240   11854
Was kann es schön'res geben
(G-B. mit noten) [SMMRRD
S, SLLDLS, SDD] AW387
                                11855
Was lebet; was schwebet (Rhein-
hardt. Choralbuch ms) [SD
DRMMSFMRMMM, RDR] E42;
F77; S7; X470; AD27a; AL
201a; BV11; BY35b   11856
-----. V [DDRMMSFMRMMM,
RDRM] AD27a   11857
Was mein Gott will (Sermisy)
[MSLSDDTD, DTLRTLS#L]
Q437; AA511; AF354 11858
-----. V [MFSLSDDTD, DTLR
DTT] AF354   11859
Washed in the blood (Hoffman)
[MSDDDSMSDDD, DRMMM]
AT192; AU111; AX276
                                11860
-----. R [MRDDTL, TLSDRM
FMR, M]   11861
Washington (Price) [DDDRRFM

RM,MFMMLSF#] I444   11862
Washington Square (Greenfield)
[DDDDDDDD,DRRRRRRD,]
Y340   11863
Wassail song (English carol) [DR
MRDRM,RDSSSS,SLL] BG15a
                                        11864
-----. R [MFSDLS,MFSDLS,MF
S]   11865
Wassail song (English carol) X
God rest you merry   11866
Watch o'er me (Barnby) [MMFS
SLDDTD,DTLSSL] BI61
                                        11867
Watch unto prayer (Warren) [SS
DMRDLD,SSDLSSMR,] AX363
                                        11868
-----. R [SSMDDL,SSDDRMMR,
SS]   11869
Watching (Doane) [SSLSDRMDL
D,SF#SLSD] AI94; AT119; AU
67; AX284   11870
-----. R [RRMRSLSDMD,LDTLS
D]   11871
Watchman (Ingham) X Dawn
                                        11872
Watchman (Leach) [DMSDMR,
SF#SDTLS,SDR] BY363b
                                        11873
Watchman (Mason) [DRMRMFS,
SMSLSMR,D] A440a; B106;
C106b; D331b; G485; H483; I
636b; J525; L355; T93; U393;
V585; Z183; AC298b; AG61a;
AH244; AJ136; AN154; AO526;
AQ283; AR124; AS99; AV263;
AW66; BA188; BD204; BE368;
BR229; BX194   11874
Watchman, blow the gospel trum-
pet (Kirkpatrick) [DRDSMSDM,
LTDTDMR,D] BB619   11875
-----. R [FRTSMRDS,DDDTDR
M,M]   11876
Watchman, tell me (Dadman) X
Is not this the land of Beulah
                                        11877
Watchman, tell us (Elvey) X St
George's Windsor   11878
Watchman! Tell us (Mason) X
Watchman   11879
Watchman's call (---) [DSDDRS
SDDRM,MDDDS] AY57   11880
Watchword (Smart) X Sion   11881

Watchword (Stainer) [DDLDDS,
SLSFM,SSLTT] D523d
                                        11882
Water-End (Shaw) [SMDRMS,
LTDRD,SMDRM] X499
                                        11883
Watermouth (Mann) [MMMRDD
T,SFFMRM,M] A349; B526;
C526b; D444b; G226; H316;
I350; J419; K361; L110; M
209; N259; O204; P4; Q352;
R307; S200; T154; U253; W
71; Y369; Z308; AB73; AC
196; AD244; AE263; AF218;
AG165; AH428; AJ228; AK271;
AL69; AM541; AO389; AP
400; AR346; AS455; AT386;
AU187; AV193; AW212; BA
526; BB288; BF424; BY119;
BZ   11884
-----. R [R#MMRDDT,SFFM
RM,]   11885
Waterspring (Bourgeois) X
Bourgeois   11886
Waterstock (Goss) [SMFSDS,
SMFSLR,RMMD] O124; W
117   11887
Watts (Brunk) [DMRDTLTD,
RMSFMRLS,] AY413   11888
Watts' Cradle song (English trad)
x Northumbria   11889
Waugh (Harrison) X Cambridge
                                        11890
Waveney (Redhead) X Metzler's
Redhead, No. 66   11891
Waverton (Jackson) [MMMFFF,
FMMLLR,MMMM] AM23
                                        11892
Wavertree (Shore) [MMMSFFF
MRD,LLLSSS] C136; D83;
AA492   11893
Way of the cross (Gabriel)
[SLDDDRDMMFM,RDTDF]
AT196; AX424   11894
-----. R [SMMMMFM,DMSS
SSLS,M]   11895
Wayland (Becket) [MRDFMRSM,
MFMLSSF#S,] AP570b
                                        11896
Wayland (Holsinger) [MMM
SSDRM,MFSLSFMR,] AQ217;
AX637; AY298   11897
We all believe in one true

God (Darmstadt G-B. 1699)
X Clausnitzer   11898
We are all enlisted (Bradbury)
[DRMRDTLSSMLS, STDR,]
BC210   11899
We are going down the valley
(Fillmore) [DRMMMMMMFRM,
DDRRR] AX615; AY496 11900
We are little gleaners (Fillmore)
[MMRRDS, DDRRM, MMRRD]
AY481   11901
We are nearing home (Sweney)
[MFSSLSMRDRMD, MSDD]
BB642   11902
-----. R [MFSLS, MSDRD,
DTTLLL]   11903
We are saved (Showalter) [SSDD
DTLLS, SSDDDTD] AI132; AR
430; AS291   11904
-----. R [SSFFMRDRM, DRMM
FSF#]   11905
We are soldiers of Christ (Ed-
wards) [SSDTLSFMMRRFL, TD
TR] AI328   11906
We are sowing (Tuckett) [DRM
MFMMD, DRMFSM, D] BC192
                                      11907
We are thy people (Beimel) [LLT
DDTRDTLM, LLTDD] BH326
                                      11908
We bless the name of Christ,
the Lord (Hastings) X Retreat
                                      11909
We build our school on thee
(Rogers) [MMMMMFMM,
FFFFFLSS,] BH254   11910
We ever pray for thee (Stephens)
[SSSSFMRMFM, LTLSFM]
BC386   11911
We give thee but thine own
(Bradley) [MMMMMM, MMRDR
M, MFFM] AS353   11912
We give thee but thine own
(Mason & Webb. Cantica laudes.)
X Heath   11913
We have an anchor (Kirkpatrick)
X Will your anchor hold?
                                      11914
We have heard (---) [SSMRMFM
MRD, SSDDDD] BB305 11915
We have heard the joyful sound
(Kirkpatrick) X Salvation
                                      11916

We join to pray (Naff) [SD
TDRMRD, DDRMFFMR] AX
552; AY296   11917
We love thy house, O God
(Robertson) [DRMSLFS,
SDTLSFM, MF] BC203
                                      11918
We march to victory (Barnby)
X To victory   11919
We meet again in gladness
(Hecht) [SDDTTDTLS,
DMDTDR, S] BH255
                                      11920
We meet again in Sabbath
School (Beesley) [SDD
RRMFS, MRDDRRM, S] BC
193   11921
We now have met (Shoemaker)
[SDRMDFMR, STDRFMRD,]
AX54; AY5   11922
We plough [plow] the fields
NOTE: Plough and plow are
interfiled as spelled plough
We plow the fields (Bay) [SM
DMSDD, DRRDTD, SMD] P
244   11924
We plough the fields (Cottman)
X Morn of gladness   11925
We plough the fields (Grimm)
[DDLTSLSF#S, SLFFMRD,]
BH195   11926
-----. R [MDTLDT, LLSRS
M, SDTD]   11927
We praise thee, O God (Hus-
band) [SDDDDDRMMMM, DM
SSS] U27; AI376; AM634;
AP718; AS16; AT205; AU155;
AV156, 328; AW437; AX417;
AY420; BY170   11928
-----. V [SSDDDDRMMRDR,
SSRR] AV156   11929
-----. R [SSLSMRDD, SSLS
MR, SS]   11930
-----. V [SSSSSLS, MMMMM
FM, RR] AV156   11931
We shall sleep, but not forever
(Vail) [SSSSMFLS, DTLLS
FM, S] N604; AI300; AY185
                                      11932
-----. R [SFMMFLSFM, SS
DDRRM]   11933
We thank thee (Batchellor) X
Onslow   11934

We thank thee (Rogers) [SSSS
LLLS, SSSLLTLS,] BH242
                              11935
We thank thee (Singer) [SDMLSFM
RD, DLLSDSF] BH193   11936
We thank thee Lord (Curry) [DM
FSRMRDFMMRMFS, L] BL68
                              11937
We thank thee, O God, for the
prophet (Norton) [DRMMRDRM
FSM, DRMMR] BC196   11938
We three kings of orient (Hopkins)
X Three kings of orient
                              11939
We would see Jesus (Belden)
[DRMFMMRDTRD, RMF#SL]
BB29   11940
We would worship (Bigelow) [DD
RRR, RSFMM, FFMRDS]
AT519   11941
Wearmouth (Steggall) [MSMFRMDR
M, FSMLSMF#] D138; AB315;
BA258   11942
Weary soul by sin oppressed
(Excell) [MMMRDLS, DDRDM
R, MMM] AS51   11943
Weather-beaten sail (Campion)
[MMRSFFMLSDRRD, MMR]
X587   11944
Webb (Webb) [SDDMDDL,
DSDRMR, SDM] A264; B99b;
C479; D252a; E581; F307b;
G487; H137; I386; J313; K230;
L347; M104; N264; O113; P255;
Q455; R99; S265a; T118; U406; V
486; W532; X646b; Y170; Z371;
AA471; AB253; AC201; AD288;
AE217; AF305; AG105; AH443;
AI329b; AJ171; AK290; AL262;
AM111; AN151; AO394; AP386;
AQ209; AR468; AS323; AT379;
AU12; AV95; AW65; AX338; AY
73; AZ151-T; BA354; BB354;
BD37; BE335; BF337; BR20;
BV586a; BX201; BY556; BZ
                              11945
Webbe (Essay on the church plain
chant. 1782) X Dulce carmen
                              11946
Webbe (Miller) [MFRDMFSSLLS,
DDTLL] B95; C95b   11947
Webbe (Webbe) X Consolation
                              11948

Weber (Flotow) X Even song
                              11949
Weber (Weber) X Jewett
                              11950
Weber (Weber) X Seymour
                              11951
Wedlock (Sacred harp. 1844)
[LTLTRMMR, TLLSMS, SL]
BZ   11952
Weeping One of Bethany
(Bushey) [MDMSSSMSDD, DL
SMMR] AY211   11953
Weighed in the balance (War-
ren) [SMMDRMMRD, DDDM
RDR,] AX294   11954
Weihnacht (Harrington) [MMS#
MSSRR, MFMFRS, MM] G99;
I120   11955
-----. R [DTLDTLDT, LSF#
SLSFM,]   11956
Weil die worte wahrheit sind
(Freylinghausen) X Truth
                              11957
Weil die worte wahrheit sind
(Herrnhut ms) X Gregor's
82d metre   11958
Weil ich Jesu schäflein bin
(Brüder. Choral buch. 1784)
[SDLLSFM, SDLLSFM, SD]
Q648; AM643; AW430 11959
Weil ich Jesu schäflein bin
Dölker. (Geistliche lieder.
1876) [DDDMRDTDR, MRM
FMRM] K556; N650   11960
Weimar (Bach, C.P.E.) [SSDTL
SFM, MRDFRMMR,] Q328;
V603; AA417; BR553   11961
Weimar (Nares) X Amsterdam
                              11962
Weimar (Pensum sacrum.
Goerlitz, 1648) X Herr Jesu
Christ   11963
Weimar (Vulpius) [MRDRMFS,
LSFMRD, MSFMR] A37; E
187; J546; Q140; S318; X215;
AA192; AB362; AZ152-B;
BR429   11964
-----. V [MRDRMFS, LSFM
RRRD, M] S318   11965
Weimar (Vulpius) X Cana
                              11966
Weisse (Wagner. Sammelung)
X Gottlob, es geht nun mehr

zum ende   11967
Weisse flaggen (Tochter Sion.
  Cologne, 1741) [DSLLSFMRD,
  DTLRDTL] AF180; BV301
                            11968
Weisse flaggen (Tochter Sion.
  Cologne, 1741) X All Saints.
  (Darmstadt G-B. 1698)   11969
Welcome (English trad) [SLTDRM,
  SDLDMRD, SLT] H438   11970
Welcome (Leach) [MDRMDLD, M
  FSMDLSMR] G395   11971
Welcome (Linton) [MMDDDLS,
  SDMDRDTD, M] AY272   11972
Welcome (Sankey) [MMMMSS
  DDDDM, LDTLS] AP407   11973
Welcome (Smart) X Vexillum
                            11974
Welcome, happy morning (Calkin)
  [SSLDDS, SFMRD, LDFFF]
  C169a; D109a; I166; BF320
                            11975
-----. R [SSDDRR, MRDTTL,
  RRRL]   11976
Welcome, happy morning (Sullivan)
  X Fortunatus   11977
Welcome, summer (Irish trad
  carol) X Valor   11978
Welcome voice (Hartsough) X I
  hear thy welcome voice 11979
Welcome, welcome Sabbath morn-
  ing (Beesley) [SF#SMDTLS, FM
  FRSFM, S] BC190   11980
Welcome Yule (Nicholson) [DLT
  DRDT, DLTDLSF, FD] BG174
                            11981
-----. R [DTL, DTLS, SFMRD
  SLS.]   11982
We'll build on the Rock (Belden)
  [SDDRMDRDLS, SDDRMD]
  BB579   11983
-----. R [MFSDRM, FMRDRM,
  MMMM]   11984
We'll never say good-by (Tenney)
  [SSMSDMDDT, LSMSDR, S]
  AU412; AX656; AY184   11985
-----. R [SSMDSLLL, LLRRMR,
  RM]   11986
We'll sing all hail (Coslett) [SM
  RDDTLSLSFFM, SLL] BC218
                            11987
We'll sing the songs of Zion
  (Mendelssohn) X Heavenly love

                            11988
We'll work till Jesus comes
  (Miller) X Land of rest
                            11989
Wellard (Whitehead) [MRDLS
  LS, SSDMR, SFMR] AL591;
  AP724   11990
Wellerd (Main) [DMSDDRTD, M
  MMRTSLS,] AO195   11991
Wellesley (Elvey) [DRMFMM
  RD, LLSSRM, DD] D615b; W
  602   11992
Wellesley (Swisher) [DSFMDRFM,
  MFSMDRMR] BD54   11993
Wellesley (Tourjée) [SDRDTS
  RMRD, LSFMRF#] G76; I98;
  L89b; R110b; T295; U18; Z
  173; AB71b; AC55; AD82;
  AE74; AG54b; AH180; AI37;
  AJ409; AL117; AR91; AS87;
  AT48; AU182; AV64; AW58;
  BB65; BF250   11994
Wellingham (Bullinger) [SMF
  SDRFM, SLSTDFML,] BY
  369   11995
Wellington Square (Warrack)
  [MLTDTLSM, LMRDTL, M]
  A265; X219; AF493; AN
  425   11996
Wells (Bortniansky) X St
  Petersburg   11997
Wells (Holdroyd) [DMSDTDLS,
  SSSSMFRD,] L439   11998
Wells (Johnson) [MFMSFMRD,
  SLSRDTLS,] BV236b   11999
Wells (Wells) X Holy Spirit,
  faithful guide   12000
Welsh carol (Welsh trad) [ML
  LLS#LTDDDTR, TDLL] BG
  59   12001
Welsh hymn (Welsh trad) X
  Ar hyd y nos   12002
Welton (Malan) [SSSDMRRM,
  LDLSDMRD] I322; L15; T
  212; V207; AJ305; AO158
                            12003
Welwyn (Scott-Gatty) [MRDTDR
  FMRDT, DLLSD] A486; E
  346; G592; J382; R150; S110;
  W648; Z497; AB36; AE407;
  AF411; AG254; AK266; AL
  129; AR211; BE57; BY621;
  BZ   12004

Wem in leidenstagen (Filitz) X
  Caswall   12005
Weman (Weman) [MMSDRRMM,
  SSLLSM] A193b   12006
Wengen (Davies) [SLTDFMFMR
  D, SLDSDL,] F65b   12007
Wenn erblick ich doch einmal
  (Flittner) X Gregor's 124th
  metre   12008
Wenn in leidenstagen (Filitz) X
  Caswall   12009
Wenn meine seel' den tag bedenket
  (Grimm. Choralbuch) X Gre-
  gor's 184th metre-C   12010
Wenn mein stündlein vorhanden
  ist (Wolff) X Naar tid og
  stund den er forhaand   12011
Wenn meine sund' (Praetorius)
  [LFLLDL#L, MSSRMFM, LD]
  Q152   12012
Wenn wir in höchsten nöthen
  sein (Bourgeois) X Command-
  ments   12013
Wennerberg I (Wennerberg) [DS
  MSLTD, SMFMRM, DSM] J378;
  N496   12014
Wennerberg II (Wennerberg) [MD
  LTDRMSF, MSSFRDR] P322
                               12015
Wentworth (Cluett) [MMMRFML,
  SFMMMF#S, MM] L56   12016
Wentworth (Maker) [SDDTLSMD,
  RMLR, MMMD] C384; D624b;
  G9; I29; J447; R409; S29; W
  441b; Y204; Z109; AB213; AC
  51; AD270; AE19; AF98; AG
  183; AH398; AI44; AK195; AL
  289; AN263; AP440; AR31; AV
  49; AW177; BA36; BB45; BF
  389; BR423; BY504; BZ
                               12017
Wer da wonet (Vehe. G-B-lein.
  1537) [DDMSMFSLS, DTLSMSF]
  E35; W88; AN350; AQ143; BN
  173; BY587   12018
Wer Gott vertraut, hat wohl
  gebaut (Calvisius) X Gregor's
  223d metre   12019
Wer hier fuer Gott will sein
  (Hermann) X O Heilege Dreifaltigkeit   12020
Wer nur den lieben Gott (---)
  [SDDMDDLLS, DTDRMFM] AW

571   12021
Wer nur den lieben Gott (Neu-
  mark) X Neumark   12022
Wer weiss, wie nahe (Bronner.
  Choral-buch. 1715) [SDSLL
  SFMD, MFMRSLL] N59; O
  445; P98   12023
-----. V [DDSLLSFMD, MFM
  RSLL] O445   12024
Wer weiss, wie nahe (Bronner.
  Choral-buch. 1715) X Win-
  chester New (Wittwe. Musik-
  alisches handbuch. 1690) X
  Crasselius (Wittwe. ibid)
                            12024a
Wer weiss, wie nahe mir mein
  ende (Meyer) X Rudolstadt
                               12025
Wer weist wie nahe mir mein
  ende. (Bronner. Choral-
  buch. 1715) X Wer weiss wie
  nahe   12026
Werde munter (Schop) X Jesu,
  joy of man's desiring   12027
We're going home tomorrow
  (Bliss) [SMR#MDDRD, LSDD,
  MMR, S] AX593   12028
-----. R [MSMMDRRRFFM,
  MSMM, D]   12029
We're marching on to glory
  (Chamberlain) [MRDSDRDTL,
  DRMMSDR,] BC194
                               12030
We're marching to Zion (Lowry)
  X Come, we that love the
  Lord   12031
We're not ashamed to own our
  Lord (Daynes) [SDMSLSFM,
  MLDMFMR, S] BC266   12032
Were you there (Negro mel)
  [SDMMMRDMRD, DMSSSL]
  A80; J500; R201; AE455;
  AF179; AG317; AH609; AR
  173; BK170; BL23; BZ
                               12033
-----. V [DDMMMRDMRD,
  MMSSSL] AE455   12034
Wesley (---) [DMRDSFMR,
  MFSLMRD, D] E588; W76b;
  AL96; AW309   12035
Wesley (Hastings) [SSSFMRS
  MD, SSLSLTD,] L6   12036

Wesley (Mason) [DTLSSSLDL
LS, MRRDT] G488; H132; J
319a; M99; N381; O112; P399;
R505; S391; T177; U408; V598;
Z523; AC303; AD380; AG259;
AH466; AJ259; AK378; AM65;
AO138a; AR561; AT453; AU248;
AV266; BA343; BB302; BF524;
12037
Wessex (Hopkins) [MMRDSSFM,
RMSLDT, TD] I473; AA18;
BE134; BR272; BX284   12038
West (West) X Moravia   12039
West Burn (Finlay) [DDRMTDLSF
M, SLSDTL] BV310, 447 12040
-----. V [DRMTDLSFM, SLS
DTLT,] BV447   12041
West Heath (Hopkins) [SMSDSLT
D, RMTDLSFM,] BA267 12042
West Milton (American trad) X
Campmeeting   12043
Westall (Worcester) [SDDDRM
FMD, DDDDLLL] BR550
12044
Westcott (Barnby) [DTLTSLSMF,
SLTDTLT] I37a; V273; Y88;
Z305; AB50; AJ182; AW52;
BF234   12045
Westgate (---) [SMMFMRMD, TL
DTLS, SM] AO147   12046
Westerly (Hopkins) [SSMFSRM,
RRDRMTD,] A230   12047
Westminster (Cooke) [SSLSFMRD,
DRMFMRDS,] F15b   12048
Westminster (Sullivan) X Propior
Deo   12049
Westminster (Turle) [MSSDDTLS,
SMTDRS, ST] B183; C183; D
189a; E441; F169; I700; W27;
X581; AL18; AP63b; AS385;
BA17; BE54; BV10; BY64
12050
Westminster Abbey (Purcell)
[MSMDFRTS, DRMRDTLS,]
F574; BV660b; BY372a   12051
Westminster College (Greiter)
X Psalm 68   12052
Westminster New (Nares) [DMMM
RMFSLLS, FMRDD] F334b;
AP350   12053
Westmoreland (Plainsong, arr by
Barnby) [MMMFMR, MDRMRD,
MMMF] L557; AB384   12054

Westmoreland (Steggall) [MFSM
SDT, DLSMMF#S, SM] Y114
12055
Weston (Roe) [MMFMRMRD,
MSSFLMR, M] D432b; I130;
M585; N140; AN553; BR28
12056
Weston (Wesley) [LTDTLTS#
L, DRMLSFM, T] W452b
12057
Westridge (Shaw) [MFSMRDL
S, DRMDR, FSL] A514;
X363; BV357; BY747   12058
Westron Wynde (Llewellyn)
[DRMFS, MSFMR, DRMRMF]
BV136   12059
Westwood (McCartney) [MFM
LMMR, DTLSLS, MFM] D68a;
J328; M325; AB274; AH315;
AV305; BF518   12060
Wetherby (Wesley) [LDLSFDR
RD, DFMMRD] A73; W513
12061
Wetterling (Wetterling) [SSD
DDDDTT, SSRRRRM,] M238;
N95   12062
Wexford carol (English carol)
[SDDTDRMFS, SFMDSLL#]
BG14   12063
Weymouth (Ferris) [SDTDR
MFS, FMDDTD, S] A401
12064
Weyse (Weyse) [DMMMSSDL
S, MLSSFRM] J299; M299;
O379; P226; Q592; AA565
12065
Weyse II (Weyse) [SDTDDRRM,
SMRDLS, DS] O611   12066
What a friend (Converse) X
Erie   12067
What a mighty God (Warren)
[SDDRRMSS, SLSMDMR, S]
AX16   12068
-----. R [DDDDRRM, MMM
MFF#S, SS]   12069
What a sea of tears (Gounod)
X Rouen   12070
What a wonderful Saviour (Hoff-
man) X Hoffman   12071
What beauteous sun surpassing
star (Schmidt) X What star
is this   12072
What did He do? (Owen) [DSL

894   Hymns and Tunes

SDTLSS, MSLRDTD,] AU385   299   12092
                            12073 What will you do with Jesus
-----. R [SMSSLSFM, DDTL,   (McKinney) [SSSMMMFFR,
RRDT,]   12074   FFFRRRS] AU101   12093
What do I owe? (Powell) [SD   -----. R [DTLSMLR, TLSRM
RMSSF#MR#M, FMRSSL] BY490   FLS, D]   12094
                            12075 What will you do with Jesus?
What glorious scenes mine eyes   (Stocks) [MMMMMMFMM,
behold (Beesley) [MMRDSFMMR   DTLLSFF] AX266   12095
DTD, MRSF#] BC197   12076   -----. R [MFSDLSM, DTLTDT,
-----. R [DMSFMDDFFM, MRD   DDD]   12096
TRF]   12078 What will your answer be?
What happiness can equal mine   (Teddlie) [SSSSSSLLL, SSSDT
(German trad) [DTLSLFMRD,   DR,] AX295   12097
DTSF#LTL] BO39; BP67   What would you give in exchange?
                            12079   (Carr) [SDMSLSMDRD, SDDMSF]
What happiness can equal mine   AX275   12098
(Schein) X Eisenach   12080   -----. R [MDRM, SF#SM, M
What joy to reach (Norwegian)   R#MSLSMD]   12099
[SDDRRMF, SMMFRD, SDD]   Wheeler (Hardy) [DRMFLS,
P330   12081   LFSMDR, RMMF#] BY116
What lovely Infant (---) [DMMMR   12100
DLS, SMMSFMRM] BO157   Wheelock (Sanders) [SSSLSMDM
                            12082   SLSM, DRDR] AQ182   12101
What mortal tongue can sing   Whelpton (Whelpton) X Hear
(Roman hymnal) [DMRDSFMR,   our prayer   12102
RMRDRDT, F] BN158; BO82   When blossoms flowered (Yon)
                            12083   [SSFMFMRMRDR, SDDRM]
What shall the harvest be? (Bliss)   BQ126   12103
[MFF#SMDDTT, TLLLSSS]   -----. R [SDTDRDS, MMRMF
AU404   12084   MR, MF]   12104
-----. R [SMFSLTDTLS, FMFRM   When Christ was born (Brown)
F]   12085   [DSMDRMFMRM, MRRRMSL]
What star is this (Schmidt) [MSM   B547; C547; BG178; BV118
DRMFS, SLDDTD, SL] BN26;   12105
BO161   12086 When Christ was born (German
What tender mercy (Ogden) [MR   mel. 14th c) X In dulce
DMRDLDSD, RRDRMM] AX26   jubilo   12106
                            12087 When Christ was born in Beth-
-----. R [RMRSMFMD, FFMM   lehem (Beesley) [DTLSFMR
RDR, M]   12088   D, RMLSMRDM] BC295
What tongue can tell (Nicolai) X   12107
Frankfort   12089 When dark and drear (Daynes)
What voice salutes the startled   [MFSF#SLSDTLSF#LSM, M]
ear (Beesley) [SSLSDDTT, SST   BC293   12108
LFM, SS] BC275   12090   When day's shadows lengthen
-----. R [SDSLL#LLL, LRLTDT   (Catholic) [MMRDFR, SSF
TT,]   12091   RDT, SSSD] BQ140   12109
What was witnessed in the heavens? When first the glorious light of
[SLTDMMRDSS, SLSRMF] BC   truth (---) [SMSSSMSS, SLD
                                       TLS, SM] BC198   12110
                                   When great St Patrick (Kelly)
                                       [SDSMFSLS, MLMRDRMM]

BN165   12111

When He cometh (Root) [DRMM
  MFSS, LMMRDD, DR] N651;
  W158a; AL614; AM651; AP794;
  AW432; BB148; BV355   12112
-----. R [DTLLDSS, LSDDRMS,
  DT]   12113
When here, O Lord (Allgemeines
  katholisches G-B. Vienna,
  1744) X Hursley   12114
When I get to the end (Tillman)
  [SDDDMFSTL, LLSTLSL]
  AU26   12115
When I see the blood (Foote) [S
  SLSMLLSS, SFSFRLS] AU70
                           12116
-----. R [MFSLSD, SDTLSS,
  MFSD]   12117
When I see the blood (Showalter)
  [MMRDSLDLS, SDRMDRR]
  AX307,564; AY240,340   12118
-----. V [MRDSLDDS, DRMDR
  RD, M] AX564   12119
-----. R [DRMDLS, DDRDRM,
  MFDR   12120
-----. V [DMSSSLSSM, DMSSS
  LS] AX564   12121
When I survey the wondrous
  cross (Plainsong M 1: arr by
  Mason) X Hamburg   12122
When in the hour of utmost need
  (Bourgeois) X Commandments
                           12123
When in the wondrous realms
  (Schreiner) [MRDFMRRM, MF#
  SLSF#F#S,] BC199   12124
When Israel, of the Lord beloved
  (Beimel) [SDTDRMFM, DSFMRD
  TD] BH119   12125
When Israel to the wilderness
  (Beimel) [DMSRMDRLTD, DFM
  RDT] BH127   12126
When, marshalled on the nightly
  plain (Calkin) X Waltham
                           12127
When morning fills the sky
  (German trad) [DMFSMD, DRM
  FSM, MRTD] BN190; BO10
                           12128
-----. V [DMFSSD, DRMFSM,
  MRTD] BO10   12129
When morning gilds the skies
  (Haydn) X O esca viatorum

                           12130
When morning gilds the skies
  (German trad) X When
  morning fills the sky   12131
When my life-work is ended
  (Sweney) X I shall know Him
                           12132
When peace, like a river
  (Bliss) X Bliss   12133
When the battle's over (---)
  [SDDMMSFM, MFMRRD, SD]
  AU395; AY122   12134
-----. R [SDDDRMFSSSFM,
  SFFF]   12135
When the book is opened
  (Smith) [SSDDLSSD, DRMSM
  DR, S] AX293; AY389
                           12136
-----. R [MMRMFRMD, TT
  LLRMR, S]   12137
When the King comes in
  (Lorenz) [SLSMRDRMD, LS
  LDTLS] BB537   12138
-----. R [RRRDRMMS, LSLD
  LS, DD]   12139
When the King shall claim His
  own (Barnes) [SDMSDSTL,
  TDRTDRM, D] BB539 12140
When the Lord turned the cap-
  tivity (Gelineau) X Defend
  me, O God   12141
When the mists have rolled
  away (Sankey) [MFSSSSSD,
  TLSSSSS, S] AU354   12142
When the morning comes
  (Tindley) X By and by
                           12143
When the roll is called (Black)
  X The roll   12144
When the rosy light of morning
  (Baird) [MFSSLSLTDS, TLS
  SFM] BC200   12145
-----. R [TDRDRM, MRDDD
  MDR, SS]   12146
When the Sabbath (Jewish trad)
  [MSLSSFMFM, SDL#LSFM]
  BH114   12147
When the shadows flee (Sellers)
  [MFSMRMDS, MFSRDMFS]
  AU429   12148
-----. R [SSDDTLTT, SSRRD
  TRD,]   12149
When the sun (French carol

mel) X Gloria   12150
When the sun shines bright
  (Reynolds) X Lura   12151
When there is peace (Binder)
  [SLTDDFFM, MLLSMDL#L,]
  BH16   12152
When they ring the golden bells
  (DeMarbelle) [SFMR#MR#MS,
  MDLTDLSD,] AU360   12153
-----. R [SSLFDLFL, DLSLSM
  MS,]   12154
When this song of praise shall
  cease (Stark) X Berkshire
                             12155
When upon life's billows (Excell)
  X Blessings   12156
When very early in the dawn
  (Cologne G-B.) X Vigiles et
  sancti   12157
When we all get to heaven (Wil-
  son) X Heaven   12158
When we walk with the Lord
  (Towner) X Trust and obey
                             12159
Where could I go? (Coats)
  [MMMMDRDDRD, DDRMMF]
  AX520   12160
Where He leads I'll follow
  (Ogden) X Sweet are the
  promises   12161
Where He leads me (Norris)
  [SDMMFMMMR, STRDMRRD,]
  AH336; AR248; AS207; AT361;
  AU164; AV338; AW500; AY115
                             12162
Where He may lead me (Black)
  [MMMMDSSS, LLLSMRMR,]
  AS249; AX507   12163
-----. R [DRMFFFFM, MFSL
  LLDT,]   12164
Where is my boy tonight (Lowry)
  [MMMFMMRD, DDDDFFM, M]
  AU89   12165
-----. R [MFDDDRM, SSRRR
  MR, RM]   12166
Where Jesus is, 'Tis heaven
  (Black) [SDRMSLDD, DTLSMM
  DR,] AX335   12167
-----. R [SFFFFMDM, MMM
  SMMDR,]   12168
Where Judah's faithful sons are
  found (Alman) [SDSDL#LSF,
  LSRSFRM, D] BH210   12169

Where shall I be? (---) [SD
  DMMDDM, DLLS, SDDM] AX
  286   12170
-----. R [MSDDMDMRDLS,
  DSDDM]   12171
Where the gates swing outward
  never) [SSDDDDRMMM,
  MRDRDL] AX569   12172
-----. R [SFMMMMRDDD,
  TLSSDM]   12173
Where we'll never grow old
  (Moore) [DRMR#MD, MFSF#S
  M, SSLD] AU348   12174
-----. R [SMSDLDLS, SSSM
  MMRD]   12175
Where will I go? (Warren)
  [MRMRDD, DRDLS, DTRDR]
  AX290   12176
Where will you spend eternity
  (Tenney) [MRDFMMDM, SFM
  RRMFM] AU290; AX268; AY
  531   12177
-----. R [MFMMSLSS, DDRM
  DRDD]   12178
Wherever He leads I'll go
  (McKinney) X Falls Creek
                             12179
While Jesus whispers to you
  (Palmer) X Come, sinner,
  come   12180
While of these emblems we
  partake (McBurney) [MSFM
  DMRD, SF#MTSF#RM,]
  BC226   12181
While of these emblems we
  partake (Schreiner) [MMM
  SFMDR, MMLLSF#M,] BC
  217   12182
While shepherds watched (Eng-
  lish mel., 18th c) X God
  rest you merry   12183
While shepherds watched their
  flocks (Willis) X Carol
                             12184
While the days are going by
  (Sankey) [MFSSLSSD, DRM
  DRRD, M] AU394; AX182
                             12185
-----. R [DRM, DLS, DMS,
  MDR, DRMM]   12186
Whisper a prayer (McKinney)
  [DTLSF#SLS, DTDMRDR, D]
  AU453   12187

-----. R [SDRM, RSRD, DTLSD,
LTD]   12188
Whispering hope (Hawthorne, pseud)
[SSSDTLSM, FFFLSFM, M]
AU466   12189
-----. R [SLTDTDRDRMS,
LTDSS]   12190
Whitburn (Baker) X Hesperus
                                12191
White (White) [SMMMRDLS, SDD
MRDR, S] BB230   12192
White fields (Bruning) [DSLMSL
LS, DDDDDRM, D] AK383
                                12193
White gates (Williams) [LLSLM
DTL, LLSMRDRM] E541; X
489; BV553a   12194
White Ladies Aston (Atkins)
[LTDRDTDLT, DTLSFML] E
400; X370   12195
White Lent (French trad) X
Quittez, pasteurs   12196
White ribbon (Sampaix) [SMFM
DMRRD, LDLSDMR] H528
                                12197
-----. R [SSLSMMRRD, LTDSD
RM,]   12198
Whitefield (Miller) [DDSLTD, SM
DLSFMMR, S] H68; I22b
                                12199
Whitehall (Lawes) [DTLDMFLS,
SLTDTLMR,] E234b; F525;
W297; X589; AN91a; BV274
                                12200
Whitehead (Whitehead) [SDRMM
SMR, MDTLTDRS] B441 12201
Whiteland (German) [DRDDTD
MRDTD, SSFMM] BR243 12202
Whiter than snow (Fischer) [SS
DRMRDRMRD, SSDRM] P267;
AI282; AO639; AR445; AS452;
AT201; AU9; AW469; AX407;
AY233; BB592   12203
-----. R [RRRRDMDLS, SLDFM
RD]   12204
Whitfield (Heber) X Calcutta
                                12205
Whitford (Lloyd) [MRDTLLS#,
MLTDRT, MRD] W390; AF315
                                12206
Whither, pilgrims (Bradbury)
[SDDTRFLS, SDTSLTD, S]
AP783   12207

Whither thus in holy rapture
(Mainz G-B. 1661) X Lady
of the visitation   12208
Whither thus in holy rapture
(Slovak hymnal) [DMLSF#
SDS, LSFFSFM, D] BQ80
                                12209
Whitner (Campbell) [MRMDSL
DS, SDTDMRDT,] V573
                                12210
Whitney (Andrews) [DTSLM
FLRDT, DTLRTS] AD377
                                12211
Whitstable (Vincent) [DSMD
SFMD, FMRLT, MTR] BY
728   12212
Whitsun (Selby) [DDRMRDTLS,
SLTDFMR] F613   12213
Whitsuntide (Gilchrist) [MLT
DML, TDTLTSM, MFS] BR
209   12214
Whittier (Maker) X Rest
                                12215
Whittingham (Parker) [SSDDM
FSLDT, LSMDRR,] B543b;
C543b   12216
Who came down (McGranahan)
[MMRDSLT, DMSMMR, MMR]
AI385   12217
-----. R [SSSSLLL, SLSMMR
R, MM]   12218
Who givest all (LeSaint) [DM
MMMMRR, MFFFFFMM,]
AR597; AS426   12219
-----. R [SDTLSDTT, DRDT
RRDD,]   12220
Who is He (Hanby) X Adora-
tion   12221
Who is like Thee (Binder) [SM
SDDDTLTD, SMSLSL] BH69
                                12222
Who knows how near (Bronner.
Choralbuch. 1715) X Wer
weiss wie nahe   12223
Who made ocean (Finnish trad)
[DDTTLDT, MMS#TLL, DDT]
BK4   12224
Who taught the bird (Binder)
[SSLSMMFR, MFSTLS, SS]
BH247   12225
Whole wide world (Kirkpatrick)
[SDSMDSS, SLSFMR, SMD]
AE355; AO524   12226

-----. R [SSSSLTDRDT, SSLT
DR]   12227
Who'll be the next (Lowry) [SS
SSSDMRDS, LLTDTL] AX258
                                 12228
-----. R [DSSS, DLLL, TTDRM
RDS]   12229
Wholly thine (Belden) [DRMDSD
MRD, TDRDRM, D] BB597
                                 12230
-----. R [SMSMDM, FMRRD
RM, SMS]   12231
Who's on the Lord's side?
(---) [SSDDRM, MMMFMR,
TSTR] BC175   12232
Whose works, O Lord, like thine
(Warren) [DMMRRSLS, SFFMDR,
RS] BH222   12233
Whosoever (Bliss) [SLSMDDLDL
S, SLSMDM] AT238; AU126;
AX220; BB571   12234
-----. R [TTTDR, DDDLS, MMM
SLS]   12235
Whosoever will (Bliss) X Who-
soever   12236
Why art thou cast down (Crueger.
Praxis pietatis melica. 1653)
X Ratisbon   12237
Why art thou cast down? (Jewish
trad) X V'al Kulom mel
                                 12238
Why art thou sorrowful (Yenn)
[SSDTDMMRLDTLS, SLT] BQ
144   12239
Why carelessly wait? (Warren)
[DMRDSLS, DMRDRMR, DM]
AX288   12240
Why do you wait? (Root) X
Sheffield   12241
Why not now? (Case) [SDTRTLSM,
LSFRSFM, S] AT218; AV333;
AX236   12242
-----. R [DTLTLS, LSFMFSM,
DTL]   12243
Why this tumult (Gelineau) [RR
FR, RRSM, RLDL, LTSL,]
BSp. 6   12244
Wiant (Chinese mel) [LLSSDSDR,
SLDRMSRR] BZ   12245
Wickliffe (Hastings) [SSDMMRFRD
TD, SLLDT] L29   12246
Wicklow (Irish trad) [DRMLSMRD
LLS, DRMRD] E157; X182

                                 12247
Wie gross ist des Allmäch-
t'gen Guete (Bach) X
Apolutrosis   12248
Wie gross ist des Allmäch-
t'gen Güten (Richter)
[SDRMDSSMD, MRSMLSF#]
AW516   12249
Wie herrlich ist's ein schoeflein
Christi werden (Grimm's
Choralbuch) X Gregor's
115th metre   12250
Wie schön ist unser Königs
Braut (Freylinghausen G-B.
1704) X Gregor's 97th me-
tre   12251
Wie schön leuchtet [der Morgen-
stern] (Nicolai) X Frankfort
                                 12252
Wie soll ich dich empfangen
(Crueger. 1653) [DMFSSF
M, FMDRRD, DMF] K51;
N65; Q58b; AA136   12253
Wie wohl ist mir (Bach) X
Dessler   12254
Wie wohl ist mir [O freund
der seelen] (Freylinghausen.
Geistreiches G-B. 1704)
X Sinner's friend   12255
Wigan (Wesley) [LDTRDF, MR
DTLS#L, DT] A338; F212;
J83   12256
Wigton (Scottish Psalter)
[MMMFMRDRD, MMRMFS, R]
E354; J384a; S234; W406;
X630; Z342; AF330; AN234a
                                 12257
Wigtown (Scottish Psalter) X
Wigton   12258
Wild bells (Lahee) [DDDTLSFM
RDDTLSFM] G537; AB398;
AW379   12259
Wilderness (Thatcher) [LDLM
MLTD, SSSTSRT] A574a;
BV595   12260
Wildersmouth (Hopkins) [DRM
MRMSF, MRDDRRM, M]
U401; V589; W573; AO429
                                 12261
Wildwood (Pitts) [SSSLSSSDRM
R, RSTDR] AG295; AH515
                                 12262
Will Jesus find us watching

(Doane) X Watching   12263
Will the circle be unbroken
    (Gabriel) [MFSSDRMM, MRD
    RDLS, M] AX613   12264
-----. R [DRMSMRDM, DTLR
    DLS, S]   12265
Will there be any stars (Sweney)
    X Stars in my crown   12266
Will you go? (---) [DRMMMM
    FLSRFMD, SDT] BB368 12267
-----. R [SFMMFSFMRDRM,
    SDTD]   12268
Will you go to Jesus (Showalter)
    [DDDRMSLS, MDSMMR, SM]
    AX238; AY220   12269
-----. R [LFFSLSMS, FRRMFM
    F#S]   12270
Will your anchor hold (Kirkpatrick)
    [DRMDLRRDTD, MMRRST]
    AL501; AU392; AW482; AX
    483; BB584; BY568   12271
-----. R [SSSSSSSLSS, MMMSSMD]
                             12272
Williams (Kingsley) X Kingsley
                             12273
Williams (Williams) [SDTRDM
    RF, MSSFMRDT,] L109a; AO
    52   12274
Williamson (German) [SMRDDTD
    R, SFMRRSFM,] AK307; AO
    322   12275
Willing (Willing) X Alstone 12276
Willing to own thee (Sea)
    [SDRMMDTLS, STRFFFD]
    AS231   12277
Willingham (Abt) [MMMRDMF
    F#SRFM, MF#RR] J496; N515;
    O549; P303; Y258; AC225; AH
    500; BB406; BE359   12278
Willington (Williams) [SDMSMDM
    LTD, RMSRSD] V260   12279
Wilma (Smyth) [SMMMMRMFM,
    SRFMRD, S] BR534   12280
Wilmar (Minns) [DMSSFRDTD,
    DDTLSLT] AB69   12281
Wilmot (Weber) [DMRDSDMRDS,
    LDSMMR] H116; I545b; L218;
    T231; U227; V107; AJ327; AO
    83; AX248; AY373; BI79
                             12282
Wilson (Mendelssohn) [SMRDTRD
    LSM, SLDTTR] I116   12283
Wilson (Wilson) X Martyrdom

                             12284
Wilton (Mann) [SMRDRMSFLLS,
    SDTLS] W171; AL119
                             12285
Wilton (Stanley) [DDDRMFM
    RD, DDMRDTL] BY519b
                             12286
Wilton Square (Watts-Hughes)
    [MDDTLSFM, MLLLTS#, MD]
    BY427b   12287
Wiltshire (Smart) [SMSDDTD
    FMRRM, SS] A441; C301a; E
    502; F290; J420; N270; S83;
    X677; AF81; AL537a; AM77d;
    AP19c; AW583; BV512; BY
    589   12288
-----. V [SSDDTDFMRRM,
    SSSSM] F290   12289
Wimbledon (Lahee) [SLSDDTT,
    MRDTTL, LLT] AP786
                             12290
Wimbledon (Wesley) [SDRFM
    RRM, FSLSFMM] A420a;
    W539; AL430a; AP504a
                             12291
Wimborne (Whitaker) [DDRM
    DSLFRDT, SDRMD] H64;
    I439; L171   12292
Winchcombe (Calkin) [SDDD,
    MMMMDS, SLLTDR,] BR222
                             12293
Winchester (Ests's Whole booke
    of Psalmes) X Winchester
    Old   12294
Winchester New. (Wittwe. Ham-
    burger Musikalisches hand-
    buch. 1690) [SDSLLSFM, MF
    MRSSF#S,] A10; B145b; C
    145b; D44a; E9; F2b; J162;
    K326; L109b; Q12; R242; S
    150b; V480; W92; X137; Y
    349; Z471; AB1; AD176; AF
    9; AH552; AK95; AL16; AM
    56; AN28; AP104; AQ246;
    AR352; AW369; AZ22-X; BA
    152; BE336; BF182; BL1; BN
    1; BR11; BV79; BX48; BY86;
    BZ   12295
-----. V [SDSLLSFM, MFM
    RSLSS,] J162   12295a
Winchester Old (Est's Whole
    booke of Psalms) [DMMRD
    FFMRMSSF#S, MLS] A13a

B71; C71b; D657; E30; F62;
G175; I181; J389; K265; L14;
O20; Q31; R381; S91; V166;
W181; X82a; AA72; AD28; AF
146; AK228; AL23; AN155b;
AP41a; AW191; AZ14-Z; BA
841; BB101; BD180; BE122;
BJ39; BN128; BO263; BR9;
BV123; BX252; BY113; BZ
2296
-----. V [DMMRDFM, RMSS
F#S, MLS] BN128   12297
Winchester Old (Wittwe. Musik-
alisches handbuch) X Winchester
New   12298
Windermere (Kroeger) [MSLSDLS,
DMMFFM, MSL] T90; AJ133
12299
Windermere (Maker) [MRMFSS
FMFSLL, SSLT] BY5a   12300
Windermere (Somervell) [SLSFS
LS, DFMRMDR, SL] E522; R553;
Sap. 31; X332; AH567; BE143;
BV499; BY530a   12301
Windham (Read) [LDRMMDTL,
LDTDMRDT,] J298b; M323;
Q612; V447; AA551; AQ154;
AY394; BZ   12302
Winding I (Winding) [MMSFM
RDDRMD, FFMLS] M130 12303
Winding II (Winding) [SSLTSDLS,
MFFFSMM, D] M286; BE332
12304
Windrush (Rouen church mel) X
Prompto gentes animo   12305
Windsor (Barnby) X Caritas
12306
Windsor (Tye) [LLTDTLLS#, DM
RDTD, DM] A284; B124a; E332;
F334a; G136; J269; M136; O314;
Q176; V682; X547b; AA502; AF
226; AM22; AN115; AP45; AQ
89; AW39; AZ14-O; BE107; BJ
53; BR280; BV142; BZ   12307
Windsor and Eton (Tye) X
Windsor   12308
Windsor Forest (Clarke) [SFSDRL
SLFM, TMF#SLD] AQ199
12309
Windy Ridge (Aufranc) [SSF#FTL
TD, SSLTLSTD,] BB335   12310
Winkworth (Barnby) [MMF#S#LL
S#L, LSLTDD] A226; B229

12311
-----. R [S#LTDRMMRM,
MRDTD]   12312
Winning souls for Jesus (Mac-
kay) [SSMFSMRDDLSM,
RMFS] AX186; AY529
12313
-----. R [SSSSSSDDMRDS,
LLLL]   12314
Winscott (Wesley, S.S.) [MM
RDLSFM, MFMRDTDR,] J
218b; W338; AL297b; AP385
12315
Winsted (Dutch trad) [SDDM
RDTLLF, RDDRMD,] Y275;
Z553   12316
Winston (Hildebrand) [MSFM
RDRM, DLTDRMRR,] AY
273   12317
Winterbourne (Barnes) [DRM
FMMRR, MFSLLRDR] BB
391   12318
Winter's snow (Goss) X See,
amid the winter's snow
12319
Winter's snow (Morris) [MRM
SLSL, LTDTLSFM, M] BG
190b   12320
Winterton (Barnby) [SLTDMM,
LRFM, SLTDMM,] Q403;
V358; AA353; AB268
12321
Winton (Lloyd) [SMSDDRD,
DFMRDMR, RM] AP256
12322
Wir christenleub (Dresden.
Neues G-B. 1593) X
Ecce agnus   12323
Wir danken dir, Herr Jesu
Christ (Bergkreyen. 1551)
[RFFMRFSL, LFSSFMMR,]
AA193   12324
Wir danken dir, Herr Jesu
Christ (Erfurt. 1663) [LTSML
LS#L, DRMRDDTD,] AA217
12325
Wir glauben all' an einen Gott
(Darmstadt G-B. 1699) X
Clausnitzer   12326
Wir glauben all 'an einen Gott
(Wagner. G-B. ms) 1742)
[DDTLSLRSM, RSF#SDTL]
Q251a; AA394b   12327

Wir glauben all an einen Gott
(Walther) X Confession 12328
Wir pflügen (Schulz) X Claudius
12329
Wir wollen alle fröhlich sein
(Nürnberg G-B. 1544) X
Betracht'n wir heut zu dieser
frist 12330
Wirak (Miller) [SLMSDRM,
FSLSMFMR,M] BB215 12331
Wireless (Barnes) [SMMRDRM,
SMDLSMDR,M] Y186 12332
Wirksworth (Chetham. Psalms,
1718) X Aylesbury 12333
Wirtemburg (Rosenmüller) X
Nassau 12334
Wirth (Bradbury) [SSDMDDLS,
DTDRDDT,S] AJ44 12335
Wisdom (Thalben-Ball) [SMRD
TLSFM,SLTDMRD] BE198
12336
Wishart (Smart) X Nachtlied
12337
Wismar (Schein) X Eisenach
12338
With all the power of heart
(Durham) [DMFSSLLS,SDTLS
LTL] BC216 12339
With gladsome feet (MacFarren)
[DDRMDS,SLTDLD,LTSD]
BR516 12340
With God and His mercy (Ahn-
felt) X Ack, saliga stunder
12341
With happy voices (Mason) X
Missionary hymn 12342
With harps and with viols (Bliss)
[MFSSLTDDTDRDLS,SS]
AM714 12343
-----. R [MRDDDTLLLRRMR,
RRM] 12344
With songs and honors sounding
(Ward) X Materna 12345
With tender greeting (Piel)
[SFMLS,RFMSFMR,MLSF#]
BP93 12346
With thankful hearts, O Lord
(Showalter) X Mohler 12347
With the voice of sweet spring
(Cowen) [DRMSSM,DRMLS
M,RDMS] BH70 12348
With wondering awe (---) [SSDD,
TLSDD,SLLFLLS,] BC209

12349
-----. R [SLSMMFRRDMRDT
D.] 12350
Wither's Rocking hymn (Wil-
liams) [MFSMRLSM,MFSMR
LTS,] BG185 12351
Within the veil (---) [DMRDD
RMFFFM,MMMMF#] BB138
12352
Wittenberg (Frech) [SDSFMLS
SFM,RDMF#SL] L451b; AJ
270 12353
-----. V [SDSMLSFM,RDM
F#SLS,S] AJ270 12354
Wittenberg (Ilse) [SDRMLSFM,
RDRTDTLS,] AA316 12355
Wittenberg (Etlich Christliche
lider. 1524) [SSSSL#LS
F,SMDRMF#SL] E478; F
366a; J259; K285; L85; M41,
594; O141; P94; Q301; X156;
AA314; AB203; AR659; AZ
132-D; BA23; BV205a
12356
-----. V [SSSSLL#LSF,SMD
RMF#LS] M594 12357
-----. V [SSSSL#LSF,SMDM
F#SLS,] M41 12358
-----. V [SSSSL#LSF,SMDM
FSLS] Q301 12359
Wittenberg (Luther) X From
heaven high 12361
Wittenberg (Luther) X Spires
12362
Wo Gott der Herr nicht bei
uns hält (Geistliche lieder.
Wittenberg, 1535) X O Jesu,
nar jag häden skall 12363
Wo Gott züm haus (Geistliche
lieder. 1535) [DSSMRMF#S,
SMSFSMRD,] Q131; AA445;
BI15 12364
-----. V [DSSFMRMF#S,SM
SFSMR] BI15 12365
Wo ist Jesus, mein verlangen
(Thommen. Christen-Schatz.
Basel, 1745) X Desire
12366
Wo soll ich fliehen hin
(Stiller) [MSLRRM,SDTLLS,
SMLL] Q57 12367
Wohlauf, thut nicht verzagen
(Helder) [DMMRDFM,SLS

FRM, DMM] E32; X322b 12368
Woking (Glynn) [DMSLSLTD, LRT
MDTL] A502   12369
Woking (Spencer-Palmer) [SDSL
FMRS, DTSLMRDR] BV332a
                                12370
Wolder (Wolder. Catechismus G-
B. 1598) [DDSMRDDRMR,
MSFMRD,] J251; M329; O162;
P51; Q69; W306; X660; AA22;
AL331; AM210; AW570; AX147
                                12371
-----. V [DDSMDTDRMSMRRD,
DD] M329   12372
-----. V [DDSMDDMR, MSFM
RD, DD] O162   12373
-----. V [DDSMDDMR, MSFMRD,
MS] W306   12374
-----. V [DDSFMRDMR, MFSF
MRD,] AW570   12376
Wolder (Wolder) X Walder
(Walder)   12377
Wolff (Wolff) [DSLDRDTL, SDRM
FRD, D] M391   12378
Wollt ihr wissen ... (Cammin.
Melodienbuch ...) [DTLSLTD,
MRDRTLS, LS] S331; AM435
                                12379
Wollt ihr wissen was mein Preis
(Reimann) X Reimann's 315th
metre   12380
Wolvercote (Ferguson) [SDFMRM
DLS, MFSMRDR] F331; W508a;
AD171; BE250; BV365; BY271
                                12381
Wolverhampton (Redhead) [SSM
RDRFFM, DMSLLS, S] J395;
M127; O243   12382
Womit soll ich dich wohl loben
(Knecht) X Gotha   12383
Wonder (Bax) [LTDTLLSL, LFSM
RFMR] X107   12384
Wonder (Poppen) [SDMFMMRD,
TLRMRD, SM] M363   12385
Wonder tidings (English trad.
15th c) [SSTLTDRTDLS, SSLSF]
BG40   12386
Wonderful grace (Lillenas) [SSS
SSLS, DMFSFM, MMM] AM702
                                12387
-----. R [DRMFSLSMSR,
DRMSDT]   12388
Wonderful grace (Pollock) [SSDT

LDS, DRMDRMR, MR] AX
324; AY234   12389
-----. R [MRDDRDLS, SDR
MDRMR]   12390
Wonderful Jesus (Denton) [MR
DMDRDLS, DRMSMSF] AX21
                                12391
-----. R [SF#SLF, FSLSM,
MR#MSMS]   12392
Wonderful love (Watson) [MMM
MDRMDFM, MRLRMR] AL
488; AM669; AP399   12393
Wonderful love (Wiseman) [M
MMSFMRMRD, LFMR, MR#]
BY411   12394
Wonderful love of Jesus
(Lorenz) [SSDDTTLL, LRSSF
FMM,] BB650   12395
-----. R [SSSSLLLL, SSSS
FMS, D]   12396
Wonderful peace (Cooper) [DR
MMMMRDRDLS, DRMM]
BB610   12397
-----. R [MDRDLS, SSDDDM
RMR, M]   12398
Wonderful peace of my Saviour
(Reynolds) X Venting   12399
Wonderful Saviour (Jacobs)
[SLSMSDDT, RMFTLS, SL]
AY392   12400
Wonderful story of love (Driver)
[DDDDTLS, DDDTRD, DDD]
AU349; AX281   12401
Wonderful, wonderful Jesus
(Sellers) X New Orleans
                                12402
Wonderful words (Bliss) [MMM
FMMRR, SRRMRDS, M] H88;
R265; Z442; AE306; AG141;
AH241; AI406; AM722; AP
761; AS184; AT181; AU233;
AV314; AW494; AX36; BB
574; BZ   12403
-----. R [SFFFFMMM, MRD
RTDMS,]   12404
Wonderful words of life (Bliss)
X Wonderful words   12405
Wondrous cross (Harmonia
perfecta, 1730) [LMDTMRD
T, MSF#MMR#M, L] AP192b;
BV156a   12406
------. V [LMDTMRDT, MTS
F#MMR#M,] BV156a 12406a

RMLSMR, RMSL] AB250
                                          12464
                                 Worship (Meineke) [MMRDMR
                                 12442   DTD, MRMTLS, R] BR106
Woolwich (Kettle) [MR#MFMR,   12465
   RD#RMRD, DRDF] L254; N503;   Worthy (---) [DDDDTLS, LLLL
   Y98; BB328   12443   SFM, DD] BB168   12466
Worcester (Playford's Whole book -----. R [SMDTLS, FMRSMD,
   of Psalms) [LTDTLRRD#, L   SMDT]   12467
   MRSF#M, MM] X323   12444   Worthy art thou, Lord (---)
Worcester (Whinfield) [DMSD   [SSDDDDD, TDRRRRR, FF]
   MRDDT, DTLSFMR] D617b;   AX6   12468
   P236; Q244; AA268   12445   -----. R [MFSMLSM, SMRFM
Word of God to earth (Elgar)   RM, MF]   12469
   X In the Light and light excell- Would men know (Sellers) [SL
   ing   12446   TDRDMD, DDTDRDS, S]
Word of life (Maker) [MMDRM   AX438   12470
   SFM, MRMFM, DLS] AP291a;   -----. R [MRDSF#SDT, F
   BY243a   12447   FFFFFM, S]   12471
Words of life (Bliss) X Wonder-   Would you live for Jesus (Nus-
   ful words   12448   baum) [SDDRMMMMMRRMF,
Words on the cross: The litany   STR] AS239; AT239; AU
   (Monk) [DDRDTLL, LDTLRDT,   122; AX277   12472
   TM] B164; D530   12449   -----. R [SSRSSRFFMM, SS
Wordsworth (---) [MMRMMDRM   RSSR]   12473
   RD, SLLSSM] BR113   12450   Would you lose your load of sin
Wordsworth (Monk) [MSMFMRD,   [DSDRMFM, SMMRDMR, DS]
   RMSLLS, SDS] F41; BE135   AI402   12474
                          12451   -----. R [SF#SLSSFF, FMF
Worgan (Lyra Davidica, 1708)   SFFMM,]   12475
   X Easter hymn   12452   Wraysbury (Hopkins) [MRDMRS
Work (Mason) X Diligence 12453   MRD, DMRSSLF#] L33; BY
Work, for the night is coming   10   12476
   (Mason) X Diligence   12454   Wreford (Carter) [MMSFMMR
Work song (Mason) X Diligence   D, D#RMFLR, SD] D25a;
                          12455   AL192; AP347a; AS448; AZ
Working (Shaw) [DMLSRFMRD,   272-B   12477
   DMLSRFM] X345   12456   Wrestling Jacob (Wesley) [DM
World invisible (Haile) [MSLLL   SRMRDRM, MMRDFFM] F
   SSSM, STDDDTT] Y192   12457   343; W416; AL312a; BY767
World to come (Hindu air) X   12478
   Happy land   12458   Write these words (---) [DDD
Worley (Rosecrans) [MFSDM   DDR, DDDLTD.] R550
   RDTD, SRMFMR, M] AS267   12479
                          12459   Wulfrun (Briggs) [DSDRMFRM,
Worship (German trad) [SDDRRM   SLLSMRDR,] X401; AF527
   SR, RSSFMRD,] A250   12460   12480
Worship (German trad) X   Wunderbarer König (Neander)
   Gregor's 159th metre 12461   X Arnsberg   12481
Worship (Harrington) [MMFSFM   Würtemburg (Rosenmüller) X
   RD, MRFMSSF#S,] G10; I14   Nassau   12482
                          12462   Wurzburg (Andächtige und auser-
-----. V [MMFSFMMRD, MRFM   lesene gesänger) [SDTDRM
   SSF#] I14   12463   RDTS, DTDRMR] E127; X
Worship (Hopkins) X Jehovah

150b; BN122; BY392   12483

Wych Cross (Routley) [DRMSM
RDLLDLSMRDM,] BV60b;
BY650   12484

Wychbold (Whinfield) [DSLSFMR
MD, RSLTDLS,] E409; O262b;
BY299   12485

Wycliff (Stainer) X Oxford 12486

Wye Valley (Mountain) X Remo
                            12487

Wyke (Heward) [MSRFMRDT,
FMLSDTLS] F359   12488

Wylde Green (Cutts) [MMMRDRM
FR, SSSFMRD] BZ   12489

Wynnstay (Lloyd) [DMSSLSSM,
DRRM, DMSS] AL547a; AM344;
AP674   12490

Wyoming (Carter) [MMFMMRD,
DDRDRR#M, MM] BR334

                            12491

Wyoming (Perkins) [DDDDDTDR
TD, DFFFMR] T267; AJ372
                            12492

Wytham (Watson) [DSSLDRM,
RFMRDR, RLR] BV397   12493

Wyvill (Wyvill) [DDRMSFMRD,
RMF#SDTL] AV304   12494

X

Xavier (Champneys) [DSLFRSM,
MMMRSTLS, LR] F485   12495

Xavier (Stainer) [DRMLSFSM, R
FMRDR, RM] D653a; F106b;
BA496; BY211b   12496

Y

Yaa'leh (Beimel) [MMS#MMMLLL
S#FMS#, MMT] BH323   12497

Yarbrough (Bradbury) [SDMMM
RDR, STRFFMRM,] AT356;
AU174; AX397; AY223   12498

Yattendon (Tye) X Yattendon 15
                            12499

Yattendon 4 (Wooldridge) [DRFM
RD, RMSFMR, MSLS] BJ4   12500

Yattendon 8 (Clark) [LLTDTDRDT
LM, SFMRM] BJ8   12501

Yattendon 11 (Wooldridge) [MMM
MRRDFFM, SSF#S, SL] BJ11
                            12502

Yattendon 12 (Bishop) X
Leicester   12503

Yattendon 15 (Tye & Wooldridge)
[SDRMFSSF#S, RFMDDT, R]
W528b; BE225; BJ15
                            12504

Yattendon 17 (Wooldridge) [S
SLTDDTT, DRMRRM, SM]
BJ17   12505

Yattendon 18 (Wooldridge)
[FLLSLTD, RRTDLLS, TT]
BJ18   12506

Yattendon 22 (Wooldridge) [M
DSFMRM, MF#SS, SMLSS]
BJ22   12507

Yattendon 46 (Wooldridge)
[DRMFFM, LSDMRD, SFM]
A481; AJ535; BJ46   12508

Ye are the light (Brunk) [DD
DDTLSM, FFFFSFM, D]
AX157; AY382   12509

Ye children, come (Sprague)
[SSMMDLFF, LSMMDR, SS]
AI405; AM656   12510

-----. R [DMSMRD, RMFFSM
R, MRD]   12511

Ye children of our God (Careless) [SSLSSFM, MDDTLS,
MMF] BC288   12512

Ye chosen Twelve (Fox) [DSF
MRDLSFM, RSFMMF] BC211
                            12513

Ye elders of Israel (---) [SDT
DRMRMFSLSM, MSF] BC
344   12514

Ye lands, to the Lord (Hoff)
X Hoff   12515

Ye messengers (Edmunds) [SM
FRMD, RMFSLR, SMFS] BL
86   12516

Ye must be born again (Stebbins) X Born again   12517

Ye simple souls who stray
(Stephens) [MMMSFMR, RRM
FRSFM, M] BC290   12518

-----. R [SSSMRDT, TTDRTMR
D, D]   12519

Ye sons and daughters (Palestrina) X Victory   12520

Ye souls of the faithful (Bragers) [MMDRMLTDRDT, RR
TRM] BP95   12521

Ye souls of the faithful (Cath-

olic) [DRMMRDM, SDTLS, RM
FF] BO145   12522

Ye souls of the faithful (Italian
hymn mel) [SMRDDTSFMRRD,
MSFM] BQ114   12523

Ye who are called to labor (---)
[SF#SDSTL, LSLFLS, SF#S] BC
345   12524

Yearning (Norwegian) [MS#LTRDLL
SM, MRTDDD] P343   12525

Years of youth (Morse) [DTRDRM
FM, SFMR, MFRM] AE446; AR
370   12526

Yes, for me He careth (Richards)
X Armstrong   12527

Yes, heaven is the prize (Mendelssohn) X Heavenly love
                 12528

Ygdrasil (Clarke) [MSFMRMFL
MM, SDTDRD] AQ197   12529

Yield not to temptation (Palmer)
[MMFMRR, DDRDT, LLTDS]
N648; U161; W704; AE258;
AG195; AH452; AI404; AM658;
AO631; AP770; AS320; AT364;
AU338; AV371; AW477; AX441;
AY445; BA835; BB498; BY569
                 12530

-----. R [SSSLSSD, RRRDRMD,
DD]   12531

Yigdal (Jewish trad) [MMMS#LT
LS#DTLS#FM, MM] BH327
                 12532

Yigdal (Jewish trad) X Leoni
                 12533

Yimloch (Sulzer) [SMMMRRD,
D#D#RMFMRDT,] BH287
                 12534

Yimloch Adonoy (Jewish trad) X
Boruch Shaym I   12535

Ymdaith Mwnge (Welsh trad)
[DLTDDSMFS, MLLMRDT]
E203; X209   12536

Yn y Glyn (Evans) [LLMMLSLTL
L, MF#SMDR] E563; W529a;
X339   12537

Yoakley (Yoakley) [DRMMFSMDR
MFFM, DMS] G222; I333; AJ
211; AZ96-K   12538

Yoeman's carol (Church Gallery
book) [SDRMFSLS, SRMFMRD
S,] BG20   12539

-----. R [FMSDLTDRTLS, DRM

FS]   12540

Yom Kippur mode (Jewish trad)
[DDDRMMRR, SDDRMSMR,]
BH163   12541

Yom Kippur prayer (Weinberg)
X Lord, what off'ring shall
we bring   12542

York (Barnes) [MMRDMFFM,
SSFMFRMF] BB144   12543

York (Harris) [SSMRDTL, SS
DTDR, SSM] D585b   12544

York (Scottish Psalter, 1615)
[DMSFLMSR, RMSSF#S, DM]
A312a; E472; F301; V92;
X628; AB325; AF95; AL630b;
AP13; BA317; BJ71; BR138;
BV89   12545

Yorkshire (Wainwright) [DDRM
FSMFSL, SLTDRMRD] A16;
B76; C76; D56a; E21; F61;
G93; J19; K24; Q84; U344;
W54; X73; Z506; AD336; AF
127; AK115; AL67; AN349b;
AP175; AR134; AW71; AZ
600-A; BA159; BR148; BV
97; BY93   12546

You can make the pathway
bright (Dungan) [SDFMR#M
D, TDMRD#RLRM] BC208
                 12547

-----. R [SSSFLFM, FMMR
RSR, MF]   12548

You can't do wrong and get by
(Ellis) [MFSSLSDRMRD,
DLLLD] AX282   12549

-----. R [DLLDDLS, SDDDDR
MR, D]   12550

Youth (Lynes) X Recessional
                 12551

Yule (Luther) X From heaven
high   12552

Z

Zachary (French trad) [SFM
FRDMR, MRDRMF#SF#]
X576   12553

Zeal (Marshall) [DDMDS, RD#
RMRDMLS, RD#] BF512
                 12554

Zebulon (Mason) [SSFMRD,
RMMFMR, SSFM] L48; AA11;
AJ358   12555

Zeige mir dein angesicht (Frey-
linghausen) X Gregor's 77th
metre   12556
Zelotes (Mozart) X Mozart II
                             12557
Zennor (Maker) [SMRDTLDTL
S, SFFMDT] U30; AI295   12558
Zeno (Morton) [MRDTDRLTR
DS, LFMRL] T8; AJ12   12559
Zephyr (Bradbury) [SSSLDLSMR,
FMRMSFM] D87b; H86; I457;
L330; T169; U70; V141; AA51;
AE327; AI214; AJ248; AO567;
AP77b; AS125; BB41; BR22
                             12560
Zerah (Mason) [SDDDMRSS, SSMF
RM, SL] H8; L227; R71; T224;
U12; V97a; AG37; AJ318; AM
163; AO131; AR123; AS106;
AX101; BB175   12561
Zeuch ein (Crueger) [MDSFMRD,
MRDTDR, MDS] Q228; AA252
                             12562
Zeuch ein zu meinen toren
(Crueger) X Zeuch ein   12563
Zeuch meinen geist (Knorr,
Neuer helicon. 1684) X St
Gregory   12564
Zinck (Zinck, Koralbog. 1801)
[DSFMRM, SDTLS, DSFMR]
M249; O26; P5; Q542   12565
Zinck (Zinck. Koralbog. 1801)
X Paa Gud alene   12566
Zinzendorf (Drese) X Rochelle
                             12567

Zion
NOTE: In English language
entries, Zion is always spelled
Sion within this index.   12568
Zion klagt (Schein) [LMMSFMR
D#,MFSFMMR, L] Q268; AA
505   12569
Zions vaegter (Nicolai) X
Sleepers, wake   12570
Zoan (Havergal) [DMRDTDD, DF
MFRM, M] A545b; B99; C99;
D323b; V584; AP60b; BR233;
BV273   12571
Zochraynu (Jewish trad) [MRM
LLLDTL, MRMTTTR] BH312
                             12572
Zoerbig (Selle) [DSFMRDSLTDT,

SLLTD] AZ142-A   12573
Zu Bethlehem geboren (Nord-
stern. Fuhrer ...) X Eia,
Eia   12574
Zu meinem herrn (Schicht)
[SLTDTDDRRMD, MRDTS]
E119; W103; AF173; AN
101   12575
Zum frieden (Bach) [MDLLF
MFM, RDFMRDT, M] E499;
W285b; X674; BE110
                             12576
Zundel (Zundel) [MRDTLTD,
DMRDDT, MRD] Eap. 68
                             12577
Zundel (Zundel) X Beecher
                             12578
Zurich (Weimar. G-B. 1681)
X Jesu, meines lebens
leben   12579
Zuversicht (Crueger. Praxis
pietatis melica. 1653) X
Ratisbon   12580
Zwingli (Knecht) [SDDDLSFM,
SLLLRDT, S] BR416   12581
Zwingli (Zwingli) [DDRMFRD,
MFSSRMF, MF] AO605
                             12582

Composers and Tune Names

Anonymous

Anonymous tunes
NOTE: Satisfactory sources could not be identified for these melodies.

A few more years shall roll;
  X11014 The pilgrim
A poor wayfaring man of grief
Ades domine
Agnus dei
Anfield
Annapolis
As swiftly my days
As wide as the skies
Atonement
Ave, Regina (19th c)
Balfern
Bamberg (17th c)
Barton X2975 Emmaus
Behold, it is the springtime of
  the year
Benediction
Benison
Bernard
Better land
Bexfield
Bingham
Birling (19th c)
Bowring
Bradbury
Cana
Caritas
Carmelite litany
Carol
Carthage
Children's friend
Christ, the Lord, is risen today
Come, all ye saints who dwell
Come, go with me, beyond the
  sea
Come, Holy Ghost, send down
  (19th c)

Come, humble sinner
Come, let us anew
Come, O thou King of Kings
Come, thou O come
Comfort
Communion
Concord
Consecration; X10642a Take my
  life and let it be
Create in this weak form of mine
Damascus
Daughter of a mighty Father
Daughter of Zion
David's harp
Deliverer; X4961 Humility;
  X10091 Sitting at the feet
Denmark; X7970 O ye moun-
  tains high
Dona nobis pacem
Down by the river's verdant
  side
Dublin
Dwight
Ecclesia
Eden
El Kader
Eleanor
Es ist noch raum
Evergreen
Expectation
Exultation
Faithful
For health and strength
Freeport
Gambold
Gaudeamus igitur
Good morning to you
Gott sprach zu dir
Gregor's 20th metre (before
  1400)
Grey
Hail the glorious golden city
Hark, hark my soul
Hark! what mean those holy

voices; X2243 Crown Him
He loves me
Hemans
He's coming
Higher than I
His bride
Home I
Home II; X5055 I hear in the air
Homeward bound; X7432 No, not one (Hugg)
Honor
How far from home
How firm a foundation
Immanuel
In the good ship
Jesus, my Lord, my God
Jesus of Nazareth
Jesus, the Light of the world
Jesus the very thought of thee
Kingo
Laurel Hill
Leaf
Ledbury
Leominster
Let each man learn
Levabo
Liberty Hall; X6756 Martyrdom (Wilson)
Light of the world
Lind
Litany
Litany No. 3
Little clusters; X8510 Pleasant pastures
Little reapers
Loyal and true
Maitland
Meet mother in the skies
Mendota; X10281 Speak gently
Middlesex
Monroe Place
Morning has come
Mountain Christians
My dearest Saviour
My God, how wonderful thou art; X7205 My God! how ought
My God, I am determined
My Shepherd
Nay, speak no ill
Need
Never alone
Newark

Newcombe
Ninety-third [Psalm]
No mortal eye hath seen
No night in heaven
Not made with hands
Now let us rejoice
O God all gracious
O Heart of Jesus
O how happy are they; X2125 Convert
O, how I love Jesus; X4928 How I love Jesus; X7896 O, save me
O Mother! most afflicted (1638)
O save me at the cross; X7749 O, how I love Jesus
O thou eternal King
O turn to Jesus, Mother
Old 148th
On the mountain's top appearing
Onward
Palestine
Palmer
Panem vivum
Parting hymn
Pastoral
Percivals
Pietas
Praise to the man
Prayer
Press on
Promise
Purity; X6377 Lord of hosts; X9756 Saviour, teach me
Refuge
Remember thy creator
Renova
Repose
Resignation (adapted by Sieboth)
Resignation
Robinson
Rowley
Sacred crown
St Barnabas
St Luke; X9485 St Luke's
St Paul's
Saviour of the nations, come (16th c)
See! amid the winter's snow
See, O God, we childrenccome
Shechem
Shepherd true
Shields

Sleep, holy Babe
Smithville
Southampton (1870)
Spring gardens
Steele
Striving onward, pressing for-
ward
Sweden (16th c North Europe)
X5064 I hoppet sig min;
X7465 Norrland
Sweet the moments; X2611 Divine
compassion
Taenk, naar engang den Taage;
X8121 One radiant morn
Tantum ergo
Tantum ergo
Taps
The convert
The hallowed spot
The righteous marching home
The Spirit of God like a Fire
Thorney Abbey
Toronto
Tubingen
Turner
Viator
Vig
Vita aeterna
Waken, Christian children
Watchman's call
We have heard
Wer nur den lieben Gott
Wesley
Westgate
What lovely infant
When first the glorious light of
truth
When the battle's over; X877
Battle hymn
Where shall I be?
Who's on the Lord's side?
Will you go?
With wondering awe
Within the veil
Wordsworth
Worthy
Worthy art thou, Lord
Write these words (ancient melody)
Ye elders of Israel; X11345
Touch not the cup
Ye who are called to labor

A

A. H. A. (A. H. Ackley?)
Jesus has died for me
A. L. B.
I cannot be idle (1907)
I've enlisted in the service
Abbey, Alonzo J., 1825-87
Cooling
Abbey, Horatio G.
Tucker
Abbot, Asahel
'Tis religion that can give;
X8583 Praise to God;
X8607 Prayer
Abbot, H.
Day
Protection
Abelard, Peter, 1079-1142
Gildas; X694 Augustine;
X9286 St Augustine
Abt, Franz, 1819-85
Pastor
Willingham
Acfield, W.
Vesper
Achron, Joseph, 1886-1943
God supreme
I lift mine eyes (1932)
O God, the Rock of Ages
(1932)
There is a mystic tie (1932)
Ackley, A. H. (A. H. A. ?)
He lives; X125 Ackley
Ackley, B. D.
Be with me (1917)
Earthly pleasures (1911)
Go as a witness (1917)
Have you prayed it through?
(1915)
Just outside the door (1912)
Only thy tender care (1916)
Adam, Adolphe-Charles, 1803-
56
O holy night
Adams, Mrs. Crosby
Montreat
Adams, Thomas, 1785-1858
Holborn
Resurgam
Adcock, John, 1838-1919
Derwent (1882)

Woodbrook
Ahle, Johann Rudolph, 1625-73
    Augsburg (1662); X3936 Gott
        ist getreu
    Liebster Jesu (1664); X574
        Arnheim; X1150 Blessed
        Jesus, at thy; X2515 Des-
        sau; X6170 Liebster Jesu,
        wir; X7585 Nuremberg;
        X10140 Spode Jesu, vi er
        Salve cordis gaudium
Ahle. Geistliche arien, 1672
    Es ist genung
Ahlström, Olof, 1756-1835
    St James' Stockholm; X4983
        Hvad röst, hvad
Ahnfelt, Oskar, 1813-82
    Ack, saliga stunder; X12341
        With God and His
    Ahnfelt
    I djupet af mitt hjärta
    Jag är främling; X5229 I'm
        a pilgrim
    O sälla land
Ahnfelt, O. Sanger.
    Hos Gud är idel gladje
Aitken, William M. H.
    Blackburn
Akeroyd, S. Divine companion,
1701
    Lambeth
Albert, Heinrich, 1604-51
    Waltham; X239 Albert; X3860
        Godesberg; X3931 Gott des
        himmels; X5885 Koenigsberg
Alcock, Walter G., 1861-
    Bryant
Alexander, Ian
    Binghampton (1927)
    Song of the pilgrims (1927)
Alexis, Gerhard Theodore, 1889-
1927
    Blessed hope (1924)
    Ishpeming (1924)
    Maria (1924)
    St Ingrid) X5342 Ingrid
    Seraphim (1923)
Allchin, William Thomas
Howell, 1843-83
    Emmaus
Alleman, Benjamin F.
    Alleman
Allen, Alfred R.

St Helena (1911)
Allen, Cecil John, 1886-
    Ewhurst
Allen, Chester G., 1838-78
    Greatorex
    Joyful song; X367 Allen;
        X8568 Praise Him! praise
    Lebanon
Allen, George Nelson, 1812-
77
    Maitland (1840); X7185
        Must Jesus bear
Allen, Hugh Percy, 1869-
1946
    Kingly vale
    Midian
    Qui laborat orat
    Valour
Alleyne, A. 1867-1949
    Vernham Dean
Allgemeines Katholisches
    gesangbuch. Vienna, 1774
    Halle
    Hursley (Long meter); X311
        All things are thine; X
        3987 Gracious God whose;
        X8546 Pour out thy spirit;
        X10499 Sun of my soul;
        X10699 Te deum; X12114
        When here, O Lord
    Te deum (78.78.77 meter)
        X1733 Christ the Lord is
        risen; X3809 God is great;
        X4180 Grosser Gott; X
        4278 Halle; X4788 Holy
        God, we praise; X4975
        Hursley; X8327 Pascal;
        X11669a Victor King
Alman, Samuel
    Believe not those (arr, 1932)
    Hymn for tabernacles (1932)
    Nishmas (1932)
    O Lord, our King (1932)
    The lifting of mine hands
        (1932)
    Where Judah's faithful sons
        are found (1932)
Alsatian traditional see Ger-
    man traditional, if anony-
    mous source
Alwood, J. K.
    Unclouded day; X11090
        The unclouded day

Ambrose, Robert S.
  Ambrose (1876); X2630 Dolce
    domum; X2721 Dulce domum;
    X8123 One sweetly solemn;
    X10514 Sunset
Ambrosian (ancient melody)
  Christus vincit
  Deus creator omnium
  Rerum deus tenax vigor
"American folk hymn"
  NOTE: Hymnal BZ uses this
  phrase for Negro Spirituals.

American Indian tribal tunes
  see Chippewa, Dakota, Omaha

American musical miscellany,
  1798
  Ganges; X4958 Hull
American traditional
  Alida (early 19th c)
  Amazing grace (1805); X973
    Behold the Saviour; X3971
    Grace; X6611 McIntosh;
    X10175 Solon; X10778
    That doleful night
  Arise (A southern mel.);
    X5137 I will arise and go
  Campmeeting; X986 Belief;
    X3038 Es ist ein born;
    X3436 Forever here my
    rest; X4937 How pleasant
    and how; X5046 I do believe;
    X7691 O God of wisdom;
    X8617 Prayer is the soul's;
    X12043 West Milton
  Cleansing fountain (early 19th
    c); X3461 Fountain; X10872
    The fountain
  Foundation; X4919 How firm a
    foundation; X4956 Huger;
    X8681 Protection
  Jordan's Banks; X8096a On
    Jordan's banks; X8672
    Promised land; V8673-75
    misfiled as Promised Land;
    X11022 The promised land
  Land of rest
  Lonesome Valley
  Millenium (before 1850)
  Müller (19th c); X769 Away
    in a manger; X6532
    Luther

  Ontario
  The wayfaring Stranger
Ampleforth, Laurence
  O Sacred Heart! Our home
Amps, William, 1824-1910
  Venice (1858)
Andächtige und auserlesene
  gesänger. Würzburg, 1703
  Würzburg; X10064 Sing
    the Holy Family's
Andernach Gesangbuch, 1608
  Andernach; X7601 O blessed
    day, when
  In natali domini
  Jesus dulcis memoria;
    X2726 Dulcis Jesu memor-
    ia
  Rex gloriose; X9009 Rex
    gloriose martyrum
  Song of the ship; X3047
    Es kommt ein schiff
  Te lucis ante terminum
  Tres magi de gentibus
Anderson, A. W.
  Omnipotence (1940)
Anderson, James Smith, 1853-
  1945
  Fingal
  Shiloh (arr)
Anderson, William K., 1888-
  Journey's end (1930)
Andrews, Carroll T.
  Queen when the earth (1958)
  Salve, Pater salvatoris
    (1958)
Andrews, Mark, 1875-
  Lauda anima
  Motherland (1927)
  Whitney (1910)
Andriessen, Hendrik, 1892-
  O Lord, in this great my-
    stery
Angell, Warren M., 1907-
  Shawnee (1951)
Angers church melody
  Lucis creator
Anglo-Genevan Psalms, 1558
  Old 25th
Anglo-Genevan Psalter (by
  John Day), 1561
  Old 18th
Anglo-Genevan Psalter, 1556.
  Old 22d

Old 44th
Anhang der Seelen-Harpff. Onolz-
bach, 1665
    Lobe den herren, o meine
Anonymous tunes see beginning
    of this index (p. 909)
Antes, John, 1740-1811
    Hope; X3237 Falckner
    Monkland
Anthes, Friedrich, Konrad, 1812-
    Anthes (1847)
Antiphonale romanum
    En clara vox redarguit M 1
    Exultet cor praecordiis M 1
        X5562 Jesu dulcis memoria;
        X7887 O salutaris Hostia
Antonio.
    Regina caeli laetare (1667)
Arcadelt, Jacques, ca 1505 - ca
60
    Arcadelt (1572); X720 Ave
    Maria
Armenian liturgy
    Armenian hymn
Armes, Philip, 1836-1908
    Armes (1875); X3567 Galilee
    Vigilantes
Armistead, John, 1877-1935
    Pro patria; X1286 Break,
        day of God
Armstrong, James, 1840-1928
    Armstrong (arr)
    Newland
Armstrong, Thomas
    Exon (1931)
Arndt, E. M.
    God speed the right; X7534
        Now to heaven our
Arne, Thomas Augustine, 1710-
78
    Arlington (1762); X413 Am I a
        soldier; X979 Behold, where,
        in a; X3295 Father, we
        come; X5232 I'm not ashamed;
        X7935 O thou, whose temple;
        X10941 The Lord be with
        us; X11202 This is the day
    Falkirk
    Shakespeare's carol I
Arnold, Robert S.
    No tears in heaven (1935)
Arnold, Samuel, 1740-1802
    Arnold

Arnold, William
    Alexandria; X5749 Judea
    Middleton
Arnold. Complete psalmodist,
1756
    Epsom
Arran, Isle of see Scottish
    traditional: Isle of Arran
Arrhenius, Jakob
    Jesus allt mitt goda är
Arsdale, P.P. van see Van
    Arsdale, P.P.
Arterbury, Joel
    My testimony
Arthur, Edward, 1874-1948
    Bodlondeb (1927)
    Llansamlet
    Lucerna laudoniae (1927)
    Lumetto
    Pax vobiscum (1927)
    St Kentigern (1927)
    St Sulien (1927)
    Tabernacle
Arundel hymns
    Ave, maris stella; X2102
        Consolator
As hymnodus sacer, Leipzig,
1625
    Ach Gott und Herr; X232
        Ak, Herre form; X274
        All glory be to God; X
        3878 Goeldel
    Breslau; X113 Ach Gott,
        wie; X1762 Christi blut;
        X4633 Herr Jesu Christ;
        X5642 Jesus my life;
        X6087 Leipsic
Ashfield, Robert James, 1911-
    Broadwalk
Ashford, Emma L.
    Evelyn (1905)
    Sutherland (1905)
Ashworth, C. Collection, 1760
    St Thomas
Asian melody
    Sri Lampang
Asper, Frank Wilson, 1892-
    God is in His holy temple
    Hear thou our hymn
    O hark! a glorious sound
    O thou, before the world
        began
    Rejoice, ye Saints of Latter-

days
Rise up, O men of God
Take courage, Saints
This house we dedicate
'Tis sweet to sing
Atkins, Ivor, 1869-1953
White Ladies Aston
Atkinson, Frederick Cook, 1841-97
Caritas perfecta (1885)
Morecambe (1870)
Thetford
Attwood, Thomas, 1765-1838
Attwood (1831); X11580 Veni
Creator, No. 1
Staines
Auber, D.F.
Mercy's free
Aufranc, D.A.R.
Pevensey (1940)
Thetford (1940)
Windy Ridge (1940)
Austrian traditional
Dolomite chant
The shepherd; X2554 Dickinson
Avis, E.C.
Thy love to me
Avison, Charles, 1709-70
Avison; X10001 Shout the
glad tidings
Aylward, T.E., 1844-
Balcom
Ayres, James Caiger, 1933-
St Aidan

B

B E W see Warren, B. Elliott
B.S.
Hibernia's patron saint
Babcock, Maltbie Davenport,
1858-1901
Prayer (1889)
Babst. Gesangbuch, 1545
Da Jesus an des kreuzes
Bach, Karl Philipp Emanuel,
1714-88
Apolutrosis; X12248 Wie
gross ist des
Weimar (1784)
Bach, Johann Sebastian, 1685-1750

Chamber music
Cöthen; X2889 Eins ist not
Crasselius
Dessler; X12254 Wie wohl
ist mir
Faithful
Ich halte treulich still;
X10965 The Lord is risen
Laus deo (1736)
Nicht so traurig; X9826
Sebastian
Now blessed thou
Potsdam; X7779 O Jesus
victim-priest
Rinkart; X5904 Kommt seelen
Zum frieden
Bach, Johann Sebastian, The
School of
Blessing and honour
Baden-Powell, James
Knightsbridge
Salve, festa dies
Song of songs
Baermann, Carl, 1839-1913
Beverly (1903)
Peace (1905)
Baessler, J.G.
Alleluia! Gott zu loben
(1826)
Bailey, E.R., 1859-1938
Canaan
Praise him; X3812 God is
love
Baillot, Pierre Marie Francois
de Sales, 1771-1842
Oliphant
Bain, James Leith Macbeth,
184?-1925
Marosa (1932); X1356
Brother James' air
Bainbridge, Leslie
Jesus! thou art coming
Baird, R.B.
Improve the shining moments
When the rosy light of morning
Baker, A.S., 1868-96
Canaan
Corner-stone
Gaudia matris
Baker, Benjamin Franklin,
1811-89

Wallace
Baker, David, 1940-
Thanksgiving
Baker, Frederick G., 1840-76
St Saviour (1876); X5753
Judson; X9726 Sauveur
Baker, Henry, 1835-1910
Hesperus (1866); X8746 Quebec
X12191 Whitburn
Baker, Henry Williams, 1821-77
St Timothy (1875); X1841
Clearway
Stephanos (1868)
Baker, Reginald, 1904-
Mansfield Road
Bales, Richard
Thee, Lord (1964)
Balle, Carl C. N., 1806-55
Emmanuel (1860); X12 A Dan-
ish tune; X801 Balle;
X2518 Det kimer nu til;
X3462 Fountain of grace;
X10776 Thanksgiving hymn;
X10898 The happy Christ-
mas
Ballet, W.
Lute-book lullaby (17th c)
Balthasar.
Ave maris stella
Tantum ergo
Tota pulchra es
Baltzell, I. and Baltzell, L.
may be the same individual.
Note carefully.
Baltzell, I.
Missionary's farewell
Baltzell, L.
I want to be a worker
Bamberg (no initials)
Sing with joy (1732)
Bambridge, William S.
St Asaph
Bancroft, H. Hugh.
Ascension (1938)
Bansbach, Philip A.
Hail, holy Queen (1940)
O sweet Infant Jesus (1940)
Barber, E. W.
San Remo
Barham-Gould, Arthur Cyril,
1891-1953
St Leonard's

Baring-Gould, Sabine, 1834-
1924
Eudoxia; X7530 Now the day
is over
Barker, Cyril
The Prince of Peace
Barker, E. R.
St John Damascene
Barnard, Mrs. Charles
Give of your best; X825
Barnard
Barnard, Charlotte Alington,
(Claribel, pseud), 1830-69
Brocklesbury (1868); X10340
Brocklesby; X6916 Mer-
ton
Pilgrimage
Barnby, Joseph, 1838-96
Afternoon (1896)
Angels of Jesus; X1537 Car-
men Coeli
Barnby I
Barnby II; X8787 Ralston
Barnby III (1872); X6557
Lux vitae
Barnby's Hymnary, Tune
101
Bethlehem
Burleigh (1872)
Caritas; X408 Alverstoke;
X409 Alverstroke; X11610
Ventnor; X12306 Windsor
Carlton; X9262 St Andrew;
X9267 St Andrews
Children's praise (1896)
Chiselhurst
Cloisters (1868); X6383
Lord of our life
Crossing the bar (1892)
Crucis umbra (1890)
Diadema (1883); X1103
Birkdale; X1407 Burnley
Diademata (1872)
Domine, nobiscum
Dulce, (1883)
Edinburgh (1872); X850
Barnby's hymnary, Tune
590; X3997 Grasmere;
X8092 Omnia
Emmaus; X7313 Neale
Eton
Eton College

Evening hymn
Faroon
Frankscot (1883); X11823
Waring
Galilean (1883)
Good Shepherd
Hearth fire (1868)
Hebron (1874); X6698 Mar
Saba
His forever (1890)
Holy, holy, Holy Lord
Holy Trinity (1861); X266
All as God wills; X2068
Coniston
Irae
Jordan (1872); X1503 Cantate
domino; X4877 Horeb
Just as I am; X829 Barnby;
X2741 Dunstan; X7121 Mor-
ris
Kirkdale; X836 Barnby's
hynary, Tune 91; X2057
Confidence; X9975 Shield;
X11234 Through the day
Laudes domini (1868); X10878
The God of harvest
Litlington Tower
Long Milford
Longwood; X1066 Bethsaida;
X7933 O thou whose power
Manna
Mansfield (1893)
Merrial (1868); X830 Barnby;
X3127 Evening; X7531 Now
the day is over; X11463
Twilight
Newnham
Nightfall (1897); X851 Barnby's
hymnary, Tune 633; X4876
Horeb; X8593 Praise ye our
Father
Paradise (1866); X7852 O
Paradise; X8307 Paradise,
No 2
Rejoice
Requiem (1869); X5981 Last
sleep; X8947 Requiescat;
X10935 The last sleep
Roseat hues
St Anatolius
St Andrew (1866); X831 Barn-
by; X844 Barnby's hymnary,
Tune 237; X7043 Monsell

St Anselm (1869); X3707
Gladness
St Boniface; X9383 St Fidelis
St Chrysostom (1871); X164
Adoro; X165 Adoro te;
X1804 Chrysostom; X2939
Ellerton; X7804 O Light,
whose beams; X11386
Tristitia
St Hilda (1861); X4697
Hilda
St Ignatius; X3915 Gordon;
X7370 New year
St Olave (1897); X4420
Havergal; X8660 Pro me
perforatus
St Polycarp (1869); X5581
Jesus, I my cross; X5622
Jesus, lover of my soul;
X8528 Polycarp; X9382
St Fabian
St Sylvester; X635 Aspiration;
X2463 Deliverance; X4831
Holy Word
Sandringham (1889); X3294
Father, to us; X7856 O
perfect love; X8428 Perfect
love
Sarum (1868); X832 Barnby;
X3413 For all the saints;
X6957 Militant; X8662
Pro omnibus sanctis; X
8944 Requiem; X9576 St
Philip
Sinai
Soho (1881); X10326 Spring-
tide hour
Stand up; X833 Barnby
Stanley (1894)
Sunset; X11251 Thy will be
done
Te deum laudamus
Tender Shepherd
The blessed name
The blessed rest
The golden chain (1887);
X3884 Golden chain
To victory (1872); X5328
Incarnation; X6702 March to
victory; X10885 The good
fight; X11919 We march to
victory
Veni, Domini Jesu

Via pacis I
Via pacis II (1889)
Vita aeterna (1868)
Watch o'er me
Westcott (1872)
   X4211 Guildhall; X9956
   Sheltering wing
Winkworth (1869)
Winterton (1892)
Woodleigh
Barnekow, Christian, 1837-1913
   Barnekow I
   Barnekow II
   Barnekow III
   Viborg
Barnes, Archie Fairbairn, 1878-
   Dunblane Cathedral
   Montague
Barnes, Edward Shippen, 1887-
   Bala Cynwyd (1937)
   Comrades of the cross (1927)
   Faithful legions (1936)
   God with us (1936)
   Holmes (1936)
   O come, let us worship (1926)
   Qui tenet (1927)
   San Vicente (1939)
   Somerset (1937)
   The Mystic (1927)
   Thine house (1937)
   Wireless (1927)
Barnes, Edwin, fl. 1886
   Heber
   Morton
   Russell
   Salisbury
   Southampton
   When the King shall claim His
      own
   Winterbourne
   York
Barraclough, Henry
   Benediction (1932)
Barrington, J.W.
   Onward
Barrows, Donald S., 1877-1951
   Conquest (1941)
   Cura dei (1941)
Barry, Charles Ainslie, 1830-
1915
   Annunciation
Barthélémon, Francois
Hippolyte, 1741-1808

Autumn (1785); X6694 Mant
Ballerma; X797 Balerma;
   X5290 In memory of the
   Saviour's
Morning hymn (1789)
Bartlett, Maro L.
Temple(1905)
Barton. Psalms, 1706
   Coleshill
Basford, Henry
   Lux coelestis
Basque traditional, etc.
   Golden sheaves; X5813
      Khanta zagun
   Swansea
   The Infant King
Bassford, William Kipp, 1839-
1902
   Thanksgiving; X1480 Can a
   little child
Basswood, W.K. see Bassford,
   William K.
Batchellor, Daniel
   Onslow (1885); X1674 Child's
      morning hymn; X11934
   We thank thee
Bate, H.A., 1899-
   Collingwood
Battishill, Jonathan, 1738-
1801
   Battishill
Baumbach, Adolph, 1830-80
   In corde meo; X6132 Let
      the words
Baume, John W.
   Emilie (1905)
Baumgartner, Hope Leroy
   Sprague Hall (1927)
Bax, Arnold Edward Trevor,
1883-1953
   Wonder (1931)
Baxter, Catherine Deisher,
1914-
   Blest moments (1958)
Bay, R.
   We plow the fields
Beale, E.D.
   Thy word have I hid
Beall, B.B.
   Lift Him up
Beatson, C.S.
   Riber
Beaty, Richard William, 1799-

1883
Caritas
Beaumont, Geoffrey, 1903-
Chesterton
Gracias
Bechler, John Christian, 1784-
1857
Bechler
Praise the Lord
Beck, Abraham Reinke, 1833-
Just as I am (1861); X942
Beck
Becker, Arthur C.
To God our Father
Becket, Robert Anderson, 1834-
1910
Wayland
Becket, Thomas à, 1843-1918
Red, white and blue; X1903
Columbia the gem; X11518
Up, awake, ye defenders
Bedford, G. L., 1912-
Bletchley
Beecher, H. W. Plymouth col-
lection, 1855
Advent
Ives
Latter day; X10784 The
alarm
Beery, Adaline H.
Hail, blessed Trinity (1894)
Beery, William, 1852-
Berne
Blessed Bible, how I love it
(1901)
Come, Holy Ghost, in love
Elgin (1950)
Huntingdon; X10641 Take my
hand and lead
Huntingdon II
Juniata (1896); X6292 Lo, a
gleam
John Nass
Love of God (1951)
Beesley, Ebenezer
God of our fathers, we come
to thee
Great is the Lord; 'tis good
High on the mountain top
Let us oft speak kind words
Lord, we ask thee
Reverently and meekly now
Sing we now at parting

The happy day has rolled on
We meet again in Sabbath
School
Welcome, welcome Sabbath
morning
What glorious scenes mine
eyes behold
What voice salutes the
startled ear
When Christ was born in
Bethlehem
Beethoven, Ludwig van, 1770-
1827
A hymn anthem; X7769 O
Jesus Christ, Redeemer
X10905 The heavens, O
God
Alsace
X1208 Bonn; X4872 Hop-
kins; X5974 Larghetto
Beethoven (from 9th sym-
phony); X4203 Guide me,
O thou great; X5002
Hymn to joy; X5724 Joy;
X8153 Onward brothers,
march
Depth of mercy
Dulcetta
Emmanuel; X2095 Consola-
tion; X2112 Contemplation;
X2615 Djupt sjun ker aret;
X7819a O Lord, our little
ones
Gorton; X6372 Lord, keep
us safe
Gracious Father, O Lord,
hear us
Mountain wave
O lead and guide us
O salutaris hostia; X9483
St Luke, No 1
Peace be to this congregation
Salome; X2991 Engedi
Sardis; X2331 Dane; X4435
Hayes; X9740 Savior,
breath an evening; X11304
To the God of all
Sidwell
Beimel, Jacob
Bow down thine ear, Lord
(1932)
Hymn for the golden age
(1932)

Unto the hills (1932)
We are thy people
When Israel, of the Lord
  beloved (1932)
When Israel to the wilderness
  (1932)
Yaa'leh
Beirly, A.
  In hymns of praise (1896)
Belcher, John W.
  Ionia
Belden, Franklin E.
  A shelter in the time of
    storm (1899)
  Belden (1900); X6338 Look
    for the beautiful
  Blessed Lord, how much I
    need thee (1886)
  Cover with His life (1899)
  Diligence (1886)
  Even at the door (1886)
  Fillmore (1886)
  Hakes (1878)
  Hold fast till He come (1886)
  Holy day, Jehovah's rest
    (1886)
  I will sing of Jesus' love
    (1886)
  Look for the waymarks
  Mason (1886)
  Oakland (1886)
  Over the line (1895)
  Robinson (1886)
  The judgment has set (1886)
  There's no other name like
    Jesus (1886)
  Verdi (1886)
  We would see Jesus (1899)
  We'll build on the Rock (1886)
  Wholly thine (1886)
Bell, John Montgomerie, 1837-
1910
  St Baldred
  St Giles
Bell, M. F.
  St Mark
Bell, William Henry, 1873-1946
  Cathcart
  Hail harbinger of morn
Beltjens, Joseph H.
  Tantum ergo
Benbow, William
  Amnos (1914)

Savonarola (1915)
Benedictine plainsong, mode
and date indicated when
known
  Adoro te devote M 5 (13th
    c); X8868 Redhead, No.
    12 (Redhead)
  Jam lucis M 6
  Jam lucis orto sidere M 8
  O blessed by God (Monte
    Cassino trad)
Bennard, George
  Old rugged cross (1913);
    X9160 Rugged cross;
    X11007 The old rugged
    cross
Benson, H. Ford, 1859-1933
  Aurora
Bentley, William W.
  Christ the Lord cometh
  Dedication
  In the rifted rock; X10612
    Sweetly resting
Benz, Johann B.
  O Queen of peerless majesty
    (1861)
Berggreen, Andreas Peter (or
Anton Peter Berggren) 1801-
80
  Amen, Jesus hanskal raade
    (1849); X427 Amen sjunge
    hvarje; X2328 Dana
  Berggren I; X3193 Expecta-
    tion; X9001 Revelation;
    X10637 Taenk, naar engang
  Berggren II
  Brorson
  Even song
  Grace
  Underbar en stjarna blid
  Vita
"Berg kreyen", 1551
  Wir danken dir, Herr Jesu
    Christ
Bergquist, John Victor, 1877-
1935
  Aline
  Donald (1924)
  Emilia (1924)
  Final rest (1903)
  Muriel (1924)
Berky, Georgia Guiney
  Dwell in me

Berlin, Irving (real name Isidor
  Balin), 1888-
    God bless America (1939)
Berridge, Arthur, 1855-
    Harvard (1905)
    Huddleston
Besler, Samuel, 1574-1625
    Herr Gott Vater
Beutler, J. B.
    In morgenrot gekleidet (1799)
Bicknell, C., 1842-1918
    Come faithful people
Bierman, J. B.
    Aus tiefer not (ca 1876)
Bigelow, James, 1920-
    Now for each yearning heart
    We would worship (1951)
Biggs, Arthur H.
    Charlotte (1941)
    Sumner (1941)
Biggs, Richard Keys
    Communion processional (1958)
    Trimphantly doth Christ
      (1958)
Bilhorn, Peter P.
    I will sing (1887); X12413
      Wondrous story
    O, the best Friend to have is
      Jesus
    Redemption
    Sweet peace (1887); X10585
      Sweet peace, the gift;
    X11135 There comes to my
Billings, William, 1746-1800
    Amherst (1770)
Bills, G. M.
    The best friend of all
Binder, Abraham Wolfe, 1895-
    Adonoy yimloch
    Again as evening's shadow falls
      (1932)
    All the world (1932)
    Arise to praise the Lord
      (1932)
    Ayn komocho
    Before the Menorah (1932)
    Blessed, blessed
    Evening prayer (1932)
    Father, see thy suppliant
      children (1932)
    Father, to thy dear name
      (1932)
    God is my strong salvation

      (1932)
    God moves in a mysterious
      way (1932)
    God of Israel (1932)
    Happy he who walketh (1932);
      X4321 Happy he that never
    Harneenu
    Here let thy people (1932)
    Hymn to mothers (1932)
    In mercy Lord, incline thine
      ear (1932)
    Kindle the taper (1932)
    Lo! the earth rejoices
      (1932)
    May the words
    Mee chomocho
    O render thanks (1932)
    O Soul Supreme (1932)
    Out of the depths, O Lord
      (1932)
    Priestly benediction
    Rest in the Lord, my soul
      (1932)
    Sabbath blessing (1932)
    Sabbath hymn; X1962
      Come, O Sabbath day
    Sh'ma Yisroayl
    Summer suns are glowing
      (1932)
    The Lord, my Shepherd still
      has been (1932)
    Va-y'dabayr moshe
    When there is peace (1932)
    Who is like thee (1932)
    Who taught the bird (1932)
Bingham, Seth, 1882-
    Madison Avenue (1943)
Bird, James
    Hurlbut (1927)
Birtchnell, Frank N.
    Heart of the Holy Child
Bischoff, J. W.
    The Lord is my light
Bishop, Henry Rowley, 1786-
1855
    Home sweet home; X4839
      Home; X6937 'Mid plea-
      sures and; X10573 Sweet
      home
Bishop, John, 1665-1737
    Illsley; X1111 Bishop; X
      5225 Ilsley
    Leicester (ca 1700); X945

Bedford; X12503 Yattendon
12
Bixel, James W., 1913-
Silent (1938)
Bixler, Marguerite
Hartville
Black, James M.
Look to the Lamb of God
(1918)
The roll; X6063 Leave it
there (Tindley, arr); X9097
Roll call; X12144 When the
roll is
Where He may lead me (1900);
X5108 I remember Calvary
Where Jesus is, 'tis heaven
Blackall, A.K., 1877-
Swanmore
Blackith, H. de la Haye
Palgrave (1893)
Blackman, G.A.
Calm on the listening ear
Blake, Leonard James, 1907-
Remission
Twyford
Blanchard, George F., 1868-
Lest we forget (1898); X8831
Recessional
Blanchard, William G., 1905-
Godwin (1934)
Blanchet, Alfred Tom, 1868-
1926
Animae hominum
Bland, A.P.
How beautiful heaven must be
Blanton, Leonard Cooper
Columbia (1951)
Blessin, G.
Blessin
Bliss, Philipp, becomes Bliss,
Philip P., or Bliss, P.P. or
Bliss, Philip Paul, 1838-76
Almost persuaded; X388 Al-
most
Bliss; X5432 It is well
X11704 Ville de Havre;
X12133 When peace, like a
Daniel; X2334 Daniel's band;
X2339 Dare to be a Daniel
Eternity
Gladness (1870); X5020 I am
so glad; X5625 Jesus loves
me

Go bury thy sorrow
Hold the fort
Holiness (1875); X7069 More
holiness give me; X7241
My prayer
I gave my life for thee
(1874); X4421 Havergal;
X5804 Kenosis; X9209
Sacrifice
Light of the world; X10937;
The Light of the world;
X11111 The whole world
was
Lower lights; X1317 Brightly
beams; X6130 Let the low-
er lights; X10000 Should
you feel
Man of sorrows; X363 Alle-
luia, what a Saviour;
X3663 Gethsemane
Once for all
Precious promise
St Cyril
We're going home tomorrow
What shall the harvest be?
Whosoever; X12236 Whoso-
ever will
With harps and with viols
Wonderful words; X10065
Sing them over again;
X12405 Wonderful words of
life; X12448 Words of life
Blomqvist, Joel
Böjd under korset
Sabbatsdag, hur skön du är
Blosser, H.C.
Only thee
Blow, William
St Agnes; X218 Agnus dei;
X1182 Blow
Blumenthal, Jacob (or Jacques),
1829-1909
Blumenthal; X4399 Haste
not! Haste not!; X11229
Though our hearts
Blunt, F.W., 1939-1921
Merrial; X4353 Hark, the
voice; X6390 Lord, thy
word abideth; X6565 Lynd-
hurst; X8936 Repose
Bode, Arnold G.H.
Laramie (1941)
Boe, V.E.

At sunset (1914)
Jesus all glorious (1931)
Bohemian Brethren.
NOTE: Publication date or
source given, when known.

Augusta (1566); X7956 O wie
  sehr lieblich!
Betracht'n wir heut zu dieser
  frist (1544); X7523 Now glad
  of heart; X12330 Wir wollen
  alle fröhlich sein
Bohemian Brethren (1566);
  X7005 Mit freuden zart;
  X10062 Sing praise to Him
Far off lands (Hemmets Koral-
  bok); X1197 Bohemian hymn
Gaude, regina gloriae (1544)
Gregor's 2d metre (1531); X
  3618 Gelobt sei Gott, der
Gregor's 54th metre (before
  1566); X1699 Christ, der du
  bist
Gregor's 520th metre (1541);
  X3942 Gott woll'n wir loben
Landskron (1531)
Lofsungur (1531)
O mensch sieh (1566); X1191
  Bohemia
Saelir (1544); X2336 Danket
  dem herrn; X8383 Peace
Savannah, see Wesley, J.
  Foundery collection, 1742
Stettin (1566); X7577 Nun seht
Unitas Fratrum (1566)
Bohemian traditional, etc.
NOTE: Wisely see also Czeck
traditional titles.

Be ye joyful; X9658 Salvator
  natus
Freuen wir uns (1457); X3504
  Freuen wir uns all in
Gladness (12th c)
Judah's Lion (ca 1600)
Kommet ihr hirten; X8003 Old
  Bohemian carol
Resurgenti Nazareno (1505)
Bolton, Fannie E.
  Bolton (1900)
Bolze, G.
  Walk with Jesus (1788); X5977
    Lasset uns mit Jesu

Bonitus, Brother
  Dear Guardian of Mary
Bonner, Carey, 1859-1938
  Doudney
  Muswell Hill II
  Sommerlied
  Tilak
Bonner, Robert
  Pastor regalis (1887)
Bontrager, Sylvia
  God is good
Booth, Ballington, 1959-1940
  The cross is not greater
Booth, Josiah, 1852-1930
  Avondale (1887)
  Baynard
  Beechwood
  Bracondale
  Commonwealth (1888)
  Cross and crown
  Earlham
  Excelsior
  Fernshaw
  Holy war
  Limpsfield
  New year
  Northrepps
  Peniel (1909)
  Remembrance
  Swainsthrope
  True-hearted
  Wardlaw
Bornschein, Franz Carl, 1879-1948
  Pax veritatis (1927)
Borthwick, R. Brown see
  Brown-Borthwick, R.
Bortniansky, Dmitri Stepanovich,
1751-1825
  St Petersburg (1825); X1222
    Bortiansky; X1637 Cherubic
    hymn; X5688 Jesus, thy
    boundless; X6457 Lowell;
    X9169 Russia; X11997
    Wells
  Vesper hymn (1818); X1223
    Bortiansky; X9177 Russian
    vesper
Bost, Paul A.I.D., 1790-1874
  Bost
  Gratitude (1837)
Bostwick, W.J.
  Father, we come to thee
Bottazzo, L.

Ave Maria (1940)
Boughton, Rutland, 1878-
  Ben Jonson's carol
Bourgeois, Loys (Louis), ca
  1510-ca 1561
  NOTE: See also Genevan
Psalter, 1551 and Goudimel (who
republished Bourgeois, etc.)

  Ascending King (1551)
  Bourgeois (1551); X599 As the
    hart; X1036 Berlin; X1876
    Coblentz; X2017 Comme un
    cerf attere; X3502 Freu dich
    sehr; X3634 Genevan Psalm
    42; X5555 Jesus, dine dybe;
    X6301 Lo, they come in glad;
    X6495 Ludwigsburg; X8030
    Old 42d; X8703 Psalm 42;
    X11194 Thirsting; X11886
    Waterspring
  Commandments (1543); X2011
    Commandemens; X4901 Hour
    of need; X6107 Les command-
    emens; X6632 Magdeburg;
    X7266 Naar vi i største;
    X12013 Wenn wir in höchsten;
    X12123 When in the hour of
  Du fort de ma detresse (ca
    1545); X2118 Contrition;
    X5482 Jeg raaber fast, O
    Herre
  Genevan Psalm 22 (1549); X8032
    Old 71st
  Holy Hill (1543)
  L'Omnipotent (1551); X3636
    Genevan Psalm 110; X8716
    Psalm 110
  Lord, to thee (1551); X8360
    Pathway
  Mon Dieu, prête-moi l'orielle
    (1543); X3635 Genevan
    Psalm 86; X8712 Psalm 86
  Nunc dimittis (1549)
  O esca viatorum (1542); X8507
    Pleading; X8697 Psalm 6
  Old 38th (1542)
  Old 100th (1551); X2602 Dis-
    miss us with thy; X2684
    Doxology; X3526 From all
    that dwell; X4027 Great
    King of saints; X7884 O
    salutaris Hostia; X8040 Old

  Hundred; X8566 Praise
    God from whom; X10633
    Tabor (Kugelmann. Concen-
    tus novi, 1540); X10916
    The hundredth Psalm;
    X11006 The Old Hundredth;
    X11311 To Thee, O Jesus
    Christ
  Old 107th (1643); X8715
    Psalm 107
  Old 124th [10.10.10.10.10
    metre] (1551); X3629
    Geneva 124; X7875 O
    sacred Heart of Jesus;
    X8010 Old hundred twenty-
    fourth
  Old 127th
  Old 136th (1551)
  Psalm 88 (1543)
  Rendez à dieu (1543); X2152
    Cornerstone; X3197 Exul-
    tation; X3637 Genevan
    Psalm 118; X7304 Navarre;
    X8717 Psalm 118
  Royal law (1551); X3628
    Geneva 119; X3638 Gene-
    van Psalm 119
  St Michael (1551); X1456
    Calvin; X8058 Old 134th
  Sion's praise (1543)
  Toulon [10.10.10.10 metre]
    (1551); X7305 Navarre;
    X7930 O thou that rulest;
    X8055 Old 124th
Bourne, Annie F. (Fanny
  Crosby??)
  Give me thy heart
Bowcher, J.
  East Hill
Bowen, J.C.
  O vision bright
Bower, John Dykes, 1905-
  Amen Court
  Elton
  Standish
Bowman, J.M.
  My Saviour guides me
  Stover
Boyce, R. Fisher
  Beautiful star of Bethlehem
    (1940)
Boyce, William, 1710-79
  Appleton (1740)

Boyce (1765); X4288 Halton
Holgate; X5497 Jersey; X
   9938 Sharon
Chant
Chapel Royal
Kingsland; X1259 Boyce
Morning hymn
Portsea
Boyd, William, 1816-68
   Pentecost (1864)
Boyle, Ina
   Enniskerry
Brackett, Lyman
   Alma
   Communion
   Guidance (1887)
   Norton (1887)
   Science
Bradbury, William Batchelder,
   1816-68
   Agawam
   Aletta (1860); X4769 Holy
     Bible, book; X8655 Prince
     of peace, control
   Amelia
   Andre
   Aughton (1864); X4472 He
     leadeth me
   Baca; X1928 Come, gracious
     Spirit
   Bloomfield chant
   Braden
   Brown; X1649 Chief shepherd;
     X4940 How sweet, how hea-
     venly; X5292 In mercy,
     Lord
   Caddo
   Clarksville
   Dalliba
   Dare to do right
   Don't forget the Sabbath
   During
   Even me; X6360 Lord, I
     hear of showers
   Fade, fade, each earthly joy
   Farewell, all earthly honors
   Fulton
   Harvey's chant; X3825 God
     moves in a
   Helena
   Jazer
   Lottie; X2674 Dove
   Mason's chant

Meroe
Monora
Morris chant
My latest sun
Newell
Olive's Brow (1853); X11274
   'Tis midnight
Oriel
Over the ocean wave
Peoria
Pleasant pastures (1859);
   X1265 Bradbury; X9748
   Savioir, like a Shepherd;
   X9958 Shepherd
Redal
Renar; X1678 China; X5626
   Jesus loves me; X11826
   Warner
Rest (1843); X631 Asleep in
   Jesus; X1266 Bradbury
Rolland
Sabaoth; X4797 Holy is the
   Lord
Salome
Silverton
Stand like the brave
Sutherland
Sweet hour (ca 1860); X10577
   Sweet hour of prayer;
   X11783 Walford
The solid rock; X7219 My
   hope is built; X10164 Solid
   Rock
There is no name; X1156
   Blessed name; X10606
   Sweetest name; X11080
   The sweetest name
Viola (1849)
We are all enlisted
Whither, pilgrims
Wirth
Woodworth (1849); X5762
   Just as I am
Yarbrough; X10643 Take my
   life, and let
Zephyr; X8448 Philadelphia
Bradley, F. L.
   We give thee but thine own
     (1920)
Bradshaw, M. L.
   Consolator
Bragers, Achille P.
   All hail, dear Conqueror

Ave, tu rex pácis
Christ the Lord is risen to-
    day
Creator Spirit, Lord of grace
Dear Angel, ever at my side
Great St Joseph (1953)
Hail noble column
Hymn to the Cross
Let every creature
O Christ, of Angel legions
O fair Creator of the skies
    (1954)
O food that weary pilgrims
    love (1953)
O Hunter blessed
O Lord, I am not worthy
    (1953)
Out of the depths
St Gabriel, O blessed youth
St Joseph, pride of heaven's
    court
Sing we triumphant (1953)
Soul of my Saviour (1953)
The divine praises (1939)
'Tis the day of resurrection
    (1953)
Ye souls of the faithful (1953)
Braham and Nathan. Hebrew
    melodies.
    Psalm 136
Brahms, Johannes, 1833-97
    Brahms; X11673 Victorious
    Lucy; X1063 Bethlehem lullaby;
        X9742 Saviour, hear us, we;
        X11333 Too late, too late
    The quest; X6721 Marias Wall-
        fahrt
Brandeis, Frederick, 1832-99
    Pray when the morn unveileth
Branscombe, Gena, 1881-
    Browning (1927)
    Chalice (1927)
    Picton (1927)
Braun, Johann G.
    Braun; X9395 St Gabriel
Breedlove, Leonard P., d ca
    1879
    Cross of Christ (1844)
Breitendich. Koralbog, 1764
    Frisk op, min sjael
Brenneman, Henry B.
    There's a beautiful, beautiful
        land; X4845 Home of the

blest
Brethren hymnal, 1901
    Lisle
Breton traditional
    Afar upon a foreign shore
    St Lo
Brewer, Alfred Herbert, 1865-
    1928
    Glovernia
Brewer, John Hyatt, 1856-
    1931
    Cuyler
Bridge, John Frederick, 1844-
    1924
    Conquest
    Ninety and nine
    Olrig Grange (1905)
    St Beatrice
Bridgers, Luther B., 1884-
    1948
    Sweetest name (1909); X4467
        He keeps me singing
Briegel, Carl Wolfgang, 1626-
    Ach wie sehnlich wart ich
        (1687)
    Liebster Jesu (1687)
Briggs, George Wallace, 1875-
    1959
    David (1929)
    Loughborough
    Loughborough College
    St Francis
    St Martin (1931)
    Springtime
    Wulfrun (1929)
Brightbill, Alvin Franz, 1903-
    Bounding heart
    Communion hymn: X7826 O
        Lord! to thee who
Bristol, Lee H., Jr., 1923-
    Sedgwick
Bristol Tune book, 1876
    Cambria
    St Austin; X708 Austin;
        X11330 Tonus peregrinus
        (Pre-reformation mel)
Brockless, George Frederick,
    1887-1957
    Fritwell
Bronner. Choral-buch, 1715
    Jesus, Jesus, nichts als
        Jesus
    Wer weiss, wie nahe mir

mein ende; X2201 Crasselius
(Wittwe. Hamburger Musik-
alisches handbuch, 1690);
H4985 Hvo ved, hvor naer
mig; X12026 Wer weist wie
nahe; X12223 Who knows
how near
Broomfield, William Robert,
1826-88
   St Kilda
Brown, Arthur Henry, 1830-1926
   All hallows (1862); X372
      Allhallows
   Gerrans
   Holy church (1862)
   Holy cross
   Holy rood (1863)
   Lammas (1868)
   Legion
   Litany
   Margaretting
   Purleigh (1856); X3189 Ex-
      mouth
   Saffron Walden (1890)
   St Anatolius (1862); X1361
      Brown
   St Anstell
   St John Damascene
   St Mabyn; X6589 Mabyn
   St Ulric
   Story of the cross
   Veni lux
   When Christ was born (1859);
      X5260 In excelsis gloria
Brown, Charles S.
   America, the beautiful (1906)
   Consecration (1901)
   Thou delightest, O Lord
Brown, Howard L.
   Follow, I will follow thee
    '(1937)
Brown, J.A.
   Pray (1922)
Brown, L.O.
   I cannot tell thee (1899)
Brown, S.R.
   Monson (before 1938)
Brown-Borthwick, Robert, 1840-
94
   Eucharist
   Grange
Browne, John Lewis, 1864-1933
   Glorious Patron (1913)

   Lord, who at Cana's wedd-
     ing feast
Browne, Mary A.
   Browne
Bruder Choral-buch, 1784
   (probably Bohemian Brethren)
   Weil ich Jesu schafflein bin
Brun, Fritz, 1878-1943
   O Virgin all lovely
Bruning, David
   White fields (1915)
Brunk, C.H.
   Father! In life's young
     morning; X3921 Gorton
   Gethsemane
Brunk, J. Claude
   O Love Divine
Brunk, J.D.
   Benediction
   Come to me
   Hagerstown
   I heard the voice of Jesus
     say (1911)
   In thy holy place
   Jesus the teacher
   Lilies of the field
   No abiding city here
   Sweetest hosannas
   Vespers
   Watts (1910)
   Ye are the light; X10938
     The light of the world
Bryan, Cornelius
   Bryan; X9903 Serenity
Brydaine, Father
   Jesus, my God; behold
Buck, Percy Carter, 1871-
1947
   Draw nigh; X8876 Refuge
   Gonfalon Royal
   Martins (1913); X9589 St
     Sebastian
   Mont Richard
   Pater noster
   Resurrection morning
   St Barnabas
Bugenhagen. Liturgy. Braun-
schweig, 1528
   Agnus dei; X1749 Christe,
     du lamm
Bull, Ole Bornemann, 1810-80
   Asleep in Jesus
Bullard, Frederick Field,

1864-1904
  Hosmer (1902)
  Longfellow
Bullinger, Ethelbert William,
1837-1913
  Geneva; X584 Art thou weary;
    X1391 Bullinger
  Samaria (1874)
  Tenterden
  Wellingham
Bullivant, G., 1883-1937
  Bow Church
Bullock, Ernest
  Berry Down (1925)
Bunnett, Edward, 1834-1923
  Agnes (1877); X6230 Litany
  Happy home
  Kirby Bedon (1887); X1703
    Christ in His word
  Litany, No. 1
  Ransom
Burder, G.
  Luton
Burgmüller, Friedrich
  Emmons
Burke, J.H.
  Burke
  Not I, but Christ (1896)
Burkett, J.C.
  Happy spirits
Burleigh, Henry Thacker, 1866-
1949
  Alston
Burnap, Uzziah Christopher, 1834-
1900
  Amesbury (1895)
  Baxter (1871)
  Boston
  Browning
  Cleveland
  Clifton
  Cochran
  Enos
  Gould
  Hinchman (1869)
  Holy Guide (1895)
  In-as-much
  Paraclete
  Seelye (1869)
    X5385 Invocation
Burney, Charles, 1726-1814
  Truro (1769); X11312 To Thee,
    O Lord

Burnham, John N.
  Veritas (1923)
Burrowes, John Freckleton,
1787-1852
  Beechmont
  Burlington (1830)
Burstall, F.H.
  Nocturn
Burt, Bates, G., 1878-1948
  Lynne (1940)
  Shaddick (1941)
Busch and Bushey
  NOTE: Composers cited with
these names are probably from
the same family, variant spell-
ing

Busch, Calvin A.
  Second Parish (1954)
Bushey, J. Calvin
  Calvin; X7955 O why not
    tonight
  Marching home
  Weeping One of Bethany
Butcher, Frank C.
  Birchington
Butcher, William U., fl 1860
  Prayer
Butler, L.T.
  St Wystan
Button, Henry Elliot, 1861-
1925
  Child Service
  Sumus tibi
  Sursum voces
Buzzard, Rufus
  As the dawn was breaking
Byers, A.L.
  Are you adorning the doc-
    trine?
  Consecration
  Fill me with thy Spirit
    (1918)
  How reads your life-book?
  I would not have my way
  Love each other
  Obedience
  Only thine (1918)
  Shall I be ashamed
  Tell what He's done for you
    (1922)
Byles, Blanche Douglas
  Thy great bounty (1925)

Byshe, Fred H.
  A clean heart

C

C. A. P.
  Sullivan (1855)
Caldbeck, George Thomas,
1852-1912?
  Pax tecum (1877); X1086
    Bickersteth
Caldicott, Alfred James, 1842-
97
  Civitas dei
  Pastor bonus
Caldwell, C. T.
  How long must we wait (1917)
Caldwell, William
  Loving kindness (before 1830);
    X763 Awake, my soul, in
Calkin, Jean Baptiste, 1827-1905
  Bradfield (1872); X9445 St John
    Baptist
  Calkin I (1887); X9762 Savoy
    Chapel
  Calkin II (1887); X9440 St
    John
  Civitas dei; X1201 Bonar
  Elim (1867); X7127 Moscow
  Golden corn; X2439 Dedication;
    X8741 Purleigh
  Munus
  Newman (1867)
  Nox praecessit (1873)
  Ramoth
  St Joseph
  Sefton (1872)
  Theoctistus (1872)
  Waltham (1872); X1473 Camden;
    X2620 Doane; X5059 I heard
    the bells; X12127 When mar-
    shalled on
  Welcome, happy morning; X816
    Baptiste
  Winchcombe
Callcott, William Hutchins, 1807-
82
  Elim (1867); X1439 Callcott;
    X8970 Rest
  Intercession (1865); X386 Al-
    mighty Father, hear (Men-
    delssohn); X5367 Interces-

cession New
Calvin, J. Psalter, 1539
  Nostre dieu
Calvisius, Sethus, 1556-1615
  Calvisius (1589); X103 Ach
    bleib bei uns
  Gregor's 223d metre (1598);
    X12019 Wer Gott vertraut
Cambra, A.
  Fierce was the wild billow
Camidge, John, 1735-1803
  O Lord, open thou our eyes
Cammin, J. Melodienbuch von
Rautenburg.
  Wollt ihr wissen was mein
    preis
Camp, Harvey
  Aylesbury
Camp, John Spencer, 1858-
1946
  Abiding grace (1905)
  Sylvester (1905)
Camp, Mabel Johnston
  He is coming again (1913)
Campbell, John P.
  Axson (1899)
  Barnett (1901)
  In memoriam (1899)
  Lacy (1899)
  Langdon (1900)
  Leslie (1899)
  Lowrance (1899)
  Milster (1899)
  Mobile (1899)
  Reed (1899)
  Resignation (1900)
  Whitner (1899)
Campbell, Leroy B.
  Hosanna (1929)
  Vision (1929)
  Warren (1930)
Campbell, Paul O.
  Holy Spirit (1939)
Campbell, Sidney Scholfield,
1909-
  Old Commons
Campbell, Thomas, 1825-
  Sagina
Campian (or Campion), Thomas
1567-1620
  Babylon's Streams (1613)
  Campian (1613); X11689

View me, Lord
Campian 2 (ca 1613)
Song of joy
Weather-beaten sail
Candlyn, Frederick H.
Rugby (1927)
Vitai lampada (1927)
Canning, Thomas, 1911-
Covenant hymn (1961)
Cannon, Tracy Y.
Come, let us sing an
evening hymn
Come, rejoice
God of power, God of right
How beautiful thy temples,
Lord
Jesus, mighty King of Sion
Praise the Lord with heart
and voice
The Lord be with us
Cantica laudis, see Mason &
Webb. Cantica laudis
Cantiques de Strasbourg, 1697
Summer in winter
Canzuns spirituaelas. Upper
Engadine, 1765.
Engadine
Il buon pastor
Careless, George
Again we meet around the
board
Arise, my soul, arise
Arise, O glorious Sion
Author of faith, Eternal Word
Behold the great Redeemer die
Hark! listen to the trumpeters
He died! the great Redeemer
I saw a mighty angel
O give me back my Prophet
dear
O Lord of Hosts
O thou kind and gracious
Father; X10143 Softly beams
the sacred
Prayer is the soul's sincere
desire
Rest, rest for the weary soul
The Lord imparted from above
The morning breaks: the
shadows flee
Thou dost not weep alone
Though deepening trials

Ye children of our God
Carey, Henry, ca 1687-1743
Carey (1723); X1522 Carey's;
X10534 Surrey
Osborne
Surrey
Carnett, Ellis L.
It is finished (1940)
Carr, Benjamin, 1768-1831
Spanish chant (arr 1824);
X3665 Gethsemane; X6231
Litany; X6620 Madrid; X
10272 Spain; X10277
Spanish hymn; X10278
Spanish melody
Carr, F.
Kirkstall
Carr, J.H.
What would you give in ex-
change?
Carter, A. Norman
Palm Sunday (1882)
Carter, Edmund S., 1845-
Slingsby (1865); X617 As-
cham; X1559 Carter;
X2386 Day by day
Wreford (1865)
Carter, J.H.
Wyoming
Carter, Olen S.
Thanksgiving (1885)
Carter, R. Kelso
Launch out into the deep
Promises (1886); X10358
Standing on the promises
Case, Charles C., 1843-1918
Why not now?
Cassel, Flora Hamilton, 1852-
1911
NOTE: See also Flora H.
Good. May be the same individ-
ual.

Lambdin; X6472 Loyalty to
Christ
Mother knows (1890)
The King's business; X1566
Cassel; X5012 I am a
stranger
Casson, J.H.
Semper aspectemus (1875);
X9881 Semper

Catholic traditional, etc.
  NOTE: These tunes are usually
modern, anonymous, and found
within the Catholic hymnals.

  Adoramus te, panem
  All praise to St Patrick
  Alleluia! Alleluia
  Cor Jesu, cor purissimum
  Daily, daily, sing to Mary
  Dear Angel! ever at my side
  Flowers of the fairest; X1321
    Bring flowers of the
  Full in the panting heart
  Green are the leaves
  Hail, Queen of the Heavens
  Hail, thou living Victim
  Holy Patron! thee saluting
  Holy Spirit, come and shine
  In this sacrament
  Jesu deus, amor meus
  Jesus, Jesus, come to me
  Jesus, my Lord, my God;
    X3223 Faith of our fathers
  Lauda Sion
  Mother dear, O pray for me
  Mother of mercy; X7620 O come
    and mourn
  Now are the days
  O come, and mourn
  O faithful cross
  O Lord, I am not worthy
  Pilgrim song
  Pone luctum (1750)
  Pray for the dead!
  Queen and Mother
  See, amid the winter's snow
  Sing, sing, ye angel bands
  Sweet Saviour! bless us
  Te, Joseph, celebrent
  The clouds hang thick
  This is the image of our Queen
  Thou warrior of the Lord
  Thou who, hero-like
  To Jesus' heart all burning
  Victoria
  Vivat! vivat!
  When day's shadows lengthen
  Ye souls of the faithful
Catholic Hymn tunes, 1849
  Lugano; X6453 Loving Shep-
    herd of thy sheep

Catholisches gesangbuch.
  Strasbourg, 1697
  Fortem virili pectore
Catholische Geistliche gesänge.
  Andernach, 1608 see Ander-
  nach Gesangbuch 1608
Catholische Kirchengesang.
  Cologne, 1623 see Cologne
  Gesang-buch. 1623 and
  NOTE: Most hymnals pub-
lished before 1650 are cited
under place of publication.
Later books are by title or
compiler, whichever applies.

Cecil, R.
  St Sebastian
Cecilia Miriam, Sr. S. N. J. M.
  Guardian of Virgins (1958)
Celestial harps. Edinburgh,
  1824
  Pax celeste
Chadwick, George Whitefield,
  1854-1931
  Armstrong (1887)
  Eaton (1888)
  Little town (1927)
  Peace (1890)
  Warfare
Chadwyck-Healey, H. P., 1889-
  Radwell
Challinor, Frederic Arthur,
  1866-1952
  Stories of Jesus (ca 1904)
Chalmers' Collection, 1749
  Aberdeen; X9556 St Paul
Chamberlain, G. B.
  Confidence (1870)
Chamberlain, John M.
  We're marching on to glory
Champness, W.
  Montgomery (1762)
Champneys, Francis Henry,
  1848-1930
  St Jerome (1889)
  St Vernonica
  Xavier
Chants ordinaires de l'office
  Divin. Paris, 1881.
  Grafton; X10671 Tantum
    ergo [sacramentum]
Chapin, Aaron and Chapin,

Amzi have not been absolutely
identified as composers or
compilers of these three tunes.
Both men are cited as "A.
Chapin" in some books. Their
active years were the same
period in U.S. history.
Chapin, Aaron
  Forest; X9082 Rockbridge
    Golden Hills (1832)
Chapin, Amzi, 1768-1835
  Melody (1823); X1629 Chelms-
    ford; X8649 Primrose
Chartres Antiphoner, 1784
  Adesto, sancta trinitas
Chauvenet Collection
  Jerusalem
Cheeswright, Frederick H.
  Shackelford (ca 1889)
Chepmell, E.
  Dinard
Cherubini, Maria Luigi Carlo
  Zenobio Salvatore, known as
  Luigi Cherubini, 1760-1842
  Dallas
  Redemption
  Veni, Jesu, amor mi
Chester, William Sidell
  Chester (1898)
Chester ms., ca 1425
  Song of the Nuns of Chester
Chetham, J. Psalmody, 1718
  Aylesbury; X12333 Wirksworth
  Marlow; X1169 Blest be the
    dear; X7829 O Lord, while
    we confess
Chevenix-Trench, May
  Name
Chinese traditional, etc.
  Hsuan P'ing see below Confucian
    Temple chant
  Hubbard
  Jasmine flower
  Le P'ing
  P'u T'o; X1680 Chinese
    melody; X9937 Shanghai
  Shanghai
  Song of the Yangtze boatmen
    (chantey)
  Wiant
Chippewa (Indian) melody
  Manitou

Chitty, Simon Comenius, 1831-
  1902
  Benjamin
  Graceham
  Wachovia (1890)
Chope, Richard Robert, 1830-
  Herbert
  St Cyprian
  Scudamore
Chope's Carols
  Chope
Chopin, Francois-Frédéric,
  1810-49
  Hear our prayer
Chord, S.H.
  Some sweet day
Choron, Alexandre Etienne,
  1771-1834
  Tynemouth (1822)
Christiansen, Frederik Melius,
  1871-1955
  As sinks beneath the ocean
  Flower of love (1919)
  One resolve (1891)
Christliche lieder. Wittenberg,
  1524
  NOTE: See also Geistliche
Gesangbüchlein. Wittenberg,
1524 and Etliche Christliche
lieder. Wittenberg, 1524

  Nun freut euch; X4105 Gre-
    gor's 132d metre-B; X
    7542 Nu fryde sig hver;
    X7565 Nun freut euch
    lieben christen ...
Church-Gallery book
  A Gallery carol
  Candlemas Eve
  Yoeman's carol
Church Hymnal
  Ferniehurst
Church of Scotland Hymn tune
  book, 1862
  Amberg
Clark (no initials)
  The unseen city
Clark, Edward, 1888-
  Barre
Clark, E.M.
  Catherine
Clark, Jeremy or Clarke,

Jeremiah, ca 1673-1707
A morning hymn
Bishopthorpe (1700); X9562
St Paul's
Brockham
Bromley (1700)
Hermon
King's Norton
St Magnus; X7507 Nottingham
Tunbridge
Uffingham; X9482 St Luke;
X10104 Sleep, downy sleep
Yattendon 8
Clark, Thomas, 1775-1859
Crediton
Essex
Grafton
Warsaw
Clarke, Harry D., 1888-
Into my heart
Clarke, Henry Leland, 1907-
Art (1959)
Valley Forge (1958
Windsor Forest (1960)
Ygdrasil (1960)
Clarke, John, 1770-1836
Clarke's
Clausener. Gesangbuch, 1653
Cordis donum
O Jesu mi dulcissimi
Clayson, William
Hope of Israel
Nearer, dear Savior to thee
O thou Rock of our Salvation
O what songs of the heart
The day dawn is breaking
To Nephi, seer of olden time
Clelland, Wilfred G.
Martha (1957)
Clemens, Charles Edwin, 1858-
1923
O Lord, save thy people
Clemens, Theodor L., 1858-
Raglan
Clemm, J. B. O.
Clemm (1895); X3250 Far and
near the fields; X4378 Harvest;
X10818 The call for reapers
Click, D. M.
God is love, His mercy; X2868
Effie
Clifton, John Charles, 1781-
1841

Clifton
Cluett, John W. A.
Wentworth
Coats, J. B.
Building for eternity (1941)
Where could I go? (1940)
Cobb, Gerard Francis, 1838-
1904
Aysgarth
Cobb; X5995   Lauda Sion;
X5999 Lauda Sion salva-
torem
Gerard
Harrogate
Moultrie; X6297 Lo! the
clouds have
Cocker, Norman, 1889-1953
Ripponden
Ryburn
Coe, William Wallace, 1862-
Beatrice (1895)
Coerne, Louis Adolphe, 1870-
1922
Son of Man
Cole, John
Geneva
Coleman, E. G., 1872-
Burning light
Coleridge-Taylor, Samuel,
1875-1912
Luconer
Coles, George, 1792-1858
Duane Street (1835);
X5572 Jesus from whom
all
A Collection of hymns and
sacred poems. Dublin, 1749
Irish; X2717 Dublin; X
11097 The venite
Coller, Percy E. B.
St Joan (1941)
Collier, Edward A.
Marchfield
Collignon, C., 1725-85
University
Cologne Gesangbuch, 1623
Cologne; X1796 Christus ist
auferstanden
Herrick's carol
Hilariter; X2558 Die ganze
welt
Hosmer; X4511 Heart's de-
sire; X6645 Mainz; X6718

Maria jung und zart
O King of Kings
Vigiles et sancti; X270 All
  creatures of our; X364 Alle-
  luias; X2788 Easter alleluya;
  X2804 Easter song; X5979
  Lasst uns erfreuen; X6119
  Let hymns of joy; X10725
  Tell us now, O Death;
  X12157 When very early
Cologne Gesangbuch, 1634
  The secret flower; X3609
  Gebor'n ist uns ein kindelein
Cologne, Symphonia Sirenum,
  1695
  I love thee, O thou Lord;
  X7646 O Deus, ego amo te
Comley, J.
  Green Hill
Conant, Albert F.
  Christmas Morn
Conant, Grace Wilbur, 1880-
  1948
  Agni (1927)
  Carry on (1927)
  Far Hills (1927)
  Fealty (1927)
  Merlin (1927)
Confucian Temple chant
  Hsuan P'ing
Congregational Church music,
  1871
  Lavington
Conkey, Ithamar, 1815-67
  Rathbun (1851); X3752 Glori-
    ous things of thee; X5301
    In the cross of Christ
Conradi, Johan G., ca 1830-96
  Alone, with Thee
Conte, Paolo, 1891-
  Redentore (1940); X4030
    Great Redeemer
Converse, Charles Crozart,
  1832-1918
  Erie (1868); X2124 Converse;
    X3510 Friend; X3517 Friend-
    ship; X5420 Israel, Israel,
    God is; X12067 What a
    friend
  Friend of sinners (1896)
  I am not worthy
  Savior! teach me

Cook, G. H.
  Heavenly sunlight
Cook, John T.
  Heaven
Cooke, Benjamin, 1734-93
  Westminster
Cooke, Greville, 1894-
  Emmaus
  Golden Grove
  Ivinghoe
  Sentinel
Cooke, H. E.
  Niles
  St Ignatius
Cooke, William Henry, 1820-
  1912
  Bath
  Sanctissimus
Cooper, Alexander Smith,
  1835-
  Sanctus
Cooper, George, 1820-76
  St Sepulchre (1836)
Cooper, W. G.
  Wonderful peace
Copes, V. Earle, 1921-
  Epworth Church (1964)
  Kingdom 1960)
  Vicar (1963)
Corbeil, Pierre de, d 1222
  Corbeil
  Orientis partibus (ca 1210);
    X2049 Concordi laetitia;
    X5657 Jesus our Brother;
    X6959 Milites crucis;
    X7445 Nomen Jesu; X8008
    Old French melody; X8869
    Redhead, No. 45 (Red-
    head); X9504 St Martin
Cornelius, Peter, 1824-74
  The Christmas tree; X1744
    Christbaum
  The Kings; X2563 Die König
Cornell, John Henry, 1828-94
  Bethel
  Cornell
  Excelsius (1872)
  I think when I read
  Triumph
Corner, D. G. Geistliche nach-
  tigall, 1649
  Corner; X1543 Carol; X2885

Ein kindlein in der; X5253 In
 der wiegen; X10850 The cradle
Heiliger Geist
Corner, D.G. Gesangbuch, 1625
 Christi mutter stund vor
 schmerzen; X6783 Mater
 dolorosa
Corner, D.G. Gesangbuch, 1631
 Omni dei
Cornish folksong see English
 traditional: Lew Trenchard
Cornysshe, William, early 16th c
 Robyn
Coslett, Joseph
 We'll sing all hail
Costa, Michael, 1806-84
 Costa; X2625 Doers
 Eli
 Jesus, Saviour, Heavenly
 Father
Costellow (no initials)
 Surrey (ca 1810)
Coster, Arthur V., 1864-1931
 City of light (1909)
Cottman, Arthur, 1842-79
 Beachley
 Dalehurst (1874)
 Eversley
 Kendal
 Millikan
 Mirfield (1874)
 Morn of gladness (1877); X
 2169 Cottman; X9131 Ros-
 well; X11925 We plough the
 fields
Coules, Reginald F.
 Dedicatio anni
Courteville, Raphael
 St James (1697)
Covell, William King, 1906-
 Pelham Street (1960)
Coward, Henry, 1849-1944
 Norfolk Park
Cowen, Frederic Hymen, 1852-
1935
 Now bless the God of all
 With the voice of sweet spring
 (1932)
Cramer, Francis, 19th c
 St Agatha
Crawford, Edward Patrick, 1846-
1912
 Jehovah nissi

Crawford, Jane Romney
 Father in heaven, we do
 believe
Crespin, Jean
 O Herre Gud, oändelig (1551)
Crespin. Psalms, 1556
 Norwich; X8061 Old 137th
 Psalm 23
Cringan, Alexander Thom,
1860-
 Harvest song
 Simcoe
Croatian carol
 Croatia (14th c)
Croft, J.B. Collection.
 Iste confessor; X492
 Angers
Croft, (or Crofts) William,
1678-1727
 All Saints (1703)
 Binchester
 Croft's 136th; X2221 Croft;
 X2224 Croft's; X2227
 Croft's 148th
 Eatington
 Hanover (1708); X2078
 Conquest; X2222 Croft;
 X2460 Delay not
 St Anne (1708); X7206
 My God, how wonderful;
 X7692 O God, our help;
 X9269 St Ann's
 St Matthew (1708)
 Southampton (1727)
Crofton, Edward Lord
 Crofton (1893)
Crook, George C.
 Minto (1918)
Crookall, Msgr.
 Dear Angel! ever at my
 side
 O come and mourn
Crosbie, Howard Augustus,
1844-1918
 St Cephas
 Sefton
Cross, Moses S., 1854-1911
 Resignation
 Waratah (1905)
Cross, Paul
 Mary, the Dawn (20th c)
Crossley, Hastings, 1846-
 Eripe me

Crossley, Thomas H.
  Anagola (1876)
Crossley, W. J.
  Woodhall (1905)
Crotch, William, 1775-1847
  Sidon
Crowfoot, W., 1724-83
  St Mark
Crueger, Johann, 1598-1662
  NOTE: Crueger's Praxis pie-
tatis melica, originally published
in Berlin, 1644, contained many
of these chorales. Reprints and
other compilations were issued
during his lifetime. Publication
date, when known, is the limit of
the citation herein.

  Auf, auf, mein Herz (1648)
  Christmas joy (1653); X3522
    Fröhlich soll mein
  Crueger
  Du, o schönes Weltegebäude
    (1649); X4123 Gregor's 168th
    metre-C; X5567 Jesus er
    mit liv i live
  Graefenberg (1653); X2268
    Crueger; X5774 Kabzeel;
    X7557 Nun danket all';
    X7559 Nun danket all' und
    bringet ehr; X10769 Thanks-
    giving
  Gregor's 79th metre (1653);
    X5357 Innsbruck (Isaak);
    X7948 O welt, sieh hier dein
  Hebron
  Herzliebster Jesu (1640); X3285
    Father most holy; X4070
    Gregor's 36th metre; X7791
    O Lamb of God, have; X10486
    Suffering Savior; X11750
    Vreden din afvend
  Holy Ghost (1639); X4551
    Heiliger Geist
  Jesus, all my gladness (1653);
    X3597 Gaudeo; X4134 Gre-
    gor's 208th metre-A; X5629
    Jesu, meine freude
  Lob sei dem Allmachtigen Gott;
    X4068 Gregor's 22d metre-C;
    X9184 Ryden
  Manger (1653); X7765 O Jesu

  Christ, dein Kripplein
Marburg
Nun danket (1647); X2270
  Crueger; X2490 Deo gra-
  tias; X4006 Gratitude;
  X4392 Harwich; X6708
  Marenzo; X7548 Nu takker
  alle Gud; X7561 Nun danket
  alle Gott; X11182 Thine
  advent Lord
O hvor salig er I dog I
  fromme (1649); X7958 O
  wie selig seid ihr
O Jesu Christ, du höchstes
  Gut (1658)
Oblation (1653); X4623 Herr,
  deinen zorn; X6306 Lobet
  den Herren
Ratisbon (1653); X1037 Ber-
  lin; X1275 Brandenberg;
  X2059 Confidence; X2891
  Eins ist noth; X3065 Et er
  nødigt; X5539 Jesus Christ,
  my sure; X5566 Jesus er
  mit haab og; X5631 Jesu,
  meine zuversicht; X6509
  Luise; X8126 One thing
  needful; X8807 Rathbon;
  X11765 Waddell; X12237
  Why art thou cast; X12580
  Zuversicht
St Nicholas (1649); X66
  Aaberg; X2448 Deep and
  glorious; X2269 Crueger;
  X4626 Herr, ich habe
  missgehandelt; X4642
  Herre, jeg har handlet;
  X8880 Regensburg
St Simon (1549); X4663
  Herzlich thut mich erfreuen
Schmuecke dich (1649);
  X2432 Deck thyself; X3928
  Gothenburg; X7547 Nu skal
  du, min sjael; X9785
  Schmuecke dich, O liebe
  seele; X11528 Upsala I;
  X11529 Upsala II
Schwing dich auf zu deinem
  Gott (1653)
Von Gott will ich nicht
  lassen (1640)
Wachet doch; erwacht (1662)

Wie soll ich dich empfangen
(1653)
Zeuch ein (1653); X12563
Zeuch ein zu meinen
Cruickshank, W. A. C.
Ter sanctus
Cuff, C. R.
Pastoral chant
Cunningham, F. Selection of
Psalm tunes, 1834
Birmingham
Currie, Edward C.
Christ the Lord is my true
Shepherd (1958)
Holy is God (1958)
Currier, Everett R.
Bourne (1941)
Curry, R. Donald
We thank thee Lord (1963)
Curwen's (John) Standard course,
1860
God is near thee
Curwen's (John) Tune book, 1842
Children of Jerusalem; X6335
Infant praise
Glory
Custance, A. F. M.
Easter flowers
Orison
Cuthbert, Elizabeth H.
Howard
Cutler, Henry Stephen, 1824-1902
All Saints new (1872); X298
All saints new; X2295 Cut-
ler; X2981 Emulation; X11707
Vindex
Cutts, Peter, 1937-
Wylde Green
Cuzens, Benjamin
Coventry
Czeck traditional, etc.
NOTE: See also entries under
Bohemian and Moravian
Rocking (1931)
The Birds (1928)

D

Dadman, J. W.
Is not this the land of Beulah;
X2383 Dawning; X11877
Watchman, tell me
Rest for the weary

Dahle, John, 1853-1931
Guidance (1911)
Jubilate (1911)
Luther Seminary
Red Wing Seminary
St Olaf (1911)
Dakota (Indian) hymn
Dakota hymn
Dale, Benjamin James, 1885-
1943
Sidmouth
Dale, Charles J.
Denby (1904)
Dale, Reginald Francis, 1845-
1919
St Catherine (1867)
Dale, W. T.
Holy City (1913)
Daley, James E.
God most truly (1958)
Damon's Psalter, 1579
Southwell; X2482 Denham
Dana, Mary S. B. (later, Mary
S. B. D. Shindler)
Flee as a bird (arr); X10273
Spain
D'Andrieux (17th c)
Prayer
Daniels, Mabel Wheeler, 1878-
Dreamers (1927)
Danish traditional, etc.
All things bright and beauti-
ful
Bairn; X6204 Lille Guds
barn
Celestia; X7743 O how beau-
tiful the sky
Galdan
Herra
Lassen
Nativity
Nature's praises
Ostergaard; X10777 That
cause can neither
Parting hymn
Release; X215 Agnus;
X5113 I see thee standing;
X5484 Jeg ser dig, søde
Lam
Salvator
Danks, Hart Pease, 1834-1903
Delphine (1901)
No night there; X5310 In the

land of fadeless
Spitta
The Lord in Zion reigneth
(1886)
Dare, Elkanah Kelsay, 1782-
1826
Kedron
Darius, Frederick R.
Ruhetag (1916)
Darke, Harold Edwin, 1888-
Cornhill
Naphill
Darley, W. H. W.
Goderich
Darms, Antonius
My Lord and I; X4957
Huguenot hymn
Darmstadt Gesang-buch,
NOTE: Several editions in-
dicated by date at end of tune
name.

All saints (1698); X306 All
saints old; X3749 Glorious
saint whose deeds immortal;
X6405 Lorrain; X11969
Weisse flaggen (Tochter Sion,
Cologne)
Clausnitzer (1699); X11898 We
all believe in one; X12326
Wir glauben all' an einen
Darmstadt (1698); X687 Auf,
seele, sei geruest't
Goldschmidt (1698); X4065
Gregor's 16th metre; X7645
O der alles [hoett' verloren];
X8580 Praise the Saviour
Gregor's 39th metre-B (1698);
X102 Ach, alles was himmel
Gregor's 101st metre(1698);
X8633 Preis, lob, ehr, ruhm
Gregor's 167th metre-E (1698);
X7650 O du Liebe meiner
Liebe
Gregor's 189th metre-B (1697);
X9791 Schönster Immanuel,
Herzog der Frommen
Gregor's 192d metre (1698);
X10130 So fuehrst du doch
Gregor's 211th metre (1687);
X6169 Liebster Jesu, lieb-
stes lieben!; X6378 Lord
of life

Luebeck (1699); X6849 Mein-
en Jesum lass' ich nicht
Nun kommt das neue (1698)
Victor
Darwall, John, 1731-97
Darwall (1770); X2354 Dar-
wall's 148th
Darwall, Leicester, 1813-
St Hubert; X4951 Hubert
Davenport, F. S. S.
Queen's College
Davidisches Harfen-un Psalter-
spiel, 1744
In allen meinen thaten
O gloriosa Virginum
Davies, David, 1810-75
Glan'rafon
Davies, Edward Thomas, 1878-
All saints
Michaelmas
Davies, Henry Walford, 1869-
1941
Ainger (1915); X8742 Purpose
Auctor vitae
Christmas carol; X11350
Town of Bethlehem
Etherington
Firmament
God be in my head (1910)
Hampstead; X6786 Matheson
Oswald's Tree
Pentatone (1923)
Plentitude
St André
Temple (1906)
Vision
Wallog
Wengen
Davies, Robert, 1814-67
Hope (1860; X3792 Gobaith
Davis, Arthur
Creevelea (1927)
Davis, F. W.
Aberavon
Davis, Frank M.
Gather the golden grain
Lead me, Saviour; X6040
Lead me; X9746 Saviour,
lead me lest
My name's written there;
X5408 Is my name written
Sleeping on guard
Davis, G.

Monmouth
Davis, J.W.
  Sitting at the feet of Jesus;
    X11395 Troubled soul, thy
  God
Davis, Katherine K., 1892-
  Massachusetts (1964)
  Surette (1964)
  Wachuset (1964)
Davis, Marchel, fl. ca 1848
  Goshen (1860); X3337 Fides;
    X8346 Pastor bonus
Davis, O.S.
  Lord, give us a vision
Davis, W.B.
  St Leonard
Dawes, Eric, 1902-
  Broome
Day, George Henry, 1883-
  Decision (1929)
  Edsall (1940)
  Geneva (1940)
  My Master (1929)
  Parce domine (1917)
  Rochester (1929)
Day, John. Psalter, 1562
  Old 81st
  St Flavian; X2411 Dear Angel,
    ever at; X3377 Flavian
  Tallis' Lamentation
Daynes, Joseph J.
  As the dew from heaven
  Behold, the mountain of the
    Lord
  Come, listen to a prophet's
    voice
  Glorious things are sung
  Great God, attend
  Hark ten thousand thousand
    voices
  If you could hie to Kolob
  Lord, accept our true devotion
  Lord, thou wilt hear me
  Now we'll sing with one accord
  We're not ashamed to own our
    Lord
  When dark and drear
Deale, Edgar Martin, 1905-
  Edwin
Dean, Harry A.
  Lord, we come before thee
  Savior, Redeemer of my soul
Dean, Joseph H.

Before thee, Lord, I bow
  my head
Deane, John H.
  Sienna (1869)
  Verona
Dearle, D.W.
  David (1926)
Dearle, Edward
  Penitentia (1880)
Decius, Nikolaus, ca 1490-
1541
  O Lamm Gottes; X221 Agnus
    dei; X5931 Lamb of God;
    X7712 O Guds Lam uskyl-
    dig; X7798 O Lamm Got-
    tes unschuldig; X10407
    Steterburg
De Fluiter, Henry
  Hail Him the King of Glory
  Mizpah
De Jong, Gerrit, jr.
  Come, sing to the Lord
de Lloyd, David, 1883-1948
  see Lloyd, David de
De Marbelle, Dion
  When they ring the golden
    bells
Demuth, John Arthur, 1848-
1920
  Oberlin (1900)
Dennis, T.
  He died of a broken heart
Denton, J.P.
  Wonderful Jesus
Depew, Arthur
  Mater (1925)
De Roo, Cornelia J.
  The tribes
Dessler, W.C., 1660-1722
  Gregor's 183d metre;
    X6840 Mein Jesu, dem
    dei seraphinen
Deutsch, M.
  Of all the thoughts of God
Deutsch kirchenampt see
  Teutsch Kirchenampt
De Vaughan, W.M.
  My Saviour cares for me
Devereux, L.
  Boardman; X2534 Devereaux
D'Hooghe, J.
  Jesus, Creator of the world
Dickey, Mark, 1885-

Pater omnipotens (1941)
Veni, anima mea
Dickinson, Charles J., 1822-83
Agape (1861); X8937 Repose;
X9691 Sanctuary
Diggle, Roland
Racine (1941)
Diggs, T. Lloyd
St Francis (1906)
Dijon Church melody
O invidenda martyrum
The Divine companion, 1709
O God of love
Divine Musical miscellany, 1754
Old 23d
Dixon, R. W.
Staincliffe
Dixon, William, 1750-1825
Lanesboro; X5491 Jehovah,
Jesus, Lord
Doane, William Howard, 1832-
1915
Arms of Jesus; X8877 Refuge;
X9216 Safe in the arms of;
X10902 The heart's refuge
Avalon (arr)
Be silent (1903); X11364
Tread softly
Cleansing; X2041 Compassion;
X2218 Crimson; X11230
Though your sins be
Come, great Deliverer
Constance
Doane I
Doane II; X1149 Blessed hour;
X4902 Hour of prayer;
X11280 'Tis the blessed
hour
Every day and hour (1899);
X3171 Every hour; X9749
Saviour, more than life
Hide me, O My Saviour;
X4681 Hide me
I am thine; X2229 Crosby;
X2686 Draw me nearer;
X5025 I am Thine, O Lord
If I come to Jesus
Jesus is passing this way
Jesus, thy name I love;
X2654 Donora
Labor on; X5308 In the har-
vest field
More like Jesus

More love to thee (1870);
X2538 Devotion; X8634
Prentiss
Near the cross; X5609
Jesus, keep me near
Now just a word for Jesus
Only a step; X8133 Only a
step to Jesus
Pass me not; X8335 Pass
me not, O gentle
Precious Name (1899);
X10644 Take the name [of
Jesus with you]; X11020
The precious name
Preston
Rescue (1870); X8953 Res-
cue the perishing
Tell me the old, old story;
X3105 Evangel; X8014
Old, old story
To God be the glory (1903)
Toiling on; X11309 To the
work
Vision (1873); X3838 God of
our strength
Watching (1904); X12263
Will Jesus find us watch-
ing; X12435 Woodstock
Dobbs, Jack Percival Baker,
1922-
Teilo sant
Dobici, L.
Soul of my Saviour
Docker, F. A. W.
Sion quadrata
Doles, Johann Friedrich,
1715-97
Ich lass dich nicht (1780)
Lichfield; X2306 Da
Christus geboren
Doles, J. F. Choralbuch.
Leipsic, 1785
Doles
Norman
Dölker. Geistliche lieder, 1876
Weil ich Jesu schäflein bin
Donizetti, Gaetano, 1797-1848
Lucia
Paulina
Savery; X1538 Carmen
naturae
Dooner, Albert J.
Tantum ergo

Doty, Abraham
  Judah
Dougall, Hugh W.
  I wander through the stilly
  night
Dougall, Neill
  Kilmarnock (1831)
Doughty, A. S.
  Soon trials and conflicts;
  X4846 Home of the soul
  (new)
Douglas, Charles Winfred, 1867-
1944
  Dexter Street (1940)
  St Dunstan's (1917)
Douglas, Sallie Hume
  Follow the gleam (1915)
Dowland, John, 1562-1626
  Galliard
Downes, Lewis Thomas, 1827-
1907
  Solitude; X4972 Hurdus
Drei schöne neue geistliche lieder.
  München, 1637
  Soll's sein
Dresden. Neuesgesangbuch, 1593
  Ecce agnus; X7176 Munich;
  X12323 Wir christenleub
Dresden Gesangbuch, 1632
  Dresden; X5978 Lasst uns alle
Dresden Gesangbuch, 1694
  So giebst Du; X2692 Dresden
Dresden mss., 1761
  St Kerrian
Drese, Adam, 1620-1701
  Rochelle (1698); X581 Arnstadt;
  X2696 Drese; X4076 Gregor's
  46th metre; X4360 Harlem;
  X4533 Heavenly guide; X5533
  Jesus, be our Guide; X5668
  Jesu, rufe mich; X5675
  Jesus, still lead on; X9861
  Seelenbrautigam; X10292
  Spire; X11063 The soul's
  Bridegroom; X11237 Thur-
  ingia; X12567 Zinzendorf
Dressler, W.
  Holy Mary, Mother mild
Dretzel, Cornelius Heinrich,
  1698-1775
  Dretzel I
  Dretzel II; X7636 O dass ich
  tausend

Dretzel, C. H. Musicalische
  harmonie, 1731
  Dieses ist der Tag der wonne
Drewett, Edwin, 1850-1924
  Elmhurst (1887)
Driver, J. M.
  Wonderful story
Drury, Miriam
  Once again to its close
  (1940)
Düben, Gustaf, 1671-1730
  Jesu; X2713 Düben; X3706
  Glädje utan Gud ej finnes;
  X3711 Gladness; X5532
  Jesus är min van den
  bäste
Dublin Troper, ca 1360
  Angelus ad Virginum
Dubois, Clément-Francois
  Theodore, 1837-1924
  Christ, we do all adore
  thee (1867)
  Tantum ergo
Duckworth, Francis, 1862-1941
  Rimington (1904)
Duguet, Abbe
  O salutaris
Dunbar, C. R.
  I'll live for him; X2734
  Dunbar; X7224 My life,
  my love, I give to
Dunbar, E. W.
  A few more years: X2733
  Dunbar; X7904 O, sing to
  me of heaven
Duncalf, Henry
  St Bartholomew (1762)
Duncan, S. E.
  Something I would tell you
Dungan, J. M.
  You can make the pathway
  bright
Dunham, Henry Morton, 1853-
1929
  Puritan (1905)
Dunhill, Thomas Frederick,
  1877-1946
  Beatus
Dunkley, Ferdinand Luis, 1869-
1956
  O God, all gracious; X8222
  Our fortress strong
Dunman, S. J. P.

St Margaret
Dupuis, Thomas Sanders, 1730-96
  Chant
Durham, Alfred M.
  Again, our dear redeeming
    Lord
  Firm as the mountains around
    us
  Sweet is the peace the Gospel
    brings
  They the builders of the nation
Durham, Lowell M.
  With all the power of heart
Durham, Thomas
  Stars of morning, shout for joy
Dussek, Ronald
  Gorran
Dutch traditional, etc.
  NOTE; Holland and Nether-
lands are unused herein. Melodies
are gathered under Dutch.

  Annunciation (1896); X2399 De
    boodschap; X10989 The mes-
    sage
  Dutch carol (1599)
  Help, Lord, the souls (1500)
  In Babilone
  Kremser (1625); X7341 Nether-
    lands; X7342 Netherlands folk-
    song; X8684 Protection;
    X10949 The Lord in His
    righteousness
  Sion's daughter
  Song of the Spirit
  The garden of Jesus (1633)
  Valerius (old hymn)
  Winsted
Dutton, Deodatus, jr., 1808-
32
  Woodstock (ca 1830)
Dvořák, Antonin, 1841-1904
  Going home
Dykes, John Bacchus, 1823-76
  Alford (1875)
  Almsgiving (1865); X2119
    Contrition; X2946 Elliott;
    X8611 Prayer
  Arundel
  Beatitudo (1875); X4007
    Gratitude
  Blairgowrie (1872); X2761

Dykes; X4369 Hartford;
  X11499 Union Square
Calm; X5206 Ilkley
Come unto me (1875)
Derry
Dies Dominica; X1282 Bread
  of heaven
Dies irae (1861)
Dominus regit me (1868);
  X1582 Cecilia; X2643
  Dominus regit
Ecce panis
Edmund
Elvet
Esca viatorum (1868); X1608
  Chapin; X4245 Hail! holy
  guide
Etiam et mihi
Faith; X1204 Bone pastor;
  X2727 Dulcis memoria
Ferrier
Fiat lux (1875)
Gerontius (1868)
Glastonbury
Glebe Field
Herald angels
Hollingside (1861); X9437
  St James the Less
Horbury (1861)
Hosanna (1865)
Hosanna we sing; X4890
  Hosanna
Intercession, arr (1853);
  X5368 Intercession old;
  X9246 St Alkmund
Jerusalem (1862)
Jesu, magister bone; X10456
  Stratford
Judea
Keble (1875); X10458 Streatham
Laud
Lindisfarne (1862)
Litany of the Passion
Lux benigna (1865); X6039
  Lead, kindly light
Mary Magdalene; X2762
  Dykes; X9508 St Mary
  Magdalene
Melita (1861)
Nicaea (1861); X2763 Dykes;
  X4792 Holy, holy, holy
Olivet (1870)

Once again
Oswestry
Oswin (1862); X9544 St Oswin
Paradise, No. 1; X8302
   Paradise
Pax dei (1868)
Prince of Peace
Requiescat (1875); X8385
   Peace
Resurrection; X2785 Easter
Rivaulx (1866)
Rock of Ages; X3666 Geth-
   semane; X11412 Trust
St Aelred
St Agnes (1866); X2745 Durham;
   X5682 Jesus the very thought;
   X5718 Joseph, our certain
St Anatolius (1862); X450
   Anatolius
St Andrew of Crete (1868);
   X2213 Crete
St Bede (1867); X10117 Slingsby;
   X11824 Waring
St Bees (1862); X1643 Chester
St Cross (1861)
St Cuthbert (1861)
St Drostane (1862); X9040 Ride
   on, ride on
St Godric (1862)
St John (1864); X2830 Ecce agnus
St Ninian (1866)
St Oswald I (1857); X2764
   Dykes; X5566 Jesus, highest
   heaven's; X8202 Oswald;
   X10619 Sychar
St Oswald II (1862)
St Sylvester (1862); X9609
   St Sylvester, No. 2; X10622
   Sylvester
St Werburgh (1862)
St Winifred
Sanctuary (1871)
Shoreham
Stabat mater
Strength and Stay (1875)
Trinity College (1857); X10770
   Thanksgiving
Veni creator, No. 2
Vesperi lux (1873)
Via bona (1862)
Via dolorosa
Visio domini (1868)
Vox angelica (1868); X478

Angels' song
   Vox dilecti (1868)
Dykes, John St. O.
   The Sacred Heart
Dyson, George, 1883-
   Atkey
   Elgin
   Frainsby
   Let thy word abide

E

Earnshaw, Robert Henry,
1856-1929
   Arizona
Eaton, Edward D.
   Be strong (1917)
Ebeling, Johann Georg, 1637-
76
   Du meine Seele singe
   Ebeling I (1666); X289 All
      my heart this night;
      X1210 Bonn; X6520 Lüne-
      burg; X11840 Warum
      sollt ich
   Ebeling II; X6593 Luene-
      burg
   Nicht so traurig, nicht so
      sehr; X2826 Ebeling
   Philippi; X2560 Die güldne
      sonne; X2825 Ebeling;
      X3131 Evening and morn-
      ing; X3474 Franconia
   Shining day (1666); X71
      Abendlied; X2503 Der tag
      mit seinem lichte
   Voller wunder
Eberhard, Karl Otto, d 1757
   Gregor's 249th metre; X2559
      Die Gottes seraphin; X9901
      Seraphim
Eberwein, Max
   Valentia
Eccard, Johannes, 1553-1611
   Herr Jesu Christ, wahr'r
      mensch und Gott (1597)
Edmunds, John, 1913-
   God is ascended (1961)
   Love of the Father (1961)
   Ye messengers (1957)
Edson, Lewis, 1748-1820
   Bridgewater (1782)
   Contrast; X2400 De Fleury

X4941 How tedious and taste-
less
Lenox; X551 Arise, my soul
arise
Edwards, A. Morris
We are soldiers of Christ
Edwards, F. Llewellyn
Kington (20th c)
Edwards, J.
Fatherland
Edwards, John, 1878-1928
Maesgwyn
Edwards, John David
Rhosymedre (ca 1840); X6446
Lovely
Edwards, Lewis D.
Come, lay his books and
papers by
I know that my Redeemer lives
Let Sion in her beauty rise
Edwards, P.C., jr.
Chignell
Forward
Racine
Edwards, R., 1797-1862
Caersalem
Edwards, T.D., 1875-1930
Rhyd-y-groes
Egbert, Father
Hail, all hail, sweet youth
Egli, Johann Heinrich, 1742-
1810
Egli (1790); X3046 Es kam die
gnadenvolle
Gott ist mein hort (1787)
Eiland, F.L.
Hold to God's unchanging hand
Ekström, A.
Jesus för varlden gifvet sitt
lif; X1648 Chief of sinners
El Nathan, pseud. see Whittle,
Daniel W., 1840-1901
Elgar, Edward William, 1857-1934
In the Light all light excelling;
X12446 Word of God to earth
Elliott, E.S.
Veni
Elliott, James William, 1833-1915
Belsize
Day of grace
Day of rest
Eucharistica
Gloria in excelsis

Hosanna
St Mark
Triumphant; X1810 Church
triumphant
Vespers
Ellis, Lethal A.
You can't do wrong and get
by (1929)
Ellis, William, 1868-1947
St Hild
St Nicholas
Ellor, James, 1819-99
Diadem (1838)
Elvey, George Job, 1816-93
Adoration
Diademata (1868)
Elvey
Illuminatio
Pilgrimage
St Crispin (1862)
St George's Windsor (1858);
X1997 Come, ye thankful;
X2964 Elvey; X4382 Har-
vest home; X9400 St
George; X9402 St George
of Windsor; X9403 St G
George's; X11878 Watch-
man, tell us
Sunninghill
Undique gloria
Urswicke
Wellesley
Emerson, Luther Orlando,
1820-1915
Addison
Ascription
Elliott
Font Hill
Goodwell
Hemingford
Home
Malone
Mandor
Mer lo (composer's acrostic)
Moravian
Peaceful rest
Redeemer
Sessions (1847); X3221 Faith
is a living power
Stearndale
Woodside
Emmelar, pseud. see Richards,
Henry Brinley, 1817-89
Enchiridion. Erfurt, 1524 see

Erfurt Gesangbuch, 1524
Enchiridion. Erfurt, 1527
    O Herre Gott
Enchiridion. Lübeck, 1545
    Sei du mir gegrüsset
Enckhausen, Heinrich Friedrich,
    1799-1885
    Schönste Sonne; X1877 Coburg
Enke, Gályarabok. Hungarian
    Galley slaves hymn, 1674
    Magyar
Englebrecht, J.C.
    The sweet story of old
English chorister
    Jesus, once of humble birth
English hymnody see early sources,
    as Day's Psalter, Est's Psalter,
    Anglo-Genevan Psalter, New
    Version, etc. Traditional tunes
    will be found under English
    traditional, which follows.
English traditional, including
    many carols.
    A babe is born
    A new dial
    A Virgin most pure I;
        X11710 Virgin unspotted II
    A virgin most pure II
    A virgin most pure III
    A virgin most pure IV; X11711
        Virgin most pure
    A virgin unspotted; X620
        Ash grove
    Agincourt (ca1415); X2489 Deo
        gracias
    All and some (ca 1450)
    All in the morning
    Anima Christi
    Ar det ringa kall att tjäna
    Boar's Head carol
    Bramley; X60 A virgin un-
        spotted II; X5338 Infinite
        light; X11710 Virgin un-
        spotted II
    Bridgwater
    Bunyan
    Butler
    Capel; X10993 The miraculous
        harvest
    Ceres
    Chanticleer
    Cherry tree; X1636 Cherry tree
        carol; X10822 The cherry

    tree carol I
    Christmas Eve I
    Christmas Eve II
    Come, come ye Saints
    Comfort; X8214 Otto
    Coventry carol (1591)
    Coverdale's carol
    Danby
    De profundis
    Decree; X10862 The decree
    Dent Dale
    Devonshire
    Diana (16th c)
    Dives and Lazarus
    Dorking
    Down in yon forest
    Dulcina
    Dunstan
    Eardisley; X2610 Dives and
        Lazarus
    East Horndon
    Eastertime; X2156 Cornish
        carol; M7193 My dancing
        day
    Effingham
    England's Lane
    Essex
    Ethnol
    Exile
    Farnaby
    Farnham
    Fitzwilliam
    Forest Green; X7806 O little
        town; X11016 The plough-
        boy's dream
    Fortunatus; X3452 Fortune
    Furry Day carol
    Garden
    Gloucestershire wassail
    God rest you merry (18th c);
        (London carol); X11866
        Wassail song; X12183
        While shepherds watched
    God rest you merry II
        (Cornwall carol)
    God's dear son
    Golden mornings
    Gosterwood
    Green growth the holly see
        Henry VIII, King of England
    Greensleeves (before 1642);
        X1727 Christ the King;
        X5845 Kings of the East

Hambridge
Hardwick
Hereford carol
Herongate
Hitchen carol; X10798 The
  bellman's song
Holy Well; X10913 The Holy
  Well
Horsham
Ignatius
Ingrave
Jacob's Ladder
Jerusalem, du Herrens nya
  stad
Job I
Job II
Job III
Joseph and Mary
Joys seven
King Herod and the cock
Kingdom of God
King's Langley (a May Day
  carol)
King's Lynn
Kingsfold; X5849 Kingsford
Langport
La Trobe's 586th metre
Leach
Lebanon
Lew Trenchard; X4824 Holy
  Spirit, truth
Lodsworth
Make we joy
Market Square
Mary, how sweetly falls that
  word
May carol
May-day garland
May song
Mendip
Monks Gate (Sussex trad)
Muswell Hill; X11069 The staff
  of faith
Newbury;   X10799 The bell-
  man's song
No room in the Inn; X11710
  Virgin unspotted II; X61
  A virgin unspotted III
Noel; X2771 Eardisley; X3650
  Gerard; X10692 Task sublime
Northumbria; X11889 Watts'
  Cradle song
Prince Rupert (1648 march)

Raise your voices, vales and
  mountains
Ramoth
Righteous judge (19th c)
Rodmell
Rosslyn
Royal Oak
Rusper
St Austin; X8724 Psalm of
  Sion
St Hugh
St Issey
St Stephen
Sandys (publ 1833); X9 A
  child this day
Sans Day carol
Sheffield
Shepton-Beauchamp
Shipston
Sir Christèmas
Somerset carol
Somerset wassail
Song of praise; X3843 God
  our Father made
Southill
Stalham
Stowey; X1671 Children's
  song of the nativity
Summercourt
Sunny Bank: X5110 I saw
  three ships; X10997 The
  mulberry bush
Sussex I; X10547 Sussex
  mummers carol
Sussex II
Sussex carol
Task sublime
Terra beata; X10753 Terra
  patris
The Angel Gabriel
The bellman's song
The carnal and the crane
The cherry tree carol I is
  entered as Cherry tree.
  See above
The cherry tree carol II
The cherry tree carol III
The cherry tree carol IV
The decree I is entered as
  Decree. See above
The decree II
The first nowell; X10869
  The first noël

The holly and the ivy
The Holy Well
The Lamb of God
The merchants' carol; X3883
  Golden
The praise of Christmas
The salutation carol (15 c)
The Saviour's work
The seven virgins
The sinner's redemption
The three traitors
The truth from above
This endris night (15th c)
This new Christmas carol
Wassail song
Welcome (a Celtic carol)
Wexford carol
Wonder tidings (15th c)
Wondrous works
Entwisle, J. Howard
  Christ will me His aid (1900)
Ephros, Gershon
  Child's evening prayer (1932)
  L'cho adonoy
Epstein, A.
  I bless thee, Father, for the
    grace
  Pledging our lives
Erfurt Gesangbuch, 1524
  Ach Gott vom Himmel
  Förlossningen ar vunnen;
    X4185 Gud Faders Søn en-
    baarne; X4622 Herr Christ
    der einig; X11008 The only
    Son from heaven
  Komm heiliger Geist, Herre
    Gott; X5889 Kom Helligaand,
    Herre Gud; X8297 Paraclete;
    X11837 Wartburg
Erfurt Gesangbuch, 1663
  Salus mortalium
  Wir danken dir, Herr Jesu
    Christ
Erskine, John, 1870-1951
  St Paul's (1917)
Esmond, A.
  Manger
Essay on the Church Plain Chant,
1782
  Dulce carmen; X351 Alleluia,
    dulce carmen; X1118 Bithy-
    nia; X2147 Corinth; X8287

Pange lingua gloriosa;
  X10059 Sing my tongue;
  X10666 Tantum ergo;
  X11946 Webbe
Essex, George
  Aberdour
Est, T. Whole book of Psalms,
1592
  Cheshire; X1641 Cheshire
    tune
  Old 25th; X7912 O spirit
    of the living God
  Old 30th
  Old 120th; X8034 Old 77th;
    X8038 Old 81st
  Old 136th
  Winchester Old; X729 Ave,
    Maris stella; X12294
    Winchester
Etlich Christliche lieder.
Wittenberg, 1524 see also
  Walther, Johann. Geistliches
  Gesangbuchlein. Wittenberg,
  1524
  Wittenberg; X3037 Es ist das
    heil; X4186 Gud har af
    sin; X4194 Guds Søn er
    kommen; X4487 He that
    believes; X9557 St Paul;
    X9647 Salvation; X9737
    Saving health; X10287
    Speratus
Ett, Kaspar. Cantica sacra.
Munich, 1840
  Oriel; X8282 Pange lingua;
    X10669 Tantum ergo;
    X11307 To the Name that
    brings
  St Martin; X730 Ave, Maris
    stella; X7986 Ocean Star,
    we greet you
Evangelisches choralbuch. Halle,
1829
  Lobt den Herrn, die morgen-
    sonne
Evans, Daniel. Hymnau a
Thonau, 1865
  Llangloffan
Evans, David, 1874-1948
  Bonifacio (1927)
  Charterhouse (1927)
  Frondeg

Henllan (1927)
Hinton-Martell
Innellan (1927)
Kildrostan (1927)
Kirkland (1927)
Llandaf
Neuadd wen
Orisons (1927)
Pisgah
Ton-mân (1912)
Yn y Glyn (1927)
Evans, David Emlyn, 1843-1913
  Cwmdu
  Hereford
  Trewen
Evans, W. J., 1866-1947
  Rhys
Everest, Charles
  Alexander
Everett, Asa B., 1828-75
  Ashville
  Free waters
  Ionia
  Knocking at the door
  Magnificence; X10053 Since
    o'er thy footstool
  Newcastle
  Richmond (1859)
  Sweetly, Lord, have we heard;
    X3411 Footsteps; X3412
    Footsteps of Jesus
Everett, L. C., 1818-67
  Everett; X10166 Solitude
  Mattie; X7717 O happy is the
    man
  Spring
Ewing, Alexander C., 1830-95
  Ewing (1853); X543 Argyle;
    X5514 Jerusalem, the golden
Ewing, J. C., 1849-1937
  Pioneer
Excell, Edwin Othello, 1851-1921
  Blessings; X12156 When upon
    life's
  Hear our prayer
  In a world where sorrow
  In the shadow of His wings
  Jesus bids us shine
  Let Him in; X11172 There's
    a stranger
  My Father knows (1896)
  Othello; X5050 I have a song;
    X10051 Since I have been

The Lord is in His holy tem-
    ple
  Weary soul by sin oppressed
    (1912)
Eyre, A. J., 1853-1919
  Selby

F

Fabisch, H.
  Happy he who walketh ever
Fabricius, Werner, 1633-79
  NOTE: Real name, Peter
Schmid, was discarded

  Gregor's 133d meter-B (1659)
    X684 Auf, auf, weil der
    tag
Fairlamb, James Remington,
  1838-1908
  Faith
  Martineau
  Vicaria (1864)
Falconer, A. Croil
  Consolator
  Harvest-tide
  St Vigian
Faning, Joseph Eaton, 1850-
  1927
  Vita
Far eastern sources see
  Asian, Chinese, etc.
Farjeon, Harry, 1878-1948
  Need (1931)
  Our brother is born
Farmer, Henry, 1819-91
  Angels holy
  Farmer
  In the field
Farrer, John Downing, 1829-
  1919
  Jubilate
  New Calabar
Faure, Jean-Baptiste, 1830-
  1914
  The Palms
Fawcett, John, 1789-1867
  Melling (1822)
  Relief (1822)
Feilden, Oswald Mosley, 1837-
  1924
  Eden
  Enon

Felton, William M.
  Hymn for Memorial Day
Ferguson, William Harold, 1874-
1950
  Cuddesdon
  Frilford
  Hominum amator
  Ladywell
  Wolvercote
Ferretti, Salvatore, 1817-74
  Salvatori; X2988 Endsleigh
Ferris, Theodore P.
  Weymouth (1941)
Fesca, Alexander Ernst, 1820-
1849
  Peace
Figulus, Wolfgang, 1520-91
  NOTE: Real name, Töpfer
  Helft mir Gott's Gute (1575)
Filby, William C., 1836-
  Epiphany
  Fortitude (1874); X8150
    Onward
  Sundridge
Filitz, Friedrich, 1804-76
  Capetown (1847); X2338 Dantzig
  Caswall (1847); X1000 Bemer-
    ton; X3759 Glory be to Jesus;
    X11728 Viva! viva! Gesu;
    X12005 Wem in leidenstagen;
    X12009 Wenn in leidenstagen
  Clewer (1847)
  Mannheim (1847); X685 Auf,
    auf, weil der tag; X8682
    Protection; X10670 Tantum
    ergo
Fillmore, Charles M.
  Abide in me
Fillmore, Fred A.
  I will early seek my Saviour
  Seeds of promise
Fillmore, James H., 1849-1941
  Be strong, O men (1920)
  Flower
  Give to the Lord
  Lord of the nations
  O wonderful word of salvation
    (1915)
  Open thou mine eyes
  Pounds; X3350 Fillmore;
    X4314 Hannah; X5077 I know
    that my Redeemer
  Purer in heart

  Resolution; X5019 I am re-
    solved
  Saviour, I would live (1923)
  The beautiful garden of
    prayer (1920)
  Turn your faces toward the
    morning
  We are going down the valley
  We are little gleaners
Fink, Gottfried Wilhelm, 1783-
1846
  Bethlehem (1842); X1831
    Claudius; X3106 Evangel;
    X3558 Gabriel; X9899
    Seraph
Finlay, Kenneth George, 1882-
  Ardgowan
  Ayrshire
  Carrick
  Cobham
  Crieff
  Farnell
  Finnart
  Ford Place
  Garelochside
  Glenfinlas
  Hamilton
  Helensburgh
  Hyndland
  Irvine Waterside
  Lyle Road
  Scotstoun
  West Burn
Finnish traditional, etc.
  Lost in the night
  Nyland
  Suomi (a 17th c cavalry
    march)
  Suomi II
  Who made ocean
Fischer, William E., 1849-
1936
  Laus regis; X9935 Shamokin
    Trewks
Fischer, William Gustavus, 1835-
1912
  Coming to the cross; X5014
    I am coming to the cross;
    X5026 I am trusting; X7532
    Now the shades of night;
    X11431 Trusting
  Hankey (ca 1872); X2820
    Eaton Square; X5094 I

love to tell the story; X
10722 Tell the story
O, I love to talk with Jesus
The Rock of refuge; X7909
  O sometimes the shadows
  are deep; X9081 Rock of
  refuge; X11034 The Rock
  that is higher
Whiter than snow (1872); X3369
  Fischer; X6370 Lord Jesus,
  I long to
Wondrous love
Fisher, Albert C. , 1886-1946
  Fisher (1912)
  Redeeming love (1956)
Fisher, Nevin W. , 1900-
  Bridgewater (1951)
  Highland Avenue (1950)
  Jesu, dulcedo cordium (1951)
  McPherson (1951)
  Praise and prayer (1951)
Fishwick, William
  Detroit (1930)
  Fishwick (1930)
  Mt Eliot (1930)
Fitzwater, A. J. , 1886-
  Riches of God (1951)
Flemish traditional, etc.
  A little child; X3382 Flemish
    carol
  Flanders; X473 Angels holy
  Jesus of the manger
  Three Kings
Flemming, Friedrich F. 1778-
1813
  Flemming (1811); X3277 Father
    in heaven; X3381 Fleming;
    X5362 Integer [vitae]
Fletcher, Douglas, 1884-
  Molleson (1924)
Fliedner. Liederbuch fur Klein-
  kinder-schulen, 1842
  Dijon; X7168 Müde bin ich
    geh zur reh
Flittner, Johann, 1618-78
  Flittner (1653); X119 Ach, was
    soll ich
  Gregor's 124th metre (1661);
    X2440 Dedication; X12008
    Wenn erblick ich doch
Flood, Edwin
  Sons of men, behold
Florian, Sr. Mary, S.S.J.

Glorious Mary (1958)
Flotow, Friedrich Ferdinand
  Adolf, 1812-83
  Even Song; X11949 Weber
    Guidance
Floyd, Alfred E. , 1870-
  Land of our birth
  Vermont
Fluiter, Henry de see De
  Fluiter, Henry
Fones, J. G.
  Beautiful Sion, built above
  For our devotions, Father
  I'll praise my Maker
Foote, Arthur William,
  1853-1937
  Easter carol
Foote, Arthur, II, 1911-
  Four winds (1958)
  Struther (1949)
Foote, J. G.
  When I see the blood
Forrest, C. H.
  Heart of Jesus
Fosbery, L. M.
  Leland
Foss, Hubert James, 1899-
1953
  Croydon
Foster, J.
  Pembroke
Foster, Myles Birket, 1851-
1922
  Crucis milites
  Crucis victoria
  Dawn
  Dedication (1890)
  Medford (by M.B.F., presumed
    to be M. B. Foster)
  Monica
  Salvator (1905)
  Vox celestis (1905)
Foster, Stephen Collins, 1826-
64
  I love Him; X8002 Old Black
    Joe
Fowles, Leonard N. , 1871-
1939
  Cavell (1918); X8454 Phoenix
    Golders Green
Fox, A. M.
  Ye chosen Twelve
Francis, M. , Sr. , P.C.

Bringing our praise (1958)
Francis, Philip
  Hark, a herald voice
Franck, César-Auguste, 1822-90
  Ave Maria
  Panis Angelicus
  St Clothilde
Franck, Johann Wolfgang, 1644-
ca 1710
  Komm, seele (1681); X4290
    Hamburg
Franck, Melchior, ca 1579-1639
  Melchior (1663); X4518; Heaven;
    X4534 Heavenly Jerusalem;
    X5500 Jerusalem; X5509
    Jerusalem, du hochgebaute
    stadt
  Morning Star (1628)
  Was fuerrechst du Feind
    Herodes (1616)
Franck, Peter, 1616-75
  Schwing dich (1657); X3249
    Fang dein werk; X3473
    Franck
Franklin Square (perhaps by S.B.
  Pond, 1850)
  The bird let loose
Franz, Robert, 1815-92
  Dedication
Frech, Johann G.
  Wittenberg; X640 Aspurg
Frederick, Donald, 1917-
  James Quinter
  Mack (1951)
  Spirit-wind
Freeman, Andrew, 1876-
  Limpsfield
Freeman, Elizabeth W.
  East Church (1899)
French Psalter, 1562 see Gen-
  evan Psalter, 1562
French traditional, liturgical,
  etc.
  Ad perennis (16th c church)
  Au clair de la lune
  Bell carol; X5477 Je sais,
    vierge Marie
  Besançon carol; X1550 Carol
    of the advent; X9968 Shep-
    herds, shake off
  Carol of service; X8677 Prompte-
    ment levez-vous
  Chartres (15th c); X5320 In

the town; X7511 Nous voici
  dans la ville
Christus vincit
City of David, Bethlehem
Collaudemus
Daily, daily; X360 Alleluia!
  Sing to Jesus; X2315
  Daily, daily sing to Mary
Delight
Destiny (16th c)
Fragrance; X1547 Carol of
  beauty; X8753 Quelle est
  cette odeur agreable?
Gevaert (13th c noel);
  X11058 The sleep of the
  Child Jesus
Gloria; X463 Angel voices;
  X469 Angels, from the;
  X485 Angels we have
  heard; X5396 Iris; X6106
  Les anges dans nos;
  X8006 Old French melody;
  X9964 Shepherds in the
  field; X12150 When the
  sun
Grace soit; X3982 Grace
  soit rendue; X8577 Praise
  the Lord in heaven; X10495
  Summer time; X11498
  Une vaine crainte
Gregor's 167th metre-B
  (1558); X4657 Herz und
  herz vereinst
Jesus the glory
Let Christian hearts (16th c)
Lille
Love is come again; X3498
  Love is come again;
  X3864 Godhead here in
  hiding; X7442 Nöel nouve-
  let
Masters in the hall
Normandy (a Norman carol)
Nous allons; X2791 Easter
  carol; X7510 Nous allons,
  ma mie
O filii et filiae (15th c
  plainsong, Solemes ver-
  sion, M 2, or modern
  version)
O God thou art (16th c)
Old French carol; X1058
  Bethlehem; X2337 Dans

cette etable
Old French noël
Patapan
Picardy (17th c); X3499 French
 carol
Quittez, Pasteurs; X12196
 White Lent
Sion's daughters
So, brother; X2407 De turlu tur-
 lutu; X3320 Fesans raijouis-
 sance
Summer carol
The band of children (16th c);
 X5929 Laissez paitre vos
 betes; X7624 O come, Divine
 Messiah
The builders; X3992 Grand Dieu!
 que de merveilles
The kingdom; X8766 Quoi, ma
 voisine?
The Maid of France (used by
 Bizet in L'Arlésienne suite)
The praises of that saint;
 X3541 From thee, illustrious
The Spirit; X2176 Courons, a
 la fete
'Tis the month of our Mother
Un flambeau; X1320 Bring a
 torch
Waking-time; X11734 Voison,
 d'où venait?
Zachary
Freudenthal, Julius
 En kelohenu; X775 Ayn kay-lo-
 hay-nu
Freylinghausen, Johann Anastasius,
1670-1739
 NOTE; Both composer and
compiler. Melodies not completely
identified, but they may be attri-
buted to these publication dates:
Gesangbuch. Halle, 1704; Neues
Geistriches Gesangbuch, 1714;
with several intervening and un-
identified dates also cited.

 Briesen (1704); X3523 Fröhlich
 soll mein herz springen
 Christe, wahres seelenlicht
 (1704); X6192 Light of the
 soul
 Conqueror (1704); X6392 Lord
 victorious; X7653 O du store

seierherre; X7654 O durch-
 brecher
Das ist meine freude
Den des vaters sinn geboren
Festus (1704); X1211 Bonn;
 X4112 Gregor's 155th
 metre; X4207 Guiding
 star; X7648 O du hueter
 Israel
Grasmere
Gregor's 77th metre (Troch-
 aic: 7. 6. 7. 6. 7. 7) (1705);
 X2394 Dayspring; X8035
 Old 77th-A; X12556 Zeige
 mir dein angesicht
Gregor's 95th metre (1710);
 X7959 O wie selig sind
 die
Gregor's 97th metre (1704);
 X9773 Scepter; X12251
 Wie schön ist unsers
Gregor's 102d metre (1704);
 X3614 Gekreuzigter, mein
 herz sucht
Gregor's 109th metre (1710);
 X3013a Er ist mein him-
 mel
Gregor's 118th metre (1704);
 X3001 Entbinde mich, mein
 Gott
Gregor's 151st metre-I (1704);
 X3027 Ermuntert euch, ihr
 frommen; X8900 Rejoice
Gregor's 156th metre (Troch-
 aic: 7. 8. 7. 8. 7. 8. 8. 7)
 (1704); X5595 Jesus ist
 das schoenste licht
Gregor's 167th metre-D
 (1704); X4638 Herr und
 Gott der tag
Gregor's 184th metre-A
 (1704); X3458 Foundation;
 X7916 O suezer Stand, O
 sel'ges leben
Gregor's 221st metre (1704);
 X2702 Du ewiger abgrund
 der seligen liebe; X10331
 Springs of salvation
Gregor's 310th metre (1704);
 X7088 Morgenstern auf
 finstre nacht
Gregor's 341st metre (1704);
 X2553 Dich, Jesu, loben

vir; X3508 Freylinghausen
Jesus ist das schönste licht;
  X6848 Meine liebe lebet
  noch
Luebeck (1704); X1524 Carinthia;
  X3938 Gott sei dank; X4003
  Gratia; X5674 Jesus, Savior,
  risen;   X8106 On this day,
  the first; X10023 Silcher I
Macht hoch die tür (1704);
  X449 Anastasius; X1785 Christ-
mas morn; X3509 Freyling-
hausen
Morgenglanz der Ewigkeit (1704);
  X2395 Dayspring; X8171
  Oremus; X8775 Radiant morn
Pressburg (1714); X7398 Nicht
  so traurig
Richter (1706); X6846 Meine
  armuth
Se Solens skjønne Lys og Pragt
  (1704); X2498 Der lieben
  Sonne licht und pracht;
  X4279 Halle; X8474 Pilgri-
  mage
Search the Scriptures
Sebastian (1714); X5632 Jesu
  meines glaubens zier
Sinner's friend (1704); X4141
  Gregor's 218th metre;
  X12255 Wie wohl ist mir
  [O freund der seelen]
Truth (1704); X11957 Weil die
  worte wahrheit sind
Tu vins, Jesus (1704); X4089
  Gregor's 83d metre; X4217
  Guter hirte [willst du nicht?]
Friedell, Harold W., 1905-58
  Finlay
Friese, Heinrich
  O Welt, sieh hier (1703)
Fritsch, Ahasuerus, 1629-1701
  Darmstadt (1679); X7702 O Gott,
  du frommer Gott; X11845
  Was frag' ich nach
  Sollt es gleich bisweillen
  scheinen
Fromm, L. E.
  Benediction (1934)
  Response (1939)
Frost, Charles Joseph, 1848-1922
  Harvest

Frost, E. H.
  Tabler
Fulda melody
  O sacrament most holy
Fuller, H. R.
  Christian soldiers
  Christians, awake
  God in heaven
Fuller Maitland, John Alexan-
  der, 1856-1936
  Luccombe
Funk, Joseph
  Lingham

G

G. E. M. G. (melody originated
  in Occupied China, World
  War II; & sung by students
  and teachers)
  Unafraid
Gabriel, Charles H., 1856-1932
  Adowa
  Americus
  Arles
  Aspinwall (1912)
  Avondale (1901)
  Behold, I stand at the door
    (1917)
  Birdstown
  Chios (1912)
  Erskine
  Glory song (1900); X10877
    The glory song
  Go to the deeps (1907)
  Hanford (1906)
  He is so precious (1902);
    X8632 Precious to me
  He lifted me (1905)
  Higher ground; X5233 I'm
    pressing on the upward way
  His eye is on the sparrow
  How marvelous; X7250 My
    Saviour's love
  I stand all amazed (1898)
  Just when I need Him (1908);
    X3559 Gabriel
  Kathrine
  Knowhead
  Lansing
  Lucile
  McCabe; X9885 Send the

light
McDaniel (1914)
Nilus
Old-time power (1912)
Pressly
Safe with Jesus (1900)
Sarah (1901)
Song of the Saviour (1893)
Sweet promise; X5144 I will
  not forget thee
Trust Him
Use me, Saviour
Way of the cross (1906);
  X11104 The way of the
  cross
Where the gates swing outward
  never (1920)
Will the circle be unbroken
Gade, Niels Vilhelm, 1817-90
  Child Jesus
  Gade
Gadsby, Henry Robert, 1842-
1907
  Joy
  St Boniface (1875)
Gaelic traditional, etc.
  Bunessan
  Killin
  St Patrick
Gaines, Samuel Richards, 1869-
1945
  The coming day (1927)
Gale, Clement R.
  Bavaria
  Galsberg; X3564a Gaisberg
Gamble, J. Collection, 1659
  Gamble
Ganss, H.G.
  Long live the Pope!
Ganther (no initials)
  St Hilary
Gardiner, William. Sacred
  melodies, 1812-15
    Belmont; X4433 Haydn, No. 2;
    X4569 Help, Lord, the souls;
    X7611 O Christ, behind the
    temple's veil; X9311 St
    Bernard; X11516 Unveil mine
    eyes; X11702 Vigils
  Dedham
  Gardiner; X1212 Bonn; X3545
    Fulda; X3656 Germany
    (Beethoven); X11811 Walton

Garratt, Charles A.
  Comfort (19th c)
Garrett, George Mursell, 1834-
97
  Advent (1891)
  Beulah
  Communion
  Crucis (1872)
  Eschol
  Forgiveness; X1909 Come;
    X3400 Follow me
  Genesis
  Hymn of glory
  Manger
  St Croix (1889)
  St John's College (1872)
  Tetworth
Garrett, Margueritte Bixler
  Brother, here's a message
  Our prayer (1925)
Garrison, Joseph
  Something for Jesus
Gastorius, Severus, d 1678
  Was Gott tut (1670); X790
    Baden; X3585 Gastorius;
    X4115 Gregor's 160th
    metre-B; X4616 Hermon;
    X4866 Hope; X7764 O
    Jesus Christ, alone to
    thee; X10707 Te lucis
    ante terminum; X11847
    Was Gott thut das ist
Gates, B. Cecil
  How long, O Lord, most
    holy
Gates, Crawford M.
  Ring out, wild bells
Gatty, Nicholas Comyn, 1874-
1946
  Laetabundus
  Midhurst
  Tugwood
Gaul, Alfred Robert, 1837-1913
  Filius dei
  Holy City; X3601 Gaul
  Holy City II; X4775 Holy
    City
  Sanctus
  O worship the Lord
Gauntlett, Henry John, 1805-76
  Ardwick
  Ascension tide; X611 Ascen-
    sion; X614 Ascension, No.

2
Beaumaris
Cobern; X4899 Houghton; X
  6011 Laudate dominum
Constance (1875)
Eternity (1849)
Evermore
Gauntlett I; X6002 Laudate do-
  minum
Gauntlett II
Gauntlett III
Hatfield; X1505 Canterbury
Hawkhurst
Hereford
I love to hear the story
Irby (1858)
Jeshurun
Newland (1858)
Presbyter
Resurrection hymn
Riseholme
St Albinus (1852); X242 Albinus
St Alphege (1852); X397 Alphege;
  X9248 St Alphage
St Ambrose (based on plain-
  song M 8)
St Fulbert (1852); X3544 Ful-
  bert
St George (1848); X3605 Gauntlett;
  X9540 St Olave
St Mark
Springfield
Triumph
University College (1852);
  X8151 Onward
Vita
Gauntlett's Comprehensive tune
  book, 1851
  Giessen
Gawler. Harmonia perfecta, 1730
  see Harmonia perfecta,
  1730
Gay, Annabeth McClelland, 1925-
  Shepherds' pipes
Gebauer, J.C.
  Maria, hun er en Jomfru ren
    X3607 Gebauer
Geer, G.J.
  Holy voices
  Marshall
Geibel, Adam, 1855-1933
  Behold! a royal army
  Lullaby

Trumpet call; X1969 Come,
  sing to the Lord; X3613
  Geibel; X10354 Stand up,
  stand up for
Geistliche gesangbuchlein-
  Wittenberg, 1524 was edited
  by Johann Walther. See note
  under his name
Geistliche gesänge. Leipzig,
  1625 see As hymnodus sacer.
  Leipzig, 1625
Geistliche kirchengesang.
  Cologne, 1599
  Rosa mystica (usually cited
    as harmonized by Michael
    Praetorius, 1609); X18
  A great and mighty wonder;
    X960 Behold a branch;
    X962 Behold a rose;
    X3039 Es ist ein ros' ent-
    sprungen; X7902 O sing a
    joyous carol; X8559 Prae-
    torius; X8885 Regina caeli
    jubila; X11136 There is a
    flower
Geistliche lieder. Wittenberg,
  1535 (often cited as Klug ...)
  Christum wir sollen loben
    schon
  Jeg raaber, Herr Jesu Krist;
    X5174 Ich ruf zu dir
  Jeus Christus, unser Heiland
  Luther; X3042 Es ist gewiss-
    lich; X4981 Hvad kan os
    komme til; X6538 Luther's
    hymn (1535); X6539 Luther's
    hymn (1531); X7039 Mon-
    mouth; X7564 Nun freut
    euch
  O Jesu när jag häden skall;
    X4106 Gregor's 132d metre-
    F; X12363 Wo Gott der
    Herr nicht bei uns
  Wo Gott zum Haus; X895; Be
    thou exalted
Geistliches gesange. Wittenberg,
  1544
  Rhau; X2566 Die seele Christi;
    X4067 Gregor's 22d metre-
    A; X7570 Nun lasst uns
    den leib
Geistliches volkslied, 1850
  Desire; X2509 Desire (min-

or reading); X7839 O mein
Jesu, ich muss; X9713 San-
tolius
Geistreiches gesangbuch. Darm-
stadt. 1698 see Darmstadt
gesangbuch, 1698
Gelineau, Joseph, S.J.
Come ring out your joy (1953)
Defend me, O God (1953);
X12141 When the Lord
turned
Have mercy on me (1953)
He who dwells (1953)
How great is your name (1953);
X7679 O give the Lord, you
I lift up my eyes (1953);
X11320 To You have I lifted
I love the Lord (1953); X5125
I trusted even when
I rejoiced when I heard
(1953)
If the Lord does not build
(1953)
Like the deer that yearns (1953)
My Shepherd is the Lord (1953)
O blessed are those (1953)
O give thanks (1953)
O praise the Lord (1953)
Out of the depths (1953);
X11305 To the Lord in the
hour
The canticle of the Blessed
Virgin I (1953)
The canticle of the Blessed
Virgin II (1953)
The Lord is King (1953);
X2280 Cry out with joy
The Lord's is the earth
(1953)
Why this tumult (1953)
Genevan Psalters
NOTE: Several psalters are in-
cluded. Date gives the edition es-
sential to melody publication.

Ainsworth 97 (1562); X9210
Sacrifice of praise; X5085
I love the Lord
Au fort de ma détresse (1542)
Autumn (1551) NOTE: This is
usually attributed to Barthélémon.
Donne secours (1551); X2006
Comfort ye; X3632 Genevan

Psalm 12; X8698 Psalm 12
Geneva (1551)
Geneva 61 (1562)
Holy Name [being the minor
reading of Louez dieu]
(1562); X6414 Louez dieu
(minor reading)
Jervaulx Abbey (1562);
X8711 Psalm 84; X10627
Tabernacles
Louez dieu [being the major
reading of Holy Name]
(1562); X4806a Holy Name
(major reading); X8721
Psalm 136
Meadow Cove [being the lat-
ter portion of Psalm 47]
(1551); X8705 Psalm 47
Ministres de l'Eternel
(1562); X8719 Psalm 135
O Seigneur (1551); X7108
Morning praise; X8696
Psalm 3
Old First (1542)
Old 117th (1551)
Psalm 93 (1562)
Psalm 138; X5742 Jubilation
Psalm 146 (Delft ed., 1602)
Genge, R.S.
Holy Comfort
George, Graham, 1912-
Grace Church, Cananoque
(1964)
The King's majesty (1940)
Gerle, Hans. Musica Teutsch.
Nürnberg, 1532
Ich dank' dir, lieber Herre
German traditional, including
many church melodies.
All morgen ist (1537)
Altenburg
Angelus; X5608 Jesu, joy of
man's desiring (Schop)
Armageddon
Badea
Baptizien (adapted by Luther
and Walther)
Bohemia (14th c)
Christmas dawn (1823);
X2892 Entracht; X7283
När juldags-morgon glim-
mer; X11238 Thuringia
Commit thy way; X955

Befiehl du deine wege
Cor dulce, cor amabile (1669);
 X6719 Maria mater gratia;
 X11648 Vexilla regis pro-
 deunt
Cyriacus (15th c); X1794 Chris-
 tum wir sollen loben schön
Das Leiden des Herrn
Dies sind die heil'gen (ca
 1200)
Dolwyddelan (1693)
Durch Adam's fall (1525); X
 5478 Jeg beder dig
Earthly friends (16th c)
Eisleben (15th c); X4553
 Heiliger Herre Gott
Electus
En främling klappar pa din
 dörr
Erfreut euch (1536); X5909
 Kreuznach
Evergreen; X1931 Come, hail
 the cause
Franconia
Freiburg (16th c); X3048 Es
 liegt ein schloss; X5068 I
 know a kingdom; X5486 Jeg
 ved et evigt himmerig;
 X5832 Kingdom
Germania
Glorious Virgin, thee we
 sing
God is ascended (16th c);
 X3620 Gen himmel auf
 gefahren ist
Gregor's 159th metre; X2500
 Der Sabbath ist um's men-
 schen will'n; X12461 Wor-
 ship
Gregor's 168th metre-B (1642);
 X5550 Jesu, der du meine
 seele
Gregor's 185th metre-A (1740);
 X2179 Covenant; X2867 Eeu-
 wig dank en eere; X4005
 Gratitude; X4637 Herr und
 aeltster deiner
Gregor's 212th metre (before
 1540); X2744 Durch Adam's
 fall ist
Herzlich thut mich erfreuen
 (mediaeval mel)
Homburgh

Ich fahr dahin; X11687
 Vienna
In dulci jubilo (14th c);
 X5485 Jeg synger Julekind;
 X5872 Klug; X12106 When
 Christ was born
Incense
I'll sing a hymn to Mary
Jag tvor pa Gud, och vet
 (1523)
Jesus lives, and Jesus
 leads; X338 Alle vögel;
 X3401 Follow me
Komm, Gott Schöpfer, heil-
 iger Geist (1524)
Kommt her zu mir (15th c);
 X889 Be not dismayed;
 X5891 Kom hid til mig,
 enhver isaer; X6258 Little
 flock
Lambs of Jesus
Laus tibi Christi (14th c);
 X6023 Laus tibi
Leonburg
Liberation
Lo! the heavens are break-
 ing
Lobet und preiset
Lux noel
Magdalena (16th c)
Mary's wandering; X6722
 Marias wanderschaft
Mecklenburg
Mendebras; X6882 Mende-
 bas; X7642 O day of rest
 and gladness
Mendon; X636 Aspiration;
 X1276 Brandenburg
Mothering Sunday (14th c);
 X5181 Ich weiss ein
 lieblich engelspiel
Naar mig min Synd vil
 kraenke (1790)
Neckar
Nu wol Gott das unser gesang
 (16th c)
O'er the silent waters
Peace makers
Pekin
Plea (16th c)
Resonet in laudibus (14th c);
 X5717 Joseph lieber,
 Joseph mein; X10235

Song of the crib
Rudolfstadt
St Basil
Sanglier
Selvin
Sheltered Dale
Siberia
Singen wir aus Herzens Grund
    (1544); X3302 Fear my child,
    thy God; X10625 Sunge vi af
    hjertens grund
Song
Stabat mater (old German);
    X5903 Kommt, ihr seelen,
    nehmt zu herzen
Stilla jag pa dig vill akta
    (18th c)
Susanni (16th c)
The Star
Thessalonica
Thule
Tredeca; X5238 Immortal Babe
Twinkling stars
Tyholland
Tysk
Wachterlied (16th c)
Wansted
What happiness can equal mine
When morning fills the sky;
    X12131 When morning gilds
Whiteland
Williamson
Woodbird; X3035 Es flog ein
    kleins waldvöglein; X5215
    I'll sing a hymn; X7903
    O sing the great apostle
Worship
Gerold, Johan Carl
    Jehovah (1800)
Gerovitch, Eliezer
    Adon olom
    Adonoy adonoy
Gersbach, Anton
    Anton
Gesang-und Notenbuch. Stuttgart,
    1744
    O Grosser Gott
Gesangbuch. Erfurt, 1663 see
    Erfurt Gesangbuch, 1663
Gesangbuch mit noten, 1890
    Aus dem himmel ferne
    Ich singe dir
    Ich weiss an wen ich glaube

O leide, leide gern
Seliger friede
So lange Jesus bleibt der
    Herr
Unter lilien jener freuden
Was kann es schön'res
    geben
Gesius, Bartholomaeus, 1555-
    1613
    Commemoration; X2335 Dank
        sei Gott [in der höhe];
        X3610 Geduld, die soll's
    Du Friedensfürst, Herr Jesu
        Christ
    Gesius; X4675 Heut' trium-
        phiret; X11393 Triumphs
        today the Lord
    Herrnhut; X2034 Communion
        hymn; X5553 Jesus, din
        lhukommelse; X6845
        Mein Seel, o Herr, muss
    O Christe, Morgensterne
        (1605)
Gether, A.
    Gether
Giardini, Felice de, 1716-96
    Athens
    Blendon
    Moscow; X3773 Glory to
        God on high; X5440 Italian
        hymn; X11088 The Trinity;
        X11380 Trinity
    Turin
Gibbons, Orlando, 1583-1625
    Angel's song (1623); X468
        Angels; X474 Angels'
        hymn; X1933 Come, Holy
        Ghost; X3671 Gibbons;
        X6188 Light divine;
        X10225 Song 34
    Bourdillon; X10227 Song 46
    Song I (1623)
    Song 3 (1623)
    Song 4
    Song 5
    Song 13 (1623); X1506
        Canterbury; X3672 Gibbons
    Song 18
    Song 20
    Song 22 (1623); X4676 Heze-
        kiah
    Song 24
    Song 31 (1623)

Song 46 (1623); X3385
Fletcher; X3673 Gibbons
Song 67 (1621)
NOTE: The bass is attributed
to Gibbons; the melody is from
Prys, Psalms, 1621; X3674
Gibbons; X9512 St Matthias
Gibbs, Cecil Armstrong, 1889-
1960
Crossings (1930)
Danbury (1925)
Herrick's Ode (1928)
Lingwood
Little Baddow (1930)
Gibson, Alexander S., 1843-
1919
Alexander (1915)
Look down on us
Gideon, Henry
How good it is to thank the
Lord (1932)
Giffe, William T.
O wonderful prayer
Sweet is the story
Gifford, Philip A.
I think, when I read; X10598
Sweet story
Gilbert, Walter Bond, 1829-
1910
Angelica; X3678 Gilbert;
X3679 Gilberts
Maidstone (1862); X477 Angels,
roll the rock
Morning
Rodigast
St Enoch
Stuyvesant
Thanksgiving
Gilchrist, William Wallace, 1846-
1916
Christmas
Communion
Easter
Evening
Merry Christmas bells
Sound over the waters (1920)
Whitsuntide
Woodland (1891)
Gilding, Edmund
St Edmund (1762); X2443
Dedication
Gill, Benjamin
Holmfirth (1905)

Gill, John
Frankfort; X7368 New St
Andrew
Gillespie, James, 1929
Harrowby
Gillis, Emma Hanford
Lead on, thou God of
Hosts (1914)
Gilmore, H. C.
St Luke, No. 2
Gilmour, H. L.
He brought me out
Love found me
Make me a blessing today
Gilmour, Robert. Psalm-
Singer's assistant, 1793
Montrose
Giornovichi (real name Jarno-
wick), Giovanni Marie, 1745-
1804
St Asaph
Gladstone, William Henry, 1840-
91
Erskine
Hammersmith
Ombersley (1872)
Glaser, Joseph
Glaser
Gläser, Carl G., 1784-1829
Azmon (ca 1839); X293 All
praise to our redeeming
Lord; X785 Azmon new;
X2481 Denfield; X3276
Father, I stretch my hands;
X7707 O grant thy servants
Glezen, E. K.
Glezen
Gluck, Christoph Willibald,
1714-87
Chant your songs
Father all-holy
Orpheus
Glynn, Franklin
Maxon (1941)
Scarborough (1941)
Woking (1941)
Gnadauer choralbuch, 1735
Marter Christi
Gnadauer choralbuch, 1784
O dass ich tausend; X7639
O das ich tausend zungen
hätte; X8045 Old 106th
Godfrey, Nathaniel S., 1817-83

Ellingham
Goerz, P.J.
O, be still
Goldfarb, I.
Sholom alaychem
Goldstein, M.
Va-anachnu
Goldsworthy, W.A.
Bouwerie (1941)
Gooch, Frederick
Baginton (1858)
Good, Flora H.
Since Jesus did appear; X5525
Jesus a wedding guest
Good, P.S.
Evening
Good, S.E.
The cleft of the Rock
Goodhart, A.M.
Etona
Goodrich, Charles G.
Shortle (1905)
Goodrich. Service and tune book
Rest
Gordon, Adoniram Judson, 1836-
99
Gordon (1864); X1528 Caritas;
X6420 Love; X7221 My
Jesus, I love thee
In tenderness
Goss, John, 1800-80
Advent (1872); X3256 Fareham
Arthur's Seat (1874)
Bevan (1853)
Dona; X9132 Rothley; X840
Barnby's hymnary,Tune 154;
X3924 Goss; X11358 Trans-
figuration
Glad tidings
Israel
Lauda anima (1869); X1009
Benedic anima mea; X2640
Dominic, Our Lady's cham-
pion; X5540 Jesus Christ,
the King of ages; X8557
Praise; X8571 Praise my
soul; X9558 St Paul
Peterborough
St Augustine (1854)
St Casimer
St Cyprian
Salvator

See, amid the winter snow
(1870); X4962 Humility;
X12319 Winter's snow
Tarsus; X9559 St Paul
Waterstock
Gotha Cantional, 1726
Jag gar mot döden, hvar
jag gar
Gottschalk, Louis Moreau,
1829-69
Mercy (1854); X3842 God,
Our Father, hear; X3956
Gottschalk; X4333 Happy
who in early youth;
X4787 Holy Ghost, with
light; X5980 Last hope;
X6685 Manna
Gottshall, Henry G., 1903-46
Christopher Sower (1938)
Goudimel, Claude, 1508-72
Goudimel; X9044 Righteous
Judge
Gregor's 205th metre; X824
Barnabas; X3612 Geht,
erhoeht die majestaet;
X3959 Goudimel
Gould, Edwin
Conjugal love; X2070 Con-
jugial love
Lord, I believe
Pax caelestis
Gould, John Edgar, 1822-75
Adrian
Bera (1849)
Hymn; X3961 Gould
Morgan
Pilot (1871); X5673 Jesus
Saviour, pilot me
Gould, Nathanael D.
Woodland
Goule (no initials)
Hail, heavenly Queen
Gounod, Charles François, 1818-
93
Alma redemptoris mater
Ave verum corpus
Evening hymn; X3966 Goun-
od's Evening hymn; X9205
Sacred Heart! in accents
Gounod
Jesus, food of angels; X170
Adoro te devote

Lovely appear
Lux prima (1872); X839 Barn-
  by's hymnary, Tune 148;
  X3965 Gounod; X4506 Heart
  of Jesus! golden chalice;
  X6556 Lux vera; X7179
  Muriel
O sacrament most holy
Olney
Orient; X6549 Lux fiat
Praise ye the Father
Radiant morn; X6543 Lux
  aeterna; X11027 The radiant
  morn
Rouen; X12070 What a sea of
  tears
Veni Emmanuel
Wondrous love that cannot
  falter
Gower, Jean Milne, 1867-
Livermore
Gower, John Henry, 1855-1922
  Angel choir (1896)
  Bonaventura
  Devotion (1895)
  Ecclesia
  Gower's Litany (1890)
    X3967 Gower; X6232 Litany
  Laus Deo
  Meditation (1890); X11138
    There is a green hill
  Ministry (1909)
  Neilson (1894)
  Petition
  Recessional (1903); X3969
    Gower's Recessional
  Reliance (1895)
  St Botolf (1890)
  Sundown
Grabowski, J.
  Jerusalem
Graham, S. J.
  Gleams of the golden morning
Grape, John T., 1833-
  All to Christ I owe; X5056
    I hear the Saviour say;
    X5658 Jesus paid it all
Grauman, Max
  Come let us sing in sweet
    accord (1932)
  God is the giver of all (1932)
  Jacob's ladder (1932)
  Lord, unto thy sacred dwelling

Our pious fathers (1932)
  Sabbath hymn (1932)
  The stars watch you (1932)
Graun, Karl Heinrich, 1704-
59
  Look up and see
Graves, F. A.
  He was nailed to the cross
  He'll never forget
Gray, Alan, 1855-1935
  Battle cry
  Hosanna
Gray, D. Vincent
  Holy Innocents (1941)
Greatorex, Henry Wellington,
1811-58
  Bemerton (1849)
  Geer
  Glory be to the Father (1851);
    X3740 Gloria patri
  Grostette
  Leighton (1849)
  St Gabriel
Greatorex, Walter, 1871-1930
  Woodlands (1919)
Greek melody
  Luke; X660 Athens; X4036
    Greek folksong; X5124 I
    think when I read; X9633
    Salamis; X10599 Sweet
    story
Green, Harold, 1871-1931
  The quiet hour; X8761
    Quietude
Green, James. Book of Psalm-
ody, 1724
  Crowle
Green, James. Psalmody, 1731
  Ferry
Green, James. Psalmody, 1744
  Althorp
Greene, Maurice, 1696-1755
  St Nicholas
Greenfield, Alfred M.
  Washington Square (1927)
Greenwood, E. Norman
  Benevolence (1932)
  Freedom (1932)
  Lansdowne (1932)
  Prayer (1932)
  Radlett (1932)
  Selworthy (1932)
  Swanage (1932)

Greenwood's Psalmody, Halifax,
1838
  Affection
Gregor, Christian Friedrich,
1723-1801
  Eden (1763)
  Gregor (1784)
  Gregor's 6th metre (1784);
    X2473 Den die Engel droben
  Gregor's 7th metre (1784);
    X334 Alle deine gaben
  Gregor's 9th metre (1784); X5541
    Jesus Christus blick dich
    an
  Gregor's 12th metre (1784);
    X4018 Great High Priest;
    X4731 Höchster priester,
    der du dich
  Gregor's 54th metre-D (1784);
    X1306 Brich durch mein
    angefachtnes herz
  Gregor's 74th metre (1784);
    X4636 Herr Jesu, ewig's
    licht
  Gregor's 99th metre (1784);
    X7592 O anblick der mir's
    herz bricht
  Gregor's 107th metre; X6841
    Mein Jesu, der du vor dem
    scheiden; X9201 Sacrament
  Gregor's 112th metre; X3014
    Er wird es thun, der fromme,
    treue Gott; X4701 Hilf Gott,
    dasz mir's gelinge!
  Gregor's 126th metre-B (1784)
  Gregor's 163d metre (1784);
    X11761 Wachet, wachet, lie-
    ben kinder
  Gregor's 208th metre-C (1784);
    X2887 Einer, ach nur einer
  Old 96th (1784); X7732 O
    Herre Gott, in meiner noth
  Old 271st (1784); X3608 Gebor'n
    ist uns der heil'ge Christ;
    X11357 Tranquillity
Greiter, Mattaeus, ca 1490-1550
  Psalm 68 (ca 1525); X4155
    Greiter; X6479 Lucerne;
    X8051 Old 113th; X8702
    Psalm 36; X12052 Westminster
    College
Grenoble Antiphoner, 1753
  Deus tuorum militum; X4157

Grenoble; X5547 Jesu,
  corona Virginum; X11444
  Tu, Christe, nostrum
Gretchaninov, Alexander Tik-
honovitch, 1864-1956
  New Russia
Grey, Francis Richard, 1813-
90
  St Aidan
Grieg, Edvard Hagerup, 1844-
1907
  Asa's death; X619 Ase's
    death
  Ave maris stella
  Fatherland song
  Hagerup; X7689 O God of
    hosts
  Springfield
  The snow lay on the ground
Griffith, William, 1867-1929
  Cuttle Mills
Grigg, Joseph
  Grigg; X3685 Give
Grigg, Thomas
  Tiverton
Griggs, Thomas C.
  Earth, with her ten thousand
    flowers
  Gently raise the sacred
    strain
Grimley, John T.
  Summerford (1887)
Grimm, Carl Hugo, 1890-
  A noble life (1932)
  Come, let us praise (1932)
  Friend after friend (1932)
  Hymn of the harvest (1932)
  It singeth low (1932)
  Prayer for wisdom (1932)
  We plough the fields (1932)
Grimm, D.J. Choralbuch,
1755
  Consolation; X7400 Nicht so
    traurig, nicht so sehr
  Gregor's 39th metre-C;
    X5172 Ich liebe dich herz-
    lich, O Jesu
  Gregor's 115th metre; X216
    Agnus Christi; X12250
    Wie herrlich ist's ein
    schoeflein
  Gregor's 172d metre; X112
    Ach Gott! was hat vor

herrlichkeit; X11091 The
Unity's march
Gregor's 184th metre-C; X
12010 Wenn meine seel' den
tag bedenket
Gregor's 244th metre; X5163
Ich blicke nach der hoehe
Grimm's 253d metre; X4552
Heil'ger Geist do tröster
mein; X6185 Light
Grimm's 265th metre; X3524
Frohlock', liebe christenheit
Grimm's 315th metre; X8844
Rede selber uns zu gut
Grimm's 349th metre; X7086
Morgenglanz der ewigkeit
Grimm's 480th metre; X11759
Wachet auf, ihr mueden geister
Grimm's 552d metre; X115
Ach Herr, wo sind nun meine
vor'gen kroefte
Old 193d; X5596 Jesu, Jehovah!
ich soch' und verlange
Old 466th; X2701 Du bist ja,
Jesu, meine freude
Saxony; X5175 Ich seh'in ban-
gen Busz-ideen
Tabor; X1117 Bist willkom-
men, liebster freund
Grimshaw, John, d 1819
Heaton Norris
Grisham, R.N.
I will never turn back
Griswold (no initials)
Griswold
Grobe, J.
Torgau (1840)
Groos, C.
Sun of grace
Grove, Albert H.
Cross of Christ, O sacred
tree
Grueber, Franz Xaver, 1787-
1863
Holy night (1818); X3705 Glade
Jul; X4183 Grüber; X10029
Silent night; X10416 Stille
nacht
Grundy, David Heywood, 1934-
College Cross
Crigglestone
Dumpton Gap
Nonington

Thornes House
Guidetti, Giovanni Domenico,
1530-92
Guidetti; X188 Aeterna
Christi munera
Guilmant, Alexander Felix,
1837-1911
Ave verum corpus
Guisborough hymnal
Aeterna caeli gloria (a
plainsong M 4)
Gustaf, Prince of Sweden,
1827-52
Till fridens hem
Gwyllt Ieuan, 1822-77 see
Roberts, John, 1822-77

H

Haas, George C.F., 1854-1927
Luther League Hymn (1893);
X8260 Pactum
St Mark's (1915)
Hackleman, W.E.M.
Others (1915)
Hadley, Patrick Arthur Sheldon,
1899-
Pembroke (1925)
Hadow, William Henry, 1859-
1937
South Cerney
Haeffner, Johann Christian
Friedrich, 1759-1833
O, du mitt hjärtas trängtan
(1808)
Haeffner, J.C.F. Koralbok
1819
Han lefver! o min ande,
känn
Haeussler, Theodore C.
Irmer (1938)
Hagen, Francis Florentine,
1815-1907
The Morning Star (1842)
Hagfors, Ernest August, 1827-
1913
Pilgrim song
Haile, Eugen, 1873-1933
God (1932)
God of grace (1932)
To thee, above all creatures'
gaze (1932)
World invisible (1927)

Hakes, D. S.
   If any little word of mine (1908)
   Lift Him up
   Like as a father
   My song (1900)
   Standard
   Sweet be thy rest
Halévy, Jacques-François Fro-
   mental-Elie, 1799-1862
   Min hamatsar; X3386 Fling
     wide the gates; X4733 Hodu
     and Ono
Hall, Americk, 1785-1827
   Devotion
Hall, Jacob Henry, 1855-
   He knoweth thy grief (1897)
   Here at thy table
   Saviour, breathe an evening
     blessing; X3151 Evening song;
     X3753 Glorious things of thee
   Sweet hour of prayer
   Sykes
   'Tis the harvest time
   Trusting in Jesus (1896)
Hall, J. Lincoln
   Does Jesus care?
Hall, Walter Henry, 1862-1935
   Aletheia (1918)
   Cecil (1917)
   Egbert (1917)
   Mallett (1918)
   Oneonta (1918)
   Reigate (1918)
   St Wilfred (1900)
Halle melody
   Petersen (1697); X3780 Glück
     zu kreuz
The Hallelujah, 1849
   Malvern; X682 Audley
Haller, Michael, 1840-1915
   I see by rays surrounded
   Queen of the Rosary
   Sub tuum praesidium
Hallman, E. S.
   O everlasting Light
Hallstrom, Henry
   Lynchburg (1941)
Halpern, M.
   Adonoy mo odom
Halstead, E.
   Snowdon (1940)
   Vesper hymn (1938)
Hamburg. Neu Catechismus-Ge-

sangbuch, 1598
   Eisleben; X5487 Jeg vil din
     pris unsjunge; X7214
     My heart its incense burn-
     ing
Hamburger Musikalisches hand-
buch. 1690 see Wittwe, Georg.
   Musikalische handbuch, 1690
Hamilton, Clarence Grant, 1865-
1935
   Wallace (1914)
Hamilton-Gell, A. W.
   Stanton
Hammer, John Beck
   Martha (1876)
Hammerschmidt, Andreas,
1612-75
   Freuet euch, ihr Christen
     (1646); X4136 Gregor's
     210th metre
   Meinen Jesum lass ich nicht
     (1658); X9767 Saxony
Hammond, Mary Jane, 1878-
   Spiritus vitae
Hammontree, Homer
   He just put Himself in my
     place (1921)
   O, my Saviour crucified
     (1940)
   Our times are in thy hand
Hampton, John, 1834-1921
   St Cecilia (1875); X11643
     Vexilla regis
Hanby, Benjamin Russell, 1833-
67
   Adoration (1866); X6465 Low-
     liness; X12221 Who is He
Hancock, B. J., 1862-1937
   Easter time
Handel, Georg Friedrich, 1685-
1759
   [H] Alleluia chorus (1742)
   Antioch (1836); X5732 Joy to
     the world
   Bede (1733)
   Brunswick
   Canons; X1497 Cannons
   Christmas (1728); X648 At
     midnight, so the sages
     tell; X762 Awake, my soul
   Desiring to love
   Dirge
   Father in heaven

Father, O hear us; X3273
  Father Almighty, we bow
  before thee
Gopsal (1750)
Halifax (1748)
Händel
Innocents (source in doubt)
Judas Maccabaeus (1747);
  X6592 Maccabaeus; X11187
  Thine is the glory
Messiah (1742); X1269 Brad-
  ford; X11730 Vivit
Messiah [Come unto me, ye
  weary] (1742); X1987
  Come unto Me; X9002
  Revelation
Milites (1727); X5496 Jericho
  tune
Samson (1742); X9682 Samp-
  son
Solomon; X10536 Sursum
  corda
Sweet hosannas
Thatcher (ca 1874); X2373
  David; X10757 Thacher
Theodora
Hanecy, J. S.
  Glorious things of Thee are
    spoken
Hann, Sidney
  Queenswood
Hansen, H. Matthias
  Hour of prayer; X5969 Lanier
Hanson, S. C.
  The open gate
Harding, H. A.
  Foel fras
Harding, James P., ca 1860-
  1911
  Morning Star (1892)
Harding, R. Y., 1859-
  Agatha
  Knowlton
Hardy, B. E.
  Wheeler
Hardy, H. W.
  Eastbourne
Harington, Henry, 1727-1816
  Harington; X8996 Retirement
Harker, J.
  Paraclete (1914)
  Simonside (1940)
Harkness, Robert

He will hold me fast
O, what a change (1905)
Such love (1929)
Harmer, Charles H., 1865-
  Memory
Harmonia perfecta, 1730
  Bucklebury
  Wondrous cross; X2955
    Eltham
Harmonia sacra, 1753
  Cradle hymn
  Mason; X8009 Old German
  People of the living God
  Resurrection
  Sion's glad morning
Harper, Earl Enyeart, 1895-
  Shirleyn (1928)
Harrington, Calvin S.
  Fisk
Harrington, Claude W.
  Asbury (1905)
Harrington, Karl Pomeroy,
  1861-1953
  Beyond (1905)
  Christmas song (1904)
  Copeland (1905)
  Evanston (1905)
  Golgotha (1938)
  Moore (1905)
  My Master (1927)
  Orono (1905)
  Palm Sunday (1905)
  Parker (1905)
  Praise (1905)
  The Lord is in His Holy
    Temple (1905); X5386
    Invocation [sentence]
  Weihnacht (1903)
  Worship (1905)
Harris, E. A.
  York
Harris, T. W.
  Glenmont
  Taconic
Harris, Thoro
  Crimea (1905)
Harris, William Henry, 1883-
  Alberta
  Gladdening light
  Kybald Twychen
  North Petherton
  Sennen Cove
Harrison, Annie F.

In the gloaming; X9760 Savior,
    while my heart is tender
Harrison, Ralph, 1748-1810
    Bankfield; X7152 Mt Olive
    Peterboro; X8436 Peterborough;
        X8437 Peterborough Old
    Stirling; X10406 Sterling
    Warrington
Harrison, Ralph. Sacred harmony,
1784
    Blackbourne
    Cambridge; X663 Athol; X
        1463 Camberwell; X3756
        Glory; X11890 Waugh
Hart, Dorothea, arr
    I have decided to follow Jesus
        (1950)
Hart, Philip, d 1749
    Hilderstone (1713)
Hart, W. H.
    Brierly
Hartmann, Emil, 1836-98
    Avis
Hartmann, Johann Peder Emilius,
1805-1900
    Dyb af Kjaerlighed
    Ingemann
    Hartmann; X7988 Odumin
    Mirabile
    Peace of God; X3483 Fred til
        bod; X4373 Hartmann;
        X8398 Peace to soothe
    Rosa
    Stegman
Hartog, Cecile
    Into thy hands
Hart's Psalter, 1615 see Scottish
    Psalter, 1615
Harts, Harry L.
    Nazareth (1927)
Hartshorn, W. Irving
    Irving
    Ruth
Hartsough, Lewis, 1820-72
    I hear thy welcome voice;
        X5013 I am coming, Lord;
        X11979 Welcome voice
    Let me go
Harwood, Basil, 1859-1949
    Alveston
    Combe Martin (1908)
    Elberton
    Hazel

Lower Marlwood
Luckington
Oldown
St Audrey
Thornbury
Harwood, Edward
    Rapture
Hassler, Hans Leo, 1564-1612
    NOTE: Certainly more than
this single Hassler melody is
within 20th century church mu-
sic! Others are probably in
compilations cited elsewhere
herein.

    Passion chorale (1601);
        X4396 Hassler; X4664
        Herzlich thut mich ver-
        langen; X6837 Mein G'mut
        ist mir; X6945 Mig hjer-
        telig nu laenges; X7207
        My God, how wonderful;
        X7719 O haupt voll blut;
        X11183 Thine arm, O
        Lord
Hastings, Eurotas P.
    Detroit
Hastings, Thomas, 1784-1872
    Arcadia
    Bartley
    Bremen; X6385 Lord of the
        Church
    Broughton
    Byefield
    Hastings; X1444 Calm
    Haven
    Invitation
    Luther
    Ortonville (1837); X5690
        Jesus, united by the grace;
        X6651 Majestic sweetness;
        X7699 O God, we pray for
        all; X8615 Prayer for all
        men
    New Haven
    Peniel
    Retreat (1842); X3527 From
        every stormy wind; X5191
        If I would be a child;
        X11909 We bless the name
        of
    Robinson
    Romberg

Sion; X470 Angels! from the realms; X4204 Guide me, O thou great; X10081 Sion stands with hills surrounded
Still water
Toplady (1832); X3177 Every morning mercies new; X9078 Rock of ages
Wesley
Wicliffe

Hasty, E.E.
Seeking for me

Hately, Thomas Legerwood, 1815-67
Leuchars
Nenthorn

Hately, Walter, 1843-1907
St Helen

Hatton, John C., d 1793
Duke Street (1793); X3525 From all that dwell below the skies

Haughey, M.T.
There is sunlight on the Hill-top

Hauser, Carl
Hymn of thanksgiving

Haven, C.A.
Beautiful land on high

Havergal, Frances Ridley, 1836-79
Caswell Bay
Eirene
Hermas (1871)
There came a little child to earth

Havergal, William Henry, 1793-1870
Consecration; X8361 Patmos
Dusseldorf (1849)
Eden; X9524 St Nicholas
Evan (1847); X819 Baptized into our Saviour's death; X1137 Blessed be the name; X3104 Evan new X4330 Happy the home when God is there; X5882 Knox; X6365 Lord, in thy presence; X7674 O for a faith that will not shrink
Haver; X788 Baca
St John (1851); X158 Adoration; X9448 St John's

Samos
Zoan (1859)

Hawaiian traditional
He lives on high [Aloha]; X392 Aloha

Hawarden, Viscountess, see Maude, Caroline

Haweis, Thomas, 1734-1820
Richmond (1792); X1645 Chesterfield

Hawkes, H.W.
God is in His holy temple

Hawkins, Gordon, 1911-
Ballards Lane

Hawley, W.A.
Harris

Haworth, F.
The dawn was purpling

Hawthorne, Alice (pseud. of Septimus Winner) 1827-1902
Whispering hope

Hay, Edyth Hillery, d 1943
Hillery; X6399 Lord, with devotion
The way is dark (1923)

Hayden, Victoria (or Victoire)
Father, I come to thee; X2061 Confirmation

Haydn (no initials)
Have mercy on us
O come, loud anthems; X159 Adoration
Rapture

Haydn, Franz Joseph, 1732-1809
Austria (1797); X711 Austrian hymn; X4434 Haydn's hymn; X8579 Praise the Lord! ye heavens
Bowen; X4432 Haydn, No. 1 X8212 Otterbourne
Bradford; X8570 Praise, Lord, for thee in Zion waits
Brownell; X1366 Brownwell
Creation (1798); X4352 Hark, the song of jubilee
Haydn (1791); X7099 Morning Petition (1801); X4430 Haydn X9537 St Olaf
St Alban; X9241 St Alban, No. 2; X9242 St Alban's
St Anthony chorale; X9276

St Anthony's choral
Haydn, Johann Michael, 1737-
1806
   Greenland (1819); X6026 Lau-
      sanne
   Hear thy children
   Lyons (from the Paderborn
      Gesangbuch, 1765 text);
      X4943 How wondrous and
      great; X7859 O praise
      ye the Lord; X7865 O
      purest of creatures; X
      7967 O, worship the King
   O esca viatorum; X7671 O food
      that weary pilgrims love;
      X12130 When morning
      gilds the skies
   Offertorium
   St Avold; X11603 Venice
   Salzburg
   Salzburg II; X4431 Haydn;
      X2565 Die sach' ist dein
   St Michel's; X3923 Goshen;
      X4429 Haydn; X5501 Jeru-
      salem; X5511 Jerusalem,
      Jerusalem; X9055 Ripon;
      X9495 St Maria
Hayes, Oleta
   Christ's return (1935)
Hayes, William, 1705-77
   Chant
   Magdalene College; X5853 King-
      ston
   New 113th
   Tranmere
Hayman, Henry, 1820-94
   Lanherne; X4156 Grenfell
Hayne, Leighton George, 1836-
83
   Buckland (1863)
   Chalvey (1868)
   St Anselm
   St Cecilia (1863); X1583 Cecilia
   St Lawrence (1863)
Haynes, D. F.
   Pontiac (1934)
Haynes, William, 1829-1902
   Feodore
   Guilford (1876)
Hays, William Shakespeare, 1837-
1907
   Salvationist; X6205 Lily of the
      valley; X10939 The Lily of

the valley
Heaton, Walter
   Patricroft (1923)
Heatwole, L. J.
   Non-resistance
   The Christian's passport
Heber, Reginald, 1783-1826
   Calcutta; X2257 Crucifix;
      X12205 Whitfield
Heberden, Arthur C.
   Evensong
Hebrew melodies see Jewish
   Traditional, etc.
Hecht, Simon
   A message sweet
   We meet again in gladness
      (1932)
Hedberg, Fredrik Gabriel,
1811-93
   Kom, huldaste förbarmare
Hedges, Anthony John, 1931-
   Starlight
Heineken, N. S.
   Heineken
Heinlein, Paul, 1626-80
   Jesu, Jesu du mein hirt;
      X10886 The Good Shep-
      herd
Heins, Francis D., 1878-
   Hereford (1930)
Heins, Nicholas
   Brecon (1900)
Helder, Bartholomäus, 1585-
1635
   Dich bitt ich, trautes Jesu-
      lein (1635)
   Wohlauf, thut nicht verzagen;
      X4558 Helder
Heller, James G., 1892-
   A new shrine (1932)
   Blest is the bond (1932)
   Into the tomb of ages (1932)
   Lord, be thou with us still
      (1932)
   Lord, do thou guide me (1932)
   O Lord, what is man!
   O Thou, whose Presence
      (1932)
   Once more the liberal year
   Opening song (1932)
   Resignation (1932)
   The cry of Israel (1932)
   Thy brother (1932)

'Tis not the large, the hjge,
the vast (1932)
'Tis winter
Hemy, Henri Frederich, 1818-
1901
Beulah (1864)
Conqueror; X1534 Carmel;
X2312 Daily, daily
Hail, glorious St Patrick
Paradise; X7853 O Paradise
St Catherine (1864); X3224
Faith of our fathers; X8651
Prince; X9384 St Finbar;
X11474 Tynemouth
Siloam; X9189 Sabbata; X9939
Sharon
Hemy, H. F. Easy hymn tunes ...
for Catholic schools. London,
1851
Stella; X4261 Hail, Queen of
heaven; X10398 Stella maris
Henderson, J. W.
He ransomed me (1916)
Hendrickson, H. N.
Alma Mater
Henle, M.
Remember Him, the only One
Henry, Prince of Battenberg,
1858-
Battenberg
Henry VIII, King of England,
1491-1547
Green grow'th the holly
Henson, J. M.
Somebody follows you
Herbert, George, 1817-1906
Burwell; X6379 Lord of life
and king; X7605 O Bread of
Heaven; X10516 Sunset;
X10594 Sweet Saviour! Bless
Holy Queen, we come; X4331
Happy we, who thus; X4812
Holy Queen, we bend
Herbert, John B.
Algiers
Lafayette
Magnus
Olena (1912)
Herbst, Martin, 1654-81 (probable
composer)
Heinlein (1676); X701 Aus der
tiefe; X3539 From the depths
we cry; X4618 Hernlein [sic]

Hereford Hymnal
Martyr Dei qui unicum
(plainsong M 4)
Hermann, Nikolaus, ca 1485-
1561
Erscheinen ist der herrlich
tag (major reading) (1560);
X4609 Hermann
Erscheinen ist der herrlich
tag (minor reading) 1560)
Hermann (1554); X5700
Joachimsthal; X6310 Lobt
Gott; X6312 Lobt Gott, ihr
Christen; X6504 Luetzen;
X6542 Lutzen; X7404 Nico-
laus; X7713 O happy day;
X8156 Op alle som paa
Jorden; X10868 The first
fruits of
Nu lader os da grave ned
O Heilige Dreifaltigkeit (1560);
X11379 Trinity; X12020
Wer hier fuer Gott
Herold, Louis-Joseph-Ferdinand,
1791-1833
Heart of Mary (1808)
Messiah (1839)
Herr, Amos
I owe the Lord a morning
song (1890); X4008 Grati-
tude
Herrmann, Christopher F.
Faith (1882)
Herrnhut ms Choral buch,
1735-45
Gregor's 37th metre; X1396a
Bunyan (Thommen. Chris-
ten-schatz); X2362 Das
wahre christenthum; X4057
Gregor
Gregor's 82d metre; X4437
Hayn; X11958 Weil die
worte wahrheit sind
Gregor's 141st metre-A;
X1044 Berthelsdorf; X2358
Das ist unbeschreiblich
Gregor's 166th metre; X2567
Die wanderschaft in; X8475
Pilgrimage
Herron, J. D.
Dummerston
Hershey, Urban Henry, 1876-
1952

Hershey

Hervey, Frederick Alfred John,
1846-1910
  Castle Rising
  Hervey's Litany; X4655 Hervey
    X6233 Litany
  Richemont

Heseltine, Philip, 1894-1930
  see his pseudonym: Warlock,
    Peter

Hesperian harp, 1840
  Bourbon

Heward, Leslie H., 1897-1943
  Wyke

Hewlett, Thomas, 1845-74
  Dalkeith; X7824 O Lord, thy
    love

Hewlett, William Henry, 1873-
1940
  Somerset (ca 1915)
  Teach me, O Lord

Hews, George, 1806-73
  Coronet
  Holley (1835); X6387 Lord,
    speak to me

Hays, John A.
  Our Father (1947)
  The Lord's Prayer (1947)

Heywood, John
  Aston
  Festival

Hibbard, S.
  Exhortation

Hickman, Roger M. fl 1917
  Aviemore

Higgs, H.M., 1855-1929
  Cara patria

Hildebrand, E.T.
  Ashburn
  Let them come to see
  Serving the Lord in song (1907)
  Winston

Hildesheim melody
  Hail, holy Queen (1937); X9669
    Salve Regina coelitum

Hiles, Henry, 1826-1904
  Birkdale (1865)
  Fiat lux
  St Leonard (1867); X4700 Hiles;
    X6101 Leonard
  Sweden

Hill, G. Everett
  Rex triumphans

Hille, Johann Georg
  Einer ist König (ca 1730)
  Gregor's 161st metre (1739);
    X7758 O ihr auserwoehl-
    ten
  Gregor's 217th metre-B;
    X6839 Mein heiland nimmt
    de

Hiller (or Hüller), Johann
Adam, 1728-1804
  Love divine

Himmel, Friedrich Heinrich,
1765-1814
  Himmel
  Light of the world

Himmels-Lust. Leipzig, 1675
  Liebster Immanuel; X2972
    Emmanuel

Hindu (Indian) air
  Happy Land; X11140 There
    is a happy land; X12458
    World to come

Hintze, Jakob, 1622-1702
  Salzburg (1678); X336 Alle
    menschen; X654 At the
    Lamb's high feast; X2709
    Du, o schönes weltege-
    baeude; X4716 Hintze;
    X5695 Jesus with thy
    Church; X7533 Now the
    world is saved; X8063
    Old 168th; X9121 Rosen-
    müller

Hirst, G.
  Salvator amicus

Hodge, C.R.
  Herbert

Hodges, Edward, 1796-1867
  Bristol (1841)
  Habakkuk
  Peace

Hodges, John Sebastian Bach,
1830-1915
  Alleluia piis edite
  Eucharistic hymn (1868);
    X3085 Eucharist; X8294
    Panis vitae
  Hodges (1869)
  Matins
  Sebastian
  Memorial

Hodson, Henry E.
  Urbs caelestis (1880)

Hoff, Erik Christian, 1830-94
  Her vil ties
  Hoff; X4193 Guds menighed,
    syng; X12515 Ye lands, to
    the Lord
Hoffman, C. Christian, 1839-
93
  Ave
  Fulfillment; X2478 Den store
    mester kommer
Hoffman, Elisha A., 1939-1929
  Hoffman; X1026 Benton Har-
    bor; X1702 Christ has for
    sin; X12071 What a wonder-
    ful
  Hoffman II; X5413 Is your all
    on the altar?
  Is thy heart right with God?
  O Lord, within my soul
  Orwigsburg; X5098 I must
    tell Jesus
  Washed in the blood; X540 Are
    you washed in the blood?
Hogan, Frederick William, 1845-
  Magherafelt
Hohenfurth ms. 1410
  Dies est laetitiae; X1260 Boye;
    X1509 Cantus ubique; X2153
    Cornfields; X2502 Der tag
    der ist [so freuden reich];
    X3066 Et lidet barn saa;
    X4139 Gregor's 215th metre;
    X10775 Thanksgiving carol;
    X11317 To us is born
  Quem pastores; X1546 Carol
    melody, 14th c; X2427 Dear-
    mer; X8755 Quem pastores
    laudavere; X9966 Shepherds
    left their flocks astraying
Holbrook, Joseph Parry, 1822-
88
  Bishop
  Church
  Clinton
  Gerhardt
  Greek hymn (1870)
  Handy
  Lyte
  Miriam
  Refuge; X5623 Jesus, lover of
    my soul
  Remsen
  Segur

  Truman
Holden, Oliver, 1765-1844
  Coronation (1793); X280 All
    hail the great Immanuel's
    name; X281 All hail the
    power; X5492 Jehovah,
    Lord of heaven and earth
Holden, O. Union harmony,
1793
  Boundless mercy
Holdroyd, Israel
  Rochester (1753)
  Wells
Holland see Dutch
Hollingshead, D.S.
  Gring
Holmes, Henry James Ernest,
1852-1938
  Eventide; X4765 Holmes
  Linton
  Pater omnium
Holsinger, George Blackburn,
1857-1908
  At the Saviour's right hand
  Be thou our guide
  Beautiful homeland (1902)
  Cross of Christ, O sacred
    tree
  Eternal source
  Hark! the voice of Jesus
    calling (1901)
  Holsinger (1901)
  Little ones like me
  Love not the world
  Purer in heart
  Rest over Jordan
  Wayland (1902); X4595 Here,
    Lord of life and
Holst, Gustav Theodore, 1874-
1934
  NOTE: Real name was Gus-
tavus Theodore von Holst, but
changed after 1914.

  Bossiney
  Brookend
  Chilswell (1927)
  Cranham (1906); X6944 Mid-
    winter
  Essex
  Hillcrest (1928)
  Lullay my liking
  Monk Street

Sheen
Stepney
Thaxted
Valiant hearts (1925)
Holyoke, Samuel, 1762-1820)
  Hingham
Hopkins, D.E., 1902-
  Buffham
Hopkins, Edward John, 1818-1901
  Abbey
  Artavia (1887)
  Children's voices (1875)
  Culford
  Christmas Morn
  Deva (1887)
  Ellers (1869); X1014 Benedic-
    tion; X2940 Ellerton; X5394
    Irene; X7860 O precious
    sign and seal; X8375 Pax
    dei
  Epiphany
  Epiphany II
  Evangel; X4543 Heber
  Feniton Court
  Hartland
  Jehovah; X12464 Worship
  Kelso; X3176 Every morning;
    X8559 Praise
  Knowsley
  Laetabundus
  Nukapu; X7051 Montgomery
  Pascal, No. 1; X8328 Pascal
  Redcliff
  Rocklands
  Sacrament
  St Athanasius (1872); X658
    Athanasius;   X3828 God of
    hosts
  St Elwyn
  St Hugh (1862)
  St Joseph
  St Philip (1852)
  St Piran
  St Raphael (1862); X8800 Raphael
  Tadcaster
  Temple (1867)
  Tideswell
  Toronto
  Tribute
  Vaughan
  Wessex
  West Heath
  Wildersmouth (1879)

Wraysbury
Hopkins, J., 1822-1900
  Allington
Hopkins, John Henry, jr., 1820-
91
  Come Holy Ghost; X11582
    Veni Creator, No. 3
  Ninety-fifth [Psalm]
  Sabaoth
  Satterlee
  Three Kings of Orient
    (1857); X5844 Kings of
    orient; X11939 We three
    Kings of orient
  Twilight; X4873 Hopkins
Hopkins, John Henry
  Grand Isle (1940)
  Westerly (1941)
Hopkins, Josiah, 1786-1862
  Expostulation
Hopkirk, James
  Bellwoods (1938)
Horne, Johann, d 1547
  Gaudeamus pariter (1544);
    X750 Ave virgo; X751
    Ave virgo virginum
Horner, B.W.
  Brotherland
Horner, E.F., 1864-1928
  Aldersgate Street
  Hampstead (1904)
Horsley, Charles Edward.
  Eighty-four church tunes, 1857
  Bodley
  St Bavon
Horsley, William, 1774-1858
  Belgrave
  Horsley (1844)
Horsman, Edward, 1873-1918
  Siloam (1903)
Hostetter, P.
  Sycamore
Hott, G.P.
  Glory gates
Houseley, Henry, 1852-1925
  Cross and crown (1896)
  Denver (1896)
Howard, Alonzo Potter, 1838-
1902
  Lonely midnight; X5312 In
    the lonely midnight
Howard, Samuel, 1710-82
  Coventry (1762)

Isleworth (1765)
Lancaster; X7119 Mornington
St Bride (1762); X9323 St
Brides; X9324 St Bride's
Smith; X2715 Dublin; X4945
Howard
Howard, Samuel, 1846-
Sunset
Howells, Herbert Norman, 1892-
Severn (1931)
Hoyte, William Stevenson, 1844-
Ellerton
Margaret Street
St Columba; X4947 Hoyte;
X9342 St Colomb
Hubbard, S.
Parsons
Hudson, Ralph E., 1843-1901
At the cross (1885); X235
Alas! and did my Saviour
bleed; X4955 Hudson
Blessed Name; X1138 Blessed
be the name
I know I love thee better
(1881)
The Lord is my Shepherd
Hudson, Robert, 1732-1815
St Olave
Huet, Pierre Daniel, 1630-1721
Diva servatrix; X885 Bayeaux
Huffaker, Perry L., 1902-
Lauree (1951)
Pine Glen
Spring Run (1951)
Hugg, George C.
A full surrender
Christ is born in Bethlehem
Christian soldier
Closer cling to Jesus
Father, lead us
God of love
Good-bye (1898)
He arose (1892)
I come to thee (1898)
Jesus knows (1892)
Just as seemeth good to Thee
May the Christ-life shine in
me
No, not one; X4860 Homeward
bound
Scattering precious seed
Send me light
Hughes, G.W., 1861-1941

Buddugoliaeth
Hughes, John (Glandŵr), 1872-
1914
Calon Lân
Hughes, John (Pontypridd),
1873-1932
Cwm Rhondda (1905); X2244
Crown Him; X4205 Guide
us, O thou great
Hughes, John (Dolgelly), 1896-
Be thou faithful
Dinas Bethlehem
Maelor
The Lord bless thee
Hughes, Thomas
Saron
Huish, O.P.
Come, all ye sons of God
Come unto Jesus
Jesus, my Saviour true
There is a land whose sunny
vales; X11542 Utah, Utah,
beautiful
Hull, Asa, 1828-
In dark Gethsemane; X7810
O Lord, Divine, we come;
X8917 Remember Me
Hull, Asa. The casket of Sun-
day School melodies, 1865
Ich weiss einen strom;
X11031 The river of life
Stella
Hullah, John Pyke, 1812-84
Benison
Bentley (1866)
Salisbury (arr); X8959
Resignation; X9721 Sarum
Hult, Adolf, 1869-
Messiah (1899)
Hultman, J.A.
Spicer
Hume, Duncan
Dare to be brave; X2171
Courage
Hume, Paul, 1915-
O Brightness (1964)
Hummel, Johann Nepomuk,
1778-1837
Hark, hark, my soul
Humperdinck, Engelberg, 1854-
1921
Hark the herald host (1893)
Humphreys, F.L.

St Mabyn
Humphreys, R.D., 1826-
   Rapture
Hungarian traditional, etc.
   Alleluia song (1855)
   Christus Urunknak (carol)
   Dallam (folk)
   Du meiner seelen' (16th c
      chorale); X11361 Transyl-
      vania
   Magyar see Éneke, Gályara-
      bok.
   O most Holy (hymn)
   Regi litania (litany)
   Thirsting for the living
      Fountain
Hunnewell, Frank S.
   Optimism (1916)
Hunt, John Eric, 1903-58
   Shrewsbury
Hunter, C.E.
   Do you love the world?
   God's way is best
   Humility
   My heart says Amen
   Saints' reward
   Seedtime and harvest
   The Good Shepherd
Huntington, C.W.
   Huntington
Hurd, Peter Wyeth
   The Saints of God (1957)
Hurley, E.G.
   Holy Queen! we bend before thee
Hurndall, W.F.
   Springhill
Hurst, John, 1859-
   Calvary (1890)
   Gulworthy
Hurst, William, 1849-
   Leicester
Hus, John, 1369-1415 supposed
composer
Herr Jesu Christ
   NOTE: See Pensum sacrum,
   Görlitz, 1648.
Husband, John J., 1760-1825
   We praise thee, O God; X362
      Alleluia, 'tis done; X8903
      Rejoice and be glad; X9006
      Revive us again; X11188
      Thine the glory
Huston, Frank C.

It pays to serve Jesus (1909)
Hutcheson, Charles, 1792-1860
   Stracathro (1832)
Hutchins. Sunday School hymnal
   A shepherd band
   Easter flowers
Hutton, James. Tunes for the
hymns, 1740-44
   Cennick
   Chelsea
   Eastham
   Lindsey House
   Ockbrook
   Old 583d; X10074 Sinners
      Redeemer
Hutton, Laura Josephine, 1852-
88
   Eternity
   Warfare
Huxtable, F.
   Tempest
Hyatt, Nathaniel Irving
   Comrade heart (1927)
   Requiem (1927)
   Torchbearers (1927)
Hymns and tunes, 1890
   Follow the path; X1235
      Bound Brook
   May the grace of Christ;
      X5156 I would love thee
Hymns for children
   Birds are singing
Hymns of the Eastern Church
   Safe home
   St Stephen the Sabaite

           I

Icelandic melody
   Iceland
Iliffe, Frederick, 1847-1928
   Autumn, No. 2
Ilse, Ludwig Herman, 1845-
1931
   Erfurt (1910)
   Wittenberg (1910)
Illsley, Frank G.
   Ilsley (1887)
Indian traditional
   NOTE: See also Marathi,
and Hindu
   Binti hamari
Ingall. Christian harmony,

1805
   I love thee
Ingalls, Jeremiah, 1764-1828
   Invitation; X1995 Come, ye
      sinners
   Fillmore
   Northfield
   The midnight call (1863);
      X7195 My dearest friends
      in bonds; X8324 Parting
      hand
   Vesper (1804)
Ingham, Thomas H., 1878-1948
   Dawn (1931); X11872 Watchman
Ireland, John Nicholson, 1879-
1962
   Eastergate
   Chelsea
   Love unknown (1948)
   New Prince, new pomp
   Sampford (1948)
Irish traditional, etc.
   Clonmel; X4540 Heavenward
   Cormac
   Daniel
   Deirdre; X9553 St Patrick
      (St Patrick)
   Dun Aluinn
   Dunaha
   Durrow
   Fanad Head
   Fingal
   Garton; X3583 Gartan
   Irish carol
   Kilgetty
   Londonderry; X5399 Irish
      melody; X6323 Londonderry
      air
   Lorica Patricii
   Marylebone
   Moville
   O Bethlehem
   O Lord, reprieve (ancient)
   Peacefield (ancient)
   Petrie
   Remember the poor
   St Columba; X1898 Columba;
      X3024 Erin; X7607 O
      breathe on me
   St Patrick; X2459 Deirdre
   St Sechnall
   Slane
   Sussex carol

   Sweet story; X987 Believe me
      if all those; X2986 Endear-
      ing young charms
   The five lesser joys
   Valor; X11978 Welcome,
      summer
   Wicklow
Irons, Herbert Stephen, 1834-
1905
   Crucifer
   Heavenly voices
   Hope
   Irons (1861); X9346 St Co-
      lumba; X9347 St Columbia
   St Chrysostom (1860)
   St Leonard (1916)
   Southwell (1861); X5402 Irons
Irvine, Jessie Seymour, 1836-
87
   Crimond
Isaacs, Lewis C.
   Praise ye the Lord (1932)
   The God that to our fathers
   The heavens, O God (1932)
Isaak, Heinrich, ca 1450-1527
   NOTE: Spelling varies great-
ly, as: Isaac, Izak, Yzacm
Ysack; Arrigo Tedesco, Arrig-
hus Tedesco
   Innsbruck; X5358 Innsbruck,
      ich musz dich lassen; X
      5359 Innsbruck new; X
      5360 Innspruck; X7543 Nu
      hviler mark og enge;
      X7576 Nun ruhen alle
      wälder; X7606 O Bread
      of life; X7659 O esca
      viatorum; X7672 O food to
      pilgrims: X7946 O welt,
      ich muss dich lassen;
      X11838 Wartburg
   Innsbruck (Bach arr);
   NOTE: See previous entry
for variant tune names.
Iszlai, Marton (19th c)
   Marton
Isle of Arran see Arran, Isle
of
Italian Association of St Cecilia
   Christus vincit
Italian traditional, liturgical,
etc.
   Ave, maris stella

From starry heaven (1755)
I'm a pilgrim; X8464 Pilgrim
Jerusalem, my happy home
Monte Cassino
Oliva speciosa (18th c)
Ye souls of the faithful
Iverson, Daniel
Spirit of the living God;
X3243 Fall fresh on me
Ivimey, John W.
Crispinian

J

J. H. H. here identified as
Hopkins, John Henry, jr.
Jackson, George K., 1745-1822
Dibden
Jackson, Robert, 1842-1914
Ashburton
Columbia
Cressbrook
Lymington
Niagara
Old Judea
Trentham (1888)
Waverton (1876)
Jackson, Thomas, ca 1715-81
Jackson; X1427 Byzantium
Jackson, William (of Exeter),
1730-1803
Exeter
Jackson, William, 1815-66
Evening hymn
Jacobs, W. K.
Gently, Lord, O, gently
Happy with Christ
I love to tell the story (1896)
Saviour, like a shepherd
Wonderful Saviour
Jacobs, William, 1796-1872
Hope; X1599 Chant; X5454
Jacobs
Jacobsen (no initials)
O gloriosa Virginum
Jacobsohn, B.
From heaven's height
Jaehnigen, C. F.
Charity; X5775 Kaerlighen fra
Gud
James, Frederick, 1858-1922
Gennesaret
Noricum

James, Philip, 1890-
Cwmafon (1927); X1907
Comavon
Faith triumphant (1927)
Tregaron (1941)
Jamouneau, Arthur J.
Lynton
Janowska, S.
Stars of glory
Japanese melody
Kimigayo
Jarman, Thomas, 1782-1862
Lyngham
Jarvis, Samuel (probable com-
poser)
Stanley (1762); X7052 Mont-
gomery
Jaspers, C.
Resonet in laudibus
Jassinowsky, Pinchos
A Succoth prayer (1932)
Morning prayer (1932)
Succoth hymn (1932)
The Torah (1932)
Thy word is to my feet a
lamp (1932)
Jeater, William, 1838-
Rossetti (1907)
Jeboult, H. A., 1871-1925
St Mary Magdalene
Jeffery, John Albert, ca 1854-
ca 1929
Albany (1886); X451 Ancient
of days
Liddon; X9233 St Agnes
School
Jeffrey, H. R.
Come home, poor sinner
The golden harvest
Jenkins, David, 1848-1915
Bod Alwyn
Penlan
Jenkins, Joseph W.
St Joseph, be our Guide
(1963)
Jenkins, Rory Donaughmore,
1914-
Cotham
Jenks, S.
Communion
Jenner, Henry Lascelles, 1820-
98
Quam dilecta (1861); X4259

Hail, ocean's beauteous Star
Jepson, Harry Benjamin, 1870-
1952
Battell Chapel
Jerusalem's Gates reopened, 1919
Peace through the cross
Jespersön, Niels. Gradual, 1573
Jespersön; X4982 Hvad ljus
öfver griften
Jesson, R.H., 1929-
Barnet
Jewish traditional, including many
temple melodies arranged for
congregational use.
NOTE: Numerous items are
indexed elsewhere under composer's
name, but notice the traditional
names in Hebrew-transliterated-
to-roman letters in this section.

Addeer hu; X3833 God of might;
X8574 Praise the Lord
Adon olam; X5374 Into the
tomb of ages
Adonoy hu ho-eloheem
Akdamus; X4942 How wondrous
All ye dwellers
Ashray yod'ay; X10974 The
Lord reigneth
Ayl hora aleelah; X3855 God,
that doest wondrously; X7335
N'eelah hymn
Az yasheer (Sephardic mel);
X7597 O bless the Lord,
my; X11399 True freedom
Bemotzoay; X2592 Dim mine
eyes with many teardrops
Blessings over the Chanukkah
lights
Bor-chu
Boruch shaym I; X12535 Yim-
loch Adonoy
Boruch shaym II
Boughs (Succos mel); X10648
Take unto you
Come, ye faithful servants
see Levenson, Boris
Duties of today
Eliyahu hanavi; X3274 Father
hear
For the mountains
Gaza
Grace after meals

Hakafos melody; X11198
This feast of the Law
Hallel; X4402 Hatikvo; X
11145 There is a mystic
tie
Hasidim
Jewish tune
Kee hinay kachomer; X11314
To Thee we give ourselves
Kee hinay kachomer II;
X6293 Lo, as the potter
molds the clay
Kiddush (Lewandowski ver-
sion); X1168 Blessings
over the Lulav
Kol nidre
Leoni; X10973 The Lord our
God we praise; X12533
Yigdal
May the words
Me chomocho I; X3535 From
heaven's heights the thun-
der peals
Me chomocho II
Me chomocho III
N'eelah melody I; X8099
On parting
N'eelah melody II; X11076
The sun goes down
Olaynu
Omnom kayn; X4996 Hymn of
glory
Ono adonoy kaper no
Oveenu malkaynu; X8098
On mighty wings; X8220
Our Father, our King
Rock of Ages; X3449 For-
tress-Rock, my God;
X6829 Mee chomocho;
X7061 Mooz [t]zur
Rosh Hashanah I; X2379
Dawn
Rosh Hashanah II; X10956
The Lord is King
Shalom (arr as a round)
Sheer hamaalos
Sheer hasheersem I; X9194
Sabbath Eve
Sheer hasheereem II; X5247
In answer to my prayer
Sh'ma Yisroayl I
Sh'ma Yisroayl II
Sh'ma Yisroayl III

Simchas Torah; X8909 Re-
joicing of the law
Sinai's Height (Akdamos mode
arr); X233 Akdamos mode;
X3536 From Sinai's height
a fountain gushes
Tal; X10236 Song of the dew
The Lord of all
The lulav; X10478 Succos
The Sabbath Bride
The torch of Israel
There is a mystic tie <u>see</u>
Achron, Joseph
Tovo l'fonecho
Un'saneh tokef
V'al kulom; X12238 Why art
thou cast down?
V'nishlach
When the Sabbath
Yigdal
Yom Kippur Mode; X3239
Forgive us, Lord
Zochraynu
Jewson, James Pentland, 1825-
89
Merton
Tudor (1876)
John Gamble's Collection, 1659
see Gamble, John. Collection,
1659
Johnson, Arthur Basil Noel, 1861-
1950
Wells
Johnson, James A.
Devotion
Johnson, Peter, 1870-
Arnold (1923)
Carolina (1922)
Cecile
Dorothea (1923)
Gloria dei (1923)
Gustavus Adolphus (1923)
Mildred (1923)
Norelius
St Paul (1924)
Johnson, William Lyman
Concord (1905)
Pleasant Street (1905)
Jones, Charles P.
All I need
Nothing like Jesus (1913)
Jones, Darius Elliott, 1815-81
Stockwell

Wood
Jones, David Hugh, 1900-
Miller Chapel (1954)
Jones, Griffith Hugh (Gutyn
Arfon), 1849-1919
Llef
Jones, J.R., 1762-1822
Ramoth
Jones, James Edmund, 1866-
1939
Belleville; X5765 Just for
today
Langemarck
Walden
Jones, John (Talysarn), 1797-
1857
Llanllyfni
Tanycastell
Jones, Lewis E,
Jones (1906)
Lean on His arms   (1903)
There is power in the blood;
X8549 Power in the blood
Jones, Owen (canon)
Dark the night
Jones, T.E.
Quinquagesima
Jones, Tom
Let the beauty of Jesus
Jones, William ("Oriental
Jones"), 1726-1800
St Stephen; X7386 Newington;
X10401 Stephens
Jordan, Charles Warwick
Domus domini
Rhodes; X1850 Clifton
Joseph, Georg
Angelus (1657); X7517 Now
at the Lamb's high royal
feast
Gregor's 225th metre (1668);
X10071 Singt dem Herrn,
nah und fern
Gregor's 298th metre (1668);
X5557 Jesu, du hoffnung
Keine Schönheit hat die welt
(1657); X1541 Carne;
X9786 Schönheit
Joseph, J.M., 1894-1929
Eskdale
Jowett, Joseph, 1784-1856
Kerry
Thanket

Joy, W.
  Holywell
Jude, William Herbert, 1851-
1922
  Galilee (1887); X5536 Jesus
    calls us; X5748 Jude
  Onward, Christian soldiers
Judefind, W. B.
  Twilight
Jutson, Charles Bentley, 1870-
1930
  The story of Jesus

K

"K"
  Hark! Are they not angels
Kaillmark, E.
  Do what is right
Kaiser, Alois
  As pants the hart
  Blessed, O blessed (1932)
  Grateful praises
  Mee chomocho
Kalhauge, Sophus Viggo Harald,
1840-1905
  Viggo
Kálmán, Farkas
  Kalman
Kasschau, Frank
  Brooklyn (1929)
Katholische Kirchengesänge.
  Paderborn, 1616
  Paderborn
Keegan, G. Kearnie
  Looking to Jesus (1940)
Keeler, Bradley
  Vittel Woods (1924)
Keeler, J. J.
  A voice hath spoken
Keeny, David E.
  He loveth me
Keller, Arnold Frederick, 1890-
  Holy manger (1958)
  Redeemer (1958)
  Springtime (1958)
Keller, Matthias, 1813-75
  American hymn; X5796 Keller's
    American hymn
Kelly, Richard A.
  Holy Spirit, led us (1940)
Kelly, Thomas C.
  Accept, kind Father (1958)

When great St Patrick (1958)
Kennedy, Amanda
  Star of the East
Kentucky Harmony, 1816
  NOTE: see also Supplement
to Kentucky Harmony.

  Salvation
  Tender thought
Kern, Jan
  Praise now your God (1964)
Kestel, Edmund, O. S. B.
  Alleluia, Christ is risen
    (1946)
  Song of the Branches (1946)
Kettle, Charles E.
  Blenden (1876)
  Exultation
  Hosanna
  Resignation
  Trust
  Woolwich; X12440 Woolich
Kidner, Frank Derek, 1913-
  Oak Hill
  Polzeath
Kieff melody
  Russian Cantakion of the de-
    parted
Kieffer, Aldine S.
  And now my soul, another
    year; X6729 Markell
  Josie
  The city of light
Kilgore, Clive Harold, 1889-
  Pax (1958)
Kimball, Edward P.
  Great God, to thee my even-
    ing song
  The wintry day, descending
Kimball, Jacob, 1761-1826
  Milton (1793)
Kinder, Ralph, 1876-1952
  Ship of State (1927)
King, A.
  Eastnor
King, Charles John, 1859-1934
  Northampton
King, Chauncey J.
  Some time we'll see
King, Oliver A., 1855-1923
  Oliver
King, Robert
  David's Harp (1722)

Kingham, Millicent Douglas,
    1866-1927
    Benson (1894); X225 Ainger
Kingo, Gradual, 1699
    I Jesu Navn skal al vor Gjern-
        ing ske
    O Jesus, for din Pine; X6367
        Lord Jesus, by thy passion
Kingsley, George, 1811-84
    Edwards (1847)
    Elizabethtown; X7673 O for a
        closer walk
    Ferguson
    Frederick
    Heber (ca 1873)
    Kingsley; X12273 Williams
    Lucius
    Mount Auburn
    Newbold
    Southport
    Tappan (1839)
    Ware
Kinross, J.
    How blest the man (1932)
Kirchen Gesange. Bremen, 1707
    Amor dei
Kirchengesangbuch. Strassburg,
    1541
    All' Ehr' und Lob
Kirchen-und haus Buch. Dresden,
    1694
    Nun lasst uns geh'n
Kirkpatrick, William J., 1838-
    1921
    A blessing in prayer
    Alone with God
    Annetta (1901)
    Cradle song; X6537 Luther's
        cradle hymn
    Dear to the heart (1899); X65
        A wonderful Saviour; X5866
        Kirkpatrick; X10844 The
        cleft of the rock
    Deeper yet (1896)
    For Christ and the Church
    Give me thy heart
    NOTE: Here filed under Annie
F. Bourne, who may have been
Fanny Crosby. Kirkpatrick published many melodies which he
did not write, without mention-
ing that fact.

Great is the Love
He hideth my soul
Heaven at last
Him that cometh unto me
How blest
I have work enough to do
Jesus comes
Kirkpatrick
Lest I forget (1921); X5829
    King of my life; X6049
    Lead me to Calvary
Lord, I'm coming home
    (1892); X2008 Coming
    home; X5446 I've wander-
    ed far away
Meet me there
Moline (1901)
No shadows yonder (1903)
Redeemed
Salvation (1882); X5670 Jesus
    saves; X11916 We have
    heard the joyful sound
Sands (1901)
Saved to the uttermost
Saxony
Stepping in the light
The Comforter has come
The promises of God
Thou spotless Lamb of God
Trust in Jesus (1881); X11277
    'Tis so sweet" X11432
    Trusting
Wait, and murmur not
Watchman, blow the gospel
    trumpet
Whole wide world; X11106
    The whole wide world
Will your anchor hold;
    X11914 We have an anchor
Kittel, Johann Christian, 1732-
1809
    Bis willkommen (1790)
    Quedlinburg; X6763 Mary
        Immaculate, Mother and
        Maid
Kjerulf, Halfdan, 1815-68
    Evening blessing
Klein, Bernhard, 1793-1832
    Löwen, lasst euch wieder-
        finden (1817)
Kleiner Liederschatz, 1901
    See the shining dewdrops

Kloss, J. F.
  Hail to thee! true Body
Klug, Joseph. Gesangbuch, 1535
  or Geistliche Lieder, Wittenberg, 1535 see Geistliche Lieder, Wittenberg, 1535
Knapp, Mrs. Joseph F., 1839-
  1908
  NOTE: Possibly is Mary A.
Bachelor Knapp (See Julian, p.
  1609, 1641)

  Albertson
  Assurance (1873); X1136
    Blessed assurance
  Behold me standing
  Cleansing wave; X10841 The
    cleansing wave
  Nearer the cross
Knapp, William, 1698-1768
  Spetisbury
  Wareham (1738); X302 All
    saints; X11391 Triumphant
    Sion
Knecht, Justin Heinrich, 1752-
  1817
  Domini clamavi (1797)
  Gotha (1797); X12383 Womit
    soll ich dich
  Herr, dir ist niemand zu ver-
    gleichen
  Knecht (1799) [Meter 7.6.7.6.]
    X863 Barton; X5883 Kocher;
    X7091 Morlaix
  St Hilda (1799, arr by Husband
    1871) [Meter 7.6.7.6.D];
    X6900 Meredith; X9367 St
    Edith
  Salvation by grace (1796); X702
    Aus gnaden soll ich
  Vienna (1797); X7997 Ohne rast
    und unverweilt; X8819
    Ravenna
  Zwingli
Knight, G.H., 1908-
  Valley
  Veryan
Knight, H.
  Stabat mater
Knorr. Neuer helicon, 1684
  St Gregory; X4154 Gregory;
    X12565 Zeuch meinen geist
Knowles, G.J.

  Balfour (18th c)
Knowlton, F.S.
  For peace and for plenty
Knox, J.C.
  Advent
Knudsen, Peder, 1819-63
  Christmas Eve
Koch, H.C. Choralbuch, 1816
  Auch jetzt macht Gott
Koch, Minna, 1845-1924
  Minna
Kocher, Conrad, 1786-1872
  Dix (1838); X3421 For the
    beauty of; X8187 Orisons;
    X11375 Treuer heiland
  Urquell aller Selig keiten
Koenen, Father
  Hail! Christ our Redeemer
Koenig, Johann Balthasar, 1691-
  1758
  Evangelists; X370 Alles ist
    an Gottes; X676 Auctor
    omnium bonorum; X4699
    Hildesheim
  Tempest
Koenig, J.B. Choralbuch, 1738
  NOTE: Title of book varies
considerably.

  Der am Kreuz
  Franconia; X6987 Miracle
  Ich singe dir
  Ich will dich lieben; X9774
    Scheffler; X11365 Trea-
    sure
  Mentzer; X2909 Elbe; X7640
    O dass ich tausand zungen
    hätte
Kolb, A.B.
  Christ is risen (1896)
  Dear Saviour, when I think of
    thee
  Grateful submission
  Love's consecration
Kolb, A.C.
  Dear Lord, I come; X10390
    Steiner
  Protection
  Shine in my heart, Lord
    Jesus
  That heavenly home
Koralbok for den Norske Kirke,
  1926

St Olaf's Sequence
Koschat, Thomas, 1845-1914
   Poland; X5906 Koschat; X10963
     The Lord is my Shepherd;
     X10964 The Lord is our
     Leader
Kotzschmar, Hermann, 1829-
1909
   Claflin
Kozeluch (or Kotzeluch), Leopold
Anton, 1752-1818
   Kozeluch
Krauth, Harriet Reynolds (Mrs.
  Adolph Spaeth), 1845-1925
   Easter Eve (1869)
Kreitmaier, J., S.J., arr
   Great King of Kings
Krieger, Adam, 1634-66
   Nun sich der Tag (1667);
     X3062 Esslingen; X7580
     Nun sich der tag geendet
     (Williams)
Kroeger, Ernest Richard, 1862-
1934
   Christine
   Elizabeth
   Fulton
   Gairney Bridge (1901)
   Josephine (1901)
   Windermere
Krossing, Peter Casper
   Nu lukker sig mit oege
Kücken, Friedrick Wilhelm, 1810-
82
   Kücker; X8938 Repose
Kugelmann, Johann. Concentus
novi, 1540
   Tabor; X6976 Min sjael, min
     sjael; X7573 Nun lob' mein'
     seel'; X8041 Old hundred
     (Bourgeois)
Kurzenknabe, J.H.
   Heavenly Father

L

Lacy, William S.
   Vernon (1891)
LaFeillée. Methode du plain chant
   Alleluia, dulce carmen (1808)
   Jesu redemptor saeculi (1782)
   Milan (1782); X6155 Lichfield
   St Ambrose (1782)

Lagergren, Johan Frederik,
1826-
   Gud var Gud; X5927 Lager-
     gren
Lagi, Rudolf, 1823-68
   I lift my eyes
Lahee, Henry, 1826-1912
   Magi
   Nativity (1855)
   St Serf
   Wild bells (ca 1875)
   Wimbledon; X5928 Lahee
Lamb, James, 1835-1904
   Invermay
Lambillotte, Louis, 1796-1855
   On this day, O beautiful
     Mother
   Panis Angelicus
   Sub tuum praesidium
   Veni, Creator Spiritus;
     X1936 Come, Holy Ghost,
     creator blest
LaMontaine, John, 1920-
   Come, my way
Lampe, John Friedrich, 1703-
51
   Kent (1746); X2537 Devonshire
Lancaster, J.
   St Silas (1860)
Landahl, Carl Wilfred, 1908-
   Invocation
Landis, A.L.
   Blessed Bible; X3460 Fount
     of glory
Lane, Spencer, 1843-1903
   Penitence (1875); X5309 In
     the hour of trial; X5952
     Lane; X6566 Lyndhurst;
     X8317 Parole; X10285
     Spencer Lane
Lang, Craig Sellar, 1891-
   Eastern monarchs
   St Keverne (1936)
   St Enodoc
Langden, W.A.
   Irvin
Langdon, Richard. Divine
harmony, 1774
   Langdon
Langford, Samuel
   God's glory
   Langford
Langran, James, 1835-1909

Deerhurst; X2426 Dearhurst
Langran (1862); X842 Barnby's
  hymnary, Tune 224; X9231
  St Agnes
Langton, Stephen
  NOTE: "The golden sequence"
is ascribed to Langton: an 11th c
plainsong M 1
  Veni Sancte Spiritus; X3890
    Golden sequence
La Salle hymnal
  Great God! whatever through
    thy church
La Scala santa, 1681
  Coleraine; X1710 Christ is
    our Head; X11665 Vicenza
Latin (mediaeval) melodies
  Christ ist erstanden (12th c);
    based on Victimae Paschali);
    X1720 Christ lag in todes-
    banden; X1730 Christ the
    Lord hath risen; X1797
    Christus ist erstanden;
    X11668 Victimi paschali;
    X11670 Victor King
  Christ lag in todesbanden
    (12th c; in Geistliches
    Gesangbüchlein. Wittenberg,
    1524); X2474 Den Herre
    Krist i dødens baand; X2665
    Dorian mode (Latin, 18th c;
    X11338 Torgau; X11668 Vic-
    timi paschali
  Christ lag in todesbanden (12th
    c; in Geistliches Gesang-
    büchlein. Wittenberg, 1524.
    Bach harm.)
  Dies irae (ca 1200)
  Kyrie, Gott Vater (ca 800;
    hymn, "Kyrie fons bonitatis")
  Nunc sancte nobis
La Tombelle, Ferdinand de, 1854-
1928
  O gloriosa virginum
LaTrobe, Christian Ignatius,
1758-1836
  Invitation (1795)
  Judgment (1795)
  LaTrobe; X2250 Croyland
  LaTrobe's 121st metre (1824)
  LaTrobe's 578th metre
LaTrobe, Peter, 1795-1863
  Courage (1852)

  LaTrobe's 166th metre (1825)
  Sweeter sounds (1854)
Laubenstein, Paul F.
  Declare, O heavens (1964)
Laudi spirituali. Florence, 14th
c (adapted by Charles Burney,
1782)
  Alta trinita beata; X333 Alla
    trinita beata
Laufenberg, H., von ms. ca
1430
  In einem Krepplein lag ein
    Kind
Laufer, Calvin Weiss, 1874-
1938
  Field (1919)
  Hall (1918)
  Hanna (1927)
  Kerr (1932)
  Percival-Smith (1933)
  Seek ye the Lord (1927)
  Stockwell, New
  The Lord is in His holy
    temple (1926)
Laurenti, Laurentius, 1660-1722
  Rejoice, all ye believers
    (ca 1700)
Lausanne Choral book
  Broadlands; X6025 Lausanne
Lavallée, Calixa, 1842-91
  O Canada (1880)
Law, John
  Montesano
Lawes, Henry, 1596-1662
  Battle
  Falkland; X10595 Sweet
    Saviour, bless us
  Farley Castle; X2126 Conway
    Psalm 32; X6029 Lawes
    Psalm 47 (1638); X6027
    Lawes' Psalm 47
  Whitehall; X9704 Sandys
    Psalm 8
Lawson, James
  Lawson
Layard, E.B.
  In medio Bello
Layriz, Friedrich, 1809-59
  Eins ist not (1849)
Layriz Collection, 1853
  Layriz; X5361 Ins feld geh
Leach, James, 1762-98
  Watchman

Leach, Rowland, 1885-
Welcome (1933)
Leatherman, M. Janie
Sweet rest in heaven
Leavitt, Joshua. Christian lyre,
1830-31
Light
Pleading Saviour
Ledington, Stanley
Benediction (1939)
Communion (1939)
For the Sabbath (1938)
Rose of Sharon (1940)
Lee, George E.
Sleep
Lee, James Vernon, 1892-1959
Eastview
Lee, John
All you who seek (1958)
Just for today (1958)
O salutaris hostia (1964)
Leech, Lida Shivers, 1873-
Giving (1923); X11428 Trust,
try, and prove me
God's way (1911)
I have made my choice (1915);
X11184 Thine for service
Lees, John
Lamb's Hill (ca 1805)
Lefebvre, Channing
Rodney (1935)
Legge, Alfred, 1843-1919
Theodora
Lehman, F.M.
The love of God (1917)
Lehmann, W.H.
Fremont (1929)
Leighton, William, d before
1614
Leighton (1614);
NOTE: Probably in his The
teares or lamentacions of a
sorrowfull soule. 1614
Leinbach, E.W., 1823-1901
Leinbach (1870)
Leipzig, Library ms., 1756
Ich sterbe täglich
Leisentrit, J. Catholicum
Hymnologium, 1584
Ave virgo virginum; X752b
Ave vivens Hostia; X4272
Hail, true Victim; X4332
Happy we who thus united

Narenza
Regina caeli jubila
Le Jeune, George Fitz-Cur-
wood, 1842-1904
Glorious things
Highest Lands
Holy Spirit (1894)
Love divine (1887); X6091 Le
Jeune; X6431 Love divine,
No. 2
Urbs beata (1887)
Lemare, Edwin Henry, 1865-
1934
Haven
Lemke, August, 1820-1913
Mach hoch die tür (1849)
Lerman, Joseph W., 1865-1935
Corwin (ca 1908)
Ilona (1908)
Le Saint, Louis
Who givest all (1920)
Leslie, C.E.
Silently, they pass away;
X10030 Silently bury the
dead
Leslie, E.
Lift your glad voices
Leslie, Ernest B.
Adsum
Greenwell
Leslie, Henry, ca 1825-76
Ephraim
Leslie, J.H.
Alpha
Lester, Thomas William, 1889-
1956
First Church
Industry (1927)
Land of our hearts (1927)
Two fatherlands (1927)
Levenson, Boris, 1884-1947
As God wills (1932)
Come, ye faithful servants
(1932)
God! send us men (1932)
Israel's song (1932)
My faith (1932)
Sing to the Sovereign of the
skies (1932)
The day is done (1932)
The voice of God is calling
(1932)
These things shall be (1932)

Lewandowski, Louis, 1821-1904
  Almighty God
  Ayn kay-lo-hay-nu (1932)
  Earth with all thy thousand
    voices (1932)
  Hayom T'am'tsaynu
  How good it is to thank the
    Lord; X6034 L'cho dodee
  Kee vayom
  Mee chomocho
  S'lach no
  Vayomer adonoy
  V'shom'ru
Lewars, Harold, 1882-1915
  Adjutor (1914)
  Froebel (1909)
  Rorate caeli (1914); X9109
    Rorate coeli
  Salve Jesu (1914)
  Septem voces, 1st (1914)
  Septem voces, 2d (1914)
  Septem voces, 3d (1914)
  Septem voces, 4th (1914)
  Septem voces, 5th (1914)
  Septem voces, 6th (1914)
  Septem voces, 7th (1914)
  Vexilla regis (1913)
Lewars, Ralph P., 1883-
  Festal day (1958)
Lewis, Freeman, 1780- 1859
  Beloved (1913); X2724 Dulcimer;
    X6822 Meditation; X7190 My
    beloved; X8855 Redeemer of
    Israel
Lewis, John S.
  Sister, thou wast mild
Lewis, Henry A.
  Mary
Lewis, T.C.
  Crux
Ley, Henry George, 1887-1962
  Ad astra
  Ottery St Mary
  Rushford (1936)
Leyda, Ida F.
  Morning prayer
Liander, C.G.
  Via dolorosa
Liefeld, Albert D.
  Liefeld (1911)
Lightwood, James Thomas, 1856-
  Lytham (1910)
Lillenas, Bertha Mae

Leave your burden (1934);
  X6065 Leave your bur-
  den at the place of prayer
Lillenas, Haldor, 1885-
  Don't turn Him away
  The peace that Jesus gives
    (1931)
  Wonderful grace (1918)
Lindeman, Ludvig Matthias,
1812-87
  Ak, Fader, lad dit Ord,
    din Aand; X7665 O Father,
    may thy word prevail
  All glory, laud
  Bryd frem, mit hjertes trang
    at lindre
  Den store hvide Flok
  Dies irae
  Easter glory; X3484 Fred
    til bod; X5676 Jesus, Sun
    of righteousness; X6493
    Ludovica
  Et Barner født i Bethlehem
  Gift of grace
  Herre Jesus Krist, min
    Frelser du est; X6369
    Lord Jesus Christ, my
    Saviour blest
  Hjem Jeg Laenges; X10461
    Stricken, smitten
  Holy mountains; X2097
    Consolation;
    X5656 Jesus only;
    X7262 Naar mit øie, traet
    af møie; X7284 Nar mit
    öie
  I denne Verdens Sorger
    saenkt
  I Himmelen, i Himmelen
  I Jesus søger jeg min Fred
  I praegtige Himle
  Jeg har min Sag til Gud
    hjemstilt
  Jesus, kom dog selv til mig
  King's land; X7799 O land
    of our King
  Kirken; X1390 Built on the
    Rock; X1806 Church;
    X5862 Kirken den er et
    gammelt hus; X6990
    Mirken
  Kjaerlighed er Lysets Kilde;
    X6187 Light; X6444 Love,

the fount of light
Lindeman; X4187 Gud skal alting
  mage; X5660 Jesus, price-
  less treasure
Ludwig; X4909 How blessed is
  the little flock; X4986 Hvor
  salig er den lille
Min Sjael, min Sjael, lov
  Herren; X7257 My soul, now
  bless
Nu er Frelsens Dag oprundet
O kom dog hver, son Synd har
  gjort
O lad din Aand nu med os
  vaere; X83 Abide among us
Op, thi Dagen nu freymbryder
Our Lady, Trondhjem; X2803
  Easter morrow; X4585 Her
  vil ties; X8330 Paschal;
  X8332 Paskemorgen slukker
  sorgen
Over Kedron
Repentance; X4643 Herre, jeg
  har handlet
Sal vil vi nu sige hver-andre
  Farvel; X457 And now we
  must bid
Som Tørstige Hjort; X589 As
  after the water-brooks
Spring of souls; X1518 Care
  for me; X7466 Norse; X10248
  Sørg, O kjaere Fader
Vaagn op, du, som sover
Lindsay, Miss
  Too late
Lindstrom, Albert Esaias, 1853-
  Mig kläd i helig prydned
  Min ljufva tröst
Linekar, Thomas Joseph, 1858-
  Colwyn Bay
Link, C.U.
  Grace, 'tis a charming sound;
    X7825 O Lord, to thee I
    cry; X8508 Pleading
  Victory
Linley, Francis
  Lord of all being
Lint, Conrad G., 1834-
  Fellowship
Linton, G.W.
  Welcome
Lissant, G.B.
  Banner

Holy Jesus
Rex regum
Lithuanian melody
  Jesus, when we go to rest
Littlewood, Ernest
  Golden Grove
Llewellyn, William Benjamin
 James, 1925-
  Majesty
  Tidings
  Westron Wynde
Lloyd, Charles Francis Am-
 brose, 1852-1917
  Ravensworth
Lloyd, Charles Harford, 1845-
 1919
  Dayspring
  Sacramentum Unitatis (1885)
  Achnasheen (1903)
  St Frideswide
Lloyd, David de, 1883-1948
  Richmond Hill
Lloyd, John Ambrose, 1815-74
  Abergele (1873)
  Brynteg
  Cromer
  Downing
  Eifionydd
  Groeswen
  Henryd
  Kilmorey
  Wynnstay
Lloyd, John Morgan, 1880-
  Colwinstone (1927)
  Nadolig (1927)
  Perth Kerry (1927)
  Pro nostris liberis (1927)
Lloyd, Richard Francis,
 1871-
  Celestial voices
  Clairvaux
  Light of ages
  Winton
Lloyd, Richard Hey, 1933-
  Sarum New
Lloyd, William, 1786-1852
  Meirionydd (1840); X6857
    Meirionnydd; X6858
    Meiromydd
Lob, Otto
  There lives a God
Lockhart, Charles, 1745-1815
  Carlisle (1769)

Loes, Harry Dixon, 1892-
  Looking unto Jesus (1933)
  Redeemer (1921); X1161
    Blessed Redeemer
Loewen, Lois
  Evening praise
Lohr, George Augustus, 1821-97
  St Frances; X1901 Columbia
Lomas, George, 1834-84
  Althorp; X1594 Chamouni
  Pentecost
  Southport
  Submission
  Sursum corda; X10540 Sursum
    corda, No. 2
  Verbum pacis
Longacre, Lindsay Bartholomew,
  1870-
  Deeper life (1928)
  Firenze (1941)
  New America
Loomis, Harvey Worthington,
  1865-1930
  Park Square (1927)
Lord, A. E.
  St Austin
Lorenz, Edmund S. (or Edward
  S.), 1854-
  Amid the trials; X11222 Thou
    thinkest, Lord, of me
  Give me the Bible
  God is love (1886)
  Joy cometh in the morning
  Tell it to Jesus
  The name of Jesus
  When the King comes in
  Wonderful love of Jesus
Lough, A. D.
  All for Jesus
Lourdes Pilgrims Hymn,
  Grenoble, 1882
  Immaculate Mary; X11301 To
    kneel at thine altar
Lovelace, Austin C., 1919-
  Hinman (1953)
Loveless, Wendell P.
  Lead me to some soul today
    (1936)
  Sweeter than the day before
    (1936)
Lowden, C. Harold, 1883-
  Geneva
  Homines Christi (1914)

Living for Jesus; X6268
  Living
Noyon (1917)
Stewart
Lowe, Albert, ca 1840-86
  Ambleside
  Praise (1876); X346 Alleluia;
    X6456 Lowe
Lowenberg, William
  Let Israel trust in God
    alone (1932)
Lowens, Irving, 1916-
  Pioneers (1955)
Löwenstern, Matthias
  Appelles von, 1594-1648
  Christe du beistand
  Lowenstern; X4674 Heut' ist
    o mensch
  Nun preiset alle (1644); X
    243 Alcaic ode; X4083
    Gregor's 70th metre
Lowry, Robert, 1826-99
  All the way (ca 1888); X
    6467 Lowry; X11483 Ulster
  Beautiful river; X4318 Han-
    some place; X9929 Shall
    we gather
  Beauty of holiness; X7969
    O worship the Lord
  Christ arose (1874)
  Come, we that love the Lord;
    X6706 Marching to Zion;
    X12031 We're marching to
  Follow on
  Heavenly Father (1878)
  Keller; X4684 Hide thou me
  Need (1872); X2493 Depend-
    ence; X5100 I need thee
    [every hour]; X6468 Low-
    ry; X11622 Vernon
  Never shone a light (1882)
  No hope in Jesus
  Nothing but the blood (1876);
    X8497 Plainfield
  One more day's work
  Paxtang (1917)
  Something for Jesus (1899);
    X2009 Coming now, O
    Lord, to; X2088 Conse-
    cration; X6469 Lowry;
    X9757 Savior, thy dying
    love; X10202 Something
    for Thee

Where is my boy tonight
Who'll be the next?
Loy, Harvey
   Avanti (1924)
   Gannett (1924)
   Risveglio (1922)
Luard-Selby, Bertram, 1853-
  1919 see Selby, Bertram
  Luard, 1853-1919
Lucas, James, ca 1762-
   Lucas (1832); X1951 Come,
    let us anew
   Swanwick
Lund, Anthony C.
   Blessed are they that have
    the faith
   Bring, heavy heart, your
    grief
Lüneburg Gesangbuch, 1648
   Ach Jesu, dessen Treu
Lüneburg Gesangbuch, 1686
   Jesu meine Lust und Wonne
   Jesu meines herzen freud
   Meinhold; X82 Abglanz aller
    magestaet
Luther, Martin, 1483-1546
   Ein' feste Burg (1529); X27
    A mighty fortress; X39 A
    safe stronghold; X49 A
    stronghold sure; X2882 Ein'
    feste burg ist unser Gott;
    X3448 Fortress; X6531 Lu-
    ther
   From heaven high (1539); X
    3019 Erfurt; X3467 Fra him-
    len hoit; X3529 From heaven
    above; X3907 Good news from
    heaven; X11739 Vom himmel
    hoch; X12361 Wittenberg;
    X12552 Yule
   Jesaia, dem Propheten (1526)
Luther, M. Christliche Gesang.
  Wittenberg, 1542
   Jam moesta
   Spires (based on Plainsong
    M 2, Jesu dulcedo cordium)
    X3022 Erhalt uns, Herr;
    X4750 Hold oppe, Gud, hos
    os dit ord; X6373 Lord
    keep us steadfast; X6530
    Luther; X12362 Wittenberg
Lutkin, Peter Christian, 1858-
  1931

Baptism (1905)
Belleville (1905)
Camp (1905)
Carman (1895)
Caryl (1905)
Charity (1927)
City Road (1905)
Copenhagen
Dublin (1927)
Father, to thee we look
  (1897)
Gleason (1905)
Joshua (1905)
Kiel (1905)
Kolding (1905)
Lanier (1905)
Olivarius (1905)
Patten (1902)
Prescott (1905)
Psalm 23; X8231 Our
  Shepherd is the Lord
Racine (1905)
Red Cross (1927)
St Barbara (1902)
Sevenfold Amen
The Highway (1927)
The Lord bless you; X1016
  Benediction
Theodore (1905)
Transfiguration (1905)
Upham (1905); X3840 God
  of the nations, near and
  far
Vox aeterna
Lutteroth, Ascan Henri Théo-
dore, 1802-89
   Bryntirion
Lutz, Wilhelm Meyer, 1822-
1903
   Stanley; X10518 Sunset
Lvov, Alexey Feodorovitch,
1798-1870
   Russia (1833); X3848 God
    save America; X3856 God
    the all-merciful; X7130
    Moscow; X9058 Rise,
    crowned with light; X9174
    Russian anthem; X9176
    Russian hymn
Lwoff, Alexis Feodorovich,
1798-1870 see Lvov, Alexey
  Feodorovitch, 1798-1870
Lynes, Frank, 1858-1913

Disciples
Sons of light
The armor of light
Lynes, T.
Recessional; X12551 Youth
Lyoff, Alexis Theodore, 1798-
1870 see Lvov, Alexey
Feodorovitch, 1798-1870
Lyon, G.W.
Fast to thine arm
Lyra Anglo-Judaica
Askenazi tune
Lyra Davidica, 1708
Easter hymn; X493 Anglia;
X1737 Christ, the Lord is
risen; X2787 Easter;
X6577 Lyra; X7081 Morgan;
X12452 Worgan [sic]
Lysberg, Charles-Samuel (real
name Bovy-Lysberg) 1821-73
Almighty Father, hear

M

M.B.F.
NOTE: See also Foster, Myles
B., 1851-1922

Melford (1886); X1158 Blessed
night, when first the plain
Maasalo, Armas, 1885-
Jesus hear
McAfee, Cleland Boyd, 1866-
1944
McAfee; X4503 Heart of God;
X7319 Near to the heart;
X11146 There is a place
Macalister, Robert Alexander
Stewart, 1870-1950
New Grange (1927)
St Darerca (1927)
Temple Bryan (1927)
McBurney, S.
Come, follow me
While of these emblems we
partake
McCartney, Robert Hyslop, 1844-
95
Jesus dilectissimi
Remembrance
Westwood
McClellan, John Jasper, 1874-
1925

Sweet is the work, my God,
my King
McConnell, J. Edwin, 1892-
1954
McConnell (1914)
McCutchan, Robert Guy (John
Porter, pseud), 1877-
All the world (1930)
De Pauw (1928)
Fowler (1929)
Masefield (1933)
Oxnam (1929)
Porter
Tiplady (1931)
MacDonald, Archibald
Warrior (1877)
MacDougall, Hamilton Craw-
ford, 1858-
Hazard (1907)
MacElree, Mary Eyre
Eyre (1947)
Macey, J.D., 1860-1933
Mayfield
Macfarlane, J.M.
Dearest children, God is
near you
MacFarlane, James
NOTE: This may be same
composer as above.
Far, far away on Judea's
plains
Macfarren, George Alexander,
1813-87
Dedication (1889); X3283
Father, let me dedicate
Evening hymn (1870)
Light of the world
Luffenham (1872); X3233
Faithfulness; X10761
Thankfulness
Lux prima
Thy life (1875); X11245 Thy
life was given
With gladsome feet
Macfarren, Walter Cecil, 1826-
1905
Barmouth (ca 1875)
Macfarren (1870)
McGranahan, James, 1840-
1907
Alleluia for the cross
By grace are ye saved
Christ returneth; X5433 It

may be at morn
Christ returneth; X5433 It
    may be at morn
El Nathan (1885); X5078 I know
    whom I have believed;
    X12408 Wondrous grace
Every day
For God so loved
Frances (1901)
He is not here, but is risen
He will hide me
His tender mercies (1890)
I'll stand by
Kinsman (1897)
McGranahan
My Redeemer; X5147 I will
    sing; X7848 O my Father
Neumeister; X1723 Christ
    receiveth sinful men; X10073
    Sinners Jesus will receive
None but Christ
Redeemed (1907)
Royal banner; X10791 The ban-
    ner of the cross
Shall you? shall I?
Showers of blessing; X11162
    There shall be showers
Some time we'll understand;
    X7497 Not now, but in the
    coming years
That will be glory for me
The crowning day; X8225 Our
    Lord is now rejected
Thy God reigneth
Thy will be done
Who came down
Would you lose your load of
    sin?
McHose, Irvine N. (late 19th -
early 20th c)
    O, such wonderful love
McIntosh, Robert M.
    Gathering home
    Tell it again
    The Kingdom coming; X10922
    The Kingdom is coming
McIntyre, Thomas
    How great the wisdom
Mackay, J.B.
    Winning souls for Jesus
McKinney, B.B., 1886-1952
    NOTE: McKinney jr and Mc
    Kinney sr, both B.B. McKin-

ney, are not clearly identified. But one set of dates is
known. Melodies are interfiled.

All on the altar (1936)
Another day is dawning
    (1940)
Awake, put on thy strength
    (1940)
Be ye doers of the Word
    (1940)
Breathe o'er our waiting
    spirits (1936)
Bryson City (1940); X1017
    Benediction
Christ for the whole wide
    world (1938)
Christian home (1949)
Coleman (1924); X6125 Let
    others see Jesus in you
Come home (1940)
Crowned or crucified (1940)
Draw near (1940)
Falls Creek (1936); X12179
    Wherever He leads I'll go
Forgive
Glorious Name (1942)
Grice
He died for me
Holcomb (1927); X10282
    Speak to my heart
I was glad when they said
In the old-time way (1937)
In thy holy temple (1940)
Into the woods (1940)
John three-Sixteen
Lead on, lead on (1940)
Leavell; X554 Arise, O
    youth of God
Lee (1931); X9908 Serve the
    Lord with gladness
Leila (1940); X6374 Lord, lay
    some soul upon my heart
Lubbock (1924); X10999 The
    nail-scarred hand
Matthews
Muskogee (1934); X4404
    Have faith in God
My Father knows (1940)
'Neath the old olive trees
    (1929)
O God eternal (1936)

Routh (1926); X9724 Satisfied
with Jesus
Somebody needs your love
(1940)
The Christian home (1940)
The Lord bless thee
The upper room (1939)
Thy will be done! (1937)
Touch me, Lord Jesus (1940)
Travis Avenue
Truett; X1291 Breathe on me
What will you do with Jesus
(1940)
Whisper a prayer (1940)

Maclagan, William Dalrymple,
1826-1910
Bread of heaven (1875)
Lichfield
Newington (1875); X6614 Mac-
lagan
Palms of glory
Prince of Peace (1884)
Troas
Maclean, Joseph
Charlotte (1899)
Craig (1899)
Dabney (1899)
Goetchius (1901)
Holly Springs (1899)
Lenoir (1899)
Plumer (1899)
Preston (1898)
Maclean,, Quentin Stuart Mor-
varen, 1896-
O King of nations (1958)
MacLeod, D. B.
The children's King
McManiman, G. E.
Sovereignty
Macmeikan, J. A.
St Regulus
MacMillan, Ernest Campbell,
1893-
Light of Light
Macmillan, Margaret, 1863-
1903
Roslyn
McNaughton, J. H.
Home (1863); X6423 Love at
home; X11151 There is
beauty all around
McPhail, John

In that day
McPhail, M. L.
The story that never grows
old (1898)
McWhood, Leonard Beecher,
1870-
Hymn of nations (1933)
McWilliams, Clement Charles,
1934-
Dulwich
Magdalen Hospital Hymns, ca
1760
Lyne
Plaistow
Magdeburg, Joachim. Christ-
liche Tischgesänge. Erfurt,
1572
Guds Godhed wil vi prise;
X3651 Gerhardt; X11741
Von Gott will ich nicht
lassen
Maher, William J., S.J. d
1677
Sing of my Savior
Mailloux, Thomas B., C.S.B.
Child of a Virgin (1958)
Main, Hubert Platt, 1839-
1926
Calling to thee
Cassidy (1895)
Clark
Emmanuel
Hold thou my hand
Keep thou my way
My Lord and I
Ninth Street
Ridgefield; X9820 Search
me, O Lord
Staunton
Wellerd
Mainz Gesangbuch, 1661
Lady of the visitation;
X12208 Whither thus in
holy rapture
Mainz; X1422 By the cross;
X10338 Stabat mater
Mainz Gesangbuch, 1833
O God, eternal Father;
X7686 O God, almighty
Father
Mainzer, Joseph, 1801-51
Humility; X6647 Mainzer
Mainzer (1841)

Maker, Frederick Charles,
1844-1927
   All this night; X7299 Nativity
   Cliftonville
   Crossing the bar
   Curfew
   Darmstadt
   Ford Cottage (1909)
   In memoriam
   Invitation (1881); X1981
      Come to the Saviour
   Julian
   Lyndhurst
   Maker; X8299 Paraclete
   Melrose
   Morgenlied (1876)
   Ravensbourne
   Rest (1887); X2958 Elton;
      X12215 Whittier
   St Christopher (1881); X1788
      Christopher; X6662 Maker
   St Germans
   Wentworth (1876)
   Windermere
   Word of life; X3950 Gottlieb
   Zennor
Malan, Henri Abraham César,
1787-1864
   Boynton
   Hendon (1827); X2089 Conse-
      cration; X4794 Holy, holy,
      holy Lord; X6395 Lord,
      we come before thee now;
      X11315 To thy pastures,
      fair
   In His love abiding(1827);
      X4363 Harre meine seele;
      X11769 Wait on God
   Nazareth
   Rosefield
   Silchester
   Welton
Malet, G.E.W., 1839-1918
   Corpus domini
Malim, A.W.
   King of Love; X7010 Mittit
Mallary, R. DeWitt
   Beecroft
   Sojourner
Malley, James
   Lytham
Malmstrom, Carl Sigurd, 1886-
   Chisago (1924)

Mann, Arthur Henry, 1850-
1929
   Allerton
   Beeforth (1885)
   Berno
   Claudius
   King's College
   Lasus (ca 1900); X7480
      Norwich
   Mann; X7372 New Year
   Orient morning (1885);
      X1018 Benediction
   St Asaph
   Silesius
   Stanley
   Valour (1889); X11003 The
      New Year
   Vesper
   Watermouth (1889); X484
      Angel's story; X2277
      Crux Christi; X7481 Nor-
      wich
   Wilton
Manookin, Robert P.
   O sons of Sion
Manx traditional, etc.
   Carol of the Kingdom
   Peel Castle
   Santwat
Marathi (India) traditional
   Tana mana dhana
March, F.K.
   College (1905)
Margetson, E.J.
   Sol justitiae
   Woodworth
Marks, Clement A., 1864-1912
   Ferdinand (1895)
Marks, J. Christopher
   Marthina
Marks, William Edie
   The last mile of the way
Marquis, Robert C.
   It must be told (1893)
Marsh, Charles H., 1886-
   Is it the crowning day (1910)
   One day; X1609 Chapman
Marsh, Simeon Butler, 1798-
1875
   Endor
   Martyn (1834); X5598 Jesus,
      Jesus, come to me; X5624
      Jesus, lover of my soul;

X9005 Reverently and meek-
ly now
Marsh, William J.
In this sacrament (1958)
Michael, prince (1958)
Marshall, John Patton, 1877-1941
Zeal
Marshall, Leonard
Prayer
Marshall, W.S.
Marshall (1876); X1160 Blessed
quietness; X4815 Holy quiet-
ness; X5734 Joys are flow-
ing
Martin, George Clement, 1844-
1916
All Hallows (1892)
Carnarvon
Chilton Foliat
Holy Faith
Israel
Per pacem
St Helen
Martin, George E.
There's a song (New) (1899)
Martin, George William, 1828-81
Leominster (1862); X9302
St Basil
Martin, S. Wesley, 1839-
The gospel bells
Martin, W.
Melmore
Martin, W. Stillman, 1862-1935
Martin (1905); X3799 God
cares; X3857 God will take
care
Mary (religious)
NOTE: The name Mary is con-
sidered as secondary in this in-
dex: e.g., Sister Mary Florian,
S.S.J. will become: Florian, Sr.
Mary, S.S.J. The secular sur-
name is ignored.

Mason, Daniel Gregory, 1873-1953
Deed (1927)
Mason, Harry Silvertone, 1881-
Beacon Hill (1925); X538 "Are
ye able"
Mason, Henry Lowell, 1864-
Exeter (1923)
Mason, John. Companion, 1847
Sion

Mason, Lowell, 1792-1872
NOTE: Some of these tunes
are associated with Mason's
name as compiler and publisher
rather than as composer. Cf.
Baker's Biographical dictionary
for list of his collections.

Admah
Alvan
Anvern
Ashwell
Bealoth (1843); X5089 I love
thy kingdom, Lord
Beethoven
Bethany (1856); X1053 Bethel;
X3183 Excelsior; X7322
Nearer, my God
Bonar
Boylston (1832); X7012
Mixolydian; X7487 Not all
the blood of beasts
Capello
Chimes
Cowper
Cyprus
Daughter of Zion
Denny; X6100 Leon
Diligence (1864); X6458
Lowell; X12453 Work;
X12454 Work, for the
night is coming; X12455
Work song
Dort (1832); X3798 God bless
our native land
Downs
El Paran
Eltham
Elton
Ernan (1850)
Evarts; X10815 The Bride-
groom soon
Gerar; X6302 Lo, what a
pleasing
Haddam
Hamburg (arr) see Plain-
song M 1, "Hamburg"
Hamden
Hartel
Harwell (1841); X7849 O my
Father
Heath (1850); X1378 Bucer
X2029 Communion; X9804

Schumann; X11913 We give
thee but thine
Hebron (1850); X1704 Christ,
in the night; X6352 Lord,
cause thy face; X6774
Mason
Henley (1854)
Herbert
Hermon
Illa
Kane
Laban (1830); X6 A charge
to keep; X7254 My soul
be on thy guard
Magister
Malvern (1847)
Melton
Mendebras (arr) see German
traditional, Mendebras
Meribah (1839); X6723 Mari-
bah
Migdol
Milton
Missionary hymn (1823);
X3528 From Greenland's
icy; X4545 Heber; X6999
Missionary; X7965 O word
of God incarnate; X12342
With happy voices
Mount Vernon; X5692 Jesus,
while our hearts; X10090
Sister, thou was mild
Nashville
Norwich (1825)
Oak; X4525 Heaven is my
home
Olden
Olivet (1833); X7198 My faith
looks up
Olney
Orford
Osgood
Ostend
Ovio
Pentonville
Ripley
Rockingham (1830); X890
Be present at our table;
X4011 Gravity; X9086
Rockingham (New)
Rodman
Sabbath (1824); X9199 Sabbath
morn; X9219 Safely through

another week
Seir
Shawmut
Soto
Sparta
Star of peace; X6190 Light
of life
Stow; X10449 Stowe
Today (1831); X7273 Nain
Unity
Uxbridge (1830); X10135
So let our lips and
Watchman (1830); X11879
Watchman! Tell us
Wesley (1833); X4269 Hail
to the brightness
Zebulon
Zerah; X11316 To us a child
of hope
Mason, Sam
Sing Glory, Hallelujah (1920);
X8667 Proclaim the tidings
Vision (1925)
Mason, Timothy Battle, 1801-61
Eden
Eshtemoa
Masser, John Thornton, 1855-
St Margaret
Mather, William, 1756-1808
Medfield; X668 Attercliffe;
X5106 I pray thee, Lord;
X9949 Sheffield
Mathias, Franz Xaver, 1871-
1939
Eintracht
Matthews, Henry E., arr, 1820.-
Children's praises (ca 1853);
X3757 Glory; X9146 Rowe
Matthews, J.H., 1859-
Belfry praise
Matthews, Timothy Richard,
1826-1910
Bromham (1886)
Chenies (1855); X4992 Hymn
for the month of May
Corfe Mullen
Ludborough (1846)
Margaret (1876); X2948
Elliott
North Coates (1862)
Reynoldstone
Storrs; X9765 Saxby
Matthews, William, 1759-1830

Madrid
Matthias, John B.
   Deliverance will come (1836)
Matthison-Hansen, L.
   Ara
Mattoni, M.
   Joseph, pure spouse
   There is an everlasting home
Maude, Caroline, i.e. Vis-
   countess Hewarden
   Evening hymn
Maunder, John H.
   Martham (1897)
   Parry
   The whole wide world (1894)
Mauro-Cottone, Melchiorre
   Regina caeli laetare (1918)
Mayence see Mainz
Mayer, Frederick Christian, 1882-
   Mayer (1930)
Means, Claude
   Seabury (1941)
Mechlin plainsong
   Stabat Mater, M 4
   Verbum supernum, M 8
      (in Antiphonarium romanum)
Méhul, Etienne-Nicholas, 1763-
1817
   Gilead; X6835 Mehul
   Joseph; X6836 Mehul
Meineke, Charles, 1782-1850
   Gloria Patri (1840)
   Morning Star
   Worship
Meiningen Gesangbuch, 1693
   Munich (Mendelssohn arr);
      X2542 Devotion; X6854 Mein-
      ingen; X7704 O Gott, du
      frommer
   O Gott, du frommer Gott;
      X108 Ach Gott, verlass
      mich; X2350 Darmstadt;
      X7175 Munich; X7697 O God,
      thou faithful; X7711 O Gud,
      du fromme Gud
   St Leonard (Bach arr); X296
      All saints; X810 Bamberg;
      X1975 Come, thou quickening
      Spirit; X2896 Eisenach;
      X3932 Gott des himmels und
      der erden; X4611 Hermanns-
      burg; X4708 Himlens Gud og
      Jordens Herre; X5897 Komm,

o kom, du Geist; X6158
   Liebe die du mich zum;
   X6860 Melanchthon; X11306
   To the Name that brings
Melish, R.
   I heard the voice of Jesus
      say; X2699 Drink to me
      only with; X3252 Far,
      far beyond
Melling, Ellen Knowles
   O say, what is truth
Melodiae Prudentianae, 1553
   Ades pater supreme
Mendelssohn, Felix, 1809-47
   NOTE: Full name, Jacob
Ludwig Felix Mendelssohn-
Bartholdy.

   Almighty Father, hear (1846);
      X381 Almighty Father;
      X897 Be thou faithful;
      X5364 Intercession ([re-
      frain] Callcott)
   Angels' song
   Aspiration
   Birmingham; X1571 Cast thy
      burden on the Lord
   Brightest and best; X1038
      Berlin; X2030 Communion;
      X2098 Consolation; X3292
      Father, to thee we look;
      X3305 Felix; X6885 Men-
      delssohn; X8827 Raynolds;
      X9014 Reynolds
   But the Lord (from St Paul)
   Constancy
   Cyprus; X9970 Sherborne
   Dauchy
   Dusseldorf
   Elijah
   Elven
   Evangelist (1836); X4932 How
      lovely are thy dwellings
   Friend
   Heavenly love; X90 Abiding;
      X5271 In heavenly love
      abiding; X7693 O God, the
      eternal Father; X8912 Re-
      liance; X9822 Seasons;
      X11988 We'll sing the
      songs of Zion; X12528 Yes,
      heaven is the prize
   Holy cross, see Wade, arr

Intercession (refrain only) (1846)
Leipzig
Lift thine eyes (from Elijah)
Lift up your heads
Lord's Day
Mendelssohn (1840); X1059 Beth-
lehem; X1423 By the first
bright Easter Day; X1773
Christmas; X3323 Festgesang;
X4350 Hark! the hearld angels;
X4588 Herald angels; X9847
See! amid the winter's snow;
X11566 Vaterland, in deinen
gauen
O rest in the Lord (from Elijah)
Selwyn; X859 Bartholdy; X3306
Felix
Stukeley; X1395 Bunyan
Trust (1840); X2113 Contempla-
tion; X3815 God is love; X6886
Mendelssohn; X8223 Our guid-
ing star; X11426 Trust, No. 1
Wilson
Meredith, Isaac Hickman, 1872-
Meredith (1900); X1558 Carson;
X9818 Seal us, O Holy Spirit
Stowell (1935)
Merrick, George Purnell, 1840-
Aldersgate
Merrill, William Pierson, 1867-
America befriend (1912); X8942
Republic
Marcus Whitman (1927)
Soldiers of Christ (1895)
Messiter, Arthur Henry, 1834-1916
Marion (1883)
Metcalfe, L. C.
Metcalfe (1925)
Methfessel, Albert Gottlieb, 1785-
1869
Courtland
Methfessel, A. G. Song book, 1818
Salem; X11084 The time is far
spent
Meurers, P.
The very Angels' Bread; X8290
Panis angelicus
Meyer, Franz Heinrich Christoph,
1705-67
Mein Schöpfer, steh mir bei (1740)
Meyer, J.D. Seelenfreud, Ulm, 1692
Es ist kein tag; X6933 Meyer
Rudolstadt; X7263 Naar synderen

ret ser; X12025 Wer weiss,
wie nahe
Meyer, S. W.
Dolut
Michaud, Joseph
Praise we Christ; the King
(1940)
Michel, Abbe
Pie Jesu
Micklem, Thomas Caryl, 1925-
Sandwith
Miles, C. Austin
In the garden (1912?)
Milford, Robin H., 1903-60
Prayers (1925)
Milgrove, Benjamin, 1731-1810
Harts; X4264 Hail! thou liv-
ing Bread; X4370 Hart-
ford; X7751 O how lovely;
X10466 Study song
Harwich (1812)
Mt Ephraim
St Helena (1861)
Millard, Harrison, 1829-95
Abide with me; 'Tis eventide
Miller (no initials)
Tantum ergo
Miller, Anne L.
Vermont (1941)
Miller, Charles Edward, 1856-
Waldrons
Miller, Edward, 1731-1807
Galway
Rockingham, arr (1790);
X1578 Caton; X2031 Com-
munion; X2276 Crux beata;
X6963 Miller; X9087 Rock-
ingham Old
Webbe, arr (ca 1790)
Whitefield
Miller, Harold A.
Branson (1939)
Collegedale (1939)
Jenkins (1939)
Massachusetts (1939)
Preston (1939)
Rogers (1939)
Schroeder (1939)
Vesper (1939)
Wirak (1939)
Woods (1939)
Miller, L. David, 1919-

Fortitudo (1958)
Miller, Robert B.
  Good Shepherd, Rosemont
Miller, Russell King
  Father, let thy blessing
  Sweet Sabbath (1932); X2514
    Despise not, Lord
Miller, Samuel Martin, 1890-
  Daystar (1922)
  Lux dei (1923)
Miller, Selden
  St Stephens' Church
Miller, Walter L.
  Peace, perfect peace
Miller, William
  Going home; X5231 I'm going
    home; X7217 My heavenly
    home is bright
  Land of rest; X7800, O land
    of rest, for thee I sigh;
    X11989 We'll work till Jesus
Milligan, Cleo Cannon
  Pax orbi (1941)
Miner, George A. See Minor,
  George A.
Minke, Emma L.
  Nativity (1899)
Minkler, Ross H.
  A prayer for grace (1936)
Minns, G.
  Wilmar
Minor, George A.
  Bringing in the sheaves; X4380
    Harvest; X10271 Sowing in
    the morning; X11052 The
    sheaves
Minshall, Edward
  Coppee; X10329 Springfield
  Horton
Mishler, Roy S.
  Close to my Savior
Mitchell, Mrs. E. T.
  Claribel, arr
Mitchell, J. S.
  Mitchell
Mitchell, S.
  Pilesgrove
Mitterer, Ignaz Martin, 1850-1924
  A priestly heart (1929)
Mitton, Samuel B.
  Awake! O ye people
Modern harp
  Logan

Moffatt, James, 1870-1944
  Ultima
Mohr, Joseph, S. J., d 1892
  Ave maris stella
  He who once in righteous
    vengeance; X10673 Tan-
    tum ergo
  O King of might and splendor
  Panis angelicus; X9211
    Sacris solemnis
Molthar, Philip Henry
  Gregor's 483d metre (1750);
    X9780 Schlaf, liebes Kind
Mombach, J. S.
  Let there be light
Monaghan, Francis E., C. S. B.
  Behold a simple tender
    Babe (1958)
A Monk of Gethsemani [Monas-
  tery]
  All of seeing
  In this your month (1958)
  Lady in sorrow (1958)
  Lord Jesus, when I think of
    thee (1958)
  Maria, mater gratia (1958)
  O God, thy soldiers' faith-
    ful Lord (1958)
  Prayer of St Francis (1958)
  Sing, my tongue (1958)
  This is the day (1958)
Monk, Edwin George, 1819-
1900
  Angel voices (1861)
  Hopkins
  Monk
  St Ninian (1862)
Monk, Mark James, 1858-
  Campfields
Monk, William Henry, 1823-
89
  Aber
  Adsis, Jesu
  All things bright and beauti-
    ful; X313 All things bright
  Alleluia perenne (1868)
  Ascension (1861); X613 As-
    cension, No. 1
  Beverly (1875); X182 Advent
  Clifton; X7100 Morning
  Colyton
  Coronae (1871); X2245 Crown
    Him

Easter hymn; X5537 Jesus
   Christ is risen today
Evelyns (1875)
Eventide (1861); X86 Abide
   with me; X7030 Monk
Litany
Merton (1850)
Minto
Nutfield (1861)
Plumptre
St Ambrose (1874); X9256
   St. Ambrose, No. 2
St Bernard
St Constantine (1861)
St Ethelwald (1861); X1553
   Carr; X2989 Energy
St Matthias (1861); X6792
   Matthias
St Medan (arr)
St Philip (1861); X7031 Monk
St Sacrament
Supplication
Unde et memores (1875)
Verbum pacis (1889)
Vigilate (1868)
Waltham; X7032 Monk
Words on the cross: The Litany
   (1889); X6249 Litany, No. 10
Wordsworth
Montani, Isabella
   Hail, full of grace (1920)
Montani, Nicola Aloysius, 1880-
1948
   A message from the Sacred
      Heart (1920)
   All ye who seek
   Angels we have heard (1920)
   Ave, regina coelorum (1920)
   By the blood that flowed (1920)
   Christ the Lord is risen today
      (1920)
   Crown Him (1920)
   Daily, daily sing to Mary
      (1920)
   Blest is the Faith
   Dear Angel! ever at my side
   Dear little One! how sweet
      (1920)
   Full of glory (1920)
   Faith of our Fathers (1920)
   Glory be to Jesus
   God of mercy and compassion
      (1920)

Hail, Jesus, hail! (1920)
Hail, Mary, full of grace
   (1920)
Hail, Rock of Ages (1920)
Hark! a mystic voice
   (1920)
Hark! hark! my soul (1920)
Heart of Jesus (1940)
I see my Jesus crucified
Ingrediente domino (1940)
Jesus Christ is risen today
   (1920)
Jesus, gentlest Saviour (1920)
Jesus, my Lord, my God
Just for today
Let the deep organ swell
   (1920)
Mother of Christ (1920)
My God, accept my heart
   (1920)
Now at the Lamb's high
   royal feast (1920)
O blessed father! sent (1920)
O come and mourn (1920)
O dearest Love divine (1920)
O Heart of Jesus
O how I love thee Jesus
   (1925)
O Jesus Christ, remember
   (1920)
O Jesus, thou the beauty art
   (1920)
O Lord, I am not worthy
O purest of creatures
O'erwhelmed in depths of
   woe
Pie Jesu (1936)
Praise to the Holiest (1920)
Praise we our God
Saint of the Sacred Heart
   (1920)
Seek ye a Patron (1920)
Spirit of grace and union
   (1920)
Sweet Saviour! bless us
Tantum ergo
Tantum ergo (1910)
The Word, descending (1920);
   X7886 O salutaris Hostia
Thee prostrate I adore
To Christ, the Prince of
   Peace
To Jesus' Heart, all burn-

ing
To the Name that brings
  salvation (1920)
Unto him, for whom, this
  day
Veni Creator Spiritus
Moody, May Whittle, 1870-
  Moment by moment
Moon, Robert M.
  I am trusting in His word
Moore. Psalm singer's pocket
  companion, 1756
  Glasgow
Moore, C. L.
  Trust in Jesus
Moore, George D.
  My soul in sad exile; X4418
    Haven of rest; X10901 The
    haven of rest
Moore, James C., 1888-
  If only you knew Him (1940)
  Moore (1956)
  Where we' ll never grow old
Moore, W.
  Confidence
Moore, William
  Holy manna; X1305 Brethren,
    we have met
Moore, Willis A.
  Motherhood
Moravian traditional hymns
  Gregor's 39th metre-A; X2053
    Confession; X5173 Ich
    ruehme mich einzig
  Hussite hymn
  Old 26th; X5203 Ihr seelen,
    sinkt, ja sinket hin
Morgan, Alfred Phillips, 1857-
  St Apollos
Morgan, G.A., 1892-1957
  Ashbourne Road
Morgan, Irvin J.
  Mant (1895)
Morice, F.D.
  Ascendit (19th c)
Moring, Karl Johan, 1832-68
  Moring
Morley, Henry L.
  Newcastle (1875)
Morley, Thomas, 1845-91
  Holborn (1891); X10077 Sion
    Muriel
  St Alban's; X2374 David

X7092 Morley
Mornington, Garret Colley
  Wellesley, Earl of, 1735-81
  Chant
  Mornington
Morris, Mrs. C.H., 1862-
1929
  I know God's promise is true
  I will be true to thee (1913)
  In His keeping (1898)
  McConnelsville; X6121 Let
    Jesus come into
  Nearer, still nearer (1898);
    X7122 Morris
  Second coming
  The fight is on (1905)
Morris, Homer F.
  I intend to go through with
    Him
Morris, Reginald Owen, 1886-
1948
  Constantia
  Hermitage
  Winter's snow
Morse, Anna J.
  Consecration (1941)
  Kemper (1941)
Morse, Charles Henry, 1853-
1927
  Seccomb (1893)
Morse, Kenneth I., 1913-
  Years of youth (1951)
Morson, W.C.T.
  Acadia
Mortimer, Alfred G.
  Round the throne of glory
    (1879)
Morton, Alexander B.
  Falconer
  Oliva
  Zeno (1901)
Moschetti, Giuseppi, 1908-
  St Francis
Mosley, T.B.
  I am trusting in my Saviour
  The Lord of glory; X1479a
    Campmeeting (American
    trad)
Moss, Edwin, 1838-
  Cullingworth (1877)
  Llandaff
Moszkowski, Moritz, 1854-
1925

Little flower
Motte, Amanda
   A call for help
Moulton, W. Fiddian
   Advent
   St Beatrice
Mountain, James, 1843-1933
   Jesus, Saviour, blessed
     centre
   O the bitter shame
   Remo; X6198 Like a river;
     X12487 Wye Valley
   Resting; X5579 Jesus, I am
     resting
Mozarabic plainsong, M 5
   Tantum ergo
Mozart, Wolfgang Amadeus, 1756-
91
   NOTE: Full name, Johannes
Chrysostomus Wolfgangus
Theophilus.

   Agnus dei
   Ariel; X7634 O, could I speak;
     X11228 Though in the out-
     ward Church
   Ave, verum corpus
   Cana; X2758 Dwelling place;
     X4924 How goodly is thy
     house; X5471 Janes; X7513
     Novalis; X8388 Peace
   Dona nobis pacem
   Easton
   Ellesdie; X2254 Crucifer;
     X2599 Disciple; X2943 Elles-
     ton; X4356 Hark! the voice
     of Jesus crying; X5582
     Jesus, I my cross; X7488
     Not alone for mighty; X8465
     Pilgrim
   Folsom
   Home
   Jubilee
   Mozart I
   Mozart II; X7508 Nottingham;
     X9500 St Mark; X12577
     Zelotes
   O Gottes Lamm
   Pa jorden är allting forander-
     ligt
   Sonata; X10374a Stars of
     glory
   Stars of glory; X10209a Sonata

Mudie, Thomas Mollison, 1809-
76
   Budleigh
Mueller, Carl F.
   Lone Acre (1941)
   Overlook Park (1939)
Muir, Alexander
   Maple leaf forever
Müller, Hermann von, 1859-
1938 see Bonner, Carey,
1859-1938
Müller, I.
   Fidelis ad mortem
Müller, J.M., 1683-
   NOTE: Associated with a
Choralbuch of the Norwegian
Church.

Müller
   Stobel
Müller, Wenzel, 1767-1835
   Abscheid
Mullinar, Michael
   Billesley (1927)
Munn, Mrs. S.E.
   Father, see thy suppliant
     children
Munson, Kenneth, 1916-
   Cole
Münster Gesangbuch, 1677
   Fairest Lord Jesus; X9788
     Schönster Herr Jesu
Muret, Marc-Antoine, 1526-
85
   Gems of day; X6036 Le ver-
     meil du soliel
Murphy, Joseph A.
   Jesus dulcis memoria (1937)
Murray, A. Gregory, O.S.B.,
1905-
   Anglorum apostolus
   O King of might (1963)
   Surrexit
Murray, J. McCrombie
   Nomen (1894)
Murray, James R., 1841-1905
   Cling to the Bible
   Eudora; X6588 Mabon
   Thanks for the Sabbath School
Murrill, Herbert Henry John,
1909-52
   Arnold
Musgrave, John T.

Evening shadows (1900)
Ford
Musikalisches handbuch Hamburg,
   1690 see Wittwe, Georg ...
Myers, S.S.
   The Lord is in His holy tem-
      ple

N

Nachtenhöfer, Casper Friedrich,
   1624-85
   Cross-bearer (1651); X10132
      So gehst du nun, mein Jesu,
      hin
Naegeli, Johann (Hans) Georg,
   1773-1836
   Dennis; X454 And are we yet
      alive; X1170 Blest be the
      tie; X4920 How gentle
      God's; X6401 Lord's Sup-
      per
   Is there any pleasure
   Naomi; X3298 Father, whate'er
      of earthly bliss
   Pastorale
   Scott
Naff, Edward D.
   We join to pray; X4305 Hand
      in hand
Nafziger, Olive
   My Lord, I'll go
Nanini (or Nanino), Giovanni
   Maria, ca 1545-1607
   Nanini; X7279 Nannini
   Stabat mater
Napleton, John, 1850-
   Woodchester
Nares, James, 1715-83
   Amsterdam (1742); X4079
      Gregor's 56th metre;
      X5184 Ich will's wagen;
      X9909 Service; X11962
      Weimar
   Aynhoe; X7286 Nares
   Westminster New (1762)
Nash, Charles Ellwood, 1855-
   1932
   Lee
Naumburg, S.
   S'u Sh'oreem
Naylor, C.W.
   Once again we come (1907)

Naylor, Edward Woodall, 1867-
   1934
   Farnboro (1894)
   From strength to strength
Naylor, John, 1838-97
   Lift up
   Ringland
Neander, Joachim, 1650-80
   Arnsberg; X3935 Gott ist
      gegenwärtig; X4176
      Gröningen; X9003 Rever-
      ence; X12481 Wunderbarer
      König
   Meine Hoffnung; X12407
      Wondrous gift
   Neander (1680); X2752 Dus-
      seldorf; X4460 He is risen;
      X8308 Paran; X8989 Res-
      urrection; X11511 Unser
      Heerscher [unser König]
   Neander II (1679); X5250
      In Christo gelebt
   Ratisbon, see Werner's
      Choralbuch, 1815
   Sieh hier bin ich, Ehren-
      könig (1679); X4593 Here
      behold me; X5479 Jeg er
      rede til at bede; X6652
      Majesty; X8065 Old 197th
Neefe, Christian Gottlob, 1748-
   98
   Meiringen
Neff, J. Raymond
   He comes
Negro spirituals
   NOTE: Called American folk
   melodies in citation Z. See
   books on Southern (U.S.) tra-
   ditional and Southern spirituals
   for further information on this
   very complicated traditional
   melodic heritage.

   And I couldn't hear nobody
      pray
   Balm in Gilead
   Behold the Star
   Communion spiritual (a Cal-
      houn melody); X6139 Let
      us break bread
   Deep River
   Go down Moses
   Go tell it on the mountains

God's heaven
Goodbye, Mourner
Great day
I have a mother over yonder
I want to be a Christian;
    X6361 Lord, I want to be
    a Christian
In-a this-a band
It's me
Jacob's ladder; X10161 Soldiers
    of the cross
Listen to the lambs
Little David
McKee
My Lord, what a mourning;
    X7230 My Lord, what a
    morning
Nobody knows
O Mary, don't you weep
Steal away
Sweet chariot
The world's desire
    NOTE: Contributed by one
of the Theological Seminaries
in Atlanta, Georgia. It is pre-
sumed to be a Negro tradition-
al spiritual.

War no more
Were you there?
Nellemann, J.
    God's plan
Netherlands . . . see Dutch
Neu Ordentlich Gesangbuch, 1646
    Steadfast; X107 Ach Gott, ver-
    lass mich nicht; X5185 Idag
    er naadens tid
Neues Geistreiches Gesangbuch.
    Halle, 1704 see Freylinghausen.
    Neues Geistreiches Gesangbuch.
    Halle, 1704
Neukomm, Sigismund Ritter von,
1778-1858
    Ames
    St Vincent
    The Seer, Joseph, the Seer
Neumark, Georg, 1621-81
    Neumark (1657); X223 Ah,
    well it is that God should
    read; X691 Augsburg; X1297
    Bremen; X4984 Hvo ene
    lader herren raade; X5195
    If thou but suffer; X12022

Wer nur den lieben Gott
Neumeister, Erdmann, 1671-
1756
    Jesus nimmt die sünder an
    (1718)
Nevin, Alice, 1837-1925
    Resurrection
Nevin, George Balch, 1859-
1933
    Easton
    Fidei defensor (1927)
    Nevin
New Version. Supplement, 1708
    Alfreton
    Folkingham
Newman, Richard S., 1850-
    Companion
    Land of rest (1877)
Newton, Frank E.
    Orwell
Nichol, Henry Ernest, 1862-
1928
    NOTE: Used an acrostic
pseudonym, Colin Sterne.

    Corelli
    Kirk Ella
    Lowell (1905)
    Message (1896); X2345
        Darkness to dawning
Nicholson, Sidney Hugo, 1875-
1947
    Aethelwold
    Airlie
    Bow Brick Hill
    Chislehurst
    Crucifer
    Cumulus
    Feniton
    Hosanna in excelsis
    Leamington
    Litany of the Passion
    Lytlington
    Music-makers (1919)
    St Nicholas
    Tenbury
    Totteridge
    Welcome Yule
    Woodchurch
Nickle, W.S.
    Jesus will bear me o'er
Nicolai, Philip, 1556-1608
    Frankfort (1599); X196 Af

høiheden oprunden er; X4914
How brightly beams; X7118
Morning Star; X7402 Nicolai;
X12089 What tongue can tell;
X12252 Wie schön leuchtet
[der Morgenstern]
  Sleepers, wake (1599); X761
Awake, arise; X4651 Herrn-
hut; X7403 Nicolai; X7527
Now let every tongue; X11758
Wachet auf!; X11772 Wake,
arise; X11773 Wake, awake;
Z12570 Zions vaegter
Nielsen, Ludolf, 1876-1939
  Nielsen
Niemeyer, Edward
  O selig Haus (1854); X4324
Happy home; X7715 O happy
home, where thou art
Nigidius, Petrus, 1501-83
  Die nacht ist kommen (1550)
Niles, John Jacob, 1892-
  Niles (1955)
Nisbet, John MacDonnell, 1857-
  Carden Place
Nitzschke, F.R., 1871-
  Grace (1908)
Noble, Thomas Tertius, 1867-
1953
  Annisquam (1938)
  Bethlem Land
  Ely Cathedral (1895)
  Euroclydon (1918)
  Mauburn (1918)
  New England (1941)
  New York (1917)
  Ora labora (1918)
  Raymond (1917)
  Recessional (1918)
  Rockport (1938)
  St Audrey (1894)
  Santa Monica (1938)
Noelsch, William
  Noelsch
Norden, Norris Lindsay, 1887-
1956
  Around the weary world (1932)
  Giver of all (1932)
  Hymn of spring (1932)
  Loud let the swelling anthems
rise (1932)
  Thy praise, O Lord (1932)
Nordstern. Führer zur Selig-keit,

1671
  Eia, Eia; X12574 Zu Beth-
lehem geboren
Norrbom, August, 1860-
  Augustana (1924)
Norris, J.S.
  Where He leads me; X3397
Follow all the way; X5037
I can hear my Savior;
X7464 Norris
Norris, Thomas, 1741-90
  Chant
Northrop, A.
  Northrop
Norton, Mrs.
  We thank thee, O God, for
the Prophet
Norwegian traditional, etc.
  NOTE: Several melodies have
been specially arranged by
Overby. These are marked
with an asterisk (*) before
the date

  Anxious heart (*1931)
  Behold a host (Grieg arr)
  Blessed host (*1932)
  Deus fortis; X5274 In His
kingdom
  Draw us to Thee
  Far verden, far vel; X11077
The sun has gone down
  Hardy Norsemen
  Hauge; X5269 In heaven
above
  Heavenly treasures (*1931);
X1148 Blessed host;
X2477 Den store, hvite
flokke; X4034 Great white
host; X8739 Purity; X10624
Symphony
  In heaven is joy
  My cross
  Norse air
  O can you sing the new
song (*1932)
  Oslo
  Precious child (*1931)
  Princess Eugenie
  Sabbath chimes (*1931)
  Visions of Christ (*1932)
  What joy to reach (*)
  Yearning (*1931)

Nottingham, S.
  Sponsa
Novello, Francis Vincent, 1781-
  1861
    Albano (1800)
    Children's prayer
    Hail! Jesus, Hail!
Nowakowsky, David
    Descend, O Sabbath Princess
      (1932)
    Evening prayer (1932)
    Sabbath hymn (1932)
Nürnberg. [Broadside publication]
  1541
    Allein zu dir, Herr Jesu
      Christ; X250 Alene til dig,
      Herre Jesus Krist; X4132
      Gregor's 202d metre
Nürnberg Gesangbuch, 1676
    O Jesu Christ, mein lebens
      licht; X4634 Herr Jesu
      Christ, meines lebens licht;
      X7771 O Jesu Christe,
      wahres licht
    Sedulius
Nusbaum, Cyrus S.
    Would you live for Jesus (1899);
      X7586 Nusbaum; X4723 His
      way with thee
Nyberg, Berndt Mikael, 1871-1940
    Nyberg
Nyberg, Hugo, 1873-
    Helsingfors
Nyland. Piae cantiones, 1582
  see Piae cantiones. Griefswald,
  Finland, 1582

                    O

Oakeley, Herbert Stanley, 1830-
  1903
    Abends (1873)
    Dominica (1875); X2637 Domen-
      ica
    Ealing
    Eastwell
    Edina (1868)
    Evangelium
Oakley, W. H.
    Penitence; X2120 Contrition
Oberammergau. Passion Play.
    Oberammergau
O'Connell, William Henry,

Cardinal, 1859-1944
    Hymn to the Holy Name
O'Connor-Morris, G.
    Faith (1932)
Ogden, William A., 1841-97
    Any where, Dear Saviour
    Baptize us anew
    Bring them in; X9959 Shep-
      herd
    Deliverance
    Lovingly, tenderly calling
    Suffer the children to come
      (1894)
    Sweet are the promises;
      X12161 Where He leads
      I'll follow
    Two little hands
    What tender mercy
Ohl, Jeremiah Franklin, 1850-
  1941
    Come and hear the grand
      old story (1886)
    Evening (1884)
    Gerhardt (1915)
    Lewars (1893)
    Pilgrim
    St Chrysostom (1910)
    Shelter (1912)
    Theodoret (1887)
    Theophilus (1885)
Ohl, Wesley Jacob, 1864-
    Trust (1887)
O'Kane, Tullius C., 1830-
  1912
    Church of God, awake
    Home over there; X7923
      O think of the home;
      X10914 The home over
      there
    Mighty rock
    O'Kane; X8097 On Jordan's
      stormy banks
Ola Olude, A. T. see Olude,
    A. T. Ola
Oldberg, Arne
    Gilder (1905)
Olds, William B.
    Fons sempiternus (1937)
    Pioneers (1937)
Oliver, George Edgar
    Albany
    Livingston
    Oliver

Oliver, Henry Kemble, 1800-85
   Federal Street (1832)
   Harmony Grove
   Merton
   Saxony
Oliver, Richard J.
   He was wounded
Olivers, Thomas, 1725-99
   Helmsley
Olsson, Otto Emanuel, 1879-
   Transfiguration
Olude, A.T. Ola
   Nigerian tune
Omaha (Indian) traditional
   Omaha Peace song
Oratory hymns [Chester?]
   Chester; X11531 Urania
Oudaen, J. Amsterdam Psalter,
 1685
   Vreuchten; X2401 De liefde vo-
     ortgebracht; X2806 Easter-
     tide; X3326 Festival carol;
     X11206 This joyful Easter-
     tide
Ouseley, Frederick Arthur Gore,
 1825-89
   Aberystwyth (1861); X10742
     Tenbury
   All things bright
   Bewdley
   Blackie
   Christchurch
   Contemplation
   Glory in the highest (1877);
     X5261 In excelsis gloria
   Hereford
   Pruen
   St Gabriel (1868); X3560
     Gabriel
   St Theoctistus (1882)
   Sharon (1875)
   Tenbury
   Woolmer's
Overby, Oscar Rudolph, 1892-
   Our Christ
Owen, Frank K.
   Knickerbocker (1941)
Owen, Morfydd, 1892-1918
   Richard
Owen, R.T.
   Open wide thy heart
Owen, William, 1814-93
   Bryn Calfaria; X1154 Blessed

   Lord, in thee; X7147
   Mount Calvary
   Prysgol
   What did He do?

P

Paderborn Gesangbuch, 1765
   O purest of creatures;
     X4236 Hail! Glorious St
     Patrick; X6576 Lyons
     (Haydn); X7603 O blessed
     St Patrick; X8264 Pader-
     born
Pados, Virginia Bogdan
   O love that nothing can efface
     (1943)
Page, Arthur, 1846-
   Lord of might
Paine, John Knowles, 1839-1906
   Harvard Hymn
   Lincoln (1873)
Paisiello, Giovanni, 1741-1816
   Vigil; X4742 Holborn
Palestrina, Giovanni Pierluigi,
 ca 1525-94
   Praeneste
   Tantum ergo, No. 2
   Victory (1588); X8268
     Palestrina; X9751 Savior,
     Redeemer, God of Love;
     X12520 Ye sons and
     daughters
Palmer, Horatio Palmer, 1834-
 1907
   Christ is knocking (1879);
     X9926 Shall I let Him in
   Come, sinner, come; X12180
     While Jesus whispers
   Follow me; X2766 Each coo-
     ing dove
   Memories of Galilee
   Peace, be still!; X6779
     Master, the tempest
   Precious Saviour, dear
     Redeemer
   Rose of Sharon
   Vincent (1887); X5768 Just
     for today; X6356 Lord,
     for tomorrow
   Yield not to temptation (1868);
     X3444 Fortitude; X8277
     Palmer

Palmer, M.
  Clair Market
Palmer, Peggy Spencer, 1900-
  see Spencer Palmer, Florence
  Margaret, 1900-
Palmer, W. St Clair
  Clolata
Palssan, Bjarna, 1857-87
  Hin maeta morgunstunden
Paris Antiphoner, 1681
  Annue Christe
  Christi sanctorum
  O quanta qualia; X5439 Itala
    X8892 Regnator orbis
  Sol praeceps rapitur (plainsong,
    M 3)
Paris Gradual, 1685
  Antiphoner
Paris Gradual, 1689
  Solemnis haec festivitas
The Parish choir, 1850
  Innocents; X600 As the sun
    doth daily; X1772 Christmas
    (Handel)
Parker, Edwin Pond, 1836-1925
  Dawn
  Love's offering (1888)
Parker, Handel, 1857-1929
  Deep harmony
Parker, Horatio William, 1836-
1919
  Ancient of Days (1903)
  Auburndale (1893)
  Clovelly (1903)
  Courage
  Foundation (1903)
  Garden City (1893); X2389
    Day of praise
  Holy Day
  Jubilate (1894); X8906 Rejoice,
    the Lord is King
  King of Glory
  Mission (1894)
  Mount Sion (1886)
  Parker (1894); X11645 Vexilla
    regis
  Pax veritatis (1918)
  Pixham (1901)
  Pro patria (1900); X1164
    Blessing and honor; X8315
    Parker
  Stella (1893); X8316 Parker
  Victor's crown (1893)

Vox aeterna (1903)
Whittingham (1887)
Parker, James Cutler Dunn,
1828-1916
  God hath sent his angels;
    X2789 Easter angels
Parker, Leonard
  Panoply of light
Parker, Robert
  St Alkmund (1868)
Parkyn, Walter A.
  Vesper
Parr, Henry, 1815-
  St Quintin (1834)
Parratt, Walter, 1841-1924
  Huddersfield
  Obiit
  Parratt (1904)
Parry, Charles Hubert Hastings,
1848-1918
  Angmering
  Bishopthorpe
  Bournemouth
  Freshwater
  Infantium laudes
  Intercessor (1904)
  Jerusalem
  Jubilate
  Laudate dominum
  Marylebone
  Nature
  Newfoundland
  Repton
  Rustington
Parry, Edwin F.
  Hail to the brightness
  O holy words of truth
Parry, Joseph, 1841-1903
  Aberystwyth (1879)
  Dinbych
  Llangristiolus
  Merthry Tydvil; X2578 Dies
    irae
  O home beloved, where'er I
    wander
  St Joseph
Parsons, Ernest J.
  Sturges (1941)
Patton, Arthur St George, 1853-
92
  St Kevin
  Vigil
Peace, Albert Lister, 1844-

1912
  Crux crudelis
  Edom (1885)
  Fight of faith
  Green Hill (1885)
  Guild
  Lux beata
  St Margaret (1885); X6443
    Love that will not let me
    go; X6711 Margaret
  Submission
Peace, Lister R., 1885-
  Nova vita (1914)
Pearce, James
  Protection
Pearsall, Robert Lucas de, 1795-
1856
  Gloria
  Pearsall (1863); X4247 Hail!
    holy Joseph
  St Hildred
Peek, Joseph Yates, 1843-1911
  Peek; X5155 I would be true
Peel, Frederick
  Heslington (1893)
  Heslington, No. 2 (1894)
Peery, Rob Roy, 1900-
  Byrd (1929)
  Stirewalt (1927)
Peloquin, C. Alexander
  O Jesu! life-spring (1959)
Penn, W.E.
  The sheltering rock
Penner, Edwin
  Trust your hand into His
Pensum Sacrum. Görlitz, 1648
  Herr Jesu Christ, dich zu uns
    wend
  NOTE: John Hus is the supposed
composer, cf books AZ and BA
herein; X312 All things are thine;
    X1508 Cantionale; X4977 Hus;
    X6368 Lord Jesus Christ,
    be present now; X8566 Prague;
    X11963 Weimar
Perkins, C.W.
  Heathfields
Perkins, E.A.
  Perkins
Perkins, Emily Swan, 1866-
  Burg (1921)
  Eastman (1937)
  Good cheer (1927)

Laufer (1925)
Peterson (1921)
Riverdale
Perkins, Henry Southwick,
1833-1914
  Victors
Perkins, Theodore Edson, 1831-
1912
  Caskey
  Freely give
  Lundie; X3207 Fade, fade,
    each earthly joy; X6823
    Meditation; X8430 Perkins
  Magill
  More love to Thee (1875)
  Nazareth
  Repentance
  Sabbath Evening
  The love of Jesus
  Wyoming
Perkins, Thomas E.
  On the radiant threshold
    (1923)
Perkins, William Oscar, 1831-
1902
  Amara
  Beyond the sunset
  Did you think to pray; X2657
    Don't forget to pray;
    X3016 Ere you left your
    room
  Guernsey
  Jesus, thou hast promised
  Only thee
Perosi, Don Lorenzo, 1872-
1956
  L'Emmanuello; X5621 Jesus,
    Lord, be thou mine own
  O cor Jesu
  O sacrum convivium
  Tantum ergo (1937)
Perry, E. Cooper
  Spes unica (1889)
  Vesalius (1895)
Perry, J.C.
  Bid them look to Christ
Perry, S.J.
  Saviour, we come to thee
Persichetti, Vincent, 1915-
  Contrition
  Lament (1956)
Peruchot, Luigi
  The heavens are Thine

Pescott, Frank Denty, 1880-
  Guernsey
Peter, Christopher, 1626-69
  Christopher; X5201 Ihr
    gestirn'
  Das herrlich hohe fest (ca 1674)
Petersen, H. H.
  O'er the gloomy hills of dark-
    ness
  There is an hour of peace
Peterson, Samuel E., 1869-
  Rondthaler
Pettet, A., ca 1785- ca 1845
  Hic breve vivitur
Pettman, Charles Edgar, 1866-
  1943
  Love incarnate
Pfautsch, Lloyd, 1921-
  Euclid (1964)
Phillips, H.
  New Sabbath (ca 1806)
Phillips, Philip, 1834-75
  Home of the soul; X5148 I will
    sing; X5151 I will sing you
    a song
  One sweetly solemn thought
  Pilgrims mission
Phillips, Thomas, 1735-1807
  Lydia
Piae Cantiones. Griefswald, Fin-
  land, 1582
    NOTE: See Oxford book of
carols, p. 291, for the history
of this book.

  Athens
  Congaudeat
  Divinum mysterium (13th c
    plainsong M 5); X2141 Corde
    natus; X2143 Corde natus ex
    parentis
  Ein kind geborn; X2419 Dear
    Maker of the starry skies;
    X5249 In Bethlehem, that
    fair city; X8726 Puer natus
  Gabriel's message
  In vernali tempore; X10323
    Spring has come
  January carol
  O mentes perfidas
  Psallat fidelis concio
  Puer nobis nascitur; X8090
    Omega and alpha; X8733

  Puer nobis nascitur;
    X9840 Sedulius; X10307
    Splendour; X11515 Unto
    us a boy is born
  Tempus adest floridum;
    X3905 Good King Wences-
    las
  The word itself
  Theodoric; X8104 On this day
    earth shall ring; X8433
    Personent hodie; X10057
    Sing aloud on this day
Piel, P.
  Ad sacratissimum cor Jesu
  Daily, daily sing to Mary
  Dear crown of all the virgin
    choir
  O heart of Mary
  With tender greeting
Pieraccini, Emilio, 1828-1902
  Santa Trinita; X1941 Come,
    Holy Ghost, who ever one;
    X11381 Trinity
Pierce, Jason Noble, 1880-
  Penfield
Pierre, Maitre, see also French
    Psalter, 1562 and Gene-
    van Psalter, 1562
  Dominus sanctus (1562)
  Gloria (1562)
  Pierre (1562)
  Sovereign grace (1562)
  Trumpet (1562)
Pierson, Hugo
  For thee, O dear, dear
    country
Pilgrimsharpan
  Mer helighet gif mig
Pilsbury. United States'
  harmony, 1799
    Bartimaeus; X1614 Charles-
    ton; X1616 Charlestown
Pincott, Frank
  Christ, my Life
Pinder, F.
  Temple Boro
Pisani, Umberto
  Armoria Biblica
  Pisani
Pitts, William S., 1829-1903
  Princethorpe; X8493 Pitts
  Wildwood; X6254 Little brown
    church

Plainsongs

NOTE: It has seemed more practical to arrange by traditional tune name (followed by mode number), than numerically by mode. Few source notes are given.

It must be remembered that countless additional plainsongs are cited under place name, rite, publication, or personal name (when presumed accurate).

A solis ortus cardine M 3
Adesto, Sancta Trinitas M 3
Aeterna Christi munera M 7
Alma redemptoris Mater M 5
Annue Christi, saeculorum Domini M 1
Attende M 5; X667 Attende, Domini
Audi, benigne conditor M 2 (major reading)
Audi, benigne conditor M 3 (minor reading)
Aurora lucis rutilat, Pt. I, M 4; X1829 Claro paschali gaudio
Ave Maria M 1
Ave, maris stella M 1
Ave, Regina caelorum M 6
Bone pastor M 7 (12th c)
Christe, qui lux es et dies (ca 600); X1747 Christe, der du bist tag und licht; X4069 Gregor's 22d metre-D; X8555 Prague
Christe qui lux es et dies M 2
Christe sanctorum decus angelorum M 8
Clarum decus jejunii M 2
Cor Jesu sacratissimum M 1
Cultor dei, memento M 8
Dies irae (13th c)
Ecce nomen Domine Emmanuel
Ecce! Panis angelorum M 8; X5998 Lauda Sion
Ecce tempus idoneum M 3
Eia, Jesu adorande M 3
Ex more docti mystico M 2
Exultet caelum laudibus M 4
Exultet caelum laudibus M 8; X2529 Deus, tuorum militum
Felix dies M 2

Gestum matris gloriosae M 2
Gloria, laus et honor M 1
Hamburg M 1 (Lowell Mason arr, 1844); X1232 Boston; X11733 Voice divine; X12122 When I survey the wondrous cross
Hostis Herodes impie M 3
In dich hab ich Gehofft, Herr (Jan Kern arr, 1964)
In manus tuas M 6
In manus tuas M 6
In manus tuas (Eastertide) M 6
Iste confessor
Iste confessor M 2
Iste confessor M 8
Jam Christus astra ascenderat M 1
Jerusalem et Sion filiae M 5
Jesu, quadragenariae M 4; X7851 O nata lux de lumina; X9646 Salutis humanae sator
Laetabundus M 5 (11th c)
Languentibus in purgatorio
Lauda Sion M 7 (12th c)
Magnae Deus potentiae M 2
Martyr Dei M 6
Mundi salus affutura M 8
Nazareth (arr by S. Webbe)
Non nobis, Domini
Nunc Sancte M 8
Nunc Sancte, nobis, Spiritus M 4
O amor quam ecstaticus M 1
O Emmanuel (major antiphon) M 2
O gloriosa virginum M 2
O salutaris Hostia M 7
O salutaris Hostia M 8
Olmutz M 7 (arr by Lowell) Mason, 1834)
Optatus votis M 4
Oremus pro Pontifice M 1
Our Father
Palm Sunday anthem M 1
Parce, Domini M 1
Paule, doctor egregie M 7
Prayer for a holy death M 1
Puer natus in Bethlehem M 1
Quem terra, pontus, aethera

M 2
Rector potens, verax Deus M 2
Regina caeli laetáre M 6
Rerum Deus tenax vigor M 4
Rorate, caeli M 1
St Gregory (arr by Joseph
  Barnby)
Salus aeterna M 7 (before
  11th c)
Salve, Mater M 5
Salve Regina M 5
Save us waking
Sponsa Christi quae per orbem
  M 1-2
Sub tuum praesidium M 7
Tantum ergo M 5
Te, Joseph, celebrent M 1
Te lucis, arr
Te lucis ante terminum M 8
To God on high (adapted, in
  Schumann, Gesangbuch, 1539)
  X249 Alene Gud i Himmerig;
  X275 All glory be to thee;
  X341 Allein Gott in der höh
  sei ehr; X669 Attolle paulum;
  X2430 Decius; X2910 Elberfeld;
  X3696 Give thanks to God;
  X4280 Halle; X6486 Lucis
  creator optime; X9565 St
  Peter
Ut queant laxis M 2
Veni Emmanuel M 1; X7631
  O come, O come, Immanuel;
  X11592 Veni, Immanuel;
  X11601 Veni, veni Emmanuel
Veni, O Sapientiae
Veni, Redemptor gentium M 1;
  X916 Beata nobis gaudia
Victimi Paschali M 1 (major
  reading) (12th c); X1712
  Christ ist erstanden; X1721
  Christ lag in todesbanden
Victimi Paschali M 1 (minor
  reading) (12th c)
Virginia proles M 8
Westmoreland (arr by Barnby)
Planque (no initials)
  O cor amoris victima
Playford, John. Whole book of
  Psalms, 1677
  Worcester
Pleyel, Ignaz Joseph, 1757-1831
  Brattle Street

Grace Church (1815); X9581
  St Polycarp
Onido
Pleyel's Hymn (1791); X8517
  Pleyel; X11185 Thine for-
  ever; God of love
Savannah
Seasons; X5975 Larue
Plymouth collection see
  Beecher, H.W. Plymouth
  collection
Poitiers Antiphoner, 1746
  Auctoritate saeculi; X5559
  Jesu, dulcedo cordium
Poitiers Vesperale, 1740
  Rouen; X5426 Iste confessor
Polack, Herman Adolph, 1862-
  1930
  Clairvaux (1910)
  Horeb (1910)
Polish traditional, etc.
  Come, O Lord Jesus
  Poland; X11583 Veni Creator
  Spiritus
  Slumber, O slumber
  Teshiniens (ca 1500)
  W Zlobie Lezy; X5334 Infant
  holy; X8526 Polish carol
  Warsaw
Polleri, G. B.
  Ecce panis angelorum; X1206
  Bone pastor
Pollock, Charles Edward, 1853-
  Abide with me, I need thee
  Bless the words; X1555 Car-
  rington; X10642 Take my
  heart, O Father
  Come to Jesus
  Come, ye wanderers
  Forever here my rest; X9212
  Sadie
  Full salvation
  Gouldie
  He knoweth the way that I
  take
  Home of the soul
  How oft, alas; X6797 May
  I bring my sins to Jesus
  I love to steal awhile away;
  X6093 Lella
  I love to think of my home;
  X7218 My home above
  I wonder

Lead me on
Morrow's Hill
My God, how endless is thy
    love; X7396 Nicholls
Nearing the port
O holy day
Often weary and worn; X8975
    Rest by and by
Open the wells of salvation
Parousia; X6294 Lo! He
    comes, with clouds descend-
    ing
Praise the Lord
Precious Jesus, O to love
    thee (1901)
Salonica
Shoemaker
Some near, near day
There are hearts that never
    falter (1901)
Thou art the way; X7278
Nannie
Violet
Walk daily with your Saviour
Wonderful grace
Pond, Sylvanus Billings, 1792-
1871
    Armenia (1835)
    Henry (1835)
    The bird let loose see Frank-
        lin Square (perhaps by S.B.
        Pond, 1850)
    The heavens
Ponsonby, A.B.
    Deo gratias (1913)
Pontius, William H.
    Eighmey (1905)
    Holy Hill (1905)
    Waiting and watching
Poole, Clement William 1828-
1924
    Petersham
Poole, Henry James, 1843-97
    St Lucy
Poppen, Emmanuel, ca 1870-1950
    Joy (1904)
    Poppen (1910)
    Sidney
    Wonder (1907)
Popple, Herbert
    St Aidan (1931)
Porter, Hugh Boring, 1897-
    Builders (1927)

Renascence (1927)
Porter, John, pseud see
    McCutchan, Robert Guy,
    1877-
Portnersches Gesangbuch, 1831
    O Christliche herzen
Portugal (or Portogallo), Mar-
    cos Antonio da Fonseca
    (real name Ascençao) 1762-
    1830.
    Sicilian Mariners (1794)
        NOTE: Sometimes attri-
buted to this author. The dates
correspond, but Baker's Bio-
graphical dictionary makes no
mention.
Portuguese melody
    Ecce panis angelorum
Poteat, Edwin McNeill, 1892-
1955
    Bow down thine ear
    Oikoumenikos
    Quest
Pothier, Joseph, O.S.B.,
1835-1923
    Thou that art so fair
Powell, C., 1855-1934
    What do I owe?
Powell, James Baden, see
    Baden-Powell, James
Powell, Joseph P.
    Sorrows
Powell, Robert J., 1932-
    Author of life (1964)
Praetorius, Michael, 1571-
1621
    NOTE: Name, originally
Schultheiss, was Latinized.

    Ach Herr
    Das alte Jahre ist nun
        dahin (1609)
    Es geh, wies woll (1610);
        X3067 Et trofast hjerte,
        Herre min
    Ich dank' dir schon (1610);
        X4064 Gregor's 15th
        metre
    Melody (1610)
    Praetorius I (1599); X3554
        Für dein empfangen speis
        und trank
    Praetorius II (1536 mel.

arr. 1609); X111 Ach Gott
vom himmelreiche; X5219
I'll Thee exalt
Wenn meine sünd (1609)
Pratt, John Barnes, 1865-
Dorothy (1929)
Presbrey, O. F.
Not half has ever been told
Price, Carl Fowler, 1881-
Ferree
Milburn (1941)
The Morning Watch (1913)
Washington (1905)
Price, John (Beulah), 1857-
Gwyneth
Price, Tom, 1857-1925
Bugail Israel
Joseph
Prichard, Rowland Hugh, 1811-87
Hyfrydol (1830); X5278 In
humility, our Saviour
Pritchard, Thomas Cuthbertson
Leithead, 1885-
Belhaven (1927)
Gifford (1927)
Leithead (1927)
Prothero, H. A.
St Ninian
Prout, Ebenezer, 1835-1909
Allen; X4052 Greenwood
Cairnbrook
Hurst Monceaux
Laus sempiterna
Raleigh
Via lucis
Prys, Edmund. Psalms, 1621
St Mary; X9510 St Mary's
The Psalmist, 1830
Halle
Psalmodia Evangelica, 1789
Bromsgrove
Psalteriolum harmonicum, 1642
Ave Maria klare
Psalterium chorale. Constance,
1510
Beata nobis gaudia; X1638
Cherubic hymn
Public School hymn book, 1929
Pax
Pullen, Alice M.
Cottingham (20th c)
Purcell, Henry, ca 1659-95
Bow down in worship

Burford
The Lord bless you
Walsall (1699)
Westminster Abbey
Purday, Charles Henry, 1799-
1885
Notting Hill
Sandon (1860)
Putman, L. G.
Christus rex
Pyper, George D.
Does the journey seem
long?

Q

Quaile, Robert Newton, 1867-
Athlone (1911)
Old Bridge (1903); X10772
Thanksgiving

R

R. E.
Boxted (1935)
R. J. C.
Calvert (1910)
Rader, Paul
Only believe (1921)
Randall, John, 1715-99
Cambridge; X1472 Cam-
bridge new; X8796 Ran-
dall
Lewes
Randall; X1601 Chant
Randegger, Alberto, 1832-1911
Evening prayer
Rappaport, S.
The Lord -- The Lord of
glory reigns
Rau, Albert George
Unami (1889)
Rau, Robert, 1844-1906
Grabesruhe (1864); X8817
Rau; X9163 Ruhe ist des
todes schlummer
Nightfall (1877)
Ravanello, Oreste, 1871-1938
Gloria, laus et honor
Tantum ergo
Ravenscroft's Psalter, 1621
Bristol; X1332 Bristol, No.
1

Durham
Gloucester
Lincoln
Norwich
Old 104th; X8821 Ravenscroft
Remember; X429 America
   (Thesaurus musicus, 1740)
St David; X9359 St David's
Salisbury
Raymond-Barker, C., S.J.
   Let the deep organ swell
Read, David (or Daniel), 1757-
1836
   Lisbon; X959 Begin the day
      with God
   Windham
Reay, Samuel, 1822-
   Brotherhood
   Chorley (1876)
   Comforter Divine
   Laus sempiterna
   Undique gloria (1872)
Recueil de cantiques
   Swiss melody; X8482 Pilgrims
      of the night
Redhead, Richard, 1820-1901
   Alma Mater
   Holy Offerings (1870)
   Lauds (1850)
   Metzler's Redhead No. 66
      (1859); X6931 Metzler;
      X8864 Redhead; X8872
      Redhead, No. 66; X11891
      Waveney
   Petra (1853); X230 Ajalon;
      X3667 Gethsemane; X8865
      Redhead; X8873 Redhead,
      No. 76
   Redhead
   Redhead, No. 1 (1870); X5430
      "It is finished"
   Redhead, No. 46; X2693 Dres-
      den; X6017 Laus deo
   St Chad
   St Ebbe (1853)
   St Nicholas (1859); X2428
      Debenham; X9531 St Nicholas;
      X10367 Star of Jacob
   St Prisca (1853); X8866 Red-
      head; X8871 Redhead, No.
      47; X8973 Rest; X9363 St
      Dunstan; X10747 Tenebrae
   St Victor

Wolverhampton
Redner, Lewis Henry, 1831-
1908
   St Louis (1868); X1060 Beth-
      lehem; X7807 O little
      town of Bethlehem
Reed, Luther Dotterer, 1873-
   Mount Airy (1958)
Rees, Gomer Christmas, 1872-
   Resolven (1915)
Rees, John Thomas, 1858-1912
   Dole
Regnart (or Regnard), Jacob,
ca 1540-99
   Göttingen (1574); X686 Auf
      meinen lieben Gott; X4085
      Gregor's 75th metre; X
      8891 Regnart; X3543 Fryd
      dig, du kristi brud
Reichardt, Louise (or Luise),
1779-1826
   Schlaf, Kindlein, schlaf;
      X10106 Sleep, holy Babe
Reimann, John Balthasar, 1702-
49
   O herre Gott, in meiner
      Not (1747)
   O Jesu (1741); X7780 O Jesu,
      warum legst
   Reimann's 315th metre (1747);
      X8895 Reimann; X12380
      Wollt ihr wissen was
Reinagle, Alexander Robert,
1799-1877
   Ben Rhydding
   Kidlington (1865)
   Leigh
   Moccas
   St Peter (1836); X7211 My
      God, I love thee; X9570
      St Peter's, Oxford
Reinecke, Carl Heinrich Car-
sten, 1824-1910
   Evening prayer
   Morning prayer
   Tenderness
Reinigius, P. Haus Kirchen
Cantorie, 1587
   O Jesu Christ
Reissiger, F.A., 1809-83
   Lord of spirits
Reissiger, Karl Gottlieb, 1798-
1859

Beloit
Reitz, Albert S., 1879-
    Reitz (1925)
Remondi, R.
    O sacrum convivium
Remsberg, Wilson L.
    Hope
Rendle, Lily, 1875-
    Ellah (1928)
    Everyland, No. 1 (1933)
    Mariners (1935)
    Pax (1928)
    Vesper hymn (1930)
Reuter, Friedrich Otto (Fritz),
    1863-1924
    New Ulm (1910)
    Reuter
The Revivalist, 1869
    Peace
Reynolds, Isham E., 1879-1949
    Jesus, my Lord, is real to
        me (1933)
    Lura; X12151 When the sun
        shines bright
    Venting (1925); X12399 Wonder-
        ful peace
Reynolds, William J., 1920-
    Create in me
Rheinberger, Josef Gabriel, 1839-
    1901
    O salutaris hostia
Rheinhardt, J.H. Choralbuch.
    Uttingen, 1754
    Was lebet, was schwebet;
        X11543 Uttingen
Rice, Elihu S.
    Shall we meet (1866)
Rich, C.B.
    Comfort (1932)
    Compassion
Richards, B.
    Let the whole creation ring
Richards, Charles H.
    Redeemer's praise
Richards, G. Darlington
    Holmbush (1938)
    Julian (1939)
Richards, Henry Brinley, 1817-89
    NOTE: Used pseud Emmelar.
    Armstrong; X9031 Richards;
        X12527 Yes, for me He
        careth
Richards, John (Isalaw), 1843-

1908
    Sanctus
Richardson, John J., 1816-79
    Again the slowly circling
        year
    Hail, thou Star of Ocean
    Love
    Tichfield; X1421 By the
        blood that flowed
Richter, Christian Friedrich,
    1676-1711
    Gregor's 114th metre (1714);
        X6843 Mein Salomo, dein
        freundliches
    Wie gross ist des allmacht'
        gen güten (1703)
Rider, H. deK.
    Angelus
    Gentle Saviour
Ridsdale, Charles Joseph, 1840-
    None other Lamb
Righini, Vincenzo, 1756-1812
    Righini
Rimbault, Edward Francis,
    1816-76
    Delhi
    Happy day (1854)
    Clarion
Rinck, Johann Christian Hein-
    rich, 1770-1846
    Alle jahre wieder
    Overberg
    St Lucian; X70 Abend [ist es
        wieder]; X3152 Evening
        sun descending; X8767
        Rabenlei
Rinder, Reuben R.
    Psalm 42 (1932)
    Thou ever present Perfect
        Friend (1932)
Rinehart, Thomas Franklin,
    1860-
    Adrian (1901)
Robbins, Howard Chandler,
    1876-1952
    Chelsea Square (1941)
Roberts, Arthur Owen, 1869-
    1952
    Blodyn
    Hoylake
Roberts, Caradog, 1878-1935
    Berwyn
    Margaret

Rachie
Roberts, David E., 1863-
    Goodwill (1925)
Roberts, J. Varley
    Elm
Roberts, John (Ieuan Gwyllt)
    1822-77
    Ardudwy
    Bethel
    Bont-Newydd
    Four Seas (1859)
    Liverpool
    Moab (1870)
    Rheidol
Roberts, John Dryhurst, 1862-
    Caergybi (1883)
Roberts, John Henry, 1848-1924
    O grant us light
Roberts, Robert, 1863-
    Alice
Roberts, Robert Edwin, 1878-
1940
    Philippine
Robertson, Leroy J., 1896-
    Go, ye messengers
    God of our fathers, known of
        old; X6376 Lord of all
        being
    Great King of heaven
    I'm a pilgrim; I'm a stranger
    Let earth's inhabitants rejoice
    Lo! on the water's brink
    O happy home! O blest abode
    The glorious gospel light
    Up! arouse thee, O beautiful
        Zion
    Upon the cross of Calvary
    We love thy House, O God
Robertson, Robert B.
    Snowden
Robinson, W. O.
    M. I. A. we hail thee
Roe, John Edward, 1838-71
    Gentle Jesus
    Onward (1870)
    Weston
Roff, Joseph
    Great King of Peace (1959)
Rogers, Benjamin, 1614-98
    Hymnus eucharisticus; X6628
        Magdalen Tower hymn;
        X10985 The Magdalen
        Tower hymn

Rogers, H. E.
    Church of God
Rogers, James Hotchkiss,
    1857-1940
    A little kingdom I possess
        (1932)
    Lo, our Father's tender
        care (1932)
    May He who kept us (1932)
    Thankful hearts (1932)
    The wise may bring their
        learning (1932)
    The worth of suffering
        (1932)
    Uplift the song of praise
        (1932)
    We build our school on thee
        (1932)
    We thank thee (1932)
Rogers, W. J.
    Humble thyself to walk
Roh, Johann, d 1547 see
    Horne, Johann, d 1547
Rolle, Johann Heinrich, 1716-
85
    Praise the Lord
Roman hymnal (date unknown)
    Consecration to Our Lady
    What mortal tongue can
        sing
The Roman hymnal, 1884
    O Mother blest
Ronan, John E.
    Out of the depths (20th c)
Rooper, J. B.
    Risby (1925)
Root, George Frederick, 1820-
95
    NOTE: Pseud Friedrich
Wurzel
    Beauteous day
    Children of Jerusalem
    Clymer
    Come to the Saviour (1870)
        X5382 Invitation
    Ellon (1871); X5092 I love
        to hear the story;
        X10443 Story of love
    Firmament
    Harvest home; X7954 O,
        where are the reapers
    In the silent midnight
        watches

Jesus loves the little children
Like a strong and raging fire;
    X9793 School thy feelings;
    X11170 There's a song
Lyra
Now to Jesus Christ
Quam dilecta
Return, O wanderer
Rialto; X2239 Crossing the
    bar
Ring the bells of heaven
Rosedale
Sheffield; X12241 Why do you
    wait?
Shining Shore; X7194 My days
    are gliding
The hem of His garment
Varina (1856); X3195 Extol
    the love of Christ; X11141
    There is a land
When He cometh (1866); X5696
    Jewels
Roper, Charles F.
    Arimathea
    Blessed morn (1883)
    Jerusalem (1872)
Rosche, George F.
    A shelter in the time of
        storm (1894)
    Have faith in God
    He keepeth me ever (1891)
Rosecrans, James H.
    Glenn (1890)
    Worley
Rosenmüller, Johann, ca 1620-
84
    Calvary (1655)
    Nassau; X1209 Bonn; X2062
        Confirmation; X6606 Mache
        dich, mein geist; X7401
        Nicolai; X9529 St Nicolai;
        X9865 Segne uns; X10243
        Songs of praise; X10453
        Straf mich nicht; X11354
        Traeder nu til Herrens
        Bord; X12334 Wirtemburg;
        X12482 Würtemburg
    Rosenmüller (1649)
Rosenroth, Christian Knorr von,
1636-89
    Old 29th; X2122 Contrition;
        X4686 Hier legt mein sinn
Ross, Roger Rowson, 1817-99

St Peter's, Manchester;
    X9567 St Peters'
Ross, William Baird, 1871-
1951
    Carillon (1925)
Rossini, Gioachino Antonio,
1792-1888
    Captain of Israel's host
    Elation
    Faith
    Linwood; X8118 One God!
    One Lord
    Manoah (1851)
    Warner
Rostacker Gesangbuch, 1659
    Gregor's 151st metre-H;
        X956 Befiehl du deine
        wege; X8686 Protector
Rostockhandboken, 1529
    Ter sanctus; X11652 Vi lofve
        dig, o store Gud; X11795
        Wallin
Rötscher, J. F.
    Exodus (1790)
Rouen church melodies
    Aeterna Christi munera
    Ave verum, M 5
    Because you live again (1728);
        X2178 Coutances
    Christi fons jugis; X9139
        Rouen
    Coelites plaudant (17th c);
        X9140 Rouen
    Jesu corona
    Prompto gentes animo;
        X12305 Windrush
    Rouen
    St Venantius
    Ut queant laxis (1681)
Rounsefell, Carrie E., 1861-
1930
    I'll go where you want me
        to go (1894); X2091 Con-
        secration; X5434 It may
        not be on the mountain;
        X6673 Manchester; X7160
        Mountain's height
Rousseau, Jean-Jacques, 1712-
78
    Greenville (1825); X1996
        Come, ye sinners; X6353
        Lord, dismiss us; X9143
        Rousseau

Routley, Erik Reginald, 1917–
  Cliff Town (1951)
  Abingdon
  Mill Brow
  Sutton Courtenay
  Varndean
  Wych Cross
Rowlands, William Penfro,
1860–1937
  Blaenwern
Rubbra, Edmund, 1901–
  The Virgin's cradle hymn
    (1925)
Rubin, A.
  Father, see thy suppliant
    children
Ruebush, J. H.
  Booker
  God knows what is best (1897)
Ruebush, W. H.
  Something to do
Rung, Henrik, 1807–71
  Jutland
  Rung I
  Rung II
Runkel, Kenneth E.
  Eternal Light (1941)
Runyan, William M., 1870–
  Faithfulness; X4022 Great is
    thy faithfulness
  Not what these hands have
    done (1935)
  Teach me thy will, O Lord
    (1935)
  What God hath promised
Rupp, H. S.
  Bringing home the sheaves
  Give me a foothold
  Jerusalem, my happy home;
    X1493 Canaan
Rusbridge, A. Ewart, 1917–
  Horfield
Rush, E. Leonard, C.S.B.
  Tantum ergo (20th c?)
Russell, E. H.
  Pittsburgh
  Seal
Russell, Frederick George,
1867–1929
  Lombard Street (1929)
Russell, S. L.
  Charing (1931)
  Stanstead (1931)

  Sutton Valence (1931)
Russian traditional, etc.
  Blessed light
  Come let us worship (19th c
    ?)
  Easter eggs; X2320 Dalalin
  Praise to God; X2805 Easter
    song
  Volga boatman
Rutström, Andreas Carl, 1721–
72
  Min blodige konung
Ruud, Gordon C., 1920–
  Madagascar (1958)
Ryley, Geoffrey Charles Edward,
1866–1947
  Canon VIII
  East Peckham
  Sarratt

S

S.M.W.V.R.
  NOTE: This is a joint initial
pseud of Martin Shaw and Ralph
Vaughan Williams; used for melody "Cobbold". The order, W. V.
R., seems to indicate this composer's preference to be known
as "Williams", rather than
"Vaughan Williams".

Sabel, S.
  Early will I seek thee
Sacred harmony. Leeds, ca 1720
  Castleford
Sacred harmony, 1780
  Derbe
Sacred harp, 1844
  Wedlock
Sacred hymns and tunes. Boston,
1880
  Eden
Sacred hymns and tunes. Bristol,
1876
  Bona patria
St Alban's Tune Book, 1866
  Holborn Hill; X2950 Elven;
    X9239 St Alban; X9240
    St Alban, No. 1; X8414
    Penitence
  Lebbaeus; X1663 Children's
    litany; X4299 Hampden–

Sidney; X6235 Litany; X6240
Litany, No. 2; X6244 Litany,
No. 5 (Hoyte); X9890 Septem
voces (Hoyte); X9898 Septem
voces
Messengers; X9238 St Alban
Mill Lane (No. 10)
St Gall Cantarium, 1845
The Lord whom earth
St Gall Gesangbuch, 1863
Harvest hymn
St Gall
St Patrick (ascribed to) 372-466
A. D.
St Patrick; X4237 Hail glorious
St Patrick; X7093 Morley;
X9555 St Patrick's Breast-
plate
St Peter Damian, +1072
Ave Maris stella
Saint-Saëns, Charles Camille,
1835-1921
Ave verum corpus
Tollite hostias
Sampaix, Leon
Allegiance
Baker Chapel
Dorothy
Elizabeth
White ribbon
Samuel, Edward
Great Arbiter of human fate
Tent-like this day
Sanders, Harry
Mighty to save
Sanders, Robert L., 1906-
Adam's Song (1961)
Binyon (1961)
Ganador (1958)
Keith (1958)
Misericorde (1932)
Pont Neuf (1961)
Promise (1932)
Wheelock (1961)
Woodlawn (1934)
Sanderson, Wilfred
Conisborough
Sandström, Israel
I know a way
Sanger, Florence Ziegler, 1906-
Communion meditation
Sankey, I. Allen
Anniversary (1907?)

Sankey, Ira David, 1840-1908
A shelter in the time of storm
Am I a soldier
Be ye strong in the Lord
Beneath the cross
Have you sought?
I am praying for you; X1869
Cluff; X5049 I have a
Savior; X5366 Intercession;
X8621 Praying for you
Newcastle
O safe to the Rock; X4685
Hiding [in Thee]; X9707
Sankey; X9954 Shelter
O, wondrous Name (1886)
Only remembered
Room for Thee (1881)
Sankey
Take me as I am
Tell it out, arr (1881)
Ten thousand times ten thou-
sand
The ninety and nine
Trusting Jesus
Under His wings (1896)
Victory; X2985 Encamped
along the hills; X3222
Faith is the victory;
X9708 Sankey
Walking in the sunshine
Welcome
When the mists have rolled
away
While the days are going by
Sargent, N. B.
Building for eternity
Sarum plainsongs
NOTE: Tune name is follow-
ed by mode, source and approx-
imate date (when known).

Ad cenam agni providi, M 8
(11th c)
Aeterna Rex, M 8 (Sarum
Antiphonal)
Aurora lucis rutilat, Pt I,
M 8 (Sarum Antiphonal)
Chorus novae Jerusalem,
M 3
Christe redemptor, M 1;
X1756 Christe, redemptor
omnium; X5563 Jesu dul-
cis memoria; X5663 Jesu
redemptor

Christe sanctorum, M 1
Conditor alme, M 4; X2052
    Conditor alme siderum;
    X2206 Creator, alme siderum;
    X6484 Lucis creator; X8499
    Plainsong M 4
Deus creator omnium, M 4
    (Sarum Antiphonal); X8498
    Plainsong
Ecce jam noctis, M 4
Gloria, laus et honor, M 1
    (Sarum Processional)
Immense caeli conditor, M 2
Lucis creator, M 8
Nocte surgentes, M 6; X8500
    Plainsong M 6
O lux beata Trinitas, M 8
O Pater Sancte, M 4 (Sarum
    Antiphonal)
Pange lingua, M 3
Primo dierum omnium, M 4
    (6th c)
Salve, festa dies, M 4
Sanctorum meritis, M 7;
    X8292 Panis angelicus
Splendor paternae, M 1; X6518
    Lumina; X7537 Nox et tene-
    brae et nubila; X10312 Splen-
    dor paternae gloriae
Te lucis, M 8
The Rosy Sequence (Sarum
    Gradual, 1527, 28, & 32);
    X3468 Fragment
Urbs beata, M 2
Veni creator, M 8
Verbum supernum, M 2
Vexilla regis, M 1; X11615
    Verbum supernum; X11649
    Vexilla regis prodeunt
Sateren, Leland Bernhard, 1913-
    Eldora (1958)
    Marlee (1958)
Schachner, J. R.
    Brompton
Schafer, Norman W.H., 1858-
    Ecclesia (1900)
Schalit, Heinrich
    A week within the Sukko green
    (1932); X9993 Sh'meenee
    atseres
    Almighty Father (1932)
    Our Father, we beseech thy
    grace (1932)

    The cry of Israel (1932)
Scheffler, Johann. Heilege
Seelenlust, 1657
    Culbach; X1726 Christ, the
    glory of the sky; X11712
    Virgin wholly marvelous
Scheffler; X4562 Helfer
    meiner armen seele; X6236
    Litany
Scheidemann, David, 1570-
1625
    Puer nobis nascitur
Scheidt, Samuel, 1587-1654
    O Jesulein süss (1623);
    X7728 O Heiliger Geist,
    O Heiliger Gott; X7805 O
    little one; X10826 The
    Child Jesus
Schein, Johann Hermann, 1586-
1630
    Der Heilige Geist hernier-
    derkam (1627)
    Eisenach (1629); X5431 It is
    no earthly summer's ray
    X6088 Leipsic; X6607
    Mach's mit mir Gott;
    X6985 "Mir nach," Spricht
    Christus, unser; X9776
    Schein; X10033 Silesius;
    X12080 What happiness
    can; X12338 Wismar
    Ravenshaw
    Zion Klagt (1623)
Schemelli, G. C. Gesangbuch,
1736
    To Thee, O Lord
Schicht, Johann Gottfried
(i.e. "Theophil"), 1753-1823
    Ascendit Deus
    Majesty (1819)
    Manna
    Mir ist erbarmung Wider-
    fahren; X3015 Erbarmung
    Mittler, schau auf sie
    hernieder (1819)
    Zu meinem herrn
Schiller, Friedrich von. Ode
an die Freude, 1799
    An die freude
Schilling, Frederick
    Beautiful Star
    Schilling (1865)

Schlicht, Ludolf E.
  Gregor's 243d metre (1744);
    X2469 Dem heiligen blute
    des herrn zu gefallen
Schmid, Bernhardt. Orgelbuch.
  Strassburg, 1577
  ——— Herzlich liebe hab ich dich, o
    Herr; X4145 Gregor's 232d
    metre; X5480 Jeg har dig
    hjerteligen kjaer
Schmidlin, Jean, fl 1796
  Swiss tune; X2694 Dresden;
    X10617 Switzerland
Schmidt, C.
  What star is this; X12072 What
    beauteous sun surpassing star
Schmidt, Johann Eusebius
  Fahre fort; X3210 Fahre fort!
    Zion, fahre fort; X4102 Greg-
    or's 119th metre; X4799 Holy
    Lord
Schmuck, Cornelius
  Jesu dulcis memoria
Schneider (or Schnyder), Fried-
  rich J.C., 1786-1853
  Halle (1829)
  Lischer
Schnyder von Wartensee, Xaver,
  1786-1868
  NOTE: Variously cited as:
  Schnyder, Xavier; Wartensee, X.S.
  von; or Schneider, with above vari-
  ations.

  Horton; X1215 Book divine
Scholefield, Clement Cotterill,
  1839-1904
  Fides
  Irene (1874)
  Litany, No. 9; X6237 Litany;
    X9315 St Blane
  St Clement (1874)
  St Nicholas (1870)
Scholfield, Jack P., 1882-
  Jesus is the Name
  Rapture (1911); X9732 Saved,
    saved
  Think on thy way
Scholinus, Friedrich Karl Ludwig,
  1772-1816
  Mamre
Schop, Johann, d 1664
  Demmin
  Eternity (1642); X7768 O Jesus

Christ our only Lord; X11756
  Wach auf, mein Geist!
Jesu joy of man's desiring
  (1642); X5731 Joy of man's
  desiring; X5940 Lamp of
  our feet; X8881 Regensburg;
  X9796 Schop; X11548 Vaer
  nu glad og vel; X12027
  Werde munter
Schop (1641); X1287 Break
  forth, O beauteous heavenly
  light; X3028 Ermuntre dich
  [mein schwacher Geist]
Sollt' ich meinem Gott (1641);
  X1504 Cantate domino; X
  4293 Hamburg; X10773
  Thanksgiving
Schorring. Koralbog, 1781
  Contentment; X1142 Blessed
  communion; X5554 Jesus,
  din søde forening et
  smage; X9797 Schörring
Schott, J.G.
  So wahr ich leb, spricht
    Gott der Herr (1603)
Schreiner, Alexander, 1901-
  Behold thy sons and daughters
  God loved us, so He sent
    His Son
  Holy temples on Mount Zion
  In memory of the Crucified
  Lead me into life eternal
  Lord, accept into thy King-
    dom
  Thy Spirit, Lord, has stirred
  Truth eternal
  When in the wondrous realms
  While of these emblems we
    partake
Schröter, Leonhart, ca 1532-
  ca 1601
  Freut, euch, ihr lieben
    (1587)
Schubert, Franz Peter, 1797-
  1828
  Abendlied
  Esterhazy
  Hymn of praise
  Jesus, ever-loving Saviour
  Jesus, thou art coming
    (ascribed to Schubert)
  Laudate Dominum

Oremus pro Pontifice
Salve, Regina
Schubert; X3214 Fairford
Schubert II
Schuler, George S., 1882-
  Schuler (1924); X6657 Make
  me a blessing
Schulthes, Wilhelm August
Ferdinand, 1816-79
  Lambeth (1871); X4232 Hail!
  Bright archangel; X4287
  Hallon; X5205 Ilfracomb
  Raise your voices, vales and
  mountains; X2139 Cor Jesu,
  salus
  Requiem
Schultz, Ferdinand
  Abendruh (20th c)
Schulz, Johann Abraham Peter,
1747-1800
  Claudius (1800); X531 Arator;
  X2695 Dresden; X8273 Palm
  Sunday; X12329 Wir pflügen
  Hvad hör jäg?
  Paedia; X4583 Her kommer
  dine arme; X9803 Schulz;
  X11246 Thy little ones
  Swahili; X11839 Warum sind
  der Thränen
  Tekna; X5202 Ihr kinderlein
  kommet; X7643 O dear
  little children
Schumacher, Bernhard, 1866-
  Baltimore (1910)
  Firm foundation (1931)
  Septem verba (1939)
Schumann, Robert Alexander,
1810-56
  Canonbury (1839); X94 Above
  the heavens, eternal God;
  X4933 How lovely are thy
  dwellings; X7360 New every
  morning; X7694 O God, the
  refuge; X11462 'Twas like a
  dream
  Fredricton
  Holy love
Schumann, V. Gesangbuch, 1539
  Old 112th; X2258 Crucifixion;
  X4916 How fair the Church;
  X7662 O Fader vor i him-
  merig; X7833 O Love how

deep; X9805 Schumann;
  X10979 The Lord's pray-
  er; X11565 Vater unser
  [im Himmelreich]
Scott, Clara H., 1841-97
  Open my eyes (1895); X9813
  Scott
Scott, J.S.
  Salonica
Scott, James King, 1839-83
  Auchincairn
Scott-Gatty, Alfred, 1847-1918
  Bodmin
  Maud
  Spirit Divine (1899); X2842
  Ecclesfield; X6784 Mater
  misericordiae
  Welwyn (1902)
Scottish Presbyterian hymnal
  Laus sempiterna
Scottish Psalters, various dates
  Abbey (1615)
  Caithness (1635)
  Culross (1634)
  Dundee (1615); X3497 French
  Dunfermline (1615)
  Elgin (1625)
  Glenluce (1635)
  Greyfriars (1635)
  London New (1635)
  Melrose (1635)
  Plaintive martyrs (1615);
  X6757 Martyrs; X8013
  Old martyrs
  Psalm 80 (1564); X8036 Old
  80th
  Wigton (1635); X12258 Wig-
  town
  York (1615); X9810 Scotch
  stilt
  67th Psalm (1615); X8707
  Psalm 67
Scottish traditional, etc.
  Caledonia; X11163 Therefore
  give us love
  Cameronian Midnight hymn
  Candler (i.e. "Bonnie Doon",
  in Hesperian Harp, 1847);
  X1213 Bonnie Doon
  Covenanters; X8492 Pisgah
  Faithful (1931)
  Fine flowers

Rorate
Selma (from Isle of Arran);
    X11078 The sun in splendor
    rose
Ward
Sea, M.A.
I belong to Jesus; X2445
    Dedication
Willing to own thee (1896)
Sederquist, G.W.
The breaking of the day
Selby, Bertram Luard, 1853-
1919
Eccles
Ivyhatch
Praises
Ramaulx (1904)
Whitsun
Selle, Thomas, 1599-1663
Zoerbig (1655); X7942 O ur-
    sprung des lebens
Sellers, Ernest O., 1869-1952
New Orleans: X12402 Wonderful,
    wonderful Jesus
Open our eyes, thy glory be-
    holding (1940)
Thy word have I hid (1908);
    X3002 Eola; X11259 Thy
    word is a lamp
When the shadows flee (1909)
Would men know
Selnecker, Nicolaus. Christliche
Psalmen, 1587
Selnecker; X4062 Gregor's
    10th metre; X7572 Nun
    lasst uns Gott; X11757 Wach
    auf, mein herz, und singe
Sens. Office de la circoncision
attributed to Pierre de Corbeil,
d 1222.
Orientis partibus
Sens Processional, 1728
Ave radix
Sephardic melodies are filed as
Jewish traditional
Serbian traditional
May the words
Sering, Friedrich Wilhelm, 1822-
1901
Sering
Sermisy, Claude (or Claudin) de,
ca 1490-1562
Was mein Gott will (1529)

Seven sobs of a sorrowful soul,
1585
Hunnys
Miserere mei
Sewall, Frank
Accrington (1893)
Austin (1893)
Bath (1893)
Come children, arr (1893)
Constance (1893)
Emmanuel (1893)
Eucharist
Keble (1893)
Morn of joy (1893)
Pentecost
Pilgrim (1893)
Praise (1893)
Rachel (1893)
Rector potens (1893)
Resurgam (1893)
St Amand (1893)
St Ambrose (1893)
St Cecilia
Skara (1893)
Speranza
Sursum corda, No. 1 (1893)
Vincenzo (1893)
Vladimir (1893)
Sewell, Hampton H., 1874-1937
Sewell
Seymour, Joseph
Uplift the voice and sing
Shann, Richard. Ms., 1611
Come, love we God
Sharpe , Evelyn
Bulstrode (1931)
Platt's Lane (1929)
Shaw, Geoffrey Turton, 1879-
1943
Dymchurch (1915)
Fairlight (1929)
Freedom (1919)
Gillam (1915)
Glynthorpe (1925)
Gresham (1915)
Hickling Broad (1931)
Langham (1925)
Lime Street
Miles animosus
Paddocks
Praise
Ring out (1925)
Rothwell

The snow lies thick
Water-end (1925)
Shaw, Knowles
I am the vine
Shaw, Martin, 1875-1958
Aldeby (1929)
All bells in Paradise
All waters (1931)
Battle Song (1915)
Belsize
Berwick Street (1929)
Birthday (1915)
Boundary
Bromley Common (1915)
Camber (1931)
Cheerful
Children all (1915)
Cobbold (with Vaughan Williams, and signed:
S. M. W. V. R.)
Dian
Door keeper (1931)
Downshire Hill (1925)
Gentle Jesus (1915)
Good-bye (1915)
Greeting (1915)
Gun Hill (1929)
Henham (1931)
Herald (melody appears for alto voice)
High Road (1915)
I sing of a Maiden (1928)
In excelsis gloria
Julius
Kings in glory
Lemon's Farm
Little Cornard (1915)
Maddermarket (1929)
Make we merry (1926)
Manor Street (1915)
Marching
Merry Christmas
Mundays (1931)
Oakridge Lynch (1925)
Oppidans Mews (1915)
Out of your sleep
Oxenbridge (1931)
Pimlico Road (1925)
Pioneers (1925)
Purpose (1931)
Riley (1915)
Royden (1929)
Swanwick (1931)

Spring (1930)
Toc H
Westridge (1929)
Working (1930)
Shearer, Winifred Jacobs,
1882-
Filia
Sheehan, Peter E., C.S.B.
Let all on earth their
voices (1958)
Sheeles, John, 1688-1761
Addison's (ca 1720); X6320
London
Sheldon, Robin Treeby, 1932-
Broadbent
Crackington
Daymer
Flora
Jonathan
Maer Down
Prims
Shelley, Harry Rowe, 1858-
1947
All things bright and beautiful (1932)
In God, the Holy (1932)
Lord, in this sacred hour
(1932)
O Lord, be near me (1932)
O Lord, thy all discerning
eyes (1932)
Thy faithful servant, Lord,
doth yearn (1932)
Shenk, J. M.
Come, heaven-bound pilgrims; X8830 Rebecca
Shepard, F.S.
My Lord and I (1898
Shephard, H. F.
Matins
Shepherd (or Shepard), James
Hallett, 1835-79
Hallett
Shepherd, Jehu, 1899-
Avondale
Shepherd, William N. B.
Give us room that we may
dwell
Sherwin, William Fisk (or
Fishe) 1826-88
Anniversary song
Battle cry; X10255 Sound
the battle cry

Better Land
Bread of Life (1877); X1289
   Break thou the bread;
   X5984 Lathbury
Chautauqua (1877); X3143
   Evening praise; X9886 Sen-
   nen
Cutting
God's love
Heavenly fold
Kelley; X937 Beautiful valley
   of Eden
Mason; X206 Agape
Monsell
Praise ye the Lord
Sherwin I (1880); X3569
   Galilee
Sherwin II
Shield, William, 1748-1829
Auld Lang Syne (ca 1782)
Shields, Elizabeth McE.
   Others (1917)
Shoemaker, Joseph Shellenberger,
   1854-1936
   Come, lost one
   Freeport
   We now have met (1889);
      X10402 Stephenson
Shore, W.
   Wavertree
Showalter, Anthony J., 1858-
1924
   God moves in a mysterious
      way; X2397 Dayton; X6425
      Love consecrates the
      humblest act
   Leaning on Jesus; X6062 Lean-
      ing on the everlasting arms;
      X10003 Showalter
   O for a heart to praise my
      God; X10167 Solitude
Showalter, B. F.
   Sleep till that morning
Showalter, J. Henry, 1864-1947
   At the golden gate of prayer
   Awake, O earth
   Broadway
   Come, just as you are
   He seeks His wandering sheep
   I need thee, precious Jesus
   In from the highways; X3589
      Gather them into the fold
   In His Name (1900)

Keep us close to Thee
Lord, this day thy children
   meet
Mohler; X12347 With thankful
   hearts
More like Thee
Mosley
Nearer the cross of Jesus
None can satisfy
O I long to see the beauty
Shall we know each other
   there
Showalter; X1292 Breathe
   upon us, Holy Spirit
Tell the sweet old story
The garden (1922); X9849
   See Him in the garden
The Lord my Shepherd is
The Lord of the harvest
   calls
There is an arm
Walk in the Light
We are saved (1899); X9034
   Riches of grace
When I see the blood; X1670
   Children's song of praise;
   X6348 Lord, a little band;
   X10809 The blood of the
   Lamb
Showalter, Jacob M.
   Will you go to Jesus
Shrubsole, William, 1760-1806
   Miles' Lane (1779); X9281
   St Asaph
Sibelius, Jan (or Jean), 1865-
1957
   NOTE: Christened Johan
Julius Christian Sibelius
   Finlandia (1894)
Sicilian melody
   Sicilian Mariners (1794, in
      Merrick's Psalms); X2603
      Dismissal; X6354 Lord,
      dismiss us; X6428 Love
      divine; X6726 Mariners;
      X7893 O sanctissima;
      X10009 Sicilian hymn;
      X10012 Sicilian mariners'
      hymn; X10013 Sicily
Sidebotham, Joseph W., 1830-
   St Eanswyth (1881)
Siedhoff, E. Elizabeth
   Boston

Silas, Edouard, 1827-1909
  Silas
Silcher, Friedrich, 1789-1860
  Gott ein Vater; X3841 God our
    Father; X8350 Pastor pastorum
  Lorelei; X796 Baldwin; X9645
    Salutas
  Morning; X10148 Soho II
  Silcher II (1825)
  So nimm denn meine Hände;
    X7918 O take my hand;
    X10025 Silcher; X10646
    Take thou my hand and
    lead me
Silesian traditional
  Heavenly Friend
  St Elizabeth (1842); X605 Asca-
    lon; X2274 Crusader's hymn;
    X2457 Deilig er Jorden;
    X3212 Fairest Lord Jesus;
    X9790 Schönster Herr Jesu
Simper, Caleb
  Elmcourt
  Give thanks
  Roland
  Rosslyn
Simpson, Margaret M.
  The regions beyond
Sims, A.J.
  The Unseen Hand
Sims, W. Hines, 1907-
  McComb (1956)
  Meridian (1951)
Singer, Jacob
  All wise, All great (1932)
  Gird us, O God (1932)
  Harvest (1932)
  Kindle the taper (1932)
  Let there be light I (1932)
  Let there be light II (1932)
  Lift up your heads
  O God, whose law from age
    to age (1932)
  Rejoice and offer thanks to
    God (1932)
  This child we dedicate (1932)
  We thank thee (1932)
Sisters of Notre Dame
  Dear St Joseph, pure
Sisters of St Joseph, Toronto
  Be thou King
Skeffington, W.S.
  Hill Bourne

Skinner, T. Stanley
  Rominger
Slater, Gordon, 1896-
  Bilsdale (1931)
  Fountain Abbey (1931)
  St Botolph
Sletten, Jacob Hveding
  Jesus, come to me (1923)
Slovak traditional, etc.
  NOTE: Hymnal BQ quotes
  from a "Slovak Hymnal" with
  no further identification. Many
  melodies below are there
  named.

  Ave Maria! O Maiden, O
    Mother
  Blessed Francis, holy father
  By the first bright Easter
    Day
  Cor, arca legem continens
  Great God, what ever through
    thy church
  Great St Joseph
  Hail, glorious St Patrick
  Heart of our Lord
  Help, Lord, the souls
  I need thee, precious Jesus
  If great wonders
  Jesus, thou art coming
  Lead us, great teacher Paul
  Lift up, ye princes
  Little King, so fair
  Man of Sorrows; X7044a
    Monsell
  O come and mourn
  O Paradise! O Paradise
  O Thou pure light
  O turn to Jesus
  Remember, holy Mary
  Resurrection (1600 ms)
  Sacred Heart of Jesus
  Slovakia
  Sweet Agnes, holy child
  Tantum ergo
  This is the image of the
    Queen
  Tranoscius
  Whither thus in holy rapture
Smallman, C. Stanley, 1894-
  Dear love
Smallwood, Williams, 1831-97
  Antwerp

Smart, George Thomas, 1776-1867
  Wiltshire (1795)
Smart, Henry, 1813-79
  Alexander (1872)
  Barnby's Hymnary, Tune 140
  Barnby's Hymnary, Tune 291
  Barnby's Hymnary, Tune 475
  Bethany (1867); X657 At thy feet;
    X2256 Crucifer; X3804 God
    incarnate, veil thy splendor
  Chebar
  Colebrooke
  Corde Natus
  Desire
  Eventide (1876); X10120 Smart
  Everton (1867)
  Gordon
  Heathlands (1866)
  Horeb
  Jamison (1866); X10501 Sunder-
    land
  Lancashire (1836); X7966 O
    word of God incarnate
  Lexington (1881)
  Misericordia
  Moredun
  Moseley (1881)
  Nachtlied (1872); X1535
    Carmel; X12337 Wishart
  Nomina
  Northumberland
  Paradise (1868)
  Pilgrims (1868); X2370
    Daughter of Sion; X111746
    Vox angelica
  Regent Square (1867) X471
    Angels, from the realms;
    X5751 Judge eternal,
    throned in splendor
  Rex gloriae (1868)
  St Leonard (1867)
  St Pancras
  Seraphim
  Sion (1872); X847 Barnby's
    hymnary, Tune 474; X3454
    Forward; X9318 St Boniface;
    X9321 St Botolph; X10121
    Smart; X11881 Watchword
  Trisagion (1868)
  Vexillum (1868); X11974 Wel-
    come
Smit, W.A.

  Tantum ergo
Smith, Alfred M.
  Assisi (1940)
  Labor (1941)
  Sursum corda (1941)
Smith, Besse E.
  Glory, praise and blessing
  O perfect love
  The Saviour reigns
Smith, Beulah
  Beulah (improvised when a
    child of five years)
Smith, David Stanley, 1877-
1949
  Fortitude (1904)
  Los Angeles (1905)
Smith, Edward J.
  University hymn (1911)
Smith, Henry Percy, 1825-98
  Maryton (1874); X10500
    Sun of my soul
Smith, Howard E., 1863-1918
  I want to love Him more
  Love lifted me (1912); X9220
    Safety
  When the Book is opened
Smith, Isaac. Collection, ca
1770
  Abridge; X9602 St Stephen
  Oxford New
  Silver Street; X3238 Falcon
    Street
Smith, John Stafford, 1750-
1836
  National anthem, arr (1771);
    X7897 O say, can you
    see!; X10370 Star-spang-
    led banner; X11071 The
    star-spangled banner
Smith, Joseph
  Radiance
Smith, Kenneth Donald, 1928-
  Raphael
Smith, Lucia May
  Ashland (1918)
Smith, R.A. Laslett, 1873-
  Forest Hill Church
Smith, R.F.
  There came three Kings
    (1875); X3007 Epiphany
Smith, Robert Archibald, 1780-
1829

St Lawrence
Smith, Samuel, 1821-1917
    Edengrove (1874); X9629
    Saints' days
    Gaudete
    Melanesia
    Newton Ferns
    Ruth (1870)
Smith. Harmonious companion,
1732
    St Bartholomew
Smucker, S.J.
    I long to be there
    Rittman
Smyth, A.C.
    Come along, come along
    Come, thou glorious day
    O, how lovely was the morn-
        ing
    Sion stands with hills sur-
        rounded
Smyth, Harper G., 1873-1945
    Euclid; X6658 Make me a
        channel
Smyth, Julian K.
    Children of the light
    Copley Square
    God's mariner
    Montrose
    Pastor bonus
    Prince of Peace
    Roll out, O song, to God;
        X11701 Vigilia
    Roxbury
    Wilma
Söderberg, Th[eodor?]
    O du Guds Lam
Södergren, Carl Johannes, 1870-
    Agatha (1924)
Sohren, Peter, ca 1630- ca 1692
    Dies ist der Tag (1676)
    Elbing (1668); X2706 Du
        lifvets bröd; X4631 Herr
        Jesu Christ, du hast bereit't;
        X4632 Herr Jesu Christ, du
        höchstes Gut
    Gute bäume bringen, arr;
        X10150 Sohren
    Sohren (1668), arr (by W. Doug-
        las (1938); X4216 Gute
        baume bringen
Somervell, Arthur, 1863-1937
    Blencathra (1925)

Dominus vobiscum
    Kendal (1906)
    Langdale
    Rugby
    Somervell; X1693 Chorus
        angelorum; X8585 Praise
        to the Holiest
    Stonethwaite (1931); X2387
        Day by day
    Windermere
Songs and tunes for education,
1861
    Haslemere
Soto de Langa, Francisco, 1539-
1619
    Langa
Souter Liedekens Ghemaect ter
Eeren Gods. Antwerp, 1539
    If ye would hear
Southern harmony (Walker's);
1835
    Complainer
    Distress
    The spiritual sailor
Southern harmony, 1855
    True happiness
Southgate, Frederic, 1824-85
    St Agatha
Southgate, Thomas Bishop, 1814-
68
    Brookfield (1887)
    Southgate
Sowerby, Leo, 1895-
    Palisades (1941)
    Perry
    Taylor Hall (1941)
Spaeth, Adolph, 1939-1910
    NOTE: Christened, Philipp
Friedrich Adolph Theodor
Spaeth.
    O Gottessohn (1885)
Spaeth, Mrs. Adolph, see
    Krauth, Harriet Reynolds,
    1845-1925
Spanish traditional
    Spanish carol
    Torches
Spanish plainsong, see Mozar-
    abic Rite
Spazier, Johann Karl Gottlieb
    (or Johann Gottlieb Karl),
    1761-1805
    Spazier

Speck, A. L.
  The blameless Church
Spee, Friedrich von. Trutz-
  Nachtigal, 1649
  NOTE: See also Corner. Geist-
  liche Nachtigall, 1649

  Nachtigall; X117 Ach! Wan doch
    Jesu liebster mein
Speer, Daniel, 1636-1707
  Speer; X9222 Sag was hilft
Spencer, W. A.
  I shall be like Him
Spencer Palmer, Florence
  Margaret (i. e. Peggy) 1900 -
    Adoramus
    Brynland
    Carmichael
    Ellasgarth
    Keynsham
    Lydbrook
    Quest
    Smitten Rock
    Woking
Spevniček, Lachmannov
  Now let the earth with joy
Spielman, John H.
  Mt Zion (1881)
  Ormiston (1881)
  Pentecost (1881)
Spiess, Johann Martin, 1715-
  ca 66
    Swabia (1745); X5099 I name
      thy hallowed Name; X10472
      Suabia; X10553 Swabia No.
      1
Spilman, Jonathan
  Illinois
Spilman, Jonathan E.
  Away in a manger (1834);
    X3390 Flow gently sweet
    Afton; X10834 The Christ-
    mas manger hymn
Spinney, Frank, 1850-88
  Holy offerings
  St Denys
Spinney, Walter
  Name of Jesus (1890)
Spohr, Louis (or Ludwig), 1784-
  1859
    Flensburg; X11749 Vox Jesu;
      X11825 Waring
    Gerald (1834); X315 All things

bright; X1271 Brady; X
  5383 Invitation; X5504 Jer-
  usalem; X10316 Sophr
Leyden; X5800 Kemerton
Spohr (1835); X1634 Cherith;
  X6631 Magdalene; X10046
  Simpson; X11044 The sanc-
  tity of sorrow
Sprague, P. J.
  Ye children, come
Spratt, Ann Baird
  Kedron (1866)
Squires, William H.
  Sacred morn
Staden, Sigmund Gottlieb
  [Theophilus?] ca 1605-55
  Die Helle Sonne
Stafford, C. C.
  I'll make it my home
Stainer, John, 1840-1901
  Author of life
  Beati (1873); X303 All saints;
    X1049 Bethabara; X6626
    Magdalen; X8974 Rest;
    X9630 Saints of God;
    X10343 Stainer
  Blessed Home (1875); X
    10806 The blessed home
  Charity (1868)
  Children offerings
  Conquest (1875); X5505
    Jerusalem
  Contrition (1882)
  Covenant (1889)
  Credo (1875)
  Crucifixion (1887); X2236
    Cross of Jesus
  Crux salutifera
  Dominus misericordiae
  Elijah
  Eucharisticus; X5574 Jesus,
    gentlest Saviour
  Evangel; X5287 In memoriam;
    X10344 Stainer
  Evening prayer (1898)
  Gloaming (1898)
  God in nature (1897)
  God so loved the world
  Grandpont
  Iona (1868)
  Laus matutina (1872); X834
    Barnby's hymnary, Tune
    53; X2381 Dawn; X8597

Praise ye the Lord
Litany, No. 6 (1875)
Love Divine (1889)
Lux prima; X835 Barnby's
  hymnary, Tune 59; X10510
  Sunrise
Magdalena (1868)
Oblations
Oxford; X273 All for Jesus;
  X5811 Keston; X12486
  Wycliff
Paschale gaudium
Pastor bonus (1875); X9426
  St Hill
Pilgrim band
Repose (1875)
Rex Regum
St Benedict
St Giles; X2854 Eden; X8319
  Parousia
St Paul's
Scientia salutis
Sebaste
Simplicity
Sudeley
Suppliant
Veni
Veni Spiritus
Vesper (1875)
Watchword
Woodlynn (1889)
Xavier (1875); X9392 St
  Francis Xavier
Stair, Patty, 1869-1926
  Bassett (1915)
Stanfield, Francis, 1836-
  Sweet Sacrament Divine
    (1860)
Stanford, Charles Villiers, 1852-
1924
  Airedale
  Engelberg (1904)
  Geronimo (1909)
  Jolwynds (1904)
  Orient
Staniforth, Thomas Worsley,
1845-1909
  Jerusalem (1866); X9878 Sel-
    wood; X10360 Staniforth
  O heart of Mary
Stanley, Samuel, 1767-1822
  Calvary
  Doversdale

Kent
Wilton
Shirland
Simeon
Stonefield
Warwick
Stanton, Walter Kendall, 1891-
  Cannock (1951)
  Crudwell
  Dolberrow
  Hampton Lucy
  Linton
  Mylor
  Northumbria
  Ready token
  Silchester
Staples, H. J., 1891-1943
  Nightingale
Stark, E. J.
  Berkshire; X12155 When this
    song of praise shall cease
  Firm this cornerstone
Stark, Josef
  P'sach Lonu
Stratham, Francis Reginald,
1844-
  Freshwater (1872)
  Thanksgiving; X943 Beddome;
    X2251 Croyland; X8940
    Repose
Statham, H. D., 1889-
  Arncliffe
Statham, Heathcote
  Tenbury (1925)
Statham, Henry Heathcote,
1839-
  St Joseph; X9232 St Agnes;
    X10378 Statham
Statham, W., 1832-98
  St Margaret
Stebbins, George Coles, 1846-
1945
  Adelaide (1907); X4410 Have
    Thine own way; X4783 Holy
    desire; X8527 Pollard;
    X10385 Stebbins; X10530
    Surrender
  Assiut (1912)
  Ben Avon
  Born again; X12517 Ye must
    be born again
  "But for a moment" (1906)
  Christian, walk carefully

Come to the fountain
Come unto Me
Eskridge
Evening prayer (1876)
Fear not
Friend (1878); X5445 I've found
   a friend; X10480 Such a
   friend
Holiness (1890); X5964 Langstaff;
   X6334 Longstaff; X10647
   Take time to be holy
Janet (1912)
Jesus, I come (1886); X8233
   Out of my bondage
Jesus is calling; X1442 Call-
   ing today; X5591 Jesus is
   tenderly calling; X10386
   Stebbins
Kinross (1901)
Lydia
Moorehead (1927)
Providence; X7184 Must I go,
   and empty-handed
Saved by grace; X10179 Some
   day the silver cord
Sialkot
Spirit so holy
The Green Hill; X4043 Green
   Hill; X10387 Stebbins;
   X11139 There is a green
   hill
The Homeland (1920)
True-hearted, whole-hearted
   (1890)
Stebbins, George Waring, 1869-
1930
   Easter flowers (1913)
   Manchester (1927)
Steffe, John William
   Battle hymn (1852); X876
      Battle hymn of the Republic;
      X10792 The battle hymn of
      the Republic
Steggall, Charles H., 1826-1905
   Christchurch (1858); X1698
      Christ Church
   Day of praise
   Help us, O God
   Lincoln's Inn (1892)
   Manger Throne (1867)
   Morwellham; X7079 Morewell-
      ham
   Orient

St Albans
St Ambrose
St Clement (1849)
St Edmund (1849); X9372
   St Edward
St Lawrence
Wearmouth (1890)
Westmoreland
Woolsey (1872)
Stein, A. Gereon
   Great St Joseph (1852)
Steinel, Irving A.
   Consecration hymn (1940)
   Evans (1939)
Steiner, Johann Ludwig, 1688-
1761
   Steiner (1735); X3941 Gott
      will's machen
Stenhammer, Per Ulrik, 1829-
75
   Grace; X4645 Herren sig i
      nad förklarer
Stephens, Charles Edward,
1821-92
   Dr. Steggall's Tune 172
      (1865)
Stephens, Evan
   All hail the glorious day
   Awake, ye Saints of God
   Come, dearest Lord
   Father, thy children to thee
      now raise
   For the strength of the
      hills
   Glory to God in the highest
   In remembrance of thy
      suffering
   Know this, that every soul
      is free
   Land of the mountains high
      (commemorating Utah's
      statehood)
   Lean on my ample arm
   Let us all press on
   Lo! the mighty God
   O awake! my slumbering
      minstrel
   O happy homes among the
      hills
   Our mountain home
   Praise ye the Lord
   Raise your voices to the
      Lord

Sacred the place of prayer
Savior, Redeemer of my soul
See, the mighty angel flying!
Shall the youth of Sion falter?
The voice of God again is heard
Today, while the sun shines
We ever pray for thee
What was witnessed in the
   heavens?
Ye simple souls who stray
Stephenson, J.
   Sandford
Stevens, David
   Millet (1921)
Stevens, Richard John Samuel,
1757-1837
   Shakespeare's Carol II
Stevenson (no initials)
   O Heart of God (1918?)
Stevenson, Frederick
   Hart (1892)
Stewart, Charles Hylton, 1884-
1932
   Corona
   Rochester
Stewart, J. W.
   Adoration
Stewart, Robert Prescott, 1825-
94
   Adrian
   Coeli enarrant; X1880 Coeli
   Eucharistica
   Garfirth (1868)
   Holyrood (1873)
   Mount Calvary (1874); X1518a;
      Caress; X9275 St Anthony,
      we turn
   Prescott (ca 1873)
   St Audoen
   St Helen's; X5926 Lafayette;
      X9417 St Helen
   Vespers
Stiastny, Johann
   Stiastny
Stieler, Kaspar. Der Busfertige
Sünder. Nürnberg, 1679
   Wo soll ich fliehen hin
Stillman, J. M.
   I want to be more like Jesus
      (1878); X7071 More like
      Jesus
Stobaeus, Johann, 1580-1646
   Lift up your heads (1634);

X6610 Macht hoch die
   Thür
Such', wer da will (1613)
Stock, Sarah Geraldina, 1838-
98
   Moel Llys (1899)
Stocks, George Gilbert, 1877-
1960
   Sunset
   Village
Stocks, M. L.
   What will you do with Jesus?
Stockton, John Hart, 1813-
77
   Glory to His name
   Great Physician, arr;
      X10609 Sweetest name;
      X10623 Sympathy; X10891
      The Great Physician [now
      is near]
   Stockton (1875); X1924 Come,
      every soul; X6978 Minerva;
      X8144 Only trust him;
      X11416 Trust
Stokes, Walter
   Ravendale
Stokowski, Leopold Antoni
   Stanislaw, 1887-
   In excelsis gloria (1908)
Stolpe, Gustav, 1833-1901
   Dig, Jesus, min dyraste
      Jesus (1892)
   Helig, helig, helig Herre
      Gud (1892)
Stone, Frank Leslie
   Sunset and evening star
      (1901)
Storer, Henry Johnson, 1860-
1935
   Brightly gleams (1890)
   Harvest home (1890)
   O Sion, haste (1894)
   Patmos (1891)
Störl, Johann Georg Christian,
1675-1719
   Störl I; X7112 Morning
      sacrifice; X7560 Nun
      danket all' und bringet
      ehr; X8640 Preservation
   Störl II; X7760 O Jerusalem
      du schöne
Störl's Wurtemberg Gesangbuch,
1710

Bremen
Stötzel, Johann Georg
   Ruhe ist das beste gut (1777)
Stötzel, Choralbuch. Stuttgart,
1744
   O wie selig seid ihr doch;
      X915 Beata
   So führst du hoch; X4843 Home
Strachauer, H.
   Hermann
   So sweet and clear
Stralsund Gesangbuch, 1665
   Praise to the Lord; X4082
      Gregor's 61st metre; X4397
      Hast du denn, Jesu; X6005
      Laudate dominum; X6304
      Lobe den Herren; X6448 Lov-
      er den Herre; X8563 Praise;
      X8569 Praise Jehovah; X8600
      Praxis pietatis
Strassburg Psalter, 1539
   Genevan 137th
   Old 130th
Strassburg Kirchenampt, 1524
   see both Teutsch Kirchenampt,
Strassburg, 1525 and Kirchenge-
sangbuch. Strassburg, 1541
Strassburger Kirchengesangbuch,
1616
   Strassburg
Strattner, Christoph Georg
(or Georg Christoph), 1650-
1705
   Posen (1691); X1736 Christ
      the Lord is risen today;
      X3159 Ever faithful; X4710
      Himmel, erde, luft und
      meer; X10457 Strattner
Straub, S.W., 1842-1899
   Providence
Streatfeild, Charlotte
   Langton
Strohm, Albert J.
   Stewart (1933)
Strom, Ralph Alvin, 1909-
(sometimes 1901-
   Beaumont (1924)
   Elmie (1924)
   Mathilda (1924)
   Name of Jesus
   St Ansgar (1924)
Strong, Thomas Banks, 1861-
1944

Hebdomadal
   Poplar
Strover, Martin Christian Tinne,
1932-
   Broadwood
   Simon
Strutt, R., 1848-1927
   St Catherine's Court
Stubbs, G. Edward, 1857-
   Asaph (1894); X3026 Erling
Stutsman, Grace May
   Waits' carol (1935)
Su Yin-lan, 1915-37
   Sheng en (1934)
Sullivan, Arthur Seymour, 1842-
1900
   All this night
   Angel voices (1872)
   Audite audientes me (1874)
   Bishopgarth (1897); X5744
      Jubilee
   Carrow (1873)
   Clarence (1874)
   Coena Domini (1874)
   NOTE: "Livorno" is an en-
largement of this melody;
      X7676 O gentle Savior
   Constance
   Courage, brother (1872);
      X857 Barony
   Emmelar
   NOTE: This name refers to
Henry Brinley Richards, Sulli-
van's contemporary in London.
   Evelyn (1874)
   Ever faithful; X3161 Ever
      faithful, ever sure
   Falfield (1874)
   Fortunatus (1872); X11977
      Welcome, happy morning
   Golden sheaves
   Hanford (1874); X70303 Nau-
      ford [sic]
   Homeland (1867); X3427 For
      thee, O dear, dear coun-
      try; X7604 O bone patria
   In memoriam
   Lacrymae (1872); X841
      Barnby's hymnary, Tune
      222; X9659 Salvator No. 1
   Livorno (see Coena Domini,
      above); X10812 The bread
      that giveth strength

Lux Eoi (1874); X359 Alleluia!
 Praise the Savior
Lux mundi (1872); X843 Barn-
 by's hymnary, Tune 225;
 X5516 Jerusalem the golden!
Marlborough, arr
Mount Sion
Propior Deo (1872); X12049
 Westminster
Resurrexit (1874)
Safe home
St Edmund (1872); X4526
 Heaven is my home
St Francis (1874)
St Francis II
St Gertrude (1871); X3540
 From the eastern mountains;
 X3660 Gertrude; X8155 On-
 ward, Christian soldiers;
 X10488 Sullivan
St Kevin (1872); X845 Barnby's
 hymnary, Tune 285
St Millicent
St Nathaniel; X7293 Nathaniel
St Patrick (1874)
St Theresa (1874); X11176
 Theresa
Saints of God (1874)
Samuel (1874); X4978 Hushed
 was the evening hymn
Shepherd
Storm-tossed
Sullivan
The long way home
Ultor omnipotens (1874)
Valete; X7871 O render thanks
Venite ad me
Sullivan, E.M.
 Tantum ergo (1940)
Sulzer, Salomon (or Solomon)
 1804-90
 Bor'chu
 Kodosh
 O Lord, my God
 Shiveesee
 Sh'ma Yisroayl I
 Sh'ma Yisroayl II; X1227
 Boruch shaym
 The Lord of all
 Va-a-nachnu
 Yimloch
Summer, John B., 1838-1918
 see Sumner, John B.

(Accuracy of spelling is not
established: both forms in pub-
lications)
Summers, J.
 Palmyra (1863); X10122 Smi-
 ley
Summers, James Lea, 1837-81
 Lea
Sumner, John B., 1838-1918
 The Child of a King; X7 A
 child of a king; X8 A
 child of the king; X1095
 Binghamton
Sunderreiter, G. Himmlischen
 Harfen. Augsburg, 1581
 In dich hab' ich gehoffet
Suomen Koraalikirja, 1738
 Finnish Song
Supplement to Kentucky Har-
 mony, 1820
 Detroy; X2521 Detroit; X7114
 Morning song (Wyeth
 Repository, 1813)
Sussex traditional see English
 traditional
Swabian folk song
 Miserere nobis (Brahms
 arr); X2021 Common ways
Swan, Timothy, 1758-1842
 China
Swedish Koralbok, 1697
 see the 1697 items filed with
Swedish traditional melodies
just below.
Swedish traditional, liturgical,
etc.
NOTE: The 1697 items were
published in the Swedish Koral-
bok, 1697. And see Then
Swenska Psalmboken. Stock-
hom, 1695

 Amicus; X5461 Jag har en
 vän
 Blomstertid (1697); X2471
 Den blomstertid nu kom-
 mer
 Dalarne
 Frälsta värld! i nodens un-
 der (1697)
 Gaa nu hen og grav min
 Grav
 Gor porten hög (1697)

Heroes hymn
I Kristi sar jag somnar in
(1689)
Jesus! du dig själf uppväckte
(1675)
Jesus, lat din rädda dufva;
X3516 Friends of Jesus
Kalmar (1676); X4557 Hela
världen fröjdes herren;
X5620 Jesus, Lord and
precious Saviour
Laurinus (1697); X1584 Celeste;
X5063 I himmelen, i himme-
len
Messiah (16th c); X1029 Bere-
den; X1030 Bereden väg för
herran
Misstrosta ej att Gud är god
(1695)
Mitt hjerta Jesu! denna dag
(in Swedish Koralbok, 1884)
O store Gud
O wonderful words
Oss Kristna bör tro och besin-
na (before 1540)
Pax (1697); X123 Ack, bliv
hos oss; X9185 Sa är full-
komnadt
Praise (1697); X195 Af himlens
Riddarholm (1697); X11526 Upp,
min tunga
St Erik (1697)
St Lawrence, Lund (17th c)
X11527 Uppfaren är var
herre
Sandell; X1660 Children of the
heavenly Father; X11442 Try-
ggare kan ingen vara
Skader, skader nu här alle
(1697)
Swedish Litany (1697)
Vigil; X4225 Haf trones lampa
färdig
Sweetser, Joseph Emerson, 1825-
73
Diman
Greenwood (1894)
Owen
Rose Hill
Sweezy, Israel B.
Palmer
Sweney, John R., 1837-99
Beulah Land

Calvary
Fill me now; X4905 Hover
o'er me, Holy Spirit;
X10613 Sweney
Give me Jesus; X10645 Take
the world, but give
Hast du Jesus ruf vernom-
men; X6380 Lord of light,
whose name outshineth
He will gather the wheat
Hyatt
I shall know Him; X7247 My
Saviour first of all;
X12132 When my life-
work
Jesus leads (1893)
More about Jesus (1887);
X10614 Sweney
Stars in my crown; X12266
Will there be any stars
Story of Jesus; X7951 O
what could my Jesus do
more; X10721 Tell me the
story
Sunshine; X11175 There's
sunshine in my soul
The Lord is my Light
Unsearchable riches; X7922
O the unsearchable riches
Victory through grace; X
2072 Conquering now
We are nearing home
Swift, James Frederick, 1847-
1931
Ernstein
Te laudant omnia
Swisher, Walter S.
Cornish (1923)
Hamilton (1923)
Lee (1924)
Newell (1923)
Wellesley (1924)
Swiss traditional
NOTE: See also the Tyrolese
traditional tunes.

Solothurn
Stillingfleet
Vaudois
Sydenham, Edwin Augustus, 1847-
91
King Edward
Sydnor, G.G.

Dawning (1926)
Sykes, Frederick H., 1826-
Holcombe
Symonds, Daniel Philip, 1929-
Mernle

T

Taddei, M.
Hail, Thou Star of Ocean
(1920)
Tai Jun Park
Korea
Taler (a Dominican, Monastery
of Strasbourg, 1361)
Jesu Redemptor omnium
Tallis (or Tallys, Talys),
Thomas, ca 1505-95
Fifth mode melody
First mode melody
Second mode melody
Seventh mode melody
Tallis' Canon (ca 1567); X1498
Canon; X3140 Evening hymn;
X7926 O thou immortal holy
Light; X10655 Tallis' Even-
ing hymn; X10658 Tallis'
Hymn
Tallis' Ordinal (ca 1567);
X8586 Praise to the Holiest
X10650 Tallis
The Second tune
The 5th tune (1560)
The 6th tune (1560)
Third mode melody (1567)
Veni Creator (ascribed to)
Tans'ur (originally Tanzer),
William, 1706-83
Bangor (1734)
Barby (1755); X9263 St Andrew
St Martin's (1740); X3563
Gainsborough
Rothwell
Tans'ur, W. Compleat melody,
1734
Colchester
Tarbutton, William A.
A little while
Briggs
Tartini, Giuseppe, 1692-1770
Stabat Mater
Tate, Laura A.
Bovina

Taylor, B. M.
Upon the first day
Taylor, Cyril Vincent, 1907-
Abbot's Leigh
Belstead
Beweley
Bushmead
Coolinge
Eirene
Libera nos
Mead House
Portland
Sheldonian
Taylor, E. G.
Latakia; X11152 There is
life for a look
Taylor, John Prentice, 1871-
Kirn
Taylor, Virgil Corydon, 1817-
91
Louvan (1847)
Warren
Tchaikowsky, Peter Ilitch,
1840-93
NOTE: Great variation in
transliteration of spelling.
Baker uses Tchaikovsky, Piotr
Ilyitch.

In aeternum
O come, let us worship
Petrograd
The Crown of Roses; X10694
Tchaikowsky's "Legend"
Tearne, T.S.
The bell cadence
Teasley, D.O.
All because we do not love
them
Be ready when He comes
Behold what love
Eternity
Glorious peace
Gone to bloom above
I know in my heart what it
means
No friend like Jesus
The last farewell; X9999
Should we meet here no
more
Teddlie, Tillet S.
Heaven holds all to me
Into our hands (1939)

What will your answer be?
(1935)
Temple Star
  Be not afraid
  Lyte
Tenney, John H.
  Beneath thy shadow hiding
  Closer to thee, My Father
  Ever will I pray
  Go to thy rest, fair child;
    X1297 Burber
  Not far from the Kingdom
  Sabbath bell
  We'll never say good-by (1889)
  Where will you spend eternity
Terry, Richard Runciman, 1865-
1938
  Christ the Lord is my true
    Shephard
  Crown Him
  Doxford
  Full of glory
  Hail, Mary, Pearl of Grace
  Highwood
  Holy Church; X356 Alleluia,
    let the holy anthem rise;
    X2846 Ecclesia
  Newman (1912); X1090 Billing
  O Godhead hid
Teschner, Melchior, 1584-1635
  St Theodulph (1615); X277 All
    glory, praise [laud] and
    honor; X9501 St Mark;
    X10754 Teschner; X11130
    Theodulph; X11554 Valet
    will dich dir geben
Teutsch Kirchenampt. Strass-
burg, 1525
  Aus tiefer not; X4639 Herr,
    wie du willst, so schik's mit
    mir; X6540 Luther's hymn;
    X7729 O helligaand, du skat;
    X7737 O Holy Ghost, thou
    gift; X10454 Strasburg
  Es woll' uns Gott genädig sein;
    X7661 O Fader var, barmher-
    tig god
  Passiontide; X447 An wasser-
    fleussen Babylon; X2886 Ein
    lamm geht hin
Thalben-Ball, George Thomas,
1896-
  Arden

Dennis
Dransfield (1932)
Egerton (1932)
Jesmian
Laudon (1932)
Llanherne
Nazareth
Stand up
Vigil
Wisdom
Walford
Warwick
Thalberg, Sigismond, 1812-71
  Thalberg
Thatcher, Reginald Sparshatt,
1888-1957
  Long Mynd (1931)
  Wilderness (1936)
Thayer, M.C.
  Wakeman
Theiss, J.A.
  Wondrous story
Then Swenska Psalmboken.
Stockholm, 1695.
  NOTE: See also Swedish
traditional melodies, 1695
items may be from this book.

Stockholm; X2499 Der mange
  skal komme; X11161
  There many shall come
Theophane, M., Sr., O.S.F.
  Blessed Francis, holy
    father (1958)
Thermignon, D.
  Creator alme siderum;
    X11587 Veni Creator
    Spiritus
Thesaurus musicus, 1740
  America; X3849 God save
    our gracious king;
    X3850 God save the
    queen; X7191 My coun-
    try 'tis of thee; X7295
    National anthem; X7818
    O Lord, our God
Thiman, Eric Harding, 1900-
  Ashford
  Beeding
  Binney's
  Goring
  Holborn
  Milton Abbas

morning comes
Leave it there, arr.
NOTE: Apparently a variant of
James Black's 'The roll".

Nothing between
Stand by me
Tinsley, W. C.
I'll go where He sendeth me
Tintner, M.
Splendor of the morning sun-
light
Tochter Sion. Cologne, 1741
St Bernard; X2189 Covert
X5578 Jesus, how good the
thought
Weisse flaggen; X300 All
saints (later form) (Darm-
stadt G-B.)
Toews, Aaron
The Lord's Prayer
Toews, Jacob D.
Come, ye weary ones, tonight
(1943)
The Beatitudes
Tomadini, Jacopo, 1820-83
Panis angelicus
Tomer, William Gould, 1832-
96
God be with you (1882); X2531
Deus vobiscum; X3257 Fare-
well; X7014 Mizpah; X11328
Tomer
Tomissön, Hans. Psalmebog, 1569.
Franzen; X524 Appeal; X7762
O Jesu! än de dina
Herre Gud Fader, du vor h∅i'
ste Tr∅st
Island; X4912 How blest are
they; X6977 Min sjael og
aand opmuntre dig; X11210
Thomisson
Mit Haab og Tr∅st og al Tillid
Thomissön
Torrance, George William, 1835-
1907
Adoration
Moredun; X1855 Clinging;
X11417 Trust
Tourjée, Eben, 1834-91
Cary
Tourjée, Lizzie Esterbrook,
1858-1913

Wellesley (1877); X11347
Tourjée
Tours, Berthold, 1838-97
Deventer; X6730 Marken
Gouda; X2722 Dulce nomen
Groningen (1872); X1043
Bertha
Holland (1875);
Rotterdam (1875)
The Wise Men (1881); X184
Advent
Tours (1872); X1045 Berthold;
X5295 In palmis; X11153
There is never a day
Towner, Daniel B., 1850-1919
Anywhere; X522 Anywhere
with Jesus
Calvary; X647 At Calvary
Marvelous grace (1910);
X3980 Grace greater than
our sin; X7057 Moody
My anchor holds
Nor silver nor gold
Only a sinner (1905)
Some sweet day
The hand that was wounded
(1905)
Towner
Trust and obey; X12159 When
we walk with the Lord
Tozer, A. Edmonds
Ave Maria! Thou Virgin and
Mother
Jazer
NOTE: This appears to be
a misprint of word "Tozer";
X331 All ye who seek
Tozer, Ferris
Stand firm
Tozer
Track, Gerhard
I shall approach the altar
(1964)
Traditional melodies
IMPORTANT NOTE: These
might have been placed in the
anonymous section, but because
of their long use within Church
or Folk music this category
was made. For traditional
melodies which may be attribu-
ted to a national or cultural
community, see the name of

that culture or community.

Ecce Agnus
Grassmere; X7908 O so bright
Homeward
How gladly
Merciful Saviour
On the wood His arms (Mediae-
val mel)
Redeemer (ca 1400); X2711
Du vaere lovet, Jesus; X3615
Gelobet seist du
Reykjavik (15th c)
Shepherds in the field abiding
(ancient)
Venite adoremus
Trappist Monks' contributions are
entered as: A Monk of Gethse-
mani
Trebel, G. H.
Godfrey (1910)
Heavenly City (1883)
Thou, whose Almighty Word
(1903)
Trebel
Trembath, Henry G., 1844-1908
Rosmore (1893)
Trier Gesangbuch, 1695
Sunrise; X2318 Daily, sing in
praise of Mary; X7136
Mother, Mary, at thy altar
Triller (no initials)
Spiritus Sancti gratia (1555)
Troup, E. Josephine
Truth
Trowbridge, J. C.
Jesus is coming
Troyte, Arthur Henry Dyke,
1811-57
Lonsdale
My God, my Father
Troyte (1860)
Troyte, No. 1; X1602 Chant
(Troyte, No. 1); X7213 My
God, my Father
Troyte, No. 2; X1603 Chant
(Troyte, No. 2)
True, Latham
Donum Dei
Truss, Ida T.
The happy story hour (1936)
Tschaikowsky, Peter Ilitch, see
Tchaikowsky, P. I.

Tscherlitzky, Johann H.
Glorification (1832); X3943
Gottes lamm ruft gnade
Tucker, Henry
Hobart
Joy-bells (1850)
Tucker, Isaac
Devizes
Tuckerman, Samuel Parkman,
1819-90
Humility
Tuckett, Henry A.
Choose the right
We are sowing
Tufts, John Wheeler, 1825-
1908
Adoration
Tullar, Grant Colfax, 1869-
1950
Face to face (1899)
Nailed to the cross
Tullar (1912); X8215 Our best
Tullidge, John
An angel from on high
Come, all ye sons of Zion
Think not, when you gather
Turle, James, 1802-82
Armagh (1861); X11456
Turle
Fairfield
Lostwithiel (1854)
St John's Westminster (1862);
X9443 St John
St Peter's Westminster
(1862); X9568 St Peter's
Westminster (1835)
Turner, Herbert B., 1852-
1927
Cushman (1905)
Earl (1893)
Turner, William, 1651-1740
Egham
Turpin, Edmund Hart, 1835-
1907
Argyle (1866)
Litany No. 1 (1875)
Litany No. 2 (1875)
Litany No. 7 (1875)
Litany No. 8 (1875)
Mansfield (1889)
Turpin's Litany; X6246
Litany, No. 7
Turton, Thomas, 1780-1864

Ely (1844)
  St Etheldreda; X9380 St Ethel-
    reda
Tye, Christopher, 1500-72
  Farrant
  Gethsemane (1553)
  Southwark
  Windsor (1553); X2737 Dundee
    (Damon's Booke of musicke,
    1591); X12308 Windsor and
    Eton
  Yattendon 15 (arr by H.E.
    Wooldridge); X12499
    Yattendon
Tyler, James Sherman, 1842-1917
  City bright
Tyrolese traditional
  NOTE: See also the Swiss
traditional tunes.

  Andreas Hofer (National song
    of the Tyrol)
  Falan-tidings; X11477 Tyrolese
  Tyrolean Cradle song

                    U

Udulutsch, Irvin, O.F.M.
  Mary Immaculate, Star
Ufford, Edwin S., 1851-1929
  I believe the Bible
  Life line; X11235 Throw out
    the life-line
Ukranian melody
  Shepherd care
Ulich, Johann
  Meinen Jesum lass ich nicht
    (1674)
Union harmony, 1793 see Holden,
  Oliver. Union Harmony, 1793
Unitas Fratrum (as author) see
  Bohemian Brethren
Unseld, Benjamin C., 1843-
  1923
  Ancyra (1901)
  Euphemia (1901)
  Gracious King enthroned (1901)
  Once more before we part
    X10572 Sweet day
Updegraff, E. Grace
  Carter
Urhan, Chrétien, 1790-1845

Rutherford (1834)

                    V

Vail, Silas Jones, 1818-84
  Close to Thee; X1132 Bless
    Jehovah; X4559 Helen;
    X11219 Thou, my ever-
    lasting
  Gates ajar; X10875 The gate
    ajar for me; X11137 There
    is a gate that stands ajar
  He died for thee
  We shall sleep, but not for-
    ever
Vale, Walter S.
  Cowley (1935)
Van Andel, Henry
  Calvin College (1928)
Van Arsdale, P.P.
  Mission song; X4355 Hark!
    the voice of Jesus
Van Damme, P.J., Canon of
  Ghent
    Adoro te, No. 2; X3670
    Ghent
Vanden Plas, E.
  Pie Jesu
Van der Werp, H.
  Passion (1911)
  Rehoboth (1911)
  Resting-place (1911)
  Van der Werp
Van Hoose, H.W.
  Increase my faith
Vassar College
  Peace I leave with you
    (1937)
Vaudois traditional see Swiss
  traditional
Vaughan, James D.
  Gathering buds
Vaughan Williams, Ralph see
  Williams, Ralph Vaughan
Vehe. Gesangbuchlein, 1537
  On Jordan's bank
  Wer da wonet; X5192 If,
    now, thou seekest miracles
Venua, Frederick Marc Antoine,
  1788-1872
  Park Street (1810)
Verdi, Fortunino Giuseppe
  Francesco, 1813-1901

Come unto Him and rest
Vetter, Daniel, d 1730
  Vetter (1713); X2363 Das walt'
    Gott [Vater]; X11642 Vetters
Vibbard, Harry
  Country lanes (1927)
Vibbert, W. H.
  Triumph, No. 2 (1896)
Vincent, Charles John, jr., 1852-
1934
  Donum Dei
  Dun Elm
  Monod (1877); X9458 St Jude
  St Ishmael
  Silksworth
  Southwick
  Whitstable
Vincent, G. F.
  Supplication (1890)
Viner, William Letton, 1790-
1867
  Dismissal (1845); X4201
    Guide me
Vitale, Tomaso
  O Lord, save thy people, arr
Vittoria, T. L., da
  Jesu dulcis memoria
Voigtländer, J.
  Vola
Vulpius, Melchior, 1560-1616
  NOTES: Unlatinized name was
Fuchs.
  The 1609 date following tune
name indicates its inclusion in
Vulpius' Gesangbuch, Jena, 1609

  Cana (1709); NOTE: This is
one of several tunes having 14
name variants in this index;
X84 Abide in grace; X104
    Ach bleib mit deiner gnade;
    X1178 Bliv med din store
    naade; X1299 Bremen; X1709
    Christ is my life; X1795
    Christus der ist mein; X
    4549 Heidelberg; X5004 Hymn
    to St Joseph; X6211 Lincoln;
    X6842 Mein leben; X7463
    Normanton; X8455 Phuvah;
    X11754 Vulpius; X11966 Wei-
    mar
  Das Neugeborne (1609); X2361
    Das neugeborne kindelein;

X5494 Jena; X9819 Search
    me, O God
  Der tag bricht an; X1288
    Break thou, O Lord, the
    bread
  Die Helle Sonn' leucht't
    (1609)
  Gelobt sei Gott (1609);
    X11753 Vulpius
  Lobet den Herrn, ihr (1609)
    X6311 Lobt Gott; X6866
    Melchior
  Lusatia
  Weimar (1609); X1691 Choral;
    X4111 Gregor's 152d
    metre-B; X5549 Jesu,
    deine passion; X5614 Jesu
    Kreuz, leiden und pein;
    X5617 Jesu leiden, pein
    und tod

W

W. C. B.
  St John's, Highlands
Wade, J. F. Cantus diversi,
1751
  Adeste fideles; X1910 Come,
    all ye faithful; X7617 O
    come, all ye faithful;
    X8540 Portuguese; X8541
    Portuguese hymn
  St Thomas; X3154 Evensong;
    X4763 Hollywood; X4835
    Holywood; X7514 Novello;
    X9444 St John; X10061
    Sing my tongue, the Sa-
    viour's glory; X10685
    Tantum ergo
Wade, James Clifft, 1847-
  Holy Cross, arr
Waghorne, William Richard, 1881-
  Greystone (1906)
Wagner, J. G. MS Gesangbuch.
  Langenöls, 1742
  Wir glauben all' an einen
    Gott; X8530 Pomerania
Wagner, J. G. Sammlung alter
und neuer, 1742
  Gottlob, es geht nunmehr
    zu Ende; X3951 Gottlob;
    X5650 Jesus, my Lord,
    my God; X11967 Weisse

Wagner, Wilhelm Richard, 1813-
83
  Da zu dir der Heiland kam;
    X6859 Meistersinger chorale
  Lohengrin (1850)
  Parsifal (1882)
  Pilgrim's chorus [sic] (1845);
    X5388 Invocation; X8469a;
    Pilgrim chorus; X11015 The
    pilgrim's chorus
  Rise, O Lord
  Temple (1868)
  The Lord God Jesus Christ
Wainwright, John, 1723-68
  Yorkshire (1750); X1782
    Christmas hymn; X10422
    Stockport
Wainwright, Robert (or Richard),
1748-82
  Liverpool
  Manchester (1791); X6676 Man-
    chester new
  Wainwright (1790)
Walch, James, 1837-1901
  Eagley
  St George's Bolton (1875)
  Sawley (1860); X7203 My God,
    accept my heart
  Tidings (1876); X466 Angelic
    songs; X7907 O Sion, haste;
    X8668 Proclamation; X11454
    Tunbridge
Walder, Johann Jakob, 1750-1817
  Walder (1788); X12377 Wolder
    (Wolder)
Waldis, Burkard
  Es muss die ganz Christenschar
    (1553); X8514 Pleasure it is
  Säll du, som dig at Gud be-
    tror (1553)
  Waldis (1553); X7710 O Gud!
    ditt rike ingen
Walenn, J. F.
  Walenn
Wales, Univ. of. Student's hymnal,
1923
  Childhood
  Courage
  Quinta
  Reunion
  Rhiw
Walker, Edward Charles, 1848-
72

  King's College
  St Marguerite (1876); X6715
    Marguerite
Walker, William. Southern
harmony, 1835 see Southern
  harmony, 1835
Wallace, William Vincent, 1814-
65
  Serenity (1856); X5384 Invita-
    tion
  Wallace
Walmisley, Thomas Attwood,
1814-56
  Walmisley
Walter, Samuel
  O love, how deep (1964)
Walter, William Henry, 1825-
93
  Festal song (1894)
Walters, E.
  Dear little One
Walther, Carl Ferdinand Wil-
helm, 1811-87
  Walther (1860)
Walther, Johannes, 1496-1570.
Geistliches Gesangbuchlein.
Wittenberg 1524.
  NOTES: Walther's original
name was Blanckenmüller.
  This was the first Protestant
singing-book: containing eight
hymns (four by Luther), and
with music edited and prepared
by Walther. Cf. both Baker
(on Walther) and Julian (on
Luther).

  Christ unser Herr zum Jor-
    dan kam; X4131 Gregor's
    201st metre
  Confession; X11653 Vi tro
    og trøste paa; X12328 Wir
    glauben all an
  De profundis; X194 Af dyb-
    sens nød; X707 Aus tiefer
    not [noth]
  Es spracht der Unweisen
    Mund
  Gott des Vater wohn'
  Lieblich, dunkel, sanft und
    stille (date uncertain)
  Mensch, willt du leben
    seliglich

Mit Fried' und Freud'
Mitten wir im Leben sind;
   X6943 Midt i livit ere vi
Soldau; X3334 Fidei unitas;
   X4080 Gregor's 58th metre;
   X7540 Nu bede vi den helli-
   gaand; X7551 Nun bitten wir
   den; X10302 Spiritus
Soldau, Pt. II; X4081 Gregor's
   58th metre, Pt. II
Venit hora (Bach arr); X3334
   Fidei unitas; X5009 Hymn to
   the sorrowful Mother; X5888
   Kom, du folkefrelser; X7566
   Nun komm der heiden;
   X11595a Veni, redemptor;
   X11597, Veni redemptor
   gentium
Walther; X3939 Gott sei gelobet;
   X4189 Gud vaere lovet evig
Wär Gott nicht mit uns
Walton, Herbert Francis Raine,
  1869-
   Children's song
Warburton, J.S.
   Spes meo in deo
Ward, Samuel Augustus, 1847-
  1903
   Materna (1882); X7595 O beau-
   tiful for spacious skies;
   X10911 The Holy City;
   X12345 With songs and
   honors
Warlock, Peter (pseud of Philip
  Heseltine), 1894-1930
   Adam lay ybounden (1925)
   Balulalow
   Tyrley, Tyrlow
Warner, Massah M., 1836-1900
   Amadeus
   Art thou weary? (1890)
   Dickson
   Proclamation
   Roepper
   Softly the night is sleeping;
   X11829 Warner
Warner, Richard, 1908-
   Ramwold
Warrack, Guy, 1900-
   Wellington Square (1931)
Warrell, Arthur Sydney, 1883-
  1939
   Farmborough

Warren, B. Elliott
   A ransom for all
   Come closer to me
   Ever lead me
   Glory to God in the highest
   His yoke is easy; X10962
     The Lord is my Shepherd
     (Hudson)
   I would be closer to thee
   Keep me near thee
   Let not your heart be
     troubled
   Long have they waited (1900)
   Lost forever
   Not dead, but sleeping
   Saviour, I'm coming
   Sin can never enter there
   Sing about Jesus
   The bond of perfectness
   The Christian's Guide
   The eventide
   The last great day
   The ninety-nine
   The temple of God
   Two little hands
   Watch unto prayer
   Weighed in the balance
   What a mighty God!
   Where will I go? (1923)
   Why carelessly wait?
Warren, George William, 1828-
  1902
   Ecce agnus
   Columbia College (1886)
   Grace
   Guide me (1884)
   Log College
   National hymn (1892); X3834
     God of our fathers; X8666
     Pro patria
   Resurrection morning
Warren, Ivor
   Whose works, O Lord, like
     Thine
Warren, Samuel Prowse, 1841-
  1914
   Bread of life; X11832 Warren
   Gould
   Unity (1886)
Wartensee, Xavier Schnyder von,
  see Schnyder von Wartensee,
    Xavier.
Wathall, Alfred G.

Ascending song (1905)
Fellowship (1905)
Festgesang (1905)
Greeting (1905)
Implicit trust (1905)
Plymouth (1905)
Stella (1905)
Watson, Adam, 1845-1912
Wonderful love
Watson, James, 1816-80
Holyrood (1867)
Watson, Lawrence White, 1860-
1927
Salve Domini (1909)
Watson, Sydney, 1903-
May Hill
Stonor
Wytham
Watts-Hughes, Megan, 1842-1907
Wilton Square
Weale, William, ca 1690-1727
see Wheall, William
Webb, George James, 1803-87
NOTE: See also Mason and
Webb. Cantica laudis.

Webb (1837); X3912 Goodwin;
X5103 I need thee, precious
Jesus; X5121 I thank the Lord
my maker; X7107 Morning
light; X10355 Stand up, stand
up for
Webbe, Samuel, 1740-1816
Behold! behold He cometh
Benevento (1792)
Consolation (1792); X375 Alma
X380 Alma redemptoris
[mater]; X1993 Come, ye
disconsolate; X2105 Consola-
tor; X2601 Disconsolate;
X8238 Out of the depths;
X11948 Webbe
Melcombe (1782); X590 As fades
the glowing orb; X7312
Nazareth; X7891 O salutaris
Hostia; X7927 O thou immor-
tal Light
Veni Sancte Spiritus (1782);
X1973 Come, thou Holy
Spirit, come; X4823 Holy
Spirit, Lord of light
Webbe, Samuel, jr., 1770-1843
is often cited as composer

in Gardiner's Sacred melo-
dies
Webbe, William Y.
King Olaf
Weber, Carl Maria Fried-
rich Ernst von, 1736-1826
Help us, O God
Jewett (1820); X2496 Der
Freyschuetz; X7220
My Jesus, as thou wilt;
X8522 Poacher; X11950
Weber
Seymour (1826); X1623
Chatham; X10144 Softly
now the light; X11951
Weber
Wilmot; X4358 Hark! what
mean those holy voices;
X6225 Listen to the
gentle promptings
Weber, Frederich Wilhelm,
1813-94
Paean; X8305 Paradise
Webster, Harry, 1878-
Nil nisi labore
Webster, Joseph Philbrick,
1819-75
Sweet by and bye (1868);
X11168 There's a land
Webster, Lorin
Ruth (1905)
Service (1905)
Webster, Mary Phillips, 1858-
Chadwick (1913)
He leads us on (1913)
Weeden, Winfield S., 1847-
1908
My mother's prayer
Sunlight
Surrender; X5120 I surren-
der all
Weekes, Samuel, 1843-
Brent
Burleigh
Weimar, Georg Peter, 1734-
1800
Allgütiger, mein Preis-
gesang; X3020 Erfurt
Brasted (1780)
Weimar Gesangbuch, 1681
Jesu, meines lebens leben;
X337 Alle menschen
müssen sterben; X2351

Darmstadt; X12579 Zurich
Weinberg, Jacob, 1879-1956
  A week within the Sukko green
    (1932); X9994 Sh'meenee
    atseres
  Grant me strength (1932)
  Hymn for Day of Atonement
    (1932)
  If our God had not befriended
    (1932)
  Lord, what offering shall we
    bring (1932); X12542 Yom
    Kippur prayer
  O Lord, where shall I find
    Thee? (1932)
  Once more, O Lord (1932)
  Psalm 119 (1932)
  Sound the loud timbrel (1932)
  Ten thousand martyrs (1932)
Weisenthal, T.V. (or F.V.)
  Salvation (1830)
Weisse, Michael, ca 1430-1534
  Michael
Weisse, M. Ave hierarchia,
  1531
    Ravenshaw; X3944 Gottes sohn
      ist kommen; X7064 Moravia;
      X8033 Old 72d
Wellesley, Garrett, 1735-81 see
  Mornington, Earl of
NOTE: Sometimes written "Wes-
ley", by other members of the
large family.
Wells, Marcus Morris, 1815-95
  Holy Spirit, faithful Guide
    X3231 Faithful guide; X4200
    Guide; C12000 Wells
Welsh traditional, and traditional
  hymn tunes (marked *)
  April; X4717 Hir oesi fair
  Ar hyd y nos; X323 All through
    the night; X12002 Welsh
    hymn
  Arfon (major reading)*
  Arfon (minor reading)*
  Ash Grove, see English
    traditional, etc.
  Blaenhafren
  Braint
  Caerlleon*
  Crugybar*
  Denbigh*

Dolgelly* (19th c)
Erfyniad*
Ffigysbren* (1840)
Glan Geirionydd*
Gwalchmai
Gwalia
Hail, Guest
Harlech
Jabez*
Llanfyllin (1865)
Llangan
Llangoedmor * (1826)
Llanilar*
Llansannan*
Lledrod* (1859); X6283
  Llangollen
Maldwyn (ca 1600)
Moriah*
Nos Galan; X2431 Deck the
  halls
O Thou who hearest prayer
Poverty; X8087 Olwen
Rhuddlan
Rhyddid*
St Denio; X5701 Joanna
Suo-gân
Talyllyn
Trefaenan
Welsh carol
Ymdaith mwnge; X7037 Monk's
  march
Weman, Henry
  Weman (1937)
Wennerberg, Gunnar, 1817-
1901
  Thy Kingdom come; X11270
    Tillkomme ditt rike
  Wennerberg I
  Wennerberg II
Werner, Arno, 1865-1955
  O salutaris hostia
Wesley, Charles, the younger,
  1757-1834
  Berkshire
  Epworth
  Lystra
Wesley, John. Foundery col-
  lection, 1742
    Savannah (from a MS choral-
      buch. Herrnhut, ca 1740)
Wesley, Samuel, 1866-1837
  Bristol

Doncaster (1837); X1061
  Bethlehem
Hierapolis
Sanctus
Wesley, Samuel Sebastian, 1810-
76
  NOTE: His European Palmist,
1872 melodies are included below.

Achill (1872)
Alcester, arr
Alleluia (1868)
Almsgiving; X9830 Sebastian
Ashburton
Aurelia (1864); X511 Another
  year is dawning; X10838
  The church's one foundation
Bowden, arr
Brecknock
Brief life is here our portion
Bude
Clevedon
Colchester (1872)
Cornwall
Dawn
Eden, W.
Ellingham
Engedi
Epworth
Eternity
Grace Dieu
Gratitude; X6877 Memoria
Gweedore
Harewood (1839); X4422
  Havewood
Hawarden
Hawkridge
Hereford (1872)
Hornsey
Lead me, Lord
Mara
Morning (see also his Streatley)
Orisons
Patmos
Philadelphia, arr
Radford
Remembrance
St Michael New
Sebastian (1872); X4900
  Houghton
Serug (1872)
Streatley, arr (see also his
  morning); X4424 Hawes

Trinity
Weston
Wetherby (1872)
Wigan (1872)
Wimbledon (1864)
Winscott
Wrestling Jacob; X8411
  Peniel
Wessnitzer, Wolfgang
  Aldwinkle (1665)
  Tviflan ur min sjal förs-
    vinne (1661)
West, Dorothy
  God's presence
West, John A.
  Godfrey
West, John Ebenezer, 1863-
1929
  Holy Cross
West, Lewis Renatus, 1753-
1826
  Moravia (1795); X11479
    Tytherton; X12039
    West
Westlake, Frederick, 1840-98
  St Ursula (1863)
Wetterling, Hampus, 1830-70
  Wetterling; X10413 Stilla,
    ja, allt mera
Weyse, Christoph Ernst Freid-
rich, 1774-1842
  Cheerfulness; X406 Altid
    frejdig naar du
  Christmas brings joy; X
    9919 Sewey
  Store Gud, som dig til
    Aere
  Weyse; X2475 Den signede
    dag; X7641 O day full
    of grace
  Weyse II (1837)
Wheall, William, ca 1690-1927
  Bedford (1723)
Wheelwright, Lorin F.
  Come all ye saints
Whelan, Ernest H.
  Lux perpetua (1891)
Whelpton, George, 1847-
1930
  Dismissal
  Hear our prayer (1897);
    X12102 Whelpton
Whinfield, Wallis Grenville,

1865-1919
Universal praise (1906)
Upwick
Worcester
Wychbold
Whitaker, John, 19th c.
NOTE: Perhaps John Whitaker,
1820-95 of Whitaker's Almanack
Wimborne
White, Benjamin Franklin
Hamilton (1844)
White, L. Meadows
Meadows
Motherhood (1899)
White, J.E. [probably John
White, 1855-1902]
Marietta (1878?)
White
White Spirituals.
Herein filed under "American
traditional" are melodies from
the Appalachian and Piedmont: as
Foundation
Amazing grace
Cleansing fountain
See also file, "Negro spirit-
uals", etc.
Whitehead, Alfred, 1887-
Wellard
Whitehead, Alfred E.
Chichester (1941)
Whitehead, H., O.P.
Hail, holy Joseph (20th c)
O Christ, thy guilty people
(20th c)
Whitehead, H.A.
Victory
Whitehead, J. Brinton, 1869-
Whitehead (1909)
Whiting, Arthur Battelle, 1861-
1936
Litany No. 4
Whitlock, Percy
Infinitas
Oblation (1932)
Presence (1932)
Satis (1932)
Whitmer, Thomas Carl, 1873-
Deed (1930)
Golden trumpets (1930)
Gratitude (1929)
Whitney, H.N.
Luella

Whitney, Samuel Brenton, 1842-
1914
Coelestis aula
Crusader (1889)
Whittington, C.J.
Arise, O Lord
City strong and mighty
Glory flaming
I bow in utter need
I come into thy house
Thy testimonies, arr
Whitwell, W.J.
Groombridge
Widdeman, E.S.
McCabe
Saviour, again to thy dear
Name; X2998 Enon
Widdemer, E.S., see Widde-
man, E.S.
Widéen, Karl Ivor Natanael,
1871-1951
Security; X11443 Tryggare
kan ingen
Skara
Wilcox, J.H., see Willocx,
John H.
Wild, A.A.
Beaufort
Wilkes, John Bernard, 1785-
1869
Lyte (1861)
Wilkin's Psalmody, 1669
Stroudwater
Wilkinson, Walter Olivant, 1852-
Presbyter (1895)
Willan, Healey, 1880-
Eternal Light
Haec Dies
Hail Mary
St Basil
Stella orientis
Willcocks, David Valentine,
1919-
Conquering love
Willcox, John Henry, 1827-75
Faben (1849)
Jesu, bone pastor; X5659 Jesu
pastor
Williams, Aaron, 1731-76
Mear; X7580 Nun sich der
tag
St Thomas (1763); X1992
Come, we that love

Williams, Benjamin, 1839-1918
 Deganwy
Williams, C.C.
 Have you any room for Jesus?
Williams, Charles Lee, 1853-
 1935
 Gloucester (1890); X1697 Christ
  by heavenly hosts
 Tibberton (1885)
 Williams
Williams, David McKinley, 1887-
 Canticum refectionis (1941)
 Christus rex (1941)
 Georgetown (1941)
 Malabar (1941)
 Non nobis Domine (1942)
 St Bartholomew's
 Trackless ways (1936)
Williams, F.W.
 Willington (1851)
Williams, J.E.
 Don't let your light burn low
Williams, J. Rhosyd, 1885-
 Overdale
Williams, John (Dolgelley),
 1740-1821
 Brynhyfryd
Williams, Ralph Vaughan, 1872-
 1958
 Abinger (1931)
 Blake's Cradle hymn (1928)
 Cumnor (1925)
 Down Ampney (1906)
 Famous men (1923)
 Guildford (1925)
 King's Weston (1925)
 Magda (1925)
 Mantegna (1931)
 Marathon (1928)
 Oakley (1925)
 Randolph
 Salve festa dies (1906)
 Sine nomine (1906)
 Snow in the street
 The call (1911)
 The golden carol (1928)
 White gates
 Wither's Rocking hymn (1928)
Williams, Robert, ca 1781-1821
 Llanfair (1817)
Williams, Thomas. Psalmody,
 ca 1770
 Durham; X2675 Dover;

X4302 Hampton;
X4953 Huddersfield
Williams, Thomas (Hafrenydd),
 1807-94
 Llandinam
 Nantmel
Williams, Thomas John, 1869-
 1944
 Ebenezer (1890); X11331
  Ton-y-botel
Williams, W.A.
 Christ is all
Williamson, J., 1868-1947
 St Katrine
Willing, Christopher E., 1830-
 1904
 Alstone (1868); X12276 Will-
  ing
Willis, J.A. (or T.A.?)
 Lucerne
Willis, Richard Storrs, 1819-
 1900
 Carol (1850); X5427 It came
  upon the midnight; X12184
  While shepherds watched
  their
 Madison
Wilms, Jan Willem, 1772-1847
 Hague; X4757 Holland; X6150
  Leyden; X11427 Trust, No.
  2
Wilson, A.W., 1869-
 Perranporth
Wilson, David Frederick Rud-
 dell, 1871-1957
 Drumcondra
Wilson, Emily D., 1865-1942
 Heaven; X12158 When we all
  get to heaven
Wilson, Hugh, 1764-1825
 Lucas
 Martyrdom (ca 1800); X100
  According to thy gracious
  word; X304 All saints;
  X757 Avon; X6153a Liber-
  ty Hall (---); X7522 Now
  from the altar of my
  heart; X7524 Now, gra-
  cious Lord, thine arm;
  X10710 Teach me the
  measure; X12284 Wilson
Wilson, Ira B.
 May God depend on you?

(1878)
Our Pilot (1907)
Wilson, Robert H.
    Seedtime
Wilson, Roger Charles, 1912-
Dayton (1958)
    Spiritus domini (1958)
Wilson, W (?)
    Arabia (1833)
Wiltberger, August, 1850-1928
    Hymn to the Holy Cross (1908)
Winchester, Caleb Thomas, 1847-
1920
    Middletown (1905)
Winding, August Henrik, 1835-99
    Winding I
    Winding II; X7340 Nestling;
        X10177 Som hønen klukker
        mindelig
Winn, William, 1828-88
    Barnby's Hymnary Tune 525
        (1872)
Winner, Septimus, 1827-1902
    see Hawthorne, Alice, pseud.
Wilson, Selection of Psalm Tunes.
1825
    Smith
Winsett, R. E.
    The Church of the living God
        (1918)
    The great reaping day
    The midnight cry
Wise, Michael, ca 1648-87
    Congleton
Wiseman, Frederick Luke, ca
1859-1944
    All Hallows
    Wonderful love
Wissmer, Pierre, 1915-
    Geneva (1939)
    Miron (1939)
Witt, Christian Friedrich, 1660-
1716
    Ach, wann werd ich dahin kom-
        men (1715)
    Stuttgart (1715); X1064 Bethle-
        hem, of noblest; X8345 Pas-
        tor benignus
Wittwe, Georg. Musikalisches
Handbuch. Hamburg, 1690
    Crasselius; X2597 Dir, dir,
        Jehova, will ich singen;
        X4095 Gregor's 106th metre;

X5162 Ich armer mensch, ich
    armer suender; X12024a Wer
    weiss, wie nahe (Bronner.
    Choralbuch, 1715)
Winchester New; X2201 Crassel-
    ius; X8096 On Jordan's bank;
    X12024a Wer weiss, wie nahe
    (Bronner. Choral-buch,
    1715); X12298 Winchester old
Wolder. Catechismus-Gesangbüch-
lein, 1598
    Wolder; X703 Aus meines her-
        zens grunde; X2903 Eiselben;
        X7065 Moravia; X8908 Rejoic-
        ing; X11067 The Spirit of the
        Lord revealeth
Wolff, J.
    Naar Tid og Stund den er forha-
        and (1560); X1454 Calvary;
        X12011 Wenn mein stündlein
        vorhanded ist
    Wolff (1568)
Wolle, John Frederick,1863-1933
    Advent
    Dies Irae I (1890)
    Dies Irae II (1890)
    Palmarum (1923)
Wolle, Theodore Frederick,
1832-85
    Asleep in Jesus (1877)
Wonnberger, C.
    Alleluia, Jesus lives
    Inita
    Wonnberger (in Schemelli.
        Gesangbuch, 1736); X5178
        Ich steh an deiner krippe
Wood, Basil
    Paddington
Wood, Charles, 1866-1926
    Cambridge (1925)
    Rangoon
    Recessional
Wood, D. J.
    Isca
    Pastor
Wood, David Duffle, 1838-1910
    St Stephen's Church (1895);
        X5759 Juniata
Wood, Thomas, 1892-1950
    St Osyth (1925)
    School house (1931)
Woodbury, Isaac Baker, 1819-
58

NOTE: Original spelling as
Woodberry.

Burton
Chopin
Desire
Dorrnance (1845); X10659 Tal-
   mar; X11200 This is not my
   place
Edmeston
Ella
Enon's Isle
Eucharist (1856); X8082 Olivet;
   X12421 Woodbury
Happy Sion
Lake Enon (1854); X6894
   Mercersburg
Life's harvest
Modena
Nearer home (1852); X6397
   Lord, when at thy command;
   X7053 Montgomery; X12422
   Woodbury
Ozrem
Rakem
Selena; X3836 God of our
   fathers, known of old
Siloam
Speed away
Woodman, Jonathan Call, 1813-
94
   State Street (1844)
Woodman, Raymond Huntington,
1861-1943
   Adoration (1893)
   Bethlehem
   Unity (1895)
   Woodman
Woods, Bertram Ernest, 1900-
   Norwick
Wooldridge, Harry Ellis, 1845-
1917
   Yattendon 4 (1891)
   Yattendon 11 (1890)
   Yattendon 17 (1899)
   Yattendon 18 (1899)
   Yattendon 22 (1887)
   Yattendon 46 (1899)
Wooler, Alfred, 1867-1937
   Incarnation (1920)
Woollen, Russell, 1923-
   Lord of nations

Worcester, John
   Westall (1893)
Worden, B. T.
   Crossing the bar (1905)
Work, Henry Clay, 1832-84
   Come, Saviour, come
Wostenholm, Maurice L., 1887-
   My Holyoke (1910)
Wright, J.B.F.
   Precious memories
Wright, Thomas, 1763-1829
   Stockton
Wrigley, W.A.
   Thirsk
Würtemberg Gesangbuch, 1784
   Ellacombe; X5588 Jesus is
   God; X7869 O Queen of
   the Holy Rosary; X11189
   Think gently of the erring
   one
Würzburg Gesangbuch, 1628
   O Traurigkeit; X548 Ari-
   mathaea; X4075 Gregor's
   45th metre; X7635 O dark-
   est woe; X7734 O hjertens
   ve; X7939 O traurigkeit!
   O herzeleid
Wyeth, John, 1770-1858
   Nettleton (1825); X1971
   Come, thou fount
Wyeth, J. Repository of sacred
   music. Pt. II; 1813
   Morning song; X2101 Consola-
   tion; X2524 Detroy (Suppl.
   to Kentucky Harmony,
   1820)
Wyvill, Z., 1762-1837
   Wyvill

                            Y

Yenn, S.M.
   Hail Virgin, dearest Mary
   Mother of mercy (1920)
   Why art thou sorrowful?
Yoakley, John, 1860-1915
   All souls
Yoakley, William, 1820-
   Yoakley (1841)
Yon, Pietro Alessandro, 1886-
1943
   St Augustine (1939)

When blossoms flowered (1917)
York Breviary
   Jesu, Salvator saeculi
Young, Alfred
   See, He comes (1953)
   Slain for my soul
Young, E. Edwin
   Jesus, revealed in me (1931)
Young, Walter E.
   Falmouth (1932)
   Fortitude (1932)
   Love (1932)
   Saviour (1932)

Z

Ziegler, Charles L.
   Church vigilant (1902)
Zeuner, Charles, 1795-1857
   see his real name, Zeuner,
   Heinrich Christoph, 1795-
   1857
Zeuner, Heinrich Christoph,
   1795-1857
   Groton
   Hummel
   Luther's Chant
   Missionary Chant
   Oaksville (1839)

Zinck, Hartnack Otto Konrad,
   1746-1832
   Congregation
   Copenhagen; X5488 Jeg vil
     mig Herren love; X7808
     O living Bread
Zinck, H. O. K. Koralbog,
   1801
   Naglet til et Kors paa Jor-
     den; X2260 Crucifixion
   Paa Gud alene; X5267 In
     God, my Saviour; X12566
     Zinck
   Paa sit Kors i Dodens
     Smerte
   Zinck; X7546 Nu rinder
     solen op; X10513 Sunrise
Zundel, John, 1815-82
   Beecher (1870); X6430 Love
     divine; X12578 Zundel
   Brooklyn (1852)
   Lebanon; X5135 I was a
     wandering sheep
   Louisville
   Zundel (ca 1855)
Zwingli, Huldrich (or Ulrich)
   1484-1531
   Zwingli

Melodies, a Systematic Index

DDD - (Multiple)

DDDDTLSM, RMFLSMS, D	5798	
DDDDTLSM, FFFFSFM, D	12509	
DDDDTLSMS, DDDDTLT	4445	
DDDDTLSFMFS, DDLLS	5989	
DDDDTLSS, MSRMFSFM,	3789	
DDDDTLSS, SSSSSSS, M	2756	
DDDDTLSLMSF, RRRRD	1853	
DDDDTLS, LLLLSFM, DD	12466	
DDDDTLLSS, SLSFSFM	34	
DDDRDDDRMFM, MSFMR	5490	
DDDRDD, DTDLSS, DDDR	9414	
DDDRDDS, LSLTDD, DD	10736	
DDDRDDT, LSSDMR, MFS	9472	
DDDRDMFSSLS, LTDSS	3555	
DDDRDTDR, RMDDRMRD,	9897	
DDDRDTSLTD, MRTDTL	1627	
DDDRDTTL, LDRMMR	641	
DDDR, RRM, MMMF, RFM.	5082	
DDDR, RRM, MMMS, MDR, MM		
	7598	
DDDRRMDDRDT, MMMMR	3383	
DDDRRMRDR, DDDRMFM	6386	
DDDRRM, MMLSMRD, SSM	4840	
DDDRRMFS, SSMLTDTL	4625	
DDDRRM, SFMMRR, RRLS	11179	
DDDRRFMRM, MFMMLSF#	11862	
DDDRRSFM, MRDDTD, DD	3627	
DDDRR#MMS, FMDMRR, MF		
	8820	
DDDRMD, DTDRMS, FSLT	5708	
DDDRMD, RTDTL, DDDRM	6764	
DDDRMD, MMMFSM, SMDL	2984	
DDDRMDMFS, DTLS, DDD	11700	
DDDRMRD, RMRSSF#S, LS	11599	
DDDRMRDR, MSLSFMRD	8999	
DDDRMR, DMRRD, DDDRM	671	
DDDRMRDTS, DSSF#SMR,	6429	
DDDRMR, SSMSLSFMFM	11732	
DDDRMMRR, MFSLTS, SD	9607	
DDDRMMRR, SDDRMSMR,	12541	
DDDRMFRD, MRRLTDRD	2571	
DDDRMFRDTD, MMFSSL	8248	
DDDRMFRM, DMFSRSF#S	482	
DDDRMFRM, DMSLSFMR,	1607	
DDDRMFRS, DMFSRSF#S,	479	
DDDRMFMRD, DDMRDTL	12286	
DDDRMFMRM, MMMF#SLS	794	
DDDRMFMR, MFSSLLS, M	9571	
DDDRMFM, MRDDTD, DDD	3507	
DDDRMFFM, SDMMF#S	9352	
DDDRMFFM, SMFSLRR, S	3720	
DDDRMFSLSM, DDDRMF	11457	
DDDRMFSL, TDRSSFR, R	782	

DDDRMSM, DDDRMMRD, D	7502	
DDDRMS, MSFMRD, DDDR	3230	
DDDRMSFMR, DDRFMRM,	6935	
DDDRMSFF, MMMRDT, TD	1294	
DDDRMS, FFFLD, DDTLS	9180	
DDDRMSLS, RRRMFSLS	5544	
DDDRMSLS, MDSMMR, SM	12269	
DDDRFMFS, SSSLLSFM	8366	
DDDRSM, MMMFMR, SSFM	11684	
DDDRTDRM, MRRRDTLS,	8680	
DDDRTD, MMMMFRM, SD	9373	
DDDRTD, MMMFRM, SDLS	9374	
DDDRTDTLS, SDRMRDT	7544	
DDDMDDDM, MMMMRDDM,	3867	
DDDMDMSDMRDS, FLFM	8589	
DDDMDFMRD, MMMRMFM	4624	
DDDMDSRM, LSMFMDS, S	4182	
DDDMDSSDTSLSM, DSL	4661	
DDDMRD, RRRFMR, MF#F#S,		
	7362	
DDDMRDRRF, RMMSFML	1296	
DDDMRDRM, MMMLSF#S, S	162	
DDDMRDFM, MMMSMRTL	4995	
DDDMRDTD, MRMFMRM	11960	
DDDMRDTDS, MMMSFMR	6553	
DDDMRDTRD, DLDLDSF	754	
DDDMRRD, DDDFMR, SSS	461	
DDDMMRRSFM, FMFRML	4473	
DDDMMM, SSSLRM, DDDL	10382	
DDDMMFFS, DDMMFFSL,	5196	
DDDMML, LSDFMR, RMSL	2548	
DDDMFS, MLLSRM, MMMM	11261	
DDDMFSSS, SLSMFS, SL	10455	
DDDMFSLS, DDDMFSLS	5257	
DDDMFSLS, SDDMFSL	5256	
DDDMSSD, DRMDRDTLS,	1696	
DDDMSSL, SMRDDTDR, R	9554	
DDDMSLSSMDTRD, DDD	3263	
DDDMSLS, SMMRDM, DDD	2044	
DDDMLSMR, DDLSSLT, S	9416	
DDDFRMFS, SLTDTDLS,	5167	
DDDFRMF#S, MFSLFSF, S	5166	
DDDFRMF#S, SLTDTLS, S	5165	
DDDFMDLTD, SDTLTDR,	8584	
DDDFMRD, DLSDMRR, DD	5799	
DDDFMRD, DLSDMRRS, D	11378	
DDDFFFFL, LLSSMSMR	10854	
DDDSDD, RRRLRR, MMMF#	1816	
DDDSDRMD, LLSDFMR, R	7087	
DDDSDRM, MRRRRMD, D, DD	285	
DDDSDRM, MMLLSF#S, DD	4159	
DDDSDRM, LSFMRDR, DD	1405	
DDDSDMRD, MMMDMSFM,	6136	

1054

DDDSDMMR, RMFFDRM, D 6807
DDDSDMSFM, MMMRFRD 4577
DDDSMFSLSD, RMRSLT 4870
DDDSMFSLS, MMMMMMF 1706
DDDSFMDLFS, SLLLFL 1173
DDDSSD, SSSSMS, MMMF# 183
DDDSSLFS, SDRMFSFM 6112
DDDSSLLS, SSDTSLLS, 7727
DDDSSLTD, DDTTLSLS, 1048
DDDSSLTD, SFSMRR, DD 6873
DDDS, SLTRDTDFMM, SF 8759
DDDSLDRD, DMDDRT, DD 6171
DDDSLDTLS, DTLSLFM 2880
DDDSLMMRD, MMRDLDR 975
DDDSLM, MFRMFS, DTLS, 6970
DDDSLS, SDRMRD, DMSM 6097
DDDSLSLD, MMRDDMS, S 4754
DDDSLTD, RRRMFMR, MM 2212
DDDSLTDS, DDDTLRS, D 467
DDDSLTDTLS, DTLSLF 2878
DDDSTDLS, DTLSLFRD, 2881
DDDSTDTLS, DTLSLFM 2879
DDDLDRTL, LTDRSLTL 1301
DDDLDRTL, LTDRSTLS, 1301a
DDDLDRTL, TDRDSTLS, 1304
DDDLDLLDL, DDDLSSS 5048
DDDLRLDTL, LTDRLDTL, 7486
DDDLFMRD, SLDSFM, MM 2561
DDDLSF#S, DDDLSF#S, TT 1624
DDDLSLD, MMMDRMR, MM 3775
DDDLLFFFLFFF, LLLL 6682
DDDLLSM, DDDSDR, RRR 9912
DDDLLSFM, SLLLLS, MF 9428
DDDLTDD, RMDRDD, MMM 1986
DDDLTDRDTL, LTDRSL 1302
DDDLTDRMD, SFMRDRD, 3926
DDDLTDRMRD, MMMLSS 4635
DDDLTDRTS, RRDTDRM 5737
DDDLTDRTL, LTDRDTD 1303
DDDTDRDRM, MMMFSSF 10696
DDDTDRD, MMMRMFM, RD 3275
DDDTDRDTD, DRMMMRD 6909
DDDTDR, RRRDRM, MMRD 11677
DDDTDRMD, SDDDTLSF 1716
DDDTDRMRD, MMMRDSM 10695
DDDTDR, MRDFMR, RRRM 5498
DDDTDMMRDTD, RRRMD 5220
DDDTMRD, DDDTTLS, FM 7382
DDDTMLLS, DFFMSSF#S, 5754
DDDTSFFM, SSMSFRDM 7163
DDDTSLLS, MDRMFSFM 2219
DDDTSLTD, MRFMRDRM, 458
DDDTLDLS, MSLSDMRD, 5462

DDDTLSDM, DRMFMMRR 5150
DDDTLS, MMMRDT, RLLS, 2760
DDDTLSFMRDDTLSFM 12259
DDDTLSFM, STDRMSFR, 7460
DDDTLSFFM, SSMSFRD 7165
DDDTLSSDDDTLS, DDD 8590
DDDTLSS, LLLLTDR, MMM 11822
DDDTLSLFMRD, SSMLT 6160
DDDTLSLFMRRD, SSML 6160a
DDDTLSLSM, DDDTLTL 8688
DDDTLSLTD, DRDTDTLS, 4281
DDDTLTD, RRMSLRT, RFM 9309
DDDTLTDL, DDDTSTSL 2289
DDDTLTRD, FMRDTLS, S 1319
DDDTLTLS, DRMSFMRD 1902
DDDTLTLS, MMMRDRT, D 2316
DDDTLTLSMF#S, DRMRD 10087
DDDTTDLS, SLDTLSFM, 6934
DDDTTRD, MMMRRFM, SS 10048
DDDTTRRMDFFFMMFM 10687
DDDTTLDLS, MMMRDR, F 1290
DDDTTLS, LLLDDDDTD, 1741
DDDTTLLS, LTLSLTLS, 4693
DDDTTLLT, TDDRDTLS 7820
DDDTTLLTTSS, SSSMM 5333
DDDTTTLS, SLTTTLTL 11336

DDR

DDRDDRDRRM, DRRDDR 5640
DDRDDTD, MRDTLLT, TD 9896
DDRDDTD, LSLSMFS, SL 6331
DDRDRMDR, LSMSFMRM, 226
DDRDRM, MSFMFS, SS#LL 1815
DDRDMMFM, SFMRMRRR 6818
DDRDMFS, MRDDD, DDRD 9430
DDRDMSFM, DRMSSF#S, S 8091
DDRDFMLS, DTLSFSM, M 7982
DDRDFSFMR, MSLSDTD 4090
DDRDSDRM, MFSFMDR, M 9506
DDRDSMSD, MRRRSDLS, 6290
DDRDLSSLDDRM, RRR 10100
DDRDLSSLDDRM, SMRR 10102
DDRDLSLDDRM, RRRRM 10101
DDRDTLLS, SSDSMDR, M 4329
DDRDTLL, LDTLRDT, TM 12449
DDRDTLTD, DDRDTLTD 10936
DDRRRDFMRD, FSLSFS 3327
DDRRR, RSFMM, FFMRDS 11941
DDRRRFFM, MMDTLTM, M 8560
DDRRR#R#FR, RRMMFFSM, 3975

1055

DDRRMDLRDT, TDRMFM	2205
DDRRMDTLS, SSLTDTL	7928
DDRRMRR, FFMRDTD, MR	736
DDRRMMRR, MSFMRRD, D	10601
DDRRMFR, MRDTLLS, SL	3160
DDRRMFMRM, MFSLTDD,	1399
DDRRMSMDDTRTS, DDR	11729
DDRRMSMR, DDMMRD, DD	1238
DDRRMSFFRRM, DDRRM	8925
DDRMDDFMRRD, SMDF	7866
DDRMDDTD, MRTLLS, RF	9255
DDRMDDTD, MMFSMRDR,	10297
DDRMDRDTD, RRMFRSM	8934
DDRMDRDT, RRTDRDTL,	2208
DDRMDRRR, RRMFTDMS,	9129
DDRMDRRMFR, MMFSSF	1854
DDRMD, RRMFMF, MMFSR	7575
DDRMD, RRMFFF, MMFSR,	7574
DDRMDRMDLL, LDDLDD	9957
DDRMDRMFMRDD, DMF	4206
DDRMDRTD, DSSLFSSM,	8183
DDRMDRTD, MFSLLS, SF	9074
DDRMDMFS, DDRMDMF	11698
DDRMDMFS, MDMSMSF#S	3321
DDRMDMFS, SFMRDMFS,	8708
DDRMDMFS, SFMRDMF#S,	8709
DDRMDMLS, DDRMMSFR,	11559
DDRMDFRD, MFMRDTDR,	2015
DDRMDFMRRD, MMFSML	4743
DDRMDFMR, RMSFMRDT,	6336
DDRMDFMR, SMLF#F#SLT	9314
DDRMDFMMR, RMFSLSF	4713
DDRMDFFMRRD, SMDFM	7867
DDRMDFFM, RMFSMFRD,	271
DDRMDSRD, SSLTSDLS,	10176
DDRMDSRM, MFLSDR, SD	9429
DDRMDSRM, MSSLFRSM,	5699
DDRMDSSS, FMFSLLSF	11777
DDRMDSS, LSMDMR, SFM	276
DDRMDS, SLSFMR, RMTD	5495
DDRMDS, SLTDLD, LTSD	12340
DDRMDSLFRDT, SDRMD	12292
DDRMDLTD, RMDTDTLS,	2965
DDRMDTDRMF, MDR, DTD,	
	1922
DDRMDTLLSL, DDR#MSF	3268
DDRMRD, RDTD, DDRMRD	7971
DDRMRDRRM, DRMFSFM	6527
DDRMRD, RRMFMR, MTLS,	11226
DDRMRDRMF, SLSLSM	9057
DDRMRD, MRMFSLS, SSL	737
DDRMRDMFS, SSLSFMF	6569
DDRMRDFR, RMF#SSF#S, D	
	3269

DDRMRDFRRMSSF#S, DF	3270
DDRMRDFMRMM, RMFMM	402
DDRMRD, FLTDD, RDTLD	5400
DDRMRDSSS, RRMFRSF	792
DDRMRDTD, DDDRDTLS#	3661
DDRMRDTD, RMFSFMMR	9369
DDRMRDTD, RMSFMR, MF	9379
DDRMRDTD, MSSLTDLS,	11544
DDRMRDTLS, SLTDFMR	12213
DDRMRRDT, RTDLSDDD,	3307
DDRMRRMF, MRDTDLS, D	3107
DDRMRMRDLS, DDRMFM	1325
DDRMRMFMRM, MMMF	4291
DDRM, RMFS, SLSMDRMR,	7945
DDRMRFRD, MFMRDTDR,	2014
DDRMRFMRD, MFMRDTD	2013
DDRMRFMRDL, SDRM, DM	240
DDRMMRD, DRMRDRR, DD	3984
DDRMMRDTTL, MMF#SSF#	
	10221
DDRMMR, RMFMRD, DMFS	9547
DDRMMRRM, SFRMMDRM,	1174
DDRMMRMRRD, MSSS	6752
DDRMMRMFMRMRDDDR	11480
DDRMMRMFFM, RDRM, MF	
	10477
DDRMMR, SFMRRD, DDRM	6844
DDRMMMRMFMRDD, DMF	505
DDRMMMRMFMRDD, MM	504
DDRMMMRMSFMRD, MM	6571
DDRMMMFS, SLSMDRMR,	4481
DDRMMFMR, MFMRDTDR	2016
DDRMMFM, RMF#SSF#S, DD	
	4147
DDRMMFFMD, DLLDLS, T	1866
DDRMMFFMR, MFMRD	2012
DDRMMFSDTD, LTRDTL	3623
DDRMMFSSFM, RRMFMS	3251
DDRMMFSLSM, DTDRMS	1087
DDRMMSM, FFMMRD, DDR	185
DDRMMSFMRMMM, RDRM	11857
DDRMMLLS#LMFMRRD, D	1760
DDRMFRD, RDLTDRD, DD	2570
DDRMFRD, RRLTDD, DDRM	2569
DDRMFRD, RRLTDTD, DD	2573
DDRMFRD, MFSSRMF, MF	12582
DDRMFRM, RRDSSF#S, RM	9461
DDRMFMDDTD, MMMSLT	7296
DDRMFMRD, DMSLSMR, D	2613
DDRMFMRD, DSSSLTDD	8729
DDRMFMRDR.	6137
DDRMFMRD, RMFSF#S, SD	7417
DDRMFMRDRM, F#SRDTL	9076
DDRMFMRD, MFSSLSFM,	9578

DDRMFMRD, MSLSDTLS 9271
DDRMFMRD, SSLSMSFM, 9252
DDRMFMRD, SSLTDTLS, 9480
DDRMFMRDTD, RMSFRM 2535
DDRMFMRDTD, MMFSMR 11122
DDRMFMRM, DMRDTDLS, 5473
DDRMFMRM, MRSSRMFM 10310
DDRMFM, RSDFR, MMMML 11821
DDRMFMRS, SLSMMRDR, 3727
DDRMFMRLMR,RSMRDT 4946
DDRMFMMD, DSLTSLTD 8731
DDRMFMM, RMRDD, RRFF 2048
DDRMFM, MMRDT, DDRMF 6765
DDRMFM, SFMRFM, MMF#S 138
DDRMFM, SSFMR, SMLS 1846
DDRMFFM, DDRMRRD, DMS 8444
DDRMFFMM, RRMMRD, DD 3710
DDRMFSDDDSTLS, DSTL 10403
DDRMFSRMF#S, FMRMFS 7520
DDRMFSMFSL, SLTDRMRD 12546
DDRMFSFM, DDTDLS, DD 2574
DDRMFS, FMRDTD, RMDF 1394
DDRMFSFMR, RMMRSTR 1068
DDRMFSFMR, RMFSLS, S 9043
DDRMFS, FMRM, SDRMFM, 10537
DDRMFSFM, LF#SSF#S, RT 11473
DDRMFSSDTSLSM, DSL 4662
DDRMFSSM, MLSSF#S, SM 2739
DDRMFSSS, FMFSFM, MM 8263
DDRMFSSS, SFMRDMR, R 9405
DDRMFS, SSSFMR, RMF 1076
DDRMFSSLTD, DDTLSR 8094
DDRMFSSLTDMR, SSF# 11504
DDRMFS, SLTDLS, DDRM 3655
DDRMFS, SL#LSSS, LFSM 2977
DDRMFSLFMRRD, SDDR 996
DDRMFSLSMS, MSMDRM 5503
DDRMFSLSFMRRD, SDD 995
DDRMFSLTD, SDDTSLM 9798
DDRMF#SSF#S, MFMRMR, D 9794
DDRMF#SSF#S, SLTDTLLS, 488
DDRMF#SLS, LTDSFMF#S, 8824
DDRMSDRMR, RMFSMRR 7767
DDRMSDLS, DDRMSDLT, 9166
DDRMSDLS, MDMRRD, DD 4365
DDRMSMD, RRRRSM, DDR 3407
DDRMSMRDLDM, LDTLS 3465
DDRMSFM, DDRMRD. 1083
DDRMSFMRD, RMF#SDTL 12494
DDRMSFMR, RDRMRDR, R 4143

DDRMSFMRRM, DDTDLS 2646
DDRMSFMR, SDTLSSF#S, 6303
DDRMSFM, MSFRMDT, DR 5352
DDRMSFM, MSSRMDT, DR 5347
DDRMSFFMDFMRRD, SL 8022
DDRMSFF, TTDRSM, DDR 11114
DDRMSFLTRD, MFRLSD 9223
DDRMSSFM, SLLLDDTL, 11353
DDRMSLDTSLS, DRMLS 4210
DDRMSLSSM, SSMRFMR 10981
DDRMSLLS, DRMSLDS, L 6964
DDRMLSFM, MMFSDM 9351
DDRMLSFM, MFSMMRDD, 7664
DDRMLSSF, MRSMDRM, D 9423
DDRMLLSFM, MSSFRD, D 1107
DDRMLLSF, FMRDRR, RS 7472
DDRMLTD, RFMDMR, DDR 8349
DDRMLTDRTS, LDTLDT 1455
DDRMTDLSFM, SLSDTL 12040
DDRFDFLS, FLFSFRD, D 10896
DDRFMMFL, SLLTDRM, M 6218
DDRFMRDR, MLTDRMF 2090
DDRFMRLS, SSFMRDRT 2023
DDRFLSFTTLSFSRM, D 8983
DDRSMRDS, LTDDDTDR, 6043
DDRSFMRD, RRLTDRD, D 2572
DDRLSM, MMF#F#S, DDSS#L 11026
DDRL, LDLSL. 10819
DDRTD, RRMFM, SSLFFS 3272
DDRTDR, MMFMRDRD 428
DDRTLS, DRMFMR, DRMD 3575
DDRTLSLSFMD, SSSLT 4129
DDRTTDRM, SFRMDTLS, 12441
DDRTTD, LDTSM, LLLSL 6206

DDM

DDMDRDLL, DDMDRDLD 3854
DDMDMMRDTD, DMSMSS 459
DDMDMMSM, RSMDTDR, D 3927
DDMDMS, DDDMRDR, SDD 5398
DDMDS, RD#RMRDMLS, RD# 12554
DDMDTRD, MMSMMRDR, F 8738
DDMRDDTD, DTDRLDTL, 10548
DDMRDDTD, FMRRD#RSM 68
DDMRDRRM, DRMFSFMRD, 6526
DDMRDRRM, DMFSMRD, D 6525
DDMRDRRM, DMFSFMRD, 6528
DDMRDRMSFM, SDLSMR, 1245
DDMRDSLS, DRMMSFMR, 8157
DDMRDTD, RMSFMR, RRM 9368

1057

DDMRDTD, MMSFMRM, SS	8278
DDMRDTL, MFRMRD, DDM	3441
DDMRR, RFMM, DTL#LSFM	
	11546
DDMRRRFM, MMRDTLS, T	5551
DDMRFMR, FMDRTD, DDM	4104
DDMRFFM, RMSFLS, SDD	10555
DDMRSSSDRT, SLTDRM	3704
DDMRLSFM, SSSDLFF	11766
DDMMRDRLTD, DDMMRR	1464
DDMMRDSS, FMDDRTLT,	6406
DDMMRRDD, D#RMFLMR, S	9293
DDMMR, RRFFM, MMSSL,	4395
DDMMRFRDTD, MMSSMD	1658
DDMMMRD, DDFFLLS, SR	868
DDMMMRDMRD, MMSSSL	12034
DDMMMMD, DDDDDLS, SF	7234
DDMMSDDTTLS, STTTD	6893
DDMMSMRD, DDDMSSLS	5128
DDMMSMRD, DDMSLSM, D	5127
DDMMSM, FFMRMR, RMFM	700
DDMMSFMR, SMFMRD, DD	6277
DDMMSFMR, SFMFMRD, D	6276
DDMMSFM, MMFLDDD, RM	2304
DDMMSSS, RRFFLLL, SM	898
DDMMSS, LLLSM, SSSSD	7395
DD, MM, LSMFSM, RRSLTL	9696
DDMMLLS#, LMFMRRD, DD	
	1761
DDMFMSDFRRD, DDFMRS	11617
DDMFSSSLDLS, SLLLS	6010
DDMFSSLLS, DLRSSTD,	3758
DDMFSS, LTDSMF#S, FR	8823
DDMFSLS, SDMSFMR, FF	314
DDMF#SLS, F#SLS, SSFFM	10118
DDMSDDLS, SDFMRMR	9625
DDMS, DFLD, DTLSF#LSM,	11108
DDMSDTLSLRS, FLSFM	573
DDMSMRTD, DDMSLFM, S	6799
DDMSMFSLS, DTLSMSF	12018
DDMSMSDDRM, DDDLSD	3703
DDMSFLDS, MMRTDDTS	6555
DDMSFLMFSMR, MFSLS	1414
DDMSSMMSFMRD, DDMS	53
DDMSSMFLS, MRDDTDR,	8683
DDMSSFMR, RMFRRM, DD	5607
DDMSSSDTLS, TTLS, RS	10476
DDMSSSMFS, TDLDSSL	1067
DDMSSSLSMD, DDDDDD	5051
DDMSSLSFS, DSFMRRM,	2181
DDMSSLSLTDD, MMF#SS	1652
DDMSLSMRD, DDFLLS, M	12409
DDMSLSMR, SSFMLF#F#M,	1745

DDMSLSLTD, MFSDRMR,	1605
DDMSLLS, MFSLRMFM, M	6243
DDMSLTDLSM, DDFMSS,	8567
DDMLDSSSM, DDMSFMR	9947
DDMLSMD, DRMRRMFM, M	1742
DDFMRDTS, DDLSFSM, R	9178
DDFMRM, RMSFMR, SDTL	4257
DDFMRS, DRRM, MMF#SLT,	
	2510
DDFFFFDRM, MMRRRF#M	5041
DDFFFFFM, MMMRLRR, S	6463
DDFFFLLLSM, MMRSSS	10893
DDFFLFMS, SRRRMFM, D	10357
DDFSLL#D, LDL#LFSF, LS	6413
DDFLSM, SRMFM, DDFLS	10566
DDSDDRRD, DFFMMRDS,	143
DDSDRMDM, FSLFMRD, D	1872
DDSDRM, DLSS, RRLRRF	8641
DDS, DRM, MMSFMRDRMD,	8582
DDSDRM, FMDMR, DDSDRM,	
	9364
DDSDRMFMRD, DDSDRM	5222
DDSDRMFMRDTD, RMRD	5104
DDSDRMFMRM, SMFSDR	5397
DDSDRMFM, SMDFMRD, D	8506
DDSDRM, SFMRRM, MMMR	4897
DDSDRS, MRMFMRD, DTL	140
DDSDRTS, MRMFMR, DDT	142
DDSDMDMS, FMFSSFMR,	2116
DDSDMDMS, FMSMRDRD,	2117
DDSDMRRD, RRTDTLS,	2583
DDSDFMRD, DRMFMRLT	7562
DDSDFMRD, DRFMRLTD	7563
DDSDFMRD, MRS#LDTLS,	9940
DDSDTLMS, SDMSMDSR	8832
DDSRSMFR, SSFMMRLS,	6547
DDSMDDDTDR, RMDRMF#	7977
DDSMDDMR, MSFMRD, DD	12373
DDSMDDMR, MSFMRD, MS	12374
DDSMDRRM, SFMRD, FFF	8884
DDSMDTDRMSMRRD, DD	12372
DDSMDTDR, SLDDTD, DD	12419
DDSMRDDRMR, MSFMRD,	12371
DDSMRDTLS, DRMRD,	8588
DDSMRDTLSLTDRD, DD	8587
DDSMMDSSFMR, RRSF#M	11809
DDSMMRDDTDR, DDSMM	7627
DDSMMRDDTDR, DSMMR	7629
DDSMFSMD, MMRMDRTS,	3111
DDSMSFMRDTDD, DDSM	4072
DDSFMRDMR, MFSFMRD,	12376
DDSSDR, RMFMFSM, SST	6260
DDSSDRMM, LSFMRRD, D	3596a

1058

DDSSDRM, LSFMRD, DD	3596
DDSSDLTD, DRMFRSF#S,	5254
DDSSFRM, RRMSLS, SLS	2691
DDSSFMRD, TDRMFS, DD	3845
DDSSFMRRD, SSMSSLS,	2609
DDSSFMMMR, DRMRD, DD	1274
DDSSFSMD, MMRRDRTS,	3110
DDSSLSMD, TDTMFS, DS	10195
DDSSLTDS, LSFMRRD, D	5600
DDSLDDTD, MMDRSDTL,	8740
DDSLDMRD, RMF#SDTLS,	7637
DDSLMSDR, MSDTLTLS	1879
DDSLSLTDFMRDTD, DR	1345
DDSLLSFMD, MFMRSLL	12024
DDSLLSFMRDS, SMRDM	7050
DDSLTDRD, DMRDTDLLS,	7721
DDSLTDRDTD, MRDTRM	8802
DDSLTDRMR, RMF#SDTL	7638
DDSLTDRMR, MRDLTDR	3192
DDSLTDRM, FSRDMR, RR	4591
DDSLTDFMRDTD, DRMD	1347
DDSLTDFMRDTDRMDT	1346
DDSLTD, SMDLSFMMR, S	12199
DDSLTDLS, FMSFMRD, D	4114
DDSLTDT, SDDMRD, DDS	2131
DDLDDS, SLSFM, SSLTT	11882
DDLDRMD, RMDMFSM, DT	6619
DDLDMRRD, DTLDRTL, D	7776
DDLRDTDSMD, DDLFMR	4128
DDLRDDLL, SSLLTD, DR	8704
DDLSDDLS, DDRMRDRS	8978
DDLSMRDRMD, DDLSMR	7501
DDLSMRRDRMLS, SSMM	11796
DDLSMRTD, DRMRTLS, D	5808
DDLSFMRDDRMFS, DDL	10196
DDLSFMRD, LSDTTD, DS	3846
DDLSTD, RRTDLS, SDRM	779
DDLS#LFMS, SSSRMFM, D	6177
DDLLMML, DDRRMML.	3376
DDLLSDRM, RSFMRFMR	7730
DDLLTSDD, MFRSSF#S, M	5777
DDLTDRMD, SFMRDRD, D	3925
DDLTDMRRD, DTLTDRD	7777
DDLTD, MMRSLTD, DTLT	10098
DDLTSLSF#S, SLFFMRD,	11926
DDTDDRRM, DFFMMRRD,	10651
DDTDDRMRDTDS, DMMM	8886
DDTDD#R, MMMFMR, SSMM	6265
DDTDR, DRMRD, MFSFM	9070
DDTDRDRM, MSFMMRDR,	9292
DDTDRRRDRM, RMRDTD	562
DDTDRRRD, MMRMFRT, DDRR	
	5873
DDTDRRRD, MMRMFRT, DTD	
	9424
DDTDRR, MMRMF, SSFSL	6298
DDTDRMD, FMRDTLTLS,	10744
DDTDRMRD, SMDMR, RRD	4803
DDTDRMMR, DFMRRD, DM	1630
DDTDRM, MFMRDT, RDLS,	1054
DDTDRM, MFLSFM, MMTD	4196
DDTDRMFMRD, MFSFMR	9071
DDTDRMFMRDTD, MFSL	146
DDTDRLTD, DFMMRDR, S	7660
DDTDRTDTLS, MRRDRS	7781
DDTDRTS, RMRDLS, DDT	5164
DDTDRTLS, RMRDTLS, D	3017
DDTDMMRRDTT, LTDSD	11201
DDTDMRRD, DFMDRM,	9385
DDTDFMMDR, DDTDFMM	2835
DDTDSMFRD, DMFSLTD	288
DDTDLDS, MDFRDTD, DD	10275
DDTDLSFM, SLDRRR, SM	9587
DDTDLSFFM, DDTDLSF#	7212
DDTDLSSD, SFMRRD, DD	8031
DDTDLS, LMLS#LT, D#TD#L	
	5830
DDTDLSLT, DRMSLLS, S	347
DDTDLLDD, DTLTDRDT	6507
DDTDLLLS, SLTDMR, SS	1039
DDTDLTD, MMRSFMRD, D	6501
DDTDLTDS, LTDFRDD, D	9584
DDTDTLS, DDTDTLS, MM	6234
DDTDTL, SSF#SFM, RDTD,	3617
DDTDTLLTT, DTDLTDR	6508
DDTRDT, RD#RFM, SSLSD	9333
DDTRDTLLS, MMMRDSF	11724
DDTRRRDM, MMMRDLS, S	5141
DDTRMLRDT, FMRSMDR	10089
DDTMDDT, LLSMMMRD, D	5571
DDTSDRMD, TDRMFRD, D	3051
DDTSFFM, SMSFRDMR, D	7167
DDTSFFM, SMSFRDMRR,	7164
DDTSLSM, DDDTLSLLT	10880
DDTSLLS, DDRMFFM, DD	3202
DDTSLTDD, RMFFMMR, D	5638
DDTSLTDD, MMFFMMR, D	5635
DDTSLTDD, MSFMRDR, D	5634
DDTSLTD, MMFFMMR, MF	5636
DDTLDRD, DDRTSDT, T	9873
DDTLDTD, DDRTTDT, TD	9874
DDTLDTLSDM, MMRDMR	11075
DDTLDTLS, MFMRFM, MR	
	10825
DDTLRDTDSFMRD, DDT	6741
DDTLMMRD, LTDTLS#, S#L	1833

DDT LM FLS#, S#LFM LT, T	3068
DDT LSDDDT LS, LT DRM	2196
DDT LSDRDTD, RMRDTD	11820
DDT LSDRM, DRRRM, DDT	8169
DDT LSDRM, DMFSMFRD,	7733
DDT LSDRM, MMMRDFMR,	8041
DDT LSDRM, MMRDDD, DD	10630
DDT LSDRM, MMMMRDTD,	10631
DDT LSDRM, MMMRMFMR,	8043
DDT LS, DRMFMR, SFMLS	9738
DDT LSDRM, SSFMRDRD	1813
DDT LSMMR, DRMRMFRM,	8985
DDT LSM, MRMFLLS, SDD	2655
DDT LSM, MMRDTD, DFFM	9539
DDT LSM, SMRDR, DDT LS	3922
DDT LSFMRDS, SLTDRT	1884
DDT LSFMSD, SDSMDMS	4678
DDT LSFFM, SMSFRDMR	7166
DDT LSS, DRMRDLTD, SL	10088
DDT LSLRSM, RSF#SDT L	12327
DDT LSLSM, SSSSLDT, D	9695
DDT LSLS, SLSMRMR, DD	9514
DDT LSLLSFM, DDT LSL	11458
DDT LSLTDD, MMFFMMR,	5637
DDT LSLTD, TRTDT LS, S	780
DDT LSLT L, SDT LSLT L,	8347
DDT LLS, RTSFFM, MSSL	9206
DDT LLSFFLSM, DDT LL	3783
DDT LLTDRSS, MMRDMR	10193
DDT LTDRD, DDRTRDT, T	9876
DDT LTDRD, DDRT LSDT	9875
DDT LTDRS, SMRD, DDT L	2166
DDT LTRDS, DMRLRR, DD	260
DDT LTS, SDTDR, RMF#LS	826
DDT LTS#, MMRDRT, TDRM	7991
DDT LTS#TDRM, MRMDRT	870
DDT LTLSFM, RDFMLSF#	8737
DDT TDDS, FFLLSSD.	1186
DDT TRRDD, MDDFMR, RR	7854
DDT TRRDD, MFMRDDT, S	3553
DDT TRRDD, MSFDRM, MM	7379
DDT TRRDD, SLLTDRRR,	9398
DDT TLDT, MMS#TLL, DDT	12224
DDT TLS, SDTDR, MMF#F#S	
	10554
DDT TLLSS, DDTT LSF#S,	7237
DDT TLLS, SLLSSFFM, D	2716
DRDDTDMRDTD, SSFMM	12202
DRDRMD, FSLSFSLFSF	5924
DRDRMFRM, RMFRDRFM	5665
DRDRMFMRDR, SFMMR	4988
DRDRMFMRFMRD, DSSL	8889
DRDRMFFSFM, MF#S#LL	99

DRDRMLS, SFMRDRRD, M	9787
DRDFMRD, MSDTS#L, LS	3180
DRDFMLS, SSMDRM, MMD	3582
DRDFFM, MSRFMR, RRMD	8701
DRDSDRDS, DMSFMRSF	8622
DRDSDRM, MSFMRRD, DR	7399
DRDSMRML, TDRFMRDR,	8650
DRDSMSDM, LTDTDMR, D	11875
DRDSF#F, DMRD, DRDSF#F,	
	5651
DRDSLDRMSFMDRF, MR	9456
DRDSLTDMRD, DRDSLT	2527
DRDLDRMR, RMFMMLS, S	3139
DRDTDRRMD, MFSFMRD	1892
DRDTDRMD, DRMFMDRM,	9017
DRDTDFSF, FDMFSLLS,	11577
DRDTRMRD, RDLTRD#RM,	3371
DRDTLSS, DRFMMRR, DR	9841
DRDTLTSD, DRRDRFRM,	7600
DRD#RMDLD, LSSDRMRD	10181
DRD#RMDLD, MSSLSMDR,	3587
DRRDDFMRM, SF#SLTMS	621
DRRDDFFMR, DRFMRDT	4790
DRRDDFFM, MRDSFM, SD	
	11045
DRRDRMS, MRRDRM, DMM	10589
DRRDSLTD, MSLSMDTL	10156
DRRDLSDDTD, MSLSMD	10157
DRRDLSDDTD, MSLSMR	10158
DRRDLSLD, MSLSMDLD	10154
DRRDLSLD, MSLSMRDL	11368
DRRDLSLTD, MSLSMDL	10155
DRRDLSTD, DMSLSMDL	11367
DRRRRRMFM, RMMMRMF	5736
DRRRMMMR, RRMMFSMD	11033
DRRRFDRFFMRMM, SFM	1830
DRRRFMRMS, SSRRFMR	3876
DRRMRDRMSSFM, LSSF	10679
DRRMRSF#MR, DRRMRSF#	7528
DRRMMFFMRDS, SLTDS	985
DRRMMSSDRRMS, FSLS	2979
DRRMFSFMRD, MRST LS	7473
DRRMFLS, SMMLSF#M, TD	2388
DRRM, SDDRRM, RMSSF#S,	690
DRRMSMR, DRMSDT LS, S	10940
DRRMSFMR, RMRDT LS, R	2436
DRRMSFMRFTRD, RFRM	3419
DRRSF, MRMRD, DRDTD.	7944
DRRSSD, LRMSFM, MF#SL	6148
DRRLL#LLLSSLSSF, LL	11596
DRR#MRDSMR, FMRDDRR#	
	10947
DRMDDDRMSFR, SFMMM	5227

DRMDDRMSFR, SFRRRR 5228
DRMDD, SLLSFM, RMFSS, 8007
DRMDRDFMRM, RDTDRM 745
DRMDRRD, DDRMDRS, RM 320
DRMDRRDFMRMM, RDTD 744
DRMDRMD, DMSMDR, DRM 10184
DRMDRMDR, MFSLSL, LD 6563
DRMDRMDRMFSLS, LTD 9329
DRMDRMRDRMFMR, DTL 5378
DRMDRMRRMRD, TLSFR 10375
DRMDRMFMMR, SFMFRD 10246
DRMDRMFM, LSFMRRD, DT
9615
DRMDRMFM, LTDRMF#S, R
10034
DRMDRMFSM, LSSMFFM, 880
DRMDRMF#SS, DTLSDDT 7315
DRMDRMSSF, LLLSRM, F# 2045
DRMDRS, DRMDRS, DDRM 8108
DRMDRTD, SSLMFSSM, M 8181
DRMDRTD, SSLMSSM, MR 8182
DRMDRTDSSLFSSM, MR 8184
DRMDMRMFSM, SSFFMR 3990
DRMDMFF#, DDTSMF#M, MM
4610
DRMDMFSM, FSLSSF#S, D 9039
DRMDMFSS, DTLSMRRD, 7314
DRMDMFSL, SSDTD, DRM 7036
DRMDMSD, LSMLSMDRM 5447
DRMDMSSFMR, MDTLSD 9151
DRMDMSLS, MRDDRMR, D 10203
DRMDFM, RDDTD, MFSML 9867
DRMDFMRD, RRMRDTLS, 2576
DRMDFMRD, RRMSSF#S, D 4836
DRMDFMR, RRMSSF#S, SM 2470
DRMDFMRMFM, SFMR 2550
DRMDFMMD, TDRDRRM, D 1072
DRMDFMMD, TDRD#RR#M, D
3643
DRMDFMMRD, DRMDFMM 10335
DRMDFMMR, DFMRDTD, D 6636
DRMDFMMR, MRRDDRM, D
11691
DRMDFMMR, TDRDMRD, D 4529
DRMDSDRMDS, DRMFSD 10491
DRMDSDMRD, TDRDRM, D 12230
DRMDSMDMRD, SDDMDL 9167
DRMDSFMRM, MFSMTTD 2519
DRMDSFM, RMFRLSFM, S 2504
DRMDSLSMFS, LTDSLS 10084
DRMDLRRDTD, MMRRST 12271
DRMDLSDDRDRM, DRMD 6635
DRMDLS, DDRDRM, MFDR 12120

DRMDLS, DDRRDRM, DRM 653
DRM, DLS, DMS, MDR, DRMM
12186
DRMDLSFMFSLRM, DRM 4680
DRMDLSLS, DRMSMS, DR 6035
DRMDLTDR, MFSDTLS, D 8994
DRMDTDR, MSFMRD, DRM 4507
DRMDTLTD, MF#STLSF#S 3830
DRMDTLTS, LTDMRDTD 6261
DRMRDDRMRR, MSDMFT 9284
DRMRDDTD, DSFFMF, FM 6210
DRMRDRDDLLSSL, MMM 10661
DRMRDR, DRMRMD, 10523
DRMRDRDLS, DRMMMSS 10568
DRMRDRDLS, DRMSMR, M 11164
DRMRDRRM, MFMDMSM, M
11148
DRMRDRM, RDSSSS, SLL 11864
DRMRDRMFMR, MRDTLS, 10691
DRMRDRMFMR, SSMFSLS, 7441
DRMRDRLSFM, MFLSMM 5944
DRMRD, MFMRD, MFSFMR 9072
DRMRDMF#S, SLSFMFRD, 6568
DRMRDMSL, DTTSLLS, T 10237
DRMRD, FMRDTRS, SMDL 9809
DRMRDFMMMR, TDRRRD 4488
DRMRDSMDRDRMS, SSD 4736
DRMRDS, MSFMRM, SSSM 9147
DRMRDSSS, LTDLRDTL 7302
DRMRDS, TDRDRM, RDDL 11029
DRMRDLRMT, RDTDRSM, 10262
DRMRDLSD, DRRRMR, DR 2621
DRMRDLS, DRMRD, TDRM 9434
DRMRDLSDRSMFRD, DR 7033
DRMRDLSM, DRMRMSR, 715
DRMRDLSFRRRR, DRMR 10451
DRMRDLS, SSDDMR, DRM 7594
DRMRDLTD, DRMFSMR, R 3010
DRMRDL, TDRRMDR, MFS 5916
DRMRDTDRD, DRMRDTD 2136
DRMRDTLS, DRMFMRD, 1241
DRMRDTLSSDD, RMF#SD 1449
DRMRDTLSSMLS, STDR, 11899
DRMRDTL, LSLDRTD, DR 3823
DRMRDTTLL, RMFMRDDT, 6688
DRMRMDDTLDLS, SSDD 10800
DRMRMFMDRS, DRMRMF 2220
DRMRMFMRDR, MDRMFM 4118
DRMRMFMRR, MFSFMRD, 5188
DRMRMFM, RMFSMFR, RR 783
DRMRMFMRSM, DDLTLS 11073
DRMRMFSMD, RMFSLSF# 1445
DRMRMFSM, LSFMRDR, M 3963

1061

DRMRMFSM, LSFMRRMS 879
DRMRMFS, SMSLSMR, D 11874
DRMRMF#SS, DDTDTLS, D 2074
DRMRMF#SS, DDTLTLLS, 2073
DRMRMF#SSF#S, SLSF, FS 2823
DRMRMSMRD, SLTDLSM 860a
DRMRMSFMR, DRSM, DRM 3128
DRMRMSFMRLSSS, MFS 6512
DRMRMSFM, MRDRLTLS, 6644
DRMRMSFM, MRDTLRDT 6952
DRMRMSFM, MRDTLRT, D 6952a
DRMRMSFM, MRDTLTLS, 6643
DRMRMSFMFLSSS, MFS 6511
DRMRMSFM, LSFMRRM, S 881
DRMRMSSF#S, SLF, FSM, D

2822
DRMRMSLS, DLSMLFMR, 1610
DRMRMSLSMDRMFMM, D 11716
DRMRMSLS, SLF, FSM, MS 2821
DRMRMLSM, SSSFMR#M, M 5428
DRMRMLSFM, LSFMRM, S 1489
DRMRMLLLLMR, SDSSF 150
DRMRFMRTD, LSFMRMD 710
DRMRFMFM, MRDRM, SFF 9603
DRMRSMRD, SLTDLSMR, 860
DRMRS, FSMDR, RSSF#MR 1611
DRMR#MDRMFMFR, MFSL 655
DRMR#MD, MFSF#SM, SSLD

12174
DRMR#MFS, SSDTLS, SSS 2622
DRMMDDTDRRT, TDRMM 2367
DRMMDMSLSM, MFRMDR 2970
DRMMDMFSFFM, RMMD 8673
DRMMDMFSFFSFM, RMM 8675
DRMMRD, DRMMSR, MFSS 7239
DRMMRD, DRSFFM, DRMM 5143
DRMMRDDMSSFM, MMFL 11418
DRMMRDR, DDDSLSMS, D 5545
DRMMRDRMFFMR, DRMF 2770
DRMMRDRMFSM, DRMMR 11938
DRMMRDMMRR, RMFSMD, 2275
DRMMRDM, SDTLS, RMFF 12522
DRMMRDMS, LLSMRDR, D 5315
DRMMRDFFFMRDLS, DD 1384
DRMMRDTLTDRT, LSS 4795
DRMMRMMRMRD, DRRSS 1512
DRMMRMFMRM, MFFMRR 4292
DRMMRMFSFMMRM, MFS 9729
DRMMRMSF, MRDDRRM, M 12261
DRMMRMSF, FMRDRMD, D 3687
DRMMRSLSLSFM, RMFM 2115
DRMMR#MMRD, DMSMR#MM

5142

DRMMMDMFSSSM, DDMR 4738
DRMMMDMSSM, DRMMSF 2618
DRMMMDMSSS, MSDDTL 2931
DRMMMRDRDS, DMSSSF 6883
DRMMMRDRDL, DLSDDT 5915
DRMMMRDRRR, RMFFFM 7274
DRMMMRDMS, SLDTLS, D 6705
DRMMMRDSD, TDRMRDL 10724
DRMMMRDSSS, LSMMRD 8109
DRMMMRDS, LDD, DMSSS 10348
DRMMMRDSLTD, DMSSS 10347
DRMMMRDLD, DRRRSSM 2947
DRMMMRDTLS, LMFSSF 11119
DRMMMRRDRR, DMSMRD 6939
DRMMMRRDMM, DMSMRD 9976
DRMMMRR, RMFFFMM, ML

8810
DRMMMRMRDS, DMSSSS 9116
DRMMMRMFMFMRMRD, 10676
DRMMMRMFFF, MFSMRD 11149
DRMMMRMFS, DSMRDFM 2864
DRMMMRMFLS, MRMFFM 1084
DRMMMRMSM, MRRRDRM,

10199
DRMMMRSMD, DRMRDL, M 2664
DRMMMR#MFMR#MD, DDFF

11102
DRMMMR#MSS, SDDRDRM, 1007
DRMMMMDMRD, MFSSSM 7258
DRMMMMRDRDLS, DRMM 12397
DRMMMMRDTR, RMFFFF 10933
DRMMMMRMFS, SSLLLS 8000
DRMMMMRMFLSSS, MR 6510
DRMMMMRMFLSSS, FMR 6513
DRMMMMR#MD, MSSSMRF 1457
DRMMMMMD, DRRTTD, DR 1434
DRMMMMDRD, MFSLSM 7504
DRMMMMM, DMSSSSS, SS 6832
DRMMMMMRDDRDDLS, D 11035
DRMMMMMRDRDDLS, DR 11037
DRMMMMMRDMDDLS, SS 5116
DRMMMMMRD, MFSSSLL 1388
DRMMMMM, RMRDDLD, DR 1415
DRMMMMMMRDD, RRMRD, 3717
DRMMMMMMFRM, DDRRR

11900
DRMMMMFSSSS, SSLL 7994
DRMMMMFMRMRR, RMFS 5122
DRMMMMFMR, TDRRMFM 4869
DRMMMMFMMRDRM, MFS 5983
DRMMMM, FMMRRDR, RMF 651
DRMMMMFSFSFM, RRMM 5713
DRMMMMFLSRFMD, SDT 12267

1062

DRMMMMS, MRDMR, RMFF 5054
DRMMMMSMMD, RDRRMS 5948
DRMMMMSMMR, DRDRRM 5946
DRMMMFMRD, DRRDRM, D 891
DRMMMFMRD, MFSSSL 1871
DRMMMFMRRR, MRDDDT 3487
DRMMMFMRRR, SF#SF#M 7104
DRMMMFMR#MD, MFSSLS 6920
DRMMMFSFFFM, RMMMF 5712
DRMM, MFSS, SDSLSFM, R 5489
DRMMMFSS, LMMRDD, DR 12112
DRMMMFS, LTDTLTS, SS 823
DRMMMS, FMRRRMF, MRD 888
DRMMMSFMRRMF, MRDDRMR
8804
DRMMMSFMRRMF, MRDMDDR
3259
DRMMMSLFF, LSRRMFM, 10263
DRMMFRS, DRMDRD, DRM 7428
DRMMFRLS, MSSFFSF 11466
DRMMFMRDRM, MFSSM 6709
DRMMFMRDRS, LTDDRD 2775
DRMMFMRDS, DRMSSFM 4538
DRMMFMR, TDRFMRD, DR 9190
DRMMFMMD, DMRMFSM, D
11907
DRMMFMMRD, MFSSLSS 2907
DRMMFMMR, RDDRRM, DR
11785
DRMMFMMR, RMFFFFFM, 130
DRMMFMMR, RMFFSFM, D 5435
DRMMFMMR, RMFLSFM, D 7757
DRMMFMMR, RMSFRMD, 6427
DRMMFMMR, MRDDRSM, S 9812
DRMMFMMR, MRDTDRMR 1424
DRMMFMMR, TDRRMRRD 157
DRMMFMMR, TDRFMRD, D 5101
DRMMFMMR, TDRFMRM, M
5273
DRMMFMLS, FMMSMR, SD 11661
DRMMFFMD, MFSSLLS, F 6176
DRMMFFMRD, DMSSLLS 8266
DRMMFFM, MMRRMFSFFM 220
DRMMFFMFM, SFMRDTD 3374
DRMMFSMDRMFFM, DMS 12538
DRMMFS, MRDDRMR, MRD 3175
DRMMFSFMM, SSFFMMR 10336
DRMMFSLSR, MMR, DDT, R 321
DRMMFSLS, MRDSSLSM 5791
DRMMFSLSFM, MFSDFM 6028
DRMMFSLSS, LLDLSSM 3743
DRMMF#SSSLLTDD, RMR 4142
DRMMSMDRMD, SSLLLR 10930

DRMMSMMR, RMFLSFFM, 9697
DRMMSFMRR, RMFFLSF 415
DRMMSFMRMFM, SSRM 12437
DRMMSLTD, TTLLSFM, R 3827
DRMMLSSFMMR, MFMRD 9107

DRMF

DRMFRDTD, RMSDLSF#S, 7418
DRMFRSLSDFFM, F#S#TL 2688
DRMFRSTD, DTRSMLSF# 9984
DRMFMDRD, MFSLSMF#S, 8565
DRMFMDRD, MSLSMFS, S 514
DRMFMDMRRDTD, TDRM 6876
DRMFMRD, DSSLTDD, DR 8730
DRMFMRDD, SLTDTLSS, 2333
DRMFMRDDTD, MRMF#S, L
6814
DRMFMRDDTD, MFSLS 11346
DRMFMRDDTD, MFSLS 8054
DDMFMRDRRRSLL#LS. 5263
DRMFMRDR, RMRDTL, RR 11647
DRMFMRDRM, MRMF#SRS 6083
DRMFMRD, RMFSLS, SDD 10151
DRMFMRDRM, F#SRDTLS, 9075
DRMFMRDR, FSLL#LSFS 11598
DRMFMRDRS, DRMFMRD 10519
DRMFMRD, SSLTDD, DRT 8732
DRMFMRD, SLSDLTD, DR 9843
DRMFMRD, SLTDTTLS, L 4819
DRMFMRDTDR, DDDL#LS 8801
DRMFMRD, TDRDFMR, DR 1809
DRMFMRDTDRM, RDTLT 8788
DRMFMR, DTDR, MMMMT
10728
DRMFMRDTD, RMSSFMM 3241
DRMFMRDTD, MF#SLSF#F#
5289
DRMFMRRD, MFSDTLS, S 405
DRMFMRRD, MFSLFR, ST 8373
DRMFMRRD, SMSDTLLS, 4508
DRMFMRRD#RMR, FFFRS 2564
DRMFMRRSFFM, SMRDR 1529
DRMFMRMRD, MFSLSMFS, 2612
DRMFMRMRD, SDTRFLS 173
DRMFMRMFM, SSDLSTL 11126
DRMFMRM, FFMSSF#S, DR 9227
DRMFMRMFSLSSF#S, SF 11751a
DRMFMRSFM, RRRSRDT 8598
DRMFMRLSDR, SF#STLS 1404
DRMFMRLTD, MFSMDTL 6961
DRMFMMRD, D#D#D#RR#M, MR
6567

1063

DRMFMMRDRD, MFSLSS 749
DRMFMMRDRDTD, MFSF 6595
DRMFMMRD, MDTLS#L, TD
4531
DRMFMMRDMSLS, SDDT 10517
DRMFMMRD, LLSSRM, DD 11992
DRMFMMRDTRD, RMF#SL
11940
DRMFMMR, RDMSLSF, LT 10621
DRMFMMRR, MFSLLRDR 12318
DRMFMMRR, SRMFM, DRM 3697
DRMFMMR, MRDRMRD, MS 1310
DRMFMMRSMRD, DFMLS 5224
DRMFMMMRDDT, RMF#SD 2817
DRMFMS, MRDRLS, SLDR 425
DRMFMSFMR, SMDTLS, 4883
DRMFMLSDT, LTDSFMF 10198
DRMFMLS, SDMTLS, FMF 2092
DRMFMLSSFM, MFSLSD 1589
DRMFMLLS, SLTDRTLS 3191
DRMFFMRD, MRDDTD, SS 8982
DRMFFM, MMMSF#M, MRTD
3315
DRMFFM, LSDMRD, SFM 12508
DRMFFFFM, MFSLLLDT, 12164
DRMFFLDFMM, SDMRRR 7243
DRMFFLSMSFMFRM, DR 4854
DRMFSDDTD, LLLSSF#S, 4150
DRMFSDS, LSFMSSR, RM 1585
DRMFS, DTLSMFSLTD, D 3847
DRMFSDTLS, LTDRMRR 11805
DRMFSDTLS, LTDRMFR 11800
DRMFSMRMD, MFSLL#L#L
2700
DRMFSMM, MFSLTDS, SL 11634
DRMFS, MSFMR, DRMRMF 12059
DRMFSM, SLDFMR, SDTS 3476
DRMFSMS, LSLFM, DRMF 10741
DRMFSFMR, DDDFMRD, L 2720
DRMFSFMRD, DRMFSFS 9345
DRMFSFMRM, MMRMFR 11292
DRMFSFSMRD, DRMFSFSL 9344
DRMFSSMD, LSFMRRD, M 2472
DRMFSSFMR, SLTDTLL 2900
DRMFSSFMSSLTDTLL 2898
DRMFSSS, FSLS, SSFFM 906
DRMFSSLRDTLS, DTDR 665
DRMFSSLSFMD, FMRR 9038
DRMFSSLS, SDRMFMRD, 7797
DRMFS, SLTDDRMFSSF 3075
DRMFSSLTD, TDRSLTL 6499
DRMFS, LRMFSM, MDTLSF, 2292
DRMFSLRSM, MFMRDMR, 4596

DRMFSLFSFM, DTLSLT 6154
DRMFSLS, DRMFSLS, SS 322
DRMFSLSD, MF#SDTS, RF 3300
DRMFSLS, DSLSFM, RFM 11221
DRMFSLSMRMFM, RMSD 5221
DRMFSLSMSR, DRMSDT 12388
DRMFSLTD, RMDLDT, LS 1099
DRMFSLTD, MRDRDTD, S 3209
DRMFLDM, F#SMDRM, MFF
4702
DRMFLSM, RMFMRD, DRM 6454
DRMFLS, MMRLTDT, RMF 714
DRMFLSM, MSDDRM, MF#F#
3429
DRMFLSFM, SLDTTLLS, 808
DRMFLSFM, SLTDLS, SL 827
DRMFLSSFM, RMSMR, DR 4994
DRMFLS, LFSMDR, RMMF# 12100
DRMFLS, LFSMDR, SMDT 7131
DRMFLS, LLFSMDR, SMD 7132
DRMFLLS, SLTDRDT, TD 7770
DRMFLLTDSD, DTDRMR 10605
DRMF#F#SRRFM, RMSSF#S,
3041
DRMF#F#SRRFM, MFLLS#L,
3040
DRMF#SLS, F#SLS, SSFFM 907
DRMSD, DRMSD, RMFLSF 1247
DRMSDRTD, MRSFMR, DR 77
DRMSDMFRRD, MFSLFS 8838
DRMSDMLD, DRMDSLR, D 4969
DRMSDLSR, MMMFMRRS, 9125
DRMSDLSMM, LSMMRMD, 8417
DRMSDTLS, FMRRD, DRM 3550
DRMSDTLSLSFMMRMR, 4202
DRMSDTLS, LTDRMRD, D 11803
DRMSDTLS, LTDRMFRD, 11802
DRMSMDRDT, RMFLSFL 199
DRMSMDRMD, SDRM, MF#S 6980
DRMSMDFM, LTDMRR, R 919
DRMSMRD, RMFLSMR, LS 10752
DRMSMRDM, DTLRDLS, S 12265
DRMSMRDL, LDLSMRDM, 12484
DRMSFRDRM, FMLSDDT 8358
DRMSFMDRM, SF#SLSMR 4966
DRMSFMDTLS, LTDRMR 11801
DRMSFMRD, RRMSSF#S, D
11461
DRMSFMRD, MF#SSLSF#S, 6350
DRMSFMRD, FMR, MF#S, FS
1783
DRMSFMRD, SLTDDT, LS 8280
DRMSFMRR, RMFLLSFM, 201

1064

1065

DMDDSSSLLTD, DSSLF	5339	DMRDDTLSMRD, SSFMM	2851
DMDRDDDTDR, MRMFMM,	4970	DMRDDTLSLFM, DTDRR	9186
DMDRRD, STSLLS, FMDL	9419	DMRDRDRMSS, MFFMDM	8217
DMDRRDTL, MRDFMRDM	1307	DMRDRDTD, RMSFMR, SD	1466
DMDRMRFMRD, MSMSFM	4641	DMRDRRRDRM, MMRMFM	594
DMDRMFRD, DMF#SRSF#S,	481	DMRDRM, DDRDLD, LSLS	10847
DMDRMFMRD, DMF#SRSF#	480	DMRDRMDTL, DSMDMRD,	10452
DMDRMSFMRD, DLFLSM	1968	DMRDRMRDR, MSSSLSM	3351
DMDRSFMRD, RRRMSSF#	2698	DMRDRMFMR, RMFSFMM	5081
DMDRTD, RMSFMR, SDDL	1467	DMRDRMS, SLSMSLL, LS	9872
DMDMDMMMD, DMDDLDDL	3903	DMRDRTDRDS, MMSSFM	10984
DMDM, DFFDRM, MRRM, SS	8998	DMRDMRD, DLRFSSS, DR	3514
DMDMDSSM, DRRRFM, DM	1040	DMRDMRDDTD, MSFMMD	10133
DMDMMRDRM, DRTRMFM	11324	DMRDMRDDTLS, SLLLS	2468
DMDMMFS, FMMSMR, DMD	805	DMRDMRDLSLS, MSLSM	3194
DMDMFS, MLMLTT, TDLT	9285	DMRDMRDTD, RMSFMR, S	1465
DMDMSD, SSMFSM, MRSF#	6019	DMRDMFSFM, RDRTLS, D	231
DMDMSSDDRTD, DMDMS	4073	DMRDMFS, SSLLSMDMR,	4443
DMDFRS, FMMRRD, DLDT	8494	DMRDMF#S, DMRDMF#S, ML	
DMDFRSF#S, DFFMRDRD	10906		3734
DMDFRLS, MDDRMR, RMM	6533	DMRDMSFM, DRMFMRM, R	7705
DMDFRTDD, MSMTLSSS,	2974	DMRDMSFM, DRMFSFMR	9943
DMDFSLLS, SRFMDMF, F	9165	DMRDMSFM, SLSFMR, RM	650
DMDFLSMRD, DMDFLSM	6313	DMRDMSLS, RMRDMSLS,	3736
DMDSDMFSM, DSMDRMF	1230	DMRDFMRDRTD, TDRM	5365
DMDS, DFFFMR, RTDLS,	10226	DMRDFLSFM, SF#STLS, S	6421
DMDSRMRD, MSSSFMR, D	4110	DMRDSDRMD, MFSLSFF	8531
DMDSRFMR, RMDLSLTD,	2552	DMRDSDMRDS, LDSMMR	12282
DMDSMD, SLSFMMR, RMD	2353	DMRDSMDRM, DDTSLTS,	7685
DMDSMD, TLSFMR, RMDL	2352	DMRDSMDS, DSRMRDTL	2995
DMDSMRDTD, RMSLSFS,	9320	DMRDSMDS, DSRMRTLS	2994
DMDSMFMRM, LRMDTLT,	534	DMRDSMFFS, FMR, RDTL	1240
DMDSMFSLS, STDRDMR	7753	DMRDSFMRD, DTLSRDT	7150
DMDS, MSLSMRD, DMDS, D	7496	DMRDSFMR, RMRDRDRT, F	12083
DMDSMLM, FSMDRM, MSM	5741	DMRDSFMR, MFSLMRD, D	12035
DMDSMLSLTD, SLSFMR	1106	DMRDSFMR, SDRMLTD, D	10782
DMDSFMRD, SLFDTLS, R	7385	DMRDSSFMRM, MRLSDF	8406
DMDSLS, STSRMR, DTLS,	2672	DMRD, SSLSFFM,	9677
DMDSLTD, RMDSFMR, RM	1990	DMRDSLDRM, MSLSDRL	3358
DMDSTD, MMRSSF#LS, SS	3648	DMRDSLDS, DMMSSR, DM	5133
DMDLLRRT, SDDRRMMR,	6686	DMRDSLS, DMRDRMR, DM	12240
DMRDDDRDR, MSMSSMR	10990	DMRDSLSMRDMR, RMMS	1724
DMRDDD, RMSLLS, FMMF	11659	DMRDSLS, SMRDMR, SMR	4770
DMRDDDL, LSMMRR, FMR	7525	DMRDSLTDRMDLR, LLT	3463
DMRDDRRM, MRDFMRDT	4687	DMRDSLTDRMR, DMLTD	1122
DMRDDRMFFFM, MMMMF#		DMRDSLTD, MRTDLS, MR	7925
	12352	DMRDSLTDS, SDRMFMR	9614
DMRDDMSSLS, DMRDDM	22	DMRDSTRD, SSMMDRMR,	13
DMRDDFRM, MRDSFFRM,	8025	DMRDLRRD, SLSLDLS, S	3888
DMRDDFMMR, SDRFMRD,	1382	DMRDLSRM, MRSF#SLTL	9561
DMRDDLRFM, MDTLSTL	1188	DMRDLSFM, MRDRMR, DT	791
DMRDDLSFM, DSFMLTD	6675	DMRDLSFM, MSDTLS, SMD	1573
DMRDDTDFFMR, RSFMR	5750	DMRDLSFM, MSSFMDR, D	9000

DMRDLS, SMMDMMR, RRR 10063
DMRDLSSS, DLRRDTD, D 9100
DMRDLSLD, DMRMSMMR, 802
DMRDLSLD, RMRMSMR, R 803
DMRDTD, DDRDLS, SRM 7333
DMRDTDD, DFMFRM, M 12571
DMRDTD, DRMFMR, RMFS 6760
DMRDTDRD, DDTLSMDR, 1870
DMRDTDRMDR, DRMLRD 1373
DMRDTDRMF, RSMF#SLT 1849
DMRDTDLS, LDTLS#L, DD 2850
DMRDTLDS, SSSSDR, LF 2132
DMRDTLSS, SLTDTRRT, 11846
DMRDTLLS, RMDMF#S, SL 8405
DMRDTLTD, RMSFMRLS, 11888
DMRRFMRD, MSSLSMF#S, 1905
DMRRFM, MMRMFMMR, DR
9932
DMRRFFMM, RMRRMR, SF 1023
DMRMDRTD, DSRMF#S, SF 10260
DMRMFMRDD, MMRMSF#S 7882
DMRMFS, DLSFFM, MF#MF#
9702
DMRMFS, MMDFRD, MRDS 8024
DMRMFSM, LSFMRM, SLT 1484
DMRMFSFM, LSFMRM, SL 1486
DMRMFSSM, LSFMRM, SL 1487
DMRMFS, SFMR, RRDRMF, 10284
DMRMFSS, SFMFSM, DMR 9204
DMRMF#SSF#S, SLSLTDT 6616
DMRMSMFMRD, MRMSFM 257
DMRMLSFM, LSFMRM, DS 1485
DMRMLSFM, LSFMRM, SL 1488
DMRFMRDRF, MLF#SSF#S, 4119
DMRFMRRD, MDLRDTLS, 6102
DMRFMSFM, RDDMRS, S#L 9711
DMRFMSFM, MRDFMR, DR 202
DMRFMLS, DTLSFM, MMM 884
DMRSFMDR, DDTLTDRM 11812
DMRSSDMRSS, SFMRMF 10391
DMRSSF#S, DSLSFMR, SM 4167
DMRTS, DMRTS, SDDRRM 7784
DMRTSLLS, DDRMSDRS, 2241
DMR#MDRMSF#LS, DMR#MD
5212
DMR#MMFMF, F#SDTLLSS,
11806
DMMDMFMRD, MSSFMRR 4858
DMMRDRDLSD, RRMRS, M 10717
DMMRDRMRMS, SSLSMR 11468
DMMRDMMR, DSSS, SLSS 7495
DMMRDFMR, DRMFRDTD 1470
DMMRDFMR, DMFRDTD, D 1469

DMMRDFM, RMSSF#S, MLS 12297
DMMRDFM, SLSFRM, DMM 12368
DMMRDFFM, RMSSF#S, MLS
12296
DMMRDFF, LSDMSRMR, D 6050
DMMRDFSFM, MMMR#MF#F#
9484
DMMRDSLS, SSDTLSM, D 10807
DMMRDSLLS, DTLSMSF# 11594
DMMRDS, LTDRM, MRMF#S
11537
DMMRDTDF, SFFMRM, SM 6881
DMMRDTRD, DTRDDTLS, 10340
DMMRDTLDT, TLTDRM, T 6224
DMMRRMFR, MFSLSMD, D 10832
DMMRRSD, DLLSFM, MMM 4539
DMMRRSLS, SFFMDR, RS 12233
DMMRMDLS, MRMFM, MSM
11223
DMMRMDTD, MSFMDMR, S 822
DMMRMRD, MSSFSFM, MR 8352
DMMRMRDTD, MSFMRDM 821
DMMRMFM, RDDRRM, SMM 3258
DMMRMF, MRRDRM, DMMR 1202
DMMRFM, RDDDMR, RMSM 14
DMMRSDMMR, SDSSFMR 6904
DMMRSDFMR, MSRRMDT 10072
DMMRSFMRDR, SDRMR 136
DMMR#MFM, RSDDTL, LSS 2662
DMMR#MFFM, DMRDTD, MR
1581
DMMR#MSF, RDDRRM, DMM
10588
DMMR#MSSLSF#S, MMRDR 9925
DMMMDRD, DDDRDLS, SS 2659
DMMMDRMD, SSSSRMFM, 11004
DMMMDRMR, DMSSDMRD, 3881
DMMMDSSS, SMDFMR, DM 6734
DMMMDLSS, MSFRRMFM, 8643
DMMMRDDD, RMSFMR, F 558
DMMMRDDD, MSSSSLLS, 1705
DMMMMRDR, DDRMMRDD, D 5242
DMMMRD, MSSSFM, SLLL 10640
DMMMRDMSSLS, MRRMF 6639
DMMMRDMSSLS, SMMMD 6357
DMMMRDFFM, DRD, MSSS 1669
DMMMRDS, FMMMRDDT, D 9407
DMMMRDLS, SMMSFMRM 12082
DMMMRDLLSFM, MMMLL 11630
DMMMRRDD, DRRRDRMS, 7748
DMMMRMDDD, DRRRDRM 7746
DMMMRMFSM, SFMFMRM 8693
DMMMRMFS, MLLLSFMR, 6903

1067

DMMMRMFSS, DMMMRDM	10951
DMMMRMFS, SLSSMFMM,	4368
DMMMRMFSLLS, FMRDD	12053
DMMMRMSM, DRRRDRM, D	1786
DMMMRS, DRRRDRM, MMM	9019
DMMMRSSS, SDSLSSMR,	3576a
DMMMRSSS, SDSLSLMR,	3576
DMMMR#MFFM, MMRDTRD,	
	967
DMMMR#MSM, DRRRMFM, D	
	4516
DMMMMD, MSSSSM, SDTL	10920
DMMMMRDS, FMMMMRDR,	4468
DMMMMRDSSSS, SLLLS	4444
DMMMMRMFFFF, MRRRR	10247
DMMMMMRDDLS, DTTTL	43
DMMMMMRD, RMSSFMR, R	2536
DMMMMMRR, MFFFFFMM,	
	12219
DMMMMFMMRM, MSSSSL	2036
DMMMMFSLSF#S, SSFMR	1220
DMMMMSMDR, DMSLSLS	2272
DMMMMSMDR, DSLSLSM	2271
DMMMFMRD, MSSSLSRM	10639
DMMMFMRRR, SF#SF#MRD	7105
DMMMFSMSLT, SDDTLS	3779
DMMMFSSDRM, SLTDDD	1175
DMMMFS, SFFMMR, RMMM	6552
DMMMFS, SSMRDR, DMMM	11220
DMMMFSSLSF#S, LLSSF	5934
DMMMSRRR, MFSLSFMM	12436
DMMMSFMRRM, DMMMSF	3330
DMMMSSDLS, MLSSFRM	12065
DMMFRDDL, LSRM, SLTR	990
DMMFRDTD, DFSLSFMR	2408
DMMFRSSS, MFRFMRD, D	11459
DMMFMRDLSS, MSSLSF	2905
DMMFMRRM, DLTDRMFR,	7106
DMMFMRMD, LSMMRRSD	5506
DMMFMRSSL, SFMFSMR	2491
DMMFMM, MRRFFM, MSSL	
	11501
DMMFMFSS, SSMFRD, DM	3481
DMMFMFLS, MSDTLS, FM	411
DMMFFMRD, MSSFMR, MR	8434
DMMFFMRSFM, MMMMRD	395
DMMFFSS, SSMFRD, DMM	3482
DMMFFSTD, RMFSF#S, SL	7133
DMMFSDRDT, DRRMFSL	642
DMMFSSFM, SMMRRD, DM	9595
DMMFSSSMRDLS, DTMM	5105
DMMFSLMRD, SLDSFFM	9467
DMMFLSM, RDDRMR, RMM	1400
DMMSDDRTSFM, MFSSL	11721
DMMSDDLS, SDMRRR, SS	10267
DMMSDRMFM, SSSLTDT,	11781
DMMSDRMFSFM, MSSTM	3091
DMMSDRMS, LLSMSMR, D	6122
DMMSDMRD, DLSMFSM, M	10315
DMMSMDTDFFM, MRSSF#	10626
DMMSMRMR, MSSDRM, MR	12427
DMMSFMRMD, DDTDRMF	7992
DMMSFMRLS, SSMDDRR	2780
DMMSSDDF, FMRDRM, MM	9181
DMMSSD, DTLSF#S, SLTD	9442
DMMSSD, SMLSMFSM, MM	8798
DMMSSDT, SLFSMR, RMM	9326
DMMSSMRD, MSLSMR, DM	7245
DMMSSFMR, SLTDTL	2897
DMMSSSLSM, DDDMMRM	8381
DMMSSLSMDMRD, MMML	11744
DMMSSLS, SDRMMFRD,	7796
DMMSSLLS, SDRTSSF#S,	6869
DMMSSLLS, SRFM, DMMS	11502
DMMSSTLS, MDDRRM, MS	9534
DMMSLS, SRRMF#S, LTSD	5161
DMMLRDT, TDRMDMR, RM	2246
DMMLSFMF, MS#LRDT, S#S#	
	2551
DMMLSFSMFR, SFMRDM	4379
DMMLLSS, FMDDTD, DMM	4857
DMFRD, DLLTDS, SSFMF	7872
DMFRDMSSLSFFM, DFM	1342
DMFRDMSLS, SDTLSS	9085
DMFRMD, RMLSF#S, SMSD	8387
DMFRMDRT, RMF#SRMRD	259
DMFRMFMRM, SSMRMFM	8026
DMFRSSFM, MRDFMR, RM	2069
DMFRSSFFMR, SLTDSF	2911
DMFRTDRM, RDTLRT, RS	2818
DMFRTDRT, RMSF#SLF#S,	28
DMFMRDRD, TLLLRDT, D	3735
DMFMRD, MSLSMR, RRRM	2417
DMFMRDSSLTD, DDDTS	10429
DMFMRDTD, SDTLSF#S, S	6731
DMFMRMDRM, LLTDTLS#	6145
DMFFMRDMRTTD, DMFF	3916
DMFSD, DMRDRD, TDSLS	526
DMFSDDTD, RMRDRF#SS	3755
DMFSDDTD, MRDTLS, DM	6216
DMFSDRDL, DTDRMFM, D	7602
DMFSDRRD, SDTLTLS, R	5681
DMFSDRMF, MRDDTD, SD	2736
DMFSDMRD, DRMRSLTL	6086
DMFSDMRDRM, MLTDDR	6339
DMFSDFMR, RMF#SF#S, DM	

DMFSLSFMRMFRD, DMF	7509
DMFSLSFM, RMSSF#S, RR	3722
DMFSLSFMRM, SLTDTL	494
DMFSLSFMR, SLTDTLS	2901
DMFSLSFM, MMRDDTLS,	6492
DMFSLSFMFMDRTD, MF	6570
DMFSLS, SSLTDSMMMF	379
DMFSLS, SLTDLT, SDTLS	8053
DMFSLLS, DRRMFM, MRS	1881
DMFSLTDRS, DTLS, LSF	3805
DMFSLTD, MFMRMF#S, SS	9060
DMFSLTD, TLMSF#M, MFR	1005
DMFSLTDTLS, SSSLS	2718
DMFLSDST, LSSLSMR, D	15
DMFLSMD, MRTTLS, DMF	318
DMFLSMSFMFRM, DMFL	4855
DMF#SDFMMRD, DLTDLR	10099
DMF#SSLDTL, SSDTDMR	10113
DMF#SSLTD, RMDTSLDT	4093

DMS

DMSDDD, MSDMMM, MMMF	9098
DMSDDD, MLDMMM, DTTM,	
	10450
DMSDDRDTD, DRDTLS, R	5176
DMSDDRMFM, SLSFMR, R	3430
DMSDDRMF, LSFMS, TDR	6464
DMSDDRLSFM, SLRT, DL	6488
DMSDDRTD, MMMRTSLS,	11991
DMSDDMRDS, DTLFLLS	11690
DMSDDTD, LLLSFMMRR	10376
DMSDDTLS, DRMRDTLS,	8486
DMSDDTLSFFM, SMSLS	7901
DMSDRM, MRSDTSLS, DF	9971
DMSDRMFMDRD, RRMRT	3281
DMSDRS, DLSSFM, RMSL	1746
DMSDRTD, MRDTLLS, DM	6416
DMSDRTD, MRSSF#S, SSF	813a
DMSDRTD, MRSTLS, SSF	813
DMSDR, TLSLS, DRMSL, S	1393
DMSDMRDDT, DTLSFMR	12445
DMSDMRDSD, DDTDTLS,	7055
DMSDMRRD, RMFSLTLS,	7384
DMSDMRR, TDSSFM, DMS	2707
DMSDMR, SF#SDTLS, SDR	11873
DMSDMRLSFM, SDTLSF#	3011
DMSDMMRDTD, RMSLSF#	3246
DMSDMFSLR, SFMF#SLT	982
DMSDMLLS, DMSDTLLS,	3055
DMSDFMRR, RMRSTLST	6309
DMSDFLS, MFSDMFRD,	2801
DMSDFLLS, MFSDFMFMRD	2800

DMSDSM, DSLSFM, SMRD	8763
DMSDSMSDMD, DRMRDT	11685
DMSDSFMRD, DMDLTDS	2528
DMSDSFMRD, RMF#SSLS	9134
DMSDSFMRD, LSF#SLDT	6267
DMSDSFM, SLLSFMR, SD	8062
DMSDSFSM, RMF#SSTLS,	11384
DMSDSLDS, FMDDTD, DM	6735
DMSDSLSFM, RMF#SDTL	5183
DMSDSLSFM, SDDDFMR,	7725
DMSDSLS, SDTDRM, MRD	9343
DMSDSLTD, DSLSSFMR	5746
DMSDSTLS, MMRDRMF#S,	6874
DMSDLDSFSMDMR, DMS	5618
DMSDLDLS, FSMDRRD, S	5619
DMSDLFFM, RMFSLTDR,	6627
DMSDLF#LS, LSRSF#FM, D	
	3751
DMSDLSRM, MMLDTLS,	7391
DMSDLS, FMDRMF#S, SRD	7063
DMSDLS, FMDMF#S, SRDT	7062
DMSDLSFM, MRSLLS, SS	8439
DMSDLSFLSMRD, MF#SL	11843
DMSDLS, LDLSMRM, D	9439
DMSDLSLSMRD, MSLDT	11842
DMSDLSLSMRD, MSLTD	11841
DMSD, LTDS, SLSSMDRR	3593
DMSDTDRR, DMRTLLS, D	1109
DMSDTDLS, SSSSMFRD,	11998
DMSDTLFM, RDMLTS, LL	10194
DMSDTLS, FMRDFMR, MS	10245
DMSDTLSFM, SDDRR#M, R	6126
DMSDTLSLDFLSM, MRD	4270
DMSDTLSLLS, SFMLS	1799
DMSDTLSLTDTLSFM,	4567
DMSRRDD#RFM, SDRDTL	8382
DMSRMDRLTD, DFMRDT	12126
DMSRMRDRM, MMRDFFM	12478
DMSRFMRD, RMRDTLLS,	9436
DMS, MDRTD, SLTDLLS, M	8576
DMSMDLDD, LLSSMR, DM	1839
DMSMDLDSD, DRMFMR, D	7380
DMSMDLFM, DRMFMDDD,	5340
DMSMRDD, DRFLSM, SDT	5057
DMSMRDDTDR, MFLSMS	10638
DMSMRDRD, MMMFSSFM	10698
DMSMRDRMFM, DMSDTL	3185
DMSMRD, RMFFSMR, MRD	12511
DMSMRDTR, MDLDTL, DM	10785
DMSMRMF#S, LSMRDDTD,	4630
DMSMRMF#S, LSFMRDRM	4629
DMSMMRRD, FFMMRDR, D	4449
DMSMFSLSR, MFSFM	8754

DMSMFSLTD, MMRDTLS, 7034
DMSMFLSR, MSFRDLTS, 4066
DMSMFLSM, SDFMRRD, D 9054
DMSMSMFSFMRD, RMRM 3187
DMSFRDRM, DFMLSTDF, 3054a
DMSFRDRM, DFMLSTDS 3054
DMSFMDDFFM, MRDTRF 12078
DMSFMDRM, DSSLDTLS, 11640
DMSFMRDRRD, SLTDTL 10538
DMSFMRD, RMFMRR#M, MS
2920
DMSFMRDMRD, DMSF#MR#
10749
DMSFMRD, SDSLSFMR, S 436
DMSFMR, RRSLTLS, F#MS
6954
DMSFMRRM, MDTLSFMR 3084
DMSFMRMDRM, SLSFMF 9620
DMSFMRFM, RDMRDTD, D 5389
DMSFMR, SLDTLS, SDRM 2963
DMSFMMRD, DLSSMR, TD 4041
DMSFMLSFM, SLSFMR, R 11355
DMSFMLLS, SFMRRMFM 7789
DMSFLMSR, RMSSF#S, DM
12545
DMSF#SM, SSLTDS, SSF#S 4847
DMSF#SLS, DSTLS, DMSL 9142
DMSSDDTDMMR, DRRMF# 452
DMSSMDRM, DSSLTDLS, 11639
DMSSMDRM, DSSLTDTLS 11641
DMSSMRDRMD, DMSDSL 5021
DMSSMRDTD, MSFMRDS 8463
DMSSMMRD, RDLSDMDR,
11094
DMSSFRDTD, DDTLSLT 12281
DMSSFM, DMRDDT, DMSD 8374
DMSSFMRD, RMF#STTLS 795
DMSSFM, RRFFMR, MRFS 8081
DMSSFMRMF, FLFSMDF# 4874
DMSSFMR, MF#SDTLS, DR 8421
DMSSFMRF, MRDLSDRM, 9056
DMSSFMMRD, DDTDSFM 9672
DMSSFF, RFLLSS, RSF#S 6612
DMSSFSM, DDTTLLS, ST 2283
DMSSFLDLSMS, DMSSF 10382
DMSSFLSM, SFMDRD, DM 2777
DMSSFLLSMRD, MRRMF 7377
DMSSFLLS, MF#SSLLS, S 6918
DMSSF#SLSDMM, MFSSF 1956
DMSSSDMMRDTD, DDFS 9103
DMSSSDMLSFR, LSMSF 5647
DMSSSDMLSFR, LSSMS 5646
DMSSSDLDS, SFM, FMR, D 3999

DMSSSDTD, SDTDSFMR 4791
DMSSSDTSLS, DSRFSM 666
DMSSSDTL, SMMFMR, DM 4513
DMSSSMDMR, RMFFFLS 7196
DMSSSMRDFF, LSFMMR 1957
DMSSSM, MMMMS, SDTLS 10828
DMSSSMSDDD, SDTLSF 4413
DMSSS, MSDDD, SSLDTL 5314
DMSSSFMDMFRTD, DMS 9709
DMSSSSSDTTL, RMFSM 9700
DMSSSSSS, DSS, SLSSS 6434
DMSSSSSL#LS, MDDRMS 11638
DMSSSS, LSFRMFFF, SM 2038
DMSSSSLSFS, RMFMSS 4258
DMSSSSLS, SDSDRMRD 10114
DMSSSSLS, SDSDRMRDTLS 10109
DMSSSSLS, SDTDMRMR 10110
DMSSSSLSLS, SDSDMR 10112
DMSSSSLL, SDTDMRDR 10111
DMSSSSLL#L#L, SLDDLSLD, 6613
DMSSSLFLD, LSMRDML 1172
DMSSSLSM, DSLLLDS, D 5306
DMSSSLSM, SSDTLLS, M 11388
DMSSSLSFMRDD, DMS 166
DMSSSLS, SDRMFMRD, D 7794
DMSSSLSSM, DMSSSLS 12121
DMSSSLSLS, SDRMFRD, 7795
DMSSSLTDD, DRMSFFM, 2146
DMSSSLTDS, DMSSSMD 10210
DMSSLMSF, MRDRM, MFS 1893
DMSSLMSS, MSDDTS#L, L 11131
DMSSLFSMRD, MRRMFM 7376
DMSSLSM, DRRDRM, DMS 3787
DMSSLSMDMSR, RMFRD 961
DMSSLSM, DTDFMMR, DMSS 7001
DMSSLSM, MMRMFFM, DM 11655
DMSSLSFMRDD, DMSSL 167
DMSSLSFMRD, RMF#SSL 8067
DMSSLSFMR, MFSDRM 5801
DMSSLSFM, MFSDMRD, S 6687
DMSSLSFS, DMSSLSFS, 10817
DMSSLSSM, DDDRDLS, D 5757
DMSSLSSM, DRRM, DMSS 12490
DMSSLS, SMFMRD, DMSL 9287
DMSSLSSM, FMRDRMR, D 9657
DMSSLSSM, SSRMFM, DM 5095
DMSSLSSFM, MRMFLR, S 2600
DMSSLS, SLDTLS, SSLD 4833
DMSSLLM, DDTF#R#D#T, DM
3762
DMSSLL, MRMFMM, DMSS 677
DMSSLLMS, SMSTLLS#S, 4406
DMSSLLF#S, LLF#S, FFRM 9083

DMSSLLS, SSSDTLTLS, 9102
DMSSLLSS, LSFMRRR, D 2151
DMSSLLLS, MSFMRDD, D 8867
DMSSLTDD, MRDTTLS, F 4171
DMSSLTDDM, LRMFFM, M 9308
DMSSLTDD, SSDLSF#S, D 7154
DMSSLTDDSSSSLTD, D 9710
DMSSLTD, RSMDTLS, SS 4306
DMSSLTDS, MRMDRM, DM 11281
DMSSLTDSS, MSLLTDR 9998
DMSSLTDS, LSSFMR, DM 3549
DMSSLTDS, LLSDSFMR, 4825
DMSSLTD, TDRTLLS, MF 6496
DMSSLTD, TRDTLLS, DM 4170
DMSSLTD, TRSTLLS, SD 6498
DMSLDLSFS, LSFSMRD 5502
DMSLMSMRM, DMSLMF#S 7143
DMSLF#S, DMSLF#S, DTLS, 4997
DMSLSDDLS, DMSSLSM 1838
DMSLSDTLSMDRM, DMS 11624
DMSLSMD, DRRDRM, DMS 324
DMSLSMDRD, DRRRSFM, 7999
DMSLSMRD, RRRRDRM, M 8480
DMSLSMRMD, DDRRDRM, 7072
DMSLSMMRD, LSDLSDR 5820
DMSLSMFS, DLTDSSFM, 11472
DMSLSFMRDDD, SLTDR 1654
DMSLSFMRMD, DMSLSM 9983
DMSLSFM, MRFMDR, DMS 1200
DMSLSFS, DDRMRDLL, D 1471
DMSLSF#SM, RDRMFLR, R 2391
DMSLSSFM, SLDSF#S, DT 2681
DMSLSS, SLSDMR, RMSL 4729
DMSLSLDTLSLSS, DSL 9670
DMSLSLTD, DDTLLSFF 550
DMSLSLTD, LRTMDTL 12369
DMSL, LSMRM, MSLD, SLS 7251
DMSLTD, DMDTLT, RRRM 2356
DMSLTDRM, MFRRRMD, D 7536
DMSLTD, MRDRDTD, SSL 3208
DMSLTDSM, SLDTLS, LT 10824
DMSLTDLS, DRMF#SLS, S 1077
DMSTLSD, SLLLSS, MFF 9296
DMLSDDRD, FMRDSSF#S, 6252
DMLSRFMRD, DMLSRFM 12456
DMLSMDRMDL, TDLM, DM 1207
DMLSMDFM, DLTDMR, RR 5062
DMLSMRDRM, SLSF#S, MS 9879
DMLSMMRDRRMFMR, DM 7066
DMLSMMRDMR, RD#RFLL 8111
DMLSMMRD, SLDDRMR, M

7444
DMLSFM, SSFMLSSF, MR 7280

DMLSF#F, LRMFSLS, DTR 10192
DMLSF#SDS, LSFFSFM, D 12209
DMLLTDD, DTDSMDRM, M 9059
DMTDFMMRD#RL, LLLSF 8077
DFRRMRDRD, DRMMSFM 5467
DFRRMRDRD, DRMFSFMR 5466
DFRMDL, LSMFRRM, DDD 11244
DFRMSL, SLTDRL, TDLT 4255
DFRSMFMRRD, DFRSD 11556
DFMRDDDRMR, RSFMS 358
DFMRDDTDR, DMSLF#S, R 91
DFMRDRS, LTDLRDDT, D 1613
DFMRDSFM, MRSLLS, SD 9386
DFMRDSS, LSDDRM, F#SD 6630
DFMRDTD, DRMF#STLS, S 5200
DFMRFMRD, MLDFRDT, S 5828
DFMMRDTD, DRMF#SLTL 3572
DFFMDRRRRDRM, SLFL 8846
DFFMDRMF, FMRDTLSF, 8056
DFFFFFFMMMM, MDDDD 7256
DFFFFLLLSF#S, MRRMF 5
DFFLFMMS, MRSF#MF#S, S 6085
DFSM, SDLFSMDTLS, RT 7411

DSD

DSDDDDD, RMRDMF#S, SS 6958a
DSDDDDD, RMDMF#S, DSM 6958
DSDDRRM, MRDMR, DSDM 3742
DSDDRSM, MSF#STLLS, F 5612
DSDDRSSDDRM, MDDDS 11880
DSDDSLSLSMD, DRMSS 3764
DSDDTDRMFFMR, RRMF 6305
DSDDTD, LDDLFF, DRTD 8060
DSDDTLSFMMR, MLSSF# 95
DSDRDTD, DFSLSDFMR, 1531
DSDRDT, DRMFMR, MMM 11560
DSDRMDMF, SLFRDRM, D 8646
DSDRMD, TDLLS, SSLTD 9378
DSDRMRDS, DFFMRMFR, D 4161
DSDRMRDS, LLSSDMR, D 5773
DSDRMRDTS, DRMFMRR 3359
DSDRMRMF, SFMR, DSDR 443
DSDRMRMFSSSFMR, DS 442a
DSDRMRMF, SLSFMR, DS 442
DSDRMR, FMDRRD, MRMS 8291
DSDRMRTS, DRMFRRD, D 10414
DSDRMMMFM, RDRMD, RM 8581
DSDRMFR, DMRTDLS, MM 4188
DSDRMFRM, SLLSMRDR, 12480
DSDRMFMRDRD, RMDMR 11695
DSDRMFMRD, RMDLRDT 6870
DSDRMFMR, SDRMFMR 9007

DSDRMFM, SMMRDMR, DS	12474
DSDRMFFM, SDMFSLMR,	5810
DSDRMSFMR, RMFRDRM,	4492
DSDRMSFM, RLTD, DSDR	10261
DSDRS, MRMFMR, DTLDR	141
DSDMDMSFMRD, MRDFM	1431
DSDMDMSLSF#SM, FSSL	11403
DSDMDTLS, SLTDTDMR	1825
DSDMRDMMF#SS, SSSDS	2888
DSDMRDFMRM, SLSFMR	8449
DSDMRD, SMSFMR, DLDM	776
DSDMRD, SLTDRDT, DMF#	8429
DSDMRDTD, DFSLSDFMR,	1530
DSDMRDTD, RMSFMR, SD	1468
DSDMMRDR, DMLSFMRD,	9024
DSDMMRDT, DLLLSL, DL	8516
DSDMMR, FLMRDT, DRMM	11742
DSDMSFMR, DSDFLS, SL	9357
DSDMLSFMR, SSLTDFR	10432
DSDFMRD, DSLRFMRD, D	9080
DSDFMRD, SLRFMRD, DS	9079
DSDSDDTDS, MMFSLSF	4349
DSDSDRDTLS, MSMSMF	8610
DSDSDRM, FRMDTDR, MF	3003
DSDSDRMFMR, SRTSTL	10379
DSDSDTDRDLT, TFSTF	11143
DSDSMD, SFRD, DTDLSD	1625
DSDSMRDR, MFSLTDR, D	4771
DSDSMFMRD, DRMFMR, M	10464
DSDSLSM, MRMSLS, DSD	9806
DSDSLTD, RRMDMF#S, RL	957
DSDTDRMD, MSSMSFM, M	7264
DSDTSLSFM, MMRMFSS	1380
DSDTLFLTDSFM, DTDR	7609
DSDTLS, SFMRMFM, DMF#	2172
DSDTLTDRMRD, MRDTL	8254
DS, RMFS, SM, SM, SM, SM, MD,	
	10796
DSRMFS, SLSSF#S, DSRM	9915
DSMDDLLS, SDTSLLS, M	4541
DSMDDTD, MRDTLLS, RR	9106
DSMDRDTDR, MFSDRMRD,	9599
DSMDRMFM, DSMLSFSM,	5542
DSMDRMFMRM, MRRMSL	12105
DSMDRSSMDR, MMTTDM	10958
DSMDRTDR, MSDMRD, MF	9601
DSMDRTLS, SDDRRM, SF	1492
DSMDMFSLLS, LSRMF#	6862
DSMDFMMR, MRDRTLS, D	5568
DSMDFMFLD, DMDSRDT	6282
DSMDSMSMDRFRD, DSM	11055
DSMDSFMD, FMRLT, MTR	12212
DSMDSFMMR, MDFMRMR	4865

DSMDSF#SLSMFSL, TTD	3702
DSMDSLDT, SDMSRD, SD	6321
DSMDSLLS, SLTDTLLS,	3478
DSMDSTD, RRMMF#MF#SR,	355
DSMDSTRFM, SMDRMSF	3644
DSMDLS, DRMFS, DDDDM	560
DSMDLTD, MRMLF#S, RSR	2357
DSMRDDRTLS, LTDDRR	4764
DSMRDDTLS, SLLSTD, M	8413
DSMRDRDTDR, MFSDRM	9600
DSMRDRMRDLS, DMSLS	10558
DSMRDRM, MMDRMF#S, S	6727
DSMRDMFSLLS, LSRMF#	6865
DSMRDFFSLS, FMF#SRR	1402
DSMRDFSL, MRMFSM, SM	3776
DSMRDSLLS, SLTDTLLS	3479
DSMRDLS, LDFMRDS, MD	9680
DSMRDTDD, MFRSSF#S, D	5556
DSMRDTDLS, DRMRDTL,	2629
DSMRDTLS, LTDRMF#S, L	6742
DSMRDTTL, RLFMRDDT,	719
DSMRSDRMFSFFMRDF	1896
DSMRSFMRDDT, LSFMS	2649
DSMRTD, MDSFRM, SMDR	9042
DSMMRDDTDR, RDSMMR	7630
DSMFRDTD, DRMFSLRR,	4891
DSMFSMRDTDRFRMDRTD,	7843
DSMFSFRM, FMDRMR, SL	6875
DSMFSLS, DLTDTLS, MF	738
DSMFSLLS, SDLTTL, D	10228
DSMFLS, DDDRM, DDTLR	10366
DSMSDRMD, FMRDTDR, M	8573
DSMSDRM, RRRDRMDS, D	4871
DSMSDRMF, SDRMRDT, D	6459
DSMSDMRDS, LTDRMRD	8295
DSMSDS, DRMFMR, DSMS	8657
DSMS, FMDR, MSF#STLS, D	2799
DSMSLS, FMSFM, STLSD	1875
DSMSLLS, MFSDRM, LMD	11564
DSMSLTD, SMFMRM, DSM	12014
DSMLFRFMD, MRDSSTL	5330
DSMLSMDR, FMSLLS, S	2746
DSMLSFMR, RMSSF#S, SS	456
DSMLSFFM, MFSDFMR, D	4814
DSMTDRMLTDR, MLSM, D	3919
DSFMDRMFSM, RSF#SSF#	4117
DSFMDRFM, MFSMDRMR	11993
DSFMDMRD, DLSFMMRD	5414
DSFMDFMR, SDRMRDR, D	6116
DSFMDS, MFSLTDRDDT,	11835
DSFMDSFM, MLDTMS#F, F	4055
DSFMRDDTLS, SSDDMR	1184
DSFMRDRD, DSF#MRSL	2190

1073

DSLMFSTD, FMRDRTLS,	1798
DSLMSLLS, DDDDDRM, D	12193
DSLFRSMD, RRMLSF#S, D	2585
DSLFRSM, MMRSTLS, LR	12495
DSLFMMMFRD, SDRMMF	11828
DSLSDDRM, MFMRDLTD,	7549
DSLSDRMD, RMFMRD#R, R	10526
DSLSDMSR, MMRSLTS, D	5871
DSLSDFSM, SDRMFFFM	9592
DSLS, DSLS, DDDD, DDDD,	349
DSLSDTDRMD, SFMFRD	6285
DSLSDTLSS, MSLRDTD,	12073
DSLSDTLS, SLDSMRD, D	9638
DSLSMRDDRDLSF, MFS	2765
DSLSMRDS, LLFMRMR, D	2075
DSLSMRMD, RMLSDT, SD	6681
DSLSMFRM, RMFSFMR, D	4386
DSLSMFMRRM, DSLS	1507
DSLSMSFRD, RMLSF#S, L	8618
DSLSFM, DRMRD, RRMRD	1396
DSLSFM, DRMMRD, MRMR	4071
DS, LSFMRDMR, RMLSFM	3713
DSLSFMRDFMRDTD, RM	6038
DSLSFMRDTDRS, LTDR	6015
DSLSFMRMD, RSLTDLS,	12485
DSLSFMRM, FSLTDRT, M	2249
DSLSFMRM, SLDTLS, DS	6494
DSLSFMFS, DRMFMRDR,	8678
DSLSFMFSDLRDTD, MR	7367
DSLSFM, SSLTDT, RSL	11478
DSLSFM, SLRMRD, MDSS	4151
DSLSFM, LTDDTD, RMRS,	7357
DSLSFMLTSDDTD, DRR	1882
DSLSSD, MRMDDDTLT, D	8768
DSLSSFF, RTDTLSS, MD	11001
DSLSSFFM, DRLSFMRR	2849
DSLLMFM, MRDRMM, MRD	723
DSLLFTRD, SMMRMFRM,	8224
DSLLSFMD, SLTDTLLS	299
DSLLSFMRD, DTLRDTL	11968
DSLLSFM, LLRDTLS, DT	4135
DSLLSSDRRMD, DSSLT	5787
DSLLSSFM, DRMRRD, DS	9161
DSLL#LSDRRD, MFSLFD	1675
DSLTDRRM, SFRMMR, DS	10629
DSLTDRMD, DLRDTLLS,	10069
DSLTDRMD, MSSMSFM, M	7265
DSLTDRMD, FLRDTLS, D	4175
DSLTDRMRD, MRDTLLS,	1279

DSLTDRMRRD, SLTDRT	345
DSLTDRM, RMFMRDDT, D	3184
DSLTDRMFM, SDTTDTL	2308
DSLTDRM, FLSMRDT, DS	2915
DSLTDRT, DRMSFMRR, M	5531
DSLTDMRD, FMRMDRM, M	1731
DSLTDMRDT, LTDRM, MM	4878
DSLTD, MMFRD, SSMF#S, M	2645
DSLTDFMMR, MDTLLS, S	6152
DSLTDFMMR, MSFRDRM,	3521
DSLTDS, MMFLS, DSLTD	10635
DSLTLSSDRMMR, RMRD	163
DSTLSSMRDR, SDMFLS	1580
DLDRMSS, LSMDRDLS, D	3310
DLDFMR, DTDRR, RTDRM	2870
DLD, SMDR, FMLSFMF#S, F	8380
DLDSLRDD, DDFMRDM	2458
DLDLSMRDR, FRMFMRR	9030
DLDLSLTD, DMSMRDR, S	11627
DLDTF, LTLSM, SFMLLL	8117
DLRDDFFMRD, SDRMMR	3633
DLRL, DLRL, DFMFMR, DL	11736
DLMFFM, MMMLTD, DDDD	6582
DLMLSFML, TMSF#TDRT,	7344
DLFRTSDMMRD, DLFRTS	9360
DLFFMMRRFD, L#LSLDR,	10446
DLFFSLS, MRRSFM, DLF	7210
DLSDDRFMR, SMMDFMR	8931
DLSDDMRD, DMSMDRMR,	3432
DLSDRM, MRDFMR, SDDD	6222
DLSDRMMR, MSFMRD, SM	3989
DLSDRMMR, MSFMRD, SF	3989a
DLSDRMMSFMRD, DLSD	10269
DLSDRMFR, SMDFMRD, D	7766
DLSDMRD, DLSDMRD, SL	1897
DLSDFFMR, SDRRM, TTD	12429
DLSMRSFM, SSLTDRDT,	3059
DLSMFRDT, DSSSFMR, D	6077
DLSMSSSDTD, DLSMFF	5241
DLSFSLSM, SFMRMFM, M	3431
DLSSLTD, SLSFMRD, DM	6979
DLSLSLSMS, SLRRDLD,	7419
DLSTLSMSFMRM, MF#LL	9811
DLS#LDTLSM, SDTLTSL	8860
DLLDDLS, SDDDDRMR, D	12550
DLLDRMFRD, DMMRM	8270
DLLDTLTD, SDRFMRDR,	6128
DLLFLLS, SFMFSM, DLL	6591
DLLSMRLTDD, DTLMSS	4571
DLLSSFFM, MRLSFM, DL	11103
DLTDDSMFS, MLLMRDT	12536
DLTDRDT, DLTDLSF, FD	11981

DLTDRM, MMMMLS#M, MDL 747
11747
DLTDMLSMM, SFMRDRR 6151
DLTDLTDRMD, MDRMDM 3138
DLTDLTDRTLS, LTDMR 6515
DLTS, FMRMRS, SDTDRD 5407
DLTS#MLTDRM, MMFMRD 5843
DLTS#MLTDRM, MFMRDD 5842
DLTTDTLT, TTMMRRD, M 9069
DL#LDDRSS, DFFMMRDR 11144

DTD

DTDDDTDD, DMRDTLS, S 2862
DTDRDRMRD, TTDRTDD 6758
DTDRDFDRM, MMRDDRD 8093
DTDRDF, MRDTDDR, RSS 6181
DTDRDFFM, LTDLSSS, D 2614
DTDRDSLT, RD#RMRRDS, 5643
DTDRDT, DRMMRDF, RMF 10520
DTDRDTD, MRDFMR, DTL 9907
DTDRDTRFMMR, MRMDT 1252
DTDRDTFMMR, MRMDTT 1253
DTDRDTLS#LTM, MLSFM 9509
DTDRRDRM, MFMRMDLS, 2769
DTDRRDRM, FMRDDRD, D 706
DTDRRDRM, FMRDTDRD, 705
DTDRRR, MDDDTD, RMRD 8293
DTDR, RFFFM, RDTRD. 10108
DTDRRLTDRM, MRDT, SR 1248
DTDRMRD, RD#RMFMR, MR
4965
DTDRMRD, SFMRMFM, MR# 7874
DTDRMRTD, MMMFMR, DT 2042
DTDRMRTDT, MMRDTSL 10339
DTDRMFRRD, SMDFMRL 4198
DTDRMFMRDDTD, MFSL 3451
DTDRMFMRD, RMRDTLL 9157
DTDRMFFM, MRSSF#S, SS 9451
DTDRMFSM, MLSMF#S, FM 8432
DTDRMFSSFMRD, FMRS 9522
DTDRMFLSFM, MRSSF#M 5000
DTDRMSMR, MRDLSDRD, 9084
DTDRMSFMR, MMMLSF#S, 9717
DTDRMLSF, MMMSFMRM, 3338
DTDRFMRMDFM, DDTLS 10206
DTDRF#S, SLSSFM, MFFM 7017
DTDRSFMR, MFSDFMRD, 3319
DTDRTDRM, MRRMF#S, SD 5280
DTDMRDDT, LRSDLLS, S 8870
DTDMRDTD, RMMLFR, RM 7111
DTDFMMRDR, RSSSFMF, 6953
DTDFMMR, MLLTDRD, MM 9259

DTDFFFMS, DMRM, MMRR 8071
DTDSDTDR, DMDLRDRT 6888
DTDSMFMR, MFSDRSM, M 9546
DTDSFMRDTDRDT, DTD 944
DTDSLSFM, MF#SLTLS, D 10771
DTDSLLS, MRDSLTD, DT 1656
DTDSLTD, RRRDTLS, DR 9814
DTDSTLS, LLSSSFM, DD 3363
DTDLDS, MDFRDTD, DTD 10276
DTDL, MRRRRRRDRDTL 11349
DTDLSDDLMMRD, SLSD 5677
DTDLSDRD, TDRRR, R#RR# 1020
DTDLSMFMRD, MFSRMD 10682
DTDLSFM, DLRDTLS, DS 4063
DTDLSFMS, SLTDTDMR 11774
DTDLS#LMM, LTDRDT, DT 25
DTDLTSLL, DDRDTLST 2580
DTDLTS, LTDRM, RMFSL 1462
DTDTDLLSS, TLTLTLS 1453
DTDTLL, SLDTD, DRMRF 10551
DTRDRMMRFMM, SMRLS 1328
DTRDRMFM, SFMR, MFRM 12526
DTRDFMRD#, RTDLS, DTL
11605
DTRDFM, RRRRR, DMRSD 8932
DTRDFMMRR, RRMRTSS, 4800
DTRDFMLS, DDRRR, SFM 10044
DTRDS, LS#TLS, MFF#SDS 16
DTRRRDMM, MRMFLS, DD 10971
DTRRRDMM, MRMFLS, MS 1479
DTRMRDM, SDLSFMSDR, 5011
DTFTRDMS, MRTLMF#S, T 2627
DTSMSLS, SDTLRTSLS, 8661
DTSLMRDMSL, RDTLSD 10043
DTSLMFLRDT, DTLRTS 12211
DTSLMSDRMS, DRMS, SL 9356
DTSLMS, DTSLMS, F#MF#S 1523
DTSLMSFM, MMMMMMRL 6111
DTSLFMRD, DFMLSDDT, 8793
DTSLFMRSS, DDRMSMR 10305
DTSLFSMR, RFMLS#L, LD 2392
DTSLSSFMMR, LSMFMM 4025
DTSLLSMF, FDRMSLTD 284
DTSLTDD, MRTDLS, SSS 724
DTSLTDRMRDTR, DTSL 3894
DTSLTD, MRTDLS, SSSL 7285
DTSLTS, DTSLTS, DDRM 12439
DTLDRD, MRDMR, DTLDR 4037
DTLDRDTS, LTTD, DTL 528
DTLDMRRD, DTLRDTL, D 7775
DTLDMFLS, SLTDTLMR, 12200
DTLDSFM, MFSLSMR, MF# 9681
DTLDSLMFRD, DFMLSD 1246

DT LDLS, DRMSDMR, MRD 8628
DT LDT LDT, LSF#SLSFM, 11956
DT LDT L, FT RMMM, LTS#L 3513
DT L, DT LS, SFMRDSLS. 11982
DT LDT LLS#, LTDDRM FM 2291
DT LDT LTM, DDDRDRM, M 2424
DT LDT LT LLS#, S#LTDRM 4221
DT LRDT LS, DT LRDT LS, 4251
DT LMRDRM, SLSMSLSM, 11321
DT LMRDTDRS#, LTDFMR 7397
DT LMRDTDLS#, TTTDRM 10729
DT LMMMMRDT L, DRMSS 10365
DT LMSLSLDT, DT LFSL 4309
DT LMSLTRDR, TRFLLT 9833
DT LMLS, RDT LS, MTMRR 5683
DT LFLS, FMRDRSS, DT L 7355
DT LF, T LSM, RF#LDT LRS 11609
DT LSDRDRM, DFMRMDR 2398
DT LSDRDRMD, FMRMRDT 5248
DT LSDRMD, MM FMDRD, D 6391
DT LSDRMMRDDT, TDRM 7356
DT LSDRM FSM, RMF#SLT 8905
DT LSDMRD, DRM FRM, MR 7479
DT LSDMRDRM, MRDSMD 1341
DT LSDMSFM, RLFMRDT, 7459
DT LSDFMRD, DT DFMRR 6482
DT LSDT LS, TDDRRM, MD 3342
DT LSDT LS, TDRMRDRT, 2635
DT LSRFFM, SLTDSRSM 208
DT LSMDRM FMR, SMRDL 6197
DT LSMRDSFM, LTDMRR 4741
DT LSMRDT, FMRMRDLT, 3081
DT LSMRRD, SSDLTDRR, 5837
DT LSMFSDRT, TDDRMT 6184
DT LSMFSLTD, RMRDT L 10233
DT LSMFT LS, MRDTDL 9763
DT LSMS, DT LSMS, F#T LS, 1900
DT LSMSMS, T LST LSLM, 11
DT LSMSF, RDD#RLS, FMF 9361
DT LSMSSFRFFM, DT LS 9091
DT LSMSLFLLSS, DT DR 7044
DT LSM LDSM, MRDLRDT 2605
DT LSM LDLSM, MRDLR 2604
DT LSM LR, T LSRMFLS, D 12094
DT LSM L, SMRDRM, MF#S# 992
DT LSM, LSFMR, MF#ST LS

10683
DT LSM L, LFMRDT, DDDR 6096
DT LSM LLS, DT LSM LLS, 4658
DT LSM LLS#, DT LSM LLS# 4660
DT LSFMRD, DT LT LS, DL 981
DT LSFMRDRM, RMF#SLT 529
DT LSFMRDRM, FFMRMF 3290
DT LSFMRD, RMLSMRDM 12107
DT LSFMRD, SLLTTD, DD 513
DT LSFM, MMMMRR, MFRS 3150
DT LSFMM, SDT LS, DT LS 4108
DT LSFM, MSFMRM, MMMF# 75
DT LSFMFSDDTD, MRDT 6621
DT LSFMFS, LSFMRMFM, 387
DT LSFMLLS, DT LSFML 4659
DT LSFFFFF, T LSFMFS 10506
DT LSF, T LSFM, MFLSDT 10532
DT LSF#S, SFFMMF#, SSSL 1478
DT LSF#SLS, DT DMRDR, D 12187
DT LSF#LLS, FMMMRDT, M 4826
DT LSSDRD, DSLSDT 11500
DT LSSDT LLS, FMMRDD 4811
DT LSSSDT LS, MMMMLS 2735
DT LSSSLDLLS, MRRDT 12037
DT LSSLDR, MRDTDRDT, 4779
DT LSSLSD, DRMFSLS, S 10811
DT LSSLSFM, RRMFMRMF 3336
DT LSSLTD, DDRSDT LS, 3616
DT LSSLTD, DRMFMR, RM 6535
DT LSSLTD, DRTDT LS, D 106
DT LSSLTD, DT LSSLTD, 4646
DT LSSLTD, RDT LTDLS, 105a
DT LSSLTD, RDT LT LS, D 106a
DT LSSLTD, RDT LT LLS, 105
DT LSLDRD, MSFRMRDM 740
DT LSLRM, DT DRSM, MRM 3325
DT LSLRFM, RSMF#SLDT 3329
DT LSLRSFMRD, SLF#SL 4033
DT LSLMRDT, DRMFMRD 1250
DT LSLFMRD, DT SF#LT L 12079
DT LSLFSMRD, MRSF#DT 5179
DT LSLSDSFM, MFMRSL 7696
DT LSL, SMRDR, SLMRDR 5058
DT LSLSM, MFSLTD, DDT 4364
DT LSLSM, LSFDRM, MF#S# 1517
DT LSLSFM, FMRDMLF#S, 1655
DT LSLSS, DT LSFRM, SF# 8105a
DT LSLLSFM, SLTDMRL 2207
DT LSLLSS, RT LST LSS, 8158
DT LSLTDRMFS, SLSMF 462
DT LSLTD, MRDRT LS, LS 12379
DT LSLTDLFMRD, DT LS 4130
DT LSLTD, TRTDT LS, SD 778

DT LSLT LS, SMLSFMR, R 3860
DT LS # DT LS #, LTDT LDT, M 9288
DT LS #, S # LTDRM, TDLRDT 5066
DT LS # LM, DT LS # L, MSFRM
        6781
DT LS #, LTRD # LTT L, LSLT 6993
DT LS # LT, LSFM, TTTTR # M,
        6714
DT LLDSS, LSDDRMS, DT 12113
DT LLMMRDT, DT LLLT L 5782
DT LLSDT LS, SFRDRM, R 7412
DT LLSS, FMRD, SFMMRR, 7042
DT LLSS, ST LF, FLSM, SD 6747
DT LLSSLTDFM, RMFSM 8558
DT LLSLTDMR, DT LLSD 10251
DT LLS # MLL, DT LLS # TM, M
        2926
DT LLS # L, SSMRTD, DT LS 645
DT LLLSDDR, DRMMRDLS, 5847
DT LLLSDRM, RMSMRDR 3227
DT LLLSLTDDR, DRMMR 5848
DT LLLLLLLSSSSM, FF 10405
DT LTDDDT, DT LTDDDT 8259
DT LTDRD, FFMRDT LS, S 3116
DT LTDR, RDTDRM, SMMM 8806
DT LTDRRT, DT RMRRD, D 2824
DT LTDRMR, MRDT RRMD 8029
DT LTDRM, MFSFMRDLT 118
DT LTDRM L, FFMLRDTD #, 2575
DT LTDRTS, SDTDRMFM 4561
DT LTDRT LSD, DDTDRM 1930
DT LTDLSS, DT LMSFMM, 5259
DT LTDLLS, DDRRRRDR 10992
DT LT, RDTD, MRDDT LSS 5585
DT LTMRDT, LRDT LT, MD 2919
DT LT FT LFM, SSFMRFL 4367
DT LTSLSMF, SLTDT LT 12045
DT LTSLSL, MFSLDRTS, 11335
DT LTSLTD, DDSSMFSF 3530
DT LTSLTD, DDSSMSFM, 3531
DT LTSLTD, DDSSFMFS 3533
DT LT LS, RDRM, RMFL, FM 3797
DT LT LSF # S, MFSLLLTD 7950
DT LT LS, LSFMFSM, DT L 12243
DT LT LSLTD, DDSSMFS 3532
DT LTT L, SDTDRSM, MMM 2547
DTTDMRRMR, RRMRSRM 9969
DTTDSMRD, MSMDRR, LR 3817
DTTDSSLSFM, LS # S # LMM 1163
DTT LF, T LLSM, RMFSLT 9145
DTT LS, DTT LS, LSMFMRM. 8888
DTT LLLT LMSS, SLT LSL 10503
DTTTDRRRDT L, DFMMR 5035

DTTTT LTDDDDT, DRRR 8481

RDD

RDDRMDRRM F, FMRDRM 595
RDRMRD, RDRMD, DT LSD 8952
RDRMMRMSF, FSLLSFR 5649
RDRFM FRMMRDRR, FMF 679
RDRFFMRMRD, RDRFFM 8949
RDRFFMRMRRDRFF, SF 5423
RDRFSFMR, SSFSFMRD 8837
RDRFSFMR, LSMSFMR, 11666
RDRFSFMR, LSLFSLL, L 10318
RDRTDLFS, STRRMDRR, 2837
RDRTDT LSFSS, STRRM 2836
RDMS, SMSD, DMDSMFSL 10146
RDTD, RDTD, DFMRSFMR, 10790
RDT LSDMD, FFLDTDR, S 7003
RDT LLS # L, FMRDTDLM, M 2279
RD # MRTSDLS, RD # MRTSD 11452
RRDRDDT L, RRDLSLSR 211
RRDRMFMR, RRDRMFMR 7027
RRDRSFSLS, DLTDDSL 2193
RRDTDLSDRFFMRM, SS 8756
RRDTR, DMRD, LLTDT LS 1967
RRDTSDMR, MRDTDD 7035
RRD # RMFRM, LRDFMRD # R 8713
RRRDRMMS, LSLDLS, DD 12139
RRRDRTDL, FMRD # TDR, R
        11209
RRRRDRMSS, LSMSMRD 5300
RRRRDMDLS, SLDFMRD 12204
RRRRRRRFR, RFRDDTD 6762
RRRRRR, SSFMRD, MRRM 2792
RRRRRMRS, SRSF # RDLS, 10188
RRRRRMF, MMMRDMR, RR 1657
RRRRMRDS, LLLLTDR, M 4412
RRRMMFRD, DFSLFFMF 6637
RRRMFM, DDDRMR, RRMF 988
RRRFFFMMLS, DDDDT L 1729
RRRSRMFM, MMMR, F # MF # S,
        5644
RRRLLSSLSFM, LLTSD, 1800
RRRLTDT LS, LTD # RLDT 3031
RRRT LS, FFFFM, SSSDR 3282
RRMRD, RRRMRD, SDDDR 7223
RRMRDTDM, RMRDT LS, M 3205
RRMRRRS, F # F # F # MRRS, RR
        567
RRMRS, MMFMD, FFFMRD 10718
RRMRSF # MF # S, RRMRSF # M
        6195
RRMRSLSDRM, FMMRDR, 5266

RRMRSLSDMD, LDTLSD   11871
RRMFRMD, DRRMML, RRM
4191
RRMFMR, DRL, LSFF#FMF
2063
RRMFMMFS, FMRDLS   8988
RRMF, MMFS, SDTLSMDM 7880
RRMFF, MMFSS, SF#SLTD 8136
RRMFFFMMFS, SSLTLS   10763
RRMFFSFM, LDLL#LSFF, 6524
RRMFSFM, RFMDRM, LDD
11042
RRMFLSFM, DDMSMR, MR
6440
RRMFLSFM, RRMFLSFM, 6110
RRMSSDSLS, DRFMRD   3425
RRFRRDFSL, LSDDRDD   5463
RRFR, RRSM, RLDL, LTSL,
12244
RRFMDMRDTL, LDDRRM 11043
RRFMRD#R, RLFSFM, RRF
9013
RRFSLTDL, LTDRDTL, R 6460
RRLSSL, LLRTDL, SLD, S 11129
RMDRML, DDTDRS, SSMR 9154
RMDSSLDS, DMMMRDR, S 5097
RMRDRMS, LFLDLSM, SL 5730
RMRDS, MFMR, MRDDTLS 8125
RMRDLDRMSMR, RMRDL 10745
RMRMRRR, RMRMLL, MSD
7695
RMRSMFMD, FFMMRDR, M
12088
RMMRDRMFS, RMMLLSF   500
RMMMDTLSFM, RMDLTD 6767
RMMMRRDD, DRRRDRMS, 5307
RMMFFFMRMFMR, MFFS   726
RMMFFSSL, LL#DLS, L#LS
7454
RMFMRMFLS, LTDTLSM   1743
RMFMFS, LLSF#S, DDDST 520
RMFMSFSFM, LFLSM, SF 1861
RMFMSLSMR, SFMRDTL 9974
RMFFMRMS, MRDDRMR, M
7756
RMFFFMRM, SSLLSMR, M 5764
RMFFSFMR, MFSLSMR, M 2421
RMFS, DLSFM, DTLSMD 8477
RMFSMSFMF, RMFSMSF 8648
RMFSFMRD, DRMFSFMR 6660
RMFSFMRMM, MRMFMSS 6753
RMFSLRMFSFMM, SLDD   48
RMFSLTDRDTL, FRMFS 8778

RMLLLSML, TMLLSML, T 6913
RFRD#RMFMR, FFFFDRF 1751
RFRRDR, FFRMMR, RLL#L 5424
RFRRDFSFSLL, FLDLS   8274
RFRLFMRL, LDLTDRL,   8501
RFMRM, DTDRSRFMRD, T 4703
RFMRFF, RMDRFF, FFF 7438
RFMRLDTL, SSDTLLS#L, 4696
RFMFSLRDFMFRDDR, R   10702
RFMSSSFM, RMFSRMRD, 2525
RFFMRFSL, LFSSFMMR, 12324
RFFMFSFMRFMR, RFSL 8728
RFSLRSFM, SLDDTLTD, 1793
RFSLSDTL, SDTLSFMR,   820
RFSLSDTL, LDTLSFMR 1739
RFSLTDTL, S#DTLSFMR, 1740
RFLSLDLS, LFLRDL, S 9770
RSFMD, MRDTDLS, MMMM 11510
RSF#MDLRDT, MMRRDRM 1229
RSLFMRM, RSLLSFM, LD 7842
RSLSDTLS, LTSMFMR   5997
RLSFMRFSL, LRDL#LSL 7590
RlSLMFMSFMRD#R, LLR 2056
RLSLMFSL, TDRDTL   11371
RLLMSFMR, RLTDRDTL, 11813
RLLSRDTL, DLDTL, LDT 7005
RLLSFMRSLTDTL, RSL 5669
RLLTSLTDTL, RDTLSD   506
RLLTSLTRDTLSL, LLR   734
RLL#LSSLSSFSSLSFMR, 3739
RLTSLTDRDTSL, RRDR 7365
RLTSLTRDTLSL, LLRM   735
RTSMMRTSS, SFRDFMR 8539
R#MMRDDT, SFFMRM,   11885
R#MMMMMSR, MFMFLFMR,
1688

MDD

MDDDDDD, MSSSSSS, SL 5213
MDDR, MFFM, SLSMRMSF 6678
MDDRMSMR, DRMSMRR, M 2651
MDDRMSSLMRD, MDDRM 8725
MDDMSFM, MSRMRDT, SD 5349
MDDMS, LFFLD, DTL, SRM 4371
MDDFMSSS, SDTDRFTT 9052
MD, DL, RSTLSF#S, SDMRD
11434
MDDL, SDTDRMMR, MDDL 6061
MDDLSSTLSSD, MDDL, S 9951
MDDTDMS, LSDSFMSFM 1403
MDDTDLS, LTDFMRDT, M 11495
MDDT, DLLS#, MMMFMRD, T

	7937
MDDT, DLLS#, MMSFMRD, T	
	7938
MDDTFRRD, SMMRMFMR	5535
MDDTLSFM, MLLLTS#, MD	
	12287
MDDTTDDL, MMS#S#L, MDD	
	3784
MDRDSTLS, SLTDRR, FM	9494
MDRDLDRM, MSMDRFM, M	5483
MDRDLD, SMRMMR, MDRD	8962
MDRDLS, RRFRM, MDRDL	9745
MDRDLSMS, DRRRDRM, S	7134
MDRDLS, SSDDDMRMR, M	12398
MDRDTSL, LDTRDM, MDR	1554
MDRRD, DRDTDMR, SFMR	11714
MDRM, DDFDRMR, DRMRR,	9988
MDRMDLD, MFSMDLSMR	11971
MDRMDLTD, RMDDRD, MD	
	11484
MDRMRDRM, DTDRDTSD,	7716
MDRMRDM, SMDTDM, FMF	214
MDRMRMSFMRD, MMF#SF#	866
MDRMMRDDTD, MDRMMR	11552
MDRMMMMDRM, DSSFMRD	476
MDRMMMMMFS, SFMRFM	6359
MDRMMMMSFM, RDDRFM,	9390
MDRMMFMR#M, MRD#RMRD	
	4929
MDRM, MFFM, RRMFMFSL,	4837
MDRMMFFFM, MRDTRFM	12077
MDRMMFFFFM, SLSMDD	1988
MDRMFRM, MSSFRMMRD	11513
MDRMFM, DRMFM, SRMFL	4465
MDRMFM, DTLS#, LSFMRD,	
	10445
MDRMFMRDTD, MMMSFM	3837
MDRMFMRM, LSTDFMMR,	6191
MDRMFM, RTMRD, MDRMF	3873
MDRMFSDMRD, MDRMFS	3153
MDRMFSFM, MFSSRMDT,	5355
MDRMFSFM, MFSSRMRDT	5356
MDRMFSFFM, MFSSRMR	5354
MDRMFS, LSMFSS, LDTS	3219
MDRMFSLS, SDRMFS, LS	1364
MDRMFSLTDT, LSSFMM	3750
MDRMFLR, RMFSSF#S, MR	2494
MDRMFLMR, DRDRM, MDR	1970
MDRMF#S, SF#MR#F#M, MRMF	
	7029
MDRMSD, LSMRMM, MDRM	3500
MDRMSDLS, LFSMSFMR,	7813
MDRMSD, TLSDMR, SMSL	999

MDRMSDTLSLM, F#SLTL	2192
MDRMSMDRDTL, MMRML	2653
MDRMSMR, MLS#LTDT, D	11329
MDRMSFMRMD, SDMSLS	6221
MDRMSFMMRD, MMRSRF	5963
MDRMSFM, MSFMRMFMR,	5351
MDRMSFM, MSSRMDT, TD	5346
MDRMSFM, SFMRRM, MDR	2705
MDRMSFFM, MSSRMDDT	5348
MDRM, SF#SM, MR#MSLSMD	
	12099
MDRMSSFM, MSSRMDT, S	5350
MDRMSLDSMRR, MDRMS	3676
MDRMSLDTLS, RTDRRM	85
MDRMSLSMRDM, MFSTL	2485
MDRMSLSMS, RMFMRDR,	5854
MDRMSLTD, RMSMRD, MD	4575
MDRMLDMSMS, SSLDMM	6517
MDRMLRTDRM, DLTDLD	3624
MDRMLSMD, TLTDRMDT,	3083
MDRFMFSFM, MDRFMFS	187
MDRMFFM, RDMSFM, MLSF	2240
MDRSDRDTS, LTDDRRM	9471a
MDRSDRTS, LTDDRSM, M	9471
MDRSDFMRM, MRDRSLS	1496
MDRSMDR, DDDDRMRD, S	6165
MDRSMDR, DDTDRMRD, M	6164
MDRSFMDR, DDLTDRMR	6166
MDRSFMRDR, DTLTDRM	6163
MDRSFMMR, DTLTDRMR	6162
MDRSSLTDRFF, RMDLS	6208
MDRTTDMRMM, MRDMRD	2990
MDRTTDFMRM, SMF#R#F#T	
	301
MDMDDLS, DDDDMMSS, L	10570
MDMDRD#RFMD, MTDLRD	873
MDMRLTRS, SLSLTDMM	5726
MDMFMRDRR, MMMLTDD	3953
MDMFMRDR, MMMLTDDT,	3952
MDMFMRDR, MLTDDT, MD	3955
MDMFMRMR, MMMLTDDT	3954
MDMFMRTD, RMRDSDDD,	9753
MDMFMMMM, MLLSMMRR,	2449
MDMFS, SLSMFR, SDTLS	8505
MDMSMDRM, DLLSFMRS,	1774
MDMSMRD, DLFMDR, MDM	7320
MDMSMRMFM, FFFMDSM	2032
MDMSFM, RDLSF#MF#S, SL	
	11612
MDMSSSDLS, SSSSDSS	11745
MDMSSSMSDD, DLSMMR	11953
MDMSSLFS, SLFSFMRM,	2051
MDMSSLSFS, SRFFMMR	7663

MDT LLLLL, LFMRRFFM, 5392
MDT LT DDRRM, LSSDDF 10748
MDT LTMM LSFS, SDT DR 11243
MDT LTS, LT DRMSF#M, DL
11558
MDT LT, TRDT LT LLLS#, L 217

MRD

MRDDDDDD, DRRRRM, RM 2466
MRDDDDDD, TDRRMMR, M 1807
MRDDDRMSFMR, RRMFM 6056
MRDDD, SLDDD, LSDRMM 817
MRDDDT LLLLRRMR, RRM 12344
MRDDDT LTTT, SSMMMR 5304
MRDDRDLS, SDRMDRMR 12390
MRDDRDT LS, TDRRRDRM, 4195
MRDDRDTT, SFFFFM, MR 8017
MRDDRRMD, DT LRDTD, M 9660
MRDDRRM, SLSMR, MRDD 10182
MRDDRRMS, LLSMRDR, M 3551
MRDDRRM, TDRT LLS, S 9775
MRDDRM, DT LLTS, SSFM 9410
MRDDRMFF, FFMSSF#S, M 3240
MRDDRMFS, SDDT LS, SS 9011
MRDDRM, LSF#MR#M, MDDT
11600
MRDDRFMR, SDTT DMRR#, 527
MRDDMRDD, SMRRMFM, M 8631
MRDDMSRR, MSLSMRD, M 7343
MRDDMSFM, RMFFRDTD, 8803
MRDDFMRDDT, RMDDDM 8946
MRDDFMRDS, DT LSMFS 4441
MRDDFMR, RRRRRDRM, M 4781
MRDDFMR, SLLSMDR, MR 6927
MRDDFMMR, RRMFLDTM 2723
MRDDFMMR, MF#SMF#S, FS
10759
MRDDSFMR, DRMFRDTD 9004
MRDDSLLS, SLTDT L, LL 6932
MRDDLS, DRMMRDR, MFS 9884
MRDDLSMRDDLS, RMFR 4393
MRDDLS, MRRDLSLL, LS 8088
MRDDLL, SDMR, MRDDL 1050
MRDDTDRDLLS, DDDMR 10141
MRDDTDRMRD, SFMMRD 7102
MRDDTDRFMR, SMRDTD 4798
MRDDTDR, SFMRDTD, MR 8423
MRDDTDRLTD, DT LSD 9327
MRDDTDSFMR, RMFT L 5930
MRDDT LSDMR, MRDDT L 8245
MRDDT LSRM, FSMLFRR, 4385
MRDDT LSFMR, MRDMRD 1105

MRDDT LS, FSMSMRR, MR 11012
MRDDT LSS, MFMMRDTD 9337
MRDDT L, SSSDMR, MRDD 2453
MRDDT LSLTD, RMRT RD 11621
MRDDT L, T LSDRMFMR, M 11861
MRDDTT, DRMSFM, RDLS, 6775
MRDDTT, DRSM, MRT RDD, 6450
MRDDTT, FMRRDD, DLLL 3885
MRDRDDMSFLDD, T LSF 10600
MRDRDS, MFSMR, MRDRD 11283
MRDRDSMSDDRM, MFSM 10373
MRDRDLDDRD, DT LT LS 743
MRDRDLS, SSLDSDMRR 3174
MRDRDLSLD, TTTT DRD 6790
MRDRDLLS, DRMRFMR, M 9641
MRDRMD, MRDRMD, LLLR 2661
MRDRMDSRDT LTDMRR 6808
MRDRMDLS, SMMR, FMRR 9217
MRDRMDT LM, MFSLSMR 4578
MRDRMRDD, DRDFM L, SD 8306
MRDRMRD, MFSFMR, M 4158
MRDRMR, DLSL, DRMFM 2378
MRDRMRMS, LSSLSMR, M 6998
MRDRMMR, FMRDDRRD, S 9895
MRDRMFR, SSFMRMRR, S 3352
MRDRMFMDL#L, MMSFL, M
6695
MRDRMFMRDTDRD, MRD 11535
MRDRMFMRMF, SFMFRD 1668
MRDRMFMMR, SLSMFRM, 10574
MRDRMFSM, MMRDR, MRD 5671
MRDRMFSM, LLSMFSM, S 9393
MRDRMFSFM, SMFMRDR 9783
MRDRMFSLDT, T LFLLS 2794
MRDRMFS, LSFMRD, MSFMR
11964
MRDRMFS, LSFMRRRD, M 11965
MRDRMFSLSFM, MRFM, M 6203
MRDRMFSLTDT LS, LT 10870
MRDRM F#SSF#S, MFMRMRD
9795
MRDRMSDLSFMRD, RMS 1042
MRDRMS, RDTDRS, DT LT 4345
MRDRMS, FMDTRD, SFMS 11438
MRDRMSFM, SMFMDMRD, 9782
MRDRMSFM, SMFMRDR 9781
MRDRMSFM, SSLSFMRD, 9784
MRDRMSFFM, MDSSRMR 5353
MRDRMSS, MRDRMSS, S#F# 731
MRDRMSSS, DSSMMR, MR 7324
MRDRMSS, LLLRDT, LSD 11421
MRDRMLMRDRM, MRDRM 4440
MRDRMLSSFM, RMF#SLT 5881

MRDRFMDT, LRMFSM, MM   12177

4993	MRDFMMRD, DRMFFF, RM 2322
MRDRFM, SMSMRD, MDLT 1713	MRDFMMRDRM, SFMMRR 1120
MRDRSDRDTS, LTDDRS 9470	MRDFMMRDRM, SLSFMR 10418
MRDRS, DRMSFM, LSTDR 10027	MRDFMMRD, SDDRRM, SS 4670
MRDRSDMRDTS, LSFMR 2167	MRDFMMRS, SLTDLSF#M, 3134
MRDRSDTLTS, SLTDRM 5756	MRDFMMRLRDT, SRRSL 7494
MRDRSMDR, DDDDRMRD, 6161	MRDFMSLS, RMFLLSF#S, 10447
MRDRSMRDR, DDDDRMR 6167	MRDFMLRR, MSFMRM, SL 6274
MRDRSLSDRM, MRDSMR 1847	MRDFMLLSRM, MF#SDTL 307
MRDRLS, SDRMFR, TMSF 11213	MRDFMLLS, SLTDLSF#S, 5341
MRDRTD, FRMDR, MRDRT 9032	MRDFMLLS, STDRMDFM 6996
MRDRTDTLT, S#LTDRDS, 625	MRDFMLTD, RMFSLR, RR 3216
MRDRTSDDRRM, MSMDT 949	MRDFML, TDSMFR, RMSF 2872
MRDMDRDRMD, DTLSDM 2616	MRDFFMRS, F#SLSTRDT 2935
MRDMDRDLS, DRMSMSF 12391	MRDFFMRS, SLTDSFMR, 3564
MRDMRD, SFMSFM, LSFM. 8887	MRDFFM, MSMDRT, RFMR 373
MRDMRDLDSD, RRDRMM 12087	MRDFFFMRS, LTDDSMF 3391
MRDMRDTD, SFMMR#M, MR	MRDFFFFM, MFSLLRDT, 8089
6680	MRDSDDTLS, SFMRTDF 9221
MRDMRSMRD, DMRSSLF#	MRDSDDTT, LSLTDRM, M 6583
12476	MRDSDRDTL, DRMMSDR, 12030
MRDMMSFM, RMDMSLS, M 728	MRDSDRMFR, MFSSMSM 3060
MRDMFSMD, MFSSFMRM 6279	MRDSDRM, SFMRDTTD, 8986
MRDMFLDD, DTLL, SFMF 1104	MRDS, DRFMRR, SFMMRR 4976
MRDMSDFMRDRD, SMR 6585	MRDSDMFM, SLSMDR, MR 566
MRDMSDTL, DLSLSMR, M 11132	MRDSDSTL, RDTDRR#M, M 5199
MRDMSFM, LTDRTLS, DT	MRDSDTDR, MRDLDDTD, 8175
11688	MRDSDTDRMSFM, DTDR 9973
MRDMSS, LLMLS, SF#MST 6725	MRDSDT, SDRMRFM, MRD 5790
MRDMSLSM, MRDDRMRD, 5910	MRDSRDRMRD, FMRDTD 604
MRDMSLSM, MRDDRMMR 5910a	MRDSRMFM, MRDRDTD, R 9995
MRDMSLSSDMFLS, SSF 7529	MRDSMDRMFMR, SMDRS 8829
MRDMLDSD, RMRTDRM, M 652	MRDSMDRFMRD, MRDRM 11775
MRDFRDTD, MMMF#LSFM,	MRDSMRDT, LSFFFM, SD 11147
5815	MRDSMRRD, MMLSMDFR, 9046
MRDFMDMR, SSLSFMR, M 9900	MRDSMRMD, DDDFFM, MR 6439
MRDFMRDMR, SFMRRFM 2442	MRDSMFMRM, MMMF#F#S, S
MRDFMRDMMR, SMRDRM 6044	1821
MRDFMRD, SFMLSFM, DD 8883	MRDSMSDT, FMRLTLSM, 1450
MRDFMRDTDR, MFRSMR 10096	MRDSMSFM, MTLSSF#SL 11816
MRDFMRDT, TDRMSSF, F 9594	MRDSFMDTLLS, SFMLS 7989
MRDFMRRM, MF#SLSF#F#S	MRDSFMRD, DLSFLM, MS 11722
12124	MRDSFMRD, RRRFRDRM, 7680
MRDFMRMDRT, DRMLSM 6272	MRDSFMRDRRM, MFSLT 2003
MRDFMRMDRTDFMRLS 1883	MRDSFMRDR, FMLRF#S, S 9585
MRDFMRMD, MRDRSMF# 9513	MRDSFMRDTDMR, RRMF 638
MRDFMRSMDL, SDTLSF 8605	MRDSFMMRDDT, RMRDS 1179
MRDFMRSM, MFMLSSF#S,	MRDSFMMRDR, MRDSFM 1311
11896	MRDSFFMRDTDMR, RRM 1314
MRDFMRSFMLS, DTLSR 10399	MRDSF#SDT, FFFFFFM, S 12471
MRDFMRSLMDRM, RSMD 5520	MRDSSDDT, LSMFSMLS 5323
MRDFMMDM, SFMRRMFM	MRDSSM, DSLSMR, MRDS 10067

MRDTTL, TDRMR, SFMRR 7801
MRDTTL, TDMMRM, MSMR 80
MRDTTLTDSSS, DTRDT 9855
MRD#RFMR#M, SFMRF#LS, F
4448
MRRDDRDDTT, FMMRTL 8857
MRRDDMSFFMM, MRFRD 10463
MRRD, DMSSFFM, DFFRR 9778
MRRDDMLLM, SSSLLTD, 1679
MRRDDTT, FMMRRDD, DT 4809
MRRDDTTL, FMMRDRM, M 925
MRRD, MSSFFM, MFFRRS 9779
MRRDFMRMRDS, SMDLS 9628
MRRDFMMR, MFSLSFM, S 2123
MRRDFMMR, SFMRDRT, F 3082
MRRDSSFFM, DTTLDLS 5459
MRRDSS, SSFDRM, MMMS 2238
MRRDLFMMR, DLTSD#RR# 4490
MRRDTDR, FMMRDRM, DD 3565
MRRRMFFMRM, MMLSF#M 2663
MRRRMFLS, MRRRMFM, S 7253
MRRMRDSRMTLF#, F#SF#M
5938
MRRMRRDRRMRDT, RRT 3737
MRRMFMRMS, SLLLLTD 5075
MRRMFS, SLSFSM, STLS, 8419
MRRFMRD, MSSLLS, MFSL 54
MRRSMDRM, MMF#SLTLS, 4758
MRRSMRD, DSSLS[M]FSL 4336
MRMDDRMF, RMSDTLT, L 3213
MRMDDRMFSM, SFSMRD 9029
MRMDDFFM, MLLSDMRR, 3179
MRMDDS, SFMR, MRMDDS, 8736
MRMDRDDTD, MF#SLF#F#M,
10680
MRMDRMM, SSSFMR, MRM 532
MRMDRM, LTTDRS, SDTL 9158
MRMDRFMMR, MRMDFMR 2161
MRMDMRMD, MLSMRDM, M
1775
MRMDMRMS, LSFMRDTD 2341
MRMDMSFM, LSMDRR, SS 282
MRMDSDRM, SFMLSSMR, 5976
MRMDSFSM, STLSMR, M 1070
MRMDSLDS, SDTDMRDT, 12210
MRMDSL, STRM, MRMDS 8679
MRMDLD, MRMDLD, MRMD 6226
MRMDLS, DRFS, MRMDLS, 4509
MRMDLS, RDRM, MRMDLS, 7075
MRMDTL, MSFMRD, TDRF 9666
MRMRDD, DRDLS, DTRDR 12176
MRMRDSDRM, DMMFMRF, 804
MRMRLSMS, MRMRLSMS, 1022

MRMMDMSMS, SSLLLLDD 455
MRMMMRMM, MMFSFMR, R
6994
MRMFRRD, SFMF#SF#M, LS
2719
MRMFRM, SLTDLT, TDSL 9577
MRMFRSDDRM, MLLSM 9203
MRMFRSD, FMDRDTD, MLL 5803
MRMFMDTDR, RD#RMR, RD 137
MRMFMRD, DRRM, RRMRD 8397
MRMFMR, DRMRS, L#LSFM 7976
MRMFMRMD, DTDMRR, RM 576
MRMFMRMDRRM, MRMFM 3356
MRMFMRM, MRDRMRD, MR
8219
MRMFMRMF, RSSSFM, MF# 1476
MRMFMMRR, LRTLSM, MR 8637
MRMFMSFMRRDTD, DTL 1955
MRMFM, SLSMRR, MSDTT 2024
MRMFFFRFMRDTL, LTD 4184
MRMFSMRD, MRMFSMRD, 114
MRMFSFMRD, SF#SLTLS 8776
MRMFSFM, SFMFMRMR, M 5691
MRMFSS, MRMFS, LSFL 9613
MRMFSSFMFSLL, SSLT 12300
MRMFSS, LDTLS, SLSFM 2532
MRMFSLSFFMM, MRDDR 5594
MRMFLRM, MFSLRRMR, S 247
MRMFLSM, MSMDRM, MRM 1125
MRMFLLS, DTSFLS, MM 1025
MRMSMRDFMR, MFMSMR 1214
MRMSMRM, SDDTLS, MRM 9093
MRMSMFMRMD, RDRMDR 3851
MRMSFRDT, DLSMRDR, M 3566
MRMSFMRD, RMF#SDTLS, 10032
MRMSFM, RDMLTDT, SLT 11611
MRMSFMRMFMRD, DDTL 9689
MRMSFMRMFMR, FMFLS 8204
MRMSSFMM, SFMRDTDR, 7890
MRMSSFMFLS, MRMSSR 8105
MRMS, SSSSF#S, MRMD, DD 4868
MRMSSLFM, MSMDRR, FF 2415
MRMS, SLSD, DTLSMFFF 1989
MRMSLSF#M, MDRMRDTL, 1719
MRMSLSL, LTDTLSFM, M 12320
MRMSLTDR, FMFLTDRM, 10296
MRMSLTTLSM, MRLR, MT 1878
MRMLSDRM, MSDTSLDT 2685
MRMLSF, LTDRD, MRMF#M 177
MRMLLDTL, LDTLSF#SL 9123
MRMLLS, DTDFFM, SDTL 8786
MRMLLLDTL, MRMTTTR 12572
MRMLTDRS, FMRDLSL, 5841

MMRMMMMRM, MSMF#F#S, ST
        3309
MMRMFR, DLSFM, MSDLS 3093
MMRMFRMD, TTLLRMR, S 12137
MMRMFR, SDRMF, DLSFF 3092
MMRMFRS, DTLSSFM, MM 6149
MMRMFM, DRDTD, MMRMF 4756
MMRMFM, RRRMDR, MMRM 5684
MMRMFMLS, DDTLSLS, S 9264
MMRMFML, TDMR, MMFSS 1586
MMRMFFMRRFLS, MMRM 10119
MMRMFFM, SSDLF#F#S 9582
MMRMFFM, SSFMFSM, MF#
        11808
MMRMFFFSM, SLTDDTL 3080
MMRMFSD, DLSFSM, MMR 3621
MMRMFSDS, MDDRFFM, M 3324
MMRMFSM, SSFMFFM, MF#
        11807
MMRMFS, SDTSLS, SFRM 8591
MMRMFLSF, MDLFR, SDT 2297
MMRMFLLS, DSMFSDMR, 846
MMRMFTD, DTDRSSF#S, S 1368
MMRMSRR, FFMFLSS, SS 3968
MMRMSFRDRM, MFMFLS 7621
MMRMSFMRD, MRMSFMR, 256
MMRMSFMRD, FFMFLSF 4505
MMRMSFF, MRMFLSS, DD 9877
MMRMSFF, FFMFLSS, DD 5597
MMRMSS, MMRD, MMRMSS, 4326
MMRMSSFMD, MMRMSSF 3731
MMRMSLM, MRMDTDL, RR 1717
MMRMSLM, MRMDTDLL, R 1712
MMRMLDTL, MFMRDT, TD
        10212
MMRMLLSM, SFMRDRM, L 2689
MMRMLLLLD, LMRDTL, M 9124
MMRFRDRFFRM, RFLSF 352
MMRFRT, SDRMSR, MMRF
        11572
MMRFMRDRT, DFMLSF#S 3423
MMRFMRRDRM, MMLRRS 5245
MMRFMRSM, MRDFMR, RR 203
MMRFMRLSF, MMMMRDF 2028
MMRFMRLL, RRD#MRD, SS 7275
MMRFMRLT, DRSMRD, MR
        10470
MMRFMRTDRS, SSFLSF 5648
MMRFMLSS, DTLSMMRR, 9605
MMRSDRT, DSLTDDTD, T 10511
MMRSDRTS, DSLTDDTD, 10512
MMRSDLSDFMR, MMRSL# 3232
MMRSMMRS, LTSSF#S, FF 2950

MMRSFMRD, DDRM, MRSF# 3372
MMRSFMRM, MSDRRD, MM 7786
MMRSFFMLSDRRD, MMR 11944
MMRSF#MRM, SLTDTLLM, 3978
MMRSSFFM, MLLSMMRR, 8409
MMRSTRD, SLDTLS, MMR 9404
MMRLDT, DDTLS, MMRRS 4504
MMRLDTRD, MRSLDT, TD 6315
MMRLSFM, DTLSMF#S, MM
        2861
MMRLTDD, RMDSFR, MMR 5628
MMRLTDRD, DDRMFFFM, 856
MMRLTD, SSFDRM, MMFM 4248
MMRTRDTL, LDRMSF#M, M
        2743
MMRTLTDS, DRMMMFMR 5117
MMR#R#MMS, SDDRRRSS, M
        6259
MMR#R#MMRD, SDRDDT, FF
        2778
MMR#MDDDRMF, FFMFRR 253
MMR#MDMLS, SLDMRDR, M 1231
MMR#MDSSF#SM, MMR#MDR
        2186
MMR#MR#DDRDL, SDTDR, R
        4243
MMR#MMFMF, RRRSFM, MM
        6590
MMR#MMSFMR#M, SMSFMF
        5960
MMR#MFMRDR, FFMFSFM 6058
MMR#MFM, RRMRRD, MMR#M
        4470
MMR#MFMMRD, DLSFSMR#
        633
MMR#MFMMRD, SSF#SDSS 10342
MMR#MFMMRR, MDDRRM, M
        1644
MMR#MFMMRL, TDD#RSFM
        10607
MMR#MFM, SDDFM, MMMF#S
        11626
MMR#MSRRDRM, LLS#LDS 6346
MMR#MSSRR, MFMFRS, MM
        11955
MMR#MSLS, SDSFML, DSS 2155
MMR#MLDTL, MSMRDM, MR
        8028
MMR#MLSSF, MRD#RSFM, S
        3973

MMM

MMMDRDLSD, SSSSLF#S,　7426
MMMDRRR, MMSFMRD, M　6751
MMMDRRMM, SLSMDMR, M　2671
MMMDRMRD, DDDRDLS, S　11440
MMMDRMRD, RFFSLLS, M　9848
MMMDRMMMFDRM, MMMR　7271
MMMDRMMF, RDMSFM, DL　7538
MMMDRMSS, LLLFSLDD,　2797
MMMD, MMMD, MSFMRFFM,　5370
MMMDMMMMF, FMRDDTT　10593
MMMDMSLSM, MFRMDRM　2969
MMMDFMR, RDRDRMD, MM　6262
MMMDFMRMD, RMFSDDM　3791
MMMDFMMD, DRMFLSFM,　8879
MMMDFMMRDRFMRD, DS　50
MMMDS, SDRMRMSM, DDR　9991
MMMDSSS, FFFRMS, MMM　6296
MMMDSLS, SLTDTLTLS,　3318
MMMDTLLLSMD, RRRSL　6409
MMMRDDD, DRRMMR, MMM　861
MMMRDDDRDL, SSDDMR　1842
MMMRDDS, DDRRMMR,　6071
MMMRDDTDR, DTLSFMR　10388
MMMRDDTD, RRRMSSF#S,　10440
MMMRDDT, DMSLSSDMR,　9077
MMMRDDT, SFFMRM, M　11884
MMMRDDTT, DRMFFM, SS　7060
MMMRDRDL, DLSDDTDR,　3347
MMMRDRDL, SSSF#MR#M, L　536
MMMRDRDT, RRRMDRM, S　6441
MMMRDRRRDL, SSDTDR　6060
MMMRDR, RFFFMRM, MSM　3748
MMMRDRMDL, FFMRDM　10544
MMMRDRMFR, SSSFMRD　12489
MMMRDRMF, MDRR, SSFM　8441
MMMRDRM, LLLRLRM, FF　6809
MMMRDRFM, MSLMSMRM　7841
MMMRDRFM, SLMSMRMD　7840
MMMRDMRDSSS, FFFMR　6127
MMMRDM, RRRDMT, LLSF　5887
MMMRDMRT, LDTMRDT, M　4582
MMMRDMM, MFSRRM, SSS　3025
MMMRDMFF#SRFM, MF#RR　12278
MMMRDMFS, DRMFMR, RR　9464
MMMRDFMR, DRRRM, MMMR　4458
MMMRDFM, RD#LRRDTLS#10945

MMMRDFFM, RSSFML, LL　4042
MMMRDF, FFFMRS, SMF#S　5858
MMMRDSFMR, DRMLSF#S,　1542
MMMRDSFF, FFFMRLSS,　5720
MMMRDSSM, RRDRM, MMM　1708
MMMRDS, SFFMRM, MRMR　616
MMMRDSLD, SDMRR, MMM　4682
MMMRDSL, RDTD, RRRRR　8164
MMMRDSLS, RMSTLR, R#M　8774
MMMRDSLLS, DRRM, MMM　3366
MMMRDLD, RRRDMR, MMM　7227
MMMRDL, FMRDT, SRMD, R　4612
MMMRDLS, DDRDMR, MMM　11943
MMMRDLSD, RRRMRDMR, S　5627
MMMRDL, SSLSS, SSSF　602
MMMRDTDLSM, SSSSDD　4706
MMMRDT, FFFMR#M, MMRL　7329
MMMRDTLSS, MLS, RLS, R　10396
MMMRDTLS, S#S#S#S#S#LTD　4181
MMMRDTLTLS, MMMRDT　10788
MMMRRDD, DFFMFR, RSS　9182
MMMRRDDDTT, LTDSSF　11836
MMMRRDD, RRRDFMR, MM　7070
MMMRRDDT, DRMFMRRD,　6426
MMMRRDDT, TDRMFRD, M　2232
MMMRRD, MMMRRDRDTL,　8310
MMMRRD, SSMLTD, DDRM,　1281
MMMRRD, SSSFM, LLLSS　6514
MMMRRFMRDRM, SMSML　12411
MMMRRFFFM, SSSFMRD　8459
MMMRMRD, RRRMRD, RRR　10159
MMMRMRDRRMM, FFMRR　7584
MMMRMRDTLTDR, MMMR　1940
MMMRMRRD, RDDTLDTL　10860
MMMRMFRM, RMFFMRM, M　5654
MMMRMFRMFSM, SSSSD　11040
MMMRMF, RN.FLSFM, MMD　3301
MMMRMFMRDDT, DD#RST　8783
MMMRMFMR, FMRDRMRM　11723
MMMRMFMLM, MSFMRDR　10967
MMMRMFFM, MLMDTL, MM　681
MMMRMFFF, FFFMRSSS,　623
MMMRMFF#S, RRRDRMD, M　2002
MMMRMFSDSM, RMFLSF　8511
MMMRMFS, RRRRDRM, FF　4707

MMMRMFSM, FFFSFMRS, 930
MMMRMFSM, LLLSDSFR, 6778
MMMRMF, LSFM, MMMF#F#S, 9502
MMMRMFTD, SSSMRR 9230
MMMRMSFM, SSS#LMF, TT 6572
MMMRMSSF, MMRDR, SL 10400
MMMRMSLS, MRRRRDRM, 11284
MMMRMSLSM, MMMMRDR, 9632
MMMRFMRDD, RMRDTDT 2137
MMMRFMRD, RRRLDTL, M 9290
MMMRFMRD, SSSFLFMR 3832
MMMRFMRD, SSLSFMR, M 7276
MMMRFM, MMMFRM, MMMF# 865
MMMRFML, SFMMMF#S, MM 12016
MMMRFFFMLLSMRDR, M 10672
MMMRSFM, LRMFM, RRSL 882
MMMRSSLDDDRDDDLD 8283
MMMRSSLTDD, DRDTLD 8284
MMMRSLSF, MSFMRFM, M 5230
MMMRSLTDS, DTLLRDT, 950
MMMRLSMRR#, MMMLDTD# 8185
MMMRLSFMRM, MMMF#TT 2934
MMMRLSLF, FMMDLS, SM 2170
MMMRLTRD, MMRSMRDT 571
MMMRLTRDS, MMRSMRD 570
MMMR#MFSM, FFFMRSM, M 7421
MMMR#MS, DFMMRR, SSST 8298
MMMR#MSRR, RRRD#RFM, M 2047
MMMR#MSFF, MRMSFM, SS 9208
MMMR#MSFL, RDTDRSM, M 9478
MMMR#MSSF#, FMDDRR, MM 8972
MMMMDD, DDDDRRM, MMM 5441
MMMMDDDR, RRMFFMRM, 787
MMMMDRDDRD, DDRMMF 12160
MMMMDRDLLS, DDDDMM 7500
MMMMDRRT, TDDDDMRM, 7000
MMMMDRRT, TDRMFMRM, 11249
MMMMDRMDFM, MRLRMR 12393
MMMMDRMD, SSSFRMDR 8069
MMMMDRM, RDLLDRMR, M 3355
MMMMDRM, MMMRMF#S, SS 12432

MMMMDRMFMM, RDDTD, D 8513
MMMMDSSS, SRMFSM, MM 11271
MMMMDSSS, LLLLSMRMR, 12163
MMMMDLLMDL, LTDRMF 10471
MMMMRD, DRRRMRD, SMM 913
MMMMRD, DRMR, MMMMRD, 4296
MMMMRD, DRMRFMRD, DR 11815
MMMMRDDF, MRDT, SSSS 1556
MMMMRDDL, SDMSMR, MM 5876
MMMMRDDTDR, FFFFMR 9733
MMMMRDRDLS, SDDDTD 10714
MMMMRDRM, MLSDRDRM, 9196
MMMMRDRM, SSSSF#MF# 9336
MMMMRDRLL, DTLS#L, MM 5970
MMMMRDMR#R, FFFFSFM, 291
MMMMRDMSSSLS, MMRD 5031
MMMMRD, FMR, MMMMRDL 3226
MMMMRDFFM, SSRMDMS 11637
MMMMRDFFF, MMMSMDR, 5693
MMMMRD, SDDRMR, FFFF 9535
MMMMRDSD, DMRTDRM, M 308
MMMMRDS, MMMMRDR, SF 5288
MMMMRD, SSSS, MMMMRD 5962
MMMMRDSS, LLLLLDRM, M 9144
MMMMRDLDRM, SSSSLT 8370
MMMMRDLDLS, TTTTLS 5575
MMMMRDL, SDTDFMR, MR 4244
MMMMRDLLS, SMDR, MMM 10610
MMMMRDLL, LSDRDRM, M 4560
MMMMRDTD, SFMRLDT, F 8779
MMMMRDTLS, DDRDTRR 9187
MMMMRDTLS#LL, MMMMR 4097
MMMMRR, DDDDTT, LLSD 578
MMMMRR, DDDDTT, LLLL 579
MMMMRRDD, DRRRDRM, M 1765
MMMMRRDDD, RRRDRMS, 5610
MMMMRRDFFM, SSF#S, SL 12502
MMMMRR, MFFMRM, LLLL 5381
MMMMRR, FFFM, SFMR#MM, 5783
MMMMRR, FFFFMM, SSSS 10325
MMMMRRFFFFM, LTLSF 3234
MMMMRR, SSSSF#F#, TT 7512
MMMMRMDDM, SMLSSML 9933
MMMMRMDLTDR, MFSLS 10709

1091

MMMMRMRD, DMFSMFFM, 7632
MMMMRMF, MDDRM, MMMM 10298
MMMMRMF, MDRM, MMMMR 10299
MMMMRMFMR, LSFMRMF 5090
MMMMRMFFFFMR, SSLT 2293
MMMMRMFSM, MMMMMRR, 9608
MMMMRMSM, RRSSFRM, M 2467
MMMMRMSSSSM, RRRRD 5115
MMMMRMSLSM, RFFFSL 3592
MMMMR, FFFFM, MSSSMF, 4500
MMMMRFTDRMR, RMMMR 7861
MMMMRS, DRMFFM, SDDR 2815
MMMMRSLS, FSFMF#SFM, 4991
MMMMRLDD, SSSTLMSS, 3470
MMMMRTDTL, DDRDRM, M 4904
MMMMR#MSS, SF#SMSDT, F3782
MMMMMDRMM, SSSSSMF# 4694
MMMMMRDR, MMMLSSF#S, 2327
MMMMMRDRM, FMRDR, MF 8154
MMMMMRDF, MMMMRRD 8418
MMMMMRDTLDRM, MMMM 1234
MMMMMR, RDDDDT, TLLL 1481
MMMMMRR, RSRMFM, MMM 3719
MMMMMRR, FFSRFMM, MF# 6554
MMMMMRRS, SSMRDDF, F 9953
MMMMMRRS, SSSSSLLT, 2007
MMMMMRMF, FFFFFSRM, 3768
MMMMMRMFSM, LSFMRD 5391
MMMMMR#, MMSSSSSF, FF 9992
MMMMMMDD, DFFMRS, SSS 6821
MMMMMMDRMSFM, FFFF 1011
MMMMMMRD, FFMRDT, SS 1598
MMMMMMRDTLS, SDMMR 7413
MMMMMMRM, MLLLTT, ML 6324
MMMMMMRMFMR, FFSLF 2598
MMMMMMRMFS, SDTLSS 10590
MMMMMMRMFS, SLLSMF 6669
MMMMMMRS, DFMRRR, MM 1015
MMMMMMMRDDT, SSSSS 4960
MMMMMMMRDR, RRRRRR 1920
MM, MM, MM, MRDL, RMFSSM 10750
MMMMMM, MRMFS, SSS#S#L 7058
MMMMMM, MMRDRM, MFFM 11912

MMMMMMMMM, MMMMMMM 9942
MMMMMMMMMM, MMF#SSS 7159
MMMMMM, MMMMM, LLSS 9265
MMMMMMMFMRM, MMMMM
MMMMMMMMFM, MSSSSS 8745
MMMMMMMMSSM, MMMMM 2642
MMMMMMM, MLLLLL, LSS 7047 / 7392
MMMMMMMF, FMDLRDT, M 7123
MMMMMMMFFF, RRM, MMM 8391
MMMMMMMFSM, LLLLLL 9825
MMMMMM, MSSSLLSM, MM 5239
MMMMM, MFDRM, SLTDMR 912
MMMMMMFRM, SSFMLTD 8861
MMMMMMFM, RRRRDRM, S 6213
MMMMMMFM, RRMRD, MMM 5319
MMMMMMFMM, DTLLSFF 12095
MMMMMMFFFFMR, FFFF 9928
MMMMMMFS, FFFFFMRM, 11396
MMMMMMSRM, LLLLLLL 3795
MMMMMMLMMSFFFDFM, 9987
MMMMMMFRS, DDRRMDSM 11593
MMMMMMFR, SFMRM, SSSS 2922
MMMMMMFMRD, SSSSSLS 8485
MMMM, MFMRDTLS#L, LMF 3057
MMMMMMFMR, SF#SMLSF#S, 629
MMMMMFMM, RDDRR#M, MM 3279
MMMMMFMM, FFFFFLSS, 11910
MMMMMF, FRRRMR, RMMS 6099
MMMMMFFM, RDDRMR, RR 1425
MMMMMFFM, LDTLSFFM, 9225
MMMMMFFF, MRRRRSFM, 10127
MMMMMFF, FFFFFM, MMM 11110
MMMMMSRR, FSLSMMRR, 12433
MMMMMS, MDDDRM, MLSF 2793
MMMMMSMDR, RDDDRM, R 2930
MMMMMSFM, DDTDRMRD 556
MMMMMSFMRRD, SSSFM 97
MMMMMSFM, RRRLSSF#S, 4589
MMMMMSFMRRM, MMMM 1857
MMMMMSF, FRRDRFM, RD 7644

MMMMMSSFDM, FFFFFF 3133
MMMMMS, SF#FMFR, DDDL 6092
MMMMMSSS, SDLFLSS, M 10882
MMMMMSSS, SLLSSS, SD 209
MMMMMSSL, SFFFFFMM 4475
MMMMMSLSFFM, MDDTL 6732
MMMMMSLSSDDM, MMMR 8122
MMMMMLTDTDL, SMLTD 245
MMMMFRM, MRDTLLT, DT 6245
MMMMFRT, DDRMSF#M, LL
6189
MMMMFMRDRM, SSSSLS 6712
MMMMFMRDRM, SLSDDT 12425
MMMMFMRD, MMMSMDFM 5781
MMMMFMRMRD, RRRRSF 10628
MMMMFMMD, MRRFMM, MM
3402
MMMMFMMR, DRMSFMR, R 8862
MMMMFMSD, FFFMLLR, S 5860
MMMMFFMD, DDDDDRM, M
10092
MMMMFFM, DDDDRRM, MF 1947
MMMMFFM, LLSSFFM, SS 9301
MMMMFFF, RRSFFMM, DD 241
MMMMFFFFFSFML, LLL 7827
MM, MMFF, FFFTLS, MMMR
8211
MMMMFFFF#, SSDSMFMR, 9148
MMMMFS, DFMR, SSFMRD,
10444
MMMMFSFMR, MFMRDRR 11595
MMMMFSSFM, RRRRSTD 9114
MMMMFSFMR, MDMLSF# 11629
MMMMFSSS, SLTDRDT, T 607
MMMMFSLR, FMRDRM, SD 3158
MMMMFSTD, DLSFMMR, R 9869
MMMMFLLS, FMMMF#LLS, 5816
MMMMSDDD, SMFSLMR, S 6022
MMMMSDRM, DTLSMR, MM 3164
MMMMSDRM, MMMMMF#F#S,
4361
MMMMSRR, RRRRFDD, D 6250
MMMMSRM, FFTLS, SSDD 9141
MMMMSMR, RLSS, SDDTM 10855
MMMMSMRFRM, MSFMMR 9119
MMMMSMRFM, LLLSMSS 4174
MMMMSMSM, MRRRMFM, M 1094
MMMMSM, LSDRM, MMMMS
10249
MMMMSFM, DDRRFMR, MM 1183
MMMMSFMDRD, DFLSMD 2035
MMMMSFMR, DDRMFRD, M 9455
MMMMSFMR, DDRMFFM, M 8995

MMMMSFM, RRRRFMR, D 3117
MMMMSFMFMFLFMR, MM 2650
MMMMSFM, SLTDTSLT, T 3738
MMMMSFFM, MRRMFFFM,
11256
MMMMSSDDDDM, LDTLS 11973
MMMMSSFMD, MMRMMSS 3732
MMMMSSFMFRFM, DTDS 9650
MMMMSSFF, FMMMDMRR, 2278
MMMMSSSM, RRRRFLLS, 5458
MMMMLDDT, TDL, SLF, ML 2302
MMMMLS#LM, RDMSFMRD, 2210
MMMFDRM, MMRLTD, DDT 8971
MMMFDM, SFMRMR, MFLS
11372
MMMFRDTRD, SSSLFMR 9136
MMMFRM, DDDRLT, DDDR 1187
MMMFRMDT, TDRMLRD#R,
10214
MMMFRSDT, DSLFFM, RM 4376
MMMFRSS, MMMFLS, SF#M 8467
MMMFRSLS, FMMFRRD, M 2109
MMMFMDLS, DFFMDR, RR 7202
MMMFMRDRD, MMRMFS, R
12257
MMMFMRD, FFFSFMR, SS 8165
MMMFMRDS, LDDRDLS, T 2660
MMMFMRD, LSDDMR, MMM 8131
MMMFMRD#RS, DDRRM, MM 465
MMMFMRR, DDDRDTT, LL 580
MMMFMRRDDT, SDRMRD 8550
MMMFMRRR, SSFMDDT 6770
MMMFMR, MDRMRD, MMMF
12054
MMMFMRMD, MMMSF#MF#S,
2216
MMMFMRM, DTLLSSMR, M 135
MMMFMRMFFFM, RRMFF 11413
MMMFMRMF, FFFSFMFS, 3097
MMMFMR, FFFSFM, MMMF 2634
MMMFMRSD, DRMFLS, SD 2925
MMMFMRSS, SDRMFMR, M 3693
MMMFMRLS, SDTLSFFM 9997
MMMFMRLSS, MFSLTDS 8533
MMMFMR#M, DTLLSSMR, M
134
MMMFMMD, RRRMRDS, MM 1921
MMMFMMRD, DDDDFFM, M 12165
MMMFMMRD, DDDRMF#F#S,
4744
MMMFMMRDD, DRRSFM, M
11470
MMMFMMRD, DDRM, SSSL 11705

1093

MMM FMMR, DDLSFM, FSD   696
MMM FMMRDRM, DRTD, M   9699
MMM FMMRDRMM, MMMFM
                        1383
MMM FMMRD, MSSSFM, MM
                       10894
MMM FMMRD, SDSFMR, TT 5293
MMM FMMRDTRD, MFMLS   9831
MMM FMMRR, RRMRRDD, L 7838
MMM FMMRR, RSRMFM, FS 9905
MMM FMMRR, RSRMFM, SS 9904
MMM FMMRRMRLS, SSST   6940
MMM FMMRR, SRRMRDS, M
                       12403
MMM FMFSF, MRDTDRMR, 11047
MMM FMSRR, MFFMRR, SD 10579
MMM FMSRM, DLSFMMRR,   2953
MMM FMSSFM, FFFMMF#F#
                        3304
MMM FMLSDRMR, SFMLS   7268
MMM FMLSFFM, DTLSLT   7076
MMM FFRRRM, MMMSSF#F#9332
MMM FFRRMFM, SSLTSS   6802
MMM FF, RSFFM, LLTDRS 3286
MMM FFMRR, RRMFRLTD,   1443
MMM FFM, MDMSSS, SFMR 2759
MMM FFF, FMMLLR, MMMM
                       11892
MMM FFFFFMFSS, LLSMM   1199
MMM FFF, SSSL, DTLSS#L 3297
MMM FFFLSFM, DTF#S, SS 4510
MMM FFSFMRM, FSDFMR   5061
MMM FFSFM, MMMRSF#F#S,
                        7138
MMM FFLFM, MLLDLS, SM   952
MMM FFTRD, DDTLSMSS   9235
MMM FF#SR, DDDFDM, MMM
                        4745
MMM FSDRM, SSDTLLS, L 5917
MMM FSM, FRMMR, MFSMF 6299
MMM FSSSD, DLSLSMR,   9278
MMM FSSSMFMF, RMFST   1165
MMM FSLSD, TLSFM, MMM 3491
MMM FLDTT, LSDRMR, RM 4301
MMM FLSM, SRMFMRM, MM 6901
MMM FTDRM, MSMRMD, RM 7809
MMM FTLTD, DRMSFMR, M 5935
MMM FTLTD, RMFSMRDT   2340
MMM F#S#LM, DDDRMF, LMM
                       11300
MMMSDRRM, MMMLMMRR, 8329
MMMSDRRM, SSSDTLL   9349
MMMSDRRM, SSSFSMFR   4673

MMMSDRM, FMLSSFFMM   5743
MMMSDRM, FFMDDTDR, M 9635
MMMSDSFM, MMLF#STLS,
                      10562
MMMSDLS, DFMRD, MMMS 6021
MMMSDTDRD, MRSFM, RR 3466
MMMSDTDR, RRRFTD, DD 9857
MMMSDTDRMFM, MMMDL   2968
MMMSRRM, DTLSSF#S, RR 9016
MMMSRMMSF, MFSSFLL   9295
MMMS, MDDRRMD, MMMSM
                     10105
MMMSMDDRRM, MDTLSD   5114
MMMSMDRDLD, SSSLSM   3590
MMMSMDRM, MMMRDLRR,   1112
MMMSMDRM, MFMFLSFM,   8785
MMMSMDRM, SSSDTLSM   11784
MMMSMDRFM, LLLSDFM   9202
MMMSMRMFSM, MMLSF   9528
MMMSMRMFSM, SSF#SDT   11792
MMMSMMRR, RDDFFM, MM 2488
MMMSMMRR, RFFFFM, MM   88
MMMSMMMDD, DDDDRRM,   5442
MMMSMMFFL, LSFMSMR,   5209
MMMSMFMDRRD, SF#SMF# 8177
MMMSMFMRDMR, MF#F#SL
                      4796
MMMSMFMR, RRRDRM, SS 5093
MMMSFM, DDDRFFM, MMM 5965
MMMSFMDRMRD, MSLS, D 1010
MMMSFMDR, MMMLLSF#M,
                     12182
MMMSFMR, DDRMRD, TTT 4576
MMMSFMRD, DRMFRSFM,   9491
MMMSFMRD, RMFSDTLS,   2309
MMMSFMRD, MSMRDTL, M 6659
MMMSFMRDFFM, MFSLR   2413
MMMSFMRD, SSSSLMFRD,   265
MMMSFMRD, SSSTLSF#S, 4784
MMMSFMR, RRMFRSFM, M
                     12518
MMMSFMR, MDDRRRSF#, F
                      8386
MMMSFMRMD, DLSFMRD   854
MMMSFMRMD, MFSLL#LS, 1895
MMMSFMRMRD, LFMR, MR#
                     12394
MMMSFMRMFM, MLLSF#   7281
MMMSFMRM, SSDMLSF#S, 8256
MMMSFM, RSFMFS, LTDT, 8226
MMMSFMMR, MFFLSFM, M 1653
MMMSFM, MRMFSM, SLSM 3790
MMMSFMMMRDTDRMD, D   5251

1094

MMMSFM, SSSLTS, SSSL 246
MMMSFMLSFMMRR, RRR 8289
MMMSFMLLS, SDSSFMM 3819
MMMSFFM, MMRMFMRD, M 6852
MMMSFFFMRD, LLLSSS 11893
MMMSSDD, DFFFSFM, MM 2093
MMMSSDDRFM, FFMRLS 10808
MMMSSDDM, RDLLRDT, S 7298
MMMSSDDMMRFM, MMMF 11242
MMMSSDDM, MRSRDMLS 1515
MMMSSDDF, FMS#LLSFM, 7934
MMMSSD, DFFLLR, RMFS 2237
MMMSSDRM, MMMFMRRD, 8561
MMMSSDRM, MFSLSFMR, 11897
MMMSS, DFFM, LLLSMMM 7323
MMMSSRRRRF, FDRDRM 5824
MMMSSRMFRM, RDDDDT 2732
MMMSSM, MRMFSM, MMMS 1264
MMMSSM, MMMDRM, MMMF#
2108
MMMSSMMSSMMDRMR, M 3870
MMMSSM, LLLLLS#L, MMMM
9941
MMMSSF, MRDRRM, MLLS 11660
MMMSSFMMRD, MMMRSD 7998
MMMSSFM, MRMSMRD, MM 3729
MMMSSFFMDR, R#MSDDT 582
MMMSSF, TDDRRM, SSSL 6016
MMMS, SSMSL, LLLD, DTS 8235
MMMSSSLMS, SLTDLT, F 9832
MMMSSLSM, MRMSFM, DS 6793
MMMSSLSFSM, MRMFMF 3087
MMMSSLSF#SM, MRMFRR 3088
MMMSSLLFLD, DTLSMS 2085
MMMSSLLFLDS, SMRDM 7738
MMMSSLTD, LSFM, MMML 8826
MMMSLDM, MMMMRD, RRM
11814
MMMSLSDRM, FMRMRDT 10056
MMMSLTDDRDT, DSMDR 12438
MMMSTDRM, SLSDMLLR, 4867
MMMSTDFMR, FFFMSSF# 693
MMMS#LTLS#DTLS#FM, MM
12532
MMMS#LTLS#S#, TTDLSF#M,
4120
MMMLMFMRD, RMRDTL, M
10086
MMMLSTDR, SMDDLLTS 815
MMMLLSFM, SSSLDTLS, 971
MMMLLS#L, LDTLTMLS#, M
3668
MMMLLLS#S#, LLDDDTT, L

8945
MMMLLTS#S#L, DDTTLLS 11547
MMMLTDRMFM, DTLTTM, 5375
MMMLTDTLM, DDMRDDT 10684
MMMLTDTLLS#L, MMF#SL
9025
MMMLTRMM, MSFMRDDT, 10674
MMMTRRD, SSSRFFM, SS 3173

MMF

MMFRDTMD, TLRTLTDM, 3831
MMFRSRRD, MRDTL, SMM 9604
MMFRLTD, RRMRRDT, RM 7387
MMFRTLLS, MMFRTLLS, 8440
MMFMDRDRMRD, MMSF 2608
MMFMDRDRM, MMMRDLS 11675
MMFMDRMFM, DRRRDDF 4565
MMFMDRMF, FRRSFMR, M 444
MMFMRDMD, RSFTDRM, M
4398
MMFMRDFMRM, SDTLSF# 1331
MMFMRDSD, RRFMR, RRR 2556
MMFMRD, SSSFMRMR, MM 9671
MMFMRDTD, MLSFRDTD, 9829
MMFMRDTL, MMTLSF#SL 148
MMFMRR, DDRDT, LLTDS 12530
MMFMRRDTLS, LLFRDT 6831
MMFMRRRMR, DDFMRMD, M
10531
MMFMRMDD, RMFSMLS, S 3108
MMFMRMRD, MMFMRDT, D 6878
MMFMRMRD, MSSFLMR, M
12056
MMFMRMRD, SSLSFSFM 3983
MMFMRM, SSLSF#S, SSSL 2520
MMFMRSRD, DTDFMRLR, 9730
MMFMRSSLDD, DRDDTL 8286
MMFMRLDTMRD, DDLTD 4235
MMFMRLLS#, LSFMLTDT 624
MMFMRLTDRMR, RMF#SS 9463
MMFMRLTL, SLTDRMSF, 1918
MMFMMRD, DDRDRR#M, MM
12491
MMFMMRDR, RMFMRDTD, 11448
MMFMMRD, RLTSDMR, MM 5223
MMFMMRD, SSLSSFM, SD 4209
MMFMMRDTD, FMRMSFM 3136
MMFMMRRD, LSRM, MMFM
10732
MMFMMRRLR, RRMRRDD 1983
MMFMMRL, RRMRRDS, MS 2779
MMFMMMR, DTLTRD, MMF 3426

1095

MMF, MFS, MSD, SFMSRSD, 5318
MMFMFLLS, DMMRDRSS 547
MMFMSDRMFS, SSMDMR, 6341
MMFMSDRM, SSLSMRR, R 4592
MMFMSSLSSDTD 11679
MMFMLS, DMSRM, MMFM 8412
MMFMLLS, MMMMMFR, MM
11697
MMFFMRRD, MFSSLLS, M 10002
MMFFFFLLSMS, MMRSS 4494
MMFFSRMS, DDT, LLS, SS 6679
MMFFSM, FFMMR, MMR 3098
MMFSDDRDRM, DRMFSF 2150
MMFSDDT, DRMFFM, MR#M6009
MMFSDDTLSS, MRRMFS 8751
MMFSDDTT, LSS#LFMR, M 2951
MMFSDRDTD, SLDLSMS 9573
MMFSDRRMFM, MRDLSS 8415
MMFSDRMRD, SSLTDTL 3190
MMFSDRMFFMR, RMF#SL 2918
MMFSDMRDLS, FMF#SRR 3317
MMFSDLSM, MSMRMRMF 4307
MMFSDLSM, SDTLRMFL 3771
MMFSDTDR, FFFTLLSS, 7236
MMFSDTDRTDS, LDLSM 7929
MMFSDTRD, TTLSRMLS, 11142
MMFSDTFL, LSSSFMMR, 2130
MMFSDTLSFMM, MMLLS 3940
MMFSDTLSFFM, MFSLS 2859
MMFSDTLL, LSDTLS, FM 858
MMFSRDRMR, RRMFSLS 6851
MMFSRM, MMLSF#M, SDTL 9261
MMFSMDRMF, MRDDRMM 1460
MMFSMDRM, FSDFFM, MM 6782
MMFSMRDDTD, MMF#STL 6335
MMFSMRDRMM, SLTDTL 6477
MMFSMRD, MMSSSMRDR, 4882
MMFSMRRM, SDDTSTLS, 10264
MMFSMRMD, DTLSSLSF#, 9316
MMFSMMR, MMMFSRDD, M
8399
MMFSMFMR, RRMFMRDM, 10864
MMFSMSFMRM, MRSMDT 8246
MMFSMLSFMR, MFSLT 3578
MMFSMLLSRM, SSDTLT 11588
MMFSFMRD, MRFMSSF#S, 12462
MMFSFMRRR, MFMRD, MM 9661
MMFSFMRRR, SFMRD, TT 4013
MMFS, FMRM, MMRD, RDTD
11397
MMFSFMR, SMFFMRS, MM 6930
MMFSFMMRD, MRFMSSF# 12463
MMFSFMLSFM, SSLTLS 646

MMFSSDDTLSM, MRDFM 5967
MMFSSDRM, LTDMRD, MM 7289
MMFSSDRM, LTDMRRD, M 7289a
MMFSSRFF, MMRDRM, SD 9411
MMFSSFM, RDDRMMRR, MM 953
MMFSSFMR, RRMFSM, MM 11215
MMFSSFMRR, MFSMRRD, 5605
MMFSSFMR, MFSMRRD, R 5606
MMFSSFFM, MRDRTTDD, 3998
MMFSSFFM, MMRMFMRD, 6853
MMFSSF#RFFMD, MRDMR 568
MMFSSSDTLSM, MRDFM 5968
MMFSSSDTLS, FMMMTL 8496
MMFSSSMFSLL, RRMFF 5955
MMFSSLDDTD, DTLSSL 11867
MMFSSLSF#SM, DTLSMR 87
MMFSSLS, SDDDMF#S, SD 10719
MMFSSLS, TTDRRRD, MM 10720
MMFSSLLDLSM, SSLSD 8318
MMFSSLLSM, MRMFRMF 394
MMFSSLLS, SDLSRFMR, 6209
MMFSSLTDRDT, TDLSL 2451
MMFSSLTD, TLSFMMR, M 4767
MMFSLD, SLFLSFM, MMM 4256
MMFSLS, DRMFMR, DTLS, 4574
MMFSLSRM, SSRMF#S, SD 716
MMFSLSMDFMRM, MF#F#S
10460
MMFSLSFM, RMSSF#S, RR 3723
MMFSLSLSM, MDSMDS, M 11059
MMFSLSLSLSFM, SFML 10341
MMFSLLSM, DDTLSF#S, L 5639
MMFSLTDS, SRSM, MMF 7587
MMFLSFFM, MSDLSF#S, M 4762
MMFLLS, MRDRM, MMSSS 3299
MMF#F#SRSLLTS, LLDTL 1343
MMF#SF#T, TDDTLSSFMM 2094
MMF#STL, RDTL, LLTDTL 6516
MMF#S#LLS#L, LSLTDD 12311
MMF#S#LT, LDLSFM, SSF#S
10248
MMSDDRFM, DLFSLSMR, 664
MMSDRD, LLDLS, FLSFM 12420
MMSDRRMM, SSLLSM 12006
MMSDRMRD, LTDRDT, T 10080
MMSDRM, RMFFMR, DDLR 733
MMSDRMFM, F#SLTLSF, M 5956
MMSDMLTD, DRFMLSF#S, 11555
MMSDSLDS, SRMFSLSF 4923
MMSDTL, SLSMRDRM, MS 8620
MMSDRDRMR, RRMSLSFM, 5652
MMSRD, FFLRDSL, MMSRD, 974
MMSRRRMF, FFMRRM, ML 11214

1096

MMSMDRMR, MSSF#S, LSF 8762
MMSMDRM, MMSMDRM, MM
    9406
MMSMDRMF, MRDTMRDT 1461
MMSMDRMF, SSTSMF#S, L
    6803
MMSMRD, RDTLS, LLDRM 176
MMSMRDRMSL, SLTDTL 9952
MMSMRDR, FFLFMRM, SS 6248
MMSMRRDMDTL, LRLMR
    10479
MMSMRRFR, DTDRMSFM 222
MMSMRMFFM, DLSMRMF#
    920
MMSMRMFFM, SSMFMRM, 3308
MMSMRMSFMMR, MFSLD 9389
MMSMMRD, MMFSLFFM, M
    9893
MMSMMRRM, FFLFMRM, S
    5311
MMSMMFRM, SDSLSSF#S, 2860
MMSMMS, MSDTLLS, RMF 6490
MMSMFLS, SSMDRMR, MM 1387
MMSMFLLS, DMMRMFMR, 7156
MMSMSS, RRSRSS, DMMS 9215
MMSFRDMRD, MRDDDRM
    11337
MMSFRDTDMR, FMLSDR 8100
MMSFRM, DDMRTD, MSF#M,
    6466
MMSFRMDR, SSSDTLLS, 2708
MMSFRLTD, RRMFMRDR 9636
MMSFRTDDM, LLRMRDT 9050
MMSFMDRMSFM, MMRMR 626
MMSFMRDDRMD, FFMLS 12303
MMSFMRD, RRRMF#SSF#S,
    5246
MMSFMRD, RRRMF#LS, DT
    10152
MMSFMRDR, MMRDRRS, M 9496
MMSFMRDRMM, SLDDTL 3266
MMSFMRDRLTD, RMF#SD
    10123
MMSFMRDRLTD, RMF#SR
    10123a
MMSFMRDT, DDTDMR, MM 1432
MMSFMRRD, RMFLSFM, M
    7141
MMSFMRRM, RMFMRRD, M
    1836
MMSFMR, MDDRRM, MFMR
    6142
MMSFMRMR, RRFMRDRD 9518

MMSFMRMF, RRFMRDRM, 10485
MMSFMRMF, FFLSFMFS, 3976
MMSFMMRD, D#RMFLR, SD
    12477
MMSFMMRR, MFLSFM, MM 1062
MMSFMF, LSF#SDDT, DLS 9686
MMSFMLS, S#S#LDRMRD, L
    11662
MMSFFM, DTDFMR, RMSS 9623
MMSF#FMDDLLDS, RSFM 4987
MMSSDDMM, LRSDFMRD. 1803
MMSSDDMM, LLTDRM, MS 6983
MMSSDDMM, LTDRMSR, M 2159
MMSSDDSS, LLSDFMMR, 155
MMSSDDS, LLSLFMM, MM 2284
MMSSDDS, LLSLFFM, MM 2285
MMSSDD, LFFSLS, SRRM 7990
MMSSDRMR, FMLSFMR, M 9421
MMSSDRM, LTDMRRD, MM 7291
MMSSDRM, LTDMRRD, SR 7288
MMSSDSFMFMMR, SSLT 9693
MMSSDLRTD, RMDLSTL 1677
MMSSDTT, FFTTRDD, SS 10760
MMSSRRMM, LLRMFFM, S 290
MMSSFR, DRMFR, FFMML 335
MMSSFRDRFFMM, DDTL 2781
MMSSFRMR, DDDTDRMR 9122
MMSSFFM, SSLSMRR, LL 9388
MMSSF#SLS, MMMMSFMR, 6868
MMSSSFMMR, DDFFMRM, 8321
MMSSSFFM, MMLSSFM, F# 7028
MMSSSF#S, SSFMDFMR, R 4554
MMSSSLSMS, MSSSLSM 5039
MMSSLMSS, SSFFSTLS, 9731
MMSSLLDDS, DDLLDS, M 6447
MMSSLTLS, MSDTLTS, M 10208
MMSLDDLSSLS, MMSLS 5474
MMSLDRM, SMDTDFMR, T 8395
MMSLMDDRMS, DDTDS, L 2329
MMSLSDRM, MS#LTDL, DT 1278
MMSLSM, DDMFR, MDLSD 7371
MMSLSMMS, DDDFMMR, R 852
MMSLSLLDR, MRMDLSMS, 3357
MM, SLTDRMSDRM, MRRD# 3435
MMSLTDMS, FFMRDRLR, 11127
MMS#MMMLLLS#FMS#, MMT
    12497
MMS#S#MRMF, MMLLS#FMF
    7197
MMLDRMRDTL, MSFM, LD 3050
MMLDRMRDTL, MSF#M, LD
    3049
MMLDMRDLT, TTMMDTL, 11657

MMLDT L, SDSMDRM, MMM 8251
MMLDT L, LSLFFFM, MMS 709
MMLRDTT L, LTDRFM, MF# 1539
MMLMLDMFMRDT L, DRD 5794
MMLFMMRM, S#LDDTD, TD 120
MMLSMDRM, MMMMDLMR# 3239
MMLSMRDR, MDTLTTS, M 2639
MMLSFMRD, MSRMMMRD 5761
MMLSFMMR, RRMRMFMR, 4032
MMLSFM, MSDRMRD, MML 7703
MMLSFM, SRFMRD, MMLS 2636
MMLSFFM, MSF#MMR#M, MS 5599
MMLSF#S, DDTDRM, MMLS 4755
MMLSSFMRDLT, MMLSS 632
MMLSSLLFLDS, SMRDM 7739
MMLSLTD, TDRMDTL, MM 9807
MMLS#LRDTLS#, S#LSFML 6078
MMLS#LTTL, DTMLLS#, MS 297
MMLLDRM, MMFRDTL, MM 10634
MML, LF#S#LMRRT, MLT 1647
MMLLSFMD, SMLSFFM, R 10020
MMLLSFM, SLSDDTD, SM 10170
MMLLSFSLR, RMSLTS, S 11359
MMLLSSMD, SMLSFFM, R 10019
MMLLSSFMD, SMLSFFM, 10018
MMLLLSL, LTDLLSFM, M 8487
MMLLLLLLLS#LDT, MMM 777
MMLLLLTDD, TLRTS#, LLL 2808
MMLLTDDT, TLLLLS#, M 11748
MMLLTTD, DLSMRFM, MM 5985
MMLLTTDTL, LRRDDT, M 6281
MMLTDDDT, DDMRDTTL, 1371
MMLTDDDT, DRMRDTTL, 1372
MMLTDDRMS, FMRDTL, L 8647
MMLTDRDT, LTDLTML, S 5193
MMLTDRM, MMF#SSF#MM, M 4556
MMLTDRM, MMSSF#F#M, MM 4555
MMLTS#LTDRTL, MRDTL 6773
MMTDRDTL, DDTLS#LT, M 4122
MMTDLS, DSFMSR, FFD#R 2774
MMTDLS, LLTDLS, MRSR 7098
MMTRD, FMTRD, MLMSFM 9198
MMTTTRLD, LTDRLTDR 5721

MFD

MFDDDRM, SSRRRMR, RM 12166
MFDMRR, RMTRDD, DTLS 9758

MFDMMFDM, MSMDRTTL 10350
MFRD, DRDTLSS, DRMSF 2894
MFRDRRMM, MFRDRRMM, 4887
MFRDMFSSLLS, DDTLL 11947
MFRDMSLS, SLSDMR, R 9304
MFRDSDRMFRD, MMMFR 7162
MFRMDRTD, RLRDDTLS 11225
MFRMMFRM, DTLR, MFRM 3728
MFRMFR, MFSDFMRD. 3166
MFRMFFSLRDS, SSSFMM 4427
MFRMFSLRTDS, SSSFM 4428
MFRSDRTD, FMLSFMFM 6147
MFRSDLSFMR, RMRSLF 8378
MFRSS#LTDFMR, MMF#SL 10288
MFRTDS, FSMDR, MMF#F#S 6981
MFMDDDRMRL, LRMSS, MF 10649
MFMDRDRD, RRSTLSLS, 9868
MFMDRDTL, LDTLLSL, D 8723
MFMDSLSM, DDRFMRM, M 1377
MFMRDDDFFFFMRS, DD 10700
MFMRDDTD, SDDFFM, MD 3354
MFMRDRFM, MFLSMRDR 2784
MFMRDFML, TDRDTD, SM 121
MFMRDLL, SDDMMR, MFM 7317
MFMRDTLS, SDMSLSR, M 1865
MFMRRRR, RMRDDDD, DT 905
MFMRRRMDRM, SLSFMM 10252
MFMRRRMRD, DDRMFML 9228
MFMRRRMRDD, DTLLLD 5023
MFMRRRMRD, DRMFMLR 9229
MFMRRMM, MFMRRMM, MF 1802
MFMRRSFMRD, RRDTLS 523
MFMR, RSFM, MMFMRMRD 8604
MFMRRSFM, SF#SLMRDT, 4425
MFMRRSFM, SLTDTLSF# 7877
MFMRMDDTL, TDRMSFM 7613
MFMRMDRDTL, TDRMSF 7614
MFMRMDRM, SMDRMFFM, 10751
MFMRMDRM, LLTDTLS# 6144
MFMRMD, TLTDRS, MFM 1672
MFMRMRDS, LTDMMR, MF 7325
MFMRMMRDRMM, MDMS 2833
MFMRSDRMFRMD, RMFS 7016
MFMRSDFMR, STLDF#S, S 4777
MFMRSRD, DRDTRMRD, M 5616
MFMRSRMRD, DDDTDRM, 5030
MFMRSRFFM, MMMMSLL 3877
MFMRSFMRD, MFMRSDT 6403
MFMRSSLD, DLDTLSS, L 10153
MFMRLDT, LSTMRS, SSD 5552
MFMRLDTLT, TDDRRM, M 1572

MFMRLR, DT LTD, MFMRL	10201a	MFFMDTLSLS, MRRMLS 9415

MFMRLR, DT LTD, MFMRL 10201a MFFMDTLSLS, MRRMLS 9415
MFMRLR, DTLTDS, MFMR 10201 MFFMRDDDFMR, TDRDS 11180
MFMRLRMRD, LTDFMMR 4417 MFFM, MRLTDR, SDRMFS, 765
MFMRLS, DDSMRDD, RML 4220 MFFMMMRRR, RMMRRRD 7837
MFMRLSFM, MSRMTDRT, 1887 MFFMMLS#LLS#, MFRTDD 8458
MFMRLLRMFFM, RSF#ML 3005 MFFMSD, TLDLLS, MFFF 1141
MFMRLLFM, MFMRSFMR 110 MFFFLDRMMMM, MFSMD 818
MFMRLTTD, MMMMFR, MF 1130 MFFSDDLS, DTLSF#S, MF 2962
MFMR#MD, RRDTD, MFMR#M MFFLFFM, RSSTLS, SLL 9305
11351 MFF#SDDTF, MMMMLLRR, 9450
MFMMRDDTD, MFSSFMM 4973 MFF#SDRMRD, STLFLSM, 6746
MFMMRD, DTLS, RRRMFS, 8735 MFF#SDLSFM, MLTDTLS 6745
MFMMRD, RDRR#M, MFMMR MFF#SMDDTT, TLLLSSS 12084
11247 MFF#SMRMFRDT, RMRSL 1722
MFMMRDRFM, SSDDTLS 7078 MFF#SMMRD, SMSTTRLL 10
MFMMRD, RSFM, MFMMRD, 3206 MFF#SMSDTLS, SRMFMR 3699
MFMMRD, SLMRDR, RMSSL 8744 MFF#SSSSLMSF, RMFLS 11493
MFMMRD, SLSSFM, RMFF 1159 MFF#SSL, LDLS, MFMMDT 7149
MFMMRDTD, RMTDRS, SL 11449 MFF#SLSMDDTLS, FSRT 6041
MFMMRRD, DRRFFM, MFM 7331 MFF#SLTDR, DTLSLSFM, 3365
MFMMRR, DRDT, LTLDRM, 3220 MFF#LSDTSF, RMFTLSR 8897
MFMMRR, RMFMRD, FRRD, 7521 MFSDDMRDLD, TLSMSDR, 6737
MFMMRRMM, SSSSSF#SS, 7277 MFSDDLSMDRM, MFSFM 9195
MFMMRFSFM, SLSSMMR 1860 MFSDDLSM, SLSMFSM, S 8471
MFMMRL, RMRRDSD, DDT 9918 MFSDDLSM, LLSLSSFM 2843
MFMMMMR, RDDTTL, LMM 1790 MFSDDTD, LTDSLRR, MF 7177
MFMMMSFF, MRDRFM, MM 8300 MFSDDTLSM, RLSDRMR 4229
MFMMFMRD, RMFRMDMR, 9274 MFSDDTLS, MSDRD, MFS 6090
MFMMFMRD, RMFMMR, MF 9273 MFSDDTLTDS, SMRMFM 7993
MFMMSLSS, DDRMDRDDD 12178 MFSDDTTL, SFMFSM, MM 2856
MFMMLLS#, S#LDTS#L, SSD 3654 MFSDRDDTTDRFMRRD 4014
MFMFFFMR#M, MSF#SDMRR, 3901 MFSDRM, DRMMMRMFS, S 3120
MFMSDRLR, RMRSSLSM 4801 MFSDRMRSFMRD, MRMF# 2916
MFMSDTLS, SDFMMRR, M 11263 MFSDRM, MFMRDMRD, SS 4320
MFMSRMFDRM, MRMRDT 6269 MFSDRM, FMRDRM, MMMM
MFMSMDLSM, MRMRLS, M 1612 11984
MFMSMRDDTD, RN RSFM 8247 MFSDRMF, MRSSFMRFM, 4372
MFMSMRMRFR, DDRRMS 10374 MFSDRMFMRLR, DTTLS 6597
MFMSFMRD, RMFSDTLS, 9452 MFSDRMFFM, SDSLMF#S 3681
MFMSFMRD, SLSRDTLS, 11999 MFSDRTD, DRMFFM, MRS 8404
MFM, SFFMRDRR, RFMR 10496 MFSDMDDT, RMFTRFFM, 6255
MFMSSRMRFF, DDRRMS 10209 MFSDMDLD, FLSDTLS, M 5937
MFMSSLSD, DTLSLFM, M 1263 MFSDMDTL, RDTRLTD, M 5198
MFMSTDRM, SLSFMR, RM 1784 MFSDMRDDL, DTLSDRM 1998
MFMLMMR, DTLSLS, MFM 12060 MFSDMRDS, LDSDTLS, T 2668
MFMLSDRM, MRSTLS, SL 6603 MFSDMRDLD, TLSMSDR, 6740
MFMLSMRMD, DTRRMFS, 4289 MFSDMRDLD, TLSLSMD 3796
MFMLSFFM, SLTDTLLS, 3343 MFSDMRDTD, SRMFMR, M 12459
MFMLS, SMTRD, LLLSDT 1985 MFSDMRD, TLSLSFFM, M 5343
MFFDRMD, MSMDRD, MR 258 MFSDMR, RMFSFM, MFSD 11326
MFFDFMR#M, RDDDRMR, S 3898 MFSDMSFMRD, MFRFS, M 4677
MFFMD, DRRM, MFFMD, RM 389 MFSDMSF#SLFMF, FMRT 6138
MFFMDFFFM, LTLSMMR 4822 MFSDFMMR, RMFRDTD, M 3121

1099

MFSDLDSM, DRMSFMR, M	9679	MFSMFS, DTLSLSFM, MF	3619
MFSDLSM, DTLTDT, DDD	12096	MFSMFSMDD, MFSSSSM,	1650
MFSDLS, MFSSDLS, MFS	11865	MFSMFS, SMDRMR, RMF	11291
MFSDLTDS, FSMDRRR, M	3170	MFSMFLSM, SFMRFM, MF	5152
MFSDTDRS, LTDFMRM, M	1143	MFSMSDDTT, RMFSLSS	6013
MFSDTDMR, SFFMRDTD	7090	MFSMSDM, RDLDDLS, MF	11616
MFSDTDLS, MFSDFMR, M	8916	MFSMSD, SSLLLSSMFS	7995
MFSDTLSDRM, MFSSSF	1771	MFSMSDT, DLSMMF#S, SM	12055
MFSDTLS, DRMSFMR, MF	5345	MFSMS, DTLFL, DLSMSD	6739
MFSDTLSM, DRMDRMRD,	11348	MFSMSSFR, FFMDMMR, S	2311
MFSDTLSM, MSMSMR, MF	1662	MFSMSLDLSM, DRMDRM	10794
MFSDTLSM, SLSRSLS, M	7453	MFSM, LSDMRR, DDTLSD	9824
MFSDTLSFMFS, LSMRM	279	MFSMLSMDMR, RMSMRF	10037
MFSDTLSLDRMR, TDRM	9792	MFSMLSM, SMRFMRM, MF	12469
MFSDTL#T, TLRFLSM, MF	1536	MFSM, LSFM, DTLSSF#S, R	472
MFSRMFLR, DTLSLFMM,	9530	MFSMLSFMRDRM, MFSM	4239
MFSRFM, RMDLT, TTDMR	1243	MFSMLSF#SM, DRMFMRM	8137
MFSMDDRMDL, SLTDFM	207	MFSMLSSMSFSMFR, MF	3115
MFSMDRMD, DTDFMMR, M	7722	MFSFMRDDRMR, RMFSF	2368
MFSMDRMD, DTTLLFMR,	3746	MFSFMR, DDRSM, LSFMS	5410
MFSMDRMD, RMF#SLT, DS	2393	MFSFMRDRMRM, FMRSF	4219
MFSMDRMD, LTDDRMFM,	7550	MFSFMRRD, MRMF#SSF#S,	5793
MFSMDRM, MFSMFMR, MF	10833	MFSFMRRR, RMFMRMMM,	3488
MFSMDRMFMR, MMFMRM	11571	MFSFMRM, DRMFMM,	6794
MFSMDRML, DRDMMF#MS,	7332	MFSFMRMMRDRFMRFM,	1694
MFSMDLSM, DRMSFMR, D	268	MFSFMRMFM, SMLSFMR,	8841
MFSMDLSM, RMFLSFM, S	7931	MFSFMFSM, MMFMRMFR,	11036
MFSMDLSM, MRMSFMR, M	2365	MFSFMFSM, SSLSFMR, S	5865
MFSMDLS, SLS, MFSMDL	6118	MFSFMFSLS, RM FMRMF	10727
MFSMDTLS, SRRMFSM, M	3137	MFSFMFLS, MFSDT, TRD	10746
MFSMDTLSSM, DRMFSS	5907	MFSF#SDMRDTDR, RMFT	10372
MFSMRD, RMRLR, MFSM	2197	MFSF#SDTLSLDRM, MFS	4668
MFSMRDRSLS, DRMMMF	5302	MFSF#SDTLS#L, TLSMSD	6738
MFSMRDMRDDLS, MFSS	10892	MFSF#SM, DRMR#MD, DRMR	
MFSMRDMLS, DRMSFMR	3886		2628
MFSMRDSLDLS, SDRMR	9037	MFSF#SMRD, MFSF#SSF#S,	929
MFSMRDLS, DRMDR, FSL	12058	MFSF#SMFSLS, MMFMRS	10356
MFSMRDLS, SSDSFMR, M	8623	MFSF#SLSDTLSF#LSM, M	12108
MFSMRDTDRM, MFSMRD	7024	MFSF#SLTRDS, DDDTDR	7493
MFSMRDTLS, DTLDMRD,	5024	MFSF#LSSSLS#TL, LSFM	8015
MFSMRR, FSLSS, LLLSF	10301	MFSSDRM, RDLDTDR, MF	7002
MFSMRMDS, MFSRDMFS	12148	MFSSDRMM, MRDRDLS, M	12264
MFSMRMRDS, MFSMDMR,	11159	MFSSDRM, SLTDTLLS, S	11439
MFSMRMM, MFSMRM, MF#S	2046	MFSSDRM, LTDMRD, RMFS	7290
MFSMRLSM, MFSMRLTS,	12351	MFSSDRM, LTDMSF#S, MF	7292
MFSMMRD, RMFLLSM, MF	5149	MFSSDMRDLD, LSSDMR,	6649
MFSMM, RDLDD, TLSDRM	2483	MFSSDMRDL, LSSDMR, M	6650
MFSMMRRDLDLDMFS, S#	6264	MFSSDS, MFSRM, DRMSD	11650
MFSMMSD, DRRRRMFM, D	1389	MFSSDLSMS, SLLRDTL	1769
MFSMMLTS#, TTTDTLSS	4094	MFSSDTLLS, MSDMRDT	5102
MFSMFRD, MFSMDLS, MF	555	MFSSDTTL, LDTLSFM, M	6800
MFSMFMR, MFSDMRD, D	3641	MFSSMDRR, FLSDMRD, M	2420
MFSMFMRM, FSLSMRDR,	6212	MFSSMDS, RMFFFFF, LT	8207

MFSSMRDDTLSRSFM, M	348
MFSSMRDTLSF, MLSSF	4400
MFSSMR, RMFFFFMRM, M	10569
MFSSMMFFMR, RMMFS[S]D	5840
MFSSFMRD, LTDDTLS, M	2725
MFSSFMRRM, MRSSLTL	10257
MFSSFMRR, MFSDRRD, M	5604
MFSSFMRR, MFSMRRD, M	5603
MFSSFMRR, MFSMRFMR	5601
MFSSFMR, MFSFMRD, MF	5602
MFSSF#SRMFFMF, DRMM	3293
MMFSSF#SLSD, TLSMSRM,	5197
MFSSF#SLSS, FMRMSFF	2127
MFSSF#LSDM, MRMFSSF	11297
MFSSSDDL, LLSLSFM, M	1976
MFSSSDDT, RMFFFLLS,	8856
MFSSSDDT, TDRRRFFM,	7752
MFSSSDRMFM, MRRMFL	3588
MFSSSDRMFM, MMRDTD	5449
MFSSSDMRD, SLDDLS, M	3826
MFSSSDMFSLS, DDTRL	9149
MFSSSDS, MRDTLS, MFS	5913
MFSSSDSSLLS, MSSFF	3
MFSSSDTLS, FMMMTLS	8495
MFSSSMRDDD, MRRSRM,	4964
MFSSSMFSSS, MMMMRM	2678
MFSSSMLLL, SMRDLSM	4544
MFSSSFMLLS, TDRRR	8997
MFSSSSDRMMMM, RMFF	11325
MFSSSSMDDDD, RRRDM	3718
MFSSSSSD, TLSSSSS, S	12142
MFSSSSSM, DDRMRRD, M	4672
MFSSSSS, SFMMMMM, RD	3071
MFSSSSLSDRMD, DTLL	10991
MFSSSSLS, MSDDDDRD,	4483
MFSSSSLLS, SMMMMFM	10620
MFSSSLDTLSM, RMFST	1685
MFSSSLSMF, RM FFFSF	10934
MFSSSLSFMRDRDLS, S	11023
MFSSSLSFM, FMRD, MFS	4252
MFSSSLSFM, FMMRD, MF	4250
MFSSSLSFFF, SMDSMM	1491
MFSSSLSF#SM, RMFFMF	3076
MFSSSLSLSF, FSLLLS	7917
MFSSSLTDDD, LRDTLS,	2486
MFSSSLTD, DRMFSLS	8987
MFSSSLTDS, MFSLSFM,	1682
MFSSLDLS, DTDRMR, RM	5036
MFSSLRDT, DSLLLSFF	8984
MFSSLMSS, DTLLDLS, L	5313
MFSSLSDRMRD, DLLLD	12549
MFSSLSDRMMFM, SDDM	6141
MFSSLSDS, SSSSLSS, M	5145
MFSSLSMD, DDDDTLS, M	10723
MFSSLSMD, SLLTDLS, M	10929
MFSSLSMRDDLS, MFSD	11028
MFSSLSM, RDRDLDS, MF	2000
MFSSLSMRDRMD, MSDD	11902
MFSSLSMSD, SLLLDLS, F	5276
MFSSLSMSDTLS, SDDD	4848
MFSSLSMS, LLSMMRDR,	5763
MFSSLSFMFMRM, MFSD	10840
MFSSLSF#SM, MRDRMFM,	3437
MFSSLSSD, DRMDRRD, M	12185
MFSSLSSD, DRMRDLS, M	8976
MFSSLSSM, DRDDLS, DR	9653
MFSSLSSM, MMSRD#RM, M	572
MFSSLSSF, MRSRMRR, S	1385
MFSSLSLTDS, TLSSFM	12145
MFSSLSLTDTL, SLTSL	5702
MFSSLLS, DTLS, MFSSL	8103
MFSSLLSM, MRDDRRM, M	1376
MFSSLLSM, SLLSF#S, DR	11786
MFSSLLLS, DRMMFFFM,	2838
MFSSLTDD, LSFLSFM, M	2890
MFSSLTDDTDRDLS, SS	12343
MFSSLTDSSSMDR, MFS	10412
MFSSLTDT, DRMRDLS, R	6704
MFSLDDTLS, SLMSSSL	7351
MFSLDR, SDSLSFS, DRS	11342
MFSLDTD, SMLLLRR, RM	7155
MFSLDTSL, SMRDSLRR,	2040
MFSLDTLDLLS, SLMSF	2067
MFSLDTL, SLTDMR, DTD	6006
MFSLRDM, SLTDLLS, MF	10216
MFSLRRM, SLTDLLS, MF	10215
MFSLRMF, FSLSMDR, MM	2549
MFSLRSSFMF, MRFMRD	8789
MFSLMLS, SDTLSFM, MF	7350
MFSLFRMFS, DRMFLTD	11269
MFSLFFMM, SRMDTDR, S	5630
MFSLFS, MRDTLT, TRMR	10371
MFSLSD, DDRRDRM, DMS	7073
MFSLSDDTD, DTLRDTT	11859
MFSLSDDT, TDRFLSM, M	7812
MFSLSDDT, TDRTLTD, D	2755
MFSLSDDTT, RMFSLTL	11362
MFSLSDRS, SFMFMSDL	92
MFSLSDRTD, DTLRDTL	420
MFSLSDM, MRDDTLLS, M	6948
MFSLSD, SDTLSS, MFSD	12117
MFSLSDLSFFM, MRSLS	4944
MFSLSDT, RMFSLTS, DR	5710
MFSLSM, DRDRM, SLSML	7736
MFSLSMD, RMFSFMR, MF	3872
MFSLSMDMRDL, LSDDD	4493

MFSLSMDFM, LTDRMFR,	7126
MFSLSMD, SSFMLLSMD	7089
MFSLSMDLS, DRMFMMR,	2191
MFSLSMRDRDLS, DRMR	11074
MFSLSMRD, MMFSMRM, M	8612
MFSLSMRMFSFR, MFSL	6389
MFSLSM, RMFSLTS, DT	10693
MFSLSMRFM, SMRDDDT	2110
MFSLSMMR, RMFLSFM, M	272
MFSLSM, MFSSSMR, MFS	6046
MFSLS, MFSDTLS, SLSL	8847
MFSLS, MSDRD, DTTLLL	11903
MFSLSFMR, DRFM, MF#SL	3446
MFSLSFMR, MFSLDTLS,	954
MFSLSFMR, MFSLSD, MF	58
MFSLSFMR, SMFSLSD, M	57
MFSLSFMR, SMFSLTD, M	57a
MFSLSFMMRDRD, DDTT	5317
MFSLSFMMR, DRMSSLS	400
MFSLSFMMM, FMRFMRM,	6594
MFSLSFMFSLTDFMRD,	2462
MFSLSSDRMRD, MFSLS	11064
MFSLSSMDFMMR, MFSL	6581
MFSLSSMRMFM, MFSLS	8174
MFSLSSFMRS, SF#SFFF	7593
MFSLS, SLTDMR, DDTLL	2294
MFSLLRDTDS, SLSFSF	6135
MFSLLRMFSS, DRMSMR	6615
MFSLLRSFM, DTLSFMR,	4766
MFSLLLLSM, MFRSSM, MF	5590
MFSLLTDRTS, LDLSMR	1237
MFSLL#LSFM, RSFMRD, M	51
MFSLTDDRMMFM, RDDL	6601
MFSLTDRDMD, DDTDRD	4463
MFSLTDMLSM, DTDFMR,	11567
MFSLTDSF, MRDRMFR, M	11631
MFSLTDS, LLSMRMFFM,	4832
MFSLTLSFMFSFF, MFS	340
MFSTDD, LSFMR, MFSTD	5836
MFSTDRM, MTDFMR, MF#S	3182
MFS#S#S#LTT, DTLS#TS#, TT	
	3996
MFLDTL, RDTDLS, SLMF	10125
MFLSDDDFMMR, MF#RST	2286
MFLSDRFM, MTDFMR, MF	1410
MFLSDMRD, FFMLLSDT	2738
MFLSDTRS, LSMDDSFM	1344
MFLSMDRMD, MMSFMDR,	4199
MFLSFM, MRDDTD, SLF#S	9401
MFLSFM, SDMRLTS, SDR	6580
MFLSFM, LTLTDDT, LSF	11098
MFLSSDMMR, RMFLSFS	1034
MFLS, SDTTLL, SMFMRD	1974

MFTR, DDTLSF#SLSSM, S	9736
MF#SF#MRDFMR, DTLMML,	
	1777
MF#SSLSMR, RLSMSF#M, L	56

MSD

MSDDDDTLSM, SLLLDT	10805
MSDDDSMSDDD, DRMMM	11860
MSDDRRFMRR, DTLSLS	1604
MSDDRM, DTLSFM, MMLL	11818
MSDDRMFM, FSLDFMR, S	8473
MSDDRFM, RSMDTLS, DD	4169
MSDDRFM, MSDRD, MSDDR	612
MSDDRSFMRD, SMLDRM	7330
MSDDMDMRDLS, DSDDM	12171
MSDRDMFMRRD, FFMSF	1953
MSDRDTD, LSTDFMR, MS	10703
MSDRRRDRM, MSDRRRM	252
MSDRMRD, RFMLSF#S, RD	951
MSDRMRDTL, LTDTLDR	9888
MSDRMFMR, MFRD, MSDR	4218
MSDRMFS, LSFMRLS, SS	9207
MSDRSLTDRM, DFMRSM	6288
MSDMRD, DMLDTL, MRRS	997
MSDMRMRDL, TDTLSFM	6598
MSDMRMRDTLSD, MSDM	5733
MSDMRMFM, FLSMRDTD	11340
MSDMRMFFM, RDDTLST	1972
MSDMRMF, LSMDRM, MSD	2624
MSDMFMRRMDS, LLTDF	3689
MSDMFSLR, FMRLDRT, S	1116
MSDMLSDMRD, TDRMFS	6076
MSDFRDTD, SDTLRSFM	1885
MSDFMRD, MFSLLR, SDM	4679
MSDFMR, RMLRDT, TDDR	11289
MSDFMRM, MLRFMRM, MS	8663
MSDFMR, MSSF#SS, LLSD	3879
MSDFMMRLS, SDTLMF#S	6273
MSDFFMD, LSDMRD, MSD	9135
MSDFSM, DRMFLR, DDTD,	3332
MSDFLD, SLSMRRRF, MS	11469
MSDSDRM, DRMFMRDMR	896
MSDSMDMR, DDLSSFMR,	2377
MSDSLDS, MRDTDMR, MS	2234
MSDSLS, MRDFFMLSFM	2382
MSDSTLSF, MFSRMFMR	5715
MSDLDDDDDDLS, DDDD	10571
MSDLSFM, RSSSLTLS, S	8692
MSDLSFM, RSSLTLS, SL	8691
MSDLSFFM, LLSLSFMR	10665
MSDTDDRMDFRR, SF#MR	4146
MSDTDF, MRLSFM, MRTT	8960

MSDTDLRSM, MMMMRDT	2375	MSMRRSMR, DMDT L, FLF	4497
MSDTRDT, STRD#MRD, DD	6801	MSMRMDT LSSTDMMR, S	5042
MSDT L, DFMR, TMRDMSF	9914	MSMRMFM, FSMLFR, SSF	5918
MSDT LSMDRRM, FFMLS	2546	MSMRMFSM, MLSFLDDR	2923
MSDT LS, MRMFSM, SDT L	9817	MSMRFMDR, DTRDLS, DL	10333
MSDT LSM, SSDDDDDTD	4520	MSMRLR, MMMRDMRRR, M	1324
MSDT LSFM, RDMLSFMR	771	MSMRLTD, RMSLLR, RMF#	6415
MSDT LSSFM, RDFMRF#S	6146	MSFMMFMR, MFMRDT LS,	7845
MSDT LSSF, MSDMRDR, R	8253	MSMMDRR, RMRDDT L.	3946
MSDT LSLFS, MSDRMFM	4813	MSMMDRRRFFM, MSMM, D	
MSDTT LS, DDT LSMM	8948		12029
MSDTT LS, MSDDT LS, TD	8578	MSMMRDRM, DLSMDRMR,	9319
MSDTT LLS, DRMFSMRR	11488	MSMMRDRM, SDT LSSLS,	2967
MSRD, DMT L, LLTDSDD, R	6438	MSMMRDFMR, RMF#SLT L	4009
MSRDDT, FTMRDS, SMRD	6587	MSMMMD, MRDSFMRS, FM	1991
MSRDFFM, SDFMRRR, MS	4313	MSMMMSRR, TDDMMS, SS	23
MSRRRSDD, DDDLDRM,	3568	MSMMFSLRR, RFMRMFS	11196
MSRMDRT, TDFMRRM, S#S#	3168	MSMFRMDRM, FSMLSMF#	11942
MSRMD, MRMSLSMS, TT L	1127	MSMFMRDRM, FSMLSMD	5285
MSRMDLSD, DDRMMRF#S,	3280	MSMFMRD, RMSLLS, SDS	12451
MSRMDLS, LDRMRRR, MS	9370	MSMFMF, RRRDTM, MRDT	6364
MSRMFRM, MSRMFRD, R	8518	MSMFSLRD, RSMFRM, SM	9299
MSRMFSLSFMRD, SFMR	7077	MSMFL, TMRDS, LDLSMM	9802
MSRMFLTDMLS, SSRSL	5437	MSMS, DMDM, LLLSMDDT	3692
MSRMSFMRD, MLSMFR, M	2114	MSMSMSDDT LLS, RMFR	6491
MSRFMRDT, FMLSDT LS	12488	MSMSLMRD, DT LSMMR, R	7146
MSRSFFM, MMTMRD, DLL	7499	MSMSLSMR, MSMLSMR, S	9981
MSMDDRDRMD, MSMDDR	10232	MSFRDM, SLSMFR, DDSF	5905
MSMDDRDRM, MSMDDRM	10231	MSFRRMSFMF, FFMR	11607
MSMDDRMFM, FSDLTDT,	10322	MSFRMDRR, SSDT LLS, S	487
MSMDRMDL, DSDRMR, MS	8652	MSFRMD, MLTDRMR, MSF	10591
MSMDRMM, TDRMLM, MSM	4862	MSFRT, DMMRDT, MDRML	722
MSMDRMFMLSLS, SDT L	968	MSFMDRMD, RMFLSDMR,	853
MSMDRMFS, SLDDTD, SL	12086	MSFMDMRD, SF#MTSF#RM,	
MSMDRMSDT LS, SMRDD	6018		12181
MSMDRS, SDRMFR, RMRM	2816	MSFMDMRD, SLDDRT, RS	9619
MSMDFRTS, DRMRDT LS,	12051	MSFMDMRD, ST LSMSFM	11590
MSMDSS, SDT LS, SSMSL	3420	MSFMDLS, SFFMSDMR, M	6975
MSMDTDRMRD, RMFSSL	9516	MSFMRDD, DT LFLS, MSF	2568
MSMDTDRM, FMRST LS, M	2454	MSFMRD, DRMFLR, MFML	9283
MSMDT L, LFMRDT, RMMS	2813	MSFMRDDRFM, MSSFMR	9391
MSMRD, DRDLLS, TTTDD	3404	MSFMRD, DFLLSS, SLF#S,	5689
MSMRDDRMSMR, SLRT L,	10743	MSFMRD, DLFR, DTDFML,	2976
MSMRDDMDLS, SSFMLD	3602	MSFMRD, DLLSFM, RMMF#	9088
MSMRDDT LS, MRDFMLS	2157	MSFMRDDT, DDRMMF#S, D	9476
MSMRDDTT, DRMFSM, SL	8304	MSFMRDDTDMR, MMMLT	4325
MSMRDRTD, SDT LSLF#S,	10361	MSFMRDDT LS, FMFMSL	6159
MSMRDMRD, FMLSFMR, R	544	MSFMRDRM, DLTDRMRR,	12317
MSMRDMSLDT LDMRT L	11545	MSFMRDRMR, SFFMRMR	6608
MSMRDL, DTDMS, SS#L	9243	MSFMRDRM, MRRSSF#LS,	5680
MSMRDLMDT L, RDLFFM,	4298	MSFMRDRMFMR, SDT L	8476
MSMRDLSFM, SDSLSSF	8923	MSFMRD, RMSFMR, MMFS	1812
MSMRDT LLS, SLTDRR, S	10006	MSFMRDRS, SLLSFMR, M	5067

MSFMRDRTD, SLSFMSF 6772
MSFMRDRT, TDDRRM, M 236
MSFMRDRT, TDRMFRD, M 10169
MSFMRDT, DRMSFM, MSF 8416
MSFMRDTD, SDTLSFMF 704
MSFMRRD, DTDFMR, RMM 6716
MSFMRRMF#S, RMRDRDT 11313
MSFMRMDR, MFSS#LTT, D 4952
MSFMRMRD, RMLSF#TLS, 9094
MSFMRMFS, MFSLFSSF, 6183
MSFMRMFLMM, SDTDRD 12529
MSFMRMF#SS, RMRDRT, M 7690
MSFMRMSF, FLSFMSFM 3974
MSFMRFMRDD, TDRMSF 52
MSFMRFFM, MMRTLSMR, 6666
MSFMMRDRMFMR, RSDT 8478
MSFMMRD, RMFMRLS, MS 6795
MSFMMRD, FMLSRRR, MM 4884
MSFMMRD, FMLSSF#S, D 213
MSFMMRDF, FLSFFMRS, 4173
MSFMMRDT, RDTLDTTT, 7708
MSFMMRRD, DTLSMLRR, 4747
MSFMMRRD, SSLTDMR, 2644
MSFMMRMFMRM, MMDTT 7924
MSFMMMRD, DDRMFSLF 2033
MSFMMMRD, SLTDRMRR, 5493
MSFMMMRMFDT, RDTDM 2103
MSFMFMRD, DLSFSMF#S, 9397
MSFMSDL, LRSFRRM, MM 8977
MSFMSDL#L, RSMDFMMR, 4253
MSFMSDTLS, SSDFMMRR, 11262
MSFMSMRD, RMSDLSFM, 1126
MSFMSFFM, MFSLFMR, R 2211
MSFMLR, RFMRS, DDRMM 998
MSFFMRRMF#F#LS, SDMM 2586
MSFFMMR, DTLSSS, SLT 4740
MSFSMSRS, MSFRDTD 11632
MSF#SMDDTDS, SSDMSM 11009
MSF#SMMMR#MD, DRRRRM
10829
MSF#SM, SLDTLLS, SF#SD, 10567
MSF#SMLSF#M, MDTLRLT 1925
MSF#LSSDTTL, LRMSFF 5296

MSS

MSSDDTLS, SMTDRS, ST 12050
MSSDRM, MRMFFM, MMSS 1563
MSSDRMRD, RMLSSLD 9816
MSSDRMFSLR, MF#F#SLT 7610
MSSDMSSD, SDTLSSF#S 7980
MSSDFFMRS, DTLSLS 8127
MSSMDRMFMRD, DRRDS 8695

MSSMDMMR, RMFRSFM, M 1133
MSSMRDRMMM, MSSMRD 5332
MSSMRD, RMSMR, MSSMR 3880
MSSMRDMR, MSSMRDR, M 11423
MSSMSS, LTDTLLS, SDD 133
MSSFRLLS, SDDTTLS 1533
MSSFMRDSLMSFM, SLT 692
MSSFFMSDTLLS, MSSF 11720
MSSFLL, SLSMMR, MFMR 7318
MSSSDS, SLSFM, MSSSL 6263
MSSSMDR, RRMSMDR, RR 8720
MSSSMRD, MMMLSMR, MS 5678
MSSSMMMMMD, DRRRRM 10827
MSSSMFSLSM, SLLDTL 5207
MSSSMS, DMMMRM, SDDD 10884
MSSSMS, DMMFMR, MFFF 7831
MSSSMSSM, SMR, MSSSM 7437
MSSSFMMR, FLRMMR, SF 8822
MSSSFFFM, MMMMRR, RF 9499
MSSSSDM, MRRFFM, RMSS 4044
MSSSSDTL, LSFMSRRD, 9631
MSSSSMSDTLS, SSLDL 2623
MSSSSSSDL, LSFMSFM 7414
MSSSSSSLSMR, MFFFF 4749
MSSSSLLT, TTTTDT, MT 11192
MSSSSLL#LFSLSSSSS 11752
MSSSLMRD, RMRMF#SDT 6838
MSSS, LSMFFM, MMMF, F#D
8353
MSSSLSFM, MFMRDR, RR 10394
MSSSLTDR, MSSSLTLS, 3893
MSSSLTDSS, MSFMRM, M 1852
MSSLDR, MRDLSMS, RRM 11400
MSSLMS, SMDTDR, MFFM 8193
MSSLSMDLS, SLTDMRL 6648
MSSLSM, RDRMF#S, SDTL 4486
MSSLSMMRD, MSSLSMM 7431
MSSLSM, MMMFMR, DDTL 5018
MSSLSMF, RFFSFMRDR 4335
MSSLSMSFMR, SLTRDL 4572
MSSLSMSLTDDT, FLLT 5244
MSSLS, LDDLS, SSDRMD 1327
MSSLLD, DMRD, DTLSF#S, 10539
MSSLLS, DMMFMR, MSSL 5134
MSSLLS, MDDFFM, MRMF 5706
MSSLLSFM, FSSLDS, FM 5336
MSSLLSFSSL, SMFSFM 3181
MSSLTDS, DDLDRM, SRD# 9662
MSSLTDTL, SDRMRDRT 8095
MSSLTDTL, TDSLMSFM, 6891
MSLDRDLDT, SFFMRDT 8208
MSLDRMMMM, SSLDDLS, 7436
MSLDSMMR, DRMLSMR, M 9468

1104

MSLDTSDRDTLTLSM,M	10783
MSLDTSLS,LTDSFMMR,	10675
MSLDTL,SMRF,LRDTLD,	2214
MSLDTLLS,MRDDLLS,M	1792
MSLRRM,SDTLLS,SMLL	12367
MSLR,LTRDL,LTRDL,RL	7858
MSLMRDD,MSLMRDR,MS	6470
MSLMRD,RMFSML,LTLS	6445
MSLMR,RFSL#L,TSF#TTD#	3489
MSLMSMDRM,MLDTRDL	10557
MSLSDD,RRMFMM,SSSS	7068
MSLSDDTD,DTLRTLS#L	11858
MSLSDFMR,STRFLSRR#	7249
MSLSDSFMRDD,DMF	3118
MSLSDLS,DMMFFM,MSL	12299
MSLSDLSM,DRMFR,MS	464
MSLSDTLS,LTSMFMR	5996
MSLSMDRM,MRSSF#S,SD	10467
MSLSMDFL,SSLSMDR,M	4328
MSLSMRDRM,SMF#SLT	5711
MSLSMRDMMFM,MSMDT	5065
MSLSMRDMM,SMSLSDM	2174
MSLSMMRD,DRMFRMFS,	10186
MSLSMMFM,MSLSMR,MS	977
MSLSMFMR,MFSFRM,SD	317
MSLSMFMMR,RSLSDTD	4401
MSLSMSFMMRD,DFDRM	9856
MSLSFMRDD,MF#SSLTD	8797
MSLSFM,MRDTD,RMF#SL	7339
MSLSFMFRD,RMF#SDTL	9497
MSLSSDFM,MRFMMRR,M	10289
MSLSSFM,DTLSMDR,MS	4760
MSLSSFM,MMRSSF#S,MS	4761
MSLSSFMFM,SDL#LSFM	12147
MSLLFFSS,MDTLSLFM	9012
MSLLSFMM,MMRFMRM,	2757
MSLLSF#SLM,DMSMRDR	9946
MSLLSSFM,DRFMRFRM	8168
MSLLSLDR,SF#MDTTLS,	9551
MSLLLSSSM,STDDDTT	12457
MSLLTDMSSM,MLLTDR	10821
MSLTDDMMRM,SLTDMR	10735
MSLTDD,TLSFM,MMFMM	1906
MSLTDRDM,SRRRRMFM,	4462
MSLTDRDL,SDMMRDR,M	11791
MSLTDRMR,FLTDRS,MM	1055
MSLTDRM,FLRDTDR,SF	9422
MSLTDTL,RDLSLFM,SS	139
MSLTDTLRDT,MRDTLS	6461
MSLTDTLM,LSDFMRM,S	2230
MSTDDLFMRD,RMMF#F#S	4098
MSTDMSLDTRD,MRFMR	6275
MSTDLSFMRM,SDMFSL	1570

MS#FMFS#,S#LTLS#LFS#M,M	6824
MS#LTDTLS#LT,LTDRM	2194
MS#LTRDLLSM,MRTDDD	12525
MS#LTRDTL,LDDRRM,MS	8718
MLDDTL,FFFF,MLDDTL,	11693
MLDMLLS#L,DTRDMFRT	4152
MLDLSMFS,LSFMRDT,L	11025
MLDTRDL,DTLS#TL,MLD	10129
MLDTSLLSM,MLDTSL,M	9967
MLDTS#LDM,DLDTS#M,ML	11046
MLDTS#LM,FMRDRM,MSR	8011
MLDTS#L,TDLDMRM,MF#S	10525
MLDTLSFMFS,DRMFSL	2730
MLDTLSLT,MLSLTD,LD	2287
MLDTLS#LTM,MDDRDRM	8229
MLDTLS#LT,MLS#LTD,SD	2288
MLDTLLSFFM,DMLSFM	6558
MLDTLTLSL,LDRMDRR	678
MLMRF#MRDLTL,DRMRS	10927
MLMFRDTL,TDRMLSF#	5417
MLMFMDRM,MFSFRDTL,	2404
MLMFLSFM,MRDFFF,RM	7815
MLMSDRM,FSMRDTLL,T	4647
MLSDDRFM,MFRSDRLT,	1499
MLSDRRM,FMRMDTLS,R	3839
MLSDTDRRM,SLTDTLS	10904
MLSRMFM,SDTF#SLS,SL#	3440
MLSMDRDT,LSDMSFMR,	1051
MLSMDRMFMRM,MDTLS	9454
MLSMRDRM,RDRDLDRD,	7233
MLSMRDRM,SDT,DLS,MM	101
MLSMRDRM,LDTL,MLSM	3518
MLSMRDRTL,RMLRRMF,	9761
MLSMRMF,MMMRDTD,RS	3113
MLSMMRD,LTDSLTS,ML	3313
MLSM,MRM,MTLT,TSM.	2455
MLSM,MRM,MTLT,TSMF#M.	5107
MLSMM,MLSMM,MLLSFM	4040
MLSMFMRDRD,MSF#SLS	7754
MLSMSFM,SMLSF#F#M,SR	10224
MLSFMRRM,TDDTLTL,M	8340
MLSFMRRM,TDDTTL,ML	8340a
MLSFMRM,TDDTLTL,ML	8337
MLSFMRM,TDDTTL,MLS	8338
MLSFMRM,TDTLS#L,MLS	8339
MLSFMLRDTD,DSFMRM	10016

MLSFSM, SDT LLS, SLTD	4501	MLLLLLSDT L, LMRDDT	11086
MLSSDTTT LS#S#, LTDLT	10473	MLLLLTDDT LT, RMFMR	2321
MLSSRRSFFM, DT LSF#S	11512	MLLLLTDLL, SFMMMMM	2844
MLSLSMDR, MLSMRDT L,	6289	MLLLTDDDT LLSM, MSL	7462
MLSLTDRMST LLSL, MS	878	MLLLTDRMM, RDT LT L	4276
MLSLTD, RMTDLSM, MLS	116	MLLLTTDRTDRMFLS#L,	9462
MLSLTDLT, TDRMDDTD,	4649	MLLTDDTS#L, TMMRDDT	8199
MLS#MMS#LDLM, LS#LTDT		MLLTDDT LDTLLS#, TDD	6665
	5886	MLLTDDT LTS#L, TDDRT	6664
MLS#LDTLS#, LSFMLLS#L,		MLLTDRMFM, TDDDRMF	11726
	9498	MLLTDL, TTLSL, MMMDR	2740
MLS#LRDT, DLRDTT L, ML	4056	MLLTD, TRRRR, DT LFM, R	9962
MLS#LMSRM, LTDTMSF#M,	6915	MLLTDT LTM, MMRRDDL	7962
MLS#LSMDT L, DMRDTLT	8913	MLLTTDT L, LRRDDT, ML	6280
MLS#LTD, DRDT LSFM, ML		MLLTTTD, MLLTTTD, LL	6182
	10381	MLTDDRRM, MRMDDT, MD	7578
MLS#LTD, DRDT LS#F#M, M		MLTDDRRM, MLDTLS#, TD	7579
	10380	MLTDDTTS, LFMRMSLT	5112
MLS#LTDRDT L, DMDTLT	6153	MLTDRDL, MMRDT L, MLT	1551
MLS#LTDMMDL, MLS#LTD	2435	MLTDRDT LSM, MLTDRM,	7113
MLS#LTDMMDT, DLS#LTD	2434	MLTDRDT L, SLLTSL, ML	6113
MLS#LTDSLFM, MSF#MRD		MLTDRM, DRMFRM, TDDD	6104
	10213	MLTDRM, DRMFSM, DDDD	6105
MLS#LTDLT, TDRMDDTD,	4650	MLTDRM, DRMFSM, TDR	6103
MLS#LTDTT LLMM, MDSD	8241	MLTDRMRD, LTDT, MLTD	989
MLS#LTDTT LLMM, SDSD	8240	MLTDRMRDT, TDTLTDR	1780
MLS#LTRDT, TDRMDRTD,	4648	MLTDRMRFM, MRMDTDL	11231
MLS#LTS#F#M, MDTDRTLS#		MLTDRMMR, LDDTLSL, M	2595
	7232	MLTDRMMSFM, RDLT, TD	9503
MLLDRDLS, MLLDRD, DR	5826	MLTDRMFM, LSMDRM, MS	4594
MLLDRDLSL, LLLDLDRM,	1239	MLTDRMLSFM, MDTLSF#	8457
MLLDRMRDT L, SSMRMS	2742	MLTDRMLS#, SDRMFSDT,	4227
MLLDMRDT L, LRMFLSL	9192	MLTDRTLTLSM, MMRTL	2188
MLLDTLMD, LLLDTLS#L,	9089	MLTDMDTLT, DDRM, DRM	8394
MLLDTLLDDMRD, MFMR	7616	MLTDMRDL#, LDTLTM, ML	
MLLDTLLS#, LSSMRRD, M	10756		2215
MLLMRDML, TDMLLT, MD	11656	MLTDMRDT, RRRMRDTL,	7940
MLLMRDT L, MLLMDRML,	9387	MLTDMRDT L, S#LDRRM, M	8078
MLLMRMML, TDRMLDTM,	8836	MLTDMMR#M, MRDTDTL, M	
MLLMMFD, DRMFRM, MLL	11236		5460
MLLMMSLSFM, MSSLTD	5784	MLTDMSMRMSL, LTDDT	5716
MLLSDFFM, DDRR, MLLS	5767	MLTDMLLLS, MDRRMF#S	5703
MLLSMFM, MRMDDT, MLL	6253	MLTDML, TDTLTSM, MFS	12214
MLLSMSDMRDDT, TRTS	9549	MLTDS#LLM, FMRDTLL, M	10988
MLLSSFMRDRM, MF#S#LT	98	MLTDLSFM, SLDRRD, ML	7261
MLLSLSFM, MLSLSFM, S	1548	MLTDLSFM, SLTDFMRD,	7267
MLLSLSFM, SFMRDT L,	496	MLTDLSLFMM, MRDTSR	2978
MLLS#MDDT, T LLS#MDLT,	29	MLTDLS#TDR, R#MTRDTL	4570
MLLS#MMDDT L, TDLTS#M	8658	MLTDLLFM, DFMRDRT L,	3396
MLLS#F#MLTD, RDT LDT L	542	MLTDLTS#L, MLTDMRDT	147
MLLS#LTDL, TLSF#M, LTD	3542	MLTDLTT, TLTDDT, MRR	7847
MLLLLSMSDMRDDT, TDR	9552	MLTDTDRMM, SSFMSFM	4127
MLLLS#LTDDDTR, TDLL	12001	MLTDTRLS#T, MMMMRDT	2961

MLTDTMRDD, TMFFMMR 4931
MLTDTLDTLS#, TDTDRM, 4615
MLTDTLFM, SSFMLLS#L, 2134
MLTDTLS, DLTDRM, MRM 672
MLTDTLS, DTLDRM, RMF# 2703
MLTDTLSM, RTLTDRM, M 2749
MLTDTLSMM, MLTDTL 7046
MLTDTLSM, MLTDRM, ML 7785
MLTDTLSM, LMRDTL, M 11996
MLTDTLSLM, MRDTMLT 10546
MLTDTLSLM, MLLSFM, M 965
MLTDTLSLM, TDDTLSL 11089
MLTDTLSTL, TDRMRDL, 3013
MLTDTLLM, MDDRMRM, D 3267
MLTDTLLSLTL, SLSM, M 10919
MLTDTLTM, MDRMFMR, D 9260
MLTDTLTSM, SSSFMLT 7349
MLTDTLTS#M, SSFMLLS# 7346
MLTDTLTS#M, SSF#MLLS# 7345
MLTDTLTLS, DTMF#SF#M, 6769
MLTDTLTLS#M, SSFMLL 7348
MLTDTLTLS#, SSFMLLS# 7347
MLTDTLTLS#, TDTDRM, M 4614
MLTDTLTTLSMRMM, ML 3248
MLTRDFMM, RSLSFMDR 10014
MLT, MLT, DTLTDRDT, ML 603
MLTS#S#F#S#, LTDT, TLSS 251
MLTS#S#S#, LTDRMMM, SDR 3211a
MLTS#S#, LTDRMM, SDDRM 3211
MTDRMRFRMM, MMMLSF 5561
MTDMFS, LMFSLT, DLSR 8529
MTDFMRRR, MFLMSRDR, 1904
MTDFMRLTDT, DRMLSF 5809
MTDFMRTDMR, STD#RMR 9041
MTDSLTDMMR, DLSDDT 8368
MTDS#LFMR, LDTLTLS, D 5034
MTDLLDTLTLS, LTDTM 475
MTDLLFMD, MTDLTSL, M 518
MTRDFDMR, DTSSS, SS#L 3626
MTRDLSLSFM, MTRDLS# 7171
MTRDTLSLLSFM, DDTR 746

FDD

FDDDFFM, LMMMLLT, LL 11522
FDRDLLLLTDL, MRDTR 11402
FDFSLSLS, FDFSLLS, 3264
FDLDRDRFD, LDSF. 4926
FRMMMMMSLLSLL#LSS 7855
FRMFSLSF, SLSFMRM, M 2875
FRTSDMSM, FFFMMMRD 1101
FRTSMRDS, DDDTDRM, M 11876

FMRDDTLS, LFSMSFMR, 483
FMRDRFSF, LDL#SLSFL 741
FMRD, FMRD, DTLS, DT 11699
FMRRRLR, MFSLSLFMR 8489
FMRRMRDD, LSFRMFM, F 7700
FMMMMFSLS, MRRRRMF 4469
FMFRMDRR, FFSFMRDM 2579
FMFSLSFRFMFMM, SLT 5661
FMFSLSFRFMFSFM, SL 5662
FMSDLTDRTLS, DRMFS 12540
FMSLSFSLSFMM, RRLL 2526
FMSLSFSLSFMM, RLLL 2526a
FFDRMM, RRDRM, MMRDS 11344
FFMMRRRSD, FFMMMRM 5235
FFMFSDTD, MFSLSFRR, 3188
FFM, SMR, MRDDRMFMRD.10183
FFFR, MMMD, DDDDTDRM
10715
FFFMRMSLFM, SLSLDD 699
FFFMMRRM, MRDLDRR 9328
FFFFDRMM, SSSMRDR, M 11441
FFFFMMMM, LLLSFMRF# 1980
FFFFMSDDDT, TTTTDL 10597
FFFFFMMM, MMMSMR, M 5694
FFFFSLLS, FSLSFRFS 5282
FFFSFFFFFMSL, LLSS 5283
FFFLSSMS, MRDSMMR, M 7326
FFSFFMRDRMMM, SSLL 3199
FFSLFSFM, SFFMRFSF, 7583
FFSLSSFM, SMFRDFFF, 5237
FFSLLSFMMR, LLTDDT 10222
FFSLL#LSL, LSDDSLL# 10309
FFLD, DDRD, DLTL, LSLF. 4925
FFLD, DDRD, DLTL, LSLF, RFSF,
FL#S 1965
FSRDLS, FFMTRRDTLM, 3781
FSMSLFRM, SLDLSLSF 9664
FSFMSSLLSFRM, FRFM 8950
FSFSLL#LSL#LSF, FDDR 8890
FSLLRDDL#LLS, LL#LLS 9108
FSLLLSTDLSLSF, FSL 10677
FSLL#LSLL, SDDSLL#LS 10311
FLDDDRD, L#LSFF, FLDD 168
FLDMSD, RRRRDT, SMMM 10983
FLLSLTD, RRTDLLS, TT 12506

SDD

SDDDDDDD, MRDMRD, SF 1949
SDDDDDD, SSDDDDTDR, 5814
SDDDDDRDLS, SSRMFT 4705
SDDDDD, RMDLLL, SLTD 9300
SDDDDDRMRDTD, DMMM 4238

SDDDDDRMRDTD, DMMM	4238	SDDDRMMRDR, SRRRMF	5129
SDDDDDRMMMM, DMSSS	11928	SDDDRM, MRDFMR, RMRM	10448
SDDDDD, RMMMMM, SDDD	5932	SDDDRMMRR, SRRRMFF	11254
SDDDDDMRDT, SDRMFR	10952	SDDDRMMM, RMFSSFMR,	8791
SDDDDDS, SLLTRD, MRR	4214	SDDDRMMM, MRMFTRD, S	3167
SDDDDDTDRM, DFMRDT,	10489	SDDDRMMM, FMDTRD, SD	5040
SDDDDDTDF, MMRDTLS#	1225	SDDDRMMM, FSSSMFMR,	172
SDDDDRDDT, DRRRRMR	7742	SDDDRMMM, FSSSLS, SL	10505
SDDDDRRR, RSF#FFMRR,	3333	SDDDRMMM, SSMDMR, MF	4963
SDDDDRRM, DFFMMRRD,	10652	SDDDRMFMD, DDDDLLL	12044
SDDDDRRMFM, DFFMMR	10653	SDDDRMFMRMS, SFRRR	3778
SDDDDR, MSFMRD, SDDD	9035	SDDDRMFMR, TDRMFSL	9924
SDDDDRMSLS, DRRRRM	4383	SDDDRMFM, SFMRDT, TT	4967
SDDDDRML, LRRRRDLS,	10781	SDDDRMFSM, DSMFMRD,	10428
SDDDDRTD, DMRDDT, SS	10876	SDDDRMFS, MMMMMFMR,	44
SDDDDRTD, RMMMDTLS,	1408	SDDDRMFSSSFM, SFFF	12135
SDDDDMDMS, LSSSSMD	393	SDDDRMFS, SLLLSFFS,	7698
SDDDDMRD, DRRDTD, DM	2949	SDDDRMFS, LMFMRDRM	3119
SDDDDMRDRRRRFMRD	5456	SDDDRMLTD, LSLSLTD,	11120
SDDDDMRD, SRRFMR, SM	2971	SDDDRTDTRL, SDDDRM,	7366
SDDDDMRD, TDRRRRFM	4850	SDDDMDRD, MSSSMDMR,	4907
SDDDDM, MRRRFMRM, SL	10888	SDDDMDSM, SMDMRRTD,	2980
SDDDDMSSSS, MFRSMD	1681	SDDDMDLS, SDDDMR, SD	6655
SDDDDSDMMMMD, MSSS	557	SDDDMRDRRRRFMRDDD	5455
SDDDDSMRDS, SRRRRD	634	SDDDMRDR, MDDMSL, LS	695
SDDDDTDRDTD, DMDDD	5182	SDDDMRDS, FMRDRRM, S	11257
SDDDDTDRDTD, DMRDD	11079	SDDDMRD, SLTDFMR, SM	9618
SDDDDTDRRRR, SMMDR	6475	SDDDMRDLS, DRRRDRM	11053
SDDDDTDRSSS, MMFMR	4692	SDDDMRRR, RMFSLSFM	10968
SDDDDTMRD, DRMFMDR,	11260	SDDDMRRR, MFSFMRDR	6452
SDDDDTLS, DMMDRMR, S	6358	SDDDMRSS, SSMFRM, SL	12561
SDDDDTLS, MRMFFMRM,	10972	SDDDMMR, RMFRDTD, SD	9673
SDDDDTLSM, SDDDSMR,	10581	SDDDMMRR, FMFRDTD, S	9674
SDDDDTLS, SDLSF#S, SS#	1426	SDDD, MMMMDS, SLLTDR,	12293
SDDDDTLSLSM, RMFMF	5586	SDDDMFS, DTDRTD, SDD	6066
SDDDDTLSLSFMMR, RL	3459	SDDDMFSSS, SDRMMRM,	6988
SDDDDTTLL, SDDRDR	4999	SDDDMFSLS, MFSDRM,	3993
SDDDDTT, TLTLLSS, SD	10766	SDDDMFSL, LLLLLTTD,	6667
SDDDRDLS, DMDMDRMR,	11093	SDDDMFSTL, LLSTLSL	12115
SDDDRDTLSLT, SDLS, SD	4689	SDDDMSMD, DRMRDRTS,	10508
SDDDRMD, DRRDTD, SDD	10883	SDDDMSMS, LSMDTDMR,	2589
SDDDRMDRRR, MFSFMD	6451	SDDDMSM, LSSFRM, SDD	4886
SDDDRMD, SRRMFM, SMR	5240	SDDDMSLS, FMDRMD, SD	8919
SDDDRMDL, RDDTTDD, S	1102	SDDDMLS, SSLSDRM, MS	10889
SDDDRMDLLLS, MSDDM	2182	SDDDSDDD, SMFSLMR, S	6020
SDDDRMDLLLS, MSSLD	2182a	SDDDSDRM, MSMRTLRS,	10250
SDDDRMRD, DRRTTD, SD	5735	SDDDSDRM, SFMRDS, SL	4861
SDDDRMRD, RMSLSFMR	11834	SDDDSMSD, SLLLLLDLS,	7449
SDDDRMRD, RSSSLTLS,	8189	SDDDSSRD, TLTDTL	283
SDDDRMRDR, SLSFMRD,	6956	SDDDSLSSSLSS, SRRR	10866
SDDDRMRD, SFMMRR, RM	5991	SDDDSLLS, SDDDSMDR	2590
SDDDRMRMFS, MFMDRRD,	3434	SDDDLSFM, SLLLRDT, S	12581
SDDDRM, RMSFMR, RMRM	4688	SDDDLTDRTLS, SDDDR	2782

SDDDLTTTDLDS, SDDD	3438
SDDDTD, DRRM, MRMDT, T	10253
SDDDTDRRR, RMMMRDR	4124
SDDDTDRMMF, MLSDRF	2682
SDDDTDR, SRRRDRM, SM	6070
SDDDTDMDDT, DRRTLT	8325
SDDDTD, MSSSF#S, MLSF	3312
SDDDTDFMMRDTLS#, SM	1224
SDDDTDS, MFFLFSSD, S	1185
SDDDTDLSDTD, MRTSL	10899
SDDDTLSRM, SDRMRDR	7022
SDDDTLSMD, SLFDTLS,	3142
SDDDTLSFM, SLDTDRD,	4938
SDDDTLSSM, SDDDTDR	4164
SDDDTLSSS, SMMMFMR	11248
SDDDTLS, SLDTRD, DRM	6962
SDDDTLTDRM, MFMRDR,	6329
SDDDTT, DRRRSM, MMM	673
SDDDTTLL, LFMRDDTT,	4892
SDDRDRMSMRD, RMRDD	1495
SDDRDTD, RMMFMR, DRM	8548
SDDRDTD, RMMFMR, DMD	8547
SDDRDTRRDRM, SMMFM	4998
SDDRDT, SRRMRD, MFSM	5298
SDDRDTLTDS, SRRMFM	9706
SDDRRMD, FMDDTD, MRR	924
SDDRRM, DFFMRD, SDD	9022
SDDRRMDLRDT, SLTDR	2204
SDDRRMDLS, STDTLS, S	592
SDDRRMRD, DFFMMR, S	6278
SDDRRMRDR, RMSFMMR,	976
SDDRRMRD, RMMFMR, SS	784
SDDRRMRD, RMSRMD, SD	316
SDDRRMRD, SLLSLS, SD	8192
SDDRRMRD, SLTDTLS, S	11218
SDDRRMRMD, MFSSFMR,	3442
SDDRRMF, RMFRDTD, SD	5180
SDDRRMFM, DFMRDR, SD	7844
SDDRRMFM, MRDDRRD, S	7846
SDDRRMFS, MRDDRRM, S	11921
SDDRRMF, SMMFRD, SDD	12081
SDDRRMFSFMMRRD, SD	941
SDDRRMSR, RSSFMRD,	12460
SDDRRMSR, FMMRDR, SD	8689
SDDRRMSFM, SFFMMR, S	9279
SDDRRMSS, SLSMDMR, S	12068
SDDRRMLS, MFSMFRDD,	1490
SDDRMDD, MFSSLF, RMF	2195
SDDRMDRDLS, SDDRMD	11983
SDDRMDMRDTD, MFMRD	10559
SDDRMDFFMR, SDDRMF	6573
SDDRMDSM, DLLSFM, SD	6562
SDDRMD, SSLDFM, DRMM	7238

SDDRMDS, SLLRLRD, RM	11532
SDDRMRD, DRRDTLS, SL	2680
SDDRMRDSFMMR, RSSL	4274
SDDRMRD, LRRMFMR, RS	5869
SDDRMMDFFMR, SDDRM	6574
SDDRMMRMDLS, RMDLS,	5838
SDDRMMMMMRRMF, STR	12472
SDDRMMMFSMRD, SDDR	7864
SDDRMMFSMRD, SDDRM	7863
SDDRMMFSLS, MMMLSF	6033
SDDRMMFSLS, SFMMRD	8654
SDDRMMFLSFMRD, SDD	7862
SDDRMMSDRTD, RMRDT	4317
SDDRMMSFMRMMM, RDR	11856
SDDRMFRMD, RMFSLFS	11070
SDDRMFMDRD, SMRDTL	8354
SDDRMFMR, DRMRDRRR	197
SDDRMFMRD, MFSSMRD	10912
SDDRMFSFM, MLLRMF, T	11239
SDDRMFSLSFS, SFRMF	7477
SDDRMFSLS, SDDRMFS	5258
SDDRMSDDLS, SDDRM	5945
SDDRMSDRTD, RMRDTD	4316
SDDRMSMDMR, MSSLSM	627
SDDRMSMR, FMDDMRTS,	10509
SDDRMSSFMMRD, SDDR	11476
SDDRMSLLTD, MRTSDM	1093
SDDRML, SMRDRM, SDDR	3485
SDDRFMRMR, RDDFMR,	8553
SDDRSMD, LSDDRD, SDD	10353
SDDRSMFMR, DLFMRDT	2983
SDDRSFMRDRRMRD, SD	10816
SDDRTDD, MRFMRD, SDD	10490
SDDRTD, LSDRM, MRMFS	5868
SDDRTDLS, MFSMSLTS,	3360
SDDMDDMRRMRD, SDDM	5234
SDDMDDL, DSDRMR, SDM	11945
SDDMDDLS, SDDMDRMR,	5331
SDDMDDLLS, DTDRMFM	12021
SDDMDS, FMRDRMR, TDD	11521
SDDMDSFM, SLTDRDT, L	10738
SDDMDLDS, MSLSMMR, S	11424
SDDMDLDS, SDMRDDT, R	2149
SDDMDLLD, LSDMDMR, S	11154
SDDMDLLD, LSSDDR, RM	8276
SDDMDLTD, MSFMRDR, M	1494
SDDMDTRTS, LSMFTD, S	3236
SDDMRDDSLDLS, SDDR	770
SDDMRDRRF, RMMSFML	1295
SDDMRDR, MFSFMFMR,	9616
SDDMRDLLDT, LSSSDM	262
SDDMRDTDR, SRMFMRM,	1781
SDDMRDTLS, DTDFMR, S	4228

SDDMRDT LLF, RDDRMD,	12316	SDDTSRRD, SMMRRLR, S	1917
SDDMRRFMSDLS, FMFR	7186	SDDTSFFM, SSLSFMMR,	8748
SDDMRRFTTRD, SDDMR	4260	SDDTSSLLSM, MTLSLS	5438
SDDMR, SRRFM, DMSMFL	3574	SDDTSLSM, SDDDTLSL	10881
SDDMMDDM, DLLS, SDDM	12170	SDDTSLTD, DTLSFMRD,	8052
SDDMMRDR, MRDMRD, R	2160	SDDT LSDRM, FMRDMRD	541
SDDMMFMRM, DRMFRM, M	3141	SDDT LSDRM, FSMLFS, M	5457
SDDMMS, MRDMRD, SDDM	424	SDDT LSM, DRMSMRD, SD	8408
SDDMMSFMRDFMRD, SL	767	SDDT LSMD, RMLR, MMMD	12017
SDDMMSFMR, MDRDTLS,	4980	SDDT LSM, SLSMRDD, RM	10740
SDDMMSFM, MFMRRD, SD	12134	SDDT LSFM, SLRDTD, SL	1057
SDDMFS, SLLLLSM, SDD	1913	SDDT LSSM, MFFSRMSR,	2476
SDDMSD, DTSSLS, SSDD	11503	SDDT LSS, SDDLDS, SDD	6174
SDDMSD, SDSDRM, MRTD	1351	SDDT LSLR, MRFMRDS, D	11125
SDDMSFMR, SDDMSFMR	8614	SDDT LSLS, DRMSFMR, S	369
SDDMSSLSMDRM, SDDM	5087	SDDT LSLS, FMSLRDT, S	9375
SDDMSSLSFMSD, SDDD	4918	SDDT LSLS, SSSFMRM, S	6384
SDDMSLS, MSMRDM, SDD	2043	SDDT LSLS, SSSLLSFM,	11524
SDDFMRD, DRMMMRDR, S	3125	SDDT LSLS, SLDSMR, RM	10908
SDDFMRDTD, RMDSLS, S	1091	SDDT LSLS, SLRDTD, S	1056
SDDSMRDTD, FMRDTLR	2877	SDDT LSLLD, DRRRDRM,	4381
SDDSMFMRD, DT LLLRD	8012	SDDT LS, LTDRMRDR, SM	587
SDDSFMRD, DTDRSTLS,	5168	SDDT LLSS, DMRRSM, SD	3033
SDDSSMD, SFMRDS, DT	1834	SDDT LTDRMF#S, MFRMM	4820
SDDSSMRD, SFMRDS, TD	8901	SDDT LTLS, LTDDRRM, M	9226
SDDSST LS, FFMRDSS, S	4735	SDDTTDRM, MDLRDTLS,	3937
SDDSST LS, FFMRRMFM	4737	SDDTTD, SFMFSLR, RMM	1362
SDDLSFFM, RMSDTLLS,	10678	SDDTTDTLS, DMDTDR, S	11920
SDDTDDSLSFM, SDDRM	6968	SDDTT, SRRDD, SMRDT, L	3726
SDDTDRDRMD, MRMSFM	11205	SDDTTL, DFFMR, DSFMR	3284
SDDTDRDS, SDDDTTDR	10944	SDDTTLDLS, DSDSFMR	10524
SDDTDRRD, DTSLLS, RM	9617	SDDTTLRR, MFMFSRM, M	8616
SDDTDRRD, RMRMFS, SL	1666	SDDTTLLS, DSFMMRR, M	11623
SDDTDRRD, MRDTRLLS,	6180	SDDTTLLS, SMRDTL, LF	6412
SDDTDRR, SRRDRM, SMM	5216	SDDTTLLS, SMMRRR, MF	8636
SDDTDRMRD, DMMRMFS	8372	SDDTTLL, LLMRDT, TDR	2263
SDDTDRMFMR, SDDTDR	11486	SDDTTLTS, SSLTDSFM	1954
SDDTDRMFS, SFMDSLL#	12063		
SDDTDR, MLLLRDT, LSD	4671	SDR	
SDDTDR, SRRDRM, SMMF	1071		
SDDTDRTS, SDDFMRDR	7618	SDRDDMFSLSSM, DRDR	9548
SDDTDMMR, SSSFMRM, S	6884	SDRDMSLSM, SMDS, SDR	3490
SDDTDS, FMRRD, MLLTD	6634	SDRDFMDRDD, MSMDFM	5510
SDDTDSSLSFFM, SDDD	3859	SDRDSDRMRD, MFSMDM	8323
SDDTDLLS, MRRDTLT, S	10049	SDRDSMFM, SMDRMFS, S	3090
SDDTDLLS, MSFRMFM, S	10734	SDRDSMFS, DMFMSLTD,	3472
SDDTDLTD, DRRMRDDT,	2355	SDRDSMSD, RMRDMR, SD	10349
SDDTDLTDS, LSSSFMM	4810	SDRDLSM, SDTDMMR, FM	7526
SDDTRFLS, SDTSLTD, S	12207	SDRDTDRRD, MSFMRDR,	8922
SDDTMRRD, SFMDRMD, S	7144	SDRDTDRRM, FFRMRMR	11654
SDDTFLLS, DMMRFMD, S	9862	SDRDTDFSFM, MRTDFM	6922
SDDTFLLS, MSFSLRDT,	3972	SDRDTSDRM, RMDRMF#S,	9489
SDDTSRD, RRFMRD#R, DM	5403	SDRDTSRMRD, MFLLDT	1262

1110

Entry	Page
SDRDTSRMRD, LSFMRF#	11994
SDRDT LSSLS, FMDMRD	1859
SDRDT LSLTD, MSLSMD	5951
SDRRMRDDTLSLS, FMS	11065
SDRRMRMFFS, FMRDTD	10094
SDRMDDLS, TTDTLS, SD	4375
SDRMDDTDR, SRMFRRD	8470
SDRMDRDRM, MFMRMDM	6419
SDRMDRDLSD, DTDRRR	8161
SDRMDRDTD, RMMSMRRR	2511
SDRMDRMFRS, MRDLTD	4880
SDRMDRMF, FMRDMRTD,	7973
SDRMDRFM, MLTDLS, RM	9435
SDRMDMRD, RI'RDRMLS,	9477
SDRMDMRD, MFMRD#R, RF	9291
SDRMDMR#MFL, DTLSDM	5371
SDRMDMFSL, SFMRM, DM	3178
SDRMDFRD, TDMRRM, MS	8699
SDRMDFRMRDTD, SDRM	10865
SDRMDFMRD, SLSLLTL	1952
SDRMDFMR, RMDTLS, SL	5942
SDRMDFMRMDL, DTLSS	1619
SDRMDFMRMRD, MRDTR	10131
SDRMDFMR, STDRFMRD,	11922
SDRMDFMMR, RM FSMMR	8773
SDRMDFFM, MLRSDTLS,	1475
SDRMDSSMD, MRSMLSF#	12249
SDRMDSSFMRD, MRMRS	4126
SDRMDLDLS, SDRMDRT	4327
SDRMDLS, DFMRDR, SDR	6193
SDRMDLLTD, DTDRDRM,	11674
SDRMDLTD, LSSDMR, SM	1360
SDRMDTRS, SLDFMMRR,	7248
SDRMDTLTD, MRSDTLS	11288
SDRMRDD, DRMMSFMMR,	1167
SDRMRDDRMF, FMRSMD	12424
SDRMRDD, SSMFSL, DTL	10241
SDRMRDRDLLS, SDMSF	4959
SDRMRDRMF#S, SDRMRD	9188
SDRMRD, MSSFMR, MDFM	3680
SDRMRDMSLSFM, MRFM	3715
SDRMRDFMR, RSFMRDR	404
SDRMRDFMR, SMLF#F#S, S	9313
SDRMRDFSLSM, RMF#SL	2265
SDRMRD, SFMRRM, RTLS,	3331
SDRMRD, SLDTLS, SLTD	764
SDRMRD, SLTDLS, SDRM	5778
SDRMRD, LDRD, SDRMRD,	3340
SDRMRDL, SDRMS, SLSM	3721
SDRMRDLS, SDRMDS, RM	3102
SDRMRDLS, SDRMF#S, SF	6872
SDRMRDLS, SLTDRMR, M	9560
SDRMRDTD, DRMSFMR, S	2874
SDRMRDTD, MRMDTLLS,	9469
SDRMRDTD, SDMSMRDR	9701
SDRMRDTLS, DTDRMD, S	2409
SDRM, RDTLSFMS, SDRM	5728
SDRMRDTLTD, MRSDTLS,	11287
SDRMRDTLTS, RMF#SMD	11083
SDRMRRSM, SDRMRRM, M	1819
SDRMRMRD, DSFMFMRR,	1673
SDRMRFMD, LSMFMRDD	10465
SDRMRFMRDR, RMFSFM	8252
SDRMRFMRD, SLSLTDT	7759
SDRMRFMMR, DDDDTRR	9880
SDRM, RSRD, DTLSD, LTD	12188
SDRMR, SRMFM, SSMSFM	7101
SDRMR, SRMFM, SSSSFM	1593
SDRMRS, SLSLDR, RRRR	6095
SDRMMDTLS, STRFFFD	12277
SDRMMRDDDTLS, STTT	3403
SDRMMRDRDRM, MSSSS	6194
SDRMMRDRDLS, SDRMM	5038
SDRMMRDLDLS, DTDR,	6545
SDRMMMRDRR, SRMFFF	7244
SDRMMMRDRR, STRFFF	7242
SDRMMMRDMR, RMRDDR	5069
SDRMMMMRML, LRMFFF	11715
SDRMMMML, SMRDDDTL,	1576
SDRMMMFDRM, MRD#RMR	7023
SDRMMMFDRM, SRMFMF	3691
SDRMMMFRMDS, DRMFS	10586
SDRMMFMR, SFMRMTDLS	399
SDRMMMFMR, SFMRMTLS	398
SDRMMMFMMR, STRFFL	8159
SDRMMMSFMR, SDRMMM	9727
SDRMMFRRTD, SLSSF#S	4989
SDRMMFM, RDTLDTLS, S	10789
SDRMMFMRMD, SDMSSL	4495
SDRMMFMRM, MRDTDRD	11019
SDRMMFMRM, MRDTDRM	11018
SDRMMSDRMM, RMFMMR	3910
SDRMMSMR, MDTLTDRS	12201
SDRMMSFDRM, MMRRRD	383
SDRMMSFM, MMDMFMRD,	2129
SDRMFRDRTD, MSRTMR	4842
SDRMFRR, SLSMRDRD, M	7282
SDRMFRMD, DDMSLSMR,	3070
SDRMFRSML, FSMRDFM	3520
SDRMFMRD, MRTRDLLS,	12417
SDRMFMRD, SDRMFMRD,	4091
SDRMFMRD, SLTDLLS, S	6596
SDRMFMRR, DRMFMRD, S	11789
SDRMFMR, MDDRDT, SDR	7516
SDRMFMRTD, RMLSF#S, R	11199
SDRMFM, SDRMFM, SSFF	4059

SDRMFSDRDTD, TLSSS	2544
SDRMFSDRMRDRD, DSS	11049
SDRMFSDFMR, RMFSFM	5088
SDRMFSDT, RSLTDLLS,	2750
SDRMFSRMFM, RMF#SLS	7681
SDRMFSRMFM, RMSSMF#	7684
SDRMFSMD, MLSFMR, SD	7718
SDRMFSM, DLSFFM, MRS	2811
SDRMFSMRDRD, SLTDR	11265
SDRMFSM, RDRMFR, SDR	2786
SDRMFS, MFLRDT, SDTL	4816
SDRMFS, MLSFSM, SDRM	4419
SDRMFSFMD, SSFMFMR	4116
SDRMFSFMRDRMFR, SD	8445
SDRMFSFMRD, SSFMFS	5204
SDRMFSFMR, RMF#SSF#S,	7761
SDRMFSFM, FMRDDT, RR	10265
SDRMFSFM, SDRMFSFM,	4088
SDRMFSFM, LSFMMRD, S	11849
SDRMFSFM, LSFMMRRD,	11852
SDRMFSFM, LSFMFMRD,	11848
SDRMFS, SDRMFS, SDRM	10998
SDRMFSSM, LSFMMRD, S	11851
SDRMFSSF#S, RFMDDT, R	12504
SDRMFSSSMRRD, SDRM	10874
SDRMFSSS, MRMFMRDR,	3447
SDRMFSS, LSMFSD, SDR	8005
SDRMFS, SLSFLSFMRD	11751
SDRMFSSLLS, MFSMFM	11771
SDRMFSSLTD, SLTSLF	1249
SDRMFSLSFMDRTD, MF	6217
SDRMFSLSFM, DMMRDS,	8206
SDRMFSLS, SRMFMRDS,	12539
SDRMFLS, DMSSFSFM, S	6223
SDRMFLSFM, SLSFMMR,	530
SDRMSDRM, MRDMRD, SD	1927
SDRMSDRM, MRMFRMFS,	6880
SDRMSDRM, MFMRDMRD,	4319
SDRMSDRM, LSMRDR, MR	4844
SDRMSRD, SDRMSRD,	9979
SDRMSMSLM, SDRMSMS	6351
SDRMSFRD, MMFMDSDR,	3086
SDRMSFMR, DRMRDSFM,	5921
SDRMSFMRDR, MFMRDT	62
SDRMSFMRMD, RDRMSL	3339
SDRMSFMR, MDTDRTS, S	1392
SDRMSFLLS, SDRMSFR	7308
SDRMSSDRMS, SDMSLL	9306
SDRMSSDFMR, FMTDDR	1162
SDRMSSF, RRRSFM, SDR	7209
SDRMSSF, MMRLTD, SSL	6997
SDRMSSF#MR#M, FMRSSL	12075
SDRMSSSMD, MRDLDDL	936

SDRMSSSLSFM, RRMFS	432
SDRMSLDD, DTLSMMDR,	12167
SDRMSLMS, TDRMDFMR,	9460
SDRMSLML, LFSLLTST,	6707
SDRMSL, SMDRMS, SLMM	855
SDRMSLSM, DRSMDLRR,	8968
SDRMSL, LRMRDT, SMRD	9490
SDRMSL, LRMFS, SDRMS	3571
SDRMSLTDTLS, SDRMS	8671
SDRMLRDT, SLTDMRD,	2912
SDRMLRRT, SLTDMRD, S	2913
SDRMLSFM, RDRTDTLS,	12355
SDRMLSFMRD, MRDTDR	8068
SDRMLSFM, LSMRRD, SD	11854
SDRMLSFM, LSFMFMRD,	11850
SDRMLSFM, LSFMFSRD,	11853
SDRMLSSFM, RMFSMRD,	354
SDRMTDRT, RFFMDMF#S,	1338
SDRFMDTRD, SFMRDS, S	4601
SDRFMRRM, FSLSFMM	12291
SDRFMLSMDRM, SDTLS	8311
SDRFFMDLRS, SDRFLS	2128
SDRSMD, MRDLS, SSDDF	9266
SDRSM, LRMLF, MTRDTL	9858
SDRTDRMFRDD, MRSF#M	9303
SDRTDRMFR, MFSSFRD,	5704
SDRTDRMFMR, MRDTL	1244
SDRTSDRM, RMDMF#S, RM	9488
SDMDDLS, SFRMDLSTL	4885
SDMDRDDL, DLSSLDD, S	5409
SDMDRDDL, DLSSLTD, S	5409a
SDMDRDDL, LLSSLTD, S	5409b
SDMDRDLD, DMSDRMR, S	7755
SDMDRMD, MFSLSMR, DR	2010
SDMDRMDS, LTDLFMMR,	1446
SDMDMRDLS, SDMDMRS,	417
SDMDMSLSMDMR, MFSF	10839
SDMDSSM, SDMDRMRD, S	2956
SDMDSLDLS, SSDRMFM	11032
SDMDLDSM, SDMDDTDR,	2796
SDMDLSDMRFM, MMFML	900
SDMDLS, SSSDMDR, SDM	8139
SDMDLSTD, DTDFMR, RM	3493
SDMDTDRD, SSTTLLS, S	6805
SDMDTRDS, DMSMDMR, S	1862
SDMDTLSDS, SLMRMF#	8808
SDMDTLS, SDRMSR, MFM	9622
SDMDTLTSDR, MF#SMMR	10995
SDMRDDTTLL, RDDTLT	5714
SDMRDRDS, LDTLDLS, S	8627
SDMRDMRDLS, SDMRDR	2027
SDMRDMR, RMFFMRM, DT	5390
SDMRDMSR, RLSMMDRR,	2298

SDMRDMSF, MMRLDRD, D   5805

SDMRDMSF, MSDDRRM, D   2941

SDMRDFLS, STDRRMFM,   649

SDMRDS, FMDRTD, MRS   2180

SDMRD, SSDMMRDT, MMM   8393

SDMRDSLDR, MFSRFMR   1474

SDMRDLD, SLSMR, MFSM   4841a

SDMRDLFMFM, SDRTLS   6923

SDMRDLS, MSFRDTD, SD   11708

SDMRDLSFMFM, SDRTL   6924

SDMRDLSS, SSSMRDR, R   9692

SDMRDLS, SLDRRD, SDM   7873

SDMRDLS, TDRSLSM, SD   11433

SDMRDLLS, SSLSDDR, M   8849

SDMRDTDRDS, DRRRRD   9033

SDMRDTDLSS, MRRD#RM   4479

SDMRDTLS, SDRMDR, RR   10039

SD, MRDTLSSF#LS, STMR   893

SDMRRM, MFLSMR, MMRD   7389

SDMRRM, SFMRRD, DTLS   9515

SDMRMDLFFSDFRRD, R   2198

SDMRMD, TDRRRSFM, MF   1701

SDMRMFSSFM, RDMSSD   4297

SDMRFMDT, SFMFSMR, S   9815

SDMRFMRD, TDRTLDTL   6820

SDMRSDRRD, SSSDTLF   3979

SDMRSLTDLS, SSFMR   2993

SDMRTDS, DMSFMRFM, MR   9066

SDMRTD, SLDTLS, DTDR   6417

SDMR#MDMFSSM, DMRRM   6473

SDMR#MRD, DDRDTLS, SD   6064

SDMR#MSMD, TDRD#RFM, S   11173

SDMMDDLL, SRFFMR, RS   6398

SDMMDRMFMD, MMRDTD,   4451

SDMMDRFF, RMDTDRSS,   2712

SDMMRD, DMSSFM, RRF#S,   753

SDMMRDDLS, TDRDRM, S   11157

SDMMRDRDTD, SDMSFM   1767

SDMMRDRR, RMFFMRM, S   5615

SDMMRDRMFSLS, MMRR   5755

SDMMRDRFFMRMSSFM   3416

SDMMRD, SFMLRR, MDRT   9698

SDMMRD, LRFFMR, RMLS   3196

SDMMRDTD, TDRRDTLS,   6156

SDMMRDTRR, SRFFMRD   10726

SDMMRRMFFM, SLTLSM   10668

SDMMRFFLFFM, MMMDD   11217

SDMMRS, SDMMRS, FMLT   8186

SDMMRLDTLS, SDMSFL   6830

SDMMR#MD, TDRMRDL, DL   904

SDMMR#M, MRFFM, SDMMR#   5950

SDMMR#MFLR, DDTDTLS   7919

SDMMMDMSSS, SMRRDRM,   7450

SDMMMDMSSS, SMRRRD   7452

SDMMMRDR, STRFFMRM,   12498

SDMMMRDMRD, DMSSSL   12033

SDMMMRDFM, MRDDRR#M,   9927

SDMMMRS, SSDDTD, SDM   5519

SDMMMMRDLD, LLSDRM   7215

SDMMMMMMMFS, SSRMF   4415

SDMMMSFF, FRTLTD, SM   5779

SDMMMLLR, SDLDRRM, R   181

SDMMFMRDRDL, LSDDM   4334

SDMMFMMRDDRD, LSDR   4

SDMMFMMR, STRDMRRD,   12162

SDMMSFRMD, DTLDLLT   4300

SDMMSSFF, FMFRDTD, S   9705

SDMMS, SLSFFM, MMSSD   9341

SDMFRDTDRMFSMR, SD   6895

SDMFRMDS, SDMSMRM, S   350

SDMFMRD#R, STRFFMR#M,   8296

SDMFMRMDLL, TDRMDR,   3645

SDMFMRMD, TLLMRR, SD   10052

SDMFMRLL, TDRMRDSS,   8858

SDMFMMRD, TLRMRD, SM   12385

SDMFSDRMMRD, DLSFM   972

SDMFS, DTDLSS, SLLDS   2687

SDMFSLSFMRM, MSDTDR   4515

SDMFSLSS, SLLSLSFM,   8904

SDMFLSM, MFSSLFS, SD   1914

SDMFLSFMMF#F#S, SSSS#   1309

SDMFLS, SLSTDR, SSDT   2652

SDMSDMRD, DRMF#SRDT   4893

SDMSDMR, DDSLSLDD, M   7406

SDMSDSTL, TDRTDRM, D   12140

SDMSMDMLTD, RMSRSD   12279

SDMSMRDRM, RDRMFMR,   4166

SDMSMRDMRD, DTLDRD   1428

SDMSMRFM, DTLSF#S, SD   6855

SDMSMRLTSD, MFLSMR   2593

SDMSMMRDRM, FMRSDM   814

SDMSMMMR, MFFFRDTD,   11061

SDMSFMRD, SDMRDTLS,   10411

SDMSFMRD, TLDTLS, DL   2648

SDMSFMR, RDDRMR, RRF#   3198

SDMSFMRMRD, MFSMRD   7723

SDMSFMFRD, MRSDTDLS,   9036

SDMSFMFS, TLSFMFSF   7588

SDMSFLMRDTLTD, MMR   204

SDMSF#F, FLSFFMM, RRM   748

SDMSSDRM, FSDLLS, TM   1268

SDMSSF, MDDTD, LTDF   9317

SDMSSFMDRMFMRD, SD   59

SDMSSFMF, STRFFMRM,	4691
SDMSSFM, SLRDTD, SDM	11694
SDMSSL, SDLMFS, SLTD	4240
SDMSSLSLS, MRDDRDR	8166
SDMSLSMDRD, SDDMSF	12098
SDMSLSMD, MRRLRR, S	8537
SDMSLS, MRDRFM, MRDS	180
SDMSLSFM, DLRDLTD, S	5270
SDMSLSFM, MLDMFMR, S	12032
SDMSLTD, DRMDFMRTD	3904
SDMSTDRM, F#SLTRDTL	8462
SDMSTRDLS, FMDMRDT	4403
SDMLRSFM, RMF#SLTLS	2433
SDMLFRDRM, LSFMRDD	3063
SDMLFRDTD, RMSDFMR	2228
SDMLFMRDR, SDMRSLT	1035
SDMLFMRD, SMRDTLS, MF	1329
SDMLSFMRD, DLLSDSF	11936
SDMLSFMRM, SDRTSLS	6115
SDMLSSFMLS, SDRTSL	4023
SDMLSLSFR, RMMMMDD	11190
SDMTLSMD, DLSDRMFR	6157
SDFMRD, MRSTLS, SSLL	1683
SDFMRDTD, RMFSDMR, S	4268
SDFMRDTLSD, DDRMRF#	3754
SDFMRMDLS, MFSMRDR	12381
SDFMRLDT, SFMDTLR, S	8180
SDFMR#MD, TDMRD#RLRM	
	12547
SDFMMRR, DDDDRRM, MF	5043
SDFFMRD, SDFFMRD, RR	1590
SDFFMRS, SDFFMR, RRS	3803

SDS

SDSDDRRM, MFFMRDMR,	8070
SDSDDMR, DDTLSSS, SD	3453
SDSDRMD, LSTRFM, SDS	7225
SDSDRMRD, DFFMRMFR,	4163
SDSDRMRD, RMRMFSFM,	5418
SDSDRMRD, MRDTLS, SD	2177
SDSDRMRD, FFFDRM, MF	1707
SDSDRMRD, SFMRRRF#S	9362
SDSDRMRD, TLTDRR, SS	10975
SDSDRMR, MFSDMRDTD,	9948
SDSDRMMR, MFRDTD, MR	10845
SDSDRM, MFMRDR, SDSD	3303
SDSDRMM, SFMRDR, SDS	8990
SDSDRMFMRD, SFM, FMR	7297
SDSDRMFS, MFSLSFMR	2667
SDSDRMSS, LSMDMRDD,	6965
SDSDMRL, TSRFLSM, SD	9772
SDSDMSM, DRMDRMSD,	2966

SDSDMS, FMMRDRD, SDS	1899
SDSDMSS, LSMRMD, SLL	10306
SDSDSDRMFS, MFSLSF	2666
SDSDSDTDSL, LRLRLR	8848
SDSDSLTD, RMMRDT, TD	1300
SDSDL#LSF, LSRSFRM, D	12169
SDSRDR, MFMRDRS, SDS	8532
SDSRSMRDR, SDTLSLS	9298
SDSMDRSD, SRTDLTSL	11050
SDSMDMMRDDT, SFRTS	20
SDSMDFM, MMMRDT, SDS	552
SDSMDSMD, DFMRDT, SD	2163
SDSMDSMRDDT, SFMRD	21
SDSMDSFM, RDSDMR, SR	10280
SDSMDSS, SLSFMR, SMD	12226
SDSMDLRDT, RMSFRDT	11366
SDSMDL, SFMFSRM, MMMF#	
	5739
SDSMRDRMSRM,DFFMR	3908
SDSMRDRFM, SDTDFLS,	608
SDSMRDFMMR, MMRMFM	8023
SDSMRDLS, MFSLTDMR	11390
SDSMRDLS, SSFMRDTD	8271
SDSMRDTL, LSSSFM, SD	6638
SDSMRRDD, DLLTDRDT,	12430
SDSMRFMRD, RSRFMSF	5994
SDSMMMRDS, SLTDRDT	30
SDSMMFSSLSSSF, LRD	8479
SDSMF, SDSMF, SDSMFS	4054
SDSMFSSLTD, RMRTST	1676
SDSMFSLS, MLMRDRMM	12111
SDSMFSLT, SLLRDTDR	4894
SDSMSDD, SLFRDT, SMT	6534
SDSMSDSM, SDDRMR, RR	4016
SDSMSRSF, STSRSDSM,	6879
SDSMSL, SLTDTLS, RM	3322
SDSMLSFM, RDMF#SLS, S	12354
SDSFMRDDT, LSLTDRM	9982
SDSFMRDSS, FMSFRDT	3254
SDSFMLSSFM, RDMF#SL	12353
SDSFSMM, MMLS#TL, SDS	3902
SDSFSMFSLR, RMSDLS	2255
SDSFSLS, DFMRDR, SLS	2865
SDSSDMRD, DDLRDLS, S	4311
SDSSMDMMRDDT, SFRT	19
SDSSMSSDDRMD, SLLL	10858
SDSSFMDTLS, FMRM, LR	11497
SDSSFMFS, SLTDSFMR,	4254
SDSSSDLTRDT, TF#MMD	721
SDSSSFMD, SSFMRRD, S	9678
SDSSLSM, FMDRMD, DFF	78
SDSLDRDRM, DFFMRDR,	10303
SDSLDRRD, MFFMDRS, F	3600

SDSLDFMRM, MLSDMRT	5344	SDLSDRMFS, LFMRDTD	6693
SDSLRDTTD, SF#SLDTT	768	SDLSDRFM, MRSLDTS, S	9808
SDSLFM, DMFSLTDT, SL	5851	SDLS, DMRDR, TRRDTSL	4644
SDSLFMRRD, RMF#SSF#S,	2914	SDLSDTDRDTL, LLSMF	127
SDSLFMRS, DTSLMRDR	12370	SDLSMDRMFSM, SDLRS	6625
SDSLFM, SDTTLS, RTSL	8066	SDLSMDRM, SLTDRT, DS	2076
SDSLSDRMDRD, SLLLD	10618	SDLSFM, DRMRRD, MRMR	11178
SDSLSDRM, MRMRD, SDS	7868	SDLSFMRMFLS, RFMLD	4377
SDSLSD, RMTDRMR, RSF	9047	SDLSFM, MRSSF#S, SDLS	8261
SDSLSDMFMRM, SDSLS	7204	SDLSLFRD, MSSLTDDT,	3044
SDSLSMFS, LSLTDS, SR	4362	SDLSTD, RFMRDTTDD, L	6343
SDSLSFM, DMFSLTDT, S	5850	SDLLSFM, SDLLSFM, SD	11959
SDSLSFMM, SFMRDD, MR	5899	SDLLLRDTS, DRMFMRR	10437
SDSLSFMM, SFMRRDD, M	5898	SDTDDRRM, SMRDLS, DS	12066
SDSLSFMM, SSFMRRD, S	9676	SDTDRDS, MMRMFMR, MF	12104
SDSLSFMFS, FMDRRD, D	2372	SDTDRDTD, DMMRDTLL	7461
SDSLSFM, SSFMRRD, SDS	9675	SDTDRDTDS, MRDTLTD	4387
SDSLSFFM, RMSLDT, SD	8519	SDTDRDTL, SDTDRS, SR	460
SDSLSSM, SLSDMS, SDS	717	SDTDRRM, SDTDRRM, SD	4060
SDSLSSFM, MSFM, MRTS	3064	SDTDRMD, DFFFFM, SDT	11389
SDSLLSMFMRM, MMFML	9481	SDTDRMD, DLFMRD, SDT	512
SDSLLSFMD, RM F#SLTD	2199	SDTDRMRD, DDRMFFMR	11917
SDSLLSFMD, MFMRSLL	12023	SDTDRMRDDT, MRDTDL	9639
SDSLLSFMRD, RMMRSL	2200b	SDTDRMRD, MRDTLTDT,	6811
SDSLLSFMRD, RMF#SLT	2200	SDTDRMRD, LFMDMR, RS	9010
SDSLLSFMRDS, SMRDS	10364	SDTDRMRDTS, DTDRMR	12483
SDSLLSFM, MFMRSSF#S,	12295	SDTDRMR, RSFMRD, SDT	2144
SDSLLSFM, MFMRSLSS,	12295a	SDTDRMRMFSLSM, MSF	12514
SDSLLSLSFMRD, RMF#S	2200a	SDTDRMR, FMDRRMR, SR	4273
SDSLL#LLL, LRLTDTTT,	12091	SDTDRMRSLTDRRD, SD	7688
SDSLTD, DFMRDDT, T	4512	SDTDRMM, RMFSSFMR, M	3537
SDSLTDRM, DRTDRMFS,	7670	SDTDRMMR, MLTDLLS, M	588
SDSLTDRM, MFMRDTLS,	5878	SDTDRM, MFFDRM, MMRR	1700
SDSLTDRM, SSMRDL, LR	2273	SDTDRMFR, MFSLRMFM,	10690
SDSLTDRSM, MMMF#S#LTD,		SDTDRMFR, SSSSS#LLR,	9717a
	867	SDTDRMFRSFM, RDDMR	6089
SDSLTDSFM, SLFRDTD	5954	SDTDRMFM, DSFMRDTD	12125
SDSLTD, SLSFMR, SDSL	4223	SDTDRMFMR, RDLRMSTL	2814
SDSTLS, SF#LSF#S, SDM	8301	SDTDRMFS, DRDTRMRD,	353
SDSTLS, SSMDMR, MRDM	6011	SDTDRMFS, DLSFMMDR,	8907
SDSTLLMF, LRDTLLSM,	6974	SDTDRMFSMD, MFSDTD	5524
SDSTLL, SRFM, SDSTLL,	7007	SDTDRMFS, FMDDTD, S	12064
SDLDRMRD, SMDFMRR, R	6713	SDTDRMFSMR, MDTDR	2810
SDLDSDRMRMS, SDLDS	3456	SDTDRMFSMR, MFMFS	17
SDLDS, MRSFMRDLLLS,	5839	SDTDRMSFMR, TRDLRM	1483
SDLDSLSFMS, DRMSFM,	6689	SDTDRFMRD, FFMSRRD,	7475
SDLRDTD, DMRDTLS, DL#	1734	SDTDRSMD,MSDTLDR, S	5523
SDLRDTDS, LTSFMLLR,	11308	SDTDRSSRD#RMD, SMRM	4348
SDL, RDT, SSLTDDTD, MM	4144	SDTDRSLTD, DTLRT, TL	3580
SDLRDT, TMDFMR, RSSF	8769	SDTDRSLTDSMRDD, DF	8899
SDLRMDM, SDLRMD, MRS	6955	SDTDRTS, SDTDRM, MRM	963
SDLSDRMRD, MSMDMR,	6754	SDTDMDMRMFTL, MMRL	3393
SDLSDRMRD, MSMRDMR,	6755	SDTDMRDRDTD, RMFSS	3362

SDTLTS, FMFSLR, RMF#S	9433
SDTLTS, LTDFMR, RMRD	6982
SDTTLRMF, LSFMSTTT,	8379
SDTTLS, SDRMRD, SDTT	4423
SDTTLLMMRD, TTLS, SD	8425
SDTTLLTLMS, SLTLSL	10502
SRDDTRDRM, DDTLLLTD	11279
SRDTD, TLLLTDR, SMR#M	4165
SRD#RMDD, SFMFFM, MSS	
	11533
SRD#RMDLS, SLLFMRDR	1451
SRRRMD, SLTDRM, MMMM	366
SRRRSMMM, SLSFRSFM,	1075
SRRMFMRDRM, MSFMMR	4452
SRMDRM, RRRMMF#SF#F, M	
	10142
SRMFRMSS, DFFMRDMR	6117
SRMFMRD, SLTDSMF#S, L	11672
SRMFSMFS, LFLRDT	5740
SRMFLSFM, RMF#SLTLS,	3733
SRMLSLDRSM, SLMMRD	535
SRSMMMLMSF, FFFMRM	11419
SRTSSMDS, SFMRDDT, S	7964

SMD

SMDDDDRDTLL, LLMRL	10050
SMDDDDSS, DDTDRLL, L	234
SMDDDDTDRD, SSSMDD	1939
SMDDDTLLS, LMFSLSF	69
SMDDDTLTLSSSLTD, S	8001
SMDDRTTD, DSMMFRRM	10903
SMDDMRD, LSMMRRR, MD	8980
SMDDSLSFM, RSDDLT	8770
SMDDLLLS, DTDRFFM, D	7658
SMDDLLLSS, DTDRFFM	7658a
SMDDTDRSFFM, MRDFR	5645
SMDDTDRTS, SSLTDLS	6605
SMDDTLSDRM, MFMRRD	9457
SMDDTLS, MFSLFMRD, S	8792
SMDRDDLS, STTLSD, SM	5073
SMDRDLS, SLLSLSM, SM	8124
SMDRDLLSSD, MRMRRM	9906
SMDRDTD, DRMFSFMR, S	7129
SMDRDTLSLTD, RMFFM	5279
SMDRMD, RMLSMR, RMSL	12442
SMDRMDFM, SSSFMMDR,	3348
SMDRM, RSMD, DDDRMMS	5593
SMDRMR, SMDR, MFSLSL	4242
SMDRMFMRD, SLSFMRD#	9644
SMDRMFMRDLTD, DMFS	917
SMDRM, FMRRD, SSLTD, S	606
SMDRMFFM, SLLSMR, SM	4908

SMDRMFSDS, SDMRD, FF	3801
SMDRMFLS, DLSMFMR, S	3349
SMDRM, SLDD, STTSSMM	11341
SMDRMS, LDTLS, MSDRM	3862
SMDRMSLMFRD, DSLTD	9193
SMDRMS, LTDRD, SMDRM	11883
SMDRMLSDRDT, MR#TTF#	1189
SMDRFMR, MDMSSFM, SL	5698
SMDRS, DLSFM, SMRSD, T	6003
SMDRTD, DRMFMR, SMDS,	7128
SMDRTDD, MSDTS#L, SDS	10950
SMDRTD, MRDTLS, RTSD	8422
SMDMDD, DTRD, SMD, MSS	10031
SMDMRD, MRSSF#S, MFFM	377
SMDMRDLS, MMMMSLSM	1441
SMDMRFMR, MDMSSFM, S	5697
SMDMRFMRM, DTDRSLT	7790
SMDMSDD, DRRDTD, SMD	11924
SMDMSDMRDMF#S, SMRD	7294
SMDMSDS, SDMRD, LMDM	3800
SMDMSD, LSDSFMR, SML	5470
SMDMSL, DFMRRD, RMRM	3604
SMDMSLS, SMDDMSLS, F	8964
SMDMSLS, SMDMSLS, FF	8966
SMDFRD, DRRMMF, RMMM	9214
SMDFRDRTD, MRMTDLS,	9887
SMDFRSFM, RDSFMMR, S	6551
SMDFRSLFM, STDRTSD	10835
SMDFMRRD, DTSDRMFS	3242
SMDFMLS, DFFMRM, SMD	1626
SMDSDRSM, SMDSSRMD.	7103
SMDSRD, DFDMMR, SDSD	5825
SMDSMRDS, LLSDSFM, S	8882
SMDS, MRDLSMRMF, MMM	6048
SMDSMRDTL, SMDMMRR,	2425
SMDSFMMRDFMLSDFM	391
SMDSSDDT, SDMFMRD, S	2066
SMDSSDRM, DFMRDTDR,	9688
SMDSSSLTDR, SMDL, LR	11186
SMDSSL, LRRSFMRD, SL	2348
SMDSLS, MDTDMR, SMDS	10498
SMDSLS, SRMFRD, RMLF#	5170
SMDSLLS, LTDTLS, SMD	8734
SMDSLTD, SFFMDR, SMR#	1267
SMDSTLSLSM, LSSFMR	1711
SMDLDS, MFSLSDDTLS	4522
SMDLRDTD, FMRSDTLS,	255
SMDLRT, DLTDFMRM, MM	2390
SMDLRTS, DLTSMF, SMF#	7484
SMDLFMRD, MRLSDTLS,	2461
SMDLS, DDTRRD, MSFMR,	537
SMDLSDRM, SMDLLS, RM	6037
SMDLSMFMDRD, SMDDT	339

SMDLSM, FMRDMR, SMFL	4267		SMRDDTDRMD, SM, SMRD	10803
SMDLSFMR, SDT LLS, M	946		SMRDDTDR, SFMRRSFM,	12275
SMDLS, FMFSLTDSS, MM	2100		SMRDDTFFMRM, SLRFS	4927
SMDLSSMDLS, DFFRSM	1873		SMRDDTSFMRRD, MSFM	12523
SMDLSS, FSLTDS, MMMFF	2099		SMRDDT, LFMRS, SDDTM	10497
SMDLSSSMDLS, DFFRS	1874		SMRDDTLSDMR, RMRDT	6316
SMDLSSLT, TDRMLR, RF	577		SMRDDTLS, MF#SLRSDT	9053
SMDL, SLSMDR, MMMMSS	6902		SMRDDTLS, FMFSLRRR,	1575
SMDLSLTDTMR, RDRMS	4226		SMRDDTLS, FMFSLR, SM	1041
SMDLSTRSSMDLSTRS	6042		SMRDDTLS, SFMSMRDR,	8818
SMDLLLF#RT, TLSDRFM	5008		SMRDDTLS, SLMF#SSF#S,	7004
SMDLLLLTDRS, SMDLL	2173		SMRDDTLSLSFFM, SLL	11987
SMDLTD, SMDLTD, RMF#S,			SMRDDTLS, TDLRTLLS,	9330
	4714		SMRDDTLLS, SSLTDTD	8072
SMDLTD, TLLLRT, SDDR	2647		SMRDDTLTD, RMF#SRDT	3861
SMDTDRD, MSMRMFM, SM	7498		SMRDDTLTS, SMDRTLS,	4805
SMDTDRD, SMRDDTDR, S	5071		SMRDRDRM, MSFMRDRD,	2999
SMDTDMR, DFMLLS, SDS	4535		SMRDRD, SLTDS, DRDLS	6640
SMDTDMRD, SFMLRR, RR	1357		SMRDRDLS, SDSMRS, SM	6907
SMDTRD, LDLLSS, SLSS,	3217		SMRDRDLS, SSLSFM, SM	7589
SMDTRDLSM, MFSRRSF	9866		SMRDRDLL, DRDRMR, SM	3686
SMDTRF, LSFMFS, DSMR	3296		SMRDRDTD, MRDTDTLS,	2541
SMDT, FRLS, SMDT, LSSS	11788		SMRDRDTT, SFMRSDRM,	1322
SMDTLSMRD, LLSMMRM,	8466		SMRDRRM, FMLSFMR, SM	869
SMDTLS, MFRMFLSSM, S	9021		SMRDRRM, SDTSSF#S, D	1379
SMDTLS, FMRSMD, SMDT	12467		SMRDRMD, RMSDTDL, LR	3581
SMDTLSLSMMR, MSDLD	6677		SMRDRMFRM, SLSSMDM	3395
SMDTLSLSSM, SRMFLS	1139		SMRDRMFS, MFSLSF#S, S	3519
SMDTLSTRFM, SLLTLS,	6355		SMRDRMFSLS, RDRMFS	4277
SMDTTLSD, FMRDTDR, S	9864		SMRDRMFSLSFM, MMFR,	5171
SMRDDDD, DRMFMRM, MR	9257		SMRDRMSFLLS, SDTLS	12285
SMRDDDFMRSS, DTS	10410		SMRDRSRMRDRS, SMFM	10556
SMRDDDTLS, SMRDDDT	7440		SMRDRT, DRRMFS, RSMR	9159
SMRDD, DTLSS, LTDRMR	3278		SMRDMDRDTL, LSLTDM	10533
SMRDDRRM, RMSLLT, S	9922		SMRDMDLS, DTRDSLR, M	175
SMRDDRRSSF, FMRSMD	1336		SMRDMRDRT, SFMRFM, L	5421
SMRDDRMFM, RMRDRDT	9823		SMRDMRDT, SFMRFMRD,	1889
SMRDDRMFM, SDRMSFM	6080		SMRDMRR, SRMFFMM, SS	3698
SMRDDRMFFM, MFSLDT	7876		SMRDMRSD, SMRDMRSD,	3165
SMRDDRMFSM, SLSFMR	371		SMRDMFSLS, TDLSFMF	5404
SMRDDRMSMSL, TDSMF	9105		SMRDMFSLLS, LSRMF#S	6864
SMRDDRMSFM, MMMDDT	2323		SMRDMFSLTDS, DTSRD	5972
SMRDDRMSFFM, MMMF#F#			SMRDMSDT, SFMRLTLS,	10583
	1047		SMRDMSDT, TTFLTLSM,	10187
SMRDDMSD, DTLSMMDS,	2492		SMRDMS, SDRDLFRT, SD	6692
SMRDDFLLS, SMSDTLSF#	5992		SMRDMSLS, MLSTDMR, R	3714
SMRDDSFM, SLDSDLRR,	1978		SMRDMSLSFM, LLSLT	2543
SMRDDLSF, FMRDTDRD	8834		SMRDMLSMDMR, RMRDM	7647
SMRDDLSFFM, SLTDMR	3964		SMRDMLSM, SLTDTLS	3909
SMRDDLLS, SDLTLSLM	564		SMRDMLSS, MSFRMD, SM	10802
SMRDDLLLS, LFRSDRM	1409a		SMRDMLLS, SFMDLTD, S	5140
SMRDDLLLS, LFRSDRF	1409		SMRDFMDM, SSRMFMRR,	4446
SMRD, DLTDRDS, SMDF, L	1943		SMRDFMRDRTD, TDDRM	7883a

SMRDFMRDRTD, TDRMF	7883
SMDRDFM, RMRDRDT, DRM	5641
SMRDFMRM, SLDDTDD, S	7008
SMRDFMRLSSF#, FFSRF	6337
SMRDFMRLTD, MSTLRF#	8410
SMRDFLS, DSLSMRDR, R	2262
SMRDSDRMFSD, SMRDS	8764
SMRDSDRMFSS, SMRDS	8765
SMRDSDLS, FMLSFMR, D	244
SMRDSDTLS, MLSFMR,	1632
SMRDSDTL, SLMFMR, MF	10483
SMRDSMRD, DFFFLLS, SM	5015
SMRDSMRD, RMSMRMS, S	6396
SMRDSMMR, DRMMSF#S,	11115
SMRDSFMR, MLTDRMLS	12426
SMRDS, SMMFMMR, LFD#R	11268
SMRDSSLDLS, DTDRMF	2438
SMRDSSL, LRRSFMRD	2347
SMRDSLDRSM, MRRDT	10054
SMRDSLDMRMD, LDRMS	1335
SMRDSLDLS, SLTDRFM	5379
SMRDSLFF, LSMMRDM	688
SMRDSLSFFM, SLTDTL	9156
SMRDSLSS, DRMSFMRD	5169
SMRDSLTDT, DSLSFMR	11620
SMRDSTLS, DRSRR#M, SM	4778
SMRDSTLSDF, LSLTDD	2418
SMRDSTLS, DLTDFMRD,	10007
SMRDSTL, STDRSM, MML	7180
SMRDLD, TDRSM, SMRMF	5033
SMRDLFMR, SLDTLSF#S,	9474
SMRDLSD, DRRDRM, SMR	1565
SMRDLSDRM, SMRDLSD	6806
SMRDL, SDMDR, MRDTDL	8334
SMRDLS, DTDFMMR, SMR	8700
SMRDLSFM, SDDTLS, TR	11779
SMRDLSLTD, TLSLMRD	5834
SMRDLLSFM, MRD#RSFM,	2626
SMRDLLLS, DTLMTLS, R	10268
SMRDTDDMRDD, DMS	8403
SMRDTDRDS, SLTDRMR,	6815
SMRDTDSRM, RDDFMRR,	3871
SMRDTDSRM, TDDFMRR	8201
SMRDTD, SFMR, RDTL	11606
SMRDTD, SLTDDRT, STL	8255
SMRDTDLS, SDMSRRM, S	10960
SMRDTRDLSM, SLDTTR	12283
SMRDTRL, DDTLSS, SMR	6946
SMRDTLDS, SDDRDM, LF	64
SMRDTLDTLS, SFFMDT	12558
SMRDTLFMDTD, RMFSS	1115
SMRDTLSD, RMRMF#S, SS	3410
SMRDTLS, DFMRDDT, SM	8443

SMRDTLSFM, SLTDMRD	12336
SMRDTLS, SDDDRMR, FM	773
SMRD, TLLLLLS, DDTRR	4343
SMRDTLTDS, STDRMSF	6703
SMRDTTLDS, SSFMMR	993
SMRDTTLS, DFMRDDT, S	8442
SMRDTTLS, SDDMRDRM,	4039
SMRDTTLL, LRDTSDRM,	36
SMRRD, DDLS, SRMRD, DM	4772
SMRRDD, MDTL, SLTDRM	9418
SMRRD, DFLS, DTLLS, DF	7434
SMRRDLSLS, SLTDDRMR,	1544
SMRRMR, SMDDRM, DRMM	2973
SMRRMFFM, DTLRSFM, L	426

SMRM

SMRMDRDS, SDDDRDRM,	539
SMRMDTDRDLS, SDDDD	601
SMRMRD, DRMFLS, SSSF	7095
SMRMRD, DSLSSFFFMR	7821
SMRMMSMRD, DLFMFRM	5373
SMRMFRT, SDMRDT, SMR	9621
SMRMFMRDLS, SSFFSM	3392
SMRMFMFS, FMFSLFMR	8685
SMRMFSDTL, SSLLRRDTD,	4830
SMRMSM, RRDRRMS, SMR	7503
SMRMSMRM, SLTLSMR, D	9563
SMRFMDS, DRMLSFMF, L	11072
SMRFMRD, SFMFSRM, SM	3653
SMRFMRD, SFMSRM, SMR	3652
SMRFMRDTLS, SSDTDL	758
SMRFMRLR, DTTDDRSM,	40
SMRSDRDTS, DRMFSFM	5448
SMRSTLDS, DTDRMMR, R	2456
SMRLTLS, SDLDFLMR, S	3477
SMRLTSS, SDLDFLMR, S	3477a
SMRTDDTT, LSDRMMRR,	2005
SMRTDLSM, SDTRDLS, S	2751
SMR#MDDRD, LSDDMMR, S	12028
SMR#MDDRDLS, SSF#SMR	7124
SMR#MRDRM, RDDRDLS, S	3897
SMR#MRDLD, LSSDRMRD	10180
SMR#MRDLS, DTTDRD, SM	5769
SMR#MRDTD, SLS#LRT, SF	7740
SMR#MMSFMDLS, DDTLT	5436
SMR#MFRD#R, SRD#RMDRM	
	1134
SMR#MFMDRDRM, SMR#MF	
	8348
SMR#MFMMRD, DDTLSMR,	9179
SMMDDRDTLS, SLTDMM	10481
SMMDDRRS, LTDDDRMF	9593

SMMDDLDLS, DDMMR, SM	6362
SMMDRDRDMS, SMMDRD	407
SMMDRDRMD, SRTSMDM	9606
SMMDRMMRD, DDDMRDR,	11954
SMMD, TDRD#RLSM, SMMD,	11174
SMMRDDD, LSFMDMRR, S	2954
SMMRDDD, TDRMR, SMMR	5363
SMMRDDF, RRMF#STLS, S	10324
SMMRDDF, RRMF#STLLS,	10324a
SMMRDDFM, DMF#SLRDL,	11264
SMMRDDLLS, SDMDR, SM	10424
SMMRDDTLDS, SSDDRM	7898
SMMRDRD, DSSLLR, RMM	1588
SMMRDRD, MFSMLFR, RM	11692
SMMRDRDLSM, SFMRMF	6906
SMMRD, RMMF#S, SDSFM, S	7316
SMMRDRM, SMDLSMDR, M	12332
SMMRDFM, RDDMRDT, SR	5515
SMMRDFFM, MMRDRM, MS	2384
SMMRDS, SFFMRM, MRMR	615
SMMRDSSLDRDTT, DMS	8536
SMMRDS, LFFMR, SDRMF	3030
SMMRDLD, SLSMR, MFSM	4841
SMMRDLSD, RMMSFMR, F	7252
SMMRDLSSFM, SLTDRM	1911
SMMRRDD, LDDLLSS, SF	9200
SMMRRDM, RMRRRDDLD,	7109
SMMRRDFM, MFSDDRMM,	2248
SMMRRD, SFFMMR, SSSF	7830
SMMRRDS, SLLDLS, SDD	11855
SMMRRD, LFFML, TSSFF	10900
SMMRMDM, RDDLDDDS, M	6602
SMMRMDS, SSSFSM, DLL	11238
SMMRMDS, SSSLSM, DLL	1776
SMMRMFMD, DRRRRMFM	3747
SMMRMFM, RDDRRM, SMM	887
SMMRMFLS, MSMDRMRD	1776a
SMMRMSS, LLDLLSS, SM	8928
SMMRSDDS, SDDRSM, MR	2812
SMMRSMMR, DDFMR, SSD	12423
SMMRTSD, DFFMDR, R#MR	9065
SMMR#R#MD, DRRFFM, SMM	9799
SMMR#MFT, TFFMRS, SSS#	4439
SMMMDDDL, SSMMDR, SS	4936
SMMMDDLD, DTDRRDRM,	3900
SMMMDFMMRR, SRMFFF	4939
SMMMRDDD, SFFFMRRR,	1074
SMMMRD, DRRRMRD, SMM	914
SMMMRDDRRMD, SMMMD	4579
SMMMRDRM, DTLSFMFS	11831
SMMMRDRMFM, SLSSMM	6172
SMMMRDRM, FSLSMMRD	10185
SMMMRDRLS, SRRRMRD,	2084

SMMMRDLD, FMMMRDRS,	8927
SMMMRDLS, DMRRMR, RF	9487
SMMMRDLS, SDDMRDR, S	12192
SMMMRDTD, SSLTDFMR,	3058
SMMMRDTRD, TLRFRMR,	8805
SMMMRDTSSS, SFFFMR	6455
SMMMRDTLTL, SMMMRD	10244
SMMMRRDD, TLLFMMRR,	3700
SMMMRRD, D#D#RMFMRDT,	
	12534
SMMMRRDMDDDLLS, DD	8018
SMMMRMFRT, SDDDTDR,	9955
SMMMRMFMRDDT, DD#RS	8784
SMMMRMFMRD, RRRRDT,	10982
SMMMRMFMRR, SRRRDR	11252
SMMMRLTDRD, DFMRDT	1349
SMMMRLTD, RMFSFMR, S	9090
SMMMR#MMDDRM, SMMMM	
	8367
SMMMR#MFMRD, SRRD#RF	
	6057
SMMMR#MSM, MDDRDRR#M	
	2908
SMMMMD, DMMMF, SFFFF	8523
SMMMMRDDLDS, SDDDD	7255
SMMMMRDMD, MSSSMDM	4906
SMMMMRD, MSSSMSR, SM	3245
SMMMMRMFM, SRFMRD, S	12280
SMMMMMRR, RMRDTD, LF	966
SMMMMMRF, LDTDMRR, S	11727
SMMMMMMRLL, LSFM, MS	8363
SMMMMMM, MMDTDFSFF	11409
SMMMMMMFMM, MRRRDR	
	11092
SMMMMMSDM, MDDRMDR	11250
SMMMMML, DDDTLD, MSS	7828
SMMMMFDM, MRMRLTDR,	7201
SMMMMFM, DMSSSSLS, M	11895
SMMMMFMR, RSLMRDRD	1113
SMMMMSDD, MLTDRM, MR	11830
SMMMMS, DTDFMMR, RFF	11570
SMMMMSSS, RDDSFMR, S	2594
SMMMFRDRM, SLTDRTL	1501
SMMMFMRDRM, SLTDRT	1500
SMMMFMRRDLS, STTTT	4461
SMMMFMRRR, MRDDRRM	11087
SMMMFSDLDS, SLSTD	357
SMMMFSDTL, SLTDRRM,	9838
SMMMFSLS, MSRMFMRM	10442
SMMMSDRM, FMDMRD, SM	5592
SMMMSMMM, SDMSDRMR,	5211
SMMMSMFFLD, LSSSDS	10813
SMMMSS, FMDDTD, MRRS	11520

SMMFMRDTDR, SFFSFM	403	SMFSDRDTL, SLTDLR, M	9236
SMMFMRMD, LSMMRR, SD	5507	SMFSDRMR#M, MRDTDRD	9917
SMMFMRMD, TLDTLS, SM	12046	SMFSDRMMD, LTDDRDL	10837
SMMFMRMD, TLRTLTD, S	1365	SMFSD, RMFSFMR, MFSL	5747
SMMFMRLS, MDDTDR, SM	5949	SMFSDRFM, SLSTDFML,	11995
SMMFMMR, DDTDRMM, SM	10915	SMFSDFMRDLD, SDRMS	3690
SMMFMSFM, SLTDRM, MR	11117	SMFSDFSLTDS, SSLTT	10431
SMMFFDRM, MRRDRMS, S	5186	SMFSDS, SMFSLR, RMMD	11887
SMMFFSSD, RMMMRDR, S	3244	SMFSDSLTDT, SLTDTL	809
SMMFSDTLS, F#F#SLTDT	3766	SMFSDLDS, DDDTDRTD,	4617
SMMFSFR, MMMRDR, MMM	5687	SMFSDLSFM, MFMRDFM	2632
SMMFSLSM, RMLSF#MF#S,	3695	SMFSDTLDLS, FRMTLS	8129
SMMFSLLD, DDDTLS, TT	1725	SMFSDT, LSDFSM, FSDT	8874
SMMFLS, MSFRFM, SMMR	8782	SMFSDTLS, MFMFSMFR,	8595
SMMFTRDDT, LSF#SLSS	9735	SMFS, DTLS, SMFSMRD, S	10482
SMMSDRRM, DFFMMR, SM	8309	SMFSDTLS, LSFMFMRM,	8075
SMMSDMRD, DLSMFSM, M	10314	SMFSDTLL, LSF#SMRR, S	1888
SMMSDMRD, MLSMFSM, M	10313	SMFSRMDFMR, RMF#SLT	7139
SMMSMDRM, RMSDMRS, S	11100	SMFSMRDS, DTDRFMR, S	1979
SMMSF, SRD#RLS, SLMFF	11410	SMFSMRDL, DSDMDR, RM	1216
SMMSSFF, STRFM, SMMS	1081	SMFSMS, DTLSFM, SLLT	8749
SMMTDDT, DLLFLS, SSS	2252	SMFSFDRM, LLSMF#MF#S,11406	
SMFRDDFLS, DDTLMLS#	561	SMFSFMDR, SMFSFMDT	8262
SMFRDMM, SMFRDMM, RS	7096	SMFSFFSDTLSM, SFRS	6914
SMFRRD, RMF#SSF#S, SLSL	10552	SMFSSDRM, SLSDDT, SM	4597
SMFRMD, RMFSLR, SMFS	12516	SMFSSDLS, MRMLSRR, S	1631
SMFRSFRDTD, MMRRF#F#	2217	SMFSSMFRRD, DMFSFM	227
SMFMDDLS, DTDFMR, SM	6449	SMFSSSDDRMFS, SMFS	8619
SMFMDMRRD, LDLSDMR	12197	SMFSSS, DTLLS, SLTDR	8951
SMFMDMR#R, SFFFFM, SM	4447	SMFSSSSLDDD, SSSDR	6327
SMFMRD, DMSLS, LTDT	9505	SMFSSLDDTD, DLDTSL	8714
SMFMRD, SDLSFM, SDTL	5936	SMFSSLMS, FRFMDR	1617
SMFMRD, MFSSLS, SLTD	1757	SMFSSLFS, SDDDTLDS,	7714
SMFMRD, MSDTLS, SLSF	1251	SMFSSLS, DDDDRM, SMF	2591
SMFMRDTD, SLTDTDLS,	1963	SMFSSLSF#S, MMRDRRR	8162
SMFMRDTLS, MFLTL	9153	SMFSSLSF#SM, MRTRDT	11664
SMFMRRMD, SLDTLS, SM	9162	SMFSSLSS, MRMFSM, SM	8200
SMFMRSDRTD, RMFSL	6579	SMFSSLLLLLS, SDDT	9720
SMFMRSRMRD, DDTLSD	10957	SMFSSLTDMMR, RMRDR	5376
SMFMMRR, SRMRRDD, SM	3725	SMFSSLTD, TDTLSLLS,	7709
SMFMFSDTL, SLRDTD, S	4829	SMFSSLTDTLS, DRMFS	1337
SMFMSMRDRLDT, LSS	9339	SMFSLDTD, RMSSF#S, SD	3918
SMFMSSRM, SSDDRDT, D	4001	SMFSLDT, LSLSFM, MRM	2924
SMFFLF#SS, DDLTSLS, S	5268	SMFSLMFS, LSMFSFM, S	9654
SMFSDDLTDL, SMFSDR,	8961	SMFSLS, DDTLLS, SM	1261
SMFSDDTL, SLSFSFMR,	8191	SMFSLS, MFRMRDRD, SS	10529
SMFSDDTLTDS, FSFMM	2313	SMFSLSMFSL, SSLTST	5284
SMFSDDTLTD, LLLSST	3029	SMFSLSMSFMRS, SMFS	10300
SMFSDDTT, DRMFMR, R	305	SMFSLS, MSFMMR, MMR#M	4471
SMFSDDTT, LSDRMMRR,	9325	SMFSLS, FRMSFM, SMFS	7097
SMFSDRDTD, SLDLSM	9572	SMFSLSFMRD, SMSDLS,	11303
SMFSDRDTD, LDLSMSF	9575	SMFSLSFM, RRMMRDT, T	11437
		SMFSLSSFM, SMRMFSM	8027

SMFSLSS, SMFSLSS, SM	3417
SMFSLLL, TLSFM, FLRD	2444
SMFSLTDD, LSDRMRD, S	8265
SMFSLTDS, LFLDTLS, D	5218
SMFSLTDTLSM, FRMFM	8116
SMFSLTDTLS, FMFRMF	12085
SMFSLTDTLS, SDRMLS	10712
SMFSLTDTLLS, SFMRM	7182
SMFSTD, DTDTLS, MFSL	2747
SMFSTLSM, FSRM, SMFS	10433
SMSDDDTLS, FMFSLR, S	3384
SMSDDDTLTD, SMSLSL	12222
SMSDDRD, DFMRDMR, RM	12322
SMSDDRRM, DTDFMRRR,	7394
SMSDDTDFMRRM, SS	12288
SMSDDTRSRFFM, SDMS	1363
SMSDDTLS, SDMRDT, RM	3169
SMSDDTTD, MDMLSS, SR	3793
SMSDRD, DLDRMR, DTLS,	6668
SMSDRD, DLDRMR, SSFM	6668a
SMSDRMM, MSFDFM, MSS	1814
SMSDRM, SLSMDR, RSF#L	639
SMSDMDLD, SMSDTRR, S	3515
SMSDMRDTD, MRSLSF#S,	9511
SMSDMR#MR, DRDLS, SSS	7353
SMSDMMR, DDTLTD, SMS	9350
SMSDMFSLR, SMF#STLS	983
SMSDMFSLR, SFMF#SLT	984
SMSDMFSLS, SRSMF#SR	1692
SMSDML, LSMMRR, RSTT	2773
SMSDFMRD, MFSMFLS, L	3546
SMSDFMR, RMF#SSF#S, SM	4109
SMSDSDRM, RMFSFMRD,	11763
SMSDSLDS, SSSFMMR, S	6697
SMSDSLSS, DTSTLS, SR	1826
SMSDS, LTDDTLS, FRST	6074
SMSDSLTD, RMTDLSFM,	12042
SMSDLDLS, SSSMMMRD	12175
SMSDLSRM, MRF#SLTDF#	9312
SMSDTDRM, SLTDRMFR,	10616
SMSDTL, SMDMF#S, SLDT	2848
SMSDTLS, FMRLSFM, SS	6047
SMSDTLTD, DSMLSMMR,	11494
SMSMDRDLS, SMSDDMR	10859
SMSMDM, MFSDMRD.	3122
SMSMDM, FMRRDRM, SMS	12231
SMSMDLDS, TDRDTLS, F	6696
SMSMRDDRDLS, SSFFL	4478
SMSMRDTL, DSDDMR, SM	6761
SMSMMRR, MTDDRLT, DD	11436
SMSM, MMRD, DDRDRDMD,	8626
SMSMMFMRDR, RRRRMF	10395
SMSMFFFMR, MMFSSLS	1843

SMSMSMRDRMM, SMSMM	10238
SMSMSM, MSFRM, LFFLS	11628
SMSMSFLR, RMFMRDRM,	5655
SMSFMRDSR, MFRLDTR	72
SMSFMRD, SLTDTLT, LS	683
SMSFMRL, DTLSFM, MSF	4485
SMSFMRTLS, DTDFDM, M	3361
SMSFM, MRMFR, DTLSTL	
	12415
SMSFSSSSSM, RRMFMR	5884
SMSSDRDTLTD, RMRDR	6617
SMSSFMRD, DRMFLTD, S	3892
SMSSFMR, RMDRDTDD, S	491
SMSSFMR, RMDFRMDD, S	490
SMSSFMFL, LTDRTD	9152
SMSSSDMD, DLSMDRM, S	4263
SMSSSMSSS, MSSLSMM	5679
SMSSSMSS, SLDTLS, SM	12110
SMSSLMMFLLTS, SMMM	1919
SMSSLSFM, DDTL, RRDT	12074
SMSLD, DMDMD, SMSLD, L	8929
SMSLDRD, DTDLSS, SMS	11793
SMSLDRMSLD, RMMSRM	374
SMSLDSFM, SDMFMRDR,	9413
SMSLDS, LDTLS, SLTDR	3603
SMSLDTS, FMDRRM, SFM	11467
SMSLMS, MRMFSMRD, DR	9073
SMSLFRFSMDMSR, SMS	8326
SMSLSDSM, SFSLSTSR,	9640
SMSLSFRM, SDTLLS, SD	10434
SMSLSFMRD, MRDRMFMR,	
	6892
SMSLSFMRM, SDTLLS, S	10435
SMSLSFM, MRDDTD, SMS	2019
SMSLSFM, MRMRRD, SMS	2018
SMSLSFSM, SDTLTSF#S	9754
SMSLSS, SFMRRD, SMSD	10417
SMSLSLTD, DTRMDTLS,	4548
SMSLLD, SMSLLD, DRMM	10397
SMSTLSDM, RTRFMRM, F	1579
SMLDSFM, RMF#SLLS, SM	5380
SMLDTLSM, DDRMSLS, S	9542
SMLRMFFFSL, LSFSFM	10230
SMLFRSMD, DTLSFRT, M	7393
SMLSDDTD, SDSLF#S, TD	9268
SMLSDDTLTDS, DTLSM	8606
SMLSDFMR, MMFMDMRD,	1459
SMLSDTLSFMRR, SDDT	4100
SMLSMDFM, MRDTDRM, S	11538
SMLSMDLS, MMMLS#LT, D	
	11204
SMLSMRDS, DTLDTLS, S	11095
SMLSMFFRSFM, SLDSD	675

SMLSMFSFMRD, RMRMS	9399	SFMRDLDDT, DRMFRSF	9923
SMLSFDFM, SRMFLSFM,	292	SFMRDLS, MRDFMR, RMF	6724
SMLSFMR, MFSFMRD, RM	10602	SFMRDLSFMR, MFSLSL	9747
SMLSFM, MFLSMR, SSSL	1334	SFMRDTDD, RMFSLSFM,	9272
SMLSFMFMR, SMLSFMF#	1664	SFMRDTD, DLTDTLSFM,	739
SMLSFM, SDFMRD, MRSF#	2506	SFMRDTDR, DSSS#LF#S, S	10124
SMLSFMSFRM, SMLSFM	3335	SFMRDTDR, MLDTRS, SL	1820
SMLSFFRSFM, MRDDFM	4782	SFMRDTDFMRM, MRF#SR	1521
SMLSFFM, DTDSFMR, SD	1514	SFMRDTDLRS, DTRSF#S,	11658
SMLSSMRMSFFM, SMLS	8670	SFMRDTLFMDTD, RMFS	1114
SMLS, SMLSMDR, SMRF, D	11539	SFMRDTL, LLTDTLS, SL	6618
SMLSSLDD, SFMLSSMR	2058	SFMRRD, MRSSF#S, DLTS	2247
SMLS, SLSMMR, SDDMDL	11425	SFMRRD, MSLR, SSMRM	5401
SMLSLTD, DTDSLLS, FF	1735	SFMRRLLSFFM, MRDDT	1032
SMLSLTDS, MFSDTLRT,	838	SFMRMDRMRDD, MSSMD	191
SMLS, TLSDS, LDLSSLS	4456	SFMRMDRMFLRS, SFMF	10797
SMLTDDT, LDSMFMRD, S	8811	SFMRMDTL, RSMLSF, RM	6908
SMLTDDT, LDLSFMRD, S	8813	SFMRMDTL, SDRM, LRDT	5337
SMLTDFMRM, MRF#SSDT	1519	SFMRMRDMS, SLSMMRD	5405
SMTDDDDRTD, DRRRRM,	5508	SFMRMFRD, MFSLLR, SL	5499
SMTDRDLSMLS, SLLLR	5123	SFMRMFM, MRSLLS, SLT	9381
SMTDRT, TDLSSS, SLTD	6966	SFMRMFSM, SLFRSFM, S	4230
SMTDMLS, FMSRSD, MLS	5045	SFMRMSFR, RMFRMSFM,	3147
SMTDSLSFM, SLTDRDT,	10507	SFMR, MSSDTLT, DLTSD	7633
SMTDLDT, RSLFMRM, SM	11212	SFMRFMRD, DRFMLSF#M,	3034
SMTDLSFM, MRSF#SLTL	5807	SFMRFMRDMRDTRDD, F	2545
SMTRDMFLSS, SDRMRD	10923	SFMRFMRD, MLSTDFMR,	8635
SMTRDLSMS, SLRMFLS,	11407	SFMRFMRD, TLSLDTD, S	1540
SMTRDLSLS, SLTDDRM	1545	SFMRFM, SFMRRD, TDTD	76
SMTRDTLS, SDDRRM, MM	5415	SFMRLSFM, DLSFFMF#S,	11227
SFDMRDMSDDTL, SSSL	7408	SFMRLSFMDTLSLF#S, S	2416
SFDMRDMSDDT, LSLSF	7407	SFMR#MR#MS, MDLTDLSD,	
SFRDRM, SDTLSMSFMF	4853		12153
SFRD, STLSFMFS, SFRD,	7200	SFMMRDDTRDTL, FMRR	1916
SFRMDRRD, FMRRD#R, RM	1330	SFMMRDDTLDLS, SDDD	10801
SFMDDMMR, RMFRRTDS,	6124	SFMMRDRDLL, SDDDRM	9859
SFMDRDLSM, MFSDMSF	10522	SFMMRDRMMF#S, SLSF#S,	1950
SFMDRMRDRS, LTDRMF	610	SFMMRDRMM, SFMFMRD	6856
SFMDRTDS, LTDLSMR, S	10008	SFMMRD, RMFM, SFMMRD,	10711
SFMDTLL, SMSFM, SFMD	3647	SFMMRDRMFFM, RFMLL	10327
SFMD#RSMRDD, SDTTLS	5770	SFMMRDRM, FSFMMRR,	1283
SFMRDDRMD, RMFRMRD	7485	SFMMRD, MRTTLS, RRMF	9331
SFMRDDRMSFM, SMDLS	11505	SFMMRDMLS, FMRRRMF	5136
SFMRDDL, DLSDMDMR, S	1153	SFMMRDLS, MRDSMR, SF	5797
SFMRDDLSFM, SDSLLT	9425	SFMMR, RRRMRD, MFMMR,	
SFMRDRD, MFSLSFMMR	7571		11762
SFMRDRMDLS, STTRRF	10587	SFMMRRMFFM, MRMSMM	8630
SFMRDMRD, SSDTDR, ML	3316	SFMMRR, LSRLSSF#, MF#R#	
SFMRDSDRMRD, SFMRD	326		8351
SFMR, DSDTLS, TDLFMR,	5988	SFMMR, RLLSFFM, MRDD	1031
SFMRD, SRRDT, SDTLSM	1587	SFMMRMMRMRD, DRRSS	1511
SFMRDSS#LLR, RMRSRR#	31	SFMMRMSF, FMRRDRM, S	5321
SFMRDSLTD, DTLSLSF	10076	SFMMRLTDRFM, RMRD, T	5859

1124

SSDDDDRDTT, TDTLLL	2464		SSDDRMFM, SMFRSRMR	6114
SSDDDDRMRTD, DRMRD	4407		SSDDRMFM, SSSFMRDT	11573
SSDDDDRMMRDR, SSRR	11929		SSDDRMFS, LSMDTDRM	7309
SSDDDDRMMM, MRDRDL	12172		SSDDRFMM, DDMMLLSS,	3123
SSDDDDRMMM, MMRRRM	6045		SSDDRFMM, DMRRTRDD,	8781
SSDDDDRMSS, SFMRDR	6521		SSDDRTD, MMFMR, SSMD	4528
SSDDDDMDS, SSLLDTL	10842		SSDDRTDS, DRMFMRDD	4323
SSDDDDMRDLDS, SSDD	7953		SSDDMDRD, MRDTLLS, S	5752
SSDDDDTDSM, DRFFMR	4598		SSDDMDRR, FLSMFRD, S	2310
SSDDDDTRR, RRDMMDR,	5096		SSDDMRDRDL, LLSSDR	5027
SSDDDDTLSF#LS, SSTL	5074		SSDDMRDR, MMSDTDRD,	4821
SSDDDRMMR, RMFFFMR	6921		SSDDMRDL, LLSDMMR, S	1140
SSDDDRMMRMD, RMRRR	5443		SSDDMRDT, LTDMSFMM	3311
SSDDDRMSSLLLTD, LL	10047		SSDDMMR, MFRLTD, MRR	3486
SSDDDRSFMD, SLLSFM	8840		SSDDMMMMRD, SLDSLL	7080
SSDDDMDSLDS, DRMSS	5052		SSDDMFSLDT, LSMDRR,	12216
SSDDDMRDTL, LRSTRS	6140		SSDDMS, DFMMRD, DSSD	8080
SSDDDMMR, DRMDMRD, S	3129		SSDDMSLS, MFLDLS, MM	7478
SSDDDMSMMR, FFMFRD	4502		SSDDFMRD, DRMMMRDR,	3124
SSDDDSDRMMM, FMRMR	6593		SSDDLSSD, DRMSMDR, S	12136
SSDDDTDRL, LLTTTTL	3095		SSDD, TDRRMFSFMRD, S	11755
SSDDDTSSFFFFM, SSL	908		SSDDTDFMRRM, SSSSM	12289
SSDDDTLSLFM, SLTDR	4222		SSDDTDLSFFM, SSSLS	2183
SSDDDTLSLS, MMSSFM	9667		SSDDTRDTLSDS, DRMR	2839
SSDDDTLLS, SSDDDTD	11904		SSDDT, SRMRD, MSSSFM	10258
SSDDDTLTDS, LTDRMS	2175		SSDDT, SRFFM, SMDR, SS	3662
SSDDDTLT, SSRRRDTD,	4464		SSDDTSSRRD, SLLFMR,	3599
SSDDDTTTLTD, DRMMM	6175		SSDD, TLSDD, SLLFLLS,	12349
SSDDRDRMD, FFMDR, SS	1964		SSDDTLSDRM, SSFFMRD	586
SSDDRDRMFF, MRDMRL	193		SSDDTLS, MMSDDRD, SS	8790
SSDDRDRMS, SLSMMRD	9930		SSDDTLS, SSLLSF#S, SS	1948
SSDDRDRM, LDLSDMRT	9120		SSDDTLTLS, SSDDDTD	1818
SSDDRDT, DRD#RR#M, SSD	9836		SSDDTLTT, SSRRDTRD,	12149
SSDDRDT, DRD#RMD, SSM	5297		SSDDTTDS, SLTDDRD, D	7158
SSDDRDT, LLRRFTD, MM	7545		SSDDTT, SSRRDD, DRLD	1052
SSDDRDTT, DRDRRM, SS	4234		SSDDTTLFTLS, SDRMD	11465
SSDDRDTT, FFRSFM, SS	11682		SSDDTTLL, LRSSFFMM,	12395
SSDDRRM, DDFMRDRMR,	4374		SSDDTTLL, LSSLSS, SS	4208
SSDDRRM, DDFMRDMR,	4374a		SSDRDDT, LSSLFM, SSD	6989
SSDDRRMD, MMSSFMR, L	7535		SSDRDRM, LTDRD, SDDD	1218
SSDDRRMD, SSLFRSM,	10469		SSDRDTD, RMRDTLS, FF	8279
SSDDRRM, DTLSLSFM, S	10474		SSDRDTDMRDT, DLTDD	9358
SSDDRR, MRDTTL, RRRL	11976		SSDRM, DDRDLS, SSDMS	7735
SSDDRRM, RMRDTLS, SS	4086		SSDRMDRDRM, MFMRMD	6418
SSDDRRM, RMRDTLS, SS	4113		SSDRMDRR, MRDRDTD, S	4294
SSDDRRMM, DDFMRDMR	4374b		SSDRMDLS#LTL, RRTDR	11323
SSDDRRMFS, SMMRFRD	446		SSDRMRDRMRD, SSDRM	12203
SSDDRRM, SSFMRRMR, S	6393		SSDRMRDSS, RMFFFFM,	6300
SSDDRMDR, MDMRDLD, L	9980		SSDRMRDL, TDRMFMR, S	2847
SSDDRMD, SSLDFM, DRM	7240		SSDRMRL, DTLTSD, SMR	3000
SSDDRMR, DLDDLS, SSS	10853		SSDRMMRR, RTDMRD, M	1369
SSDDRM, MMMFMR, TSTR	12232		SSDRMMMRDDT, SSLTD	8400
SSDDRMFMRDT, SSLMF	508		SSDRMMFDRM, MMRLTD	9768

SSDRMMSFDRM, MMFLT	10959	SSDMSDDTLTD, DDTLS	124
SSDRMMLL, LLRMFFTT,	5327	SSDMSMSFRSM, SLFLS	8424
SSDRMFMRS, DRMSDRD,	4303	SSDMSSFR, FMDTDR, SS	3172
SSDRMFFSSS, SLL#L, SF	11569	SSDMSSTT, STRFLLSS, S	4476
SSDRMFS, MSFMDRD, MR	4806	SSDMSLSSM, MFMMRLS	11339
SSDRMFSLMSM, SSDRM	11118	SSDFMR, DDTLS, LLTDR	5833
SSDRMF#S, SSSMLMSR, S	8488	SSDFMRRD, SLRRMR, SS	6654
SSDRMS, MMRDL, SSDRM	3573	SSDFMMRD, TLDFLS, SS	8074
SSDRMSFMR, MF#SDTSL,	11536	SSDFFM, RRSDDT, TDDR	8957
SSDRMSS, FMRDRDTL, S	9130	SSDSDRMD, FMRDTLS, S	6813
SSDRMSLSMR, MFMRMR	4748	SSDSDRMRD, MFSSFMR,	5864
SSDRSM, RDDRDT, TLSS	6789	SSDSDRM, SSSMDR, SSD	9649
SSDRS, SSDRMF, MFSDL	10197	SSDSDMRR, SSSDMRD, S	4391
SSDRLSFM, SMSLDT, DS	9394	SSDSDMSDMSDMSDM, D	10689
SSDRTD, DMSFMR, TDMR	2831	SSDSMMRD, DRMFLTRD,	10362
SSDMDDLS, DTDRDDT, S	12335	SSDSMMSM, DRRM, SSDS	3853
SSDMDDLS, SSDMDR	3103	SSDSMMSM, MMRMFMR, S	5316
SSDMDDLSSS, DSFMSD	6075	SSDSMFMR, RMRTDRDT,	10337
SSDMDRDDLS, SSDRMF	1157	SSDSMFFR, RDRMDSMM	1280
SSDMDRDL, LSDMDMRR,	3821	SSDSMFSRFM, SMRDTS	2106
SSDMDRMRMR, SSDMDM	9739	SSDSMFSM, SDTTLLS, M	8624
SSDMDRTD, DDMSMFRM,	517	SSDSMFS, SSLLLLS, SS	7188
SSDMDRTDTS, MFSMDD	2148	SSDSMFSLLS, SDTSTR	8669
SSDMDMMRLTDS, SSDM	5017	SSDSMFLS, DRMFLSFM	10308
SSDMDSSLS, SFFMDR, T	3424	SSDSMLSS, SDTTLTD, S	6604
SSDMDLDS, DRSSDRM, M	8140	SSDSFMRD, SFMMRDS,	1078
SSDMDLDS, SDDDDMDR,	42	SSDSFML, RRSFMRM, SS	486
SSDMDLTD, RRDTLSFM,	9191	SSDSSMFFF, FFTLSFM	1166
SSDMDTLDLLS, SSLSM	3291	SSDSSFFM, RMFSMRDR,	1738
SSDMRDDT, SSTFMRMD,	8230	SSDSSFFM, LLSMRDR, S	6548
SSDMRDDTLS, FMDLSF#	7816	SSDSLDR, MRDMRLTS, S	6215
SSDMRDDTT, TDRFMRR	2465	SSDSLSSM, SSFRSFM, S	1073
SSDMRDMSF, MMRLDRD,	5806	SSDSLLS, MRDTLLS, SS	4793
SSDMRDSD, RDRM, RDDL	5795	SSDSTLS, RRDLSF#S, TT	1146
SSDMRDLD, SSDLSSMR,	11868	SSDSTLS, MFSLSFMR, S	4286
SSDMRDLS, SSDMDR, FM	3101	SSDLDS, MMMFDRM, SSS	6736
SSDMRDTDRMFFM, MMR	9197	SSDLRDTD, MRMRDTDR	6947
SSDMRDTDLS, DDTR, FL	7914	SSDLSDMRRD, RMSMRD	5745
SSDMRMFM, MFSLSMDM	2385	SSDLSMFRD, D#RMFSMR,	3078
SSDMRMFS, MRDRSLDT,	4881	SSDLSM, FMRDR, MMFLS	4266
SSDMRMSDFMR, SLSFM	6559	SSDLSMFSDLTLS, SSR	5119
SSDMRLLS, SFMSF#MR#M,	8939	SSDLSFSM, MSDTLS, SM	5453
SSDMMDDDLL, LSDMFM	11282	SSDLSSMRD, SDDMSLS	4621
SSDMMDLS, DRRDRM, MS	9883	SSDLLD, RRDLDLS, LLS	3346
SSDMMRD, MMLSFMR, MM	1851	SSDLTDS, SLLSFM, MFS	7783
SSDMMRDS, SDMSSDMR	4721	SSDTDRMRMFSMD, MFS	10716
SSDMMRDL, RDLSDMDR,	4690	SSDTDRM, MMSMRDR, MM	2104
SSDMMRFRDTD, SLLDT	12246	SSDTDRMFRM, SFMRMR	10494
SSDMMRFM, MRFMRDTD	11177	SSDTDRMSFMR, TRDLR	1482
SSDMMFMRR, SSTRFFF	5856	SSDTDRLR, DTDRD#RMD,	969
SSDMMSMRFTD, SSDMM	4004	SSDTDRTD, MRTDLSF#S,	434
SSDMFMRR, SSTRMD, SS	9715	SSDTDMMRLDTLS, SLT	12239
SSDMFMMRMFSFM, DDT	766	SSDTDFRM, MMTLTSSS	161

SSDT DSLS, SSSSDRMR	11817
SSDTRDTD, TDRR#MFT, S	9851
SSDTRDT LS, LSMMRD	689
SSDT, RFLS, DMFSLSMR,	4482
SSDT FFLS, SSDTTLS, D	7979
SSDT SRFM, DTLRSLS, S	10439
SSDT SLT, RDTDT LS, SS	9703
SSDT LDDS, MMRDT LS, S	9431
SSDT LDS, DRMDRMR, MR	12389
SSDT LRDDT LTDS, MMR	9280
SSDT LSRDT, SSRT LST	3370
SSDT LSMDRM, MRSLT	670
SSDT LSMM, RDDMRDLS,	11193
SSDT LSFMRMRDS, SSL	3829
SSDT LSFM, MRDFRMMR,	11961
SSDT LSFMMRFL, TDTR	11906
SSDT LSFM, MMRSSF#S, S	11447
SSDT LSFM, MMSDMRMD,	8178
SSDT LSFM, SDLRSLT L	2533
SSDT LSFSFM, MF#SDT L	5451
SSDT LSFSFM, MSDT LS	5452
SSDT LSSFM, LDMRDT L	2317
SSDT LS, SSMFMR, SSDT	3072
SSDT LS, SSFFM, SLTDD	5685
SSDT LS, SSLSFM, MFSS	11430
SSDT LS, SLLLLL, LRT L	2772
SSDT LSTLS, SSFMRDM	4409
SSDT LTDS, DRMDFMR, S	806
SSDT LTDS, SLSLLTM, S	309
SSDT LT, SSRDTD, SMRD	4457
SSDT TTLTD, SLTDRDT	10969
SSRDR, MRDDLS, DRMRM	10849
SSRDMFLS, RMSDT LF#R,	9722
SSRDT LSDM, SSRDT LS	4653
SSRDT LSFMD, DDRDMR	10739
SSRRDRMRD, SSRRDRM,	11273
SSRRRD#RMDM, SSRRRD	5210
SSRRMRDM, MRRMRR, SS	1561
SSRRMRDS, SSLDTDR, S	11096
SSRRMR, SSMMFM, SDDM	510
SSRRSSMM, MMRSF#S, MF	7381
SSRFMRDTMRRD, TLMM	6012
SSRFMM, LLMSFF, SLTD	3235
SSRSSRFFMM, SSRSSR	12473

SSM

SSMDDDRMFM, MMRDT L	10768
SSMDDRMSF, FMRDMDR	8859
SSMDDRFM, SSMSDT LM	10946
SSMDDSMMRMD, DDT LS	224
SSM, DDS, MFFFFSFMMF	38
SSMDDSMSFRM, SSMDD	8257

SSMDDS, MSSSS, SLDDD	892
SSMDDLDD, DMDSMR, SS	4480
SSMDDL, SSDDRMMR, SS	11869
SSMDDL, LSSDT LS, SSM	5208
SSMDDT LS, MFSMFR, MM	3314
SSMDDT LSFM, MRMFRS	8544
SSMDDT LLSFM, MMLTD	7117
SSMDRDRMDS, SSMDRD	9769
SSMDRDLLS, SDDDMRD	6656
SSMDRMRD, RMSSF#S, RM	4000
SSMDRMR, SSMDRMR, SM	4804
SSMDRMFMR, SSMDRMF	445
SSMDRMFS, SSDMDRD, S	4028
SSMDRMFLS, SDT LSMR	2168
SSMDRM, SDSLFM, SFMR,	1937
SSMDRM, SFMRRD, SSLF	789
SSMDRM, SLDT LS, SMSD	3863
SSMDRML, SDFMDMR, MD	6478
SSMDRSRMRD, MSM FRD	1805
SSMDMDDT L, LLSF#FMR	6317
SSMDMSSLLS, SSFSDF	5518
SSMDFLS, SSMDFLS, DS	8896
SSMDSMFMRFLS, SSMD	11794
SSMDSMSLFRM, SDDMR	2729
SSMDSSSFRS, SSMDDT	3611
SSMDSSSSMDMRRRMF	938
SSMDSLLL, LLRRMR, RM	11986
SSMDLDSD, RMRDRMR, S	948
SSMDLSMS, SDDMDR, RM	618
SSMDTDMRTS, SLSTRF	6972
SSMDTDMRTS, LSTRFT	6973
SSMDTRRD, DTTLDLS, S	6480
SSMDTLMRDT, RTSMRD	10994
SSMDT LS, MFRMFLSSM,	9020
SSMDTT LL, LRRSFM, SS	6487
SSMRDDRMFM, SDRMSF	6079
SSMRDDMST LMS, SLFM	2507
SSMRDDLF#S, SLLLTDR,	4971
SSMRDDT, DRD#RR#M, DDS	4863
SSMRDDT, LSFMRRD, T L	10830
SSMRDD#RFMR, RSFMRD	10345
SSMRDRDT, DDLSFMR, S	3995
SSMRDRDT, TDFMMRM, M	2133
SSMRDRFFM, DMSLLS, S	12382
SSMRDMFSLLS, LSRMF#	6863
SSMRDS, DDRSM, SSM	10078
SSMRDS, DFSDL, LSFS	10079
SSMRDSS, DDLFLD, TLS	11420
SSMRDSSMFS, DT LFST	5070
SSMRDSSFMMR, SDRML	7045
SSMRDSLS, DRMFRDD, S	6051
SSMRDS, LLDDS, S#S#LDM	559
SSMRDSLLS, LTDSLSF	10068

SSMRDLLS, SSSLDT LS,	6744	
SSMRDTD, SSSSLTDT, S	3368	
SSMRDTRDLS, SLRDTD,	8954	
SSMRDT L, SSDT DR, SSM	12544	
SSMRRDLSMS, SSRDT F	7021	
SSMRRDLS, SST LSLSF#	1155	
SSMRRDLLSS, SSFRMR	7687	
SSMRMRD, D#RMFLS, FMM	9270	
SSMRMFMMRD, SSDDDD	11915	
SSMRLT, SDDDDLS, FMD	3985	
SSMRTDS, SLDFLS, DDT	6950	
SSMRT FFF, LSMRTDRM	12416	
SSMMDDSLTLSLTLS, S	7336	
SSMMDDL, LSMMDR, SSM	7018	
SSMMDRDLS, SDDMDR, S	10970	
SSMMDRDTT, SSFFRMR	438	
SSMMDR, SLF#S, SSMMSL,	11322	
SSMMDLFF, LSMMDR, SS	12510	
SSMMRD, SSFFMR, RMSS	5930	
SSMMRDS, SLDDTD, SSM	1633	
SSMMRDLL, DSDDRMR, S	7425	
SSMMRDT F, MRDDRR#M, M	4654	
SSMMRRD, DDDTTL, MMR	2396	
SSMMRRD, DDFFMR, RRL	1437	
SSMMRRDD, LLDDLLS, S	6030	
SSMMRRD, LLFFMR, DTS	6270	
SSMMRMDS, SSMMRMD, L	7151	
SSMMRMFLS, SDRMRMF	12414	
SSMMRM, SSMMRD, SLLD	6411	
SSMMMDDDTDMMR, RMF	545	
SSMMMDDRDLS, SSDMS	9063	
SSMMMD, DRSRMFM, SSM	8141	
SSMMMDDTRFFM, SSDT	546	
SSMMMRDDT, LSSDRDT,	8645	
SSMMMRDRMFL, TLSFF	10205	
SSMMMRDLRR, TTTTLS	7960	
SSMMMSFR, FMSDLS, SS	3960	
SSMMFMRR, DTLSLSD, S	3512	
SSMMSSRR, MFSLTS, SS	6785	
SSMMSSFF, FFMRMFM, S	7383	
SSMFRDDFMRM, MRF#SL	5835	
SSMFMRRD, SSMF#SLLS,	376	
SSMFSDDT LS, SSFMRF	3006	
SSMFSDDT, LLSDRMRD.	6710	
SSMFSDDTLLS, SSTDR	26	
SSMFSDDTT, LSLFSM, S	2530	
SSMFSDRDTD, SLDLSM	9574	
SSMFSDRM, RDDDRDLD	5303	
SSMFSDMDRD, MFFFFS	37	
SSMFSDTLS, SSMFSDT	3229	
SSMFSDTTLS, SSRMFF	11778	
SSMFSRM, RRDRMTD,	12047	
SSMFSMDR, FMRMFLS, M	6400	

SSMFSM, DTDR, MSDRMF	4231
SSMFSMRDDD, TLSSLS	3414
SSMFSMRDDLSM, RMFS	12313
SSMFSMRDR, TDDRMFM	10545
SSMFSMM, DDMRTD, SSM	9110
SSMFSSDS, SLSMDR, SS	10848
SSMFSSM, MSSMFSSM, M	11374
SSMFSSM, SSMFSSM, MM	11373
SSMFSSSLDLS, SSMFS	10980
SSMFSLMSF#F, FFRMFT	10897
SSMFSLFMRD, RMRTSL	872
SSMFSLS, DTLTLS, SLL	1418
SSMFSLSM, SLLTTD, MR	7652
SSMFSLSM, LLLDDLS, S	9741
SSMFSLSF, FFRMFSFM,	7920
SSMFSLSSS, LMF#SRDT	11581
SSMFSLS, SLDTLSFM, D	10026
SSMFSLLSD, DRRRRDR	7491
SSMFSL, LSDMRD, DTLT	515
SSMFSLLS, SDTLMF#S, S	4162
SSMFSLL, LLF#SLTT, DD	2795
SSMFSLTDTLS, SSFMR	10393
SSMFLSM, DDFSLR, SSM	5941
SSMFLSMRDTLS, FMSD	9396
SSMFLSM, SDDRRMSDT	73
SSMFL, SSMMR, SSMFL, S	1945
SSMFLS, SSFRM, DDTDR	9446
SSMSDDRMDRM, MRRRS	10351
SSMSDDSD, MRDMRD, SS	7041
SSMSDDLD, TLSMFRM, L	11551
SSMSDDLS, MLSMDMR, S	3586
SSMSDRD, LSDSSFM, SS	8331
SSMSDRMDDTTTDRD, S	4934
SSMSDMDDT, LSMSDR, S	11985
SSMSDSMSFSFR, FFRF	7456
SSMSDSMSSFFM, SSMS	1354
SSMSRMDL, LDSDTDR, S	11158
SSMSMDSD, RMRSMRDR,	7596
SSMSMDLS, DDMS, SSMS	6257
SSMSMSLSF, FFRFRFS	11285
SSMSFRFMF, MR, RMFSL	575
SSMSSDDT LS, SFMRMF	10392a
SSMSSDDT LS, SSFMRM	10392
SSMSSDRM, MRDMRDL, D	6804
SSMSSMSDMRDT LSL, T	11066
SSMSSMSFRFM, MMFLS	4838
SSMSSMSFRFM, SSMSS	10713
SSMSSFMF, FFMRLSFM,	7802
SSMSSFFFF, FTLTDSS	11768
SSMSLDRMRDDLS, SSM	10085
SSMSLR, FFRFSM, SSMM,	439
SSMSLF, LSDRMR, RMMF	5016
SSMSLS, FFTLLS, DSMD	3874

SSMSLSSM, DRMDMMR, D	10204		SSFMMMRD, SLTDTLS, L	9882
SSMSLSLDD, RMRRDLS,	781		SSFMMMRMSF, FFMRRL	8525a
SSMSLLDTLS, SSSDSM	8609		SSFMMMMRD, SLTDFMR,	793
SSMSL, LSSSDRRM, FMM	7492		SSFMMMMRMSF, FFMRR	8525
SSMLMSFM, DRMFLS, DT	430		SSFMMMMRMSF, STRSS	4341
SSMLFSSMLFSMSRMD,	5900		SSFMMMFSLSFR, RRDT	7881
SSMLS, MMMRFM, SDTLT	5377		SSFMFR, LSFMRM, DTRD	9564
SSMLSSRR, MFSLTDSS,	8799		SSFMFMRD, DFMSFTDR,	10042
SSMLSSFMSR, RMDFRS	10220		SSFMFMRD, LSFRMFR, S	9310
SSMLSSFF, MMRDRM, SL	9910		SSFMFMRMRDR, SDDRM	12103
SSMLSLTD, RMDTLS, RT	9475		SSFMFMMFSDTTLL, LM	7968
SSFRMDS, DMRMFRS, SS	6674		SSFMFSD, DTLTD, SSFM	2754
SSFMDDSS, SLSFMR, SS	7208		SSFMFS, DTDFMR, SSFM	8085
SSFMDDT, DTLSLLS, SS	9583		SSFMFSMR, MFFLFM, SF#	4773
SSFMDDTL, LSLSMR, SS	7963		SSFMFSMM, MMMTDLR, S	4530
SSFMDRMD, DFFDRM, SS	6084		SSFMFS, LSFMRMFM, SS	1828
SSFMDRMF, FFFFLSFM,	6202		SSFMFSLS, LSFMRD, SS	6750
SSFM, DLTDLS, MFMR, SM	3534		SSFMSDDRTD, MRRMRD	11833
SSFMDTLS, LSMFRRM, M	6134		SSFMSDRM, SLTDTLLS,	2135
SSFMDTLL, LSMSFM, SS	3646		SSFMSDTL, LSMDDR, DR	6887
SSFMRD, DTLSLSFM, FF	7120		SSFMSMTRD, DLSDLSF	7405
SSFMRDRD, RRMF#SSF#S,	7170		SSFMSFMRMFS, SSFMDR	3089
SSFMRDRMR, SSFMRDR	9728		SSFMSFMR, FMDLRDT, S	9517
SSFMRD, RMMFMR, SSFM	12555		SSFMSSLSFMMRMMF#F#	8281
SSFMRDS, SLDRDS, SSF	509		SSFMSLSDMFSFM, DTL	4099
SSFMRDS, TDRMFR, SSF	6926		SSFMSLSFMR, SSFMSL	154
SSFMRDS, TDRMFSS, SS	6925		SSFMSLTD, DDTLDTLS,	7870
SSFMRDLS, SDTLSSF#S,	6867		SSFMLSMFMRDS, SDDR	1932
SSFMRDTDFMR, FMLF#F#	5959		SSFMLSFM, DTLSFM, SS	5060
SSFMRDTD, SDTLSMDR	1003		SSFMLSFMRFM, MMMLL	6967
SSFMRDT, SSFMRDT, DR	9842		SSFFMRDRM, DRMMFSF#	11905
SSFMRDTLFMR, MSF#MF#	7701		SSFFMMDRMRDD, SSFF	5569
SSFMRDD, RRMRMLF#S, D	3557		SSFFMMRD, DRMFLS, FM	6422
SSFMRRD, LLLSFM, DTL	3480		SSFFMSSDDRDDT, TDT	662
SSFMRMRDRR, MFMLSF	8438		SSFSDLLSFSD, RRRMF	11296
SSFMRMRD, TDRMFS, SL	11392		SSFSMR, MSSLS, DDTLS	3642
SSFMRMLSL, TDMSFM, R	8777		SSFLFFM, MMRLFLS, SD	8209
SSFMRFM, SLTDTLLS, R	1628		SSF#MRTSL, TDLLS#LTS	4047
SSFMRLLSFM, SDTMF#S	11618		SSF#FTLTD, SSLTLSTD,	12310
SSFMRTSL, TDLLS#LTS	4048		SSF#SDRDDT, LSTDRMF	5472
SSFMMRDDL, DSSDMMS	7961		SSF#SDMMR#MFM, MRD#RL	
SSFMMRDDTLS, SSLSS	7169			10918
SSFMMRDDTLS, SLTDF	5475		SSF#SDLS, DDTDRRR, SS	6242
SSFMMRDDTLTD, DFML	7879		SSF#SRSSR#DSR#R#FSR#D,	
SSFMMRDMR, SSFMMRD	1008			5786
SSFMMRDLLLS, SSFMM	4454		SSF#SMDRFMRRD, DSFM	9624
SSFMMRRD, SLTDSLLS,	11671		SSF#SMRDDDTT, SSSLT	8243
SSFMMRMFLSFM, SDTL	1176		SSF#SMRDDTLS, SSFMF	10780
SSFMMR, FFMRM, SSLTD	3475		SSF#SMRDMFM, SLSMDM	1088
SSFMMMRD, DFFFMRM, M	9118		SSF#SMRDL, DSDDMMRR	3820
SSFMMMRD, DTLDFLS, S	5925		SSF#SMRDLD, LSDDDRM	1942
SSFMMMRD, MFMRDR, SD	5513		SSF#SMFFF, FMR#MDRRR	200
SSFMMMRD, MFSLLSMR,	5852		SSF#SLMSFR, RMFSTLS	10851

SSF#SLFM, MMMRTSRD, S	3405
SSF#SLSDSM, SMRMFML	9777
SSF#SLSMFM, SSF#SLSM	1984
SSF#SLSMSF#F, LLS#LTL	6347
SSF#SLSF#SM, DDTDRDL	11770
SSF#SLSSSDRM, MRTSR,	3394
SSF#SLTDRM, MRMFMRD	2364
SSF#LSMRDLD, LSSDRM	5157
SSF#TLSM, DTLSF, MRMT	8935

SSSD

SSSDDDDR, RRRMFSMR,	10279
SSSDDDDL, LTTTDRM, S	5154
SSSDDD, RRRDRM, SSSD	2452
SSSDDDRMRD, MMMRTS	837
SSSDDDRM, MMMMMMF#S,	1181
SSSDDD, MFFS, LTDRMM	2349
SSSDDRRRRM, DTLS, SL	11496
SSSDDRMD, SLFDLS, SS	533
SSSDDRMM, MFMDRRD, S	10681
SSSDDRMFM, RRRMF#SL	516
SSSDDMD, DRMFMRD, MS	3649
SSSDDMRD, MDMSMDMR,	1690
SSSDDLS, SSSMMRR, TD	9365
SSSDDLLL, LLLRDDT, S	8365
SSSDDTDRDDT, SSSRR	10592
SSSDDTDRMRD, MMMFM	8384
SSSDRRRM, MRMS, FMMF	11584
SSSDRRMS, SSLSDMR, M	3816
SSSDRMD, LSDRTD, DRR	10352
SSSDRMMRRD, MMFSSD	10211
SSSDRM, MRMFRT, SLTD	2641
SSSDRMFRD, MF#F#SMDD	5548
SSSDRMFMRMM, SMMMS	378
SSSDRM, SFMMRD, MSSD	8794
SSSDMRDS, DTLTDRSM	6481
SSSDMRDLDDT, SLLLR	6178
SSSDMRDT, DRMDLRRS,	9453
SSSDMRRM, LDLSDMRD	12003
SSSDMRLTD, DDDDDDT	7125
SSSDMFSLSM, FFFMRM	4519
SSSDMFLS, DRFMRM, SM	3917
SSSDFMRS, SDLRSLTL	10774
SSSDFMMRD, RRMDSFM,	7011
SSSDF, FFMRDSFM, MMM	8594
SSSDSMRD, MDMSMDMR,	1689
SSSDSMFS, SLDTDRLT,	8538
SSSDSFMR, FFFTLSFM,	9095
SSSDSSMR, FFFRTLTD,	8969
SSSDSSFMRM, SSSDRM	8644
SSSDSSFM, MRMFFS, SS	448
SSSDSSS, DMFSLTL, RL	1065

SSSDSS, LSFMRFMLLS	11327
SSSDSLMFSRM, SDDDR	12428
SSSDSLSS, DRMFMRM, S	862
SSSDSLLS, SDRMDRDT	8435
SSSDSLLLS, SSSLDTT	664
SSSDSL, LLLRLT, SSSD	10160
SSSDSTLS, MDRMDTLS,	5943
SSSDSTLL, FFMFLSM, S	8303
SSSDLLS, SRD#RR#M, DDD	2253
SSSDTDRD, RMFMR, DRM	8138
SSSDTDRSD, DLTDMRD	10035
SSSDTDR, SSRRDRM, MR	1069
SSSDTRDD, DDFMRSM, M	4720
SSSDTLSM, FFFLSFM, M	12189
SSSDTLSM, FSLSMDRR	126
SSSDTLSMS, MFRRMFM	2807
SSSDTLS, FFFSSM, SSS	4020
SSSDTLSSM, SLTDRDD	7835
SSSDTLSLSM, SSFFFM	4724
SSSDTLLS, LFSMDTLS,	6646
SSSDTLLLR, TTDRMMR	10116
SSSRRRMFM, MMMRRLT	928
SSSMDDDS, DDMRDMR, R	8250a
SSSMDDDS, DRMRDMR, R	8250
SSSMDDDSMR, RMFMRM	3818
SSSMDDDS, SSLLLLS, S	8148
SSSMDDTLDS, RRRRRR	11011
SSSMDDT, LLSDTLS, SS	6671
SSSMDS, DTLFM, SSMSD	10843
SSSMDSLS, DDRRDTD, S	10075
SSSMDLD, SSSMRRR, SS	9755
SSSMDTLS, SLLTRR, SS	7300
SSSMDTLS, SLTDDLFM	2410
SSSMDTTL, FFFRTLS, S	911
SSSMRD, DRRDRM, MFFF	7321
SSSMRDLS, SSSDTDR, R	6889
SSSMRDLS, SSSFMRDR,	10688
SSSMRDLLD, LSSDTDR,	6890
SSSMRDTDLS, SSMLSF	6307
SSSMRDTLSLTD, SDDD	1915
SSSMRDT, TTDRTMRD, D	12519
SSSMRMDS, SSFLSFFM,	3203
SSSMR, TLTRTLS, SSSM	3794
SSSMMRDSLTT, SSSFF	1824
SSSM, MRDL, DLSSSDRM	6345
SSSMMRDLS, SDDMMR, S	5299
SSSMMMFFR, FFFRRRS	12093
SSSMMFSLS, SSSRFMR	7490
SSSMFRM, FSLTDSSFF	8128
SSSMFMMR, SSSMFMMR	9668
SSSMFS, DDDTLS, SSSR	7328
SSSMFSMR, SLTDTLSF	7172
SSSMFSM, SSLLSMR, FF	11276

SSSMFSM, SSLLSMR, FF	11276
SSSMFSSSLFLS, SSSF	7327
SSSMFSLS, SDTDTLS, S	1837
SSSMFSLLLD, MMDRMD,	5411
SSSMFSLLLS, MFRRMF	4725
SSSMFSL, LLLRMFS, FM	1221
SSSMFLS, DDTLSF#S, SS	7059
SSSMSDDD, RRRDMMM, S	7894
SSSMSDDTT, DRSSLTD,	2083
SSSMSDMR, DLSSDRR, R	4587
SSSMSDMR#M, RDDRDLS,	7352
SS, SMSSF#FMFSM, MLMM	10409
SSSM, SSSLLFL, LLLSM	7913
SSSMSLD, LLLSLTD, MM	1435
SSSMSLD, LLLSLTD, MF	1436
SSSMSLDT, LSSFSM, SS	5047
SSSMSLLS, SMSFMRD, S	11780
SSSMLSF, FFFRSFM, SS	7429
SSSMLSSM, MFSLDTLS,	8878
SSSMLSS, FRRLSS, SSS	8575
SSSMLLSM, DRMSFMRM,	3744
SSSFMDLSM, FFFMRSF	8687
SSSFMRD, DTLSMDR, RR	7539
SSSFMRDRML, SDDMMS,	7972
SSSFMRDM, SDDT, DTLS	6788
SSSFMRRD, DRRRDRM, M	3511
SSSFMRRM, MSLLSFM, M	5322
SSSFMRSMD, SSLSLTD,	12036
SSSFMR#R#M, DDLDRDM, M	
	5429
SSSFMMDDTTL, FFFMR	725
SSSFMMR, FFFMRM, SSS	1359
SSSFMMMR, DRMMSFMR	3148
SSSFMMMMRD, DLSDMS	1661
SSSFMFS, SSSFMFS, DR	9844
SSSFMFSLS, TTTLSFM	1452
SSSFMSMLS, DR#R#MDR#R#	
	3770
SSSFMSSS, SMMRMFSM	8825
SSSFFMMDRMRDD, SSF	5570
SSSFFMMR, MFSMRRR, M	9828
SSSFLFM, FMMRRSR, MF	12548
SSSF#FM, MMDRRM, SSLS	2539
SSSF#SDS, MSSFRM, SSS	1006
SSSF#SM, MMMR#MD, DDDT	
	5857
SSSF#SLMSF, FMFLSFM	7941
SSSF#SLSD, MFMRLSFM,	11767
SSSF#SLSM, MFMRMFSM,	6871
SSSF#SLSSD, DRDTLSF	6123
SSSF#SLS, SSDRLT, DDD	396
SSSF#SLTD, MMMRDTLT,	7420
SSSF#LSM, DRMFFM, MD	9335

SSSF#LS, MMMR#FM, MMMR	
	7272
SSSSDDDMD, MSSSFFM	10887
SSSS, DDTDDRRM, DDTD	10654
SSSSDDTLT, SDRMDR, D	9569
SSSSDRM, SSRD, MMSMD	7110
SSSSDRTD, RLTLLS, SD	5177
SSSSDMMM, SDDDRM, SS	11563
SSSSDS, MFSRM, MSDTL	11651
SSSSDSSS, DRRLLSFM,	8343
SSSSDLLS, DDTSLSF#M,	6928
SSSSDT, DTLSF#S, FFSM	11507
SSSSDTLS, DMMMSFMR,	11005
SSSSDTLS, FMLSMFR	5993
SSSSDTLL, LFRDTRD, S	4337
SSSSDTLL, LLLLRDTT,	10857
SSSSRD, TLTDTDFMRD,	9062
SSSSMDRD, DFSLFR, RR	8004
SSSSMDSM, FFFSFRM, S	10115
SSSSMRDDDRMM, LLTD	6340
SSSSMRDRM, FSLDLLS	5771
SSSSMRDS, RMFRMFM, M	597
SSSSMRDLL, SSSRSDR	3709
SSSSMRRD, SSSMRRD, D	7424
SSSSMFSLS, MMMSSFM	7427
SSSSMFSLLLL, RRRRR	11608
SSSSMFSLTD, DTLT, LS	5584
SSSSMFLS, DTLLSFM, S	11932
SSSSMSDDDD, RRRDDR	11509
SSSSMSDD, DDSMSDMR	4566
SSSSMSDRMS, DTTTTD	6599
SSSSMSFMR, FFFFRLS	8851
SSSSMSFMFSFM, DRRM	3408
SSSSMSLSSF, FMFRRS	5372
SSSSMLSSFM, DRMMMS	7451
SSSSFMR, DRRM, SSSSF	132
SSSSFMRD, RMSLDTLS,	3991
SSSSFMRD, LLLLSSFL	5419
SSSSFMRRR, RRMFSLS	3866
SSSSFMRMFM, LTLSFM	11911
SSSSFMRS, SLLLSS, SS	5469
SSSSFMR#M, DTLSSLDT	6546
SSSSFMMMRDDDTD. DD	3418
SSSSFMFMRD, MMMMRD	6308
SSSSFMFSM, RLSSF#S, D	732
SSSSFMSDRMMMRD, D	874
SSSSFMS, LLLSMMR, MM	5611
SSSSF#SM, SLLLDS, SSM	365

SSSSSD

SSSSSDRM, SDTTLS, MF	8795
SSSSSDRM, SSSDTLLS,	525

SSSSSDRM, SSSDTLLS,	525	SSSSS, LSFMLS, DDSL#L	1355
SSSSSDRM, LLLDLS, SS	628	SSSSSLSFS, SLLL#L#	1934
SSSSSDMRDS, LLTDTL	12228	SSSSSLSSM, DRRRRDR	3875
SSSSSDS, MRRSFM, RMM	4045	SSSSSLSS, SSMRDDTT,	991
SSSSSMRD, MSDDTLSL	5003	SSSS, SLSS, SSSSSSSSL	3986
SSSSSMSSS, SSSSTTL	6227	SSSSSLLS, DDDTLSF#S,	10134
SSSSSMLSFMRMDRMF	5922	SSSSSLLS, DDLRMFFM,	9064
SSSSSMLSFMR, FFFFF	1406	SSSSSLLS, SDRMSFMR,	11450
SSSSSFMR, RMMF#F#SS, S	5187	SSSSSLLS, SLTDTLL, T	10787
SS, SS, SFMRMRD	6728	SSSSSLLLSS, SDRMRD	8377
SSSSSFMR, LLLLLSF	4310	SSSSSLLL, LSMMDMMR,	11062
SSSSSFSLTD, DTLLSF	11275	SSSSSLTDS, DRRRRDR	8845
SSSSSF#SM, MMMMMR#MD,		SSSSSLTD, LSDRDRM, S	2658
	4722	SSSSSLTD, TDTLTLLS,	7569
SSSSSSDDMRDS, LLLL	12314	SSSSS#LSFFM, SSS#LMR	10017
SSSSSSDD, LSMSFMR, R	4002	SSSSLDDD, RRRRFMMM,	7067
SSSSSSDDT, DLSMDR, S	2928	SSSSLDRD, DTLMTDRM,	6691
SSSSSS, DRDM, MMMRDM	5325	SSSSLDR, MRDLSMS, DR	7744
SSSSSSDRM, MFFFFMS	4384	SSSSLDSM, MRDRMF#S,	9376
SSSSSSDS, SSSSMRDR	5083	SSSSLDLSMSLD, MRDL	10334
SSSSSSDSSSSLS, SLL	10438	SSSSLDTLS, FMLSSFM	11455
SSSSSS, DTDRD, DMRDD	4911	SSSSLMS, SDTRLTD, SS	2235
SSSSSSDT, TDLSFM, MM	1912	SSSSLFMRM, MMMRRD, D	6991
SSSSSS, MSLLDDTDD	1177	SSSSLS, DDTLS, SSSSL	1192
SSSSSSFM, SLTTLS, DD	1597	SSSSLSDRM, MMRLT, SS	1012
SSSSSSF#SLS, MRMSFM,	10907	SSSSLSDTMLS, SLLT	237
SSSSSSSDRM, RRRRRD	3708	SSSSLSM, DDDFFM, MFM	5139
SSSSSSSSDTLL, LSFMR	11485	SSSSLS, MMMMFM, DMFS	4466
SSSSSSSSSD, SLLLDS, D	6776	SSSSLS, FMRRD, SSSSL	6024
SSSSSSSSSM, DLLDLS, D	2748	SSSSLS, FFMMR, MMRRD	8926
SSSSSS, SSMRDTLS, SS	964	SSSSLSFS, SSSLDTLT,	3835
SSSSSSSSSF#SM, MMMR#	10283	SSSSLSSD, SSSSLSR, S	6199
SSSSSSSSSS, SLLDRM	11319	SSSSLSSM, DDDLTLS, D	5758
SSSSSSSSS, SSLLLLL	7363	SSSSLLSM, RRRRDRM, S	10093
SSSSSSSS, SSLTDRM, S	4346	SSSSLLSM, SMRMR, MRD	9218
SSSSSSS, SLLLTDT, DS	6410	SSSSLLSS, DDTLTD, SM	6055
SSSSSSSLLSMR, MMFF#	423	SSSSLLS, SRRRDRM, SS	6748
SSSSSSSLTDS, DTLLL	6344	SSSSLLLS, SSSLLTLS,	11935
SSSSSSSLS, MF#STLSFM,	1564	SSSSLLL, SLSMMRR, MM	12218
SSSSSSLSS, MMMSSMD	12272	SSSSLLLL, SSSSFMS, D	12396
SSSSSS, LLS#LTLD, DDT	6910	SSSSLLL, LLDLDTTTT	7878
SSSSSSLLLS, DTRD#R, D	11156	SSSSLLLL, TTTTDDD, M	5789
SSSSSS, LLLSMR, MMFF#	422	SSSSLL#LSF, SMDRMF#SLS	
SSSSSSL, LLSSDDR, DR	156		12357
SSSSSSLLL, SSSDTDR,	12097	SSSSLTDD, DTLSMDFM	11718
SSSSSSLTD, DRRDSLT	2584	SSSSLTDDT, TTTTDR	9492
SSSSSSLTD, DTLSSMD	8835	SSSSLTDRDT, SSLTDR	12227
SSSSSSLTD, LLLLLLT	4459	SSSSLTDRMD, LTRDLS	11676
SSSSSLDD, LSDMRD, SS	7222	SSSSLTDMRD, DDTLSD	3364
SSSSSLSD, DTDRRDRM,	1577	SSSSLTDMRD, SLLLT	7153
SSSSSLS, DMFSFM, MMM	12387	SSSSLTDS, TTTTDRD, L	10004
SSSSSLS, RRDRM, DMS	9408	SSSSL#LSF, SMDRMF#SL	12356
SSSSSLS, MMMMMFM, RR	11931	SSSSL#LSF, SMDMFSLS	12359

SSSSL#LSF, SMDMF#SLS,	12358
SSSLDR, MDDDLS, DRMR	7745
SSSLDLSMR. FMRMSFM	12560
SSSLDTLS, SSSDDTDR, SSS	10578
SSSLDTLS, SSSLDTDR, MDD	
	8833
SSSLRMFM, DFR, SSSLR	6207
SSSLRMFFM, MMLSFM, F#	2845
SSSLMRDTLS, MRDTLS	6825
SSSLM, MMMSM, DDDS#D, D	
	6905
SSSLMFFSRM, DDRM, MS	7390
SSSLMSFF, FTLSFM, SD	8084
SSSLFFSLSM, SSSSMM	4537
SSSLFSM, SSSTLS, SSS	11725
SSSLF#SS, MMMSTD, SSS	10758
SSSLS, DDDTLS, LTDSM	4153
SSSLSDRD, DTRMRDLS,	8854
SSSLSDRD, TRMRDLS, S	8853
SSSLSDRDTLS, LDSFM	11810
SSSLSDRM, MDDRDDRM,	8130
SSSLSDRMMRMFS, LLL	10259
SSSLSDMRDS, SSSLSD	9771
SSSLSDMR, RDDDMSRS	11819
SSSLSDS, DRMDLS, SLS	8119
SSSLSD, SSSLSR, SSSL	6199a
SSSLSMD, DDDRDLS, SS	6408
SSSLSM, DDDRDL, SSSL	1326
SSSLSMDMSLSM, DRDR	12101
SSSLSMD, TLSSSSLS, S	6833
SSSLSMRD, DRFMRDS, S	11081
SSSLSMR, DMRMSS, SSS	5947
SSSLSMRDLD, LSDDMR	7915
SSSLSMMDFMRD, DMSS	7433
SSSLSMMR, FFFMRDTD,	9068
SSSLS, MMMFM, RRRRDR	6173
SSSLSMF, FFFSFRM, SS	6522
SSSLSFM, RMDFMR, RFM	7811
SSSLSFMFSDD, LLLTD	8676
SSSLSFMS, RMMMRDR, DR	11681
SSSLSFSM, DRMFFM, SL	332
SSSLSFSM, SFMRDR, RM	6787
SSSLSSDDDD, RRRRDD	6328
SSSLSSD, DRRRRDRM, S	9950
SSSLSSD, RRRDRMD, DD	12531
SSSLSSDRM, FMRMDRS	10055
SSSLSSD, SSSLSSR, SM	8120
SSSLSSM, MMRMFFM, SS	11107
SSSLSSM, FMRDTD, SSS	9111
SSSLSSM, FMRRDDTD, S	9112
SSSLSSFMS, MMMMMMR	11678
SSSLSSF#S, TTDRDDTD,	9870
SSSLSSSDRMR, RSTDR	12262

SSSLSSSM, MRDRMM, SS	9113
SSSLSSSSSLS, SDMSM	2617
SSSLSSLSM, MMMMMSF	9168
SSSLSS, LLTMD, DDTLS	848
SSSLLDDD, MRDT, SSSL	4249
SSSLLDDD, SS#LTDRR, S	2026
SSSLLDTD, DDDRMFMR	8115
SSSLLDTLS, DMRDRTD,	7228
SSSLLMFSS, DRMSMFM	10953
SSSLLS, DDDDDR, MMMD	5412
SSSLLS, MFMRDTD, SSS	7554
SSSLLS, MFMRMRD, SSS	7553
SSSLLS, MSLDT, TDLSF#	4879
SSSLLSFMRD#RS, SSSL	6325
SSSLLS, SMFMRD, RRRM	7555
SSSLLSSFRM, SDTDRM	8236
SSSLLS, SFMRMRD, SS	7552
SSSLLS, SFMRSFMRD, S	7556
SSSLLSSS, DDDRMRRD,	8079
SSSLLS, SSSDDR, RMMD	3920
SSSLLSSS, SDTLLLRD	2606
SSSLLLS, MMMMSFMR, M	4704
SSSLLLL, LSFM, LLLD	1447
SSSL, LTTD, MMRMF#S, SD	3130
SSSLTD, DDDTLS, S#LLL	1417
SSSLTDRMRDLS, SSTL	11169
SSSLTDRM, MRMFSM, DL	2669
SSSLTDRMFMR#M, D#MRL	934
SSSLTDRSD, MMRRMFL	6505
SSSLTDRSS, MMRRMFL	6506
SSSLTD, MRMFSM, SSSL	2904
SSSLTDMFSRS, LTLSL	1687
SSSLTDSM, MSSFFM, SL	11121
SSSLTDSMS, DDRRFFM,	8638
SSSLTDSS, DMFMRLRD#	10363
SSSLTDS, SSSLTDS, LL	10909
SSSLTDS, LLDTLS, SRR	6073
SSSLTDTDFLDM, MMRL	11216
SSSLTDTLS, LFSMSDT	8314
SSSLTDTTL, LLLTD#R	1642
SSSLTLS, SDDRRM, MFF	5879
SSSL#L#LSFSS, DSMSFM	742
SSSTLS, SDDRRD, MSMD	2927
SSSTLTLSD, SSSTLLL	5076
SSSTTLSD, MRMFSTLS,	10925
SSS#LTDRMF, MDRM, SSS#	1082

SSL

SSLD, DDDR, DDDL, LFSL	5194
SSLD, DDDR, DDDL, LLLS,	10977
SSLD, DDDL, LLLS.	10955
SSLD, DDR, DDDL, LRD, SS	6201

1133

SSLDDDRR, DRFFMRRM,	9061	SSLSDMMR, DSSMDR, MS	10423
SSLDDDS, FMRDMRR,	179	SSLSDSFMRD, MRSSLT	11562
SSLDDDLS, MRDDDMR, S	8625	SSLSDSL, LLTDTLS, TT	6241
SSLDDRRDMRDL, SSLD	4802	SSLSDTRD, DRMFLSM, S	7375
SSLDDRMD, LLSDDMR, M	11181	SSLSDTRD, MRFMMRL, L	6476
SSLDDS, SFMRD, LDFFF	11975	SSLSDT, RFSTLS, MMFS	6342
SSLDDTLS, SLRDTD, MM	1024	SSLSDTLSF, FMMRDRM,	6402
SSLDRDRM, LSDMFMRD	4295	SSLSDTLS, LSFMRRM, S	5006
SSLDRMDL, SLSDMR, SS	7506	SSLSDTLL, LFRDTTD, S	7467
SSLDRFMR, DDTDRLS, S	9687	SSLSMDDL, SDMDSMR, S	3023
SSLDRSDDTLS, SLTDR	718	SSLSMDDT, RDTLSLS, S	3204
SSLDRSSLDMS, RFFMS	10996	SSLSMDDT, SSLSFTLS,	5029
SSLDMRRD, DDRMFFM, M	4212	SSLSMDRDLTD, TDRDM	9049
SSLDMMRDRRDSFMFF	10733	SSLSMD, RMFS, SSLSMD	5275
SSLDMSFMRM, MSLSMR	11429	SSLSMDRM, SSMDMMR, S	10810
SSLDFMMR, SDTDRF#S, S	6238	SSLSMD, RLTLS, SSLSM	8149
SSLDLDT, TRLTLS, SSL	11109	SSLSMD, MRDDDRMR, SS	8602
SSLDTS, SSLDT, DDTDM	1560	SSLSMDMR, DDRMSFR, R	1532
SSLDTLS, DDRMFMRM, M	11460	SSLSMDSLSM, FSLSTD	8073
SSLDTLSM, MMRLSFM, S	8512	SSLSMDLS, DRRDTD, RR	7378
SSLDTLSM, MFSSDRMR	5028	SSLSMDLTDS, SLTDSM	10961
SSLDTLSFLSLTLSFS,	7889	SSLSMRDDM, SSLSMRD	10580
SSLRTDR, MSRSLTS, LL	1079	SSLSMRDD, SSLSMR, SS	11930
SSLMMRMM, MMFRDRM, S		SSLSMRDRRM, MRDSF	11385
	4347	SSLSMRDRMSDTLS, SS	11530
SSLMSSLM, MFSLLTDR	11318	SSLSMRDTD, DMRTRDT	5776
SSLMSLSM, SSLMSLSM,	9250	SSLSMRMRD, TLDLSF	947
SSLFDLFL, DLSLSMMS,	12154	SSLSMRMFM, MDTLSF#S,	8956
SSLFMR, DMRT, DSLFMR,	145	SSLSMMRD, DRRSRM, DM	11787
SSLFMM, DTSLSS, SRMF	507	SSLSMMRRD, LTDSDRM,	12198
SSLFMMMFRD, SDRMMF	11827	SSLSMMRR, SSLSRRDD,	1323
SSLFFLSMM, MRRRRMF#	11010	SSLSMMMFMT, DRMTLD	6489
SSLFLSF#SM, MMRRRRD	9117	SSLSMMFR, MFSTLS, SS	12225
SSLFLLSSM, DDMDDDR	41	SSLS, MMFM, DDDDDDMR	11167
SSLF#SDMR, FFMRRLL, L	6271	SSLSMMFM, MFSLSFMR,	433
SSLSDDDTLS, SSLTDT	4910	SSLSMMSM, DDRRMSMR,	926
SSLSDDTD, DSLSDDTL	10083	SSLSMMSFD#R, MDDSFM	6661
SSLSDDTDRM, DDRDM	2937	SSLSMFSDRDL, SSLSF	10404
SSLSDDTDRMM, DDRDM	2938	SSLSMFSDT, LSDFRM, M	7474
SSLSDDT, RRMFTDR, MM	5395	SSLSMFSDTLS, MRDTT	11401
SSLSDDTT, SSTLFM, SS	12090	SSLSMFSF, RSDTLT, SS	9960
SSLSDRMDLD, SF#SLSD	11870	SSLSMFSFMRMD, SS	5908
SSLSDRMDLS, TTDRMR,	5265	SSLSMFLSFM, STLTRD	4453
SSLSDRMMRD, LTDDRD	10836	SSLSMS, DDRDLD, LSLS	10846
SSLSDRMMR, DTDRSLF#	4389	SSLSMS, MMRDMR, MMRD	10190
SSLSDRMFRTD, MRDRM	6936	SSLSMSFFF, FFSFRFM	5053
SSLSDRMFMR, DTDRMR	5131	SSLSMLLSS, SFSFRLS	12116
SSLSDRMFMR, MDLSDR	7409	SSLSMT, RDSDT, RRD#RF	6586
SSLSDRM, SSLSFMF, MM	8911	SSLSFDDS, MMDTDRMD	11589
SSLSDMRD, RMFSLSM	401	SSLSFMDLLS, SSLSFM	10663
SSLSDMRD, MRDMMRR, S	8535	SSLSFMRD, DDTLSFMF	6541
SSLSDMRDT, LTDFMRD,	11414	SSLSFMRD, DRMFMRDS,	12048
SSLSDMR, RRMFMRM, SF	6239	SSLSFMRD, MRDFMR, MF	6529

1134

SSLSFMRD, MLDTLS, LM 8653
SSLSFMRMFSLT, DSSF 10389
SSLSFMFS, SRDDFFMM 5785
SSLSFMSM, SFMMFMRR, 1763
SSLSFM, SFRMRD, RMF#S, 8450
SSLSFM, SFRMRD, MFSL 8451
SSLSFM, SFRMMR, DTLS, 8452
SSLSFM, SSLSFM, MFSL 11487
SSLSFSFM, RRTLSF#S, S 4709
SSLSFSLSL, DDDDRD 5465
SSLSFLTL, SSFMLT, DF 8102
SSLSF#SDS, MSLSFMR, M 2557
SSLSF#SDSLSF#S, SFFF 5727
SSLSF#SMM, MMRRDRM, M 596
SSLSSDDDTLS, SLDDD 3228
SSLSSDRDRM, MFMRMD 67
SSLSSDRD, SMMRDRM, M 1732
SSLSSDRM, MMRDLSFM, 886
SSLSSDMMRDRMS, SSM 1827
SSLSSDSLSS, DLTDRF 11134
SSLSSMDMSRD, MFFFL 927
SSLSSMMFFS, SSLSSL 6828
SSLSSMSLDLS, SDRML 8955
SSLSSFMRR, MFSDRRM, 6941
SSLSSFM, MDDTLS, MMF 12512
SSL, SSFMF, FFS, FFMR#M, 4930
SSLSSSMDM, SMMRDR, S 11165
SSLSSTMRDTLS, SSDR 4954
SSLSSTLTDSS, MSDLS 8197
SSLSLDTD, MMRSLTDT, 5911
SSLSLTTD, SSLSTDR, M 8981
SSLSTDRMR, MFMRMTL 1205
SSLSTLSDTLSM, RDRM 8203
SSLSTL, SSFFM, SSLST 5243
SSLSTLLMS, SDDDTLS 3808
SSLLDDL, FSSLLM, SMM 4477
SSLLDD, TTDLS, DDMMS 7468
SSLLDDTT, LSRRR#M, MM 2231
SSLLDTLT, DDFMMRR, R 3253
SSLLFSLSM, SFMRRRD 416
SSLLFLSM, MMRRMF#S, D 3688
SSLLFLLSSMS, MMRMF 10932
SSLLFLLSSM, SSFFFM 2619
SSLLSDDT, DRMDTLS, S 4580
SSLLSDDT, DTDRSM, MF 10978
SSLLSDRM, MSFMRDRM 5780
SSLLSDMMR, DTLSSTL 1124
SSLLSRD, DDTLLS, MMM 10873
SSLLSMDRMFS, FMRMF 519
SSLLS, MMDRM, RMFRMF 9427
SSLLSMMF, MMRSRRDD, 4474
SSLLSSM, FFRRMFS, SS 286
SSLLSS, SFLLS, LTDDS 1695

SSLLLFSLSM, MFSSSM 7259
SSLLLFLS, SSF#RRMF#S 6474
SSLLLLLDTLLS, MFSL 7505
SSLLLLL, SMRRMMF, MD 1867
SSLLLLLSSSS, MRDDS 8110
SSLLLLLLS, SSDTLLT 4564
SSLLLLTLLSMS, SLLL 4739
SSLLTLS, LLTTDLR, DT 9744
SSLLTTD, RRDDTTLS, S 6850
SSLL, TTDS, MMRSDRT, T 1121
SSLTDDDT, LLSFMFRM 8815
SSLTDDRM, MSRMRTDT, 2555
SSLTDDLT, DD#MRSM, MM 435
SSLTDDT, DRD#RR#M, SM 8362
SSLTDDTDRMFM, MSFM 10948
SSLTDDTDR, FMSF#MRS, 10147
SSLTDDT, LDSMFRD, MM 8809
SSLTDDT, LDSMFMRD, S 3929
SSLTDDT, LSMMRDT, TM 4789
SSLTD, DTLSLS, SSLTD, 11408
SSLTDDTL, TDRLSFM, S 7009
SSLTDDTT, DRMRRM, SM 12505
SSLTDDTT, LDSFMFRD, 8816
SSLTDDTT, LLSMFRD, S 8814
SSLTDRDRM, MFMRMDR, 9985
SSLTDRDT, DDRRFMRM, 5880
SSLTDRMDL, RDTLTDT, 9853
SSLTDRMMRD, LLDFLS, 2767
SSLTDRMMFD#R, SSLTD 994
SSLTDRMF, MRDTLTD, S 10239
SSLTDRMSFRFM, MRLF 5109
SSLTDRFFM, DDMRDTL 5476
SSLTDMDTLSLSRS, SS 7056
SSLTDMFRM, SFM, SSLT 11133
SSLTDMLSS, SSDTLLT 8076
SSLTDS, DDRTD, SSLTD 3981
SSLTDSDRSRM, MFLFM 11290
SSLTDS, MDLRDT, SSFM 9353
SSLTDSS, FMFLSMS, SM 6069
SSLTDLS, DSMFMRD, MS 4265
SSLTDLSMS, SLTDRDT, 2952
SSLTDLSFMRRFMFSS, 4898
SSLTDLSFM, MMSDTLL 5564
SSLTDLSFLSLTDTLSL 192
SSLTDLT, DRMRD, SSLT 5923
SSLTDTDMRTD, TRDLS, 4734
SSLTDT, DSMFR, SSLTD 3930
SSLTDTRDLS, MMRRRD 9712
SSLTDTLDTLS, SSDRM 2893
SSLTDTLS, DDDTSLDD 698
SSLTDTLS, MFD#RLSR#M, 5126
SSLTSDLS, MFFFSMM, D 12304

SSLTSLTDT, RRRRRRR	46
SSLTSLTDT, SSDTTLS	47
SSLTSLTDTLSS, SLTD	190
SSLTTSLTDTLSS, ST	189
SSTDRMR, SSTDMR, SSM	11101
SSTDRMFFM, MFSRMFR	1033
SSTDRMSFM, RMMMLSF#	4780
SSTRMRD, DDFFFFM, MS	4312
SSTRFTDMS, SSTRFSM,	9854
SSTLTDRTDLS, SSLSF	12386

SLD

SLDD, DDDRMRDD, RRRR	10863
SLDDDDMRRDDDD, MFS	2037
SLDDDDMRRD, MFSSSS	2039
SLDDDRD, DDTDLLS, SL	9251
SLDDDRDMMFM, RDTDF	11894
SLDDDRM, DRMFSS, SLD	9447
SLDDDMDLS, SDDDMS, S	11030
SLD, DDSLSSSSLM, MMM	4013
SLDDRDTT, LTDRRDD, R	10664
SLDDLDR, MRMDRDRT, T	7678
SLDDLSMSLD, DRDMRD,	7374
SLDDTD, DRRDLS, SLLD	8520
SLDDTD, DLTDLS, SDLT	3958a
SLDDTD, DLTTLS, SDLT	3958
SLDDTDRD, FFMRDRM, S	10317
SLDDTD, TDMMR#M, SFMR	2261
SLDDTRDTDLSS, SLDD	9297
SLDDTLSS#LFFM, MRMF	7905
SLDDTLS, LDRD, SLDDT	2802
SLDDTLSTRTLS, MRDD	7981
SLDRMDTLSDFMRDD, D	9944
SLDRMFR, MDLSFS, SLDR	1128
SLDRMSLDRM, RRDTLS	9027
SLDRMSLS, MRDDRTL, S	565
SLDRFMRD, DMFSDR, RM	10942
SLDMDMRDLSS, SLDMD	419
SLDMDMRDLS, SLDMDM	418
SLDMRD, SLDMRD, MSRR	3579
SLDMMMMRDFFF, FMRF	10924
SLDFMRMDL, LRTSDFM	3899
SLDFMRMR, RSDDDF, FM	10036
SLDFMMR, MDTDRT, DRM	1817
SLDSMRDRR, MFSLSFM	8484
SLDS, SLDFMRM, DFFRR	10943
SLDSLFSMR, MSF#STDL	1370
SLDLDSD, DMDMS, SLDL	3455
SLDLDSDDMRMS, SLDL	3457
SLDLDL, LSLDLDL, RDT	10820
SLDLRDLS, SLDLDRMR	7416
SLDLSMRD, MSLSMDR, M	6332

SLDLSLDD, SDRMDRLD,	2540
SLDLTDDSLSFMR, SLD	10701
SLDLTDTDRD, DRMTDR	3225
SLDTD, RMSF#S, MFSSFM,	10550
SLDTDRSS, MFMRDR	7359
SLDTMRRD, FMRDTLLS,	10541
SLDTMR, TDMRLS, SDTL	1646
SLDTFFFLTS, MRDSLD	7949
SLDTSDRM, MMMFMRDT,	5760
SLDTSFS, SS#DL#SFS, SL	1420
SLDTSLDT, SLTDRRR, F	497
SLDTSLLL, SMSMRM, DR	3061
SLDT, STRD, DTLS, DDLT	7183
SLDTLSMD, DRMFMRMD	11038
SLDTLSMFLSFM, DTLS	3548
SLDTLSM, SLDTLSM, RM	1591
SLDTLSFM, RMSFMRDT,	6129
SLDTLSLL, SLDRTDTL,	10234
SLRDTDRM, DFFMRDRT	6330
SLRDT, DFFFMMRLTDD	384
SLRDT, TDFFF, FMMRLT	385
SLRMFSM, SLRMFSM, SS	2366
SLRSDFTM, MMTDDRMR,	1135
SLRSSFM, DRMDRRD, MF#	4715
SLMDRDDLD, SLMDRRR	1416
SLMRDTLS, MRDTLSDD	6826
SLMRMDS, DRMFSDRMR,	6435
SLMRTDLSMDR, MF#LRS	4695
SLMMDTLS, MRMFLSRM,	8930
SLMFMRRD, MFSLLSFM,	10706
SLMFSFMR, FMSLTDLS,	7724
SLMFSLTDDRD, RRMDT	7612
SLMSDRM, FSLSMFMR, M	12331
SLMSFF, FSRFMM, MFMR	9759
SLMSFF, FSRFMM, LLTD	11683
SLMSLTDDR, SMRDTLS	8599
SLFDTLLSSMS, MFSLS	4669
SLFMRRD, MFLSMS, SLF	1516
SLFMRS, DTLS, LFMRD	8320
SLF, FSM, DDDDDRDTLS	3814
SLF#SDRMMR, DTLSSLS	9800
SLSDDDTLS, STRFRMD	8147
SLSDDRDT, DRMRR, MFS	585
SLSDDRM, MRDSMRD, MR	8992
SLSDDTDR, RMRDMRTD,	1313
SLSDDTDRMR, MDLFMR	2299
SLSDDTDRMR, MFSFRD	2300
SLSDDTLS, LTDRMRDR,	5831
SLSDDTT, MRDTTL, LLT	12290
SLSDRD, DTDLLS, SLSD	8083
SLSDRDTDMDDT, SLSR	10137
SLSDRMR, FMRDRT, SLS	11123
SLSDRMRSMR, LRMFMD	8639

SLSDRM, MRDR, SLSDRM,	7074
SLSDRM, MFMRLT, SLS	2480
SLSDRMFS, DFMRDR, FM	11523
SLSDRMFSMRDR, SDTL	10430
SLSDRMSRMRDRL, LRM	7984
SLSDRM, SRSM, FSLMRS	5406
SLSDRLTLS, DSFMRSF#	6560
SLSDMRDT, LSSLMS, SM	5725
SLSDMRDT, TDRMSSF#S,	2025
SLSDMRLTLS, DDMRLR,	3622
SLSDMMRD, DDDTDRMR	6896
SLSDMMRD, DTDDMRMR	6898
SLSDMMRD, DTDDSMRM	6897
SLSDMMRDT, DRDTLS, F	3911
SLSDMFML, RSDFMR, MF	9449
SLSDFMR, DRMFLS, SL	9258
SLSDFMR, RMLSF#S, SLS	7443
SLSDSDMR, RMRDLS, SL	7675
SLSDSDTLS, SLSDMRD	3162
SLSDSLSDRM, RRMRRM	9913
SLSDSLLS, SDMRTDTL	7892
SLSDLT, SSSDMS, SLSD	1787
SLSDTDRD, RMRDTLS, S	9590
SLSDTD, MLTDDT, SLTD	7469
SLSDT, SLSRD, SSMDTL,	3906
SLSDTLSD, DLTDFR, MD	1129
SLSDTLSMFSMR, DRDS	727
SLSDTLSF, MRDSFMRF	8839
SLSDTL, SFMMRD, DRDS	2004
SLSDTLS, SS#S#LFR, MR#M	10021
SLSDTLSLSFM, RMFSF	2369
SLSDTLLS, FMFSLSSM,	4411
SLSDTLLS, FMFLSFM, S	6349
SLSDTLLS, SMRDRMRD,	3012
SLSRRMFMRM, MSLSF#S	4213
SLSMDDDLS, SLSMRRR	11024
SLSMDDLDLS, SLSMDM	12234
SLSMDDTT, RRDSMMR, L	8772
SLSMDRDLS, DMSFRDR	4035
SLSMDRDLSLSMR, SLS	4751
SLSMDR, RMF#SSFS, SDT	8376
SLSMDRMDR, SLTDSMS	2154
SLSMDRMRD, MSMLSSF#	6068
SLSM, DRMFMSM, DLSM	9545
SLSMDRM, FSMRDRT, DT	1277
SLSMDRM, FSLDDS, SFM	4719
SLSMDRM, FLSMSFR, MD	9533
SLSMDRLL, TLSFFM, SL	9921
SLSMDMD, SLSMRDMMR,	11491
SLSMDM, FDRM, MLTDTL,	5653
SLSMDFMMR, RMRDRMS	11160
SLSMDSF, TDDMRDR, SL	7338
SLSMD, SLSMR, SLSMDT	325
SLSMDLDD, DRRRDRMS,	10931
SLSMDLS, DRMRDTD, T	11334
SLSMDLSM, DRMFSLSF	4521
SLSMDLSM, DLSMDRM, R	5990
SLSMD, LTDSM, SLSSMD	3443
SLSMDTLTDS, SDMRST	1254
SLSMRDDTLS, MMFSLT	3004
SLSMRD, RDRMS, SLSMR	6519
SLSMRD, RDRSFM, RMFL	5526
SLSMRDRDM, SLL#TSMF#	7013
SLSMRDRMD, LSLDTLS	12138
SLSMRDRMRD, DTLSFM	980
SLSMRDRFM, MRDTLTD	122
SLSMRDFFF, RMFTLS, S	8227
SLSMRD, SMRDR, RMFLS	6683
SLSMRDST, LSMSFM, MS	1358
SLSMRDTS, SLSFMRD, S	5272
SLSMRDTL, DLSDDTDR,	10487
SLSMRDTL, LLRDTDR, S	6462
SLSMRRM, DTLSSF#S, RR	9015
SLSMRRM, RMLDDTD, MS	9340
SLSMRMM, SMFSLDD, MR	8420
SLSMRMFM, SLTLSF#SF#	4590
SLSMRMFS, SLSRFMRD,	5895
SLSMMRDDLS, DDRMRD	8979
SLSMMRDS, SLLDLS, SS	12410
SLSMMRD, SLFMRDT, SL	8893
SLSMMRD, LLDDFMR, SL	6228
SLSMMRD, LTDSFMR, SL	8472
SLSMMRRD, LDSDMRR, S	11352
SLSMMFRRDMRDTD.	12350
SLSMFR, MDMRLR, SLSM	9694
SLSMFMDRD, MDTMMLS	9837
SLSMFMRDRM, FSMR, SL	10564
SLSMFMRDRM, SLSMFM	3373
SLSMFMRR, MSLFMRD, S	1651
SLSMFMMRSRD, LFLSM	10082
SLSMFFMM, FMRDDTLS	4107
SLSMFSMD, RSSF#MF#S, S	9734
SLSMFS, MRDTDTL, LLR	7519
SLSMFSM, MRDDSFMR, S	10045
SLSMFSSLFLDTLS, D	5425
SLSMFS, SL#DLSF, LS, SR	583
SLSMFS, LSSLTTDS, DM	1217
SLSMFSL, TDRFMFLS, S	933
SLSMFLS, DRDLTRD, DM	7741
SLSMF#S, DFMRRD, SSML	3913
SLSMSDDT, RMFTLS, SL	12400
SLSMSDRDL, TTDRMDT	1982
SLSMSDTLLS, SRMFSL	1440
SLSMSRMF#S, SLSRFMR,	5894
SLSMSMFMDM, RD#RMFS	10015
SLSMSFMFRD, DMFSSL	8020

SLSMSFFM, DLDMSFM, S	5305	
SLSMSFFM, RMFSFMRD,	8341	
SLSMSSFR, MDDRSM, SL	8910	
SLSMSLSM, DDMDLTD,	11370	
SLSMLSM, RRTDDS, LL	4807	
SLSMSLS, MFMDRMD, SL	7354	
SLSMSLSM, SLSMRDR, S	11369	
SLSMSLSM, SLSMSR, SD	8690	
SLSMSLS, SLTDRT, LTL	6437	
SLSM, SLLDLS, MRMFSM,	3045	
SLSFRMFSFM, SSLFMRD.	12412	
SLSFMDRM, TDRMFTLR,	6623	
SLSFMR, DRMFMR, MSLS	3934	
SLSFMRD, MFSMSFMRM	563	
SLSFMRD, FMRDTLS, SD	899	
SLSFMRDL, DRMSDLS, L	4351	
SLSFMRDT, DRMFSMR, S	10427	
SLSFMRRM, MDDRSM, SL	2267	
SLSFMRR, MFMRMD, SLS	11740	
SLSFMRM, MDDRSM, SLS	2266	
SLSFMRMFM, DDRMFMR	11602	
SLSFMRMF#S, SLSRFMR	5896	
SLSFMRMS, LLDLSMR, S	4354	
SLSFMR, FMDRRD, DS	7581	
SLSFMM, RMFFFM, SDTL	2997	
SLSFMMR, MFSM, SLSFM	10136	
SLSFMM, FSFMR, SLSFM	11776	
SLSFMFRMFSLLSS, S	7836	
SLSFMFRMFS, LTDTLS	3594	
SLSFMFMRD, RMF#SSF#S,	674	
SLSFMFMR, MFMRSLSF#	9289	
SLSFMFMRMS, SLSFMF	10575	
SLSFMFSRRD, MRMF#SR	9438	
SLSFMFSFMRMFMR	3730	
SLSFMFSFFM, RMFSFM	8342	
SLSFMFSLSFM, SSLTD	10010	
SLSFMSD, TLSFMLS, SL	6133	
SLSFMSSFFMF, TL#TLS	5709	
SLSFMSLSFM, SSLTDT	10011	
SLSFSDRD, DSLTDRMM	11578	
SLSFSDRD, DSTDRMMR,	11576	
SLSFSDTLSMD, RMRMF#	6749	
SLSFSMFMR, STLSLFS	2422	
SLSFSLSDRDD, DSLDR	11574	
SLSFSLSDRRD, DSLDR	11575	
SLSFSLS, DFMRMDR, SL	12301	
SLSFSLSLTDTLSS, TR	7888	
SLSFLDDSLSFSS, SR	6485	
SLSF#RFSFM, MFMRLRR	569	
SLSF#SMSMRDFDM, MRD	2790	
SLSF#SSMRD, LS#LTDTL	1808	
SLSSDDTT, SLSSRRDD,	328	
SLSSDRRD, SLSSDMRR,	6008	

SLSSDMRD, DRMSLS, DR	10320	
SLSSDMRL, DTLSFSM, S	8390	
SLSSDTDRMRDTDLSS	8172	
SLSS, DTLSMLLSFS, M	8170	
SLSSRF, MMRRLT, RSF#	1592	
SLSSMDDTLSLS, FSFM	1562	
SLSSMRD, DDLDRM, SLS	7226	
SLSSMRDRDL, LSDRMR	10762	
SLSSMMMFMMR, SLSSR	10636	
SLSS, MMMFMM, SLTDSF	7720	
SLSSMFRSFFM, SLSSM	2001	
SLSSMFMRRM, DMSLLS	11713	
SLSSMSFFMF, LTLLRS	4308	
SLSSFMS, MMMMRDR, SS	11680	
SLSSF#LDDDT, SDMSFM	1413	
SLSSSSSLTD, TLTS, SL	6544	
SLSSSLTDMRDT, RDTD	11625	
SLSSLS, DDLSFMRDR, S	909	
SLSSLS, SSLSDRM, RMF	6052	
SLSSTDDRML, LL#L#LD#R	923	
SLSLDTDLS, SLMSLTT	10667	
SLSLDTLSMFS, STDRD	11613	
SLSLSDRMFMRMFS, LSL	755	
SLSLSDRMFS, SSLSLS	756	
SLSLSSSS, DDDDDTD, S	8392	
SLSLTDD, LLSSMRDR, M	5792	
SLSLTDMLSRMD, SLSL	1108	
SLSLTDS, DTRDMR, SMR	6670	
SLSLTD, SFMSFMR, SF#M	3659	
SLSLTDTDRS, SMRDRS,	7608	
SLSTDLSFFM, SLSTDS	2325	

SLL

SLLDMRDLLL, SLLDLS	8389	
SLLDTRDMR, MFSSLSS,	7415	
SLLDTLSM, DRRRDRMS,	10200	
SLLDTLSM, SRSTTLS, D	4517	
SLLFLDLSMS, MMRD#RS	5158	
SLLFLS, MSLSMR, DMMS	7246	
SLLSDRM, SRMFMRDDT,	11635	
SLLSDFFM, RDFMLDDT,	3077	
SLLSDTDR, SDDFMMR, R	1285	
SLLSMD, DDDTLS, LFSM	9171	
SLLSMD, DDTLS, LFSMM	9173	
SLLSM, DDTLS, LFSMMM	9172	
SLLSMD, DTLSL, FSSMM	9170	
SLLSFMMR, DRMSDLS, S	9527	
SLLSF#S, SRSDRM, MFDR	935	
SLLSSDDT, DLSSLTLR	3149	
SLLSSDDT, LLSDSFM, S	6407	
SLLSSLRRMR, TLTDRT	7337	
SLLSLDTD, RMFMRRD.	4498	

SLLLLDDSS, MRMFLLSS,	1840
SLLLLDTLLS, MFMFSSR	1958
SLLLRRRSD, DDFFFLS	7625
SLLLSFMFSLS, LTDSS	3556
SLLLLLSMS, SLLSMMR, S	11155
SLLLLLS, MSLSMR, MSS	978
SLLLLLLTLSSS, MFFFS	45
SLLLLLTDSSSSM, SLLL	10921
SLL, LTT, SSLDMSL, MFM	4888
SLLTLSSSM, DLLSSSD	4499
SLL#SLF, RMFSM, TDRMD	8167
SLL#SL#LFLLS, SLL#SL#L	9846
SLTDDDDD, DRRMMDFR,	3682
SLTDDDDD, SDRMMMRM	1938
SLTDDDRMLL, LTDRRR	8629
SLTDDDTDRM, LTD#RRR	894
SLTDDDTLLS, SLTDDD	8112
SLTDDRRMD, DRMFMRD	1144
SLTDDRRMD, FMRMRDL	1353
SLTDDRRMFM, MRDRSS	6375
SLTDDRMFM, SFMRMDT	8758
SLTDDRMFM, SFMRMRD	5982
SLTDDMRD, DTDRRM, MM	79
SLTDDMRDRS, SLSMDM	4536
SLTDDFFM, MLLSMDL#L,	12152
SLTDDLTDFMR, DRMFM	10041
SLTDDLT, RFMRDLS, MF	4656
SLTDDTDRS, SSSRMFM,	11686
SLTDDTR, DDTSM, MRDT	9579
SLTDDT, SSLSS, LTDMM	6911
SLTDDTSLTRRD, LTDM	598
SLTDDTLS, MRMFFMRM,	1085
SLTDDTLSM, SSSSLSS,	5146
SLTDDTLTD, RFM, SSSF	2145
SLTDDTLTF, FFTTLFM,	7457
SLTDD#RS, SLTDMRFFM	9127
SLTDRDDT, RD#RMRDLL	1525
SLTDRDDT, RSSS#LFM, L	7040
SLTDRDMD, DDTDRDS, S	12470
SLTDRD, SLTDRM, TDRM	6771
SLTDRDT, DDLFMRM, MS	8920
SLTDRDT, DLFMRM, MSM	8921
SLTDRDTRSM, SLTDRD	902
SLTDRDTRLLS, DDDDM	1848
SLTDRDT, SFMRDMRD, R	4338
SLTDRDT, STDRMRD, DD	3869
SLTDRDT, TFLTLS, SLT	7229
SLTDRDTTTLSLS, SLT	3577
SLTDRMDD, MRDTLS, RD	6919
SLTDRMD, DMLSF#S, SSS	9911
SLTDRMDDTTD, DTTLT	6992
SLTDRMDL, LRTDLSF#S,	2959
SLTDRMRD, DDMDFR, SL	3957

SLTDRMRD, MRMDTLLS,	4125
SLTDRMRD, MSFMDR, SL	3018
SLTDRMRRRMFSLS, SF	11224
SLTDRMMRD, LLDFLS, S	2768
SLTDRMFRDT, RMFSDT	4271
SLTDRMFR, SFMRMRRD,	2107
SLTDRMFMRM, SFMRM	6642
SLTDRM, FSFMRR, RRMF	2380
SLTDRMFS, FMRMRDTD,	4058
SLTDRMF#S, SLTDRMDR,	10582
SLTDRMF#S, LSFSM, SFR	7115
SLTDRM, SDSFMR, STLS,	10420
SLTDRM, SDLDMRD, SLT	11970
SLTDRM, SFMRDT, TDRM	849
SLTDRMSFMR, MRDLTD	7311
SLTDRFM, RDLSS, RRSF	9626
SLTDRS, LTDR, SMTDLS	7906
SLTDRLTD, DMFSFSR, R	7142
SLTDMDLT, STDRFMRM,	958
SLTDMRDRMR, RMFSFM	6984
SLTDMRD, FMRDTLS, S	9282
SLTDMRDS, TD#R#MSF#MS	
	1766
SLTDMRDTD, SDRMSFM	11360
SLTDMRDTLT, LTDSDM	3096
SLTDMRDT, TDTLSSM, D	10786
SLTDMRSD, DRMF#SF#M, T	
	11782
SLTDMMRD, FFMRMRR, R	4426
SLTDMMRDSS, SLSRMF	12092
SLTDMMRDTRD, MMRDM	8447
SLTDMMRLDT, DTLSDR	205
SLTDMMMSF#SF#SF#F, SL	
	10603
SLTDMM, LRFM, SLTDMM,	12321
SLTDMSFM, RDDTLS, SS	8608
SLTDMSF, MRMFFM, SLT	2077
SLTDMSFM, MMRDMRD, S	697
SLTDMSSS, DMMFS, SLT	8431
SLTDMSTT, SLLFFM, MM	7307
SLTDML, SMRDLM, DRM	6796
SLTDFMRD, SFRSSF#LS,	10270
SLTDFMRM, LMRMSFM, M	2783
SLTDFM, MSDRM, RMFSL	2858
SLTDFMFMRD, SLDSDL,	12007
SLTDFMLR, DTDDRSLS,	7181
SLTDFF, MDDRM, SLTDF	2281
SLTDFF, MRDRM, SLTDM	2282
SLTDFF, MRDTM, RRMRS	8101
SLTDFT, SRSR#M, SLTDR	10608
SLTDSDRDT, SLTRTRD	11255
SLTDSDRMD, MLSMRDL,	7455
SLTDS, DTLSSFMFR, MF	152

1139

SLTDSRMD, DT LSRFM, S	11203
SLTDSMDRD, DT LST LS	3970
SLTDSMR#MF, FSLSFRR#	8898
SLTDSM FS, DFMMR, SLT	5766
SLTDSLSD, TLSMDLS, M	6131
SLTDST LS, SLTDST LS,	4029
SLTDLSMSFMRD, SLTD	4711
SLTDLSFM, MRTDRDLT,	6536
SLTDLS, SDLSFM, LSFM	2324
SLTDTDDRRMD, MRDTS	12575
SLTDTDRDRMS, LTDSS	12190
SLTDTDRM, MSFMDFMR,	609
SLTDTDRMFM, FSMDRL	6382
SLTDTLMSS, SLTDTLM	10867
SLTDTLSM, DFLSMDS, S	6471
SLTDTLSLFS, TRDTRD	3200
SLTDTTL, LSSDDR, SRR	9978
SLTRDMFSFM, SDMLRF	712
SLTR, TLMRMF#, SLTRMR	11099
SLTSSLTDRM, FMRMRD	4010
SLT, LDDTLLS, LLSFMM	5912
SLTLSRDS, MMRSDRT, T	11128
SLTLSFMRDMLS, SLTL	10795
SLTLSFMRM, FSMRMDT	921
SLTTLDTLSLT, STSLM	2840
STDDDTDRRD, DMSMMR	5393
STDDRMRMDTLTS, SLL#	8918
STDRD#RMDS, DMFSMRD	970
STDRRTDRMMR, RRDLD	10475
STDRMDR, SLTDTLSLS,	9690
STDR, SDRM, F#F#F#S, SDMS	
	6951
STDMRDTLSS, TMRDLD	7054
STRMRD, DFFMRDMR, SS	9150
STRFMRD, DRDTLTSF, M	6949
STRSFMD, STRFLSM, SF	9860
STRTDRMFSMDT, SDRM	1147
STLSFMFS, SLLSF#S, FM	10895
STLTSM, FSLSLRMF, SR	3409
STTLSLSS, MSRFFM, SD	89
STTLTDS, SLDTLS, SSD	3415
STTTTTDS, SRDTLSFM, M	11298
STTTTLTDTLS, SFMFR	4455
S#S#LLSSSS, DDDRDDT, T	10686
S#LTDRMDRDT, TDTDRM,	9598
S#LTDRMMRM, MRDTD	12312
S#LTDTLLS#LTDTDLTD	9821

LDD

LDDDDRDT, LLLLTTL	10705
LDDDTS, MLLS#LTDTT, T	7822
LDDDTL, LDDDTL, LTLS	7943

LDDRDDT, S#LTDTRD, LT	2917
LDDRRMMRDTL, LDDRR	10561
LDDRRMMFRMM, SDDRR	4160
LDDRMMLTDTTL, LTDT	11208
LDDMRDLD, DDDMMSLS,	6326
LDDSLSFM, LDRMRDTD,	9894
LDDTDRDT, LDTL, LDRM	8727
LDDTLRD, DTTTDLS#, MT	10879
LDDTLSTRRML, SLSFRD	11051
LDDTTL, MRRDDT, TDDR	2828
LDDTTL, LDDRRM, MSSF	10266
LDRDFMRDTDD, MSLSF	5966
LDRDLSLL#L, SLDFSMR	11060
LDRDLLDRDL, MRDMRD	10242
LDRDTDTL, DMMRDRTL,	10656
LDRRDRFS, DTLFMMRD,	9550
LDRMDRDLSL, LDRMSL,	2523
LDRMDRDLS#L, LDRMS#L,	2522
LDRMDRDTL, LDRMDRD	7669
LDRMRDRDTL, LDRMR	7666
LDRMRDRML, SDRMRDR	7974
LDRMRDLSL, RMSLLSM	2607
LDRMRDTLS#L, TDLTMR	3021
LDRMRMDTL, LSLTLSF#	5546
LDRMRFMRD, MRDTMRT	2301
LDRMMDTL, LDTDMRDT,	12302
LDRMMRDT, TDRMMRRD,	786
LDRMMRMDL, LRRRLDR	11105
LDRMMMDR, MTDRMDTL,	6371
LDRMMMRMF#SM, SMRDR	3631
LDRMMFRM, DMFSSLF	5914
LDRMMFMD, DTLS#LRMF	7515
LDRMMFFM, MFDRRD, DM	7483
LDRMMLMRDTL, DMF#SL	2895
LDRMML, SMDRML, DTLS	6256
LDRMFMRTSL, TDLLS#LT	4046
LDRMSDRMR, RMFSMRR	9839
LDRMSMRD, MSMDRDTL,	2753
LDRMLDRML, DRMMRDT	11550
LDRMLMRDTL, LDRMLS	3712
LDRMLSMR, DFSMRDDF	10126
LDRMLS, SMRDRTL, DRM	2290
LDRMLLS#L, DRMFMRDT,	3914
LDRMLLS#LL, DTLSFFM	10172
LDRMLTDTL, DRMFMMR	1375
LDRMTDRT, SLTF#SMR#M,	
	5079
LDRFMLDRDTL, LTDM	10926
LDRTDTLS#, LRDDTD, DR	4968
LDMRDRDT, LRDTL, LDM	4178
LDMRDMMRTD, LTDTLT	7192
LDMRDT, DMLSF#M, F#MR#M,	
	8963

1140

LDMRDTLT, DMRDRM, M	10468
LDMRMFMRDT, TDRTMD	1151
LDMMRDRMRDLL, LDM	6318
LDMMMRFMRD, RMDLDR	11591
LDMLMFMRDT, DLTDRM,	9525
LDMLMFMRRD, TLTDRM, M	9526
LDMLMLTMRDTL, MMMR	8064
LDMLSMRM, MFSMRDRL,	3262
LDMLSFMRDR, MLSL, LD	7269
LDMLSFFM, RDTLLDDT,	5044
LDMTRTLLSM, SLTRMT	2233
LDFLF, SDMSM, STRFSF	4496
LDLRDFFM, RLDTTL, MM	7987
LDLMDTLM, MSMFLM, MS	8503
LDLMDTLM, MSMF#SLM, M	8502
LDLMMLTD, SSSTSRT	12260
LDLSFDRRD, DFMMRD	12061
LDLSLDDLSM, SSLSLD	549
LDLSLDTL, DRRMDRRM	10294
LDLS#LDTL, DRRMDRRM	10295
LDLLS#LTS#M, RDTLS#F#S#	10028
LDLLTDLL, LLTDTLSL	10708
LDTDRDT, DRMFMRD, MD	4786
LDTDRM, MRDTT, TMRRD	9213
LDTDLS#LSFM, SSMLTD	2065
LDTDLTDR, MMRDTL, MM	4061
LDTDLTTLLSLTTL, LR	9835
LDTDTDRMFM, RDRMRD	7682
LDTD#RDT, DRMFMRD, MD	4785
LDTRDF, MRDTLS#L, DT	12256
LDTMDTL, TDTLDTL, LD	5819
LDTMM, MMLS#TL, MLDTM	3145
LDTMFRM, DMRSLTD, ML	11453
LDTSMLLM, MF#SLF#TTS,	11585
LDTSLDSM, MLFTSD, DT	8216
LDTS#TLDRM, MRTRDLD	5005
LDTLDDLTSLDD, DDD	7439
LDTLDMRM, MDDFMRD#R	6032
LDTLDMRL, DSMRDR, RS	2121
LDTLMDRFMR, RMSF#S, D	8044
LDTLM, RDTLT, MMFSLT	11568
LDTLMRDT, TDTLMMR#M,	8371
LDTLMMRDTL, DLS#LTD	11798
LDTLMMRDTL, DTLS#LT	11799
LDTLMM, LDTLM, FMMRD,	131
LDTLMFT, DRMMRRD, SS	4864
LDTLMLSFMD, DRMFSF	11017
LDTLSDRM, MMMRMDDT	7731
LDTLSDRM, MMMMRDTD,	10632
LDTLSLMLL, DRDTLTD	9138
LDTLSLTD, DRMFDTL, T	5294
LDTLS#LMM, F#SMSFM, LD	4913

LDTLS#LTDTL, DDDDSD	1752
LDTLS#LTL, TDTDRDRM,	11376
LDTLS#LT, TDRMDTL, TD	10070
LDTLLRTM, DRMFSM, ML	9377
LDTLLSFM, MSDMRD, MS	9507
LDTLLLS#L, DTLLS#L, DF	11048
LDTLLTTDDRDTLSL, L	6404
LDTLTM, LRMFMLS#L, LD	6733
LRDLSFSLR, LRDLSFS	1004
LRDTLDLDTL, LDLDLS	10737
LRDTLSFS, RRRM, MFFS	10856
LRRDFMRD, FMRD#, LDLR	3630
LRRMFRMMFS, SRDL, LR	9934
LRMDLDRM, LRMDLDRM,	8239
LRMFMRD, FRMFSL, LS#L	2704
LRMFMRD, FMRFSL, SLT	8057
LRLLFSLTD, LRLLFSL	5264
LRTDLTSL, DRTDLTSS,	6912
LRTDTLS#LTM, LLSSFF	10022
LRTLSTMDTL, LDRFMR	2798
LM, DDRMMRDTTL, MMF#S	10223
LMDDRFTLLS#, LS#, DS#LR#	4438
LMDDTLS#LTDTLRDRM,	8694
LMDRMLDTLSM, LMDRM	8491
LMDRMLTDRDTL, LMDR	9137
LMDLRM, LDTLT, RTDRM	6624
LMDLTLS#L, LDTLMRDT,	6284
LMDTMRDT, MSF#MMR#M, L	12406
LMDTMRDT, MTSF#MMR#M,	12406a
LMDTLLT, DSMDRRD, R	1477
LMRDDT, DRDTTL, DLSF	3496
LMRDRDTL, LLTDRM, SD	1119
LMRDLDRM, MLSFMRMR	940
LMRDTDTLS#L, DTLTDR	2242
LMRDTLDRM, F#S#LTDTL	10097
LMRDTL, MSFMRM, DTLM	774
LMRDTL, MSF#MR#M, MMRM	2633
LMRDTLMLFMRMDTL, L	4101
LMRDTLS#L, DRMFMRDD,	11446
LMRDTLS#LL, DDRMFMR	11445
LMRDTL, LSLFFM, LSLF	9441
LMRDTLTLS#, RDFMMRM	261
LMRMDRDTL, LLSFFM,	11619
LMRMDTL, LLLRSSLM, L	4394
LMRMFM, LLD#TD#RD#, S#ML	6827
LMRMTDTRDTLS#L, MMF	2055

1141

LMRMTDT L, MMLSF#MSF#	2054	
LMMDLLLS#, MLSFMRRM,	5481	
LMMRDR, MRDTDTLS#, LM	6780	
LMMRDT, DT LLS#L, TDT L	6287	
LMMRDTMLSS, LTTDRF	1779	
LMMRDT L, DSSFMRM, DR	9892	
LMMRRDDT, LTDRDT, TD	6014	
LMMRRDDT, TDRMDRTS	11475	
LMMRMLDRDT L, LRDLD	8710	
LMMRMT, LMMRMT, DTDR	4979	
LMMMDFMRM, RDT LTS#, S#	1096	

LMMMRDT, TDRMRSM, ML 2596
LMMMRTDT L, TDDRDRM 4903
LMMMMRDRD, DT LSLLM 9850
LMMMMMD, DMMMRR, RFF 9493
LMMMFRM, SLMDTM, LMM 2690
LMMMFMMRDT, LDDRR#R# 3379
LMMMFMMRDT, LDDRR#R#MT, L 3380
LMMMFMMT, LDDRR#MT, L 3378
LMMMLLSDT LS, TDTLS# 10421
LMMMTRDLSL, DRRMSF 11764
LMMFMRDRL, LMSFMRD 11039
LMMFMRLDT L, LDLMF#S 2501
LMMSFMRD#, MFSFMMR, L 12569
LM, MSF#MRDLM, MF#LMRD 1273
LMMLMMSRRSR, MLTDM 4489
LMMTDRR, LDRTDL, LMM 1622
LMMTRDT L, LFFMLSF#M, 7623
LMFMDDMRRD, TLDFML 10256
LMFMRDT, MLDTS#LT, DD 5543
LMFFMLLS#, LMFFSRFM, 8757
LMF#RMD, RRMDT L, LMF#R 6436
LMF#SLSF#M, LT LMF#M, MS 8047
LMSLLS, LDT L, DDSLTD, 6266
LMS#LTDRT, DSTDRMFR 1502
LMS#LTDT L, DTLTDRM, L 9520a
LMLDT L, DSDMRD, MRD 9322
LMLSSDLS, DMDRDT L, 6186
LMLLTDT, DLLSFM, MLM 11068
LMLLTSF#M, DMRDTT L, L 2710
LMLTDRD, TLLS#L, LM 8656
LMLTDLTD, RRDTLS#L, L 5576
LMLTDTLS#M, TDRDTT L, 2495
LMLTRDT L, DSDRMRD, L 6641
LMTDRDT L, DRMFMRM, M 2184
LMTDLRMFM, TDRMSFM 8504
LFRMMLLS, DTMSF#M, LF 3562
LFRSFMM, MFFSSLL, LT 7947

LFMRDLTS#, LTDDRRM, L 3865
LFMRRL#SFMM, DTMLLT 3135
LFMFMRMDR, MSFLSDT 7773
LFFMDRMFMRD, MSLTS 3625
LFFSLSMS, FRRMFMF#S, 12270
LFSM, RFSL, RDRL, LDT L, 4408
LFSM, FSL, RDRL, LDTDT 5085
LFLLDL#L, MSSRMFM, LD 12012
LFLLSSSLSMR, MMMMR 10611
LSDDTDD, LSDDTD, D#RM 319
LSDRMRM, RMFMMRD, RM 3561
LSDRMSFM, DRMFRD, DT 8356
LSMDLDRM, SDRMRDL, L 5973
LSMRDRM, DTSLMFS, SL# 1080
LSMRSSM, DT LSFM, MMM 593
LSMFSM, LSMFSM, LS#LT 2902
LSMSL, DLSLM, LDLDR, M 4949
LSMLTDDT, MRDTLT, TD 4568
LSFMDLSFMD, LTDRMM 2581
LSFMDTLS#, MMRDRDTD, 11482
LSFMRDRMDT, LSFMRD 1430
LSFMRS, DT LSLSFMRR 3858
LSFMMFLDDT L, LSFMM 5369
LSFMFRMDT, LTDRMLT 8539
LSFMFMF, SFMR#MR#M, DD 11013
LSLDDT LT LSLTDD, RD 11541
LSLDRDT LMRTRDT L, M 11667
LSLDRDT L, LFSLSFMR 1721
LSLDRL, LSLFMFR, MMR 1714
LSLDT LSL, DRDT LSLL, 680
LSLMRDT L, TDRMF#F#S, L 1868
LSLMRMLLS, DRMSMRD 11719
LSLSFMFRDSSFSLL, 1758
LSLTDRD, LSLFRM, LSL 1333
LSLTDRMRDT L, DT LSL 6319
LSLTDT L, DT LTDRM, FM 4366
LSLTRT L, TRMRMLF#MR, 5822
LSLTLDRMRFMRLL, MF 8562
LSLT L, DLTRM, SRMRR, T 1886
LSLTTDTLT, LSLTSLS 5560
LS#F#MDRDTT L, TDRMLR 248
LS#STDRDT L, DTLTDRM, 9521a
LS#S#LTDTLLS#, LLSFMM 6442
LS#LDTLS#, DDTLS#LS#LT 9175
LS#LMDTLS#, SLMFSRMR 8642
LS#LMFMRDRMRDR, DRM 9597
LS#LMLRDT L, LSFMFSD 7049
LS#LTDDTM, LSFMRRD, L 6847
LS#LTDDTM, LSFMRRM, L 6847a

LS # LTDDTL, DTLTDRM, M	9521	LLMMTDRR, LTDRTDL, L	1621
LS # LTDRTL, DTLTDRM, M	9520	LLMLS#S#LL, DTLSLF#M, L	
LS # LTDRTL, DTLTDRM, L	9520b		10171
LS # LTDRTL, MFMDRDT, L	9018	LLMLLSSM, MFMDRD, LL	8046
LS # LTDSMS, FMFMRMFS,	5132	LLMLTDRDTDL, MRDTL	5817
LS # LTDLTM, SSFMRRM, S	4137	LLMLTDTDLM, DRMFMR	10986
LS # LTDT, DMRDTL, DDT, M	8991	LLMTDTLS#L, DDRMDRL	1198
LS # LTDTDT, DRMRDTL, L	5450	LLMTRDTL, MMF#SF#MF#R	
LS # LTTD, DTDRRM, MRSF	2841		5255
		LLSDRMML, MLSDRMML,	10852
		LLSDSLLM, DMRDSD, DM	1891
LLD		LLSDTLS#L, DMRDTD, DM	2714
		LLSDTLTL, LDRDRMD, D	11604b
LLDDRRMD, SSFMRRD, R	3387	LLSDTLTL, LTDRDRMD,	11604
LLDDRRM, MRFMRRM, MS	9891	LLSDTTL, LDRDRMD, DR	11604a
LLDDRRM, MSFMRRD, RR	3388	LLSMDRM, MMLDT, RDTL	6143
LLDDMFSR, MMDTLLR, T	10060	LLSMRMFSFM, LTDMSF	2314
LLDRMLRT, DDRMFFM,	129	LLSMRSLDDTLT, LRRT	7683
LLDRTMLRRRMR, MMMR	151	LLSMSFMRMM, LLSMSF	3375
LLDMRDTD, MMSMDTD, M	4550	LLSMSSM, FFMMRF#S, DM	4450
LLDMLMF#M#F#RM, DLDML		LLSFMDTLTLS#, LLS#LT	1123
	7819	LLSFMRMFSLTT, DDTL	2111
LLDMLM, SSRRM, LLDMF	3760	LLSFMMRR, FSLLSSF, M	3505
LLDFRM, MSMRDT, TMF#S	6622	LLSFMMR, LRDTLLS#, LT	1226
LLDLM, FMRDL, LRRDRM	3215	LLSFMTDTLS#, MMMRDR	11481
LLDLSDRM, RSLSF#MRM	6483	LLSSDSDR, SLDRMSRR	12245
LLDLSMSDDLSM, SSLS	9936	LLSLDRL, LSLFMFR, SS	1715
LLDLTDRMM, DRMRMF#S	2577	LLSLDMRDRDT, DLLLT	382
LLDTDLSM, MFMFMFMF	931	LLSLMDTL, LLSMRDRM	12194
LLDTSLTD, TDRMDRD, L	3036	LLSLS, MSMSMSM, DMSS	10383
LLDTLS, DDLTDR, TDMR	3464	LLSLSSFM, LLSMRMRL	210
LLDTLSDR, MMSFR, RRS	6960	LLSLSSF#M, LLSMRMRL	212
LLDTLS, LDDTT, DDLTD	7015	LLSL, SLTSL, LSLL, SLT	6766
LLDTLS#TL, DDMRDTTD,	828	LLSLLTDD, TDRFMRD, R	7161
LLRD#RMRDL#L, RFSLTD#	3806	LLSLL, TLSLL, LSLMM, S	1801
LLRD#RMRDTL, RFSLTD#	3807	LLSLTDRTL, LMMDRM, M	63
LL, RR, MMRMMRDL, DLLD	3785	LLSLTDTL, LLSLTDTL,	7025
LLMDRDTL, DDTDDRM, L	3471	LLSLTLTDTLL, LSLTL	2996
LLMDLDRM, MF#SMDRTL,	5861	LLS#LDTTM, MLDTTL, LL	8021
LLMRDDRMRT, RDTLSF#	6798	LLS#LDTTLS#, LTDRTL, M	2185
LLMRDRMDL, LTDRMDT	9714	LLS#LMMRM,MF#SLTLSF	11579
LLMRMDTL, MLTDTLSL	1	LLS#LTD, DTMMR#M, LLS#L	
LLMMRDR, LLDRTL, LLL	1219		7932
LLMMRDTL, SLTDRM, L	3844	LLS#LTDRM, MRDTLS#, TD	4599
LLMMRDTLS#, LTDDRR	8198	LLS#LTDLT, MMRDTLS#, L	6672
LLMMRMDR, TDRTLTL, L	6777	LLS#LTDTL, LLS#LTDTL,	7026
LLMMRMD, TDRT, MDT, TD	8355	LLS#LTDT, MMRDDT, LL	6672a
LLMMRM, MMRDDT, TDRM	3945	LLLDDMD, LTDLTDLM, M	2022
LLMMMRMFM, MMSDRMF	3422	LLLDDTDR, MDLLS#L, LL	4563
LLMMFSM, LLMMFSM, LM	2809	LLLDDTL, DSLSFM, SDD	871
LLMMF#F#L, LLMMF#F#L, LL		LLLDRDTL, DRRMMRDT,	6291
	1960	LLLDRRDT, LDTLS#L, LL	10408
LLMMLSLTLL, MF#SMDR	12537	LLLDMRDR, SMSFMRDT	11253
LLMMTDRR, LLDRTDL,	1620		

LLLDSSSM, MFSMR, RRR 8132
LLLDLSFM, DTLSMFRD, 5416
LLLDLL, LSFL, LLLLDTL, 3100
LLLDTLR, DTTSSLTDR 2202
LLLDTLS, DTLLRM, TDM 287
LLLDTL, SSLTS#M, LLLD 8914
LLLDTLTM, LLLDTLS#, S# 630
LLLMRDMRDT, MMF#SF#M 2360
LLLMRDTLTDDRRM, MF 3094
LLLMRMDT, LDTDRMRD 5901
LLLMRMDT, LDTDMRDT, 5902
LLLMMFFM, DRMFMRRD, 2497
LLLMMFFM, MTDRMRDTD 10304
LLLMMSFM, MMMRRRDTL. 264
LLLMFMMRD, RRTLTL, L 2319
LLLMFMMRDT, RRRRDT 2359
LLLMFSMRD, RMMFSM, D 4640
LLLMF#SF#MRMF#S#LMSF# 3032
LLLMSF#M#R, RF#MF#S#LM, L 11356
LLLMLSF#M, MLSFMR#M, L 7006
LLLFL, DDDSS, F#F#F#F#SF# 5933
LLLFLSF#SM, RRRF#MRS, 4746
LLLSDDRMM, MFSFFMR 8285
LLLSMR, DTTL, LLLLSMR, 9133
LLLSMMLLSM, MDDTDR 3353
LLLSM, LTDDRT, TDRMD, 4665
LLLSFSLLR, FSMFRD 11534
LLLSSDRM, MFMRDRRD, 7763
LLLSSLDTD, MMSFM 7656
LLLSLDTD, MMSFMRRD, 7657
LLLSLDTL, DRRDRMMM, 10704
LLLSLSFMR, LDRLTDT 4138
LLLSL#LSFF, SLSFMFM 2138
LLLS#M, LTDDRDT, TDRM 4667
LLLS#F#M, LTDDRDT, TDR 4666
LLLS#LDTT, TTMMR#M, MM 3367
LLLLDTL, LSFSLL, MMM 5538
LLLLDTL, LLSFM, LLLL 4828
LLLLRFMR, LLTSLDTL, 3201
LLLLFD, SSSSMS, F#MRL 5772
LLLLFLLLSM, SSSSRS 8852
LLLLSF#M, RLLF#SF#MR, S 2140
LLLLSSSS, SRMFSM, LL 11272
LLLLS#L, LLTDRM, DRD 7448
LLLLLDTL, LS#LDMS, FF 3684
LLLLLSM, SLSSMR, MMM 5877
LLLLLLLS, LLLLSLLL 7582

LLLLLLLS#F#S#L, DDDDD 2162
LLL, LLL, LLDDRM, MMDL 9986
LLLLLLLT, DDDL#LSF, M 4586
LLLLLTTLSL, LLLSSS 8958
LLLLTDRM, LSFMLLT 3606
LLLLTDTRT, TLTDRTR 8221
LLLLTTDL, DRMRDTT, L 8213
LLLTDRM, MMMRDDT, TT 4990
LLLTDTLSM, FFFMRSM, 7422
LLLTDTLSF#M, MMRDTL 11056
LLLTDTLSLL, LLTDTL 5118
LLLTDTL, LTDMRDT, DT 622
LLLTDTL, TTTDRDT, D 1823
LLLTDTTL, LDDDRRSM, 1640
LLLTLS, LLLTLS, LTDT 6653
LLLTLTDMMRDT, DDRM 1098
LLLTTDRM, MRRLTD, DM 10240
LLLTTDLS, SDRDTD, DD 2884
LLLTTDLS, SDMRRDDD, 2883
LLTDDT, DTLSL, DDRMM 8234
LLTDDTRDTLM, LLTDD 11908
LLTDDTLT, TDRMMMRM, 1429
LLTDDTTL, LDDRSM, MM 1639
LLTDRMDR, LDMF#RMM, M
LLTDRMDTL, DTLS#LT 81
LLTDRMRD, MSFMRDTL, 10139
LLTDRMRDT, S#LTDRMM 1398
LLTDRMRDTLLS#,S#S#LT 5010
LLTDRM, MRRDDT, TDRM 3949
LLTDRM, MRRDDT, TDRM, MR 4084
LLTDRM, MMRDDT, TDRM 3948
LLTDRM, MMRDRT, TDRM 3947
LLTDRMM, MLLS#L, LLT 10149
LLTDRMM, SMLS#L, LLTD 4215
LLTDRM, SFMRRM, SMSL 713
LLTDRMT, TDTLDT, S#LT 5821
LLTDRTD, LLTDRTM, DD 4776
LLTDRTS, SLLTTM, LLT 4190
LLTDMRDT, DRFMRDTD, 5987
LLTDMRDT, DLTDRM, MR 9465
LLTDMRDTLSSL, TDRM 8924
LLTDMMMFMRM, MRMFM 9048
LLTDMTL, TMRDDT, TMT 7772
LLTDFMRDTL, MLTDRM, 8196
LLTDLDRM, SLSMDRRM, 7885
LLTDLMMM, LMMRDRM, L 3669
LLTDLTDRM, MMMSMRR 4077
LLTDLTS, SLLTTM, LLT 4192
LLTDLTTLLSLTTL, LR 9834
LLTDTDRDTLM, SFMRR 12501
LLTDTMF#SLFM, SF#MRR 1748

1144

LLTDT LDFMLL, DDRR#R	6942
LLTDT LMRDT, LLTDT L	3450
LLTDT LFL, TDRMRS, SL	8752
LLTDT LS, SDMRRM, LLT	4388
LLTDT LSLM, MRMFMRMD,	2064
LLTDT LSLLL, DDRFM	2863
LLTDT LS#LTML, S#LTLT	2876
LLTDT LLS#, DMRDTD, DM	12307
LLTDT L, TDRMRM, MRDT	2479
LLTDT LTTDRDT L, MR	2827
LLTD#RM, RFRDL#L, DDTD	10219
LLTLS, LDTLM, TDTL.	7667
LLTLS#, LTDTLTM, TDRM	7668
LLTLTDRT, LDMRMFMR,	6995
LLTTDDS, LLMMFSSF	4282
LLTTDDT, LTDDDTLS#, L	8460
LLTTTDRM, MRRLLTDD	5664
LTDDRDTL, DRMMLSLM	4573
LTDDRDTT, DTLTLS#LL	2508
LTDDRRDD, LTDRMFRM	2402
LTDDRRM, DRMMF#F#S, LS	9889
LTDDRRMM, MDTDRDTT,	7270
LTDDRMDSSS, MRDDL	8275
LTDDSFSFM, LTDDSSS	4342
LTDDTSLLLLTDDRM, MR	10871
LTDDTLS, FMRLSFMFS,	5277
LTDDTLS#L, LLSMSFM, L	6394
LTDRDTDLT, DTLSFML	12195
LTDRDTLDTLSLL, LMS	9538
LTDRMRDRT, LTDTLLS	7814
LTDRMRDTDT, LTDDRM	8407
LTDRMRDT, RDLDTSL, L	3891
LTDRMMRDTLS#S#, LTDT	2371
LTDRMMRMM, MMFSFM	8456
LTDRMMFMFRM, MDDRR	4283
LTDRMMFMFLM, RRTDD	4284
LTDRMFFM, MRDTLLS#, L	6366
LTDRMFS#, LTDDRRD, LT	1789
LTDRMSMRTL, RMLDRM,	10346
LTDRMSF#M, MMMRDRM, L	6286
LTDRMLRMFML, LLSSS	10319
LTDRMLRDTSLSL, LSD	8534
LTDRMLRT, DDRMFFM,	128
LTDRMLSF, MMRDTT	10527
LTDRMLLS#LL, DTLSFF	10173
LTDRMLLS#LTL, LTDRM	1549
LTDRMT, RMF#SLM, SF#RT,	2728
LTDRSF#SMLSMRDLTL,	55
LTDRLTLTD, DTLSMMF#	10560
LTDRTM, RTDLTL, LLTD	3683
LTDRTLS, DRMFMRD, LT	8592
LTDMRDT, MF#SMLSF#M, L	6168

LTDMRDT, SDRMFFM, LT	2096
LTDMRDTTT, RDRMFMR	7260
LTDMMRDDT, LTDRMRD	2344
LTDMMRDTL, LTDTLS#	1242
LTDMM, LTDMM, FMRTLL	4619
LTDMLDTL, DRMMRRD, L	4121
LTDLDRMD, MFSMRRD, M	4728
LTDLMMM, MMRDTL, LTD	11124
LTDLFFFM, LLSFMRDT,	4322
LTDLSMS#LLTD, RMMRD	1946
LTDLTDL, DDRMRDT, RR	7626
LTDTDRMM, LTDTLLS#L, D	3895
LTDTDRMM, LTDTLLS#L, L	3895a
LTDTDLMM, LTDTDRM, M	1002
LTDTLDTLSLM, LTDTL	9965
LTDTLRRD#, LMRSF#M, MM	12444
LTDTLRMFFM, MMRDTL	5091
LTDTLS, RRMFLSFMFS,	1686
LTDTLS, MMF#LS#L, SSLS	269
LTDTLSM, SDTLSL, LTD	8743
LTDTLSM, SLTLSL, LTD	10274
LTDTLSM, LSFMDRM,	8369
LTDTLSL, DRMMFMFRM,	3503
LTDTLSLS, DRMDRRD, D	10359
LTDTLS, LTDRL, DRMM	5846
LTDTLS#L, DRMRDTD, MM	7482
LTDTLS#L, DRMFMRM, FM	4168
LTDTLS#LTDTL, DRRMDRRM,	10293
LTDTLL, DDTLSLLLM, SL	4613
LTDTLLRMFMR, RDMTM	9945
LTDTLLSL, LFSMRFMR	12384
LTDTLLS#L, MMRRDDT, T	1448
LTDTLLS#LT, DRDT, LTL	800
LTDTL, LTDTL, MRDT, TD	2829
LTDTLTS#M, MLRDTTL, L	4547
LTDTLTS#L, DRMLSFM, T	12057
LTDTLTL, DDRMDR, RMF	9961
LTDTTLLSM, LTDTTLL	6720
LTRDSSFM, MF#LSDTLS,	7518
LTRRTRMFM, MLSLM, DD	1097
LTRLTRDTDL, DRMMRD	5326
LTMRDTLS#L, TDDRRM, M	2638
LTSDTLSL, MLTLDDTD,	8059
LTSMLLS#L, DRMRDDTD,	12325
LTLSLTDTLT, MLTLSL	2679
LTLS#LDTLLS#, S#LLSLS	5565
LTLS#LTDT, TDRMRDTL,	10755
LTLS#TDTL, DRMDRMD, D	9580

LT LTDDRDRM, MSFMMR	11286
LT LTDRDT, LDTT LSL, L	5080
LT LTRMMR, T LLSMS, SL	11952
LTTD, DDRM, FMMRDTT L,	8603
LTTDS#LTDRDT L, TDTD	4172
LTTDLLRTDLL, DDRMD	8572
LTTDLTSL, LT RDTDLT,	11514

TDD

TDDT LSM, SSSFR, LLLS	939
TDRDRM, MRDDDMDR, SS	12146
TDRDRM, MFFFMSMR, SF	4851
TDRDRMMFFFLSM, DRM	503
TDRRDRMD, SSLDT LS, M	1977
TDRRDRMM, RMFFMDR, S	6031
TDRRDRMMMFMR, MFS	901
TDRRRDRMD, RMRDT LS,	1999
TDRRRRDRM, SSLLLDT	4849
TDRRRRDTD, DT LLLDT	8016
TDRRRRRT, LTDDDRDS,	4484
TDRRRRFMRDS, DRMMM	7216
TDRRFMRDR, SRRFMRD	7619
TDRRFTDD, MFSSSMR, S	1864
TDRMRM LSMRDL, DMFS	6322
TDRFTD, MFSSMR, SDMM	1863
TDMSSLSDM, SFRT FMR	4921
TDSMDLL, LLLTDT L, SD	1401

TDTDRMRDT, SDDSRM, L	1778
TDT LMRDT, RDT LRDT L,	109
TDT LTDRDT LS#, MLLTD	4727
TDT LTDRDT LS#MLTDR	4726
TDT LTRDT, RDTDLSFM,	3052
TDT LTRDT, TDTDLLFM,	2307
TDT LTRMRDT, RDTDLS	3053
TRDDDSDLD, DDDSDL	11233
TRDM, MMMMMRDRRRRD	3868
TRMRDT LTT, SLTTTTT	7447
TRMTSS, LDT LSTSLS,	9643
TMRT RDT LTDDRDRM, M	2429
TMS#LTRDT, TDLTS#LT, T	10095
TMTDTSLT, TDRDLSFM,	2403
TMTDT LSLT, TDRDT LS	2406
TMTDT LS#LT, TRRDT LS	2405
TSDD, RR, MFSFMRD.	1667
TSFR#RR#FR#RDS, SLDRM	327
T LSDSLLLLS, F#MRDF#F#	2187
T LSDS, T LSM, MFMMRD	11267
T L#LFFMSM, MRSR, RDSD,	3406
TTDMMRM, MRD#RLLL, LL	6247
TTRTDT, LDT LS, DSSSL	5190
TTLT, TTSL, DDTD, DDLT,	4491
TTTDDRS, DDRRM, MMMD	4021
TTTDR, DDDLS, MMMSLS	12235
TTTDT LTDR, DRMLTDR	10987

APPENDIXES

APPENDIX A

GLOSSARY

Author: That person, institution, publisher, compiler, anthology, or tradition responsible for writing, approval, or transmittal to others of the earliest verified text of the hymn (as poem).

Chorus: See Refrain

Citation: Directive to a named hymnal, a very specified numbered hymn or tune, or to a page on which that hymn or tune is printed. For purposes of this Index, citations are made only to the item numbers (see below) which are chronologically representative of the first appearance of the text of hymn or tune within each hymnal as analyzed.

Composer: See Author, and substitute "of the tune (as music)" for the underlined words.

Congregational song: Vocal music, varying greatly from sect to sect and from meeting to meeting, used at community worship in an act of community participation. Modern literature of this nature is predominantly secular in origin, social in nature, and dedicated to Man's decision to meet the Divine Ideal.

Descant: Contrasting and decorative melody, usually a soprano solo, which becomes a vocal accompaniment to the hymn tune. In common practice it is used with selected stanzas only: in a short hymn, perhaps at the third or fourth stanza; in a long hymn, perhaps near the middle of the hymn, and again at the final or near final stanza. Descants are not indexed.

Diatonic scale: The melodic eight-tone scale used in most western music, proceeding naturally without chromatic interruption, and in any key. The relative musical intervals and syllable names are constant, no matter the key of the printed score.

First line: Usually the first line of the poetical hymn, but occasionally enlarged to avoid confusion with similar phrases.

1149

First phrases of melody: Here determined as approximately the sixteen opening tones of the score as sung to the accompanying
words, and recorded in the tonic sol-fa syllables.

Flats: See Sharps; also the schedule on p.viii.

Gospel song: Poem (usually sung) encouraging man to offer honor,
worship, praise to God. See also Hymn.

Hymn: Poem (usually sung) in praise to God. See also Gospel song.

Hymn tune: A musical setting of a hymn or psalm, usually in four-
part harmony, and intended for use in public worship. See also
Hymn, and Tune.

Item number: The specific number, within a specific hymnal, that
identifies desirable information exactly; as BQ3 points to Book
BQ, according to the symboloc terminology of this Index, and to
the particular content numbered Three (3). It may be used to indicate a rendering of a hymn, a hymn tune, a tune name, or a
variant of any of these three.

Liturgy: That portion of the act of public worship which is formal
in nature, and chiefly dominated by the clergy rather than the congregation; but in which a priest-and-people antiphonal question-
and-answer, statement-and-response is elemental. Originally used
to describe the Mass, and the directives and rubrics pertaining
thereto.

Melody: A series of single notes arranged in musically expressive
succession. (O.U.D.)

Movable Do: See the illustrations, Appendix D. Notice that the
syllable names follow regularly as the scale opening tone varies.
The intervals are constant, the tone names are constant no matter
the key of the score.

Refrain of hymn or tune: The words or the melody repetitively sung
between formal poetical stanzas of the hymn. Citations are not
made to refrains; simply records of their texts, and references
by use of letter R to the Standard First Line or the Standard
Tune Name.

Serial number: The chronological entry number in Index I or Index
III, beginning respectively with 100001 (Index I) and 1 (Index III).

These numbers are used in Indexes II and IV, respectively, to
assemble related materials alphabetically displayed in Indexes
I and III. The numbers found at Index V relate to those at Index
III. (Some serial numbers are eliminated because of resolved
conflicts.)

Sharps: The symbols used to indicate a half-step rise in the physical value of a musical tone. The character is #. Sharps are
used in these Indexes when indicated by the score; and when
used in substitution for flats (according to the schedule on viii.
Flats are not represented herein, except by way of the relative
sharped (raised) tone instead of its printed lowered counterpart
tone. This procedure was adopted to expedite the mechanical work
involved within the Index. Musical purists will be unhappy! The
piano will sing the same sounds.

Solfaing: See Solmization

Solmization: Singing melodies to the syllables of the tonic sol-fa
scale.

Source: Book in which required materials are included.

Primary source: The original book or manuscript containing the
text as it was set at the time of its composition.

Secondary sources: Books, such as the seventy-eight hymnals
herein analyzed, with reprint of words and music. Except for a
handful of sources, quoted within these hymnals, everything is
from Secondary Sources. Several manuscripts, the Church Gallery
Book, and a few of the very earliest hymnals are mostly what
might be here called Primary Sources. Consequently, the term
Sources is usually used.

Standard: For purposes of this Index only, Standard indicates the
hymn or tune as printed in the book in which it was initially discovered as the cataloging progressed. This might have been at
Book A, or Book BZ.

Standard first line: The reading of the first line of a hymn (poem)
as it was initially recorded within the cumulation of this Index.
Citations to this are made as they appear during the progress of
the indexing.

Standard melody: The reading of the first phrase of the melody as it
was initially recorded during the cumulation of this Index. Citations to this are made as they appear during the progress of the
indexing.

Standard tune name: The name associated with a melody as it was
initially recorded during the cumulation of this Index. The standard tune name serves as a label to identify the standard melody
with which it is associated. Citations, apparently to the standard
tune name, are in reality attributed to the standard melody.

Standard first line, melody, or tune name: The second to be established: When a variant of any of these is sufficient to cause
identification and discrimination difficulties, a second reading
is established as standard, and citations are made to it as they
occur during the progress of the indexing.

Syllables: The tone names associated with the intervals in the diatonic musical scale, which is not dependent on Fixed-Do, and is
based on the simple scale without chromatic intrusion.

Tonic Solfa scale: Syllable names of the diatonic scale are Do(D),
Re(R), Mi(M), Fa(F), Sol(S), La(L), and Ti(T), with the sequence
repeating. Letters in parentheses are the symbols used for melodic record in this Index. In case a tone is raised one-half step,
it is marked as: S#

Tune: A rhythmical succession of musical tones, here referring to
the tones to which a hymn is set for use in congregational singing.

Tune name: Name assigned to a melody. Established tradition in the
association of melody with tune name is usually weak, as indicated
by the large number of variants in Index IV. Nevertheless, all
assigned tune names have herein been accepted as tune names,
have been recorded, and references inserted to tie the related
tune names to the standard tune name for the purposes of the
index.

Variant first line, melody: Slight deviant rendering of text or tune
which does not cause confusion in identification. Citations are
limited to one time only (that first), with X symbolizing refer-

ence to standard first line in Index I; and V symbolizing reference to standard melody in Index III.

Variant tune name: Name for a melody which differs from the
standard tune name. No citations are made, simply a reference
X to the established or standard tune name is made at Index III.

APPENDIX B

ABBREVIATIONS

abr	abridged	O.U.D.	tionary on historical principles. 3d ed. rev. Oxford [1955]
arr	arranged, arranger		
Baker	Baker's Biographical dictionary of musicians, 5th ed., rev. by Slonimsky. Schirmer [c 1958]	p	page
		pseud	pseudonym
		publ	published
		R	Re (syllable) refrain (chorus)
c	century		
ca	circa	S	Sol (syllable)
cf	compare	Sr	Senior Sister (nun)
comp	compiled, compiler		
d	died	suppl	supplement
D	Do (syllable)	T	Ti (syllable)
F	Fa (syllable)	tr	translated, translator
fl	flourished	trad	traditional
Fr	Father (priest)	univ	university
G-B	Gesangbuch	V	variant reading volume
harm	harmony	S	see; see also (rare)
Jr	Junior	A-Z, AA-AZ, and BA-BZ	symbols used to identify hymnals analyzed (see List of books indexed)
Julian	Julian. A dictionary of hymnology. Dover [1957] 2 v		
K-G	Kirchengesangbuch	#	sharp
L	La (syllable)	♭	flat (unused symbol)
M	Mi (syllable) mode (plainchant): M is frequently followed by arabic number 1-8, to indicate the melodic mode to which the tune is set	,	musical phrase ending
		.	melodic ending
		?	authorship disputed
		??	authorship ascribed
mel	melody	( )	encloses source, or author, in Indexes I and III
OUD, or	Oxford Universal dic-		

[ ]   unintentionally a very   1-8   following M (as M2)
      few were allowed to   indicates plainchant
      stand in the melodic   in Mode Two; etc.
      redaction as indication
      of notes not always   I, II,   arbitrarily added to
      used: normal proce-   III   tune names to serve
      dure was to make an   as identification sym-
      additional variant entry.   bols for sorting pur-
                                       poses.

APPENDIX C

ARBITRARY DECISIONS ADOPTED IN THIS INDEX

Always use Alleluia, Jam, O, and Sion; no other spelling accepted
either as entry word or within the text where filing order
would be affected except in the case of Zion in German.

Always interfile Savior and Saviour, Jesu and Jesus; but spell as
printed.

Always use The, A, or An when presented as initial words in Indexes I and III; and recognize them in filing sequences.

Never use The, A, or An when presented as initial words in titles
of books, except for the purposes of clarification; and always
disregard them for purposes of filing.

Initialisms, i.e., persons known by initials only, are entered
straightforward only; never inverted. Reference from inverted
order is not made.

Pseudonyms are occasionally identified, and some references are
made. Additional identification is now and then included in
special notes within Indexes II and IV.

Traditional hymns and tunes (carols, folk songs, diocesan tunes)
are attributed to the tradition, if possible the date is given,
and the mode indicated when it is known for Gregorian plainsongs and for Jewish melodies.

Anonymity was a final resort only. It has been possible, even
here, to occasionally indicate approximate date or region from
which the material sprung.

Hymns and tunes which fall into these impersonal categories
(initialisms, pseudonymous, traditional, and anonymous) were
usually not subdivided. Rather the list is alphabetical, with
some sorting device (as date, mode, etc.) after the name.
This seemed more practical for the reader, and required but
little more space to delineate.

Dates of birth and death of author or composer, of publication, of
   era of origin; full names of authors and composers (including
   unused forenames when known) have been included in Indexes
   II and IV. Julian and Baker have been combed almost name-
   by-name; indexes of sources within all hymnals have been
   consistently used; and special attention has been paid to information within recently published hymnals for verification and
   for completing biographical notes.

Honorifics (as, Lord, Sir, Rev.) are infrequently used; members
   of the Catholic hierarchy are usually identified (as, Innocent
   IV, Pope); and saints are named by use of "St" as opening
   term. This is a departure from most library practice, from
   Catholic practice. It is adopted here because congregational
   song has been, historically, a Protestant manifestation. The
   literature of hymnody since the Protestant Reformation, from
   Protestant sources, tends to follow the practice here utilized.

Exclude Hymnal C from the citation record of hymns. They are absolute duplication of items and item numbers found in Book B.
   The tunes, however, differ and are indexed fully.

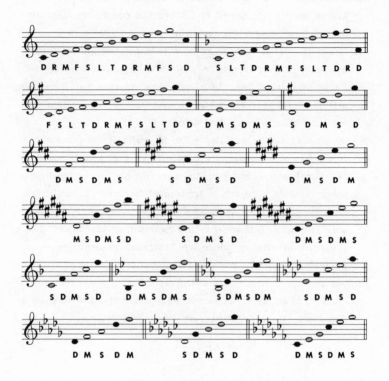

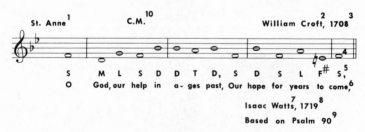

St. Anne C.M.   William Croft, 1708

S M L S D   D T D, S   D S L F[#] S,

O   God, our help in a-ges past, Our hope for years to come,

Isaac Watts, 1719

Based on Psalm 90

APPENDIX D

THE SCALES

1) Tune name; 2) Composer; 3) Date; 4) Notation; 5) Solmization;
6) Hymn; 7) Author; 8) Date; 9) Original source; 10) Common meter

1158

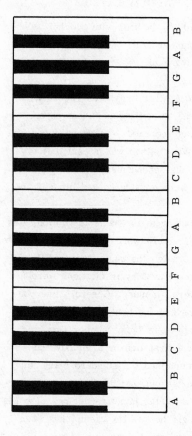

APPENDIX E

PIANO KEYBOARD

The musical scale with neither sharps nor flats is known as Key C. It begins on key marked C.

The hymn illustrated in Appendix D is in Key of B Flat, and the first piano key struck is that marked F.

When a musical tone is raised by one-half step (a sharp), the note next closest to the right is struck, rather than the note bearing the usual syllable name. Notice the example near to the end of the illustration in Appendix D.

APPENDIX F
HOW THIS BOOK WAS CUMULATED

Beginning with The Hymnal, 1940 (A), a book with which I was
very familiar, and with Hymn Number One, "Come, thou long-expected Jesus" by Witt (1715), the hymns were taken one-by-one
and book-by-book.

Poetry (i.e., the poets and the first lines) was recorded --
card-by-card, citation-by-citation. Then the music (composer,
melodic sequence, tune name) was recorded -- card-by-card, citation-by-citation, book-by-book. When either was repeated (i.e.,
absolute identity) within a book, the second mention was not made.
When variants were quoted they were considered and cited if ap-
propriate to the Index.

When Book B, an earlier book from the same institution, was
studied, variants appeared. By C, there were still further variants.
In fact, all of the poetry of C repeated the same order of B; and
the music was variant throughout. The C hymn citations were not
made; the C melodic citations were all made. Generally the rou-
tine of completing both the hymns and the tunes within a single
book was followed, always item-by-item from Number One.

That book (hymnal) in which a first line or a melody was
noticed originally (first time) determined the standard entry for
this Index. It may not have been the original reading, but it served as the base around which to pivot the many renderings of words
and of music in these seventy-eight books. No attempt has been
made, ever! to identify or to reconstruct texts; but a seriously
consistent effort has been made to cite as source that person, institution, publisher, compiler, anthology, or culture originally responsible for its inception or its transmission; and to relate materials which belong together. When a closely variant rendering appeared, two citations were made: (1) at the main, or standard,

1160

entry (as tune name, or at first line respectively) and (2) at the independent secondary entry with this special variation recorded, and with
a reference to the standard form.

A refrain or chorus, as part of hymn or tune, required full quotation of first line and also of first sixteen notes of the melody. Refrain
cards bear no citations, simply references to standard entry.

Variants to the refrain, either words or melody, were cited
one time only and in the same manner as variants to the standard
entry (as indicated in second paragraph above).

Thus far only one standard form has been considered. Variants
appeared which were both too severe, and too popular, to treat as
secondary items. Alternate forms were established as standard, as
those found under Whittier's name (Index II, as author) or the several Cherry Tree Carols (Index IV, as English traditional).

At the end of the work, when Book BZ had been completed,
most of the poetry had been automatically sorted. The problem
was the music.

Up to this time four indexes were being made concurrently:
two for the hymns (first line and author); two for the music (tune
name and composer). And up to this time musical relationships
could be assured only when human memory was assisted by citation
similarities. Tune names and tune sources had long since been discarded as definitive. They are irregular. They are inexact. They
are capriciously applied. Melodic similarities could not be completely trusted, no matter how like seemed the labels.

The only solution was to immediately create Index V out of
what is here displayed as Index III, and to do it immediately.
Simple tune name references were eliminated. All the others were
arranged as published in Index V. Identical melodies were found.
Many of these had been attributed to both real and anonymous
sources, to both real and traditional sources, to different published sources, to different diocesan (see) sources. This sorting
reduced both the German traditional and the English traditional
sections by at least twenty-five percent. The various gesangbuchs,
Walther, Luther, Bourgeois, and Psalter entries were cumulated.

Syllabic reading of the melodies proved to be effective in every instance except one. That was early in the study, and no record was retained of the melodies involved -- but they were of secondary importance so far as common usage was concerned. It has thus proved necessary, only in the ratio of 1:12582 instances, to record the time signature, note value, or high and low tones in order to completely identify melodies of songs which people ordinarily sing.

When apparently identical or closely variant melodies were found, hymnals had to be studied to verify similarity. Then all references were collected and directed to that form determined as standard (once again identifying the initial citation chronologically within this Index). Some of these variants required hours of work. I hope the reader will find few unresolved references. Fourteen tune names to what are here standardised as "Cana" and "Ratisbon", both of them old German melodies, are the extreme. Only when the very final editing was being done, and after many pages had already been put into final form by the Scarecrow Press typist, could the two pairs of "14" be appropriately filed.

Index V, "Melodies, a systematic index" was typed after the duplicates had been removed and serial numeration confirmed. Cards then had to be returned to order for Index III. It was at this time that information could be gathered to enlarge Index IV's value -- just as similar information was cumulated from Index I to enlarge Index II.

When thirty-five books had been completed only these twelve poems were found common:

Abide with me (Lyte)
Adeste fideles (Latin, 18th c., and in several translations)
All hail the power (Perronet)
Hark! the herald angels (Wesley)
Holy, holy, holy (Heber)
Jesus, lover of my soul (Wesley)
Jesus shall reign (Watts)
O [Our] God, our help in ages past (Watts)
Saviour again to thy dear name (Ellerton)
Sun of my soul (Keble)
The church's one foundation (Stone)

When I survey the wondrous cross (Watts)

With Book #36, AJ, two of these fell out. As the Jewish, the less orthodox and more dissident Christian books and the widely differing Catholic hymnals were surveyed, the number of constantly recurring words and music was reduced. But accretion improved. The Church of Jesus Christ of Latter-Day Saints, the Moravians, the Christian Scientists each forced new entries for a very, very large number of hymns and tunes. The earlier of the two Moravian books (AZ) contains more than 1500 hymns. There is a relatively small number of melodies -- but each has at least two distinguishing tune names!

The usual portion of words and tunes new to the Index in the later analyses was close to fifteen percent. Constant tallying pointed to a very wide range of congregational song known only to a particular institution. The specific instances which follow are illustrative:

Union hymnal (BH) and The Oxford Book of carols (BG) each introduced materials which were well analyzed. Every Catholic book was rich in texts and in scores not recorded earlier, but the sources (i.e., the authors and the composers) were less regularly reported than in many of the counterpart liturgical Protestant hymnals.

Anglican Hymn book (BV) melodies included ninety-five new ones (14 percent) and its new hymns numbered eighty-three (12.5 per cent). The melodic index arranged metrically with the initial measures of the score quoted is an innovation to hymnals.

The Baptist hymn book (BY) presented 103 new hymns and 244 new tunes, or 13.38 and 26.5 percent respectively. Both BV and BY are books from Britain, published within the recent five years.

A letter from The Methodist Publishing House and dated February 16, 1966 gives this information:

"Our plans now are to release this new Hymnal sometime in July, 1966.

"The title page reads as follows:

THE METHODIST HYMNAL

Official Hymnal of The Methodist Church
The Methodist Publishing House
Nashville, Tennessee"

The final book indexed (BZ) is representative of the hymnal just
recorded. By close comparison of the Report, i.e. BZ, and the
1935 edition (G) it was found that twenty-six new melodies and twenty-
eight new poems were added to the Index file. There are to be,
according to the Report's statistics, 402 tunes and 539 hymns in
the 1966 edition.

It would seem by comparing and contrasting editorial arrangements made for books BV, BY, and BZ that there was a basic
difference. Anglican Hymn book had a Committee of twelve members; The Baptist hymn book, a Committee of twenty members;
and Report to the 1964 General Conference, which is representative of The Methodist hymnal [1966] had forty-two named persons
and a battery of questionnaires sent to 22,000 ministers -- more
than half of whom responded. Relative contrast with books such as
X, Y, BG, BH, and BJ -- where individuals or a small editorial
committee were free to work untrammeled by public and institutional opinion -- show a peculiar earthy freshness added. Some of
this may pass, or be congregationally neglected; other will have
had the opportunity to prove itself good. On the other hand it must
be said that The Methodist hymnal [1966] editorial policy stated
a serious intent of returning Wesleyan hymns to the people. This
has been done. It does not show in statistics here published, because the hymns had been recorded from older publications.

Coming from a childhood in Lancaster County, Pennsylvania,
I knew this region as anvil and crucible for religion. The Swedes
(Lutherans) had almost reached us; Penn's influence was there in
the Quaker Meeting House south of Quarryville; the Scottish-Irish-
English were evident in the southern section -- where there were
Methodist and Presbyterian congregations, often joined by Friends;
just a small Baptist congregation in the county seat. There were
United Brethren (not Unitas Fratrum), Evangelical, River Brethren,
Dunkard, Amish, New Mennonite, Mennonite, Church of the Breth-
ren, Church of God. Anglican influence was strongest in Lancaster

City and in the old iron mining community of Mt. Hope. The Re-
formed-Lutheran Union churches, common to the counties just east
of Lancaster, were here separate institutions with separate places
of worship. Lititz has its strong Moravian community, its Linden
Hall -- the oldest women's college in the U.S.A., now an academy
only. Roman Catholic churches were at the county seat; quite recently a large Greek Orthodox community has immigrated. Lancaster City has had an active Unitarian congregation for many years;
and the Jewish congregation in the City is large and strong.

This personal note explains the presence of certain hymnals
which are easily overlooked. It particularly explains Ausbund (BU)
which originated in 1570. The Amish people love to sing, their
young people past sixteen years of age have their Saturday evening
"singings", and their services on Sundays are three to four hours
long. When you consider that Hans Betz's hymn (BU106) "Ihr Christen g'mein" has forty-six eight-line stanzas, it is necessary to allow a bit of time!

Just one Ausbund hymn (BU131) was found elsewhere: "Our
Father God, thy name we praise", at BY362. In its original form
it is used at every Sunday morning service as the second hymn,
according to a letter from M.E. Ressler (Secretary to Music,
Lancaster Mennonite Conference, September 14, 1965). The
British Baptists sing their three stanzas to the tune "Mit freunden
zart"; the Amish sing their four stanzas to "Aus tiefer noth",
which is indicated as alternate tune in BY.

Tying for first place as most generally used tune are Bourgeois's "Old 100th" (associated with either Praise God, from whom
all blessings flow, or All people that on earth do dwell) and "Adeste
fideles", found in Wade's Cantus diversi. These are in seventy of
the books examined.

Second place, as in sixty-seven books, is held by "St Anne",
by Croft (associated with O God, our help in ages past).

In tie for third, in sixty-six books, are "Moscow" by Giardini
(associated with Come thou almighty king) and Dykes's "Niceae"
which is closely associated with Holy, holy, holy, holy, Lord God.

The most used hymn, as might be surmised, is the 18th century Latin "Adeste fideles" when it is completely reckoned. Latin
text, translations beginning, "Come hither", "Ye faithful, come
hither", "Come, all ye faithful", "O come, all ye faithful", etc.
are found in seventy hymnals. Actually, had it been in more than
seventy books, it would have been somewhat misplaced: several
books include pre-18th century hymns only, one is a book of carols (this is a composed poem), one is a Jewish hymnal, one is
Christian Science hymnal, one a psalter, one a secondary book to
its partner.

"O God, our help in ages past", Isaac Watts' metrical paraphrase of the 90th Psalm, is in sixty-seven books: a perfect mat-
ing with tune "St Anne", in the same manner as "Adeste fideles"
words and tune are perfectly mated.

Found under fourteen different tune names are the melodies
standardized here as "Cana," by Vulpius, and "Ratisbon", published by Crueger. The greatest number of actual melodic variants
has not been sought, but would most probably exist in some one of
the early German hymn tunes which proved popular and singable.

Serial numeration in the first line file (Index I) indicates 11979
entry lines (numbering begins with 100001).

Parallel Index III is serially numbered from 1 to 12582.

By adding the number of hymns published in each of these
hymnals, there is a total of 39,373 printed hymns in the seventy-
eight books. This means that at least that many exact citations are
recorded with the Index I entries.

Comparably, after considering that a great many hymns are
set to two or even three tunes, it is most likely that about the
same number of tunes were examined, but cited only once per
tune per hymnal (total citations for tunes are fewer in Index III,
than for first lines in Index I).

If a guess may be hazarded, I would estimate that about 3200
references are made to variant tune names; 2500 references to
variant first lines; 1000 to first lines of refrains; 1000 to first
phrases of refrain melody; and 1000 to variants of the standard

melody. In other words, there are almost 24,500 first line and melody entries. Of these, approximately 8700 are references of one sort or another. The ratio is approximately 1:2 as references and primary entries are counted. It is symbolic, very symbolic, of the nearly insurmountable indexing and musicological literary confusion which had to be cleared. Hopefully there is a bit more consistency!

APPENDIX G
General Survey of Hymnals As Books of Reference

	A	B	C	D	E	F	G	H	I	J	K	L	M	N	O	P	Q	R	S	T	U	V	W	X	Y	Z
Title page with authority symbol	*	*	*	*	*	*	*	*	*	*	*	*	*	*	*	*	*	*	*	*	*	*	*	*	*	*
Table of contents	*	*	*	*	*	*	*	*	*	*	*	*	*	*	*	*	*	*	*	*	*	*	*	*	*	*
Sources acknowledged fully	*	*	*	*	*	*					*	*	*				*					*	*	*	*	*
Birth/Death dates of Author/Composer	*	*			*	*				*	*	*	*	*		*	*	*			*	*	*	*		*
HYMNS (Poetry)																										
First line index	*	*	*	*	*	*	*	*	*	*	*	*	*	*	*	*	*	*	*	*	*	*	*	*	*	*
Author index	*	*	*	*	*	*	*	*	*	*	*	*	*	*	*	*	*	*	*	*	*	*	*	*	*	*
Hymns of the historical faith	*	*	*	*	*	*	*	*	*	*	*	*	*	*	*	*	*	*	*	*			*	*		
Psalter in meter	*	*					*			*	*						*	*				*	*			
19th-20th century hymns	*	*	*	*			*	*			*	*	*	*				*				*	*	*	*	*
Children's hymns named	*	*					*	*					*	*	*	*							*			
TUNES (Music)																										
Tune name index, alphabetical	*	*	*	*	*	*	*	*	*	*	*	*	*	*	*	*	*	*	*	*	*	*	*	*	*	*
Tune name index, metrical	*	*	*	*	*	*	*	*	*	*	*	*	*	*	*	*	*	*	*	*	*	*	*	*	*	*
Composer index	*	*	*	*	*	*	*	*	*	*	*	*	*	*	*	*	*	*	*	*	*	*	*	*	*	*
Plainsongs included	*			*	*	*	*	*			*	*						*	*				*			*
Reformation tunes	*			*	*	*	*	*			*	*	*	*				*	*				*			
Folk tunes, all cultures							*	*													*					
Gospel songs																										
EDITORIAL POLICIES, etc.																										
Preface (or other) Statement on Song	*	*		*		*				*	*	*	*	*	*	*	*	*					*	*		
Specialties of the book	*	*	*	*	*		*	*	*	*	*	*	*	*	*	*	*	*								
Liturgical section							*			*	*	*	*	*	*	*	*	*		*		*	*	*	*	*
Prayer book section (or substitute)							*			*	*	*	*	*	*	*	*									
Documents of the historical faith							*			31						32		33								

	AA	AB	AC	AD	AE	AF	AG	AH	AI	AJ	AK	AL	AM	AN	AO	AP	AQ	AR	AS	AT	AU	AV	AW	AX	AY	AZ
Title page with authority symbol	*	*						*			*	*	*	*	*	*	*	*	*	*	*	*	*	*	*	*
Table of contents	*	*						*			*	*	*	*	*	*	*	*	*	*	*	*	*	*	*	*
Sources acknowledged fully		*			*	*																				
Birth/Death dates of Author/ Composer	*			*			*	*				*		*			*			*	*					*
HYMNS (Poetry)																										
First line index	*	*	*	*	*	*		*	*		*	*	*	*	*	*	*	*	*	*	*	*	*	*	*	*
Author index		*	*	*	*	*	*	*	*		*	*	*	*	*	*	*	*	*	*	*	*	*	*	*	*
Hymns of the historical faith	*					*		*	*	*	*	*	*	*	*	*	*	*	*		*	*	*	*		*
Psalter in meter							*	*	*	*	*	*	*													
19th-20th century hymns		*		*	*	*		*		*	*	*	*	*	*	*	*		*	*	*	*	*	*	*	
Children's hymns named	*			*	*	*	*		*	*	*	*	*	*	*				*		*	*				
TUNES (Music)																										
Tune name index, alphabetical	*	*	*	*	*	*		*	*		*	*	*	*	*	*	*			*	*				*	*
Tune name index, metrical	*	*	*	*	*	*		*	*		*	*	*	*	*	*	*			*	*				*	*
Composer index																	*			*	*					*
Plainsongs included																										
Reformation tunes	*	*	*	*	*	*	*	*	*	*	*	*	*			*	*			*	*		*		*	*
Folk tunes, all cultures		*	*	*	*	*	*	*	*	*	*	*	*	*	*	*	*			*	*		*		*	*
Gospel songs				*				*					*				*	*		*	*		*	*	*	
EDITORIAL POLICIES																										
Preface (or other) statement on song	7	8	9			10	11		12	13		*	14			15	*								16	17
Specialties of the book	*										*		*	*	*	*	*	*	*	*	*	*	*	*	*	*
Liturgical section	*	*	*	*	*	*	*	*	*				*				*	*	*			*				*
Prayer book section (or substitute)	*		*	*	*	*	*	*	*				*				*									
Documents of the Historical faith									34				35													

General Survey of Hymnals As Books of Reference - Appendix G

General Survey of Hymnals As Books of Reference - Appendix G

	BA	BB	BC	BD	BE	BF	BG	BH	BI	BJ	BK	BL	BM	BN	BO	BP	BQ	BR	BS	BT	BU	BV	BW	BX	BY	BZ	B?
Title page with authority symbol	*	*	*		*	*	*	*	*	*	*	*	*	*	*	*	*	*	*	*	*	*	*	*	*	*	?
Table of contents				*	*	*	*	*	*	*	*	*	*	*	*	*	*	*			*	*	*	*	*	*	*
Sources acknowledged fully						*	*											*									
Birth/Death dates of Author/Composer	*		*					*				*			*		*								*		
HYMNS (Poetry)																											
First line index	*	*	*	*	*	*	*	*	*	*	*	*	*	*	*	*	*	*	*	*	*	*	*	*	*	*	*
Author index	*	*	*	*	*	*	*	*	*	*		*	*	*	*	*	*	*	*	*	*	*	*	*	*	*	*
Hymns of the historical faith								*	*	*	*	*	*	*							*						
Psalter in meter												*	*					*									
19th-20th century hymns	*			*	*	*	*	*	*	*	*	*	*	*	*	*	*	*	*	*	*	*	*	*	*	*	
Children's hymns named				*	*	*		*	*	*		*	*		*	*	*	*			*	*	*				
TUNES (Music)																											
Tune name index, alphabetical	*	*	*	*	*	*	*	*		*	*	*	*	*	*	*	*	*	*	*	*	*	*	*	*	*	*
Tune name index, metrical	*	*	*	*	*	*		*		*		*	*	*	*	*	*	*	*	*		*	*				
Composer index	*	*	*	*	*	*	*	*	*	*	*	*	*	*	*	*	*	*	*	*	*	*	*	*	*	*	*
Plainsongs included									*	*	*	*	*	*	*	*	*			*	*						
Reformation tunes	*			*	*			*				*	*	*		*			*	*	*	*					
Folk tunes, all cultures			*	*	*	*	*	*							*						*	*	*	*	*	*	*
Gospel songs		*	*	*																							
EDITORIAL POLICIES; etc.																											
Preface (or other) statement on Song	*							*	*	*		*			*		*		*	*	*	*	*	*	*	*	
Specialties of the book	18		19	20			21	22	23	24		25							26	27		28	29		30		
Liturgical section	*	*	*	*	*		*	*	*	*	*	*	*	*	*	*	*	*	*	*	*	*	*	*	*	*	*
Prayer book section (or sub.)	*		*	*				*			*	*	*		*												
Documents of the historical faith				36				37	38										39	40					41		

NOTES.   (Note number is followed by the book symbol)

1 K   Brief history of Lutheran music, p 306-8.

2 Q   Glossary of liturgical terms, p 168-9.

3 V   Extensive index of hymns and related Bible text, pre-
           liminary pages.

4 W   Index of Hymns for the Young, p 913-17.

5 Y   Newly composed "Sacraments of common life" and
           "Prayers", with the college and university student in
           mind, p 428-41.

6 Z   Index of Hymns for use with children, 9-12, p 538.

7 AA   List of translated hymns with author and date, p 534-37.

8 AM   Notes on hymns and tunes, p 433-82.

9 AC   "Prayers and high resolves", "Devotional poetry and
           prose", recently composed or translated p 307-40.

10 AF   Detailed acknowledgements, p 550-58.

11 AG   Tri-liturgical text: Protestant, Catholic, Jewish service
           music; also a general hymnal section.

12 AJ   Psalter. (Books T and AM contain many Psalms, but
           they also contain modern hymns. Book AJ is entirely
           metrical Psalms).

13 AK)
14 AN)   Acknowledgements, pp vi-x; and xv-xxi respectively.

15 AQ   Acknowledgements, p 475-77; Notes on hymns, tunes,
           and readings, p   415-74.

16 AY   Contains a small section of post-Reformation German
           Mennonite hymns, fifty texts and a handful of melodies.

17 AZ   Great store of traditional Unitas Fratrum hymnody; as-
           signing the long-used metre numeration from Gregor's
           Tune book, etc.; economy of space achieved by arrang-
           ing all hymns and tunes with similar metre together,
           thus permitting ease in exchange of tune, and avoiding
           every opportunity to reprint the music.

18 BA   Inter-coded with Book AZ; but rather than the brilliant
           economy of space in that book, BA is lavish in white
           space on the page and reprinting of melody as desired.
           Rearrangement of hymns, by liturgical use, required

the deliberate format change.

19 BC   Mormon hymns show strong geographical influence; set-
          tings arranged for variant voice groups and congrega-
          tional song.

20 BE   Except for the first hymn (Tate & Brady: Be thou, O
          God, exalted high) the entire series is arranged alpha-
          betically by first line; lavish use of white space on the
          page.

21 BG   Historical notes about text and tune are as useful for
          church and community song as for literary and musicolog-
          ical studies.

22 BH   Since at least 1961 publications, this book is now in two
          sections: Parts I and III are in the larger volume; Part
          II, "Musical services", is issued separately with its own
          index. Earlier printings (from c1932) were in one vol-
          ume.

23 BI   Full service with music, several anthems (i. e. Psalms
          set to music); and the only Hebrew (untransliterated)
          texts set to music printed from right-to-left of the
          page; and the only Greek (untransliterated) texts. Neither
          of these has been indexed.

24 BJ   Literary and historical notes on these hundred hymns--
          perhaps the most significant contribution to Twentieth
          Century hymnology that has been made -- are set in
          exquisite design; musical notation recalls original tunes.

25 BL   One hundred hymns, mutually approved by Catholic and
          Protestant and set in type to the Protestant, rather than
          the Catholic, tradition. Use requires musical literacy.

26 BS   Small paper-back, translations by the Ladies of the Grail,
          England. One of the Psalms, "Like the deer that yearns",
          (Ps. 41 in Catholic tradition; Ps. 42 in others) is found
          also in BL; otherwise these are distinct within the Index.

27 BT   Full texts of hymns in German.

28 BV   Instead of a numerical and tune name metrical index,
          this book contains a metrical index with opening melody in
          score.

29 BW   Survey of Mennonite music, p xii-xxxix.

30 BY I   Influenced by Anglican hymns and tunes in contents,
          format, and general tone; in contrast to the Baptist
          books from the U.S. which contain great quantities of
          gospel song, this has little.

- - - - - - -

31 L   Augsburg Confession; Formula for government; Constitution of the General Synod of the Evangelical Lutheran Church in the U.S.

32 O   Augsburg Confession; Athanasian Creed, Luther's Small catechism.

33 S   Brief statement of the Reformed Faith.

34 AJ   Doctrinal standards; Liturgy; and Church order; also Heidelberg Confession; Canons of Dordrecht; Forms for both ex-communication and re-admission.

35 AM   Westminster Confession.

36 BE   Six hymns by the Reverend Mary Baker Eddy included.

37 BH   Traditional Jewish texts (transliterated), several of which -- as in the Christian tradition -- are frequently heard in secular music (the Kol Nidre, and the Dies Irae) See Note 22 above.

38 BI   General Confessions of faith; Advent of Our Lord, etc.

39 BT   Texts of some of the very earliest German Lutheran hymns, given in German parallel to their English translations; in full in both languages.

40 BU   Oldest Protestant hymnal in use in the U.S.A.; little changed since 1570. No compilation exists for the melodies which are said to be the same plainchant used four hundred years ago in Europe. Several authors have been identified; several are named in the hymn itself; but the bulk of poetry must remain cited as Ausbund, in lieu of known author.
           Includes also "Confession, oder bekenntnitz" and the "Defensiones oppositionum"; and "Wahrhaftiger bericht von den Brüdern im Schweitzerland . . . von dem 1635-sten bis in das 1645ste Jahr". This latter is biographical.

41 BZ   Revives the use of some Wesley hymns long omitted from books, uses phrase "American folk hymn" for hymns and tunes usually known as "Negro spirituals".

APPENDIX H

MATERIALS EXCLUDED FROM THESE INDEXES

(but included in hymnals analyzed)

Stated institutional liturgy; variants to that liturgy: as, The Magnificat, Te deum, Responses, Psalms.

This is not an index to the liturgies of worship, the interplay
between priest and people. This is an index to the united worship
in song by the priest and the people. It is, consequently, of more
recent date than the Jewish Holy Day service music, than the
Mass, and the services derived from the Mass. However, when
this material (either texts or tunes) appears in versions used for
true congregational song it is included.

Attempts to prove and to cite the original text of word or melody:
as, Which version of the "Passion chorale" was the original
version?

This is neither an exercise in literary criticism nor in
musicological history. This is an index to items as they appear
in the printed books listed elsewhere within the Introduction, books
which have been officially adopted for institutional use, or which
have sprung from institutional life (as the Army and Navy, universities) and which have been used at worship during part of the
time from the year 1900 through the year 1965.

This is an index to the particular poetry and song quoted in
seventy-six hymnals and in two hymnal companions. Relationships
are many; those which it was possible to make within a very formal index have been made. Others must be left to the reader.

References to intermediate editorial history: as, Who recorded the
words and songs to folksongs, or who revised the plainsongs?
However, when these have become established versions with
known authorship, credit is acknowledged.

Full information about versions, revisions, editing to deliber-
ately delete certain words from entire hymnals (as: blood, Trinity,
Catholic) requires lengthy verbal discussion. John Julian has done
it well, but his work is three-quarters of a century old! No one
has published a comparable study of melodies and tune names.
Though Robert Guy McCutchan's Hymn tune names (Abingdon, 1957)
appeared shortly after this work was begun, it includes only about
two thousand names and far less than half as many melodies.

The Hymn Society of America and the British Hymn Society
are working on indexes to revise and enlarge Julian's Dictionary.
They have mutually agreed that the Americans shall remain within
their province, and the British within theirs: with enough for each
to do and with duplication avoided. According to the Annual report
of the Hymn Society of America for 1965, based on the activities
of the Society reviewed at the Forty-third annual meeting, May 1,
1965 at Princeton, Dr. Leonard Ellinwood stated that 187,765 first-
line cards from 1,070 hymnals were prepared. This was more
than ten years of work, and but one-third of the hymnals intended
for analysis were completed. Biographical materials will have to
wait for completion of the analytical indexing.

Hymns and tunes is far smaller, of more limited scope -- so
far as background data and poetry are concerned. Hymns and
tunes is peculiar, and of very different scope -- because of its
inclusion of both poetry and melody. Musical information about
Key, Time signature, Phraseology, and Note value: as indicated
on the printed page.

Because this Index does not intend to serve as a means for
reproducing the melody, but simply for identifying it, the above
items of information are not essential.

Variant readings of both hymn and tune after the first are not cited
separately: as, The several versions of "Holy night" are each
identified at first appearance at variant entry and at main entry; thereafter citation is always and only made with the main
entry record.

This decision had to be made in the interests of brevity. The

fact of a variant rendering is established; it can be found in print
if desired; and associated readings are closely enough related by
reference symbols so that it is usually possible to use the different
versions within a single congregational singing group without diffi-
culty. Extreme variants are here included as separate items.
Some of the German chorales, for example, fall into the category
of extreme variants.

Original Latin names of the Office Hymns, etc.; and the unquoted
    names of Latin, German, Greek, Jewish, and other non-Eng-
    lish hymns or tunes are not included; except only when they
    have been included as part of the proper textual material
    indexed.

As an example, "Adeste fideles" is occasionally quoted in Latin, and has been fully indexed under its Latin first line. Hymns
ancient and modern uses the Latin words as titles to hymns derived
from the Latin. The hymn is quoted in English; the Latin words
are therefore omitted.

Attempts to associate words and music: as, What books quote "The
    King of love my shepherd is" to the tune "Dominus regit me"?
    Such association is completely outside the purview of this In-
dex. Gospel songs, usually known by some portion of the hymn's
words, are the only items where an association of this kind may
be found -- as a result of the nature of the materials and not the
result of intention.

Relative meter of hymn and of tune: as, Which tunes are in Com-
    mon Meter? and Which hymns can be sung to this tune?
    This record is outside the intention of the Index. It may be
found in individual hymnal indexes. We leave the compilation to a
braver soul!

Descants found in Books F, X, BV, and BY are not identified --
    either the hymn utilizing a descant, or the tune and composer.

APPENDIX I

HYMNALS ANALYZED
ARRANGED ACCORDING TO DATE OF ISSUE*

ISSUE DATE   CODE

1570 &   Ausbund; das ist: Etliche shöne Christliche Lieder, wie
1962   sie in dem Gesängnis zu Passau in dem Schloss von
           den Schweizer-Brüdern und von anderen rechtgläubi-
           gen Christen hin und her gedichtet worden, melcher
           religion sie seien, unpartheiisch sehr nützlich. Nebst
           einem Anhang von sechs Liedern. 13. Aufl. Verlag
           von den Amischen Gemeinden in Lancaster County,
           Pa. [Lancaster] 1962.
           140 hymns and 6 liedern. Text only.   BU

1876 &   Offices of worship and hymns (with tunes). 3d ed., rev.
1891   and enl. [1891] Bound with The Liturgy and the Offices
           of worship of the American Province of the Unitas
           Fratrum, or The Moravian Church. Winston Salem
           [Pref. 1876, 1908; c1908]
           1564 hymns with tunes   AZ

1893   The Church hymnal, rev. and enl., in accordance with
           the action of the General Convention of the Protestant
           Episcopal Church in the U.S.A. Boston [c1893]
           679 hymns with tunes   D

1893   The Magnificat. Hymns with tunes, compiled for the use
           of the New-Church. 6th ed. New York [c1893] 1901.
           566 hymns with tunes   BR

1899   Book of worship with hymns and tunes. General Synod
           of the Evangelical Lutheran Church in the U.S.
           Philadelphia [c1899]
           607 hymns with tunes   L

1899 &   Hymns: The Yattendon hymnal, ed. by Robert Bridges
1920   and H. Ellis Wooldridge. London and Oxford [1899]
           1920.
           100 hymns with tunes, and ample notes   BJ

---

* The hymnals, arranged by letter citation symbol, will be
found at the beginning of the volume.

1901   The Methodist Protestant hymnal. Board of Publication of
            the Methodist Protestant Church. Baltimore [c1901]
            531 hymns with tunes   H

1901   The New Psalms and hymns with supplement, published
            by authority of the General Assembly of the Presby-
            terian Church in the U.S. Richmond, Va., 1901.
            770 hymns with tunes   V

1902   Church and Sunday school hymnal. Comp. and publ.
            under the direction of the Committee appointed by
            Mennonite Conferences. J.D. Brunk, musical ed.
            Scottdale, Pa., [c1902, c1911]
            412 hymns and tunes in English; Suppl. #413-532;
            and 50 German hymns with some tunes   AY

1905   The Methodist hymnal, official hymnal of the Methodist
            Episcopal Church, South, and the Methodist Episcopal
            Church. Nashville [c1905]
            748 hymns with tunes   I

1913   The Lutheran hymnary, including the Symbols of the
            Evangelical Lutheran Church. Minneapolis [c1913,
            1935]
            618 hymns with tunes   O

1914   The New hymn and tune book. 1914. Bound with Services
            for congregational worship. Boston, American Unitar-
            ian Asso., 1914.
            546 hymns with tunes   BX

1916   The Hymnal, as authorized for use by the General
            Convention of the Protestant Episcopal Church in the
            U.S.A. New York [c1916]
            561 hymns with tunes   B

1918   The Book of praise, authorised by the General Assembly
            of the Presbyterian Church in Canada. Toronto [1918]
            816 hymns with tunes   AP

1918   Common service book of the Lutheran Church, authorized
            by the United Lutheran Church in America. Philadel-
            phia [c1918]
            578 hymns with tunes   K

1920   Hymnal and Liturgies of the Moravian Church (Unitas
            Fratrum). Published by authority of the Provincial
            Synod, Bethlehem, 1920.
            952 hymns with tunes   BA

1924   The Beacon hymnal for church schools. [Unitarian]
            Boston [c1924]
            250 hymns with tunes   BD

1924   Evangelical Lutheran hymn-book. Edition of 1924. St.
            Louis, 1924
            567 hymns with tunes   AA

1925   The Hymnal and Order of service, authorized by the
            Evangelical Lutheran Augustana Synod. Lectionary ed.
            Rock Island, Ill. [1925]
            682 hymns with tunes   N

1925   Hymnal, Church of the Brethren, by authority of the
            General Conference. Elgin, Ill. [c1925]
            499 hymns with tunes   AS

1925 &   St. Basil's hymnal, 39th ed. Comp. by the Basilian
1935   Fathers. Chicago [c1935; imprimature, Toronto 1925]
            301 hymns with tunes   BO

1926 &   New Baptist hymnal, containing standard and gospel
1958   hymns. Philadelphia [c1926, 1958]
            407 hymns with tunes   AV

1927   The Church hymnary. Rev. ed. Authorized for use in
            public worship by the Church of Scotland, the United
            Free Church of Scotland [and the Presbyterian
            Churches of Ireland, England, Wales, Australia, New
            Zealand, and Southern Africa] London [pref.1927]
            713 hymns with tunes   W

1927   The Presbyterian hymnal, published by authority of the
            Presbyterian Church in the U.S. Richmond, Va.
            [c1927]
            500 hymns with tunes   U

1927   The Psalter hymnal of the United Presbyterian Board of
            Publication and Bible School work. Pittsburgh [c1927]
            458 hymns with tunes   T

1928   The American student hymnal, ed. by H. Augustine
            Smith. New York and London [c1928]
            385 hymns with tunes   Y

1929   The Book of worship for the Reformed Church in the U.
            S. Philadelphia, 1929.
            660 hymns with tunes   AO

1929   The New Christian hymnal, ed. by H.J. Kuiper. Grand
            Rapids, c1929.
            451 hymns with tunes   AI

1930   American Lutheran hymnal. Columbus [c1930]
            651 hymns with tunes   M

1930   The Hymnary. Authorized by the General Council of the
                 United Church of Canada. Toronto [c1930]
                 691 hymns with tunes   AL

1930   The New Hymnal for American youth. Ed. by H.
                 Augustine Smith. New York [c1930]|
                 344 hymns with tunes

                                                                                         AC

1931 &   Songs of praise, enlarged ed. [Words ed.: Percy Dear-
1958   mer; Music eds.: Ralph Vaughan Williams and Martin
                 Shaw] London [c1931, 1958]
                 705 hymns with tunes   X

1932   The Concordia hymnal. Minneapolis [c1932]
                 434 hymns with tunes   P

1932 &   Union hymnal: Songs and prayers for Jewish worship.
                 3d ed., rev. and enl. [New York, 1932] 1957.
                 341 hymns with tunes   BH

1933   The English hymnal. London, 1933.
                 656 hymns with tunes; Appendix of 72 tunes   E

1933   The Hymnal, published by authority of the General As-
                 sembly of the Presbyterian Church in the U.S.A.
                 Philadelphia, 1933.
                 513 hymns with tunes   S

1935   The Methodist hymnal. Nashville [c1935]
                 564 hymns with tunes   G

1936 &   The Hymnal as authorized for use by the General Con-
1916   vention of the Protestant Episcopal Church in the
                 U.S.A. in . . .1916. Boston [c1936]
                 561 hymns, with tunes which vary from the New
                 York ed. of 1916   C

1937   Christian Science hymnal, with seven hymns written
                 by the Reverend Mary Baker Eddy. Boston, c1937
                 429 hymns with tunes   BE

1937   Hymns of the Spirit, for use in the Free Churches of
                 America. Boston [c1937, 1960]
                 568 hymns with tunes, and eight additional tunes
                                                                                         AN

1937   The New church hymnal, ed. by H. Augustine Smith
                 [and others] New York [c1937]
                 492 hymns with tunes   AD

1937   The Student hymnary, ed. by Edward Dwight Eaton.
                 New York, 1937.

416 hymns with tunes   AB

1939   Christian worship and praise, ed. by Henry Hallam
            Tweedy under the direction of the Commission for
            Christian Worship and Praise [of the Reformed
            Church in America] New York, 1939.
            Nos. 167-700 being hymns with tunes.   BF

1939   Liturgy and Hymnal, for the use of the General Church
            of the New Jerusalem. 4th and rev. ed. Bryn Athyn,
            Pa., 1939.
            64 doxologies, etc. with tunes: 117 hymns with tunes. BI

1940   The Broadman hymnal; B. B. McKinney, music ed.
            Nashville, c1940.
            480 hymns with tunes   AU

1940   The Church hymnal. Official hymnal of the Seventh-Day
            Advent Church. Takoma Park, Washington, D.C.
            [c1940]
            703 hymns with tunes   BB

1940   Hymnal for Christian worship. [Richmond, Va., c1940]
            340 hymns with tunes   AG

1940   The Mennonite hymnary. Published by the Board of
            Publication of the General Conference. Berne,
            Indiana, and Newton, Kansas [c1940]
            623 hymns with tunes   AW

1941   Christian worship, a hymnal. [Baptists and Disciples]
            St. Louis [c1941]
            Nos. 94-651 being hymns with tunes   Z

1941   The Hymnal, containing complete orders of worship.
            Authorized by the General Synod of the Evangelical
            and Reformed Church. St. Louis [c1941]
            481 hymns with tunes   AK

1941   The Lutheran hymnal, authorized by the Evangelical
            Lutheran Synodical Conference of North America.
            St. Louis [c1941]
            660 hymns with tunes; and accompanied by the
            book next below: Q

1942 &   The Handbook to the Lutheran Hymnal. 3d and rev. ed.
1958   by W. G. Polack. St. Louis [c1942, c1958]
            Accompanies the Lutheran Hymnal, just above, and
            includes full texts in original script and language
            of many of the hymns; also biographical and literary
            notes concerning authors, translators, composers,
            and arrangers.   BT

1942   The Hymnal, Army and Navy, ed. by Ivan L. Bennett,
            New York, 1942.
            625 hymns with tunes for Roman Catholic, Jewish, and
            and Protestant worship.   AH

1943   The Hymnal of the Protestant Episcopal Church in the
            U.S., 1940. New York [c1943]
            600 hymns with tunes   A

1947 &   The Psalter [as prepared and published by the United
1927   Presbyterian Church]. Grand Rapids [c1927, rev. ed.
            1947]
            434 hymns with tunes   AJ

1947 &   The St. Gregory hymnal and Catholic choir book. Com-
1920   piled by Nicola A. Montani. Philadelphia, c1920,
            c1947 [Imprimature, Philadelphia 1920? and Supple-
            ment approval 1941]
            283 hymns with tunes; also 1947 supplement containing
            materials chiefly liturgical. Nos. 4 and 251 are the
            only variants from the 1920 ed.   BQ

1948   Hymns of the Church of Jesus Christ of Latter-Day
            Saints. Salt Lake City [c1948]
            387 hymns with tunes   BC

1949   Handbook to the Mennonite Hymnary, by Lester Hostetler.
            Newton, Kansas, 1949.
            Accompanies the Mennonite Hymnary (1940, above),
            and includes both English and German language
            hymns, some literary and much biographical informa-
            tion related to hymnal contents.   BW

1950   Hymns ancient and modern, rev. 1950. London, 1950.
            636 hymns with tunes   F

1951   The Brethren hymnal, authorized by Annual Conference,
            Church of the Brethren. Elgin, Ill. [c1951]
            614 hymns with tunes   AR

1954   The Monastery hymnal. Comp., arr., and ed. by Achille
            P. Bragers. Boston [c1954; imprimature New York,
            1954]
            107 hymns with tunes; part English, part Latin
            texts   BP

1955   A Hymnal for Friends. Philadelphia, 1955.
            176 hymns with tunes   BK

1955   The Hymnbook, published by Presbyterian Church in the
            U.S., Presbyterian Church in the U.S.A., United
            Presbyterian Church of North America, Reformed
            Church in America. New York [c1955]

      557 hymns with tunes   R

1955   Twenty four Psalms and a Canticle translated from the
        Hebrew and arranged for singing to the Psalmody of
        Joseph Gelineau. [Tr. under direction of The Grail,
        England] Toledo, Ohio [1955; Paris, 1953; imprima-
        ture Westminster, 1955]
        25 hymns in new translation with tunes   BS

1956   Baptist hymnal, ed. by Walter Hines Sims. Nashville
        [c1956]
        513 hymns with tunes   AT

1957   The Hymnal [of the Evangelical United Brethren
        Church]. Dayton, Ohio [c1957]
        474 hymns with tunes   AE

1958   The New Saint Basil hymnal, comp., arr., and ed. by
        the Basilian Fathers. Cincinnati, 1958. [imprimature
        Toronto, 1958]
        210 hymns with tunes; approximately two-thirds are
        English, and one-third Latin   BN

1958   The Pilgrim hymnal. [Congregational] Boston [c1958]
        584 hymns (bits of service music interspersed) with
        tunes   AF

1959   Christian hymnal [authorized by the General Conference
        of the Church of God in Christ, Mennonite] Hesston,
        Kansas, 1959.
        657 hymns with tunes   AX

1959   Our parish prays and sings [with] organ accompaniment
        including masses contained in the Parish Kyriale, by
        Rev. Irvin Udulutsch, OFM. Cap. Collegeville, Minn.
        [c1959; imprimature St. Cloud, 1959]
        97 hymns with tunes   BM

1961   Trinity hymnal [of the Orthodox Presbyterian Church].
        Philadelphia, 1961.
        730 hymns with tunes   AM

1962   The Baptist hymn book, with music. London [1962]
        777 hymns with tunes   BY

1964   Hymnal of Christian unity, ed. by Clifford A. Bennett
        and Paul Hume. Toledo, Ohio [c1964; imprimature
        Toledo, 1964]
        100 hymns with tunes   BL

1964   Hymns for the celebration of life [by the Unitarian
        Universalist Hymnbook Commission] Boston [c1964]
        327 hymns with tunes; and ample notes   AQ

1964 &   The Oxford book of carols, ed. by Percy Dearmer,
1928   Ralph Vaughan Williams, and Martin Shaw. London
              [reset 1964 with changes]
              197 carols with tunes; and ample notes   BG

1964 &   Report of the Hymnal Committee of the Commission on
1966*   Worship, to the 1964 General Conference of the Meth-
              odist Church. [c1964] Forms the Preliminary draft
              and Final report concerning
              539 hymns and 402 tunes proposed for inclusion in
              the 1966 Methodist hymnal.*   BZ

1965   Anglican hymn book. London [1965]
              663 hymns with tunes; metrical index in score   BV

*1966   The Methodist Hymnal, Official hymnal of The Methodist
              Church. Nashville [1966]
              In press. Information on contents secured from book
              second above. Information on title secured from pub-
              lisher.

APPENDIX J

BIBLIOGRAPHY

In addition to the vast amount of information contained within the indexes of the hymnals analyzed, small searches for facts were made in several college and university libraries. Four basic reference books have been constantly by my side. A fifth, released very much too late to be helpful to this work, is marked with an asterisk.

Baker's Biographical dictionary of musicians. 5th ed., rev. by
    Nicolas Slonimsky. New York, Schirmer [c1958]

Julian, John, ed. A dictionary of hymnology. New York, Dover
    Publications [2d rev. ed. reprint, 1957] 2 v.

McCutchan, Robert Guy. Hymn tune names, their sources and
    significance. New York, Abingdon Pr. [1957]

*McDormand, Thomas B., and Frederick S. Crossman. Judson
    Concordance to hymns. Valley Forge, Judson Pr.[c1965]

Riemenschneider, Albert. 371 Harmonized chorales and 69 Chorale
    melodies with figured bass by Johann Sebastian Bach;
    Rev., corr., ed. and annotated. New York, Schirmer,
    c1941

For definitions quoted exactly or repeated less formally:

The Oxford Universal dictionary on historical principles. 3d ed.,
    rev. with addenda. Oxford, Clarendon Pr. [1955]